CW01480963

THE INTERLINEAR

NRSV-NIV

PARALLEL
NEW TESTAMENT
IN GREEK
AND ENGLISH

THE INTERLINEAR NRSV-NIV PARALLEL NEW TESTAMENT IN GREEK AND ENGLISH

ALFRED MARSHALL

ZondervanPublishingHouse
Academic and Professional Books
Grand Rapids, Michigan

A Division of HarperCollins*Publishers*

Requests for information should be addressed to:
Zondervan Publishing House
Grand Rapids, Michigan 49530

Library of Congress Cataloging-in-Publication Data

Bible. N. T. Greek. 1993
The interlinear NRSV-NIV parallel New Testament in Greek and English
p. cm.
ISBN 0-310-40160-7
1. Bible. N. T.—Interlinear translations, English. I. Marshall, Alfred. II. Bible. N. T. English. New Revised Standard. 1993. III. Bible. N. T. English. New International. 1993. IV. Title.
BS1965.5 19993
225.4'8–dc20 93-37364
CIP

Previously published in 1990 as The NRSV-NIV Parallel New Testament in Greek and English.

Printed in the United States of America

97 98 99 / DH / 10 9 8 7 6 5 4 3

This edition is printed on acid-free paper and meets the American National Standards Institute Z39.48 standard.

Introduction to the Interlinear Greek Text and Translation

The Greek Text

The text of the Greek New Testament has come down to us in various manuscripts, printing not being invented until the fifteenth century and Erasmus not publishing his Greek New Testament until 1516. Some of these manuscripts are more important than others (age not necessarily being indicative of importance). The study of the various manuscript copies, and the assessment of their individual value in attempting to reconstruct the original as nearly as possible, constitutes the science of textual criticism. For those who wish to study this seriously there are many books available; it is sufficient to say here that, after Erasmus, a great number of scholars have, over a long period, applied themselves to the task of constructing a reliable text out of the mass of various readings that have arisen from copying and making copies from copies of the old manuscripts (scholars such as Mill, Stephens, Griesbach, Lachmann, Tischendorf, Tregelles, and Alford).

The Greek text used in this book is that of the 21st edition of Eberhard Nestle's *Novum Testamentum Graece,* based on the study and critical research of generations of scholars, except that John 7:53–8:11 is not in that text but is relegated to the foot of the page as a critical note. It is here retained in the text. The critical notes of Nestle's work, which enable students to follow the reasons for variations in the text, have been omitted as being outside the scope of this publication. The student who requires these critical notes is referred to the Greek edition published in Great Britain by the British and Foreign Bible Society and in Germany (Stuttgart) by Privilegierte Württembergische Bibelanstalt, by whose permission this recension is used.

Square brackets are found in certain places in the Greek text.

These indicate only that, according to Nestle, some editors include and others omit the word or words so enclosed. Translation has been made here in the usual way.

Avoiding interpretation, then, we give some details of how we have proceeded in the matter of a literal translation. These should be studied and understood if proper use is to be made of this attempt to promote an intelligent reading of the Greek New Testament.

The English Translation

The Wording in General

The relationship between the Greek text and the interlinear English is as follows: Greek words not required in the translation into English are (*a*) represented by a short dash, as for example the definite article with proper names. Alternatively (*b*) italic type is used to show that words or even in some cases letters are not really needed for an idiomatic English rendering. For example, "man" is sometimes redundant (as in Matt. 20:1; Acts 2:22). On the other hand, words supplied in English for which there is no Greek equivalent are placed in square brackets [. . .]. Naturally, there will be differences of judgment as to this practice in the passages involved.

The modern form for the third person singular of verbs (present indicative) has been used (loves) in place of the now obsolete -(e)th (loveth); but the older "ye" has been retained for the nominative ("you" for the oblique cases) of the second person plural pronoun; and "thou" (thee), not "you," for the second person singular. It is a loss that in modern English these differences have disappeared; so unaccustomed are we now to them that even the average reader of the Authorized Version misses the point of Luke 22:31. The loss is even more to be regretted when God is addressed as "You."

Where some word other than the strictly literal one seems to be needed in the translation, the former is printed in parentheses immediately after the latter—e.g., Matthew 10:17, "beware from (of) men."

Occasionally it is not feasible to give a literal rendering without undue explanation; some idiomatic word or phrase has to be used. There are only a few of such passages, and they are indicated by the mark †.

There are a number of Greek phrases, other than where † is used, which are to be taken as a whole, not word for word:

ἐπὶ τὸ αὐτό = "on the same" = "together"
διὰ τοῦτο = "because-of this" = "therefore"
ἵνα μή = "in-order-that not" = "lest"
καθ' ὑπερβολήν = "by-way-of excess" = "excessively"

Εὐαγγελίζω. This and its cognate noun have been anglicized (evangelize, evangel). But while we can "evangelize" a city, we do not "evangelize" a person or a subject; so we must speak of "preaching (good tidings) to" a person or of "preaching" a subject. We can, of course, speak of "evangelizing" absolutely as in 1 Corinthians 1:17. Ellicott on 1 Thessalonians 3:6 has some useful information for the student.

Verbs

The ending of a Greek verb normally indicates the person (1st, 2nd, or 3rd, sing. or pl.). If the pronoun is separately expressed, this can be clearly seen in the interlinear translation.

Where there is more than one subject of a verb, Greek will often put the verb in the singular to agree with the nearest subject. This is not in accordance with English grammar, which requires a plural verb if there is more than one subject. In Revelation 9:2, "sun" and "air" call for the plural "were darkened," as in the Authorized Version. But the Greek verb is in the singular. It is sometimes typographically possible to indicate the difference of grammatical usage.

A peculiarity of Greek construction is that a neuter plural subject may take a singular verb; but this is by no means invariable, and there appears to be no rule to go by. In translating, the position is sometimes shown by the use of an italic letter for the ending of the verb ([they] commit*s*); at other times the alternative is given in parenthesis (is(are)). But there are places where neither course is possible without taking up too much space, and the matter is left to the intelligence of the reader.

The subjunctive mood is dying out in English, and no attempt has been made to represent consistently the Greek mood, except by the use of the analytic form "I may . . . ," with its related optative (of which latter there are only thirty-seven examples in the New Testament, fifteen of these being the familiar γένοιτο = "may it be"). But such words as ἵνα and compounds of ἄν (ὅταν, ἐάν), etc., introducing a subjective or hypothetical element into a verbal idea, must be followed by the subjunctive mood.

The Greek perfect can generally be taken as represented by an English present—a past action continuing in its effect down to the present, in contrast to an action wholly in the past. But in a literal translation the English perfect has been retained. In John 11:27, the Authorized Version is idiomatically correct, but the Revised Version is literally so (πεπίστευκα = "I have believed"); compare 2 Timothy 1:12, where the Authorized Version adopts the literal equivalent. So, for example, τετέλεσται = "it has been finished" = "it is finished." In participles, italics show that the auxiliary verbs may be dispensed with in English.

The interlinear translation has introduced a comma after "Behold" in a number of places. The reason for this is as follows. The Greek ἰδού (or other form), properly an imperative of the defective verb ὁράω, is used as an exclamation, as is its English equivalent. That is to say, it is not then an active verb taking a direct object in the accusative case; it is simply exclamatory and is followed by a noun in the nominative, with its predicate or complement understood. For example, in John 1:29, there is no command to behold the Lamb of God; instead, the idea is, "Look! [there goes]. . . ." The position is different in such passages as Matthew 28:6 and Romans 11:22, where there is a command.

Greek will often use a preposition in a compound verb and then repeat it (or use one similar) before a noun in the same sentence; in such passages the preposition would not be used twice in English. But in such a phrase as *εἰσέρχεσθαι εἰς οἶκον* we can say "to enter into a house" (the counterpart in French being *entrer dans une maison*). We can indeed say simply "to enter a house." Another exception would be *ἀπέρχεσθαι ἀπό* ("to go away from"). But *διαφέρειν διὰ τοῦ ἱεροῦ* means "to carry *through* through the temple" (e.g., Mark 11:16).

Necessity or compulsion is most frequently expressed by the use of an impersonal verb (or a verb used impersonally), with the person concerned in the accusative as the object of the verb (δεῖ με = "it behoves me" = "I must").

Participles

Greek is "a participle-loving language," said the late A. T. Robertson, and it uses this part of speech much more frequently than we do, and in different ways.

To begin with, it is absolutely essential to grasp the distinction between *continuous, momentary,* and *completed* action. The first is commonly, but wrongly, spoken of as a present participle, the second as an aorist (which does not mean "past"), and the third as a perfect. (There is a rare future participle—continuous in the future.)

1. A participle may be used as an adjective qualifying a noun,

just as in English (e.g., 1 Thess. 1:9—"a living God"; Heb. 7:8—"dying men"). This is so simple as not to need further remark.

2. A participle may be used, again as in English, as a verb to describe some action (e.g., Acts 9:39—"all the widows stood by . . . weeping and showing. . .").

3. A participle may be used, with the definite article, with, say, "one" understood, where we should use a noun or a relative phrase (e.g., frequently, *ὁ πιστεύων* = "the [one] believing" = "the believer" *or* "he who believes"). Here the participle is continuous; in Luke 1:45, it is momentary (and, naturally, feminine in gender, referring to Mary's one act of faith at the Annunciation). If two participles are used with but one definite article, as in John 5:24, the meaning is that one person is doubly described, not two persons doing two things. This feature has been preserved in our translation.

4. Very frequently indeed, where in English we use two or more finite verbs to describe associated actions, Greek will use participles and only one finite verb for the main action. But here judgment is necessary to distinguish two (or more) simultaneous actions from consecutive ones; and as we have no aorist participle in English the matter is not always free from difficulty. In Acts 10:34 ("Peter opening his mouth said") the two actions were obviously simultaneous! Likewise, Acts 1:24 ("Praying they said"). But sometimes one action must be completed before another could begin (e.g., Luke 22:17—"having given thanks, he said . . ."). Here the act of giving thanks to God would be complete before Jesus addressed His disciples; therefore the aorist participle must be represented in English by the analytic "having given thanks." That this is not unimportant is shown by Matthew 26:30 ("having sung a hymn they went out"). To translate the aorist participle here by "singing a hymn" would certainly convey the idea that the singing occurred as they went out. In Acts 21:14, it is not easy to see how the keeping silence and the saying could be contemporaneous ("Having said, The will of the Lord be done, we kept silence"). These few examples should, we think, suffice to show the principles involved.

Negatives

As the negatives *οὐ(κ)* (categorical) and *μή* (hypothetical) are easily recognizable, it has not been thought necessary always to render them separately, but they are included with any verb with which they may be used. But whereas in English the negative follows the verb, in Greek it precedes (e.g., Matt. 3:11). If such a phrase happens to be broken at the end of a line, this course has not been feasible.

The double negative *οὐ μή* has been consistently rendered "by no means."

Incidentally, though of importance, these two negative particles, or their compounds, when introducing questions, expect different answers. *οὐ* appeals to the fact, anticipating "Yes, it is so" (e.g., John 11:9, "Are there not twelve hours of the day?"). The answer would be "Yes, there are." On the contrary, *μή* denies the suggestion and expects the reply "No, it is not so"; or, if not so explicit as that, doubts whether it is so (e.g., John 18:35). The form of the question in the Authorized Version and the Revised Version indicates that Pilate was asking for information, whereas he was rejecting the idea with scorn and contempt—"I am not a Jew [am I]?" The answer, if any, would be—"No, certainly not." This distinction is largely overlooked in the English Versions. To assist to the correct nuance of thought, in such places the latter negative in the interlinear translation is italicized, and the reader must read into the original what is intended; the result is sometimes surprising. An article in *The Bible Translator* for January 1953 may be consulted.

While on the subject of negatives, Greek favors the use of two such, one strengthening the other. In such sentences the second negative has to be replaced in English by a positive (e.g., Matt. 22:46).

Nouns

In familiar proper names there will appear some inconsistency, a compromise between the actual spellings preferred by Nestle and the Authorized Version; but this is of no great importance.

In Greek, gender belongs to the word and not necessarily to what is indicated by the word; whereas, of course, in English we keep the ideas of masculine, feminine, and neuter to men, women, and inanimate things respectively—English, by the way, being the only great modern language to do so. Allowance must be made for this in translating; sometimes it is possible to transfer the idea from one language to another. The note to Revelation 13:1 may be consulted.

It has not been considered necessary always to indicate the order of a noun and its adjective; a knowledge of English is sufficient for this. But where there is any risk of ambiguity, small superior figures indicate the order in which the words should be read.

Adjectives

The construction of the demonstrative adjectives is peculiar in Greek. The definite article is used as well as the demonstrative adjective in one of two possible positions: either—

οὗτος *ὁ* οἶκος
this *the* house

or—

ὁ οἶκος οὗτος
the house this

The definite article is of course not wanted in English, and the proper translation of the phrase is obvious—"this house." Similarly ἐκεῖνος ("that"). It is sometimes possible typographically to treat the three-word phrase as a whole, with the idiomatic translation underneath.

There is no indefinite article in Greek. The use of it in translation is a matter of individual judgment. The numeral "one" is sometimes found; whether this means that just one, and no more, is to be understood is again open to argument (e.g., Matt. 21:19; 26:69). We have inserted "a" or "an" as a matter of course where it seems called for.

The definite article must sometimes be rendered by a pronoun or a possessive adjective. This is particularly so where parts of the body are indicated (e.g., Matt. 8:3). Sometimes it is used "pronominally"—that is, it must be rendered "he" (or otherwise according to the gender) or "they" (e.g., Mark 10:4).

Similarly, the definite article is used in Greek with a possessive adjective, as in Matthew 18:20—

εἰς *τὸ* ἐμὸν ὄνομα
in *the* my name

or, alternatively, the construction may be, say—

εἰς *τὸ* ὄνομα *τὸ* ἐμόν
in *the* name *the* my

This remark applies only to the first and second persons, singular and plural, not to the third, where the only possible construction in this respect would be "in the name of him/her/them." This has been followed literally, as the reader can always make the necessary English construction for himself. Occasionally such a construction as "in the name of me" will be found, meaning the same thing.

The neuter form of an adjective may be used as an adverb. In John 19:35, ἀληθῆ is the neuter of ἀληθής ("true") and must be rendered "truly." So πρῶτον ("firstly"), though "first" is quite often used in English as an adverb. Conversely, an adverb may be used as an adjective (e.g., *νῦν*, "now" = "present").

The word *ταῦτα* ("these things," neuter plural) might be rendered by the singular "this," as in the common phrase *μετὰ ταῦτα* ("after this"); but this liberty has not been taken in the present literal translation.

The gender of an adjective may demand "man," "woman," or "thing" to be supplied (e.g., Matt. 9:27—"two blind men").

There is the *genitive of quality,* of which there are many examples in the New Testament. If in English we say "a man of courage" or "an act of kindness," this is equivalent to "a courageous man" or "a kind act" respectively. We have translated literally, with an occasional footnote where this construction is not generally recognized.

As "first" is used as an adverb as well as "firstly," it has not been thought necessary always to print "first*ly*"; the matter is of no great importance.

Particles

A number of Greek particles are said to be "post-positive"—that is to say, they cannot stand as the first word in a sentence but are found in the second, third, or even the fourth place. Such words must of course be taken first in English; but it has not been thought necessary to show this, as the construction is sufficiently obvious. They include *γάρ* ("for"), *δέ* ("and, but, now"), *οὖν* ("therefore," which can be post-positive in English), *τις* (a certain), *μέν* (indeed), and *γε* ("really"—generally too subtle to be reproduced in English).

μέν . . . δέ. These two particles, in contrasted clauses, are not translatable literally, unless "indeed . . . but" be used, as we have done in some places. But by adopting the phrases "on the one hand . . . on the other" the contrast is brought out. These particles are, in fact, somewhat elusive as to their force. See John 19:24, 32, where *μέν* has been left untranslated—an example of the difficulty of rendering it satisfactorily in a literal translation.

The word *ὅτι* as a conjunction, when meaning "that," is used to introduce spoken words as recorded; it is then known as the "recitative *ὅτι.*" In English the original present tense of any verb would in such a construction ("indirect speech") be changed to the past—e.g., "He said that the man was a liar." But Greek retains the original tense as actually used. What the speaker really said was "The man is a liar." The conjunction thus becomes superfluous and the reported words would in modern usage be put within quotation marks, as above. These, however, are not used in this translation (e.g., Matt. 21:3).

Strictly speaking, ἵνα is a "telic" particle—that is, it denotes purpose (τέλος, "an end"); hence a full translation is "in order that." But inasmuch as in New Testament times there was a tendency to use it where ὅτι would be expected, it sometimes means no more than the conjunction "that" (e.g., Matt. 5:29). Sometimes, then, where there may be room for difference of opinion as to its precise force, or even where there is none, "*in order* that" will be found in the literal translation.

Idiomatic constructions

There are five idiomatic Greek constructions that, being of frequent occurrence, call for explanation.

a. The *genitive absolute*. This is made up of a participle and a noun or pronoun, both in the genitive case and agreeing otherwise as well but having no grammatical relation to the context. It is used to indicate time during which, at which, or connected with which something takes place. The close of such a Greek phrase is shown by the superior letter [a] (e.g., Luke 3:1). There are variations of this. In Luke 12:36, two participles are used with no noun; it has to be supplied from the context. So also 2 Corinthians 7:15, and see the note on Romans 9:11 under "Notes on Particular Passages" below.

b. The *accusative* (or other case) *and infinitive*. Here what is in English the subject of the verb (the doer of the action) is put in the accusative (or other) case, and the verb itself is put in the infinitive. A superior letter [b] closes such a phrase (e.g., Luke 1:21).

c. The *dative of possession*. The possessor is put in the dative case. The idea may be grasped by comparing our English way of saying that a thing "belongs to so-and-so." The superior letter [c] shows this idiom (e.g., Luke 1:5, 7, 14).

d. The *genitive of purpose* or *result*. The infinitive of a verb is in the genitive case, as shown by the preceding definite article. The article itself can be ignored. Again the appropriate letter [d] shows the existence of the idiom (e.g., Matt. 2:13). The same idea can be shown without any article (e.g., Matt. 4:1).

e. The *dative of time*. This shows a point of time "in" or "at" which a thing happens (ἐν may or may not be used). The letter [e] indicates this (e.g., Luke 2:43; 18:35).

The constructions b and e can sometimes be combined (e.g., Luke 1:8).

Notes on Particular Passages

Mark 10:11—An article by Dr. Nigel Turner in *The Bible Translator* for October 1956 gives good reasons for understanding the verse thus, *αὐτήν* referring to the last woman mentioned (*ἄλλην*).

Mark 14:6—The *ἐν* here is somewhat puzzling. The parallel in Matthew (26:10) has *εἰς*, which would mean "to," "toward," or "for"; and Mark's *ἐν* must then be taken as equivalent in meaning to *εἰς*. This may throw light on 1 John 4:16.

Luke 7:14—It does not seem right to insist here on the passive voice of *ἐγέρθητι* (cf. 8:54 and, in another connection, 11:8). But our Lord "was raised," as are the dead generally; they do not "rise"; (see 1 Cor. 15, etc.).

John 8:25—"The answer of Jesus is one of the most disputed passages in the Gospel" (Godet). Nestle punctuates as a question; hence we have given what appears to be a reasonable rendering interrogatively.

Acts 7:46—The word *οἴκῳ* is a manuscript variant for *θεῷ*. There is some uncertainty as to how this reading arose; see the Authorized Version. Has Psalm 24:6, text and margin, any bearing on the matter?

Acts 18:10—The words *λαὸς πολύς* must not be understood as meaning "many persons." *λαός* is the regular word for the chosen people, Israel (almost without exception). Here in Corinth was to be a new community, taking the place of the Jewish population. So translate it "a great people."

Romans 1:12—This refers to their faith (= "confidence") in one another—Paul and his readers. "Mutual" is correct in Authorized Version, but it is generally misunderstood as being equivalent to "common," which it is not.

Romans 9:11—There is no noun agreeing with the two participles. But it is nevertheless a "genitive absolute" construction. The Authorized Version supplies the subject.

2 Corinthians 11:28—There is another view of Paul's words here. The word *ἐπίστασις* occurs in the New Testament only here and in Acts 24:12. The related noun *ἐπιστάτης* ("one standing over,"

"superintendent," "master") is peculiar to Luke (six times in his Gospel). Then there is a variant reading in our verse, *μου* instead of *μοι*. So the meaning may be—"my daily superintendence *or* attention." This would bring it into line with the remainder of the verse.

Philippians 3:16—This is, according to Burton, the only certain use in the New Testament of the "imperatival infinitive," Romans 12:15 being a probable example. Moulton thinks it highly probable in Titus 2:1–10. The epistolary *χαίρειν* (Acts 15:23; 23:26; James 1:1) is said to be the same in origin, though a verb of bidding may be assumed, as in fact we do find in 2 John 10, 11. Compare the French warning in railway carriages—*Ne pas se pencher au dehors*. In English we have such a full expression as "You are 'to do' so and so" (e.g., 2 Thess. 3:14). If Nestle's text is accepted here, it is an additional instance to those given under Philippians 3:16 above, though with a negative as a prohibition. (Textus Receptus, etc., give a plain imperative.) But perhaps we may insert "so as" ("mark this man, so as not to mix with him").

2 Timothy 4:3—The construction of the last three words of this verse is difficult. "Having itching ears" may be a workable paraphrase, but it cannot be said to represent literally the actual Greek. There is no word for "having"; and there is nothing corresponding to "itching" as a participial adjective qualifying "ears." *τὴν ἀκοήν* is accusative singular, the object of a verb—and the only verb is the participle that precedes. This is masculine plural, agreeing with *διδασκάλους*, and, while this latter is accusative, whereas the participle is nominative, this must be taken as an example of rational rather than grammatical concord. It is the teachers who "tickle" the ears of those concerned.

Hebrews 2:10—That is, it is God who perfected Jesus Christ (the author, or captain, of our salvation) by means of sufferings, whose work it is to lead many sons to glory; *ἀγαγόντα* ("leading," referring to Jesus) agrees with *ἀρχηγόν*, not with *αὐτῷ* ("him," i.e., God). Besides, there is a parallel between Joshua and Jesus, as both leaders of their peoples. In fine, it is the function of a captain to lead, and Jesus is the leader here.

Hebrews 9:16–17—We are aware of the problem in regard to *διαθήκη* in this passage; but this translation is no place for purporting to settle a question that has divided commentators. It must suffice to say that we have translated the word consistently as "covenant"; the idea of a legatee receiving something on the death of a testator by reason of the latter's having made a "testament" or "will" is, so far as we can see, quite non-biblical. The covenant victim, then, is "the one making covenant," unless the person establishing the covenant is to be understood as identifying himself with it; and the covenant is in fact ratified over the dead body or bodies. But other views are taken of the matter.

James 2:1—This is an example of two genitives in apposition. There are other instances of such a construction. In Colossians 1:18, the meaning must be "of the body (,) *of* the church"—the body is the church, as verse 24 says. Colossians 2:2 has "of God, of Christ." For Romans 11:17, see the note at that place. Regarding John 8:44 ("of the father (,) *of* the devil"), their father was the Devil.

Revelation 16:14—The word "Almighty" is not an adjective but another noun in apposition.

NOTE on Matthew 16:3; 27:65; Luke 12:56; Acts 21:37; 1 Thessalonians 4:4; 1 Timothy 3:5; James 4:17; 2 Peter 2:9—As in French, so in the Greek of the New Testament, we have the idea of "to know (how) to do" a thing as being the same as "to be able to do" it. But while the French use only *savoir*, not *connaître*, in this way, both *γινώσκω* and *οἶδα* have this meaning in the New Testament. In fact, it is the former in Matthew 16:3 and the latter in the parallel in Luke (12:56). So, in French, *Savez-vous nager?* = Know you to swim? = Can you swim? In all the above passages this seems to be the meaning. It may be noted that the Authorized Version so renders the verbs in some passages, in others giving "know how." The instance in James 4:17 may be arguable. Philippians 4:12 also may be considered, and Matthew 7:11 = Luke 11:13.

The New Revised Standard Version

To the Reader

This preface is addressed to you by the Committee of translators, who wish to explain, as briefly as possible, the origin and character of our work. The publication of our revision is yet another step in the long, continual process of making the Bible available in the form of the English language that is most widely current in our day. To summarize in a single sentence: the New Revised Standard Version of the Bible is an authorized revision of the Revised Standard Version, published in 1952, which was a revision of the American Standard Version, published in 1901, which, in turn, embodied earlier revisions of the King James Version, published in 1611.

The need for issuing a revision of the Revised Standard Version of the Bible arises from three circumstances: (*a*) the acquisition of still older Biblical manuscripts, (*b*) further investigation of linguistic features of the text, and (*c*) changes in preferred English usage. Consequently, in 1974 the Policies Committee of the Revised Standard Version, which is a standing committee of the National Council of the Churches of Christ in the U.S.A., authorized the preparation of a revision of the entire RSV Bible.

For the New Testament the Committee has based its work on the most recent edition of *The Greek New Testament,* prepared by an interconfessional and international committee and published by the United Bible Societies (1966; 3rd ed. corrected, 1983; information concerning changes to be introduced into the critical apparatus of the forthcoming 4th edition was available to the Committee). As in that edition, double brackets are used to enclose a few passages that are generally regarded to be later additions to their text, but which we have retained because of their evident antiquity and their importance in the textual tradition. Only in very rare instances have we replaced the text or the punctuation of the Bible Societies' edition by an alternative that seemed to us to be superior. Here and there in the footnotes the phrase, "Other ancient authorities read," identifies alternative readings preserved by Greek manuscripts and early versions. Alternative renderings of the text are indicated by the word "Or."

As for the style of English adopted for the present revision, among the mandates given to the Committee in 1980 by the Division of Education and Ministry of the National Council of Churches of Christ (which now holds the copyright of the RSV Bible) was the directive to continue in the tradition of the King James Bible, but to introduce such changes as are warranted on the basis of accuracy, clarity, euphony, and current English usage. Within the constraints set by the original texts and by the mandates of the Division, the Committee has followed the maxim, "As literal as possible, as free as necessary." As a consequence, the New Revised Standard Version (NRSV) remains essentially a literal translation. Paraphrastic renderings have been adopted only sparingly, and then chiefly to compensate for a deficiency in the English language—the lack of a common gender third person singular pronoun.

During the almost half a century since the publication of the RSV, many in the churches have become sensitive to the danger of linguistic sexism arising from the inherent bias of the English language towards the masculine gender, a bias that in the case of the Bible has often restricted or obscured the meaning of the original text. The mandates from the Division specified that, in references to men and women, masculine-oriented language should be eliminated as far as this can be done without altering passages that reflect the historical situation of ancient patriarchal culture. As can be appreciated, more than once the Committee found that the several, mandates stood in tension and even in conflict. The various concerns had to be balanced case by case in order to provide a faithful and acceptable rendering without using contrived English. In the vast majority of cases, however, inclusiveness has been attained by simple rephrasing or by introducing plural forms when this does not distort the meaning of the passage. Of course, in narrative and in parable no attempt was made to generalize the sex of individual persons.

It will be seen that in prayers addressed to God the archaic second person singular pronouns (*thee, thou, thine*) and verb forms (*art, hast, hadst*) are no longer used. Although some readers may regret this change, it should be pointed out that in the original languages neither the Old Testament nor the New makes any linguistic distinction between addressing a human being and addressing the Deity. Furthermore, in the tradition of the King James Version one will not expect to find the use of capital letters for pronouns that refer to the Deity—such capitalization is an unnecessary innovation that has only recently been introduced into a few

English translations of the Bible. Finally, we have left to the discretion of the licensed publishers such matters as section headings, cross-references, and clues to the pronunciation of proper names.

This new version seeks to preserve all that is best in the English Bible as it has been known and used through the years. It is intended for use in public reading and congregational worship, as well as in private study, instruction, and meditation. We have resisted the temptation to introduce terms and phrases that merely reflect current moods, and have tried to put the message of the Scriptures in simple, enduring words and expressions that are worthy to stand in the great tradition of the King James Bible and its predecessors. It is the hope and prayer of the translators that this version of the Bible may continue to hold a large place in congregational life and to speak to all readers, young and old alike, helping them to understand and believe and respond to its message.

For the Committee,
BRUCE M. METZGER

The New International Version

The New International Version of the New Testament, first published in 1973, is a completely new translation made by many scholars working directly from the Greek. The Greek text used in the work of translation was an eclectic one. Where existing texts differ, the translators made their choice of readings in accord with sound principles of textual criticism. Footnotes call attention to places where there was uncertainty about what constituted the original text. These have been introduced by the phrase "Some MSS add (*or* omit *or* read)."

As in all translations of the Scriptures, the precise meaning of the original text could not in every case be determined. In important instances of this kind, footnotes introduced by "Or" suggest an alternate rendering of the text. In the translation itself, brackets were occasionally used to indicate words or phrases supplied for clarification.

Certain convictions and aims guided the translators. They were all committed to the full authority and complete trustworthiness of the Scriptures. Therefore, their first concern was the accuracy of the translation and its fidelity to the thought of the New Testament writers. While they weighed the significance of the lexical and grammatical details of the Greek text, they strove for more than a word-for-word translation. Because thought patterns and syntax differ from language to language, faithful communication of the meaning of the writers of the New Testament demanded frequent modifications in sentence structure and constant regard for the contextual meanings of words.

Concern for clarity of style—that it should be idiomatic without being idiosyncratic, contemporary without being dated—also motivated the translators and their consultants. They consistently aimed at simplicity of expression, with sensitive attention to the connotation and sound of the chosen word. At the same time, they endeavored to avoid a sameness of style in order to reflect the varied styles and moods of the New Testament writers.

As for the omission of the pronouns "thou," "thee," and

"thine" in reference to the Deity, the translators felt that to retain these archaisms (along with the strange verb forms, such as *doest, wouldest,* and *hadst*) would have violated their aim of faithful translation. The Greek text uses no special pronouns to express reverence for God and Christ. Scripture is not enhanced by keeping, as a special mode of addressing Deity, forms that in the day of the King James Bible were simply the regular pronouns and verbs used in everyday speech, whether referring to God or to man.

The Greek Alphabet

Α	α	Alpha	a	
Β	β	Beta	b	
Γ	γ	Gamma	g	hard, as in be*g*in[1]
Δ	δ	Delta	d	
Ε	ε	Epsilon	e	short, as in m*e*t
Ζ	ζ	Zeta	z	
Η	η	Eta	e	long, as in sc*e*ne
Θ	θ	Theta	th	as in *th*in
Ι	ι	Iota	i	
Κ	κ	Kappa	k	
Λ	λ	Lambda	l	
Μ	μ	Mu	m	
Ν	ν	Nu	n	
Ξ	ξ	Xi	x	
Ο	ο	Omicron	o	short, as in l*o*t
Π	π	Pi	p	
Ρ	ρ	Rho	r	
Σ	σ, *final s*	Sigma	s[2]	
Τ	τ	Tau	t	
Υ	υ	Upsilon	u	
Φ	φ	Phi	ph	
Χ	χ	Chi	ch	hard, as in lo*ch*
Ψ	ψ	Psi	ps	
Ω	ω	Omega	o	long, as in thr*o*ne

[1] Except that before κ, χ or another γ, it is nasal—ng, as in a*nch*or.
[2] Sharp as in thi*s*, but flat before β or μ, as in a*s*bestos, di*s*mal.

The left-hand column contains the NRSV text, the right-hand column, the NIV text.

The Gospel According
to
Matthew
Chapter 1
The Genealogy of Jesus the Messiah

AN account of the gene-
alogy[a] of Jesus the
Messiah,[b] the son of David, the son of Abraham.
2 Abraham was the fa-
ther of Isaac, and Isaac the
father of Jacob, and Jacob
the father of Judah and his
brothers, 3 and Judah the
father of Perez and Zerah
by Tamar, and Perez the father of Hezron, and Hez-
ron the father of Aram,
4 and Aram the father of
Aminadab, and Aminadab
the father of Nahshon, and
Nahshon the father of Salmon, 5 and Salmon the fa-
ther of Boaz by Rahab, and
Boaz the father of Obed by
Ruth, and Obed the father
of Jesse, 6 and Jesse the father of King David.
And David was the fa-
ther of Solomon by the wife
of Uriah, 7 and Solomon the
father of Rehoboam, and
Rehoboam the father of
Abijah, and Abijah the father of Asaph,[c] 8 and
Asaph[c] the father of Jehoshaphat, and Jehosha-
phat the father of Joram,
and Joram the father of Uzziah, 9 and Uzziah the father of Jotham, and Jotham
the father of Ahaz, and
Ahaz the father of Hezekiah, 10 and Hezekiah the father of Manasseh, and Ma-
nasseh the father of
Amos,[d] and Amos[d] the father of Josiah, 11 and Josiah
the father of Jechoniah and
his brothers, at the time of
the deportation to Babylon.
12 And after the depor-
tation to Babylon: Jechoniah was the father of Salathiel, and Salathiel the father
of Zerubbabel, 13 and Ze-
rubbabel the father of Abiud, and Abiud the father of
Eliakim, and Eliakim the

[a] Or *birth*
[b] Or *Jesus Christ*
[c] Other ancient authorities read *Asa*
[d] Other ancient authorities read *Amon*

ΚΑΤΑ ΜΑΘΘΑΙΟΝ
According to Matthew

1 Βίβλος γενέσεως Ἰησοῦ Χριστοῦ
[The] book of [the] generation of Jesus Christ
υἱοῦ Δαυὶδ υἱοῦ Ἀβραάμ.
son of David son of Abraham.

2 Ἀβραὰμ ἐγέννησεν τὸν Ἰσαάκ, Ἰσαὰκ δὲ
Abraham begat – Isaac, and Isaac
ἐγέννησεν τὸν Ἰακώβ, Ἰακὼβ δὲ ἐγέννησεν τὸν
begat – Jacob, and Jacob begat –
Ἰούδαν καὶ τοὺς ἀδελφοὺς αὐτοῦ, **3** Ἰούδας δὲ
Judas and the brothers of him, and Judas
ἐγέννησεν τὸν Φάρες καὶ τὸν Ζάρα ἐκ τῆς
begat – Phares and – Zara out of –
Θαμάρ, Φάρες δὲ ἐγέννησεν τὸν Ἑσρώμ,
Thamar, and Phares begat – Esrom,
Ἑσρὼμ δὲ ἐγέννησεν τὸν Ἀράμ, **4** Ἀρὰμ δὲ
and Esrom begat – Aram, and Aram
ἐγέννησεν τὸν Ἀμιναδάβ, Ἀμιναδὰβ δὲ
begat – Aminadab, and Aminadab
ἐγέννησεν τὸν Ναασσών, Ναασσὼν δὲ ἐγέννησεν
begat – Naasson, and Naasson begat
τὸν Σαλμών, **5** Σαλμὼν δὲ ἐγέννησεν τὸν Βόες
– Salmon, and Salmon begat – Booz
ἐκ τῆς Ῥαχάβ, Βόες δὲ ἐγέννησεν τὸν Ἰωβὴδ
out of – Rachab, and Booz begat – Obed
ἐκ τῆς Ῥούθ, Ἰωβὴδ δὲ ἐγέννησεν τὸν Ἰεσσαί,
out of – Ruth, and Obed begat – Jesse,
6 Ἰεσσαὶ δὲ ἐγέννησεν τὸν Δαυὶδ τὸν βασιλέα.
and Jesse begat – David the king.
Δαυὶδ δὲ ἐγέννησεν τὸν Σολομῶνα ἐκ τῆς
And David begat – Solomon out of the

τοῦ Οὐρίου, **7** Σολομὼν δὲ ἐγέννησεν
[one who had been the wife] – of Uriah, and Solomon begat
τὸν Ῥοβοάμ, Ῥοβοὰμ δὲ ἐγέννησεν τὸν
– Roboam, and Roboam begat –
Ἀβιά, Ἀβιὰ δὲ ἐγέννησεν τὸν Ἀσάφ, **8** Ἀσὰφ
Abia, and Abia begat – Asaph, and Asaph
δὲ ἐγέννησεν τὸν Ἰωσαφάτ, Ἰωσαφὰτ δὲ
begat – Josaphat, and Josaphat
ἐγέννησεν τὸν Ἰωράμ, Ἰωρὰμ δὲ ἐγέννησεν τὸν
begat – Joram, and Joram begat –
Ὀζίαν, **9** Ὀζίας δὲ ἐγέννησεν τὸν Ἰωαθάμ,
Ozias, and Ozias begat – Joatham,
Ἰωαθὰμ δὲ ἐγέννησεν τὸν Ἀχάζ, Ἀχὰζ δὲ
and Joatham begat – Achaz, and Achaz
ἐγέννησεν τὸν Ἑζεκίαν, **10** Ἑζεκίας δὲ
begat – Hezekias, and Hezekias
ἐγέννησεν τὸν Μανασσῆ, Μανασσῆς δὲ ἐγέννησεν
begat – Manasses, and Manasses begat
τὸν Ἀμώς, Ἀμὼς δὲ ἐγέννησεν τὸν Ἰωσίαν,
– Amos, and Amos begat – Josias,
11 Ἰωσίας δὲ ἐγέννησεν τὸν Ἰεχονίαν καὶ
and Josias begat – Jechonias and
τοὺς ἀδελφοὺς αὐτοῦ ἐπὶ τῆς μετοικεσίας
the brothers of him at the deportation
Βαβυλῶνος. **12** Μετὰ δὲ τὴν μετοικεσίαν
of Babylon. And after the deportation
Βαβυλῶνος Ἰεχονίας ἐγέννησεν τὸν Σαλαθιήλ,
of Babylon Jechonias begat – Salathiel,
Σαλαθιὴλ δὲ ἐγέννησεν τὸν Ζοροβαβέλ,
and Salathiel begat – Zorobabel,
13 Ζοροβαβὲλ δὲ ἐγέννησεν τὸν Ἀβιούδ,
and Zorobabel begat – Abiud,
Ἀβιοὺδ δὲ ἐγέννησεν τὸν Ἐλιακίμ, Ἐλιακὶμ δὲ
and Abiud begat – Eliakim, and Eliakim

Matthew
Chapter 1
The Genealogy of Jesus

A RECORD of the gene-
alogy of Jesus Christ
the son of David, the son of
Abraham:

2 Abraham was the father of Isaac,
Isaac the father of Jacob,
Jacob the father of Judah and his brothers,
3 Judah the father of Perez and Zerah, whose mother was Tamar,
Perez the father of Hezron,
Hezron the father of Ram,
4 Ram the father of Amminadab,
Amminadab the father of Nahshon,
Nahshon the father of Salmon,
5 Salmon the father of Boaz, whose mother was Rahab,
Boaz the father of Obed, whose mother was Ruth,
Obed the father of Jesse,
6 and Jesse the father of King David.

David was the father of Solomon, whose mother had been Uriah's wife,
7 Solomon the father of Rehoboam,
Rehoboam the father of Abijah,
Abijah the father of Asa,
8 Asa the father of Jehoshaphat,
Jehoshaphat the father of Jehoram,
Jehoram the father of Uzziah,
9 Uzziah the father of Jotham,
Jotham the father of Ahaz,
Ahaz the father of Hezekiah,
10 Hezekiah the father of Manasseh,
Manasseh the father of Amon,
Amon the father of Josiah,
11 and Josiah the father of Jeconiah[a] and his brothers at the time of the exile to Babylon.

12 After the exile to Babylon:
Jeconiah was the father of Shealtiel,
Shealtiel the father of Zerubbabel,
13 Zerubbabel the father of Abiud,
Abiud the father of Eliakim,
Eliakim the father of

[a] *11* That is, Jehoiachin; also in verse 12

father of Azor, 14 and Azor
the father of Zadok, and
Zadok the father of Achim,
and Achim the father of Eliud, 15 and Eliud the father
of Eleazar, and Eleazar the
father of Matthan, and
Matthan the father of Ja-
cob, 16 and Jacob the father
of Joseph the husband of
Mary, of whom Jesus was
born, who is called the
Messiah.[e]
17 So all the generations
from Abraham to David are
fourteen generations; and
from David to the deportation to Babylon, fourteen
generations; and from the
deportation to Babylon to
the Messiah,[e] fourteen
generations.

The Birth of Jesus the Messiah

18 Now the birth of
Jesus the Messiah[b] took
place in this way. When his
mother Mary had been en-
gaged to Joseph, but before
they lived together, she
was found to be with child
from the Holy Spirit. 19 Her
husband Joseph, being a
righteous man and unwill-
ing to expose her to public
disgrace, planned to dis-
miss her quietly. 20 But just
when he had resolved to do
this, an angel of the Lord
appeared to him in a dream
and said, "Joseph, son of
David, do not be afraid to
take Mary as your wife, for
the child conceived in her is
from the Holy Spirit. 21 She
will bear a son, and you are
to name him Jesus, for he
will save his people from
their sins." 22 All this took
place to fulfill what had
been spoken by the Lord
through the prophet:
23 "Look, the virgin
shall conceive
and bear a son,

[e] Or *the Christ*

ἐγέννησεν τὸν Ἀζώρ, 14 Ἀζὼρ δὲ ἐγέννησεν
begat – Azor, and Azor begat
τὸν Σαδώκ, Σαδὼκ δὲ ἐγέννησεν τὸν Ἀχίμ,
– Sadoc, and Sadoc begat – Achim,
Ἀχὶμ δὲ ἐγέννησεν τὸν Ἐλιούδ, 15 Ἐλιοὺδ δὲ
and Achim begat – Eliud, and Eliud
ἐγέννησεν τὸν Ἐλεαζάρ, Ἐλεαζὰρ δὲ ἐγέννησεν
begat – Eleazar, and Eleazar begat
τὸν Μαθθάν, Μαθθὰν δὲ ἐγέννησεν τὸν Ἰακώβ,
– Matthan, and Matthan begat – Jacob,
16 Ἰακὼβ δὲ ἐγέννησεν τὸν Ἰωσὴφ τὸν ἄνδρα
and Jacob begat – Joseph the husband
Μαρίας, ἐξ ἧς ἐγεννήθη Ἰησοῦς ὁ λεγόμενος
of Mary, of whom was born Jesus the [one] called
Χριστός.
Christ.
17 Πᾶσαι οὖν αἱ γενεαὶ ἀπὸ Ἀβραὰμ
Therefore all the generations from Abraham
ἕως Δαυὶδ γενεαὶ δεκατέσσαρες, καὶ ἀπὸ
until David generations fourteen, and from
Δαυὶδ ἕως τῆς μετοικεσίας Βαβυλῶνος γενεαὶ
David until the deportation of Babylon generations
δεκατέσσαρες, καὶ ἀπὸ τῆς μετοικεσίας Βαβυ-
fourteen, and from the deportation of Baby-
λῶνος ἕως τοῦ Χριστοῦ γενεαὶ δεκατέσσαρες.
lon until the Christ generations fourteen.
18 Τοῦ δὲ Ἰησοῦ Χριστοῦ ἡ γένεσις
– Now [3]of Jesus [4]Christ [1]the [2]birth
οὕτως ἦν. μνηστευθείσης τῆς μητρὸς αὐτοῦ
[5]thus [6]was. Being betrothed the mother of him
=When his mother Mary was betrothed
Μαρίας τῷ Ἰωσήφ, πρὶν ἢ συνελθεῖν αὐτοὺς
Mary[a] – to Joseph, before to come together them[b]
=before they came together
εὑρέθη ἐν γαστρὶ ἔχουσα ἐκ πνεύματος
[1]she was found [3]in [4]womb [2]having of(by) [the] Spirit
= she was pregnant
ἁγίου. 19 Ἰωσὴφ δὲ ὁ ἀνὴρ αὐτῆς,
Holy. Now Joseph the husband of her,
δίκαιος ὢν καὶ μὴ θέλων αὐτὴν δειγμα-
[2]just [1]being and not wishing her to hold up as an
τίσαι, ἐβουλήθη λάθρα ἀπολῦσαι αὐτήν.
example, resolved secretly to dismiss her.
20 ταῦτα δὲ αὐτοῦ ἐνθυμηθέντος, ἰδοὺ
But these things him thinking on,[a] behold
=while he thought on these things,
ἄγγελος κυρίου κατ' ὄναρ ἐφάνη
an angel of [the] Lord by a dream appeared
αὐτῷ λέγων· Ἰωσὴφ υἱὸς Δαυίδ, μὴ
to him saying: Joseph son of David, [2]not
φοβηθῇς παραλαβεῖν Μαρίαν τὴν
[1]fear thou to take Mary the
γυναῖκά σου· τὸ γὰρ ἐν αὐτῇ γεννηθὲν
wife of thee: for the thing in her begotten
ἐκ πνεύματός ἐστιν ἁγίου. 21 τέξεται δὲ
[2]of [3][the] [5]Spirit [1]is [4]Holy. And she will bear
υἱόν, καὶ καλέσεις τὸ ὄνομα αὐτοῦ
a son, and thou shalt call the name of him
Ἰησοῦν· αὐτὸς γὰρ σώσει τὸν λαὸν
Jesus; for he will save the people
αὐτοῦ ἀπὸ τῶν ἁμαρτιῶν αὐτῶν. 22 Τοῦτο δὲ
of him from the sins of them. Now [2]this
ὅλον γέγονεν ἵνα πληρωθῇ τὸ ῥηθὲν
[1]all has occurred in order that might be fulfilled the [thing] spoken
ὑπὸ κυρίου διὰ τοῦ προφήτου λέγοντος·
by [the] Lord through the prophet saying:
23 ἰδοὺ ἡ παρθένος ἐν γαστρὶ ἕξει
Behold the virgin [2]in [3]womb [1]will have

Azor,
14 Azor the father of Za-
dok,
Zadok the father of
Akim,
Akim the father of Eli-
ud,
15 Eliud the father of Eleazar,
Eleazar the father of
Matthan,
Matthan the father of
Jacob,
16 and Jacob the father of
Joseph, the husband
of Mary, of whom
was born Jesus, who
is called Christ.
17 Thus there were four-
teen generations in all from
Abraham to David, four-
teen from David to the exile
to Babylon, and fourteen
from the exile to the
Christ.[b]

The Birth of Jesus Christ

18 This is how the birth of
Jesus Christ came about:
His mother Mary was
pledged to be married to Joseph, but before they came
together, she was found to
be with child through the
Holy Spirit. 19 Because Joseph her husband was a
righteous man and did not
want to expose her to public disgrace, he had in mind
to divorce her quietly.
20 But after he had considered this, an angel of the
Lord appeared to him in a
dream and said, "Joseph
son of David, do not be
afraid to take Mary home
as your wife, because what
is conceived in her is from
the Holy Spirit. 21 She will
give birth to a son, and you
are to give him the name
Jesus,[c] because he will
save his people from their
sins."
22 All this took place to
fulfill what the Lord had
said through the prophet:
23 "The virgin will be with
child and will give birth to
a son, and they will call

[b] 17 Or *Messiah*. "The Christ" (Greek) and "the Messiah" (Hebrew) both mean "the Anointed One."

[c] 21 *Jesus* is the Greek form of *Joshua*, which means *the LORD saves*.

and they shall name
him
Emmanuel,"
which means, "God is with
us." 24 When Joseph awoke
from sleep, he did as the
angel of the Lord com-
manded him; he took her as
his wife, 25 but had no marital relations with her until
she had borne a son;[f] and
he named him Jesus.

καὶ τέξεται υἱόν, καὶ καλέσουσιν τὸ
and will bear a son, and they will call the
ὄνομα αὐτοῦ Ἐμμανουήλ, ὅ ἐστιν
name of him Emmanuel, which is
μεθερμηνευόμενον μεθ᾽ ἡμῶν ὁ θεός.
being interpreted with us - God.
24 ἐγερθεὶς δὲ [ὁ] Ἰωσὴφ ἀπὸ τοῦ
Then [2]being raised - [1]Joseph from the(his)
ὕπνου ἐποίησεν ὡς προσέταξεν αὐτῷ ὁ
sleep did as bade him the
ἄγγελος κυρίου, καὶ παρέλαβεν τὴν
angel of [the] Lord, and took the
γυναῖκα αὐτοῦ· 25 καὶ οὐκ ἐγίνωσκεν
wife of him; and knew not
αὐτὴν ἕως [οὗ] ἔτεκεν υἱόν· καὶ ἐκάλεσεν
her until she bore a son; and he called
τὸ ὄνομα αὐτοῦ Ἰησοῦν.
the name of him Jesus.

him Immanuel"[d]—which
means, "God with us."
24When Joseph woke up,
he did what the angel of the
Lord had commanded him
and took Mary home as his
wife. 25But he had no union
with her until she gave birth
to a son. And he gave him
the name Jesus.

Chapter 2

The Visit of the Wise Men

IN the time of King Her-
od, after Jesus was born
in Bethlehem of Judea,
wise men[g] from the East
came to Jerusalem, 2ask-
ing, "Where is the child
who has been born king of
the Jews? For we observed
his star at its rising,[h] and
have come to pay him hom-
age." 3When King Herod
heard this, he was frightened, and all Jerusalem
with him; 4and calling together all the chief priests
and scribes of the people,
he inquired of them where
the Messiah[e] was to be
born. 5They told him, "In
Bethlehem of Judea; for so
it has been written by the
prophet:
6 'And you, Bethlehem,
in the land
of Judah,
are by no means
least among the
rulers of Judah;
for from you shall
come a ruler
who is to shepherd[i]
my
people Israel.' "
7 Then Herod secretly
called for the wise men[j]
and learned from them the
exact time when the star
had appeared. 8Then he
sent them to Bethlehem,
saying, "Go and search dili-

2 Τοῦ δὲ Ἰησοῦ γεννηθέντος ἐν Βηθλέεμ
- Now Jesus having been born[a] in Bethlehem
=when Jesus was born
τῆς Ἰουδαίας ἐν ἡμέραις Ἡρῴδου τοῦ
- of Judæa in [the] days of Herod the
βασιλέως, ἰδοὺ μάγοι ἀπὸ ἀνατολῶν
king, behold magi from [the] east
παρεγένοντο εἰς Ἱεροσόλυμα 2 λέγοντες·
arrived in Jerusalem saying:
ποῦ ἐστιν ὁ τεχθεὶς βασιλεὺς τῶν
Where is the [one] born king of the
Ἰουδαίων; εἴδομεν γὰρ αὐτοῦ τὸν ἀστέρα
Jews? for we saw of him the star
ἐν τῇ ἀνατολῇ, καὶ ἤλθομεν προσκυνῆσαι
in the east, and came to worship
αὐτῷ. 3 ἀκούσας δὲ ὁ βασιλεὺς Ἡρῴδης
him. Now hearing [this] the king Herod
ἐταράχθη, καὶ πᾶσα Ἱεροσόλυμα μετ᾽
was troubled, and all Jerusalem with
αὐτοῦ, 4 καὶ συναγαγὼν πάντας τοὺς
him, and having assembled all the
ἀρχιερεῖς καὶ γραμματεῖς τοῦ λαοῦ
chief priests and scribes of the people
ἐπυνθάνετο παρ᾽ αὐτῶν ποῦ ὁ χριστὸς
he inquired from them where the Christ
γεννᾶται. 5 οἱ δὲ εἶπαν αὐτῷ· ἐν
is being born. And they told him: In
Βηθλέεμ τῆς Ἰουδαίας· οὕτως γὰρ
Bethlehem - of Judæa; for thus
γέγραπται διὰ τοῦ προφήτου· 6 καὶ
it has been written through the prophet: And
σὺ Βηθλέεμ, γῆ Ἰούδα, οὐδαμῶς ἐλαχίστη
thou Bethlehem, land of Juda, [2]not at all [3]least
εἶ ἐν τοῖς ἡγεμόσιν Ἰούδα. ἐκ σοῦ γὰρ
[1]art among the governors of Juda. For out of thee
ἐξελεύσεται ἡγούμενος, ὅστις ποιμανεῖ
will come forth a governor, who will shepherd
τὸν λαόν μου τὸν Ἰσραήλ.
the people of me - Israel.
7 Τότε Ἡρῴδης λάθρα καλέσας τοὺς
Then Herod secretly calling the
μάγους ἠκρίβωσεν παρ᾽ αὐτῶν τὸν
magi inquired carefully from them the
χρόνον τοῦ φαινομένου ἀστέρος, 8 καὶ
time of the appearing star, and
πέμψας αὐτοὺς εἰς Βηθλέεμ εἶπεν·
sending them to Bethlehem said:

Chapter 2

The Visit of the Magi

AFTER Jesus was born in
Bethlehem in Judea,
during the time of King
Herod, Magi[e] from the
east came to Jerusalem
2and asked, "Where is the
one who has been born king
of the Jews? We saw his
star in the east[f] and have
come to worship him."
3When King Herod heard
this he was disturbed, and
all Jerusalem with him.
4When he had called to-
gether all the people's chief
priests and teachers of the
law, he asked them where
the Christ[g] was to be born.
5"In Bethlehem in Judea,"
they replied, "for this is
what the prophet has written:

6" 'But you, Bethlehem,
in the land of Judah,
are by no means least
among the rulers of
Judah;
for out of you will come
a ruler
who will be the
shepherd of my
people Israel.'[h]"

7Then Herod called the
Magi secretly and found
out from them the exact
time the star had appeared.
8He sent them to Bethle-
hem and said, "Go and

[f]Other ancient authorities read *her firstborn son*
[g]Or *astrologers*; Gk *magi*
[h]Or *in the East*
[i]Or *rule*
[j]Or *astrologers*; Gk *magi*

[d]23 Isaiah 7:14
[e]1 Traditionally *Wise Men*
[f]2 Or *star when it rose*
[g]4 Or *Messiah*
[h]6 Micah 5:2

gently for the child; and when you have found him, bring me word so that I may also go and pay him homage." 9 When they had heard the king, they set out; and there, ahead of them, went the star that they had seen at its rising,[k] until it stopped over the place where the child was. 10 When they saw that the star had stopped,[l] they were overwhelmed with joy. 11 On entering the house, they saw the child with Mary his mother; and they knelt down and paid him homage. Then, opening their treasure chests, they offered him gifts of gold, frankincense, and myrrh. 12 And having been warned in a dream not to return to Herod, they left for their own country by another road.

The Escape to Egypt

13 Now after they had left, an angel of the Lord appeared to Joseph in a dream and said, "Get up, take the child and his mother, and flee to Egypt, and remain there until I tell you; for Herod is about to search for the child, to destroy him." 14 Then Joseph[m] got up, took the child and his mother by night, and went to Egypt, 15 and remained there until the death of Herod. This was to fulfill what had been spoken by the Lord through the prophet, "Out of Egypt I have called my son."

The Massacre of the Infants

16 When Herod saw that he had been tricked by the wise men,[j] he was infuriated, and he sent and killed all the children in and around Bethlehem who

[k] Or *in the East*
[l] Gk *saw the star*
[m] Gk *he*

πορευθέντες ἐξετάσατε ἀκριβῶς περὶ τοῦ
Going question ye carefully concerning the
παιδίου· ἐπὰν δὲ εὕρητε, ἀπαγγείλατέ
child; and when ye find, report
μοι, ὅπως κἀγὼ ἐλθὼν προσκυνήσω αὐτῷ.
to me, so that I also coming may worship him.
9 οἱ δὲ ἀκούσαντες τοῦ βασιλέως ἐπορεύθησαν·
So they hearing the king went;
καὶ ἰδοὺ ὁ ἀστήρ, ὃν εἶδον ἐν τῇ
and behold the star, which they saw in the
ἀνατολῇ, προῆγεν αὐτοὺς ἕως ἐλθὼν
east, went before them until coming
ἐστάθη ἐπάνω οὗ ἦν τὸ παιδίον. **10** ἰδόντες
it stood over where was the child. ²seeing
δὲ τὸν ἀστέρα ἐχάρησαν χαρὰν μεγάλην
¹And the star they rejoiced [with] a joy great
σφόδρα. **11** καὶ ἐλθόντες εἰς τὴν οἰκίαν
exceedingly. And coming into the house
εἶδον τὸ παιδίον μετὰ Μαρίας τῆς μητρὸς
they saw the child with Mary the mother
αὐτοῦ, καὶ πεσόντες προσεκύνησαν αὐτῷ,
of him, and falling they worshipped him,
καὶ ἀνοίξαντες τοὺς θησαυροὺς αὐτῶν
and opening the treasures of them
προσήνεγκαν αὐτῷ δῶρα, χρυσὸν καὶ
they offered to him gifts, gold and
λίβανον καὶ σμύρναν. **12** καὶ χρηματισθέντες
frankincense and myrrh. And having been warned
κατ' ὄναρ μὴ ἀνακάμψαι πρὸς Ἡρῴδην,
by a dream not to return to Herod,
δι' ἄλλης ὁδοῦ ἀνεχώρησαν εἰς τὴν
by another way they departed to the
χώραν αὐτῶν.
country of them.
13 Ἀναχωρησάντων δὲ αὐτῶν, ἰδοὺ
Now having departed them,* behold
= when they had departed,
ἄγγελος κυρίου φαίνεται κατ' ὄναρ τῷ
an angel of [the] Lord appears by a dream –
Ἰωσὴφ λέγων· ἐγερθεὶς παράλαβε τὸ
to Joseph saying: Rising take thou the
παιδίον καὶ τὴν μητέρα αὐτοῦ, καὶ φεῦγε
child and the mother of him, and flee
εἰς Αἴγυπτον, καὶ ἴσθι ἐκεῖ ἕως ἂν εἴπω
into Egypt, and be there until I tell
σοι· μέλλει γὰρ Ἡρῴδης ζητεῖν τὸ παιδίον τοῦ
thee; for ²is about ¹Herod to seek the child –
ἀπολέσαι αὐτό. **14** ὁ δὲ ἐγερθεὶς παρέλαβεν
to destroy[d] him. So he rising took
τὸ παιδίον καὶ τὴν μητέρα αὐτοῦ
the child and the mother of him
νυκτὸς καὶ ἀνεχώρησεν εἰς Αἴγυπτον,
of(by) night and departed to Egypt,
15 καὶ ἦν ἐκεῖ ἕως τῆς τελευτῆς Ἡρῴδου·
and was there until the death of Herod;
ἵνα πληρωθῇ τὸ ῥηθὲν ὑπὸ κυρίου
in order that might be fulfilled the [thing] spoken by [the] Lord
διὰ τοῦ προφήτου λέγοντος· ἐξ
through the prophet saying: Out of
Αἰγύπτου ἐκάλεσα τὸν υἱόν μου.
Egypt I called the son of me.
16 Τότε Ἡρῴδης ἰδὼν ὅτι ἐνεπαίχθη
Then Herod seeing that he was mocked
ὑπὸ τῶν μάγων ἐθυμώθη λίαν, καὶ
by the magi was angered exceedingly, and
ἀποστείλας ἀνεῖλεν πάντας τοὺς παῖδας
sending killed all the boy-children

make a careful search for the child. As soon as you find him, report to me, so that I too may go and worship him."

9 After they had heard the king, they went on their way, and the star they had seen in the east[i] went ahead of them until it stopped over the place where the child was. 10 When they saw the star, they were overjoyed. 11 On coming to the house, they saw the child with his mother Mary, and they bowed down and worshiped him. Then they opened their treasures and presented him with gifts of gold and of incense and of myrrh. 12 And having been warned in a dream not to go back to Herod, they returned to their country by another route.

The Escape to Egypt

13 When they had gone, an angel of the Lord appeared to Joseph in a dream. "Get up," he said, "take the child and his mother and escape to Egypt. Stay there until I tell you, for Herod is going to search for the child to kill him."

14 So he got up, took the child and his mother during the night and left for Egypt, 15 where he stayed until the death of Herod. And so was fulfilled what the Lord had said through the prophet: "Out of Egypt I called my son."[j]

16 When Herod realized that he had been outwitted by the Magi, he was furious, and he gave orders to kill all the boys in Bethle-

[i] *9* Or *seen when it rose*
[j] *15* Hosea 11:1

were two years old or un-
der, according to the time
that he had learned from
the wise men.[j] 17Then was
fulfilled what had been spoken through the prophet
Jeremiah:

18 "A voice was heard in
Ramah,
wailing and loud
lamentation,
Rachel weeping for
her children;
she refused to be
consoled,
because they are
no more."

The Return from Egypt

19 When Herod died, an
angel of the Lord suddenly
appeared in a dream to Joseph in Egypt and said,
20"Get up, take the child
and his mother, and go to
the land of Israel, for those
who were seeking the
child's life are dead."
21Then Joseph[m] got up,
took the child and his mother, and went to the land of
Israel. 22But when he
heard that Archelaus was
ruling over Judea in place
of his father Herod, he was
afraid to go there. And after
being warned in a dream,
he went away to the district
of Galilee. 23There he
made his home in a town
called Nazareth, so that
what had been spoken
through the prophets might
be fulfilled, "He will be
called a Nazorean."

τοὺς ἐν Βηθλέεμ καὶ ἐν πᾶσι τοῖς
– in Bethlehem and in all the
ὁρίοις αὐτῆς ἀπὸ διετοῦς καὶ κατωτέρω,
districts of it from two years and under,
κατὰ τὸν χρόνον ὃν ἠκρίβωσεν παρὰ τῶν
according to the time which he strictly inquired from the
μάγων. **17** τότε ἐπληρώθη τὸ ῥηθὲν διὰ
magi. Then was fulfilled the [thing] spoken through
Ἰερεμίου τοῦ προφήτου λέγοντος· **18** φωνὴ
Jeremiah the prophet saying: A voice
ἐν Ῥαμὰ ἠκούσθη, κλαυθμὸς καὶ ὀδυρμὸς
in Rama was heard, weeping and mourning
πολύς· Ῥαχὴλ κλαίουσα τὰ τέκνα αὐτῆς,
much; Rachel weeping for the children of her,
καὶ οὐκ ἤθελεν παρακληθῆναι, ὅτι
and would not *to* be comforted, because
οὐκ εἰσίν.
they are not.

19 Τελευτήσαντος δὲ τοῦ Ἡρῴδου, ἰδοὺ
But dying – Herod,[a] behold
= Herod having died,
ἄγγελος κυρίου φαίνεται κατ' ὄναρ τῷ
an angel of [the] Lord appears by a dream
Ἰωσὴφ ἐν Αἰγύπτῳ **20** λέγων· ἐγερθεὶς
to Joseph in Egypt saying: Rising
παράλαβε τὸ παιδίον καὶ τὴν μητέρα
take thou the child and the mother
αὐτοῦ, καὶ πορεύου εἰς γῆν Ἰσραήλ·
of him, and go into [the] land of Israel;
τεθνήκασιν γὰρ οἱ ζητοῦντες τὴν ψυχὴν
for have died the [ones] seeking the life
τοῦ παιδίου. **21** ὁ δὲ ἐγερθεὶς παρέλαβεν
of the child. So he rising took
τὸ παιδίον καὶ τὴν μητέρα αὐτοῦ καὶ
the child and the mother of him and
εἰσῆλθεν εἰς γῆν Ἰσραήλ. **22** ἀκούσας δὲ
entered into [the] land of Israel. But hearing
ὅτι Ἀρχέλαος βασιλεύει τῆς Ἰουδαίας
that Archelaus reigns over – Judæa
ἀντὶ τοῦ πατρὸς αὐτοῦ Ἡρῴδου ἐφοβήθη
instead of the father of him Herod he feared
ἐκεῖ ἀπελθεῖν· χρηματισθεὶς δὲ κατ'
there to go; and being warned by
ὄναρ ἀνεχώρησεν εἰς τὰ μέρη τῆς
a dream he departed into the parts –
Γαλιλαίας, **23** καὶ ἐλθὼν κατῴκησεν εἰς
of Galilee, and coming dwelt in
πόλιν λεγομένην Ναζαρέθ· ὅπως πληρωθῇ
a city called Nazareth; so that was fulfilled
τὸ ῥηθὲν διὰ τῶν προφητῶν ὅτι
the [thing] spoken through the prophets[,] –
Ναζωραῖος κληθήσεται.
A Nazarene he shall be called.

hem and its vicinity who
were two years old and under, in accordance with the
time he had learned from
the Magi. 17Then what was
said through the prophet
Jeremiah was fulfilled:

18"A voice is heard in
Ramah,
weeping and great
mourning,
Rachel weeping for her
children
and refusing to be
comforted,
because they are no
more."[k]

The Return to Nazareth

19After Herod died, an
angel of the Lord appeared
in a dream to Joseph in
Egypt 20and said, "Get up,
take the child and his mother and go to the land of Israel, for those who were trying to take the child's life
are dead."

21So he got up, took the
child and his mother and
went to the land of Israel.
22But when he heard that
Archelaus was reigning in
Judea in place of his father
Herod, he was afraid to go
there. Having been warned
in a dream, he withdrew to
the district of Galilee, 23and
he went and lived in a town
called Nazareth. So was
fulfilled what was said
through the prophets: "He
will be called a Nazarene."

Chapter 3

The Proclamation of John the Baptist

IN those days John the
Baptist appeared in the
wilderness of Judea, pro-
claiming, 2"Repent, for the
kingdom of heaven has
come near."[n] 3This is the
one of whom the prophet
Isaiah spoke when he said,
"The voice of one
crying out in

[n] Or *is at hand*

3 Ἐν δὲ ταῖς ἡμέραις ἐκείναις παραγίνεται
Now in – days those arrives
Ἰωάννης ὁ βαπτιστὴς κηρύσσων ἐν τῇ
John the Baptist proclaiming in the
ἐρήμῳ τῆς Ἰουδαίας, **2** λέγων· μετανοεῖτε·
wilderness – of Judæa, saying: Repent ye;
ἤγγικεν γὰρ ἡ βασιλεία τῶν οὐρανῶν.
for has come near the kingdom of the heavens.
3 οὗτος γάρ ἐστιν ὁ ῥηθεὶς διὰ Ἠσαΐου
For this is the [one] spoken [of] through Isaiah
τοῦ προφήτου λέγοντος· φωνὴ βοῶντος
the prophet saying: A voice of [one] crying

Chapter 3

John the Baptist Prepares the Way

IN those days John the
Baptist came, preaching
in the Desert of Judea 2and
saying, "Repent, for the
kingdom of heaven is
near." 3This is he who was
spoken of through the
prophet Isaiah:

"A voice of one calling

[k] 18 Jer. 31:15

the wilderness:
'Prepare the way of
the Lord,
make his paths
straight.' "

[4]Now John wore clothing of camel's hair with a leather belt around his waist, and his food was locusts and wild honey. [5]Then the people of Jerusalem and all Judea were going out to him, and all the region along the Jordan, [6]and they were baptized by him in the river Jordan, confessing their sins.

7 But when he saw many Pharisees and Sadducees coming for baptism, he said to them, "You brood of vipers! Who warned you to flee from the wrath to come? [8]Bear fruit worthy of repentance. [9]Do not presume to say to yourselves, 'We have Abraham as our ancestor'; for I tell you, God is able from these stones to raise up children to Abraham. [10]Even now the ax is lying at the root of the trees; every tree therefore that does not bear good fruit is cut down and thrown into the fire.

11 "I baptize you with[o] water for repentance, but one who is more powerful than I is coming after me; I am not worthy to carry his sandals. He will baptize you with[o] the Holy Spirit and fire. [12]His winnowing fork is in his hand, and he will clear his threshing floor and will gather his wheat into the granary; but the chaff he will burn with unquenchable fire."

[o] Or *in*

ἐν τῇ ἐρήμῳ· ἑτοιμάσατε τὴν ὁδὸν
in the wilderness: Prepare ye the way
κυρίου, εὐθείας ποιεῖτε τὰς τρίβους
of [the] Lord, straight make the paths
αὐτοῦ. **4** Αὐτὸς δὲ ὁ Ἰωάννης εἶχεν
of him. Now [2]himself – [1]John had
τὸ ἔνδυμα αὐτοῦ ἀπὸ τριχῶν καμήλου
the raiment of him from hairs of a camel
καὶ ζώνην δερματίνην περὶ τὴν ὀσφὺν
and a girdle leathern round the loin[s]
αὐτοῦ· ἡ δὲ τροφὴ ἦν αὐτοῦ ἀκρίδες
of him; and the food [2]was [1]of him locusts
καὶ μέλι ἄγριον. **5** Τότε ἐξεπορεύετο πρὸς
and honey wild. Then went out to
αὐτὸν Ἱεροσόλυμα καὶ πᾶσα ἡ Ἰουδαία
him Jerusalem and all – Judæa
καὶ πᾶσα ἡ περίχωρος τοῦ Ἰορδάνου,
and all the neighbourhood of the Jordan,
6 καὶ ἐβαπτίζοντο ἐν τῷ Ἰορδάνῃ ποταμῷ
and were baptized in the Jordan river
ὑπ' αὐτοῦ ἐξομολογούμενοι τὰς ἁμαρτίας
by him confessing the sins
αὐτῶν. **7** Ἰδὼν δὲ πολλοὺς τῶν
of them. And seeing many of the
Φαρισαίων καὶ Σαδδουκαίων ἐρχομένους
Pharisees and Sadducees coming
ἐπὶ τὸ βάπτισμα εἶπεν αὐτοῖς· γεννήματα
to the baptism he said to them: Offspring
ἐχιδνῶν, τίς ὑπέδειξεν ὑμῖν φυγεῖν ἀπὸ
of vipers, who warned you to flee from
τῆς μελλούσης ὀργῆς; **8** ποιήσατε οὖν
the coming wrath? Produce therefore
καρπὸν ἄξιον τῆς μετανοίας· **9** καὶ
fruit worthy – of repentance; and
μὴ δόξητε λέγειν ἐν ἑαυτοῖς· πατέρα
think not to say among [your]selves: [2][as] father
ἔχομεν τὸν Ἀβραάμ· λέγω γὰρ ὑμῖν ὅτι
[1]We have – [2]Abraham; for I tell you that
δύναται ὁ θεὸς ἐκ τῶν λίθων τούτων
[2]is able – [1]God out of – stones these
ἐγεῖραι τέκνα τῷ Ἀβραάμ. **10** ἤδη δὲ
to raise children – to Abraham. And already
ἡ ἀξίνη πρὸς τὴν ῥίζαν τῶν δένδρων
the axe at the root of the trees
κεῖται· πᾶν οὖν δένδρον μὴ ποιοῦν
is laid; therefore every tree not producing
καρπὸν καλὸν ἐκκόπτεται καὶ εἰς πῦρ
fruit good is cut down and into [the] fire
βάλλεται. **11** ἐγὼ μὲν ὑμᾶς βαπτίζω
is cast. I indeed you baptize
ἐν ὕδατι εἰς μετάνοιαν· ὁ δὲ
in water to repentance; but the [one]
ὀπίσω μου ἐρχόμενος ἰσχυρότερός μού
after me coming [3]stronger [2][than] [4]I
ἐστιν, οὗ οὐκ εἰμὶ ἱκανὸς τὰ ὑποδήματα
[1]is, of whom I am not worthy the sandals
βαστάσαι· αὐτὸς ὑμᾶς βαπτίσει ἐν πνεύματι
to bear; he [2]you [1]will baptize in [the] Spirit
ἁγίῳ καὶ πυρί· **12** οὗ τὸ πτύον ἐν τῇ
Holy and fire; of whom the fan [is] in the
χειρὶ αὐτοῦ, καὶ διακαθαριεῖ τὴν ἅλωνα
hand of him, and he will thoroughly cleanse the threshing-floor
αὐτοῦ, καὶ συνάξει τὸν σῖτον αὐτοῦ
of him, and will gather the wheat of him
εἰς τὴν ἀποθήκην, τὸ δὲ ἄχυρον κατα-
into the barn, but the chaff he will

in the desert,
'Prepare the way for the
Lord,
make straight paths for
him.' "[l]

[4]John's clothes were made of camel's hair, and he had a leather belt around his waist. His food was locusts and wild honey. [5]People went out to him from Jerusalem and all Judea and the whole region of the Jordan. [6]Confessing their sins, they were baptized by him in the Jordan River.

[7]But when he saw many of the Pharisees and Sadducees coming to where he was baptizing, he said to them: "You brood of vipers! Who warned you to flee from the coming wrath? [8]Produce fruit in keeping with repentance. [9]And do not think you can say to yourselves, 'We have Abraham as our father.' I tell you that out of these stones God can raise up children for Abraham. [10]The ax is already at the root of the trees, and every tree that does not produce good fruit will be cut down and thrown into the fire.

[11]"I baptize you with[m] water for repentance. But after me will come one who is more powerful than I, whose sandals I am not fit to carry. He will baptize you with the Holy Spirit and with fire. [12]His winnowing fork is in his hand, and he will clear his threshing floor, gathering his wheat into the barn and burning up the chaff with

[l] *3* Isaiah 40:3
[m] *11* Or *in*

The Baptism of Jesus

13 Then Jesus came
from Galilee to John at the
Jordan, to be baptized by
him. 14 John would have
prevented him, saying, "I
need to be baptized by you,
and do you come to me?"
15 But Jesus answered him,
"Let it be so now; for it is
proper for us in this way to
fulfill all righteousness."
Then he consented. 16 And
when Jesus had been bap-
tized, just as he came up
from the water, suddenly
the heavens were opened
to him and he saw the Spirit
of God descending like a
dove and alighting on him.
17 And a voice from heaven
said, "This is my Son, the
Beloved,[p] with whom I am
well pleased."

κατακαύσει πυρὶ ἀσβέστῳ.
consume with fire unquenchable.

13 Τότε παραγίνεται ὁ Ἰησοῦς ἀπὸ τῆς
Then arrives – Jesus from –

Γαλιλαίας ἐπὶ τὸν Ἰορδάνην πρὸς τὸν
Galilee at the Jordan to –

Ἰωάννην τοῦ βαπτισθῆναι ὑπ' αὐτοῦ.
John – to be baptized[d] by him.

14 ὁ δὲ διεκώλυεν αὐτὸν λέγων· ἐγὼ
But he forbade him saying: I

χρείαν ἔχω ὑπὸ σοῦ βαπτισθῆναι, καὶ σὺ
[2]need [1]have [4]by [5]thee [3]to be baptized, and thou

ἔρχῃ πρός με; 15 ἀποκριθεὶς δὲ ὁ
comest to me? But answering –

Ἰησοῦς εἶπεν αὐτῷ· ἄφες ἄρτι· οὕτως γὰρ
Jesus said to him: Permit now; for thus

πρέπον ἐστὶν ἡμῖν πληρῶσαι πᾶσαν
[2]fitting [1]it is to us to fulfil all

δικαιοσύνην. τότε ἀφίησιν αὐτόν.
righteousness. Then he permits him.

16 βαπτισθεὶς δὲ ὁ Ἰησοῦς εὐθὺς ἀνέβη
And having been baptized – Jesus immediately went up

ἀπὸ τοῦ ὕδατος· καὶ ἰδοὺ ἠνεῴχθησαν
from the water; and behold [3]were opened

οἱ οὐρανοί, καὶ εἶδεν πνεῦμα θεοῦ
[1]the [2]heavens, and he saw [the] Spirit of God

καταβαῖνον ὡσεὶ περιστεράν, ἐρχόμενον ἐπ'
coming down as a dove, coming upon

αὐτόν· 17 καὶ ἰδοὺ φωνὴ ἐκ τῶν
him; and behold a voice out of the

οὐρανῶν λέγουσα· οὗτός ἐστιν ὁ υἱός
heavens saying: This is the son

μου ὁ ἀγαπητός, ἐν ᾧ εὐδόκησα.
of me the beloved, in whom I was well pleased.

unquenchable fire."

The Baptism of Jesus

13 Then Jesus came from
Galilee to the Jordan to be
baptized by John. 14 But
John tried to deter him,
saying, "I need to be baptized by you, and do you
come to me?"
15 Jesus replied, "Let it be
so now; it is proper for us to
do this to fulfill all righteousness." Then John con-
sented.
16 As soon as Jesus was
baptized, he went up out of
the water. At that moment
heaven was opened, and he
saw the Spirit of God de-
scending like a dove and
lighting on him. 17 And a
voice from heaven said,
"This is my Son, whom I
love; with him I am well
pleased."

Chapter 4

The Temptation of Jesus

THEN Jesus was led up
by the Spirit into the
wilderness to be tempted
by the devil. 2 He fasted
forty days and forty nights,
and afterwards he was fam-
ished. 3 The tempter came
and said to him, "If you are
the Son of God, command
these stones to become
loaves of bread." 4 But he
answered, "It is written,
'One does not live by
bread alone,
but by every word
that comes from
the mouth of
God.' "
5 Then the devil took
him to the holy city and
placed him on the pinnacle
of the temple, 6 saying to
him, "If you are the Son of

4 Τότε ὁ Ἰησοῦς ἀνήχθη εἰς τὴν
Then – Jesus was led up into the

ἔρημον ὑπὸ τοῦ πνεύματος πειρασθῆναι
wilderness by the Spirit to be tempted

ὑπὸ τοῦ διαβόλου. 2 καὶ νηστεύσας ἡμέρας
by the devil. And having fasted days

τεσσεράκοντα καὶ τεσσεράκοντα νύκτας
forty and forty nights

ὕστερον ἐπείνασεν. 3 καὶ προσελθὼν ὁ
afterward he hungered. And approaching the

πειράζων εἶπεν αὐτῷ· εἰ υἱὸς εἶ τοῦ
tempting [one] said to him: If Son thou art –

θεοῦ, εἰπὲ ἵνα οἱ λίθοι οὗτοι ἄρτοι
of God, say *in order* that – stones these [2]loaves

γένωνται. 4 ὁ δὲ ἀποκριθεὶς εἶπεν·
[1]may become. But he answering said:

γέγραπται· οὐκ ἐπ' ἄρτῳ μόνῳ ζήσεται
It has been written: Not on bread only shall live

ὁ ἄνθρωπος, ἀλλ' ἐπὶ παντὶ ῥήματι
– man, but on every word

ἐκπορευομένῳ διὰ στόματος θεοῦ. 5 Τότε
proceeding through [the] mouth of God. Then

παραλαμβάνει αὐτὸν ὁ διάβολος εἰς τὴν
takes him the devil into the

ἁγίαν πόλιν, καὶ ἔστησεν αὐτὸν ἐπὶ τὸ
holy city, and stood him on the

πτερύγιον τοῦ ἱεροῦ, 6 καὶ λέγει αὐτῷ·
wing of the temple, and says to him:

Chapter 4

The Temptation of Jesus

THEN Jesus was led by
the Spirit into the des-
ert to be tempted by the
devil. 2 After fasting forty
days and forty nights, he
was hungry. 3 The tempter
came to him and said, "If
you are the Son of God, tell
these stones to become
bread."
4 Jesus answered, "It is
written: 'Man does not live
on bread alone, but on every word that comes from
the mouth of God.'[n]"
5 Then the devil took him
to the holy city and had him
stand on the highest point
of the temple. 6 "If you are

[p] Or *my beloved Son*

[n]4 Deut. 8:3

God, throw yourself down;
for it is written,
'He will command his angels concerning you,'
and 'On their hands they will bear you up,
so that you will not dash your foot against a stone.' "
7 Jesus said to him, "Again
it is written, 'Do not put the
Lord your God to the
test.' "
8 Again, the devil took
him to a very high mountain and showed him all the
kingdoms of the world and
their splendor; 9 and he said
to him, "All these I will give
you, if you will fall down
and worship me." 10 Jesus
said to him, "Away with
you, Satan! for it is written,
'Worship the Lord your God,
and serve only him.' "
11 Then the devil left him,
and suddenly angels came
and waited on him.

Jesus Begins His Ministry in Galilee

12 Now when Jesus[q]
heard that John had been
arrested, he withdrew to
Galilee. 13 He left Nazareth
and made his home in Capernaum by the sea, in the
territory of Zebulun and
Naphtali, 14 so that what
had been spoken through
the prophet Isaiah might be
fulfilled:
15 "Land of Zebulun, land of Naphtali,
on the road by the sea, across the Jordan, Galilee of the Gentiles—
16 the people who sat in darkness
have seen a great light,
and for those who sat in the region and shadow of death
light has dawned."
17 From that time Jesus began to proclaim, "Repent,
for the kingdom of heaven
has come near."[r]

εἰ υἱὸς εἶ τοῦ θεοῦ, βάλε σεαυτὸν
If Son thou art – of God, cast thyself
κάτω· γέγραπται γὰρ ὅτι τοῖς ἀγγέλοις
down; for it has been written[,] – To the angels
αὐτοῦ ἐντελεῖται περὶ σοῦ καὶ ἐπὶ χειρῶν
of him he will give command concerning thee and on hands
ἀροῦσίν σε, μήποτε προσκόψῃς πρὸς
they will bear thee, lest thou strike against
λίθον τὸν πόδα σου. 7 ἔφη αὐτῷ ὁ
a stone the foot of thee. Said to him –
Ἰησοῦς· πάλιν γέγραπται· οὐκ ἐκπειράσεις
Jesus: Again it has been written: Not overtempt shalt thou
κύριον τὸν θεόν σου. 8 Πάλιν παρα-
[the] Lord the God of thee. Again
λαμβάνει αὐτὸν ὁ διάβολος εἰς ὄρος
takes him the devil to a mountain
ὑψηλὸν λίαν, καὶ δείκνυσιν αὐτῷ πάσας
high exceedingly, and shows him all
τὰς βασιλείας τοῦ κόσμου καὶ τὴν
the kingdoms of the world and the
δόξαν αὐτῶν, 9 καὶ εἶπεν αὐτῷ· ταῦτά
glory of them, and said to him: These things
σοι πάντα δώσω, ἐὰν πεσὼν προσκυνήσῃς
to thee all I will give, if falling thou wilt worship
μοι. 10 τότε λέγει αὐτῷ ὁ Ἰησοῦς·
me. Then says to him – Jesus:
ὕπαγε, σατανᾶ· γέγραπται γάρ· κύριον
Go, Satan; for it has been written: [The] Lord
τὸν θεόν σου προσκυνήσεις καὶ αὐτῷ
the God of thee thou shalt worship and him
μόνῳ λατρεύσεις. 11 Τότε ἀφίησιν αὐτὸν
only thou shalt serve. Then leaves him
ὁ διάβολος, καὶ ἰδοὺ ἄγγελοι προσῆλθον
the devil, and behold angels approached
καὶ διηκόνουν αὐτῷ.
and ministered to him.
12 Ἀκούσας δὲ ὅτι Ἰωάννης παρεδόθη
Now hearing that John was delivered up
ἀνεχώρησεν εἰς τὴν Γαλιλαίαν. 13 καὶ
he departed to – Galilee. And
καταλιπὼν τὴν Ναζαρὰ ἐλθὼν κατῴκησεν
leaving – Nazareth coming he dwelt
εἰς Καφαρναοὺμ τὴν παραθαλασσίαν ἐν
in Capernaum – beside the sea in [the]
ὁρίοις Ζαβουλὼν καὶ Νεφθαλίμ· 14 ἵνα
districts of Zebulon and Naphthali; in order that
πληρωθῇ τὸ ῥηθὲν διὰ Ἠσαΐου
might be fulfilled the [thing] spoken through Isaiah
τοῦ προφήτου λέγοντος· 15 γῆ Ζαβουλὼν
the prophet saying: Land of Zebulon
καὶ γῆ Νεφθαλίμ, ὁδὸν θαλάσσης,
and land of Naphthali, way of [the] sea,
πέραν τοῦ Ἰορδάνου, Γαλιλαία τῶν ἐθνῶν,
beyond the Jordan, Galilee of the nations,
16 ὁ λαὸς ὁ καθήμενος ἐν σκοτίᾳ φῶς
the people – sitting in darkness [2]light
εἶδεν μέγα, καὶ τοῖς καθημένοις ἐν
[1]saw [3]a great, and to the [ones] sitting in
χώρᾳ καὶ σκιᾷ θανάτου, φῶς ἀνέτειλεν
a land and shadow of death, light sprang up
αὐτοῖς.
to them.
17 Ἀπὸ τότε ἤρξατο ὁ Ἰησοῦς κηρύσσειν
From then began – Jesus to proclaim
καὶ λέγειν· μετανοεῖτε· ἤγγικεν γὰρ
and to say: Repent ye; for has drawn near

the Son of God," he said,
"throw yourself down. For
it is written:
" 'He will command his angels concerning you,
and they will lift you up in their hands,
so that you will not strike your foot against a stone.'[o]"
7 Jesus answered him, "It
is also written: 'Do not put
the Lord your God to the
test.'[p]"
8 Again, the devil took
him to a very high mountain and showed him all the
kingdoms of the world and
their splendor. 9 "All this I
will give you," he said, "if
you will bow down and
worship me."
10 Jesus said to him,
"Away from me, Satan!
For it is written: 'Worship
the Lord your God, and
serve him only.'[q]"
11 Then the devil left him,
and angels came and attended him.

Jesus Begins to Preach

12 When Jesus heard that
John had been put in prison, he returned to Galilee.
13 Leaving Nazareth, he
went and lived in Capernaum, which was by the lake
in the area of Zebulun and
Naphtali— 14 to fulfill what
was said through the
prophet Isaiah:
15 "Land of Zebulun and land of Naphtali,
the way to the sea, along the Jordan,
Galilee of the Gentiles—
16 the people living in darkness
have seen a great light;
on those living in the land of the shadow of death
a light has dawned."[r]
17 From that time on Jesus
began to preach, "Repent,
for the kingdom of heaven
is near."

[q] Gk *he*
[r] Or *is at hand*

[o] *6* Psalm 91:11,12
[p] *7* Deut. 6:16
[q] *10* Deut. 6:13
[r] *16* Isaiah 9:1,2

Jesus Calls the First Disciples

18 As he walked by the
Sea of Galilee, he saw two
brothers, Simon, who is
called Peter, and Andrew
his brother, casting a net
into the sea—for they were
fishermen. 19 And he said to
them, "Follow me, and I
will make you fish for people." 20 Immediately they
left their nets and followed
him. 21 As he went from
there, he saw two other
brothers, James son of
Zebedee and his brother
John, in the boat with their
father Zebedee, mending
their nets, and he called
them. 22 Immediately they
left the boat and their father, and followed him.

Jesus Ministers to Crowds of People

23 Jesus[s] went
throughout Galilee, teaching in their synagogues and
proclaiming the good
news[t] of the kingdom and
curing every disease and
every sickness among the
people. 24 So his fame
spread throughout all Syria, and they brought to him
all the sick, those who were
afflicted with various diseases and pains, demoni-
acs, epileptics, and paralytics, and he cured them.
25 And great crowds fol-
lowed him from Galilee,
the Decapolis, Jerusalem,
Judea, and from beyond
the Jordan.

Chapter 5

The Beatitudes

WHEN Jesus[q] saw the
crowds, he went up
the mountain; and after he

[s] Gk *He*
[t] Gk *gospel*

ἡ βασιλεία τῶν οὐρανῶν.
the kingdom of the heavens.
18 Περιπατῶν δὲ παρὰ τὴν θάλασσαν
And walking beside the sea
τῆς Γαλιλαίας εἶδεν δύο ἀδελφούς, Σίμωνα
– of Galilee he saw two brothers, Simon
τὸν λεγόμενον Πέτρον καὶ Ἀνδρέαν τὸν
– called Peter and Andrew the
ἀδελφὸν αὐτοῦ, βάλλοντας ἀμφίβληστρον εἰς
brother of him, casting a net into
τὴν θάλασσαν· ἦσαν γὰρ ἁλεεῖς. **19** καὶ
the sea; for they were fishers. And
λέγει αὐτοῖς· δεῦτε ὀπίσω μου, καὶ
he says to them: Come after me, and
ποιήσω ὑμᾶς ἁλεεῖς ἀνθρώπων. **20** οἱ
I will make you fishers of men. [2]they
δὲ εὐθέως ἀφέντες τὰ δίκτυα ἠκολούθη-
[1]And immediately leaving the nets fol-
σαν αὐτῷ. **21** Καὶ προβὰς ἐκεῖθεν εἶδεν
lowed him. And going on thence he saw
ἄλλους δύο ἀδελφούς, Ἰάκωβον τὸν τοῦ
other two brothers, James the [son] –
Ζεβεδαίου καὶ Ἰωάννην τὸν ἀδελφὸν
of Zebedee and John the brother
αὐτοῦ, ἐν τῷ πλοίῳ μετὰ Ζεβεδαίου τοῦ
of him, in the boat with Zebedee the
πατρὸς αὐτῶν καταρτίζοντας τὰ δίκτυα
father of them mending the nets
αὐτῶν· καὶ ἐκάλεσεν αὐτούς. **22** οἱ δὲ
of them; and he called them. And they
εὐθέως ἀφέντες τὸ πλοῖον καὶ τὸν
immediately leaving the boat and the
πατέρα αὐτῶν ἠκολούθησαν αὐτῷ.
father of them followed him.
23 Καὶ περιῆγεν ἐν ὅλῃ τῇ Γαλιλαίᾳ,
And he went about in all – Galilee,
διδάσκων ἐν ταῖς συναγωγαῖς αὐτῶν
teaching in the synagogues of them
καὶ κηρύσσων τὸ εὐαγγέλιον τῆς βασιλείας
and proclaiming the gospel of the kingdom
καὶ θεραπεύων πᾶσαν νόσον καὶ πᾶσαν
and healing every disease and every
μαλακίαν ἐν τῷ λαῷ. **24** καὶ ἀπῆλθεν ἡ
illness among the people. And went the
ἀκοὴ αὐτοῦ εἰς ὅλην τὴν Συρίαν· καὶ
report of him into all – Syria; and
προσήνεγκαν αὐτῷ πάντας τοὺς κακῶς
they brought to him all the [ones] [2]ill
=those who were ill
ἔχοντας ποικίλαις νόσοις καὶ βασάνοις
[1]having [2]various [3]diseases [4]and [5]tortures
συνεχομένους, δαιμονιζομένους καὶ σεληνιαζ-
[1]suffering from, demon-possessed and luna-
ομένους καὶ παραλυτικούς, καὶ ἐθεράπευσεν
tics and paralysed, and he healed
αὐτούς. **25** καὶ ἠκολούθησαν αὐτῷ ὄχλοι
them. And [3]followed [4]him [2]crowds
πολλοὶ ἀπὸ τῆς Γαλιλαίας καὶ Δεκαπόλεως
[1]many from – Galilee and Decapolis
καὶ Ἱεροσολύμων καὶ Ἰουδαίας καὶ πέραν
and Jerusalem and Judæa and beyond
τοῦ Ἰορδάνου.
the Jordan.

5 Ἰδὼν δὲ τοὺς ὄχλους ἀνέβη εἰς
And seeing the crowds he went up into

The Calling of the First Disciples

18As Jesus was walking
beside the Sea of Galilee,
he saw two brothers, Si-
mon called Peter and his
brother Andrew. They
were casting a net into the
lake, for they were fishermen. 19"Come, follow
me," Jesus said, "and I
will make you fishers of
men." 20At once they left
their nets and followed
him.
21Going on from there, he
saw two other brothers,
James son of Zebedee and
his brother John. They
were in a boat with their father Zebedee, preparing
their nets. Jesus called
them, 22and immediately
they left the boat and their
father and followed him.

Jesus Heals the Sick

23Jesus went throughout
Galilee, teaching in their
synagogues, preaching the
good news of the kingdom,
and healing every disease
and sickness among the
people. 24News about him
spread all over Syria, and
people brought to him all
who were ill with various
diseases, those suffering
severe pain, the demon-
possessed, those having
seizures, and the para-
lyzed, and he healed them.
25Large crowds from Gali-
lee, the Decapolis,[s] Jerusalem, Judea and the region
across the Jordan followed
him.

Chapter 5

The Beatitudes

NOW when he saw the
crowds, he went up

[s]*25* That is, the Ten Cities

sat down, his disciples
came to him. 2 Then he began to speak, and taught
them, saying:
3 "Blessed are the poor
in spirit, for theirs is the
kingdom of heaven.
4 "Blessed are those
who mourn, for they will be
comforted.
5 "Blessed are the
meek, for they will inherit
the earth.
6 "Blessed are those
who hunger and thirst for
righteousness, for they will
be filled.
7 "Blessed are the mer-
ciful, for they will receive
mercy.
8 "Blessed are the pure
in heart, for they will see
God.
9 "Blessed are the
peacemakers, for they will
be called children of God.
10 "Blessed are those
who are persecuted for
righteousness' sake, for
theirs is the kingdom of
heaven.
11 "Blessed are you
when people revile you and
persecute you and utter all
kinds of evil against you
falsely[u] on my account.
12 Rejoice and be glad, for
your reward is great in
heaven, for in the same
way they persecuted the
prophets who were before
you.

Salt and Light

13 "You are the salt of
the earth; but if salt has lost
its taste, how can its saltiness be restored? It is no
longer good for anything,
but is thrown out and trampled under foot.
14 "You are the light of
the world. A city built on a
hill cannot be hid. 15 No one
after lighting a lamp puts it
under the bushel basket,
but on the lampstand, and it
gives light to all in the
house. 16 In the same way,

[u] Other ancient authorities lack *falsely*

τὸ ὄρος· καὶ καθίσαντος αὐτοῦ προσῆλθαν
the mountain; and sitting him[a] [4]approached
=when he sat
αὐτῷ οἱ μαθηταὶ αὐτοῦ· 2 καὶ ἀνοίξας τὸ
[5]*to* him [1]the [2]disciples [3]of him; and opening the
στόμα αὐτοῦ ἐδίδασκεν αὐτοὺς λέγων·
mouth of him he taught them saying:
3 Μακάριοι οἱ πτωχοὶ τῷ πνεύματι,
Blessed [are] the poor – in spirit,
ὅτι αὐτῶν ἐστιν ἡ βασιλεία τῶν οὐρανῶν.
for of them is the kingdom of the heavens.
4 μακάριοι οἱ πενθοῦντες, ὅτι αὐτοὶ
Blessed [are] the mourning [ones], for they
παρακληθήσονται. 5 μακάριοι οἱ πραεῖς,
shall be comforted. Blessed [are] the meek,
ὅτι αὐτοὶ κληρονομήσουσιν τὴν γῆν.
for they shall inherit the earth.
6 μακάριοι οἱ πεινῶντες καὶ διψῶντες
Blessed [are] the hungering and thirsting [ones] [after]
τὴν δικαιοσύνην, ὅτι αὐτοὶ χορτασ-
– righteousness, for they shall be
θήσονται. 7 μακάριοι οἱ ἐλεήμονες, ὅτι
satisfied. Blessed [are] the merciful, for
αὐτοὶ ἐλεηθήσονται. 8 μακάριοι οἱ καθαροὶ
they shall obtain mercy. Blessed [are] the clean
τῇ καρδίᾳ, ὅτι αὐτοὶ τὸν θεὸν ὄψονται.
– in heart, for they – [2]God [1]shall see.
9 μακάριοι οἱ εἰρηνοποιοί, ὅτι [αὐτοὶ]
Blessed [are] the peacemakers, for they
υἱοὶ θεοῦ κληθήσονται. 10 μακάριοι οἱ
sons of God shall be called. Blessed [are] the [ones]
δεδιωγμένοι ἕνεκεν δικαιοσύνης, ὅτι αὐτῶν
having been persecuted for the sake of righteousness, for of them
ἐστιν ἡ βασιλεία τῶν οὐρανῶν. 11 μακάριοί
is the kingdom of the heavens. Blessed
ἐστε ὅταν ὀνειδίσωσιν ὑμᾶς καὶ διώξωσιν
are ye when they reproach you and persecute
καὶ εἴπωσιν πᾶν πονηρὸν καθ' ὑμῶν
and say all evil against you
ψευδόμενοι ἕνεκεν ἐμοῦ. 12 χαίρετε
lying for the sake of me. Rejoice
καὶ ἀγαλλιᾶσθε, ὅτι ὁ μισθὸς ὑμῶν
and be glad, because the reward of you [is]
πολὺς ἐν τοῖς οὐρανοῖς· οὕτως γὰρ
much in the heavens; for thus
ἐδίωξαν τοὺς προφήτας τοὺς πρὸ
they persecuted the prophets – before
ὑμῶν.
you.
13 Ὑμεῖς ἐστε τὸ ἅλας τῆς γῆς· ἐὰν δὲ
Ye are the salt of the earth; but if
τὸ ἅλας μωρανθῇ, ἐν τίνι ἁλισθήσεται;
the salt be tainted, by what shall it be salted?
εἰς οὐδὲν ἰσχύει ἔτι εἰ μὴ βληθὲν ἔξω
for nothing is it strong longer except being cast out
καταπατεῖσθαι ὑπὸ τῶν ἀνθρώπων. 14 Ὑμεῖς
to be trodden down by – men. Ye
ἐστε τὸ φῶς τοῦ κόσμου. οὐ δύναται
are the light of the world. [6]Not [5]can
πόλις κρυβῆναι ἐπάνω ὄρους κειμένη·
[1]a city [7]*to* be hid [3]on [4]a mountain [2]set;
15 οὐδὲ καίουσιν λύχνον καὶ τιθέασιν
nor do they light a lamp and place
αὐτὸν ὑπὸ τὸν μόδιον, ἀλλ' ἐπὶ τὴν
it under the bushel, but on the
λυχνίαν, καὶ λάμπει πᾶσιν τοῖς ἐν τῇ
lampstand, and it lightens all the [ones] in the

on a mountainside and sat
down. His disciples came
to him, 2 and he began to
teach them, saying:

3 "Blessed are the poor in
spirit,
for theirs is the
kingdom of heaven.
4 Blessed are those who
mourn,
for they will be
comforted.
5 Blessed are the meek,
for they will inherit the
earth.
6 Blessed are those who
hunger and thirst for
righteousness,
for they will be filled.
7 Blessed are the merciful,
for they will be shown
mercy.
8 Blessed are the pure in
heart,
for they will see God.
9 Blessed are the
peacemakers,
for they will be called
sons of God.
10 Blessed are those who
are persecuted
because of
righteousness,
for theirs is the
kingdom of heaven.

11 "Blessed are you when
people insult you, perse-
cute you and falsely say all
kinds of evil against you because of me. 12 Rejoice and
be glad, because great is
your reward in heaven, for
in the same way they persecuted the prophets who
were before you.

Salt and Light

13 "You are the salt of the
earth. But if the salt loses
its saltiness, how can it be
made salty again? It is no
longer good for anything,
except to be thrown out
and trampled by men.
14 "You are the light of the
world. A city on a hill cannot be hidden. 15 Neither do
people light a lamp and put
it under a bowl. Instead
they put it on its stand, and
it gives light to everyone in

let your light shine before
others, so that they may
see your good works and
give glory to your Father in
heaven.

The Law and the Prophets

17 "Do not think that I
have come to abolish the
law or the prophets; I have
come not to abolish but to
fulfill. 18 For truly I tell you,
until heaven and earth pass
away, not one letter,[v] not
one stroke of a letter, will
pass from the law until all is
accomplished. 19 There-
fore, whoever breaks[w] one
of the least of these commandments, and teaches
others to do the same, will
be called least in the kingdom of heaven; but whoev-
er does them and teaches
them will be called great in
the kingdom of heaven.
20 For I tell you, unless
your righteousness ex-
ceeds that of the scribes
and Pharisees, you will
never enter the kingdom of
heaven.

Concerning Anger

21 "You have heard that
it was said to those of ancient times, 'You shall not
murder'; and 'whoever
murders shall be liable to
judgment.' 22 But I say to
you that if you are angry
with a brother or sister,[x]
you will be liable to judgment; and if you insult[y] a
brother or sister,[z] you will
be liable to the council; and
if you say, 'You fool,' you
will be liable to the hell[a] of
fire. 23 So when you are offering your gift at the altar,
if you remember that your
brother or sister[b] has
something against you,

οἰκίᾳ. **16** οὕτως λαμψάτω τὸ φῶς ὑμῶν
house. Thus let shine the light of you
ἔμπροσθεν τῶν ἀνθρώπων, ὅπως ἴδωσιν
before – men, so that they may see
ὑμῶν τὰ καλὰ ἔργα καὶ δοξάσωσιν
of you the good works and may glorify
τὸν πατέρα ὑμῶν τὸν ἐν τοῖς οὐρανοῖς.
the Father of you – in the heavens.
17 Μὴ νομίσητε ὅτι ἦλθον καταλῦσαι
Think not that I came to destroy
τὸν νόμον ἢ τοὺς προφήτας· οὐκ ἦλθον
the law or the prophets; I came not
καταλῦσαι ἀλλὰ πληρῶσαι. **18** ἀμὴν γὰρ
to destroy but to fulfil. For truly
λέγω ὑμῖν, ἕως ἂν παρέλθῃ ὁ οὐρανὸς
I say to you, until pass away the heaven
καὶ ἡ γῆ, ἰῶτα ἓν ἢ μία κεραία οὐ
and the earth, iota one or one point by no
μὴ παρέλθῃ ἀπὸ τοῦ νόμου, ἕως ἂν
means shall pass away from the law, until
πάντα γένηται. **19** ὃς ἐὰν οὖν λύσῃ
all things come to pass. [2]Whoever [1]therefore breaks
μίαν τῶν ἐντολῶν τούτων τῶν ἐλαχίστων
one – commandments of these the least
καὶ διδάξῃ οὕτως τοὺς ἀνθρώπους, ἐλάχιστος
and teaches thus – men, least
κληθήσεται ἐν τῇ βασιλείᾳ τῶν οὐρανῶν·
he shall be called in the kingdom of the heavens;
ὃς δ' ἂν ποιήσῃ καὶ διδάξῃ, οὗτος
but whoever does and teaches, this [one]
μέγας κληθήσεται ἐν τῇ βασιλείᾳ τῶν
great shall be called in the kingdom of the
οὐρανῶν. **20** λέγω γὰρ ὑμῖν ὅτι ἐὰν μὴ
heavens. For I tell you that except
περισσεύσῃ ὑμῶν ἡ δικαιοσύνη πλεῖον
shall exceed of you the righteousness more [than] [that]
τῶν γραμματέων καὶ Φαρισαίων, οὐ μὴ
of the scribes and Pharisees, by no means
εἰσέλθητε εἰς τὴν βασιλείαν τῶν οὐρανῶν.
shall ye enter into the kingdom of the heavens.
21 Ἠκούσατε ὅτι ἐρρέθη τοῖς ἀρχαίοις·
Ye heard that it was said to the ancients:
οὐ φονεύσεις· ὃς δ' ἂν φονεύσῃ,
Thou shalt not kill; and whoever kills,
ἔνοχος ἔσται τῇ κρίσει. **22** ἐγὼ δὲ
liable shall be to the judgment. But I
λέγω ὑμῖν ὅτι πᾶς ὁ ὀργιζόμενος τῷ
tell you that everyone being angry with the
ἀδελφῷ αὐτοῦ ἔνοχος ἔσται τῇ κρίσει·
brother of him liable shall be to the judgment;
ὃς δ' ἂν εἴπῃ τῷ ἀδελφῷ αὐτοῦ ῥακά,
and whoever says to the brother of him[,] Raca,
ἔνοχος ἔσται τῷ συνεδρίῳ· ὃς δ' ἂν εἴπῃ
liable shall be to the council; and whoever says[,]
μωρέ, ἔνοχος ἔσται εἰς τὴν γέενναν
Fool, liable shall be to the gehenna
τοῦ πυρός. **23** ἐὰν οὖν προσφέρῃς τὸ
– of fire. Therefore if thou bringest the
δῶρόν σου ἐπὶ τὸ θυσιαστήριον κἀκεῖ
gift of thee to the altar and there
μνησθῇς ὅτι ὁ ἀδελφός σου ἔχει τι
rememberest that the brother of thee has something
κατὰ σοῦ, **24** ἄφες ἐκεῖ τὸ δῶρόν σου
against thee, leave there the gift of thee
ἔμπροσθεν τοῦ θυσιαστηρίου, καὶ ὕπαγε
before the altar, and go

the house. 16In the same
way, let your light shine before men, that they may see
your good deeds and praise
your Father in heaven.

The Fulfillment of the Law

17"Do not think that I
have come to abolish the
Law or the Prophets; I have
not come to abolish them
but to fulfill them. 18I tell
you the truth, until heaven
and earth disappear, not
the smallest letter, not the
least stroke of a pen, will by
any means disappear from
the Law until everything is
accomplished. 19Anyone
who breaks one of the least
of these commandments
and teaches others to do
the same will be called least
in the kingdom of heaven,
but whoever practices and
teaches these commands
will be called great in the
kingdom of heaven. 20For I
tell you that unless your
righteousness surpasses
that of the Pharisees and
the teachers of the law, you
will certainly not enter the
kingdom of heaven.

Murder

21"You have heard that it
was said to the people long
ago, 'Do not murder,[t] and
anyone who murders will
be subject to judgment.'
22But I tell you that anyone
who is angry with his brother[u] will be subject to judgment. Again, anyone who
says to his brother,
'Raca,[v]' is answerable to
the Sanhedrin. But anyone
who says, 'You fool!' will
be in danger of the fire of
hell.
23"Therefore, if you are
offering your gift at the altar and there remember
that your brother has something against you, 24leave

[v] Gk *one iota*
[w] Or *annuls*
[x] Gk *a brother*; other ancient authorities add *without cause*
[y] Gk *say Raca to* (an obscure term of abuse)
[z] Gk *a brother*
[a] Gk *Gehenna*
[b] Gk *your brother*

[t] *21* Exodus 20:13
[u] *22* Some manuscripts *brother without cause*
[v] *22* An Aramaic term of contempt

24leave your gift there before the altar and go; first
be reconciled to your
brother or sister,[b] and then
come and offer your gift.
25Come to terms quickly
with your accuser while
you are on the way to
court[c] with him, or your
accuser may hand you over
to the judge, and the judge
to the guard, and you will
be thrown into prison.
26Truly I tell you, you will
never get out until you have
paid the last penny.

Concerning Adultery

27 "You have heard that
it was said, 'You shall not
commit adultery.' 28But I
say to you that everyone
who looks at a woman with
lust has already committed
adultery with her in his
heart. 29If your right eye
causes you to sin, tear it out
and throw it away; it is better for you to lose one of
your members than for
your whole body to be
thrown into hell.[a] 30And if
your right hand causes you
to sin, cut it off and throw
it away; it is better for you
to lose one of your mem-
bers than for your whole
body to go into hell.[a]

Concerning Divorce

31 "It was also said,
'Whoever divorces his
wife, let him give her a certificate of divorce.' 32But I
say to you that anyone who
divorces his wife, except
on the ground of unchastity, causes her to commit
adultery; and whoever
marries a divorced woman
commits adultery.

Concerning Oaths

33 "Again, you have
heard that it was said to
those of ancient times,
'You shall not swear falsely, but carry out the vows
you have made to the
Lord.' 34But I say to you,
Do not swear at all, either
by heaven, for it is the
throne of God, 35or by the

[c] Gk lacks *to court*

πρῶτον διαλλάγηθι τῷ ἀδελφῷ σου, καὶ
first be reconciled to the brother of thee, and
τότε ἐλθὼν πρόσφερε τὸ δῶρόν σου.
then coming offer the gift of thee.
25 ἴσθι εὐνοῶν τῷ ἀντιδίκῳ σου
Be well disposed to the opponent of thee
ταχὺ ἕως ὅτου εἶ μετ' αὐτοῦ ἐν τῇ
quickly while thou art with him in the
ὁδῷ· μήποτέ σε παραδῷ ὁ ἀντίδικος τῷ
way; lest [4]thee [3]deliver [1]the [2]opponent to the
κριτῇ καὶ ὁ κριτὴς τῷ ὑπηρέτῃ, καὶ
judge and the judge to the attendant, and
εἰς φυλακὴν βληθήσῃ· **26** ἀμὴν λέγω
into prison thou be cast; truly I say
σοι, οὐ μὴ ἐξέλθῃς ἐκεῖθεν ἕως ἂν
to thee, by no means shalt thou come out thence until
ἀποδῷς τὸν ἔσχατον κοδράντην.
thou repayest the last farthing.
27 Ἠκούσατε ὅτι ἐρρέθη· οὐ μοιχεύσεις.
Ye heard that it was said: Thou shalt not commit adultery.
28 ἐγὼ δὲ λέγω ὑμῖν ὅτι πᾶς ὁ βλέπων
But I tell you that everyone seeing
γυναῖκα πρὸς τὸ ἐπιθυμῆσαι [αὐτὴν]
a woman with a view – to desire her
ἤδη ἐμοίχευσεν αὐτὴν ἐν τῇ καρδίᾳ
already committed adultery with her in the heart
αὐτοῦ. **29** εἰ δὲ ὁ ὀφθαλμός σου ὁ δεξιὸς
of him. So if the [2]eye [3]of thee – [1]right
σκανδαλίζει σε, ἔξελε αὐτὸν καὶ βάλε
[4]causes [6]to stumble [5]thee, pluck out it and cast
ἀπὸ σοῦ· συμφέρει γάρ σοι ἵνα ἀπόληται
from thee; for it is expedient for thee that [5]perish
ἓν τῶν μελῶν σου καὶ μὴ ὅλον τὸ
[1]one [2]of the [3]members [4]of thee and not all the
σῶμά σου βληθῇ εἰς γέενναν. **30** καὶ
body of thee be cast into gehenna. And
εἰ ἡ δεξιά σου χεὶρ σκανδαλίζει σε, ἔκκοψον
if the [1]right [3]of thee [2]hand [4]causes [6]to stumble [5]thee, cut out
αὐτὴν καὶ βάλε ἀπὸ σοῦ· συμφέρει γάρ
it and cast from thee; for it is expedient
σοι ἵνα ἀπόληται ἓν τῶν μελῶν σου
for thee that [5]perish [1]one [2]of the [3]members [4]of thee
καὶ μὴ ὅλον τὸ σῶμά σου εἰς γέενναν
and not all the body of thee into gehenna
ἀπέλθῃ. **31** Ἐρρέθη δέ· ὃς ἂν ἀπολύσῃ
go away. And it was said: Whoever dismisses
τὴν γυναῖκα αὐτοῦ, δότω αὐτῇ ἀποστάσιον.
the wife of him, let him give her a bill of divorce.
32 ἐγὼ δὲ λέγω ὑμῖν ὅτι πᾶς ὁ ἀπολύων
But I tell you that everyone dismissing
τὴν γυναῖκα αὐτοῦ παρεκτὸς λόγου
the wife of him apart from a matter
πορνείας ποιεῖ αὐτὴν μοιχευθῆναι,
of fornication makes her *to* commit adultery,
καὶ ὃς ἐὰν ἀπολελυμένην γαμήσῃ,
and whoever [2]a dismissed [woman] [1]marries,
μοιχᾶται. **33** Πάλιν ἠκούσατε ὅτι ἐρρέθη
commits adultery. Again ye heard that it was said
τοῖς ἀρχαίοις· οὐκ ἐπιορκήσεις, ἀποδώσεις
to the ancients: Thou shalt not perjure, [2]shalt repay
δὲ τῷ κυρίῳ τοὺς ὅρκους σου. **34** ἐγὼ δὲ
[1]but to the Lord the oaths of thee. But I
λέγω ὑμῖν μὴ ὀμόσαι ὅλως· μήτε ἐν τῷ
tell you not to swear at all; neither by the
οὐρανῷ, ὅτι θρόνος ἐστὶν τοῦ θεοῦ·
heaven, because [the] throne it is – of God;

your gift there in front of
the altar. First go and be
reconciled to your brother;
then come and offer your
gift.
25"Settle matters quickly
with your adversary who is
taking you to court. Do it
while you are still with him
on the way, or he may hand
you over to the judge, and
the judge may hand you
over to the officer, and you
may be thrown into prison.
26I tell you the truth, you
will not get out until you
have paid the last penny.[w]

Adultery

27"You have heard that it
was said, 'Do not commit
adultery.'[x] 28But I tell you
that anyone who looks at a
woman lustfully has al-
ready committed adultery
with her in his heart. 29If
your right eye causes you
to sin, gouge it out and
throw it away. It is better
for you to lose one part of
your body than for your
whole body to be thrown
into hell. 30And if your right
hand causes you to sin, cut
it off and throw it away. It
is better for you to lose one
part of your body than for
your whole body to go into
hell.

Divorce

31"It has been said, 'Anyone who divorces his wife
must give her a certificate
of divorce.'[y] 32But I tell
you that anyone who di-
vorces his wife, except for
marital unfaithfulness,
causes her to become an
adulteress, and anyone
who marries the divorced
woman commits adultery.

Oaths

33"Again, you have heard
that it was said to the people long ago, 'Do not break
your oath, but keep the
oaths you have made to the
Lord.' 34But I tell you, Do
not swear at all: either by
heaven, for it is God's
throne; 35or by the earth,

[w] *26* Greek *kodrantes*
[x] *27* Exodus 20:14
[y] *31* Deut. 24:1

earth, for it is his footstool,
or by Jerusalem, for it is the
city of the great King.
36And do not swear by
your head, for you cannot
make one hair white or
black. 37Let your word be
'Yes, Yes' or 'No, No';
anything more than this
comes from the evil one.[d]

Concerning Retaliation

38 "You have heard that
it was said, 'An eye for an
eye and a tooth for a tooth.'
39But I say to you, Do not
resist an evildoer. But if
anyone strikes you on the
right cheek, turn the other
also; 40and if anyone wants
to sue you and take your
coat, give your cloak as
well; 41and if anyone forces
you to go one mile, go also
the second mile. 42Give to
everyone who begs from
you, and do not refuse anyone who wants to borrow
from you.

Love for Enemies

43 "You have heard that
it was said, 'You shall love
your neighbor and hate
your enemy.' 44But I say to
you, Love your enemies
and pray for those who persecute you, 45so that you
may be children of your Father in heaven; for he
makes his sun rise on the
evil and on the good, and
sends rain on the righteous
and on the unrighteous.
46For if you love those who
love you, what reward do
you have? Do not even the
tax collectors do the same?
47And if you greet only
your brothers and sisters,[e]
what more are you doing
than others? Do not even

[d] Or *evil*
[e] Gk *your brothers*

35 μήτε ἐν τῇ γῇ, ὅτι ὑποπόδιόν
nor by the earth, because footstool

ἐστιν τῶν ποδῶν αὐτοῦ· μήτε εἰς
it is of the feet of him; nor by

Ἰεροσόλυμα, ὅτι πόλις ἐστὶν τοῦ μεγάλου
Jerusalem, because city it is of the great

βασιλέως· **36** μήτε ἐν τῇ κεφαλῇ σου
King; nor by the head of thee

ὀμόσῃς, ὅτι οὐ δύνασαι μίαν τρίχα
swear, because thou canst not one hair

λευκὴν ποιῆσαι ἢ μέλαιναν. **37** ἔστω
white *to* make or black. [2]let [6]be

δὲ ὁ λόγος ὑμῶν ναὶ ναί, οὒ οὔ·
[1]But [3]the [4]word [5]of you Yes yes, No no;

τὸ δὲ περισσὸν τούτων ἐκ τοῦ πονηροῦ
for the excess of these of – evil

ἐστιν. **38** Ἠκούσατε ὅτι ἐρρέθη· ὀφθαλμὸν
is. Ye heard that it was said: An eye

ἀντὶ ὀφθαλμοῦ καὶ ὀδόντα ἀντὶ ὀδόντος.
instead of an eye and a tooth instead of a tooth.

39 ἐγὼ δὲ λέγω ὑμῖν μὴ ἀντιστῆναι
But I tell you not to oppose

τῷ πονηρῷ· ἀλλ' ὅστις σε ῥαπίζει εἰς
– evil; but who thee strikes on

τὴν δεξιὰν σιαγόνα [σου], στρέψον αὐτῷ
the right cheek of thee, turn to him

καὶ τὴν ἄλλην· **40** καὶ τῷ θέλοντί
also the other; and to the [one] wishing

σοι κριθῆναι καὶ τὸν χιτῶνά σου λαβεῖν,
thee to judge and the tunic of thee to take,

ἄφες αὐτῷ καὶ τὸ ἱμάτιον· **41** καὶ
allow him also the [outer] garment; and

ὅστις σε ἀγγαρεύσει μίλιον ἕν, ὕπαγε
who [2]thee [1]shall impress [4]mile [3]one, go

μετ' αὐτοῦ δύο. **42** τῷ αἰτοῦντί
with him two. To the [one] asking

σε δός, καὶ τὸν θέλοντα ἀπὸ σοῦ
thee give, and the [one] wishing from thee

δανείσασθαι μὴ ἀποστραφῇς. **43** Ἠκούσατε
to borrow turn not away. Ye heard

ὅτι ἐρρέθη· ἀγαπήσεις τὸν πλησίον σου
that it was said: Thou shalt love the neighbour of thee

καὶ μισήσεις τὸν ἐχθρόν σου. **44** ἐγὼ
and thou shalt hate the enemy of thee. [2]I

δὲ λέγω ὑμῖν· ἀγαπᾶτε τοὺς ἐχθροὺς
[1]But tell you: Love ye the enemies

ὑμῶν καὶ προσεύχεσθε ὑπὲρ τῶν
of you and pray ye for the [ones]

διωκόντων ὑμᾶς· **45** ὅπως γένησθε υἱοὶ
persecuting you; so that ye may become sons

τοῦ πατρὸς ὑμῶν τοῦ ἐν οὐρανοῖς,
of the Father of you – in heavens,

ὅτι τὸν ἥλιον αὐτοῦ ἀνατέλλει ἐπὶ
because the sun of him he makes to rise on

πονηροὺς καὶ ἀγαθοὺς καὶ βρέχει ἐπὶ
evil men and good and rains on

δικαίους καὶ ἀδίκους. **46** ἐὰν γὰρ
just men and unjust. For if

ἀγαπήσητε τοὺς ἀγαπῶντας ὑμᾶς, τίνα
ye love the [ones] loving you, what

μισθὸν ἔχετε; οὐχὶ καὶ οἱ τελῶναι τὸ
reward have ye? [2]not [3]even [4]the [5]tax-collectors [6]the

αὐτὸ ποιοῦσιν; **47** καὶ ἐὰν ἀσπάσησθε
[7]same [1]do? and if ye greet

τοὺς ἀδελφοὺς ὑμῶν μόνον, τί περισσὸν
the brothers of you only, what excess

for it is his footstool; or by
Jerusalem, for it is the city
of the Great King. 36And do
not swear by your head, for
you cannot make even one
hair white or black. 37Sim-
ply let your 'Yes' be 'Yes,'
and your 'No,' 'No'; any-
thing beyond this comes
from the evil one.

An Eye for an Eye

38"You have heard that it
was said, 'Eye for eye, and
tooth for tooth.'[z] 39But I
tell you, Do not resist an
evil person. If someone
strikes you on the right
cheek, turn to him the other
also. 40And if someone
wants to sue you and take
your tunic, let him have
your cloak as well. 41If
someone forces you to go
one mile, go with him two
miles. 42Give to the one
who asks you, and do not
turn away from the one
who wants to borrow from
you.

Love for Enemies

43"You have heard that it
was said, 'Love your
neighbor[a] and hate your
enemy.' 44But I tell you:
Love your enemies[b] and
pray for those who perse-
cute you, 45that you may be
sons of your Father in
heaven. He causes his sun
to rise on the evil and the
good, and sends rain on the
righteous and the unrighteous. 46If you love those
who love you, what reward
will you get? Are not even
the tax collectors doing
that? 47And if you greet
only your brothers, what
are you doing more than
others? Do not even pagans

[z] *38* Exodus 21:24; Lev. 24:20; Deut. 19:21
[a] *43* Lev. 19:18
[b] *44* Some late manuscripts *enemies, bless those who curse you, do good to those who hate you*

the Gentiles do the same? 48 Be perfect, therefore, as your heavenly Father is perfect.

ποιεῖτε; οὐχὶ καὶ οἱ ἐθνικοὶ τὸ αὐτὸ
do ye? [2]not [3]even [4]the [5]gentiles [6]the [7]same
ποιοῦσιν; 48 Ἔσεσθε οὖν ὑμεῖς τέλειοι
[1]do? Be therefore ye perfect
ὡς ὁ πατὴρ ὑμῶν ὁ οὐράνιος τέλειός
as the [2]Father [3]of you – [1]heavenly perfect
ἐστιν.
is.

do that? 48 Be perfect, therefore, as your heavenly Father is perfect.

Chapter 6

Concerning Almsgiving

"BEWARE of practicing your piety before others in order to be seen by them; for then you have no reward from your Father in heaven.

2 "So whenever you give alms, do not sound a trumpet before you, as the hypocrites do in the synagogues and in the streets, so that they may be praised by others. Truly I tell you, they have received their reward. 3 But when you give alms, do not let your left hand know what your right hand is doing, 4 so that your alms may be done in secret; and your Father who sees in secret will reward you.[f]

Concerning Prayer

5 "And whenever you pray, do not be like the hypocrites; for they love to stand and pray in the synagogues and at the street corners, so that they may be seen by others. Truly I tell you, they have received their reward. 6 But whenever you pray, go into your room and shut the door and pray to your Father who is in secret; and your Father who sees in secret will reward you.[f]

7 "When you are praying, do not heap up empty phrases as the Gentiles do; for they think that they will be heard because of their many words. 8 Do not be

[f]Other ancient authorities add *openly*

6 Προσέχετε δὲ τὴν δικαιοσύνην ὑμῶν
And take ye heed the righteousness of you
μὴ ποιεῖν ἔμπροσθεν τῶν ἀνθρώπων πρὸς
not to do in front of – men with a view to
τὸ θεαθῆναι αὐτοῖς· εἰ δὲ μή γε, μισθὸν
– to be seen by them; otherwise, reward
οὐκ ἔχετε παρὰ τῷ πατρὶ ὑμῶν τῷ
ye have not with the Father of you –
ἐν τοῖς οὐρανοῖς. 2 Ὅταν οὖν ποιῇς
in the heavens. [2]When [1]therefore thou doest
ἐλεημοσύνην, μὴ σαλπίσῃς ἔμπροσθέν σου,
alms, sound not a trumpet before thee,
ὥσπερ οἱ ὑποκριταὶ ποιοῦσιν ἐν ταῖς
as the hypocrites do in the
συναγωγαῖς καὶ ἐν ταῖς ῥύμαις, ὅπως
synagogues and in the streets, so that
δοξασθῶσιν ὑπὸ τῶν ἀνθρώπων· ἀμὴν
they may be glorified by – men; truly
λέγω ὑμῖν, ἀπέχουσιν τὸν μισθὸν αὐτῶν.
I tell you, they have the reward of them.
3 σοῦ δὲ ποιοῦντος ἐλεημοσύνην μὴ
But thee doing* alms not
= when thou doest
γνώτω ἡ ἀριστερά σου τί ποιεῖ ἡ
let know the left [hand] of thee what does the
δεξιά σου, 4 ὅπως ᾖ σου ἡ ἐλεημοσύνη
right of thee, so that [4]may be [3]of thee [1]the [2]alms
ἐν τῷ κρυπτῷ· καὶ ὁ πατήρ σου
in – secret; and the Father of thee
ὁ βλέπων ἐν τῷ κρυπτῷ ἀποδώσει σοι.
the [one] seeing in – secret will repay thee.
5 Καὶ ὅταν προσεύχησθε, οὐκ ἔσεσθε
And when ye pray, be not ye
ὡς οἱ ὑποκριταί· ὅτι φιλοῦσιν ἐν ταῖς
as the hypocrites; because they love in the
συναγωγαῖς καὶ ἐν ταῖς γωνίαις τῶν
synagogues and in the corners of the
πλατειῶν ἑστῶτες προσεύχεσθαι, ὅπως
open streets standing to pray, so that
φανῶσιν τοῖς ἀνθρώποις· ἀμὴν λέγω
they may appear – to men; truly I tell
ὑμῖν, ἀπέχουσιν τὸν μισθὸν αὐτῶν. 6 σὺ
you, they have the reward of them. [2]thou
δὲ ὅταν προσεύχῃ, εἴσελθε εἰς τὸ ταμιεῖόν
[1]But [3]when [4]prayest, enter into the private room
σου καὶ κλείσας τὴν θύραν σου πρόσευξαι
of thee and having shut the door of thee pray
τῷ πατρί σου τῷ ἐν τῷ κρυπτῷ·
to the Father of thee the [one] in – secret;
καὶ ὁ πατήρ σου ὁ βλέπων ἐν τῷ
and the Father of thee the [one] seeing in –
κρυπτῷ ἀποδώσει σοι. 7 Προσευχόμενοι δὲ
secret will repay thee. But praying
μὴ βατταλογήσητε ὥσπερ οἱ ἐθνικοί·
do not utter empty words as the gentiles;
δοκοῦσιν γὰρ ὅτι ἐν τῇ πολυλογίᾳ αὐτῶν
for they think that in the much speaking of them

Chapter 6

Giving to the Needy

"BE careful not to do your 'acts of righteousness' before men, to be seen by them. If you do, you will have no reward from your Father in heaven.

2 "So when you give to the needy, do not announce it with trumpets, as the hypocrites do in the synagogues and on the streets, to be honored by men. I tell you the truth, they have received their reward in full. 3 But when you give to the needy, do not let your left hand know what your right hand is doing, 4 so that your giving may be in secret. Then your Father, who sees what is done in secret, will reward you.

Prayer

5 "And when you pray, do not be like the hypocrites, for they love to pray standing in the synagogues and on the street corners to be seen by men. I tell you the truth, they have received their reward in full. 6 But when you pray, go into your room, close the door and pray to your Father, who is unseen. Then your Father, who sees what is done in secret, will reward you. 7 And when you pray, do not keep on babbling like pagans, for they think they will be heard because of their many words. 8 Do

like them, for your Father
knows what you need be-
fore you ask him.
9 "Pray then in this
way:
Our Father in heaven,
hallowed be your
name.
10 Your kingdom
come.
Your will be done,
on earth as it is in
heaven.
11 Give us this day our
daily bread.[g]
12 And forgive us our
debts,
as we also have
forgiven
our debtors.
13 And do not bring us
to the time of
trial,[h]
but rescue us from
the evil one.[i]
14 For if you forgive others
their trespasses, your heavenly Father will also forgive you; 15 but if you do
not forgive others, neither
will your Father forgive
your trespasses.

Concerning Fasting

16 "And whenever you
fast, do not look dismal,
like the hypocrites, for they
disfigure their faces so as to
show others that they are
fasting. Truly I tell you,
they have received their reward. 17 But when you fast,
put oil on your head and
wash your face, 18 so that
your fasting may be seen
not by others but by your
Father who is in secret; and
your Father who sees in secret will reward you.[f]

Concerning Treasures

19 "Do not store up for
yourselves treasures on
earth, where moth and
rust[j] consume and where
thieves break in and steal;
20 but store up for your-

[g] Or *our bread for tomorrow*
[h] Or *us into temptation*
[i] Or *from evil.* Other ancient authorities add, in some form, *For the kingdom and the power and the glory are yours forever. Amen.*
[j] Gk *eating*

εἰσακουσθήσονται. 8 μὴ οὖν ὁμοιωθῆτε
they will be heard. Not therefore be ye like
αὐτοῖς· οἶδεν γὰρ [ὁ θεὸς] ὁ πατὴρ
them; for [5]knows – [1]God [2]the [3]Father
ὑμῶν ὧν χρείαν ἔχετε πρὸ τοῦ ὑμᾶς
[4]of you of what things [2]need [1]ye have before – you
αἰτῆσαι αὐτόν. 9 οὕτως οὖν προσεύχεσθε
to ask[b] him. [2]Thus [1]therefore pray
ὑμεῖς· Πάτερ ἡμῶν ὁ ἐν τοῖς οὐρανοῖς·
ye: Father of us the [one] in the heavens:
Ἁγιασθήτω τὸ ὄνομά σου· 10 ἐλθάτω
Let it be hallowed the name of thee; let it come
ἡ βασιλεία σου· γενηθήτω τὸ θέλημά σου,
the kingdom of thee; let it come about the will of thee,
ὡς ἐν οὐρανῷ καὶ ἐπὶ γῆς· 11 Τὸν
as in heaven also on earth; The
ἄρτον ἡμῶν τὸν ἐπιούσιον δὸς ἡμῖν
[2]bread [3]of us – [1]daily give to us
σήμερον· 12 καὶ ἄφες ἡμῖν τὰ ὀφειλή-
to-day; and forgive us the debts
ματα ἡμῶν, ὡς καὶ ἡμεῖς ἀφήκαμεν
of us, as indeed we forgave
τοῖς ὀφειλέταις ἡμῶν· 13 καὶ μὴ εἰσενέγκῃς
the debtors of us; and not bring
ἡμᾶς εἰς πειρασμόν, ἀλλὰ ῥῦσαι ἡμᾶς ἀπὸ
us into temptation, but rescue us from
τοῦ πονηροῦ. 14 Ἐὰν γὰρ ἀφῆτε τοῖς
– evil. For if ye forgive –
ἀνθρώποις τὰ παραπτώματα αὐτῶν, ἀφήσει
men the trespasses of them, will forgive
καὶ ὑμῖν ὁ πατὴρ ὑμῶν ὁ οὐράνιος·
also you the [2]Father [3]of you – [1]heavenly;
15 ἐὰν δὲ μὴ ἀφῆτε τοῖς ἀνθρώποις,
but if ye forgive not – men,
οὐδὲ ὁ πατὴρ ὑμῶν ἀφήσει τὰ παραπτώ-
neither the Father of you will forgive the tres-
ματα ὑμῶν. 16 Ὅταν δὲ νηστεύητε,
passes of you. And when ye fast,
μὴ γίνεσθε ὡς οἱ ὑποκριταὶ σκυθρωποί·
be not as the hypocrites gloomy;
ἀφανίζουσιν γὰρ τὰ πρόσωπα αὐτῶν
for they disfigure the faces of them
ὅπως φανῶσιν τοῖς ἀνθρώποις νηστεύοντες·
so that they may appear – to men fasting;
ἀμὴν λέγω ὑμῖν, ἀπέχουσιν τὸν μισθὸν
truly I tell you, they have the reward
αὐτῶν. 17 σὺ δὲ νηστεύων ἄλειψαί σου
of them. But thou fasting anoint of thee
τὴν κεφαλὴν καὶ τὸ πρόσωπόν σου νίψαι,
the head and the face of thee wash,
18 ὅπως μὴ φανῇς τοῖς ἀνθρώποις νηστεύων
so that thou appearest not – to men fasting
ἀλλὰ τῷ πατρί σου τῷ ἐν τῷ κρυφαίῳ·
but to the Father of thee the [one] in – secret;
καὶ ὁ πατήρ σου ὁ βλέπων ἐν τῷ
and the Father of thee the [one] seeing in –
κρυφαίῳ ἀποδώσει σοι.
secret will repay thee.
19 Μὴ θησαυρίζετε ὑμῖν θησαυροὺς
Do not lay up *treasure* for you treasures
ἐπὶ τῆς γῆς, ὅπου σὴς καὶ βρῶσις
on the earth, where moth and rust
ἀφανίζει, καὶ ὅπου κλέπται διορύσσουσιν
removes, and where thieves dig through
καὶ κλέπτουσιν· 20 θησαυρίζετε δὲ ὑμῖν
and steal; but lay up *treasure* for you

not be like them, for your
Father knows what you
need before you ask him.
9 "This, then, is how you
should pray:

" 'Our Father in heaven,
hallowed be your name,
10 your kingdom come,
your will be done
on earth as it is in
heaven.
11 Give us today our daily
bread.
12 Forgive us our debts,
as we also have
forgiven our
debtors.
13 And lead us not into
temptation,
but deliver us from the
evil one.[c]'

14 For if you forgive men
when they sin against you,
your heavenly Father will
also forgive you. 15 But if
you do not forgive men
their sins, your Father will
not forgive your sins.

Fasting

16 "When you fast, do not
look somber as the hypo-
crites do, for they disfigure
their faces to show men
they are fasting. I tell you
the truth, they have re-
ceived their reward in full.
17 But when you fast, put oil
on your head and wash
your face, 18 so that it will
not be obvious to men that
you are fasting, but only to
your Father, who is un-
seen; and your Father, who
sees what is done in secret,
will reward you.

Treasures in Heaven

19 "Do not store up for
yourselves treasures on
earth, where moth and rust
destroy, and where thieves
break in and steal. 20 But
store up for yourselves

[c] 13 Or *from evil*; some late manuscripts *one, / for yours is the kingdom and the power and the glory forever. Amen.*

selves treasures in heaven,
where neither moth nor
rust[j] consumes and where
thieves do not break in and
steal. 21 For where your
treasure is, there your
heart will be also.

The Sound Eye

22 "The eye is the lamp
of the body. So, if your eye
is healthy, your whole
body will be full of light;
23 but if your eye is un-
healthy, your whole body
will be full of darkness. If
then the light in you is darkness, how great is the darkness!

Serving Two Masters

24 "No one can serve
two masters; for a slave
will either hate the one and
love the other, or be devoted to the one and despise
the other. You cannot
serve God and wealth.[k]

Do Not Worry

25 "Therefore I tell you,
do not worry about your
life, what you will eat or
what you will drink,[l] or
about your body, what you
will wear. Is not life more
than food, and the body
more than clothing?
26 Look at the birds of the
air; they neither sow nor
reap nor gather into barns,
and yet your heavenly Fa-
ther feeds them. Are you
not of more value than
they? 27 And can any of you
by worrying add a single
hour to your span of life?[m]
28 And why do you worry
about clothing? Consider
the lilies of the field, how
they grow; they neither toil
nor spin, 29 yet I tell you,
even Solomon in all his glory was not clothed like one
of these. 30 But if God so
clothes the grass of the

θησαυροὺς ἐν οὐρανῷ, ὅπου οὔτε σὴς
treasures in heaven, where neither moth
οὔτε βρῶσις ἀφανίζει, καὶ ὅπου κλέπται
nor rust removes, and where thieves
οὐ διορύσσουσιν οὐδὲ κλέπτουσιν· 21 ὅπου
do not dig through nor steal; [2]where
γάρ ἐστιν ὁ θησαυρός σου, ἐκεῖ
[1]for is the treasure of thee, there
ἔσται καὶ ἡ καρδία σου. 22 Ὁ λύχνος
will be also the heart of thee. The lamp
τοῦ σώματός ἐστιν ὁ ὀφθαλμός. ἐὰν οὖν
of the body is the eye. [2]If [1]therefore
ᾖ ὁ ὀφθαλμός σου ἁπλοῦς, ὅλον τὸ σῶμά
[6]be [3]the [4]eye [5]of thee single, all the body
σου φωτεινὸν ἔσται· 23 ἐὰν δὲ ὁ
of thee shining will be; but if the
ὀφθαλμός σου πονηρὸς ᾖ, ὅλον τὸ σῶμά
eye of thee evil be, all the body
σου σκοτεινὸν ἔσται. εἰ οὖν τὸ φῶς
of thee dark will be. [2]If [1]therefore the light
τὸ ἐν σοὶ σκότος ἐστίν, τὸ σκότος
– in thee darkness is, the darkness
πόσον. 24 Οὐδεὶς δύναται δυσὶ κυρίοις
how great. No one can two lords
δουλεύειν· ἢ γὰρ τὸν ἕνα μισήσει καὶ
to serve; for either the one he will hate and
τὸν ἕτερον ἀγαπήσει, ἢ ἑνὸς ἀνθέξεται
the other he will love, or one he will hold to
καὶ τοῦ ἑτέρου καταφρονήσει. οὐ δύνασθε
and the other he will despise. Ye cannot
θεῷ δουλεύειν καὶ μαμωνᾷ. 25 Διὰ
God *to* serve and mammon. There-
τοῦτο λέγω ὑμῖν· μὴ μεριμνᾶτε τῇ
fore I say to you: Be not anxious for the
ψυχῇ ὑμῶν τί φάγητε [ἢ τί πίητε],
life of you[,] what ye may eat or what ye may drink,
μηδὲ τῷ σώματι ὑμῶν τί ἐνδύσησθε.
nor for the body of you[,] what ye may put on.
οὐχὶ ἡ ψυχὴ πλεῖόν ἐστιν τῆς τροφῆς καὶ τὸ
[2]not [3]the [4]life [5]more [1]Is [than] the food and the
σῶμα τοῦ ἐνδύματος; 26 ἐμβλέψατε εἰς
body [than] the raiment? Look ye at
τὰ πετεινὰ τοῦ οὐρανοῦ, ὅτι οὐ σπείρουσιν
the birds – of heaven, that they sow not
οὐδὲ θερίζουσιν οὐδὲ συνάγουσιν εἰς
nor reap nor gather into
ἀποθήκας, καὶ ὁ πατὴρ ὑμῶν ὁ οὐράνιος
barns, and the [2]Father [3]of you – [1]heavenly
τρέφει αὐτά· οὐχ ὑμεῖς μᾶλλον διαφέρετε
feeds them; do not ye more excel
αὐτῶν; 27 τίς δὲ ἐξ ὑμῶν μεριμνῶν
them? But who of you being anxious
δύναται προσθεῖναι ἐπὶ τὴν ἡλικίαν αὐτοῦ
can *to* add to the stature of him
πῆχυν ἕνα; 28 καὶ περὶ ἐνδύματος τί
cubit one? and concerning clothing why
μεριμνᾶτε; καταμάθετε τὰ κρίνα τοῦ ἀγροῦ,
be ye anxious? consider the lilies of the field,
πῶς αὐξάνουσιν· οὐ κοπιῶσιν οὐδὲ
how they grow; they labour not nor
νήθουσιν· 29 λέγω δὲ ὑμῖν ὅτι οὐδὲ Σολομὼν
spin; but I tell you that not Solomon
ἐν πάσῃ τῇ δόξῃ αὐτοῦ περιεβάλετο ὡς
in all the glory of him was clothed as
ἓν τούτων. 30 εἰ δὲ τὸν χόρτον τοῦ
one of these. But if the grass of the

treasures in heaven, where
moth and rust do not de-
stroy, and where thieves do
not break in and steal.
21For where your treasure
is, there your heart will be
also.
22"The eye is the lamp of
the body. If your eyes are
good, your whole body will
be full of light. 23But if your
eyes are bad, your whole
body will be full of darkness. If then the light within
you is darkness, how great
is that darkness!
24"No one can serve two
masters. Either he will hate
the one and love the other,
or he will be devoted to the
one and despise the other.
You cannot serve both God
and Money.

Do Not Worry

25"Therefore I tell you,
do not worry about your
life, what you will eat or
drink; or about your body,
what you will wear. Is not
life more important than
food, and the body more
important than clothes?
26Look at the birds of the
air; they do not sow or reap
or store away in barns, and
yet your heavenly Father
feeds them. Are you not
much more valuable than
they? 27Who of you by worrying can add a single hour
to his life[d]?
28"And why do you wor-
ry about clothes? See how
the lilies of the field grow.
They do not labor or spin.
29Yet I tell you that not
even Solomon in all his
splendor was dressed like
one of these. 30If that is

[k] Gk *mammon*
[l] Other ancient authorities lack *or what you will drink*
[m] Or *add one cubit to your height*

[d] 27 Or *single cubit to his height*

field, which is alive today
and tomorrow is thrown
into the oven, will he not
much more clothe you—
you of little faith? 31 Therefore do not worry, saying,
'What will we eat?' or
'What will we drink?' or
'What will we wear?' 32 For
it is the Gentiles who strive
for all these things; and indeed your heavenly Father
knows that you need all
these things. 33 But strive
first for the kingdom of
God[n] and his[o] righteousness, and all these things
will be given to you as well.
34 "So do not worry
about tomorrow, for to-
morrow will bring worries
of its own. Today's trouble
is enough for today.

Chapter 7

Judging Others

"Do not judge, so
that you may not
be judged. 2 For with the
judgment you make you
will be judged, and the
measure you give will be
the measure you get. 3 Why
do you see the speck in
your neighbor's[p] eye, but
do not notice the log in your
own eye? 4 Or how can you
say to your neighbor,[q] 'Let
me take the speck out of
your eye,' while the log is
in your own eye? 5 You
hypocrite, first take the log
out of your own eye, and
then you will see clearly to
take the speck out of your
neighbor's[p] eye.

Profaning the Holy

6 "Do not give what is
holy to dogs; and do not
throw your pearls before
swine, or they will trample
them under foot and turn
and maul you.

Ask, Search, Knock

7 "Ask, and it will be
given you; search, and you

[n] Other ancient authorities lack *of God*
[o] Or *its*
[p] Gk *brother's*
[q] Gk *brother*

ἀγροῦ σήμερον ὄντα καὶ αὔριον εἰς
field to-day being and to-morrow into
κλίβανον βαλλόμενον ὁ θεὸς οὕτως
an oven being thrown - God thus
ἀμφιέννυσιν, οὐ πολλῷ μᾶλλον ὑμᾶς,
clothes, not much more you,
ὀλιγόπιστοι; 31 μὴ οὖν μεριμνήσητε
little-faiths? Therefore be ye not anxious
λέγοντες· τί φάγωμεν; ἤ· τί
saying: What may we eat? or: What
πίωμεν; ἤ· τί περιβαλώμεθα; 32 πάντα
may we drink? or: What may we put on? ³all
γὰρ ταῦτα τὰ ἔθνη ἐπιζητοῦσιν· οἶδεν
¹for these things the nations seek after; ⁶knows
γὰρ ὁ πατὴρ ὑμῶν ὁ οὐράνιος ὅτι
¹for ²the ⁴Father ⁵of you – ³heavenly that
χρῄζετε τούτων ἁπάντων. 33 ζητεῖτε δὲ
ye need these things *of* all. But seek ye
πρῶτον τὴν βασιλείαν καὶ τὴν δικαιοσύνην
first the kingdom and the righteousness
αὐτοῦ, καὶ ταῦτα πάντα προστεθήσεται
of him, and these things all shall be added
ὑμῖν. 34 μὴ οὖν μεριμνήσητε εἰς τὴν
to you. Therefore be ye not anxious for the
αὔριον, ἡ γὰρ αὔριον μεριμνήσει
morrow, for the morrow will be anxious
ἑαυτῆς· ἀρκετὸν τῇ ἡμέρᾳ ἡ κακία αὐτῆς.
of itself; sufficient to the day the evil of it.

7 Μὴ κρίνετε, ἵνα μὴ κριθῆτε· 2 ἐν ᾧ
Judge not, lest ye be judged; ²with ³what
γὰρ κρίματι κρίνετε κριθήσεσθε, καὶ
¹for judgment ye judge ye shall be judged, and
ἐν ᾧ μέτρῳ μετρεῖτε μετρηθήσεται ὑμῖν.
with what measure ye measure it shall be measured to you.
3 τί δὲ βλέπεις τὸ κάρφος τὸ ἐν
And why seest thou the chip – in
τῷ ὀφθαλμῷ τοῦ ἀδελφοῦ σου, τὴν
the eye of the brother of thee, ²the
δὲ ἐν τῷ σῷ ὀφθαλμῷ δοκὸν οὐ κατα-
¹but ⁴in – ⁵thine ⁶eye ³beam thou consider-
νοεῖς; 4 ἢ πῶς ἐρεῖς τῷ ἀδελφῷ σου·
est not? or how wilt thou say to the brother of thee:
ἄφες ἐκβάλω τὸ κάρφος ἐκ τοῦ ὀφθαλμοῦ
Allow [that] I may pluck *out* the chip out of the eye
σου, καὶ ἰδοὺ ἡ δοκὸς ἐν τῷ ὀφθαλμῷ
of thee, and behold the beam in the eye
σου; 5 ὑποκριτά, ἔκβαλε πρῶτον ἐκ τοῦ
of thee? hypocrite, pluck *out* first out of the
ὀφθαλμοῦ σου τὴν δοκόν, καὶ τότε
eye of thee the beam, and then
διαβλέψεις ἐκβαλεῖν τὸ κάρφος ἐκ
thou wilt see clearly to pluck *out* the chip out of
τοῦ ὀφθαλμοῦ τοῦ ἀδελφοῦ σου. 6 Μὴ
the eye of the brother of thee. not
δῶτε τὸ ἅγιον τοῖς κυσίν, μηδὲ βάλητε
Give the holy to the dogs, neither cast
τοὺς μαργαρίτας ὑμῶν ἔμπροσθεν τῶν
the pearls of you before the
χοίρων, μήποτε καταπατήσουσιν αὐτοὺς
pigs, lest they will trample them
ἐν τοῖς ποσὶν αὐτῶν καὶ στραφέντες
with the feet of them and turning
ῥήξωσιν ὑμᾶς. 7 Αἰτεῖτε, καὶ δοθήσεται
may rend you. Ask, and it shall be given

how God clothes the grass
of the field, which is here
today and tomorrow is
thrown into the fire, will he
not much more clothe you,
O you of little faith? 31 So do
not worry, saying, 'What
shall we eat?' or 'What
shall we drink?' or 'What
shall we wear?' 32 For the
pagans run after all these
things, and your heavenly
Father knows that you
need them. 33 But seek first
his kingdom and his righteousness, and all these
things will be given to you
as well. 34 Therefore do not
worry about tomorrow, for
tomorrow will worry about
itself. Each day has enough
trouble of its own.

Chapter 7

Judging Others

"Do not judge, or you
too will be judged.
2 For in the same way you
judge others, you will be
judged, and with the mea-
sure you use, it will be measured to you.
3 "Why do you look at the
speck of sawdust in your
brother's eye and pay no
attention to the plank in
your own eye? 4 How can
you say to your brother,
'Let me take the speck out
of your eye,' when all the
time there is a plank in your
own eye? 5 You hypocrite,
first take the plank out of
your own eye, and then you
will see clearly to remove
the speck from your brother's eye.
6 "Do not give dogs what
is sacred; do not throw
your pearls to pigs. If you
do, they may trample them
under their feet, and then
turn and tear you to pieces.

Ask, Seek, Knock

7 "Ask and it will be given

will find; knock, and the door will be opened for you. 8 For everyone who asks receives, and everyone who searches finds, and for everyone who knocks, the door will be opened. 9 Is there anyone among you who, if your child asks for bread, will give a stone? 10 Or if the child asks for a fish, will give a snake? 11 If you then, who are evil, know how to give good gifts to your children, how much more will your Father in heaven give good things to those who ask him!

The Golden Rule

12 "In everything do to others as you would have them do to you; for this is the law and the prophets.

The Narrow Gate

13 "Enter through the narrow gate; for the gate is wide and the road is easy[r] that leads to destruction, and there are many who take it. 14 For the gate is narrow and the road is hard that leads to life, and there are few who find it.

A Tree and Its Fruit

15 "Beware of false prophets, who come to you in sheep's clothing but inwardly are ravenous wolves. 16 You will know them by their fruits. Are grapes gathered from thorns, or figs from thistles? 17 In the same way, every good tree bears good fruit, but the bad tree bears bad fruit. 18 A good tree cannot bear bad fruit, nor can a bad tree bear good fruit. 19 Every tree that

[r] Other ancient authorities read *for the road is wide and easy*

ὑμῖν· ζητεῖτε, καὶ εὑρήσετε· κρούετε,
to you; seek, and ye shall find; knock,

καὶ ἀνοιγήσεται ὑμῖν. 8 πᾶς γὰρ ὁ αἰτῶν
and it shall be opened to you. For every asking [one]

λαμβάνει, καὶ ὁ ζητῶν εὑρίσκει, καὶ
receives, and the seeking [one] finds, and

τῷ κρούοντι ἀνοιγήσεται. 9 ἢ τίς ἐστιν
to the knocking [one] it shall be opened. Or 1what 2is there

ἐξ ὑμῶν ἄνθρωπος, ὃν αἰτήσει ὁ υἱὸς
4of 5you 3man, whom 4will ask 1the 2son

αὐτοῦ ἄρτον, μὴ λίθον ἐπιδώσει αὐτῷ;
3of him 5a loaf, *not* a stone he will give him?

10 ἢ καὶ ἰχθὺν αἰτήσει, μὴ ὄφιν ἐπιδώσει
or also a fish he will ask, *not* a serpent he will give

αὐτῷ; 11 εἰ οὖν ὑμεῖς πονηροὶ ὄντες
him? If therefore ye 2evil 1being

οἴδατε δόματα ἀγαθὰ διδόναι τοῖς τέκνοις
know 3gifts 2good 1to give to the children

ὑμῶν, πόσῳ μᾶλλον ὁ πατὴρ ὑμῶν ὁ
of you, how much more the Father of you –

ἐν τοῖς οὐρανοῖς δώσει ἀγαθὰ τοῖς
in the heavens will give good things to the [ones]

αἰτοῦσιν αὐτόν. 12 Πάντα οὖν ὅσα ἐὰν
asking him. All things therefore as many soever as

θέλητε ἵνα ποιῶσιν ὑμῖν οἱ ἄνθρωποι,
ye wish that may do to you – men,

οὕτως καὶ ὑμεῖς ποιεῖτε αὐτοῖς· οὗτος
thus also ye do to them; 2this

γάρ ἐστιν ὁ νόμος καὶ οἱ προφῆται.
1for is the law and the prophets.

13 Εἰσέλθατε διὰ τῆς στενῆς πύλης·
Enter ye in through the narrow gate;

ὅτι πλατεῖα [ἡ πύλη] καὶ εὐρύχωρος
because wide the gate and broad

ἡ ὁδὸς ἡ ἀπάγουσα εἰς τὴν ἀπώλειαν,
the way – leading away to – destruction,

καὶ πολλοί εἰσιν οἱ εἰσερχόμενοι δι᾽
and many are the [ones] going in through

αὐτῆς· 14 ὅτι στενὴ ἡ πύλη καὶ τεθλιμ-
it; because strait the gate and made

μένη ἡ ὁδὸς ἡ ἀπάγουσα εἰς τὴν ζωήν,
narrow the way – leading away to – life,

καὶ ὀλίγοι εἰσὶν οἱ εὑρίσκοντες αὐτήν.
and few are the [ones] finding it.

15 Προσέχετε ἀπὸ τῶν ψευδοπροφητῶν,
Beware from(of) – false prophets,

οἵτινες ἔρχονται πρὸς ὑμᾶς ἐν ἐνδύμασι
who come to you in clothes

προβάτων, ἔσωθεν δέ εἰσιν λύκοι ἅρπαγες.
of sheep, but within are wolves greedy.

16 ἀπὸ τῶν καρπῶν αὐτῶν ἐπιγνώσεσθε
From the fruits of them ye will know

αὐτούς. μήτι συλλέγουσιν ἀπὸ ἀκανθῶν σταφυλὰς
them. They do not gather from thorns grapes

ἢ ἀπὸ τριβόλων σῦκα; 17 οὕτως πᾶν
or from thistles figs? So 1every

δένδρον ἀγαθὸν καρποὺς καλοὺς ποιεῖ,
3tree 2good 6fruits 5good 4produces,

τὸ δὲ σαπρὸν δένδρον καρποὺς πονηροὺς
but the corrupt tree fruits evil

ποιεῖ. 18 οὐ δύναται δένδρον ἀγαθὸν
produces. 3Cannot 2tree 1a good

καρποὺς πονηροὺς ἐνεγκεῖν, οὐδὲ δένδρον
6fruits 5evil 4*to* bear, nor 2tree

σαπρὸν καρποὺς καλοὺς ἐνεγκεῖν. 19 πᾶν
1a corrupt 5fruits 4good 3*to* bear. Every

to you; seek and you will find; knock and the door will be opened to you. 8 For everyone who asks receives; he who seeks finds; and to him who knocks, the door will be opened.

9 "Which of you, if his son asks for bread, will give him a stone? 10 Or if he asks for a fish, will give him a snake? 11 If you, then, though you are evil, know how to give good gifts to your children, how much more will your Father in heaven give good gifts to those who ask him! 12 So in everything, do to others what you would have them do to you, for this sums up the Law and the Prophets.

The Narrow and Wide Gates

13 "Enter through the narrow gate. For wide is the gate and broad is the road that leads to destruction, and many enter through it. 14 But small is the gate and narrow the road that leads to life, and only a few find it.

A Tree and Its Fruit

15 "Watch out for false prophets. They come to you in sheep's clothing, but inwardly they are ferocious wolves. 16 By their fruit you will recognize them. Do people pick grapes from thornbushes, or figs from thistles? 17 Likewise every good tree bears good fruit, but a bad tree bears bad fruit. 18 A good tree cannot bear bad fruit, and a bad tree cannot bear good fruit.

does not bear good fruit is
cut down and thrown into
the fire. 20 Thus you will
know them by their fruits.

Concerning Self-Deception

21 "Not everyone who
says to me, 'Lord, Lord,'
will enter the kingdom of
heaven, but only the one
who does the will of my Father in heaven. 22 On that
day many will say to me,
'Lord, Lord, did we not
prophesy in your name,
and cast out demons in
your name, and do many
deeds of power in your
name?' 23 Then I will de-
clare to them, 'I never
knew you; go away from
me, you evildoers.'

Hearers and Doers

24 "Everyone then who
hears these words of mine
and acts on them will be
like a wise man who built
his house on rock. 25 The
rain fell, the floods came,
and the winds blew and
beat on that house, but it
did not fall, because it had
been founded on rock.
26 And everyone who hears
these words of mine and
does not act on them will be
like a foolish man who built
his house on sand. 27 The
rain fell, and the floods
came, and the winds blew
and beat against that
house, and it fell—and
great was its fall!"
28 Now when Jesus had
finished saying these

δένδρον μὴ ποιοῦν καρπὸν καλὸν ἐκκόπτεται
tree not producing fruit good is cut down
καὶ εἰς πῦρ βάλλεται. **20** ἄρα γε ἀπὸ
and into fire is cast. Therefore from
τῶν καρπῶν αὐτῶν ἐπιγνώσεσθε αὐτούς.
the fruits of them ye will know them.
21 Οὐ πᾶς ὁ λέγων μοι κύριε κύριε,
Not everyone saying to me Lord[,] Lord,
εἰσελεύσεται εἰς τὴν βασιλείαν τῶν οὐρανῶν,
will enter into the kingdom of the heavens,
ἀλλ' ὁ ποιῶν τὸ θέλημα τοῦ πατρός
but the [one] doing the will of the Father
μου τοῦ ἐν τοῖς οὐρανοῖς. **22** πολλοὶ
of me – in the heavens. Many
ἐροῦσίν μοι ἐν ἐκείνῃ τῇ ἡμέρᾳ· κύριε
will say to me in that – day· Lord[,]
κύριε, οὐ τῷ σῷ ὀνόματι ἐπροφητεύσαμεν,
Lord, not – in thy name we prophesied,
καὶ τῷ σῷ ὀνόματι δαιμόνια ἐξεβάλομεν,
and – in thy name demons we expelled,
καὶ τῷ σῷ ὀνόματι δυνάμεις πολλὰς
and – in thy name mighty works many
ἐποιήσαμεν; **23** καὶ τότε ὁμολογήσω
did? and then I will declare
αὐτοῖς ὅτι οὐδέποτε ἔγνων ὑμᾶς· ἀπο-
to them[,] – Never I knew you; de-
χωρεῖτε ἀπ' ἐμοῦ οἱ ἐργαζόμενοι τὴν
part from me the [ones] working –
ἀνομίαν.
lawlessness.
24 Πᾶς οὖν ὅστις ἀκούει μου τοὺς
Everyone therefore who hears of me –
λόγους τούτους καὶ ποιεῖ αὐτούς,
words these and does them,
ὁμοιωθήσεται ἀνδρὶ φρονίμῳ, ὅστις ᾠκοδό-
shall be likened man to a prudent, who built
μησεν αὐτοῦ τὴν οἰκίαν ἐπὶ τὴν πέτραν.
of him the house on the rock.
25 καὶ κατέβη ἡ βροχὴ καὶ ἦλθον οἱ
And came down the rain and came the
ποταμοὶ καὶ ἔπνευσαν οἱ ἄνεμοι καὶ
rivers and blew the winds and
προσέπεσαν τῇ οἰκίᾳ ἐκείνῃ, καὶ οὐκ
fell against – house that, and not
ἔπεσεν· τεθεμελίωτο γὰρ ἐπὶ τὴν
it fell; for it had been founded on the
πέτραν. **26** καὶ πᾶς ὁ ἀκούων μου
rock. And everyone hearing of me
τοὺς λόγους τούτους καὶ μὴ ποιῶν
– words these and not doing
αὐτοὺς ὁμοιωθήσεται ἀνδρὶ μωρῷ, ὅστις
them shall be likened man to a foolish, who
ᾠκοδόμησεν αὐτοῦ τὴν οἰκίαν ἐπὶ τὴν
built of him the house on the
ἄμμον. **27** καὶ κατέβη ἡ βροχὴ καὶ
sand. And came down the rain and
ἦλθον οἱ ποταμοὶ καὶ ἔπνευσαν οἱ
came the rivers and blew the
ἄνεμοι καὶ προσέκοψαν τῇ οἰκίᾳ ἐκείνῃ,
winds and beat against – house that,
καὶ ἔπεσεν, καὶ ἦν ἡ πτῶσις αὐτῆς
and it fell, and was the fall of it
μεγάλη.
great.
28 Καὶ ἐγένετο ὅτε ἐτέλεσεν ὁ Ἰησοῦς
And it came to pass when finished – Jesus

19 Every tree that does not
bear good fruit is cut down
and thrown into the fire.
20 Thus, by their fruit you
will recognize them.
21 "Not everyone who
says to me, 'Lord, Lord,'
will enter the kingdom of
heaven, but only he who
does the will of my Father
who is in heaven. 22 Many
will say to me on that day,
'Lord, Lord, did we not
prophesy in your name,
and in your name drive out
demons and perform many
miracles?' 23 Then I will tell
them plainly, 'I never knew
you. Away from me, you
evildoers!'

The Wise and Foolish Builders

24 "Therefore everyone
who hears these words of
mine and puts them into
practice is like a wise man
who built his house on the
rock. 25 The rain came
down, the streams rose,
and the winds blew and
beat against that house; yet
it did not fall, because it
had its foundation on the
rock. 26 But everyone who
hears these words of mine
and does not put them into
practice is like a foolish
man who built his house on
sand. 27 The rain came
down, the streams rose,
and the winds blew and
beat against that house,
and it fell with a great
crash."

28 When Jesus had fin-

things, the crowds were astounded at his teaching,
29for he taught them as one
having authority, and not
as their scribes.

Chapter 8

Jesus Cleanses a Leper

WHEN Jesus[s] had
come down from the
mountain, great crowds followed him; 2and there was
a leper[t] who came to him
and knelt before him, saying, "Lord, if you choose,
you can make me clean."
3He stretched out his hand
and touched him, saying, "I
do choose. Be made
clean!" Immediately his
leprosy[t] was cleansed.
4Then Jesus said to him,
"See that you say nothing
to anyone; but go, show
yourself to the priest, and
offer the gift that Moses
commanded, as a testimo-
ny to them."

Jesus Heals a Centurion's Servant

5 When he entered Ca-
pernaum, a centurion came
to him, appealing to him
6and saying, "Lord, my
servant is lying at home
paralyzed, in terrible distress." 7And he said to him,
"I will come and cure him."
8The centurion answered,
"Lord, I am not worthy to
have you come under my
roof; but only speak the
word, and my servant will
be healed. 9For I also am a
man under authority, with
soldiers under me; and I
say to one, 'Go,' and he
goes, and to another,
'Come,' and he comes, and
to my slave, 'Do this,' and
the slave does it." 10When
Jesus heard him, he was
amazed and said to those
who followed him, "Truly I
tell you, in no one[u] in Isra-

[s] Gk *he*
[t] The terms *leper* and *leprosy* can refer to several diseases
[u] Other ancient authorities read *Truly I tell you, not even*

τοὺς λόγους τούτους, ἐξεπλήσσοντο οἱ
– words these, were astounded the
ὄχλοι ἐπὶ τῇ διδαχῇ αὐτοῦ· 29 ἦν γὰρ
crowds at the teaching of him; for he was
διδάσκων αὐτοὺς ὡς ἐξουσίαν ἔχων, καὶ
teaching them as authority having, and
οὐχ ὡς οἱ γραμματεῖς αὐτῶν.
not as the scribes of them.

8 Καταβάντος δὲ αὐτοῦ ἀπὸ τοῦ ὄρους
And coming down him[a] from the mountain
=as he came down
ἠκολούθησαν αὐτῷ ὄχλοι πολλοί. 2 καὶ
followed him crowds many. And
ἰδοὺ λεπρὸς προσελθὼν προσεκύνει αὐτῷ
behold a leper approaching worshipped him
λέγων· κύριε, ἐὰν θέλῃς, δύνασαί με
saying: Lord, if thou art willing, thou art able me
καθαρίσαι. 3 καὶ ἐκτείνας τὴν χεῖρα
to cleanse. And stretching out the(his) hand
ἥψατο αὐτοῦ λέγων· θέλω, καθαρίσθητι.
he touched him saying: I am willing, be thou cleansed.
καὶ εὐθέως ἐκαθαρίσθη αὐτοῦ ἡ λέπρα.
And immediately was cleansed of him the leprosy.
4 καὶ λέγει αὐτῷ ὁ Ἰησοῦς· ὅρα μηδενὶ
And says to him – Jesus: See *to* no one
εἴπῃς, ἀλλὰ ὕπαγε σεαυτὸν δεῖξον τῷ
thou tellest, but go thyself show to the
ἱερεῖ καὶ προσένεγκον τὸ δῶρον ὃ
priest and offer the gift which
προσέταξεν Μωϋσῆς, εἰς μαρτύριον αὐτοῖς.
commanded Moses, for a testimony to them.
5 Εἰσελθόντος δὲ αὐτοῦ εἰς Καφαρναοὺμ
And entering him[a] into Capernaum,
=as he entered
προσῆλθεν αὐτῷ ἑκατόνταρχος παρακαλῶν
approached *to* him a centurion beseeching
αὐτὸν 6 καὶ λέγων· κύριε, ὁ παῖς μου
him and saying: Lord, the boy of me
βέβληται ἐν τῇ οἰκίᾳ παραλυτικός,
has been laid [aside] in the house a paralytic,
δεινῶς βασανιζόμενος. 7 λέγει αὐτῷ·
terribly *being* tortured. He says to him:
ἐγὼ ἐλθὼν θεραπεύσω αὐτόν. 8 ἀποκριθεὶς
I coming will heal him. answering
δὲ ὁ ἑκατόνταρχος ἔφη· κύριε, οὐκ εἰμὶ
But the centurion said: Lord, I am not
ἱκανὸς ἵνα μου ὑπὸ τὴν στέγην εἰσέλθῃς·
worthy that of me under the roof thou mayest enter;
ἀλλὰ μόνον εἰπὲ λόγῳ, καὶ ἰαθήσεται ὁ παῖς
but only say in a word, and will be healed the boy
μου. 9 καὶ γὰρ ἐγὼ ἄνθρωπός εἰμι
of me. [3]also [1]For [2]I [5]a man [4]am
ὑπὸ ἐξουσίαν, ἔχων ὑπ᾽ ἐμαυτὸν στρατιώτας,
under authority, having under myself soldiers,
καὶ λέγω τούτῳ· πορεύθητι, καὶ πορεύεται,
and I say to this: Go, and he goes,
καὶ ἄλλῳ· ἔρχου, καὶ ἔρχεται, καὶ τῷ
and to another: Come, and he comes, and to the
δούλῳ μου· ποίησον τοῦτο, καὶ ποιεῖ.
slave of me: Do this, and he does [it].
10 ἀκούσας δὲ ὁ Ἰησοῦς ἐθαύμασεν
And hearing – Jesus marvelled
καὶ εἶπεν τοῖς ἀκολουθοῦσιν· ἀμὴν λέγω
and said to the [ones] following: Truly I tell

ished saying these things,
the crowds were amazed at
his teaching, 29because he
taught as one who had au-
thority, and not as their
teachers of the law.

Chapter 8

The Man With Leprosy

WHEN he came down
from the mountain-
side, large crowds followed
him. 2A man with leprosy[e]
came and knelt before him
and said, "Lord, if you are
willing, you can make me
clean."
3Jesus reached out his
hand and touched the man.
"I am willing," he said.
"Be clean!" Immediately
he was cured[f] of his leprosy. 4Then Jesus said to him,
"See that you don't tell
anyone. But go, show
yourself to the priest and
offer the gift Moses com-
manded, as a testimony to
them."

The Faith of the Centurion

5When Jesus had entered
Capernaum, a centurion
came to him, asking for
help. 6"Lord," he said,
"my servant lies at home
paralyzed and in terrible
suffering."
7Jesus said to him, "I will
go and heal him."
8The centurion replied,
"Lord, I do not deserve to
have you come under my
roof. But just say the word,
and my servant will be
healed. 9For I myself am a
man under authority, with
soldiers under me. I tell this
one, 'Go,' and he goes; and
that one, 'Come,' and he
comes. I say to my servant,
'Do this,' and he does it."
10When Jesus heard this,
he was astonished and said
to those following him, "I
tell you the truth, I have not

[e] 2 The Greek word was used for various diseases affecting the skin—not necessarily leprosy.
[f] 3 Greek *made clean*

el have I found such faith.
11 I tell you, many will
come from east and west
and will eat with Abraham
and Isaac and Jacob in the
kingdom of heaven,
12 while the heirs of the
kingdom will be thrown
into the outer darkness,
where there will be weep-
ing and gnashing of teeth."
13 And to the centurion
Jesus said, "Go; let it be
done for you according to
your faith." And the ser-
vant was healed in that
hour.

Jesus Heals Many at Peter's House

14 When Jesus entered
Peter's house, he saw his
mother-in-law lying in bed
with a fever; 15 he touched
her hand, and the fever left
her, and she got up and began to serve him. 16 That
evening they brought to
him many who were pos-
sessed with demons; and
he cast out the spirits with
a word, and cured all who
were sick. 17 This was to
fulfill what had been spoken through the prophet
Isaiah, "He took our infirmities and bore our dis-
eases."

Would-Be Followers of Jesus

18 Now when Jesus saw
great crowds around him,
he gave orders to go over to
the other side. 19 A scribe
then approached and said,
"Teacher, I will follow you
wherever you go." 20 And
Jesus said to him, "Foxes
have holes, and birds of the
air have nests; but the Son
of Man has nowhere to lay

ὑμῖν, παρ' οὐδενὶ τοσαύτην πίστιν ἐν τῷ
you, from no one such faith in –
'Ισραὴλ εὗρον. 11 λέγω δὲ ὑμῖν ὅτι
Israel I found. And I tell you that
πολλοὶ ἀπὸ ἀνατολῶν καὶ δυσμῶν ἥξουσιν
many from east and west will come
καὶ ἀνακλιθήσονται μετὰ 'Αβραὰμ καὶ
and will recline with Abraham and
'Ισαὰκ καὶ 'Ιακὼβ ἐν τῇ βασιλείᾳ τῶν
Isaac and Jacob in the kingdom of the
οὐρανῶν· 12 οἱ δὲ υἱοὶ τῆς βασιλείας
heavens; but the sons of the kingdom
ἐκβληθήσονται εἰς τὸ σκότος τὸ ἐξώτερον·
will be cast out into the darkness – outer;
ἐκεῖ ἔσται ὁ κλαυθμὸς καὶ ὁ βρυγμὸς
there will be the weeping and the gnashing
τῶν ὀδόντων. 13 καὶ εἶπεν ὁ 'Ιησοῦς τῷ
of the teeth. And said – Jesus to the
ἑκατοντάρχῃ· ὕπαγε, ὡς ἐπίστευσας γενη-
centurion: Go, as thou believedst let it
θήτω σοι. καὶ ἰάθη ὁ παῖς ἐν τῇ
be to thee. And was healed the boy in –
ὥρᾳ ἐκείνῃ.
hour that.

14 Καὶ ἐλθὼν ὁ 'Ιησοῦς εἰς τὴν οἰκίαν
And coming – Jesus into the house
Πέτρου εἶδεν τὴν πενθερὰν αὐτοῦ βεβλη-
of Peter he saw the mother-in-law of him *having been*
μένην καὶ πυρέσσουσαν· 15 καὶ ἥψατο
laid [aside] and fever-stricken; and he touched
τῆς χειρὸς αὐτῆς, καὶ ἀφῆκεν αὐτὴν ὁ
the hand of her, and left her the
πυρετός· καὶ ἠγέρθη, καὶ διηκόνει αὐτῷ.
fever; and she arose, and ministered to him.
16 'Οψίας δὲ γενομένης προσήνεγκαν
And evening coming[a] they brought
=when evening came
αὐτῷ δαιμονιζομένους πολλούς· καὶ ἐξέβαλεν
to him *being* demon-possessed many; and he expelled
τὰ πνεύματα λόγῳ, καὶ πάντας τοὺς
the spirits with a word, and all the [ones]
=those
κακῶς ἔχοντας ἐθεράπευσεν· 17 ὅπως
ill having he healed; so that
who were ill
πληρωθῇ τὸ ῥηθὲν διὰ 'Ησαΐου τοῦ
was fulfilled the [thing] spoken through Isaiah the
προφήτου λέγοντος· αὐτὸς τὰς ἀσθενείας
prophet saying: He the weaknesses
ἡμῶν ἔλαβεν καὶ τὰς νόσους ἐβάστασεν.
of us took and the diseases he bore.
18 'Ιδὼν δὲ ὁ 'Ιησοῦς ὄχλον περὶ
But [2]seeing – [1]Jesus a crowd around
αὐτὸν ἐκέλευσεν ἀπελθεῖν εἰς τὸ πέραν.
him commanded to go away to the other side.
19 Καὶ προσελθὼν εἷς γραμματεὺς εἶπεν
And approaching one scribe said
αὐτῷ· διδάσκαλε, ἀκολουθήσω σοι
to him: Teacher, I will follow thee
ὅπου ἐὰν ἀπέρχῃ. 20 καὶ λέγει αὐτῷ
wherever thou mayest go. And says to him
ὁ 'Ιησοῦς· αἱ ἀλώπεκες φωλεοὺς ἔχουσιν
– Jesus: The foxes holes have
καὶ τὰ πετεινὰ τοῦ οὐρανοῦ κατα-
and the birds of the heaven nests,
σκηνώσεις, ὁ δὲ υἱὸς τοῦ ἀνθρώπου
but the Son – of man

found anyone in Israel with
such great faith. 11 I say to
you that many will come
from the east and the west,
and will take their places at
the feast with Abraham,
Isaac and Jacob in the kingdom of heaven. 12 But the
subjects of the kingdom
will be thrown outside, into
the darkness, where there
will be weeping and gnashing of teeth."
13 Then Jesus said to the
centurion, "Go! It will be
done just as you believed it
would." And his servant
was healed at that very
hour.

Jesus Heals Many

14 When Jesus came into
Peter's house, he saw Pe-
ter's mother-in-law lying in
bed with a fever. 15 He
touched her hand and the
fever left her, and she got
up and began to wait on
him.
16 When evening came,
many who were demon-
possessed were brought to
him, and he drove out the
spirits with a word and
healed all the sick. 17 This
was to fulfill what was spoken through the prophet
Isaiah:

"He took up our infirmities
and carried our diseases."[g]

The Cost of Following Jesus

18 When Jesus saw the
crowd around him, he gave
orders to cross to the other
side of the lake. 19 Then a
teacher of the law came to
him and said, "Teacher, I
will follow you wherever
you go."
20 Jesus replied, "Foxes
have holes and birds of the
air have nests, but the Son
of Man has no place to lay

[g] 17 Isaiah 53:4

his head." 21 Another of his
disciples said to him,
"Lord, first let me go and
bury my father." 22 But
Jesus said to him, "Follow
me, and let the dead bury
their own dead."

Jesus Stills the Storm

23 And when he got into
the boat, his disciples followed him. 24 A windstorm
arose on the sea, so great
that the boat was being
swamped by the waves; but
he was asleep. 25 And they
went and woke him up,
saying, "Lord, save us! We
are perishing!" 26 And he
said to them, "Why are you
afraid, you of little faith?"
Then he got up and rebuked
the winds and the sea; and
there was a dead calm.
27 They were amazed, say-
ing, "What sort of man is
this, that even the winds
and the sea obey him?"

Jesus Heals the Gadarene Demoniacs

28 When he came to the
other side, to the country of
the Gadarenes,[v] two de-
moniacs coming out of the
tombs met him. They were
so fierce that no one could
pass that way. 29 Suddenly
they shouted, "What have
you to do with us, Son of
God? Have you come here
to torment us before the
time?" 30 Now a large herd
of swine was feeding at
some distance from them.
31 The demons begged him,
"If you cast us out, send us
into the herd of swine."

[v] Other ancient authorities read *Gergesenes*; others, *Gerasenes*

οὐκ ἔχει ποῦ τὴν κεφαλὴν κλίνῃ.
has not where the(his) head he may lay.
21 ἕτερος δὲ τῶν μαθητῶν εἶπεν
And another of the disciples said
αὐτῷ· κύριε, ἐπίτρεψόν μοι πρῶτον
to him: Lord, allow me first
ἀπελθεῖν καὶ θάψαι τὸν πατέρα μου.
to go away and bury the father of me.
22 ὁ δὲ Ἰησοῦς λέγει αὐτῷ· ἀκολούθει
– But Jesus says to him: Follow thou
μοι, καὶ ἄφες τοὺς νεκροὺς θάψαι τοὺς
me, and leave the dead to bury the
ἑαυτῶν νεκρούς.
of themselves dead.
23 Καὶ ἐμβάντι αὐτῷ εἰς τὸ πλοῖον,
And embarking him[a] in the ship,
=as he embarked
ἠκολούθησαν αὐτῷ οἱ μαθηταὶ αὐτοῦ.
followed him the disciples of him.
24 καὶ ἰδοὺ σεισμὸς μέγας ἐγένετο ἐν
And behold storm a great there was in
τῇ θαλάσσῃ, ὥστε τὸ πλοῖον καλύπτ-
the sea, so as the ship to be en-
εσθαι ὑπὸ τῶν κυμάτων· αὐτὸς δὲ ἐκάθευδεν.
veloped by the waves; but he was sleeping.
25 καὶ προσελθόντες ἤγειραν αὐτὸν λέγοντες·
And approaching they roused him saying:
κύριε, σῶσον, ἀπολλύμεθα. 26 καὶ λέγει
Lord, save, we are perishing. And he says
αὐτοῖς· τί δειλοί ἐστε, ὀλιγόπιστοι;
to them: Why fearful are ye, little-faiths?
τότε ἐγερθεὶς ἐπετίμησεν τοῖς ἀνέμοις καὶ
Then rising he rebuked the winds and
τῇ θαλάσσῃ, καὶ ἐγένετο γαλήνη μεγάλη.
the sea, and there was calm a great.
27 οἱ δὲ ἄνθρωποι ἐθαύμασαν λέγοντες·
And the men marvelled saying:
ποταπός ἐστιν οὗτος, ὅτι καὶ οἱ ἄνεμοι
Of what sort is this [man], that even the winds
καὶ ἡ θάλασσα αὐτῷ ὑπακούουσιν;
and the sea him obey?
28 Καὶ ἐλθόντος αὐτοῦ εἰς τὸ πέραν εἰς
And coming him[a] to the other side into
=when he came
τὴν χώραν τῶν Γαδαρηνῶν ὑπήντησαν
the country of the Gadarenes met
αὐτῷ δύο δαιμονιζόμενοι ἐκ τῶν μνημείων
him two demon-possessed out of the tombs
ἐξερχόμενοι, χαλεποὶ λίαν, ὥστε μὴ
coming *out*, dangerous exceedingly, so as not
ἰσχύειν τινὰ παρελθεῖν διὰ τῆς ὁδοῦ
to be able anyone[b] to pass through – way
ἐκείνης. 29 καὶ ἰδοὺ ἔκραξαν λέγοντες·
that. And behold they cried out saying:
τί ἡμῖν καὶ σοί, υἱὲ τοῦ θεοῦ; ἦλθες
What to us and to thee, Son – of God? camest thou
ὧδε προ καιροῦ βασανίσαι ἡμᾶς; 30 ἦν
here before [the] time to torture us? there was
δὲ μακρὰν ἀπ' αὐτῶν ἀγέλη χοίρων
Now far off from them a herd pigs
πολλῶν βοσκομένη. 31 οἱ δὲ δαίμονες
of many feeding. And the demons
παρεκάλουν αὐτὸν λέγοντες· εἰ ἐκβάλλεις
besought him saying: If thou expellest
ἡμᾶς, ἀπόστειλον ἡμᾶς εἰς τὴν ἀγέλην
us, send us into the herd

his head."
21 Another disciple said to
him, "Lord, first let me go
and bury my father."
22 But Jesus told him,
"Follow me, and let the
dead bury their own dead."

Jesus Calms the Storm

23 Then he got into the
boat and his disciples followed him. 24 Without
warning, a furious storm
came up on the lake, so that
the waves swept over the
boat. But Jesus was sleeping. 25 The disciples went
and woke him, saying,
"Lord, save us! We're go-
ing to drown!"
26 He replied, "You of little faith, why are you so
afraid?" Then he got up
and rebuked the winds and
the waves, and it was completely calm.
27 The men were amazed
and asked, "What kind of
man is this? Even the winds
and the waves obey him!"

The Healing of Two Demon-possessed Men

28 When he arrived at the
other side in the region of
the Gadarenes,[h] two de-
mon-possessed men com-
ing from the tombs met
him. They were so violent
that no one could pass that
way. 29 "What do you want
with us, Son of God?" they
shouted. "Have you come
here to torture us before
the appointed time?"
30 Some distance from
them a large herd of pigs
was feeding. 31 The demons
begged Jesus, "If you drive
us out, send us into the
herd of pigs."

[h] 28 Some manuscripts *Gergesenes*; others *Gerasenes*

32And he said to them,
"Go!" So they came out
and entered the swine; and
suddenly, the whole herd
rushed down the steep
bank into the sea and perished in the water. 33The
swineherds ran off, and on
going into the town, they
told the whole story about
what had happened to the
demoniacs. 34Then the
whole town came out to
meet Jesus; and when they
saw him, they begged him
to leave their neighbor-
hood. 1And after getting
into a boat he crossed the
sea and came to his own
town.

Jesus Heals a Paralytic

2 And just then some
people were carrying a paralyzed man lying on a bed.
When Jesus saw their faith,
he said to the paralytic,
"Take heart, son; your sins
are forgiven." 3Then some
of the scribes said to themselves, "This man is blaspheming." 4But Jesus, perceiving their thoughts,
said, "Why do you think
evil in your hearts? 5For
which is easier, to say,
'Your sins are forgiven,' or
to say, 'Stand up and
walk'? 6But so that you
may know that the Son of
Man has authority on earth
to forgive sins"—he then
said to the paralytic—
"Stand up, take your bed
and go to your home."
7And he stood up and went
to his home. 8When the
crowds saw it, they were
filled with awe, and they
glorified God, who had giv-
en such authority to human
beings.

τῶν χοίρων. **32** καὶ εἶπεν αὐτοῖς·
of the pigs. And he said to them:
ὑπάγετε. οἱ δὲ ἐξελθόντες ἀπῆλθον εἰς
Go ye. So the coming out [ones] went away into
τοὺς χοίρους· καὶ ἰδοὺ ὥρμησεν πᾶσα ἡ
the pigs; and behold rushed all the
ἀγέλη κατὰ τοῦ κρημνοῦ εἰς τὴν θάλασσαν,
herd down the precipice into the sea,
καὶ ἀπέθανον ἐν τοῖς ὕδασιν. **33** οἱ
and died in the waters. the
δὲ βόσκοντες ἔφυγον, καὶ ἀπελθόντες
But feeding [ones] fled, and going away
εἰς τὴν πόλιν ἀπήγγειλαν πάντα καὶ
into the city reported all things and
τὰ τῶν δαιμονιζομένων. **34** καὶ ἰδοὺ
the [things] of the demon-possessed [ones]. And behold
πᾶσα ἡ πόλις ἐξῆλθεν εἰς ὑπάντησιν
all the city came out with a view to a meeting [with]
τῷ Ἰησοῦ, καὶ ἰδόντες αὐτὸν παρεκάλεσαν
– Jesus, and seeing ²him ¹besought
ὅπως μεταβῇ ἀπὸ τῶν ὁρίων αὐτῶν.
so that he might remove from the borders of them.

9 Καὶ ἐμβὰς εἰς πλοῖον διεπέρασεν,
And embarking in a ship he crossed over,
καὶ ἦλθεν εἰς τὴν ἰδίαν πόλιν. **2** Καὶ
and came into the(his) own city. And
ἰδοὺ προσέφερον αὐτῷ παραλυτικὸν ἐπὶ
behold they brought to him a paralytic on
κλίνης βεβλημένον. καὶ ἰδὼν ὁ Ἰησοῦς
a mattress *having been* laid. And ²seeing – ¹Jesus
τὴν πίστιν αὐτῶν εἶπεν τῷ παραλυτικῷ·
the faith of them said to the paralytic:
θάρσει, τέκνον, ἀφίενταί σου αἱ ἁμαρτίαι.
Be of good cheer, child, are forgiven of thee the sins.
3 καὶ ἰδού τινες τῶν γραμματέων εἶπαν
And behold some of the scribes said
ἐν ἑαυτοῖς· οὗτος βλασφημεῖ. **4** καὶ
among themselves: This [man] blasphemes. And
εἰδὼς ὁ Ἰησοῦς τὰς ἐνθυμήσεις αὐτῶν
³knowing – ¹Jesus the thoughts of them
εἶπεν· ἱνατί ἐνθυμεῖσθε πονηρὰ ἐν ταῖς
said: Why think ye evil things in the
καρδίαις ὑμῶν; **5** τί γάρ ἐστιν εὐκοπώ-
hearts of you? for which is easier,
τερον, εἰπεῖν· ἀφίενταί σου αἱ ἁμαρτίαι, ἢ
to say: ⁴are forgiven ³of thee ¹The ²sins, or
εἰπεῖν· ἔγειρε καὶ περιπάτει; **6** ἵνα δὲ
to say: Rise and walk? But in order that
εἰδῆτε ὅτι ἐξουσίαν ἔχει ὁ υἱὸς τοῦ
ye may know that authority has the Son –
ἀνθρώπου ἐπὶ τῆς γῆς ἀφιέναι ἁμαρτίας
of man on the earth to forgive sins—
τότε λέγει τῷ παραλυτικῷ· ἔγειρε ἆρόν
then he says to the paralytic: Rise[,] take
σου τὴν κλίνην καὶ ὕπαγε εἰς τὸν οἶκόν
of thee the mattress and go to the house
σου. **7** καὶ ἐγερθεὶς ἀπῆλθεν εἰς τὸν
of thee. And rising he went away to the
οἶκον αὐτοῦ. **8** ἰδόντες δὲ οἱ ὄχλοι
house of him. But seeing the crowds
ἐφοβήθησαν καὶ ἐδόξασαν τὸν θεὸν τὸν
feared and glorified – God the [one]
δόντα ἐξουσίαν τοιαύτην τοῖς ἀνθρώποις.
giving ²authority ¹such – to men.

32He said to them, "Go!"
So they came out and went
into the pigs, and the whole
herd rushed down the steep
bank into the lake and died
in the water. 33Those tending the pigs ran off, went
into the town and reported
all this, including what had
happened to the demon-
possessed men. 34Then the
whole town went out to
meet Jesus. And when they
saw him, they pleaded with
him to leave their region.

Chapter 9

Jesus Heals a Paralytic

JESUS stepped into a
boat, crossed over and
came to his own town.
2Some men brought to him
a paralytic, lying on a mat.
When Jesus saw their faith,
he said to the paralytic,
"Take heart, son; your sins
are forgiven."
3At this, some of the
teachers of the law said to
themselves, "This fellow is
blaspheming!"
4Knowing their thoughts,
Jesus said, "Why do you
entertain evil thoughts in
your hearts? 5Which is easier: to say, 'Your sins are
forgiven,' or to say, 'Get up
and walk'? 6But so that you
may know that the Son of
Man has authority on earth
to forgive sins. . . ." Then
he said to the paralytic,
"Get up, take your mat and
go home." 7And the man
got up and went home.
8When the crowd saw this,
they were filled with awe;
and they praised God, who
had given such authority to
men.

The Call of Matthew

9 As Jesus was walking along, he saw a man called Matthew sitting at the tax booth; and he said to him, "Follow me." And he got up and followed him.

10 And as he sat at dinner[w] in the house, many tax collectors and sinners came and were sitting[x] with him and his disciples. 11 When the Pharisees saw this, they said to his disciples, "Why does your teacher eat with tax collectors and sinners?" 12 But when he heard this, he said, "Those who are well have no need of a physician, but those who are sick. 13 Go and learn what this means, 'I desire mercy, not sacrifice.' For I have come to call not the righteous but sinners."

The Question about Fasting

14 Then the disciples of John came to him, saying, "Why do we and the Pharisees fast often,[y] but your disciples do not fast?" 15 And Jesus said to them, "The wedding guests cannot mourn as long as the bridegroom is with them, can they? The days will come when the bridegroom is taken away from them, and then they will fast. 16 No one sews a piece of unshrunk cloth on an old cloak, for the patch pulls away from the cloak, and a worse tear is made. 17 Neither is new wine put into old wineskins; otherwise, the skins burst, and the

[w] Gk *reclined*
[x] Gk *were reclining*
[y] Other ancient authorities lack *often*

9 Καὶ παράγων ὁ Ἰησοῦς ἐκεῖθεν εἶδεν
And [2]passing by – [1]Jesus thence saw
ἄνθρωπον καθήμενον ἐπὶ τὸ τελώνιον,
a man sitting at the custom house,
Μαθθαῖον λεγόμενον, καὶ λέγει αὐτῷ·
Matthew named, and says to him:
Ἀκολούθει μοι. καὶ ἀναστὰς ἠκολούθησεν
Follow me. And rising up he followed
αὐτῷ. 10 Καὶ ἐγένετο αὐτοῦ ἀνακει-
him. And it came to pass him reclin-
=as he was reclining
μένου ἐν τῇ οἰκίᾳ, καὶ ἰδοὺ πολλοὶ
ing[a] in the house, and behold many
τελῶναι καὶ ἁμαρτωλοὶ ἐλθόντες συνανέκειντο
tax-collectors and sinners coming reclined at table with
τῷ Ἰησοῦ καὶ τοῖς μαθηταῖς αὐτοῦ.
– Jesus and the disciples of him.
11 καὶ ἰδόντες οἱ Φαρισαῖοι ἔλεγον τοῖς
And [2]seeing [1]the [1]Pharisees said to the
μαθηταῖς αὐτοῦ· διὰ τί μετὰ τῶν τελωνῶν
disciples of him: Why with – tax-collectors
καὶ ἁμαρτωλῶν ἐσθίει ὁ διδάσκαλος ὑμῶν;
and sinners eats the teacher of you?
12 ὁ δὲ ἀκούσας εἶπεν· οὐ χρείαν
But he hearing said: Not need
ἔχουσιν οἱ ἰσχύοντες ἰατροῦ ἀλλ' οἱ
have the [ones] being strong of a physician but the [ones]
=those
κακῶς ἔχοντες. 13 πορευθέντες δὲ μάθετε
ill having. But going learn ye
who are ill.
τί ἐστιν· ἔλεος θέλω καὶ οὐ θυσίαν· οὐ
what it is: Mercy I desire and not sacrifice; not
γὰρ ἦλθον καλέσαι δικαίους ἀλλὰ
for I came to call righteous [people] but
ἁμαρτωλούς.
sinners.

14 Τότε προσέρχονται αὐτῷ οἱ μαθηταὶ
Then approach *to* him the disciples
Ἰωάννου λέγοντες· διὰ τί ἡμεῖς καὶ οἱ
of John saying: Why we and the
Φαρισαῖοι νηστεύομεν, οἱ δὲ μαθηταί
Pharisees fast, but the disciples
σου οὐ νηστεύουσιν; 15 καὶ εἶπεν
of thee fast not? And said
αὐτοῖς ὁ Ἰησοῦς· μὴ δύνανται οἱ
to them – Jesus: *not* Can the
υἱοὶ τοῦ νυμφῶνος πενθεῖν, ἐφ' ὅσον
sons of the bridechamber *to* mourn, so long as
μετ' αὐτῶν ἐστιν ὁ νυμφίος; ἐλεύσονται
with them is the bridegroom? [2]will come
δὲ ἡμέραι ὅταν ἀπαρθῇ ἀπ' αὐτῶν ὁ
[1]but [2]days when is taken away from them the
νυμφίος, καὶ τότε νηστεύσουσιν. 16 οὐδεὶς
bridegroom, and then they will fast. no one
δὲ ἐπιβάλλει ἐπίβλημα ῥάκους ἀγνάφου
Now puts *on* a patch cloth of unfulled
ἐπὶ ἱματίῳ παλαιῷ· αἴρει γὰρ τὸ
on garment an old; for takes away the
πλήρωμα αὐτοῦ ἀπὸ τοῦ ἱματίου, καὶ
fullness of it from the garment, and
χεῖρον σχίσμα γίνεται. 17 οὐδὲ
a worse rent becomes. Neither
βάλλουσιν οἶνον νέον εἰς ἀσκοὺς
do they put wine new into wineskins
παλαιούς· εἰ δὲ μή γε, ῥήγνυνται
old; otherwise, are burst

The Calling of Matthew

9 As Jesus went on from there, he saw a man named Matthew sitting at the tax collector's booth. "Follow me," he told him, and Matthew got up and followed him.

10 While Jesus was having dinner at Matthew's house, many tax collectors and "sinners" came and ate with him and his disciples. 11 When the Pharisees saw this, they asked his disciples, "Why does your teacher eat with tax collectors and 'sinners'?"

12 On hearing this, Jesus said, "It is not the healthy who need a doctor, but the sick. 13 But go and learn what this means: 'I desire mercy, not sacrifice.'[i] For I have not come to call the righteous, but sinners."

Jesus Questioned About Fasting

14 Then John's disciples came and asked him, "How is it that we and the Pharisees fast, but your disciples do not fast?"

15 Jesus answered, "How can the guests of the bridegroom mourn while he is with them? The time will come when the bridegroom will be taken from them; then they will fast.

16 "No one sews a patch of unshrunk cloth on an old garment, for the patch will pull away from the garment, making the tear worse. 17 Neither do men pour new wine into old wineskins. If they do, the skins will burst, the wine

[i] *13* Hosea 6:6

wine is spilled, and the
skins are destroyed; but
new wine is put into fresh
wineskins, and so both are
preserved."

*A Girl Restored to Life
and a Woman Healed*

18 While he was saying
these things to them, suddenly a leader of the synagogue[z] came in and knelt
before him, saying, "My
daughter has just died; but
come and lay your hand on
her, and she will live."
19 And Jesus got up and followed him, with his disciples. 20 Then suddenly a
woman who had been suf-
fering from hemorrhages
for twelve years came up
behind him and touched the
fringe of his cloak, 21 for
she said to herself, "If I
only touch his cloak, I will
be made well." 22 Jesus
turned, and seeing her he
said, "Take heart, daugh-
ter; your faith has made
you well." And instantly
the woman was made well.
23 When Jesus came to the
leader's house and saw the
flute players and the crowd
making a commotion, 24 he
said, "Go away; for the girl
is not dead but sleeping."
And they laughed at him.
25 But when the crowd had
been put outside, he went
in and took her by the hand,
and the girl got up. 26 And
the report of this spread
throughout that district.

*Jesus Heals Two Blind
Men*

27 As Jesus went on
from there, two blind men
followed him, crying loudly, "Have mercy on us, Son
of David!" 28 When he en-
tered the house, the blind

[z] Gk lacks *of the synagogue*

οἱ ἀσκοί, καὶ ὁ οἶνος ἐκχεῖται καὶ
the wineskins, and the wine is poured out and
οἱ ἀσκοὶ ἀπόλλυνται. ἀλλὰ βάλλουσιν
the wineskins are destroyed. But they put
οἶνον νέον εἰς ἀσκοὺς καινούς, καὶ
wine new into wineskins fresh, and
ἀμφότεροι συντηροῦνται.
both are preserved.
18 Ταῦτα αὐτοῦ λαλοῦντος αὐτοῖς,
These things him speaking[a] to them,
=As he was speaking these things
ἰδοὺ ἄρχων [εἷς] προσελθὼν προσ-
behold ruler one approaching wor-
εκύνει αὐτῷ λέγων ὅτι ἡ θυγάτηρ
shipped him saying[,] – The daughter
μου ἄρτι ἐτελεύτησεν· ἀλλὰ ἐλθὼν
of me just now died; but coming
ἐπίθες τὴν χεῖρά σου ἐπ' αὐτήν,
lay *on* the hand of thee on her,
καὶ ζήσεται. 19 καὶ ἐγερθεὶς ὁ Ἰησοῦς
and she will live. And rising – Jesus
ἠκολούθει αὐτῷ καὶ οἱ μαθηταὶ αὐτοῦ.
followed him[,] also the disciples of him.
20 Καὶ ἰδοὺ γυνὴ αἱμορροοῦσα
And behold a woman suffering from a flow of blood
δώδεκα ἔτη προσελθοῦσα ὄπισθεν ἥψατο
twelve years approaching behind touched
τοῦ κρασπέδου τοῦ ἱματίου αὐτοῦ·
the fringe of the garment of him;
21 ἔλεγεν γὰρ ἐν ἑαυτῇ· ἐὰν μόνον
for she was saying in herself: If only
ἅψωμαι τοῦ ἱματίου αὐτοῦ, σωθήσομαι.
I may touch the garment of him, I shall be healed.
22 ὁ δὲ Ἰησοῦς στραφεὶς καὶ ἰδὼν
– And Jesus turning and seeing
αὐτὴν εἶπεν· θάρσει, θύγατερ· ἡ
her said: Be of good cheer, daughter; the
πίστις σου σέσωκέν σε. καὶ ἐσώθη
faith of thee has healed thee. And was healed
ἡ γυνὴ ἀπὸ τῆς ὥρας ἐκείνης. 23 Καὶ
the woman from – hour that. And
ἐλθὼν ὁ Ἰησοῦς εἰς τὴν οἰκίαν τοῦ ἄρχοντος
coming – Jesus into the house of the ruler
καὶ ἰδὼν τοὺς αὐλητὰς καὶ τὸν ὄχλον
and seeing the flute-players and the crowd
θορυβούμενον 24 ἔλεγεν· ἀναχωρεῖτε· οὐ
terrified he said: Depart ye; not
γὰρ ἀπέθανεν τὸ κοράσιον ἀλλὰ καθεύδει.
for died the girl but sleeps.
καὶ κατεγέλων αὐτοῦ. 25 ὅτε δὲ
And they ridiculed him. But when
ἐξεβλήθη ὁ ὄχλος, εἰσελθὼν ἐκράτησεν
was put out the crowd, entering he took hold of
τῆς χειρὸς αὐτῆς, καὶ ἠγέρθη τὸ κορα-
the hand of her, and was raised the girl.
σιον. 26 καὶ ἐξῆλθεν ἡ φήμη αὕτη
And went out – report this
εἰς ὅλην τὴν γῆν ἐκείνην. 27 Καὶ
into all – land that. And
παράγοντι ἐκεῖθεν τῷ Ἰησοῦ ἠκολούθησαν
passing by thence – Jesus[e] followed
=as Jesus passed by thence
δύο τυφλοὶ κράζοντες καὶ λέγοντες· ἐλέησον
two blind men crying out and saying: Pity
ἡμᾶς, υἱὸς Δαυίδ. 28 ἐλθόντι δὲ εἰς
us, son of David. And coming[e] into
=when he came

will run out and the wineskins will be ruined. No,
they pour new wine into
new wineskins, and both
are preserved."

*A Dead Girl and a Sick
Woman*

18 While he was saying
this, a ruler came and knelt
before him and said, "My
daughter has just died. But
come and put your hand on
her, and she will live."
19 Jesus got up and went
with him, and so did his disciples.
20 Just then a woman who
had been subject to bleeding for twelve years came
up behind him and touched
the edge of his cloak. 21 She
said to herself, "If I only
touch his cloak, I will be
healed."
22 Jesus turned and saw
her. "Take heart, daugh-
ter," he said, "your faith
has healed you." And the
woman was healed from
that moment.
23 When Jesus entered the
ruler's house and saw the
flute players and the noisy
crowd, 24 he said, "Go
away. The girl is not dead
but asleep." But they
laughed at him. 25 After the
crowd had been put out-
side, he went in and took
the girl by the hand, and
she got up. 26 News of this
spread through all that region.

*Jesus Heals the Blind and
Mute*

27 As Jesus went on from
there, two blind men fol-
lowed him, calling out,
"Have mercy on us, Son of
David!"
28 When he had gone in-
doors, the blind men came

men came to him; and
Jesus said to them, "Do
you believe that I am able
to do this?" They said to
him, "Yes, Lord." 29 Then
he touched their eyes and
said, "According to your
faith let it be done to you."
30 And their eyes were
opened. Then Jesus sternly
ordered them, "See that no
one knows of this." 31 But
they went away and spread
the news about him
throughout that district.

Jesus Heals One Who Was Mute

32 After they had gone
away, a demoniac who was
mute was brought to him.
33 And when the demon had
been cast out, the one who
had been mute spoke; and
the crowds were amazed
and said, "Never has any-
thing like this been seen in
Israel." 34 But the Pharisees
said, "By the ruler of the
demons he casts out the demons."[a]

The Harvest Is Great, the Laborers Few

35 Then Jesus went
about all the cities and villages, teaching in their synagogues, and proclaiming
the good news of the kingdom, and curing every disease and every sickness.
36 When he saw the crowds,
he had compassion for
them, because they were
harassed and helpless, like
sheep without a shepherd.
37 Then he said to his disciples, "The harvest is plentiful, but the laborers are
few; 38 therefore ask the
Lord of the harvest to send
out laborers into his harvest."

[a] Other ancient authorities lack this verse

τὴν οἰκίαν προσῆλθον αὐτῷ οἱ τυφλοί,
the house approached *to* him the blind men,

καὶ λέγει αὐτοῖς ὁ Ἰησοῦς· πιστεύετε
and says to them – Jesus: Believe ye

ὅτι δύναμαι τοῦτο ποιῆσαι; λέγουσιν
that I can this *to* do? They say

αὐτῷ· ναί, κύριε. 29 τότε ἥψατο τῶν
to him: Yes, Lord. Then he touched the

ὀφθαλμῶν αὐτῶν λέγων· κατὰ τὴν
eyes of them saying: According to the

πίστιν ὑμῶν γενηθήτω ὑμῖν. 30 καὶ
faith of you let it be to you. And

ἠνεῴχθησαν αὐτῶν οἱ ὀφθαλμοί. καὶ
were opened of them the eyes. And

ἐνεβριμήθη αὐτοῖς ὁ Ἰησοῦς λέγων·
sternly admonished them – Jesus saying:

ὁρᾶτε μηδεὶς γινωσκέτω. 31 οἱ δὲ
See [2]no one [1]let [3]know. But they

ἐξελθόντες διεφήμισαν αὐτὸν ἐν ὅλῃ
going out spread about him in all

τῇ γῇ ἐκείνῃ. 32 Αὐτῶν δὲ ἐξερχομένων,
– land that. And them going out,[a]
=as they were going out,

ἰδοὺ προσήνεγκαν αὐτῷ κωφὸν δαι-
behold they brought to him a dumb man *being*

μονιζόμενον. 33 καὶ ἐκβληθέντος τοῦ
demon-possessed. And being expelled the
=when the demon was expelled

δαιμονίου ἐλάλησεν ὁ κωφός. καὶ ἐθαύμασαν
demon[a] spoke the dumb man. And marvelled

οἱ ὄχλοι λέγοντες· οὐδέποτε ἐφάνη οὕτως
the crowds saying: Never it appeared thus

ἐν τῷ Ἰσραήλ. 34 οἱ δὲ Φαρισαῖοι
in – Israel. But the Pharisees

ἔλεγον· ἐν τῷ ἄρχοντι τῶν δαιμονίων
said: By the ruler of the demons

ἐκβάλλει τὰ δαιμόνια.
he expels the demons.

35 Καὶ περιῆγεν ὁ Ἰησοῦς τὰς
And went about – Jesus the

πόλεις πάσας καὶ τὰς κώμας, διδάσκων
cities all and the villages, teaching

ἐν ταῖς συναγωγαῖς αὐτῶν καὶ κηρύσσων
in the synagogues of them and proclaiming

τὸ εὐαγγέλιον τῆς βασιλείας καὶ θεραπεύων
the gospel of the kingdom and healing

πᾶσαν νόσον καὶ πᾶσαν μαλακίαν.
every disease and every illness.

36 Ἰδὼν δὲ τοὺς ὄχλους ἐσπλαγχνίσθη
And seeing the crowds he was filled with tenderness

περὶ αὐτῶν, ὅτι ἦσαν ἐσκυλμένοι καὶ
concerning them, because they were distressed and

ἐρριμμένοι ὡσεὶ πρόβατα μὴ ἔχοντα
prostrate as sheep not having

ποιμένα. 37 τότε λέγει τοῖς μαθηταῖς
a shepherd. Then he says to the disciples

αὐτοῦ· ὁ μὲν θερισμὸς πολύς, οἱ δὲ
of him: Indeed the harvest [is] much, but the

ἐργάται ὀλίγοι· 38 δεήθητε οὖν τοῦ κυρίου
workmen few; pray ye therefore the Lord

τοῦ θερισμοῦ ὅπως ἐκβάλῃ
of the harvest so that he may thrust forth

ἐργάτας εἰς τὸν θερισμὸν αὐτοῦ. 10 Καὶ
workmen into the harvest of him. And

to him, and he asked them,
"Do you believe that I am
able to do this?"
"Yes, Lord," they re-
plied.
29 Then he touched their
eyes and said, "According
to your faith will it be done
to you"; 30 and their sight
was restored. Jesus warned
them sternly, "See that no
one knows about this."
31 But they went out and
spread the news about him
all over that region.
32 While they were going
out, a man who was de-
mon-possessed and could
not talk was brought to
Jesus. 33 And when the demon was driven out, the
man who had been mute
spoke. The crowd was
amazed and said, "Nothing
like this has ever been seen
in Israel."
34 But the Pharisees said,
"It is by the prince of demons that he drives out demons."

The Workers Are Few

35 Jesus went through all
the towns and villages,
teaching in their syna-
gogues, preaching the good
news of the kingdom and
healing every disease and
sickness. 36 When he saw
the crowds, he had com-
passion on them, because
they were harassed and
helpless, like sheep without
a shepherd. 37 Then he said
to his disciples, "The harvest is plentiful but the
workers are few. 38 Ask the
Lord of the harvest, therefore, to send out workers
into his harvest field."

Chapter 10

The Twelve Apostles

THEN Jesus[b] sum-
moned his twelve dis-
ciples and gave them au-
thority over unclean spirits, to cast them out, and to
cure every disease and every sickness. 2 These are
the names of the twelve
apostles: first, Simon, also
known as Peter, and his
brother Andrew; James son
of Zebedee, and his brother
John; 3 Philip and Bartholomew; Thomas and Mat-
thew the tax collector;
James son of Alphaeus,
and Thaddaeus;[c] 4 Simon
the Cananaean, and Judas
Iscariot, the one who be-
trayed him.

The Mission of the Twelve

5 These twelve Jesus
sent out with the following
instructions: "Go nowhere
among the Gentiles, and
enter no town of the Samaritans, 6 but go rather to the
lost sheep of the house of
Israel. 7 As you go, pro-
claim the good news, 'The
kingdom of heaven has
come near.'[d] 8 Cure the
sick, raise the dead,
cleanse the lepers,[e] cast
out demons. You received
without payment; give
without payment. 9 Take no
gold, or silver, or copper in
your belts, 10 no bag for
your journey, or two tu-
nics, or sandals, or a staff;
for laborers deserve their
food. 11 Whatever town or
village you enter, find out
who in it is worthy, and
stay there until you leave.

[b] Gk *he*
[c] Other ancient authorities read *Lebbaeus*, or *Lebbaeus called Thaddaeus*
[d] Or *is at hand*
[e] The terms *leper* and *leprosy* can refer to several diseases

προσκαλεσάμενος τοὺς δώδεκα μαθητὰς
calling forward the twelve disciples

αὐτοῦ ἔδωκεν αὐτοῖς ἐξουσίαν πνευμάτων
of him he gave to them authority of(over) spirits

ἀκαθάρτων ὥστε ἐκβάλλειν αὐτά, καὶ
unclean so as to expel them, and

θεραπεύειν πᾶσαν νόσον καὶ πᾶσαν μαλα-
to heal every disease and every ill-

κίαν. 2 Τῶν δὲ δώδεκα ἀποστόλων
ness. Now of the twelve apostles

τὰ ὀνόματά ἐστιν ταῦτα· πρῶτος Σίμων
the names is(are) these: first Simon

ὁ λεγόμενος Πέτρος καὶ Ἀνδρέας ὁ
the [one] named Peter and Andrew the

ἀδελφὸς αὐτοῦ, καὶ Ἰάκωβος ὁ τοῦ
brother of him, and James the [son] –

Ζεβεδαίου καὶ Ἰωάννης ὁ ἀδελφὸς αὐτοῦ,
of Zebedee and John the brother of him,

3 Φίλιππος καὶ Βαρθολομαῖος, Θωμᾶς
Philip and Bartholomew, Thomas

καὶ Μαθθαῖος ὁ τελώνης, Ἰάκωβος
and Matthew the tax-collector, James

ὁ τοῦ Ἁλφαίου καὶ Θαδδαῖος, 4 Σίμων
the [son] – of Alphæus and Thaddæus, Simon

ὁ Καναναῖος καὶ Ἰούδας ὁ Ἰσκαριώτης
the Cananæan and Judas – Iscariot

ὁ καὶ παραδοὺς αὐτόν. 5 Τούτους
the [one] also betraying him. These

τοὺς δώδεκα ἀπέστειλεν ὁ Ἰησοῦς
– twelve sent forth – Jesus

παραγγείλας αὐτοῖς λέγων·
giving charge to them saying:

Εἰς ὁδὸν ἐθνῶν μὴ ἀπέλθητε, καὶ
Into [the] way of [the] nations go ye not, and

εἰς πόλιν Σαμαριτῶν μὴ εἰσέλθητε·
into a city of Samaritans enter not;

6 πορεύεσθε δὲ μᾶλλον πρὸς τὰ πρόβατα
but go rather unto the sheep

τὰ ἀπολωλότα οἴκου Ἰσραήλ. 7 πορευ-
the lost of [the] house of Israel. And

όμενοι δὲ κηρύσσετε λέγοντες ὅτι ἤγγικεν
going proclaim ye saying[,] – has drawn near

ἡ βασιλεία τῶν οὐρανῶν. 8 ἀσθενοῦντας
The kingdom of the heavens. Ailing [ones]

θεραπεύετε, νεκροὺς ἐγείρετε, λεπροὺς
heal ye, dead [ones] raise, lepers

καθαρίζετε, δαιμόνια ἐκβάλλετε· δωρεὰν
cleanse, demons expel; freely

ἐλάβετε, δωρεὰν δότε. 9 Μὴ κτήσησθε
ye received, freely give. Do not provide

χρυσὸν μηδὲ ἄργυρον μηδὲ χαλκὸν εἰς
gold nor silver nor brass in

τὰς ζώνας ὑμῶν, 10 μὴ πήραν εἰς ὁδὸν
the girdles of you, not a wallet for [the] way

μηδὲ δύο χιτῶνας μηδὲ ὑποδήματα μηδὲ
nor two tunics nor sandals nor

ῥάβδον· ἄξιος γὰρ ὁ ἐργάτης τῆς
a staff; for worthy [is] the workman of the

τροφῆς αὐτοῦ. 11 εἰς ἣν δ' ἂν πόλιν
food of him. And into whatever city

ἢ κώμην εἰσέλθητε, ἐξετάσατε τίς ἐν
or village ye may enter, inquire who in

αὐτῇ ἄξιός ἐστιν· κἀκεῖ μείνατε ἕως ἂν
it worthy is; and there remain until

Chapter 10

Jesus Sends Out the Twelve

HE called his twelve dis-
ciples to him and gave
them authority to drive out
evil[j] spirits and to heal every disease and sickness.
2 These are the names of
the twelve apostles: first,
Simon (who is called Peter)
and his brother Andrew;
James son of Zebedee, and
his brother John; 3 Philip
and Bartholomew; Thomas
and Matthew the tax col-
lector; James son of Al-
phaeus, and Thaddaeus;
4 Simon the Zealot and Judas Iscariot, who betrayed
him.
5 These twelve Jesus sent
out with the following instructions: "Do not go
among the Gentiles or enter
any town of the Samari-
tans. 6 Go rather to the lost
sheep of Israel. 7 As you go,
preach this message: 'The
kingdom of heaven is near.'
8 Heal the sick, raise the
dead, cleanse those who
have leprosy,[k] drive out
demons. Freely you have
received, freely give. 9 Do
not take along any gold or
silver or copper in your
belts; 10 take no bag for the
journey, or extra tunic, or
sandals or a staff; for the
worker is worth his keep.
11 "Whatever town or vil-
lage you enter, search for
some worthy person there
and stay at his house until

[j] 1 Greek *unclean*
[k] 8 The Greek word was used for various diseases affecting the skin—not necessarily leprosy.

12 As you enter the house, greet it. 13 If the house is worthy, let your peace come upon it; but if it is not worthy, let your peace return to you. 14 If anyone will not welcome you or listen to your words, shake off the dust from your feet as you leave that house or town. 15 Truly I tell you, it will be more tolerable for the land of Sodom and Gomorrah on the day of judgment than for that town.

Coming Persecutions

16 "See, I am sending you out like sheep into the midst of wolves; so be wise as serpents and innocent as doves. 17 Beware of them, for they will hand you over to councils and flog you in their synagogues; 18 and you will be dragged before governors and kings because of me, as a testimony to them and the Gentiles. 19 When they hand you over, do not worry about how you are to speak or what you are to say; for what you are to say will be given to you at that time; 20 for it is not you who speak, but the Spirit of your Father speaking through you. 21 Brother will betray brother to death, and a father his child, and children will rise against parents and have them put to death; 22 and you will be hated by all because of my name. But the one who endures to the end will be saved. 23 When they persecute you in one town, flee

ἐξέλθητε. **12** εἰσερχόμενοι δὲ εἰς τὴν
ye may go out. And entering into the

οἰκίαν ἀσπάσασθε αὐτήν· **13** καὶ ἐὰν μὲν
house greet it; and if indeed

ᾖ ἡ οἰκία ἀξία, ἐλθάτω ἡ εἰρήνη ὑμῶν
be the house worthy, let come the peace of you

ἐπ' αὐτήν· ἐὰν δὲ μὴ ᾖ ἀξία, ἡ εἰρήνη
on it; but if it be not worthy, the peace

ὑμῶν πρὸς ὑμᾶς ἐπιστραφήτω. **14** καὶ
of you unto you let return. And

ὃς ἂν μὴ δέξηται ὑμᾶς μηδὲ ἀκούσῃ
whoever may not receive you nor hear

τοὺς λόγους ὑμῶν, ἐξερχόμενοι ἔξω
the words of you, going *out* outside

τῆς οἰκίας ἢ τῆς πόλεως ἐκείνης ἐκτινά-
– house or – city that shake

ξατε τὸν κονιορτὸν τῶν ποδῶν ὑμῶν.
off the dust of the feet of you.

15 ἀμὴν λέγω ὑμῖν, ἀνεκτότερον ἔσται
Truly I tell you, more tolerable it will be [for]

γῇ Σοδόμων καὶ Γομόρρων ἐν ἡμέρᾳ κρίσεως
[the] land of Sodom and Gomorra in [the] day of judgment

ἢ τῇ πόλει ἐκείνῃ. **16** Ἰδοὺ ἐγὼ
than [for] – city that. Behold I

ἀποστέλλω ὑμᾶς ὡς πρόβατα ἐν μέσῳ
send forth you as sheep in [the] midst

λύκων· γίνεσθε οὖν φρόνιμοι ὡς οἱ
of wolves; be ye therefore prudent as –

ὄφεις καὶ ἀκέραιοι ὡς αἱ περιστεραί.
serpents and harmless as – doves.

17 Προσέχετε δὲ ἀπὸ τῶν ἀνθρώπων·
And beware from(of) – men;

παραδώσουσιν γὰρ ὑμᾶς εἰς συνέδρια,
for they will deliver up you to councils,

καὶ ἐν ταῖς συναγωγαῖς αὐτῶν μαστιγώ-
and in the synagogues of them they will

σουσιν ὑμᾶς· **18** καὶ ἐπὶ ἡγεμόνας δὲ καὶ
scourge you; and before leaders and also

βασιλεῖς ἀχθήσεσθε ἕνεκεν ἐμοῦ, εἰς
kings ye will be led for the sake of me, for

μαρτύριον αὐτοῖς καὶ τοῖς ἔθνεσιν.
a testimony to them and to the nations.

19 ὅταν δὲ παραδῶσιν ὑμᾶς, μὴ μεριμνή-
But when they deliver up you, do not be

σητε πῶς ἢ τί λαλήσητε· δοθήσεται
anxious how or what ye may say; 'it will be given

γὰρ ὑμῖν ἐν ἐκείνῃ τῇ ὥρᾳ τί λαλήσητε·
'for to you in that – hour what ye may say;

20 οὐ γὰρ ὑμεῖς ἐστε οἱ λαλοῦντες,
for not ye are the [ones] speaking,

ἀλλὰ τὸ πνεῦμα τοῦ πατρὸς ὑμῶν τὸ
but the Spirit of the Father of you the [one]

λαλοῦν ἐν ὑμῖν. **21** παραδώσει δὲ
speaking in you. And 'will deliver up

ἀδελφὸς • ἀδελφὸν εἰς θάνατον καὶ πατὴρ
'brother brother to death and father

τέκνον, καὶ ἐπαναστήσονται τέκνα ἐπὶ
child, and will stand up children against

γονεῖς καὶ θανατώσουσιν αὐτούς. **22** καὶ
parents and put to death them. And

ἔσεσθε μισούμενοι ὑπὸ πάντων διὰ
ye will be *being* hated by all men on account of

τὸ ὄνομά μου· ὁ δὲ ὑπομείνας εἰς
the name of me; but the [one] enduring to

τέλος, οὗτος σωθήσεται. **23** ὅταν δὲ
[the] end, this will be saved. But when

you leave. 12 As you enter the home, give it your greeting. 13 If the home is deserving, let your peace rest on it; if it is not, let your peace return to you. 14 If anyone will not welcome you or listen to your words, shake the dust off your feet when you leave that home or town. 15 I tell you the truth, it will be more bearable for Sodom and Gomorrah on the day of judgment than for that town. 16 I am sending you out like sheep among wolves. Therefore be as shrewd as snakes and as innocent as doves.

17 "Be on your guard against men; they will hand you over to the local councils and flog you in their synagogues. 18 On my account you will be brought before governors and kings as witnesses to them and to the Gentiles. 19 But when they arrest you, do not worry about what to say or how to say it. At that time you will be given what to say, 20 for it will not be you speaking, but the Spirit of your Father speaking through you.

21 "Brother will betray brother to death, and a father his child; children will rebel against their parents and have them put to death. 22 All men will hate you because of me, but he who stands firm to the end will be saved. 23 When you are

to the next; for truly I tell
you, you will not have gone
through all the towns of Israel before the Son of Man
comes.
24 "A disciple is not
above the teacher, nor a
slave above the master; 25 it
is enough for the disciple to
be like the teacher, and the
slave like the master. If
they have called the master
of the house Beelzebul,
how much more will they
malign those of his household!

Whom to Fear

26 "So have no fear of
them; for nothing is cov-
ered up that will not be uncovered, and nothing se-
cret that will not become
known. 27 What I say to you
in the dark, tell in the light;
and what you hear whis-
pered, proclaim from the
housetops. 28 Do not fear
those who kill the body but
cannot kill the soul; rather
fear him who can destroy
both soul and body in
hell.[f] 29 Are not two sparrows sold for a penny? Yet
not one of them will fall to
the ground apart from your
Father. 30 And even the
hairs of your head are all
counted. 31 So do not be
afraid; you are of more value than many sparrows.
32 "Everyone therefore
who acknowledges me be-
fore others, I also will acknowledge before my Fa-
ther in heaven; 33 but whoever denies me before
others, I also will deny before my Father in heaven.

[f] Gk *Gehenna*

διώκωσιν ὑμᾶς ἐν τῇ πόλει ταύτῃ,
they persecute you in – city this,
φεύγετε εἰς τὴν ἑτέραν· ἀμὴν γὰρ
flee ye to – [an]other; for truly
λέγω ὑμῖν, οὐ μὴ τελέσητε τὰς πόλεις
I tell you, by no means ye will complete the cities
[τοῦ] Ἰσραὴλ ἕως ἔλθῃ ὁ υἱὸς τοῦ ἀν-
– of Israel until comes the Son – of
θρώπου. **24** Οὐκ ἔστιν μαθητὴς ὑπὲρ
man. not is A disciple above
τὸν διδάσκαλον οὐδὲ δοῦλος ὑπὲρ τὸν
the teacher nor a slave above the
κύριον αὐτοῦ. **25** ἀρκετὸν τῷ μαθητῇ
lord of him. Enough for the disciple
ἵνα γένηται ὡς ὁ διδάσκαλος αὐτοῦ,
that he be as the teacher of him,
καὶ ὁ δοῦλος ὡς ὁ κύριος αὐτοῦ. εἰ
and the slave as the lord of him. If
τὸν οἰκοδεσπότην Βεεζεβοὺλ ἐπεκάλεσαν,
the housemaster Beelzebub they called,
πόσῳ μᾶλλον τοὺς οἰκιακοὺς αὐτοῦ.
how much more the members of [the] household of him.
26 μὴ οὖν φοβηθῆτε αὐτούς· οὐδὲν γάρ
Therefore fear ye not them; for nothing
ἐστιν κεκαλυμμένον ὃ οὐκ ἀποκαλυφ-
is *having been* veiled which will not be un-
θήσεται, καὶ κρυπτὸν ὃ οὐ γνωσθήσεται.
veiled, and hidden which will not be made known.
27 ὃ λέγω ὑμῖν ἐν τῇ σκοτίᾳ, εἴπατε
What I say to you in the darkness, say ye
ἐν τῷ φωτί· καὶ ὃ εἰς τὸ οὖς ἀκούετε,
in the light; and what in the ear ye hear,
κηρύξατε ἐπὶ τῶν δωμάτων. **28** καὶ
proclaim on the housetops. And
μὴ φοβεῖσθε ἀπὸ τῶν ἀποκτεννόντων
do not fear – the [ones] killing
τὸ σῶμα, τὴν δὲ ψυχὴν μὴ δυναμένων
the body, but the soul not *being* able
ἀποκτεῖναι· φοβεῖσθε δὲ μᾶλλον τὸν
to kill; but fear ye rather the [one]
δυνάμενον καὶ ψυχὴν καὶ σῶμα ἀπολέσαι
***being* able both soul and body to destroy**
ἐν γεέννῃ. **29** οὐχὶ δύο στρουθία ἀσσα-
in gehenna. Not two sparrows of(for) a
ρίου πωλεῖται; καὶ ἓν ἐξ αὐτῶν οὐ
farthing are sold? and one of them not
πεσεῖται ἐπὶ τὴν γῆν ἄνευ τοῦ πατρὸς
will fall on the earth without the Father
ὑμῶν. **30** ὑμῶν δὲ καὶ αἱ τρίχες τῆς
of you. But of you even the hairs of the
κεφαλῆς πᾶσαι ἠριθμημέναι εἰσίν. **31** μὴ
head all *having been* numbered are. not
οὖν φοβεῖσθε· πολλῶν στρουθίων διαφέρετε
Therefore fear ye; [3]many [4]sparrows [2]excel
ὑμεῖς. **32** Πᾶς οὖν ὅστις ὁμολογήσει
[1]ye. Everyone therefore who shall confess
ἐν ἐμοὶ ἔμπροσθεν τῶν ἀνθρώπων,
– me before – men,
ὁμολογήσω κἀγὼ ἐν αὐτῷ ἔμπροσθεν
will confess I also – him before
τοῦ πατρός μου τοῦ ἐν τοῖς οὐρανοῖς·
the Father of me – in the heavens;
33 ὅστις δ' ἂν ἀρνήσηταί με ἔμπροσθεν
and whoever denies me before
τῶν ἀνθρώπων, ἀρνήσομαι κἀγὼ αὐτὸν
– men, will deny I also him

persecuted in one place,
flee to another. I tell you
the truth, you will not finish
going through the cities of
Israel before the Son of
Man comes.
24 "A student is not above
his teacher, nor a servant
above his master. 25 It is
enough for the student to
be like his teacher, and the
servant like his master. If
the head of the house has
been called Beelzebub,[l]
how much more the mem-
bers of his household!
26 "So do not be afraid of
them. There is nothing concealed that will not be disclosed, or hidden that will
not be made known.
27 What I tell you in the
dark, speak in the daylight;
what is whispered in your
ear, proclaim from the
roofs. 28 Do not be afraid of
those who kill the body but
cannot kill the soul. Rather, be afraid of the One who
can destroy both soul and
body in hell. 29 Are not two
sparrows sold for a pen-
ny[m]? Yet not one of them
will fall to the ground apart
from the will of your Fa-
ther. 30 And even the very
hairs of your head are all
numbered. 31 So don't be
afraid; you are worth more
than many sparrows.
32 "Whoever acknowl-
edges me before men, I will
also acknowledge him be-
fore my Father in heaven.
33 But whoever disowns me
before men, I will disown

[l] 25 Greek *Beezeboul* or *Beelzeboul*
[m] 29 Greek *an assarion*

Not Peace, but a Sword

34 "Do not think that I have come to bring peace to the earth; I have not come to bring peace, but a sword.
35 For I have come to
set a man
against his
father,
and a daughter against
her mother,
and a daughter-in-law
against her
mother-in-law;
36 and one's foes will be
members of
one's own
household.
37 Whoever loves father or
mother more than me is not
worthy of me; and whoever
loves son or daughter more
than me is not worthy of
me; 38 and whoever does
not take up the cross and
follow me is not worthy of
me. 39 Those who find their
life will lose it, and those
who lose their life for my
sake will find it.

Rewards

40 "Whoever welcomes
you welcomes me, and
whoever welcomes me wel-
comes the one who sent
me. 41 Whoever welcomes
a prophet in the name of a
prophet will receive a
prophet's reward; and
whoever welcomes a righ-
teous person in the name of
a righteous person will receive the reward of the
righteous; 42 and whoever
gives even a cup of cold water to one of these little
ones in the name of a
disciple—truly I tell you,
none of these will lose their
reward."

ἔμπροσθεν τοῦ πατρός μου τοῦ ἐν
before the Father of me – in

τοῖς οὐρανοῖς. **34** Μὴ νομίσητε ὅτι
the heavens. Do not suppose that

ἦλθον βαλεῖν εἰρήνην ἐπὶ τὴν γῆν· οὐκ ἦλθον
I came to bring peace on the earth; I came not

βαλεῖν εἰρήνην ἀλλὰ μάχαιραν. **35** ἦλθον γὰρ
to bring peace but a sword. For I came

διχάσαι ἄνθρωπον κατὰ τοῦ πατρὸς
to make hostile a man against the father

αὐτοῦ καὶ θυγατέρα κατὰ τῆς μητρὸς
of him and a daughter against the mother

αὐτῆς καὶ νύμφην κατὰ τῆς πενθερᾶς
of her and a bride against the mother-in-law

αὐτῆς, **36** καὶ ἐχθροὶ τοῦ ἀνθρώπου οἱ
of her, and [the] enemies – of a man the

οἰκιακοὶ αὐτοῦ. **37** Ὁ φιλῶν πατέρα
members of [the] household of him. The [one] loving father

ἢ μητέρα ὑπὲρ ἐμὲ οὐκ ἔστιν μου ἄξιος·
or mother beyond me is not of me worthy;

καὶ ὁ φιλῶν υἱὸν ἢ θυγατέρα ὑπὲρ
and the [one] loving son or daughter beyond

ἐμὲ οὐκ ἔστιν μου ἄξιος· **38** καὶ ὃς
me is not of me worthy; and [he] who

οὐ λαμβάνει τὸν σταυρὸν αὐτοῦ καὶ
takes not the cross of him and

ἀκολουθεῖ ὀπίσω μου, οὐκ ἔστιν μου
follows after me, is not of me

ἄξιος. **39** ὁ εὑρὼν τὴν ψυχὴν αὐτοῦ
worthy. The [one] finding the life of him

ἀπολέσει αὐτήν, καὶ ὁ ἀπολέσας τὴν
will lose it, and the [one] losing the

ψυχὴν αὐτοῦ ἕνεκεν ἐμοῦ εὑρήσει αὐτήν.
life of him for the sake of me will find it.

40 Ὁ δεχόμενος ὑμᾶς ἐμὲ δέχεται, καὶ
The [one] receiving you me receives, and

ὁ ἐμὲ δεχόμενος δέχεται τὸν
the [one] me receiving receives the [one]

ἀποστείλαντά με. **41** ὁ δεχόμενος προ-
having sent me. The [one] receiving a pro-

φήτην εἰς ὄνομα προφήτου μισθὸν
phet in [the] name of a prophet [the] reward

προφήτου λήμψεται, καὶ ὁ δεχόμενος
of a prophet will receive, and the [one] receiving

δίκαιον εἰς ὄνομα δικαίου μισθὸν
a righteous man in [the] name of a righteous man [the] reward

δικαίου λήμψεται. **42** καὶ ὃς ἐὰν ποτίσῃ
of a righteous man will receive. And whoever gives to drink

ἕνα τῶν μικρῶν τούτων ποτήριον ψυχροῦ
one – of these little [ones] a cup of cold water

μόνον εἰς ὄνομα μαθητοῦ, ἀμὴν λέγω ὑμῖν,
only in [the] name of a disciple, truly I tell you,

οὐ μὴ ἀπολέσῃ τὸν μισθὸν αὐτοῦ.
on no account will he lose the reward of him.

him before my Father in
heaven.
34 "Do not suppose that I
have come to bring peace
to the earth. I did not come
to bring peace, but a sword.
35 For I have come to turn

" 'a man against his
father,
a daughter against her
mother,
a daughter-in-law against
her mother-in-law—
36 a man's enemies will
be the members of
his own
household.'[n]

37 "Anyone who loves his
father or mother more than
me is not worthy of me;
anyone who loves his son
or daughter more than me
is not worthy of me; 38 and
anyone who does not take
his cross and follow me is
not worthy of me. 39 Who-
ever finds his life will lose
it, and whoever loses his
life for my sake will find it.
40 "He who receives you
receives me, and he who
receives me receives the
one who sent me. 41 Anyone
who receives a prophet because he is a prophet will
receive a prophet's reward,
and anyone who receives a
righteous man because he
is a righteous man will receive a righteous man's reward. 42 And if anyone
gives even a cup of cold water to one of these little
ones because he is my disciple, I tell you the truth, he
will certainly not lose his
reward."

Chapter 11

Now when Jesus had finished instructing his twelve disciples, he went on from there to teach and proclaim his message in their cities.

11 Καὶ ἐγένετο ὅτε ἐτέλεσεν ὁ
And it came to pass when ended –

Ἰησοῦς διατάσσων τοῖς δώδεκα μαθηταῖς
Jesus giving charge to the twelve disciples

αὐτοῦ, μετέβη ἐκεῖθεν τοῦ διδάσκειν
of him, he removed thence – to teach[d]

καὶ κηρύσσειν ἐν ταῖς πόλεσιν αὐτῶν.
and to proclaim[d] in the cities of them.

Chapter 11

Jesus and John the Baptist

After Jesus had finished instructing his twelve disciples, he went on from there to teach and preach in the towns of Galilee.[o]

[n] 36 Micah 7:6
[o] 1 Greek *in their towns*

Messengers from John the Baptist

2 When John heard in
prison what the Messiah[g]
was doing, he sent word by
his[h] disciples 3 and said to
him, "Are you the one who
is to come, or are we to
wait for another?" 4 Jesus
answered them, "Go and
tell John what you hear and
see: 5 the blind receive their
sight, the lame walk, the
lepers[i] are cleansed, the
deaf hear, the dead are
raised, and the poor have
good news brought to
them. 6 And blessed is anyone who takes no offense at
me."

Jesus Praises John the Baptist

7 As they went away,
Jesus began to speak to the
crowds about John: "What
did you go out into the wilderness to look at? A reed
shaken by the wind? 8 What
then did you go out to see?
Someone[j] dressed in soft
robes? Look, those who
wear soft robes are in royal
palaces. 9 What then did
you go out to see? A prophet?[k] Yes, I tell you, and
more than a prophet.
10 This is the one about
whom it is written,

'See, I am sending my
messenger
ahead of you,
who will prepare
your way
before you.'

11 Truly I tell you, among
those born of women no
one has arisen greater than
John the Baptist; yet the
least in the kingdom of
heaven is greater than he.
12 From the days of John
the Baptist until now the
kingdom of heaven has suffered violence,[l] and the violent take it by force. 13 For
all the prophets and the law
prophesied until John

[g] Or *the Christ*
[h] Other ancient authorities read *two of his*
[i] The terms *leper* and *leprosy* can refer to several diseases
[j] Or *Why then did you go out? To see someone*
[k] Other ancient authorities read *Why then did you go out? To see a prophet?*
[l] Or *has been coming violently*

2 Ὁ δὲ Ἰωάννης ἀκούσας ἐν τῷ
– But John hearing in the
δεσμωτηρίῳ τὰ ἔργα τοῦ Χριστοῦ,
prison the works – of Christ,
πέμψας διὰ τῶν μαθητῶν αὐτοῦ 3 εἶπεν
sending through the disciples of him said
αὐτῷ· σὺ εἶ ὁ ἐρχόμενος, ἢ ἕτερον
to him: Thou art the coming [one], or another
προσδοκῶμεν; 4 καὶ ἀποκριθεὶς ὁ
may we expect? And answering –
Ἰησοῦς εἶπεν αὐτοῖς· πορευθέντες ἀπαγ-
Jesus said to them: Going report
γείλατε Ἰωάννῃ ἃ ἀκούετε καὶ βλέπετε·
ye to John [the things] which ye hear and see:
5 τυφλοὶ ἀναβλέπουσιν καὶ χωλοὶ
blind men see again and lame men
περιπατοῦσιν, λεπροὶ καθαρίζονται καὶ κωφοὶ
walk, lepers are cleansed and deaf men
ἀκούουσιν, καὶ νεκροὶ ἐγείρονται καὶ
hear, and dead men are raised and
πτωχοὶ εὐαγγελίζονται· 6 καὶ μακάριός
poor men are evangelized; and blessed
ἐστιν ὃς ἐὰν μὴ σκανδαλισθῇ ἐν ἐμοί.
is whoever is not offended in me.
7 Τούτων δὲ πορευομένων ἤρξατο ὁ
And these going* began –
*= as these were going
Ἰησοῦς λέγειν τοῖς ὄχλοις περὶ Ἰωάννου·
Jesus to say to the crowds concerning John:
τί ἐξήλθατε εἰς τὴν ἔρημον θεάσασθαι;
What went ye out into the wilderness to see?
κάλαμον ὑπὸ ἀνέμου σαλευόμενον; 8 ἀλλὰ
a reed by wind being shaken? But
τί ἐξήλθατε ἰδεῖν; ἄνθρωπον ἐν μαλακοῖς
what went ye out to see? a man in soft material
ἠμφιεσμένον; ἰδοὺ οἱ τὰ μαλακὰ
having been clothed? Behold[,] the [ones] – soft material
φοροῦντες ἐν τοῖς οἴκοις τῶν βασιλέων. 9 ἀλλὰ
wearing [are] in the houses – of kings. But
τί ἐξήλθατε; προφήτην ἰδεῖν; ναὶ λέγω
why went ye out? a prophet to see? Yes[,] I tell
ὑμῖν, καὶ περισσότερον προφήτου. 10 οὗτός
you, and more [than] a prophet. This
ἐστιν περὶ οὗ γέγραπται· ἰδοὺ ἐγὼ
is he concerning whom it has been written: Behold[,] I
ἀποστέλλω τὸν ἄγγελόν μου πρὸ προσώπου
send forth the messenger of me before [the] face
σου, ὃς κατασκευάσει τὴν ὁδόν σου
of thee, who will prepare the way of thee
ἔμπροσθέν σου. 11 ἀμὴν λέγω ὑμῖν,
before thee. Truly I tell you,
οὐκ ἐγήγερται ἐν γεννητοῖς γυναικῶν
there has not arisen among [those] born of women
μείζων Ἰωάννου τοῦ βαπτιστοῦ· ὁ δὲ
a greater [than] John the Baptist; but the
μικρότερος ἐν τῇ βασιλείᾳ τῶν οὐρανῶν
lesser in the kingdom of the heavens
μείζων αὐτοῦ ἐστιν. 12 ἀπὸ δὲ τῶν
greater [than] he is. And from the
ἡμερῶν Ἰωάννου τοῦ βαπτιστοῦ ἕως
days of John the Baptist until
ἄρτι ἡ βασιλεία τῶν οὐρανῶν βιάζεται,
now the kingdom of the heavens is forcibly treated,
καὶ βιασταὶ ἁρπάζουσιν αὐτήν. 13 πάντες γὰρ
and forceful men seize it. For all
οἱ προφῆται καὶ ὁ νόμος ἕως
the prophets and the law until

2 When John heard in prison what Christ was doing,
he sent his disciples 3 to ask
him, "Are you the one who
was to come, or should we
expect someone else?"
4 Jesus replied, "Go back
and report to John what
you hear and see: 5 The
blind receive sight, the
lame walk, those who have
leprosy[p] are cured, the
deaf hear, the dead are
raised, and the good news
is preached to the poor.
6 Blessed is the man who
does not fall away on ac-
count of me."
7 As John's disciples were
leaving, Jesus began to
speak to the crowd about
John: "What did you go out
into the desert to see? A
reed swayed by the wind?
8 If not, what did you go out
to see? A man dressed in
fine clothes? No, those
who wear fine clothes are
in kings' palaces. 9 Then
what did you go out to see?
A prophet? Yes, I tell you,
and more than a prophet.
10 This is the one about
whom it is written:

"'I will send my
messenger ahead of
you,
who will prepare your
way before you.'[q]

11 I tell you the truth:
Among those born of wom-
en there has not risen anyone greater than John the
Baptist; yet he who is least
in the kingdom of heaven is
greater than he. 12 From the
days of John the Baptist until now, the kingdom of
heaven has been forcefully
advancing, and forceful
men lay hold of it. 13 For all
the Prophets and the Law
prophesied until John.

[p] *5* The Greek word was used for various diseases affecting the skin—not necessarily leprosy.
[q] *10* Mal. 3:1

came; 14 and if you are willing to accept it, he is Elijah who is to come. 15 Let anyone with ears[m] listen!

16 "But to what will I compare this generation? It is like children sitting in the marketplaces and calling to one another,

17 'We played the flute for you, and you did not dance;
we wailed, and you did not mourn.'

18 For John came neither eating nor drinking, and they say, 'He has a demon'; 19 the Son of Man came eating and drinking, and they say, 'Look, a glutton and a drunkard, a friend of tax collectors and sinners!' Yet wisdom is vindicated by her deeds."[n]

Woes to Unrepentant Cities

20 Then he began to reproach the cities in which most of his deeds of power had been done, because they did not repent. 21 "Woe to you, Chorazin! Woe to you, Bethsaida! For if the deeds of power done in you had been done in Tyre and Sidon, they would have repented long ago in sackcloth and ashes. 22 But I tell you, on the day of judgment it will be more tolerable for Tyre and Sidon than for you. 23 And you, Capernaum,

will you be exalted to heaven?
No, you will be brought down to Hades.

For if the deeds of power done in you had been done in Sodom, it would have remained until this day. 24 But I tell you that on the day of judgment it will be more tolerable for the land of Sodom than for you."

Jesus Thanks His Father

25 At that time Jesus said, "I thank[o] you, Fa-

[m] Other ancient authorities add *to hear*
[n] Other ancient authorities read *children*
[o] Or *praise*

Ἰωάννου ἐπροφήτευσαν· **14** καὶ εἰ θέλετε
John prophesied; and if ye are willing
δέξασθαι, αὐτός ἐστιν Ἠλίας ὁ μέλλων
to receive [it *or* him], he is Elias the [one] about
ἔρχεσθαι. **15** ὁ ἔχων ὦτα ἀκουέτω.
to come. The [one] having ears let him hear.
16 Τίνι δὲ ὁμοιώσω τὴν γενεὰν ταύτην;
But to what shall I liken – generation this?
ὁμοία ἐστὶν παιδίοις καθημένοις ἐν ταῖς
Like it is to children sitting in the
ἀγοραῖς ἃ προσφωνοῦντα τοῖς ἑτέροις
marketplaces who calling to the others
17 λέγουσιν· ηὐλήσαμεν ὑμῖν καὶ οὐκ
say: We piped to you and not
ὠρχήσασθε· ἐθρηνήσαμεν καὶ οὐκ ἐκόψασθε.
ye did dance; we lamented and ye did not mourn.
18 ἦλθεν γὰρ Ἰωάννης μήτε ἐσθίων μήτε
For came John neither eating nor
πίνων, καὶ λέγουσιν· δαιμόνιον ἔχει.
drinking, and they say: a demon He has.
19 ἦλθεν ὁ υἱὸς τοῦ ἀνθρώπου ἐσθίων καὶ
Came the Son – of man eating and
πίνων, καὶ λέγουσιν· ἰδοὺ ἄνθρωπος
drinking, and they say: Behold[,] a man
φάγος καὶ οἰνοπότης, τελωνῶν φίλος καὶ
gluttonous and a wine-drinker, of tax-collectors a friend and
ἁμαρτωλῶν. καὶ ἐδικαιώθη ἡ σοφία ἀπὸ
of sinners. And was(is) justified – wisdom from(by)
τῶν ἔργων αὐτῆς.
the works of her.
20 Τότε ἤρξατο ὀνειδίζειν τὰς πόλεις
Then he began to reproach the cities
ἐν αἷς ἐγένοντο αἱ πλεῖσται δυνάμεις
in which happened the very many powerful deeds
αὐτοῦ, ὅτι οὐ μετενόησαν· **21** οὐαί σοι,
of him, because they repented not: Woe to thee,
Χοραζίν· οὐαί σοι, Βηθσαϊδά· ὅτι εἰ
Chorazin; woe to thee, Bethsaida; because if
ἐν Τύρῳ καὶ Σιδῶνι ἐγένοντο αἱ δυνάμεις
in Tyre and Sidon happened the powerful deeds
αἱ γενόμεναι ἐν ὑμῖν, πάλαι ἂν
– having happened in you, long ago –
ἐν σάκκῳ καὶ σποδῷ μετενόησαν.
in sackcloth and ashes they would have repented.
22 πλὴν λέγω ὑμῖν, Τύρῳ καὶ Σιδῶνι
However I tell you, For Tyre and for Sidon
ἀνεκτότερον ἔσται ἐν ἡμέρᾳ κρίσεως ἢ
more tolerable it will be in [the] day of judgment than
ὑμῖν. **23** καὶ σύ, Καφαρναούμ, μὴ
for you. And thou, Capernaum, *not*
ἕως οὐρανοῦ ὑψωθήσῃ; ἕως ᾅδου
as far as heaven wast thou exalted? as far as hades
καταβήσῃ· ὅτι εἰ ἐν Σοδόμοις ἐγενήθησαν
thou shalt descend; because if in Sodom happened
αἱ δυνάμεις αἱ γενόμεναι ἐν σοί,
the powerful deeds – having happened in thee,
ἔμεινεν ἂν μέχρι τῆς σήμερον. **24** πλὴν
it would have remained until – to-day. However
λέγω ὑμῖν ὅτι γῇ Σοδόμων ἀνεκτότερον
I tell you that for [the] land of Sodom more tolerable
ἔσται ἐν ἡμέρᾳ κρίσεως ἢ σοί.
it will be in [the] day of judgment than for thee.
25 Ἐν ἐκείνῳ τῷ καιρῷ ἀποκριθεὶς
At that – time answering
ὁ Ἰησοῦς εἶπεν· ἐξομολογοῦμαί σοι,
– Jesus said: I give thanks to thee,

14 And if you are willing to accept it, he is the Elijah who was to come. 15 He who has ears, let him hear.

16 "To what can I compare this generation? They are like children sitting in the marketplaces and calling out to others:

17 " 'We played the flute for you,
and you did not dance;
we sang a dirge,
and you did not mourn.'

18 For John came neither eating nor drinking, and they say, 'He has a demon.' 19 The Son of Man came eating and drinking, and they say, 'Here is a glutton and a drunkard, a friend of tax collectors and "sinners." ' But wisdom is proved right by her actions."

Woe on Unrepentant Cities

20 Then Jesus began to denounce the cities in which most of his miracles had been performed, because they did not repent. 21 "Woe to you, Korazin! Woe to you, Bethsaida! If the miracles that were performed in you had been performed in Tyre and Sidon, they would have repented long ago in sackcloth and ashes. 22 But I tell you, it will be more bearable for Tyre and Sidon on the day of judgment than for you. 23 And you, Capernaum, will you be lifted up to the skies? No, you will go down to the depths.[r] If the miracles that were performed in you had been performed in Sodom, it would have remained to this day. 24 But I tell you that it will be more bearable for Sodom on the day of judgment than for you."

Rest for the Weary

25 At that time Jesus said, "I praise you, Father, Lord

[r] 23 Greek *Hades*

ther, Lord of heaven and
earth, because you have
hidden these things from
the wise and the intelligent
and have revealed them to
infants; 26 yes, Father, for
such was your gracious
will.[p] 27 All things have
been handed over to me by
my Father; and no one
knows the Son except the
Father, and no one knows
the Father except the Son
and anyone to whom the
Son chooses to reveal him.
28 "Come to me, all you
that are weary and are carrying heavy burdens, and I
will give you rest. 29 Take
my yoke upon you, and
learn from me; for I am gentle and humble in heart, and
you will find rest for your
souls. 30 For my yoke is
easy, and my burden is
light."

Chapter 12

Plucking Grain on the Sabbath

At that time Jesus went
through the grain-
fields on the sabbath; his
disciples were hungry, and
they began to pluck heads
of grain and to eat. 2 When
the Pharisees saw it, they
said to him, "Look, your
disciples are doing what is
not lawful to do on the sabbath." 3 He said to them,
"Have you not read what
David did when he and his
companions were hungry?
4 He entered the house of
God and ate the bread of
the Presence, which it was
not lawful for him or his
companions to eat, but
only for the priests. 5 Or
have you not read in the

[p] Or *for so it was well-pleasing in your sight*

πάτερ, κύριε τοῦ οὐρανοῦ καὶ τῆς γῆς,
Father, lord of the heaven and of the earth,

ὅτι ἔκρυψας ταῦτα ἀπὸ σοφῶν καὶ συνε-
because thou hiddest these things from wise and intel-

τῶν, καὶ ἀπεκάλυψας αὐτὰ νηπίοις·
ligent men, and didst reveal them to infants;

26 ναί, ὁ πατήρ, ὅτι οὕτως εὐδοκία
yes, – Father, because thus good pleasure

ἐγένετο ἔμπροσθέν σου. 27 Πάντα μοι
it was before thee. All things to me

παρεδόθη ὑπὸ τοῦ πατρός μου, καὶ
were delivered by the Father of me, and

οὐδεὶς ἐπιγινώσκει τὸν υἱὸν εἰ μὴ ὁ
no one fully knows the Son except the

πατήρ, οὐδὲ τὸν πατέρα τις ἐπιγινώσκει
Father, neither the Father anyone fully knows

εἰ μὴ ὁ υἱὸς καὶ ᾧ ἐὰν βούληται ὁ
except the Son and [he] to whom if wills the

υἱὸς ἀποκαλύψαι. 28 Δεῦτε πρός με
Son to reveal. Come unto me

πάντες οἱ κοπιῶντες καὶ πεφορτισμένοι,
all the [ones] labouring and *having been* burdened,

κἀγὼ ἀναπαύσω ὑμᾶς. 29 ἄρατε τὸν
and I will rest you. Take the

ζυγόν μου ἐφ' ὑμᾶς καὶ μάθετε ἀπ'
yoke of me on you and learn from

ἐμοῦ, ὅτι πραΰς εἰμι καὶ ταπεινὸς τῇ
me, because meek I am and lowly –

καρδίᾳ, καὶ εὑρήσετε ἀνάπαυσιν ταῖς
in heart, and ye will find rest to the

ψυχαῖς ὑμῶν· 30 ὁ γὰρ ζυγός μου
souls of you; for the yoke of me

χρηστὸς καὶ τὸ φορτίον μου ἐλαφρόν
gentle and the burden of me light

ἐστιν.
is.

12 Ἐν ἐκείνῳ τῷ καιρῷ ἐπορεύθη ὁ
At that – time went –

Ἰησοῦς τοῖς σάββασιν διὰ τῶν σπορίμων·
Jesus on the sabbath through the cornfields;

οἱ δὲ μαθηταὶ αὐτοῦ ἐπείνασαν, καὶ
and the disciples of him hungered, and

ἤρξαντο τίλλειν στάχυας καὶ ἐσθίειν.
began to pluck ears [of corn] and to eat.

2 οἱ δὲ Φαρισαῖοι ἰδόντες εἶπαν αὐτῷ·
But the Pharisees seeing said to him:

ἰδοὺ οἱ μαθηταί σου ποιοῦσιν ὃ οὐκ
Behold[,] the disciples of thee are doing what not

ἔξεστιν ποιεῖν ἐν σαββάτῳ. 3 ὁ δὲ
it is lawful to do on a sabbath. And he

εἶπεν αὐτοῖς· οὐκ ἀνέγνωτε τί ἐποίησεν
said to them: Did ye not read what did

Δαυίδ, ὅτε ἐπείνασεν καὶ οἱ μετ'
David, when he hungered and the [ones] with

αὐτοῦ; 4 πῶς εἰσῆλθεν εἰς τὸν οἶκον
him? how he entered into the house

τοῦ θεοῦ καὶ τοὺς ἄρτους τῆς προ-
– of God and the loaves of the set-

θέσεως ἔφαγον, ὃ οὐκ ἐξὸν ἦν αὐτῷ
ting forth ate, which not lawful it was for him

φαγεῖν οὐδὲ τοῖς μετ' αὐτοῦ, εἰ μὴ
to eat neither the [ones] with him, except

τοῖς ἱερεῦσιν μόνοις; 5 ἢ οὐκ ἀνέγνωτε
for the priests only? or did ye not read

of heaven and earth, be-
cause you have hidden
these things from the wise
and learned, and revealed
them to little children.
26 Yes, Father, for this was
your good pleasure.
27 "All things have been
committed to me by my Fa-
ther. No one knows the
Son except the Father, and
no one knows the Father
except the Son and those to
whom the Son chooses to
reveal him.
28 "Come to me, all you
who are weary and bur-
dened, and I will give you
rest. 29 Take my yoke upon
you and learn from me, for
I am gentle and humble in
heart, and you will find rest
for your souls. 30 For my
yoke is easy and my burden
is light."

Chapter 12

Lord of the Sabbath

At that time Jesus went
through the grain-
fields on the Sabbath. His
disciples were hungry and
began to pick some heads
of grain and eat them.
2 When the Pharisees saw
this, they said to him,
"Look! Your disciples are
doing what is unlawful on
the Sabbath."
3 He answered, "Haven't
you read what David did
when he and his compan-
ions were hungry? 4 He entered the house of God, and
he and his companions ate
the consecrated bread—
which was not lawful for
them to do, but only for the
priests. 5 Or haven't you

law that on the sabbath the
priests in the temple break
the sabbath and yet are
guiltless? 6 I tell you, something greater than the temple is here. 7 But if you had
known what this means, 'I
desire mercy and not sacrifice, you would not have
condemned the guiltless.
8 For the Son of Man is lord
of the sabbath."

The Man with a Withered Hand

9 He left that place and
entered their synagogue;
10 a man was there with a
withered hand, and they
asked him, "Is it lawful to
cure on the sabbath?" so
that they might accuse him.
11 He said to them, "Sup-
pose one of you has only
one sheep and it falls into a
pit on the sabbath; will you
not lay hold of it and lift it
out? 12 How much more
valuable is a human being
than a sheep! So it is lawful
to do good on the sabbath."
13 Then he said to the man,
"Stretch out your hand."
He stretched it out, and it
was restored, as sound as
the other. 14 But the Pharisees went out and con-
spired against him, how to
destroy him.

God's Chosen Servant

15 When Jesus became
aware of this, he departed.
Many crowds[a] followed
him, and he cured all of
them, 16 and he ordered
them not to make him
known. 17 This was to fulfill
what had been spoken
through the prophet Isaiah:
18 "Here is my servant,
whom I
have chosen,
my beloved, with
whom my soul
is well pleased.
I will put my Spirit
upon him,

[a] Other ancient authorities lack *crowds*

ἐν τῷ νόμῳ ὅτι τοῖς σάββασιν οἱ
in the law that on the sabbaths the
ἱερεῖς ἐν τῷ ἱερῷ τὸ σάββατον βεβηλοῦ-
priests in the temple the sabbath pro-
σιν καὶ ἀναίτιοί εἰσιν; 6 λέγω δὲ
fane and guiltless are? And I tell
ὑμῖν ὅτι τοῦ ἱεροῦ μεῖζόν ἐστιν ὧδε.
you that [than] the temple a greater [thing] is here.
7 εἰ δὲ ἐγνώκειτε τί ἐστιν· ἔλεος
But if ye had known what it is: Mercy
θέλω καὶ οὐ θυσίαν, οὐκ ἂν κατε-
I desire and not sacrifice, ye would not have
δικάσατε τοὺς ἀναιτίους. 8 κύριος γάρ
condemned the guiltless. For Lord
ἐστιν τοῦ σαββάτου ὁ υἱὸς τοῦ ἀνθρώπου.
is of the sabbath the Son – of man.
9 Καὶ μεταβὰς ἐκεῖθεν ἦλθεν εἰς τὴν
And removing thence he came into the
συναγωγὴν αὐτῶν. 10 καὶ ἰδοὺ ἄνθρωπος
synagogue of them. And behold[,] a man
χεῖρα ἔχων ξηράν· καὶ ἐπηρώτησαν αὐτὸν
³[his] hand ¹having ²withered; and they questioned him
λέγοντες· εἰ ἔξεστιν τοῖς σάββασιν
saying: If it is lawful on the sabbaths
θεραπεῦσαι; ἵνα κατηγορήσωσιν αὐτοῦ.
to heal? in order that they might accuse him.
11 ὁ δὲ εἶπεν αὐτοῖς· τίς ἔσται ἐξ
So he said to them: ¹What ³will there be ⁴of
ὑμῶν ἄνθρωπος ὃς ἕξει πρόβατον ἕν,
⁵you ²man who will have sheep one,
καὶ ἐὰν ἐμπέσῃ τοῦτο τοῖς σάββασιν
and if ²fall *in* ¹this on the sabbaths
εἰς βόθυνον, οὐχὶ κρατήσει αὐτὸ καὶ
into a ditch, will he not lay hold of it and
ἐγερεῖ; 12 πόσῳ οὖν διαφέρει ἄνθρωπος
raise? By how much then surpasses a man
προβάτου. ὥστε ἔξεστιν τοῖς σάββασιν
a sheep. So that it is lawful on the sabbaths
καλῶς ποιεῖν. 13 τότε λέγει τῷ ἀνθρώπῳ·
well to do. Then he says to the man:
ἔκτεινόν σου τὴν χεῖρα. καὶ ἐξέτεινεν,
Stretch forth of thee the hand. And he stretched forth,
καὶ ἀπεκατεστάθη ὑγιὴς ὡς ἡ ἄλλη.
and it was restored healthy as the other.
14 ἐξελθόντες δὲ οἱ Φαρισαῖοι συμβούλιον
And going out the Pharisees counsel
ἔλαβον κατ' αὐτοῦ, ὅπως αὐτὸν ἀπολέ-
took against him, so as him they might
σωσιν. 15 Ὁ δὲ Ἰησοῦς γνοὺς ἀνε-
destroy. – But Jesus knowing de-
χώρησεν ἐκεῖθεν. καὶ ἠκολούθησαν αὐτῷ
parted thence. And followed him
πολλοί, καὶ ἐθεράπευσεν αὐτοὺς πάντας,
many, and he healed them all,
16 καὶ ἐπετίμησεν αὐτοῖς ἵνα μὴ φανερὸν
and warned them that ³not ⁴manifest
αὐτὸν ποιήσωσιν· 17 ἵνα πληρωθῇ τὸ
²him ¹they ⁵should ⁶make; that might be fulfilled the [thing]
ῥηθὲν διὰ Ἠσαΐου τοῦ προφήτου
spoken through Isaiah the prophet
λέγοντος· 18 ἰδοὺ ὁ παῖς μου ὃν
saying: Behold[,] the servant of me whom
ᾑρέτισα, ὁ ἀγαπητός μου ὃν εὐδόκησεν
I chose, the beloved of me [with] whom was well pleased
ἡ ψυχή μου· θήσω τὸ πνεῦμά μου ἐπ'
the soul of me; I will put the spirit of me on

read in the Law that on the
Sabbath the priests in the
temple desecrate the day
and yet are innocent? 6I tell
you that one[s] greater than
the temple is here. 7If you
had known what these
words mean, 'I desire mercy, not sacrifice,'[t] you
would not have condemned
the innocent. 8For the Son
of Man is Lord of the Sabbath."
9Going on from that
place, he went into their
synagogue, 10and a man
with a shriveled hand was
there. Looking for a reason
to accuse Jesus, they asked
him, "Is it lawful to heal on
the Sabbath?"
11He said to them, "If any
of you has a sheep and it
falls into a pit on the Sabbath, will you not take hold
of it and lift it out? 12How
much more valuable is a
man than a sheep! There-
fore it is lawful to do good
on the Sabbath."
13Then he said to the
man, "Stretch out your
hand." So he stretched it
out and it was completely
restored, just as sound as
the other. 14But the Pharisees went out and plotted
how they might kill Jesus.

God's Chosen Servant

15Aware of this, Jesus
withdrew from that place.
Many followed him, and he
healed all their sick,
16warning them not to tell
who he was. 17This was to
fulfill what was spoken
through the prophet Isaiah:

18"Here is my servant
whom I have
chosen,
the one I love, in
whom I delight;
I will put my Spirit on
him,

[s] 6 Or *something*; also in verses 41 and 42
[t] 7 Hosea 6:6

and he will proclaim
justice to the
Gentiles.
19 He will not wrangle
or cry aloud,
nor will anyone hear
his voice in the
streets.
20 He will not break a
bruised reed
or quench a
smoldering wick
until he brings justice
to victory.
21 And in his name the
Gentiles will
hope."

Jesus and Beelzebul

22 Then they brought to
him a demoniac who was
blind and mute; and he
cured him, so that the one
who had been mute could
speak and see. 23 All the
crowds were amazed and
said, "Can this be the Son
of David?" 24 But when the
Pharisees heard it, they
said, "It is only by Beelzebul, the ruler of the de-
mons, that this fellow casts
out the demons." 25 He
knew what they were
thinking and said to them,
"Every kingdom divided
against itself is laid waste,
and no city or house divided against itself will stand.
26 If Satan casts out Satan,
he is divided against himself; how then will his kingdom stand? 27 If I cast out
demons by Beelzebul, by
whom do your own exor-
cists[r] cast them out?
Therefore they will be your
judges. 28 But if it is by the
Spirit of God that I cast out
demons, then the kingdom
of God has come to you.
29 Or how can one enter a
strong man's house and
plunder his property, with-

[r] Gk *sons*

αὐτόν, καὶ κρίσιν τοῖς ἔθνεσιν ἀπαγγελεῖ.
him, and judgment to the nations he will announce.
19 οὐκ ἐρίσει οὐδὲ κραυγάσει, οὐδὲ
He will not strive nor *will* shout, nor
ἀκούσει τις ἐν ταῖς πλατείαις τὴν
will hear anyone in the streets the
φωνὴν αὐτοῦ. 20 κάλαμον συντετριμμένον
voice of him. A reed *having been* bruised
οὐ κατεάξει καὶ λίνον τυφόμενον οὐ
he will not break and flax smoking not
σβέσει, ἕως ἂν ἐκβάλῃ εἰς νῖκος τὴν
he will quench, until he put forth to victory –
κρίσιν. 21 καὶ τῷ ὀνόματι αὐτοῦ ἔθνη
judgment. And in the name of him nations
ἐλπιοῦσιν.
will hope.

22 Τότε προσηνέχθη αὐτῷ δαιμονιζ-
Then was brought to him a demon-
όμενος τυφλὸς καὶ κωφός· καὶ ἐθεράπευσεν
possessed man blind and dumb; and he healed
αὐτόν, ὥστε τὸν κωφὸν λαλεῖν καὶ
him, so as the dumb to speak and
βλέπειν. 23 καὶ ἐξίσταντο πάντες οἱ
to see[b]. And were astonished all the
ὄχλοι καὶ ἔλεγον· μήτι οὗτός ἐστιν ὁ
crowds and said: *not* This is the
υἱὸς Δαυίδ; 24 οἱ δὲ Φαρισαῖοι ἀκού-
son of David? But the Pharisees hear-
σαντες εἶπον· οὗτος οὐκ ἐκβάλλει τὰ
ing said: This man does not expel the
δαιμόνια εἰ μὴ ἐν τῷ Βεεζεβοὺλ ἄρχοντι
demons except by – Beelzebub ruler
τῶν δαιμονίων. 25 εἰδὼς δὲ τὰς ἐνθυμήσεις
of the demons. But knowing the thoughts
αὐτῶν εἶπεν αὐτοῖς· πᾶσα βασιλεία
of them he said to them: Every kingdom
μερισθεῖσα καθ' ἑαυτῆς ἐρημοῦται,
divided against itself is brought to desolation,
καὶ πᾶσα πόλις ἢ οἰκία μερισθεῖσα καθ'
and every city or house divided against
ἑαυτῆς οὐ σταθήσεται. 26 καὶ εἰ
itself will not stand. And if
ὁ σατανᾶς τὸν σατανᾶν ἐκβάλλει, ἐφ'
– Satan – *Satan ¹expels, against
ἑαυτὸν ἐμερίσθη· πῶς οὖν σταθή-
himself he was (is) divided; how therefore will
σεται ἡ βασιλεία αὐτοῦ; 27 καὶ εἰ
stand the kingdom of him? And if
ἐγὼ ἐν Βεεζεβοὺλ ἐκβάλλω τὰ δαιμόνια,
I by Beelzebub expel the demons,
οἱ υἱοὶ ὑμῶν ἐν τίνι ἐκβάλλουσιν;
the sons of you by what do they expel?
διὰ τοῦτο αὐτοὶ κριταὶ ἔσονται ὑμῶν.
therefore they judges shall be of you.
28 εἰ δὲ ἐν πνεύματι θεοῦ ἐγὼ
But if by [the] Spirit of God I
ἐκβάλλω τὰ δαιμόνια, ἄρα ἔφθασεν
expel the demons, then came
ἐφ' ὑμᾶς ἡ βασιλεία τοῦ θεοῦ. 29 ἢ
upon you the kingdom – of God. Or
πῶς δύναταί τις εἰσελθεῖν εἰς τὴν
how can anyone *to* enter into the
οἰκίαν τοῦ ἰσχυροῦ καὶ τὰ σκεύη αὐτοῦ
house of the strong man and the vessels of him

and he will proclaim
justice to the
nations.
19 He will not quarrel or
cry out;
no one will hear his
voice in the streets.
20 A bruised reed he will
not break,
and a smoldering wick
he will not snuff out,
till he leads justice to
victory.
21 In his name the nations
will put their
hope."[u]

Jesus and Beelzebub

22 Then they brought him
a demon-possessed man
who was blind and mute,
and Jesus healed him, so
that he could both talk and
see. 23 All the people were
astonished and said,
"Could this be the Son of
David?"
24 But when the Pharisees
heard this, they said, "It is
only by Beelzebub,[v] the
prince of demons, that this
fellow drives out demons."
25 Jesus knew their
thoughts and said to them,
"Every kingdom divided
against itself will be ruined,
and every city or house-
hold divided against itself
will not stand. 26 If Satan
drives out Satan, he is divided against himself. How
then can his kingdom
stand? 27 And if I drive out
demons by Beelzebub, by
whom do your people drive
them out? So then, they
will be your judges. 28 But if
I drive out demons by the
Spirit of God, then the
kingdom of God has come
upon you.
29 "Or again, how can
anyone enter a strong
man's house and carry off

[u] *21* Isaiah 42:1-4
[v] *24* Greek *Beezeboul* or *Beelzeboul*; also in verse 27

out first tying up the strong
man? Then indeed the
house can be plundered.
30 Whoever is not with me
is against me, and whoever
does not gather with me
scatters. 31 Therefore I tell
you, people will be forgiv-
en for every sin and blasphemy, but blasphemy
against the Spirit will not be
forgiven. 32 Whoever
speaks a word against the
Son of Man will be forgiv-
en, but whoever speaks
against the Holy Spirit will
not be forgiven, either in
this age or in the age to
come.

A Tree and Its Fruit

33 "Either make the
tree good, and its fruit
good; or make the tree bad,
and its fruit bad; for the tree
is known by its fruit. 34 You
brood of vipers! How can
you speak good things,
when you are evil? For out
of the abundance of the
heart the mouth speaks.
35 The good person brings
good things out of a good
treasure, and the evil person brings evil things out of
an evil treasure. 36 I tell
you, on the day of judg-
ment you will have to give
an account for every care-
less word you utter; 37 for
by your words you will be
justified, and by your
words you will be con-
demned."

The Sign of Jonah

38 Then some of the
scribes and Pharisees said
to him, "Teacher, we wish
to see a sign from you."

ἁρπάσαι, ἐὰν μὴ πρῶτον δήσῃ τὸν
to seize, if not first he binds the

ἰσχυρόν; καὶ τότε τὴν οἰκίαν αὐτοῦ
strong man? and then the house of him

διαρπάσει. **30** ὁ μὴ ὢν μετ' ἐμοῦ
he will plunder. The [one] not being with me

κατ' ἐμοῦ ἐστιν, καὶ ὁ μὴ συνάγων μετ'
against me is, and the [one] not gathering with

ἐμοῦ σκορπίζει. **31** Διὰ τοῦτο λέγω
me scatters. Therefore I tell

ὑμῖν, πᾶσα ἁμαρτία καὶ βλασφημία
you, all sin and blasphemy

ἀφεθήσεται τοῖς ἀνθρώποις, ἡ δὲ τοῦ
will be forgiven – to men, but the of the

πνεύματος βλασφημία οὐκ ἀφεθήσεται.
Spirit blasphemy will not be forgiven.

32 καὶ ὃς ἐὰν εἴπῃ λόγον κατὰ τοῦ
And whoever speaks a word against the

υἱοῦ τοῦ ἀνθρώπου, ἀφεθήσεται αὐτῷ·
Son – of man, it will be forgiven *to* him;

ὃς δ' ἂν εἴπῃ κατὰ τοῦ πνεύματος
but whoever speaks against the Spirit

τοῦ ἁγίου, οὐκ ἀφεθήσεται αὐτῷ
– Holy, it will not be forgiven *to* him

οὔτε ἐν τούτῳ τῷ αἰῶνι οὔτε ἐν τῷ
neither in this – age nor in the [one]

μέλλοντι. **33** Ἢ ποιήσατε τὸ δένδρον
coming. Either make the tree

καλὸν καὶ τὸν καρπὸν αὐτοῦ καλόν,
good and the fruit of it good,

ἢ ποιήσατε τὸ δένδρον σαπρὸν καὶ τὸν
or make the tree bad and the

καρπὸν αὐτοῦ σαπρόν· ἐκ γὰρ τοῦ
fruit of it bad; for of(by) the

καρποῦ τὸ δένδρον γινώσκεται. **34** γεννή-
fruit the tree is known. Off-

ματα ἐχιδνῶν, πῶς δύνασθε ἀγαθὰ λαλεῖν
spring of vipers, how can ye good things *to* speak

πονηροὶ ὄντες; ἐκ γὰρ τοῦ περισ-
[2]evil [1]being? for out of the abund-

σεύματος τῆς καρδίας τὸ στόμα λαλεῖ.
ance of the heart the mouth speaks.

35 ὁ ἀγαθὸς ἄνθρωπος ἐκ τοῦ ἀγαθοῦ
The good man out of the good

θησαυροῦ ἐκβάλλει ἀγαθά, καὶ ὁ πονηρὸς
treasure puts forth good things, and the evil

ἄνθρωπος ἐκ τοῦ πονηροῦ θησαυροῦ
man out of the evil treasure

ἐκβάλλει πονηρά. **36** λέγω δὲ
puts forth evil things. But I tell

ὑμῖν ὅτι πᾶν ῥῆμα ἀργὸν ὃ λαλήσουσιν
you that every word idle which will speak

οἱ ἄνθρωποι, ἀποδώσουσιν περὶ αὐτοῦ
– men, they will render concerning it

λόγον ἐν ἡμέρᾳ κρίσεως· **37** ἐκ γὰρ
account in [the] day of judgment; for of(by)

τῶν λόγων σου δικαιωθήσῃ, καὶ ἐκ
the words of thee thou wilt be justified, and of(by)

τῶν λόγων σου καταδικασθήσῃ.
the words of thee thou wilt be condemned.

38 Τότε ἀπεκρίθησαν αὐτῷ τινες τῶν
Then answered him some of the

γραμματέων καὶ Φαρισαίων λέγοντες·
scribes and Pharisees saying:

διδάσκαλε, θέλομεν ἀπὸ σοῦ σημεῖον ἰδεῖν.
Teacher, we wish from thee a sign to see.

his possessions unless he
first ties up the strong man?
Then he can rob his house.
30 "He who is not with me
is against me, and he who
does not gather with me
scatters. 31 And so I tell
you, every sin and blasphemy will be forgiven men,
but the blasphemy against
the Spirit will not be forgiv-
en. 32 Anyone who speaks a
word against the Son of
Man will be forgiven, but
anyone who speaks against
the Holy Spirit will not be
forgiven, either in this age
or in the age to come.
33 "Make a tree good and
its fruit will be good, or
make a tree bad and its fruit
will be bad, for a tree is recognized by its fruit. 34 You
brood of vipers, how can
you who are evil say any-
thing good? For out of the
overflow of the heart the
mouth speaks. 35 The good
man brings good things out
of the good stored up in
him, and the evil man
brings evil things out of the
evil stored up in him. 36 But
I tell you that men will have
to give account on the day
of judgment for every care-
less word they have spo-
ken. 37 For by your words
you will be acquitted, and
by your words you will be
condemned."

The Sign of Jonah

38 Then some of the Pharisees and teachers of the law
said to him, "Teacher, we
want to see a miraculous
sign from you."

39 But he answered them,
"An evil and adulterous
generation asks for a sign,
but no sign will be given to
it except the sign of the
prophet Jonah. 40 For just
as Jonah was three days
and three nights in the belly
of the sea monster, so for
three days and three nights
the Son of Man will be in
the heart of the earth.
41 The people of Nineveh
will rise up at the judgment
with this generation and
condemn it, because they
repented at the proclamation of Jonah, and see,
something greater than Jonah is here! 42 The queen of
the South will rise up at the
judgment with this generation and condemn it, because she came from the
ends of the earth to listen to
the wisdom of Solomon,
and see, something greater
than Solomon is here!

The Return of the Unclean Spirit

43 "When the unclean
spirit has gone out of a person, it wanders through
waterless regions looking
for a resting place, but it
finds none. 44 Then it says,
'I will return to my house
from which I came.' When
it comes, it finds it empty,
swept, and put in order.
45 Then it goes and brings
along seven other spirits
more evil than itself, and
they enter and live there;
and the last state of that
person is worse than the
first. So will it be also with
this evil generation."

The True Kindred of Jesus

46 While he was still
speaking to the crowds, his

39 ὁ δὲ ἀποκριθεὶς εἶπεν αὐτοῖς·
But he answering said to them:
γενεὰ πονηρὰ καὶ μοιχαλὶς σημεῖον
generation An evil and adulterous a sign
ἐπιζητεῖ, καὶ σημεῖον οὐ δοθήσεται
seeks, and a sign shall not be given
αὐτῇ εἰ μὴ τὸ σημεῖον Ἰωνᾶ τοῦ
to it except the sign of Jonas the
προφήτου. 40 ὥσπερ γὰρ ἦν Ἰωνᾶς
prophet. For as was Jonas
ἐν τῇ κοιλίᾳ τοῦ κήτους τρεῖς ἡμέρας
in the belly of the sea monster three days
καὶ τρεῖς νύκτας, οὕτως ἔσται ὁ υἱὸς
and three nights, so will be the Son
τοῦ ἀνθρώπου ἐν τῇ καρδίᾳ τῆς γῆς
– of man in the heart of the earth
τρεῖς ἡμέρας καὶ τρεῖς νύκτας. 41 ἄνδρες
three days and three nights. *Men*
Νινευῖται ἀναστήσονται ἐν τῇ κρίσει
Ninevites will stand up in the judgment
μετὰ τῆς γενεᾶς ταύτης καὶ κατα-
with – generation this and will
κρινοῦσιν αὐτήν· ὅτι μετενόησαν εἰς τὸ
condemn it; because they repented at the
κήρυγμα Ἰωνᾶ, καὶ ἰδοὺ πλεῖον Ἰωνᾶ
proclamation of Jonas, and behold a greater thing [than] Jonas
ὧδε. 42 βασίλισσα νότου ἐγερθήσεται
[is] here. [The] queen of [the] south will be raised
ἐν τῇ κρίσει μετὰ τῆς γενεᾶς ταύτης
in the judgment with – generation this
καὶ κατακρινεῖ αὐτήν· ὅτι ἦλθεν ἐκ
and will condemn it; because she came out of
τῶν περάτων τῆς γῆς ἀκοῦσαι τὴν σοφίαν
the limits of the earth to hear the wisdom
Σολομῶνος, καὶ ἰδοὺ πλεῖον Σολομῶνος
of Solomon, and behold a greater thing [than] Solomon
ὧδε. 43 Ὅταν δὲ τὸ ἀκάθαρτον πνεῦμα
[is] here. Now when the unclean spirit
ἐξέλθῃ ἀπὸ τοῦ ἀνθρώπου, διέρχεται δι'
goes out from – a man, he goes through
ἀνύδρων τόπων ζητοῦν ἀνάπαυσιν, καὶ
dry places seeking rest, and
οὐχ εὑρίσκει. 44 τότε λέγει· Εἰς τὸν
finds not. Then he says: Into the
οἶκόν μου ἐπιστρέψω ὅθεν ἐξῆλθον·
house of me I will return whence I came out;
καὶ ἐλθὸν εὑρίσκει σχολάζοντα [καὶ]
and coming he finds [it] standing empty and
σεσαρωμένον καὶ κεκοσμημένον. 45 τότε
having been swept and *having been* furnished. Then
πορεύεται καὶ παραλαμβάνει μεθ' ἑαυτοῦ
he goes and takes with him*self*
ἑπτὰ ἕτερα πνεύματα πονηρότερα ἑαυτοῦ,
seven other spirits more evil [than] himself,
καὶ εἰσελθόντα κατοικεῖ ἐκεῖ· καὶ
and entering dwells there; and
γίνεται τὰ ἔσχατα τοῦ ἀνθρώπου ἐκείνου
become*s* the last things – man of that
χείρονα τῶν πρώτων. οὕτως ἔσται
worse [than] the first. Thus it will be
καὶ τῇ γενεᾷ ταύτῃ τῇ πονηρᾷ.
also – [2]generation [1]to this – [3]evil.
46 Ἔτι αὐτοῦ λαλοῦντος τοῖς ὄχλοις,
Yet him speaking* to the crowds,
=While he was still speaking

39 He answered, "A wicked and adulterous generation asks for a miraculous
sign! But none will be given
it except the sign of the
prophet Jonah. 40 For as Jonah was three days and
three nights in the belly of a
huge fish, so the Son of
Man will be three days and
three nights in the heart of
the earth. 41 The men of
Nineveh will stand up at
the judgment with this generation and condemn it; for
they repented at the
preaching of Jonah, and
now one[w] greater than Jonah is here. 42 The Queen of
the South will rise at the
judgment with this generation and condemn it; for she
came from the ends of the
earth to listen to Solomon's
wisdom, and now one
greater than Solomon is
here.
43 "When an evil[x] spirit
comes out of a man, it goes
through arid places seeking
rest and does not find it.
44 Then it says, 'I will return
to the house I left.' When it
arrives, it finds the house
unoccupied, swept clean
and put in order. 45 Then it
goes and takes with it seven
other spirits more wicked
than itself, and they go in
and live there. And the final
condition of that man is
worse than the first. That is
how it will be with this
wicked generation."

Jesus' Mother and Brothers

46 While Jesus was still
talking to the crowd, his

[w] *41* Or *something*; also in verse 42
[x] *43* Greek *unclean*

mother and his brothers
were standing outside,
wanting to speak to him.
47 Someone told him,
"Look, your mother and
your brothers are standing
outside, wanting to speak
to you."[s] 48 But to the one
who had told him this,
Jesus[t] replied, "Who is my
mother, and who are my
brothers?" 49 And pointing
to his disciples, he said,
"Here are my mother and
my brothers! 50 For whoever does the will of my Father in heaven is my brother and sister and mother."

Chapter 13

The Parable of the Sower

THAT same day Jesus
went out of the house
and sat beside the sea.
2 Such great crowds gath-
ered around him that he got
into a boat and sat there,
while the whole crowd
stood on the beach. 3 And
he told them many things in
parables, saying: "Listen!
A sower went out to sow.
4 And as he sowed, some
seeds fell on the path, and
the birds came and ate
them up. 5 Other seeds fell
on rocky ground, where
they did not have much
soil, and they sprang up
quickly, since they had no
depth of soil. 6 But when
the sun rose, they were
scorched; and since they
had no root, they withered
away. 7 Other seeds fell
among thorns, and the
thorns grew up and choked

[s] Other ancient authorities lack verse 47
[t] Gk *he*

ἰδοὺ ἡ μήτηρ καὶ οἱ ἀδελφοὶ αὐτοῦ
behold the mother and the brothers of him
εἱστήκεισαν ἔξω ζητοῦντες αὐτῷ λαλῆσαι.
stood outside seeking to him to speak.
47 [εἶπεν δέ τις αὐτῷ· ἰδοὺ ἡ μήτηρ
And said someone to him: Behold[,] the mother
σου καὶ οἱ ἀδελφοί σου ἔξω ἑστήκασιν
of thee and the brothers of thee outside are standing
ζητοῦντές σοι λαλῆσαι.] 48 ὁ δὲ
seeking to thee to speak. And he
ἀποκριθεὶς εἶπεν τῷ λέγοντι αὐτῷ· τίς
answering said to the [one] saying to him: Who
ἐστιν ἡ μήτηρ μου, καὶ τίνες εἰσὶν οἱ
is the mother of me, and who are the
ἀδελφοί μου; 49 καὶ ἐκτείνας τὴν
brothers of me? And stretching forth the
χεῖρα [αὐτοῦ] ἐπὶ τοὺς μαθητὰς αὐτοῦ
hand of him on the disciples of him
εἶπεν· ἰδοὺ ἡ μήτηρ μου καὶ οἱ ἀδελφοί
he said: Behold[,] the mother of me and the brothers
μου. 50 ὅστις γὰρ ἂν ποιήσῃ τὸ θέλημα
of me. For whoever does the will
τοῦ πατρός μου τοῦ ἐν οὐρανοῖς, αὐτός
of the Father of me – in heavens, he
μου ἀδελφὸς καὶ ἀδελφὴ καὶ μήτηρ ἐστίν.
of me brother and sister and mother is.

13 Ἐν τῇ ἡμέρᾳ ἐκείνῃ ἐξελθὼν ὁ
On – day that [1]going out of –
Ἰησοῦς τῆς οἰκίας ἐκάθητο παρὰ τὴν
[1]Jesus of the house sat beside the
θάλασσαν· 2 καὶ συνήχθησαν πρὸς αὐτὸν
sea; and were assembled to him
ὄχλοι πολλοί, ὥστε αὐτὸν εἰς πλοῖον
crowds many, so as him in a ship
=so that embarking in a ship he sat,
ἐμβάντα καθῆσθαι, καὶ πᾶς ὁ ὄχλος
embarking to sit[b], and all the crowd
ἐπὶ τὸν αἰγιαλὸν εἱστήκει. 3 καὶ ἐλάλησεν
on the beach stood. And he spoke
αὐτοῖς πολλὰ ἐν παραβολαῖς λέγων·
to them many things in parables saying:
Ἰδοὺ ἐξῆλθεν ὁ σπείρων τοῦ σπείρειν.
Behold went out the [one] sowing – to sow[d].
4 καὶ ἐν τῷ σπείρειν αὐτὸν ἃ μὲν
And in the to sow him[e] some indeed
=as he sowed
ἔπεσεν παρὰ τὴν ὁδόν, καὶ ἐλθόντα τὰ
fell beside the way, and coming the
πετεινὰ κατέφαγεν αὐτά. 5 ἄλλα δὲ
birds devoured them. But others
ἔπεσεν ἐπὶ τὰ πετρώδη ὅπου οὐκ
fell on the rocky places where not
εἶχεν γῆν πολλήν, καὶ εὐθέως ἐξανέτειλεν
it had earth much, and immediately it sprang up
διὰ τὸ μὴ ἔχειν βάθος γῆς· 6 ἡλίου
on account of the not to have depth of earth; [the] sun
=because it had not
δὲ ἀνατείλαντος ἐκαυματίσθη, καὶ διὰ
But having risen[a] it was scorched, and on account of
=when the sun rose =because
τὸ μὴ ἔχειν ῥίζαν ἐξηράνθη. 7 ἄλλα δὲ
the not to have root it was dried up. But others
it had not
ἔπεσεν ἐπὶ τὰς ἀκάνθας, καὶ ἀνέβησαν
fell on the thorns, and came up

mother and brothers stood
outside, wanting to speak
to him. 47 Someone told
him, "Your mother and
brothers are standing outside, wanting to speak to
you."[y]
48 He replied to him,
"Who is my mother, and
who are my brothers?"
49 Pointing to his disciples,
he said, "Here are my
mother and my brothers.
50 For whoever does the will
of my Father in heaven is
my brother and sister and
mother."

Chapter 13

The Parable of the Sower

THAT same day Jesus
went out of the house
and sat by the lake. 2 Such
large crowds gathered
around him that he got into
a boat and sat in it, while all
the people stood on the
shore. 3 Then he told them
many things in parables,
saying: "A farmer went out
to sow his seed. 4 As he was
scattering the seed, some
fell along the path, and the
birds came and ate it up.
5 Some fell on rocky places,
where it did not have much
soil. It sprang up quickly,
because the soil was shallow. 6 But when the sun
came up, the plants were
scorched, and they with-
ered because they had no
root. 7 Other seed fell
among thorns, which grew

[y] 47 Some manuscripts do not have verse 47.

them. 8Other seeds fell on
good soil and brought forth
grain, some a hundredfold,
some sixty, some thirty.
9Let anyone with ears[u] listen!"

The Purpose of the Parables

10 Then the disciples
came and asked him, "Why
do you speak to them in
parables?" 11He answered,
"To you it has been given to
know the secrets[v] of the
kingdom of heaven, but to
them it has not been given.
12For to those who have,
more will be given, and
they will have an abun-
dance; but from those who
have nothing, even what
they have will be taken
away. 13The reason I speak
to them in parables is that
'seeing they do not per-
ceive, and hearing they do
not listen, nor do they understand.' 14With them indeed is fulfilled the prophecy of Isaiah that says:

'You will indeed
listen, but never
understand,
and you will indeed
look, but never
perceive.
15 For this people's
heart has
grown dull,
and their ears are
hard of hearing,
and they have
shut their eyes;
so that they might
not look with
their eyes,
and listen with their
ears,
and understand with
their heart and
turn—
and I would heal
them.'

16But blessed are your
eyes, for they see, and your
ears, for they hear. 17Truly
I tell you, many prophets
and righteous people
longed to see what you see,
but did not see it, and to
hear what you hear, but did
not hear it.

[u] Other ancient authorities add *to hear*
[v] Or *mysteries*

αἱ ἄκανθαι καὶ ἀπέπνιξαν αὐτά. 8 ἄλλα δὲ
the thorns and choked them. And others
ἔπεσεν ἐπὶ τὴν γῆν τὴν καλὴν καὶ
fell on the earth - good and
ἐδίδου καρπόν, ὃ μὲν ἑκατόν, ὃ δὲ
gave fruit, the one a hundred, the other
ἑξήκοντα, ὃ δὲ τριάκοντα. 9 ὁ ἔχων
sixty, the other thirty. The [one] having
ὦτα ἀκουέτω. 10 Καὶ προσελθόντες οἱ
ears let him hear. And approaching the
μαθηταὶ εἶπαν αὐτῷ· διὰ τί ἐν παρα-
disciples said to him: Why in par-
βολαῖς λαλεῖς αὐτοῖς; 11 ὁ δὲ
ables speakest thou to them? And he
ἀποκριθεὶς εἶπεν· ὅτι ὑμῖν δέδοται
answering said: Because to you it has been given
γνῶναι τὰ μυστήρια τῆς βασιλείας τῶν
to know the mysteries of the kingdom of the
οὐρανῶν, ἐκείνοις δὲ οὐ δέδοται. 12 ὅστις
heavens, but to those it has not been given. [he] who
γὰρ ἔχει, δοθήσεται αὐτῷ καὶ περισ-
For has, it will be given to him and he will
σευθήσεται· ὅστις δὲ οὐκ ἔχει, καὶ
have abundance; but [he] who has not, even
ὃ ἔχει ἀρθήσεται ἀπ᾽ αὐτοῦ. 13 διὰ
what he has will be taken from him. There-
τοῦτο ἐν παραβολαῖς αὐτοῖς λαλῶ, ὅτι
fore in parables to them I speak, because
βλέποντες οὐ βλέπουσιν καὶ ἀκούοντες
seeing they see not and hearing
οὐκ ἀκούουσιν οὐδὲ συνιοῦσιν. 14 καὶ
they hear not neither understand. And
ἀναπληροῦται αὐτοῖς ἡ προφητεία Ἠσαΐου
is fulfilled in them the prophecy of Isaiah
ἡ λέγουσα· ἀκοῇ ἀκούσετε καὶ οὐ μὴ
- saying: In hearing ye will hear and by no means
συνῆτε, καὶ βλέποντες βλέψετε
understand, and seeing ye will see
καὶ οὐ μὴ ἴδητε. 15 ἐπαχύνθη γὰρ
and by no means perceive. For waxed gross
ἡ καρδία τοῦ λαοῦ τούτου, καὶ τοῖς
the heart people of this, and with the
ὠσὶν βαρέως ἤκουσαν, καὶ τοὺς ὀφθαλμοὺς
ears heavily they heard, and the eyes
αὐτῶν ἐκάμμυσαν· μήποτε ἴδωσιν τοῖς
of them they closed; lest they see with the
ὀφθαλμοῖς καὶ τοῖς ὠσὶν ἀκούσωσιν
eyes and with the ears hear
καὶ τῇ καρδίᾳ συνῶσιν καὶ ἐπιστρέψωσιν,
and with the heart understand and turn back,
καὶ ἰάσομαι αὐτούς. 16 ὑμῶν δὲ μακάριοι
and I will heal them. But of you blessed
οἱ ὀφθαλμοὶ ὅτι βλέπουσιν, καὶ τὰ
the eyes because they see, and the
ὦτα [ὑμῶν] ὅτι ἀκούουσιν. 17 ἀμὴν
ears of you because they hear. truly
γὰρ λέγω ὑμῖν ὅτι πολλοὶ προφῆται καὶ
For I say to you that many prophets and
δίκαιοι ἐπεθύμησαν ἰδεῖν ἃ
righteous men desired to see [the things] which
βλέπετε καὶ οὐκ εἶδαν, καὶ ἀκοῦσαι
ye see and did not see, and to hear
ἃ ἀκούετε καὶ οὐκ ἤκουσαν.
[the things] which ye hear and did not hear.

up and choked the plants.
8Still other seed fell on
good soil, where it pro-
duced a crop—a hundred,
sixty or thirty times what
was sown. 9He who has
ears, let him hear."
10The disciples came to
him and asked, "Why do
you speak to the people in
parables?"
11He replied, "The
knowledge of the secrets of
the kingdom of heaven has
been given to you, but not
to them. 12Whoever has
will be given more, and he
will have an abundance.
Whoever does not have,
even what he has will be
taken from him. 13This is
why I speak to them in parables:

"Though seeing, they do
not see;
though hearing, they
do not hear or
understand.

14In them is fulfilled the
prophecy of Isaiah:

" 'You will be ever
hearing but never
understanding;
you will be ever seeing
but never
perceiving.
15For this people's heart
has become
calloused;
they hardly hear with
their ears,
and they have closed
their eyes.
Otherwise they might
see with their eyes,
hear with their ears,
understand with their
hearts
and turn, and I would
heal them.'[z]

16But blessed are your eyes
because they see, and your
ears because they hear.
17For I tell you the truth,
many prophets and right-
eous men longed to see
what you see but did not
see it, and to hear what you
hear but did not hear it.

[z] 15 Isaiah 6:9,10

The Parable of the Sower Explained

18 "Hear then the para-
ble of the sower. 19 When
anyone hears the word of
the kingdom and does not
understand it, the evil one
comes and snatches away
what is sown in the heart;
this is what was sown on
the path. 20 As for what was
sown on rocky ground, this
is the one who hears the
word and immediately re-
ceives it with joy; 21 yet
such a person has no root,
but endures only for a
while, and when trouble or
persecution arises on ac-
count of the word, that person immediately falls
away.[w] 22 As for what was
sown among thorns, this is
the one who hears the
word, but the cares of the
world and the lure of
wealth choke the word, and
it yields nothing. 23 But as
for what was sown on good
soil, this is the one who
hears the word and under-
stands it, who indeed bears
fruit and yields, in one case
a hundredfold, in another
sixty, and in another thirty."

The Parable of Weeds among the Wheat

24 He put before them
another parable: "The kingdom of heaven may be
compared to someone who
sowed good seed in his
field; 25 but while everybody was asleep, an enemy
came and sowed weeds
among the wheat, and then
went away. 26 So when the
plants came up and bore
grain, then the weeds ap-
peared as well. 27 And the
slaves of the householder
came and said to him,

[w] Gk *stumbles*

18 Ὑμεῖς οὖν ἀκούσατε τὴν παραβολὴν
[2]Ye [3]therefore [1]hear the parable

τοῦ σπείραντος. **19** Παντὸς ἀκούοντος
of the sowing [one]. Everyone hearing[a]
=When anyone hears

τὸν λόγον τῆς βασιλείας καὶ μὴ συνιέντος
the word of the kingdom and not understanding[a]
=does not understand

ἔρχεται ὁ πονηρὸς καὶ ἁρπάζει τὸ
comes the evil one and seizes the [thing]

ἐσπαρμένον ἐν τῇ καρδίᾳ αὐτοῦ· οὗτός
having been sown in the heart of him; this

ἐστιν ὁ παρὰ τὴν ὁδὸν σπαρείς. **20** ὁ
is the [word] by the way sown. the [word]

δὲ ἐπὶ τὰ πετρώδη σπαρείς, οὗτός ἐστιν
And on the rocky places sown, this is

ὁ τὸν λόγον ἀκούων καὶ εὐθὺς μετὰ
the [one] [2]the [3]word [1]hearing and immediately with

χαρᾶς λαμβάνων αὐτόν· **21** οὐκ ἔχει δὲ
joy receiving it; but he has not

ῥίζαν ἐν ἑαυτῷ ἀλλὰ πρόσκαιρός ἐστιν,
root in himself but short-lived is,

γενομένης δὲ θλίψεως ἢ διωγμοῦ
and occurring tribulation or persecution[a]
=when tribulation or persecution occurs

διὰ τὸν λόγον εὐθὺς σκανδαλίζεται.
on account of the word immediately he is offended.

22 ὁ δὲ εἰς τὰς ἀκάνθας σπαρείς, οὗτός
But the [word] in the thorns sown, this

ἐστιν ὁ τὸν λόγον ἀκούων, καὶ ἡ
is the [one] [2]the [3]word [1]hearing, and the

μέριμνα τοῦ αἰῶνος καὶ ἡ ἀπάτη
anxiety of the age and the deceit

τοῦ πλούτου συμπνίγει τὸν λόγον, καὶ
– of riches chokes the word, and

ἄκαρπος γίνεται. **23** ὁ δὲ ἐπὶ τὴν
unfruitful it becomes. And the [word] on the

καλὴν γῆν σπαρείς, οὗτός ἐστιν ὁ
good earth sown, this is the [one]

τὸν λόγον ἀκούων καὶ συνιείς, ὃς
[4]the [5]word [1]hearing [2]and [3]understanding, who

δὴ καρποφορεῖ καὶ ποιεῖ ὃ μὲν ἑκατόν,
indeed bears fruit and produces one indeed a hundred,

ὃ δὲ ἑξήκοντα, ὃ δὲ τριάκοντα.
the other sixty, the other thirty.

24 Ἄλλην παραβολὴν παρέθηκεν αὐτοῖς
Another parable he set before them

λέγων· ὡμοιώθη ἡ βασιλεία τῶν
saying: was(is) likened The kingdom of the

οὐρανῶν ἀνθρώπῳ σπείραντι καλὸν σπέρμα
heavens to a man sowing good seed

ἐν τῷ ἀγρῷ αὐτοῦ. **25** ἐν δὲ τῷ
in the field of him. But in the
=while men slept

καθεύδειν τοὺς ἀνθρώπους ἦλθεν αὐτοῦ
to sleep – men[e] came of him

ὁ ἐχθρὸς καὶ ἐπέσπειρεν ζιζάνια ἀνὰ μέσον
the enemy and oversowed tares in between

τοῦ σίτου καὶ ἀπῆλθεν. **26** ὅτε δὲ
the wheat and went away. But when

ἐβλάστησεν ὁ χόρτος καὶ καρπὸν
sprouted the grass and fruit

ἐποίησεν, τότε ἐφάνη καὶ τὰ ζιζάνια.
produced, then appeared also the tares.

27 προσελθόντες δὲ οἱ δοῦλοι τοῦ οἰκο-
So approaching the slaves of the house-

18"Listen then to what
the parable of the sower
means: 19When anyone
hears the message about
the kingdom and does not
understand it, the evil one
comes and snatches away
what was sown in his heart.
This is the seed sown along
the path. 20The one who received the seed that fell on
rocky places is the man
who hears the word and at
once receives it with joy.
21But since he has no root,
he lasts only a short time.
When trouble or persecu-
tion comes because of the
word, he quickly falls
away. 22The one who re-
ceived the seed that fell
among the thorns is the
man who hears the word,
but the worries of this life
and the deceitfulness of
wealth choke it, making it
unfruitful. 23But the one
who received the seed that
fell on good soil is the man
who hears the word and understands it. He produces a
crop, yielding a hundred,
sixty or thirty times what
was sown."

The Parable of the Weeds

24Jesus told them another
parable: "The kingdom of
heaven is like a man who
sowed good seed in his
field. 25But while everyone
was sleeping, his enemy
came and sowed weeds
among the wheat, and went
away. 26When the wheat
sprouted and formed
heads, then the weeds also
appeared.
27"The owner's servants
came to him and said, 'Sir,

'Master, did you not sow
good seed in your field?
Where, then, did these
weeds come from?' 28He
answered, 'An enemy has
done this.' The slaves said
to him, 'Then do you want
us to go and gather them?'
29But he replied, 'No; for
in gathering the weeds you
would uproot the wheat
along with them. 30Let
both of them grow together
until the harvest; and at
harvest time I will tell the
reapers, Collect the weeds
first and bind them in bundles to be burned, but gather the wheat into my
barn.' "

The Parable of the Mustard Seed

31 He put before them
another parable: "The kingdom of heaven is like a
mustard seed that someone
took and sowed in his field;
32it is the smallest of all the
seeds, but when it has
grown it is the greatest of
shrubs and becomes a tree,
so that the birds of the air
come and make nests in its
branches."

The Parable of the Yeast

33 He told them another
parable: "The kingdom of
heaven is like yeast that a
woman took and mixed in
with[x] three measures of
flour until all of it was leavened."

The Use of Parables

34 Jesus told the crowds
all these things in parables;
without a parable he told
them nothing. 35This was
to fulfill what had been spoken through the prophet:[y]
"I will open my
mouth to speak
in parables;

[x] Gk *hid in*
[y] Other ancient authorities read *the prophet Isaiah*

δεσπότου εἶπον αὐτῷ· κύριε, οὐχὶ καλὸν
master said to him: Lord, not good
σπέρμα ἔσπειρας ἐν τῷ σῷ ἀγρῷ;
seed sowedst thou in – thy field?
πόθεν οὖν ἔχει ζιζάνια; 28 ὁ δὲ ἔφη
whence then has it tares? And he said
αὐτοῖς· ἐχθρὸς ἄνθρωπος τοῦτο ἐποίησεν.
to them: An enemy man this did.
οἱ δὲ δοῦλοι αὐτῷ λέγουσιν· θέλεις
So the slaves to him say: Willest thou
οὖν ἀπελθόντες συλλέξωμεν αὐτά; 29 ὁ
then going away we may collect them? he
δέ φησιν· οὔ, μήποτε συλλέγοντες τὰ
But says: No, lest collecting the
ζιζάνια ἐκριζώσητε ἅμα αὐτοῖς τὸν
tares ye should root up together with them the
σῖτον. 30 ἄφετε συναυξάνεσθαι ἀμφότερα
wheat. Leave to grow together both
ἕως τοῦ θερισμοῦ· καὶ ἐν καιρῷ τοῦ
until the harvest; and in time of the
θερισμοῦ ἐρῶ τοῖς θερισταῖς· συλλέξατε
harvest I will say to the reapers: Collect ye
πρῶτον τὰ ζιζάνια καὶ δήσατε αὐτὰ
first the tares and bind them
εἰς δέσμας πρὸς τὸ κατακαῦσαι αὐτά,
in bundles – – to burn them,
τὸν δὲ σῖτον συναγάγετε εἰς τὴν ἀποθήκην
but the wheat gather ye into the barn
μου. 31 Ἄλλην παραβολὴν παρέθηκεν
of me. Another parable he set before
αὐτοῖς λέγων· ὁμοία ἐστὶν ἡ βασιλεία
them saying: Like is the kingdom
τῶν οὐρανῶν κόκκῳ σινάπεως, ὃν
of the heavens to a grain of mustard, which
λαβὼν ἄνθρωπος ἔσπειρεν ἐν τῷ ἀγρῷ
[2]taking [1]a man sowed in the field
αὐτοῦ· 32 ὃ μικρότερον μέν ἐστιν
of him; which less indeed is
πάντων τῶν σπερμάτων, ὅταν δὲ
[than] all the seeds, but when
αὐξηθῇ, μεῖζον τῶν λαχάνων ἐστὶν
it grows, greater [than] the herbs it is
καὶ γίνεται δένδρον, ὥστε ἐλθεῖν τὰ
and becomes a tree, so as to come the
πετεινὰ τοῦ οὐρανοῦ καὶ κατασκηνοῦν
birds of the heaven and dwell
ἐν τοῖς κλάδοις αὐτοῦ. 33 Ἄλλην
in the branches of it. Another
παραβολὴν ἐλάλησεν αὐτοῖς· ὁμοία
parable he spoke to them: Like
ἐστὶν ἡ βασιλεία τῶν οὐρανῶν ζύμῃ,
is the kingdom of the heavens to leaven,
ἣν λαβοῦσα γυνὴ ἐνέκρυψεν εἰς ἀλεύρου
which [2]taking [1]a woman hid in [3]of meal
σάτα τρία, ἕως οὗ ἐζυμώθη ὅλον.
[2]measures [1]three, until was leavened [the] whole.
34 Ταῦτα πάντα ἐλάλησεν ὁ Ἰησοῦς ἐν
These things all spoke – Jesus in
παραβολαῖς τοῖς ὄχλοις, καὶ χωρὶς παραβολῆς
parables to the crowds, and without a parable
οὐδὲν ἐλάλει αὐτοῖς· 35 ὅπως πληρωθῇ
nothing he spoke to them; so that was fulfilled
τὸ ῥηθὲν διὰ τοῦ προφήτου λέγοντος·
the [thing] spoken through the prophet saying:
ἀνοίξω ἐν παραβολαῖς τὸ στόμα μου,
I will open in parables the mouth of me,

didn't you sow good seed in
your field? Where then did
the weeds come from?'
28" 'An enemy did this,'
he replied.
"The servants asked him,
'Do you want us to go and
pull them up?'
29" 'No,' he answered,
'because while you are
pulling the weeds, you may
root up the wheat with
them. 30Let both grow to-
gether until the harvest. At
that time I will tell the harvesters: First collect the
weeds and tie them in bundles to be burned; then
gather the wheat and bring
it into my barn.' "

The Parables of the Mustard Seed and the Yeast

31He told them another
parable: "The kingdom of
heaven is like a mustard
seed, which a man took and
planted in his field.
32Though it is the smallest
of all your seeds, yet when
it grows, it is the largest of
garden plants and becomes
a tree, so that the birds of
the air come and perch in
its branches."
33He told them still another parable: "The kingdom
of heaven is like yeast that
a woman took and mixed
into a large amount[a] of
flour until it worked all
through the dough."
34Jesus spoke all these
things to the crowd in parables; he did not say any-
thing to them without using
a parable. 35So was fulfilled
what was spoken through
the prophet:

"I will open my mouth
in parables,

[a] *33* Greek *three satas* (probably about 1/2 bushel or 22 liters)

I will proclaim what
has been hidden
from the
foundation of
the world."[z]

Jesus Explains the Parable of the Weeds

36 Then he left the
crowds and went into the
house. And his disciples
approached him, saying,
"Explain to us the parable
of the weeds of the field."
37 He answered, "The one
who sows the good seed is
the Son of Man; 38 the field
is the world, and the good
seed are the children of the
kingdom; the weeds are the
children of the evil one,
39 and the enemy who
sowed them is the devil; the
harvest is the end of the
age, and the reapers are angels. 40 Just as the weeds
are collected and burned up
with fire, so will it be at the
end of the age. 41 The Son
of Man will send his angels,
and they will collect out of
his kingdom all causes of
sin and all evildoers, 42 and
they will throw them into
the furnace of fire, where
there will be weeping and
gnashing of teeth. 43 Then
the righteous will shine like
the sun in the kingdom of
their Father. Let anyone
with ears[a] listen!

Three Parables

44 "The kingdom of
heaven is like treasure hid-

[z] Other ancient authorities lack *of the world*
[a] Other ancient authorities add *to hear*

ἐρεύξομαι κεκρυμμένα ἀπὸ καταβολῆς.
I will utter things having been hidden from [the] foundation.

36 Τότε ἀφεὶς τοὺς ὄχλους ἦλθεν
Then sending away the crowds he came

εἰς τὴν οἰκίαν. Καὶ προσῆλθον αὐτῷ
into the house. And approached *to* him

οἱ μαθηταὶ αὐτοῦ λέγοντες· διασάφησον
the disciples of him saying: Explain thou

ἡμῖν τὴν παραβολὴν τῶν ζιζανίων τοῦ
to us the parable of the tares of the

ἀγροῦ. 37 ὁ δὲ ἀποκριθεὶς εἶπεν· ὁ
field. And he answering said: The [one]

σπείρων τὸ καλὸν σπέρμα ἐστὶν ὁ
sowing the good seed is the

υἱὸς τοῦ ἀνθρώπου· 38 ὁ δὲ ἀγρός
Son – of man; and the field

ἐστιν ὁ κόσμος· τὸ δὲ καλὸν σπέρμα,
is the world; and the good seed,

οὗτοί εἰσιν οἱ υἱοὶ τῆς βασιλείας· τὰ δὲ
these are the sons of the kingdom; and the

ζιζάνιά εἰσιν οἱ υἱοὶ τοῦ πονηροῦ, 39 ὁ
tares are the sons of the evil [one], the

δὲ ἐχθρὸς ὁ σπείρας αὐτά ἐστιν ὁ
and enemy the [one] sowing them is the

διάβολος· ὁ δὲ θερισμὸς συντέλεια
devil; and the harvest [the] completion

αἰῶνός ἐστιν, οἱ δὲ θερισταὶ ἄγγελοί
of [the] age is, and the reapers angels

εἰσιν. 40 ὥσπερ οὖν συλλέγεται τὰ
are. As therefore are collected the

ζιζάνια καὶ πυρὶ κατακαίεται, οὕτως
tares and with fire are consumed, thus

ἔσται ἐν τῇ συντελείᾳ τοῦ αἰῶνος·
it will be at the completion of the age;

41 ἀποστελεῖ ὁ υἱὸς τοῦ ἀνθρώπου
will send forth the Son – of man

τοὺς ἀγγέλους αὐτοῦ, καὶ συλλέξουσιν
the angels of him, and they will collect

ἐκ τῆς βασιλείας αὐτοῦ πάντα
out of the kingdom of him all

τὰ σκάνδαλα καὶ τοὺς ποιοῦντας
the things leading to sin and the [ones] doing

τὴν ἀνομίαν, 42 καὶ βαλοῦσιν αὐτοὺς εἰς
– lawlessness, and will cast them into

τὴν κάμινον τοῦ πυρός· ἐκεῖ ἔσται ὁ
the furnace – of fire; there will be the

κλαυθμὸς καὶ ὁ βρυγμὸς τῶν ὀδόντων.
wailing and the gnashing of the teeth.

43 τότε οἱ δίκαιοι ἐκλάμψουσιν ὡς ὁ
Then the righteous will shine forth as the

ἥλιος ἐν τῇ βασιλείᾳ τοῦ πατρὸς
sun in the kingdom of the Father

αὐτῶν. ὁ ἔχων ὦτα ἀκουέτω.
of them. The [one] having ears let him hear.

44 Ὁμοία ἐστὶν ἡ βασιλεία τῶν
Like is the kingdom of the

οὐρανῶν θησαυρῷ κεκρυμμένῳ ἐν τῷ
heavens to treasure *having been* hidden in the

ἀγρῷ, ὃν εὑρὼν ἄνθρωπος ἔκρυψεν, καὶ
field, which [2]finding [1]a man hid, and

ἀπὸ τῆς χαρᾶς αὐτοῦ ὑπάγει καὶ πωλεῖ
from the joy of him goes and sells

ὅσα ἔχει καὶ ἀγοράζει τὸν ἀγρὸν
what things he has and buys – field

ἐκεῖνον. 45 Πάλιν ὁμοία ἐστὶν ἡ
that. Again like is the

I will utter things
hidden since the
creation of the
world."[b]

The Parable of the Weeds Explained

36 Then he left the crowd
and went into the house.
His disciples came to him
and said, "Explain to us
the parable of the weeds in
the field."
37 He answered, "The one
who sowed the good seed is
the Son of Man. 38 The field
is the world, and the good
seed stands for the sons of
the kingdom. The weeds
are the sons of the evil one,
39 and the enemy who sows
them is the devil. The harvest is the end of the age,
and the harvesters are angels.
40 "As the weeds are
pulled up and burned in the
fire, so it will be at the end
of the age. 41 The Son of
Man will send out his an-
gels, and they will weed out
of his kingdom everything
that causes sin and all who
do evil. 42 They will throw
them into the fiery furnace,
where there will be weep-
ing and gnashing of teeth.
43 Then the righteous will
shine like the sun in the
kingdom of their Father.
He who has ears, let him
hear.

The Parables of the Hidden Treasure and the Pearl

44 "The kingdom of heav-

[b] *35* Psalm 78:2

den in a field, which someone found and hid; then in
his joy he goes and sells all
that he has and buys that
field.
45 "Again, the kingdom
of heaven is like a merchant
in search of fine pearls;
46 on finding one pearl of
great value, he went and
sold all that he had and
bought it.
47 "Again, the kingdom
of heaven is like a net that
was thrown into the sea and
caught fish of every kind;
48 when it was full, they
drew it ashore, sat down,
and put the good into baskets but threw out the bad.
49 So it will be at the end of
the age. The angels will
come out and separate the
evil from the righteous
50 and throw them into the
furnace of fire, where there
will be weeping and gnashing of teeth.

Treasures New and Old

51 "Have you under-
stood all this?" They an-
swered, "Yes." 52 And he
said to them, "Therefore
every scribe who has been
trained for the kingdom of
heaven is like the master of
a household who brings out
of his treasure what is new
and what is old." 53 When
Jesus had finished these
parables, he left that place.

The Rejection of Jesus at Nazareth

54 He came to his
hometown and began to
teach the people[b] in their
synagogue, so that they
were astounded and said,
"Where did this man get
this wisdom and these
deeds of power? 55 Is not
this the carpenter's son? Is
not his mother called
Mary? And are not his
brothers James and Joseph
and Simon and Judas?

[b] Gk *them*

βασιλεία τῶν οὐρανῶν ἐμπόρῳ ζητοῦντι
kingdom of the heavens to a merchant seeking
καλοὺς μαργαρίτας· **46** εὑρὼν δὲ ἕνα πολύτιμον
beautiful pearls; and finding one valuable
μαργαρίτην ἀπελθὼν πέπρακεν πάντα
pearl going away sold all things
ὅσα εἶχεν καὶ ἠγόρασεν αὐτόν.
what he had and bought it.
47 Πάλιν ὁμοία ἐστὶν ἡ βασιλεία τῶν
Again like is the kingdom of the
οὐρανῶν σαγήνῃ βληθείσῃ εἰς τὴν θάλασσαν
heavens to a net cast into the sea
καὶ ἐκ παντὸς γένους συναγαγούσῃ·
and of every kind gathering;
48 ἣν ὅτε ἐπληρώθη ἀναβιβάσαντες ἐπὶ
which when it was filled bringing up onto
τὸν αἰγιαλὸν καὶ καθίσαντες συνέλεξαν
the shore and sitting collected
τὰ καλὰ εἰς ἄγγη, τὰ δὲ σαπρὰ ἔξω
the good into vessels, but the bad out
ἔβαλον. **49** οὕτως ἔσται ἐν τῇ συντελείᾳ
cast. Thus it will be at the completion
τοῦ αἰῶνος· ἐξελεύσονται οἱ ἄγγελοι καὶ
of the age: will go forth the angels and
ἀφοριοῦσιν τοὺς πονηροὺς ἐκ μέσου
will separate the evil men from [the] midst
τῶν δικαίων, **50** καὶ βαλοῦσιν αὐτοὺς
of the righteous, and will cast them
εἰς τὴν κάμινον τοῦ πυρός· ἐκεῖ
into the furnace – of fire; there
ἔσται ὁ κλαυθμὸς καὶ ὁ βρυγμὸς τῶν
will be the wailing and the gnashing of the
ὀδόντων. **51** Συνήκατε ταῦτα πάντα;
teeth. Did ye understand [a]these things [a]all?
λέγουσιν αὐτῷ· ναί. **52** ὁ δὲ εἶπεν
They say to him: Yes. So he said
αὐτοῖς· διὰ τοῦτο πᾶς γραμματεὺς
to them: Therefore every scribe
μαθητευθεὶς τῇ βασιλείᾳ τῶν οὐρανῶν
made a disciple to the kingdom of the heavens
ὅμοιός ἐστιν ἀνθρώπῳ οἰκοδεσπότῃ,
like is to *a man* a housemaster,
ὅστις ἐκβάλλει ἐκ τοῦ θησαυροῦ
who puts forth out of the treasure
αὐτοῦ καινὰ καὶ παλαιά.
of him new and old things.
53 Καὶ ἐγένετο ὅτε ἐτέλεσεν ὁ
And it came to pass when ended –
Ἰησοῦς τὰς παραβολὰς ταύτας, μετῆρεν
Jesus – parables these, he removed
ἐκεῖθεν. **54** καὶ ἐλθὼν εἰς τὴν πατρίδα
thence. And coming into the native town
αὐτοῦ ἐδίδασκεν αὐτοὺς ἐν τῇ συνα-
of him he taught them in the syna-
γωγῇ αὐτῶν, ὥστε ἐκπλήσσεσθαι αὐτοὺς
gogue of them, so as to be astounded them
=so that they were astounded
καὶ λέγειν· πόθεν τούτῳ ἡ σοφία αὕτη
and to say[b]: Whence to this man – wisdom this
and said:
καὶ αἱ δυνάμεις; **55** οὐχ οὗτός ἐστιν
and the powerful deeds? not this man is
ὁ τοῦ τέκτονος υἱός; οὐχ ἡ μήτηρ
the of the carpenter son? not the mother
αὐτοῦ λέγεται Μαριὰμ καὶ οἱ ἀδελφοὶ
of him called Mary and the brothers
αὐτοῦ Ἰάκωβος καὶ Ἰωσὴφ καὶ Σίμων
of him James and Joseph and Simon

en is like treasure hidden in
a field. When a man found
it, he hid it again, and then
in his joy went and sold all
he had and bought that
field.
45 "Again, the kingdom of
heaven is like a merchant
looking for fine pearls.
46 When he found one of
great value, he went away
and sold everything he had
and bought it.

The Parable of the Net

47 "Once again, the king-
dom of heaven is like a net
that was let down into the
lake and caught all kinds of
fish. 48 When it was full, the
fishermen pulled it up on
the shore. Then they sat
down and collected the
good fish in baskets, but
threw the bad away. 49 This
is how it will be at the end
of the age. The angels will
come and separate the
wicked from the righteous
50 and throw them into the
fiery furnace, where there
will be weeping and gnashing of teeth.
51 "Have you understood
all these things?" Jesus
asked.
"Yes," they replied.
52 He said to them,
"Therefore every teacher
of the law who has been instructed about the kingdom
of heaven is like the owner
of a house who brings out
of his storeroom new treasures as well as old."

A Prophet Without Honor

53 When Jesus had fin-
ished these parables, he
moved on from there.
54 Coming to his hometown,
he began teaching the people in their synagogue, and
they were amazed. "Where
did this man get this wisdom and these miraculous
powers?" they asked.
55 "Isn't this the carpenter's son? Isn't his mother's name Mary, and aren't
his brothers James, Joseph,

56 And are not all his sisters
with us? Where then did
this man get all this?"
57 And they took offense at
him. But Jesus said to
them, "Prophets are not
without honor except in
their own country and in
their own house." 58 And he
did not do many deeds of
power there, because of
their unbelief.

Chapter 14

The Death of John the Baptist

AT that time Herod the
ruler[c] heard reports
about Jesus; 2 and he said to
his servants, "This is John
the Baptist; he has been
raised from the dead, and
for this reason these powers are at work in him."
3 For Herod had arrested
John, bound him, and put
him in prison on account of
Herodias, his brother Philip's wife,[d] 4 because John
had been telling him, "It is
not lawful for you to have
her." 5 Though Herod[e]
wanted to put him to death,
he feared the crowd, be-
cause they regarded him as
a prophet. 6 But when Herod's birthday came, the
daughter of Herodias
danced before the compa-
ny, and she pleased Herod
7 so much that he promised
on oath to grant her whatever she might ask.
8 Prompted by her mother,
she said, "Give me the head
of John the Baptist here on
a platter." 9 The king was
grieved, yet out of regard
for his oaths and for the
guests, he commanded it to
be given; 10 he sent and had
John beheaded in the pris-

[c] Gk *tetrarch*
[d] Other ancient authorities read *his brother's wife*
[e] Gk *he*

καὶ Ἰούδας; **56** καὶ αἱ ἀδελφαὶ αὐτοῦ
and Judas? and the sisters of him
οὐχὶ πᾶσαι πρὸς ἡμᾶς εἰσιν; πόθεν
not all with us are? Whence
οὖν τούτῳ ταῦτα πάντα; **57** καὶ
then to this man these things all? And
ἐσκανδαλίζοντο ἐν αὐτῷ. ὁ δὲ Ἰησοῦς
they were offended in him. – But Jesus
εἶπεν αὐτοῖς· οὐκ ἔστιν προφήτης
said to them: [3]not [2]is [1]A prophet
ἄτιμος εἰ μὴ ἐν τῇ πατρίδι καὶ
unhonoured except in the(his) native town and
ἐν τῇ οἰκίᾳ αὐτοῦ. **58** καὶ οὐκ ἐποίησεν ἐκεῖ
in the house of him. And not he did there
δυνάμεις πολλὰς διὰ τὴν ἀπιστίαν αὐτῶν.
powerful deeds many because of the unbelief of them.

14 Ἐν ἐκείνῳ τῷ καιρῷ ἤκουσεν
At that – time heard
Ἡρῴδης ὁ τετραάρχης τὴν ἀκοὴν Ἰησοῦ,
Herod the tetrarch the report of Jesus,
2 καὶ εἶπεν τοῖς παισὶν αὐτοῦ· οὗτός
and said to the servants of him: This
ἐστιν Ἰωάννης ὁ βαπτιστής· αὐτὸς
is John the Baptist; he
ἠγέρθη ἀπὸ τῶν νεκρῶν, καὶ διὰ τοῦτο
was raised from the dead, and therefore
αἱ δυνάμεις ἐνεργοῦσιν ἐν αὐτῷ.
the powerful deeds operate in him.
3 Ὁ γὰρ Ἡρῴδης κρατήσας τὸν Ἰωάννην
– For Herod seizing – John
ἔδησεν καὶ ἐν φυλακῇ ἀπέθετο διὰ
bound and in prison put away on account of
Ἡρῳδιάδα τὴν γυναῖκα Φιλίππου τοῦ
Herodias the wife of Philip the
ἀδελφοῦ αὐτοῦ· **4** ἔλεγεν γὰρ ὁ Ἰωάννης
brother of him; for said – John
αὐτῷ· οὐκ ἔξεστίν σοι ἔχειν αὐτήν.
to him: It is not lawful for thee to have her.
5 καὶ θέλων αὐτὸν ἀποκτεῖναι ἐφοβήθη
And wishing him to kill he feared
τὸν ὄχλον, ὅτι ὡς προφήτην αὐτὸν
the crowd, because as a prophet him
εἶχον. **6** γενεσίοις δὲ γενομένοις τοῦ
they had. Now on the birthday occurring° –
Ἡρῴδου ὠρχήσατο ἡ θυγάτηρ τῆς
of Herod danced the daughter –
Ἡρῳδιάδος ἐν τῷ μέσῳ καὶ ἤρεσεν
of Herodias in the midst and pleased
τῷ Ἡρῴδῃ, **7** ὅθεν μεθ' ὅρκου ὡμολόγησεν
– Herod, whence with an oath he promised
αὐτῇ δοῦναι ὃ ἐὰν αἰτήσηται. **8** ἡ δὲ
[2]her [1]to give whatever she might ask. So she
προβιβασθεῖσα ὑπὸ τῆς μητρὸς αὐτῆς·
being instructed by the mother of her:
δός μοι, φησίν, ὧδε ἐπὶ πίνακι τὴν
Give me, she says, here on a platter the
κεφαλὴν Ἰωάννου τοῦ βαπτιστοῦ. **9** καὶ
head of John the Baptist. And
λυπηθεὶς ὁ βασιλεὺς διὰ τοὺς
being grieved the king on account of the
ὅρκους καὶ τοὺς συνανακειμένους
oaths and the [ones] reclining at table with [him]
ἐκέλευσεν δοθῆναι, **10** καὶ πέμψας
he commanded to be given, and sending

Simon and Judas? 56 Aren't
all his sisters with us?
Where then did this man
get all these things?" 57 And
they took offense at him.
But Jesus said to them,
"Only in his hometown and
in his own house is a prophet without honor."
58 And he did not do many
miracles there because of
their lack of faith.

Chapter 14

John the Baptist Beheaded

AT that time Herod the
tetrarch heard the re-
ports about Jesus, 2 and he
said to his attendants,
"This is John the Baptist;
he has risen from the dead!
That is why miraculous
powers are at work in
him."
3 Now Herod had arrested
John and bound him and
put him in prison because
of Herodias, his brother
Philip's wife, 4 for John had
been saying to him: "It is
not lawful for you to have
her." 5 Herod wanted to kill
John, but he was afraid of
the people, because they
considered him a prophet.
6 On Herod's birthday the
daughter of Herodias
danced for them and
pleased Herod so much
7 that he promised with an
oath to give her whatever
she asked. 8 Prompted by
her mother, she said,
"Give me here on a platter
the head of John the Bap-
tist." 9 The king was distressed, but because of his
oaths and his dinner guests,
he ordered that her request
be granted 10 and had John

on. 11The head was
brought on a platter and
given to the girl, who
brought it to her mother.
12His disciples came and
took the body and buried it;
then they went and told
Jesus.

Feeding the Five Thousand

13 Now when Jesus
heard this, he withdrew
from there in a boat to a
deserted place by himself.
But when the crowds heard
it, they followed him on
foot from the towns.
14When he went ashore, he
saw a great crowd; and he
had compassion for them
and cured their sick.
15When it was evening, the
disciples came to him and
said, "This is a deserted
place, and the hour is now
late; send the crowds away
so that they may go into the
villages and buy food for
themselves." 16Jesus said
to them, "They need not go
away; you give them some-
thing to eat." 17They re-
plied, "We have nothing
here but five loaves and
two fish." 18And he said,
"Bring them here to me."
19Then he ordered the
crowds to sit down on the
grass. Taking the five
loaves and the two fish, he
looked up to heaven, and
blessed and broke the
loaves, and gave them to
the disciples, and the disciples gave them to the
crowds. 20And all ate and
were filled; and they took
up what was left over of the

ἀπεκεφάλισεν Ἰωάννην ἐν τῇ φυλακῇ.
beheaded John in the prison.
11 καὶ ἠνέχθη ἡ κεφαλὴ αὐτοῦ ἐπὶ
And was brought the head of him on
πίνακι καὶ ἐδόθη τῷ κορασίῳ, καὶ
a platter and was given to the maid, and
ἤνεγκεν τῇ μητρὶ αὐτῆς. 12 καὶ
she brought [it] to the mother of her. And
προσελθόντες οἱ μαθηταὶ αὐτοῦ ἦραν τὸ
[4]approaching [1]the [2]disciples [3]of him took the
πτῶμα καὶ ἔθαψαν αὐτόν, καὶ ἐλθόντες
corpse and buried him, and coming
ἀπήγγειλαν τῷ Ἰησοῦ. 13 Ἀκούσας δὲ
reported – to Jesus. And [2]hearing
ὁ Ἰησοῦς ἀνεχώρησεν ἐκεῖθεν ἐν
– [1]Jesus departed thence in
πλοίῳ εἰς ἔρημον τόπον κατ' ἰδίαν·
a ship to a desert place privately;
καὶ ἀκούσαντες οἱ ὄχλοι ἠκολούθησαν
and [3]hearing [1]the [2]crowds followed
αὐτῷ πεζῇ ἀπὸ τῶν πόλεων. 14 Καὶ
him afoot from the cities. And
ἐξελθὼν εἶδεν πολὺν ὄχλον, καὶ
going forth he saw a much crowd, and
ἐσπλαγχνίσθη ἐπ' αὐτοῖς καὶ
was filled with tenderness over them and
ἐθεράπευσεν τοὺς ἀρρώστους αὐτῶν.
healed the sick of them.
15 ὀψίας δὲ γενομένης προσῆλθον αὐτῷ
Now evening coming on* approached to him
*=when evening came on
οἱ μαθηταὶ λέγοντες· ἔρημός ἐστιν ὁ
the disciples saying: Desert is the
τόπος καὶ ἡ ὥρα ἤδη παρῆλθεν·
place and the hour already passed;
ἀπόλυσον οὖν τοὺς ὄχλους, ἵνα ἀπελθόντες
dismiss therefore the crowds, that going away
εἰς τὰς κώμας ἀγοράσωσιν ἑαυτοῖς
into the villages they may buy for themselves
βρώματα. 16 ὁ δὲ Ἰησοῦς εἶπεν αὐτοῖς·
foods. – But Jesus said to them:
οὐ χρείαν ἔχουσιν ἀπελθεῖν· δότε
Not need they have to go away; give
αὐτοῖς ὑμεῖς φαγεῖν. 17 οἱ δὲ λέγουσιν
them ye to eat. But they say
αὐτῷ· οὐκ ἔχομεν ὧδε εἰ μὴ πέντε
to him: We have not here except five
ἄρτους καὶ δύο ἰχθύας. 18 ὁ δὲ εἶπεν·
loaves and two fishes. And he said:
φέρετέ μοι ὧδε αὐτούς. 19 καὶ κελεύσας
Bring to me here them. And having commanded
τοὺς ὄχλους ἀνακλιθῆναι ἐπὶ τοῦ χόρτου,
the crowds to recline on the grass,
λαβὼν τοὺς πέντε ἄρτους καὶ τοὺς δύο
taking the five loaves and the two
ἰχθύας, ἀναβλέψας εἰς τὸν οὐρανὸν
fishes, looking up to – heaven
εὐλόγησεν, καὶ κλάσας ἔδωκεν τοῖς
he blessed, and breaking gave to the
μαθηταῖς τοὺς ἄρτους, οἱ δὲ μαθηταὶ
disciples the loaves, and the disciples
τοῖς ὄχλοις. 20 καὶ ἔφαγον πάντες καὶ
to the crowds. And ate all and
ἐχορτάσθησαν· καὶ ἦραν τὸ περισσεῦον
were satisfied; and they took the excess

beheaded in the prison.
11His head was brought in
on a platter and given to the
girl, who carried it to her
mother. 12John's disciples
came and took his body and
buried it. Then they went
and told Jesus.

Jesus Feeds the Five Thousand

13When Jesus heard what
had happened, he withdrew
by boat privately to a solitary place. Hearing of this,
the crowds followed him on
foot from the towns.
14When Jesus landed and
saw a large crowd, he had
compassion on them and
healed their sick.
15As evening ap-
proached, the disciples
came to him and said,
"This is a remote place,
and it's already getting late.
Send the crowds away, so
they can go to the villages
and buy themselves some
food."
16Jesus replied, "They do
not need to go away. You
give them something to
eat."
17"We have here only
five loaves of bread and
two fish," they answered.
18"Bring them here to
me," he said. 19And he directed the people to sit
down on the grass. Taking
the five loaves and the two
fish and looking up to heav-
en, he gave thanks and
broke the loaves.Then he
gave them to the disciples,
and the disciples gave them
to the people. 20They all ate
and were satisfied, and the
disciples picked up twelve

broken pieces, twelve baskets full. 21 And those who
ate were about five thou-
sand men, besides women
and children.

Jesus Walks on the Water

22 Immediately he
made the disciples get into
the boat and go on ahead to
the other side, while he dismissed the crowds. 23 And
after he had dismissed the
crowds, he went up the
mountain by himself to
pray. When evening came,
he was there alone, 24 but
by this time the boat, bat-
tered by the waves, was far
from the land,[f] for the
wind was against them.
25 And early in the morning
he came walking toward
them on the sea. 26 But
when the disciples saw him
walking on the sea, they
were terrified, saying, "It is
a ghost!" And they cried
out in fear. 27 But immediately Jesus spoke to them
and said, "Take heart, it is
I; do not be afraid."
28 Peter answered him,
"Lord, if it is you, com-
mand me to come to you on
the water." 29 He said,
"Come." So Peter got out
of the boat, started walking
on the water, and came toward Jesus. 30 But when he
noticed the strong wind,[g]
he became frightened, and
beginning to sink, he cried
out, "Lord, save me!"
31 Jesus immediately
reached out his hand and
caught him, saying to him,
"You of little faith, why did

[f] Other ancient authorities read *was out on the sea*

[g] Other ancient authorities read *the wind*

τῶν κλασμάτων, δώδεκα κοφίνους πλήρεις.
of the fragments, twelve baskets full.

21 οἱ δὲ ἐσθίοντες ἦσαν ἄνδρες ὡσεὶ
And the [ones] eating were men about

πεντακισχίλιοι χωρὶς γυναικῶν καὶ
five thousand apart from women and

παιδίων. 22 Καὶ [εὐθέως] ἠνάγκασεν
children. And immediately he constrained

τοὺς μαθητὰς ἐμβῆναι εἰς τὸ πλοῖον
the disciples to embark in the ship

καὶ προάγειν αὐτὸν εἰς τὸ πέραν,
and to go before him to the other side,

ἕως οὗ ἀπολύσῃ τοὺς ὄχλους. 23 Καὶ
until he should dismiss the crowds. And

ἀπολύσας τοὺς ὄχλους ἀνέβη εἰς τὸ
having dismissed the crowds he went up into the

ὄρος κατ' ἰδίαν προσεύξασθαι. ὀψίας
mountain privately to pray. evening
=And when

δὲ γενομένης μόνος ἦν ἐκεῖ. 24 τὸ δὲ
And coming on* alone he was there. But the
evening came on

πλοῖον ἤδη σταδίους πολλοὺς ἀπὸ τῆς
ship now furlongs many from the

γῆς ἀπεῖχεν, βασανιζόμενον ὑπὸ τῶν
land was away, being distressed by the

κυμάτων, ἦν γὰρ ἐναντίος ὁ ἄνεμος.
waves, [4]was [1]for [5]contrary [2]the [3]wind.

25 τετάρτῃ δὲ φυλακῇ τῆς νυκτὸς
Now in [the] fourth watch of the night

ἦλθεν πρὸς αὐτοὺς περιπατῶν ἐπὶ τὴν
he came toward them walking on the

θάλασσαν. 26 οἱ δὲ μαθηταὶ ἰδόντες
sea. And the disciples seeing

αὐτὸν ἐπὶ τῆς θαλάσσης περιπατοῦντα
him on the sea walking

ἐταράχθησαν λέγοντες ὅτι φάντασμά
were troubled saying[,] – A phantasm

ἐστιν, καὶ ἀπὸ τοῦ φόβου ἔκραξαν.
it is, and from – fear they cried out.

27 εὐθὺς δὲ ἐλάλησεν [ὁ Ἰησοῦς]
But immediately spoke – Jesus

αὐτοῖς λέγων· θαρσεῖτε, ἐγώ εἰμι·
to them saying: Be of good cheer, I am;

μὴ φοβεῖσθε. 28 ἀποκριθεὶς δὲ αὐτῷ ὁ
do not fear. And answering him –

Πέτρος εἶπεν· κύριε, εἰ σὺ εἶ, κέλευσόν
Peter said: Lord, if thou art, command

με ἐλθεῖν πρὸς σὲ ἐπὶ τὰ ὕδατα. 29 ὁ
me to come to thee on the waters. he

δὲ εἶπεν· ἐλθέ. καὶ καταβὰς ἀπὸ τοῦ
And said: Come. And going down from the

πλοίου Πέτρος περιεπάτησεν ἐπὶ τὰ ὕδατα
ship Peter walked on the waters

καὶ ἦλθεν πρὸς τὸν Ἰησοῦν. 30 βλέπων δὲ
and came toward – Jesus. But seeing

τὸν ἄνεμον ἐφοβήθη, καὶ ἀρξάμενος
the wind he was afraid, and beginning

καταποντίζεσθαι ἔκραξεν λέγων·
to sink he cried out saying:

κύριε, σῶσόν με. 31 εὐθέως δὲ ὁ
Lord, save me. And immediately –

Ἰησοῦς ἐκτείνας τὴν χεῖρα ἐπελάβετο
Jesus stretching out the(his) hand took hold

αὐτοῦ, καὶ λέγει αὐτῷ· ὀλιγόπιστε,
of him, and says to him: Little-faith,

basketfuls of broken pieces
that were left over. 21 The
number of those who ate
was about five thousand
men, besides women and
children.

Jesus Walks on the Water

22 Immediately Jesus
made the disciples get into
the boat and go on ahead of
him to the other side, while
he dismissed the crowd.
23 After he had dismissed
them, he went up on a
mountainside by himself to
pray. When evening came,
he was there alone, 24 but
the boat was already a considerable distance[c] from
land, buffeted by the waves
because the wind was
against it.
25 During the fourth watch
of the night Jesus went out
to them, walking on the
lake. 26 When the disciples
saw him walking on the
lake, they were terrified.
"It's a ghost," they said,
and cried out in fear.
27 But Jesus immediately
said to them: "Take cour-
age! It is I. Don't be
afraid."
28 "Lord, if it's you," Peter replied, "tell me to
come to you on the water."
29 "Come," he said.
Then Peter got down out
of the boat, walked on the
water and came toward
Jesus. 30 But when he saw
the wind, he was afraid
and, beginning to sink,
cried out, "Lord, save
me!"
31 Immediately Jesus
reached out his hand and
caught him. "You of little

[c] 24 Greek *many stadia*

you doubt?" 32When they
got into the boat, the wind
ceased. 33And those in the
boat worshiped him, say-
ing, "Truly you are the Son
of God."

Jesus Heals the Sick in Gennesaret

34 When they had
crossed over, they came to
land at Gennesaret. 35After
the people of that place recognized him, they sent
word throughout the region
and brought all who were
sick to him, 36and begged
him that they might touch
even the fringe of his cloak;
and all who touched it were
healed.

Chapter 15

The Tradition of the Elders

THEN Pharisees and
scribes came to Jesus
from Jerusalem and said,
2"Why do your disciples
break the tradition of the elders? For they do not wash
their hands before they
eat." 3He answered them,
"And why do you break the
commandment of God for
the sake of your tradition?
4For God said,[h] 'Honor
your father and your mother,' and, 'Whoever speaks
evil of father or mother
must surely die.' 5But you
say that whoever tells father or mother, 'Whatever
support you might have
had from me is given to
God,'[i] then that person
need not honor the father.[j]
6So, for the sake of your
tradition, you make void
the word[k] of God. 7You
hypocrites! Isaiah prophesied rightly about you when
he said:
8 'This people honors
me with

[h] Other ancient authorities read *commanded, saying*
[i] Or *is an offering*
[j] Other ancient authorities add *or the mother*
[k] Other ancient authorities read *law*; others, *commandment*

εἰς τί ἐδίστασας; 32 καὶ ἀναβάντων
why didst thou doubt? And going up
=as they went up
αὐτῶν εἰς τὸ πλοῖον ἐκόπασεν ὁ ἄνεμος.
them* into the ship ceased the wind.
33 οἱ δὲ ἐν τῷ πλοίῳ προσεκύνησαν αὐτῷ
And the [ones] in the ship worshipped him
λέγοντες· ἀληθῶς θεοῦ υἱὸς εἶ. 34 Καὶ
saying: Truly of God Son thou art. And
διαπεράσαντες ἦλθον ἐπὶ τὴν γῆν εἰς
crossing over they came onto the land to
Γεννησαρέτ. 35 καὶ ἐπιγνόντες αὐτὸν
Gennesaret. And recognizing him
οἱ ἄνδρες τοῦ τόπου ἐκείνου ἀπέστειλαν
the men – place of that sent
εἰς ὅλην τὴν περίχωρον ἐκείνην, καὶ
into all – neighbourhood that, and
προσήνεγκαν αὐτῷ πάντας τοὺς κακῶς
brought to him all the [ones] ill
=those who were ill,
ἔχοντας, 36 καὶ παρεκάλουν αὐτὸν ἵνα
having, and besought him that
μόνον ἅψωνται τοῦ κρασπέδου τοῦ
only they might touch the fringe of the
ἱματίου αὐτοῦ· καὶ ὅσοι ἥψαντο διεσώθησαν.
garment of him; and as many as touched were completely healed.

15 Τότε προσέρχονται τῷ Ἰησοῦ
Then approach – to Jesus
ἀπὸ Ἱεροσολύμων Φαρισαῖοι καὶ γραμματεῖς
from Jerusalem Pharisees and scribes
λέγοντες· 2 διὰ τί οἱ μαθηταί σου
saying: Why the disciples of thee
παραβαίνουσιν τὴν παράδοσιν τῶν
transgress the tradition of the
πρεσβυτέρων; οὐ γὰρ νίπτονται τὰς χεῖρας
elders? for not they wash the(ir) hands
ὅταν ἄρτον ἐσθίωσιν. 3 ὁ δὲ ἀπο-
whenever bread they eat. And he answer-
κριθεὶς εἶπεν αὐτοῖς· διὰ τί καὶ ὑμεῖς
ing said to them: Why indeed ye
παραβαίνετε τὴν ἐντολὴν τοῦ θεοῦ
transgress the commandment – of God
διὰ τὴν παράδοσιν ὑμῶν; 4 ὁ γὰρ
on account of the tradition of you? – For
θεὸς εἶπεν· τίμα τὸν πατέρα καὶ τὴν
God said: Honour the father and the
μητέρα, καί· ὁ κακολογῶν πατέρα
mother, and: The [one] speaking evil of father
ἢ μητέρα θανάτῳ τελευτάτω. 5 ὑμεῖς δὲ
or mother by death let him die. But ye
λέγετε· ὃς ἂν εἴπῃ τῷ πατρὶ ἢ
say: Whoever says to the(his) father or
τῇ μητρί· δῶρον ὃ ἐὰν ἐξ ἐμοῦ
to the(his) mother: A gift whatever by me
ὠφελήθῃς, 6 οὐ μὴ τιμήσει τὸν
thou mightest be owed, by no means shall he honour the
πατέρα αὐτοῦ ἢ τὴν μητέρα αὐτοῦ·
father of him or the mother of him;
καὶ ἠκυρώσατε τὸν λόγον τοῦ θεοῦ
and ye annulled the word – of God
διὰ τὴν παράδοσιν ὑμῶν. 7 ὑποκρι-
on account of the tradition of you. Hypocrites,
ταί, καλῶς ἐπροφήτευσεν περὶ ὑμῶν
well prophesied concerning you
Ἡσαΐας λέγων· 8 ὁ λαὸς οὗτος τοῖς
Isaiah saying: This people with the

faith," he said, "why did
you doubt?"
32And when they climbed
into the boat, the wind died
down. 33Then those who
were in the boat worshiped
him, saying, "Truly you
are the Son of God."
34When they had crossed
over, they landed at Gen-
nesaret. 35And when the
men of that place recog-
nized Jesus, they sent word
to all the surrounding country. People brought all their
sick to him 36and begged
him to let the sick just
touch the edge of his cloak,
and all who touched him
were healed.

Chapter 15

Clean and Unclean

THEN some Pharisees
and teachers of the law
came to Jesus from Jerusalem and asked, 2"Why do
your disciples break the
tradition of the elders?
They don't wash their
hands before they eat!"
3Jesus replied, "And why
do you break the command
of God for the sake of your
tradition? 4For God said,
'Honor your father and
mother'[d] and 'Anyone
who curses his father or
mother must be put to
death.'[e] 5But you say that
if a man says to his father or
mother, 'Whatever help
you might otherwise have
received from me is a gift
devoted to God,' 6he is not
to 'honor his father[f]' with
it. Thus you nullify the
word of God for the sake of
your tradition. 7You hypocrites! Isaiah was right
when he prophesied about
you:
8" 'These people honor

[d] 4 Exodus 20:12; Deut. 5:16
[e] 4 Exodus 21:17; Lev. 20:9
[f] 6 Some manuscripts *father or his mother*

their lips,
but their hearts are
far from me;
9 in vain do they
worship me,
teaching human
precepts as
doctrines.' "

Things That Defile

10 Then he called the
crowd to him and said to
them, "Listen and under-
stand: 11 it is not what goes
into the mouth that defiles a
person, but it is what
comes out of the mouth
that defiles." 12 Then the
disciples approached and
said to him, "Do you know
that the Pharisees took offense when they heard
what you said?" 13 He an-
swered, "Every plant that
my heavenly Father has
not planted will be uprooted. 14 Let them alone; they
are blind guides of the
blind.[i] And if one blind
person guides another,
both will fall into a pit."
15 But Peter said to him,
"Explain this parable to
us." 16 Then he said, "Are
you also still without understanding? 17 Do you not
see that whatever goes into
the mouth enters the stomach, and goes out into the
sewer? 18 But what comes
out of the mouth proceeds
from the heart, and this is
what defiles. 19 For out of
the heart come evil intentions, murder, adultery,
fornication, theft, false witness, slander. 20 These are
what defile a person, but to
eat with unwashed hands
does not defile."

The Canaanite Woman's Faith

21 Jesus left that place
and went away to the dis-
trict of Tyre and Sidon.

[i] Other ancient authorities lack *of the blind*

χείλεσίν με τιμᾷ, ἡ δὲ καρδία αὐτῶν
lips me honours, but the heart of them
πόρρω ἀπέχει ἀπ' ἐμοῦ· 9 μάτην δὲ
far is away from me; and vainly
σέβονταί με, διδάσκοντες διδασκαλίας
they worship me, teaching teachings
ἐντάλματα ἀνθρώπων. 10 Καὶ προσκαλε-
ordinances of men. And calling
σάμενος τὸν ὄχλον εἶπεν αὐτοῖς·
forward the crowd he said to them:
ἀκούετε καὶ συνίετε· 11 οὐ τὸ εἰσερχ-
Hear ye and understand: Not the [thing] enter-
όμενον εἰς τὸ στόμα κοινοῖ τὸν ἄνθρωπον,
ing into the mouth defiles the man,
ἀλλὰ τὸ ἐκπορευόμενον ἐκ τοῦ στόματος,
but the [thing] coming forth out of the mouth,
τοῦτο κοινοῖ τὸν ἄνθρωπον. 12 Τότε
this defiles the man. Then
προσελθόντες οἱ μαθηταὶ λέγουσιν αὐτῷ·
approaching the disciples say to him:
οἶδας ὅτι οἱ Φαρισαῖοι ἀκούσαντες τὸν
Dost thou know that the Pharisees hearing the
λόγον ἐσκανδαλίσθησαν; 13 ὁ δὲ ἀπο-
saying were offended? And he answer-
κριθεὶς εἶπεν· πᾶσα φυτεία ἣν οὐκ
ing said: Every plant which not
ἐφύτευσεν ὁ πατήρ μου ὁ οὐράνιος ἐκριζω-
planted the Father of me – heavenly shall be
θήσεται. 14 ἄφετε αὐτούς· τυφλοί εἰσιν
uprooted. Leave them; blind they are
ὁδηγοὶ τυφλῶν· τυφλὸς δὲ τυφλὸν
leaders of blind; ³a blind man ¹and ⁵a blind man
ἐὰν ὁδηγῇ, ἀμφότεροι εἰς βόθυνον πεσοῦνται.
²if ⁴leads, both into a ditch will fall.
15 Ἀποκριθεὶς δὲ ὁ Πέτρος εἶπεν αὐτῷ·
And answering – Peter said to him:
φράσον ἡμῖν τὴν παραβολήν. 16 ὁ δὲ
Explain to us the parable. So he
εἶπεν· ἀκμὴν καὶ ὑμεῖς ἀσύνετοί
said: Thus also ye unintelligent
ἐστε; 17 οὐ νοεῖτε ὅτι πᾶν τὸ
are? Do ye not understand that everything
εἰσπορευόμενον εἰς τὸ στόμα εἰς τὴν
entering into the mouth into the
κοιλίαν χωρεῖ καὶ εἰς ἀφεδρῶνα ἐκβάλλεται;
stomach goes and into a drain is cast out?
18 τὰ δὲ ἐκπορευόμενα ἐκ τοῦ
but the things coming forth out of the
στόματος ἐκ τῆς καρδίας ἐξέρχεται,
mouth out of the heart comes forth,
κἀκεῖνα κοινοῖ τὸν ἄνθρωπον. 19 ἐκ
and those defiles the man. out of
γὰρ τῆς καρδίας ἐξέρχονται διαλογισμοὶ
For the heart come forth thoughts
πονηροί, φόνοι, μοιχεῖαι, πορνεῖαι, κλοπαί,
evil, murders, adulteries, fornications, thefts,
ψευδομαρτυρίαι, βλασφημίαι. 20 ταῦτά
false witnessings, blasphemies. These things
ἐστιν τὰ κοινοῦντα τὸν ἄνθρωπον·
is(are) the [ones] defiling the man;
τὸ δὲ ἀνίπτοις χερσὶν φαγεῖν οὐ
– but with unwashed hands to eat not
κοινοῖ τὸν ἄνθρωπον.
defiles the man.
21 Καὶ ἐξελθὼν ἐκεῖθεν ὁ Ἰησοῦς
And going forth thence – Jesus

me with their lips,
but their hearts are far
from me.
9 They worship me in
vain;
their teachings are but
rules taught by
men.'[g]"
10 Jesus called the crowd
to him and said, "Listen
and understand. 11 What
goes into a man's mouth
does not make him 'un-
clean,' but what comes out
of his mouth, that is what
makes him 'unclean.'"
12 Then the disciples came
to him and asked, "Do you
know that the Pharisees
were offended when they
heard this?"
13 He replied, "Every
plant that my heavenly Father has not planted will be
pulled up by the roots.
14 Leave them; they are
blind guides.[h] If a blind
man leads a blind man,
both will fall into a pit."
15 Peter said, "Explain the
parable to us."
16 "Are you still so dull?"
Jesus asked them.
17 "Don't you see that
whatever enters the mouth
goes into the stomach and
then out of the body? 18 But
the things that come out of
the mouth come from the
heart, and these make a
man 'unclean.' 19 For out of
the heart come evil
thoughts, murder, adul-
tery, sexual immorality,
theft, false testimony, slander. 20 These are what make
a man 'unclean'; but eating
with unwashed hands does
not make him 'unclean.'"

The Faith of the Canaanite Woman

21 Leaving that place,
Jesus withdrew to the re-

[g] 9 Isaiah 29:13
[h] 14 Some manuscripts *guides of the blind*

22 Just then a Canaanite
woman from that region
came out and started shouting, "Have mercy on me,
Lord, Son of David; my
daughter is tormented by a
demon." 23 But he did not
answer her at all. And his
disciples came and urged
him, saying, "Send her
away, for she keeps shouting after us." 24 He an-
swered, "I was sent only to
the lost sheep of the house
of Israel." 25 But she came
and knelt before him, saying, "Lord, help me." 26 He
answered, "It is not fair to
take the children's food
and throw it to the dogs."
27 She said, "Yes, Lord, yet
even the dogs eat the
crumbs that fall from their
masters' table." 28 Then
Jesus answered her,
"Woman, great is your
faith! Let it be done for you
as you wish." And her
daughter was healed in-
stantly.

Jesus Cures Many People

29 After Jesus had left
that place, he passed along
the Sea of Galilee, and he
went up the mountain,
where he sat down. 30 Great
crowds came to him, bringing with them the lame, the
maimed, the blind, the
mute, and many others.
They put them at his feet,
and he cured them, 31 so
that the crowd was amazed
when they saw the mute
speaking, the maimed

ἀνεχώρησεν εἰς τὰ μέρη Τύρου καὶ
departed into the parts of Tyre and
Σιδῶνος. **22** καὶ ἰδοὺ γυνὴ Χαναναία
Sidon. And behold woman a Canaanite
ἀπὸ τῶν ὁρίων ἐκείνων ἐξελθοῦσα
from – borders those coming forth
ἔκραζεν λέγουσα· ἐλέησόν με, κύριε
cried out saying: Pity me, Lord[,]
υἱὸς Δαυίδ· ἡ θυγάτηρ μου κακῶς
son of David; the daughter of me badly
δαιμονίζεται. **23** ὁ δὲ οὐκ ἀπεκρίθη
is demon-possessed. But he answered not
αὐτῇ λόγον. καὶ προσελθόντες οἱ μαθηταὶ
her a word. And approaching the disciples
αὐτοῦ ἠρώτων αὐτὸν λέγοντες· ἀπόλυσον
of him besought him saying: Dismiss
αὐτήν, ὅτι κράζει ὄπισθεν ἡμῶν. **24** ὁ
her, because she is crying out behind us. he
δὲ ἀποκριθεὶς εἶπεν· οὐκ ἀπεστάλην
But answering said: I was not sent
εἰ μὴ εἰς τὰ πρόβατα τὰ ἀπολωλότα
except to the sheep – lost
οἴκου Ἰσραήλ. **25** ἡ δὲ ἐλθοῦσα
of [the] house of Israel. But she coming
προσεκύνει αὐτῷ λέγουσα· κύριε, βοήθει
worshipped him saying: Lord, help
μοι. **26** ὁ δὲ ἀποκριθεὶς εἶπεν· οὐκ
me. But he answering said: not
ἔστιν καλὸν λαβεῖν τὸν ἄρτον τῶν τέκνων
It is good to take the bread of the children
καὶ βαλεῖν τοῖς κυναρίοις. **27** ἡ δὲ
and to throw to the dogs. And she
εἶπεν· ναί, κύριε· καὶ γὰρ τὰ κυνάρια
said: Yes, Lord; but even the dogs
ἐσθίει ἀπὸ τῶν ψιχίων τῶν πιπτόντων
eats from the crumbs – falling
ἀπὸ τῆς τραπέζης τῶν κυρίων αὐτῶν.
from the table of the masters of them.
28 τότε ἀποκριθεὶς ὁ Ἰησοῦς εἶπεν αὐτῇ·
Then answering – Jesus said to her:
ὦ γύναι, μεγάλη σου ἡ πίστις· γενηθήτω
O woman, great of thee the faith; let it be
σοι ὡς θέλεις. καὶ ἰάθη ἡ
to thee as thou desirest. And was healed the
θυγάτηρ αὐτῆς ἀπὸ τῆς ὥρας ἐκείνης.
daughter of her from – hour that.
29 Καὶ μεταβὰς ἐκεῖθεν ὁ Ἰησοῦς
And removing thence – Jesus
ἦλθεν παρὰ τὴν θάλασσαν τῆς Γαλιλαίας,
came by the sea – of Galilee,
καὶ ἀναβὰς εἰς τὸ ὄρος ἐκάθητο ἐκεῖ.
and going up into the mountain he sat there.
30 καὶ προσῆλθον αὐτῷ ὄχλοι πολλοὶ ἔχοντες
And approached *to* him crowds many having
μεθ' ἑαυτῶν χωλούς, κυλλούς, τυφλούς,
with them*selves* lame, maimed, blind,
κωφούς, καὶ ἑτέρους πολλούς, καὶ ἔρριψαν
dumb, and others many, and cast
αὐτοὺς παρὰ τοὺς πόδας αὐτοῦ· καὶ
them at the feet of him; and
ἐθεράπευσεν αὐτούς· **31** ὥστε τὸν ὄχλον
he healed them; so as the crowd
=so that the crowd marvelled
θαυμάσαι βλέποντας κωφοὺς λαλοῦντας,
to marvel[b] seeing dumb men speaking,

gion of Tyre and Sidon. 22 A
Canaanite woman from
that vicinity came to him,
crying out, "Lord, Son of
David, have mercy on me!
My daughter is suffering
terribly from demon-pos-
session."
23 Jesus did not answer a
word. So his disciples came
to him and urged him,
"Send her away, for she
keeps crying out after us."
24 He answered, "I was
sent only to the lost sheep
of Israel."
25 The woman came and
knelt before him. "Lord,
help me!" she said.
26 He replied, "It is not
right to take the children's
bread and toss it to their
dogs."
27 "Yes, Lord," she said,
"but even the dogs eat the
crumbs that fall from their
masters' table."
28 Then Jesus answered,
"Woman, you have great
faith! Your request is granted." And her daughter was
healed from that very hour.

Jesus Feeds the Four Thousand

29 Jesus left there and
went along the Sea of Galilee. Then he went up on a
mountainside and sat
down. 30 Great crowds
came to him, bringing the
lame, the blind, the crippled, the mute and many
others, and laid them at his
feet; and he healed them.
31 The people were amazed
when they saw the mute
speaking, the crippled

whole, the lame walking,
and the blind seeing. And
they praised the God of Israel.

Feeding the Four Thousand

32 Then Jesus called his
disciples to him and said, "I
have compassion for the
crowd, because they have
been with me now for three
days and have nothing to
eat; and I do not want to
send them away hungry,
for they might faint on the
way." 33 The disciples said
to him, "Where are we to
get enough bread in the
desert to feed so great a
crowd?" 34 Jesus asked
them, "How many loaves
have you?" They said,
"Seven, and a few small
fish." 35 Then ordering the
crowd to sit down on the
ground, 36 he took the sev-
en loaves and the fish; and
after giving thanks he
broke them and gave them
to the disciples, and the disciples gave them to the
crowds. 37 And all of them
ate and were filled; and
they took up the broken
pieces left over, seven baskets full. 38 Those who had
eaten were four thousand
men, besides women and
children. 39 After sending
away the crowds, he got
into the boat and went to
the region of Magadan.[m]

κυλλοὺς ὑγιεῖς καὶ χωλοὺς περιπατοῦντας
maimed whole and lame walking

καὶ τυφλοὺς βλέποντας· καὶ ἐδόξασαν
and blind seeing; and they glorified

τὸν θεὸν Ἰσραήλ. 32 Ὁ δὲ Ἰησοῦς
the God of Israel. – And Jesus

προσκαλεσάμενος τοὺς μαθητὰς αὐτοῦ
calling forward the disciples of him

εἶπεν· σπλαγχνίζομαι ἐπὶ τὸν ὄχλον,
said: I am filled with tenderness over the crowd,

ὅτι ἤδη ἡμέραι τρεῖς προσμένουσίν
because now days three they remain

μοι καὶ οὐκ ἔχουσιν τί φάγωσιν·
with me and have not anything they may eat;

καὶ ἀπολῦσαι αὐτοὺς νήστεις οὐ θέλω,
and to dismiss them without food I am not willing,

μήποτε ἐκλυθῶσιν ἐν τῇ ὁδῷ. 33 καὶ
lest they fail in the way. And

λέγουσιν αὐτῷ οἱ μαθηταί· πόθεν
say to him the disciples: Whence

ἡμῖν ἐν ἐρημίᾳ ἄρτοι τοσοῦτοι ὥστε
to us in a desert loaves so many so as

χορτάσαι ὄχλον τοσοῦτον; 34 καὶ λέγει
to satisfy a crowd so great? And says

αὐτοῖς ὁ Ἰησοῦς· πόσους ἄρτους ἔχετε;
to them – Jesus: How many loaves have ye?

οἱ δὲ εἶπαν· ἑπτά, καὶ ὀλίγα ἰχθύδια.
And they said: Seven, and a few fishes.

35 καὶ παραγγείλας τῷ ὄχλῳ ἀναπεσεῖν
And having enjoined the crowd to recline

ἐπὶ τὴν γῆν 36 ἔλαβεν τοὺς ἑπτὰ
on the ground he took the seven

ἄρτους καὶ τοὺς ἰχθύας καὶ εὐχαριστήσας
loaves and the fishes and giving thanks

ἔκλασεν καὶ ἐδίδου τοῖς μαθηταῖς, οἱ δὲ
he broke and gave to the disciples, and the

μαθηταὶ τοῖς ὄχλοις. 37 καὶ ἔφαγον πάντες
disciples to the crowds. And ate all

καὶ ἐχορτάσθησαν, καὶ τὸ περισσεῦον τῶν
and were satisfied, and the excess of the

κλασμάτων ἦραν, ἑπτὰ σπυρίδας πλήρεις.
fragments they took, seven baskets full.

38 οἱ δὲ ἐσθίοντες ἦσαν τετρακισχίλιοι
And the [ones] eating were four thousand

ἄνδρες χωρὶς γυναικῶν καὶ παιδίων.
men apart from women and children.

39 Καὶ ἀπολύσας τοὺς ὄχλους ἐνέβη εἰς
And having dismissed the crowds he embarked in

τὸ πλοῖον, καὶ ἦλθεν εἰς τὰ ὅρια Μαγαδάν.
the ship, and came into the borders of Magadan.

made well, the lame walk-
ing and the blind seeing.
And they praised the God
of Israel.
32Jesus called his disci-
ples to him and said, "I
have compassion for these
people; they have already
been with me three days
and have nothing to eat. I
do not want to send them
away hungry, or they may
collapse on the way."
33His disciples answered,
"Where could we get
enough bread in this re-
mote place to feed such a
crowd?"
34"How many loaves do
you have?" Jesus asked.
"Seven," they replied,
"and a few small fish."
35He told the crowd to sit
down on the ground.
36Then he took the seven
loaves and the fish, and
when he had given thanks,
he broke them and gave
them to the disciples, and
they in turn to the people.
37They all ate and were satisfied. Afterward the disciples picked up seven bas-
ketfuls of broken pieces
that were left over. 38The
number of those who ate
was four thousand, besides
women and children. 39Af-
ter Jesus had sent the
crowd away, he got into the
boat and went to the vicinity of Magadan.

Chapter 16

The Demand for a Sign

THE Pharisees and Sad-
ducees came, and to
test Jesus[n] they asked him
to show them a sign from
heaven. 2 He answered
them, "When it is evening,
you say, 'It will be fair
weather, for the sky is red.'
3 And in the morning, 'It
will be stormy today, for
the sky is red and threatening.' You know how to in-
terpret the appearance of
the sky, but you cannot in-

[m] Other ancient authorities read *Magdala* or *Magdalan*
[n] Gk *him*

16 Καὶ προσελθόντες οἱ Φαρισαῖοι καὶ
And approaching the Pharisees and

Σαδδουκαῖοι πειράζοντες ἐπηρώτησαν αὐτὸν
Sadducees tempting asked him

σημεῖον ἐκ τοῦ οὐρανοῦ ἐπιδεῖξαι
a sign out of *the* heaven to show

αὐτοῖς. 2 ὁ δὲ ἀποκριθεὶς εἶπεν αὐτοῖς·
to them. But he answering said to them:

[ὀψίας γενομένης λέγετε· εὐδία,
Evening coming on* ye say: Fair weather,
=When evening comes on

πυρράζει γὰρ ὁ οὐρανός· 3 καὶ πρωΐ·
for is red the heaven(sky); and in the morning:

σήμερον χειμών, πυρράζει γὰρ στυγνάζων
To-day stormy weather, for is red being overcast

Chapter 16

The Demand for a Sign

THE Pharisees and Sad-
ducees came to Jesus
and tested him by asking
him to show them a sign
from heaven.
2He replied,[i] "When
evening comes, you say, 'It
will be fair weather, for the
sky is red,' 3and in the

[i] 2 Some early manuscripts do not have the rest of verse 2 and all of verse 3.

terpret the signs of the
times.[o] 4An evil and adulterous generation asks for a
sign, but no sign will be giv-
en to it except the sign of
Jonah." Then he left them
and went away.

The Yeast of the Pharisees and Sadducees

5 When the disciples
reached the other side,
they had forgotten to bring
any bread. 6Jesus said to
them, "Watch out, and be-
ware of the yeast of the
Pharisees and Sadducees."
7They said to one another,
"It is because we have
brought no bread." 8And
becoming aware of it, Jesus
said, "You of little faith,
why are you talking about
having no bread? 9Do you
still not perceive? Do you
not remember the five
loaves for the five thou-
sand, and how many bas-
kets you gathered? 10Or
the seven loaves for the
four thousand, and how
many baskets you gath-
ered? 11How could you fail
to perceive that I was not
speaking about bread? Be-
ware of the yeast of the
Pharisees and Sadducees!"
12Then they understood
that he had not told them to
beware of the yeast of
bread, but of the teaching
of the Pharisees and Sadducees.

Peter's Declaration about Jesus

13 Now when Jesus
came into the district of
Caesarea Philippi, he asked
his disciples, "Who do people say that the Son of Man
is?" 14And they said,
"Some say John the Bap-
tist, but others Elijah, and
still others Jeremiah or one
of the prophets." 15He said
to them, "But who do you

[o] Other ancient authorities lack *2When it is . . . of the times*

ὁ οὐρανός. τὸ μὲν πρόσωπον τοῦ
the heaven(sky). The – face of the
οὐρανοῦ γινώσκετε διακρίνειν, τὰ δὲ
heaven(sky) ye know* to discern, but the
σημεῖα τῶν καιρῶν οὐ δύνασθε;] 4 γενεὰ
signs of the times can ye not? A generation
πονηρὰ καὶ μοιχαλὶς σημεῖον ἐπιζητεῖ,
evil and adulterous a sign seeks,
καὶ σημεῖον οὐ δοθήσεται αὐτῇ εἰ μὴ
and a sign shall not be given to it except
τὸ σημεῖον Ἰωνᾶ. καὶ καταλιπὼν αὐτοὺς
the sign of Jonah. And leaving them
ἀπῆλθεν. 5 Καὶ ἐλθόντες οἱ μαθηταὶ εἰς
he went away. And coming the disciples to
τὸ πέραν ἐπελάθοντο ἄρτους λαβεῖν.
the other side they forgot loaves to take.
ὁ δὲ Ἰησοῦς εἶπεν αὐτοῖς· 6 ὁρᾶτε καὶ
– And Jesus said to them: Beware and
προσέχετε ἀπὸ τῆς ζύμης τῶν Φαρισαίων
take heed from the leaven of the Pharisees
καὶ Σαδδουκαίων. 7 οἱ δὲ διελογίζοντο
and Sadducees. But they reasoned
ἐν ἑαυτοῖς λέγοντες ὅτι ἄρτους οὐκ
among themselves saying[:] – Loaves not
ἐλάβομεν. 8 γνοὺς δὲ ὁ Ἰησοῦς εἶπεν·
we took. But knowing – Jesus said:
τί διαλογίζεσθε ἐν ἑαυτοῖς, ὀλιγόπιστοι,
Why reason ye among yourselves, little-faiths,
ὅτι ἄρτους οὐκ ἔχετε; 9 οὔπω νοεῖτε,
because loaves ye have not? Do ye not yet understand,
οὐδὲ μνημονεύετε τοὺς πέντε ἄρτους τῶν
neither remember ye the five loaves of the
πεντακισχιλίων καὶ πόσους κοφίνους
five thousand and how many baskets
ἐλάβετε; 10 οὐδὲ τοὺς ἑπτὰ ἄρτους τῶν
ye took? Neither the seven loaves of the
τετρακισχιλίων καὶ πόσας σπυρίδας
four thousand and how many baskets
ἐλάβετε; 11 πῶς οὐ νοεῖτε ὅτι οὐ
ye took? How do ye not understand that not
περὶ ἄρτων εἶπον ὑμῖν; προσέχετε δὲ ἀπὸ
concerning loaves I said to you? But take heed from
τῆς ζύμης τῶν Φαρισαίων καὶ Σαδ-
the leaven of the Pharisees and Sad-
δουκαίων. 12 τότε συνῆκαν ὅτι οὐκ
ducees. Then they understood that not
εἶπεν προσέχειν ἀπὸ τῆς ζύμης [τῶν
he said to take heed from the leaven of the
ἄρτων], ἀλλὰ ἀπὸ τῆς διδαχῆς τῶν
loaves, but from the teaching of the
Φαρισαίων καὶ Σαδδουκαίων.
Pharisees and Sadducees.
13 Ἐλθὼν δὲ ὁ Ἰησοῦς εἰς τὰ μέρη
And coming – Jesus into the parts
Καισαρείας τῆς Φιλίππου ἠρώτα τοὺς
of Cæsarea – of Philip he questioned the
μαθητὰς αὐτοῦ λέγων· τίνα λέγουσιν οἱ
disciples of him saying: Whom say –
ἄνθρωποι εἶναι τὸν υἱὸν τοῦ ἀνθρώπου;
men to be the Son – of man?
14 οἱ δὲ εἶπαν· οἱ μὲν Ἰωάννην τὸν
And they said: Some indeed John the
βαπτιστήν, ἄλλοι δὲ Ἠλίαν, ἕτεροι δὲ
Baptist, and others Elias, and others
Ἰερεμίαν ἢ ἕνα τῶν προφητῶν. 15 λέγει
Jeremias or one of the prophets. He says

*See note on page xvi. Note the use in the next line of δύνασθε.

morning, 'Today it will be
stormy, for the sky is red
and overcast.' You know
how to interpret the ap-
pearance of the sky, but
you cannot interpret the
signs of the times. 4A wicked and adulterous genera-
tion looks for a miraculous
sign, but none will be given
it except the sign of Jo-
nah." Jesus then left them
and went away.

The Yeast of the Pharisees and Sadducees

5When they went across
the lake, the disciples forgot to take bread. 6"Be
careful," Jesus said to
them. "Be on your guard
against the yeast of the
Pharisees and Sadducees."
7They discussed this
among themselves and
said, "It is because we
didn't bring any bread."
8Aware of their discus-
sion, Jesus asked, "You of
little faith, why are you
talking among yourselves
about having no bread? 9Do
you still not understand?
Don't you remember the
five loaves for the five
thousand, and how many
basketfuls you gathered?
10Or the seven loaves for
the four thousand, and how
many basketfuls you gath-
ered? 11How is it you don't
understand that I was not
talking to you about bread?
But be on your guard
against the yeast of the
Pharisees and Sadducees."
12Then they understood
that he was not telling them
to guard against the yeast
used in bread, but against
the teaching of the Pharisees and Sadducees.

Peter's Confession of Christ

13When Jesus came to the
region of Caesarea Philippi,
he asked his disciples,
"Who do people say the
Son of Man is?"
14They replied, "Some
say John the Baptist; others
say Elijah; and still others,
Jeremiah or one of the
prophets."

say that I am?" 16 Simon
Peter answered, "You are
the Messiah,[p] the Son of
the living God." 17 And
Jesus answered him,
"Blessed are you, Simon
son of Jonah! For flesh and
blood has not revealed this
to you, but my Father in
heaven. 18 And I tell you,
you are Peter,[q] and on this
rock[r] I will build my
church, and the gates of
Hades will not prevail
against it. 19 I will give you
the keys of the kingdom of
heaven, and whatever you
bind on earth will be bound
in heaven, and whatever
you loose on earth will be
loosed in heaven." 20 Then
he sternly ordered the disciples not to tell anyone
that he was[s] the Messi-
ah.[p]

Jesus Foretells His Death and Resurrection

21 From that time on,
Jesus began to show his
disciples that he must go to
Jerusalem and undergo
great suffering at the hands
of the elders and chief
priests and scribes, and be
killed, and on the third day
be raised. 22 And Peter took
him aside and began to rebuke him, saying, "God
forbid it, Lord! This must
never happen to you."
23 But he turned and said to
Peter, "Get behind me, Satan! You are a stumbling
block to me; for you are
setting your mind not on divine things but on human
things."

The Cross and Self-Denial

24 Then Jesus told his
disciples, "If any want to

[p] Or *the Christ*
[q] Gk *Petros*
[r] Gk *petra*
[s] Other ancient authorities add *Jesus*

αὐτοῖς· ὑμεῖς δὲ τίνα με λέγετε εἶναι;
to them: But [3]ye [1]whom [4]me [2]say to be?
16 ἀποκριθεὶς δὲ Σίμων Πέτρος εἶπεν·
And answering Simon Peter said:
17 σὺ εἶ ὁ χριστὸς ὁ υἱὸς τοῦ θεοῦ
Thou art the Christ the Son - *of* God
τοῦ ζῶντος. ἀποκριθεὶς δὲ ὁ Ἰησοῦς
of the living. And answering - Jesus
εἶπεν αὐτῷ· μακάριος εἶ, Σίμων
said to him: Blessed art thou, Simon
Βαριωνά, ὅτι σὰρξ καὶ αἷμα οὐκ ἀπεκά-
Barjonas, because flesh and blood did not
λυψέν σοι ἀλλ' ὁ πατήρ μου ὁ ἐν
reveal to thee but the Father of me - in
τοῖς οὐρανοῖς. 18 κἀγὼ δέ σοι λέγω
the heavens. And I also to thee say[,]
ὅτι σὺ εἶ Πέτρος, καὶ ἐπὶ ταύτῃ τῇ
- Thou art Peter, and on this -
πέτρᾳ οἰκοδομήσω μου τὴν ἐκκλησίαν,
rock I will build of me the church,
καὶ πύλαι ᾅδου οὐ κατισχύσουσιν
and [the] gates of hades will not prevail against
αὐτῆς. 19 δώσω σοι τὰς κλεῖδας τῆς
it. I will give thee the keys of the
βασιλείας τῶν οὐρανῶν, καὶ ὃ ἐὰν
kingdom of the heavens, and whatever
δήσῃς ἐπὶ τῆς γῆς ἔσται δεδεμένον ἐν τοῖς
thou bindest on the earth shall be *having been* bound in the
οὐρανοῖς, καὶ ὃ ἐὰν λύσῃς ἐπὶ τῆς
heavens, and whatever thou loosest on the
γῆς ἔσται λελυμένον ἐν τοῖς οὐρανοῖς.
earth shall be *having been* loosed in the heavens.
20 τότε ἐπετίμησεν τοῖς μαθηταῖς ἵνα
Then he warned the disciples that
μηδενὶ εἴπωσιν ὅτι αὐτός ἐστιν ὁ
to no one they should tell that he is the
χριστός.
Christ.
21 Ἀπὸ τότε ἤρξατο Ἰησοῦς Χριστὸς
From then began Jesus Christ
δεικνύειν τοῖς μαθηταῖς αὐτοῦ ὅτι δεῖ
to show to the disciples of him that it behoves
αὐτὸν εἰς Ἰεροσόλυμα ἀπελθεῖν καὶ
him to Jerusalem to go and
πολλὰ παθεῖν ἀπὸ τῶν πρεσβυτέρων καὶ
many things to suffer from the elders and
ἀρχιερέων καὶ γραμματέων καὶ ἀποκτανθῆναι
chief priests and scribes and to be killed
καὶ τῇ τρίτῃ ἡμέρᾳ ἐγερθῆναι. 22 καὶ
and on the third day to be raised. And
προσλαβόμενος αὐτὸν ὁ Πέτρος ἤρξατο
taking him - Peter began
ἐπιτιμᾶν αὐτῷ λέγων· ἵλεώς σοι,
to rebuke him saying: Propitious to thee, =May God help thee,
κύριε· οὐ μὴ ἔσται σοι τοῦτο. 23 ὁ δὲ
Lord: by no means shall be to thee this. But he
στραφεὶς εἶπεν τῷ Πέτρῳ· ὕπαγε ὀπίσω
turning said to Peter: Go behind
μου, σατανᾶ· σκάνδαλον εἶ ἐμοῦ,
me, Satan; an offence thou art of me,
ὅτι οὐ φρονεῖς τὰ τοῦ θεοῦ
because thou thinkest not the things - of God
ἀλλὰ τὰ τῶν ἀνθρώπων. 24 Τότε ὁ
but the things - of men. Then -
Ἰησοῦς εἶπεν τοῖς μαθηταῖς αὐτοῦ· εἴ
Jesus said to the disciples of him: If

15 "But what about you?"
he asked. "Who do you say
I am?"
16 Simon Peter answered,
"You are the Christ,[j] the
Son of the living God."
17 Jesus replied, "Blessed
are you, Simon son of Jo-
nah, for this was not re-
vealed to you by man, but
by my Father in heaven.
18 And I tell you that you are
Peter,[k] and on this rock I
will build my church, and
the gates of Hades[l] will not
overcome it.[m] 19 I will give
you the keys of the king-
dom of heaven; whatever
you bind on earth will be[n]
bound in heaven, and whatever you loose on earth will
be[n] loosed in heaven."
20 Then he warned his disciples not to tell anyone that
he was the Christ.

Jesus Predicts His Death

21 From that time on Jesus
began to explain to his disciples that he must go to Jerusalem and suffer many
things at the hands of the
elders, chief priests and
teachers of the law, and
that he must be killed and
on the third day be raised to
life.
22 Peter took him aside
and began to rebuke him.
"Never, Lord!" he said.
"This shall never happen
to you!"
23 Jesus turned and said to
Peter, "Get behind me, Satan! You are a stumbling
block to me; you do not
have in mind the things of
God, but the things of
men."
24 Then Jesus said to his
disciples, "If anyone

[j] *16* Or *Messiah*; also in verse 20
[k] *18 Peter* means *rock*.
[l] *18* Or *hell*
[m] *18* Or *not prove stronger than it*
[n] *19* Or *have been*

become my followers, let them deny themselves and take up their cross and follow me. [25]For those who want to save their life will lose it, and those who lose their life for my sake will find it. [26]For what will it profit them if they gain the whole world but forfeit their life? Or what will they give in return for their life?

27 "For the Son of Man is to come with his angels in the glory of his Father, and then he will repay everyone for what has been done. [28]Truly I tell you, there are some standing here who will not taste death before they see the Son of Man coming in his kingdom."

τις θέλει ὀπίσω μου ἐλθεῖν, ἀπαρνησάσθω
anyone wishes after me to come, let him deny

ἑαυτὸν καὶ ἀράτω τὸν σταυρὸν αὐτοῦ,
himself and let him take the cross of him,

καὶ ἀκολουθείτω μοι. **25** ὃς γὰρ ἐὰν
and let him follow me. For whoever

θέλῃ τὴν ψυχὴν αὐτοῦ σῶσαι, ἀπολέσει
wishes the life of him to save, he will lose

αὐτήν· ὃς δ' ἂν ἀπολέσῃ τὴν ψυχὴν
it; and whoever loses the life

αὐτοῦ ἕνεκεν ἐμοῦ, εὑρήσει αὐτήν. **26** τί
of him for the sake of me, he will find it. what

γὰρ ὠφεληθήσεται ἄνθρωπος, ἐὰν τὸν
For will be benefited a man, if the

κόσμον ὅλον κερδήσῃ, τὴν δὲ ψυχὴν
world whole he should gain, but the soul

αὐτοῦ ζημιωθῇ; ἢ τί δώσει ἄνθρωπος
of him loses? or what will give a man

ἀντάλλαγμα τῆς ψυχῆς αὐτοῦ; **27** μέλλει
an exchange of the soul of him? is about

γὰρ ὁ υἱὸς τοῦ ἀνθρώπου ἔρχεσθαι ἐν τῇ
For the Son – of man to come in the

δόξῃ τοῦ πατρὸς αὐτοῦ μετὰ τῶν ἀγγέλων
glory of the Father of him with the angels

αὐτοῦ, καὶ τότε ἀποδώσει ἑκάστῳ
of him, and then he will reward *to* each man

κατὰ τὴν πρᾶξιν αὐτοῦ. **28** ἀμὴν λέγω
according to the conduct of him. Truly I say

ὑμῖν ὅτι εἰσίν τινες τῶν ὧδε ἑστώτων
to you[,] – There are some of the [ones] here standing

οἵτινες οὐ μὴ γεύσωνται θανάτου ἕως ἂν
who by no means may taste of death until

ἴδωσιν τὸν υἱὸν τοῦ ἀνθρώπου ἐρχόμενον
they see the Son – of man coming

ἐν τῇ βασιλείᾳ αὐτοῦ.
in the kingdom of him.

would come after me, he must deny himself and take up his cross and follow me. [25]For whoever wants to save his life[o] will lose it, but whoever loses his life for me will find it. [26]What good will it be for a man if he gains the whole world, yet forfeits his soul? Or what can a man give in exchange for his soul? [27]For the Son of Man is going to come in his Father's glory with his angels, and then he will reward each person according to what he has done. [28]I tell you the truth, some who are standing here will not taste death before they see the Son of Man coming in his kingdom."

Chapter 17

The Transfiguration

SIX days later, Jesus took with him Peter and James and his brother John and led them up a high mountain, by themselves. [2]And he was transfigured before them, and his face shone like the sun, and his clothes became dazzling white. [3]Suddenly there appeared to them Moses and Elijah, talking with him. [4]Then Peter said to Jesus, "Lord, it is good for us to be here; if you wish, I[t] will make three dwellings[u] here, one for you, one for Moses, and one for Elijah." [5]While he was still speak-

17 Καὶ μεθ' ἡμέρας ἓξ παραλαμβάνει ὁ
And after days six takes –

Ἰησοῦς τὸν Πέτρον καὶ Ἰάκωβον καὶ
Jesus – Peter and James and

Ἰωάννην τὸν ἀδελφὸν αὐτοῦ, καὶ ἀναφέρει
John the brother of him, and leads up

αὐτοὺς εἰς ὄρος ὑψηλὸν κατ' ἰδίαν. **2** καὶ
them to mountain a high privately. And

μετεμορφώθη ἔμπροσθεν αὐτῶν, καὶ
he was transfigured before them, and

ἔλαμψεν τὸ πρόσωπον αὐτοῦ ὡς ὁ ἥλιος,
shone the face of him as the sun,

τὰ δὲ ἱμάτια αὐτοῦ ἐγένετο λευκὰ ὡς
and the garments of him became white as

τὸ φῶς. **3** καὶ ἰδοὺ ὤφθη αὐτοῖς Μωϋσῆς
the light. And behold was seen by them Moses

καὶ Ἠλίας συλλαλοῦντες μετ' αὐτοῦ.
and Elias conversing with him.

4 ἀποκριθεὶς δὲ ὁ Πέτρος εἶπεν τῷ
And answering – Peter said –

Ἰησοῦ· κύριε, καλόν ἐστιν ἡμᾶς ὧδε
to Jesus: Lord, good it is us here

εἶναι· εἰ θέλεις, ποιήσω ὧδε τρεῖς
to be; if thou willest, I will make here three

σκηνάς, σοὶ μίαν καὶ Μωϋσεῖ
tents, for thee one and for Moses

μίαν καὶ Ἠλίᾳ μίαν. **5** ἔτι αὐτοῦ
one and for Elias one. Yet him
=While he was yet

Chapter 17

The Transfiguration

AFTER six days Jesus took with him Peter, James and John the brother of James, and led them up a high mountain by themselves. [2]There he was transfigured before them. His face shone like the sun, and his clothes became as white as the light. [3]Just then there appeared before them Moses and Elijah, talking with Jesus.

[4]Peter said to Jesus, "Lord, it is good for us to be here. If you wish, I will put up three shelters—one for you, one for Moses and one for Elijah."

[5]While he was still speak-

[t] Other ancient authorities read *we*
[u] Or *tents*

[o] 25 The Greek word means either *life* or *soul*; also in verse 26.

ing, suddenly a bright cloud
overshadowed them, and
from the cloud a voice said,
"This is my Son, the Be-
loved;[v] with him I am well
pleased; listen to him!"
6 When the disciples heard
this, they fell to the ground
and were overcome by
fear. 7 But Jesus came and
touched them, saying, "Get
up and do not be afraid."
8 And when they looked up,
they saw no one except
Jesus himself alone.
9 As they were coming
down the mountain, Jesus
ordered them, "Tell no one
about the vision until after
the Son of Man has been
raised from the dead."
10 And the disciples asked
him, "Why, then, do the
scribes say that Elijah must
come first?" 11 He replied,
"Elijah is indeed coming
and will restore all things;
12 but I tell you that Elijah
has already come, and they
did not recognize him, but
they did to him whatever
they pleased. So also the
Son of Man is about to suffer at their hands." 13 Then
the disciples understood
that he was speaking to
them about John the Bap-
tist.

Jesus Cures a Boy with a Demon

14 When they came to
the crowd, a man came to
him, knelt before him,
15 and said, "Lord, have
mercy on my son, for he is
an epileptic and he suffers
terribly; he often falls into
the fire and often into the
water. 16 And I brought him
to your disciples, but they
could not cure him."

λαλοῦντος, ἰδοὺ νεφέλη φωτεινὴ ἐπεσκίασεν
speaking[a], behold cloud a bright overshadowed
speaking,
αὐτούς, καὶ ἰδοὺ φωνὴ ἐκ τῆς νεφέλης
them, and behold a voice out of the cloud
λέγουσα· οὗτός ἐστιν ὁ υἱός μου ὁ
saying: This is the son of me the
ἀγαπητός, ἐν ᾧ εὐδόκησα· ἀκούετε
beloved, in whom I was well pleased; hear ye
αὐτοῦ. 6 καὶ ἀκούσαντες οἱ μαθηταὶ
him. And hearing the disciples
ἔπεσαν ἐπὶ πρόσωπον αὐτῶν καὶ
fell on [the] face[s] of them and
ἐφοβήθησαν σφόδρα. 7 καὶ προσῆλθεν ὁ
feared exceedingly. And approached –
Ἰησοῦς καὶ ἁψάμενος αὐτῶν εἶπεν·
Jesus and touching them said:
ἐγέρθητε καὶ μὴ φοβεῖσθε. 8 ἐπάραντες δὲ
Rise and do not fear. And lifting up
τοὺς ὀφθαλμοὺς αὐτῶν οὐδένα εἶδον εἰ
the eyes of them no one they saw ex-
μὴ αὐτὸν Ἰησοῦν μόνον. 9 Καὶ κατα-
cept himself Jesus only. And com-
=as
βαινόντων αὐτῶν ἐκ τοῦ ὄρους ἐνετείλατο
ing down them[a] out of the mountain enjoined
they were coming down
αὐτοῖς ὁ Ἰησοῦς λέγων· μηδενὶ εἴπητε
them – Jesus saying: To no one tell
τὸ ὅραμα ἕως οὗ ὁ υἱὸς τοῦ ἀνθρώπου
the vision until the Son – of man
ἐκ νεκρῶν ἐγερθῇ. 10 Καὶ ἐπηρώτησαν
out of dead be raised. And questioned
αὐτὸν οἱ μαθηταὶ λέγοντες· τί οὖν
him the disciples saying: Why then
οἱ γραμματεῖς λέγουσιν ὅτι Ἠλίαν δεῖ
the scribes say that [s]Elias [1]it behoves
ἐλθεῖν πρῶτον; 11 ὁ δὲ ἀποκριθεὶς εἶπεν·
to come first? And he answering said:
Ἠλίας μὲν ἔρχεται καὶ ἀποκαταστήσει
Elias indeed is coming and will restore
πάντα· 12 λέγω δὲ ὑμῖν ὅτι Ἠλίας
all things; but I tell you that Elias
ἤδη ἦλθεν, καὶ οὐκ ἐπέγνωσαν
already came, and they did not recognize
αὐτόν, ἀλλ' ἐποίησαν ἐν αὐτῷ ὅσα
him, but did by him whatever things
ἠθέλησαν· οὕτως καὶ ὁ υἱὸς τοῦ ἀνθρώπου
they wished; thus also the Son – of man
μέλλει πάσχειν ὑπ' αὐτῶν. 13 τότε
is about to suffer by them. Then
συνῆκαν οἱ μαθηταὶ ὅτι περὶ
understood the disciples that concerning
Ἰωάννου τοῦ βαπτιστοῦ εἶπεν αὐτοῖς.
John the Baptist he spoke to them.
14 Καὶ ἐλθόντων πρὸς τὸν ὄχλον προσ-
And [they] coming to the crowd ap-
ῆλθεν αὐτῷ ἄνθρωπος γονυπετῶν αὐτὸν
proached to him a man falling on knees to him
15 καὶ λέγων· κύριε, ἐλέησόν μου τὸν
and saying: Lord, pity of me the
υἱόν, ὅτι σεληνιάζεται καὶ κακῶς ἔχει·
son, because he is moonstruck and ill has;
=is ill;
πολλάκις γὰρ πίπτει εἰς τὸ πῦρ καὶ
for often he falls into the fire and
πολλάκις εἰς τὸ ὕδωρ. 16 καὶ προσήνεγκα
often into the water. And I brought
αὐτὸν τοῖς μαθηταῖς σου, καὶ οὐκ
him to the disciples of thee, and not

ing, a bright cloud enveloped them, and a voice
from the cloud said, "This
is my Son, whom I love;
with him I am well pleased.
Listen to him!"
6 When the disciples
heard this, they fell face-
down to the ground, terrified. 7 But Jesus came and
touched them. "Get up,"
he said. "Don't be afraid."
8 When they looked up,
they saw no one except
Jesus.
9 As they were coming
down the mountain, Jesus
instructed them, "Don't
tell anyone what you have
seen, until the Son of Man
has been raised from the
dead."
10 The disciples asked
him, "Why then do the
teachers of the law say that
Elijah must come first?"
11 Jesus replied, "To be
sure, Elijah comes and will
restore all things. 12 But I
tell you, Elijah has already
come, and they did not recognize him, but have done
to him everything they
wished. In the same way
the Son of Man is going to
suffer at their hands."
13 Then the disciples understood that he was talking to
them about John the Bap-
tist.

The Healing of a Boy With a Demon

14 When they came to the
crowd, a man approached
Jesus and knelt before him.
15 "Lord, have mercy on
my son," he said. "He has
seizures and is suffering
greatly. He often falls into
the fire or into the water.
16 I brought him to your disciples, but they could not

[v] Or *my beloved Son*

17 Jesus answered, "You faithless and perverse generation, how much longer must I be with you? How much longer must I put up with you? Bring him here to me." 18 And Jesus rebuked the demon,[w] and it[x] came out of him, and the boy was cured instantly. 19 Then the disciples came to Jesus privately and said, "Why could we not cast it out?" 20 He said to them, "Because of your little faith. For truly I tell you, if you have faith the size of a[y] mustard seed, you will say to this mountain, 'Move from here to there,' and it will move; and nothing will be impossible for you."[z]

Jesus Again Foretells His Death and Resurrection

22 As they were gathering[a] in Galilee, Jesus said to them, "The Son of Man is going to be betrayed into human hands, 23 and they will kill him, and on the third day he will be raised." And they were greatly distressed.

Jesus and the Temple Tax

24 When they reached Capernaum, the collectors of the temple tax[b] came to Peter and said, "Does your teacher not pay the temple tax?"[b] 25 He said, "Yes, he does." And when he came home, Jesus spoke of it first, asking, "What do you think, Simon? From whom do kings of the earth take toll or tribute? From their children or from others?"

[w] Gk *it* or *him*
[x] Gk *the demon*
[y] Gk *faith as a grain of*
[z] Other ancient authorities add verse 21, *But this kind does not come out except by prayer and fasting*
[a] Other ancient authorities read *living*
[b] Gk *didrachma*

ἠδυνήθησαν αὐτὸν θεραπεῦσαι. **17** ἀπο-
they were able him to heal. an-
κριθεὶς δὲ ὁ Ἰησοῦς εἶπεν· ὦ γενεὰ
swering And – Jesus said: O generation
ἄπιστος καὶ διεστραμμένη, ἕως πότε
unbelieving and *having been* perverted, until when
μεθ' ὑμῶν ἔσομαι; ἕως πότε
with you shall I be? until when
ἀνέξομαι ὑμῶν; φέρετέ μοι αὐτὸν
shall I endure you? bring to me him
ὧδε. **18** καὶ ἐπετίμησεν αὐτῷ ὁ Ἰησοῦς,
here. And rebuked it – Jesus,
καὶ ἐξῆλθεν ἀπ' αὐτοῦ τὸ δαιμόνιον,
and came out from him the demon,
καὶ ἐθεραπεύθη ὁ παῖς ἀπὸ τῆς ὥρας
and was healed the boy from – hour
ἐκείνης. **19** Τότε προσελθόντες οἱ μαθηταὶ
that. Then [3]approaching [1]the [2]disciples
τῷ Ἰησοῦ κατ' ἰδίαν εἶπον· διὰ
– *to* Jesus privately said: Why
τί ἡμεῖς οὐκ ἠδυνήθημεν ἐκβαλεῖν αὐτό;
we were not able to expel it?
20 ὁ δὲ λέγει αὐτοῖς· διὰ τὴν ὀλιγο-
And he says to them: Because of the little
πιστίαν ὑμῶν· ἀμὴν γὰρ λέγω ὑμῖν, ἐὰν
faith of you; for truly I say to you, if
ἔχητε πίστιν ὡς κόκκον σινάπεως,
ye have faith as a grain of mustard,
ἐρεῖτε τῷ ὄρει τούτῳ· μετάβα
ye will say – mountain to this: Remove
ἔνθεν ἐκεῖ, καὶ μεταβήσεται, καὶ οὐδὲν
hence there, and it will be removed, and nothing
ἀδυνατήσει ὑμῖν. ‡
will be impossible to you.
22 Συστρεφομένων δὲ αὐτῶν ἐν τῇ
And strolling them[a] in –
=as they were strolling
Γαλιλαίᾳ εἶπεν αὐτοῖς ὁ Ἰησοῦς· μέλλει
Galilee said to them – Jesus: is about
ὁ υἱὸς τοῦ ἀνθρώπου παραδίδοσθαι εἰς
The Son – of man to be delivered into
χεῖρας ἀνθρώπων, **23** καὶ ἀποκτενοῦσιν
[the] hands of men, and they will kill
αὐτόν, καὶ τῇ τρίτῃ ἡμέρᾳ ἐγερθήσεται.
him, and on the third day he will be raised.
καὶ ἐλυπήθησαν σφόδρα.
And they were grieved exceedingly.
24 Ἐλθόντων δὲ αὐτῶν εἰς Καφαρναοὺμ
And coming them[a] to Capernaum
=when they came
προσῆλθον οἱ τὰ δίδραχμα λαμβάνοντες
approached the [ones] the didrachmæ receiving
τῷ Πέτρῳ καὶ εἶπαν· ὁ διδάσκαλος
– Peter and said: The teacher
ὑμῶν οὐ τελεῖ δίδραχμα; λέγει· ναί.
of you not pays drachmae? He says: Yes.
25 καὶ ἐλθόντα εἰς τὴν οἰκίαν προ-
And [4]coming [5]into [6]the [7]house [2]pre-
έφθασεν αὐτὸν ὁ Ἰησοῦς λέγων· τί σοι
ceded [3]him – [1]Jesus saying: What to thee
δοκεῖ, Σίμων; οἱ βασιλεῖς τῆς γῆς
seems it, Simon? the kings of the earth
ἀπὸ τίνων λαμβάνουσιν τέλη ἢ κῆνσον;
from whom do they take toll or poll-tax?
ἀπὸ τῶν υἱῶν αὐτῶν ἢ ἀπὸ τῶν ἀλλοτρίων;
from the sons of them or from – strangers?

‡ Verse 21 omitted by Nestle; *cf.* NIV

heal him."

17 "O unbelieving and perverse generation," Jesus replied, "how long shall I stay with you? How long shall I put up with you? Bring the boy here to me." 18 Jesus rebuked the demon, and it came out of the boy, and he was healed from that moment.

19 Then the disciples came to Jesus in private and asked, "Why couldn't we drive it out?"

20 He replied, "Because you have so little faith. I tell you the truth, if you have faith as small as a mustard seed, you can say to this mountain, 'Move from here to there' and it will move. Nothing will be impossible for you.[p]"

22 When they came together in Galilee, he said to them, "The Son of Man is going to be betrayed into the hands of men. 23 They will kill him, and on the third day he will be raised to life." And the disciples were filled with grief.

The Temple Tax

24 After Jesus and his disciples arrived in Capernaum, the collectors of the two-drachma tax came to Peter and asked, "Doesn't your teacher pay the temple tax[q]?"

25 "Yes, he does," he replied.

When Peter came into the house, Jesus was the first to speak. "What do you think, Simon?" he asked. "From whom do the kings of the earth collect duty and taxes—from their own sons or from others?"

[p] 20 Some manuscripts *you*. [21] *But this kind does not go out except by prayer and fasting.*
[q] 24 Greek *the two drachmas*

26When Peter[c] said,
"From others," Jesus said
to him, "Then the children
are free. 27However, so
that we do not give offense
to them, go to the sea and
cast a hook; take the first
fish that comes up; and
when you open its mouth,
you will find a coin;[d] take
that and give it to them for
you and me."

Chapter 18

True Greatness

AT that time the disciples
came to Jesus and
asked, "Who is the greatest
in the kingdom of heaven?"
2He called a child, whom
he put among them, 3and
said, "Truly I tell you, unless you change and be-
come like children, you will
never enter the kingdom of
heaven. 4Whoever be-
comes humble like this
child is the greatest in the
kingdom of heaven. 5Who-
ever welcomes one such
child in my name welcomes
me.

Temptations to Sin

6 "If any of you put a
stumbling block before one
of these little ones who believe in me, it would be better for you if a great millstone were fastened around
your neck and you were
drowned in the depth of the
sea. 7Woe to the world because of stumbling blocks!
Occasions for stumbling
are bound to come, but woe
to the one by whom the
stumbling block comes!
8 "If your hand or your
foot causes you to stumble,
cut it off and throw it away;

[c] Gk *he*
[d] Gk *stater*; the stater was worth two didrachmas

26 εἰπόντος δέ· ἀπὸ τῶν ἀλλο-
and [he] saying*: = when he said: From – strangers,
τρίων, ἔφη αὐτῷ ὁ Ἰησοῦς· ἄρα γε
said to him – Jesus: Then
ἐλεύθεροί εἰσιν οἱ υἱοί. 27 ἵνα δὲ μὴ
free are the sons. But lest
σκανδαλίσωμεν αὐτούς, πορευθεὶς εἰς
we should offend them, going to
θάλασσαν βάλε ἄγκιστρον καὶ τὸν
[the] sea cast a hook and the
ἀναβάντα πρῶτον ἰχθὺν ἆρον, καὶ ἀνοίξας
[3]coming up [2]first [1]fish take, and opening
τὸ στόμα αὐτοῦ εὑρήσεις στατῆρα·
the mouth of it thou wilt find a stater;
ἐκεῖνον λαβὼν δὸς αὐτοῖς ἀντὶ ἐμοῦ καὶ
that taking give them for me and
σοῦ.
thee.

18 Ἐν ἐκείνῃ τῇ ὥρᾳ προσῆλθον οἱ
In that – hour approached the
μαθηταὶ τῷ Ἰησοῦ λέγοντες· τίς ἄρα
disciples – *to* Jesus saying: Who then
μείζων ἐστὶν ἐν τῇ βασιλείᾳ τῶν οὐρανῶν;
greater is in the kingdom of the heavens?
2 καὶ προσκαλεσάμενος παιδίον ἔστησεν
And calling forward a child he set
αὐτὸ ἐν μέσῳ αὐτῶν 3 καὶ εἶπεν· ἀμὴν
him in [the] midst of them and said: Truly
λέγω ὑμῖν, ἐὰν μὴ στραφῆτε καὶ
I say to you, except ye turn and
γένησθε ὡς τὰ παιδία, οὐ μὴ
become as – children, by no means
εἰσέλθητε εἰς τὴν βασιλείαν τῶν
may ye enter into the kingdom of the
οὐρανῶν. 4 ὅστις οὖν ταπεινώσει ἑαυτὸν
heavens. [2][he] who [1]Therefore will humble himself
ὡς τὸ παιδίον τοῦτο, οὗτός ἐστιν ὁ
as – child this, this [one] is the
μείζων ἐν τῇ βασιλείᾳ τῶν οὐρανῶν.
greater in the kingdom of the heavens.
5 καὶ ὃς ἐὰν δέξηται ἓν παιδίον
And whoever receives one child
τοιοῦτο ἐπὶ τῷ ὀνόματί μου, ἐμὲ δέχεται·
such on(in) the name of me, me receives;
6 ὃς δ' ἂν σκανδαλίσῃ ἕνα τῶν
and whoever offends one –
μικρῶν τούτων τῶν πιστευόντων εἰς ἐμέ,
little [ones] of these – believing in me,
συμφέρει αὐτῷ ἵνα κρεμασθῇ μύλος
it is expedient for him that be hanged an upper
ὀνικὸς περὶ τὸν τράχηλον αὐτοῦ καὶ
millstone round the neck of him and
καταποντισθῇ ἐν τῷ πελάγει τῆς θαλάσσης.
he be drowned in the depth of the sea.
7 Οὐαὶ τῷ κόσμῳ ἀπὸ τῶν σκανδάλων·
Woe to the world from – offences;
ἀνάγκη γὰρ ἐλθεῖν τὰ σκάνδαλα, πλὴν
for [it is] a necessity to come – offences, but
οὐαὶ τῷ ἀνθρώπῳ δι' οὗ τὸ σκάνδαλον
woe to the man through whom the offence
ἔρχεται. 8 Εἰ δὲ ἡ χείρ σου ἢ ὁ
comes. Now if the hand of thee or the
πούς σου σκανδαλίζει σε, ἔκκοψον αὐτὸν
foot of thee offends thee, cut off it

26"From others," Peter
answered.
"Then the sons are ex-
empt," Jesus said to him.
27"But so that we may not
offend them, go to the lake
and throw out your line.
Take the first fish you
catch; open its mouth and
you will find a four-drach-
ma coin. Take it and give it
to them for my tax and
yours."

Chapter 18

The Greatest in the Kingdom of Heaven

AT that time the disciples
came to Jesus and
asked, "Who is the great-
est in the kingdom of heav-
en?"
2He called a little child
and had him stand among
them. 3And he said: "I tell
you the truth, unless you
change and become like little children, you will never
enter the kingdom of heav-
en. 4Therefore, whoever
humbles himself like this
child is the greatest in the
kingdom of heaven.
5"And whoever wel-
comes a little child like this
in my name welcomes me.
6But if anyone causes one
of these little ones who believe in me to sin, it would
be better for him to have a
large millstone hung
around his neck and to be
drowned in the depths of
the sea.
7"Woe to the world be-
cause of the things that
cause people to sin! Such
things must come, but woe
to the man through whom
they come! 8If your hand or
your foot causes you to sin
cut it off and throw it away.

it is better for you to enter life maimed or lame than to have two hands or two feet and to be thrown into the eternal fire. 9 And if your eye causes you to stumble, tear it out and throw it away; it is better for you to enter life with one eye than to have two eyes and to be thrown into the hell[e] of fire.

The Parable of the Lost Sheep

10 "Take care that you do not despise one of these little ones; for, I tell you, in heaven their angels continually see the face of my Father in heaven.[f] 12 What do you think? If a shepherd has a hundred sheep, and one of them has gone astray, does he not leave the ninety-nine on the mountains and go in search of the one that went astray? 13 And if he finds it, truly I tell you, he rejoices over it more than over the ninety-nine that never went astray. 14 So it is not the will of your[g] Father in heaven that one of these little ones should be lost.

Reproving Another Who Sins

15 "If another member of the church[h] sins against you,[i] go and point out the fault when the two of you are alone. If the member listens to you, you have regained that one.[j] 16 But if you are not listened to, take one or two others along with you, so that every word may be confirmed by the evidence of two or three witnesses. 17 If the member refuses to listen to them, tell it to the church; and if the offender refuses

καὶ βάλε ἀπὸ σοῦ· καλόν σοί ἐστιν
and cast from thee; good for thee it is
εἰσελθεῖν εἰς τὴν ζωὴν κυλλὸν ἢ χωλόν,
to enter into – life maimed or lame,
ἢ δύο χεῖρας ἢ δύο πόδας ἔχοντα βληθῆναι
than two hands or two feet having to be cast
εἰς τὸ πῦρ τὸ αἰώνιον. 9 καὶ εἰ ὁ
into the fire – eternal. And if the
ὀφθαλμός σου σκανδαλίζει σε, ἔξελε αὐτὸν
eye of thee offends thee, pluck out it
καὶ βάλε ἀπὸ σοῦ· καλόν σοί ἐστιν
and cast from thee; good for thee it is
μονόφθαλμον εἰς τὴν ζωὴν εἰσελθεῖν, ἢ
one-eyed into *the* life to enter, than
δύο ὀφθαλμοὺς ἔχοντα βληθῆναι εἰς
two eyes having to be cast into
τὴν γέενναν τοῦ πυρός. 10 Ὁρᾶτε μὴ
the gehenna – of fire. See [that] not
καταφρονήσητε ἑνὸς τῶν μικρῶν τούτων·
ye despise one – little [ones] of these;
λέγω γὰρ ὑμῖν ὅτι οἱ ἄγγελοι αὐτῶν
for I tell you that the angels of them
ἐν οὐρανοῖς διὰ παντὸς βλέπουσι τὸ
in heaven*s* always see the
πρόσωπον τοῦ πατρός μου τοῦ ἐν οὐρανοῖς.‡
face of the Father of me – in heaven*s*.
12 Τί ὑμῖν δοκεῖ; ἐὰν γένηταί τινι
What to you seems it? if there be to any
=any man has
ἀνθρώπῳ ἑκατὸν πρόβατα καὶ πλανηθῇ
man[c] a hundred sheep and wanders
ἓν ἐξ αὐτῶν, οὐχὶ ἀφήσει τὰ ἐνενήκοντα
one of them, will he not leave the ninety-
ἐννέα ἐπὶ τὰ ὄρη καὶ πορευθεὶς ζητεῖ τὸ
nine on the mountains and going seeks the
πλανώμενον; 13 καὶ ἐὰν γένηται
wandering [one]? And if he happens
εὑρεῖν αὐτό, ἀμὴν λέγω ὑμῖν ὅτι
to find it, truly I say to you that
χαίρει ἐπ' αὐτῷ μᾶλλον ἢ ἐπὶ τοῖς
he rejoices over it more than over the
ἐνενήκοντα ἐννέα τοῖς μὴ πεπλανημένοις.
ninety-nine – not having wandered.
14 οὕτως οὐκ ἔστιν θέλημα ἔμπροσθεν
So it is not [the] will before
τοῦ πατρὸς ὑμῶν τοῦ ἐν οὐρανοῖς ἵνα
the Father of you – in heaven*s* that
ἀπόληται ἓν τῶν μικρῶν τούτων.
should perish one – little [ones] of these.
15 Ἐὰν δὲ ἁμαρτήσῃ ὁ ἀδελφός σου,
Now if sins the brother of thee,
ὕπαγε ἔλεγξον αὐτὸν μεταξὺ σοῦ καὶ
go reprove him between thee and
αὐτοῦ μόνου. ἐάν σου ἀκούσῃ, ἐκέρδησας
him alone. If thee he hears, thou gainedst
τὸν ἀδελφόν σου· 16 ἐὰν δὲ μὴ
the brother of thee; but if not
ἀκούσῃ, παράλαβε μετὰ σοῦ ἔτι ἕνα ἢ
he hears, take with thee more one or
δύο, ἵνα ἐπὶ στόματος δύο μαρτύρων
two, that on(by) [the] mouth of two witnesses
ἢ τριῶν σταθῇ πᾶν ῥῆμα· 17 ἐὰν δὲ
or three may be established every word; but if
παρακούσῃ αὐτῶν, εἰπὸν τῇ ἐκκλησίᾳ
he refuses to hear them, tell *to* the church;

‡ Ver. 11 omitted by Nestle; *cf.* NIV note.

It is better for you to enter life maimed or crippled than to have two hands or two feet and be thrown into eternal fire. 9 And if your eye causes you to sin, gouge it out and throw it away. It is better for you to enter life with one eye than to have two eyes and be thrown into the fire of hell.

The Parable of the Lost Sheep

10 "See that you do not look down on one of these little ones. For I tell you that their angels in heaven always see the face of my Father in heaven.[r]

12 "What do you think? If a man owns a hundred sheep, and one of them wanders away, will he not leave the ninety-nine on the hills and go to look for the one that wandered off? 13 And if he finds it, I tell you the truth, he is happier about that one sheep than about the ninety-nine that did not wander off. 14 In the same way your Father in heaven is not willing that any of these little ones should be lost.

A Brother Who Sins Against You

15 "If your brother sins against you,[s] go and show him his fault, just between the two of you. If he listens to you, you have won your brother over. 16 But if he will not listen, take one or two others along, so that 'every matter may be established by the testimony of two or three witnesses.'[t] 17 If he refuses to listen to them, tell it to the

[e] Gk *Gehenna*
[f] Other ancient authorities add verse 11, *For the Son of Man came to save the lost*
[g] Other ancient authorities read *my*
[h] Gk *If your brother*
[i] Other ancient authorities lack *against you*
[j] Gk *the brother*

[r] *10* Some manuscripts *heaven. 11The Son of Man came to save what was lost.*
[s] *15* Some manuscripts do not have *against you.*
[t] *16* Deut. 19:15

to listen even to the church,
let such a one be to you as
a Gentile and a tax collector. [18]Truly I tell you,
whatever you bind on earth
will be bound in heaven,
and whatever you loose on
earth will be loosed in
heaven. [19]Again, truly I tell
you, if two of you agree on
earth about anything you
ask, it will be done for you
by my Father in heaven.
[20]For where two or three
are gathered in my name, I
am there among them."

Forgiveness

21 Then Peter came and
said to him, "Lord, if another member of the
church[k] sins against me,
how often should I forgive?
As many as seven times?"
[22]Jesus said to him, "Not
seven times, but, I tell you,
seventy-seven[l] times.

The Parable of the Unforgiving Servant

23 "For this reason the
kingdom of heaven may be
compared to a king who
wished to settle accounts
with his slaves. [24]When he
began the reckoning, one
who owed him ten thou-
sand talents[m] was brought
to him; [25]and, as he could
not pay, his lord ordered
him to be sold, together
with his wife and children
and all his possessions, and
payment to be made. [26]So
the slave fell on his knees
before him, saying, 'Have
patience with me, and I will
pay you everything.' [27]And
out of pity for him, the lord
of that slave released him
and forgave him the debt.

ἐὰν δὲ καὶ τῆς ἐκκλησίας παρακούσῃ,
and if even the church he refuses to hear,
ἔστω σοι ὥσπερ ὁ ἐθνικὸς καὶ
let him be to thee as the gentile and
ὁ τελώνης. **18** Ἀμὴν λέγω ὑμῖν,
the tax-collector. Truly I say to you,
ὅσα ἐὰν δήσητε ἐπὶ τῆς γῆς ἔσται
whatever things ye bind on the earth shall be
δεδεμένα ἐν οὐρανῷ, καὶ ὅσα ἐὰν
having been bound in heaven, and whatever things
λύσητε ἐπὶ τῆς γῆς ἔσται λελυμένα
ye loose on the earth shall be *having been* loosed
ἐν οὐρανῷ. **19** Πάλιν [ἀμὴν] λέγω
in heaven. Again truly I say
ὑμῖν ὅτι ἐὰν δύο συμφωνήσωσιν ἐξ
to you that if two agree of
ὑμῶν ἐπὶ τῆς γῆς περὶ παντὸς πράγ-
you on the earth concerning every
ματος οὗ ἐὰν αἰτήσωνται, γενήσεται
thing whatever they ask, it shall be
αὐτοῖς παρὰ τοῦ πατρός μου τοῦ ἐν
to them from the Father of me – in
οὐρανοῖς. **20** οὗ γάρ εἰσιν δύο ἢ τρεῖς
heavens. For where are two or three
συνηγμένοι εἰς τὸ ἐμὸν ὄνομα, ἐκεῖ εἰμι
having been assembled in – my name, there I am
ἐν μέσῳ αὐτῶν.
in [the] midst of them.
21 Τότε προσελθὼν ὁ Πέτρος εἶπεν
Then approaching – Peter said
αὐτῷ· κύριε, ποσάκις ἁμαρτήσει εἰς
to him: Lord, how often will sin against
ἐμὲ ὁ ἀδελφός μου καὶ ἀφήσω αὐτῷ;
me the brother of me and I will forgive him?
ἕως ἑπτάκις; **22** λέγει αὐτῷ ὁ Ἰησοῦς·
until seven times? says to him – Jesus:
οὐ λέγω σοι ἕως ἑπτάκις, ἀλλὰ
I tell not *to* thee until seven times, but
ἕως ἑβδομηκοντάκις ἑπτά. **23** Διὰ τοῦτο
until seventy times seven. Therefore
ὡμοιώθη ἡ βασιλεία τῶν οὐρανῶν
was(is) likened the kingdom of the heavens
ἀνθρώπῳ βασιλεῖ, ὃς ἠθέλησεν συνᾶραι
to *a man* a king, who wished to take
λόγον μετὰ τῶν δούλων αὐτοῦ. **24** ἀρξα-
account with the slaves of him. And
μένου δὲ αὐτοῦ συναίρειν, προσήχθη
beginning him* to take, [5]was brought forward
=as he began
εἷς αὐτῷ ὀφειλέτης μυρίων ταλάντων.
[1]one [6]to him [2]debtor [3]of ten thousand [4]talents.
25 μὴ ἔχοντος δὲ αὐτοῦ ἀποδοῦναι, ἐκέλευσεν
And not having him* to repay, commanded
=as he had not
αὐτὸν ὁ κύριος πραθῆναι καὶ τὴν
him the lord to be sold and the(his)
γυναῖκα καὶ τὰ τέκνα καὶ πάντα ὅσα
wife and – children and all things whatever
ἔχει, καὶ ἀποδοθῆναι. **26** πεσὼν οὖν ὁ
he has, and to be repaid. Falling therefore the
δοῦλος προσεκύνει αὐτῷ λέγων· μακρο-
slave did obeisance to him saying: Defer
θύμησον ἐπ' ἐμοί, καὶ πάντα ἀποδώσω
anger over me, and all things I will repay
σοι. **27** σπλαγχνισθεὶς δὲ ὁ κύριος τοῦ
thee. And filled with tenderness the lord –
δούλου ἐκείνου ἀπέλυσεν αὐτόν, καὶ τὸ
slave of that released him, and the

church; and if he refuses to
listen even to the church,
treat him as you would a
pagan or a tax collector.
[18]"I tell you the truth,
whatever you bind on earth
will be[u] bound in heaven,
and whatever you loose on
earth will be[u] loosed in
heaven.
[19]"Again, I tell you that if
two of you on earth agree
about anything you ask for,
it will be done for you by
my Father in heaven. [20]For
where two or three come
together in my name, there
am I with them."

The Parable of the Unmerciful Servant

[21]Then Peter came to
Jesus and asked, "Lord,
how many times shall I forgive my brother when he
sins against me? Up to sev-
en times?"
[22]Jesus answered, "I tell
you, not seven times, but
seventy-seven times.[v]
[23]"Therefore, the king-
dom of heaven is like a king
who wanted to settle ac-
counts with his servants.
[24]As he began the settle-
ment, a man who owed him
ten thousand talents[w] was
brought to him. [25]Since he
was not able to pay, the
master ordered that he and
his wife and his children
and all that he had be sold
to repay the debt.
[26]"The servant fell on his
knees before him. 'Be pa-
tient with me,' he begged,
'and I will pay back everything.' [27]The servant's
master took pity on him,

[k] Gk *if my brother*
[l] Or *seventy times seven*
[m] A talent was worth more than fifteen years' wages of a laborer

[u] 18 Or *have been*
[v] 22 Or *seventy times seven*
[w] 24 That is, millions of dollars

28 But that same slave, as
he went out, came upon
one of his fellow slaves
who owed him a hundred
denarii;[n] and seizing him
by the throat, he said, 'Pay
what you owe.' 29 Then his
fellow slave fell down and
pleaded with him, 'Have
patience with me, and I will
pay you.' 30 But he refused;
then he went and threw him
into prison until he would
pay the debt. 31 When his
fellow slaves saw what had
happened, they were greatly distressed, and they
went and reported to their
lord all that had taken
place. 32 Then his lord summoned him and said to him,
'You wicked slave! I for-
gave you all that debt because you pleaded with me.
33 Should you not have had
mercy on your fellow
slave, as I had mercy on
you?' 34 And in anger his
lord handed him over to be
tortured until he would pay
his entire debt. 35 So my
heavenly Father will also
do to every one of you, if
you do not forgive your
brother or sister[o] from
your heart."

δάνειον ἀφῆκεν αὐτῷ. 28 ἐξελθὼν δὲ
loan forgave him. But going out
ὁ δοῦλος ἐκεῖνος εὗρεν ἕνα τῶν
– slave that found one of the
συνδούλων αὐτοῦ, ὃς ὤφειλεν αὐτὸν ἑκατὸν
fellow-slaves of him, who owed him a hundred
δηνάρια, καὶ κρατήσας αὐτὸν ἔπνιγεν
denarii, and seizing him throttled
λέγων· ἀπόδος εἴ τι ὀφείλεις.
saying: Repay if something thou owest.
29 πεσὼν οὖν ὁ σύνδουλος αὐτοῦ παρε-
Falling therefore the fellow-slave of him be-
κάλει αὐτὸν λέγων· μακροθύμησον ἐπ'
sought him saying: Defer anger over
ἐμοί, καὶ ἀποδώσω σοι. 30 ὁ δὲ οὐκ
me, and I will repay thee. But he not
ἤθελεν, ἀλλὰ ἀπελθὼν ἔβαλεν αὐτὸν εἰς
wished, but going away threw him into
φυλακὴν ἕως ἀποδῷ τὸ ὀφειλόμενον.
prison until he should repay the thing owing.
31 ἰδόντες οὖν οἱ σύνδουλοι αὐτοῦ τὰ
Seeing therefore the fellow-slaves of him the things
γενόμενα ἐλυπήθησαν σφόδρα, καὶ
having taken place they were grieved exceedingly, and
ἐλθόντες διεσάφησαν τῷ κυρίῳ ἑαυτῶν
coming explained to the lord of them*selves*
πάντα τὰ γενόμενα. 32 τότε προσ-
all the things having taken place. Then [1]call-
καλεσάμενος αὐτὸν ὁ κύριος αὐτοῦ λέγει
ing [2]forward [3]him the lord of him says
αὐτῷ· δοῦλε πονηρέ, πᾶσαν τὴν ὀφειλὴν
to him: [2]Slave [1]wicked, all – debt
ἐκείνην ἀφῆκά σοι, ἐπεὶ παρεκάλεσάς με·
that I forgave thee, since thou besoughtest me;
33 οὐκ ἔδει καὶ σὲ ἐλεῆσαι τὸν
did it not behove also thee to pity the
σύνδουλόν σου, ὡς κἀγὼ σὲ ἠλέησα;
fellow-slave of thee, as I also thee pitied?
34 καὶ ὀργισθεὶς ὁ κύριος αὐτοῦ
And being angry the lord of him
παρέδωκεν αὐτὸν τοῖς βασανισταῖς ἕως οὗ
delivered him to the tormentors until
ἀποδῷ πᾶν τὸ ὀφειλόμενον αὐτῷ.
he should repay all the thing owing to him.
35 Οὕτως καὶ ὁ πατήρ μου ὁ οὐράνιος
Thus also the Father of me – heavenly
ποιήσει ὑμῖν, ἐὰν μὴ ἀφῆτε ἕκαστος
will do to you, unless ye forgive each one
τῷ ἀδελφῷ αὐτοῦ ἀπὸ τῶν καρδιῶν
the brother of him from the hearts
ὑμῶν.
of you.

canceled the debt and let
him go.
28 "But when that servant
went out, he found one of
his fellow servants who
owed him a hundred denar-
ii.[x] He grabbed him and began to choke him. 'Pay
back what you owe me!' he
demanded.
29 "His fellow servant fell
to his knees and begged
him, 'Be patient with me,
and I will pay you back.'
30 "But he refused. In-
stead, he went off and had
the man thrown into prison
until he could pay the debt.
31 When the other servants
saw what had happened,
they were greatly dis-
tressed and went and told
their master everything
that had happened.
32 "Then the master called
the servant in. 'You wicked
servant,' he said, 'I canceled all that debt of yours
because you begged me to.
33 Shouldn't you have had
mercy on your fellow ser-
vant just as I had on you?'
34 In anger his master
turned him over to the jail-
ers to be tortured, until he
should pay back all he
owed.
35 "This is how my heav-
enly Father will treat each
of you unless you forgive
your brother from your
heart."

Chapter 19

Teaching about Divorce

WHEN Jesus had fin-
ished saying these
things, he left Galilee and
went to the region of Judea
beyond the Jordan. 2 Large
crowds followed him, and
he cured them there.

19 Καὶ ἐγένετο ὅτε ἐτέλεσεν ὁ
And it came to pass when ended –
Ἰησοῦς τοὺς λόγους τούτους, μετῆρεν
Jesus – words these, he removed
ἀπὸ τῆς Γαλιλαίας καὶ ἦλθεν εἰς τὰ
from – Galilee and came into the
ὅρια τῆς Ἰουδαίας πέραν τοῦ Ἰορδάνου.
borders – of Judæa across the Jordan.
2 καὶ ἠκολούθησαν αὐτῷ ὄχλοι πολλοί,
And followed him crowds many,
καὶ ἐθεράπευσεν αὐτοὺς ἐκεῖ.
and he healed them there.

Chapter 19

Divorce

WHEN Jesus had fin-
ished saying these
things, he left Galilee and
went into the region of Judea to the other side of the
Jordan. 2 Large crowds followed him, and he healed
them there.

[n] The denarius was the usual day's wage for a laborer
[o] Gk *brother*

[x] *28* That is, a few dollars

3 Some Pharisees came to him, and to test him they asked, "Is it lawful for a man to divorce his wife for any cause?" 4 He answered, "Have you not read that the one who made them at the beginning 'made them male and female,' 5 and said, 'For this reason a man shall leave his father and mother and be joined to his wife, and the two shall become one flesh'? 6 So they are no longer two, but one flesh. Therefore what God has joined together, let no one separate." 7 They said to him, "Why then did Moses command us to give a certificate of dismissal and to divorce her?" 8 He said to them, "It was because you were so hard-hearted that Moses allowed you to divorce your wives, but from the beginning it was not so. 9 And I say to you, whoever divorces his wife, except for unchastity, and marries another commits adultery."[p]

10 His disciples said to him, "If such is the case of a man with his wife, it is better not to marry." 11 But he said to them, "Not everyone can accept this teaching, but only those to whom it is given. 12 For there are eunuchs who have been so from birth, and there are eunuchs who have been made eunuchs by others, and there are eunuchs who have made themselves eunuchs for the sake of the kingdom of heaven. Let anyone accept this who can."

[p] Other ancient authorities read *except on the ground of unchastity, causes her to commit adultery*; others add at the end of the verse *and he who marries a divorced woman commits adultery*

3 Καὶ προσῆλθον αὐτῷ Φαρισαῖοι
And approached *to* him Pharisees

πειράζοντες αὐτὸν καὶ λέγοντες· εἰ ἔξεστιν
tempting him and saying: If it is lawful

ἀπολῦσαι τὴν γυναῖκα αὐτοῦ κατὰ πᾶσαν
to dismiss the wife of him for every

αἰτίαν; **4** ὁ δὲ ἀποκριθεὶς εἶπεν· οὐκ
cause? And he answering said: not

ἀνέγνωτε ὅτι ὁ κτίσας ἀπ'
Did ye read that the [one] creating from

ἀρχῆς ἄρσεν καὶ θῆλυ ἐποίησεν αὐτούς;
[the] beginning male and female made them?

5 καὶ εἶπεν· ἕνεκα τούτου καταλείψει
And he said: For the sake of this shall leave

ἄνθρωπος τὸν πατέρα καὶ τὴν μητέρα
a man the(his) father and the(his) mother

καὶ κολληθήσεται τῇ γυναικὶ αὐτοῦ,
and shall cleave to the wife of him,

καὶ ἔσονται οἱ δύο εἰς σάρκα μίαν·
and ³shall be ¹the ²two ⁴in ⁶flesh ⁵one;

6 ὥστε οὐκέτι εἰσὶν δύο ἀλλὰ σὰρξ μία.
so as no longer are they two but flesh one.

ὃ οὖν ὁ θεὸς συνέζευξεν, ἄνθρωπος
What therefore – God yoked together, a man

μὴ χωριζέτω. **7** λέγουσιν αὐτῷ· τί οὖν
let not separate. They say to him: Why then

Μωϋσῆς ἐνετείλατο δοῦναι βιβλίον ἀπο-
²Moses ¹did ³enjoin to give a document of

στασίου καὶ ἀπολῦσαι; **8** λέγει αὐτοῖς·
divorce and to dismiss? He says to them:

ὅτι Μωϋσῆς πρὸς τὴν σκληροκαρδίαν
– Moses in view of the obduracy

ὑμῶν ἐπέτρεψεν ὑμῖν ἀπολῦσαι τὰς
of you allowed you to dismiss the

γυναῖκας ὑμῶν· ἀπ' ἀρχῆς δὲ οὐ
wives of you; but from [the] beginning not

γέγονεν οὕτως. **9** λέγω δὲ ὑμῖν ὅτι
it has been so. But I say to you that

ὃς ἂν ἀπολύσῃ τὴν γυναῖκα αὐτοῦ
whoever dismisses the wife of him

μὴ ἐπὶ πορνείᾳ καὶ γαμήσῃ ἄλλην,
not of(for) fornication and marries another,

μοιχᾶται. **10** λέγουσιν αὐτῷ οἱ μαθηταί·
commits adultery. Say to him the disciples:

εἰ οὕτως ἐστὶν ἡ αἰτία τοῦ ἀνθρώπου
If so is the cause of the man

μετὰ τῆς γυναικός, οὐ συμφέρει γαμῆσαι.
with the wife, it is not expedient to marry.

11 ὁ δὲ εἶπεν αὐτοῖς· οὐ πάντες χωροῦσιν
And he said to them: Not all men grasp

τὸν λόγον τοῦτον, ἀλλ' οἷς δέδοται.
– saying this, but [those] to whom it has been given.

12 εἰσὶν γὰρ εὐνοῦχοι οἵτινες ἐκ κοιλίας
For there are eunuchs who from [the] womb

μητρὸς ἐγεννήθησαν οὕτως, καὶ εἰσὶν
of a mother were born so, and there are

εὐνοῦχοι οἵτινες εὐνουχίσθησαν ὑπὸ τῶν
eunuchs who were made eunuchs by –

ἀνθρώπων, καὶ εἰσὶν εὐνοῦχοι οἵτινες
men. and there are eunuchs who

εὐνούχισαν ἑαυτοὺς διὰ τὴν
made eunuchs themselves on account of the

βασιλείαν τῶν οὐρανῶν. ὁ δυνάμενος
kingdom of the heavens. The [one] *being* able

χωρεῖν χωρείτω.
to grasp [it] let him grasp.

3 Some Pharisees came to him to test him. They asked, "Is it lawful for a man to divorce his wife for any and every reason?"

4 "Haven't you read," he replied, "that at the beginning the Creator 'made them male and female,'[y] 5 and said, 'For this reason a man will leave his father and mother and be united to his wife, and the two will become one flesh'[z]? 6 So they are no longer two, but one. Therefore what God has joined together, let man not separate."

7 "Why then," they asked, "did Moses command that a man give his wife a certificate of divorce and send her away?"

8 Jesus replied, "Moses permitted you to divorce your wives because your hearts were hard. But it was not this way from the beginning. 9 I tell you that anyone who divorces his wife, except for marital unfaithfulness, and marries another woman commits adultery."

10 The disciples said to him, "If this is the situation between a husband and wife, it is better not to marry."

11 Jesus replied, "Not everyone can accept this word, but only those to whom it has been given. 12 For some are eunuchs because they were born that way; others were made that way by men; and others have renounced marriage[a] because of the kingdom of heaven. The one who can accept this should accept it."

[y] 4 Gen. 1:27
[z] 5 Gen. 2:24
[a] 12 Or *have made themselves eunuchs*

Jesus Blesses Little Children

13 Then little children
were being brought to him
in order that he might lay
his hands on them and
pray. The disciples spoke
sternly to those who
brought them; 14 but Jesus
said, "Let the little children
come to me, and do not
stop them; for it is to such
as these that the kingdom
of heaven belongs." 15 And
he laid his hands on them
and went on his way.

The Rich Young Man

16 Then someone came
to him and said, "Teacher,
what good deed must I do
to have eternal life?" 17 And
he said to him, "Why do
you ask me about what is
good? There is only one
who is good. If you wish to
enter into life, keep the
commandments." 18 He
said to him, "Which ones?"
And Jesus said, "You shall
not murder; You shall not
commit adultery; You shall
not steal; You shall not
bear false witness; 19 Honor
your father and mother;
also, You shall love your
neighbor as yourself."
20 The young man said to
him, "I have kept all
these;[q] what do I still
lack?" 21 Jesus said to him,
"If you wish to be perfect,
go, sell your possessions,
and give the money[r] to the
poor, and you will have
treasure in heaven; then
come, follow me." 22 When
the young man heard this
word, he went away griev-
ing, for he had many pos-
sessions.
23 Then Jesus said to
his disciples, "Truly I tell
you, it will be hard for a
rich person to enter the
kingdom of heaven.
24 Again I tell you, it is easier for a camel to go through
the eye of a needle than for

[q] Other ancient authorities add *from my youth*
[r] Gk lacks *the money*

13 Τότε προσηνέχθησαν αὐτῷ παιδία,
Then were brought to him children,

ἵνα τὰς χεῖρας ἐπιθῇ αὐτοῖς καὶ
that the(his) hands he should put on them and

προσεύξηται· οἱ δὲ μαθηταὶ ἐπετίμησαν
pray; but the disciples rebuked

αὐτοῖς. 14 ὁ δὲ Ἰησοῦς εἶπεν· ἄφετε
them. – But Jesus said: Permit

τὰ παιδία καὶ μὴ κωλύετε αὐτὰ ἐλθεῖν
the children and do not prevent them to come

πρός με· τῶν γὰρ τοιούτων ἐστὶν ἡ
unto me; – for of such is the

βασιλεία τῶν οὐρανῶν. 15 καὶ ἐπιθεὶς
kingdom of the heavens. And putting on

τὰς χεῖρας αὐτοῖς ἐπορεύθη ἐκεῖθεν.
the(his) hands *on* them he went thence.

16 Καὶ ἰδοὺ εἷς προσελθὼν αὐτῷ εἶπεν·
And behold one approaching *to* him said:

διδάσκαλε, τί ἀγαθὸν ποιήσω ἵνα
Teacher, what good thing may I do that

σχῶ ζωὴν αἰώνιον; ὁ δὲ εἶπεν αὐτῷ·
I may have life eternal? And he said to him:

17 τί με ἐρωτᾷς περὶ τοῦ ἀγαθοῦ;
Why me questionest thou concerning the good?

εἷς ἐστιν ὁ ἀγαθός· εἰ δὲ θέλεις εἰς
one is the good; but if thou wishest into

τὴν ζωὴν εἰσελθεῖν, τήρει τὰς ἐντολάς.
– life to enter, keep the commandments.

18 λέγει αὐτῷ· ποίας; ὁ δὲ Ἰησοῦς
He says to him: Which? – And Jesus

ἔφη· τὸ οὐ φονεύσεις, οὐ μοιχεύσεις,
said: – Thou shalt not kill, Thou shalt not commit adultery,

οὐ κλέψεις, οὐ ψευδομαρτυρήσεις,
Thou shalt not steal, Thou shalt not bear false witness,

19 τίμα τὸν πατέρα καὶ τὴν μητέρα,
Honour the(thy) father and the(thy) mother,

καὶ ἀγαπήσεις τὸν πλησίον σου ὡς
and Thou shalt love the neighbour of thee as

σεαυτόν. 20 λέγει αὐτῷ ὁ νεανίσκος·
thyself. Says to him the young man:

ταῦτα πάντα ἐφύλαξα· τί ἔτι ὑστερῶ;
[2]These things [1]all I kept; what yet do I lack?

21 ἔφη αὐτῷ ὁ Ἰησοῦς· εἰ θέλεις τέλειος
Said to him – Jesus: If thou wishest perfect

εἶναι, ὕπαγε πώλησόν σου τὰ ὑπάρχοντα
to be, go sell of thee the belongings

καὶ δὸς πτωχοῖς, καὶ ἕξεις
and give to [the] poor, and thou shalt have

θησαυρὸν ἐν οὐρανοῖς, καὶ δεῦρο ἀκολούθει
treasure in heavens, and come follow

μοι. 22 ἀκούσας δὲ ὁ νεανίσκος τὸν
me. But hearing the young man –

λόγον [τοῦτον] ἀπῆλθεν λυπούμενος·
word this went away grieving;

ἦν γὰρ ἔχων κτήματα πολλά. 23 Ὁ
for he was having possessions many. –

δὲ Ἰησοῦς εἶπεν τοῖς μαθηταῖς αὐτοῦ·
So Jesus said to the disciples of him:

ἀμὴν λέγω ὑμῖν ὅτι πλούσιος δυσκόλως
Truly I tell you that a rich man hardly

εἰσελεύσεται εἰς τὴν βασιλείαν τῶν
will enter into the kingdom of the

οὐρανῶν. 24 πάλιν δὲ λέγω ὑμῖν,
heavens. And again I tell you,

εὐκοπώτερόν ἐστιν κάμηλον διὰ τρήματος
easier it is a camel through [the] eye

The Little Children and Jesus

13 Then little children
were brought to Jesus for
him to place his hands on
them and pray for them.
But the disciples rebuked
those who brought them.
14 Jesus said, "Let the little children come to me,
and do not hinder them, for
the kingdom of heaven be-
longs to such as these."
15 When he had placed his
hands on them, he went on
from there.

The Rich Young Man

16 Now a man came up to
Jesus and asked, "Teach-
er, what good thing must I
do to get eternal life?"
17 "Why do you ask me
about what is good?" Jesus
replied. "There is only One
who is good. If you want to
enter life, obey the com-
mandments."
18 "Which ones?" the
man inquired.
Jesus replied, " 'Do not
murder, do not commit
adultery, do not steal, do
not give false testimony,
19 honor your father and
mother,'[b] and 'love your
neighbor as yourself.'[c]"
20 "All these I have
kept," the young man said.
"What do I still lack?"
21 Jesus answered, "If
you want to be perfect, go,
sell your possessions and
give to the poor, and you
will have treasure in heav-
en. Then come, follow
me."
22 When the young man
heard this, he went away
sad, because he had great
wealth.
23 Then Jesus said to his
disciples, "I tell you the
truth, it is hard for a rich
man to enter the kingdom
of heaven. 24 Again I tell
you, it is easier for a camel
to go through the eye of a

[b] *19* Exodus 20:12-16; Deut. 5:16-20
[c] *19* Lev. 19:18

someone who is rich to enter the kingdom of God."
25When the disciples heard
this, they were greatly astounded and said, "Then
who can be saved?" 26But
Jesus looked at them and
said, "For mortals it is impossible, but for God all
things are possible."
27 Then Peter said in re-
ply, "Look, we have left
everything and followed
you. What then will we
have?" 28Jesus said to
them, "Truly I tell you, at
the renewal of all things,
when the Son of Man is
seated on the throne of his
glory, you who have fol-
lowed me will also sit on
twelve thrones, judging the
twelve tribes of Israel.
29And everyone who has
left houses or brothers or
sisters or father or mother
or children or fields, for my
name's sake, will receive a
hundredfold,[s] and will inherit eternal life. 30But
many who are first will be
last, and the last will be
first.

ῥαφίδος εἰσελθεῖν ἢ πλούσιον εἰς τὴν
of a needle to enter than a rich man into the
βασιλείαν τοῦ θεοῦ. 25 ἀκούσαντες δὲ
kingdom – of God. And hearing
οἱ μαθηταὶ ἐξεπλήσσοντο σφόδρα
the disciples were astounded exceedingly
λέγοντες· τίς ἄρα δύναται σωθῆναι;
saying: Who then can *to* be saved?
26 ἐμβλέψας δὲ ὁ Ἰησοῦς εἶπεν
And looking upon – Jesus said
αὐτοῖς· παρὰ ἀνθρώποις τοῦτο ἀδύνατόν
to them: With men this impossible
ἐστιν, παρὰ δὲ θεῷ πάντα δυνατά.
is, but with God all things [are] possible.
27 Τότε ἀποκριθεὶς ὁ Πέτρος εἶπεν αὐτῷ·
Then answering – Peter said to him:
ἰδοὺ ἡμεῖς ἀφήκαμεν πάντα καὶ
Behold we left all things and
ἠκολουθήσαμέν σοι· τί ἄρα ἔσται
followed thee; what then shall be =shall we have?
ἡμῖν; 28 ὁ δὲ Ἰησοῦς εἶπεν αὐτοῖς·
to us[c]? – And Jesus said to them:
ἀμὴν λέγω ὑμῖν ὅτι ὑμεῖς οἱ ἀκολουθή-
Truly I tell you that ye the [ones] having
σαντές μοι, ἐν τῇ παλιγγενεσίᾳ, ὅταν
followed me, in the regeneration, when
καθίσῃ ὁ υἱὸς τοῦ ἀνθρώπου ἐπὶ θρόνου
sits the Son – of man on [the] throne
δόξης αὐτοῦ, καθήσεσθε καὶ αὐτοὶ ἐπὶ
of glory of him, ye will sit also [your]selves on
δώδεκα θρόνους κρίνοντες τὰς δώδεκα
twelve thrones judging the twelve
φυλὰς τοῦ Ἰσραήλ. 29 καὶ πᾶς ὅστις
tribes – of Israel. And everyone who
ἀφῆκεν οἰκίας ἢ ἀδελφοὺς ἢ ἀδελφὰς ἢ
left houses or brothers or sisters or
πατέρα ἢ μητέρα ἢ τέκνα ἢ ἀγροὺς
father or mother or children or fields
ἕνεκεν τοῦ ἐμοῦ ὀνόματος, πολλαπλα-
for the sake of – my name, mani-
σίονα λήμψεται καὶ ζωὴν αἰώνιον
fold will receive and life eternal
κληρονομήσει. 30 Πολλοὶ δὲ ἔσονται πρῶτοι
will inherit. But many [3]will be [1]first
ἔσχατοι καὶ ἔσχατοι πρῶτοι.
[2]last and last first.

needle than for a rich man
to enter the kingdom of
God."
25When the disciples
heard this, they were greatly astonished and asked,
"Who then can be saved?"
26Jesus looked at them
and said, "With man this is
impossible, but with God
all things are possible."
27Peter answered him,
"We have left everything
to follow you! What then
will there be for us?"
28Jesus said to them, "I
tell you the truth, at the renewal of all things, when
the Son of Man sits on his
glorious throne, you who
have followed me will also
sit on twelve thrones, judging the twelve tribes of Israel. 29And everyone who
has left houses or brothers
or sisters or father or mother[d] or children or fields for
my sake will receive a hundred times as much and will
inherit eternal life. 30But
many who are first will be
last, and many who are last
will be first.

Chapter 20

The Laborers in the Vineyard

"FOR the kingdom of
heaven is like a
landowner who went out
early in the morning to hire
laborers for his vineyard.
2After agreeing with the laborers for the usual daily
wage,[t] he sent them into
his vineyard. 3When he
went out about nine
o'clock, he saw others
standing idle in the marketplace; 4and he said to them,

20 Ὁμοία γάρ ἐστιν ἡ βασιλεία τῶν
For like is the kingdom of the
οὐρανῶν ἀνθρώπῳ οἰκοδεσπότῃ, ὅστις
heavens to *a man* a housemaster, who
ἐξῆλθεν ἅμα πρωῒ μισθώσασθαι
went out early in the morning to hire
ἐργάτας εἰς τὸν ἀμπελῶνα αὐτοῦ. 2 συμ-
workmen in the vineyard of him. And
φωνήσας δὲ μετὰ τῶν ἐργατῶν ἐκ δηναρίου
agreeing with the workmen out of(for) a denarius
τὴν ἡμέραν ἀπέστειλεν αὐτοὺς εἰς τὸν
the day he sent them into the
ἀμπελῶνα αὐτοῦ. 3 καὶ ἐξελθὼν περὶ
vineyard of him. And going out about
τρίτην ὥραν εἶδεν ἄλλους ἑστῶτας
[the] third hour he saw others standing
ἐν τῇ ἀγορᾷ ἀργούς, 4 καὶ ἐκείνοις
in the marketplace idle, and to those

Chapter 20

The Parable of the Workers in the Vineyard

"FOR the kingdom of
heaven is like a
landowner who went out
early in the morning to hire
men to work in his vine-
yard. 2He agreed to pay
them a denarius for the day
and sent them into his vineyard.
3"About the third hour he
went out and saw others
standing in the marketplace
doing nothing. 4He told
them, 'You also go and

[s] Other ancient authorities read *manifold*
[t] Gk *a denarius*

[d]29 Some manuscripts *mother or wife*

'You also go into the vineyard, and I will pay you
whatever is right.' So they
went. 5 When he went out
again about noon and about
three o'clock, he did the
same. 6 And about five
o'clock he went out and
found others standing
around; and he said to
them, 'Why are you stand-
ing here idle all day?'
7 They said to him, 'Be-
cause no one has hired us.'
He said to them, 'You also
go into the vineyard.'
8 When evening came, the
owner of the vineyard said
to his manager, 'Call the laborers and give them their
pay, beginning with the last
and then going to the first.'
9 When those hired about
five o'clock came, each of
them received the usual
daily wage.[u] 10 Now when
the first came, they thought
they would receive more;
but each of them also re-
ceived the usual daily
wage.[u] 11 And when they
received it, they grumbled
against the landowner,
12 saying, 'These last
worked only one hour, and
you have made them equal
to us who have borne the
burden of the day and the
scorching heat.' 13 But he
replied to one of them,
'Friend, I am doing you no
wrong; did you not agree
with me for the usual daily
wage?[u] 14 Take what be-
longs to you and go; I
choose to give to this last
the same as I give to you.
15 Am I not allowed to do
what I choose with what
belongs to me? Or are you
envious because I am gen-
erous?'[v] 16 So the last will

[u] Gk *a denarius*
[v] Gk *is your eye evil because I am good?*

εἶπεν· ὑπάγετε καὶ ὑμεῖς εἰς τὸν
said: Go also ye into the

ἀμπελῶνα, καὶ ὃ ἐὰν ᾖ δίκαιον δώσω
vineyard, and whatever may be just I will give

ὑμῖν. οἱ δὲ ἀπῆλθον. 5 πάλιν [δὲ]
you. And they went. And again

ἐξελθὼν περὶ ἕκτην καὶ ἐνάτην ὥραν
going out about [the] sixth and [the] ninth hour

ἐποίησεν ὡσαύτως. 6 περὶ δὲ τὴν
he did similarly. And about the

ἑνδεκάτην ἐξελθὼν εὗρεν ἄλλους ἑστῶτας,
eleventh going out he found others standing,

καὶ λέγει αὐτοῖς· τί ὧδε ἑστήκατε
and says to them: Why here stand ye

ὅλην τὴν ἡμέραν ἀργοί; 7 λέγουσιν αὐτῷ·
all the day idle? They say to him:

ὅτι οὐδεὶς ἡμᾶς ἐμισθώσατο. λέγει αὐτοῖς·
Because no one us hired. He says to them:

ὑπάγετε καὶ ὑμεῖς εἰς τὸν ἀμπελῶνα.
Go also ye into the vineyard.

8 ὀψίας δὲ γενομένης λέγει ὁ κύριος
And evening having come[a] says the lord
=when evening had come

τοῦ ἀμπελῶνος τῷ ἐπιτρόπῳ αὐτοῦ·
of the vineyard to the steward of him:

κάλεσον τοὺς ἐργάτας καὶ ἀπόδος τὸν
Call the workmen and pay the

μισθόν, ἀρξάμενος ἀπὸ τῶν ἐσχάτων
wage, beginning from the last ones

ἕως τῶν πρώτων. 9 ἐλθόντες δὲ οἱ
until the first. And coming the [ones]

περὶ τὴν ἑνδεκάτην ὥραν ἔλαβον ἀνὰ
about the eleventh hour received each

δηνάριον. 10 καὶ ἐλθόντες οἱ πρῶτοι
a denarius. And coming the first

ἐνόμισαν ὅτι πλεῖον λήμψονται· καὶ
supposed that more they will receive; and

ἔλαβον τὸ ἀνὰ δηνάριον καὶ αὐτοί.
they received the [2]each [1]denarius also [them]selves.

11 λαβόντες δὲ ἐγόγγυζον κατὰ τοῦ
And receiving they grumbled against the

οἰκοδεσπότου λέγοντες· 12 οὗτοι οἱ ἔσχατοι
housemaster saying: These – last

μίαν ὥραν ἐποίησαν, καὶ ἴσους αὐτοὺς
one hour wrought, and equal them

ἡμῖν ἐποίησας τοῖς βαστάσασι τὸ
to us thou madest the [ones] having borne the

βάρος τῆς ἡμέρας καὶ τὸν καύσωνα.
burden of the day and the heat.

13 ὁ δὲ ἀποκριθεὶς ἑνὶ αὐτῶν εἶπεν·
But he answering one of them said:

ἑταῖρε, οὐκ ἀδικῶ σε· οὐχὶ
Comrade, I do not injure thee; not

δηναρίου συνεφώνησάς μοι; 14 ἆρον
of(for) a denarius thou didst agree with me? take

τὸ σὸν καὶ ὕπαγε· θέλω δὲ
the thine and go; but I wish
=that which is thine

τούτῳ τῷ ἐσχάτῳ δοῦναι ὡς καὶ
to this – last man to give as also

σοί· 15 οὐκ ἔξεστίν μοι ὃ θέλω
to thee; is it not lawful to me what I wish

ποιῆσαι ἐν τοῖς ἐμοῖς; ἢ ὁ
to do among *the* my things? or the

ὀφθαλμός σου πονηρός ἐστιν ὅτι ἐγὼ
eye of thee evil is because I

work in my vineyard, and I
will pay you whatever is
right.' 5 So they went.
"He went out again about
the sixth hour and the ninth
hour and did the same
thing. 6 About the eleventh
hour he went out and found
still others standing
around. He asked them,
'Why have you been stand-
ing here all day long doing
nothing?'
7 " 'Because no one has
hired us,' they answered.
"He said to them, 'You
also go and work in my
vineyard.'
8 "When evening came,
the owner of the vineyard
said to his foreman, 'Call
the workers and pay them
their wages, beginning with
the last ones hired and going on to the first.'
9 "The workers who were
hired about the eleventh
hour came and each re-
ceived a denarius. 10 So
when those came who were
hired first, they expected to
receive more. But each one
of them also received a denarius. 11 When they re-
ceived it, they began to
grumble against the land-
owner. 12 'These men who
were hired last worked
only one hour,' they said,
'and you have made them
equal to us who have borne
the burden of the work and
the heat of the day.'
13 "But he answered one
of them, 'Friend, I am not
being unfair to you. Didn't
you agree to work for a denarius? 14 Take your pay
and go. I want to give the
man who was hired last the
same as I gave you. 15 Don't
I have the right to do what I
want with my own money?
Or are you envious because
I am generous?'

be first, and the first will be last."[w]

A Third Time Jesus Foretells His Death and Resurrection

17 While Jesus was going up to Jerusalem, he took the twelve disciples aside by themselves, and said to them on the way, 18 "See, we are going up to Jerusalem, and the Son of Man will be handed over to the chief priests and scribes, and they will condemn him to death; 19 then they will hand him over to the Gentiles to be mocked and flogged and crucified; and on the third day he will be raised."

The Request of the Mother of James and John

20 Then the mother of the sons of Zebedee came to him with her sons, and kneeling before him, she asked a favor of him. 21 And he said to her, "What do you want?" She said to him, "Declare that these two sons of mine will sit, one at your right hand and one at your left, in your kingdom." 22 But Jesus answered, "You do not know what you are asking. Are you able to drink the cup that I am about to drink?"[x] They said to him, "We are able." 23 He said to them, "You will indeed drink my cup, but to sit at my right hand and at my left, this is not mine to grant, but it is for those for whom it has been prepared by my Father."

24 When the ten heard it, they were angry with the two brothers. 25 But Jesus called them to him and said, "You know that the rulers of the Gentiles lord it over them, and their great

[w] Other ancient authorities add *for many are called but few are chosen*

[x] Other ancient authorities add *or to be baptized with the baptism that I am baptized with?*

ἀγαθός εἰμι; **16** Οὕτως ἔσονται οἱ ἔσχατοι
good am? Thus will be the last [ones]

πρῶτοι καὶ οἱ πρῶτοι ἔσχατοι.
first and the first last.

17 Μέλλων δὲ ἀναβαίνειν Ἰησοῦς εἰς
And being about to go up Jesus to

Ἱεροσόλυμα παρέλαβεν τοὺς δώδεκα κατ'
Jerusalem he took the twelve private-

ἰδίαν, καὶ ἐν τῇ ὁδῷ εἶπεν αὐτοῖς·
ly, and in the way said to them:

18 ἰδοὺ ἀναβαίνομεν εἰς Ἱεροσόλυμα, καὶ
Behold we are going up to Jerusalem, and

ὁ υἱὸς τοῦ ἀνθρώπου παραδοθήσεται τοῖς
the Son – of man will be delivered to the

ἀρχιερεῦσιν καὶ γραμματεῦσιν, καὶ κατα-
chief priests and scribes, and they will

κρινοῦσιν αὐτὸν εἰς θάνατον, **19** καὶ
condemn him to death, and

παραδώσουσιν αὐτὸν τοῖς ἔθνεσιν εἰς
they will deliver him to the nations *for*

τὸ ἐμπαῖξαι καὶ μαστιγῶσαι καὶ
– to mock and to scourge and

σταυρῶσαι, καὶ τῇ τρίτῃ ἡμέρᾳ ἐγερθή-
to crucify, and on the third day he will be

σεται.
raised.

20 Τότε προσῆλθεν αὐτῷ ἡ μήτηρ τῶν
Then approached *to* him the mother of the

υἱῶν Ζεβεδαίου μετὰ τῶν υἱῶν αὐτῆς
sons of Zebedee with the sons of her

προσκυνοῦσα καὶ αἰτοῦσά τι ἀπ' αὐτοῦ.
doing obeisance and asking something from him.

21 ὁ δὲ εἶπεν αὐτῇ· τί θέλεις; λέγει
And he said to her: What wishest thou? She says

αὐτῷ· εἰπὲ ἵνα καθίσωσιν οὗτοι οἱ
to him: Say that may sit these the

δύο υἱοί μου εἷς ἐκ δεξιῶν καὶ εἷς
two sons of me one on [the] right and one

ἐξ εὐωνύμων σου ἐν τῇ βασιλείᾳ
on [the] left of thee in the kingdom

σου. **22** ἀποκριθεὶς δὲ ὁ Ἰησοῦς
of thee. And answering – Jesus

εἶπεν· οὐκ οἴδατε τί αἰτεῖσθε.
said: Ye know not what ye ask.

δύνασθε πιεῖν τὸ ποτήριον ὃ ἐγὼ
Can ye *to* drink the cup which I

μέλλω πίνειν; λέγουσιν αὐτῷ· δυνάμεθα.
am about to drink? They say to him: We can.

23 λέγει αὐτοῖς· τὸ μὲν ποτήριόν μου
He says to them: Indeed the cup of me

πίεσθε, τὸ δὲ καθίσαι ἐκ δεξιῶν
ye shall drink, – but to sit on [the] right

μου καὶ ἐξ εὐωνύμων οὐκ ἔστιν
of me and on [the] left is not

ἐμὸν τοῦτο δοῦναι, ἀλλ' οἷς ἡτοί-
mine this to give, but to whom it has

μασται ὑπὸ τοῦ πατρός μου. **24** καὶ
been prepared by the Father of me. And

ἀκούσαντες οἱ δέκα ἠγανάκτησαν περὶ
hearing the ten were incensed about

τῶν δύο ἀδελφῶν. **25** ὁ δὲ Ἰησοῦς
the two brothers. – So Jesus

προσκαλεσάμενος αὐτοὺς εἶπεν· οἴδατε
calling forward them said: Ye know

ὅτι οἱ ἄρχοντες τῶν ἐθνῶν κατακυριεύουσιν
that the rulers of the nations lord it over

16 "So the last will be first, and the first will be last."

Jesus Again Predicts His Death

17 Now as Jesus was going up to Jerusalem, he took the twelve disciples aside and said to them, 18 "We are going up to Jerusalem, and the Son of Man will be betrayed to the chief priests and the teachers of the law. They will condemn him to death 19 and will turn him over to the Gentiles to be mocked and flogged and crucified. On the third day he will be raised to life!"

A Mother's Request

20 Then the mother of Zebedee's sons came to Jesus with her sons and, kneeling down, asked a favor of him.

21 "What is it you want?" he asked.

She said, "Grant that one of these two sons of mine may sit at your right and the other at your left in your kingdom."

22 "You don't know what you are asking," Jesus said to them. "Can you drink the cup I am going to drink?"

"We can," they answered.

23 Jesus said to them, "You will indeed drink from my cup, but to sit at my right or left is not for me to grant. These places belong to those for whom they have been prepared by my Father."

24 When the ten heard about this, they were indignant with the two brothers. 25 Jesus called them together and said, "You know that the rulers of the Gentiles lord it over them, and

ones are tyrants over them.
26It will not be so among
you; but whoever wishes to
be great among you must
be your servant, 27and
whoever wishes to be first
among you must be your
slave; 28just as the Son of
Man came not to be served
but to serve, and to give his
life a ransom for many."

Jesus Heals Two Blind Men

29 As they were leaving
Jericho, a large crowd followed him. 30There were
two blind men sitting by the
roadside. When they heard
that Jesus was passing by,
they shouted, "Lord,[y]
have mercy on us, Son of
David!" 31The crowd sternly ordered them to be quiet;
but they shouted even
more loudly, "Have mercy
on us, Lord, Son of Da-
vid!" 32Jesus stood still and
called them, saying, "What
do you want me to do for
you?" 33They said to him,
"Lord, let our eyes be
opened." 34Moved with
compassion, Jesus touched
their eyes. Immediately
they regained their sight
and followed him.

Chapter 21

Jesus' Triumphal Entry into Jerusalem

WHEN they had come
near Jerusalem and
had reached Bethphage, at
the Mount of Olives, Jesus
sent two disciples, 2saying
to them, "Go into the village ahead of you, and immediately you will find a
donkey tied, and a colt with
her; untie them and bring
them to me. 3If anyone
says anything to you, just

[y] Other ancient authorities lack *Lord*

αὐτῶν καὶ οἱ μεγάλοι κατεξουσιάζουσιν
them and the great ones have authority over

αὐτῶν. 26 οὐχ οὕτως ἐστὶν ἐν ὑμῖν·
them. Not thus is it among you;

ἀλλ' ὃς ἐὰν θέλῃ ἐν ὑμῖν μέγας γενέσθαι,
but whoever wishes among you great to become,

ἔσται ὑμῶν διάκονος, 27 καὶ ὃς ἂν
will be of you servant, and whoever

θέλῃ ἐν ὑμῖν εἶναι πρῶτος, ἔσται ὑμῶν
wishes among you to be first, he shall be of you

δοῦλος· 28 ὥσπερ ὁ υἱὸς τοῦ ἀνθρώπου
slave; as the Son – of man

οὐκ ἦλθεν διακονηθῆναι, ἀλλὰ διακο-
came not to be served, but to

νῆσαι καὶ δοῦναι τὴν ψυχὴν αὐτοῦ
serve and to give the life of him

λύτρον ἀντὶ πολλῶν.
a ransom instead of many.

29 Καὶ ἐκπορευομένων αὐτῶν ἀπὸ Ἰεριχὼ
And going out them* from Jericho
=as they were going out

ἠκολούθησεν αὐτῷ ὄχλος πολύς. 30 καὶ
followed him crowd a much. And

ἰδοὺ δύο τυφλοὶ καθήμενοι παρὰ τὴν
behold two blind men sitting beside the

ὁδόν, ἀκούσαντες ὅτι Ἰησοῦς παράγει,
way, hearing that Jesus is passing by,

ἔκραξαν λέγοντες· κύριε, ἐλέησον ἡμᾶς,
cried out saying: Lord, pity us,

υἱὸς Δαυίδ. 31 ὁ δὲ ὄχλος ἐπετίμησεν
son of David. But the crowd rebuked

αὐτοῖς ἵνα σιωπήσωσιν· οἱ δὲ μεῖζον
them that they should be silent; but they more

ἔκραξαν λέγοντες· κύριε, ἐλέησον ἡμᾶς,
cried out saying: Lord, pity us,

υἱὸς Δαυίδ. 32 καὶ στὰς ὁ Ἰησοῦς
son of David. And standing – Jesus

ἐφώνησεν αὐτοὺς καὶ εἶπεν· τί θέλετε
called them and said: What wish ye

ποιήσω ὑμῖν; 33 λέγουσιν αὐτῷ· κύριε,
I may do to you? They say to him: Lord,

ἵνα ἀνοιγῶσιν οἱ ὀφθαλμοὶ ἡμῶν.
that may be opened the eyes of us.

34 σπλαγχνισθεὶς δὲ ὁ Ἰησοῦς ἥψατο
And being filled with tenderness – Jesus touched

τῶν ὀμμάτων αὐτῶν, καὶ εὐθέως ἀνέβλεψαν
the eyes of them, and immediately they saw again

καὶ ἠκολούθησαν αὐτῷ.
and followed him.

21 Καὶ ὅτε ἤγγισαν εἰς Ἱεροσόλυμα
And when they drew near to Jerusalem

καὶ ἦλθον εἰς Βηθφαγὴ εἰς τὸ ὄρος τῶν
and came to Bethphage to the mount of the

ἐλαιῶν, τότε Ἰησοῦς ἀπέστειλεν δύο
olives, then Jesus sent two

μαθητὰς 2 λέγων αὐτοῖς· πορεύεσθε εἰς
disciples telling them: Go ye into

τὴν κώμην τὴν κατέναντι ὑμῶν, καὶ εὐθὺς
the village – opposite you, and at once

εὑρήσετε ὄνον δεδεμένην καὶ πῶλον μετ'
ye will find an ass *having been* tied and a colt with

αὐτῆς· λύσαντες ἀγάγετέ μοι. 3 καὶ ἐάν
her/it; loosening bring to me. And if

τις ὑμῖν εἴπῃ τι, ἐρεῖτε ὅτι ὁ
anyone to you says anything, ye shall say[,] – The

their high officials exercise
authority over them. 26Not
so with you. Instead, whoever wants to become great
among you must be your
servant, 27and whoever
wants to be first must be
your slave— 28just as the
Son of Man did not come to
be served, but to serve, and
to give his life as a ransom
for many."

Two Blind Men Receive Sight

29As Jesus and his disci-
ples were leaving Jericho, a
large crowd followed him.
30Two blind men were sit-
ting by the roadside, and
when they heard that Jesus
was going by, they shout-
ed, "Lord, Son of David,
have mercy on us!"
31The crowd rebuked
them and told them to be
quiet, but they shouted all
the louder, "Lord, Son of
David, have mercy on us!"
32Jesus stopped and
called them. "What do you
want me to do for you?" he
asked.
33"Lord," they an-
swered, "we want our
sight."
34Jesus had compassion
on them and touched their
eyes. Immediately they received their sight and followed him.

Chapter 21

The Triumphal Entry

AS they approached Jeru-
salem and came to
Bethphage on the Mount of
Olives, Jesus sent two disciples, 2saying to them,
"Go to the village ahead of
you, and at once you will
find a donkey tied there,
with her colt by her. Untie
them and bring them to me.
3If anyone says anything to
you, tell him that the Lord

say this, 'The Lord needs
them.' And he will send
them immediately.[z]"
4This took place to fulfill
what had been spoken
through the prophet, say-
ing,
5 "Tell the daughter of
Zion,
Look, your king is
coming to you,
humble, and
mounted on
a donkey,
and on a colt, the
foal of
a donkey."
6The disciples went and did
as Jesus had directed them;
7they brought the donkey
and the colt, and put their
cloaks on them, and he sat
on them. 8A very large
crowd[a] spread their cloaks
on the road, and others cut
branches from the trees
and spread them on the
road. 9The crowds that
went ahead of him and that
followed were shouting,
"Hosanna to the Son
of David!
Blessed is the one
who comes in
the name of the
Lord!
Hosanna in the
highest heaven!"
10When he entered Jerusa-
lem, the whole city was in
turmoil, asking, "Who is
this?" 11The crowds were
saying, "This is the prophet
Jesus from Nazareth in
Galilee."

Jesus Cleanses the Temple

12 Then Jesus entered
the temple[b] and drove out
all who were selling and
buying in the temple, and
he overturned the tables of
the money changers and
the seats of those who sold
doves. 13He said to them,
"It is written,
'My house shall be
called a house
of prayer';
but you are making
it a den
of robbers."
14 The blind and the
lame came to him in the

[z] Or *'The Lord needs them and will send them back immediately.'*

[a] Or *Most of the crowd*

[b] Other ancient authorities add *of God*

κύριος αὐτῶν χρείαν ἔχει· εὐθὺς δὲ
Lord of them need has; and immediately
ἀποστελεῖ αὐτούς. **4** Τοῦτο δὲ γέγονεν
he will send them. Now this has happened
ἵνα πληρωθῇ τὸ ῥηθὲν διὰ τοῦ
that might be fulfilled the thing spoken through the
προφήτου λέγοντος· **5** εἴπατε τῇ θυγατρὶ
prophet saying: Tell ye the daughter
Σιών· ἰδοὺ ὁ βασιλεύς σου ἔρχεταί σοι
of Zion: Behold[,] the king of thee comes to thee
πραῢς καὶ ἐπιβεβηκὼς ἐπὶ ὄνον καὶ ἐπὶ
meek and having mounted on an ass and on
πῶλον υἱὸν ὑποζυγίου. **6** πορευθέντες δὲ
a colt son(foal) of an ass. And going
οἱ μαθηταὶ καὶ ποιήσαντες καθὼς συνέταξεν
the disciples and doing as directed
αὐτοῖς ὁ Ἰησοῦς **7** ἤγαγον τὴν ὄνον καὶ
them – Jesus they brought the ass and
τὸν πῶλον, καὶ ἐπέθηκαν ἐπ᾽ αὐτῶν
the colt, and put *on* on them
τὰ ἱμάτια, καὶ ἐπεκάθισεν ἐπάνω αὐτῶν.
the(ir) garments, and he sat *on* on them.
8 ὁ δὲ πλεῖστος ὄχλος ἔστρωσαν ἑαυτῶν
And the very large crowd strewed of them*selves*
τὰ ἱμάτια ἐν τῇ ὁδῷ, ἄλλοι δὲ ἔκοπτον
the garments in the way, and others cut
κλάδους ἀπὸ τῶν δένδρων καὶ ἐστρών-
branches from the trees and strewed
νυον ἐν τῇ ὁδῷ. **9** οἱ δὲ ὄχλοι οἱ
in the way. And the crowds the [ones]
προάγοντες αὐτὸν καὶ οἱ ἀκολουθοῦντες
going before him and the [ones] following
ἔκραζον λέγοντες· ὡσαννὰ τῷ υἱῷ Δαυίδ·
cried out saying: Hosanna to the son of David;
εὐλογημένος ὁ ἐρχόμενος ἐν ὀνόματι
blessed the [one] coming in [the] name
κυρίου· ὡσαννὰ ἐν τοῖς ὑψίστοις. **10** καὶ
of [the] Lord; hosanna in the highest [places]. And
εἰσελθόντος αὐτοῦ εἰς Ἱεροσόλυμα ἐσείσθη
entering him[a] into Jerusalem was shaken
=as he entered
πᾶσα ἡ πόλις λέγουσα· τίς ἐστιν οὗτος;
all the city saying: Who is this?
11 οἱ δὲ ὄχλοι ἔλεγον· οὗτός ἐστιν ὁ
And the crowds said: This is the
προφήτης Ἰησοῦς ὁ ἀπὸ Ναζαρὲθ τῆς
prophet Jesus the [one] from Nazareth –
Γαλιλαίας.
of Galilee.
12 Καὶ εἰσῆλθεν Ἰησοῦς εἰς τὸ ἱερὸν
And entered Jesus into the temple
καὶ ἐξέβαλεν πάντας τοὺς πωλοῦντας καὶ
and cast out all the [ones] selling and
ἀγοράζοντας ἐν τῷ ἱερῷ, καὶ τὰς τραπέζας
buying in the temple, and the tables
τῶν κολλυβιστῶν κατέστρεψεν καὶ τὰς
of the money-changers he overturned and the
καθέδρας τῶν πωλούντων τὰς περιστεράς,
seats of the [ones] selling the doves,
13 καὶ λέγει αὐτοῖς· γέγραπται· ὁ οἶκός
and says to them: It has been written: The house
μου οἶκος προσευχῆς κληθήσεται, ὑμεῖς
of me a house of prayer shall be called, [2]ye
δὲ αὐτὸν ποιεῖτε σπήλαιον λῃστῶν. **14** Καὶ
[1]but [4]it [3]are making a den of robbers. And
προσῆλθον αὐτῷ τυφλοὶ καὶ χωλοὶ ἐν τῷ
approached *to* him blind and lame [ones] in the

needs them, and he will
send them right away."
4This took place to fulfill
what was spoken through
the prophet:

5"Say to the Daughter of
Zion,
'See, your king comes
to you,
gentle and riding on a
donkey,
on a colt, the foal of a
donkey.'"[e]

6The disciples went and
did as Jesus had instructed
them. 7They brought the
donkey and the colt, placed
their cloaks on them, and
Jesus sat on them. 8A very
large crowd spread their
cloaks on the road, while
others cut branches from
the trees and spread them
on the road. 9The crowds
that went ahead of him and
those that followed shouted,

"Hosanna[f] to the Son of
David!"

"Blessed is he who
comes in the name
of the Lord!"[g]

"Hosanna[f] in the
highest!"

10When Jesus entered Je-
rusalem, the whole city
was stirred and asked,
"Who is this?"
11The crowds answered,
"This is Jesus, the prophet
from Nazareth in Galilee."

Jesus at the Temple

12Jesus entered the tem-
ple area and drove out all
who were buying and sell-
ing there. He overturned
the tables of the money
changers and the benches
of those selling doves. 13"It
is written," he said to
them, " 'My house will be
called a house of prayer,'[h]
but you are making it a 'den
of robbers.'[i]"
14The blind and the lame
came to him at the temple,

[e] *5* Zech. 9:9

[f] *9* A Hebrew expression meaning "Save!" which became an exclamation of praise; also in verse 15

[g] *9* Psalm 118:26

[h] *13* Isaiah 56:7

[i] *13* Jer. 7:11

temple, and he cured them.
15 But when the chief
priests and the scribes saw
the amazing things that he
did, and heard[c] the children crying out in the temple, "Hosanna to the Son of
David," they became angry
16 and said to him, "Do you
hear what these are say-
ing?" Jesus said to them,
"Yes; have you never read,
'Out of the mouths of
infants and
nursing babies
you have prepared
praise for
yourself'?"
17 He left them, went out of
the city to Bethany, and
spent the night there.

Jesus Curses the Fig Tree

18 In the morning, when
he returned to the city, he
was hungry. 19 And seeing a
fig tree by the side of the
road, he went to it and
found nothing at all on it
but leaves. Then he said to
it, "May no fruit ever come
from you again!" And the
fig tree withered at once.
20 When the disciples saw
it, they were amazed, saying, "How did the fig tree
wither at once?" 21 Jesus
answered them, "Truly I
tell you, if you have faith
and do not doubt, not only
will you do what has been
done to the fig tree, but
even if you say to this
mountain, 'Be lifted up and
thrown into the sea,' it will
be done. 22 Whatever you
ask for in prayer with faith,
you will receive."

The Authority of Jesus Questioned

23 When he entered the
temple, the chief priests
and the elders of the people
came to him as he was
teaching, and said, "By
what authority are you doing these things, and who
gave you this authority?"

[c] Gk lacks *heard*

ἱερῷ, καὶ ἐθεράπευσεν αὐτούς. 15 ἰδόντες
temple, and he healed them. [7]seeing
δὲ οἱ ἀρχιερεῖς καὶ οἱ γραμματεῖς τὰ
[1]But [2]the [3]chief priests [4]and [5]the [6]scribes the
θαυμάσια ἃ ἐποίησεν καὶ τοὺς παῖδας
marvels which he did and the children
τοὺς κράζοντας ἐν τῷ ἱερῷ καὶ λέγοντας·
– crying out in the temple and saying:
ὡσαννὰ τῷ υἱῷ Δαυίδ, ἠγανάκτησαν, 16 καὶ
Hosanna to the son of David, they were incensed, and
εἶπαν αὐτῷ· ἀκούεις τί οὗτοι λέγουσιν;
said to him: Hearest thou what these are saying?
ὁ δὲ Ἰησοῦς λέγει αὐτοῖς· ναί· οὐδέποτε
– And Jesus says to them: Yes; never
ἀνέγνωτε ὅτι ἐκ στόματος νηπίων καὶ
did ye read[,] – Out of [the] mouth of infants and
θηλαζόντων κατηρτίσω αἶνον; 17 Καὶ
sucking [ones] thou didst prepare praise? And
καταλιπὼν αὐτοὺς ἐξῆλθεν ἔξω τῆς
leaving them he went forth outside the
πόλεως εἰς Βηθανίαν, καὶ ηὐλίσθη ἐκεῖ.
city to Bethany, and lodged there.
18 Πρωῒ δὲ ἐπαναγαγὼν εἰς τὴν πόλιν
Now early going up to the city
ἐπείνασεν. 19 καὶ ἰδὼν συκῆν μίαν ἐπὶ τῆς
he hungered. And seeing fig-tree one on the
ὁδοῦ ἦλθεν ἐπ' αὐτήν, καὶ οὐδὲν εὗρεν
way he went up(to) it, and nothing found
ἐν αὐτῇ εἰ μὴ φύλλα μόνον, καὶ λέγει
in it except leaves only, and says
αὐτῇ· οὐ μηκέτι ἐκ σοῦ καρπὸς γένηται
to it: Never of thee fruit may be
εἰς τὸν αἰῶνα. καὶ ἐξηράνθη παραχρῆμα
to the age. And was dried up instantly
ἡ συκῆ. 20 καὶ ἰδόντες οἱ μαθηταὶ
the fig-tree. And seeing the disciples
ἐθαύμασαν λέγοντες· πῶς παραχρῆμα
marvelled saying: How instantly
ἐξηράνθη ἡ συκῆ; 21 ἀποκριθεὶς δὲ ὁ
was withered the fig-tree? And answering –
Ἰησοῦς εἶπεν αὐτοῖς· ἀμὴν λέγω ὑμῖν,
Jesus said to them: Truly I say to you,
ἐὰν ἔχητε πίστιν καὶ μὴ διακριθῆτε,
If ye have faith and do not doubt,
οὐ μόνον τὸ τῆς συκῆς ποιήσετε, ἀλλὰ
not only the* of the fig-tree ye will do, but
κἂν τῷ ὄρει τούτῳ εἴπητε· ἄρθητι
also if – mountain to this ye say: Be thou taken
καὶ βλήθητι εἰς τὴν θάλασσαν, γενήσεται·
and cast into the sea, it shall be;
22 καὶ πάντα ὅσα ἂν αἰτήσητε ἐν τῇ
and all things whatever ye may ask in –
προσευχῇ πιστεύοντες λήμψεσθε.
prayer believing ye shall receive.
23 Καὶ ἐλθόντος αὐτοῦ εἰς τὸ ἱερὸν
And coming him* into the temple
=as he came
προσῆλθον αὐτῷ διδάσκοντι οἱ ἀρχιερεῖς
approached *to* him teaching* the chief priests
=while he taught
καὶ οἱ πρεσβύτεροι τοῦ λαοῦ λέγοντες·
and the elders of the people saying:
ἐν ποίᾳ ἐξουσίᾳ ταῦτα ποιεῖς; καὶ
By what authority these things doest thou? and
τίς σοι ἔδωκεν τὴν ἐξουσίαν ταύτην;
who thee gave – authority this?

and he healed them. 15But
when the chief priests and
the teachers of the law saw
the wonderful things he did
and the children shouting in
the temple area, "Hosanna
to the Son of David," they
were indignant.
16"Do you hear what
these children are saying?"
they asked him.
"Yes," replied Jesus,
"have you never read,

" 'From the lips of
children and infants
you have ordained
praise'[j]?"

17And he left them and
went out of the city to Bethany, where he spent the
night.

The Fig Tree Withers

18Early in the morning, as
he was on his way back to
the city, he was hungry.
19Seeing a fig tree by the
road, he went up to it but
found nothing on it except
leaves. Then he said to it,
"May you never bear fruit
again!" Immediately the
tree withered.
20When the disciples saw
this, they were amazed.
"How did the fig tree wither so quickly?" they asked.
21Jesus replied, "I tell
you the truth, if you have
faith and do not doubt, not
only can you do what was
done to the fig tree, but also
you can say to this moun-
tain, 'Go, throw yourself
into the sea,' and it will be
done. 22If you believe, you
will receive whatever you
ask for in prayer."

The Authority of Jesus Questioned

23Jesus entered the tem-
ple courts, and, while he
was teaching, the chief
priests and the elders of the
people came to him. "By
what authority are you doing these things?" they
asked. "And who gave you
this authority?"

[j] *16* Psalm 8:2

24 Jesus said to them, "I will
also ask you one question;
if you tell me the answer,
then I will also tell you by
what authority I do these
things. 25 Did the baptism
of John come from heaven,
or was it of human origin?"
And they argued with one
another, "If we say, 'From
heaven,' he will say to us,
'Why then did you not be-
lieve him?' 26 But if we say,
'Of human origin,' we are
afraid of the crowd; for all
regard John as a prophet."
27 So they answered Jesus,
"We do not know." And he
said to them, "Neither will
I tell you by what authority
I am doing these things.

The Parable of the Two Sons

28 "What do you think?
A man had two sons; he
went to the first and said,
'Son, go and work in the
vineyard today.' 29 He answered, 'I will not'; but later he changed his mind and
went. 30 The father[d] went
to the second and said the
same; and he answered, 'I
go, sir'; but he did not go.
31 Which of the two did the
will of his father?" They
said, "The first." Jesus said
to them, "Truly I tell you,
the tax collectors and the
prostitutes are going into
the kingdom of God ahead
of you. 32 For John came to
you in the way of righteousness and you did not be-
lieve him, but the tax collectors and the prostitutes
believed him; and even after you saw it, you did not
change your minds and be-
lieve him.

The Parable of the Wicked Tenants

33 "Listen to another
parable. There was a land-

[d] Gk *He*

24 ἀποκριθεὶς δὲ ὁ Ἰησοῦς εἶπεν αὐτοῖς·
And answering – Jesus said to them:
ἐρωτήσω ὑμᾶς κἀγὼ λόγον ἕνα, ὃν
will question you I also word one, which
ἐὰν εἴπητέ μοι, κἀγὼ ὑμῖν ἐρῶ ἐν ποίᾳ
if ye tell me, I also you will tell by what
ἐξουσίᾳ ταῦτα ποιῶ· **25** τὸ βάπτισμα
authority these things I do: The baptism
τὸ Ἰωάννου πόθεν ἦν; ἐξ οὐρανοῦ ἢ
– of John whence was it? from heaven or
ἐξ ἀνθρώπων; οἱ δὲ διελογίζοντο ἐν
from men? And they reasoned among
ἑαυτοῖς λέγοντες· ἐὰν εἴπωμεν· ἐξ οὐρανοῦ,
themselves saying: If we say: From heaven,
ἐρεῖ ἡμῖν· διὰ τί οὖν οὐκ ἐπιστεύσατε
he will say to us: Why then believed ye not
αὐτῷ; **26** ἐὰν δὲ εἴπωμεν· ἐξ ἀνθρώπων,
him? But if we say: From men,
φοβούμεθα τὸν ὄχλον· πάντες γὰρ ὡς
we fear the crowd: for all as
προφήτην ἔχουσιν τὸν Ἰωάννην. **27** καὶ
a prophet have – John. And
ἀποκριθέντες τῷ Ἰησοῦ εἶπαν· οὐκ
answering – Jesus they said: We do
οἴδαμεν. ἔφη αὐτοῖς καὶ αὐτός· οὐδὲ
not know. said to them also He: Neither
ἐγὼ λέγω ὑμῖν ἐν ποίᾳ ἐξουσίᾳ ταῦτα
I tell you by what authority these things
ποιῶ. **28** Τί δὲ ὑμῖν δοκεῖ; ἄνθρωπος
I do. But what to you seems it? A man
εἶχεν τέκνα δύο· προσελθὼν τῷ πρώτῳ
had children two; approaching *to* the first
εἶπεν· τέκνον, ὕπαγε σήμερον ἐργάζου ἐν
he said: Child, go to-day work in
τῷ ἀμπελῶνι. **29** ὁ δὲ ἀποκριθεὶς εἶπεν·
the vineyard. But he answering said:
ἐγὼ κύριε, καὶ οὐκ ἀπῆλθεν. **30** προσ-
I [go], lord, and went not. And
ελθὼν δὲ τῷ δευτέρῳ εἶπεν ὡσαύτως.
approaching *to* the second he said similarly.
ὁ δὲ ἀποκριθεὶς εἶπεν· οὐ θέλω, ὕστερον
And he answering said: I will not, later
μεταμεληθεὶς ἀπῆλθεν. **31** τίς ἐκ τῶν δύο
repenting he went. Which of the two
ἐποίησεν τὸ θέλημα τοῦ πατρός; λέγουσιν·
did the will of the father? They say:
ὁ ὕστερος. λέγει αὐτοῖς ὁ Ἰησοῦς· ἀμὴν
The latter. Says to them – Jesus: Truly
λέγω ὑμῖν ὅτι οἱ τελῶναι καὶ αἱ πόρναι
I tell you[,] – The tax-collectors and the harlots
προάγουσιν ὑμᾶς εἰς τὴν βασιλείαν τοῦ
are going before you into the kingdom –
θεοῦ. **32** ἦλθεν γὰρ Ἰωάννης πρὸς ὑμᾶς
of God. For came John to you
ἐν ὁδῷ δικαιοσύνης, καὶ οὐκ ἐπιστεύσατε
in a way of righteousness, and ye believed not
αὐτῷ· οἱ δὲ τελῶναι καὶ αἱ πόρναι
him; but the tax-collectors and the harlots
ἐπίστευσαν αὐτῷ· ὑμεῖς δὲ ἰδόντες οὐδὲ
believed him; but ye seeing not
μετεμελήθητε ὕστερον τοῦ πιστεῦσαι αὐτῷ.
repented later – to believe[d] him.
[d] =so as to believe
33 Ἄλλην παραβολὴν ἀκούσατε. Ἄνθρωπος
Another parable hear ye. *A man*

* Some such word as 'sign' must be supplied.

24 Jesus replied, "I will
also ask you one question.
If you answer me, I will tell
you by what authority I am
doing these things. 25 John's
baptism—where did it
come from? Was it from
heaven, or from men?"
They discussed it among
themselves and said, "If
we say, 'From heaven,' he
will ask, 'Then why didn't
you believe him?' 26 But if
we say, 'From men'—we
are afraid of the people, for
they all hold that John was
a prophet."
27 So they answered
Jesus, "We don't know."
Then he said, "Neither
will I tell you by what authority I am doing these
things.

The Parable of the Two Sons

28 "What do you think?
There was a man who had
two sons. He went to the
first and said, 'Son, go and
work today in the vine-
yard.'
29 " 'I will not,' he an-
swered, but later he
changed his mind and
went.
30 "Then the father went
to the other son and said
the same thing. He an-
swered, 'I will, sir,' but he
did not go.
31 "Which of the two did
what his father wanted?"
"The first," they an-
swered.
Jesus said to them, "I tell
you the truth, the tax collectors and the prostitutes
are entering the kingdom of
God ahead of you. 32 For
John came to you to show
you the way of righteous-
ness, and you did not be-
lieve him, but the tax collectors and the prostitutes
did. And even after you
saw this, you did not repent
and believe him.

The Parable of the Tenants

33 "Listen to another parable: There was a landown-

owner who planted a vine-
yard, put a fence around it,
dug a wine press in it, and
built a watchtower. Then
he leased it to tenants and
went to another country.
34 When the harvest time
had come, he sent his
slaves to the tenants to collect his produce. 35 But the
tenants seized his slaves
and beat one, killed another, and stoned another.
36 Again he sent other
slaves, more than the first;
and they treated them in
the same way. 37 Finally he
sent his son to them, saying, 'They will respect my
son.' 38 But when the tenants saw the son, they said
to themselves, 'This is the
heir; come, let us kill him
and get his inheritance.'
39 So they seized him,
threw him out of the vineyard, and killed him.
40 Now when the owner of
the vineyard comes, what
will he do to those ten-
ants?" 41 They said to him,
"He will put those
wretches to a miserable
death, and lease the vineyard to other tenants who
will give him the produce at
the harvest time."
42 Jesus said to them,
"Have you never read in
the scriptures:

'The stone that the
builders rejected
has become the
cornerstone;[e]
this was the Lord's
doing,
and it is amazing in
our eyes'?

43 Therefore I tell you, the
kingdom of God will be tak-
en away from you and giv-
en to a people that pro-

[e] Or *keystone*

ἦν οἰκοδεσπότης ὅστις ἐφύτευσεν ἀμπελῶνα,
there was a housemaster who planted a vineyard,
καὶ φραγμὸν αὐτῷ περιέθηκεν καὶ ὤρυξεν
and [3]a hedge [2]it [1]put round and dug
ἐν αὐτῷ ληνὸν καὶ ᾠκοδόμησεν πύργον,
in it a winepress and built a tower,
καὶ ἐξέδοτο αὐτὸν γεωργοῖς, καὶ ἀπεδή-
and let it to husbandmen, and departed.
μησεν. 34 ὅτε δὲ ἤγγισεν ὁ καιρὸς τῶν
And when drew near the time of the
καρπῶν, ἀπέστειλεν τοὺς δούλους αὐτοῦ
fruits, he sent the slaves of him
πρὸς τοὺς γεωργοὺς λαβεῖν τοὺς καρποὺς
to the husbandmen to receive the fruits
αὐτοῦ. 35 καὶ λαβόντες οἱ γεωργοὶ
of it. And [3]taking [1]the [2]husbandmen
τοὺς δούλους αὐτοῦ ὃν μὲν ἔδειραν, ὃν
the slaves of him this one they flogged, that
δὲ ἀπέκτειναν, ὃν δὲ ἐλιθοβόλησαν. 36 πάλιν
one they killed, another they stoned. Again
ἀπέστειλεν ἄλλους δούλους πλείονας τῶν
he sent other slaves more [than] the
πρώτων, καὶ ἐποίησαν αὐτοῖς ὡσαύτως.
first [ones], and they did to them similarly.
37 ὕστερον δὲ ἀπέστειλεν πρὸς αὐτοὺς
But later he sent to them
τὸν υἱὸν αὐτοῦ λέγων· ἐντραπήσονται
the son of him saying: They will reverence
τὸν υἱόν μου. 38 οἱ δὲ γεωργοὶ ἰδόντες
the son of me. But the husbandmen seeing
τὸν υἱὸν εἶπον ἐν ἑαυτοῖς· οὗτός ἐστιν
the son said among themselves: This is
ὁ κληρονόμος· δεῦτε ἀποκτείνωμεν αὐτὸν
the heir; come[,] let us kill him
καὶ σχῶμεν τὴν κληρονομίαν αὐτοῦ·
and let us possess the inheritance of him;
39 καὶ λαβόντες αὐτὸν ἐξέβαλον ἔξω τοῦ
and taking [2]him [1]they cast *out* outside the
ἀμπελῶνος καὶ ἀπέκτειναν. 40 ὅταν οὖν
vineyard and killed. When therefore
ἔλθῃ ὁ κύριος τοῦ ἀμπελῶνος, τί ποιήσει
comes the lord of the vineyard, what will he do
τοῖς γεωργοῖς ἐκείνοις; 41 λέγουσιν αὐτῷ·
– husbandmen to those? They say to him:
κακοὺς κακῶς ἀπολέσει αὐτούς, καὶ τὸν
Bad men badly he will destroy them, and the
ἀμπελῶνα ἐκδώσεται ἄλλοις γεωργοῖς,
vineyard he will give out to other husbandmen,
οἵτινες ἀποδώσουσιν αὐτῷ τοὺς καρποὺς
who will render to him the fruits
ἐν τοῖς καιροῖς αὐτῶν. 42 λέγει αὐτοῖς ὁ
in the seasons of them. Says to them –
Ἰησοῦς· οὐδέποτε ἀνέγνωτε ἐν ταῖς
Jesus: Did ye never read in the
γραφαῖς· λίθον ὃν ἀπεδοκίμασαν οἱ
scriptures: A stone which rejected the
οἰκοδομοῦντες, οὗτος ἐγενήθη εἰς κεφαλὴν
building [ones], this became – head
γωνίας· παρὰ κυρίου ἐγένετο αὕτη, καὶ
of [the] corner; from [the] Lord became this, and
ἔστιν θαυμαστὴ ἐν ὀφθαλμοῖς ἡμῶν; 43 διὰ
it is marvellous in [the] eyes of us? There-
τοῦτο λέγω ὑμῖν ὅτι ἀρθήσεται ἀφ' ὑμῶν
fore I tell you[,] – will be taken from you
ἡ βασιλεία τοῦ θεοῦ καὶ δοθήσεται
The kingdom – of God and will be given

er who planted a vineyard.
He put a wall around it, dug
a winepress in it and built a
watchtower. Then he rent-
ed the vineyard to some
farmers and went away on
a journey. 34 When the harvest time approached, he
sent his servants to the tenants to collect his fruit.
35 "The tenants seized his
servants; they beat one,
killed another, and stoned a
third. 36 Then he sent other
servants to them, more
than the first time, and the
tenants treated them the
same way. 37 Last of all, he
sent his son to them. 'They
will respect my son,' he
said.
38 "But when the tenants
saw the son, they said to
each other, 'This is the
heir. Come, let's kill him
and take his inheritance.'
39 So they took him and
threw him out of the vineyard and killed him.
40 "Therefore, when the
owner of the vineyard
comes, what will he do to
those tenants?"
41 "He will bring those
wretches to a wretched
end," they replied, "and
he will rent the vineyard to
other tenants, who will give
him his share of the crop at
harvest time."
42 Jesus said to them,
"Have you never read in
the Scriptures:

" 'The stone the builders
rejected
has become the
capstone[k];
the Lord has done this,
and it is marvelous in
our eyes'[l]?

43 "Therefore I tell you
that the kingdom of God
will be taken away from
you and given to a people

[k] 42 Or *cornerstone*
[l] 42 Psalm 118:22,23

duces the fruits of the kingdom.[f] 44 The one who falls
on this stone will be broken
to pieces; and it will crush
anyone on whom it falls."[g]
45 When the chief
priests and the Pharisees
heard his parables, they realized that he was speaking
about them. 46 They wanted
to arrest him, but they
feared the crowds, because
they regarded him as a
prophet.

ἔθνει ποιοῦντι τοὺς καρποὺς αὐτῆς.
to a nation producing the fruits of it.
44 [καὶ ὁ πεσὼν ἐπὶ τὸν λίθον τοῦτον
And the [one] falling on – stone this
συνθλασθήσεται· ἐφ' ὃν δ' ἂν πέσῃ,
will be broken in pieces; but on whomever it falls,
λικμήσει αὐτόν.] 45 Καὶ ἀκούσαντες οἱ
it will crush to powder him. And hearing the
ἀρχιερεῖς καὶ οἱ Φαρισαῖοι τὰς παραβολὰς
chief priests and the Pharisees the parables
αὐτοῦ ἔγνωσαν ὅτι περὶ αὐτῶν λέγει·
of him they knew that concerning them he tells;
46 καὶ ζητοῦντες αὐτὸν κρατῆσαι ἐφοβήθησαν
and seeking him to seize they feared
τοὺς ὄχλους, ἐπεὶ εἰς προφήτην αὐτὸν εἶχον.
the crowds, since for a prophet him they had.

who will produce its fruit.
44He who falls on this stone
will be broken to pieces,
but he on whom it falls will
be crushed."[m]
45When the chief priests
and the Pharisees heard
Jesus' parables, they knew
he was talking about them.
46They looked for a way to
arrest him, but they were
afraid of the crowd because
the people held that he was
a prophet.

Chapter 22

The Parable of the Wedding Banquet

ONCE more Jesus
spoke to them in par-
ables, saying: 2 "The kingdom of heaven may be
compared to a king who
gave a wedding banquet for
his son. 3 He sent his slaves
to call those who had been
invited to the wedding banquet, but they would not
come. 4 Again he sent other
slaves, saying, 'Tell those
who have been invited:
Look, I have prepared my
dinner, my oxen and my fat
calves have been slaugh-
tered, and everything is
ready; come to the wedding
banquet.' 5 But they made
light of it and went away,
one to his farm, another to
his business, 6 while the
rest seized his slaves, mistreated them, and killed
them. 7 The king was en-
raged. He sent his troops,
destroyed those murder-
ers, and burned their city.
8 Then he said to his slaves,
'The wedding is ready, but
those invited were not worthy. 9 Go therefore into the
main streets, and invite everyone you find to the wed-

22 Καὶ ἀποκριθεὶς ὁ Ἰησοῦς πάλιν
And answering – Jesus again
εἶπεν ἐν παραβολαῖς αὐτοῖς λέγων·
spoke in parables to them saying:
2 ὡμοιώθη ἡ βασιλεία τῶν οὐρανῶν
Was(is) likened the kingdom of the heavens
ἀνθρώπῳ βασιλεῖ, ὅστις ἐποίησεν γάμους
to *a man* a king, who made a wedding feast
τῷ υἱῷ αὐτοῦ. 3 καὶ ἀπέστειλεν τοὺς
for the son of him. And he sent the
δούλους αὐτοῦ καλέσαι τοὺς κεκλημένους
slaves of him to call the [ones] *having been* invited
εἰς τοὺς γάμους, καὶ οὐκ ἤθελον ἐλθεῖν.
to the feast, and they wished not to come.
4 πάλιν ἀπέστειλεν ἄλλους δούλους λέγων·
Again he sent other slaves saying:
εἴπατε τοῖς κεκλημένοις· ἰδοὺ τὸ
Tell the [ones] *having been* invited: Behold[,] the
ἄριστόν μου ἡτοίμακα, οἱ ταῦροί μου
supper of me I have prepared, the oxen of me
καὶ τὰ σιτιστὰ τεθυμένα, καὶ πάντα
and the fatted beasts having been killed, and all things
ἕτοιμα· δεῦτε εἰς τοὺς γάμους. 5 οἱ δὲ
[are] ready; come to the feast. But they
ἀμελήσαντες ἀπῆλθον, ὃς μὲν εἰς τὸν
not caring went off, one to the(his)
ἴδιον ἀγρόν, ὃς δὲ ἐπὶ τὴν ἐμπορίαν
own field, another on the trading
αὐτοῦ· 6 οἱ δὲ λοιποὶ κρατήσαντες
of him; and the rest seizing
τοὺς δούλους αὐτοῦ ὕβρισαν καὶ ἀπέκτειναν.
the slaves of him insulted and killed.
7 ὁ δὲ βασιλεὺς ὠργίσθη, καὶ πέμψας
So the king became angry, and sending
τὰ στρατεύματα αὐτοῦ ἀπώλεσεν τοὺς
the armies of him destroyed –
φονεῖς ἐκείνους καὶ τὴν πόλιν αὐτῶν
murderers those and the city of them
ἐνέπρησεν. 8 τότε λέγει τοῖς δούλοις
burned. Then he says to the slaves
αὐτοῦ· ὁ μὲν γάμος ἕτοιμός ἐστιν, οἱ δὲ
of him: Indeed the feast ready is, but the [ones]
κεκλημένοι οὐκ ἦσαν ἄξιοι· 9 πορεύεσθε
having been invited were not worthy; go ye
οὖν ἐπὶ τὰς διεξόδους τῶν ὁδῶν, καὶ
therefore onto the partings of the ways, and
ὅσους ἐὰν εὕρητε καλέσατε εἰς τοὺς
as many as ye find call to the

Chapter 22

The Parable of the Wedding Banquet

JESUS spoke to them
again in parables, say-
ing: 2"The kingdom of
heaven is like a king who
prepared a wedding ban-
quet for his son. 3He sent
his servants to those who
had been invited to the banquet to tell them to come,
but they refused to come.
4"Then he sent some
more servants and said,
'Tell those who have been
invited that I have prepared
my dinner: My oxen and
fattened cattle have been
butchered, and everything
is ready. Come to the wedding banquet.'
5"But they paid no atten-
tion and went off—one to
his field, another to his
business. 6The rest seized
his servants, mistreated
them and killed them. 7The
king was enraged. He sent
his army and destroyed
those murderers and
burned their city.
8"Then he said to his servants, 'The wedding ban-
quet is ready, but those I
invited did not deserve to
come. 9Go to the street corners and invite to the banquet anyone you find.' 10So

[f] Gk *the fruits of it*
[g] Other ancient authorities lack verse 44

[m] 44 Some manuscripts do not have verse 44.

ding banquet.' 10 Those
slaves went out into the
streets and gathered all
whom they found, both
good and bad; so the wed-
ding hall was filled with
guests.
11 "But when the king
came in to see the guests,
he noticed a man there who
was not wearing a wedding
robe, 12 and he said to him,
'Friend, how did you get in
here without a wedding
robe?' And he was speech-
less. 13 Then the king said
to the attendants, 'Bind
him hand and foot, and
throw him into the outer
darkness, where there will
be weeping and gnashing of
teeth.' 14 For many are
called, but few are cho-
sen."

The Question about Paying Taxes

15 Then the Pharisees
went and plotted to entrap
him in what he said. 16 So
they sent their disciples to
him, along with the Herodians, saying, "Teacher, we
know that you are sincere,
and teach the way of God in
accordance with truth, and
show deference to no one;
for you do not regard people with partiality. 17 Tell
us, then, what you think. Is
it lawful to pay taxes to the
emperor, or not?" 18 But
Jesus, aware of their malice, said, "Why are you
putting me to the test, you
hypocrites? 19 Show me the
coin used for the tax." And
they brought him a denarius. 20 Then he said to them,
"Whose head is this, and
whose title?" 21 They an-
swered, "The emperor's."

γάμους. 10 καὶ ἐξελθόντες οἱ δοῦλοι
feast. And going forth – slaves

ἐκεῖνοι εἰς τὰς ὁδοὺς συνήγαγον πάντας
those into the ways assembled all

οὓς εὗρον, πονηρούς τε καὶ ἀγαθούς·
whom they found, both bad and good;

καὶ ἐπλήσθη ὁ νυμφὼν ἀνακειμένων.
and was filled the wedding chamber of(with) reclining [ones].

11 εἰσελθὼν δὲ ὁ βασιλεὺς θεάσασθαι
But entering the king to behold

τοὺς ἀνακειμένους εἶδεν ἐκεῖ
the reclining [ones] he saw there

ἄνθρωπον οὐκ ἐνδεδυμένον ἔνδυμα γάμου·
a man not *having been* dressed[in] a dress of wedding;

12 καὶ λέγει αὐτῷ· ἑταῖρε, πῶς
and he says to him: Comrade, how

εἰσῆλθες ὧδε μὴ ἔχων ἔνδυμα γάμου;
enteredst thou here not having a dress of wedding?

ὁ δὲ ἐφιμώθη. 13 τότε ὁ βασιλεὺς
And he was silenced. Then the king

εἶπεν τοῖς διακόνοις· δήσαντες αὐτοῦ
said to the servants: Binding of him

πόδας καὶ χεῖρας ἐκβάλετε αὐτὸν
feet and hands throw out him

εἰς τὸ σκότος τὸ ἐξώτερον· ἐκεῖ ἔσται
into the darkness – outer; there will be

ὁ κλαυθμὸς καὶ ὁ βρυγμὸς τῶν
the wailing and the gnashing of the

ὀδόντων. 14 Πολλοὶ γάρ εἰσιν κλητοί,
teeth. For many are called,

ὀλίγοι δὲ ἐκλεκτοί.
but few chosen.

15 Τότε πορευθέντες οἱ Φαρισαῖοι συμ-
Then going the Pharisees coun-

βούλιον ἔλαβον ὅπως αὐτὸν παγιδεύσωσιν
sel took so as him they might ensnare

ἐν λόγῳ. 16 καὶ ἀποστέλλουσιν αὐτῷ
in a word. And they send to him

τοὺς μαθητὰς αὐτῶν μετὰ τῶν Ἡρῳ-
the disciples of them with the Hero-

διανῶν λέγοντας· διδάσκαλε, οἴδαμεν
dians saying: Teacher, we know

ὅτι ἀληθὴς εἶ καὶ τὴν ὁδὸν τοῦ
that truthful thou art and the way –

θεοῦ ἐν ἀληθείᾳ διδάσκεις, καὶ οὐ
of God in truth thou teachest, and not

μέλει σοι περὶ οὐδενός, οὐ γὰρ
it concerns *to* thee about no one(anyone), ²not ¹for

βλέπεις εἰς πρόσωπον ἀνθρώπων·
³thou lookest to face of men;

17 εἰπὸν οὖν ἡμῖν, τί σοι δοκεῖ;
tell therefore us, what to thee seems it?

ἔξεστιν δοῦναι κῆνσον Καίσαρι ἢ οὔ;
is it lawful to give tribute to Cæsar or no?

18 γνοὺς δὲ ὁ Ἰησοῦς τὴν πονηρίαν
But knowing – Jesus the wickedness

αὐτῶν εἶπεν· τί με πειράζετε, ὑποκριταί;
of them said: Why me tempt ye, hypocrites?

19 ἐπιδείξατέ μοι τὸ νόμισμα τοῦ κήνσου.
Show me the money of the tribute.

οἱ δὲ προσήνεγκαν αὐτῷ δηνάριον. 20 καὶ
And they brought to him a denarius. And

λέγει αὐτοῖς· τίνος ἡ εἰκὼν αὕτη
he says to them: Of whom – image this

καὶ ἡ ἐπιγραφή; 21 λέγουσιν· Καίσαρος.
and – superscription? They say: Of Cæsar.

the servants went out into
the streets and gathered all
the people they could find,
both good and bad, and the
wedding hall was filled with
guests.
11 "But when the king
came in to see the guests,
he noticed a man there who
was not wearing wedding
clothes. 12 'Friend,' he
asked, 'how did you get in
here without wedding
clothes?' The man was
speechless.
13 "Then the king told the
attendants, 'Tie him hand
and foot, and throw him
outside, into the darkness,
where there will be weep-
ing and gnashing of teeth.'
14 "For many are invited,
but few are chosen."

Paying Taxes to Caesar

15 Then the Pharisees
went out and laid plans to
trap him in his words.
16 They sent their disciples
to him along with the Herodians. "Teacher," they
said, "we know you are a
man of integrity and that
you teach the way of God in
accordance with the truth.
You aren't swayed by men,
because you pay no atten-
tion to who they are. 17 Tell
us then, what is your opinion? Is it right to pay taxes
to Caesar or not?"
18 But Jesus, knowing
their evil intent, said, "You
hypocrites, why are you
trying to trap me? 19 Show
me the coin used for paying
the tax." They brought him
a denarius, 20 and he asked
them, "Whose portrait is
this? And whose inscrip-
tion?"
21 "Caesar's," they re-
plied.
Then he said to them,

Then he said to them,
"Give therefore to the emperor the things that are the
emperor's, and to God the
things that are God's."
22 When they heard this,
they were amazed; and
they left him and went
away.

The Question about the Resurrection

23 The same day some
Sadducees came to him,
saying there is no resurrection;[h] and they asked him a
question, saying,
24 "Teacher, Moses said, 'If
a man dies childless, his
brother shall marry the
widow, and raise up chil-
dren for his brother.'
25 Now there were seven
brothers among us; the first
married, and died childless,
leaving the widow to his
brother. 26 The second did
the same, so also the third,
down to the seventh.
27 Last of all, the woman
herself died. 28 In the resurrection, then, whose wife
of the seven will she be?
For all of them had married
her."
29 Jesus answered
them, "You are wrong, be-
cause you know neither the
scriptures nor the power of
God. 30 For in the resurrection they neither marry nor
are given in marriage, but
are like angels[i] in heaven.
31 And as for the resurrection of the dead, have you
not read what was said to
you by God, 32 'I am the
God of Abraham, the God
of Isaac, and the God of Jacob'? He is God not of the
dead, but of the living."
33 And when the crowd
heard it, they were as-
tounded at his teaching.

The Greatest Commandment

34 When the Pharisees
heard that he had silenced

[h] Other ancient authorities read *who say that there is no resurrection*

[i] Other ancient authorities add *of God*

τότε λέγει αὐτοῖς· ἀπόδοτε οὖν τὰ
Then he says to them: Render then the things
Καίσαρος Καίσαρι καὶ τὰ τοῦ θεοῦ
of Cæsar to Cæsar and the things – of God
τῷ θεῷ. **22** καὶ ἀκούσαντες ἐθαύμασαν,
– to God. And hearing they marvelled,
καὶ ἀφέντες αὐτὸν ἀπῆλθαν.
and leaving him went away.
23 Ἐν ἐκείνῃ τῇ ἡμέρᾳ προσῆλθον
On that – day approached
αὐτῷ Σαδδουκαῖοι, λέγοντες μὴ εἶναι
to him Sadducees, saying not to be
ἀνάστασιν, καὶ ἐπηρώτησαν αὐτὸν
a resurrection, and questioned him
24 λέγοντες· διδάσκαλε, Μωϋσῆς εἶπεν·
saying: Teacher, Moses said:
ἐάν τις ἀποθάνῃ μὴ ἔχων τέκνα,
If any man dies not having children,
ἐπιγαμβρεύσει ὁ ἀδελφὸς αὐτοῦ τὴν
shall take to wife after the brother of him the
γυναῖκα αὐτοῦ καὶ ἀναστήσει σπέρμα
wife of him and shall raise up seed
τῷ ἀδελφῷ αὐτοῦ. **25** ἦσαν δὲ παρ'
to the brother of him. Now there were with
ἡμῖν ἑπτὰ ἀδελφοί· καὶ ὁ πρῶτος
us seven brothers; and the first
γήμας ἐτελεύτησεν, καὶ μὴ ἔχων
having married died, and not having
σπέρμα ἀφῆκεν τὴν γυναῖκα αὐτοῦ τῷ
seed left the wife of him to the
ἀδελφῷ αὐτοῦ· **26** ὁμοίως καὶ ὁ δεύτερος
brother of him; likewise also the second
καὶ ὁ τρίτος, ἕως τῶν ἑπτά. **27** ὕστερον
and the third, until the seven. last
δὲ πάντων ἀπέθανεν ἡ γυνή. **28** ἐν τῇ
And of all died the woman. In the
ἀναστάσει οὖν τίνος τῶν ἑπτὰ ἔσται
resurrection then of which of the seven will she be
γυνή; πάντες γὰρ ἔσχον αὐτήν. **29** ἀπο-
wife? for all had her. an-
κριθεὶς δὲ ὁ Ἰησοῦς εἶπεν αὐτοῖς·
swering And – Jesus said to them:
πλανᾶσθε μὴ εἰδότες τὰς γραφὰς μηδὲ
Ye err not knowing the scriptures nor
τὴν δύναμιν τοῦ θεοῦ. **30** ἐν γὰρ τῇ
the power – of God. For in the
ἀναστάσει οὔτε γαμοῦσιν οὔτε γαμίζονται,
resurrection neither they marry nor are given in marriage,
ἀλλ' ὡς ἄγγελοι ἐν τῷ οὐρανῷ εἰσιν.
but as angels in *the* heaven are.
31 περὶ δὲ τῆς ἀναστάσεως τῶν νεκρῶν
But concerning the resurrection of the dead
οὐκ ἀνέγνωτε τὸ ῥηθὲν ὑμῖν ὑπὸ
did ye not read the thing said to you by
τοῦ θεοῦ λέγοντος· **32** ἐγώ εἰμι ὁ θεὸς
– God saying: I am the God
Ἀβραὰμ καὶ ὁ θεὸς Ἰσαὰκ καὶ ὁ θεὸς
of Abraham and the God of Isaac and the God
Ἰακώβ; οὐκ ἔστιν [ὁ] θεὸς νεκρῶν
of Jacob? He is not the God of dead men
ἀλλὰ ζώντων. **33** καὶ ἀκούσαντες οἱ ὄχλοι
but of living [ones]. And hearing the crowds
ἐξεπλήσσοντο ἐπὶ τῇ διδαχῇ αὐτοῦ.
were astounded over(at) the teaching of him.
34 Οἱ δὲ Φαρισαῖοι ἀκούσαντες ὅτι
But the Pharisees hearing that

"Give to Caesar what is
Caesar's, and to God what
is God's."
22When they heard this,
they were amazed. So they
left him and went away.

Marriage at the Resurrection

23That same day the Sad-
ducees, who say there is no
resurrection, came to him
with a question. 24"Teacher," they said, "Moses told
us that if a man dies without
having children, his brother
must marry the widow and
have children for him.
25Now there were seven
brothers among us. The
first one married and died,
and since he had no chil-
dren, he left his wife to his
brother. 26The same thing
happened to the second
and third brother, right on
down to the seventh. 27Fi-
nally, the woman died.
28Now then, at the resur-
rection, whose wife will
she be of the seven, since
all of them were married to
her?"
29Jesus replied, "You are
in error because you do not
know the Scriptures or the
power of God. 30At the resurrection people will neither marry nor be given in
marriage; they will be like
the angels in heaven. 31But
about the resurrection of
the dead—have you not
read what God said to you,
32'I am the God of Abra-
ham, the God of Isaac, and
the God of Jacob'[n]? He is
not the God of the dead but
of the living."
33When the crowds heard
this, they were astonished
at his teaching.

The Greatest Commandment

34Hearing that Jesus had
silenced the Sadducees, the

[n] *32* Exodus 3:6

the Sadducees, they gathered together, [35]and one of them, a lawyer, asked him a question to test him. [36]"Teacher, which commandment in the law is the greatest?" [37]He said to him, " 'You shall love the Lord your God with all your heart, and with all your soul, and with all your mind.' [38]This is the greatest and first commandment. [39]And a second is like it: 'You shall love your neighbor as yourself.' [40]On these two commandments hang all the law and the prophets."

The Question about David's Son

41 Now while the Pharisees were gathered together, Jesus asked them this question: [42]"What do you think of the Messiah?[j] Whose son is he?" They said to him, "The son of David." [43]He said to them, "How is it then that David by the Spirit[k] calls him Lord, saying,

[44] 'The Lord said to my Lord,
"Sit at my right hand,
until I put your enemies under your feet" '?

[45]If David thus calls him Lord, how can he be his son?" [46]No one was able to give him an answer, nor from that day did anyone dare to ask him any more questions.

ἐφίμωσεν τοὺς Σαδδουκαίους, συνήχθησαν
he silenced the Sadducees, were assembled

ἐπὶ τὸ αὐτό, 35 καὶ ἐπηρώτησεν εἷς
together, and [5]questioned [1]one

ἐξ αὐτῶν νομικὸς πειράζων αὐτόν· 36 δι-
[2]of [3]them [4]a lawyer [6]tempting him: Teach-

δάσκαλε, ποία ἐντολὴ μεγάλη ἐν τῷ
er, what commandment [is] great in the

νόμῳ; 37 ὁ δὲ ἔφη αὐτῷ· ἀγαπήσεις
law? And he said to him: Thou shalt love

κύριον τὸν θεόν σου ἐν ὅλῃ τῇ καρδίᾳ
[the] Lord the God of thee with all the heart

σου καὶ ἐν ὅλῃ τῇ ψυχῇ σου καὶ ἐν
of thee and with all the soul of thee and with

ὅλῃ τῇ διανοίᾳ σου. 38 αὕτη ἐστὶν ἡ
all the understanding of thee. This is the

μεγάλη καὶ πρώτη ἐντολή. 39 δευτέρα
great and first commandment. [The] second

ὁμοία αὐτῇ· ἀγαπήσεις τὸν πλησίον σου
[is] like to it: Thou shalt love the neighbour of thee

ὡς σεαυτόν. 40 ἐν ταύταις ταῖς δυσὶν ἐντολαῖς
as thyself. In(on) these – two commandments

ὅλος ὁ νόμος κρέμαται καὶ οἱ προφῆται.
all the law hangs and the prophets.

41 Συνηγμένων δὲ τῶν Φαρισαίων
And having assembled the Pharisees[a]
=when the Pharisees were assembled

ἐπηρώτησεν αὐτοὺς ὁ Ἰησοῦς 42 λέγων· τι
questioned them – Jesus saying: What

ὑμῖν δοκεῖ περὶ τοῦ χριστοῦ; τίνος
to you seems it concerning the Christ? of whom

υἱός ἐστιν; λέγουσιν αὐτῷ· τοῦ Δαυίδ.
son is he? They say to him: – Of David.

43 λέγει αὐτοῖς· πῶς οὖν Δαυὶδ ἐν
He says to them: How then David in

πνεύματι καλεῖ αὐτὸν κύριον λέγων·
spirit calls him Lord saying:

44 εἶπεν κύριος τῷ κυρίῳ μου·
Said [the] LORD to the Lord of me:

κάθου ἐκ δεξιῶν μου ἕως ἂν θῶ τοὺς
Sit on [the] right of me until I put the

ἐχθρούς σου ὑποκάτω τῶν ποδῶν σου;
enemies of thee underneath the feet of thee?

45 εἰ οὖν Δαυὶδ καλεῖ αὐτὸν κύριον, πῶς
If then David calls him Lord, how

υἱὸς αὐτοῦ ἐστιν; 46 καὶ οὐδεὶς ἐδύνατο
son of him is he? And no one was able

ἀποκριθῆναι αὐτῷ λόγον οὐδὲ ἐτόλμησέν
to answer him a word nor dared

τις ἀπ' ἐκείνης τῆς ἡμέρας ἐπερωτῆσαι
anyone from that – day *to* question

αὐτὸν οὐκέτι.
him no(any) more.

Pharisees got together. [35]One of them, an expert in the law, tested him with this question: [36]"Teacher, which is the greatest commandment in the Law?"

[37]Jesus replied: " 'Love the Lord your God with all your heart and with all your soul and with all your mind.'[o] [38]This is the first and greatest commandment. [39]And the second is like it: 'Love your neighbor as yourself.'[p] [40]All the Law and the Prophets hang on these two commandments."

Whose Son Is the Christ?

[41]While the Pharisees were gathered together, Jesus asked them, [42]"What do you think about the Christ[q]? Whose son is he?"

"The son of David," they replied.

[43]He said to them, "How is it then that David, speaking by the Spirit, calls him 'Lord'? For he says,

[44]" 'The Lord said to my Lord:
"Sit at my right hand
until I put your enemies under your feet." '[r]

[45]If then David calls him 'Lord,' how can he be his son?" [46]No one could say a word in reply, and from that day on no one dared to ask him any more questions.

Chapter 23

Jesus Denounces Scribes and Pharisees

THEN Jesus said to the crowds and to his disciples, [2]"The scribes and the Pharisees sit on Moses' seat; [3]therefore, do whatever they teach you and follow it; but do not do as they do, for they do not practice

23 Τότε ὁ Ἰησοῦς ἐλάλησεν τοῖς ὄχλοις
Then – Jesus spoke to the crowds

καὶ τοῖς μαθηταῖς αὐτοῦ 2 λέγων· ἐπὶ
and to the disciples of him saying: On

τῆς Μωϋσέως καθέδρας ἐκάθισαν οἱ
the of Moses seat sat the

γραμματεῖς καὶ οἱ Φαρισαῖοι. 3 πάντα
scribes and the Pharisees. All things

οὖν ὅσα ἐὰν εἴπωσιν ὑμῖν ποιήσατε
therefore whatever they may tell you do ye

καὶ τηρεῖτε, κατὰ δὲ τὰ ἔργα αὐτῶν
and keep, but according to the works of them

Chapter 23

Seven Woes

THEN Jesus said to the crowds and to his disciples: [2]"The teachers of the law and the Pharisees sit in Moses' seat. [3]So you must obey them and do everything they tell you. But do not do what they do, for

[j] Or *Christ*
[k] Gk *in spirit*

[o]37 Deut. 6:5
[p]39 Lev. 19:18
[q]42 Or *Messiah*
[r]44 Psalm 110:1

what they teach. 4They tie
up heavy burdens, hard to
bear,[l] and lay them on the
shoulders of others; but
they themselves are unwilling to lift a finger to move
them. 5They do all their
deeds to be seen by others;
for they make their phylacteries broad and their
fringes long. 6They love to
have the place of honor at
banquets and the best seats
in the synagogues, 7and to
be greeted with respect in
the marketplaces, and to
have people call them rabbi. 8But you are not to be
called rabbi, for you have
one teacher, and you are all
students.[m] 9And call no
one your father on earth,
for you have one Father—
the one in heaven. 10Nor
are you to be called instruc-
tors, for you have one instructor, the Messiah.[n]
11The greatest among you
will be your servant. 12All
who exalt themselves will
be humbled, and all who
humble themselves will be
exalted.
13 "But woe to you,
scribes and Pharisees, hypocrites! For you lock people out of the kingdom of
heaven. For you do not go
in yourselves, and when
others are going in, you
stop them.[o] 15Woe to you,
scribes and Pharisees, hypocrites! For you cross sea
and land to make a single
convert, and you make the
new convert twice as much
a child of hell[p] as yourselves.
16 "Woe to you, blind

[l] Other ancient authorities lack *hard to bear*
[m] Gk *brothers*
[n] Or *the Christ*
[o] Other authorities add here (or after verse 12) verse 14, *Woe to you, scribes and Pharisees, hypocrites! For you devour widows' houses and for the sake of appearance you make long prayers; therefore you will receive the greater condemnation*
[p] Gk *Gehenna*

μὴ ποιεῖτε· λέγουσιν γὰρ καὶ οὐ ποιοῦσιν.
do ye not; for they say and do not.
4 δεσμεύουσιν δὲ φορτία βαρέα καὶ
And they bind burdens heavy and
ἐπιτιθέασιν ἐπὶ τοὺς ὤμους τῶν ἀνθρώπων,
put *on* on the shoulders – of men,
αὐτοὶ δὲ τῷ δακτύλῳ αὐτῶν οὐ
but they with the finger of them not
θέλουσιν κινῆσαι αὐτά. 5 πάντα δὲ
are willing to move them. But all
τὰ ἔργα αὐτῶν ποιοῦσιν πρὸς τὸ θεαθῆναι
the works of them they do *for* – to be seen
τοῖς ἀνθρώποις· πλατύνουσιν γὰρ τὰ
– by men; for they broaden the
φυλακτήρια αὐτῶν καὶ μεγαλύνουσιν τὰ
phylacteries of them and enlarge the
κράσπεδα, 6 φιλοῦσιν δὲ τὴν πρωτο-
fringes, and they like the chief
κλισίαν ἐν τοῖς δείπνοις καὶ τὰς πρωτο-
place in the suppers and the chief
καθεδρίας ἐν ταῖς συναγωγαῖς 7 καὶ τοὺς
seats in the synagogues . and the
ἀσπασμοὺς ἐν ταῖς ἀγοραῖς καὶ
greetings in the marketplaces and
καλεῖσθαι ὑπὸ τῶν ἀνθρώπων ῥαββί.
to be called by – men rabbi.
8 ὑμεῖς δὲ μὴ κληθῆτε ῥαββί· εἷς γάρ
But ye be not called rabbi; for one
ἐστιν ὑμῶν ὁ διδάσκαλος, πάντες δὲ ὑμεῖς
is of you the teacher, and all ye
ἀδελφοί ἐστε. 9 καὶ πατέρα μὴ καλέσητε
brothers are. And father call ye not
ὑμῶν ἐπὶ τῆς γῆς· εἷς γάρ ἐστιν
of you on the earth; for one is
ὑμῶν ὁ πατὴρ ὁ οὐράνιος. 10 μηδὲ
of you the Father – heavenly. Neither
κληθῆτε καθηγηταί, ὅτι καθηγητὴς
be ye called leaders, because leader
ὑμῶν ἐστιν εἷς ὁ Χριστός. 11 ὁ δὲ
of you is one the Christ. And the
μείζων ὑμῶν ἔσται ὑμῶν διάκονος.
greater of you shall be of you servant.
12 Ὅστις δὲ ὑψώσει ἑαυτὸν ταπεινωθήσεται,
And [he] who will exalt himself shall be humbled,
καὶ ὅστις ταπεινώσει ἑαυτὸν ὑψωθήσεται.
and [he] who will humble himself shall be exalted.
13 Οὐαὶ δὲ ὑμῖν, γραμματεῖς καὶ Φαρισαῖοι
But woe to you, scribes and Pharisees
ὑποκριταί, ὅτι κλείετε τὴν βασιλείαν
hypocrites, because ye shut the kingdom
τῶν οὐρανῶν ἔμπροσθεν τῶν ἀνθρώπων
of the heavens before – men;
ὑμεῖς γὰρ οὐκ εἰσέρχεσθε, οὐδὲ τοὺς
for ye do not enter, nor the [ones]
εἰσερχομένους ἀφίετε εἰσελθεῖν.‡ 15 Οὐαὶ
entering do ye allow to enter. Woe
ὑμῖν, γραμματεῖς καὶ Φαρισαῖοι ὑποκριταί,
to you, scribes and Pharisees hypocrites,
ὅτι περιάγετε τὴν θάλασσαν καὶ τὴν
because ye go about the sea and the
ξηρὰν ποιῆσαι ἕνα προσήλυτον, καὶ ὅταν
dry [land] to make one proselyte, and when
γένηται, ποιεῖτε αὐτὸν υἱὸν γεέννης διπλό-
he becomes, ye make him a son of gehenna twofold
τερον ὑμῶν. 16 Οὐαὶ ὑμῖν, ὁδηγοὶ τυφλοὶ
more [than] you. Woe to you, leaders blind

they do not practice what
they preach. 4They tie up
heavy loads and put them
on men's shoulders, but
they themselves are not
willing to lift a finger to
move them.
5"Everything they do is
done for men to see: They
make their phylacteries[s]
wide and the tassels on
their garments long; 6they
love the place of honor at
banquets and the most im-
portant seats in the synagogues; 7they love to be
greeted in the marketplaces
and to have men call them
'Rabbi.'
8"But you are not to be
called 'Rabbi,' for you
have only one Master and
you are all brothers. 9And
do not call anyone on earth
'father,' for you have one
Father, and he is in heaven.
10Nor are you to be called
'teacher,' for you have one
Teacher, the Christ.[t]
11The greatest among you
will be your servant. 12For
whoever exalts himself will
be humbled, and whoever
humbles himself will be exalted.
13"Woe to you, teachers
of the law and Pharisees,
you hypocrites! You shut
the kingdom of heaven in
men's faces. You your-
selves do not enter, nor will
you let those enter who are
trying to.[u]
15"Woe to you, teachers
of the law and Pharisees,
you hypocrites! You travel
over land and sea to win a
single convert, and when
he becomes one, you make
him twice as much a son of
hell as you are.
16"Woe to you, blind

[s] 5 That is, boxes containing Scripture verses, worn on forehead and arm
[t] 10 Or *Messiah*
[u] 13 Some manuscripts *to.* 14*Woe to you, teachers of the law and Pharisees, you hypocrites! You devour widows' houses and for a show make lengthy prayers. Therefore you will be punished more severely.*

guides, who say, 'Whoever swears by the sanctuary is bound by nothing, but whoever swears by the gold of the sanctuary is bound by the oath.' 17 You blind fools! For which is greater, the gold or the sanctuary that has made the gold sacred? 18 And you say, 'Whoever swears by the altar is bound by nothing, but whoever swears by the gift that is on the altar is bound by the oath.' 19 How blind you are! For which is greater, the gift or the altar that makes the gift sacred? 20 So whoever swears by the altar, swears by it and by everything on it; 21 and whoever swears by the sanctuary, swears by it and by the one who dwells in it; 22 and whoever swears by heaven, swears by the throne of God and by the one who is seated upon it.

23 "Woe to you, scribes and Pharisees, hypocrites! For you tithe mint, dill, and cummin, and have neglected the weightier matters of the law: justice and mercy and faith. It is these you ought to have practiced without neglecting the others. 24 You blind guides! You strain out a gnat but swallow a camel!

25 "Woe to you, scribes and Pharisees, hypocrites! For you clean the outside of the cup and of the plate, but inside they are full of greed and self-indulgence. 26 You blind Pharisee! First clean the inside of the cup,[q] so that the outside also may become clean.

27 "Woe to you, scribes and Pharisees, hypocrites! For you are like whitewashed tombs, which on

οἱ λέγοντες· ὃς ἂν ὀμόσῃ ἐν τῷ ναῷ,
the [ones] saying: Whoever swears by the shrine,
οὐδέν ἐστιν· ὃς δ' ἂν ὀμόσῃ ἐν τῷ χρυσῷ
nothing it is; but whoever swears by the gold
τοῦ ναοῦ, ὀφείλει. **17** μωροὶ καὶ τυφλοί,
of the shrine, he owes. Fools and blind,
τίς γὰρ μείζων ἐστιν, ὁ χρυσὸς ἢ ὁ ναὸς
for which greater is, the gold or the shrine
ὁ ἁγιάσας τὸν χρυσόν; **18** καί· ὃς ἂν
– sanctifying the gold? And: whoever
ὀμόσῃ ἐν τῷ θυσιαστηρίῳ, οὐδέν ἐστιν·
swears by the altar, nothing it is;
ὃς δ' ἂν ὀμόσῃ ἐν τῷ δώρῳ τῷ ἐπάνω
but whoever swears by the gift – upon
αὐτοῦ, ὀφείλει. **19** τυφλοί, τί γὰρ μεῖζον,
it, he owes. Blind, for which [is] greater,
τὸ δῶρον ἢ τὸ θυσιαστήριον τὸ
the gift or the altar –
ἁγιάζον τὸ δῶρον; **20** ὁ οὖν ὀμόσας
sanctifying the gift? Therefore the [one] swearing
ἐν τῷ θυσιαστηρίῳ ὀμνύει ἐν αὐτῷ καὶ
by the altar swears by it and
ἐν πᾶσι τοῖς ἐπάνω αὐτοῦ· **21** καὶ ὁ
by all the things upon it; and the [one]
ὀμόσας ἐν τῷ ναῷ ὀμνύει ἐν αὐτῷ
swearing by the shrine swears by it
καὶ ἐν τῷ κατοικοῦντι αὐτόν· **22** καὶ
and by the [one] inhabiting it; and
ὁ ὀμόσας ἐν τῷ οὐρανῷ ὀμνύει ἐν τῷ
the [one] swearing by *the* heaven swears by the
θρόνῳ τοῦ θεοῦ καὶ ἐν τῷ καθημένῳ
throne – of God and by the [one] sitting
ἐπάνω αὐτοῦ. **23** Οὐαὶ ὑμῖν, γραμματεῖς
upon it. Woe to you, scribes
καὶ Φαρισαῖοι ὑποκριταί, ὅτι ἀποδεκατοῦτε
and Pharisees hypocrites, because ye tithe
τὸ ἡδύοσμον καὶ τὸ ἄνηθον καὶ τὸ
the mint and the dill and the
κύμινον, καὶ ἀφήκατε τὰ βαρύτερα
cummin, and ye [have] left the heavier things
τοῦ νόμου, τὴν κρίσιν καὶ τὸ ἔλεος
of the law, – judgment and – mercy
καὶ τὴν πίστιν· ταῦτα δὲ ἔδει ποιῆσαι
and – faith; but these things it behoved to do
κἀκεῖνα μὴ ἀφεῖναι. **24** ὁδηγοὶ τυφλοί,
and those not to leave. Leaders blind,
οἱ διϋλίζοντες τὸν κώνωπα, τὴν δὲ
the [ones] straining the gnat, but ^{2}the
κάμηλον καταπίνοντες. **25** Οὐαὶ ὑμῖν,
^{3}camel ^{1}swallowing. Woe to you,
γραμματεῖς καὶ Φαρισαῖοι ὑποκριταί, ὅτι
scribes and Pharisees hypocrites, because
καθαρίζετε τὸ ἔξωθεν τοῦ ποτηρίου καὶ
ye cleanse the outside of the cup and
τῆς παροψίδος, ἔσωθεν δὲ γέμουσιν ἐξ
the dish, but within they are full of
ἁρπαγῆς καὶ ἀκρασίας. **26** Φαρισαῖε τυφλέ,
robbery and intemperance. Pharisee blind,
καθάρισον πρῶτον τὸ ἐντὸς τοῦ ποτηρίου
cleanse thou first the inside of the cup
ἵνα γένηται καὶ τὸ ἐκτὸς αὐτοῦ καθαρόν.
that may be also the outside of it clean.
27 Οὐαὶ ὑμῖν, γραμματεῖς καὶ Φαρισαῖοι
Woe to you, scribes and Pharisees
ὑποκριταί, ὅτι παρομοιάζετε τάφοις κεκονια-
hypocrites, because ye resemble graves *having been*

guides! You say, 'If anyone swears by the temple, it means nothing; but if anyone swears by the gold of the temple, he is bound by his oath.' 17 You blind fools! Which is greater: the gold, or the temple that makes the gold sacred? 18 You also say, 'If anyone swears by the altar, it means nothing; but if anyone swears by the gift on it, he is bound by his oath.' 19 You blind men! Which is greater: the gift, or the altar that makes the gift sacred? 20 Therefore, he who swears by the altar swears by it and by everything on it. 21 And he who swears by the temple swears by it and by the one who dwells in it. 22 And he who swears by heaven swears by God's throne and by the one who sits on it.

23 "Woe to you, teachers of the law and Pharisees, you hypocrites! You give a tenth of your spices—mint, dill and cummin. But you have neglected the more important matters of the law—justice, mercy and faithfulness. You should have practiced the latter, without neglecting the former. 24 You blind guides! You strain out a gnat but swallow a camel.

25 "Woe to you, teachers of the law and Pharisees, you hypocrites! You clean the outside of the cup and dish, but inside they are full of greed and self-indulgence. 26 Blind Pharisee! First clean the inside of the cup and dish, and then the outside also will be clean.

27 "Woe to you, teachers of the law and Pharisees, you hypocrites! You are like whitewashed tombs,

[q] Other ancient authorities add *and of the plate*

‡ **Ver. 14 omitted by Nestle;** *cf.* **NIV footnote.**

the outside look beautiful,
but inside they are full of
the bones of the dead and of
all kinds of filth. 28So you
also on the outside look
righteous to others, but inside you are full of hypocrisy and lawlessness.
29 "Woe to you, scribes
and Pharisees, hypocrites!
For you build the tombs of
the prophets and decorate
the graves of the righteous,
30and you say, 'If we had
lived in the days of our ancestors, we would not have
taken part with them in
shedding the blood of the
prophets.' 31Thus you testify against yourselves that
you are descendants of
those who murdered the
prophets. 32Fill up, then,
the measure of your ancestors. 33You snakes, you
brood of vipers! How can
you escape being sen-
tenced to hell?[r] 34There-
fore I send you prophets,
sages, and scribes, some of
whom you will kill and crucify, and some you will flog
in your synagogues and
pursue from town to town,
35so that upon you may
come all the righteous
blood shed on earth, from
the blood of righteous Abel
to the blood of Zechariah
son of Barachiah, whom
you murdered between the
sanctuary and the altar.
36Truly I tell you, all this
will come upon this generation.

The Lament over Jerusalem

37 "Jerusalem, Jerusa-
lem, the city that kills the
prophets and stones those
who are sent to it! How often have I desired to gather
your children together as a

[r] Gk *Gehenna*

μένοις, οἵτινες ἔξωθεν μὲν φαίνονται
whitewashed, who(which) outwardly indeed appear

ὡραῖοι, ἔσωθεν δὲ γέμουσιν ὀστέων
beautiful, but within they are full of bones

νεκρῶν καὶ πάσης ἀκαθαρσίας. 28 οὕτως
of dead men and of all uncleanness. Thus

καὶ ὑμεῖς ἔξωθεν μὲν φαίνεσθε τοῖς
also ye outwardly indeed appear –

ἀνθρώποις δίκαιοι, ἔσωθεν δέ ἐστε μεστοὶ
to men righteous, but within ye are full

ὑποκρίσεως καὶ ἀνομίας. 29 Οὐαὶ ὑμῖν,
of hypocrisy and of lawlessness. Woe to you

γραμματεῖς καὶ Φαρισαῖοι ὑποκριταί,
scribes and Pharisees hypocrites,

ὅτι οἰκοδομεῖτε τοὺς τάφους τῶν προφητῶν
because ye build the graves of the prophets

καὶ κοσμεῖτε τὰ μνημεῖα τῶν δικαίων,
and adorn the monuments of the righteous,

30 καὶ λέγετε· εἰ ἤμεθα ἐν ταῖς ἡμέραις
and say: If we were in the days

τῶν πατέρων ἡμῶν, οὐκ ἂν ἤμεθα
of the fathers of us, we would not have been

αὐτῶν κοινωνοὶ ἐν τῷ αἵματι τῶν προ-
of them partakers in the blood of the pro-

φητῶν. 31 ὥστε μαρτυρεῖτε ἑαυτοῖς ὅτι
phets. So ye witness to [your]selves that

υἱοί ἐστε τῶν φονευσάντων τοὺς προφήτας.
sons ye are of the [ones] having killed the prophets.

32 καὶ ὑμεῖς πληρώσατε τὸ μέτρον τῶν
And ²ye ¹fulfil the measure of the

πατέρων ὑμῶν. 33 ὄφεις, γεννήματα ἐχιδνῶν,
fathers of you. Serpents, offspring of vipers,

πῶς φύγητε ἀπὸ τῆς κρίσεως τῆς γεέννης;
how escape ye from the judgment – of gehenna?

34 διὰ τοῦτο ἰδοὺ ἐγὼ ἀποστέλλω πρὸς
Therefore behold I send to

ὑμᾶς προφήτας καὶ σοφοὺς καὶ γραμ-
you prophets and wise men and scribes;

ματεῖς· ἐξ αὐτῶν ἀποκτενεῖτε καὶ
of them ye will kill and

σταυρώσετε, καὶ ἐξ αὐτῶν μαστιγώσετε
will crucify, and of them ye will scourge

ἐν ταῖς συναγωγαῖς ὑμῶν καὶ διώξετε
in the synagogues of you and will persecute

ἀπὸ πόλεως εἰς πόλιν· 35 ὅπως ἔλθῃ
from city to city; so comes

ἐφ' ὑμᾶς πᾶν αἷμα δίκαιον ἐκχυννόμενον
on you all blood righteous being shed

ἐπὶ τῆς γῆς ἀπὸ τοῦ αἵματος Ἅβελ τοῦ
on the earth from the blood of Abel the

δικαίου ἕως τοῦ αἵματος Ζαχαρίου υἱοῦ
righteous until the blood of Zacharias son

Βαραχίου, ὃν ἐφονεύσατε μεταξὺ τοῦ ναοῦ
Barachias, whom ye murdered between the shrine

καὶ τοῦ θυσιαστηρίου. 36 ἀμὴν λέγω
and the altar. Truly I tell

ὑμῖν, ἥξει ταῦτα πάντα ἐπὶ τὴν
you, will come all these things on –

γενεὰν ταύτην. 37 Ἰερουσαλὴμ Ἰερουσαλήμ,
generation this. Jerusalem Jerusalem,

ἡ ἀποκτείνουσα τοὺς προφήτας καὶ
the [one] killing the prophets and

λιθοβολοῦσα τοὺς ἀπεσταλμένους πρὸς αὐτήν,
stoning the [ones] sent to her,

ποσάκις ἠθέλησα ἐπισυναγαγεῖν τὰ τέκνα
how often I wished to gather the children

which look beautiful on the
outside but on the inside
are full of dead men's
bones and everything un-
clean. 28In the same way,
on the outside you appear
to people as righteous but
on the inside you are full of
hypocrisy and wickedness.
29"Woe to you, teachers
of the law and Pharisees,
you hypocrites! You build
tombs for the prophets and
decorate the graves of the
righteous. 30And you say,
'If we had lived in the days
of our forefathers, we
would not have taken part
with them in shedding the
blood of the prophets.' 31So
you testify against your-
selves that you are the descendants of those who
murdered the prophets.
32Fill up, then, the measure
of the sin of your forefathers!
33"You snakes! You
brood of vipers! How will
you escape being con-
demned to hell? 34There-
fore I am sending you
prophets and wise men and
teachers. Some of them
you will kill and crucify;
others you will flog in your
synagogues and pursue
from town to town. 35And
so upon you will come all
the righteous blood that has
been shed on earth, from
the blood of righteous Abel
to the blood of Zechariah
son of Berekiah, whom you
murdered between the tem-
ple and the altar. 36I tell you
the truth, all this will come
upon this generation.
37"O Jerusalem, Jerusa-
lem, you who kill the
prophets and stone those
sent to you, how often I
have longed to gather your

hen gathers her brood un-
der her wings, and you
were not willing! 38 See,
your house is left to you,
desolate.[s] 39 For I tell you,
you will not see me again
until you say, 'Blessed is
the one who comes in the
name of the Lord.' "

Chapter 24

The Destruction of the Temple Foretold

AS Jesus came out of the
temple and was going
away, his disciples came to
point out to him the buildings of the temple. 2 Then
he asked them, "You see all
these, do you not? Truly I
tell you, not one stone will
be left here upon another;
all will be thrown down."

Signs of the End of the Age

3 When he was sitting
on the Mount of Olives, the
disciples came to him privately, saying, "Tell us,
when will this be, and what
will be the sign of your
coming and of the end of
the age?" 4 Jesus answered
them, "Beware that no one
leads you astray. 5 For
many will come in my
name, saying, 'I am the
Messiah!'[t] and they will
lead many astray. 6 And
you will hear of wars and
rumors of wars; see that
you are not alarmed; for
this must take place, but
the end is not yet. 7 For nation will rise against nation,
and kingdom against king-
dom, and there will be famines[u] and earthquakes in
various places: 8 all this is
but the beginning of the
birthpangs.

Persecutions Foretold

9 "Then they will hand
you over to be tortured and
will put you to death, and

[s] Other ancient authorities lack *desolate*
[t] Or *the Christ*
[u] Other ancient authorities add *and pestilences*

σου, ὃν τρόπον ὄρνις ἐπισυνάγει τὰ
of thee, as a bird gathers the
νοσσία [αὐτῆς] ὑπὸ τὰς πτέρυγας, καὶ
young of her under the(her) wings, and
οὐκ ἠθελήσατε. 38 ἰδοὺ ἀφίεται ὑμῖν ὁ
ye wished not. Behold is left to you the
οἶκος ὑμῶν. 39 λέγω γὰρ ὑμῖν, οὐ μή
house of you. For I tell you, by no means
με ἴδητε ἀπ' ἄρτι ἕως ἂν εἴπητε·
me ye see from now until ye say:
εὐλογημένος ὁ ἐρχόμενος ἐν ὀνόματι
Blessed the [one] coming in [the] name
κυρίου.
of [the] Lord.

24 Καὶ ἐξελθὼν ὁ Ἰησοῦς ἀπὸ τοῦ
And going forth – Jesus from the
ἱεροῦ ἐπορεύετο, καὶ προσῆλθον οἱ μαθηταὶ
temple went, and [4]approached [1]the [2]disciples
αὐτοῦ ἐπιδεῖξαι αὐτῷ τὰς οἰκοδομὰς
[3]of him to show him the buildings
τοῦ ἱεροῦ. 2 ὁ δὲ ἀποκριθεὶς εἶπεν
of the temple. And he answering said
αὐτοῖς· οὐ βλέπετε ταῦτα πάντα; ἀμὴν
to them: See ye not all these things? Truly
λέγω ὑμῖν, οὐ μὴ ἀφεθῇ ὧδε λίθος ἐπὶ
I tell you, by no means will be left here stone on
λίθον ὃς οὐ καταλυθήσεται. 3 Καθημένου
stone which shall not be overthrown. sitting
δὲ αὐτοῦ ἐπὶ τοῦ ὄρους τῶν ἐλαιῶν
and him[a] on the mount of the olives
= And as he sat
προσῆλθον αὐτῷ οἱ μαθηταὶ κατ' ἰδίαν
approached to him the disciples privately
λέγοντες· εἰπὲ ἡμῖν, πότε ταῦτα ἔσται,
saying: Tell us, when these things will be,
καὶ τί τὸ σημεῖον τῆς σῆς παρουσίας
and what the sign – of thy presence
καὶ συντελείας τοῦ αἰῶνος; 4 καὶ ἀπο-
and of [the] completion of the age? And answer-
κριθεὶς ὁ Ἰησοῦς εἶπεν αὐτοῖς· βλέπετε
ing – Jesus said to them: See ye
μή τις ὑμᾶς πλανήσῃ. 5 πολλοὶ γὰρ
not(lest) anyone [2]you [1]cause [3]to err. For many
ἐλεύσονται ἐπὶ τῷ ὀνόματί μου λέγοντες·
will come on(in) the name of me saying:
ἐγώ εἰμι ὁ χριστός, καὶ πολλοὺς πλανή-
I am the Christ, and [2]many [1]will cause
σουσιν. 6 μελλήσετε δὲ ἀκούειν πολέ-
[3]to err. But ye will be about to hear [of]
μους καὶ ἀκοὰς πολέμων· ὁρᾶτε μὴ
wars and rumours of wars; see not
θροεῖθε· δεῖ γὰρ γενέσθαι, ἀλλ'
ye are disturbed; for it behoves to happen, but
οὔπω ἐστὶν τὸ τέλος. 7 ἐγερθήσεται γὰρ
not yet is the end. For will be raised
ἔθνος ἐπὶ ἔθνος καὶ βασιλεία ἐπὶ βασιλείαν,
nation against nation and kingdom against kingdom,
καὶ ἔσονται λιμοὶ καὶ σεισμοὶ
and there will be famines and earthquakes
κατὰ τόπους· 8 πάντα δὲ ταῦτα ἀρχὴ
throughout places; but all these things [are] beginning
ὠδίνων. 9 τότε παραδώσουσιν ὑμᾶς
of birth-pangs. Then they will deliver you
εἰς θλῖψιν καὶ ἀποκτενοῦσιν ὑμᾶς,
to affliction and will kill you,

children together, as a hen
gathers her chicks under
her wings, but you were not
willing. 38 Look, your house
is left to you desolate.
39 For I tell you, you will not
see me again until you say,
'Blessed is he who comes
in the name of the Lord.'[v] "

Chapter 24

Signs of the End of the Age

JESUS left the temple
and was walking away
when his disciples came up
to him to call his attention
to its buildings. 2 "Do you
see all these things?" he
asked. "I tell you the truth,
not one stone here will be
left on another; every one
will be thrown down."
3 As Jesus was sitting on
the Mount of Olives, the
disciples came to him privately. "Tell us," they
said, "when will this happen, and what will be the
sign of your coming and of
the end of the age?"
4 Jesus answered: "Watch
out that no one deceives
you. 5 For many will come
in my name, claiming, 'I am
the Christ,[w]' and will deceive many. 6 You will hear
of wars and rumors of
wars, but see to it that you
are not alarmed. Such
things must happen, but the
end is still to come. 7 Nation
will rise against nation, and
kingdom against kingdom.
There will be famines and
earthquakes in various
places. 8 All these are the
beginning of birth pains.
9 "Then you will be hand-
ed over to be persecuted
and put to death, and you

[v] 39 Psalm 118:26
[w] 5 Or *Messiah*: also in verse 23

you will be hated by all nations because of my name.
10 Then many will fall
away,[v] and they will betray one another and hate
one another. 11 And many
false prophets will arise
and lead many astray.
12 And because of the in-
crease of lawlessness, the
love of many will grow
cold. 13 But the one who endures to the end will be
saved. 14 And this good
news[w] of the kingdom will
be proclaimed throughout
the world, as a testimony to
all the nations; and then the
end will come.

The Desolating Sacrilege

15 "So when you see the
desolating sacrilege standing in the holy place, as was
spoken of by the prophet
Daniel (let the reader understand), 16 then those in
Judea must flee to the
mountains; 17 the one on
the housetop must not go
down to take what is in the
house; 18 the one in the field
must not turn back to get a
coat. 19 Woe to those who
are pregnant and to those
who are nursing infants in
those days! 20 Pray that
your flight may not be in
winter or on a sabbath.
21 For at that time there will
be great suffering, such as
has not been from the be-
ginning of the world until
now, no, and never will be.
22 And if those days had not
been cut short, no one
would be saved; but for the
sake of the elect those days
will be cut short. 23 Then if
anyone says to you, 'Look!
Here is the Messiah!'[x] or

καὶ ἔσεσθε μισούμενοι ὑπὸ πάντων
and ye will be *being* hated by all

τῶν ἐθνῶν διὰ τὸ ὄνομά μου.
the nations because of the name of me.

10 καὶ τότε σκανδαλισθήσονται πολλοὶ καὶ
And then will be offended many and

ἀλλήλους παραδώσουσιν καὶ μισήσουσιν
one another will deliver and they will hate

ἀλλήλους· 11 καὶ πολλοὶ ψευδοπροφῆται
one another; and many false prophets

ἐγερθήσονται καὶ πλανήσουσιν πολλούς·
will be raised and will cause to err many;

12 καὶ διὰ τὸ πληθυνθῆναι τὴν
and because of – to be increased the

ἀνομίαν ψυγήσεται ἡ ἀγάπη τῶν
lawlessness will grow cold the love of the

πολλῶν. 13 ὁ δὲ ὑπομείνας εἰς τέλος,
many. But the [one] enduring to [the] end,

οὗτος σωθήσεται. 14 καὶ κηρυχθήσεται
this will be saved. And will be proclaimed

τοῦτο τὸ εὐαγγέλιον τῆς βασιλείας
this – gospel of the kingdom

ἐν ὅλῃ τῇ οἰκουμένῃ εἰς μαρτύριον
in all the inhabited earth for a testimony

πᾶσιν τοῖς ἔθνεσιν, καὶ τότε ἥξει τὸ
to all the nations, and then will come the

τέλος. 15 Ὅταν οὖν ἴδητε τὸ
end. When therefore ye see the

βδέλυγμα τῆς ἐρημώσεως τὸ ῥηθὲν διὰ
abomination – of desolation – spoken through

Δανιὴλ τοῦ προφήτου ἑστὸς ἐν τόπῳ
Daniel the prophet stand in place

ἁγίῳ, ὁ ἀναγινώσκων νοείτω,
holy, the [one] reading let him understand,

16 τότε οἱ ἐν τῇ Ἰουδαίᾳ φευγέτωσαν
then the [ones] in – Judæa let them flee

εἰς τὰ ὄρη, 17 ὁ ἐπὶ τοῦ δώματος μὴ
to the mountains, the [one] on the housetop let him

καταβάτω ἆραι τὰ ἐκ τῆς οἰκίας αὐτοῦ,
not come down to take the things out of the house of him,

18 καὶ ὁ ἐν τῷ ἀγρῷ μὴ ἐπιστρεψάτω
and the [one] in the field let him not turn back

ὀπίσω ἆραι τὸ ἱμάτιον αὐτοῦ. 19 οὐαὶ
behind to take the garment of him. woe

δὲ ταῖς ἐν γαστρὶ ἐχούσαις καὶ ταῖς
And to the women in womb having and to the [ones]
=the pregnant women

θηλαζούσαις ἐν ἐκείναις ταῖς ἡμέραις.
giving suck in those – days.

20 προσεύχεσθε δὲ ἵνα μὴ γένηται ἡ
And pray ye lest happen the

φυγὴ ὑμῶν χειμῶνος μηδὲ σαββάτῳ·
flight of you of(in) winter nor on a sabbath;

21 ἔσται γὰρ τότε θλῖψις μεγάλη, οἵα οὐ
for will be then affliction great, such as not

γέγονεν ἀπ' ἀρχῆς κόσμου ἕως
has happened from [the] beginning of [the] world until

τοῦ νῦν οὐδ' οὐ μὴ γένηται. 22 καὶ
– now neither by no means may happen. And

εἰ μὴ ἐκολοβώθησαν αἱ ἡμέραι ἐκεῖναι,
except were cut short – days those,

οὐκ ἂν ἐσώθη πᾶσα σάρξ· διὰ δὲ τοὺς
not – was saved all flesh; but on account of the
=no flesh would be saved;

ἐκλεκτοὺς κολοβωθήσονται αἱ ἡμέραι ἐκεῖναι.
chosen will be cut short – days those.

23 τότε ἐάν τις ὑμῖν εἴπῃ· ἰδοὺ ὧδε
Then if anyone to you says: Behold here

will be hated by all nations
because of me. 10 At that
time many will turn away
from the faith and will betray and hate each other,
11 and many false prophets
will appear and deceive
many people. 12 Because of
the increase of wickedness,
the love of most will grow
cold, 13 but he who stands
firm to the end will be
saved. 14 And this gospel of
the kingdom will be
preached in the whole
world as a testimony to all
nations, and then the end
will come.
15 "So when you see
standing in the holy place
'the abomination that
causes desolation,'[x] spoken of through the prophet
Daniel—let the reader un-
derstand—16 then let those
who are in Judea flee to the
mountains. 17 Let no one on
the roof of his house go
down to take anything out
of the house. 18 Let no one
in the field go back to get
his cloak. 19 How dreadful it
will be in those days for
pregnant women and nurs-
ing mothers! 20 Pray that
your flight will not take
place in winter or on the
Sabbath. 21 For then there
will be great distress, un-
equaled from the beginning
of the world until now—
and never to be equaled
again. 22 If those days had
not been cut short, no one
would survive, but for the
sake of the elect those days
will be shortened. 23 At that
time if anyone says to you,
'Look, here is the Christ!'

[v] Or *stumble*
[w] Or *gospel*
[x] Or *the Christ*

[x] *15* Daniel 9:27; 11:31; 12:11

'There he is!'—do not be-
lieve it. 24 For false messi-
ahs[y] and false prophets
will appear and produce
great signs and omens, to
lead astray, if possible,
even the elect. 25 Take
note, I have told you be-
forehand. 26 So, if they say
to you, 'Look! He is in the
wilderness,' do not go out.
If they say, 'Look! He is in
the inner rooms,' do not believe it. 27 For as the lightning comes from the east
and flashes as far as the
west, so will be the coming
of the Son of Man. 28 Wherever the corpse is, there the
vultures will gather.

The Coming of the Son of Man

29 "Immediately after
the suffering of those days
the sun will be
darkened,
and the moon will
not give
its light;
the stars will fall from
heaven,
and the powers of
heaven will
be shaken.
30 Then the sign of the Son
of Man will appear in heav-
en, and then all the tribes of
the earth will mourn, and
they will see 'the Son of
Man coming on the clouds
of heaven' with power and
great glory. 31 And he will
send out his angels with a
loud trumpet call, and they
will gather his elect from
the four winds, from one
end of heaven to the other.

The Lesson of the Fig Tree

32 "From the fig tree
learn its lesson: as soon as
its branch becomes tender
and puts forth its leaves,
you know that summer is
near. 33 So also, when you

y Or *christs*

ὁ χριστός, ἤ· ὧδε, μὴ πιστεύσητε·
the Christ, or: Here, do not believe;
24 ἐγερθήσονται γὰρ ψευδόχριστοι καὶ
for will be raised false Christs and
ψευδοπροφῆται, καὶ δώσουσιν σημεῖα μεγάλα
false prophets, and they will give signs great
καὶ τέρατα, ὥστε πλανῆσαι, εἰ δυνατόν,
and marvels, so as to cause to err, if possible,
καὶ τοὺς ἐκλεκτούς. 25 ἰδοὺ προείρηκα
even the chosen. Behold I have before told
ὑμῖν. 26 ἐὰν οὖν εἴπωσιν ὑμῖν· ἰδοὺ
you. If therefore they say to you: Behold
ἐν τῇ ἐρήμῳ ἐστίν, μὴ ἐξέλθητε· ἰδοὺ
in the desert he is, go not ye forth; Behold
ἐν τοῖς ταμιείοις, μὴ πιστεύσητε·
in the private rooms, do not ye believe;
27 ὥσπερ γὰρ ἡ ἀστραπὴ ἐξέρχεται ἀπὸ
for as the lightning comes forth from
ἀνατολῶν καὶ φαίνεται ἕως δυσμῶν,
[the] east and shines unto [the] west,
οὕτως ἔσται ἡ παρουσία τοῦ υἱοῦ
so will be the presence of the Son
τοῦ ἀνθρώπου· 28 ὅπου ἐὰν ᾖ τὸ
– of man; wherever may be the
πτῶμα, ἐκεῖ συναχθήσονται οἱ ἀετοί.
carcase, there will be assembled the eagles.
29 Εὐθέως δὲ μετὰ τὴν θλῖψιν τῶν
And immediately after the affliction –
ἡμερῶν ἐκείνων ὁ ἥλιος σκοτισθήσεται,
days of those the sun will be darkened,
καὶ ἡ σελήνη οὐ δώσει τὸ φέγγος
and the moon will not give the light
αὐτῆς, καὶ οἱ ἀστέρες πεσοῦνται ἀπὸ τοῦ
of her, and the stars will fall from –
οὐρανοῦ, καὶ αἱ δυνάμεις τῶν οὐρανῶν
heaven, and the powers of *the* heavens
σαλευθήσονται. 30 καὶ τότε φανήσεται
will be shaken. And then will appear
τὸ σημεῖον τοῦ υἱοῦ τοῦ ἀνθρώπου ἐν
the sign of the Son – of man in
οὐρανῷ, καὶ τότε κόψονται πᾶσαι αἱ
heaven, and then will bewail all the
φυλαὶ τῆς γῆς καὶ ὄψονται τὸν υἱὸν
tribes of the land and they will see the Son
τοῦ ἀνθρώπου ἐρχόμενον ἐπὶ τῶν
– of man coming on the
νεφελῶν τοῦ οὐρανοῦ μετὰ δυνάμεως καὶ
clouds – of heaven with power and
δόξης πολλῆς· 31 καὶ ἀποστελεῖ τοὺς
glory much; and he will send the
ἀγγέλους αὐτοῦ μετὰ σάλπιγγος μεγάλης,
angels of him with trumpet a great,
καὶ ἐπισυνάξουσιν τοὺς ἐκλεκτοὺς αὐτοῦ
and they will assemble the chosen of him
ἐκ τῶν τεσσάρων ἀνέμων ἀπ' ἄκρων
out of the four winds from [the] extremities
οὐρανῶν ἕως [τῶν] ἄκρων αὐτῶν. 32 Ἀπὸ
of [the] heavens unto the extremities of them. from
δὲ τῆς συκῆς μάθετε τὴν παραβολήν·
Now the fig-tree learn ye the parable:
ὅταν ἤδη ὁ κλάδος αὐτῆς γένηται ἁπαλὸς
When now the branch of it becomes tender
καὶ τὰ φύλλα ἐκφύῃ, γινώσκετε ὅτι
and the leaves it puts forth, ye know that
ἐγγὺς τὸ θέρος· 33 οὕτως καὶ ὑμεῖς
near [is] the summer; so also ye

or, 'There he is!' do not believe it. 24 For false Christs
and false prophets will appear and perform great
signs and miracles to de-
ceive even the elect—if
that were possible. 25 See, I
have told you ahead of
time.
26 "So if anyone tells you,
'There he is, out in the desert,' do not go out; or,
'Here he is, in the inner
rooms,' do not believe it.
27 For as lightning that
comes from the east is visible even in the west, so will
be the coming of the Son of
Man. 28 Wherever there is a
carcass, there the vultures
will gather.
29 "Immediately after the
distress of those days

" 'the sun will be
darkened,
and the moon will not
give its light;
the stars will fall from
the sky,
and the heavenly
bodies will be
shaken.'[y]

30 "At that time the sign of
the Son of Man will appear
in the sky, and all the nations of the earth will
mourn. They will see the
Son of Man coming on the
clouds of the sky, with
power and great glory.
31 And he will send his angels with a loud trumpet
call, and they will gather
his elect from the four
winds, from one end of the
heavens to the other.
32 "Now learn this lesson
from the fig tree: As soon as
its twigs get tender and its
leaves come out, you know
that summer is near.
33 Even so, when you see all

y29 Isaiah 13:10; 34:4

see all these things, you know that he[z] is near, at the very gates. 34 Truly I tell you, this generation will not pass away until all these things have taken place. 35 Heaven and earth will pass away, but my words will not pass away.

The Necessity for Watchfulness

36 "But about that day and hour no one knows, neither the angels of heaven, nor the Son,[a] but only the Father. 37 For as the days of Noah were, so will be the coming of the Son of Man. 38 For as in those days before the flood they were eating and drinking, marrying and giving in marriage, until the day Noah entered the ark, 39 and they knew nothing until the flood came and swept them all away, so too will be the coming of the Son of Man. 40 Then two will be in the field; one will be taken and one will be left. 41 Two women will be grinding meal together; one will be taken and one will be left. 42 Keep awake therefore, for you do not know on what day[b] your Lord is coming. 43 But understand this: if the owner of the house had known in what part of the night the thief was coming, he would have stayed awake and would not have let his house be broken into. 44 Therefore you also must be ready, for the Son of Man is coming at an unexpected hour.

The Faithful or the Unfaithful Slave

45 "Who then is the faithful and wise slave, whom his master has put in charge of his household, to

[z] Or *it*
[a] Other ancient authorities lack *nor the Son*
[b] Other ancient authorities read *at what hour*

ὅταν ἴδητε πάντα ταῦτα, γινώσκετε ὅτι
when ye see all these things, know that
ἐγγύς ἐστιν ἐπὶ θύραις. **34** ἀμὴν λέγω
near it is on(at) [the] doors. Truly I tell
ὑμῖν ὅτι οὐ μὴ παρέλθῃ ἡ γενεὰ
you that by no means passes away – generation
αὕτη ἕως ἂν πάντα ταῦτα γένηται.
this until all these things happen*s*.
35 ὁ οὐρανὸς καὶ ἡ γῆ παρελεύσεται, οἱ
The heaven and the earth will pass away, [2]the
δὲ λόγοι μου οὐ μὴ παρέλθωσιν. **36** Περὶ
[1]but words of me by no means may pass away. concerning
δὲ τῆς ἡμέρας ἐκείνης καὶ ὥρας οὐδεὶς
But – day that and hour no one
οἶδεν, οὐδὲ οἱ ἄγγελοι τῶν οὐρανῶν
knows, neither the angels of *the* heaven*s*
οὐδὲ ὁ υἱός, εἰ μὴ ὁ πατὴρ μόνος.
nor the Son, except the Father only.
37 ὥσπερ γὰρ αἱ ἡμέραι τοῦ Νῶε, οὕτως
For as the days – of Noah, so
ἔσται ἡ παρουσία τοῦ υἱοῦ τοῦ ἀνθρώπου.
will be the presence of the Son – of man.
38 ὡς γὰρ ἦσαν ἐν ταῖς ἡμέραις
For as they were in – days
[ἐκείναις] ταῖς πρὸ τοῦ κατακλυσμοῦ
those the [ones] before the flood
τρώγοντες καὶ πίνοντες, γαμοῦντες καὶ
eating and drinking, marrying and
γαμίζοντες, ἄχρι ἧς ἡμέρας εἰσῆλθεν
being given in marriage, until which day entered
Νῶε εἰς τὴν κιβωτόν, **39** καὶ οὐκ ἔγνωσαν
Noah into the ark, and knew not
ἕως ἦλθεν ὁ κατακλυσμὸς καὶ ἦρεν
until came the flood and took
ἅπαντας, οὕτως ἔσται καὶ ἡ παρουσία
all, so will be also the presence
τοῦ υἱοῦ τοῦ ἀνθρώπου **40** τότε ἔσονται
of the Son – of man. Then will be
δύο ἐν τῷ ἀγρῷ, εἷς παραλαμβάνεται
two men in the field, one is taken
καὶ εἷς ἀφίεται· **41** δύο ἀλήθουσαι
and one is left; two women grinding
ἐν τῷ μύλῳ, μία παραλαμβάνεται καὶ
in(at) the mill, one is taken and
μία ἀφίεται. **42** γρηγορεῖτε οὖν, ὅτι
one is left. Watch ye therefore, because
οὐκ οἴδατε ποίᾳ ἡμέρᾳ ὁ κύριος
ye know not on what day the lord
ὑμῶν ἔρχεται. **43** Ἐκεῖνο δὲ γινώσκετε
of you is coming. And that know ye
ὅτι εἰ ᾔδει ὁ οἰκοδεσπότης ποίᾳ
that if knew the housemaster in what
φυλακῇ ὁ κλέπτης ἔρχεται, ἐγρηγόρησεν
watch the thief is coming, he would have
ἂν καὶ οὐκ ἂν εἴασεν διορυχθῆναι
watched and would not have allowed to be dug through
τὴν οἰκίαν αὐτοῦ. **44** διὰ τοῦτο καὶ
the house of him. Therefore also
ὑμεῖς γίνεσθε ἕτοιμοι, ὅτι ᾗ οὐ δοκεῖτε
ye be ready, because [1]in which [3]ye think not
ὥρᾳ ὁ υἱὸς τοῦ ἀνθρώπου ἔρχεται. **45** Τίς
[2]hour the Son – of man comes. Who
ἄρα ἐστὶν ὁ πιστὸς δοῦλος καὶ φρόνιμος
then is the faithful slave and prudent
ὃν κατέστησεν ὁ κύριος ἐπὶ τῆς οἰκετείας
whom appointed the lord over the household

these things, you know that it[z] is near, right at the door. 34 I tell you the truth, this generation[a] will certainly not pass away until all these things have happened. 35 Heaven and earth will pass away, but my words will never pass away.

The Day and Hour Unknown

36 "No one knows about that day or hour, not even the angels in heaven, nor the Son,[b] but only the Father. 37 As it was in the days of Noah, so it will be at the coming of the Son of Man. 38 For in the days before the flood, people were eating and drinking, marrying and giving in marriage, up to the day Noah entered the ark; 39 and they knew nothing about what would happen until the flood came and took them all away. That is how it will be at the coming of the Son of Man. 40 Two men will be in the field; one will be taken and the other left. 41 Two women will be grinding with a hand mill; one will be taken and the other left.

42 "Therefore keep watch, because you do not know on what day your Lord will come. 43 But understand this: If the owner of the house had known at what time of night the thief was coming, he would have kept watch and would not have let his house be broken into. 44 So you also must be ready, because the Son of Man will come at an hour when you do not expect him.

45 "Who then is the faithful and wise servant, whom the master has put in charge of the servants in his

[z] *33* Or *he*
[a] *34* Or *race*
[b] *36* Some manuscripts do not have *nor the Son*.

give the other slaves[c] their
allowance of food at the
proper time? 46 Blessed is
that slave whom his master
will find at work when he
arrives. 47 Truly I tell you,
he will put that one in
charge of all his posses-
sions. 48 But if that wicked
slave says to himself, 'My
master is delayed,' 49 and
he begins to beat his fellow
slaves, and eats and drinks
with drunkards, 50 the master of that slave will come
on a day when he does not
expect him and at an hour
that he does not know.
51 He will cut him in
pieces[d] and put him with
the hypocrites, where there
will be weeping and gnashing of teeth.

Chapter 25

The Parable of the Ten Bridesmaids

"THEN the kingdom
of heaven will be
like this. Ten bridesmaids[e]
took their lamps and went
to meet the bridegroom.[f]
2 Five of them were foolish,
and five were wise. 3 When
the foolish took their
lamps, they took no oil with
them; 4 but the wise took
flasks of oil with their
lamps. 5 As the bridegroom
was delayed, all of them became drowsy and slept.
6 But at midnight there was
a shout, 'Look! Here is the
bridegroom! Come out to
meet him.' 7 Then all those
bridesmaids[e] got up and

[c] Gk *to give them*
[d] Or *cut him off*
[e] Gk *virgins*
[f] Other ancient authorities add *and the bride*

αὐτοῦ τοῦ δοῦναι αὐτοῖς τὴν τροφὴν ἐν
of him – to give[d] to them the food in

καιρῷ; 46 μακάριος ὁ δοῦλος ἐκεῖνος ὃν
season? blessed [is] – slave that whom

ἐλθὼν ὁ κύριος αὐτοῦ εὑρήσει οὕτως
coming the lord of him will find so

ποιοῦντα· 47 ἀμὴν λέγω ὑμῖν ὅτι ἐπὶ
doing; truly I tell you that over

πᾶσιν τοῖς ὑπάρχουσιν αὐτοῦ καταστήσει
all the goods of him he will appoint

αὐτόν. 48 ἐὰν δὲ εἴπῃ ὁ κακὸς δοῦλος
him. But if says – wicked slave

ἐκεῖνος ἐν τῇ καρδίᾳ αὐτοῦ· χρονίζει
that in the heart of him: Delays

μου ὁ κύριος, 49 καὶ ἄρξηται τύπτειν
of me the lord, and begins to strike

τοὺς συνδούλους αὐτοῦ, ἐσθίῃ δὲ καὶ
the fellow-slaves of him, and eats and

πίνῃ μετὰ τῶν μεθυόντων, 50 ἥξει ὁ
drinks with the [ones] being drunk, will come the

κύριος τοῦ δούλου ἐκείνου ἐν ἡμέρᾳ ᾗ
lord – slave of that on a day on which

οὐ προσδοκᾷ καὶ ἐν ὥρᾳ ᾗ οὐ
he does not expect and in an hour in which not

γινώσκει, 51 καὶ διχοτομήσει αὐτόν,
he knows, and will cut asunder him,

καὶ τὸ μέρος αὐτοῦ μετὰ τῶν
and the portion of him with the

ὑποκριτῶν θήσει· ἐκεῖ ἔσται ὁ
hypocrites will place; there will be the

κλαυθμὸς καὶ ὁ βρυγμὸς τῶν ὀδόντων.
wailing and the gnashing of the teeth.

25 Τότε ὁμοιωθήσεται ἡ βασιλεία
Then shall be likened the kingdom

τῶν οὐρανῶν δέκα παρθένοις, αἵτινες
of the heavens to ten virgins, who

λαβοῦσαι τὰς λαμπάδας ἑαυτῶν ἐξῆλθον
taking the lamps of them* went forth

εἰς ὑπάντησιν τοῦ νυμφίου. 2 πέντε δὲ
to a meeting of the bridegroom. Now five

ἐξ αὐτῶν ἦσαν μωραὶ καὶ πέντε φρόνιμοι.
of them were foolish and five prudent.

3 αἱ γὰρ μωραὶ λαβοῦσαι τὰς λαμπάδας
For the foolish [ones] taking the lamps

οὐκ ἔλαβον μεθ' ἑαυτῶν ἔλαιον.
did not take with them oil.

4 αἱ δὲ φρόνιμοι ἔλαβον ἔλαιον ἐν
But the prudent [ones] took oil in

τοῖς ἀγγείοις μετὰ τῶν λαμπάδων ἑαυτῶν.
the vessels with the lamps of them.

5 χρονίζοντος δὲ τοῦ νυμφίου ἐνύσταξαν
But delaying the bridegroom* slumbered
=while the bridegroom delayed

πᾶσαι καὶ ἐκάθευδον. 6 μέσης δὲ
all and slept. And of(in) [the] middle

νυκτὸς κραυγὴ γέγονεν· ἰδοὺ ὁ
of [the] night a cry there has been: Behold[,] the

νυμφίος, ἐξέρχεσθε εἰς ἀπάντησιν. 7 τότε
bridegroom, go ye forth to a meeting. Then

ἠγέρθησαν πᾶσαι αἱ παρθένοι ἐκεῖναι
were raised all – virgins those

*Here, and in the three following occurrences, as elsewhere, the strict meaning is emphatic or reflexive—'of themselves'; but this cannot be insisted on.

household to give them
their food at the proper
time? 46 It will be good for
that servant whose master
finds him doing so when he
returns. 47 I tell you the
truth, he will put him in
charge of all his posses-
sions. 48 But suppose that
servant is wicked and says
to himself, 'My master is
staying away a long time,'
49 and he then begins to beat
his fellow servants and to
eat and drink with drunk-
ards. 50 The master of that
servant will come on a day
when he does not expect
him and at an hour he is not
aware of. 51 He will cut him
to pieces and assign him a
place with the hypocrites,
where there will be weep-
ing and gnashing of teeth.

Chapter 25

The Parable of the Ten Virgins

"AT that time the king-
dom of heaven
will be like ten virgins who
took their lamps and went
out to meet the bride-
groom. 2 Five of them were
foolish and five were wise.
3 The foolish ones took their
lamps but did not take any
oil with them. 4 The wise,
however, took oil in jars
along with their lamps.
5 The bridegroom was a
long time in coming, and
they all became drowsy
and fell asleep.
6 "At midnight the cry
rang out: 'Here's the bridegroom! Come out to meet
him!'
7 "Then all the virgins

trimmed their lamps. 8 The
foolish said to the wise,
'Give us some of your oil,
for our lamps are going
out.' 9 But the wise replied,
'No! there will not be
enough for you and for us;
you had better go to the
dealers and buy some for
yourselves.' 10 And while
they went to buy it, the
bridegroom came, and
those who were ready went
with him into the wedding
banquet; and the door was
shut. 11 Later the other
bridesmaids[g] came also,
saying, 'Lord, lord, open to
us.' 12 But he replied, 'Truly I tell you, I do not know
you.' 13 Keep awake therefore, for you know neither
the day nor the hour.[h]

The Parable of the Talents

14 "For it is as if a man,
going on a journey, sum-
moned his slaves and en-
trusted his property to
them; 15 to one he gave five
talents,[i] to another two, to
another one, to each ac-
cording to his ability. Then
he went away. 16 The one
who had received the five
talents went off at once and
traded with them, and
made five more talents.
17 In the same way, the one
who had the two talents
made two more talents.
18 But the one who had received the one talent went
off and dug a hole in the
ground and hid his master's
money. 19 After a long time
the master of those slaves
came and settled accounts
with them. 20 Then the one

[g] Gk *virgins*
[h] Other ancient authorities add *in which the Son of Man is coming*
[i] A talent was worth more than fifteen years' wages of a laborer

καὶ ἐκόσμησαν τὰς λαμπάδας ἑαυτῶν.
and trimmed the lamps of them.
8 αἱ δὲ μωραὶ ταῖς φρονίμοις εἶπαν·
So the foolish [ones] to the prudent said:
δότε ἡμῖν ἐκ τοῦ ἐλαίου ὑμῶν, ὅτι
Give us of the oil of you, because
αἱ λαμπάδες ἡμῶν σβέννυνται. **9** ἀπεκρί-
the lamps of us are being quenched. But
θησαν δὲ αἱ φρόνιμοι λέγουσαι· μήποτε
answered the prudent saying: Lest
οὐ μὴ ἀρκέσῃ ἡμῖν καὶ ὑμῖν·
by no means it suffices to us and to you;
πορεύεσθε μᾶλλον πρὸς τοὺς πωλοῦντας
go ye rather to the [ones] selling
καὶ ἀγοράσατε ἑαυταῖς. **10** ἀπερχομένων
and buy for [your]selves. And going =as they
δὲ αὐτῶν ἀγοράσαι ἦλθεν ὁ νυμφίος,
away them[a] were going away to buy came the bridegroom,
καὶ αἱ ἕτοιμοι εἰσῆλθον μετ' αὐτοῦ
and the ready [ones] went in with him
εἰς τοὺς γάμους, καὶ ἐκλείσθη ἡ
to the wedding festivities, and was shut the
θύρα. **11** ὕστερον δὲ ἔρχονται καὶ αἱ
door. Then later come also the
λοιπαὶ παρθένοι λέγουσαι· κύριε κύριε,
remaining virgins saying: Lord[,] Lord,
ἄνοιξον ἡμῖν. **12** ὁ δὲ ἀποκριθεὶς εἶπεν·
open to us. But he answering said:
ἀμὴν λέγω ὑμῖν, οὐκ οἶδα ὑμᾶς.
Truly I say to you, I know not you.
13 Γρηγορεῖτε οὖν, ὅτι οὐκ οἴδατε
Watch ye therefore, because ye know not
τὴν ἡμέραν οὐδὲ τὴν ὥραν. **14** Ὥσπερ
the day nor the hour. as
γὰρ ἄνθρωπος ἀποδημῶν ἐκάλεσεν
For a man going from home called
τοὺς ἰδίους δούλους καὶ παρέδωκεν αὐτοῖς
the(his) own slaves and delivered to them
τὰ ὑπάρχοντα αὐτοῦ, **15** καὶ ᾧ μὲν ἔδωκεν
the goods of him, and to one he gave
πέντε τάλαντα, ᾧ δὲ δύο, ᾧ δὲ
five talents, to another two, to another
ἕν, ἑκάστῳ κατὰ τὴν ἰδίαν δύναμιν,
one, to each according to the(his) own ability,
καὶ ἀπεδήμησεν. **16** εὐθέως πορευθεὶς
and went from home. Immediately going
ὁ τὰ πέντε τάλαντα λαβὼν ἠργάσατο
the [one] the five talents receiving traded
ἐν αὐτοῖς καὶ ἐκέρδησεν ἄλλα
in them and gained other
πέντε· **17** ὡσαύτως ὁ τὰ δύο ἐκέρδησεν
five; similarly the [one] [receiving] the two gained
ἄλλα δύο. **18** ὁ δὲ τὸ ἓν λαβὼν
other two. But the [one] the one receiving
ἀπελθὼν ὤρυξεν γῆν καὶ ἔκρυψεν
going away dug earth and hid
τὸ ἀργύριον τοῦ κυρίου αὐτοῦ.
the silver of the lord of him.
19 μετὰ δὲ πολὺν χρόνον ἔρχεται ὁ
Then after much time comes the
κύριος τῶν δούλων ἐκείνων καὶ συναίρει
lord – slaves of those and takes
λόγον μετ' αὐτῶν. **20** καὶ προσελθὼν
account with them. And approaching

woke up and trimmed their
lamps. 8 The foolish ones
said to the wise, 'Give us
some of your oil; our lamps
are going out.'
9 " 'No,' they replied,
'there may not be enough
for both us and you. In-
stead, go to those who sell
oil and buy some for yourselves.'
10 "But while they were
on their way to buy the oil,
the bridegroom arrived.
The virgins who were
ready went in with him to
the wedding banquet. And
the door was shut.
11 "Later the others also
came. 'Sir! Sir!' they said.
'Open the door for us!'
12 "But he replied, 'I tell
you the truth, I don't know
you.'
13 "Therefore keep
watch, because you do not
know the day or the hour.

The Parable of the Talents

14 "Again, it will be like a
man going on a journey,
who called his servants and
entrusted his property to
them. 15 To one he gave five
talents[c] of money, to another two talents, and to
another one talent, each according to his ability. Then
he went on his journey.
16 The man who had re-
ceived the five talents went
at once and put his money
to work and gained five
more. 17 So also, the one
with the two talents gained
two more. 18 But the man
who had received the one
talent went off, dug a hole
in the ground and hid his
master's money.
19 "After a long time the
master of those servants returned and settled accounts

[c] *15* A talent was worth more than a thousand dollars.

who had received the five
talents came forward,
bringing five more talents,
saying, 'Master, you handed over to me five talents;
see, I have made five more
talents.' 21 His master said
to him, 'Well done, good
and trustworthy slave; you
have been trustworthy in a
few things, I will put you in
charge of many things; enter into the joy of your master.' 22 And the one with the
two talents also came forward, saying, 'Master, you
handed over to me two talents; see, I have made two
more talents.' 23 His master
said to him, 'Well done,
good and trustworthy
slave; you have been trustworthy in a few things, I
will put you in charge of
many things; enter into the
joy of your master.' 24 Then
the one who had received
the one talent also came
forward, saying, 'Master, I
knew that you were a harsh
man, reaping where you
did not sow, and gathering
where you did not scatter
seed; 25 so I was afraid, and
I went and hid your talent
in the ground. Here you
have what is yours.' 26 But
his master replied, 'You
wicked and lazy slave! You
knew, did you, that I reap
where I did not sow, and
gather where I did not scatter? 27 Then you ought to
have invested my money
with the bankers, and on
my return I would have received what was my own
with interest. 28 So take the
talent from him, and give it
to the one with the ten talents. 29 For to all those who
have, more will be given,

ὁ τὰ πέντε τάλαντα λαβὼν προσ-
the [one] the five talents receiving brought
ἤνεγκεν ἄλλα πέντε τάλαντα λέγων· κύριε,
other five talents saying: Lord,
πέντε τάλαντά μοι παρέδωκας· ἴδε ἄλλα
five talents to me thou deliveredst; behold other
πέντε τάλαντα ἐκέρδησα. 21 ἔφη αὐτῷ
five talents I gained. Said to him
ὁ κύριος αὐτοῦ· εὖ, δοῦλε ἀγαθὲ καὶ
the lord of him: Well, slave good and
πιστέ, ἐπὶ ὀλίγα ἦς πιστός,
faithful, over a few things thou wast faithful,
ἐπὶ πολλῶν σε καταστήσω· εἴσελθε
over many thee I will set; enter thou
εἰς τὴν χαρὰν τοῦ κυρίου σου. 22 προσ-
into the joy of the lord of thee. Ap-
ελθὼν καὶ ὁ τὰ δύο τάλαντα
proaching also the [one] the two talents
[having received]
εἶπεν· κύριε, δύο τάλαντά μοι
said: Lord, two talents to me
παρέδωκας· ἴδε ἄλλα δύο τάλαντα
thou deliveredst; behold other two talents
ἐκέρδησα. 23 ἔφη αὐτῷ ὁ κύριος αὐτοῦ·
I gained. Said to him the lord of him:
εὖ, δοῦλε ἀγαθὲ καὶ πιστέ, ἐπὶ
Well, slave good and faithful, over
ὀλίγα ἦς πιστός, ἐπὶ πολλῶν
a few things thou wast faithful, over many
σε καταστήσω· εἴσελθε εἰς τὴν
thee I will set; enter thou into the
χαρὰν τοῦ κυρίου σου. 24 προσ-
joy of the lord of thee. ap-
ελθὼν δὲ καὶ ὁ τὸ ἓν τάλαντον
proaching And also the [one] the one talent
εἰληφὼς εἶπεν· κύριε, ἔγνων σε
having received said: Lord, I knew thee
ὅτι σκληρὸς εἶ ἄνθρωπος, θερίζων
that [2]a hard [1]thou art [3]man, reaping
ὅπου οὐκ ἔσπειρας, καὶ συνάγων
where thou didst not sow, and gathering
ὅθεν οὐ διεσκόρπισας· 25 καὶ φοβηθεὶς
whence thou didst not scatter; and fearing
ἀπελθὼν ἔκρυψα τὸ τάλαντόν σου
going away I hid the talent of thee
ἐν τῇ γῇ· ἴδε ἔχεις τὸ σόν.
in the earth; behold thou hast the thine.
26 ἀποκριθεὶς δὲ ὁ κύριος αὐτοῦ εἶπεν
And answering the lord of him said
αὐτῷ· πονηρὲ δοῦλε καὶ ὀκνηρέ,
to him: Evil slave and slothful,
ᾔδεις ὅτι θερίζω ὅπου οὐκ ἔσπειρα,
thou knewest that I reap where I sowed not,
καὶ συνάγω ὅθεν οὐ διεσκόρπισα;
and I gather whence I did not scatter?
27 ἔδει σε οὖν βαλεῖν τὰ ἀργύριά
it behoved thee therefore to put the silver pieces
μου τοῖς τραπεζίταις, καὶ ἐλθὼν ἐγὼ
of me to the bankers, and coming I
ἐκομισάμην ἂν τὸ ἐμὸν σὺν τόκῳ.
would have received the mine with interest.
28 ἄρατε οὖν ἀπ' αὐτοῦ τὸ τάλαντον
Take therefore from him the talent
καὶ δότε τῷ ἔχοντι τὰ δέκα τάλαντα·
and give to the [one] having the ten talents;
29 τῷ γὰρ ἔχοντι παντὶ δοθήσεται καὶ
for to [2]having [1]everyone will be given and

with them. 20The man who
had received the five talents brought the other five.
'Master,' he said, 'you entrusted me with five tal-
ents. See, I have gained
five more.'
21"His master replied,
'Well done, good and faithful servant! You have been
faithful with a few things; I
will put you in charge of
many things. Come and
share your master's happi-
ness!'
22"The man with the two
talents also came. 'Mas-
ter,' he said, 'you entrusted
me with two talents; see, I
have gained two more.'
23"His master replied,
'Well done, good and faithful servant! You have been
faithful with a few things; I
will put you in charge of
many things. Come and
share your master's happi-
ness!'
24"Then the man who had
received the one talent
came. 'Master,' he said, 'I
knew that you are a hard
man, harvesting where you
have not sown and gather-
ing where you have not
scattered seed. 25So I was
afraid and went out and hid
your talent in the ground.
See, here is what belongs to
you.'
26"His master replied,
'You wicked, lazy servant!
So you knew that I harvest
where I have not sown and
gather where I have not
scattered seed? 27Well
then, you should have put
my money on deposit with
the bankers, so that when I
returned I would have re-
ceived it back with interest.
28"'Take the talent from
him and give it to the one
who has the ten talents.
29For everyone who has
will be given more, and he

and they will have an abundance; but from those who
have nothing, even what
they have will be taken
away. 30 As for this worthless slave, throw him into
the outer darkness, where
there will be weeping and
gnashing of teeth.'

The Judgment of the Nations

31 "When the Son of
Man comes in his glory,
and all the angels with him,
then he will sit on the
throne of his glory. 32 All
the nations will be gathered
before him, and he will separate people one from an-
other as a shepherd sepa-
rates the sheep from the
goats, 33 and he will put the
sheep at his right hand and
the goats at the left. 34 Then
the king will say to those at
his right hand, 'Come, you
that are blessed by my Father, inherit the kingdom
prepared for you from the
foundation of the world;
35 for I was hungry and you
gave me food, I was thirsty
and you gave me something
to drink, I was a stranger
and you welcomed me, 36 I
was naked and you gave me
clothing, I was sick and you
took care of me, I was in
prison and you visited me.'
37 Then the righteous will
answer him, 'Lord, when
was it that we saw you hungry and gave you food, or
thirsty and gave you something to drink? 38 And when
was it that we saw you a
stranger and welcomed
you, or naked and gave you
clothing? 39 And when was
it that we saw you sick or in
prison and visited you?'
40 And the king will answer
them, 'Truly I tell you, just

περισσευθήσεται· τοῦ δὲ μὴ ἔχοντος
he will have abundance; but from the [one] not having
καὶ ὃ ἔχει ἀρθήσεται ἀπ' αὐτοῦ.
even what he has will be taken from him.
30 καὶ τὸν ἀχρεῖον δοῦλον ἐκβάλετε εἰς
And the useless slave cast ye out into
τὸ σκότος τὸ ἐξώτερον· ἐκεῖ ἔσται ὁ
the darkness – outer; there will be the
κλαυθμὸς καὶ ὁ βρυγμὸς τῶν ὀδόντων
wailing and the gnashing of the teeth.
31 Ὅταν δὲ ἔλθῃ ὁ υἱὸς τοῦ ἀνθρώπου
And when comes the Son – of man
ἐν τῇ δόξῃ αὐτοῦ καὶ πάντες οἱ ἄγγελοι
in the glory of him and all the angels
μετ' αὐτοῦ, τότε καθίσει ἐπὶ θρόνου
with him, then he will sit on a throne
δόξης αὐτοῦ· 32 καὶ συναχθήσονται
of glory of him; and will be assembled
ἔμπροσθεν αὐτοῦ πάντα τὰ ἔθνη, καὶ
before him all the nations, and
ἀφορίσει αὐτοὺς ἀπ' ἀλλήλων, ὥσπερ
he will separate them from one another, as
ὁ ποιμὴν ἀφορίζει τὰ πρόβατα ἀπὸ
the shepherd separates the sheep from
τῶν ἐρίφων, 33 καὶ στήσει τὰ μὲν
the goats, and will set the –
πρόβατα ἐκ δεξιῶν αὐτοῦ, τὰ δὲ ἐρίφια
sheep on [the] right of him, but the goats
ἐξ εὐωνύμων. 34 τότε ἐρεῖ ὁ
on [the] left. Then will say the
βασιλεὺς τοῖς ἐκ δεξιῶν αὐτοῦ·
king to the [ones] on [the] right of him:
δεῦτε οἱ εὐλογημένοι τοῦ πατρός μου,
Come the [ones] blessed of the Father of me,
κληρονομήσατε τὴν ἡτοιμασμένην ὑμῖν
inherit ye the [3]having been prepared [2]for you
βασιλείαν ἀπὸ καταβολῆς κόσμου.
[1]kingdom from [the] foundation of [the] world.
35 ἐπείνασα γὰρ καὶ ἐδώκατέ μοι
For I hungered and ye gave me
φαγεῖν, ἐδίψησα καὶ ἐποτίσατέ με,
to eat, I thirsted and ye gave [2]drink [1]me,
ξένος ἤμην καὶ συνηγάγετέ με,
a stranger I was and ye entertained me,
36 γυμνὸς καὶ περιεβάλετέ με, ἠσθένησα
naked and ye clothed me, I ailed
καὶ ἐπεσκέψασθέ με, ἐν φυλακῇ ἤμην
and ye visited me, in prison I was
καὶ ἤλθατε πρός με. 37 τότε ἀποκριθή-
and ye came to me. Then will
σονται αὐτῷ οἱ δίκαιοι λέγοντες· κύριε,
answer him the righteous saying: Lord,
πότε σε εἴδομεν πεινῶντα καὶ ἐθρέψαμεν,
when thee saw we hungering and fed,
ἢ διψῶντα καὶ ἐποτίσαμεν; 38 πότε δέ
or thirsting and gave drink? and when
σε εἴδομεν ξένον καὶ συνηγάγομεν,
thee saw we a stranger and entertained,
ἢ γυμνὸν καὶ περιεβάλομεν; 39 πότε δέ
or naked and clothed? and when
σε εἴδομεν ἀσθενοῦντα ἢ ἐν φυλακῇ καὶ
thee saw we ailing or in prison and
ἤλθομεν πρός σέ; 40 καὶ ἀποκριθεὶς ὁ
came to thee? And answering the
βασιλεὺς ἐρεῖ αὐτοῖς· ἀμὴν λέγω
king will say to them: Truly I tell

will have an abundance.
Whoever does not have,
even what he has will be
taken from him. 30 And
throw that worthless ser-
vant outside, into the darkness, where there will be
weeping and gnashing of
teeth.'

The Sheep and the Goats

31 "When the Son of Man
comes in his glory, and all
the angels with him, he will
sit on his throne in heavenly glory. 32 All the nations
will be gathered before
him, and he will separate
the people one from another as a shepherd separates
the sheep from the goats.
33 He will put the sheep on
his right and the goats on
his left.
34 "Then the King will say
to those on his right,
'Come, you who are
blessed by my Father; take
your inheritance, the kingdom prepared for you since
the creation of the world.
35 For I was hungry and you
gave me something to eat, I
was thirsty and you gave
me something to drink, I
was a stranger and you invited me in, 36 I needed
clothes and you clothed
me, I was sick and you
looked after me, I was in
prison and you came to visit me.'
37 "Then the righteous
will answer him, 'Lord,
when did we see you hun-
gry and feed you, or thirsty
and give you something to
drink? 38 When did we see
you a stranger and invite
you in, or needing clothes
and clothe you? 39 When did
we see you sick or in prison
and go to visit you?'
40 "The King will reply, 'I
tell you the truth, whatever

as you did it to one of the
least of these who are members of my family,[j] you did
it to me.' 41 Then he will say
to those at his left hand,
'You that are accursed, depart from me into the eternal fire prepared for the
devil and his angels; 42 for I
was hungry and you gave
me no food, I was thirsty
and you gave me nothing to
drink, 43 I was a stranger
and you did not welcome
me, naked and you did not
give me clothing, sick and
in prison and you did not
visit me.' 44 Then they also
will answer, 'Lord, when
was it that we saw you hungry or thirsty or a stranger
or naked or sick or in prison, and did not take care of
you?' 45 Then he will an-
swer them, 'Truly I tell
you, just as you did not do
it to one of the least of
these, you did not do it to
me.' 46 And these will go
away into eternal punish-
ment, but the righteous into
eternal life."

ὑμῖν, ἐφ' ὅσον ἐποιήσατε ἑνὶ τούτων
you, inasmuch as ye did to one of these
τῶν ἀδελφῶν μου τῶν ἐλαχίστων, ἐμοὶ
– brothers of me the least, to me
ἐποιήσατε. 41 τότε ἐρεῖ καὶ τοῖς ἐξ
ye did. Then he will say also to the [ones] on
εὐωνύμων· πορεύεσθε ἀπ' ἐμοῦ κατ-
[the] left: Go from me *having been*
ηραμένοι εἰς τὸ πῦρ τὸ αἰώνιον
cursed [ones] into the fire – eternal
τὸ ἡτοιμασμένον τῷ διαβόλῳ καὶ τοῖς
– *having been* prepared for the devil and the
ἀγγέλοις αὐτοῦ. 42 ἐπείνασα γὰρ καὶ
angels of him. For I hungered and
οὐκ ἐδώκατέ μοι φαγεῖν, ἐδίψησα
ye gave not me to eat, I thirsted
καὶ οὐκ ἐποτίσατέ με, 43 ξένος
and ye [1]gave [3]not [4]drink [2]me, a stranger
ἤμην καὶ οὐ συνηγάγετέ με, γυμνὸς
I was and ye entertained not me, naked
καὶ οὐ περιεβάλετέ με, ἀσθενὴς καὶ ἐν
and ye clothed not me, ill and in
φυλακῇ καὶ οὐκ ἐπεσκέψασθέ με. 44 τότε
prison and ye visited not me. Then
ἀποκριθήσονται καὶ αὐτοὶ λέγοντες· κύριε,
will answer also they saying: Lord,
πότε σε εἴδομεν πεινῶντα ἢ διψῶντα ἢ
when thee saw we hungering or thirsting or
ξένον ἢ γυμνὸν ἢ ἀσθενῆ ἢ ἐν φυλακῇ
a stranger or naked or ill or in prison
καὶ οὐ διηκονήσαμέν σοι; 45 τότε
and did not minister to thee? Then
ἀποκριθήσεται αὐτοῖς λέγων· ἀμὴν λέγω
he will answer them saying: Truly I tell
ὑμῖν, ἐφ' ὅσον οὐκ ἐποιήσατε ἑνὶ
you, inasmuch as ye did not to one
τούτων τῶν ἐλαχίστων, οὐδὲ ἐμοὶ
of these – least [ones], neither to me
ἐποιήσατε. 46 καὶ ἀπελεύσονται οὗτοι εἰς
ye did. And will go away these into
κόλασιν αἰώνιον, οἱ δὲ δίκαιοι εἰς
punishment eternal, but the righteous into
ζωὴν αἰώνιον.
life eternal.

you did for one of the least
of these brothers of mine,
you did for me.'
41 "Then he will say to
those on his left, 'Depart
from me, you who are
cursed, into the eternal fire
prepared for the devil and
his angels. 42 For I was hungry and you gave me noth-
ing to eat, I was thirsty and
you gave me nothing to
drink, 43 I was a stranger
and you did not invite me
in, I needed clothes and
you did not clothe me, I
was sick and in prison and
you did not look after me.'
44 "They also will answer,
'Lord, when did we see you
hungry or thirsty or a
stranger or needing clothes
or sick or in prison, and did
not help you?'
45 "He will reply, 'I tell
you the truth, whatever
you did not do for one of
the least of these, you did
not do for me.'
46 "Then they will go
away to eternal punish-
ment, but the righteous to
eternal life."

Chapter 26

The Plot to Kill Jesus

WHEN Jesus had fin-
ished saying all
these things, he said to his
disciples, 2 "You know that
after two days the Passover
is coming, and the Son of
Man will be handed over to
be crucified."
3 Then the chief priests
and the elders of the people
gathered in the palace of
the high priest, who was
called Caiaphas, 4 and they
conspired to arrest Jesus

26 Καὶ ἐγένετο ὅτε ἐτέλεσεν ὁ
And it came to pass when ended –
Ἰησοῦς πάντας τοὺς λόγους τούτους,
Jesus all – words these,
εἶπεν τοῖς μαθηταῖς αὐτοῦ· 2 οἴδατε
he said to the disciples of him: Ye know
ὅτι μετὰ δύο ἡμέρας τὸ πάσχα γίνεται,
that after two days the passover occurs,
καὶ ὁ υἱὸς τοῦ ἀνθρώπου παραδίδοται εἰς
and the Son – of man is delivered –
τὸ σταυρωθῆναι. 3 Τότε συνήχθησαν οἱ
– to be crucified. Then were assembled the
ἀρχιερεῖς καὶ οἱ πρεσβύτεροι τοῦ λαοῦ
chief priests and the elders of the people
εἰς τὴν αὐλὴν τοῦ ἀρχιερέως τοῦ
in the court of the high priest –
λεγομένου Καϊαφᾶ, 4 καὶ συνεβουλεύ-
named Caiaphas, and con-
σαντο ἵνα τὸν Ἰησοῦν δόλῳ κρατή-
sulted that – Jesus by guile they might

Chapter 26

The Plot Against Jesus

WHEN Jesus had fin-
ished saying all these
things, he said to his disciples, 2 "As you know, the
Passover is two days away
—and the Son of Man will
be handed over to be crucified."
3 Then the chief priests
and the elders of the people
assembled in the palace of
the high priest, whose
name was Caiaphas, 4 and
they plotted to arrest Jesus

[j] Gk *these my brothers*

by stealth and kill him.
5 But they said, "Not during
the festival, or there may
be a riot among the peo-
ple."

The Anointing at Bethany

6 Now while Jesus was
at Bethany in the house of
Simon the leper,[k] 7 a woman came to him with an alabaster jar of very costly
ointment, and she poured it
on his head as he sat at the
table. 8 But when the disciples saw it, they were angry
and said, "Why this waste?
9 For this ointment could
have been sold for a large
sum, and the money given
to the poor." 10 But Jesus,
aware of this, said to them,
"Why do you trouble the
woman? She has per-
formed a good service for
me. 11 For you always have
the poor with you, but you
will not always have me.
12 By pouring this ointment
on my body she has pre-
pared me for burial. 13 Truly I tell you, wherever this
good news[l] is proclaimed
in the whole world, what
she has done will be told in
remembrance of her."

Judas Agrees to Betray Jesus

14 Then one of the
twelve, who was called Judas Iscariot, went to the
chief priests 15 and said,
"What will you give me if I
betray him to you?" They
paid him thirty pieces of silver. 16 And from that mo-
ment he began to look for
an opportunity to betray
him.

The Passover with the Disciples

17 On the first day of
Unleavened Bread the dis-
ciples came to Jesus, saying, "Where do you want us
to make the preparations
for you to eat the Pass-
over?" 18 He said, "Go into

[k] The terms *leper* and *leprosy* can refer to several diseases
[l] Or *gospel*

σωσιν καὶ ἀποκτείνωσιν· 5 ἔλεγον δέ·
seize and might kill; but they said:
μὴ ἐν τῇ ἑορτῇ, ἵνα μὴ θόρυβος
Not at the feast, lest a disturbance
γένηται ἐν τῷ λαῷ.
occurs among the people.
6 Τοῦ δὲ Ἰησοῦ γενομένου ἐν Βηθανίᾳ
– And Jesus being[a] in Bethany
[a] =when Jesus was
ἐν οἰκίᾳ Σίμωνος τοῦ λεπροῦ,
in [the] house of Simon the leper,
7 προσῆλθεν αὐτῷ γυνὴ ἔχουσα ἀλάβαστρον
approached *to* him a woman having an alabaster phial
μύρου βαρυτίμου καὶ κατέχεεν ἐπὶ
of ointment very expensive and poured [it] on
τῆς κεφαλῆς αὐτοῦ ἀνακειμένου. 8 ἰδόντες
the head of him reclining. And see-
δὲ οἱ μαθηταὶ ἠγανάκτησαν λέγοντες·
ing the disciples were angry saying:
εἰς τί ἡ ἀπώλεια αὕτη; 9 ἐδύνατο γὰρ
To what – waste this? for could
τοῦτο πραθῆναι πολλοῦ καὶ δοθῆναι
this *to* be sold of(for) much and *to* be given
πτωχοῖς. 10 γνοὺς δὲ ὁ Ἰησοῦς εἶπεν
to poor. And knowing – Jesus said
αὐτοῖς· τί κόπους παρέχετε τῇ γυναικί;
to them: Why trouble ye the woman?
ἔργον γὰρ καλὸν ἠργάσατο εἰς ἐμέ·
for work a good she wrought to me:
11 πάντοτε γὰρ τοὺς πτωχοὺς ἔχετε μεθ'
for always the poor ye have with
ἑαυτῶν, ἐμὲ δὲ οὐ πάντοτε ἔχετε·
yourselves, but me not always ye have;
12 βαλοῦσα γὰρ αὕτη τὸ μύρον τοῦτο
for [2]putting [1]this woman – [4]ointment [3]this
ἐπὶ τοῦ σώματός μου πρὸς τὸ ἐνταφιάσαι
on the body of me for – to bury
με ἐποίησεν. 13 ἀμὴν λέγω ὑμῖν, ὅπου
me she did. Truly I tell you, wher-
ἐὰν κηρυχθῇ τὸ εὐαγγέλιον τοῦτο ἐν
ever is proclaimed – gospel this in
ὅλῳ τῷ κόσμῳ, λαληθήσεται καὶ ὃ
all the world, will be spoken also what
ἐποίησεν αὕτη εἰς μνημόσυνον αὐτῆς.
did this woman for a memorial of her.
14 Τότε πορευθεὶς εἷς τῶν δώδεκα, ὁ
Then going one of the twelve, the [one]
λεγόμενος Ἰούδας Ἰσκαριώτης, πρὸς
named Judas Iscariot, to
τοὺς ἀρχιερεῖς 15 εἶπεν· τί θέλετέ μοι
the chief priests he said: What are ye willing me
δοῦναι, κἀγὼ ὑμῖν παραδώσω αὐτόν;
to give, and I to you will deliver him?
οἱ δὲ ἔστησαν αὐτῷ τριάκοντα ἀργύρια.
And they weighed him thirty pieces of silver.
16 καὶ ἀπὸ τότε ἐζήτει εὐκαιρίαν ἵνα
And from then he sought opportunity that
αὐτὸν παραδῷ.
him he might deliver.
17 Τῇ δὲ πρώτῃ τῶν ἀζύμων
Now on the first [day] – of unleavened bread
προσῆλθον οἱ μαθηταὶ τῷ Ἰησοῦ
approached the disciples – *to* Jesus
λέγοντες· ποῦ θέλεις ἑτοιμάσωμέν
saying: Where willest thou we may prepare
σοι φαγεῖν τὸ πάσχα; 18 ὁ δὲ
for thee to eat the passover? So he

in some sly way and kill
him. 5 "But not during the
Feast," they said, "or
there may be a riot among
the people."

Jesus Anointed at Bethany

6 While Jesus was in Bethany in the home of a man
known as Simon the Leper,
7 a woman came to him with
an alabaster jar of very expensive perfume, which
she poured on his head as
he was reclining at the table.
8 When the disciples saw
this, they were indignant.
"Why this waste?" they
asked. 9 "This perfume
could have been sold at a
high price and the money
given to the poor."
10 Aware of this, Jesus
said to them, "Why are you
bothering this woman? She
has done a beautiful thing
to me. 11 The poor you will
always have with you, but
you will not always have
me. 12 When she poured this
perfume on my body, she
did it to prepare me for
burial. 13 I tell you the truth,
wherever this gospel is
preached throughout the
world, what she has done
will also be told, in memory
of her."

Judas Agrees to Betray Jesus

14 Then one of the Twelve
—the one called Judas Is-
cariot—went to the chief
priests 15 and asked, "What
are you willing to give me if
I hand him over to you?"
So they counted out for him
thirty silver coins. 16 From
then on Judas watched for
an opportunity to hand him
over.

The Lord's Supper

17 On the first day of the
Feast of Unleavened
Bread, the disciples came
to Jesus and asked,
"Where do you want us to
make preparations for you
to eat the Passover?"

the city to a certain man, and say to him, 'The Teacher says, My time is near; I will keep the Passover at your house with my disciples.' " 19 So the disciples did as Jesus had directed them, and they prepared the Passover meal.

20 When it was evening, he took his place with the twelve;[m] 21 and while they were eating, he said, "Truly I tell you, one of you will betray me." 22 And they became greatly distressed and began to say to him one after another, "Surely not I, Lord?" 23 He answered, "The one who has dipped his hand into the bowl with me will betray me. 24 The Son of Man goes as it is written of him, but woe to that one by whom the Son of Man is betrayed! It would have been better for that one not to have been born." 25 Judas, who betrayed him, said, "Surely not I, Rabbi?" He replied, "You have said so."

The Institution of the Lord's Supper

26 While they were eating, Jesus took a loaf of bread, and after blessing it he broke it, gave it to the disciples, and said, "Take, eat; this is my body." 27 Then he took a cup, and after giving thanks he gave it to them, saying, "Drink from it, all of you; 28 for this is my blood of the[n] covenant, which is poured out for many for the forgiveness of sins. 29 I tell you, I

[m] Other ancient authorities add *disciples*
[n] Other ancient authorities add *new*

εἶπεν· ὑπάγετε εἰς τὴν πόλιν πρὸς
said: Go ye into the city to
τὸν δεῖνα καὶ εἴπατε αὐτῷ· ὁ
such a one and say to him: The
διδάσκαλος λέγει· ὁ καιρός μου
teacher says: The time of me
ἐγγύς ἐστιν· πρὸς σὲ ποιῶ τὸ πάσχα
near is; with thee I make the passover
μετὰ τῶν μαθητῶν μου. **19** καὶ ἐποίησαν
with the disciples of me. And did
οἱ μαθηταὶ ὡς συνέταξεν αὐτοῖς ὁ
the disciples as enjoined them –
Ἰησοῦς, καὶ ἡτοίμασαν τὸ πάσχα. **20** Ὀψίας
Jesus, and prepared the passover. evening
δὲ γενομένης ἀνέκειτο μετὰ τῶν δώδεκα
And coming[a] he reclined with the twelve
=when evening came
[μαθητῶν]. **21** καὶ ἐσθιόντων αὐτῶν εἶπεν·
disciples. And eating them[a] he said:
=as they were eating
ἀμὴν λέγω ὑμῖν ὅτι εἷς ἐξ ὑμῶν παρα-
Truly I tell you that one of you will
δώσει με. **22** καὶ λυπούμενοι σφόδρα
betray me. And grieving exceedingly
ἤρξαντο λέγειν αὐτῷ εἷς ἕκαστος·
they began to say to him [1]one [1]each:
μήτι ἐγώ εἰμι, κύριε; **23** ὁ δὲ ἀποκριθεὶς
Not I am, Lord? And he answering
=It is not I,
εἶπεν· ὁ ἐμβάψας μετ' ἐμοῦ τὴν
said: The [one] dipping with me the(his)
χεῖρα ἐν τῷ τρυβλίῳ, οὗτός με παρα-
hand in the dish, this man me will
δώσει. **24** ὁ μὲν υἱὸς τοῦ ἀνθρώπου
betray. Indeed the Son – of man
ὑπάγει καθὼς γέγραπται περὶ αὐτοῦ,
goes as it has been written concerning him,
οὐαὶ δὲ τῷ ἀνθρώπῳ ἐκείνῳ δι'
but woe – man to that through
οὗ ὁ υἱὸς τοῦ ἀνθρώπου παραδίδοται·
whom the Son – of man is betrayed;
καλὸν ἦν αὐτῷ εἰ οὐκ ἐγεννήθη
good were it for him if was not born
ὁ ἄνθρωπος ἐκεῖνος. **25** ἀποκριθεὶς δὲ
– man that. And answering
Ἰούδας ὁ παραδιδοὺς αὐτὸν εἶπεν·
Judas the [one] betraying him said:
μήτι ἐγώ εἰμι, ῥαββί; λέγει αὐτῷ·
Not I am, rabbi? He says to him:
=It is not I,
σὺ εἶπας. **26** Ἐσθιόντων δὲ αὐτῶν
Thou saidst. And eating them[a]
=as they were eating
λαβὼν ὁ Ἰησοῦς ἄρτον καὶ εὐλογήσας
taking – Jesus a loaf and blessing
ἔκλασεν καὶ δοὺς τοῖς μαθηταῖς εἶπεν·
he broke and giving to the disciples said:
λάβετε φάγετε· τοῦτό ἐστιν τὸ σῶμά
Take ye[,] eat ye; this is the body
μου. **27** καὶ λαβὼν ποτήριον καὶ εὐχαρι-
of me. And taking a cup and giving
στήσας ἔδωκεν αὐτοῖς λέγων· πίετε ἐξ
thanks he gave to them saying: Drink ye of
αὐτοῦ πάντες· **28** τοῦτο γάρ ἐστιν τὸ
it all; for this is the
αἷμά μου τῆς διαθήκης τὸ περὶ πολλῶν
blood of me of the covenant the [blood] concerning many
ἐκχυννόμενον εἰς ἄφεσιν ἁμαρτιῶν. **29** λέγω
being shed for forgiveness of sins. I tell

18 He replied, "Go into the city to a certain man and tell him, 'The Teacher says: My appointed time is near. I am going to celebrate the Passover with my disciples at your house.' " 19 So the disciples did as Jesus had directed them and prepared the Passover.

20 When evening came, Jesus was reclining at the table with the Twelve. 21 And while they were eating, he said, "I tell you the truth, one of you will betray me."

22 They were very sad and began to say to him one after the other, "Surely not I, Lord?"

23 Jesus replied, "The one who has dipped his hand into the bowl with me will betray me. 24 The Son of Man will go just as it is written about him. But woe to that man who betrays the Son of Man! It would be better for him if he had not been born."

25 Then Judas, the one who would betray him, said, "Surely not I, Rabbi?"

Jesus answered, "Yes, it is you."[d]

26 While they were eating, Jesus took bread, gave thanks and broke it, and gave it to his disciples, saying, "Take and eat; this is my body."

27 Then he took the cup, gave thanks and offered it to them, saying, "Drink from it, all of you. 28 This is my blood of the[e] covenant, which is poured out for many for the forgiveness of

[d] 25 Or *"You yourself have said it"*
[e] 28 Some manuscripts *the new*

will never again drink of
this fruit of the vine until
that day when I drink it new
with you in my Father's
kingdom."
30 When they had sung
the hymn, they went out to
the Mount of Olives.

Peter's Denial Foretold

31 Then Jesus said to
them, "You will all become
deserters because of me
this night; for it is written,
'I will strike the
shepherd,
and the sheep of the
flock will
be scattered.'
32 But after I am raised up,
I will go ahead of you to
Galilee." 33 Peter said to
him, "Though all become
deserters because of you, I
will never desert you."
34 Jesus said to him, "Truly
I tell you, this very night,
before the cock crows, you
will deny me three times."
35 Peter said to him, "Even
though I must die with you,
I will not deny you." And
so said all the disciples.

Jesus Prays in Gethsemane

36 Then Jesus went
with them to a place called
Gethsemane; and he said to
his disciples, "Sit here
while I go over there and
pray." 37 He took with him
Peter and the two sons of
Zebedee, and began to be
grieved and agitated.
38 Then he said to them, "I
am deeply grieved, even to
death; remain here, and
stay awake with me."
39 And going a little farther,
he threw himself on the
ground and prayed, "My
Father, if it is possible, let

δὲ ὑμῖν, οὐ μὴ πίω ἀπ' ἄρτι ἐκ
And you, by no means will I drink from now of
τούτου τοῦ γενήματος τῆς ἀμπέλου ἕως
this – fruit of the vine until
τῆς ἡμέρας ἐκείνης ὅταν αὐτὸ πίνω μεθ'
– day that when it I drink with
ὑμῶν καινὸν ἐν τῇ βασιλείᾳ τοῦ πατρός
you new in the kingdom of the Father
μου.
of me.
30 Καὶ ὑμνήσαντες ἐξῆλθον εἰς τὸ
And having sung a hymn they went forth to the
ὄρος τῶν ἐλαιῶν. 31 Τότε λέγει αὐτοῖς ὁ
mount of the olives. Then says to them –
Ἰησοῦς· πάντες ὑμεῖς σκανδαλισθήσεσθε
Jesus: All ye will be offended
ἐν ἐμοὶ ἐν τῇ νυκτὶ ταύτῃ· γέγραπται
in me to-night; it has been written
γάρ· πατάξω τὸν ποιμένα, καὶ δια-
for: I will strike the shepherd, and will
σκορπισθήσονται τὰ πρόβατα τῆς ποίμνης·
be scattered the sheep of the flock;
32 μετὰ δὲ τὸ ἐγερθῆναί με προάξω
but after the to be raised me[b] I will go before
=I am raised
ὑμᾶς εἰς τὴν Γαλιλαίαν. 33 ἀποκριθεὶς
you to – Galilee. answering
δὲ ὁ Πέτρος εἶπεν αὐτῷ· εἰ πάντες
And – Peter said to him: If all men
σκανδαλισθήσονται ἐν σοί, ἐγὼ οὐδέποτε
shall be offended in thee, I never
σκανδαλισθήσομαι. 34 ἔφη αὐτῷ ὁ Ἰησοῦς·
will be offended. Said to him – Jesus:
ἀμὴν λέγω σοι ὅτι ἐν ταύτῃ τῇ νυκτὶ
Truly I tell thee that to-night
πρὶν ἀλέκτορα φωνῆσαι τρὶς ἀπαρνήσῃ
before a cock to crow[b] three times thou wilt deny
με. 35 λέγει αὐτῷ ὁ Πέτρος· κἂν
me. Says to him – Peter: Even if
δέῃ με σὺν σοὶ ἀποθανεῖν, οὐ μή σε
it behoves me with thee to die, by no means thee
=I must die with thee.
ἀπαρνήσομαι. ὁμοίως καὶ πάντες οἱ
I will deny. Likewise also all the
μαθηταὶ εἶπαν.
disciples said.
36 Τότε ἔρχεται μετ' αὐτῶν ὁ Ἰησοῦς
Then comes with them – Jesus
εἰς χωρίον λεγόμενον Γεθσημανί, καὶ λέγει
to a piece of land called Gethsemane, and says
τοῖς μαθηταῖς· καθίσατε αὐτοῦ ἕως οὗ
to the disciples: Sit ye here until
ἀπελθὼν ἐκεῖ προσεύξωμαι. 37 καὶ παρα-
going away there I may pray. And tak-
λαβὼν τὸν Πέτρον καὶ τοὺς δύο υἱοὺς
ing – Peter and the two sons
Ζεβεδαίου ἤρξατο λυπεῖσθαι καὶ ἀδημονεῖν.
of Zebedee he began to grieve and to be distressed.
38 τότε λέγει αὐτοῖς· περίλυπός ἐστιν
Then he says to them: Deeply grieved is
ἡ ψυχή μου ἕως θανάτου· μείνατε
the soul of me unto death; remain ye
ὧδε καὶ γρηγορεῖτε μετ' ἐμοῦ. 39 καὶ
here and watch ye with me. And
προελθὼν μικρὸν ἔπεσεν ἐπὶ πρόσωπον
going forward a little he fell on [the] face
αὐτοῦ προσευχόμενος καὶ λέγων· πάτερ
of him praying and saying: Father

sins. 29 I tell you, I will not
drink of this fruit of the vine
from now on until that day
when I drink it anew with
you in my Father's king-
dom."
30 When they had sung a
hymn, they went out to the
Mount of Olives.

Jesus Predicts Peter's Denial

31 Then Jesus told them,
"This very night you will
all fall away on account of
me, for it is written:
"'I will strike the
shepherd,
and the sheep of the
flock will be
scattered.'[f]
32 But after I have risen, I
will go ahead of you into
Galilee."
33 Peter replied, "Even if
all fall away on account of
you, I never will."
34 "I tell you the truth,"
Jesus answered, "this very
night, before the rooster
crows, you will disown me
three times."
35 But Peter declared,
"Even if I have to die with
you, I will never disown
you." And all the other disciples said the same.

Gethsemane

36 Then Jesus went with
his disciples to a place
called Gethsemane, and he
said to them, "Sit here
while I go over there and
pray." 37 He took Peter and
the two sons of Zebedee
along with him, and he began to be sorrowful and
troubled. 38 Then he said to
them, "My soul is over-
whelmed with sorrow to
the point of death. Stay
here and keep watch with
me."
39 Going a little farther, he
fell with his face to the
ground and prayed, "My

[f] 31 Zech. 13:7

this cup pass from me; yet
not what I want but what
you want." 40 Then he came
to the disciples and found
them sleeping; and he said
to Peter, "So, could you
not stay awake with me one
hour? 41 Stay awake and
pray that you may not
come into the time of trial;[o] the spirit indeed is
willing, but the flesh is
weak." 42 Again he went
away for the second time
and prayed, "My Father, if
this cannot pass unless I
drink it, your will be done."
43 Again he came and found
them sleeping, for their
eyes were heavy. 44 So
leaving them again, he
went away and prayed for
the third time, saying the
same words. 45 Then he
came to the disciples and
said to them, "Are you still
sleeping and taking your
rest? See, the hour is at
hand, and the Son of Man is
betrayed into the hands of
sinners. 46 Get up, let us be
going. See, my betrayer is
at hand."

The Betrayal and Arrest of Jesus

47 While he was still
speaking, Judas, one of the
twelve, arrived; with him
was a large crowd with
swords and clubs, from the
chief priests and the elders
of the people. 48 Now the
betrayer had given them a
sign, saying, "The one I
will kiss is the man; arrest
him." 49 At once he came
up to Jesus and said,
"Greetings, Rabbi!" and
kissed him. 50 Jesus said to

[o] Or *into temptation*

μου, εἰ δυνατόν ἐστιν, παρελθάτω ἀπ'
of me, if possible it is, let pass from
ἐμοῦ τὸ ποτήριον τοῦτο· πλὴν οὐχ
me – cup this; yet not
ὡς ἐγὼ θέλω ἀλλ' ὡς σύ. **40** καὶ
as I will but as thou. And
ἔρχεται πρὸς τοὺς μαθητὰς καὶ εὑρίσκει
he comes to the disciples and finds
αὐτοὺς καθεύδοντας, καὶ λέγει τῷ Πέτρῳ·
them sleeping, and says – to Peter:
οὕτως οὐκ ἰσχύσατε μίαν ὥραν
So were ye not able one hour
γρηγορῆσαι μετ' ἐμοῦ; **41** γρηγορεῖτε καὶ
to watch with me? Watch ye and
προσεύχεσθε, ἵνα μὴ εἰσέλθητε εἰς
pray, lest ye enter into
πειρασμόν· τὸ μὲν πνεῦμα πρόθυμον,
temptation; indeed the spirit [is] eager,
ἡ δὲ σὰρξ ἀσθενής. **42** πάλιν ἐκ
but the flesh weak. Again –
δευτέρου ἀπελθὼν προσηύξατο λέγων·
second [time] going away he prayed saying:
πάτερ μου, εἰ οὐ δύναται τοῦτο παρελθεῖν
Father of me, if cannot this *to* pass away
ἐὰν μὴ αὐτὸ πίω, γενηθήτω τὸ θέλημά
except it I drink, let be done the will
σου. **43** καὶ ἐλθὼν πάλιν εὗρεν αὐτοὺς
of thee. And coming again he found them
καθεύδοντας, ἦσαν γὰρ αὐτῶν οἱ ὀφθαλμοὶ
sleeping, for were of them the eyes
βεβαρημένοι. **44** καὶ ἀφεὶς αὐτοὺς πάλιν
having been burdened. And leaving them again
ἀπελθὼν προσηύξατο ἐκ τρίτου, τὸν
going away he prayed a third [time], the
αὐτὸν λόγον εἰπὼν πάλιν. **45** τότε ἔρχεται
same word saying again. Then he comes
πρὸς τοὺς μαθητὰς καὶ λέγει αὐτοῖς·
to the disciples and says to them:
καθεύδετε λοιπὸν καὶ ἀναπαύεσθε·
Sleep ye now and rest;
ἰδοὺ ἤγγικεν ἡ ὥρα καὶ ὁ υἱὸς τοῦ
behold has drawn near the hour and the Son –
ἀνθρώπου παραδίδοται εἰς χεῖρας
of man is betrayed into [the] hands
ἁμαρτωλῶν. **46** ἐγείρεσθε, ἄγωμεν· ἰδοὺ
of sinners. Rise ye, let us be going; behold
ἤγγικεν ὁ παραδιδούς με.
has drawn near the [one] betraying me.

47 Καὶ ἔτι αὐτοῦ λαλοῦντος, ἰδοὺ
And still him speaking,[a] behold
[a] = while he was still speaking,
Ἰούδας εἷς τῶν δώδεκα ἦλθεν, καὶ μετ'
Judas one of the twelve came, and with
αὐτοῦ ὄχλος πολὺς μετὰ μαχαιρῶν καὶ
him crowd a much with swords and
ξύλων ἀπὸ τῶν ἀρχιερέων καὶ πρεσβυτέρων
clubs from the chief priests and elders
τοῦ λαοῦ. **48** ὁ δὲ παραδιδοὺς αὐτὸν ἔδωκεν
of the people. Now the [one] betraying him gave
αὐτοῖς σημεῖον λέγων· ὃν ἂν φιλήσω
them a sign saying: Whomever I may kiss
αὐτός ἐστιν· κρατήσατε αὐτόν. **49** καὶ
he it is; seize ye him. And
εὐθέως προσελθὼν τῷ Ἰησοῦ εἶπεν· χαῖρε,
immediately approaching – *to* Jesus he said: Hail,
ῥαββί, καὶ κατεφίλησεν αὐτόν. **50** ὁ
rabbi, and affectionately kissed him. –

Father, if it is possible, may
this cup be taken from me.
Yet not as I will, but as you
will."
40 Then he returned to his
disciples and found them
sleeping. "Could you men
not keep watch with me for
one hour?" he asked Peter.
41 "Watch and pray so that
you will not fall into temptation. The spirit is willing,
but the body is weak."
42 He went away a second
time and prayed, "My Fa-
ther, if it is not possible for
this cup to be taken away
unless I drink it, may your
will be done."
43 When he came back, he
again found them sleeping,
because their eyes were
heavy. 44 So he left them
and went away once more
and prayed the third time,
saying the same thing.
45 Then he returned to the
disciples and said to them,
"Are you still sleeping and
resting? Look, the hour is
near, and the Son of Man is
betrayed into the hands of
sinners. 46 Rise, let us go!
Here comes my betrayer!"

Jesus Arrested

47 While he was still
speaking, Judas, one of the
Twelve, arrived. With him
was a large crowd armed
with swords and clubs, sent
from the chief priests and
the elders of the people.
48 Now the betrayer had arranged a signal with them:
"The one I kiss is the man;
arrest him." 49 Going at
once to Jesus, Judas said,
"Greetings, Rabbi!" and
kissed him.

him, "Friend, do what you
are here to do." Then they
came and laid hands on
Jesus and arrested him.
51 Suddenly, one of those
with Jesus put his hand on
his sword, drew it, and
struck the slave of the high
priest, cutting off his ear.
52 Then Jesus said to him,
"Put your sword back into
its place; for all who take
the sword will perish by the
sword. 53 Do you think that
I cannot appeal to my Fa-
ther, and he will at once
send me more than twelve
legions of angels? 54 But
how then would the scrip-
tures be fulfilled, which say
it must happen in this
way?" 55 At that hour Jesus
said to the crowds, "Have
you come out with swords
and clubs to arrest me as
though I were a bandit?
Day after day I sat in the
temple teaching, and you
did not arrest me. 56 But all
this has taken place, so that
the scriptures of the prophets may be fulfilled." Then
all the disciples deserted
him and fled.

Jesus before the High Priest

57 Those who had ar-
rested Jesus took him to
Caiaphas the high priest, in
whose house the scribes
and the elders had gath-
ered. 58 But Peter was following him at a distance, as
far as the courtyard of the
high priest; and going inside, he sat with the guards
in order to see how this
would end. 59 Now the
chief priests and the whole
council were looking for
false testimony against

δὲ Ἰησοῦς εἶπεν αὐτῷ· ἑταῖρε,
But Jesus said to him: Comrade, [do that]
ἐφ' ὃ πάρει. τότε προσελθόντες ἐπέβαλον
on what thou art here. Then approaching they laid *on*
τὰς χεῖρας ἐπὶ τὸν Ἰησοῦν καὶ ἐκράτησαν
the(ir) hands on – Jesus and seized
αὐτόν. 51 καὶ ἰδοὺ εἷς τῶν μετὰ
him. And behold one of the [ones] with
Ἰησοῦ ἐκτείνας τὴν χεῖρα ἀπέσπασεν
Jesus stretching out the(his) hand drew
τὴν μάχαιραν αὐτοῦ, καὶ πατάξας τὸν
the sword of him, and striking the
δοῦλος τοῦ ἀρχιερέως ἀφεῖλεν αὐτοῦ τὸ
slave of the high priest cut off of him the
ὠτίον. 52 τότε λέγει αὐτῷ ὁ Ἰησοῦς·
ear. Then says to him – Jesus:
ἀπόστρεψον τὴν μάχαιράν σου εἰς τὸν
Put back the sword of thee into the
τόπον αὐτῆς· πάντες γὰρ οἱ λαβόντες
place of it; for all the [ones] taking
μάχαιραν ἐν μαχαίρῃ ἀπολοῦνται. 53 ἢ
a sword by a sword will perish. Or
δοκεῖς ὅτι οὐ δύναμαι παρακαλέσαι
thinkest thou that I cannot *to* ask
τὸν πατέρα μου, καὶ παραστήσει μοι
the Father of me, and he will provide me
ἄρτι πλείω δώδεκα λεγιῶνας ἀγγέλων;
now more [than] twelve legions of angels?
54 πῶς οὖν πληρωθῶσιν αἱ γραφαὶ ὅτι
how then may be fulfilled the scriptures that
οὕτως δεῖ γενέσθαι; 55 Ἐν ἐκείνῃ τῇ ὥρᾳ
thus it must be? In that – hour
εἶπεν ὁ Ἰησοῦς τοῖς ὄχλοις· ὡς ἐπὶ
said – Jesus to the crowds: As against
λῃστὴν ἐξήλθατε μετὰ μαχαιρῶν καὶ
a robber came ye forth with swords and
ξύλων συλλαβεῖν με; καθ' ἡμέραν ἐν
clubs to take me? daily in
τῷ ἱερῷ ἐκαθεζόμην διδάσκων, καὶ οὐκ
the temple I sat teaching, and not
ἐκρατήσατέ με. 56 τοῦτο δὲ ὅλον
ye seized me. But this all
γέγονεν ἵνα πληρωθῶσιν αἱ γραφαὶ
has come to pass that may be fulfilled the scriptures
τῶν προφητῶν. Τότε οἱ μαθηταὶ πάντες
of the prophets. Then the disciples all
ἀφέντες αὐτὸν ἔφυγον.
leaving him fled.

57 Οἱ δὲ κρατήσαντες τὸν Ἰησοῦν
But the [ones] having seized – Jesus
ἀπήγαγον πρὸς Καϊαφᾶν τὸν ἀρχιερέα,
led [him] away to Caiaphas the high priest,
ὅπου οἱ γραμματεῖς καὶ οἱ πρεσβύτεροι
where the scribes and the elders
συνήχθησαν. 58 ὁ δὲ Πέτρος ἠκολούθει
were assembled. – And Peter followed
αὐτῷ [ἀπὸ] μακρόθεν ἕως τῆς αὐλῆς
him from afar up to the court
τοῦ ἀρχιερέως, καὶ εἰσελθὼν ἔσω ἐκάθητο
of the high priest, and entering within sat
μετὰ τῶν ὑπηρετῶν ἰδεῖν τὸ τέλος.
with the attendants to see the end.
59 Οἱ δὲ ἀρχιερεῖς καὶ τὸ συνέδριον
And the chief priests and the council
ὅλον ἐζήτουν ψευδομαρτυρίαν κατὰ τοῦ
whole sought false witness against –

50 Jesus replied, "Friend,
do what you came for."[g]
Then the men stepped
forward, seized Jesus and
arrested him. 51 With that,
one of Jesus' companions
reached for his sword,
drew it out and struck the
servant of the high priest,
cutting off his ear.
52 "Put your sword back
in its place," Jesus said to
him, "for all who draw the
sword will die by the
sword. 53 Do you think I
cannot call on my Father,
and he will at once put at
my disposal more than
twelve legions of angels?
54 But how then would the
Scriptures be fulfilled that
say it must happen in this
way?"
55 At that time Jesus said
to the crowd, "Am I lead-
ing a rebellion, that you
have come out with swords
and clubs to capture me?
Every day I sat in the temple courts teaching, and
you did not arrest me.
56 But this has all taken
place that the writings of
the prophets might be fulfilled." Then all the disciples deserted him and fled.

Before the Sanhedrin

57 Those who had arrested
Jesus took him to Caia-
phas, the high priest, where
the teachers of the law and
the elders had assembled.
58 But Peter followed him at
a distance, right up to the
courtyard of the high
priest. He entered and sat
down with the guards to see
the outcome.
59 The chief priests and
the whole Sanhedrin were
looking for false evidence
against Jesus so that they

[g]50 Or *"Friend, why have you come?"*

Jesus so that they might put
him to death, 60 but they
found none, though many
false witnesses came for-
ward. At last two came forward 61 and said, "This fellow said, 'I am able to destroy the temple of God and
to build it in three days.' "
62 The high priest stood up
and said, "Have you no answer? What is it that they
testify against you?" 63 But
Jesus was silent. Then the
high priest said to him, "I
put you under oath before
the living God, tell us if you
are the Messiah,[p] the Son
of God." 64 Jesus said to
him, "You have said so.
But I tell you,

From now on you will
see the
Son of Man
seated at the right
hand of Power
and coming on the
clouds
of heaven."

65 Then the high priest tore
his clothes and said, "He
has blasphemed! Why do
we still need witnesses?
You have now heard his
blasphemy. 66 What is your
verdict?" They answered,
"He deserves death."
67 Then they spat in his face
and struck him; and some
slapped him, 68 saying,
"Prophesy to us, you Mes-
siah![p] Who is it that struck
you?"

Peter's Denial of Jesus

69 Now Peter was sit-
ting outside in the courtyard. A servant-girl came
to him and said, "You also
were with Jesus the Galilean." 70 But he denied it before all of them, saying, "I
do not know what you are
talking about." 71 When he
went out to the porch, another servant-girl saw him,
and she said to the bystand-

[p] Or *Christ*

Ἰησου ὅπως αὐτὸν θανατώσωσιν, 60 καὶ
Jesus so as him they might put to death, and

οὐχ εὗρον πολλῶν προσελθόντων
did not find[,] many approaching
=when many false witnesses approached.

ψευδομαρτύρων. ὕστερον δὲ προσελθόντες
false witnesses[*]. But later approaching

δύο 61 εἶπαν· οὗτος ἔφη· δύναμαι κατα-
two said: This man said: I can *to* de-

λῦσαι τὸν ναὸν τοῦ θεοῦ καὶ διὰ τριῶν
stroy the shrine – of God and through(after) three

ἡμερῶν οἰκοδομῆσαι. 62 καὶ ἀναστὰς
days *to* build. And standing up

ὁ ἀρχιερεὺς εἶπεν αὐτῷ· οὐδὲν
the high priest said to him: Nothing

ἀποκρίνῃ, τί οὗτοί σου κατα-
answerest thou, what these men thee give

μαρτυροῦσιν; 63 ὁ δὲ Ἰησοῦς ἐσιώπα.
evidence against? – But Jesus remained silent.

καὶ ὁ ἀρχιερεὺς εἶπεν αὐτῷ· ἐξορκίζω
And the high priest said to him: I adjure

σε κατὰ τοῦ θεοῦ τοῦ ζῶντος ἵνα ἡμῖν
thee by – God the living that us

εἴπῃς εἰ σὺ εἶ ὁ χριστὸς ὁ υἱὸς τοῦ
thou tell if thou art the Christ the Son –

θεοῦ. 64 λέγει αὐτῷ ὁ Ἰησοῦς· σὺ εἶπας·
of God. Says to him – Jesus: Thou saidst;

πλὴν λέγω ὑμῖν, ἀπ' ἄρτι ὄψεσθε τὸν
yet I tell you, from now ye will see the

υἱὸν τοῦ ἀνθρώπου καθήμενον ἐκ
Son – of man sitting on [the]

δεξιῶν τῆς δυνάμεως καὶ ἐρχόμενον
right [hand] of the power and coming

ἐπὶ τῶν νεφελῶν τοῦ οὐρανοῦ. 65 τότε
on the clouds – of heaven. Then

ὁ ἀρχιερεὺς διέρρηξεν τὰ ἱμάτια αὐτοῦ
the high priest rent the garments of him

λέγων· ἐβλασφήμησεν· τί ἔτι χρείαν ἔχομεν
saying: He blasphemed; what yet need have we

μαρτύρων; ἴδε νῦν ἠκούσατε τὴν βλασφη-
of witnesses? behold now ye heard the blas-

μίαν· 66 τί ὑμῖν δοκεῖ; οἱ δὲ ἀπο-
phemy; what to you seems it? And they answer-

κριθέντες εἶπαν· ἔνοχος θανάτου ἐστίν.
ing said: Liable of(to) death he is.

67 Τότε ἐνέπτυσαν εἰς τὸ πρόσωπον αὐτοῦ
Then they spat in the face of him

καὶ ἐκολάφισαν αὐτόν, οἱ δὲ
and violently maltreated him, and they

ἐρράπισαν 68 λέγοντες· προφήτευσον ἡμῖν,
slapped [him] saying: Prophesy thou to us,

χριστέ, τίς ἐστιν ὁ παίσας σε;
Christ, who is it the [one] having struck thee?

69 Ὁ δὲ Πέτρος ἐκάθητο ἔξω ἐν
– And Peter sat outside in

τῇ αὐλῇ· καὶ προσῆλθεν αὐτῷ μία
the court; and approached *to* him one

παιδίσκη λέγουσα· καὶ σὺ ἦσθα μετὰ
maidservant saying: Also thou wast with

Ἰησοῦ τοῦ Γαλιλαίου. 70 ὁ δὲ ἠρνήσατο
Jesus the Galilæan. But he denied

ἔμπροσθεν πάντων λέγων· οὐκ οἶδα
before all saying: I know not

τί λέγεις. 71 ἐξελθόντα δὲ εἰς τὸν
what thou sayest. And [4]going out [5]into [6]the

πυλῶνα εἶδεν αὐτὸν ἄλλη καὶ λέγει
[7]porch [2]saw [3]him [1]another and says

could put him to death.
60 But they did not find any,
though many false wit-
nesses came forward.
Finally two came forward
61 and declared, "This fellow said, 'I am able to destroy the temple of God and
rebuild it in three days.' "
62 Then the high priest
stood up and said to Jesus,
"Are you not going to an-
swer? What is this testimony that these men are bringing against you?" 63 But
Jesus remained silent.
The high priest said to
him, "I charge you under
oath by the living God: Tell
us if you are the Christ,[h]
the Son of God."
64 "Yes, it is as you say,"
Jesus replied. "But I say to
all of you: In the future you
will see the Son of Man sitting at the right hand of the
Mighty One and coming on
the clouds of heaven."
65 Then the high priest
tore his clothes and said,
"He has spoken blasphe-
my! Why do we need any
more witnesses? Look,
now you have heard the
blasphemy. 66 What do you
think?"
"He is worthy of death,"
they answered.
67 Then they spit in his
face and struck him with
their fists. Others slapped
him 68 and said, "Prophesy
to us, Christ. Who hit
you?"

Peter Disowns Jesus

69 Now Peter was sitting
out in the courtyard, and a
servant girl came to him.
"You also were with Jesus
of Galilee," she said.
70 But he denied it before
them all. "I don't know
what you're talking
about," he said.
71 Then he went out to the
gateway, where another
girl saw him and said to the

[h] 63 Or *Messiah*; also in verse 68

ers, "This man was with Jesus of Nazareth."[q] 72 Again he denied it with an oath, "I do not know the man." 73 After a little while the bystanders came up and said to Peter, "Certainly you are also one of them, for your accent betrays you." 74 Then he began to curse, and he swore an oath, "I do not know the man!" At that moment the cock crowed. 75 Then Peter remembered what Jesus had said: "Before the cock crows, you will deny me three times." And he went out and wept bitterly.

τοῖς ἐκεῖ· οὗτος ἦν μετὰ Ἰησοῦ τοῦ
to the [ones] there: This man was with Jesus the

Ναζωραίου. 72 καὶ πάλιν ἠρνήσατο
Nazarene. And again he denied

μετὰ ὅρκου ὅτι οὐκ οἶδα τὸν ἄνθρωπον.
with an oath[,] – I know not the man.

73 μετὰ μικρὸν δὲ προσελθόντες οἱ
And after a little approaching the [ones]

ἑστῶτες εἶπον τῷ Πέτρῳ· ἀληθῶς καὶ
standing said – to Peter: Truly also

σὺ ἐξ αὐτῶν εἶ, καὶ γὰρ ἡ λαλιά σου
thou of them art, for indeed the speech of thee

δῆλόν σε ποιεῖ. 74 τότε ἤρξατο καταθε-
manifest thee makes. Then he began to

ματίζειν καὶ ὀμνύειν ὅτι οὐκ οἶδα τὸν
curse and to swear[,] – I know not the

ἄνθρωπον. καὶ εὐθὺς ἀλέκτωρ ἐφώνησεν.
man. And immediately a cock crowed.

75 καὶ ἐμνήσθη ὁ Πέτρος τοῦ ῥήματος
And remembered – Peter the word

Ἰησοῦ εἰρηκότος ὅτι πρὶν ἀλέκτορα
of Jesus having said[,] – Before a cock

φωνῆσαι τρὶς ἀπαρνήσῃ με· καὶ
to crow[b] three times thou wilt deny me; and

ἐξελθὼν ἔξω ἔκλαυσεν πικρῶς.
going forth outside he wept bitterly.

people there, "This fellow was with Jesus of Nazareth."

72 He denied it again, with an oath: "I don't know the man!"

73 After a little while, those standing there went up to Peter and said, "Surely you are one of them, for your accent gives you away."

74 Then he began to call down curses on himself and he swore to them, "I don't know the man!"

Immediately a rooster crowed. 75 Then Peter remembered the word Jesus had spoken: "Before the rooster crows, you will disown me three times." And he went outside and wept bitterly.

Chapter 27

Jesus Brought before Pilate

WHEN morning came, all the chief priests and the elders of the people conferred together against Jesus in order to bring about his death. 2 They bound him, led him away, and handed him over to Pilate the governor.

The Suicide of Judas

3 When Judas, his betrayer, saw that Jesus[r] was condemned, he repented and brought back the thirty pieces of silver to the chief priests and the elders. 4 He said, "I have sinned by betraying innocent[s] blood." But they said, "What is that to us? See to it yourself." 5 Throwing down the pieces of silver in the temple, he departed; and he went and hanged himself. 6 But the chief priests, taking the pieces of silver, said, "It is not lawful to put them into the treasury, since they are blood money." 7 After conferring together, they used them to buy the potter's field as a place to bury for-

[q] Gk *the Nazorean*
[r] Gk *he*
[s] Other ancient authorities read *righteous*

27 Πρωΐας δὲ γενομένης συμβούλιον
And early morning coming[a] counsel
= when early morning came

ἔλαβον πάντες οἱ ἀρχιερεῖς καὶ οἱ
took all the chief priests and the

πρεσβύτεροι τοῦ λαοῦ κατὰ τοῦ
elders of the people against –

Ἰησοῦ ὥστε θανατῶσαι αὐτόν· 2 καὶ
Jesus so as to put to death him; and

δήσαντες αὐτὸν ἀπήγαγον καὶ παρ-
having bound him they led away and de-

έδωκαν Πιλάτῳ τῷ ἡγεμόνι. 3 Τότε
livered to Pilate the governor. Then

ἰδὼν Ἰούδας ὁ παραδοὺς αὐτὸν
[5]seeing [1]Judas [2]the [one] [3]having betrayed [4]him

ὅτι κατεκρίθη, μεταμεληθεὶς ἔστρεψεν τὰ
that he was condemned, repenting returned the

τριάκοντα ἀργύρια τοῖς ἀρχιερεῦσιν
thirty pieces of silver to the chief priests

καὶ πρεσβυτέροις 4 λέγων· ἥμαρτον
and elders saying: I sinned

παραδοὺς αἷμα ἀθῷον. οἱ δὲ εἶπαν·
betraying blood innocent. But they said:

τί πρὸς ἡμᾶς; σὺ ὄψῃ. 5 καὶ ῥίψας
What to us? thou shalt see [to it]. And tossing

τὰ ἀργύρια εἰς τὸν ναὸν ἀν-
the pieces of silver into the shrine he

εχώρησεν, καὶ ἀπελθὼν ἀπήγξατο. 6 οἱ
departed, and going away hanged himself. the

δὲ ἀρχιερεῖς λαβόντες τὰ ἀργύρια εἶπαν·
But chief priests taking the pieces of silver said:

οὐκ ἔξεστιν βαλεῖν αὐτὰ εἰς τὸν
It is not lawful to put them into the

κορβανᾶν, ἐπεὶ τιμὴ αἵματός ἐστιν.
treasury, since price of blood it is.

7 συμβούλιον δὲ λαβόντες ἠγόρασαν ἐξ
So counsel taking they bought of(with)

αὐτῶν τὸν ἀγρὸν τοῦ κεραμέως εἰς ταφὴν
them the field of the potter for burial

Chapter 27

Judas Hangs Himself

EARLY in the morning, all the chief priests and the elders of the people came to the decision to put Jesus to death. 2 They bound him, led him away and handed him over to Pilate, the governor.

3 When Judas, who had betrayed him, saw that Jesus was condemned, he was seized with remorse and returned the thirty silver coins to the chief priests and the elders. 4 "I have sinned," he said, "for I have betrayed innocent blood."

"What is that to us?" they replied. "That's your responsibility."

5 So Judas threw the money into the temple and left. Then he went away and hanged himself.

6 The chief priests picked up the coins and said, "It is against the law to put this into the treasury, since it is blood money." 7 So they decided to use the money to buy the potter's field as a burial place for foreigners.

eigners. 8For this reason
that field has been called
the Field of Blood to this
day. 9Then was fulfilled
what had been spoken
through the prophet Jere-
miah,[t] "And they took[u]
the thirty pieces of silver,
the price of the one on
whom a price had been
set,[v] on whom some of the
people of Israel had set a
price, 10and they gave[w]
them for the potter's field,
as the Lord commanded
me."

Pilate Questions Jesus

11 Now Jesus stood be-
fore the governor; and the
governor asked him, "Are
you the King of the Jews?"
Jesus said, "You say so."
12But when he was accused
by the chief priests and elders, he did not answer.
13Then Pilate said to him,
"Do you not hear how
many accusations they
make against you?" 14But
he gave him no answer, not
even to a single charge, so
that the governor was
greatly amazed.

Barabbas or Jesus?

15 Now at the festival
the governor was accus-
tomed to release a prisoner
for the crowd, anyone
whom they wanted. 16At
that time they had a notorious prisoner, called Jesus[x]
Barabbas. 17So after they
had gathered, Pilate said to
them, "Whom do you want
me to release for you,
Jesus[x] Barabbas or Jesus
who is called the Messi-
ah?"[y] 18For he realized
that it was out of jealousy
that they had handed him
over. 19While he was sit-
ting on the judgment seat,
his wife sent word to him,
"Have nothing to do with
that innocent man, for to-
day I have suffered a great
deal because of a dream

[t] Other ancient authorities read *Zechariah* or *Isaiah*
[u] Or *I took*
[v] Or *the price of the precious One*
[w] Other ancient authorities read *I gave*
[x] Other ancient authorities lack *Jesus*
[y] Or *the Christ*

τοῖς ξένοις. **8** διὸ ἐκλήθη ὁ ἀγρὸς
for the strangers. Wherefore was called – field
ἐκεῖνος ἀγρὸς αἵματος ἕως τῆς σήμερον.
that Field of blood until – to-day.
9 τότε ἐπληρώθη τὸ ῥηθὲν διὰ
Then was fulfilled the [thing] spoken through
Ἰερεμίου τοῦ προφήτου λέγοντος· καὶ
Jeremiah the prophet saying: And
ἔλαβον τὰ τριάκοντα ἀργύρια, τὴν
they took the thirty pieces of silver, the
τιμὴν τοῦ τετιμημένου ὃν ἐτιμήσαντο
price of the [one] *having been* priced whom they priced
ἀπὸ υἱῶν Ἰσραήλ, **10** καὶ ἔδωκαν
from [the] sons of Israel, and gave
αὐτὰ εἰς τὸν ἀγρὸν τοῦ κεραμέως, καθὰ
them for the field of the potter, as
συνέταξέν μοι κύριος. **11** Ὁ δὲ
directed me [the] Lord. – And
Ἰησοῦς ἐστάθη ἔμπροσθεν τοῦ ἡγεμόνος·
Jesus stood before the governor;
καὶ ἐπηρώτησεν αὐτὸν ὁ ἡγεμὼν λέγων·
and questioned him the governor saying:
σὺ εἶ ὁ βασιλεὺς τῶν Ἰουδαίων; ὁ δὲ
Thou art the king of the Jews? – And
Ἰησοῦς ἔφη· σὺ λέγεις. **12** καὶ ἐν
Jesus said: Thou sayest. And in
τῷ κατηγορεῖσθαι αὐτὸν ὑπὸ τῶν
the to be accused him[e] by the
=as he was accused
ἀρχιερέων καὶ πρεσβυτέρων οὐδὲν
chief priests and elders nothing
ἀπεκρίνατο. **13** τότε λέγει αὐτῷ ὁ Πιλᾶτος·
he answered. Then says to him – Pilate:
οὐκ ἀκούεις πόσα σου κατα-
Hearest thou not what things [3]thee [1]they
μαρτυροῦσιν; **14** καὶ οὐκ ἀπεκρίθη αὐτῷ
[2]give evidence against? And he answered not him
πρὸς οὐδὲ ἓν ῥῆμα, ὥστε θαυμάζειν
to not one word, so as to marvel
=so that the governor marvelled
τὸν ἡγεμόνα λίαν. **15** Κατὰ δὲ ἑορτὴν
the governor[b] exceedingly. Now at a feast
εἰώθει ὁ ἡγεμὼν ἀπολύειν ἕνα τῷ ὄχλῳ
was accustomed the governor to release [3]one [1]to the [2]crowd
δέσμιον ὃν ἤθελον. **16** εἶχον δὲ τότε
[4]prisoner whom they wished. And they had then
δέσμιον ἐπίσημον λεγόμενον Βαραββᾶν
prisoner a notable named Barabbas.
17 συνηγμένων οὖν αὐτῶν εἶπεν αὐτοῖς
Therefore having assembled them[a] said to them
=when they were assembled
ὁ Πιλᾶτος· τίνα θέλετε ἀπολύσω
– Pilate: Whom do ye wish I may release
ὑμῖν, [τὸν] Βαραββᾶν ἢ Ἰησοῦν τὸν
to you, – Barabbas or Jesus –
λεγόμενον χριστόν; **18** ᾔδει γὰρ ὅτι
called Christ? for he knew that
διὰ φθόνον παρέδωκαν αὐτόν. **19** Καθη-
because of envy they delivered him. sit-
μένου δὲ αὐτοῦ ἐπὶ τοῦ βήματος
ting Now him[a] on the tribunal
= Now as he sat
ἀπέστειλεν πρὸς αὐτὸν ἡ γυνὴ αὐτοῦ
sent to him the wife of him
λέγουσα· μηδὲν σοὶ καὶ τῷ δικαίῳ
saying: Nothing to thee and – just man
ἐκείνῳ· πολλὰ γὰρ ἔπαθον σήμερον κατ'
to that; for many things I suffered to-day by

8That is why it has been
called the Field of Blood to
this day. 9Then what was
spoken by Jeremiah the
prophet was fulfilled:
"They took the thirty silver
coins, the price set on him
by the people of Israel,
10and they used them to
buy the potter's field, as
the Lord commanded
me."[i]

Jesus Before Pilate

11Meanwhile Jesus stood
before the governor, and
the governor asked him,
"Are you the king of the
Jews?"
"Yes, it is as you say,"
Jesus replied.
12When he was accused
by the chief priests and the
elders, he gave no answer.
13Then Pilate asked him,
"Don't you hear the testimony they are bringing
against you?" 14But Jesus
made no reply, not even to
a single charge—to the
great amazement of the
governor.
15Now it was the gover-
nor's custom at the Feast to
release a prisoner chosen
by the crowd. 16At that
time they had a notorious
prisoner, called Barabbas.
17So when the crowd had
gathered, Pilate asked
them, "Which one do you
want me to release to you:
Barabbas, or Jesus who is
called Christ?" 18For he
knew it was out of envy
that they had handed Jesus
over to him.
19While Pilate was sitting
on the judge's seat, his wife
sent him this message:
"Don't have anything to do
with that innocent man, for
I have suffered a great deal

[i] *10* See Zech. 11:12,13; Jer. 19:1-13; 32:6-9.

about him." 20 Now the
chief priests and the elders
persuaded the crowds to
ask for Barabbas and to
have Jesus killed. 21 The
governor again said to
them, "Which of the two do
you want me to release for
you?" And they said, "Barabbas." 22 Pilate said to
them, "Then what should I
do with Jesus who is called
the Messiah?"[y] All of them
said, "Let him be cruci-
fied!" 23 Then he asked,
"Why, what evil has he
done?" But they shouted
all the more, "Let him be
crucified!"

Pilate Hands Jesus over to Be Crucified

24 So when Pilate saw
that he could do nothing,
but rather that a riot was
beginning, he took some
water and washed his
hands before the crowd,
saying, "I am innocent of
this man's blood;[z] see to it
yourselves." 25 Then the
people as a whole an-
swered, "His blood be on
us and on our children!"
26 So he released Barabbas
for them; and after flogging
Jesus, he handed him over
to be crucified.

The Soldiers Mock Jesus

27 Then the soldiers of
the governor took Jesus
into the governor's head-
quarters,[a] and they gathered the whole cohort
around him. 28 They
stripped him and put a scarlet robe on him, 29 and after
twisting some thorns into a
crown, they put it on his
head. They put a reed in his
right hand and knelt before
him and mocked him, say-
ing, "Hail, King of the
Jews!" 30 They spat on him,
and took the reed and
struck him on the head.
31 After mocking him, they

ὄναρ δι' αὐτόν. 20 Οἱ δὲ ἀρχιερεῖς
a dream because of him. But the chief priests

καὶ οἱ πρεσβύτεροι ἔπεισαν τοὺς
and the elders persuaded the

ὄχλους ἵνα αἰτήσωνται τὸν Βαραββᾶν,
crowds that they should ask – Barabbas,

τὸν δὲ Ἰησοῦν ἀπολέσωσιν. 21 ἀπο-
– and Jesus should destroy. So

κριθεὶς δὲ ὁ ἡγεμὼν εἶπεν αὐτοῖς·
answering the governor said to them:

τίνα θέλετε ἀπὸ τῶν δύο ἀπολύσω
Which do ye wish from the two I may release

ὑμῖν; οἱ δὲ εἶπαν· τὸν Βαραββᾶν.
to you? And they said: – Barabbas.

22 λέγει αὐτοῖς ὁ Πιλᾶτος· τί οὖν
Says to them – Pilate: What then

ποιήσω Ἰησοῦν τὸν λεγόμενον χριστόν;
may I do [to] Jesus – called Christ?

λέγουσιν πάντες· σταυρωθήτω. 23 ὁ δὲ
They say all: Let him be crucified. But he

ἔφη· τί γὰρ κακὸν ἐποίησεν; οἱ δὲ
said: Why what evil did he? But they

περισσῶς ἔκραζον λέγοντες· σταυρω-
more cried out saying: Let him be

θήτω. 24 ἰδὼν δὲ ὁ Πιλᾶτος ὅτι οὐδὲν
crucified. And seeing – Pilate that nothing

ὠφελεῖ ἀλλὰ μᾶλλον θόρυβος γίνεται,
is gained but rather an uproar occurs,

λαβὼν ὕδωρ ἀπενίψατο τὰς χεῖρας
taking water he washed the(his) hands

κατέναντι τοῦ ὄχλου λέγων· ἀθῷός
in front of the crowd saying: Innocent

εἰμι ἀπὸ τοῦ αἵματος τούτου· ὑμεῖς
I am from the blood of this man; ye

ὄψεσθε. 25 καὶ ἀποκριθεὶς πᾶς ὁ λαὸς
will see [to it]. And answering all the people

εἶπεν· τὸ αἷμα αὐτοῦ ἐφ' ἡμᾶς καὶ
said: The blood of him on us and

ἐπὶ τὰ τέκνα ἡμῶν. 26 τότε ἀπέλυσεν
on the children of us. Then he released

αὐτοῖς τὸν Βαραββᾶν, τὸν δὲ Ἰησοῦν
to them – Barabbas, – but Jesus

φραγελλώσας παρέδωκεν ἵνα σταυρωθῇ.
having scourged he delivered that he might be crucified.

27 Τότε οἱ στρατιῶται τοῦ ἡγεμόνος
Then the soldiers of the governor

παραλαβόντες τὸν Ἰησοῦν εἰς τὸ πραιτώ-
having taken – Jesus into the præ-

ριον συνήγαγον ἐπ' αὐτὸν ὅλην τὴν
torium assembled against him all the

σπεῖραν. 28 καὶ ἐκδύσαντες αὐτὸν χλαμύδα
band. And stripping him cloak

κοκκίνην περιέθηκαν αὐτῷ, 29 καὶ
a purple they placed round him, and

πλέξαντες στέφανον ἐξ ἀκανθῶν ἐπέθηκαν
having plaited a crown of thorns they placed [it] *on*

ἐπὶ τῆς κεφαλῆς αὐτοῦ καὶ κάλαμον
on the head of him and a reed

ἐν τῇ δεξιᾷ αὐτοῦ, καὶ γονυπετή-
in the right [hand] of him, and bowing

σαντες ἔμπροσθεν αὐτοῦ ἐνέπαιξαν αὐτῷ
the knee in front of him mocked at him

λέγοντες· χαῖρε, βασιλεῦ τῶν Ἰουδαίων,
saying: Hail, king of the Jews,

30 καὶ ἐμπτύσαντες εἰς αὐτὸν ἔλαβον
and spitting at him took

today in a dream because of
him."

20 But the chief priests and
the elders persuaded the
crowd to ask for Barabbas
and to have Jesus execut-
ed.

21 "Which of the two do
you want me to release to
you?" asked the governor.

"Barabbas," they an-
swered.

22 "What shall I do, then,
with Jesus who is called
Christ?" Pilate asked.

They all answered, "Cru-
cify him!"

23 "Why? What crime has
he committed?" asked Pi-
late.

But they shouted all the
louder, "Crucify him!"

24 When Pilate saw that he
was getting nowhere, but
that instead an uproar was
starting, he took water and
washed his hands in front
of the crowd. "I am inno-
cent of this man's blood,"
he said. "It is your responsibility!"

25 All the people an-
swered, "Let his blood be
on us and on our children!"

26 Then he released Bar-
abbas to them. But he had
Jesus flogged, and handed
him over to be crucified.

The Soldiers Mock Jesus

27 Then the governor's
soldiers took Jesus into the
Praetorium and gathered
the whole company of sol-
diers around him. 28 They
stripped him and put a scarlet robe on him, 29 and then
twisted together a crown of
thorns and set it on his
head. They put a staff in his
right hand and knelt in front
of him and mocked him.
"Hail, king of the Jews!"
they said. 30 They spit on
him, and took the staff and
struck him on the head
again and again. 31 After
they had mocked him, they

[z] Other ancient authorities read *this righteous blood*, or *this righteous man's blood*
[a] Gk *the praetorium*

stripped him of the robe
and put his own clothes on
him. Then they led him
away to crucify him.

The Crucifixion of Jesus

32 As they went out,
they came upon a man from
Cyrene named Simon; they
compelled this man to carry his cross. 33 And when
they came to a place called
Golgotha (which means
Place of a Skull), 34 they offered him wine to drink,
mixed with gall; but when
he tasted it, he would not
drink it. 35 And when they
had crucified him, they divided his clothes among
themselves by casting
lots;[b] 36 then they sat down
there and kept watch over
him. 37 Over his head they
put the charge against him,
which read, "This is Jesus,
the King of the Jews."
38 Then two bandits
were crucified with him,
one on his right and one on
his left. 39 Those who
passed by derided[c] him,
shaking their heads 40 and
saying, "You who would
destroy the temple and
build it in three days, save
yourself! If you are the Son
of God, come down from
the cross." 41 In the same
way the chief priests also,
along with the scribes and
elders, were mocking him,
saying, 42 "He saved oth-
ers; he cannot save him-
self.[d] He is the King of Israel; let him come down
from the cross now, and we
will believe in him. 43 He
trusts in God; let God deliv-

[b] Other ancient authorities add *in order that what had been spoken through the prophet might be fulfilled, "They divided my clothes among themselves, and for my clothing they cast lots."*
[c] Or *blasphemed*
[d] Or *is he unable to save himself?*

τὸν κάλαμον καὶ ἔτυπτον εἰς τὴν κεφαλὴν
the reed and struck at the head
αὐτοῦ. **31** καὶ ὅτε ἐνέπαιξαν αὐτῷ,
of him. And when they mocked at him,
ἐξέδυσαν αὐτὸν τὴν χλαμύδα καὶ ἐνέδυσαν
they took off him the cloak and put on
αὐτὸν τὰ ἱμάτια αὐτοῦ, καὶ ἀπήγαγον
him the garments of him, and led away
αὐτὸν εἰς τὸ σταυρῶσαι. **32** Ἐξερχόμενοι
him – – to crucify. going forth
δὲ εὗρον ἄνθρωπον Κυρηναῖον, ὀνό-
And they found *a man* a Cyrenian, by
ματι Σίμωνα· τοῦτον ἠγγάρευσαν ἵνα
name Simon; this man they impressed that
ἄρῃ τὸν σταυρὸν αὐτοῦ. **33** Καὶ
he should bear the cross of him. And
ἐλθόντες εἰς τόπον λεγόμενον Γολγοθά,
coming to a place called Golgotha,
ὅ ἐστιν κρανίου τόπος λεγόμενος,
which is [3]of a skull [2]A place [1]called,
34 ἔδωκαν αὐτῷ πιεῖν οἶνον μετὰ
they gave him to drink wine with
χολῆς μεμιγμένον· καὶ γευσάμενος οὐκ
gall *having been* mixed; and tasting not
ἠθέλησεν πιεῖν. **35** σταυρώσαντες δὲ
he would *to* drink. And having crucified
αὐτὸν διεμερίσαντο τὰ ἱμάτια αὐτοῦ
him they divided the garments of him
βάλλοντες κλῆρον, **36** καὶ καθήμενοι ἐτήρουν
casting a lot, and sitting they guarded
αὐτὸν ἐκεῖ. **37** καὶ ἐπέθηκαν ἐπάνω
him there. And they placed *on* above
τῆς κεφαλῆς αὐτοῦ τὴν αἰτίαν αὐτοῦ
the head of him the charge of him
γεγραμμένην· ΟΥΤΟΣ ΕΣΤΙΝ ΙΗΣΟΥΣ
having been written: THIS IS JESUS
Ο ΒΑΣΙΛΕΥΣ ΤΩΝ ΙΟΥΔΑΙΩΝ. **38** Τότε
THE KING OF THE JEWS. Then
σταυροῦνται σὺν αὐτῷ δύο λῃσταί,
are crucified with him two robbers,
εἷς ἐκ δεξιῶν καὶ εἷς ἐξ εὐωνύμων.
one on [the] right and one on [the] left.
39 Οἱ δὲ παραπορευόμενοι ἐβλασφήμουν
And the [ones] passing by blasphemed
αὐτὸν κινοῦντες τὰς κεφαλὰς αὐτῶν
him wagging the heads of them
40 καὶ λέγοντες· ὁ καταλύων τὸν ναὸν
and saying: The [one] destroying the shrine
καὶ ἐν τρισὶν ἡμέραις οἰκοδομῶν,
and in three days building [it],
σῶσον σεαυτόν, εἰ υἱὸς εἶ τοῦ θεοῦ,
save thyself, if Son thou art – of God,
καὶ κατάβηθι ἀπὸ τοῦ σταυροῦ. **41** ὁμοίως
and come down from the cross. Likewise
[καὶ] οἱ ἀρχιερεῖς ἐμπαίζοντες μετὰ
also the chief priests mocking with
τῶν γραμματέων καὶ πρεσβυτέρων ἔλεγον
the scribes and elders said:
42 ἄλλους ἔσωσεν, ἑαυτὸν οὐ δύναται
Others he saved, himself he cannot
σῶσαι· βασιλεὺς Ἰσραήλ ἐστιν,
to save; King of Israel he is,
καταβάτω νῦν ἀπὸ τοῦ σταυροῦ καὶ
let him come down now from the cross and
πιστεύσομεν ἐπ᾽ αὐτόν. **43** πέποιθεν
we will believe on him. He has trusted

took off the robe and put
his own clothes on him.
Then they led him away to
crucify him.

The Crucifixion

32 As they were going out,
they met a man from Cyre-
ne, named Simon, and they
forced him to carry the
cross. 33 They came to a
place called Golgotha
(which means The Place of
the Skull). 34 There they offered Jesus wine to drink,
mixed with gall; but after
tasting it, he refused to
drink it. 35 When they had
crucified him, they divided
up his clothes by casting
lots.[j] 36 And sitting down,
they kept watch over him
there. 37 Above his head
they placed the written
charge against him: THIS IS
JESUS, THE KING OF THE
JEWS. 38 Two robbers were
crucified with him, one on
his right and one on his left.
39 Those who passed by
hurled insults at him, shaking their heads 40 and saying, "You who are going to
destroy the temple and
build it in three days, save
yourself! Come down from
the cross, if you are the Son
of God!"
41 In the same way the
chief priests, the teachers
of the law and the elders
mocked him. 42 "He saved
others," they said, "but he
can't save himself! He's
the King of Israel! Let him
come down now from the
cross, and we will believe
in him. 43 He trusts in God.

[j] 35 A few late manuscripts *lots that the word spoken by the prophet might be fulfilled: "They divided my garments among themselves and cast lots for my clothing"* (Psalm 22:18)

er him now, if he wants to; for he said, 'I am God's Son.' " 44 The bandits who were crucified with him also taunted him in the same way.

The Death of Jesus

45 From noon on, darkness came over the whole land[e] until three in the afternoon. 46 And about three o'clock Jesus cried with a loud voice, "Eli, Eli, lema sabachthani?" that is, "My God, my God, why have you forsaken me?" 47 When some of the bystanders heard it, they said, "This man is calling for Elijah." 48 At once one of them ran and got a sponge, filled it with sour wine, put it on a stick, and gave it to him to drink. 49 But the others said, "Wait, let us see whether Elijah will come to save him."[f] 50 Then Jesus cried again with a loud voice and breathed his last.[g] 51 At that moment the curtain of the temple was torn in two, from top to bottom. The earth shook, and the rocks were split. 52 The tombs also were opened, and many bodies of the saints who had fallen asleep were raised. 53 After his resurrection they came out of the tombs and entered the holy city and appeared to many. 54 Now when the centurion and those with him, who were keeping watch over Jesus, saw the earthquake and what took place, they were terrified and said, "Truly this man was God's Son!"[h]

55 Many women were

[e] Or *earth*

[f] Other ancient authorities add *And another took a spear and pierced his side, and out came water and blood*

[g] Or *gave up his spirit*

[h] Or *a son of God*

ἐπὶ τὸν θεόν, ῥυσάσθω νῦν εἰ θέλει
on – God, let him rescue now if he wants

αὐτόν· εἶπεν γὰρ ὅτι θεοῦ εἰμι υἱός.
him; for he said[,] – of God I am Son.

44 τὸ δ' αὐτὸ καὶ οἱ λῃσταὶ οἱ συσταυρω-
And the same also the robbers – crucified

θέντες σὺν αὐτῷ ὠνείδιζον αὐτόν. **45** Ἀπὸ
with with him reproached him. from

δὲ ἕκτης ὥρας σκότος ἐγένετο ἐπὶ
Now [the] sixth hour darkness occurred over

πᾶσαν τὴν γῆν ἕως ὥρας ἐνάτης.
all the land until hour [the] ninth.

46 περὶ δὲ τὴν ἐνάτην ὥραν ἀνεβόησεν ὁ
And about the ninth hour cried out –

Ἰησοῦς φωνῇ μεγάλῃ λέγων· ηλι ηλι
Jesus voice with a great saying: Eli Eli

λεμα σαβαχθάνι; τοῦτ' ἔστιν· θεέ μου
lema sabachthani? this is: God of me[,]

θεέ μου, ἱνατί με ἐγκατέλιπες; **47** τινὲς
God of me, why me didst thou forsake? some

δὲ τῶν ἐκεῖ ἑστηκότων ἀκούσαντες
And of the [ones] there standing hearing

ἔλεγον ὅτι Ἠλίαν φωνεῖ οὗτος.
said[,] – [2]Elias [3]calls [1]this man.

48 καὶ εὐθέως δραμὼν εἷς ἐξ αὐτῶν καὶ
And immediately running one of them and

λαβὼν σπόγγον πλήσας τε ὄξους καὶ
taking a sponge and filling of(with) vinegar and

περιθεὶς καλάμῳ ἐπότιζεν αὐτόν.
putting [it] round a reed gave to drink him.

49 οἱ δὲ λοιποὶ εἶπαν· ἄφες ἴδωμεν
But the rest said: Leave[,] let us see

εἰ ἔρχεται Ἠλίας σώσων αὐτόν. **50** ὁ
if comes Elias saving him. –

δὲ Ἰησοῦς πάλιν κράξας φωνῇ
And Jesus again crying out voice

μεγάλῃ ἀφῆκεν τὸ πνεῦμα. **51** Καὶ
with a great released the(his) spirit. And

ἰδοὺ τὸ καταπέτασμα τοῦ ναοῦ ἐσχίσθη
behold the veil of the shrine was rent

[ἀπ'] ἄνωθεν ἕως κάτω εἰς δύο, καὶ ἡ
from above to below in two, and the

γῆ ἐσείσθη, καὶ αἱ πέτραι ἐσχίσ-
earth was shaken, and the rocks were

θησαν, **52** καὶ τὰ μνημεῖα ἀνεῴχθησαν
rent, and the tombs were opened

καὶ πολλὰ σώματα τῶν κεκοιμημένων
and many bodies of the having fallen asleep

ἁγίων ἠγέρθησαν· **53** καὶ ἐξελθόντες
saints were raised; and coming forth

ἐκ τῶν μνημείων μετὰ τὴν ἔγερσιν
out of the tombs after the rising

αὐτοῦ εἰσῆλθον εἰς τὴν ἁγίαν πόλιν καὶ
of him entered into the holy city and

ἐνεφανίσθησαν πολλοῖς. **54** Ὁ δὲ ἑκατόν-
appeared to many. And the centu-

ταρχος καὶ οἱ μετ' αὐτοῦ τηροῦντες
rion and the [ones] with him guarding

τὸν Ἰησοῦν ἰδόντες τὸν σεισμὸν καὶ
– Jesus seeing the earthquake and

τὰ γινόμενα ἐφοβήθησαν σφόδρα,
the things happening feared exceedingly,

λέγοντες· ἀληθῶς θεοῦ υἱὸς ἦν οὗτος.
saying: Truly [4]of God [3]Son [2]was [1]this man.

55 Ἦσαν δὲ ἐκεῖ γυναῖκες πολλαὶ
Now there were there women many

Let God rescue him now if he wants him, for he said, 'I am the Son of God.' " 44 In the same way the robbers who were crucified with him also heaped insults on him.

The Death of Jesus

45 From the sixth hour until the ninth hour darkness came over all the land. 46 About the ninth hour Jesus cried out in a loud voice, *"Eloi, Eloi,*[k] *lama sabachthani?"*—which means, "My God, my God, why have you forsaken me?"[l]

47 When some of those standing there heard this, they said, "He's calling Elijah."

48 Immediately one of them ran and got a sponge. He filled it with wine vinegar, put it on a stick, and offered it to Jesus to drink. 49 The rest said, "Now leave him alone. Let's see if Elijah comes to save him."

50 And when Jesus had cried out again in a loud voice, he gave up his spirit.

51 At that moment the curtain of the temple was torn in two from top to bottom. The earth shook and the rocks split. 52 The tombs broke open and the bodies of many holy people who had died were raised to life. 53 They came out of the tombs, and after Jesus' resurrection they went into the holy city and appeared to many people.

54 When the centurion and those with him who were guarding Jesus saw the earthquake and all that had happened, they were terrified, and exclaimed, "Surely he was the Son[m] of God!"

55 Many women were

[k] 46 Some manuscripts *Eli, Eli*

[l] 46 Psalm 22:1

[m] 54 Or *a son*

also there, looking on from
a distance; they had fol-
lowed Jesus from Galilee
and had provided for him.
56 Among them were Mary
Magdalene, and Mary the
mother of James and Jo-
seph, and the mother of the
sons of Zebedee.

The Burial of Jesus

57 When it was evening,
there came a rich man from
Arimathea, named Joseph,
who was also a disciple of
Jesus. 58 He went to Pilate
and asked for the body of
Jesus; then Pilate ordered it
to be given to him. 59 So Joseph took the body and
wrapped it in a clean linen
cloth 60 and laid it in his
own new tomb, which he
had hewn in the rock. He
then rolled a great stone to
the door of the tomb and
went away. 61 Mary Magda-
lene and the other Mary
were there, sitting opposite
the tomb.

The Guard at the Tomb

62 The next day, that is,
after the day of Prepara-
tion, the chief priests and
the Pharisees gathered before Pilate 63 and said, "Sir,
we remember what that im-
postor said while he was
still alive, 'After three days
I will rise again.' 64 Therefore command the tomb to
be made secure until the
third day; otherwise his
disciples may go and steal
him away, and tell the people, 'He has been raised
from the dead,' and the last
deception would be worse
than the first." 65 Pilate said
to them, "You have a

ἀπὸ μακρόθεν θεωροῦσαι, αἵτινες ἠκολού-
from afar beholding, who followed

θησαν τῷ Ἰησοῦ ἀπὸ τῆς Γαλιλαίας
– Jesus from – Galilee

διακονοῦσαι αὐτῷ· 56 ἐν αἷς ἦν
ministering to him; among whom was

Μαρία ἡ Μαγδαληνή, καὶ Μαρία ἡ
Mary the Magdalene, and Mary the

τοῦ Ἰακώβου καὶ Ἰωσὴφ μήτηρ, καὶ ἡ
– of James and of Joseph mother, and the

μήτηρ τῶν υἱῶν Ζεβεδαίου.
mother of the sons of Zebedee.

57 Ὀψίας δὲ γενομένης ἦλθεν ἄνθρωπος
Now evening having come* came man
= when evening had come

πλούσιος ἀπὸ Ἁριμαθαίας, τοὔνομα Ἰωσήφ,
a rich from Arimathæa, the name Joseph,

ὃς καὶ αὐτὸς ἐμαθητεύθη τῷ Ἰησοῦ·
who also himself was discipled – to Jesus;

58 οὗτος προσελθὼν τῷ Πιλάτῳ ᾐτήσατο
this man approaching – *to* Pilate asked

τὸ σῶμα τοῦ Ἰησοῦ. τότε ὁ Πιλᾶτος
the body – of Jesus. Then – Pilate

ἐκέλευσεν ἀποδοθῆναι. 59 καὶ λαβὼν
commanded [it] to be given [him]. And taking

τὸ σῶμα ὁ Ἰωσὴφ ἐνετύλιξεν αὐτὸ [ἐν]
the body – Joseph wrapped it in

σινδόνι καθαρᾷ, 60 καὶ ἔθηκεν αὐτὸ ἐν
sheet a clean, and placed it in

τῷ καινῷ αὐτοῦ μνημείῳ ὃ ἐλατό-
the new of him tomb which he

μησεν ἐν τῇ πέτρᾳ, καὶ προσκυλίσας
hewed in the rock, and having rolled *to*

λίθον μέγαν τῇ θύρᾳ τοῦ μνημείου
stone a great to the door of the tomb

ἀπῆλθεν. 61 Ἦν δὲ ἐκεῖ Μαριὰμ
went away. And there was there Mary

ἡ Μαγδαληνὴ καὶ ἡ ἄλλη Μαρία,
the Magdalene and the other Mary,

καθήμεναι ἀπέναντι τοῦ τάφου. 62 Τῇ
sitting opposite the grave. on the

δὲ ἐπαύριον, ἥτις ἐστὶν μετὰ τὴν παρα-
And morrow, which is after the prepara

σκευήν, συνήχθησαν οἱ ἀρχιερεῖς
tion, were assembled the chief priests

καὶ οἱ Φαρισαῖοι πρὸς Πιλᾶτον 63 λέ-
and the Pharisees to Pilate say-

γοντες· κύριε, ἐμνήσθημεν ὅτι ἐκεῖνος
ing: Sir, we remembered that that

ὁ πλάνος εἶπεν ἔτι ζῶν· μετὰ τρεῖς
– deceiver said yet living: After three

ἡμέρας ἐγείρομαι. 64 κέλευσον οὖν
days I am raised. Command therefore

ἀσφαλισθῆναι τὸν τάφον ἕως τῆς
to be made fast the grave until the

τρίτης ἡμέρας, μήποτε ἐλθόντες οἱ μαθηταὶ
third day, lest coming the disciples

κλέψωσιν αὐτὸν καὶ εἴπωσιν τῷ λαῷ·
may steal him and may say to the people:

ἠγέρθη ἀπὸ τῶν νεκρῶν, καὶ ἔσται
He was raised from the dead, and will be

ἡ ἐσχάτη πλάνη χείρων τῆς πρώτης.
the last deceit worse [than] the first.

65 ἔφη αὐτοῖς ὁ Πιλᾶτος· ἔχετε κου-
Said to them – Pilate: Ye have a

there, watching from a distance. They had followed
Jesus from Galilee to care
for his needs. 56 Among
them were Mary Magda-
lene, Mary the mother of
James and Joses, and the
mother of Zebedee's sons.

The Burial of Jesus

57 As evening ap-
proached, there came a
rich man from Arimathea,
named Joseph, who had
himself become a disciple
of Jesus. 58 Going to Pilate,
he asked for Jesus' body,
and Pilate ordered that it be
given to him. 59 Joseph took
the body, wrapped it in a
clean linen cloth, 60 and
placed it in his own new
tomb that he had cut out of
the rock. He rolled a big
stone in front of the en-
trance to the tomb and
went away. 61 Mary Magda-
lene and the other Mary
were sitting there opposite
the tomb.

The Guard at the Tomb

62 The next day, the one
after Preparation Day, the
chief priests and the Pharisees went to Pilate.
63 "Sir," they said, "we remember that while he was
still alive that deceiver
said, 'After three days I
will rise again.' 64 So give
the order for the tomb to be
made secure until the third
day. Otherwise, his disciples may come and steal
the body and tell the people
that he has been raised
from the dead. This last deception will be worse than
the first."
65 "Take a guard," Pilate
answered. "Go, make the

guard[i] of soldiers; go,
make it as secure as you
can."[j] 66 So they went with
the guard and made the
tomb secure by sealing the
stone.

Chapter 28

The Resurrection of Jesus

AFTER the sabbath, as
the first day of the
week was dawning, Mary
Magdalene and the other
Mary went to see the tomb.
2 And suddenly there was a
great earthquake; for an angel of the Lord, descending
from heaven, came and
rolled back the stone and
sat on it. 3 His appearance
was like lightning, and his
clothing white as snow.
4 For fear of him the guards
shook and became like
dead men. 5 But the angel
said to the women, "Do not
be afraid; I know that you
are looking for Jesus who
was crucified. 6 He is not
here; for he has been
raised, as he said. Come,
see the place where he[k]
lay. 7 Then go quickly and
tell his disciples, 'He has
been raised from the
dead,[l] and indeed he is going ahead of you to Galilee;
there you will see him.'
This is my message for
you." 8 So they left the
tomb quickly with fear and
great joy, and ran to tell his
disciples. 9 Suddenly Jesus
met them and said, "Greetings!" And they came to
him, took hold of his feet,
and worshiped him. 10 Then

[i] Or *Take a guard*
[j] Gk *you know how*
[k] Other ancient authorities read *the Lord*
[l] Other ancient authorities lack *from the dead*

στωδίαν· ὑπάγετε ἀσφαλίσασθε ὡς οἴδατε.
guard; go ye make fast as ye know*.

66 οἱ δὲ πορευθέντες ἠσφαλίσαντο τὸν
And they going made fast the

τάφον σφραγίσαντες τὸν λίθον μετὰ τῆς
grave sealing the stone with the

κουστωδίας.
guard.

28 Ὀψὲ δὲ σαββάτων, τῇ ἐπιφωσκούσῃ
But late of [the] sabbaths, at the drawing on

εἰς μίαν σαββάτων, ἦλθεν Μαριὰμ ἡ
toward one of [the] sabbaths, came Mary the
=the first day of the week,

Μαγδαληνὴ καὶ ἡ ἄλλη Μαρία θεωρῆσαι
Magdalene and the other Mary to view

τὸν τάφον. 2 καὶ ἰδοὺ σεισμὸς ἐγένετο
the grave. And behold earthquake occurred

μέγας· ἄγγελος γὰρ κυρίου καταβὰς
a great; for an angel of [the] Lord descending

ἐξ οὐρανοῦ καὶ προσελθὼν ἀπεκύλισεν
out of heaven and approaching rolled away

τὸν λίθον καὶ ἐκάθητο ἐπάνω αὐτοῦ.
the stone and sat upon it.

3 ἦν δὲ ἡ εἰδέα αὐτοῦ ὡς ἀστραπή,
And was the appearance of him as lightning,

καὶ τὸ ἔνδυμα αὐτοῦ λευκὸν ὡς χιών.
and the dress of him white as snow.

4 ἀπὸ δὲ τοῦ φόβου αὐτοῦ ἐσείσθησαν
And from the fear of him were shaken

οἱ τηροῦντες καὶ ἐγενήθησαν ὡς
the [ones] guarding and they became as

νεκροί. 5 ἀποκριθεὶς δὲ ὁ ἄγγελος
dead. And answering the angel

εἶπεν ταῖς γυναιξίν· μὴ φοβεῖσθε ὑμεῖς·
said to the women: Fear not ye;

οἶδα γὰρ ὅτι Ἰησοῦν τὸν ἐσταυρω-
for I know that Jesus the [one] *having been*

μένον ζητεῖτε· 6 οὐκ ἔστιν ὧδε·
crucified ye seek; he is not here;

ἠγέρθη γὰρ καθὼς εἶπεν· δεῦτε ἴδετε τὸν
for he was raised as he said; come see ye the

τόπον ὅπου ἔκειτο. 7 καὶ ταχὺ πορευθεῖσαι
place where he lay. And quickly going

εἴπατε τοῖς μαθηταῖς αὐτοῦ ὅτι ἠγέρθη
tell the disciples of him that he was raised

ἀπὸ τῶν νεκρῶν, καὶ ἰδοὺ προάγει ὑμᾶς
from the dead, and behold he goes before you

εἰς τὴν Γαλιλαίαν, ἐκεῖ αὐτὸν ὄψεσθε.
to – Galilee, there him ye will see.

ἰδοὺ εἶπον ὑμῖν. 8 καὶ ἀπελθοῦσαι ταχὺ
Behold I told you. And going away quickly

ἀπὸ τοῦ μνημείου μετὰ φόβου καὶ χαρᾶς
from the tomb with fear and joy

μεγάλης ἔδραμον ἀπαγγεῖλαι τοῖς
great they ran to announce to the

μαθηταῖς αὐτοῦ. 9 καὶ ἰδοὺ Ἰησοῦς
disciples of him. And behold Jesus

ὑπήντησεν αὐταῖς λέγων· χαίρετε. αἱ δὲ
met them saying: Hail. And they

προσελθοῦσαι ἐκράτησαν αὐτοῦ τοὺς πόδας
approaching held of him the feet

καὶ προσεκύνησαν αὐτῷ. 10 τότε λέγει
and worshipped him. Then says

*** can. See note on page xviii.**

tomb as secure as you
know how." 66 So they
went and made the tomb
secure by putting a seal on
the stone and posting the
guard.

Chapter 28

The Resurrection

AFTER the Sabbath, at
dawn on the first day
of the week, Mary Magda-
lene and the other Mary
went to look at the tomb.
2 There was a violent
earthquake, for an angel of
the Lord came down from
heaven and, going to the
tomb, rolled back the stone
and sat on it. 3 His appearance was like lightning, and
his clothes were white as
snow. 4 The guards were so
afraid of him that they
shook and became like
dead men.
5 The angel said to the
women, "Do not be afraid,
for I know that you are
looking for Jesus, who was
crucified. 6 He is not here;
he has risen, just as he said.
Come and see the place
where he lay. 7 Then go
quickly and tell his disciples: 'He has risen from the
dead and is going ahead of
you into Galilee. There you
will see him.' Now I have
told you."
8 So the women hurried
away from the tomb, afraid
yet filled with joy, and ran
to tell his disciples. 9 Suddenly Jesus met them.
"Greetings," he said. They
came to him, clasped his
feet and worshiped him.

Jesus said to them, "Do not
be afraid; go and tell my
brothers to go to Galilee;
there they will see me."

The Report of the Guard

11 While they were go-
ing, some of the guard went
into the city and told the
chief priests everything
that had happened. 12 After
the priests[m] had assembled
with the elders, they de-
vised a plan to give a large
sum of money to the sol-
diers, 13 telling them, "You
must say, 'His disciples
came by night and stole him
away while we were
asleep.' 14 If this comes to
the governor's ears, we will
satisfy him and keep you
out of trouble." 15 So they
took the money and did as
they were directed. And
this story is still told among
the Jews to this day.

The Commissioning of the Disciples

16 Now the eleven dis-
ciples went to Galilee, to
the mountain to which
Jesus had directed them.
17 When they saw him, they
worshiped him; but some
doubted. 18 And Jesus came
and said to them, "All authority in heaven and on
earth has been given to me.
19 Go therefore and make
disciples of all nations,
baptizing them in the name
of the Father and of the Son
and of the Holy Spirit,
20 and teaching them to
obey everything that I have
commanded you. And re-
member, I am with you al-
ways, to the end of the
age."[n]

[m] Gk *they*
[n] Other ancient authorities add *Amen*

αὐταῖς ὁ Ἰησοῦς· μὴ φοβεῖσθε· ὑπάγετε
to them – Jesus: Fear ye not; go ye
ἀπαγγείλατε τοῖς ἀδελφοῖς μου ἵνα
announce to the brothers of me that
ἀπέλθωσιν εἰς τὴν Γαλιλαίαν, κἀκεῖ
they may go away into – Galilee, and there
με ὄψονται. **11** Πορευομένων δὲ αὐτῶν
me they will see. And going them[a]
= as they were going
ἰδού τινες τῆς κουστωδίας ἐλθόντες εἰς
behold some of the guard coming into
τὴν πόλιν ἀπήγγειλαν τοῖς ἀρχιερεῦσιν
the city announced to the chief priests
ἅπαντα τὰ γενόμενα. **12** καὶ συν-
all the things having happened. And being
αχθέντες μετὰ τῶν πρεσβυτέρων συμβούλιόν
assembled with the elders [3]counsel
τε λαβόντες ἀργύρια ἱκανὰ ἔδωκαν τοῖς
[1]and [2]taking silver enough gave to the
στρατιώταις, **13** λέγοντες· εἴπατε ὅτι οἱ
soldiers, saying: Say ye that the
μαθηταὶ αὐτοῦ νυκτὸς ἐλθόντες ἔκλεψαν
disciples of him of(by) night coming stole
αὐτὸν ἡμῶν κοιμωμένων. **14** καὶ ἐὰν
him we sleeping.[a] And if
= while we slept.
ἀκουσθῇ τοῦτο ἐπὶ τοῦ ἡγεμόνος,
be heard this before the governor,
ἡμεῖς πείσομεν καὶ ὑμᾶς ἀμερίμνους
we will persuade and you free from anxiety
ποιήσομεν. **15** οἱ δὲ λαβόντες ἀργύρια
we will make. And they taking silver
ἐποίησαν ὡς ἐδιδάχθησαν. Καὶ διεφη-
did as they were taught. And was spread
μίσθη ὁ λόγος οὗτος παρὰ Ἰουδαίοις
about – saying this by Jews
μέχρι τῆς σήμερον [ἡμέρας]. **16** Οἱ δὲ
until to-day. So the
ἕνδεκα μαθηταὶ ἐπορεύθησαν εἰς τὴν
eleven disciples went to –
Γαλιλαίαν, εἰς τὸ ὄρος οὗ ἐτάξατο
Galilee, to the mountain where appointed
αὐτοῖς ὁ Ἰησοῦς, **17** καὶ ἰδόντες αὐτὸν
them – Jesus, and seeing him
προσεκύνησαν, οἱ δὲ ἐδίστασαν. **18** καὶ
they worshipped, but some doubted. And
προσελθὼν ὁ Ἰησοῦς ἐλάλησεν αὐτοῖς
approaching – Jesus talked with them
λέγων· ἐδόθη μοι πᾶσα ἐξουσία ἐν
saying: was given to me All authority in
οὐρανῷ καὶ ἐπὶ [τῆς] γῆς. **19** πορευθέντες
heaven and on the earth. Going
οὖν μαθητεύσατε πάντα τὰ ἔθνη, βαπτίζ-
therefore disciple ye all the nations, baptiz-
οντες αὐτοὺς εἰς τὸ ὄνομα τοῦ πατρὸς
ing them in the name of the Father
καὶ τοῦ υἱοῦ καὶ τοῦ ἁγίου πνεύματος,
and of the Son and of the Holy Spirit,
20 διδάσκοντες αὐτοὺς τηρεῖν πάντα
teaching them to observe all things
ὅσα ἐνετειλάμην ὑμῖν· καὶ ἰδοὺ ἐγὼ
whatever I gave command to you; and behold I
μεθ' ὑμῶν εἰμι πάσας τὰς ἡμέρας ἕως
with you am all the days until
τῆς συντελείας τοῦ αἰῶνος.
the completion of the age.

10Then Jesus said to them,
"Do not be afraid. Go and
tell my brothers to go to
Galilee; there they will see
me."

The Guards' Report

11While the women were
on their way, some of the
guards went into the city
and reported to the chief
priests everything that had
happened. 12When the
chief priests had met with
the elders and devised a
plan, they gave the soldiers
a large sum of money,
13telling them, "You are to
say, 'His disciples came
during the night and stole
him away while we were
asleep.' 14If this report gets
to the governor, we will
satisfy him and keep you
out of trouble." 15So the
soldiers took the money
and did as they were in-
structed. And this story has
been widely circulated
among the Jews to this very
day.

The Great Commission

16Then the eleven disci-
ples went to Galilee, to the
mountain where Jesus had
told them to go. 17When
they saw him, they wor-
shiped him; but some
doubted. 18Then Jesus
came to them and said,
"All authority in heaven
and on earth has been given
to me. 19Therefore go and
make disciples of all na-
tions, baptizing them in[n]
the name of the Father and
of the Son and of the Holy
Spirit, 20and teaching them
to obey everything I have
commanded you. And
surely I am with you al-
ways, to the very end of the
age."

[n] *19* Or *into*; see Acts 8:16; 19:5; Romans 6:3; 1 Cor. 1:13; 10:2 and Gal. 3:27.

The Gospel According
to
Mark

Chapter 1

The Proclamation of John the Baptist

THE beginning of the
good news[a] of Jesus
Christ, the Son of God.[b]
2 As it is written in the
prophet Isaiah,[c]
"See, I am sending
my messenger
ahead of you,[d]
who will prepare
your way;
3 the voice of one
crying out in the
wilderness:
'Prepare the way of
the Lord,
make his paths
straight,' "
4 John the baptizer ap-
peared[e] in the wilderness,
proclaiming a baptism of
repentance for the forgiveness of sins. 5 And people
from the whole Judean
countryside and all the people of Jerusalem were going
out to him, and were bap-
tized by him in the river
Jordan, confessing their
sins. 6 Now John was
clothed with camel's hair,
with a leather belt around
his waist, and he ate locusts
and wild honey. 7 He pro-
claimed, "The one who is
more powerful than I is
coming after me; I am not
worthy to stoop down and
untie the thong of his sandals. 8 I have baptized you
with[f] water; but he will
baptize you with[f] the Holy
Spirit."

The Baptism of Jesus

9 In those days Jesus
came from Nazareth of
Galilee and was baptized
by John in the Jordan.
10 And just as he was coming up out of the water, he
saw the heavens torn apart
and the Spirit descending
like a dove on him. 11 And a
voice came from heaven,
"You are my Son, the Be-
loved;[g] with you I am well
pleased."

The Temptation of Jesus

12 And the Spirit imme-
diately drove him out into
the wilderness. 13 He was in
the wilderness forty days,
tempted by Satan; and he
was with the wild beasts;
and the angels waited on
him.

[a] Or *gospel*
[b] Other ancient authorities lack *the Son of God*
[c] Other ancient authorities read *in the prophets*
[d] Gk *before your face*
[e] Other ancient authorities read *John was baptizing*
[f] Or *in*
[g] Or *my beloved Son*

ΚΑΤΑ ΜΑΡΚΟΝ
According to Mark

1 Ἀρχὴ τοῦ εὐαγγελίου Ἰησοῦ Χριστοῦ.
[The] beginning of the gospel of Jesus Christ.
2 Καθὼς γέγραπται ἐν τῷ Ἠσαΐᾳ τῷ
As it has been written in – Isaiah the
προφήτῃ· ἰδοὺ ἀποστέλλω τὸν ἄγγελόν μου
prophet: Behold[,] I send the messenger of me
πρὸ προσώπου σου, ὃς κατασκευάσει τὴν ὁδόν
before [the] face of thee, who will prepare the way
σου· **3** φωνὴ βοῶντος ἐν τῇ ἐρήμῳ· ἑτοιμάσατε
of thee; a voice of [one] crying in the desert: Prepare ye
τὴν ὁδὸν κυρίου, εὐθείας ποιεῖτε τὰς τρίβους
the way of [the] Lord, straight make the paths
αὐτοῦ, **4** ἐγένετο Ἰωάννης ὁ βαπτίζων ἐν τῇ
of him, came John the [one] baptizing in the
ἐρήμῳ κηρύσσων βάπτισμα μετανοίας εἰς
desert proclaiming a baptism of repentance for
ἄφεσιν ἁμαρτιῶν. **5** καὶ ἐξεπορεύετο πρὸς
forgiveness of sins. And went out to
αὐτὸν πᾶσα ἡ Ἰουδαία χώρα καὶ οἱ Ἱεροσο-
him all the Judæan country and the Jerusa-
λυμῖται πάντες, καὶ ἐβαπτίζοντο ὑπ᾽ αὐτοῦ
lemites all, and were baptized by him
ἐν τῷ Ἰορδάνῃ ποταμῷ ἐξομολογούμενοι τὰς
in the Jordan river confessing the
ἁμαρτίας αὐτῶν. **6** καὶ ἦν ὁ Ἰωάννης
sins of them. And was – John
ἐνδεδυμένος τρίχας καμήλου καὶ ζώνην
having been clothed [in] hairs of a camel and girdle
δερματίνην περὶ τὴν ὀσφὺν αὐτοῦ, καὶ ἔσθων
a leathern round the loin[s] of him, and eating
ἀκρίδας καὶ μέλι ἄγριον. **7** καὶ ἐκήρυσσεν
locusts and honey wild. And he proclaimed
λέγων· ἔρχεται ὁ ἰσχυρότερός μου ὀπίσω
saying: Comes the [one] stronger of me after
=than I
[μου], οὗ οὐκ εἰμὶ ἱκανὸς κύψας λῦσαι
me, of whom I am not competent stooping to loosen
τὸν ἱμάντα τῶν ὑποδημάτων αὐτοῦ. **8** ἐγὼ
the thong of the sandals of him. I
ἐβάπτισα ὑμᾶς ὕδατι, αὐτὸς δὲ βαπτίσει ὑμᾶς
baptized you in water, but he will baptize you
πνεύματι ἁγίῳ.
Spirit in [the] Holy.
9 Καὶ ἐγένετο ἐν ἐκείναις ταῖς ἡμέραις
And it came to pass in those – days
ἦλθεν Ἰησοῦς ἀπὸ Ναζαρὲθ τῆς Γαλιλαίας
came Jesus from Nazareth – of Galilee
καὶ ἐβαπτίσθη εἰς τὸν Ἰορδάνην ὑπὸ
and was baptized in the Jordan by
Ἰωάννου. **10** καὶ εὐθὺς ἀναβαίνων ἐκ τοῦ
John. And immediately going up out of the
ὕδατος εἶδεν σχιζομένους τοὺς οὐρανοὺς
water he saw being rent the heavens
καὶ τὸ πνεῦμα ὡς περιστερὰν καταβαῖνον
and the Spirit as a dove coming down
εἰς αὐτόν· **11** καὶ φωνὴ [ἐγένετο] ἐκ τῶν
to him; and a voice there was out of the
οὐρανῶν· σὺ εἶ ὁ υἱός μου ὁ ἀγαπητός,
heavens: Thou art the Son of me the beloved,
ἐν σοὶ εὐδόκησα. **12** Καὶ εὐθὺς τὸ
in thee I was well pleased. And immediately the
πνεῦμα αὐτὸν ἐκβάλλει εἰς τὴν ἔρημον.
Spirit him thrusts forth into the desert.
13 καὶ ἦν ἐν τῇ ἐρήμῳ τεσσεράκοντα
And he was in the desert forty
ἡμέρας πειραζόμενος ὑπὸ τοῦ σατανᾶ, καὶ
days being tempted by – Satan, and
ἦν μετὰ τῶν θηρίων, καὶ οἱ ἄγγελοι
was with the wild beasts, and the angels

Mark

Chapter 1

John the Baptist Prepares the Way

THE beginning of the
gospel about Jesus
Christ, the Son of God.[a]

2 It is written in Isaiah the
prophet:

"I will send my
messenger ahead of
you,
who will prepare your
way"[b]—
3 "a voice of one calling in
the desert,
'Prepare the way for the
Lord,
make straight paths for
him.' "[c]

4 And so John came, baptizing in the desert region and
preaching a baptism of repentance for the forgive-
ness of sins. 5 The whole Judean countryside and all
the people of Jerusalem
went out to him. Confess-
ing their sins, they were
baptized by him in the Jordan River. 6 John wore
clothing made of camel's
hair, with a leather belt
around his waist, and he ate
locusts and wild honey.
7 And this was his message:
"After me will come one
more powerful than I, the
thongs of whose sandals I
am not worthy to stoop
down and untie. 8 I baptize
you with[d] water, but he
will baptize you with the
Holy Spirit."

The Baptism and Temptation of Jesus

9 At that time Jesus came
from Nazareth in Galilee
and was baptized by John
in the Jordan. 10 As Jesus
was coming up out of the
water, he saw heaven being
torn open and the Spirit descending on him like a
dove. 11 And a voice came
from heaven: "You are my
Son, whom I love; with you
I am well pleased."
12 At once the Spirit sent
him out into the desert,
13 and he was in the desert
forty days, being tempted
by Satan. He was with the
wild animals, and angels attended him.

[a] *1* Some manuscripts do not have *the Son of God.*
[b] *2* Mal. 3:1
[c] *3* Isaiah 40:3
[d] *8* Or *in*

The Beginning of the Galilean Ministry

14 Now after John was
arrested, Jesus came to
Galilee, proclaiming the
good news[a] of God,[h]
15and saying, "The time is
fulfilled, and the kingdom
of God has come near;[i] repent, and believe in the
good news."[a]

Jesus Calls the First Disciples

16 As Jesus passed
along the Sea of Galilee, he
saw Simon and his brother
Andrew casting a net into
the sea—for they were
fishermen. 17And Jesus
said to them, "Follow me
and I will make you fish for
people." 18And immediate-
ly they left their nets and
followed him. 19As he went
a little farther, he saw
James son of Zebedee and
his brother John, who were
in their boat mending the
nets. 20Immediately he
called them; and they left
their father Zebedee in the
boat with the hired men,
and followed him.

The Man with an Unclean Spirit

21 They went to Caper-
naum; and when the sab-
bath came, he entered the
synagogue and taught.
22They were astounded at
his teaching, for he taught
them as one having authority, and not as the scribes.
23Just then there was in
their synagogue a man with
an unclean spirit, 24and he
cried out, "What have you
to do with us, Jesus of Nazareth? Have you come to
destroy us? I know who
you are, the Holy One of
God." 25But Jesus rebuked
him, saying, "Be silent, and

[h] Other ancient authorities read *of the kingdom*
[i] Or *is at hand*

διηκόνουν αὐτῷ.
ministered to him.

14 Καὶ μετὰ τὸ παραδοθῆναι τὸν
And after the to be delivered –
= after John was delivered

Ἰωάννην ἦλθεν ὁ Ἰησοῦς εἰς τὴν Γαλιλαίαν
John[b] came – Jesus into – Galilee

κηρύσσων τὸ εὐαγγέλιον τοῦ θεοῦ 15 [καὶ
proclaiming the gospel – of God and

λέγων], ὅτι πεπλήρωται ὁ καιρὸς καὶ
saying, – Has been fulfilled the time and

ἤγγικεν ἡ βασιλεία τοῦ θεοῦ· μετανοεῖτε
has drawn near the kingdom – of God; repent ye

καὶ πιστεύετε ἐν τῷ εὐαγγελίῳ. 16 Καὶ
and believe in the gospel. And

παράγων παρὰ τὴν θάλασσαν τῆς Γαλιλαίας
passing along beside the sea – of Galilee

εἶδεν Σίμωνα καὶ Ἀνδρέαν τὸν ἀδελφὸν
he saw Simon and Andrew the brother

Σίμωνος ἀμφιβάλλοντας ἐν τῇ θαλάσσῃ·
of Simon casting [a net] in the sea;

ἦσαν γὰρ ἁλεεῖς. 17 καὶ εἶπεν αὐτοῖς
for they were fishers. And said to them

ὁ Ἰησοῦς· δεῦτε ὀπίσω μου, καὶ ποιήσω
– Jesus: Come after me, and I will make

ὑμᾶς γενέσθαι ἁλεεῖς ἀνθρώπων. 18 καὶ
you to become fishers of men. And

εὐθὺς ἀφέντες τὰ δίκτυα ἠκολούθησαν
immediately leaving the nets they followed

αὐτῷ. 19 Καὶ προβὰς ὀλίγον εἶδεν
him. And going forward a little he saw

Ἰάκωβον τὸν τοῦ Ζεβεδαίου καὶ Ἰωάννην
James the [son] – of Zebedee and John

τὸν ἀδελφὸν αὐτοῦ καὶ αὐτοὺς ἐν τῷ
the brother of him even them in the

πλοίῳ καταρτίζοντας τὰ δίκτυα. 20 καὶ
ship mending the nets. And

εὐθὺς ἐκάλεσεν αὐτούς· καὶ ἀφέντες τὸν
immediately he called them; and leaving the

πατέρα αὐτῶν Ζεβεδαῖον ἐν τῷ πλοίῳ
father of them Zebedee in the ship

μετὰ τῶν μισθωτῶν ἀπῆλθον ὀπίσω αὐτοῦ.
with the hired servants they went after him.

21 Καὶ εἰσπορεύονται εἰς Καφαρναούμ·
And they enter into Capernaum;

καὶ εὐθὺς τοῖς σάββασιν εἰσελθὼν
and immediately on the sabbaths entering

εἰς τὴν συναγωγὴν ἐδίδασκεν. 22 καὶ
into the synagogue he taught. And

ἐξεπλήσσοντο ἐπὶ τῇ διδαχῇ αὐτοῦ· ἦν
they were astounded on(at) the teaching of him; [2]he was

γὰρ διδάσκων αὐτοὺς ὡς ἐξουσίαν ἔχων,
[1]for teaching them as authority having,

καὶ οὐχ ὡς οἱ γραμματεῖς. 23 Καὶ εὐθὺς
and not as the scribes. And immediately

ἦν ἐν τῇ συναγωγῇ αὐτῶν ἄνθρωπος
there was in the synagogue of them a man

ἐν πνεύματι ἀκαθάρτῳ, καὶ ἀνέκραξεν
in spirit an unclean, and he cried out

24 λέγων· τί ἡμῖν καὶ σοί, Ἰησοῦ
saying: What to us and to thee, Jesus

Ναζαρηνέ; ἦλθες ἀπολέσαι ἡμᾶς; οἶδά
Nazarene? camest thou to destroy us? I know

σε τίς εἶ, ὁ ἅγιος τοῦ θεοῦ. 25 καὶ
thee who thou art, the holy [one] – of God. And

ἐπετίμησεν αὐτῷ ὁ Ἰησοῦς [λέγων]·
rebuked him – Jesus saying:

The Calling of the First Disciples

14After John was put in
prison, Jesus went into
Galilee, proclaiming the
good news of God. 15"The
time has come," he said.
"The kingdom of God is
near. Repent and believe
the good news!"
16As Jesus walked beside
the Sea of Galilee, he saw
Simon and his brother An-
drew casting a net into the
lake, for they were fishermen. 17"Come, follow
me," Jesus said, "and I
will make you fishers of
men." 18At once they left
their nets and followed
him.
19When he had gone a lit-
tle farther, he saw James
son of Zebedee and his
brother John in a boat, preparing their nets. 20Without
delay he called them, and
they left their father Zebedee in the boat with the
hired men and followed
him.

Jesus Drives Out an Evil Spirit

21They went to Caperna-
um, and when the Sabbath
came, Jesus went into the
synagogue and began to
teach. 22The people were
amazed at his teaching, because he taught them as
one who had authority, not
as the teachers of the law.
23Just then a man in their
synagogue who was pos-
sessed by an evil[e] spirit
cried out, 24"What do you
want with us, Jesus of Nazareth? Have you come to
destroy us? I know who
you are—the Holy One of
God!"
25"Be quiet!" said Jesus

[e] 23 Greek *unclean*; also in verses 26 and 27

come out of him!" 26 And
the unclean spirit, convulsing him and crying with a
loud voice, came out of
him. 27 They were all
amazed, and they kept on
asking one another, "What
is this? A new teaching—
with authority! He[j] commands even the unclean
spirits, and they obey
him." 28 At once his fame
began to spread throughout
the surrounding region of
Galilee.

Jesus Heals Many at Simon's House

29 As soon as they[k] left
the synagogue, they en-
tered the house of Simon
and Andrew, with James
and John. 30 Now Simon's
mother-in-law was in bed
with a fever, and they told
him about her at once.
31 He came and took her by
the hand and lifted her up.
Then the fever left her, and
she began to serve them.
32 That evening, at sun-
down, they brought to him
all who were sick or pos-
sessed with demons. 33 And
the whole city was gath-
ered around the door.
34 And he cured many who
were sick with various diseases, and cast out many
demons; and he would not
permit the demons to
speak, because they knew
him.

A Preaching Tour in Galilee

35 In the morning, while
it was still very dark, he got
up and went out to a deserted place, and there he
prayed. 36 And Simon and
his companions hunted for
him. 37 When they found
him, they said to him, "Everyone is searching for
you." 38 He answered, "Let
us go on to the neighboring

[j] Or *A new teaching! With authority he*
[k] Other ancient authorities read *he*

φιμώθητι καὶ ἔξελθε [ἐξ αὐτοῦ]. 26 καὶ
Be quiet and come *out* out of him. And
σπαράξαν αὐτὸν τὸ πνεῦμα τὸ ἀκάθαρτον
throwing him the spirit – unclean
καὶ φωνῆσαν φωνῇ μεγάλῃ ἐξῆλθεν ἐξ
and shouting voice with a great he came *out* out of
αὐτοῦ. 27 καὶ ἐθαμβήθησαν ἅπαντες, ὥστε
him. And were astounded all, so as = so that
συζητεῖν αὐτοὺς λέγοντας· τί ἐστιν τοῦτο;
to debate them[b] saying: What is this? they debated
διδαχὴ καινὴ κατ' ἐξουσίαν· καὶ τοῖς
teaching a new by authority; and the
πνεύμασι τοῖς ἀκαθάρτοις ἐπιτάσσει, καὶ
spirits – unclean he commands, and
ὑπακούουσιν αὐτῷ. 28 καὶ ἐξῆλθεν ἡ
they obey him. And went forth the
ἀκοὴ αὐτοῦ εὐθὺς πανταχοῦ εἰς ὅλην
report of him immediately everywhere into all
τὴν περίχωρον τῆς Γαλιλαίας. 29 Καὶ
the neighbourhood – of Galilee. And
εὐθὺς ἐκ τῆς συναγωγῆς ἐξελθόντες ἦλθον
immediately out of the synagogue going forth they came
εἰς τὴν οἰκίαν Σίμωνος καὶ Ἀνδρέου
into the house of Simon and Andrew
μετὰ Ἰακώβου καὶ Ἰωάννου. 30 ἡ δὲ
with James and John. Now the
πενθερὰ Σίμωνος κατέκειτο πυρέσσουσα,
mother-in-law of Simon was laid [aside] fever-stricken,
καὶ εὐθὺς λέγουσιν αὐτῷ περὶ αὐτῆς.
and immediately they tell him about her.
31 καὶ προσελθὼν ἤγειρεν αὐτὴν κρατήσας
And approaching he raised her holding
τῆς χειρός καὶ ἀφῆκεν αὐτὴν ὁ πυρετός,
the(her) hand; and left her the fever,
καὶ διηκόνει αὐτοῖς. 32 Ὀψίας δὲ γενο-
and she served them. And evening com- = when evening
μένης, ὅτε ἔδυσεν ὁ ἥλιος, ἔφερον πρὸς
ing,[a] when set the sun, they brought to came,
αὐτὸν πάντας τοὺς κακῶς ἔχοντας καὶ
him all the [ones] ill having and = those who were ill
τοὺς δαιμονιζομένους· 33 καὶ ἦν ὅλη ἡ
the being demon-possessed; and was all the
πόλις ἐπισυνηγμένη πρὸς τὴν θύραν.
city *having been* assembled at the door.
34 καὶ ἐθεράπευσεν πολλοὺς κακῶς ἔχοντας
And he healed many ill having = who were ill
ποικίλαις νόσοις, καὶ δαιμόνια πολλὰ
with various diseases, and demons many
ἐξέβαλεν, καὶ οὐκ ἤφιεν λαλεῖν τὰ δαιμόνια,
he expelled, and did not allow to speak the demons,
ὅτι ᾔδεισαν αὐτόν. 35 Καὶ πρωῒ ἔννυχα
because they knew him. And [3]early [4]in the night
λίαν ἀναστὰς ἐξῆλθεν καὶ ἀπῆλθεν εἰς
[2]very [1]rising up he went out and went away to
ἔρημον τόπον, κἀκεῖ προσηύχετο. 36 καὶ
a desert place, and there prayed. And
κατεδίωξεν αὐτὸν Σίμων καὶ οἱ μετ'
hunted down him Simon and the [ones] with
αὐτοῦ, καὶ εὗρον αὐτὸν καὶ λέγουσιν
him, and found him and say
αὐτῷ 37 ὅτι πάντες ζητοῦσίν σε. 38 καὶ
to him[,] – All are seeking thee. And
λέγει αὐτοῖς· ἄγωμεν ἀλλαχοῦ εἰς τὰς
he says to them: Let us go elsewhere into the

sternly. "Come out of
him!" 26 The evil spirit
shook the man violently
and came out of him with a
shriek.
27 The people were all so
amazed that they asked
each other, "What is this?
A new teaching—and with
authority! He even gives
orders to evil spirits and
they obey him." 28 News
about him spread quickly
over the whole region of
Galilee.

Jesus Heals Many

29 As soon as they left the
synagogue, they went with
James and John to the
home of Simon and An-
drew. 30 Simon's mother-in-
law was in bed with a fever,
and they told Jesus about
her. 31 So he went to her,
took her hand and helped
her up. The fever left her
and she began to wait on
them.
32 That evening after sun-
set the people brought to
Jesus all the sick and demon-possessed. 33 The
whole town gathered at the
door, 34 and Jesus healed
many who had various dis-
eases. He also drove out
many demons, but he
would not let the demons
speak because they knew
who he was.

Jesus Prays in a Solitary Place

35 Very early in the morning, while it was still dark,
Jesus got up, left the house
and went off to a solitary
place, where he prayed.
36 Simon and his compan-
ions went to look for him,
37 and when they found him,
they exclaimed: "Every-
one is looking for you!"
38 Jesus replied, "Let us
go somewhere else—to the

towns, so that I may pro-
claim the message there
also; for that is what I came
out to do." 39 And he went
throughout Galilee, pro-
claiming the message in
their synagogues and casting out demons.

Jesus Cleanses a Leper

40 A leper[l] came to
him begging him, and
kneeling[m] he said to him,
"If you choose, you can
make me clean." 41 Moved
with pity,[n] Jesus[o]
stretched out his hand and
touched him, and said to
him, "I do choose. Be made
clean!" 42 Immediately the
leprosy[l] left him, and he
was made clean. 43 After
sternly warning him he sent
him away at once, 44 saying
to him, "See that you say
nothing to anyone; but go,
show yourself to the priest,
and offer for your cleansing
what Moses commanded,
as a testimony to them."
45 But he went out and began to proclaim it freely,
and to spread the word, so
that Jesus[o] could no longer
go into a town openly, but
stayed out in the country;
and people came to him
from every quarter.

Chapter 2

Jesus Heals a Paralytic

WHEN he returned to
Capernaum after
some days, it was reported
that he was at home. 2 So
many gathered around that
there was no longer room
for them, not even in front
of the door; and he was
speaking the word to them.
3 Then some people[p] came,
bringing to him a paralyzed
man, carried by four of
them. 4 And when they
could not bring him to
Jesus because of the
crowd, they removed the
roof above him; and after
having dug through it, they
let down the mat on which

[l] The terms *leper* and *leprosy* can refer to several diseases
[m] Other ancient authorities lack *kneeling*
[n] Other ancient authorities read *anger*
[o] Gk *he*
[p] Gk *they*

ἐχομένας κωμοπόλεις, ἵνα καὶ ἐκεῖ
neighbouring towns, that also there
κηρύξω· εἰς τοῦτο γὰρ ἐξῆλθον. 39 καὶ
I may proclaim; for for this [purpose] I came forth. And
ἦλθεν κηρύσσων εἰς τὰς συναγωγὰς αὐτῶν
he came proclaiming in the synagogues of them
εἰς ὅλην τὴν Γαλιλαίαν καὶ τὰ δαιμόνια
in all – Galilee and the demons
ἐκβάλλων.
expelling.

40 Καὶ ἔρχεται πρὸς αὐτὸν λεπρὸς
And comes to him a leper
παρακαλῶν αὐτὸν καὶ γονυπετῶν λέγων
beseeching him and falling on [his] knees saying
αὐτῷ ὅτι ἐὰν θέλῃς δύνασαί με καθαρίσαι.
to him[,] – If thou art willing thou art able me to cleanse.
41 καὶ σπλαγχνισθεὶς ἐκτείνας τὴν
And being filled with tenderness stretching forth the(his)
χεῖρα αὐτοῦ ἥψατο καὶ λέγει αὐτῷ· θέλω,
hand ²him ¹he touched and says to him: I am willing,
καθαρίσθητι. 42 καὶ εὐθὺς ἀπῆλθεν ἀπ'
be thou cleansed. And immediately departed from
αὐτοῦ ἡ λέπρα, καὶ ἐκαθαρίσθη. 43 καὶ
him the leprosy, and he was cleansed. And
ἐμβριμησάμενος αὐτῷ εὐθὺς ἐξέβαλεν αὐτόν,
sternly admonishing him immediately he put out him,
44 καὶ λέγει αὐτῷ· ὅρα μηδενὶ μηδὲν
and says to him: See no one no(any)thing
εἴπῃς, ἀλλὰ ὕπαγε σεαυτὸν δεῖξον τῷ
thou tellest, but go thyself show to the
ἱερεῖ καὶ προσένεγκε περὶ τοῦ καθαρισμοῦ σου
priest and offer concerning the cleansing of thee
ἃ προσέταξεν Μωϋσῆς, εἰς μαρτύριον
[the things] which commanded Moses, for a testimony
αὐτοῖς. 45 ὁ δὲ ἐξελθὼν ἤρξατο κηρύσσειν
to them. But he going out began to proclaim
πολλὰ καὶ διαφημίζειν τὸν λόγον, ὥστε
many things and to spread about the matter, so as = so that
μηκέτι αὐτὸν δύνασθαι φανερῶς εἰς πόλιν
no longer him to be able[b] openly into a city
he was no longer able
εἰσελθεῖν, ἀλλ' ἔξω ἐπ' ἐρήμοις τόποις
to enter, but outside on(in) desert places
ἦν· καὶ ἤρχοντο πρὸς αὐτὸν πάντοθεν.
he was; and they came to him from all directions.

2 Καὶ εἰσελθὼν πάλιν εἰς Καφαρναοὺμ
And entering again into Capernaum
δι' ἡμερῶν ἠκούσθη ὅτι ἐν οἴκῳ ἐστίν.
through days it was heard that at home he is(was).
= after [some] days
2 καὶ συνήχθησαν πολλοί, ὥστε μηκέτι
And were assembled many, so as no longer
χωρεῖν μηδὲ τὰ πρὸς τὴν θύραν, καὶ
to have room not – at the door, and
ἐλάλει αὐτοῖς τὸν λόγον. 3 καὶ ἔρχονται
he spoke to them the word. And they come
φέροντες πρὸς αὐτὸν παραλυτικὸν αἰρόμενον
carrying to him a paralytic being borne
ὑπὸ τεσσάρων. 4 καὶ μὴ δυνάμενοι
by four [men]. And not being able
προσενέγκαι αὐτῷ διὰ τὸν ὄχλον
to bring to him because of the crowd
ἀπεστέγασαν τὴν στέγην ὅπου ἦν, καὶ
they unroofed the roof where he was, and
ἐξορύξαντες χαλῶσι τὸν κράβατον ὅπου ὁ
having opened up they lower the mattress where the

nearby villages—so I can
preach there also. That is
why I have come." 39 So he
traveled throughout Gali-
lee, preaching in their synagogues and driving out demons.

A Man With Leprosy

40 A man with leprosy[f]
came to him and begged
him on his knees, "If you
are willing, you can make
me clean."
41 Filled with compassion,
Jesus reached out his hand
and touched the man. "I
am willing," he said. "Be
clean!" 42 Immediately the
leprosy left him and he was
cured.
43 Jesus sent him away at
once with a strong warning:
44 "See that you don't tell
this to anyone. But go,
show yourself to the priest
and offer the sacrifices that
Moses commanded for
your cleansing, as a testimony to them." 45 Instead
he went out and began to
talk freely, spreading the
news. As a result, Jesus
could no longer enter a
town openly but stayed
outside in lonely places.
Yet the people still came to
him from everywhere.

Chapter 2

Jesus Heals a Paralytic

A FEW days later, when
Jesus again entered
Capernaum, the people
heard that he had come
home. 2 So many gathered
that there was no room left,
not even outside the door,
and he preached the word
to them. 3 Some men came,
bringing to him a paralytic,
carried by four of them.
4 Since they could not get
him to Jesus because of the
crowd, they made an open-
ing in the roof above Jesus
and, after digging through
it, lowered the mat the par

[f] 40 The Greek word was used for various diseases affecting the skin—not necessarily leprosy.

the paralytic lay. 5When
Jesus saw their faith, he
said to the paralytic, "Son,
your sins are forgiven."
6Now some of the scribes
were sitting there, ques-
tioning in their hearts,
7"Why does this fellow
speak in this way? It is blasphemy! Who can forgive
sins but God alone?" 8At
once Jesus perceived in his
spirit that they were discussing these questions
among themselves; and he
said to them, "Why do you
raise such questions in
your hearts? 9Which is easier, to say to the paralytic,
'Your sins are forgiven,' or
to say, 'Stand up and take
your mat and walk'? 10But
so that you may know that
the Son of Man has authority on earth to forgive
sins"—he said to the
paralytic— 11"I say to you,
stand up, take your mat and
go to your home." 12And
he stood up, and immedi-
ately took the mat and went
out before all of them; so
that they were all amazed
and glorified God, saying,
"We have never seen any-
thing like this!"

Jesus Calls Levi

13 Jesus[q] went out
again beside the sea; the
whole crowd gathered
around him, and he taught
them. 14As he was walking
along, he saw Levi son of
Alphaeus sitting at the tax
booth, and he said to him,
"Follow me." And he got
up and followed him.
15 And as he sat at din-
ner[r] in Levi's[s] house,
many tax collectors and

παραλυτικὸς κατέκειτο. **5** καὶ ἰδὼν ὁ
paralytic was lying. And seeing –

Ἰησοῦς τὴν πίστιν αὐτῶν λέγει τῷ
Jesus the faith of them he says to the

παραλυτικῷ· τέκνον, ἀφίενταί σου αἱ
paralytic: Child, are forgiven of thee the

ἁμαρτίαι. **6** ἦσαν δέ τινες τῶν γραμματέων
sins. Now there were some of the scribes

ἐκεῖ καθήμενοι καὶ διαλογιζόμενοι ἐν ταῖς
there sitting and reasoning in the

καρδίαις αὐτῶν· **7** τί οὗτος οὕτως λαλεῖ;
hearts of them: Why this [man] thus speaks?

βλασφημεῖ· τίς δύναται ἀφιέναι ἁμαρτίας
he blasphemes; who can *to* forgive sins

εἰ μὴ εἷς ὁ θεός; **8** καὶ εὐθὺς ἐπιγνοὺς
except one[,] – God? And immediately knowing

ὁ Ἰησοῦς τῷ πνεύματι αὐτοῦ ὅτι οὕτως
– Jesus in the spirit of him that thus

διαλογίζονται ἐν ἑαυτοῖς, λέγει αὐτοῖς·
they reason among themselves, he says to them:

τί ταῦτα διαλογίζεσθε ἐν ταῖς καρδίαις
Why these things reason ye in the hearts

ὑμῶν; **9** τί ἐστιν εὐκοπώτερον, εἰπεῖν
of you? What is easier, to say

τῷ παραλυτικῷ· ἀφίενταί σου αἱ ἁμαρτίαι,
to the paralytic: are forgiven of thee the sins,

ἢ εἰπεῖν· ἔγειρε καὶ ἆρον τὸν κράβατόν
or to say: Rise and take the mattress

σου καὶ περιπάτει; **10** ἵνα δὲ εἰδῆτε
of thee and walk? But that ye may know

ὅτι ἐξουσίαν ἔχει ὁ υἱὸς τοῦ ἀνθρώπου
that authority has the Son – of man

ἀφιέναι ἁμαρτίας ἐπὶ τῆς γῆς,—λέγει τῷ
to forgive sins on the earth,—he says to the

παραλυτικῷ· **11** σοὶ λέγω, ἔγειρε ἆρον
paralytic: To thee I say, rise[,] take

τὸν κράβατόν σου καὶ ὕπαγε εἰς τὸν
the mattress of thee and go to the

οἶκόν σου. **12** καὶ ἠγέρθη καὶ εὐθὺς
house of thee. And he arose and immediately

ἄρας τὸν κράβατον ἐξῆλθεν ἔμπροσθεν
taking the mattress he went forth before

πάντων, ὥστε ἐξίστασθαι πάντας καὶ
all, so as to be astonished all and
= so that they were all astonished and glorified

δοξάζειν τὸν θεὸν λέγοντας ὅτι οὕτως
to glorify[b] – God saying[,] – Thus

οὐδέποτε εἴδαμεν.
never we saw.

13 Καὶ ἐξῆλθεν πάλιν παρὰ τὴν θάλασσαν·
And he went forth again by the sea;

καὶ πᾶς ὁ ὄχλος ἤρχετο πρὸς αὐτόν,
and all the crowd came to him,

καὶ ἐδίδασκεν αὐτούς. **14** Καὶ παράγων
and he taught them. And passing along

εἶδεν Λευὶν τὸν τοῦ Ἁλφαίου καθήμενον
he saw Levi the [son] – Alphæus sitting

ἐπὶ τὸ τελώνιον, καὶ λέγει αὐτῷ· ἀκολούθει
on(in *or* at) the custom house, and says to him: Follow

μοι. καὶ ἀναστὰς ἠκολούθησεν αὐτῷ.
me. And rising up he followed him.

15 Καὶ γίνεται κατακεῖσθαι αὐτὸν ἐν τῇ
And it comes to pass to recline him[b] in the
= he reclines

οἰκίᾳ αὐτοῦ, καὶ πολλοὶ τελῶναι καὶ
house of him, and many tax-collectors and

alyzed man was lying on.
5When Jesus saw their
faith, he said to the paralytic, "Son, your sins are forgiven."
6Now some teachers of
the law were sitting there,
thinking to themselves,
7"Why does this fellow talk
like that? He's blasphem-
ing! Who can forgive sins
but God alone?"
8Immediately Jesus knew
in his spirit that this was
what they were thinking in
their hearts, and he said to
them, "Why are you think-
ing these things? 9Which is
easier: to say to the paralytic, 'Your sins are forgiven,'
or to say, 'Get up, take
your mat and walk'? 10But
that you may know that
the Son of Man has authority on earth to forgive
sins . . . ." He said to the
paralytic, 11"I tell you, get
up, take your mat and go
home." 12He got up, took
his mat and walked out in
full view of them all. This
amazed everyone and they
praised God, saying, "We
have never seen anything
like this!"

The Calling of Levi

13Once again Jesus went
out beside the lake. A large
crowd came to him, and he
began to teach them. 14As
he walked along, he saw
Levi son of Alphaeus sit-
ting at the tax collector's
booth. "Follow me," Jesus
told him, and Levi got up
and followed him.
15While Jesus was having
dinner at Levi's house,
many tax collectors and

[q] Gk *He*
[r] Gk *reclined*
[s] Gk *his*

sinners were also sitting[t]
with Jesus and his
disciples—for there were
many who followed him.
16 When the scribes of[u] the
Pharisees saw that he was
eating with sinners and tax
collectors, they said to his
disciples, "Why does he
eat[v] with tax collectors
and sinners?" 17 When
Jesus heard this, he said to
them, "Those who are well
have no need of a physi-
cian, but those who are
sick; I have come to call not
the righteous but sinners."

The Question about Fasting

18 Now John's disciples
and the Pharisees were
fasting; and people[p] came
and said to him, "Why do
John's disciples and the
disciples of the Pharisees
fast, but your disciples do
not fast?" 19 Jesus said to
them, "The wedding guests
cannot fast while the bridegroom is with them, can
they? As long as they have
the bridegroom with them,
they cannot fast. 20 The
days will come when the
bridegroom is taken away
from them, and then they
will fast on that day.
21 "No one sews a piece
of unshrunk cloth on an old
cloak; otherwise, the patch
pulls away from it, the new
from the old, and a worse
tear is made. 22 And no one
puts new wine into old
wineskins; otherwise, the
wine will burst the skins,
and the wine is lost, and so
are the skins; but one puts
new wine into fresh wine-
skins."[w]

Pronouncement about the Sabbath

23 One sabbath he was
going through the grain-

[t] Gk *reclining*
[u] Other ancient authorities read *and*
[v] Other ancient authorities add *and drink*
[w] Other ancient authorities lack *but one puts new wine into fresh wineskins*

ἁμαρτωλοὶ συνανέκειντο τῷ Ἰησοῦ καὶ
sinners reclined with – Jesus and
τοῖς μαθηταῖς αὐτοῦ· ἦσαν γὰρ πολλοί,
the disciples of him; for there were many,
καὶ ἠκολούθουν αὐτῷ. 16 καὶ οἱ γραμματεῖς
and they followed him. And the scribes
τῶν Φαρισαίων ἰδόντες ὅτι ἐσθίει
of the Pharisees seeing that he eats(ate)
μετὰ τῶν ἁμαρτωλῶν καὶ τελωνῶν ἔλεγον
with – sinners and tax-collectors said
τοῖς μαθηταῖς αὐτοῦ· ὅτι μετὰ τῶν
to the disciples of him: – With –
τελωνῶν καὶ ἁμαρτωλῶν ἐσθίει; 17 καὶ
tax-collectors and sinners does he eat? And
ἀκούσας ὁ Ἰησοῦς λέγει αὐτοῖς [ὅτι] οὐ
hearing – Jesus says to them[,] – Not
χρείαν ἔχουσιν οἱ ἰσχύοντες ἰατροῦ ἀλλ'
need have the [ones] being strong of a physician but
οἱ κακῶς ἔχοντες· οὐκ ἦλθον καλέσαι
the [ones] ill having; I came not to call
= those who are ill;
δικαίους ἀλλὰ ἁμαρτωλούς. 18 Καὶ ἦσαν
righteous men but sinners. And [7]were
οἱ μαθηταὶ Ἰωάννου καὶ οἱ Φαρισαῖοι
[1]the [2]disciples [3]of John [4]and [5]the [6]Pharisees
νηστεύοντες. καὶ ἔρχονται καὶ λέγουσιν
[8]fasting. And they come and say
αὐτῷ· διὰ τί οἱ μαθηταὶ Ἰωάννου καὶ
to him: Why the disciples of John and
οἱ μαθηταὶ τῶν Φαρισαίων νηστεύουσιν,
the disciples of the Pharisees fast,
οἱ δὲ σοὶ μαθηταὶ οὐ νηστεύουσιν; 19 καὶ
– but thy disciples do not fast? And
εἶπεν αὐτοῖς ὁ Ἰησοῦς· μὴ δύνανται οἱ
said to them – Jesus: *not* can the
υἱοὶ τοῦ νυμφῶνος, ἐν ᾧ ὁ νυμφίος
sons of the bridechamber, while† the bridegroom
μετ' αὐτῶν ἐστιν, νηστεύειν; ὅσον χρόνον
with them is, *to* fast? what time
ἔχουσιν τὸν νυμφίον μετ' αὐτῶν, οὐ
they have the bridegroom with them, not
δύνανται νηστεύειν. 20 ἐλεύσονται δὲ ἡμέραι
they can *to* fast. But will come days
ὅταν ἀπαρθῇ ἀπ' αὐτῶν ὁ νυμφίος, καὶ
when taken away from them the bridegroom, and
τότε νηστεύσουσιν ἐν ἐκείνῃ τῇ ἡμέρᾳ.
then they will fast in that – day.
21 Οὐδεὶς ἐπίβλημα ῥάκους ἀγνάφου ἐπιράπτει
No one a patch cloth of unfulled sews
ἐπὶ ἱμάτιον παλαιόν· εἰ δὲ μή, αἴρει
on garment an old; otherwise, [5]takes
τὸ πλήρωμα ἀπ' αὐτοῦ τὸ καινὸν τοῦ
[6]the [7]fulness [8]from [9]itself [1]the [2]new [3]the
παλαιοῦ, καὶ χεῖρον σχίσμα γίνεται. 22 καὶ
[4]old, and a worse rent occurs. And
οὐδεὶς βάλλει οἶνον νέον εἰς ἀσκοὺς παλαιούς·
no one puts wine new into wineskins old;
εἰ δὲ μή, ῥήξει ὁ οἶνος τοὺς ἀσκούς,
otherwise, [3]will burst [1]the [2]wine the wineskins,
καὶ ὁ οἶνος ἀπόλλυται καὶ οἱ ἀσκοί.
and the wine perishes and the wineskins.
[ἀλλὰ οἶνον νέον εἰς ἀσκοὺς καινούς.]
But wine new into wineskins fresh.
23 Καὶ ἐγένετο αὐτὸν ἐν τοῖς σάββασιν
And it came to pass him on the sabbaths
= as he passed on the sabbath

"sinners" were eating with
him and his disciples, for
there were many who fol-
lowed him. 16 When the
teachers of the law who
were Pharisees saw him
eating with the "sinners"
and tax collectors, they
asked his disciples: "Why
does he eat with tax collectors and 'sinners'?"
17 On hearing this, Jesus
said to them, "It is not the
healthy who need a doctor,
but the sick. I have not
come to call the righteous,
but sinners."

Jesus Questioned About Fasting

18 Now John's disciples
and the Pharisees were
fasting. Some people came
and asked Jesus, "How is it
that John's disciples and
the disciples of the Pharisees are fasting, but yours
are not?"
19 Jesus answered, "How
can the guests of the bridegroom fast while he is with
them? They cannot, so long
as they have him with
them. 20 But the time will
come when the bridegroom
will be taken from them,
and on that day they will
fast.
21 "No one sews a patch
of unshrunk cloth on an old
garment. If he does, the
new piece will pull away
from the old, making the
tear worse. 22 And no one
pours new wine into old
wineskins. If he does, the
wine will burst the skins,
and both the wine and the
wineskins will be ruined.
No, he pours new wine into
new wineskins."

Lord of the Sabbath

23 One Sabbath Jesus was
going through the grain-

fields; and as they made
their way his disciples began to pluck heads of grain.
24 The Pharisees said to
him, "Look, why are they
doing what is not lawful on
the sabbath?" 25 And he
said to them, "Have you
never read what David did
when he and his compan-
ions were hungry and in
need of food? 26 He entered
the house of God, when
Abiathar was high priest,
and ate the bread of the
Presence, which it is not
lawful for any but the
priests to eat, and he gave
some to his companions."
27 Then he said to them,
"The sabbath was made for
humankind, and not hu-
mankind for the sabbath;
28 so the Son of Man is lord
even of the sabbath."

παραπορεύεσθαι διὰ τῶν σπορίμων, καὶ
to pass[b] through the cornfields, and
οἱ μαθηταὶ αὐτοῦ ἤρξαντο ὁδὸν ποιεῖν
the disciples of him began way to make
τίλλοντες τοὺς στάχυας. 24 καὶ οἱ Φαρισαῖοι
plucking the ears of corn. And the Pharisees
ἔλεγον αὐτῷ· ἴδε τί ποιοῦσιν τοῖς σάββασιν
said to him: Behold[,] why do on the sabbaths
ὃ οὐκ ἔξεστιν; 25 καὶ λέγει αὐτοῖς·
what is not lawful? And he says to them:
οὐδέποτε ἀνέγνωτε τί ἐποίησεν Δαυίδ,
never read ye what did David,
ὅτε χρείαν ἔσχεν καὶ ἐπείνασεν αὐτὸς
when need he had and hungered he
καὶ οἱ μετ' αὐτοῦ; 26 [πῶς] εἰσῆλθεν
and the [ones] with him? how he entered
εἰς τὸν οἶκον τοῦ θεοῦ ἐπὶ Ἀβιαθὰρ
into the house – of God on (in the days of) Abiathar
ἀρχιερέως καὶ τοὺς ἄρτους τῆς προθέσεως
high priest and the loaves of the setting forth
ἔφαγεν, οὓς οὐκ ἔξεστιν φαγεῖν εἰ μὴ
ate, which it is not lawful to eat except
τοὺς ἱερεῖς, καὶ ἔδωκεν καὶ τοῖς σὺν
the priests, and gave also to the [ones] with
αὐτῷ οὖσιν; 27 καὶ ἔλεγεν αὐτοῖς·
him being? And he said to them:
τὸ σάββατον διὰ τὸν ἄνθρωπον ἐγένετο,
The sabbath on account of – man was,
καὶ οὐχ ὁ ἄνθρωπος διὰ τὸ σάββατον·
and not – man on account of the sabbath;
28 ὥστε κύριός ἐστιν ὁ υἱὸς τοῦ ἀνθρώπου
so as Lord is the Son – of man
καὶ τοῦ σαββάτου.
also of the sabbath.

fields, and as his disciples
walked along, they began
to pick some heads of
grain. 24 The Pharisees said
to him, "Look, why are
they doing what is unlawful
on the Sabbath?"
25 He answered, "Have
you never read what David
did when he and his com-
panions were hungry and in
need? 26 In the days of Abiathar the high priest, he entered the house of God and
ate the consecrated bread,
which is lawful only for
priests to eat. And he also
gave some to his compan-
ions."
27 Then he said to them,
"The Sabbath was made
for man, not man for the
Sabbath. 28 So the Son of
Man is Lord even of the
Sabbath."

Chapter 3

The Man with a Withered Hand

AGAIN he entered the
synagogue, and a man
was there who had a with-
ered hand. 2 They watched
him to see whether he
would cure him on the sabbath, so that they might accuse him. 3 And he said to
the man who had the with-
ered hand, "Come for-
ward." 4 Then he said to
them, "Is it lawful to do
good or to do harm on the
sabbath, to save life or to
kill?" But they were silent.
5 He looked around at them
with anger; he was grieved
at their hardness of heart
and said to the man,
"Stretch out your hand."
He stretched it out, and his
hand was restored. 6 The
Pharisees went out and immediately conspired with

3 Καὶ εἰσῆλθεν πάλιν εἰς συναγωγήν.
And he entered again into a synagogue.
καὶ ἦν ἐκεῖ ἄνθρωπος ἐξηραμμένην ἔχων
And there was there a man [4]having been withered [1]having
τὴν χεῖρα· 2 καὶ παρετήρουν αὐτὸν εἰ
[2]the [3]hand; and they watched carefully him if
τοῖς σάββασιν θεραπεύσει αὐτόν, ἵνα
on the sabbaths he will heal him, that
κατηγορήσωσιν αὐτοῦ. 3 καὶ λέγει τῷ
they might accuse him. And he says to the
ἀνθρώπῳ τῷ τὴν χεῖρα ἔχοντι ξηράν·
man – the hand having dry:
ἔγειρε εἰς τὸ μέσον. 4 καὶ λέγει αὐτοῖς·
Rise into the midst. And he says to them:
ἔξεστιν τοῖς σάββασιν ἀγαθὸν ποιῆσαι
Lawful on the sabbaths good to do
ἢ κακοποιῆσαι, ψυχὴν σῶσαι ἢ ἀποκτεῖναι;
or to do evil, life to save or to kill?
οἱ δὲ ἐσιώπων. 5 καὶ περιβλεψάμενος
But they were silent. And looking round
αὐτοὺς μετ' ὀργῆς, συλλυπούμενος ἐπὶ
[on] them with anger, being greatly grieved on(at)
τῇ πωρώσει τῆς καρδίας αὐτῶν, λέγει
the hardness of the heart of them, he says
τῷ ἀνθρώπῳ· ἔκτεινον τὴν χεῖρα. καὶ
to the man: Stretch forth the hand. And
ἐξέτεινεν, καὶ ἀπεκατεστάθη ἡ χεὶρ αὐτοῦ.
he stretched forth, and was restored the hand of him.
6 καὶ ἐξελθόντες οἱ Φαρισαῖοι εὐθὺς μετὰ
And going forth the Pharisees immediately with

Chapter 3

ANOTHER time he went
into the synagogue,
and a man with a shriveled
hand was there. 2 Some of
them were looking for a
reason to accuse Jesus, so
they watched him closely
to see if he would heal him
on the Sabbath. 3 Jesus said
to the man with the shriveled hand, "Stand up in
front of everyone."
4 Then Jesus asked them,
"Which is lawful on the
Sabbath: to do good or to
do evil, to save life or to
kill?" But they remained silent.
5 He looked around at
them in anger and, deeply
distressed at their stubborn
hearts, said to the man,
"Stretch out your hand."
He stretched it out, and his
hand was completely re-
stored. 6 Then the Pharisees
went out and began to plot

the Herodians against him,
how to destroy him.

A Multitude at the Seaside

7 Jesus departed with
his disciples to the sea, and
a great multitude from Galilee followed him; 8 hearing
all that he was doing, they
came to him in great num-
bers from Judea, Jerusa-
lem, Idumea, beyond the
Jordan, and the region
around Tyre and Sidon.
9 He told his disciples to
have a boat ready for him
because of the crowd, so
that they would not crush
him; 10 for he had cured
many, so that all who had
diseases pressed upon him
to touch him. 11 Whenever
the unclean spirits saw
him, they fell down before
him and shouted, "You are
the Son of God!" 12 But he
sternly ordered them not to
make him known.

Jesus Appoints the Twelve

13 He went up the
mountain and called to him
those whom he wanted,
and they came to him.
14 And he appointed
twelve, whom he also
named apostles,[x] to be
with him, and to be sent out
to proclaim the message,
15 and to have authority to
cast out demons. 16 So he
appointed the twelve:[y] Simon (to whom he gave the
name Peter); 17 James son
of Zebedee and John the
brother of James (to whom
he gave the name Boaner-
ges, that is, Sons of Thunder); 18 and Andrew, and
Philip, and Bartholomew,
and Matthew, and Thomas,
and James son of Alphae-
us, and Thaddaeus, and Si-

[x] Other ancient authorities lack *whom he also named apostles*
[y] Other ancient authorities lack *So he appointed the twelve*

τῶν Ἡρῳδιανῶν συμβούλιον ἐδίδουν κατ'
the Herodians counsel gave against
αὐτοῦ, ὅπως αὐτὸν ἀπολέσωσιν.
him, that him they might destroy.
7 Καὶ ὁ Ἰησοῦς μετὰ τῶν μαθητῶν
And – Jesus with the disciples
αὐτοῦ ἀνεχώρησεν πρὸς τὴν θάλασσαν·
of him departed to the sea;
καὶ πολὺ πλῆθος ἀπὸ τῆς Γαλιλαίας
and a much(great) multitude from – Galilee
ἠκολούθησεν· καὶ ἀπὸ τῆς Ἰουδαίας **8** καὶ
followed; and from – Judæa and
ἀπὸ Ἱεροσολύμων καὶ ἀπὸ τῆς Ἰδουμαίας
from Jerusalem and from – Idumæa
καὶ πέραν τοῦ Ἰορδάνου καὶ περὶ Τύρον
and beyond the Jordan and round Tyre
καὶ Σιδῶνα, πλῆθος πολύ, ἀκούοντες ὅσα
and Sidon, multitude a much(great), hearing what things
ποιεῖ, ἦλθον πρὸς αὐτόν. **9** καὶ εἶπεν
he does, came to him. And he told
τοῖς μαθηταῖς αὐτοῦ ἵνα πλοιάριον προσκαρτέρῃ
the disciples of him that a boat should remain near
αὐτῷ διὰ τὸν ὄχλον, ἵνα μὴ θλίβωσιν
him because of the crowd, lest they should press upon
αὐτόν· **10** πολλοὺς γὰρ ἐθεράπευσεν, ὥστε
him; for many he healed, so as
ἐπιπίπτειν αὐτῷ ἵνα αὐτοῦ ἅψωνται
to fall upon him that him they might touch
ὅσοι εἶχον μάστιγας. **11** καὶ τὰ πνεύματα
as many as had plagues. And the spirits
τὰ ἀκάθαρτα, ὅταν αὐτὸν ἐθεώρουν, προσέπιπτον
– unclean, when him they saw, fell before
αὐτῷ καὶ ἔκραζον λέγοντα ὅτι σὺ εἶ ὁ
him and cried out saying[,] – Thou art the
υἱὸς τοῦ θεοῦ. **12** καὶ πολλὰ ἐπετίμα
Son – of God. And much he warned
αὐτοῖς ἵνα μὴ αὐτὸν φανερὸν ποιήσωσιν.
them that not him manifest they should make.
13 Καὶ ἀναβαίνει εἰς τὸ ὄρος, καὶ
And he goes up into the mountain, and
προσκαλεῖται οὓς ἤθελεν αὐτός, καὶ
calls to [him] [those] whom wished he, and
ἀπῆλθον πρὸς αὐτόν. **14** καὶ ἐποίησεν δώδεκα
they went to him. And he made twelve
ἵνα ὦσιν μετ' αὐτοῦ, καὶ ἵνα ἀποστέλλῃ
that they might be with him, and that he might send
αὐτοὺς κηρύσσειν **15** καὶ ἔχειν ἐξουσίαν
them to proclaim and to have authority
ἐκβάλλειν τὰ δαιμόνια· **16** καὶ ἐποίησεν
to expel the demons; and he made
τοὺς δώδεκα, καὶ ἐπέθηκεν ὄνομα τῷ
the twelve, and he added a name –
Σίμωνι Πέτρον· **17** καὶ Ἰάκωβον τὸν τοῦ
to Simon[,] Peter; and James the [son] –
Ζεβεδαίου καὶ Ἰωάννην τὸν ἀδελφὸν τοῦ
of Zebedee and John the brother –
Ἰακώβου, καὶ ἐπέθηκεν αὐτοῖς ὄνομα
of James, and he added to them a name[,]
Βοανηργές, ὅ ἐστιν υἱοὶ βροντῆς· **18** καὶ
Boanerges, which is sons of thunder; and
Ἀνδρέαν καὶ Φίλιππον καὶ Βαρθολομαῖον
Andrew and Philip and Bartholomew
καὶ Μαθθαῖον καὶ Θωμᾶν καὶ Ἰάκωβον
and Matthew and Thomas and James
τὸν τοῦ Ἁλφαίου καὶ Θαδδαῖον καὶ
the [son] – of Alphæus and Thaddæus and

with the Herodians how
they might kill Jesus.

Crowds Follow Jesus

7 Jesus withdrew with his
disciples to the lake, and a
large crowd from Galilee
followed. 8 When they
heard all he was doing,
many people came to him
from Judea, Jerusalem, Idumea, and the regions
across the Jordan and
around Tyre and Sidon.
9 Because of the crowd he
told his disciples to have a
small boat ready for him, to
keep the people from
crowding him. 10 For he had
healed many, so that those
with diseases were pushing
forward to touch him.
11 Whenever the evil[g] spirits saw him, they fell down
before him and cried out,
"You are the Son of God."
12 But he gave them strict
orders not to tell who he
was.

The Appointing of the Twelve Apostles

13 Jesus went up on a
mountainside and called to
him those he wanted, and
they came to him. 14 He appointed twelve—designat-
ing them apostles[h]—that
they might be with him and
that he might send them out
to preach 15 and to have authority to drive out de-
mons. 16 These are the
twelve he appointed: Si-
mon (to whom he gave the
name Peter); 17 James son of
Zebedee and his brother
John (to them he gave the
name Boanerges, which
means Sons of Thunder);
18 Andrew, Philip, Bartholomew, Matthew, Thomas,
James son of Alphaeus,
Thaddaeus, Simon the

[g] *11* Greek *unclean*; also in verse 30
[h] *14* Some manuscripts do not have *designating them apostles*.

mon the Cananaean, 19and
Judas Iscariot, who be-
trayed him.

Jesus and Beelzebul

Then he went home;
20and the crowd came to-
gether again, so that they
could not even eat. 21When
his family heard it, they
went out to restrain him,
for people were saying,
"He has gone out of his
mind." 22And the scribes
who came down from Jeru-
salem said, "He has Beel-
zebul, and by the ruler of
the demons he casts out demons." 23And he called
them to him, and spoke to
them in parables, "How
can Satan cast out Satan?
24If a kingdom is divided
against itself, that kingdom
cannot stand. 25And if a
house is divided against itself, that house will not be
able to stand. 26And if Satan has risen up against
himself and is divided, he
cannot stand, but his end
has come. 27But no one can
enter a strong man's house
and plunder his property
without first tying up the
strong man; then indeed
the house can be plun-
dered.
28 "Truly I tell you,
people will be forgiven for
their sins and whatever
blasphemies they utter;
29but whoever blasphemes
against the Holy Spirit can
never have forgiveness, but
is guilty of an eternal sin"—
30for they had said, "He
has an unclean spirit."

The True Kindred of Jesus

31 Then his mother and
his brothers came; and
standing outside, they sent
to him and called him. 32A

Σίμωνα τὸν Καναναῖον 19 καὶ Ἰούδαν
Simon the Cananæan and Judas
Ἰσκαριώθ, ὃς καὶ παρέδωκεν αὐτόν.
Iscariot, who indeed betrayed him.
20 Καὶ ἔρχεται εἰς οἶκον· καὶ συνέρχεται
And he comes into a house; and comes together
πάλιν [ὁ] ὄχλος, ὥστε μὴ δύνασθαι
again the crowd, so as not to be able
= so that they were not able
αὐτοὺς μηδὲ ἄρτον φαγεῖν. 21 καὶ ἀκούσαντες
them[b] *not* bread to eat. And hearing
οἱ παρ' αὐτοῦ ἐξῆλθον κρατῆσαι αὐτόν·
the[ones] with him went forth to seize him;
= his relations
ἔλεγον γὰρ ὅτι ἐξέστη. 22 καὶ οἱ
for they said[,] – He is beside himself. And the
γραμματεῖς οἱ ἀπὸ Ἱεροσολύμων καταβάντες
scribes – from Jerusalem coming down
ἔλεγον ὅτι Βεεζεβοὺλ ἔχει, καὶ ὅτι ἐν
said[,] – Beelzebub he has, and[,] – By
τῷ ἄρχοντι τῶν δαιμονίων ἐκβάλλει τὰ
the ruler of the demons he expels the
δαιμόνια. 23 καὶ προσκαλεσάμενος αὐτοὺς
demons. And calling to [him] them
ἐν παραβολαῖς ἔλεγεν αὐτοῖς· πῶς δύναται
in parables he said to them: How can
σατανᾶς σατανᾶν ἐκβάλλειν; 24 καὶ ἐὰν
Satan ^{2}Satan ^{1}*to* expel ? and if
βασιλεία ἐφ' ἑαυτὴν μερισθῇ, οὐ δύναται
a kingdom against itself be divided, cannot
σταθῆναι ἡ βασιλεία ἐκείνη· 25 καὶ ἐὰν
stand – kingdom that; and if
οἰκία ἐφ' ἑαυτὴν μερισθῇ, οὐ δυνήσεται
a house against itself be divided, will not be able
ἡ οἰκία ἐκείνη στῆναι. 26 καὶ εἰ ὁ
– house that to stand. And if –
σατανᾶς ἀνέστη ἐφ' ἑαυτὸν καὶ ἐμερίσθη,
Satan stood up against himself and was divided,
οὐ δύναται στῆναι ἀλλὰ τέλος ἔχει.
he cannot *to* stand but an end has.
27 ἀλλ' οὐ δύναται οὐδεὶς εἰς τὴν οἰκίαν
But cannot no(any)one into the house
τοῦ ἰσχυροῦ εἰσελθὼν τὰ σκεύη αὐτοῦ
of the strong man entering the goods of him
διαρπάσαι, ἐὰν μὴ πρῶτον τὸν ἰσχυρὸν
to plunder, unless first the strong man
δήσῃ, καὶ τότε τὴν οἰκίαν αὐτοῦ διαρπάσει.
he bind, and then the house of him he will plunder.
28 Ἀμὴν λέγω ὑμῖν ὅτι πάντα ἀφεθήσεται
Truly I tell you that all will be forgiven
τοῖς υἱοῖς τῶν ἀνθρώπων τὰ ἁμαρτήματα
to the sons – of men the sins
καὶ αἱ βλασφημίαι, ὅσα ἐὰν βλασφημήσωσιν·
and the blasphemies, whatever they may blaspheme;
29 ὃς δ' ἂν βλασφημήσῃ εἰς τὸ πνεῦμα
but whoever blasphemes against the Spirit
τὸ ἅγιον, οὐκ ἔχει ἄφεσιν εἰς τὸν αἰῶνα,
– Holy, has not forgiveness unto the age,
ἀλλὰ ἔνοχός ἐστιν αἰωνίου ἁμαρτήματος.
but liable is of an eternal sin.
30 ὅτι ἔλεγον· πνεῦμα ἀκάθαρτον ἔχει.
Because they said: spirit an unclean he has.
31 Καὶ ἔρχονται ἡ μήτηρ αὐτοῦ καὶ οἱ
And come the mother of him and the
ἀδελφοὶ αὐτοῦ, καὶ ἔξω στήκοντες ἀπέστειλαν
brothers of him, and outside standing sent
πρὸς αὐτὸν καλοῦντες αὐτόν. 32 καὶ
to him calling him. And

Zealot 19and Judas Iscariot,
who betrayed him.

Jesus and Beelzebub

20Then Jesus entered a
house, and again a crowd
gathered, so that he and his
disciples were not even
able to eat. 21When his family heard about this, they
went to take charge of him,
for they said, "He is out of
his mind."
22And the teachers of the
law who came down from
Jerusalem said, "He is possessed by Beelzebub[i]! By
the prince of demons he is
driving out demons."
23So Jesus called them
and spoke to them in parables: "How can Satan drive
out Satan? 24If a kingdom is
divided against itself, that
kingdom cannot stand. 25If
a house is divided against
itself, that house cannot
stand. 26And if Satan op-
poses himself and is divided, he cannot stand; his end
has come. 27In fact, no one
can enter a strong man's
house and carry off his possessions unless he first ties
up the strong man. Then he
can rob his house. 28I tell
you the truth, all the sins
and blasphemies of men
will be forgiven them. 29But
whoever blasphemes
against the Holy Spirit will
never be forgiven; he is
guilty of an eternal sin."
30He said this because
they were saying, "He has
an evil spirit."

Jesus' Mother and Brothers

31Then Jesus' mother and
brothers arrived. Standing
outside, they sent someone
in to call him. 32A crowd

[i]22 Greek *Beezeboul* or *Beelzeboul*

crowd was sitting around him; and they said to him, "Your mother and your brothers and sisters[z] are outside, asking for you." 33 And he replied, "Who are my mother and my brothers?" 34 And looking at those who sat around him, he said, "Here are my mother and my brothers! 35 Whoever does the will of God is my brother and sister and mother."

ἐκάθητο περὶ αὐτὸν ὄχλος, καὶ λέγουσιν
sat round him a crowd, and they say

αὐτῷ· ἰδοὺ ἡ μήτηρ σου καὶ οἱ ἀδελφοί
to him: Behold[,] the mother of thee and the brothers

σου καὶ αἱ ἀδελφαί σου ἔξω ζητοῦσίν σε.
of thee and the sisters of thee outside seek thee.

33 καὶ ἀποκριθεὶς αὐτοῖς λέγει· τίς ἐστιν
And answering them he says: Who is

ἡ μήτηρ μου καὶ οἱ ἀδελφοί; 34 καὶ
the mother of me and the brothers? And

περιβλεψάμενος τοὺς περὶ αὐτὸν κύκλῳ
looking round [at] the [ones] round him in a circle

καθημένους λέγει· ἴδε ἡ μήτηρ μου
sitting he says: Behold[,] the mother of me

καὶ οἱ ἀδελφοί μου. 35 ὃς ἂν ποιήσῃ τὸ
and the brothers of me. Whoever does the

θέλημα τοῦ θεοῦ, οὗτος ἀδελφός μου
will - of God, this one brother of me

καὶ ἀδελφὴ καὶ μήτηρ ἐστίν.
and sister and mother is.

was sitting around him, and they told him, "Your mother and brothers are outside looking for you."
33 "Who are my mother and my brothers?" he asked.
34 Then he looked at those seated in a circle around him and said, "Here are my mother and my brothers! 35 Whoever does God's will is my brother and sister and mother."

Chapter 4

The Parable of the Sower

AGAIN he began to teach beside the sea. Such a very large crowd gathered around him that he got into a boat on the sea and sat there, while the whole crowd was beside the sea on the land. 2 He began to teach them many things in parables, and in his teaching he said to them: 3 "Listen! A sower went out to sow. 4 And as he sowed, some seed fell on the path, and the birds came and ate it up. 5 Other seed fell on rocky ground, where it did not have much soil, and it sprang up quickly, since it had no depth of soil. 6 And when the sun rose, it was scorched; and since it had no root, it withered away. 7 Other seed fell among thorns, and the thorns grew up and choked it, and it yielded no grain. 8 Other seed fell into good soil and brought forth

4 Καὶ πάλιν ἤρξατο διδάσκειν παρὰ τὴν
And again he began to teach by the

θάλασσαν· καὶ συνάγεται πρὸς αὐτὸν ὄχλος
sea; and is assembled to him crowd

πλεῖστος, ὥστε αὐτὸν εἰς πλοῖον ἐμβάντα
a very large, so as him in a ship embarking
= so that embarking in a ship he sat

καθῆσθαι ἐν τῇ θαλάσσῃ, καὶ πᾶς ὁ
to sit[b] in the sea, and all the

ὄχλος πρὸς τὴν θάλασσαν ἐπὶ τῆς γῆς
crowd toward the sea on the land

ἦσαν. 2 καὶ ἐδίδασκεν αὐτοὺς ἐν παραβολαῖς
were. And he taught them in parables

πολλά, καὶ ἔλεγεν αὐτοῖς ἐν τῇ διδαχῇ
many things, and said to them in the teaching

αὐτοῦ· 3 ἀκούετε. ἰδοὺ ἐξῆλθεν ὁ σπείρων
of him: Hear ye. Behold[,] went out the [one] sowing

σπεῖραι. 4 καὶ ἐγένετο ἐν τῷ σπείρειν
to sow. And it came to pass in the to sow[e]
= as he sowed

ὃ μὲν ἔπεσεν παρὰ τὴν ὁδόν, καὶ ἦλθεν
some fell by the way, and came

τὰ πετεινὰ καὶ κατέφαγεν αὐτό. 5 καὶ
the birds and devoured it. And

ἄλλο ἔπεσεν ἐπὶ τὸ πετρῶδες ὅπου οὐκ
other fell on the rocky place where not

εἶχεν γῆν πολλήν, καὶ εὐθὺς ἐξανέτειλεν
it had earth much, and immediately it sprang up

διὰ τὸ μὴ ἔχειν βάθος γῆς·
on account of the not to have depth of earth;
= because it had no depth of earth;

6 καὶ ὅτε ἀνέτειλεν ὁ ἥλιος ἐκαυματίσθη, καὶ
and when rose the sun it was scorched, and

διὰ τὸ μὴ ἔχειν ῥίζαν ἐξηράνθη. 7 καὶ
on account of the not to have root it was withered. And
= because it had no root

ἄλλο ἔπεσεν εἰς τὰς ἀκάνθας, καὶ ἀνέβησαν
other fell among the thorns, and came up

αἱ ἄκανθαι καὶ συνέπνιξαν αὐτό, καὶ
the thorns and choked it, and

καρπὸν οὐκ ἔδωκεν. 8 καὶ ἄλλα ἔπεσεν
fruit it gave not. And others fell

εἰς τὴν γῆν τὴν καλὴν καὶ ἐδίδου καρπὸν
into the earth - good and gave fruit

Chapter 4

The Parable of the Sower

AGAIN Jesus began to teach by the lake. The crowd that gathered around him was so large that he got into a boat and sat in it out on the lake, while all the people were along the shore at the water's edge. 2 He taught them many things by parables, and in his teaching said: 3 "Listen! A farmer went out to sow his seed. 4 As he was scattering the seed, some fell along the path, and the birds came and ate it up. 5 Some fell on rocky places, where it did not have much soil. It sprang up quickly, because the soil was shallow. 6 But when the sun came up, the plants were scorched, and they withered because they had no root. 7 Other seed fell among thorns, which grew up and choked the plants, so that they did not bear grain. 8 Still other seed fell on good soil. It came up,

[z] Other ancient authorities lack *and sisters*

grain, growing up and increasing and yielding thirty and sixty and a hundredfold." 9And he said, "Let anyone with ears to hear listen!"

The Purpose of the Parables

10 When he was alone, those who were around him along with the twelve asked him about the parables. 11And he said to them, "To you has been given the secret[a] of the kingdom of God, but for those outside, everything comes in parables; 12in order that

'they may indeed
look, but not
perceive,
and may indeed
listen, but not
understand;
so that they may not
turn again and
be forgiven.'"

13 And he said to them, "Do you not understand this parable? Then how will you understand all the parables? 14The sower sows the word. 15These are the ones on the path where the word is sown: when they hear, Satan immediately comes and takes away the word that is sown in them. 16And these are the ones sown on rocky ground: when they hear the word, they immediately receive it with joy. 17But they have no root, and endure only for a while; then, when trouble or persecution arises on account of the word, immediately they fall away.[b] 18And others are those sown among the thorns: these are the ones who hear the word, 19but the cares of the world, and the lure of wealth, and the desire for other things come in and choke the word, and it yields nothing. 20And these are the ones

[a] Or *mystery*
[b] Or *stumble*

ἀναβαίνοντα καὶ αὐξανόμενα καὶ ἔφερεν
coming up and growing and bore

εἰς τριάκοντα καὶ ἐν ἑξήκοντα καὶ ἐν
in thirty and in sixty and in

ἑκατόν. **9** καὶ ἔλεγεν· ὃς ἔχει ὦτα
a hundred. And he said: Who has ears

ἀκούειν ἀκουέτω. **10** Καὶ ὅτε ἐγένετο
to hear let him hear. And when he was

κατὰ μόνας, ἠρώτων αὐτὸν οἱ περὶ
alone,† asked him the [ones] round

αὐτὸν σὺν τοῖς δώδεκα τὰς παραβολάς.
him with the twelve the parables.

11 καὶ ἔλεγεν αὐτοῖς· ὑμῖν τὸ μυστήριον
And he said to them: To you the mystery

δέδοται τῆς βασιλείας τοῦ θεοῦ· ἐκείνοις δὲ
has been given of the kingdom – of God; but to those

τοῖς ἔξω ἐν παραβολαῖς τὰ πάντα
the [ones] outside in parables – all things

γίνεται, **12** ἵνα βλέποντες βλέπωσιν καὶ
is(are), that seeing they may see and

μὴ ἴδωσιν, καὶ ἀκούοντες ἀκούωσιν καὶ
not perceive, and hearing they may hear and

μὴ συνιῶσιν, μήποτε ἐπιστρέψωσιν καὶ
not understand, lest they should turn and

ἀφεθῇ αὐτοῖς. **13** καὶ λέγει αὐτοῖς·
it should be forgiven them. And he says to them:

οὐκ οἴδατε τὴν παραβολὴν ταύτην, καὶ πῶς
Know ye not – parable this, and how

πάσας τὰς παραβολὰς γνώσεσθε; **14** ὁ
all the parables will ye know? The [one]

σπείρων τὸν λόγον σπείρει. **15** οὗτοι δέ εἰσιν
sowing [2]the [3]word [1]sows. And these are

οἱ παρὰ τὴν ὁδόν, ὅπου σπείρεται ὁ
the [ones] by the way, where is sown the

λόγος, καὶ ὅταν ἀκούσωσιν, εὐθὺς ἔρχεται
word, and when they hear, immediately comes

ὁ σατανᾶς καὶ αἴρει τὸν λόγον τὸν
– Satan and takes the word –

ἐσπαρμένον εἰς αὐτούς. **16** καὶ οὗτοί εἰσιν
having been sown in them. And these are

ὁμοίως οἱ ἐπὶ τὰ πετρώδη σπειρόμενοι,
likewise the [ones] on the rocky places being sown,

οἳ ὅταν ἀκούσωσιν τὸν λόγον εὐθὺς
who when they hear the word immediately

μετὰ χαρᾶς λαμβάνουσιν αὐτόν, **17** καὶ
with joy receive it, and

οὐκ ἔχουσιν ῥίζαν ἐν ἑαυτοῖς ἀλλὰ
have not root in themselves but

πρόσκαιροί εἰσιν, εἶτα γενομένης θλίψεως
shortlived are, then happening affliction
= when affliction or persecution happens

ἢ διωγμοῦ διὰ τὸν λόγον εὐθὺς
or persecution[a] on account of the word immediately

σκανδαλίζονται. **18** καὶ ἄλλοι εἰσὶν οἱ εἰς
they are offended. And others are the [ones] among

τὰς ἀκάνθας σπειρόμενοι· οὗτοί εἰσιν οἱ
the thorns being sown; these are the [ones]

τὸν λόγον ἀκούσαντες, **19** καὶ αἱ μέριμναι
the word hearing, and the cares

τοῦ αἰῶνος καὶ ἡ ἀπάτη τοῦ πλούτου
of the age and the deceitfulness – of riches

καὶ αἱ περὶ τὰ λοιπὰ ἐπιθυμίαι
and [1]the [3]about [4]the [5]other things [2]desires

εἰσπορευόμεναι συμπνίγουσιν τὸν λόγον, καὶ
coming in choke the word, and

ἄκαρπος γίνεται. **20** καὶ ἐκεῖνοί εἰσιν
unfruitful it becomes. And those are

grew and produced a crop, multiplying thirty, sixty, or even a hundred times."

9Then Jesus said, "He who has ears to hear, let him hear."

10When he was alone, the Twelve and the others around him asked him about the parables. 11He told them, "The secret of the kingdom of God has been given to you. But to those on the outside everything is said in parables 12so that,

" 'they may be ever
seeing but never
perceiving,
and ever hearing but
never
understanding;
otherwise they might
turn and be
forgiven!'[j]"

13Then Jesus said to them, "Don't you understand this parable? How then will you understand any parable? 14The farmer sows the word. 15Some people are like seed along the path, where the word is sown. As soon as they hear it, Satan comes and takes away the word that was sown in them. 16Others, like seed sown on rocky places, hear the word and at once receive it with joy. 17But since they have no root, they last only a short time. When trouble or persecution comes because of the word, they quickly fall away. 18Still others, like seed sown among thorns, hear the word; 19but the worries of this life, the deceitfulness of wealth and the desires for other things come in and choke the word, making it unfruitful. 20Others, like seed sown on

[j] *12* Isaiah 6:9,10

sown on the good soil: they hear the word and accept it and bear fruit, thirty and sixty and a hundredfold."

A Lamp under a Bushel Basket

21 He said to them, "Is a lamp brought in to be put under the bushel basket, or under the bed, and not on the lampstand? 22 For there is nothing hidden, except to be disclosed; nor is anything secret, except to come to light. 23 Let anyone with ears to hear listen!" 24 And he said to them, "Pay attention to what you hear; the measure you give will be the measure you get, and still more will be given you. 25 For to those who have, more will be given; and from those who have nothing, even what they have will be taken away."

The Parable of the Growing Seed

26 He also said, "The kingdom of God is as if someone would scatter seed on the ground, 27 and would sleep and rise night and day, and the seed would sprout and grow, he does not know how. 28 The earth produces of itself, first the stalk, then the head, then the full grain in the head. 29 But when the grain is ripe, at once he goes in with his sickle, because the harvest has come."

The Parable of the Mustard Seed

30 He also said, "With what can we compare the kingdom of God, or what parable will we use for it? 31 It is like a mustard seed, which, when sown upon the ground, is the smallest of all the seeds on earth; 32 yet when it is sown it grows up and becomes the greatest of all shrubs, and puts forth large branches,

οἱ ἐπὶ τὴν γῆν τὴν καλὴν σπαρέντες,
the [ones] on the earth – good sown,
οἵτινες ἀκούουσιν τὸν λόγον καὶ παραδέχονται
who hear the word and welcome [it]
καὶ καρποφοροῦσιν ἐν τριάκοντα καὶ ἐν
and bear fruit in thirty and in
ἑξήκοντα καὶ ἐν ἑκατόν. 21 Καὶ ἔλεγεν
sixty and in a hundred. And he said
αὐτοῖς ὅτι μήτι ἔρχεται ὁ λύχνος ἵνα
to them[,] – *not* Comes the lamp that
ὑπὸ τὸν μόδιον τεθῇ ἢ ὑπὸ τὴν
under the bushel it may be placed or under the
κλίνην; οὐχ ἵνα ἐπὶ τὴν λυχνίαν
couch? not that on the lampstand
τεθῇ; 22 οὐ γάρ ἐστίν τι κρυπτόν,
it may be placed? For there is not anything hidden,
ἐὰν μὴ ἵνα φανερωθῇ· οὐδὲ ἐγένετο
except that it may be manifested; nor became
ἀπόκρυφον, ἀλλ' ἵνα ἔλθῃ εἰς φανερόν.
covered, but that it may come into [the] open.
23 εἴ τις ἔχει ὦτα ἀκούειν ἀκουέτω.
If anyone has ears to hear let him hear.
24 Καὶ ἔλεγεν αὐτοῖς· βλέπετε τί
And he said to them: Take heed what
ἀκούετε. ἐν ᾧ μέτρῳ μετρεῖτε
ye hear. With what measure ye measure
μετρηθήσεται ὑμῖν, καὶ προστεθήσεται ὑμῖν.
it will be measured to you, and it will be added to you.
25 ὃς γὰρ ἔχει, δοθήσεται αὐτῷ· καὶ ὃς
For [he] who has, it will be given to him; and who
οὐκ ἔχει, καὶ ὃ ἔχει ἀρθήσεται ἀπ'
has not, even what he has will be taken from
αὐτοῦ. 26 Καὶ ἔλεγεν· οὕτως ἐστὶν ἡ
him. And he said: Thus is the
βασιλεία τοῦ θεοῦ, ὡς ἄνθρωπος βάλῃ
kingdom – of God, as a man might cast
τὸν σπόρον ἐπὶ τῆς γῆς, 27 καὶ καθεύδῃ
the seed on the earth, and might sleep
καὶ ἐγείρηται νύκτα καὶ ἡμέραν, καὶ ὁ
and rise night and day, and the
σπόρος βλαστᾷ καὶ μηκύνηται ὡς οὐκ
seed sprouts and lengthens as not
οἶδεν αὐτός. 28 αὐτομάτη ἡ γῆ καρποφορεῖ,
knows he. Of its own accord the earth bears fruit,
πρῶτον χόρτον, εἶτεν στάχυν, εἶτεν πλήρης
first grass, then an ear, then full
σῖτος ἐν τῷ στάχυϊ. 29 ὅταν δὲ παραδοῖ
corn in the ear. But when permits
ὁ καρπός, εὐθὺς ἀποστέλλει τὸ δρέπανον,
the fruit, immediately he sends(puts) forth the sickle,
ὅτι παρέστηκεν ὁ θερισμός. 30 Καὶ ἔλεγεν·
because has come the harvest. And he said:
πῶς ὁμοιώσωμεν τὴν βασιλείαν τοῦ θεοῦ,
How may we liken the kingdom – of God,
ἢ ἐν τίνι αὐτὴν παραβολῇ θῶμεν; 31 ὡς
or by [1]what [4]it [2]parable [3]may we place? As
κόκκῳ σινάπεως, ὃς ὅταν σπαρῇ ἐπὶ τῆς
a grain of mustard, which when it is sown on the
γῆς, μικρότερον ὂν πάντων τῶν σπερμάτων
earth, smaller being [than] all the seeds
τῶν ἐπὶ τῆς γῆς, 32 καὶ ὅταν σπαρῇ,
– on the earth, and when it is sown,
ἀναβαίνει καὶ γίνεται μεῖζον πάντων τῶν
comes up and becomes greater [than] all the
λαχάνων, καὶ ποιεῖ κλάδους μεγάλους,
herbs, and makes branches great,

good soil, hear the word, accept it, and produce a crop—thirty, sixty or even a hundred times what was sown."

A Lamp on a Stand

21 He said to them, "Do you bring in a lamp to put it under a bowl or a bed? Instead, don't you put it on its stand? 22 For whatever is hidden is meant to be disclosed, and whatever is concealed is meant to be brought out into the open. 23 If anyone has ears to hear, let him hear."

24 "Consider carefully what you hear," he continued. "With the measure you use, it will be measured to you—and even more. 25 Whoever has will be given more; whoever does not have, even what he has will be taken from him."

The Parable of the Growing Seed

26 He also said, "This is what the kingdom of God is like. A man scatters seed on the ground. 27 Night and day, whether he sleeps or gets up, the seed sprouts and grows, though he does not know how. 28 All by itself the soil produces grain—first the stalk, then the head, then the full kernel in the head. 29 As soon as the grain is ripe, he puts the sickle to it, because the harvest has come."

The Parable of the Mustard Seed

30 Again he said, "What shall we say the kingdom of God is like, or what parable shall we use to describe it? 31 It is like a mustard seed, which is the smallest seed you plant in the ground. 32 Yet when planted, it grows and becomes the largest of all garden plants,

so that the birds of the air
can make nests in its
shade."

The Use of Parables

33 With many such par-
ables he spoke the word to
them, as they were able to
hear it; 34 he did not speak
to them except in parables,
but he explained every-
thing in private to his disciples.

Jesus Stills a Storm

35 On that day, when
evening had come, he said
to them, "Let us go across
to the other side." 36 And
leaving the crowd behind,
they took him with them in
the boat, just as he was.
Other boats were with him.
37 A great windstorm arose,
and the waves beat into the
boat, so that the boat was
already being swamped.
38 But he was in the stern,
asleep on the cushion; and
they woke him up and said
to him, "Teacher, do you
not care that we are perishing?" 39 He woke up and rebuked the wind, and said to
the sea, "Peace! Be still!"
Then the wind ceased, and
there was a dead calm.
40 He said to them, "Why
are you afraid? Have you
still no faith?" 41 And they
were filled with great awe
and said to one another,
"Who then is this, that even
the wind and the sea obey
him?"

Chapter 5

Jesus Heals the Gerasene Demoniac

THEY came to the other
side of the sea, to the
country of the Gerasenes.[c]
2 And when he had stepped
out of the boat, immediately a man out of the tombs

[c] Other ancient authorities read *Gergesenes*; others, *Gadarenes*

ὥστε δύνασθαι ὑπὸ τὴν σκιὰν αὐτοῦ τὰ
so as to be able under the shade of it the
= so that the birds of heaven are able to dwell under its shade.

πετεινὰ τοῦ οὐρανοῦ κατασκηνοῦν. 33 Καὶ
birds – of heaven to dwell.[b] And

τοιαύταις παραβολαῖς πολλαῖς ἐλάλει αὐτοῖς
[s]such [s]parables [1]in many he spoke to them

τὸν λόγον, καθὼς ἠδύναντο ἀκούειν·
the word, as they were able to hear;

34 χωρὶς δὲ παραβολῆς οὐκ ἐλάλει αὐτοῖς,
and without a parable he spoke not to them,

κατ' ἰδίαν δὲ τοῖς ἰδίοις μαθηταῖς ἐπέλυεν
but privately to the(his) own disciples he explained

πάντα.
all things.

35 Καὶ λέγει αὐτοῖς ἐν ἐκείνῃ τῇ
And he says to them on that –

ἡμέρᾳ ὀψίας γενομένης· διέλθωμεν εἰς τὸ
day evening having come[a]: Let us pass over to the
= when evening had come:

πέραν. 36 καὶ ἀφέντες τὸν ὄχλον
other side. And leaving the crowd

παραλαμβάνουσιν αὐτὸν ὡς ἦν ἐν τῷ
they take him as he was in the

πλοίῳ, καὶ ἄλλα πλοῖα ἦν μετ' αὐτοῦ.
ship, and other ships were with him.

37 καὶ γίνεται λαῖλαψ μεγάλη ἀνέμου,
And occurs storm a great of wind,

καὶ τὰ κύματα ἐπέβαλλεν εἰς τὸ πλοῖον,
and the waves struck into the ship,

ὥστε ἤδη γεμίζεσθαι τὸ πλοῖον. 38 καὶ
so as now to be filled the ship.[b] And

αὐτὸς ἦν ἐν τῇ πρύμνῃ ἐπὶ τὸ
he was in the stern on the

προσκεφάλαιον καθεύδων. καὶ ἐγείρουσιν
pillow sleeping. And they rouse

αὐτὸν καὶ λέγουσιν αὐτῷ· διδάσκαλε, οὐ μέλει
him and say to him: Teacher, matters it not

σοι ὅτι ἀπολλύμεθα; 39 καὶ διεγερθεὶς
to thee that we are perishing? And being roused

ἐπετίμησεν τῷ ἀνέμῳ καὶ εἶπεν τῇ
he rebuked the wind and said to the

θαλάσσῃ· σιώπα, πεφίμωσο. καὶ ἐκόπασεν
sea: Be quiet, be muzzled. And dropped

ὁ ἄνεμος, καὶ ἐγένετο γαλήνη μεγάλη.
the wind, and there was calm a great.

40 καὶ εἶπεν αὐτοῖς· τί δειλοί ἐστε
And he said to them: Why fearful are ye

οὕτως; πῶς οὐκ ἔχετε πίστιν; 41 καὶ
thus? how have ye not faith? And

ἐφοβήθησαν φόβον μέγαν, καὶ ἔλεγον πρὸς
they feared fear a great, and said to

ἀλλήλους· τίς ἄρα οὗτός ἐστιν, ὅτι καὶ
one another: Who then this man is, that both

ὁ ἄνεμος καὶ ἡ θάλασσα ὑπακούει αὐτῷ;
the wind and the sea obeys him?

5 Καὶ ἦλθον εἰς τὸ πέραν τῆς θαλάσσης
And they came to the other side of the sea

εἰς τὴν χώραν τῶν Γερασηνῶν. 2 καὶ
into the country of the Gerasenes. And

ἐξελθόντος αὐτοῦ ἐκ τοῦ πλοίου, [εὐθὺς]
coming *out* him[a] out of the ship, immediately
= as he came *out*

ὑπήντησεν αὐτῷ ἐκ τῶν μνημείων ἄνθρωπος
met him out of the tombs a man

with such big branches that
the birds of the air can
perch in its shade."
33 With many similar parables Jesus spoke the word
to them, as much as they
could understand. 34 He did
not say anything to them
without using a parable.
But when he was alone
with his own disciples, he
explained everything.

Jesus Calms the Storm

35 That day when evening
came, he said to his disciples, "Let us go over to the
other side." 36 Leaving the
crowd behind, they took
him along, just as he was, in
the boat. There were also
other boats with him. 37 A
furious squall came up, and
the waves broke over the
boat, so that it was nearly
swamped. 38 Jesus was in
the stern, sleeping on a
cushion. The disciples
woke him and said to him,
"Teacher, don't you care if
we drown?"
39 He got up, rebuked the
wind and said to the waves,
"Quiet! Be still!" Then the
wind died down and it was
completely calm.
40 He said to his disciples,
"Why are you so afraid?
Do you still have no faith?"
41 They were terrified and
asked each other, "Who is
this? Even the wind and the
waves obey him!"

Chapter 5

The Healing of a Demon-possessed Man

THEY went across the
lake to the region of
the Gerasenes.[k] 2 When
Jesus got out of the boat, a
man with an evil[l] spirit
came from the tombs to

[k] 1 Some manuscripts *Gadarenes*; other manuscripts *Gergesenes*
[l] 2 Greek *unclean*; also in verses 8 and 13

with an unclean spirit met
him. 3 He lived among the
tombs; and no one could restrain him any more, even
with a chain; 4 for he had
often been restrained with
shackles and chains, but
the chains he wrenched
apart, and the shackles he
broke in pieces; and no one
had the strength to subdue
him. 5 Night and day among
the tombs and on the mountains he was always howl-
ing and bruising himself
with stones. 6 When he saw
Jesus from a distance, he
ran and bowed down be-
fore him; 7 and he shouted
at the top of his voice,
"What have you to do with
me, Jesus, Son of the Most
High God? I adjure you by
God, do not torment me."
8 For he had said to him,
"Come out of the man, you
unclean spirit!" 9 Then
Jesus[d] asked him, "What is
your name?" He replied,
"My name is Legion; for
we are many." 10 He
begged him earnestly not to
send them out of the country. 11 Now there on the
hillside a great herd of
swine was feeding; 12 and
the unclean spirits[e] begged
him, "Send us into the
swine; let us enter them."
13 So he gave them permission. And the unclean spirits came out and entered
the swine; and the herd,
numbering about two thou-
sand, rushed down the
steep bank into the sea, and
were drowned in the sea.
14 The swineherds ran
off and told it in the city and
in the country. Then people
came to see what it was that

[d] Gk *he*
[e] Gk *they*

ἐν πνεύματι ἀκαθάρτῳ, 3 ὃς τὴν κατοίκησιν
in(with) spirit an unclean, who the(his) dwelling
εἶχεν ἐν τοῖς μνήμασιν, καὶ οὐδὲ ἁλύσει
had among the tombs, and not with a chain
=no one any more
οὐκέτι οὐδεὶς ἐδύνατο αὐτὸν δῆσαι, 4 διὰ
no longer no one was able him to bind, on account of
was able to bind him with a chain, = because
τὸ αὐτὸν πολλάκις πέδαις καὶ ἁλύσεσιν
the him often with fetters and chains
he had often been bound with fetters and chains, and . . .
δεδέσθαι, καὶ διεσπάσθαι ὑπ' αὐτοῦ τὰς
to have been bound, and to be burst by him the
ἁλύσεις καὶ τὰς πέδας συντετρῖφθαι, καὶ
chains and the fetters to have been broken, and
οὐδεὶς ἴσχυεν αὐτὸν δαμάσαι· 5 καὶ
no one was able him to subdue; and
διὰ παντὸς νυκτὸς καὶ ἡμέρας ἐν τοῖς μνήμασιν
always of(by) night and day among the tombs
καὶ ἐν τοῖς ὄρεσιν ἦν κράζων καὶ
and in the mountains he was crying out and
κατακόπτων ἑαυτὸν λίθοις. 6 καὶ ἰδὼν
cutting himself with stones. And seeing
τὸν Ἰησοῦν ἀπὸ μακρόθεν ἔδραμεν καὶ
– Jesus from afar he ran and
προσεκύνησεν αὐτόν, 7 καὶ κράξας φωνῇ
worshipped him, and crying out with a voice
μεγάλῃ λέγει· τί ἐμοὶ καὶ σοί, Ἰησοῦ
great(loud) he says: What to me and to thee, Jesus
υἱὲ τοῦ θεοῦ τοῦ ὑψίστου; ὁρκίζω σε
Son – of God the most high? I adjure thee
τὸν θεόν, μή με βασανίσῃς. 8 ἔλεγεν
– by God, not me thou mayest torment. he said
γὰρ αὐτῷ· ἔξελθε τὸ πνεῦμα τὸ ἀκάθαρτον
For to him: Come *out* the spirit – unclean
ἐκ τοῦ ἀνθρώπου. 9 καὶ ἐπηρώτα αὐτόν·
out of the man. And he questioned him:
τί ὄνομά σοι; καὶ λέγει αὐτῷ· λεγιὼν
What name to thee?[c] And he says to him: Legion
= What name hast thou ? = My
ὄνομά μοι, ὅτι πολλοί ἐσμεν. 10 καὶ
name to me,[c] because many we are. And
name is Legion,
παρεκάλει αὐτὸν πολλὰ ἵνα μὴ αὐτὰ
he besought him much that not them
ἀποστείλῃ ἔξω τῆς χώρας. 11 ἦν δὲ
he would send outside the country. Now there was
ἐκεῖ πρὸς τῷ ὄρει ἀγέλη χοίρων μεγάλη
there near the mountain herd of pigs a great
βοσκομένη· 12 καὶ παρεκάλεσαν αὐτὸν
feeding; and they besought him
λέγοντες· πέμψον ἡμᾶς εἰς τοὺς χοίρους,
saying: Send us into the pigs,
ἵνα εἰς αὐτοὺς εἰσέλθωμεν. 13 καὶ ἐπέτρεψεν
that into them we may enter. And he allowed
αὐτοῖς. καὶ ἐξελθόντα τὰ πνεύματα τὰ
them. And coming out the spirits –
ἀκάθαρτα εἰσῆλθον εἰς τοὺς χοίρους, καὶ
unclean entered into the pigs, and
ὥρμησεν ἡ ἀγέλη κατὰ τοῦ κρημνοῦ εἰς
rushed the herd down the precipice into
τὴν θάλασσαν, ὡς δισχίλιοι, καὶ ἐπνίγοντο
the sea, about two thousand, and were choked
ἐν τῇ θαλάσσῃ. 14 καὶ οἱ βόσκοντες
in the sea. And the [ones] feeding
αὐτοὺς ἔφυγον καὶ ἀπήγγειλαν εἰς τὴν
them fled and reported in the
πόλιν καὶ εἰς τοὺς ἀγρούς· καὶ ἦλθον
city and in the fields; and they came

meet him. 3 This man lived
in the tombs, and no one
could bind him any more,
not even with a chain. 4 For
he had often been chained
hand and foot, but he tore
the chains apart and broke
the irons on his feet. No
one was strong enough to
subdue him. 5 Night and
day among the tombs and
in the hills he would cry out
and cut himself with
stones.
6 When he saw Jesus from
a distance, he ran and fell
on his knees in front of him.
7 He shouted at the top of
his voice, "What do you
want with me, Jesus, Son
of the Most High God?
Swear to God that you
won't torture me!" 8 For
Jesus had said to him,
"Come out of this man,
you evil spirit!"
9 Then Jesus asked him,
"What is your name?"
"My name is Legion," he
replied, "for we are
many." 10 And he begged
Jesus again and again not to
send them out of the area.
11 A large herd of pigs was
feeding on the nearby hillside. 12 The demons begged
Jesus, "Send us among the
pigs; allow us to go into
them." 13 He gave them
permission, and the evil
spirits came out and went
into the pigs. The herd,
about two thousand in
number, rushed down the
steep bank into the lake and
were drowned.
14 Those tending the pigs
ran off and reported this in
the town and countryside,
and the people went out to

had happened. 15They
came to Jesus and saw the
demoniac sitting there,
clothed and in his right
mind, the very man who
had had the legion; and
they were afraid. 16Those
who had seen what had
happened to the demoniac
and to the swine reported
it. 17Then they began to
beg Jesus[f] to leave their
neighborhood. 18As he was
getting into the boat, the
man who had been pos-
sessed by demons begged
him that he might be with
him. 19But Jesus[d] refused,
and said to him, "Go home
to your friends, and tell
them how much the Lord
has done for you, and what
mercy he has shown you."
20And he went away and
began to proclaim in the
Decapolis how much Jesus
had done for him; and ev-
eryone was amazed.

A Girl Restored to Life and a Woman Healed

21 When Jesus had
crossed again in the boat[g]
to the other side, a great
crowd gathered around
him; and he was by the sea.
22Then one of the leaders
of the synagogue named Jairus came and, when he
saw him, fell at his feet
23and begged him repeatedly, "My little daughter is at
the point of death. Come
and lay your hands on her,
so that she may be made
well, and live." 24So he
went with him.
And a large crowd fol-
lowed him and pressed in
on him. 25Now there was a
woman who had been suf-
fering from hemorrhages
for twelve years. 26She had
endured much under many
physicians, and had spent
all that she had; and she
was no better, but rather

[f]Gk *him*
[g]Other ancient authorities lack *in the boat*

ἰδεῖν τί ἐστιν τὸ γεγονός. 15 καὶ
to see what is the thing having happened. And

ἔρχονται πρὸς τὸν Ἰησοῦν, καὶ θεωροῦσιν τὸν
they come to – Jesus, and see the

δαιμονιζόμενον καθήμενον ἱματισμένον καὶ
demon-possessed man sitting *having been* clothed and

σωφρονοῦντα, τὸν ἐσχηκότα τὸν λεγιῶνα,
being in his senses, the man having had the legion,

καὶ ἐφοβήθησαν. 16 καὶ διηγήσαντο αὐτοῖς οἱ
and they were afraid. And related to them the [ones]

ἰδόντες πῶς ἐγένετο τῷ δαιμονιζομένῳ
seeing how it happened to the demon-possessed man

καὶ περὶ τῶν χοίρων. 17 καὶ ἤρξαντο
and about the pigs. And they began

παρακαλεῖν αὐτὸν ἀπελθεῖν ἀπὸ τῶν ὁρίων
to beseech him to depart from the territory

αὐτῶν. 18 καὶ ἐμβαίνοντος αὐτοῦ εἰς τὸ
of them. And embarking him* in the
= as he embarked

πλοῖον παρεκάλει αὐτὸν ὁ δαιμονισθεὶς
ship besought him the [one] demon-possessed

ἵνα μετ' αὐτοῦ ᾖ. 19 καὶ οὐκ ἀφῆκεν
that with him he might be. And he permitted not

αὐτόν, ἀλλὰ λέγει αὐτῷ· ὕπαγε εἰς τὸν
him, but says to him: Go to the

οἶκόν σου πρὸς τοὺς σούς, καὶ ἀπάγγειλον
house of thee to the thine, and report
= thy people,

αὐτοῖς ὅσα ὁ κύριός σοι πεποίηκεν καὶ
to them what things the Lord to thee has done and

ἠλέησέν σε. 20 καὶ ἀπῆλθεν καὶ ἤρξατο
pitied thee. And he departed and began

κηρύσσειν ἐν τῇ Δεκαπόλει ὅσα ἐποίησεν
to proclaim in – Decapolis what things did

αὐτῷ ὁ Ἰησοῦς, καὶ πάντες ἐθαύμαζον.
to him – Jesus, and all men marvelled.

21 Καὶ διαπεράσαντος τοῦ Ἰησοῦ ἐν τῷ
And crossing over – Jesus* in the
= when Jesus had crossed over

πλοίῳ πάλιν εἰς τὸ πέραν συνήχθη ὄχλος
ship again to the other side was assembled crowd

πολὺς ἐπ' αὐτόν, καὶ ἦν παρὰ τὴν θάλασσαν.
a much(great) to him, and he was by the sea.

22 Καὶ ἔρχεται εἷς τῶν ἀρχισυναγώγων,
And comes one of the synagogue chiefs,

ὀνόματι Ἰάϊρος, καὶ ἰδὼν αὐτὸν πίπτει
by name Jairus, and seeing him falls

πρὸς τοὺς πόδας αὐτοῦ, 23 καὶ παρακαλεῖ
at the feet of him, and beseeches

αὐτὸν πολλὰ λέγων ὅτι τὸ θυγάτριόν μου
him much saying[,] – The daughter of me

ἐσχάτως ἔχει, ἵνα ἐλθὼν ἐπιθῇς
is at the point of death,† that coming thou mayest lay *on*

τὰς χεῖρας αὐτῇ, ἵνα σωθῇ καὶ ζήσῃ.
the(thy) hands on her, that she may be healed and may live.

24 καὶ ἀπῆλθεν μετ' αὐτοῦ. καὶ ἠκολούθει αὐτῷ
And he went with him. And followed him

ὄχλος πολύς, καὶ συνέθλιβον αὐτόν. 25 Καὶ
crowd a much(great), and pressed upon him. And

γυνὴ οὖσα ἐν ῥύσει αἵματος δώδεκα
a woman being in a flow of blood twelve
= having

ἔτη, 26 καὶ πολλὰ παθοῦσα ὑπὸ πολλῶν
years, and many things suffering by many

ἰατρῶν καὶ δαπανήσασα τὰ παρ' αὐτῆς
physicians and having spent *the* with her

πάντα, καὶ μηδὲν ὠφεληθεῖσα ἀλλὰ μᾶλλον
all things, and nothing having been profited but rather

see what had happened.
15When they came to Jesus,
they saw the man who had
been possessed by the le-
gion of demons, sitting
there, dressed and in his
right mind; and they were
afraid. 16Those who had
seen it told the people what
had happened to the de-
mon-possessed man—and
told about the pigs as well.
17Then the people began to
plead with Jesus to leave
their region.
18As Jesus was getting
into the boat, the man who
had been demon-possessed
begged to go with him.
19Jesus did not let him, but
said, "Go home to your
family and tell them how
much the Lord has done for
you, and how he has had
mercy on you." 20So the
man went away and began
to tell in the Decapolis[m]
how much Jesus had done
for him. And all the people
were amazed.

A Dead Girl and a Sick Woman

21When Jesus had again
crossed over by boat to the
other side of the lake, a
large crowd gathered
around him while he was by
the lake. 22Then one of the
synagogue rulers, named
Jairus, came there. Seeing
Jesus, he fell at his feet
23and pleaded earnestly
with him, "My little daughter is dying. Please come
and put your hands on her
so that she will be healed
and live." 24So Jesus went
with him.
A large crowd followed
and pressed around him.
25And a woman was there
who had been subject to
bleeding for twelve years.
26She had suffered a great
deal under the care of many
doctors and had spent all

[m]20 That is, the Ten Cities

grew worse. 27 She had
heard about Jesus, and
came up behind him in the
crowd and touched his
cloak, 28 for she said, "If I
but touch his clothes, I will
be made well." 29 Immedi-
ately her hemorrhage
stopped; and she felt in her
body that she was healed of
her disease. 30 Immediately
aware that power had gone
forth from him, Jesus
turned about in the crowd
and said, "Who touched
my clothes?" 31 And his disciples said to him, "You see
the crowd pressing in on
you; how can you say,
'Who touched me?' " 32 He
looked all around to see
who had done it. 33 But the
woman, knowing what had
happened to her, came in
fear and trembling, fell
down before him, and told
him the whole truth. 34 He
said to her, "Daughter,
your faith has made you
well; go in peace, and be
healed of your disease."
35 While he was still
speaking, some people
came from the leader's
house to say, "Your daughter is dead. Why trouble the
teacher any further?" 36 But
overhearing[h] what they
said, Jesus said to the leader of the synagogue, "Do
not fear, only believe."
37 He allowed no one to follow him except Peter,
James, and John, the brother of James. 38 When they
came to the house of the
leader of the synagogue, he
saw a commotion, people
weeping and wailing loud-
ly. 39 When he had entered,
he said to them, "Why do
you make a commotion and
weep? The child is not dead

[h] Or *ignoring*; other ancient authorities read *hearing*

εἰς τὸ χεῖρον ἐλθοῦσα, 27 ἀκούσασα τὰ
to the worse having come, hearing the things
περὶ τοῦ Ἰησοῦ, ἐλθοῦσα ἐν τῷ ὄχλῳ
about – Jesus, coming in the crowd
ὄπισθεν ἥψατο τοῦ ἱματίου αὐτοῦ· 28 ἔλεγεν
behind touched the garment of him; she said[,]
γὰρ ὅτι ἐὰν ἅψωμαι κἂν τῶν ἱματίων
for – If I may touch even the garments
αὐτοῦ, σωθήσομαι. 29 καὶ εὐθὺς ἐξηράνθη
of him, I shall be healed. And immediately was dried up
ἡ πηγὴ τοῦ αἵματος αὐτῆς, καὶ ἔγνω
the fountain of the blood of her, and she knew
τῷ σώματι ὅτι ἴαται ἀπὸ τῆς
in the(her) body that she is(was) cured from the
μάστιγος. 30 καὶ εὐθὺς ὁ Ἰησοῦς ἐπιγνοὺς ἐν
plague. And immediately – Jesus knowing in
ἑαυτῷ τὴν ἐξ αὐτοῦ δύναμιν ἐξελθοῦσαν,
himself ¹the ⁴out of ⁵him ²power ³going forth,
ἐπιστραφεὶς ἐν τῷ ὄχλῳ ἔλεγεν· τίς μου ἥψατο τῶν
turning in the crowd said: Who of me touched the
ἱματίων; 31 καὶ ἔλεγον αὐτῷ οἱ μαθηταὶ
garments? And said to him the disciples
αὐτοῦ· βλέπεις τὸν ὄχλον συνθλίβοντά σε,
of him: Thou seest the crowd pressing upon thee,
καὶ λέγεις· τίς μου ἥψατο; 32 καὶ
and thou sayest: Who me touched? And
περιεβλέπετο ἰδεῖν τὴν τοῦτο ποιήσασαν.
he looked round to see the [one] this having done.
33 ἡ δὲ γυνὴ φοβηθεῖσα καὶ τρέμουσα,
And the woman fearing and trembling,
εἰδυῖα ὃ γέγονεν αὐτῇ, ἦλθεν καὶ προσέ-
knowing what has happened to her, came and fell
πεσεν αὐτῷ καὶ εἶπεν αὐτῷ πᾶσαν τὴν ἀλήθειαν.
before him and told him all the truth.
34 ὁ δὲ εἶπεν αὐτῇ· θυγάτηρ, ἡ πίστις
And he said to her: Daughter, the faith
σου σέσωκέν σε· ὕπαγε εἰς εἰρήνην, καὶ
of thee has healed thee; go in peace, and
ἴσθι ὑγιὴς ἀπὸ τῆς μάστιγός σου. 35 Ἔτι
be whole from the plague of thee. Still
— While
αὐτοῦ λαλοῦντος ἔρχονται ἀπὸ τοῦ
him speaking* they come from the
he was still speaking
ἀρχισυναγώγου λέγοντες ὅτι ἡ θυγάτηρ
synagogue chief saying[,] – The daughter
σου ἀπέθανεν· τί ἔτι σκύλλεις τὸν διδάσκαλον;
of thee died; why still troublest thou the teacher?
36 ὁ δὲ Ἰησοῦς παρακούσας τὸν λόγον
But Jesus overhearing the word
λαλούμενον λέγει τῷ ἀρχισυναγώγῳ· μὴ
being spoken says to the synagogue chief: not
φοβοῦ, μόνον πίστευε. 37 καὶ οὐκ ἀφῆκεν
Fear, only believe. And he allowed not
οὐδένα μετ' αὐτοῦ συνακολουθῆσαι εἰ μὴ
no(any)one with him to accompany except
τὸν Πέτρον καὶ Ἰάκωβον καὶ Ἰωάννην
– Peter and James and John
τὸν ἀδελφὸν Ἰακώβου. 38 καὶ ἔρχονται
the brother of James. And they come
εἰς τὸν οἶκον τοῦ ἀρχισυναγώγου, καὶ
into the house of the synagogue chief, and
θεωρεῖ θόρυβον, καὶ κλαίοντας καὶ
he sees an uproar, and [men] weeping and
ἀλαλάζοντας πολλά, 39 καὶ εἰσελθὼν λέγει
crying aloud much, and entering he says
αὐτοῖς· τί θορυβεῖσθε καὶ κλαίετε; τὸ
to them: Why make ye an uproar and weep? the

she had, yet instead of getting better she grew worse.
27 When she heard about
Jesus, she came up behind
him in the crowd and
touched his cloak, 28 be-
cause she thought, "If I
just touch his clothes, I will
be healed." 29 Immediately
her bleeding stopped and
she felt in her body that she
was freed from her suffering.
30 At once Jesus realized
that power had gone out
from him. He turned
around in the crowd and
asked, "Who touched my
clothes?"
31 "You see the people
crowding against you," his
disciples answered, "and
yet you can ask, 'Who
touched me?' "
32 But Jesus kept looking
around to see who had
done it. 33 Then the woman,
knowing what had hap-
pened to her, came and fell
at his feet and, trembling
with fear, told him the
whole truth. 34 He said to
her, "Daughter, your faith
has healed you. Go in
peace and be freed from
your suffering."
35 While Jesus was still
speaking, some men came
from the house of Jairus,
the synagogue ruler. "Your
daughter is dead," they
said. "Why bother the
teacher any more?"
36 Ignoring what they said,
Jesus told the synagogue
ruler, "Don't be afraid; just
believe."
37 He did not let anyone
follow him except Peter,
James and John the brother
of James. 38 When they
came to the home of the
synagogue ruler, Jesus saw
a commotion, with people
crying and wailing loudly.
39 He went in and said to
them, "Why all this com-

but sleeping." 40 And they
laughed at him. Then he put
them all outside, and took
the child's father and mother and those who were with
him, and went in where the
child was. 41 He took her by
the hand and said to her,
"Talitha cum," which
means, "Little girl, get up!"
42 And immediately the girl
got up and began to walk
about (she was twelve
years of age). At this they
were overcome with
amazement. 43 He strictly
ordered them that no one
should know this, and told
them to give her something
to eat.

παιδίον οὐκ ἀπέθανεν ἀλλὰ καθεύδει.
child did not die but sleeps.

40 καὶ κατεγέλων αὐτοῦ. αὐτὸς δὲ ἐκβαλὼν
And they ridiculed him. But he putting out

πάντας παραλαμβάνει τὸν πατέρα τοῦ
all takes the father of the

παιδίου καὶ τὴν μητέρα καὶ τοὺς μετ'
child and the mother and the [ones] with

αὐτοῦ, καὶ εἰσπορεύεται ὅπου ἦν τὸ
him, and goes in where was the

παιδίον. **41** καὶ κρατήσας τῆς χειρὸς
child. And taking hold of the hand

τοῦ παιδίου λέγει αὐτῇ· ταλιθὰ κοῦμ, ὅ
of the child he says to her: Talitha koum, which

ἐστιν μεθερμηνευόμενον· τὸ κοράσιον, σοὶ
is being interpreted: – Maid, to thee

λέγω, ἔγειρε. **42** καὶ εὐθὺς ἀνέστη τὸ
I say, arise. And immediately rose up the

κοράσιον καὶ περιεπάτει· ἦν γὰρ
maid and walked; for she was

ἐτῶν δώδεκα. καὶ ἐξέστησαν εὐθὺς
[of the age] of years twelve. And they were astonished immediately
=immediately they were exceedingly astonished.

ἐκστάσει μεγάλῃ. **43** καὶ διεστείλατο
astonishment with a great. And he ordered

αὐτοῖς πολλὰ ἵνα μηδεὶς γνοῖ τοῦτο, καὶ
them much that no one should know this, and

εἶπεν δοθῆναι αὐτῇ φαγεῖν.
told to be given to her to eat.
=[them] to give her [something] to eat.

motion and wailing? The
child is not dead but
asleep." 40 But they
laughed at him.
After he put them all out,
he took the child's father
and mother and the disci-
ples who were with him,
and went in where the child
was. 41 He took her by the
hand and said to her, "*Talitha koum!*" (which means,
"Little girl, I say to you,
get up!"). 42 Immediately
the girl stood up and
walked around (she was
twelve years old). At this
they were completely as-
tonished. 43 He gave strict
orders not to let anyone
know about this, and told
them to give her something
to eat.

Chapter 6

The Rejection of Jesus at Nazareth

He left that place and
came to his home-
town, and his disciples followed him. 2 On the sab-
bath he began to teach in
the synagogue, and many
who heard him were as-
tounded. They said,
"Where did this man get all
this? What is this wisdom
that has been given to him?
What deeds of power are
being done by his hands!
3 Is not this the carpenter,
the son of Mary[i] and
brother of James and Joses
and Judas and Simon, and
are not his sisters here with
us?" And they took of-
fense[j] at him. 4 Then Jesus
said to them, "Prophets are
not without honor, except
in their hometown, and
among their own kin, and in
their own house." 5 And he
could do no deed of power

[i] Other ancient authorities read *son of the carpenter and of Mary*
[j] Or *stumbled*

6 Καὶ ἐξῆλθεν ἐκεῖθεν, καὶ ἔρχεται εἰς
And he went forth thence, and comes into

τὴν πατρίδα αὐτοῦ, καὶ ἀκολουθοῦσιν
the native place of him, and follow

αὐτῷ οἱ μαθηταὶ αὐτοῦ. **2** καὶ γενομένου
him the disciples of him. And coming
= when

σαββάτου ἤρξατο διδάσκειν ἐν τῇ συναγωγῇ·
a sabbath[a] he began to teach in the synagogue;
a sabbath came

καὶ οἱ πολλοὶ ἀκούοντες ἐξεπλήσσοντο
and the many hearing were astonished

λέγοντες· πόθεν τούτῳ ταῦτα, καὶ τίς ἡ
saying: Whence to this man these things, and what the

σοφία ἡ δοθεῖσα τούτῳ; καὶ αἱ δυνάμεις
wisdom – given to this(him)? And *the* powerful deeds

τοιαῦται διὰ τῶν χειρῶν αὐτοῦ γινόμεναι;
such through the hands of him coming about?

3 οὐχ οὗτός ἐστιν ὁ τέκτων, ὁ υἱὸς
[2]Not [3]this man [1]is the carpenter, the son

τῆς Μαρίας καὶ ἀδελφὸς Ἰακώβου καὶ
of Mary and brother of James and

Ἰωσῆτος καὶ Ἰούδα καὶ Σίμωνος; καὶ
Joses and Judas and Simon? and

οὐκ εἰσὶν αἱ ἀδελφαὶ αὐτοῦ ὧδε πρὸς
[2]not [1]are the sisters of him here with

ἡμᾶς; καὶ ἐσκανδαλίζοντο ἐν αὐτῷ. **4** καὶ
us? And they were offended in(at) him. And

ἔλεγεν αὐτοῖς ὁ Ἰησοῦς ὅτι οὐκ ἔστιν
said to them – Jesus[,] – [3]not [2]is

προφήτης ἄτιμος εἰ μὴ ἐν τῇ πατρίδι
[1]A prophet unhonoured except in the native place

αὐτοῦ καὶ ἐν τοῖς συγγενεῦσιν αὐτοῦ
of him and among the relatives of him

καὶ ἐν τῇ οἰκίᾳ αὐτοῦ. **5** καὶ οὐκ
and in the house of him. And not

Chapter 6

A Prophet Without Honor

Jesus left there and
went to his hometown,
accompanied by his disci-
ples. 2 When the Sabbath
came, he began to teach in
the synagogue, and many
who heard him were
amazed.
"Where did this man get
these things?" they asked.
"What's this wisdom that
has been given him, that he
even does miracles! 3 Isn't
this the carpenter? Isn't
this Mary's son and the
brother of James, Joseph,[n]
Judas and Simon? Aren't
his sisters here with us?"
And they took offense at
him.
4 Jesus said to them,
"Only in his hometown,
among his relatives and in
his own house is a prophet
without honor." 5 He could

[n] 3 Greek *Joses*, a variant of *Joseph*

there, except that he laid
his hands on a few sick people and cured them. 6 And
he was amazed at their unbelief.

The Mission of the Twelve

Then he went about
among the villages teach-
ing. 7 He called the twelve
and began to send them out
two by two, and gave them
authority over the unclean
spirits. 8 He ordered them
to take nothing for their
journey except a staff; no
bread, no bag, no money in
their belts; 9 but to wear
sandals and not to put on
two tunics. 10 He said to
them, "Wherever you enter
a house, stay there until
you leave the place. 11 If
any place will not welcome
you and they refuse to hear
you, as you leave, shake off
the dust that is on your feet
as a testimony against
them." 12 So they went out
and proclaimed that all
should repent. 13 They cast
out many demons, and
anointed with oil many who
were sick and cured them.

The Death of John the Baptist

14 King Herod heard of
it, for Jesus'[k] name had become known. Some were[l]
saying, "John the baptizer
has been raised from the
dead; and for this reason
these powers are at work in
him." 15 But others said, "It
is Elijah." And others said,
"It is a prophet, like one of
the prophets of old." 16 But
when Herod heard of it, he
said, "John, whom I be-
headed, has been raised."
17 For Herod himself
had sent men who arrested
John, bound him, and put

[k] Gk *his*
[l] Other ancient authorities read *He was*

ἐδύνατο ἐκεῖ ποιῆσαι οὐδεμίαν δύναμιν,
he could there *to* do no(any) powerful deed,

εἰ μὴ ὀλίγοις ἀρρώστοις ἐπιθεὶς τὰς
except *on* a few sick [ones] laying on the(his)

χεῖρας ἐθεράπευσεν. 6 καὶ ἐθαύμασεν διὰ
hands he healed. And he marvelled because of

τὴν ἀπιστίαν αὐτῶν.
the unbelief of them.

Καὶ περιῆγεν τὰς κώμας κύκλῳ
And he went round the villages in circuit

διδάσκων. 7 Καὶ προσκαλεῖται τοὺς δώδεκα,
teaching. And he calls to [him] the twelve,

καὶ ἤρξατο αὐτοὺς ἀποστέλλειν δύο δύο,
and began them to send forth two [by] two,

καὶ ἐδίδου αὐτοῖς ἐξουσίαν τῶν πνευμάτων
and gave them authority the spirits

τῶν ἀκαθάρτων, 8 καὶ παρήγγειλεν αὐτοῖς
– of(over) unclean, and charged them

ἵνα μηδὲν αἴρωσιν εἰς ὁδὸν εἰ μὴ ῥάβδον
that nothing they should take in [the] way except a staff

μόνον, μὴ ἄρτον, μὴ πήραν, μὴ εἰς τὴν
only, not bread, not a wallet, not in the

ζώνην χαλκόν, 9 ἀλλὰ ὑποδεδεμένους σανδάλια,
girdle copper [money], but having had tied on sandals,

καὶ μὴ ἐνδύσησθε δύο χιτῶνας. 10 καὶ
and do not put on two tunics. And

ἔλεγεν αὐτοῖς· ὅπου ἐὰν εἰσέλθητε εἰς
he said to them: Wherever ye enter into

οἰκίαν, ἐκεῖ μένετε ἕως ἂν ἐξέλθητε
a house, there remain until ye go out

ἐκεῖθεν. 11 καὶ ὃς ἂν τόπος μὴ δέξηται
thence. And whatever place receives not

ὑμᾶς μηδὲ ἀκούσωσιν ὑμῶν, ἐκπορευόμενοι
you nor they hear you, going out

ἐκεῖθεν ἐκτινάξατε τὸν χοῦν τὸν ὑποκάτω
thence shake off the dust – under

τῶν ποδῶν ὑμῶν εἰς μαρτύριον αὐτοῖς.
the feet of you for a testimony to them.

12 Καὶ ἐξελθόντες ἐκήρυξαν ἵνα μετανοῶσιν,
And going forth they proclaimed that men should repent,

13 καὶ δαιμόνια πολλὰ ἐξέβαλλον, καὶ
and demons many they expelled, and

ἤλειφον ἐλαίῳ πολλοὺς ἀρρώστους καὶ
anointed with oil many sick [ones] and

ἐθεράπευον.
healed.

14 Καὶ ἤκουσεν ὁ βασιλεὺς Ἡρῴδης,
And heard the king Herod,

φανερὸν γὰρ ἐγένετο τὸ ὄνομα αὐτοῦ, καὶ
for manifest became the name of him, and

ἔλεγον ὅτι Ἰωάννης ὁ βαπτίζων ἐγήγερται
they said[,] – John the baptizing [one] has been raised

ἐκ νεκρῶν, καὶ διὰ τοῦτο ἐνεργοῦσιν αἱ
from [the] dead, and therefore operate the

δυνάμεις ἐν αὐτῷ. 15 ἄλλοι δὲ ἔλεγον
powerful deeds in him. But others said[,]

ὅτι Ἠλίας ἐστίν· ἄλλοι δὲ ἔλεγον ὅτι
– Elias it/he is; and [yet] others said[,] –

προφήτης ὡς εἷς τῶν προφητῶν. 16 ἀκούσας δὲ
A prophet as one of the prophets. But hearing

ὁ Ἡρῴδης ἔλεγεν· ὃν ἐγὼ ἀπεκεφάλισα
– Herod said: [2]whom [3]I [4]beheaded

Ἰωάννην, οὗτος ἠγέρθη. 17 Αὐτὸς γὰρ ὁ
[1]John, this was raised. For [2]himself –

Ἡρῴδης ἀποστείλας ἐκράτησεν τὸν Ἰωάννην
[1]Herod sending seized – John

not do any miracles there,
except lay his hands on a
few sick people and heal
them. 6 And he was amazed
at their lack of faith.

Jesus Sends Out the Twelve

Then Jesus went around
teaching from village to village. 7 Calling the Twelve to
him, he sent them out two
by two and gave them au-
thority over evil[o] spirits.
8 These were his instruc-
tions: "Take nothing for
the journey except a staff
—no bread, no bag, no
money in your belts. 9 Wear
sandals but not an extra tunic. 10 Whenever you enter
a house, stay there until
you leave that town. 11 And
if any place will not welcome you or listen to you,
shake the dust off your feet
when you leave, as a testimony against them."
12 They went out and
preached that people
should repent. 13 They
drove out many demons
and anointed many sick
people with oil and healed
them.

John the Baptist Beheaded

14 King Herod heard
about this, for Jesus' name
had become well known.
Some were saying,[p] "John
the Baptist has been raised
from the dead, and that is
why miraculous powers are
at work in him."
15 Others said, "He is Elijah."
And still others claimed,
"He is a prophet, like one
of the prophets of long
ago."
16 But when Herod heard
this, he said, "John, the
man I beheaded, has been
raised from the dead!"
17 For Herod himself had
given orders to have John

[o] 7 Greek *unclean*
[p] 14 Some early manuscripts *He was saying*

him in prison on account of
Herodias, his brother Philip's wife, because Herod[m]
had married her. 18 For
John had been telling Herod, "It is not lawful for you
to have your brother's
wife." 19 And Herodias had
a grudge against him, and
wanted to kill him. But she
could not, 20 for Herod
feared John, knowing that
he was a righteous and holy
man, and he protected him.
When he heard him, he was
greatly perplexed;[n] and
yet he liked to listen to him.
21 But an opportunity came
when Herod on his birth-
day gave a banquet for his
courtiers and officers and
for the leaders of Galilee.
22 When his daughter Herodias[o] came in and danced,
she pleased Herod and his
guests; and the king said to
the girl, "Ask me for whatever you wish, and I will
give it." 23 And he solemnly
swore to her, "Whatever
you ask me, I will give you,
even half of my kingdom."
24 She went out and said to
her mother, "What should I
ask for?" She replied, "The
head of John the baptizer."
25 Immediately she rushed
back to the king and re-
quested, "I want you to
give me at once the head of
John the Baptist on a platter." 26 The king was deeply
grieved; yet out of regard
for his oaths and for the
guests, he did not want to
refuse her. 27 Immediately
the king sent a soldier of the

καὶ ἔδησεν αὐτὸν ἐν φυλακῇ διὰ Ἡρῳδιάδα
and bound him in prison because of Herodias

τὴν γυναῖκα Φιλίππου τοῦ ἀδελφοῦ αὐτοῦ,
the wife of Philip the brother of him,

ὅτι αὐτὴν ἐγάμησεν· 18 ἔλεγεν γὰρ ὁ
because her he married; for said –

Ἰωάννης τῷ Ἡρῴδῃ ὅτι οὐκ ἔξεστίν
John – to Herod[,] – It is not lawful

σοι ἔχειν τὴν γυναῖκα τοῦ ἀδελφοῦ σου.
for thee to have the wife of the brother of thee.

19 ἡ δὲ Ἡρῳδιὰς ἐνεῖχεν αὐτῷ καὶ
– Now Herodias had a grudge against him and

ἤθελεν αὐτὸν ἀποκτεῖναι, καὶ οὐκ ἠδύνατο·
wished [2]him [1]to kill, and could not;

20 ὁ γὰρ Ἡρῴδης ἐφοβεῖτο τὸν Ἰωάννην,
– for Herod feared – John.

εἰδὼς αὐτὸν ἄνδρα δίκαιον καὶ ἅγιον, καὶ
knowing him a man just and holy, and

συνετήρει αὐτόν, καὶ ἀκούσας αὐτοῦ πολλὰ
kept safe him, and hearing him much = was

ἠπόρει, καὶ ἡδέως αὐτοῦ ἤκουεν. 21 καὶ
was in difficulties, and gladly him heard. And
in great difficulties,

γενομένης ἡμέρας εὐκαίρου ὅτε Ἡρῴδης
coming day a suitable[a] when Herod
= when a suitable day came

τοῖς γενεσίοις αὐτοῦ δεῖπνον ἐποίησεν τοῖς
on the birthday festivities of him a supper made for the

μεγιστᾶσιν αὐτοῦ καὶ τοῖς χιλιάρχοις καὶ
courtiers of him and the chiliarchs and

τοῖς πρώτοις τῆς Γαλιλαίας, 22 καὶ
the chief men – of Galilee, and

εἰσελθούσης τῆς θυγατρὸς αὐτῆς τῆς
entering the daughter [2]*of* herself –
= when the daughter of Herodias herself entered and danced,

Ἡρῳδιάδος καὶ ὀρχησαμένης, ἤρεσεν τῷ
[1]of Herodias and dancing,[a] she pleased –

Ἡρῴδῃ καὶ τοῖς συνανακειμένοις. ὁ δὲ
Herod and the [ones] reclining with [him]. And the

βασιλεὺς εἶπεν τῷ κορασίῳ· αἴτησόν με
king said to the girl: Ask me

ὃ ἐὰν θέλῃς, καὶ δώσω σοι· 23 καὶ
whatever thou wishest, and I will give thee; and

ὤμοσεν αὐτῇ ὅτι ὃ ἐὰν αἰτήσῃς δώσω
he swore to her[,] – Whatever thou askest I will give

σοι ἕως ἡμίσους τῆς βασιλείας μου.
thee up to half of the kingdom of me.

24 καὶ ἐξελθοῦσα εἶπεν τῇ μητρὶ αὐτῆς·
And going out she said to the mother of her:

τί αἰτήσωμαι; ἡ δὲ εἶπεν· τὴν κεφαλὴν
What may I ask? And she said: The head

Ἰωάννου τοῦ βαπτίζοντος. 25 καὶ
of John the [one] baptizing. And

εἰσελθοῦσα εὐθὺς μετὰ σπουδῆς πρὸς τὸν
entering immediately with haste to the

βασιλέα ἠτήσατο λέγουσα· θέλω ἵνα ἐξαυτῆς
king she asked saying: I wish that at once

δῷς μοι ἐπὶ πίνακι τὴν κεφαλὴν Ἰωάννου
thou mayest give me on a dish the head of John

τοῦ βαπτιστοῦ. 26 καὶ περίλυπος γενόμενος
the Baptist. And deeply grieved becoming

ὁ βασιλεὺς διὰ τοὺς ὅρκους καὶ τοὺς
the king because of the oaths and the [ones]

ἀνακειμένους οὐκ ἠθέλησεν ἀθετῆσαι αὐτήν.
reclining did not wish to reject her.

27 καὶ εὐθὺς ἀποστείλας ὁ βασιλεὺς
And immediately [3]sending [1]the [2]king

arrested, and he had him
bound and put in prison.
He did this because of Herodias, his brother Philip's
wife, whom he had mar-
ried. 18For John had been
saying to Herod, "It is not
lawful for you to have your
brother's wife." 19So He-
rodias nursed a grudge
against John and wanted to
kill him. But she was not
able to, 20because Herod
feared John and protected
him, knowing him to be a
righteous and holy man.
When Herod heard John,
he was greatly puzzled[q];
yet he liked to listen to him.
21Finally the opportune
time came. On his birthday
Herod gave a banquet for
his high officials and military commanders and the
leading men of Galilee.
22When the daughter of Herodias came in and danced,
she pleased Herod and his
dinner guests.

The king said to the girl,
"Ask me for anything you
want, and I'll give it to
you." 23And he promised
her with an oath, "Whatever you ask I will give you,
up to half my kingdom."

24She went out and said to
her mother, "What shall I
ask for?"

"The head of John the
Baptist," she answered.

25At once the girl hurried
in to the king with the request: "I want you to give
me right now the head of
John the Baptist on a platter."

26The king was greatly
distressed, but because of
his oaths and his dinner
guests, he did not want to
refuse her. 27So he immediately sent an executioner

[m] Gk *he*
[n] Other ancient authorities read *he did many things*
[o] Other ancient authorities read *the daughter of Herodias herself*

[q]20 Some early manuscripts *he did many things*

guard with orders to bring
John's[p] head. He went and
beheaded him in the prison,
28 brought his head on a
platter, and gave it to the
girl. Then the girl gave it to
her mother. 29 When his
disciples heard about it,
they came and took his
body, and laid it in a tomb.

Feeding the Five Thousand

30 The apostles gath-
ered around Jesus, and told
him all that they had done
and taught. 31 He said to
them, "Come away to a de-
serted place all by your-
selves and rest a while."
For many were coming and
going, and they had no leisure even to eat. 32 And
they went away in the boat
to a deserted place by
themselves. 33 Now many
saw them going and recog-
nized them, and they hur-
ried there on foot from all
the towns and arrived
ahead of them. 34 As he
went ashore, he saw a great
crowd; and he had compas-
sion for them, because they
were like sheep without a
shepherd; and he began to
teach them many things.
35 When it grew late, his
disciples came to him and
said, "This is a deserted
place, and the hour is now
very late; 36 send them
away so that they may go
into the surrounding country and villages and buy
something for themselves
to eat." 37 But he answered
them, "You give them
something to eat." They
said to him, "Are we to go

σπεκουλάτορα ἐπέταξεν ἐνέγκαι τὴν κεφαλὴν
an executioner gave order to bring the head

αὐτοῦ. καὶ ἀπελθὼν ἀπεκεφάλισεν αὐτὸν
of him. And going he beheaded him

ἐν τῇ φυλακῇ, 28 καὶ ἤνεγκεν τὴν κεφαλὴν
in the prison, and brought the head

αὐτοῦ ἐπὶ πίνακι καὶ ἔδωκεν αὐτὴν τῷ
of him on a dish and gave it to the

κορασίῳ, καὶ τὸ κοράσιον ἔδωκεν αὐτὴν
girl, and the girl gave it

τῇ μητρὶ αὐτῆς. 29 καὶ ἀκούσαντες οἱ
to the mother of her. And hearing the

μαθηταὶ αὐτοῦ ἦλθαν καὶ ἦραν τὸ πτῶμα
disciples of him went and took the corpse

αὐτοῦ καὶ ἔθηκαν αὐτὸ ἐν μνημείῳ.
of him and put it in a tomb.

30 Καὶ συνάγονται οἱ ἀπόστολοι πρὸς
And assemble the apostles to

τὸν Ἰησοῦν, καὶ ἀπήγγειλαν αὐτῷ πάντα
– Jesus, and reported to him all things

ὅσα ἐποίησαν καὶ ὅσα ἐδίδαξαν. 31 καὶ
which they did and which they taught. And

λέγει αὐτοῖς· δεῦτε ὑμεῖς αὐτοὶ κατ'
he says to them: Come ye [your]selves pri-

ἰδίαν εἰς ἔρημον τόπον καὶ ἀναπαύσασθε ὀλίγον.
vately to a desert place and rest a little.

ἦσαν γὰρ οἱ ἐρχόμενοι καὶ οἱ
For [2]were [3]the [ones] [4]coming [5]and [6]the [ones]

ὑπάγοντες πολλοί, καὶ οὐδὲ φαγεῖν
[7]going [1]many, and not to eat

εὐκαίρουν. 32 καὶ ἀπῆλθον ἐν τῷ πλοίῳ
they had opportunity. And they went away in the ship

εἰς ἔρημον τόπον κατ' ἰδίαν. 33 καὶ
to a desert place privately. And

εἶδον αὐτοὺς ὑπάγοντας καὶ ἐπέγνωσαν
[2]saw [3]them [4]going [5]and [6]knew

πολλοί, καὶ πεζῇ ἀπὸ πασῶν τῶν πόλεων
[1]many, and on foot from all the cities

συνέδραμον ἐκεῖ καὶ προῆλθον αὐτούς.
ran together there and came before them.

34 Καὶ ἐξελθὼν εἶδεν πολὺν ὄχλον, καὶ
And going forth he saw a much(great) crowd, and

ἐσπλαγχνίσθη ἐπ' αὐτοὺς ὅτι ἦσαν ὡς
had compassion on them because they were as

πρόβατα μὴ ἔχοντα ποιμένα, καὶ ἤρξατο
sheep not having a shepherd, and he began

διδάσκειν αὐτοὺς πολλά. 35 Καὶ ἤδη ὥρας
to teach them many things. And now an hour
= it being

πολλῆς γενομένης προσελθόντες αὐτῷ οἱ
much coming[a] approaching *to* him the
late

μαθηταὶ αὐτοῦ ἔλεγον ὅτι ἔρημός ἐστιν
disciples of him said[,] – Desert is

ὁ τόπος καὶ ἤδη ὥρα πολλή· 36 ἀπόλυσον
the place and now hour a much; dismiss
= it is late;

αὐτούς, ἵνα ἀπελθόντες εἰς τοὺς κύκλῳ
them, that going away to the round about

ἀγροὺς καὶ κώμας ἀγοράσωσιν ἑαυτοῖς τί
fields and villages they may buy for themselves what

φάγωσιν. 37 ὁ δὲ ἀποκριθεὶς εἶπεν αὐτοῖς·
they may eat. But he answering said to them:

δότε αὐτοῖς ὑμεῖς φαγεῖν. καὶ λέγουσιν
Give them ye to eat. And they say

with orders to bring John's
head. The man went, be-
headed John in the prison,
28 and brought back his
head on a platter. He presented it to the girl, and she
gave it to her mother. 29 On
hearing of this, John's disciples came and took his
body and laid it in a tomb.

Jesus Feeds the Five Thousand

30 The apostles gathered
around Jesus and reported
to him all they had done
and taught. 31 Then, be-
cause so many people were
coming and going that they
did not even have a chance
to eat, he said to them,
"Come with me by your-
selves to a quiet place and
get some rest."
32 So they went away by
themselves in a boat to a
solitary place. 33 But many
who saw them leaving rec-
ognized them and ran on
foot from all the towns and
got there ahead of them.
34 When Jesus landed and
saw a large crowd, he had
compassion on them, be-
cause they were like sheep
without a shepherd. So he
began teaching them many
things.
35 By this time it was late
in the day, so his disciples
came to him. "This is a remote place," they said,
"and it's already very late.
36 Send the people away so
they can go to the sur-
rounding countryside and
villages and buy them-
selves something to eat."
37 But he answered, "You
give them something to
eat."
They said to him, "That

[p] Gk *his*

and buy two hundred de-
narii[q] worth of bread, and
give it to them to eat?"
38 And he said to them,
"How many loaves have
you? Go and see." When
they had found out, they
said, "Five, and two fish."
39 Then he ordered them to
get all the people to sit
down in groups on the
green grass. 40 So they sat
down in groups of hun-
dreds and of fifties. 41 Taking the five loaves and the
two fish, he looked up to
heaven, and blessed and
broke the loaves, and gave
them to his disciples to set
before the people; and he
divided the two fish among
them all. 42 And all ate and
were filled; 43 and they took
up twelve baskets full of
broken pieces and of the
fish. 44 Those who had eat-
en the loaves numbered
five thousand men.

Jesus Walks on the Water

45 Immediately he
made his disciples get into
the boat and go on ahead to
the other side, to Bethsaida, while he dismissed the
crowd. 46 After saying farewell to them, he went up on
the mountain to pray.
47 When evening came,
the boat was out on the sea,
and he was alone on the
land. 48 When he saw that
they were straining at the
oars against an adverse
wind, he came towards
them early in the morning,
walking on the sea. He intended to pass them by.
49 But when they saw him
walking on the sea, they
thought it was a ghost and
cried out; 50 for they all saw

αὐτῷ· ἀπελθόντες ἀγοράσωμεν δηναρίων
to him: Going away may we buy [2]of(for) [4]denarii

διακοσίων ἄρτους, καὶ δώσομεν αὐτοῖς
[3]two hundred [1]loaves, and shall we give them

φαγεῖν; 38 ὁ δὲ λέγει αὐτοῖς· πόσους
to eat? And he says to them: How many

ἔχετε ἄρτους; ὑπάγετε ἴδετε. καὶ γνόντες
have ye loaves? Go see. And knowing

λέγουσιν· πέντε, καὶ δύο ἰχθύας. 39 καὶ
they say: Five, and two fishes. And

ἐπέταξεν αὐτοῖς ἀνακλιθῆναι πάντας συμπόσια
he instructed them to recline all companies

συμπόσια ἐπὶ τῷ χλωρῷ χόρτῳ. 40 καὶ
companies on the green grass. And

ἀνέπεσαν πρασιαὶ πρασιαὶ κατὰ ἑκατὸν
they reclined groups groups by a hundred

καὶ κατὰ πεντήκοντα. 41 καὶ λαβὼν τοὺς
and by fifty. And taking the

πέντε ἄρτους καὶ τοὺς δύο ἰχθύας,
five loaves and the two fishes,

ἀναβλέψας εἰς τὸν οὐρανὸν εὐλόγησεν καὶ
looking up to – heaven he blessed and

κατέκλασεν τοὺς ἄρτους καὶ ἐδίδου τοῖς
broke the loaves and gave to the

μαθηταῖς ἵνα παρατιθῶσιν αὐτοῖς, καὶ
disciples that they might set before them, and

τοὺς δύο ἰχθύας ἐμέρισεν πᾶσιν. 42 καὶ
the two fishes he divided to all. And

ἔφαγον πάντες καὶ ἐχορτάσθησαν, 43 καὶ
they ate all and were satisfied, and

ἦραν κλάσματα δώδεκα κοφίνων πληρώματα
they took fragments twelve [2]of baskets [1]fullnesses

καὶ ἀπὸ τῶν ἰχθύων 44 καὶ ἦσαν οἱ
and from the fishes. And were the

φαγόντες τοὺς ἄρτους πεντακισχίλιοι ἄνδρες.
[ones] eating the loaves five thousand males.

45 Καὶ εὐθὺς ἠνάγκασεν τοὺς μαθητὰς
And immediately he constrained the disciples

αὐτοῦ ἐμβῆναι εἰς τὸ πλοῖον καὶ προάγειν
of him to embark in the ship and to go before

εἰς τὸ πέραν πρὸς Βηθσαϊδάν, ἕως αὐτὸς
to the other side to Bethsaida, until he

ἀπολύει τὸν ὄχλον. 46 καὶ ἀποταξάμενος
dismisses the crowd. And having said farewell

αὐτοῖς ἀπῆλθεν εἰς τὸ ὄρος προσεύξασθαι.
to them he went away to the mountain to pray.

47 καὶ ὀψίας γενομένης ἦν τὸ πλοῖον ἐν
And evening coming on[a] was the ship in
= when evening came on

μέσῳ τῆς θαλάσσης, καὶ αὐτὸς μόνος ἐπὶ
[the] midst of the sea, and he alone on

τῆς γῆς. 48 καὶ ἰδὼν αὐτοὺς βασανιζομένους
the land. And seeing them being distressed

ἐν τῷ ἐλαύνειν, ἦν γὰρ ὁ ἄνεμος ἐναντίος
in the to row, [4]was [1]for [2]the [3]wind contrary
= rowing,

αὐτοῖς, περὶ τετάρτην φυλακὴν τῆς νυκτὸς
to them, about [the] fourth watch of the night

ἔρχεται πρὸς αὐτοὺς περιπατῶν ἐπὶ τῆς
he comes toward them walking on the

θαλάσσης· καὶ ἤθελεν παρελθεῖν αὐτούς.
sea; and wished to go by them.

49 οἱ δὲ ἰδόντες αὐτὸν ἐπὶ τῆς θαλάσσης
But they seeing him on the sea

περιπατοῦντα ἔδοξαν ὅτι φάντασμά ἐστιν,
walking thought that a phantasm it is(was),

would take eight months of
a man's wages[r]! Are we to
go and spend that much on
bread and give it to them to
eat?"
38 "How many loaves do
you have?" he asked. "Go
and see."
When they found out,
they said, "Five—and two
fish."
39 Then Jesus directed
them to have all the people
sit down in groups on the
green grass. 40 So they sat
down in groups of hun-
dreds and fifties. 41 Taking
the five loaves and the two
fish and looking up to heav-
en, he gave thanks and
broke the loaves. Then he
gave them to his disciples
to set before the people. He
also divided the two fish
among them all. 42 They all
ate and were satisfied,
43 and the disciples picked
up twelve basketfuls of
broken pieces of bread and
fish. 44 The number of the
men who had eaten was
five thousand.

Jesus Walks on the Water

45 Immediately Jesus
made his disciples get into
the boat and go on ahead of
him to Bethsaida, while he
dismissed the crowd. 46 After leaving them, he went
up on a mountainside to
pray.
47 When evening came,
the boat was in the middle
of the lake, and he was
alone on land. 48 He saw the
disciples straining at the
oars, because the wind was
against them. About the
fourth watch of the night he
went out to them, walking
on the lake. He was about
to pass by them, 49 but
when they saw him walking
on the lake, they thought he
was a ghost. They cried

[q] The denarius was the usual day's wage for a laborer

[r] 37 Greek *take two hundred denarii*

him and were terrified. But
immediately he spoke to
them and said, "Take
heart, it is I; do not be
afraid." 51 Then he got into
the boat with them and the
wind ceased. And they
were utterly astounded,
52 for they did not understand about the loaves, but
their hearts were hardened.

Healing the Sick in Gennesaret

53 When they had
crossed over, they came to
land at Gennesaret and
moored the boat. 54 When
they got out of the boat,
people at once recognized
him, 55 and rushed about
that whole region and be-
gan to bring the sick on
mats to wherever they
heard he was. 56 And wherever he went, into villages
or cities or farms, they laid
the sick in the market-
places, and begged him that
they might touch even the
fringe of his cloak; and all
who touched it were
healed.

καὶ ἀνέκραξαν· 50 πάντες γὰρ αὐτὸν εἶδαν
and cried out; for all him saw
καὶ ἐταράχθησαν. ὁ δὲ εὐθὺς ἐλάλησεν
and were troubled. But he immediately talked
μετ' αὐτῶν, καὶ λέγει αὐτοῖς· θαρσεῖτε,
with them, and says to them: Be of good cheer,
ἐγώ εἰμι· μὴ φοβεῖσθε. 51 καὶ ἀνέβη
I am; be ye not afraid. And he went up
πρὸς αὐτοὺς εἰς τὸ πλοῖον, καὶ ἐκόπασεν
to them into the ship, and ceased
ὁ ἄνεμος· καὶ λίαν ἐκ περισσοῦ ἐν ἑαυτοῖς
the wind; and very much exceedingly in themselves
ἐξίσταντο· 52 οὐ γὰρ συνῆκαν ἐπὶ
they were astonished; for they did not understand concerning
τοῖς ἄρτοις ἀλλ' ἦν αὐτῶν ἡ καρδία
the loaves, but was of them the heart
πεπωρωμένη. 53 Καὶ διαπεράσαντες ἐπὶ
having been hardened. And crossing over [2]onto
τὴν γῆν ἦλθον εἰς Γεννησαρὲτ καὶ
[3]the [4]land [1]they came to Gennesaret and
προσωρμίσθησαν. 54 καὶ ἐξελθόντων αὐτῶν
anchored. And coming *out* them[a]
= as they came
ἐκ τοῦ πλοίου εὐθὺς ἐπιγνόντες αὐτὸν
out of the ship immediately knowing him
55 περιέδραμον ὅλην τὴν χώραν ἐκείνην
they ran round all – country that
καὶ ἤρξαντο ἐπὶ τοῖς κραβάτοις τοὺς
and began on the pallets the [ones]
= those
κακῶς ἔχοντας περιφέρειν, ὅπου ἤκουον
ill having to carry round, where they heard
who were ill
ὅτι ἐστίν. 56 καὶ ὅπου ἂν εἰσεπορεύετο
that he is(was). And wherever he entered
εἰς κώμας ἢ εἰς πόλεις ἢ εἰς ἀγρούς,
into villages or into cities or into country,
ἐν ταῖς ἀγοραῖς ἐτίθεσαν τοὺς ἀσθενοῦντας,
in the marketplaces they put the ailing [ones],
καὶ παρεκάλουν αὐτὸν ἵνα κἂν τοῦ
and besought him that if even the
κρασπέδου τοῦ ἱματίου αὐτοῦ ἅψωνται·
fringe of the garment of him they might touch;
καὶ ὅσοι ἂν ἥψαντο αὐτοῦ ἐσῴζοντο.
and as many as touched him were healed.

out, 50 because they all saw
him and were terrified.
Immediately he spoke to
them and said, "Take courage! It is I. Don't be
afraid." 51 Then he climbed
into the boat with them,
and the wind died down.
They were completely
amazed, 52 for they had not
understood about the
loaves; their hearts were
hardened.
53 When they had crossed
over, they landed at Gen-
nesaret and anchored
there. 54 As soon as they got
out of the boat, people recognized Jesus. 55 They ran
throughout that whole re-
gion and carried the sick on
mats to wherever they
heard he was. 56 And
wherever he went—into
villages, towns or countryside—they placed the sick
in the marketplaces. They
begged him to let them
touch even the edge of his
cloak, and all who touched
him were healed.

Chapter 7

The Tradition of the Elders

NOW when the Phari-
sees and some of the
scribes who had come from
Jerusalem gathered around
him, 2 they noticed that
some of his disciples were
eating with defiled hands,
that is, without washing
them. 3 (For the Pharisees,
and all the Jews, do not eat
unless they thoroughly
wash their hands,[r] thus
observing the tradition of
the elders; 4 and they do not
eat anything from the market unless they wash it;[s]
and there are also many

7 Καὶ συνάγονται πρὸς αὐτὸν οἱ Φαρισαῖοι
And assemble to him the Pharisees
καί τινες τῶν γραμματέων ἐλθόντες ἀπὸ
and some of the scribes coming from
Ἱεροσολύμων. 2 καὶ ἰδόντες τινὰς τῶν
Jerusalem. And seeing some of the
μαθητῶν αὐτοῦ ὅτι κοιναῖς χερσίν, τοῦτ'
disciples of him that with unclean hands, this
ἔστιν ἀνίπτοις, ἐσθίουσιν τοὺς ἄρτους,
is unwashed, they eat bread,
3 — οἱ γὰρ Φαρισαῖοι καὶ πάντες οἱ
— for the Pharisees and all the
Ἰουδαῖοι ἐὰν μὴ πυγμῇ νίψωνται τὰς
Jews unless with [the] fist they wash the
= ? carefully
χεῖρας οὐκ ἐσθίουσιν, κρατοῦντες τὴν
hands eat not, holding the
παράδοσιν τῶν πρεσβυτέρων, 4 καὶ ἀπ'
tradition of the elders, and from
ἀγορᾶς ἐὰν μὴ ῥαντίσωνται οὐκ ἐσθίουσιν, καὶ
marketplaces unless they sprinkle they eat not, and

Chapter 7

Clean and Unclean

THE Pharisees and some
of the teachers of the
law who had come from Je-
rusalem gathered around
Jesus and 2 saw some of his
disciples eating food with
hands that were "un-
clean," that is, unwashed.
3 (The Pharisees and all the
Jews do not eat unless they
give their hands a ceremonial washing, holding to the
tradition of the elders.
4 When they come from the
marketplace they do not
eat unless they wash. And

[r] Meaning of Gk uncertain
[s] Other ancient authorities read *and when they come from the marketplace, they do not eat unless they purify themselves*

other traditions that they
observe, the washing of
cups, pots, and bronze kettles.[t]) 5So the Pharisees
and the scribes asked him,
"Why do your disciples not
live[u] according to the tradition of the elders, but eat
with defiled hands?" 6He
said to them, "Isaiah
prophesied rightly about
you hypocrites, as it is written,

'This people honors
me with
their lips,
but their hearts are
far from me;
7 in vain do they
worship me,
teaching human
precepts as
doctrines.'

8You abandon the com-
mandment of God and hold
to human tradition."
9 Then he said to them,
"You have a fine way of rejecting the commandment
of God in order to keep
your tradition! 10For Mo-
ses said, 'Honor your fa-
ther and your mother'; and,
'Whoever speaks evil of father or mother must surely
die.' 11But you say that if
anyone tells father or mother, 'Whatever support you
might have had from me is
Corban' (that is, an offering
to God[v])— 12then you no
longer permit doing any-
thing for a father or mother,
13thus making void the
word of God through your
tradition that you have
handed on. And you do
many things like this."
14 Then he called the
crowd again and said to
them, "Listen to me, all of
you, and understand:
15there is nothing outside a
person that by going in can
defile, but the things that
come out are what de-
file."[w]

[t]Other ancient authorities add *and beds*
[u]Gk *walk*
[v]Gk lacks *to God*
[w]Other ancient authorities add verse 16, *"Let anyone with ears to hear listen"*

ἄλλα πολλά ἐστιν ἃ παρέλαβον κρατεῖν,
other things many there are which they received to hold,
βαπτισμοὺς ποτηρίων καὶ ξεστῶν καὶ
washings of cups and of utensils and
χαλκίων, — 5 καὶ ἐπερωτῶσιν αὐτὸν οἱ
of bronze vessels, — and questioned him the
Φαρισαῖοι καὶ οἱ γραμματεῖς· διὰ τί
Pharisees and the scribes: Why
οὐ περιπατοῦσιν οἱ μαθηταί σου κατὰ τὴν
walk not the disciples of thee according to the
παράδοσιν τῶν πρεσβυτέρων, ἀλλὰ κοιναῖς
tradition of the elders, but with unclean
χερσὶν ἐσθίουσιν τὸν ἄρτον; 6 ὁ δὲ εἶπεν
hands eat – bread ? And he said
αὐτοῖς· καλῶς ἐπροφήτευσεν Ἠσαΐας περὶ
to them: Well prophesied Esaias concerning
ὑμῶν τῶν ὑποκριτῶν, ὡς γέγραπται ὅτι
you *the* hypocrites, as it has been written[:] –
οὗτος ὁ λαὸς τοῖς χείλεσίν με τιμᾷ,
This – people with the lips me honours,
ἡ δὲ καρδία αὐτῶν πόρρω ἀπέχει ἀπ'
but the heart of them [2]far [1]is [3]away from
ἐμοῦ· 7 μάτην δὲ σέβονταί με, διδάσκοντες
me; and in vain they worship me, teaching
διδασκαλίας ἐντάλματα ἀνθρώπων. 8 ἀφέντες
teachings [which are] commands of men. Leaving
τὴν ἐντολὴν τοῦ θεοῦ κρατεῖτε τὴν
the commandment – of God ye hold the
παράδοσιν τῶν ἀνθρώπων. 9 καὶ ἔλεγεν
tradition – of men. And he said
αὐτοῖς· καλῶς ἀθετεῖτε τὴν ἐντολὴν τοῦ
to them: Well ye set aside the commandment –
θεοῦ, ἵνα τὴν παράδοσιν ὑμῶν τηρήσητε.
of God, that the tradition of you ye may keep.
10 Μωϋσῆς γὰρ εἶπεν· τίμα τὸν πατέρα σου
For Moses said: Honour the father of thee
καὶ τὴν μητέρα σου, καί· ὁ κακολογῶν
and the mother of thee, and: The [one] speaking evil of
πατέρα ἢ μητέρα θανάτῳ τελευτάτω. 11 ὑμεῖς
father or mother by death let him end(die). ye
δὲ λέγετε· ἐὰν εἴπῃ ἄνθρωπος τῷ πατρὶ
But say: If says a man to the(his) father
ἢ τῇ μητρί· κορβᾶν, ὅ ἐστιν δῶρον,
or to the mother: Korban, which is a gift,
ὃ ἐὰν ἐξ ἐμοῦ ὠφεληθῇς, 12 οὐκέτι ἀφίετε
whatever by me thou mightest profit, no longer ye allow
αὐτὸν οὐδὲν ποιῆσαι τῷ πατρὶ ἢ τῇ
him no(any)thing to do for the father or the
μητρί, 13 ἀκυροῦντες τὸν λόγον τοῦ θεοῦ
mother, annulling the word – of God
τῇ παραδόσει ὑμῶν ᾗ παρεδώκατε· καὶ
by the tradition of you which ye received; and
παρόμοια τοιαῦτα πολλὰ ποιεῖτε. 14 Καὶ
[3]similar things [2]such [1]many ye do. And
προσκαλεσάμενος πάλιν τὸν ὄχλον ἔλεγεν
calling to [him] again the crowd he said
αὐτοῖς· ἀκούσατέ μου πάντες καὶ σύνετε.
to them: Hear ye me all and understand.
15 οὐδέν ἐστιν ἔξωθεν τοῦ ἀνθρώπου
Nothing there is from without – a man
εἰσπορευόμενον εἰς αὐτὸν ὃ δύναται κοινῶσαι
entering into him which can *to* defile
αὐτόν· ἀλλὰ τὰ ἐκ τοῦ ἀνθρώπου ἐκπο-
him; but the things out of – a man coming

they observe many other
traditions, such as the
washing of cups, pitchers
and kettles.[s])
5So the Pharisees and
teachers of the law asked
Jesus, "Why don't your
disciples live according to
the tradition of the elders
instead of eating their food
with 'unclean' hands?"
6He replied, "Isaiah was
right when he prophesied
about you hypocrites; as it
is written:

" 'These people honor
me with their lips,
but their hearts are far
from me.
7They worship me in
vain;
their teachings are but
rules taught by
men.'[t]

8You have let go of the
commands of God and are
holding on to the traditions
of men."
9And he said to them:
"You have a fine way of
setting aside the commands
of God in order to observe[u]
your own traditions! 10For
Moses said, 'Honor your
father and your mother,'[v]
and, 'Anyone who curses
his father or mother must
be put to death.'[w] 11But
you say that if a man says
to his father or mother:
'Whatever help you might
otherwise have received
from me is Corban' (that is,
a gift devoted to God),
12then you no longer let him
do anything for his father or
mother. 13Thus you nullify
the word of God by your
tradition that you have
handed down. And you do
many things like that."
14Again Jesus called the
crowd to him and said,
"Listen to me, everyone,
and understand this.
15Nothing outside a man
can make him 'unclean' by
going into him. Rather, it is
what comes out of a man

[s]*4* Some early manuscripts *pitchers, kettles and dining couches*
[t]*6,7* Isaiah 29:13
[u]*9* Some manuscripts *set up*
[v]*10* Exodus 20:12; Deut. 5:16
[w]*10* Exodus 21:17; Lev. 20:9

17 When he had left the crowd and entered the house, his disciples asked him about the parable. 18 He said to them, "Then do you also fail to understand? Do you not see that whatever goes into a person from outside cannot defile, 19 since it enters, not the heart but the stomach, and goes out into the sewer?" (Thus he declared all foods clean.) 20 And he said, "It is what comes out of a person that defiles. 21 For it is from within, from the human heart, that evil intentions come: fornication, theft, murder, 22 adultery, avarice, wickedness, deceit, licentiousness, envy, slander, pride, folly. 23 All these evil things come from within, and they defile a person."

The Syrophoenician Woman's Faith

24 From there he set out and went away to the region of Tyre.[x] He entered a house and did not want anyone to know he was there. Yet he could not escape notice, 25 but a woman whose little daughter had an unclean spirit immediately heard about him, and she came and bowed down at his feet. 26 Now the woman was a Gentile, of Syrophoenician origin. She begged him to cast the demon out of her daughter. 27 He said to her, "Let the children be fed first, for it is not fair to take the children's food and throw it to the dogs." 28 But she an-

[x] Other ancient authorities add *and Sidon*

ρευόμενά ἐστιν τὰ κοινοῦντα τὸν ἄνθρωπον.‡
forth are the [ones] defiling – a man.
17 Καὶ ὅτε εἰσῆλθεν εἰς οἶκον ἀπὸ τοῦ
And when he entered into a house from the
ὄχλου, ἐπηρώτων αὐτὸν οἱ μαθηταὶ αὐτοῦ
crowd, questioned him the disciples of him
τὴν παραβολήν. 18 καὶ λέγει αὐτοῖς·
the parable. And he says to them:
οὕτως καὶ ὑμεῖς ἀσύνετοί ἐστε; οὐ
Thus also ye undiscerning are? do ye not
νοεῖτε ὅτι πᾶν τὸ ἔξωθεν εἰσπορευόμενον
understand that everything from without entering
εἰς τὸν ἄνθρωπον οὐ δύναται αὐτὸν
into – a man cannot him
κοινῶσαι, 19 ὅτι οὐκ εἰσπορεύεται αὐτοῦ
to defile, because it enters not of him
εἰς τὴν καρδίαν ἀλλ' εἰς τὴν κοιλίαν,
into the heart but into the belly,
καὶ εἰς τὸν ἀφεδρῶνα ἐκπορεύεται, καθα-
and into the drain goes out, purg-
ρίζων πάντα τὰ βρώματα; 20 ἔλεγεν δὲ
ing all – foods? And he said[,]
ὅτι τὸ ἐκ τοῦ ἀνθρώπου ἐκπορευόμενον,
– The thing out of – a man coming forth,
ἐκεῖνο κοινοῖ τὸν ἄνθρωπον. 21 ἔσωθεν
that defiles – a man. from within
γὰρ ἐκ τῆς καρδίας τῶν ἀνθρώπων
For out of the heart – of men
οἱ διαλογισμοὶ οἱ κακοὶ ἐκπορεύονται,
– thoughts – evil come forth,
πορνεῖαι, κλοπαί, φόνοι, 22 μοιχεῖαι,
fornications, thefts, murders, adulteries,
πλεονεξίαι, πονηρίαι, δόλος, ἀσέλγεια, ὀφθαλμὸς
greedinesses, iniquities, deceit, lewdness, eye
πονηρός, βλασφημία, ὑπερηφανία, ἀφροσύνη·
an evil, blasphemy, arrogance, foolishness;
23 πάντα ταῦτα τὰ πονηρὰ ἔσωθεν ἐκπορεύεται
all these – evil things from within comes forth
καὶ κοινοῖ τὸν ἄνθρωπον.
and defile – a man.
24 Ἐκεῖθεν δὲ ἀναστὰς ἀπῆλθεν εἰς τὰ ὅρια
And thence rising up he went away into the district
Τύρου. Καὶ εἰσελθὼν εἰς οἰκίαν οὐδένα ἤθελεν
of Tyre. And entering into a house no one he wished
γνῶναι, καὶ οὐκ ἠδυνάσθη λαθεῖν· 25 ἀλλ'
to know, and could not *to* be hidden; but
εὐθὺς ἀκούσασα γυνὴ περὶ αὐτοῦ, ἧς
immediately [2]hearing [1]a woman about him, of whom = whose
εἶχεν τὸ θυγάτριον αὐτῆς πνεῦμα ἀκάθαρτον,
had the daughter of her spirit an unclean, daughter had
ἐλθοῦσα προσέπεσεν πρὸς τοὺς πόδας αὐτοῦ·
coming fell at the feet of him;
26 ἡ δὲ γυνὴ ἦν Ἑλληνίς, Συροφοινίκισσα
and the woman was a Greek, a Syrophenician
τῷ γένει· καὶ ἠρώτα αὐτὸν ἵνα τὸ
– by race; and she asked him that the
δαιμόνιον ἐκβάλῃ ἐκ τῆς θυγατρὸς αὐτῆς.
demon he would expel out of the daughter of her.
27 καὶ ἔλεγεν αὐτῇ· ἄφες πρῶτον
And he said to her: Permit first
χορτασθῆναι τὰ τέκνα· οὐ γάρ ἐστιν καλὸν
to be satisfied the children; for it is not good
λαβεῖν τὸν ἄρτον τῶν τέκνων καὶ τοῖς
to take the bread of the children and to the

‡ Verse 16 omitted by Nestle; *cf.* NIV footnote.

that makes him 'unclean.'[x]"
17 After he had left the crowd and entered the house, his disciples asked him about this parable. 18 "Are you so dull?" he asked. "Don't you see that nothing that enters a man from the outside can make him 'unclean'? 19 For it doesn't go into his heart but into his stomach, and then out of his body." (In saying this, Jesus declared all foods "clean.")
20 He went on: "What comes out of a man is what makes him 'unclean.' 21 For from within, out of men's hearts, come evil thoughts, sexual immorality, theft, murder, adultery, 22 greed, malice, deceit, lewdness, envy, slander, arrogance and folly. 23 All these evils come from inside and make a man 'unclean.' "

The Faith of a Syrophoenician Woman

24 Jesus left that place and went to the vicinity of Tyre.[y] He entered a house and did not want anyone to know it; yet he could not keep his presence secret. 25 In fact, as soon as she heard about him, a woman whose little daughter was possessed by an evil[z] spirit came and fell at his feet. 26 The woman was a Greek, born in Syrian Phoenicia. She begged Jesus to drive the demon out of her daughter.
27 "First let the children eat all they want," he told her, "for it is not right to take the children's bread and toss it to their dogs."

[x] *15* Some early manuscripts *'unclean.' 16 If anyone has ears to hear, let him hear.*
[y] *24* Many early manuscripts *Tyre and Sidon*
[z] *25* Greek *unclean*

swered him, "Sir,[y] even the dogs under the table eat the children's crumbs." [29]Then he said to her, "For saying that, you may go—the demon has left your daughter." [30]So she went home, found the child lying on the bed, and the demon gone.

Jesus Cures a Deaf Man

31 Then he returned from the region of Tyre, and went by way of Sidon towards the Sea of Galilee, in the region of the Decapolis. [32]They brought to him a deaf man who had an impediment in his speech; and they begged him to lay his hand on him. [33]He took him aside in private, away from the crowd, and put his fingers into his ears, and he spat and touched his tongue. [34]Then looking up to heaven, he sighed and said to him, "Ephphatha," that is, "Be opened." [35]And immediately his ears were opened, his tongue was released, and he spoke plainly. [36]Then Jesus[z] ordered them to tell no one; but the more he ordered them, the more zealously they proclaimed it. [37]They were astounded beyond measure, saying, "He has done everything well; he even makes the deaf to hear and the mute to speak."

Chapter 8

Feeding the Four Thousand

IN those days when there was again a great crowd without anything to eat, he called his disciples and said to them, [2]"I have compassion for the crowd, because

[y] Or *Lord*; other ancient authorities prefix *Yes*
[z] Gk *he*

κυναρίοις βαλεῖν. **28** ἡ δὲ ἀπεκρίθη καὶ
dogs to throw [it]. And she answered and
λέγει αὐτῷ· ναί, κύριε· καὶ τὰ κυνάρια
says to him: Yes, Lord; and yet the dogs
ὑποκάτω τῆς τραπέζης ἐσθίουσιν ἀπὸ τῶν
under the table eat from the
ψιχίων τῶν παιδίων. **29** καὶ εἶπεν αὐτῇ·
crumbs of the children. And he said to her:
διὰ τοῦτον τὸν λόγον ὕπαγε, ἐξελήλυθεν
Because of this – word go, has gone forth
ἐκ τῆς θυγατρός σου τὸ δαιμόνιον. **30** καὶ
out of the daughter of thee the demon. And
ἀπελθοῦσα εἰς τὸν οἶκον αὐτῆς εὗρεν τὸ
going away to the house of her she found the
παιδίον βεβλημένον ἐπὶ τὴν κλίνην καὶ τὸ
child *having been* laid on the couch and the
δαιμόνιον ἐξεληλυθός. **31** Καὶ πάλιν ἐξελθὼν
demon having gone forth. And again going forth
ἐκ τῶν ὁρίων Τύρου ἦλθεν διὰ Σιδῶνος
out of the district of Tyre he came through Sidon
εἰς τὴν θάλασσαν τῆς Γαλιλαίας ἀνὰ
to the sea – of Galilee in the
μέσον τῶν ὁρίων Δεκαπόλεως. **32** Καὶ
midst of the district of Decapolis. And
φέρουσιν αὐτῷ κωφὸν καὶ μογιλάλον, καὶ
they bring to him a man deaf and speaking with difficulty, and
παρακαλοῦσιν αὐτὸν ἵνα ἐπιθῇ αὐτῷ τὴν
they beseech him that he would put *on* on him the(his)
χεῖρα. **33** καὶ ἀπολαβόμενος αὐτὸν ἀπὸ
hand. And taking away him from
τοῦ ὄχλου κατ' ἰδίαν ἔβαλεν τοὺς δακτύλους
the crowd privately he put the fingers
αὐτοῦ εἰς τὰ ὦτα αὐτοῦ καὶ πτύσας
of him into the ears of him and spitting
ἥψατο τῆς γλώσσης αὐτοῦ, **34** καὶ
he touched the tongue of him, and
ἀναβλέψας εἰς τὸν οὐρανὸν ἐστέναξεν,
looking up to – heaven he groaned,
καὶ λέγει αὐτῷ· ἐφφαθά, ὅ ἐστιν διανοίχθητι.
and says to him: Ephphatha, which is Be thou opened.
35 καὶ ἠνοίγησαν αὐτοῦ αἱ ἀκοαί, καὶ
And were opened of him the ears, and
εὐθὺς ἐλύθη ὁ δεσμὸς τῆς γλώσσης αὐτοῦ,
immediately was loosened the bond of the tongue of him,
καὶ ἐλάλει ὀρθῶς. **36** καὶ διεστείλατο
and he spoke correctly. And he ordered
αὐτοῖς ἵνα μηδενὶ λέγωσιν· ὅσον δὲ
them that no one they should tell; but as much as
αὐτοῖς διεστέλλετο, αὐτοὶ μᾶλλον περισσότερον
them he ordered, they more exceedingly
ἐκήρυσσον. **37** καὶ ὑπερπερισσῶς ἐξεπλήσσοντο
proclaimed. And most exceedingly they were astounded
λέγοντες· καλῶς πάντα πεποίηκεν, καὶ
saying: Well all things he has done, both
τοὺς κωφοὺς ποιεῖ ἀκούειν καὶ ἀλάλους
the deaf he makes to hear and dumb
λαλεῖν.
to speak.

8 Ἐν ἐκείναις ταῖς ἡμέραις πάλιν πολλοῦ
In those – days again a much(great)
= there being
ὄχλου ὄντος καὶ μὴ ἐχόντων τί φάγωσιν,
crowd being* and not having* anything they might eat,
a great crowd
προσκαλεσάμενος τοὺς μαθητὰς λέγει αὐτοῖς·
calling to [him] the disciples he says to them:

[28]"Yes, Lord," she replied, "but even the dogs under the table eat the children's crumbs."

[29]Then he told her, "For such a reply, you may go; the demon has left your daughter."

[30]She went home and found her child lying on the bed, and the demon gone.

The Healing of a Deaf and Mute Man

[31]Then Jesus left the vicinity of Tyre and went through Sidon, down to the Sea of Galilee and into the region of the Decapolis.[a] [32]There some people brought to him a man who was deaf and could hardly talk, and they begged him to place his hand on the man.

[33]After he took him aside, away from the crowd, Jesus put his fingers into the man's ears. Then he spit and touched the man's tongue. [34]He looked up to heaven and with a deep sigh said to him, *"Ephphatha!"* (which means, "Be opened!"). [35]At this, the man's ears were opened, his tongue was loosened and he began to speak plainly.

[36]Jesus commanded them not to tell anyone. But the more he did so, the more they kept talking about it. [37]People were overwhelmed with amazement. "He has done everything well," they said. "He even makes the deaf hear and the mute speak."

Chapter 8

Jesus Feeds the Four Thousand

DURING those days another large crowd gathered. Since they had nothing to eat, Jesus called his disciples to him and

[a] *31* That is, the Ten Cities

they have been with me now for three days and have nothing to eat. [3]If I send them away hungry to their homes, they will faint on the way—and some of them have come from a great distance." [4]His disciples replied, "How can one feed these people with bread here in the desert?" [5]He asked them, "How many loaves do you have?" They said, "Seven." [6]Then he ordered the crowd to sit down on the ground; and he took the seven loaves, and after giving thanks he broke them and gave them to his disciples to distribute; and they distributed them to the crowd. [7]They had also a few small fish; and after blessing them, he ordered that these too should be distributed. [8]They ate and were filled; and they took up the broken pieces left over, seven baskets full. [9]Now there were about four thousand people. And he sent them away. [10]And immediately he got into the boat with his disciples and went to the district of Dalmanutha.[a]

The Demand for a Sign

11 The Pharisees came and began to argue with him, asking him for a sign from heaven, to test him. [12]And he sighed deeply in his spirit and said, "Why does this generation ask for a sign? Truly I tell you, no sign will be given to this generation." [13]And he left them, and getting into the boat again, he went across to the other side.

The Yeast of the Pharisees and of Herod

14 Now the disciples[b] had forgotten to bring any bread; and they had only one loaf with them in the boat. [15]And he cautioned them, saying, "Watch

[a] Other ancient authorities read *Mageda* or *Magdala*
[b] Gk *they*

2 σπλαγχνίζομαι ἐπὶ τὸν ὄχλον, ὅτι ἤδη
I have compassion on the crowd, because now
ἡμέραι τρεῖς προσμένουσίν μοι καὶ οὐκ
days three they remain with me and not
ἔχουσιν τί φάγωσιν· **3** καὶ ἐὰν ἀπολύσω
they have anything they may eat; and if I dismiss
αὐτοὺς νήστεις εἰς οἶκον αὐτῶν, ἐκλυθήσονται
them fasting to house of them, they will faint
ἐν τῇ ὁδῷ· καί τινες αὐτῶν ἀπὸ μακρόθεν
in the way; and some of them from afar
εἰσίν. **4** καὶ ἀπεκρίθησαν αὐτῷ οἱ μαθηταὶ
are. And answered him the disciples
αὐτοῦ ὅτι πόθεν τούτους δυνήσεταί τις
of him[,] – [1]Whence [6]these people [3]will [4]be able [2]anyone
ὧδε χορτάσαι ἄρτων ἐπ᾽ ἐρημίας; **5** καὶ
[8]here [5]to satisfy [7]of(with) loaves [9]on(in) [10]a desert ? And
ἠρώτα αὐτούς· πόσους ἔχετε ἄρτους;
he asked them: How many have ye loaves ?
οἱ δὲ εἶπαν· ἑπτά. **6** καὶ παραγγέλλει τῷ
And they said: Seven. And he commands the
ὄχλῳ ἀναπεσεῖν ἐπὶ τῆς γῆς· καὶ λαβὼν
crowd to recline on the ground; and taking
τοὺς ἑπτὰ ἄρτους εὐχαριστήσας ἔκλασεν
the seven loaves giving thanks he broke
καὶ ἐδίδου τοῖς μαθηταῖς αὐτοῦ ἵνα
and gave to the disciples of him that
παρατιθῶσιν, καὶ παρέθηκαν τῷ ὄχλῳ.
they might serve, and they served the crowd.
7 καὶ εἶχον ἰχθύδια ὀλίγα· καὶ εὐλογήσας
And they had fishes a few; and blessing
αὐτὰ εἶπεν καὶ ταῦτα παρατιθέναι. **8** καὶ
them he told also these to be served. And
ἔφαγον καὶ ἐχορτάσθησαν, καὶ ἦραν
they ate and were satisfied, and took
περισσεύματα κλασμάτων, ἑπτὰ σπυρίδας.
excesses of fragments, seven baskets.
9 ἦσαν δὲ ὡς τετρακισχίλιοι. καὶ ἀπέλυσεν
Now they were about four thousand. And he dismissed
αὐτούς. **10** Καὶ εὐθὺς ἐμβὰς εἰς τὸ
them. And immediately embarking in the
πλοῖον μετὰ τῶν μαθητῶν αὐτοῦ
ship with the disciples of him
ἦλθεν εἰς τὰ μέρη Δαλμανουθά.
he came into the region of Dalmanutha.
11 Καὶ ἐξῆλθον οἱ Φαρισαῖοι καὶ ἤρξαντο
And came forth the Pharisees and began
συζητεῖν αὐτῷ, ζητοῦντες παρ᾽ αὐτοῦ
to debate with him, seeking from him
σημεῖον ἀπὸ τοῦ οὐρανοῦ, πειράζοντες
a sign from – heaven, tempting
αὐτόν. **12** καὶ ἀναστενάξας τῷ πνεύματι
him. And groaning in the spirit
αὐτοῦ λέγει· τί ἡ γενεὰ αὕτη ζητεῖ
of him he says: Why – [3]generation [2]this [1]does [4]seek
σημεῖον; ἀμὴν λέγω ὑμῖν, εἰ δοθήσεται
a sign ? Truly I tell you, if will be given
τῇ γενεᾷ ταύτῃ σημεῖον. **13** καὶ ἀφεὶς
– generation to this a sign. And leaving
αὐτοὺς πάλιν ἐμβὰς ἀπῆλθεν εἰς τὸ
them again embarking he went away to the
πέραν. **14** Καὶ ἐπελάθοντο λαβεῖν ἄρτους,
other side. And they forgot to take loaves,
καὶ εἰ μὴ ἕνα ἄρτον οὐκ εἶχον μεθ᾽
and except one loaf they had not with
ἑαυτῶν ἐν τῷ πλοίῳ. **15** καὶ διεστέλλετο
them*selves* in the ship. And he charged

said, [2]"I have compassion for these people; they have already been with me three days and have nothing to eat. [3]If I send them home hungry, they will collapse on the way, because some of them have come a long distance."

[4]His disciples answered, "But where in this remote place can anyone get enough bread to feed them?"

[5]"How many loaves do you have?" Jesus asked.

"Seven," they replied.

[6]He told the crowd to sit down on the ground. When he had taken the seven loaves and given thanks, he broke them and gave them to his disciples to set before the people, and they did so. [7]They had a few small fish as well; he gave thanks for them also and told the disciples to distribute them. [8]The people ate and were satisfied. Afterward the disciples picked up seven basketfuls of broken pieces that were left over. [9]About four thousand men were present. And having sent them away, [10]he got into the boat with his disciples and went to the region of Dalmanutha.

[11]The Pharisees came and began to question Jesus. To test him, they asked him for a sign from heaven. [12]He sighed deeply and said, "Why does this generation ask for a miraculous sign? I tell you the truth, no sign will be given to it." [13]Then he left them, got back into the boat and crossed to the other side.

The Yeast of the Pharisees and Herod

[14]The disciples had forgotten to bring bread, except for one loaf they had with them in the boat. [15]"Be careful," Jesus

out—beware of the yeast of the Pharisees and the yeast of Herod."[c] 16 They said to one another, "It is because we have no bread." 17 And becoming aware of it, Jesus said to them, "Why are you talking about having no bread? Do you still not perceive or understand? Are your hearts hardened? 18 Do you have eyes, and fail to see? Do you have ears, and fail to hear? And do you not remember? 19 When I broke the five loaves for the five thousand, how many baskets full of broken pieces did you collect?" They said to him, "Twelve." 20 "And the seven for the four thousand, how many baskets full of broken pieces did you collect?" And they said to him, "Seven." 21 Then he said to them, "Do you not yet understand?"

Jesus Cures a Blind Man at Bethsaida

22 They came to Bethsaida. Some people[d] brought a blind man to him and begged him to touch him. 23 He took the blind man by the hand and led him out of the village; and when he had put saliva on his eyes and laid his hands on him, he asked him, "Can you see anything?" 24 And the man[e] looked up and said, "I can see people, but they look like trees, walking." 25 Then Jesus[e] laid his hands on his eyes again; and he looked intently and his sight was restored, and he saw everything clearly. 26 Then he sent him away to his home, saying, "Do not even go into the village."[f]

Peter's Declaration about Jesus

27 Jesus went on with his disciples to the villages of Caesarea Philippi; and

[c] Other ancient authorities read *the Herodians*
[d] Gk *They*
[e] Gk *he*
[f] Other ancient authorities add *or tell anyone in the village*

αὐτοῖς λέγων· ὁρᾶτε, βλέπετε ἀπὸ τῆς
them saying: See, look ye from the
=Beware of
ζύμης τῶν Φαρισαίων καὶ τῆς ζύμης
leaven of the Pharisees and of the leaven
Ἡρῴδου. 16 καὶ διελογίζοντο πρὸς ἀλλήλους
of Herod. And they reasoned with one another
ὅτι ἄρτους οὐκ ἔχουσιν. 17 καὶ γνοὺς
because loaves they have(had) not. And knowing
λέγει αὐτοῖς· τί διαλογίζεσθε ὅτι ἄρτους
he says to them: Why reason ye because loaves
οὐκ ἔχετε; οὔπω νοεῖτε οὐδὲ συνίετε;
ye have not? not yet understand ye nor realize?
πεπωρωμένην ἔχετε τὴν καρδίαν ὑμῶν;
having been hardened have ye the heart of you?
18 ὀφθαλμοὺς ἔχοντες οὐ βλέπετε, καὶ
eyes having see ye not, and
ὦτα ἔχοντες οὐκ ἀκούετε; καὶ
ears having hear ye not? and
οὐ μνημονεύετε, 19 ὅτε τοὺς πέντε ἄρτους
do ye not remember, when the five loaves
ἔκλασα εἰς τοὺς πεντακισχιλίους, πόσους
I broke to the five thousand, how many
κοφίνους κλασμάτων πλήρεις ἤρατε; λέγουσιν
baskets of fragments full ye took? They say
αὐτῷ· δώδεκα. 20 ὅτε τοὺς ἑπτὰ εἰς
to him: Twelve. When the seven to
τοὺς τετρακισχιλίους, πόσων σπυρίδων
the four thousand, [2]of how many [3]baskets
πληρώματα κλασμάτων ἤρατε; καὶ λέγουσιν·
[1]fullnesses [4]of fragments ye took? And they say:
ἑπτά. 21 καὶ ἔλεγεν αὐτοῖς· οὔπω συνίετε;
Seven. And he said to them: Not yet do ye realize?
22 Καὶ ἔρχονται εἰς Βηθσαϊδάν. Καὶ
And they come to Bethsaida. And
φέρουσιν αὐτῷ τυφλόν, καὶ παρακαλοῦσιν
they bring to him a blind man, and beseech
αὐτὸν ἵνα αὐτοῦ ἅψηται. 23 καὶ ἐπιλαβόμενος
him that him he would touch. And laying hold of
τῆς χειρὸς τοῦ τυφλοῦ ἐξήνεγκεν αὐτὸν
the hand of the blind man he led forth him
ἔξω τῆς κώμης, καὶ πτύσας εἰς τὰ
outside the village, and spitting in the
ὄμματα αὐτοῦ, ἐπιθεὶς τὰς χεῖρας αὐτῷ,
eyes of him, putting *on* the hands on him,
ἐπηρώτα αὐτόν· εἴ τι βλέπεις; 24 καὶ
questioned him: If anything thou seest? And
ἀναβλέψας ἔλεγεν· βλέπω τοὺς ἀνθρώπους,
looking up he said: I see – men,
ὅτι ὡς δένδρα ὁρῶ περιπατοῦντας.
that as trees I behold walking.
25 εἶτα πάλιν ἐπέθηκεν τὰς χεῖρας ἐπὶ
Then again he put *on* the hands on
τοὺς ὀφθαλμοὺς αὐτοῦ, καὶ διέβλεψεν καὶ
the eyes of him, and he looked steadily and
ἀπεκατέστη, καὶ ἐνέβλεπεν τηλαυγῶς ἅπαντα.
was restored, and saw clearly all things.
26 καὶ ἀπέστειλεν αὐτὸν εἰς οἶκον αὐτοῦ
And he sent him to house of him
λέγων· μηδὲ εἰς τὴν κώμην εἰσέλθῃς.
saying: Not into the village thou mayest enter.
27 Καὶ ἐξῆλθεν ὁ Ἰησοῦς καὶ οἱ μαθηταὶ
And went forth – Jesus and the disciples
αὐτοῦ εἰς τὰς κώμας Καισαρείας τῆς
of him to the villages of Cæsarea –

warned them. "Watch out for the yeast of the Pharisees and that of Herod."

16 They discussed this with one another and said, "It is because we have no bread."

17 Aware of their discussion, Jesus asked them: "Why are you talking about having no bread? Do you still not see or understand? Are your hearts hardened? 18 Do you have eyes but fail to see, and ears but fail to hear? And don't you remember? 19 When I broke the five loaves for the five thousand, how many basketfuls of pieces did you pick up?"

"Twelve," they replied.

20 "And when I broke the seven loaves for the four thousand, how many basketfuls of pieces did you pick up?"

They answered, "Seven."

21 He said to them, "Do you still not understand?"

The Healing of a Blind Man at Bethsaida

22 They came to Bethsaida, and some people brought a blind man and begged Jesus to touch him. 23 He took the blind man by the hand and led him outside the village. When he had spit on the man's eyes and put his hands on him, Jesus asked, "Do you see anything?"

24 He looked up and said, "I see people; they look like trees walking around."

25 Once more Jesus put his hands on the man's eyes. Then his eyes were opened, his sight was restored, and he saw everything clearly. 26 Jesus sent him home, saying, "Don't go into the village.[b]"

Peter's Confession of Christ

27 Jesus and his disciples went on to the villages around Caesarea Philippi.

[b] 26 Some manuscripts *Don't go and tell anyone in the village*

on the way he asked his disciples, "Who do people say
that I am?" 28 And they answered him, "John the
Baptist; and others, Elijah;
and still others, one of the
prophets." 29 He asked
them, "But who do you say
that I am?" Peter answered
him, "You are the Messi-
ah."[g] 30 And he sternly ordered them not to tell anyone about him.

Jesus Foretells His Death and Resurrection

31 Then he began to
teach them that the Son of
Man must undergo great
suffering, and be rejected
by the elders, the chief
priests, and the scribes,
and be killed, and after
three days rise again. 32 He
said all this quite openly.
And Peter took him aside
and began to rebuke him.
33 But turning and looking
at his disciples, he rebuked
Peter and said, "Get behind
me, Satan! For you are setting your mind not on di-
vine things but on human
things."
34 He called the crowd
with his disciples, and said
to them, "If any want to become my followers, let
them deny themselves and
take up their cross and follow me. 35 For those who
want to save their life will
lose it, and those who lose
their life for my sake, and
for the sake of the gospel,[h]
will save it. 36 For what will
it profit them to gain the
whole world and forfeit
their life? 37 Indeed, what
can they give in return for
their life? 38 Those who are

[g] Or *the Christ*
[h] Other ancient authorities read *lose their life for the sake of the gospel*

Φιλίππου· καὶ ἐν τῇ ὁδῷ ἐπηρώτα τοὺς
of Philip; and in the way he questioned the
μαθητὰς αὐτοῦ λέγων αὐτοῖς· τίνα με
disciples of him saying to them: Whom me
λέγουσιν οἱ ἄνθρωποι εἶναι; 28 οἱ δὲ
say – men to be? And they
εἶπαν αὐτῷ λέγοντες ὅτι Ἰωάννην τὸν
told him saying[,] – John the
βαπτιστήν, καὶ ἄλλοι Ἠλίαν, ἄλλοι δὲ
Baptist, and others Elias, but others[,]
ὅτι εἷς τῶν προφητῶν. 29 καὶ αὐτὸς
– one of the prophets. And he
ἐπηρώτα αὐτούς· ὑμεῖς δὲ τίνα με λέγετε
questioned them: But ye whom me say ye
εἶναι; ἀποκριθεὶς ὁ Πέτρος λέγει αὐτῷ·
to be? Answering – Peter says to him:
σὺ εἶ ὁ χριστός. 30 καὶ ἐπετίμησεν
Thou art the Christ. And he warned
αὐτοῖς ἵνα μηδενὶ λέγωσιν περὶ αὐτοῦ.
them that no one they might tell about him.
31 Καὶ ἤρξατο διδάσκειν αὐτοὺς ὅτι δεῖ
And he began to teach them that it behoves
τὸν υἱὸν τοῦ ἀνθρώπου πολλὰ παθεῖν,
the Son – of man many things to suffer,
καὶ ἀποδοκιμασθῆναι ὑπὸ τῶν πρεσβυτέρων
and to be rejected by the elders
καὶ τῶν ἀρχιερέων καὶ τῶν γραμματέων
and the chief priests and the scribes
καὶ ἀποκτανθῆναι καὶ μετὰ τρεῖς ἡμέρας
and to be killed and after three days
ἀναστῆναι· 32 καὶ παρρησίᾳ τὸν λόγον
to rise again; and openly the word
ἐλάλει. καὶ προσλαβόμενος ὁ Πέτρος
he spoke. And [2]taking [4]aside – [1]Peter
αὐτὸν ἤρξατο ἐπιτιμᾶν αὐτῷ. 33 ὁ δὲ
[3]him began to rebuke him. But he
ἐπιστραφεὶς καὶ ἰδὼν τοὺς μαθητὰς αὐτοῦ
turning round and seeing the disciples of him
ἐπετίμησεν Πέτρῳ καὶ λέγει· ὕπαγε ὀπίσω
rebuked Peter and says: Go behind
μου, σατανᾶ, ὅτι οὐ φρονεῖς τὰ τοῦ
me, Satan, because thou mindest not the things –
θεοῦ ἀλλὰ τὰ τῶν ἀνθρώπων. 34 Καὶ
of God but the things – of men. And
προσκαλεσάμενος τὸν ὄχλον σὺν τοῖς μαθηταῖς
calling to [him] the crowd with the disciples
αὐτοῦ εἶπεν αὐτοῖς· εἴ τις θέλει ὀπίσω
of him he said to them: If anyone wishes after
μου ἐλθεῖν, ἀπαρνησάσθω ἑαυτὸν καὶ ἀράτω
me to come, let him deny himself and take
τὸν σταυρὸν αὐτοῦ, καὶ ἀκολουθείτω μοι.
the cross of him, and let him follow me.
35 ὃς γὰρ ἐὰν θέλῃ τὴν ψυχὴν αὐτοῦ σῶ-
For whoever wishes the life of him to
σαι, ἀπολέσει αὐτήν· ὃς δ' ἂν ἀπολέσει
save, will lose it; but whoever will lose
τὴν ψυχὴν αὐτοῦ ἕνεκεν ἐμοῦ καὶ τοῦ
the life of him for the sake of me and the
εὐαγγελίου, σώσει αὐτήν. 36 τί γὰρ ὠφελεῖ
gospel, will save it. For what profits
ἄνθρωπον κερδῆσαι τὸν κόσμον ὅλον καὶ
a man to gain the world whole and
ζημιωθῆναι τὴν ψυχὴν αὐτοῦ; 37 τί γὰρ
to be fined the soul of him? For what
δοῖ ἄνθρωπος ἀντάλλαγμα τῆς ψυχῆς αὐτοῦ;
might give a man an exchange of the soul of him?

On the way he asked them,
"Who do people say I
am?"
28 They replied, "Some
say John the Baptist; others
say Elijah; and still others,
one of the prophets."
29 "But what about you?"
he asked. "Who do you say
I am?"
Peter answered, "You
are the Christ.[c]"
30 Jesus warned them not
to tell anyone about him.

Jesus Predicts His Death

31 He then began to teach
them that the Son of Man
must suffer many things
and be rejected by the elders, chief priests and
teachers of the law, and
that he must be killed and
after three days rise again.
32 He spoke plainly about
this, and Peter took him
aside and began to rebuke
him.
33 But when Jesus turned
and looked at his disciples,
he rebuked Peter. "Get behind me, Satan!" he said.
"You do not have in mind
the things of God, but the
things of men."
34 Then he called the
crowd to him along with his
disciples and said: "If anyone would come after me,
he must deny himself and
take up his cross and follow
me. 35 For whoever wants
to save his life[d] will lose it,
but whoever loses his life
for me and for the gospel
will save it. 36 What good is
it for a man to gain the
whole world, yet forfeit his
soul? 37 Or what can a man
give in exchange for his
soul? 38 If anyone is

[c] 29 Or *Messiah*. "The Christ" (Greek) and "the Messiah" (Hebrew) both mean "the Anointed One."
[d] 35 The Greek word means either *life* or *soul*; also in verse 36.

ashamed of me and of my words[i] in this adulterous and sinful generation, of them the Son of Man will also be ashamed when he comes in the glory of his Father with the holy angels." 1 And he said to them, "Truly I tell you, there are some standing here who will not taste death until they see that the kingdom of God has come with[j] power."

The Transfiguration

2 Six days later, Jesus took with him Peter and James and John, and led them up a high mountain apart, by themselves. And he was transfigured before them, 3 and his clothes became dazzling white, such as no one[k] on earth could bleach them. 4 And there appeared to them Elijah with Moses, who were talking with Jesus. 5 Then Peter said to Jesus, "Rabbi, it is good for us to be here; let us make three dwellings,[l] one for you, one for Moses, and one for Elijah." 6 He did not know what to say, for they were terrified. 7 Then a cloud overshadowed them, and from the cloud there came a voice, "This is my Son, the Beloved;[m] listen to him!" 8 Suddenly when they looked around, they saw no one with them any more, but only Jesus.

The Coming of Elijah

9 As they were coming down the mountain, he ordered them to tell no one

[i] Other ancient authorities read *and of mine*
[j] Or *in*
[k] Gk *no fuller*
[l] Or *tents*
[m] Or *my beloved Son*

38 ὃς γὰρ ἐὰν ἐπαισχυνθῇ με καὶ
For whoever is ashamed of me and
τοὺς ἐμοὺς λόγους ἐν τῇ γενεᾷ ταύτῃ
– my words in – generation this
τῇ μοιχαλίδι καὶ ἁμαρτωλῷ, καὶ ὁ
– adulterous and sinful, also the
υἱὸς τοῦ ἀνθρώπου ἐπαισχυνθήσεται αὐτόν,
Son – of man will be ashamed of him,
ὅταν ἔλθῃ ἐν τῇ δόξῃ τοῦ πατρὸς
when he comes in the glory of the Father
αὐτοῦ μετὰ τῶν ἀγγέλων τῶν ἁγίων.
of him with the angels – holy.

9 καὶ ἔλεγεν αὐτοῖς· ἀμὴν λέγω ὑμῖν
And he said to them: Truly I tell you
ὅτι εἰσίν τινες ὧδε τῶν ἑστηκότων
that there are some here of the [ones] standing
οἵτινες οὐ μὴ γεύσωνται θανάτου ἕως ἂν
who by no means may taste of death until
ἴδωσιν τὴν βασιλείαν τοῦ θεοῦ ἐληλυθυῖαν
they see the kingdom – of God having come
ἐν δυνάμει.
in power.
2 Καὶ μετὰ ἡμέρας ἓξ παραλαμβάνει
And after days six takes
ὁ Ἰησοῦς τὸν Πέτρον καὶ τὸν Ἰάκωβον
– Jesus – Peter and – James
καὶ Ἰωάννην, καὶ ἀναφέρει αὐτοὺς εἰς
and John, and leads up them into
ὄρος ὑψηλὸν κατ' ἰδίαν μόνους. καὶ
mountain a high privately alone. And
μετεμορφώθη ἔμπροσθεν αὐτῶν, 3 καὶ τὰ
he was transfigured before them, and the
ἱμάτια αὐτοῦ ἐγένετο στίλβοντα λευκὰ λίαν,
garments of him became gleaming white exceedingly,
οἷα γναφεὺς ἐπὶ τῆς γῆς οὐ δύναται
such as fuller on the earth cannot
οὕτως λευκᾶναι. 4 καὶ ὤφθη αὐτοῖς Ἡλίας
so *to* whiten. And appeared to them Elias
σὺν Μωϋσεῖ, καὶ ἦσαν συλλαλοῦντες τῷ
with Moses, and they were conversing with –
Ἰησοῦ. 5 καὶ ἀποκριθεὶς ὁ Πέτρος λέγει
Jesus. And answering – Peter says
τῷ Ἰησοῦ· ῥαββί, καλόν ἐστιν ἡμᾶς ὧδε
– to Jesus: Rabbi, good it is us here
εἶναι, καὶ ποιήσωμεν τρεῖς σκηνάς, σοὶ
to be, and let us make three tents, for thee
μίαν καὶ Μωϋσεῖ μίαν καὶ Ἠλίᾳ μίαν.
one and for Moses one and for Elias one.
6 οὐ γὰρ ᾔδει τί ἀποκριθῇ· ἔκφοβοι γὰρ
For he knew not what he answered; for exceedingly afraid
ἐγένοντο. 7 καὶ ἐγένετο νεφέλη ἐπισκιάζουσα
they became. And there came a cloud overshadowing
αὐτοῖς, καὶ ἐγένετο φωνὴ ἐκ τῆς νεφέλης·
them, and there came a voice out of the cloud:
οὗτός ἐστιν ὁ υἱός μου ὁ ἀγαπητός,
This is the Son of me *the* beloved,
ἀκούετε αὐτοῦ. 8 καὶ ἐξάπινα περιβλεψάμενοι
hear ye him. And suddenly looking round
οὐκέτι οὐδένα εἶδον εἰ μὴ τὸν Ἰησοῦν
no longer no(any)one they saw except – Jesus
μόνον μεθ' ἑαυτῶν. 9 Καὶ καταβαινόντων
only with themselves. And coming down
= as they came down
αὐτῶν ἐκ τοῦ ὄρους διεστείλατο αὐτοῖς
them* out of the mountain he ordered them

ashamed of me and my words in this adulterous and sinful generation, the Son of Man will be ashamed of him when he comes in his Father's glory with the holy angels."

Chapter 9

AND he said to them, "I tell you the truth, some who are standing here will not taste death before they see the kingdom of God come with power."

The Transfiguration

2 After six days Jesus took Peter, James and John with him and led them up a high mountain, where they were all alone. There he was transfigured before them. 3 His clothes became dazzling white, whiter than anyone in the world could bleach them. 4 And there appeared before them Elijah and Moses, who were talking with Jesus.

5 Peter said to Jesus, "Rabbi, it is good for us to be here. Let us put up three shelters—one for you, one for Moses and one for Elijah." 6 (He did not know what to say, they were so frightened.)

7 Then a cloud appeared and enveloped them, and a voice came from the cloud: "This is my Son, whom I love. Listen to him!"

8 Suddenly, when they looked around, they no longer saw anyone with them except Jesus.

9 As they were coming down the mountain, Jesus gave them orders not to tell

about what they had seen,
until after the Son of Man
had risen from the dead.
10So they kept the matter
to themselves, questioning
what this rising from the
dead could mean. 11Then
they asked him, "Why do
the scribes say that Elijah
must come first?" 12He
said to them, "Elijah is indeed coming first to restore
all things. How then is it
written about the Son of
Man, that he is to go
through many sufferings
and be treated with con-
tempt? 13But I tell you that
Elijah has come, and they
did to him whatever they
pleased, as it is written
about him."

The Healing of a Boy with a Spirit

14 When they came to
the disciples, they saw a
great crowd around them,
and some scribes arguing
with them. 15When the
whole crowd saw him, they
were immediately over-
come with awe, and they
ran forward to greet him.
16He asked them, "What
are you arguing about with
them?" 17Someone from
the crowd answered him,
"Teacher, I brought you
my son; he has a spirit that
makes him unable to speak;
18and whenever it seizes
him, it dashes him down;
and he foams and grinds his
teeth and becomes rigid;
and I asked your disciples
to cast it out, but they could
not do so." 19He answered
them, "You faithless generation, how much longer
must I be among you? How
much longer must I put up
with you? Bring him to
me." 20And they brought
the boy[n] to him. When the
spirit saw him, immediately
it convulsed the boy,[n] and

[n] Gk *him*

ἵνα μηδενὶ ἃ εἶδον διηγήσωνται,
that to no one [the] things which they saw they should relate,
εἰ μὴ ὅταν ὁ υἱὸς τοῦ ἀνθρώπου ἐκ νεκρῶν
except when the Son – of man out of [the] dead
ἀναστῇ. 10 καὶ τὸν λόγον ἐκράτησαν πρὸς
should rise. And the word they held to
ἑαυτοὺς συζητοῦντες τί ἐστιν τὸ ἐκ
themselves debating what is the "out of
νεκρῶν ἀναστῆναι. 11 Καὶ ἐπηρώτων αὐτὸν
[the] dead to rise." And they questioned him
λέγοντες· ὅτι λέγουσιν οἱ γραμματεῖς ὅτι
saying: Why say the scribes that
Ἠλίαν δεῖ ἐλθεῖν πρῶτον; 12 ὁ δὲ ἔφη
Elias it behoves to come first? And he said
αὐτοῖς· Ἠλίας μὲν ἐλθὼν πρῶτον
to them: Elias indeed coming first
ἀποκαθιστάνει πάντα· καὶ πῶς γέγραπται
restores all things; and how has it been written
ἐπὶ τὸν υἱὸν τοῦ ἀνθρώπου, ἵνα πολλὰ
on(concerning) the Son – of man, that many things
πάθῃ καὶ ἐξουδενηθῇ; 13 ἀλλὰ λέγω ὑμῖν
he should suffer and be set at naught? But I tell you
ὅτι καὶ Ἠλίας ἐλήλυθεν, καὶ ἐποίησαν
that indeed Elias has come, and they did
αὐτῷ ὅσα ἤθελον, καθὼς γέγραπται
to him what they wished, as it has been written
ἐπ' αὐτόν.
on(concerning) him.

14 Καὶ ἐλθόντες πρὸς τοὺς μαθητὰς
And coming to the disciples
εἶδον ὄχλον πολὺν περὶ αὐτοὺς καὶ
they saw crowd a much(great) around them and
γραμματεῖς συζητοῦντας πρὸς αὐτούς.
scribes debating with them.
15 καὶ εὐθὺς πᾶς ὁ ὄχλος ἰδόντες αὐτὸν
And immediately all the crowd seeing him
ἐξεθαμβήθησαν, καὶ προστρέχοντες ἠσπάζοντο
were greatly astonished, and running up to greeted
αὐτόν. 16 καὶ ἐπηρώτησεν αὐτούς· τί
him. And he questioned them: What
συζητεῖτε πρὸς αὐτούς; 17 καὶ ἀπεκρίθη
are ye debating with them? And answered
αὐτῷ εἷς ἐκ τοῦ ὄχλου· διδάσκαλε,
him one of the crowd: Teacher,
ἤνεγκα τὸν υἱόν μου πρὸς σέ, ἔχοντα
I brought the son of me to thee, having
πνεῦμα ἄλαλον· 18 καὶ ὅπου ἐὰν αὐτὸν
spirit a dumb; and wherever him
καταλάβῃ, ῥήσσει αὐτόν, καὶ ἀφρίζει καὶ
it seizes, it tears him, and he foams and
τρίζει τοὺς ὀδόντας καὶ ξηραίνεται· καὶ
grinds the(his) teeth and he wastes away; and
εἶπα τοῖς μαθηταῖς σου ἵνα αὐτὸ
I told the disciples of thee that it
ἐκβάλωσιν, καὶ οὐκ ἴσχυσαν. 19 ὁ δὲ
they might expel, and they were not able. And he
ἀποκριθεὶς αὐτοῖς λέγει· ὦ γενεὰ ἄπιστος,
answering them says: O generation unbelieving,
ἕως πότε πρὸς ὑμᾶς ἔσομαι; ἕως πότε
until when with you shall I be? how long
= how long
ἀνέξομαι ὑμῶν; φέρετε αὐτὸν πρός με.
shall I endure you? bring him to me.
20 καὶ ἤνεγκαν αὐτὸν πρὸς αὐτόν. καὶ
And they brought him to him. And
ἰδὼν αὐτὸν τὸ πνεῦμα εὐθὺς συνεσπάραξεν
seeing him the spirit immediately violently threw

anyone what they had seen
until the Son of Man had
risen from the dead. 10They
kept the matter to them-
selves, discussing what
"rising from the dead"
meant.
11And they asked him,
"Why do the teachers of
the law say that Elijah must
come first?"
12Jesus replied, "To be
sure, Elijah does come
first, and restores all
things. Why then is it written that the Son of Man
must suffer much and be rejected? 13But I tell you, Elijah has come, and they
have done to him every-
thing they wished, just as it
is written about him."

The Healing of a Boy With an Evil Spirit

14When they came to the
other disciples, they saw a
large crowd around them
and the teachers of the law
arguing with them. 15As
soon as all the people saw
Jesus, they were over-
whelmed with wonder and
ran to greet him.
16"What are you arguing
with them about?" he
asked.
17A man in the crowd an-
swered, "Teacher, I
brought you my son, who is
possessed by a spirit that
has robbed him of speech.
18Whenever it seizes him, it
throws him to the ground.
He foams at the mouth,
gnashes his teeth and be-
comes rigid. I asked your
disciples to drive out the
spirit, but they could not."
19"O unbelieving genera-
tion," Jesus replied, "how
long shall I stay with you?
How long shall I put up
with you? Bring the boy to
me."
20So they brought him.
When the spirit saw Jesus,
it immediately threw the
boy into a convulsion. He

he fell on the ground and
rolled about, foaming at the
mouth. 21 Jesus[o] asked the
father, "How long has this
been happening to him?"
And he said, "From child-
hood. 22 It has often cast
him into the fire and into
the water, to destroy him;
but if you are able to do
anything, have pity on us
and help us." 23 Jesus said
to him, "If you are able!—
All things can be done for
the one who believes."
24 Immediately the father of
the child cried out,[p] "I believe; help my unbelief!"
25 When Jesus saw that a
crowd came running to-
gether, he rebuked the unclean spirit, saying to it,
"You spirit that keeps this
boy from speaking and
hearing, I command you,
come out of him, and never
enter him again!" 26 After
crying out and convulsing
him terribly, it came out,
and the boy was like a
corpse, so that most of
them said, "He is dead."
27 But Jesus took him by the
hand and lifted him up, and
he was able to stand.
28 When he had entered the
house, his disciples asked
him privately, "Why could
we not cast it out?" 29 He
said to them, "This kind
can come out only through
prayer."[q]

Jesus Again Foretells His Death and Resurrection

30 They went on from
there and passed through
Galilee. He did not want
anyone to know it; 31 for he
was teaching his disciples,
saying to them, "The Son
of Man is to be betrayed
into human hands, and they
will kill him, and three days
after being killed, he will
rise again." 32 But they did

αὐτόν, καὶ πεσὼν ἐπὶ τῆς γῆς ἐκυλίετο
him, and falling on the earth he wallowed
ἀφρίζων. 21 καὶ ἐπηρώτησεν τὸν πατέρα
foaming. And he questioned the father
αὐτοῦ· πόσος χρόνος ἐστὶν ὡς τοῦτο
of him: What time is it while this
γέγονεν αὐτῷ; ὁ δὲ εἶπεν· ἐκ παιδιόθεν·
has happened to him? And he said: From childhood;
22 καὶ πολλάκις καὶ εἰς πῦρ αὐτὸν
and often both into fire him
ἔβαλεν καὶ εἰς ὕδατα ἵνα ἀπολέσῃ αὐτόν· ἀλλ'
it threw and into waters that it may destroy him; but
εἴ τι δύνῃ, βοήθησον ἡμῖν σπλαγχνισθεὶς
if anything thou canst, help us having compassion
ἐφ' ἡμᾶς. 23 ὁ δὲ Ἰησοῦς εἶπεν αὐτῷ· τὸ εἰ
on us. – And Jesus said to him: The "if
δύνῃ, πάντα δυνατὰ τῷ πιστεύοντι.
thou canst," all things possible to the [one] believing.
24 εὐθὺς κράξας ὁ πατὴρ τοῦ παιδίου
Immediately crying out the father of the child
ἔλεγεν· πιστεύω· βοήθει μου τῇ ἀπιστίᾳ.
said: I believe; help thou of me the unbelief.
25 ἰδὼν δὲ ὁ Ἰησοῦς ὅτι ἐπισυντρέχει
And [2]seeing – [1]Jesus that is(was) running together
ὄχλος, ἐπετίμησεν τῷ πνεύματι τῷ ἀκαθάρτῳ
a crowd, rebuked the spirit – unclean
λέγων αὐτῷ· τὸ ἄλαλον καὶ κωφὸν
saying to it: – Dumb and deaf
πνεῦμα, ἐγὼ ἐπιτάσσω σοι, ἔξελθε ἐξ
spirit, I command thee, come forth out of
αὐτοῦ καὶ μηκέτι εἰσέλθῃς εἰς αὐτόν.
him and no more mayest thou enter into him.
26 καὶ κράξας καὶ πολλὰ σπαράξας
And crying out and much convulsing [him]
ἐξῆλθεν· καὶ ἐγένετο ὡσεὶ νεκρός, ὥστε
it came out; and he was as dead, so as
τοὺς πολλοὺς λέγειν ὅτι ἀπέθανεν. 27 ὁ
– many to say[b] that he died. –
= many said
δὲ Ἰησοῦς κρατήσας τῆς χειρὸς αὐτοῦ
But Jesus taking hold of the hand of him
ἤγειρεν αὐτόν, καὶ ἀνέστη. 28 καὶ
raised him, and he stood up. And
εἰσελθόντος αὐτοῦ εἰς οἶκον οἱ μαθηταὶ
entering him[a] into a house the disciples
=when he entered
αὐτοῦ κατ' ἰδίαν ἐπηρώτων αὐτόν· ὅτι
of him privately questioned him: Why
ἡμεῖς οὐκ ἠδυνήθημεν ἐκβαλεῖν αὐτό;
we were not able to expel it?
29 καὶ εἶπεν αὐτοῖς· τοῦτο τὸ γένος ἐν
And he told them: This – kind by
οὐδενὶ δύναται ἐξελθεῖν εἰ μὴ ἐν προσευχῇ.
nothing can *to* come out except by prayer.
30 Κἀκεῖθεν ἐξελθόντες παρεπορεύοντο διὰ
And thence going forth they passed through
τῆς Γαλιλαίας, καὶ οὐκ ἤθελεν ἵνα
– Galilee, and he wished not that
τις γνοῖ· 31 ἐδίδασκεν γὰρ τοὺς μαθητὰς
anyone should know; for he was teaching the disciples
αὐτοῦ, καὶ ἔλεγεν αὐτοῖς ὅτι ὁ υἱὸς τοῦ
of him, and told them[,] – The Son –
ἀνθρώπου παραδίδοται εἰς χεῖρας ἀνθρώπων,
of man is betrayed into [the] hands of men,
καὶ ἀποκτενοῦσιν αὐτόν, καὶ ἀποκτανθεὶς
and they will kill him, and being killed
μετὰ τρεῖς ἡμέρας ἀναστήσεται. 32 οἱ
after three days he will rise up. they

fell to the ground and rolled
around, foaming at the
mouth.
21 Jesus asked the boy's
father, "How long has he
been like this?"
"From childhood," he
answered. 22 "It has often
thrown him into fire or water to kill him. But if you
can do anything, take pity
on us and help us."
23 " 'If you can'?" said
Jesus. "Everything is possible for him who be-
lieves."
24 Immediately the boy's
father exclaimed, "I do believe; help me overcome
my unbelief!"
25 When Jesus saw that a
crowd was running to the
scene, he rebuked the evil[e]
spirit. "You deaf and mute
spirit," he said, "I com-
mand you, come out of him
and never enter him
again."
26 The spirit shrieked,
convulsed him violently
and came out. The boy
looked so much like a
corpse that many said,
"He's dead." 27 But Jesus
took him by the hand and
lifted him to his feet, and he
stood up.
28 After Jesus had gone in-
doors, his disciples asked
him privately, "Why
couldn't we drive it out?"
29 He replied, "This kind
can come out only by
prayer.[f]"
30 They left that place and
passed through Galilee.
Jesus did not want anyone
to know where they were,
31 because he was teaching
his disciples. He said to
them, "The Son of Man is
going to be betrayed into
the hands of men. They will
kill him, and after three
days he will rise." 32 But

[o] Gk *He*
[p] Other ancient authorities add *with tears*
[q] Other ancient authorities add *and fasting*

[e] 25 Greek *unclean*
[f] 29 Some manuscripts *prayer and fasting*

not understand what he was saying and were afraid to ask him.

Who Is the Greatest?

33 Then they came to Capernaum; and when he was in the house he asked them, "What were you arguing about on the way?" 34 But they were silent, for on the way they had argued with one another who was the greatest. 35 He sat down, called the twelve, and said to them, "Whoever wants to be first must be last of all and servant of all." 36 Then he took a little child and put it among them; and taking it in his arms, he said to them, 37 "Whoever welcomes one such child in my name welcomes me, and whoever welcomes me welcomes not me but the one who sent me."

Another Exorcist

38 John said to him, "Teacher, we saw someone[r] casting out demons in your name, and we tried to stop him, because he was not following us." 39 But Jesus said, "Do not stop him; for no one who does a deed of power in my name will be able soon afterward to speak evil of me. 40 Whoever is not against us is for us. 41 For truly I tell you, whoever gives you a cup of water to drink because you bear the name of Christ will by no means lose the reward.

Temptations to Sin

42 "If any of you put a stumbling block before one of these little ones who believe in me,[s] it would be better for you if a great millstone were hung around your neck and you were thrown into the sea. 43 If your hand causes you to stumble, cut it off; it is better for you to enter life

δὲ ἠγνόουν τὸ ῥῆμα, καὶ ἐφοβοῦντο
But did not know the word, and feared

αὐτὸν ἐπερωτῆσαι.
him to question.

33 Καὶ ἦλθον εἰς Καφαρναούμ. Καὶ
And they came to Capernaum. And

ἐν τῇ οἰκίᾳ γενόμενος ἐπηρώτα αὐτούς·
in the house being he questioned them:

τί ἐν τῇ ὁδῷ διελογίζεσθε; **34** οἱ δὲ
What in the way were ye debating? And they

ἐσιώπων· πρὸς ἀλλήλους γὰρ διελέχθησαν
were silent; [2]with [3]one another [1]for they debated

ἐν τῇ ὁδῷ τίς μείζων. **35** καὶ καθίσας
in the way who [was] greater. And sitting

ἐφώνησεν τοὺς δώδεκα καὶ λέγει αὐτοῖς·
he called the twelve and says to them:

εἴ τις θέλει πρῶτος εἶναι, ἔσται πάντων
If anyone wishes first to be, he shall be of all

ἔσχατος καὶ πάντων διάκονος. **36** καὶ
last and of all servant. And

λαβὼν παιδίον ἔστησεν αὐτὸ ἐν μέσῳ
taking a child he set it(him) in [the] midst

αὐτῶν, καὶ ἐναγκαλισάμενος αὐτὸ εἶπεν
of them, and folding in [his] arms it he said

αὐτοῖς· **37** ὃς ἂν ἓν τῶν τοιούτων παιδίων
to them: Whoever one – of such children

δέξηται ἐπὶ τῷ ὀνόματί μου, ἐμὲ δέχεται·
receives on(in) the name of me, me receives;

καὶ ὃς ἂν ἐμὲ δέχηται, οὐχ ἐμὲ δέχεται
and whoever me receives, not me receives

ἀλλὰ τὸν ἀποστείλαντά με. **38** Ἔφη αὐτῷ
but the [one] having sent me. Said to him

ὁ Ἰωάννης· διδάσκαλε, εἴδομέν τινα ἐν
– John: Teacher, we saw someone in

τῷ ὀνόματί σου ἐκβάλλοντα δαιμόνια, ὃς
the name of thee expelling demons, who

οὐκ ἀκολουθεῖ ἡμῖν, καὶ ἐκωλύομεν αὐτόν,
does not follow us, and we forbade him,

ὅτι οὐκ ἠκολούθει ἡμῖν. **39** ὁ δὲ Ἰησοῦς
because he was not following us. – But Jesus

εἶπεν· μὴ κωλύετε αὐτόν· οὐδεὶς γάρ
said: Do not forbid him: for no one

ἐστιν ὃς ποιήσει δύναμιν ἐπὶ τῷ ὀνόματί
there is who shall do a mighty work on(in) the name

μου καὶ δυνήσεται ταχὺ κακολογῆσαί με·
of me and will be able quickly to speak evil of me;

40 ὃς γὰρ οὐκ ἔστιν καθ' ἡμῶν, ὑπὲρ
for who is not against us, for

ἡμῶν ἐστιν. **41** Ὃς γὰρ ἂν ποτίσῃ
us is. For whoever [1]gives [3]drink

ὑμᾶς ποτήριον ὕδατος ἐν ὀνόματι, ὅτι
[2]you a cup of water in [the] name, because

Χριστοῦ ἐστε, ἀμὴν λέγω ὑμῖν ὅτι
of Christ ye are, truly I tell you that

οὐ μὴ ἀπολέσῃ τὸν μισθὸν αὐτοῦ. **42** Καὶ
by no means he will lose the reward of him. And

ὃς ἂν σκανδαλίσῃ ἕνα τῶν μικρῶν τούτων
whoever offends one – [3]little [ones] [1]of these

τῶν πιστευόντων, καλόν ἐστιν αὐτῷ μᾶλλον
– [2]believing, good is it for him rather

εἰ περίκειται μύλος ὀνικὸς περὶ τὸν
if be laid *round* a [heavy] millstone round the

τράχηλον αὐτοῦ καὶ βέβληται εἰς τὴν
neck of him and he be thrown into the

θάλασσαν. **43** Καὶ ἐὰν σκανδαλίσῃ σε ἡ
sea. And if offends thee the

they did not understand what he meant and were afraid to ask him about it.

Who Is the Greatest?

33 They came to Capernaum. When he was in the house, he asked them, "What were you arguing about on the road?" 34 But they kept quiet because on the way they had argued about who was the greatest.

35 Sitting down, Jesus called the Twelve and said, "If anyone wants to be first, he must be the very last, and the servant of all."

36 He took a little child and had him stand among them. Taking him in his arms, he said to them, 37 "Whoever welcomes one of these little children in my name welcomes me; and whoever welcomes me does not welcome me but the one who sent me."

Whoever Is Not Against Us Is for Us

38 "Teacher," said John, "we saw a man driving out demons in your name and we told him to stop, because he was not one of us."

39 "Do not stop him," Jesus said. "No one who does a miracle in my name can in the next moment say anything bad about me, 40 for whoever is not against us is for us. 41 I tell you the truth, anyone who gives you a cup of water in my name because you belong to Christ will certainly not lose his reward.

Causing to Sin

42 "And if anyone causes one of these little ones who believe in me to sin, it would be better for him to be thrown into the sea with a large millstone tied around his neck. 43 If your hand causes you to sin, cut

[r] Other ancient authorities add *who does not follow us*
[s] Other ancient authorities lack *in me*

maimed than to have two
hands and to go to hell,[t] to
the unquenchable fire.[u]
45 And if your foot causes
you to stumble, cut it off; it
is better for you to enter life
lame than to have two feet
and to be thrown into
hell.[t, u] 47 And if your eye
causes you to stumble, tear
it out; it is better for you to
enter the kingdom of God
with one eye than to have
two eyes and to be thrown
into hell,[t] 48 where their
worm never dies, and the
fire is never quenched.
49 "For everyone will
be salted with fire.[v] 50 Salt
is good; but if salt has lost
its saltiness, how can you
season it?[w] Have salt in
yourselves, and be at peace
with one another."

Chapter 10

Teaching about Divorce

HE left that place and
went to the region of
Judea and[x] beyond the Jordan. And crowds again
gathered around him; and,
as was his custom, he again
taught them.
2 Some Pharisees came,
and to test him they asked,
"Is it lawful for a man to
divorce his wife?" 3 He answered them, "What did
Moses command you?"
4 They said, "Moses al-
lowed a man to write a certificate of dismissal and to
divorce her." 5 But Jesus
said to them, "Because of
your hardness of heart he
wrote this commandment
for you. 6 But from the beginning of creation, 'God
made them male and fe-
male.' 7 'For this reason a

[t] Gk *Gehenna*
[u] Verses 44 and 46 (which are identical with verse 48) are lacking in the best ancient authorities
[v] Other ancient authorities either add or substitute *and every sacrifice will be salted with salt*
[w] Or *how can you restore its saltiness?*
[x] Other ancient authorities lack *and*

χείρ σου, ἀπόκοψον αὐτήν· καλόν ἐστίν
hand of thee, cut off it; good is it
σε κυλλὸν εἰσελθεῖν εἰς τὴν ζωήν, ἢ τὰς
thee maimed to enter into – life, than the
δύο χεῖρας ἔχοντα ἀπελθεῖν εἰς τὴν
two hands having to go away into –
γέενναν, εἰς τὸ πῦρ τὸ ἄσβεστον.‡ 45 καὶ
gehenna, into the fire *the* unquenchable. And
ἐὰν ὁ πούς σου σκανδαλίζῃ σε, ἀπόκοψον
if the foot of thee offends thee, cut off
αὐτόν· καλόν ἐστίν σε εἰσελθεῖν εἰς τὴν
it; good is it thee to enter into –
ζωὴν χωλόν, ἢ τοὺς δύο πόδας ἔχοντα
life lame, than the two feet having
βληθῆναι εἰς τὴν γέενναν.‡ 47 καὶ ἐὰν ὁ
to be cast into – gehenna. And if the
ὀφθαλμός σου σκανδαλίζῃ σε, ἔκβαλε αὐτόν·
eye of thee offends thee, cast out it;
καλόν σέ ἐστιν μονόφθαλμον εἰσελθεῖν εἰς
good thee is it one-eyed to enter into
τὴν βασιλείαν τοῦ θεοῦ, ἢ δύο ὀφθαλμοὺς
the kingdom – of God, than two eyes
ἔχοντα βληθῆναι εἰς τὴν γέενναν, 48 ὅπου
having to be cast into – gehenna, where
ὁ σκώληξ αὐτῶν οὐ τελευτᾷ καὶ τὸ
the worm of them dies not and the
πῦρ οὐ σβέννυται. 49 Πᾶς γὰρ πυρὶ
fire is not quenched. For everyone with fire
ἁλισθήσεται. 50 καλὸν τὸ ἅλας· ἐὰν δὲ
shall be salted. Good [is] – salt; but if
τὸ ἅλας ἄναλον γένηται, ἐν τίνι αὐτὸ
– salt saltless becomes, by what it
ἀρτύσετε; ἔχετε ἐν ἑαυτοῖς ἅλα καὶ
will ye season ? Have in yourselves salt and
εἰρηνεύετε ἐν ἀλλήλοις.
be at peace among one another.

10 Καὶ ἐκεῖθεν ἀναστὰς ἔρχεται εἰς τὰ
And thence rising up he comes into the
ὅρια τῆς Ἰουδαίας καὶ πέραν τοῦ
territory – of Judæa and beyond the
Ἰορδάνου, καὶ συμπορεύονται πάλιν ὄχλοι
Jordan, and ³go *with* ¹again ²crowds
πρὸς αὐτόν, καὶ ὡς εἰώθει πάλιν ἐδίδασκεν
⁴with ⁵him, and as he was wont again he taught
αὐτούς. 2 Καὶ προσελθόντες Φαρισαῖοι
them. And ²approaching ¹Pharisees
ἐπηρώτων αὐτὸν εἰ ἔξεστιν ἀνδρὶ γυναῖκα
questioned him if it is(was) lawful for a man a wife
ἀπολῦσαι, πειράζοντες αὐτόν. 3 ὁ δὲ
to dismiss, testing him. And he
ἀποκριθεὶς εἶπεν αὐτοῖς· 4 τί ὑμῖν ἐνετείλατο
answering said to them: What you ordered
Μωϋσῆς; οἱ δὲ εἶπαν· ἐπέτρεψεν Μωϋσῆς
Moses ? And they said: permitted Moses
βιβλίον ἀποστασίου γράψαι καὶ ἀπολῦσαι.
a roll of divorce to write and to dismiss.
5 ὁ δὲ Ἰησοῦς εἶπεν αὐτοῖς· πρὸς τὴν
– And Jesus said to them: For the
σκληροκαρδίαν ὑμῶν ἔγραψεν ὑμῖν τὴν
hardheartedness of you he wrote to you –
ἐντολὴν ταύτην. 6 ἀπὸ δὲ ἀρχῆς κτίσεως
this commandment. But from [the] beginning of creation

‡ Verse 44 omitted by Nestle; *cf.* NIV footnote.

‡ Verse 46 omitted by Nestle; *cf.* NIV footnote.

it off. It is better for you to
enter life maimed than with
two hands to go into hell,
where the fire never goes
out.[g] 45 And if your foot
causes you to sin, cut it off.
It is better for you to enter
life crippled than to have
two feet and be thrown into
hell.[h] 47 And if your eye
causes you to sin, pluck it
out. It is better for you to
enter the kingdom of God
with one eye than to have
two eyes and be thrown
into hell, 48 where

" 'their worm does not
die,
and the fire is not
quenched.'[i]

49 Everyone will be salted
with fire.
50 "Salt is good, but if it
loses its saltiness, how can
you make it salty again?
Have salt in yourselves,
and be at peace with each
other."

Chapter 10

Divorce

JESUS then left that
place and went into the
region of Judea and across
the Jordan. Again crowds
of people came to him, and
as was his custom, he
taught them.
2 Some Pharisees came
and tested him by asking,
"Is it lawful for a man to
divorce his wife?"
3 "What did Moses com-
mand you?" he replied.
4 They said, "Moses per-
mitted a man to write a certificate of divorce and send
her away."
5 "It was because your
hearts were hard that Mo-
ses wrote you this law,"
Jesus replied. 6 "But at the
beginning of creation God

[g] *43* Some manuscripts *out, [44] where / " 'their worm does not die, / and the fire is not quenched.'*
[h] *45* Some manuscripts *hell, [46] where / " 'their worm does not die, / and the fire is not quenched.'*
[i] *48* Isaiah 66:24

man shall leave his father
and mother and be joined to
his wife,[y] 8and the two
shall become one flesh.' So
they are no longer two, but
one flesh. 9Therefore what
God has joined together, let
no one separate."
10 Then in the house the
disciples asked him again
about this matter. 11He
said to them, "Whoever divorces his wife and marries
another commits adultery
against her; 12and if she divorces her husband and
marries another, she commits adultery."

Jesus Blesses Little Children

13 People were bringing
little children to him in order that he might touch
them; and the disciples
spoke sternly to them.
14But when Jesus saw this,
he was indignant and said
to them, "Let the little children come to me; do not
stop them; for it is to such
as these that the kingdom
of God belongs. 15Truly I
tell you, whoever does not
receive the kingdom of God
as a little child will never
enter it." 16And he took
them up in his arms, laid his
hands on them, and blessed
them.

The Rich Man

17 As he was setting out
on a journey, a man ran up
and knelt before him, and
asked him, "Good Teacher,
what must I do to inherit
eternal life?" 18Jesus said
to him, "Why do you call
me good? No one is good
but God alone. 19You
know the commandments:
'You shall not murder; You
shall not commit adultery;
You shall not steal; You
shall not bear false witness;
You shall not defraud;
Honor your father and
mother.'" 20He said to
him, "Teacher, I have kept
all these since my youth."

[y] Other ancient authorities lack *and be joined to his wife*

ἄρσεν καὶ θῆλυ ἐποίησεν αὐτούς· 7 ἕνεκεν
male and female he made them; for the sake of
τούτου καταλείψει ἄνθρωπος τὸν πατέρα
this shall leave a man the father
αὐτοῦ καὶ τὴν μητέρα, 8 καὶ ἔσονται
of him and the mother, and shall be
οἱ δύο εἰς σάρκα μίαν· ὥστε οὐκέτι
the two – flesh one; so as no longer
εἰσὶν δύο ἀλλὰ μία σάρξ. 9 ὃ οὖν ὁ
are they two but one flesh. What then –
θεὸς συνέζευξεν, ἄνθρωπος μὴ χωριζέτω.
God yoked together, ³man ²not ¹let ⁴separate.
10 καὶ εἰς τὴν οἰκίαν πάλιν οἱ μαθηταὶ
And in the house again the disciples
περὶ τούτου ἐπηρώτων αὐτόν. 11 καὶ
about this questioned him. And
λέγει αὐτοῖς· ὃς ἂν ἀπολύσῃ τὴν γυναῖκα
he says to them: Whoever dismisses the wife
αὐτοῦ καὶ γαμήσῃ ἄλλην, μοιχᾶται ἐπ'
of him and marries another, commits adultery with
αὐτήν· 12 καὶ ἐὰν αὐτὴ ἀπολύσασα τὸν
her; and if she having dismissed the
ἄνδρα αὐτῆς γαμήσῃ ἄλλον, μοιχᾶται.
husband of her marries another, she commits adultery.
13 Καὶ προσέφερον αὐτῷ παιδία ἵνα
And they brought to him children that
αὐτῶν ἅψηται· οἱ δὲ μαθηταὶ ἐπετίμησαν
them he might touch; but the disciples rebuked
αὐτοῖς. 14 ἰδὼν δὲ ὁ Ἰησοῦς ἠγανάκτησεν
them. But ²seeing – ¹Jesus was angry
καὶ εἶπεν αὐτοῖς· ἄφετε τὰ παιδία
and said to them: Allow the children
ἔρχεσθαι πρός με, μὴ κωλύετε αὐτά·
to come to me, do not prevent them;
τῶν γὰρ τοιούτων ἐστὶν ἡ βασιλεία τοῦ
– for of such is the kingdom –
θεοῦ. 15 ἀμὴν λέγω ὑμῖν, ὃς ἂν
of God. Truly I tell you, whoever
μὴ δέξηται τὴν βασιλείαν τοῦ θεοῦ ὡς
receives not the kingdom – of God as
παιδίον, οὐ μὴ εἰσέλθῃ εἰς αὐτήν. 16 καὶ
a child, by no means may enter into it. And
ἐναγκαλισάμενος αὐτὰ κατευλόγει τιθεὶς τὰς
folding in [his] arms them he blesses putting the(his)
χεῖρας ἐπ' αὐτά.
hands on them.
17 Καὶ ἐκπορευομένου αὐτοῦ εἰς ὁδὸν
And going forth him[a] into [the] way
— as he went forth
προσδραμὼν εἷς καὶ γονυπετήσας αὐτὸν
running to one and kneeling to him
ἐπηρώτα αὐτόν· διδάσκαλε ἀγαθέ, τί ποιήσω
questioned him: Teacher good, what may I do
ἵνα ζωὴν αἰώνιον κληρονομήσω; 18 ὁ δὲ
that life eternal I may inherit? – And
Ἰησοῦς εἶπεν αὐτῷ· τί με λέγεις ἀγαθόν;
Jesus said to him: Why me callest thou good?
οὐδεὶς ἀγαθὸς εἰ μὴ εἷς ὁ θεός. 19 τὰς ἐντολὰς
no one good except one – God. The commandments
οἶδας· μὴ φονεύσῃς, μὴ μοιχεύσῃς,
thou knowest: Do not kill, Do not commit adultery,
μὴ κλέψῃς, μὴ ψευδομαρτυρήσῃς, μὴ
Do not steal, Do not bear false witness, Do
ἀποστερήσῃς, τίμα τὸν πατέρα σου καὶ
not defraud, Honour the father of thee and
τὴν μητέρα. 20 ὁ δὲ ἔφη αὐτῷ· διδάσκαλε,
the mother. And he said to him: Teacher,

'made them male and female.'[j] 7'For this reason a
man will leave his father
and mother and be united
to his wife,[k] 8and the two
will become one flesh.'[l] So
they are no longer two, but
one. 9Therefore what God
has joined together, let man
not separate."
10When they were in the
house again, the disciples
asked Jesus about this.
11He answered, "Anyone
who divorces his wife and
marries another woman
commits adultery against
her. 12And if she divorces
her husband and marries
another man, she commits
adultery."

The Little Children and Jesus

13People were bringing
little children to Jesus to
have him touch them, but
the disciples rebuked them.
14When Jesus saw this, he
was indignant. He said to
them, "Let the little children come to me, and do
not hinder them, for the
kingdom of God belongs to
such as these. 15I tell you
the truth, anyone who will
not receive the kingdom of
God like a little child will
never enter it." 16And he
took the children in his
arms, put his hands on
them and blessed them.

The Rich Young Man

17As Jesus started on his
way, a man ran up to him
and fell on his knees before
him. "Good teacher," he
asked, "what must I do to
inherit eternal life?"
18"Why do you call me
good?" Jesus answered.
"No one is good—except
God alone. 19You know the
commandments: 'Do not
murder, do not commit
adultery, do not steal, do
not give false testimony, do
not defraud, honor your father and mother.'[m]"
20"Teacher," he declared, "all these I have

[j] 6 Gen. 1:27
[k] 7 Some early manuscripts do not have *and be united to his wife.*
[l] 8 Gen. 2:24
[m] 19 Exodus 20:12-16; Deut. 5:16-20

21 Jesus, looking at him,
loved him and said, "You
lack one thing; go, sell what
you own, and give the money[z] to the poor, and you
will have treasure in heav-
en; then come, follow me."
22 When he heard this, he
was shocked and went
away grieving, for he had
many possessions.
23 Then Jesus looked
around and said to his disciples, "How hard it will be
for those who have wealth
to enter the kingdom of
God!" 24 And the disciples
were perplexed at these
words. But Jesus said to
them again, "Children, how
hard it is[a] to enter the kingdom of God! 25 It is easier
for a camel to go through
the eye of a needle than for
someone who is rich to enter the kingdom of God."
26 They were greatly as-
tounded and said to one another,[b] "Then who can be
saved?" 27 Jesus looked at
them and said, "For mor-
tals it is impossible, but not
for God; for God all things
are possible."
28 Peter began to say to
him, "Look, we have left
everything and followed
you." 29 Jesus said, "Truly I
tell you, there is no one
who has left house or
brothers or sisters or mother or father or children or
fields, for my sake and for
the sake of the good
news,[c] 30 who will not receive a hundredfold now in
this age—houses, brothers
and sisters, mothers and

[z] Gk lacks *the money*
[a] Other ancient authorities add *for those who trust in riches*
[b] Other ancient authorities read *to him*
[c] Or *gospel*

ταῦτα πάντα ἐφυλαξάμην ἐκ νεότητός μου.
all these things I observed from youth of me.
21 ὁ δὲ Ἰησοῦς ἐμβλέψας αὐτῷ ἠγάπησεν
– But Jesus looking at him loved
αὐτὸν καὶ εἶπεν αὐτῷ· ἕν σε ὑστερεῖ·
him and said to him: One thing thee is wanting:
ὕπαγε, ὅσα ἔχεις πώλησον καὶ δὸς [τοῖς]
go, what things thou hast sell and give to the
πτωχοῖς, καὶ ἕξεις θησαυρὸν ἐν οὐρανῷ,
poor, and thou wilt have treasure in heaven,
καὶ δεῦρο ἀκολούθει μοι. 22 ὁ δὲ στυγνάσας
and come follow me. But he being sad
ἐπὶ τῷ λόγῳ ἀπῆλθεν λυπούμενος, ἦν
at the word went away grieving, ¹he was
γὰρ ἔχων κτήματα πολλά. 23 Καὶ
¹for having possessions many. And
περιβλεψάμενος ὁ Ἰησοῦς λέγει τοῖς
looking round – Jesus says to the
μαθηταῖς αὐτοῦ· πῶς δυσκόλως οἱ τὰ
disciples of him: How hardly the [ones] the
χρήματα ἔχοντες εἰς τὴν βασιλείαν τοῦ
riches having into the kingdom –
θεοῦ εἰσελεύσονται. 24 οἱ δὲ μαθηταὶ
of God shall enter. And the disciples
ἐθαμβοῦντο ἐπὶ τοῖς λόγοις αὐτοῦ. ὁ δὲ
were amazed at the words of him. – And
Ἰησοῦς πάλιν ἀποκριθεὶς λέγει αὐτοῖς·
Jesus again answering says to them:
τέκνα, πῶς δύσκολόν ἐστιν εἰς τὴν
Children, how hard it is into the
βασιλείαν τοῦ θεοῦ εἰσελθεῖν· 25 εὐκοπώτερόν
kingdom – of God to enter; easier
ἐστιν κάμηλον διὰ τῆς τρυμαλιᾶς τῆς
it is a camel through the eye –
ῥαφίδος διελθεῖν ἢ πλούσιον εἰς τὴν
of a needle to go *through* than a rich man into the
βασιλείαν τοῦ θεοῦ εἰσελθεῖν. 26 οἱ δὲ
kingdom – of God to enter. But they
περισσῶς ἐξεπλήσσοντο λέγοντες πρὸς
exceedingly were astonished saying to
ἑαυτούς· καὶ τίς δύναται σωθῆναι;
themselves: And who can *to* be saved?
27 ἐμβλέψας αὐτοῖς ὁ Ἰησοῦς λέγει· παρὰ
Looking at them – Jesus says: With
ἀνθρώποις ἀδύνατον, ἀλλ' οὐ παρὰ θεῷ·
men [it is] impossible, but not with God;
πάντα γὰρ δυνατὰ παρὰ τῷ θεῷ. 28 Ἤρξατο
for all things [are] possible with – God. Began
λέγειν ὁ Πέτρος αὐτῷ· ἰδοὺ ἡμεῖς ἀφήκαμεν
to say – Peter to him: Behold [,] we left
πάντα καὶ ἠκολουθήκαμέν σοι. 29 ἔφη ὁ
all things and have followed thee. Said –
Ἰησοῦς· ἀμὴν λέγω ὑμῖν, οὐδείς ἐστιν
Jesus: Truly I tell you, no one there is
ὃς ἀφῆκεν οἰκίαν ἢ ἀδελφοὺς ἢ ἀδελφὰς
who left house or brothers or sisters
ἢ μητέρα ἢ πατέρα ἢ τέκνα ἢ ἀγροὺς
or mother or father or children or fields
ἕνεκεν ἐμοῦ καὶ ἕνεκεν τοῦ εὐαγγελίου,
for the sake of me and for the sake of the gospel,
30 ἐὰν μὴ λάβῃ ἑκατονταπλασίονα νῦν
but he receives a hundredfold now
ἐν τῷ καιρῷ τούτῳ οἰκίας καὶ ἀδελφοὺς
in – time this houses and brothers
καὶ ἀδελφὰς καὶ μητέρας καὶ τέκνα καὶ
and sisters and mothers and children and

kept since I was a boy."
21 Jesus looked at him and
loved him. "One thing you
lack," he said. "Go, sell
everything you have and
give to the poor, and you
will have treasure in heav-
en. Then come, follow
me."
22 At this the man's face
fell. He went away sad, because he had great wealth.
23 Jesus looked around
and said to his disciples,
"How hard it is for the rich
to enter the kingdom of
God!"
24 The disciples were
amazed at his words. But
Jesus said again, "Chil-
dren, how hard it is[n] to enter the kingdom of God! 25 It
is easier for a camel to go
through the eye of a needle
than for a rich man to enter
the kingdom of God."
26 The disciples were even
more amazed, and said to
each other, "Who then can
be saved?"
27 Jesus looked at them
and said, "With man this is
impossible, but not with
God; all things are possible
with God."
28 Peter said to him, "We
have left everything to follow you!"
29 "I tell you the truth,"
Jesus replied, "no one who
has left home or brothers or
sisters or mother or father
or children or fields for me
and the gospel 30 will fail to
receive a hundred times as
much in this present age
(homes, brothers, sisters,
mothers, children and

[n] 24 Some manuscripts *is for those who trust in riches*

children, and fields with
persecutions—and in the
age to come eternal life.
31 But many who are first
will be last, and the last will
be first."

A Third Time Jesus Foretells His Death and Resurrection

32 They were on the
road, going up to Jerusa-
lem, and Jesus was walking
ahead of them; they were
amazed, and those who followed were afraid. He took
the twelve aside again and
began to tell them what was
to happen to him, 33 saying,
"See, we are going up to
Jerusalem, and the Son of
Man will be handed over to
the chief priests and the
scribes, and they will condemn him to death; then
they will hand him over to
the Gentiles; 34 they will
mock him, and spit upon
him, and flog him, and kill
him; and after three days he
will rise again."

The Request of James and John

35 James and John, the
sons of Zebedee, came forward to him and said to
him, "Teacher, we want
you to do for us whatever
we ask of you." 36 And he
said to them, "What is it
you want me to do for
you?" 37 And they said to
him, "Grant us to sit, one at
your right hand and one at
your left, in your glory."
38 But Jesus said to them,
"You do not know what
you are asking. Are you
able to drink the cup that I
drink, or be baptized with
the baptism that I am baptized with?" 39 They re-
plied, "We are able." Then
Jesus said to them, "The
cup that I drink you will
drink; and with the baptism
with which I am baptized,
you will be baptized; 40 but

ἀγροὺς μετὰ διωγμῶν, καὶ ἐν τῷ αἰῶνι
fields with persecutions, and in the age
τῷ ἐρχομένῳ ζωὴν αἰώνιον. 31 πολλοὶ δὲ
– coming life eternal. And [1]many
ἔσονται πρῶτοι ἔσχατοι καὶ οἱ ἔσχατοι
[3]will be [2]first [4]last and the last
πρῶτοι.
first.

32 [T]Ἦσαν δὲ ἐν τῇ ὁδῷ ἀναβαίνοντες
Now they were in the way going up
εἰς Ἱεροσόλυμα, καὶ ἦν προάγων αὐτοὺς
to Jerusalem, and was going before them
ὁ Ἰησοῦς, καὶ ἐθαμβοῦντο, οἱ δὲ
– Jesus, and they were astonished, and the
ἀκολουθοῦντες ἐφοβοῦντο. καὶ παραλαβὼν
[ones] following were afraid. And taking
πάλιν τοὺς δώδεκα ἤρξατο αὐτοῖς λέγειν
again the twelve he began them to tell
τὰ μέλλοντα αὐτῷ συμβαίνειν, 33 ὅτι ἰδοὺ
the things about to him to happen, – Behold
ἀναβαίνομεν εἰς Ἱεροσόλυμα, καὶ ὁ υἱὸς
we are going up to Jerusalem, and the Son
τοῦ ἀνθρώπου παραδοθήσεται τοῖς
– of man will be betrayed to the
ἀρχιερεῦσιν καὶ τοῖς γραμματεῦσιν, καὶ
chief priests and to the scribes, and
κατακρινοῦσιν αὐτὸν θανάτῳ καὶ παραδώσουσιν
they will condemn him to death and will deliver
αὐτὸν τοῖς ἔθνεσιν 34 καὶ ἐμπαίξουσιν
him to the nations and they will mock
αὐτῷ καὶ ἐμπτύσουσιν αὐτῷ καὶ μαστι-
him and will spit at him and will
γώσουσιν αὐτὸν καὶ ἀποκτενοῦσιν, καὶ
scourge him and will kill, and
μετὰ τρεῖς ἡμέρας ἀναστήσεται.
after three days he will rise again.

35 Καὶ προσπορεύονται αὐτῷ Ἰάκωβος
And approach *to* him James
καὶ Ἰωάννης οἱ [δύο] υἱοὶ Ζεβεδαίου
and John the two sons of Zebedee
λέγοντες αὐτῷ· διδάσκαλε, θέλομεν ἵνα ὃ ἐὰν
saying to him: Teacher, we wish that whatever
αἰτήσωμέν σε ποιήσῃς ἡμῖν. 36 ὁ
we may ask thee thou mayest do for us. he
δὲ εἶπεν αὐτοῖς· τί θέλετέ με ποιήσω
And said to them: What wish ye me I may do
ὑμῖν; 37 οἱ δὲ εἶπαν αὐτῷ· δὸς ἡμῖν
for you ? And they said to him: Give us
ἵνα εἷς σου ἐκ δεξιῶν καὶ εἷς ἐξ
that one of thee out of(on) [the] right and one on
= on thy right
ἀριστερῶν καθίσωμεν ἐν τῇ δόξῃ σου.
[thy] left we may sit in the glory of thee.
38 ὁ δὲ Ἰησοῦς εἶπεν αὐτοῖς· οὐκ οἴδατε
– And Jesus said to them: Ye know not
τί αἰτεῖσθε. δύνασθε πιεῖν τὸ ποτήριον
what ye ask. Can ye *to* drink the cup
ὃ ἐγὼ πίνω, ἢ τὸ βάπτισμα ὃ ἐγὼ
which I drink, or the baptism which I
βαπτίζομαι βαπτισθῆναι; 39 οἱ δὲ εἶπαν
am baptized *to* be baptized [with] ? And they said
αὐτῷ· δυνάμεθα. ὁ δὲ Ἰησοῦς εἶπεν
to him: We can. – And Jesus said
αὐτοῖς· τὸ ποτήριον ὃ ἐγὼ πίνω πίεσθε,
to them: The cup which I drink shall ye drink,
καὶ τὸ βάπτισμα ὃ ἐγὼ βαπτίζομαι
and the baptism which I am baptized [with]

fields—and with them, persecutions) and in the age to
come, eternal life. 31 But
many who are first will be
last, and the last first."

Jesus Again Predicts His Death

32 They were on their way
up to Jerusalem, with Jesus
leading the way, and the
disciples were astonished,
while those who followed
were afraid. Again he took
the Twelve aside and told
them what was going to
happen to him. 33 "We are
going up to Jerusalem," he
said, "and the Son of Man
will be betrayed to the chief
priests and teachers of the
law. They will condemn
him to death and will hand
him over to the Gentiles,
34 who will mock him and
spit on him, flog him and
kill him. Three days later
he will rise."

The Request of James and John

35 Then James and John,
the sons of Zebedee, came
to him. "Teacher," they
said, "we want you to do
for us whatever we ask."
36 "What do you want me
to do for you?" he asked.
37 They replied, "Let one
of us sit at your right and
the other at your left in
your glory."
38 "You don't know what
you are asking," Jesus
said. "Can you drink the
cup I drink or be baptized
with the baptism I am baptized with?"
39 "We can," they an-
swered.
Jesus said to them, "You
will drink the cup I drink
and be baptized with the
baptism I am baptized

to sit at my right hand or at
my left is not mine to grant,
but it is for those for whom
it has been prepared."
41 When the ten heard
this, they began to be angry
with James and John. 42 So
Jesus called them and said
to them, "You know that
among the Gentiles those
whom they recognize as
their rulers lord it over
them, and their great ones
are tyrants over them.
43 But it is not so among
you; but whoever wishes to
become great among you
must be your servant,
44 and whoever wishes to
be first among you must be
slave of all. 45 For the Son
of Man came not to be
served but to serve, and to
give his life a ransom for
many."

The Healing of Blind Bartimaeus

46 They came to Jeri-
cho. As he and his disciples
and a large crowd were
leaving Jericho, Bartimaeus son of Timaeus, a blind
beggar, was sitting by the
roadside. 47 When he heard
that it was Jesus of Nazareth, he began to shout out
and say, "Jesus, Son of David, have mercy on me!"
48 Many sternly ordered
him to be quiet, but he cried
out even more loudly, "Son
of David, have mercy on
me!" 49 Jesus stood still and
said, "Call him here." And
they called the blind man,
saying to him, "Take heart;
get up, he is calling you."
50 So throwing off his cloak,
he sprang up and came to
Jesus. 51 Then Jesus said to
him, "What do you want
me to do for you?" The

βαπτισθήσεσθε· **40** τὸ δὲ καθίσαι ἐκ δεξιῶν
ye shall be baptized; – but to sit on right
μου ἢ ἐξ εὐωνύμων οὐκ ἔστιν ἐμὸν
of me or on [my] left is not mine
δοῦναι, ἀλλ' οἷς ἡτοίμασται. **41** Καὶ
to give, but for whom it has been prepared. And
ἀκούσαντες οἱ δέκα ἤρξαντο ἀγανακτεῖν
[3]hearing [1]the [2]ten began to be incensed
περὶ Ἰακώβου καὶ Ἰωάννου. **42** καὶ
about James and John. And
προσκαλεσάμενος αὐτοὺς ὁ Ἰησοῦς λέγει
[1]calling [3]to [4][him] [2]them – Jesus says
αὐτοῖς· οἴδατε ὅτι οἱ δοκοῦντες ἄρχειν
to them: Ye know that the [ones] thinking to rule
τῶν ἐθνῶν κατακυριεύουσιν αὐτῶν καὶ
the nations lord it over them and
οἱ μεγάλοι αὐτῶν κατεξουσιάζουσιν αὐτῶν.
the great [ones] of them exercise authority over them.
43 οὐχ οὕτως δέ ἐστιν ἐν ὑμῖν· ἀλλ'
[2]not [3]so [1]But is it among you; but
ὃς ἂν θέλῃ μέγας γενέσθαι ἐν ὑμῖν,
whoever wishes great to become among you,
ἔσται ὑμῶν διάκονος, **44** καὶ ὃς ἂν
shall be of you servant, and whoever
θέλῃ ἐν ὑμῖν εἶναι πρῶτος, ἔσται πάντων
wishes among you to be first, shall be of all
δοῦλος· **45** καὶ γὰρ ὁ υἱὸς τοῦ ἀνθρώπου
slave; for even the Son – of man
οὐκ ἦλθεν διακονηθῆναι ἀλλὰ διακονῆσαι
did not come to be served but to serve
καὶ δοῦναι τὴν ψυχὴν αὐτοῦ λύτρον ἀντὶ
and to give the life of him a ransom instead of
πολλῶν.
many.
46 Καὶ ἔρχονται εἰς Ἰεριχώ. Καὶ
And they come to Jericho. And
ἐκπορευομένου αὐτοῦ ἀπὸ Ἰεριχὼ καὶ τῶν
going out him[a] from Jericho and the
= as he was going out
μαθητῶν αὐτοῦ καὶ ὄχλου ἱκανοῦ ὁ υἱὸς
disciples[a] of him and crowd a considerable[a] the son
Τιμαίου Βαρτιμαῖος, τυφλὸς προσαίτης,
of Timæus Bartimæus, a blind beggar,
ἐκάθητο παρὰ τὴν ὁδόν. **47** καὶ ἀκούσας
sat by the way. And hearing
ὅτι Ἰησοῦς ὁ Ναζαρηνός ἐστιν ἤρξατο
that Jesus the Nazarene it is(was) he began
κράζειν καὶ λέγειν· υἱὲ Δαυὶδ Ἰησοῦ,
to cry out and to say: Son of David Jesus,
ἐλέησόν με. **48** καὶ ἐπετίμων αὐτῷ πολλοὶ
pity me. And rebuked him many
ἵνα σιωπήσῃ· ὁ δὲ πολλῷ μᾶλλον ἔκραζεν·
that he should be quiet. But he much more cried out:
υἱὲ Δαυίδ, ἐλέησόν με. **49** καὶ στὰς
Son of David, pity me. And standing
ὁ Ἰησοῦς εἶπεν· φωνήσατε αὐτόν. καὶ
– Jesus said: Call him. And
φωνοῦσιν τὸν τυφλὸν λέγοντες αὐτῷ·
they call the blind man saying to him:
θάρσει, ἔγειρε, φωνεῖ σε. **50** ὁ δὲ
Be of good courage, rise, he calls thee. So he
ἀποβαλὼν τὸ ἱμάτιον αὐτοῦ ἀναπηδήσας ἦλθεν
throwing away the garment of him leaping up came
πρὸς τὸν Ἰησοῦν. **51** καὶ ἀποκριθεὶς αὐτῷ ὁ
to – Jesus. And answering him –
Ἰησοῦς εἶπεν· τί σοι θέλεις ποιήσω;
Jesus said: What for thee wishest thou I may do?

with, 40 but to sit at my right
or left is not for me to grant.
These places belong to
those for whom they have
been prepared."
41 When the ten heard
about this, they became indignant with James and
John. 42 Jesus called them
together and said, "You
know that those who are regarded as rulers of the Gentiles lord it over them, and
their high officials exercise
authority over them. 43 Not
so with you. Instead, whoever wants to become great
among you must be your
servant, 44 and whoever
wants to be first must be
slave of all. 45 For even the
Son of Man did not come to
be served, but to serve, and
to give his life as a ransom
for many."

Blind Bartimaeus Receives His Sight

46 Then they came to Jericho. As Jesus and his disciples, together with a large
crowd, were leaving the
city, a blind man, Barti-
maeus (that is, the Son of
Timaeus), was sitting by
the roadside begging.
47 When he heard that it was
Jesus of Nazareth, he be-
gan to shout, "Jesus, Son
of David, have mercy on
me!"
48 Many rebuked him and
told him to be quiet, but he
shouted all the more, "Son
of David, have mercy on
me!"
49 Jesus stopped and said,
"Call him."
So they called to the blind
man, "Cheer up! On your
feet! He's calling you."
50 Throwing his cloak aside,
he jumped to his feet and
came to Jesus.
51 "What do you want me
to do for you?" Jesus asked
him.

blind man said to him, "My
teacher,[d] let me see
again." 52 Jesus said to him,
"Go; your faith has made
you well." Immediately he
regained his sight and followed him on the way.

ὁ δὲ τυφλὸς εἶπεν αὐτῷ· ῥαββουνί, ἵνα
And the blind man said to him: Rabboni, that
ἀναβλέψω. 52 καὶ ὁ Ἰησοῦς εἶπεν αὐτῷ·
I may see again. And – Jesus said to him:
ὕπαγε, ἡ πίστις σου σέσωκέν σε. καὶ
Go, the faith of thee has healed thee. And
εὐθὺς ἀνέβλεψεν, καὶ ἠκολούθει αὐτῷ ἐν
immediately he saw again, and followed him in
τῇ ὁδῷ.
the way.

The blind man said,
"Rabbi, I want to see."
52 "Go," said Jesus,
"your faith has healed
you." Immediately he re-
ceived his sight and fol-
lowed Jesus along the road.

Chapter 11

Jesus' Triumphal Entry into Jerusalem

WHEN they were ap-
proaching Jerusa-
lem, at Bethphage and
Bethany, near the Mount of
Olives, he sent two of his
disciples 2 and said to them,
"Go into the village ahead
of you, and immediately as
you enter it, you will find
tied there a colt that has
never been ridden; untie it
and bring it. 3 If anyone
says to you, 'Why are you
doing this?' just say this,
'The Lord needs it and will
send it back here immedi-
ately.' " 4 They went away
and found a colt tied near a
door, outside in the street.
As they were untying it,
5 some of the bystanders
said to them, "What are
you doing, untying the
colt?" 6 They told them
what Jesus had said; and
they allowed them to take
it. 7 Then they brought the
colt to Jesus and threw
their cloaks on it; and he sat
on it. 8 Many people spread
their cloaks on the road,
and others spread leafy
branches that they had cut
in the fields. 9 Then those
who went ahead and those
who followed were shout-
ing,

"Hosanna!
Blessed is the one who comes in the name of the Lord!
10 Blessed is the coming kingdom of our ancestor David!
Hosanna in the highest heaven!"

11 Καὶ ὅτε ἐγγίζουσιν εἰς Ἱεροσόλυμα
And when they draw near to Jerusalem
εἰς Βηθφαγὴ καὶ Βηθανίαν πρὸς τὸ
to Bethphage and Bethany at the
ὄρος τῶν ἐλαιῶν, ἀποστέλλει δύο τῶν
mount of the olives, he sends two of the
μαθητῶν αὐτοῦ 2 καὶ λέγει αὐτοῖς· ὑπάγετε
disciples of him and tells them: Go ye
εἰς τὴν κώμην τὴν κατέναντι ὑμῶν, καὶ
into the village – opposite you, and
εὐθὺς εἰσπορευόμενοι εἰς αὐτὴν εὑρήσετε
immediately entering into it ye will find
πῶλον δεδεμένον ἐφ' ὃν οὐδεὶς οὔπω
a colt *having been* tied on which [1]no one [2]*not* yet
ἀνθρώπων ἐκάθισεν· λύσατε αὐτὸν καὶ
[3]of men [4]sat; loosen it and
φέρετε. 3 καὶ ἐάν τις ὑμῖν εἴπῃ· τί
bring. And if anyone to you says: Why
ποιεῖτε τοῦτο; εἴπατε· ὁ κύριος αὐτοῦ
do ye this? say: The Lord of it
χρείαν ἔχει, καὶ εὐθὺς αὐτὸν ἀποστέλλει
need has, and immediately it he sends
πάλιν ὧδε. 4 καὶ ἀπῆλθον καὶ εὗρον
again here. And they went and found
πῶλον δεδεμένον πρὸς θύραν ἔξω ἐπὶ
a colt *having been* tied at a door outside on
τοῦ ἀμφόδου, καὶ λύουσιν αὐτόν. 5 καὶ
the open street, and they loosen it. And
τινες τῶν ἐκεῖ ἑστηκότων ἔλεγον αὐτοῖς·
some of the [ones] there standing said to them:
τί ποιεῖτε λύοντες τὸν πῶλον; 6 οἱ δὲ
What do ye loosening the colt? And they
εἶπαν αὐτοῖς καθὼς εἶπεν ὁ Ἰησοῦς·
said to them as said – Jesus;
καὶ ἀφῆκαν αὐτούς. 7 καὶ φέρουσιν τὸν
and they let go them. And they bring the
πῶλον πρὸς τὸν Ἰησοῦν, καὶ ἐπιβάλλουσιν
colt to – Jesus, and they throw on
αὐτῷ τὰ ἱμάτια αὐτῶν, καὶ ἐκάθισεν
it the garments of them, and he sat
ἐπ' αὐτόν. 8 καὶ πολλοὶ τὰ ἱμάτια αὐτῶν
on it. And many the garments of them
ἔστρωσαν εἰς τὴν ὁδόν, ἄλλοι δὲ στιβάδας,
strewed in the way, and others wisps of twigs,
κόψαντες ἐκ τῶν ἀγρῶν. 9 καὶ οἱ
cutting out of the fields. And the [ones]
προάγοντες καὶ οἱ ἀκολουθοῦντες ἔκραζον·
going before and the [ones] following cried out:
ὡσαννά· εὐλογημένος ὁ ἐρχόμενος ἐν
Hosanna; blessed the [one] coming in
ὀνόματι κυρίου· 10 εὐλογημένη ἡ ἐρχομένη
[the] name of [the] Lord; blessed the coming
βασιλεία τοῦ πατρὸς ἡμῶν Δαυίδ· ὡσαννὰ
kingdom of the father of us David; Hosanna

Chapter 11

The Triumphal Entry

AS they approached Jeru-
salem and came to
Bethphage and Bethany at
the Mount of Olives, Jesus
sent two of his disciples,
2 saying to them, "Go to the
village ahead of you, and
just as you enter it, you will
find a colt tied there, which
no one has ever ridden. Untie it and bring it here. 3 If
anyone asks you, 'Why are
you doing this?' tell him,
'The Lord needs it and will
send it back here short-
ly.' "
4 They went and found a
colt outside in the street,
tied at a doorway. As they
untied it, 5 some people
standing there asked,
"What are you doing, untying that colt?" 6 They answered as Jesus had told
them to, and the people let
them go. 7 When they
brought the colt to Jesus
and threw their cloaks over
it, he sat on it. 8 Many people spread their cloaks on
the road, while others
spread branches they had
cut in the fields. 9 Those
who went ahead and those
who followed shouted,

"Hosanna![o]"

"Blessed is he who comes in the name of the Lord!"[p]

10 "Blessed is the coming kingdom of our father David!"

"Hosanna in the highest!"

[d] Aramaic *Rabbouni*

[o] 9 A Hebrew expression meaning "Save!" which became an exclamation of praise; also in verse 10

[p] 9 Psalm 118:25,26

11 Then he entered Je-
rusalem and went into the
temple; and when he had
looked around at every-
thing, as it was already late,
he went out to Bethany
with the twelve.

Jesus Curses the Fig Tree

12 On the following
day, when they came from
Bethany, he was hungry.
13 Seeing in the distance a
fig tree in leaf, he went to
see whether perhaps he
would find anything on it.
When he came to it, he
found nothing but leaves,
for it was not the season for
figs. 14 He said to it, "May
no one ever eat fruit from
you again." And his disciples heard it.

Jesus Cleanses the Temple

15 Then they came to
Jerusalem. And he entered
the temple and began to
drive out those who were
selling and those who were
buying in the temple, and
he overturned the tables of
the money changers and
the seats of those who sold
doves; 16 and he would not
allow anyone to carry anything through the temple.
17 He was teaching and saying, "Is it not written,
'My house shall be
called a house
of prayer for all
the nations'?
But you have made
it a den
of robbers."
18 And when the chief
priests and the scribes
heard it, they kept looking
for a way to kill him; for
they were afraid of him, because the whole crowd was
spellbound by his teaching.
19 And when evening came,
Jesus and his disciples[e]
went out of the city.

The Lesson from the Withered Fig Tree

20 In the morning as
they passed by, they saw
the fig tree withered away
to its roots. 21 Then Peter
remembered and said to
him, "Rabbi, look! The fig
tree that you cursed has
withered." 22 Jesus an-

[e] Gk *they*: other ancient authorities read *he*

ἐν τοῖς ὑψίστοις. 11 Καὶ εἰσῆλθεν εἰς
in the highest [places]. And he entered into
Ἱεροσόλυμα εἰς τὸ ἱερόν· καὶ περιβλεψάμενος
Jerusalem into the temple; and looking round at
πάντα, ὀψὲ ἤδη οὔσης τῆς ὥρας, ἐξῆλθεν
all things, [5]late [4]now [3]being [1]the [2]hour,[a] he went forth
εἰς Βηθανίαν μετὰ τῶν δώδεκα.
to Bethany with the twelve.
12 Καὶ τῇ ἐπαύριον ἐξελθόντων αὐτῶν
And on the morrow going forth them[a]
= as they went forth
ἀπὸ Βηθανίας ἐπείνασεν. 13 καὶ ἰδὼν
from Bethany he hungered. And seeing
συκῆν ἀπὸ μακρόθεν ἔχουσαν φύλλα ἦλθεν
a fig-tree from afar having leaves he came
εἰ ἄρα τι εὑρήσει ἐν αὐτῇ, καὶ ἐλθὼν
if perhaps something he will find in it, and coming
ἐπ' αὐτὴν οὐδὲν εὗρεν εἰ μὴ φύλλα·
upon it nothing he found except leaves;
ὁ γὰρ καιρὸς οὐκ ἦν σύκων. 14 καὶ
for the time was not of figs. And
ἀποκριθεὶς εἶπεν αὐτῇ· μηκέτι εἰς τὸν
answering he said to it: No more to the
αἰῶνα ἐκ σοῦ μηδεὶς καρπὸν φάγοι.
age of thee no one fruit may eat.
= May no one eat fruit of thee for ever.
καὶ ἤκουον οἱ μαθηταὶ αὐτοῦ. 15 Καὶ
And [4]heard [1]the [2]disciples [3]of him. And
ἔρχονται εἰς Ἱεροσόλυμα. Καὶ εἰσελθὼν
they come to Jerusalem. And entering
εἰς τὸ ἱερὸν ἤρξατο ἐκβάλλειν τοὺς
into the temple he began to cast out the [ones]
πωλοῦντας καὶ τοὺς ἀγοράζοντας ἐν τῷ
selling and the [ones] buying in the
ἱερῷ, καὶ τὰς τραπέζας τῶν κολλυβιστῶν
temple, and the tables of the moneychangers
καὶ τὰς καθέδρας τῶν πωλούντων τὰς
and the seats of the [ones] selling the
περιστερὰς κατέστρεψεν, 16 καὶ οὐκ ἤφιεν
doves he overturned, and did not permit
ἵνα τις διενέγκῃ σκεῦος διὰ τοῦ
that anyone should carry *through* a vessel through the
ἱεροῦ, 17 καὶ ἐδίδασκεν καὶ ἔλεγεν αὐτοῖς· οὐ
temple, and taught and said to them: Not
γέγραπται ὅτι ὁ οἶκός μου οἶκος προσευχῆς
has it been written that the house of me a house of prayer
κληθήσεται πᾶσιν τοῖς ἔθνεσιν; ὑμεῖς δὲ
shall be called for all the nations ? but ye
πεποιήκατε αὐτὸν σπήλαιον λῃστῶν. 18 καὶ
have made it a den of robbers. And
ἤκουσαν οἱ ἀρχιερεῖς καὶ οἱ γραμματεῖς,
[6]heard [1]the [2]chief priests [3]and [4]the [5]scribes,
καὶ ἐζήτουν πῶς αὐτὸν ἀπολέσωσιν·
and they sought how him they might destroy;
ἐφοβοῦντο γὰρ αὐτόν, πᾶς γὰρ ὁ ὄχλος
for they feared him, for all the crowd
ἐξεπλήσσετο ἐπὶ τῇ διδαχῇ αὐτοῦ. 19 Καὶ
was astounded at the teaching of him. And
ὅταν ὀψὲ ἐγένετο, ἐξεπορεύοντο ἔξω τῆς
when late it became, they went forth outside the
πόλεως. 20 Καὶ παραπορευόμενοι πρωῒ
city. And passing along early
εἶδον τὴν συκῆν ἐξηραμμένην ἐκ ῥιζῶν.
they saw the fig-tree *having been* withered from [the] roots.
21 καὶ ἀναμνησθεὶς ὁ Πέτρος λέγει αὐτῷ·
And [2]remembering – [1]Peter says to him:
ῥαββί, ἴδε ἡ συκῆ ἣν κατηράσω
Rabbi, behold[,] the fig-tree which thou cursedst

11 Jesus entered Jerusa-
lem and went to the temple.
He looked around at everything, but since it was already late, he went out to
Bethany with the Twelve.

Jesus Clears the Temple

12 The next day as they
were leaving Bethany,
Jesus was hungry. 13 Seeing
in the distance a fig tree in
leaf, he went to find out if it
had any fruit. When he
reached it, he found nothing but leaves, because it
was not the season for figs.
14 Then he said to the tree,
"May no one ever eat fruit
from you again." And his
disciples heard him say it.
15 On reaching Jerusalem,
Jesus entered the temple
area and began driving out
those who were buying and
selling there. He over-
turned the tables of the
money changers and the
benches of those selling
doves, 16 and would not allow anyone to carry mer-
chandise through the tem-
ple courts. 17 And as he
taught them, he said, "Is it
not written:

" 'My house will be
called
a house of prayer for
all nations'[q]?

But you have made it 'a den
of robbers.'[r]"
18 The chief priests and
the teachers of the law
heard this and began looking for a way to kill him, for
they feared him, because
the whole crowd was
amazed at his teaching.
19 When evening came,
they[s] went out of the city.

The Withered Fig Tree

20 In the morning, as they
went along, they saw the fig
tree withered from the
roots. 21 Peter remembered
and said to Jesus, "Rabbi,
look! The fig tree you
cursed has withered!"

[q] *17* Isaiah 56:7
[r] *17* Jer. 7:11
[s] *19* Some early manuscripts *he*

swered them, "Have[f] faith
in God. 23 Truly I tell you, if
you say to this mountain,
'Be taken up and thrown
into the sea,' and if you do
not doubt in your heart, but
believe that what you say
will come to pass, it will be
done for you. 24 So I tell
you, whatever you ask for
in prayer, believe that you
have received[g] it, and it
will be yours.
25 "Whenever you
stand praying, forgive, if
you have anything against
anyone; so that your Fa-
ther in heaven may also forgive you your tres-
passes."[h]

Jesus' Authority Is Questioned

27 Again they came to
Jerusalem. As he was walking in the temple, the chief
priests, the scribes, and the
elders came to him 28 and
said, "By what authority
are you doing these things?
Who gave you this authority to do them?" 29 Jesus
said to them, "I will ask you
one question; answer me,
and I will tell you by what
authority I do these things.
30 Did the baptism of John
come from heaven, or was
it of human origin? Answer
me." 31 They argued with
one another, "If we say,
'From heaven,' he will say,
'Why then did you not be-
lieve him?' 32 But shall we
say, 'Of human origin'?"—
they were afraid of the
crowd, for all regarded
John as truly a prophet.
33 So they answered Jesus,
"We do not know." And
Jesus said to them, "Nei-
ther will I tell you by what
authority I am doing these
things."

[f] Other ancient authorities read *"If you have*

[g] Other ancient authorities read *are receiving*

[h] Other ancient authorities add verse 26. *"But if you do not forgive, neither will your Father in heaven forgive your trespasses."*

ἐξήρανται. **22** καὶ ἀποκριθεὶς ὁ Ἰησοῦς λέγει
has been withered. And answering – Jesus says
αὐτοῖς· ἔχετε πίστιν θεοῦ. **23** ἀμὴν λέγω ὑμῖν
to them: Have [the] faith of God. Truly I tell you
ὅτι ὃς ἂν εἴπῃ τῷ ὄρει τούτῳ· ἄρθητι
that whoever says – mountain to this: Be thou taken
καὶ βλήθητι εἰς τὴν θάλασσαν, καὶ μὴ
and be thou cast into the sea, and not
διακριθῇ ἐν τῇ καρδίᾳ αὐτοῦ ἀλλὰ πιστεύῃ
doubts in the heart of him but believes
ὅτι ὃ λαλεῖ γίνεται, ἔσται αὐτῷ. **24** διὰ
that what he says happens, it will be to him.[c] There-
= he will have it.
τοῦτο λέγω ὑμῖν, πάντα ὅσα προσεύχεσθε
fore I tell you, all things which ye pray
καὶ αἰτεῖσθε, πιστεύετε ὅτι ἐλάβετε, καὶ
and ask, believe that ye received, and
ἔσται ὑμῖν. **25** καὶ ὅταν στήκετε
it will be to you.[c] And when ye stand
= ye will have it.
προσευχόμενοι, ἀφίετε εἴ τι ἔχετε κατά
praying, forgive if anything ye have against
τινος, ἵνα καὶ ὁ πατὴρ ὑμῶν ὁ ἐν τοῖς
anyone, that also the Father of you – in the
οὐρανοῖς ἀφῇ ὑμῖν τὰ παραπτώματα ὑμῶν.‡
heavens may forgive you the trespasses of you.
27 Καὶ ἔρχονται πάλιν εἰς Ἰεροσόλυμα.
And they come again to Jerusalem.
καὶ ἐν τῷ ἱερῷ περιπατοῦντος αὐτοῦ
And in the temple walking him[a]
=as he walked
ἔρχονται πρὸς αὐτὸν οἱ ἀρχιερεῖς καὶ οἱ
come to him the chief priests and the
γραμματεῖς καὶ οἱ πρεσβύτεροι, **28** καὶ
scribes and the elders, and
ἔλεγον αὐτῷ· ἐν ποίᾳ ἐξουσίᾳ ταῦτα
said to him: By what authority these things
ποιεῖς; ἢ τίς σοι ἔδωκεν τὴν ἐξουσίαν
doest thou? or who thee gave – authority
ταύτην ἵνα ταῦτα ποιῇς; **29** ὁ δὲ Ἰησοῦς
this that these things thou mayest do? – And Jesus
εἶπεν αὐτοῖς· ἐπερωτήσω ὑμᾶς ἕνα λόγον,
said to them: I will question you one word,
καὶ ἀποκρίθητέ μοι, καὶ ἐρῶ ὑμῖν ἐν
and answer ye me, and I will tell you by
ποίᾳ ἐξουσίᾳ ταῦτα ποιῶ. **30** τὸ βάπτισμα
what authority these things I do. The baptism
τὸ Ἰωάννου ἐξ οὐρανοῦ ἦν ἢ ἐξ ἀνθρώπων;
– of John of heaven was it or of men?
ἀποκρίθητέ μοι. **31** καὶ διελογίζοντο πρὸς
answer ye me. And they debated with
ἑαυτοὺς λέγοντες· ἐὰν εἴπωμεν· ἐξ οὐρανοῦ,
themselves saying: If we say: Of heaven,
ἐρεῖ· διὰ τί οὖν οὐκ ἐπιστεύσατε αὐτῷ;
he will say: Why then did ye not believe him?
32 ἀλλὰ εἴπωμεν· ἐξ ἀνθρώπων;—ἐφοβοῦντο
But may we say: Of men? — they feared
τὸν ὄχλον· ἅπαντες γὰρ εἶχον τὸν Ἰωάννην
the crowd; for all men held – John
ὄντως ὅτι προφήτης ἦν. **33** καὶ
[3]really [1]that [4]a prophet [2]he was. And
ἀποκριθέντες τῷ Ἰησοῦ λέγουσιν· οὐκ
answering – Jesus they say: not
οἴδαμεν. καὶ ὁ Ἰησοῦς λέγει αὐτοῖς·
We know. And – Jesus says to them:
οὐδὲ ἐγὼ λέγω ὑμῖν ἐν ποίᾳ ἐξουσίᾳ
Neither I tell you by what authority

‡ Verse 26 omitted by Nestle; *cf.* NIV footnote.

22 "Have[t] faith in God,"
Jesus answered. 23 "I tell
you the truth, if anyone
says to this mountain, 'Go,
throw yourself into the
sea,' and does not doubt in
his heart but believes that
what he says will happen, it
will be done for him.
24 Therefore I tell you,
whatever you ask for in
prayer, believe that you
have received it, and it will
be yours. 25 And when you
stand praying, if you hold
anything against anyone,
forgive him, so that your
Father in heaven may for-
give you your sins.[u]"

The Authority of Jesus Questioned

27 They arrived again in
Jerusalem, and while Jesus
was walking in the temple
courts, the chief priests,
the teachers of the law and
the elders came to him.
28 "By what authority are
you doing these things?"
they asked. "And who
gave you authority to do
this?"
29 Jesus replied, "I will
ask you one question. An-
swer me, and I will tell you
by what authority I am doing these things. 30 John's
baptism—was it from
heaven, or from men? Tell
me!"
31 They discussed it
among themselves and
said, "If we say, 'From
heaven,' he will ask, 'Then
why didn't you believe
him?' 32 But if we say,
'From men' . . . ." (They
feared the people, for everyone held that John really was a prophet.)
33 So they answered
Jesus, "We don't know."
Jesus said, "Neither will
I tell you by what authority
I am doing these things."

[t] 22 Some early manuscripts *If you have*

[u] 25 Some manuscripts *sins. 26 But if you do not forgive, neither will your Father who is in heaven forgive your sins.*

Chapter 12

The Parable of the Wicked Tenants

THEN he began to speak to them in parables. "A man planted a vineyard, put a fence around it, dug a pit for the wine press, and built a watchtower; then he leased it to tenants and went to another country. 2When the season came, he sent a slave to the tenants to collect from them his share of the produce of the vineyard. 3But they seized him, and beat him, and sent him away empty-handed. 4And again he sent another slave to them; this one they beat over the head and insulted. 5Then he sent another, and that one they killed. And so it was with many others; some they beat, and others they killed. 6He had still one other, a beloved son. Finally he sent him to them, saying, 'They will respect my son.' 7But those tenants said to one another, 'This is the heir; come, let us kill him, and the inheritance will be ours.' 8So they seized him, killed him, and threw him out of the vineyard. 9What then will the owner of the vineyard do? He will come and destroy the tenants and give the vineyard to others. 10Have you not read this scripture:

'The stone that the builders rejected
has become the cornerstone;[i]
11 this was the Lord's doing,
and it is amazing in our eyes'?"

12 When they realized that he had told this parable against them, they wanted to arrest him, but they

[i] Or *keystone*

ταῦτα ποιῶ. **12** Καὶ ἤρξατο αὐτοῖς ἐν
these things I do. And he began to them in
παραβολαῖς λαλεῖν. ἀμπελῶνα ἄνθρωπος
parables to speak. ³a vineyard ¹A man
ἐφύτευσεν, καὶ περιέθηκεν φραγμὸν καὶ ὤρυξεν
²planted, and put round [it] a hedge and dug
ὑπολήνιον καὶ ᾠκοδόμησεν πύργον, καὶ
a winepress and built a tower, and
ἐξέδοτο αὐτὸν γεωργοῖς, καὶ ἀπεδήμησεν.
let out it to husbandmen, and went away.
2 καὶ ἀπέστειλεν πρὸς τοὺς γεωργοὺς τῷ
And he sent to the husbandmen at the
καιρῷ δοῦλον, ἵνα παρὰ τῶν γεωργῶν
time a slave, that from the husbandmen
λάβῃ ἀπὸ τῶν καρπῶν τοῦ ἀμπελῶνος·
he might receive from(of) the fruits of the vineyard;
3 καὶ λαβόντες αὐτὸν ἔδειραν καὶ ἀπέστειλαν
And taking him they beat and sent away
κενόν. **4** καὶ πάλιν ἀπέστειλεν πρὸς αὐτοὺς
empty. And again he sent to them
ἄλλον δοῦλον· κἀκεῖνον ἐκεφαλαίωσαν καὶ
another slave; and that one they wounded in the head and
ἠτίμασαν. **5** καὶ ἄλλον ἀπέστειλεν· κἀκεῖνον
insulted. And another he sent; and that one
ἀπέκτειναν, καὶ πολλοὺς ἄλλους, οὓς μὲν
they killed, and many others, ²some
δέροντες, οὓς δὲ ἀποκτέννοντες. **6** ἔτι ἕνα
¹beating, ²others ¹killing. Still one
εἶχεν, υἱὸν ἀγαπητόν· ἀπέστειλεν αὐτὸν
he had, a son beloved; he sent him
ἔσχατον πρὸς αὐτοὺς λέγων ὅτι ἐντραπήσονται
last to them saying[,] – They will reverence
τὸν υἱόν μου. **7** ἐκεῖνοι δὲ οἱ γεωργοὶ
the son of me. But those – husbandmen
πρὸς ἑαυτοὺς εἶπαν ὅτι οὗτός ἐστιν ὁ
to themselves said[,] – This is the
κληρονόμος· δεῦτε ἀποκτείνωμεν αὐτόν, καὶ
heir; come[,] let us kill him, and
ἡμῶν ἔσται ἡ κληρονομία. **8** καὶ λαβόντες
of us will be the inheritance. And taking
ἀπέκτειναν αὐτόν, καὶ ἐξέβαλον αὐτὸν
they killed him, and cast *out* him
ἔξω τοῦ ἀμπελῶνος. **9** τί ποιήσει ὁ
outside the vineyard. What will do the
κύριος τοῦ ἀμπελῶνος; ἐλεύσεται καὶ
lord of the vineyard ? he will come and
ἀπολέσει τοὺς γεωργούς, καὶ δώσει τὸν
will destroy the husbandmen, and will give the
ἀμπελῶνα ἄλλοις. **10** οὐδὲ τὴν γραφὴν
vineyard to others. ²not – ⁴scripture
ταύτην ἀνέγνωτε· λίθον ὃν ἀπεδοκίμασαν
³this ¹Read ye : A stone which ³rejected
οἱ οἰκοδομοῦντες, οὗτος ἐγενήθη εἰς κεφαλὴν
¹the [ones] ²building, this became for head
γωνίας· **11** παρὰ κυρίου ἐγένετο αὕτη,
of corner; from [the] Lord was this,
καὶ ἔστιν θαυμαστὴ ἐν ὀφθαλμοῖς ἡμῶν;
and it is marvellous in eyes of us ?
12 Καὶ ἐζήτουν αὐτὸν κρατῆσαι, καὶ
And they sought him to seize, and
ἐφοβήθησαν τὸν ὄχλον· ἔγνωσαν γὰρ
feared the crowd; for they knew
ὅτι πρὸς αὐτοὺς τὴν παραβολὴν
that to them the parable

Chapter 12

The Parable of the Tenants

HE then began to speak to them in parables: "A man planted a vineyard. He put a wall around it, dug a pit for the winepress and built a watchtower. Then he rented the vineyard to some farmers and went away on a journey. 2At harvest time he sent a servant to the tenants to collect from them some of the fruit of the vineyard. 3But they seized him, beat him and sent him away empty-handed. 4Then he sent another servant to them; they struck this man on the head and treated him shamefully. 5He sent still another, and that one they killed. He sent many others; some of them they beat, others they killed.

6"He had one left to send, a son, whom he loved. He sent him last of all, saying, 'They will respect my son.'

7"But the tenants said to one another, 'This is the heir. Come, let's kill him, and the inheritance will be ours.' 8So they took him and killed him, and threw him out of the vineyard.

9"What then will the owner of the vineyard do? He will come and kill those tenants and give the vineyard to others. 10Haven't you read this scripture:

" 'The stone the builders rejected
has become the capstone[v];
11the Lord has done this,
and it is marvelous in our eyes'[w]?"

12Then they looked for a way to arrest him because they knew he had spoken the parable against them.

[v] *10* Or *cornerstone*
[w] *11* Psalm 118:22,23

feared the crowd. So they left him and went away.

The Question about Paying Taxes

13 Then they sent to him some Pharisees and some Herodians to trap him in what he said. 14 And they came and said to him, "Teacher, we know that you are sincere, and show deference to no one; for you do not regard people with partiality, but teach the way of God in accordance with truth. Is it lawful to pay taxes to the emperor, or not? 15 Should we pay them, or should we not?" But knowing their hypocrisy, he said to them, "Why are you putting me to the test? Bring me a denarius and let me see it." 16 And they brought one. Then he said to them, "Whose head is this, and whose title?" They answered, "The emperor's." 17 Jesus said to them, "Give to the emperor the things that are the emperor's, and to God the things that are God's." And they were utterly amazed at him.

The Question about the Resurrection

18 Some Sadducees, who say there is no resurrection, came to him and asked him a question, saying, 19 "Teacher, Moses wrote for us that 'if a man's brother dies, leaving a wife but no child, the man[j] shall marry the widow and raise up children for his brother.' 20 There were seven brothers; the first married and, when he died, left no children; 21 and the second married her and died, leaving no children; and the third likewise; 22 none of the seven left children. Last of all the woman herself died. 23 In the resurrection[k] whose wife will she

[j] Gk *his brother*
[k] Other ancient authorities add *when they rise*

εἶπεν. καὶ ἀφέντες αὐτὸν ἀπῆλθον.
he told. And leaving him they went away.

13 Καὶ ἀποστέλλουσιν πρὸς αὐτόν τινας τῶν
And they send to him some of the

Φαρισαίων καὶ τῶν Ἡρῳδιανῶν ἵνα αὐτὸν
Pharisees and of the Herodians that him

ἀγρεύσωσιν λόγῳ. 14 καὶ ἐλθόντες
they might catch in a word. And coming

λέγουσιν αὐτῷ· διδάσκαλε, οἴδαμεν ὅτι
they say to him: Teacher, we know that

ἀληθὴς εἶ καὶ οὐ μέλει σοι περὶ
true thou art and it matters not to thee about

οὐδενός· οὐ γὰρ βλέπεις εἰς πρόσωπον
no(any)one; for thou lookest not at [the] face

ἀνθρώπων, ἀλλ' ἐπ' ἀληθείας τὴν ὁδὸν
of men, but on(in) truth the way

τοῦ θεοῦ διδάσκεις· ἔξεστιν δοῦναι κῆνσον
– of God teachest; is it lawful to give tribute

Καίσαρι ἢ οὔ; δῶμεν ἢ μὴ δῶμεν;
to Cæsar or no? may we give or may we not give?

15 ὁ δὲ εἰδὼς αὐτῶν τὴν ὑπόκρισιν εἶπεν
But he knowing of them the hypocrisy said

αὐτοῖς· τί με πειράζετε; φέρετέ μοι
to them: Why me tempt ye? bring me

δηνάριον ἵνα ἴδω. 16 οἱ δὲ ἤνεγκαν. καὶ
a denarius that I may see. And they brought. And

λέγει αὐτοῖς· τίνος ἡ εἰκὼν αὕτη καὶ ἡ
he says to them: Of whom – image this and –

ἐπιγραφή; οἱ δὲ εἶπαν αὐτῷ· Καίσαρος.
superscription? And they tell him: Of Cæsar.

17 ὁ δὲ Ἰησοῦς εἶπεν αὐτοῖς· τὰ Καίσαρος
– So Jesus said to them: The things of Cæsar

ἀπόδοτε Καίσαρι καὶ τὰ τοῦ θεοῦ τῷ
render to Cæsar and the things – of God –

θεῷ. καὶ ἐξεθαύμαζον ἐπ' αὐτῷ.
to God. And they marvelled at him.

18 Καὶ ἔρχονται Σαδδουκαῖοι πρὸς αὐτόν,
And come Sadducees to him,

οἵτινες λέγουσιν ἀνάστασιν μὴ εἶναι, καὶ
who say resurrection not to be, and
= that there is no resurrection,

ἐπηρώτων αὐτὸν λέγοντες· 19 διδάσκαλε,
questioned him saying: Teacher,

Μωϋσῆς ἔγραψεν ἡμῖν ὅτι ἐάν τινος
Moses wrote to us that if of anyone

ἀδελφὸς ἀποθάνῃ καὶ καταλίπῃ γυναῖκα
a brother should die and leave behind a wife

καὶ μὴ ἀφῇ τέκνον, ἵνα λάβῃ ὁ ἀδελφὸς
and leave not a child, – [4]may take [1]the [2]brother

αὐτοῦ τὴν γυναῖκα καὶ ἐξαναστήσῃ σπέρμα
[3]of him the wife and may raise up seed

τῷ ἀδελφῷ αὐτοῦ. 20 ἑπτὰ ἀδελφοὶ ἦσαν·
to the brother of him. Seven brothers there were;

καὶ ὁ πρῶτος ἔλαβεν γυναῖκα, καὶ
and the first took a wife, and

ἀποθνῄσκων οὐκ ἀφῆκεν σπέρμα· 21 καὶ
dying left not seed; and

ὁ δεύτερος ἔλαβεν αὐτήν, καὶ ἀπέθανεν μὴ
the second took her, and died not

καταλιπὼν σπέρμα· καὶ ὁ τρίτος ὡσαύτως·
leaving behind seed; and the third similarly;

22 καὶ οἱ ἑπτὰ οὐκ ἀφῆκαν σπέρμα.
and the seven left not seed.

ἔσχατον πάντων καὶ ἡ γυνὴ ἀπέθανεν.
Last of all also the wife died.

23 ἐν τῇ ἀναστάσει, ὅταν ἀναστῶσιν,
In the resurrection, when they rise again,

But they were afraid of the crowd; so they left him and went away.

Paying Taxes to Caesar

13 Later they sent some of the Pharisees and Herodians to Jesus to catch him in his words. 14 They came to him and said, "Teacher, we know you are a man of integrity. You aren't swayed by men, because you pay no attention to who they are; but you teach the way of God in accordance with the truth. Is it right to pay taxes to Caesar or not? 15 Should we pay or shouldn't we?"

But Jesus knew their hypocrisy. "Why are you trying to trap me?" he asked. "Bring me a denarius and let me look at it." 16 They brought the coin, and he asked them, "Whose portrait is this? And whose inscription?"

"Caesar's," they replied.

17 Then Jesus said to them, "Give to Caesar what is Caesar's and to God what is God's."

And they were amazed at him.

Marriage at the Resurrection

18 Then the Sadducees, who say there is no resurrection, came to him with a question. 19 "Teacher," they said, "Moses wrote for us that if a man's brother dies and leaves a wife but no children, the man must marry the widow and have children for his brother. 20 Now there were seven brothers. The first one married and died without leaving any children. 21 The second one married the widow, but he also died, leaving no child. It was the same with the third. 22 In fact, none of the seven left any children. Last of all, the woman died too. 23 At the resurrection[x] whose

[x] 23 Some manuscripts *resurrection, when men rise from the dead,*

be? For the seven had married her."
24 Jesus said to them,
"Is not this the reason you
are wrong, that you know
neither the scriptures nor
the power of God? 25 For
when they rise from the
dead, they neither marry
nor are given in marriage,
but are like angels in heav-
en. 26 And as for the dead
being raised, have you not
read in the book of Moses,
in the story about the bush,
how God said to him, 'I am
the God of Abraham, the
God of Isaac, and the God
of Jacob'? 27 He is God not
of the dead, but of the living; you are quite wrong."

The First Commandment

28 One of the scribes
came near and heard them
disputing with one another,
and seeing that he an-
swered them well, he asked
him, "Which command-
ment is the first of all?"
29 Jesus answered, "The
first is, 'Hear, O Israel: the
Lord our God, the Lord is
one; 30 you shall love the
Lord your God with all
your heart, and with all
your soul, and with all your
mind, and with all your
strength.' 31 The second is
this, 'You shall love your
neighbor as yourself.'
There is no other com-
mandment greater than
these." 32 Then the scribe
said to him, "You are right,
Teacher; you have truly
said that 'he is one, and besides him there is no other';
33 and 'to love him with all
the heart, and with all the
understanding, and with all
the strength,' and 'to love
one's neighbor as
oneself,'—this is much

τίνος αὐτῶν ἔσται γυνή; οἱ γὰρ ἑπτὰ
of which of them will she be wife? for the seven
ἔσχον αὐτὴν γυναῖκα. 24 ἔφη αὐτοῖς ὁ
had her [as] wife. Said to them –
Ἰησοῦς· οὐ διὰ τοῦτο πλανᾶσθε μὴ
Jesus: [3]not [4]therefore [1]Do [2]ye [5]err not
εἰδότες τὰς γραφὰς μηδὲ τὴν δύναμιν
knowing the scriptures nor the power
τοῦ θεοῦ; 25 ὅταν γὰρ ἐκ νεκρῶν
– of God? for when out of [the] dead
ἀναστῶσιν, οὔτε γαμοῦσιν οὔτε γαμίζονται,
they rise again, they neither marry nor are given in marriage,
ἀλλ' εἰσὶν ὡς ἄγγελοι ἐν τοῖς οὐρανοῖς.
but are as angels in the heavens.
26 περὶ δὲ τῶν νεκρῶν ὅτι ἐγείρονται,
But concerning the dead that they are raised,
οὐκ ἀνέγνωτε ἐν τῇ βίβλῳ Μωϋσέως ἐπὶ
did ye not read in the roll of Moses at
τοῦ βάτου πῶς εἶπεν αὐτῷ ὁ θεὸς λέγων·
the bush how said to him – God saying:
ἐγὼ ὁ θεὸς Ἀβραὰμ καὶ θεὸς Ἰσαὰκ
I [am] the God of Abraham and God of Isaac
καὶ θεὸς Ἰακώβ; 27 οὐκ ἔστιν θεὸς
and God of Jacob? he is not God
νεκρῶν ἀλλὰ ζώντων. πολὺ πλανᾶσθε.
of dead [persons] but of living [ones]. Much ye err.
28 Καὶ προσελθὼν εἷς τῶν γραμματέων,
And [4]approaching [1]one [2]of the [3]scribes,
ἀκούσας αὐτῶν συζητούντων, εἰδὼς ὅτι
hearing them debating, knowing that
καλῶς ἀπεκρίθη αὐτοῖς, ἐπηρώτησεν αὐτόν·
well he answered them, questioned him:
ποία ἐστὶν ἐντολὴ πρώτη πάντων;
What is [the] commandment first of all?
29 ἀπεκρίθη ὁ Ἰησοῦς ὅτι πρώτη ἐστίν·
Answered – Jesus[,] – [The] first is:
ἄκουε, Ἰσραήλ, κύριος ὁ θεὸς ἡμῶν κύριος
Hear, Israel, Lord the God of us Lord
= The Lord our God is one Lord,
εἷς ἐστιν, 30 καὶ ἀγαπήσεις κύριον τὸν
one is, and thou shalt love Lord the
θεόν σου ἐξ ὅλης τῆς καρδίας σου καὶ
God of thee from(with) all the heart of thee and
ἐξ ὅλης τῆς ψυχῆς σου καὶ ἐξ ὅλης
with all the soul of thee and with all
τῆς διανοίας σου καὶ ἐξ ὅλης τῆς ἰσχύος
the mind of thee and with all the strength
σου. 31 δευτέρα αὕτη· ἀγαπήσεις τὸν
of thee. [The] second [is] this: Thou shalt love the
πλησίον σου ὡς σεαυτόν. μείζων τούτων
neighbour of thee as thyself. Greater [than] these
ἄλλη ἐντολὴ οὐκ ἔστιν. 32 καὶ εἶπεν
other commandment there is not. And said
αὐτῷ ὁ γραμματεύς· καλῶς, διδάσκαλε, ἐπ'
to him the scribe: Well, teacher, on(in)
ἀληθείας εἶπες ὅτι εἷς ἐστιν καὶ οὐκ
truth thou sayest that one there is and not
ἔστιν ἄλλος πλὴν αὐτοῦ· 33 καὶ τὸ
there is another besides him; and –
ἀγαπᾶν αὐτὸν ἐξ ὅλης τῆς καρδίας καὶ ἐξ
to love him with all the heart and with
ὅλης τῆς συνέσεως καὶ ἐξ ὅλης τῆς
all the understanding and with all the
ἰσχύος, καὶ τὸ ἀγαπᾶν τὸν πλησίον ὡς
strength, and – to love the(one's) neighbour as

wife will she be, since the
seven were married to
her?"
24 Jesus replied, "Are you
not in error because you do
not know the Scriptures or
the power of God? 25 When
the dead rise, they will neither marry nor be given in
marriage; they will be like
the angels in heaven.
26 Now about the dead rising—have you not read in
the book of Moses, in the
account of the bush, how
God said to him, 'I am the
God of Abraham, the God
of Isaac, and the God of Jacob'[y]? 27 He is not the God
of the dead, but of the living. You are badly mistak-
en!"

The Greatest Commandment

28 One of the teachers of
the law came and heard
them debating. Noticing
that Jesus had given them a
good answer, he asked
him, "Of all the command-
ments, which is the most
important?"
29 "The most important
one," answered Jesus, "is
this: 'Hear, O Israel, the
Lord our God, the Lord is
one.[z] 30 Love the Lord
your God with all your
heart and with all your soul
and with all your mind and
with all your strength.'[a]
31 The second is this: 'Love
your neighbor as your-
self.'[b] There is no commandment greater than
these."
32 "Well said, teacher,"
the man replied. "You are
right in saying that God is
one and there is no other
but him. 33 To love him with
all your heart, with all your
understanding and with all
your strength, and to love
your neighbor as yourself is

[y] *26* Exodus 3:6
[z] *29* Or *the Lord our God is one Lord*
[a] *30* Deut. 6:4,5
[b] *31* Lev. 19:18

more important than all
whole burnt offerings and
sacrifices." 34 When Jesus
saw that he answered wisely, he said to him, "You are
not far from the kingdom of
God." After that no one
dared to ask him any question.

The Question about David's Son

35 While Jesus was
teaching in the temple, he
said, "How can the scribes
say that the Messiah[l] is
the son of David? 36 David
himself, by the Holy Spirit,
declared,
'The Lord said to my
Lord,
"Sit at my right hand,
until I put your
enemies under
your feet." '
37 David himself calls him
Lord; so how can he be his
son?" And the large crowd
was listening to him with
delight.

Jesus Denounces the Scribes

38 As he taught, he said,
"Beware of the scribes,
who like to walk around in
long robes, and to be greeted with respect in the marketplaces, 39 and to have
the best seats in the synagogues and places of honor
at banquets! 40 They devour
widows' houses and for the
sake of appearance say
long prayers. They will receive the greater condem-
nation."

The Widow's Offering

41 He sat down oppo-
site the treasury, and
watched the crowd putting
money into the treasury.
Many rich people put in
large sums. 42 A poor widow came and put in two
small copper coins, which
are worth a penny. 43 Then
he called his disciples and
said to them, "Truly I tell
you, this poor widow has
put in more than all those

[l] Or *the Christ*

ἑαυτὸν περισσότερόν ἐστιν πάντων τῶν
himself more is [than] all the
ὁλοκαυτωμάτων καὶ θυσιῶν. 34 καὶ ὁ
burnt offerings and sacrifices. And –
Ἰησοῦς, ἰδὼν αὐτὸν ὅτι νουνεχῶς ἀπεκρίθη,
Jesus, seeing him that sensibly he answered,
εἶπεν αὐτῷ· οὐ μακρὰν εἶ ἀπὸ τῆς
said to him: Not far thou art from the
βασιλείας τοῦ θεοῦ. καὶ οὐδεὶς οὐκέτι
kingdom – of God. And no one no(any) more
ἐτόλμα αὐτὸν ἐπερωτῆσαι.
dared him to question.
35 Καὶ ἀποκριθεὶς ὁ Ἰησοῦς ἔλεγεν
And answering – Jesus said
διδάσκων ἐν τῷ ἱερῷ· πῶς λέγουσιν οἱ
teaching in the temple: How say the
γραμματεῖς ὅτι ὁ χριστὸς υἱὸς Δαυίδ
scribes that the Christ son of David
ἐστιν; 36 αὐτὸς Δαυὶδ εἶπεν ἐν τῷ πνεύματι
is? himself David said by the Spirit
τῷ ἁγίῳ· εἶπεν κύριος τῷ κυρίῳ μου·
– Holy: said [the] LORD to the Lord of me:
κάθου ἐκ δεξιῶν μου ἕως ἂν θῶ τοὺς
Sit at [the] right [hand] of me until I put the
ἐχθρούς σου ὑποκάτω τῶν ποδῶν σου.
enemies of thee under the feet of thee.
37 αὐτὸς Δαυὶδ λέγει αὐτὸν κύριον, καὶ
himself David says(calls) him Lord, and
πόθεν αὐτοῦ ἐστιν υἱός;
whence of him is he son ?
Καὶ ὁ πολὺς ὄχλος ἤκουεν αὐτοῦ
And the much crowd heard him
ἡδέως. 38 Καὶ ἐν τῇ διδαχῇ αὐτοῦ
gladly. And in the teaching of him
ἔλεγεν· βλέπετε ἀπὸ τῶν γραμματέων
he said: Beware from(of) the scribes
τῶν θελόντων ἐν στολαῖς περιπατεῖν καὶ
the [ones] wishing in robes to walk about and
ἀσπασμοὺς ἐν ταῖς ἀγοραῖς 39 καὶ
greetings in the marketplaces and
πρωτοκαθεδρίας ἐν ταῖς συναγωγαῖς καὶ
chief seats in the synagogues and
πρωτοκλισίας ἐν τοῖς δείπνοις· 40 οἱ
chief places in the dinners; the [ones]
κατέσθοντες τὰς οἰκίας τῶν χηρῶν καὶ
devouring the houses of the widows and
προφάσει μακρὰ προσευχόμενοι, οὗτοι
under pretence long praying, these
λήμψονται περισσότερον κρίμα. 41 Καὶ
will receive greater condemnation. And
καθίσας κατέναντι τοῦ γαζοφυλακείου ἐθεώρει
sitting opposite the treasury he beheld
πῶς ὁ ὄχλος βάλλει χαλκὸν εἰς τὸ
how the crowd puts copper money into the
γαζοφυλακεῖον· καὶ πολλοὶ πλούσιοι ἔβαλλον
treasury; and many rich men put
πολλά· 42 καὶ ἐλθοῦσα μία χήρα πτωχὴ
much; and coming one widow poor
ἔβαλεν λεπτὰ δύο, ὅ ἐστιν κοδράντης.
put lepta two, which is a quadrans.
43 καὶ προσκαλεσάμενος τοὺς μαθητὰς αὐτοῦ
And calling to [him] the disciples of him
εἶπεν αὐτοῖς· ἀμὴν λέγω ὑμῖν ὅτι
he said to them: Truly I tell you that
ἡ χήρα αὕτη ἡ πτωχὴ πλεῖον πάντων
– [3]widow [1]this – [2]poor [5]more [than] [6]all

more important than all
burnt offerings and sacrifices."
34 When Jesus saw that he
had answered wisely, he
said to him, "You are not
far from the kingdom of
God." And from then on no
one dared ask him any
more questions.

Whose Son Is the Christ?

35 While Jesus was teach-
ing in the temple courts, he
asked, "How is it that the
teachers of the law say that
the Christ[c] is the son of
David? 36 David himself,
speaking by the Holy Spirit, declared:
" 'The Lord said to my
Lord:
"Sit at my right hand
until I put your enemies
under your feet." '[d]
37 David himself calls him
'Lord.' How then can he be
his son?"
The large crowd listened
to him with delight.
38 As he taught, Jesus
said, "Watch out for the
teachers of the law. They
like to walk around in flowing robes and be greeted in
the marketplaces, 39 and
have the most important
seats in the synagogues and
the places of honor at banquets. 40 They devour widows' houses and for a show
make lengthy prayers.
Such men will be punished
most severely."

The Widow's Offering

41 Jesus sat down opposite
the place where the offerings were put and watched
the crowd putting their
money into the temple treasury. Many rich people
threw in large amounts.
42 But a poor widow came
and put in two very small
copper coins,[e] worth only
a fraction of a penny.[f]
43 Calling his disciples to
him, Jesus said, "I tell you
the truth, this poor widow

[c] 35 Or *Messiah*
[d] 36 Psalm 110:1
[e] 42 Greek *two lepta*
[f] 42 Greek *kodrantes*

who are contributing to the
treasury. 44 For all of them
have contributed out of
their abundance; but she
out of her poverty has put
in everything she had, all
she had to live on."

Chapter 13

The Destruction of the Temple Foretold

AS he came out of the
temple, one of his dis-
ciples said to him, "Look,
Teacher, what large stones
and what large buildings!"
2 Then Jesus asked him,
"Do you see these great
buildings? Not one stone
will be left here upon another; all will be thrown
down."
3 When he was sitting
on the Mount of Olives opposite the temple, Peter,
James, John, and Andrew
asked him privately, 4 "Tell
us, when will this be, and
what will be the sign that all
these things are about to be
accomplished?" 5 Then
Jesus began to say to them,
"Beware that no one leads
you astray. 6 Many will
come in my name and say,
'I am he!'[m] and they will
lead many astray. 7 When
you hear of wars and ru-
mors of wars, do not be
alarmed; this must take
place, but the end is still to
come. 8 For nation will rise
against nation, and king-
dom against kingdom;
there will be earthquakes in
various places; there will
be famines. This is but the
beginning of the birth-
pangs.

Persecution Foretold

9 "As for yourselves,
beware; for they will hand
you over to councils; and
you will be beaten in synagogues; and you will stand
before governors and kings
because of me, as a testimony to them. 10 And the

[m] Gk *I am*

ἔβαλεν τῶν βαλλόντων εἰς τὸ γαζοφυλακεῖον·
[4]put the [ones] putting into the treasury;

44 πάντες γὰρ ἐκ τοῦ περισσεύοντος αὐτοῖς
for all out of the abounding to them[c]
= their abundance

ἔβαλον, αὕτη δὲ ἐκ τῆς ὑστερήσεως αὐτῆς
put, but this woman out of the want of her

πάντα ὅσα εἶχεν ἔβαλεν, ὅλον τὸν βίον
[3]all things [2]how many [4]she had [1]put, all the living

αὐτῆς.
of her.

Chapter 13

13 Καὶ ἐκπορευομένου αὐτοῦ ἐκ τοῦ
And going forth him[a] out of the
= as he went forth

ἱεροῦ λέγει αὐτῷ εἷς τῶν μαθητῶν αὐτοῦ·
temple says to him one of the disciples of him:

διδάσκαλε, ἴδε ποταποὶ λίθοι καὶ ποταπαὶ
Teacher, behold[,] what great stones and what great

οἰκοδομαί. 2 καὶ ὁ Ἰησοῦς εἶπεν αὐτῷ·
buildings. And – Jesus said to him:

βλέπεις ταύτας τὰς μεγάλας οἰκοδομάς;
Seest thou these – great buildings?

οὐ μὴ ἀφεθῇ λίθος ἐπὶ λίθον ὃς οὐ
by no means be left stone on stone which by no
= there shall by no means be left stone on stone which will not

μὴ καταλυθῇ. 3 Καὶ καθημένου αὐτοῦ
means be overthrown. And sitting him[a]
be overthrown. = as he sat

εἰς τὸ ὄρος τῶν ἐλαιῶν κατέναντι τοῦ
in(on) the mount of the olives opposite the

ἱεροῦ, ἐπηρώτα αὐτὸν κατ' ἰδίαν Πέτρος
temple, questioned him privately Peter

καὶ Ἰάκωβος καὶ Ἰωάννης καὶ Ἀνδρέας·
and James and John and Andrew:

4 εἰπὸν ἡμῖν, πότε ταῦτα ἔσται, καὶ τί
Tell us, when these things will be, and what

τὸ σημεῖον ὅταν μέλλῃ ταῦτα συντελεῖσθαι
the sign when [3]are about [2]these things [4]to be completed

πάντα; 5 ὁ δὲ Ἰησοῦς ἤρξατο λέγειν
[1]all? – And Jesus began to say

αὐτοῖς· βλέπετε μή τις ὑμᾶς πλανήσῃ.
to them: See lest anyone you lead astray.

6 πολλοὶ ἐλεύσονται ἐπὶ τῷ ὀνόματί μου
Many will come on(in) the name of me

λέγοντες ὅτι ἐγώ εἰμι, καὶ πολλοὺς
saying[,] – I am, and many

πλανήσουσιν. 7 ὅταν δὲ ἀκούσητε πολέμους
they will lead astray. But when ye hear [of] wars

καὶ ἀκοὰς πολέμων, μὴ θροεῖσθε· δεῖ
and rumours of wars, be not disturbed; it behoves

γενέσθαι, ἀλλ' οὔπω τὸ τέλος. 8 ἐγερθήσεται
to happen, but not yet the end. will be raised

γὰρ ἔθνος ἐπ' ἔθνος καὶ βασιλεία ἐπὶ
For nation against nation and kingdom against

βασιλείαν. ἔσονται σεισμοὶ κατὰ τόπους,
kingdom. There will be earthquakes in places,

ἔσονται λιμοί· ἀρχὴ ὠδίνων ταῦτα.
there will be famines; beginning of birth-pangs these things [are].

9 Βλέπετε δὲ ὑμεῖς ἑαυτούς· παραδώσουσιν
But see ye yourselves; they will deliver

ὑμᾶς εἰς συνέδρια καὶ εἰς συναγωγὰς
you to councils and in synagogues

δαρήσεσθε καὶ ἐπὶ ἡγεμόνων καὶ βασιλέων
ye will be beaten and before rulers and kings

σταθήσεσθε ἕνεκεν ἐμοῦ, εἰς μαρτύριον
ye will stand for the sake of me, for a testimony

has put more into the treasury than all the others.
44 They all gave out of their
wealth; but she, out of her
poverty, put in everything
—all she had to live on."

Chapter 13

Signs of the End of the Age

AS he was leaving the
temple, one of his dis-
ciples said to him, "Look,
Teacher! What massive
stones! What magnificent
buildings!"
2 "Do you see all these
great buildings?" replied
Jesus. "Not one stone here
will be left on another; every one will be thrown
down."
3 As Jesus was sitting on
the Mount of Olives oppo-
site the temple, Peter,
James, John and Andrew
asked him privately, 4 "Tell
us, when will these things
happen? And what will be
the sign that they are all
about to be fulfilled?"
5 Jesus said to them:
"Watch out that no one deceives you. 6 Many will
come in my name, claim-
ing, 'I am he,' and will deceive many. 7 When you
hear of wars and rumors of
wars, do not be alarmed.
Such things must happen,
but the end is still to come.
8 Nation will rise against nation, and kingdom against
kingdom. There will be
earthquakes in various
places, and famines. These
are the beginning of birth
pains.
9 "You must be on your
guard. You will be handed
over to the local councils
and flogged in the syna-
gogues. On account of me
you will stand before governors and kings as wit-

good news[n] must first be
proclaimed to all nations.
11 When they bring you to
trial and hand you over, do
not worry beforehand
about what you are to say;
but say whatever is given
you at that time, for it is not
you who speak, but the
Holy Spirit. 12 Brother will
betray brother to death,
and a father his child, and
children will rise against
parents and have them put
to death; 13 and you will be
hated by all because of my
name. But the one who en-
dures to the end will be
saved.

The Desolating Sacrilege

14 "But when you see
the desolating sacrilege set
up where it ought not to be
(let the reader understand),
then those in Judea must
flee to the mountains; 15 the
one on the housetop must
not go down or enter the
house to take anything
away; 16 the one in the field
must not turn back to get a
coat. 17 Woe to those who
are pregnant and to those
who are nursing infants in
those days! 18 Pray that it
may not be in winter. 19 For
in those days there will be
suffering, such as has not
been from the beginning of
the creation that God created until now, no, and never
will be. 20 And if the Lord
had not cut short those
days, no one would be
saved; but for the sake of
the elect, whom he chose,
he has cut short those days.
21 And if anyone says to
you at that time, 'Look!
Here is the Messiah!'[o] or
'Look! There he is!'—do
not believe it. 22 False mes-

[n] Gk *gospel*
[o] Or *the Christ*

αὐτοῖς. 10 καὶ εἰς πάντα τὰ ἔθνη πρῶτον
to them. And to all the nations first
δεῖ κηρυχθῆναι τὸ εὐαγγέλιον. 11 καὶ ὅταν
it behoves to be proclaimed the gospel. And when
= the gospel must be proclaimed.
ἄγωσιν ὑμᾶς παραδιδόντες, μὴ προμεριμνᾶτε
they lead you delivering, be not anxious beforehand
τί λαλήσητε, ἀλλ' ὃ ἐὰν δοθῇ ὑμῖν ἐν
what ye speak, but whatever is given you in
ἐκείνῃ τῇ ὥρᾳ, τοῦτο λαλεῖτε· οὐ γάρ
that – hour. this speak ye; for not
ἐστε ὑμεῖς οἱ λαλοῦντες ἀλλὰ τὸ πνεῦμα
are ye the [ones] speaking but the Spirit
τὸ ἅγιον. 12 καὶ παραδώσει ἀδελφὸς
– Holy. And [2]will deliver [1]a brother
ἀδελφὸν εἰς θάνατον καὶ πατὴρ τέκνον, καὶ
a brother to death and a father a child, and
ἐπαναστήσονται τέκνα ἐπὶ γονεῖς καὶ
[2]will rise *against* [1]children against parents and
θανατώσουσιν αὐτούς· 13 καὶ ἔσεσθε
will put to death them; and ye will be
μισούμενοι ὑπὸ πάντων διὰ τὸ ὄνομά
being hated by all men on account of the name
μου· ὁ δὲ ὑπομείνας εἰς τέλος, οὗτος
of me; but the [one] enduring to [the] end, this
σωθήσεται. 14 Ὅταν δὲ ἴδητε τὸ βδέλυγμα
will be saved. But when ye see the abomination
τῆς ἐρημώσεως ἑστηκότα ὅπου οὐ δεῖ, ὁ
– of desolation stand where he (it) behoves not, the
ἀναγινώσκων νοείτω, τότε οἱ ἐν τῇ
[one] reading let him understand, then the [ones] in –
Ἰουδαίᾳ φευγέτωσαν εἰς τὰ ὄρη, 15 ὁ ἐπὶ
Judæa let them flee to the mountains, the [one] on
τοῦ δώματος μὴ καταβάτω μηδὲ εἰσελθάτω
the roof let him not come down nor let him enter
τι ἆραι ἐκ τῆς οἰκίας αὐτοῦ, 16 καὶ ὁ
anything to take out of the house of him, and the [one]
εἰς τὸν ἀγρὸν μὴ ἐπιστρεψάτω εἰς τὰ
in the field let him not return to the things
ὀπίσω ἆραι τὸ ἱμάτιον αὐτοῦ. 17 οὐαὶ
behind to take the garment of him. woe
δὲ ταῖς ἐν γαστρὶ ἐχούσαις καὶ ταῖς
But to the women pregnant† and to the
θηλαζούσαις ἐν ἐκείναις ταῖς ἡμέραις.
[ones] giving suck in those – days.
18 προσεύχεσθε δὲ ἵνα μὴ γένηται χειμῶνος·
But pray ye that it may not happen of(in) winter;
19 ἔσονται γὰρ αἱ ἡμέραι ἐκεῖναι θλῖψις, οἵα
for [3]will be – [2]days [1]those [4]affliction, of such a kind
οὐ γέγονεν τοιαύτη ἀπ' ἀρχῆς κτίσεως
[2]has not happened [1]as from [the] beginning of [the] creation
ἣν ἔκτισεν ὁ θεὸς ἕως τοῦ νῦν καὶ οὐ
which created – God until – now and by
μὴ γένηται. 20 καὶ εἰ μὴ ἐκολόβωσεν
no means may be. And unless [2]shortened
κύριος τὰς ἡμέρας, οὐκ ἂν ἐσώθη πᾶσα
[1][the] Lord the days, would not be saved all
= no flesh would be saved;
σάρξ· ἀλλὰ διὰ τοὺς ἐκλεκτοὺς οὓς
flesh; but on account of the chosen whom
ἐξελέξατο ἐκολόβωσεν τὰς ἡμέρας. 21 καὶ
he chose he shortened the days. And
τότε ἐάν τις ὑμῖν εἴπῃ· ἴδε ὧδε ὁ
then if anyone [2]you [1]tells: Behold here [is] the
χριστός, ἴδε ἐκεῖ, μὴ πιστεύετε· 22 ἐγερθή-
Christ, behold there, believe ye not; [5]will be

nesses to them. 10 And the
gospel must first be
preached to all nations.
11 Whenever you are arrested and brought to trial, do
not worry beforehand
about what to say. Just say
whatever is given you at
the time, for it is not you
speaking, but the Holy
Spirit.
12 "Brother will betray
brother to death, and a father his child. Children will
rebel against their parents
and have them put to death.
13 All men will hate you because of me, but he who
stands firm to the end will
be saved.
14 "When you see 'the
abomination that causes
desolation'[g] standing
where it[h] does not belong
—let the reader under-
stand—then let those who
are in Judea flee to the
mountains. 15 Let no one on
the roof of his house go
down or enter the house to
take anything out. 16 Let no
one in the field go back to
get his cloak. 17 How dreadful it will be in those days
for pregnant women and
nursing mothers! 18 Pray
that this will not take place
in winter, 19 because those
will be days of distress un-
equaled from the begin-
ning, when God created the
world, until now—and
never to be equaled again.
20 If the Lord had not cut
short those days, no one
would survive. But for the
sake of the elect, whom he
has chosen, he has short-
ened them. 21 At that time if
anyone says to you, 'Look,
here is the Christ[i]!' or,
'Look, there he is!' do not
believe it. 22 For false

[g] 14 Daniel 9:27; 11:31; 12:11
[h] 14 Or *he;* also in verse 29
[i] 21 Or *Messiah*

siahs[p] and false prophets
will appear and produce
signs and omens, to lead
astray, if possible, the
elect. 23 But be alert; I have
already told you every-
thing.

The Coming of the Son of Man

24 "But in those days,
after that suffering,
the sun will be
darkened,
and the moon will
not give
its light,
25 and the stars will be
falling
from heaven,
and the powers in
the heavens will
be shaken.
26 Then they will see 'the
Son of Man coming in
clouds' with great power
and glory. 27 Then he will
send out the angels, and
gather his elect from the
four winds, from the ends
of the earth to the ends of
heaven.

The Lesson of the Fig Tree

28 "From the fig tree
learn its lesson: as soon as
its branch becomes tender
and puts forth its leaves,
you know that summer is
near. 29 So also, when you
see these things taking
place, you know that he[q] is
near, at the very gates.
30 Truly I tell you, this generation will not pass away
until all these things have
taken place. 31 Heaven and
earth will pass away, but
my words will not pass
away.

The Necessity for Watchfulness

32 "But about that day
or hour no one knows, neither the angels in heaven,
nor the Son, but only the
Father. 33 Beware, keep
alert;[r] for you do not know
when the time will come.
34 It is like a man going on a
journey, when he leaves
home and puts his slaves in
charge, each with his work,
and commands the door-

[p] Or *christs*
[q] Or *it*
[r] Other ancient authorities add *and pray*

σονται δὲ ψευδόχριστοι καὶ ψευδοπροφῆται
raised [1]and [2]false Christs [3]and [4]false prophets
καὶ ποιήσουσιν σημεῖα καὶ τέρατα πρὸς
and they will do signs and wonders *for*
τὸ ἀποπλανᾶν, εἰ δυνατόν, τοὺς ἐκλεκτούς.
– to lead astray, if possible, the chosen.
23 ὑμεῖς δὲ βλέπετε· προείρηκα ὑμῖν πάντα.
But [2]ye [1]see; [1]I have told [4]before [2]you [3]all things.
24 Ἀλλὰ ἐν ἐκείναις ταῖς ἡμέραις μετὰ
But in those – days after
τὴν θλῖψιν ἐκείνην ὁ ἥλιος σκοτισθήσεται,
– affliction that the sun will be darkened,
καὶ ἡ σελήνη οὐ δώσει τὸ φέγγος αὐτῆς,
and the moon will not give the light of her,
25 καὶ οἱ ἀστέρες ἔσονται ἐκ τοῦ οὐρανοῦ
and the stars [1]will be [3]out of – [4]heaven
πίπτοντες, καὶ αἱ δυνάμεις αἱ ἐν τοῖς
[2]falling, and the powers – in the
οὐρανοῖς σαλευθήσονται. 26 καὶ τότε ὄψονται
heavens will be shaken. And then they will see
τὸν υἱὸν τοῦ ἀνθρώπου ἐρχόμενον ἐν
the Son – of man coming in
νεφέλαις μετὰ δυνάμεως πολλῆς καὶ δόξης.
clouds with power much and glory.
27 καὶ τότε ἀποστελεῖ τοὺς ἀγγέλους καὶ
And then he will send the angels and
ἐπισυνάξει τοὺς ἐκλεκτοὺς [αὐτοῦ] ἐκ τῶν
they will assemble the chosen of him out of the
τεσσάρων ἀνέμων ἀπ' ἄκρου γῆς ἕως
four winds from [the] extremity of earth to
ἄκρου οὐρανοῦ. 28 Ἀπὸ δὲ τῆς συκῆς
[the] extremity of heaven. Now from the fig-tree
μάθετε τὴν παραβολήν· ὅταν ἤδη ὁ
learn the parable; when now the
κλάδος αὐτῆς ἁπαλὸς γένηται καὶ ἐκφύῃ
branch of it tender becomes and puts forth
τὰ φύλλα, γινώσκετε ὅτι ἐγγὺς τὸ θέρος
the leaves, ye know that near the summer
ἐστίν· 29 οὕτως καὶ ὑμεῖς, ὅταν ἴδητε
is; so also ye, when ye see
ταῦτα γινόμενα, γινώσκετε ὅτι ἐγγύς ἐστιν
these things happening, know that near he/it is
ἐπὶ θύραις. 30 ἀμὴν λέγω ὑμῖν ὅτι οὐ
at [the] doors. Truly I tell you that by no
μὴ παρέλθῃ ἡ γενεὰ αὕτη μέχρις οὗ
means passes – generation this until
ταῦτα πάντα γένηται. 31 ὁ οὐρανὸς καὶ
these things all happen. The heaven and
ἡ γῆ παρελεύσονται, οἱ δὲ λόγοι μου
the earth will pass away, but the words of me
οὐ παρελεύσονται. 32 Περὶ δὲ τῆς ἡμέρας
will not pass away. But concerning – day
ἐκείνης ἢ τῆς ὥρας οὐδεὶς οἶδεν, οὐδὲ
that or – hour no one knows, not
οἱ ἄγγελοι ἐν οὐρανῷ οὐδὲ ὁ υἱός, εἰ
the angels in heaven neither the Son, ex-
μὴ ὁ πατήρ. 33 Βλέπετε, ἀγρυπνεῖτε·
cept the Father. Look, be wakeful;
οὐκ οἴδατε γὰρ πότε ὁ καιρός ἐστιν.
for ye know not when the time is.
34 ὡς ἄνθρωπος ἀπόδημος ἀφεὶς τὴν οἰκίαν
As a man away from home leaving the house
αὐτοῦ καὶ δοὺς τοῖς δούλοις αὐτοῦ τὴν
of him and giving to the slaves of him –
ἐξουσίαν, ἑκάστῳ τὸ ἔργον αὐτοῦ, καὶ
authority, to each the work of him, and

Christs and false prophets
will appear and perform
signs and miracles to de-
ceive the elect—if that
were possible. 23 So be on
your guard; I have told you
everything ahead of time.
24 "But in those days, following that distress,

" 'the sun will be
darkened,
and the moon will not
give its light;
25 the stars will fall from
the sky,
and the heavenly
bodies will be
shaken.'[j]

26 "At that time men will
see the Son of Man coming
in clouds with great power
and glory. 27 And he will
send his angels and gather
his elect from the four
winds, from the ends of the
earth to the ends of the
heavens.
28 "Now learn this lesson
from the fig tree: As soon as
its twigs get tender and its
leaves come out, you know
that summer is near.
29 Even so, when you see
these things happening,
you know that it is near,
right at the door. 30 I tell you
the truth, this generation[k]
will certainly not pass away
until all these things have
happened. 31 Heaven and
earth will pass away, but
my words will never pass
away.

The Day and Hour Unknown

32 "No one knows about
that day or hour, not even
the angels in heaven, nor
the Son, but only the Fa-
ther. 33 Be on guard! Be
alert[l]! You do not know
when that time will come.
34 It's like a man going
away: He leaves his house
and puts his servants in
charge, each with his as-
signed task, and tells the

[j] 25 Isaiah 13:10; 34:4
[k] 30 Or *race*
[l] 33 Some manuscripts *alert and pray*

keeper to be on the watch.
35Therefore, keep awake—
for you do not know when
the master of the house will
come, in the evening, or at
midnight, or at cockcrow,
or at dawn, 36or else he
may find you asleep when
he comes suddenly. 37And
what I say to you I say to
all: Keep awake."

Chapter 14

The Plot to Kill Jesus

IT was two days before
the Passover and the
festival of Unleavened
Bread. The chief priests
and the scribes were looking for a way to arrest
Jesus[s] by stealth and kill
him; 2for they said, "Not
during the festival, or there
may be a riot among the
people."

The Anointing at Bethany

3 While he was at Beth-
any in the house of Simon
the leper,[t] as he sat at the
table, a woman came with
an alabaster jar of very
costly ointment of nard,
and she broke open the jar
and poured the ointment on
his head. 4But some were
there who said to one an-
other in anger, "Why was
the ointment wasted in this
way? 5For this ointment
could have been sold for
more than three hundred
denarii,[u] and the money
given to the poor." And
they scolded her. 6But
Jesus said, "Let her alone;
why do you trouble her?
She has performed a good
service for me. 7For you always have the poor with
you, and you can show
kindness to them whenever
you wish; but you will not
always have me. 8She has
done what she could; she
has anointed my body be-
forehand for its burial.
9Truly I tell you, wherever

[s] Gk *him*
[t] The terms *leper* and *leprosy* can refer to several diseases
[u] The denarius was the usual day's wage for a laborer

τῷ θυρωρῷ ἐνετείλατο ἵνα γρηγορῇ.
the doorkeeper he commanded that he should watch.
35 γρηγορεῖτε οὖν· οὐκ οἴδατε γὰρ πότε
Watch ye therefore; for ye know not when
ὁ κύριος τῆς οἰκίας ἔρχεται, ἢ ὀψὲ ἢ
the lord of the house comes, either late or
μεσονύκτιον ἢ ἀλεκτοροφωνίας ἢ πρωΐ·
at midnight or at cock-crowing or early;
36 μὴ ἐλθὼν ἐξαίφνης εὕρῃ ὑμᾶς καθεύδ-
lest coming suddenly he find you sleep-
οντας. 37 ὃ δὲ ὑμῖν λέγω, πᾶσιν λέγω,
ing. And what to you I say, to all I say,
γρηγορεῖτε.
watch ye.

14 Ἦν δὲ τὸ πάσχα καὶ τὰ ἄζυμα
Now it was the Passover and [the feast of] the unleavened bread†
μετὰ δύο ἡμέρας. καὶ ἐζήτουν οἱ ἀρχιερεῖς
after two days. And sought the chief priests
καὶ οἱ γραμματεῖς πῶς αὐτὸν ἐν δόλῳ
and the scribes how ²him ³by ⁴guile
κρατήσαντες ἀποκτείνωσιν. 2 ἔλεγον γάρ·
¹seizing they might kill. For they said:
μὴ ἐν τῇ ἑορτῇ, μήποτε ἔσται θόρυβος
Not at the feast, lest there will be a disturbance
τοῦ λαοῦ.
of the people.
3 Καὶ ὄντος αὐτοῦ ἐν Βηθανίᾳ ἐν τῇ
And being him* in Bethany in the
= when he was
οἰκίᾳ Σίμωνος τοῦ λεπροῦ, κατακειμένου
house of Simon the leper, reclining
= as he reclined
αὐτοῦ ἦλθεν γυνὴ ἔχουσα ἀλάβαστρον
him* came a woman having an alabaster phial
μύρου νάρδου πιστικῆς πολυτελοῦς·
of ointment ²nard ¹of pure ³costly;
συντρίψασα τὴν ἀλάβαστρον κατέχεεν αὐτοῦ
breaking the alabaster phial she poured over of him
τῆς κεφαλῆς. 4 ἦσαν δέ τινες ἀγανακτοῦντες
the head. Now there were some being angry
πρὸς ἑαυτούς· εἰς τί ἡ ἀπώλεια αὕτη
with themselves: Why – waste this
τοῦ μύρου γέγονεν; 5 ἠδύνατο γὰρ τοῦτο
of the ointment has occurred? for ³could ¹this
τὸ μύρον πραθῆναι ἐπάνω δηναρίων
– ²ointment to be sold [for] over denarii
τριακοσίων καὶ δοθῆναι τοῖς πτωχοῖς·
three hundred and to be given to the poor;
καὶ ἐνεβριμῶντο αὐτῇ. 6 ὁ δὲ Ἰησοῦς
and they were indignant with her. – But Jesus
εἶπεν· ἄφετε αὐτήν· τί αὐτῇ κόπους
said: Leave her; why ³to her ²troubles
παρέχετε; καλὸν ἔργον ἠργάσατο ἐν ἐμοί.
¹cause ye? a good work she wrought in me.
7 πάντοτε γὰρ τοὺς πτωχοὺς ἔχετε μεθ'
For always the poor ye have with
ἑαυτῶν, καὶ ὅταν θέλητε δύνασθε αὐτοῖς
yourselves, and whenever ye wish ye can to them
εὖ ποιῆσαι, ἐμὲ δὲ οὐ πάντοτε ἔχετε.
well to do, but me not always ye have.
8 ὃ ἔσχεν ἐποίησεν· προέλαβεν μυρίσαι τὸ
What she had she did; she was beforehand to anoint the
σῶμά μου εἰς τὸν ἐνταφιασμόν. 9 ἀμὴν
body of me for the burial. truly

one at the door to keep
watch.
35"Therefore keep watch
because you do not know
when the owner of the
house will come back—
whether in the evening, or
at midnight, or when the
rooster crows, or at dawn.
36If he comes suddenly, do
not let him find you sleeping. 37What I say to you, I
say to everyone:
'Watch!' "

Chapter 14

Jesus Anointed at Bethany

NOW the Passover and
the Feast of Unleav-
ened Bread were only two
days away, and the chief
priests and the teachers of
the law were looking for
some sly way to arrest
Jesus and kill him. 2"But
not during the Feast," they
said, "or the people may
riot."
3While he was in Betha-
ny, reclining at the table in
the home of a man known
as Simon the Leper, a
woman came with an ala-
baster jar of very expensive
perfume, made of pure
nard. She broke the jar and
poured the perfume on his
head.
4Some of those present
were saying indignantly to
one another, "Why this
waste of perfume? 5It could
have been sold for more
than a year's wages[m] and
the money given to the
poor." And they rebuked
her harshly.
6"Leave her alone," said
Jesus. "Why are you both-
ering her? She has done a
beautiful thing to me. 7The
poor you will always have
with you, and you can help
them any time you want.
But you will not always
have me. 8She did what she
could. She poured perfume
on my body beforehand to
prepare for my burial. 9I

[m]5 Greek *than three hundred denarii*

the good news[v] is pro-
claimed in the whole world,
what she has done will be
told in remembrance of
her."

Judas Agrees to Betray Jesus

10 Then Judas Iscariot,
who was one of the twelve,
went to the chief priests in
order to betray him to
them. 11 When they heard
it, they were greatly
pleased, and promised to
give him money. So he be-
gan to look for an opportunity to betray him.

The Passover with the Disciples

12 On the first day of
Unleavened Bread, when
the Passover lamb is sacrificed, his disciples said to
him, "Where do you want
us to go and make the preparations for you to eat the
Passover?" 13 So he sent
two of his disciples, saying
to them, "Go into the city,
and a man carrying a jar of
water will meet you; follow
him, 14 and wherever he enters, say to the owner of the
house, 'The Teacher asks,
Where is my guest room
where I may eat the Pass-
over with my disciples?'
15 He will show you a large
room upstairs, furnished
and ready. Make prepara-
tions for us there." 16 So the
disciples set out and went
to the city, and found everything as he had told
them; and they prepared
the Passover meal.
17 When it was evening,
he came with the twelve.
18 And when they had taken
their places and were eating, Jesus said, "Truly I tell
you, one of you will betray
me, one who is eating with
me." 19 They began to be
distressed and to say to him
one after another, "Surely,
not I?" 20 He said to them,
"It is one of the twelve, one
who is dipping bread[w] into
the bowl[x] with me. 21 For

[v] Or *gospel*
[w] Gk lacks *bread*
[x] Other ancient authorities read *same bowl*

δὲ λέγω ὑμῖν, ὅπου ἐὰν κηρυχθῇ τὸ
And I tell you, wherever is proclaimed the
εὐαγγέλιον εἰς ὅλον τὸν κόσμον, καὶ ὃ
gospel in all the world, also what
ἐποίησεν αὕτη λαληθήσεται εἰς μνημόσυνον
did this woman will be spoken for a memorial
αὐτῆς. 10 Καὶ Ἰούδας Ἰσκαριώθ, ὁ εἷς
of her. And Judas Iscariot, the one
τῶν δώδεκα, ἀπῆλθεν πρὸς τοὺς ἀρχιερεῖς
of the twelve, went to the chief priests
ἵνα αὐτὸν παραδοῖ αὐτοῖς. 11 οἱ δὲ
that him he might betray to them. And they
ἀκούσαντες ἐχάρησαν καὶ ἐπηγγείλαντο αὐτῷ
hearing rejoiced and promised him
ἀργύριον δοῦναι. καὶ ἐζήτει πῶς αὐτὸν
silver to give. And he sought how him
εὐκαίρως παραδοῖ.
opportunely he might betray.

12 Καὶ τῇ πρώτῃ ἡμέρᾳ τῶν ἀζύμων,
And on the first day of unleavened bread,†
ὅτε τὸ πάσχα ἔθυον, λέγουσιν αὐτῷ οἱ
when the passover they sacrificed, say to him the
μαθηταὶ αὐτοῦ· ποῦ θέλεις ἀπελθόντες
disciples of him: Where wishest thou , going
ἑτοιμάσωμεν ἵνα φάγῃς τὸ πάσχα; 13 καὶ
we may prepare that thou eatest the passover? And
ἀποστέλλει δύο τῶν μαθητῶν αὐτοῦ καὶ
he sends two of the disciples of him and
λέγει αὐτοῖς· ὑπάγετε εἰς τὴν πόλιν, καὶ
tells them: Go ye into the city, and
ἀπαντήσει ὑμῖν ἄνθρωπος κεράμιον ὕδατος
will meet you a man a pitcher of water
βαστάζων· ἀκολουθήσατε αὐτῷ, 14 καὶ ὅπου
carrying; follow him, and wher-
ἐὰν εἰσέλθῃ εἴπατε τῷ οἰκοδεσπότῃ ὅτι ὁ
ever he enters tell the housemaster[,] – The
διδάσκαλος λέγει· ποῦ ἐστιν τὸ κατάλυμά
teacher says: Where is the guest room
μου, ὅπου τὸ πάσχα μετὰ τῶν μαθητῶν
of me, where the passover with the disciples
μου φάγω; 15 καὶ αὐτὸς ὑμῖν δείξει
of me I may eat? And he you will show
ἀνάγαιον μέγα ἐστρωμένον ἕτοιμον· καὶ
upper room a large *having been* spread ready; and
ἐκεῖ ἑτοιμάσατε ἡμῖν. 16 καὶ ἐξῆλθον οἱ
there prepare ye for us. And went forth the
μαθηταὶ καὶ ἦλθον εἰς τὴν πόλιν καὶ
disciples and came into the city and
εὗρον καθὼς εἶπεν αὐτοῖς, καὶ ἡτοίμασαν
found as he told them, and they prepared
τὸ πάσχα. 17 Καὶ ὀψίας γενομένης ἔρχεται
the passover. And evening coming[a] he comes
= when evening came
μετὰ τῶν δώδεκα. 18 καὶ ἀνακειμένων
with the twelve. And reclining
= as they reclined and ate
αὐτῶν καὶ ἐσθιόντων ὁ Ἰησοῦς εἶπεν·
them and eating[a] – Jesus said:
ἀμὴν λέγω ὑμῖν ὅτι εἷς ἐξ ὑμῶν παραδώσει
Truly I tell you that one of you will betray
με, ὁ ἐσθίων μετ' ἐμοῦ. 19 ἤρξαντο
me, the [one] eating with me. They began
λυπεῖσθαι καὶ λέγειν αὐτῷ εἷς κατὰ εἷς·
to grieve and to say to him one by one:
μήτι ἐγώ; 20 ὁ δὲ εἶπεν αὐτοῖς· εἷς τῶν
Not I? And he said to them: One of the
δώδεκα, ὁ ἐμβαπτόμενος μετ' ἐμοῦ εἰς
twelve, the [one] dipping with me in

tell you the truth, wherever
the gospel is preached
throughout the world, what
she has done will also be
told, in memory of her."
10Then Judas Iscariot,
one of the Twelve, went to
the chief priests to betray
Jesus to them. 11They were
delighted to hear this and
promised to give him mon-
ey. So he watched for an
opportunity to hand him
over.

The Lord's Supper

12On the first day of the
Feast of Unleavened
Bread, when it was cus-
tomary to sacrifice the
Passover lamb, Jesus' disciples asked him, "Where
do you want us to go and
make preparations for you
to eat the Passover?"
13So he sent two of his
disciples, telling them, "Go
into the city, and a man carrying a jar of water will
meet you. Follow him.
14Say to the owner of the
house he enters, 'The
Teacher asks: Where is my
guest room, where I may
eat the Passover with my
disciples?' 15He will show
you a large upper room,
furnished and ready. Make
preparations for us there."
16The disciples left, went
into the city and found
things just as Jesus had told
them. So they prepared the
Passover.
17When evening came,
Jesus arrived with the
Twelve. 18While they were
reclining at the table eating,
he said, "I tell you the
truth, one of you will betray me—one who is eating
with me."
19They were saddened,
and one by one they said to
him, "Surely not I?"
20"It is one of the
Twelve," he replied, "one
who dips bread into the

the Son of Man goes as it is
written of him, but woe to
that one by whom the Son
of Man is betrayed! It
would have been better for
that one not to have been
born."

The Institution of the Lord's Supper

22 While they were eat-
ing, he took a loaf of bread,
and after blessing it he
broke it, gave it to them,
and said, "Take; this is my
body." 23 Then he took a
cup, and after giving thanks
he gave it to them, and all
of them drank from it. 24 He
said to them, "This is my
blood of the[y] covenant,
which is poured out for
many. 25 Truly I tell you, I
will never again drink of the
fruit of the vine until that
day when I drink it new in
the kingdom of God."

Peter's Denial Foretold

26 When they had sung
the hymn, they went out to
the Mount of Olives. 27 And
Jesus said to them, "You
will all become deserters;
for it is written,

'I will strike the shepherd,
and the sheep will be scattered.'

28 But after I am raised up,
I will go before you to Galilee." 29 Peter said to him,
"Even though all become
deserters, I will not."
30 Jesus said to him, "Truly
I tell you, this day, this
very night, before the cock
crows twice, you will deny
me three times." 31 But he
said vehemently, "Even
though I must die with you,
I will not deny you." And
all of them said the same.

Jesus Prays in Gethsemane

32 They went to a place

[y] Other ancient authorities add *new*

τὸ [ἓν] τρύβλιον. 21 ὅτι ὁ μὲν υἱὸς τοῦ
the one dish. Because indeed the Son –
ἀνθρώπου ὑπάγει καθὼς γέγραπται περὶ
of man is going as it has been written concerning
αὐτοῦ· οὐαὶ δὲ τῷ ἀνθρώπῳ ἐκείνῳ δι'
him; but woe – man to that through
οὗ ὁ υἱὸς τοῦ ἀνθρώπου παραδίδοται·
whom the Son – of man is betrayed;
καλὸν αὐτῷ εἰ οὐκ ἐγεννήθη ὁ ἄνθρωπος
good for him if was not born – man
ἐκεῖνος. 22 Καὶ ἐσθιόντων αὐτῶν λαβὼν
that. And eating them[a] taking
= as they were eating
ἄρτον εὐλογήσας ἔκλασεν καὶ ἔδωκεν αὐτοῖς
a loaf blessing he broke and gave to them
καὶ εἶπεν· λάβετε· τοῦτό ἐστιν τὸ σῶμά
and said: Take ye; this is the body
μου. 23 καὶ λαβὼν ποτήριον εὐχαριστήσας
of me. And taking a cup giving thanks
ἔδωκεν αὐτοῖς, καὶ ἔπιον ἐξ αὐτοῦ πάντες.
he gave to them, and drank of it all.
24 καὶ εἶπεν αὐτοῖς· τοῦτό ἐστιν τὸ αἷμά
And he said to them: This is the blood
μου τῆς διαθήκης τὸ ἐκχυννόμενον ὑπὲρ
of me of the covenant – being shed for
πολλῶν. 25 ἀμὴν λέγω ὑμῖν ὅτι οὐκέτι
many. Truly I tell you[,] – No more
οὐ μὴ πίω ἐκ τοῦ γενήματος τῆς ἀμπέλου
by no(any) means will I drink of the fruit of the vine
ἕως τῆς ἡμέρας ἐκείνης ὅταν αὐτὸ πίνω
until – day that when it I drink
καινὸν ἐν τῇ βασιλείᾳ τοῦ θεοῦ.
new in the kingdom – of God.
26 Καὶ ὑμνήσαντες ἐξῆλθον εἰς τὸ
And having sung a hymn they went forth to the
ὄρος τῶν ἐλαιῶν. 27 Καὶ λέγει αὐτοῖς ὁ
mount of the olives. And says to them –
Ἰησοῦς ὅτι πάντες σκανδαλισθήσεσθε, ὅτι
Jesus[,] – [2]All [1]ye [3]will [4]be offended, because
γέγραπται· πατάξω τὸν ποιμένα, καὶ τὰ
it has been written: I will strike the shepherd, and the
πρόβατα διασκορπισθήσονται. 28 ἀλλὰ μετὰ
sheep will be scattered. But after
τὸ ἐγερθῆναί με προάξω ὑμᾶς εἰς τὴν
the to be raised me[b] I will go before you to –
= I am raised
Γαλιλαίαν. 29 ὁ δὲ Πέτρος ἔφη αὐτῷ·
Galilee. – And Peter said to him:
εἰ καὶ πάντες σκανδαλισθήσονται, ἀλλ'
If even all men shall be offended, yet
οὐκ ἐγώ. 30 καὶ λέγει αὐτῷ ὁ Ἰησοῦς·
not I. And says to him – Jesus:
ἀμὴν λέγω σοι ὅτι σὺ σήμερον ταύτῃ τῇ
Truly I tell thee[,] – Thou to-day in this –
νυκτὶ πρὶν ἢ δὶς ἀλέκτορα φωνῆσαι τρίς
night before twice a cock to sound[b] thrice
με ἀπαρνήσῃ. 31 ὁ δὲ ἐκπερισσῶς ἐλάλει·
me thou wilt deny. But he more exceedingly said:
ἐὰν δέῃ με συναποθανεῖν σοι, οὐ μή
If it should behove me *to* die with thee, by no means
= I must
σε ἀπαρνήσομαι. ὡσαύτως [δὲ] καὶ πάντες
thee will I deny. And similarly also all
ἔλεγον.
said.
32 Καὶ ἔρχονται εἰς χωρίον οὗ τὸ
And they come to a piece of land of which the

bowl with me. 21 The Son of
Man will go just as it is written about him. But woe to
that man who betrays the
Son of Man! It would be
better for him if he had not
been born."
22 While they were eating,
Jesus took bread, gave
thanks and broke it, and
gave it to his disciples, saying, "Take it; this is my
body."
23 Then he took the cup,
gave thanks and offered it
to them, and they all drank
from it.
24 "This is my blood of
the[n] covenant, which is
poured out for many," he
said to them. 25 "I tell you
the truth, I will not drink
again of the fruit of the vine
until that day when I drink
it anew in the kingdom of
God."
26 When they had sung a
hymn, they went out to the
Mount of Olives.

Jesus Predicts Peter's Denial

27 "You will all fall
away," Jesus told them,
"for it is written:

" 'I will strike the shepherd,
and the sheep will be scattered.'[o]

28 But after I have risen, I
will go ahead of you into
Galilee."
29 Peter declared, "Even
if all fall away, I will not."
30 "I tell you the truth,"
Jesus answered, "today—
yes, tonight—before the
rooster crows twice[p] you
yourself will disown me
three times."
31 But Peter insisted em-
phatically, "Even if I have
to die with you, I will never
disown you." And all the
others said the same.

Gethsemane

32 They went to a place

[n] 24 Some manuscripts *the new*
[o] 27 Zech. 13:7
[p] 30 Some early manuscripts do not have *twice*.

called Gethsemane; and he
said to his disciples, "Sit
here while I pray." 33 He
took with him Peter and
James and John, and began
to be distressed and agitated. 34 And said to them, "I
am deeply grieved, even to
death; remain here, and
keep awake." 35 And going
a little farther, he threw
himself on the ground and
prayed that, if it were possible, the hour might pass
from him. 36 He said,
"Abba,[z] Father, for you all
things are possible; remove
this cup from me; yet, not
what I want, but what you
want." 37 He came and
found them sleeping; and
he said to Peter, "Simon,
are you asleep? Could you
not keep awake one hour?
38 Keep awake and pray
that you may not come into
the time of trial;[a] the spirit
indeed is willing, but the
flesh is weak." 39 And again
he went away and prayed,
saying the same words.
40 And once more he came
and found them sleeping,
for their eyes were very
heavy; and they did not
know what to say to him.
41 He came a third time and
said to them, "Are you still
sleeping and taking your
rest? Enough! The hour has
come; the Son of Man is betrayed into the hands of sinners. 42 Get up, let us be going. See, my betrayer is at
hand."

The Betrayal and Arrest of Jesus

43 Immediately, while
he was still speaking, Judas, one of the twelve, arrived; and with him there
was a crowd with swords
and clubs, from the chief
priests, the scribes, and the

[z] Aramaic for *Father*
[a] Or *into temptation*

ὄνομα Γεθσημανί, καὶ λέγει τοῖς μαθηταῖς
name [was] Gethsemane, and he says to the disciples
αὐτοῦ· καθίσατε ὧδε ἕως προσεύξωμαι.
of him: Sit ye here while I pray.
33 καὶ παραλαμβάνει τὸν Πέτρον καὶ τὸν
And he takes – Peter and –
Ἰάκωβον καὶ τὸν Ἰωάννην μετ' αὐτοῦ,
James and – John with him,
καὶ ἤρξατο ἐκθαμβεῖσθαι καὶ ἀδημονεῖν,
and began to be greatly astonished and to be distressed,
34 καὶ λέγει αὐτοῖς· περίλυπός ἐστιν ἡ
and says to them: Deeply grieved is the
ψυχή μου ἕως θανάτου· μείνατε ὧδε καὶ
soul of me unto death; remain ye here and
γρηγορεῖτε. **35** καὶ προελθὼν μικρὸν ἔπιπτεν
watch. And going forward a little he fell
ἐπὶ τῆς γῆς, καὶ προσηύχετο ἵνα εἰ
on the ground, and prayed that if
δυνατόν ἐστιν παρέλθῃ ἀπ' αὐτοῦ ἡ ὥρα,
possible it is might pass away from him the hour,
36 καὶ ἔλεγεν· ἀββὰ ὁ πατήρ, πάντα
and said: Abba – Father, all things
δυνατά σοι· παρένεγκε τὸ ποτήριον τοῦτο
[are] possible to thee; remove – cup this
ἀπ' ἐμοῦ· ἀλλ' οὐ τί ἐγὼ θέλω ἀλλὰ
from me; but not what I wish but
τί σύ. **37** καὶ ἔρχεται καὶ εὑρίσκει
what thou. And he comes and finds
αὐτοὺς καθεύδοντας, καὶ λέγει τῷ Πέτρῳ·
them sleeping, and says – to Peter:
Σίμων, καθεύδεις; οὐκ ἴσχυσας μίαν ὥραν
Simon, sleepest thou? couldest thou not one hour
γρηγορῆσαι; **38** γρηγορεῖτε καὶ προσεύχεσθε,
to watch? Watch ye and pray,
ἵνα μὴ ἔλθητε εἰς πειρασμόν· τὸ μὲν
lest ye come into temptation; indeed the
πνεῦμα πρόθυμον, ἡ δὲ σὰρξ ἀσθενής.
spirit [is] eager, but the flesh weak.
39 καὶ πάλιν ἀπελθὼν προσηύξατο τὸν
And again going away he prayed ²the
αὐτὸν λόγον εἰπών. **40** καὶ πάλιν ἐλθὼν
³same ⁴word ¹saying. And again coming
εὗρεν αὐτοὺς καθεύδοντας, ἦσαν γὰρ αὐτῶν
he found them sleeping, for were of them
οἱ ὀφθαλμοὶ καταβαρυνόμενοι, καὶ οὐκ
the eyes becoming heavy, and not
ᾔδεισαν τί ἀποκριθῶσιν αὐτῷ. **41** καὶ
they knew what they might answer him. And
ἔρχεται τὸ τρίτον καὶ λέγει αὐτοῖς·
he comes the third [time] and says to them:
καθεύδετε τὸ λοιπὸν καὶ ἀναπαύεσθε·
Sleep ye now† and rest;
ἀπέχει· ἦλθεν ἡ ὥρα, ἰδοὺ παραδίδοται ὁ
it is enough; came the hour, behold is betrayed the
υἱὸς τοῦ ἀνθρώπου εἰς τὰς χεῖρας τῶν
Son – man into the hands –
ἁμαρτωλῶν. **42** ἐγείρεσθε, ἄγωμεν· ἰδοὺ ὁ
of sinners. Rise ye, let us go; behold the
παραδιδούς με ἤγγικεν. **43** Καὶ εὐθὺς ἔτι
[one] betraying me has drawn near. And immediately yet
αὐτοῦ λαλοῦντος παραγίνεται [ὁ] Ἰούδας
him speaking[a] arrives – Judas
= while he was still speaking
εἷς τῶν δώδεκα, καὶ μετ' αὐτοῦ ὄχλος
one of the twelve, and with him a crowd
μετὰ μαχαιρῶν καὶ ξύλων παρὰ τῶν
with swords and clubs from the

called Gethsemane, and
Jesus said to his disciples,
"Sit here while I pray."
33 He took Peter, James and
John along with him, and
he began to be deeply distressed and troubled.
34 "My soul is over-
whelmed with sorrow to
the point of death," he said
to them. "Stay here and
keep watch."
35 Going a little farther, he
fell to the ground and
prayed that if possible the
hour might pass from him.
36 "*Abba*,[q] Father," he
said, "everything is possible for you. Take this cup
from me. Yet not what I
will, but what you will."
37 Then he returned to his
disciples and found them
sleeping. "Simon," he said
to Peter, "are you asleep?
Could you not keep watch
for one hour? 38 Watch and
pray so that you will not fall
into temptation. The spirit
is willing, but the body is
weak."
39 Once more he went
away and prayed the same
thing. 40 When he came
back, he again found them
sleeping, because their
eyes were heavy. They did
not know what to say to
him.
41 Returning the third
time, he said to them, "Are
you still sleeping and resting? Enough! The hour has
come. Look, the Son of
Man is betrayed into the
hands of sinners. 42 Rise!
Let us go! Here comes my
betrayer!"

Jesus Arrested

43 Just as he was speaking,
Judas, one of the Twelve,
appeared. With him was a
crowd armed with swords
and clubs, sent from the

[q] 36 Aramaic for *Father*

elders. 44 Now the betrayer
had given them a sign, saying, "The one I will kiss is
the man; arrest him and
lead him away under
guard." 45 So when he
came, he went up to him at
once and said, "Rabbi!"
and kissed him. 46 Then
they laid hands on him and
arrested him. 47 But one of
those who stood near drew
his sword and struck the
slave of the high priest, cutting off his ear. 48 Then
Jesus said to them, "Have
you come out with swords
and clubs to arrest me as
though I were a bandit?
49 Day after day I was with
you in the temple teaching,
and you did not arrest me.
But let the scriptures be fulfilled." 50 All of them deserted him and fled.
51 A certain young man
was following him, wearing
nothing but a linen cloth.
They caught hold of him,
52 but he left the linen cloth
and ran off naked.

Jesus before the Council

53 They took Jesus to
the high priest; and all the
chief priests, the elders,
and the scribes were as-
sembled. 54 Peter had followed him at a distance,
right into the courtyard of
the high priest; and he was
sitting with the guards,
warming himself at the fire.
55 Now the chief priests and
the whole council were
looking for testimony
against Jesus to put him to
death; but they found none.
56 For many gave false testimony against him, and
their testimony did not
agree. 57 Some stood up

ἀρχιερέων καὶ τῶν γραμματέων καὶ τῶν
chief priests and the scribes and the
πρεσβυτέρων. **44** δεδώκει δὲ ὁ παραδιδοὺς
elders. [1]Now [5]had given [2]the [one] [3]betraying
αὐτὸν σύσσημον αὐτοῖς λέγων· ὃν ἂν
[4]him [7]a signal [6]them saying: Whomever
φιλήσω αὐτός ἐστιν· κρατήσατε αὐτὸν καὶ
I may kiss he is; seize ye him and
ἀπάγετε ἀσφαλῶς. **45** καὶ ἐλθὼν εὐθὺς
lead away securely. And coming immediately
προσελθὼν αὐτῷ λέγει· ῥαββί, καὶ
approaching *to* him he says: Rabbi, and
κατεφίλησεν αὐτόν· **46** οἱ δὲ ἐπέβαλαν τὰς
fervently kissed him; and they [1]laid [4]on [2]the(their)
χεῖρας αὐτῷ καὶ ἐκράτησαν αὐτόν. **47** εἷς
[3]hands him and seized him. [2]one
δέ τις τῶν παρεστηκότων σπασάμενος
[1]But [3]a certain of the [ones] standing by drawing
τὴν μάχαιραν ἔπαισεν τὸν δοῦλον τοῦ ἀρχιερέως
the sword struck the slave of the high priest
καὶ ἀφεῖλεν αὐτοῦ τὸ ὠτάριον. **48** καὶ
and cut off of him the ear. And
ἀποκριθεὶς ὁ Ἰησοῦς εἶπεν αὐτοῖς· ὡς
answering – Jesus said to them: As
ἐπὶ λῃστὴν ἐξήλθατε μετὰ μαχαιρῶν καὶ
against a robber came ye forth with swords and
ξύλων συλλαβεῖν με; **49** καθ᾽ ἡμέραν ἤμην
clubs to arrest me? Daily I was
πρὸς ὑμᾶς ἐν τῷ ἱερῷ διδάσκων, καὶ οὐκ
with you in the temple teaching, and not
ἐκρατήσατέ με· ἀλλ᾽ ἵνα πληρωθῶσιν αἱ
ye did seize me; but that may be fulfilled the
γραφαί. **50** καὶ ἀφέντες αὐτὸν ἔφυγον
scriptures. And leaving him they fled
πάντες. **51** Καὶ νεανίσκος τις συνηκολούθει
all. And a certain young man accompanied
αὐτῷ περιβεβλημένος σινδόνα ἐπὶ γυμνοῦ,
him *having been* clothed [in] a nightgown over [his] naked [body],
καὶ κρατοῦσιν αὐτόν· **52** ὁ δὲ καταλιπὼν
and they seize him; and he leaving
τὴν σινδόνα γυμνὸς ἔφυγεν.
the nightgown naked fled.

53 Καὶ ἀπήγαγον τὸν Ἰησοῦν πρὸς τὸν
And they led away – Jesus to the
ἀρχιερέα, καὶ συνέρχονται πάντες οἱ
high priest, and come together all the
ἀρχιερεῖς καὶ οἱ πρεσβύτεροι καὶ οἱ
chief priests and the elders and the
γραμματεῖς. **54** καὶ ὁ Πέτρος ἀπὸ μακρόθεν
scribes. And – Peter from afar
ἠκολούθησεν αὐτῷ ἕως ἔσω εἰς τὴν αὐλὴν
followed him until within *in* the court
τοῦ ἀρχιερέως, καὶ ἦν συγκαθήμενος μετὰ
of the high priest, and was sitting *with* with
τῶν ὑπηρετῶν καὶ θερμαινόμενος πρὸς τὸ
the attendants and warming himself by the
φῶς. **55** Οἱ δὲ ἀρχιερεῖς καὶ ὅλον τὸ
bright fire. Now the chief priests and all the
συνέδριον ἐζήτουν κατὰ τοῦ Ἰησοῦ
council sought against – Jesus
μαρτυρίαν εἰς τὸ θανατῶσαι αὐτόν, καὶ
witness for the to put to death him, and
= so as
οὐχ ηὕρισκον· **56** πολλοὶ γὰρ ἐψευδομαρτύρουν
found not; for many falsely witnessed
κατ᾽ αὐτοῦ, καὶ ἴσαι αἱ μαρτυρίαι οὐκ
against him, and [4]identical [1]the [2]testimonies [3]not

chief priests, the teachers
of the law, and the elders.
44 Now the betrayer had
arranged a signal with
them: "The one I kiss is the
man; arrest him and lead
him away under guard."
45 Going at once to Jesus,
Judas said, "Rabbi!" and
kissed him. 46 The men
seized Jesus and arrested
him. 47 Then one of those
standing near drew his
sword and struck the ser-
vant of the high priest, cutting off his ear.
48 "Am I leading a rebel-
lion," said Jesus, "that you
have come out with swords
and clubs to capture me?
49 Every day I was with
you, teaching in the temple
courts, and you did not arrest me. But the Scriptures
must be fulfilled." 50 Then
everyone deserted him and
fled.
51 A young man, wearing
nothing but a linen gar-
ment, was following Jesus.
When they seized him, 52 he
fled naked, leaving his garment behind.

Before the Sanhedrin

53 They took Jesus to the
high priest, and all the chief
priests, elders and teachers
of the law came together.
54 Peter followed him at a
distance, right into the
courtyard of the high
priest. There he sat with
the guards and warmed
himself at the fire.
55 The chief priests and
the whole Sanhedrin were
looking for evidence
against Jesus so that they
could put him to death, but
they did not find any.
56 Many testified falsely
against him, but their state-
ments did not agree.

and gave false testimony
against him, saying, 58 "We
heard him say, 'I will destroy this temple that is
made with hands, and in
three days I will build another, not made with
hands.'" 59 But even on
this point their testimony
did not agree. 60 Then the
high priest stood up before
them and asked Jesus,
"Have you no answer?
What is it that they testify
against you?" 61 But he was
silent and did not answer.
Again the high priest asked
him, "Are you the Messi-
ah,[b] the Son of the Blessed
One?" 62 Jesus said, "I am;
and
'you will see the Son
of Man
seated at the right
hand of
the Power,'
and 'coming with the
clouds
of heaven.'"
63 Then the high priest tore
his clothes and said, "Why
do we still need witnesses?
64 You have heard his blasphemy! What is your deci-
sion?" All of them con-
demned him as deserving
death. 65 Some began to
spit on him, to blindfold
him, and to strike him, saying to him, "Prophesy!"
The guards also took him
over and beat him.

Peter Denies Jesus

66 While Peter was be-
low in the courtyard, one of
the servant-girls of the high
priest came by. 67 When
she saw Peter warming
himself, she stared at him
and said, "You also were
with Jesus, the man from
Nazareth." 68 But he denied
it, saying, "I do not know
or understand what you are
talking about." And he
went out into the fore-
court.[c] Then the cock

ἦσαν. **57** καί τινες ἀναστάντες ἐψευδομαρτύρουν
[2]were. And some standing up falsely witnessed
κατ' αὐτοῦ λέγοντες **58** ὅτι ἡμεῖς ἠκούσαμεν
against him saying[,] – We heard
αὐτοῦ λέγοντος ὅτι ἐγὼ καταλύσω τὸν
him saying[,] – I will overthrow –
ναὸν τοῦτον τὸν χειροποίητον καὶ διὰ
[3]shrine [1]this – [2]handmade and through(after)
τριῶν ἡμερῶν ἄλλον ἀχειροποίητον οἰκο-
three days another not handmade I will
δομήσω. **59** καὶ οὐδὲ οὕτως ἴση ἦν ἡ
build. And not so identical was the
μαρτυρία αὐτῶν. **60** καὶ ἀναστὰς ὁ
witness of them. And standing up the
ἀρχιερεὺς εἰς μέσον ἐπηρώτησεν τὸν Ἰησοῦν
high priest in [the] midst questioned – Jesus
λέγων· οὐκ ἀποκρίνῃ οὐδὲν τί οὗτοί σου
saying: Answerest thou not no(any)thing what these men [2]thee
καταμαρτυροῦσιν; **61** ὁ δὲ ἐσιώπα καὶ
[1]testify against ? But he was silent and
οὐκ ἀπεκρίνατο οὐδέν. πάλιν ὁ ἀρχιερεὺς
answered not no(any)thing. Again the high priest
ἐπηρώτα αὐτὸν καὶ λέγει αὐτῷ· σὺ εἶ ὁ
questioned him and says to him: Thou art the
χριστὸς ὁ υἱὸς τοῦ εὐλογητοῦ; **62** ὁ δὲ
Christ the Son of the Blessed [one] ? – And
Ἰησοῦς εἶπεν· ἐγώ εἰμι, καὶ ὄψεσθε
Jesus said: I am, and ye will see
τὸν υἱὸν τοῦ ἀνθρώπου ἐκ δεξιῶν καθήμενον
the Son – of man [2]at [the] right [hand] [1]sitting
τῆς δυνάμεως καὶ ἐρχόμενον μετὰ τῶν
of the Power and coming with the
νεφελῶν τοῦ οὐρανοῦ. **63** ὁ δὲ ἀρχιερεὺς
clouds – of heaven. And the high priest
διαρήξας τοὺς χιτῶνας αὐτοῦ λέγει· τί
rending the tunics of him says: What
ἔτι χρείαν ἔχομεν μαρτύρων; **64** ἠκούσατε
more need have we of witnesses ? ye heard
τῆς βλασφημίας· τί ὑμῖν φαίνεται; οἱ δὲ
the blasphemy; what to you appears it ? And they
πάντες κατέκριναν αὐτὸν ἔνοχον εἶναι
all condemned him liable to be
θανάτου. **65** Καὶ ἤρξαντό τινες ἐμπτύειν
of(to) death. And began some to spit at
αὐτῷ καὶ περικαλύπτειν αὐτοῦ τὸ πρόσωπον
him and to cover of him the face
καὶ κολαφίζειν αὐτὸν καὶ λέγειν αὐτῷ·
and to maltreat him and to say to him:
προφήτευσον, καὶ οἱ ὑπηρέται ῥαπίσμασιν
Prophesy, and the attendants with slaps
αὐτὸν ἔλαβον. **66** Καὶ ὄντος τοῦ Πέτρου
[2]him [1]took. And being – Peter[a]
= as Peter was
κάτω ἐν τῇ αὐλῇ ἔρχεται μία τῶν
below in the court comes one of the
παιδισκῶν τοῦ ἀρχιερέως, **67** καὶ ἰδοῦσα
maidservants of the high priest, and seeing
τὸν Πέτρον θερμαινόμενον ἐμβλέψασα αὐτῷ
– Peter warming himself looking at him
λέγει· καὶ σὺ μετὰ τοῦ Ναζαρηνοῦ ἦσθα
says: And [1]thou [3]with [4]the [5]Nazarene [2]wast
τοῦ Ἰησοῦ. **68** ὁ δὲ ἠρνήσατο λέγων· οὔτε
– [6]Jesus. But he denied saying: [2]neither
οἶδα οὔτε ἐπίσταμαι σὺ τί λέγεις. καὶ
[1]I [3]know [4]nor [5]understand [7]thou [6]what [8]sayest. And
ἐξῆλθεν ἔξω εἰς τὸ προαύλιον· **69** καὶ ἡ
he went forth outside into the forecourt; and the

57 Then some stood up
and gave this false testimony against him: 58 "We
heard him say, 'I will destroy this man-made tem-
ple and in three days will
build another, not made by
man.'" 59 Yet even then
their testimony did not
agree.
60 Then the high priest
stood up before them and
asked Jesus, "Are you not
going to answer? What is
this testimony that these
men are bringing against
you?" 61 But Jesus re-
mained silent and gave no
answer.
Again the high priest
asked him, "Are you the
Christ,[r] the Son of the
Blessed One?"
62 "I am," said Jesus.
"And you will see the Son
of Man sitting at the right
hand of the Mighty One and
coming on the clouds of
heaven."
63 The high priest tore his
clothes. "Why do we need
any more witnesses?" he
asked. 64 "You have heard
the blasphemy. What do
you think?"
They all condemned him
as worthy of death. 65 Then
some began to spit at him;
they blindfolded him,
struck him with their fists,
and said, "Prophesy!" And
the guards took him and
beat him.

Peter Disowns Jesus

66 While Peter was below
in the courtyard, one of the
servant girls of the high
priest came by. 67 When she
saw Peter warming himself,
she looked closely at him.
"You also were with that
Nazarene, Jesus," she
said.
68 But he denied it. "I
don't know or understand
what you're talking
about," he said, and went
out into the entryway.[s]

[b] Or *the Christ*
[c] Or *gateway*

[r] 61 Or *Messiah*
[s] 68 Some early manuscripts *entryway and the rooster crowed*

crowed.[d] 69And the
servant-girl, on seeing him,
began again to say to the
bystanders, "This man is
one of them." 70But again
he denied it. Then after a
little while the bystanders
again said to Peter, "Certainly you are one of them;
for you are a Galilean."
71But he began to curse,
and he swore an oath, "I do
not know this man you are
talking about." 72At that
moment the cock crowed
for the second time. Then
Peter remembered that
Jesus had said to him, "Before the cock crows twice,
you will deny me three
times." And he broke down
and wept.

παιδίσκη ἰδοῦσα αὐτὸν ἤρξατο πάλιν λέγειν
maidservant seeing him began again to say
τοῖς παρεστῶσιν ὅτι οὗτος ἐξ αὐτῶν ἐστιν.
to the [ones] standing by[,] – This man of them is.
70 ὁ δὲ πάλιν ἠρνεῖτο. καὶ μετὰ μικρὸν
But he again denied. And after a little
πάλιν οἱ παρεστῶτες ἔλεγον τῷ Πέτρῳ·
again the [ones] standing by said – to Peter:
ἀληθῶς ἐξ αὐτῶν εἶ· καὶ γὰρ Γαλιλαῖος
Truly of them thou art; [2]indeed [1]for [4]a Galilæan
εἶ. 71 ὁ δὲ ἤρξατο ἀναθεματίζειν καὶ
[3]thou art. And he began to curse and
ὀμνύναι ὅτι οὐκ οἶδα τὸν ἄνθρωπον
to swear[,] – I know not – man
τοῦτον ὃν λέγετε. 72 καὶ εὐθὺς ἐκ
this whom ye say. And immediately a
δευτέρου ἀλέκτωρ ἐφώνησεν. καὶ ἀνεμνήσθη
second time a cock crew. And remembered
ὁ Πέτρος τὸ ῥῆμα ὡς εἶπεν αὐτῷ ὁ
– Peter the word as said to him –
Ἰησοῦς ὅτι πρὶν ἀλέκτορα δὶς φωνῆσαι
Jesus[,] – Before a cock twice *to* crow[b]
τρίς με ἀπαρνήσῃ· καὶ ἐπιβαλὼν ἔκλαιεν.
thrice me thou wilt deny; and thinking thereon he wept.

69When the servant girl
saw him there, she said
again to those standing
around, "This fellow is one
of them." 70Again he de-
nied it.
After a little while, those
standing near said to Peter,
"Surely you are one of
them, for you are a Galilean."
71He began to call down
curses on himself, and he
swore to them, "I don't
know this man you're talking about."
72Immediately the rooster
crowed the second time.[t]
Then Peter remembered
the word Jesus had spoken
to him: "Before the rooster
crows twice[u] you will disown me three times." And
he broke down and wept.

Chapter 15

Jesus before Pilate

As soon as it was morn-
ing, the chief priests
held a consultation with the
elders and scribes and the
whole council. They bound
Jesus, led him away, and
handed him over to Pilate.
2Pilate asked him, "Are
you the King of the Jews?"
He answered him, "You
say so." 3Then the chief
priests accused him of
many things. 4Pilate asked
him again, "Have you no
answer? See how many
charges they bring against
you." 5But Jesus made no
further reply, so that Pilate
was amazed.

Pilate Hands Jesus over to Be Crucified

6 Now at the festival he
used to release a prisoner
for them, anyone for whom
they asked. 7Now a man
called Barabbas was in
prison with the rebels who
had committed murder dur-
ing the insurrection. 8So
the crowd came and began
to ask Pilate to do for them
according to his custom.
9Then he answered them,
"Do you want me to release

[d]Other ancient authorities lack *Then the cock crowed*

15 Καὶ εὐθὺς πρωῒ συμβούλιον ἑτοιμάσαντες
And immediately early [2]a council [1]preparing
οἱ ἀρχιερεῖς μετὰ τῶν πρεσβυτέρων καὶ
the chief priests with the elders and
γραμματέων καὶ ὅλον τὸ συνέδριον, δήσαντες
scribes and all the council, having bound
τὸν Ἰησοῦν ἀπήνεγκαν καὶ παρέδωκαν
– Jesus led [him] away and delivered [him]
Πιλάτῳ. 2 καὶ ἐπηρώτησεν αὐτὸν ὁ
to Pilate. And questioned him –
Πιλᾶτος· σὺ εἶ ὁ βασιλεὺς τῶν Ἰουδαίων;
Pilate: Thou art the king of the Jews?
ὁ δὲ ἀποκριθεὶς αὐτῷ λέγει· σὺ λέγεις.
And he answering him says: Thou sayest.
3 καὶ κατηγόρουν αὐτοῦ οἱ ἀρχιερεῖς πολλά.
And accused him the chief priests many things.
4 ὁ δὲ Πιλᾶτος πάλιν ἐπηρώτα αὐτὸν [λέγων]·
– But Pilate again questioned him saying:
οὐκ ἀποκρίνῃ οὐδέν; ἴδε πόσα
Answerest thou not no(any)thing? Behold how many things
σου κατηγοροῦσιν. 5 ὁ δὲ Ἰησοῦς οὐκ-
thee they accuse. – But Jesus no(any)
ἔτι οὐδὲν ἀπεκρίθη, ὥστε θαυμάζειν
more nothing answered, so as to marvel
= so that Pilate marvelled.
τὸν Πιλᾶτον. 6 Κατὰ δὲ ἑορτὴν ἀπέλυεν
– Pilate[b]. Now at a feast he released
αὐτοῖς ἕνα δέσμιον ὃν παρῃτοῦντο. 7 ἦν δὲ
to them one prisoner whom they begged. Now there was
ὁ λεγόμενος Βαραββᾶς μετὰ τῶν
the [one] named Barabbas with the
στασιαστῶν δεδεμένος, οἵτινες ἐν τῇ στάσει
rebels *having been* bound, who* in the rebellion
φόνον πεποιήκεισαν. 8 καὶ ἀναβὰς ὁ ὄχλος
murder had done. And going up the crowd
ἤρξατο αἰτεῖσθαι καθὼς ἐποίει αὐτοῖς.
began to ask as he used to do for them.
9 ὁ δὲ Πιλᾶτος ἀπεκρίθη αὐτοῖς λέγων·
– But Pilate answered them saying:

* Note the plural.

Chapter 15

Jesus Before Pilate

Very early in the
morning, the chief
priests, with the elders, the
teachers of the law and the
whole Sanhedrin, reached
a decision. They bound
Jesus, led him away and
handed him over to Pilate.
2"Are you the king of the
Jews?" asked Pilate.
"Yes, it is as you say,"
Jesus replied.
3The chief priests ac-
cused him of many things.
4So again Pilate asked him,
"Aren't you going to an-
swer? See how many things
they are accusing you of."
5But Jesus still made no
reply, and Pilate was
amazed.
6Now it was the custom at
the Feast to release a prisoner whom the people re-
quested. 7A man called
Barabbas was in prison
with the insurrectionists
who had committed murder
in the uprising. 8The crowd
came up and asked Pilate to
do for them what he usually
did.
9"Do you want me to re-
lease to you the king of the

[t]72 Some early manuscripts do not have *the second time*.
[u]72 Some early manuscripts do not have *twice*.

for you the King of the Jews?" 10 For he realized that it was out of jealousy that the chief priests had handed him over. 11 But the chief priests stirred up the crowd to have him release Barabbas for them instead. 12 Pilate spoke to them again, "Then what do you wish me to do[e] with the man you call[f] the King of the Jews?" 13 They shouted back, "Crucify him!" 14 Pilate asked them, "Why, what evil has he done?" But they shouted all the more, "Crucify him!" 15 So Pilate, wishing to satisfy the crowd, released Barabbas for them; and after flogging Jesus, he handed him over to be crucified.

The Soldiers Mock Jesus

16 Then the soldiers led him into the courtyard of the palace (that is, the governor's headquarters[g]); and they called together the whole cohort. 17 And they clothed him in a purple cloak; and after twisting some thorns into a crown, they put it on him. 18 And they began saluting him, "Hail, King of the Jews!" 19 They struck his head with a reed, spat upon him, and knelt down in homage to him. 20 After mocking him, they stripped him of the purple cloak and put his own clothes on him. Then they led him out to crucify him.

The Crucifixion of Jesus

21 They compelled a passer-by, who was coming in from the country, to carry his cross; it was Simon of Cyrene, the father of Alexander and Rufus. 22 Then they brought Jesus[h] to the place called Golgotha (which means the place of a skull). 23 And they offered

[e] Other ancient authorities read *what should I do*
[f] Other ancient authorities lack *the man you call*
[g] Gk *the praetorium*
[h] Gk *him*

θέλετε ἀπολύσω ὑμῖν τὸν βασιλέα τῶν
Do ye wish I may release to you the king of the
Ἰουδαίων; **10** ἐγίνωσκεν γὰρ ὅτι διὰ φθόνον
Jews ? For he knew that on account of envy
παραδεδώκεισαν αὐτὸν οἱ ἀρχιερεῖς. **11** οἱ
had delivered him the chief priests. the
δὲ ἀρχιερεῖς ἀνέσεισαν τὸν ὄχλον ἵνα
But chief priests stirred up the crowd that
μᾶλλον τὸν Βαραββᾶν ἀπολύσῃ αὐτοῖς.
rather - Barabbas he should release to them.
12 ὁ δὲ Πιλᾶτος πάλιν ἀποκριθεὶς ἔλεγεν
- So Pilate again answering said
αὐτοῖς· τί οὖν ποιήσω [ὃν] λέγετε τὸν
to them: What then may I do [to him] whom ye call the
βασιλέα τῶν Ἰουδαίων; **13** οἱ δὲ πάλιν
king of the Jews ? And they again
ἔκραξαν· σταύρωσον αὐτόν. **14** ὁ δὲ
cried out: Crucify him. - But
Πιλᾶτος ἔλεγεν αὐτοῖς· τί γὰρ ἐποίησεν
Pilate said to them: Indeed what ˢdid he
κακόν; οἱ δὲ περισσῶς ἔκραξαν· σταύρωσον
ˡevil ? and they more cried out: Crucify
αὐτόν. **15** ὁ δὲ Πιλᾶτος βουλόμενος τῷ
him. - And Pilate resolving the
ὄχλῳ τὸ ἱκανὸν ποιῆσαι ἀπέλυσεν αὐτοῖς
crowd to satisfy† released to them
τὸν Βαραββᾶν, καὶ παρέδωκεν τὸν Ἰησοῦν
- Barabbas, and delivered - Jesus
φραγελλώσας ἵνα σταυρωθῇ.
having scourged [him] that he might be crucified.
16 Οἱ δὲ στρατιῶται ἀπήγαγον αὐτὸν
Then the soldiers led away him
ἔσω τῆς αὐλῆς, ὅ ἐστιν πραιτώριον, καὶ
inside the court, which is prætorium, and
συγκαλοῦσιν ὅλην τὴν σπεῖραν. **17** καὶ
they call together all the cohort. And
ἐνδιδύσκουσιν αὐτὸν πορφύραν καὶ περιτιθέασιν
they put on him a purple [robe] and place round
αὐτῷ πλέξαντες ἀκάνθινον στέφανον· **18** καὶ
him plaiting a thorny crown; and
ἤρξαντο ἀσπάζεσθαι αὐτόν· χαῖρε, βασιλεῦ
they began to salute him: Hail, king
τῶν Ἰουδαίων· **19** καὶ ἔτυπτον αὐτοῦ τὴν
of the Jews; and they struck of him the
κεφαλὴν καλάμῳ καὶ ἐνέπτυον αὐτῷ, καὶ
head with a reed and spat at him, and
τιθέντες τὰ γόνατα προσεκύνουν αὐτῷ.
placing(bending) the(their) knees worshipped him.
20 καὶ ὅτε ἐνέπαιξαν αὐτῷ, ἐξέδυσαν
And when they mocked him, they took off
αὐτὸν τὴν πορφύραν καὶ ἐνέδυσαν αὐτὸν
him the purple [robe] and put on him
τὰ ἱμάτια αὐτοῦ. Καὶ ἐξάγουσιν αὐτὸν
the garments of him. And they lead forth him
ἵνα σταυρώσωσιν αὐτόν. **21** καὶ ἀγγαρεύουσιν
that they might crucify him. And they impress
παράγοντά τινα Σίμωνα Κυρηναῖον ἐρχόμενον
passing by a certain Simon a Cyrenian coming
ἀπ' ἀγροῦ, τὸν πατέρα Ἀλεξάνδρου καὶ
from [the] country, the father of Alexander and
Ῥούφου, ἵνα ἄρῃ τὸν σταυρὸν αὐτοῦ.
of Rufus, that he might bear the cross of him.
22 καὶ φέρουσιν αὐτὸν ἐπὶ τὸν Γολγοθᾶν
And they bring him to the Golgotha
τόπον, ὅ ἐστιν μεθερμηνευόμενος κρανίου
place, which is being interpreted of a skull

Jews?" asked Pilate, 10 knowing it was out of envy that the chief priests had handed Jesus over to him. 11 But the chief priests stirred up the crowd to have Pilate release Barabbas instead.

12 "What shall I do, then, with the one you call the king of the Jews?" Pilate asked them.

13 "Crucify him!" they shouted.

14 "Why? What crime has he committed?" asked Pilate.

But they shouted all the louder, "Crucify him!"

15 Wanting to satisfy the crowd, Pilate released Barabbas to them. He had Jesus flogged, and handed him over to be crucified.

The Soldiers Mock Jesus

16 The soldiers led Jesus away into the palace (that is, the Praetorium) and called together the whole company of soldiers. 17 They put a purple robe on him, then twisted together a crown of thorns and set it on him. 18 And they began to call out to him, "Hail, king of the Jews!" 19 Again and again they struck him on the head with a staff and spit on him. Falling on their knees, they paid homage to him. 20 And when they had mocked him, they took off the purple robe and put his own clothes on him. Then they led him out to crucify him.

The Crucifixion

21 A certain man from Cyrene, Simon, the father of Alexander and Rufus, was passing by on his way in from the country, and they forced him to carry the cross. 22 They brought Jesus to the place called Golgotha (which means The Place of the Skull).

him wine mixed with
myrrh; but he did not take
it. 24 And they crucified
him, and divided his
clothes among them, cast-
ing lots to decide what each
should take.
25 It was nine o'clock in
the morning when they crucified him. 26 The inscription of the charge against
him read, "The King of the
Jews." 27 And with him
they crucified two bandits,
one on his right and one on
his left.[i] 29 Those who
passed by derided[j] him,
shaking their heads and
saying, "Aha! You who
would destroy the temple
and build it in three days,
30 save yourself, and come
down from the cross!" 31 In
the same way the chief
priests, along with the
scribes, were also mocking
him among themselves and
saying, "He saved others;
he cannot save himself.
32 Let the Messiah,[k] the
King of Israel, come down
from the cross now, so that
we may see and believe."
Those who were crucified
with him also taunted him.

The Death of Jesus

33 When it was noon,
darkness came over the
whole land[l] until three in
the afternoon. 34 At three
o'clock Jesus cried out
with a loud voice, "Eloi,
Eloi, lema sabachthani?"
which means, "My God,
my God, why have you for-
saken me?"[m] 35 When some
of the bystanders heard it,
they said, "Listen, he is
calling for Elijah." 36 And
someone ran, filled a
sponge with sour wine, put
it on a stick, and gave it to
him to drink, saying,
"Wait, let us see whether
Elijah will come to take him
down." 37 Then Jesus gave

[i] Other ancient authorities add verse 28, *And the scripture was fulfilled that says, "And he was counted among the lawless."*
[j] Or *blasphemed*
[k] Or *the Christ*
[l] Or *earth*
[m] Other ancient authorities read *made me a reproach*

τόπος. 23 καὶ ἐδίδουν αὐτῷ ἐσμυρνισμένον
place. And they gave him [2]*having been* spiced with myrrh

οἶνον· ὃς δὲ οὐκ ἔλαβεν. 24 καὶ σταυροῦσιν
[1]wine; but who(he) received not. And they crucify

αὐτόν, καὶ διαμερίζονται τὰ ἱμάτια αὐτοῦ,
him, and divide the garments of him,

βάλλοντες κλῆρον ἐπ' αὐτὰ τίς τί ἄρῃ.
casting a lot on them [2]one [1]what might take.

25 ἦν δὲ ὥρα τρίτη καὶ ἐσταύρωσαν
Now it was hour third and they crucified

αὐτόν. 26 καὶ ἦν ἡ ἐπιγραφὴ τῆς αἰτίας
him. And was the superscription of the accusation

αὐτοῦ ἐπιγεγραμμένη· Ο ΒΑΣΙΛΕΥΣ ΤΩΝ
of him *having been* written over: THE KING OF THE

ΙΟΥΔΑΙΩΝ. 27 Καὶ σὺν αὐτῷ σταυροῦσιν
JEWS. And with him they crucify

δύο λῃστάς, ἕνα ἐκ δεξιῶν καὶ ἕνα ἐξ
two robbers, one on [the] right and one on

εὐωνύμων αὐτοῦ.‡ 29 Καὶ οἱ παραπορευόμενοι
[the] left of him. And the [ones] passing by

ἐβλασφήμουν αὐτὸν κινοῦντες τὰς κεφαλὰς
blasphemed him wagging the heads

αὐτῶν καὶ λέγοντες· οὐὰ ὁ καταλύων
of them and saying: Ah the [one] overthrowing

τὸν ναὸν καὶ οἰκοδομῶν [ἐν] τρισὶν
the shrine and building in three

ἡμέραις, 30 σῶσον σεαυτὸν καταβὰς ἀπὸ
days, save thyself coming down from

τοῦ σταυροῦ. 31 ὁμοίως καὶ οἱ ἀρχιερεῖς
the cross. Likewise also the chief priests

ἐμπαίζοντες πρὸς ἀλλήλους μετὰ τῶν
mocking to one another with the

γραμματέων ἔλεγον· ἄλλους ἔσωσεν, ἑαυτὸν
scribes said: Others he saved, himself

οὐ δύναται σῶσαι· 32 ὁ χριστὸς ὁ βασιλεὺς
he cannot *to* save; the Christ the king

Ἰσραὴλ καταβάτω νῦν ἀπὸ τοῦ σταυροῦ,
of Israel let come down now from the cross,

ἵνα ἴδωμεν καὶ πιστεύσωμεν. καὶ οἱ
that we may see and believe. And the

συνεσταυρωμένοι σὺν αὐτῷ ὠνείδιζον αὐτόν.
[ones] crucified *with* with him reproached him.

33 Καὶ γενομένης ὥρας ἕκτης σκότος
And becoming hour sixth* darkness
= when it was the sixth hour

ἐγένετο ἐφ' ὅλην τὴν γῆν ἕως ὥρας
came over all the land until [the] hour

ἐνάτης. 34 καὶ τῇ ἐνάτῃ ὥρᾳ ἐβόησεν ὁ
ninth. And at the ninth hour cried –

Ἰησοῦς φωνῇ μεγάλῃ· ἐλωῒ ἐλωῒ λαμὰ
Jesus with a voice great(loud): Eloi[,] Eloi[,] lama

σαβαχθάνι; ὅ ἐστιν μεθερμηνευόμενον· ὁ
sabachthani ? which is being interpreted: The

θεός μου ὁ θεός μου, εἰς τί ἐγκατέλιπές
God of me[,] the God of me, why didst thou forsake

με; 35 καί τινες τῶν παρεστηκότων
me ? And some of the [ones] standing by

ἀκούσαντες ἔλεγον· ἴδε Ἠλίαν φωνεῖ.
hearing said: Behold Elias he calls.

36 δραμὼν δέ τις γεμίσας σπόγγον ὄξους
And running one having filled a sponge of(with) vinegar

περιθεὶς καλάμῳ ἐπότιζεν αὐτόν, λέγων·
placing it round a reed [1]gave [3]to drink [2]him, saying:

ἄφετε ἴδωμεν εἰ ἔρχεται Ἠλίας καθελεῖν
Leave[,] let us see if comes Elias [1]to take [2]down

‡ Verse 28 omitted by Nestle; *cf.* NIV footnote.

23 Then they offered him
wine mixed with myrrh,
but he did not take it. 24 And
they crucified him. Dividing up his clothes, they cast
lots to see what each would
get.
25 It was the third hour
when they crucified him.
26 The written notice of the
charge against him read:
THE KING OF THE JEWS.
27 They crucified two robbers with him, one on his
right and one on his left.[v]
29 Those who passed by
hurled insults at him, shaking their heads and saying,
"So! You who are going to
destroy the temple and
build it in three days,
30 come down from the
cross and save yourself!"
31 In the same way the
chief priests and the teachers of the law mocked him
among themselves. "He
saved others," they said,
"but he can't save himself!
32 Let this Christ,[w] this
King of Israel, come down
now from the cross, that we
may see and believe."
Those crucified with him
also heaped insults on him.

The Death of Jesus

33 At the sixth hour darkness came over the whole
land until the ninth hour.
34 And at the ninth hour
Jesus cried out in a loud
voice, *"Eloi, Eloi, lama
sabachthani?"* — which
means, "My God, my God,
why have you forsaken
me?"[x]
35 When some of those
standing near heard this,
they said, "Listen, he's
calling Elijah."
36 One man ran, filled a
sponge with wine vinegar,
put it on a stick, and offered
it to Jesus to drink. "Now
leave him alone. Let's see
if Elijah comes to take him
down," he said.

[v] 27 Some manuscripts *left,* [28] *and the scripture was fulfilled which says, "He was counted with the lawless ones"* (Isaiah 53:12)
[w] 32 Or *Messiah*
[x] 34 Psalm 22:1

a loud cry and breathed his
last. 38 And the curtain of
the temple was torn in two,
from top to bottom. 39 Now
when the centurion, who
stood facing him, saw that
in this way he[n] breathed
his last, he said, "Truly this
man was God's Son!"[o]
40 There were also
women looking on from a
distance; among them were
Mary Magdalene, and
Mary the mother of James
the younger and of Joses,
and Salome. 41 These used
to follow him and provided
for him when he was in Galilee; and there were many
other women who had
come up with him to Jeru-
salem.

The Burial of Jesus

42 When evening had
come, and since it was the
day of Preparation, that is,
the day before the sabbath,
43 Joseph of Arimathea, a
respected member of the
council, who was also himself waiting expectantly for
the kingdom of God, went
boldly to Pilate and asked
for the body of Jesus.
44 Then Pilate wondered if
he were already dead; and
summoning the centurion,
he asked him whether he
had been dead for some
time. 45 When he learned
from the centurion that he
was dead, he granted the
body to Joseph. 46 Then Joseph[p] bought a linen cloth,
and taking down the
body,[q] wrapped it in the
linen cloth, and laid it in a
tomb that had been hewn
out of the rock. He then
rolled a stone against the
door of the tomb. 47 Mary
Magdalene and Mary the
mother of Joses saw where
the body[q] was laid.

[n] Other ancient authorities add *cried out and*
[o] Or *a son of God*
[p] Gk *he*
[q] Gk *it*

αὐτόν. 37 ὁ δὲ Ἰησοῦς ἀφεὶς φωνὴν
²him. – But Jesus letting go voice
μεγάλην ἐξέπνευσεν. 38 Καὶ τὸ καταπέτασμα
a great(loud) expired. And the veil
τοῦ ναοῦ ἐσχίσθη εἰς δύο ἀπ' ἄνωθεν
of the shrine was rent in two from top
ἕως κάτω. 39 Ἰδὼν δὲ ὁ κεντυρίων ὁ
to bottom. And ⁶seeing ¹the ²centurion –
παρεστηκὼς ἐξ ἐναντίας αὐτοῦ ὅτι οὕτως
³standing by ⁴opposite ⁵him that thus
ἐξέπνευσεν, εἶπεν· ἀληθῶς οὗτος ὁ ἄνθρωπος
he expired, said: Truly this – man
υἱὸς θεοῦ ἦν. 40 Ἦσαν δὲ καὶ γυναῖκες
son of God was. Now there were also women
ἀπὸ μακρόθεν θεωροῦσαι, ἐν αἷς καὶ
from afar beholding, among whom both
Μαρία ἡ Μαγδαληνὴ καὶ Μαρία ἡ
Mary the Magdalene and Mary ¹the
Ἰακώβου τοῦ μικροῦ καὶ Ἰωσῆτος μήτηρ
³of James ⁴the ⁵little ⁶and ⁷of Joses ²mother
καὶ Σαλώμη, 41 αἳ ὅτε ἦν ἐν τῇ Γαλιλαίᾳ
and Salome, who when he was in – Galilee
ἠκολούθουν αὐτῷ καὶ διηκόνουν αὐτῷ, καὶ
followed him and served him, and
ἄλλαι πολλαὶ αἱ συναναβᾶσαι αὐτῷ εἰς
others many – having come up with him to
Ἱεροσόλυμα.
Jerusalem.
42 Καὶ ἤδη ὀψίας γενομένης, ἐπεὶ ἦν
And now evening coming,[a] since it was
= when it was evening,
παρασκευή, ὅ ἐστιν προσάββατον, 43 ἐλθὼν
[the] preparation, which is the day before the sabbath, coming
Ἰωσὴφ ὁ ἀπὸ Ἁριμαθαίας, εὐσχήμων
Joseph the [one] from Arimathæa, an honourable
βουλευτής, ὃς καὶ αὐτὸς ἦν προσδεχόμενος
councillor, who also [him]self was expecting
τὴν βασιλείαν τοῦ θεοῦ, τολμήσας εἰσῆλθεν
the kingdom – of God, taking courage went in
πρὸς τὸν Πιλᾶτον καὶ ᾐτήσατο τὸ σῶμα
to – Pilate and asked the body
τοῦ Ἰησοῦ. 44 ὁ δὲ Πιλᾶτος ἐθαύμασεν
– of Jesus. – And Pilate marvelled
εἰ ἤδη τέθνηκεν, καὶ προσκαλεσάμενος τὸν
if already he has died, and calling to [him] the
κεντυρίωνα ἐπηρώτησεν αὐτὸν εἰ πάλαι
centurion questioned him if long ago
ἀπέθανεν· 45 καὶ γνοὺς ἀπὸ τοῦ κεντυρίωνος
he died; and knowing from the centurion
ἐδωρήσατο τὸ πτῶμα τῷ Ἰωσήφ. 46 καὶ
he granted the corpse – to Joseph. And
ἀγοράσας σινδόνα καθελὼν αὐτὸν ἐνείλησεν
having bought a piece of unused linen taking down him he wrapped
τῇ σινδόνι καὶ κατέθηκεν αὐτὸν ἐν μνήματι
with the linen and deposited him in a tomb
ὃ ἦν λελατομημένον ἐκ πέτρας, καὶ
which was *having been* hewn out of rock, and
προσεκύλισεν λίθον ἐπὶ τὴν θύραν τοῦ
rolled a stone against the door of the
μνημείου. 47 ἡ δὲ Μαρία ἡ Μαγδαληνὴ
tomb. – And Mary the Magdalene
καὶ Μαρία ἡ Ἰωσῆτος ἐθεώρουν ποῦ
and Mary the [mother] of Joses beheld where
τέθειται.
he has been laid.

37 With a loud cry, Jesus
breathed his last.
38 The curtain of the temple was torn in two from
top to bottom. 39 And when
the centurion, who stood
there in front of Jesus,
heard his cry and[y] saw how
he died, he said, "Surely
this man was the Son[z] of
God!"
40 Some women were
watching from a distance.
Among them were Mary
Magdalene, Mary the
mother of James the youn-
ger and of Joses, and Salome. 41 In Galilee these
women had followed him
and cared for his needs.
Many other women who
had come up with him to
Jerusalem were also there.

The Burial of Jesus

42 It was Preparation Day
(that is, the day before the
Sabbath). So as evening approached, 43 Joseph of Arimathea, a prominent mem-
ber of the Council, who
was himself waiting for the
kingdom of God, went
boldly to Pilate and asked
for Jesus' body. 44 Pilate
was surprised to hear that
he was already dead. Sum-
moning the centurion, he
asked him if Jesus had already died. 45 When he
learned from the centurion
that it was so, he gave the
body to Joseph. 46 So Jo-
seph bought some linen
cloth, took down the body,
wrapped it in the linen, and
placed it in a tomb cut out
of rock. Then he rolled a
stone against the entrance
of the tomb. 47 Mary Mag-
dalene and Mary the moth-
er of Joses saw where he
was laid.

[y] 39 Some manuscripts do not have *heard his cry and.*
[z] 39 Or *a son*

Chapter 16

The Resurrection of Jesus

WHEN the sabbath
was over, Mary
Magdalene, and Mary the
mother of James, and Salome bought spices, so that
they might go and anoint
him. 2 And very early on
the first day of the week,
when the sun had risen,
they went to the tomb.
3 They had been saying to
one another, "Who will roll
away the stone for us from
the entrance to the tomb?"
4 When they looked up,
they saw that the stone,
which was very large, had
already been rolled back.
5 As they entered the tomb,
they saw a young man,
dressed in a white robe, sitting on the right side; and
they were alarmed. 6 But he
said to them, "Do not be
alarmed; you are looking
for Jesus of Nazareth, who
was crucified. He has been
raised; he is not here.
Look, there is the place
they laid him. 7 But go, tell
his disciples and Peter that
he is going ahead of you to
Galilee; there you will see
him, just as he told you."
8 So they went out and fled
from the tomb, for terror
and amazement had seized
them; and they said nothing
to anyone, for they were
afraid.[r]

THE SHORTER ENDING OF MARK

⟦And all that had been
commanded them they told
briefly to those around Peter. And afterward Jesus
himself sent out through
them, from east to west,
the sacred and imperish-
able proclamation of eternal salvation.[s]⟧

THE LONGER ENDING OF MARK

Jesus Appears to Mary Magdalene

9 ⟦Now after he rose
early on the first day of the
week, he appeared first to
Mary Magdalene, from
whom he had cast out sev-
en demons. 10 She went out
and told those who had
been with him, while they
were mourning and weep-
ing. 11 But when they heard
that he was alive and had
been seen by her, they
would not believe it.

[r] Some of the most ancient authorities bring the book to a close at the end of verse 8. One authority concludes the book with the shorter ending; others include the shorter ending and then continue with verses 9-20. In most authorities verses 9-20 follow immediately after verse 8, though in some of these authorities the passage is marked as being doubtful.

[s] Other ancient authorities add *Amen*

16 Καὶ διαγενομένου τοῦ σαββάτου [ἡ]
And passing the sabbath[a] –
= when the sabbath was past
Μαρία ἡ Μαγδαληνὴ καὶ Μαρία ἡ [τοῦ]
Mary the Magdalene and Mary the [mother] –
Ἰακώβου καὶ Σαλώμη ἠγόρασαν ἀρώματα
of James and Salome bought spices
ἵνα ἐλθοῦσαι ἀλείψωσιν αὐτόν. **2** καὶ λίαν
that coming they might anoint him. And very
πρωῒ [τῇ] μιᾷ τῶν σαββάτων ἔρχονται
early on the first day of the week† they come
ἐπὶ τὸ μνῆμα, ἀνατείλαντος τοῦ ἡλίου.
upon the tomb, rising the sun.[a]
= as the sun rose.
3 καὶ ἔλεγον πρὸς ἑαυτάς· τίς ἀποκυλίσει
And they said to themselves: Who will roll away
ἡμῖν τὸν λίθον ἐκ τῆς θύρας τοῦ μνημείου;
for us the stone out of the door of the tomb?
4 καὶ ἀναβλέψασαι θεωροῦσιν ὅτι ἀνακεκύλισται
And looking up they behold that has been rolled back
ὁ λίθος· ἦν γὰρ μέγας σφόδρα. **5** καὶ
the stone; for it was great exceedingly. And
εἰσελθοῦσαι εἰς τὸ μνημεῖον εἶδον νεανίσκον
entering into the tomb they saw a young man
καθήμενον ἐν τοῖς δεξιοῖς περιβεβλημένον
sitting on the right *having been* clothed
στολὴν λευκήν, καὶ ἐξεθαμβήθησαν. **6** ὁ δὲ
robe [in] a white, and they were greatly astonished. But he
λέγει αὐταῖς· μὴ ἐκθαμβεῖσθε· Ἰησοῦν
says to them: Be not greatly astonished; Jesus
ζητεῖτε τὸν Ναζαρηνὸν τὸν ἐσταυρωμένον·
ye seek the Nazarene – *having been* crucified;
ἠγέρθη, οὐκ ἔστιν ὧδε· ἴδε ὁ τόπος
he was raised, he is not here; behold[,] the place
ὅπου ἔθηκαν αὐτόν. **7** ἀλλὰ ὑπάγετε εἴπατε
where they put him. But go ye tell
τοῖς μαθηταῖς αὐτοῦ καὶ τῷ Πέτρῳ ὅτι
the disciples of him and – Peter that
προάγει ὑμᾶς εἰς τὴν Γαλιλαίαν· ἐκεῖ
he goes before you to – Galilee; there
αὐτὸν ὄψεσθε, καθὼς εἶπεν ὑμῖν. **8** καὶ
him ye will see, as he told you. And
ἐξελθοῦσαι ἔφυγον ἀπὸ τοῦ μνημείου, εἶχεν
going forth they fled from the tomb, [5]had
γὰρ αὐτὰς τρόμος καὶ ἔκστασις· καὶ
[1]for [6]them [2]trembling [3]and [4]bewilderment; and
οὐδενὶ οὐδὲν εἶπαν· ἐφοβοῦντο γάρ.
no one no(any)thing they told; for they were afraid.
9 Ἀναστὰς δὲ πρωῒ πρώτῃ σαββάτου
And rising early on the first day of the week†
ἐφάνη πρῶτον Μαρίᾳ τῇ Μαγδαληνῇ, παρ'
he appeared first to Mary the Magdalene, from
ἧς ἐκβεβλήκει ἑπτὰ δαιμόνια. **10** ἐκείνη
whom he had expelled seven demons. That [one]
= She
πορευθεῖσα ἀπήγγειλεν τοῖς μετ' αὐτοῦ
going reported to the [ones] with him
= those who had been with him
γενομένοις πενθοῦσι καὶ κλαίουσιν· **11** κἀκεῖνοι
having been mourning and weeping; and those
ἀκούσαντες ὅτι ζῇ καὶ ἐθεάθη ὑπ' αὐτῆς
hearing that he lives and was seen by her

Chapter 16

The Resurrection

WHEN the Sabbath
was over, Mary
Magdalene, Mary the
mother of James, and Salome bought spices so that
they might go to anoint
Jesus' body. 2 Very early on
the first day of the week,
just after sunrise, they
were on their way to the
tomb 3 and they asked each
other, "Who will roll the
stone away from the en-
trance of the tomb?"
4 But when they looked
up, they saw that the stone,
which was very large, had
been rolled away. 5 As they
entered the tomb, they saw
a young man dressed in a
white robe sitting on the
right side, and they were
alarmed.
6 "Don't be alarmed," he
said. "You are looking for
Jesus the Nazarene, who
was crucified. He has ris-
en! He is not here. See the
place where they laid him.
7 But go, tell his disciples
and Peter, 'He is going
ahead of you into Galilee.
There you will see him, just
as he told you.' "
8 Trembling and bewil-
dered, the women went out
and fled from the tomb.
They said nothing to any-
one, because they were
afraid.

[The most reliable early manuscripts and other ancient witnesses do not have Mark 16:9–20.]

9 When Jesus rose early
on the first day of the week,
he appeared first to Mary
Magdalene, out of whom
he had driven seven de-
mons. 10 She went and told
those who had been with
him and who were mourn-
ing and weeping. 11 When
they heard that Jesus was
alive and that she had seen
him, they did not believe it.

Jesus Appears to Two Disciples

12 After this he ap-
peared in another form to
two of them, as they were
walking into the country.
13 And they went back and
told the rest, but they did
not believe them.

Jesus Commissions the Disciples

14 Later he appeared to
the eleven themselves as
they were sitting at the table; and he upbraided them
for their lack of faith and
stubbornness, because
they had not believed those
who saw him after he had
risen.[t] 15 And he said to
them, "Go into all the
world and proclaim the
good news[u] to the whole
creation. 16 The one who
believes and is baptized
will be saved; but the one
who does not believe will
be condemned. 17 And
these signs will accompany
those who believe: by using
my name they will cast out
demons; they will speak in
new tongues; 18 they will
pick up snakes in their
hands,[v] and if they drink
any deadly thing, it will not
hurt them; they will lay
their hands on the sick, and
they will recover."

The Ascension of Jesus

19 So then the Lord
Jesus, after he had spoken
to them, was taken up into
heaven and sat down at the
right hand of God. 20 And
they went out and pro-
claimed the good news ev-
erywhere, while the Lord
worked with them and con-
firmed the message by the
signs that accompanied
it.[w]]]

[t] Other ancient authorities add, in whole or in part, *And they excused themselves, saying, "This age of lawlessness and unbelief is under Satan, who does not allow the truth and power of God to prevail over the unclean things of the spirits. Therefore reveal your righteousness now"—thus they spoke to Christ. And Christ replied to them, "The term of years of Satan's power has been fulfilled, but other terrible things draw near. And for those who have sinned I was handed over to death, that they may return to the truth and sin no more, that they may inherit the spiritual and imperishable glory of righteousness that is in heaven."*

[u] Or *gospel*

[v] Other ancient authorities lack *in their hands*

[w] Other ancient authorities add *Amen*

ἠπίστησαν. **12** Μετὰ δὲ ταῦτα δυσὶν ἐξ
disbelieved. And after these things to two of

αὐτῶν περιπατοῦσιν ἐφανερώθη ἐν ἑτέρᾳ
them walking he was manifested in a different

μορφῇ πορευομένοις εἰς ἀγρόν· **13** κἀκεῖνοι
form going into [the] country; and those

ἀπελθόντες ἀπήγγειλαν τοῖς λοιποῖς· οὐδὲ
going reported to the rest; neither

ἐκείνοις ἐπίστευσαν. **14** Ὕστερον [δὲ]
those they believed. And later

ἀνακειμένοις αὐτοῖς τοῖς ἕνδεκα ἐφανερώθη,
to the reclining them the eleven he was manifested,
= to the eleven as they reclined

καὶ ὠνείδισεν τὴν ἀπιστίαν αὐτῶν καὶ
and reproached the disbelief of them and

σκληροκαρδίαν ὅτι τοῖς θεασαμένοις αὐτὸν
hardness of heart because the [ones] beholding him

ἐγηγερμένον οὐκ ἐπίστευσαν. **15** καὶ εἶπεν
having been raised they did not believe. And he said

αὐτοῖς· πορευθέντες εἰς τὸν κόσμον ἅπαντα
to them: Going into [2]the [3]world [1]all

κηρύξατε τὸ εὐαγγέλιον πάσῃ τῇ κτίσει.
proclaim ye the gospel to all the creation.

16 ὁ πιστεύσας καὶ βαπτισθεὶς σωθήσεται,
The [one] believing and being baptized will be saved,

ὁ δὲ ἀπιστήσας κατακριθήσεται. **17** σημεῖα
but the [one] disbelieving will be condemned. [3]signs

δὲ τοῖς πιστεύσασιν ταῦτα παρακολουθήσει·
[1]And [5]the [ones] [6]believing [2]these [4]will follow:

ἐν τῷ ὀνόματί μου δαιμόνια ἐκβαλοῦσιν,
in the name of me demons they will expel,

γλώσσαις λαλήσουσιν καιναῖς, **18** ὄφεις
[3]tongues [1]they will speak [2]with new, serpents

ἀροῦσιν κἂν θανάσιμόν τι πίωσιν
they will take and if [3]deadly [2]anything [1]they drink

οὐ μὴ αὐτοὺς βλάψῃ, ἐπὶ ἀρρώστους χεῖρας
by no means them it will hurt, on sick [ones] hands

ἐπιθήσουσιν καὶ καλῶς ἕξουσιν. **19** Ὁ μὲν
they will place *on* and well they will have. [1]The [4]there-
=they will recover.

οὖν κύριος [Ἰησοῦς] μετὰ τὸ λαλῆσαι
fore [2]Lord [3]Jesus after the to speak
= speaking

αὐτοῖς ἀνελήμφθη εἰς τὸν οὐρανὸν καὶ
to them was taken up into – heaven and

ἐκάθισεν ἐκ δεξιῶν τοῦ θεοῦ. **20** ἐκεῖνοι
sat at [the] right [hand] – of God. those

δὲ ἐξελθόντες ἐκήρυξαν πανταχοῦ, τοῦ
But going forth proclaimed everywhere, the

κυρίου συνεργοῦντος καὶ τὸν λόγον
Lord working with and the word
= while the Lord worked with [them] and confirmed the word

βεβαιοῦντος διὰ τῶν ἐπακολουθούντων
confirming[a] through the accompanying

σημείων.
signs.

12 Afterward Jesus ap-
peared in a different form
to two of them while they
were walking in the coun-
try. 13 These returned and
reported it to the rest; but
they did not believe them
either.

14 Later Jesus appeared to
the Eleven as they were
eating; he rebuked them for
their lack of faith and their
stubborn refusal to believe
those who had seen him after he had risen.

15 He said to them, "Go
into all the world and
preach the good news to all
creation. 16 Whoever be-
lieves and is baptized will
be saved, but whoever
does not believe will be
condemned. 17 And these
signs will accompany those
who believe: In my name
they will drive out demons;
they will speak in new
tongues; 18 they will pick up
snakes with their hands;
and when they drink deadly
poison, it will not hurt them
at all; they will place their
hands on sick people, and
they will get well."

19 After the Lord Jesus
had spoken to them, he was
taken up into heaven and
he sat at the right hand of
God. 20 Then the disciples
went out and preached ev-
erywhere, and the Lord
worked with them and con-
firmed his word by the
signs that accompanied it.

The Gospel According
to

Luke

Chapter 1

Dedication to Theophilus

SINCE many have un-
dertaken to set down
an orderly account of the
events that have been fulfilled among us, 2just as
they were handed on to us
by those who from the be-
ginning were eyewitnesses
and servants of the word,
3I too decided, after inves-
tigating everything carefully from the very first,[a] to
write an orderly account
for you, most excellent
Theophilus, 4so that you
may know the truth con-
cerning the things about
which you have been in-
structed.

The Birth of John the Baptist Foretold

5 In the days of King
Herod of Judea, there was
a priest named Zechariah,
who belonged to the priestly order of Abijah. His wife
was a descendant of Aaron,
and her name was Eliza-
beth. 6Both of them were
righteous before God, living blamelessly according
to all the commandments
and regulations of the
Lord. 7But they had no
children, because Eliza-
beth was barren, and both
were getting on in years.
8 Once when he was
serving as priest before
God and his section was on
duty, 9he was chosen by
lot, according to the custom of the priesthood, to
enter the sanctuary of the
Lord and offer incense.
10Now at the time of the incense offering, the whole
assembly of the people was
praying outside. 11Then
there appeared to him an
angel of the Lord, standing
at the right side of the altar
of incense. 12When Zecha-
riah saw him, he was terrified; and fear overwhelmed
him. 13But the angel said to
him, "Do not be afraid,
Zechariah, for your prayer
has been heard. Your wife

[a] Or *for a long time*

ΚΑΤΑ ΛΟΥΚΑΝ

According to Luke

1 Ἐπειδήπερ πολλοὶ ἐπεχείρησαν ἀνατάξασθαι
Since many took in hand to draw up
διήγησιν περὶ τῶν πεπληροφορημένων
a narrative concerning 1the 3having been fully carried out
ἐν ἡμῖν πραγμάτων, **2** καθὼς παρέδοσαν ἡμῖν
4among 5us 2matters, as delivered to us
οἱ ἀπ' ἀρχῆς αὐτόπται καὶ ὑπηρέται
the [ones] from [the] beginning eyewitnesses and attendants
γενόμενοι τοῦ λόγου, **3** ἔδοξε κἀμοὶ
becoming of the Word, it seemed good to me also
παρηκολουθηκότι ἄνωθεν πᾶσιν ἀκριβῶς
having investigated from their source all things accurately
καθεξῆς σοι γράψαι, κράτιστε Θεόφιλε,
3in order 2to thee 1to write, most excellent Theophilus,
4 ἵνα ἐπιγνῷς περὶ ὧν
that thou mightest know 4concerning 5which
κατηχήθης λόγων τὴν ἀσφάλειαν.
6thou wast instructed 3of [the] things 1the 2reliability.
5 Ἐγένετο ἐν ταῖς ἡμέραις
There was in the days
Ἡρῴδου βασιλέως τῆς Ἰουδαίας ἱερεύς
of Herod king – of Judæa 2priest
τις ὀνόματι Ζαχαρίας ἐξ ἐφημερίας Ἀβιά,
1a certain by name Zacharias of [the] course of Abia,
καὶ γυνὴ αὐτῷ ἐκ τῶν θυγατέρων Ἀαρών,
and wife to him[c] of the daughters of Aaron,
=his wife
καὶ τὸ ὄνομα αὐτῆς Ἐλισάβετ. **6** ἦσαν δὲ
and the name of her Elisabeth. And they were
δίκαιοι ἀμφότεροι ἐναντίον τοῦ θεοῦ,
righteous both before – God,
πορευόμενοι ἐν πάσαις ταῖς ἐντολαῖς καὶ
going in all the commandments and
δικαιώμασιν τοῦ κυρίου ἄμεμπτοι. **7** καὶ
ordinances of the Lord blameless. And
οὐκ ἦν αὐτοῖς τέκνον, καθότι ἦν ἡ
there was not to them a child,[c] because 2was –
=they had no child,
Ἐλισάβετ στεῖρα, καὶ ἀμφότεροι προβεβηκότες
1Elisabeth barren, and both having advanced
ἐν ταῖς ἡμέραις αὐτῶν ἦσαν. **8** Ἐγένετο
in the days of them were. it came to pass
δὲ ἐν τῷ ἱερατεύειν αὐτὸν ἐν τῇ τάξει
Now in the to serve as priest him[be] in the order
=while he served as priest
τῆς ἐφημερίας αὐτοῦ ἔναντι τοῦ θεοῦ,
of the course of him before – God,
9 κατὰ τὸ ἔθος τῆς ἱερατείας ἔλαχε τοῦ
according to the custom of the priesthood his lot was –
θυμιᾶσαι εἰσελθὼν εἰς τὸν ναὸν τοῦ κυρίου,
to burn incense[d] entering into the shrine of the Lord,
10 καὶ πᾶν τὸ πλῆθος ἦν τοῦ λαοῦ
and all 1the 2multitude 5was 3of the 4people
προσευχόμενον ἔξω τῇ ὥρᾳ τοῦ θυμιάματος.
praying outside at the hour – of incense.
11 ὤφθη δὲ αὐτῷ ἄγγελος κυρίου ἑστὼς
And there appeared to him an angel of [the] Lord standing
ἐκ δεξιῶν τοῦ θυσιαστηρίου τοῦ θυμιάματος.
on [the] right of the altar – of incense.
12 καὶ ἐταράχθη Ζαχαρίας ἰδών, καὶ φόβος
And was troubled Zacharias seeing, and fear
ἐπέπεσεν ἐπ' αὐτόν. **13** εἶπεν δὲ πρὸς
fell *on* upon him. But said to
αὐτὸν ὁ ἄγγελος· μὴ φοβοῦ, Ζαχαρία,
him the angel: Fear not, Zacharias,
διότι εἰσηκούσθη ἡ δέησίς σου, καὶ ἡ
because was heard the request of thee, and the

Luke

Chapter 1

Introduction

MANY have undertak-
en to draw up an ac-
count of the things that
have been fulfilled[a] among
us, 2just as they were handed down to us by those who
from the first were eyewitnesses and servants of the
word. 3Therefore, since I
myself have carefully in-
vestigated everything from
the beginning, it seemed
good also to me to write an
orderly account for you,
most excellent Theophilus,
4so that you may know the
certainty of the things you
have been taught.

The Birth of John the Baptist Foretold

5In the time of Herod king
of Judea there was a priest
named Zechariah, who be-
longed to the priestly division of Abijah; his wife
Elizabeth was also a de-
scendant of Aaron. 6Both
of them were upright in the
sight of God, observing all
the Lord's commandments
and regulations blamelessly. 7But they had no children, because Elizabeth
was barren; and they were
both well along in years.
8Once when Zechariah's
division was on duty and he
was serving as priest before
God, 9he was chosen by
lot, according to the custom of the priesthood, to go
into the temple of the Lord
and burn incense. 10And
when the time for the burning of incense came, all the
assembled worshipers
were praying outside.
11Then an angel of the
Lord appeared to him,
standing at the right side of
the altar of incense.
12When Zechariah saw
him, he was startled and
was gripped with fear.
13But the angel said to him:
"Do not be afraid, Zechariah; your prayer has been
heard. Your wife Elizabeth

[a] 1 Or *been surely believed*

Elizabeth will bear you a son, and you will name him John. 14 You will have joy and gladness, and many will rejoice at his birth, 15 for he will be great in the sight of the Lord. He must never drink wine or strong drink; even before his birth he will be filled with the Holy Spirit. 16 He will turn many of the people of Israel to the Lord their God. 17 With the spirit and power of Elijah he will go before him, to turn the hearts of parents to their children, and the disobedient to the wisdom of the righteous, to make ready a people prepared for the Lord." 18 Zechariah said to the angel, "How will I know that this is so? For I am an old man, and my wife is getting on in years." 19 The angel replied, "I am Gabriel. I stand in the presence of God, and I have been sent to speak to you and to bring you this good news. 20 But now, because you did not believe my words, which will be fulfilled in their time, you will become mute, unable to speak, until the day these things occur."

21 Meanwhile the people were waiting for Zechariah, and wondered at his delay in the sanctuary. 22 When he did come out, he could not speak to them, and they realized that he had seen a vision in the sanctuary. He kept motioning to them and remained unable to speak. 23 When

γυνή σου Ἐλισάβετ γεννήσει υἱόν σοι,
wife of thee Elisabeth will bear a son to thee,

καὶ καλέσεις τὸ ὄνομα αὐτοῦ Ἰωάννην·
and thou shalt call the name of him John;

14 καὶ ἔσται χαρά σοι καὶ ἀγαλλίασις,
and there shall be joy to thee and gladness,[c]
=thou shalt have joy and gladness,

καὶ πολλοὶ ἐπὶ τῇ γενέσει αὐτοῦ χαρή-
and many over the birth of him will

σονται. 15 ἔσται γὰρ μέγας ἐνώπιον
rejoice. For he will be great in the eyes of

κυρίου, καὶ οἶνον καὶ σίκερα οὐ μὴ
[the] Lord, and wine and strong drink by no means

πίῃ, καὶ πνεύματος ἁγίου πλησθήσεται
may he drink, and of(with) Spirit [the] Holy he will be filled

ἔτι ἐκ κοιλίας μητρὸς αὐτοῦ, 16 καὶ
even from [the] womb of [the] mother of him, and

πολλοὺς τῶν υἱῶν Ἰσραὴλ ἐπιστρέψει ἐπὶ κύριον
many of the sons of Israel he will turn to [the] Lord

τὸν θεὸν αὐτῶν· 17 καὶ αὐτὸς προελεύσεται
the God of them; and he will go *before*

ἐνώπιον αὐτοῦ ἐν πνεύματι καὶ δυνάμει
before him in [the] spirit and power

Ἠλίου, ἐπιστρέψαι καρδίας πατέρων ἐπὶ
of Elias, to turn [the] hearts of fathers to

τέκνα καὶ ἀπειθεῖς ἐν φρονήσει
children and disobedient [ones] to [the] understanding

δικαίων, ἑτοιμάσαι κυρίῳ λαὸν κατεσκευασ-
of [the] just, to prepare for [the] Lord a people *having been*

μένον. 18 καὶ εἶπεν Ζαχαρίας πρὸς τὸν ἄγγελον·
prepared. And said Zacharias to the angel:

κατὰ τί γνώσομαι τοῦτο; ἐγὼ γάρ εἰμι
By what shall I know this? for I am

πρεσβύτης καὶ ἡ γυνή μου προβεβηκυῖα
old and the wife of me *having* advanced

ἐν ταῖς ἡμέραις αὐτῆς. 19 καὶ ἀποκριθεὶς
in the days of her. And answering

ὁ ἄγγελος εἶπεν αὐτῷ· ἐγώ εἰμι Γαβριὴλ
the angel said to him: I am Gabriel

ὁ παρεστηκὼς ἐνώπιον τοῦ θεοῦ, καὶ
the [one] standing before – God, and

ἀπεστάλην λαλῆσαι πρὸς σὲ καὶ εὐαγ-
I was sent to speak to thee and to

γελίσασθαί σοι ταῦτα· 20 καὶ ἰδοὺ
announce to thee these things; and behold

ἔσῃ σιωπῶν καὶ μὴ δυνάμενος λαλῆσαι
thou shalt be being silent and not being able to speak

ἄχρι ἧς ἡμέρας γένηται ταῦτα, ἀνθ' ὧν οὐκ
until which day happens these things, because not
=the day when these things happen,

ἐπίστευσας τοῖς λόγοις μου, οἵτινες πληρω-
thou believedst the words of me, which will be

θήσονται εἰς τὸν καιρὸν αὐτῶν. 21 καὶ ἦν
fulfilled in the time of them. And was

ὁ λαὸς προσδοκῶν τὸν Ζαχαρίαν, καὶ
the people expecting – Zacharias, and

ἐθαύμαζον ἐν τῷ χρονίζειν ἐν τῷ ναῷ
they marvelled in(at) the to delay in the shrine
=when he delayed in the shrine.

αὐτόν. 22 ἐξελθὼν δὲ οὐκ ἐδύνατο λαλῆσαι
him.[be] And going out he was not able to speak

αὐτοῖς καὶ ἐπέγνωσαν ὅτι ὀπτασίαν ἑώρακεν
to them, and they knew that a vision he has(had) seen

ἐν τῷ ναῷ· καὶ αὐτὸς ἦν διανεύων
in the shrine; and he was beckoning

αὐτοῖς, καὶ διέμενεν κωφός. 23 καὶ
to them, and remained dumb. And

will bear you a son, and you are to give him the name John. 14 He will be a joy and delight to you, and many will rejoice because of his birth, 15 for he will be great in the sight of the Lord. He is never to take wine or other fermented drink, and he will be filled with the Holy Spirit even from birth.[b] 16 Many of the people of Israel will he bring back to the Lord their God. 17 And he will go on before the Lord, in the spirit and power of Elijah, to turn the hearts of the fathers to their children and the disobedient to the wisdom of the righteous—to make ready a people prepared for the Lord."

18 Zechariah asked the angel, "How can I be sure of this? I am an old man and my wife is well along in years."

19 The angel answered, "I am Gabriel. I stand in the presence of God, and I have been sent to speak to you and to tell you this good news. 20 And now you will be silent and not able to speak until the day this happens, because you did not believe my words, which will come true at their proper time."

21 Meanwhile, the people were waiting for Zechariah and wondering why he stayed so long in the temple. 22 When he came out, he could not speak to them. They realized he had seen a vision in the temple, for he kept making signs to them but remained unable to speak.

[b] 15 Or *from his mother's womb*

his time of service was ended, he went to his home.
24 After those days his
wife Elizabeth conceived,
and for five months she remained in seclusion. She
said, 25 "This is what the
Lord has done for me when
he looked favorably on me
and took away the disgrace
I have endured among my
people."

The Birth of Jesus Foretold

26 In the sixth month
the angel Gabriel was sent
by God to a town in Galilee
called Nazareth, 27 to a virgin engaged to a man whose
name was Joseph, of the
house of David. The vir-
gin's name was Mary.
28 And he came to her and
said, "Greetings, favored
one! The Lord is with
you."[b] 29 But she was
much perplexed by his
words and pondered what
sort of greeting this might
be. 30 The angel said to her,
"Do not be afraid, Mary,
for you have found favor
with God. 31 And now, you
will conceive in your womb
and bear a son, and you will
name him Jesus. 32 He will
be great, and will be called
the Son of the Most High,
and the Lord God will give
to him the throne of his ancestor David. 33 He will
reign over the house of Jacob forever, and of his
kingdom there will be no
end." 34 Mary said to the
angel, "How can this be,
since I am a virgin?"[c]
35 The angel said to her,
"The Holy Spirit will come
upon you, and the power of
the Most High will over-
shadow you; therefore the

[b] Other ancient authorities add *Blessed are you among women*
[c] Gk *I do not know a man*

ἐγένετο ὡς ἐπλήσθησαν αἱ ἡμέραι τῆς
it came to pass when were fulfilled the days of the
λειτουργίας αὐτοῦ, ἀπῆλθεν εἰς τὸν οἶκον
service of him, he went away to the house
αὐτοῦ. **24** Μετὰ δὲ ταύτας τὰς ἡμέρας
of him. And after these – days
συνέλαβεν Ἐλισάβετ ἡ γυνὴ αὐτοῦ, καὶ
conceived Elisabeth the wife of him, and
περιέκρυβεν ἑαυτὴν μῆνας πέντε, λέγουσα
hid herself months five, saying[,]
25 ὅτι οὕτως μοι πεποίηκεν κύριος ἐν
– Thus to me has done [the] Lord in
ἡμέραις αἷς ἐπεῖδεν ἀφελεῖν ὄνειδός
days in which he looked upon to take away reproach
μου ἐν ἀνθρώποις.
of me among men.
26 Ἐν δὲ τῷ μηνὶ τῷ ἕκτῳ ἀπεστάλη
Now in the month – sixth was sent
ὁ ἄγγελος Γαβριὴλ ἀπὸ τοῦ θεοῦ εἰς
the angel Gabriel from – God to
πόλιν τῆς Γαλιλαίας ᾗ ὄνομα Ναζαρέθ,
a city – of Galilee to which name[e] Nazareth,
= the name of which [was]
27 πρὸς παρθένον ἐμνηστευμένην ἀνδρὶ ᾧ ὄνομα
to a virgin *having been* betrothed to a man to whom name[e]
Ἰωσήφ, ἐξ οἴκου Δαυίδ, καὶ τὸ ὄνομα
Joseph, of [the] house of David, and the name
τῆς παρθένου Μαριάμ. **28** καὶ εἰσελθὼν
of the virgin [was] Mary. And entering
πρὸς αὐτὴν εἶπεν· χαῖρε, κεχαριτωμένη, ὁ
to her he said: Hail, *having been* favoured [one], the
κύριος μετὰ σοῦ. **29** ἡ δὲ ἐπὶ τῷ λόγῳ
Lord [is] with thee. And she at the saying
διεταράχθη, καὶ διελογίζετο ποταπὸς εἴη
was greatly disturbed, and considered of what sort [2]might be
ὁ ἀσπασμὸς οὗτος. **30** καὶ εἶπεν ὁ ἄγγελος
– [3]greeting [1]this. And said the angel
αὐτῇ· μὴ φοβοῦ, Μαριάμ· εὗρες γὰρ
to her: Fear not, Mary: for thou didst find
χάριν παρὰ τῷ θεῷ. **31** καὶ ἰδοὺ συλλήμψῃ
favour with – God. And behold thou wilt conceive
ἐν γαστρὶ καὶ τέξῃ υἱόν, καὶ καλέσεις τὸ
in womb and bear a son, and thou shalt call the
ὄνομα αὐτοῦ Ἰησοῦν. **32** οὗτος ἔσται μέγας
name of him Jesus. This will be great
καὶ υἱὸς ὑψίστου κληθήσεται, καὶ δώσει
and Son of [the] Most High will be called, and will give
αὐτῷ κύριος ὁ θεὸς τὸν θρόνον Δαυὶδ
him [the] Lord – God the throne of David
τοῦ πατρὸς αὐτοῦ, **33** καὶ βασιλεύσει ἐπὶ
the father of him, and he will reign over
τὸν οἶκον Ἰακὼβ εἰς τοὺς αἰῶνας, καὶ
the house of Jacob unto the ages, and
=for ever,
τῆς βασιλείας αὐτοῦ οὐκ ἔσται τέλος.
of the kingdom of him there will not be an end.
34 εἶπεν δὲ Μαριὰμ πρὸς τὸν ἄγγελον·
And said Mary to the angel:
πῶς ἔσται τοῦτο, ἐπεὶ ἄνδρα οὐ γινώσκω;
How will be this, since a man I know not?
35 καὶ ἀποκριθεὶς ὁ ἄγγελος εἶπεν αὐτῇ·
And answering the angel said to her:
πνεῦμα ἅγιον ἐπελεύσεται ἐπὶ σέ, καὶ
[1][The] [3]Spirit [2]Holy will come *upon* upon thee, and
δύναμις ὑψίστου ἐπισκιάσει σοι· διὸ
[the] power of [the] Most High will overshadow thee; wherefore

23 When his time of ser-
vice was completed, he returned home. 24 After this
his wife Elizabeth became
pregnant and for five
months remained in seclu-
sion. 25 "The Lord has done
this for me," she said. "In
these days he has shown
his favor and taken away
my disgrace among the
people."

The Birth of Jesus Foretold

26 In the sixth month, God
sent the angel Gabriel to
Nazareth, a town in Gali-
lee, 27 to a virgin pledged to
be married to a man named
Joseph, a descendant of
David. The virgin's name
was Mary. 28 The angel
went to her and said,
"Greetings, you who are
highly favored! The Lord is
with you."
29 Mary was greatly trou-
bled at his words and wondered what kind of greeting
this might be. 30 But the angel said to her, "Do not be
afraid, Mary, you have
found favor with God.
31 You will be with child and
give birth to a son, and you
are to give him the name
Jesus. 32 He will be great
and will be called the Son of
the Most High. The Lord
God will give him the
throne of his father David,
33 and he will reign over the
house of Jacob forever; his
kingdom will never end."
34 "How will this be,"
Mary asked the angel,
"since I am a virgin?"
35 The angel answered,
"The Holy Spirit will come
upon you, and the power of
the Most High will over-
shadow you. So the holy

child to be born[d] will be
holy; he will be called Son
of God. 36 And now, your
relative Elizabeth in her old
age has also conceived a
son; and this is the sixth
month for her who was said
to be barren. 37 For nothing
will be impossible with
God." 38 Then Mary said,
"Here am I, the servant of
the Lord; let it be with me
according to your word."
Then the angel departed
from her.

Mary Visits Elizabeth

39 In those days Mary
set out and went with haste
to a Judean town in the hill
country, 40 where she en-
tered the house of Zechariah and greeted Elizabeth.
41 When Elizabeth heard
Mary's greeting, the child
leaped in her womb. And
Elizabeth was filled with
the Holy Spirit 42 and exclaimed with a loud cry,
"Blessed are you among
women, and blessed is the
fruit of your womb. 43 And
why has this happened to
me, that the mother of my
Lord comes to me? 44 For
as soon as I heard the
sound of your greeting, the
child in my womb leaped
for joy. 45 And blessed is
she who believed that there
would be[e] a fulfillment of
what was spoken to her by
the Lord."

Mary's Song of Praise

46 And Mary[f] said,
47 "My soul magnifies
the Lord,
and my spirit
rejoices in God
my Savior,
48 for he has looked with
favor on the
lowliness of his
servant.
Surely, from now
on all
generations will
call me blessed;
49 for the Mighty One
has done great
things for me,

καὶ τὸ γεννώμενον ἅγιον κληθήσεται υἱὸς θεοῦ.
also the thing being born holy will be called[,] Son of God.
36 καὶ ἰδοὺ Ἐλισάβετ ἡ συγγενίς σου καὶ
And behold Elisabeth the relative of thee also
αὐτὴ συνείληφεν υἱὸν ἐν γήρει αὐτῆς, καὶ
she conceived a son in old age of her, and
οὗτος μὴν ἕκτος ἐστὶν αὐτῇ τῇ καλουμένῃ
this month sixth is with her the [one] *being* called
στείρᾳ· **37** ὅτι οὐκ ἀδυνατήσει παρὰ τοῦ
barren; because will not be impossible with –
θεοῦ πᾶν ῥῆμα. **38** εἶπεν δὲ Μαριάμ· ἰδοὺ ἡ
God every word. And said Mary: Behold[,] the
δούλη κυρίου· γένοιτό μοι κατὰ
handmaid of [the] Lord; may it be to me according to
τὸ ῥῆμά σου. καὶ ἀπῆλθεν ἀπ' αὐτῆς
the word of thee. And went away from her
ὁ ἄγγελος. **39** Ἀναστᾶσα δὲ Μαριὰμ ἐν
the angel. And rising up Mary in
ταῖς ἡμέραις ταύταις ἐπορεύθη εἰς τὴν
– days these she went to the
ὀρεινὴν μετὰ σπουδῆς εἰς πόλιν Ἰούδα,
mountain country with haste to a city of Juda,
40 καὶ εἰσῆλθεν εἰς τὸν οἶκον Ζαχαρίου
and entered into the house of Zacharias
καὶ ἠσπάσατο τὴν Ἐλισάβετ. **41** καὶ
and greeted – Elisabeth. And
ἐγένετο ὡς ἤκουσεν τὸν ἀσπασμὸν τῆς
it came to pass when [2]heard [3]the [4]greeting –
Μαρίας ἡ Ἐλισάβετ, ἐσκίρτησεν τὸ βρέφος
[5]of Mary – [1]Elisabeth, leaped the babe
ἐν τῇ κοιλίᾳ αὐτῆς, καὶ ἐπλήσθη πνεύματος
in the womb of her, and [2]was filled [3]of(with) [5]Spirit
ἁγίου ἡ Ἐλισάβετ, **42** καὶ ἀνεφώνησεν
[4][the] Holy – [1]Elisabeth, and she called out
κραυγῇ μεγάλῃ καὶ εἶπεν· εὐλογημένη
cry with a great and said: Blessed [art]
σὺ ἐν γυναιξίν, καὶ εὐλογημένος ὁ καρπὸς
thou among women, and blessed [is] the fruit
τῆς κοιλίας σου. **43** καὶ πόθεν μοι τοῦτο
of the womb of thee. And whence to me this
ἵνα ἔλθῃ ἡ μήτηρ τοῦ κυρίου μου πρὸς
that comes the mother of the Lord of me to
ἐμέ; **44** ἰδοὺ γὰρ ὡς ἐγένετο ἡ φωνὴ τοῦ
me? For behold when came the sound of the
ἀσπασμοῦ σου εἰς τὰ ὦτά μου, ἐσκίρτησεν
greeting of thee in the ears of me, leaped
ἐν ἀγαλλιάσει τὸ βρέφος ἐν τῇ κοιλίᾳ
in gladness the babe in the womb
μου. **45** καὶ μακαρία ἡ πιστεύσασα ὅτι
of me. And blessed the [one] believing because
ἔσται τελείωσις τοῖς λελαλημένοις αὐτῇ
there shall be a completion to the things *having been* spoken to her
παρὰ κυρίου. **46** Καὶ εἶπεν Μαριάμ·
from [the] Lord. And said Mary:
Μεγαλύνει ἡ ψυχή μου τὸν κύριον, **47** καὶ
Magnifies the soul of me the Lord, and
ἠγαλλίασεν τὸ πνεῦμά μου ἐπὶ τῷ θεῷ
exulted the spirit of me in – God
τῷ σωτῆρί μου· **48** ὅτι ἐπέβλεψεν ἐπὶ τὴν
the saviour of me; because he looked *on* upon the
ταπείνωσιν τῆς δούλης αὐτοῦ. ἰδοὺ γὰρ
humiliation of the handmaid of him. For behold
ἀπὸ τοῦ νῦν μακαριοῦσίν με πᾶσαι αἱ
from – now [4]will [5]deem [7]blessed [6]me [1]all [2]the
γενεαί· **49** ὅτι ἐποίησέν μοι μεγάλα ὁ
[3]generations; because did to me great things the

one to be born will be
called[c] the Son of God.
36 Even Elizabeth your relative is going to have a child
in her old age, and she who
was said to be barren is in
her sixth month. 37 For
nothing is impossible with
God."
38 "I am the Lord's ser-
vant," Mary answered.
"May it be to me as you
have said." Then the angel
left her.

Mary Visits Elizabeth

39 At that time Mary got
ready and hurried to a town
in the hill country of Judea,
40 where she entered Zechariah's home and greeted
Elizabeth. 41 When Eliza-
beth heard Mary's greet-
ing, the baby leaped in her
womb, and Elizabeth was
filled with the Holy Spirit.
42 In a loud voice she exclaimed: "Blessed are you
among women, and blessed
is the child you will bear!
43 But why am I so favored,
that the mother of my Lord
should come to me? 44 As
soon as the sound of your
greeting reached my ears,
the baby in my womb
leaped for joy. 45 Blessed is
she who has believed that
what the Lord has said to
her will be accomplished!"

Mary's Song

46 And Mary said:
"My soul glorifies the
Lord
47 and my spirit rejoices
in God my Savior,
48 for he has been mindful
of the humble state of
his servant.
From now on all
generations will call
me blessed,
49 for the Mighty One has
done great things for
me—

[d] Other ancient authorities add *of you*
[e] Or *believed, for there will be*
[f] Other ancient authorities read *Elizabeth*

[c] 35 Or *So the child to be born will be called holy.*

and holy is his
name.
50 His mercy is for those
who fear him
from generation to
generation.
51 He has shown
strength with
his arm;
he has scattered the
proud in the
thoughts of their
hearts.
52 He has brought down
the powerful
from their
thrones,
and lifted up the
lowly;
53 he has filled the
hungry with
good things,
and sent the rich
away empty.
54 He has helped his
servant Israel,
in remembrance of
his mercy,
55 according to the
promise he
made to our
ancestors,
to Abraham and to
his descendants
forever."
56 And Mary remained
with her about three
months and then returned
to her home.

The Birth of John the Baptist

57 Now the time came
for Elizabeth to give birth,
and she bore a son. 58 Her
neighbors and relatives
heard that the Lord had
shown his great mercy to
her, and they rejoiced with
her.
59 On the eighth day
they came to circumcise
the child, and they were going to name him Zechariah
after his father. 60 But his
mother said, "No; he is to
be called John." 61 They
said to her, "None of your
relatives has this name."
62 Then they began motioning to his father to find out
what name he wanted to
give him. 63 He asked for a
writing tablet and wrote,
"His name is John." And all
of them were amazed.
64 Immediately his mouth
was opened and his tongue

δυνατός. καὶ ἅγιον τὸ ὄνομα αὐτοῦ,
Mighty [one]. And holy the name of him,
50 καὶ τὸ ἔλεος αὐτοῦ εἰς γενεὰς καὶ
and the mercy of him to generations and
γενεὰς τοῖς φοβουμένοις αὐτόν. **51** Ἐποίησεν
generations to the [ones] fearing him. He did
κράτος ἐν βραχίονι αὐτοῦ, διεσκόρπισεν
might with [the] arm of him, he scattered
ὑπερηφάνους διανοίᾳ καρδίας αὐτῶν·
haughty [ones] in [the] understanding of [the] heart of them;
52 καθεῖλεν δυνάστας ἀπὸ θρόνων καὶ ὕψω-
he pulled down potentates from thrones and exalt-
σεν ταπεινούς, **53** πεινῶντας ἐνέπλησεν
ed humble [ones], hungering [ones] he filled
ἀγαθῶν καὶ πλουτοῦντας ἐξαπέστειλεν
of(with) good things and rich [ones] he sent away
κενούς. **54** ἀντελάβετο Ἰσραὴλ παιδὸς αὐτοῦ,
empty. He succoured Israel servant of him,
μνησθῆναι ἐλέους, **55** καθὼς ἐλάλησεν
to remember mercy, as he spoke
πρὸς τοὺς πατέρας ἡμῶν, τῷ Ἀβραὰμ
to the fathers of us, – to Abraham
καὶ τῷ σπέρματι αὐτοῦ εἰς τὸν αἰῶνα.
and to the seed of him unto the age.
=for ever.

56 Ἔμεινεν δὲ Μαριὰμ σὺν αὐτῇ ὡς
And remained Mary with her about
μῆνας τρεῖς, καὶ ὑπέστρεψεν εἰς τὸν
months three, and returned to the
οἶκον αὐτῆς.
house of her.

57 Τῇ δὲ Ἐλισάβετ ἐπλήσθη ὁ χρόνος
– Now [4]to Elisabeth [3]was fulfilled [1]the [2]time
τοῦ τεκεῖν αὐτήν, καὶ ἐγέννησεν υἱόν.
– to bear her,[bd] and she brought forth a son.
=that she should bear,
58 καὶ ἤκουσαν οἱ περίοικοι καὶ οἱ
And heard the neighbours and the
συγγενεῖς αὐτῆς ὅτι ἐμεγάλυνεν κύριος τὸ
relatives of her that magnified [the] Lord the
ἔλεος αὐτοῦ μετ' αὐτῆς, καὶ συνέχαιρον
mercy of him with her, and they rejoiced with
αὐτῇ. **59** Καὶ ἐγένετο ἐν τῇ ἡμέρᾳ τῇ
her. And it came to pass on the day –
ὀγδόῃ ἦλθον περιτεμεῖν τὸ παιδίον, καὶ
eighth they came to circumcise the child, and
ἐκάλουν αὐτὸ ἐπὶ τῷ ὀνόματι τοῦ πατρὸς
were calling it(him) by the name of the father
αὐτοῦ Ζαχαρίαν. **60** καὶ ἀποκριθεῖσα ἡ
of him Zacharias. And answering the
μήτηρ αὐτοῦ εἶπεν· οὐχί, ἀλλὰ κληθήσεται
mother of him said : No, but he shall be called
Ἰωάννης. **61** καὶ εἶπαν πρὸς αὐτὴν ὅτι
John. And they said to her[,] –
οὐδείς ἐστιν ἐκ τῆς συγγενείας σου ὃς
No one there is of the kindred of thee who
καλεῖται τῷ ὀνόματι τούτῳ. **62** ἐνένευον
is called – name by this. they nodded
δὲ τῷ πατρὶ αὐτοῦ τὸ τί ἂν θέλοι
And to the father of him – what he might wish
καλεῖσθαι αὐτό. **63** καὶ αἰτήσας πινακίδιον
[2]to be called [1]him. And asking for a tablet
ἔγραψεν λέγων· Ἰωάννης ἐστὶν ὄνομα
he wrote saying : John is name
αὐτοῦ. καὶ ἐθαύμασαν πάντες. **64** ἀνεῴχθη δὲ
of him. And they marvelled all. And was opened
τὸ στόμα αὐτοῦ παραχρῆμα καὶ ἡ
the mouth of him instantly and the

holy is his name.
50 His mercy extends to
those who fear him,
from generation to
generation.
51 He has performed
mighty deeds with
his arm;
he has scattered those
who are proud in
their inmost
thoughts.
52 He has brought down
rulers from their
thrones
but has lifted up the
humble.
53 He has filled the hungry
with good things
but has sent the rich
away empty.
54 He has helped his
servant Israel,
remembering to be
merciful
55 to Abraham and his
descendants
forever,
even as he said to our
fathers."

56 Mary stayed with Elizabeth for about three
months and then returned
home.

The Birth of John the Baptist

57 When it was time for
Elizabeth to have her baby,
she gave birth to a son.
58 Her neighbors and relatives heard that the Lord
had shown her great mer-
cy, and they shared her joy.
59 On the eighth day they
came to circumcise the
child, and they were going
to name him after his father
Zechariah, 60 but his mother
spoke up and said, "No!
He is to be called John."
61 They said to her,
"There is no one among
your relatives who has that
name."
62 Then they made signs to
his father, to find out what
he would like to name the
child. 63 He asked for a writing tablet, and to every-
one's astonishment he
wrote, "His name is
John." 64 Immediately his
mouth was opened and his

freed, and he began to speak, praising God. 65 Fear came over all their neighbors, and all these things were talked about throughout the entire hill country of Judea. 66 All who heard them pondered them and said, "What then will this child become?" For, indeed, the hand of the Lord was with him.

Zechariah's Prophecy

67 Then his father Zechariah was filled with the Holy Spirit and spoke this prophecy:

68 "Blessed be the Lord God of Israel,
for he has looked favorably on his people and redeemed them.
69 He has raised up a mighty savior[g] for us
in the house of his servant David,
70 as he spoke through the mouth of his holy prophets from of old,
71 that we would be saved from our enemies and from the hand of all who hate us.
72 Thus he has shown the mercy promised to our ancestors,
and has remembered his holy covenant,
73 the oath that he swore to our ancestor Abraham,
to grant us 74 that we, being rescued from the hands of our enemies,
might serve him without fear,
75 in holiness and righteousness before him all our days.
76 And you, child, will be called the prophet of the Most High;
for you will go before the Lord to prepare his ways,
77 to give knowledge of salvation to his people
by the forgiveness of their sins.
78 By the tender mercy of our God,
the dawn from on high will break upon[h] us,
79 to give light to those who sit in darkness and in the shadow of death,

[g] Gk *a horn of salvation*
[h] Other ancient authorities read *has broken upon*

γλῶσσα αὐτοῦ, καὶ ἐλάλει εὐλογῶν τὸν
tongue of him, and he spoke blessing –
θεόν. 65 Καὶ ἐγένετο ἐπὶ πάντας φόβος
God. And [3]came [2]on [4]all [1]fear
τοὺς περιοικοῦντας αὐτούς, καὶ ἐν ὅλῃ τῇ
the [ones] dwelling round them, and in all the
ὀρεινῇ τῆς Ἰουδαίας διελαλεῖτο πάντα
mountain country – of Judæa [4]were talked over [1]all
τὰ ῥήματα ταῦτα, 66 καὶ ἔθεντο πάντες
– [3]facts [2]these, and [4]put [1]all
οἱ ἀκούσαντες ἐν τῇ καρδίᾳ αὐτῶν,
[2]the [ones] [3]hearing in the heart of them,
λέγοντες· τί ἄρα τὸ παιδίον τοῦτο ἔσται;
saying: What then – child this will be?
καὶ γὰρ χεὶρ κυρίου ἦν μετ' αὐτοῦ.
for indeed [the] hand of [the] Lord was with him.
67 Καὶ Ζαχαρίας ὁ πατὴρ αὐτοῦ ἐπλήσθη
And Zacharias the father of him was filled
πνεύματος ἁγίου καὶ ἐπροφήτευσεν λέγων·
of(with) Spirit [the] Holy and prophesied saying:
68 Εὐλογητὸς κύριος ὁ θεὸς τοῦ Ἰσραήλ,
Blessed [be] [the] Lord the God – of Israel,
ὅτι ἐπεσκέψατο καὶ ἐποίησεν λύτρωσιν τῷ
because he visited and wrought redemption for the
λαῷ αὐτοῦ, 69 καὶ ἤγειρεν κέρας σωτηρίας
people of him, and raised a horn of salvation
ἡμῖν ἐν οἴκῳ Δαυὶδ παιδὸς αὐτοῦ, 70 καθὼς
for us in [the] house of David servant of him, as
ἐλάλησεν διὰ στόματος τῶν ἁγίων ἀπ'
he spoke through [the] mouth of the [1]holy [4]from
αἰῶνος προφητῶν αὐτοῦ, 71 σωτηρίαν ἐξ
[5][the] age [2]prophets [3]of him, salvation out of
ἐχθρῶν ἡμῶν καὶ ἐκ χειρὸς πάντων τῶν
[the] enemies of us and out of [the] hand of all the [ones]
μισούντων ἡμᾶς, 72 ποιῆσαι ἔλεος μετὰ
hating us, to perform mercy with
τῶν πατέρων ἡμῶν καὶ μνησθῆναι διαθήκης
the fathers of us and to remember [the] covenant
ἁγίας αὐτοῦ, 73 ὅρκον ὃν ὤμοσεν πρὸς Ἀβραὰμ
holy of him, [the] oath which he swore to Abraham
τὸν πατέρα ἡμῶν, 74 τοῦ δοῦναι ἡμῖν
the father of us, – to give[d] us
ἀφόβως ἐκ χειρὸς ἐχθρῶν ῥυσθέντας
[5]fearlessly [2]out of [3][the] hand [4]of [our] enemies [1]having been delivered
λατρεύειν αὐτῷ 75 ἐν ὁσιότητι καὶ δικαιοσύνῃ
[6]to serve him in holiness and righteousness
ἐνώπιον αὐτοῦ πάσαις ταῖς ἡμέραις ἡμῶν.
before him all the days[e] of us.
76 Καὶ σὺ δέ, παιδίον, προφήτης ὑψίστου
And thou also, child, a prophet of [the] Most High
κληθήσῃ· προπορεύσῃ γὰρ ἐνώπιον κυρίου
wilt be called; for thou wilt go *before* before [the] Lord
ἑτοιμάσαι ὁδοὺς αὐτοῦ, 77 τοῦ δοῦναι
to prepare [the] ways of him, – to give[d]
γνῶσιν σωτηρίας τῷ λαῷ αὐτοῦ ἐν
a knowledge of salvation to the people of him by
ἀφέσει ἁμαρτιῶν αὐτῶν, 78 διὰ σπλάγχνα
forgiveness of sins of them, because of [the] bowels
ἐλέους θεοῦ ἡμῶν, ἐν οἷς ἐπισκέψεται
of mercy of God of us, whereby will visit
ἡμᾶς ἀνατολὴ ἐξ ὕψους, 79 ἐπιφᾶναι τοῖς
us a [sun]rising from [the] height, to appear [1]to the [ones]
ἐν σκότει καὶ σκιᾷ θανάτου καθημένοις,
[3]in [4]darkness [5]and [6]in a shadow [7]of death [2]sitting,

tongue was loosed, and he began to speak, praising God. 65 The neighbors were all filled with awe, and throughout the hill country of Judea people were talking about all these things. 66 Everyone who heard this wondered about it, asking, "What then is this child going to be?" For the Lord's hand was with him.

Zechariah's Song

67 His father Zechariah was filled with the Holy Spirit and prophesied:

68 "Praise be to the Lord, the God of Israel,
because he has come and has redeemed his people.
69 He has raised up a horn[d] of salvation for us
in the house of his servant David
70 (as he said through his holy prophets of long ago),
71 salvation from our enemies
and from the hand of all who hate us—
72 to show mercy to our fathers
and to remember his holy covenant,
73 the oath he swore to our father Abraham:
74 to rescue us from the hand of our enemies,
and to enable us to serve him without fear
75 in holiness and righteousness before him all our days.

76 And you, my child, will be called a prophet of the Most High;
for you will go on before the Lord to prepare the way for him,
77 to give his people the knowledge of salvation
through the forgiveness of their sins,
78 because of the tender mercy of our God,
by which the rising sun will come to us from heaven
79 to shine on those living in darkness
and in the shadow of death,

[d] 69 *Horn* here symbolizes strength.

to guide our feet
into the way
of peace."
80 The child grew and
became strong in spirit, and
he was in the wilderness
until the day he appeared
publicly to Israel.

Chapter 2

The Birth of Jesus

IN those days a decree
went out from Emperor
Augustus that all the world
should be registered. 2 This
was the first registration
and was taken while Qui-
rinius was governor of Syria. 3 All went to their own
towns to be registered. 4 Joseph also went from the
town of Nazareth in Galilee
to Judea, to the city of David called Bethlehem, be-
cause he was descended
from the house and family
of David. 5 He went to be
registered with Mary, to
whom he was engaged and
who was expecting a child.
6 While they were there, the
time came for her to deliver
her child. 7 And she gave
birth to her firstborn son
and wrapped him in bands
of cloth, and laid him in a
manger, because there was
no place for them in the inn.

The Shepherds and the Angels

8 In that region there
were shepherds living in
the fields, keeping watch
over their flock by night.
9 Then an angel of the Lord
stood before them, and the
glory of the Lord shone
around them, and they
were terrified. 10 But the
angel said to them, "Do not
be afraid; for see—I am
bringing you good news of

τοῦ κατευθῦναι τοὺς πόδας ἡμῶν εἰς ὁδὸν
– to guide[d] the feet of us into a way
εἰρήνης.
of peace.
80 Τὸ δὲ παιδίον ηὔξανεν καὶ ἐκραταιοῦτο
And the child grew and became strong
πνεύματι, καὶ ἦν ἐν ταῖς ἐρήμοις ἕως
in spirit, and was in the deserts until
ἡμέρας ἀναδείξεως αὐτοῦ πρὸς τὸν Ἰσραήλ.
[the] days of showing of him to – Israel.

2 Ἐγένετο δὲ ἐν ταῖς ἡμέραις ἐκείναις
Now it came to pass in – days those
ἐξῆλθεν δόγμα παρὰ Καίσαρος Αὐγούστου
went out a decree from Cæsar Augustus
ἀπογράφεσθαι πᾶσαν τὴν οἰκουμένην. 2 αὕτη
to be enrolled all the inhabited earth. This
ἀπογραφὴ πρώτη ἐγένετο ἡγεμονεύοντος τῆς
²enrolment ¹first was governing –
=when Cyrenius governed Syria.
Συρίας Κυρηνίου. 3 καὶ ἐπορεύοντο πάντες
Syria Cyrenius.[a] And went all
ἀπογράφεσθαι, ἕκαστος εἰς τὴν ἑαυτοῦ
to be enrolled, each man to the of himself
πόλιν. 4 Ἀνέβη δὲ καὶ Ἰωσὴφ ἀπὸ τῆς
city. So went up also Joseph from –
Γαλιλαίας ἐκ πόλεως Ναζαρὲθ εἰς τὴν
Galilee out of a city Nazareth to –
Ἰουδαίαν εἰς πόλιν Δαυὶδ ἥτις καλεῖται Βηθλέεμ,
Judæa to a city of David which is called Bethlehem,
διὰ τὸ εἶναι αὐτὸν ἐξ οἴκου καὶ
because of the to be him[b] *out* of [the] house and
=because he was
πατριᾶς Δαυίδ, 5 ἀπογράψασθαι σὺν Μαριὰμ
family of David, to be enrolled with Mary
τῇ ἐμνηστευμένῃ αὐτῷ, οὔσῃ ἐγκύῳ.
the[one] *having been* betrothed to him, being pregnant.
6 Ἐγένετο δὲ ἐν τῷ εἶναι αὐτοὺς ἐκεῖ
And it came to pass in the to be them[be] there
=while they were
ἐπλήσθησαν αἱ ἡμέραι τοῦ τεκεῖν αὐτήν,
were fulfilled the days – to bear her,[bd]
=for her to bear,
7 καὶ ἔτεκεν τὸν υἱὸν αὐτῆς τὸν πρωτότοκον,
and she bore the son of her the firstborn,
καὶ ἐσπαργάνωσεν αὐτὸν καὶ ἀνέκλινεν
and she swathed him and laid
αὐτὸν ἐν φάτνῃ, διότι οὐκ ἦν αὐτοῖς
him in a manger, because there was not for them
τόπος ἐν τῷ καταλύματι. 8 Καὶ ποιμένες
place in the inn. And shepherds
ἦσαν ἐν τῇ χώρᾳ τῇ αὐτῇ ἀγραυλοῦντες
there were in the country – same living in the fields
καὶ φυλάσσοντες φυλακὰς τῆς νυκτὸς ἐπὶ
and keeping guard of(in) the night over
τὴν ποίμνην αὐτῶν. 9 καὶ ἄγγελος κυρίου
the flock of them. And an angel of [the] Lord
ἐπέστη αὐτοῖς καὶ δόξα κυρίου περιέλαμψεν
came upon them and [the] glory of [the] Lord shone around
αὐτούς, καὶ ἐφοβήθησαν φόβον μέγαν.
them, and they feared fear a great.
=exceedingly.
10 καὶ εἶπεν αὐτοῖς ὁ ἄγγελος· μὴ
And said to them the angel: not
φοβεῖσθε· ἰδοὺ γὰρ εὐαγγελίζομαι ὑμῖν
Fear ye; for behold I announce to you

to guide our feet into the
path of peace."
80 And the child grew and
became strong in spirit; and
he lived in the desert until
he appeared publicly to Israel.

Chapter 2

The Birth of Jesus

IN those days Caesar Au-
gustus issued a decree
that a census should be tak-
en of the entire Roman
world. 2 (This was the first
census that took place
while Quirinius was governor of Syria.) 3 And everyone went to his own town
to register.
4 So Joseph also went up
from the town of Nazareth
in Galilee to Judea, to Bethlehem the town of David,
because he belonged to the
house and line of David.
5 He went there to register
with Mary, who was
pledged to be married to
him and was expecting a
child. 6 While they were
there, the time came for the
baby to be born, 7 and she
gave birth to her firstborn,
a son. She wrapped him in
cloths and placed him in a
manger, because there was
no room for them in the inn.

The Shepherds and the Angels

8 And there were shep-
herds living out in the fields
nearby, keeping watch
over their flocks at night.
9 An angel of the Lord appeared to them, and the
glory of the Lord shone
around them, and they
were terrified. 10 But the angel said to them, "Do not
be afraid. I bring you good

great joy for all the people:
11 to you is born this day in
the city of David a Savior,
who is the Messiah,[i] the
Lord. 12 This will be a sign
for you: you will find a
child wrapped in bands of
cloth and lying in a man-
ger." 13 And suddenly there
was with the angel a multitude of the heavenly host,[j]
praising God and saying,
14 "Glory to God in the
highest heaven,
and on earth peace
among those
whom he
favors!"[k]

15 When the angels had
left them and gone into
heaven, the shepherds said
to one another, "Let us go
now to Bethlehem and see
this thing that has taken
place, which the Lord has
made known to us." 16 So
they went with haste and
found Mary and Joseph,
and the child lying in the
manger. 17 When they saw
this, they made known
what had been told them
about this child; 18 and all
who heard it were amazed
at what the shepherds told
them. 19 But Mary trea-
sured all these words and
pondered them in her
heart. 20 The shepherds returned, glorifying and
praising God for all they
had heard and seen, as it
had been told them.

Jesus Is Named

21 After eight days had passed, it was time to circumcise the child; and he was called Jesus, the name given by the angel before he was conceived in the womb.

Jesus Is Presented in the Temple

22 When the time came for their purification ac-

[i] Or *the Christ*
[j] Gk *army*
[k] Other ancient authorities read *peace, good will among people*

χαρὰν μεγάλην, ἥτις ἔσται παντὶ τῷ λαῷ,
joy a great, which will be to all the people,

11 ὅτι ἐτέχθη ὑμῖν σήμερον σωτήρ, ὅς
because was born to you to-day a Saviour, who

ἐστιν χριστὸς κύριος, ἐν πόλει Δαυίδ.
is Christ [the] Lord, in a city of David.

12 καὶ τοῦτο ὑμῖν σημεῖον, εὑρήσετε βρέφος
And this to you a sign, ye will find a babe

ἐσπαργανωμένον καὶ κείμενον ἐν φάτνῃ.
having been swathed and lying in a manger.

13 καὶ ἐξαίφνης ἐγένετο σὺν τῷ ἀγγέλῳ
And suddenly there was with the angel

πλῆθος στρατιᾶς οὐρανίου αἰνούντων τὸν
a multitude army of a heavenly praising –

θεὸν καὶ λεγόντων· 14 δόξα ἐν ὑψίστοις
God and saying: Glory in highest [places]

θεῷ καὶ ἐπὶ γῆς εἰρήνη ἐν ἀνθρώποις
to God and on earth peace among men

εὐδοκίας. 15 Καὶ ἐγένετο ὡς ἀπῆλθον
of goodwill. And it came to pass when went away

ἀπ' αὐτῶν εἰς τὸν οὐρανὸν οἱ ἄγγελοι,
from them to – heaven the angels,

οἱ ποιμένες ἐλάλουν πρὸς ἀλλήλους·
the shepherds said to one another:

διέλθωμεν δὴ ἕως Βηθλέεμ καὶ ἴδωμεν
Let us go then unto Bethlehem and let us see

τὸ ῥῆμα τοῦτο τὸ γεγονὸς ὃ ὁ κύριος
– thing this – having happened which the Lord

ἐγνώρισεν ἡμῖν. 16 καὶ ἦλθαν σπεύσαντες,
made known to us. And they came hastening,

καὶ ἀνεῦραν τήν τε Μαριὰμ καὶ τὸν
and found – both Mary and –

Ἰωσὴφ καὶ τὸ βρέφος κείμενον ἐν τῇ
Joseph and the babe lying in the

φάτνῃ· 17 ἰδόντες δὲ ἐγνώρισαν περὶ τοῦ
manger; and seeing they made known concerning the

ῥήματος τοῦ λαληθέντος αὐτοῖς περὶ τοῦ
word – spoken to them concerning –

παιδίου τούτου. 18 καὶ πάντες οἱ ἀκούσαντες
child this. And all the [ones] hearing

ἐθαύμασαν περὶ τῶν λαληθέντων ὑπὸ τῶν
marvelled concerning the things spoken by the

ποιμένων πρὸς αὐτούς· 19 ἡ δὲ Μαρία
shepherds to them; – but Mary

πάντα συνετήρει τὰ ῥήματα ταῦτα συμβάλλουσα
[2]all [1]kept – [4]things [3]these pondering

ἐν τῇ καρδίᾳ αὐτῆς. 20 καὶ ὑπέστρεψαν
in the heart of her. And returned

οἱ ποιμένες δοξάζοντες καὶ αἰνοῦντες τὸν
the shepherds glorifying and praising –

θεὸν ἐπὶ πᾶσιν οἷς ἤκουσαν καὶ εἶδον
God at all things which they heard and saw

καθὼς ἐλαλήθη πρὸς αὐτούς.
as was spoken to them.

21 Καὶ ὅτε ἐπλήσθησαν ἡμέραι ὀκτὼ
And when were completed days eight

τοῦ περιτεμεῖν αὐτόν, καὶ ἐκλήθη τὸ
– to circumcise him[d], *and* was called the

ὄνομα αὐτοῦ Ἰησοῦς, τὸ κληθὲν ὑπὸ τοῦ
name of him Jesus, the [name] called by the

ἀγγέλου πρὸ τοῦ συλλημφθῆναι αὐτὸν ἐν
angel before the to be conceived him[b] in
=he was conceived

τῇ κοιλίᾳ.
the womb.

22 Καὶ ὅτε ἐπλήσθησαν αἱ ἡμέραι τοῦ
And when were completed the days of the

news of great joy that will
be for all the people. 11 To-
day in the town of David a
Savior has been born to
you; he is Christ[e] the Lord.
12 This will be a sign to you:
You will find a baby
wrapped in cloths and lying
in a manger."
13 Suddenly a great com-
pany of the heavenly host
appeared with the angel,
praising God and saying,
14 "Glory to God in the
highest,
and on earth peace to
men on whom his
favor rests."

15 When the angels had
left them and gone into
heaven, the shepherds said
to one another, "Let's go
to Bethlehem and see this
thing that has happened,
which the Lord has told us
about."
16 So they hurried off and
found Mary and Joseph,
and the baby, who was ly-
ing in the manger. 17 When
they had seen him, they
spread the word concern-
ing what had been told
them about this child, 18 and
all who heard it were
amazed at what the shep-
herds said to them. 19 But
Mary treasured up all these
things and pondered them
in her heart. 20 The shepherds returned, glorifying
and praising God for all the
things they had heard and
seen, which were just as
they had been told.

Jesus Presented in the Temple

21 On the eighth day, when it was time to circumcise him, he was named Jesus, the name the angel had given him before he had been conceived.

22 When the time of their

[e] 11 Or *Messiah*. "The Christ" (Greek) and "the Messiah" (Hebrew) both mean "the Anointed One"; also in verse 26.

cording to the law of Mo-
ses, they brought him up to
Jerusalem to present him to
the Lord [23](as it is written
in the law of the Lord, "Every firstborn male shall be
designated as holy to the
Lord"), [24]and they offered
a sacrifice according to
what is stated in the law of
the Lord, "a pair of turtledoves or two young pi-
geons."
25 Now there was a man
in Jerusalem whose name
was Simeon;[l] this man
was righteous and devout,
looking forward to the consolation of Israel, and the
Holy Spirit rested on him.
[26]It had been revealed to
him by the Holy Spirit that
he would not see death before he had seen the Lord's
Messiah.[m] [27]Guided by the
Spirit, Simeon[n] came into
the temple; and when the
parents brought in the child
Jesus, to do for him what
was customary under the
law, [28]Simeon[o] took him
in his arms and praised
God, saying,
"Master, now you
are dismissing
your servant[p] in
peace,
according to your
word;
30 for my eyes have seen
your salvation,
31 which you have
prepared in the
presence of all
peoples,
32 a light for revelation
to the Gentiles
and for glory to
your people
Israel."
33 And the child's fa-
ther and mother were
amazed at what was being
said about him. [34]Then
Simeon[q] blessed them and
said to his mother Mary,
"This child is destined for
the falling and the rising of
many in Israel, and to be a

[l] Gk *Symeon*
[m] Or *the Lord's Christ*
[n] Gk *In the Spirit, he*
[o] Gk *he*
[p] Gk *slave*

καθαρισμοῦ αὐτῶν κατὰ τὸν νόμον
cleansing of them according to the law
Μωϋσέως, ἀνήγαγον αὐτὸν εἰς Ἰεροσόλυμα
of Moses, they took up him to Jerusalem
παραστῆσαι τῷ κυρίῳ, 23 καθὼς γέγραπται
to present to the Lord, as it has been written
ἐν νόμῳ κυρίου ὅτι πᾶν ἄρσεν διανοῖγον
in [the] law of the Lord[,] – Every male opening
μήτραν ἅγιον τῷ κυρίῳ κληθήσεται, 24 καὶ
a womb holy to the Lord shall be called, and
τοῦ δοῦναι θυσίαν κατὰ τὸ εἰρημένον ἐν
– to give[d] a sacrifice according to the thing said in
τῷ νόμῳ κυρίου, ζεῦγος τρυγόνων ἢ δύο
the law of [the] Lord, a pair of turtledoves or two
νοσσοὺς περιστερῶν. 25 Καὶ ἰδοὺ ἄνθρωπος
nestlings of doves. And behold[,] a man
ἦν ἐν Ἰερουσαλὴμ ᾧ ὄνομα Συμεών, καὶ
was in Jerusalem to whom name[c] Simeon, and
=whose name was
ὁ ἄνθρωπος οὗτος δίκαιος καὶ εὐλαβής,
– man this [was] just and devout,
προσδεχόμενος παράκλησιν τοῦ Ἰσραήλ, καὶ
expecting [the] consolation – of Israel, and
πνεῦμα ἦν ἅγιον ἐπ' αὐτόν· 26 καὶ ἦν
[1][the] [3]Spirit [4]was [2]Holy upon him; and it was
αὐτῷ κεχρηματισμένον ὑπὸ τοῦ πνεύματος
to him *having been* communicated by the Spirit
τοῦ ἁγίου μὴ ἰδεῖν θάνατον πρὶν ἢ ἂν
– Holy not to see death before
ἴδῃ τὸν χριστὸν κυρίου. 27 καὶ ἦλθεν
he should see the Christ of [the] Lord. And he came
ἐν τῷ πνεύματι εἰς τὸ ἱερόν· καὶ ἐν τῷ
by the Spirit into the temple; and in the
=as the(his) parents brought in
εἰσαγαγεῖν τοὺς γονεῖς τὸ παιδίον Ἰησοῦν
to bring in the parents[be] the child Jesus
τοῦ ποιῆσαι αὐτοὺς κατὰ τὸ εἰθισμένον
– to do them[bd] according to the custom
=for them to do
τοῦ νόμου περὶ αὐτοῦ, 28 καὶ αὐτὸς
of the law concerning him, *and* he
ἐδέξατο αὐτὸ εἰς τὰς ἀγκάλας καὶ
received him in the(his) arms and
εὐλόγησεν τὸν θεὸν καὶ εἶπεν· 29 νῦν
blessed – God and said : Now
ἀπολύεις τὸν δοῦλόν σου, δέσποτα, κατὰ
thou releasest the slave of thee, Master, according to
τὸ ῥῆμά σου ἐν εἰρήνῃ· 30 ὅτι εἶδον οἱ
the word of thee in peace; because saw the
ὀφθαλμοί μου τὸ σωτήριόν σου, 31 ὃ
eyes of me the salvation of thee, which
ἡτοίμασας κατὰ πρόσωπον πάντων τῶν
thou didst prepare before [the] face of all the
λαῶν, 32 φῶς εἰς ἀποκάλυψιν ἐθνῶν καὶ
peoples, a light for a revelation of [the] nations and
δόξαν λαοῦ σου Ἰσραήλ. 33 καὶ ἦν
a glory of [the] people of thee Israel. And [7]was(were)
ὁ πατὴρ αὐτοῦ καὶ ἡ μήτηρ θαυμάζοντες
[1]the [2]father [3]of him [4]and [5]the [6]mother [8]marvelling
ἐπὶ τοῖς λαλουμένοις περὶ αὐτοῦ. 34 καὶ
at the things being said concerning him. And
εὐλόγησεν αὐτοὺς Συμεὼν καὶ εἶπεν πρὸς
blessed them Simeon and said to
Μαριὰμ τὴν μητέρα αὐτοῦ· ἰδοὺ οὗτος
Mary the mother of him : Behold[,] this
κεῖται εἰς πτῶσιν καὶ ἀνάστασιν πολλῶν
is set for fall and rising again of many

purification according to
the Law of Moses had been
completed, Joseph and
Mary took him to Jerusa-
lem to present him to the
Lord [23](as it is written
in the Law of the Lord,
"Every firstborn male is
to be consecrated to the
Lord"[f]), [24]and to offer a
sacrifice in keeping with
what is said in the Law of
the Lord: "a pair of doves
or two young pigeons."[g]
[25]Now there was a man in
Jerusalem called Simeon,
who was righteous and de-
vout. He was waiting for
the consolation of Israel,
and the Holy Spirit was
upon him. [26]It had been revealed to him by the Holy
Spirit that he would not die
before he had seen the
Lord's Christ. [27]Moved by
the Spirit, he went into the
temple courts. When the
parents brought in the child
Jesus to do for him what the
custom of the Law re-
quired, [28]Simeon took him
in his arms and praised
God, saying:
29 "Sovereign Lord, as you
have promised,
you now dismiss[h] your
servant in peace.
30 For my eyes have seen
your salvation,
31 which you have
prepared in the sight
of all people,
32 a light for revelation to
the Gentiles
and for glory to your
people Israel."
33 The child's father and
mother marveled at what
was said about him. [34]Then
Simeon blessed them and
said to Mary, his mother:
"This child is destined to
cause the falling and rising
of many in Israel, and to be

[f] *23* Exodus 13:2,12
[g] *24* Lev. 12:8
[h] *29* Or *promised, / now dismiss*

sign that will be opposed
35 so that the inner thoughts of many will be revealed—and a sword will pierce your own soul too."

36 There was also a prophet, Anna[r] the daughter of Phanuel, of the tribe of Asher. She was of a great age, having lived with her husband seven years after her marriage, 37 then as a widow to the age of eighty-four. She never left the temple but worshiped there with fasting and prayer night and day. 38 At that moment she came, and began to praise God and to speak about the child[s] to all who were looking for the redemption of Jerusalem.

The Return to Nazareth

39 When they had finished everything required by the law of the Lord, they returned to Galilee, to their own town of Nazareth. 40 The child grew and became strong, filled with wisdom; and the favor of God was upon him.

The Boy Jesus in the Temple

41 Now every year his parents went to Jerusalem for the festival of the Passover. 42 And when he was twelve years old, they went up as usual for the festival. 43 When the festival was ended and they started to return, the boy Jesus stayed behind in Jerusalem, but his parents did not know it. 44 Assuming that he was in the group of travelers, they went a day's journey. Then they started to look for him among their relatives and friends. 45 When they did not find him, they returned to Jeru-

[q] Gk *Symeon*
[r] Gk *Hanna*

ἐν τῷ Ἰσραὴλ καὶ εἰς σημεῖον ἀντιλεγ-
in – Israel and for a sign spoken

όμενον — 35 καὶ σοῦ δὲ αὐτῆς τὴν ψυχὴν
against — and [5]of thee [7]also [6][thy]self [3]the [4]soul

διελεύσεται ῥομφαία—, ὅπως ἂν ἀποκαλυφθῶσιν
[2]will go through [1]a sword —, so as – may be revealed

ἐκ πολλῶν καρδιῶν διαλογισμοί. 36 Καὶ
of many hearts [the] thoughts. And

ἦν Ἄννα προφῆτις, θυγάτηρ Φανουήλ, ἐκ
there was Anna a prophetess, a daughter of Phanuel, of

φυλῆς Ἀσήρ· αὕτη προβεβηκυῖα ἐν ἡμέραις
[the] tribe of Asher; this having advanced in days

πολλαῖς, ζήσασα μετὰ ἀνδρὸς ἔτη ἑπτὰ
many, having lived with a husband years seven

ἀπὸ τῆς παρθενίας αὐτῆς, 37 καὶ αὐτὴ
from the virginity of her, and she [was]

χήρα ἕως ἐτῶν ὀγδοήκοντα τεσσάρων, ἣ
a widow until years eighty-four, who

οὐκ ἀφίστατο τοῦ ἱεροῦ νηστείαις καὶ
withdrew not from the temple with fastings and

δεήσεσιν λατρεύουσα νύκτα καὶ ἡμέραν.
petitionings serving night and day.

38 καὶ αὐτῇ τῇ ὥρᾳ ἐπιστᾶσα ἀνθωμολογεῖτο
And at the very hour* coming upon she gave thanks

τῷ θεῷ καὶ ἐλάλει περὶ αὐτοῦ πᾶσιν τοῖς
– to God and spoke about him to all the [ones]

προσδεχομένοις λύτρωσιν Ἰερουσαλήμ. 39 Καὶ
expecting redemption in Jerusalem. And

ὡς ἐτέλεσαν πάντα τὰ κατὰ τὸν νόμον
when they finished all things – according to the law

κυρίου, ἐπέστρεψαν εἰς τὴν Γαλιλαίαν εἰς
of [the] Lord, they returned to – Galilee to

πόλιν ἑαυτῶν Ναζαρέθ.
a city of them*selves* Nazareth.

40 Τὸ δὲ παιδίον ηὔξανεν καὶ ἐκραταιοῦτο
And the child grew and became strong

πληρούμενον σοφίᾳ, καὶ χάρις θεοῦ ἦν ἐπ'
being filled with wisdom, and [the] grace of God was upon

αὐτό.
him.

41 Καὶ ἐπορεύοντο οἱ γονεῖς αὐτοῦ κατ'
And went the parents of him year

ἔτος εἰς Ἰερουσαλὴμ τῇ ἑορτῇ τοῦ πάσχα.
by year† to Jerusalem at the feast of the Passover.

42 Καὶ ὅτε ἐγένετο ἐτῶν δώδεκα, ἀναβαινόντων
And when he became of years twelve, going up
=as they went up

αὐτῶν κατὰ τὸ ἔθος τῆς ἑορτῆς, 43 καὶ
them[a] according to the custom of the feast, and

τελειωσάντων τὰς ἡμέρας, ἐν τῷ ὑποστρέφειν
fulfilling[a] the days, in the to return
=when they returned

αὐτοὺς ὑπέμεινεν Ἰησοῦς ὁ παῖς ἐν
them[be] [4]remained [3]Jesus [1]the [2]boy in

Ἰερουσαλήμ, καὶ οὐκ ἔγνωσαν οἱ γονεῖς
Jerusalem, and [4]knew not [1]the [2]parents

αὐτοῦ. 44 νομίσαντες δὲ αὐτὸν εἶναι ἐν
[3]of him. But supposing him to be in

τῇ συνοδίᾳ ἦλθον ἡμέρας ὁδὸν καὶ ἀνεζήτουν
the company they went of a day a journey and sought

αὐτὸν ἐν τοῖς συγγενεῦσιν καὶ τοῖς
him among the(ir) relatives and the(ir)

γνωστοῖς, 45 καὶ μὴ εὑρόντες ὑπέστρεψαν
acquaintances, and not finding returned

*** Strictly, this construction should mean "the hour itself"; but the context demands "the same hour". See 10. 7, 21; 12. 12; 13. 1, 31; 20. 19; 23. 12; 24. 13. "Luke seems to be the only N.T. writer who affects the construction" (C. F. D. Moule). See also Acts 16. 18; 22. 13. Of course there is not a great difference between "the hour itself", "the very hour", and "the same hour".**

a sign that will be spoken against, 35 so that the thoughts of many hearts will be revealed. And a sword will pierce your own soul too."

36 There was also a prophetess, Anna, the daughter of Phanuel, of the tribe of Asher. She was very old; she had lived with her husband seven years after her marriage, 37 and then was a widow until she was eighty-four.[i] She never left the temple but worshiped night and day, fasting and praying. 38 Coming up to them at that very moment, she gave thanks to God and spoke about the child to all who were looking forward to the redemption of Jerusalem.

39 When Joseph and Mary had done everything required by the Law of the Lord, they returned to Galilee to their own town of Nazareth. 40 And the child grew and became strong; he was filled with wisdom, and the grace of God was upon him.

The Boy Jesus at the Temple

41 Every year his parents went to Jerusalem for the Feast of the Passover. 42 When he was twelve years old, they went up to the Feast, according to the custom. 43 After the Feast was over, while his parents were returning home, the boy Jesus stayed behind in Jerusalem, but they were unaware of it. 44 Thinking he was in their company, they traveled on for a day. Then they began looking for him among their relatives and friends. 45 When they did not find him, they

[i] 37 Or *widow for eighty-four years*

salem to search for him.
46 After three days they
found him in the temple,
sitting among the teachers,
listening to them and asking them questions. 47 And
all who heard him were
amazed at his understand-
ing and his answers.
48 When his parents[t] saw
him they were astonished;
and his mother said to him,
"Child, why have you
treated us like this? Look,
your father and I have been
searching for you in great
anxiety." 49 He said to
them, "Why were you
searching for me? Did you
not know that I must be in
my Father's house?"[u]
50 But they did not understand what he said to them.
51 Then he went down with
them and came to Naza-
reth, and was obedient to
them. His mother treasured
all these things in her heart.
52 And Jesus increased
in wisdom and in years,[v]
and in divine and human favor.

Chapter 3

The Proclamation of John the Baptist

IN the fifteenth year of
the reign of Emperor Ti-
berius, when Pontius Pilate
was governor of Judea, and
Herod was ruler[w] of Galilee, and his brother Philip
ruler[w] of the region of Itu-
raea and Trachonitis, and
Lysanias ruler[w] of Abilene, 2 during the high priesthood of Annas and Caia-
phas, the word of God
came to John son of Zechariah in the wilderness. 3 He
went into all the region

[s] Gk *him*
[t] Gk *they*
[u] Or *be about my Father's interests?*
[v] Or *in stature*
[w] Gk *tetrarch*

εἰς Ἰερουσαλὴμ ἀναζητοῦντες αὐτόν. **46** καὶ
to Jerusalem seeking him. And

ἐγένετο μετὰ ἡμέρας τρεῖς εὗρον αὐτὸν
it came to pass after days three they found him

ἐν τῷ ἱερῷ καθεζόμενον ἐν μέσῳ τῶν
in the temple sitting in [the] midst of the

διδασκάλων καὶ ἀκούοντα αὐτῶν καὶ
teachers both hearing them and

ἐπερωτῶντα αὐτούς· **47** ἐξίσταντο δὲ πάντες
questioning them; and were astonished all

οἱ ἀκούοντες αὐτοῦ ἐπὶ τῇ συνέσει καὶ
the [ones] hearing him at the intelligence and

ταῖς ἀποκρίσεσιν αὐτοῦ. **48** καὶ ἰδόντες
the answers of him. And seeing

αὐτὸν ἐξεπλάγησαν, καὶ εἶπεν πρὸς αὐτὸν
him they were astounded, and said to him

ἡ μήτηρ αὐτοῦ· τέκνον, τί ἐποίησας ἡμῖν
the mother of him: Child, why didst thou to us

οὕτως; ἰδοὺ ὁ πατήρ σου κἀγὼ ὀδυνώμενοι
thus? behold[,] the father of thee and I greatly distressed

ζητοῦμέν σε. **49** καὶ εἶπεν πρὸς αὐτούς·
are seeking thee. And he said to them:

τί ὅτι ἐζητεῖτέ με; οὐκ ᾔδειτε ὅτι ἐν
Why [is it] that ye sought me? did ye not know that in =I

τοῖς τοῦ πατρός μου δεῖ εἶναί με;
the [affairs] of the Father of me it behoves to be me?
must be about my Father's business?

50 καὶ αὐτοὶ οὐ συνῆκαν τὸ ῥῆμα ὃ
And they did not understand the word which

ἐλάλησεν αὐτοῖς. **51** καὶ κατέβη μετ'
he spoke to them. And he went down with

αὐτῶν καὶ ἦλθεν εἰς Ναζαρέθ, καὶ ἦν
them and came to Nazareth, and was

ὑποτασσόμενος αὐτοῖς. καὶ ἡ μήτηρ
being subject to them. And the mother

αὐτοῦ διετήρει πάντα τὰ ῥήματα ἐν τῇ
of him carefully kept all the matters in the

καρδίᾳ αὐτῆς. **52** Καὶ Ἰησοῦς προέκοπτεν
heart of her. And Jesus progressed

ἐν τῇ σοφίᾳ καὶ ἡλικίᾳ καὶ χάριτι παρὰ
in – wisdom and age and favour before

θεῷ καὶ ἀνθρώποις.
God and men.

3 Ἐν ἔτει δὲ πεντεκαιδεκάτῳ τῆς
Now in [the] year fifteenth of the

ἡγεμονίας Τιβερίου Καίσαρος, ἡγεμονεύοντος
government of Tiberius Cæsar, governing
=while Pontius Pilate

Ποντίου Πιλάτου τῆς Ἰουδαίας, καὶ
Pontius Pilate[a] – of Judæa, and
was governing

τετρααρχοῦντος τῆς Γαλιλαίας Ἡρῴδου,
ruling as tetrarch – of Galilee Herod,[a]
=while Herod was ruling as tetrarch of Galilee,

Φιλίππου δὲ τοῦ ἀδελφοῦ αὐτοῦ τετρα-
and Philip the brother of him ruling

αρχοῦντος τῆς Ἰτουραίας καὶ Τραχωνίτιδος
as tetrarch[a] [1]of the [2]of Ituræa [4]and [5]of Trachonitis

χώρας, καὶ Λυσανίου τῆς Ἀβιληνῆς
[3]country, and Lysanias – of Abilene

τετρααρχοῦντος, **2** ἐπὶ ἀρχιερέως Ἅννα
ruling as tetrarch[a], in the time of [the] high priest Anna

καὶ Καϊαφᾶ, ἐγένετο ῥῆμα θεοῦ ἐπὶ Ἰωάννην
and Caiaphas, came a word of God to John

τὸν Ζαχαρίου υἱὸν ἐν τῇ ἐρήμῳ. **3** καὶ
the of Zacharias son in the desert. And

went back to Jerusalem to
look for him. 46 After three
days they found him in the
temple courts, sitting
among the teachers, listening to them and asking
them questions. 47 Every-
one who heard him was
amazed at his understand-
ing and his answers.
48 When his parents saw
him, they were astonished.
His mother said to him,
"Son, why have you treat-
ed us like this? Your father
and I have been anxiously
searching for you."
49 "Why were you search-
ing for me?" he asked.
"Didn't you know I had to
be in my Father's house?"
50 But they did not understand what he was saying to
them.
51 Then he went down to
Nazareth with them and
was obedient to them. But
his mother treasured all
these things in her heart.
52 And Jesus grew in wis-
dom and stature, and in favor with God and men.

Chapter 3

John the Baptist Prepares the Way

IN the fifteenth year of
the reign of Tiberius
Caesar—when Pontius Pi-
late was governor of Judea,
Herod tetrarch of Galilee,
his brother Philip tetrarch
of Iturea and Traconitis,
and Lysanias tetrarch of
Abilene—2 during the high
priesthood of Annas and
Caiaphas, the word of God
came to John son of Zechariah in the desert. 3 He went

around the Jordan, pro-
claiming a baptism of re-
pentance for the forgive-
ness of sins, 4 as it is written
in the book of the words of
the prophet Isaiah,
"The voice of one
crying out in
the wilderness:
'Prepare the way of
the Lord,
make his paths
straight.
5 Every valley shall be
filled,
and every mountain
and hill shall be
made low,
and the crooked shall
be made
straight,
and the rough ways
made smooth;
6 and all flesh shall see
the salvation of
God.'"
7 John said to the
crowds that came out to be
baptized by him, "You
brood of vipers! Who
warned you to flee from the
wrath to come? 8 Bear
fruits worthy of repen-
tance. Do not begin to say
to yourselves, 'We have
Abraham as our ancestor';
for I tell you, God is able
from these stones to raise
up children to Abraham.
9 Even now the ax is lying at
the root of the trees; every
tree therefore that does not
bear good fruit is cut down
and thrown into the fire."
10 And the crowds
asked him, "What then
should we do?" 11 In reply
he said to them, "Whoever
has two coats must share
with anyone who has none;
and whoever has food must
do likewise." 12 Even tax
collectors came to be baptized, and they asked him,
"Teacher, what should we
do?" 13 He said to them,
"Collect no more than the
amount prescribed for
you." 14 Soldiers also asked
him, "And we, what should
we do?" He said to them,

ἦλθεν εἰς πᾶσαν τὴν περίχωρον τοῦ
he came into all the neighbourhood of the
Ἰορδάνου κηρύσσων βάπτισμα μετανοίας
Jordan proclaiming a baptism of repentance
εἰς ἄφεσιν ἁμαρτιῶν, 4 ὡς γέγραπται ἐν
for forgiveness of sins, as it has been written in
βίβλῳ λόγων Ἠσαΐου τοῦ προφήτου·
[the] roll of [the] words of Esaias the prophet :
φωνὴ βοῶντος ἐν τῇ ἐρήμῳ· ἑτοιμάσατε
Voice of [one] crying in the desert : Prepare ye
τὴν ὁδὸν κυρίου, εὐθείας ποιεῖτε τὰς
the way of [the] Lord, straight make the
τρίβους αὐτοῦ· 5 πᾶσα φάραγξ πληρωθήσεται
paths of him; every valley shall be filled up
καὶ πᾶν ὄρος καὶ βουνὸς ταπεινωθήσεται,
and every mountain and hill shall be laid low,
καὶ ἔσται τὰ σκολιὰ εἰς εὐθείας καὶ αἱ
and shall be the crooked [places] into straight [ones] and the
τραχεῖαι εἰς ὁδοὺς λείας· 6 καὶ ὄψεται
rough [places] into ways smooth; and [2]shall see
πᾶσα σὰρξ τὸ σωτήριον τοῦ θεοῦ.
[1]all [2]flesh the salvation – of God.
7 Ἔλεγεν οὖν τοῖς ἐκπορευομένοις ὄχλοις
He said therefore to the [2]going out [1]crowds
βαπτισθῆναι ὑπ᾽ αὐτοῦ· γεννήματα ἐχιδνῶν,
to be baptized by him : Offspring of vipers,
τίς ὑπέδειξεν ὑμῖν φυγεῖν ἀπὸ τῆς
who warned you to flee from the
μελλούσης ὀργῆς; 8 ποιήσατε οὖν καρποὺς
coming wrath? Produce therefore fruits
ἀξίους τῆς μετανοίας· καὶ μὴ ἄρξησθε
worthy – of repentance; and do not begin
λέγειν ἐν ἑαυτοῖς· πατέρα ἔχομεν τὸν
to say among yourselves : Father we have –
Ἀβραάμ· λέγω γὰρ ὑμῖν ὅτι δύναται ὁ
Abraham; for I tell you that [2]can –
θεὸς ἐκ τῶν λίθων τούτων ἐγεῖραι τέκνα
[1]God out of – stones these to raise children
τῷ Ἀβραάμ. 9 ἤδη δὲ καὶ ἡ ἀξίνη πρὸς
– to Abraham. And [2]already [1]even the axe at
τὴν ῥίζαν τῶν δένδρων κεῖται· πᾶν οὖν
the root of the trees is laid; [2]every [1]therefore
δένδρον μὴ ποιοῦν καρπὸν καλὸν
tree not producing fruit good
ἐκκόπτεται καὶ εἰς πῦρ βάλλεται. 10 Καὶ
is being cut down and into fire is being cast. And
ἐπηρώτων αὐτὸν οἱ ὄχλοι λέγοντες· τί
asked him the crowds saying : What
οὖν ποιήσωμεν; 11 ἀποκριθεὶς δὲ ἔλεγεν
then may we do? And answering he told
αὐτοῖς· ὁ ἔχων δύο χιτῶνας μεταδότω
them : The [one] having two tunics let him impart
τῷ μὴ ἔχοντι, καὶ ὁ ἔχων βρώματα
to the [one] not having, and the [one] having foods
ὁμοίως ποιείτω. 12 ἦλθον δὲ καὶ τελῶναι
likewise let him do. And there came also tax-collectors
βαπτισθῆναι καὶ εἶπαν πρὸς αὐτόν·
to be baptized and they said to him :
διδάσκαλε, τί ποιήσωμεν; 13 ὁ δὲ εἶπεν
Teacher, what may we do? And he said
πρὸς αὐτούς· μηδὲν πλέον παρὰ τὸ
to them : Nothing more besides the [thing]
διατεταγμένον ὑμῖν πράσσετε. 14 ἐπηρώτων δὲ
having been commanded you do ye. And asked
αὐτὸν καὶ στρατευόμενοι λέγοντες· τί
him also men serving in the army saying : What

into all the country around
the Jordan, preaching a
baptism of repentance for
the forgiveness of sins. 4 As
is written in the book of the
words of Isaiah the prophet:
"A voice of one calling
in the desert,
'Prepare the way for the
Lord,
make straight paths for
him.
5 Every valley shall be
filled in,
every mountain and hill
made low.
The crooked roads shall
become straight,
the rough ways
smooth.
6 And all mankind will see
God's salvation.'"[j]
7 John said to the crowds
coming out to be baptized
by him, "You brood of vi-
pers! Who warned you to
flee from the coming
wrath? 8 Produce fruit in
keeping with repentance.
And do not begin to say to
yourselves, 'We have
Abraham as our father.'
For I tell you that out of
these stones God can raise
up children for Abraham.
9 The ax is already at the
root of the trees, and every
tree that does not produce
good fruit will be cut down
and thrown into the fire."
10 "What should we do
then?" the crowd asked.
11 John answered, "The
man with two tunics should
share with him who has
none, and the one who has
food should do the same."
12 Tax collectors also
came to be baptized.
"Teacher," they asked,
"what should we do?"

j 6 Isaiah 40:3-5

"Do not extort money from
anyone by threats or false
accusation, and be satisfied
with your wages."
15 As the people were
filled with expectation, and
all were questioning in their
hearts concerning John,
whether he might be the
Messiah,[x] 16 John an-
swered all of them by saying, "I baptize you with water; but one who is more
powerful than I is coming; I
am not worthy to untie the
thong of his sandals. He
will baptize you with[y] the
Holy Spirit and fire. 17 His
winnowing fork is in his
hand, to clear his threshing
floor and to gather the
wheat into his granary; but
the chaff he will burn with
unquenchable fire."
18 So, with many other
exhortations, he pro-
claimed the good news to
the people. 19 But Herod
the ruler,[z] who had been
rebuked by him because of
Herodias, his brother's
wife, and because of all the
evil things that Herod had
done, 20 added to them all
by shutting up John in prison.

The Baptism of Jesus

21 Now when all the
people were baptized, and
when Jesus also had been
baptized and was praying,
the heaven was opened,
22 and the Holy Spirit descended upon him in bodily
form like a dove. And a
voice came from heaven,
"You are my Son, the Be-
loved;[a] with you I am well
pleased."[b]

The Ancestors of Jesus

23 Jesus was about thir-
ty years old when he began
his work. He was the son
(as was thought) of Joseph

[x] Or *the Christ*
[y] Or *in*
[z] Gk *tetrarch*
[a] Or *my beloved Son*
[b] Other ancient authorities read *You are my Son, today I have begotten you*

ποιήσωμεν καὶ ἡμεῖς; καὶ εἶπεν αὐτοῖς·
may do also we? And he told them :
μηδένα διασείσητε μηδὲ συκοφαντήσητε,
No one intimidate nor accuse falsely,
καὶ ἀρκεῖσθε τοῖς ὀψωνίοις ὑμῶν.
and be satisfied with the pay of you.
15 Προσδοκῶντος δὲ τοῦ λαοῦ καὶ
Now expecting the people[a] and
=while the people were expecting and all were debating
διαλογιζομένων πάντων ἐν ταῖς καρδίαις
debating all[a] in the hearts
αὐτῶν περὶ τοῦ Ἰωάννου, μήποτε αὐτὸς
of them concerning – John, perhaps he
εἴη ὁ χριστός, **16** ἀπεκρίνατο λέγων πᾶσιν
might be the Christ, [2]answered [3]saying [4]to all
ὁ Ἰωάννης· ἐγὼ μὲν ὕδατι βαπτίζω ὑμᾶς·
– [1]John : I indeed with water baptize you;
ἔρχεται δὲ ὁ ἰσχυρότερός μου, οὗ οὐκ
but there comes the [one] stronger of me, of whom not
=than I,
εἰμὶ ἱκανὸς λῦσαι τὸν ἱμάντα τῶν ὑποδημά-
I am competent to loosen the thong of the san-
των αὐτοῦ· αὐτὸς ὑμᾶς βαπτίσει ἐν
dals of him; he you will baptize with
πνεύματι ἁγίῳ καὶ πυρί· **17** οὗ τὸ πτύον
Spirit [the] Holy and fire; of whom the fan [is]
ἐν τῇ χειρὶ αὐτοῦ διακαθᾶραι τὴν ἅλωνα
in the hand of him thoroughly to cleanse the threshing-floor
αὐτοῦ καὶ συναγαγεῖν τὸν σῖτον εἰς τὴν
of him and to gather the wheat into the
ἀποθήκην αὐτοῦ, τὸ δὲ ἄχυρον κατακαύσει
barn of him, but the chaff he will burn up
πυρὶ ἀσβέστῳ. **18** Πολλὰ μὲν οὖν καὶ
with fire unquenchable. Many things indeed therefore and
ἕτερα παρακαλῶν εὐηγγελίζετο τὸν λαόν·
different exhorting he evangelized the people;
19 ὁ δὲ Ἡρῴδης ὁ τετραάρχης, ἐλεγχόμενος
– but Herod the tetrarch, being reproved
ὑπ᾽ αὐτοῦ περὶ Ἡρῳδιάδος τῆς γυναικὸς
by him concerning Herodias the wife
τοῦ ἀδελφοῦ αὐτοῦ καὶ περὶ πάντων ὧν
of the brother of him and concerning [1]all [3]things [4]which
ἐποίησεν πονηρῶν ὁ Ἡρῴδης, **20** προσέθηκεν
[6]did [2]evil – [5]Herod, added
καὶ τοῦτο ἐπὶ πᾶσιν, κατέκλεισεν τὸν
also this above all, he shut up
Ἰωάννην ἐν φυλακῇ.
John in prison.
21 Ἐγένετο δὲ ἐν τῷ βαπτισθῆναι ἅπαντα
Now it came to pass in the to be baptized all
=when all the people were baptized
τὸν λαὸν καὶ Ἰησοῦ βαπτισθέντος καὶ
the people[be] and Jesus being baptized and
=as Jesus had been baptized and was praying
προσευχομένου ἀνεῳχθῆναι τὸν οὐρανὸν **22** καὶ
praying[a] to be opened the heaven and
=the heaven was opened and the Holy Spirit came down
καταβῆναι τὸ πνεῦμα τὸ ἅγιον σωματικῷ
to come down the Spirit – Holy[b] in a bodily
εἴδει ὡς περιστερὰν ἐπ᾽ αὐτόν, καὶ φωνὴν
form as a dove upon him, and a voice
ἐξ οὐρανοῦ γενέσθαι· σὺ εἶ ὁ υἱός μου
out of heaven to come[b] : Thou art the Son of me
ὁ ἀγαπητός, ἐν σοὶ εὐδόκησα. **23** Καὶ
– beloved, in thee I was well pleased. And
αὐτὸς ἦν Ἰησοῦς ἀρχόμενος ὡσεὶ ἐτῶν
[2]himself [3]was [1]Jesus [4]beginning about years

13 "Don't collect any
more than you are required
to," he told them.
14 Then some soldiers
asked him, "And what
should we do?"
He replied, "Don't extort
money and don't accuse
people falsely—be content
with your pay."
15 The people were wait-
ing expectantly and were
all wondering in their
hearts if John might possibly be the Christ.[k] 16 John
answered them all, "I baptize you with[l] water. But
one more powerful than I
will come, the thongs of
whose sandals I am not
worthy to untie. He will
baptize you with the Holy
Spirit and with fire. 17 His
winnowing fork is in his
hand to clear his threshing
floor and to gather the
wheat into his barn, but he
will burn up the chaff with
unquenchable fire." 18 And
with many other words
John exhorted the people
and preached the good
news to them.
19 But when John rebuked
Herod the tetrarch because
of Herodias, his brother's
wife, and all the other evil
things he had done, 20 Herod added this to them all:
He locked John up in prison.

The Baptism and Genealogy of Jesus

21 When all the people
were being baptized, Jesus
was baptized too. And as
he was praying, heaven
was opened 22 and the Holy
Spirit descended on him in
bodily form like a dove.
And a voice came from
heaven: "You are my Son,
whom I love; with you I am
well pleased."
23 Now Jesus himself was
about thirty years old when
he began his ministry. He

[k] *15* Or *Messiah*
[l] *16* Or *in*

son of Heli, 24 son of Matthat, son of Levi, son of
Melchi, son of Jannai, son
of Joseph, 25 son of Mattathias, son of Amos, son of
Nahum, son of Esli, son of
Naggai, 26 son of Maath,
son of Mattathias, son of
Semein, son of Josech, son
of Joda, 27 son of Joanan,
son of Rhesa, son of Zerubbabel, son of Shealtiel,[c]
son of Neri, 28 son of Melchi, son of Addi, son of Cosam, son of Elmadam, son
of Er, 29 son of Joshua, son
of Eliezer, son of Jorim,
son of Matthat, son of
Levi, 30 son of Simeon, son
of Judah, son of Joseph,
son of Jonam, son of Eliakim, 31 son of Melea, son of
Menna, son of Mattatha,
son of Nathan, son of Da-
vid, 32 son of Jesse, son of
Obed, son of Boaz, son of
Sala,[d] son of Nahshon,
33 son of Amminadab, son
of Admin, son of Arni,[e]
son of Hezron, son of Pe-
rez, son of Judah, 34 son of
Jacob, son of Isaac, son of
Abraham, son of Terah,
son of Nahor, 35 son of Serug, son of Reu, son of Peleg, son of Eber, son of
Shelah, 36 son of Cainan,
son of Arphaxad, son of
Shem, son of Noah, son of
Lamech, 37 son of Methuselah, son of Enoch, son of
Jared, son of Mahalaleel,
son of Cainan, 38 son of
Enos, son of Seth, son of
Adam, son of God.

τριάκοντα, ὢν υἱός, ὡς ἐνομίζετο, Ἰωσήφ,
thirty, being son, as was supposed, of Joseph,

τοῦ Ἠλὶ 24 τοῦ Ματθὰτ τοῦ Λευὶ τοῦ
– of Eli – of Matthat – of Levi –

Μελχὶ τοῦ Ἰανναὶ τοῦ Ἰωσὴφ 25 τοῦ
of Melchi – of Jannai – of Joseph –

Ματταθίου τοῦ Ἀμὼς τοῦ Ναοὺμ τοῦ
of Mattathias – of Amos – of Naum –

Ἑσλὶ τοῦ Ναγγαὶ 26 τοῦ Μάαθ τοῦ
of Hesli – of Naggai – of Maath –

Ματταθίου τοῦ Σεμεῒν τοῦ Ἰωσὴχ τοῦ
of Mattathias – of Semein – of Josech –

Ἰωδὰ 27 τοῦ Ἰωανὰν τοῦ Ῥησὰ τοῦ
of Jodah – of Joanan – of Rhesa –

Ζοροβαβὲλ τοῦ Σαλαθιὴλ τοῦ Νηρὶ 28 τοῦ
of Zorobabel – of Salathiel – of Neri –

Μελχὶ τοῦ Ἀδδὶ τοῦ Κωσὰμ τοῦ
of Melchi – of Addi – of Kosam –

Ἐλμαδὰμ τοῦ Ἢρ 29 τοῦ Ἰησοῦ τοῦ
of Elmadam – of Er – of Jesus –

Ἐλιέζερ τοῦ Ἰωρὶμ τοῦ Μαθθὰτ τοῦ
of Eliezer – of Jorim – of Matthat –

Λευὶ 30 τοῦ Συμεὼν τοῦ Ἰούδα τοῦ
of Levi – of Simeon – of Juda –

Ἰωσὴφ τοῦ Ἰωνὰμ τοῦ Ἐλιακὶμ 31 τοῦ
of Joseph – of Jonam – of Eliakim –

Μελεὰ τοῦ Μεννὰ τοῦ Ματταθὰ τοῦ
of Melea – of Menna – of Mattatha –

Ναθὰμ τοῦ Δαυὶδ 32 τοῦ Ἰεσσαὶ τοῦ
of Natham – of David – of Jesse –

Ἰωβὴδ τοῦ Βόος τοῦ Σάλα τοῦ Ναασσὼν
of Jobed – of Boos – of Sala – of Naasson

33 τοῦ Ἀμιναδὰβ τοῦ Ἀδμὶν τοῦ Ἀρνὶ
– of Aminadab – of Admin – of Arni

τοῦ Ἑσρὼμ τοῦ Φάρες τοῦ Ἰούδα
– of Hesrom – of Phares – of Juda

34 τοῦ Ἰακὼβ τοῦ Ἰσαὰκ τοῦ Ἀβραὰμ
– of Jacob – of Isaac – of Abraham

τοῦ Θάρα τοῦ Ναχὼρ 35 τοῦ Σεροὺχ
– of Thara – of Nachor – of Seruch

τοῦ Ῥαγαὺ τοῦ Φάλεκ τοῦ Ἔβερ τοῦ
– of Rhagau – of Phalek – of Eber –

Σάλα 36 τοῦ Καϊνὰμ τοῦ Ἀρφαξὰδ τοῦ
of Sala – of Cainam – of Arphaxad –

Σὴμ τοῦ Νῶε τοῦ Λάμεχ 37 τοῦ Μαθουσάλα
of Sem – of Noe – of Lamech – of Mathusala

τοῦ Ἑνὼχ τοῦ Ἰάρετ τοῦ Μαλελεὴλ
– of Henoch – of Jaret – of Maleleel

τοῦ Καϊνὰμ 38 τοῦ Ἐνὼς τοῦ Σὴθ τοῦ
– of Cainam – of Enos – of Seth –

Ἀδὰμ τοῦ θεοῦ.
of Adam – of God.

was the son, so it was
thought, of Joseph,
the son of Heli, 24the
son of Matthat,
the son of Levi, the son
of Melki,
the son of Jannai, the
son of Joseph,
25the son of Mattathias,
the son of Amos,
the son of Nahum, the
son of Esli,
the son of Naggai, 26the
son of Maath,
the son of Mattathias,
the son of Semein,
the son of Josech, the
son of Joda,
27the son of Joanan, the
son of Rhesa,
the son of Zerubbabel,
the son of Shealtiel,
the son of Neri, 28the
son of Melki,
the son of Addi, the son
of Cosam,
the son of Elmadam,
the son of Er,
29the son of Joshua, the
son of Eliezer,
the son of Jorim, the
son of Matthat,
the son of Levi, 30the
son of Simeon,
the son of Judah, the
son of Joseph,
the son of Jonam, the
son of Eliakim,
31the son of Melea, the
son of Menna,
the son of Mattatha, the
son of Nathan,
the son of David, 32the
son of Jesse,
the son of Obed, the son
of Boaz,
the son of Salmon,[m] the
son of Nahshon,
33the son of Amminadab,
the son of Ram,[n]
the son of Hezron, the
son of Perez,
the son of Judah, 34the
son of Jacob,
the son of Isaac, the son
of Abraham,
the son of Terah, the
son of Nahor,
35the son of Serug, the
son of Reu,
the son of Peleg, the son
of Eber,
the son of Shelah, 36the
son of Cainan,
the son of Arphaxad,
the son of Shem,
the son of Noah, the son
of Lamech,
37the son of Methuselah,
the son of Enoch,
the son of Jared, the son
of Mahalalel,
the son of Kenan, 38the
son of Enosh,
the son of Seth, the son
of Adam,
the son of God.

Chapter 4

The Temptation of Jesus

JESUS, full of the Holy
Spirit, returned from
the Jordan and was led by
the Spirit in the wilderness,
2 where for forty days he
was tempted by the devil.

[c] Gk *Salathiel*
[d] Other ancient authorities read *Salmon*
[e] Other ancient authorities read *Amminadab, son of Aram*; others vary widely

4 Ἰησοῦς δὲ πλήρης πνεύματος ἁγίου
And Jesus full of ¹[the] ³Spirit ²Holy

ὑπέστρεψεν ἀπὸ τοῦ Ἰορδάνου, καὶ ἤγετο
returned from the Jordan, and was led

ἐν τῷ πνεύματι ἐν τῇ ἐρήμῳ 2 ἡμέρας
by the Spirit in the desert days

τεσσεράκοντα πειραζόμενος ὑπὸ τοῦ διαβόλου.
forty being tempted by the devil.

[m] *32* Some early manuscripts *Sala*
[n] *33* Some manuscripts *Amminadab, the son of Admin, the son of Arni*; other manuscripts vary widely.

He ate nothing at all during
those days, and when they
were over, he was fam-
ished. 3 The devil said to
him, "If you are the Son of
God, command this stone
to become a loaf of bread."
4 Jesus answered him, "It is
written, 'One does not live
by bread alone.' "
5 Then the devil[f] led
him up and showed him in
an instant all the kingdoms
of the world. 6 And the
devil[f] said to him, "To you
I will give their glory and all
this authority; for it has
been given over to me, and
I give it to anyone I please.
7 If you, then, will worship
me, it will all be yours."
8 Jesus answered him, "It is
written,

'Worship the Lord
your God,
and serve only
him.' "

9 Then the devil[f] took
him to Jerusalem, and
placed him on the pinnacle
of the temple, saying to
him, "If you are the Son of
God, throw yourself down
from here, 10 for it is written,

'He will command his
angels
concerning you,
to protect you,'

11 and

'On their hands they
will bear
you up,
so that you will not
dash your foot
against a
stone.' "

12 Jesus answered him, "It
is said, 'Do not put the
Lord your God to the
test.' " 13 When the devil
had finished every test, he
departed from him until an
opportune time.

The Beginning of the Galilean Ministry

14 Then Jesus, filled
with the power of the Spirit, returned to Galilee, and
a report about him spread
through all the surrounding
country. 15 He began to
teach in their synagogues

[f] Gk *he*

Καὶ οὐκ ἔφαγεν οὐδὲν ἐν ταῖς ἡμέραις
And he ate not no(any)thing in – days
ἐκείναις, καὶ συντελεσθεισῶν αὐτῶν ἐπεί-
those, and being ended them[a] he
=when they were ended
νασεν. 3 εἶπεν δὲ αὐτῷ ὁ διάβολος·
hungered. And said to him the devil :
εἰ υἱὸς εἶ τοῦ θεοῦ, εἰπὲ τῷ λίθῳ
If Son thou art – of God, tell – stone
τούτῳ ἵνα γένηται ἄρτος. 4 καὶ ἀπεκρίθη
this that it become a loaf. And made answer
πρὸς αὐτὸν ὁ Ἰησοῦς· γέγραπται ὅτι
to him – Jesus : It has been written[,] –
οὐκ ἐπ᾽ ἄρτῳ μόνῳ ζήσεται ὁ ἄνθρωπος.
Not on bread only shall live – man.
5 Καὶ ἀναγαγὼν αὐτὸν ἔδειξεν αὐτῷ πάσας
And leading up him he showed him all
τὰς βασιλείας τῆς οἰκουμένης ἐν στιγμῇ
the kingdoms of the inhabited earth in a moment
χρόνου. 6 καὶ εἶπεν αὐτῷ ὁ διάβολος·
of time. And said to him the devil :
σοὶ δώσω τὴν ἐξουσίαν ταύτην ἅπασαν καὶ
To thee I will give – authority this all and
τὴν δόξαν αὐτῶν, ὅτι ἐμοὶ παραδέδοται
the glory of them, because to me it has been delivered
καὶ ᾧ ἐὰν θέλω δίδωμι αὐτήν· 7 σὺ οὖν
and to whomever I wish I give it; [a]thou [1]therefore
ἐὰν προσκυνήσῃς ἐνώπιον ἐμοῦ, ἔσται σοῦ
[a]if worship before me, will be of thee
πᾶσα. 8 καὶ ἀποκριθεὶς ὁ Ἰησοῦς εἶπεν
all. And answering – Jesus said
αὐτῷ· γέγραπται· προσκυνήσεις κύριον τὸν
to him : It has been written: Thou shalt worship [the] Lord the
θεόν σου καὶ αὐτῷ μόνῳ λατρεύσεις.
God of thee and him only shalt thou serve.
9 Ἤγαγεν δὲ αὐτὸν εἰς Ἰερουσαλὴμ καὶ
And he led him to Jerusalem and
ἔστησεν ἐπὶ τὸ πτερύγιον τοῦ ἱεροῦ, καὶ
set on the gable of the temple, and
εἶπεν αὐτῷ· εἰ υἱὸς εἶ τοῦ θεοῦ, βάλε
said to him : If Son thou art – of God, throw
σεαυτὸν ἐντεῦθεν κάτω· 10 γέγραπται γὰρ ὅτι
thyself hence down; for it has been written[,] –
τοῖς ἀγγέλοις αὐτοῦ ἐντελεῖται περὶ
The angels of him he will command concerning
σοῦ τοῦ διαφυλάξαι σε, 11 καὶ ὅτι ἐπὶ
thee – to preserve[d] thee, and – on
χειρῶν ἀροῦσίν σε, μήποτε προσκόψῃς
[their] hands they will bear thee, lest thou dash
πρὸς λίθον τὸν πόδα σου. 12 καὶ
against a stone the foot of thee. And
ἀποκριθεὶς εἶπεν αὐτῷ ὁ Ἰησοῦς ὅτι
answering said to him – Jesus[,] –
εἴρηται· οὐκ ἐκπειράσεις κύριον τὸν
It has been said : Thou shalt not overtempt [the] Lord the
θεόν σου. 13 Καὶ συντελέσας πάντα πειρασμὸν
God of thee. And having finished every temptation
ὁ διάβολος ἀπέστη ἀπ᾽ αὐτοῦ ἄχρι καιροῦ.
the devil went away from him until a season.
14 Καὶ ὑπέστρεψεν ὁ Ἰησοῦς ἐν τῇ
And returned – Jesus in the
δυνάμει τοῦ πνεύματος εἰς τὴν Γαλιλαίαν·
power of the Spirit to – Galilee;
καὶ φήμη ἐξῆλθεν καθ᾽ ὅλης τῆς περιχώρου
and a rumour went forth throughout all the neighbourhood
περὶ αὐτοῦ. 15 καὶ αὐτὸς ἐδίδασκεν ἐν
concerning him. And he taught in

Chapter 4

The Temptation of Jesus

JESUS, full of the Holy
Spirit, returned from
the Jordan and was led by
the Spirit in the desert,
2 where for forty days he
was tempted by the devil.
He ate nothing during those
days, and at the end of
them he was hungry.
3 The devil said to him, "If
you are the Son of God, tell
this stone to become
bread."
4 Jesus answered, "It is
written: 'Man does not live
on bread alone.'[o]"
5 The devil led him up to a
high place and showed him
in an instant all the kingdoms of the world. 6 And he
said to him, "I will give you
all their authority and
splendor, for it has been
given to me, and I can give
it to anyone I want to. 7 So if
you worship me, it will all
be yours."
8 Jesus answered, "It is
written: 'Worship the Lord
your God and serve him
only.'[p]"
9 The devil led him to Jerusalem and had him stand
on the highest point of the
temple. "If you are the Son
of God," he said, "throw
yourself down from here.
10 For it is written:

" 'He will command his
angels concerning
you
to guard you carefully;
11 they will lift you up in
their hands,
so that you will not
strike your foot
against a stone.'[q]"

12 Jesus answered, "It
says: 'Do not put the Lord
your God to the test.'[r]"
13 When the devil had finished all this tempting, he
left him until an opportune
time.

Jesus Rejected at Nazareth

14 Jesus returned to Galilee in the power of the Spirit, and news about him
spread through the whole
countryside. 15 He taught in

[o] *4* Deut. 8:3
[p] *8* Deut. 6:13
[q] *11* Psalm 91:11,12
[r] *12* Deut. 6:16

and was praised by every-
one.

The Rejection of Jesus at Nazareth

16 When he came to
Nazareth, where he had
been brought up, he went
to the synagogue on the
sabbath day, as was his
custom. He stood up to
read, 17 and the scroll of the
prophet Isaiah was given to
him. He unrolled the scroll
and found the place where
it was written:
18 "The Spirit of the
Lord is upon
me,
because he has
anointed me
to bring good
news to the
poor.
He has sent me to
proclaim release
to the captives
and recovery of
sight to the
blind,
to let the
oppressed go
free,
19 to proclaim the year
of the Lord's
favor."
20 And he rolled up the
scroll, gave it back to the
attendant, and sat down.
The eyes of all in the synagogue were fixed on him.
21 Then he began to say to
them, "Today this scripture
has been fulfilled in your
hearing." 22 All spoke well
of him and were amazed at
the gracious words that
came from his mouth. They
said, "Is not this Joseph's
son?" 23 He said to them,
"Doubtless you will quote
to me this proverb, 'Doc-
tor, cure yourself!' And
you will say, 'Do here also
in your hometown the
things that we have heard
you did at Capernaum.'"
24 And he said, "Truly I tell
you, no prophet is accepted
in the prophet's hometown.
25 But the truth is, there
were many widows in Isra-
el in the time of Elijah,
when the heaven was shut
up three years and six

ταῖς συναγωγαῖς αὐτῶν, δοξαζόμενος ὑπὸ
the synagogues of them, being glorified by
πάντων.
all.
16 Καὶ ἦλθεν εἰς Ναζαρά, οὗ ἦν
And he came to Nazareth, where he was
τεθραμμένος, καὶ εἰσῆλθεν κατὰ τὸ εἰωθὸς
having been brought up, and entered according to the custom =his custom
αὐτῷ ἐν τῇ ἡμέρᾳ τῶν σαββάτων εἰς τὴν
to him[c] on the day of the sabbaths into the
συναγωγήν, καὶ ἀνέστη ἀναγνῶναι. 17 καὶ
synagogue, and stood up to read. And
ἐπεδόθη αὐτῷ βιβλίον τοῦ προφήτου
was handed to him a roll of the prophet
Ἠσαΐου, καὶ ἀνοίξας τὸ βιβλίον εὗρεν
Esaias, and having opened the roll he found
[τὸν] τόπον οὗ ἦν γεγραμμένον· 18 πνεῦμα
the place where it was *having been* written : [The] Spirit
κυρίου ἐπ' ἐμέ, οὗ εἵνεκεν ἔχρισέν με
of [the] Lord [is] upon me, wherefore he anointed me
εὐαγγελίσασθαι πτωχοῖς, ἀπέσταλκέν με
to evangelize [the] poor, he has sent me
κηρῦξαι αἰχμαλώτοις ἄφεσιν καὶ τυφλοῖς
to proclaim to captives release and to blind [ones]
ἀνάβλεψιν, ἀποστεῖλαι τεθραυσμένους ἐν
sight, to send away *having been* crushed [ones] in
ἀφέσει, 19 κηρῦξαι ἐνιαυτὸν κυρίου δεκτόν.
release, to proclaim a year of [the] Lord acceptable.
20 καὶ πτύξας τὸ βιβλίον ἀποδοὺς τῷ
And having closed the roll returning [it] to the
ὑπηρέτῃ ἐκάθισεν· καὶ πάντων οἱ ὀφθαλμοὶ
attendant he sat; and of all the eyes
ἐν τῇ συναγωγῇ ἦσαν ἀτενίζοντες αὐτῷ.
in the synagogue were gazing at him.
21 ἤρξατο δὲ λέγειν πρὸς αὐτοὺς ὅτι
And he began to say to them[,] –
σήμερον πεπλήρωται ἡ γραφὴ αὕτη ἐν
To-day has been fulfilled – scripture this in
τοῖς ὠσὶν ὑμῶν. 22 καὶ πάντες ἐμαρτύρουν
the ears of you. And all bore witness
αὐτῷ καὶ ἐθαύμαζον ἐπὶ τοῖς λόγοις τῆς
to him and marvelled at the words –
χάριτος τοῖς ἐκπορευομένοις ἐκ τοῦ στόματος
of grace – proceeding out of the mouth
αὐτοῦ, καὶ ἔλεγον· οὐχὶ υἱός ἐστιν Ἰωσὴφ
of him, and they said : [2]not [4]son [1]Is [5]of Joseph
οὗτος; 23 καὶ εἶπεν πρὸς αὐτούς· πάντως
[3]this man? And he said to them : To be sure
ἐρεῖτέ μοι τὴν παραβολὴν ταύτην· ἰατρέ,
ye will say to me – parable this : Physician,
θεράπευσον σεαυτόν· ὅσα ἠκούσαμεν γεν-
heal thyself; what things we heard hap-
όμενα εἰς τὴν Καφαρναούμ, ποίησον καὶ
pening in – Capernaum, do also
ὧδε ἐν τῇ πατρίδι σου. 24 εἶπεν δέ·
here in the native place of thee. And he said :
ἀμὴν λέγω ὑμῖν ὅτι οὐδεὶς προφήτης
Truly I tell you that no prophet
δεκτός ἐστιν ἐν τῇ πατρίδι αὐτοῦ. 25 ἐπ'
acceptable is in the native place of him. [2]on(in)
ἀληθείας δὲ λέγω ὑμῖν, πολλαὶ χῆραι ἦσαν
[3]truth [1]But I tell you, many widows were
ἐν ταῖς ἡμέραις Ἠλίου ἐν τῷ Ἰσραήλ,
in the days of Elias in – Israel,
ὅτε ἐκλείσθη ὁ οὐρανὸς ἐπὶ ἔτη τρία καὶ
when was shut up the heaven over years three and

their synagogues, and ev-
eryone praised him.
16 He went to Nazareth,
where he had been brought
up, and on the Sabbath day
he went into the syna-
gogue, as was his custom.
And he stood up to read.
17 The scroll of the prophet
Isaiah was handed to him.
Unrolling it, he found the
place where it is written:
18 "The Spirit of the Lord
is on me,
because he has
anointed me
to preach good news to
the poor.
He has sent me to
proclaim freedom
for the prisoners
and recovery of sight
for the blind,
to release the oppressed,
19 to proclaim the year of
the Lord's favor."[s]
20 Then he rolled up the
scroll, gave it back to the
attendant and sat down.
The eyes of everyone in the
synagogue were fastened
on him, 21 and he began by
saying to them, "Today
this scripture is fulfilled in
your hearing."
22 All spoke well of him
and were amazed at the
gracious words that came
from his lips. "Isn't this Joseph's son?" they asked.
23 Jesus said to them,
"Surely you will quote this
proverb to me: 'Physician,
heal yourself! Do here in
your hometown what we
have heard that you did in
Capernaum.'"
24 "I tell you the truth,"
he continued, "no prophet
is accepted in his home-
town. 25 I assure you that
there were many widows in
Israel in Elijah's time,
when the sky was shut for
three and a half years and

[s] 19 Isaiah 61:1,2

months, and there was a severe famine over all the
land; 26 yet Elijah was sent
to none of them except to a
widow at Zarephath in Si-
don. 27 There were also
many lepers[g] in Israel in
the time of the prophet Elisha, and none of them was
cleansed except Naaman
the Syrian." 28 When they
heard this, all in the synagogue were filled with rage.
29 They got up, drove him
out of the town, and led him
to the brow of the hill on
which their town was built,
so that they might hurl him
off the cliff. 30 But he
passed through the midst of
them and went on his way.

The Man with an Unclean Spirit

31 He went down to Ca-
pernaum, a city in Galilee,
and was teaching them on
the sabbath. 32 They were
astounded at his teaching,
because he spoke with au-
thority. 33 In the synagogue
there was a man who had
the spirit of an unclean demon, and he cried out with
a loud voice, 34 "Let us
alone! What have you to do
with us, Jesus of Nazareth?
Have you come to destroy
us? I know who you are,
the Holy One of God."
35 But Jesus rebuked him,
saying, "Be silent, and
come out of him!" When
the demon had thrown him
down before them, he came
out of him without having
done him any harm. 36 They
were all amazed and kept
saying to one another,
"What kind of utterance is
this? For with authority
and power he commands
the unclean spirits, and out
they come!" 37 And a report
about him began to reach
every place in the region.

[g] The terms *leper* and *leprosy* can refer to several diseases

μῆνας ἕξ, ὡς ἐγένετο λιμὸς μέγας ἐπὶ
months six, when came famine a great over
πᾶσαν τὴν γῆν, **26** καὶ πρὸς οὐδεμίαν
all the land, and to not one
αὐτῶν ἐπέμφθη Ἠλίας εἰ μὴ εἰς Σάρεπτα
of them was sent Elias except to Sarepta
τῆς Σιδωνίας πρὸς γυναῖκα χήραν. **27** καὶ
– of Sidon to a woman a widow. And
πολλοὶ λεπροὶ ἦσαν ἐν τῷ Ἰσραὴλ ἐπὶ
many lepers were in – Israel during
Ἐλισαίου τοῦ προφήτου, καὶ οὐδεὶς αὐτῶν
Elisæus the prophet, and not one of them
ἐκαθαρίσθη εἰ μὴ Ναιμὰν ὁ Σύρος.
was cleansed except Naaman the Syrian.
28 καὶ ἐπλήσθησαν πάντες θυμοῦ ἐν τῇ
And [2]were filled [1]all of(with) anger in the
συναγωγῇ ἀκούοντες ταῦτα, **29** καὶ ἀναστάντες
synagogue hearing these things, and rising up
ἐξέβαλον αὐτὸν ἔξω τῆς πόλεως, καὶ
they cast *out* him outside the city, and
ἤγαγον αὐτὸν ἕως ὀφρύος τοῦ ὄρους ἐφ'
led him to a brow of the hill on
οὗ ἡ πόλις ᾠκοδόμητο αὐτῶν, ὥστε
which the city was built of them, so as
κατακρημνίσαι αὐτόν· **30** αὐτὸς δὲ διελθὼν
to throw down him; but he passing *through*
διὰ μέσου αὐτῶν ἐπορεύετο.
through [the] midst of them went.

31 Καὶ κατῆλθεν εἰς Καφαρναοὺμ πόλιν
And he went down to Capernaum a city
τῆς Γαλιλαίας. καὶ ἦν διδάσκων αὐτοὺς
– of Galilee. And he was teaching them
ἐν τοῖς σάββασιν· **32** καὶ ἐξεπλήσσοντο
on the sabbaths; and they were astounded
ἐπὶ τῇ διδαχῇ αὐτοῦ, ὅτι ἐν ἐξουσίᾳ
at the teaching of him, because with authority
ἦν ὁ λόγος αὐτοῦ. **33** καὶ ἐν τῇ συναγωγῇ
was the word of him. And in the synagogue
ἦν ἄνθρωπος ἔχων πνεῦμα δαιμονίου
there was a man having a spirit [2]demon
ἀκαθάρτου, καὶ ἀνέκραξεν φωνῇ μεγάλῃ·
[1]of an unclean, and he shouted voice with a great :
34 ἔα, τί ἡμῖν καὶ σοί, Ἰησοῦ Ναζαρηνέ;
Ah, what to us and to thee, Jesus Nazarene?
ἦλθες ἀπολέσαι ἡμᾶς; οἶδά σε τίς εἶ,
Camest thou to destroy us? I know thee who thou art,
ὁ ἅγιος τοῦ θεοῦ. **35** καὶ ἐπετίμησεν αὐτῷ
the holy one – of God. And rebuked him
ὁ Ἰησοῦς λέγων· φιμώθητι καὶ ἔξελθε
– Jesus saying : Be muzzled and come out
ἀπ' αὐτοῦ. καὶ ῥίψαν αὐτὸν τὸ δαιμόνιον
from him. And [3]throwing [4]him [1]the [2]demon
εἰς τὸ μέσον ἐξῆλθεν ἀπ' αὐτοῦ μηδὲν
in the midst came out from him nothing
βλάψαν αὐτόν. **36** καὶ ἐγένετο θάμβος
injuring him. And came astonishment
ἐπὶ πάντας, καὶ συνελάλουν πρὸς ἀλλήλους
on all, and they spoke to one another
λέγοντες· τίς ὁ λόγος οὗτος, ὅτι ἐν
saying : What [is] – word this, because with
ἐξουσίᾳ καὶ δυνάμει ἐπιτάσσει τοῖς
authority and power he commands the
ἀκαθάρτοις πνεύμασιν καὶ ἐξέρχονται; **37** καὶ
unclean spirits and they come out? And
ἐξεπορεύετο ἦχος περὶ αὐτοῦ εἰς πάντα
went forth a rumour concerning him into every

there was a severe famine
throughout the land. 26 Yet
Elijah was not sent to any
of them, but to a widow in
Zarephath in the region of
Sidon. 27 And there were
many in Israel with leprosy[t] in the time of Elisha the
prophet, yet not one of
them was cleansed—only
Naaman the Syrian."
28 All the people in the
synagogue were furious
when they heard this.
29 They got up, drove him
out of the town, and took
him to the brow of the hill
on which the town was
built, in order to throw him
down the cliff. 30 But he
walked right through the
crowd and went on his
way.

Jesus Drives Out an Evil Spirit

31 Then he went down to
Capernaum, a town in Galilee, and on the Sabbath began to teach the people.
32 They were amazed at his
teaching, because his message had authority.
33 In the synagogue there
was a man possessed by a
demon, an evil[u] spirit. He
cried out at the top of his
voice, 34 "Ha! What do you
want with us, Jesus of Nazareth? Have you come to
destroy us? I know who
you are—the Holy One of
God!"
35 "Be quiet!" Jesus said
sternly. "Come out of
him!" Then the demon
threw the man down before
them all and came out without injuring him.
36 All the people were
amazed and said to each
other, "What is this teaching? With authority and
power he gives orders to
evil spirits and they come
out!" 37 And the news about

[t] 27 The Greek word was used for various diseases affecting the skin—not necessarily leprosy.
[u] 33 Greek *unclean*; also in verse 36

Healings at Simon's House

38 After leaving the
synagogue he entered Si-
mon's house. Now Simon's
mother-in-law was suffer-
ing from a high fever, and
they asked him about her.
39 Then he stood over her
and rebuked the fever, and
it left her. Immediately she
got up and began to serve
them.
40 As the sun was set-
ting, all those who had any
who were sick with various
kinds of diseases brought
them to him; and he laid his
hands on each of them and
cured them. 41 Demons also
came out of many, shout-
ing, "You are the Son of
God!" But he rebuked them
and would not allow them
to speak, because they
knew that he was the Mes-
siah.[h]

Jesus Preaches in the Synagogues

42 At daybreak he de-
parted and went into a deserted place. And the
crowds were looking for
him; and when they
reached him, they wanted
to prevent him from leaving
them. 43 But he said to
them, "I must proclaim the
good news of the kingdom
of God to the other cities
also; for I was sent for this
purpose." 44 So he continued proclaiming the mes-
sage in the synagogues of
Judea.[i]

τόπον τῆς περιχώρου. **38** Ἀναστὰς δὲ
place of the neighbourhood. And rising up

ἀπὸ τῆς συναγωγῆς εἰσῆλθεν εἰς τὴν
from the synagogue he entered into the

οἰκίαν Σίμωνος. πενθερὰ δὲ τοῦ Σίμωνος
house of Simon. And [the] mother-in-law – of Simon

ἦν συνεχομένη πυρετῷ μεγάλῳ, καὶ
was being seized fever with a great, and

ἠρώτησαν αὐτὸν περὶ αὐτῆς. **39** καὶ
they ask him about her. And

ἐπιστὰς ἐπάνω αὐτῆς ἐπετίμησεν τῷ πυρετῷ,
standing over her he rebuked the fever,

καὶ ἀφῆκεν αὐτήν· παραχρῆμα δὲ ἀναστᾶσα
and it left her; and at once rising up

διηκόνει αὐτοῖς. **40** Δύνοντος δὲ τοῦ
she served them. And setting the
=as the sun was setting

ἡλίου ἅπαντες ὅσοι εἶχον ἀσθενοῦντας
sun[a] all as many as had ailing [ones]

νόσοις ποικίλαις ἤγαγον αὐτοὺς πρὸς αὐτόν·
diseases with various brought them to him;

ὁ δὲ ἑνὶ ἑκάστῳ αὐτῶν τὰς χεῖρας
and he [5]one [4]on each [6]of them [2]the(his) [3]hands

ἐπιτιθεὶς ἐθεράπευεν αὐτούς. **41** ἐξήρχετο
[1]putting *on* healed them. came out

δὲ καὶ δαιμόνια ἀπὸ πολλῶν, κραυγάζοντα
And also demons from many, crying out

καὶ λέγοντα ὅτι σὺ εἶ ὁ υἱὸς τοῦ θεοῦ.
and saying[,] – Thou art the Son – of God.

καὶ ἐπιτιμῶν οὐκ εἴα αὐτὰ λαλεῖν, ὅτι
And rebuking he allowed not them to speak, because

ᾔδεισαν τὸν χριστὸν αὐτὸν εἶναι. **42** Γενομένης
they knew [3]the [4]Christ [1]him [2]to be. coming
=And when

δὲ ἡμέρας ἐξελθὼν ἐπορεύθη εἰς ἔρημον
And day[a] going forth he went to a desert
day came

τόπον· καὶ οἱ ὄχλοι ἐπεζήτουν αὐτόν, καὶ
place; and the crowds sought him, and

ἦλθον ἕως αὐτοῦ, καὶ κατεῖχον αὐτὸν
came up to him, and detained him

τοῦ μὴ πορεύεσθαι ἀπ' αὐτῶν. **43** ὁ δὲ
– not to go[d] from them. And he
=so that he should not go

εἶπεν πρὸς αὐτοὺς ὅτι καὶ ταῖς ἑτέραις
said to them[,] – Also to the other

πόλεσιν εὐαγγελίσασθαί με δεῖ τὴν
cities [3]to preach [2]me [1]it behoves the

βασιλείαν τοῦ θεοῦ, ὅτι ἐπὶ τοῦτο ἀπεστάλην.
kingdom – of God, because on this I was sent.

44 καὶ ἦν κηρύσσων εἰς τὰς συναγωγὰς
And he was proclaiming in the synagogues

τῆς Ἰουδαίας.
– of Judæa.

him spread throughout the
surrounding area.

Jesus Heals Many

38 Jesus left the synagogue
and went to the home of Simon. Now Simon's moth-
er-in-law was suffering
from a high fever, and they
asked Jesus to help her.
39 So he bent over her and
rebuked the fever, and it
left her. She got up at once
and began to wait on them.
40 When the sun was set-
ting, the people brought to
Jesus all who had various
kinds of sickness, and laying his hands on each one,
he healed them. 41 More-
over, demons came out of
many people, shouting,
"You are the Son of God!"
But he rebuked them and
would not allow them to
speak, because they knew
he was the Christ.[v]
42 At daybreak Jesus went
out to a solitary place. The
people were looking for
him and when they came to
where he was, they tried to
keep him from leaving
them. 43 But he said, "I
must preach the good news
of the kingdom of God to
the other towns also, be-
cause that is why I was
sent." 44 And he kept on
preaching in the syna-
gogues of Judea.[w]

Chapter 5

Jesus Calls the First Disciples

ONCE while Jesus[j]
was standing beside
the lake of Gennesaret, and
the crowd was pressing in
on him to hear the word of
God, 2 he saw two boats
there at the shore of the
lake; the fishermen had
gone out of them and were
washing their nets. 3 He got
into one of the boats, the

5 Ἐγένετο δὲ ἐν τῷ τον ὄχλον ἐπικεῖσθαι
Now it came to pass in the the crowd to press upon
=as the crowd pressed upon him and heard

αὐτῷ καὶ ἀκούειν τὸν λόγον τοῦ θεοῦ,
him and to hear[be] the word – of God,

καὶ αὐτὸς ἦν ἑστὼς παρὰ τὴν λίμνην
and he was standing by the lake

Γεννησαρέτ, **2** καὶ εἶδεν δύο πλοιάρια
Gennesaret, and saw two boats

ἑστῶτα παρὰ τὴν λίμνην· οἱ δὲ ἁλεεῖς
standing by the lake; but the fishermen

ἀπ' αὐτῶν ἀποβάντες ἔπλυνον τὰ δίκτυα.
from them having gone away were washing the nets.

Chapter 5

The Calling of the First Disciples

ONE day as Jesus was
standing by the Lake
of Gennesaret,[x] with the
people crowding around
him and listening to the
word of God, 2 he saw at the
water's edge two boats, left
there by the fishermen,
who were washing their

[h] Or *the Christ*
[i] Other ancient authorities read *Galilee*
[j] Gk *he*

[v] 41 Or *Messiah*
[w] 44 Or *the land of the Jews*; some manuscripts *Galilee*
[x] 1 That is, Sea of Galilee

one belonging to Simon,
and asked him to put out a
little way from the shore.
Then he sat down and
taught the crowds from the
boat. 4 When he had fin-
ished speaking, he said to
Simon, "Put out into the
deep water and let down
your nets for a catch." 5 Simon answered, "Master,
we have worked all night
long but have caught nothing. Yet if you say so, I will
let down the nets." 6 When
they had done this, they
caught so many fish that
their nets were beginning to
break. 7 So they signaled
their partners in the other
boat to come and help
them. And they came and
filled both boats, so that
they began to sink. 8 But
when Simon Peter saw it,
he fell down at Jesus'
knees, saying, "Go away
from me, Lord, for I am a
sinful man!" 9 For he and all
who were with him were
amazed at the catch of fish
that they had taken; 10 and
so also were James and
John, sons of Zebedee,
who were partners with Simon. Then Jesus said to Simon, "Do not be afraid;
from now on you will be
catching people." 11 When
they had brought their
boats to shore, they left everything and followed him.

Jesus Cleanses a Leper

12 Once, when he was
in one of the cities, there
was a man covered with
leprosy.[k] When he saw
Jesus, he bowed with his
face to the ground and
begged him, "Lord, if you

[k] The terms *leper* and *leprosy* can refer to several diseases

3 ἐμβὰς δὲ εἰς ἓν τῶν πλοίων, ὃ ἦν
And embarking in one of the boats, which was

Σίμωνος, ἠρώτησεν αὐτὸν ἀπὸ τῆς γῆς
of Simon, he asked him from the land

ἐπαναγαγεῖν ὀλίγον· καθίσας δὲ ἐκ τοῦ
to put out a little; and sitting [4]out of [5]the

πλοίου ἐδίδασκεν τοὺς ὄχλους. **4** ὡς δὲ
[6]boat [1]he taught [2]the [3]crowds. And when

ἐπαύσατο λαλῶν, εἶπεν πρὸς τὸν Σίμωνα·
he ceased speaking, he said to – Simon :

ἐπανάγαγε εἰς τὸ βάθος, καὶ χαλάσατε
Put out into the deep, and let down

τὰ δίκτυα ὑμῶν εἰς ἄγραν. **5** καὶ
the nets of you for a draught. And

ἀποκριθεὶς Σίμων εἶπεν· ἐπιστάτα, δι'
answering Simon said : Master, through

ὅλης νυκτὸς κοπιάσαντες οὐδὲν ἐλάβομεν·
[the] whole night labouring nothing we took;

ἐπὶ δὲ τῷ ῥήματί σου χαλάσω τὰ δίκτυα.
but at the word of thee I will let down the nets.

6 καὶ τοῦτο ποιήσαντες συνέκλεισαν πλῆθος
And this doing they enclosed multitude

ἰχθύων πολύ· διερρήσσετο δὲ τὰ δίκτυα
of fishes a much; and were being torn the nets

αὐτῶν. **7** καὶ κατένευσαν τοῖς μετόχοις
of them. And they nodded to the(ir) partners

ἐν τῷ ἑτέρῳ πλοίῳ τοῦ ἐλθόντας
in the other boat – coming
=that they should come

συλλαβέσθαι αὐτοῖς· καὶ ἦλθαν, καὶ ἔπλησαν
to help[d] them; and they came, and filled

ἀμφότερα τὰ πλοῖα ὥστε βυθίζεσθαι αὐτά.
both the boats so as to be sinking them.[b]
=so that they were sinking.

8 ἰδὼν δὲ Σίμων Πέτρος προσέπεσεν τοῖς
And seeing Simon Peter fell at the

γόνασιν Ἰησοῦ λέγων· ἔξελθε ἀπ' ἐμοῦ,
knees of Jesus saying : Depart from me,

ὅτι ἀνὴρ ἁμαρτωλός εἰμι, κύριε. **9** θάμβος
because man a sinful I am, Lord. astonishment

γὰρ περιέσχεν αὐτὸν καὶ πάντας τοὺς
For seized him and all the [ones]

σὺν αὐτῷ ἐπὶ τῇ ἄγρᾳ τῶν ἰχθύων ᾗ
with him at the draught of the fishes which

συνέλαβον, **10** ὁμοίως δὲ καὶ Ἰάκωβον καὶ
they took, and likewise both James and

Ἰωάννην υἱοὺς Ζεβεδαίου, οἳ ἦσαν κοινωνοὶ
John sons of Zebedee, who were sharers

τῷ Σίμωνι. καὶ εἶπεν πρὸς τὸν Σίμωνα
– with Simon. And said to – Simon

ὁ Ἰησοῦς· μὴ φοβοῦ· ἀπὸ τοῦ νῦν
– Jesus: Fear thou not; from – now

ἀνθρώπους ἔσῃ ζωγρῶν. **11** καὶ καταγαγόντες
men thou wilt be taking alive. And bringing down

τὰ πλοῖα ἐπὶ τὴν γῆν, ἀφέντες πάντα
the boats onto the land, leaving all things

ἠκολούθησαν αὐτῷ.
they followed him.

12 Καὶ ἐγένετο ἐν τῷ εἶναι αὐτὸν ἐν
And it came to pass in the to be him[be] in
=as he was

μιᾷ τῶν πόλεων καὶ ἰδοὺ ἀνὴρ πλήρης
one of the cities *and* behold[,] a man full

λέπρας· ἰδὼν δὲ τὸν Ἰησοῦν, πεσὼν ἐπὶ
of leprosy; and seeing — Jesus, falling on

πρόσωπον ἐδεήθη αὐτοῦ λέγων· κύριε,
[his] face he begged him saying : Lord,

nets. 3 He got into one of the
boats, the one belonging to
Simon, and asked him to
put out a little from shore.
Then he sat down and
taught the people from the
boat.

4 When he had finished
speaking, he said to Simon,
"Put out into deep water,
and let down[y] the nets for a
catch."

5 Simon answered, "Mas-
ter, we've worked hard all
night and haven't caught
anything. But because you
say so, I will let down the
nets."

6 When they had done so,
they caught such a large
number of fish that their
nets began to break. 7 So
they signaled their partners
in the other boat to come
and help them, and they
came and filled both boats
so full that they began to
sink.

8 When Simon Peter saw
this, he fell at Jesus' knees
and said, "Go away from
me, Lord; I am a sinful
man!" 9 For he and all his
companions were aston-
ished at the catch of fish
they had taken, 10 and so
were James and John, the
sons of Zebedee, Simon's
partners.

Then Jesus said to Simon,
"Don't be afraid; from now
on you will catch men."
11 So they pulled their boats
up on shore, left everything
and followed him.

The Man With Leprosy

12 While Jesus was in one
of the towns, a man came
along who was covered
with leprosy.[z] When he
saw Jesus, he fell with his
face to the ground and
begged him, "Lord, if you

[y] *4* The Greek verb is plural.
[z] *12* The Greek word was used for various diseases affecting the skin—not necessarily leprosy.

choose, you can make me clean." 13 Then Jesus[j] stretched out his hand, touched him, and said, "I do choose. Be made clean." Immediately the leprosy[k] left him. 14 And he ordered him to tell no one. "Go," he said, "and show yourself to the priest, and, as Moses commanded, make an offering for your cleansing, for a testimony to them." 15 But now more than ever the word about Jesus[l] spread abroad; many crowds would gather to hear him and to be cured of their diseases. 16 But he would withdraw to deserted places and pray.

Jesus Heals a Paralytic

17 One day, while he was teaching, Pharisees and teachers of the law were sitting near by (they had come from every village of Galilee and Judea and from Jerusalem); and the power of the Lord was with him to heal.[m] 18 Just then some men came, carrying a paralyzed man on a bed. They were trying to bring him in and lay him before Jesus;[l] 19 but finding no way to bring him in because of the crowd, they went up on the roof and let him down with his bed through the tiles into the middle of the crowd[n] in front of Jesus. 20 When he saw their faith, he said, "Friend,[o] your sins are forgiven you." 21 Then the scribes and the Pharisees began to question, "Who is this who is speaking blasphemies? Who can forgive sins but God alone?" 22 When Jesus perceived their questionings, he an-

[l] Gk *him*
[m] Other ancient authorities read *was present to heal them*
[n] Gk *into the midst*
[o] Gk *Man*

ἐὰν θέλῃς, δύνασαί με καθαρίσαι. **13** καὶ
if thou willest, thou canst me *to* cleanse. And
ἐκτείνας τὴν χεῖρα ἥψατο αὐτοῦ λέγων·
stretching out the(his) hand he touched him saying:
θέλω, καθαρίσθητι· καὶ εὐθέως ἡ λέπρα
I am willing, be thou cleansed; and immediately the leprosy
ἀπῆλθεν ἀπ' αὐτοῦ. **14** καὶ αὐτὸς παρήγγειλεν
departed from him. And he charged
αὐτῷ μηδενὶ εἰπεῖν, ἀλλὰ ἀπελθὼν δεῖξον
him no one to tell, but going away show
σεαυτὸν τῷ ἱερεῖ, καὶ προσένεγκε περὶ
thyself to the priest, and offer concerning
τοῦ καθαρισμοῦ σου καθὼς προσέταξεν
the cleansing of thee as commanded
Μωϋσῆς, εἰς μαρτύριον αὐτοῖς. **15** διήρχετο
Moses, for a testimony to them. went
δὲ μᾶλλον ὁ λόγος περὶ αὐτοῦ, καὶ
But rather the word concerning him, and
συνήρχοντο ὄχλοι πολλοὶ ἀκούειν καὶ
³accompanied ²crowds ¹many to hear and
θεραπεύεσθαι ἀπὸ τῶν ἀσθενειῶν αὐτῶν·
to be healed from the infirmities of them;
16 αὐτὸς δὲ ἦν ὑποχωρῶν ἐν ταῖς ἐρήμοις
but he was withdrawing in the deserts
καὶ προσευχόμενος.
and praying.

17 Καὶ ἐγένετο ἐν μιᾷ τῶν ἡμερῶν καὶ
And it came to pass on one of the days *and*
αὐτὸς ἦν διδάσκων, καὶ ἦσαν καθήμενοι
he was teaching, and were sitting
Φαρισαῖοι καὶ νομοδιδάσκαλοι οἳ ἦσαν
Pharisees and law-teachers who were
ἐληλυθότες ἐκ πάσης κώμης τῆς Γαλιλαίας
having come out of every village – of Galilee
καὶ Ἰουδαίας καὶ Ἰερουσαλήμ· καὶ δύναμις
and Judæa and Jerusalem; and [the] power
κυρίου ἦν εἰς τὸ ἰᾶσθαι αὐτόν. **18** καὶ
of [the] Lord was ¹in – ³to cure ²him. And
ἰδοὺ ἄνδρες φέροντες ἐπὶ κλίνης ἄνθρωπον
behold[,] men bearing on a couch a man
ὃς ἦν παραλελυμένος, καὶ ἐζήτουν αὐτὸν
who was *having been* paralysed, and they sought ²him
εἰσενεγκεῖν καὶ θεῖναι [αὐτὸν] ἐνώπιον
¹to carry in and to lay him before
αὐτοῦ. **19** καὶ μὴ εὑρόντες ποίας εἰσ-
him. And not finding how† they
ενέγκωσιν αὐτὸν διὰ τὸν ὄχλον, ἀναβάντες
might carry in him because of the crowd, going up
ἐπὶ τὸ δῶμα διὰ τῶν κεράμων καθῆκαν
onto the roof through the tiles they let down
αὐτὸν σὺν τῷ κλινιδίῳ εἰς τὸ μέσον
him with the couch into the midst
ἔμπροσθεν τοῦ Ἰησοῦ. **20** καὶ ἰδὼν τὴν
in front of – Jesus. And seeing the
πίστιν αὐτῶν εἶπεν· ἄνθρωπε, ἀφέωνταί
faith of them he said: Man, have been forgiven
σοι αἱ ἁμαρτίαι σου. **21** καὶ ἤρξαντο
thee the sins of thee. And began
διαλογίζεσθαι οἱ γραμματεῖς καὶ οἱ Φαρισαῖοι
to reason the scribes and the Pharisees
λέγοντες· τίς ἐστιν οὗτος ὃς λαλεῖ
saying: Who is this man who speaks
βλασφημίας; τίς δύναται ἁμαρτίας ἀφεῖναι
blasphemies? Who can sins *to* forgive
εἰ μὴ μόνος ὁ θεός; **22** ἐπιγνοὺς δὲ ὁ
except only – God? But knowing –

are willing, you can make me clean."

13 Jesus reached out his hand and touched the man. "I am willing," he said. "Be clean!" And immediately the leprosy left him.

14 Then Jesus ordered him, "Don't tell anyone, but go, show yourself to the priest and offer the sacrifices that Moses commanded for your cleansing, as a testimony to them."

15 Yet the news about him spread all the more, so that crowds of people came to hear him and to be healed of their sicknesses. 16 But Jesus often withdrew to lonely places and prayed.

Jesus Heals a Paralytic

17 One day as he was teaching, Pharisees and teachers of the law, who had come from every village of Galilee and from Judea and Jerusalem, were sitting there. And the power of the Lord was present for him to heal the sick. 18 Some men came carrying a paralytic on a mat and tried to take him into the house to lay him before Jesus. 19 When they could not find a way to do this because of the crowd, they went up on the roof and lowered him on his mat through the tiles into the middle of the crowd, right in front of Jesus.

20 When Jesus saw their faith, he said, "Friend, your sins are forgiven."

21 The Pharisees and the teachers of the law began thinking to themselves, "Who is this fellow who speaks blasphemy? Who can forgive sins but God alone?"

22 Jesus knew what they

swered them, "Why do you raise such questions in your hearts? 23 Which is easier, to say, 'Your sins are forgiven you,' or to say, 'Stand up and walk'? 24 But so that you may know that the Son of Man has authority on earth to forgive sins"—he said to the one who was paralyzed—"I say to you, stand up and take your bed and go to your home." 25 Immediately he stood up before them, took what he had been lying on, and went to his home, glorifying God. 26 Amazement seized all of them, and they glorified God and were filled with awe, saying, "We have seen strange things today."

Jesus Calls Levi

27 After this he went out and saw a tax collector named Levi, sitting at the tax booth; and he said to him, "Follow me." 28 And he got up, left everything, and followed him.

29 Then Levi gave a great banquet for him in his house; and there was a large crowd of tax collectors and others sitting at the table[p] with them. 30 The Pharisees and their scribes were complaining to his disciples, saying, "Why do you eat and drink with tax collectors and sinners?" 31 Jesus answered, "Those who are well have no need of a physician, but those who are sick; 32 I have come to call not the righteous but sinners to repentance."

The Question about Fasting

33 Then they said to him, "John's disciples, like the disciples of the Pharisees, frequently fast and pray, but your disciples eat

[p] Gk *reclining*

Ἰησοῦς τοὺς διαλογισμοὺς αὐτῶν, ἀποκριθεὶς
Jesus the reasonings of them, answering
εἶπεν πρὸς αὐτούς· τί διαλογίζεσθε ἐν
said to them: Why reason ye in
ταῖς καρδίαις ὑμῶν; 23 τί ἐστιν εὐκοπώτερον,
the hearts of you? What is easier,
εἰπεῖν· ἀφέωνταί σοι αἱ ἁμαρτίαι σου, ἢ
to say: Have been forgiven thee the sins of thee, or
εἰπεῖν· ἔγειρε καὶ περιπάτει; 24 ἵνα δὲ
to say: Rise and walk? but that
εἰδῆτε ὅτι ὁ υἱὸς τοῦ ἀνθρώπου ἐξουσίαν
ye may know that the Son – of man authority
ἔχει ἐπὶ τῆς γῆς ἀφιέναι ἁμαρτίας, —
has on the earth to forgive sins, —
εἶπεν τῷ παραλελυμένῳ· σοὶ λέγω, ἔγειρε
he said to the paralysed [one]: To thee I say, rise
καὶ ἄρας τὸ κλινίδιόν σου πορεύου εἰς
and taking the pallet of thee go to
τὸν οἶκόν σου. 25 καὶ παραχρῆμα ἀναστὰς
the house of thee. And at once rising up
ἐνώπιον αὐτῶν, ἄρας ἐφ' ὃ κατέκειτο,
before them, taking [that] on which he was lying,
ἀπῆλθεν εἰς τὸν οἶκον αὐτοῦ δοξάζων τὸν
he went away to the house of him glorifying –
θεόν. 26 καὶ ἔκστασις ἔλαβεν ἅπαντας, καὶ
God. And bewilderment took all, and
ἐδόξαζον τὸν θεόν, καὶ ἐπλήσθησαν φόβου
they glorified – God, and were filled of(with) fear
λέγοντες ὅτι εἴδομεν παράδοξα σήμερον.
saying[,] – We saw wonderful things to-day.
27 Καὶ μετὰ ταῦτα ἐξῆλθεν, καὶ ἐθεάσατο
And after these things he went forth, and saw
τελώνην ὀνόματι Λευὶν καθήμενον ἐπὶ τὸ
a tax-collector by name Levi sitting on(in) the
τελώνιον, καὶ εἶπεν αὐτῷ· ἀκολούθει μοι.
custom house, and said to him: Follow me.
28 καὶ καταλιπὼν πάντα ἀναστὰς ἠκολούθει
And abandoning all things rising up he followed
αὐτῷ. 29 Καὶ ἐποίησεν δοχὴν μεγάλην
him. And [2]made [4]feast [3]a great
Λευὶς αὐτῷ ἐν τῇ οἰκίᾳ αὐτοῦ· καὶ ἦν
[1]Levi for him in the house of him; and there was
ὄχλος πολὺς τελωνῶν καὶ ἄλλων οἳ ἦσαν
crowd a much of tax-collectors and of others who were
μετ' αὐτῶν κατακείμενοι. 30 καὶ ἐγόγγυζον
[2]with [3]them [1]reclining. And grumbled
οἱ Φαρισαῖοι καὶ οἱ γραμματεῖς αὐτῶν
the Pharisees and the scribes of them
πρὸς τοὺς μαθητὰς αὐτοῦ λέγοντες· διὰ
at the disciples of him saying: Why
τί μετὰ τῶν τελωνῶν καὶ ἁμαρτωλῶν
with the tax-collectors and sinners
ἐσθίετε καὶ πίνετε; 31 καὶ ἀποκριθεὶς ὁ
eat ye and drink ye? And answering –
Ἰησοῦς εἶπεν πρὸς αὐτούς· οὐ χρείαν
Jesus said to them: not need
ἔχουσιν οἱ ὑγιαίνοντες ἰατροῦ ἀλλὰ οἱ
have the [ones] being healthy of a physician but the
=those who are ill;
κακῶς ἔχοντες· 32 οὐκ ἐλήλυθα καλέσαι
[ones] ill having; I have not come to call
δικαίους ἀλλὰ ἁμαρτωλοὺς εἰς μετάνοιαν.
righteous persons but sinners to repentance.
33 Οἱ δὲ εἶπαν πρὸς αὐτόν· οἱ μαθηταὶ
And they said to him: The disciples
Ἰωάννου νηστεύουσιν πυκνὰ καὶ δεήσεις
of John fast often and prayers

were thinking and asked, "Why are you thinking these things in your hearts? 23 Which is easier: to say, 'Your sins are forgiven,' or to say, 'Get up and walk'? 24 But that you may know that the Son of Man has authority on earth to forgive sins. . . ." He said to the paralyzed man, "I tell you, get up, take your mat and go home." 25 Immediately he stood up in front of them, took what he had been lying on and went home praising God. 26 Everyone was amazed and gave praise to God. They were filled with awe and said, "We have seen remarkable things today."

The Calling of Levi

27 After this, Jesus went out and saw a tax collector by the name of Levi sitting at his tax booth. "Follow me," Jesus said to him, 28 and Levi got up, left everything and followed him.

29 Then Levi held a great banquet for Jesus at his house, and a large crowd of tax collectors and others were eating with them. 30 But the Pharisees and the teachers of the law who belonged to their sect complained to his disciples, "Why do you eat and drink with tax collectors and 'sinners'?"

31 Jesus answered them, "It is not the healthy who need a doctor, but the sick. 32 I have not come to call the righteous, but sinners to repentance."

Jesus Questioned About Fasting

33 They said to him, "John's disciples often fast and pray, and so do the dis

and drink. 34 Jesus said to
them, "You cannot make
wedding guests fast while
the bridegroom is with
them, can you? 35 The days
will come when the bride-
groom will be taken away
from them, and then they
will fast in those days."
36 He also told them a parable: "No one tears a piece
from a new garment and
sews it on an old garment;
otherwise the new will be
torn, and the piece from the
new will not match the old.
37 And no one puts new
wine into old wineskins;
otherwise the new wine
will burst the skins and will
be spilled, and the skins
will be destroyed. 38 But
new wine must be put into
fresh wineskins. 39 And no
one after drinking old wine
desires new wine, but says,
'The old is good.'"[q]

Chapter 6

The Question about the Sabbath

ONE sabbath[r] while
Jesus[s] was going
through the grainfields, his
disciples plucked some
heads of grain, rubbed
them in their hands, and ate
them. 2 But some of the
Pharisees said, "Why are
you doing what is not lawful[t] on the sabbath?"
3 Jesus answered, "Have
you not read what David
did when he and his com-
panions were hungry? 4 He
entered the house of God
and took and ate the bread
of the Presence, which it is
not lawful for any but the
priests to eat, and gave

[q] Other ancient authorities read *better*; others lack verse 39
[r] Other ancient authorities read *On the second first sabbath*
[s] Gk *he*
[t] Other ancient authorities add *to do*

ποιοῦνται, ὁμοίως καὶ οἱ τῶν Φαρισαίων,
make, likewise also those of the Pharisees,

οἱ δὲ σοὶ ἐσθίουσιν καὶ πίνουσιν. 34 ὁ
but those to thee[e] eat and drink. –
=but thine

δὲ Ἰησοῦς εἶπεν πρὸς αὐτούς· μὴ δύνασθε
And Jesus said to them: *not* [1]Can ye

τοὺς υἱοὺς τοῦ νυμφῶνος, ἐν ᾧ ὁ νυμφίος
[2]the [4]sons [5]of the [6]bride-chamber, [8]while [9]the [10]bridegroom

μετ᾽ αὐτῶν ἐστιν, ποιῆσαι νηστεῦσαι;
[11]with [12]them [11]is, [3]*to* make [7]to fast?

35 ἐλεύσονται δὲ ἡμέραι, καὶ ὅταν ἀπαρθῇ
but will come days, and when is taken away

ἀπ᾽ αὐτῶν ὁ νυμφίος, τότε νηστεύσουσιν
from them the bridegroom, then they will fast

ἐν ἐκείναις ταῖς ἡμέραις. 36 Ἔλεγεν δὲ
in those – days. And he told

καὶ παραβολὴν πρὸς αὐτοὺς ὅτι οὐδεὶς
also a parable to them[:] – No one

ἐπίβλημα ἀπὸ ἱματίου καινοῦ σχίσας
[2]a patch [3]from [5]garment [4]a new [1]tearing

ἐπιβάλλει ἐπὶ ἱμάτιον παλαιόν· εἰ δὲ μή γε,
[6]puts [it] [7]on [9]a garment [8]an old; otherwise,

καὶ τὸ καινὸν σχίσει καὶ τῷ παλαιῷ
both the new will tear and [7]with the [8]old

οὐ συμφωνήσει τὸ ἐπίβλημα τὸ ἀπὸ τοῦ
[6]will not agree [1]the [2]patch – [3]from [4]the

καινοῦ. 37 καὶ οὐδεὶς βάλλει οἶνον νέον
[5]new. And no one puts wine new

εἰς ἀσκοὺς παλαιούς· εἰ δὲ μή γε, ῥήξει
into wineskins old; otherwise, [4]will burst

ὁ οἶνος ὁ νέος τοὺς ἀσκούς, καὶ αὐτὸς
[1]the [3]wine – [2]new [5]the [6]wineskins, and it

ἐκχυθήσεται καὶ οἱ ἀσκοὶ ἀπολοῦνται.
will be poured out and the wineskins will perish.

38 ἀλλὰ οἶνον νέον εἰς ἀσκοὺς καινοὺς
But wine new into wineskins new

βλητέον. 39 καὶ οὐδεὶς πιὼν παλαιὸν
one must put. And no one having drunk old

θέλει νέον· λέγει γάρ· ὁ παλαιὸς χρηστός
desires new; for he says: The old good

ἐστιν.
is.

6 Ἐγένετο δὲ ἐν σαββάτῳ διαπορεύεσθαι
And it came to pass on a sabbath to go through
=he went through

αὐτὸν διὰ σπορίμων, καὶ ἔτιλλον οἱ
him[b] *through* cornfields, and [4]plucked [1]the

μαθηταὶ αὐτοῦ καὶ ἤσθιον τοὺς στάχυας
[2]disciples [3]of him and ate the ears

ψώχοντες ταῖς χερσίν. 2 τινὲς δὲ τῶν
rubbing with the(ir) hands. And some of the

Φαρισαίων εἶπαν· τί ποιεῖτε ὃ οὐκ ἔξεστιν
Pharisees said: Why do ye what is not lawful

τοῖς σάββασιν; 3 καὶ ἀποκριθεὶς πρὸς
on the sabbaths? And replying to

αὐτοὺς εἶπεν ὁ Ἰησοῦς· οὐδὲ τοῦτο ἀνέγνωτε
them said – Jesus: [2]not [3]this [1]read ye

ὃ ἐποίησεν Δαυίδ, ὁπότε ἐπείνασεν αὐτὸς
which did David, when hungered he

καὶ οἱ μετ᾽ αὐτοῦ ὄντες; 4 ὡς εἰσῆλθεν
and the [ones] with him being? how he entered

εἰς τὸν οἶκον τοῦ θεοῦ καὶ τοὺς ἄρτους
into the house – of God and the loaves

τῆς προθέσεως λαβὼν ἔφαγεν καὶ ἔδωκεν
of the setting forth taking he ate and gave

ciples of the Pharisees, but
yours go on eating and
drinking."
34 Jesus answered, "Can
you make the guests of the
bridegroom fast while he is
with them? 35 But the time
will come when the bride-
groom will be taken from
them; in those days they
will fast."
36 He told them this parable: "No one tears a patch
from a new garment and
sews it on an old one. If he
does, he will have torn the
new garment, and the patch
from the new will not
match the old. 37 And no
one pours new wine into
old wineskins. If he does,
the new wine will burst the
skins, the wine will run out
and the wineskins will be
ruined. 38 No, new wine
must be poured into new
wineskins. 39 And no one after drinking old wine wants
the new, for he says, 'The
old is better.'"

Chapter 6

Lord of the Sabbath

ONE Sabbath Jesus was
going through the
grainfields, and his disciples began to pick some
heads of grain, rub them in
their hands and eat the ker-
nels. 2 Some of the Pharisees asked, "Why are you
doing what is unlawful on
the Sabbath?"
3 Jesus answered them,
"Have you never read
what David did when he
and his companions were
hungry? 4 He entered the
house of God, and taking
the consecrated bread, he
ate what is lawful only for

some to his companions?" [5]Then he said to them, "The Son of Man is lord of the sabbath."

The Man with a Withered Hand

6 On another sabbath he entered the synagogue and taught, and there was a man there whose right hand was withered. [7]The scribes and the Pharisees watched him to see whether he would cure on the sabbath, so that they might find an accusation against him. [8]Even though he knew what they were thinking, he said to the man who had the withered hand, "Come and stand here." He got up and stood there. [9]Then Jesus said to them, "I ask you, is it lawful to do good or to do harm on the sabbath, to save life or to destroy it?" [10]After looking around at all of them, he said to him, "Stretch out your hand." He did so, and his hand was restored. [11]But they were filled with fury and discussed with one another what they might do to Jesus.

Jesus Chooses the Twelve Apostles

12 Now during those days he went out to the mountain to pray; and he spent the night in prayer to God. [13]And when day came, he called his disciples and chose twelve of them, whom he also named apostles: [14]Simon, whom he named Peter, and his brother Andrew, and James, and John, and Philip, and Bartholomew, [15]and Matthew, and Thomas, and James son of Al-

τοῖς μετ' αὐτοῦ, οὓς οὐκ ἔξεστιν φαγεῖν
to the [ones] with him, which it is not lawful to eat

εἰ μὴ μόνους τοὺς ἱερεῖς; 5 καὶ ἔλεγεν
except only the priests? And he said

αὐτοῖς· κύριός ἐστιν τοῦ σαββάτου ὁ
to them: Lord is of the sabbath the

υἱὸς τοῦ ἀνθρώπου. 6 Ἐγένετο δὲ ἐν
Son – of man. And it came to pass on

ἑτέρῳ σαββάτῳ εἰσελθεῖν αὐτὸν εἰς τὴν
another sabbath to enter him into the
=he entered into the synagogue and

συναγωγὴν καὶ διδάσκειν· καὶ ἦν ἄνθρωπος
synagogue and to teach[b]; and there was a man
taught;

ἐκεῖ καὶ ἡ χεὶρ αὐτοῦ ἡ δεξιὰ ἦν ξηρά·
there and the [2]hand [3]of him – [1]right was withered;

7 παρετηροῦντο δὲ αὐτὸν οἱ γραμματεῖς
and carefully watched him the scribes

καὶ οἱ Φαρισαῖοι εἰ ἐν τῷ σαββάτῳ
and the Pharisees if on the sabbath

θεραπεύει, ἵνα εὕρωσιν κατηγορεῖν αὐτοῦ.
he heals, that they might find to accuse him.

8 αὐτὸς δὲ ᾔδει τοὺς διαλογισμοὺς αὐτῶν,
But he knew the reasonings of them,

εἶπεν δὲ τῷ ἀνδρὶ τῷ ξηρὰν ἔχοντι τὴν
and said to the man – [3]withered [1]having [2]the

χεῖρα· ἔγειρε καὶ στῆθι εἰς τὸ μέσον·
[4]hand: Rise and stand in the midst;

καὶ ἀναστὰς ἔστη. 9 εἶπεν δὲ ὁ Ἰησοῦς
and rising up he stood. And said – Jesus

πρὸς αὐτούς· ἐπερωτῶ ὑμᾶς εἰ ἔξεστιν
to them: I ask you if it is lawful

τῷ σαββάτῳ ἀγαθοποιῆσαι ἢ κακοποιῆσαι,
on the sabbath to do good or to do evil,

ψυχὴν σῶσαι ἢ ἀπολέσαι; 10 καὶ περι-
life to save or to destroy? And looking

βλεψάμενος πάντας αὐτοὺς εἶπεν αὐτῷ·
round at all them he said to him:

ἔκτεινον τὴν χεῖρά σου. ὁ δὲ ἐποίησεν,
Stretch out the hand of thee. And he did,

καὶ ἀπεκατεστάθη ἡ χεὶρ αὐτοῦ. 11 αὐτοὶ
and was restored the hand of him. they

δὲ ἐπλήσθησαν ἀνοίας, καὶ διελάλουν πρὸς
But were filled of(with) madness, and talked to

ἀλλήλους τί ἂν ποιήσαιεν τῷ Ἰησοῦ.
one another what they might do – to Jesus.

12 Ἐγένετο δὲ ἐν ταῖς ἡμέραις ταύταις
Now it came to pass in – days these

ἐξελθεῖν αὐτὸν εἰς τὸ ὄρος προσεύξασθαι,
to go forth him[b] to the mountain to pray,
=he went forth

καὶ ἦν διανυκτερεύων ἐν τῇ προσευχῇ τοῦ
and was spending the whole night in the prayer –

θεοῦ. 13 καὶ ὅτε ἐγένετο ἡμέρα, προσεφώνησεν
of God. And when it became day, he called to [him]

τοὺς μαθητὰς αὐτοῦ, καὶ ἐκλεξάμενος ἀπ'
the disciples of him, and choosing from

αὐτῶν δώδεκα, οὓς καὶ ἀποστόλους ὠνόμασεν,
them twelve, whom also apostles he named,

14 Σίμωνα, ὃν καὶ ὠνόμασεν Πέτρον, καὶ
Simon, whom also he named Peter, and

Ἀνδρέαν τὸν ἀδελφὸν αὐτοῦ, καὶ Ἰάκωβον
Andrew the brother of him, and James

καὶ Ἰωάννην, καὶ Φίλιππον καὶ Βαρθο-
and John, and Philip and Bartho-

λομαῖον, 15 καὶ Μαθθαῖον καὶ Θωμᾶν,
lomew, and Matthew and Thomas,

priests to eat. And he also gave some to his companions." [5]Then Jesus said to them, "The Son of Man is Lord of the Sabbath."

[6]On another Sabbath he went into the synagogue and was teaching, and a man was there whose right hand was shriveled. [7]The Pharisees and the teachers of the law were looking for a reason to accuse Jesus, so they watched him closely to see if he would heal on the Sabbath. [8]But Jesus knew what they were thinking and said to the man with the shriveled hand, "Get up and stand in front of everyone." So he got up and stood there.

[9]Then Jesus said to them, "I ask you, which is lawful on the Sabbath: to do good or to do evil, to save life or to destroy it?"

[10]He looked around at them all, and then said to the man, "Stretch out your hand." He did so, and his hand was completely restored. [11]But they were furious and began to discuss with one another what they might do to Jesus.

The Twelve Apostles

[12]One of those days Jesus went out to a mountainside to pray, and spent the night praying to God. [13]When morning came, he called his disciples to him and chose twelve of them, whom he also designated apostles: [14]Simon (whom he named Peter), his brother Andrew, James, John, Philip, Bartholomew, [15]Matthew, Thomas, James son of Alphaeus, Si-

phaeus, and Simon, who
was called the Zealot,
16 and Judas son of James,
and Judas Iscariot, who became a traitor.

Jesus Teaches and Heals

17 He came down with
them and stood on a level
place, with a great crowd of
his disciples and a great
multitude of people from all
Judea, Jerusalem, and the
coast of Tyre and Sidon.
18 They had come to hear
him and to be healed of
their diseases; and those
who were troubled with unclean spirits were cured.
19 And all in the crowd were
trying to touch him, for
power came out from him
and healed all of them.

Blessings and Woes

20 Then he looked up at
his disciples and said:
"Blessed are you who
are poor,
for yours is the
kingdom of
God.
21 "Blessed are you who
are hungry now,
for you will be
filled.
"Blessed are you who
weep now,
for you will laugh.
22 "Blessed are you
when people hate you, and
when they exclude you, revile you, and defame you[u]
on account of the Son of
Man. 23 Rejoice in that day
and leap for joy, for surely
your reward is great in
heaven; for that is what
their ancestors did to the
prophets.
24 "But woe to you who
are rich,
for you have
received your
consolation.
25 "Woe to you who are
full now,
for you will be
hungry.
"Woe to you who are
laughing now,
for you will mourn
and weep.
26 "Woe to you when all

[u] Gk *cast out your name as evil*

[καὶ] Ἰάκωβον Ἁλφαίου καὶ Σίμωνα τὸν
and James [son] of Alphæus and Simon the [one]
καλούμενον ζηλωτήν, 16 καὶ Ἰούδαν Ἰακώβου,
being called a Zealot, and Judas of James,
καὶ Ἰούδαν Ἰσκαριώθ, ὃς ἐγένετο προδότης,
and Judas Iscariot, who became betrayer,
17 καὶ καταβὰς μετ' αὐτῶν ἔστη ἐπὶ
and coming down with them he stood on
τόπου πεδινοῦ, καὶ ὄχλος πολὺς μαθητῶν
place a level, and crowd a much of disciples
αὐτοῦ, καὶ πλῆθος πολὺ τοῦ λαοῦ ἀπὸ
of him, and multitude a much of the people from
πάσης τῆς Ἰουδαίας καὶ Ἰερουσαλὴμ καὶ
all – Judæa and Jerusalem and
τῆς παραλίου Τύρου καὶ Σιδῶνος, 18 οἳ
the coast country of Tyre and Sidon, who
ἦλθον ἀκοῦσαι αὐτοῦ καὶ ἰαθῆναι ἀπὸ
came to hear him and to be cured from
τῶν νόσων αὐτῶν, καὶ οἱ ἐνοχλούμενοι
the diseases of them, and the [ones] being tormented
ἀπὸ πνευμάτων ἀκαθάρτων ἐθεραπεύοντο.
from spirits unclean were healed.
19 καὶ πᾶς ὁ ὄχλος ἐζήτουν ἅπτεσθαι
And all the crowd sought to touch
αὐτοῦ, ὅτι δύναμις παρ' αὐτοῦ ἐξήρχετο
him, because power from him went forth
καὶ ἰᾶτο πάντας. 20 Καὶ αὐτὸς ἐπάρας
and cured all. And he lifting up
τοὺς ὀφθαλμοὺς αὐτοῦ εἰς τοὺς μαθητὰς
the eyes of him to the disciples
αὐτοῦ ἔλεγεν·
of him said :
Μακάριοι οἱ πτωχοί, ὅτι ὑμετέρα ἐστὶν
Blessed [are] the poor, because yours is
ἡ βασιλεία τοῦ θεοῦ. 21 μακάριοι οἱ
the kingdom – of God. Blessed [are] the [ones]
πεινῶντες νῦν, ὅτι χορτασθήσεσθε. μακάριοι
hungering now, because ye will be satisfied. Blessed [are]
οἱ κλαίοντες νῦν, ὅτι γελάσετε. 22 μακάριοί
the [ones] weeping now, because ye will laugh. Blessed
ἐστε ὅταν μισήσωσιν ὑμᾶς οἱ ἄνθρωποι,
are ye when [2]hate [3]you – [1]men,
καὶ ὅταν ἀφορίσωσιν ὑμᾶς καὶ ὀνειδίσωσιν
and when they separate you and reproach
καὶ ἐκβάλωσιν τὸ ὄνομα ὑμῶν ὡς πονηρὸν
and cast out the name of you as evil
ἕνεκα τοῦ υἱοῦ τοῦ ἀνθρώπου. 23 χάρητε
for the sake of the Son – of man. Rejoice
ἐν ἐκείνῃ τῇ ἡμέρᾳ καὶ σκιρτήσατε·
in that – day and leap for joy;
ἰδοὺ γὰρ ὁ μισθὸς ὑμῶν πολὺς ἐν τῷ
for behold[,] the reward of you much in –
οὐρανῷ· κατὰ τὰ αὐτὰ γὰρ ἐποίουν τοῖς
heaven; for according to the same things [4]did [5]to the
=in the same way
προφήταις οἱ πατέρες αὐτῶν.
[6]prophets [1]the [2]fathers [3]of them.
24 Πλὴν οὐαὶ ὑμῖν τοῖς πλουσίοις, ὅτι
But woe to you the rich [ones], because
ἀπέχετε τὴν παράκλησιν ὑμῶν. 25 οὐαὶ ὑμῖν,
ye have the consolation of you. Woe to you,
οἱ ἐμπεπλησμένοι νῦν, ὅτι πεινάσετε.
the [ones] *having been* filled up now, because ye will hunger.
οὐαί, οἱ γελῶντες νῦν, ὅτι πενθήσετε
Woe, the [ones] laughing now, because ye will mourn
καὶ κλαύσετε. 26 οὐαὶ ὅταν καλῶς ὑμᾶς
and lament. Woe when well [of] you

mon who was called the
Zealot, 16 Judas son of
James, and Judas Iscariot,
who became a traitor.

Blessings and Woes

17 He went down with
them and stood on a level
place. A large crowd of his
disciples was there and a
great number of people
from all over Judea, from
Jerusalem, and from the
coast of Tyre and Sidon,
18 who had come to hear
him and to be healed of
their diseases. Those troubled by evil[a] spirits were
cured, 19 and the people all
tried to touch him, because
power was coming from
him and healing them all.
20 Looking at his disci-
ples, he said:

"Blessed are you who
are poor,
for yours is the
kingdom of God.
21 Blessed are you who
hunger now,
for you will be
satisfied.
Blessed are you who
weep now,
for you will laugh.
22 Blessed are you when
men hate you,
when they exclude you
and insult you
and reject your name
as evil,
because of the Son of
Man.

23 "Rejoice in that day
and leap for joy, because
great is your reward in
heaven. For that is how
their fathers treated the
prophets.

24 "But woe to you who
are rich,
for you have already
received your
comfort.
25 Woe to you who are well
fed now,
for you will go hungry.
Woe to you who laugh
now,
for you will mourn and
weep.
26 Woe to you when all

[a] 18 Greek *unclean*

speak well of you, for that
is what their ancestors did
to the false prophets.

Love for Enemies

27 "But I say to you that
listen, Love your enemies,
do good to those who hate
you, 28 bless those who
curse you, pray for those
who abuse you. 29 If any-
one strikes you on the
cheek, offer the other also;
and from anyone who takes
away your coat do not
withhold even your shirt.
30 Give to everyone who
begs from you; and if anyone takes away your
goods, do not ask for them
again. 31 Do to others as
you would have them do to
you.
32 "If you love those
who love you, what credit
is that to you? For even sinners love those who love
them. 33 If you do good to
those who do good to you,
what credit is that to you?
For even sinners do the
same. 34 If you lend to those
from whom you hope to re-
ceive, what credit is that to
you? Even sinners lend to
sinners, to receive as much
again. 35 But love your enemies, do good, and lend,
expecting nothing in re-
turn.[v] Your reward will be
great, and you will be children of the Most High; for
he is kind to the ungrateful
and the wicked. 36 Be merciful, just as your Father is
merciful.

Judging Others

37 "Do not judge, and
you will not be judged; do

[v] Other ancient authorities read *despairing of no one*

εἴπωσιν πάντες οἱ ἄνθρωποι· κατὰ τὰ
say all – men; for according to
=in the same way

αὐτὰ γὰρ ἐποίουν τοῖς ψευδοπροφήταις οἱ
the same things did to the false prophets the

πατέρες αὐτῶν. 27 Ἀλλὰ ὑμῖν λέγω
fathers of them. But you I tell

τοῖς ἀκούουσιν· ἀγαπᾶτε τοὺς ἐχθροὺς
the [ones] hearing: Love ye the enemies

ὑμῶν, καλῶς ποιεῖτε τοῖς μισοῦσιν ὑμᾶς,
of you, ²well ¹do to the [ones] hating you,

28 εὐλογεῖτε τοὺς καταρωμένους ὑμᾶς,
bless the [ones] cursing you,

προσεύχεσθε περὶ τῶν ἐπηρεαζόντων ὑμᾶς.
pray about the [ones] insulting you.

29 τῷ τύπτοντί σε ἐπὶ τὴν σιαγόνα
To the [one] striking thee on the cheek

πάρεχε καὶ τὴν ἄλλην, καὶ ἀπὸ τοῦ
turn also the other, and from the [one]

αἴροντός σου τὸ ἱμάτιον καὶ τὸν χιτῶνα
taking of thee the garment also the tunic

μὴ κωλύσῃς. 30 παντὶ αἰτοῦντί σε δίδου,
do not prevent. To everyone asking thee give,

καὶ ἀπὸ τοῦ αἴροντος τὰ σὰ μὴ ἀπαίτει.
and from the [one] taking thy things do not ask back.

31 καὶ καθὼς θέλετε ἵνα ποιῶσιν ὑμῖν
And as ye wish that may do to you

οἱ ἄνθρωποι, ποιεῖτε αὐτοῖς ὁμοίως. 32 καὶ
– men, do ye to them likewise. And

εἰ ἀγαπᾶτε τοὺς ἀγαπῶντας ὑμᾶς, ποία
if ye love the [ones] loving you, what

ὑμῖν χάρις ἐστίν; καὶ γὰρ οἱ ἁμαρτωλοὶ
to you thanks is there?[c] for even – sinners
=thanks have ye?

τοὺς ἀγαπῶντας αὐτοὺς ἀγαπῶσιν. 33 καὶ
²the [ones] ³loving ⁴them ¹love. even

γὰρ ἐὰν ἀγαθοποιῆτε τοὺς ἀγαθοποιοῦντας
For if ye do good to the [ones] doing good to

ὑμᾶς, ποία ὑμῖν χάρις ἐστίν; καὶ οἱ
you, what to you thanks is there?[c] even –
=thanks have ye?

ἁμαρτωλοὶ τὸ αὐτὸ ποιοῦσιν. 34 καὶ ἐὰν
sinners the same thing do. And if

δανείσητε παρ' ὧν ἐλπίζετε λαβεῖν, ποία
ye lend from whom ye hope to receive, what

ὑμῖν χάρις [ἐστίν]; καὶ ἁμαρτωλοὶ
to you thanks is there?[c] even sinners
=thanks have ye?

ἁμαρτωλοῖς δανείζουσιν ἵνα ἀπολάβωσιν τὰ
to sinners lend that they may receive back the

ἴσα. 35 πλὴν ἀγαπᾶτε τοὺς ἐχθροὺς ὑμῶν
equal things. But love ye the enemies of you

καὶ ἀγαθοποιεῖτε καὶ δανείζετε μηδὲν
and do good and lend nothing

ἀπελπίζοντες· καὶ ἔσται ὁ μισθὸς ὑμῶν
despairing; and will be the reward of you
=despairing not at all;

πολύς, καὶ ἔσεσθε υἱοὶ ὑψίστου, ὅτι
much, and ye will be sons of [the] Most High, because

αὐτὸς χρηστός ἐστιν ἐπὶ τοὺς ἀχαρίστους
he kind is to the unthankful

καὶ πονηρούς. 36 Γίνεσθε οἰκτίρμονες,
and evil. Be ye compassionate,

καθὼς ὁ πατὴρ ὑμῶν οἰκτίρμων ἐστίν.
as the Father of you compassionate is.

37 καὶ μὴ κρίνετε, καὶ οὐ μὴ κριθῆτε· καὶ
And do not judge, and by no means ye may be judged; and

men speak well of
you,
for that is how their
fathers treated the
false prophets.

Love for Enemies

27 "But I tell you who hear
me: Love your enemies, do
good to those who hate
you, 28 bless those who
curse you, pray for those
who mistreat you. 29 If
someone strikes you on
one cheek, turn to him the
other also. If someone
takes your cloak, do not
stop him from taking your
tunic. 30 Give to everyone
who asks you, and if any-
one takes what belongs to
you, do not demand it
back. 31 Do to others as you
would have them do to you.
32 "If you love those who
love you, what credit is that
to you? Even 'sinners' love
those who love them.
33 And if you do good to
those who are good to you,
what credit is that to you?
Even 'sinners' do that.
34 And if you lend to those
from whom you expect re-
payment, what credit is
that to you? Even 'sinners'
lend to 'sinners,' expecting
to be repaid in full. 35 But
love your enemies, do good
to them, and lend to them
without expecting to get
anything back. Then your
reward will be great, and
you will be sons of the Most
High, because he is kind to
the ungrateful and wicked.
36 Be merciful, just as your
Father is merciful.

Judging Others

37 "Do not judge, and you
will not be judged. Do not

not condemn, and you will
not be condemned. For-
give, and you will be forgiv-
en; 38 give, and it will be
given to you. A good mea-
sure, pressed down, shak-
en together, running over,
will be put into your lap; for
the measure you give will
be the measure you get
back."

39 He also told them a
parable: "Can a blind person guide a blind person?
Will not both fall into a pit?
40 A disciple is not above
the teacher, but everyone
who is fully qualified will
be like the teacher. 41 Why
do you see the speck in
your neighbor's[w] eye, but
do not notice the log in your
own eye? 42 Or how can
you say to your neighbor,[x]
'Friend,[x] let me take out
the speck in your eye,'
when you yourself do not
see the log in your own
eye? You hypocrite, first
take the log out of your own
eye, and then you will see
clearly to take the speck
out of your neighbor's[w]
eye.

A Tree and Its Fruit

43 "No good tree bears
bad fruit, nor again does a
bad tree bear good fruit;
44 for each tree is known by
its own fruit. Figs are not
gathered from thorns, nor
are grapes picked from a
bramble bush. 45 The good
person out of the good treasure of the heart produces
good, and the evil person
out of evil treasure pro-
duces evil; for it is out of
the abundance of the heart
that the mouth speaks.

[w] Gk *brother's*
[x] Gk *brother*

μὴ καταδικάζετε, καὶ οὐ μὴ καταδικασθῆτε.
do not condemn, and by no means ye may be condemned.

ἀπολύετε, καὶ ἀπολυθήσεσθε· 38 δίδοτε, καὶ
Forgive, and ye will be forgiven; give, and

δοθήσεται ὑμῖν· μέτρον καλὸν πεπιεσμένον
it will be given to you; measure good *having been* pressed down

σεσαλευμένον ὑπερεκχυννόμενον δώσουσιν εἰς
having been shaken running over they will give into

τὸν κόλπον ὑμῶν· ᾧ γὰρ μέτρῳ μετρεῖτε
the bosom of you; for in what measure ye measure

ἀντιμετρηθήσεται ὑμῖν. 39 Εἶπεν δὲ καὶ
it will be measured in return to you. And he told also

παραβολὴν αὐτοῖς· μήτι δύναται τυφλὸς
a parable to them: *Not* can a blind man

τυφλὸν ὁδηγεῖν; οὐχὶ ἀμφότεροι εἰς βόθυνον
[2]a blind man [1]guide? not both into a ditch

ἐμπεσοῦνται; 40 οὐκ ἔστιν μαθητὴς ὑπὲρ
will fall *in*? [2]not [3]is [1]A disciple above

τὸν διδάσκαλον· κατηρτισμένος δὲ πᾶς
the teacher; [1]but [4]*having been* perfected [2]everyone

ἔσται ὡς ὁ διδάσκαλος αὐτοῦ. 41 Τί δὲ
[3]will be as the teacher of him. And why

βλέπεις τὸ κάρφος τὸ ἐν τῷ ὀφθαλμῷ
seest thou the mote – in the eye

τοῦ ἀδελφοῦ σου, τὴν δὲ δοκὸν τὴν ἐν
of the brother of thee, but the beam – in

τῷ ἰδίῳ ὀφθαλμῷ οὐ κατανοεῖς; 42 πῶς
thine own eye thou considerest not? how

δύνασαι λέγειν τῷ ἀδελφῷ σου· ἀδελφέ,
canst thou *to* say to the brother of thee: Brother,

ἄφες ἐκβάλω τὸ κάρφος τὸ ἐν τῷ
allow I may take out the mote – in the
=allow me to take out

ὀφθαλμῷ σου, αὐτὸς τὴν ἐν τῷ ὀφθαλμῷ
eye of thee, [1][thy]self [4]the [6]in [7]the [8]eye

σου δοκὸν οὐ βλέπων; ὑποκριτά, ἔκβαλε
[9]of thee [5]beam [2]not [3]seeing? hypocrite, take *out*

πρῶτον τὴν δοκὸν ἐκ τοῦ ὀφθαλμοῦ σου,
first the beam out of the eye of thee,

καὶ τότε διαβλέψεις τὸ κάρφος τὸ ἐν τῷ
and then thou wilt see clearly the mote – in the

ὀφθαλμῷ τοῦ ἀδελφοῦ σου ἐκβαλεῖν. 43 Οὐ
eye of the brother of thee to take out. [2]no

γάρ ἐστιν δένδρον καλὸν ποιοῦν καρπὸν
[1]For [3]there is [5]tree [4]good producing fruit

σαπρόν, οὐδὲ πάλιν δένδρον σαπρὸν ποιοῦν
bad, nor again tree a bad producing

καρπὸν καλόν. 44 ἕκαστον γὰρ δένδρον
fruit good. For each tree

ἐκ τοῦ ἰδίου καρποῦ γινώσκεται· οὐ γὰρ
by the(its) own fruit is known; for not

ἐξ ἀκανθῶν συλλέγουσιν σῦκα, οὐδὲ ἐκ
of thorns do they gather figs, nor of

βάτου σταφυλὴν τρυγῶσιν. 45 ὁ ἀγαθὸς
a thorn bush a grape do they pick. The good

ἄνθρωπος ἐκ τοῦ ἀγαθοῦ θησαυροῦ τῆς
man out of the good treasure of the(his)

καρδίας προφέρει τὸ ἀγαθόν, καὶ ὁ
heart brings forth the good, and the
=that which is good,

πονηρὸς ἐκ τοῦ πονηροῦ προφέρει τὸ
evil man out of the evil brings forth the

πονηρόν· ἐκ γὰρ περισσεύματος καρδίας
evil; for out of [the] abundance of [his] heart
=that which is evil;

condemn, and you will not
be condemned. Forgive,
and you will be forgiven.
38 Give, and it will be given
to you. A good measure,
pressed down, shaken to-
gether and running over,
will be poured into your
lap. For with the measure
you use, it will be measured
to you."

39 He also told them this
parable: "Can a blind man
lead a blind man? Will they
not both fall into a pit? 40 A
student is not above his
teacher, but everyone who
is fully trained will be like
his teacher.

41 "Why do you look at
the speck of sawdust in
your brother's eye and pay
no attention to the plank in
your own eye? 42 How can
you say to your brother,
'Brother, let me take the
speck out of your eye,'
when you yourself fail to
see the plank in your own
eye? You hypocrite, first
take the plank out of your
eye, and then you will see
clearly to remove the speck
from your brother's eye.

A Tree and Its Fruit

43 "No good tree bears
bad fruit, nor does a bad
tree bear good fruit. 44 Each
tree is recognized by its
own fruit. People do not
pick figs from thornbushes,
or grapes from briers.
45 The good man brings
good things out of the good
stored up in his heart, and
the evil man brings evil
things out of the evil stored
up in his heart. For out of
the overflow of his heart his
mouth speaks.

The Two Foundations

46 "Why do you call me
'Lord, Lord,' and do not do
what I tell you? 47 I will
show you what someone is
like who comes to me,
hears my words, and acts
on them. 48 That one is like
a man building a house,
who dug deeply and laid the
foundation on rock; when a
flood arose, the river burst
against that house but
could not shake it, because
it had been well built.[y]
49 But the one who hears
and does not act is like a
man who built a house on
the ground without a foundation. When the river
burst against it, immediately it fell, and great was the
ruin of that house."

λαλεῖ τὸ στόμα αὐτοῦ. 46 Τί δέ με καλεῖτε·
speaks the mouth of him. And why me call ye:
κύριε κύριε, καὶ οὐ ποιεῖτε ἃ
Lord[,] Lord, and do not [the things] which
λέγω; 47 Πᾶς ὁ ἐρχόμενος πρός με καὶ
I say? Everyone coming to me and
ἀκούων μου τῶν λόγων καὶ ποιῶν αὐτούς,
hearing of me the words and doing them,
ὑποδείξω ὑμῖν τίνι ἐστὶν ὅμοιος. 48 ὅμοιός
I will show you to whom he is like. Like
ἐστιν ἀνθρώπῳ οἰκοδομοῦντι οἰκίαν, ὃς
he is to a man building a house, who
ἔσκαψεν καὶ ἐβάθυνεν καὶ ἔθηκεν θεμέλιον
dug and deepened and laid a foundation
ἐπὶ τὴν πέτραν· πλημμύρης δὲ γενομένης
on the rock; and a flood occurring[a]
=when a flood occurred
προσέρρηξεν ὁ ποταμὸς τῇ οἰκίᾳ ἐκείνῃ,
[3]dashed against [1]the [2]river – house that,
καὶ οὐκ ἴσχυσεν σαλεῦσαι αὐτὴν διὰ
and was not able to shake it because of
τὸ καλῶς οἰκοδομῆσθαι αὐτήν. 49 ὁ δὲ
the well to be built it.[b] But the [one]
=because it was well built.
ἀκούσας καὶ μὴ ποιήσας ὅμοιός ἐστιν
hearing and not doing [2]like [1]is
ἀνθρώπῳ οἰκοδομήσαντι οἰκίαν ἐπὶ τὴν
a man having built a house on the
γῆν χωρὶς θεμελίου, ᾗ προσέρρηξεν ὁ
earth without a foundation, [2]which [5]dashed [1]against [3]the
ποταμός, καὶ εὐθὺς συνέπεσεν, καὶ ἐγένετο
[4]river, and immediately it collapsed, and [5]was
τὸ ῥῆγμα τῆς οἰκίας ἐκείνης μέγα.
[1]the [2]ruin – [4]house [3]of that [6]great.

The Wise and Foolish Builders

46 "Why do you call me,
'Lord, Lord,' and do not do
what I say? 47 I will show
you what he is like who
comes to me and hears my
words and puts them into
practice. 48 He is like a man
building a house, who dug
down deep and laid the
foundation on rock. When
a flood came, the torrent
struck that house but could
not shake it, because it was
well built. 49 But the one
who hears my words and
does not put them into
practice is like a man who
built a house on the ground
without a foundation. The
moment the torrent struck
that house, it collapsed and
its destruction was com-
plete."

Chapter 7

Jesus Heals a Centurion's Servant

AFTER Jesus[z] had fin-
ished all his sayings in
the hearing of the people,
he entered Capernaum. 2 A
centurion there had a slave
whom he valued highly,
and who was ill and close to
death. 3 When he heard
about Jesus, he sent some
Jewish elders to him, asking him to come and heal
his slave. 4 When they
came to Jesus, they ap-
pealed to him earnestly,
saying, "He is worthy of
having you do this for him,
5 for he loves our people,
and it is he who built our
synagogue for us." 6 And
Jesus went with them, but
when he was not far from
the house, the centurion
sent friends to say to him,

7 Ἐπειδὴ ἐπλήρωσεν πάντα τὰ ῥήματα
When he completed all the words
αὐτοῦ εἰς τὰς ἀκοὰς τοῦ λαοῦ, εἰσῆλθεν
of him in the ears of the people, he entered
εἰς Καφαρναούμ. 2 Ἑκατοντάρχου δέ
into Capernaum. Now [2]of [3]a [5]centurion
τινος δοῦλος κακῶς ἔχων ἤμελλεν τελευτᾶν,
[4]certain [1]a slave [7]ill [6]having(being) [12]was about [13]to die,
ὃς ἦν αὐτῷ ἔντιμος. 3 ἀκούσας δὲ περὶ
[8]who [9]was [11]to him [10]dear. And hearing about
τοῦ Ἰησοῦ ἀπέστειλεν πρὸς αὐτὸν πρε-
– Jesus he sent to him eld-
σβυτέρους τῶν Ἰουδαίων, ἐρωτῶν αὐτὸν
ers of the Jews, asking him
ὅπως ἐλθὼν διασώσῃ τὸν δοῦλον αὐτοῦ.
that coming he might recover the slave of him.
4 οἱ δὲ παραγενόμενοι πρὸς τὸν Ἰησοῦν
And they coming to – Jesus
παρεκάλουν αὐτὸν σπουδαίως, λέγοντες ὅτι ἄξιός
besought him earnestly, saying[,] – Worthy
ἐστιν ᾧ παρέξῃ τοῦτο· 5 ἀγαπᾷ γὰρ
he is for whom thou shouldest grant this; for he loves
τὸ ἔθνος ἡμῶν καὶ τὴν συναγωγὴν
the nation of us and the synagogue
αὐτὸς ᾠκοδόμησεν ἡμῖν. 6 ὁ δὲ Ἰησοῦς
he built for us. – And Jesus
ἐπορεύετο σὺν αὐτοῖς. ἤδη δὲ αὐτοῦ οὐ
went with them. And yet him not
=while he was yet
μακρὰν ἀπέχοντος ἀπὸ τῆς οἰκίας, ἔπεμψεν
far being away[a] from the house, sent
not far away

Chapter 7

The Faith of the Centurion

WHEN Jesus had fin-
ished saying all this
in the hearing of the people,
he entered Capernaum.
2 There a centurion's servant, whom his master valued highly, was sick and
about to die. 3 The centurion heard of Jesus and sent
some elders of the Jews to
him, asking him to come
and heal his servant.
4 When they came to Jesus,
they pleaded earnestly with
him, "This man deserves
to have you do this, 5 because he loves our nation
and has built our syna-
gogue." 6 So Jesus went
with them.
He was not far from the
house when the centurion

[y] Other ancient authorities read *founded upon the rock*
[z] Gk *he*

"Lord, do not trouble yourself, for I am not worthy to
have you come under my
roof; 7 therefore I did not
presume to come to you.
But only speak the word,
and let my servant be
healed. 8 For I also am a
man set under authority,
with soldiers under me; and
I say to one, 'Go,' and he
goes, and to another,
'Come,' and he comes, and
to my slave, 'Do this,' and
the slave does it." 9 When
Jesus heard this he was
amazed at him, and turning
to the crowd that followed
him, he said, "I tell you, not
even in Israel have I found
such faith." 10 When those
who had been sent returned
to the house, they found
the slave in good health.

Jesus Raises the Widow's Son at Nain

11 Soon afterwards[a] he
went to a town called Nain,
and his disciples and a large
crowd went with him. 12 As
he approached the gate of
the town, a man who had
died was being carried out.
He was his mother's only
son, and she was a widow;
and with her was a large
crowd from the town.
13 When the Lord saw her,
he had compassion for her
and said to her, "Do not
weep." 14 Then he came
forward and touched the
bier, and the bearers stood
still. And he said, "Young
man, I say to you, rise!"
15 The dead man sat up and
began to speak, and Jesus[b]
gave him to his mother.
16 Fear seized all of them;
and they glorified God,
saying, "A great prophet
has risen among us!" and
"God has looked favorably

[a] Other ancient authorities read *Next day*
[b] Gk *he*

φίλους ὁ ἑκατοντάρχης λέγων αὐτῷ· κύριε,
friends the centurion saying to him : Lord,
μὴ σκύλλου· οὐ γὰρ ἱκανός εἰμι ἵνα ὑπὸ
do not trouble; for not worthy am I that under
τὴν στέγην μου εἰσέλθῃς· 7 διὸ οὐδὲ
the roof of me thou shouldest enter; wherefore not
ἐμαυτὸν ἠξίωσα πρὸς σὲ ἐλθεῖν· ἀλλὰ εἰπὲ
myself I accounted worthy to thee to come; but say
λόγῳ, καὶ ἰαθήτω ὁ παῖς μου. 8 καὶ
in a word, and let be cured the servant of me. [2]also
γὰρ ἐγὼ ἄνθρωπός εἰμι ὑπὸ ἐξουσίαν
[1]For [3]I [5]a man [4]am [7]under [8]authority
τασσόμενος, ἔχων ὑπ᾽ ἐμαυτὸν στρατιώτας,
[6]*being* set, having under myself soldiers,
καὶ λέγω τούτῳ· πορεύθητι, καὶ πορεύεται,
and I tell this one : Go, and he goes,
καὶ ἄλλῳ· ἔρχου, καὶ ἔρχεται, καὶ τῷ
and another : Come, and he comes, and the
δούλῳ μου· ποίησον τοῦτο, καὶ ποιεῖ.
slave of me : Do this, and he does.
9 ἀκούσας δὲ ταῦτα ὁ Ἰησοῦς ἐθαύμασεν
And hearing these [words] – Jesus marvelled at
αὐτόν, καὶ στραφεὶς τῷ ἀκολουθοῦντι αὐτῷ
him, and turning to the [2]following [3]him
ὄχλῳ εἶπεν· λέγω ὑμῖν, οὐδὲ ἐν τῷ
[1]crowd said : I tell you, not in –
Ἰσραὴλ τοσαύτην πίστιν εὗρον. 10 καὶ
Israel such faith I found. And
ὑποστρέψαντες εἰς τὸν οἶκον οἱ πεμφθέντες
returning to the house the [ones] sent
εὗρον τὸν δοῦλον ὑγιαίνοντα. 11 Καὶ
found the slave well. And
ἐγένετο ἐν τῷ ἑξῆς ἐπορεύθη εἰς πόλιν
it came to pass on the next day he went into a city
καλουμένην Ναΐν, καὶ συνεπορεύοντο αὐτῷ
being called Nain, and went with him
οἱ μαθηταὶ αὐτοῦ καὶ ὄχλος πολύς.
the disciples of him and crowd a much.
12 ὡς δὲ ἤγγισεν τῇ πύλῃ τῆς πόλεως, καὶ
And as he drew near to the gate of the city, *and*
ἰδοὺ ἐξεκομίζετο τεθνηκὼς μονογενὴς
behold was being carried out [for burial] having died an only born
υἱὸς τῇ μητρὶ αὐτοῦ, καὶ αὐτὴ ἦν χήρα,
son to the mother of him, and this was a widow,
καὶ ὄχλος τῆς πόλεως ἱκανὸς ἦν σὺν
and a [2]crowd [3]of the [4]city [1]considerable was with
αὐτῇ. 13 καὶ ἰδὼν αὐτὴν ὁ κύριος
her. And seeing her the Lord
ἐσπλαγχνίσθη ἐπ᾽ αὐτῇ καὶ εἶπεν αὐτῇ·
felt compassion over her and said to her :
μὴ κλαῖε. 14 καὶ προσελθὼν ἥψατο τῆς
Do not weep. And approaching he touched the
σοροῦ, οἱ δὲ βαστάζοντες ἔστησαν, καὶ
bier, and the [ones] bearing stood, and
εἶπεν· νεανίσκε, σοὶ λέγω, ἐγέρθητι. 15 καὶ
he said : Young man, to thee I say, Arise. And
ἀνεκάθισεν ὁ νεκρὸς καὶ ἤρξατο λαλεῖν,
sat up the dead man and began to speak,
καὶ ἔδωκεν αὐτὸν τῇ μητρὶ αὐτοῦ.
and he gave him to the mother of him.
16 ἔλαβεν δὲ φόβος πάντας, καὶ ἐδόξαζον
And [2]took [1]fear [3]all, and they glorified
τὸν θεὸν λέγοντες ὅτι προφήτης μέγας
– God saying[,] – prophet A great
ἠγέρθη ἐν ἡμῖν, καὶ ὅτι ἐπεσκέψατο ὁ
was raised among us, and[,] – [2]visited –

sent friends to say to him:
"Lord, don't trouble yourself, for I do not deserve to
have you come under my
roof. 7 That is why I did not
even consider myself wor-
thy to come to you. But say
the word, and my servant
will be healed. 8 For I myself am a man under authority, with soldiers under me.
I tell this one, 'Go,' and he
goes; and that one, 'Come,'
and he comes. I say to my
servant, 'Do this,' and he
does it."
9 When Jesus heard this,
he was amazed at him, and
turning to the crowd fol-
lowing him, he said, "I tell
you, I have not found such
great faith even in Israel."
10 Then the men who had
been sent returned to the
house and found the ser-
vant well.

Jesus Raises a Widow's Son

11 Soon afterward, Jesus
went to a town called Nain,
and his disciples and a large
crowd went along with
him. 12 As he approached
the town gate, a dead person was being carried out
—the only son of his mother, and she was a widow.
And a large crowd from the
town was with her. 13 When
the Lord saw her, his heart
went out to her and he said,
"Don't cry."
14 Then he went up and
touched the coffin, and
those carrying it stood still.
He said, "Young man, I
say to you, get up!" 15 The
dead man sat up and began
to talk, and Jesus gave him
back to his mother.
16 They were all filled with
awe and praised God. "A
great prophet has appeared
among us," they said.

on his people!" 17This
word about him spread
throughout Judea and all
the surrounding country.

Messengers from John the Baptist

18 The disciples of John
reported all these things to
him. So John summoned
two of his disciples 19and
sent them to the Lord to
ask, "Are you the one who
is to come, or are we to
wait for another?" 20When
the men had come to him,
they said, "John the Baptist
has sent us to you to ask,
'Are you the one who is to
come, or are we to wait for
another?'" 21Jesus[c] had
just then cured many peo-
ple of diseases, plagues,
and evil spirits, and had
given sight to many who
were blind. 22And he an-
swered them, "Go and tell
John what you have seen
and heard: the blind re-
ceive their sight, the lame
walk, the lepers[d] are
cleansed, the deaf hear, the
dead are raised, the poor
have good news brought to
them. 23And blessed is
anyone who takes no of-
fense at me."
24 When John's mes-
sengers had gone, Jesus[b]
began to speak to the
crowds about John:[e]
"What did you go out into
the wilderness to look at? A
reed shaken by the wind?
25What then did you go out
to see? Someone[f] dressed
in soft robes? Look, those
who put on fine clothing
and live in luxury are in
royal palaces. 26What then
did you go out to see? A
prophet? Yes, I tell you,
and more than a prophet.
27This is the one about
whom it is written,

θεὸς τὸν λαὸν αὐτοῦ. 17 καὶ ἐξῆλθεν ὁ
[1]God the people of him. And went forth –
λόγος οὗτος ἐν ὅλῃ τῇ Ἰουδαίᾳ περὶ
word this in all – Judæa [5]concerning
αὐτοῦ καὶ πάσῃ τῇ περιχώρῳ.
[6]him [1]and [2]all [3]the [4]neighbourhood.
18 Καὶ ἀπήγγειλαν Ἰωάννῃ οἱ μαθηταὶ
And reported to John the disciples
αὐτοῦ περὶ πάντων τούτων. καὶ
of him about all these things. And
προσκαλεσάμενος δύο τινὰς τῶν μαθητῶν
calling to [him] [2]two [1]a certain of the disciples
αὐτοῦ ὁ Ἰωάννης 19 ἔπεμψεν πρὸς τὸν
of him – John sent to the
κύριον λέγων· σὺ εἶ ὁ ἐρχόμενος, ἢ ἄλλον
Lord saying: Thou art the coming [one], or another
προσδοκῶμεν; 20 παραγενόμενοι δὲ πρὸς
may we expect? And coming to
αὐτὸν οἱ ἄνδρες εἶπαν· Ἰωάννης ὁ βαπτιστὴς
him the men said: John the Baptist
ἀπέστειλεν ἡμᾶς πρὸς σὲ λέγων· σὺ εἶ ὁ
sent us to thee saying: Thou art the
ἐρχόμενος, ἢ ἄλλον προσδοκῶμεν; 21 ἐν
coming [one], or another may we expect? In
ἐκείνῃ τῇ ὥρᾳ ἐθεράπευσεν πολλοὺς ἀπὸ
that – hour he healed many from(of)
νόσων καὶ μαστίγων καὶ πνευμάτων πονηρῶν,
diseases and plagues and spirits evil,
καὶ τυφλοῖς πολλοῖς ἐχαρίσατο βλέπειν.
and blind persons to many he gave to see.
22 καὶ ἀποκριθεὶς εἶπεν αὐτοῖς· πορευθέντες
And answering he said to them: Going
ἀπαγγείλατε Ἰωάννῃ ἃ εἴδετε καὶ
report to John [the things] which ye saw and
ἠκούσατε· τυφλοὶ ἀναβλέπουσιν, χωλοὶ
heard: blind men see again, lame men
περιπατοῦσιν, λεπροὶ καθαρίζονται, καὶ κωφοὶ
walk, lepers are being cleansed, and deaf men
ἀκούουσιν, νεκροὶ ἐγείρονται, πτωχοὶ
hear, dead men are raised, poor people
εὐαγγελίζονται· 23 καὶ μακάριός ἐστιν ὃς ἐὰν
are evangelized; and blessed is whoever
μὴ σκανδαλισθῇ ἐν ἐμοί. 24 Ἀπελθόντων δὲ
is not offended in me. And going away
=as the
τῶν ἀγγέλων Ἰωάννου ἤρξατο λέγειν πρὸς
the messengers of John[*] he began to say to
messengers of John went away
τοὺς ὄχλους περὶ Ἰωάννου· τί ἐξήλθατε
the crowds concerning John: What went ye forth
εἰς τὴν ἔρημον θεάσασθαι; κάλαμον ὑπὸ
into the desert to see? a reed by
ἀνέμου σαλευόμενον; 25 ἀλλὰ τί ἐξήλθατε
wind being shaken? But what went ye forth
ἰδεῖν; ἄνθρωπον ἐν μαλακοῖς ἱματίοις
to see? a man in soft garments
ἠμφιεσμένον; ἰδοὺ οἱ ἐν ἱματισμῷ ἐνδόξῳ
having been behold[,] the [1]in [3]raiment [2]splendid
clothed? [ones]
καὶ τρυφῇ ὑπάρχοντες ἐν τοῖς βασιλείοις
[4]and [5]in luxury [6]being [8]in – [9]royal palaces
εἰσίν. 26 ἀλλὰ τί ἐξήλθατε ἰδεῖν; προφήτην;
[7]are. But what went ye forth to see? a prophet?
ναὶ λέγω ὑμῖν, καὶ περισσότερον προφήτου.
yes I tell you, and more [than] a prophet.
27 οὗτός ἐστιν περὶ οὗ γέγραπται· ἰδοὺ
This is he concerning whom it has been written: Behold

"God has come to help his
people." 17This news about
Jesus spread throughout
Judea[b] and the surrounding country.

Jesus and John the Baptist

18John's disciples told
him about all these things.
Calling two of them, 19he
sent them to the Lord to
ask, "Are you the one who
was to come, or should we
expect someone else?"
20When the men came to
Jesus, they said, "John the
Baptist sent us to you to
ask, 'Are you the one who
was to come, or should we
expect someone else?'"
21At that very time Jesus
cured many who had dis-
eases, sicknesses and evil
spirits, and gave sight to
many who were blind. 22So
he replied to the messen-
gers, "Go back and report
to John what you have seen
and heard: The blind re-
ceive sight, the lame walk,
those who have leprosy[c]
are cured, the deaf hear,
the dead are raised, and the
good news is preached to
the poor. 23Blessed is the
man who does not fall away
on account of me."
24After John's messen-
gers left, Jesus began to
speak to the crowd about
John: "What did you go out
into the desert to see? A
reed swayed by the wind?
25If not, what did you go
out to see? A man dressed
in fine clothes? No, those
who wear expensive
clothes and indulge in luxury are in palaces. 26But
what did you go out to see?
A prophet? Yes, I tell you,
and more than a prophet.
27This is the one about
whom it is written:

[c] Gk *He*
[d] The terms *leper* and *leprosy* can refer to several diseases
[e] Gk *him*
[f] Or *Why then did you go out? To see someone*

[b] 17 Or *the land of the Jews*
[c] 22 The Greek word was used for various diseases affecting the skin—not necessarily leprosy.

'See, I am sending my
messenger
ahead of you,
who will prepare
your way
before you.'
28 I tell you, among those
born of women no one is
greater than John; yet the
least in the kingdom of God
is greater than he." 29 (And
all the people who heard
this, including the tax collectors, acknowledged the
justice of God,[g] because
they had been baptized
with John's baptism. 30 But
by refusing to be baptized
by him, the Pharisees and
the lawyers rejected God's
purpose for themselves.)
31 "To what then will I
compare the people of this
generation, and what are
they like? 32 They are like
children sitting in the marketplace and calling to one
another,
'We played the flute
for you, and you
did not dance;
we wailed, and you
did not weep.'
33 For John the Baptist has
come eating no bread and
drinking no wine, and you
say, 'He has a demon';
34 the Son of Man has come
eating and drinking, and
you say, 'Look, a glutton
and a drunkard, a friend of
tax collectors and sinners!'
35 Nevertheless, wisdom is
vindicated by all her children."

A Sinful Woman Forgiven

36 One of the Pharisees
asked Jesus[e] to eat with
him, and he went into the
Pharisee's house and took
his place at the table.
37 And a woman in the city,
who was a sinner, having
learned that he was eating
in the Pharisee's house,
brought an alabaster jar of
ointment. 38 She stood behind him at his feet, weeping, and began to bathe his
feet with her tears and to
dry them with her hair.

[g] Or *praised God*

ἀποστέλλω τὸν ἄγγελόν μου πρὸ προσώπου
I send the messenger of me before [the] face
σου, ὃς κατασκευάσει τὴν ὁδόν σου
of thee, who will prepare the way of thee
ἔμπροσθέν σου. **28** λέγω ὑμῖν, μείζων
before thee. I tell you, [6]greater
ἐν γεννητοῖς γυναικῶν Ἰωάννου οὐδείς
[1]among [2][those] born [3]of women [[7]than] [8]John [4]no one
ἐστιν· ὁ δὲ μικρότερος ἐν τῇ βασιλείᾳ τοῦ
[5]is; but the less in the kingdom –
θεοῦ μείζων αὐτοῦ ἐστιν. **29** καὶ πᾶς ὁ
of God greater [than] he is. And all the
λαὸς ἀκούσας καὶ οἱ τελῶναι ἐδικαίωσαν
people hearing and the tax-collectors justified
τὸν θεόν, βαπτισθέντες τὸ βάπτισμα
– God, being baptized [with] the baptism
Ἰωάννου· **30** οἱ δὲ Φαρισαῖοι καὶ οἱ
of John; but the Pharisees and the
νομικοὶ τὴν βουλὴν τοῦ θεοῦ ἠθέτησαν εἰς
lawyers [4]the [5]counsel – [6]of God [1]rejected [2]for
ἑαυτούς, μὴ βαπτισθέντες ὑπ' αὐτοῦ. **31** Τίνι
[3]themselves, not being baptized by him. To what
οὖν ὁμοιώσω τοὺς ἀνθρώπους τῆς γενεᾶς
then may I liken the men – generation
ταύτης, καὶ τίνι εἰσὶν ὅμοιοι; **32** ὅμοιοί εἰσιν
of this, and to what are they like? Like are they
παιδίοις τοῖς ἐν ἀγορᾷ καθημένοις καὶ
to children – in a marketplace sitting and
προσφωνοῦσιν ἀλλήλοις ἃ λέγει· ηὐλήσαμεν
calling to one another who says: We piped
ὑμῖν καὶ οὐκ ὠρχήσασθε· ἐθρηνήσαμεν καὶ
to you and ye did not dance; we mourned and
οὐκ ἐκλαύσατε. **33** ἐλήλυθεν γὰρ Ἰωάννης
ye did not weep. For has come John
ὁ βαπτιστὴς μὴ ἐσθίων ἄρτον μήτε πίνων
the Baptist not eating bread nor drinking
οἶνον, καὶ λέγετε· δαιμόνιον ἔχει.
wine, and ye say: A demon he has.
34 ἐλήλυθεν ὁ υἱὸς τοῦ ἀνθρώπου ἐσθίων
Has come the Son – of man eating
καὶ πίνων, καὶ λέγετε· ἰδοὺ ἄνθρωπος
and drinking, and ye say: Behold[,] a man
φάγος καὶ οἰνοπότης, φίλος τελωνῶν καὶ
a glutton and a winebibber, a friend of tax-collectors and
ἁμαρτωλῶν. **35** καὶ ἐδικαιώθη ἡ σοφία
of sinners. And was(is) justified – wisdom
ἀπὸ πάντων τῶν τέκνων αὐτῆς.
from(by) all the children of her.
36 Ἠρώτα δέ τις αὐτὸν τῶν Φαρισαίων
And [4]asked [1]a certain one [5]him [2]of the [3]Pharisees
ἵνα φάγῃ μετ' αὐτοῦ· καὶ εἰσελθὼν εἰς
that he would eat with him; and entering into
τὸν οἶκον τοῦ Φαρισαίου κατεκλίθη. **37** καὶ
the house of the Pharisee he reclined. And[,]
ἰδοὺ γυνὴ ἥτις ἦν ἐν τῇ πόλει ἁμαρτωλός,
behold[,] a woman who was in the city a sinner,
καὶ ἐπιγνοῦσα ὅτι κατάκειται ἐν τῇ
and knowing that he reclines in the
οἰκίᾳ τοῦ Φαρισαίου, κομίσασα ἀλάβαστρον
house of the Pharisee, bringing an alabaster box
μύρου **38** καὶ στᾶσα ὀπίσω παρὰ τοὺς
of ointment and standing behind at the
πόδας αὐτοῦ κλαίουσα, τοῖς δάκρυσιν
feet of him weeping, with the(her) tears
ἤρξατο βρέχειν τοὺς πόδας αὐτοῦ, καὶ
began to wet the feet of him, and

" 'I will send my
messenger ahead of
you,
who will prepare your
way before you.'[d]
28 I tell you, among those
born of women there is no
one greater than John; yet
the one who is least in the
kingdom of God is greater
than he."
29 (All the people, even
the tax collectors, when
they heard Jesus' words,
acknowledged that God's
way was right, because
they had been baptized by
John. 30 But the Pharisees
and experts in the law rejected God's purpose for
themselves, because they
had not been baptized by
John.)
31 "To what, then, can I
compare the people of this
generation? What are they
like? 32 They are like children sitting in the marketplace and calling out to
each other:

" 'We played the flute
for you,
and you did not dance;
we sang a dirge,
and you did not cry.'

33 For John the Baptist
came neither eating bread
nor drinking wine, and you
say, 'He has a demon.'
34 The Son of Man came
eating and drinking, and
you say, 'Here is a glutton
and a drunkard, a friend of
tax collectors and "sin-
ners." ' 35 But wisdom is
proved right by all her children."

Jesus Anointed by a Sinful Woman

36 Now one of the Phari-
sees invited Jesus to have
dinner with him, so he went
to the Pharisee's house and
reclined at the table.
37 When a woman who had
lived a sinful life in that
town learned that Jesus
was eating at the Pharisee's
house, she brought an alabaster jar of perfume, 38 and
as she stood behind him at
his feet weeping, she began
to wet his feet with her

[d] 27 Mal. 3:1

Then she continued kissing
his feet and anointing them
with the ointment. 39 Now
when the Pharisee who had
invited him saw it, he said
to himself, "If this man
were a prophet, he would
have known who and what
kind of woman this is who
is touching him—that she
is a sinner." 40 Jesus spoke
up and said to him, "Simon,
I have something to say to
you." "Teacher," he re-
plied, "Speak." 41 "A certain creditor had two debtors; one owed five hundred
denarii,[h] and the other fifty. 42 When they could not
pay, he canceled the debts
for both of them. Now
which of them will love him
more?" 43 Simon answered,
"I suppose the one for
whom he canceled the
greater debt." And Jesus[b]
said to him, "You have
judged rightly." 44 Then
turning toward the woman,
he said to Simon, "Do you
see this woman? I entered
your house; you gave me
no water for my feet, but
she has bathed my feet with
her tears and dried them
with her hair. 45 You gave
me no kiss, but from the
time I came in she has not
stopped kissing my feet.
46 You did not anoint my
head with oil, but she has
anointed my feet with ointment. 47 Therefore, I tell
you, her sins, which were
many, have been forgiven;
hence she has shown great
love. But the one to whom
little is forgiven, loves little." 48 Then he said to her,
"Your sins are forgiven."
49 But those who were at
the table with him began to
say among themselves,
"Who is this who even for-

[h] The denarius was the usual day's wage for a laborer

ταῖς θριξὶν τῆς κεφαλῆς αὐτῆς ἐξέμασσεν,
with the hairs of the head of her wiped off,
καὶ κατεφίλει τοὺς πόδας αὐτοῦ καὶ
and fervently kissed the feet of him and
ἤλειφεν τῷ μύρῳ. 39 ἰδὼν δὲ ὁ Φαρισαῖος
anointed with the ointment. But [5]seeing [1]the [2]Pharisee
ὁ καλέσας αὐτὸν εἶπεν ἐν ἑαυτῷ λέγων·
– [3]having invited [4]him spoke within himself saying :
οὗτος εἰ ἦν [ὁ] προφήτης, ἐγίνωσκεν ἂν
This man if he was the prophet, would have known
τίς καὶ ποταπὴ ἡ γυνὴ ἥτις ἅπτεται
who and what sort the woman who is touching
αὐτοῦ, ὅτι ἁμαρτωλός ἐστιν. 40 καὶ
him, because a sinner she is. And
ἀποκριθεὶς ὁ Ἰησοῦς εἶπεν πρὸς αὐτόν·
answering – Jesus said to him :
Σίμων, ἔχω σοί τι εἰπεῖν. ὁ δέ· διδάσκαλε,
Simon, I have to thee something to say. And he : Teacher,
εἰπέ, φησίν. 41 δύο χρεοφειλέται ἦσαν
say, says. Two debtors were
=A certain creditor had two debtors;
δανειστῇ τινι· ὁ εἷς ὤφειλεν δηνάρια
creditor to a certain;[c] the one owed denarii
πεντακόσια, ὁ δὲ ἕτερος πεντήκοντα. 42 μὴ
five hundred, and the other fifty. Not
=As they had no[thing]
ἐχόντων αὐτῶν ἀποδοῦναι ἀμφοτέροις
having them[a] to repay [2]both
ἐχαρίσατο. τίς οὖν αὐτῶν πλεῖον ἀγαπήσει
[1]he freely forgave. Who then of them more will love
αὐτόν; 43 ἀποκριθεὶς Σίμων εἶπεν·
him? Answering Simon said :
ὑπολαμβάνω ὅτι ᾧ τὸ πλεῖον ἐχαρίσατο.
I suppose[,] – to whom the more he freely forgave.
ὁ δὲ εἶπεν αὐτῷ· ὀρθῶς ἔκρινας. 44 καὶ
And he said to him : Rightly thou didst judge. And
στραφεὶς πρὸς τὴν γυναῖκα τῷ Σίμωνι
turning to the woman – to Simon
ἔφη· βλέπεις ταύτην τὴν γυναῖκα; εἰσῆλθόν
he said : Seest thou this – woman? I entered
σου εἰς τὴν οἰκίαν, ὕδωρ μοι ἐπὶ πόδας
of thee into the house, water to me on(for) [my] feet
οὐκ ἔδωκας· αὕτη δὲ τοῖς δάκρυσιν
thou gavest not; but this woman with the(her) tears
ἔβρεξέν μου τοὺς πόδας καὶ ταῖς θριξὶν
wet of me the feet and with the hairs
αὐτῆς ἐξέμαξεν. 45 φίλημά μοι οὐκ ἔδωκας·
of her wiped off. A kiss to me thou gavest not;
αὕτη δὲ ἀφ' ἧς εἰσῆλθον οὐ διέλειπεν
but this woman from [the time] I entered ceased not
which
καταφιλοῦσά μου τοὺς πόδας. 46 ἐλαίῳ
fervently kissing of me the feet. With oil
τὴν κεφαλήν μου οὐκ ἤλειψας· αὕτη δὲ
the head of me thou didst not anoint; but this woman
μύρῳ ἤλειψεν τοὺς πόδας μου. 47 οὗ
with ointment anointed the feet of me. Of which
=Wherefore
χάριν λέγω σοι, ἀφέωνται αἱ ἁμαρτίαι
for the sake *of* I tell thee, [3]have been forgiven [1]the [2]sins
αὐτῆς αἱ πολλαί, ὅτι ἠγάπησεν πολύ·
[4]of her – [5]many, because she loved much;
ᾧ δὲ ὀλίγον ἀφίεται, ὀλίγον ἀγαπᾷ.
but to whom little is forgiven, little he loves.
48 εἶπεν δὲ αὐτῇ· ἀφέωνταί σου αἱ
And he said to her : Have been forgiven of thee the
ἁμαρτίαι. 49 καὶ ἤρξαντο οἱ συνανακείμενοι
sins. And began the [ones] reclining with [him]

tears. Then she wiped them
with her hair, kissed them
and poured perfume on
them.
39 When the Pharisee who
had invited him saw this, he
said to himself, "If this
man were a prophet, he
would know who is touch-
ing him and what kind of
woman she is—that she is a
sinner."
40 Jesus answered him,
"Simon, I have something
to tell you."
"Tell me, teacher," he
said.
41 "Two men owed money
to a certain moneylender.
One owed him five hundred
denarii,[e] and the other fifty. 42 Neither of them had
the money to pay him back,
so he canceled the debts of
both. Now which of them
will love him more?"
43 Simon replied, "I sup-
pose the one who had the
bigger debt canceled."
"You have judged cor-
rectly," Jesus said.
44 Then he turned toward
the woman and said to Si-
mon, "Do you see this
woman? I came into your
house. You did not give me
any water for my feet, but
she wet my feet with her
tears and wiped them with
her hair. 45 You did not give
me a kiss, but this woman,
from the time I entered, has
not stopped kissing my
feet. 46 You did not put oil
on my head, but she has
poured perfume on my
feet. 47 Therefore, I tell you,
her many sins have been
forgiven—for she loved
much. But he who has been
forgiven little loves little."
48 Then Jesus said to her,
"Your sins are forgiven."
49 The other guests began
to say among themselves,

[e] *41* A denarius was a coin worth about a day's wages.

gives sins?" 50And he said
to the woman, "Your faith
has saved you; go in
peace."

Chapter 8

Some Women Accompany Jesus

SOON afterwards he
went on through cities
and villages, proclaiming
and bringing the good news
of the kingdom of God. The
twelve were with him, 2as
well as some women who
had been cured of evil spirits and infirmities: Mary,
called Magdalene, from
whom seven demons had
gone out, 3and Joanna, the
wife of Herod's steward
Chuza, and Susanna, and
many others, who provided
for them[i] out of their resources.

The Parable of the Sower

4 When a great crowd
gathered and people from
town after town came to
him, he said in a parable:
5"A sower went out to sow
his seed; and as he sowed,
some fell on the path and
was trampled on, and the
birds of the air ate it up.
6Some fell on the rock; and
as it grew up, it withered
for lack of moisture. 7Some
fell among thorns, and the
thorns grew with it and
choked it. 8Some fell into
good soil, and when it
grew, it produced a hun-
dredfold." As he said this,
he called out, "Let anyone
with ears to hear listen!"

[i]Other ancient authorities read *him*

λέγειν ἐν ἑαυτοῖς· τίς οὗτός ἐστιν, ὃς καὶ
to say among themselves : Who this is, who even
ἁμαρτίας ἀφίησιν; **50** εἶπεν δὲ πρὸς τὴν
sins forgives? But he said to the
γυναῖκα· ἡ πίστις σου σέσωκέν σε·
woman : The faith of thee has saved thee;
πορεύου εἰς εἰρήνην.
go in peace.

8 Καὶ ἐγένετο ἐν τῷ καθεξῆς καὶ αὐτὸς
And it came to pass afterwards *and* he
διώδευεν κατὰ πόλιν καὶ κώμην κηρύσσων
journeyed through every† city and village proclaiming
καὶ εὐαγγελιζόμενος τὴν βασιλείαν τοῦ
and preaching the kingdom –
θεοῦ, καὶ οἱ δώδεκα σὺν αὐτῷ, **2** καὶ
of God, and the twelve with him, and
γυναῖκές τινες αἳ ἦσαν τεθεραπευμέναι ἀπὸ
women certain who were having been healed from
πνευμάτων πονηρῶν καὶ ἀσθενειῶν, Μαρία
spirits evil and infirmities, Mary
ἡ καλουμένη Μαγδαληνή, ἀφ' ἧς δαιμόνια
– *being* called Magdalene, from whom demons
ἑπτὰ ἐξεληλύθει, **3** καὶ Ἰωάννα γυνὴ Χουζᾶ
seven had gone out, and Joanna wife of Chuza
ἐπιτρόπου Ἡρῴδου καὶ Σουσάννα καὶ
steward of Herod and Susanna and
ἕτεραι πολλαί, αἵτινες διηκόνουν αὐτοῖς
others many, who ministered to them
ἐκ τῶν ὑπαρχόντων αὐταῖς.
out of the possessions to them.[c]

4 Συνιόντος δὲ ὄχλου πολλοῦ καὶ τῶν
And coming together crowd a much and the [ones]
=when a great crowd came together and people in each city
κατὰ πόλιν ἐπιπορευομένων πρὸς αὐτὸν
in each city† resorting[a] to him
resorted
εἶπεν διὰ παραβολῆς· **5** ἐξῆλθεν ὁ σπείρων
he said by a parable : Went forth the [one] sowing
τοῦ σπεῖραι τὸν σπόρον αὐτοῦ. καὶ ἐν τῷ
– to sow[d] the seed of him. And in the
σπείρειν αὐτὸν ὃ μὲν ἔπεσεν παρὰ τὴν
to sow him[be] this fell by the
=as he sowed
ὁδὸν καὶ κατεπατήθη, καὶ τὰ πετεινὰ τοῦ
way and was trodden down, and the birds of the
οὐρανοῦ κατέφαγεν αὐτό. **6** καὶ ἕτερον
heaven(air) devoured it. And other [seed]
κατέπεσεν ἐπὶ τὴν πέτραν, καὶ φυὲν
fell on the rock, and grown
ἐξηράνθη διὰ τὸ μὴ ἔχειν ἰκμάδα.
it was withered because of the not to have moisture.
=because it had no moisture.
7 καὶ ἕτερον ἔπεσεν ἐν μέσῳ τῶν ἀκανθῶν, καὶ
And other fell in [the] midst of the thorns, and
συμφυεῖσαι αἱ ἄκανθαι ἀπέπνιξαν αὐτό.
growing up with [it] the thorns choked it.
8 καὶ ἕτερον ἔπεσεν εἰς τὴν γῆν τὴν
And other fell in the soil –
ἀγαθὴν καὶ φυὲν ἐποίησεν καρπὸν
good and grown it produced fruit
ἑκατονταπλασίονα. ταῦτα λέγων ἐφώνει· ὁ
a hundredfold. These things saying he called: The [one]
ἔχων ὦτα ἀκούειν ἀκουέτω. **9** Ἐπηρώτων δὲ
having ears to hear let him hear. And questioned

"Who is this who even forgives sins?"
50Jesus said to the wom-
an, "Your faith has saved
you; go in peace."

Chapter 8

The Parable of the Sower

AFTER this, Jesus trav-
eled about from one
town and village to another, proclaiming the good
news of the kingdom of
God. The Twelve were
with him, 2and also some
women who had been
cured of evil spirits and diseases: Mary (called Magdalene) from whom seven de-
mons had come out; 3Joan-
na the wife of Cuza, the
manager of Herod's house-
hold; Susanna; and many
others. These women were
helping to support them out
of their own means.
4While a large crowd was
gathering and people were
coming to Jesus from town
after town, he told this parable: 5"A farmer went out
to sow his seed. As he was
scattering the seed, some
fell along the path; it was
trampled on, and the birds
of the air ate it up. 6Some
fell on rock, and when it
came up, the plants with-
ered because they had no
moisture. 7Other seed fell
among thorns, which grew
up with it and choked the
plants. 8Still other seed fell
on good soil. It came up
and yielded a crop, a hundred times more than was
sown."
When he said this, he
called out, "He who has
ears to hear, let him hear."

The Purpose of the Parables

9 Then his disciples
asked him what this para-
ble meant. 10 He said, "To
you it has been given to
know the secrets[j] of the
kingdom of God; but to others I speak[k] in parables, so
that
'looking they may not
perceive,
and listening they
may not
understand.'

The Parable of the Sower Explained

11 "Now the parable is
this: The seed is the word
of God. 12 The ones on the
path are those who have
heard; then the devil comes
and takes away the word
from their hearts, so that
they may not believe and
be saved. 13 The ones on
the rock are those who,
when they hear the word,
receive it with joy. But
these have no root; they believe only for a while and in
a time of testing fall away.
14 As for what fell among
the thorns, these are the
ones who hear; but as they
go on their way, they are
choked by the cares and
riches and pleasures of life,
and their fruit does not mature. 15 But as for that in the
good soil, these are the
ones who, when they hear
the word, hold it fast in an
honest and good heart, and
bear fruit with patient endurance.

A Lamp under a Jar

16 "No one after light-
ing a lamp hides it under a
jar, or puts it under a bed,
but puts it on a lampstand,
so that those who enter
may see the light. 17 For
nothing is hidden that will
not be disclosed, nor is
anything secret that will
not become known and
come to light. 18 Then pay
attention to how you listen;
for to those who have,
more will be given; and
from those who do not
have, even what they seem
to have will be taken
away."

The True Kindred of Jesus

19 Then his mother and
his brothers came to him,

[j] Or *mysteries*
[k] Gk lacks *I speak*

αὐτὸν οἱ μαθηταὶ αὐτοῦ τίς αὕτη εἴη ἡ
him the disciples of him what [1]this [3]might be –
παραβολή. 10 ὁ δὲ εἶπεν· ὑμῖν δέδοται
[2]parable. And he said : To you it has been given
γνῶναι τὰ μυστήρια τῆς βασιλείας τοῦ
to know the mysteries of the kingdom –
θεοῦ, τοῖς δὲ λοιποῖς ἐν παραβολαῖς, ἵνα
of God, but to the rest in parables, that
βλέποντες μὴ βλέπωσιν καὶ ἀκούοντες μὴ
seeing they may not see and hearing not
συνιῶσιν. 11 ἔστιν δὲ αὕτη ἡ παραβολή.
they may understand. [4]is [1]Now [2]this – [3]parable.
ὁ σπόρος ἐστὶν ὁ λόγος τοῦ θεοῦ.
The seed is the word – of God.
12 οἱ δὲ παρὰ τὴν ὁδόν εἰσιν οἱ ἀκούσαντες,
And the [ones] by the way are the [ones] hearing,
εἶτα ἔρχεται ὁ διάβολος καὶ αἴρει τὸν
then comes the devil and takes the
λόγον ἀπὸ τῆς καρδίας αὐτῶν, ἵνα μὴ
word from the heart of them, lest
πιστεύσαντες σωθῶσιν. 13 οἱ δὲ ἐπὶ τῆς
believing they may be saved. And the [ones] on the
πέτρας οἳ ὅταν ἀκούσωσιν μετὰ χαρᾶς
rock who when they hear with joy
δέχονται τὸν λόγον· καὶ οὗτοι ῥίζαν
receive the word; and these root
οὐκ ἔχουσιν, οἳ πρὸς καιρὸν πιστεύουσιν
have not, who for a time believe
καὶ ἐν καιρῷ πειρασμοῦ ἀφίστανται. 14 τὸ
and in time of trial withdraw. the [one]
δὲ εἰς τὰς ἀκάνθας πεσόν, οὗτοί εἰσιν
And in the thorns falling, these are
οἱ ἀκούσαντες, καὶ ὑπὸ μεριμνῶν καὶ
the [ones] hearing, [1]and [4]by [5]cares [6]and
πλούτου καὶ ἡδονῶν τοῦ βίου πορευόμενοι
[7]riches [8]and [9]pleasures – [10]of life [2]going
συμπνίγονται καὶ οὐ τελεσφοροῦσιν. 15 τὸ
[3]are choked and do not bear [fruit] to maturity. the [one]
δὲ ἐν τῇ καλῇ γῇ, οὗτοί εἰσιν οἵτινες ἐν
And in the good soil, these are [those] who in
καρδίᾳ καλῇ καὶ ἀγαθῇ ἀκούσαντες τὸν
heart a worthy and good hearing the
λόγον κατέχουσιν καὶ καρποφοροῦσιν ἐν
word hold fast and bear fruit in
ὑπομονῇ. 16 Οὐδεὶς δὲ λύχνον ἅψας
patience. Now no one a lamp having lit
καλύπτει αὐτὸν σκεύει ἢ ὑποκάτω κλίνης
hides it with a vessel or underneath a couch
τίθησιν, ἀλλ᾽ ἐπὶ λυχνίας τίθησιν, ἵνα οἱ
puts, but on a lampstand puts, that the
εἰσπορευόμενοι βλέπωσιν τὸ φῶς. 17 οὐ
[ones] coming in may see the light. not
γάρ ἐστιν κρυπτὸν ὃ οὐ φανερὸν
For [anything] is hidden which [3]not [4]manifest
γενήσεται, οὐδὲ ἀπόκρυφον ὃ οὐ μὴ
[1]will [2]become, nor secret which by no means
γνωσθῇ καὶ εἰς φανερὸν ἔλθῃ. 18 βλέπετε
will be known and to [be] manifest come. See
οὖν πῶς ἀκούετε· ὃς ἂν γὰρ ἔχῃ,
therefore how ye hear; for whoever has,
δοθήσεται αὐτῷ· καὶ ὃς ἂν μὴ ἔχῃ,
it will be given to him; and whoever has not,
καὶ ὃ δοκεῖ ἔχειν ἀρθήσεται ἀπ᾽ αὐτοῦ.
even what he seems to have will be taken from him.
19 Παρεγένετο δὲ πρὸς αὐτὸν ἡ μήτηρ
And came to him the mother

9 His disciples asked him
what this parable meant.
10 He said, "The knowledge
of the secrets of the kingdom of God has been given
to you, but to others I
speak in parables, so that,

" 'though seeing, they
may not see;
though hearing, they
may not
understand.'[f]

11 "This is the meaning of
the parable: The seed is the
word of God. 12 Those along
the path are the ones who
hear, and then the devil
comes and takes away the
word from their hearts, so
that they may not believe
and be saved. 13 Those on
the rock are the ones who
receive the word with joy
when they hear it, but they
have no root. They believe
for a while, but in the time
of testing they fall away.
14 The seed that fell among
thorns stands for those who
hear, but as they go on their
way they are choked by
life's worries, riches and
pleasures, and they do not
mature. 15 But the seed on
good soil stands for those
with a noble and good
heart, who hear the word,
retain it, and by persever-
ing produce a crop.

A Lamp on a Stand

16 "No one lights a lamp
and hides it in a jar or puts it
under a bed. Instead, he
puts it on a stand, so that
those who come in can see
the light. 17 For there is
nothing hidden that will not
be disclosed, and nothing
concealed that will not be
known or brought out into
the open. 18 Therefore consider carefully how you listen. Whoever has will be
given more; whoever does
not have, even what he
thinks he has will be taken
from him."

Jesus' Mother and Brothers

19 Now Jesus' mother and
brothers came to see him,

[f] 10 Isaiah 6:9

but they could not reach
him because of the crowd.
20 And he was told, "Your
mother and your brothers
are standing outside, wanting to see you." 21 But he
said to them, "My mother
and my brothers are those
who hear the word of God
and do it."

Jesus Calms a Storm

22 One day he got into a
boat with his disciples, and
he said to them, "Let us go
across to the other side of
the lake." So they put out,
23 and while they were sailing he fell asleep. A windstorm swept down on the
lake, and the boat was filling with water, and they
were in danger. 24 They
went to him and woke him
up, shouting, "Master,
Master, we are perishing!"
And he woke up and re-
buked the wind and the raging waves; they ceased,
and there was a calm. 25 He
said to them, "Where is
your faith?" They were
afraid and amazed, and
said to one another, "Who
then is this, that he commands even the winds and
the water, and they obey
him?"

Jesus Heals the Gerasene Demoniac

26 Then they arrived at
the country of the Gera-
senes,[l] which is opposite
Galilee. 27 As he stepped
out on land, a man of the
city who had demons met
him. For a long time he had
worn[m] no clothes, and he
did not live in a house but in
the tombs. 28 When he saw
Jesus, he fell down before
him and shouted at the top
of his voice, "What have
you to do with me, Jesus,
Son of the Most High God?
I beg you, do not torment

[l] Other ancient authorities read *Gadarenes*; others, *Gergesenes*
[m] Other ancient authorities read *a man of the city who had had demons for a long time met him. He wore*

καὶ οἱ ἀδελφοὶ αὐτοῦ, καὶ οὐκ ἠδύναντο
and the brothers of him, and were not able
συντυχεῖν αὐτῷ διὰ τὸν ὄχλον. 20 ἀπηγγέλη δὲ
to come up with him be- cause of the crowd. And it was reported
αὐτῷ· ἡ μήτηρ σου καὶ οἱ ἀδελφοί σου
to him: The mother of thee and the brothers of thee
ἑστήκασιν ἔξω ἰδεῖν θέλοντές σε. 21 ὁ δὲ
are standing outside [2]to see [1]wishing thee. But he
ἀποκριθεὶς εἶπεν πρὸς αὐτούς· μήτηρ μου
answering said to them: Mother of me
καὶ ἀδελφοί μου οὗτοί εἰσιν οἱ τὸν λόγον
and brothers of me [2]these [1]are [3]the [ones] [7]the [8]word
τοῦ θεοῦ ἀκούοντες καὶ ποιοῦντες.
– [9]of God [4]hearing [5]and [6]doing.
22 Ἐγένετο δὲ ἐν μιᾷ τῶν ἡμερῶν καὶ
And it came to pass on one of the days *and*
αὐτὸς ἐνέβη εἰς πλοῖον καὶ οἱ μαθηταὶ
he embarked in a boat and the disciples
αὐτοῦ, καὶ εἶπεν πρὸς αὐτούς· διέλθωμεν
of him, and he said to them; Let us go over
εἰς τὸ πέραν τῆς λίμνης· καὶ ἀνήχθησαν.
to the other side of the lake; and they put to sea.
23 πλεόντων δὲ αὐτῶν ἀφύπνωσεν. καὶ
And sailing =as they sailed them[a] he fell asleep. And
κατέβη λαῖλαψ ἀνέμου εἰς τὴν λίμνην, καὶ
came down a storm of wind to the lake, and
συνεπληροῦντο καὶ ἐκινδύνευον. 24 προσ-
they were filling up and were in danger. ap-
ελθόντες δὲ διήγειραν αὐτὸν λέγοντες·
proaching And they awoke him saying:
ἐπιστάτα ἐπιστάτα, ἀπολλύμεθα. ὁ δὲ
Master[,] Master, we are perishing. But he
διεγερθεὶς ἐπετίμησεν τῷ ἀνέμῳ καὶ τῷ
being awakened rebuked the wind and the
κλύδωνι τοῦ ὕδατος· καὶ ἐπαύσαντο, καὶ ἐγένετο
roughness of the water; and they ceased, and there was
γαλήνη. 25 εἶπεν δὲ αὐτοῖς· ποῦ ἡ πίστις ὑμῶν;
a calm. Then he said to them: Where the faith of you?
φοβηθέντες δὲ ἐθαύμασαν, λέγοντες πρὸς
And fearing they marvelled, saying to
ἀλλήλους· τίς ἄρα οὗτός ἐστιν, ὅτι καὶ
one another: Who then [2]this man [1]is, that [3]even
τοῖς ἀνέμοις ἐπιτάσσει καὶ τῷ ὕδατι, καὶ
[5]the [6]winds [4]he commands and the water, and
ὑπακούουσιν αὐτῷ; 26 Καὶ κατέπλευσαν εἰς
they obey him? And they sailed down to
τὴν χώραν τῶν Γερασηνῶν, ἥτις ἐστὶν
the country of the Gerasenes, which is
ἀντιπέρα τῆς Γαλιλαίας. 27 ἐξελθόντι δὲ
opposite – Galilee. And going out =as he went out
αὐτῷ ἐπὶ τὴν γῆν ὑπήντησεν ἀνήρ τις
him[e] onto the land met [him] man a certain
ἐκ τῆς πόλεως ἔχων δαιμόνια, καὶ χρόνῳ
out of the city having demons, and [2]time
ἱκανῷ οὐκ ἐνεδύσατο ἱμάτιον, καὶ ἐν οἰκίᾳ
[1]for a considerable put not on a garment, and in a house
οὐκ ἔμενεν ἀλλ' ἐν τοῖς μνήμασιν. 28 ἰδὼν
remained not but among the tombs. seeing
δὲ τὸν Ἰησοῦν ἀνακράξας προσέπεσεν αὐτῷ
And – Jesus crying out he fell prostrate before him
καὶ φωνῇ μεγάλῃ εἶπεν· τί ἐμοὶ καὶ σοί,
and voice in a great(loud) said: What to me and to thee,
Ἰησοῦ υἱὲ τοῦ θεοῦ τοῦ ὑψίστου; δέομαί
Jesus Son – of God – most high? I beg

but they were not able to
get near him because of the
crowd. 20 Someone told
him, "Your mother and
brothers are standing outside, wanting to see you."
21 He replied, "My moth-
er and brothers are those
who hear God's word and
put it into practice."

Jesus Calms the Storm

22 One day Jesus said to
his disciples, "Let's go
over to the other side of the
lake." So they got into a
boat and set out. 23 As they
sailed, he fell asleep. A
squall came down on the
lake, so that the boat was
being swamped, and they
were in great danger.
24 The disciples went and
woke him, saying, "Mas-
ter, Master, we're going to
drown!"
He got up and rebuked
the wind and the raging waters; the storm subsided,
and all was calm. 25 "Where
is your faith?" he asked his
disciples.
In fear and amazement
they asked one another,
"Who is this? He com-
mands even the winds and
the water, and they obey
him."

The Healing of a Demon-possessed Man

26 They sailed to the re-
gion of the Gerasenes,[g]
which is across the lake
from Galilee. 27 When Jesus
stepped ashore, he was met
by a demon-possessed man
from the town. For a long
time this man had not worn
clothes or lived in a house,
but had lived in the tombs.
28 When he saw Jesus, he
cried out and fell at his feet,
shouting at the top of his
voice, "What do you want
with me, Jesus, Son of the
Most High God? I beg you,

[g] 26 Some manuscripts *Gadarenes*; other manuscripts *Gergesenes*; also in verse 37

me"— 29for Jesus[n] had commanded the unclean spirit to come out of the man. (For many times it had seized him; he was kept under guard and bound with chains and shackles, but he would break the bonds and be driven by the demon into the wilds.) 30Jesus then asked him, "What is your name?" He said, "Legion"; for many demons had entered him. 31They begged him not to order them to go back into the abyss.

32 Now there on the hillside a large herd of swine was feeding; and the demons[o] begged Jesus[p] to let them enter these. So he gave them permission. 33Then the demons came out of the man and entered the swine, and the herd rushed down the steep bank into the lake and was drowned.

34 When the swineherds saw what had happened, they ran off and told it in the city and in the country. 35Then people came out to see what had happened, and when they came to Jesus, they found the man from whom the demons had gone sitting at the feet of Jesus, clothed and in his right mind. And they were afraid. 36Those who had seen it told them how the one who had been possessed by demons had been healed. 37Then all the people of the surrounding country of the Gerasenes[l] asked Jesus[p] to leave them; for they were seized with great fear. So he got into the boat and returned.

[n] Gk *he*
[o] Gk *they*
[p] Gk *him*

σου, μή με βασανίσῃς. 29 παρήγγελλεν
of thee, do not me torment. he charged

γὰρ τῷ πνεύματι τῷ ἀκαθάρτῳ ἐξελθεῖν
For the spirit – unclean to come out

ἀπὸ τοῦ ἀνθρώπου. πολλοῖς γὰρ χρόνοις
from the man. For many times

συνηρπάκει αὐτόν, καὶ ἐδεσμεύετο ἁλύσεσιν
it had seized him, and he was bound with chains

καὶ πέδαις φυλασσόμενος, καὶ διαρήσσων
and fetters being guarded, and tearing asunder

τὰ δεσμὰ ἠλαύνετο ἀπὸ τοῦ δαιμονίου εἰς
the bonds he was driven from(by) the demon into

τὰς ἐρήμους. 30 ἐπηρώτησεν δὲ αὐτὸν ὁ
the deserts. And questioned him. –

Ἰησοῦς· τί σοι ὄνομά ἐστιν; ὁ δὲ εἶπεν·
Jesus : What to thee name is?[c] And he said :

λεγιών, ὅτι εἰσῆλθεν δαιμόνια πολλὰ εἰς
Legion, because [3]entered [2]demons [1]many into

αὐτόν. 31 καὶ παρεκάλουν αὐτὸν ἵνα μὴ
him. And they besought him that not

ἐπιτάξῃ αὐτοῖς εἰς τὴν ἄβυσσον ἀπελθεῖν.
he would order them into the abyss to go away.

32 ἦν δὲ ἐκεῖ ἀγέλη χοίρων ἱκανῶν
Now there was there a herd pigs of many

βοσκομένη ἐν τῷ ὄρει· καὶ παρεκάλεσαν
feeding in the mountain; and they besought

αὐτὸν ἵνα ἐπιτρέψῃ αὐτοῖς εἰς ἐκείνους
him that he would allow them into those

εἰσελθεῖν· καὶ ἐπέτρεψεν αὐτοῖς. 33 ἐξελθόντα
to enter; and he allowed them. [4]coming out

δὲ τὰ δαιμόνια ἀπὸ τοῦ ἀνθρώπου εἰσῆλθον
[1]So [2]the [3]demons from the man entered

εἰς τοὺς χοίρους, καὶ ὥρμησεν ἡ ἀγέλη
into the pigs, and rushed the herd

κατὰ τοῦ κρημνοῦ εἰς τὴν λίμνην καὶ
down the precipice into the lake and

ἀπεπνίγη. 34 ἰδόντες δὲ οἱ βόσκοντες
was choked. And [3]seeing [1]the [ones] [2]feeding

τὸ γεγονὸς ἔφυγον καὶ ἀπήγγειλαν εἰς
[4]the thing [5]having happened fled and reported in
=what had happened

τὴν πόλιν καὶ εἰς τοὺς ἀγρούς. 35 ἐξῆλθον
the city and in the farms they went out

δὲ ἰδεῖν τὸ γεγονός, καὶ ἦλθον πρὸς τὸν
And to see the thing having happened, and came to –
=what had happened,

Ἰησοῦν, καὶ εὗρον καθήμενον τὸν ἄνθρωπον
Jesus, and found sitting the man

ἀφ' οὗ τὰ δαιμόνια ἐξῆλθεν ἱματισμένον
from whom the demons went out having been clothed

καὶ σωφρονοῦντα παρὰ τοὺς πόδας τοῦ
and being in his senses by the feet –

Ἰησοῦ, καὶ ἐφοβήθησαν. 36 ἀπήγγειλαν δὲ
of Jesus, and they were afraid. And [3]reported

αὐτοῖς οἱ ἰδόντες πῶς ἐσώθη ὁ δαιμο-
[4]to them [1]the [ones] [2]seeing [5]how [6]was healed [6]the [7]demon-

νισθείς. 37 καὶ ἠρώτησεν αὐτὸν ἅπαν τὸ
possessed. And asked him all the

πλῆθος τῆς περιχώρου τῶν Γερασηνῶν
multitude of the neighbourhood of the Gerasenes

ἀπελθεῖν ἀπ' αὐτῶν, ὅτι φόβῳ μεγάλῳ
to go away from them, because fear with a great

συνείχοντο· αὐτὸς δὲ ἐμβὰς εἰς πλοῖον
they were seized; so he embarking in a boat

don't torture me!" 29For Jesus had commanded the evil[h] spirit to come out of the man. Many times it had seized him, and though he was chained hand and foot and kept under guard, he had broken his chains and had been driven by the demon into solitary places.

30Jesus asked him, "What is your name?"

"Legion," he replied, because many demons had gone into him. 31And they begged him repeatedly not to order them to go into the Abyss.

32A large herd of pigs was feeding there on the hillside. The demons begged Jesus to let them go into them, and he gave them permission. 33When the demons came out of the man, they went into the pigs, and the herd rushed down the steep bank into the lake and was drowned.

34When those tending the pigs saw what had happened, they ran off and reported this in the town and countryside, 35and the people went out to see what had happened. When they came to Jesus, they found the man from whom the demons had gone out, sitting at Jesus' feet, dressed and in his right mind; and they were afraid. 36Those who had seen it told the people how the demon-possessed man had been cured. 37Then all the people of the region of the Gerasenes asked Jesus to leave them, because they were overcome with fear. So he got into the boat and left.

[h]29 Greek *unclean*

[38]The man from whom the
demons had gone begged
that he might be with him;
but Jesus[n] sent him away,
saying, [39]"Return to your
home, and declare how
much God has done for
you." So he went away,
proclaiming throughout the
city how much Jesus had
done for him.

A Girl Restored to Life and a Woman Healed

40 Now when Jesus re-
turned, the crowd wel-
comed him, for they were
all waiting for him. [41]Just
then there came a man
named Jairus, a leader of
the synagogue. He fell at
Jesus' feet and begged him
to come to his house, [42]for
he had an only daughter,
about twelve years old,
who was dying.
As he went, the crowds
pressed in on him. [43]Now
there was a woman who
had been suffering from
hemorrhages for twelve
years; and though she had
spent all she had on physicians,[q] no one could cure
her. [44]She came up behind
him and touched the fringe
of his clothes, and immediately her hemorrhage
stopped. [45]Then Jesus
asked, "Who touched me?"
When all denied it, Peter[r]
said, "Master, the crowds
surround you and press in
on you." [46]But Jesus said,
"Someone touched me; for
I noticed that power had
gone out from me."
[47]When the woman saw
that she could not remain
hidden, she came trem-
bling; and falling down before him, she declared in
the presence of all the people why she had touched
him, and how she had been

[q] Other ancient authorities lack *and had spent all she had on physicians*

[r] Other ancient authorities add *and those who were with him*

ὑπέστρεψεν. **38** ἐδεῖτο δὲ αὐτοῦ ὁ ἀνὴρ
returned. And begged of him the man

ἀφ' οὗ ἐξεληλύθει τὰ δαιμόνια εἶναι σὺν
from whom had gone out the demons to be with

αὐτῷ· ἀπέλυσεν δὲ αὐτὸν λέγων· **39** ὑπόστρεφε
him; but he dismissed him saying : Return

εἰς τὸν οἶκόν σου, καὶ διηγοῦ ὅσα σοι
to the house of thee, and relate what things [a]to thee

ἐποίησεν ὁ θεός. καὶ ἀπῆλθεν καθ' ὅλην
[a]did – [1]God. And he went away throughout all

τὴν πόλιν κηρύσσων ὅσα ἐποίησεν αὐτῷ
the city proclaiming what things [a]did [a]to him

ὁ Ἰησοῦς.
– [1]Jesus.

40 Ἐν δὲ τῷ ὑποστρέφειν τὸν Ἰησοῦν
Now in the to return – Jesus[be]
=when Jesus returned

ἀπεδέξατο αὐτὸν ὁ ὄχλος· ἦσαν γὰρ
welcomed him the crowd; for they were

πάντες προσδοκῶντες αὐτόν. **41** καὶ ἰδοὺ
all expecting him. And behold

ἦλθεν ἀνὴρ ᾧ ὄνομα Ἰάϊρος, καὶ οὗτος
came a man to whom name Jairus,[c] and this man

ἄρχων τῆς συναγωγῆς ὑπῆρχεν· καὶ πεσὼν
a ruler of the synagogue was; and falling

παρὰ τοὺς πόδας Ἰησοῦ παρεκάλει αὐτὸν
at the feet of Jesus he besought him

εἰσελθεῖν εἰς τὸν οἶκον αὐτοῦ, **42** ὅτι
to enter into the house of him, because

θυγάτηρ μονογενὴς ἦν αὐτῷ ὡς ἐτῶν
daughter an only born was to him[c] about of years
=he had an only daughter

δώδεκα καὶ αὕτη ἀπέθνῃσκεν. Ἐν δὲ τῷ
twelve and this(she) was dying. Now in the
=as he went

ὑπάγειν αὐτὸν οἱ ὄχλοι συνέπνιγον αὐτόν.
to go him[be] the crowds pressed upon him.

43 καὶ γυνὴ οὖσα ἐν ῥύσει αἵματος ἀπὸ
And a woman being in a flow of blood from
=having

ἐτῶν δώδεκα, ἥτις οὐκ ἴσχυσεν ἀπ'
years twelve, who was not able from

οὐδενὸς θεραπευθῆναι, **44** προσελθοῦσα ὄπισθεν
no(any)one to be healed, approaching behind

ἥψατο τοῦ κρασπέδου τοῦ ἱματίου αὐτοῦ,
touched the fringe of the garment of him,

καὶ παραχρῆμα ἔστη ἡ ῥύσις τοῦ αἵματος
and at once stood the flow of the blood

αὐτῆς. **45** καὶ εἶπεν ὁ Ἰησοῦς· τίς ὁ
of her. And said – Jesus : Who the

ἁψάμενός μου; ἀρνουμένων δὲ πάντων
[one] touching me? And denying all[a]
=when all denied

εἶπεν ὁ Πέτρος· ἐπιστάτα, οἱ ὄχλοι
said – Peter : Master, the crowds

συνέχουσίν σε καὶ ἀποθλίβουσιν. **46** ὁ δὲ
press upon thee and jostle. – But

Ἰησοῦς εἶπεν· ἥψατό μού τις· ἐγὼ γὰρ
Jesus said : Touched me someone; for I

ἔγνων δύναμιν ἐξεληλυθυῖαν ἀπ' ἐμοῦ.
knew power having gone forth from me.

47 ἰδοῦσα δὲ ἡ γυνὴ ὅτι οὐκ ἔλαθεν,
And [3]seeing [1]the [2]woman that she was not hidden,

τρέμουσα ἦλθεν καὶ προσπεσοῦσα αὐτῷ δι'
trembling came and prostrating before him [6]for

ἣν αἰτίαν ἥψατο αὐτοῦ ἀπήγγειλεν ἐνώπιον
[7]what [8]cause [9]she touched [10]him [1]declared [3]before

[38]The man from whom
the demons had gone out
begged to go with him, but
Jesus sent him away, say-
ing, [39]"Return home and
tell how much God has
done for you." So the man
went away and told all over
town how much Jesus had
done for him.

A Dead Girl and a Sick Woman

[40]Now when Jesus re-
turned, a crowd welcomed
him, for they were all expecting him. [41]Then a man
named Jairus, a ruler of the
synagogue, came and fell at
Jesus' feet, pleading with
him to come to his house
[42]because his only daughter, a girl of about twelve,
was dying.
As Jesus was on his way,
the crowds almost crushed
him. [43]And a woman was
there who had been subject
to bleeding for twelve
years,[i] but no one could
heal her. [44]She came up behind him and touched the
edge of his cloak, and immediately her bleeding
stopped.
[45]"Who touched me?"
Jesus asked.
When they all denied it,
Peter said, "Master, the
people are crowding and
pressing against you."
[46]But Jesus said, "Someone touched me; I know
that power has gone out
from me."
[47]Then the woman, see-
ing that she could not go
unnoticed, came trembling
and fell at his feet. In the
presence of all the people,
she told why she had
touched him and how she

[i]43 Many manuscripts *years, and she had spent all she had on doctors*

immediately healed. 48 He
said to her, "Daughter,
your faith has made you
well; go in peace."
49 While he was still
speaking, someone came
from the leader's house to
say, "Your daughter is
dead; do not trouble the
teacher any longer."
50 When Jesus heard this,
he replied, "Do not fear.
Only believe, and she will
be saved." 51 When he
came to the house, he did
not allow anyone to enter
with him, except Peter,
John, and James, and the
child's father and mother.
52 They were all weeping
and wailing for her; but he
said, "Do not weep; for she
is not dead but sleeping."
53 And they laughed at him,
knowing that she was dead.
54 But he took her by the
hand and called out,
"Child, get up!" 55 Her spirit returned, and she got up
at once. Then he directed
them to give her something
to eat. 56 Her parents were
astounded; but he ordered
them to tell no one what
had happened.

Chapter 9

The Mission of the Twelve

THEN Jesus[n] called the
twelve together and
gave them power and au-
thority over all demons and
to cure diseases, 2 and he
sent them out to proclaim
the kingdom of God and to
heal. 3 He said to them,
"Take nothing for your
journey, no staff, nor bag,
nor bread, nor money—not
even an extra tunic. 4 What-

παντὸς τοῦ λαοῦ, καὶ ὡς ἰάθη παραχρῆμα.
[3]all [4]the [5]people, and how she was cured at once.
48 ὁ δὲ εἶπεν αὐτῇ· θυγάτηρ, ἡ πίστις
And he said to her : Daughter, the faith
σου σέσωκέν σε· πορεύου εἰς εἰρήνην.
of thee has healed thee; go in peace.
49 Ἔτι αὐτοῦ λαλοῦντος ἔρχεταί τις παρὰ
Yet him speaking[a] comes someone from
[a]=While he was yet speaking
τοῦ ἀρχισυναγώγου λέγων ὅτι τέθνηκεν
the synagogue ruler saying[,] – Has died
ἡ θυγάτηρ σου· μηκέτι σκύλλε τὸν
the daughter of thee; no more trouble the
διδάσκαλον. 50 ὁ δὲ Ἰησοῦς ἀκούσας
teacher. – But Jesus hearing
ἀπεκρίθη αὐτῷ· μὴ φοβοῦ· μόνον πίστευσον,
answered him : Fear thou not; only believe,
καὶ σωθήσεται. 51 ἐλθὼν δὲ εἰς τὴν
and she will be healed. And coming into the
οἰκίαν οὐκ ἀφῆκεν εἰσελθεῖν τινα σὺν
house he allowed not to enter anyone with
αὐτῷ εἰ μὴ Πέτρον καὶ Ἰωάννην καὶ
him except Peter and John and
Ἰάκωβον καὶ τὸν πατέρα τῆς παιδὸς καὶ
James and the father of the maid and
τὴν μητέρα. 52 ἔκλαιον δὲ πάντες καὶ
the mother. And were weeping all and
ἐκόπτοντο αὐτήν. ὁ δὲ εἶπεν· μὴ κλαίετε·
bewailing her. But he said : Weep ye not;
οὐκ ἀπέθανεν ἀλλὰ καθεύδει. 53 καὶ
she did not die but sleeps. And
κατεγέλων αὐτοῦ, εἰδότες ὅτι ἀπέθανεν.
they ridiculed him, knowing that she died.
54 αὐτὸς δὲ κρατήσας τῆς χειρὸς αὐτῆς
But he holding the hand of her
ἐφώνησεν λέγων· ἡ παῖς, ἔγειρε. 55 καὶ
called saying : – Maid, arise. And
ἐπέστρεψεν τὸ πνεῦμα αὐτῆς, καὶ ἀνέστη
returned the spirit of her, and she rose up
παραχρῆμα, καὶ διέταξεν αὐτῇ δοθῆναι
at once, and he commanded [2]to her [1]to be given
φαγεῖν. 56 καὶ ἐξέστησαν οἱ γονεῖς
to eat. And were amazed the parents
αὐτῆς· ὁ δὲ παρήγγειλεν αὐτοῖς μηδενὶ
of her; but he enjoined them [2]no one
εἰπεῖν τὸ γεγονός.
[1]to tell the thing having happened.
=what had happened.

9 Συγκαλεσάμενος δὲ τοὺς δώδεκα ἔδωκεν
And having called together the twelve he gave
αὐτοῖς δύναμιν καὶ ἐξουσίαν ἐπὶ πάντα τὰ
them power and authority over all the
δαιμόνια καὶ νόσους θεραπεύειν· 2 καὶ
demons and diseases to heal; and
ἀπέστειλεν αὐτοὺς κηρύσσειν τὴν βασιλείαν
sent them to proclaim the kingdom
τοῦ θεοῦ καὶ ἰᾶσθαι, 3 καὶ εἶπεν πρὸς
– of God and to cure, and said to
αὐτούς· μηδὲν αἴρετε εἰς τὴν ὁδόν, μήτε
them : Nothing take ye for the way, neither
ῥάβδον μήτε πήραν μήτε ἄρτον μήτε
staff nor wallet nor bread nor
ἀργύριον μήτε ἀνὰ δύο χιτῶνας ἔχειν.
silver nor each two tunics to have.

had been instantly healed.
48 Then he said to her,
"Daughter, your faith has
healed you. Go in peace."
49 While Jesus was still
speaking, someone came
from the house of Jairus,
the synagogue ruler. "Your
daughter is dead," he said.
"Don't bother the teacher
any more."
50 Hearing this, Jesus said
to Jairus, "Don't be afraid;
just believe, and she will be
healed."
51 When he arrived at the
house of Jairus, he did not
let anyone go in with him
except Peter, John and
James, and the child's father and mother. 52 Mean-
while, all the people were
wailing and mourning for
her. "Stop wailing," Jesus
said. "She is not dead but
asleep."
53 They laughed at him,
knowing that she was dead.
54 But he took her by the
hand and said, "My child,
get up!" 55 Her spirit returned, and at once she
stood up. Then Jesus told
them to give her something
to eat. 56 Her parents were
astonished, but he ordered
them not to tell anyone
what had happened.

Chapter 9

Jesus Sends Out the Twelve

WHEN Jesus had
called the Twelve to-
gether, he gave them power
and authority to drive out
all demons and to cure diseases, 2 and he sent them
out to preach the kingdom
of God and to heal the sick.
3 He told them: "Take nothing for the journey—no
staff, no bag, no bread, no
money, no extra tunic.

ever house you enter, stay
there, and leave from
there. 5Wherever they do
not welcome you, as you
are leaving that town shake
the dust off your feet as a
testimony against them."
6They departed and went
through the villages, bringing the good news and curing diseases everywhere.

Herod's Perplexity

7 Now Herod the ruler[s]
heard about all that had
taken place, and he was
perplexed, because it was
said by some that John had
been raised from the dead,
8by some that Elijah had
appeared, and by others
that one of the ancient
prophets had arisen. 9Her-
od said, "John I beheaded;
but who is this about whom
I hear such things?" And he
tried to see him.

Feeding the Five Thousand

10 On their return the
apostles told Jesus[t] all
they had done. He took
them with him and with-
drew privately to a city
called Bethsaida. 11When
the crowds found out about
it, they followed him; and
he welcomed them, and
spoke to them about the
kingdom of God, and
healed those who needed to
be cured.
12 The day was drawing
to a close, and the twelve
came to him and said,
"Send the crowd away, so
that they may go into the
surrounding villages and
countryside, to lodge and
get provisions; for we are
here in a deserted place."
13But he said to them,
"You give them something
to eat." They said, "We
have no more than five
loaves and two fish—

[s] Gk *tetrarch*
[t] Gk *him*

4 καὶ εἰς ἣν ἂν οἰκίαν εἰσέλθητε, ἐκεῖ
And into whatever house ye may enter, there
μένετε καὶ ἐκεῖθεν ἐξέρχεσθε. 5 καὶ
remain and thence go forth. And
ὅσοι ἂν μὴ δέχωνται ὑμᾶς, ἐξερχόμενοι
as many as may not receive you, going forth
ἀπὸ τῆς πόλεως ἐκείνης τὸν κονιορτὸν
from – city that the dust
ἀπὸ τῶν ποδῶν ὑμῶν ἀποτινάσσετε εἰς
from the feet of you shake off for
μαρτύριον ἐπ' αὐτούς. 6 ἐξερχόμενοι δὲ
a testimony against them. And going forth
διήρχοντο κατὰ τὰς κώμας εὐαγγελιζόμενοι
they went through throughout the villages evangelizing
καὶ θεραπεύοντες πανταχοῦ. 7 Ἤκουσεν
and healing everywhere. [5]heard
δὲ Ἡρῴδης ὁ τετραάρχης τὰ γινόμενα
[1]And [2]Herod [3]the [4]tetrarch the things happening
πάντα, καὶ διηπόρει διὰ τὸ λέγεσθαι
all, and was in perplexity because of the to be said
=because it was said
ὑπό τινων ὅτι Ἰωάννης ἠγέρθη ἐκ νεκρῶν,
by some that John was raised from [the] dead,
8 ὑπό τινων δὲ ὅτι Ἠλίας ἐφάνη, ἄλλων
and by some that Elias appeared, [2]others
δὲ ὅτι προφήτης τις τῶν ἀρχαίων ἀνέστη.
[1]but that prophet a certain of the ancients rose again.
9 εἶπεν δὲ [ὁ] Ἡρῴδης· Ἰωάννην ἐγὼ
But said – Herod : John I
ἀπεκεφάλισα· τίς δέ ἐστιν οὗτος περὶ οὗ
beheaded; but who is this about whom
ἀκούω τοιαῦτα; καὶ ἐζήτει ἰδεῖν αὐτόν.
I hear such things? And he sought to see him.
10 Καὶ ὑποστρέψαντες οἱ ἀπόστολοι
And having returned the apostles
διηγήσαντο αὐτῷ ὅσα ἐποίησαν. Καὶ
narrated to him what things they did. And
παραλαβὼν αὐτοὺς ὑπεχώρησεν κατ' ἰδίαν
taking them he departed privately
εἰς πόλιν καλουμένην Βηθσαϊδά. 11 οἱ δὲ
to a city *being* called Bethsaida. But the
ὄχλοι γνόντες ἠκολούθησαν αὐτῷ· καὶ
crowds knowing followed him; and
ἀποδεξάμενος αὐτοὺς ἐλάλει αὐτοῖς περὶ
welcoming them he spoke to them about
τῆς βασιλείας τοῦ θεοῦ, καὶ τοὺς χρείαν
the kingdom – of God, and the [ones] [2]need
ἔχοντας θεραπείας ἰᾶτο. 12 Ἡ δὲ ἡμέρα
[1]having of healing he cured. But the day
ἤρξατο κλίνειν· προσελθόντες δὲ οἱ δώδεκα
began to decline; and approaching the twelve
εἶπαν αὐτῷ· ἀπόλυσον τὸν ὄχλον, ἵνα
said to him : Dismiss the crowd, that
πορευθέντες εἰς τὰς κύκλῳ κώμας καὶ
going to [1]the [5]around [2]villages [3]and
ἀγροὺς καταλύσωσιν καὶ εὕρωσιν ἐπισιτισμόν,
[4]farms they may lodge and may find provisions,
ὅτι ὧδε ἐν ἐρήμῳ τόπῳ ἐσμέν. 13 εἶπεν
because here in a desert place we are. he said
δὲ πρὸς αὐτούς· δότε αὐτοῖς φαγεῖν
And to them : [1]Give [3]them [4]to eat
ὑμεῖς. οἱ δὲ εἶπαν· οὐκ εἰσὶν ἡμῖν
[2]ye. But they said : There are not to us[c]
=We have not
πλεῖον ἢ ἄρτοι πέντε καὶ ἰχθύες δύο, εἰ
more than loaves five and fishes two, un-

4Whatever house you en-
ter, stay there until you
leave that town. 5If people
do not welcome you, shake
the dust off your feet when
you leave their town, as a
testimony against them."
6So they set out and went
from village to village,
preaching the gospel and
healing people every-
where.
7Now Herod the tetrarch
heard about all that was going on. And he was per-
plexed, because some were
saying that John had been
raised from the dead, 8oth-
ers that Elijah had ap-
peared, and still others that
one of the prophets of long
ago had come back to life.
9But Herod said, "I be-
headed John. Who, then, is
this I hear such things
about?" And he tried to see
him.

Jesus Feeds the Five Thousand

10When the apostles re-
turned, they reported to
Jesus what they had done.
Then he took them with
him and they withdrew by
themselves to a town called
Bethsaida, 11but the
crowds learned about it and
followed him. He wel-
comed them and spoke to
them about the kingdom of
God, and healed those who
needed healing.
12Late in the afternoon
the Twelve came to him
and said, "Send the crowd
away so they can go to the
surrounding villages and
countryside and find food
and lodging, because we
are in a remote place
here."
13He replied, "You give
them something to eat."
They answered, "We
have only five loaves of
bread and two fish—unless

unless we are to go and buy
food for all these people."
14 For there were about five
thousand men. And he said
to his disciples, "Make
them sit down in groups of
about fifty each." 15 They
did so and made them all sit
down. 16 And taking the
five loaves and the two
fish, he looked up to heav-
en, and blessed and broke
them, and gave them to the
disciples to set before the
crowd. 17 And all ate and
were filled. What was left
over was gathered up,
twelve baskets of broken
pieces.

Peter's Declaration about Jesus

18 Once when Jesus[u]
was praying alone, with
only the disciples near him,
he asked them, "Who do
the crowds say that I am?"
19 They answered, "John
the Baptist; but others, Elijah; and still others, that
one of the ancient prophets
has arisen." 20 He said to
them, "But who do you say
that I am?" Peter an-
swered, "The Messiah[v] of
God."

Jesus Foretells His Death and Resurrection

21 He sternly ordered
and commanded them not
to tell anyone, 22 saying,
"The Son of Man must un-
dergo great suffering, and
be rejected by the elders,
chief priests, and scribes,
and be killed, and on the
third day be raised."
23 Then he said to them
all, "If any want to become
my followers, let them
deny themselves and take
up their cross daily and fol-

[u] Gk *he*
[v] Or *The Christ*

μήτι πορευθέντες ἡμεῖς ἀγοράσωμεν εἰς
less going we may buy for
πάντα τὸν λαὸν τοῦτον βρώματα. 14 ἦσαν
all – people this foods. there were
γὰρ ὡσεὶ ἄνδρες πεντακισχίλιοι. εἶπεν δὲ
For about men five thousand. And he said
πρὸς τοὺς μαθητὰς αὐτοῦ· κατακλίνατε
to the disciples of him : [1]Make [3]to recline
αὐτοὺς κλισίας ὡσεὶ ἀνὰ πεντήκοντα.
[2]them [in] groups [1]about [3]each [2]fifty.
15 καὶ ἐποίησαν οὕτως καὶ κατέκλιναν
And they did so and made to recline
ἅπαντας. 16 λαβὼν δὲ τοὺς πέντε ἄρτους
all. And taking the five loaves
καὶ τοὺς δύο ἰχθύας, ἀναβλέψας εἰς τὸν
and the two fishes, looking up to –
οὐρανὸν εὐλόγησεν αὐτοὺς καὶ κατέκλασεν,
heaven he blessed them and broke,
καὶ ἐδίδου τοῖς μαθηταῖς παραθεῖναι τῷ
and gave to the disciples to set before the
ὄχλῳ. 17 καὶ ἔφαγον καὶ ἐχορτάσθησαν
crowd. And they ate and were satisfied
πάντες· καὶ ἤρθη τὸ περισσεῦσαν αὐτοῖς
all; and were taken the excess to them
κλασμάτων κόφινοι δώδεκα.
of fragments baskets twelve.
18 Καὶ ἐγένετο ἐν τῷ εἶναι αὐτὸν
And it came to pass in the to be him[be]
=as he was
προσευχόμενον κατὰ μόνας συνῆσαν αὐτῷ
praying alone were with him
οἱ μαθηταί, καὶ ἐπηρώτησεν αὐτοὺς λέγων·
the disciples, and he questioned them saying :
τίνα με οἱ ὄχλοι λέγουσιν εἶναι; 19 οἱ δὲ
Whom me the crowds say to be? And they
=Whom do the crowds say that I am?
ἀποκριθέντες εἶπαν· Ἰωάννην τὸν βαπτιστήν,
answering said : John the Baptist,
ἄλλοι δὲ Ἠλίαν, ἄλλοι δὲ ὅτι προφήτης
but others Elias, and others that prophet
τις τῶν ἀρχαίων ἀνέστη. 20 εἶπεν δὲ
a certain of the ancients rose again. And he said
αὐτοῖς· ὑμεῖς δὲ τίνα με λέγετε εἶναι;
to them ; But ye whom me say to be?
=whom say ye that I am?
Πέτρος δὲ ἀποκριθεὶς εἶπεν· τὸν χριστὸν
And Peter answering said: The Christ
τοῦ θεοῦ. 21 ὁ δὲ ἐπιτιμήσας αὐτοῖς
– of God. But he warning [2]them
παρήγγειλεν μηδενὶ λέγειν τοῦτο, 22 εἰπὼν
[1]charged [4]no one [3]to tell [5]this, saying
ὅτι δεῖ τὸν υἱὸν τοῦ ἀνθρώπου πολλὰ
that it behoves the Son – of man many things
παθεῖν καὶ ἀποδοκιμασθῆναι ἀπὸ τῶν
to suffer and to be rejected from(by) the
πρεσβυτέρων καὶ ἀρχιερέων καὶ γραμματέων
elders and chief priests and scribes
καὶ ἀποκτανθῆναι καὶ τῇ τρίτῃ ἡμέρᾳ
and to be killed and on the third day
ἐγερθῆναι. 23 Ἔλεγεν δὲ πρὸς πάντας·
to be raised. And he said to all :
εἴ τις θέλει ὀπίσω μου ἔρχεσθαι, ἀρνησάσθω
If anyone wishes after me to come, let him deny
ἑαυτὸν καὶ ἀράτω τὸν σταυρὸν
himself and take the cross
αὐτοῦ καθ' ἡμέραν, καὶ ἀκολουθείτω μοι.
of him daily, and let him follow me.

we go and buy food for all
this crowd." 14(About five
thousand men were there.)
But he said to his disci-
ples, "Have them sit down
in groups of about fifty
each." 15The disciples did
so, and everybody sat
down. 16Taking the five
loaves and the two fish and
looking up to heaven, he
gave thanks and broke
them. Then he gave them to
the disciples to set before
the people. 17They all ate
and were satisfied, and the
disciples picked up twelve
basketfuls of broken pieces
that were left over.

Peter's Confession of Christ

18Once when Jesus was
praying in private and his
disciples were with him, he
asked them, "Who do the
crowds say I am?"
19They replied, "Some
say John the Baptist; others
say Elijah; and still others,
that one of the prophets of
long ago has come back to
life."
20"But what about you?"
he asked. "Who do you say
I am?"
Peter answered, "The
Christ[j] of God."
21Jesus strictly warned
them not to tell this to anyone. 22And he said, "The
Son of Man must suffer
many things and be rejected by the elders, chief
priests and teachers of the
law, and he must be killed
and on the third day be
raised to life."
23Then he said to them all:
"If anyone would come af-
ter me, he must deny him-
self and take up his cross
daily and follow me. 24For

[j] 20 Or *Messiah*

low me. 24 For those who
want to save their life will
lose it, and those who lose
their life for my sake will
save it. 25 What does it profit them if they gain the
whole world, but lose or
forfeit themselves?
26 Those who are ashamed
of me and of my words, of
them the Son of Man will be
ashamed when he comes in
his glory and the glory of
the Father and of the holy
angels. 27 But truly I tell
you, there are some standing here who will not taste
death before they see the
kingdom of God."

The Transfiguration

28 Now about eight
days after these sayings
Jesus[u] took with him Peter
and John and James, and
went up on the mountain to
pray. 29 And while he was
praying, the appearance of
his face changed, and his
clothes became dazzling
white. 30 Suddenly they
saw two men, Moses and
Elijah, talking to him.
31 They appeared in glory
and were speaking of his
departure, which he was
about to accomplish at Jerusalem. 32 Now Peter and
his companions were
weighed down with sleep;
but since they had stayed
awake,[w] they saw his glory
and the two men who stood
with him. 33 Just as they
were leaving him, Peter
said to Jesus, "Master, it is
good for us to be here; let
us make three dwellings,[x]

24 ὃς γὰρ ἐὰν θέλῃ τὴν ψυχὴν αὐτοῦ
For whoever wishes the life of him
σῶσαι, ἀπολέσει αὐτήν· ὃς δ' ἂν ἀπολέσῃ
to save, he will lose it; but whoever loses
τὴν ψυχὴν αὐτοῦ ἕνεκεν ἐμοῦ, οὗτος
the life of him for the sake of me, this [one]
σώσει αὐτήν. **25** τί γὰρ ὠφελεῖται
will save it. For what is profited
ἄνθρωπος κερδήσας τὸν κόσμον ὅλον ἑαυτὸν
a man gaining the world whole [3]himself
δὲ ἀπολέσας ἢ ζημιωθείς; **26** ὃς γὰρ ἂν
[1]but [2]losing or suffering loss? For whoever
ἐπαισχυνθῇ με καὶ τοὺς ἐμοὺς λόγους,
is ashamed of me and – my words,
τοῦτον ὁ υἱὸς τοῦ ἀνθρώπου ἐπαι-
this [one] the Son – of man will be
σχυνθήσεται, ὅταν ἔλθῃ ἐν τῇ δόξῃ
ashamed of, when he comes in the glory
αὐτοῦ καὶ τοῦ πατρὸς καὶ τῶν ἁγίων
of him and of the Father and of the holy
ἀγγέλων. **27** λέγω δὲ ὑμῖν ἀληθῶς,
angels. But I tell you truly,
εἰσίν τινες τῶν αὐτοῦ ἑστηκότων οἳ
there are some of the [ones] here standing who
οὐ μὴ γεύσωνται θανάτου ἕως ἂν ἴδωσιν
by no means may taste of death until they see
τὴν βασιλείαν τοῦ θεοῦ.
the kingdom – of God.

28 Ἐγένετο δὲ μετὰ τοὺς λόγους τούτους
And it came to pass [4]after – [6]sayings [5]these
ὡσεὶ ἡμέραι ὀκτώ, καὶ παραλαβὼν Πέτρον
[1]about [3]days [2]eight, *and* taking Peter
καὶ Ἰωάννην καὶ Ἰάκωβον ἀνέβη εἰς τὸ
and John and James he went up into the
ὄρος προσεύξασθαι. **29** καὶ ἐγένετο ἐν τῷ
mountain to pray. And [9]became in the
=[1]as [2]he [3]prayed
προσεύχεσθαι αὐτὸν τὸ εἶδος τοῦ προσώπου
to pray him[be] [4]the [5]appearance [6]of the [7]face
αὐτοῦ ἕτερον καὶ ὁ ἱματισμὸς αὐτοῦ
[8]of him [10]different and the raiment of him
λευκὸς ἐξαστράπτων. **30** καὶ ἰδοὺ ἄνδρες
[2]white [1]gleaming. And[,] behold[,] men
δύο συνελάλουν αὐτῷ, οἵτινες ἦσαν Μωϋσῆς
two conversed with him, who were Moses
καὶ Ἠλίας, **31** οἳ ὀφθέντες ἐν δόξῃ ἔλεγον
and Elias, who appearing in glory spoke of
τὴν ἔξοδον αὐτοῦ, ἣν ἤμελλεν πληροῦν
the exodus of him, which he was about to accomplish
ἐν Ἰερουσαλήμ. **32** ὁ δὲ Πέτρος καὶ οἱ
in Jerusalem. – But Peter and the [ones]
σὺν αὐτῷ ἦσαν βεβαρημένοι ὕπνῳ· δια-
with him were *having been* burdened with sleep; [2]wak-
γρηγορήσαντες δὲ εἶδαν τὴν δόξαν αὐτοῦ
ing thoroughly [1]but they saw the glory of him
καὶ τοὺς δύο ἄνδρας τοὺς συνεστῶτας
and the two men – standing with
αὐτῷ. **33** καὶ ἐγένετο ἐν τῷ διαχωρίζεσθαι
him. And it came to pass in the to part
=when they parted
αὐτοὺς ἀπ' αὐτοῦ εἶπεν ὁ Πέτρος πρὸς
them[be] from him said – Peter to
τὸν Ἰησοῦν· ἐπιστάτα, καλόν ἐστιν ἡμᾶς
– Jesus: Master, good it is [for] us
ὧδε εἶναι, καὶ ποιήσωμεν σκηνὰς τρεῖς,
here to be, and let us make tents three,

whoever wants to save his
life will lose it, but whoever
loses his life for me will
save it. 25 What good is it for
a man to gain the whole
world, and yet lose or forfeit his very self? 26 If anyone is ashamed of me and
my words, the Son of Man
will be ashamed of him
when he comes in his glory
and in the glory of the Father and of the holy angels.
27 I tell you the truth, some
who are standing here will
not taste death before they
see the kingdom of God."

The Transfiguration

28 About eight days after
Jesus said this, he took Peter, John and James with
him and went up onto a
mountain to pray. 29 As he
was praying, the appear-
ance of his face changed,
and his clothes became as
bright as a flash of lightning. 30 Two men, Moses
and Elijah, 31 appeared in
glorious splendor, talking
with Jesus. They spoke
about his departure, which
he was about to bring to fulfillment at Jerusalem. 32 Peter and his companions
were very sleepy, but when
they became fully awake,
they saw his glory and the
two men standing with him.
33 As the men were leaving
Jesus, Peter said to him,
"Master, it is good for us to
be here. Let us put up three
shelters—one for you, one

[w] Or *but when they were fully awake*
[x] Or *tents*

one for you, one for Moses,
and one for Elijah"—not
knowing what he said.
34 While he was saying this,
a cloud came and over-
shadowed them; and they
were terrified as they entered the cloud. 35 Then
from the cloud came a
voice that said, "This is my
Son, my Chosen;[y] listen to
him!" 36 When the voice
had spoken, Jesus was
found alone. And they kept
silent and in those days told
no one any of the things
they had seen.

Jesus Heals a Boy with a Demon

37 On the next day,
when they had come down
from the mountain, a great
crowd met him. 38 Just then
a man from the crowd
shouted, "Teacher, I beg
you to look at my son; he is
my only child. 39 Suddenly
a spirit seizes him, and all
at once he[z] shrieks. It con-
vulses him until he foams at
the mouth; it mauls him and
will scarcely leave him. 40 I
begged your disciples to
cast it out, but they could
not." 41 Jesus answered,
"You faithless and per-
verse generation, how
much longer must I be with
you and bear with you?
Bring your son here."
42 While he was coming, the
demon dashed him to the
ground in convulsions. But
Jesus rebuked the unclean
spirit, healed the boy, and
gave him back to his father.
43 And all were astounded

[y] Other ancient authorities read *my Beloved*

[z] Or *it*

μίαν σοὶ καὶ μίαν Μωϋσεῖ καὶ μίαν
one for thee and one for Moses and one

Ἠλίᾳ, μὴ εἰδὼς ὃ λέγει. 34 ταῦτα δὲ
for Elias, not knowing what he says. And these things

αὐτοῦ λέγοντος ἐγένετο νεφέλη καὶ
him saying[a] came a cloud and
=while he said these things

ἐπεσκίαζεν αὐτούς· ἐφοβήθησαν δὲ ἐν τῷ
overshadowed them; and they feared in the
=as they entered

εἰσελθεῖν αὐτοὺς εἰς τὴν νεφέλην. 35 καὶ
to enter them[be] into the cloud. And

φωνὴ ἐγένετο ἐκ τῆς νεφέλης λέγουσα·
a voice came out of the cloud saying :

οὗτός ἐστιν ὁ υἱός μου ὁ ἐκλελεγμένος,
This is the Son of me – *having been* chosen,

αὐτοῦ ἀκούετε, 36 καὶ ἐν τῷ γενέσθαι
him hear ye, and in the to become
=when the voice came

τὴν φωνὴν εὑρέθη Ἰησοῦς μόνος. καὶ
the voice[be] was found Jesus alone. And

αὐτοὶ ἐσίγησαν καὶ οὐδενὶ ἀπήγγειλαν ἐν ἐκείναις
they were silent and to no one reported in those

ταῖς ἡμέραις οὐδὲν ὧν ἑώρακαν.
– days no(any) thing of [the things] which they have (had) seen.

37 Ἐγένετο δὲ τῇ ἑξῆς ἡμέρᾳ κατελ-
And it came to pass on the following day coming

θόντων αὐτῶν ἀπὸ τοῦ ὄρους συνήντησεν
down them[a] from the mountain met
=as they came down

αὐτῷ ὄχλος πολύς. 38 καὶ ἰδοὺ ἀνὴρ
him crowd a much. And[,] behold[,] a man

ἀπὸ τοῦ ὄχλου ἐβόησεν λέγων· διδάσκαλε,
from the crowd called aloud saying : Teacher,

δέομαί σου ἐπιβλέψαι ἐπὶ τὸν υἱόν μου,
I beg of thee to look *at* at the son of me,

ὅτι μονογενής μοί ἐστιν, 39 καὶ ἰδοὺ
because only born to me he is, and[,] behold[,]

πνεῦμα λαμβάνει αὐτόν, καὶ ἐξαίφνης
a spirit takes him, and suddenly

κράζει καὶ σπαράσσει αὐτὸν μετὰ ἀφροῦ,
cries out and throws him with foam,

καὶ μόλις ἀποχωρεῖ ἀπ' αὐτοῦ συντρῖβον
and scarcely departs from him bruising

αὐτόν· 40 καὶ ἐδεήθην τῶν μαθητῶν σου
him; and I begged of the disciples of thee

ἵνα ἐκβάλωσιν αὐτό, καὶ οὐκ ἠδυνήθησαν.
that they would expel it, and they were not able.

41 ἀποκριθεὶς δὲ ὁ Ἰησοῦς εἶπεν· ὦ
And answering – Jesus said : O

γενεὰ ἄπιστος καὶ διεστραμμένη, ἕως πότε
generation unbelieving and *having been* perverted, until when

ἔσομαι πρὸς ὑμᾶς καὶ ἀνέξομαι ὑμῶν;
shall I be with you and endure you?

προσάγαγε ὧδε τὸν υἱόν σου. 42 ἔτι
Bring here the son of thee. yet

δὲ προσερχομένου αὐτοῦ ἔρρηξεν αὐτὸν τὸ
But approaching him[a] tore him the
=But while he was yet approaching

δαιμόνιον καὶ συνεσπάραξεν· ἐπετίμησεν δὲ
demon and threw violently; but [2]rebuked

ὁ Ἰησοῦς τῷ πνεύματι τῷ ἀκαθάρτῳ, καὶ
– [1]Jesus [3]the [5]spirit – [4]unclean, and

ἰάσατο τὸν παῖδα καὶ ἀπέδωκεν αὐτὸν τῷ
cured the boy and restored him to the

πατρὶ αὐτοῦ. 43 ἐξεπλήσσοντο δὲ πάντες
father of him. And were astounded all

for Moses and one for Elijah." (He did not know
what he was saying.)
34 While he was speaking,
a cloud appeared and en-
veloped them, and they
were afraid as they entered
the cloud. 35 A voice came
from the cloud, saying,
"This is my Son, whom I
have chosen; listen to
him." 36 When the voice
had spoken, they found
that Jesus was alone. The
disciples kept this to themselves, and told no one at
that time what they had
seen.

The Healing of a Boy With an Evil Spirit

37 The next day, when
they came down from the
mountain, a large crowd
met him. 38 A man in the
crowd called out, "Teach-
er, I beg you to look at my
son, for he is my only child.
39 A spirit seizes him and he
suddenly screams; it
throws him into convul-
sions so that he foams at
the mouth. It scarcely ever
leaves him and is destroying him. 40 I begged your
disciples to drive it out, but
they could not."
41 "O unbelieving and perverse generation," Jesus
replied, "how long shall I
stay with you and put up
with you? Bring your son
here."
42 Even while the boy was
coming, the demon threw
him to the ground in a convulsion. But Jesus rebuked
the evil[k] spirit, healed the
boy and gave him back to
his father. 43 And they were

[k] 42 Greek *unclean*

at the greatness of God.

Jesus Again Foretells His Death

While everyone was
amazed at all that he was
doing, he said to his disciples, 44 "Let these words
sink into your ears: The
Son of Man is going to be
betrayed into human
hands." 45 But they did not
understand this saying; its
meaning was concealed
from them, so that they
could not perceive it. And
they were afraid to ask him
about this saying.

True Greatness

46 An argument arose
among them as to which
one of them was the greatest. 47 But Jesus, aware of
their inner thoughts, took a
little child and put it by his
side, 48 and said to them,
"Whoever welcomes this
child in my name welcomes
me, and whoever wel-
comes me welcomes the
one who sent me; for the
least among all of you is the
greatest."

Another Exorcist

49 John answered,
"Master, we saw someone
casting out demons in your
name, and we tried to stop
him, because he does not
follow with us." 50 But
Jesus said to him, "Do not
stop him; for whoever is
not against you is for you."

A Samaritan Village Refuses to Receive Jesus

51 When the days drew
near for him to be taken up,
he set his face to go to Jerusalem. 52 And he sent messengers ahead of him. On
their way they entered a
village of the Samaritans to
make ready for him; 53 but
they did not receive him,

ἐπὶ τῇ μεγαλειότητι τοῦ θεοῦ.
at the majesty - of God.
Πάντων δὲ θαυμαζόντων ἐπὶ πᾶσιν οἷς
And all marvelling[a] at all things which
=while all marvelled
ἐποίει εἶπεν πρὸς τοὺς μαθητὰς αὐτοῦ·
he did he said to the disciples of him :
44 Θέσθε ὑμεῖς εἰς τὰ ὦτα ὑμῶν τοὺς
Lay ye in the ears of you -
λόγους τούτους· ὁ γὰρ υἱὸς τοῦ ἀνθρώπου
sayings these; for the Son - of man
μέλλει παραδίδοσθαι εἰς χεῖρας ἀνθρώπων.
is about to be betrayed into [the] hands of men.
45 οἱ δὲ ἠγνόουν τὸ ῥῆμα τοῦτο, καὶ ἦν
But they knew not - word this, and it was
παρακεκαλυμμένον ἀπ' αὐτῶν ἵνα μὴ
having been veiled from them lest
αἴσθωνται αὐτό, καὶ ἐφοβοῦντο ἐρωτῆσαι
they should perceive it, and they feared to ask
αὐτὸν περὶ τοῦ ῥήματος τούτου. 46 Εἰσῆλθεν
him about - word this. entered
δὲ διαλογισμὸς ἐν αὐτοῖς, τὸ τίς ἂν εἴη
And a debate among them, - who might be
=a debate arose
μείζων αὐτῶν. 47 ὁ δὲ Ἰησοῦς εἰδὼς τὸν
greater(est) of them. - And Jesus knowing the
διαλογισμὸν τῆς καρδίας αὐτῶν, ἐπιλαβόμενος
debate of the heart of them, taking
παιδίον ἔστησεν αὐτὸ παρ' ἑαυτῷ, 48 καὶ
a child stood it(him) beside himself, and
εἶπεν αὐτοῖς· ὃς ἐὰν δέξηται τοῦτο τὸ
said to them : Whoever receives this -
παιδίον ἐπὶ τῷ ὀνόματί μου, ἐμὲ δέχεται·
child on(in) the name of me, me receives;
καὶ ὃς ἂν ἐμὲ δέξηται, δέχεται τὸν
and whoever me receives, receives the [one]
ἀποστείλαντά με· ὁ γὰρ μικρότερος ἐν
having sent me; for [1]the [one] [3]lesser [4]among
πᾶσιν ὑμῖν ὑπάρχων, οὗτός ἐστιν μέγας.
[6]all [5]you [2]being, this [one] is great.
49 Ἀποκριθεὶς δὲ ὁ Ἰωάννης εἶπεν· ἐπιστάτα,
And answering - John said : Master,
εἴδομέν τινα ἐν τῷ ὀνόματί σου ἐκβάλλοντα
we saw someone in the name of thee expelling
δαιμόνια, καὶ ἐκωλύομεν αὐτόν, ὅτι
demons, and we prevented him, because
οὐκ ἀκολουθεῖ μεθ' ἡμῶν. 50 εἶπεν δὲ πρὸς
he does not follow with us. And said to
αὐτὸν Ἰησοῦς· μὴ κωλύετε· ὃς γὰρ οὐκ
him Jesus: Do not prevent; for [he] who not
ἔστιν καθ' ὑμῶν, ὑπὲρ ὑμῶν ἐστιν.
is against you, for you is.
51 Ἐγένετο δὲ ἐν τῷ συμπληροῦσθαι
And it came to pass in the to be fulfilled
τὰς ἡμέρας τῆς ἀναλήμψεως αὐτοῦ καὶ
the days of the assumption of him[be] *and*
=as the days of his assumption were fulfilled
αὐτὸς τὸ πρόσωπον ἐστήρισεν τοῦ
he the(his) face set -
πορεύεσθαι εἰς Ἰερουσαλήμ, 52 καὶ ἀπέστειλεν
to go[d] to Jerusalem, and sent
ἀγγέλους πρὸ προσώπου αὐτοῦ. καὶ
messengers before face of him. And
πορευθέντες εἰσῆλθον εἰς κώμην Σαμαριτῶν,
going they entered into a village of Samaritans,
ὥστε ἑτοιμάσαι αὐτῷ· 53 καὶ οὐκ ἐδέξαντο
so as to prepare for him; and they did not receive

all amazed at the greatness
of God.
While everyone was mar-
veling at all that Jesus did,
he said to his disciples,
44 "Listen carefully to what
I am about to tell you: The
Son of Man is going to be
betrayed into the hands of
men." 45 But they did not
understand what this
meant. It was hidden from
them, so that they did not
grasp it, and they were
afraid to ask him about it.

Who Will Be the Greatest?

46 An argument started
among the disciples as to
which of them would be the
greatest. 47 Jesus, knowing
their thoughts, took a little
child and had him stand beside him. 48 Then he said to
them, "Whoever wel-
comes this little child in my
name welcomes me; and
whoever welcomes me wel-
comes the one who sent
me. For he who is least
among you all—he is the
greatest."
49 "Master," said John,
"we saw a man driving out
demons in your name and
we tried to stop him, be-
cause he is not one of us."
50 "Do not stop him,"
Jesus said, "for whoever is
not against you is for you."

Samaritan Opposition

51 As the time approached
for him to be taken up to
heaven, Jesus resolutely
set out for Jerusalem.
52 And he sent messengers
on ahead, who went into a
Samaritan village to get
things ready for him; 53 but
the people there did not

because his face was set toward Jerusalem. 54When
his disciples James and
John saw it, they said,
"Lord, do you want us to
command fire to come
down from heaven and
consume them?"[a] 55But he
turned and rebuked them.
56Then[b] they went on to
another village.

Would-Be Followers of Jesus

57 As they were going
along the road, someone
said to him, "I will follow
you wherever you go."
58And Jesus said to him,
"Foxes have holes, and
birds of the air have nests;
but the Son of Man has nowhere to lay his head."
59To another he said, "Follow me." But he said,
"Lord, first let me go and
bury my father." 60But
Jesus[c] said to him, "Let
the dead bury their own
dead; but as for you, go and
proclaim the kingdom of
God." 61Another said, "I
will follow you, Lord; but
let me first say farewell to
those at my home." 62Jesus
said to him, "No one who
puts a hand to the plow and
looks back is fit for the
kingdom of God."

Chapter 10

The Mission of the Seventy

AFTER this the Lord ap-
pointed seventy[d]
others and sent them on
ahead of him in pairs to every town and place where
he himself intended to go.
2He said to them, "The harvest is plentiful, but the laborers are few; therefore

[a] Other ancient authorities add *as Elijah did*
[b] Other ancient authorities read *rebuked them, and said, "You do not know what spirit you are of, 56for the Son of Man has not come to destroy the lives of human beings but to save them." Then*
[c] Gk *he*
[d] Other ancient authorities read *seventy-two*

αὐτόν, ὅτι τὸ πρόσωπον αὐτοῦ ἦν
him, because the face of him was
πορευόμενον εἰς Ἰερουσαλήμ. **54** ἰδόντες
going to Jerusalem. [6]seeing
δὲ οἱ μαθηταὶ Ἰάκωβος καὶ Ἰωάννης
And [1]the [2]disciples [3]James [4]and [5]John
εἶπαν· κύριε, θέλεις εἴπωμεν πῦρ κατα-
[7]said : Lord, wilt thou we may tell fire to come
βῆναι ἀπὸ τοῦ οὐρανοῦ καὶ ἀναλῶσαι
down from – heaven and to destroy
αὐτούς; **55** στραφεὶς δὲ ἐπετίμησεν αὐτοῖς.
them? But turning he rebuked them.
56 καὶ ἐπορεύθησαν εἰς ἑτέραν κώμην.
And they went to another village.
57 Καὶ πορευομένων αὐτῶν ἐν τῇ ὁδῷ
And going them* in the way
*=as they went
εἶπέν τις πρὸς αὐτόν· ἀκολουθήσω σοι
said one to him : I will follow thee
ὅπου ἐὰν ἀπέρχῃ. **58** καὶ εἶπεν αὐτῷ ὁ
wherever thou goest. And said to him –
Ἰησοῦς· αἱ ἀλώπεκες φωλεοὺς ἔχουσιν καὶ
Jesus : The foxes holes have and
τὰ πετεινὰ τοῦ οὐρανοῦ κατασκηνώσεις, ὁ
the birds – of heaven nests, [2]the
δὲ υἱὸς τοῦ ἀνθρώπου οὐκ ἔχει ποῦ τὴν
[1]but Son – of man has not where the(his)
κεφαλὴν κλίνῃ. **59** Εἶπεν δὲ πρὸς ἕτερον·
head he may lay. And he said to another :
ἀκολούθει μοι. ὁ δὲ εἶπεν· ἐπίτρεψόν μοι
Follow me. But he said : Allow me
πρῶτον ἀπελθόντι θάψαι τὸν πατέρα μου.
first going to bury the father of me.
60 εἶπεν δὲ αὐτῷ· ἄφες τοὺς νεκροὺς
But he said to him : Leave the dead
θάψαι τοὺς ἑαυτῶν νεκρούς, σὺ δὲ ἀπελθὼν
to bury the of themselves dead, but thou going
=their own dead,
διάγγελλε τὴν βασιλείαν τοῦ θεοῦ. **61** Εἶπεν
announce the kingdom – of God. said
δὲ καὶ ἕτερος· ἀκολουθήσω σοι, κύριε·
And also another : I will follow thee, Lord;
πρῶτον δὲ ἐπίτρεψόν μοι ἀποτάξασθαι τοῖς
but first allow me to say farewell to the [ones]
εἰς τὸν οἶκόν μου. **62** εἶπεν δὲ [πρὸς
in the house of me. But said to
αὐτὸν] ὁ Ἰησοῦς· οὐδεὶς ἐπιβαλὼν τὴν
him – Jesus : No one putting *on* the(his)
χεῖρα ἐπ' ἄροτρον καὶ βλέπων εἰς τὰ
hand on a plough and looking at the things
ὀπίσω εὔθετός ἐστιν τῇ βασιλείᾳ τοῦ θεοῦ.
behind fit is for the kingdom – of God.

10 Μετὰ δὲ ταῦτα ἀνέδειξεν ὁ κύριος
Now after these things appointed the Lord
ἑτέρους ἑβδομήκοντα [δύο], καὶ ἀπέστειλεν
others seventy-two, and sent
αὐτοὺς ἀνὰ δύο πρὸ προσώπου αὐτοῦ εἰς
them two by two† before face of him into
πᾶσαν πόλιν καὶ τόπον οὗ ἤμελλεν αὐτὸς
every city and place where [2]was about [1]he
ἔρχεσθαι. **2** ἔλεγεν δὲ πρὸς αὐτούς· ὁ
to come. And he said to them : the
μὲν θερισμὸς πολύς, οἱ δὲ ἐργάται ὀλίγοι·
Indeed harvest much, but the workmen few;

welcome him, because he
was heading for Jerusalem.
54When the disciples James
and John saw this, they
asked, "Lord, do you want
us to call fire down from
heaven to destroy them[l]?"
55But Jesus turned and rebuked them, 56and[m] they
went to another village.

The Cost of Following Jesus

57As they were walking
along the road, a man said
to him, "I will follow you
wherever you go."
58Jesus replied, "Foxes
have holes and birds of the
air have nests, but the Son
of Man has no place to lay
his head."
59He said to another man,
"Follow me."
But the man replied,
"Lord, first let me go and
bury my father."
60Jesus said to him, "Let
the dead bury their own
dead, but you go and pro-
claim the kingdom of
God."
61Still another said, "I
will follow you, Lord; but
first let me go back and say
good-by to my family."
62Jesus replied, "No one
who puts his hand to the
plow and looks back is fit
for service in the kingdom
of God."

Chapter 10

Jesus Sends Out the Seventy-two

AFTER this the Lord ap-
pointed seventy-two[n]
others and sent them two
by two ahead of him to every town and place where
he was about to go. 2He
told them, "The harvest is
plentiful, but the workers

[l] 54 Some manuscripts *them, even as Elijah did*
[m] 55,56 Some manuscripts *them. And he said, "You do not know what kind of spirit you are of, for the Son of Man did not come to destroy men's lives, but to save them." 56And*
[n] 1 Some manuscripts *seventy*; also in verse 17

ask the Lord of the harvest
to send out laborers into his
harvest. 3 Go on your way.
See, I am sending you out
like lambs into the midst of
wolves. 4 Carry no purse,
no bag, no sandals; and
greet no one on the road.
5 Whatever house you en-
ter, first say, 'Peace to this
house!' 6 And if anyone is
there who shares in peace,
your peace will rest on that
person; but if not, it will return to you. 7 Remain in the
same house, eating and
drinking whatever they
provide, for the laborer de
serves to be paid. Do no
move about from house to
house. 8 Whenever you en-
ter a town and its people
welcome you, eat what is
set before you; 9 cure the
sick who are there, and say
to them, 'The kingdom of
God has come near to
you.'[e] 10 But whenever
you enter a town and they
do not welcome you, go out
into its streets and say,
11 'Even the dust of your
town that clings to our feet,
we wipe off in protest
against you. Yet know this:
the kingdom of God has
come near.'[f] 12 I tell you,
on that day it will be more
tolerable for Sodom than
for that town.

Woes to Unrepentant Cities

13 "Woe to you, Chora-
zin! Woe to you, Bethsai-
da! For if the deeds of power done in you had been
done in Tyre and Sidon,
they would have repented
long ago, sitting in sackcloth and ashes. 14 But at

δεήθητε οὖν τοῦ κυρίου τοῦ θερισμοῦ
beg ye therefore of the Lord of the harvest
ὅπως ἐργάτας ἐκβάλῃ εἰς τὸν θερισμὸν
that workmen he would thrust forth into the harvest
αὐτοῦ. 3 ὑπάγετε· ἰδοὺ ἀποστέλλω ὑμᾶς
of him. Go ye; behold I send you
ὡς ἄρνας ἐν μέσῳ λύκων. 4 μὴ βαστάζετε
as lambs in [the] midst of wolves. Do not carry
βαλλάντιον, μὴ πήραν, μὴ ὑποδήματα· καὶ
a purse, nor a wallet, nor sandals; and
μηδένα κατὰ τὴν ὁδὸν ἀσπάσησθε. 5 εἰς
no one by the way greet. [2]into
ἣν δ' ἂν εἰσέλθητε οἰκίαν, πρῶτον λέγετε·
[1]And [3]whatever [5]ye enter [4]house, first say:
εἰρήνη τῷ οἴκῳ τούτῳ. 6 καὶ ἐὰν ἐκεῖ
Peace – house to this. And if there
ᾖ υἱὸς εἰρήνης, ἐπαναπαήσεται ἐπ' αὐτὸν
there is a son of peace, shall rest on it(?him)
ἡ εἰρήνη ὑμῶν· εἰ δὲ μή γε, ἐφ' ὑμᾶς
the peace of you; otherwise, on you
ἀνακάμψει. 7 ἐν αὐτῇ δὲ τῇ οἰκίᾳ μένετε,
it shall return. [2]in [4]same [1]And [3]the house* remain,
ἔσθοντες καὶ πίνοντες τὰ παρ' αὐτῶν·
eating and drinking the things with them;
ἄξιος γὰρ ὁ ἐργάτης τοῦ μισθοῦ αὐτοῦ.
for worthy [is] the workman of the pay of him.
μὴ μεταβαίνετε ἐξ οἰκίας εἰς οἰκίαν.
Do not remove from house to house.
8 καὶ εἰς ἣν ἂν πόλιν εἰσέρχησθε καὶ
And into whatever city ye enter and
δέχωνται ὑμᾶς, ἐσθίετε τὰ παρατιθέμενα
they receive you, eat the things being set before
ὑμῖν, 9 καὶ θεραπεύετε τοὺς ἐν αὐτῇ
you, and heal the [2]in [3]it
ἀσθενεῖς, καὶ λέγετε αὐτοῖς· ἤγγικεν ἐφ'
[1]sick, and tell them: Has drawn near on(to)
ὑμᾶς ἡ βασιλεία τοῦ θεοῦ. 10 εἰς ἣν δ'
you the kingdom – of God. And into what-
ἂν πόλιν εἰσέλθητε καὶ μὴ δέχωνται ὑμᾶς,
ever city ye enter and they do not receive you,
ἐξελθόντες εἰς τὰς πλατείας αὐτῆς εἴπατε·
going forth into the streets of it say:
11 καὶ τὸν κονιορτὸν τὸν κολληθέντα ἡμῖν
Even the dust – adhering to us
=the dust of your city adhering to us, on our feet,
ἐκ τῆς πόλεως ὑμῶν εἰς τοὺς πόδας
of the city of you on the(our) feet
ἀπομασσόμεθα ὑμῖν· πλὴν τοῦτο γινώσκετε,
we shake off to you; nevertheless this know ye,
ὅτι ἤγγικεν ἡ βασιλεία τοῦ θεοῦ. 12 λέγω
that has drawn near the kingdom – of God. I tell
ὑμῖν ὅτι Σοδόμοις ἐν τῇ ἡμέρᾳ ἐκείνῃ
you that for Sodom in – day that
ἀνεκτότερον ἔσται ἢ τῇ πόλει ἐκείνῃ.
more endurable it will be than – city for that.
13 Οὐαί σοι, Χοραζίν, οὐαί σοι, Βηθσαϊδά·
Woe to thee, Chorazin, woe to thee, Bethsaida;
ὅτι εἰ ἐν Τύρῳ καὶ Σιδῶνι ἐγενήθησαν αἱ
because if in Tyre and Sidon happened the
δυνάμεις αἱ γενόμεναι ἐν ὑμῖν, πάλαι ἂν ἐν
powerful deeds – happening in you, long ago – in
σάκκῳ καὶ σποδῷ καθήμενοι μετενόησαν.
sackcloth and ashes sitting they would have repented.

are few. Ask the Lord of
the harvest, therefore, to
send out workers into his
harvest field. 3Go! I am
sending you out like lambs
among wolves. 4Do not
take a purse or bag or sandals; and do not greet anyone on the road.
5"When you enter a
house, first say, 'Peace to
this house.' 6If a man of
peace is there, your peace
will rest on him; if not, it
will return to you. 7Stay in
that house, eating and
drinking whatever they
give you, for the worker deserves his wages. Do not
move around from house to
house.
8"When you enter a town
and are welcomed, eat
what is set before you.
9Heal the sick who are
there and tell them, 'The
kingdom of God is near
you.' 10But when you enter
a town and are not wel-
comed, go into its streets
and say, 11'Even the dust of
your town that sticks to our
feet we wipe off against
you. Yet be sure of this:
The kingdom of God is
near.' 12I tell you, it will be
more bearable on that day
for Sodom than for that
town.
13"Woe to you, Korazin!
Woe to you, Bethsaida!
For if the miracles that
were performed in you had
been performed in Tyre
and Sidon, they would
have repented long ago, sitting in sackcloth and ashes.

* Luke here, and in 2. 38; 10. 21; 12. 12; 13. 31; 24. 13, as well as in Acts 16. 18; 22. 13, ignores the strict idiomatic construction of αὐτός when in apposition. The words here should mean "in the house itself" but obviously do mean "in the same house". So elsewhere. See note on Luke 2. 38.

[e] Or *is at hand for you*
[f] Or *is at hand*

the judgment it will be more tolerable for Tyre and Sidon than for you. [15]And you, Capernaum,
will you be exalted to heaven?
No, you will be brought down to Hades.

16 "Whoever listens to you listens to me, and whoever rejects you rejects me, and whoever rejects me rejects the one who sent me."

The Return of the Seventy

17 The seventy[g] returned with joy, saying, "Lord, in your name even the demons submit to us!" [18]He said to them, "I watched Satan fall from heaven like a flash of lightning. [19]See, I have given you authority to tread on snakes and scorpions, and over all the power of the enemy; and nothing will hurt you. [20]Nevertheless, do not rejoice at this, that the spirits submit to you, but rejoice that your names are written in heaven."

Jesus Rejoices

21 At that same hour Jesus[h] rejoiced in the Holy Spirit[i] and said, "I thank[j] you, Father, Lord of heaven and earth, because you have hidden these things from the wise and the intelligent and have revealed them to infants; yes, Father, for such was your gracious will.[k] [22]All things have been handed over to me by my Father; and no one knows who the Son is except the Father, or who the Father is except the Son and anyone to whom the Son chooses to reveal him."

23 Then turning to the disciples, Jesus[h] said to them privately, "Blessed are the eyes that see what you see! [24]For I tell you

[g] Other ancient authorities read *seventy-two*
[h] Gk *he*
[i] Other authorities read *in the spirit*
[j] Or *praise*
[k] Or *for so it was well-pleasing in your sight*

14 πλὴν Τύρῳ καὶ Σιδῶνι ἀνεκτότερον
Nevertheless for Tyre and Sidon more endurable
ἔσται ἐν τῇ κρίσει ἢ ὑμῖν. **15** καὶ σύ,
it will be in the judgment than for you. And thou,
Καφαρναούμ, μὴ ἕως οὐρανοῦ ὑψωθήσῃ;
Capernaum, *not* to heaven wast thou lifted?
ἕως τοῦ ᾅδου καταβήσῃ. **16** Ὁ ἀκούων
to – hades thou shalt come down. The [one] hearing
ὑμῶν ἐμοῦ ἀκούει, καὶ ὁ ἀθετῶν ὑμᾶς
you me hears, and the [one] rejecting you
ἐμὲ ἀθετεῖ· ὁ δὲ ἐμὲ ἀθετῶν ἀθετεῖ τὸν
me rejects; and the [one] me rejecting rejects the [one]
ἀποστείλαντά με. **17** Ὑπέστρεψαν δὲ οἱ
having sent me. And returned the
ἑβδομήκοντα [δύο] μετὰ χαρᾶς λέγοντες·
seventy-two with joy saying :
κύριε, καὶ τὰ δαιμόνια ὑποτάσσεται ἡμῖν
Lord, even the demons submit*s* to us
ἐν τῷ ὀνόματί σου. **18** εἶπεν δὲ αὐτοῖς·
in the name of thee. And he said to them :
ἐθεώρουν τὸν σατανᾶν ὡς ἀστραπὴν ἐκ
I beheld – Satan as lightning out of
τοῦ οὐρανοῦ πεσόντα. **19** ἰδοὺ δέδωκα
– heaven fall. Behold I have given
ὑμῖν τὴν ἐξουσίαν τοῦ πατεῖν ἐπάνω
you the authority – to tread[d] on
ὄφεων καὶ σκορπίων, καὶ ἐπὶ πᾶσαν τὴν
serpents and scorpions, and on all the
δύναμιν τοῦ ἐχθροῦ, καὶ οὐδὲν ὑμᾶς οὐ μὴ
power of the enemy, and nothing you by no(any) means
ἀδικήσει. **20** πλὴν ἐν τούτῳ μὴ χαίρετε
shall hurt. Nevertheless in this rejoice not
ὅτι τὰ πνεύματα ὑμῖν ὑποτάσσεται, χαίρετε
that the spirits to you submit*s*, ²rejoice
δὲ ὅτι τὰ ὀνόματα ὑμῶν ἐγγέγραπται ἐν
¹but that the names of you have been enrolled in
τοῖς οὐρανοῖς. **21** Ἐν αὐτῇ τῇ ὥρᾳ
the heavens. In ²same ¹the hour
ἠγαλλιάσατο τῷ πνεύματι τῷ ἁγίῳ καὶ
he exulted in(?by) the Spirit – Holy and
εἶπεν· ἐξομολογοῦμαί σοι, πάτερ, κύριε
said: I praise thee, Father, Lord
τοῦ οὐρανοῦ καὶ τῆς γῆς, ὅτι ἀπέκρυψας
– of heaven and – of earth, because thou didst hide
ταῦτα ἀπὸ σοφῶν καὶ συνετῶν, καὶ
these things from wise and intelligent [ones], and
ἀπεκάλυψας αὐτὰ νηπίοις· ναί, ὁ πατήρ,
didst reveal them to infants; yes – Father,
ὅτι οὕτως εὐδοκία ἐγένετο ἔμπροσθέν σου.
because thus good pleasure it was before thee.
22 πάντα μοι παρεδόθη ὑπὸ τοῦ πατρός
All things to me were delivered by the Father
μου, καὶ οὐδεὶς γινώσκει τίς ἐστιν ὁ
of me, and no one knows who is the
υἱὸς εἰ μὴ ὁ πατήρ, καὶ τίς ἐστιν ὁ πατὴρ
Son except the Father, and who is the Father
εἰ μὴ ὁ υἱὸς καὶ ᾧ ἐὰν βούληται
except the Son and [he] to whomever wills
ὁ υἱὸς ἀποκαλύψαι. **23** Καὶ στραφεὶς
the Son to reveal [him]. And turning
πρὸς τοὺς μαθητὰς κατ' ἰδίαν εἶπεν·
to the disciples privately he said :
μακάριοι οἱ ὀφθαλμοὶ οἱ βλέποντες ἃ
Blessed the eyes – seeing the things which
βλέπετε. **24** λέγω γὰρ ὑμῖν ὅτι πολλοὶ
ye see. For I tell you that many

[14]But it will be more bearable for Tyre and Sidon at the judgment than for you. [15]And you, Capernaum, will you be lifted up to the skies? No, you will go down to the depths.[o]

[16]"He who listens to you listens to me; he who rejects you rejects me; but he who rejects me rejects him who sent me."

[17]The seventy-two returned with joy and said, "Lord, even the demons submit to us in your name."

[18]He replied, "I saw Satan fall like lightning from heaven. [19]I have given you authority to trample on snakes and scorpions and to overcome all the power of the enemy; nothing will harm you. [20]However, do not rejoice that the spirits submit to you, but rejoice that your names are written in heaven."

[21]At that time Jesus, full of joy through the Holy Spirit, said, "I praise you, Father, Lord of heaven and earth, because you have hidden these things from the wise and learned, and revealed them to little children. Yes, Father, for this was your good pleasure.

[22]"All things have been committed to me by my Father. No one knows who the Son is except the Father, and no one knows who the Father is except the Son and those to whom the Son chooses to reveal him."

[23]Then he turned to his disciples and said privately, "Blessed are the eyes that see what you see. [24]For I tell you that many

[o] 15 Greek *Hades*

that many prophets and
kings desired to see what
you see, but did not see it,
and to hear what you hear,
but did not hear it."

The Parable of the Good Samaritan

25 Just then a lawyer
stood up to test Jesus.[l]
"Teacher," he said, "what
must I do to inherit eternal
life?" 26He said to him,
"What is written in the law?
What do you read there?"
27He answered, "You shall
love the Lord your God
with all your heart, and
with all your soul, and with
all your strength, and with
all your mind; and your
neighbor as yourself."
28And he said to him, "You
have given the right an-
swer; do this, and you will
live."
29 But wanting to justi-
fy himself, he asked Jesus,
"And who is my neigh-
bor?" 30Jesus replied, "A
man was going down from
Jerusalem to Jericho, and
fell into the hands of robbers, who stripped him,
beat him, and went away,
leaving him half dead.
31Now by chance a priest
was going down that road;
and when he saw him, he
passed by on the other side.
32So likewise a Levite,
when he came to the place
and saw him, passed by on
the other side. 33But a Samaritan while traveling
came near him; and when
he saw him, he was moved
with pity. 34He went to him
and bandaged his wounds,
having poured oil and wine
on them. Then he put him
on his own animal, brought
him to an inn, and took care
of him. 35The next day he
took out two denarii,[m] gave
them to the innkeeper, and
said, 'Take care of him; and

προφῆται καὶ βασιλεῖς ἠθέλησαν ἰδεῖν ἃ
prophets and kings desired to see the things which
ὑμεῖς βλέπετε καὶ οὐκ εἶδαν, καὶ ἀκοῦσαι
ye see and did not see, and to hear
ἃ ἀκούετε καὶ οὐκ ἤκουσαν.
the things which ye hear and did not hear.
25 Καὶ ἰδοὺ νομικός τις ἀνέστη
And[,] behold[,] lawyer a certain stood up
ἐκπειράζων αὐτὸν λέγων· διδάσκαλε, τί
tempting him saying: Teacher, what
ποιήσας ζωὴν αἰώνιον κληρονομήσω; 26 ὁ
doing 5life 4eternal 3I 1may 2inherit? he
δὲ εἶπεν πρὸς αὐτόν· ἐν τῷ νόμῳ τί
And said to him: In the law what
γέγραπται; πῶς ἀναγινώσκεις; 27 ὁ δὲ
has been written? how readest thou? And he
ἀποκριθεὶς εἶπεν· ἀγαπήσεις κύριον τὸν
answering said: Thou shalt love [the] Lord the
θεόν σου ἐξ ὅλης τῆς καρδίας σου καὶ
God of thee from all the heart of thee and
ἐν ὅλῃ τῇ ψυχῇ σου καὶ ἐν ὅλῃ τῇ
with all the soul of thee and with all the
ἰσχύϊ σου καὶ ἐν ὅλῃ τῇ διανοίᾳ σου,
strength of thee and with all the mind of thee,
καὶ τὸν πλησίον σου ὡς σεαυτόν. 28 εἶπεν
and the neighbour of thee as thyself. he said
δὲ αὐτῷ· ὀρθῶς ἀπεκρίθης· τοῦτο ποίει
And to him: Rightly thou didst answer; this do
καὶ ζήσῃ. 29 ὁ δὲ θέλων δικαιῶσαι ἑαυτὸν
and thou shalt live. But he wishing to justify himself
εἶπεν πρὸς τὸν Ἰησοῦν· καὶ τίς ἐστίν
said to – Jesus: And who is
μου πλησίον; 30 ὑπολαβὼν ὁ Ἰησοῦς
of me neighbour? Taking [him] up – Jesus
εἶπεν· ἄνθρωπός τις κατέβαινεν ἀπὸ
said: A certain man was going down from
Ἰερουσαλὴμ εἰς Ἰεριχώ, καὶ λησταῖς
Jerusalem to Jericho, and 2robbers
περιέπεσεν, οἳ καὶ ἐκδύσαντες αὐτὸν καὶ
1fell in with, who both stripping him and
πληγὰς ἐπιθέντες ἀπῆλθον ἀφέντες ἡμιθανῆ.
2blows 1laying 3on 4[him] went away leaving [him] half dead.
31 κατὰ συγκυρίαν δὲ ἱερεύς τις κατέβαινεν
And by a coincidence a certain priest was going down
ἐν τῇ ὁδῷ ἐκείνῃ, καὶ ἰδὼν αὐτὸν
in – way that, and seeing him
ἀντιπαρῆλθεν. 32 ὁμοίως δὲ καὶ Λευίτης
passed by opposite. And likewise also a Levite
κατὰ τὸν τόπον ἐλθὼν καὶ ἰδὼν
upon the place coming and seeing
ἀντιπαρῆλθεν. 33 Σαμαρίτης δέ τις ὁδεύων
passed by opposite. And a certain Samaritan journeying
ἦλθεν κατ' αὐτὸν καὶ ἰδὼν ἐσπλαγχνίσθη,
came upon him and seeing was filled with pity,
34 καὶ προσελθὼν κατέδησεν τὰ τραύματα
and approaching bound up the wounds
αὐτοῦ ἐπιχέων ἔλαιον καὶ οἶνον, ἐπιβιβάσας
of him pouring on oil and wine, 2placing
δὲ αὐτὸν ἐπὶ τὸ ἴδιον κτῆνος ἤγαγεν
1and him on the(his) own beast brought
αὐτὸν εἰς πανδοχεῖον καὶ ἐπεμελήθη αὐτοῦ.
him to an inn and cared for him.
35 καὶ ἐπὶ τὴν αὔριον ἐκβαλὼν δύο
And on the morrow taking out two
δηνάρια ἔδωκεν τῷ πανδοχεῖ καὶ εἶπεν·
denarii he gave to the innkeeper and said:

prophets and kings wanted
to see what you see but did
not see it, and to hear what
you hear but did not hear
it."

The Parable of the Good Samaritan

25On one occasion an ex-
pert in the law stood up to
test Jesus. "Teacher," he
asked, "what must I do to
inherit eternal life?"
26"What is written in the
Law?" he replied. "How
do you read it?"
27He answered: " 'Love
the Lord your God with all
your heart and with all your
soul and with all your
strength and with all your
mind'[p]; and, 'Love your
neighbor as yourself.'[q]"
28"You have answered
correctly," Jesus replied.
"Do this and you will
live."
29But he wanted to justify
himself, so he asked Jesus,
"And who is my neigh-
bor?"
30In reply Jesus said: "A
man was going down from
Jerusalem to Jericho, when
he fell into the hands of robbers. They stripped him of
his clothes, beat him and
went away, leaving him
half dead. 31A priest happened to be going down the
same road, and when he
saw the man, he passed by
on the other side. 32So too,
a Levite, when he came to
the place and saw him,
passed by on the other side.
33But a Samaritan, as he
traveled, came where the
man was; and when he saw
him, he took pity on him.
34He went to him and ban-
daged his wounds, pouring
on oil and wine. Then he
put the man on his own
donkey, took him to an inn
and took care of him. 35The
next day he took out two
silver coins[r] and gave
them to the innkeeper.
'Look after him,' he said,

[l] Gk *him*
[m] The denarius was the usual day's wage for a laborer

[p] 27 Deut. 6:5
[q] 27 Lev. 19:18
[r] 35 Greek *two denarii*

when I come back, I will
repay you whatever more
you spend.' 36 Which of
these three, do you think,
was a neighbor to the man
who fell into the hands of
the robbers?" 37 He said,
"The one who showed him
mercy." Jesus said to him,
"Go and do likewise."

Jesus Visits Martha and Mary

38 Now as they went on
their way, he entered a certain village, where a woman named Martha wel-
comed him into her home.
39 She had a sister named
Mary, who sat at the
Lord's feet and listened to
what he was saying. 40 But
Martha was distracted by
her many tasks; so she
came to him and asked,
"Lord, do you not care that
my sister has left me to do
all the work by myself? Tell
her then to help me." 41 But
the Lord answered her,
"Martha, Martha, you are
worried and distracted by
many things; 42 there is
need of only one thing.[n]
Mary has chosen the better
part, which will not be tak-
en away from her."

Chapter 11

The Lord's Prayer

HE was praying in a cer-
tain place, and after
he had finished, one of his
disciples said to him,
"Lord, teach us to pray, as
John taught his disciples."
2 He said to them, "When
you pray, say:
Father,[o] hallowed be

[n] Other ancient authorities read *few things are necessary, or only one*

[o] Other ancient authorities read *Our Father in heaven*

ἐπιμελήθητι αὐτοῦ, καὶ ὅ τι ἂν προσδα-
Care thou for him, and whatever thou spendest
πανήσῃς ἐγὼ ἐν τῷ ἐπανέρχεσθαί με
in addition I in the to return me[be]
=when I return
ἀποδώσω σοι. **36** τίς τούτων τῶν τριῶν πλησίον
will repay thee. Who of these – three [4]neighbour
δοκεῖ σοι γεγονέναι τοῦ ἐμπεσόντος
[1]seems it [2]to thee [3]to have become of the [one] falling *into*
εἰς τοὺς λῃστάς; **37** ὁ δὲ εἶπεν· ὁ ποιήσας
among the robbers? And he said: The [one] doing
τὸ ἔλεος μετ' αὐτοῦ. εἶπεν δὲ αὐτῷ ὁ
the mercy with him. And said to him
Ἰησοῦς· πορεύου καὶ σὺ ποίει ὁμοίως.
Jesus: Go and thou do likewise.
38 Ἐν δὲ τῷ πορεύεσθαι αὐτοὺς αὐτὸς
And in the to go them[be] he
=as they went
εἰσῆλθεν εἰς κώμην τινά· γυνὴ δέ τις
entered into a certain village; and a certain woman
ὀνόματι Μάρθα ὑπεδέξατο αὐτὸν εἰς τὴν
by name Martha received him into the
οἰκίαν. **39** καὶ τῇδε ἦν ἀδελφὴ καλουμένη
house. And to this was a sister[c] *being* called
=she had a sister
Μαριάμ, ἣ καὶ παρακαθεσθεῖσα πρὸς τοὺς
Mary, who also sitting beside at the
πόδας τοῦ κυρίου ἤκουεν τὸν λόγον αὐτοῦ.
feet of the Lord heard the word of him.
40 ἡ δὲ Μάρθα περιεσπᾶτο περὶ πολλὴν
– But Martha was distracted about much
διακονίαν· ἐπιστᾶσα δὲ εἶπεν· κύριε, οὐ
serving; and coming upon [him] she said: Lord, not
μέλει σοι ὅτι ἡ ἀδελφή μου μόνην με
matters it to thee that the sister of me [3]alone [2]me
κατέλειπεν διακονεῖν; εἰπὸν οὖν αὐτῇ ἵνα
[1]left to serve? tell therefore her that
μοι συναντιλάβηται. **41** ἀποκριθεὶς δὲ εἶπεν
[2]me [1]she may help. And answering said
αὐτῇ ὁ κύριος· Μάρθα Μάρθα, μεριμνᾷς
to her the Lord: Martha[,] Martha, thou art anxious
καὶ θορυβάζῃ περὶ πολλά, **42** ὀλίγων δέ
and disturbed about many things, but of few things
ἔστιν χρεία ἢ ἑνός· Μαριὰμ γὰρ τὴν
there is need or of one; for Mary the
ἀγαθὴν μερίδα ἐξελέξατο, ἥτις οὐκ
good part chose, which not
ἀφαιρεθήσεται αὐτῆς.
shall be taken from her.

11 Καὶ ἐγένετο ἐν τῷ εἶναι αὐτὸν ἐν
And it came to pass in the to be him[be] in
=when he was
τόπῳ τινὶ προσευχόμενον, ὡς ἐπαύσατο,
a certain place praying, as he ceased,
εἶπέν τις τῶν μαθητῶν αὐτοῦ πρὸς
said a certain one of the disciples of him to
αὐτόν· κύριε, δίδαξον ἡμᾶς προσεύχεσθαι,
him: Lord, teach us to pray,
καθὼς καὶ Ἰωάννης ἐδίδαξεν τοὺς μαθητὰς
even as also John taught the disciples
αὐτοῦ. **2** εἶπεν δὲ αὐτοῖς· ὅταν
of him. And he said to them: When
προσεύχησθε, λέγετε· Πάτερ, ἁγιασθήτω τὸ
ye pray, say: Father, let be hallowed the

'and when I return, I will
reimburse you for any ex-
tra expense you may have.'
36 "Which of these three
do you think was a neigh-
bor to the man who fell into
the hands of robbers?"
37 The expert in the law replied, "The one who had
mercy on him."
Jesus told him, "Go and
do likewise."

At the Home of Martha and Mary

38 As Jesus and his disciples were on their way, he
came to a village where a
woman named Martha
opened her home to him.
39 She had a sister called
Mary, who sat at the
Lord's feet listening to
what he said. 40 But Martha
was distracted by all the
preparations that had to be
made. She came to him and
asked, "Lord, don't you
care that my sister has left
me to do the work by my-
self? Tell her to help me!"
41 "Martha, Martha," the
Lord answered, "you are
worried and upset about
many things, 42 but only one
thing is needed.[s] Mary has
chosen what is better, and
it will not be taken away
from her."

Chapter 11

Jesus' Teaching on Prayer

ONE day Jesus was
praying in a certain
place. When he finished,
one of his disciples said to
him, "Lord, teach us to
pray, just as John taught his
disciples."
2 He said to them, "When
you pray, say:

" 'Father,[t]
hallowed be your name,

[s] 42 Some manuscripts *but few things are needed—or only one*

[t] 2 Some manuscripts *Our Father in heaven*

your name.
Your kingdom
come.[p]
3 Give us each day
our daily
bread.[q]
4 And forgive us our
sins,
for we ourselves
forgive everyone
indebted to us.
And do not bring us
to the time of
trial."[r]

Perseverance in Prayer

5 And he said to them,
"Suppose one of you has a
friend, and you go to him at
midnight and say to him,
'Friend, lend me three
loaves of bread; 6for a
friend of mine has arrived,
and I have nothing to set
before him.' 7And he an-
swers from within, 'Do not
bother me; the door has already been locked, and my
children are with me in bed;
I cannot get up and give
you anything.' 8I tell you,
even though he will not get
up and give him anything
because he is his friend, at
least because of his persistence he will get up and
give him whatever he
needs.
9 "So I say to you, Ask,
and it will be given you;
search, and you will find;
knock, and the door will be
opened for you. 10For ev-
eryone who asks receives,
and everyone who searches
finds, and for everyone
who knocks, the door will
be opened. 11Is there anyone among you who, if
your child asks for[s] a fish,
will give a snake instead of
a fish? 12Or if the child asks
for an egg, will give a scorpion? 13If you then, who
are evil, know how to give
good gifts to your children,
how much more will the
heavenly Father give the
Holy Spirit[t] to those who
ask him!"

Jesus and Beelzebul

14 Now he was casting
out a demon that was mute;
when the demon had gone
out, the one who had been

ὄνομά σου· ἐλθάτω ἡ βασιλεία σου·
name of thee; let come the kingdom of thee;
3 τὸν ἄρτον ἡμῶν τὸν ἐπιούσιον δίδου
the bread of us – belonging to the morrow give
ἡμῖν τὸ καθ' ἡμέραν· 4 καὶ ἄφες ἡμῖν τὰς
us each day†; and forgive us the
ἁμαρτίας ἡμῶν, καὶ γὰρ αὐτοὶ ἀφίομεν
sins of us, for indeed [our]selves we forgive
παντὶ ὀφείλοντι ἡμῖν· καὶ μὴ εἰσενέγκῃς
everyone owing to us; and lead not
ἡμᾶς εἰς πειρασμόν. 5 Καὶ εἶπεν πρὸς
us into temptation. And he said to
αὐτούς· τίς ἐξ ὑμῶν ἕξει φίλον, καὶ
them : Who of you shall have a friend, and
πορεύσεται πρὸς αὐτὸν μεσονυκτίου καὶ
will come to him at midnight and
εἴπῃ αὐτῷ· φίλε, χρῆσόν μοι τρεῖς ἄρτους,
say to him : Friend, lend me three loaves,
6 ἐπειδὴ φίλος μου παρεγένετο ἐξ ὁδοῦ
since a friend of me arrived off a journey
πρός με καὶ οὐκ ἔχω ὃ παραθήσω αὐτῷ·
to me and I have not what I may set before him;
7 κἀκεῖνος ἔσωθεν ἀποκριθεὶς εἴπῃ· μή
and that one within answering may say : Not
μοι κόπους πάρεχε· ἤδη ἡ θύρα κέκλεισται,
me troubles cause; now the door has been shut,
καὶ τὰ παιδία μου μετ' ἐμοῦ εἰς τὴν
and the children of me with me in the
κοίτην εἰσίν· οὐ δύναμαι ἀναστὰς δοῦναί
bed are; I cannot rising up *to* give
σοι. 8 λέγω ὑμῖν, εἰ καὶ οὐ δώσει
thee. I tell you, if even he will not give
αὐτῷ ἀναστὰς διὰ τὸ εἶναι φίλον αὐτοῦ,
him rising up on account of the to be friend of him,
=because he is his friend,
διά γε τὴν ἀναίδειαν αὐτοῦ ἐγερθεὶς
yet on account of the importunity of him rising
δώσει αὐτῷ ὅσων χρῄζει. 9 Κἀγὼ ὑμῖν
he will give him as many as he needs. And I [2]you
λέγω, αἰτεῖτε, καὶ δοθήσεται ὑμῖν· ζητεῖτε,
[1]tell, ask, and it will be given you; seek,
καὶ εὑρήσετε· κρούετε, καὶ ἀνοιγήσεται
and ye will find; knock, and it will be opened
ὑμῖν. 10 πᾶς γὰρ ὁ αἰτῶν λαμβάνει, καὶ
to you. For everyone asking receives, and
ὁ ζητῶν εὑρίσκει, καὶ τῷ κρούοντι
the [one] seeking finds, and to the [one] knocking
ἀνοιγήσεται. 11 τίνα δὲ ἐξ ὑμῶν τὸν
it will be opened. And [1]what [4]of [5]you –
πατέρα αἰτήσει ὁ υἱὸς ἰχθύν, μὴ
[6]father [3][is there] [2][of whom] [9]will ask [7]the [8]son [10]a fish, *not*
ἀντὶ ἰχθύος ὄφιν αὐτῷ ἐπιδώσει; 12 ἢ
instead of a fish [3]a serpent [2]to him [1]will hand? or
καὶ αἰτήσει ᾠόν, ἐπιδώσει αὐτῷ σκορπίον;
even he will ask an egg, will hand to him a scorpion?
13 εἰ οὖν ὑμεῖς πονηροὶ ὑπάρχοντες οἴδατε δόματα
If therefore ye [2]evil [1]being know gifts
ἀγαθὰ διδόναι τοῖς τέκνοις ὑμῶν, πόσῳ
good to give to the children of you, how much
μᾶλλον ὁ πατὴρ ὁ ἐξ οὐρανοῦ δώσει
more the Father – of heaven will give
πνεῦμα ἅγιον τοῖς αἰτοῦσιν αὐτόν.
Spirit [the] Holy to the [ones] asking him.
14 Καὶ ἦν ἐκβάλλων δαιμόνιον, καὶ αὐτὸ
And he was expelling a demon, and it
ἦν κωφόν· ἐγένετο δὲ τοῦ δαιμονίου
was dumb; and it came to pass the demon
=as the demon went out

your kingdom come.[u]
3Give us each day our
daily bread.
4Forgive us our sins,
for we also forgive
everyone who sins
against us.[v]
And lead us not into
temptation.[w]' "

5Then he said to them,
"Suppose one of you has a
friend, and he goes to him
at midnight and says,
'Friend, lend me three
loaves of bread, 6because a
friend of mine on a journey
has come to me, and I have
nothing to set before him.'
7"Then the one inside an-
swers, 'Don't bother me.
The door is already locked,
and my children are with
me in bed. I can't get up
and give you anything.' 8I
tell you, though he will not
get up and give him the
bread because he is his
friend, yet because of the
man's boldness[x] he will get
up and give him as much as
he needs.
9"So I say to you: Ask
and it will be given to you;
seek and you will find;
knock and the door will be
opened to you. 10For ev-
eryone who asks receives;
he who seeks finds; and to
him who knocks, the door
will be opened.
11"Which of you fathers,
if your son asks for[y] a fish,
will give him a snake in-
stead? 12Or if he asks for an
egg, will give him a scorpion? 13If you then, though
you are evil, know how to
give good gifts to your children, how much more will
your Father in heaven give
the Holy Spirit to those
who ask him!"

Jesus and Beelzebub

14Jesus was driving out a
demon that was mute.
When the demon left, the

[p] A few ancient authorities read *Your Holy Spirit come upon us and cleanse us.* Other ancient authorities add *Your will be done, on earth as in heaven*
[q] Or *our bread for tomorrow*
[r] Or *us into temptation.* Other ancient authorities add *but rescue us from the evil one* (or *from evil*)
[s] Other ancient authorities add *bread, will give a stone; or if your child asks for*
[t] Other ancient authorities read *the Father give the Holy Spirit from heaven*

[u]2 Some manuscripts *come. May your will be done on earth as it is in heaven.*
[v]4 Greek *everyone who is indebted to us*
[w]4 Some manuscripts *temptation but deliver us from the evil one*
[x]8 Or *persistence*
[y]11 Some manuscripts *for bread, will give him a stone; or if he asks for*

mute spoke, and the
crowds were amazed.
15 But some of them said,
"He casts out demons by
Beelzebul, the ruler of the
demons." 16 Others, to test
him, kept demanding from
him a sign from heaven.
17 But he knew what they
were thinking and said to
them, "Every kingdom di-
vided against itself be-
comes a desert, and house
falls on house. 18 If Satan
also is divided against himself, how will his kingdom
stand? —for you say that I
cast out the demons by Beelzebul. 19 Now if I cast out
the demons by Beelzebul,
by whom do your exor-
cists[u] cast them out?
Therefore they will be your
judges. 20 But if it is by the
finger of God that I cast out
the demons, then the kingdom of God has come to
you. 21 When a strong man,
fully armed, guards his cas-
tle, his property is safe.
22 But when one stronger
than he attacks him and
overpowers him, he takes
away his armor in which he
trusted and divides his
plunder. 23 Whoever is not
with me is against me, and
whoever does not gather
with me scatters.

The Return of the Unclean Spirit

24 "When the unclean
spirit has gone out of a person, it wanders through
waterless regions looking
for a resting place, but not
finding any, it says, 'I will
return to my house from
which I came.' 25 When it
comes, it finds it swept and
put in order. 26 Then it goes
and brings seven other spirits more evil than itself, and

ἐξελθόντος ἐλάλησεν ὁ κωφός· καὶ
going out[a] spoke the dumb man; and

ἐθαύμασαν οἱ ὄχλοι· 15 τινὲς δὲ ἐξ
marvelled the crowds; but some of

αὐτῶν εἶπαν· ἐν Βεεζεβοὺλ τῷ ἄρχοντι
them said: By Beelzebub the chief

τῶν δαιμονίων ἐκβάλλει τὰ δαιμόνια·
of the demons he expels the demons;

16 ἕτεροι δὲ πειράζοντες σημεῖον ἐξ οὐρανοῦ
and others tempting a sign out of heaven

ἐζήτουν παρ' αὐτοῦ. 17 αὐτὸς δὲ εἰδὼς
sought from him. But he knowing

αὐτῶν τὰ διανοήματα εἶπεν αὐτοῖς· πᾶσα
of them the thoughts said to them: Every

βασιλεία ἐφ' ἑαυτὴν διαμερισθεῖσα ἐρημοῦται,
kingdom against itself divided is made desolate,

καὶ οἶκος ἐπὶ οἶκον πίπτει. 18 εἰ δὲ
and a house against a house falls. And if

καὶ ὁ σατανᾶς ἐφ' ἑαυτὸν διεμερίσθη,
also – Satan against himself was divided,

πῶς σταθήσεται ἡ βασιλεία αὐτοῦ; ὅτι
how will stand the kingdom of him? because

λέγετε ἐν Βεεζεβοὺλ ἐκβάλλειν με τὰ
ye say by Beelzebub to expel me[b] the
=[that] by Beelzebub I expel

δαιμόνια. 19 εἰ δὲ ἐγὼ ἐν Βεεζεβοὺλ
demons. But if I by Beelzebub

ἐκβάλλω τὰ δαιμόνια, οἱ υἱοὶ ὑμῶν ἐν
expel the demons, the sons of you by

τίνι ἐκβάλλουσιν; διὰ τοῦτο αὐτοὶ ὑμῶν
what do they expel? therefore they of you

κριταὶ ἔσονται. 20 εἰ δὲ ἐν δακτύλῳ
judges shall be. But if by [the] finger

θεοῦ [ἐγὼ] ἐκβάλλω τὰ δαιμόνια, ἄρα
of God I expel the demons, then

ἔφθασεν ἐφ' ὑμᾶς ἡ βασιλεία τοῦ θεοῦ.
came upon you the kingdom – of God.

21 ὅταν ὁ ἰσχυρὸς καθωπλισμένος φυλάσσῃ
When the strong man *having been* well armed guards

τὴν ἑαυτοῦ αὐλήν, ἐν εἰρήνῃ ἐστὶν τὰ
the of him*self* palace, in peace is(are) the

ὑπάρχοντα αὐτοῦ· 22 ἐπὰν δὲ ἰσχυρότερος
goods of him; but when a stronger

αὐτοῦ ἐπελθὼν νικήσῃ αὐτόν, τὴν πανοπλίαν
[than] him coming upon overcomes him, the armour

αὐτοῦ αἴρει, ἐφ' ᾗ ἐπεποίθει, καὶ τὰ
of him he takes, on which he had relied, and the

σκῦλα αὐτοῦ διαδίδωσιν. 23 Ὁ μὴ ὢν
arms of him distributes. The [one] not being

μετ' ἐμοῦ κατ' ἐμοῦ ἐστιν, καὶ ὁ μὴ
with me against me is, and the [one] not

συνάγων μετ' ἐμοῦ σκορπίζει. 24 Ὅταν
gathering with me scatters. When

τὸ ἀκάθαρτον πνεῦμα ἐξέλθῃ ἀπὸ τοῦ
the unclean spirit goes out from the

ἀνθρώπου, διέρχεται δι' ἀνύδρων τόπων
man, he goes *through* through dry places

ζητοῦν ἀνάπαυσιν, καὶ μὴ εὑρίσκον λέγει·
seeking rest, and not finding says:

ὑποστρέψω εἰς τὸν οἶκόν μου ὅθεν ἐξῆλθον·
I will return to the house of me whence I came out;

25 καὶ ἐλθὸν εὑρίσκει σεσαρωμένον καὶ
and coming he finds [it] *having been* swept and

κεκοσμημένον. 26 τότε πορεύεται καὶ
having been furnished. Then he goes and

παραλαμβάνει ἕτερα πνεύματα πονηρότερα
takes other spirits more wicked

man who had been mute
spoke, and the crowd was
amazed. 15 But some of
them said, "By Beelze-
bub,[z] the prince of de-
mons, he is driving out demons." 16 Others tested
him by asking for a sign
from heaven.
17 Jesus knew their
thoughts and said to them:
"Any kingdom divided
against itself will be ruined,
and a house divided against
itself will fall. 18 If Satan is
divided against himself,
how can his kingdom
stand? I say this because
you claim that I drive out
demons by Beelzebub.
19 Now if I drive out de-
mons by Beelzebub, by
whom do your followers
drive them out? So then,
they will be your judges.
20 But if I drive out demons
by the finger of God, then
the kingdom of God has
come to you.
21 "When a strong man,
fully armed, guards his own
house, his possessions are
safe. 22 But when someone
stronger attacks and overpowers him, he takes away
the armor in which the man
trusted and divides up the
spoils.
23 "He who is not with me
is against me, and he who
does not gather with me,
scatters.
24 "When an evil[a] spirit
comes out of a man, it goes
through arid places seeking
rest and does not find it.
Then it says, 'I will return
to the house I left.' 25 When
it arrives, it finds the house
swept clean and put in order. 26 Then it goes and
takes seven other spirits
more wicked than itself,

[u] Gk *sons*

[z] *15* Greek *Beezeboul* or *Beelzeboul*; also in verses 18 and 19
[a] *24* Greek *unclean*

they enter and live there;
and the last state of that
person is worse than the
first."

True Blessedness

27 While he was saying
this, a woman in the crowd
raised her voice and said to
him, "Blessed is the womb
that bore you and the
breasts that nursed you!"
28 But he said, "Blessed
rather are those who hear
the word of God and obey
it!"

The Sign of Jonah

29 When the crowds
were increasing, he began
to say, "This generation is
an evil generation; it asks
for a sign, but no sign will
be given to it except the
sign of Jonah. 30 For just as
Jonah became a sign to the
people of Nineveh, so the
Son of Man will be to this
generation. 31 The queen of
the South will rise at the
judgment with the people
of this generation and condemn them, because she
came from the ends of the
earth to listen to the wisdom of Solomon, and see,
something greater than Solomon is here! 32 The people
of Nineveh will rise up at
the judgment with this generation and condemn it, because they repented at the
proclamation of Jonah, and
see, something greater than
Jonah is here!

The Light of the Body

33 "No one after light-
ing a lamp puts it in a cel-
lar,[v] but on the lampstand
so that those who enter
may see the light. 34 Your
eye is the lamp of your
body. If your eye is
healthy, your whole body
is full of light; but if it is not
healthy, your body is full of
darkness. 35 Therefore con-

[v] Other ancient authorities add *or under the bushel basket*

ἑαυτοῦ ἑπτά, καὶ εἰσελθόντα κατοικεῖ
[than] himself seven, and entering he dwells
ἐκεῖ· καὶ γίνεται τὰ ἔσχατα τοῦ ἀνθρώπου
there; and becomes the last things – man
ἐκείνου χείρονα τῶν πρώτων. 27 Ἐγένετο
of that worse [than] the first. it came to pass
δὲ ἐν τῷ λέγειν αὐτὸν ταῦτα ἐπάρασά τις
And in the to say him[be] these things [6]lifting up [1]a certain
=as he said
φωνὴν γυνὴ ἐκ τοῦ ὄχλου εἶπεν αὐτῷ·
[7][her] [8]voice [2]woman [3]of [4]the [5]crowd said to him:
μακαρία ἡ κοιλία ἡ βαστάσασά σε καὶ
Blessed the womb – having borne thee and
μαστοὶ οὓς ἐθήλασας. 28 αὐτὸς δὲ εἶπεν·
[the] breasts which thou didst suck. But he said:
μενοῦν μακάριοι οἱ ἀκούοντες τὸν λόγον
Nay rather blessed the [ones] hearing the word
τοῦ θεοῦ καὶ φυλάσσοντες.
– of God and keeping.
29 Τῶν δὲ ὄχλων ἐπαθροιζομένων ἤρξατο
And the crowds pressing upon[a] he began
=as the crowds pressed upon [him]
λέγειν· ἡ γενεὰ αὕτη γενεὰ πονηρά ἐστιν·
to say: – [2]generation [1]This [3]generation [4]an evil [5]is;
σημεῖον ζητεῖ, καὶ σημεῖον οὐ δοθήσεται
a sign it seeks, and a sign will not be given
αὐτῇ εἰ μὴ τὸ σημεῖον Ἰωνᾶ. 30 καθὼς
to it except the sign of Jonas. even as
γὰρ ἐγένετο [ὁ] Ἰωνᾶς τοῖς Νινευίταις
For [2]became – [1]Jonas [4]to the [5]Ninevites
σημεῖον, οὕτως ἔσται καὶ ὁ υἱὸς τοῦ
[3]a sign, so will be also the Son –
ἀνθρώπου τῇ γενεᾷ ταύτῃ. 31 βασίλισσα
of man – generation to this. [The] queen
νότου ἐγερθήσεται ἐν τῇ κρίσει μετὰ τῶν
of [the] south will be raised in the judgment with the
ἀνδρῶν τῆς γενεᾶς ταύτης καὶ κατακρινεῖ
men – generation of this and will condemn
αὐτούς· ὅτι ἦλθεν ἐκ τῶν περάτων τῆς
them; because she came from the extremities of the
γῆς ἀκοῦσαι τὴν σοφίαν Σολομῶνος, καὶ
earth to hear the wisdom of Solomon, and
ἰδοὺ πλεῖον Σολομῶνος ὧδε. 32 ἄνδρες
behold a greater [than] Solomon [is] here. Men
Νινευῖται ἀναστήσονται ἐν τῇ κρίσει μετὰ
Ninevites will rise up in the judgment with
τῆς γενεᾶς ταύτης καὶ κατακρινοῦσιν αὐτήν·
– generation this and will condemn it;
ὅτι μετενόησαν εἰς τὸ κήρυγμα Ἰωνᾶ, καὶ
because they repented at the proclamation of Jonas, and
ἰδοὺ πλεῖον Ἰωνᾶ ὧδε. 33 Οὐδεὶς λύχνον
behold a greater [than] Jonas [is] here. No one [2]a lamp
ἅψας εἰς κρύπτην τίθησιν οὐδὲ ὑπὸ τὸν
[1]having lit [4]in [5]secret [3]places [it] nor under the
μόδιον, ἀλλ' ἐπὶ τὴν λυχνίαν, ἵνα οἱ
bushel, but on the lampstand, that the
εἰσπορευόμενοι τὸ φέγγος βλέπωσιν. 34 ὁ
ones] entering the light may see. The
λύχνος τοῦ σώματός ἐστιν ὁ ὀφθαλμός σου.
lamp of the body is the eye of thee.
ὅταν ὁ ὀφθαλμός σου ἁπλοῦς ᾖ, καὶ
When the eye of thee single is, also
ὅλον τὸ σῶμά σου φωτεινόν ἐστιν· ἐπὰν
all the body of thee bright is; [2]when
δὲ πονηρὸς ᾖ, καὶ τὸ σῶμά σου σκοτεινόν.
[1]but evil it is, also the body of thee [is] dark.

and they go in and live
there. And the final condition of that man is worse
than the first."
27 As Jesus was saying
these things, a woman in
the crowd called out,
"Blessed is the mother
who gave you birth and
nursed you."
28 He replied, "Blessed
rather are those who hear
the word of God and obey
it."

The Sign of Jonah

29 As the crowds in-
creased, Jesus said, "This
is a wicked generation. It
asks for a miraculous sign,
but none will be given it except the sign of Jonah.
30 For as Jonah was a sign to
the Ninevites, so also will
the Son of Man be to this
generation. 31 The Queen of
the South will rise at the
judgment with the men of
this generation and con-
demn them; for she came
from the ends of the earth
to listen to Solomon's wisdom, and now one[b] greater
than Solomon is here.
32 The men of Nineveh will
stand up at the judgment
with this generation and
condemn it; for they re-
pented at the preaching of
Jonah, and now one greater
than Jonah is here.

The Lamp of the Body

33 "No one lights a lamp
and puts it in a place where
it will be hidden, or under a
bowl. Instead he puts it on
its stand, so that those who
come in may see the light.
34 Your eye is the lamp of
your body. When your
eyes are good, your whole
body also is full of light.
But when they are bad,
your body also is full of

[b] 31 Or *something*; also in verse 32

sider whether the light in you is not darkness. 36 If then your whole body is full of light, with no part of it in darkness, it will be as full of light as when a lamp gives you light with its rays."

Jesus Denounces Pharisees and Lawyers

37 While he was speaking, a Pharisee invited him to dine with him; so he went in and took his place at the table. 38 The Pharisee was amazed to see that he did not first wash before dinner. 39 Then the Lord said to him, "Now you Pharisees clean the outside of the cup and of the dish, but inside you are full of greed and wickedness. 40 You fools! Did not the one who made the outside make the inside also? 41 So give for alms those things that are within; and see, everything will be clean for you.

42 "But woe to you Pharisees! For you tithe mint and rue and herbs of all kinds, and neglect justice and the love of God; it is these you ought to have practiced, without neglecting the others. 43 Woe to you Pharisees! For you love to have the seat of honor in the synagogues and to be greeted with respect in the marketplaces. 44 Woe to you! For you are like unmarked graves, and people walk over them without realizing it."

45 One of the lawyers answered him, "Teacher, when you say these things, you insult us too." 46 And he said, "Woe also to you lawyers! For you load people with burdens hard to bear, and you yourselves do not lift a finger to ease

35 σκόπει οὖν μὴ τὸ φῶς τὸ ἐν σοὶ
Watch therefore lest the light – in thee

σκότος ἐστίν. **36** εἰ οὖν τὸ σῶμά σου
darkness is. If therefore [1]the [2]body [3]of thee

ὅλον φωτεινόν, μὴ ἔχον μέρος τι σκοτεινόν,
[4]whole [is] bright, not having [2]part [1]any dark,

ἔσται φωτεινὸν ὅλον ὡς ὅταν ὁ λύχνος
[2]will be [3]bright [1]all as when the lamp

τῇ ἀστραπῇ φωτίζῃ σε.
with the(its) shining enlightens thee.

37 Ἐν δὲ τῷ λαλῆσαι ἐρωτᾷ αὐτὸν
Now in the to speak[e] asks him
=as [he] spoke

Φαρισαῖος ὅπως ἀριστήσῃ παρ' αὐτῷ·
a Pharisee that he would dine with him;

εἰσελθὼν δὲ ἀνέπεσεν. **38** ὁ δὲ Φαρισαῖος
and entering he reclined. But the Pharisee

ἰδὼν ἐθαύμασεν ὅτι οὐ πρῶτον ἐβαπτίσθη
seeing marvelled that not first he washed

πρὸ τοῦ ἀρίστου. **39** εἶπεν δὲ ὁ κύριος
before the dinner. But said the Lord

πρὸς αὐτόν· νῦν ὑμεῖς οἱ Φαρισαῖοι τὸ
to him: Now ye – Pharisees the

ἔξωθεν τοῦ ποτηρίου καὶ τοῦ πίνακος
outside of the cup and of the dish

καθαρίζετε, τὸ δὲ ἔσωθεν ὑμῶν γέμει
cleanse, but the inside of you is full

ἁρπαγῆς καὶ πονηρίας. **40** ἄφρονες, οὐχ
of robbery and wickedness. Foolish men, not

ὁ ποιήσας τὸ ἔξωθεν καὶ τὸ ἔσωθεν
the [one] making the outside also the inside

ἐποίησεν; **41** πλὴν τὰ ἐνόντα δότε
made? Nevertheless the things being within give

ἐλεημοσύνην, καὶ ἰδοὺ πάντα καθαρὰ ὑμῖν
alms, and behold all things clean to you

ἐστιν. **42** ἀλλὰ οὐαὶ ὑμῖν τοῖς Φαρισαίοις,
is(are). But woe to you – Pharisees,

ὅτι ἀποδεκατοῦτε τὸ ἡδύοσμον καὶ τὸ
because ye tithe the mint and the

πήγανον καὶ πᾶν λάχανον, καὶ παρέρχεσθε
rue and every herb, and pass by

τὴν κρίσιν καὶ τὴν ἀγάπην τοῦ θεοῦ·
the judgment and the love – of God;

ταῦτα δὲ ἔδει ποιῆσαι κἀκεῖνα μὴ
but these things it behoved to do and those not

παρεῖναι. **43** οὐαὶ ὑμῖν τοῖς Φαρισαίοις,
to pass by. Woe to you – Pharisees,

ὅτι ἀγαπᾶτε τὴν πρωτοκαθεδρίαν ἐν ταῖς
because ye love the chief seat in the

συναγωγαῖς καὶ τοὺς ἀσπασμοὺς ἐν ταῖς
synagogues and the greetings in the

ἀγοραῖς. **44** οὐαὶ ὑμῖν, ὅτι ἐστὲ ὡς τὰ
marketplaces. Woe to you, because ye are as the

μνημεῖα τὰ ἄδηλα, καὶ οἱ ἄνθρωποι οἱ
tombs – unseen, and the men –

περιπατοῦντες ἐπάνω οὐκ οἴδασιν.
walking over do not know.

45 Ἀποκριθεὶς δέ τις τῶν νομικῶν λέγει
And answering one of the lawyers says

αὐτῷ· διδάσκαλε, ταῦτα λέγων καὶ ἡμᾶς
to him: Teacher, these things saying also us

ὑβρίζεις. **46** ὁ δὲ εἶπεν· καὶ ὑμῖν τοῖς
thou insultest. And he said: Also to you –

νομικοῖς οὐαί, ὅτι φορτίζετε τοὺς ἀνθρώπους
lawyers woe, because ye burden – men

φορτία δυσβάστακτα, καὶ αὐτοὶ ἑνὶ τῶν
[with] burdens difficult to carry, and [your]selves with one of the

darkness. 35 See to it, then, that the light within you is not darkness. 36 Therefore, if your whole body is full of light, and no part of it dark, it will be completely lighted, as when the light of a lamp shines on you."

Six Woes

37 When Jesus had finished speaking, a Pharisee invited him to eat with him; so he went in and reclined at the table. 38 But the Pharisee, noticing that Jesus did not first wash before the meal, was surprised.

39 Then the Lord said to him, "Now then, you Pharisees clean the outside of the cup and dish, but inside you are full of greed and wickedness. 40 You foolish people! Did not the one who made the outside make the inside also? 41 But give what is inside ⌞the dish⌟[c] to the poor, and everything will be clean for you.

42 "Woe to you Pharisees, because you give God a tenth of your mint, rue and all other kinds of garden herbs, but you neglect justice and the love of God. You should have practiced the latter without leaving the former undone.

43 "Woe to you Pharisees, because you love the most important seats in the synagogues and greetings in the marketplaces.

44 "Woe to you, because you are like unmarked graves, which men walk over without knowing it."

45 One of the experts in the law answered him, "Teacher, when you say these things, you insult us also."

46 Jesus replied, "And you experts in the law, woe to you, because you load people down with burdens they can hardly carry, and you yourselves will not lift

[c] 41 Or *what you have*

them. 47 Woe to you! For you build the tombs of the prophets whom your ancestors killed. 48 So you are witnesses and approve of the deeds of your ancestors; for they killed them, and you build their tombs. 49 Therefore also the Wisdom of God said, 'I will send them prophets and apostles, some of whom they will kill and persecute,' 50 so that this generation may be charged with the blood of all the prophets shed since the foundation of the world, 51 from the blood of Abel to the blood of Zechariah, who perished between the altar and the sanctuary. Yes, I tell you, it will be charged against this generation. 52 Woe to you lawyers! For you have taken away the key of knowledge; you did not enter yourselves, and you hindered those who were entering."

53 When he went outside, the scribes and the Pharisees began to be very hostile toward him and to cross-examine him about many things, 54 lying in wait for him, to catch him in something he might say.

δακτύλων ὑμῶν οὐ προσψαύετε τοῖς φορτίοις.
fingers of you ye do not touch the burdens.
47 οὐαὶ ὑμῖν, ὅτι οἰκοδομεῖτε τὰ μνημεῖα
Woe to you, because ye build the tombs
τῶν προφητῶν, οἱ δὲ πατέρες ὑμῶν
of the prophets, and the fathers of you
ἀπέκτειναν αὐτούς. **48** ἄρα μάρτυρές ἐστε
killed them. Therefore witnesses ye are
καὶ συνευδοκεῖτε τοῖς ἔργοις τῶν πατέρων
and ye entirely approve the works of the fathers
ὑμῶν, ὅτι αὐτοὶ μὲν ἀπέκτειναν αὐτούς,
of you, because they on one hand killed them,
ὑμεῖς δὲ οἰκοδομεῖτε. **49** διὰ τοῦτο καὶ
ye on the other hand build. Therefore also
ἡ σοφία τοῦ θεοῦ εἶπεν· ἀποστελῶ εἰς
the Wisdom – of God said: I will send to
αὐτοὺς προφήτας καὶ ἀποστόλους, καὶ ἐξ
them prophets and apostles, and of
αὐτῶν ἀποκτενοῦσιν καὶ διώξουσιν, **50** ἵνα
them they will kill and persecute, that
ἐκζητηθῇ τὸ αἷμα πάντων τῶν προφητῶν
[11]may be required [1]the [2]blood [3]of all [4]the [5]prophets
τὸ ἐκκεχυμένον ἀπὸ καταβολῆς κόσμου
– [6]*having been* shed [7]from [8][the] [9]foundation [10]of [the] world
ἀπὸ τῆς γενεᾶς ταύτης, **51** ἀπὸ αἵματος
[12]from – generation this, from [the] blood
[a]Ἄβελ ἕως αἵματος Ζαχαρίου τοῦ
of Abel to [the] blood of Zacharias –
ἀπολομένου μεταξὺ τοῦ θυσιαστηρίου καὶ
destroyed between the altar and
τοῦ οἴκου· ναὶ λέγω ὑμῖν, ἐκζητηθήσεται
the house; yes I tell you, it will be required
ἀπὸ τῆς γενεᾶς ταύτης. **52** οὐαὶ ὑμῖν τοῖς
from – generation this. Woe to you –
νομικοῖς, ὅτι ἤρατε τὴν κλεῖδα τῆς
lawyers, because ye took the key –
γνώσεως· αὐτοὶ οὐκ εἰσήλθατε καὶ τοὺς
of knowledge; [your]selves ye did not enter and the
εἰσερχομένους ἐκωλύσατε. **53** Κἀκεῖθεν ἐξελ-
[ones] entering ye prevented. And thence going
=as he went forth thence
θόντος αὐτοῦ ἤρξαντο οἱ γραμματεῖς καὶ
forth him[a] began the scribes and
οἱ Φαρισαῖοι δεινῶς ἐνέχειν καὶ ἀποστοματίζειν
the Pharisees [2]terribly [1]to be [3]angry and to [1]draw [3]out
αὐτὸν περὶ πλειόνων, **54** ἐνεδρεύοντες
[2]him concerning a great number of things, lying in wait for
αὐτὸν θηρεῦσαί τι ἐκ τοῦ στόματος αὐτοῦ.
him to catch something out of the mouth of him.

one finger to help them.

47 "Woe to you, because you build tombs for the prophets, and it was your forefathers who killed them. 48 So you testify that you approve of what your forefathers did; they killed the prophets, and you build their tombs. 49 Because of this, God in his wisdom said, 'I will send them prophets and apostles, some of whom they will kill and others they will persecute.' 50 Therefore this generation will be held responsible for the blood of all the prophets that has been shed since the beginning of the world, 51 from the blood of Abel to the blood of Zechariah, who was killed between the altar and the sanctuary. Yes, I tell you, this generation will be held responsible for it all.

52 "Woe to you experts in the law, because you have taken away the key to knowledge. You yourselves have not entered, and you have hindered those who were entering."

53 When Jesus left there, the Pharisees and the teachers of the law began to oppose him fiercely and to besiege him with questions, 54 waiting to catch him in something he might say.

Chapter 12

A Warning against Hypocrisy

MEANWHILE, when the crowd gathered by the thousands, so that they trampled on one another, he began to speak first to his disciples, "Beware of the yeast of the Pharisees, that is, their hypocrisy. 2 Nothing is covered up that will not be uncovered, and nothing secret that will not become

12 Ἐν οἷς ἐπισυναχθεισῶν τῶν μυριάδων
In which things being assembled the thousands
= Meanwhile as the thousands of the crowd were assembled,
τοῦ ὄχλου, ὥστε καταπατεῖν ἀλλήλους,
of the crowd,[a] so as to tread on one another,
ἤρξατο λέγειν πρὸς τοὺς μαθητὰς αὐτοῦ
he began to say to the disciples of him
πρῶτον· προσέχετε ἑαυτοῖς ἀπὸ τῆς ζύμης,
first: Take heed to yourselves from the leaven,
ἥτις ἐστὶν ὑπόκρισις, τῶν Φαρισαίων.
which is hypocrisy, of the Pharisees.
2 οὐδὲν δὲ συγκεκαλυμμένον ἐστὶν ὃ οὐκ
And [2]nothing [3]*having been* completely covered [1]there is which not
ἀποκαλυφθήσεται, καὶ κρυπτὸν ὃ οὐ γνωσθήσεται.
will be uncovered, and hidden which will not be known.

Chapter 12

Warnings and Encouragements

MEANWHILE, when a crowd of many thousands had gathered, so that they were trampling on one another, Jesus began to speak first to his disciples, saying: "Be on your guard against the yeast of the Pharisees, which is hypocrisy. 2 There is nothing concealed that will not be disclosed, or hidden that will not be made known. 3 What

known. 3Therefore what-
ever you have said in the
dark will be heard in the
light, and what you have
whispered behind closed
doors will be proclaimed
from the housetops.

Exhortation to Fearless Confession

4 "I tell you, my friends,
do not fear those who kill
the body, and after that can
do nothing more. 5But I
will warn you whom to
fear: fear him who, after he
has killed, has authority[w]
to cast into hell.[x] Yes, I tell
you, fear him! 6Are not five
sparrows sold for two pen-
nies? Yet not one of them is
forgotten in God's sight.
7But even the hairs of your
head are all counted. Do
not be afraid; you are of
more value than many
sparrows.
8 "And I tell you, every-
one who acknowledges me
before others, the Son of
Man also will acknowledge
before the angels of God;
9but whoever denies me
before others will be denied
before the angels of God.
10And everyone who
speaks a word against the
Son of Man will be forgiv-
en; but whoever blas-
phemes against the Holy
Spirit will not be forgiven.
11When they bring you be-
fore the synagogues, the
rulers, and the authorities,
do not worry about how[y]
you are to defend your-
selves or what you are to
say; 12for the Holy Spirit
will teach you at that very
hour what you ought to
say."

The Parable of the Rich Fool

13 Someone in the
crowd said to him, "Teacher, tell my brother to divide
the family inheritance with

[w] Or *power*
[x] Gk *Gehenna*
[y] Other ancient authorities add *or what*

3 ἀνθ' ὧν ὅσα ἐν τῇ σκοτίᾳ εἴπατε ἐν
Therefore what things in the darkness ye said in
τῷ φωτὶ ἀκουσθήσεται, καὶ ὃ πρὸς τὸ
the light will be heard, and what to the
οὖς ἐλαλήσατε ἐν τοῖς ταμιείοις κηρυχθήσεται
ear ye spoke in the private rooms will be proclaimed
ἐπὶ τῶν δωμάτων. **4** Λέγω δὲ ὑμῖν τοῖς
on the roofs. And I say to you the
φίλοις μου, μὴ φοβηθῆτε ἀπὸ τῶν
friends of me, do not be afraid from(of) the [ones]
ἀποκτεννόντων τὸ σῶμα καὶ μετὰ ταῦτα
killing the body and after these things
μὴ ἐχόντων περισσότερόν τι ποιῆσαι.
not having anything more to do.
5 ὑποδείξω δὲ ὑμῖν τίνα φοβηθῆτε·
But I will warn you whom ye may fear :
φοβήθητε τὸν μετὰ τὸ ἀποκτεῖναι ἔχοντα
¹fear ²the [one] ⁵after *the* ⁶*to* kill(killing) ³having
ἐξουσίαν ἐμβαλεῖν εἰς τὴν γέενναν. ναί
⁴authority ⁷to cast *in* into – gehenna. Yes[,]
λέγω ὑμῖν, τοῦτον φοβήθητε. **6** οὐχὶ
I say to you, this one fear ye. Not
πέντε στρουθία πωλοῦνται ἀσσαρίων δύο;
five sparrows are sold of(for) farthings two?
καὶ ἓν ἐξ αὐτῶν οὐκ ἔστιν ἐπιλελησμένον
and one of them is not *having been* forgotten
ἐνώπιον τοῦ θεοῦ. **7** ἀλλὰ καὶ αἱ τρίχες
before – God. But even the hairs
τῆς κεφαλῆς ὑμῶν πᾶσαι ἠρίθμηνται.
of the head of you all have been numbered.
μὴ φοβεῖσθε· πολλῶν στρουθίων διαφέρετε.
Fear ye not; from many sparrows ye differ.
8 λέγω δὲ ὑμῖν, πᾶς ὃς ἂν ὁμολογήσῃ
But I tell you, everyone whoever confesses
ἐν ἐμοὶ ἔμπροσθεν τῶν ἀνθρώπων, καὶ ὁ
– me before – men, also the
υἱὸς τοῦ ἀνθρώπου ὁμολογήσει ἐν αὐτῷ
Son – of man will confess – him
ἔμπροσθεν τῶν ἀγγέλων τοῦ θεοῦ· **9** ὁ δὲ
before the angels – of God; and the
ἀρνησάμενός με ἐνώπιον τῶν ἀνθρώπων
[one] denying me before – men
ἀπαρνηθήσεται ἐνώπιον τῶν ἀγγέλων τοῦ
will be denied before the angels –
θεοῦ. **10** καὶ πᾶς ὃς ἐρεῖ λόγον εἰς τὸν
of God. And everyone who shall say a word against the
υἱὸν τοῦ ἀνθρώπου, ἀφεθήσεται αὐτῷ· τῷ
Son – of man, it will be forgiven him; ²the [one]
δὲ εἰς τὸ ἅγιον πνεῦμα βλασφημήσαντι
¹but against the Holy Spirit blaspheming
οὐκ ἀφεθήσεται. **11** ὅταν δὲ εἰσφέρωσιν
will not be forgiven. And when they bring in
ὑμᾶς ἐπὶ τὰς συναγωγὰς καὶ τὰς ἀρχὰς
you before – synagogues and – rulers
καὶ τὰς ἐξουσίας, μὴ μεριμνήσητε πῶς ἢ
and – authorities, do not be anxious how or
τί ἀπολογήσησθε ἢ τί εἴπητε· **12** τὸ γὰρ
what ye may answer or what ye may say; for the
ἅγιον πνεῦμα διδάξει ὑμᾶς ἐν αὐτῇ τῇ
Holy Spirit will teach you in ²same ¹the
ὥρᾳ ἃ δεῖ εἰπεῖν. **13** Εἶπεν δέ τις
hour what things it behoves [you] to say. And said someone
ἐκ τοῦ ὄχλου αὐτῷ· διδάσκαλε, εἰπὲ τῷ
out of the crowd to him : Teacher, tell the
ἀδελφῷ μου μερίσασθαι μετ' ἐμοῦ τὴν
brother of me to divide with me the

you have said in the dark
will be heard in the day-
light, and what you have
whispered in the ear in the
inner rooms will be pro-
claimed from the roofs.
4"I tell you, my friends,
do not be afraid of those
who kill the body and after
that can do no more. 5But I
will show you whom you
should fear: Fear him who,
after the killing of the body,
has power to throw you
into hell. Yes, I tell you,
fear him. 6Are not five
sparrows sold for two pen-
nies[d]? Yet not one of them
is forgotten by God. 7In-
deed, the very hairs of your
head are all numbered.
Don't be afraid; you are
worth more than many
sparrows.
8"I tell you, whoever ac-
knowledges me before
men, the Son of Man will
also acknowledge him be-
fore the angels of God. 9But
he who disowns me before
men will be disowned be-
fore the angels of God.
10And everyone who
speaks a word against the
Son of Man will be forgiv-
en, but anyone who blas-
phemes against the Holy
Spirit will not be forgiven.
11"When you are brought
before synagogues, rulers
and authorities, do not
worry about how you will
defend yourselves or what
you will say, 12for the Holy
Spirit will teach you at that
time what you should say."

The Parable of the Rich Fool

13Someone in the crowd
said to him, "Teacher, tell
my brother to divide the inheritance with me."

[d]6 Greek *two assaria*

me." 14 But he said to him,
"Friend, who set me to be a
judge or arbitrator over
you?" 15 And he said to
them, "Take care! Be on
your guard against all kinds
of greed; for one's life does
not consist in the abun-
dance of possessions."
16 Then he told them a parable: "The land of a rich man
produced abundantly.
17 And he thought to him-
self, 'What should I do, for
I have no place to store my
crops?' 18 Then he said, 'I
will do this: I will pull down
my barns and build larger
ones, and there I will store
all my grain and my goods.
19 And I will say to my soul,
'Soul, you have ample
goods laid up for many
years; relax, eat, drink, be
merry.' 20 But God said to
him, 'You fool! This very
night your life is being demanded of you. And the
things you have prepared,
whose will they be?' 21 So it
is with those who store up
treasures for themselves
but are not rich toward
God."

Do Not Worry

22 He said to his disci-
ples, "Therefore I tell you,
do not worry about your
life, what you will eat, or
about your body, what you
will wear. 23 For life is more
than food, and the body
more than clothing. 24 Consider the ravens: they neither sow nor reap, they
have neither storehouse
nor barn, and yet God feeds
them. Of how much more
value are you than the
birds! 25 And can any of you
by worrying add a single
hour to your span of life?[z]

[z]Or *add a cubit to your stature*

κληρονομίαν. 14 ὁ δὲ εἶπεν αὐτῷ· ἄνθρωπε,
inheritance. But he said to him: Man,

τίς με κατέστησεν κριτὴν ἢ μεριστὴν ἐφ'
who me appointed a judge or a divider over

ὑμᾶς; 15 εἶπεν δὲ πρὸς αὐτούς· ὁρᾶτε
you? And he said to them: Beware

καὶ φυλάσσεσθε ἀπὸ πάσης πλεονεξίας,
and guard from(against) all covetousness,

ὅτι οὐκ ἐν τῷ περισσεύειν τινὶ ἡ ζωὴ
because [5]not [6]in [7]the [8]to abound [9]to anyone [1]the [2]life

αὐτοῦ ἐστιν ἐκ τῶν ὑπαρχόντων αὐτῷ.
[3]of him [4]is [10]of the things existing to him.[c]
=[11]his [12]possessions.

16 Εἶπεν δὲ παραβολὴν πρὸς αὐτοὺς λέγων·
And he told a parable to them saying:

ἀνθρώπου τινὸς πλουσίου εὐφόρησεν ἡ
[3]of a certain [5]man [4]rich [6]bore well [1]The

χώρα. 17 καὶ διελογίζετο ἐν ἑαυτῷ λέγων·
[2]land. And he reasoned in himself saying:

τί ποιήσω, ὅτι οὐκ ἔχω ποῦ συνάξω τοὺς
What may I do, because I have not where I may gather the

καρπούς μου; 18 καὶ εἶπεν· τοῦτο ποιήσω·
fruits of me? And he said: This will I do:

καθελῶ μου τὰς ἀποθήκας καὶ μείζονας
I will pull down of me the barns and larger ones

οἰκοδομήσω, καὶ συνάξω ἐκεῖ πάντα τὸν
I will build, and I will gather there all the

σῖτον καὶ τὰ ἀγαθά μου, 19 καὶ ἐρῶ τῇ
wheat and the goods of me, and I will say to the

ψυχῇ μου· ψυχή, ἔχεις πολλὰ ἀγαθὰ
soul of me: Soul, thou hast many goods

κείμενα εἰς ἔτη πολλά· ἀναπαύου, φάγε,
laid [up] for years many; take rest, eat,

πίε, εὐφραίνου. 20 εἶπεν δὲ αὐτῷ ὁ
drink, be glad. But said to him –

θεός· ἄφρων, ταύτῃ τῇ νυκτὶ τὴν ψυχήν
God: Foolish man, in this – night the soul

σου ἀπαιτοῦσιν ἀπὸ σοῦ· ἃ δὲ
of thee they demand from thee; then [the] things which

ἡτοίμασας, τίνι ἔσται; 21 οὕτως ὁ
thou preparedst, to whom will they be?[c] So the [one]
=whose will they be?

θησαυρίζων αὐτῷ καὶ μὴ εἰς θεὸν πλουτῶν.
treasuring to himself and not toward God being rich.

22 Εἶπεν δὲ πρὸς τοὺς μαθητὰς [αὐτοῦ]· διὰ τοῦτο
And he said to the disciples of him: Therefore

λέγω ὑμῖν· μὴ μεριμνᾶτε τῇ ψυχῇ τί
I tell you: Do not be anxious for the life what

φάγητε, μηδὲ τῷ σώματι [ὑμῶν] τί
ye may eat, nor for the body of you what

ἐνδύσησθε. 23 ἡ γὰρ ψυχὴ πλεῖόν ἐστιν
ye may put on. For the life more is

τῆς τροφῆς καὶ τὸ σῶμα τοῦ ἐνδύματος.
[than] the food and the body [than] the clothing.

24 κατανοήσατε τοὺς κόρακας, ὅτι οὔτε
Consider ye the ravens, that neither

σπείρουσιν οὔτε θερίζουσιν, οἷς οὐκ ἔστιν
they sow nor reap, to which is not[c]
=which have not

ταμιεῖον οὐδὲ ἀποθήκη, καὶ ὁ θεὸς τρέφει
storehouse nor barn, and – God feeds

αὐτούς· πόσῳ μᾶλλον ὑμεῖς διαφέρετε τῶν
them; by how much rather ye differ from the

πετεινῶν. 25 τίς δὲ ἐξ ὑμῶν μεριμνῶν
birds. And who of you being anxious

δύναται ἐπὶ τὴν ἡλικίαν αὐτοῦ προσθεῖναι
can on the stature of him *to* add

14 Jesus replied, "Man,
who appointed me a judge
or an arbiter between
you?" 15 Then he said to
them, "Watch out! Be on
your guard against all kinds
of greed; a man's life does
not consist in the abun-
dance of his possessions."
16 And he told them this
parable: "The ground of a
certain rich man produced
a good crop. 17 He thought
to himself, 'What shall I
do? I have no place to store
my crops.'
18 "Then he said, 'This is
what I'll do. I will tear
down my barns and build
bigger ones, and there I will
store all my grain and my
goods. 19 And I'll say to myself, "You have plenty of
good things laid up for
many years. Take life easy;
eat, drink and be merry." '
20 "But God said to him,
'You fool! This very night
your life will be demanded
from you. Then who will
get what you have prepared
for yourself?'
21 "This is how it will be
with anyone who stores up
things for himself but is not
rich toward God."

Do Not Worry

22 Then Jesus said to his
disciples: "Therefore I tell
you, do not worry about
your life, what you will eat;
or about your body, what
you will wear. 23 Life is
more than food, and the
body more than clothes.
24 Consider the ravens:
They do not sow or reap,
they have no storeroom or
barn; yet God feeds them.
And how much more valu-
able you are than birds!
25 Who of you by worrying
can add a single hour to his

26 If then you are not able to
do so small a thing as that,
why do you worry about
the rest? 27 Consider the lilies, how they grow: they
neither toil nor spin;[a] yet I
tell you, even Solomon in
all his glory was not clothed
like one of these. 28 But if
God so clothes the grass of
the field, which is alive to-
day and tomorrow is
thrown into the oven, how
much more will he clothe
you—you of little faith!
29 And do not keep striving
for what you are to eat and
what you are to drink, and
do not keep worrying.
30 For it is the nations of the
world that strive after all
these things, and your Father knows that you need
them. 31 Instead, strive for
his[b] kingdom, and these
things will be given to you
as well.
32 "Do not be afraid, little flock, for it is your Father's good pleasure to give
you the kingdom. 33 Sell
your possessions, and give
alms. Make purses for
yourselves that do not wear
out, an unfailing treasure in
heaven, where no thief
comes near and no moth
destroys. 34 For where your
treasure is, there your
heart will be also.

Watchful Slaves

35 "Be dressed for ac-
tion and have your lamps
lit; 36 be like those who are
waiting for their master to
return from the wedding
banquet, so that they may
open the door for him as
soon as he comes and
knocks. 37 Blessed are
those slaves whom the
master finds alert when he
comes; truly I tell you, he
will fasten his belt and have
them sit down to eat, and
he will come and serve
them. 38 If he comes during

[a] Other ancient authorities read *Consider the lilies; they neither spin nor weave*
[b] Other ancient authorities read *God's*

πῆχυν; **26** εἰ οὖν οὐδὲ ἐλάχιστον δύνασθε,
a cubit? If therefore not [the] least ye can,
τί περὶ τῶν λοιπῶν μεριμνᾶτε; **27** κατα-
why concerning the other things are ye anxious? Con-
νοήσατε τὰ κρίνα, πῶς οὔτε νήθει οὔτε
sider ye the lilies, how neither they spin nor
ὑφαίνει· λέγω δὲ ὑμῖν, οὐδὲ Σολομὼν ἐν
weave; but I tell you, not Solomon in
πάσῃ τῇ δόξῃ αὐτοῦ περιεβάλετο ὡς ἓν
all the glory of him was arrayed as one
τούτων. **28** εἰ δὲ ἐν ἀγρῷ τὸν χόρτον
of these. [1]And [2]if [9]in [10]a field [6]the [7]grass
ὄντα σήμερον καὶ αὔριον εἰς κλίβανον
[8]being [11]to-day [12]and [13]tomorrow [15]into [16]an oven
βαλλόμενον ὁ θεὸς οὕτως ἀμφιάζει, πόσῳ
[14]being thrown – [3]God [4]so [5]clothes, by how much
μᾶλλον ὑμᾶς, ὀλιγόπιστοι. **29** καὶ ὑμεῖς
rather you, little-faiths. And ye
μὴ ζητεῖτε τί φάγητε καὶ τί πίητε, καὶ
do not seek what ye may eat and what ye may drink, and
μὴ μετεωρίζεσθε· **30** ταῦτα γὰρ πάντα τὰ
do not be in suspense; for these things all the
ἔθνη τοῦ κόσμου ἐπιζητοῦσιν· ὑμῶν δὲ
nations of the world seek after; but of you
ὁ πατὴρ οἶδεν ὅτι χρῄζετε τούτων·
the Father knows that ye have need of them;
31 πλὴν ζητεῖτε τὴν βασιλείαν αὐτοῦ, καὶ
but seek ye the kingdom of him, and
ταῦτα προστεθήσεται ὑμῖν. **32** Μὴ φοβοῦ,
these things will be added to you. Fear not,
τὸ μικρὸν ποίμνιον· ὅτι εὐδόκησεν ὁ
– little flock; because was well pleased the
πατὴρ ὑμῶν δοῦναι ὑμῖν τὴν βασιλείαν.
Father of you to give you the kingdom.
33 Πωλήσατε τὰ ὑπάρχοντα ὑμῶν καὶ
Sell the possessions of you and
δότε ἐλεημοσύνην· ποιήσατε ἑαυτοῖς βαλ-
give alms; make for yourselves
λάντια μὴ παλαιούμενα, θησαυρὸν ἀνέκλειπτον
purses not becoming old, a treasure unfailing
ἐν τοῖς οὐρανοῖς, ὅπου κλέπτης οὐκ
in the heavens, where a thief not
ἐγγίζει οὐδὲ σὴς διαφθείρει· **34** ὅπου γάρ
comes near nor moth corrupts; for where
ἐστιν ὁ θησαυρὸς ὑμῶν, ἐκεῖ καὶ ἡ
is the treasure of you, there also the
καρδία ὑμῶν ἔσται. **35** Ἔστωσαν ὑμῶν αἱ
heart of you will be. Let be of you the
ὀσφύες περιεζωσμέναι καὶ οἱ λύχνοι
loins *having been* girded and the lamps
καιόμενοι· **36** καὶ ὑμεῖς ὅμοιοι ἀνθρώποις
burning; and ye like men
προσδεχομένοις τὸν κύριον ἑαυτῶν, πότε
awaiting the lord of them*selves*, when
ἀναλύσῃ ἐκ τῶν γάμων, ἵνα ἐλθόντος
he returns from the wedding festivities, that coming[a]
καὶ κρούσαντος εὐθέως ἀνοίξωσιν αὐτῷ.
and knocking[a] immediately they may open to him.
37 μακάριοι οἱ δοῦλοι ἐκεῖνοι, οὓς ἐλθὼν
Blessed – slaves those, whom coming
ὁ κύριος εὑρήσει γρηγοροῦντας· ἀμὴν λέγω
the lord will find watching; truly I tell
ὑμῖν ὅτι περιζώσεται καὶ ἀνακλινεῖ αὐτοὺς
you that he will gird himself and [1]make [3]to recline [2]them
καὶ παρελθὼν διακονήσει αὐτοῖς. **38** κἂν
and coming up to will serve them. And if

life[c]? 26Since you cannot
do this very little thing,
why do you worry about
the rest?
27"Consider how the lil-
ies grow. They do not labor
or spin. Yet I tell you, not
even Solomon in all his
splendor was dressed like
one of these. 28If that is
how God clothes the grass
of the field, which is here
today, and tomorrow is
thrown into the fire, how
much more will he clothe
you, O you of little faith!
29And do not set your heart
on what you will eat or
drink; do not worry about
it. 30For the pagan world
runs after all such things,
and your Father knows that
you need them. 31But seek
his kingdom, and these
things will be given to you
as well.
32"Do not be afraid, little
flock, for your Father has
been pleased to give you
the kingdom. 33Sell your
possessions and give to the
poor. Provide purses for
yourselves that will not
wear out, a treasure in
heaven that will not be exhausted, where no thief
comes near and no moth
destroys. 34For where your
treasure is, there your
heart will be also.

Watchfulness

35"Be dressed ready for
service and keep your
lamps burning, 36like men
waiting for their master to
return from a wedding banquet, so that when he
comes and knocks they can
immediately open the door
for him. 37It will be good for
those servants whose mas-
ter finds them watching
when he comes. I tell you
the truth, he will dress himself to serve, will have
them recline at the table
and will come and wait on

[c]25 Or *single cubit to his height*

the middle of the night, or
near dawn, and finds them
so, blessed are those
slaves.
39 "But know this: if the
owner of the house had
known at what hour the
thief was coming, he[c]
would not have let his
house be broken into.
40 You also must be ready,
for the Son of Man is coming at an unexpected hour."

The Faithful or the Unfaithful Slave

41 Peter said, "Lord,
are you telling this parable
for us or for everyone?"
42 And the Lord said, "Who
then is the faithful and prudent manager whom his
master will put in charge of
his slaves, to give them
their allowance of food at
the proper time? 43 Blessed
is that slave whom his master will find at work when
he arrives. 44 Truly I tell
you, he will put that one in
charge of all his posses-
sions. 45 But if that slave
says to himself, 'My master
is delayed in coming,' and
if he begins to beat the other slaves, men and women,
and to eat and drink and get
drunk, 46 the master of that
slave will come on a day
when he does not expect
him and at an hour that he
does not know, and will cut
him in pieces,[d] and put him
with the unfaithful. 47 That
slave who knew what his
master wanted, but did not
prepare himself or do what
was wanted, will receive a
severe beating. 48 But the
one who did not know and
did what deserved a beat-
ing will receive a light beating. From everyone to
whom much has been giv-
en, much will be required;
and from the one to whom

[c] Other ancient authorities add *would have watched and*
[d] Or *cut him off*

ἐν τῇ δευτέρᾳ κἂν ἐν τῇ τρίτῃ φυλακῇ
in the second and if in the third watch
ἔλθῃ καὶ εὕρῃ οὕτως, μακάριοί εἰσιν
he comes and finds so, blessed are
ἐκεῖνοι. **39** τοῦτο δὲ γινώσκετε, ὅτι εἰ
those [slaves]. But this know ye, that if
ᾔδει ὁ οἰκοδεσπότης ποίᾳ ὥρᾳ ὁ κλέπτης
knew the house-master in what hour the thief
ἔρχεται, οὐκ ἂν ἀφῆκεν διορυχθῆναι τὸν
comes, he would not have allowed to be dug through the
οἶκον αὐτοῦ. **40** καὶ ὑμεῖς γίνεσθε ἕτοιμοι,
house of him. And [2]ye [1]be prepared,
ὅτι ᾗ ὥρᾳ οὐ δοκεῖτε ὁ υἱὸς τοῦ
because in what hour ye think not the Son –
ἀνθρώπου ἔρχεται. **41** Εἶπεν δὲ ὁ Πέτρος·
of man comes. And said – Peter :
κύριε, πρὸς ἡμᾶς τὴν παραβολὴν ταύτην
Lord, to us – parable this
λέγεις ἢ καὶ πρὸς πάντας; **42** καὶ εἶπεν
sayest thou or also to all? And said
ὁ κύριος· τίς ἄρα ἐστὶν ὁ πιστὸς
the Lord : Who then is the faithful
οἰκονόμος ὁ φρόνιμος, ὃν καταστήσει ὁ
steward the prudent, whom will appoint the
κύριος ἐπὶ τῆς θεραπείας αὐτοῦ τοῦ
lord over the household attendants of him –
διδόναι ἐν καιρῷ [τὸ] σιτομέτριον;
to give[d] in season the portion of food?
43 μακάριος ὁ δοῦλος ἐκεῖνος, ὃν ἐλθὼν
Blessed – slave that, whom coming
ὁ κύριος αὐτοῦ εὑρήσει ποιοῦντα οὕτως.
the lord of him will find doing so.
44 ἀληθῶς λέγω ὑμῖν ὅτι ἐπὶ πᾶσιν τοῖς
Truly I tell you that over all the
ὑπάρχουσιν αὐτοῦ καταστήσει αὐτόν. **45** ἐὰν
possessions of him he will appoint him. if
δὲ εἴπῃ ὁ δοῦλος ἐκεῖνος ἐν τῇ καρδίᾳ
But says – slave that in the heart
αὐτοῦ· χρονίζει ὁ κύριός μου ἔρχεσθαι,
of him : Delays the lord of me to come,
καὶ ἄρξηται τύπτειν τοὺς παῖδας καὶ τὰς
and begins to strike the menservants and the
παιδίσκας, ἐσθίειν τε καὶ πίνειν καὶ
maidservants, [2]to eat [1]both and to drink and
μεθύσκεσθαι, **46** ἥξει ὁ κύριος τοῦ δούλου
to become drunk, will come the lord – slave
ἐκείνου ἐν ἡμέρᾳ ᾗ οὐ προσδοκᾷ καὶ ἐν
of that in a day in which he does not expect and in
ὥρᾳ ᾗ οὐ γινώσκει, καὶ διχοτομήσει
an hour *in* which he knows not, and will cut asunder
αὐτόν, καὶ τὸ μέρος αὐτοῦ μετὰ τῶν
him, and the portion of him with the
ἀπίστων θήσει. **47** ἐκεῖνος δὲ ὁ δοῦλος
unbelievers will place. But that – slave
ὁ γνοὺς τὸ θέλημα τοῦ κυρίου αὐτοῦ
– having known the will of the lord of him
καὶ μὴ ἑτοιμάσας ἢ ποιήσας πρὸς τὸ θέλημα
and not having prepared or done according to the will
αὐτοῦ δαρήσεται πολλάς· **48** ὁ δὲ
of him will be beaten [with] many [stripes]; but the [one]
μὴ γνούς, ποιήσας δὲ ἄξια πληγῶν,
not having known, but having done things worthy of stripes,
δαρήσεται ὀλίγας. παντὶ δὲ ᾧ
will be beaten [with] few [stripes]. But to everyone to whom
ἐδόθη πολύ, πολὺ ζητηθήσεται παρ' αὐτοῦ, καὶ
was given much, much will be demanded from him, and

them. 38 It will be good for
those servants whose mas-
ter finds them ready, even
if he comes in the second or
third watch of the night.
39 But understand this: If
the owner of the house had
known at what hour the
thief was coming, he would
not have let his house be
broken into. 40 You also
must be ready, because the
Son of Man will come at an
hour when you do not ex-
pect him."
41 Peter asked, "Lord, are
you telling this parable to
us, or to everyone?"
42 The Lord answered,
"Who then is the faithful
and wise manager, whom
the master puts in charge of
his servants to give them
their food allowance at the
proper time? 43 It will be
good for that servant whom
the master finds doing so
when he returns. 44 I tell
you the truth, he will put
him in charge of all his possessions. 45 But suppose the
servant says to himself,
'My master is taking a long
time in coming,' and he
then begins to beat the
menservants and maidser-
vants and to eat and drink
and get drunk. 46 The master of that servant will
come on a day when he
does not expect him and at
an hour he is not aware of.
He will cut him to pieces
and assign him a place with
the unbelievers.
47 "That servant who
knows his master's will and
does not get ready or does
not do what his master
wants will be beaten with
many blows. 48 But the one
who does not know and
does things deserving punishment will be beaten with
few blows. From everyone
who has been given much,
much will be demanded;

much has been entrusted,
even more will be demand-
ed.

Jesus the Cause of Division

49 "I came to bring fire
to the earth, and how I wish
it were already kindled! 50 I
have a baptism with which
to be baptized, and what
stress I am under until it is
completed! 51 Do you think
that I have come to bring
peace to the earth? No, I
tell you, but rather division! 52 From now on five in
one household will be di-
vided, three against two
and two against three;
53 they will be divided:
father against son
and son against father,
mother against daughter
and daughter against mother,
mother-in-law against her daughter-in-law
and daughter-in-law against mother-in-law."

Interpreting the Time

54 He also said to the
crowds, "When you see a
cloud rising in the west,
you immediately say, 'It is
going to rain'; and so it happens. 55 And when you see
the south wind blowing,
you say, 'There will be
scorching heat'; and it happens. 56 You hypocrites!
You know how to interpret
the appearance of earth and
sky, but why do you not
know how to interpret the
present time?

Settling with Your Opponent

57 "And why do you not
judge for yourselves what
is right? 58 Thus, when you
go with your accuser be-
fore a magistrate, on the
way make an effort to settle
the case,[e] or you may be
dragged before the judge,
and the judge hand you
over to the officer, and the
officer throw you in prison.
59 I tell you, you will never
get out until you have paid
the very last penny."

Chapter 13

Repent or Perish

At that very time there
were some present
who told him about the Galileans whose blood Pilate

[e] Gk *settle with him*

ᾧ παρέθεντο πολύ, περισσότερον αἰτήσουσιν
with whom was deposited much, more exceedingly they will ask
αὐτόν. 49 Πῦρ ἦλθον βαλεῖν ἐπὶ τὴν γῆν,
him. Fire I came to cast on the earth,
καὶ τί θέλω εἰ ἤδη ἀνήφθη. 50 βάπτισμα
and what will I if already it was kindled. [3]a baptism
δὲ ἔχω βαπτισθῆναι, καὶ πῶς συνέχομαι
[1]And [2]I have to be baptized [with], and how am I pressed
ἕως ὅτου τελεσθῇ. 51 δοκεῖτε ὅτι εἰρήνην
until it is accomplished. Think ye that peace
παρεγενόμην δοῦναι ἐν τῇ γῇ; οὐχί, λέγω
I came to give in the earth? No, I tell
ὑμῖν, ἀλλ' ἢ διαμερισμόν. 52 ἔσονται γὰρ
you, but rather division. For there will be
ἀπὸ τοῦ νῦν πέντε ἐν ἑνὶ οἴκῳ διαμεμε-
from – now five in one house *having been*
ρισμένοι, τρεῖς ἐπὶ δυσὶν καὶ δύο ἐπὶ
divided, three against two and two against
τρισὶν 53 διαμερισθήσονται, πατὴρ ἐπὶ υἱῷ
three will be divided, father against son
καὶ υἱὸς ἐπὶ πατρί, μήτηρ ἐπὶ θυγατέρα
and son against father, mother against daughter
καὶ θυγάτηρ ἐπὶ τὴν μητέρα, πενθερὰ
and daughter against the mother, mother-in-law
ἐπὶ τὴν νύμφην αὐτῆς καὶ νύμφη ἐπὶ
against the daughter-in-law of her and daughter-in-law against
τὴν πενθεράν. 54 Ἔλεγεν δὲ καὶ τοῖς
the mother-in-law. And he said also to the
ὄχλοις· ὅταν ἴδητε νεφέλην ἀνατέλλουσαν
crowds: When ye see a cloud rising
ἐπὶ δυσμῶν, εὐθέως λέγετε ὅτι ὄμβρος
over [the] west, immediately ye say that a storm
ἔρχεται, καὶ γίνεται οὕτως· 55 καὶ ὅταν
is coming, and it becomes so; and when
νότον πνέοντα, λέγετε ὅτι καύσων ἔσται,
a south wind blowing, ye say that heat there will be,
καὶ γίνεται. 56 ὑποκριταί, τὸ πρόσωπον
and it becomes. Hypocrites, the face
τῆς γῆς καὶ τοῦ οὐρανοῦ οἴδατε δοκιμάζειν,
of the earth and of the heaven ye know* to discern,
τὸν καιρὸν δὲ τοῦτον πῶς οὐ δοκιμάζετε;
– [2]time [1]but [3]this how do ye not discern?
57 Τί δὲ καὶ ἀφ' ἑαυτῶν οὐ κρίνετε
And why even from yourselves do ye not judge
τὸ δίκαιον; 58 ὡς γὰρ ὑπάγεις μετὰ τοῦ
the righteous thing? For as thou goest with the
ἀντιδίκου σου ἐπ' ἄρχοντα, ἐν τῇ ὁδῷ
adversary of thee to a ruler, in the way
δὸς ἐργασίαν ἀπηλλάχθαι ἀπ' αὐτοῦ, μήποτε
give(take) pains to be rid from(of) him, lest
κατασύρῃ σε πρὸς τὸν κριτήν, καὶ ὁ
he drag thee to the judge, and the
κριτής σε παραδώσει τῷ πράκτορι, καὶ ὁ
judge thee will deliver to the usher, and the
πράκτωρ σε βαλεῖ εἰς φυλακήν. 59 λέγω
usher thee will cast into prison. I tell
σοι, οὐ μὴ ἐξέλθῃς ἐκεῖθεν ἕως
thee, by no means mayest thou come out thence until
καὶ τὸ ἔσχατον λεπτὸν ἀποδῷς.
even the last lepton thou payest.

13 Παρῆσαν δέ τινες ἐν αὐτῷ τῷ
And there were present some at [2]same [1]the
καιρῷ ἀπαγγέλλοντες αὐτῷ περὶ τῶν
time reporting to him about the

* can, as Mat. 16. 3.

and from the one who has
been entrusted with much,
much more will be asked.

Not Peace but Division

49 "I have come to bring
fire on the earth, and how I
wish it were already kin-
dled! 50 But I have a baptism to undergo, and how
distressed I am until it is
completed! 51 Do you think
I came to bring peace on
earth? No, I tell you, but
division. 52 From now on
there will be five in one
family divided against each
other, three against two
and two against three.
53 They will be divided, father against son and son
against father, mother
against daughter and
daughter against mother,
mother-in-law against
daughter-in-law and daughter-in-law against mother-
in-law."

Interpreting the Times

54 He said to the crowd:
"When you see a cloud rising in the west, immediately you say, 'It's going to
rain,' and it does. 55 And
when the south wind
blows, you say, 'It's going
to be hot,' and it is. 56 Hypocrites! You know how to
interpret the appearance of
the earth and the sky. How
is it that you don't know
how to interpret this present time?
57 "Why don't you judge
for yourselves what is
right? 58 As you are going
with your adversary to the
magistrate, try hard to be
reconciled to him on the
way, or he may drag you off
to the judge, and the judge
turn you over to the officer,
and the officer throw you
into prison. 59 I tell you, you
will not get out until you
have paid the last pen-
ny.[f]"

Chapter 13

Repent or Perish

NOW there were some
present at that time
who told Jesus about the

[f] 59 Greek *lepton*

had mingled with their sacrifices. 2He asked them,
"Do you think that because
these Galileans suffered in
this way they were worse
sinners than all other Galileans? 3No, I tell you; but
unless you repent, you will
all perish as they did. 4Or
those eighteen who were
killed when the tower of Siloam fell on them—do you
think that they were worse
offenders than all the others living in Jerusalem?
5No, I tell you; but unless
you repent, you will all perish just as they did."

The Parable of the Barren Fig Tree

6 Then he told this para-
ble: "A man had a fig tree
planted in his vineyard; and
he came looking for fruit on
it and found none. 7So he
said to the gardener, 'See
here! For three years I have
come looking for fruit on
this fig tree, and still I find
none. Cut it down! Why
should it be wasting the
soil?' 8He replied, 'Sir, let
it alone for one more year,
until I dig around it and put
manure on it. 9If it bears
fruit next year, well and
good; but if not, you can
cut it down.' "

Jesus Heals a Crippled Woman

10 Now he was teaching
in one of the synagogues on
the sabbath. 11And just
then there appeared a
woman with a spirit that
had crippled her for eighteen years. She was bent
over and was quite unable
to stand up straight.
12When Jesus saw her, he
called her over and said,
"Woman, you are set free
from your ailment."
13When he laid his hands

Γαλιλαίων ὧν τὸ αἷμα Πιλᾶτος ἔμιξεν
Galilæans of whom the blood Pilate mixed

μετὰ τῶν θυσιῶν αὐτῶν. 2 καὶ ἀποκριθεὶς
with the sacrifices of them. And answering

εἶπεν αὐτοῖς· δοκεῖτε ὅτι οἱ Γαλιλαῖοι
he said to them: Think ye that – Galilæans

οὗτοι ἁμαρτωλοὶ παρὰ πάντας τοὺς Γαλι-
these sinners above all the Gali-

λαίους ἐγένοντο, ὅτι ταῦτα πεπόνθασιν;
læans were, because these things they have suffered?

3 οὐχί, λέγω ὑμῖν, ἀλλ' ἐὰν μὴ μετανοῆτε,
No, I tell you, but unless ye repent,

πάντες ὁμοίως ἀπολεῖσθε. 4 ἢ ἐκεῖνοι οἱ
all likewise ye will perish. Or those –

δεκαοκτὼ ἐφ' οὓς ἔπεσεν ὁ πύργος ἐν
eighteen on whom fell the tower in

τῷ Σιλωὰμ καὶ ἀπέκτεινεν αὐτούς, δοκεῖτε
– Siloam and killed them, think ye

ὅτι αὐτοὶ ὀφειλέται ἐγένοντο παρὰ πάντας
that they debtors were above all

τοὺς ἀνθρώπους τοὺς κατοικοῦντας Ἰερου-
the men – dwelling in Jeru-

σαλήμ; 5 οὐχί, λέγω ὑμῖν, ἀλλ' ἐὰν μὴ
salem? No, I tell you, but unless

μετανοήσητε, πάντες ὡσαύτως ἀπολεῖσθε.
ye repent, all similarly ye will perish.

6 Ἔλεγεν δὲ ταύτην τὴν παραβολήν. συκῆν
And he told this – parable. [2]A fig-tree

εἶχέν τις πεφυτευμένην ἐν τῷ ἀμπελῶνι
[3]had [1]a certain man *having been* planted in the vineyard

αὐτοῦ, καὶ ἦλθεν ζητῶν καρπὸν ἐν αὐτῇ
of him, and came seeking fruit in it

καὶ οὐχ εὗρεν. 7 εἶπεν δὲ πρὸς τὸν
and found not. And he said to the

ἀμπελουργόν· ἰδοὺ τρία ἔτη ἀφ' οὗ
vinedresser: Behold[,] three years [it is] since

ἔρχομαι ζητῶν καρπὸν ἐν τῇ συκῇ ταύτῃ
I come seeking fruit in – fig-tree this

καὶ οὐχ εὑρίσκω· ἔκκοψον αὐτήν· ἱνατί
and find not; cut down it; why

καὶ τὴν γῆν καταργεῖ; 8 ὁ δὲ ἀποκριθεὶς
even the ground it spoils? But he answering

λέγει αὐτῷ· κύριε, ἄφες αὐτὴν καὶ τοῦτο
says to him: Lord, leave it also this

τὸ ἔτος, ἕως ὅτου σκάψω περὶ αὐτὴν καὶ
– year, until I may dig round it and

βάλω κόπρια, 9 κἂν μὲν ποιήσῃ καρπὸν
may throw dung, and if indeed it makes fruit

εἰς τὸ μέλλον· εἰ δὲ μή γε, ἐκκόψεις
in the future; otherwise, thou shalt cut down

αὐτήν.
it.

10 Ἦν δὲ διδάσκων ἐν μιᾷ τῶν συναγωγῶν
And he was teaching in one of the synagogues

ἐν τοῖς σάββασιν. 11 καὶ ἰδοὺ γυνὴ
on the sabbaths. And[,] behold[,] a woman

πνεῦμα ἔχουσα ἀσθενείας ἔτη δεκαοκτώ,
[2]a spirit [1]having of infirmity years eighteen,

καὶ ἦν συγκύπτουσα καὶ μὴ δυναμένη
and was bending double and not being able

ἀνακῦψαι εἰς τὸ παντελές. 12 ἰδὼν δὲ
to become erect entirely.† And seeing

αὐτὴν ὁ Ἰησοῦς προσεφώνησεν καὶ εἶπεν
her – Jesus called to [him] and said

αὐτῇ· γύναι, ἀπολέλυσαι τῆς ἀσθενείας
to her: Woman, thou hast been loosed from the infirmity

Galileans whose blood Pi-
late had mixed with their
sacrifices. 2Jesus an-
swered, "Do you think that
these Galileans were worse
sinners than all the other
Galileans because they suffered this way? 3I tell you,
no! But unless you repent,
you too will all perish. 4Or
those eighteen who died
when the tower in Siloam
fell on them—do you think
they were more guilty than
all the others living in Jerusalem? 5I tell you, no! But
unless you repent, you too
will all perish."
6Then he told this para-
ble: "A man had a fig tree,
planted in his vineyard, and
he went to look for fruit on
it, but did not find any. 7So
he said to the man who took
care of the vineyard, 'For
three years now I've been
coming to look for fruit on
this fig tree and haven't
found any. Cut it down!
Why should it use up the
soil?'
8" 'Sir,' the man replied,
'leave it alone for one more
year, and I'll dig around it
and fertilize it. 9If it bears
fruit next year, fine! If not,
then cut it down.' "

A Crippled Woman Healed on the Sabbath

10On a Sabbath Jesus was
teaching in one of the synagogues, 11and a woman was
there who had been crip-
pled by a spirit for eighteen
years. She was bent over
and could not straighten up
at all. 12When Jesus saw
her, he called her forward
and said to her, "Woman,
you are set free from your

on her, immediately she
stood up straight and began
praising God. [14]But the
leader of the synagogue, indignant because Jesus had
cured on the sabbath, kept
saying to the crowd,
"There are six days on
which work ought to be
done; come on those days
and be cured, and not on
the sabbath day." [15]But the
Lord answered him and
said, "You hypocrites!
Does not each of you on the
sabbath untie his ox or his
donkey from the manger,
and lead it away to give it
water? [16]And ought not
this woman, a daughter of
Abraham whom Satan
bound for eighteen long
years, be set free from this
bondage on the sabbath
day?" [17]When he said this,
all his opponents were put
to shame; and the entire
crowd was rejoicing at all
the wonderful things that
he was doing.

The Parable of the Mustard Seed

18 He said therefore,
"What is the kingdom of
God like? And to what
should I compare it? [19]It is
like a mustard seed that
someone took and sowed in
the garden; it grew and became a tree, and the birds
of the air made nests in its
branches."

The Parable of the Yeast

20 And again he said,
"To what should I compare
the kingdom of God? [21]It is
like yeast that a woman
took and mixed in with[f]
three measures of flour until all of it was leavened."

The Narrow Door

22 Jesus[g] went through
one town and village after
another, teaching as he
made his way to Jerusalem.
[23]Someone asked him,

[f] Gk *hid in*
[g] Gk *He*

σου, **13** καὶ ἐπέθηκεν αὐτῇ τὰς χεῖρας·
of thee, and he put on her the(his) hands;
καὶ παραχρῆμα ἀνωρθώθη, καὶ ἐδόξαζεν
and at once she was straightened, and glorified
τὸν θεόν. **14** ἀποκριθεὶς δὲ ὁ ἀρχι-
– God. But answering the syn-
συνάγωγος, ἀγανακτῶν ὅτι τῷ σαββάτῳ
agogue ruler, being angry that [3]on the [4]sabbath
ἐθεράπευσεν ὁ Ἰησοῦς, ἔλεγεν τῷ ὄχλῳ
[2]healed – [1]Jesus, said to the crowd[,]
ὅτι ἓξ ἡμέραι εἰσὶν ἐν αἷς δεῖ ἐργάζεσθαι·
– six days there are on which it behoves to work;
ἐν αὐταῖς οὖν ἐρχόμενοι θεραπεύεσθε καὶ
on them therefore coming be ye healed and
μὴ τῇ ἡμέρᾳ τοῦ σαββάτου. **15** ἀπεκρίθη δὲ
not on the day of the sabbath. But answered
αὐτῷ ὁ κύριος καὶ εἶπεν· ὑποκριταί,
him the Lord and said: Hypocrites,
ἕκαστος ὑμῶν τῷ σαββάτῳ οὐ λύει τὸν
each one of you on the sabbath does he not loosen the
βοῦν αὐτοῦ ἢ τὸν ὄνον ἀπὸ τῆς φάτνης
ox of him or the ass from the manger
καὶ ἀπαγαγὼν ποτίζει; **16** ταύτην δὲ
and leading [it] away give drink? And this woman
θυγατέρα Ἀβραὰμ οὖσαν, ἣν ἔδησεν ὁ
a daughter of Abraham being, whom bound –
σατανᾶς ἰδοὺ δέκα καὶ ὀκτὼ ἔτη, οὐκ ἔδει
Satan behold ten and eight years, behoved it not
λυθῆναι ἀπὸ τοῦ δεσμοῦ τούτου τῇ
to be loosened from – bond this on the
ἡμέρᾳ τοῦ σαββάτου; **17** καὶ ταῦτα λέγοντος
day of the sabbath? And these things saying
=when he said these things
αὐτοῦ κατῃσχύνοντο πάντες οἱ ἀντικείμενοι
him[a] were put to shame all the [ones] opposing
αὐτῷ, καὶ πᾶς ὁ ὄχλος ἔχαιρεν ἐπὶ
him, and all the crowd rejoiced over
πᾶσιν τοῖς ἐνδόξοις τοῖς γινομένοις ὑπ'
all the glorious things – happening by
αὐτοῦ. **18** Ἔλεγεν οὖν· τίνι ὁμοία ἐστὶν ἡ
him. He said therefore: To what like is the
βασιλεία τοῦ θεοῦ, καὶ τίνι ὁμοιώσω
kingdom – of God, and to what may I liken
αὐτήν; **19** ὁμοία ἐστὶν κόκκῳ σινάπεως, ὃν
it? Like it is to a grain of mustard, which
λαβὼν ἄνθρωπος ἔβαλεν εἰς κῆπον ἑαυτοῦ,
[2]taking [1]a man cast into a garden of him*self*,
καὶ ηὔξησεν καὶ ἐγένετο εἰς δένδρον, καὶ
and it grew and became into a tree, and
τὰ πετεινὰ τοῦ οὐρανοῦ κατεσκήνωσεν
the birds of the heaven(air) lodged
ἐν τοῖς κλάδοις αὐτοῦ. **20** Καὶ πάλιν
in the branches of it. And again
εἶπεν· τίνι ὁμοιώσω τὴν βασιλείαν τοῦ
he said: To what may I liken the kingdom –
θεοῦ; **21** ὁμοία ἐστὶν ζύμῃ, ἣν λαβοῦσα
of God? Like it is to leaven, which [2]taking
γυνὴ ἔκρυψεν εἰς ἀλεύρου σάτα τρία,
[1]a woman hid in of meal measures three,
ἕως οὗ ἐζυμώθη ὅλον.
until was leavened all.

22 Καὶ διεπορεύετο κατὰ πόλεις καὶ
And he journeyed *through* throughout cities and
κώμας διδάσκων καὶ πορείαν ποιούμενος
villages teaching and journey making
εἰς Ἱεροσόλυμα. **23** Εἶπεν δέ τις αὐτῷ·
to Jerusalem. And said someone to him:

infirmity." [13]Then he put
his hands on her, and im-
mediately she straightened
up and praised God.
[14]Indignant because
Jesus had healed on the
Sabbath, the synagogue
ruler said to the people,
"There are six days for
work. So come and be
healed on those days, not
on the Sabbath."
[15]The Lord answered
him, "You hypocrites!
Doesn't each of you on the
Sabbath untie his ox or
donkey from the stall and
lead it out to give it water?
[16]Then should not this
woman, a daughter of
Abraham, whom Satan has
kept bound for eighteen
long years, be set free on
the Sabbath day from what
bound her?"
[17]When he said this, all
his opponents were humiliated, but the people were
delighted with all the wonderful things he was doing.

The Parables of the Mustard Seed and the Yeast

[18]Then Jesus asked,
"What is the kingdom of
God like? What shall I compare it to? [19]It is like a mustard seed, which a man
took and planted in his garden. It grew and became a
tree, and the birds of the air
perched in its branches."
[20]Again he asked, "What
shall I compare the king-
dom of God to? [21]It is like
yeast that a woman took
and mixed into a large
amount[g] of flour until it
worked all through the
dough."

The Narrow Door

[22]Then Jesus went
through the towns and villages, teaching as he made
his way to Jerusalem.
[23]Someone asked him,

[g]*21* Greek *three satas* (probably about 1/2 bushel or 22 liters)

"Lord, will only a few be
saved?" He said to them,
24 "Strive to enter through
the narrow door; for many,
I tell you, will try to enter
and will not be able.
25 When once the owner of
the house has got up and
shut the door, and you begin to stand outside and to
knock at the door, saying,
'Lord, open to us,' then in
reply he will say to you, 'I
do not know where you
come from.' 26 Then you
will begin to say, 'We ate
and drank with you, and
you taught in our streets.'
27 But he will say, 'I do not
know where you come
from; go away from me, all
you evildoers!' 28 There
will be weeping and gnashing of teeth when you see
Abraham and Isaac and Ja-
cob and all the prophets in
the kingdom of God, and
you yourselves thrown out.
29 Then people will come
from east and west, from
north and south, and will
eat in the kingdom of God.
30 Indeed, some are last
who will be first, and some
are first who will be last."

The Lament over Jerusalem

31 At that very hour
some Pharisees came and
said to him, "Get away
from here, for Herod wants
to kill you." 32 He said to
them, "Go and tell that fox
for me,[h] 'Listen, I am casting out demons and per-
forming cures today and tomorrow, and on the third
day I finish my work. 33 Yet
today, tomorrow, and the
next day I must be on my
way, because it is impossible for a prophet to be
killed outside of Jerusa-
lem.' 34 Jerusalem, Jerusalem, the city that kills the

[h] Gk lacks *for me*

κύριε, εἰ ὀλίγοι οἱ σῳζόμενοι; ὁ δὲ εἶπεν
Lord, if few the [ones] being saved? And he said

πρὸς αὐτούς· **24** ἀγωνίζεσθε εἰσελθεῖν διὰ
to them: Struggle to enter through

τῆς στενῆς θύρας, ὅτι πολλοί, λέγω ὑμῖν,
the strait door, because many, I tell you,

ζητήσουσιν εἰσελθεῖν καὶ οὐκ ἰσχύσουσιν.
will seek to enter and will not be able.

25 ἀφ' οὗ ἂν ἐγερθῇ ὁ οἰκοδεσπότης καὶ
From [the time] when is risen the house-master and

ἀποκλείσῃ τὴν θύραν, καὶ ἄρξησθε ἔξω
he shuts the door, and ye begin outside

ἑστάναι καὶ κρούειν τὴν θύραν λέγοντες·
to stand and to knock the door saying:

κύριε, ἄνοιξον ἡμῖν, καὶ ἀποκριθεὶς ἐρεῖ
Lord, open to us, and answering he will say

ὑμῖν· οὐκ οἶδα ὑμᾶς πόθεν ἐστέ. **26** τότε
to you: I know not you whence ye are. Then

ἄρξεσθε λέγειν· ἐφάγομεν ἐνώπιόν σου καὶ
ye will begin to say: We ate before thee and

ἐπίομεν, καὶ ἐν ταῖς πλατείαις ἡμῶν
drank, and in the streets of us

ἐδίδαξας· **27** καὶ ἐρεῖ λέγων ὑμῖν· οὐκ
thou didst teach; and he will say telling you: not

οἶδα πόθεν ἐστέ· ἀποστητε ἀπ' ἐμοῦ
I know whence ye are; stand away from me

πάντες ἐργάται ἀδικίας. **28** ἐκεῖ ἔσται ὁ
all workers of unrighteousness. There will be the

κλαυθμὸς καὶ ὁ βρυγμὸς τῶν ὀδόντων,
weeping and the gnashing of the teeth,

ὅταν ὄψησθε Ἀβραὰμ καὶ Ἰσαὰκ καὶ
when ye see Abraham and Isaac and

Ἰακὼβ καὶ πάντας τοὺς προφήτας ἐν τῇ
Jacob and all the prophets in the

βασιλείᾳ τοῦ θεοῦ, ὑμᾶς δὲ ἐκβαλλομένους
kingdom – of God, but you being thrust *out*

ἔξω. **29** καὶ ἥξουσιν ἀπὸ ἀνατολῶν καὶ
outside. And they will come from east and

δυσμῶν καὶ ἀπὸ βορρᾶ καὶ νότου, καὶ
west and from north and south, and

ἀνακλιθήσονται ἐν τῇ βασιλείᾳ τοῦ θεοῦ.
will recline in the kingdom – of God.

30 καὶ ἰδοὺ εἰσὶν ἔσχατοι οἳ ἔσονται
And behold there are last [ones] who will be

πρῶτοι, καὶ εἰσὶν πρῶτοι οἳ ἔσονται
first, and there are first [ones] who will be

ἔσχατοι. **31** Ἐν αὐτῇ τῇ ὥρᾳ προσῆλθάν
last. In [2]same [1]the hour approached

τινες Φαρισαῖοι λέγοντες αὐτῷ· ἔξελθε καὶ
some Pharisees saying to him: Depart and

πορεύου ἐντεῦθεν, ὅτι Ἡρῴδης θέλει σε
go hence, because Herod wishes thee

ἀποκτεῖναι. **32** καὶ εἶπεν αὐτοῖς· πορευθέντες
to kill. And he said to them: Going

εἴπατε τῇ ἀλώπεκι ταύτῃ· ἰδοὺ ἐκβάλλω
tell – fox this: Behold I expel

δαιμόνια καὶ ἰάσεις ἀποτελῶ σήμερον καὶ
demons and [2]cures [1]accomplish to-day and

αὔριον, καὶ τῇ τρίτῃ τελειοῦμαι. **33** πλὴν
to-morrow, and on the third [day] I am perfected. Nevertheless

δεῖ με σήμερον καὶ αὔριον καὶ τῇ ἐχομένῃ
it behoves me to-day and to-morrow and on the following [day]

πορεύεσθαι, ὅτι οὐκ ἐνδέχεται προφήτην
to journey, because it is not possible a prophet

ἀπολέσθαι ἔξω Ἰερουσαλήμ. **34** Ἰερουσαλὴμ
to perish outside Jerusalem. Jerusalem[,]

"Lord, are only a few people going to be saved?"
He said to them, 24 "Make
every effort to enter
through the narrow door,
because many, I tell you,
will try to enter and will not
be able to. 25 Once the owner of the house gets up and
closes the door, you will
stand outside knocking and
pleading, 'Sir, open the
door for us.'
"But he will answer, 'I
don't know you or where
you come from.'
26 "Then you will say,
'We ate and drank with
you, and you taught in our
streets.'
27 "But he will reply, 'I
don't know you or where
you come from. Away from
me, all you evildoers!'
28 "There will be weeping
there, and gnashing of
teeth, when you see Abra-
ham, Isaac and Jacob and
all the prophets in the kingdom of God, but you your-
selves thrown out. 29 People
will come from east and
west and north and south,
and will take their places at
the feast in the kingdom of
God. 30 Indeed there are
those who are last who will
be first, and first who will
be last."

Jesus' Sorrow for Jerusalem

31 At that time some Pharisees came to Jesus and
said to him, "Leave this
place and go somewhere
else. Herod wants to kill
you."
32 He replied, "Go tell
that fox, 'I will drive out
demons and heal people to-
day and tomorrow, and on
the third day I will reach
my goal.' 33 In any case, I
must keep going today and
tomorrow and the next day
—for surely no prophet can
die outside Jerusalem!
34 "O Jerusalem, Jerusa-

prophets and stones those
who are sent to it! How often have I desired to gather
your children together as a
hen gathers her brood un-
der her wings, and you
were not willing! 35 See,
your house is left to you.
And I tell you, you will not
see me until the time comes
when[i] you say, 'Blessed is
the one who comes in the
name of the Lord.' "

Chapter 14

Jesus Heals the Man with Dropsy

ON one occasion when
Jesus[j] was going to
the house of a leader of the
Pharisees to eat a meal on
the sabbath, they were
watching him closely. 2 Just
then, in front of him, there
was a man who had dropsy.
3 And Jesus asked the lawyers and Pharisees, "Is it
lawful to cure people on the
sabbath, or not?" 4 But they
were silent. So Jesus[j] took
him and healed him, and
sent him away. 5 Then he
said to them, "If one of you
has a child[k] or an ox that
has fallen into a well, will
you not immediately pull it
out on a sabbath day?"
6 And they could not reply
to this.

Humility and Hospitality

7 When he noticed how
the guests chose the places
of honor, he told them a
parable. 8 "When you are
invited by someone to a
wedding banquet, do not sit
down at the place of honor,
in case someone more dis-
tinguished than you has
been invited by your host;
9 and the host who invited
both of you may come and
say to you, 'Give this person your place,' and then in
disgrace you would start to
take the lowest place.

[i] Other ancient authorities lack *the time comes when*
[j] Gk *he*
[k] Other ancient authorities read *a donkey*

Ἰερουσαλήμ, ἡ ἀποκτείνουσα τοὺς προφήτας
Jerusalem, the [one] killing the prophets

καὶ λιθοβολοῦσα τοὺς ἀπεσταλμένους πρὸς
and stoning the [ones] *having been* sent to

αὐτήν, ποσάκις ἠθέλησα ἐπισυνάξαι τὰ
her, how often I wished to gather the

τέκνα σου ὃν τρόπον ὄρνις τὴν ἑαυτῆς
children of thee as † a bird the of herself

νοσσιὰν ὑπὸ τὰς πτέρυγας, καὶ οὐκ
brood under the(her) wings, and not

ἠθελήσατε. 35 ἰδοὺ ἀφίεται ὑμῖν ὁ οἶκος
ye wished. Behold is left to you the house

ὑμῶν. λέγω [δὲ] ὑμῖν, οὐ μὴ ἴδητέ με
of you. And I tell you, by no means ye may see me

ἕως ἥξει ὅτε εἴπητε· εὐλογημένος ὁ
until shall come [the time] when ye say : Blessed the

ἐρχόμενος ἐν ὀνόματι κυρίου.
[one] coming in [the] name of [the] Lord.

14 Καὶ ἐγένετο ἐν τῷ ἐλθεῖν αὐτὸν εἰς
And it came to pass in the to go him[be] into =as he went

οἶκόν τινος τῶν ἀρχόντων τῶν Φαρισαίων
a house of one of the leaders of the Pharisees

σαββάτῳ φαγεῖν ἄρτον, καὶ αὐτοὶ ἦσαν
on a sabbath to eat bread, *and* they were

παρατηρούμενοι αὐτόν. 2 καὶ ἰδοὺ ἄνθρωπός
carefully watching him. And[,] behold[,] man

τις ἦν ὑδρωπικὸς ἔμπροσθεν αὐτοῦ. 3 καὶ
a certain was dropsical before him. And

ἀποκριθεὶς ὁ Ἰησοῦς εἶπεν πρὸς τοὺς
answering – Jesus spoke to the

νομικοὺς καὶ Φαρισαίους λέγων· ἔξεστιν
lawyers and Pharisees saying : Is it lawful

τῷ σαββάτῳ θεραπεῦσαι ἢ οὔ; 4 οἱ δὲ
on the sabbath to heal or not? And they

ἡσύχασαν. καὶ ἐπιλαβόμενος ἰάσατο αὐτὸν
were silent. And taking he cured him

καὶ ἀπέλυσεν. 5 καὶ πρὸς αὐτοὺς εἶπεν·
and dismissed. And to them he said:

τίνος ὑμῶν υἱὸς ἢ βοῦς εἰς φρέαρ πεσεῖται,
Of whom of you a son or an ox into a pit shall fall,

καὶ οὐκ εὐθέως ἀνασπάσει αὐτὸν ἐν
and not immediately he will pull up it on

ἡμέρᾳ τοῦ σαββάτου; 6 καὶ οὐκ ἴσχυσαν
a day of the sabbath? And they were not able

ἀνταποκριθῆναι πρὸς ταῦτα. 7 Ἔλεγεν δὲ
to reply against these things. And he said

πρὸς τοὺς κεκλημένους παραβολήν, ἐπέχων
to the [ones] *having been* invited a parable, noting

πῶς τὰς πρωτοκλισίας ἐξελέγοντο, λέγων
how ²the ³chief seats ¹they were choosing, saying

πρὸς αὐτούς· 8 ὅταν κληθῇς ὑπό τινος εἰς
to them : When thou art invited by anyone to

γάμους, μὴ κατακλιθῇς εἰς τὴν πρωτοκλισίαν,
wedding festivities, do not recline in the chief seat,

μήποτε ἐντιμότερός σου ᾖ κεκλημένος ὑπ'
lest a more honour-able [than] thou be *having been* invited by

αὐτοῦ, 9 καὶ ἐλθὼν ὁ σὲ καὶ αὐτὸν καλέσας
him, and coming ¹the [one] ³thee ⁴and ⁵him ²inviting

ἐρεῖ σοι· δὸς τούτῳ τόπον, καὶ τότε
will say to thee : Give this man place, and then

ἄρξῃ μετὰ αἰσχύνης τὸν ἔσχατον τόπον
thou wilt begin with shame the last place

lem, you who kill the
prophets and stone those
sent to you, how often I
have longed to gather your
children together, as a hen
gathers her chicks under
her wings, but you were not
willing! 35 Look, your house
is left to you desolate. I tell
you, you will not see me
again until you say,
'Blessed is he who comes
in the name of the Lord.'[h]"

Chapter 14

Jesus at a Pharisee's House

ONE Sabbath, when
Jesus went to eat in
the house of a prominent
Pharisee, he was being
carefully watched. 2 There
in front of him was a man
suffering from dropsy.
3 Jesus asked the Pharisees
and experts in the law, "Is
it lawful to heal on the Sabbath or not?" 4 But they remained silent. So taking
hold of the man, he healed
him and sent him away.
5 Then he asked them, "If
one of you has a son[i] or an
ox that falls into a well on
the Sabbath day, will you
not immediately pull him
out?" 6 And they had nothing to say.
7 When he noticed how
the guests picked the
places of honor at the table,
he told them this parable:
8 "When someone invites
you to a wedding feast, do
not take the place of honor,
for a person more distin-
guished than you may have
been invited. 9 If so, the
host who invited both of
you will come and say to
you, 'Give this man your
seat.' Then, humiliated,
you will have to take the
least important place. 10 But

[h] 35 Psalm 118:26
[i] 5 Some manuscripts *donkey*

10But when you are invited, go and sit down at the lowest place, so that when your host comes, he may say to you, 'Friend, move up higher'; then you will be honored in the presence of all who sit at the table with you.
11For all who exalt themselves will be humbled, and those who humble themselves will be exalted."
12 He said also to the one who had invited him, "When you give a luncheon or a dinner, do not invite your friends or your brothers or your relatives or rich neighbors, in case they may invite you in return, and you would be repaid.
13But when you give a banquet, invite the poor, the crippled, the lame, and the blind.
14And you will be blessed, because they cannot repay you, for you will be repaid at the resurrection of the righteous."

The Parable of the Great Dinner

15 One of the dinner guests, on hearing this, said to him, "Blessed is the one who will eat bread in the kingdom of God!"
16Then Jesus[j] said to him, "Someone gave a great dinner and invited many.
17At the time for the dinner he sent his slave to say to those who had been invited, 'Come; for everything is ready now.'
18But they all alike began to make excuses. The first said to him, 'I have bought a piece of land, and I must go out and see it; please accept my regrets.'
19Another said, 'I have bought five yoke of oxen, and I am going to try them out; please accept my regrets.'
20Another said, 'I have just been married, and

κατέχειν. 10 ἀλλ' ὅταν κληθῇς, πορευθεὶς
to take. But when thou art invited, going
ἀνάπεσε εἰς τὸν ἔσχατον τόπον, ἵνα ὅταν ἔλθῃ
recline in the last place, that when 4comes
ὁ κεκληκώς σε ἐρεῖ σοι· φίλε,
1the [one] 2having invited 3thee he will say to thee : Friend,
προσανάβηθι ἀνώτερον· τότε ἔσται σοι δόξα
go up higher; then there will be to thee[c] glory
ἐνώπιον πάντων τῶν συνανακειμένων σοι.
before all the [ones] reclining with thee.
11 ὅτι πᾶς ὁ ὑψῶν ἑαυτὸν ταπεινωθήσεται,
Because everyone exalting himself will be humbled,
καὶ ὁ ταπεινῶν ἑαυτὸν ὑψωθήσεται.
and the [one] humbling himself will be exalted.
12 Ἔλεγεν δὲ καὶ τῷ κεκληκότι αὐτόν·
And he said also to the [one] having invited him :
ὅταν ποιῇς ἄριστον ἢ δεῖπνον, μὴ φώνει
When thou makest a dinner or a supper, do not call
τοὺς φίλους σου μηδὲ τοὺς ἀδελφούς
the friends of thee nor the brothers
σου μηδὲ τοὺς συγγενεῖς σου μηδὲ
of thee nor the relatives of thee nor
γείτονας πλουσίους, μήποτε καὶ αὐτοὶ
neighbours rich, lest also they
ἀντικαλέσωσίν σε καὶ γένηται ἀνταπόδομά
1invite 3in 4return 2thee and it becomes a recompence
σοι. 13 ἀλλ' ὅταν δοχὴν ποιῇς, κάλει
to thee. But when a party thou makest, invite
πτωχούς, ἀναπήρους, χωλούς, τυφλούς·
poor [persons], maimed, lame, blind;
14 καὶ μακάριος ἔσῃ, ὅτι οὐκ ἔχουσιν
and blessed thou shalt be, because they have not
ἀνταποδοῦναί σοι· ἀνταποδοθήσεται γάρ σοι
to recompense thee; for it will be recompensed to thee
ἐν τῇ ἀναστάσει τῶν δικαίων. 15 Ἀκούσας
in the resurrection of the just. 3hearing
δέ τις τῶν συνανακειμένων ταῦτα εἶπεν
1And 4one 5of the [ones] 6reclining with 2these things said
αὐτῷ· μακάριος ὅστις φάγεται ἄρτον ἐν
to him : Blessed [is he] who shall eat bread in
τῇ βασιλείᾳ τοῦ θεοῦ. 16 ὁ δὲ εἶπεν
the kingdom – of God. And he said
αὐτῷ· ἄνθρωπός τις ἐποίει δεῖπνον μέγα,
to him : A certain man made supper a great,
καὶ ἐκάλεσεν πολλούς, 17 καὶ ἀπέστειλεν
and invited many, and sent
τὸν δοῦλον αὐτοῦ τῇ ὥρᾳ τοῦ δείπνου
the slave of him at the hour of the supper
εἰπεῖν τοῖς κεκλημένοις· ἔρχεσθε, ὅτι ἤδη
to say to the [ones] having been invited : Come, because 2now
ἕτοιμά ἐστιν. 18 καὶ ἤρξαντο ἀπὸ μιᾶς
3prepared 1it is. And they began from one [mind]
πάντες παραιτεῖσθαι. ὁ πρῶτος εἶπεν
all to beg off. The first said
αὐτῷ· ἀγρὸν ἠγόρασα, καὶ ἔχω ἀνάγκην
to him : 2A farm 1I bought, and I am obliged†
ἐξελθὼν ἰδεῖν αὐτόν· ἐρωτῶ σε, ἔχε με
going out to see it; I ask thee, have me
παρῃτημένον. 19 καὶ ἕτερος εἶπεν· ζεύγη
begged off. And another said : 3Yoke
βοῶν ἠγόρασα πέντε, καὶ πορεύομαι
4of oxen 1I bought 2five, and I am going
δοκιμάσαι αὐτά· ἐρωτῶ σε, ἔχε με
to prove them; I ask thee, have me
παρῃτημένον. 20 καὶ ἕτερος εἶπεν· γυναῖκα
begged off. And another said : 2A wife

when you are invited, take the lowest place, so that when your host comes, he will say to you, 'Friend, move up to a better place.' Then you will be honored in the presence of all your fellow guests.
11For everyone who exalts himself will be humbled, and he who humbles himself will be exalted."
12Then Jesus said to his host, "When you give a luncheon or dinner, do not invite your friends, your brothers or relatives, or your rich neighbors; if you do, they may invite you back and so you will be repaid.
13But when you give a banquet, invite the poor, the crippled, the lame, the blind,
14and you will be blessed. Although they cannot repay you, you will be repaid at the resurrection of the righteous."

The Parable of the Great Banquet

15When one of those at the table with him heard this, he said to Jesus, "Blessed is the man who will eat at the feast in the kingdom of God."
16Jesus replied: "A certain man was preparing a great banquet and invited many guests.
17At the time of the banquet he sent his servant to tell those who had been invited, 'Come, for everything is now ready.'
18"But they all alike began to make excuses. The first said, 'I have just bought a field, and I must go and see it. Please excuse me.'
19"Another said, 'I have just bought five yoke of oxen, and I'm on my way to try them out. Please excuse me.'
20"Still another said, 'I

therefore I cannot come.'
21 So the slave returned and
reported this to his master.
Then the owner of the
house became angry and
said to his slave, 'Go out at
once into the streets and
lanes of the town and bring
in the poor, the crippled,
the blind, and the lame.'
22 And the slave said, 'Sir,
what you ordered has been
done, and there is still
room.' 23 Then the master
said to the slave, 'Go out
into the roads and lanes,
and compel people to come
in, so that my house may be
filled. 24 For I tell you,[l]
none of those who were invited will taste my din-
ner.' "

The Cost of Discipleship

25 Now large crowds
were traveling with him;
and he turned and said to
them, 26 "Whoever comes
to me and does not hate father and mother, wife and
children, brothers and sisters, yes, and even life itself, cannot be my disciple.
27 Whoever does not carry
the cross and follow me
cannot be my disciple.
28 For which of you, intending to build a tower, does
not first sit down and esti-
mate the cost, to see
whether he has enough to
complete it? 29 Otherwise,
when he has laid a foundation and is not able to finish, all who see it will begin
to ridicule him, 30 saying,
'This fellow began to build
and was not able to finish.'
31 Or what king, going out
to wage war against anoth-

[l] The Greek word for *you* here is plural

ἔγημα, καὶ διὰ τοῦτο οὐ δύναμαι ἐλθεῖν.
¹I married, and therefore I cannot *to* come.
21 καὶ παραγενόμενος ὁ δοῦλος ἀπήγγειλεν
And coming up the slave reported
τῷ κυρίῳ αὐτοῦ ταῦτα. τότε ὀργισθεὶς ὁ
to the lord of him these things. Then being angry the
οἰκοδεσπότης εἶπεν τῷ δούλῳ αὐτοῦ· ἔξελθε
house-master told the slave of him : Go out
ταχέως εἰς τὰς πλατείας καὶ ῥύμας τῆς
quickly into the streets and lanes of the
πόλεως, καὶ τοὺς πτωχοὺς καὶ ἀναπήρους
city, and the poor and maimed
καὶ τυφλοὺς καὶ χωλοὺς εἰσάγαγε ὧδε.
and blind and lame bring in here.
22 καὶ εἶπεν ὁ δοῦλος· κύριε, γέγονεν ὃ
And said the slave : Lord, has happened what
ἐπέταξας, καὶ ἔτι τόπος ἐστίν. 23 καὶ
thou didst command, and yet room there is. And
εἶπεν ὁ κύριος πρὸς τὸν δοῦλον· ἔξελθε εἰς
said the lord to the slave : Go out into
τὰς ὁδοὺς καὶ φραγμοὺς καὶ ἀνάγκασον
the ways and hedges and compel
εἰσελθεῖν, ἵνα γεμισθῇ μου ὁ οἶκος·
to come in, that may be filled of me the house ;
24 λέγω γὰρ ὑμῖν ὅτι οὐδεὶς τῶν ἀνδρῶν
for I tell you that not one – men
ἐκείνων τῶν κεκλημένων γεύσεταί μου
of those – having been invited shall taste of me
τοῦ δείπνου.
the supper.
25 Συνεπορεύοντο δὲ αὐτῷ ὄχλοι πολλοί,
And came together to him crowds many,
καὶ στραφεὶς εἶπεν πρὸς αὐτούς· 26 εἴ τις
and turning he said to them : If anyone
ἔρχεται πρός με καὶ οὐ μισεῖ τὸν πατέρα
comes to me and hates not the father
αὐτοῦ καὶ τὴν μητέρα καὶ τὴν γυναῖκα
of him and the mother and the wife
καὶ τὰ τέκνα καὶ τοὺς ἀδελφοὺς καὶ τὰς
and the children and the brothers and the
ἀδελφάς, ἔτι τε καὶ τὴν ψυχὴν ἑαυτοῦ,
sisters, and besides also the life of himself,
οὐ δύναται εἶναί μου μαθητής. 27 ὅστις
he cannot *to* be of me a disciple. Who
οὐ βαστάζει τὸν σταυρὸν ἑαυτοῦ καὶ
bears not the cross of himself and
ἔρχεται ὀπίσω μου, οὐ δύναται εἶναί μου
comes after me, he cannot *to* be of me
μαθητής. 28 Τίς γὰρ ἐξ ὑμῶν θέλων
a disciple. For who of you wishing
πύργον οἰκοδομῆσαι οὐχὶ πρῶτον καθίσας
a tower to build not first sitting
ψηφίζει τὴν δαπάνην, εἰ ἔχει εἰς ἀπαρ-
counts the cost, if he has for com-
τισμόν; 29 ἵνα μή ποτε θέντος αὐτοῦ
pletion? Lest when laying him[a]
=he has laid
θεμέλιον καὶ μὴ ἰσχύοντος ἐκτελέσαι πάντες
a foundation and not being able[a] to finish all
οἱ θεωροῦντες ἄρξωνται αὐτῷ ἐμπαίζειν
the [ones] seeing begin him to mock
30 λέγοντες ὅτι οὗτος ὁ ἄνθρωπος ἤρξατο
saying[,] – This – man began
οἰκοδομεῖν καὶ οὐκ ἴσχυσεν ἐκτελέσαι.
to build and was not able to finish.
31 Ἢ τίς βασιλεὺς πορευόμενος ἑτέρῳ βασιλεῖ
Or what king ¹going ⁵another ⁶king

just got married, so I can't
come.'
21 "The servant came
back and reported this to
his master. Then the owner
of the house became angry
and ordered his servant,
'Go out quickly into the
streets and alleys of the
town and bring in the poor,
the crippled, the blind and
the lame.'
22 " 'Sir,' the servant
said, 'what you ordered has
been done, but there is still
room.'
23 "Then the master told
his servant, 'Go out to the
roads and country lanes
and make them come in, so
that my house will be full.
24 I tell you, not one of those
men who were invited will
get a taste of my ban-
quet.' "

The Cost of Being a Disciple

25 Large crowds were
traveling with Jesus, and
turning to them he said:
26 "If anyone comes to me
and does not hate his father
and mother, his wife and
children, his brothers and
sisters—yes, even his own
life—he cannot be my dis-
ciple. 27 And anyone who
does not carry his cross and
follow me cannot be my
disciple.
28 "Suppose one of you
wants to build a tower. Will
he not first sit down and es-
timate the cost to see if he
has enough money to com-
plete it? 29 For if he lays the
foundation and is not able
to finish it, everyone who
sees it will ridicule him,
30 saying, 'This fellow began to build and was not
able to finish.'
31 "Or suppose a king is
about to go to war against

er king, will not sit down first and consider whether he is able with ten thousand to oppose the one who comes against him with twenty thousand? 32 If he cannot, then, while the other is still far away, he sends a delegation and asks for the terms of peace. 33 So therefore, none of you can become my disciple if you do not give up all your possessions.

About Salt

34 "Salt is good; but if salt has lost its taste, how can its saltiness be restored?[m] 35 It is fit neither for the soil nor for the manure pile; they throw it away. Let anyone with ears to hear listen!"

Chapter 15

The Parable of the Lost Sheep

NOW all the tax collectors and sinners were coming near to listen to him. 2 And the Pharisees and the scribes were grumbling and saying, "This fellow welcomes sinners and eats with them."

3 So he told them this parable: 4 "Which one of you, having a hundred sheep and losing one of them, does not leave the ninety-nine in the wilderness and go after the one that is lost until he finds it? 5 When he has found it, he lays it on his shoulders and rejoices. 6 And when he comes home, he calls together his friends and neighbors, saying to them, 'Rejoice with me, for I have found my sheep that was lost.' 7 Just so, I tell you, there will be more joy in heaven over one sinner who repents than over ninety-nine righteous per-

συμβαλεῖν εἰς πόλεμον οὐχὶ καθίσας πρῶτον
³to attack ⁴in ⁵war not sitting first
βουλεύσεται εἰ δυνατός ἐστιν ἐν δέκα
will deliberate if able he is with ten
χιλιάσιν ὑπαντῆσαι τῷ μετὰ εἴκοσι χιλιάδων
thousands to meet ¹the [one] ⁵with ⁶twenty ⁷thousands
ἐρχομένῳ ἐπ' αὐτόν; 32 εἰ δὲ μή γε, ἔτι
²coming ³upon ⁴him? Otherwise, yet =while
αὐτοῦ πόρρω ὄντος πρεσβείαν ἀποστείλας
him afar being[a] a delegation sending
he is yet at a distance
ἐρωτᾷ τὰ πρὸς εἰρήνην. 33 οὕτως οὖν
he asks the things for peace. So therefore
πᾶς ἐξ ὑμῶν ὃς οὐκ ἀποτάσσεται πᾶσιν
everyone of you who does not say farewell to all
τοῖς ἑαυτοῦ ὑπάρχουσιν οὐ δύναται εἶναί
¹the ³of himself ²possessions cannot *to* be
μου μαθητής. 34 Καλὸν οὖν τὸ ἅλας·
of me a disciple. Good therefore the salt;
ἐὰν δὲ καὶ τὸ ἅλας μωρανθῇ, ἐν τίνι
but if even the salt becomes useless, with what
ἀρτυθήσεται; 35 οὔτε εἰς γῆν οὔτε εἰς
will it be seasoned? neither for soil nor for
κοπρίαν εὔθετόν ἐστιν· ἔξω βάλλουσιν
manure suitable is it; outside they cast
αὐτό. ὁ ἔχων ὦτα ἀκούειν ἀκουέτω.
it The [one] having ears to hear let him hear.

15 Ἦσαν δὲ αὐτῷ ἐγγίζοντες πάντες
Now there were to him drawing near all
οἱ τελῶναι καὶ οἱ ἁμαρτωλοὶ ἀκούειν
the tax-collectors and the sinners to hear
αὐτοῦ. 2 καὶ διεγόγγυζον οἵ τε Φαρισαῖοι
him. And greatly murmured both the Pharisees
καὶ οἱ γραμματεῖς λέγοντες ὅτι οὗτος
and the scribes saying[,] – This man
ἁμαρτωλοὺς προσδέχεται καὶ συνεσθίει αὐτοῖς.
sinners receives and eats with them.
3 εἶπεν δὲ πρὸς αὐτοὺς τὴν παραβολὴν
And he spoke to them – parable
ταύτην λέγων· 4 τίς ἄνθρωπος ἐξ
this saying : What man of
ὑμῶν ἔχων ἑκατὸν πρόβατα καὶ ἀπολέσας
you having a hundred sheep and losing
ἐξ αὐτῶν ἓν οὐ καταλείπει τὰ ἐνενήκοντα
of them one does not leave the ninety-
ἐννέα ἐν τῇ ἐρήμῳ καὶ πορεύεται ἐπὶ
nine in the desert and goes after
τὸ ἀπολωλὸς ἕως εὕρῃ αὐτό; 5 καὶ
the [one] having been lost until he finds it? and
εὑρὼν ἐπιτίθησιν ἐπὶ τοὺς ὤμους αὐτοῦ
finding places *on* [it] on the shoulders of him
χαίρων, 6 καὶ ἐλθὼν εἰς τὸν οἶκον
rejoicing, and coming into the house
συγκαλεῖ τοὺς φίλους καὶ τοὺς γείτονας,
he calls together the friends and the neighbours,
λέγων αὐτοῖς· συγχάρητέ μοι, ὅτι εὗρον
saying to them : Rejoice with me, because I found
τὸ πρόβατόν μου τὸ ἀπολωλός. 7 λέγω
the sheep of me – having been lost. I tell
ὑμῖν ὅτι οὕτως χαρὰ ἐν τῷ οὐρανῷ
you that thus joy in – heaven
ἔσται ἐπὶ ἑνὶ ἁμαρτωλῷ μετανοοῦντι ἢ
will be over one sinner repenting than
ἐπὶ ἐνενήκοντα ἐννέα δικαίοις οἵτινες οὐ
over ninety-nine just men who no

another king. Will he not first sit down and consider whether he is able with ten thousand men to oppose the one coming against him with twenty thousand? 32 If he is not able, he will send a delegation while the other is still a long way off and will ask for terms of peace. 33 In the same way, any of you who does not give up everything he has cannot be my disciple.

34 "Salt is good, but if it loses its saltiness, how can it be made salty again? 35 It is fit neither for the soil nor for the manure pile; it is thrown out.

"He who has ears to hear, let him hear."

Chapter 15

The Parable of the Lost Sheep

NOW the tax collectors and "sinners" were all gathering around to hear him. 2 But the Pharisees and the teachers of the law muttered, "This man welcomes sinners and eats with them."

3 Then Jesus told them this parable: 4 "Suppose one of you has a hundred sheep and loses one of them. Does he not leave the ninety-nine in the open country and go after the lost sheep until he finds it? 5 And when he finds it, he joyfully puts it on his shoulders 6 and goes home. Then he calls his friends and neighbors together and says, 'Rejoice with me; I have found my lost sheep.' 7 I tell you that in the same way there will be more rejoicing in heaven over one sinner who repents than over ninety-nine righteous

[m] Or *how can it be used for seasoning?*

sons who need no repen-
tance.

The Parable of the Lost Coin

8 "Or what woman hav-
ing ten silver coins,[n] if she
loses one of them, does not
light a lamp, sweep the
house, and search carefully
until she finds it? 9 When
she has found it, she calls
together her friends and
neighbors, saying, 'Rejoice
with me, for I have found
the coin that I had lost.'
10 Just so, I tell you, there is
joy in the presence of the
angels of God over one sinner who repents."

The Parable of the Prodigal and His Brother

11 Then Jesus[o] said,
"There was a man who had
two sons. 12 The younger of
them said to his father, 'Father, give me the share of
the property that will belong to me.' So he divided
his property between them.
13 A few days later the
younger son gathered all he
had and traveled to a distant country, and there he
squandered his property in
dissolute living. 14 When he
had spent everything, a severe famine took place
throughout that country,
and he began to be in need.
15 So he went and hired
himself out to one of the citizens of that country, who
sent him to his fields to feed
the pigs. 16 He would gladly
have filled himself with[p]
the pods that the pigs were
eating; and no one gave him
anything. 17 But when he
came to himself he said,
'How many of my father's
hired hands have bread
enough and to spare, but
here I am dying of hunger!
18 I will get up and go to my
father, and I will say to
him, "Father, I have sinned
against heaven and before
you; 19 I am no longer worthy to be called your son;

[n] Gk *drachmas*, each worth about a day's wage for a laborer
[o] Gk *he*
[p] Other ancient authorities read *filled his stomach with*

χρείαν ἔχουσιν μετανοίας. 8 Ἢ τίς γυνὴ
need have of repentance. Or what woman

δραχμὰς ἔχουσα δέκα, ἐὰν ἀπολέσῃ
[3]drachmae [1]having [2]ten, if she loses

δραχμὴν μίαν, οὐχὶ ἅπτει λύχνον καὶ
drachma one, does not light a lamp and

σαροῖ τὴν οἰκίαν καὶ ζητεῖ ἐπιμελῶς
sweep the house and seek carefully

ἕως οὗ εὕρῃ; 9 καὶ εὑροῦσα συγκαλεῖ
until she finds? and finding she calls together

τὰς φίλας καὶ γείτονας λέγουσα· συγχάρητέ
the friends and neighbours saying: Rejoice with

μοι, ὅτι εὗρον τὴν δραχμὴν ἣν ἀπώλεσα.
me, because I found the drachma which I lost.

10 οὕτως, λέγω ὑμῖν, γίνεται χαρὰ ἐνώπιον
So, I tell you, there is joy before

τῶν ἀγγέλων τοῦ θεοῦ ἐπὶ ἑνὶ ἁμαρτωλῷ
the angels – of God over one sinner

μετανοοῦντι. 11 Εἶπεν δέ· ἄνθρωπός τις
repenting. And he said: A certain man

εἶχεν δύο υἱούς. 12 καὶ εἶπεν ὁ νεώτερος
had two sons. And said the younger

αὐτῶν τῷ πατρί· πάτερ, δός μοι τὸ
of them to the father: Father, give me the

ἐπιβάλλον μέρος τῆς οὐσίας. ὁ δὲ διεῖλες
falling upon share of the property. And he divided
=share of the property falling to [me].

αὐτοῖς τὸν βίον. 13 καὶ μετ' οὐ πολλὰς
to them the living. And after not many

ἡμέρας συναγαγὼν πάντα ὁ νεώτερος υἱὸς
days having gathered all things the younger son

ἀπεδήμησεν εἰς χώραν μακράν, καὶ ἐκεῖ
departed to country a far, and there

διεσκόρπισεν τὴν οὐσίαν αὐτοῦ ζῶν ἀσώτως.
scattered the property of him living prodigally.

14 δαπανήσαντος δὲ αὐτοῦ πάντα ἐγένετο
But having spent him* all things there came
=when he had spent

λιμὸς ἰσχυρὰ κατὰ τὴν χώραν ἐκείνην,
famine a severe throughout – country that,

καὶ αὐτὸς ἤρξατο ὑστερεῖσθαι. 15 καὶ
and he began to be in want. And

πορευθεὶς ἐκολλήθη ἑνὶ τῶν πολιτῶν τῆς
going he was joined to one of the citizens –

χώρας ἐκείνης, καὶ ἔπεμψεν αὐτὸν εἰς
country of that, and he sent him into

τοὺς ἀγροὺς αὐτοῦ βόσκειν χοίρους· 16 καὶ
the fields of him to feed pigs; and

ἐπεθύμει γεμίσαι τὴν κοιλίαν αὐτοῦ ἐκ
he longed to fill the stomach of him out of(with)

τῶν κερατίων ὧν ἤσθιον οἱ χοῖροι, καὶ
the husks which [3]ate [1]the [2]pigs, and

οὐδεὶς ἐδίδου αὐτῷ. 17 εἰς ἑαυτὸν δὲ
no one gave to him. [3]to [4]himself [1]But

ἐλθὼν ἔφη· πόσοι μίσθιοι τοῦ πατρός μου
[2]coming he said: How many hired servants of the father of me

περισσεύονται ἄρτων, ἐγὼ δὲ λιμῷ ὧδε
abound of loaves, but I with famine here
=have abundance of bread,

ἀπόλλυμαι. 18 ἀναστὰς πορεύσομαι πρὸς
am perishing. Rising up I will go to

τὸν πατέρα μου καὶ ἐρῶ αὐτῷ· πάτερ,
the father of me and I will say to him: Father,

ἥμαρτον εἰς τὸν οὐρανὸν καὶ ἐνώπιόν σου,
I sinned against – heaven and before thee,

19 οὐκέτι εἰμὶ ἄξιος κληθῆναι υἱός σου·
no longer am I worthy to be called a son of thee;

persons who do not need to
repent.

The Parable of the Lost Coin

8 "Or suppose a woman
has ten silver coins[j] and
loses one. Does she not
light a lamp, sweep the
house and search carefully
until she finds it? 9 And
when she finds it, she calls
her friends and neighbors
together and says, 'Rejoice
with me; I have found my
lost coin.' 10 In the same
way, I tell you, there is rejoicing in the presence of
the angels of God over one
sinner who repents."

The Parable of the Lost Son

11 Jesus continued:
"There was a man who had
two sons. 12 The younger
one said to his father, 'Father, give me my share of
the estate.' So he divided
his property between them.
13 "Not long after that,
the younger son got together all he had, set off for a
distant country and there
squandered his wealth in
wild living. 14 After he had
spent everything, there was
a severe famine in that
whole country, and he be-
gan to be in need. 15 So he
went and hired himself out
to a citizen of that country,
who sent him to his fields to
feed pigs. 16 He longed to
fill his stomach with the
pods that the pigs were eating, but no one gave him
anything.
17 "When he came to his
senses, he said, 'How
many of my father's hired
men have food to spare,
and here I am starving to
death! 18 I will set out and
go back to my father and
say to him: Father, I have
sinned against heaven and
against you. 19 I am no longer worthy to be called

[j] 8 Greek *ten drachmas*, each worth about a day's wages

treat me like one of your
hired hands." ' 20 So he set
off and went to his father.
But while he was still far
off, his father saw him and
was filled with compassion;
he ran and put his arms
around him and kissed him.
21 Then the son said to him,
'Father, I have sinned
against heaven and before
you; I am no longer worthy
to be called your son.'[q]
22 But the father said to his
slaves, 'Quickly, bring out
a robe—the best one—and
put it on him; put a ring on
his finger and sandals on
his feet. 23 And get the fatted calf and kill it, and let us
eat and celebrate; 24 for this
son of mine was dead and is
alive again; he was lost and
is found!' And they began
to celebrate.
25 "Now his elder son
was in the field; and when
he came and approached
the house, he heard music
and dancing. 26 He called
one of the slaves and asked
what was going on. 27 He
replied, 'Your brother has
come, and your father has
killed the fatted calf, because he has got him back
safe and sound.' 28 Then he
became angry and refused
to go in. His father came
out and began to plead with
him. 29 But he answered his
father, 'Listen! For all
these years I have been
working like a slave for
you, and I have never disobeyed your command; yet
you have never given me
even a young goat so that I
might celebrate with my
friends. 30 But when this
son of yours came back,
who has devoured your
property with prostitutes,

[q] Other ancient authorities add *treat me as one of your hired servants*

ποίησόν με ὡς ἕνα τῶν μισθίων σου.
make me as one of the hired servants of thee.
20 καὶ ἀναστὰς ἦλθεν πρὸς τὸν πατέρα
And rising up he came to the father
ἑαυτοῦ. ἔτι δὲ αὐτοῦ μακρὰν ἀπέχοντος
of him*self*. But yet him afar being away[a]
=while he was yet far away
εἶδεν αὐτὸν ὁ πατὴρ αὐτοῦ καὶ ἐσπλαγχνίσθη,
saw him the father of him and was moved with pity,
καὶ δραμὼν ἐπέπεσεν ἐπὶ τὸν τράχηλον
and running fell *on* on the neck
αὐτοῦ καὶ κατεφίλησεν αὐτόν. 21 εἶπεν δὲ
of him and fervently kissed him. And said
ὁ υἱὸς αὐτῷ· πάτερ, ἥμαρτον εἰς τὸν
the son to him: Father, I sinned against –
οὐρανὸν καὶ ἐνώπιόν σου, οὐκέτι εἰμὶ
heaven and before thee, no longer am I
ἄξιος κληθῆναι υἱός σου. 22 εἶπεν δὲ
worthy to be called a son of thee. But said
ὁ πατὴρ πρὸς τοὺς δούλους αὐτοῦ· ταχὺ
the father to the slaves of him: Quickly
ἐξενέγκατε στολὴν τὴν πρώτην καὶ ἐνδύσατε
bring ye out a robe the first and clothe
αὐτόν, καὶ δότε δακτύλιον εἰς τὴν χεῖρα
him, and give(put) a ring to the hand
αὐτοῦ καὶ ὑποδήματα εἰς τοὺς πόδας,
of him and sandals to the feet,
23 καὶ φέρετε τὸν μόσχον τὸν σιτευτόν,
and bring the calf – fattened,
θύσατε, καὶ φαγόντες εὐφρανθῶμεν, 24 ὅτι
kill, and eating let us be merry, because
οὗτος ὁ υἱός μου νεκρὸς ἦν καὶ ἀνέζησεν,
this – son of me dead was and lived again,
ἦν ἀπολωλὼς καὶ εὑρέθη. καὶ ἤρξαντο
was *having been* lost and was found. And they began
εὐφραίνεσθαι. 25 ἦν δὲ ὁ υἱὸς αὐτοῦ
to be merry. But was the son of him
ὁ πρεσβύτερος ἐν ἀγρῷ· καὶ ὡς ἐρχόμενος
– older in a field; and as coming
ἤγγισεν τῇ οἰκίᾳ, ἤκουσεν συμφωνίας καὶ
he drew near to the house, he heard music and
χορῶν, 26 καὶ προσκαλεσάμενος ἕνα τῶν
dances, and calling to [him] one of the
παίδων ἐπυνθάνετο τί ἂν εἴη ταῦτα.
lads he inquired what might be these things.
27 ὁ δὲ εἶπεν αὐτῷ ὅτι ὁ ἀδελφός σου
And he said to him[,] – The brother of thee
ἥκει, καὶ ἔθυσεν ὁ πατήρ σου τὸν μόσχον τὸν
has come, and [4]killed [1]the [2]father [3]of thee [5]the [7]calf –
σιτευτόν, ὅτι ὑγιαίνοντα αὐτὸν ἀπέλαβεν.
[6]fattened, because [5]being in health [3]him [1]he [2]received [4]back.
28 ὠργίσθη δὲ καὶ οὐκ ἤθελεν εἰσελθεῖν·
But he was angry and did not wish to enter;
ὁ δὲ πατὴρ αὐτοῦ ἐξελθὼν παρεκάλει
so the father of him coming out besought
αὐτόν. 29 ὁ δὲ ἀποκριθεὶς εἶπεν τῷ
him. But he answering said to the
πατρί· ἰδοὺ τοσαῦτα ἔτη δουλεύω σοι καὶ
father: Behold[,] so many years I serve thee and
οὐδέποτε ἐντολήν σου παρῆλθον, καὶ ἐμοὶ
never a command of thee I transgressed, and to me
οὐδέποτε ἔδωκας ἔριφον ἵνα μετὰ τῶν
never thou gavest a goat that with the
φίλων μου εὐφρανθῶ· 30 ὅτε δὲ ὁ υἱός
friends of me I might be merry; but when – [2]son
σου οὗτος ὁ καταφαγών σου τὸν βίον
[3]of thee [1]this – having devoured of thee the living

your son; make me like one
of your hired men.' 20 So he
got up and went to his father.
"But while he was still a
long way off, his father saw
him and was filled with
compassion for him; he ran
to his son, threw his arms
around him and kissed him.
21 "The son said to him,
'Father, I have sinned
against heaven and against
you. I am no longer worthy
to be called your son.[k]'
22 "But the father said to
his servants, 'Quick! Bring
the best robe and put it on
him. Put a ring on his finger
and sandals on his feet.
23 Bring the fattened calf
and kill it. Let's have a
feast and celebrate. 24 For
this son of mine was dead
and is alive again; he was
lost and is found.' So they
began to celebrate.
25 "Meanwhile, the older
son was in the field. When
he came near the house, he
heard music and dancing.
26 So he called one of the
servants and asked him
what was going on. 27 'Your
brother has come,' he re-
plied, 'and your father has
killed the fattened calf because he has him back safe
and sound.'
28 "The older brother be-
came angry and refused to
go in. So his father went out
and pleaded with him.
29 But he answered his father, 'Look! All these years
I've been slaving for you
and never disobeyed your
orders. Yet you never gave
me even a young goat so I
could celebrate with my
friends. 30 But when this
son of yours who has
squandered your property

[k] 21 Some early manuscripts *son. Make me like one of your hired men.*

you killed the fatted calf for him!' 31 Then the father[r] said to him, 'Son, you are always with me, and all that is mine is yours. 32 But we had to celebrate and rejoice, because this brother of yours was dead and has come to life; he was lost and has been found.' "

Chapter 16

The Parable of the Dishonest Manager

THEN Jesus[r] said to the disciples, "There was a rich man who had a manager, and charges were brought to him that this man was squandering his property. 2 So he summoned him and said to him, 'What is this that I hear about you? Give me an accounting of your management, because you cannot be my manager any longer.' 3 Then the manager said to himself, 'What will I do, now that my master is taking the position away from me? I am not strong enough to dig, and I am ashamed to beg. 4 I have decided what to do so that, when I am dismissed as manager, people may welcome me into their homes.' 5 So, summoning his master's debtors one by one, he asked the first, 'How much do you owe my master?' 6 He answered, 'A hundred jugs of olive oil.' He said to him, 'Take your bill, sit down quickly, and make it fifty.' 7 Then he asked another, 'And how much do you owe?' He replied, 'A hundred containers of wheat.' He said to him, 'Take your bill and make it eighty.' 8 And his master commended the dishonest manager because he had acted shrewdly; for the children of this age are

[r] Gk *he*

μετὰ πορνῶν ἦλθεν, ἔθυσας αὐτῷ τὸν
with harlots came, thou killedst for him the
σιτευτὸν μόσχον. **31** ὁ δὲ εἶπεν αὐτῷ·
fattened calf. And he said to him:
τέκνον, σὺ πάντοτε μετ' ἐμοῦ εἶ, καὶ
Child, thou always with me art, and
πάντα τὰ ἐμὰ σά ἐστιν· **32** εὐφρανθῆναι
[1]all [3]things – [2]my [5]thine [4]is(are); [3]to be merry
δὲ καὶ χαρῆναι ἔδει, ὅτι ὁ ἀδελφός
[1]And [4]and [5]to rejoice [2]it behoved [us], because – [2]brother
σου οὗτος νεκρὸς ἦν καὶ ἔζησεν, καὶ ἀπο-
[3]of thee [1]this [5]dead [4]was and came to life, and having
λωλὼς καὶ εὑρέθη.
been lost also was found.

16 Ἔλεγεν δὲ καὶ πρὸς τοὺς μαθητάς·
And he said also to the disciples:
ἄνθρωπός τις ἦν πλούσιος ὃς εἶχεν
[3]A certain [4]man [1]there was [2]rich who had
οἰκονόμον, καὶ οὗτος διεβλήθη αὐτῷ ὡς
a steward, and this was complained of to him as
διασκορπίζων τὰ ὑπάρχοντα αὐτοῦ. **2** καὶ
wasting the possessions of him. And
φωνήσας αὐτὸν εἶπεν αὐτῷ· τί τοῦτο
calling him he said to him: What [is] this
ἀκούω περὶ σοῦ; ἀπόδος τὸν λόγον τῆς
I hear about thee? render the account of the
οἰκονομίας σου· οὐ γὰρ δύνῃ ἔτι οἰκονομεῖν.
stewardship of thee; for thou canst not longer *to* be steward.
3 εἶπεν δὲ ἐν ἑαυτῷ ὁ οἰκονόμος· τί
And said in himself the steward: What
ποιήσω, ὅτι ὁ κύριός μου ἀφαιρεῖται τὴν
may I do, because the lord of me takes away the
οἰκονομίαν ἀπ' ἐμοῦ; σκάπτειν οὐκ ἰσχύω,
stewardship from me? to dig I am not able,
ἐπαιτεῖν αἰσχύνομαι. **4** ἔγνων τί ποιήσω,
to beg I am ashamed. I knew(know) what I may do,
ἵνα ὅταν μετασταθῶ ἐκ τῆς οἰκονομίας
that when I am removed out of the stewardship
δέξωνταί με εἰς τοὺς οἴκους ἑαυτῶν.
they may receive me into the houses of them*selves*.
5 καὶ προσκαλεσάμενος ἕνα ἕκαστον τῶν
And calling to [him] [2]one [1]each of the
χρεοφειλετῶν τοῦ κυρίου ἑαυτοῦ ἔλεγεν τῷ
debtors of the lord of him*self* he said to the
πρώτῳ· πόσον ὀφείλεις τῷ κυρίῳ μου;
first: How much owest thou to the lord of me?
6 ὁ δὲ εἶπεν· ἑκατὸν βάτους ἐλαίου. ὁ δὲ
And he said: A hundred baths of oil. And he
εἶπεν αὐτῷ· δέξαι σου τὰ γράμματα καὶ
told him: Take of thee the letters(bill) and
καθίσας ταχέως γράψον πεντήκοντα. **7** ἔπειτα
sitting quickly write fifty. Then
ἑτέρῳ εἶπεν· σὺ δὲ πόσον ὀφείλεις; ὁ δὲ
to another he said: [4]thou [1]And [2]how much [3]owest? And he
εἶπεν· ἑκατὸν κόρους σίτου. λέγει αὐτῷ·
said: A hundred cors of wheat. He tells him:
δέξαι σου τὰ γράμματα καὶ γράψον
Take of thee the bill and write
ὀγδοήκοντα. **8** καὶ ἐπῄνεσεν ὁ κύριος τὸν
eighty. And [3]praised [1]the [2]lord the
οἰκονόμον τῆς ἀδικίας ὅτι φρονίμως
steward – of unrighteousness because prudently
ἐποίησεν· ὅτι οἱ υἱοὶ τοῦ αἰῶνος τούτου
he acted; because the sons – age of this

with prostitutes comes home, you kill the fattened calf for him!'

31 " 'My son,' the father said, 'you are always with me, and everything I have is yours. 32 But we had to celebrate and be glad, because this brother of yours was dead and is alive again; he was lost and is found.' "

Chapter 16

The Parable of the Shrewd Manager

JESUS told his disciples: "There was a rich man whose manager was accused of wasting his possessions. 2 So he called him in and asked him, 'What is this I hear about you? Give an account of your management, because you cannot be manager any longer.'

3 "The manager said to himself, 'What shall I do now? My master is taking away my job. I'm not strong enough to dig, and I'm ashamed to beg— 4 I know what I'll do so that, when I lose my job here, people will welcome me into their houses.'

5 "So he called in each one of his master's debtors. He asked the first, 'How much do you owe my master?'

6 " 'Eight hundred gallons[l] of olive oil,' he replied.

"The manager told him, 'Take your bill, sit down quickly, and make it four hundred.'

7 "Then he asked the second, 'And how much do you owe?'

" 'A thousand bushels[m] of wheat,' he replied.

"He told him, 'Take your bill and make it eight hundred.'

8 "The master commended the dishonest manager because he had acted shrewdly. For the people of

[l] 6 Greek *one hundred batous* (probably about 3 kiloliters)
[m] 7 Greek *one hundred korous* (probably about 35 kiloliters)

more shrewd in dealing
with their own generation
than are the children of
light. 9 And I tell you, make
friends for yourselves by
means of dishonest
wealth[s] so that when it is
gone, they may welcome
you into the eternal
homes.[t]
10 "Whoever is faithful
in a very little is faithful
also in much; and whoever
is dishonest in a very little
is dishonest also in much.
11 If then you have not been
faithful with the dishonest
wealth,[s] who will entrust
to you the true riches?
12 And if you have not been
faithful with what belongs
to another, who will give
you what is your own?
13 No slave can serve two
masters; for a slave will either hate the one and love
the other, or be devoted to
the one and despise the other. You cannot serve God
and wealth."[s]

The Law and the Kingdom of God

14 The Pharisees, who
were lovers of money,
heard all this, and they ridiculed him. 15 So he said to
them, "You are those who
justify yourselves in the
sight of others; but God
knows your hearts; for
what is prized by human
beings is an abomination in
the sight of God.
16 "The law and the
prophets were in effect until John came; since then
the good news of the kingdom of God is proclaimed,
and everyone tries to enter
it by force.[u] 17 But it is easier for heaven and earth to
pass away, than for one
stroke of a letter in the law
to be dropped.
18 "Anyone who di-
vorces his wife and marries
another commits adultery,
and whoever marries a

[s] Gk *mammon*
[t] Gk *tents*
[u] Or *everyone is strongly urged to enter it*

φρονιμώτεροι ὑπὲρ τοὺς υἱοὺς τοῦ φωτὸς
more prudent than the sons of the light

εἰς τὴν γενεὰν τὴν ἑαυτῶν εἰσιν. **9** Καὶ
in the generation – of them*selves* are. And

ἐγὼ ὑμῖν λέγω, ἑαυτοῖς ποιήσατε φίλους
I [2]you [1]tell, To yourselves make friends

ἐκ τοῦ μαμωνᾶ τῆς ἀδικίας, ἵνα ὅταν
by the mammon – of unrighteousness, that when

ἐκλίπῃ δέξωνται ὑμᾶς εἰς τὰς αἰωνίους
it fails they may receive you into the eternal

σκηνάς. **10** ὁ πιστὸς ἐν ἐλαχίστῳ καὶ ἐν
tabernacles. The man faithful in least also in

πολλῷ πιστός ἐστιν, καὶ ὁ ἐν ἐλαχίστῳ
much faithful is, and the man in least

ἄδικος καὶ ἐν πολλῷ ἄδικός ἐστιν. **11** εἰ
unrighteous also in much unrighteous is. If

οὖν ἐν τῷ ἀδίκῳ μαμωνᾷ πιστοὶ οὐκ
therefore in the unrighteous mammon faithful not

ἐγένεσθε, τὸ ἀληθινὸν τίς ὑμῖν πιστεύσει;
ye were, the true who to you will entrust ?

12 καὶ εἰ ἐν τῷ ἀλλοτρίῳ πιστοὶ οὐκ
And if in the thing belonging to another faithful not

ἐγένεσθε, τὸ ἡμέτερον τίς δώσει ὑμῖν;
ye were, the ours who will give you?
=that which is ours

13 Οὐδεὶς οἰκέτης δύναται δυσὶ κυρίοις
No household slave can two lords

δουλεύειν· ἢ γὰρ τὸν ἕνα μισήσει καὶ τὸν
to serve; for either the one he will hate and the

ἕτερον ἀγαπήσει, ἢ ἑνὸς ἀνθέξεται καὶ
other he will love, or one he will hold fast to and

τοῦ ἑτέρου καταφρονήσει. οὐ δύνασθε
the other he will despise. Ye cannot

θεῷ δουλεύειν καὶ μαμωνᾷ. **14** Ἤκουον
God *to* serve and mammon. [6]heard

δὲ ταῦτα πάντα οἱ Φαρισαῖοι φιλάργυροι
[1]Now [8]these things [7]all [2]the [3]Pharisees [5]moneylovers

ὑπάρχοντες, καὶ ἐξεμυκτήριζον αὐτόν. **15** καὶ
[4]being, and they scoffed at him. And

εἶπεν αὐτοῖς· ὑμεῖς ἐστε οἱ δικαιοῦντες
he said to them : Ye are the [ones] justifying

ἑαυτοὺς ἐνώπιον τῶν ἀνθρώπων, ὁ δὲ
yourselves before – men, – but

θεὸς γινώσκει τὰς καρδίας ὑμῶν· ὅτι τὸ
God knows the hearts of you; because the thing

ἐν ἀνθρώποις ὑψηλὸν βδέλυγμα ἐνώπιον
[2]among [3]men [1]lofty [is] an abomination before

τοῦ θεοῦ. **16** Ὁ νόμος καὶ οἱ προφῆται
– God. The law and the prophets

μέχρι Ἰωάννου· ἀπὸ τότε ἡ βασιλεία τοῦ
[were] until John; from then the kingdom –

θεοῦ εὐαγγελίζεται καὶ πᾶς εἰς αὐτὴν
of God is being preached and everyone into it

βιάζεται. **17** εὐκοπώτερον δέ ἐστιν τὸν οὐρανὸν
is pressing. But easier it is the heaven

καὶ τὴν γῆν παρελθεῖν ἢ τοῦ νόμου μίαν
and the earth to pass away than of the law one

κεραίαν πεσεῖν. **18** Πᾶς ὁ ἀπολύων τὴν
little horn* to fall. Everyone dismissing the

γυναῖκα αὐτοῦ καὶ γαμῶν ἑτέραν μοιχεύει,
wife of him and marrying another commits adultery,

καὶ ὁ ἀπολελυμένην ἀπὸ
and [1]the [one] [3]a woman having been dismissed [4]from

* The little projection which distinguishes some Hebrew letters from those otherwise similar.

this world are more shrewd
in dealing with their own
kind than are the people of
the light. 9 I tell you, use
worldly wealth to gain
friends for yourselves, so
that when it is gone, you
will be welcomed into eternal dwellings.
10 "Whoever can be trust-
ed with very little can also
be trusted with much, and
whoever is dishonest with
very little will also be dishonest with much. 11 So if
you have not been trust-
worthy in handling worldly
wealth, who will trust you
with true riches? 12 And if
you have not been trust-
worthy with someone
else's property, who will
give you property of your
own?
13 "No servant can serve
two masters. Either he will
hate the one and love the
other, or he will be devoted
to the one and despise the
other. You cannot serve
both God and Money."
14 The Pharisees, who
loved money, heard all this
and were sneering at Jesus.
15 He said to them, "You
are the ones who justify
yourselves in the eyes of
men, but God knows your
hearts. What is highly valued among men is detest-
able in God's sight.

Additional Teachings

16 "The Law and the
Prophets were proclaimed
until John. Since that time,
the good news of the kingdom of God is being
preached, and everyone is
forcing his way into it. 17 It
is easier for heaven and
earth to disappear than for
the least stroke of a pen to
drop out of the Law.
18 "Anyone who divorces
his wife and marries another woman commits adul-
tery, and the man who marries a divorced woman
commits adultery.

woman divorced from her
husband commits adultery.

The Rich Man and Lazarus

19 "There was a rich
man who was dressed in
purple and fine linen and
who feasted sumptuously
every day. 20 And at his
gate lay a poor man named
Lazarus, covered with
sores, 21 who longed to satisfy his hunger with what
fell from the rich man's table; even the dogs would
come and lick his sores.
22 The poor man died and
was carried away by the angels to be with Abraham.[v]
The rich man also died and
was buried. 23 In Hades,
where he was being tor-
mented, he looked up and
saw Abraham far away
with Lazarus by his side.[w]
24 He called out, 'Father
Abraham, have mercy on
me, and send Lazarus to
dip the tip of his finger in
water and cool my tongue;
for I am in agony in these
flames.' 25 But Abraham
said, 'Child, remember that
during your lifetime you received your good things,
and Lazarus in like manner
evil things; but now he is
comforted here, and you
are in agony. 26 Besides all
this, between you and us a
great chasm has been fixed,
so that those who might
want to pass from here to
you cannot do so, and no
one can cross from there to
us.' 27 He said, 'Then, father, I beg you to send him
to my father's house—
28 for I have five brothers—
that he may warn them, so
that they will not also come
into this place of torment.'

[v] Gk *to Abraham's bosom*
[w] Gk *in his bosom*

ἀνδρὸς γαμῶν μοιχεύει. 19 Ἄνθρωπος δέ
[3]a husband [2]marrying [1]commits adultery. Now a certain

τις ἦν πλούσιος, καὶ ἐνεδιδύσκετο πορφύραν
man was rich, and used to put on a purple robe

καὶ βύσσον εὐφραινόμενος καθ' ἡμέραν
and fine linen being merry every day†

λαμπρῶς. 20 πτωχὸς δέ τις ὀνόματι
splendidly. And a certain poor man by name

Λάζαρος ἐβέβλητο πρὸς τὸν πυλῶνα αὐτοῦ
Lazarus had been placed at the gate of him

εἱλκωμένος 21 καὶ ἐπιθυμῶν χορτασθῆναι
being covered with sores and desiring to be satisfied

ἀπὸ τῶν πιπτόντων ἀπὸ τῆς τραπέζης
from the things falling from the table

τοῦ πλουσίου· ἀλλὰ καὶ οἱ κύνες ἐρχόμενοι
of the rich man; but even the dogs coming

ἐπέλειχον τὰ ἕλκη αὐτοῦ. 22 ἐγένετο δὲ
licked the sores of him. And it came to pass

ἀποθανεῖν τὸν πτωχὸν καὶ ἀπενεχθῆναι
to die the poor man and to be carried away
=that the poor man died and he was carried away

αὐτὸν ὑπὸ τῶν ἀγγέλων εἰς τὸν κόλπον
him[b] by the angels into the bosom

Ἀβραάμ· ἀπέθανεν δὲ καὶ ὁ πλούσιος καὶ
of Abraham; and died also the rich man and

ἐτάφη. 23 καὶ ἐν τῷ ᾅδῃ ἐπάρας τοὺς
was buried. And in – hades lifting up the

ὀφθαλμοὺς αὐτοῦ, ὑπάρχων ἐν βασάνοις,
eyes of him, being in torments,

ὁρᾷ Ἀβραὰμ ἀπὸ μακρόθεν καὶ Λάζαρον
he sees Abraham from afar and Lazarus

ἐν τοῖς κόλποις αὐτοῦ. 24 καὶ αὐτὸς
in the bosoms of him. And he

φωνήσας εἶπεν· πάτερ Ἀβραάμ, ἐλέησόν
calling said: Father Abraham, pity

με καὶ πέμψον Λάζαρον ἵνα βάψῃ τὸ
me and send Lazarus that he may dip the

ἄκρον τοῦ δακτύλου αὐτοῦ ὕδατος καὶ
tip of the finger of him of(in) water and

καταψύξῃ τὴν γλῶσσάν μου, ὅτι ὀδυνῶμαι
may cool the tongue of me, because I am suffering

ἐν τῇ φλογὶ ταύτῃ. 25 εἶπεν δὲ Ἀβραάμ·
in – flame this. But said Abraham:

τέκνον, μνήσθητι ὅτι ἀπέλαβες τὰ ἀγαθά
Child, remember that thou didst receive the good things

σου ἐν τῇ ζωῇ σου, καὶ Λάζαρος ὁμοίως
of thee in the life of thee, and Lazarus likewise

τὰ κακά· νῦν δὲ ὧδε παρακαλεῖται, σὺ δὲ
the bad; but now here he is comforted, but thou

ὀδυνᾶσαι. 26 καὶ ἐν πᾶσι τούτοις μεταξὺ
art suffering. And among all these things between

ἡμῶν καὶ ὑμῶν χάσμα μέγα ἐστήρικται,
us and you chasm a great has been firmly fixed,

ὅπως οἱ θέλοντες διαβῆναι ἔνθεν πρὸς
so that the [ones] wishing to pass hence to

ὑμᾶς μὴ δύνωνται, μηδὲ ἐκεῖθεν πρὸς
you cannot, neither thence to

ἡμᾶς διαπερῶσιν. 27 εἶπεν δέ· ἐρωτῶ
us may they cross over. And he said: I ask

σε οὖν, πάτερ, ἵνα πέμψῃς αὐτὸν εἰς
thee therefore, father, that thou mayest send him to

τὸν οἶκον τοῦ πατρός μου· 28 ἔχω γὰρ
the house of the father of me; for I have

πέντε ἀδελφούς· ὅπως διαμαρτύρηται αὐτοῖς,
five brothers; so that he may witness to them,

ἵνα μὴ καὶ αὐτοὶ ἔλθωσιν εἰς τὸν τόπον
lest also they come to – place

The Rich Man and Lazarus

19 "There was a rich man
who was dressed in purple
and fine linen and lived in
luxury every day. 20 At his
gate was laid a beggar
named Lazarus, covered
with sores 21 and longing to
eat what fell from the rich
man's table. Even the dogs
came and licked his sores.
22 "The time came when
the beggar died and the angels carried him to Abra-
ham's side. The rich man
also died and was buried.
23 In hell,[n] where he was in
torment, he looked up and
saw Abraham far away,
with Lazarus by his side.
24 So he called to him, 'Father Abraham, have pity on
me and send Lazarus to dip
the tip of his finger in water
and cool my tongue, be-
cause I am in agony in this
fire.'
25 "But Abraham replied,
'Son, remember that in
your lifetime you received
your good things, while
Lazarus received bad
things, but now he is comforted here and you are in
agony. 26 And besides all
this, between us and you a
great chasm has been fixed,
so that those who want to
go from here to you cannot,
nor can anyone cross over
from there to us.'
27 "He answered, 'Then I
beg you, father, send Lazarus to my father's house,
28 for I have five brothers.
Let him warn them, so that
they will not also come to

[n] 23 Greek *Hades*

[29]Abraham replied, 'They
have Moses and the proph-
ets; they should listen to
them.' [30]He said, 'No, father Abraham; but if someone goes to them from the
dead, they will repent.'
[31]He said to him, 'If they
do not listen to Moses and
the prophets, neither will
they be convinced even if
someone rises from the
dead.' "

τοῦτον τῆς βασάνου. 29 λέγει δὲ Ἀβραάμ·
this – of torment. But says Abraham :
ἔχουσι Μωϋσέα καὶ τοὺς προφήτας·
They have Moses and the prophets;
ἀκουσάτωσαν αὐτῶν. 30 ὁ δὲ εἶπεν·
let them hear them. But he said :
οὐχί, πάτερ Ἀβραάμ, ἀλλ' ἐάν τις ἀπὸ
No, father Abraham, but if someone from
νεκρῶν πορευθῇ πρὸς αὐτούς, μετανοήσουσιν.
[the] dead should go to them, they will repent.
31 εἶπεν δὲ αὐτῷ· εἰ Μωϋσέως καὶ τῶν
But he said to him : If Moses and the
προφητῶν οὐκ ἀκούουσιν, οὐδὲ ἐάν τις
prophets they do not hear, neither if someone
ἐκ νεκρῶν ἀναστῇ πεισθήσονται.
out of [the] dead should rise again will they be persuaded.

this place of torment.'
[29]"Abraham replied,
'They have Moses and the
Prophets; let them listen to
them.'
[30]" 'No, father Abra-
ham,' he said, 'but if someone from the dead goes to
them, they will repent.'
[31]"He said to him, 'If
they do not listen to Moses
and the Prophets, they will
not be convinced even if
someone rises from the
dead.' "

Chapter 17

Some Sayings of Jesus

JESUS[x] said to his disciples, "Occasions for
stumbling are bound to
come, but woe to anyone
by whom they come! [2]It
would be better for you if a
millstone were hung
around your neck and you
were thrown into the sea
than for you to cause one of
these little ones to stumble.
[3]Be on your guard! If another disciple[y] sins, you
must rebuke the offender,
and if there is repentance,
you must forgive. [4]And if
the same person sins
against you seven times a
day, and turns back to you
seven times and says, 'I repent,' you must forgive."
5 The apostles said to
the Lord, "Increase our
faith!" [6]The Lord replied,
"If you had faith the size of
a[z] mustard seed, you could
say to this mulberry tree,
'Be uprooted and planted
in the sea,' and it would
obey you.
7 "Who among you
would say to your slave
who has just come in from
plowing or tending sheep in
the field, 'Come here at
once and take your place at
the table'? [8]Would you not
rather say to him, 'Prepare
supper for me, put on your
apron and serve me while I
eat and drink; later you
may eat and drink'? [9]Do
you thank the slave for doing what was commanded?

[x] Gk *He*
[y] Gk *your brother*
[z] Gk *faith as a grain of*

17 Εἶπεν δὲ πρὸς τοὺς μαθητὰς αὐτοῦ·
And he said to the disciples of him :
ἀνένδεκτόν ἐστιν τοῦ τὰ σκάνδαλα μὴ ἐλθεῖν,
Impossible it is – the offences not to come,[d]
οὐαὶ δὲ δι' οὗ ἔρχεται· 2 λυσιτελεῖ
but woe [to him] through whom they come; it profits
αὐτῷ εἰ λίθος μυλικὸς περίκειται περὶ
him if a millstone is put *round* round
τὸν τράχηλον αὐτοῦ καὶ ἔρριπται εἰς τὴν
the neck of him and he has been thrown into the
θάλασσαν, ἢ ἵνα σκανδαλίσῃ τῶν μικρῶν
sea, than that he should offend – [2]little ones
τούτων ἕνα. 3 προσέχετε ἑαυτοῖς. ἐὰν
[3]of these [1]one. Take heed to yourselves. If
ἁμάρτῃ ὁ ἀδελφός σου, ἐπιτίμησον αὐτῷ,
sins the brother of thee, rebuke him,
καὶ ἐὰν μετανοήσῃ, ἄφες αὐτῷ. 4 καὶ
and if he repents, forgive him. And
ἐὰν ἑπτάκις τῆς ἡμέρας ἁμαρτήσῃ εἰς σὲ
if seven times of(in) the day he sins against thee
καὶ ἑπτάκις ἐπιστρέψῃ πρὸς σὲ λέγων·
and seven times turns to thee saying :
μετανοῶ, ἀφήσεις αὐτῷ. 5 Καὶ εἶπαν οἱ
I repent, thou shalt forgive him. And said the
ἀπόστολοι τῷ κυρίῳ· πρόσθες ἡμῖν πίστιν.
apostles to the Lord : Add to us faith.
6 εἶπεν δὲ ὁ κύριος· εἰ ἔχετε πίστιν ὡς
And said the Lord : If ye have faith as
κόκκον σινάπεως, ἐλέγετε ἂν τῇ συκαμίνῳ
a grain of mustard, ye would have said – sycamine-tree
ταύτῃ· ἐκριζώθητι καὶ φυτεύθητι ἐν τῇ
to this : Be thou uprooted and be thou planted in the
θαλάσσῃ· καὶ ὑπήκουσεν ἂν ὑμῖν. 7 Τίς
sea; and it would have obeyed you. who
δὲ ἐξ ὑμῶν δοῦλον ἔχων ἀροτριῶντα ἢ
But of you [2]a slave [1]having ploughing or
ποιμαίνοντα, ὃς εἰσελθόντι ἐκ τοῦ ἀγροῦ
herding, who on [his] coming in• out of the farm
ἐρεῖ αὐτῷ· εὐθέως παρελθὼν ἀνάπεσε,
will say to him : Immediately coming up recline,
8 ἀλλ' οὐχὶ ἐρεῖ αὐτῷ· ἑτοίμασον τί
but will not say to him : Prepare something
δειπνήσω, καὶ περιζωσάμενος διακόνει μοι
I may dine, and having girded thyself serve me
ἕως φάγω καὶ πίω, καὶ μετὰ ταῦτα
until I eat and drink, and after these things
φάγεσαι καὶ πίεσαι σύ; 9 μὴ ἔχει χάριν
eat and drink thou? *Not* he has thanks

Chapter 17

Sin, Faith, Duty

JESUS said to his disci-
ples: "Things that cause
people to sin are bound to
come, but woe to that person through whom they
come. [2]It would be better
for him to be thrown into
the sea with a millstone tied
around his neck than for
him to cause one of these
little ones to sin. [3]So watch
yourselves.
"If your brother sins, rebuke him, and if he repents,
forgive him. [4]If he sins
against you seven times in a
day, and seven times
comes back to you and
says, 'I repent,' forgive
him."
[5]The apostles said to the
Lord, "Increase our
faith!"
[6]He replied, "If you have
faith as small as a mustard
seed, you can say to this
mulberry tree, 'Be uprooted and planted in the sea,'
and it will obey you.
[7]"Suppose one of you
had a servant plowing or
looking after the sheep.
Would he say to the servant
when he comes in from the
field, 'Come along now and
sit down to eat'? [8]Would he
not rather say, 'Prepare my
supper, get yourself ready
and wait on me while I eat
and drink; after that you
may eat and drink'?
[9]Would he thank the ser-

10 So you also, when you
have done all that you were
ordered to do, say, 'We are
worthless slaves; we have
done only what we ought to
have done!' "

Jesus Cleanses Ten Lepers

11 On the way to Jeru-
salem Jesus[a] was going
through the region between
Samaria and Galilee. 12 As
he entered a village, ten
lepers[b] approached him.
Keeping their distance,
13 they called out, saying,
"Jesus, Master, have mer-
cy on us!" 14 When he saw
them, he said to them, "Go
and show yourselves to the
priests." And as they went,
they were made clean.
15 Then one of them, when
he saw that he was healed,
turned back, praising God
with a loud voice. 16 He
prostrated himself at
Jesus'[c] feet and thanked
him. And he was a Samari-
tan. 17 Then Jesus asked,
"Were not ten made clean?
But the other nine, where
are they? 18 Was none of
them found to return and
give praise to God except
this foreigner?" 19 Then he
said to him, "Get up and go
on your way; your faith has
made you well."

The Coming of the Kingdom

20 Once Jesus[a] was
asked by the Pharisees
when the kingdom of God
was coming, and he an-
swered, "The kingdom of
God is not coming with
things that can be ob-
served; 21 nor will they say,
'Look, here it is!' or 'There
it is!' For, in fact, the kingdom of God is among[d]
you."
22 Then he said to the
disciples, "The days are

τῷ δούλῳ ὅτι ἐποίησεν τὰ διαταχθέντα;
to the slave because he did the things commanded?

10 οὕτως καὶ ὑμεῖς, ὅταν ποιήσητε πάντα
So also ye, when ye do all

τὰ διαταχθέντα ὑμῖν, λέγετε ὅτι δοῦλοι
the things commanded you, say[,] – Slaves

ἀχρεῖοί ἐσμεν, ὃ ὠφείλομεν ποιῆσαι
unprofitable we are, what we ought to do

πεποιήκαμεν.
we have done.

11 Καὶ ἐγένετο ἐν τῷ πορεύεσθαι εἰς
And it came to pass in the to go[e] to
=as [he] went

Ἰερουσαλήμ, καὶ αὐτὸς διήρχετο διὰ μέσον
Jerusalem, *and* he passed *through* through [the] midst

Σαμαρείας καὶ Γαλιλαίας. **12** καὶ εἰσερχομένου
of Samaria and Galilee. And entering
=as he entered

αὐτοῦ εἴς τινα κώμην ἀπήντησαν δέκα
him[a] into a certain village met [him] ten

λεπροὶ ἄνδρες, οἳ ἔστησαν πόρρωθεν, **13** καὶ
leprous men, who stood afar off, and

αὐτοὶ ἦραν φωνὴν λέγοντες· Ἰησοῦ
they lifted voice saying : Jesus

ἐπιστάτα, ἐλέησον ἡμᾶς. **14** καὶ ἰδὼν εἶπεν
Master, pity us. And seeing he said

αὐτοῖς· πορευθέντες ἐπιδείξατε ἑαυτοὺς τοῖς
to them : Going show yourselves to the

ἱερεῦσιν. καὶ ἐγένετο ἐν τῷ ὑπάγειν
priests. And it came to pass in the to go
= as they went

αὐτοὺς ἐκαθαρίσθησαν. **15** εἷς δὲ ἐξ
them[be] they were cleansed. But one of

αὐτῶν, ἰδὼν ὅτι ἰάθη, ὑπέστρεψεν μετὰ
them, seeing that he was cured, returned with

φωνῆς μεγάλης δοξάζων τὸν θεόν, **16** καὶ
voice a great glorifying – God, and

ἔπεσεν ἐπὶ πρόσωπον παρὰ τοὺς πόδας
fell on [his] face at the feet

αὐτοῦ εὐχαριστῶν αὐτῷ· καὶ αὐτὸς ἦν
of him thanking him; and he was

Σαμαρίτης. **17** ἀποκριθεὶς δὲ ὁ Ἰησοῦς
a Samaritan. And answering – Jesus

εἶπεν· οὐχ οἱ δέκα ἐκαθαρίσθησαν; οἱ [δὲ]
said : Not the ten were cleansed? but the

ἐννέα ποῦ; **18** οὐχ εὑρέθησαν ὑποστρέψαντες
nine where? were there not found returning

δοῦναι δόξαν τῷ θεῷ εἰ μὴ ὁ ἀλλογενὴς
to give glory – to God only – stranger

οὗτος; **19** καὶ εἶπεν αὐτῷ· ἀναστὰς πορεύου·
this ? And he said to him : Rising up go;

ἡ πίστις σου σέσωκέν σε.
the faith of thee has healed thee.

20 Ἐπερωτηθεὶς δὲ ὑπὸ τῶν Φαρισαίων
And being questioned by the Pharisees

πότε ἔρχεται ἡ βασιλεία τοῦ θεοῦ,
when comes the kingdom – of God,

ἀπεκρίθη αὐτοῖς καὶ εἶπεν· οὐκ ἔρχεται
he answered them and said : Comes not

ἡ βασιλεία τοῦ θεοῦ μετὰ παρατηρήσεως,
the kingdom – of God with observation,

21 οὐδὲ ἐροῦσιν· ἰδοὺ ὧδε ἤ· ἐκεῖ· ἰδοὺ
nor will they say : Behold[,] here or: there; [a]behold

γὰρ ἡ βασιλεία τοῦ θεοῦ ἐντὸς ὑμῶν
[f]for the kingdom – of God within you

ἐστιν. **22** Εἶπεν δὲ πρὸς τοὺς μαθητάς·
is. And he said to the disciples :

vant because he did what
he was told to do? 10 So you
also, when you have done
everything you were told to
do, should say, 'We are unworthy servants; we have
only done our duty.' "

Ten Healed of Leprosy

11 Now on his way to Jerusalem, Jesus traveled along
the border between Samar-
ia and Galilee. 12 As he was
going into a village, ten
men who had leprosy[o] met
him. They stood at a dis-
tance 13 and called out in a
loud voice, "Jesus, Mas-
ter, have pity on us!"
14 When he saw them, he
said, "Go, show your-
selves to the priests." And
as they went, they were
cleansed.
15 One of them, when he
saw he was healed, came
back, praising God in a
loud voice. 16 He threw
himself at Jesus' feet and
thanked him—and he was a
Samaritan.
17 Jesus asked, "Were not
all ten cleansed? Where are
the other nine? 18 Was no
one found to return and
give praise to God except
this foreigner?" 19 Then he
said to him, "Rise and go;
your faith has made you
well."

The Coming of the Kingdom of God

20 Once, having been
asked by the Pharisees
when the kingdom of God
would come, Jesus replied,
"The kingdom of God does
not come with your careful
observation, 21 nor will people say, 'Here it is,' or
'There it is,' because the
kingdom of God is within[p]
you."
22 Then he said to his dis-

[a] Gk *he*
[b] The terms *leper* and *leprosy* can refer to several diseases
[c] Gk *his*
[d] Or *within*

[o] *12* The Greek word was used for various diseases affecting the skin—not necessarily leprosy.
[p] *21* Or *among*

coming when you will long
to see one of the days of the
Son of Man, and you will
not see it. 23 They will say
to you, 'Look there!' or
'Look here!' Do not go, do
not set off in pursuit. 24 For
as the lightning flashes and
lights up the sky from one
side to the other, so will the
Son of Man be in his day.[e]
25 But first he must endure
much suffering and be re-
jected by this generation.
26 Just as it was in the days
of Noah, so too it will be in
the days of the Son of Man.
27 They were eating and
drinking, and marrying and
being given in marriage,
until the day Noah entered
the ark, and the flood came
and destroyed all of them.
28 Likewise, just as it was in
the days of Lot: they were
eating and drinking, buying
and selling, planting and
building, 29 but on the day
that Lot left Sodom, it
rained fire and sulfur from
heaven and destroyed all of
them 30—it will be like that
on the day that the Son of
Man is revealed. 31 On that
day, anyone on the house-
top who has belongings in
the house must not come
down to take them away;
and likewise anyone in the
field must not turn back.
32 Remember Lot's wife.
33 Those who try to make
their life secure will lose it,
but those who lose their life
will keep it. 34 I tell you, on
that night there will be two
in one bed; one will be tak-
en and the other left.

ἐλεύσονται ἡμέραι ὅτε ἐπιθυμήσετε μίαν
Will come days when ye will long one
τῶν ἡμερῶν τοῦ υἱοῦ τοῦ ἀνθρώπου ἰδεῖν
of the days of the Son – of man to see
καὶ οὐκ ὄψεσθε. 23 καὶ ἐροῦσιν ὑμῖν·
and will not see. And they will say to you :
ἰδοὺ ἐκεῖ, ἰδοὺ ὧδε· μὴ ἀπέλθητε μηδὲ
Behold there, behold here; do not go away nor
διώξητε. 24 ὥσπερ γὰρ ἡ ἀστραπὴ
follow. For as the lightning
ἀστράπτουσα ἐκ τῆς ὑπὸ τὸν οὐρανὸν
flashing out of the [one part] under – heaven
εἰς τὴν ὑπ' οὐρανὸν λάμπει, οὕτως ἔσται
to the [other part] under heaven shines, so will be
ὁ υἱὸς τοῦ ἀνθρώπου ἐν τῇ ἡμέρᾳ αὐτοῦ.
the Son – of man in the day of him.
25 πρῶτον δὲ δεῖ αὐτὸν πολλὰ παθεῖν καὶ
But first it behoves him many things to suffer and
ἀποδοκιμασθῆναι ἀπὸ τῆς γενεᾶς ταύτης.
to be rejected from – generation this.
26 καὶ καθὼς ἐγένετο ἐν ταῖς ἡμέραις
And as it was in the days
Νῶε, οὕτως ἔσται καὶ ἐν ταῖς ἡμέραις
of Noah, so it will be also in the days
τοῦ υἱοῦ τοῦ ἀνθρώπου· 27 ἤσθιον, ἔπινον,
of the Son – of man; they were eating, drinking,
ἐγάμουν, ἐγαμίζοντο, ἄχρι ἧς ἡμέρας
marrying, giving in marriage, until which day
=the day when
εἰσῆλθεν Νῶε εἰς τὴν κιβωτόν, καὶ
entered Noah into the ark, and
ἦλθεν ὁ κατακλυσμὸς καὶ ἀπώλεσεν πάντας.
came the flood and destroyed all.
28 ὁμοίως καθὼς ἐγένετο ἐν ταῖς ἡμέραις
Likewise as it was in the days
Λώτ· ἤσθιον, ἔπινον, ἠγόραζον, ἐπώλουν,
of Lot; they were eating, drinking, buying, selling,
ἐφύτευον, ᾠκοδόμουν· 29 ᾗ δὲ ἡμέρᾳ ἐξῆλθεν
planting, building; but on which day went forth
Λὼτ ἀπὸ Σοδόμων, ἔβρεξεν πῦρ καὶ
Lot from Sodom, it rained fire and
θεῖον ἀπ' οὐρανοῦ καὶ ἀπώλεσεν πάντας.
brimstone from heaven and destroyed all.
30 κατὰ τὰ αὐτὰ ἔσται ᾗ ἡμέρᾳ ὁ υἱὸς
According to the same things it will be in which day the Son
=In the same way =on the day when
τοῦ ἀνθρώπου ἀποκαλύπτεται. 31 ἐν ἐκείνῃ
– of man is revealed. In that
τῇ ἡμέρᾳ ὃς ἔσται ἐπὶ τοῦ δώματος καὶ
– day who will be on the roof and
τὰ σκεύη αὐτοῦ ἐν τῇ οἰκίᾳ, μὴ καταβάτω
the goods of him in the house, let him not come down
ἆραι αὐτά, καὶ ὁ ἐν ἀγρῷ ὁμοίως μὴ
to take them, and the [one] in a field likewise not
ἐπιστρεψάτω εἰς τὰ ὀπίσω. 32 μνημονεύετε
let him turn back to the things behind. Remember
τῆς γυναικὸς Λώτ. 33 ὃς ἐὰν ζητήσῃ
the wife of Lot. Whoever seeks
τὴν ψυχὴν αὐτοῦ περιποιήσασθαι, ἀπολέσει
the life of him to preserve, he will lose
αὐτήν, καὶ ὃς ἂν ἀπολέσει, ζῳογονήσει
it, and whoever will lose, will preserve
αὐτήν. 34 λέγω ὑμῖν, ταύτῃ τῇ νυκτὶ
it. I tell you, in this – night
ἔσονται δύο ἐπὶ κλίνης μιᾶς, ὁ εἷς
there will be two men on couch one, the one
παραλημφθήσεται καὶ ὁ ἕτερος ἀφεθήσεται·
will be taken and the other will be left;

ciples, "The time is coming
when you will long to see
one of the days of the Son
of Man, but you will not see
it. 23 Men will tell you,
'There he is!' or 'Here he
is!' Do not go running off
after them. 24 For the Son of
Man in his day[q] will be like
the lightning, which flashes
and lights up the sky from
one end to the other. 25 But
first he must suffer many
things and be rejected by
this generation.

26 "Just as it was in the
days of Noah, so also will it
be in the days of the Son of
Man. 27 People were eating,
drinking, marrying and being given in marriage up to
the day Noah entered the
ark. Then the flood came
and destroyed them all.

28 "It was the same in the
days of Lot. People were
eating and drinking, buying
and selling, planting and
building. 29 But the day Lot
left Sodom, fire and sulfur
rained down from heaven
and destroyed them all.

30 "It will be just like this
on the day the Son of Man
is revealed. 31 On that day
no one who is on the roof of
his house, with his goods
inside, should go down to
get them. Likewise, no one
in the field should go back
for anything. 32 Remember
Lot's wife! 33 Whoever tries
to keep his life will lose it,
and whoever loses his life
will preserve it. 34 I tell you,
on that night two people
will be in one bed; one will
be taken and the other left.

[e] Other ancient authorities lack *in his day*

[q] 24 Some manuscripts do not have *in his day*.

[35]There will be two women grinding meal together; one will be taken and the other left."[f] [37]Then they asked him, "Where, Lord?" He said to them, "Where the corpse is, there the vultures will gather."

35 ἔσονται δύο ἀλήθουσαι ἐπὶ τὸ αὐτό, ἡ
there will be two women grinding together,† the
μία παραλημφθήσεται ἡ δὲ ἑτέρα ἀφεθήσεται.‡
one will be taken but the other will be left.
37 καὶ ἀποκριθέντες λέγουσιν αὐτῷ· ποῦ,
And answering they say to him : Where,
κύριε; ὁ δὲ εἶπεν αὐτοῖς· ὅπου τὸ σῶμα,
Lord? And he said to them : Where the body,
ἐκεῖ καὶ οἱ ἀετοὶ ἐπισυναχθήσονται.
there also the eagles will be gathered together.

[35]Two women will be grinding grain together; one will be taken and the other left.[r]"
[37]"Where, Lord?" they asked.
He replied, "Where there is a dead body, there the vultures will gather."

Chapter 18

The Parable of the Widow and the Unjust Judge

THEN Jesus[g] told them a parable about their need to pray always and not to lose heart. [2]He said, "In a certain city there was a judge who neither feared God nor had respect for people. [3]In that city there was a widow who kept coming to him and saying, 'Grant me justice against my opponent.' [4]For a while he refused; but later he said to himself, 'Though I have no fear of God and no respect for anyone, [5]yet because this widow keeps bothering me, I will grant her justice, so that she may not wear me out by continually coming.'"[h] [6]And the Lord said, "Listen to what the unjust judge says. [7]And will not God grant justice to his chosen ones who cry to him day and night? Will he delay long in helping them? [8]I tell you, he will quickly grant justice to them. And yet, when the Son of Man comes, will he find faith on earth?"

The Parable of the Pharisee and the Tax Collector

[9] He also told this parable to some who trusted in themselves that they were righteous and regarded others with contempt: [10]"Two

18 Ἔλεγεν δὲ παραβολὴν αὐτοῖς πρὸς
And he told [2]a parable [1]them to =that
τὸ δεῖν πάντοτε προσεύχεσθαι αὐτοὺς καὶ
the [1]to behove [3]always [4]to pray [2]them and
they must always pray and not faint,
μὴ ἐγκακεῖν, **2** λέγων· κριτής τις ἦν ἐν
not to faint, saying : [3]judge [2]a certain [1]There was [4]in
τινι πόλει τὸν θεὸν μὴ φοβούμενος καὶ
[5]a certain [6]city – [3]God [1]not [2]fearing and
ἄνθρωπον μὴ ἐντρεπόμενος. **3** χήρα δὲ ἦν
[3]man [1]not [2]regarding. And [2]a widow [1]there was
ἐν τῇ πόλει ἐκείνῃ, καὶ ἤρχετο πρὸς
in – city that, and she came to
αὐτὸν λέγουσα· ἐκδίκησόν με ἀπὸ τοῦ
him saying : Vindicate me from the
ἀντιδίκου μου. **4** καὶ οὐκ ἤθελεν ἐπὶ
opponent of me. And he would not for
χρόνον· μετὰ ταῦτα δὲ εἶπεν ἐν ἑαυτῷ·
a time; but after these things he said in himself :
εἰ καὶ τὸν θεὸν οὐ φοβοῦμαι οὐδὲ ἄνθρωπον
If indeed – God I fear not nor man
ἐντρέπομαι, **5** διά γε τὸ παρέχειν
regard, at least because of – to cause
=because this widow causes me trouble
μοι κόπον τὴν χήραν ταύτην ἐκδικήσω αὐτήν,
me trouble – widow this[b] I will vindicate her,
ἵνα μὴ εἰς τέλος ἐρχομένη ὑπωπιάζῃ με.
lest in [the] end coming she exhausts me.
6 Εἶπεν δὲ ὁ κύριος· ἀκούσατε τί ὁ κριτὴς
And said the Lord : Hear ye what the judge
τῆς ἀδικίας λέγει· **7** ὁ δὲ θεὸς οὐ μὴ
– of unrighteousness says; – and God by no means
ποιήσῃ τὴν ἐκδίκησιν τῶν ἐκλεκτῶν
will he make the vindication of the chosen [ones]
αὐτοῦ τῶν βοώντων αὐτῷ ἡμέρας καὶ
of him – crying to him day and
νυκτός, καὶ μακροθυμεῖ ἐπ' αὐτοῖς; **8** λέγω
night, and be patient over them? I tell
ὑμῖν ὅτι ποιήσει τὴν ἐκδίκησιν αὐτῶν
you that he will make the vindication of them
ἐν τάχει. πλὴν ὁ υἱὸς τοῦ ἀνθρώπου ἐλθὼν
quickly. Nevertheless the Son – of man coming
ἆρα εὑρήσει τὴν πίστιν ἐπὶ τῆς γῆς;
then will he find the faith on the earth?
9 Εἶπεν δὲ καὶ πρός τινας τοὺς
And he said also to some the [ones]
πεποιθότας ἐφ' ἑαυτοῖς ὅτι εἰσὶν
relying on themselves that they are
δίκαιοι καὶ ἐξουθενοῦντας τοὺς λοιποὺς
righteous and despising the rest
τὴν παραβολὴν ταύτην. **10** Ἄνθρωποι δύο
– parable this. Men two

Chapter 18

The Parable of the Persistent Widow

THEN Jesus told his disciples a parable to show them that they should always pray and not give up. [2]He said: "In a certain town there was a judge who neither feared God nor cared about men. [3]And there was a widow in that town who kept coming to him with the plea, 'Grant me justice against my adversary.'

[4]"For some time he refused. But finally he said to himself, 'Even though I don't fear God or care about men, [5]yet because this widow keeps bothering me, I will see that she gets justice, so that she won't eventually wear me out with her coming!'"

[6]And the Lord said, "Listen to what the unjust judge says. [7]And will not God bring about justice for his chosen ones, who cry out to him day and night? Will he keep putting them off? [8]I tell you, he will see that they get justice, and quickly. However, when the Son of Man comes, will he find faith on the earth?"

The Parable of the Pharisee and the Tax Collector

[9]To some who were confident of their own righteousness and looked down on everybody else, Jesus told this parable: [10]"Two

[f]Other ancient authorities add verse 36, *"Two will be in the field; one will be taken and the other left."*
[g]Gk *he*
[h]Or *so that she may not finally come and slap me in the face*

‡ Verse 36 omitted by Nestle; *cf.* NIV footnote.

[r]35 Some manuscripts *left.* [36]*Two men will be in the field; one will be taken and the other left.*

men went up to the temple to pray, one a Pharisee and the other a tax collector. 11 The Pharisee, standing by himself, was praying thus, 'God, I thank you that I am not like other people: thieves, rogues, adulterers, or even like this tax collector. 12 I fast twice a week; I give a tenth of all my income.' 13 But the tax collector, standing far off, would not even look up to heaven, but was beating his breast and saying, 'God, be merciful to me, a sinner!' 14 I tell you, this man went down to his home justified rather than the other; for all who exalt themselves will be humbled, but all who humble themselves will be exalted."

Jesus Blesses Little Children

15 People were bringing even infants to him that he might touch them; and when the disciples saw it, they sternly ordered them not to do it. 16 But Jesus called for them and said, "Let the little children come to me, and do not stop them; for it is to such as these that the kingdom of God belongs. 17 Truly I tell you, whoever does not receive the kingdom of God as a little child will never enter it."

The Rich Ruler

18 A certain ruler asked him, "Good Teacher, what must I do to inherit eternal life?" 19 Jesus said to him, "Why do you call me good? No one is good but God alone. 20 You know the commandments: 'You shall not commit adultery; You shall not murder; You shall not steal; You shall not bear false witness; Honor

ἀνέβησαν εἰς τὸ ἱερὸν προσεύξασθαι, ὁ εἷς
went up to the temple to pray, the one

Φαρισαῖος καὶ ὁ ἕτερος τελώνης. 11 ὁ
a Pharisee and the other a tax-collector. The

Φαρισαῖος σταθεὶς ταῦτα πρὸς ἑαυτὸν
Pharisee standing these things to himself

προσηύχετο· ὁ θεός, εὐχαριστῶ σοι ὅτι
prayed : – God, I thank thee that

οὐκ εἰμὶ ὥσπερ οἱ λοιποὶ τῶν ἀνθρώπων,
I am not as the rest – of men,

ἅρπαγες, ἄδικοι, μοιχοί, ἢ καὶ ὡς οὗτος
rapacious, unjust, adulterers, or even as this

ὁ τελώνης· 12 νηστεύω δὶς τοῦ σαββάτου,
– tax-collector; I fast twice of(in) the week,

ἀποδεκατεύω πάντα ὅσα κτῶμαι. 13 ὁ δὲ
I tithe all things how many I get. But the

τελώνης μακρόθεν ἑστὼς οὐκ ἤθελεν οὐδὲ
tax-collector far off standing would not *not* even

τοὺς ὀφθαλμοὺς ἐπᾶραι εἰς τὸν οὐρανόν,
the(his) eyes *to* lift up to – heaven,

ἀλλ' ἔτυπτεν τὸ στῆθος αὐτοῦ λέγων· ὁ
but smote the breast of him saying : –

θεός, ἱλάσθητί μοι τῷ ἁμαρτωλῷ. 14 λέγω
God, be propitious to me the sinner. I tell

ὑμῖν, κατέβη οὗτος δεδικαιωμένος εἰς τὸν
you, went down this man having been justified to the

οἶκον αὐτοῦ παρ' ἐκεῖνον· ὅτι πᾶς ὁ
house of him [rather] than that one; because everyone

ὑψῶν ἑαυτὸν ταπεινωθήσεται, ὁ δὲ ταπεινῶν
exalting himself will be humbled, and the [one] humbling

ἑαυτὸν ὑψωθήσεται.
himself will be exalted.

15 Προσέφερον δὲ αὐτῷ καὶ τὰ βρέφη
And they brought to him also the babes

ἵνα αὐτῶν ἅπτηται· ἰδόντες δὲ οἱ μαθηταὶ
that them he might touch; but [3]seeing [1]the [2]disciples

ἐπετίμων αὐτοῖς. 16 ὁ δὲ Ἰησοῦς
rebuked them. – But Jesus

προσεκαλέσατο αὐτὰ λέγων· ἄφετε τὰ
called to [him] them* saying : Allow the

παιδία ἔρχεσθαι πρός με καὶ μὴ κωλύετε
children to come to me and do not prevent

αὐτά· τῶν γὰρ τοιούτων ἐστὶν ἡ βασιλεία
them; – for of such is the kingdom

τοῦ θεοῦ. 17 ἀμὴν λέγω ὑμῖν, ὃς ἂν
– of God. Truly I tell you, whoever

μὴ δέξηται τὴν βασιλείαν τοῦ θεοῦ ὡς
does not receive the kingdom – of God as

παιδίον, οὐ μὴ εἰσέλθῃ εἰς αὐτήν.
a child, by no means enters into it.

18 Καὶ ἐπηρώτησέν τις αὐτὸν ἄρχων
And [3]questioned [1]a certain [4]him [2]ruler

λέγων· διδάσκαλε ἀγαθέ, τί ποιήσας ζωὴν
saying : Teacher good, what doing life

αἰώνιον κληρονομήσω; 19 εἶπεν δὲ αὐτῷ
eternal may I inherit? And said to him

ὁ Ἰησοῦς· τί με λέγεις ἀγαθόν; οὐδεὶς
– Jesus : Why me sayest thou good? no one

ἀγαθὸς εἰ μὴ εἷς [ὁ] θεός. 20 τὰς ἐντολὰς
[is] good except one[,] – God. The commandments

οἶδας· μὴ μοιχεύσῃς, μὴ φονεύσῃς,
thou knowest : Do not commit adultery, Do not kill,

μὴ κλέψῃς, μὴ ψευδομαρτυρήσῃς, τίμα
Do not steal, Do not bear false witness, Honour

* That is, "the babes" (τὰ βρέφη in ver. 15).

men went up to the temple to pray, one a Pharisee and the other a tax collector. 11 The Pharisee stood up and prayed about[s] himself: 'God, I thank you that I am not like other men—robbers, evildoers, adulterers—or even like this tax collector. 12 I fast twice a week and give a tenth of all I get.'

13 "But the tax collector stood at a distance. He would not even look up to heaven, but beat his breast and said, 'God, have mercy on me, a sinner.'

14 "I tell you that this man, rather than the other, went home justified before God. For everyone who exalts himself will be humbled, and he who humbles himself will be exalted."

The Little Children and Jesus

15 People were also bringing babies to Jesus to have him touch them. When the disciples saw this, they rebuked them. 16 But Jesus called the children to him and said, "Let the little children come to me, and do not hinder them, for the kingdom of God belongs to such as these. 17 I tell you the truth, anyone who will not receive the kingdom of God like a little child will never enter it."

The Rich Ruler

18 A certain ruler asked him, "Good teacher, what must I do to inherit eternal life?"

19 "Why do you call me good?" Jesus answered. "No one is good—except God alone. 20 You know the commandments: 'Do not commit adultery, do not murder, do not steal, do not give false testimony, honor

[s] 11 Or *to*

your father and mother.' "
[21]He replied, "I have kept
all these since my youth."
[22]When Jesus heard this,
he said to him, "There is
still one thing lacking. Sell
all that you own and dis-
tribute the money[i] to the
poor, and you will have
treasure in heaven; then
come, follow me." [23]But
when he heard this, he became sad; for he was very
rich. [24]Jesus looked at him
and said, "How hard it is
for those who have wealth
to enter the kingdom of
God! [25]Indeed, it is easier
for a camel to go through
the eye of a needle than for
someone who is rich to enter the kingdom of God."
26 Those who heard it
said, "Then who can be
saved?" [27]He replied,
"What is impossible for
mortals is possible for
God."
28 Then Peter said,
"Look, we have left our
homes and followed you."
[29]And he said to them,
"Truly I tell you, there is no
one who has left house or
wife or brothers or parents
or children, for the sake of
the kingdom of God, [30]who
will not get back very much
more in this age, and in the
age to come eternal life."

A Third Time Jesus Foretells His Death and Resurrection

31 Then he took the
twelve aside and said to
them, "See, we are going
up to Jerusalem, and everything that is written about
the Son of Man by the
prophets will be accom-
plished. [32]For he will be
handed over to the Gen-
tiles; and he will be mocked
and insulted and spat upon.
[33]After they have flogged
him, they will kill him, and
on the third day he will rise

τὸν πατέρα σου καὶ τὴν μητέρα. **21** ὁ δὲ
the father of thee and the mother. And he
εἶπεν· ταῦτα πάντα ἐφύλαξα ἐκ νεότητος.
said : All these things I kept from youth.
22 ἀκούσας δὲ ὁ Ἰησοῦς εἶπεν αὐτῷ· ἔτι
But hearing – Jesus said to him : Yet
ἕν σοι λείπει· πάντα ὅσα ἔχεις
one thing to thee is lacking; all things how many thou hast
πώλησον καὶ διάδος πτωχοῖς, καὶ ἕξεις
sell and distribute to poor people, and thou wilt have
θησαυρὸν ἐν [τοῖς] οὐρανοῖς, καὶ δεῦρο
treasure in – heavens, and come
ἀκολούθει μοι. **23** ὁ δὲ ἀκούσας ταῦτα
follow me. But he hearing these things
περίλυπος ἐγενήθη, ἦν γὰρ πλούσιος σφόδρα.
very grieved became, for he was rich exceedingly.
24 ἰδὼν δὲ αὐτὸν ὁ Ἰησοῦς εἶπεν· πῶς
And seeing him – Jesus said : How
δυσκόλως οἱ τὰ χρήματα ἔχοντες εἰς τὴν
hardly [1]the [ones] – [3]property [2]having into the
βασιλείαν τοῦ θεοῦ εἰσπορεύονται· **25** εὐκο-
kingdom – of God go *in*; [1]easi-
πώτερον γάρ ἐστιν κάμηλον διὰ τρήματος
er [1]for it is [for] a camel through [the] eye
βελόνης εἰσελθεῖν ἢ πλούσιον εἰς τὴν
of a needle to enter than a rich man into the
βασιλείαν τοῦ θεοῦ εἰσελθεῖν. **26** εἶπαν
kingdom – of God to enter. said
δὲ οἱ ἀκούσαντες· καὶ τίς δύναται
And the [ones] hearing : And who can
σωθῆναι; **27** ὁ δὲ εἶπεν· τὰ ἀδύνατα παρὰ
***to* be saved? And he said : The things impossible with**
ἀνθρώποις δυνατὰ παρὰ τῷ θεῷ ἐστιν.
men possible with – God is(are).
28 Εἶπεν δὲ ὁ Πέτρος· ἰδοὺ ἡμεῖς ἀφέντες
And said – Peter : Behold[,] we leaving
τὰ ἴδια ἠκολουθήσαμέν σοι. **29** ὁ δὲ
our own things followed thee. And he
εἶπεν αὐτοῖς· ἀμὴν λέγω ὑμῖν ὅτι οὐδείς
said to them : Truly I tell you that no one
ἐστιν ὃς ἀφῆκεν οἰκίαν ἢ γυναῖκα ἢ
there is who left house or wife or
ἀδελφοὺς ἢ γονεῖς ἢ τέκνα εἵνεκεν τῆς
brothers or parents or children for the sake of the
βασιλείας τοῦ θεοῦ, **30** ὃς οὐχὶ μὴ λάβῃ
kingdom – of God, who by no means receives
πολλαπλασίονα ἐν τῷ καιρῷ τούτῳ καὶ ἐν
many times over in – time this and in
τῷ αἰῶνι τῷ ἐρχομένῳ ζωὴν αἰώνιον.
the age – coming life eternal.
31 Παραλαβὼν δὲ τοὺς δώδεκα εἶπεν πρὸς
And taking the twelve he said to
αὐτούς· ἰδοὺ ἀναβαίνομεν εἰς Ἰερουσαλήμ,
them : Behold we are going up to Jerusalem,
καὶ τελεσθήσεται πάντα τὰ γεγραμ-
and will be accomplished all things – having been
μένα διὰ τῶν προφητῶν τῷ υἱῷ τοῦ
written through the prophets to the Son –
ἀνθρώπου· **32** παραδοθήσεται γὰρ τοῖς ἔθνεσιν
of man; for he will be delivered to the nations
καὶ ἐμπαιχθήσεται καὶ ὑβρισθήσεται καὶ
and will be mocked and *will be* insulted and
ἐμπτυσθήσεται, **33** καὶ μαστιγώσαντες
***will be* spit at, and having scourged**
ἀποκτενοῦσιν αὐτόν, καὶ τῇ ἡμέρᾳ τῇ
they will kill him, and on the day –

your father and mother.'[t] "
[21]"All these I have kept
since I was a boy," he said.
[22]When Jesus heard this,
he said to him, "You still
lack one thing. Sell everything you have and give to
the poor, and you will have
treasure in heaven. Then
come, follow me."
[23]When he heard this, he
became very sad, because
he was a man of great
wealth. [24]Jesus looked at
him and said, "How hard it
is for the rich to enter the
kingdom of God! [25]Indeed,
it is easier for a camel to go
through the eye of a needle
than for a rich man to enter
the kingdom of God."
[26]Those who heard this
asked, "Who then can be
saved?"
[27]Jesus replied, "What is
impossible with men is possible with God."
[28]Peter said to him, "We
have left all we had to follow you!"
[29]"I tell you the truth,"
Jesus said to them, "no one
who has left home or wife
or brothers or parents or
children for the sake of the
kingdom of God [30]will fail
to receive many times as
much in this age and, in the
age to come, eternal life."

Jesus Again Predicts His Death

[31]Jesus took the Twelve
aside and told them, "We
are going up to Jerusalem,
and everything that is written by the prophets about
the Son of Man will be fulfilled. [32]He will be handed
over to the Gentiles. They
will mock him, insult him,
spit on him, flog him and

[i]Gk lacks *the money*

[t]20 Exodus 20:12-16; Deut. 5:16-20

again." 34 But they understood nothing about all
these things; in fact, what
he said was hidden from
them, and they did not
grasp what was said.

Jesus Heals a Blind Beggar Near Jericho

35 As he approached
Jericho, a blind man was
sitting by the roadside begging. 36 When he heard a
crowd going by, he asked
what was happening.
37 They told him, "Jesus of
Nazareth[j] is passing by."
38 Then he shouted, "Jesus,
Son of David, have mercy
on me!" 39 Those who were
in front sternly ordered him
to be quiet; but he shouted
even more loudly, "Son of
David, have mercy on me!"
40 Jesus stood still and ordered the man to be
brought to him; and when
he came near, he asked
him, 41 "What do you want
me to do for you?" He said,
"Lord, let me see again."
42 Jesus said to him, "Receive your sight; your faith
has saved you." 43 Immediately he regained his sight
and followed him, glorifying God; and all the people,
when they saw it, praised
God.

τρίτῃ ἀναστήσεται. **34** καὶ αὐτοὶ οὐδὲν
third he will rise again. And they none

τούτων συνῆκαν, καὶ ἦν τὸ ῥῆμα τοῦτο
of these things understood, and [3]was – [2]utterance [1]this

κεκρυμμένον ἀπ' αὐτῶν, καὶ οὐκ ἐγίνωσκον
[4]*having been* hidden from them, and they knew not

τὰ λεγόμενα.
the things being said.

35 Ἐγένετο δὲ ἐν τῷ ἐγγίζειν αὐτὸν εἰς
And it came to pass in the to draw near him[be] to
=as he drew near

Ἰεριχὼ τυφλός τις ἐκάθητο παρὰ τὴν ὁδὸν
Jericho a certain blind man sat by the way

ἐπαιτῶν. **36** ἀκούσας δὲ ὄχλου διαπορευομένου
begging. And hearing a crowd passing through

ἐπυνθάνετο τί εἴη τοῦτο. **37** ἀπήγγειλαν
he inquired what [2]might be [1]this. And they re-

δὲ αὐτῷ ὅτι Ἰησοῦς ὁ Ναζωραῖος
ported to him[,] – Jesus the Nazarene

παρέρχεται. **38** καὶ ἐβόησεν λέγων· Ἰησοῦ
is passing by. And he cried saying: Jesus

υἱὲ Δαυίδ, ἐλέησόν με. **39** καὶ οἱ
son of David, pity me. And the [ones]

προάγοντες ἐπετίμων αὐτῷ ἵνα σιγήσῃ·
going before rebuked him that he should be quiet;

αὐτὸς δὲ πολλῷ μᾶλλον ἔκραζεν· υἱὲ
but he by much more cried out: Son

Δαυίδ, ἐλέησόν με. **40** σταθεὶς δὲ ὁ
of David, pity me. And standing –

Ἰησοῦς ἐκέλευσεν αὐτὸν ἀχθῆναι πρὸς
Jesus commanded him to be brought to

αὐτόν. ἐγγίσαντος δὲ αὐτοῦ ἐπηρώτησεν
him. And drawing near him[a] he questioned
=as he drew near

αὐτόν· **41** τί σοι θέλεις ποιήσω; ὁ δὲ
him: What for thee wishest thou I may do? And he

εἶπεν· κύριε, ἵνα ἀναβλέψω. **42** καὶ ὁ Ἰησοῦς
said: Lord, that I may see again. And – Jesus

εἶπεν αὐτῷ· ἀνάβλεψον· ἡ πίστις σου
said to him: See again; the faith of thee

σέσωκέν σε. **43** καὶ παραχρῆμα ἀνέβλεψεν,
has healed thee. And at once he saw again,

καὶ ἠκολούθει αὐτῷ δοξάζων τὸν θεόν.
and followed him glorifying – God.

καὶ πᾶς ὁ λαὸς ἰδὼν ἔδωκεν αἶνον τῷ
And all the people seeing gave praise –

θεῷ.
to God.

kill him. 33 On the third day
he will rise again."

34 The disciples did not
understand any of this. Its
meaning was hidden from
them, and they did not
know what he was talking
about.

A Blind Beggar Receives His Sight

35 As Jesus approached
Jericho, a blind man was
sitting by the roadside begging. 36 When he heard the
crowd going by, he asked
what was happening.
37 They told him, "Jesus of
Nazareth is passing by."

38 He called out, "Jesus,
Son of David, have mercy
on me!"

39 Those who led the way
rebuked him and told him
to be quiet, but he shouted
all the more, "Son of Da-
vid, have mercy on me!"

40 Jesus stopped and or-
dered the man to be
brought to him. When he
came near, Jesus asked
him, 41 "What do you want
me to do for you?"

"Lord, I want to see," he
replied.

42 Jesus said to him, "Receive your sight; your faith
has healed you." 43 Imme-
diately he received his sight
and followed Jesus, praising God. When all the people saw it, they also praised
God.

Chapter 19

Jesus and Zacchaeus

HE entered Jericho and
was passing through
it. 2 A man was there named
Zacchaeus; he was a chief
tax collector and was rich.
3 He was trying to see who
Jesus was, but on account
of the crowd he could not,
because he was short in
stature. 4 So he ran ahead
and climbed a sycamore
tree to see him, because he
was going to pass that way.

[j] Gk *the Nazorean*

19 Καὶ εἰσελθὼν διήρχετο τὴν Ἰεριχώ.
And having entered he passed through – Jericho.

2 Καὶ ἰδοὺ ἀνὴρ ὀνόματι καλούμενος
And behold[,] a man by name *being* called

Ζακχαῖος, καὶ αὐτὸς ἦν ἀρχιτελώνης, καὶ
Zacchæus, and he was a chief tax-collector, and

αὐτὸς πλούσιος· **3** καὶ ἐζήτει ἰδεῖν τὸν
he [was] rich; and he sought to see –

Ἰησοῦν τίς ἐστιν, καὶ οὐκ ἠδύνατο ἀπὸ
Jesus who he is(was), and was not able from

τοῦ ὄχλου, ὅτι τῇ ἡλικίᾳ μικρὸς ἦν.
the crowd, because – [3]in stature [2]little [1]he was.

4 καὶ προδραμὼν εἰς τὸ ἔμπροσθεν ἀνέβη
And having run forward to the front he went up

ἐπὶ συκομορέαν, ἵνα ἴδῃ αὐτόν, ὅτι
onto a sycamore-tree, that he might see him, because

ἐκείνης ἤμελλεν διέρχεσθαι. **5** καὶ ὡς
[3]that [way] [1]he was about [2]to pass along. And as

Chapter 19

Zacchaeus the Tax Collector

JESUS entered Jericho
and was passing
through. 2 A man was there
by the name of Zacchaeus;
he was a chief tax collector
and was wealthy. 3 He
wanted to see who Jesus
was, but being a short man
he could not, because of
the crowd. 4 So he ran
ahead and climbed a syca-
more-fig tree to see him,
since Jesus was coming
that way.

5 When Jesus came to the
place, he looked up and
said to him, "Zacchaeus,
hurry and come down; for I
must stay at your house to-
day." 6 So he hurried down
and was happy to welcome
him. 7 All who saw it began
to grumble and said, "He
has gone to be the guest of
one who is a sinner." 8 Zacchaeus stood there and said
to the Lord, "Look, half of
my possessions, Lord, I
will give to the poor; and if
I have defrauded anyone of
anything, I will pay back
four times as much." 9 Then
Jesus said to him, "Today
salvation has come to this
house, because he too is a
son of Abraham. 10 For the
Son of Man came to seek
out and to save the lost."

The Parable of the Ten Pounds

11 As they were listen-
ing to this, he went on to
tell a parable, because he
was near Jerusalem, and
because they supposed that
the kingdom of God was to
appear immediately. 12 So
he said, "A nobleman went
to a distant country to get
royal power for himself and
then return. 13 He sum-
moned ten of his slaves,
and gave them ten
pounds,[k] and said to them,
'Do business with these until I come back.' 14 But the
citizens of his country hated him and sent a delegation
after him, saying, 'We
do not want this man to rule
over us.' 15 When he re-
turned, having received

ἦλθεν ἐπὶ τὸν τόπον, ἀναβλέψας ὁ Ἰησοῦς
he came upon the place, looking up – Jesus
εἶπεν πρὸς αὐτόν· Ζακχαῖε, σπεύσας
said to him : Zacchæus, making haste
κατάβηθι· σήμερον γὰρ ἐν τῷ οἴκῳ σου
come down; for to-day in the house of thee
δεῖ με μεῖναι. 6 καὶ σπεύσας κατέβη,
it behoves me to remain. And making haste he came down,
καὶ ὑπεδέξατο αὐτὸν χαίρων. 7 καὶ
and welcomed him rejoicing. And
ἰδόντες πάντες διεγόγγυζον λέγοντες ὅτι
seeing all murmured saying[,] –
παρὰ ἁμαρτωλῷ ἀνδρὶ εἰσῆλθεν καταλῦσαι.
With a sinful man he entered to lodge.
8 σταθεὶς δὲ Ζακχαῖος εἶπεν πρὸς τὸν
And standing Zacchæus said to the
κύριον· ἰδοὺ τὰ ἡμίση μου τῶν ὑπαρχόντων,
Lord : Behold[,] the half of me of the possessions,
κύριε, τοῖς πτωχοῖς δίδωμι, καὶ εἴ τινός
Lord, to the poor I give, and if anyone
τι ἐσυκοφάντησα, ἀποδίδωμι τετραπλοῦν.
anything I accused falsely, I restore fourfold.
9 εἶπεν δὲ πρὸς αὐτὸν ὁ Ἰησοῦς ὅτι
And said to him – Jesus[,] –
σήμερον σωτηρία τῷ οἴκῳ τούτῳ ἐγένετο,
To-day salvation – house to this came,
καθότι καὶ αὐτὸς υἱὸς Ἀβραάμ [ἐστιν]·
because even he a son of Abraham is;
10 ἦλθεν γὰρ ὁ υἱὸς τοῦ ἀνθρώπου ζητῆσαι
for came the Son – of man to seek
καὶ σῶσαι τὸ ἀπολωλός.
and to save the thing having been lost.
11 Ἀκουόντων δὲ αὐτῶν ταῦτα προσθεὶς
And hearing them[a] these things adding
=as they heard
εἶπεν παραβολήν, διὰ τὸ ἐγγὺς εἶναι
he told a parable, because of the near to be
=because he was near to Jerusalem and they thought
Ἰερουσαλὴμ αὐτὸν καὶ δοκεῖν αὐτοὺς ὅτι
Jerusalem him and to think them[b] that
παραχρῆμα μέλλει ἡ βασιλεία τοῦ θεοῦ
at once is(was) about the kingdom – of God
ἀναφαίνεσθαι· 12 εἶπεν οὖν· ἄνθρωπός τις
to appear; he said therefore : A certain man
εὐγενὴς ἐπορεύθη εἰς χώραν μακρὰν λαβεῖν
well born went to country a far to receive
ἑαυτῷ βασιλείαν καὶ ὑποστρέψαι. 13 καλέσας
for himself a kingdom and to return. having called
δὲ δέκα δούλους ἑαυτοῦ ἔδωκεν αὐτοῖς
And ten slaves of him*self* he gave them
δέκα μνᾶς, καὶ εἶπεν πρὸς αὐτούς·
ten minas, and said to them :
πραγματεύσασθε ἐν ᾧ ἔρχομαι. 14 οἱ δὲ
Trade ye while I am coming.* But the
πολῖται αὐτοῦ ἐμίσουν αὐτόν, καὶ ἀπέστειλαν
citizens of him hated him, and sent
πρεσβείαν ὀπίσω αὐτοῦ λέγοντες· οὐ θέλομεν
a delegation after him saying : We do not wish
τοῦτον βασιλεῦσαι ἐφ' ἡμᾶς. 15 καὶ
this man to reign over us. And
ἐγένετο ἐν τῷ ἐπανελθεῖν αὐτὸν λαβόντα
it came to pass in the to return him[be] having received
=when he returned

5 When Jesus reached the
spot, he looked up and said
to him, "Zacchaeus, come
down immediately. I must
stay at your house today."
6 So he came down at once
and welcomed him gladly.
7 All the people saw this
and began to mutter, "He
has gone to be the guest of a
'sinner.'"
8 But Zacchaeus stood up
and said to the Lord,
"Look, Lord! Here and
now I give half of my possessions to the poor, and if
I have cheated anybody out
of anything, I will pay back
four times the amount."
9 Jesus said to him, "To-
day salvation has come to
this house, because this
man, too, is a son of Abraham. 10 For the Son of Man
came to seek and to save
what was lost."

The Parable of the Ten Minas

11 While they were listening to this, he went on to
tell them a parable, be-
cause he was near Jerusa-
lem and the people thought
that the kingdom of God
was going to appear at
once. 12 He said: "A man of
noble birth went to a distant country to have him-
self appointed king and
then to return. 13 So he
called ten of his servants
and gave them ten minas.[u]
'Put this money to work,'
he said, 'until I come back.'
14 "But his subjects hated
him and sent a delegation
after him to say, 'We don't
want this man to be our
king.'
15 "He was made king,

[k] The mina, rendered here by *pound*, was about three months' wages for a laborer

* That is, "again." The present of this verb often has a futurist significance; *cf.* John 14. 3.

[u] *13* A mina was about three months' wages.

royal power, he ordered
these slaves, to whom he
had given the money, to be
summoned so that he might
find out what they had
gained by trading. 16The
first came forward and
said, 'Lord, your pound
has made ten more
pounds.' 17He said to him,
'Well done, good slave! Because you have been trustworthy in a very small
thing, take charge of ten
cities.' 18Then the second
came, saying, 'Lord, your
pound has made five
pounds.' 19He said to him,
'And you, rule over five cities.' 20Then the other
came, saying, 'Lord, here
is your pound. I wrapped it
up in a piece of cloth, 21for
I was afraid of you, be-
cause you are a harsh man;
you take what you did not
deposit, and reap what you
did not sow.' 22He said to
him, 'I will judge you by
your own words, you wick-
ed slave! You knew, did
you, that I was a harsh
man, taking what I did not
deposit and reaping what I
did not sow? 23Why then
did you not put my money
into the bank? Then when I
returned, I could have collected it with interest.'
24He said to the bystand-
ers, 'Take the pound from
him and give it to the one
who has ten pounds.'
25(And they said to him,
'Lord, he has ten pounds!')
26'I tell you, to all those
who have, more will be giv-
en; but from those who
have nothing, even what
they have will be taken
away. 27But as for these
enemies of mine who did
not want me to be king over
them—bring them here and
slaughter them in my presence.' "

Jesus' Triumphal Entry into Jerusalem

28 After he had said
this, he went on ahead, going up to Jerusalem.

τὴν βασιλείαν καὶ εἶπεν φωνηθῆναι αὐτῷ
the kingdom *and* he said to be called to him
τοὺς δούλους τούτους οἷς δεδώκει τὸ
– slaves these to whom he had given the
ἀργύριον, ἵνα γνοῖ τίς τί
money, that he might know [2]anyone [1]what
διεπραγματεύσατο. **16** παρεγένετο δὲ ὁ πρῶτος
gained by trading. And came the first
λέγων· κύριε, ἡ μνᾶ σου δέκα προσηργάσατο
saying: Lord, the mina of thee [2]ten [1]gained
μνᾶς. **17** καὶ εἶπεν αὐτῷ· εὖ γε, ἀγαθὲ δοῦλε,
[3]minas. And he said to him: Well, good slave,
ὅτι ἐν ἐλαχίστῳ πιστὸς ἐγένου, ἴσθι
because in a least thing faithful thou wast, be thou
ἐξουσίαν ἔχων ἐπάνω δέκα πόλεων. **18** καὶ
[2]authority [1]having over ten cities. And
ἦλθεν ὁ δεύτερος λέγων· ἡ μνᾶ σου,
came the second saying: The mina of thee,
κύριε, ἐποίησεν πέντε μνᾶς. **19** εἶπεν δὲ
lord, made five minas. And he said
καὶ τούτῳ· καὶ σὺ ἐπάνω γίνου πέντε
also to this one: And [2]thou [3]over [1]be five
πόλεων. **20** καὶ ὁ ἕτερος ἦλθεν λέγων·
cities. And the other came saying:
κύριε, ἰδοὺ ἡ μνᾶ σου, ἣν εἶχον
Lord, behold[,] the mina of thee, which I had
ἀποκειμένην ἐν σουδαρίῳ· **21** ἐφοβούμην γάρ
being put away in a napkin; for I feared
σε, ὅτι ἄνθρωπος αὐστηρὸς εἶ, αἴρεις ὃ
thee, because man an exacting thou art, thou takest what
οὐκ ἔθηκας, καὶ θερίζεις ὃ οὐκ ἔσπειρας.
thou didst not lay, and thou reapest what thou didst not sow.
22 λέγει αὐτῷ· ἐκ τοῦ στόματός σου
He says to him: Out of the mouth of thee
κρινῶ σε, πονηρὲ δοῦλε. ᾔδεις ὅτι ἐγὼ
I will judge thee, wicked slave. Knewest thou that I
ἄνθρωπος αὐστηρός εἰμι, αἴρων ὃ οὐκ
man an exacting am, taking what not
ἔθηκα, καὶ θερίζων ὃ οὐκ ἔσπειρα; **23** καὶ
I laid, and reaping what I sowed not? And
διὰ τί οὐκ ἔδωκάς μου τὸ ἀργύριον ἐπὶ
why didst thou not give of me the money on
τράπεζαν; κἀγὼ ἐλθὼν σὺν τόκῳ ἂν
a table?* And I coming with interest –
αὐτὸ ἔπραξα. **24** καὶ τοῖς παρεστῶσιν
it would have exacted. And to the [ones] standing by
εἶπεν· ἄρατε ἀπ' αὐτοῦ τὴν μνᾶν καὶ
he said: Take from him the mina and
δότε τῷ τὰς δέκα μνᾶς ἔχοντι. **25** καὶ
give [1]to the [one] [3]the [4]ten [5]minas [2]having. And
εἶπαν αὐτῷ· κύριε, ἔχει δέκα μνᾶς.
they said to him: Lord, he has ten minas.
26 λέγω ὑμῖν ὅτι παντὶ τῷ ἔχοντι
I tell you that to everyone having
δοθήσεται, ἀπὸ δὲ τοῦ μὴ ἔχοντος καὶ
it will be given, and from the [one] not having even
ὃ ἔχει ἀρθήσεται. **27** πλὴν τοὺς ἐχθρούς
what he has will be taken. Nevertheless – enemies
μου τούτους τοὺς μὴ θελήσαντάς με
of me these the [ones] not wishing me
βασιλεῦσαι ἐπ' αὐτοὺς ἀγάγετε ὧδε καὶ
to reign over them bring ye here and
κατασφάξατε αὐτοὺς ἔμπροσθέν μου.
slay them before me.
28 Καὶ εἰπὼν ταῦτα ἐπορεύετο ἔμπροσθεν
And having said these things he went in front

* That is, a moneychanger's or banker's table.

however, and returned
home. Then he sent for the
servants to whom he had
given the money, in order
to find out what they had
gained with it.
16"The first one came and
said, 'Sir, your mina has
earned ten more.'
17" 'Well done, my good
servant!' his master re-
plied. 'Because you have
been trustworthy in a very
small matter, take charge
of ten cities.'
18"The second came and
said, 'Sir, your mina has
earned five more.'
19"His master answered,
'You take charge of five cities.'
20"Then another servant
came and said, 'Sir, here is
your mina; I have kept it
laid away in a piece of
cloth. 21I was afraid of you,
because you are a hard
man. You take out what
you did not put in and reap
what you did not sow.'
22"His master replied, 'I
will judge you by your own
words, you wicked ser-
vant! You knew, did you,
that I am a hard man, taking
out what I did not put in,
and reaping what I did not
sow? 23Why then didn't
you put my money on de-
posit, so that when I came
back, I could have collected it with interest?'
24"Then he said to those
standing by, 'Take his mina
away from him and give it
to the one who has ten minas.'
25" 'Sir,' they said, 'he already has ten!'
26"He replied, 'I tell you
that to everyone who has,
more will be given, but as
for the one who has noth-
ing, even what he has will
be taken away. 27But those
enemies of mine who did
not want me to be king over
them—bring them here and
kill them in front of me.' "

The Triumphal Entry

28After Jesus had said
this, he went on ahead, go-

29 When he had come
near Bethphage and Betha-
ny, at the place called the
Mount of Olives, he sent
two of the disciples, 30 saying, "Go into the village
ahead of you, and as you
enter it you will find tied
there a colt that has never
been ridden. Untie it and
bring it here. 31 If anyone
asks you, 'Why are you untying it?' just say this, 'The
Lord needs it.' " 32 So those
who were sent departed
and found it as he had told
them. 33 As they were untying the colt, its owners
asked them, "Why are you
untying the colt?" 34 They
said, "The Lord needs it."
35 Then they brought it to
Jesus; and after throwing
their cloaks on the colt,
they set Jesus on it. 36 As he
rode along, people kept
spreading their cloaks on
the road. 37 As he was now
approaching the path down
from the Mount of Olives,
the whole multitude of the
disciples began to praise
God joyfully with a loud
voice for all the deeds of
power that they had seen,
38 saying,

"Blessed is the king
who comes in the
name of
the Lord!
Peace in heaven,
and glory in the
highest heaven!"

39 Some of the Pharisees in
the crowd said to him,
"Teacher, order your disciples to stop." 40 He an-
swered, "I tell you, if these
were silent, the stones
would shout out."

ἀναβαίνων εἰς Ἰεροσόλυμα. 29 Καὶ ἐγένετο
going up to Jerusalem. And it came to pass

ὡς ἤγγισεν εἰς Βηθφαγὴ καὶ Βηθανίαν
as he drew near to Bethphage and Bethany

πρὸς τὸ ὄρος τὸ καλούμενον ἐλαιών,
toward the mount – *being* called of olives,

ἀπέστειλεν δύο τῶν μαθητῶν λέγων·
he sent two of the disciples saying :

30 ὑπάγετε εἰς τὴν κατέναντι κώμην, ἐν ᾗ
Go ye into the opposite village, in which

εἰσπορευόμενοι εὑρήσετε πῶλον δεδεμένον,
entering ye will find a colt *having been* tied,

ἐφ' ὃν οὐδεὶς πώποτε ἀνθρώπων ἐκάθισεν,
on which no one ever yet of men sat,

καὶ λύσαντες αὐτὸν ἀγάγετε. 31 καὶ ἐάν
and loosening it bring. And if

τις ὑμᾶς ἐρωτᾷ· διὰ τί λύετε; οὕτως
anyone you asks : Why loosen ye? thus

ἐρεῖτε· ὅτι ὁ κύριος αὐτοῦ χρείαν ἔχει.
shall ye say : Because the Lord of it need has.

32 ἀπελθόντες δὲ οἱ ἀπεσταλμένοι εὗρον
And going the [ones] *having been* sent found

καθὼς εἶπεν αὐτοῖς. 33 λυόντων δὲ
as he told them. And loosening =as they were

αὐτῶν τὸν πῶλον εἶπαν οἱ κύριοι αὐτοῦ
them[a] loosening the colt said the owners of it

πρὸς αὐτούς· τί λύετε τὸν πῶλον; 34 οἱ
to them : Why loosen ye the colt? [2]they

δὲ εἶπαν· ὅτι ὁ κύριος αὐτοῦ χρείαν ἔχει.
[1]And said : Because the Lord of it need has.

35 καὶ ἤγαγον αὐτὸν πρὸς τὸν Ἰησοῦν,
And they led it to – Jesus,

καὶ ἐπιρίψαντες αὐτῶν τὰ ἱμάτια ἐπὶ τὸν
and throwing *on* of them the garments on the

πῶλον ἐπεβίβασαν τὸν Ἰησοῦν. 36 πορευ-
colt they put on [it] – Jesus. And

ομένου δὲ αὐτοῦ ὑπεστρώννυον τὰ ἱμάτια
going him[a] they strewed the garments
=as he went

ἑαυτῶν ἐν τῇ ὁδῷ. 37 ἐγγίζοντος δὲ
of them*selves* in the way. And drawing near
=as he drew near

αὐτοῦ ἤδη πρὸς τῇ καταβάσει τοῦ ὄρους
him[a] now to the descent of the mount

τῶν ἐλαιῶν ἤρξαντο ἅπαν τὸ πλῆθος τῶν
of the olives began all the multitude of the

μαθητῶν χαίροντες αἰνεῖν τὸν θεὸν φωνῇ
disciples rejoicing to praise – God voice

μεγάλῃ περὶ πασῶν ὧν εἶδον δυνάμεων,
with a great about [1]all [3]which [4]they saw [2][the] powerful deeds,

38 λέγοντες· εὐλογημένος ὁ ἐρχόμενος, ὁ
saying : Blessed the coming [one], the

βασιλεὺς ἐν ὀνόματι κυρίου· ἐν οὐρανῷ
king in [the] name of [the] Lord; in heaven

εἰρήνη καὶ δόξα ἐν ὑψίστοις. 39 καί
peace and glory in highest places. And

τινες τῶν Φαρισαίων ἀπὸ τοῦ ὄχλου
some of the Pharisees from the crowd

εἶπαν πρὸς αὐτόν· διδάσκαλε, ἐπιτίμησον
said to him : Teacher, rebuke

τοῖς μαθηταῖς σου. 40 καὶ ἀποκριθεὶς
the disciples of thee. And answering

εἶπεν· λέγω ὑμῖν, ἐὰν οὗτοι σιωπήσουσιν,
he said : I tell you, if these shall(should) be silent,

ing up to Jerusalem. 29 As
he approached Bethphage
and Bethany at the hill
called the Mount of Olives,
he sent two of his disciples,
saying to them, 30 "Go to
the village ahead of you,
and as you enter it, you will
find a colt tied there, which
no one has ever ridden. Untie it and bring it here. 31 If
anyone asks you, 'Why are
you untying it?' tell him,
'The Lord needs it.' "
32 Those who were sent
ahead went and found it
just as he had told them.
33 As they were untying the
colt, its owners asked
them, "Why are you unty-
ing the colt?"
34 They replied, "The
Lord needs it."
35 They brought it to
Jesus, threw their cloaks
on the colt and put Jesus on
it. 36 As he went along, people spread their cloaks on
the road.
37 When he came near the
place where the road goes
down the Mount of Olives,
the whole crowd of disci-
ples began joyfully to
praise God in loud voices
for all the miracles they had
seen:

38 "Blessed is the king who
comes in the name
of the Lord!" [v]

"Peace in heaven and
glory in the
highest!"

39 Some of the Pharisees
in the crowd said to Jesus,
"Teacher, rebuke your disciples!"
40 "I tell you," he replied,
"if they keep quiet, the

[v]38 Psalm 118:26

Jesus Weeps over Jerusalem

41 As he came near and
saw the city, he wept over
it, 42 saying, "If you, even
you, had only recognized
on this day the things that
make for peace! But now
they are hidden from your
eyes. 43 Indeed, the days
will come upon you, when
your enemies will set up
ramparts around you and
surround you, and hem you
in on every side. 44 They
will crush you to the
ground, you and your children within you, and they
will not leave within you
one stone upon another;
because you did not recognize the time of your visitation from God."[l]

Jesus Cleanses the Temple

45 Then he entered the
temple and began to drive
out those who were selling
things there; 46 and he said,
"It is written,

'My house shall be a house of prayer';
but you have made it a den of robbers."

47 Every day he was
teaching in the temple. The
chief priests, the scribes,
and the leaders of the people kept looking for a way
to kill him; 48 but they did
not find anything they
could do, for all the people
were spellbound by what
they heard.

Chapter 20

The Authority of Jesus Questioned

ONE day, as he was
teaching the people in
the temple and telling the
good news, the chief
priests and the scribes
came with the elders 2 and
said to him, "Tell us, by
what authority are you doing these things? Who is it
who gave you this authority?" 3 He answered them,
"I will also ask you a question, and you tell me: 4 Did
the baptism of John come
from heaven, or was it of

[l] Gk lacks *from God*

οἱ λίθοι κράξουσιν. 41 Καὶ ὡς ἤγγισεν,
the stones will cry out. And as he drew near,
ἰδὼν τὴν πόλιν ἔκλαυσεν ἐπ' αὐτήν,
seeing the city he wept over it,
42 λέγων ὅτι εἰ ἔγνως ἐν τῇ ἡμέρᾳ
saying[,] – If thou knewest in – day
ταύτῃ καὶ σὺ τὰ πρὸς εἰρήνην· νῦν δὲ
this even thou the things for peace; but now
ἐκρύβη ἀπὸ ὀφθαλμῶν σου. 43 ὅτι ἥξουσιν
they were hidden from eyes of thee. Because will come
ἡμέραι ἐπὶ σὲ καὶ παρεμβαλοῦσιν οἱ
days upon thee and [4]will raise up [1]the
ἐχθροί σου χάρακά σοι καὶ περικυκλώσουσίν
[2]enemies [3]of thee [5]a rampart to thee and will surround
σε καὶ συνέξουσίν σε πάντοθεν, 44 καὶ
thee and will press thee on all sides, and
ἐδαφιοῦσίν σε καὶ τὰ τέκνα σου ἐν σοί,
dash to the ground thee and the children of thee in thee,
καὶ οὐκ ἀφήσουσιν λίθον ἐπὶ λίθον ἐν σοί,
and will not leave stone upon stone in thee,
ἀνθ' ὧν οὐκ ἔγνως τὸν καιρὸν τῆς
because† thou knewest not the time of the
ἐπισκοπῆς σου. 45 Καὶ εἰσελθὼν εἰς τὸ
visitation of thee. And entering into the
ἱερὸν ἤρξατο ἐκβάλλειν τοὺς πωλοῦντας,
temple he began to expel the [ones] selling,
46 λέγων αὐτοῖς· γέγραπται· καὶ ἔσται ὁ
telling them: It has been written: And shall be the
οἶκός μου οἶκος προσευχῆς· ὑμεῖς δὲ
house of me a house of prayer; but ye
αὐτὸν ἐποιήσατε σπήλαιον λῃστῶν.
it made a den of robbers.
47 Καὶ ἦν διδάσκων τὸ καθ' ἡμέραν ἐν
And he was teaching daily† in
τῷ ἱερῷ· οἱ δὲ ἀρχιερεῖς καὶ οἱ
the temple; but the chief priests and the
γραμματεῖς ἐζήτουν αὐτὸν ἀπολέσαι καὶ οἱ
scribes [6]sought [8]him [7]to destroy [1]and [2]the
πρῶτοι τοῦ λαοῦ, 48 καὶ οὐχ εὕρισκον
[3]chief men [4]of the [5]people, and did not find
τὸ τί ποιήσωσιν· ὁ λαὸς γὰρ ἅπας
– what they might do; [2]the [4]people [1]for [3]all
ἐξεκρέματο αὐτοῦ ἀκούων.
hung upon him hearing.

20 Καὶ ἐγένετο ἐν μιᾷ τῶν ἡμερῶν
And it came to pass on one of the days
διδάσκοντος αὐτοῦ τὸν λαὸν ἐν τῷ ἱερῷ
teaching him[a] the people in the temple
=as he was teaching
καὶ εὐαγγελιζομένου ἐπέστησαν οἱ ἀρχιερεῖς
and preaching good news[a] came upon [him] the chief priests
καὶ οἱ γραμματεῖς σὺν τοῖς πρεσβυτέροις,
and the scribes with the elders,
2 καὶ εἶπαν λέγοντες πρὸς αὐτόν· εἰπὸν
and spoke, saying to him: Tell
ἡμῖν ἐν ποίᾳ ἐξουσίᾳ ταῦτα ποιεῖς, ἢ τίς
us by what authority these things thou doest, or who
ἐστιν ὁ δούς σοι τὴν ἐξουσίαν ταύτην;
is the [one] having given thee – authority this?
3 ἀποκριθεὶς δὲ εἶπεν πρὸς αὐτούς·
And answering he said to them:
ἐρωτήσω ὑμᾶς κἀγὼ λόγον, καὶ εἴπατέ
Will ask you I also a word, and tell ye
μοι· 4 τὸ βάπτισμα Ἰωάννου ἐξ οὐρανοῦ
me: The baptism of John from heaven

stones will cry out."
41 As he approached Jeru-
salem and saw the city, he
wept over it 42 and said, "If
you, even you, had only
known on this day what
would bring you peace—
but now it is hidden from
your eyes. 43 The days will
come upon you when your
enemies will build an em-
bankment against you and
encircle you and hem you
in on every side. 44 They
will dash you to the ground,
you and the children within
your walls. They will not
leave one stone on another,
because you did not recognize the time of God's coming to you."

Jesus at the Temple

45 Then he entered the
temple area and began driving out those who were selling. 46 "It is written," he
said to them, " 'My house
will be a house of prayer'[w];
but you have made it 'a den
of robbers.'[x]"
47 Every day he was
teaching at the temple. But
the chief priests, the teachers of the law and the leaders among the people were
trying to kill him. 48 Yet
they could not find any way
to do it, because all the people hung on his words.

Chapter 20

The Authority of Jesus Questioned

ONE day as he was
teaching the people in
the temple courts and
preaching the gospel, the
chief priests and the teachers of the law, together
with the elders, came up to
him. 2 "Tell us by what authority you are doing these
things," they said. "Who
gave you this authority?"
3 He replied, "I will also
ask you a question. Tell
me, 4 John's baptism—was
it from heaven, or from
men?"

[w] 46 Isaiah 56:7
[x] 46 Jer. 7:11

human origin?" [5]They discussed it with one another, saying, "If we say, 'From heaven,' he will say, 'Why did you not believe him?' [6]But if we say, 'Of human origin,' all the people will stone us; for they are convinced that John was a prophet." [7]So they answered that they did not know where it came from. [8]Then Jesus said to them, "Neither will I tell you by what authority I am doing these things."

The Parable of the Wicked Tenants

9 He began to tell the people this parable: "A man planted a vineyard, and leased it to tenants, and went to another country for a long time. [10]When the season came, he sent a slave to the tenants in order that they might give him his share of the produce of the vineyard; but the tenants beat him and sent him away empty-handed. [11]Next he sent another slave; that one also they beat and insulted and sent away empty-handed. [12]And he sent still a third; this one also they wounded and threw out. [13]Then the owner of the vineyard said, 'What shall I do? I will send my beloved son; perhaps they will respect him.' [14]But when the tenants saw him, they discussed it among themselves and said, 'This is the heir; let us kill him so that the inheritance may be ours.' [15]So they threw him out of the vineyard and killed him. What then will the owner of the vineyard do to them? [16]He will come and destroy those tenants and give the vineyard to others." When they heard this, they said, "Heaven

ἦν ἢ ἐξ ἀνθρώπων; **5** οἱ δὲ συνελογίσαντο
was it or from men? And they debated

πρὸς ἑαυτοὺς λέγοντες ὅτι ἐὰν εἴπωμεν·
with themselves saying[,] – If we say:

ἐξ οὐρανοῦ, ἐρεῖ· διὰ τί οὐκ ἐπιστεύσατε
From heaven, he will say: Why did ye not believe

αὐτῷ; **6** ἐὰν δὲ εἴπωμεν· ἐξ ἀνθρώπων, ὁ
him? And if we say: From men, the

λαὸς ἅπας καταλιθάσει ἡμᾶς· πεπεισμένος
people all will stone us; for having been per-

γάρ ἐστιν Ἰωάννην προφήτην εἶναι. **7** καὶ
suaded it is* John a prophet to be. And

ἀπεκρίθησαν μὴ εἰδέναι πόθεν. **8** καὶ ὁ
they answered not to know whence. And –

Ἰησοῦς εἶπεν αὐτοῖς· οὐδὲ ἐγὼ λέγω
Jesus said to them: Neither I tell

ὑμῖν ἐν ποίᾳ ἐξουσίᾳ ταῦτα ποιῶ. **9** Ἤρξατο
you by what authority these things I do. he began

δὲ πρὸς τὸν λαὸν λέγειν τὴν παραβολὴν
And to the people to tell – parable

ταύτην. ἄνθρωπος ἐφύτευσεν ἀμπελῶνα,
this. A man planted a vineyard,

καὶ ἐξέδοτο αὐτὸν γεωργοῖς, καὶ ἀπεδή-
and let out it to husbandmen, and went

μησεν χρόνους ἱκανούς. **10** καὶ καιρῷ
away periods for considerable. And in time
=a long time.

ἀπέστειλεν πρὸς τοὺς γεωργοὺς δοῦλον,
he sent to the husbandmen a slave,

ἵνα ἀπὸ τοῦ καρποῦ τοῦ ἀμπελῶνος
that from the fruit of the vineyard

δώσουσιν αὐτῷ· οἱ δὲ γεωργοὶ ἐξαπέστειλαν
they will give him; but the husbandmen [3]sent [4]away out

αὐτὸν δείραντες κενόν. **11** καὶ προσέθετο
[2]him [1]beating [5]empty. And he added

ἕτερον πέμψαι δοῦλον· οἱ δὲ κἀκεῖνον
[2]another [1]to send slave; but they that one also
=he sent another slave in addition;

δείραντες καὶ ἀτιμάσαντες ἐξαπέστειλαν
beating and insulting sent away out

κενόν. **12** καὶ προσέθετο τρίτον πέμψαι·
empty. And he added a third to send;

οἱ δὲ καὶ τοῦτον τραυματίσαντες ἐξέβαλον.
but they also this one wounding threw out.

13 εἶπεν δὲ ὁ κύριος τοῦ ἀμπελῶνος· τί
And said the owner of the vineyard: What

ποιήσω; πέμψω τὸν υἱόν μου τὸν ἀγαπητόν·
may I do? I will send the son of me – beloved;

ἴσως τοῦτον ἐντραπήσονται. **14** ἰδόντες δὲ
perhaps this one they will regard. But seeing

αὐτὸν οἱ γεωργοὶ διελογίζοντο πρὸς
him the husbandmen debated with

ἀλλήλους λέγοντες· οὗτός ἐστιν ὁ κληρονόμος·
one another saying: This is the heir;

ἀποκτείνωμεν αὐτόν, ἵνα ἡμῶν γένηται
let us kill him, that of us may become

ἡ κληρονομία. **15** καὶ ἐκβαλόντες αὐτὸν
the inheritance. And throwing out him

ἔξω τοῦ ἀμπελῶνος ἀπέκτειναν. τί οὖν
outside the vineyard they killed. What therefore

ποιήσει αὐτοῖς ὁ κύριος τοῦ ἀμπελῶνος;
will do to them the owner of the vineyard?

16 ἐλεύσεται καὶ ἀπολέσει τοὺς γεωργοὺς
he will come and *will* destroy – husbandmen

τούτους, καὶ δώσει τὸν ἀμπελῶνα ἄλλοις.
these, and will give the vineyard to others.

* That is, the people (a collective singular) have been (=are) persuaded.

[5]They discussed it among themselves and said, "If we say, 'From heaven,' he will ask, 'Why didn't you believe him?' [6]But if we say, 'From men,' all the people will stone us, because they are persuaded that John was a prophet."

[7]So they answered, "We don't know where it was from."

[8]Jesus said, "Neither will I tell you by what authority I am doing these things."

The Parable of the Tenants

[9]He went on to tell the people this parable: "A man planted a vineyard, rented it to some farmers and went away for a long time. [10]At harvest time he sent a servant to the tenants so they would give him some of the fruit of the vineyard. But the tenants beat him and sent him away empty-handed. [11]He sent another servant, but that one also they beat and treated shamefully and sent away empty-handed. [12]He sent still a third, and they wounded him and threw him out.

[13]"Then the owner of the vineyard said, 'What shall I do? I will send my son, whom I love; perhaps they will respect him.'

[14]"But when the tenants saw him, they talked the matter over. 'This is the heir,' they said. 'Let's kill him, and the inheritance will be ours.' [15]So they threw him out of the vineyard and killed him.

"What then will the owner of the vineyard do to them? [16]He will come and kill those tenants and give the vineyard to others."

When the people heard

forbid!" [17]But he looked at
them and said, "What then
does this text mean:
'The stone that the
builders rejected
has become the
cornerstone'?[m]
[18]Everyone who falls on
that stone will be broken to
pieces; and it will crush
anyone on whom it falls."
[19]When the scribes and
chief priests realized that
he had told this parable
against them, they wanted
to lay hands on him at that
very hour, but they feared
the people.

The Question about Paying Taxes

20 So they watched him
and sent spies who pre-
tended to be honest, in order to trap him by what he
said, so as to hand him over
to the jurisdiction and authority of the governor.
[21]So they asked him,
"Teacher, we know that
you are right in what you
say and teach, and you
show deference to no one,
but teach the way of God in
accordance with truth. [22]Is
it lawful for us to pay taxes
to the emperor, or not?"
[23]But he perceived their
craftiness and said to them,
[24]"Show me a denarius.
Whose head and whose ti-
tle does it bear?" They
said, "The emperor's."
[25]He said to them, "Then
give to the emperor the
things that are the emper-
or's, and to God the things
that are God's." [26]And
they were not able in the
presence of the people to
trap him by what he said;
and being amazed by his
answer, they became si-
lent.

The Question about the Resurrection

27 Some Sadducees,
those who say there is no
resurrection, came to him

ἀκούσαντες δὲ εἶπαν· μὴ γένοιτο. **17** ὁ δὲ
And hearing they said : May it not be. And he

ἐμβλέψας αὐτοῖς εἶπεν· τί οὖν ἐστιν τὸ
looking at them said : What therefore is –

γεγραμμένον τοῦτο· λίθον ὃν ἀπεδοκίμασαν
***having been* written this : [The] stone which [3]rejected**

οἱ οἰκοδομοῦντες, οὗτος ἐγενήθη εἰς κεφαλὴν
[1]the [ones] [2]building, this came to be for [the] head

γωνίας; **18** πᾶς ὁ πεσὼν ἐπ' ἐκεῖνον τὸν
of [the] corner? Everyone falling on that –

λίθον συνθλασθήσεται· ἐφ' ὃν δ' ἂν πέσῃ,
stone will be broken in pieces; but on whomever it falls,

λικμήσει αὐτόν. **19** Καὶ ἐζήτησαν οἱ
it will crush to powder him. And sought the

γραμματεῖς καὶ οἱ ἀρχιερεῖς ἐπιβαλεῖν ἐπ'
scribes and the chief priests to lay *on* on

αὐτὸν τὰς χεῖρας ἐν αὐτῇ τῇ ὥρᾳ, καὶ
him the(ir) hands in [2]same [1]the hour, and

ἐφοβήθησαν τὸν λαόν· ἔγνωσαν γὰρ ὅτι
feared the people; for they knew that

πρὸς αὐτοὺς εἶπεν τὴν παραβολὴν ταύτην.
at them he told – parable this.

20 Καὶ παρατηρήσαντες ἀπέστειλαν ἐγκαθέτους
And watching carefully they sent spies

ὑποκρινομένους ἑαυτοὺς δικαίους εἶναι, ἵνα
pretending themselves righteous to be, that

ἐπιλάβωνται αὐτοῦ λόγου, ὥστε παραδοῦναι
they might seize of him a word, so as to deliver

αὐτὸν τῇ ἀρχῇ καὶ τῇ ἐξουσίᾳ τοῦ
him to the rule and to the authority of the

ἡγεμόνος. **21** καὶ ἐπηρώτησαν αὐτὸν
governor. And they questioned him

λέγοντες· διδάσκαλε, οἴδαμεν ὅτι ὀρθῶς
saying : Teacher, we know that [4]rightly

λέγεις καὶ διδάσκεις καὶ οὐ λαμβάνεις
[1]thou speakest [2]and [3]teachest and receivest not
=regardest not persons,

πρόσωπον, ἀλλ' ἐπ' ἀληθείας τὴν ὁδὸν τοῦ
a face, but on [the basis of] truth the way –

θεοῦ διδάσκεις· **22** ἔξεστιν ἡμᾶς Καίσαρι
of God teachest; is it lawful for us to Cæsar

φόρον δοῦναι ἢ οὔ; **23** κατανοήσας δὲ
tribute to give or not? And perceiving

αὐτῶν τὴν πανουργίαν εἶπεν πρὸς αὐτούς·
of them the cleverness he said to them :

24 δείξατέ μοι δηνάριον· τίνος ἔχει εἰκόνα
Show me a denarius; of whom has it an image

καὶ ἐπιγραφήν; οἱ δὲ εἶπαν· Καίσαρος.
and superscription? And they said : Of Cæsar.

25 ὁ δὲ εἶπεν πρὸς αὐτούς· τοίνυν ἀπόδοτε
And he said to them : So render

τὰ Καίσαρος Καίσαρι καὶ τὰ τοῦ θεοῦ
the things of Cæsar to Cæsar and the things – of God

τῷ θεῷ. **26** καὶ οὐκ ἴσχυσαν ἐπιλαβέσθαι
– to God. And they were not able to seize

αὐτοῦ ῥήματος ἐναντίον τοῦ λαοῦ, καὶ
of him a word in the presence of the people, and

θαυμάσαντες ἐπὶ τῇ ἀποκρίσει αὐτοῦ
marvelling at the answer of him

ἐσίγησαν.
they were silent.

27 Προσελθόντες δέ τινες τῶν Σαδ-
And [4]approaching [1]some [2]of the [3]Sad-

δουκαίων, οἱ ἀντιλέγοντες ἀνάστασιν μὴ
ducees, the [ones] saying in opposition* a resurrection not

this, they said, "May this
never be!"
[17]Jesus looked directly at
them and asked, "Then
what is the meaning of that
which is written:

" 'The stone the builders
rejected
has become the
capstone'[y] [z]?

[18]Everyone who falls on
that stone will be broken to
pieces, but he on whom it
falls will be crushed."
[19]The teachers of the law
and the chief priests looked
for a way to arrest him immediately, because they
knew he had spoken this
parable against them. But
they were afraid of the people.

Paying Taxes to Caesar

[20]Keeping a close watch
on him, they sent spies,
who pretended to be hon-
est. They hoped to catch
Jesus in something he said
so that they might hand him
over to the power and au-
thority of the governor.
[21]So the spies questioned
him: "Teacher, we know
that you speak and teach
what is right, and that you
do not show partiality but
teach the way of God in accordance with the truth.
[22]Is it right for us to pay
taxes to Caesar or not?"
[23]He saw through their
duplicity and said to them,
[24]"Show me a denarius.
Whose portrait and inscription are on it?"
[25]"Caesar's," they re-
plied.
He said to them, "Then
give to Caesar what is Caesar's, and to God what is
God's."
[26]They were unable to
trap him in what he had said
there in public. And astonished by his answer, they
became silent.

The Resurrection and Marriage

[27]Some of the Sadducees,
who say there is no resurrection, came to Jesus with

[m] Or *keystone*

***That is, to the Pharisees and to the generally held opinion.**

[y] *17* Or *cornerstone*
[z] *17* Psalm 118:22

28and asked him a ques-
tion, "Teacher, Moses
wrote for us that if a man's
brother dies, leaving a wife
but no children, the man[n]
shall marry the widow and
raise up children for his
brother. 29Now there were
seven brothers; the first
married, and died childless;
30then the second 31and the
third married her, and so in
the same way all seven died
childless. 32Finally the
woman also died. 33In the
resurrection, therefore,
whose wife will the woman
be? For the seven had married her."
34 Jesus said to them,
"Those who belong to this
age marry and are given in
marriage; 35but those who
are considered worthy of a
place in that age and in the
resurrection from the dead
neither marry nor are given
in marriage. 36Indeed they
cannot die anymore, be-
cause they are like angels
and are children of God,
being children of the resurrection. 37And the fact that
the dead are raised Moses
himself showed, in the story about the bush, where he
speaks of the Lord as the
God of Abraham, the God
of Isaac, and the God of Jacob. 38Now he is God not
of the dead, but of the living; for to him all of them
are alive." 39Then some of
the scribes answered,
"Teacher, you have spoken
well." 40For they no longer
dared to ask him another
question.

The Question about David's Son

41 Then he said to them,
"How can they say that the
Messiah[o] is David's son?
42For David himself says in
the book of Psalms,

[n] Gk *his brother*
[o] Or *the Christ*

εἶναι, ἐπηρώτησαν αὐτὸν **28** λέγοντες·
to be, they questioned him saying :

διδάσκαλε, Μωϋσῆς ἔγραψεν ἡμῖν, ἐάν
Teacher, Moses wrote to us, If

τινος ἀδελφὸς ἀποθάνῃ ἔχων γυναῖκα, καὶ
of anyone a brother dies having a wife, and

οὗτος ἄτεκνος ᾖ, ἵνα λάβῃ ὁ ἀδελφὸς
this man childless is, that [4]should take [1]the [2]brother

αὐτοῦ τὴν γυναῖκα καὶ ἐξαναστήσῃ σπέρμα
[3]of him [5]the [6]wife and raise up seed

τῷ ἀδελφῷ αὐτοῦ. **29** ἑπτὰ οὖν ἀδελφοὶ
to the brother of him. Seven therefore brothers

ἦσαν· καὶ ὁ πρῶτος λαβὼν γυναῖκα
there were; and the first having taken a wife

ἀπέθανεν ἄτεκνος· **30** καὶ ὁ δεύτερος **31** καὶ
died childless; and the second and

ὁ τρίτος ἔλαβεν αὐτήν, ὡσαύτως δὲ καὶ
the third took her, and similarly also

οἱ ἑπτὰ οὐ κατέλιπον τέκνα καὶ ἀπέθανον.
the seven did not leave children and died.

32 ὕστερον καὶ ἡ γυνὴ ἀπέθανεν. **33** ἡ
Lastly also the woman died. The

γυνὴ οὖν ἐν τῇ ἀναστάσει τίνος αὐτῶν
woman therefore in the resurrection of which of them

γίνεται γυνή; οἱ γὰρ ἑπτὰ ἔσχον αὐτὴν
becomes she wife? for the seven had her

γυναῖκα. **34** καὶ εἶπεν αὐτοῖς ὁ Ἰησοῦς·
[as] wife. And said to them – Jesus :

οἱ υἱοὶ τοῦ αἰῶνος τούτου γαμοῦσιν καὶ
The sons – age of this marry and

γαμίσκονται, **35** οἱ δὲ καταξιωθέντες τοῦ
are given in marriage, but the [ones] counted worthy –

αἰῶνος ἐκείνου τυχεῖν καὶ τῆς ἀναστάσεως
[3]age [2]*of* that [1]to obtain and *of* the resurrection

τῆς ἐκ νεκρῶν οὔτε γαμοῦσιν οὔτε
– out of [the] dead neither marry nor

γαμίζονται· **36** οὐδὲ γὰρ ἀποθανεῖν ἔτι
are given in marriage; for not even *to* die more

δύνανται, ἰσάγγελοι γάρ εἰσιν, καὶ υἱοί
can they, for equal to angels they are, and [2]sons

εἰσιν θεοῦ τῆς ἀναστάσεως υἱοὶ ὄντες.
[1]they are [3]of God [6]of the [7]resurrection [5]sons [4]being.

37 ὅτι δὲ ἐγείρονται οἱ νεκροί, καὶ
But that are raised the dead, even

Μωϋσῆς ἐμήνυσεν ἐπὶ τῆς βάτου, ὡς
Moses pointed out at the bush, as

λέγει κύριον τὸν θεὸν Ἀβραὰμ καὶ θεὸν
he calls [the] Lord the God of Abraham and God

Ἰσαὰκ καὶ θεὸν Ἰακώβ· **38** θεὸς δὲ οὐκ
of Isaac and God of Jacob; but God not

ἔστιν νεκρῶν ἀλλὰ ζώντων· πάντες γὰρ
he is of dead persons but of living; for all

αὐτῷ ζῶσιν. **39** ἀποκριθέντες δέ τινες
to him live. And answering some

τῶν γραμματέων εἶπαν· διδάσκαλε, καλῶς
of the scribes said : Teacher, well

εἶπας. **40** οὐκέτι γὰρ ἐτόλμων ἐπερωτᾶν
thou sayest. For no more dared they *to* question

αὐτὸν οὐδέν.
him no(any)thing.

41 Εἶπεν δὲ πρὸς αὐτούς· πῶς λέγουσιν
And he said to them : How say they

τὸν χριστὸν εἶναι Δαυὶδ υἱόν; **42** αὐτὸς
the Christ to be of David son? himself

γὰρ Δαυὶδ λέγει ἐν βίβλῳ ψαλμῶν·
For David says in [the] roll of psalms :

a question. 28"Teacher,"
they said, "Moses wrote
for us that if a man's brother dies and leaves a wife but
no children, the man must
marry the widow and have
children for his brother.
29Now there were seven
brothers. The first one married a woman and died
childless. 30The second
31and then the third married
her, and in the same way
the seven died, leaving no
children. 32Finally, the
woman died too. 33Now
then, at the resurrection
whose wife will she be,
since the seven were mar-
ried to her?"
34Jesus replied, "The
people of this age marry
and are given in marriage.
35But those who are considered worthy of taking part
in that age and in the resurrection from the dead will
neither marry nor be given
in marriage, 36and they can
no longer die; for they are
like the angels. They are
God's children, since they
are children of the resurrection. 37But in the ac-
count of the bush, even
Moses showed that the
dead rise, for he calls the
Lord 'the God of Abraham,
and the God of Isaac, and
the God of Jacob.'[a] 38He is
not the God of the dead, but
of the living, for to him all
are alive."
39Some of the teachers of
the law responded, "Well
said, teacher!" 40And no
one dared to ask him any
more questions.

Whose Son Is the Christ?

41Then Jesus said to
them, "How is it that they
say the Christ[b] is the Son
of David? 42David himself
declares in the Book of

[a]37 Exodus 3:6
[b]41 Or *Messiah*

'The Lord said to my
Lord,
"Sit at my right hand,
43 until I make your
enemies your
footstool." '
44 David thus calls him Lord; so how can he be his son?"

Jesus Denounces the Scribes

45 In the hearing of all the people he said to the[p] disciples, 46 "Beware of the scribes, who like to walk around in long robes, and love to be greeted with respect in the marketplaces, and to have the best seats in the synagogues and places of honor at banquets. 47 They devour widows' houses and for the sake of appearance say long prayers. They will receive the greater condemnation."

εἶπεν κύριος τῷ κυρίῳ μου· κάθου ἐκ
Said [the] LORD to the Lord of me: Sit thou at

δεξιῶν μου 43 ἕως ἂν θῶ τοὺς ἐχθρούς σου
[the] right of me until I put the enemies of thee

ὑποπόδιον τῶν ποδῶν σου. 44 Δαυὶδ
a footstool of the feet of thee. David

οὖν αὐτὸν κύριον καλεῖ, καὶ πῶς αὐτοῦ
therefore him Lord calls, and how of him

υἱός ἐστιν;
son is he?

45 Ἀκούοντος δὲ παντὸς τοῦ λαοῦ εἶπεν
And hearing all the people[a] he said
=as all the people heard

τοῖς μαθηταῖς· 46 προσέχετε ἀπὸ τῶν
to the disciples: Beware from(of) the

γραμματέων τῶν θελόντων περιπατεῖν ἐν
scribes – wishing to walk about in

στολαῖς καὶ φιλούντων ἀσπασμοὺς ἐν ταῖς
robes and liking greetings in the

ἀγοραῖς καὶ πρωτοκαθεδρίας ἐν ταῖς
marketplaces and chief seats in the

συναγωγαῖς καὶ πρωτοκλισίας ἐν τοῖς
synagogues and chief couches in the

δείπνοις, 47 οἳ κατεσθίουσιν τὰς οἰκίας
suppers, who devour the houses

τῶν χηρῶν καὶ προφάσει μακρὰ προσεύχονται·
of the widows and under pretence long pray;

οὗτοι λήμψονται περισσότερον κρίμα.
these will receive severer judgment.

Psalms:

" 'The Lord said to my
Lord:
"Sit at my right hand
43 until I make your
enemies
a footstool for your
feet." '[c]

44 David calls him 'Lord.' How then can he be his son?"

45 While all the people were listening, Jesus said to his disciples, 46 "Beware of the teachers of the law. They like to walk around in flowing robes and love to be greeted in the marketplaces and have the most important seats in the synagogues and the places of honor at banquets. 47 They devour widows' houses and for a show make lengthy prayers. Such men will be punished most severely."

Chapter 21

The Widow's Offering

HE looked up and saw rich people putting their gifts into the treasury; 2 he also saw a poor widow put in two small copper coins. 3 He said, "Truly I tell you, this poor widow has put in more than all of them; 4 for all of them have contributed out of their abundance, but she out of her poverty has put in all she had to live on."

The Destruction of the Temple Foretold

5 When some were speaking about the temple, how it was adorned with beautiful stones and gifts dedicated to God, he said, 6 "As for these things that you see, the days will come when not one stone will be left upon another; all will be thrown down."

Signs and Persecutions

7 They asked him, "Teacher, when will this be, and what will be the sign that this is about to take place?" 8 And he said,

21 Ἀναβλέψας δὲ εἶδεν τοὺς βάλλοντας
And looking up he saw [1]the [3]putting

εἰς τὸ γαζοφυλακεῖον τὰ δῶρα αὐτῶν
[4]into [5]the [6]treasury [7]the [8]gifts [9]of them

πλουσίους. 2 εἶδεν δέ τινα χήραν πενιχρὰν
[2]rich [ones]. And he saw a certain widow poor

βάλλουσαν ἐκεῖ λεπτὰ δύο, 3 καὶ εἶπεν·
putting there lepta two, and he said:

ἀληθῶς λέγω ὑμῖν ὅτι ἡ χήρα αὕτη ἡ
Truly I tell you that – [3]widow [1]this –

πτωχὴ πλεῖον πάντων ἔβαλεν· 4 πάντες
[2]poor more [than] all put; [2]all

γὰρ οὗτοι ἐκ τοῦ περισσεύοντος αὐτοῖς
[1]for these out of the abounding to them[e]
=their abundance

ἔβαλον εἰς τὰ δῶρα, αὕτη δὲ ἐκ τοῦ
put into the gifts, but this woman out of the

ὑστερήματος αὐτῆς πάντα τὸν βίον ὃν
want of her [2]all [3]the [4]living [5]which

εἶχεν ἔβαλεν.
[6]she had [1]put.

5 Καί τινων λεγόντων περὶ τοῦ ἱεροῦ, ὅτι
And some speaking[a] about the temple, that
=as some spoke

λίθοις καλοῖς καὶ ἀναθήμασιν κεκόσμηται,
with stones beautiful and gifts it has(had) been adorned,

εἶπεν· 6 ταῦτα ἃ θεωρεῖτε, ἐλεύσονται
he said: These things which ye behold, will come

ἡμέραι ἐν αἷς οὐκ ἀφεθήσεται λίθος ἐπὶ
days in which there will not be left stone on

λίθῳ ὃς οὐ καταλυθήσεται. 7 ἐπηρώτησαν δὲ
stone which will not be overthrown. And they questioned

αὐτὸν λέγοντες· διδάσκαλε, πότε οὖν
him saying: Teacher, when therefore

ταῦτα ἔσται; καὶ τί τὸ σημεῖον ὅταν
these things will be? And what [will be] the sign when

Chapter 21

The Widow's Offering

AS he looked up, Jesus saw the rich putting their gifts into the temple treasury. 2 He also saw a poor widow put in two very small copper coins.[d] 3 "I tell you the truth," he said, "this poor widow has put in more than all the others. 4 All these people gave their gifts out of their wealth; but she out of her poverty put in all she had to live on."

Signs of the End of the Age

5 Some of his disciples were remarking about how the temple was adorned with beautiful stones and with gifts dedicated to God. But Jesus said, 6 "As for what you see here, the time will come when not one stone will be left on another; every one of them will be thrown down."

7 "Teacher," they asked, "when will these things happen? And what will be the sign that they are about

[p] Other ancient authorities read *his*

[c] 43 Psalm 110:1
[d] 2 Greek *two lepta*

"Beware that you are not
led astray; for many will
come in my name and say,
'I am he!'[q] and, 'The time
is near!'[r] Do not go after
them.
9 "When you hear of
wars and insurrections, do
not be terrified; for these
things must take place first,
but the end will not follow
immediately." 10 Then he
said to them, "Nation will
rise against nation, and
kingdom against kingdom;
11 there will be great earthquakes, and in various
places famines and
plagues; and there will be
dreadful portents and great
signs from heaven.
12 "But before all this
occurs, they will arrest you
and persecute you; they
will hand you over to synagogues and prisons, and
you will be brought before
kings and governors be-
cause of my name. 13 This
will give you an opportunity to testify. 14 So make up
your minds not to prepare
your defense in advance;
15 for I will give you words[s]
and a wisdom that none of
your opponents will be able
to withstand or contradict.
16 You will be betrayed
even by parents and brothers, by relatives and
friends; and they will put
some of you to death.
17 You will be hated by all
because of my name. 18 But
not a hair of your head will
perish. 19 By your endur-
ance you will gain your
souls.

The Destruction of Jerusalem Foretold

20 "When you see Jeru-
salem surrounded by ar-
mies, then know that its
desolation has come near.[t]
21 Then those in Judea must
flee to the mountains, and
those inside the city must

μέλλῃ ταῦτα γίνεσθαι; **8** ὁ δὲ εἶπεν·
³are about ¹these things ²to happen? And he said:
βλέπετε μὴ πλανηθῆτε· πολλοὶ γὰρ
Beware lest ye be led astray; for many
ἐλεύσονται ἐπὶ τῷ ὀνόματί μου λέγοντες·
will come on(in) the name of me saying:
ἐγώ εἰμι, καί· ὁ καιρὸς ἤγγικεν· μὴ
I am, and: The time has drawn near; not
πορευθῆτε ὀπίσω αὐτῶν. **9** ὅταν δὲ
go ye after them. And when
ἀκούσητε πολέμους καὶ ἀκαταστασίας, μὴ
ye hear [of] wars and commotions, not
πτοηθῆτε· δεῖ γὰρ ταῦτα γενέσθαι
be ye scared; for it behoves these things to happen
πρῶτον, ἀλλ' οὐκ εὐθέως τὸ τέλος. **10** Τότε
first, but not immediately the end. Then
ἔλεγεν αὐτοῖς· ἐγερθήσεται ἔθνος ἐπ' ἔθνος
he said to them: Will be raised nation against nation
καὶ βασιλεία ἐπὶ βασιλείαν, **11** σεισμοί τε
and kingdom against kingdom, and earthquakes
μεγάλοι καὶ κατὰ τόπους λοιμοὶ καὶ λιμοὶ
great and from place to place† pestilences and famines
ἔσονται, φόβητρά τε καὶ ἀπ' οὐρανοῦ
there will be, and terrors and ³from ⁴heaven
σημεῖα μεγάλα ἔσται. **12** πρὸ δὲ τούτων
²signs ¹great there will be. But before these things
πάντων ἐπιβαλοῦσιν ἐφ' ὑμᾶς τὰς χεῖρας
all they will lay *on* on you the hands
αὐτῶν καὶ διώξουσιν, παραδιδόντες εἰς τὰς
of them and will persecute, delivering to the
συναγωγὰς καὶ φυλακάς, ἀπαγομένους ἐπὶ
synagogues and prisons, being led away on(before)
βασιλεῖς καὶ ἡγεμόνας ἕνεκεν τοῦ ὀνόματός
kings and governors for the sake of the name
μου· **13** ἀποβήσεται ὑμῖν εἰς μαρτύριον.
of me; it will turn out to you for a testimony.
14 θέτε οὖν ἐν ταῖς καρδίαις ὑμῶν μὴ
Put therefore in the hearts of you not
προμελετᾶν ἀπολογηθῆναι· **15** ἐγὼ γὰρ
to practise beforehand to defend [yourselves]; for I
δώσω ὑμῖν στόμα καὶ σοφίαν, ᾗ οὐ
will give you a mouth and wisdom, which not
δυνήσονται ἀντιστῆναι ἢ ἀντειπεῖν ἅπαντες οἱ
will be able to withstand or to contradict all the
ἀντικείμενοι ὑμῖν. **16** παραδοθήσεσθε δὲ καὶ
[ones] opposing you. And ye will be betrayed also
ὑπὸ γονέων καὶ ἀδελφῶν καὶ συγγενῶν
by parents and brothers and relatives
καὶ φίλων, καὶ θανατώσουσιν ἐξ ὑμῶν,
and friends, and they will put to death [some] of you,
17 καὶ ἔσεσθε μισούμενοι ὑπὸ πάντων διὰ
and ye will be *being* hated by all men because of
τὸ ὄνομά μου. **18** καὶ θρὶξ ἐκ τῆς
the name of me. And a hair of the
κεφαλῆς ὑμῶν οὐ μὴ ἀπόληται· **19** ἐν τῇ
head of you by no means will perish; in the
ὑπομονῇ ὑμῶν κτήσεσθε τὰς ψυχὰς ὑμῶν.
endurance of you ye will gain the souls of you.
20 Ὅταν δὲ ἴδητε κυκλουμένην ὑπὸ
But when ye see ²being surrounded ³by
στρατοπέδων Ἰερουσαλήμ, τότε γνῶτε ὅτι
⁴camps ¹Jerusalem, then know ye that
ἤγγικεν ἡ ἐρήμωσις αὐτῆς. **21** τότε οἱ ἐν
has drawn near the desolation of it. Then the [ones] in
τῇ Ἰουδαίᾳ φευγέτωσαν εἰς τὰ ὄρη, καὶ
– Judæa let them flee to the mountains, and

to take place?"
8 He replied: "Watch out
that you are not deceived.
For many will come in my
name, claiming, 'I am he,'
and, 'The time is near.' Do
not follow them. 9 When
you hear of wars and revo-
lutions, do not be frightened. These things must
happen first, but the end
will not come right away."
10 Then he said to them:
"Nation will rise against
nation, and kingdom
against kingdom. 11 There
will be great earthquakes,
famines and pestilences in
various places, and fearful
events and great signs from
heaven.
12 "But before all this,
they will lay hands on you
and persecute you. They
will deliver you to syna-
gogues and prisons, and
you will be brought before
kings and governors, and
all on account of my name.
13 This will result in your
being witnesses to them.
14 But make up your mind
not to worry beforehand
how you will defend your-
selves. 15 For I will give you
words and wisdom that
none of your adversaries
will be able to resist or contradict. 16 You will be betrayed even by parents,
brothers, relatives and
friends, and they will put
some of you to death. 17 All
men will hate you because
of me. 18 But not a hair of
your head will perish. 19 By
standing firm you will gain
life.
20 "When you see Jerusa-
lem being surrounded by
armies, you will know that
its desolation is near.
21 Then let those who are in
Judea flee to the moun-
tains, let those in the city

[q] Gk *I am*
[r] Or *at hand*
[s] Gk *a mouth*
[t] Or *is at hand*

leave it, and those out in
the country must not enter
it; 22 for these are days of
vengeance, as a fulfillment
of all that is written. 23 Woe
to those who are pregnant
and to those who are nursing infants in those days!
For there will be great distress on the earth and wrath
against this people; 24 they
will fall by the edge of the
sword and be taken away
as captives among all na-
tions; and Jerusalem will be
trampled on by the Gen-
tiles, until the times of the
Gentiles are fulfilled.

The Coming of the Son of Man

25 "There will be signs
in the sun, the moon, and
the stars, and on the earth
distress among nations
confused by the roaring of
the sea and the waves.
26 People will faint from
fear and foreboding of what
is coming upon the world,
for the powers of the heavens will be shaken. 27 Then
they will see 'the Son of
Man coming in a cloud'
with power and great glory.
28 Now when these things
begin to take place, stand
up and raise your heads,
because your redemption is
drawing near."

The Lesson of the Fig Tree

29 Then he told them a
parable: "Look at the fig
tree and all the trees; 30 as
soon as they sprout leaves
you can see for yourselves
and know that summer is
already near. 31 So also,
when you see these things
taking place, you know that
the kingdom of God is near.
32 Truly I tell you, this generation will not pass away
until all things have taken
place. 33 Heaven and earth
will pass away, but my
words will not pass away.

οἱ ἐν μέσῳ αὐτῆς ἐκχωρείτωσαν, καὶ
the [ones] in [the] midst of it let them depart out, and

οἱ ἐν ταῖς χώραις μὴ εἰσερχέσθωσαν εἰς
the [ones] in the districts let them not enter into

αὐτήν, 22 ὅτι ἡμέραι ἐκδικήσεως αὗταί
it, because days of vengeance these

εἰσιν τοῦ πλησθῆναι πάντα τὰ γεγραμμένα.
are – to be fulfilled[d] all the things having been written.

23 οὐαὶ ταῖς ἐν γαστρὶ ἐχούσαις καὶ ταῖς
Woe to the pregnant women† and to the

θηλαζούσαις ἐν ἐκείναις ταῖς ἡμέραις·
[ones] giving suck in those – days;

ἔσται γὰρ ἀνάγκη μεγάλη ἐπὶ τῆς γῆς
for there will be distress great on the land

καὶ ὀργὴ τῷ λαῷ τούτῳ, 24 καὶ πεσοῦνται
and wrath – people to this, and they will fall

στόματι μαχαίρης καὶ αἰχμαλωτισθή-
by [the] mouth(edge) of [the] sword and will be led

σονται εἰς τὰ ἔθνη πάντα, καὶ Ἰερουσαλὴμ
captive to the nations all, and Jerusalem

ἔσται πατουμένη ὑπὸ ἐθνῶν, ἄχρι οὗ
will be *being* trodden down by nations, until

πληρωθῶσιν καιροὶ ἐθνῶν. 25 Καὶ ἔσονται
are accomplished [the] times of [the] nations. And there will be

σημεῖα ἐν ἡλίῳ καὶ σελήνῃ καὶ ἄστροις,
signs in sun and moon and stars,

καὶ ἐπὶ τῆς γῆς συνοχὴ ἐθνῶν ἐν ἀπορίᾳ
and on the earth anxiety of nations in perplexity

ἤχους θαλάσσης καὶ σάλου, 26 ἀποψυχόντων
of [the] sound of [the] sea and surf, fainting
=while men faint

ἀνθρώπων ἀπὸ φόβου καὶ προσδοκίας τῶν
men* from fear and expectation of the

ἐπερχομένων τῇ οἰκουμένῃ· αἱ γὰρ δυνάμεις
things coming on the inhabited earth; for the powers

τῶν οὐρανῶν σαλευθήσονται. 27 καὶ τότε
of the heavens will be shaken. And then

ὄψονται τὸν υἱὸν τοῦ ἀνθρώπου ἐρχόμενον
they will see the Son – of man coming

ἐν νεφέλῃ μετὰ δυνάμεως καὶ δόξης
in a cloud with power and glory

πολλῆς. 28 ἀρχομένων δὲ τούτων γίνεσθαι
much(great). And beginning these things* to happen
=when these things begin

ἀνακύψατε καὶ ἐπάρατε τὰς κεφαλὰς ὑμῶν,
stand erect and lift up the heads of you,

διότι ἐγγίζει ἡ ἀπολύτρωσις ὑμῶν. 29 Καὶ
because draws near the redemption of you. And

εἶπεν παραβολὴν αὐτοῖς· ἴδετε τὴν συκῆν
he told [2]a parable [1]them : Ye see the fig-tree

καὶ πάντα τὰ δένδρα· 30 ὅταν προβάλωσιν
and all the trees; when [2]they burst into leaf

ἤδη, βλέποντες ἀφ' ἑαυτῶν γινώσκετε ὅτι
now, seeing from(of) yourselves ye know that

ἤδη ἐγγὺς τὸ θέρος ἐστίν· 31 οὕτως καὶ
now near the summer is; so also

ὑμεῖς, ὅταν ἴδητε ταῦτα γινόμενα,
ye, when ye see these things happening,

γινώσκετε ὅτι ἐγγύς ἐστιν ἡ βασιλεία
know that near is the kingdom

τοῦ θεοῦ. 32 ἀμὴν λέγω ὑμῖν ὅτι οὐ μὴ
– of God. Truly I tell you that by no means

παρέλθῃ ἡ γενεὰ αὕτη ἕως ἂν πάντα
will pass away – generation this until all things

γένηται. 33 ὁ οὐρανὸς καὶ ἡ γῆ παρ-
happens. The heaven and the earth will

ελεύσονται, οἱ δὲ λόγοι μου οὐ μὴ παρελεύ-
pass away, but the words of me by no means will pass

get out, and let those in the
country not enter the city.
22 For this is the time of
punishment in fulfillment of
all that has been written.
23 How dreadful it will be in
those days for pregnant
women and nursing moth-
ers! There will be great distress in the land and wrath
against this people. 24 They
will fall by the sword and
will be taken as prisoners to
all the nations. Jerusalem
will be trampled on by the
Gentiles until the times of
the Gentiles are fulfilled.
25 "There will be signs in
the sun, moon and stars.
On the earth, nations will
be in anguish and perplexity at the roaring and tossing
of the sea. 26 Men will faint
from terror, apprehensive
of what is coming on the
world, for the heavenly
bodies will be shaken. 27 At
that time they will see the
Son of Man coming in a
cloud with power and great
glory. 28 When these things
begin to take place, stand
up and lift up your heads,
because your redemption is
drawing near."
29 He told them this parable: "Look at the fig tree
and all the trees. 30 When
they sprout leaves, you can
see for yourselves and
know that summer is near.
31 Even so, when you see
these things happening,
you know that the kingdom
of God is near.
32 "I tell you the truth,
this generation[e] will certainly not pass away until
all these things have happened. 33 Heaven and earth
will pass away, but my
words will never pass
away.

[e]32 Or *race*

Exhortation to Watch

34 "Be on guard so that your hearts are not weighed down with dissipation and drunkenness and the worries of this life, and that day catch you unexpectedly, 35 like a trap. For it will come upon all who live on the face of the whole earth. 36 Be alert at all times, praying that you may have the strength to escape all these things that will take place, and to stand before the Son of Man."

37 Every day he was teaching in the temple, and at night he would go out and spend the night on the Mount of Olives, as it was called. 38 And all the people would get up early in the morning to listen to him in the temple.

σονται. **34** Προσέχετε δὲ ἑαυτοῖς μήποτε
away. And take heed to yourselves lest

βαρηθῶσιν ὑμῶν αἱ καρδίαι ἐν κραιπάλῃ
become burdened of you the hearts with surfeiting

καὶ μέθῃ καὶ μερίμναις βιωτικαῖς, καὶ
and deep drinking and anxieties of life,† and

ἐπιστῇ ἐφ' ὑμᾶς αἰφνίδιος ἡ ἡμέρα ἐκείνη
come *on* on you suddenly – day that

35 ὡς παγίς· ἐπεισελεύσεται γὰρ ἐπὶ πάντας
as a snare; for it will come in *on* on all

τοὺς καθημένους ἐπὶ πρόσωπον πάσης τῆς
the [ones] sitting on [the] face of all the

γῆς. **36** ἀγρυπνεῖτε δὲ ἐν παντὶ καιρῷ
earth. But be ye watchful at every time

δεόμενοι ἵνα κατισχύσητε ἐκφυγεῖν ταῦτα
begging that ye may be able to escape these things

πάντα τὰ μέλλοντα γίνεσθαι, καὶ σταθῆναι
all – being about to happen, and to stand

ἔμπροσθεν τοῦ υἱοῦ τοῦ ἀνθρώπου.
before the Son – of man.

37 Ἦν δὲ τὰς ἡμέρας ἐν τῷ ἱερῷ
Now he was [in] the days in the temple

διδάσκων, τὰς δὲ νύκτας ἐξερχόμενος
teaching, and [in] the nights going forth

ηὐλίζετο εἰς τὸ ὄρος τὸ καλούμενον
he lodged in the mountain – *being* called

ἐλαιών. **38** καὶ πᾶς ὁ λαὸς ὤρθριζεν
of olives. And all the people came in the morning

πρὸς αὐτὸν ἐν τῷ ἱερῷ ἀκούειν αὐτοῦ.
to him in the temple to hear him.

34"Be careful, or your hearts will be weighed down with dissipation, drunkenness and the anxieties of life, and that day will close on you unexpectedly like a trap. 35For it will come upon all those who live on the face of the whole earth. 36Be always on the watch, and pray that you may be able to escape all that is about to happen, and that you may be able to stand before the Son of Man."

37Each day Jesus was teaching at the temple, and each evening he went out to spend the night on the hill called the Mount of Olives, 38and all the people came early in the morning to hear him at the temple.

Chapter 22

The Plot to Kill Jesus

NOW the festival of Unleavened Bread, which is called the Passover, was near. 2 The chief priests and the scribes were looking for a way to put Jesus[u] to death, for they were afraid of the people.

3 Then Satan entered into Judas called Iscariot, who was one of the twelve; 4 he went away and conferred with the chief priests and officers of the temple police about how he might betray him to them. 5 They were greatly pleased and agreed to give him money. 6 So he consented and began to look for an opportunity to betray him to them when no crowd was present.

The Preparation of the Passover

7 Then came the day of Unleavened Bread, on which the Passover lamb had to be sacrificed. 8 So Jesus[v] sent Peter and John, saying, "Go and prepare the Passover meal for us that we may eat it." 9 They asked him, "Where do you want us to make preparations for it?"

22 Ἤγγιζεν δὲ ἡ ἑορτὴ τῶν ἀζύμων ἡ
Now drew near the feast of unleavened bread –

λεγομένη πάσχα. **2** καὶ ἐζήτουν οἱ ἀρχιερεῖς
being called Passover. And [5]sought [1]the [2]chief priests

καὶ οἱ γραμματεῖς τὸ πῶς ἀνέλωσιν
[3]and [4]the [6]scribes – how they might destroy

αὐτόν· ἐφοβοῦντο γὰρ τὸν λαόν. **3** Εἰσῆλθεν δὲ
him; for they feared the people. And entered

σατανᾶς εἰς Ἰούδαν τὸν καλούμενον
Satan into Judas – *being* called

Ἰσκαριώτην, ὄντα ἐκ τοῦ ἀριθμοῦ τῶν
Iscariot, being of the number of the

δώδεκα· **4** καὶ ἀπελθὼν συνελάλησεν τοῖς
twelve; and going he conversed with the

ἀρχιερεῦσιν καὶ στρατηγοῖς τὸ πῶς αὐτοῖς
chief priests and captains – how to them

παραδῷ αὐτόν. **5** καὶ ἐχάρησαν, καὶ
he might betray him. And they rejoiced, and

συνέθεντο αὐτῷ ἀργύριον δοῦναι. **6** καὶ
they agreed [3]him [2]money [1]to give. And

ἐξωμολόγησεν, καὶ ἐζήτει εὐκαιρίαν τοῦ
he fully consented, and sought opportunity –

παραδοῦναι αὐτὸν ἄτερ ὄχλου αὐτοῖς.
to betray[d] him apart from a crowd to them.

7 Ἦλθεν δὲ ἡ ἡμέρα τῶν ἀζύμων, ᾗ
And came the day of unleavened bread, on which

ἔδει θύεσθαι τὸ πάσχα· **8** καὶ ἀπέστειλεν
it behoved to kill the passover [lamb]; and he sent

Πέτρον καὶ Ἰωάννην εἰπών· πορευθέντες
Peter and John saying: Going

ἑτοιμάσατε ἡμῖν τὸ πάσχα, ἵνα φάγωμεν. **9** οἱ
prepare ye for us the passover, that we may eat. they

δὲ εἶπαν αὐτῷ· ποῦ θέλεις ἑτοιμάσωμεν;
And said to him: Where wishest thou [that] we may prepare?

Chapter 22

Judas Agrees to Betray Jesus

NOW the Feast of Unleavened Bread, called the Passover, was approaching, 2and the chief priests and the teachers of the law were looking for some way to get rid of Jesus, for they were afraid of the people. 3Then Satan entered Judas, called Iscariot, one of the Twelve. 4And Judas went to the chief priests and the officers of the temple guard and discussed with them how he might betray Jesus. 5They were delighted and agreed to give him money. 6He consented, and watched for an opportunity to hand Jesus over to them when no crowd was present.

The Last Supper

7Then came the day of Unleavened Bread on which the Passover lamb had to be sacrificed. 8Jesus sent Peter and John, saying, "Go and make preparations for us to eat the Passover."

9"Where do you want us to prepare for it?" they asked.

[u] Gk *him*
[v] Gk *he*

10"Listen," he said to
them, "when you have en-
tered the city, a man carrying a jar of water will meet
you; follow him into the
house he enters 11and say
to the owner of the house,
'The teacher asks you,
"Where is the guest room,
where I may eat the Pass-
over with my disciples?" '
12He will show you a large
room upstairs, already furnished. Make preparations
for us there." 13So they
went and found everything
as he had told them; and
they prepared the Passover
meal.

The Institution of the Lord's Supper

14 When the hour came,
he took his place at the table, and the apostles with
him. 15He said to them, "I
have eagerly desired to eat
this Passover with you before I suffer; 16for I tell
you, I will not eat it[w] until
it is fulfilled in the kingdom
of God." 17Then he took a
cup, and after giving thanks
he said, "Take this and divide it among yourselves;
18for I tell you that from
now on I will not drink of
the fruit of the vine until the
kingdom of God comes."
19Then he took a loaf of
bread, and when he had
given thanks, he broke it
and gave it to them, saying,
"This is my body, which is
given for you. Do this in remembrance of me." 20And
he did the same with the
cup after supper, saying,
"This cup that is poured out
for you is the new covenant
in my blood.[x] 21But see,
the one who betrays me is
with me, and his hand is on

[w] Other ancient authorities read *never eat it again*

[x] Other ancient authorities lack, in whole or in part, verses 19b-20 (*which is given . . . in my blood*)

10 ὁ δὲ εἶπεν αὐτοῖς· ἰδοὺ εἰσελθόντων
And he told them : Behold[,] entering =as ye enter
ὑμῶν εἰς τὴν πόλιν συναντήσει ὑμῖν
you[a] into the city will meet you
ἄνθρωπος κεράμιον ὕδατος βαστάζων·
a man a pitcher of water bearing;
ἀκολουθήσατε αὐτῷ εἰς τὴν οἰκίαν εἰς ἣν
follow him into the house into which
εἰσπορεύεται· 11 καὶ ἐρεῖτε τῷ οἰκοδεσπότῃ
he enters; and ye will say to the *house*-master
τῆς οἰκίας· λέγει σοι ὁ διδάσκαλος·
of the house : Says to thee the teacher :
ποῦ ἐστιν τὸ κατάλυμα ὅπου τὸ πάσχα
Where is the guest room where the passover
μετὰ τῶν μαθητῶν μου φάγω; 12 κἀκεῖνος
with the disciples of me I may eat ? And that man
ὑμῖν δείξει ἀνάγαιον μέγα ἐστρωμένον·
you will show upper room a large *having been* spread;•
ἐκεῖ ἑτοιμάσατε. 13 ἀπελθόντες δὲ εὗρον
there prepare ye. And going they found
καθὼς εἰρήκει αὐτοῖς, καὶ ἡτοίμασαν τὸ
as he had told them, and they prepared the
πάσχα. 14 Καὶ ὅτε ἐγένετο ἡ ὥρα,
passover. And, when came the hour,
ἀνέπεσεν, καὶ οἱ ἀπόστολοι σὺν αὐτῷ.
he reclined, and the apostles with him.
15 καὶ εἶπεν πρὸς αὐτούς· ἐπιθυμίᾳ
And he said to them : With desire
ἐπεθύμησα τοῦτο τὸ πάσχα φαγεῖν μεθ'
I desired this – passover to eat with
ὑμῶν πρὸ τοῦ με παθεῖν· 16 λέγω γὰρ
you before the me to suffer;[b] for I tell
=I suffer ;
ὑμῖν ὅτι οὐκέτι οὐ μὴ φάγω αὐτὸ
you that no more by no(any) means I eat it
ἕως ὅτου πληρωθῇ ἐν τῇ βασιλείᾳ τοῦ θεοῦ.
until it is fulfilled in the kingdom – of God.
17 καὶ δεξάμενος ποτήριον εὐχαριστήσας
And taking a cup having given thanks
εἶπεν· λάβετε τοῦτο καὶ διαμερίσατε εἰς
he said : Take this and divide among
ἑαυτούς· 18 λέγω γὰρ ὑμῖν, οὐ μὴ πίω
yourselves; for I tell you, by no means I drink
ἀπὸ τοῦ νῦν ἀπὸ τοῦ γενήματος τῆς
from – now [on] from the produce of the
ἀμπέλου ἕως οὗ ἡ βασιλεία τοῦ θεοῦ
vine until the kingdom – of God
ἔλθῃ. 19 καὶ λαβὼν ἄρτον εὐχαριστήσας
comes. And taking a loaf having given thanks
ἔκλασεν καὶ ἔδωκεν αὐτοῖς λέγων· τοῦτό
he broke and gave to them saying : This
ἐστιν τὸ σῶμά μου [τὸ ὑπὲρ ὑμῶν
is the body of me – for you
διδόμενον· τοῦτο ποιεῖτε εἰς τὴν ἐμὴν
being given; this do ye for – my
ἀνάμνησιν. 20 καὶ τὸ ποτήριον ὡσαύτως
memorial. And the cup similarly
μετὰ τὸ δειπνῆσαι, λέγων· τοῦτο τὸ
after the to sup, saying : This –
ποτήριον ἡ καινὴ διαθήκη ἐν τῷ αἵματί
cup [is] the new covenant in the blood
μου, τὸ ὑπὲρ ὑμῶν ἐκχυννόμενον.] 21 πλὴν
of me, – for you being shed. However
ἰδοὺ ἡ χεὶρ τοῦ παραδιδόντος με μετ'
behold[,] the hand of the [one] betraying me with

• That is, with carpets, and the dining couches supplied with cushions.

10He replied, "As you en-
ter the city, a man carrying
a jar of water will meet you.
Follow him to the house
that he enters, 11and say to
the owner of the house,
'The Teacher asks: Where
is the guest room, where I
may eat the Passover with
my disciples?' 12He will
show you a large upper
room, all furnished. Make
preparations there."
13They left and found
things just as Jesus had told
them. So they prepared the
Passover.
14When the hour came,
Jesus and his apostles reclined at the table. 15And
he said to them, "I have eagerly desired to eat this
Passover with you before I
suffer. 16For I tell you, I
will not eat it again until it
finds fulfillment in the kingdom of God."
17After taking the cup, he
gave thanks and said,
"Take this and divide it
among you. 18For I tell you
I will not drink again of the
fruit of the vine until the
kingdom of God comes."
19And he took bread,
gave thanks and broke it,
and gave it to them, saying,
"This is my body given for
you; do this in remem-
brance of me."
20In the same way, after
the supper he took the cup,
saying, "This cup is the
new covenant in my blood,
which is poured out for
you. 21But the hand of him
who is going to betray me is

the table. 22 For the Son of
Man is going as it has been
determined, but woe to that
one by whom he is be-
trayed!" 23 Then they began
to ask one another, which
one of them it could be who
would do this.

The Dispute about Greatness

24 A dispute also arose
among them as to which
one of them was to be re-
garded as the greatest.
25 But he said to them, "The
kings of the Gentiles lord it
over them; and those in authority over them are called
benefactors. 26 But not so
with you; rather the greatest among you must be-
come like the youngest,
and the leader like one who
serves. 27 For who is greater, the one who is at the
table or the one who
serves? Is it not the one at
the table? But I am among
you as one who serves.
28 "You are those who
have stood by me in my trials; 29 and I confer on you,
just as my Father has conferred on me, a kingdom,
30 so that you may eat and
drink at my table in my
kingdom, and you will sit
on thrones judging the
twelve tribes of Israel.

Jesus Predicts Peter's Denial

31 "Simon, Simon, lis-
ten! Satan has demanded[y]
to sift all of you like wheat,
32 but I have prayed for you
that your own faith may not
fail; and you, when once
you have turned back,
strengthen your brothers."
33 And he said to him,
"Lord, I am ready to go
with you to prison and to
death!" 34 Jesus[z] said, "I
tell you, Peter, the cock
will not crow this day, until
you have denied three
times that you know me."

[y] Or *has obtained permission*
[z] Gk *He*

ἐμοῦ ἐπὶ τῆς τραπέζης. 22 ὅτι ὁ υἱὸς μὲν
me on the table. Because [2]the [3]Son [1]indeed
τοῦ ἀνθρώπου κατὰ τὸ ὡρισμένον
– of man according to the [thing] having been determined
πορεύεται, πλὴν οὐαὶ τῷ ἀνθρώπῳ ἐκείνῳ
goes, nevertheless woe – man to that
δι' οὗ παραδίδοται. 23 καὶ αὐτοὶ ἤρξαντο
through whom he is betrayed. And they began
συζητεῖν πρὸς ἑαυτοὺς τὸ τίς ἄρα εἴη
to debate with themselves – who then it might be
ἐξ αὐτῶν ὁ τοῦτο μέλλων πράσσειν.
of them the [one] [3]this [1]being about [2]to do.
24 Ἐγένετο δὲ καὶ φιλονεικία ἐν αὐτοῖς,
And there was also a rivalry among them,
τὸ τίς αὐτῶν δοκεῖ εἶναι μείζων. 25 ὁ δὲ
– who of them seems to be greater. So he
εἶπεν αὐτοῖς· οἱ βασιλεῖς τῶν ἐθνῶν
said to them: The kings of the nations
κυριεύουσιν αὐτῶν, καὶ οἱ ἐξουσιάζοντες
lord it over them, and the [ones] having authority over
αὐτῶν εὐεργέται καλοῦνται. 26 ὑμεῖς δὲ
them benefactors are called. But ye
οὐχ οὕτως, ἀλλ' ὁ μείζων ἐν ὑμῖν
not so, but the greater among you
γινέσθω ὡς ὁ νεώτερος, καὶ ὁ ἡγούμενος
let him become as the younger, and the [one] governing
ὡς ὁ διακονῶν. 27 τίς γὰρ μείζων, ὁ
as the [one] serving. For who [is] greater, the
ἀνακείμενος ἢ ὁ διακονῶν; οὐχὶ ὁ
[one] reclining or the [one] serving? not the
ἀνακείμενος; ἐγὼ δὲ ἐν μέσῳ ὑμῶν εἰμι
[one] reclining? But I in [the] midst of you am
ὡς ὁ διακονῶν. 28 ὑμεῖς δέ ἐστε οἱ
as the [one] serving. But ye are the [ones]
διαμεμενηκότες μετ' ἐμοῦ ἐν τοῖς πειρα-
having remained throughout with me in the tempta-
σμοῖς μου· 29 κἀγὼ διατίθεμαι ὑμῖν καθὼς
tions of me; and I appoint to you as
διέθετό μοι ὁ πατήρ μου βασιλείαν,
appointed to me the Father of me a kingdom,
30 ἵνα ἔσθητε καὶ πίνητε ἐπὶ τῆς τραπέζης
that ye may eat and drink at the table
μου ἐν τῇ βασιλείᾳ μου, καὶ καθήσεσθε
of me in the kingdom of me, and ye will sit
ἐπὶ θρόνων τὰς δώδεκα φυλὰς κρίνοντες
on thrones [2]the [3]twelve [4]tribes [1]judging
τοῦ Ἰσραήλ. 31 Σίμων Σίμων, ἰδοὺ ὁ
– of Israel. Simon[,] Simon, behold[,] –
σατανᾶς ἐξῃτήσατο ὑμᾶς τοῦ σινιάσαι ὡς
Satan begged earnestly for you – to sift[d] as
τὸν σῖτον· 32 ἐγὼ δὲ ἐδεήθην περὶ σοῦ
the wheat; but I requested concerning thee
ἵνα μὴ ἐκλίπῃ ἡ πίστις σου· καὶ σύ
that might not fail the faith of thee; and thou
ποτε ἐπιστρέψας στήρισον τοὺς ἀδελφούς
when having turned support the brothers
σου. 33 ὁ δὲ εἶπεν αὐτῷ· κύριε, μετὰ
of thee. And he said to him: Lord, with
σοῦ ἕτοιμός εἰμι καὶ εἰς φυλακὴν καὶ εἰς
thee prepared I am both to prison and to
θάνατον πορεύεσθαι. 34 ὁ δὲ εἶπεν· λέγω
death to go. But he said: I tell
σοι, Πέτρε, οὐ φωνήσει σήμερον ἀλέκτωρ
thee, Peter, will not sound to-day a cock
ἕως τρίς με ἀπαρνήσῃ μὴ εἰδέναι. 35 Καὶ
until thrice me thou wilt deny not to know. And

with mine on the table.
22 The Son of Man will go as
it has been decreed, but
woe to that man who be-
trays him." 23 They began
to question among them-
selves which of them it
might be who would do
this.
24 Also a dispute arose
among them as to which of
them was considered to be
greatest. 25 Jesus said to
them, "The kings of the
Gentiles lord it over them;
and those who exercise authority over them call
themselves Benefactors.
26 But you are not to be like
that. Instead, the greatest
among you should be like
the youngest, and the one
who rules like the one who
serves. 27 For who is greater, the one who is at the
table or the one who
serves? Is it not the one
who is at the table? But I
am among you as one who
serves. 28 You are those
who have stood by me in
my trials. 29 And I confer on
you a kingdom, just as my
Father conferred one on
me, 30 so that you may eat
and drink at my table in my
kingdom and sit on
thrones, judging the twelve
tribes of Israel.
31 "Simon, Simon, Satan
has asked to sift you[f] as
wheat. 32 But I have prayed
for you, Simon, that your
faith may not fail. And
when you have turned
back, strengthen your
brothers."
33 But he replied, "Lord, I
am ready to go with you to
prison and to death."
34 Jesus answered, "I tell
you, Peter, before the
rooster crows today, you
will deny three times that
you know me."

[f] 31 The Greek is plural.

Purse, Bag, and Sword

35 He said to them,
"When I sent you out without a purse, bag, or san-
dals, did you lack any-
thing?" They said, "No,
not a thing." 36 He said to
them, "But now, the one
who has a purse must take
it, and likewise a bag. And
the one who has no sword
must sell his cloak and buy
one. 37 For I tell you, this
scripture must be fulfilled
in me, 'And he was counted
among the lawless'; and indeed what is written about
me is being fulfilled."
38 They said, "Lord, look,
here are two swords." He
replied, "It is enough."

Jesus Prays on the Mount of Olives

39 He came out and
went, as was his custom, to
the Mount of Olives; and
the disciples followed him.
40 When he reached the
place, he said to them,
"Pray that you may not
come into the time of trial."[a] 41 Then he withdrew
from them about a stone's
throw, knelt down, and
prayed, 42 "Father, if you
are willing, remove this cup
from me; yet, not my will
but yours be done."
⟦43 Then an angel from
heaven appeared to him
and gave him strength. 44 In
his anguish he prayed more
earnestly, and his sweat became like great drops of
blood falling down on the
ground.⟧[b] 45 When he got
up from prayer, he came to
the disciples and found
them sleeping because of
grief, 46 and he said to
them, "Why are you sleep-
ing? Get up and pray that
you may not come into the
time of trial."[a]

The Betrayal and Arrest of Jesus

47 While he was still
speaking, suddenly a
crowd came, and the one
called Judas, one of the

[a] Or *into temptation*
[b] Other ancient authorities lack verses 43 and 44

εἶπεν αὐτοῖς· ὅτε ἀπέστειλα ὑμᾶς ἄτερ
he said to them: When I sent you without
βαλλαντίου καὶ πήρας καὶ ὑποδημάτων, μή
a purse and a wallet and sandals, *not*
τινος ὑστερήσατε; οἱ δὲ εἶπαν· οὐθενός.
of anything were ye short? And they said: Of nothing.
36 εἶπεν δὲ αὐτοῖς· ἀλλὰ νῦν ὁ ἔχων
And he said to them: But now the [one] having
βαλλάντιον ἀράτω, ὁμοίως καὶ πήραν, καὶ
a purse let him take [it], likewise also a wallet, and
ὁ μὴ ἔχων πωλησάτω τὸ ἱμάτιον αὐτοῦ
the [one] not having let him sell the garment of him
καὶ ἀγορασάτω μάχαιραν. 37 λέγω γὰρ
and let him buy a sword. For I tell
ὑμῖν ὅτι τοῦτο τὸ γεγραμμένον δεῖ
you that this – having been written it behoves
τελεσθῆναι ἐν ἐμοί, τό· καὶ μετὰ ἀνόμων
to be finished in me, – And with lawless men
ἐλογίσθη· καὶ γὰρ τὸ περὶ ἐμοῦ τέλος
he was reckoned; for indeed the thing concerning me an end
ἔχει. 38 οἱ δὲ εἶπαν· κύριε, ἰδοὺ μάχαιραι
has. And they said: Lord, behold[,] swords
ὧδε δύο. ὁ δὲ εἶπεν αὐτοῖς· ἱκανόν ἐστιν.
here two. And he said to them: Enough it is.
39 Καὶ ἐξελθὼν ἐπορεύθη κατὰ τὸ ἔθος
And going forth he went according to the(his) habit
εἰς τὸ ὄρος τῶν ἐλαιῶν· ἠκολούθησαν δὲ
to the mountain of the olives; and [4]followed
αὐτῷ καὶ οἱ μαθηταί. 40 γενόμενος δὲ
[5]him [3]also [1]the [2]disciples. And coming
ἐπὶ τοῦ τόπου εἶπεν αὐτοῖς· προσεύχεσθε
upon the place he said to them: Pray ye
μὴ εἰσελθεῖν εἰς πειρασμόν. 41 καὶ αὐτὸς
not to enter into temptation. And he
ἀπεσπάσθη ἀπ' αὐτῶν ὡσεὶ λίθου βολήν,
was withdrawn from them about of a stone a throw,
καὶ θεὶς τὰ γόνατα προσηύχετο 42 λέγων·
and placing the knees he prayed saying:
πάτερ, εἰ βούλει παρένεγκε τοῦτο τὸ
Father, if thou wilt take away this –
ποτήριον ἀπ' ἐμοῦ· πλὴν μὴ τὸ θέλημά
cup from me; nevertheless not the will
μου ἀλλὰ τὸ σὸν γινέσθω. 43 [ὤφθη δὲ
of me but – thine let be. And appeared
αὐτῷ ἄγγελος ἀπ' οὐρανοῦ ἐνισχύων αὐτόν.
to him an angel from heaven strengthening him.
44 καὶ γενόμενος ἐν ἀγωνίᾳ ἐκτενέστερον
And becoming in an agony more earnestly
προσηύχετο· καὶ ἐγένετο ὁ ἱδρὼς αὐτοῦ
he prayed; and became the sweat of him
ὡσεὶ θρόμβοι αἵματος καταβαίνοντες ἐπὶ
as drops of blood falling down onto
τὴν γῆν.] 45 καὶ ἀναστὰς ἀπὸ τῆς
the earth. And rising up from the
προσευχῆς, ἐλθὼν πρὸς τοὺς μαθητὰς
prayer, coming to the disciples
εὗρεν κοιμωμένους αὐτοὺς ἀπὸ τῆς λύπης,
he found [2]sleeping [1]them from the grief,
46 καὶ εἶπεν αὐτοῖς· τί καθεύδετε;
and said to them: Why sleep ye?
ἀναστάντες προσεύχεσθε, ἵνα μὴ εἰσέλθητε
rising up pray ye, lest ye enter
εἰς πειρασμόν. 47 Ἔτι αὐτοῦ λαλοῦντος
into temptation. Yet him speaking[a]
=While he was yet speaking
ἰδοὺ ὄχλος, καὶ ὁ λεγόμενος Ἰούδας εἷς
behold[,] a crowd, and the [one] *being* named Judas one

35 Then Jesus asked them,
"When I sent you without
purse, bag or sandals, did
you lack anything?"
"Nothing," they an-
swered.
36 He said to them, "But
now if you have a purse,
take it, and also a bag; and
if you don't have a sword,
sell your cloak and buy
one. 37 It is written: 'And he
was numbered with the
transgressors'[g]; and I tell
you that this must be fulfilled in me. Yes, what is
written about me is reaching its fulfillment."
38 The disciples said,
"See, Lord, here are two
swords."
"That is enough," he re-
plied.

Jesus Prays on the Mount of Olives

39 Jesus went out as usual
to the Mount of Olives, and
his disciples followed him.
40 On reaching the place, he
said to them, "Pray that
you will not fall into temptation." 41 He withdrew
about a stone's throw be-
yond them, knelt down and
prayed, 42 "Father, if you
are willing, take this cup
from me; yet not my will,
but yours be done." 43 An
angel from heaven ap-
peared to him and strengthened him. 44 And being in
anguish, he prayed more
earnestly, and his sweat
was like drops of blood falling to the ground.[h]
45 When he rose from
prayer and went back to the
disciples, he found them
asleep, exhausted from sorrow. 46 "Why are you sleeping?" he asked them. "Get
up and pray so that you will
not fall into temptation."

Jesus Arrested

47 While he was still
speaking a crowd came up,
and the man who was
called Judas, one of the

[g] *37* Isaiah 53:12
[h] *44* Some early manuscripts do not have verses 43 and 44.

twelve, was leading them.
He approached Jesus to
kiss him; 48 but Jesus said
to him, "Judas, is it with a
kiss that you are betraying
the Son of Man?" 49 When
those who were around him
saw what was coming, they
asked, "Lord, should we
strike with the sword?"
50 Then one of them struck
the slave of the high priest
and cut off his right ear.
51 But Jesus said, "No more
of this!" And he touched
his ear and healed him.
52 Then Jesus said to the
chief priests, the officers of
the temple police, and the
elders who had come for
him, "Have you come out
with swords and clubs as if
I were a bandit? 53 When I
was with you day after day
in the temple, you did not
lay hands on me. But this is
your hour, and the power
of darkness!"

Peter Denies Jesus

54 Then they seized him
and led him away, bringing
him into the high priest's
house. But Peter was fol-
lowing at a distance.
55 When they had kindled a
fire in the middle of the
courtyard and sat down together, Peter sat among
them. 56 Then a servant-
girl, seeing him in the firelight, stared at him and
said, "This man also was
with him." 57 But he denied
it, saying, "Woman, I do
not know him." 58 A little
later someone else, on seeing him, said, "You also are
one of them." But Peter
said, "Man, I am not!"
59 Then about an hour later
still another kept insisting,

τῶν δώδεκα προήρχετο αὐτούς, καὶ ἤγγισεν
of the twelve came before them, and drew near

τῷ Ἰησοῦ φιλῆσαι αὐτόν. 48 Ἰησοῦς δὲ
– to Jesus to kiss him. But Jesus

εἶπεν αὐτῷ· Ἰούδα, φιλήματι τὸν υἱὸν
said to him: Judas, with a kiss the Son

τοῦ ἀνθρώπου παραδίδως; 49 ἰδόντες δὲ
– of man betrayest thou? And [4]seeing

οἱ περὶ αὐτὸν τὸ ἐσόμενον εἶπαν· κύριε,
[1]the [ones] [2]round [3]him the thing going to be said: Lord,

εἰ πατάξομεν ἐν μαχαίρῃ; 50 καὶ ἐπάταξεν
if we shall strike with a sword? And [4]struck

εἷς τις ἐξ αὐτῶν τοῦ ἀρχιερέως τὸν
[1]a certain one [2]of [3]them [7]of the [8]high priest [5]the

δοῦλον καὶ ἀφεῖλεν τὸ οὖς αὐτοῦ τὸ
[6]slave and cut off [1]the [3]ear [4]of him –

δεξιόν. 51 ἀποκριθεὶς δὲ ὁ Ἰησοῦς εἶπεν·
[2]right. And answering – Jesus said:

ἐᾶτε ἕως τούτου· καὶ ἁψάμενος τοῦ
Permit ye until this; and touching the

ὠτίου ἰάσατο αὐτόν. 52 Εἶπεν δὲ Ἰησοῦς
ear he cured him. And said Jesus

πρὸς τοὺς παραγενομένους ἐπ' αὐτὸν
to [1]the [9]coming [10]upon [11]him

ἀρχιερεῖς καὶ στρατηγοὺς τοῦ ἱεροῦ καὶ
[2]chief priests [3]and [4]captains [5]of the [6]temple [7]and

πρεσβυτέρους· ὡς ἐπὶ λῃστὴν ἐξήλθατε
[8]elders: As against a robber came ye out

μετὰ μαχαιρῶν καὶ ξύλων; 53 καθ' ἡμέραν
with swords and clubs? daily

ὄντος μου μεθ' ὑμῶν ἐν τῷ ἱερῷ οὐκ
being me[a] with you in the temple not
=while I was

ἐξετείνατε τὰς χεῖρας ἐπ' ἐμέ· ἀλλ' αὕτη
ye stretched out the(your) hands against me; but this

ἐστὶν ὑμῶν ἡ ὥρα καὶ ἡ ἐξουσία τοῦ
is of you the hour and the authority of the

σκότους.
darkness.

54 Συλλαβόντες δὲ αὐτὸν ἤγαγον καὶ
And having arrested him they led and

εἰσήγαγον εἰς τὴν οἰκίαν τοῦ ἀρχιερέως·
brought *in* into the house of the high priest;

ὁ δὲ Πέτρος ἠκολούθει μακρόθεν. 55 περι-
– and Peter followed afar off. light-

αψάντων δὲ πῦρ ἐν μέσῳ τῆς αὐλῆς καὶ
ing And a fire in [the] centre of the court and
=when they had lit a fire . . . and had sat down together

συγκαθισάντων ἐκάθητο ὁ Πέτρος μέσος
sitting down together[a] sat – Peter among

αὐτῶν. 56 ἰδοῦσα δὲ αὐτὸν παιδίσκη τις
them. And [3]seeing [4]him [1]a certain maidservant

καθήμενον πρὸς τὸ φῶς καὶ ἀτενίσασα
sitting near the light and gazing at

αὐτῷ εἶπεν· καὶ οὗτος σὺν αὐτῷ ἦν. 57 ὁ
him said: And this man with him was. he

δὲ ἠρνήσατο λέγων· οὐκ οἶδα αὐτόν,
But denied saying: I know not him,

γύναι. 58 καὶ μετὰ βραχὺ ἕτερος ἰδὼν
woman. And after a short while another seeing

αὐτὸν ἔφη· καὶ σὺ ἐξ αὐτῶν εἶ. ὁ
him said: And thou of them art. –

δὲ Πέτρος ἔφη· ἄνθρωπε, οὐκ εἰμί.
But Peter said: Man, I am not.

59 καὶ διαστάσης ὡσεὶ ὥρας μιᾶς ἄλλος
And intervening about hour one[a] [2]other man
=when about an hour had intervened

Twelve, was leading them.
He approached Jesus to
kiss him, 48 but Jesus asked
him, "Judas, are you be-
traying the Son of Man with
a kiss?"
49 When Jesus' followers
saw what was going to happen, they said, "Lord,
should we strike with our
swords?" 50 And one of
them struck the servant of
the high priest, cutting off
his right ear.
51 But Jesus answered,
"No more of this!" And he
touched the man's ear and
healed him.
52 Then Jesus said to the
chief priests, the officers of
the temple guard, and the
elders, who had come for
him, "Am I leading a rebellion, that you have come
with swords and clubs?
53 Every day I was with you
in the temple courts, and
you did not lay a hand on
me. But this is your hour—
when darkness reigns."

Peter Disowns Jesus

54 Then seizing him, they
led him away and took him
into the house of the high
priest. Peter followed at a
distance. 55 But when they
had kindled a fire in the
middle of the courtyard and
had sat down together, Peter sat down with them. 56 A
servant girl saw him seated
there in the firelight. She
looked closely at him and
said, "This man was with
him."
57 But he denied it.
"Woman, I don't know
him," he said.
58 A little later someone
else saw him and said,
"You also are one of
them."
"Man, I am not!" Peter
replied.
59 About an hour later another asserted, "Certainly

"Surely this man also was
with him; for he is a Galilean." 60 But Peter said,
"Man, I do not know what
you are talking about!" At
that moment, while he was
still speaking, the cock
crowed. 61 The Lord turned
and looked at Peter. Then
Peter remembered the
word of the Lord, how he
had said to him, "Before
the cock crows today, you
will deny me three times."
62 And he went out and
wept bitterly.

The Mocking and Beating of Jesus

63 Now the men who
were holding Jesus began
to mock him and beat him;
64 they also blindfolded him
and kept asking him,
"Prophesy! Who is it that
struck you?" 65 They kept
heaping many other insults
on him.

Jesus before the Council

66 When day came, the
assembly of the elders of
the people, both chief
priests and scribes, gathered together, and they
brought him to their council. 67 They said, "If you are
the Messiah,[c] tell us." He
replied, "If I tell you, you
will not believe; 68 and if I
question you, you will not
answer. 69 But from now on
the Son of Man will be seated at the right hand of the
power of God." 70 All of
them asked, "Are you,
then, the Son of God?" He
said to them, "You say that
I am." 71 Then they said,
"What further testimony do
we need? We have heard it
ourselves from his own
lips!"

τις διϊσχυρίζετο λέγων· ἐπ' ἀληθείας καὶ
[1]a cer- emphatically saying : Of a truth also
tain asserted

οὗτος μετ' αὐτοῦ ἦν, καὶ γὰρ Γαλιλαῖός
this man with him was, for indeed a Galilæan

ἐστιν. 60 εἶπεν δὲ ὁ Πέτρος· ἄνθρωπε,
he is. But said – Peter : Man,

οὐκ οἶδα ὃ λέγεις. καὶ παραχρῆμα ἔτι
I know not what thou sayest. And at once yet

λαλοῦντος αὐτοῦ ἐφώνησεν ἀλέκτωρ. 61 καὶ
speaking him[a] sounded a cock. And
=while he was yet speaking

στραφεὶς ὁ κύριος ἐνέβλεψεν τῷ Πέτρῳ,
turning the Lord looked at – Peter,

καὶ ὑπεμνήσθη ὁ Πέτρος τοῦ λόγου τοῦ
and remembered – Peter the word of the

κυρίου, ὡς εἶπεν αὐτῷ ὅτι πρὶν ἀλέκτορα
Lord, as he told him that before a cock

φωνῆσαι σήμερον ἀπαρνήσῃ με τρίς. 62 καὶ
to sound[b] to-day thou wilt deny me thrice. And

ἐξελθὼν ἔξω ἔκλαυσεν πικρῶς. 63 Καὶ οἱ
going *out* outside he wept bitterly. And the

ἄνδρες οἱ συνέχοντες αὐτὸν ἐνέπαιζον αὐτῷ
men – having in charge him* mocked him

δέροντες, 64 καὶ περικαλύψαντες αὐτὸν
beating, and covering over him

ἐπηρώτων λέγοντες· προφήτευσον, τίς ἐστιν
questioned saying : Prophesy, who is

ὁ παίσας σε; 65 καὶ ἕτερα πολλὰ
the [one] playing thee? And other things many

βλασφημοῦντες ἔλεγον εἰς αὐτόν.
blaspheming they said against him.

66 Καὶ ὡς ἐγένετο ἡμέρα, συνήχθη τὸ
And when came day, was assembled the

πρεσβυτέριον τοῦ λαοῦ, ἀρχιερεῖς τε καὶ
body of elders of the people, both chief priests and

γραμματεῖς, καὶ ἀπήγαγον αὐτὸν εἰς τὸ
scribes, and led away him to the

συνέδριον αὐτῶν, 67 λέγοντες· εἰ σὺ εἶ ὁ
council of them, saying : If thou art the

χριστός, εἰπὸν ἡμῖν. εἶπεν δὲ αὐτοῖς·
Christ, tell us. And he said to them :

ἐὰν ὑμῖν εἴπω, οὐ μὴ πιστεύσητε· 68 ἐὰν
If you I tell, by no means will ye believe; [2]if

δὲ ἐρωτήσω, οὐ μὴ ἀποκριθῆτε. 69 ἀπὸ
[1]and I question, by no means will ye answer. [2]from

τοῦ νῦν δὲ ἔσται ὁ υἱὸς τοῦ ἀνθρώπου
– [3]now [1]But [7]will be [4]the [5]Son – [6]of man

καθήμενος ἐκ δεξιῶν τῆς δυνάμεως τοῦ
[8]sitting at [the] right of the power –

θεοῦ. 70 εἶπαν δὲ πάντες· σὺ οὖν εἶ ὁ
of God. And they said all : Thou therefore art the

υἱὸς τοῦ θεοῦ; ὁ δὲ πρὸς αὐτοὺς ἔφη·
Son – of God? And he to them said :

ὑμεῖς λέγετε ὅτι ἐγώ εἰμι. 71 οἱ δὲ
Ye say that I am. And they

εἶπαν· τί ἔτι ἔχομεν μαρτυρίας χρείαν;
said : Why yet have we of witness need ?

αὐτοὶ γὰρ ἠκούσαμεν ἀπὸ τοῦ στόματος
for [our]selves we heard from the mouth

αὐτοῦ.
of him.

this fellow was with him,
for he is a Galilean."
60 Peter replied, "Man, I
don't know what you're
talking about!" Just as he
was speaking, the rooster
crowed. 61 The Lord turned
and looked straight at Peter. Then Peter remem-
bered the word the Lord
had spoken to him: "Be-
fore the rooster crows to-
day, you will disown me
three times." 62 And he
went outside and wept bitterly.

The Soldiers Mock Jesus

63 The men who were
guarding Jesus began
mocking and beating him.
64 They blindfolded him and
demanded, "Prophesy!
Who hit you?" 65 And they
said many other insulting
things to him.

Jesus Before Pilate and Herod

66 At daybreak the council
of the elders of the people,
both the chief priests and
teachers of the law, met together, and Jesus was led
before them. 67 "If you are
the Christ,[i]" they said,
"tell us."
Jesus answered, "If I tell
you, you will not believe
me, 68 and if I asked you,
you would not answer.
69 But from now on, the Son
of Man will be seated at the
right hand of the mighty
God."
70 They all asked, "Are
you then the Son of God?"
He replied, "You are
right in saying I am."
71 Then they said, "Why
do we need any more testimony? We have heard it
from his own lips."

[c] Or *the Christ*

* That is, Jesus (as some texts have it).

[i] 67 Or *Messiah*

Chapter 23

Jesus before Pilate

THEN the assembly
rose as a body and
brought Jesus[d] before Pilate. 2 They began to accuse
him, saying, "We found
this man perverting our nation, forbidding us to pay
taxes to the emperor, and
saying that he himself is the
Messiah, a king."[e] 3 Then
Pilate asked him, "Are you
the king of the Jews?" He
answered, "You say so."
4 Then Pilate said to the
chief priests and the
crowds, "I find no basis for
an accusation against this
man." 5 But they were in-
sistent and said, "He stirs
up the people by teaching
throughout all Judea, from
Galilee where he began
even to this place."

Jesus before Herod

6 When Pilate heard
this, he asked whether the
man was a Galilean. 7 And
when he learned that he
was under Herod's juris-
diction, he sent him off to
Herod, who was himself in
Jerusalem at that time.
8 When Herod saw Jesus,
he was very glad, for he had
been wanting to see him for
a long time, because he had
heard about him and was
hoping to see him perform
some sign. 9 He questioned
him at some length, but
Jesus[f] gave him no an-
swer. 10 The chief priests
and the scribes stood by,
vehemently accusing him.
11 Even Herod with his soldiers treated him with contempt and mocked him;
then he put an elegant robe
on him, and sent him back
to Pilate. 12 That same day

[d] Gk *him*
[e] Or *is an anointed king*
[f] Gk *he*

23 Καὶ ἀναστὰν ἅπαν τὸ πλῆθος αὐτῶν
And rising up all the multitude of them

ἤγαγον αὐτὸν ἐπὶ τὸν Πιλᾶτον. **2** ἤρξαντο
led him before – Pilate. they began

δὲ κατηγορεῖν αὐτοῦ λέγοντες· τοῦτον
And to accuse him saying : This man

εὕραμεν διαστρέφοντα τὸ ἔθνος ἡμῶν καὶ
we found perverting the nation of us and

κωλύοντα φόρους Καίσαρι διδόναι, καὶ
forbidding tribute to Cæsar to give, and

λέγοντα ἑαυτὸν χριστὸν βασιλέα εἶναι.
saying himself Christ a king to be.

3 ὁ δὲ Πιλᾶτος ἠρώτησεν αὐτὸν λέγων·
– And Pilate questioned him saying :

σὺ εἶ ὁ βασιλεὺς τῶν Ἰουδαίων; ὁ δὲ
Thou art the king of the Jews? And he

ἀποκριθεὶς αὐτῷ ἔφη· σὺ λέγεις. **4** ὁ δὲ
answering him said : Thou sayest. – And

Πιλᾶτος εἶπεν πρὸς τοὺς ἀρχιερεῖς καὶ
Pilate said to the chief priests and

τοὺς ὄχλους· οὐδὲν εὑρίσκω αἴτιον ἐν
the crowds : [3]No [1]I find [2]crime in

τῷ ἀνθρώπῳ τούτῳ. **5** οἱ δὲ ἐπίσχυον λέγοντες
– man this. But they insisted saying[,]

ὅτι ἀνασείει τὸν λαόν, διδάσκων καθ'
– He excites the people, teaching throughout

ὅλης τῆς Ἰουδαίας, καὶ ἀρξάμενος ἀπὸ
all – Judæa, even beginning from

τῆς Γαλιλαίας ἕως ὧδε. **6** Πιλᾶτος δὲ
– Galilee to here. And Pilate

ἀκούσας ἐπηρώτησεν εἰ ὁ ἄνθρωπος
hearing questioned if the man

Γαλιλαῖός ἐστιν, **7** καὶ ἐπιγνοὺς ὅτι ἐκ
a Galilæan is(was), and perceiving that of

τῆς ἐξουσίας Ἡρῴδου ἐστίν, ἀνέπεμψεν
the authority of Herod he is(was), he sent up

αὐτὸν πρὸς Ἡρῴδην, ὄντα καὶ αὐτὸν ἐν
him to Herod, being also him(he) in

Ἱεροσολύμοις ἐν ταύταις ταῖς ἡμέραις.
Jerusalem in these – days.

8 ὁ δὲ Ἡρῴδης ἰδὼν τὸν Ἰησοῦν ἐχάρη
– And Herod seeing – Jesus rejoiced

λίαν· ἦν γὰρ ἐξ ἱκανῶν χρόνων θέλων
greatly; for he was of a long times wishing

ἰδεῖν αὐτὸν διὰ τὸ ἀκούειν περὶ αὐτοῦ,
to see him because of the to hear[b] about him,
=because he had heard

καὶ ἤλπιζέν τι σημεῖον ἰδεῖν ὑπ' αὐτοῦ
and he hoped some sign to see by him

γινόμενον. **9** ἐπηρώτα δὲ αὐτὸν ἐν λόγοις
brought about. And he questioned him in words

ἱκανοῖς· αὐτὸς δὲ οὐδὲν ἀπεκρίνατο αὐτῷ.
many; but he nothing answered him.

10 εἱστήκεισαν δὲ οἱ ἀρχιερεῖς καὶ οἱ
And stood the chief priests and the

γραμματεῖς εὐτόνως κατηγοροῦντες αὐτοῦ.
scribes vehemently accusing him.

11 ἐξουθενήσας δὲ αὐτὸν ὁ Ἡρῴδης σὺν
And despising him – Herod with

τοῖς στρατεύμασιν αὐτοῦ καὶ ἐμπαίξας,
the soldiery of him and mocking,

περιβαλὼν ἐσθῆτα λαμπρὰν ἀνέπεμψεν αὐτὸν
throwing round clothing splendid sent back him

τῷ Πιλάτῳ. **12** ἐγένοντο δὲ φίλοι ὅ τε
– to Pilate. And became friends – both

Chapter 23

THEN the whole assem-
bly rose and led him
off to Pilate. 2And they began to accuse him, saying,
"We have found this man
subverting our nation. He
opposes payment of taxes
to Caesar and claims to be
Christ,[j] a king."
3So Pilate asked Jesus,
"Are you the king of the
Jews?"
"Yes, it is as you say,"
Jesus replied.
4Then Pilate announced
to the chief priests and the
crowd, "I find no basis for
a charge against this man."
5But they insisted, "He
stirs up the people all over
Judea[k] by his teaching. He
started in Galilee and has
come all the way here."
6On hearing this, Pilate
asked if the man was a Galilean. 7When he learned that
Jesus was under Herod's
jurisdiction, he sent him to
Herod, who was also in Jerusalem at that time.
8When Herod saw Jesus,
he was greatly pleased, because for a long time he had
been wanting to see him.
From what he had heard
about him, he hoped to see
him perform some miracle.
9He plied him with many
questions, but Jesus gave
him no answer. 10The chief
priests and the teachers of
the law were standing
there, vehemently accusing
him. 11Then Herod and his
soldiers ridiculed and
mocked him. Dressing him
in an elegant robe, they
sent him back to Pilate.

[j]2 Or *Messiah*; also in verses 35 and 39
[k]5 Or *over the land of the Jews*

Herod and Pilate became
friends with each other; before this they had been enemies.

Jesus Sentenced to Death

13 Pilate then called to-
gether the chief priests, the
leaders, and the people,
14and said to them, "You
brought me this man as one
who was perverting the
people; and here I have examined him in your pres-
ence and have not found
this man guilty of any of
your charges against him.
15Neither has Herod, for
he sent him back to us. Indeed, he has done nothing
to deserve death. 16I will
therefore have him flogged
and release him."[g]
18 Then they all shout-
ed out together, "Away
with this fellow! Release
Barabbas for us!" 19(This
was a man who had been
put in prison for an insurrection that had taken place
in the city, and for murder.)
20Pilate, wanting to release
Jesus, addressed them
again; 21but they kept
shouting, "Crucify, crucify
him!" 22A third time he said
to them, "Why, what evil
has he done? I have found
in him no ground for the
sentence of death; I will
therefore have him flogged
and then release him."
23But they kept urgently
demanding with loud
shouts that he should be
crucified; and their voices
prevailed. 24So Pilate gave
his verdict that their demand should be granted.
25He released the man they
asked for, the one who had
been put in prison for insurrection and murder, and he
handed Jesus over as they
wished.

[g] Here, or after verse 19, other ancient authorities add verse 17, *Now he was obliged to release someone for them at the festival*

Ἡρῴδης καὶ ὁ Πιλᾶτος ἐν αὐτῇ τῇ
Herod and – Pilate on [2]same [1]the
ἡμέρᾳ μετ' ἀλλήλων· προϋπῆρχον γὰρ ἐν
day with each other; for they were previously in
ἔχθρᾳ ὄντες πρὸς αὐτούς. **13** Πιλᾶτος δὲ
enmity being with themselves. And Pilate
συγκαλεσάμενος τοὺς ἀρχιερεῖς καὶ τοὺς
calling together the chief priests and the
ἄρχοντας καὶ τὸν λαὸν **14** εἶπεν πρὸς
leaders and the people said to
αὐτούς· προσηνέγκατέ μοι τὸν ἄνθρωπον
them: Ye brought to me – man
τοῦτον ὡς ἀποστρέφοντα τὸν λαόν, καὶ
this as perverting the people, and
ἰδοὺ ἐγὼ ἐνώπιον ὑμῶν ἀνακρίνας οὐθὲν
behold I [2]before [3]you [1]examining [5]*nothing*
εὗρον ἐν τῷ ἀνθρώπῳ τούτῳ αἴτιον ὧν
[4]found [7]in – [8]man [9]this [6]crime of the [things] which
κατηγορεῖτε κατ' αὐτοῦ. **15** ἀλλ' οὐδὲ
ye bring accusation against him. And neither
Ἡρῴδης· ἀνέπεμψεν γὰρ αὐτὸν πρὸς ἡμᾶς·
Herod; for he sent back him to us;
καὶ ἰδοὺ οὐδὲν ἄξιον θανάτου ἐστὶν
and behold nothing worthy of death is
πεπραγμένον αὐτῷ· **16** παιδεύσας οὖν αὐτὸν
having been done by him; chastising therefore him
ἀπολύσω.‡ **18** ἀνέκραγον δὲ παμπληθεὶ
I will release. But they shouted with the whole multitude
λέγοντες· αἶρε τοῦτον, ἀπόλυσον δὲ ἡμῖν
saying: Take this man, and release to us
τὸν Βαραββᾶν· **19** ὅστις ἦν διὰ στάσιν
– Barabbas; who was because of [2]insurrection
τινὰ γενομένην ἐν τῇ πόλει καὶ φόνον
[1]some happening in the city and murder
βληθεὶς ἐν τῇ φυλακῇ. **20** πάλιν δὲ
thrown in the prison. But again
ὁ Πιλᾶτος προσεφώνησεν αὐτοῖς, θέλων
– Pilate called to them, wishing
ἀπολῦσαι τὸν Ἰησοῦν. **21** οἱ δὲ ἐπεφώνουν
to release – Jesus. But they shouted
λέγοντες· σταύρου σταύρου αὐτόν. **22** ὁ δὲ
saying: Crucify[,] crucify thou him. But he
τρίτον εἶπεν πρὸς αὐτούς· τί γὰρ κακὸν
a third time said to them: But what evil
ἐποίησεν οὗτος; οὐδὲν αἴτιον θανάτου
did this man? no*thing* cause of death
εὗρον ἐν αὐτῷ· παιδεύσας οὖν αὐτὸν
I found in him; chastising therefore him
ἀπολύσω. **23** οἱ δὲ ἐπέκειντο φωναῖς
I will release. But they insisted voices
μεγάλαις αἰτούμενοι αὐτὸν σταυρωθῆναι,
with great asking him to be crucified,
καὶ κατίσχυον αἱ φωναὶ αὐτῶν. **24** καὶ
and prevailed the voices of them. And
Πιλᾶτος ἐπέκρινεν γενέσθαι τὸ αἴτημα
Pilate decided to be [carried out] the request
αὐτῶν· **25** ἀπέλυσεν δὲ τὸν διὰ στάσιν
of them; and he released the [one] because of insurrection
καὶ φόνον βεβλημένον εἰς φυλακήν, ὃν
and murder having been thrown into prison, whom
ᾐτοῦντο, τὸν δὲ Ἰησοῦν παρέδωκεν τῷ
they asked, – but Jesus he delivered to the
θελήματι αὐτῶν.
will of them.

‡ Ver. 17 omitted by Nestle; *cf.* NIV footnote.

12That day Herod and Pi-
late became friends—be-
fore this they had been enemies.
13Pilate called together
the chief priests, the rulers
and the people, 14and said
to them, "You brought me
this man as one who was
inciting the people to rebellion. I have examined him
in your presence and have
found no basis for your
charges against him. 15Nei-
ther has Herod, for he sent
him back to us; as you can
see, he has done nothing to
deserve death. 16There-
fore, I will punish him and
then release him.[l]"
18With one voice they
cried out, "Away with this
man! Release Barabbas to
us!" 19(Barabbas had been
thrown into prison for an
insurrection in the city, and
for murder.)
20Wanting to release
Jesus, Pilate appealed to
them again. 21But they kept
shouting, "Crucify him!
Crucify him!"
22For the third time he
spoke to them: "Why?
What crime has this man
committed? I have found in
him no grounds for the
death penalty. Therefore I
will have him punished and
then release him."
23But with loud shouts
they insistently demanded
that he be crucified, and
their shouts prevailed. 24So
Pilate decided to grant their
demand. 25He released the
man who had been thrown
into prison for insurrection
and murder, the one they
asked for, and surrendered
Jesus to their will.

[l]16 Some manuscripts *him."* 17*Now he was obliged to release one man to them at the Feast.*

The Crucifixion of Jesus

26 As they led him
away, they seized a man,
Simon of Cyrene, who was
coming from the country,
and they laid the cross on
him, and made him carry it
behind Jesus. 27 A great
number of the people fol-
lowed him, and among
them were women who
were beating their breasts
and wailing for him. 28 But
Jesus turned to them and
said, "Daughters of Jerusalem, do not weep for me,
but weep for yourselves
and for your children.
29 For the days are surely
coming when they will say,
'Blessed are the barren,
and the wombs that never
bore, and the breasts that
never nursed.' 30 Then they
will begin to say to the
mountains, 'Fall on us';
and to the hills, 'Cover us.'
31 For if they do this when
the wood is green, what
will happen when it is dry?"
32 Two others also,
who were criminals, were
led away to be put to death
with him. 33 When they
came to the place that is
called The Skull, they crucified Jesus[h] there with the
criminals, one on his right
and one on his left. [[34 Then
Jesus said, "Father, forgive
them; for they do not know
what they are doing."]][i]
And they cast lots to divide
his clothing. 35 And the
people stood by, watching;
but the leaders scoffed at
him, saying, "He saved
others; let him save himself
if he is the Messiah[j] of
God, his chosen one!"
36 The soldiers also mocked
him, coming up and offer-
ing him sour wine, 37 and

[h] Gk *him*
[i] Other ancient authorities lack the sentence *Then Jesus . . . what they are doing*
[j] Or *the Christ*

26 Καὶ ὡς ἀπήγαγον αὐτόν, ἐπιλαβόμενοι
And as they led away him, seizing

Σίμωνά τινα Κυρηναῖον ἐρχόμενον ἀπ'
Simon a certain Cyrenian coming from

ἀγροῦ ἐπέθηκαν αὐτῷ τὸν σταυρὸν φέρειν
[the] country they placed on him the cross to carry

ὄπισθεν τοῦ Ἰησοῦ. **27** Ἠκολούθει δὲ
behind – Jesus. And followed

αὐτῷ πολὺ πλῆθος τοῦ λαοῦ καὶ γυναικῶν
him a much multitude of the people and of women

αἳ ἐκόπτοντο καὶ ἐθρήνουν αὐτόν. **28** στρα-
who mourned and lamented him. turn

φεὶς δὲ πρὸς αὐτὰς Ἰησοῦς εἶπεν·
ing And to them Jesus said :

θυγατέρες Ἰερουσαλήμ, μὴ κλαίετε ἐπ'
Daughters of Jerusalem, do not weep over

ἐμέ· πλὴν ἐφ' ἑαυτὰς κλαίετε καὶ ἐπὶ
me; but over yourselves weep and over

τὰ τέκνα ὑμῶν, **29** ὅτι ἰδοὺ ἔρχονται
the children of you, because behold come

ἡμέραι ἐν αἷς ἐροῦσιν· μακάριαι αἱ
days in which they will say : Blessed the

στεῖραι, καὶ αἱ κοιλίαι αἳ οὐκ ἐγέννησαν,
barren, and the wombs which bare not,

καὶ μαστοὶ οἳ οὐκ ἔθρεψαν. **30** τότε
and breasts which gave not suck. Then

ἄρξονται λέγειν τοῖς ὄρεσιν· πέσατε ἐφ'
they will begin to say to the mountains : Fall on

ἡμᾶς, καὶ τοῖς βουνοῖς· καλύψατε ἡμᾶς·
us, and to the hills : Cover us;

31 ὅτι εἰ ἐν ὑγρῷ ξύλῳ ταῦτα ποιοῦσιν,
because if in ²full of sap ¹a tree these things they do,

ἐν τῷ ξηρῷ τί γένηται; **32** Ἤγοντο δὲ
in the dry what may happen? And were led

καὶ ἕτεροι κακοῦργοι δύο σὺν αὐτῷ
also others* criminals two with him

ἀναιρεθῆναι. **33** Καὶ ὅτε ἦλθον ἐπὶ τὸν
to be killed. And when they came upon the

τόπον τὸν καλούμενον Κρανίον, ἐκεῖ ἐσταύ-
place – *being* called Skull, there they

ρωσαν αὐτὸν καὶ τοὺς κακούργους, ὃν μὲν
crucified him and the criminals, one†

ἐκ δεξιῶν ὃν δὲ ἐξ ἀριστερῶν. **34** [ὁ δὲ
on [the] right and one† on [the] left. – And

Ἰησοῦς ἔλεγεν· πάτερ, ἄφες αὐτοῖς· οὐ
Jesus said : Father, forgive them; ³not

γὰρ οἴδασιν τί ποιοῦσιν.] διαμεριζόμενοι
¹for ²they know what they are doing. dividing

δὲ τὰ ἱμάτια αὐτοῦ ἔβαλον κλήρους.
And the garments of him they cast lots.

35 καὶ εἱστήκει ὁ λαὸς θεωρῶν. ἐξεμυκ-
And stood the people beholding. scoff-

τήριζον δὲ καὶ οἱ ἄρχοντες λέγοντες·
ed And also the rulers saying :

ἄλλους ἔσωσεν, σωσάτω ἑαυτόν, εἰ οὗτός
Others he saved, let him save himself, if this man

ἐστιν ὁ χριστὸς τοῦ θεοῦ ὁ ἐκλεκτός.
is the Christ – of God the chosen [one].

36 ἐνέπαιξαν δὲ αὐτῷ καὶ οἱ στρατιῶται
And mocked him also the soldiers

προσερχόμενοι, ὄξος προσφέροντες αὐτῷ
approaching, vinegar offering *to* him

***** **Luke uses ἕτεροι here with strict accuracy = "different." Jesus was not himself a criminal. Note punctuation of A.V. *Cf.* Acts 28. 1.**

The Crucifixion

26As they led him away,
they seized Simon from
Cyrene, who was on his
way in from the country,
and put the cross on him
and made him carry it be-
hind Jesus. 27A large number of people followed him,
including women who
mourned and wailed for
him. 28Jesus turned and
said to them, "Daughters
of Jerusalem, do not weep
for me; weep for your-
selves and for your chil-
dren. 29For the time will
come when you will say,
'Blessed are the barren
women, the wombs that
never bore and the breasts
that never nursed!' 30Then

"'they will say to the mountains, "Fall on us!"
and to the hills, "Cover us!"'[m]

31For if men do these things
when the tree is green,
what will happen when it is
dry?"
32Two other men, both
criminals, were also led out
with him to be executed.
33When they came to the
place called the Skull, there
they crucified him, along
with the criminals—one on
his right, the other on his
left. 34Jesus said, "Father,
forgive them, for they do
not know what they are doing."[n] And they divided up
his clothes by casting lots.
35The people stood
watching, and the rulers
even sneered at him. They
said, "He saved others; let
him save himself if he is the
Christ of God, the Chosen
One."
36The soldiers also came
up and mocked him. They
offered him wine vinegar

[m] *30* Hosea 10:8
[n] *34* Some early manuscripts do not have this sentence.

saying, "If you are the King
of the Jews, save yourself!"
38 There was also an in-
scription over him,[k] "This
is the King of the Jews."
39 One of the criminals
who were hanged there
kept deriding[l] him and
saying, "Are you not the
Messiah?[j] Save yourself
and us!" 40 But the other rebuked him, saying, "Do
you not fear God, since you
are under the same sen-
tence of condemnation?
41 And we indeed have been
condemned justly, for we
are getting what we de-
serve for our deeds, but
this man has done nothing
wrong." 42 Then he said,
"Jesus, remember me when
you come into[m] your kingdom." 43 He replied, "Truly
I tell you, today you will be
with me in Paradise."

The Death of Jesus

44 It was now about
noon, and darkness came
over the whole land[n] until
three in the afternoon,
45 while the sun's light
failed;[o] and the curtain of
the temple was torn in two.
46 Then Jesus, crying with a
loud voice, said, "Father,
into your hands I commend
my spirit." Having said
this, he breathed his last.
47 When the centurion saw
what had taken place, he
praised God and said,
"Certainly this man was innocent."[p] 48 And when all
the crowds who had gath-
ered there for this spectacle
saw what had taken place,
they returned home, beat-
ing their breasts. 49 But all
his acquaintances, including the women who had followed him from Galilee,
stood at a distance, watching these things.

The Burial of Jesus

50 Now there was a
good and righteous man
named Joseph, who,
though a member of the

[k] Other ancient authorities add *written in Greek and Latin and Hebrew* (that is, *Aramaic*)
[l] Or *blaspheming*
[m] Other ancient authorities read *in*
[n] Or *earth*
[o] Or *the sun was eclipsed*. Other ancient authorities read *the sun was darkened*
[p] Or *righteous*

37 καὶ λέγοντες· εἰ σὺ εἶ ὁ βασιλεὺς
and saying : If thou art the king
τῶν Ἰουδαίων, σῶσον σεαυτόν. **38** ἦν δὲ
of the Jews, save thyself. And there was
καὶ ἐπιγραφὴ ἐπ' αὐτῷ· Ο ΒΑΣΙΛΕΥΣ
also a superscription over him : THE KING
ΤΩΝ ΙΟΥΔΑΙΩΝ ΟΥΤΟΣ. **39** Εἷς δὲ
OF THE JEWS THIS. And one
τῶν κρεμασθέντων κακούργων ἐβλασφήμει
of the hanged criminals blasphemed
αὐτόν· οὐχὶ σὺ εἶ ὁ χριστός; σῶσον
him : Not thou art the Christ? save
σεαυτὸν καὶ ἡμᾶς **40** ἀποκριθεὶς δὲ ὁ
thyself and us. But answering the
ἕτερος ἐπιτιμῶν αὐτῷ ἔφη· οὐδὲ φοβῇ σὺ
other rebuking him said : Not fearest thou
τὸν θεόν, ὅτι ἐν τῷ αὐτῷ κρίματι εἶ;
– God, because in the same judgment thou art?
41 καὶ ἡμεῖς μὲν δικαίως, ἄξια γὰρ ὧν
And we indeed justly, for things worthy of what
ἐπράξαμεν ἀπολαμβάνομεν· οὗτος δὲ οὐδὲν
we did we receive back; but this man nothing
ἄτοπον ἔπραξεν. **42** καὶ ἔλεγεν Ἰησοῦ,
amiss did. And he said : Jesus,
μνήσθητί μου ὅταν ἔλθῃς εἰς τὴν βασιλείαν
remember me when thou comest into the kingdom
σου. **43** καὶ εἶπεν αὐτῷ· ἀμήν σοι λέγω,
of thee. And he said to him. Truly thee I tell,
σήμερον μετ' ἐμοῦ ἔσῃ ἐν τῷ παραδείσῳ.
to-day with me thou wilt be in the paradise.
44 Καὶ ἦν ἤδη ὡσεὶ ὥρα ἕκτη καὶ
And it was now about hour sixth and
σκότος ἐγένετο ἐφ' ὅλην τὴν γῆν ἕως
darkness came over all the land until
ὥρας ἐνάτης **45** τοῦ ἡλίου ἐκλιπόντος·
hour ninth the sun failing;[a]
=as the sun failed;
ἐσχίσθη δὲ τὸ καταπέτασμα τοῦ ναοῦ
and was torn the veil of the shrine
μέσον. **46** καὶ φωνήσας φωνῇ μεγάλῃ ὁ
in the middle. And crying voice with a great –
Ἰησοῦς εἶπεν· πάτερ, εἰς χεῖράς σου
Jesus said : Father, into hands of thee
παρατίθεμαι τὸ πνεῦμά μου. τοῦτο δὲ
I commit the spirit of me. And this
εἰπὼν ἐξέπνευσεν. **47** ἰδὼν δὲ ὁ ἑκατον-
saying he expired. And [3]seeing [1]the [2]cen-
τάρχης τὸ γενόμενον ἐδόξαζεν τὸν θεὸν
turion the thing happening glorified – God
λέγων· ὄντως ὁ ἄνθρωπος οὗτος δίκαιος
saying : Really – man this righteous
ἦν. **48** καὶ πάντες οἱ συμπαραγενόμενοι
was. And all [1]the [3]arriving together
ὄχλοι ἐπὶ τὴν θεωρίαν ταύτην, θεωρήσαντες τὰ
[2]crowds at – sight this, beholding the things
γενόμενα, τύπτοντες τὰ στήθη ὑπέστρεφον.
happening, smiting the(ir) breasts returned.
49 εἱστήκεισαν δὲ πάντες οἱ γνωστοὶ αὐτῷ
And [5]stood [1]all [2]the [ones] [3]known [4]to him
ἀπὸ μακρόθεν, καὶ γυναῖκες αἱ συνακο-
[6]afar off, and women the [ones] accom-
λουθοῦσαι αὐτῷ ἀπὸ τῆς Γαλιλαίας, ὁρῶσαι
panying him from – Galilee, seeing
ταῦτα.
these things.
50 Καὶ ἰδοὺ ἀνὴρ ὀνόματι Ἰωσὴφ
And behold[,] a man by name Joseph

37and said, "If you are the
king of the Jews, save yourself."
38There was a written no-
tice above him, which read:
THIS IS THE KING OF THE
JEWS.
39One of the criminals
who hung there hurled in-
sults at him: "Aren't you
the Christ? Save yourself
and us!"
40But the other criminal
rebuked him. "Don't you
fear God," he said, "since
you are under the same
sentence? 41We are pun-
ished justly, for we are getting what our deeds de-
serve. But this man has
done nothing wrong."
42Then he said, "Jesus,
remember me when you
come into your king-
dom.[o]"
43Jesus answered him, "I
tell you the truth, today
you will be with me in paradise."

Jesus' Death

44It was now about the
sixth hour, and darkness
came over the whole land
until the ninth hour, 45for
the sun stopped shining.
And the curtain of the temple was torn in two. 46Jesus
called out with a loud
voice, "Father, into your
hands I commit my spirit."
When he had said this, he
breathed his last.
47The centurion, seeing
what had happened,
praised God and said,
"Surely this was a right-
eous man." 48When all the
people who had gathered to
witness this sight saw what
took place, they beat their
breasts and went away.
49But all those who knew
him, including the women
who had followed him from
Galilee, stood at a distance,
watching these things.

Jesus' Burial

50Now there was a man
named Joseph, a member

[o]42 Some manuscripts *come with your kingly power*

council, 51 had not agreed
to their plan and action. He
came from the Jewish town
of Arimathea, and he was
waiting expectantly for the
kingdom of God. 52 This
man went to Pilate and
asked for the body of Jesus.
53 Then he took it down,
wrapped it in a linen cloth,
and laid it in a rock-hewn
tomb where no one had
ever been laid. 54 It was the
day of Preparation, and the
sabbath was beginning.[q]
55 The women who had
come with him from Galilee
followed, and they saw the
tomb and how his body was
laid. 56 Then they returned,
and prepared spices and
ointments.

On the sabbath they rested according to the commandment.

Chapter 24

The Resurrection of Jesus

BUT on the first day of
the week, at early
dawn, they came to the
tomb, taking the spices that
they had prepared. 2 They
found the stone rolled away
from the tomb, 3 but when
they went in, they did not
find the body.[r] 4 While
they were perplexed about
this, suddenly two men in
dazzling clothes stood beside them. 5 The women[s]
were terrified and bowed
their faces to the ground,
but the men[t] said to them,
"Why do you look for the
living among the dead? He
is not here, but has risen.[u]
6 Remember how he told
you, while he was still in
Galilee, 7 that the Son of
Man must be handed over
to sinners, and be cruci-
fied, and on the third day

[q] Gk *was dawning*
[r] Other ancient authorities add *of the Lord Jesus*
[s] Gk *They*
[t] Gk *but they*
[u] Other ancient authorities lack *He is not here, but has risen*

βουλευτὴς ὑπάρχων, ἀνὴρ ἀγαθὸς καὶ
a councillor being, a man good and
δίκαιος, — 51 οὗτος οὐκ ἦν συγκατατεθειμένος
righteous, — this man was not agreeing with
τῇ βουλῇ καὶ τῇ πράξει αὐτῶν, — ἀπὸ
the counsel and the action of them, — from
Ἁριμαθαίας πόλεως τῶν Ἰουδαίων, ὃς
Arimathæa a city of the Jews, who
προσεδέχετο τὴν βασιλείαν τοῦ θεοῦ,
was awaiting the kingdom – of God,
52 οὗτος προσελθὼν τῷ Πιλάτῳ ᾐτήσατο
this man approaching – *to* Pilate asked
τὸ σῶμα τοῦ Ἰησοῦ, 53 καὶ καθελὼν
the body – of Jesus, and taking down
ἐνετύλιξεν αὐτὸ σινδόνι, καὶ ἔθηκεν αὐτὸν
wrapped it in linen, and placed him
ἐν μνήματι λαξευτῷ, οὗ οὐκ ἦν οὐδεὶς
in tomb a hewn, where was not no(any)one
οὔπω κείμενος. 54 καὶ ἡμέρα ἦν παρασκευῆς,
not yet laid. And day it was of preparation,
καὶ σάββατον ἐπέφωσκεν. 55 Κατακολουθήσασαι
and a sabbath was coming on. 4following after
δὲ αἱ γυναῖκες, αἵτινες ἦσαν συνεληλυθυῖαι
1And 2the 3women, who were 1having come *with*
ἐκ τῆς Γαλιλαίας αὐτῷ, ἐθεάσαντο τὸ
3out of – 4Galilee 2with him, beheld the
μνημεῖον καὶ ὡς ἐτέθη τὸ σῶμα αὐτοῦ,
tomb and how was placed the body of him,
56 ὑποστρέψασαι δὲ ἡτοίμασαν ἀρώματα καὶ
and returning prepared spices and
μύρα.
ointment.

Καὶ τὸ μὲν σάββατον ἡσύχασαν κατὰ
And [on] the 2indeed 1sabbath they rested according to
τὴν ἐντολήν. 24 τῇ δὲ μιᾷ τῶν σαββάτων
the commandment. But on the one of the week
ὄρθρου βαθέως ἐπὶ τὸ μνῆμα ἦλθον φέρουσαι
while still very early† upon the tomb they came carrying
ἃ ἡτοίμασαν ἀρώματα. 2 εὗρον δὲ τὸν
2which 3they prepared 1spices. And they found the
λίθον ἀποκεκυλισμένον ἀπὸ τοῦ μνημείου,
stone *having been* rolled away from the tomb,
3 εἰσελθοῦσαι δὲ οὐχ εὗρον τὸ σῶμα
and entering they found not the body
τοῦ κυρίου Ἰησοῦ. 4 καὶ ἐγένετο ἐν τῷ
of the Lord Jesus. And it was in the
=as they were perplexed
ἀπορεῖσθαι αὐτὰς περὶ τούτου καὶ ἰδοὺ
to be perplexed them[be] about this *and* behold[,]
ἄνδρες δύο ἐπέστησαν αὐταῖς ἐν ἐσθῆτι
men two stood by them in clothing
ἀστραπτούσῃ· 5 ἐμφόβων δὲ γενομένων
shining; and terrified becoming
=as they became terrified and bent their faces
αὐτῶν καὶ κλινουσῶν τὰ πρόσωπα εἰς τὴν
them and bending the(ir) faces to the
γῆν, εἶπαν πρὸς αὐτάς· τί ζητεῖτε τὸν
earth, they said to them: Why seek ye the
ζῶντα μετὰ τῶν νεκρῶν; 6 [οὐκ ἔστιν
living [one] with the dead [ones]? He is not
ὧδε, ἀλλὰ ἠγέρθη.] μνήσθητε ὡς ἐλάλησεν
here, but was raised. Remember how he spoke
ὑμῖν ἔτι ὢν ἐν τῇ Γαλιλαίᾳ, 7 λέγων
to you yet being in – Galilee, saying[,]
τὸν υἱὸν τοῦ ἀνθρώπου ὅτι δεῖ παραδο-
The Son – of man – it behoves to be de-
θῆναι εἰς χεῖρας ἀνθρώπων ἁμαρτωλῶν καὶ
livered into hands men of sinful and

of the Council, a good and
upright man, 51 who had not
consented to their decision
and action. He came from
the Judean town of Arima-
thea and he was waiting for
the kingdom of God. 52 Going to Pilate, he asked for
Jesus' body. 53 Then he
took it down, wrapped it in
linen cloth and placed it in a
tomb cut in the rock, one in
which no one had yet been
laid. 54 It was Preparation
Day, and the Sabbath was
about to begin.

55 The women who had
come with Jesus from Galilee followed Joseph and
saw the tomb and how his
body was laid in it. 56 Then
they went home and pre-
pared spices and perfumes.
But they rested on the Sabbath in obedience to the
commandment.

Chapter 24

The Resurrection

ON the first day of the
week, very early in
the morning, the women
took the spices they had
prepared and went to the
tomb. 2 They found the
stone rolled away from the
tomb, 3 but when they en-
tered, they did not find the
body of the Lord Jesus.
4 While they were wonder-
ing about this, suddenly
two men in clothes that
gleamed like lightning
stood beside them. 5 In their
fright the women bowed
down with their faces to the
ground, but the men said to
them, "Why do you look
for the living among the
dead? 6 He is not here; he
has risen! Remember how
he told you, while he was
still with you in Galilee:
7 'The Son of Man must be
delivered into the hands of

rise again." 8Then they remembered his words, 9and
returning from the tomb,
they told all this to the elev-
en and to all the rest.
10Now it was Mary Magda-
lene, Joanna, Mary the
mother of James, and the
other women with them
who told this to the apostles. 11But these words
seemed to them an idle tale,
and they did not believe
them. 12But Peter got up
and ran to the tomb; stooping and looking in, he saw
the linen cloths by them-
selves; then he went home,
amazed at what had hap-
pened.[v]

The Walk to Emmaus

13 Now on that same
day two of them were going
to a village called Emmaus,
about seven miles[w] from
Jerusalem, 14and talking
with each other about all
these things that had happened. 15While they were
talking and discussing,
Jesus himself came near
and went with them, 16but
their eyes were kept from
recognizing him. 17And he
said to them, "What are
you discussing with each
other while you walk
along?" They stood still,
looking sad.[x] 18Then one
of them, whose name was
Cleopas, answered him,
"Are you the only stranger
in Jerusalem who does not
know the things that have
taken place there in these
days?" 19He asked them,
"What things?" They re-
plied, "The things about
Jesus of Nazareth,[y] who
was a prophet mighty in
deed and word before God
and all the people, 20and
how our chief priests and
leaders handed him over to
be condemned to death and

[v] Other ancient authorities lack verse 12
[w] Gk *sixty stadia;* other ancient authorities read *a hundred sixty stadia*
[x] Other ancient authorities read *walk along, looking sad?"*
[y] Other ancient authorities read *Jesus the Nazorean*

σταυρωθῆναι καὶ τῇ τρίτῃ ἡμέρᾳ ἀναστῆναι.
to be crucified and on the third day to rise again.

8 καὶ ἐμνήσθησαν τῶν ῥημάτων αὐτοῦ,
And they remembered the words of him,

9 καὶ ὑποστρέψασαι ἀπὸ τοῦ μνημείου
and returning from the tomb

ἀπήγγειλαν ταῦτα πάντα τοῖς ἕνδεκα καὶ
reported these things all to the eleven and

πᾶσιν τοῖς λοιποῖς. 10 ἦσαν δὲ ἡ
to all the rest. Now they were the

Μαγδαληνὴ Μαρία καὶ Ἰωάννα καὶ Μαρία
Magdalene Mary and Joanna and Mary

ἡ Ἰακώβου· καὶ αἱ λοιπαὶ* σὺν αὐταῖς*
the [mother] of James; and the rest with them

ἔλεγον πρὸς τοὺς ἀποστόλους ταῦτα. 11 καὶ
told to the apostles these things. And

ἐφάνησαν ἐνώπιον αὐτῶν ὡσεὶ λῆρος
seemed before them as folly

τὰ ῥήματα ταῦτα, καὶ ἠπίστουν αὐταῖς.* ‡
– words these, and they disbelieved them.

13 Καὶ ἰδοὺ δύο ἐξ αὐτῶν ἐν αὐτῇ τῇ
And behold[,] two of them on same the

ἡμέρᾳ ἦσαν πορευόμενοι εἰς κώμην ἀπέχουσαν
day were journeying to a village being distant

σταδίους ἑξήκοντα ἀπὸ Ἰερουσαλήμ, ᾗ
furlongs sixty from Jerusalem, to which

ὄνομα Ἐμμαοῦς, 14 καὶ αὐτοὶ ὡμίλουν
name Emmaus, and they talked

πρὸς ἀλλήλους περὶ πάντων τῶν συμβεβηκότων
to each other about all – ²having occurred

τούτων. 15 καὶ ἐγένετο ἐν τῷ ὁμιλεῖν
¹these things. And it came to pass in the to talk

αὐτοὺς καὶ συζητεῖν, καὶ αὐτὸς Ἰησοῦς
them and to discuss[be], *and* [him]self Jesus
=as they talked and discussed,

ἐγγίσας συνεπορεύετο αὐτοῖς· 16 οἱ δὲ
drawing near journeyed with them; but the

ὀφθαλμοὶ αὐτῶν ἐκρατοῦντο τοῦ μὴ
eyes of them were held – not

ἐπιγνῶναι αὐτόν. 17 εἶπεν δὲ πρὸς αὐτούς·
to recognize[d] him. And he said to them:

τίνες οἱ λόγοι οὗτοι οὓς ἀντιβάλλετε
What – words these which ye exchange

πρὸς ἀλλήλους περιπατοῦντες; καὶ ἐστάθησαν
with each other walking? And they stood

σκυθρωποί. 18 ἀποκριθεὶς δὲ εἷς ὀνόματι
sad-faced. And answering one by name

Κλεοπᾶς εἶπεν πρὸς αὐτόν· σὺ μόνος
Cleopas said to him: Thou only

παροικεῖς Ἰερουσαλὴμ καὶ οὐκ ἔγνως τὰ
a stranger in Jerusalem and knewest not the things

γενόμενα ἐν αὐτῇ ἐν ταῖς ἡμέραις ταύταις;
happening in it in – days these?

19 καὶ εἶπεν αὐτοῖς· ποῖα; οἱ δὲ εἶπαν
And he said to them: What things? And they said

αὐτῷ· τὰ περὶ Ἰησοῦ τοῦ Ναζαρηνοῦ, ὃς
to him: The things about Jesus the Nazarene, who

ἐγένετο ἀνὴρ προφήτης δυνατὸς ἐν ἔργῳ
was a *man* prophet powerful in work

καὶ λόγῳ ἐναντίον τοῦ θεοῦ καὶ παντὸς
and word before – God and all

τοῦ λαοῦ, 20 ὅπως τε παρέδωκαν αὐτὸν οἱ
the people, how both ⁷delivered ⁸him ¹the

ἀρχιερεῖς καὶ οἱ ἄρχοντες ἡμῶν εἰς
²chief priests ³and ⁴the ⁵rulers ⁶of us to

* Note the feminines.
‡ Verse 12 omitted by Nestle.

sinful men, be crucified and
on the third day be raised
again.'" 8Then they re-
membered his words.
9When they came back
from the tomb, they told all
these things to the Eleven
and to all the others. 10It
was Mary Magdalene, Jo-
anna, Mary the mother of
James, and the others with
them who told this to the
apostles. 11But they did not
believe the women, be-
cause their words seemed
to them like nonsense.
12Peter, however, got up
and ran to the tomb. Bending over, he saw the strips
of linen lying by them-
selves, and he went away,
wondering to himself what
had happened.

On the Road to Emmaus

13Now that same day two
of them were going to a village called Emmaus, about
seven miles[p] from Jerusalem. 14They were talking
with each other about ev-
erything that had hap-
pened. 15As they talked and
discussed these things with
each other, Jesus himself
came up and walked along
with them; 16but they were
kept from recognizing him.
17He asked them, "What
are you discussing together
as you walk along?"
They stood still, their
faces downcast. 18One of
them, named Cleopas,
asked him, "Are you only a
visitor to Jerusalem and do
not know the things that
have happened there in
these days?"
19"What things?" he
asked.
"About Jesus of Naza-
reth," they replied. "He
was a prophet, powerful in
word and deed before God
and all the people. 20The
chief priests and our rulers
handed him over to be sen-

[p] 13 Greek *sixty stadia* (about 11 kilometers)

crucified him. 21But we
had hoped that he was the
one to redeem Israel.[z]
Yes, and besides all this, it
is now the third day since
these things took place.
22Moreover, some women
of our group astounded us.
They were at the tomb early this morning, 23and
when they did not find his
body there, they came back
and told us that they had
indeed seen a vision of angels who said that he was
alive. 24Some of those who
were with us went to the
tomb and found it just as
the women had said; but
they did not see him."
25Then he said to them,
"Oh, how foolish you are,
and how slow of heart to
believe all that the prophets
have declared! 26Was it not
necessary that the Messi-
ah[a] should suffer these
things and then enter into
his glory?" 27Then begin-
ning with Moses and all the
prophets, he interpreted to
them the things about himself in all the scriptures.
28 As they came near
the village to which they
were going, he walked
ahead as if he were going
on. 29But they urged him
strongly, saying, "Stay
with us, because it is almost evening and the day is
now nearly over." So he
went in to stay with them.
30When he was at the table
with them, he took bread,
blessed and broke it, and
gave it to them. 31Then
their eyes were opened,
and they recognized him;
and he vanished from their
sight. 32They said to each
other, "Were not our hearts

[z] Or *to set Israel free*
[a] Or *the Christ*

κρίμα θανάτου καὶ ἐσταύρωσαν αὐτόν.
[the] judgment of death and crucified him.
21 ἡμεῖς δὲ ἠλπίζομεν ὅτι αὐτός ἐστιν
But we were hoping that he it is(was)
ὁ μέλλων λυτροῦσθαι τὸν Ἰσραήλ· ἀλλά
the [one] being about to redeem – Israel; but
γε καὶ σὺν πᾶσιν τούτοις τρίτην ταύτην
– also with all these things third this
=this is the third day
ἡμέραν ἄγει ἀφ' οὗ ταῦτα ἐγένετο.
day it leads since these things happened.
22 ἀλλὰ καὶ γυναῖκές τινες ἐξ ἡμῶν
But also [2]women [1]some of us
ἐξέστησαν ἡμᾶς, γενόμεναι ὀρθριναὶ ἐπὶ τὸ
astonished us, being early at the
μνημεῖον, 23 καὶ μὴ εὑροῦσαι τὸ σῶμα
tomb, and not finding the body
αὐτοῦ ἦλθον λέγουσαι καὶ ὀπτασίαν ἀγγέλων
of him came saying also a vision of angels
ἑωρακέναι, οἳ λέγουσιν αὐτὸν ζῆν. 24 καὶ
to have seen, who say him to live. And
=that he lives.
ἀπῆλθόν τινες τῶν σὺν ἡμῖν ἐπὶ τὸ
[5]went [1]some [2]of the [ones] [3]with [4]us to the
μνημεῖον, καὶ εὗρον οὕτως καθὼς καὶ αἱ
tomb, and found so as indeed the
γυναῖκες εἶπον, αὐτὸν δὲ οὐκ εἶδον.
women said, but him they saw not.
25 καὶ αὐτὸς εἶπεν πρὸς αὐτούς· ὦ
And he said to them: O
ἀνόητοι καὶ βραδεῖς τῇ καρδίᾳ τοῦ πιστεύειν
foolish [ones] and slow – in heart – to believe[d]
ἐπὶ πᾶσιν οἷς ἐλάλησαν οἱ προφῆται·
on(in) all things which spoke the prophets:
26 οὐχὶ ταῦτα ἔδει παθεῖν τὸν χριστὸν καὶ
[2]not [6]these things [1]behoved it [5]to suffer [3]the [4]Christ and
εἰσελθεῖν εἰς τὴν δόξαν αὐτοῦ; 27 καὶ
to enter into the glory of him? And
ἀρξάμενος ἀπὸ Μωϋσέως καὶ ἀπὸ πάντων
beginning from Moses and from all
τῶν προφητῶν διηρμήνευσεν αὐτοῖς ἐν
the prophets he explained to them in
πάσαις ταῖς γραφαῖς τὰ περὶ ἑαυτοῦ.
all the scriptures the things concerning himself.
28 Καὶ ἤγγισαν εἰς τὴν κώμην οὗ
And they drew near to the village whither
ἐπορεύοντο, καὶ αὐτὸς προσεποιήσατο
they were journeying, and he pretended
πορρώτερον πορεύεσθαι. 29 καὶ παρε-
farther to journey. And they
βιάσαντο αὐτὸν λέγοντες· μεῖνον μεθ'
urged him saying: Remain with
ἡμῶν, ὅτι πρὸς ἑσπέραν ἐστὶν καὶ κέκλικεν
us, because toward evening it is and has declined
ἤδη ἡ ἡμέρα. καὶ εἰσῆλθεν τοῦ μεῖναι
now the day. And he went in – to remain[d]
σὺν αὐτοῖς. 30 καὶ ἐγένετο ἐν τῷ
with them. And it came to pass in the
=as he reclined
κατακλιθῆναι αὐτὸν μετ' αὐτῶν λαβὼν τὸν
to recline him[be] with them taking the
ἄρτον εὐλόγησεν καὶ κλάσας ἐπεδίδου
loaf he blessed and having broken he handed
αὐτοῖς· 31 αὐτῶν δὲ διηνοίχθησαν οἱ
to them; and of them were opened up the
ὀφθαλμοί, καὶ ἐπέγνωσαν αὐτόν· καὶ αὐτὸς
eyes, and they recognized him; and he
ἄφαντος ἐγένετο ἀπ' αὐτῶν. 32 καὶ
invisible became from them. And

tenced to death, and they
crucified him; 21but we had
hoped that he was the one
who was going to redeem
Israel. And what is more, it
is the third day since all this
took place. 22In addition,
some of our women
amazed us. They went to
the tomb early this morning
23but didn't find his body.
They came and told us that
they had seen a vision of
angels, who said he was
alive. 24Then some of our
companions went to the
tomb and found it just as
the women had said, but
him they did not see."
25He said to them, "How
foolish you are, and how
slow of heart to believe all
that the prophets have spoken! 26Did not the Christ[a]
have to suffer these things
and then enter his glory?"
27And beginning with Mo-
ses and all the Prophets, he
explained to them what
was said in all the Scriptures concerning himself.
28As they approached the
village to which they were
going, Jesus acted as if he
were going farther. 29But
they urged him strongly,
"Stay with us, for it is nearly evening; the day is almost over." So he went in
to stay with them.
30When he was at the ta-
ble with them, he took
bread, gave thanks, broke
it and began to give it to
them. 31Then their eyes
were opened and they rec-
ognized him, and he disappeared from their sight.
32They asked each other,

[a]26 Or *Messiah*; also in verse 46

burning within us[b] while
he was talking to us on the
road, while he was opening
the scriptures to us?"
33 That same hour they got
up and returned to Jerusalem; and they found the
eleven and their compan-
ions gathered together.
34 They were saying, "The
Lord has risen indeed, and
he has appeared to Simon!"
35 Then they told what had
happened on the road, and
how he had been made
known to them in the
breaking of the bread.

Jesus Appears to His Disciples

36 While they were talk-
ing about this, Jesus himself stood among them and
said to them, "Peace be
with you."[c] 37 They were
startled and terrified, and
thought that they were seeing a ghost. 38 He said to
them, "Why are you frightened, and why do doubts
arise in your hearts?
39 Look at my hands and
my feet; see that it is I myself. Touch me and see; for
a ghost does not have flesh
and bones as you see that I
have." 40 And when he had
said this, he showed them
his hands and his feet.[d]
41 While in their joy they
were disbelieving and still
wondering, he said to
them, "Have you anything
here to eat?" 42 They gave
him a piece of broiled fish,
43 and he took it and ate in
their presence.
44 Then he said to them,
"These are my words that I
spoke to you while I was
still with you—that everything written about me in
the law of Moses, the
prophets, and the psalms
must be fulfilled." 45 Then
he opened their minds to
understand the scriptures,
46 and he said to them,
"Thus it is written, that the
Messiah[e] is to suffer and to

[b] Other ancient authorities lack *within us*
[c] Other ancient authorities lack *and said to them, "Peace be with you."*
[d] Other ancient authorities lack verse 40
[e] Or *the Christ*

εἶπαν πρὸς ἀλλήλους· οὐχὶ ἡ καρδία
they said to each other : Not the heart
ἡμῶν καιομένη ἦν ἐν ἡμῖν, ὡς ἐλάλει
of us burning was in us, as he spoke
ἡμῖν ἐν τῇ ὁδῷ, ὡς διήνοιγεν ἡμῖν τὰς
to us in the way, as he opened up to us the
γραφάς; 33 Καὶ ἀναστάντες αὐτῇ τῇ ὥρᾳ
scriptures? And rising up [2]same [1]in the hour
ὑπέστρεψαν εἰς Ἰερουσαλήμ, καὶ εὗρον
they returned to Jerusalem, and found
ἠθροισμένους τοὺς ἕνδεκα καὶ τοὺς σὺν
having been collected the eleven and the [ones] with
αὐτοῖς, 34 λέγοντας ὅτι ὄντως ἠγέρθη ὁ
them, saying[,] – Really was raised the
κύριος καὶ ὤφθη Σίμωνι. 35 καὶ αὐτοὶ ἐξηγοῦντο
Lord and appeared to Simon. And they related
τὰ ἐν τῇ ὁδῷ καὶ ὡς ἐγνώσθη
the things in the way and how he was known
αὐτοῖς ἐν τῇ κλάσει τοῦ ἄρτου. 36 Ταῦτα
by them in the breaking of the loaf. these things
δὲ αὐτῶν λαλούντων αὐτὸς ἔστη ἐν
And them saying[a] he stood in
=as they said these things
μέσῳ αὐτῶν. 37 πτοηθέντες δὲ καὶ
[the] midst of them. But scared and
ἔμφοβοι γενόμενοι ἐδόκουν πνεῦμα θεωρεῖν.
terrified becoming they thought a spirit to behold.
38 καὶ εἶπεν αὐτοῖς· τί τεταραγμένοι ἐστέ,
And he said to them : Why *having been* troubled are ye,
καὶ διὰ τί διαλογισμοὶ ἀναβαίνουσιν ἐν
and why thoughts come up in
τῇ καρδίᾳ ὑμῶν; 39 ἴδετε τὰς χεῖράς
the heart of you? See the hands
μου καὶ τοὺς πόδας μου, ὅτι ἐγώ εἰμι
of me and the feet of me, that I am
αὐτός· ψηλαφήσατέ με καὶ ἴδετε, ὅτι
[my]self; feel me and see, because
πνεῦμα σάρκα καὶ ὀστέα οὐκ ἔχει καθὼς
a spirit flesh and bones has not as
ἐμὲ θεωρεῖτε ἔχοντα.‡ 41 ἔτι δὲ ἀπιστούντων
me ye behold having. And yet disbelieving
=while they yet disbelieved
αὐτῶν ἀπὸ τῆς χαρᾶς καὶ θαυμαζόντων,
them[a] from the joy and marvelling[a],
εἶπεν αὐτοῖς· ἔχετέ τι βρώσιμον ἐνθάδε;
he said to them : Have ye any food here?
42 οἱ δὲ ἐπέδωκαν αὐτῷ ἰχθύος ὀπτοῦ
And they handed to him [3]fish [2]of a broiled
μέρος· 43 καὶ λαβὼν ἐνώπιον αὐτῶν ἔφαγεν.
[1]part; and taking before them he ate.
44 Εἶπεν δὲ πρὸς αὐτούς· οὗτοι οἱ λόγοι
And he said to them : These – words
μου οὓς ἐλάλησα πρὸς ὑμᾶς ἔτι ὢν σὺν
of me which I spoke to you yet being with
ὑμῖν, ὅτι δεῖ πληρωθῆναι πάντα τὰ
you, that it behoves to be fulfilled all the things
γεγραμμένα ἐν τῷ νόμῳ Μωϋσέως καὶ
having been written in the law of Moses and
τοῖς προφήταις καὶ ψαλμοῖς περὶ ἐμοῦ.
the prophets and psalms concerning me.
45 τότε διήνοιξεν αὐτῶν τὸν νοῦν τοῦ
Then he opened up of them the mind –
συνιέναι τὰς γραφάς· 46 καὶ εἶπεν αὐτοῖς
to understand[d] the scriptures; and said to them[,]
ὅτι οὕτως γέγραπται παθεῖν τὸν χριστὸν
– Thus it has been written [3]to suffer [1]the [2]Christ

‡ Verse 40 omitted by Nestle.

"Were not our hearts burning within us while he
talked with us on the road
and opened the Scriptures
to us?"
33 They got up and re-
turned at once to Jerusa-
lem. There they found the
Eleven and those with
them, assembled together
34 and saying, "It is true!
The Lord has risen and has
appeared to Simon."
35 Then the two told what
had happened on the way,
and how Jesus was recog-
nized by them when he
broke the bread.

Jesus Appears to the Disciples

36 While they were still
talking about this, Jesus
himself stood among them
and said to them, "Peace
be with you."
37 They were startled and
frightened, thinking they
saw a ghost. 38 He said to
them, "Why are you trou-
bled, and why do doubts
rise in your minds? 39 Look
at my hands and my feet. It
is I myself! Touch me and
see; a ghost does not have
flesh and bones, as you see
I have."
40 When he had said this,
he showed them his hands
and feet. 41 And while they
still did not believe it because of joy and amaze-
ment, he asked them, "Do
you have anything here to
eat?" 42 They gave him a
piece of broiled fish, 43 and
he took it and ate it in their
presence.
44 He said to them, "This
is what I told you while I
was still with you: Everything must be fulfilled that
is written about me in the
Law of Moses, the Proph-
ets and the Psalms."
45 Then he opened their
minds so they could understand the Scriptures. 46 He
told them, "This is what is
written: The Christ will suf-

rise from the dead on the
third day, 47 and that repentance and forgiveness of
sins is to be proclaimed in
his name to all nations,[f]
beginning from Jerusalem.
48 You are witnesses of
these things. 49 And see, I
am sending upon you what
my Father promised; so
stay here in the city until
you have been clothed with
power from on high."

The Ascension of Jesus

50 Then he led them out
as far as Bethany, and, lifting up his hands, he blessed
them. 51 While he was
blessing them, he withdrew
from them and was carried
up into heaven.[g] 52 And
they worshiped him, and[h]
returned to Jerusalem with
great joy; 53 and they were
continually in the temple
blessing God.[i]

καὶ ἀναστῆναι ἐκ νεκρῶν τῇ τρίτῃ ἡμέρᾳ,
and to rise again out of [the] dead on the third day,

47 καὶ κηρυχθῆναι ἐπὶ τῷ ὀνόματι αὐτοῦ
and to be proclaimed on(in) the name of him

μετάνοιαν εἰς ἄφεσιν ἁμαρτιῶν εἰς πάντα
repentance unto forgiveness of sins to all

τὰ ἔθνη, — ἀρξάμενοι ἀπὸ Ἰερουσαλήμ.
the nations, — beginning from Jerusalem.

48 ὑμεῖς μάρτυρες τούτων. **49** καὶ ἰδοὺ
Ye [are] witnesses of these things. And behold

ἐγὼ ἐξαποστέλλω τὴν ἐπαγγελίαν τοῦ
I send forth the promise of the

πατρός μου ἐφ' ὑμᾶς· ὑμεῖς δὲ καθίσατε
Father of me on you; but ye sit

ἐν τῇ πόλει ἕως οὗ ἐνδύσησθε ἐξ ὕψους
in the city until [1]ye are clothed[with][3]out of [4]height

δύναμιν.
[2]power.

50 Ἐξήγαγεν δὲ αὐτοὺς ἕως πρὸς
And he led out them until toward

Βηθανίαν, καὶ ἐπάρας τὰς χεῖρας αὐτοῦ
Bethany, and lifting up the hands of him

εὐλόγησεν αὐτούς. **51** καὶ ἐγένετο ἐν τῷ
he blessed them. And it came to pass in the

εὐλογεῖν αὐτὸν αὐτοὺς διέστη ἀπ' αὐτῶν.
to bless him[be] them he withdrew from them.
=while he blessed

52 καὶ αὐτοὶ ὑπέστρεψαν εἰς Ἰερουσαλὴμ
And they returned to Jerusalem

μετὰ χαρᾶς μεγάλης, **53** καὶ ἦσαν διὰ παντὸς
with joy great, and were continually

ἐν τῷ ἱερῷ εὐλογοῦντες τὸν θεόν.
in the temple blessing – God.

fer and rise from the dead
on the third day, 47 and repentance and forgiveness
of sins will be preached in
his name to all nations, beginning at Jerusalem.
48 You are witnesses of
these things. 49 I am going
to send you what my Fa-
ther has promised; but stay
in the city until you have
been clothed with power
from on high."

The Ascension

50 When he had led them
out to the vicinity of Bethany, he lifted up his hands
and blessed them. 51 While
he was blessing them, he
left them and was taken up
into heaven. 52 Then they
worshiped him and re-
turned to Jerusalem with
great joy. 53 And they
stayed continually at the
temple, praising God.

[f] Or *nations. Beginning from Jerusalem you are witnesses*
[g] Other ancient authorities lack *and was carried up into heaven*
[h] Other ancient authorities lack *worshiped him, and*
[i] Other ancient authorities add *Amen*

The Gospel According
to
John

Chapter 1

The Word Became Flesh

IN the beginning was the
Word, and the Word
was with God, and the
Word was God. 2 He was in
the beginning with God.
3 All things came into being
through him, and without
him not one thing came into
being. What has come into
being 4 in him was life,[a]
and the life was the light of
all people. 5 The light
shines in the darkness, and
the darkness did not overcome it.
6 There was a man sent
from God, whose name
was John. 7 He came as a
witness to testify to the
light, so that all might believe through him. 8 He
himself was not the light,
but he came to testify to the
light. 9 The true light, which
enlightens everyone, was
coming into the world.[b]
10 He was in the world,
and the world came into being through him; yet the
world did not know him.
11 He came to what was his
own,[c] and his own people
did not accept him. 12 But
to all who received him,
who believed in his name,
he gave power to become
children of God, 13 who
were born, not of blood or
of the will of the flesh or of
the will of man, but of God.
14 And the Word be-
came flesh and lived among
us, and we have seen his
glory, the glory as of a father's only son,[d] full of
grace and truth. 15 (John
testified to him and cried
out, "This was he of whom
I said, 'He who comes after
me ranks ahead of me be-

[a] Or [3] *through him. And without him not one thing came into being that has come into being.* [4] *In him was life*
[b] Or *He was the true light that enlightens everyone coming into the world*
[c] Or *to his own home*
[d] Or *the Father's only Son*

ΚΑΤΑ ΙΩΑΝΝΗΝ
According to John

1 Ἐν ἀρχῇ ἦν ὁ λόγος, καὶ ὁ λόγος
In [the] beginning was the Word, and the Word
ἦν πρὸς τὸν θεόν, καὶ θεὸς ἦν ὁ λόγος.
was with – God, and God was the Word.*
2 οὗτος ἦν ἐν ἀρχῇ πρὸς τὸν θεόν.
This one was in [the] beginning with – God.
3 πάντα δι' αὐτοῦ ἐγένετο, καὶ χωρὶς
All things through him became, and without
αὐτοῦ ἐγένετο οὐδὲ ἕν ὃ γέγονεν. 4 ἐν
him became not one thing which has become. In
αὐτῷ ζωὴ ἦν, καὶ ἡ ζωὴ ἦν τὸ φῶς
him life was, and the life was the light
τῶν ἀνθρώπων· 5 καὶ τὸ φῶς ἐν τῇ
– of men; and the light in the
σκοτίᾳ φαίνει, καὶ ἡ σκοτία αὐτὸ οὐ
darkness shines, and the darkness it not
κατέλαβεν. 6 Ἐγένετο ἄνθρωπος, ἀπεσταλμένος
overtook. There was a man, *having been* sent
παρὰ θεοῦ, ὄνομα αὐτῷ Ἰωάννης· 7 οὗτος
from God, name to him[e] John; this man
ἦλθεν εἰς μαρτυρίαν, ἵνα μαρτυρήσῃ περὶ
came for witness, that he might witness concerning
τοῦ φωτός, ἵνα πάντες πιστεύσωσιν δι'
the light, that all men might believe through
αὐτοῦ. 8 οὐκ ἦν ἐκεῖνος τὸ φῶς, ἀλλ' ἵνα
him. He was not that – light, but that
μαρτυρήσῃ περὶ τοῦ φωτός. 9 Ἦν τὸ φῶς
he might witness concerning the light. It was the light
τὸ ἀληθινόν, ὃ φωτίζει πάντα ἄνθρωπον,
– true, which enlightens every man,
ἐρχόμενον εἰς τὸν κόσμον. 10 ἐν τῷ
coming into the world. In the
κόσμῳ ἦν, καὶ ὁ κόσμος δι' αὐτοῦ
world he was, and the world through him
ἐγένετο, καὶ ὁ κόσμος αὐτὸν οὐκ ἔγνω.
became, and the world him knew not.
11 εἰς τὰ ἴδια ἦλθεν, καὶ οἱ ἴδιοι αὐτὸν
To his own things he came, and his own people him
οὐ παρέλαβον. 12 ὅσοι δὲ ἔλαβον αὐτόν,
received not. But as many as received him,
ἔδωκεν αὐτοῖς ἐξουσίαν τέκνα θεοῦ γεν-
he gave to them right children of God to be-
έσθαι, τοῖς πιστεύουσιν εἰς τὸ ὄνομα αὐτοῦ,
come, to the [ones] believing in the name of him,
13 οἳ οὐκ ἐξ αἱμάτων οὐδὲ ἐκ θελήματος
who not of bloods nor of [the] will
σαρκὸς οὐδὲ ἐκ θελήματος ἀνδρὸς ἀλλ'
of [the] flesh nor of [the] will of a man but
ἐκ θεοῦ ἐγεννήθησαν. 14 Καὶ ὁ λόγος
of God were born. And the Word
σὰρξ ἐγένετο καὶ ἐσκήνωσεν ἐν ἡμῖν,
flesh became and tabernacled among us,
καὶ ἐθεασάμεθα τὴν δόξαν αὐτοῦ, δόξαν
and we beheld the glory of him, glory
ὡς μονογενοῦς παρὰ πατρός, πλήρης χάριτος
as of an only begotten from a father, full of grace
καὶ ἀληθείας. 15 Ἰωάννης μαρτυρεῖ περὶ
and of truth. John witnesses concerning
αὐτοῦ καὶ κέκραγεν λέγων· οὗτος ἦν ὃν
him and has cried out saying: This man was he whom
εἶπον· ὁ ὀπίσω μου ἐρχόμενος ἔμπροσθέν
I said: The [one] after me coming before

* But note that the subject has the article and the predicate has it not; hence translate—"the Word was God."

John

Chapter 1

The Word Became Flesh

IN the beginning was the
Word, and the Word
was with God, and the
Word was God. 2He was
with God in the beginning.
3Through him all things
were made; without him
nothing was made that has
been made. 4In him was
life, and that life was the
light of men. 5The light
shines in the darkness, but
the darkness has not understood[a] it.
6There came a man who
was sent from God; his
name was John. 7He came
as a witness to testify concerning that light, so that
through him all men might
believe. 8He himself was
not the light; he came only
as a witness to the light.
9The true light that gives
light to every man was
coming into the world.[b]
10He was in the world,
and though the world was
made through him, the
world did not recognize
him. 11He came to that
which was his own, but his
own did not receive him.
12Yet to all who received
him, to those who believed
in his name, he gave the
right to become children of
God— 13children born not
of natural descent,[c] nor of
human decision or a hus-
band's will, but born of
God.
14The Word became flesh
and made his dwelling
among us. We have seen
his glory, the glory of the
One and Only,[d] who came
from the Father, full of
grace and truth.
15John testifies concern-
ing him. He cries out, saying, "This was he of whom
I said, 'He who comes after

[a] 5 Or *darkness, and the darkness has not overcome*
[b] 9 Or *This was the true light that gives light to every man who comes into the world*
[c] 13 Greek *of bloods*
[d] 14,18 Or *the Only Begotten*

cause he was before me.' ")
16 From his fullness we
have all received, grace
upon grace. 17 The law indeed was given through
Moses; grace and truth
came through Jesus Christ.
18 No one has ever seen
God. It is God the only
Son,[e] who is close to the
Father's heart,[f] who has
made him known.

The Testimony of John the Baptist

19 This is the testimony
given by John when the
Jews sent priests and Le-
vites from Jerusalem to ask
him, "Who are you?" 20 He
confessed and did not deny
it, but confessed, "I am not
the Messiah."[g] 21 And they
asked him, "What then?
Are you Elijah?" He said,
"I am not." "Are you the
prophet?" He answered,
"No." 22 Then they said to
him, "Who are you? Let us
have an answer for those
who sent us. What do you
say about yourself?" 23 He
said,

"I am the voice of
one crying out
in the
wilderness,
'Make straight the
way of
the Lord,' "

as the prophet Isaiah said.
24 Now they had been
sent from the Pharisees.
25 They asked him, "Why
then are you baptizing if
you are neither the Messiah,[g] nor Elijah, nor the
prophet?" 26 John an-
swered them, "I baptize
with water. Among you
stands one whom you do
not know, 27 the one who is
coming after me; I am not
worthy to untie the thong of
his sandal." 28 This took
place in Bethany across the
Jordan where John was
baptizing.

The Lamb of God

29 The next day he saw

[e] Other ancient authorities read *It is an only Son, God,* or *It is the only Son*
[f] Gk *bosom*
[g] Or *the Christ*

μου γέγονεν, ὅτι πρῶτός μου ἦν. 16 ὅτι
me has become, because first of me he was. Because
ἐκ τοῦ πληρώματος αὐτοῦ ἡμεῖς πάντες
of the fulness of him we all
ἐλάβομεν, καὶ χάριν ἀντὶ χάριτος· 17 ὅτι
received, and grace instead of grace; because
ὁ νόμος διὰ Μωϋσέως ἐδόθη, ἡ χάρις καὶ
the law through Moses was given, the grace and
ἡ ἀλήθεια διὰ Ἰησοῦ Χριστοῦ ἐγένετο.
the truth through Jesus Christ became.
18 Θεὸν οὐδεὶς ἑώρακεν πώποτε· μονογενὴς
God no man has seen never; [the] only begotten
θεὸς ὁ ὢν εἰς τὸν κόλπον τοῦ πατρός,
God the [one] being in the bosom of the Father,
ἐκεῖνος ἐξηγήσατο.
that one declared [?him].
19 Καὶ αὕτη ἐστὶν ἡ μαρτυρία τοῦ
And this is the witness –
Ἰωάννου, ὅτε ἀπέστειλαν πρὸς αὐτὸν οἱ
of John, when [3]sent [4]to [5]him [1]the
Ἰουδαῖοι ἐξ Ἱεροσολύμων ἱερεῖς καὶ Λευίτας
[2]Jews [9]from [10]Jerusalem [6]priests [7]and [8]Levites
ἵνα ἐρωτήσωσιν αὐτόν· σὺ τίς εἶ; 20 καὶ
that they might ask him: Thou who art? And
ὡμολόγησεν καὶ οὐκ ἠρνήσατο, καὶ
he confessed and denied not, and
ὡμολόγησεν ὅτι ἐγὼ οὐκ εἰμὶ ὁ χριστός.
he confessed[,] – I am not the Christ.
21 καὶ ἠρώτησαν αὐτόν· τί οὖν; Ἠλίας εἶ
And they asked him: What then? Elias art
σύ; καὶ λέγει· οὐκ εἰμί. ὁ προφήτης εἶ σύ;
thou? And he says: I am not. The prophet art thou?
καὶ ἀπεκρίθη· οὔ. 22 εἶπαν οὖν αὐτῷ·
And he answered: No. They said therefore to him:
τίς εἶ; ἵνα ἀπόκρισιν δῶμεν τοῖς
Who art thou? that an answer we may give to the [ones]
πέμψασιν ἡμᾶς· τί λέγεις περὶ σεαυτοῦ;
having sent us; What sayest thou concerning thyself?
23 ἔφη· ἐγὼ φωνὴ βοῶντος ἐν τῇ ἐρήμῳ·
He said: I [am] a voice of [one] crying in the desert:
εὐθύνατε τὴν ὁδὸν κυρίου, καθὼς εἶπεν
Make straight the way of [the] Lord, as said
Ἠσαΐας ὁ προφήτης. 24 Καὶ ἀπεσταλμένοι
Esaias the prophet. And [the ones] *having been* sent
ἦσαν ἐκ τῶν Φαρισαίων. 25 καὶ ἠρώτησαν
were of the Pharisees. And they asked
αὐτὸν καὶ εἶπαν αὐτῷ· τι οὖν βαπτίζεις
him and said to him: Why then baptizest thou
εἰ σὺ οὐκ εἶ ὁ χριστὸς οὐδὲ Ἠλίας
if thou art not the Christ nor Elias
οὐδὲ ὁ προφήτης; 26 ἀπεκρίθη αὐτοῖς ὁ
nor the prophet? Answered them –
Ἰωάννης λέγων· ἐγὼ βαπτίζω ἐν ὕδατι·
John saying: I baptize in water;
μέσος ὑμῶν στήκει ὃν ὑμεῖς οὐκ οἴδατε,
among you stands [one] whom ye know not,
27 ὁ ὀπίσω μου ἐρχόμενος, οὗ οὐκ εἰμὶ
the [one] after me coming, of whom am not
ἐγὼ ἄξιος ἵνα λύσω αὐτοῦ τὸν ἱμάντα
I worthy that I should loosen of him the thong
τοῦ ὑποδήματος. 28 Ταῦτα ἐν Βηθανίᾳ
of the sandal. These things in Bethany
ἐγένετο πέραν τοῦ Ἰορδάνου, ὅπου ἦν ὁ
happened beyond the Jordan, where was –
Ἰωάννης βαπτίζων. 29 Τῇ ἐπαύριον βλέπει
John baptizing. On the morrow he sees

me has surpassed me be-
cause he was before me.' "
16 From the fullness of his
grace we have all received
one blessing after another.
17 For the law was given
through Moses; grace and
truth came through Jesus
Christ. 18 No one has ever
seen God, but God the One
and Only,[d] [e]who is at the
Father's side, has made
him known.

John the Baptist Denies Being the Christ

19 Now this was John's
testimony when the Jews of
Jerusalem sent priests and
Levites to ask him who he
was. 20 He did not fail to
confess, but confessed
freely, "I am not the
Christ.[f]"
21 They asked him, "Then
who are you? Are you Eli-
jah?"
He said, "I am not."
"Are you the Prophet?"
He answered, "No."
22 Finally they said, "Who
are you? Give us an answer
to take back to those who
sent us. What do you say
about yourself?"
23 John replied in the
words of Isaiah the prophet, "I am the voice of one
calling in the desert, 'Make
straight the way for the
Lord.' "[g]
24 Now some Pharisees
who had been sent 25 questioned him, "Why then do
you baptize if you are not
the Christ, nor Elijah, nor
the Prophet?"
26 "I baptize with[h] wa-
ter," John replied, "but
among you stands one you
do not know. 27 He is the
one who comes after me,
the thongs of whose san-
dals I am not worthy to untie."
28 This all happened at
Bethany on the other side
of the Jordan, where John
was baptizing.

Jesus the Lamb of God

29 The next day John saw

[e] *18* Some manuscripts *but the only* (or *only begotten*) *Son*
[f] *20* Or *Messiah.* "The Christ" (Greek) and "the Messiah" (Hebrew) both mean "the Anointed One"; also in verse 25.
[g] *23* Isaiah 40:3
[h] *26* Or *in*; also in verses 31 and 33

Jesus coming toward him
and declared, "Here is the
Lamb of God who takes
away the sin of the world!
30This is he of whom I said,
'After me comes a man
who ranks ahead of me be-
cause he was before me.'
31I myself did not know
him; but I came baptizing
with water for this reason,
that he might be revealed to
Israel." 32And John testified, "I saw the Spirit descending from heaven like
a dove, and it remained on
him. 33I myself did not
know him, but the one who
sent me to baptize with water said to me, 'He on
whom you see the Spirit descend and remain is the one
who baptizes with the Holy
Spirit.' 34And I myself
have seen and have testi-
fied that this is the Son of
God."[h]

The First Disciples of Jesus

35 The next day John
again was standing with
two of his disciples, 36and
as he watched Jesus walk
by, he exclaimed, "Look,
here is the Lamb of God!"
37The two disciples heard
him say this, and they followed Jesus. 38When Jesus
turned and saw them fol-
lowing, he said to them,
"What are you looking
for?" They said to him,
"Rabbi" (which translated
means Teacher), "where
are you staying?" 39He said
to them, "Come and see."
They came and saw where
he was staying, and they re-

[h] Other ancient authorities read *is God's chosen one*

τὸν Ἰησοῦν ἐρχόμενον πρὸς αὐτόν, καὶ
– Jesus coming toward him, and

λέγει· ἴδε ὁ ἀμνὸς τοῦ θεοῦ ὁ αἴρων
says : Behold[,] the Lamb – of God – taking

τὴν ἁμαρτίαν τοῦ κόσμου. 30 οὗτός ἐστιν
the sin of the world. This is he

ὑπὲρ οὗ ἐγὼ εἶπον· ὀπίσω μου ἔρχεται
as to whom I said : After me comes

ἀνὴρ ὃς ἔμπροσθέν μου γέγονεν, ὅτι
a man who before me has become, because

πρῶτός μου ἦν. 31 κἀγὼ οὐκ ᾔδειν
first of me he was. And I knew not

αὐτόν, ἀλλ' ἵνα φανερωθῇ τῷ Ἰσραήλ,
him, but that he might be manifested – to Israel,

διὰ τοῦτο ἦλθον ἐγὼ ἐν ὕδατι βαπτίζων.
therefore came I in water baptizing.

32 Καὶ ἐμαρτύρησεν Ἰωάννης λέγων ὅτι
And witnessed John saying[,] –

τεθέαμαι τὸ πνεῦμα καταβαῖνον ὡς
I have beheld the Spirit coming down as

περιστερὰν ἐξ οὐρανοῦ, καὶ ἔμεινεν ἐπ'
a dove out of heaven, and he remained on

αὐτόν. 33 κἀγὼ οὐκ ᾔδειν αὐτόν, ἀλλ'
him. And I knew not him, but

ὁ πέμψας με βαπτίζειν ἐν ὕδατι, ἐκεῖνός
the [one] having sent me to baptize in water, that [one].

μοι εἶπεν· ἐφ' ὃν ἂν ἴδῃς τὸ πνεῦμα
to me said: On whomever thou seest the Spirit

καταβαῖνον καὶ μένον ἐπ' αὐτόν, οὗτός
coming down and remaining on him, this

ἐστιν ὁ βαπτίζων ἐν πνεύματι ἁγίῳ.
is the [one] baptizing in Spirit Holy.

34 κἀγὼ ἑώρακα, καὶ μεμαρτύρηκα ὅτι
And I have seen, and have witnessed that

οὗτός ἐστιν ὁ υἱὸς τοῦ θεοῦ.
this [one] is the Son – of God.

35 Τῇ ἐπαύριον πάλιν εἱστήκει ὁ Ἰωάννης
On the morrow again stood – John

καὶ ἐκ τῶν μαθητῶν αὐτοῦ δύο, 36 καὶ
and of the disciples of him two, and

ἐμβλέψας τῷ Ἰησοῦ περιπατοῦντι λέγει·
looking at – Jesus walking he says:

ἴδε ὁ ἀμνὸς τοῦ θεοῦ. 37 καὶ ἤκουσαν
Behold[,] the Lamb – of God. And [4]heard

οἱ δύο μαθηταὶ αὐτοῦ λαλοῦντος καὶ
[1]the [2]two [3]disciples [5]him [6]speaking and

ἠκολούθησαν τῷ Ἰησοῦ. 38 στραφεὶς δὲ
they followed – Jesus. And [2]turning

ὁ Ἰησοῦς καὶ θεασάμενος αὐτοὺς ἀκολουθοῦντας
– [1]Jesus and beholding them following

λέγει αὐτοῖς· τί ζητεῖτε; οἱ δὲ εἶπαν
says to them : What seek ye? And they said

αὐτῷ· ῥαββί (ὃ λέγεται μεθερμηνευόμενον
to him : Rabbi (which is called being translated

διδάσκαλε), ποῦ μένεις; 39 λέγει αὐτοῖς·
Teacher), where remainest thou? He says to them :

ἔρχεσθε καὶ ὄψεσθε. ἦλθαν οὖν καὶ εἶδαν
Come and ye will see. They went therefore and saw

ποῦ μένει, καὶ παρ' αὐτῷ ἔμειναν τὴν
where he remains(ed), and with him remained –

ἡμέραν ἐκείνην· ὥρα ἦν ὡς δεκάτη.
day that; hour was about tenth.

40 Ἦν Ἀνδρέας ὁ ἀδελφὸς Σίμωνος Πέτρου
It was Andrew the brother of Simon Peter

εἷς ἐκ τῶν δύο τῶν ἀκουσάντων παρὰ
one of the two – hearing from

Jesus coming toward him
and said, "Look, the Lamb
of God, who takes away the
sin of the world! 30This is
the one I meant when I
said, 'A man who comes after me has surpassed me
because he was before me.'
31I myself did not know
him, but the reason I came
baptizing with water was
that he might be revealed to
Israel."
32Then John gave this testimony: "I saw the Spirit
come down from heaven as
a dove and remain on him.
33I would not have known
him, except that the one
who sent me to baptize
with water told me, 'The
man on whom you see the
Spirit come down and re-
main is he who will baptize
with the Holy Spirit.' 34I
have seen and I testify that
this is the Son of God."

Jesus' First Disciples

35The next day John was
there again with two of his
disciples. 36When he saw
Jesus passing by, he said,
"Look, the Lamb of God!"
37When the two disciples
heard him say this, they followed Jesus. 38Turning
around, Jesus saw them
following and asked,
"What do you want?"
They said, "Rabbi"
(which means Teacher),
"where are you staying?"
39"Come," he replied,
"and you will see."
So they went and saw

mained with him that day.
It was about four o'clock in
the afternoon. 40 One of the
two who heard John speak
and followed him was An-
drew, Simon Peter's brother. 41 He first found his
brother Simon and said to
him, "We have found the
Messiah" (which is trans-
lated Anointed[i]). 42 He
brought Simon[j] to Jesus,
who looked at him and
said, "You are Simon son
of John. You are to be
called Cephas" (which is
translated Peter[k]).

Jesus Calls Philip and Nathanael

43 The next day Jesus
decided to go to Galilee. He
found Philip and said to
him, "Follow me." 44 Now
Philip was from Bethsaida,
the city of Andrew and Peter. 45 Philip found Nathanael and said to him, "We
have found him about
whom Moses in the law and
also the prophets wrote,
Jesus son of Joseph from
Nazareth." 46 Nathanael
said to him, "Can anything
good come out of Naza-
reth?" Philip said to him,
"Come and see." 47 When
Jesus saw Nathanael com-
ing toward him, he said of
him, "Here is truly an Israelite in whom there is no
deceit!" 48 Nathanael asked
him, "Where did you get to
know me?" Jesus an-
swered, "I saw you under
the fig tree before Philip
called you." 49 Nathanael
replied, "Rabbi, you are
the Son of God! You are the
King of Israel!" 50 Jesus answered, "Do you believe
because I told you that I
saw you under the fig tree?
You will see greater things
than these." 51 And he said
to him, "Very truly, I tell
you,[l] you will see heaven
opened and the angels of

[i] Or *Christ*
[j] Gk *him*
[k] From the word for *rock* in Aramaic (*kepha*) and Greek (*petra*), respectively
[l] Both instances of the Greek word for *you* in this verse are plural

Ἰωάννου καὶ ἀκολουθησάντων αὐτῷ·
John and following him;

41 εὑρίσκει οὗτος πρῶτον τὸν ἀδελφὸν τὸν
[3]finds [1]this one [2]first [4]the(his) [6]brother –

ἴδιον Σίμωνα καὶ λέγει αὐτῷ· εὑρήκαμεν
[5]own Simon and tells him : We have found

τὸν Μεσσίαν (ὅ ἐστιν μεθερμηνευόμενον
the Messiah (which is being translated

χριστός). 42 ἤγαγεν αὐτὸν πρὸς τὸν
Christ). He led him to –

Ἰησοῦν. ἐμβλέψας αὐτῷ ὁ Ἰησοῦς εἶπεν·
Jesus. Looking at him – Jesus said :

σὺ εἶ Σίμων ὁ υἱὸς Ἰωάννου, σὺ κληθήσῃ
Thou art Simon the son of John, thou shalt be called

Κηφᾶς (ὃ ἑρμηνεύεται Πέτρος). 43 Τῇ
Cephas (which is translated Peter). On the

ἐπαύριον ἠθέλησεν ἐξελθεῖν εἰς τὴν Γαλιλαίαν,
morrow he wished to go forth into – Galilee,

καὶ εὑρίσκει Φίλιππον. καὶ λέγει αὐτῷ ὁ
and finds Philip. And says to him –

Ἰησοῦς· ἀκολούθει μοι. 44 ἦν δὲ ὁ
Jesus : Follow me. Now was –

Φίλιππος ἀπὸ Βηθσαϊδά, ἐκ τῆς πόλεως
Philip from Bethsaida, of the city

Ἀνδρέου καὶ Πέτρου. 45 εὑρίσκει Φίλιππος
of Andrew and of Peter. [2]Finds [1]Philip

τὸν Ναθαναὴλ καὶ λέγει αὐτῷ· ὃν ἔγραψεν
– [3]Nathanael and tells him : [He] whom wrote

Μωϋσῆς ἐν τῷ νόμῳ καὶ οἱ προφῆται
Moses in the law and the prophets

εὑρήκαμεν, Ἰησοῦν υἱὸν τοῦ Ἰωσὴφ τὸν
we have found, Jesus son – of Joseph –

ἀπὸ Ναζαρέθ. 46 καὶ εἶπεν αὐτῷ
from Nazareth. And said to him

Ναθαναήλ· ἐκ Ναζαρὲθ δύναταί τι ἀγαθὸν
Nathanael : Out of Nazareth can anything good

εἶναι; λέγει αὐτῷ ὁ Φίλιππος· ἔρχου καὶ
to be? Says to him – Philip : Come and

ἴδε. 47 εἶδεν Ἰησοῦς τὸν Ναθαναὴλ
see. [2]Saw [1]Jesus – [3]Nathanael

ἐρχόμενον πρὸς αὐτὸν καὶ λέγει περὶ
coming toward him and says concerning

αὐτοῦ· ἴδε ἀληθῶς Ἰσραηλίτης, ἐν ᾧ
him: Behold[,] truly an Israelite, in whom

δόλος οὐκ ἔστιν. 48 λέγει αὐτῷ Ναθαναήλ·
guile is not. Says to him Nathanael :

πόθεν με γινώσκεις; ἀπεκρίθη Ἰησοῦς καὶ
Whence me knowest thou? Answered Jesus and

εἶπεν αὐτῷ· πρὸ τοῦ σε Φίλιππον φωνῆσαι
said to him : Before *the* thee Philip to call[b]
=Philip called thee

ὄντα ὑπὸ τὴν συκῆν εἶδόν σε. 49 ἀπεκρίθη
being under the fig-tree I saw thee. Answered

αὐτῷ Ναθαναήλ· ῥαββί, σὺ εἶ ὁ υἱὸς τοῦ
him Nathanael : Rabbi, thou art the Son –

θεοῦ, σὺ βασιλεὺς εἶ τοῦ Ἰσραήλ.
of God, thou king art – of Israel.

50 ἀπεκρίθη Ἰησοῦς καὶ εἶπεν αὐτῷ·
Answered Jesus and said to him :

ὅτι εἶπόν σοι ὅτι εἶδόν σε ὑποκάτω τῆς
Because I told thee that I saw thee underneath the

συκῆς, πιστεύεις; μείζω τούτων ὄψῃ.
fig-tree, believest thou? greater [than] these things thou shalt see.

51 καὶ λέγει αὐτῷ· ἀμὴν ἀμὴν λέγω
And he says to him : Truly truly I tell

ὑμῖν, ὄψεσθε τὸν οὐρανὸν ἀνεῳγότα καὶ
you, ye shall see the heaven *having been* opened and

where he was staying, and
spent that day with him. It
was about the tenth hour.
40Andrew, Simon Peter's
brother, was one of the two
who heard what John had
said and who had followed
Jesus. 41The first thing Andrew did was to find his
brother Simon and tell him,
"We have found the Messi-
ah" (that is, the Christ).
42And he brought him to
Jesus.
Jesus looked at him and
said, "You are Simon son
of John. You will be called
Cephas" (which, when
translated, is Peter[i]).

Jesus Calls Philip and Nathanael

43The next day Jesus de-
cided to leave for Galilee.
Finding Philip, he said to
him, "Follow me."
44Philip, like Andrew and
Peter, was from the town of
Bethsaida. 45Philip found
Nathanael and told him,
"We have found the one
Moses wrote about in the
Law, and about whom the
prophets also wrote—
Jesus of Nazareth, the son
of Joseph."
46"Nazareth! Can any-
thing good come from
there?" Nathanael asked.
"Come and see," said
Philip.
47When Jesus saw Na-
thanael approaching, he
said of him, "Here is a true
Israelite, in whom there is
nothing false."
48"How do you know
me?" Nathanael asked.
Jesus answered, "I saw
you while you were still under the fig tree before Philip
called you."
49Then Nathanael de-
clared, "Rabbi, you are the
Son of God; you are the
King of Israel."
50Jesus said, "You be-
lieve[j] because I told you I
saw you under the fig tree.
You shall see greater things
than that." 51He then added, "I tell you[k] the truth,
you[k] shall see heaven

[i]42 Both *Cephas* (Aramaic) and *Peter* (Greek) mean *rock*.
[j]50 Or *Do you believe . . . ?*
[k]51 The Greek is plural.

God ascending and de-
scending upon the Son of
Man."

Chapter 2

The Wedding at Cana

ON the third day there
was a wedding in
Cana of Galilee, and the
mother of Jesus was there.
2 Jesus and his disciples had
also been invited to the
wedding. 3 When the wine
gave out, the mother of
Jesus said to him, "They
have no wine." 4 And Jesus
said to her, "Woman, what
concern is that to you and
to me? My hour has not yet
come." 5 His mother said to
the servants, "Do whatever
he tells you." 6 Now standing there were six stone water jars for the Jewish rites
of purification, each holding twenty or thirty gallons.
7 Jesus said to them, "Fill
the jars with water." And
they filled them up to the
brim. 8 He said to them,
"Now draw some out, and
take it to the chief steward." So they took it.
9 When the steward tasted
the water that had become
wine, and did not know
where it came from (though
the servants who had
drawn the water knew), the
steward called the bride-
groom 10 and said to him,
"Everyone serves the good
wine first, and then the inferior wine after the guests
have become drunk. But
you have kept the good
wine until now." 11 Jesus
did this, the first of his
signs, in Cana of Galilee,
and revealed his glory; and
his disciples believed in
him.
12 After this he went
down to Capernaum with

τοὺς ἀγγέλους τοῦ θεοῦ ἀναβαίνοντας καὶ
the angels – of God going up and
καταβαίνοντας ἐπὶ τὸν υἱὸν τοῦ ἀνθρώπου.
coming down on the Son – of man.

2 Καὶ τῇ ἡμέρᾳ τῇ τρίτῃ γάμος ἐγένετο
And on the day – third a wedding there was
ἐν Κανὰ τῆς Γαλιλαίας, καὶ ἦν ἡ μήτηρ
in Cana – of Galilee, and was the mother
τοῦ Ἰησοῦ ἐκεῖ· 2 ἐκλήθη δὲ καὶ ὁ
– of Jesus there; and was invited both –
Ἰησοῦς καὶ οἱ μαθηταὶ αὐτοῦ εἰς τὸν
Jesus and the disciples of him to the
γάμον. 3 καὶ ὑστερήσαντος οἴνου λέγει ἡ
wedding. And lacking wine[a] says the
=when wine was lacking
μήτηρ τοῦ Ἰησοῦ πρὸς αὐτόν· οἶνον
mother – of Jesus to him : Wine
οὐκ ἔχουσιν. 4 καὶ λέγει αὐτῇ ὁ Ἰησοῦς·
they have not. And says to her – Jesus :
τί ἐμοὶ καὶ σοί, γύναι; οὔπω ἥκει ἡ
What to me and to thee, woman? not yet is come the
ὥρα μου. 5 λέγει ἡ μήτηρ αὐτοῦ τοῖς
hour of me. Says the mother of him to the
διακόνοις· ὅ τι ἂν λέγῃ ὑμῖν, ποιήσατε.
servants: Whatever he tells you, do ye.
6 ἦσαν δὲ ἐκεῖ λίθιναι ὑδρίαι ἓξ κατὰ
Now there were there stone water-pots six according to
τὸν καθαρισμὸν τῶν Ἰουδαίων κείμεναι,
the purifying of the Jews lying,
χωροῦσαι ἀνὰ μετρητὰς δύο ἢ τρεῖς.
containing each† measures two or three.
7 λέγει αὐτοῖς ὁ Ἰησοῦς· γεμίσατε τὰς
Tells them – Jesus : Fill ye the
ὑδρίας ὕδατος. καὶ ἐγέμισαν αὐτὰς ἕως
water-pots of(with) water. And they filled them up to
ἄνω. 8 καὶ λέγει αὐτοῖς· ἀντλήσατε νῦν
[the] top. And he tells them : Draw now
καὶ φέρετε τῷ ἀρχιτρικλίνῳ. οἱ δὲ
and carry to the master of the feast. And they
ἤνεγκαν. 9 ὡς δὲ ἐγεύσατο ὁ ἀρχιτρίκλινος
carried. But when tasted the master of the feast
τὸ ὕδωρ οἶνον γεγενημένον, καὶ οὐκ ᾔδει
the water [2]wine [1]having become, and did not know
πόθεν ἐστίν, οἱ δὲ διάκονοι ᾔδεισαν οἱ
whence it is(was), but the servants knew the [ones]
ἠντληκότες τὸ ὕδωρ, φωνεῖ τὸν νυμφίον
having drawn the water, [3]calls [4]the [5]bridegroom
ὁ ἀρχιτρίκλινος 10 καὶ λέγει αὐτῷ· πᾶς
[1]the [2]master of the feast and says to him : Every
ἄνθρωπος πρῶτον τὸν καλὸν οἶνον τίθησιν,
man first the good wine sets forth,
καὶ ὅταν μεθυσθῶσιν τὸν ἐλάσσω· σὺ
and when they become drunk the worse; thou
τετήρηκας τὸν καλὸν οἶνον ἕως ἄρτι.
hast kept the good wine until now.
11 Ταύτην ἐποίησεν ἀρχὴν τῶν σημείων ὁ
[1]This [5]did [2]beginning [3]of the [4]signs –
Ἰησοῦς ἐν Κανὰ τῆς Γαλιλαίας καὶ
Jesus in Cana – of Galilee and
ἐφανέρωσεν τὴν δόξαν αὐτοῦ, καὶ ἐπίστευσαν
manifested the glory of him, and believed
εἰς αὐτὸν οἱ μαθηταὶ αὐτοῦ.
in him the disciples of him.
12 Μετὰ τοῦτο κατέβη εἰς Καφαρναοὺμ
After this went down to Capernaum

open, and the angels of God
ascending and descending
on the Son of Man."

Chapter 2

Jesus Changes Water to Wine

ON the third day a wed-
ding took place at
Cana in Galilee. Jesus'
mother was there, 2and
Jesus and his disciples had
also been invited to the
wedding. 3When the wine
was gone, Jesus' mother
said to him, "They have no
more wine."
4"Dear woman, why do
you involve me?" Jesus replied. "My time has not yet
come."
5His mother said to the
servants, "Do whatever he
tells you."
6Nearby stood six stone
water jars, the kind used by
the Jews for ceremonial
washing, each holding from
twenty to thirty gallons.[l]
7Jesus said to the ser-
vants, "Fill the jars with
water"; so they filled them
to the brim.
8Then he told them,
"Now draw some out and
take it to the master of the
banquet."
They did so, 9and the
master of the banquet tasted the water that had been
turned into wine. He did
not realize where it had
come from, though the servants who had drawn the
water knew. Then he called
the bridegroom aside 10and
said, "Everyone brings out
the choice wine first and
then the cheaper wine after
the guests have had too
much to drink; but you
have saved the best till
now."
11This, the first of his miraculous signs, Jesus performed in Cana of Galilee.
He thus revealed his glory,
and his disciples put their
faith in him.

Jesus Clears the Temple

12After this he went down
to Capernaum with his

l6 Greek *two to three metretes* (probably about 75 to 115 liters)

his mother, his brothers, and his disciples; and they remained there a few days.

Jesus Cleanses the Temple

13 The Passover of the Jews was near, and Jesus went up to Jerusalem. [14]In the temple he found people selling cattle, sheep, and doves, and the money changers seated at their tables. [15]Making a whip of cords, he drove all of them out of the temple, both the sheep and the cattle. He also poured out the coins of the money changers and overturned their tables. [16]He told those who were selling the doves, "Take these things out of here! Stop making my Father's house a marketplace!" [17]His disciples remembered that it was written, "Zeal for your house will consume me." [18]The Jews then said to him, "What sign can you show us for doing this?" [19]Jesus answered them, "Destroy this temple, and in three days I will raise it up." [20]The Jews then said, "This temple has been under construction for forty-six years, and will you raise it up in three days?" [21]But he was speaking of the temple of his body. [22]After he was raised from the dead, his disciples remembered that he had said this; and they believed the scripture and the word that Jesus had spoken.

23 When he was in Jerusalem during the Passover festival, many believed in his name because they saw

αὐτὸς καὶ ἡ μήτηρ αὐτοῦ καὶ
he and the mother of him and
οἱ ἀδελφοὶ καὶ οἱ μαθηταὶ αὐτοῦ, καὶ
the brothers and the disciples of him, and
ἐκεῖ ἔμειναν οὐ πολλὰς ἡμέρας.
there remained not many days.

13 Καὶ ἐγγὺς ἦν τὸ πάσχα τῶν Ἰουδαίων,
And near was the Passover of the Jews,
καὶ ἀνέβη εἰς Ἱεροσόλυμα ὁ Ἰησοῦς.
and went up to Jerusalem – Jesus.
14 καὶ εὗρεν ἐν τῷ ἱερῷ τοὺς πωλοῦντας
And he found in the temple the [ones] selling
βόας καὶ πρόβατα καὶ περιστερὰς καὶ τοὺς
oxen and sheep and doves and the
κερματιστὰς καθημένους, **15** καὶ ποιήσας
coindealers sitting, and having made
φραγέλλιον ἐκ σχοινίων πάντας ἐξέβαλεν
a lash out of ropes [2]all [1]he expelled
ἐκ τοῦ ἱεροῦ, τά τε πρόβατα καὶ τοὺς
out of the temple, both the sheep and the
βόας, καὶ τῶν κολλυβιστῶν ἐξέχεεν τὰ
oxen, and [4]of the [5]moneychangers [1]poured out [2]the
κέρματα καὶ τὰς τραπέζας ἀνέτρεψεν,
[3]coins [6]and [8]the [9]tables [7]overturned,
16 καὶ τοῖς τὰς περιστερὰς πωλοῦσιν
and [2]to the [ones] [4]the [5]doves [3]selling
εἶπεν· ἄρατε ταῦτα ἐντεῦθεν, μὴ ποιεῖτε
[1]said : Take these things hence, do not make
τὸν οἶκον τοῦ πατρός μου οἶκον ἐμπορίου.
the house of the Father of me a house of merchandise.
17 ἐμνήσθησαν οἱ μαθηταὶ αὐτοῦ ὅτι
Remembered the disciples of him that
γεγραμμένον ἐστίν· ὁ ζῆλος τοῦ οἴκου
having been written it is : The zeal of the house
σου καταφάγεταί με. **18** ἀπεκρίθησαν οὖν
of thee will consume me. Answered therefore
οἱ Ἰουδαῖοι καὶ εἶπαν αὐτῷ· τί σημεῖον
the Jews and said to him: What sign
δεικνύεις ἡμῖν, ὅτι ταῦτα ποιεῖς;
showest thou to us, because these things thou doest?
19 ἀπεκρίθη Ἰησοῦς καὶ εἶπεν αὐτοῖς· λύσατε τὸν
Answered Jesus and said to them: Destroy –
ναὸν τοῦτον, καὶ ἐν τρισὶν ἡμέραις ἐγερῶ αὐτόν.
shrine this, and in three days I will raise it.
20 εἶπαν οὖν οἱ Ἰουδαῖοι· τεσσεράκοντα
Said therefore the Jews : In forty
καὶ ἓξ ἔτεσιν οἰκοδομήθη ὁ ναὸς οὗτος,
and six years was built – shrine this,
καὶ σὺ ἐν τρισὶν ἡμέραις ἐγερεῖς αὐτόν;
and thou in three days wilt raise it?
21 ἐκεῖνος δὲ ἔλεγεν περὶ τοῦ ναοῦ τοῦ
But that [one]* spoke about the shrine of the
σώματος αὐτοῦ. **22** ὅτε οὖν ἠγέρθη ἐκ
body of him. When therefore he was raised from
νεκρῶν, ἐμνήσθησαν οἱ μαθηταὶ αὐτοῦ
[the] dead, remembered the disciples of him
ὅτι τοῦτο ἔλεγεν, καὶ ἐπίστευσαν τῇ
that this he said, and they believed the
γραφῇ καὶ τῷ λόγῳ ὃν εἶπεν ὁ Ἰησοῦς.
scripture and the word which said – Jesus.

23 Ὡς δὲ ἦν ἐν τοῖς Ἱεροσολύμοις ἐν
And when he was in – Jerusalem at
τῷ πάσχα ἐν τῇ ἑορτῇ, πολλοὶ ἐπίστευσαν
the Passover at the feast, many believed
εἰς τὸ ὄνομα αὐτοῦ, θεωροῦντες αὐτοῦ τὰ
in the name of him, beholding of him the

* John repeatedly uses the demonstrative adjective ἐκεῖνος in the sense of "he," referring to Christ.

mother and brothers and his disciples. There they stayed for a few days.

[13]When it was almost time for the Jewish Passover, Jesus went up to Jerusalem. [14]In the temple courts he found men selling cattle, sheep and doves, and others sitting at tables exchanging money. [15]So he made a whip out of cords, and drove all from the temple area, both sheep and cattle; he scattered the coins of the money changers and overturned their tables. [16]To those who sold doves he said, "Get these out of here! How dare you turn my Father's house into a market!"

[17]His disciples remembered that it is written: "Zeal for your house will consume me."[m]

[18]Then the Jews demanded of him, "What miraculous sign can you show us to prove your authority to do all this?"

[19]Jesus answered them, "Destroy this temple, and I will raise it again in three days."

[20]The Jews replied, "It has taken forty-six years to build this temple, and you are going to raise it in three days?" [21]But the temple he had spoken of was his body. [22]After he was raised from the dead, his disciples recalled what he had said. Then they believed the Scripture and the words that Jesus had spoken.

[23]Now while he was in Jerusalem at the Passover Feast, many people saw

[m]17 Psalm 69:9

the signs that he was doing.
24But Jesus on his part
would not entrust himself
to them, because he knew
all people 25and needed no
one to testify about any-
one; for he himself knew
what was in everyone.

Chapter 3

Nicodemus Visits Jesus

NOW there was a Phari-
see named Nicode-
mus, a leader of the Jews.
2He came to Jesus[m] by
night and said to him,
"Rabbi, we know that you
are a teacher who has come
from God; for no one can
do these signs that you do
apart from the presence of
God." 3Jesus answered
him, "Very truly, I tell you,
no one can see the kingdom
of God without being born
from above."[n] 4Nicode-
mus said to him, "How can
anyone be born after hav-
ing grown old? Can one enter a second time into the
mother's womb and be
born?" 5Jesus answered,
"Very truly, I tell you, no
one can enter the kingdom
of God without being born
of water and Spirit. 6What
is born of the flesh is flesh,
and what is born of the
Spirit is spirit.[o] 7Do not be
astonished that I said to
you, 'You[p] must be born
from above.'[q] 8The wind[o]
blows where it chooses,
and you hear the sound of
it, but you do not know
where it comes from or
where it goes. So it is with
everyone who is born of the
Spirit." 9Nicodemus said
to him, "How can these

[m] Gk *him*
[n] Or *born anew*
[o] The same Greek word means both *wind* and *spirit*
[p] The Greek word for *you* here is plural
[q] Or *anew*

σημεῖα ἃ ἐποίει· **24** αὐτὸς δὲ Ἰησοῦς
signs which he was doing; [1]but [3][him]self, [2]Jesus
οὐκ ἐπίστευεν αὐτὸν αὐτοῖς διὰ τὸ αὐτὸν
did not commit himself to them because of the him
=because he knew
γινώσκειν πάντας, **25** καὶ ὅτι οὐ χρείαν εἶχεν
to know[b] all men, and because no need he had
ἵνα τις μαρτυρήσῃ περὶ τοῦ ἀνθρώπου·
that anyone should witness concerning – man;
αὐτὸς γὰρ ἐγίνωσκεν τί ἦν ἐν τῷ ἀνθρώπῳ.
for he knew what was in – man.
3 Ἦν δὲ ἄνθρωπος ἐκ τῶν Φαρισαίων,
Now there was a man of the Pharisees,
Νικόδημος ὄνομα αὐτῷ, ἄρχων τῶν
Nicodemus name to him[c], a ruler of the
=his name,
Ἰουδαίων· **2** οὗτος ἦλθεν πρὸς αὐτὸν νυκτὸς
Jews; this man came to him of(by) night
καὶ εἶπεν αὐτῷ· ῥαββί, οἴδαμεν ὅτι ἀπὸ
and said to him: Rabbi, we know that from
θεοῦ ἐλήλυθας διδάσκαλος· οὐδεὶς γὰρ
God thou hast come a teacher; for no one
δύναται ταῦτα τὰ σημεῖα ποιεῖν ἃ σὺ
can these – signs *to* do which thou
ποιεῖς, ἐὰν μὴ ᾖ ὁ θεὸς μετ' αὐτοῦ.
doest, except [2]is – [1]God with him.
3 ἀπεκρίθη Ἰησοῦς καὶ εἶπεν αὐτῷ· ἀμὴν
Answered Jesus and said to him: Truly
ἀμὴν λέγω σοι, ἐὰν μή τις γεννηθῇ
truly I tell thee, except anyone is born
ἄνωθεν, οὐ δύναται ἰδεῖν τὴν βασιλείαν
from above, he cannot *to* see the kingdom
τοῦ θεοῦ. **4** λέγει πρὸς αὐτὸν ὁ Νικόδημος·
– of God. Says to him – Nicodemus:
πῶς δύναται ἄνθρωπος γεννηθῆναι γέρων ὤν;
How can a man *to* be born old being?
μὴ δύναται εἰς τὴν κοιλίαν τῆς μητρὸς
not can he into the womb of the mother
αὐτοῦ δεύτερον εἰσελθεῖν καὶ γεννηθῆναι;
of him secondly *to* enter and *to* be born?
5 ἀπεκρίθη Ἰησοῦς· ἀμὴν ἀμὴν λέγω σοι,
Answered Jesus: Truly truly I tell thee,
ἐὰν μή τις γεννηθῇ ἐξ ὕδατος καὶ
except anyone is born of water and
πνεύματος, οὐ δύναται εἰσελθεῖν εἰς τὴν
spirit, he cannot *to* enter into the
βασιλείαν τοῦ θεοῦ. **6** τὸ γεγεννημένον ἐκ
kingdom – of God. The thing *having been* born of
τῆς σαρκὸς σάρξ ἐστιν, καὶ τὸ γεγεννημένον
the flesh flesh is, and the thing *having been* born
ἐκ τοῦ πνεύματος πνεῦμά ἐστιν. **7** μὴ
of the Spirit spirit is. not
θαυμάσῃς ὅτι εἶπόν σοι· δεῖ ὑμᾶς
Marvel because I told thee: It behoves you
γεννηθῆναι ἄνωθεν. **8** τὸ πνεῦμα ὅπου θέλει
to be born from above. The spirit(?wind) where it wishes
πνεῖ, καὶ τὴν φωνὴν αὐτοῦ ἀκούεις, ἀλλ'
blows, and the sound of it thou hearest, but
οὐκ οἶδας πόθεν ἔρχεται καὶ ποῦ ὑπάγει·
thou knowest not whence it comes and whither it goes;
οὕτως ἐστὶν πᾶς ὁ γεγεννημένος ἐκ τοῦ
so is everyone *having been* born of the
πνεύματος. **9** ἀπεκρίθη Νικόδημος καὶ
Spirit. Answered Nicodemus and
εἶπεν αὐτῷ· πῶς δύναται ταῦτα γενέσθαι;
said to him: How can these things *to* come about?

the miraculous signs he
was doing and believed in
his name.[n] 24But Jesus
would not entrust himself
to them, for he knew all
men. 25He did not need
man's testimony about
man, for he knew what was
in a man.

Chapter 3

Jesus Teaches Nicodemus

NOW there was a man
of the Pharisees
named Nicodemus, a mem-
ber of the Jewish ruling
council. 2He came to Jesus
at night and said, "Rabbi,
we know you are a teacher
who has come from God.
For no one could perform
the miraculous signs you
are doing if God were not
with him."
3In reply Jesus declared,
"I tell you the truth, no one
can see the kingdom of God
unless he is born again.[o]"
4"How can a man be born
when he is old?" Nicode-
mus asked. "Surely he cannot enter a second time into
his mother's womb to be
born!"
5Jesus answered, "I tell
you the truth, no one can
enter the kingdom of God
unless he is born of water
and the Spirit. 6Flesh gives
birth to flesh, but the Spirit[p] gives birth to spirit.
7You should not be sur-
prised at my saying, 'You[q]
must be born again.' 8The
wind blows wherever it
pleases. You hear its
sound, but you cannot tell
where it comes from or
where it is going. So it is
with everyone born of the
Spirit."
9"How can this be?" Nic-
odemus asked.

[n] 23 Or *and believed in him*
[o] 3 Or *born from above*; also in verse 7
[p] 6 Or *but spirit*
[q] 7 The Greek is plural.

things be?" 10Jesus an-
swered him, "Are you a
teacher of Israel, and yet
you do not understand
these things?
11 "Very truly, I tell
you, we speak of what we
know and testify to what
we have seen; yet you[r] do
not receive our testimony.
12If I have told you about
earthly things and you do
not believe, how can you
believe if I tell you about
heavenly things? 13No one
has ascended into heaven
except the one who de-
scended from heaven, the
Son of Man.[s] 14And just as
Moses lifted up the serpent
in the wilderness, so must
the Son of Man be lifted up,
15that whoever believes in
him may have eternal life.[t]
16 "For God so loved
the world that he gave his
only Son, so that everyone
who believes in him may
not perish but may have
eternal life.
17 "Indeed, God did not
send the Son into the world
to condemn the world, but
in order that the world
might be saved through
him. 18Those who believe
in him are not condemned;
but those who do not be-
lieve are condemned al-
ready, because they have
not believed in the name of
the only Son of God. 19And
this is the judgment, that
the light has come into the
world, and people loved
darkness rather than light
because their deeds were
evil. 20For all who do evil
hate the light and do not
come to the light, so that
their deeds may not be exposed. 21But those who do
what is true come to the
light, so that it may be
clearly seen that their

[r]The Greek word for *you* here and in verse 12 is plural
[s]Other ancient authorities add *who is in heaven*
[t]Some interpreters hold that the quotation concludes with verse 15

10 ἀπεκρίθη Ἰησοῦς καὶ εἶπεν αὐτῷ· σὺ
Answered Jesus and said to him : Thou
εἶ ὁ διδάσκαλος τοῦ Ἰσραὴλ καὶ ταῦτα
art the teacher – of Israel and these things
οὐ γινώσκεις; 11 ἀμὴν ἀμὴν λέγω σοι ὅτι
knowest not? Truly truly I tell thee[,] –
ὃ οἴδαμεν λαλοῦμεν καὶ ὃ ἑωράκαμεν
What we know we speak and what we have seen
μαρτυροῦμεν, καὶ τὴν μαρτυρίαν ἡμῶν
we witness, and the witness of us
οὐ λαμβάνετε. 12 εἰ τὰ ἐπίγεια εἶπον
ye receive not. If the earthly things I told
ὑμῖν καὶ οὐ πιστεύετε, πῶς ἐὰν εἴπω
you and ye believe not, how if I tell
ὑμῖν τὰ ἐπουράνια πιστεύσετε; 13 καὶ
you the heavenly things will ye believe? And
οὐδεὶς ἀναβέβηκεν εἰς τὸν οὐρανὸν εἰ μὴ
no man has gone up into – heaven except
ὁ ἐκ τοῦ οὐρανοῦ καταβάς, ὁ υἱὸς
the [one] out of – heaven having come down, the Son
τοῦ ἀνθρώπου. 14 Καὶ καθὼς Μωϋσῆς ὕψωσεν
– of man. And as Moses lifted up
τὸν ὄφιν ἐν τῇ ἐρήμῳ, οὕτως ὑψωθῆναι
the serpent in the desert, so to be lifted up
δεῖ τὸν υἱὸν τοῦ ἀνθρώπου, 15 ἵνα πᾶς ὁ
it behoves the Son – of man, that everyone
πιστεύων ἐν αὐτῷ ἔχῃ ζωὴν αἰώνιον.
believing in him may have life eternal.
16 οὕτως γὰρ ἠγάπησεν ὁ θεὸς τὸν
For thus [2]loved – [1]God the
κόσμον, ὥστε τὸν υἱὸν τὸν μονογενῆ
world, so as the Son the only begotten
ἔδωκεν, ἵνα πᾶς ὁ πιστεύων εἰς αὐτὸν
he gave, that everyone believing in him
μὴ ἀπόληται ἀλλ' ἔχῃ ζωὴν αἰώνιον.
may not perish but may have life eternal.
17 οὐ γὰρ ἀπέστειλεν ὁ θεὸς τὸν υἱὸν
For [3]not [2]sent – [1]God the Son
εἰς τὸν κόσμον ἵνα κρίνῃ τὸν κόσμον,
into the world that he might judge the world,
ἀλλ' ἵνα σωθῇ ὁ κόσμος δι' αὐτοῦ.
but that [3]might be saved [1]the [2]world through him.
18 ὁ πιστεύων εἰς αὐτὸν οὐ κρίνεται·
The [one] believing in him is not judged;
ὁ μὴ πιστεύων ἤδη κέκριται, ὅτι
the[one]not believing already has been judged, because
μὴ πεπίστευκεν εἰς τὸ ὄνομα τοῦ μονογενοῦς
he has not believed in the name of the only begotten
υἱοῦ τοῦ θεοῦ. 19 αὕτη δέ ἐστιν ἡ
Son – of God. And this is the
κρίσις, ὅτι τὸ φῶς ἐλήλυθεν εἰς τὸν
judgment, that the light has come into the
κόσμον καὶ ἠγάπησαν οἱ ἄνθρωποι μᾶλλον
world and [2]loved – [1]men [5]rather
τὸ σκότος ἢ τὸ φῶς· ἦν γὰρ αὐτῶν
[3]the [4]darkness [6]than the light; for was(were) of them
πονηρὰ τὰ ἔργα. 20 πᾶς γὰρ ὁ φαῦλα
evil the works. For everyone evil things
πράσσων μισεῖ τὸ φῶς καὶ οὐκ ἔρχεται
doing hates the light and does not come
πρὸς τὸ φῶς, ἵνα μὴ ἐλεγχθῇ τὰ ἔργα
to the light, lest is(are) reproved the works
αὐτοῦ· 21 ὁ δὲ ποιῶν τὴν ἀλήθειαν ἔρχεται
of him; but the [one] doing the truth comes
πρὸς τὸ φῶς, ἵνα φανερωθῇ αὐτοῦ τὰ
to the light, that may be manifested of him the

10"You are Israel's teacher," said Jesus, "and do
you not understand these
things? 11I tell you the
truth, we speak of what we
know, and we testify to
what we have seen, but still
you people do not accept
our testimony. 12I have
spoken to you of earthly
things and you do not be-
lieve; how then will you believe if I speak of heavenly
things? 13No one has ever
gone into heaven except
the one who came from
heaven—the Son of Man.[r]
14Just as Moses lifted up
the snake in the desert, so
the Son of Man must be lifted up, 15that everyone who
believes in him may have
eternal life.[s]
16"For God so loved the
world that he gave his one
and only Son,[t] that whoever believes in him shall not
perish but have eternal life.
17For God did not send his
Son into the world to condemn the world, but to save
the world through him.
18Whoever believes in him
is not condemned, but
whoever does not believe
stands condemned already
because he has not be-
lieved in the name of God's
one and only Son.[u] 19This
is the verdict: Light has
come into the world, but
men loved darkness instead
of light because their deeds
were evil. 20Everyone who
does evil hates the light,
and will not come into the
light for fear that his deeds
will be exposed. 21But whoever lives by the truth
comes into the light, so that
it may be seen plainly that

[r]13 Some manuscripts *Man, who is in heaven*
[s]15 Or *believes may have eternal life in him*
[t]16 Or *his only begotten Son*
[u]18 Or *God's only begotten Son*

deeds have been done in
God."[t]

Jesus and John the Baptist

22 After this Jesus and
his disciples went into the
Judean countryside, and he
spent some time there with
them and baptized. 23John
also was baptizing at Ae-
non near Salim because
water was abundant there;
and people kept coming
and were being baptized
24—John, of course, had
not yet been thrown into
prison.
25 Now a discussion
about purification arose between John's disciples and
a Jew.[u] 26They came to
John and said to him, "Rabbi, the one who was with
you across the Jordan, to
whom you testified, here
he is baptizing, and all are
going to him." 27John an-
swered, "No one can re-
ceive anything except what
has been given from heav-
en. 28You yourselves are
my witnesses that I said, 'I
am not the Messiah,[v] but I
have been sent ahead of
him.' 29He who has the
bride is the bridegroom.
The friend of the bride-
groom, who stands and
hears him, rejoices greatly
at the bridegroom's voice.
For this reason my joy has
been fulfilled. 30He must
increase, but I must de-
crease."[w]

The One Who Comes from Heaven

31 The one who comes
from above is above all; the
one who is of the earth belongs to the earth and
speaks about earthly
things. The one who comes
from heaven is above all.
32He testifies to what he
has seen and heard, yet no
one accepts his testimony.
33Whoever has accepted

[u] Other ancient authorities read *the Jews*
[v] Or *the Christ*
[w] Some interpreters hold that the quotation continues through verse 36

ἔργα ὅτι ἐν θεῷ ἐστιν εἰργασμένα.
works that in God they are *having been* wrought.
22 Μετὰ ταῦτα ἦλθεν ὁ Ἰησοῦς καὶ οἱ
After these things came – Jesus and the
μαθηταὶ αὐτοῦ εἰς τὴν Ἰουδαίαν γῆν, καὶ
disciples of him into *the* Judæan *land,* and
ἐκεῖ διέτριβεν μετ' αὐτῶν καὶ ἐβάπτιζεν.
there continued with them and baptized.
23 ἦν δὲ καὶ Ἰωάννης βαπτίζων ἐν
And was also John baptizing in
Αἰνὼν ἐγγὺς τοῦ Σαλίμ, ὅτι ὕδατα
Ainon near – Salim, because waters
πολλὰ ἦν ἐκεῖ, καὶ παρεγίνοντο καὶ
many was(were) there, and they came and
ἐβαπτίζοντο· 24 οὔπω γὰρ ἦν βεβλημένος
were baptized; for ³not yet ²was ⁴*having been* cast
εἰς τὴν φυλακὴν Ἰωάννης. 25 Ἐγένετο
⁵into ⁶the ⁷prison ¹John. There was
οὖν ζήτησις ἐκ τῶν μαθητῶν Ἰωάννου
therefore a questioning of the disciples of John
μετὰ Ἰουδαίου περὶ καθαρισμοῦ. 26 καὶ
with a Jew about purifying. And
ἦλθον πρὸς τὸν Ἰωάννην καὶ εἶπαν αὐτῷ·
they came to – John and said to him :
ῥαββί, ὃς ἦν μετὰ σοῦ πέραν τοῦ
Rabbi, [he] who was with thee beyond the
Ἰορδάνου, ᾧ σὺ μεμαρτύρηκας, ἴδε
Jordan, to whom thou hast borne witness, behold[,]
οὗτος βαπτίζει καὶ πάντες ἔρχονται πρὸς
this man baptizes and all men are coming to
αὐτόν. 27 ἀπεκρίθη Ἰωάννης καὶ εἶπεν·
him. Answered John and said :
οὐ δύναται ἄνθρωπος λαμβάνειν οὐδὲν ἐὰν μὴ
Cannot a man *to* receive no(any)thing unless
ᾖ δεδομένον αὐτῷ ἐκ τοῦ οὐρανοῦ.
it is *having been* given to him out of – heaven.
28 αὐτοὶ ὑμεῖς μοι μαρτυρεῖτε ὅτι εἶπον·
[Your]selves ye to me bear witness that I said :
οὐκ εἰμὶ ἐγὼ ὁ χριστός, ἀλλ' ὅτι
³not ²am ¹I the Christ, but that
ἀπεσταλμένος εἰμὶ ἔμπροσθεν ἐκείνου. 29 ὁ
having been sent I am before that one.* The [one]
ἔχων τὴν νύμφην νυμφίος ἐστίν· ὁ δὲ
having the bride a bridegroom is; but the
φίλος τοῦ νυμφίου, ὁ ἑστηκὼς καὶ ἀκούων
friend of the bridegroom, – standing and hearing
αὐτοῦ, χαρᾷ χαίρει διὰ τὴν φωνὴν τοῦ
him, with joy rejoices because of the voice of the
νυμφίου. αὕτη οὖν ἡ χαρὰ ἡ ἐμὴ
bridegroom. ²This ¹therefore – ⁴joy – ³my
πεπλήρωται. 30 ἐκεῖνον δεῖ αὐξάνειν, ἐμὲ
has been fulfilled. That one it behoves to increase, ²me
δὲ ἐλαττοῦσθαι. 31 Ὁ ἄνωθεν ἐρχόμενος
¹but to decrease. The [one] from above coming
ἐπάνω πάντων ἐστίν· ὁ ὢν ἐκ τῆς γῆς
over all is; the [one] being of the earth
ἐκ τῆς γῆς ἐστιν καὶ ἐκ τῆς γῆς λαλεῖ.
of the earth is and of the earth speaks.
ὁ ἐκ τοῦ οὐρανοῦ ἐρχόμενος ἐπάνω
The [one] of – heaven coming over
πάντων ἐστίν· 32 ὃ ἑώρακεν καὶ ἤκουσεν,
all is; what he has seen and heard,
τοῦτο μαρτυρεῖ, καὶ τὴν μαρτυρίαν αὐτοῦ
this he witnesses [to], and the witness of him
οὐδεὶς λαμβάνει. 33 ὁ λαβὼν αὐτοῦ τὴν
no man receives. The [one] receiving of him the

* See note to 2. 21.

what he has done has been
done through God."[v]

John the Baptist's Testimony About Jesus

22After this, Jesus and his
disciples went out into the
Judean countryside, where
he spent some time with
them, and baptized. 23Now
John also was baptizing at
Aenon near Salim, because
there was plenty of water,
and people were constantly
coming to be baptized.
24(This was before John
was put in prison.) 25An argument developed between
some of John's disciples
and a certain Jew[w] over the
matter of ceremonial washing. 26They came to John
and said to him, "Rabbi,
that man who was with you
on the other side of the Jordan—the one you testified
about—well, he is baptiz-
ing, and everyone is going
to him."
27To this John replied,
"A man can receive only
what is given him from
heaven. 28You yourselves
can testify that I said, 'I am
not the Christ[x] but am sent
ahead of him.' 29The bride
belongs to the bridegroom.
The friend who attends the
bridegroom waits and lis-
tens for him, and is full of
joy when he hears the
bridegroom's voice. That
joy is mine, and it is now
complete. 30He must be-
come greater; I must be-
come less.
31"The one who comes
from above is above all; the
one who is from the earth
belongs to the earth, and
speaks as one from the
earth. The one who comes
from heaven is above all.
32He testifies to what he
has seen and heard, but no
one accepts his testimony.
33The man who has accept-

[v] *21* Some interpreters end the quotation after verse 15.
[w] *25* Some manuscripts *and certain Jews*
[x] *28* Or *Messiah*

his testimony has certi-
fied[x] this, that God is true.
34 He whom God has sent
speaks the words of God,
for he gives the Spirit without measure. 35 The Father
loves the Son and has
placed all things in his
hands. 36 Whoever believes
in the Son has eternal life;
whoever disobeys the Son
will not see life, but must
endure God's wrath.

μαρτυρίαν ἐσφράγισεν ὅτι ὁ θεὸς ἀληθής
witness sealed that – God true
ἐστιν. 34 ὃν γὰρ ἀπέστειλεν ὁ θεὸς τὰ
is. For [he] whom [2]sent – [1]God the
ῥήματα τοῦ θεοῦ λαλεῖ· οὐ γὰρ ἐκ
words – of God speaks; for not by
μέτρου δίδωσιν τὸ πνεῦμα. 35 ὁ πατὴρ
measure he gives the Spirit. The Father
ἀγαπᾷ τὸν υἱόν, καὶ πάντα δέδωκεν ἐν
loves the Son, and all things has given in[to]
τῇ χειρὶ αὐτοῦ. 36 ὁ πιστεύων εἰς τὸν
the hand of him. The [one] believing in the
υἱὸν ἔχει ζωὴν αἰώνιον· ὁ δὲ ἀπειθῶν
Son has life eternal; but the [one] disobeying
τῷ υἱῷ οὐκ ὄψεται ζωήν, ἀλλ᾽ ἡ ὀργὴ
the Son will not see life, but the wrath
τοῦ θεοῦ μένει ἐπ᾽ αὐτόν.
– of God remains on him.

ed it has certified that God
is truthful. 34 For the one
whom God has sent speaks
the words of God, for God[y]
gives the Spirit without limit. 35 The Father loves the
Son and has placed every-
thing in his hands. 36 Whoever believes in the Son has
eternal life, but whoever
rejects the Son will not see
life, for God's wrath re-
mains on him."[z]

Chapter 4

Jesus and the Woman of Samaria

NOW when Jesus[y]
learned that the Phar-
isees had heard, "Jesus is
making and baptizing more
disciples than John"
2 —although it was not
Jesus himself but his disciples who baptized— 3 he
left Judea and started back
to Galilee. 4 But he had to
go through Samaria. 5 So he
came to a Samaritan city
called Sychar, near the plot
of ground that Jacob had
given to his son Joseph.
6 Jacob's well was there,
and Jesus, tired out by his
journey, was sitting by the
well. It was about noon.
7 A Samaritan woman
came to draw water, and
Jesus said to her, "Give me
a drink." 8 (His disciples
had gone to the city to buy
food.) 9 The Samaritan
woman said to him, "How
is it that you, a Jew, ask a
drink of me, a woman of
Samaria?" (Jews do not
share things in common
with Samaritans.)[z] 10 Jesus
answered her, "If you
knew the gift of God, and

4 Ὡς οὖν ἔγνω ὁ κύριος ὅτι ἤκουσαν
[2]When [1]therefore [5]knew [3]the [4]Lord [6]that [9]heard
οἱ Φαρισαῖοι ὅτι Ἰησοῦς πλείονας μαθητὰς
[7]the [8]Pharisees that Jesus more disciples
ποιεῖ καὶ βαπτίζει ἢ Ἰωάννης, — 2 καίτοι γε
makes and baptizes than John, — though
Ἰησοῦς αὐτὸς οὐκ ἐβάπτιζεν ἀλλ᾽ οἱ
Jesus [him]self baptized not but the
μαθηταὶ αὐτοῦ, — 3 ἀφῆκεν τὴν Ἰουδαίαν
disciples of him, — he left – Judæa
καὶ ἀπῆλθεν πάλιν εἰς τὴν Γαλιλαίαν.
and went away again into – Galilee.
4 Ἔδει δὲ αὐτὸν διέρχεσθαι διὰ τῆς
And it behoved him to pass through *through* –
Σαμαρείας. 5 ἔρχεται οὖν εἰς πόλιν τῆς
Samaria. He comes therefore to a city –
Σαμαρείας λεγομένην Συχάρ, πλησίον τοῦ
of Samaria *being* called Sychar, near the
χωρίου ὃ ἔδωκεν Ἰακὼβ [τῷ] Ἰωσὴφ
piece of land which [2]gave [1]Jacob – to Joseph
τῷ υἱῷ αὐτοῦ· 6 ἦν δὲ ἐκεῖ πηγὴ τοῦ
the son of him; and was there a fountain –
Ἰακώβ. ὁ οὖν Ἰησοῦς κεκοπιακὼς ἐκ
of Jacob. – Therefore Jesus having become wearied from
τῆς ὁδοιπορίας ἐκαθέζετο οὕτως ἐπὶ τῇ
the journey sat thus at the
πηγῇ· ὥρα ἦν ὡς ἕκτη. 7 ἔρχεται γυνὴ
fountain; [the] hour was about sixth. Comes a woman
ἐκ τῆς Σαμαρείας ἀντλῆσαι ὕδωρ. λέγει
of – Samaria to draw water. Says
αὐτῇ ὁ Ἰησοῦς· δός μοι πεῖν. 8 οἱ γὰρ
to her – Jesus : Give me to drink. For the
μαθηταὶ αὐτοῦ ἀπεληλύθεισαν εἰς τὴν
disciples of him had gone away into the
πόλιν, ἵνα τροφὰς ἀγοράσωσιν. 9 λέγει
city, that foods they might buy. Says
οὖν αὐτῷ ἡ γυνὴ ἡ Σαμαρῖτις· πῶς
therefore to him the woman – Samaritan : How
σὺ Ἰουδαῖος ὢν παρ᾽ ἐμοῦ πεῖν
thou [2]a Jew [1]being [5]from [6]me [4]to drink
αἰτεῖς γυναικὸς Σαμαρίτιδος οὔσης;
[3]askest [9]woman [8]a Samaritan [7]being?
[οὐ γὰρ συγχρῶνται Ἰουδαῖοι Σαμαρίταις.]
[1]For [4]not [3]associate [2]Jews [5]with Samaritans.
10 ἀπεκρίθη Ἰησοῦς καὶ εἶπεν αὐτῇ· εἰ ᾔδεις
Answered Jesus and said to her : If thou knewest

Chapter 4

Jesus Talks With a Samaritan Woman

THE Pharisees heard
that Jesus was gaining
and baptizing more disci-
ples than John, 2 although in
fact it was not Jesus who
baptized, but his disciples.
3 When the Lord learned of
this, he left Judea and went
back once more to Galilee.
4 Now he had to go
through Samaria. 5 So he
came to a town in Samaria
called Sychar, near the plot
of ground Jacob had given
to his son Joseph. 6 Jacob's
well was there, and Jesus,
tired as he was from the
journey, sat down by the
well. It was about the sixth
hour.
7 When a Samaritan wom-
an came to draw water,
Jesus said to her, "Will you
give me a drink?" 8 (His disciples had gone into the
town to buy food.)
9 The Samaritan woman
said to him, "You are a Jew
and I am a Samaritan wom-
an. How can you ask me for
a drink?" (For Jews do not
associate with Samari-
tans.[a])
10 Jesus answered her, "If
you knew the gift of God

[x] Gk *set a seal to*
[y] Other ancient authorities read *the Lord*
[z] Other ancient authorities lack this sentence

[y]34 Greek *he*
[z]36 Some interpreters end the quotation after verse 30.
[a]9 Or *do not use dishes Samaritans have used*

who it is that is saying to
you, 'Give me a drink,' you
would have asked him, and
he would have given you
living water." 11 The woman said to him, "Sir, you
have no bucket, and the
well is deep. Where do you
get that living water? 12 Are
you greater than our ancestor Jacob, who gave us the
well, and with his sons and
his flocks drank from it?"
13 Jesus said to her, "Everyone who drinks of this
water will be thirsty again,
14 but those who drink of
the water that I will give
them will never be thirsty.
The water that I will give
will become in them a
spring of water gushing up
to eternal life." 15 The
woman said to him, "Sir,
give me this water, so that
I may never be thirsty or
have to keep coming here
to draw water."
16 Jesus said to her,
"Go, call your husband,
and come back." 17 The
woman answered him, "I
have no husband." Jesus
said to her, "You are right
in saying, 'I have no husband'; 18 for you have had
five husbands, and the one
you have now is not your
husband. What you have
said is true!" 19 The woman
said to him, "Sir, I see that
you are a prophet. 20 Our
ancestors worshiped on
this mountain, but you[a]
say that the place where
people must worship is in
Jerusalem." 21 Jesus said to
her, "Woman, believe me,
the hour is coming when
you will worship the Father
neither on this mountain
nor in Jerusalem. 22 You

[a] The Greek word for *you* here and in verses 21 and 22 is plural

τὴν δωρεὰν τοῦ θεοῦ, καὶ τίς ἐστιν ὁ
the gift – of God, and who is the [one]
λέγων σοι· δός μοι πεῖν, σὺ ἂν ᾔτησας
saying to thee: Give me to drink, thou wouldest have asked
αὐτὸν καὶ ἔδωκεν ἄν σοι ὕδωρ ζῶν.
him and he would have given thee water living.
11 λέγει αὐτῷ· κύριε, οὔτε ἄντλημα ἔχεις
She says to him: Sir, no pail thou hast
καὶ τὸ φρέαρ ἐστὶν βαθύ· πόθεν οὖν
and the well is deep; whence then
ἔχεις τὸ ὕδωρ τὸ ζῶν; 12 μὴ σὺ μείζων
hast thou the water – living? *not* thou greater
εἶ τοῦ πατρὸς ἡμῶν Ἰακώβ, ὃς ἔδωκεν
art [than] the father of us Jacob, who gave
ἡμῖν τὸ φρέαρ, καὶ αὐτὸς ἐξ αὐτοῦ
us the well, and [him]self of it
ἔπιεν καὶ οἱ υἱοὶ αὐτοῦ καὶ τὰ θρέμματα
drank and the sons of him and the cattle
αὐτοῦ; 13 ἀπεκρίθη Ἰησοῦς καὶ εἶπεν αὐτῇ·
of him? Answered Jesus and said to her:
πᾶς ὁ πίνων ἐκ τοῦ ὕδατος τούτου
Everyone drinking of – water this
διψήσει πάλιν· 14 ὃς δ' ἂν πίῃ ἐκ τοῦ
will thirst again; but whoever drinks of the
ὕδατος οὗ ἐγὼ δώσω αὐτῷ, οὐ μὴ
water which I will give him, by no means
διψήσει εἰς τὸν αἰῶνα, ἀλλὰ τὸ ὕδωρ ὃ
will thirst unto the age, but the water which
δώσω αὐτῷ γενήσεται ἐν αὐτῷ πηγὴ
I will give him will become in him a fountain
ὕδατος ἁλλομένου εἰς ζωὴν αἰώνιον. 15 λέγει
of water springing to life eternal. Says
πρὸς αὐτὸν ἡ γυνή· κύριε, δός μοι
to him the woman: Sir, give me
τοῦτο τὸ ὕδωρ, ἵνα μὴ διψῶ μηδὲ
this – water, that I thirst not nor
διέρχωμαι ἐνθάδε ἀντλεῖν. 16 λέγει αὐτῇ·
come through hither to draw. He says to her:
ὕπαγε φώνησον τὸν ἄνδρα σου καὶ ἐλθὲ
Go call the husband of thee and come
ἐνθάδε. 17 ἀπεκρίθη ἡ γυνὴ καὶ εἶπεν·
hither. Answered the woman and said:
οὐκ ἔχω ἄνδρα. λέγει αὐτῇ ὁ Ἰησοῦς·
I have not a husband. Says to her – Jesus:
καλῶς εἶπες ὅτι ἄνδρα οὐκ ἔχω· 18 πέντε
Well sayest thou[,] – A husband I have not; [2]five
γὰρ ἄνδρας ἔσχες, καὶ νῦν ὃν ἔχεις
[1]for husbands thou hadst, and now [he] whom thou hast
οὐκ ἔστιν σου ἀνήρ· τοῦτο ἀληθὲς εἴρηκας.
is not of thee husband; this truly thou hast said.
19 λέγει αὐτῷ ἡ γυνή· κύριε, θεωρῶ
Says to him the woman: Sir, I perceive
ὅτι προφήτης εἶ σύ. 20 οἱ πατέρες
that a prophet art thou. The fathers
ἡμῶν ἐν τῷ ὄρει τούτῳ προσεκύνησαν·
of us in – mountain this worshipped;
καὶ ὑμεῖς λέγετε ὅτι ἐν Ἱεροσολύμοις
and ye say that in Jerusalem
ἐστὶν ὁ τόπος ὅπου προσκυνεῖν δεῖ.
is the place where to worship it behoves.
21 λέγει αὐτῇ ὁ Ἰησοῦς· πίστευέ μοι,
Says to her – Jesus: Believe me,
γύναι, ὅτι ἔρχεται ὥρα ὅτε οὔτε ἐν
woman, that is coming an hour when neither in
τῷ ὄρει τούτῳ οὔτε ἐν Ἱεροσολύμοις
– mountain this nor in Jerusalem

and who it is that asks you
for a drink, you would have
asked him and he would
have given you living wa-
ter."
11 "Sir," the woman said,
"you have nothing to draw
with and the well is deep.
Where can you get this living water? 12 Are you greater than our father Jacob,
who gave us the well and
drank from it himself, as
did also his sons and his
flocks and herds?"
13 Jesus answered, "Ev-
eryone who drinks this water will be thirsty again,
14 but whoever drinks the
water I give him will never
thirst. Indeed, the water I
give him will become in him
a spring of water welling up
to eternal life."
15 The woman said to him,
"Sir, give me this water so
that I won't get thirsty and
have to keep coming here
to draw water."
16 He told her, "Go, call
your husband and come
back."
17 "I have no husband,"
she replied.
Jesus said to her, "You
are right when you say you
have no husband. 18 The
fact is, you have had five
husbands, and the man you
now have is not your hus-
band. What you have just
said is quite true."
19 "Sir," the woman said,
"I can see that you are a
prophet. 20 Our fathers worshiped on this mountain,
but you Jews claim that the
place where we must wor-
ship is in Jerusalem."
21 Jesus declared, "Be-
lieve me, woman, a time is
coming when you will wor-
ship the Father neither on

worship what you do not
know; we worship what we
know, for salvation is from
the Jews. 23 But the hour is
coming, and is now here,
when the true worshipers
will worship the Father in
spirit and truth, for the Father seeks such as these to
worship him. 24 God is spirit, and those who worship
him must worship in spirit
and truth." 25 The woman
said to him, "I know that
Messiah is coming" (who is
called Christ). "When he
comes, he will proclaim all
things to us." 26 Jesus said
to her, "I am he,[b] the one
who is speaking to you."
27 Just then his disci-
ples came. They were as-
tonished that he was speaking with a woman, but no
one said, "What do you
want?" or, "Why are you
speaking with her?" 28 Then
the woman left her water
jar and went back to the
city. She said to the people,
29 "Come and see a man
who told me everything I
have ever done! He cannot
be the Messiah,[c] can he?"
30 They left the city and
were on their way to him.
31 Meanwhile the disci-
ples were urging him,
"Rabbi, eat something."
32 But he said to them, "I
have food to eat that you do
not know about." 33 So the
disciples said to one another, "Surely no one has
brought him something to
eat?" 34 Jesus said to them,
"My food is to do the will of
him who sent me and to
complete his work. 35 Do
you not say, 'Four months
more, then comes the har-

[b] Gk *I am*
[c] Or *the Christ*

προσκυνήσετε τῷ πατρί. **22** ὑμεῖς προσκυ-
will ye worship the Father. Ye wor-
νεῖτε ὃ οὐκ οἴδατε, ἡμεῖς προσκυνοῦμεν ὃ
ship what ye know not, we worship what
οἴδαμεν, ὅτι ἡ σωτηρία ἐκ τῶν Ἰουδαίων
we know, because – salvation of the Jews
ἐστίν· **23** ἀλλὰ ἔρχεται ὥρα καὶ νῦν
is; but is coming an hour and now
ἐστιν, ὅτε οἱ ἀληθινοὶ προσκυνηταὶ προσκυνή-
is, when the true worshippers will
σουσιν τῷ πατρὶ ἐν πνεύματι καὶ ἀληθείᾳ·
worship the Father in spirit and truth;
καὶ γὰρ ὁ πατὴρ τοιούτους ζητεῖ τοὺς
for indeed the Father [2]such [1]seeks the [ones]
προσκυνοῦντας αὐτόν· **24** πνεῦμα ὁ θεός,
worshipping him; God [is] spirit,*
καὶ τοὺς προσκυνοῦντας ἐν πνεύματι καὶ
and [2]the [ones] [3]worshipping [4]in [6]spirit [7]and
ἀληθείᾳ δεῖ προσκυνεῖν. **25** λέγει αὐτῷ
[8]truth [1]it behoves [5]to worship. Says to him
ἡ γυνή· οἶδα ὅτι Μεσσίας ἔρχεται, ὁ
the woman: I know that Messiah is coming, the [one]
λεγόμενος χριστός· ὅταν ἔλθῃ ἐκεῖνος,
being called Christ; when comes that one,
ἀναγγελεῖ ἡμῖν ἅπαντα. **26** λέγει αὐτῇ
he will announce to us all things. Says to her
ὁ Ἰησοῦς· ἐγώ εἰμι, ὁ λαλῶν σοι.
– Jesus: I am, the [one] speaking to thee.
27 Καὶ ἐπὶ τούτῳ ἦλθαν οἱ μαθηταὶ
And on this came the disciples
αὐτοῦ, καὶ ἐθαύμαζον ὅτι μετὰ γυναικὸς
of him, and marvelled that with a woman
ἐλάλει· οὐδεὶς μέντοι εἶπεν· τί ζητεῖς
he was speaking; no one however said: What seekest thou
ἢ τί λαλεῖς μετ' αὐτῆς; **28** ἀφῆκεν οὖν
or why speakest thou with her? [4]Left [3]therefore
τὴν ὑδρίαν αὐτῆς ἡ γυνὴ καὶ ἀπῆλθεν
[5]the [6]waterpot [7]of her [1]the [2]woman and went away
εἰς τὴν πόλιν, καὶ λέγει τοῖς ἀνθρώποις·
into the city, and says to the men:
29 δεῦτε ἴδετε ἄνθρωπον ὃς εἶπέν μοι
Come see a man who told me
πάντα ἃ ἐποίησα· μήτι οὗτός ἐστιν ὁ
all things which I did; *not* this is the
χριστός; **30** ἐξῆλθον ἐκ τῆς πόλεως καὶ
Christ? They went forth out of the city and
ἤρχοντο πρὸς αὐτόν. **31** Ἐν τῷ μεταξὺ
came to him. In the meantime
ἠρώτων αὐτὸν οἱ μαθηταὶ λέγοντες· ῥαββί,
asked him the disciples saying: Rabbi,
φάγε. **32** ὁ δὲ εἶπεν αὐτοῖς· ἐγὼ βρῶσιν
eat. But he said to them: I food
ἔχω φαγεῖν ἣν ὑμεῖς οὐκ οἴδατε. **33** ἔλεγον
have to eat which ye do not know. Said
οὖν οἱ μαθηταὶ πρὸς ἀλλήλους· μή τις
therefore the disciples to one another: *Not* anyone
ἤνεγκεν αὐτῷ φαγεῖν; **34** λέγει αὐτοῖς ὁ
brought him to eat? Says to them –
Ἰησοῦς· ἐμὸν βρῶμά ἐστιν ἵνα ποιῶ τὸ
Jesus: My food is that I may do the
θέλημα τοῦ πέμψαντός με καὶ τελειώσω
will of the [one] having sent me and may finish
αὐτοῦ τὸ ἔργον. **35** οὐχ ὑμεῖς λέγετε ὅτι
of him the work. [3]Not [2]ye [1]say that

* See note on 1. 1.

this mountain nor in Jerusalem. 22 You Samaritans
worship what you do not
know; we worship what we
do know, for salvation is
from the Jews. 23 Yet a time
is coming and has now
come when the true wor-
shipers will worship the Father in spirit and truth, for
they are the kind of wor-
shipers the Father seeks.
24 God is spirit, and his worshipers must worship in
spirit and in truth."
25 The woman said, "I
know that Messiah" (called
Christ) "is coming. When
he comes, he will explain
everything to us."
26 Then Jesus declared, "I
who speak to you am he."

The Disciples Rejoin Jesus

27 Just then his disciples
returned and were sur-
prised to find him talking
with a woman. But no one
asked, "What do you
want?" or "Why are you
talking with her?"
28 Then, leaving her water
jar, the woman went back
to the town and said to the
people, 29 "Come, see a
man who told me every-
thing I ever did. Could this
be the Christ[b]?" 30 They
came out of the town and
made their way toward
him.
31 Meanwhile his disciples
urged him, "Rabbi, eat
something."
32 But he said to them, "I
have food to eat that you
know nothing about."
33 Then his disciples said
to each other, "Could
someone have brought him
food?"
34 "My food," said Jesus,
"is to do the will of him
who sent me and to finish
his work. 35 Do you not say,

[b] 29 Or *Messiah*

vest'? But I tell you, look
around you, and see how
the fields are ripe for harvesting. 36The reaper is already receiving[d] wages
and is gathering fruit for
eternal life, so that sower
and reaper may rejoice together. 37For here the saying holds true, 'One sows
and another reaps.' 38I sent
you to reap that for which
you did not labor. Others
have labored, and you have
entered into their labor."
39 Many Samaritans
from that city believed in
him because of the wom-
an's testimony, "He told
me everything I have ever
done." 40So when the Sa-
maritans came to him, they
asked him to stay with
them; and he stayed there
two days. 41And many
more believed because of
his word. 42They said to
the woman, "It is no longer
because of what you said
that we believe, for we
have heard for ourselves,
and we know that this is
truly the Savior of the
world."

Jesus Returns to Galilee

43 When the two days
were over, he went from
that place to Galilee 44(for
Jesus himself had testified
that a prophet has no honor
in the prophet's own country). 45When he came to
Galilee, the Galileans welcomed him, since they had
seen all that he had done in
Jerusalem at the festival;
for they too had gone to the
festival.

Jesus Heals an Official's Son

46 Then he came again
to Cana in Galilee where he

[d]Or [35]. . . *the fields are already ripe for harvesting.* [36]*The reaper is receiving*

ἔτι τετράμηνός ἐστιν καὶ ὁ θερισμὸς
yet four months it is and the harvest
ἔρχεται; ἰδοὺ λέγω ὑμῖν, ἐπάρατε τοὺς
comes? Behold I tell you, lift up the
ὀφθαλμοὺς ὑμῶν καὶ θεάσασθε τὰς χώρας,
eyes of you and behold the fields,
ὅτι λευκαί εἰσιν πρὸς θερισμόν. ἤδη
because white they are to harvest. Already
36 ὁ θερίζων μισθὸν λαμβάνει καὶ συνάγει
the [one] reaping wages receives and gathers
καρπὸν εἰς ζωὴν αἰώνιον, ἵνα ὁ σπείρων
fruit to life eternal, that [1]the [one] [2]sowing
ὁμοῦ χαίρῃ καὶ ὁ θερίζων. 37 ἐν γὰρ
[7]together [6]may rejoice [3]and [4]the [one] [5]reaping. For in
τούτῳ ὁ λόγος ἐστὶν ἀληθινὸς ὅτι ἄλλος
this the word is true that another(one)
ἐστὶν ὁ σπείρων καὶ ἄλλος ὁ θερίζων.
is the[one] sowing and another the [one] reaping.
38 ἐγὼ ἀπέστειλα ὑμᾶς θερίζειν ὃ οὐχ
I sent you to reap what not
ὑμεῖς κεκοπιάκατε· ἄλλοι κεκοπιάκασιν, καὶ
ye have laboured; others have laboured, and
ὑμεῖς εἰς τὸν κόπον αὐτῶν εἰσεληλύθατε.
ye into the labour of them have entered.
39 Ἐκ δὲ τῆς πόλεως ἐκείνης πολλοὶ
And out of – city that many
ἐπίστευσαν εἰς αὐτὸν τῶν Σαμαριτῶν διὰ
believed in him of the Samaritans because of
τὸν λόγον τῆς γυναικὸς μαρτυρούσης ὅτι
the word of the woman witnessing[,] –
εἶπέν μοι πάντα ἃ ἐποίησα. 40 ὡς
He told me all things which I did. When
οὖν ἦλθον πρὸς αὐτὸν οἱ Σαμαρῖται,
therefore came to him the Samaritans,
ἠρώτων αὐτὸν μεῖναι παρ' αὐτοῖς· καὶ
they asked him to remain with them; and
ἔμεινεν ἐκεῖ δύο ἡμέρας. 41 καὶ πολλῷ
he remained there two days. And [2]more
πλείους ἐπίστευσαν διὰ τὸν λόγον αὐτοῦ,
[1]many believed because of the word of him,
42 τῇ τε γυναικὶ ἔλεγον ὅτι οὐκέτι διὰ
and to the woman they said[,] – No longer because of
τὴν σὴν λαλιὰν πιστεύομεν· αὐτοὶ γὰρ
– thy talk we believe; for [our]selves
ἀκηκόαμεν, καὶ οἴδαμεν ὅτι οὗτός ἐστιν
we have heard, and we know that this man is
ἀληθῶς ὁ σωτὴρ τοῦ κόσμου.
truly the Saviour of the world.
43 Μετὰ δὲ τὰς δύο ἡμέρας ἐξῆλθεν
And after the two days he went forth
ἐκεῖθεν εἰς τὴν Γαλιλαίαν. 44 αὐτὸς γὰρ
thence into – Galilee. For [2][him]self
Ἰησοῦς ἐμαρτύρησεν ὅτι προφήτης ἐν
[1]Jesus witnessed that a prophet in
τῇ ἰδίᾳ πατρίδι τιμὴν οὐκ ἔχει. 45 ὅτε
the(his) own native place honour has not. When
οὖν ἦλθεν εἰς τὴν Γαλιλαίαν, ἐδέξαντο
therefore he came into – Galilee, received
αὐτὸν οἱ Γαλιλαῖοι, πάντα ἑωρακότες
him the Galilæans, all things having seen
ὅσα ἐποίησεν ἐν Ἰεροσολύμοις ἐν τῇ
which he did in Jerusalem at the
ἑορτῇ· καὶ αὐτοὶ γὰρ ἦλθον εἰς τὴν
feast; [3]also [2]they [1]for went to the
ἑορτήν. 46 Ἦλθεν οὖν πάλιν εἰς τὴν
feast. He came therefore again to –

'Four months more and
then the harvest'? I tell
you, open your eyes and
look at the fields! They are
ripe for harvest. 36Even
now the reaper draws his
wages, even now he har-
vests the crop for eternal
life, so that the sower and
the reaper may be glad together. 37Thus the saying
'One sows and another
reaps' is true. 38I sent you
to reap what you have not
worked for. Others have
done the hard work, and
you have reaped the bene-
fits of their labor."

Many Samaritans Believe

39Many of the Samaritans
from that town believed in
him because of the wom-
an's testimony, "He told
me everything I ever did."
40So when the Samaritans
came to him, they urged
him to stay with them, and
he stayed two days. 41And
because of his words many
more became believers.
42They said to the wom-
an, "We no longer believe
just because of what you
said; now we have heard
for ourselves, and we know
that this man really is the
Savior of the world."

Jesus Heals the Official's Son

43After the two days he
left for Galilee. 44(Now
Jesus himself had pointed
out that a prophet has no
honor in his own country.)
45When he arrived in Galilee, the Galileans wel-
comed him. They had seen
all that he had done in Jerusalem at the Passover
Feast, for they also had
been there.
46Once more he visited
Cana in Galilee, where he

had changed the water into
wine. Now there was a royal official whose son lay ill
in Capernaum. 47 When he
heard that Jesus had come
from Judea to Galilee, he
went and begged him to
come down and heal his
son, for he was at the point
of death. 48 Then Jesus said
to him, "Unless you[e] see
signs and wonders you will
not believe." 49 The official
said to him, "Sir, come
down before my little boy
dies." 50 Jesus said to him,
"Go; your son will live."
The man believed the word
that Jesus spoke to him and
started on his way. 51 As he
was going down, his slaves
met him and told him that
his child was alive. 52 So he
asked them the hour when
he began to recover, and
they said to him, "Yesterday at one in the afternoon
the fever left him." 53 The
father realized that this was
the hour when Jesus had
said to him, "Your son will
live." So he himself be-
lieved, along with his
whole household. 54 Now
this was the second sign
that Jesus did after coming
from Judea to Galilee.

Κανὰ τῆς Γαλιλαίας, ὅπου ἐποίησεν τὸ
Cana – of Galilee, where he made the

ὕδωρ οἶνον. καὶ ἦν τις βασιλικὸς
water wine. And there was a certain courtier

οὗ ὁ υἱὸς ἠσθένει ἐν Καφαρναούμ· 47 οὗτος
of whom the son ailed in Capernaum; this man

ἀκούσας ὅτι Ἰησοῦς ἥκει ἐκ τῆς Ἰουδαίας
hearing that Jesus comes(came) out of – Judæa

εἰς τὴν Γαλιλαίαν, ἀπῆλθεν πρὸς αὐτὸν καὶ
into – Galilee, went to him and

ἠρώτα ἵνα καταβῇ καὶ ἰάσηται αὐτοῦ
asked that he would come down and would cure of him

τὸν υἱόν· ἤμελλεν γὰρ ἀποθνήσκειν. 48 εἶπεν
the son; for he was about to die. Said

οὖν ὁ Ἰησοῦς πρὸς αὐτόν· ἐὰν μὴ σημεῖα
therefore – Jesus to him: Except signs

καὶ τέρατα ἴδητε, οὐ μὴ πιστεύσητε.
and prodigies ye see, by no means ye believe.

49 λέγει πρὸς αὐτὸν ὁ βασιλικός· κύριε,
Says to him the courtier: Sir,

κατάβηθι πρὶν ἀποθανεῖν τὸ παιδίον μου.
come down before to die the child[b] of me.

50 λέγει αὐτῷ ὁ Ἰησοῦς· πορεύου, ὁ
Tells him – Jesus: Go, the

υἱός σου ζῇ. ἐπίστευσεν ὁ ἄνθρωπος τῷ
son of thee lives. 3Believed 1the 2man 4the

λόγῳ ὃν εἶπεν αὐτῷ ὁ Ἰησοῦς, καὶ
5word 6which 8said 9to him – 7Jesus, and

ἐπορεύετο. 51 ἤδη δὲ αὐτοῦ καταβαίνοντος
went. And already him going down[a]
=while he was going down

οἱ δοῦλοι ὑπήντησαν αὐτῷ λέγοντες ὅτι
the slaves met him saying that

ὁ παῖς αὐτοῦ ζῇ. 52 ἐπύθετο οὖν τὴν
the boy of him lives. He inquired therefore the

ὥραν παρ' αὐτῶν ἐν ᾗ κομψότερον ἔσχεν·
hour from them in which better he had;
=he got better;

εἶπαν οὖν αὐτῷ ὅτι ἐχθὲς ὥραν ἑβδόμην
they said therefore to him[.] – Yesterday [at] hour seventh

ἀφῆκεν αὐτὸν ὁ πυρετός. 53 ἔγνω οὖν
left him the fever. Knew therefore

ὁ πατὴρ ὅτι ἐκείνῃ τῇ ὥρᾳ ἐν ᾗ εἶπεν
the father that in that – hour in which told

αὐτῷ ὁ Ἰησοῦς· ὁ υἱός σου ζῇ· καὶ
him – Jesus: The son of thee lives; and

ἐπίστευσεν αὐτὸς καὶ ἡ οἰκία αὐτοῦ ὅλη.
believed he and the household of him whole.

54 Τοῦτο [δὲ] πάλιν δεύτερον σημεῖον
And this again a second sign

ἐποίησεν ὁ Ἰησοῦς ἐλθὼν ἐκ τῆς Ἰουδαίας
did – Jesus having come out of – Judæa

εἰς τὴν Γαλιλαίαν.
into – Galilee.

had turned the water into
wine. And there was a certain royal official whose
son lay sick at Capernaum.
47 When this man heard that
Jesus had arrived in Galilee
from Judea, he went to him
and begged him to come
and heal his son, who was
close to death.
48 "Unless you people see
miraculous signs and won-
ders," Jesus told him,
"you will never believe."
49 The royal official said,
"Sir, come down before
my child dies."
50 Jesus replied, "You
may go. Your son will
live."
The man took Jesus at his
word and departed.
51 While he was still on the
way, his servants met him
with the news that his boy
was living. 52 When he inquired as to the time when
his son got better, they said
to him, "The fever left him
yesterday at the seventh
hour."
53 Then the father realized
that this was the exact time
at which Jesus had said to
him, "Your son will live."
So he and all his household
believed.
54 This was the second miraculous sign that Jesus
performed, having come
from Judea to Galilee.

Chapter 5

Jesus Heals on the Sabbath

AFTER this there was a
festival of the Jews,
and Jesus went up to Jerusalem.
2 Now in Jerusalem by
the Sheep Gate there is a
pool, called in Hebrew[f]

5 Μετὰ ταῦτα ἦν ἑορτὴ τῶν Ἰουδαίων,
After these things there was a feast of the Jews,

καὶ ἀνέβη Ἰησοῦς εἰς Ἱεροσόλυμα. 2 ἔστιν
and went up Jesus to Jerusalem. there is

δὲ ἐν τοῖς Ἱεροσολύμοις ἐπὶ τῇ προβατικῇ
Now in – Jerusalem at the sheepgate

κολυμβήθρα, ἡ ἐπιλεγομένη Ἑβραϊστὶ
a pool, the [one] *being* called in Hebrew

Chapter 5

The Healing at the Pool

SOME time later, Jesus
went up to Jerusalem
for a feast of the Jews.
2 Now there is in Jerusalem
near the Sheep Gate a pool,
which in Aramaic is called

[e] Both instances of the Greek word for *you* in this verse are plural
[f] That is, *Aramaic*

Beth-zatha,[g] which has
five porticoes. 3 In these lay
many invalids—blind,
lame, and paralyzed.[h]
5 One man was there who
had been ill for thirty-eight
years. 6 When Jesus saw
him lying there and knew
that he had been there a
long time, he said to him,
"Do you want to be made
well?" 7 The sick man an-
swered him, "Sir, I have no
one to put me into the pool
when the water is stirred
up; and while I am making
my way, someone else
steps down ahead of me."
8 Jesus said to him, "Stand
up, take your mat and
walk." 9 At once the man
was made well, and he took
up his mat and began to
walk.
Now that day was a sab-
bath. 10 So the Jews said to
the man who had been
cured, "It is the sabbath; it
is not lawful for you to carry your mat." 11 But he answered them, "The man
who made me well said to
me, 'Take up your mat and
walk.' " 12 They asked him,
"Who is the man who said
to you, 'Take it up and
walk'?" 13 Now the man
who had been healed did
not know who it was, for
Jesus had disappeared in[i]
the crowd that was there.
14 Later Jesus found him in
the temple and said to him,
"See, you have been made
well! Do not sin any more,
so that nothing worse happens to you." 15 The man
went away and told the
Jews that it was Jesus who
had made him well.

Βηθζαθά, πέντε στοὰς ἔχουσα. 3 ἐν
Bethzatha, five porches having. In
ταύταις κατέκειτο πλῆθος τῶν ἀσθενούντων,
these lay a multitude of the ailing [ones],
τυφλῶν, χωλῶν, ξηρῶν. ‡ 5 ἦν δέ τις
blind, lame, withered. And there was a
ἄνθρωπος ἐκεῖ τριάκοντα καὶ ὀκτὼ ἔτη
certain man there thirty-eight years
ἔχων ἐν τῇ ἀσθενείᾳ αὐτοῦ· 6 τοῦτον
having in the ailment of him; [5]this man
ἰδὼν ὁ Ἰησοῦς κατακείμενον, καὶ γνοὺς
[2]seeing – [1]Jesus [4]lying, and knowing
ὅτι πολὺν ἤδη χρόνον ἔχει, λέγει αὐτῷ·
that [3]much [2]already [4]time [1]he has, says to him:
θέλεις ὑγιὴς γενέσθαι; 7 ἀπεκρίθη αὐτῷ
Wishest thou whole to become? Answered him
ὁ ἀσθενῶν· κύριε, ἄνθρωπον οὐκ ἔχω,
the ailing [one]: Sir, a man I have not,
ἵνα ὅταν ταραχθῇ τὸ ὕδωρ βάλῃ με εἰς
that when is troubled the water he may put me into
τὴν κολυμβήθραν· ἐν ᾧ δὲ ἔρχομαι ἐγώ,
the pool; but while am coming I,
ἄλλος πρὸ ἐμοῦ καταβαίνει. 8 λέγει αὐτῷ
another before me goes down. Says to him
ὁ Ἰησοῦς· ἔγειρε ἆρον τὸν κράβατόν
– Jesus: Rise[,] take the mattress
σου καὶ περιπάτει. 9 καὶ εὐθέως ἐγένετο
of thee and walk. And immediately became
ὑγιὴς ὁ ἄνθρωπος, καὶ ἦρεν τὸν κράβατον
whole the man, and took the mattress
αὐτοῦ καὶ περιεπάτει. Ἦν δὲ σάββατον
of him and walked. And it was a sabbath
ἐν ἐκείνῃ τῇ ἡμέρᾳ. 10 ἔλεγον οὖν οἱ
on that – day. Said therefore the
Ἰουδαῖοι τῷ τεθεραπευμένῳ· σάββατόν ἐστιν,
Jews to the [one] having been healed: A sabbath it is,
καὶ οὐκ ἔξεστίν σοι ἆραι τὸν κράβατον.
and it is not lawful for thee to take the mattress.
11 ὃς δὲ ἀπεκρίθη αὐτοῖς· ὁ ποιήσας
But who(he) answered them: The [one] making
με ὑγιῆ, ἐκεῖνός μοι εἶπεν· ἆρον τὸν
me whole, that one me told: Take the
κράβατόν σου καὶ περιπάτει. 12 ἠρώτησαν
mattress of thee and walk. They asked
αὐτόν· τίς ἐστιν ὁ ἄνθρωπος ὁ εἰπών
him: Who is the man – telling
σοι· ἆρον καὶ περιπάτει; 13 ὁ δὲ ἰαθεὶς
thee: Take and walk? But the [one] cured
οὐκ ᾔδει τίς ἐστιν· ὁ γὰρ Ἰησοῦς
did not know who it is(was); – for Jesus
ἐξένευσεν ὄχλου ὄντος ἐν τῷ τόπῳ.
withdrew a crowd being[a] in the place.
=as there was a crowd
14 μετὰ ταῦτα εὑρίσκει αὐτὸν ὁ Ἰησοῦς
After these things finds him – Jesus
ἐν τῷ ἱερῷ καὶ εἶπεν αὐτῷ· ἴδε ὑγιὴς
in the temple and said to him: Behold[,] whole
γέγονας· μηκέτι ἁμάρτανε, ἵνα μὴ χεῖρόν
thou hast become; no longer sin, lest [2]worse
σοί τι γένηται. 15 ἀπῆλθεν ὁ ἄνθρωπος
[4]to thee [1]something [3]happens. Went away the man
καὶ εἶπεν τοῖς Ἰουδαίοις ὅτι Ἰησοῦς
and told the Jews that Jesus
ἐστιν ὁ ποιήσας αὐτὸν ὑγιῆ. 16 καὶ διὰ
it is(was) the [one] having made him whole. And there-

‡ End of ver. 3 and ver. 4 omitted by Nestle; *cf.* NIV footnote.

Bethesda[c] and which is
surrounded by five covered
colonnades. 3 Here a great
number of disabled people
used to lie—the blind, the
lame, the paralyzed.[d] 5 One
who was there had been an
invalid for thirty-eight
years. 6 When Jesus saw
him lying there and learned
that he had been in this condition for a long time, he
asked him, "Do you want
to get well?"
7 "Sir," the invalid re-
plied, "I have no one to
help me into the pool when
the water is stirred. While I
am trying to get in, someone else goes down ahead
of me."
8 Then Jesus said to him,
"Get up! Pick up your mat
and walk." 9 At once the
man was cured; he picked
up his mat and walked.
The day on which this
took place was a Sabbath,
10 and so the Jews said to
the man who had been
healed, "It is the Sabbath;
the law forbids you to carry
your mat."
11 But he replied, "The
man who made me well
said to me, 'Pick up your
mat and walk.' "
12 So they asked him,
"Who is this fellow who
told you to pick it up and
walk?"
13 The man who was
healed had no idea who it
was, for Jesus had slipped
away into the crowd that
was there.
14 Later Jesus found him
at the temple and said to
him, "See, you are well
again. Stop sinning or
something worse may hap-
pen to you." 15 The man
went away and told the
Jews that it was Jesus who
had made him well.

[g] Other ancient authorities read *Bethesda*, others *Bethsaida*
[h] Other ancient authorities add, wholly or in part, *waiting for the stirring of the water; 4 for an angel of the Lord went down at certain seasons into the pool, and stirred up the water; whoever stepped in first after the stirring of the water was made well from whatever disease that person had.*
[i] Or *had left because of*

[c] 2 Some manuscripts *Bethzatha*; other manuscripts *Bethsaida*
[d] 3 Some less important manuscripts *paralyzed—and they waited for the moving of the waters. 4 From time to time an angel of the Lord would come down and stir up the waters. The first one into the pool after each such disturbance would be cured of whatever disease he had.*

16 Therefore the Jews started persecuting Jesus, be-
cause he was doing such
things on the sabbath.
17 But Jesus answered
them, "My Father is still
working, and I also am
working." 18 For this reason the Jews were seeking
all the more to kill him, because he was not only
breaking the sabbath, but
was also calling God his
own Father, thereby mak-
ing himself equal to God.

The Authority of the Son

19 Jesus said to them,
"Very truly, I tell you, the
Son can do nothing on his
own, but only what he sees
the Father doing; for whatever the Father[j] does, the
Son does likewise. 20 The
Father loves the Son and
shows him all that he himself is doing; and he will
show him greater works
than these, so that you will
be astonished. 21 Indeed,
just as the Father raises the
dead and gives them life, so
also the Son gives life to
whomever he wishes.
22 The Father judges no one
but has given all judgment
to the Son, 23 so that all may
honor the Son just as they
honor the Father. Anyone
who does not honor the
Son does not honor the Father who sent him. 24 Very
truly, I tell you, anyone
who hears my word and be-
lieves him who sent me has
eternal life, and does not
come under judgment, but
has passed from death to
life.

[j] Gk *that one*

τοῦτο ἐδίωκον οἱ Ἰουδαῖοι τὸν Ἰησοῦν,
fore 3persecuted 1the 2Jews – 4Jesus,
ὅτι ταῦτα ἐποίει ἐν σαββάτῳ. 17 ὁ δὲ
because these things he did on a sabbath. But he
ἀπεκρίνατο αὐτοῖς· ὁ πατήρ μου ἕως
answered them : The Father of me until
ἄρτι ἐργάζεται, κἀγὼ ἐργάζομαι· 18 διὰ
now works, and I work; because of
τοῦτο οὖν μᾶλλον ἐζήτουν αὐτὸν οἱ
this therefore 4the more 3sought 6him 1the
Ἰουδαῖοι ἀποκτεῖναι, ὅτι οὐ μόνον ἔλυεν
2Jews 5to kill, because not only he broke
τὸ σάββατον, ἀλλὰ καὶ πατέρα ἴδιον
the sabbath, but also Father [his] own
ἔλεγεν τὸν θεόν, ἴσον ἑαυτὸν ποιῶν τῷ
said – God [to be], equal himself making –
θεῷ. 19 Ἀπεκρίνατο οὖν ὁ Ἰησοῦς καὶ
to God. Answered therefore – Jesus and
ἔλεγεν αὐτοῖς· ἀμὴν ἀμὴν λέγω ὑμῖν,
said to them : Truly truly I say to you,
οὐ δύναται ὁ υἱὸς ποιεῖν ἀφ' ἑαυτοῦ
cannot the Son *to* do from himself
οὐδέν, ἂν μή τι βλέπῃ τὸν πατέρα
no(any)thing, except what he sees the Father
ποιοῦντα· ἃ γὰρ ἂν ἐκεῖνος ποιῇ, ταῦτα
doing; for whatever things that one does, these
καὶ ὁ υἱὸς ὁμοίως ποιεῖ. 20 ὁ γὰρ
also the Son likewise does. For the
πατὴρ φιλεῖ τὸν υἱὸν καὶ πάντα δείκνυσιν
Father loves the Son and all things shows
αὐτῷ ἃ αὐτὸς ποιεῖ, καὶ μείζονα τούτων
him which he does, and 1greater 3[than] 4these
δείξει αὐτῷ ἔργα, ἵνα ὑμεῖς θαυμάζητε.
5he will show 6him 2works, that ye may marvel.
21 ὥσπερ γὰρ ὁ πατὴρ ἐγείρει τοὺς
For as the Father raises the
νεκροὺς καὶ ζωοποιεῖ, οὕτως καὶ ὁ υἱὸς
dead and quickens, so also the Son
οὓς θέλει ζωοποιεῖ. 22 οὐδὲ γὰρ ὁ
whom he wills quickens. For not the
πατὴρ κρίνει οὐδένα, ἀλλὰ τὴν κρίσιν
Father judges no(any) one, but – judgment
πᾶσαν δέδωκεν τῷ υἱῷ, 23 ἵνα πάντες
all he has given to the Son, that all men
τιμῶσι τὸν υἱὸν καθὼς τιμῶσι τὸν πατέρα.
may honour the Son as they honour the Father.
ὁ μὴ τιμῶν τὸν υἱὸν οὐ τιμᾷ τὸν πατέρα
The [one] not honouring the Son honours not the Father
τὸν πέμψαντα αὐτόν. 24 Ἀμὴν ἀμὴν
– having sent him. Truly truly
λέγω ὑμῖν ὅτι ὁ τὸν λόγον μου ἀκούων
I say to you[,] – The [one] the word of me hearing
καὶ πιστεύων τῷ πέμψαντί με ἔχει
and believing the [one] having sent me has
ζωὴν αἰώνιον, καὶ εἰς κρίσιν οὐκ ἔρχεται
life eternal, and into judgment comes not
ἀλλὰ μεταβέβηκεν ἐκ τοῦ θανάτου εἰς
but has passed over out of – death into
τὴν ζωήν. 25 ἀμὴν ἀμὴν λέγω ὑμῖν ὅτι
– life. Truly truly I say to you[,] –
ἔρχεται ὥρα καὶ νῦν ἐστιν ὅτε οἱ νεκροὶ
Comes an hour and now is when the dead
ἀκούσουσιν τῆς φωνῆς τοῦ υἱοῦ τοῦ
will hear the voice of the Son –
θεοῦ καὶ οἱ ἀκούσαντες ζήσουσιν. 26 ὥσπερ
of God and the [ones] hearing will live. as

Life Through the Son

16 So, because Jesus was
doing these things on the
Sabbath, the Jews perse-
cuted him. 17 Jesus said to
them, "My Father is al-
ways at his work to this
very day, and I, too, am
working." 18 For this reason the Jews tried all the
harder to kill him; not only
was he breaking the Sab-
bath, but he was even calling God his own Father,
making himself equal with
God.

19 Jesus gave them this answer: "I tell you the truth,
the Son can do nothing by
himself; he can do only
what he sees his Father doing, because whatever the
Father does the Son also
does. 20 For the Father
loves the Son and shows
him all he does. Yes, to
your amazement he will
show him even greater
things than these. 21 For just
as the Father raises the
dead and gives them life,
even so the Son gives life to
whom he is pleased to give
it. 22 Moreover, the Father
judges no one, but has entrusted all judgment to the
Son, 23 that all may honor
the Son just as they honor
the Father. He who does
not honor the Son does not
honor the Father, who sent
him.

24 "I tell you the truth,
whoever hears my word
and believes him who sent
me has eternal life and will
not be condemned; he has
crossed over from death to

25 "Very truly, I tell
you, the hour is coming,
and is now here, when the
dead will hear the voice of
the Son of God, and those
who hear will live. 26 For
just as the Father has life in
himself, so he has granted
the Son also to have life in
himself; 27 and he has given
him authority to execute
judgment, because he is the
Son of Man. 28 Do not be
astonished at this; for the
hour is coming when all
who are in their graves will
hear his voice 29 and will
come out—those who have
done good, to the resurrection of life, and those who
have done evil, to the resurrection of condemnation.

Witnesses to Jesus

30 "I can do nothing on
my own. As I hear, I judge;
and my judgment is just,
because I seek to do not my
own will but the will of him
who sent me.
31 "If I testify about
myself, my testimony is not
true. 32 There is another
who testifies on my behalf,
and I know that his testimony to me is true. 33 You sent
messengers to John, and he
testified to the truth. 34 Not
that I accept such human
testimony, but I say these
things so that you may be
saved. 35 He was a burning
and shining lamp, and you
were willing to rejoice for a
while in his light. 36 But I
have a testimony greater
than John's. The works
that the Father has given
me to complete, the very
works that I am doing, testify on my behalf that the
Father has sent me. 37 And
the Father who sent me has
himself testified on my behalf. You have never heard
his voice or seen his form,

γὰρ ὁ πατὴρ ἔχει ζωὴν ἐν ἑαυτῷ, οὕτως
For the Father has life in himself, so
καὶ τῷ υἱῷ ἔδωκεν ζωὴν ἔχειν ἐν ἑαυτῷ.
also to the Son he gave life to have in himself.
27 καὶ ἐξουσίαν ἔδωκεν αὐτῷ κρίσιν ποιεῖν,
And authority he gave him judgment to do,
ὅτι υἱὸς ἀνθρώπου ἐστίν. 28 μὴ θαυμάζετε
because son of man* he is. Marvel not [at]
τοῦτο, ὅτι ἔρχεται ὥρα ἐν ᾗ πάντες οἱ
this, because comes an hour in which all the [ones]
ἐν τοῖς μνημείοις ἀκούσουσιν τῆς φωνῆς
in the tombs will hear the voice
αὐτοῦ 29 καὶ ἐκπορεύσονται οἱ τὰ ἀγαθὰ
of him and will come forth the [ones] the good things
ποιήσαντες εἰς ἀνάστασιν ζωῆς, οἱ τὰ
having done to a resurrection of life, the [ones] the
φαῦλα πράξαντες εἰς ἀνάστασιν κρίσεως.
evil things having done to a resurrection of judgment.
30 Οὐ δύναμαι ἐγὼ ποιεῖν ἀπ' ἐμαυτοῦ
Cannot I *to* do from myself
οὐδέν· καθὼς ἀκούω κρίνω, καὶ ἡ κρίσις
no(any)thing; as I hear I judge, and – judgment
ἡ ἐμὴ δικαία ἐστίν, ὅτι οὐ ζητῶ τὸ
– my just is, because I seek not –
θέλημα τὸ ἐμὸν ἀλλὰ τὸ θέλημα τοῦ
will – my but the will of the [one]
πέμψαντός με. 31 Ἐὰν ἐγὼ μαρτυρῶ
having sent me. If I witness
περὶ ἐμαυτοῦ, ἡ μαρτυρία μου οὐκ ἔστιν
concerning myself, the witness of me is not
ἀληθής· 32 ἄλλος ἐστὶν ὁ μαρτυρῶν περὶ
true; another there is the [one] witnessing concerning
ἐμοῦ, καὶ οἶδα ὅτι ἀληθής ἐστιν ἡ
me, and I know that true is the
μαρτυρία ἣν μαρτυρεῖ περὶ ἐμοῦ. 33 ὑμεῖς
witness which he witnesses concerning me. Ye
ἀπεστάλκατε πρὸς Ἰωάννην, καὶ μεμαρ-
have sent to John, and he has
τύρηκεν τῇ ἀληθείᾳ· 34 ἐγὼ δὲ οὐ παρὰ
witnessed to the truth; but I not from
ἀνθρώπου τὴν μαρτυρίαν λαμβάνω, ἀλλὰ
man the witness receive, but
ταῦτα λέγω ἵνα ὑμεῖς σωθῆτε. 35 ἐκεῖνος
these things I say that ye may be saved. That man
ἦν ὁ λύχνος ὁ καιόμενος καὶ φαίνων,
was the lamp – burning and shining,
ὑμεῖς δὲ ἠθελήσατε ἀγαλλιαθῆναι πρὸς
and ye were willing to exult for
ὥραν ἐν τῷ φωτὶ αὐτοῦ. 36 Ἐγὼ δὲ
an hour in the light of him. But I
ἔχω τὴν μαρτυρίαν μείζω τοῦ Ἰωάννου·
have the witness greater [than] – of John;
τὰ γὰρ ἔργα ἃ δέδωκέν μοι ὁ πατὴρ ἵνα
for the works which has given me the Father that
τελειώσω αὐτά, αὐτὰ τὰ ἔργα ἃ ποιῶ,
I may finish them, [3][them]selves [1]the [2]works which I do,
μαρτυρεῖ περὶ ἐμοῦ ὅτι ὁ πατήρ με
witness*es* concerning me that the Father me
ἀπέσταλκεν. 37 καὶ ὁ πέμψας με πατήρ,
has sent. And [1]the [3]having sent [4]me [2]Father,
ἐκεῖνος μεμαρτύρηκεν περὶ ἐμοῦ. οὔτε
that [one] has witnessed concerning me. Neither
φωνὴν αὐτοῦ πώποτε ἀκηκόατε οὔτε εἶδος
voice of him *n*ever ye have heard nor form

* Note the absence of the definite article here. See also Rev. 1. 13 and 14. 14.

life. 25 I tell you the truth, a
time is coming and has now
come when the dead will
hear the voice of the Son of
God and those who hear
will live. 26 For as the Father has life in himself, so
he has granted the Son to
have life in himself. 27 And
he has given him authority
to judge because he is the
Son of Man.
28 "Do not be amazed at
this, for a time is coming
when all who are in their
graves will hear his voice
29 and come out—those
who have done good will
rise to live, and those who
have done evil will rise to
be condemned. 30 By my-
self I can do nothing; I
judge only as I hear, and
my judgment is just, for I
seek not to please myself
but him who sent me.

Testimonies About Jesus

31 "If I testify about myself, my testimony is not
valid. 32 There is another
who testifies in my favor,
and I know that his testimony about me is valid.
33 "You have sent to John
and he has testified to the
truth. 34 Not that I accept
human testimony; but I
mention it that you may be
saved. 35 John was a lamp
that burned and gave light,
and you chose for a time to
enjoy his light.
36 "I have testimony
weightier than that of John.
For the very work that the
Father has given me to finish, and which I am doing,
testifies that the Father has
sent me. 37 And the Father
who sent me has himself
testified concerning me.
You have never heard his
voice nor seen his form,

[38]and you do not have his
word abiding in you, be-
cause you do not believe
him whom he has sent.
39 "You search the
scriptures because you
think that in them you have
eternal life; and it is they
that testify on my behalf.
[40]Yet you refuse to come to
me to have life. [41]I do not
accept glory from human
beings. [42]But I know that
you do not have the love of
God in[k] you. [43]I have
come in my Father's name,
and you do not accept me;
if another comes in his own
name, you will accept him.
[44]How can you believe
when you accept glory
from one another and do
not seek the glory that
comes from the one who
alone is God? [45]Do not
think that I will accuse you
before the Father; your accuser is Moses, on whom
you have set your hope.
[46]If you believed Moses,
you would believe me, for
he wrote about me. [47]But if
you do not believe what he
wrote, how will you believe
what I say?"

αὐτοῦ ἑωράκατε, 38 καὶ τὸν λόγον αὐτοῦ
of him ye have seen, and the word of him
οὐκ ἔχετε ἐν ὑμῖν μένοντα, ὅτι ὃν
ye have not in you remaining, because [he] whom
ἀπέστειλεν ἐκεῖνος, τούτῳ ὑμεῖς οὐ πιστεύετε.
²sent ¹that [one], this [one] ye do not believe.
39 ἐρευνᾶτε τὰς γραφάς, ὅτι ὑμεῖς δοκεῖτε
Ye search the scriptures, because ye think
ἐν αὐταῖς ζωὴν αἰώνιον ἔχειν· καὶ ἐκεῖναί
in them life eternal to have; and those
εἰσιν αἱ μαρτυροῦσαι περὶ ἐμοῦ· 40 καὶ
are the [ones] witnessing concerning me; and
οὐ θέλετε ἐλθεῖν πρός με ἵνα ζωὴν
ye wish not to come to me that life
ἔχητε. 41 Δόξαν παρὰ ἀνθρώπων οὐ
ye may have. Glory from men not
λαμβάνω, 42 ἀλλὰ ἔγνωκα ὑμᾶς ὅτι τὴν
I receive, but I have known you that the
ἀγάπην τοῦ θεοῦ οὐκ ἔχετε ἐν ἑαυτοῖς.
love – of God ye have not in *yourselves.*
43 ἐγὼ ἐλήλυθα ἐν τῷ ὀνόματι τοῦ πατρός
I have come in the name of the Father
μου, καὶ οὐ λαμβάνετέ με· ἐὰν ἄλλος
of me, and ye receive not me; if another
ἔλθῃ ἐν τῷ ὀνόματι τῷ ἰδίῳ, ἐκεῖνον
comes in – name the(his) own, that [one]
λήμψεσθε. 44 πῶς δύνασθε ὑμεῖς πιστεῦσαι,
ye will receive. How can ye *to* believe,
δόξαν παρὰ ἀλλήλων λαμβάνοντες, καὶ
glory from one another receiving, and
τὴν δόξαν τὴν παρὰ τοῦ μόνου θεοῦ
the glory – from the only God
οὐ ζητεῖτε; 45 μὴ δοκεῖτε ὅτι ἐγὼ κατηγορήσω
ye seek not? Do not think that I will accuse
ὑμῶν πρὸς τὸν πατέρα· ἔστιν ὁ κατηγορῶν
you to the Father; there is the [one] accusing
ὑμῶν Μωϋσῆς, εἰς ὃν ὑμεῖς ἠλπίκατε. 46 εἰ
you[,] Moses, in whom ye have hoped. if
γὰρ ἐπιστεύετε Μωϋσεῖ, ἐπιστεύετε ἂν
For ye believed Moses, ye would have believed
ἐμοί· περὶ γὰρ ἐμοῦ ἐκεῖνος ἔγραψεν.
me; for concerning me that [one] wrote.
47 εἰ δὲ τοῖς ἐκείνου γράμμασιν οὐ
But ¹if ⁴the ⁵of that [one] ⁶letters ²not
πιστεύετε, πῶς τοῖς ἐμοῖς ῥήμασιν
³ye believe, how – my words
πιστεύσετε;
will ye believe?

[38]nor does his word dwell
in you, for you do not believe the one he sent. [39]You
diligently study[e] the Scriptures because you think
that by them you possess
eternal life. These are the
Scriptures that testify
about me, [40]yet you refuse
to come to me to have life.
[41]"I do not accept praise
from men, [42]but I know
you. I know that you do not
have the love of God in
your hearts. [43]I have come
in my Father's name, and
you do not accept me; but if
someone else comes in his
own name, you will accept
him. [44]How can you be-
lieve if you accept praise
from one another, yet make
no effort to obtain the
praise that comes from the
only God[f]?
[45]"But do not think I will
accuse you before the Fa-
ther. Your accuser is Mo-
ses, on whom your hopes
are set. [46]If you believed
Moses, you would believe
me, for he wrote about me.
[47]But since you do not believe what he wrote, how
are you going to believe
what I say?"

Chapter 6

Feeding the Five Thousand

AFTER this Jesus went
to the other side of
the Sea of Galilee, also
called the Sea of Tiberi-
as.[l] [2]A large crowd kept
following him, because
they saw the signs that he
was doing for the sick.
[3]Jesus went up the mountain and sat down there
with his disciples. [4]Now
the Passover, the festival of
the Jews, was near. [5]When
he looked up and saw a

6 Μετὰ ταῦτα ἀπῆλθεν ὁ Ἰησοῦς πέραν
After these things went away – Jesus across
τῆς θαλάσσης τῆς Γαλιλαίας τῆς Τιβεριάδος.
the sea – of Galilee[,] – of Tiberias.
2 ἠκολούθει δὲ αὐτῷ ὄχλος πολύς, ὅτι
And followed him crowd a much, because
ἑώρων τὰ σημεῖα ἃ ἐποίει ἐπὶ τῶν
they saw the signs which he did on the
ἀσθενούντων. 3 ἀνῆλθεν δὲ εἰς τὸ ὄρος
ailing [ones]. And went up to the mountain
Ἰησοῦς, καὶ ἐκεῖ ἐκάθητο μετὰ τῶν
Jesus, and there sat with the
μαθητῶν αὐτοῦ. 4 ἦν δὲ ἐγγὺς τὸ πάσχα,
disciples of him. And was near the Passover,
ἡ ἑορτὴ τῶν Ἰουδαίων. 5 ἐπάρας οὖν
the feast of the Jews. Lifting up therefore

Chapter 6

Jesus Feeds the Five Thousand

SOME time after this,
Jesus crossed to the far
shore of the Sea of Galilee
(that is, the Sea of Tiberias), [2]and a great crowd of
people followed him be-
cause they saw the miraculous signs he had per-
formed on the sick. [3]Then
Jesus went up on a moun-
tainside and sat down with
his disciples. [4]The Jewish
Passover Feast was near.
[5]When Jesus looked up

[k] Or *among*
[l] Gk *of Galilee of Tiberius*

[e]39 Or *Study diligently* (the imperative)
[f]44 Some early manuscripts *the Only One*

large crowd coming toward
him, Jesus said to Philip,
"Where are we to buy
bread for these people to
eat?" 6 He said this to test
him, for he himself knew
what he was going to do.
7 Philip answered him, "Six
months' wages[m] would not
buy enough bread for each
of them to get a little."
8 One of his disciples, Andrew, Simon Peter's brother, said to him, 9 "There is a
boy here who has five barley loaves and two fish. But
what are they among so
many people?" 10 Jesus
said, "Make the people sit
down." Now there was a
great deal of grass in the
place; so they[n] sat down,
about five thousand in all.
11 Then Jesus took the
loaves, and when he had
given thanks, he distributed them to those who were
seated; so also the fish, as
much as they wanted.
12 When they were satis-
fied, he told his disciples,
"Gather up the fragments
left over, so that nothing
may be lost." 13 So they
gathered them up, and from
the fragments of the five
barley loaves, left by those
who had eaten, they filled
twelve baskets. 14 When
the people saw the sign that
he had done, they began to
say, "This is indeed the
prophet who is to come into
the world."
15 When Jesus realized
that they were about to
come and take him by force
to make him king, he withdrew again to the mountain
by himself.

[m] Gk *Two hundred denarii*; the denarius was the usual day's wage for a laborer
[n] Gk *the men*

τοὺς ὀφθαλμοὺς ὁ Ἰησοῦς καὶ θεασάμενος
the(his) eyes – Jesus and beholding

ὅτι πολὺς ὄχλος ἔρχεται πρὸς αὐτόν,
that a much crowd is(was) coming toward him,

λέγει πρὸς Φίλιππον· πόθεν ἀγοράσωμεν
he says to Philip : Whence may we buy

ἄρτους ἵνα φάγωσιν οὗτοι; 6 τοῦτο δὲ
loaves that may eat these? And this

ἔλεγεν πειράζων αὐτόν· αὐτὸς γὰρ ᾔδει
he said testing him; for he knew

τί ἔμελλεν ποιεῖν. 7 ἀπεκρίθη αὐτῷ ὁ
what he was about to do. Answered him –

Φίλιππος· διακοσίων δηναρίων ἄρτοι οὐκ
Philip : [2]Of two hundred [3]denarii [1]loaves not

ἀρκοῦσιν αὐτοῖς, ἵνα ἕκαστος βραχύ τι
are enough for them, that each a little

λάβῃ. 8 λέγει αὐτῷ εἷς ἐκ τῶν μαθητῶν
may take. Says to him one of the disciples

αὐτοῦ, Ἀνδρέας ὁ ἀδελφὸς Σίμωνος
of him, Andrew the brother of Simon

Πέτρου· 9 ἔστιν παιδάριον ὧδε ὃς ἔχει
Peter : There is a lad here who has

πέντε ἄρτους κριθίνους καὶ δύο ὀψάρια·
five loaves barley and two fishes;

ἀλλὰ ταῦτα τί ἐστιν εἰς τοσούτους;
but [3]these [1]what [2]is(are) among so many?

10 εἶπεν ὁ Ἰησοῦς· ποιήσατε τοὺς ἀνθρώπους
Said – Jesus : Make the men*

ἀναπεσεῖν. ἦν δὲ χόρτος πολὺς ἐν τῷ
to recline. Now there was grass much in the

τόπῳ. ἀνέπεσαν οὖν οἱ ἄνδρες τὸν ἀριθμὸν
place. Reclined therefore the men the number

ὡς πεντακισχίλιοι. 11 ἔλαβεν οὖν τοὺς
about five thousand. Took therefore the

ἄρτους ὁ Ἰησοῦς καὶ εὐχαριστήσας
loaves – Jesus and having given thanks

διέδωκεν τοῖς ἀνακειμένοις, ὁμοίως καὶ
distributed to the [ones] lying down, likewise also

ἐκ τῶν ὀψαρίων ὅσον ἤθελον. 12 ὡς δὲ
of the fishes as much as they wished. Now when

ἐνεπλήσθησαν, λέγει τοῖς μαθηταῖς αὐτοῦ·
they were filled, he tells the disciples of him:

συναγάγετε τὰ περισσεύσαντα κλάσματα, ἵνα
Gather ye the left over fragments, that

μή τι ἀπόληται. 13 συνήγαγον οὖν, καὶ
not anything is lost. They gathered therefore, and

ἐγέμισαν δώδεκα κοφίνους κλασμάτων ἐκ
filled twelve baskets of fragments of

τῶν πέντε ἄρτων τῶν κριθίνων ἃ ἐπερίσσευσαν
the five loaves – barley which were left over

τοῖς βεβρωκόσιν. 14 Οἱ οὖν ἄνθρωποι
to the [ones] having eaten. Therefore the men*

ἰδόντες ὃ ἐποίησεν σημεῖον ἔλεγον ὅτι
seeing [1]what [3]he did [2]sign said[,] –

οὗτός ἐστιν ἀληθῶς ὁ προφήτης ὁ
This is truly the prophet –

ἐρχόμενος εἰς τὸν κόσμον. 15 Ἰησοῦς
coming into the world. Jesus

οὖν γνοὺς ὅτι μέλλουσιν ἔρχεσθαι καὶ
therefore knowing that they are(were) about to come and

ἁρπάζειν αὐτὸν ἵνα ποιήσωσιν βασιλέα,
seize him that they might make a king,

ἀνεχώρησεν πάλιν εἰς τὸ ὄρος αὐτὸς
departed again to the mountain [him]self

* That is, people. Compare ἄνδρες in ver. 10.

and saw a great crowd coming toward him, he said to
Philip, "Where shall we
buy bread for these people
to eat?" 6 He asked this
only to test him, for he already had in mind what he
was going to do.
7 Philip answered him,
"Eight months' wages[g]
would not buy enough
bread for each one to have
a bite!"
8 Another of his disciples,
Andrew, Simon Peter's
brother, spoke up, 9 "Here
is a boy with five small barley loaves and two small
fish, but how far will they
go among so many?"
10 Jesus said, "Have the
people sit down." There
was plenty of grass in that
place, and the men sat
down, about five thousand
of them. 11 Jesus then took
the loaves, gave thanks,
and distributed to those
who were seated as much
as they wanted. He did the
same with the fish.
12 When they had all had
enough to eat, he said to his
disciples, "Gather the
pieces that are left over.
Let nothing be wasted."
13 So they gathered them
and filled twelve baskets
with the pieces of the five
barley loaves left over by
those who had eaten.
14 After the people saw
the miraculous sign that
Jesus did, they began to
say, "Surely this is the
Prophet who is to come
into the world." 15 Jesus,
knowing that they intended
to come and make him king
by force, withdrew again to
a mountain by himself.

[g] 7 Greek *two hundred denarii*

Jesus Walks on the Water

16 When evening came, his disciples went down to the sea, 17 got into a boat, and started across the sea to Capernaum. It was now dark, and Jesus had not yet come to them. 18 The sea became rough because a strong wind was blowing. 19 When they had rowed about three or four miles,[o] they saw Jesus walking on the sea and coming near the boat, and they were terrified. 20 But he said to them, "It is I;[p] do not be afraid." 21 Then they wanted to take him into the boat, and immediately the boat reached the land toward which they were going.

The Bread from Heaven

22 The next day the crowd that had stayed on the other side of the sea saw that there had been only one boat there. They also saw that Jesus had not got into the boat with his disciples, but that his disciples had gone away alone. 23 Then some boats from Tiberias came near the place where they had eaten the bread after the Lord had given thanks.[q] 24 So when the crowd saw that neither Jesus nor his disciples were there, they themselves got into the boats and went to Capernaum looking for Jesus.

25 When they found him on the other side of the sea, they said to him, "Rabbi, when did you come here?" 26 Jesus answered them, "Very truly, I tell you, you are looking for me, not because you saw

[o] Gk *about twenty-five or thirty stadia*
[p] Gk *I am*
[q] Other ancient authorities lack *after the Lord had given thanks*

μόνος. 16 Ὡς δὲ ὀψία ἐγένετο, κατέβησαν
alone. And when evening came, went down

οἱ μαθηταὶ αὐτοῦ ἐπὶ τὴν θάλασσαν,
the disciples of him to the sea,

17 καὶ ἐμβάντες εἰς πλοῖον ἤρχοντο πέραν
and embarking in a boat came across

τῆς θαλάσσης εἰς Καφαρναούμ. καὶ
the sea to Capernaum. And

σκοτία ἤδη ἐγεγόνει καὶ οὔπω ἐληλύθει
darkness now had come and not yet had come

πρὸς αὐτοὺς ὁ Ἰησοῦς, 18 ἥ τε θάλασσα
to them – Jesus, and the sea

ἀνέμου μεγάλου πνέοντος διηγείρετο.
wind a great blowing[a] was roused.
=as a great wind blew

19 ἐληλακότες οὖν ὡς σταδίους εἴκοσι
Having rowed therefore about furlongs twenty-

πέντε ἢ τριάκοντα θεωροῦσιν τὸν Ἰησοῦν
five or thirty they behold – Jesus

περιπατοῦντα ἐπὶ τῆς θαλάσσης καὶ ἐγγὺς
walking on the sea and near

τοῦ πλοίου γινόμενον, καὶ ἐφοβήθησαν.
the boat becoming, and they feared.

20 ὁ δὲ λέγει αὐτοῖς· ἐγώ εἰμι· μὴ
But he says to them : I am; not

φοβεῖσθε. 21 ἤθελον οὖν λαβεῖν αὐτὸν εἰς
fear ye. They wished therefore to take him into

τὸ πλοῖον, καὶ εὐθέως ἐγένετο τὸ πλοῖον
the boat, and immediately was the boat

ἐπὶ τῆς γῆς εἰς ἣν ὑπῆγον.
at the land to which they were going.

22 Τῇ ἐπαύριον ὁ ὄχλος ὁ ἑστηκὼς
On the morrow the crowd – standing

πέραν τῆς θαλάσσης εἶδον ὅτι πλοιάριον
across the sea saw that boat

ἄλλο οὐκ ἦν ἐκεῖ εἰ μὴ ἕν, καὶ ὅτι
other was not there except one, and that

οὐ συνεισῆλθεν τοῖς μαθηταῖς αὐτοῦ ὁ
[2]did not come *in* with [3]the [4]disciples [5]of him –

Ἰησοῦς εἰς τὸ πλοῖον ἀλλὰ μόνοι οἱ
[1]Jesus in the boat but alone the

μαθηταὶ αὐτοῦ ἀπῆλθον· 23 ἄλλα ἦλθεν
disciples of him went away; [1]other [3]came

πλοιάρια ἐκ Τιβεριάδος ἐγγὺς τοῦ τόπου
[2]boats from Tiberias near the place

ὅπου ἔφαγον τὸν ἄρτον εὐχαριστήσαντος
where they ate the bread having given thanks

τοῦ κυρίου. 24 ὅτε οὖν εἶδεν ὁ ὄχλος
the Lord.[a] When therefore saw the crowd
=when the Lord had given thanks.

ὅτι Ἰησοῦς οὐκ ἔστιν ἐκεῖ οὐδὲ οἱ
that Jesus is(was) not there nor the

μαθηταὶ αὐτοῦ, ἐνέβησαν αὐτοὶ εἰς τὰ
disciples of him, embarked they in the

πλοιάρια καὶ ἦλθον εἰς Καφαρναοὺμ
boats and came to Capernaum

ζητοῦντες τὸν Ἰησοῦν. 25 καὶ εὑρόντες
seeking – Jesus. And finding

αὐτὸν πέραν τῆς θαλάσσης εἶπον αὐτῷ·
him across the sea they said to him :

ῥαββί, πότε ὧδε γέγονας; 26 ἀπεκρίθη
Rabbi, when here hast thou come? Answered

αὐτοῖς ὁ Ἰησοῦς καὶ εἶπεν· ἀμὴν ἀμὴν
them – Jesus and said: Truly truly

λέγω ὑμῖν, ζητεῖτέ με οὐχ ὅτι εἴδετε
I say to you, ye seek me not because ye saw

Jesus Walks on the Water

16 When evening came, his disciples went down to the lake, 17 where they got into a boat and set off across the lake for Capernaum. By now it was dark, and Jesus had not yet joined them. 18 A strong wind was blowing and the waters grew rough. 19 When they had rowed three or three and a half miles,[h] they saw Jesus approaching the boat, walking on the water; and they were terrified. 20 But he said to them, "It is I; don't be afraid." 21 Then they were willing to take him into the boat, and immediately the boat reached the shore where they were heading.

22 The next day the crowd that had stayed on the opposite shore of the lake realized that only one boat had been there, and that Jesus had not entered it with his disciples, but that they had gone away alone. 23 Then some boats from Tiberias landed near the place where the people had eaten the bread after the Lord had given thanks. 24 Once the crowd realized that neither Jesus nor his disciples were there, they got into the boats and went to Capernaum in search of Jesus.

Jesus the Bread of Life

25 When they found him on the other side of the lake, they asked him, "Rabbi, when did you get here?"

26 Jesus answered, "I tell you the truth, you are looking for me, not because you

[h] 19 Greek *rowed twenty-five or thirty stadia* (about 5 or 6 kilometers)

signs, but because you ate
your fill of the loaves. 27 Do
not work for the food that
perishes, but for the food
that endures for eternal
life, which the Son of Man
will give you. For it is on
him that God the Father
has set his seal." 28 Then
they said to him, "What
must we do to perform the
works of God?" 29 Jesus answered them, "This is the
work of God, that you be-
lieve in him whom he has
sent." 30 So they said to
him, "What sign are you
going to give us then, so
that we may see it and believe you? What work are
you performing? 31 Our ancestors ate the manna in the
wilderness; as it is written,
'He gave them bread from
heaven to eat.'" 32 Then
Jesus said to them, "Very
truly, I tell you, it was not
Moses who gave you the
bread from heaven, but it is
my Father who gives you
the true bread from heav-
en. 33 For the bread of God
is that which[r] comes down
from heaven and gives life
to the world." 34 They said
to him, "Sir, give us this
bread always."
35 Jesus said to them, "I
am the bread of life. Whoever comes to me will never be hungry, and whoever
believes in me will never be
thirsty. 36 But I said to you
that you have seen me and
yet do not believe. 37 Everything that the Father
gives me will come to me,
and anyone who comes to
me I will never drive away;
38 for I have come down

[r]Or *he who*

σημεῖα, ἀλλʼ ὅτι ἐφάγετε ἐκ τῶν ἄρτων
signs, but because ye ate of the loaves
καὶ ἐχορτάσθητε. 27 ἐργάζεσθε μὴ τὴν
and were satisfied. Work not [for] the
βρῶσιν τὴν ἀπολλυμένην, ἀλλὰ τὴν βρῶσιν
food – perishing, but [for] the food
τὴν μένουσαν εἰς ζωὴν αἰώνιον, ἣν ὁ
– remaining to life eternal, which the
υἱὸς τοῦ ἀνθρώπου ὑμῖν δώσει· τοῦτον γὰρ
Son – of man you will give; for this [one]
ὁ πατὴρ ἐσφράγισεν ὁ θεός. 28 εἶπον
[2]the [3]Father [4]sealed – [1]God. They said
οὖν πρὸς αὐτόν· τί ποιῶμεν ἵνα ἐργαζ-
therefore to him: What may we do that we may
ώμεθα τὰ ἔργα τοῦ θεοῦ; 29 ἀπεκρίθη
work the works – of God? Answered
Ἰησοῦς καὶ εἶπεν αὐτοῖς· τοῦτό ἐστιν τὸ
Jesus and said to them: This is the
ἔργον τοῦ θεοῦ, ἵνα πιστεύητε εἰς ὃν
work – of God, that ye believe in [him] whom
ἀπέστειλεν ἐκεῖνος. 30 εἶπον οὖν αὐτῷ·
sent that [one]. They said therefore to him:
τί οὖν ποιεῖς σὺ σημεῖον, ἵνα ἴδωμεν
[1]What [2]then [3]doest [4]thou [5]sign, that we may see
καὶ πιστεύσωμέν σοι; τί ἐργάζῃ; 31 οἱ
and believe thee? what workest thou? The
πατέρες ἡμῶν τὸ μάννα ἔφαγον ἐν τῇ
fathers of us the manna ate in the
ἐρήμῳ, καθώς ἐστιν γεγραμμένον· ἄρτον
desert, as it is *having been* written: Bread
ἐκ τοῦ οὐρανοῦ ἔδωκεν αὐτοῖς φαγεῖν.
out of – heaven he gave them to eat.
32 Εἶπεν οὖν αὐτοῖς ὁ Ἰησοῦς· ἀμὴν
Said therefore to them – Jesus: Truly
ἀμὴν λέγω ὑμῖν, οὐ Μωϋσῆς δέδωκεν
truly I say to you, not Moses has given
ὑμῖν τὸν ἄρτον ἐκ τοῦ οὐρανοῦ, ἀλλʼ ὁ
you the bread out of – heaven, but the
πατήρ μου δίδωσιν ὑμῖν τὸν ἄρτον ἐκ
Father of me gives you [1]the [3]bread [4]out of
τοῦ οὐρανοῦ τὸν ἀληθινόν· 33 ὁ γὰρ ἄρτος
– [5]heaven *the* [2]true; for the bread
τοῦ θεοῦ ἐστιν ὁ καταβαίνων ἐκ τοῦ
– of God is the [one] coming down out of –
οὐρανοῦ καὶ ζωὴν διδοὺς τῷ κόσμῳ.
heaven and life giving to the world.
34 εἶπον οὖν πρὸς αὐτόν· κύριε, πάντοτε
They said therefore to him: Lord, always
δὸς ἡμῖν τὸν ἄρτον τοῦτον. 35 εἶπεν
give us – bread this. Said
αὐτοῖς ὁ Ἰησοῦς· ἐγώ εἰμι ὁ ἄρτος τῆς
to them – Jesus: I am the bread –
ζωῆς· ὁ ἐρχόμενος πρὸς ἐμὲ οὐ μὴ
of life; the [one] coming to me by no means
πεινάσῃ, καὶ ὁ πιστεύων εἰς ἐμὲ οὐ μὴ
hungers, and the [one] believing in me by no means
διψήσει πώποτε. 36 Ἀλλʼ εἶπον ὑμῖν ὅτι
will thirst *never*. But I told you that
καὶ ἑωράκατέ [με] καὶ οὐ πιστεύετε.
both ye have seen me and do not believe.
37 πᾶν ὃ δίδωσίν μοι ὁ πατὴρ πρὸς
All which gives to me the Father to
ἐμὲ ἥξει, καὶ τὸν ἐρχόμενον πρός με
me will come, and the [one] coming to me
οὐ μὴ ἐκβάλω ἔξω, 38 ὅτι καταβέβηκα
by no means I will cast *out* outside, because I have come down

saw miraculous signs but
because you ate the loaves
and had your fill. 27Do not
work for food that spoils,
but for food that endures to
eternal life, which the Son
of Man will give you. On
him God the Father has
placed his seal of approval."
28Then they asked him,
"What must we do to do
the works God requires?"
29Jesus answered, "The
work of God is this: to believe in the one he has
sent."
30So they asked him,
"What miraculous sign
then will you give that we
may see it and believe you?
What will you do? 31Our
forefathers ate the manna
in the desert; as it is written: 'He gave them bread
from heaven to eat.'[i]"
32Jesus said to them, "I
tell you the truth, it is not
Moses who has given you
the bread from heaven, but
it is my Father who gives
you the true bread from
heaven. 33For the bread of
God is he who comes down
from heaven and gives life
to the world."
34"Sir," they said, "from
now on give us this bread."
35Then Jesus declared, "I
am the bread of life. He
who comes to me will never
go hungry, and he who be-
lieves in me will never be
thirsty. 36But as I told you,
you have seen me and still
you do not believe. 37All
that the Father gives me
will come to me, and who-
ever comes to me I will
never drive away. 38For I
have come down from

[i]*31* Exodus 16:4; Neh. 9:15; Psalm 78:24,25

from heaven, not to do my
own will, but the will of him
who sent me. 39 And this is
the will of him who sent
me, that I should lose nothing of all that he has given
me, but raise it up on the
last day. 40 This is indeed
the will of my Father, that
all who see the Son and believe in him may have eternal life; and I will raise
them up on the last day."
41 Then the Jews began
to complain about him be-
cause he said, "I am the
bread that came down from
heaven." 42 They were saying, "Is not this Jesus, the
son of Joseph, whose fa-
ther and mother we know?
How can he now say, 'I
have come down from
heaven'?" 43 Jesus an-
swered them, "Do not com-
plain among yourselves.
44 No one can come to me
unless drawn by the Father
who sent me; and I will
raise that person up on the
last day. 45 It is written in
the prophets, 'And they
shall all be taught by God.'
Everyone who has heard
and learned from the Fa-
ther comes to me. 46 Not
that anyone has seen the
Father except the one who
is from God; he has seen
the Father. 47 Very truly, I
tell you, whoever believes
has eternal life. 48 I am the
bread of life. 49 Your ancestors ate the manna in the
wilderness, and they died.
50 This is the bread that
comes down from heaven,
so that one may eat of it and

ἀπὸ τοῦ οὐρανοῦ οὐχ ἵνα ποιῶ τὸ θέλημα
from – heaven not that I may do *the* [2]will
τὸ ἐμὸν ἀλλὰ τὸ θέλημα τοῦ πέμψαντός
– [1]my but the will of the [one] having sent
με. 39 τοῦτο δέ ἐστιν τὸ θέλημα τοῦ
me. And this is the will of the [one]
πέμψαντός με, ἵνα πᾶν ὃ δέδωκέν μοι
having sent me, that all which he has given me
μὴ ἀπολέσω ἐξ αὐτοῦ, ἀλλὰ ἀναστήσω
I shall not lose of it, but shall raise up
αὐτὸ ἐν τῇ ἐσχάτῃ ἡμέρᾳ. 40 τοῦτο
it in the last day. this
γάρ ἐστιν τὸ θέλημα τοῦ πατρός μου,
For is the will of the Father of me,
ἵνα πᾶς ὁ θεωρῶν τὸν υἱὸν καὶ πιστεύων
that everyone beholding the Son and believing
εἰς αὐτὸν ἔχῃ ζωὴν αἰώνιον, καὶ ἀναστήσω
in him may have life eternal, and will raise up
αὐτὸν ἐγὼ ἐν τῇ ἐσχάτῃ ἡμέρᾳ. 41 Ἐγόγ-
him I in the last day. Mur-
γυζον οὖν οἱ Ἰουδαῖοι περὶ αὐτοῦ ὅτι
mured therefore the Jews about him because
εἶπεν· ἐγώ εἰμι ὁ ἄρτος ὁ καταβὰς ἐκ
he said : I am the bread – having come down out
τοῦ οὐρανοῦ, 42 καὶ ἔλεγον· οὐχ οὗτός
– of heaven, and they said: Not this man
ἐστιν Ἰησοῦς ὁ υἱὸς Ἰωσήφ, οὗ ἡμεῖς
is Jesus the son of Joseph, of whom we
οἴδαμεν τὸν πατέρα καὶ τὴν μητέρα;
know the father and the mother?
πῶς νῦν λέγει ὅτι ἐκ τοῦ οὐρανοῦ
how now says he[,] – Out of – heaven
καταβέβηκα; 43 ἀπεκρίθη Ἰησοῦς καὶ εἶπεν
I have come down? Answered Jesus and said
αὐτοῖς· μὴ γογγύζετε μετ' ἀλλήλων.
to them: Do not murmur with one another.
44 Οὐδεὶς δύναται ἐλθεῖν πρός με ἐὰν μὴ
No one can *to* come to me unless
ὁ πατὴρ ὁ πέμψας με ἑλκύσῃ αὐτόν,
the Father the [one] having sent me should draw him,
κἀγὼ ἀναστήσω αὐτὸν ἐν τῇ ἐσχάτῃ
and I will raise up him in the last
ἡμέρᾳ. 45 ἔστιν γεγραμμένον ἐν τοῖς
day. It is *having been* written in the
προφήταις· καὶ ἔσονται πάντες διδακτοὶ
prophets : And they shall be all taught
θεοῦ· πᾶς ὁ ἀκούσας παρὰ τοῦ πατρὸς
of God; everyone hearing from the Father
καὶ μαθὼν ἔρχεται πρὸς ἐμέ. 46 οὐχ
and learning comes to me. Not
ὅτι τὸν πατέρα ἑώρακέν τις, εἰ μὴ ὁ
that [3]the [4]Father [2]has seen [1]anyone, except the [one]
ὢν παρὰ τοῦ θεοῦ, οὗτος ἑώρακεν τὸν
being from – God, this [one] has seen the
πατέρα. 47 ἀμὴν ἀμὴν λέγω ὑμῖν, ὁ
Father. Truly truly I say to you, the
πιστεύων ἔχει ζωὴν αἰώνιον. 48 Ἐγώ
[one] believing has life eternal. I
εἰμι ὁ ἄρτος τῆς ζωῆς. 49 οἱ πατέρες
am the bread – of life. The fathers
ὑμῶν ἔφαγον ἐν τῇ ἐρήμῳ τὸ μάννα καὶ
of you ate in the desert the manna and
ἀπέθανον· 50 οὗτός ἐστιν ὁ ἄρτος ὁ ἐκ
died ; this is the bread – out of
τοῦ οὐρανοῦ καταβαίνων, ἵνα τις ἐξ
– heaven coming down, that anyone of

heaven not to do my will
but to do the will of him
who sent me. 39 And this is
the will of him who sent
me, that I shall lose none of
all that he has given me, but
raise them up at the last
day. 40 For my Father's will
is that everyone who looks
to the Son and believes in
him shall have eternal life,
and I will raise him up at
the last day."
41 At this the Jews began
to grumble about him be-
cause he said, "I am the
bread that came down from
heaven." 42 They said, "Is
this not Jesus, the son of
Joseph, whose father and
mother we know? How can
he now say, 'I came down
from heaven'?"
43 "Stop grumbling among
yourselves," Jesus an-
swered. 44 "No one can
come to me unless the Fa-
ther who sent me draws
him, and I will raise him up
at the last day. 45 It is written in the Prophets: 'They
will all be taught by God.'[j]
Everyone who listens to
the Father and learns from
him comes to me. 46 No one
has seen the Father except
the one who is from God;
only he has seen the Fa-
ther. 47 I tell you the truth,
he who believes has ever-
lasting life. 48 I am the bread
of life. 49 Your forefathers
ate the manna in the desert,
yet they died. 50 But here is
the bread that comes down
from heaven, which a man
may eat and not die. 51 I am

[j]45 Isaiah 54:13

not die. 51 I am the living
bread that came down from
heaven. Whoever eats of
this bread will live forever;
and the bread that I will
give for the life of the world
is my flesh."
52 The Jews then dis-
puted among themselves,
saying, "How can this man
give us his flesh to eat?"
53 So Jesus said to them,
"Very truly, I tell you, unless you eat the flesh of the
Son of Man and drink his
blood, you have no life in
you. 54 Those who eat my
flesh and drink my blood
have eternal life, and I will
raise them up on the last
day; 55 for my flesh is true
food and my blood is true
drink. 56 Those who eat my
flesh and drink my blood
abide in me, and I in them.
57 Just as the living Father
sent me, and I live because
of the Father, so whoever
eats me will live because of
me. 58 This is the bread that
came down from heaven,
not like that which your ancestors ate, and they died.
But the one who eats this
bread will live forever."
59 He said these things
while he was teaching in
the synagogue at Caperna-
um.

The Words of Eternal Life

60 When many of his
disciples heard it, they
said, "This teaching is difficult; who can accept it?"
61 But Jesus, being aware
that his disciples were complaining about it, said to
them, "Does this offend
you? 62 Then what if you

αὐτοῦ φάγῃ καὶ μὴ ἀποθάνῃ. 51 ἐγώ
it may eat and may not die. I
εἰμι ὁ ἄρτος ὁ ζῶν ὁ ἐκ τοῦ οὐρανοῦ
am the bread – living the [one] out of – heaven
καταβάς· ἐάν τις φάγῃ ἐκ τούτου τοῦ
having come down; if anyone eats of this –
ἄρτου, ζήσει εἰς τὸν αἰῶνα· καὶ ὁ ἄρτος
bread, he will live to the age; [2]indeed [3]the [4]bread
δὲ ὃν ἐγὼ δώσω ἡ σάρξ μού ἐστιν
[1]and which I will give the flesh of me is
ὑπὲρ τῆς τοῦ κόσμου ζωῆς. 52 Ἐμάχοντο
for [1]the [3]of the [4]world [2]life. Fought
οὖν πρὸς ἀλλήλους οἱ Ἰουδαῖοι λέγοντες·
therefore with one another the Jews saying :
πῶς δύναται οὗτος ἡμῖν δοῦναι τὴν
How can this man us *to* give the(his)
σάρκα φαγεῖν; 53 εἶπεν οὖν αὐτοῖς ὁ
flesh to eat? Said therefore to them –
Ἰησοῦς· ἀμὴν ἀμὴν λέγω ὑμῖν, ἐὰν μὴ
Jesus : Truly truly I say to you, unless
φάγητε τὴν σάρκα τοῦ υἱοῦ τοῦ ἀνθρώπου
ye eat the flesh of the Son – of man
καὶ πίητε αὐτοῦ τὸ αἷμα, οὐκ ἔχετε
and drink of him the blood, ye have not
ζωὴν ἐν ἑαυτοῖς. 54 ὁ τρώγων μου τὴν
life in yourselves. The [one] eating of me the
σάρκα καὶ πίνων μου τὸ αἷμα ἔχει ζωὴν
flesh and drinking of me the blood has life
αἰώνιον, κἀγὼ ἀναστήσω αὐτὸν τῇ ἐσχάτῃ
eternal, and I will raise up him in the last
ἡμέρᾳ. 55 ἡ γὰρ σάρξ μου ἀληθής
day. For the flesh of me [2]true
ἐστιν βρῶσις, καὶ τὸ αἷμά μου ἀληθής
[1]is [3]food, and the blood of me [2]true
ἐστιν πόσις. 56 ὁ τρώγων μου τὴν
[1]is [3]drink. The [one] eating of me the
σάρκα καὶ πίνων μου τὸ αἷμα ἐν ἐμοὶ
flesh and drinking of me the blood in me
μένει κἀγὼ ἐν αὐτῷ. 57 καθὼς ἀπέστειλέν
remains and I in him. As sent
με ὁ ζῶν πατὴρ κἀγὼ ζῶ διὰ τὸν
me the living Father and I live because of the
πατέρα, καὶ ὁ τρώγων με κἀκεῖνος
Father, also the [one] eating me even that one
ζήσει δι' ἐμέ. 58 οὗτός ἐστιν ὁ ἄρτος ὁ
will live because of me. This is the bread –
ἐξ οὐρανοῦ καταβάς, οὐ καθὼς ἔφαγον
out of heaven having come down, not as ate
οἱ πατέρες καὶ ἀπέθανον· ὁ τρώγων
the fathers and died; the [one] eating
τοῦτον τὸν ἄρτον ζήσει εἰς τὸν αἰῶνα.
this – bread will live unto the age.
59 Ταῦτα εἶπεν ἐν συναγωγῇ διδάσκων ἐν
These things he said in a synagogue teaching in
Καφαρναούμ. 60 Πολλοὶ οὖν ἀκούσαντες
Capernaum. [2]Many [1]therefore [7]hearing
ἐκ τῶν μαθητῶν αὐτοῦ εἶπαν· σκληρός
[3]of [4]the [5]disciples [6]of him said : Hard
ἐστιν ὁ λόγος οὗτος· τίς δύναται αὐτοῦ
is – word this; who can it
ἀκούειν; 61 εἰδὼς δὲ ὁ Ἰησοῦς ἐν ἑαυτῷ
to hear? But knowing – Jesus in himself
ὅτι γογγύζουσιν περὶ τούτου οἱ μαθηταὶ
that [4]are murmuring [5]about [6]this [1]the [2]disciples
αὐτοῦ, εἶπεν αὐτοῖς· τοῦτο ὑμᾶς σκανδαλίζει;
[3]of him, said to them : This you offends?

the living bread that came
down from heaven. If any-
one eats of this bread, he
will live forever. This bread
is my flesh, which I will
give for the life of the
world."
52 Then the Jews began to
argue sharply among them-
selves, "How can this man
give us his flesh to eat?"
53 Jesus said to them, "I
tell you the truth, unless
you eat the flesh of the Son
of Man and drink his blood,
you have no life in you.
54 Whoever eats my flesh
and drinks my blood has
eternal life, and I will raise
him up at the last day. 55 For
my flesh is real food and my
blood is real drink. 56 Whoever eats my flesh and
drinks my blood remains in
me, and I in him. 57 Just as
the living Father sent me
and I live because of the
Father, so the one who
feeds on me will live be-
cause of me. 58 This is the
bread that came down from
heaven. Your forefathers
ate manna and died, but he
who feeds on this bread will
live forever." 59 He said
this while teaching in the
synagogue in Capernaum.

Many Disciples Desert Jesus

60 On hearing it, many of
his disciples said, "This is a
hard teaching. Who can accept it?"
61 Aware that his disciples
were grumbling about this,
Jesus said to them, "Does
this offend you? 62 What if

were to see the Son of Man ascending to where he was before? 63 It is the spirit that gives life; the flesh is useless. The words that I have spoken to you are spirit and life. 64 But among you there are some who do not believe." For Jesus knew from the first who were the ones that did not believe, and who was the one that would betray him. 65 And he said, "For this reason I have told you that no one can come to me unless it is granted by the Father."

66 Because of this many of his disciples turned back and no longer went about with him. 67 So Jesus asked the twelve, "Do you also wish to go away?" 68 Simon Peter answered him, "Lord, to whom can we go? You have the words of eternal life. 69 We have come to believe and know that you are the Holy One of God."[s] 70 Jesus answered them, "Did I not choose you, the twelve? Yet one of you is a devil." 71 He was speaking of Judas son of Simon Iscariot,[t] for he, though one of the twelve, was going to betray him.

Chapter 7

The Unbelief of Jesus' Brothers

AFTER this Jesus went about in Galilee. He did not wish[u] to go about in Judea because the Jews were looking for an opportunity to kill him. 2 Now the Jewish festival of Booths[v] was near. 3 So his brothers said to him, "Leave here

[s] Other ancient authorities read *the Christ, the Son of the living God*
[t] Other ancient authorities read *Judas Iscariot son of Simon;* others, *Judas son of Simon from Karyot* (Kerioth)
[u] Other ancient authorities read *was not at liberty*
[v] Or *Tabernacles*

62 ἐὰν οὖν θεωρῆτε τὸν υἱὸν τοῦ ἀνθρώπου
If then ye behold the Son – of man

ἀναβαίνοντα ὅπου ἦν τὸ πρότερον; **63** τὸ
ascending where he was at first? † The

πνεῦμά ἐστιν τὸ ζωοποιοῦν, ἡ σὰρξ οὐκ
spirit is the [thing] quickening, the flesh not

ὠφελεῖ οὐδέν· τὰ ῥήματα ἃ ἐγὼ λελάληκα
profits no(any)thing; the words which I have spoken

ὑμῖν πνεῦμά ἐστιν καὶ ζωή ἐστιν. **64** ἀλλ'
to you spirit is(are) and life is(are). But

εἰσὶν ἐξ ὑμῶν τινες οἳ οὐ πιστεύουσιν. ᾔδει
there are of you some who do not believe. knew

γὰρ ἐξ ἀρχῆς ὁ Ἰησοῦς τίνες εἰσὶν
For from [the] beginning – Jesus who are(were)

οἱ μὴ πιστεύοντες καὶ τίς ἐστιν ὁ
the [ones] not believing and who is(was) the

παραδώσων αὐτόν. **65** καὶ ἔλεγεν·
[one] betraying him. And he said :

διὰ τοῦτο εἴρηκα ὑμῖν ὅτι οὐδεὶς δύναται
Therefore I have told you that no one can

ἐλθεῖν πρός με ἐὰν μὴ ᾖ δεδομένον
to come to me unless it is *having been* given

αὐτῷ ἐκ τοῦ πατρός.
to him of the Father.

66 Ἐκ τούτου πολλοὶ τῶν μαθητῶν
From this many of the disciples

αὐτοῦ ἀπῆλθον εἰς τὰ ὀπίσω καὶ οὐκέτι
of him went away back† and no longer

μετ' αὐτοῦ περιεπάτουν. **67** εἶπεν οὖν ὁ
with him walked. Said therefore –

Ἰησοῦς τοῖς δώδεκα· μὴ καὶ ὑμεῖς
Jesus to the twelve : *Not* also ye

θέλετε ὑπάγειν; **68** ἀπεκρίθη αὐτῷ Σίμων
wish to go? Answered him Simon

Πέτρος· κύριε, πρὸς τίνα ἀπελευσόμεθα;
Peter : Lord, to whom shall we go away?

ῥήματα ζωῆς αἰωνίου ἔχεις· **69** καὶ ἡμεῖς
words of life eternal thou hast; and we

πεπιστεύκαμεν καὶ ἐγνώκαμεν ὅτι σὺ εἶ
have believed and have known that thou art

ὁ ἅγιος τοῦ θεοῦ. **70** ἀπεκρίθη αὐτοῖς ὁ
the holy one – of God. Answered them –

Ἰησοῦς· οὐκ ἐγὼ ὑμᾶς τοὺς δώδεκα
Jesus : [3]Not [2]I [4]you [5]the [6]twelve

ἐξελεξάμην; καὶ ἐξ ὑμῶν εἷς διάβολός
[1]chose? and of you one a devil

ἐστιν. **71** ἔλεγεν δὲ τὸν Ἰούδαν Σίμωνος
is. Now he spoke [of] – Judas [son] of Simon

Ἰσκαριώτου· οὗτος γὰρ ἔμελλεν παραδιδόναι
Iscariot; for this one was about to betray

αὐτόν, εἷς ἐκ τῶν δώδεκα.
him, one of the twelve.

7 Καὶ μετὰ ταῦτα περιεπάτει ὁ Ἰησοῦς
And after these things walked – Jesus

ἐν τῇ Γαλιλαίᾳ· οὐ γὰρ ἤθελεν ἐν τῇ
in – Galilee; for he did not wish in –

Ἰουδαίᾳ περιπατεῖν, ὅτι ἐζήτουν αὐτὸν οἱ
Judæa to walk, because [3]were seeking [4]him [1]the

Ἰουδαῖοι ἀποκτεῖναι. **2** ἦν δὲ ἐγγὺς ἡ
[2]Jews [5]to kill. Now was near the

ἑορτὴ τῶν Ἰουδαίων ἡ σκηνοπηγία. **3** εἶπον
feast of the Jews the Tabernacles. Said

οὖν πρὸς αὐτὸν οἱ ἀδελφοὶ αὐτοῦ·
therefore to him the brothers of him :

you see the Son of Man ascend to where he was before! 63 The Spirit gives life; the flesh counts for nothing. The words I have spoken to you are spirit[k] and they are life. 64 Yet there are some of you who do not believe." For Jesus had known from the beginning which of them did not believe and who would betray him. 65 He went on to say, "This is why I told you that no one can come to me unless the Father has enabled him."

66 From this time many of his disciples turned back and no longer followed him.

67 "You do not want to leave too, do you?" Jesus asked the Twelve.

68 Simon Peter answered him, "Lord, to whom shall we go? You have the words of eternal life. 69 We believe and know that you are the Holy One of God."

70 Then Jesus replied, "Have I not chosen you, the Twelve? Yet one of you is a devil!" 71 (He meant Judas, the son of Simon Iscariot, who, though one of the Twelve, was later to betray him.)

Chapter 7

Jesus Goes to the Feast of Tabernacles

AFTER this, Jesus went around in Galilee, purposely staying away from Judea because the Jews there were waiting to take his life. 2 But when the Jewish Feast of Tabernacles was near, 3 Jesus' brothers said to him, "You

[k] *63 Or Spirit*

and go to Judea so that your
disciples also may see the
works you are doing; 4for
no one who wants[w] to be
widely known acts in se-
cret. If you do these things,
show yourself to the
world." 5(For not even his
brothers believed in him.)
6Jesus said to them, "My
time has not yet come, but
your time is always here.
7The world cannot hate
you, but it hates me be-
cause I testify against it
that its works are evil. 8Go
to the festival yourselves. I
am not[x] going to this festival, for my time has not yet
fully come." 9After saying
this, he remained in Galilee.

Jesus at the Festival of Booths

10 But after his brothers
had gone to the festival,
then he also went, not publicly but as it were[y] in secret. 11The Jews were
looking for him at the festival and saying, "Where is
he?" 12And there was con-
siderable complaining
about him among the
crowds. While some were
saying, "He is a good
man," others were saying,
"No, he is deceiving the
crowd." 13Yet no one
would speak openly about
him for fear of the Jews.
14 About the middle of
the festival Jesus went up
into the temple and began
to teach. 15The Jews were
astonished at it, saying,
"How does this man have
such learning,[z] when he
has never been taught?"
16Then Jesus answered
them, "My teaching is not

[w] Other ancient authorities read *wants it*
[x] Other ancient authorities add *yet*
[y] Other ancient authorities lack *as it were*
[z] Or *this man know his letters*

μετάβηθι ἐντεῦθεν καὶ ὕπαγε εἰς τὴν Ἰουδαίαν,
Depart hence and go into – Judæa,

ἵνα καὶ οἱ μαθηταί σου θεωρήσουσιν τὰ
that also the disciples of thee will behold the

ἔργα σου ἃ ποιεῖς· 4 οὐδεὶς γάρ τι ἐν
works of thee which thou doest; for no one anything in

κρυπτῷ ποιεῖ καὶ ζητεῖ αὐτὸς ἐν παρρησίᾳ
secret does and seeks [him]self in [the] open

εἶναι. εἰ ταῦτα ποιεῖς, φανέρωσον σεαυτὸν
to be. If these things thou doest, manifest thyself

τῷ κόσμῳ. 5 οὐδὲ γὰρ οἱ ἀδελφοὶ
to the world. For not the brothers

αὐτοῦ ἐπίστευον εἰς αὐτόν. 6 λέγει οὖν
of him believed in him. Says therefore

αὐτοῖς ὁ Ἰησοῦς· ὁ καιρὸς ὁ ἐμὸς
to them – Jesus: *The* [2]time – [1]my

οὔπω πάρεστιν, ὁ δὲ καιρὸς ὁ ὑμέτερος
not yet is arrived, but *the* [2]time – [1]your

πάντοτέ ἐστιν ἕτοιμος. 7 οὐ δύναται ὁ
always is ready. Cannot the

κόσμος μισεῖν ὑμᾶς, ἐμὲ δὲ μισεῖ, ὅτι
world *to* hate you, but me it hates, because

ἐγὼ μαρτυρῶ περὶ αὐτοῦ ὅτι τὰ ἔργα
I witness about it that the works

αὐτοῦ πονηρά ἐστιν. 8 ὑμεῖς ἀνάβητε εἰς
of it evil is(are). [3]Ye [1]go [2]up to

τὴν ἑορτήν· ἐγὼ οὐκ ἀναβαίνω εἰς τὴν
the feast; I am not going up to –

ἑορτὴν ταύτην, ὅτι ὁ ἐμὸς καιρὸς οὔπω
feast this, because *the* my time not yet

πεπλήρωται. 9 ταῦτα δὲ εἰπὼν αὐτοῖς
has been fulfilled. And these things saying to them

ἔμεινεν ἐν τῇ Γαλιλαίᾳ. 10 Ὡς δὲ
he remained in – Galilee. But when

ἀνέβησαν οἱ ἀδελφοὶ αὐτοῦ εἰς τὴν ἑορτήν,
went up the brothers of him to the feast,

τότε καὶ αὐτὸς ἀνέβη, οὐ φανερῶς ἀλλὰ
then also he went up, not manifestly but

ὡς ἐν κρυπτῷ. 11 οἱ οὖν Ἰουδαῖοι
as in secret. Therefore the Jews

ἐζήτουν αὐτὸν ἐν τῇ ἑορτῇ καὶ ἔλεγον·
sought him at the feast and said:

ποῦ ἐστιν ἐκεῖνος; 12 καὶ γογγυσμὸς περὶ
Where is that man? And [3]murmuring [4]about

αὐτοῦ ἦν πολὺς ἐν τοῖς ὄχλοις· οἱ μὲν
[5]him [1]there was [2]much in the crowds; some

ἔλεγον ὅτι ἀγαθός ἐστιν· ἄλλοι [δὲ]
said[,] – A good man he is; but others

ἔλεγον· οὔ, ἀλλὰ πλανᾷ τὸν ὄχλον.
said: No, but he deceives the crowd.

13 οὐδεὶς μέντοι παρρησίᾳ ἐλάλει περὶ
No one however openly spoke about

αὐτοῦ διὰ τὸν φόβον τῶν Ἰουδαίων.
him because of the fear of the Jews.

14 Ἤδη δὲ τῆς ἑορτῆς μεσούσης ἀνέβη
But now the feast being in [its] middle[a] went up
[a] = in the middle of the feast

Ἰησοῦς εἰς τὸ ἱερὸν καὶ ἐδίδασκεν.
Jesus to the temple and taught.

15 ἐθαύμαζον οὖν οἱ Ἰουδαῖοι λέγοντες·
Marvelled therefore the Jews saying:

πῶς οὗτος γράμματα οἶδεν μὴ μεμαθηκώς;
How this man letters knows not having learned?

16 ἀπεκρίθη οὖν αὐτοῖς Ἰησοῦς καὶ εἶπεν·
Answered therefore them Jesus and said:

ought to leave here and go
to Judea, so that your disciples may see the miracles
you do. 4No one who wants
to become a public figure
acts in secret. Since you
are doing these things,
show yourself to the
world." 5For even his own
brothers did not believe in
him.
6Therefore Jesus told
them, "The right time for
me has not yet come; for
you any time is right. 7The
world cannot hate you, but
it hates me because I testify
that what it does is evil.
8You go to the Feast. I am
not yet[l] going up to this
Feast, because for me the
right time has not yet
come." 9Having said this,
he stayed in Galilee.
10However, after his
brothers had left for the
Feast, he went also, not
publicly, but in secret.
11Now at the Feast the
Jews were watching for
him and asking, "Where is
that man?"
12Among the crowds
there was widespread whispering about him. Some
said, "He is a good man."
Others replied, "No, he
deceives the people."
13But no one would say
anything publicly about
him for fear of the Jews.

Jesus Teaches at the Feast

14Not until halfway
through the Feast did Jesus
go up to the temple courts
and begin to teach. 15The
Jews were amazed and
asked, "How did this man
get such learning without
having studied?"
16Jesus answered, "My

[l] 8 Some early manuscripts do not have *yet*.

mine but his who sent me. 17 Anyone who resolves to do the will of God will know whether the teaching is from God or whether I am speaking on my own. 18 Those who speak on their own seek their own glory; but the one who seeks the glory of him who sent him is true, and there is nothing false in him.

19 "Did not Moses give you the law? Yet none of you keeps the law. Why are you looking for an opportunity to kill me?" 20 The crowd answered, "You have a demon! Who is trying to kill you?" 21 Jesus answered them, "I performed one work, and all of you are astonished. 22 Moses gave you circumcision (it is, of course, not from Moses, but from the patriarchs), and you circumcise a man on the sabbath. 23 If a man receives circumcision on the sabbath in order that the law of Moses may not be broken, are you angry with me because I healed a man's whole body on the sabbath? 24 Do not judge by appearances, but judge with right judgment."

Is This the Christ?

25 Now some of the people of Jerusalem were saying, "Is not this the man whom they are trying to kill? 26 And here he is, speaking openly, but they say nothing to him! Can it be that the authorities really know that this is the Messiah?[a] 27 Yet we know where this man is from; but when the Messiah[a] comes, no one will know where he is from." 28 Then Jesus cried out as he was teaching in the temple, "You

[a] Or *the Christ*

ἡ ἐμὴ διδαχὴ οὐκ ἔστιν ἐμὴ ἀλλὰ τοῦ
The my teaching is not mine but of the
πέμψαντός με· 17 ἐάν τις θέλῃ τὸ θέλημα
[one] having sent me; if anyone wishes the will
αὐτοῦ ποιεῖν, γνώσεται περὶ τῆς διδαχῆς,
of him to do, he will know concerning the teaching,
πότερον ἐκ τοῦ θεοῦ ἐστιν ἢ ἐγὼ ἀπ'
whether of – God it is or I from
ἐμαυτοῦ λαλῶ. 18 ὁ ἀφ' ἑαυτοῦ λαλῶν
myself speak. The [one] from himself speaking
τὴν δόξαν τὴν ἰδίαν ζητεῖ· ὁ δὲ ζητῶν
his own glory seeks; but the [one] seeking
τὴν δόξαν τοῦ πέμψαντος αὐτόν, οὗτος
the glory of the [one] having sent him, this man
ἀληθής ἐστιν καὶ ἀδικία ἐν αὐτῷ οὐκ
true is and unrighteousness in him not
ἔστιν. 19 οὐ Μωϋσῆς ἔδωκεν ὑμῖν τὸν
is. Not Moses gave you the
νόμον; καὶ οὐδεὶς ἐξ ὑμῶν ποιεῖ τὸν
law? and no one of you does the
νόμον. τί με ζητεῖτε ἀποκτεῖναι;
law. Why me seek ye to kill?
20 ἀπεκρίθη ὁ ὄχλος· δαιμόνιον ἔχεις·
Answered the crowd: A demon thou hast;
τίς σε ζητεῖ ἀποκτεῖναι; 21 ἀπεκρίθη
who thee seeks to kill? Answered
Ἰησοῦς καὶ εἶπεν αὐτοῖς· ἓν ἔργον ἐποίησα
Jesus and said to them: One work I did
καὶ πάντες θαυμάζετε. 22 διὰ τοῦτο
and all ye marvel. Because of this
Μωϋσῆς δέδωκεν ὑμῖν τὴν περιτομήν, —
Moses has given you – circumcision, —
οὐχ ὅτι ἐκ τοῦ Μωϋσέως ἐστὶν ἀλλ' ἐκ
not that of – Moses it is but of
τῶν πατέρων, — καὶ ἐν σαββάτῳ
the fathers, — and on a sabbath
περιτέμνετε ἄνθρωπον 23 εἰ περιτομὴν
ye circumcise a man. If [3]circumcision
λαμβάνει [ὁ] ἄνθρωπος ἐν σαββάτῳ ἵνα
[2]receives – [1]a man on a sabbath that
μὴ λυθῇ ὁ νόμος Μωϋσέως, ἐμοὶ χολᾶτε,
is not broken the law of Moses, with me are ye angry
ὅτι ὅλον ἄνθρωπον ὑγιῆ ἐποίησα ἐν
because a whole man healthy I made on
σαββάτῳ; 24 μὴ κρίνετε κατ' ὄψιν, ἀλλὰ
a sabbath? Judge not according to face, but
τὴν δικαίαν κρίσιν κρίνατε. 25 Ἔλεγον
– righteous judgment judge. Said
οὖν τινες ἐκ τῶν Ἱεροσολυμιτῶν· οὐχ
therefore some of the Jerusalemites: [2]Not
οὗτός ἐστιν ὃν ζητοῦσιν ἀποκτεῖναι; 26 καὶ
[3]this man [1]is it whom they are seeking to kill? and
ἴδε παρρησίᾳ λαλεῖ, καὶ οὐδὲν αὐτῷ
behold openly he speaks, and nothing to him
λέγουσιν. μήποτε ἀληθῶς ἔγνωσαν οἱ
they say. Perhaps indeed knew the
ἄρχοντες ὅτι οὗτός ἐστιν ὁ χριστός;
rulers that this is the Christ?*
27 ἀλλὰ τοῦτον οἴδαμεν πόθεν ἐστίν· ὁ δὲ
But this man we know whence he is; but [2]the
χριστὸς ὅταν ἔρχηται, οὐδεὶς γινώσκει
[3]Christ [1]when comes, no one knows
πόθεν ἐστίν. 28 ἔκραξεν οὖν ἐν τῷ ἱερῷ
whence he is. [3]Cried out [2]therefore [4]in [5]the [6]temple

* As this question is introduced by μήποτε, a negative answer is expected; see page xiii, and note ver. 31 below.

teaching is not my own. It comes from him who sent me. 17 If anyone chooses to do God's will, he will find out whether my teaching comes from God or whether I speak on my own. 18 He who speaks on his own does so to gain honor for himself, but he who works for the honor of the one who sent him is a man of truth; there is nothing false about him. 19 Has not Moses given you the law? Yet not one of you keeps the law. Why are you trying to kill me?"

20 "You are demon-possessed," the crowd answered. "Who is trying to kill you?"

21 Jesus said to them, "I did one miracle, and you are all astonished. 22 Yet, because Moses gave you circumcision (though actually it did not come from Moses, but from the patriarchs), you circumcise a child on the Sabbath. 23 Now if a child can be circumcised on the Sabbath so that the law of Moses may not be broken, why are you angry with me for healing the whole man on the Sabbath? 24 Stop judging by mere appearances, and make a right judgment."

Is Jesus the Christ?

25 At that point some of the people of Jerusalem began to ask, "Isn't this the man they are trying to kill? 26 Here he is, speaking publicly, and they are not saying a word to him. Have the authorities really concluded that he is the Christ[m]? 27 But we know where this man is from; when the Christ comes, no one will know where he is from."

28 Then Jesus, still teaching in the temple courts,

[m] 26 Or *Messiah;* also in verses 27, 31, 41 and 42

know me, and you know
where I am from. I have not
come on my own. But the
one who sent me is true,
and you do not know him.
29 I know him, because I am
from him, and he sent me."
30 Then they tried to arrest
him, but no one laid hands
on him, because his hour
had not yet come. 31 Yet
many in the crowd believed
in him and were saying,
"When the Messiah[a]
comes, will he do more
signs than this man has
done?"[b]

Officers Are Sent to Arrest Jesus

32 The Pharisees heard
the crowd muttering such
things about him, and the
chief priests and Pharisees
sent temple police to arrest
him. 33 Jesus then said, "I
will be with you a little
while longer, and then I am
going to him who sent me.
34 You will search for me,
but you will not find me;
and where I am, you cannot
come." 35 The Jews said to
one another, "Where does
this man intend to go that
we will not find him? Does
he intend to go to the Dispersion among the Greeks
and teach the Greeks?
36 What does he mean by
saying, 'You will search for
me and you will not find
me' and 'Where I am, you
cannot come'?"

Rivers of Living Water

37 On the last day of the
festival, the great day,
while Jesus was standing
there, he cried out, "Let
anyone who is thirsty come
to me, 38 and let the one
who believes in me drink.
As[c] the scripture has said,
'Out of the believer's

διδάσκων ὁ Ἰησοῦς καὶ λέγων· κἀμὲ
[7]teaching – [1]Jesus [8]and [9]saying : Both me

οἴδατε καὶ οἴδατε πόθεν εἰμί· καὶ ἀπ'
ye know and ye know whence I am; and from

ἐμαυτοῦ οὐκ ἐλήλυθα, ἀλλ' ἔστιν ἀληθινὸς
myself I have not come, but he is true

ὁ πέμψας με, ὃν ὑμεῖς οὐκ οἴδατε·
the [one] having sent me, whom ye know not;

29 ἐγὼ οἶδα αὐτόν, ὅτι παρ' αὐτοῦ εἰμι
I know him, because [2]from [3]him [1]I am

κἀκεῖνός με ἀπέστειλεν. **30** Ἐζήτουν οὖν
[4]and that one [6]me [5]sent. They sought therefore

αὐτὸν πιάσαι, καὶ οὐδεὶς ἐπέβαλεν ἐπ'
him to arrest, and no one laid *on* on

αὐτὸν τὴν χεῖρα, ὅτι οὔπω ἐληλύθει ἡ
him the hand, because not yet had come the

ὥρα αὐτοῦ. **31** Ἐκ τοῦ ὄχλου δὲ πολλοὶ
hour of him. [3]of [4]the [5]crowd [1]But [2]many

ἐπίστευσαν εἰς αὐτόν, καὶ ἔλεγον· ὁ
believed in him, and said : [2]The

χριστὸς ὅταν ἔλθῃ, μὴ πλείονα σημεῖα
[3]Christ [1]when [4]comes, *not* more signs

ποιήσει ὧν οὗτος ἐποίησεν; **32** ἤκουσαν
will he do [than] which this man did? [2]Heard

οἱ Φαρισαῖοι τοῦ ὄχλου γογγύζοντος περὶ
[1]the [2]Pharisees [4]the [5]crowd [3]murmuring [8]about

αὐτοῦ ταῦτα, καὶ ἀπέστειλαν οἱ ἀρχιερεῖς
[9]him [7]these things, and [6]sent [1]the [2]chief priests

καὶ οἱ Φαρισαῖοι ὑπηρέτας ἵνα πιάσωσιν
[3]and [4]the [5]Pharisees [7]attendants that they might arrest

αὐτόν. **33** εἶπεν οὖν ὁ Ἰησοῦς· ἔτι
him. Said therefore – Jesus : Yet

χρόνον μικρὸν μεθ' ὑμῶν εἰμι καὶ ὑπάγω
time a little with you I am and I go

πρὸς τὸν πέμψαντά με. **34** ζητήσετέ με
to the [one] having sent me. Ye will seek me

καὶ οὐχ εὑρήσετε, καὶ ὅπου εἰμὶ ἐγὼ
and will not find, and where am I

ὑμεῖς οὐ δύνασθε ἐλθεῖν. **35** εἶπον οὖν
ye cannot *to* come. Said therefore

οἱ Ἰουδαῖοι πρὸς ἑαυτούς· ποῦ οὗτος
the Jews to themselves : Where this man

μέλλει πορεύεσθαι, ὅτι ἡμεῖς οὐχ εὑρήσομεν
is about to go, that we will not find

αὐτόν; μὴ εἰς τὴν διασπορὰν τῶν Ἑλλήνων
him? *not* to the dispersion of the Greeks

μέλλει πορεύεσθαι καὶ διδάσκειν τοὺς
is he about to go and to teach the

Ἕλληνας; **36** τίς ἐστιν ὁ λόγος οὗτος
Greeks? What is – word this

ὃν εἶπεν· ζητήσετέ με καὶ οὐχ εὑρήσετε,
which he said : Ye will seek me and will not find,

καὶ ὅπου εἰμὶ ἐγὼ ὑμεῖς οὐ δύνασθε
and where am I ye cannot

ἐλθεῖν;
to come?

37 Ἐν δὲ τῇ ἐσχάτῃ ἡμέρᾳ τῇ μεγάλῃ
Now in the last day the great [day]

τῆς ἑορτῆς εἱστήκει ὁ Ἰησοῦς καὶ ἔκραξεν
of the feast stood – Jesus and cried out

λέγων· ἐάν τις διψᾷ, ἐρχέσθω πρός με
saying : If anyone thirsts, let him come to me

καὶ πινέτω. **38** ὁ πιστεύων εἰς ἐμέ,
and drink. The [one] believing in me,

καθὼς εἶπεν ἡ γραφή, ποταμοὶ ἐκ τῆς
as said the scripture, [1]rivers [5]out of [6]the

cried out, "Yes, you know
me, and you know where I
am from. I am not here on
my own, but he who sent
me is true. You do not
know him, 29 but I know
him because I am from him
and he sent me."
30 At this they tried to
seize him, but no one laid a
hand on him, because his
time had not yet come.
31 Still, many in the crowd
put their faith in him. They
said, "When the Christ
comes, will he do more miraculous signs than this
man?"
32 The Pharisees heard the
crowd whispering such
things about him. Then the
chief priests and the Pharisees sent temple guards to
arrest him.
33 Jesus said, "I am with
you for only a short time,
and then I go to the one
who sent me. 34 You will
look for me, but you will
not find me; and where I
am, you cannot come."
35 The Jews said to one another, "Where does this
man intend to go that we
cannot find him? Will he go
where our people live scattered among the Greeks,
and teach the Greeks?
36 What did he mean when
he said, 'You will look for
me, but you will not find
me,' and 'Where I am, you
cannot come'?"
37 On the last and greatest
day of the Feast, Jesus
stood and said in a loud
voice, "If anyone is
thirsty, let him come to me
and drink. 38 Whoever be-
lieves in me, as[n] the Scripture has said, streams of

[b] Other ancient authorities read *is doing*

[c] Or *come to me and drink.* [38] *The one who believes in me, as*

[n] *37,38* Or / *If anyone is thirsty, let him come to me.* / *And let him drink,* [38] *who believes in me.* / *As*

heart[d] shall flow rivers of
living water.' " 39 Now he
said this about the Spirit,
which believers in him
were to receive; for as yet
there was no Spirit,[e] because Jesus was not yet
glorified.

Division among the People

40 When they heard
these words, some in the
crowd said, "This is really
the prophet." 41 Others
said, "This is the Messi-
ah."[f] But some asked,
"Surely the Messiah[f] does
not come from Galilee,
does he? 42 Has not the
scripture said that the Messiah[f] is descended from
David and comes from
Bethlehem, the village
where David lived?" 43 So
there was a division in the
crowd because of him.
44 Some of them wanted to
arrest him, but no one laid
hands on him.

The Unbelief of Those in Authority

45 Then the temple po-
lice went back to the chief
priests and Pharisees, who
asked them, "Why did you
not arrest him?" 46 The police answered, "Never has
anyone spoken like this!"
47 Then the Pharisees re-
plied, "Surely you have not
been deceived too, have
you? 48 Has any one of the
authorities or of the Pharisees believed in him? 49 But
this crowd, which does not
know the law—they are ac-
cursed." 50 Nicodemus,
who had gone to Jesus[g] before, and who was one of
them, asked, 51 "Our law
does not judge people without first giving them a hearing to find out what they are
doing, does it?" 52 They replied, "Surely you are not
also from Galilee, are you?
Search and you will see
that no prophet is to arise
from Galilee."

[d] Gk *out of his belly*
[e] Other ancient authorities read *for as yet the Spirit* (others, *Holy Spirit*) *had not been given*
[f] Or *the Christ*
[g] Gk *him*

κοιλίας αὐτοῦ ῥεύσουσιν ὕδατος ζῶντος.
[7]belly [8]of him [4]will flow [2]water [3]of living.

39 τοῦτο δὲ εἶπεν περὶ τοῦ πνεύματος
But this he said concerning the Spirit

οὗ ἔμελλον λαμβάνειν οἱ πιστεύσαντες
whom were about to receive the [ones] believing

εἰς αὐτόν· οὔπω γὰρ ἦν πνεῦμα, ὅτι
in him; for not yet was [?the] Spirit, because

Ἰησοῦς οὐδέπω ἐδοξάσθη. **40** Ἐκ τοῦ
Jesus not yet was glorified. [Some] of the

ὄχλου οὖν ἀκούσαντες τῶν λόγων τούτων
crowd therefore hearing – words these

ἔλεγον [ὅτι]· οὗτός ἐστιν ἀληθῶς ὁ
said – : This man is truly the

προφήτης· **41** ἄλλοι ἔλεγον· οὗτός ἐστιν ὁ
prophet; Others said : This man is the

χριστός· οἱ δὲ ἔλεγον· μὴ γὰρ ἐκ τῆς
Christ; But others† said : *Not* then out of –

Γαλιλαίας ὁ χριστὸς ἔρχεται; **42** οὐχ ἡ
Galilee the Christ comes? not the

γραφὴ εἶπεν ὅτι ἐκ τοῦ σπέρματος Δαυίδ,
scripture said that of the seed of David,

καὶ ἀπὸ Βηθλέεμ τῆς κώμης ὅπου ἦν
and from Bethlehem the village where was

Δαυίδ, ἔρχεται ὁ χριστός; **43** σχίσμα
David, comes the Christ? A division

οὖν ἐγένετο ἐν τῷ ὄχλῳ δι' αὐτόν·
therefore became in the crowd because of him;

44 τινὲς δὲ ἤθελον ἐξ αὐτῶν πιάσαι αὐτόν,
and [1]some [4]wished [2]of [3]them to arrest him,

ἀλλ' οὐδεὶς ἐπέβαλεν ἐπ' αὐτὸν τὰς χεῖρας.
but no one laid *on* on him the(his) hands.

45 Ἦλθον οὖν οἱ ὑπηρέται πρὸς τοὺς
Came therefore the attendants to the

ἀρχιερεῖς καὶ Φαρισαίους, καὶ εἶπον αὐτοῖς
chief priests and Pharisees, and [3]said [2]to them

ἐκεῖνοι· διὰ τί οὐκ ἠγάγετε αὐτόν;
[1]those: Why did ye not bring him?

46 ἀπεκρίθησαν οἱ ὑπηρέται· οὐδέποτε
Answered the attendants : Never

ἐλάλησεν οὕτως ἄνθρωπος, ὡς οὗτος λαλεῖ
spoke so a man, as [1]this [3]speaks

ὁ ἄνθρωπος. **47** ἀπεκρίθησαν οὖν αὐτοῖς
– [2]man. Answered therefore them

οἱ Φαρισαῖοι· μὴ καὶ ὑμεῖς πεπλάνησθε;
the Pharisees : *Not* also ye have been deceived?

48 μή τις ἐκ τῶν ἀρχόντων ἐπίστευσεν
not anyone of the rulers believed

εἰς αὐτὸν ἢ ἐκ τῶν Φαρισαίων; **49** ἀλλὰ
in him or of the Pharisees? But

ὁ ὄχλος οὗτος ὁ μὴ γινώσκων τὸν
– crowd this – not knowing the

νόμον ἐπάρατοί εἰσιν. **50** λέγει Νικόδημος
law cursed are. Says Nicodemus

πρὸς αὐτούς, ὁ ἐλθὼν πρὸς αὐτὸν πρότερον,
to them, the [one] having come to him firstly,

εἷς ὢν ἐξ αὐτῶν· **51** μὴ ὁ νόμος ἡμῶν
[2]one [1]being of them : *Not* the law of us

κρίνει τὸν ἄνθρωπον ἐὰν μὴ ἀκούσῃ
judges the man unless it hears

πρῶτον παρ' αὐτοῦ καὶ γνῷ τί ποιεῖ;
first from him and knows what he does?

52 ἀπεκρίθησαν καὶ εἶπαν αὐτῷ· μὴ καὶ
They answered and said to him : *Not* also

σὺ ἐκ τῆς Γαλιλαίας εἶ; ἐρεύνησον καὶ
thou of – Galilee art? search and

living water will flow from
within him." 39 By this he
meant the Spirit, whom
those who believed in him
were later to receive. Up to
that time the Spirit had not
been given, since Jesus had
not yet been glorified.
40 On hearing his words,
some of the people said,
"Surely this man is the
Prophet."
41 Others said, "He is the
Christ."
Still others asked, "How
can the Christ come from
Galilee? 42 Does not the
Scripture say that the
Christ will come from Da-
vid's family[o] and from
Bethlehem, the town where
David lived?" 43 Thus the
people were divided be-
cause of Jesus. 44 Some
wanted to seize him, but no
one laid a hand on him.

Unbelief of the Jewish Leaders

45 Finally the temple
guards went back to the
chief priests and Pharisees,
who asked them, "Why
didn't you bring him in?"
46 "No one ever spoke the
way this man does," the
guards declared.
47 "You mean he has de-
ceived you also?" the Pharisees retorted. 48 "Has any
of the rulers or of the Pharisees believed in him? 49 No!
But this mob that knows
nothing of the law—there
is a curse on them."
50 Nicodemus, who had
gone to Jesus earlier and
who was one of their own
number, asked, 51 "Does
our law condemn anyone
without first hearing him to
find out what he is doing?"
52 They replied, "Are you
from Galilee, too? Look

[o] 42 Greek *seed*

The Woman Caught in Adultery

⟦53 Then each of them went
home, 1 while Jesus went to
the Mount of Olives. 2 Early in the morning he came
again to the temple. All the
people came to him and he
sat down and began to
teach them. 3 The scribes
and the Pharisees brought a
woman who had been
caught in adultery; and
making her stand before all
of them, 4 they said to him,
"Teacher, this woman was
caught in the very act of
committing adultery.
5 Now in the law Moses
commanded us to stone
such women. Now what do
you say?" 6 They said this
to test him, so that they
might have some charge to
bring against him. Jesus
bent down and wrote with
his finger on the ground.
7 When they kept on ques-
tioning him, he straight-
ened up and said to them,
"Let anyone among you
who is without sin be the
first to throw a stone at
her." 8 And once again he
bent down and wrote on the
ground.[h] 9 When they
heard it, they went away,
one by one, beginning with
the elders; and Jesus was
left alone with the woman
standing before him.
10 Jesus straightened up and
said to her, "Woman,
where are they? Has no one
condemned you?" 11 She
said, "No one, sir."[i] And
Jesus said, "Neither do I
condemn you. Go your
way, and from now on do
not sin again."⟧[j]

Jesus the Light of the World

12 Again Jesus spoke to
them, saying, "I am the
light of the world. Whoever
follows me will never walk

[h] Other ancient authorities add *the sins of each of them*
[i] Or *Lord*
[j] The most ancient authorities lack 7.53—8.11; other authorities add the passage here or after 7.36 or after 21.25 or after Luke 21.38, with variations of text; some mark the passage as doubtful.

ἴδε ὅτι ἐκ τῆς Γαλιλαίας προφήτης οὐκ
see that out of – Galilee a prophet not
ἐγείρεται.
is raised.
53 Καὶ ἐπορεύθησαν ἕκαστος εἰς τὸν οἶκον
And they went each one to the house
αὐτοῦ, 8 Ἰησοῦς δὲ ἐπορεύθη εἰς τὸ
of him, but Jesus went to the
Ὄρος τῶν Ἐλαιῶν. 2 Ὄρθρου δὲ πάλιν
Mount of the Olives. And at dawn again
παρεγένετο εἰς τὸ ἱερόν [, καὶ πᾶς ὁ
he arrived in the temple, and all the
λαὸς ἤρχετο πρὸς αὐτόν, καὶ καθίσας
people came to him, and sitting
ἐδίδασκεν αὐτούς]. 3 Ἄγουσιν δὲ οἱ
he taught them. And lead the
γραμματεῖς καὶ οἱ Φαρισαῖοι γυναῖκα ἐπὶ
scribes and the Pharisees a woman in
μοιχείᾳ κατειλημμένην, καὶ στήσαντες αὐτὴν
adultery *having been* caught, and standing her
ἐν μέσῳ 4 λέγουσιν αὐτῷ Διδάσκαλε,
in [the] midst they say to him[,] Teacher,
αὕτη ἡ γυνὴ κατείληπται ἐπ' αὐτοφώρῳ
this – woman has been caught in the act
μοιχευομένη· 5 ἐν δὲ τῷ νόμῳ [ἡμῖν]
committing adultery; now in the law to us[e]
Μωϋσῆς ἐνετείλατο τὰς τοιαύτας λιθάζειν·
Moses enjoined – [2]such [1]to stone;
σὺ οὖν τί λέγεις; 6 [τοῦτο δὲ ἔλεγον
thou therefore what sayest thou? But this they said
πειράζοντες αὐτόν, ἵνα ἔχωσιν κατηγορεῖν
tempting him, that they might have to accuse
αὐτοῦ.] ὁ δὲ Ἰησοῦς κάτω κύψας τῷ
him. – But Jesus down stooping with the
δακτύλῳ κατέγραφεν εἰς τὴν γῆν. 7 ὡς δὲ
finger wrote in the earth. But as
ἐπέμενον ἐρωτῶντες [αὐτόν], ἀνέκυψεν καὶ
they remained questioning him, he stood erect and
εἶπεν [αὐτοῖς] Ὁ ἀναμάρτητος ὑμῶν
said to them[,] The [one] sinless of you
πρῶτος ἐπ' αὐτὴν βαλέτω λίθον. 8 καὶ
first on her let him cast a stone. And
πάλιν κατακύψας ἔγραφεν εἰς τὴν γῆν.
again stooping down he wrote in the earth.
9 οἱ δὲ ἀκούσαντες ἐξήρχοντο εἷς καθ'
And they hearing went out one by
εἷς ἀρξάμενοι ἀπὸ τῶν πρεσβυτέρων, καὶ
one beginning from the older ones, and
κατελείφθη μόνος, καὶ ἡ γυνὴ ἐν μέσῳ
he was left alone, and the woman in [the] midst
οὖσα. 10 ἀνακύψας δὲ ὁ Ἰησοῦς εἶπεν
being. And standing erect – Jesus said
αὐτῇ Γύναι, ποῦ εἰσιν; οὐδείς σε κατέκρινεν;
to her[,] Woman, where are they? no one thee condemned?
11 ἡ δὲ εἶπεν Οὐδείς, κύριε. εἶπεν δὲ
And she said[,] No one, sir. So said
ὁ Ἰησοῦς Οὐδὲ ἐγώ σε κατακρίνω·
– Jesus[,] Neither I thee condemn;
πορεύου, ἀπὸ τοῦ νῦν μηκέτι ἁμάρτανε.
go, from – now no longer sin.
12 Πάλιν οὖν αὐτοῖς ἐλάλησεν ὁ Ἰησοῦς
Again therefore to them spoke – Jesus
λέγων· ἐγώ εἰμι τὸ φῶς τοῦ κόσμου·
saying: I am the light of the world;
ὁ ἀκολουθῶν μοι οὐ μὴ περιπατήσῃ ἐν
the [one] following me by no means will walk in

into it, and you will find
that a prophet[p] does not
come out of Galilee."

[The earliest and most reliable manuscripts and other ancient witnesses do not have John 7:53–8:11.]

53 Then each went to his
own home.

Chapter 8

BUT Jesus went to the
Mount of Olives. 2 At
dawn he appeared again in
the temple courts, where
all the people gathered
around him, and he sat
down to teach them. 3 The
teachers of the law and the
Pharisees brought in a
woman caught in adultery.
They made her stand be-
fore the group 4 and said to
Jesus, "Teacher, this woman was caught in the act of
adultery. 5 In the Law Moses commanded us to stone
such women. Now what do
you say?" 6 They were us-
ing this question as a trap,
in order to have a basis for
accusing him.
But Jesus bent down and
started to write on the
ground with his finger.
7 When they kept on ques-
tioning him, he straight-
ened up and said to them,
"If any one of you is without sin, let him be the first
to throw a stone at her."
8 Again he stooped down
and wrote on the ground.
9 At this, those who heard
began to go away one at a
time, the older ones first,
until only Jesus was left,
with the woman still standing there. 10 Jesus straightened up and asked her,
"Woman, where are they?
Has no one condemned
you?"
11 "No one, sir," she said.
"Then neither do I con-
demn you," Jesus de-
clared. "Go now and leave
your life of sin."

The Validity of Jesus' Testimony

12 When Jesus spoke again
to the people, he said, "I
am the light of the world.
Whoever follows me will
never walk in darkness, but

[p] 52 Two early manuscripts *the Prophet*

in darkness but will have
the light of life." 13 Then the
Pharisees said to him,
"You are testifying on your
own behalf; your testimony
is not valid." 14 Jesus answered, "Even if I testify
on my own behalf, my testimony is valid because I
know where I have come
from and where I am going,
but you do not know where
I come from or where I am
going. 15 You judge by human standards;[k] I judge no
one. 16 Yet even if I do
judge, my judgment is valid; for it is not I alone who
judge, but I and the Fa-
ther[l] who sent me. 17 In
your law it is written that
the testimony of two wit-
nesses is valid. 18 I testify
on my own behalf, and the
Father who sent me testi-
fies on my behalf." 19 Then
they said to him, "Where is
your Father?" Jesus an-
swered, "You know neither
me nor my Father. If you
knew me, you would know
my Father also." 20 He
spoke these words while he
was teaching in the trea-
sury of the temple, but no
one arrested him, because
his hour had not yet come.

Jesus Foretells His Death

21 Again he said to
them, "I am going away,
and you will search for me,
but you will die in your sin.
Where I am going, you cannot come." 22 Then the
Jews said, "Is he going to
kill himself? Is that what he
means by saying, 'Where I
am going, you cannot
come'?" 23 He said to them,
"You are from below, I am
from above; you are of this

[k] Gk *according to the flesh*
[l] Other ancient authorities read *he*

τῇ σκοτίᾳ, ἀλλ' ἕξει τὸ φῶς τῆς ζωῆς.
the darkness, but will have the light – of life.
13 εἶπον οὖν αὐτῷ οἱ Φαρισαῖοι· σὺ περὶ
Said therefore to him the Pharisees; Thou concerning
σεαυτοῦ μαρτυρεῖς· ἡ μαρτυρία σου οὐκ
thyself witnessest; the witness of thee not
ἔστιν ἀληθής. **14** ἀπεκρίθη Ἰησοῦς καὶ
is true. Answered Jesus and
εἶπεν αὐτοῖς· κἂν ἐγὼ μαρτυρῶ περὶ
said to them: Even if I witness concerning
ἐμαυτοῦ, ἀληθής ἐστιν ἡ μαρτυρία μου,
myself, true is the witness of me,
ὅτι οἶδα πόθεν ἦλθον καὶ ποῦ ὑπάγω·
because I know whence I came and where I go;
ὑμεῖς δὲ οὐκ οἴδατε πόθεν ἔρχομαι ἢ
but ye know not whence I come or
ποῦ ὑπάγω. **15** ὑμεῖς κατὰ τὴν σάρκα
where I go. Ye according to the flesh
κρίνετε, ἐγὼ οὐ κρίνω οὐδένα. **16** καὶ
judge, I judge not no(any)one. [2]even
ἐὰν κρίνω δὲ ἐγώ, ἡ κρίσις ἡ ἐμὴ
[3]if [5]judge [1]But [4]I, *the* [2]judgment – [1]my
ἀληθινή ἐστιν, ὅτι μόνος οὐκ εἰμί, ἀλλ'
true is, because alone I am not, but
ἐγὼ καὶ ὁ πέμψας με. **17** καὶ ἐν τῷ
I and the [one] having sent me. [2]even [3]in *the*
νόμῳ δὲ τῷ ὑμετέρῳ γέγραπται ὅτι δύο
[5]law [1]And – [4]your it has been written that of two
ἀνθρώπων ἡ μαρτυρία ἀληθής ἐστιν.
men the witness true is.
18 ἐγώ εἰμι ὁ μαρτυρῶν περὶ ἐμαυτοῦ,
I am the [one] witnessing concerning myself,
καὶ μαρτυρεῖ περὶ ἐμοῦ ὁ πέμψας με
and witnesses concerning me [1]the [3]having sent [4]me
πατήρ. **19** ἔλεγον οὖν αὐτῷ· ποῦ ἐστιν ὁ
[2]Father. They said therefore to him: Where is the
πατήρ σου; ἀπεκρίθη Ἰησοῦς· οὔτε ἐμὲ
Father of thee? Answered Jesus: Neither me
οἴδατε οὔτε τὸν πατέρα μου· εἰ ἐμὲ
ye know nor the Father of me; if me
ᾔδειτε, καὶ τὸν πατέρα μου ἂν ᾔδειτε.
ye knew, also the Father of me ye would have known.
20 Ταῦτα τὰ ῥήματα ἐλάλησεν ἐν τῷ
These – words he spoke in the
γαζοφυλακείῳ διδάσκων ἐν τῷ ἱερῷ· καὶ
treasury teaching in the temple; and
οὐδεὶς ἐπίασεν αὐτόν, ὅτι οὔπω ἐληλύθει
no one seized him, because not yet had come
ἡ ὥρα αὐτοῦ.
the hour of him.

21 Εἶπεν οὖν πάλιν αὐτοῖς· ἐγὼ ὑπάγω
He said therefore again to them: I go
καὶ ζητήσετέ με, καὶ ἐν τῇ ἁμαρτίᾳ
and ye will seek me, and in the sin
ὑμῶν ἀποθανεῖσθε· ὅπου ἐγὼ ὑπάγω ὑμεῖς
of you ye will die; where I go ye
οὐ δύνασθε ἐλθεῖν. **22** ἔλεγον οὖν οἱ
cannot *to* come. Said therefore the
Ἰουδαῖοι· μήτι ἀποκτενεῖ ἑαυτόν, ὅτι
Jews: *Not* will he kill himself, because
λέγει· ὅπου ἐγὼ ὑπάγω ὑμεῖς οὐ δύνασθε
he says: Where I go ye cannot
ἐλθεῖν; **23** καὶ ἔλεγεν αὐτοῖς· ὑμεῖς ἐκ
to come? And he said to them: Ye of
τῶν κάτω ἐστέ, ἐγὼ ἐκ τῶν ἄνω εἰμί·
the things below are, I of the things above am;

will have the light of life."
13The Pharisees chal-
lenged him, "Here you are,
appearing as your own witness; your testimony is not
valid."
14Jesus answered, "Even
if I testify on my own behalf, my testimony is valid,
for I know where I came
from and where I am going.
But you have no idea where
I come from or where I am
going. 15You judge by hu-
man standards; I pass judgment on no one. 16But if I
do judge, my decisions are
right, because I am not
alone. I stand with the Father, who sent me. 17In
your own Law it is written
that the testimony of two
men is valid. 18I am one
who testifies for myself; my
other witness is the Father,
who sent me."
19Then they asked him,
"Where is your father?"
"You do not know me or
my Father," Jesus replied.
"If you knew me, you
would know my Father
also." 20He spoke these
words while teaching in the
temple area near the place
where the offerings were
put. Yet no one seized him,
because his time had not
yet come.
21Once more Jesus said to
them, "I am going away,
and you will look for me,
and you will die in your sin.
Where I go, you cannot
come."
22This made the Jews ask,
"Will he kill himself? Is
that why he says, 'Where I
go, you cannot come'?"
23But he continued, "You
are from below; I am from
above. You are of this

world. I am not of this
world. 24 I told you that you
would die in your sins, for
you will die in your sins unless you believe that I am
he."[m] 25 They said to him,
"Who are you?" Jesus said
to them, "Why do I speak
to you at all?[n] 26 I have
much to say about you and
much to condemn; but the
one who sent me is true,
and I declare to the world
what I have heard from
him." 27 They did not un-
derstand that he was speaking to them about the Fa-
ther. 28 So Jesus said,
"When you have lifted up
the Son of Man, then you
will realize that I am he,[m]
and that I do nothing on my
own, but I speak these
things as the Father in-
structed me. 29 And the one
who sent me is with me; he
has not left me alone, for I
always do what is pleasing
to him." 30 As he was saying these things, many believed in him.

True Disciples

31 Then Jesus said to
the Jews who had believed
in him, "If you continue in
my word, you are truly my
disciples; 32 and you will
know the truth, and the
truth will make you free."
33 They answered him, "We
are descendants of Abra-
ham and have never been
slaves to anyone. What do
you mean by saying, 'You
will be made free'?"
34 Jesus answered
them, "Very truly, I tell
you, everyone who com-
mits sin is a slave to sin.
35 The slave does not have a
permanent place in the
household; the son has a

[m] Gk *I am*
[n] Or *What I have told you from the beginning*

ὑμεῖς ἐκ τούτου τοῦ κόσμου ἐστέ, ἐγὼ
ye of this – world are, I
οὐκ εἰμὶ ἐκ τοῦ κόσμου τούτου. **24** εἶπον
am not of – world this. I said
οὖν ὑμῖν ὅτι ἀποθανεῖσθε ἐν ταῖς ἁμαρτίαις
therefore to you that ye will die in the sins
ὑμῶν· ἐὰν γὰρ μὴ πιστεύσητε ὅτι ἐγώ
of you; for if ye believe not that I
εἰμι, ἀποθανεῖσθε ἐν ταῖς ἁμαρτίαις ὑμῶν.
am, ye will die in the sins of you.
25 ἔλεγον οὖν αὐτῷ· σὺ τίς εἶ; εἶπεν
They said therefore to him: [2]Thou [1]who [3]art? Said
αὐτοῖς ὁ Ἰησοῦς· τὴν ἀρχὴν ὅ τι καὶ
to them – Jesus: [5]at all † [1]Why [2]indeed
λαλῶ ὑμῖν; **26** πολλὰ ἔχω περὶ ὑμῶν
[3]speak I [4]to you? Many things I have about you
λαλεῖν καὶ κρίνειν· ἀλλ' ὁ πέμψας με
to speak and to judge; but the [one] having sent me
ἀληθής ἐστιν, κἀγὼ ἃ ἤκουσα παρ'
true is, and I what I heard from
αὐτοῦ, ταῦτα λαλῶ εἰς τὸν κόσμον.
him, these things I speak in the world.
27 οὐκ ἔγνωσαν ὅτι τὸν πατέρα αὐτοῖς
They did not know that [2]the [3]Father [4]to them
ἔλεγεν. **28** εἶπεν οὖν ὁ Ἰησοῦς· ὅταν
[1]he spoke [of]. Said therefore – Jesus: When
ὑψώσητε τὸν υἱὸν τοῦ ἀνθρώπου, τότε
ye lift up the Son – of man, then
γνώσεσθε ὅτι ἐγώ εἰμι, καὶ ἀπ' ἐμαυτοῦ
ye will know that I am, and from myself
ποιῶ οὐδέν, ἀλλὰ καθὼς ἐδίδαξέν με ὁ
I do nothing, but as taught me the
πατήρ, ταῦτα λαλῶ. **29** καὶ ὁ πέμψας
Father, these things I speak. And the [one] having sent
με μετ' ἐμοῦ ἐστιν· οὐκ ἀφῆκέν με
me with me is; he did not leave me
μόνον, ὅτι ἐγὼ τὰ ἀρεστὰ αὐτῷ ποιῶ
alone, because I the things pleasing to him do
πάντοτε.
always.
30 Ταῦτα αὐτοῦ λαλοῦντος πολλοὶ ἐπίσ-
These things him saying[a] many be-
=As he said these things
τευσαν εἰς αὐτόν. **31** ἔλεγεν οὖν ὁ Ἰησοῦς
lieved in him. Said therefore – Jesus
πρὸς τοὺς πεπιστευκότας αὐτῷ Ἰουδαίους·
to [1]the [3]having believed [4]him [2]Jews:
ἐὰν ὑμεῖς μείνητε ἐν τῷ λόγῳ τῷ ἐμῷ,
If ye continue in *the* [2]word – [1]my,
ἀληθῶς μαθηταί μού ἐστε, **32** καὶ γνώσεσθε
truly disciples of me ye are, and ye will know
τὴν ἀλήθειαν, καὶ ἡ ἀλήθεια ἐλευθερώσει
the truth, and the truth will free
ὑμᾶς. **33** ἀπεκρίθησαν πρὸς αὐτόν· σπέρμα
you. They answered *to* him: Seed
Ἀβραάμ ἐσμεν, καὶ οὐδενὶ δεδουλεύκαμεν
of Abraham we are, and to no one have we been enslaved
πώποτε· πῶς σὺ λέγεις ὅτι ἐλεύθεροι
*n*ever; how thou sayest that free
γενήσεσθε; **34** ἀπεκρίθη αὐτοῖς ὁ Ἰησοῦς·
ye will become? Answered them – Jesus:
ἀμὴν ἀμὴν λέγω ὑμῖν ὅτι πᾶς ὁ ποιῶν
Truly truly I tell you that everyone doing
τὴν ἁμαρτίαν δοῦλός ἐστιν τῆς ἁμαρτίας.
– sin a slave is – of sin.
35 ὁ δὲ δοῦλος οὐ μένει ἐν τῇ οἰκίᾳ
But the slave does not remain in the house

world; I am not of this
world. 24I told you that you
would die in your sins; if
you do not believe that I am
⌊the one I claim to be⌋,[q] you
will indeed die in your
sins."
25"Who are you?" they
asked.
"Just what I have been
claiming all along," Jesus
replied. 26"I have much to
say in judgment of you. But
he who sent me is reliable,
and what I have heard from
him I tell the world."
27They did not under-
stand that he was telling
them about his Father. 28So
Jesus said, "When you
have lifted up the Son of
Man, then you will know
that I am ⌊the one I claim to
be⌋ and that I do nothing on
my own but speak just what
the Father has taught me.
29The one who sent me is
with me; he has not left me
alone, for I always do what
pleases him." 30Even as he
spoke, many put their faith
in him.

The Children of Abraham

31To the Jews who had
believed him, Jesus said,
"If you hold to my teach-
ing, you are really my disciples. 32Then you will know
the truth, and the truth will
set you free."
33They answered him,
"We are Abraham's de-
scendants[r] and have never
been slaves of anyone.
How can you say that we
shall be set free?"
34Jesus replied, "I tell
you the truth, everyone
who sins is a slave to sin.
35Now a slave has no per-
manent place in the family,

[q]24 Or *I am he*; also in verse 28
[r]33 Greek *seed*; also in verse 37

place there forever. 36 So if
the Son makes you free,
you will be free indeed. 37 I
know that you are descen-
dants of Abraham; yet you
look for an opportunity to
kill me, because there is no
place in you for my word.
38 I declare what I have
seen in the Father's presence; as for you, you
should do what you have
heard from the Father."[o]

Jesus and Abraham

39 They answered him,
"Abraham is our father."
Jesus said to them, "If you
were Abraham's children,
you would be doing[p] what
Abraham did, 40 but now
you are trying to kill me, a
man who has told you the
truth that I heard from
God. This is not what Abraham did. 41 You are indeed
doing what your father
does." They said to him,
"We are not illegitimate
children; we have one fa-
ther, God himself." 42 Jesus
said to them, "If God were
your Father, you would
love me, for I came from
God and now I am here. I
did not come on my own,
but he sent me. 43 Why do
you not understand what I
say? It is because you cannot accept my word. 44 You
are from your father the
devil, and you choose to do
your father's desires. He
was a murderer from the
beginning and does not
stand in the truth, because
there is no truth in him.
When he lies, he speaks according to his own nature,
for he is a liar and the father
of lies. 45 But because I tell
the truth, you do not be-
lieve me. 46 Which of you

[o] Other ancient authorities read *you do what you have heard from your father*

[p] Other ancient authorities read *If you are Abraham's children, then do*

εἰς τὸν αἰῶνα· ὁ υἱὸς μένει εἰς τὸν
unto the age; the son remains unto the
αἰῶνα. 36 ἐὰν οὖν ὁ υἱὸς ὑμᾶς ἐλευθερώσῃ,
age. If therefore the Son you frees,
ὄντως ἐλεύθεροι ἔσεσθε. 37 Οἶδα ὅτι
really free ye will be. I know that
σπέρμα Ἀβραάμ ἐστε· ἀλλὰ ζητεῖτέ με
seed of Abraham ye are; but ye seek me
ἀποκτεῖναι, ὅτι ὁ λόγος ὁ ἐμὸς οὐ χωρεῖ
to kill, because *the* [2]word – [1]my finds no room
ἐν ὑμῖν. 38 ἃ ἐγὼ ἑώρακα παρὰ τῷ
in you. What I have seen with the
πατρὶ λαλῶ· καὶ ὑμεῖς οὖν ἃ ἠκού-
Father I speak; and ye therefore what ye
σατε παρὰ τοῦ πατρὸς ποιεῖτε. 39 ἀπεκρί-
heard from the father ye do. They
θησαν καὶ εἶπαν αὐτῷ· ὁ πατὴρ ἡμῶν Ἀβραάμ
answered and said to him: The father of us Abraham
ἐστιν. λέγει αὐτοῖς ὁ Ἰησοῦς· εἰ τέκνα
is. Says to them – Jesus : If children
τοῦ Ἀβραάμ ἐστε, τὰ ἔργα τοῦ Ἀβραὰμ
– of Abraham ye are, the works – of Abraham
ποιεῖτε· 40 νῦν δὲ ζητεῖτέ με ἀποκτεῖναι,
ye do; but now ye seek me to kill,
ἄνθρωπον ὃς τὴν ἀλήθειαν ὑμῖν λελάληκα,
a man who the truth to you has spoken,
ἣν ἤκουσα παρὰ τοῦ θεοῦ· τοῦτο Ἀβραὰμ
which I heard from – God; this Abraham
οὐκ ἐποίησεν. 41 ὑμεῖς ποιεῖτε τὰ ἔργα
did not. Ye do the works
τοῦ πατρὸς ὑμῶν. εἶπαν αὐτῷ· ἡμεῖς ἐκ
of the father of you. They said to him : We of
πορνείας οὐκ ἐγεννήθημεν, ἕνα πατέρα
fornication were not born, one father
ἔχομεν τὸν θεόν. 42 εἶπεν αὐτοῖς ὁ
we have[,] – God. Said to them –
Ἰησοῦς· εἰ ὁ θεὸς πατὴρ ὑμῶν ἦν,
Jesus : If – God father of you was,
ἠγαπᾶτε ἂν ἐμέ· ἐγὼ γὰρ ἐκ τοῦ θεοῦ
ye would have loved me; for I of – God
ἐξῆλθον καὶ ἥκω· οὐδὲ γὰρ ἀπ' ἐμαυτοῦ
came forth and have come; for not from myself
ἐλήλυθα, ἀλλ' ἐκεῖνός με ἀπέστειλεν. 43 διὰ τί
I have come, but that one me sent. Why
τὴν λαλιὰν τὴν ἐμὴν οὐ γινώσκετε;
the [2]speech – [1]my know ye not?
ὅτι οὐ δύνασθε ἀκούειν τὸν λόγον τὸν
because ye cannot *to* hear *the* [2]word –
ἐμόν. 44 ὑμεῖς ἐκ τοῦ πατρὸς τοῦ
[1]my. Ye of the father *of* the
διαβόλου ἐστὲ καὶ τὰς ἐπιθυμίας τοῦ
devil are and the desires of the
πατρὸς ὑμῶν θέλετε ποιεῖν. ἐκεῖνος
father of you ye wish to do. That one
ἀνθρωποκτόνος ἦν ἀπ' ἀρχῆς, καὶ ἐν
a murderer was from [the] beginning, and in
τῇ ἀληθείᾳ οὐκ ἔστηκεν, ὅτι οὐκ ἔστιν
the truth stood not, because not is
ἀλήθεια ἐν αὐτῷ. ὅταν λαλῇ τὸ ψεῦδος,
truth in him. When he speaks the lie,
ἐκ τῶν ἰδίων λαλεῖ, ὅτι ψεύστης ἐστὶν
out of his own things he speaks, because a liar he is
καὶ ὁ πατὴρ αὐτοῦ. 45 ἐγὼ δὲ ὅτι τὴν
and the father of it. But [2]I [1]because [4]the
ἀλήθειαν λέγω, οὐ πιστεύετέ μοι. 46 τίς
[5]truth [3]say, ye do not believe me. Who

but a son belongs to it forever. 36 So if the Son sets
you free, you will be free
indeed. 37 I know you are
Abraham's descendants.
Yet you are ready to kill
me, because you have no
room for my word. 38 I am
telling you what I have seen
in the Father's presence,
and you do what you have
heard from your father.[s]"
39 "Abraham is our fa-
ther," they answered.
"If you were Abraham's
children," said Jesus,
"then you would[t] do the
things Abraham did. 40 As it
is, you are determined to
kill me, a man who has told
you the truth that I heard
from God. Abraham did
not do such things. 41 You
are doing the things your
own father does."
"We are not illegitimate
children," they protested.
"The only Father we have
is God himself."

The Children of the Devil

42 Jesus said to them, "If
God were your Father, you
would love me, for I came
from God and now am
here. I have not come on
my own; but he sent me.
43 Why is my language not
clear to you? Because you
are unable to hear what I
say. 44 You belong to your
father, the devil, and you
want to carry out your father's desire. He was a
murderer from the begin-
ning, not holding to the
truth, for there is no truth in
him. When he lies, he
speaks his native language,
for he is a liar and the father
of lies. 45 Yet because I tell
the truth, you do not be-

[s] 38 Or *presence. Therefore do what you have heard from the Father.*

[t] 39 Some early manuscripts *"If you are Abraham's children," said Jesus, "then*

convicts me of sin? If I tell
the truth, why do you not
believe me? 47 Whoever is
from God hears the words
of God. The reason you do
not hear them is that you
are not from God."
48 The Jews answered
him, "Are we not right in
saying that you are a Sa-
maritan and have a de-
mon?" 49 Jesus answered,
"I do not have a demon; but
I honor my Father, and you
dishonor me. 50 Yet I do not
seek my own glory; there is
one who seeks it and he is
the judge. 51 Very truly, I
tell you, whoever keeps my
word will never see death."
52 The Jews said to him,
"Now we know that you
have a demon. Abraham
died, and so did the prophets; yet you say, 'Whoever
keeps my word will never
taste death.' 53 Are you
greater than our father
Abraham, who died? The
prophets also died. Who do
you claim to be?" 54 Jesus
answered, "If I glorify myself, my glory is nothing. It
is my Father who glorifies
me, he of whom you say,
'He is our God,' 55 though
you do not know him. But
I know him; if I would say
that I do not know him, I
would be a liar like you.
But I do know him and I
keep his word. 56 Your ancestor Abraham rejoiced
that he would see my day;
he saw it and was glad."
57 Then the Jews said to

ἐξ ὑμῶν ἐλέγχει με περὶ ἁμαρτίας; εἰ
of you reproves me concerning sin? If
ἀλήθειαν λέγω, διὰ τί ὑμεῖς οὐ πιστεύετέ
truth I say, why [2]ye [1]do not believe
μοι; **47** ὁ ὢν ἐκ τοῦ θεοῦ τὰ ῥήματα
me? The [one] being of – God the words
τοῦ θεοῦ ἀκούει· διὰ τοῦτο ὑμεῖς οὐκ
– of God hears; therefore ye not
ἀκούετε, ὅτι ἐκ τοῦ θεοῦ οὐκ ἐστέ.
hear, because of – God ye are not.
48 Ἀπεκρίθησαν οἱ Ἰουδαῖοι καὶ εἶπαν
Answered the Jews and said
αὐτῷ· οὐ καλῶς λέγομεν ἡμεῖς ὅτι
to him: [3]Not [4]well [1]say [2]we [5]that
Σαμαρίτης εἶ σὺ καὶ δαιμόνιον ἔχεις;
[8]a Samaritan [7]art [6]thou [9]and [11]a demon [10]hast?
49 ἀπεκρίθη Ἰησοῦς· ἐγὼ δαιμόνιον οὐκ
Answered Jesus: I a demon not
ἔχω, ἀλλὰ τιμῶ τὸν πατέρα μου, καὶ
have, but I honour the Father of me, and
ὑμεῖς ἀτιμάζετέ με. **50** ἐγὼ δὲ οὐ ζητῶ
ye dishonour me. But I seek not
τὴν δόξαν μου· ἔστιν ὁ ζητῶν καὶ
the glory of me; there is the [one] seeking and
κρίνων. **51** ἀμὴν ἀμὴν λέγω ὑμῖν, ἐάν
judging. Truly truly I tell you, if
τις τὸν ἐμὸν λόγον τηρήσῃ, θάνατον
anyone – my word keeps, death
οὐ μὴ θεωρήσῃ εἰς τὸν αἰῶνα. **52** εἶπαν
by no means will he behold unto the age. Said
αὐτῷ οἱ Ἰουδαῖοι· νῦν ἐγνώκαμεν ὅτι
to him the Jews: Now we have known that
δαιμόνιον ἔχεις. Ἀβραὰμ ἀπέθανεν καὶ οἱ
a demon thou hast. Abraham died and the
προφῆται, καὶ σὺ λέγεις· ἐάν τις τὸν
prophets, and thou sayest: If anyone the
λόγον μου τηρήσῃ, οὐ μὴ γεύσηται
word of me keeps, by no means will he taste
θανάτου εἰς τὸν αἰῶνα. **53** μὴ σὺ μείζων
of death unto the age. *Not* thou greater
εἶ τοῦ πατρὸς ἡμῶν Ἀβραάμ, ὅστις
art [than] the father of us Abraham, who
ἀπέθανεν; καὶ οἱ προφῆται ἀπέθανον· τίνα
died? and the prophets died;. whom
σεαυτὸν ποιεῖς; **54** ἀπεκρίθη Ἰησοῦς· ἐὰν
thyself makest thou? Answered Jesus: If
ἐγὼ δοξάσω ἐμαυτόν, ἡ δόξα μου οὐδέν
I glorify myself, the glory of me nothing
ἐστιν· ἔστιν ὁ πατήρ μου ὁ δοξάζων με,
is; [4]is [1]the [2]Father [3]of me the [one] glorifying me,
ὃν ὑμεῖς λέγετε ὅτι θεὸς ἡμῶν ἐστιν,
whom ye say[,] – God of us he is,
55 καὶ οὐκ ἐγνώκατε αὐτόν, ἐγὼ δὲ
and ye have not known him, but I
οἶδα αὐτόν. κἂν εἴπω ὅτι οὐκ οἶδα
know him. Even if I say that I know not
αὐτόν, ἔσομαι ὅμοιος ὑμῖν ψεύστης· ἀλλὰ
him, I shall be like you a liar; but
οἶδα αὐτὸν καὶ τὸν λόγον αὐτοῦ τηρῶ.
I know him and the word of him I keep.
56 Ἀβραὰμ ὁ πατὴρ ὑμῶν ἠγαλλιάσατο
Abraham the father of you was glad
ἵνα ἴδῃ τὴν ἡμέραν τὴν ἐμήν, καὶ εἶδεν
that he should see *the* [2]day – [1]my, and he saw
καὶ ἐχάρη. **57** εἶπαν οὖν οἱ Ἰουδαῖοι
and rejoiced. Said therefore the Jews

lieve me! 46 Can any of you
prove me guilty of sin? If I
am telling the truth, why
don't you believe me? 47 He
who belongs to God hears
what God says. The reason
you do not hear is that you
do not belong to God."

The Claims of Jesus About Himself

48 The Jews answered
him, "Aren't we right in
saying that you are a Sa-
maritan and demon-pos-
sessed?"
49 "I am not possessed by
a demon," said Jesus, "but
I honor my Father and you
dishonor me. 50 I am not
seeking glory for myself;
but there is one who seeks
it, and he is the judge. 51 I
tell you the truth, if anyone
keeps my word, he will
never see death."
52 At this the Jews ex-
claimed, "Now we know
that you are demon-pos-
sessed! Abraham died and
so did the prophets, yet you
say that if anyone keeps
your word, he will never
taste death. 53 Are you
greater than our father
Abraham? He died, and so
did the prophets. Who do
you think you are?"
54 Jesus replied, "If I glorify myself, my glory
means nothing. My Father,
whom you claim as your
God, is the one who glorifies me. 55 Though you do
not know him, I know him.
If I said I did not, I would
be a liar like you, but I do
know him and keep his
word. 56 Your father Abraham rejoiced at the thought
of seeing my day; he saw it
and was glad."
57 "You are not yet fifty

him, "You are not yet fifty years old, and have you seen Abraham?"[q] 58 Jesus said to them, "Very truly, I tell you, before Abraham was, I am." 59 So they picked up stones to throw at him, but Jesus hid himself and went out of the temple.

πρὸς αὐτόν· πεντήκοντα ἔτη οὔπω ἔχεις
to him : Fifty years not yet thou hast

καὶ Ἀβραὰμ ἑώρακας; **58** εἶπεν αὐτοῖς
and Abraham hast thou seen? Said to them

Ἰησοῦς· ἀμὴν ἀμὴν λέγω ὑμῖν, πρὶν
Jesus: Truly truly I tell you, before

Ἀβραὰμ γενέσθαι ἐγὼ εἰμί. **59** ἦραν
Abraham to become[b] =became I am. They took

οὖν λίθους ἵνα βάλωσιν ἐπ' αὐτόν·
therefore stones that they might cast on him;

Ἰησοῦς δὲ ἐκρύβη καὶ ἐξῆλθεν ἐκ τοῦ
but Jesus was hidden and went forth out of the

ἱεροῦ.
temple.

years old," the Jews said to him, "and you have seen Abraham!"

58 "I tell you the truth," Jesus answered, "before Abraham was born, I am!" 59 At this, they picked up stones to stone him, but Jesus hid himself, slipping away from the temple grounds.

Chapter 9

A Man Born Blind Receives Sight

AS he walked along, he saw a man blind from birth. 2 His disciples asked him, "Rabbi, who sinned, this man or his parents, that he was born blind?" 3 Jesus answered, "Neither this man nor his parents sinned; he was born blind so that God's works might be revealed in him. 4 We[r] must work the works of him who sent me[s] while it is day; night is coming when no one can work. 5 As long as I am in the world, I am the light of the world." 6 When he had said this, he spat on the ground and made mud with the saliva and spread the mud on the man's eyes, 7 saying to him, "Go, wash in the pool of Siloam" (which means Sent). Then he went and washed and came back able to see. 8 The neighbors and those who had seen him before as a beggar began to ask, "Is this not the man who used to sit and beg?" 9 Some were saying, "It is he." Others were saying, "No, but it is someone like him." He kept saying, "I am the man." 10 But they kept asking him, "Then how were your eyes opened?" 11 He answered, "The man called

9 Καὶ παράγων εἶδεν ἄνθρωπον τυφλὸν
And passing along he saw a man blind

ἐκ γενετῆς. **2** καὶ ἠρώτησαν αὐτὸν οἱ
from birth. And asked him the

μαθηταὶ αὐτοῦ λέγοντες· ῥαββί, τίς ἥμαρτεν,
disciples of him saying : Rabbi, who sinned,

οὗτος ἢ οἱ γονεῖς αὐτοῦ, ἵνα τυφλὸς
this man or the parents of him, that blind

γεννηθῇ; **3** ἀπεκρίθη Ἰησοῦς· οὔτε οὗτος
he was born? Answered Jesus : Neither this man

ἥμαρτεν οὔτε οἱ γονεῖς αὐτοῦ, ἀλλ' ἵνα
sinned nor the parents of him, but that

φανερωθῇ τὰ ἔργα τοῦ θεοῦ ἐν αὐτῷ.
might be manifested the works – of God in him.

4 ἡμᾶς δεῖ ἐργάζεσθαι τὰ ἔργα τοῦ
Us it behoves to work the works of the

πέμψαντός με ἕως ἡμέρα ἐστίν· ἔρχεται
[one] having sent me while day it is; comes

νὺξ ὅτε οὐδεὶς δύναται ἐργάζεσθαι. **5** ὅταν
night when no one can *to* work. When

ἐν τῷ κόσμῳ ὦ, φῶς εἰμι τοῦ κόσμου.
in the world I am, light I am of the world.

6 ταῦτα εἰπὼν ἔπτυσεν χαμαὶ καὶ ἐποίησεν
These things having said he spat on the ground and made

πηλὸν ἐκ τοῦ πτύσματος, καὶ ἐπέθηκεν
clay out of the spittle, and [1]put *on*

αὐτοῦ τὸν πηλὸν ἐπὶ τοὺς ὀφθαλμούς,
[7]of him [2]the [3]clay [4]on [5]the [6]eyes,

7 καὶ εἶπεν αὐτῷ· ὕπαγε νίψαι εἰς τὴν
and said to him : Go wash in the

κολυμβήθραν τοῦ Σιλωάμ (ὃ ἑρμηνεύεται
pool – of Siloam (which is translated

ἀπεσταλμένος). ἀπῆλθεν οὖν καὶ ἐνίψατο,
having been sent). He went therefore and washed,

καὶ ἦλθεν βλέπων. **8** Οἱ οὖν γείτονες
and came seeing. Therefore the neighbours

καὶ οἱ θεωροῦντες αὐτὸν τὸ πρότερον,
and the [ones] beholding him formerly, †

ὅτι προσαίτης ἦν, ἔλεγον· οὐχ οὗτός
that a beggar he was, said : [2]Not [3]this man

ἐστιν ὁ καθήμενος καὶ προσαιτῶν; **9** ἄλλοι
[1]is the [one] sitting and begging? Some

ἔλεγον ὅτι οὗτός ἐστιν· ἄλλοι ἔλεγον·
said[,] – This is he; others said :

οὐχί, ἀλλὰ ὅμοιος αὐτῷ ἐστιν. ἐκεῖνος
No, but like *to* him he is. That [one]

ἔλεγεν ὅτι ἐγώ εἰμι. **10** ἔλεγον οὖν
said[,] – I am. They said therefore

αὐτῷ· πῶς [οὖν] ἠνεῴχθησάν σου οἱ
to him : How then were opened of thee the

Chapter 9

Jesus Heals a Man Born Blind

AS he went along, he saw a man blind from birth. 2 His disciples asked him, "Rabbi, who sinned, this man or his parents, that he was born blind?"

3 "Neither this man nor his parents sinned," said Jesus, "but this happened so that the work of God might be displayed in his life. 4 As long as it is day, we must do the work of him who sent me. Night is coming, when no one can work. 5 While I am in the world, I am the light of the world."

6 Having said this, he spit on the ground, made some mud with the saliva, and put it on the man's eyes. 7 "Go," he told him, "wash in the Pool of Siloam" (this word means Sent). So the man went and washed, and came home seeing.

8 His neighbors and those who had formerly seen him begging asked, "Isn't this the same man who used to sit and beg?" 9 Some claimed that he was.

Others said, "No, he only looks like him."

But he himself insisted, "I am the man."

10 "How then were your eyes opened?" they demanded.

[q] Other ancient authorities read *has Abraham seen you?*
[r] Other ancient authorities read *I*
[s] Other ancient authorities read *us*

Jesus made mud, spread it
on my eyes, and said to me,
'Go to Siloam and wash.'
Then I went and washed
and received my sight."
12 They said to him,
"Where is he?" He said, "I
do not know."

The Pharisees Investigate the Healing

13 They brought to the
Pharisees the man who had
formerly been blind.
14 Now it was a sabbath day
when Jesus made the mud
and opened his eyes.
15 Then the Pharisees also
began to ask him how he
had received his sight. He
said to them, "He put mud
on my eyes. Then I
washed, and now I see."
16 Some of the Pharisees
said, "This man is not from
God, for he does not ob-
serve the sabbath." But
others said, "How can a
man who is a sinner per-
form such signs?" And they
were divided. 17 So they
said again to the blind man,
"What do you say about
him? It was your eyes he
opened." He said, "He is a
prophet."
18 The Jews did not be-
lieve that he had been blind
and had received his sight
until they called the parents
of the man who had re-
ceived his sight 19 and
asked them, "Is this your
son, who you say was born
blind? How then does he
now see?" 20 His parents
answered, "We know that
this is our son, and that he
was born blind; 21 but we do
not know how it is that now
he sees, nor do we know

ὀφθαλμοί; **11** ἀπεκρίθη ἐκεῖνος· ὁ ἄνθρωπος
eyes? Answered that [one] : The man
ὁ λεγόμενος Ἰησοῦς πηλὸν ἐποίησεν καὶ
– *being* named Jesus clay made and
ἐπέχρισέν μου τοὺς ὀφθαλμοὺς καὶ εἶπέν
anointed of me the eyes and told
μοι ὅτι ὕπαγε εἰς τὸν Σιλωὰμ καὶ
me[,] – Go to – Siloam and
νίψαι· ἀπελθὼν οὖν καὶ νιψάμενος ἀνέβλεψα.
wash; going therefore and washing I saw.
12 καὶ εἶπαν αὐτῷ· ποῦ ἐστιν ἐκεῖνος;
And they said to him : Where is that [one]?
λέγει· οὐκ οἶδα. **13** Ἄγουσιν αὐτὸν
He says: I do not know. They lead him
πρὸς τοὺς Φαρισαίους, τόν ποτε τυφλόν.
to the Pharisees, the at one time blind.
14 ἦν δὲ σάββατον ἐν ᾗ ἡμέρᾳ τὸν
Now it was a sabbath on which day [3]the
πηλὸν ἐποίησεν ὁ Ἰησοῦς καὶ ἀνέῳξεν
[4]clay [2]made – [1]Jesus and opened
αὐτοῦ τοὺς ὀφθαλμούς. **15** πάλιν οὖν
of him the eyes. Again therefore
ἠρώτων αὐτὸν καὶ οἱ Φαρισαῖοι πῶς
[4]asked [5]him [3]also [1]the [2]Pharisees how
ἀνέβλεψεν. ὁ δὲ εἶπεν αὐτοῖς· πηλὸν
he saw. And he said to them : Clay
ἐπέθηκέν μου ἐπὶ τοὺς ὀφθαλμούς, καὶ
he put *on* [4]of me [1]on [2]the [3]eyes, and
ἐνιψάμην, καὶ βλέπω. **16** ἔλεγον οὖν ἐκ
I washed, and I see. Said therefore of
τῶν Φαρισαίων τινές· οὐκ ἔστιν οὗτος
the Pharisees some : [4]not [3]is [1]This
παρὰ θεοῦ ὁ ἄνθρωπος, ὅτι τὸ σάββατον
[5]from [6]God – [2]man, because the sabbath
οὐ τηρεῖ. ἄλλοι [δὲ] ἔλεγον· πῶς δύναται
he keeps not. But others said : How can
ἄνθρωπος ἁμαρτωλὸς τοιαῦτα σημεῖα ποιεῖν;
man a sinful such signs *to* do?
καὶ σχίσμα ἦν ἐν αὐτοῖς. **17** λέγουσιν
And a division there was among them. They say
οὖν τῷ τυφλῷ πάλιν· τί σὺ λέγεις
therefore to the blind man again : What thou sayest
περὶ αὐτοῦ, ὅτι ἠνέῳξέν σου τοὺς
about him, because he opened of thee the
ὀφθαλμούς; ὁ δὲ εἶπεν ὅτι προφήτης ἐστίν.
eyes? And he said[,] – A prophet he is.
18 οὐκ ἐπίστευσαν οὖν οἱ Ἰουδαῖοι περὶ
Did not believe therefore the Jews about
αὐτοῦ ὅτι ἦν τυφλὸς καὶ ἀνέβλεψεν,
him that he was blind and saw,
ἕως ὅτου ἐφώνησαν τοὺς γονεῖς αὐτοῦ
until they called the parents of him
τοῦ ἀναβλέψαντος **19** καὶ ἠρώτησαν αὐτοὺς
of the [one] having seen and asked them
λέγοντες· οὗτός ἐστιν ὁ υἱὸς ὑμῶν, ὃν
saying : This is the son of you, whom
ὑμεῖς λέγετε ὅτι τυφλὸς ἐγεννήθη; πῶς
ye say that blind he was born? how
οὖν βλέπει ἄρτι; **20** ἀπεκρίθησαν οὖν οἱ
then sees he now? Answered therefore the
γονεῖς αὐτοῦ καὶ εἶπαν· οἴδαμεν ὅτι
parents of him and said : We know that
οὗτός ἐστιν ὁ υἱὸς ἡμῶν καὶ ὅτι τυφλὸς
this is the son of us and that blind
ἐγεννήθη· **21** πῶς δὲ νῦν βλέπει οὐκ
he was born; but how now he sees not

11 He replied, "The man
they call Jesus made some
mud and put it on my eyes.
He told me to go to Siloam
and wash. So I went and
washed, and then I could
see."
12 "Where is this man?"
they asked him.
"I don't know," he said.

The Pharisees Investigate the Healing

13 They brought to the
Pharisees the man who had
been blind. 14 Now the day
on which Jesus had made
the mud and opened the
man's eyes was a Sabbath.
15 Therefore the Pharisees
also asked him how he had
received his sight. "He put
mud on my eyes," the man
replied, "and I washed,
and now I see."
16 Some of the Pharisees
said, "This man is not from
God, for he does not keep
the Sabbath."
But others asked, "How
can a sinner do such miraculous signs?" So they were
divided.
17 Finally they turned
again to the blind man,
"What have you to say
about him? It was your
eyes he opened."
The man replied, "He is a
prophet."
18 The Jews still did not
believe that he had been
blind and had received his
sight until they sent for the
man's parents. 19 "Is this
your son?" they asked. "Is
this the one you say was
born blind? How is it that
now he can see?"
20 "We know he is our
son," the parents an-
swered, "and we know he
was born blind. 21 But how

who opened his eyes. Ask him; he is of age. He will speak for himself." 22 His parents said this because they were afraid of the Jews; for the Jews had already agreed that anyone who confessed Jesus[t] to be the Messiah[u] would be put out of the synagogue. 23 Therefore his parents said, "He is of age; ask him."

24 So for the second time they called the man who had been blind, and they said to him, "Give glory to God! We know that this man is a sinner." 25 He answered, "I do not know whether he is a sinner. One thing I do know, that though I was blind, now I see." 26 They said to him, "What did he do to you? How did he open your eyes?" 27 He answered them, "I have told you already, and you would not listen. Why do you want to hear it again? Do you also want to become his disciples?" 28 Then they reviled him, saying, "You are his disciple, but we are disciples of Moses. 29 We know that God has spoken to Moses, but as for this man, we do not know where he comes from." 30 The man answered, "Here is an astonishing thing! You do not know where he comes from, and yet he opened my eyes. 31 We know that God does not listen to sinners, but he does listen to one who worships him and obeys his will. 32 Never since the world began has it been heard that anyone opened the eyes of a person

οἴδαμεν, ἢ τίς ἤνοιξεν αὐτοῦ τοὺς ὀφθαλμοὺς
we know, or who opened of him the eyes

ἡμεῖς οὐκ οἴδαμεν· αὐτὸν ἐρωτήσατε,
we know not; him ask ye,

ἡλικίαν ἔχει, αὐτὸς περὶ ἑαυτοῦ λαλήσει.
age he has, he about himself will speak.

22 ταῦτα εἶπαν οἱ γονεῖς αὐτοῦ ὅτι ἐφο-
These things said the parents of him because they

βοῦντο τοὺς Ἰουδαίους· ἤδη γὰρ συνετέθειντο
feared the Jews; for already had agreed

οἱ Ἰουδαῖοι ἵνα ἐάν τις αὐτὸν ὁμολογήσῃ
the Jews that if anyone him should acknowledge

χριστόν, ἀποσυνάγωγος γένηται.
[to be] Christ, put away from [the] synagogue he would be.

23 διὰ τοῦτο οἱ γονεῖς αὐτοῦ εἶπαν ὅτι
Therefore the parents of him said[,] –

ἡλικίαν ἔχει, αὐτὸν ἐπερωτήσατε. **24** Ἐφώνησαν
Age he has, him question ye. They called

οὖν τὸν ἄνθρωπον ἐκ δευτέρου ὃς ἦν
therefore the man a second time who was

τυφλός, καὶ εἶπαν αὐτῷ· δὸς δόξαν τῷ
blind, and said to him: Give glory –

θεῷ· ἡμεῖς οἴδαμεν ὅτι οὗτος ὁ ἄνθρωπος
to God; we know that this – man

ἁμαρτωλός ἐστιν. **25** ἀπεκρίθη οὖν ἐκεῖνος·
sinful is. Answered therefore that [one]:

εἰ ἁμαρτωλός ἐστιν οὐκ οἶδα· ἓν οἶδα,
If sinful he is I know not; one thing I know,

ὅτι τυφλὸς ὢν ἄρτι βλέπω. **26** εἶπαν
that blind being now I see. They said

οὖν αὐτῷ· τί ἐποίησέν σοι; πῶς ἤνοιξέν
therefore to him: What did he to thee? how opened he

σου τοὺς ὀφθαλμούς; **27** ἀπεκρίθη αὐτοῖς·
of thee the eyes? He answered them:

εἶπον ὑμῖν ἤδη καὶ οὐκ ἠκούσατε· τί
I told you already and ye heard not; why

πάλιν θέλετε ἀκούειν; μὴ καὶ ὑμεῖς
again wish ye to hear? *not* also ye

θέλετε αὐτοῦ μαθηταὶ γενέσθαι; **28** καὶ
wish of him disciples to become? And

ἐλοιδόρησαν αὐτὸν καὶ εἶπαν· σὺ μαθητὴς
they reviled him and said: Thou a disciple

εἶ ἐκείνου, ἡμεῖς δὲ τοῦ Μωϋσέως ἐσμὲν
art of that man, but we – of Moses are

μαθηταί· **29** ἡμεῖς οἴδαμεν ὅτι Μωϋσεῖ
disciples; we know that by Moses

λελάληκεν ὁ θεός, τοῦτον δὲ οὐκ οἴδαμεν
has spoken – God, but this man we know not

πόθεν ἐστίν. **30** ἀπεκρίθη ὁ ἄνθρωπος
whence he is. Answered the man

καὶ εἶπεν αὐτοῖς· ἐν τούτῳ γὰρ τὸ
and said to them: In this then the

θαυμαστόν ἐστιν, ὅτι ὑμεῖς οὐκ οἴδατε
marvellous thing is, that ye do not know

πόθεν ἐστίν, καὶ ἤνοιξέν μου τοὺς
whence he is, and he opened of me the

ὀφθαλμούς. **31** οἴδαμεν ὅτι ὁ θεὸς
eyes. We know that – God

ἁμαρτωλῶν οὐκ ἀκούει, ἀλλ' ἐάν τις
sinful men does not hear, but if anyone

θεοσεβὴς ᾖ καὶ τὸ θέλημα αὐτοῦ ποιῇ,
godfearing is and the will of him does,

τούτου ἀκούει. **32** ἐκ τοῦ αἰῶνος οὐκ
this man he hears. From the age not

ἠκούσθη ὅτι ἠνέῳξέν τις ὀφθαλμοὺς τυφλοῦ
it was heard that ²opened ¹anyone eyes of a blind man

he can see now, or who opened his eyes, we don't know. Ask him. He is of age; he will speak for himself." 22 His parents said this because they were afraid of the Jews, for already the Jews had decided that anyone who acknowledged that Jesus was the Christ[u] would be put out of the synagogue. 23 That was why his parents said, "He is of age; ask him."

24 A second time they summoned the man who had been blind. "Give glory to God,[v]" they said. "We know this man is a sinner."

25 He replied, "Whether he is a sinner or not, I don't know. One thing I do know. I was blind but now I see!"

26 Then they asked him, "What did he do to you? How did he open your eyes?"

27 He answered, "I have told you already and you did not listen. Why do you want to hear it again? Do you want to become his disciples, too?"

28 Then they hurled insults at him and said, "You are this fellow's disciple! We are disciples of Moses! 29 We know that God spoke to Moses, but as for this fellow, we don't even know where he comes from."

30 The man answered, "Now that is remarkable! You don't know where he comes from, yet he opened my eyes. 31 We know that God does not listen to sinners. He listens to the godly man who does his will. 32 Nobody has ever heard of opening the eyes of a man born blind. 33 If this man

[t] Gk *him*
[u] Or *the Christ*

[u] 22 Or *Messiah*
[v] 24 A solemn charge to tell the truth (see Joshua 7:19)

born blind. 33 If this man
were not from God, he
could do nothing." 34 They
answered him, "You were
born entirely in sins, and
are you trying to teach us?"
And they drove him out.

Spiritual Blindness

35 Jesus heard that they
had driven him out, and
when he found him, he
said, "Do you believe in the
Son of Man?"[v] 36 He an-
swered, "And who is he,
sir?[w] Tell me, so that I may
believe in him." 37 Jesus
said to him, "You have
seen him, and the one
speaking with you is he."
38 He said, "Lord,[w] I believe." And he worshiped
him. 39 Jesus said, "I came
into this world for judg-
ment so that those who do
not see may see, and those
who do see may become
blind." 40 Some of the Pharisees near him heard this
and said to him, "Surely we
are not blind, are we?"
41 Jesus said to them, "If
you were blind, you would
not have sin. But now that
you say, 'We see,' your sin
remains.

γεγεννημένου· 33 εἰ μὴ ἦν οὗτος παρὰ
having been born; if [2]not [3]was [1]this man from

θεοῦ, οὐκ ἠδύνατο ποιεῖν οὐδέν. 34 ἀπεκρίθησαν
God, he could not *to* do no(any)thing. They answered

καὶ εἶπαν αὐτῷ· ἐν ἁμαρτίαις σὺ ἐγεννήθης
and said to him: In sins thou wast born

ὅλος, καὶ σὺ διδάσκεις ἡμᾶς; καὶ ἐξέβαλον
wholly, and thou teachest us? and they cast *out*

αὐτὸν ἔξω. 35 Ἤκουσεν Ἰησοῦς ὅτι
him outside. Heard Jesus that

ἐξέβαλον αὐτὸν ἔξω, καὶ εὑρὼν αὐτὸν
they cast *out* him outside, and finding him

εἶπεν· σὺ πιστεύεις εἰς τὸν υἱὸν τοῦ
said: Thou believest in the Son –

ἀνθρώπου; 36 ἀπεκρίθη ἐκεῖνος καὶ εἶπεν·
of man? Answered that [one] and said:

καὶ τίς ἐστιν, κύριε, ἵνα πιστεύσω εἰς
And who is he, sir, that I may believe in

αὐτόν; 37 εἶπεν αὐτῷ ὁ Ἰησοῦς· καὶ
him? Said to him – Jesus: Both

ἑώρακας αὐτὸν καὶ ὁ λαλῶν μετὰ σοῦ
thou hast seen him and the [one] speaking with thee

ἐκεῖνός ἐστιν. 38 ὁ δὲ ἔφη· πιστεύω, κύριε·
that [one] is. And he said: I believe, sir;

καὶ προσεκύνησεν αὐτῷ. 39 καὶ εἶπεν ὁ
and he worshipped him. And said –

Ἰησοῦς· εἰς κρίμα ἐγὼ εἰς τὸν κόσμον
Jesus: For judgment I into – world

τοῦτον ἦλθον, ἵνα οἱ μὴ βλέποντες
this came, that the [ones] not seeing

βλέπωσιν καὶ οἱ βλέποντες τυφλοὶ γένωνται.
may see and the [ones] seeing blind may become.

40 Ἤκουσαν ἐκ τῶν Φαρισαίων ταῦτα
[5]heard [1][Some] [2]of [3]the [4]Pharisees [6]these things

οἱ μετ᾽ αὐτοῦ ὄντες, καὶ εἶπαν αὐτῷ·
– [8]with [9]him [7]being, and they said to him:

μὴ καὶ ἡμεῖς τυφλοί ἐσμεν; 41 εἶπεν
Not also we blind are? Said

αὐτοῖς ὁ Ἰησοῦς· εἰ τυφλοὶ ἦτε, οὐκ
to them – Jesus: If blind ye were, not

ἂν εἴχετε ἁμαρτίαν· νῦν δὲ λέγετε ὅτι
ye would have had sin; but now ye say[,] –

βλέπομεν· ἡ ἁμαρτία ὑμῶν μένει.
We see; the sin of you remains.

were not from God, he
could do nothing."
34 To this they replied,
"You were steeped in sin at
birth; how dare you lecture
us!" And they threw him
out.

Spiritual Blindness

35 Jesus heard that they
had thrown him out, and
when he found him, he
said, "Do you believe in
the Son of Man?"
36 "Who is he, sir?" the
man asked. "Tell me so
that I may believe in him."
37 Jesus said, "You have
now seen him; in fact, he is
the one speaking with
you."
38 Then the man said,
"Lord, I believe," and he
worshiped him.
39 Jesus said, "For judg-
ment I have come into this
world, so that the blind will
see and those who see will
become blind."
40 Some Pharisees who
were with him heard him
say this and asked, "What?
Are we blind too?"
41 Jesus said, "If you were
blind, you would not be
guilty of sin; but now that
you claim you can see,
your guilt remains.

Chapter 10

Jesus the Good Shepherd

"VERY truly, I tell
you, anyone who
does not enter the sheep-
fold by the gate but climbs
in by another way is a thief
and a bandit. 2 The one who
enters by the gate is the
shepherd of the sheep.
3 The gatekeeper opens the
gate for him, and the sheep
hear his voice. He calls his
own sheep by name and
leads them out. 4 When he
has brought out all his own,
he goes ahead of them, and

[v] Other ancient authorities read *the Son of God*

[w] *Sir* and *Lord* translate the same Greek word

10 Ἀμὴν ἀμὴν λέγω ὑμῖν, ὁ μὴ
Truly truly I say to you, the [one] not

εἰσερχόμενος διὰ τῆς θύρας εἰς τὴν
entering through the door into the

αὐλὴν τῶν προβάτων ἀλλὰ ἀναβαίνων
fold of the sheep but going up

ἀλλαχόθεν, ἐκεῖνος κλέπτης ἐστὶν καὶ
by another way, that [one] a thief is and

λῃστής· 2 ὁ δὲ εἰσερχόμενος διὰ τῆς
a robber; but the [one] entering through the

θύρας ποιμήν ἐστιν τῶν προβάτων. 3 τούτῳ
door shepherd is of the sheep. To this [one]

ὁ θυρωρὸς ἀνοίγει, καὶ τὰ πρόβατα τῆς
the doorkeeper opens, and the sheep the

φωνῆς αὐτοῦ ἀκούει, καὶ τὰ ἴδια πρόβατα
voice of him hears, and the(his) own sheep

φωνεῖ κατ᾽ ὄνομα καὶ ἐξάγει αὐτά.
he calls by name and leads out them.

4 ὅταν τὰ ἴδια πάντα ἐκβάλῃ, ἔμπροσθεν
When the(his) own all he puts forth, in front of

Chapter 10

The Shepherd and His Flock

"I TELL you the
truth, the man who
does not enter the sheep
pen by the gate, but climbs
in by some other way, is a
thief and a robber. 2 The
man who enters by the gate
is the shepherd of his
sheep. 3 The watchman
opens the gate for him, and
the sheep listen to his
voice. He calls his own
sheep by name and leads
them out. 4 When he has

the sheep follow him be-
cause they know his voice.
5 They will not follow a
stranger, but they will run
from him because they do
not know the voice of
strangers." 6 Jesus used this
figure of speech with them,
but they did not understand
what he was saying to
them.
7 So again Jesus said to
them, "Very truly, I tell
you, I am the gate for the
sheep. 8 All who came be-
fore me are thieves and
bandits; but the sheep did
not listen to them. 9 I am the
gate. Whoever enters by
me will be saved, and will
come in and go out and find
pasture. 10 The thief comes
only to steal and kill and
destroy. I came that they
may have life, and have it
abundantly.
11 "I am the good shep-
herd. The good shepherd
lays down his life for the
sheep. 12 The hired hand,
who is not the shepherd
and does not own the
sheep, sees the wolf com-
ing and leaves the sheep
and runs away—and the
wolf snatches them and
scatters them. 13 The hired
hand runs away because a
hired hand does not care
for the sheep. 14 I am the
good shepherd. I know my
own and my own know me,
15 just as the Father knows
me and I know the Father.
And I lay down my life for
the sheep. 16 I have other
sheep that do not belong to
this fold. I must bring them

αὐτῶν πορεύεται, καὶ τὰ πρόβατα αὐτῷ
them he goes, and the sheep him
ἀκολουθεῖ, ὅτι οἴδασιν τὴν φωνὴν αὐτοῦ·
follows, because they know the voice of him;
5 ἀλλοτρίῳ δὲ οὐ μὴ ἀκολουθήσουσιν,
but a stranger by no means will they follow,
ἀλλὰ φεύξονται ἀπ' αὐτοῦ, ὅτι οὐκ
but will flee from him, because not
οἴδασιν τῶν ἀλλοτρίων τὴν φωνήν.
they know of the strangers the voice.
6 Ταύτην τὴν παροιμίαν εἶπεν αὐτοῖς ὁ
This – allegory told them –
Ἰησοῦς· ἐκεῖνοι δὲ οὐκ ἔγνωσαν τίνα
Jesus; but those men knew not what things
ἦν ἃ ἐλάλει αὐτοῖς. 7 Εἶπεν οὖν πάλιν
they were which he spoke to them. Said therefore again
ὁ Ἰησοῦς· ἀμὴν ἀμὴν λέγω ὑμῖν ὅτι
– Jesus: Truly truly I say to you that
ἐγώ εἰμι ἡ θύρα τῶν προβάτων. 8 πάντες
I am the door of the sheep. All
ὅσοι ἦλθον πρὸ ἐμοῦ κλέπται εἰσὶν καὶ
who came before me thieves are and
λῃσταί· ἀλλ' οὐκ ἤκουσαν αὐτῶν τὰ
robbers; but did not hear them the
πρόβατα. 9 ἐγώ εἰμι ἡ θύρα· δι' ἐμοῦ
sheep. I am the door; through me
ἐάν τις εἰσέλθῃ, σωθήσεται, καὶ εἰσελεύ-
if anyone enters, he will be saved, and will go
σεται καὶ ἐξελεύσεται καὶ νομὴν εὑρήσει.
in and *will* go out and pasture *will* find.
10 ὁ κλέπτης οὐκ ἔρχεται εἰ μὴ ἵνα
The thief comes not except that
κλέψῃ καὶ θύσῃ καὶ ἀπολέσῃ· ἐγὼ ἦλθον
he may steal and kill and destroy; I came
ἵνα ζωὴν ἔχωσιν καὶ περισσὸν ἔχωσιν.
that life they may have and abundantly *they* may have.
11 Ἐγώ εἰμι ὁ ποιμὴν ὁ καλός. ὁ
I am the shepherd – good. The
ποιμὴν ὁ καλὸς τὴν ψυχὴν αὐτοῦ τίθησιν
shepherd – good the life of him lays down
ὑπὲρ τῶν προβάτων· 12 ὁ μισθωτὸς καὶ
for the sheep; the hireling and
οὐκ ὢν ποιμήν, οὗ οὐκ ἔστιν τὰ πρόβατα
not being a shepherd, of whom is(are) not the sheep
ἴδια, θεωρεῖ τὸν λύκον ἐρχόμενον καὶ
[his] own, beholds the wolf coming and
ἀφίησιν τὰ πρόβατα καὶ φεύγει, — καὶ
leaves the sheep and flees, — and
ὁ λύκος ἁρπάζει αὐτὰ καὶ σκορπίζει· —
the wolf seizes them and scatters; —
13 ὅτι μισθωτός ἐστιν καὶ οὐ μέλει
because a hireling he is and it matters not
αὐτῷ περὶ τῶν προβάτων. 14 ἐγώ εἰμι
to him about the sheep. I am
ὁ ποιμὴν ὁ καλός, καὶ γινώσκω τὰ
the shepherd – good, and I know –
ἐμὰ καὶ γινώσκουσί με τὰ ἐμά, 15 καθὼς
mine and [2]know [3]me – [1]mine, as
γινώσκει με ὁ πατὴρ κἀγὼ γινώσκω τὸν
[3]knows [4]me [1]the [2]Father and I know the
πατέρα, καὶ τὴν ψυχήν μου τίθημι ὑπὲρ
Father, and the life of me I lay down for
τῶν προβάτων. 16 καὶ ἄλλα πρόβατα
the sheep. And other sheep
ἔχω ἃ οὐκ ἔστιν ἐκ τῆς αὐλῆς ταύτης·
I have which is(are) not of – fold this;

brought out all his own, he
goes on ahead of them, and
his sheep follow him be-
cause they know his voice.
5 But they will never follow
a stranger; in fact, they will
run away from him because
they do not recognize a
stranger's voice." 6 Jesus
used this figure of speech,
but they did not understand
what he was telling them.
7 Therefore Jesus said
again, "I tell you the truth,
I am the gate for the sheep.
8 All who ever came before
me were thieves and rob-
bers, but the sheep did not
listen to them. 9 I am the
gate; whoever enters
through me will be saved.[w]
He will come in and go out,
and find pasture. 10 The
thief comes only to steal
and kill and destroy; I have
come that they may have
life, and have it to the full.
11 "I am the good shep-
herd. The good shepherd
lays down his life for the
sheep. 12 The hired hand is
not the shepherd who owns
the sheep. So when he sees
the wolf coming, he aban-
dons the sheep and runs
away. Then the wolf at-
tacks the flock and scatters
it. 13 The man runs away because he is a hired hand and
cares nothing for the sheep.
14 "I am the good shep-
herd; I know my sheep and
my sheep know me— 15 just
as the Father knows me
and I know the Father—
and I lay down my life for
the sheep. 16 I have other
sheep that are not of this

w 9 Or *kept safe*

also, and they will listen to
my voice. So there will be
one flock, one shepherd.
17For this reason the Fa-
ther loves me, because I lay
down my life in order to
take it up again. 18No one
takes[x] it from me, but I lay
it down of my own accord.
I have power to lay it down,
and I have power to take it
up again. I have received
this command from my Fa-
ther."
19 Again the Jews were
divided because of these
words. 20Many of them
were saying, "He has a demon and is out of his mind.
Why listen to him?" 21Oth-
ers were saying, "These are
not the words of one who
has a demon. Can a demon
open the eyes of the blind?"

Jesus Is Rejected by the Jews

22 At that time the festival of the Dedication took
place in Jerusalem. It was
winter, 23and Jesus was
walking in the temple, in
the portico of Solomon.
24So the Jews gathered
around him and said to him,
"How long will you keep us
in suspense? If you are the
Messiah,[y] tell us plainly."
25Jesus answered, "I have
told you, and you do not
believe. The works that I
do in my Father's name testify to me; 26but you do not
believe, because you do
not belong to my sheep.
27My sheep hear my voice.
I know them, and they follow me. 28I give them eternal life, and they will never

[x] Other ancient authorities read *has taken*
[y] Or *the Christ*

κἀκεῖνα δεῖ με ἀγαγεῖν, καὶ τῆς φωνῆς
those also it behoves me to bring, and the voice
μου ἀκούσουσιν, καὶ γενήσεται μία ποίμνη,
of me they will hear, and there will become one flock,
εἷς ποιμήν. 17 διὰ τοῦτό με ὁ πατὴρ
one shepherd. Therefore me the Father
ἀγαπᾷ ὅτι ἐγὼ τίθημι τὴν ψυχήν μου,
loves because I lay down the life of me,
ἵνα πάλιν λάβω αὐτήν. 18 οὐδεὶς ἦρεν
that again I may take it. No one took
αὐτὴν ἀπ' ἐμοῦ, ἀλλ' ἐγὼ τίθημι αὐτὴν
it from me, but I lay down it
ἀπ' ἐμαυτοῦ. ἐξουσίαν ἔχω θεῖναι αὐτήν,
from myself. Authority I have to lay down it,
καὶ ἐξουσίαν ἔχω πάλιν λαβεῖν αὐτήν·
and authority I have again to take it;
ταύτην τὴν ἐντολὴν ἔλαβον παρὰ τοῦ
this – commandment I received from the
πατρός μου. 19 Σχίσμα πάλιν ἐγένετο ἐν
Father of me. A division again there was among
τοῖς Ἰουδαίοις διὰ τοὺς λόγους τούτους.
the Jews because of – words these.
20 ἔλεγον δὲ πολλοὶ ἐξ αὐτῶν· δαιμόνιον
And said many of them : A demon
ἔχει καὶ μαίνεται· τί αὐτοῦ ἀκούετε;
he has and raves; why him hear ye?
21 ἄλλοι ἔλεγον· ταῦτα τὰ ῥήματα οὐκ
Others said : These – words not
ἔστιν δαιμονιζομένου· μὴ δαιμόνιον δύναται
is(are) of one demon-possessed; *not* a demon can
τυφλῶν ὀφθαλμοὺς ἀνοῖξαι;
of blind men eyes *to* open?
22 Ἐγένετο τότε τὰ ἐγκαίνια ἐν τοῖς
There was then the Dedication in –
Ἱεροσολύμοις· χειμὼν ἦν· 23 καὶ περιεπάτει
Jerusalem; winter it was; and walked
ὁ Ἰησοῦς ἐν τῷ ἱερῷ ἐν τῇ στοᾷ τοῦ
– Jesus in the temple in the porch –
Σολομῶνος. 24 ἐκύκλωσαν οὖν αὐτὸν οἱ
of Solomon. Surrounded therefore him the
Ἰουδαῖοι καὶ ἔλεγον αὐτῷ· ἕως πότε
Jews and said to him: Until when
τὴν ψυχὴν ἡμῶν αἴρεις; εἰ σὺ εἶ
the life(soul) of us holdest thou * ? if thou art
ὁ χριστός, εἰπὸν ἡμῖν παρρησίᾳ. 25 ἀπεκρίθη
the Christ, tell us plainly. Answered
αὐτοῖς ὁ Ἰησοῦς· εἶπον ὑμῖν, καὶ
them – Jesus : I told you, and
οὐ πιστεύετε· τὰ ἔργα ἃ ἐγὼ ποιῶ ἐν τῷ
ye do not believe; the works which I do in the
ὀνόματι τοῦ πατρός μου, ταῦτα μαρτυρεῖ
name of the Father of me, these witness*es*
περὶ ἐμοῦ· 26 ἀλλὰ ὑμεῖς οὐ πιστεύετε,
concerning me; but ye do not believe,
ὅτι οὐκ ἐστὲ ἐκ τῶν προβάτων τῶν
because ye are not of *the* [s]sheep –
ἐμῶν. 27 τὰ πρόβατα τὰ ἐμὰ τῆς φωνῆς
[l]my. *the* sheep – My the voice
μου ἀκούουσιν, κἀγὼ γινώσκω αὐτά, καὶ
of me hear, and I know them, and
ἀκολουθοῦσίν μοι, 28 κἀγὼ δίδωμι αὐτοῖς
they follow me, and I give to them
ζωὴν αἰώνιον, καὶ οὐ μὴ ἀπόλωνται εἰς
life eternal, and by no means they perish unto

* That is, in suspense.

sheep pen. I must bring
them also. They too will listen to my voice, and there
shall be one flock and one
shepherd. 17The reason my
Father loves me is that I lay
down my life—only to take
it up again. 18No one takes
it from me, but I lay it down
of my own accord. I have
authority to lay it down and
authority to take it up
again. This command I re-
ceived from my Father."
19At these words the Jews
were again divided. 20Many
of them said, "He is de-
mon-possessed and raving
mad. Why listen to him?"
21But others said, "These
are not the sayings of a man
possessed by a demon. Can
a demon open the eyes of
the blind?"

The Unbelief of the Jews

22Then came the Feast of
Dedication[x] at Jerusalem.
It was winter, 23and Jesus
was in the temple area
walking in Solomon's Col-
onnade. 24The Jews gath-
ered around him, saying,
"How long will you keep
us in suspense? If you are
the Christ,[y] tell us plainly."
25Jesus answered, "I did
tell you, but you do not believe. The miracles I do in
my Father's name speak
for me, 26but you do not believe because you are not
my sheep. 27My sheep lis-
ten to my voice; I know
them, and they follow me.
28I give them eternal life,
and they shall never perish;

[x]22 That is, Hanukkah
[y]24 Or *Messiah*

perish. No one will snatch
them out of my hand.
29 What my Father has giv-
en me is greater than all
else, and no one can snatch
it out of the Father's
hand.[z] 30 The Father and I
are one."
31 The Jews took up
stones again to stone him.
32 Jesus replied, "I have
shown you many good
works from the Father. For
which of these are you going to stone me?" 33 The
Jews answered, "It is not
for a good work that we are
going to stone you, but for
blasphemy, because you,
though only a human being,
are making yourself God."
34 Jesus answered, "Is it not
written in your law,[a] 'I
said, you are gods'? 35 If
those to whom the word of
God came were called
'gods'—and the scripture
cannot be annulled— 36 can
you say that the one whom
the Father has sanctified
and sent into the world is
blaspheming because I
said, 'I am God's Son'? 37 If
I am not doing the works of
my Father, then do not believe me. 38 But if I do
them, even though you do
not believe me, believe the
works, so that you may
know and understand[b] that
the Father is in me and I am
in the Father." 39 Then they
tried to arrest him again,
but he escaped from their
hands.
40 He went away again
across the Jordan to the
place where John had been
baptizing earlier, and he remained there. 41 Many
came to him, and they were

τὸν αἰῶνα, καὶ οὐχ ἁρπάσει τις αὐτὰ
the age, and ²shall not seize ¹anyone them
ἐκ τῆς χειρός μου. 29 ὁ πατήρ μου ὃ
out of the hand of me. The Father of me who
δέδωκέν μοι πάντων μεῖζόν ἐστιν, καὶ
has given to me [than] all greater is, and
οὐδεὶς δύναται ἁρπάζειν ἐκ τῆς χειρὸς
no one can *to* seize out of the hand
τοῦ πατρός. 30 ἐγὼ καὶ ὁ πατὴρ ἕν
of the Father. I and the Father one
ἐσμεν. 31 Ἐβάστασαν πάλιν λίθους οἱ
we are. Lifted again stones the
Ἰουδαῖοι ἵνα λιθάσωσιν αὐτόν. 32 ἀπ-
Jews that they might stone him. An-
εκρίθη αὐτοῖς ὁ Ἰησοῦς· πολλὰ ἔργα
swered them – Jesus : Many ³works
ἔδειξα ὑμῖν καλὰ ἐκ τοῦ πατρός· διὰ
⁴I showed ⁵you ²good of the Father; because of
ποῖον αὐτῶν ἔργον ἐμὲ λιθάζετε;
which ²of them ³work ⁴me ¹stone ye?
33 ἀπεκρίθησαν αὐτῷ οἱ Ἰουδαῖοι· περὶ
Answered him the Jews : Concerning
καλοῦ ἔργου οὐ λιθάζομέν σε ἀλλὰ περὶ
a good work we do not stone thee but concerning
βλασφημίας, καὶ ὅτι σὺ ἄνθρωπος ὢν
blasphemy, and because thou a man being
ποιεῖς σεαυτὸν θεόν. 34 ἀπεκρίθη αὐτοῖς
makest thyself God. Answered them
ὁ Ἰησοῦς· οὐκ ἔστιν γεγραμμένον ἐν τῷ
– Jesus : Is it not *having been* written in the
νόμῳ ὑμῶν ὅτι ἐγὼ εἶπα· θεοί ἐστε;
law of you[,] – I said : Gods ye are?
35 εἰ ἐκείνους εἶπεν θεοὺς πρὸς οὓς ὁ
¹if ³those ²he called ⁴gods with whom the
λόγος τοῦ θεοῦ ἐγένετο, καὶ οὐ δύναται
word – of God was, and cannot
λυθῆναι ἡ γραφή, 36 ὃν ὁ πατὴρ
to be broken the scripture, ³[him] whom ⁴the ⁵Father
ἡγίασεν καὶ ἀπέστειλεν εἰς τὸν κόσμον
⁶sanctified ⁷and ⁸sent ⁹into ¹⁰the ¹¹world
ὑμεῖς λέγετε ὅτι βλασφημεῖς, ὅτι εἶπον·
²ye ¹tell[,] – Thou blasphemest, because I said :
υἱὸς τοῦ θεοῦ εἰμι; 37 εἰ οὐ ποιῶ τὰ ἔργα
Son – of God I am? If I do not the works
τοῦ πατρός μου, μὴ πιστεύετέ μοι· 38 εἰ δὲ
of the Father of me, do not believe me; but if
ποιῶ, κἂν ἐμοὶ μὴ πιστεύητε, τοῖς ἔργοις
I do, even if me ye do not believe, the works
πιστεύετε, ἵνα γνῶτε καὶ γινώσκητε
believe, that ye may know• and continue to know•
ὅτι ἐν ἐμοὶ ὁ πατὴρ κἀγὼ ἐν τῷ πατρί.
that in me the Father [is] and I in the Father.
39 Ἐζήτουν οὖν αὐτὸν πάλιν πιάσαι· καὶ
They sought therefore him again to arrest; and
ἐξῆλθεν ἐκ τῆς χειρὸς αὐτῶν.
he went forth out of the hand of them.
40 Καὶ ἀπῆλθεν πάλιν πέραν τοῦ
And he went away again across the
Ἰορδάνου εἰς τὸν τόπον ὅπου ἦν Ἰωάννης
Jordan to the place where was John
τὸ πρῶτον βαπτίζων, καὶ ἔμενεν ἐκεῖ.
at first baptizing, and remained there.
41 καὶ πολλοὶ ἦλθον πρὸς αὐτὸν καὶ
And many came to him and

no one can snatch them out
of my hand. 29 My Father,
who has given them to me,
is greater than all[z]; no one
can snatch them out of my
Father's hand. 30 I and the
Father are one."
31 Again the Jews picked
up stones to stone him,
32 but Jesus said to them, "I
have shown you many
great miracles from the Father. For which of these do
you stone me?"
33 "We are not stoning
you for any of these," replied the Jews, "but for
blasphemy, because you, a
mere man, claim to be
God."
34 Jesus answered them,
"Is it not written in your
Law, 'I have said you are
gods'[a]? 35 If he called them
'gods,' to whom the word
of God came—and the
Scripture cannot be broken
—36 what about the one
whom the Father set apart
as his very own and sent
into the world? Why then
do you accuse me of blas-
phemy because I said, 'I
am God's Son'? 37 Do not
believe me unless I do what
my Father does. 38 But if I
do it, even though you do
not believe me, believe the
miracles, that you may
know and understand that
the Father is in me, and I in
the Father." 39 Again they
tried to seize him, but he
escaped their grasp.
40 Then Jesus went back
across the Jordan to the
place where John had been
baptizing in the early days.
Here he stayed 41 and many
people came to him. They

[z] Other ancient authorities read *My Father who has given them to me is greater than all, and no one can snatch them out of the Father's hand*

[a] Other ancient authorities read *in the law*

[b] Other ancient authorities lack *and understand*; others read *and believe*

• Different tenses (aorist and present) of the same verb.

[z] 29 Many early manuscripts *What my Father has given me is greater than all*

[a] 34 Psalm 82:6

saying, "John performed
no sign, but everything that
John said about this man
was true." 42 And many believed in him there.

Chapter 11

The Death of Lazarus

NOW a certain man was
ill, Lazarus of Betha-
ny, the village of Mary and
her sister Martha. 2 Mary
was the one who anointed
the Lord with perfume and
wiped his feet with her hair;
her brother Lazarus was ill.
3 So the sisters sent a message to Jesus,[c] "Lord, he
whom you love is ill." 4 But
when Jesus heard it, he
said, "This illness does not
lead to death; rather it is for
God's glory, so that the
Son of God may be glori-
fied through it." 5 Accordingly, though Jesus loved
Martha and her sister and
Lazarus, 6 after having
heard that Lazarus[d] was
ill, he stayed two days longer in the place where he
was.
7 Then after this he said
to the disciples, "Let us go
to Judea again." 8 The disciples said to him, "Rabbi,
the Jews were just now trying to stone you, and are
you going there again?"
9 Jesus answered, "Are
there not twelve hours of
daylight? Those who walk
during the day do not stumble, because they see the
light of this world. 10 But
those who walk at night
stumble, because the light
is not in them." 11 After
saying this, he told them,
"Our friend Lazarus has

[c] Gk *him*
[d] Gk *he*

ἔλεγον ὅτι Ἰωάννης μὲν σημεῖον ἐποίησεν
said[,] – John indeed sign did
οὐδέν, πάντα δὲ ὅσα εἶπεν Ἰωάννης περὶ
none, but all things how many said John about
τούτου ἀληθῆ ἦν. **42** καὶ πολλοὶ ἐπίστευσαν
this man true was(were). And many believed
εἰς αὐτὸν ἐκεῖ.
in him there.

11 Ἦν δέ τις ἀσθενῶν, Λάζαρος ἀπὸ
Now there was a certain [man] ailing, Lazarus from
Βηθανίας, ἐκ τῆς κώμης Μαρίας καὶ
Bethany, of the village of Mary and
Μάρθας τῆς ἀδελφῆς αὐτῆς. **2** ἦν δὲ
Martha the sister of her. And it was
Μαριὰμ ἡ ἀλείψασα τὸν κύριον μύρῳ
Mary the [one] anointing the Lord with ointment
καὶ ἐκμάξασα τοὺς πόδας αὐτοῦ ταῖς
and wiping off the feet of him with the
θριξὶν αὐτῆς, ἧς ὁ ἀδελφὸς Λάζαρος
hairs of her, of whom the brother Lazarus
ἠσθένει. **3** ἀπέστειλαν οὖν αἱ ἀδελφαὶ
ailed. Sent therefore the sisters
πρὸς αὐτὸν λέγουσαι· κύριε, ἴδε ὃν
to him saying : Lord, behold[,] [he] whom
φιλεῖς ἀσθενεῖ. **4** ἀκούσας δὲ ὁ Ἰησοῦς
thou lovest ails. And hearing – Jesus
εἶπεν· αὕτη ἡ ἀσθένεια οὐκ ἔστιν πρὸς
said: This – ailment is not to
θάνατον ἀλλ' ὑπὲρ τῆς δόξης τοῦ θεοῦ,
death but for the glory – of God,
ἵνα δοξασθῇ ὁ υἱὸς τοῦ θεοῦ δι' αὐτῆς.
that may be glorified the Son – of God through it.
5 ἠγάπα δὲ ὁ Ἰησοῦς τὴν Μάρθαν καὶ
Now [2]loved – [1]Jesus – Martha and
τὴν ἀδελφὴν αὐτῆς καὶ τὸν Λάζαρον.
the sister of her and – Lazarus.
6 ὡς οὖν ἤκουσεν ὅτι ἀσθενεῖ, τότε μὲν
When therefore he heard that he ails(ed), then –
ἔμεινεν ἐν ᾧ ἦν τόπῳ δύο ἡμέρας·
he remained [1]in [2]which [4]he was [3]place two days;
7 ἔπειτα μετὰ τοῦτο λέγει τοῖς μαθηταῖς·
then after this he says to the disciples :
ἄγωμεν εἰς τὴν Ἰουδαίαν πάλιν. **8** λέγουσιν
Let us go into – Judæa again. Say
αὐτῷ οἱ μαθηταί· ῥαββί, νῦν ἐζήτουν
to him the disciples : Rabbi, [4]now [5]were [6]seeking
σε λιθάσαι οἱ Ἰουδαῖοι, καὶ πάλιν ὑπάγεις
[7]thee [8]to stone [1]the [2]Jews, and again goest thou
ἐκεῖ; **9** ἀπεκρίθη Ἰησοῦς· οὐχὶ δώδεκα
there? Answered Jesus : Not twelve
ὧραί εἰσιν τῆς ἡμέρας; ἐάν τις περιπατῇ
hours are there of the day? if anyone walks
ἐν τῇ ἡμέρᾳ, οὐ προσκόπτει, ὅτι τὸ φῶς
in the day, he does not stumble, because the light
τοῦ κόσμου τούτου βλέπει· **10** ἐὰν δέ
– world of this he sees; but if
τις περιπατῇ ἐν τῇ νυκτί, προσκόπτει,
anyone walks in the night, he stumbles,
ὅτι τὸ φῶς οὐκ ἔστιν ἐν αὐτῷ. **11** ταῦτα
because the light is not in him. These things
εἶπεν, καὶ μετὰ τοῦτο λέγει αὐτοῖς·
he said, and after this he says to them :
Λάζαρος ὁ φίλος ἡμῶν κεκοίμηται· ἀλλὰ
Lazarus the friend of us has fallen asleep; but

said, "Though John never
performed a miraculous
sign, all that John said
about this man was true."
42 And in that place many
believed in Jesus.

Chapter 11

The Death of Lazarus

NOW a man named Laz-
arus was sick. He was
from Bethany, the village
of Mary and her sister Martha. 2 This Mary, whose
brother Lazarus now lay
sick, was the same one who
poured perfume on the
Lord and wiped his feet
with her hair. 3 So the sisters sent word to Jesus,
"Lord, the one you love is
sick."
4 When he heard this,
Jesus said, "This sickness
will not end in death. No, it
is for God's glory so that
God's Son may be glorified
through it." 5 Jesus loved
Martha and her sister and
Lazarus. 6 Yet when he
heard that Lazarus was
sick, he stayed where he
was two more days.
7 Then he said to his disciples, "Let us go back to Judea."
8 "But Rabbi," they said,
"a short while ago the Jews
tried to stone you, and yet
you are going back there?"
9 Jesus answered, "Are
there not twelve hours of
daylight? A man who walks
by day will not stumble, for
he sees by this world's
light. 10 It is when he walks
by night that he stumbles,
for he has no light."
11 After he had said this,
he went on to tell them,
"Our friend Lazarus has

fallen asleep, but I am going there to awaken him."
12 The disciples said to him,
"Lord, if he has fallen
asleep, he will be all right."
13 Jesus, however, had
been speaking about his
death, but they thought
that he was referring merely to sleep. 14 Then Jesus
told them plainly, "Lazarus
is dead. 15 For your sake I
am glad I was not there, so
that you may believe. But
let us go to him." 16 Thomas, who was called the
Twin,[e] said to his fellow
disciples, "Let us also go,
that we may die with him."

Jesus the Resurrection and the Life

17 When Jesus arrived,
he found that Lazarus[d] had
already been in the tomb
four days. 18 Now Bethany
was near Jerusalem, some
two miles[f] away, 19 and
many of the Jews had come
to Martha and Mary to console them about their
brother. 20 When Martha
heard that Jesus was com-
ing, she went and met him,
while Mary stayed at
home. 21 Martha said to
Jesus, "Lord, if you had
been here, my brother
would not have died. 22 But
even now I know that God
will give you whatever you
ask of him." 23 Jesus said to
her, "Your brother will rise
again." 24 Martha said to
him, "I know that he will
rise again in the resurrection on the last day."
25 Jesus said to her, "I am
the resurrection and the
life.[g] Those who believe in
me, even though they die,
will live, 26 and everyone
who lives and believes in
me will never die. Do you
believe this?" 27 She said to

[e] Gk *Didymus*
[f] Gk *fifteen stadia*
[g] Other ancient authorities lack *and the life*

πορεύομαι ἵνα ἐξυπνίσω αὐτόν. 12 εἶπαν
I am going that I may awaken him. Said

οὖν οἱ μαθηταὶ αὐτῷ· κύριε, εἰ κεκοίμηται,
there- fore the disciples to him: Lord, if he has fallen asleep,

σωθήσεται. 13 εἰρήκει δὲ ὁ Ἰησοῦς περὶ
he will be healed. Now had spoken – Jesus concerning

τοῦ θανάτου αὐτοῦ· ἐκεῖνοι δὲ ἔδοξαν ὅτι
the death of him; but those men thought that

περὶ τῆς κοιμήσεως τοῦ ὕπνου λέγει.
concerning the sleep – of slumber he says.

14 τότε οὖν εἶπεν αὐτοῖς ὁ Ἰησοῦς
Then therefore told them – Jesus

παρρησίᾳ· Λάζαρος ἀπέθανεν, 15 καὶ χαίρω
plainly: Lazarus died, and I rejoice

δι' ὑμᾶς, ἵνα πιστεύσητε, ὅτι οὐκ ἤμην
because of you, that ye may believe, that I was not

ἐκεῖ· ἀλλὰ ἄγωμεν πρὸς αὐτόν. 16 εἶπεν
there; but let us go to him. Said

οὖν Θωμᾶς ὁ λεγόμενος Δίδυμος τοῖς
therefore Thomas – *being* called Twin to the(his)

συμμαθηταῖς· ἄγωμεν καὶ ἡμεῖς ἵνα
fellow-disciples: Let go also we(us) that

ἀποθάνωμεν μετ' αὐτοῦ. 17 Ἐλθὼν οὖν
we may die with him. Coming therefore

ὁ Ἰησοῦς εὗρεν αὐτὸν τέσσαρας ἤδη
– Jesus found him [2]four [1]already

ἡμέρας ἔχοντα ἐν τῷ μνημείῳ. 18 ἦν δὲ
[3]days having(being) in the tomb. Now was

Βηθανία ἐγγὺς τῶν Ἱεροσολύμων ὡς ἀπὸ
Bethany near – Jerusalem about [3]away

σταδίων δεκαπέντε. 19 πολλοὶ δὲ ἐκ τῶν
[2]furlongs [1]fifteen. And many of the

Ἰουδαίων ἐληλύθεισαν πρὸς τὴν Μάρθαν
Jews had come to – Martha

καὶ Μαριάμ, ἵνα παραμυθήσωνται αὐτὰς
and Mary, that they might console them

περὶ τοῦ ἀδελφοῦ. 20 ἡ οὖν Μάρθα ὡς
concerning the(ir) brother. – Therefore Martha when

ἤκουσεν ὅτι Ἰησοῦς ἔρχεται, ὑπήντησεν
she heard that Jesus is(was) coming, met

αὐτῷ· Μαριὰμ δὲ ἐν τῷ οἴκῳ ἐκαθέζετο.
him; but Mary in the house sat.

21 εἶπεν οὖν ἡ Μάρθα πρὸς Ἰησοῦν·
Said therefore – Martha to Jesus:

κύριε, εἰ ἦς ὧδε, οὐκ ἂν ἀπέθανεν ὁ
Lord, if thou wast here, would not have died the

ἀδελφός μου. 22 καὶ νῦν οἶδα ὅτι ὅσα ἂν
brother of me. And now I know that whatever things

αἰτήσῃ τὸν θεὸν δώσει σοι ὁ θεός.
thou askest – God [2]will give [3]thee – [1]God.

23 λέγει αὐτῇ ὁ Ἰησοῦς· ἀναστήσεται ὁ
Says to her – Jesus: Will rise again the

ἀδελφός σου. 24 λέγει αὐτῷ ἡ Μάρθα·
brother of thee. Says to him – Martha:

οἶδα ὅτι ἀναστήσεται ἐν τῇ ἀναστάσει
I know that he will rise again in the resurrection

ἐν τῇ ἐσχάτῃ ἡμέρᾳ. 25 εἶπεν αὐτῇ ὁ
in the last day. Said to her –

Ἰησοῦς· ἐγώ εἰμι ἡ ἀνάστασις καὶ ἡ
Jesus: I am the resurrection and the

ζωή· ὁ πιστεύων εἰς ἐμὲ κἂν ἀποθάνῃ
life; the [one] believing in me even if he should die

ζήσεται, 26 καὶ πᾶς ὁ ζῶν καὶ πιστεύων
will live, and everyone living and believing

εἰς ἐμὲ οὐ μὴ ἀποθάνῃ εἰς τὸν αἰῶνα·
in me by no means dies unto the age:

fallen asleep; but I am going
there to wake him up."
12 His disciples replied,
"Lord, if he sleeps, he will
get better." 13 Jesus had
been speaking of his death,
but his disciples thought he
meant natural sleep.
14 So then he told them
plainly, "Lazarus is dead,
15 and for your sake I am
glad I was not there, so that
you may believe. But let us
go to him."
16 Then Thomas (called
Didymus) said to the rest of
the disciples, "Let us also
go, that we may die with
him."

Jesus Comforts the Sisters

17 On his arrival, Jesus
found that Lazarus had already been in the tomb for
four days. 18 Bethany was
less than two miles[b] from
Jerusalem, 19 and many
Jews had come to Martha
and Mary to comfort them
in the loss of their brother.
20 When Martha heard that
Jesus was coming, she
went out to meet him, but
Mary stayed at home.
21 "Lord," Martha said to
Jesus, "if you had been
here, my brother would not
have died. 22 But I know
that even now God will give
you whatever you ask."
23 Jesus said to her,
"Your brother will rise
again."
24 Martha answered, "I
know he will rise again in
the resurrection at the last
day."
25 Jesus said to her, "I am
the resurrection and the
life. He who believes in me
will live, even though he
dies; 26 and whoever lives
and believes in me will never die. Do you believe
this?"

[b] 18 Greek *fifteen stadia* (about 3 kilometers)

him, "Yes, Lord, I believe
that you are the Messiah,[h]
the Son of God, the one
coming into the world."

Jesus Weeps

28 When she had said
this, she went back and
called her sister Mary, and
told her privately, "The
Teacher is here and is calling for you." 29 And when
she heard it, she got up
quickly and went to him.
30 Now Jesus had not yet
come to the village, but was
still at the place where Martha had met him. 31 The
Jews who were with her in
the house, consoling her,
saw Mary get up quickly
and go out. They followed
her because they thought
that she was going to the
tomb to weep there.
32 When Mary came where
Jesus was and saw him, she
knelt at his feet and said to
him, "Lord, if you had been
here, my brother would not
have died." 33 When Jesus
saw her weeping, and the
Jews who came with her
also weeping, he was greatly disturbed in spirit and
deeply moved. 34 He said,
"Where have you laid
him?" They said to him,
"Lord, come and see."
35 Jesus began to weep.
36 So the Jews said, "See
how he loved him!" 37 But
some of them said, "Could
not he who opened the eyes
of the blind man have kept
this man from dying?"

Jesus Raises Lazarus to Life

38 Then Jesus, again
greatly disturbed, came to
the tomb. It was a cave,
and a stone was lying

[h] Or *the Christ*

πιστεύεις τοῦτο; 27 λέγει αὐτῷ· ναί, κύριε·
believest thou this? She says to him : Yes, Lord;

ἐγὼ πεπίστευκα ὅτι σὺ εἶ ὁ χριστὸς ὁ
I have believed that thou art the Christ the

υἱὸς τοῦ θεοῦ ὁ εἰς τὸν κόσμον ἐρχόμενος.
Son – of God [1]the [3]into [4]the [5]world [2][one] coming.

28 καὶ τοῦτο εἰποῦσα ἀπῆλθεν καὶ ἐφώνησεν
And this saying she went away and called

Μαριὰμ τὴν ἀδελφὴν αὐτῆς λάθρα εἰποῦσα·
Mary the sister of her secretly saying :

ὁ διδάσκαλος πάρεστιν καὶ φωνεῖ σε.
The Teacher is here and calls thee.

29 ἐκείνη δὲ ὡς ἤκουσεν, ἐγείρεται ταχὺ
And that [one] when she heard, rose quickly

καὶ ἤρχετο πρὸς αὐτόν· 30 οὔπω δὲ
and came to him; now not yet

ἐληλύθει ὁ Ἰησοῦς εἰς τὴν κώμην, ἀλλ'
had come – Jesus into the village, but

ἦν ἔτι ἐν τῷ τόπῳ ὅπου ὑπήντησεν
was still in the place where met

αὐτῷ ἡ Μάρθα. 31 οἱ οὖν Ἰουδαῖοι
him – Martha. Therefore the Jews

οἱ ὄντες μετ' αὐτῆς ἐν τῇ οἰκίᾳ καὶ
the [ones] being with her in the house and

παραμυθούμενοι αὐτήν, ἰδόντες τὴν Μαριὰμ
consoling her, seeing – Mary

ὅτι ταχέως ἀνέστη καὶ ἐξῆλθεν,
that quickly she rose up and went out,

ἠκολούθησαν αὐτῇ, δόξαντες ὅτι ὑπάγει
followed her, thinking[,] – She is going

εἰς τὸ μνημεῖον ἵνα κλαύσῃ ἐκεῖ. 32 ἡ
to the tomb that she may weep there. –

οὖν Μαριὰμ ὡς ἦλθεν ὅπου ἦν Ἰησοῦς,
Therefore Mary when she came where was Jesus,

ἰδοῦσα αὐτὸν ἔπεσεν αὐτοῦ πρὸς τοὺς
seeing him fell of him at the

πόδας, λέγουσα αὐτῷ· κύριε, εἰ ἦς ὧδε,
feet, saying to him : Lord, if thou wast here,

οὐκ ἄν μου ἀπέθανεν ὁ ἀδελφός.
[4]would not [3]of me [5]have died [1]the [2]brother.

33 Ἰησοῦς οὖν ὡς εἶδεν αὐτὴν κλαίουσαν
Jesus therefore when he saw her weeping

καὶ τοὺς συνελθόντας αὐτῇ Ἰουδαίους
and [1]the [3]coming with [4]her [2]Jews

κλαίοντας, ἐνεβριμήσατο τῷ πνεύματι καὶ
weeping, groaned in the(his) spirit and

ἐτάραξεν ἑαυτόν, 34 καὶ εἶπεν· ποῦ
troubled himself, and said : Where

τεθείκατε αὐτόν; λέγουσιν αὐτῷ· κύριε,
have ye put him? They say to him : Lord,

ἔρχου καὶ ἴδε. 35 ἐδάκρυσεν ὁ Ἰησοῦς.
come and see. Shed tears – Jesus.

36 ἔλεγον οὖν οἱ Ἰουδαῖοι· ἴδε πῶς
Said therefore the Jews : See how

ἐφίλει αὐτόν. 37 τινὲς δὲ ἐξ αὐτῶν
he loved him. But some of them

εἶπαν· οὐκ ἐδύνατο οὗτος ὁ ἀνοίξας
said : Could not this man the [one] opening

τοὺς ὀφθαλμοὺς τοῦ τυφλοῦ ποιῆσαι ἵνα
the eyes of the blind man *to* cause that

καὶ οὗτος μὴ ἀποθάνῃ; 38 Ἰησοῦς οὖν
even this man should not die ? Jesus therefore

πάλιν ἐμβριμώμενος ἐν ἑαυτῷ ἔρχεται
again groaning in himself comes

εἰς τὸ μνημεῖον· ἦν δὲ σπήλαιον, καὶ
to the tomb; now it was a cave, and

27"Yes, Lord," she told
him, "I believe that you are
the Christ,[c] the Son of
God, who was to come into
the world."
28And after she had said
this, she went back and
called her sister Mary
aside. "The Teacher is
here," she said, "and is
asking for you." 29When
Mary heard this, she got up
quickly and went to him.
30Now Jesus had not yet
entered the village, but was
still at the place where Martha had met him. 31When
the Jews who had been
with Mary in the house,
comforting her, noticed
how quickly she got up and
went out, they followed
her, supposing she was going to the tomb to mourn
there.
32When Mary reached the
place where Jesus was and
saw him, she fell at his feet
and said, "Lord, if you had
been here, my brother
would not have died."
33When Jesus saw her
weeping, and the Jews who
had come along with her
also weeping, he was deeply moved in spirit and troubled. 34"Where have you
laid him?" he asked.
"Come and see, Lord,"
they replied.
35Jesus wept.
36Then the Jews said,
"See how he loved him!"
37But some of them said,
"Could not he who opened
the eyes of the blind man
have kept this man from
dying?"

Jesus Raises Lazarus From the Dead

38Jesus, once more deep-
ly moved, came to the
tomb. It was a cave with a
stone laid across the en-

[c] 27 Or *Messiah*

against it. 39 Jesus said,
"Take away the stone."
Martha, the sister of the
dead man, said to him,
"Lord, already there is a
stench because he has been
dead four days." 40 Jesus
said to her, "Did I not tell
you that if you believed,
you would see the glory of
God?" 41 So they took away
the stone. And Jesus
looked upward and said,
"Father, I thank you for
having heard me. 42 I knew
that you always hear me,
but I have said this for the
sake of the crowd standing
here, so that they may believe that you sent me."
43 When he had said this, he
cried with a loud voice,
"Lazarus, come out!"
44 The dead man came out,
his hands and feet bound
with strips of cloth, and his
face wrapped in a cloth.
Jesus said to them, "Un-
bind him, and let him go."

The Plot to Kill Jesus

45 Many of the Jews
therefore, who had come
with Mary and had seen
what Jesus did, believed in
him. 46 But some of them
went to the Pharisees and
told them what he had
done. 47 So the chief priests
and the Pharisees called a
meeting of the council, and
said, "What are we to do?
This man is performing
many signs. 48 If we let him
go on like this, everyone
will believe in him, and the
Romans will come and de-
stroy both our holy place[i]
and our nation." 49 But one
of them, Caiaphas, who
was high priest that year,
said to them, "You know

[i] Or *our temple*; Greek *our place*

λίθος ἐπέκειτο ἐπ' αὐτῷ. 39 λέγει ὁ
a stone was lying *on* on it. Says –
Ἰησοῦς· ἄρατε τὸν λίθον. λέγει αὐτῷ
Jesus : Lift ye the stone. Says to him
ἡ ἀδελφὴ τοῦ τετελευτηκότος Μάρθα·
the sister of the [one] having died Martha :
κύριε, ἤδη ὄζει· τεταρταῖος γάρ ἐστιν.
Lord, now he smells; for fourth [day] it is.
40 λέγει αὐτῇ ὁ Ἰησοῦς· οὐκ εἶπόν
Says to her – Jesus : Not I told
σοι ὅτι ἐὰν πιστεύσῃς ὄψῃ τὴν δόξαν
thee that if thou believest thou wilt see the glory
τοῦ θεοῦ; 41 ἦραν οὖν τὸν λίθον. ὁ
– of God? They lifted therefore the stone. –
δὲ Ἰησοῦς ἦρεν τοὺς ὀφθαλμοὺς ἄνω
And Jesus lifted the(his) eyes up
καὶ εἶπεν· πάτερ, εὐχαριστῶ σοι ὅτι
and said : Father, I thank thee that
ἤκουσάς μου. 42 ἐγὼ δὲ ᾔδειν ὅτι
thou didst hear me. And I knew that
πάντοτέ μου ἀκούεις· ἀλλὰ διὰ τὸν
always me thou hearest; but because of the
ὄχλον τὸν περιεστῶτα εἶπον, ἵνα
crowd – standing round I said, that
πιστεύσωσιν ὅτι σύ με ἀπέστειλας.
they may believe that thou me didst send.
43 καὶ ταῦτα εἰπὼν φωνῇ μεγάλῃ
And these things saying voice with a great
ἐκραύγασεν· Λάζαρε, δεῦρο ἔξω. 44 ἐξῆλθεν
he cried out : Lazarus, come out. Came out
ὁ τεθνηκὼς δεδεμένος τοὺς πόδας καὶ
the [one] having died *having been* bound the feet and
τὰς χεῖρας κειρίαις, καὶ ἡ ὄψις αὐτοῦ
the hands with bandages, and the face of him
σουδαρίῳ περιεδέδετο. λέγει αὐτοῖς ὁ
with a napkin had been bound round. Says to them –
Ἰησοῦς· λύσατε αὐτὸν καὶ ἄφετε αὐτὸν ὑπάγειν.
Jesus : Loosen him and let him *to* go.
45 Πολλοὶ οὖν ἐκ τῶν Ἰουδαίων, οἱ
Many therefore of the Jews, the [ones]
ἐλθόντες πρὸς τὴν Μαριὰμ καὶ θεασάμενοι
having come to – Mary and having beheld
ὃ ἐποίησεν, ἐπίστευσαν εἰς αὐτόν· 46 τινὲς δὲ
what he did, believed in him; but some
ἐξ αὐτῶν ἀπῆλθον πρὸς τοὺς Φαρισαίους
of them went away to the Pharisees
καὶ εἶπαν αὐτοῖς ἃ ἐποίησεν Ἰησοῦς.
and told them what things did Jesus.
47 συνήγαγον οὖν οἱ ἀρχιερεῖς καὶ οἱ
Assembled therefore the chief priests and the
Φαρισαῖοι συνέδριον, καὶ ἔλεγον· τί
Pharisees a council, and said : What
ποιοῦμεν, ὅτι οὗτος ὁ ἄνθρωπος πολλὰ
are we doing, because this – man [2]many
ποιεῖ σημεῖα; 48 ἐὰν ἀφῶμεν αὐτὸν οὕτως,
[1]does [3]signs? If we leave him thus,
πάντες πιστεύσουσιν εἰς αὐτόν, καὶ
all men will believe in him, and
ἐλεύσονται οἱ Ῥωμαῖοι καὶ ἀροῦσιν ἡμῶν
will come the Romans and will take of us
καὶ τὸν τόπον καὶ τὸ ἔθνος. 49 εἷς
both the place and the nation. [2]one
δέ τις ἐξ αὐτῶν Καϊάφας, ἀρχιερεὺς
[1]But [3]a certain of them[,] Caiaphas, high priest
ὢν τοῦ ἐνιαυτοῦ ἐκείνου, εἶπεν αὐτοῖς·
being – year of that, said to them :

trance. 39 "Take away the
stone," he said.
"But, Lord," said Mar-
tha, the sister of the dead
man, "by this time there is
a bad odor, for he has been
there four days."
40 Then Jesus said, "Did I
not tell you that if you believed, you would see the
glory of God?"
41 So they took away the
stone. Then Jesus looked
up and said, "Father, I
thank you that you have
heard me. 42 I knew that
you always hear me, but I
said this for the benefit of
the people standing here,
that they may believe that
you sent me."
43 When he had said this,
Jesus called in a loud voice,
"Lazarus, come out!"
44 The dead man came out,
his hands and feet wrapped
with strips of linen, and a
cloth around his face.
Jesus said to them, "Take
off the grave clothes and let
him go."

The Plot to Kill Jesus

45 Therefore many of the
Jews who had come to visit
Mary, and had seen what
Jesus did, put their faith in
him. 46 But some of them
went to the Pharisees and
told them what Jesus had
done. 47 Then the chief
priests and the Pharisees
called a meeting of the Sanhedrin.
"What are we accom-
plishing?" they asked.
"Here is this man performing many miraculous signs.
48 If we let him go on like
this, everyone will believe
in him, and then the Ro-
mans will come and take
away both our place[d] and
our nation."
49 Then one of them,
named Caiaphas, who was
high priest that year, spoke

[d] 48 Or *temple*

nothing at all! 50 You do not understand that it is better for you to have one man die for the people than to have the whole nation destroyed." 51 He did not say this on his own, but being high priest that year he prophesied that Jesus was about to die for the nation, 52 and not for the nation only, but to gather into one the dispersed children of God. 53 So from that day on they planned to put him to death.

54 Jesus therefore no longer walked about openly among the Jews, but went from there to a town called Ephraim in the region near the wilderness; and he remained there with the disciples.

55 Now the Passover of the Jews was near, and many went up from the country to Jerusalem before the Passover to purify themselves. 56 They were looking for Jesus and were asking one another as they stood in the temple, "What do you think? Surely he will not come to the festival, will he?" 57 Now the chief priests and the Pharisees had given orders that anyone who knew where Jesus[j] was should let them know, so that they might arrest him.

Chapter 12

Mary Anoints Jesus

SIX days before the Passover Jesus came to Bethany, the home of Lazarus, whom he had raised from the dead. 2 There they gave a dinner for him. Martha served, and Lazarus was one of those at the table with him. 3 Mary took a pound of

[j] Gk *he*

ὑμεῖς οὐκ οἴδατε οὐδέν, **50** οὐδὲ λογίζεσθε
Ye know not no(any)thing, nor reckon
ὅτι συμφέρει ὑμῖν ἵνα εἷς ἄνθρωπος
that it is expedient for us that one man
ἀποθάνῃ ὑπὲρ τοῦ λαοῦ καὶ μὴ ὅλον
should die for the people and not all
τὸ ἔθνος ἀπόληται. **51** τοῦτο δὲ ἀφ'
the nation perish. But this from
ἑαυτοῦ οὐκ εἶπεν, ἀλλὰ ἀρχιερεὺς ὢν
himself he said not, but high priest being
τοῦ ἐνιαυτοῦ ἐκείνου ἐπροφήτευσεν ὅτι
– year of that he prophesied that
ἔμελλεν Ἰησοῦς ἀποθνῄσκειν ὑπὲρ τοῦ
was about Jesus to die for the
ἔθνους, **52** καὶ οὐχ ὑπὲρ τοῦ ἔθνους
nation, and not for the nation
μόνον, ἀλλ' ἵνα καὶ τὰ τέκνα τοῦ θεοῦ
only, but that also the children – of God
τὰ διεσκορπισμένα συναγάγῃ εἰς ἕν.
– *having been* scattered he might gather into one.
53 ἀπ' ἐκείνης οὖν τῆς ἡμέρας ἐβουλεύσαντο
From [1]that [3]therefore – [2]day they took counsel
ἵνα ἀποκτείνωσιν αὐτόν. **54** Ὁ οὖν
that they might kill him. – Therefore
Ἰησοῦς οὐκέτι παρρησίᾳ περιεπάτει ἐν
Jesus no longer openly walked among
τοῖς Ἰουδαίοις, ἀλλὰ ἀπῆλθεν ἐκεῖθεν εἰς
the Jews, but went away thence into
τὴν χώραν ἐγγὺς τῆς ἐρήμου, εἰς Ἐφραὶμ
the country near the desert, to [2]Ephraim
λεγομένην πόλιν, κἀκεῖ ἔμεινεν μετὰ τῶν
[3]*being* called [1]a city, and there remained with the
μαθητῶν.
disciples.

55 Ἦν δὲ ἐγγὺς τὸ πάσχα τῶν
Now was near the Passover of the
Ἰουδαίων, καὶ ἀνέβησαν πολλοὶ εἰς
Jews, and went up many to
Ἱεροσόλυμα ἐκ τῆς χώρας πρὸ τοῦ
Jerusalem out of the country before the
πάσχα, ἵνα ἁγνίσωσιν ἑαυτούς.
Passover, that they might purify themselves.
56 ἐζήτουν οὖν τὸν Ἰησοῦν καὶ ἔλεγον
They sought therefore – Jesus and said
μετ' ἀλλήλων ἐν τῷ ἱερῷ ἑστηκότες·
with one another in the temple standing :
τί δοκεῖ ὑμῖν; ὅτι οὐ μὴ ἔλθῃ εἰς
What seems it to you? that by no means he comes to
τὴν ἑορτήν; **57** δεδώκεισαν δὲ οἱ ἀρχιερεῖς
the feast? Now had given the chief priests
καὶ οἱ Φαρισαῖοι ἐντολὰς ἵνα ἐάν τις
and the Pharisees commands that if anyone
γνῷ ποῦ ἐστιν μηνύσῃ, ὅπως πιάσωσιν
knew where he is (was) he should inform, so as they might arrest
αὐτόν. **12** Ὁ οὖν Ἰησοῦς πρὸ ἓξ ἡμερῶν
him. – Therefore Jesus [2]before [1]six [3]days
τοῦ πάσχα ἦλθεν εἰς Βηθανίαν, ὅπου
the Passover came to Bethany, where
ἦν Λάζαρος, ὃν ἤγειρεν ἐκ νεκρῶν
was Lazarus, whom [2]raised [3]out of [the] [4]dead
Ἰησοῦς. **2** ἐποίησαν οὖν αὐτῷ δεῖπνον ἐκεῖ,
[1]Jesus. They made therefore for him a supper there,
καὶ ἡ Μάρθα διηκόνει, ὁ δὲ Λάζαρος εἷς
and – Martha served, – but Lazarus one
ἦν ἐκ τῶν ἀνακειμένων σὺν αὐτῷ· **3** ἡ
was of the [ones] reclining with him; –

up, "You know nothing at all! 50 You do not realize that it is better for you that one man die for the people than that the whole nation perish."

51 He did not say this on his own, but as high priest that year he prophesied that Jesus would die for the Jewish nation, 52 and not only for that nation but also for the scattered children of God, to bring them together and make them one. 53 So from that day on they plotted to take his life.

54 Therefore Jesus no longer moved about publicly among the Jews. Instead he withdrew to a region near the desert, to a village called Ephraim, where he stayed with his disciples.

55 When it was almost time for the Jewish Passover, many went up from the country to Jerusalem for their ceremonial cleansing before the Passover. 56 They kept looking for Jesus, and as they stood in the temple area they asked one another, "What do you think? Isn't he coming to the Feast at all?" 57 But the chief priests and Pharisees had given orders that if anyone found out where Jesus was, he should report it so that they might arrest him.

Chapter 12

Jesus Anointed at Bethany

SIX days before the Passover, Jesus arrived at Bethany, where Lazarus lived, whom Jesus had raised from the dead. 2 Here a dinner was given in Jesus' honor. Martha served, while Lazarus was among those reclining at the table with him. 3 Then

costly perfume made of pure nard, anointed Jesus' feet, and wiped them[k] with her hair. The house was filled with the fragrance of the perfume. 4 But Judas Iscariot, one of his disciples (the one who was about to betray him), said, 5 "Why was this perfume not sold for three hundred denarii[l] and the money given to the poor?" 6 (He said this not because he cared about the poor, but because he was a thief; he kept the common purse and used to steal what was put into it.) 7 Jesus said, "Leave her alone. She bought it[m] so that she might keep it for the day of my burial. 8 You always have the poor with you, but you do not always have me."

The Plot to Kill Lazarus

9 When the great crowd of the Jews learned that he was there, they came not only because of Jesus but also to see Lazarus, whom he had raised from the dead. 10 So the chief priests planned to put Lazarus to death as well, 11 since it was on account of him that many of the Jews were deserting and were believing in Jesus.

Jesus' Triumphal Entry into Jerusalem

12 The next day the great crowd that had come to the festival heard that Jesus was coming to Jerusalem. 13 So they took branches of palm trees and went out to meet him, shouting,

"Hosanna!
Blessed is the one
who comes in
the name
of the Lord—

[k] Gk *his feet*
[l] Three hundred denarii would be nearly a year's wages for a laborer
[m] Gk lacks *She bought it*

οὖν Μαριὰμ λαβοῦσα λίτραν μύρου
therefore Mary taking a pound ³ointment
νάρδου πιστικῆς πολυτίμου ἤλειψεν τοὺς
⁴of spikenard ¹of pure ²costly anointed the
πόδας τοῦ Ἰησοῦ καὶ ἐξέμαξεν ταῖς
feet – of Jesus and wiped off with the
θριξὶν αὐτῆς τοὺς πόδας αὐτοῦ· ἡ δὲ
hairs of her the feet of him; and the
οἰκία ἐπληρώθη ἐκ τῆς ὀσμῆς τοῦ
house was filled of(with) the odour of the
μύρου. **4** λέγει δὲ Ἰούδας ὁ Ἰσκαριώτης
ointment. And says Judas the Iscariot
εἷς τῶν μαθητῶν αὐτοῦ, ὁ μέλλων
one of the disciples of him, the [one] being about
αὐτὸν παραδιδόναι· **5** διὰ τί τοῦτο τὸ
him to betray: Why this –
μύρον οὐκ ἐπράθη τριακοσίων δηναρίων
ointment not was sold of(for) three hundred denarii
καὶ ἐδόθη πτωχοῖς; **6** εἶπεν δὲ τοῦτο
and given to [the] poor? But he said this
οὐχ ὅτι περὶ τῶν πτωχῶν ἔμελεν αὐτῷ,
not because about the poor it mattered to him,
ἀλλ' ὅτι κλέπτης ἦν καὶ τὸ γλωσσόκομον
but because a thief he was and ²the ³bag
ἔχων τὰ βαλλόμενα ἐβάσταζεν.
¹having ⁵the things ⁶being put [in] ⁴carried. *
7 εἶπεν οὖν ὁ Ἰησοῦς· ἄφες αὐτήν,
Said therefore – Jesus: Leave her,
ἵνα εἰς τὴν ἡμέραν τοῦ ἐνταφιασμοῦ
that to the day of the burial
μου τηρήσῃ αὐτό· **8** τοὺς πτωχοὺς γὰρ
of me she may keep it; ²the ³poor ¹for
πάντοτε ἔχετε μεθ' ἑαυτῶν, ἐμὲ δὲ
always ye have with yourselves, but me
οὐ πάντοτε ἔχετε. **9** Ἔγνω οὖν ὁ ὄχλος
not always ye have. Knew therefore the crowd
πολὺς ἐκ τῶν Ἰουδαίων ὅτι ἐκεῖ ἐστιν,
great of the Jews that there he is(was),
καὶ ἦλθον οὐ διὰ τὸν Ἰησοῦν μόνον,
and they came not because of – Jesus only,
ἀλλ' ἵνα καὶ τὸν Λάζαρον ἴδωσιν ὃν
but that also – Lazarus they might see whom
ἤγειρεν ἐκ νεκρῶν. **10** ἐβουλεύσαντο δὲ
he raised out of [the] dead. But took counsel
οἱ ἀρχιερεῖς ἵνα καὶ τὸν Λάζαρον
the chief priests that also – Lazarus
ἀποκτείνωσιν, **11** ὅτι πολλοὶ δι' αὐτὸν
they might kill, because ¹many ⁴because of ⁵him
ὑπῆγον τῶν Ἰουδαίων καὶ ἐπίστευον εἰς
⁴went ²of the ³Jews and believed in
τὸν Ἰησοῦν.
– Jesus.

12 Τῇ ἐπαύριον ὁ ὄχλος πολὺς ὁ
On the morrow the crowd much –
ἐλθὼν εἰς τὴν ἑορτήν, ἀκούσαντες ὅτι
coming to the feast, hearing that
ἔρχεται Ἰησοῦς εἰς Ἱεροσόλυμα, **13** ἔλαβον
is(was) coming Jesus to Jerusalem, took
τὰ βαΐα τῶν φοινίκων καὶ ἐξῆλθον εἰς
the branches of the palm-trees and went out to
ὑπάντησιν αὐτῷ, καὶ ἐκραύγαζον· ὡσαννά,
a meeting with him, and cried out: Hosanna,
εὐλογημένος ὁ ἐρχόμενος ἐν ὀνόματι
being blessed the [one] coming in [the] name

* This may mean "stole"; *cf.* our euphemism for "steal"—to "lift" a thing.

Mary took about a pint[e] of pure nard, an expensive perfume; she poured it on Jesus' feet and wiped his feet with her hair. And the house was filled with the fragrance of the perfume.

4 But one of his disciples, Judas Iscariot, who was later to betray him, objected, 5 "Why wasn't this perfume sold and the money given to the poor? It was worth a year's wages.[f]" 6 He did not say this because he cared about the poor but because he was a thief; as keeper of the money bag, he used to help himself to what was put into it.

7 "Leave her alone," Jesus replied. "It was intended that she should save this perfume for the day of my burial. 8 You will always have the poor among you, but you will not always have me."

9 Meanwhile a large crowd of Jews found out that Jesus was there and came, not only because of him but also to see Lazarus, whom he had raised from the dead. 10 So the chief priests made plans to kill Lazarus as well, 11 for on account of him many of the Jews were going over to Jesus and putting their faith in him.

The Triumphal Entry

12 The next day the great crowd that had come for the Feast heard that Jesus was on his way to Jerusalem. 13 They took palm branches and went out to meet him, shouting,

"Hosanna![g]"

"Blessed is he who
comes in the name
of the Lord!"[h]

[e] *3* Greek *a litra* (probably about 0.5 liter)
[f] *5* Greek *three hundred denarii*
[g] *13* A Hebrew expression meaning "Save!" which became an exclamation of praise
[h] *13* Psalm 118:25, 26

the King of Israel!"
14 Jesus found a young donkey and sat on it; as it is
written:
15 "Do not be afraid,
daughter of
Zion.
Look, your king is
coming,
sitting on a
donkey's colt!"
16 His disciples did not understand these things at
first; but when Jesus was
glorified, then they remembered that these things had
been written of him and had
been done to him. 17 So the
crowd that had been with
him when he called Laza-
rus out of the tomb and
raised him from the dead
continued to testify.[n] 18 It
was also because they
heard that he had per-
formed this sign that the
crowd went to meet him.
19 The Pharisees then said
to one another, "You see,
you can do nothing. Look,
the world has gone after
him!"

Some Greeks Wish to See Jesus

20 Now among those
who went up to worship at
the festival were some
Greeks. 21 They came to
Philip, who was from Bethsaida in Galilee, and said to
him, "Sir, we wish to see
Jesus." 22 Philip went and
told Andrew; then Andrew
and Philip went and told
Jesus. 23 Jesus answered
them, "The hour has come
for the Son of Man to be
glorified. 24 Very truly, I
tell you, unless a grain of
wheat falls into the earth
and dies, it remains just a
single grain; but if it dies, it
bears much fruit. 25 Those
who love their life lose it,

[n] Other ancient authorities read *with him began to testify that he had called . . from the dead*

κυρίου, καὶ ὁ βασιλεὺς τοῦ Ἰσραήλ.
of [the] Lord, even the king – of Israel.
14 εὑρὼν δὲ ὁ Ἰησοῦς ὀνάριον ἐκάθισεν
And [a]having found – [1]Jesus a young ass sat
ἐπ' αὐτό, καθώς ἐστιν γεγραμμένον·
on it, as it is *having been* written :
15 μὴ φοβοῦ, θυγάτηρ Σιών· ἰδοὺ ὁ
Fear not, daughter of Sion : behold[,] the
βασιλεύς σου ἔρχεται, καθήμενος ἐπὶ
king of thee comes, sitting on
πῶλον ὄνου. 16 ταῦτα οὐκ ἔγνωσαν
a foal of an ass. These things knew not
αὐτοῦ οἱ μαθηταὶ τὸ πρῶτον, ἀλλ' ὅτε
of him the disciples at first, but when
ἐδοξάσθη Ἰησοῦς, τότε ἐμνήσθησαν ὅτι
was glorified Jesus, then they remembered that
ταῦτα ἦν ἐπ' αὐτῷ γεγραμμένα καὶ
these things were on him *having been* written and
ταῦτα ἐποίησαν αὐτῷ. 17 ἐμαρτύρει οὖν
these things they did to him. Witnessed therefore
ὁ ὄχλος ὁ ὢν μετ' αὐτοῦ ὅτε τὸν
the crowd – being with him when –
Λάζαρον ἐφώνησεν ἐκ τοῦ μνημείου καὶ
Lazarus he called out of the tomb and
ἤγειρεν αὐτὸν ἐκ νεκρῶν. 18 διὰ τοῦτο
raised him out of [the] dead. Therefore
καὶ ὑπήντησεν αὐτῷ ὁ ὄχλος, ὅτι
also met him the crowd, because
ἤκουσαν τοῦτο αὐτὸν πεποιηκέναι τὸ
[1]they heard [4]this [2]him [3]to have done[b] –
σημεῖον. 19 οἱ οὖν Φαρισαῖοι εἶπαν
[5]sign. Therefore the Pharisees said
πρὸς ἑαυτούς· θεωρεῖτε ὅτι οὐκ ὠφελεῖτε
to themselves : Behold ye that ye profit not
οὐδέν· ἴδε ὁ κόσμος ὀπίσω αὐτοῦ ἀπῆλθεν.
no(any)thing; see[,] the world after him went(is gone).
20 [a]Ἦσαν δὲ [a]Ἕλληνές τινες ἐκ τῶν
Now there were [2]Greeks [1]some of the
ἀναβαινόντων ἵνα προσκυνήσωσιν ἐν τῇ
[ones] going up that they might worship at the
ἑορτῇ· 21 οὗτοι οὖν προσῆλθον Φιλίππῳ
feast; these therefore approached *to* Philip
τῷ ἀπὸ Βηθσαϊδὰ τῆς Γαλιλαίας, καὶ
the [one] from Bethsaida – of Galilee, and
ἠρώτων αὐτὸν λέγοντες· κύριε, θέλομεν
asked him saying : Sir, we wish
τὸν Ἰησοῦν ἰδεῖν. 22 ἔρχεται ὁ Φίλιππος
– Jesus to see. Comes – Philip
καὶ λέγει τῷ Ἀνδρέᾳ· ἔρχεται Ἀνδρέας
and tells – Andrew; comes Andrew
καὶ Φίλιππος καὶ λέγουσιν τῷ Ἰησοῦ.
and Philip and tell – Jesus.
23 ὁ δὲ Ἰησοῦς ἀποκρίνεται αὐτοῖς λέγων·
– And Jesus answers them saying:
ἐλήλυθεν ἡ ὥρα ἵνα δοξασθῇ ὁ υἱὸς τοῦ
Has come the hour that is glorified the Son –
ἀνθρώπου. 24 ἀμὴν ἀμὴν λέγω ὑμῖν,
of man. Truly truly I say to you,
ἐὰν μὴ ὁ κόκκος τοῦ σίτου πεσὼν εἰς
unless the grain – of wheat falling into
τὴν γῆν ἀποθάνῃ, αὐτὸς μόνος μένει·
the ground dies, it alone remains;
ἐὰν δὲ ἀποθάνῃ, πολὺν καρπὸν φέρει.
but if it dies, much fruit it bears.
25 ὁ φιλῶν τὴν ψυχὴν αὐτοῦ ἀπολλύει
The [one] loving the life of him loses

"Blessed is the King of
Israel!"
14 Jesus found a young donkey and sat upon it, as it is
written,
15 "Do not be afraid, O
Daughter of Zion;
see, your king is
coming,
seated on a donkey's
colt."[i]
16 At first his disciples did
not understand all this.
Only after Jesus was glorified did they realize that
these things had been written about him and that they
had done these things to
him.
17 Now the crowd that
was with him when he
called Lazarus from the
tomb and raised him from
the dead continued to
spread the word. 18 Many
people, because they had
heard that he had given this
miraculous sign, went out
to meet him. 19 So the Pharisees said to one another,
"See, this is getting us nowhere. Look how the
whole world has gone after
him!"

Jesus Predicts His Death

20 Now there were some
Greeks among those who
went up to worship at the
Feast. 21 They came to Philip, who was from Bethsai-
da in Galilee, with a re-
quest. "Sir," they said,
"we would like to see
Jesus." 22 Philip went to tell
Andrew; Andrew and Phil-
ip in turn told Jesus.
23 Jesus replied, "The
hour has come for the Son
of Man to be glorified. 24 I
tell you the truth, unless a
kernel of wheat falls to the
ground and dies, it remains
only a single seed. But if it
dies, it produces many
seeds. 25 The man who
loves his life will lose it,

[i] *15* Zech. 9:9

and those who hate their
life in this world will keep it
for eternal life. 26 Whoever
serves me must follow me,
and where I am, there will
my servant be also. Who-
ever serves me, the Father
will honor.

Jesus Speaks about His Death

27 "Now my soul is
troubled. And what should
I say—'Father, save me
from this hour'? No, it is
for this reason that I have
come to this hour. 28 Fa-
ther, glorify your name."
Then a voice came from
heaven, "I have glorified it,
and I will glorify it again."
29 The crowd standing there
heard it and said that it was
thunder. Others said, "An
angel has spoken to him."
30 Jesus answered, "This
voice has come for your
sake, not for mine. 31 Now
is the judgment of this
world; now the ruler of this
world will be driven out.
32 And I, when I am lifted
up from the earth, will draw
all people[o] to myself."
33 He said this to indicate
the kind of death he was to
die. 34 The crowd answered
him, "We have heard from
the law that the Messiah[p]
remains forever. How can
you say that the Son of Man
must be lifted up? Who is
this Son of Man?" 35 Jesus
said to them, "The light is
with you for a little longer.
Walk while you have the
light, so that the darkness
may not overtake you. If
you walk in the darkness,
you do not know where you
are going. 36 While you

[o] Other ancient authorities read *all things*
[p] Or *the Christ*

αὐτήν, καὶ ὁ μισῶν τὴν ψυχὴν αὐτοῦ
it, and the [one] hating the life of him
ἐν τῷ κόσμῳ τούτῳ εἰς ζωὴν αἰώνιον
in – world this unto life eternal
φυλάξει αὐτήν. 26 ἐάν ἐμοί τις διακονῇ,
will keep it. If me anyone serves,
ἐμοὶ ἀκολουθείτω, καὶ ὅπου εἰμὶ ἐγώ,
me let him follow, and where am I,
ἐκεῖ καὶ ὁ διάκονος ὁ ἐμὸς ἔσται·
there also *the* ²servant – ¹my will be;
ἐάν τις ἐμοὶ διακονῇ, τιμήσει αὐτὸν
if anyone me serves, will honour him
ὁ πατήρ. 27 νῦν ἡ ψυχή μου τετάρακται,
the Father. Now the soul of me has been troubled,
καὶ τί εἴπω; πάτερ, σῶσόν με ἐκ
and what may I say? Father, save me out of
τῆς ὥρας ταύτης. ἀλλὰ διὰ τοῦτο ἦλθον
– hour this. But therefore I came
εἰς τὴν ὥραν ταύτην. 28 πάτερ, δόξασόν
to – hour this. Father, glorify
σου τὸ ὄνομα. ἦλθεν οὖν φωνὴ ἐκ
of thee the name. Came therefore a voice out of
τοῦ οὐρανοῦ· καὶ ἐδόξασα καὶ πάλιν
– heaven : Both I glorified and again
δοξάσω. 29 ὁ οὖν ὄχλος ὁ ἑστὼς καὶ
I will glorify. Therefore the crowd – standing and
ἀκούσας ἔλεγεν βροντὴν γεγονέναι· ἄλλοι
hearing said thunder to have happened; others
ἔλεγον· ἄγγελος αὐτῷ λελάληκεν.
said : An angel to him has spoken.
30 ἀπεκρίθη Ἰησοῦς καὶ εἶπεν· οὐ δι' ἐμὲ
Answered Jesus and said : Not because of me
ἡ φωνὴ αὕτη γέγονεν ἀλλὰ δι' ὑμᾶς.
– voice this has happened but because of you.
31 νῦν κρίσις ἐστὶν τοῦ κόσμου τούτου·
Now judgment is – world of this ;
νῦν ὁ ἄρχων τοῦ κόσμου τούτου
now the ruler – world of this
ἐκβληθήσεται ἔξω· 32 κἀγὼ ἐὰν ὑψωθῶ
shall be cast *out* outside; and I if I am lifted up
ἐκ τῆς γῆς, πάντας ἑλκύσω πρὸς
out of the earth, all men will draw to
ἐμαυτόν. 33 τοῦτο δὲ ἔλεγεν σημαίνων
myself. And this he said signifying
ποίῳ θανάτῳ ἤμελλεν ἀποθνήσκειν.
by what kind of death he was about to die.
34 ἀπεκρίθη οὖν αὐτῷ ὁ ὄχλος· ἡμεῖς
Answered therefore him the crowd : We
ἠκούσαμεν ἐκ τοῦ νόμου ὅτι ὁ χριστὸς
heard out of the law that the Christ
μένει εἰς τὸν αἰῶνα, καὶ πῶς λέγεις
remains unto the age, and how sayest
σὺ ὅτι δεῖ ὑψωθῆναι τὸν υἱὸν τοῦ
thou that it behoves to be lifted up the Son –
ἀνθρώπου; τίς ἐστιν οὗτος ὁ υἱὸς τοῦ
of man? who is this – Son –
ἀνθρώπου; 35 εἶπεν οὖν αὐτοῖς ὁ Ἰησοῦς·
of man? Said therefore to them – Jesus :
ἔτι μικρὸν χρόνον τὸ φῶς ἐν ὑμῖν
Yet a little time the light among you
ἐστιν. περιπατεῖτε ὡς τὸ φῶς ἔχετε,
is. Walk while the light ye have,
ἵνα μὴ σκοτία ὑμᾶς καταλάβῃ· καὶ
lest darkness you overtakes; and
ὁ περιπατῶν ἐν τῇ σκοτίᾳ οὐκ οἶδεν
the [one] walking in the darkness knows not

while the man who hates
his life in this world will
keep it for eternal life.
26 Whoever serves me must
follow me; and where I am,
my servant also will be. My
Father will honor the one
who serves me.
27 "Now my heart is trou-
bled, and what shall I say?
'Father, save me from this
hour'? No, it was for this
very reason I came to this
hour. 28 Father, glorify your
name!"
Then a voice came from
heaven, "I have glorified
it, and will glorify it again."
29 The crowd that was there
and heard it said it had
thundered; others said an
angel had spoken to him.
30 Jesus said, "This voice
was for your benefit, not
mine. 31 Now is the time for
judgment on this world;
now the prince of this
world will be driven out.
32 But I, when I am lifted up
from the earth, will draw all
men to myself." 33 He said
this to show the kind of
death he was going to die.
34 The crowd spoke up,
"We have heard from the
Law that the Christ[j] will
remain forever, so how can
you say, 'The Son of Man
must be lifted up'? Who is
this 'Son of Man'?"
35 Then Jesus told them,
"You are going to have the
light just a little while longer. Walk while you have
the light, before darkness
overtakes you. The man
who walks in the dark does
not know where he is go-

[j] 34 Or *Messiah*

have the light, believe in
the light, so that you may
become children of light."

The Unbelief of the People

After Jesus had said this,
he departed and hid from
them. 37 Although he had
performed so many signs in
their presence, they did not
believe in him. 38 This was
to fulfill the word spoken
by the prophet Isaiah:
"Lord, who has
believed our
message,
and to whom has
the arm of the
Lord been
revealed?"
39 And so they could not believe, because Isaiah also
said,
40 "He has blinded their
eyes
and hardened their
heart,
so that they might not
look with their
eyes,
and understand with
their heart and
turn—
and I would heal
them."
41 Isaiah said this because[q]
he saw his glory and spoke
about him. 42 Nevertheless
many, even of the authorities, believed in him. But
because of the Pharisees
they did not confess it, for
fear that they would be put
out of the synagogue; 43 for
they loved human glory
more than the glory that
comes from God.

Summary of Jesus' Teaching

44 Then Jesus cried
aloud: "Whoever believes
in me believes not in me but
in him who sent me. 45 And
whoever sees me sees him
who sent me. 46 I have
come as light into the
world, so that everyone
who believes in me should
not remain in the darkness.
47 I do not judge anyone
who hears my words and
does not keep them, for I
came not to judge the
world, but to save the

[q] Other ancient witnesses read *when*

ποῦ ὑπάγει. **36** ὡς τὸ φῶς ἔχετε,
where he is going. While the light ye have,
πιστεύετε εἰς τὸ φῶς, ἵνα υἱοὶ φωτὸς
believe in the light, that sons of light
γένησθε.
ye may become.
Ταῦτα ἐλάλησεν Ἰησοῦς, καὶ ἀπελθὼν
These things spoke Jesus, and going away
ἐκρύβη ἀπ᾽ αὐτῶν. **37** Τοσαῦτα δὲ αὐτοῦ
was hidden from them. But so many him
σημεῖα πεποιηκότος ἔμπροσθεν αὐτῶν οὐκ
signs having done[a] before them not
=But while he did so many signs
ἐπίστευον εἰς αὐτόν, **38** ἵνα ὁ λόγος
they believed in him, that the word
Ἠσαΐου τοῦ προφήτου πληρωθῇ ὃν
of Esaias the prophet might be fulfilled which
εἶπεν· κύριε, τίς ἐπίστευσεν τῇ ἀκοῇ
he said: Lord, who believed the report
ἡμῶν; καὶ ὁ βραχίων κυρίου τίνι
of us? and the arm of [the] Lord to whom
ἀπεκαλύφθη; **39** διὰ τοῦτο οὐκ ἠδύναντο
was it revealed? Therefore they could not
πιστεύειν, ὅτι πάλιν εἶπεν Ἠσαΐας·
to believe, because again said Esaias:
40 τετύφλωκεν αὐτῶν τοὺς ὀφθαλμοὺς καὶ
He has blinded of them the eyes and
ἐπώρωσεν αὐτῶν τὴν καρδίαν, ἵνα
hardened of them the heart, that
μὴ ἴδωσιν τοῖς ὀφθαλμοῖς καὶ νοήσωσιν
they might not see with the eyes and understand
τῇ καρδίᾳ καὶ στραφῶσιν, καὶ ἰάσομαι
with the heart and might turn, and I will cure
αὐτούς. **41** ταῦτα εἶπεν Ἠσαΐας ὅτι
them. These things said Esaias because
εἶδεν τὴν δόξαν αὐτοῦ, καὶ ἐλάλησεν
he saw the glory of him, and spoke
περὶ αὐτοῦ. **42** ὅμως μέντοι καὶ ἐκ
about him. Nevertheless however even of
τῶν ἀρχόντων πολλοὶ ἐπίστευσαν εἰς αὐτόν,
the rulers many believed in him,
ἀλλὰ διὰ τοὺς Φαρισαίους οὐχ ὡμολόγουν,
but because of the Pharisees did not confess,
ἵνα μὴ ἀποσυνάγωγοι γένωνται·
lest put out of [the] synagogue they should become;
43 ἠγάπησαν γὰρ τὴν δόξαν τῶν ἀνθρώπων
for they loved the glory – of men
μᾶλλον ἤπερ τὴν δόξαν τοῦ θεοῦ.
more than the glory – of God.
44 Ἰησοῦς δὲ ἔκραξεν καὶ εἶπεν· ὁ
But Jesus cried out and said: The
πιστεύων εἰς ἐμὲ οὐ πιστεύει εἰς ἐμὲ
[one] believing in me believes not in me
ἀλλὰ εἰς τὸν πέμψαντά με, **45** καὶ ὁ
but in the [one] having sent me, and the
θεωρῶν ἐμὲ θεωρεῖ τὸν πέμψαντά με.
[one] beholding me beholds the [one] having sent me.
46 ἐγὼ φῶς εἰς τὸν κόσμον ἐλήλυθα,
I a light into the world have come,
ἵνα πᾶς ὁ πιστεύων εἰς ἐμὲ ἐν τῇ
that everyone believing in me in the
σκοτίᾳ μὴ μείνῃ. **47** καὶ ἐάν τίς μου
darkness may not remain. And if anyone of me
ἀκούσῃ τῶν ῥημάτων καὶ μὴ φυλάξῃ,
hears the words and keeps not,
ἐγὼ οὐ κρίνω αὐτόν· οὐ γὰρ ἦλθον
I do not judge him; for I came not

ing. 36 Put your trust in the
light while you have it, so
that you may become sons
of light." When he had finished speaking, Jesus left
and hid himself from them.

The Jews Continue in Their Unbelief

37 Even after Jesus had
done all these miraculous
signs in their presence,
they still would not believe
in him. 38 This was to fulfill
the word of Isaiah the
prophet:

"Lord, who has believed
our message
and to whom has the
arm of the Lord
been revealed?"[k]

39 For this reason they
could not believe, because,
as Isaiah says elsewhere:

40 "He has blinded their
eyes
and deadened their
hearts,
so they can neither see
with their eyes,
nor understand with
their hearts,
nor turn—and I would
heal them."[l]

41 Isaiah said this because
he saw Jesus' glory and
spoke about him.
42 Yet at the same time
many even among the lead-
ers believed in him. But because of the Pharisees they
would not confess their
faith for fear they would be
put out of the synagogue;
43 for they loved praise from
men more than praise from
God.
44 Then Jesus cried out,
"When a man believes in
me, he does not believe in
me only, but in the one who
sent me. 45 When he looks
at me, he sees the one who
sent me. 46 I have come into
the world as a light, so that
no one who believes in me
should stay in darkness.
47 "As for the person who
hears my words but does
not keep them, I do not
judge him. For I did not

[k] *38* Isaiah 53:1
[l] *40* Isaiah 6:10

world. 48The one who re-
jects me and does not re-
ceive my word has a judge;
on the last day the word
that I have spoken will
serve as judge, 49for I have
not spoken on my own, but
the Father who sent me has
himself given me a com-
mandment about what to
say and what to speak.
50And I know that his commandment is eternal life.
What I speak, therefore, I
speak just as the Father has
told me."

ἵνα κρίνω τὸν κόσμον, ἀλλ' ἵνα σώσω
that I might judge the world, but that I might save
τὸν κόσμον. **48** ὁ ἀθετῶν ἐμὲ καὶ μὴ
the world. The [one] rejecting me and not
λαμβάνων τὰ ῥήματά μου ἔχει τὸν
receiving the words of me has the
κρίνοντα αὐτόν· ὁ λόγος ὃν ἐλάλησα,
[one] judging him; the word which I spoke,
ἐκεῖνος κρινεῖ αὐτὸν ἐν τῇ ἐσχάτῃ ἡμέρᾳ.
that will judge him in the last day.
49 ὅτι ἐγὼ ἐξ ἐμαυτοῦ οὐκ ἐλάλησα,
Because I of myself did not speak,
ἀλλ' ὁ πέμψας με πατὴρ αὐτός μοι
but [1]the [3]having sent [4]me [2]Father [5]he [7]me
ἐντολὴν δέδωκεν τί εἴπω καὶ τί
[8]commandment [6]has given what I may say and what
λαλήσω. **50** καὶ οἶδα ὅτι ἡ ἐντολὴ
I may speak. And I know that the commandment
αὐτοῦ ζωὴ αἰώνιός ἐστιν. ἃ οὖν ἐγὼ
of him life eternal is. What things therefore I
λαλῶ, καθὼς εἴρηκέν μοι ὁ πατήρ,
speak, as has said to me the Father,
οὕτως λαλῶ.
so I speak.

come to judge the world,
but to save it. 48There is a
judge for the one who re-
jects me and does not ac-
cept my words; that very
word which I spoke will
condemn him at the last
day. 49For I did not speak
of my own accord, but the
Father who sent me com-
manded me what to say and
how to say it. 50I know that
his command leads to eternal life. So whatever I say
is just what the Father has
told me to say."

Chapter 13

Jesus Washes the Disciples' Feet

NOW before the festival
of the Passover,
Jesus knew that his hour
had come to depart from
this world and go to the Father. Having loved his own
who were in the world, he
loved them to the end.
2The devil had already put
it into the heart of Judas
son of Simon Iscariot to betray him. And during sup-
per 3Jesus, knowing that
the Father had given all
things into his hands, and
that he had come from God
and was going to God, 4got
up from the table,[r] took off
his outer robe, and tied a
towel around himself.
5Then he poured water into
a basin and began to wash
the disciples' feet and to
wipe them with the towel
that was tied around him.
6He came to Simon Peter,
who said to him, "Lord, are
you going to wash my
feet?" 7Jesus answered,

13 Πρὸ δὲ τῆς ἑορτῆς τοῦ πάσχα
Now before the feast of the Passover
εἰδὼς ὁ Ἰησοῦς ὅτι ἦλθεν αὐτοῦ ἡ
[2]knowing – [1]Jesus that came of him the
ὥρα ἵνα μεταβῇ ἐκ τοῦ κόσμου τούτου
hour that he should remove out of – world this
πρὸς τὸν πατέρα, ἀγαπήσας τοὺς ἰδίους
to the Father, loving the(his) own
τοὺς ἐν τῷ κόσμῳ, εἰς τέλος ἠγάπησεν
– in the world, to [the] end he loved
αὐτούς. **2** καὶ δείπνου γινομένου, τοῦ
them. And supper taking place,[a] the
=during supper,
διαβόλου ἤδη βεβληκότος εἰς τὴν καρδίαν
devil now having put[a] into the heart
=as the devil had now put
ἵνα παραδοῖ αὐτὸν Ἰούδας Σίμωνος
that [4]should betray [5]him [1]Judas [2][son] of Simon
Ἰσκαριώτης, **3** εἰδὼς ὅτι πάντα ἔδωκεν
[3]Iscariot, knowing* that all things gave
αὐτῷ ὁ πατὴρ εἰς τὰς χεῖρας, καὶ
him the Father into the(his) hands, and
ὅτι ἀπὸ θεοῦ ἐξῆλθεν καὶ πρὸς τὸν
that from God he came forth and to –
θεὸν ὑπάγει, **4** ἐγείρεται ἐκ τοῦ δείπνου
God goes, he rises out of(from) the supper
καὶ τίθησιν τὰ ἱμάτια, καὶ λαβὼν
and places [aside] the(his) garments, and taking
λέντιον διέζωσεν ἑαυτόν· **5** εἶτα βάλλει
a towel he girded himself; then he puts
ὕδωρ εἰς τὸν νιπτῆρα, καὶ ἤρξατο νίπτειν
water into the basin, and began to wash
τοὺς πόδας τῶν μαθητῶν καὶ ἐκμάσσειν
the feet of the disciples and to wipe off
τῷ λεντίῳ ᾧ ἦν διεζωσμένος.
with the towel with which he was *having been* girded.
6 ἔρχεται οὖν πρὸς Σίμωνα Πέτρον·
He comes therefore to Simon Peter;
λέγει αὐτῷ· κύριε, σύ μου νίπτεις τοὺς
he says to him: Lord, thou of me washest the

Chapter 13

Jesus Washes His Disciples' Feet

IT was just before the
Passover Feast. Jesus
knew that the time had
come for him to leave this
world and go to the Father.
Having loved his own who
were in the world, he now
showed them the full extent
of his love.[m]
2The evening meal was
being served, and the devil
had already prompted Ju-
das Iscariot, son of Simon,
to betray Jesus. 3Jesus
knew that the Father had
put all things under his
power, and that he had
come from God and was re-
turning to God; 4so he got
up from the meal, took off
his outer clothing, and
wrapped a towel around his
waist. 5After that, he
poured water into a basin
and began to wash his disciples' feet, drying them with
the towel that was wrapped
around him.
6He came to Simon Peter,
who said to him, "Lord,
are you going to wash my
feet?"

[r] Gk *from supper*

* Repeated from ver. 1; the subject is therefore again "Jesus".

[m] 1 Or *he loved them to the last*

"You do not know now
what I am doing, but later
you will understand." 8 Peter said to him, "You will
never wash my feet." Jesus
answered, "Unless I wash
you, you have no share
with me." 9 Simon Peter
said to him, "Lord, not my
feet only but also my hands
and my head!" 10 Jesus said
to him, "One who has
bathed does not need to
wash, except for the feet,[s]
but is entirely clean. And
you[t] are clean, though not
all of you." 11 For he knew
who was to betray him; for
this reason he said, "Not all
of you are clean."
12 After he had washed
their feet, had put on his
robe, and had returned to
the table, he said to them,
"Do you know what I have
done to you? 13 You call me
Teacher and Lord—and
you are right, for that is
what I am. 14 So if I, your
Lord and Teacher, have
washed your feet, you also
ought to wash one anoth-
er's feet. 15 For I have set
you an example, that you
also should do as I have
done to you. 16 Very truly,
I tell you, servants[u] are not
greater than their master,
nor are messengers greater
than the one who sent
them. 17 If you know these
things, you are blessed if
you do them. 18 I am not
speaking of all of you; I
know whom I have chosen.
But it is to fulfill the scripture, 'The one who ate my
bread[v] has lifted his heel

[s] Other ancient authorities lack *except for the feet*
[t] The Greek word for *you* here is plural
[u] Gk *slaves*
[v] Other ancient authorities read *ate bread with me*

πόδας; 7 ἀπεκρίθη Ἰησοῦς καὶ εἶπεν αὐτῷ·
feet? Answered Jesus and said to him :
ὃ ἐγὼ ποιῶ σὺ οὐκ οἶδας ἄρτι,
What I am doing thou knowest not yet,
γνώσῃ δὲ μετὰ ταῦτα. 8 λέγει αὐτῷ
but thou wilt know after these things. Says to him
Πέτρος· οὐ μὴ νίψῃς μου τοὺς πόδας
Peter : By no means shalt thou wash of me the feet
εἰς τὸν αἰῶνα. ἀπεκρίθη Ἰησοῦς αὐτῷ·
unto the age. [2]Answered [1]Jesus [3]him :
ἐὰν μὴ νίψω σε, οὐκ ἔχεις μέρος μετ'
Unless I wash thee, thou hast no part with
ἐμοῦ. 9 λέγει αὐτῷ Σίμων Πέτρος·
me. Says to him Simon Peter :
κύριε, μὴ τοὺς πόδας μου μόνον ἀλλὰ
Lord, not the feet of me only but
καὶ τὰς χεῖρας καὶ τὴν κεφαλήν. 10 λέγει
also the hands and the head. Says
αὐτῷ Ἰησοῦς· ὁ λελουμένος οὐκ ἔχει
to him Jesus : The [one] having been bathed has not
χρείαν [εἰ μὴ τοὺς πόδας] νίψασθαι,
need except the feet to wash,
ἀλλ' ἔστιν καθαρὸς ὅλος· καὶ ὑμεῖς
but is clean wholly; and ye
καθαροί ἐστε, ἀλλ' οὐχὶ πάντες. 11 ᾔδει
clean are, but not all. he knew
γὰρ τὸν παραδιδόντα αὐτόν· διὰ τοῦτο
For the [one] betraying him; therefore
εἶπεν ὅτι οὐχὶ πάντες καθαροί ἐστε.
he said[,] – Not all clean ye are.
12 Ὅτε οὖν ἔνιψεν τοὺς πόδας αὐτῶν
When therefore he washed the feet of them
καὶ ἔλαβεν τὰ ἱμάτια αὐτοῦ καὶ ἀνέπεσεν
and took the garments of him and reclined
πάλιν, εἶπεν αὐτοῖς· γινώσκετε τί πε-
again, he said to them : Do ye know what I
ποίηκα ὑμῖν; 13 ὑμεῖς φωνεῖτέ με· ὁ
have done to you? Ye call me : The
διδάσκαλος καὶ ὁ κύριος, καὶ καλῶς
Teacher and the Lord, and well
λέγετε· εἰμὶ γάρ. 14 εἰ οὖν ἐγὼ ἔνιψα
ye say; for I am. If therefore I washed
ὑμῶν τοὺς πόδας ὁ κύριος καὶ ὁ
of you the feet the Lord and the
διδάσκαλος, καὶ ὑμεῖς ὀφείλετε ἀλλήλων
Teacher, also ye ought of one another
νίπτειν τοὺς πόδας· 15 ὑπόδειγμα γὰρ
to wash the feet; for an example
ἔδωκα ὑμῖν ἵνα καθὼς ἐγὼ ἐποίησα
I gave you that as I did
ὑμῖν καὶ ὑμεῖς ποιῆτε. 16 ἀμὴν ἀμὴν
to you also ye may do. Truly truly
λέγω ὑμῖν, οὐκ ἔστιν δοῦλος μείζων
I tell you, is not a slave greater [than]
τοῦ κυρίου αὐτοῦ, οὐδὲ ἀπόστολος μείζων
the lord of him, nor a sent one greater [than]
τοῦ πέμψαντος αὐτόν. 17 εἰ ταῦτα
the [one] sending him. If these things
οἴδατε, μακάριοί ἐστε ἐὰν ποιῆτε αὐτά.
ye know, blessed are ye if ye do them.
18 Οὐ περὶ πάντων ὑμῶν λέγω· ἐγὼ
Not concerning [2]all [1]you I speak; I
οἶδα τίνας ἐξελεξάμην· ἀλλ' ἵνα ἡ
know whom I chose; but that the
γραφὴ πληρωθῇ· ὁ τρώγων μου τὸν
scripture may be fulfilled : The [one] eating of me the

7 Jesus replied, "You do
not realize now what I am
doing, but later you will understand."
8 "No," said Peter, "you
shall never wash my feet."
Jesus answered, "Unless
I wash you, you have no
part with me."
9 "Then, Lord," Simon
Peter replied, "not just my
feet but my hands and my
head as well!"
10 Jesus answered, "A
person who has had a bath
needs only to wash his feet;
his whole body is clean.
And you are clean, though
not every one of you."
11 For he knew who was going to betray him, and that
was why he said not every
one was clean.
12 When he had finished
washing their feet, he put
on his clothes and returned
to his place. "Do you un-
derstand what I have done
for you?" he asked them.
13 "You call me 'Teacher'
and 'Lord,' and rightly so,
for that is what I am. 14 Now
that I, your Lord and
Teacher, have washed your
feet, you also should wash
one another's feet. 15 I have
set you an example that
you should do as I have
done for you. 16 I tell you
the truth, no servant is
greater than his master, nor
is a messenger greater than
the one who sent him.
17 Now that you know these
things, you will be blessed
if you do them.

Jesus Predicts His Betrayal

18 "I am not referring to
all of you; I know those I
have chosen. But this is to
fulfill the scripture: 'He
who shares my bread has

against me.' 19 I tell you this
now, before it occurs, so
that when it does occur,
you may believe that I am
he.[w] 20 Very truly, I tell
you, whoever receives one
whom I send receives me;
and whoever receives me
receives him who sent me."

Jesus Foretells His Betrayal

21 After saying this
Jesus was troubled in spirit, and declared, "Very truly, I tell you, one of you
will betray me." 22 The disciples looked at one another, uncertain of whom he
was speaking. 23 One of his
disciples—the one whom
Jesus loved—was reclining
next to him; 24 Simon Peter
therefore motioned to him
to ask Jesus of whom he
was speaking. 25 So while
reclining next to Jesus, he
asked him, "Lord, who is
it?" 26 Jesus answered, "It
is the one to whom I give
this piece of bread when I
have dipped it in the
dish."[x] So when he had
dipped the piece of bread,
he gave it to Judas son of
Simon Iscariot.[y] 27 After
he received the piece of
bread,[z] Satan entered into
him. Jesus said to him, "Do
quickly what you are going
to do." 28 Now no one at the
table knew why he said this
to him. 29 Some thought
that, because Judas had the
common purse, Jesus was
telling him, "Buy what we
need for the festival"; or,
that he should give some-
thing to the poor. 30 So, after receiving the piece of
bread, he immediately

ἄρτον ἐπῆρεν ἐπ' ἐμὲ τὴν πτέρναν αὐτοῦ.
bread lifted up against me the heel of him.
19 ἀπ' ἄρτι λέγω ὑμῖν πρὸ τοῦ γενέσθαι,
From now I tell you before the to happen, =it happens,
ἵνα πιστεύητε ὅταν γένηται ὅτι ἐγώ
that ye may believe when it happens that I
εἰμι. 20 ἀμὴν ἀμὴν λέγω ὑμῖν, ὁ
am. Truly truly I say to you, the
λαμβάνων ἄν τινα πέμψω ἐμὲ λαμβάνει,
[one] receiving whomever I may send me receives,
ὁ δὲ ἐμὲ λαμβάνων λαμβάνει τὸν
and the [one] me receiving receives the [one]
πέμψαντά με. 21 ταῦτα εἰπὼν Ἰησοῦς
having sent me. These things saying Jesus
ἐταράχθη τῷ πνεύματι καὶ ἐμαρτύρησεν
was troubled in the(his) spirit and witnessed
καὶ εἶπεν· ἀμὴν ἀμὴν λέγω ὑμῖν ὅτι
and said: Truly truly I tell you that
εἷς ἐξ ὑμῶν παραδώσει με. 22 ἔβλεπον
one of you will betray me. Looked
εἰς ἀλλήλους οἱ μαθηταὶ ἀπορούμενοι περὶ
at one another the disciples being perplexed about
τίνος λέγει. 23 ἦν ἀνακείμενος εἷς ἐκ
whom he speaks. Was reclining one of
τῶν μαθητῶν αὐτοῦ ἐν τῷ κόλπῳ τοῦ
the disciples of him in the bosom –
Ἰησοῦ, ὃν ἠγάπα ὁ Ἰησοῦς· 24 νεύει
of Jesus, whom [2]loved – [1]Jesus; nods
οὖν τούτῳ Σίμων Πέτρος καὶ λέγει
therefore to this one Simon Peter and says
αὐτῷ· εἰπὲ τίς ἐστιν περὶ οὗ λέγει.
to him: Say who it is about whom he speaks.
25 ἀναπεσὼν ἐκεῖνος οὕτως ἐπὶ τὸ
Falling back that one thus on the
στῆθος τοῦ Ἰησοῦ λέγει αὐτῷ· κύριε,
breast – of Jesus he says to him: Lord,
τίς ἐστιν; 26 ἀποκρίνεται οὖν ὁ Ἰησοῦς·
who is it? Answers therefore – Jesus:
ἐκεῖνός ἐστιν ᾧ ἐγὼ βάψω τὸ ψωμίον
That one it is to whom I shall dip the morsel
καὶ δώσω αὐτῷ. βάψας οὖν [τὸ]
and shall give him. Dipping therefore the
ψωμίον λαμβάνει καὶ δίδωσιν Ἰούδᾳ
morsel he takes and gives to Judas
Σίμωνος Ἰσκαριώτου. 27 καὶ μετὰ τὸ
[son] of Simon Iscariot. And after the
ψωμίον τότε εἰσῆλθεν εἰς ἐκεῖνον ὁ
morsel then entered into that one –
σατανᾶς. λέγει οὖν αὐτῷ Ἰησοῦς· ὃ
Satan. Says therefore to him Jesus: What
ποιεῖς ποίησον τάχιον. 28 τοῦτο [δὲ]
thou doest do quickly. But this
οὐδεὶς ἔγνω τῶν ἀνακειμένων πρὸς τί
no one knew of the [ones] reclining for what
εἶπεν αὐτῷ· 29 τινὲς γὰρ ἐδόκουν, ἐπεὶ
he told him; for some thought, since
τὸ γλωσσόκομον εἶχεν Ἰούδας, ὅτι λέγει
[2]the [3]bag [4]had [1]Judas, that tells
αὐτῷ Ἰησοῦς· ἀγόρασον ὧν χρείαν
him Jesus: Buy [the] things of which need
ἔχομεν εἰς τὴν ἑορτήν, ἢ τοῖς πτωχοῖς
we have for the feast, or to the poor
ἵνα τι δῷ. 30 λαβὼν οὖν τὸ
that something he should give. Having taken therefore the

lifted up his heel against
me.'[n]
19 "I am telling you now
before it happens, so that
when it does happen you
will believe that I am He.
20 I tell you the truth, whoever accepts anyone I send
accepts me; and whoever
accepts me accepts the one
who sent me."
21 After he had said this,
Jesus was troubled in spirit
and testified, "I tell you the
truth, one of you is going to
betray me."
22 His disciples stared at
one another, at a loss to
know which of them he
meant. 23 One of them, the
disciple whom Jesus loved,
was reclining next to him.
24 Simon Peter motioned to
this disciple and said, "Ask
him which one he means."
25 Leaning back against
Jesus, he asked him,
"Lord, who is it?"
26 Jesus answered, "It is
the one to whom I will give
this piece of bread when I
have dipped it in the dish."
Then, dipping the piece of
bread, he gave it to Judas
Iscariot, son of Simon.
27 As soon as Judas took the
bread, Satan entered into
him.
"What you are about to
do, do quickly," Jesus told
him, 28 but no one at the
meal understood why Jesus
said this to him. 29 Since Judas had charge of the money, some thought Jesus was
telling him to buy what was
needed for the Feast, or to
give something to the poor.
30 As soon as Judas had tak-

[w] Gk *I am*
[x] Gk *dipped it*
[y] Other ancient authorities read *Judas Iscariot son of Simon*; others, *Judas son of Simon from Karyot* (Kerioth)
[z] Gk *After the piece of bread*

[n] *18* Psalm 41:9

went out. And it was night.

The New Commandment

31 When he had gone
out, Jesus said, "Now the
Son of Man has been glorified, and God has been glorified in him. 32 If God has
been glorified in him,[a] God
will also glorify him in himself and will glorify him at
once. 33 Little children, I
am with you only a little
longer. You will look for
me; and as I said to the
Jews so now I say to you,
'Where I am going, you
cannot come.' 34 I give you
a new commandment, that
you love one another. Just
as I have loved you, you
also should love one another. 35 By this everyone will
know that you are my disciples, if you have love for
one another."

Jesus Foretells Peter's Denial

36 Simon Peter said to
him, "Lord, where are you
going?" Jesus answered,
"Where I am going, you
cannot follow me now; but
you will follow afterward."
37 Peter said to him, "Lord,
why can I not follow you
now? I will lay down my
life for you." 38 Jesus answered, "Will you lay
down your life for me?
Very truly, I tell you, before the cock crows, you
will have denied me three
times.

Chapter 14

Jesus the Way to the Father

"DO not let your
hearts be trou-
bled. Believe[b] in God, believe also in me. 2 In my Father's house there are
many dwelling places. If it
were not so, would I have
told you that I go to prepare
a place for you?[c] 3 And if I
go and prepare a place for

[a] Other ancient authorities lack *If God has been glorified in him*

[b] Or *You believe*

[c] Or *If it were not so, I would have told you; for I go to prepare a place for you*

ψωμίον ἐκεῖνος ἐξῆλθεν εὐθύς· ἦν δὲ
morsel that one went out immediately; and it was

νύξ.
night.

31 Ὅτε οὖν ἐξῆλθεν, λέγει Ἰησοῦς·
When therefore he went out, says Jesus :

νῦν ἐδοξάσθη ὁ υἱὸς τοῦ ἀνθρώπου,
Now was(is) glorified the Son – of man,

καὶ ὁ θεὸς ἐδοξάσθη ἐν αὐτῷ· 32 εἰ
and – God was(is) glorified in him; if

ὁ θεὸς ἐδοξάσθη ἐν αὐτῷ, καὶ ὁ θεὸς
– God was(is) glorified in him, both – God

δοξάσει αὐτὸν ἐν αὐτῷ, καὶ εὐθὺς
will glorify him in him, and immediately

δοξάσει αὐτόν. 33 τεκνία, ἔτι μικρὸν
will glorify him. Children, yet a little while

μεθ' ὑμῶν εἰμι· ζητήσετέ με, καὶ καθὼς
with you I am; ye will seek me, and as

εἶπον τοῖς Ἰουδαίοις ὅτι ὅπου ἐγὼ
I said to the Jews that where I

ὑπάγω ὑμεῖς οὐ δύνασθε ἐλθεῖν, καὶ
go ye cannot *to* come, also

ὑμῖν λέγω ἄρτι. 34 Ἐντολὴν καινὴν
to you I say now. commandment A new

δίδωμι ὑμῖν, ἵνα ἀγαπᾶτε ἀλλήλους,
I give you, that ye love one another,

καθὼς ἠγάπησα ὑμᾶς ἵνα καὶ ὑμεῖς
as I loved you that also ye

ἀγαπᾶτε ἀλλήλους. 35 ἐν τούτῳ γνώσονται
love one another. By this will know

πάντες ὅτι ἐμοὶ μαθηταί ἐστε, ἐὰν
all men that to me[e] disciples ye are, if

ἀγάπην ἔχητε ἐν ἀλλήλοις. 36 Λέγει
love ye have among one another. Says

αὐτῷ Σίμων Πέτρος· κύριε, ποῦ ὑπάγεις;
to him Simon Peter : Lord, where goest thou?

ἀπεκρίθη Ἰησοῦς· ὅπου ὑπάγω οὐ δύνασαί
Answered Jesus : Where I go thou canst not

μοι νῦν ἀκολουθῆσαι, ἀκολουθήσεις δὲ
me now *to* follow, but thou wilt follow

ὕστερον. 37 λέγει αὐτῷ [ὁ] Πέτρος·
later. Says to him – Peter :

κύριε, διὰ τί οὐ δύναμαί σοι ἀκολουθῆσαι
Lord, why can I not thee *to* follow

ἄρτι; τὴν ψυχήν μου ὑπὲρ σοῦ θήσω.
yet? the life of me for thee I will lay down.

38 ἀποκρίνεται Ἰησοῦς· τὴν ψυχήν σου
Answers Jesus : The life of thee

ὑπὲρ ἐμοῦ θήσεις; ἀμὴν ἀμὴν λέγω
for me wilt thou lay down? truly truly I tell

σοι, οὐ μὴ ἀλέκτωρ φωνήσῃ ἕως οὗ
thee, by no means a cock crows until

ἀρνήσῃ με τρίς. 14 Μὴ ταρασσέσθω
thou deniest me thrice. Let not be troubled

ὑμῶν ἡ καρδία· πιστεύετε εἰς τὸν θεόν, καὶ
of you the heart; believe in – God, also

εἰς ἐμὲ πιστεύετε. 2 ἐν τῇ οἰκίᾳ τοῦ
in me believe. In the house of the

πατρός μου μοναὶ πολλαί εἰσιν· εἰ δὲ μή,
Father of me abodes many there are; otherwise,

εἶπον ἂν ὑμῖν· ὅτι πορεύομαι ἑτοιμάσαι
I would have told you; because I go to prepare

τόπον ὑμῖν· 3 καὶ ἐὰν πορευθῶ καὶ
a place for you; and if I go and

en the bread, he went out.
And it was night.

Jesus Predicts Peter's Denial

31 When he was gone,
Jesus said, "Now is the
Son of Man glorified and
God is glorified in him. 32 If
God is glorified in him,[o]
God will glorify the Son in
himself, and will glorify
him at once.
33 "My children, I will be
with you only a little longer. You will look for me,
and just as I told the Jews,
so I tell you now: Where I
am going, you cannot
come.
34 "A new command I
give you: Love one anoth-
er. As I have loved you, so
you must love one another.
35 By this all men will know
that you are my disciples, if
you love one another."
36 Simon Peter asked him,
"Lord, where are you go-
ing?"
Jesus replied, "Where I
am going, you cannot fol-
low now, but you will follow later."
37 Peter asked, "Lord,
why can't I follow you
now? I will lay down my life
for you."
38 Then Jesus answered,
"Will you really lay down
your life for me? I tell you
the truth, before the rooster crows, you will disown
me three times!

Chapter 14

Jesus Comforts His Disciples

"DO not let your
hearts be trou-
bled. Trust in God[p]; trust
also in me. 2 In my Father's
house are many rooms; if it
were not so, I would have
told you. I am going there
to prepare a place for you.
3 And if I go and prepare a

[o] 32 Many early manuscripts do not have *If God is glorified in him.*

[p] 1 Or *You trust in God*

you, I will come again and
will take you to myself, so
that where I am, there you
may be also. 4 And you
know the way to the place
where I am going."[d]
5 Thomas said to him,
"Lord, we do not know
where you are going. How
can we know the way?"
6 Jesus said to him, "I am
the way, and the truth, and
the life. No one comes to
the Father except through
me. 7 If you know me, you
will know[e] my Father also.
From now on you do know
him and have seen him."
8 Philip said to him,
"Lord, show us the Father,
and we will be satisfied."
9 Jesus said to him, "Have I
been with you all this time,
Philip, and you still do not
know me? Whoever has
seen me has seen the Fa-
ther. How can you say,
'Show us the Father'? 10 Do
you not believe that I am in
the Father and the Father is
in me? The words that I say
to you I do not speak on my
own; but the Father who
dwells in me does his
works. 11 Believe me that I
am in the Father and the
Father is in me; but if you
do not, then believe me because of the works them-
selves. 12 Very truly, I tell
you, the one who believes
in me will also do the works
that I do and, in fact, will
do greater works than
these, because I am going
to the Father. 13 I will do
whatever you ask in my
name, so that the Father
may be glorified in the Son.
14 If in my name you ask
me[f] for anything, I will do
it.

[d] Other ancient authorities read *Where I am going you know, and the way you know*
[e] Other ancient authorities read *If you had known me, you would have known*
[f] Other ancient authorities lack *me*

ἑτοιμάσω τόπον ὑμῖν, πάλιν ἔρχομαι καὶ
prepare a place for you, again I come and
παραλήμψομαι ὑμᾶς πρὸς ἐμαυτόν, ἵνα
will receive you to myself, that
ὅπου εἰμὶ ἐγὼ καὶ ὑμεῖς ἦτε. **4** Καὶ
where am I also ye may be. And
ὅπου ἐγὼ ὑπάγω οἴδατε τὴν ὁδόν.
where I go ye know the way.
5 λέγει αὐτῷ Θωμᾶς· κύριε, οὐκ οἴδαμεν
Says to him Thomas: Lord, we know not
ποῦ ὑπάγεις· πῶς οἴδαμεν τὴν ὁδόν;
where thou goest; how do we know the way?
6 λέγει αὐτῷ Ἰησοῦς· ἐγώ εἰμι ἡ ὁδὸς
Says to him Jesus: I am the way
καὶ ἡ ἀλήθεια καὶ ἡ ζωή· οὐδεὶς ἔρχεται
and the truth and the life; no one comes
πρὸς τὸν πατέρα εἰ μὴ δι' ἐμοῦ. **7** εἰ
to the Father except through me. If
ἐγνώκειτέ με, καὶ τὸν πατέρα μου
ye had known me, also the Father of me
ἂν ᾔδειτε. ἀπ' ἄρτι γινώσκετε αὐτὸν
ye would have known. From now ye know him
καὶ ἑωράκατε. **8** Λέγει αὐτῷ Φίλιππος·
and have seen. Says to him Philip:
κύριε, δεῖξον ἡμῖν τὸν πατέρα, καὶ
Lord, show us the Father, and
ἀρκεῖ ἡμῖν. **9** λέγει αὐτῷ ὁ Ἰησοῦς·
it suffices for us. Says to him – Jesus:
τοσοῦτον χρόνον μεθ' ὑμῶν εἰμι καὶ
So long time with you I am and
οὐκ ἔγνωκάς με, Φίλιππε; ὁ ἑωρακὼς
thou hast not known me, Philip? The [one] having seen
ἐμὲ ἑώρακεν τὸν πατέρα· πῶς σὺ λέγεις·
me has seen the Father; how thou sayest:
δεῖξον ἡμῖν τὸν πατέρα; **10** οὐ πιστεύεις
Show us the Father? believest thou not
ὅτι ἐγὼ ἐν τῷ πατρὶ καὶ ὁ πατὴρ
that I in the Father and the Father
ἐν ἐμοί ἐστιν; τὰ ῥήματα ἃ ἐγὼ λέγω
in me is? the words which I say
ὑμῖν ἀπ' ἐμαυτοῦ οὐ λαλῶ· ὁ δὲ πατὴρ
to you from myself I speak not; but the Father
ἐν ἐμοὶ μένων ποιεῖ τὰ ἔργα αὐτοῦ.
in me remaining does the works of him.
11 πιστεύετέ μοι ὅτι ἐγὼ ἐν τῷ πατρὶ
Believe ye me that I in the Father
καὶ ὁ πατὴρ ἐν ἐμοί· εἰ δὲ μή, διὰ
and the Father in me; otherwise, because of
τὰ ἔργα αὐτὰ πιστεύετε. **12** ἀμὴν ἀμὴν
the works [them]selves believe ye. Truly truly
λέγω ὑμῖν, ὁ πιστεύων εἰς ἐμὲ τὰ
I tell you, the [one] believing in me the
ἔργα ἃ ἐγὼ ποιῶ κἀκεῖνος ποιήσει,
works which I do that one also will do,
καὶ μείζονα τούτων ποιήσει, ὅτι ἐγὼ
and greater [than] these he will do, because I
πρὸς τὸν πατέρα πορεύομαι· **13** καὶ ὅ τι
to the Father am going; and what-
ἂν αἰτήσητε ἐν τῷ ὀνόματί μου, τοῦτο
ever ye ask in the name of me, this
ποιήσω, ἵνα δοξασθῇ ὁ πατὴρ ἐν τῷ
I will do, that may be glorified the Father in the
υἱῷ. **14** ἐάν τι αἰτήσητέ με ἐν τῷ
Son. If anything ye ask me in the
ὀνόματί μου, ἐγὼ ποιήσω. **15** Ἐὰν
name of me, I will do. If

place for you, I will come
back and take you to be
with me that you also may
be where I am. 4 You know
the way to the place where
I am going."

Jesus the Way to the Father

5 Thomas said to him,
"Lord, we don't know
where you are going, so
how can we know the
way?"
6 Jesus answered, "I am
the way and the truth and
the life. No one comes to
the Father except through
me. 7 If you really knew me,
you would know[q] my Fa-
ther as well. From now on,
you do know him and have
seen him."
8 Philip said, "Lord, show
us the Father and that will
be enough for us."
9 Jesus answered: "Don't
you know me, Philip, even
after I have been among
you such a long time? Anyone who has seen me has
seen the Father. How can
you say, 'Show us the Fa-
ther'? 10 Don't you believe
that I am in the Father, and
that the Father is in me?
The words I say to you are
not just my own. Rather, it
is the Father, living in me,
who is doing his work.
11 Believe me when I say
that I am in the Father and
the Father is in me; or at
least believe on the evi-
dence of the miracles themselves. 12 I tell you the
truth, anyone who has faith
in me will do what I have
been doing. He will do even
greater things than these,
because I am going to the
Father. 13 And I will do
whatever you ask in my
name, so that the Son may
bring glory to the Father.
14 You may ask me for anything in my name, and I will
do it.

[q] 7 Some early manuscripts *If you really have known me, you will know*

The Promise of the Holy Spirit

15 "If you love me, you
will keep[g] my command-
ments. 16 And I will ask the
Father, and he will give you
another Advocate,[h] to be
with you forever. 17 This is
the Spirit of truth, whom
the world cannot receive,
because it neither sees him
nor knows him. You know
him, because he abides
with you, and he will be in[i]
you.
18 "I will not leave you
orphaned; I am coming to
you. 19 In a little while the
world will no longer see
me, but you will see me;
because I live, you also will
live. 20 On that day you will
know that I am in my Fa-
ther, and you in me, and I
in you. 21 They who have
my commandments and
keep them are those who
love me; and those who
love me will be loved by my
Father, and I will love them
and reveal myself to them."
22 Judas (not Iscariot) said
to him, "Lord, how is it that
you will reveal yourself to
us, and not to the world?"
23 Jesus answered him,
"Those who love me will
keep my word, and my Fa-
ther will love them, and we
will come to them and
make our home with them.
24 Whoever does not love
me does not keep my
words; and the word that
you hear is not mine, but is
from the Father who sent
me.
25 "I have said these

[g] Other ancient authorities read *me, keep*
[h] Or *Helper*
[i] Or *among*

ἀγαπᾶτέ με, τὰς ἐντολὰς τὰς ἐμὰς
ye love me, *the* [2]commandments – [1]my
τηρήσετε. **16** κἀγὼ ἐρωτήσω τὸν πατέρα
ye will keep. And I will request the Father
καὶ ἄλλον παράκλητον δώσει ὑμῖν, ἵνα
and another Comforter he will give you, that
ᾖ μεθ' ὑμῶν εἰς τὸν αἰῶνα, **17** τὸ
he may be with you unto the age, the
πνεῦμα τῆς ἀληθείας, ὃ ὁ κόσμος
Spirit – of truth, which* the world
οὐ δύναται λαβεῖν, ὅτι οὐ θεωρεῖ αὐτὸ
cannot *to* receive, because it beholds not it*
οὐδὲ γινώσκει· ὑμεῖς γινώσκετε αὐτό,
nor knows; ye know it,*
ὅτι παρ' ὑμῖν μένει καὶ ἐν ὑμῖν ἔσται.
because with you he remains and in you will be.
18 Οὐκ ἀφήσω ὑμᾶς ὀρφανούς, ἔρχομαι
I will not leave you orphans, I am coming
πρὸς ὑμᾶς. **19** ἔτι μικρὸν καὶ ὁ κόσμος
to you. Yet a little and the world
με οὐκέτι θεωρεῖ, ὑμεῖς δὲ θεωρεῖτέ
me no longer beholds, but ye behold
με, ὅτι ἐγὼ ζῶ καὶ ὑμεῖς ζήσετε.
me, because I live also ye will live.
20 ἐν ἐκείνῃ τῇ ἡμέρᾳ γνώσεσθε ὑμεῖς
In that – day will know ye
ὅτι ἐγὼ ἐν τῷ πατρί μου καὶ ὑμεῖς
that I in the Father of me and ye
ἐν ἐμοὶ κἀγὼ ἐν ὑμῖν. **21** Ὁ ἔχων
in me and I in you. The [one] having
τὰς ἐντολάς μου καὶ τηρῶν αὐτάς,
the commandments of me and keeping them,
ἐκεῖνός ἐστιν ὁ ἀγαπῶν με· ὁ δὲ ἀγαπῶν
that is the [one] loving me; and the [one] loving
με ἀγαπηθήσεται ὑπὸ τοῦ πατρός μου,
me will be loved by the Father of me,
κἀγὼ ἀγαπήσω αὐτὸν καὶ ἐμφανίσω αὐτῷ
and I will love him and will manifest to him
ἐμαυτόν. **22** λέγει αὐτῷ Ἰούδας, οὐχ
myself. Says to him Judas, not
ὁ Ἰσκαριώτης· κύριε, καὶ τί γέγονεν
the Iscariot: Lord, and what has happened
ὅτι ἡμῖν μέλλεις ἐμφανίζειν σεαυτὸν καὶ
that to us thou art about to manifest thyself and
οὐχὶ τῷ κόσμῳ; **23** ἀπεκρίθη Ἰησοῦς
not to the world? Answered Jesus
καὶ εἶπεν αὐτῷ· ἐάν τις ἀγαπᾷ με,
and said to him: If anyone loves me,
τὸν λόγον μου τηρήσει, καὶ ὁ πατήρ
the word of me he will keep, and the Father
μου ἀγαπήσει αὐτόν, καὶ πρὸς αὐτὸν
of me will love him, and to him
ἐλευσόμεθα καὶ μονὴν παρ' αὐτῷ
we will come and abode with him
ποιησόμεθα. **24** ὁ μὴ ἀγαπῶν με τοὺς
we will make. The [one] not loving me the
λόγους μου οὐ τηρεῖ· καὶ ὁ λόγος ὃν
words of me keeps not; and the word which
ἀκούετε οὐκ ἔστιν ἐμὸς ἀλλὰ τοῦ
ye hear is not mine but [1]of the
πέμψαντός με πατρός. **25** Ταῦτα λελάληκα
[3]having sent [4]me [2]Father. These things I have spoken

*** The gender of these pronouns agrees, of course, with the antecedent πνεῦμα (neuter); and this has been kept though the personal Spirit of God is meant. Elsewhere, masculine pronouns are in fact used.**

Jesus Promises the Holy Spirit

15 "If you love me, you
will obey what I command.
16 And I will ask the Father,
and he will give you another Counselor to be with you
forever— 17 the Spirit of
truth. The world cannot accept him, because it neither
sees him nor knows him.
But you know him, for he
lives with you and will be[r]
in you. 18 I will not leave
you as orphans; I will come
to you. 19 Before long, the
world will not see me anymore, but you will see me.
Because I live, you also
will live. 20 On that day you
will realize that I am in my
Father, and you are in me,
and I am in you. 21 Whoever
has my commands and
obeys them, he is the one
who loves me. He who
loves me will be loved by
my Father, and I too will
love him and show myself
to him."
22 Then Judas (not Judas
Iscariot) said, "But, Lord,
why do you intend to show
yourself to us and not to the
world?"
23 Jesus replied, "If anyone loves me, he will obey
my teaching. My Father
will love him, and we will
come to him and make our
home with him. 24 He who
does not love me will not
obey my teaching. These
words you hear are not my
own; they belong to the Father who sent me.
25 "All this I have spoken

[r] *17* Some early manuscripts *and is*

things to you while I am
still with you. 26 But the
Advocate,[h] the Holy Spirit, whom the Father will
send in my name, will teach
you everything, and remind
you of all that I have said to
you. 27 Peace I leave with
you; my peace I give to
you. I do not give to you as
the world gives. Do not let
your hearts be troubled,
and do not let them be
afraid. 28 You heard me say
to you, 'I am going away,
and I am coming to you.' If
you loved me, you would
rejoice that I am going to
the Father, because the Father is greater than I. 29 And
now I have told you this before it occurs, so that when
it does occur, you may believe. 30 I will no longer talk
much with you, for the ruler of this world is coming.
He has no power over me;
31 but I do as the Father has
commanded me, so that the
world may know that I love
the Father. Rise, let us be
on our way.

ὑμῖν παρ' ὑμῖν μένων· **26** ὁ δὲ παρά-
to you with you remaining; but the Com-

κλητος, τὸ πνεῦμα τὸ ἅγιον ὃ πέμψει ὁ
forter, the Spirit – Holy which will send the

πατὴρ ἐν τῷ ὀνόματί μου, ἐκεῖνος ὑμᾶς
Father in the name of me, that one you

διδάξει πάντα καὶ ὑπομνήσει ὑμᾶς πάντα
will teach all things and remind you [of] all things

ἃ εἶπον ὑμῖν ἐγώ. **27** Εἰρήνην ἀφίημι
which [2]told [3]you [1]I. Peace I leave

ὑμῖν, εἰρήνην τὴν ἐμὴν δίδωμι ὑμῖν·
to you, [2]peace – [1]my I give you;

οὐ καθὼς ὁ κόσμος δίδωσιν ἐγὼ δίδωμι
not as the world gives I give

ὑμῖν. μὴ ταρασσέσθω ὑμῶν ἡ καρδία
you. Let not be troubled of you the heart

μηδὲ δειλιάτω. **28** ἠκούσατε ὅτι ἐγὼ
nor let it be fearful. Ye heard that I

εἶπον ὑμῖν· ὑπάγω καὶ ἔρχομαι πρὸς
told you: I go and come to

ὑμᾶς. εἰ ἠγαπᾶτέ με, ἐχάρητε ἂν ὅτι
you. If ye loved me, ye would have rejoiced that

πορεύομαι πρὸς τὸν πατέρα, ὅτι ὁ πατὴρ
I am going to the Father, because the Father

μείζων μού ἐστιν. **29** καὶ νῦν εἴρηκα
greater [than] me(I) is. And now I have told

ὑμῖν πρὶν γενέσθαι, ἵνα ὅταν γένηται
you before to happen, =it happens, that when it happens

πιστεύσητε. **30** οὐκέτι πολλὰ λαλήσω μεθ'
ye may believe. No longer many things I will speak with

ὑμῶν, ἔρχεται γὰρ ὁ τοῦ κόσμου ἄρχων·
you, for [5]is coming [1]the [3]of the [4]world [2]ruler;

καὶ ἐν ἐμοὶ οὐκ ἔχει οὐδέν, **31** ἀλλ'
and in me he has not no(any)thing, but

ἵνα γνῷ ὁ κόσμος ὅτι ἀγαπῶ τὸν
that may know the world that I love the

πατέρα, καὶ καθὼς ἐνετείλατό μοι ὁ
Father, and as commanded me the

πατήρ, οὕτως ποιῶ. Ἐγείρεσθε, ἄγωμεν
Father, so I do. Rise, let us go

ἐντεῦθεν.
hence.

while still with you. 26But
the Counselor, the Holy
Spirit, whom the Father
will send in my name, will
teach you all things and will
remind you of everything I
have said to you. 27Peace I
leave with you; my peace I
give you. I do not give to
you as the world gives. Do
not let your hearts be troubled and do not be afraid.
28"You heard me say, 'I
am going away and I am
coming back to you.' If you
loved me, you would be
glad that I am going to the
Father, for the Father is
greater than I. 29I have told
you now before it happens,
so that when it does happen
you will believe. 30I will not
speak with you much lon-
ger, for the prince of this
world is coming. He has no
hold on me, 31but the world
must learn that I love the
Father and that I do exactly
what my Father has com-
manded me.
"Come now; let us leave.

Chapter 15

Jesus the True Vine

"I am the true vine,
and my Father is the
vinegrower. 2He removes
every branch in me that
bears no fruit. Every
branch that bears fruit he
prunes[j] to make it bear
more fruit. 3You have al-
ready been cleansed[j] by
the word that I have spoken
to you. 4Abide in me as I
abide in you. Just as the
branch cannot bear fruit by
itself unless it abides in the
vine, neither can you un-
less you abide in me. 5I am

15 Ἐγώ εἰμι ἡ ἄμπελος ἡ ἀληθινή,
I am the vine – true,

καὶ ὁ πατήρ μου ὁ γεωργός ἐστιν.
and the Father of me the husbandman is.

2 πᾶν κλῆμα ἐν ἐμοὶ μὴ φέρον καρπόν,
Every branch in me not bearing fruit,

αἴρει αὐτό, καὶ πᾶν τὸ καρπὸν φέρον,
he takes it, and every [branch] the fruit bearing,

καθαίρει αὐτὸ ἵνα καρπὸν πλείονα φέρῃ.
he prunes it that fruit more it may bear.

3 ἤδη ὑμεῖς καθαροί ἐστε διὰ τὸν λόγον
Now ye clean are because of the word

ὃν λελάληκα ὑμῖν· **4** μείνατε ἐν ἐμοί,
which I have spoken to you; remain in me,

κἀγὼ ἐν ὑμῖν. καθὼς τὸ κλῆμα
and I in you. As the branch

οὐ δύναται καρπὸν φέρειν ἀφ' ἑαυτοῦ ἐὰν μὴ
cannot fruit *to* bear from itself unless

μένῃ ἐν τῇ ἀμπέλῳ, οὕτως οὐδὲ ὑμεῖς
it remains in the vine, so not ye

ἐὰν μὴ ἐν ἐμοὶ μένητε. **5** ἐγώ εἰμι
unless in me ye remain. I am

Chapter 15

The Vine and the Branches

"I AM the true vine,
and my Father is the
gardener. 2He cuts off every branch in me that bears
no fruit, while every
branch that does bear fruit
he prunes[s] so that it will be
even more fruitful. 3You
are already clean because
of the word I have spoken
to you. 4Remain in me, and
I will remain in you. No
branch can bear fruit by itself; it must remain in the
vine. Neither can you bear
fruit unless you remain in
me.

[j]The same Greek root refers to pruning and cleansing

[s]2 The Greek for *prunes* also means *cleans*.

the vine, you are the
branches. Those who abide
in me and I in them bear
much fruit, because apart
from me you can do noth-
ing. 6 Whoever does not
abide in me is thrown away
like a branch and withers;
such branches are gath-
ered, thrown into the fire,
and burned. 7 If you abide
in me, and my words abide
in you, ask for whatever
you wish, and it will be
done for you. 8 My Father
is glorified by this, that you
bear much fruit and be-
come[k] my disciples. 9 As
the Father has loved me, so
I have loved you; abide in
my love. 10 If you keep my
commandments, you will
abide in my love, just as I
have kept my Father's
commandments and abide
in his love. 11 I have said
these things to you so that
my joy may be in you, and
that your joy may be com-
plete.
12 "This is my com-
mandment, that you love
one another as I have loved
you. 13 No one has greater
love than this, to lay down
one's life for one's friends.
14 You are my friends if you
do what I command you.
15 I do not call you ser-
vants[l] any longer, because
the servant[m] does not
know what the master is
doing; but I have called you
friends, because I have
made known to you every-
thing that I have heard from
my Father. 16 You did not
choose me but I chose you.
And I appointed you to go
and bear fruit, fruit that will

[k] Or *be*
[l] Gk *slaves*
[m] Gk *slave*

ἡ ἄμπελος, ὑμεῖς τὰ κλήματα. ὁ μένων
the vine, ye the branches. The [one] remaining
ἐν ἐμοὶ κἀγὼ ἐν αὐτῷ, οὗτος φέρει
in me and I in him, this one bears
καρπὸν πολύν, ὅτι χωρὶς ἐμοῦ οὐ δύνασθε
fruit much, because apart from me ye cannot
ποιεῖν οὐδέν. 6 ἐὰν μή τις μένῃ ἐν
to do no(any)thing. Unless anyone remains in
ἐμοί, ἐβλήθη ἔξω ὡς τὸ κλῆμα καὶ
me, he was(is) cast outside as the branch and
ἐξηράνθη, καὶ συνάγουσιν αὐτὰ καὶ εἰς
was(is) dried, and they gather them and into
τὸ πῦρ βάλλουσιν, καὶ καίεται. 7 ἐὰν
the fire they cast, and they are burned. If
μείνητε ἐν ἐμοὶ καὶ τὰ ῥήματά μου
ye remain in me and the words of me
ἐν ὑμῖν μείνῃ, ὃ ἐὰν θέλητε αἰτήσασθε,
in you remains, whatever ye wish ask,
καὶ γενήσεται ὑμῖν. 8 ἐν τούτῳ ἐδοξάσθη
and it shall happen to you. By this was glorified
ὁ πατήρ μου, ἵνα καρπὸν πολὺν φέρητε
the Father of me, that fruit much ye bear
καὶ γενήσεσθε ἐμοὶ μαθηταί. 9 καθὼς
and ye will be to me[e] disciples. As
ἠγάπησέν με ὁ πατήρ, κἀγὼ ὑμᾶς
loved me the Father, I also you
ἠγάπησα· μείνατε ἐν τῇ ἀγάπῃ τῇ ἐμῇ.
loved; remain ye in *the* [2]love – [1]my.
10 ἐὰν τὰς ἐντολάς μου τηρήσητε, μενεῖτε
If the commandments of me ye keep, ye will remain
ἐν τῇ ἀγάπῃ μου, καθὼς ἐγὼ τοῦ πατρός
in the love of me, as I of the Father
μου τὰς ἐντολὰς τετήρηκα καὶ μένω
of me the commandments have kept and remain
αὐτοῦ ἐν τῇ ἀγάπῃ. 11 Ταῦτα λελάληκα
of him in the love. These things I have spoken
ὑμῖν ἵνα ἡ χαρὰ ἡ ἐμὴ ἐν ὑμῖν ᾖ
to you that *the* [2]joy – [1]my in you may be
καὶ ἡ χαρὰ ὑμῶν πληρωθῇ. 12 αὕτη
and the joy of you may be filled. This
ἐστὶν ἡ ἐντολὴ ἡ ἐμή, ἵνα ἀγαπᾶτε
is *the* [2]commandment – [1]my, that ye love
ἀλλήλους καθὼς ἠγάπησα ὑμᾶς. 13 μείζονα
one another as I loved you. [1]Greater
ταύτης ἀγάπην οὐδεὶς ἔχει, ἵνα τις
[[3]than] [4]this [2]love no one has, that anyone
τὴν ψυχὴν αὐτοῦ θῇ ὑπὲρ τῶν φίλων
the life of him should lay down for the friends
αὐτοῦ. 14 ὑμεῖς φίλοι μού ἐστε, ἐὰν
of him. Ye friends of me are, if
ποιῆτε ὃ ἐγὼ ἐντέλλομαι ὑμῖν. 15 οὐκέτι
ye do what I command you. No longer
λέγω ὑμᾶς δούλους, ὅτι ὁ δοῦλος οὐκ οἶδεν
I call you slaves, because the slave knows not
τί ποιεῖ αὐτοῦ ὁ κύριος· ὑμᾶς δὲ
what does of him the lord; but you
εἴρηκα φίλους, ὅτι πάντα ἃ ἤκουσα
I have called friends, because all things which I heard
παρὰ τοῦ πατρός μου ἐγνώρισα ὑμῖν.
from the Father of me I made known to you.
16 οὐχ ὑμεῖς με ἐξελέξασθε, ἀλλ' ἐγὼ
Not ye me chose, but I
ἐξελεξάμην ὑμᾶς, καὶ ἔθηκα ὑμᾶς ἵνα
chose you, and appointed you that
ὑμεῖς ὑπάγητε καὶ καρπὸν φέρητε καὶ
ye should go and fruit should bear and

5 "I am the vine; you are
the branches. If a man remains in me and I in him, he
will bear much fruit; apart
from me you can do noth-
ing. 6 If anyone does not remain in me, he is like a
branch that is thrown away
and withers; such branches
are picked up, thrown into
the fire and burned. 7 If you
remain in me and my words
remain in you, ask whatever you wish, and it will be
given you. 8 This is to my
Father's glory, that you
bear much fruit, showing
yourselves to be my disciples.
9 "As the Father has
loved me, so have I loved
you. Now remain in my
love. 10 If you obey my
commands, you will remain
in my love, just as I have
obeyed my Father's com-
mands and remain in his
love. 11 I have told you this
so that my joy may be in
you and that your joy may
be complete. 12 My com-
mand is this: Love each
other as I have loved you.
13 Greater love has no one
than this, that he lay down
his life for his friends.
14 You are my friends if you
do what I command. 15 I no
longer call you servants,
because a servant does not
know his master's busi-
ness. Instead, I have called
you friends, for everything
that I learned from my Father I have made known to
you. 16 You did not choose
me, but I chose you and appointed you to go and bear

last, so that the Father will
give you whatever you ask
him in my name. 17 I am giving you these commands so
that you may love one an-
other.

The World's Hatred

18 "If the world hates
you, be aware that it hated
me before it hated you. 19 If
you belonged to the
world,[n] the world would
love you as its own. Be-
cause you do not belong to
the world, but I have chosen you out of the world—
therefore the world hates
you. 20 Remember the word
that I said to you, 'Ser-
vants[o] are not greater than
their master.' If they persecuted me, they will persecute you; if they kept my
word, they will keep yours
also. 21 But they will do all
these things to you on account of my name, because
they do not know him who
sent me. 22 If I had not
come and spoken to them,
they would not have sin;
but now they have no ex-
cuse for their sin. 23 Whoever hates me hates my Father also. 24 If I had not
done among them the
works that no one else did,
they would not have sin.
But now they have seen
and hated both me and my
Father. 25 It was to fulfill
the word that is written in
their law, 'They hated me
without a cause.'
26 "When the Advo-
cate[p] comes, whom I will
send to you from the Fa-
ther, the Spirit of truth who
comes from the Father, he
will testify on my behalf.
27 You also are to testify because you have been with
me from the beginning.

[n] Gk *were of the world*
[o] Gk *Slaves*
[p] Or *Helper*

ὁ καρπὸς ὑμῶν μένῃ, ἵνα ὅ τι ἂν
the fruit of you should remain, that whatever
αἰτήσητε τὸν πατέρα ἐν τῷ ὀνόματί
ye may ask the Father in the name
μου δῷ ὑμῖν. 17 ταῦτα ἐντέλλομαι ὑμῖν,
of me he may give you. These things I command you,
ἵνα ἀγαπᾶτε ἀλλήλους. 18 Εἰ ὁ κόσμος
that ye love one another. If the world
ὑμᾶς μισεῖ, γινώσκετε ὅτι ἐμὲ πρῶτον
you hates, ye know that me before
ὑμῶν μεμίσηκεν. 19 εἰ ἐκ τοῦ κόσμου ἦτε,
you it has hated. If of the world ye were,
ὁ κόσμος ἂν τὸ ἴδιον ἐφίλει· ὅτι δὲ
the world [1]would [3]the(its) [4]own [2]have loved; but because
ἐκ τοῦ κόσμου οὐκ ἐστέ, ἀλλ' ἐγὼ
of the world ye are not, but I
ἐξελεξάμην ὑμᾶς ἐκ τοῦ κόσμου, διὰ τοῦτο
chose you out of the world, therefore
μισεῖ ὑμᾶς ὁ κόσμος. 20 μνημονεύετε
hates you the world. Remember ye
τοῦ λόγου οὗ ἐγὼ εἶπον ὑμῖν· οὐκ
the word which I said to you: Not
ἔστιν δοῦλος μείζων τοῦ κυρίου αὐτοῦ.
is a slave greater [than] the lord of him.
εἰ ἐμὲ ἐδίωξαν, καὶ ὑμᾶς διώξουσιν·
If me they persecuted, also you they will persecute;
εἰ τὸν λόγον μου ἐτήρησαν, καὶ τὸν
if the word of me they kept, also –
ὑμέτερον τηρήσουσιν. 21 ἀλλὰ ταῦτα πάντα
yours they will keep. But these things all
ποιήσουσιν εἰς ὑμᾶς διὰ τὸ ὄνομά μου,
they will do to you because of the name of me,
ὅτι οὐκ οἴδασιν τὸν πέμψαντά με.
because they know not the [one] having sent me.
22 εἰ μὴ ἦλθον καὶ ἐλάλησα αὐτοῖς, ἁμαρτίαν
Unless I came and spoke to them, sin
οὐκ εἴχοσαν· νῦν δὲ πρόφασιν οὐκ ἔχουσιν
they had not had; but now cloak they have not
περὶ τῆς ἁμαρτίας αὐτῶν. 23 ὁ ἐμὲ
concerning the sin of them. The [one] me
μισῶν καὶ τὸν πατέρα μου μισεῖ. 24 εἰ
hating also the Father of me hates. If
τὰ ἔργα μὴ ἐποίησα ἐν αὐτοῖς ἃ οὐδεὶς
the works I did not among them which no man
ἄλλος ἐποίησεν, ἁμαρτίαν οὐκ εἴχοσαν·
other did, sin they had not had;
νῦν δὲ καὶ ἑωράκασιν καὶ μεμισήκασιν
but now both they have seen and have hated
καὶ ἐμὲ καὶ τὸν πατέρα μου. 25 ἀλλ'
both me and the Father of me. But
ἵνα πληρωθῇ ὁ λόγος ὁ ἐν τῷ νόμῳ
that may be fulfilled the word – in the law
αὐτῶν γεγραμμένος ὅτι ἐμίσησάν με
of them *having been* written[,] – They hated me
δωρεάν. 26 Ὅταν ἔλθῃ ὁ παράκλητος
freely. When comes the Comforter
ὃν ἐγὼ πέμψω ὑμῖν παρὰ τοῦ πατρός,
whom I will send to you from the Father,
τὸ πνεῦμα τῆς ἀληθείας ὃ παρὰ τοῦ
the Spirit – of truth which from the
πατρὸς ἐκπορεύεται, ἐκεῖνος μαρτυρήσει
Father proceeds, that one will witness
περὶ ἐμοῦ· 27 καὶ ὑμεῖς δὲ μαρτυρεῖτε,
concerning me; [3]also [2]ye [1]and witness,
ὅτι ἀπ' ἀρχῆς μετ' ἐμοῦ ἐστε.
because from [the] beginning with me ye are.

fruit—fruit that will last.
Then the Father will give
you whatever you ask in
my name. 17 This is my
command: Love each oth-
er.

The World Hates the Disciples

18 "If the world hates you,
keep in mind that it hated
me first. 19 If you belonged
to the world, it would love
you as its own. As it is, you
do not belong to the world,
but I have chosen you out
of the world. That is why
the world hates you. 20 Remember the words I spoke
to you: 'No servant is
greater than his master.'[t]
If they persecuted me, they
will persecute you also. If
they obeyed my teaching,
they will obey yours also.
21 They will treat you this
way because of my name,
for they do not know the
One who sent me. 22 If I had
not come and spoken to
them, they would not be
guilty of sin. Now, however, they have no excuse for
their sin. 23 He who hates
me hates my Father as
well. 24 If I had not done
among them what no one
else did, they would not be
guilty of sin. But now they
have seen these miracles,
and yet they have hated
both me and my Father.
25 But this is to fulfill what is
written in their Law: 'They
hated me without reason.'[u]
26 "When the Counselor
comes, whom I will send to
you from the Father, the
Spirit of truth who goes out
from the Father, he will testify about me. 27 And you
also must testify, for you
have been with me from the
beginning.

[t] *20* John 13:16
[u] *25* Psalms 35:19; 69:4

Chapter 16

"I have said these
things to you to
keep you from stumbling.
2They will put you out of
the synagogues. Indeed, an
hour is coming when those
who kill you will think that
by doing so they are offering worship to God. 3And
they will do this because
they have not known the
Father or me. 4But I have
said these things to you so
that when their hour comes
you may remember that I
told you about them.

The Work of the Spirit

"I did not say these
things to you from the beginning, because I was with
you. 5But now I am going
to him who sent me; yet
none of you asks me,
'Where are you going?'
6But because I have said
these things to you, sorrow
has filled your hearts.
7Nevertheless I tell you the
truth: it is to your advantage that I go away, for if I
do not go away, the Advo-
cate[p] will not come to you;
but if I go, I will send him
to you. 8And when he
comes, he will prove the
world wrong about[q] sin
and righteousness and
judgment: 9about sin, be-
cause they do not believe in
me; 10about righteousness,
because I am going to the
Father and you will see me
no longer; 11about judg-
ment, because the ruler of
this world has been con-
demned.
12 "I still have many
things to say to you, but
you cannot bear them now.
13When the Spirit of truth
comes, he will guide you
into all the truth; for he will
not speak on his own, but
will speak whatever he
hears, and he will declare
to you the things that are to
come. 14He will glorify me,

[q] Or *convict the world of*

16 Ταῦτα λελάληκα ὑμῖν ἵνα μὴ
These things I have spoken to you that not
σκανδαλισθῆτε. **2** ἀποσυναγώγους ποιή-
ye be offended. Put away from [the] synagogue they
σουσιν ὑμᾶς· ἀλλ' ἔρχεται ὥρα ἵνα πᾶς ὁ
will make you; but comes an hour that everyone
ἀποκτείνας ὑμᾶς δόξῃ λατρείαν προσφέρειν
killing you thinks service to offer
τῷ θεῷ. **3** καὶ ταῦτα ποιήσουσιν ὅτι
– to God. And these things they will do because
οὐκ ἔγνωσαν τὸν πατέρα οὐδὲ ἐμέ.
they knew not the Father nor me.
4 ἀλλὰ ταῦτα λελάληκα ὑμῖν ἵνα ὅταν
But these things I have spoken to you that when
ἔλθῃ ἡ ὥρα αὐτῶν μνημονεύητε αὐτῶν,
comes the hour of them ye may remember them,
ὅτι ἐγὼ εἶπον ὑμῖν. Ταῦτα δὲ ὑμῖν
that I told you. And these things to you
ἐξ ἀρχῆς οὐκ εἶπον, ὅτι μεθ' ὑμῶν
from [the] beginning I said not, because with you
ἤμην. **5** νῦν δὲ ὑπάγω πρὸς τὸν πέμψαντά
I was. But now I am going to the [one] having sent
με, καὶ οὐδεὶς ἐξ ὑμῶν ἐρωτᾷ με·
me, and not one of you asks me:
ποῦ ὑπάγεις; **6** ἀλλ' ὅτι ταῦτα λελάληκα
Where goest thou? but because these things I have spoken
ὑμῖν, ἡ λύπη πεπλήρωκεν ὑμῶν τὴν
to you, – grief has filled of you the
καρδίαν. **7** ἀλλ' ἐγὼ τὴν ἀλήθειαν λέγω
heart. But I the truth tell
ὑμῖν, συμφέρει ὑμῖν ἵνα ἐγὼ ἀπέλθω.
you, it is expedient for you that I should go away.
ἐὰν γὰρ μὴ ἀπέλθω, ὁ παράκλητος
For if I go not away, the Comforter
οὐ μὴ ἔλθῃ πρὸς ὑμᾶς· ἐὰν δὲ πορευθῶ,
by no means comes to you; but if I go,
πέμψω αὐτὸν πρὸς ὑμᾶς. **8** καὶ ἐλθὼν
I will send him to you. And coming
ἐκεῖνος ἐλέγξει τὸν κόσμον περὶ ἁμαρτίας
that one will reprove the world concerning sin
καὶ περὶ δικαιοσύνης καὶ περὶ κρίσεως·
and concerning righteousness and concerning judgment;
9 περὶ ἁμαρτίας μέν, ὅτι οὐ πιστεύουσιν
concerning sin, – because they believe not
εἰς ἐμέ· **10** περὶ δικαιοσύνης δέ, ὅτι
in me; concerning righteousness, – because
πρὸς τὸν πατέρα ὑπάγω καὶ οὐκέτι
to the Father I am going and no longer
θεωρεῖτέ με· **11** περὶ δὲ κρίσεως, ὅτι
ye behold me; concerning – judgment, because
ὁ ἄρχων τοῦ κόσμου τούτου κέκριται.
the ruler – world of this has been judged.
12 Ἔτι πολλὰ ἔχω ὑμῖν λέγειν, ἀλλ'
Yet many things I have you to tell, but
οὐ δύνασθε βαστάζειν ἄρτι· **13** ὅταν δὲ
ye cannot *to* bear now; but when
ἔλθῃ ἐκεῖνος, τὸ πνεῦμα τῆς ἀληθείας,
comes that one, the Spirit – of truth,
ὁδηγήσει ὑμᾶς εἰς τὴν ἀλήθειαν πᾶσαν·
he will guide you into the truth all;
οὐ γὰρ λαλήσει ἀφ' ἑαυτοῦ, ἀλλ' ὅσα
for not will he speak from himself, but what things
ἀκούει λαλήσει, καὶ τὰ ἐρχόμενα
he hears he will speak, and the coming things
ἀναγγελεῖ ὑμῖν. **14** ἐκεῖνος ἐμὲ δοξάσει,
he will announce to you. That one me will glorify,

Chapter 16

"ALL this I have told
you so that you
will not go astray. 2They
will put you out of the synagogue; in fact, a time is
coming when anyone who
kills you will think he is offering a service to God.
3They will do such things
because they have not
known the Father or me. 4I
have told you this, so that
when the time comes you
will remember that I
warned you. I did not tell
you this at first because I
was with you.

The Work of the Holy Spirit

5"Now I am going to him
who sent me, yet none of
you asks me, 'Where are
you going?' 6Because I
have said these things, you
are filled with grief. 7But I
tell you the truth: It is for
your good that I am going
away. Unless I go away,
the Counselor will not
come to you; but if I go, I
will send him to you.
8When he comes, he will
convict the world of guilt[v]
in regard to sin and righteousness and judgment: 9in
regard to sin, because men
do not believe in me; 10in
regard to righteousness,
because I am going to the
Father, where you can see
me no longer; 11and in regard to judgment, because
the prince of this world
now stands condemned.
12"I have much more to
say to you, more than you
can now bear. 13But when
he, the Spirit of truth,
comes, he will guide you
into all truth. He will not
speak on his own; he will
speak only what he hears,
and he will tell you what is

[v] 8 Or *will expose the guilt of the world*

because he will take what is
mine and declare it to you.
15 All that the Father has is
mine. For this reason I said
that he will take what is
mine and declare it to you.

Sorrow Will Turn into Joy

16 "A little while, and
you will no longer see me,
and again a little while, and
you will see me." 17 Then
some of his disciples said to
one another, "What does
he mean by saying to us, 'A
little while, and you will no
longer see me, and again a
little while, and you will see
me'; and 'Because I am going to the Father'?" 18 They
said, "What does he mean
by this 'a little while'? We
do not know what he is
talking about." 19 Jesus
knew that they wanted to
ask him, so he said to them,
"Are you discussing among
yourselves what I meant
when I said, 'A little while,
and you will no longer see
me, and again a little while,
and you will see me'?
20 Very truly, I tell you, you
will weep and mourn, but
the world will rejoice; you
will have pain, but your
pain will turn into joy.
21 When a woman is in la-
bor, she has pain, because
her hour has come. But
when her child is born, she
no longer remembers the
anguish because of the joy
of having brought a human
being into the world. 22 So
you have pain now; but I
will see you again, and your
hearts will rejoice, and no
one will take your joy from
you. 23 On that day you will
ask nothing of me.[r] Very
truly, I tell you, if you ask
anything of the Father in
my name, he will give it to

ὅτι ἐκ τοῦ ἐμοῦ λήμψεται καὶ ἀναγγελεῖ
because of the of me* he will receive and will announce

ὑμῖν. 15 πάντα ὅσα ἔχει ὁ πατὴρ ἐμά
to you. All things which has the Father mine

ἐστιν· διὰ τοῦτο εἶπον ὅτι ἐκ τοῦ ἐμοῦ
is(are); therefore I said that of the of me*

λαμβάνει καὶ ἀναγγελεῖ ὑμῖν. 16 Μικρὸν
he receives and will announce to you. A little while

καὶ οὐκέτι θεωρεῖτέ με, καὶ πάλιν
and no longer ye behold me, and again

μικρὸν καὶ ὄψεσθέ με. 17 εἶπαν οὖν
a little while and ye will see me. Said therefore

ἐκ τῶν μαθητῶν αὐτοῦ πρὸς ἀλλήλους·
[some] of the disciples of him to one another:

τί ἐστιν τοῦτο ὃ λέγει ἡμῖν· μικρὸν
What is this which he tells us: A little while

καὶ οὐ θεωρεῖτέ με, καὶ πάλιν μικρὸν
and ye behold not me, and again a little while

καὶ ὄψεσθέ με; καί· ὅτι ὑπάγω
and ye will see me? and: Because I am going

πρὸς τὸν πατέρα; 18 ἔλεγον οὖν· τοῦτο
to the Father? They said therefore: [2]This

τί ἐστιν ὃ λέγει τὸ μικρόν; οὐκ οἴδαμεν
[1]what [3]is which he says[,] the "little while"? We do not know

τί λαλεῖ. 19 ἔγνω Ἰησοῦς ὅτι ἤθελον
what he speaks. Knew Jesus that they wished

αὐτὸν ἐρωτᾶν, καὶ εἶπεν αὐτοῖς· περὶ
him to question, and said to them: Concerning

τούτου ζητεῖτε μετ' ἀλλήλων ὅτι εἶπον·
this seek ye with one another because I said:

μικρὸν καὶ οὐ θεωρεῖτέ με, καὶ πάλιν
A little while and ye behold not me, and again

μικρὸν καὶ ὄψεσθέ με; 20 ἀμὴν ἀμὴν
a little while and ye will see me? Truly truly

λέγω ὑμῖν ὅτι κλαύσετε καὶ θρηνήσετε
I tell you that will weep and will lament

ὑμεῖς, ὁ δὲ κόσμος χαρήσεται· ὑμεῖς
ye, and the world will rejoice; ye

λυπηθήσεσθε, ἀλλ' ἡ λύπη ὑμῶν εἰς
will be grieved, but the grief of you into

χαρὰν γενήσεται. 21 ἡ γυνὴ ὅταν τίκτῃ
joy will become. The woman when she gives birth

λύπην ἔχει, ὅτι ἦλθεν ἡ ὥρα αὐτῆς·
grief has, because came the hour of her;

ὅταν δὲ γεννήσῃ τὸ παιδίον, οὐκέτι
but when she brings forth the child, no longer

μνημονεύει τῆς θλίψεως διὰ τὴν χαρὰν
she remembers the distress because of the joy

ὅτι ἐγεννήθη ἄνθρωπος εἰς τὸν κόσμον.
that was born a man into the world.

22 καὶ ὑμεῖς οὖν νῦν μὲν λύπην ἔχετε·
And ye therefore now indeed grief have;

πάλιν δὲ ὄψομαι ὑμᾶς, καὶ χαρήσεται
but again I will see you, and [4]will rejoice

ὑμῶν ἡ καρδία, καὶ τὴν χαρὰν ὑμῶν
[3]of you [1]the [2]heart, and the joy of you

οὐδεὶς αἴρει ἀφ' ὑμῶν. 23 καὶ ἐν ἐκείνῃ τῇ
no one takes from you. And in that –

ἡμέρᾳ ἐμὲ οὐκ ἐρωτήσετε οὐδέν.
day me ye will not question no(any)thing.

ἀμὴν ἀμὴν λέγω ὑμῖν, ἄν τι αἰτήσητε
Truly truly I tell you, whatever ye ask

τὸν πατέρα δώσει ὑμῖν ἐν τῷ ὀνόματί
the Father he will give you in the name

yet to come. 14 He will bring
glory to me by taking from
what is mine and making it
known to you. 15 All that
belongs to the Father is
mine. That is why I said the
Spirit will take from what is
mine and make it known to
you.
16 "In a little while you
will see me no more, and
then after a little while you
will see me."

The Disciples' Grief Will Turn to Joy

17 Some of his disciples
said to one another, "What
does he mean by saying, 'In
a little while you will see
me no more, and then after
a little while you will see
me,' and 'Because I am going to the Father'?" 18 They
kept asking, "What does
he mean by 'a little while'?
We don't understand what
he is saying."
19 Jesus saw that they
wanted to ask him about
this, so he said to them,
"Are you asking one an-
other what I meant when I
said, 'In a little while you
will see me no more, and
then after a little while you
will see me'? 20 I tell you the
truth, you will weep and
mourn while the world re-
joices. You will grieve, but
your grief will turn to joy.
21 A woman giving birth to a
child has pain because her
time has come; but when
her baby is born she forgets
the anguish because of her
joy that a child is born into
the world. 22 So with you:
Now is your time of grief,
but I will see you again and
you will rejoice, and no one
will take away your joy.
23 In that day you will no
longer ask me anything. I
tell you the truth, my Father will give you whatever
you ask in my name. 24 Un-

[r] Or *will ask me no question*

* Understand "that which is mine".

you.[s] 24Until now you
have not asked for anything
in my name. Ask and you
will receive, so that your
joy may be complete.

Peace for the Disciples

25 "I have said these
things to you in figures of
speech. The hour is coming
when I will no longer speak
to you in figures, but will
tell you plainly of the Father. 26On that day you will
ask in my name. I do not
say to you that I will ask the
Father on your behalf;
27for the Father himself
loves you, because you
have loved me and have believed that I came from
God.[t] 28I came from the
Father and have come into
the world; again, I am leaving the world and am going
to the Father."
29 His disciples said,
"Yes, now you are speak-
ing plainly, not in any figure of speech! 30Now we
know that you know all
things, and do not need to
have anyone question you;
by this we believe that you
came from God." 31Jesus
answered them, "Do you
now believe? 32The hour is
coming, indeed it has
come, when you will be
scattered, each one to his
home, and you will leave
me alone. Yet I am not
alone because the Father is
with me. 33I have said this
to you, so that in me you
may have peace. In the
world you face persecu-
tion. But take courage; I
have conquered the
world!"

Chapter 17

Jesus Prays for His Disciples

AFTER Jesus had spo-
ken these words, he
looked up to heaven and
said, "Father, the hour has
come; glorify your Son so

[s] Other ancient authorities read *Father, he will give it to you in my name*

[t] Other ancient authorities read *the Father*

μου. 24 ἕως ἄρτι οὐκ ᾐτήσατε οὐδὲν
of me. Until now ye asked not no(any)thing

ἐν τῷ ὀνόματί μου· αἰτεῖτε, καὶ λήμψεσθε,
in the name of me; ask, and ye will receive,

ἵνα ἡ χαρὰ ὑμῶν ᾖ πεπληρωμένη.
that the joy of you may be *having been* filled.

25 Ταῦτα ἐν παροιμίαις λελάληκα ὑμῖν·
These things in allegories I have spoken to you;

ἔρχεται ὥρα ὅτε οὐκέτι ἐν παροιμίαις
comes an hour when no longer in allegories

λαλήσω ὑμῖν, ἀλλὰ παρρησίᾳ περὶ τοῦ
I will speak to you, but plainly concerning the

πατρὸς ἀπαγγελῶ ὑμῖν. 26 ἐν ἐκείνῃ τῇ
Father will declare to you. In that –

ἡμέρᾳ ἐν τῷ ὀνόματί μου αἰτήσεσθε,
day in the name of me ye will ask,

καὶ οὐ λέγω ὑμῖν ὅτι ἐγὼ ἐρωτήσω
and I tell not you that I will request

τὸν πατέρα περὶ ὑμῶν· 27 αὐτὸς γὰρ
the Father concerning you; for [him]self

ὁ πατὴρ φιλεῖ ὑμᾶς, ὅτι ὑμεῖς ἐμὲ
the Father loves you, because ye me

πεφιλήκατε καὶ πεπιστεύκατε ὅτι ἐγὼ
have loved and have believed that I

παρὰ τοῦ θεοῦ ἐξῆλθον. 28 ἐξῆλθον
from – God came forth. I came forth

ἐκ τοῦ πατρὸς καὶ ἐλήλυθα εἰς τὸν
out of the Father and have come into the

κόσμον· πάλιν ἀφίημι τὸν κόσμον καὶ
world; again I leave the world and

πορεύομαι πρὸς τὸν πατέρα. 29 Λέγουσιν
go to the Father. Say

οἱ μαθηταὶ αὐτοῦ· ἴδε νῦν ἐν παρρησίᾳ
the disciples of him: Behold[,] now in plainness

λαλεῖς, καὶ παροιμίαν οὐδεμίαν λέγεις.
thou speakest, and [2]allegory [1]no thou sayest.

30 νῦν οἴδαμεν ὅτι οἶδας πάντα καὶ
Now we know that thou knowest all things and

οὐ χρείαν ἔχεις ἵνα τίς σε ἐρωτᾷ· ἐν
no need hast that anyone thee should question; by

τούτῳ πιστεύομεν ὅτι ἀπὸ θεοῦ ἐξῆλθες.
this we believe that from God thou camest forth.

31 ἀπεκρίθη αὐτοῖς Ἰησοῦς· ἄρτι πιστεύετε;
Answered them Jesus: Now believe ye?

32 ἰδοὺ ἔρχεται ὥρα καὶ ἐλήλυθεν ἵνα
behold[,] comes an hour and has come that

σκορπισθῆτε ἕκαστος εἰς τὰ ἴδια κἀμὲ
ye are scattered each one to the(his) own and me

μόνον ἀφῆτε· καὶ οὐκ εἰμὶ μόνος, ὅτι
alone ye leave; and I am not alone, because

ὁ πατὴρ μετ' ἐμοῦ ἐστιν. 33 ταῦτα
the Father with me is. These things

λελάληκα ὑμῖν ἵνα ἐν ἐμοὶ εἰρήνην
I have spoken to you that in me peace

ἔχητε. ἐν τῷ κόσμῳ θλῖψιν ἔχετε·
ye may have. In the world distress ye have;

ἀλλὰ θαρσεῖτε, ἐγὼ νενίκηκα τὸν κόσμον.
but cheer ye up, I have overcome the world.

17 Ταῦτα ἐλάλησεν Ἰησοῦς, καὶ ἐπάρας
These things spoke Jesus, and lifting up

τοὺς ὀφθαλμοὺς αὐτοῦ εἰς τὸν οὐρανὸν
the eyes of him to – heaven

εἶπεν· πάτερ, ἐλήλυθεν ἡ ὥρα· δόξασόν
said: Father, has come the hour; glorify

til now you have not asked
for anything in my name.
Ask and you will receive,
and your joy will be com-
plete.
25"Though I have been
speaking figuratively, a
time is coming when I will
no longer use this kind of
language but will tell you
plainly about my Father.
26In that day you will ask in
my name. I am not saying
that I will ask the Father on
your behalf. 27No, the Father himself loves you because you have loved me
and have believed that I
came from God. 28I came
from the Father and en-
tered the world; now I am
leaving the world and going
back to the Father."
29Then Jesus' disciples
said, "Now you are speak-
ing clearly and without figures of speech. 30Now we
can see that you know all
things and that you do not
even need to have anyone
ask you questions. This
makes us believe that you
came from God."
31"You believe at last!"[w]
Jesus answered. 32"But a
time is coming, and has
come, when you will be
scattered, each to his own
home. You will leave me all
alone. Yet I am not alone,
for my Father is with me.
33"I have told you these
things, so that in me you
may have peace. In this
world you will have trou-
ble. But take heart! I have
overcome the world."

Chapter 17

Jesus Prays for Himself

AFTER Jesus said this,
he looked toward
heaven and prayed:

"Father, the time has
come. Glorify your

[w] 31 Or *"Do you now believe?"*

that the Son may glorify
you, 2 since you have given
him authority over all people,[u] to give eternal life to
all whom you have given
him. 3 And this is eternal
life, that they may know
you, the only true God, and
Jesus Christ whom you
have sent. 4 I glorified you
on earth by finishing the
work that you gave me to
do. 5 So now, Father, glorify me in your own presence
with the glory that I had in
your presence before the
world existed.
6 "I have made your
name known to those
whom you gave me from
the world. They were
yours, and you gave them
to me, and they have kept
your word. 7 Now they
know that everything you
have given me is from you;
8 for the words that you
gave to me I have given to
them, and they have re-
ceived them and know in
truth that I came from you;
and they have believed that
you sent me. 9 I am asking
on their behalf; I am not
asking on behalf of the
world, but on behalf of
those whom you gave me,
because they are yours.
10 All mine are yours, and
yours are mine; and I have
been glorified in them.
11 And now I am no longer
in the world, but they are in
the world, and I am coming
to you. Holy Father, pro-
tect them in your name
that[v] you have given me,
so that they may be one, as
we are one. 12 While I was
with them, I protected
them in your name that[v]
you have given me. I guard-

[u] Gk *flesh*
[v] Other ancient authorities read *protected in your name those whom*

σου τὸν υἱόν, ἵνα ὁ υἱὸς δοξάσῃ σέ,
of thee the Son, that the Son may glorify thee,
2 καθὼς ἔδωκας αὐτῷ ἐξουσίαν πάσης
as thou gavest him authority of(over) all
σαρκός, ἵνα πᾶν ὃ δέδωκας αὐτῷ δώσῃ
flesh, that all which thou hast given him he may give
αὐτοῖς ζωὴν αἰώνιον. **3** αὕτη δέ ἐστιν
to them life eternal. And this is
ἡ αἰώνιος ζωή, ἵνα γινώσκωσιν σὲ τὸν
– eternal life, that they may know thee the
μόνον ἀληθινὸν θεὸν καὶ ὃν ἀπέστειλας
only true God and [he] whom thou didst send
Ἰησοῦν Χριστόν. **4** ἐγώ σε ἐδόξασα
Jesus Christ. I thee glorified
ἐπὶ τῆς γῆς, τὸ ἔργον τελειώσας ὃ
on the earth, the work finishing which
δέδωκάς μοι ἵνα ποιήσω· **5** καὶ νῦν
thou hast given to me that I should do; and now
δόξασόν με σύ, πάτερ, παρὰ σεαυτῷ
glorify me thou, Father, with thyself
τῇ δόξῃ ᾗ εἶχον πρὸ τοῦ τὸν κόσμον
with the glory which I had before *the* the world
=before the world was
εἶναι παρὰ σοί. **6** Ἐφανέρωσά σου τὸ
to be[b] with thee. I manifested of thee the
ὄνομα τοῖς ἀνθρώποις οὓς ἔδωκάς μοι
name to the men whom thou gavest to me
ἐκ τοῦ κόσμου. σοὶ ἦσαν κἀμοὶ αὐτοὺς
out of the world. To thee[c] they were and to me them
=Thine
ἔδωκας, καὶ τὸν λόγον σου τετήρηκαν.
thou gavest, and the word of thee they have kept.
7 νῦν ἔγνωκαν ὅτι πάντα ὅσα δέδωκάς
Now they have known that all things as many as thou hast given
μοι παρὰ σοῦ εἰσιν· **8** ὅτι τὰ ῥήματα
to me from thee are; because the words
ἃ ἔδωκάς μοι δέδωκα αὐτοῖς, καὶ αὐτοὶ
which thou gavest to me I have given to them, and they
ἔλαβον, καὶ ἔγνωσαν ἀληθῶς ὅτι παρὰ
received, and knew truly that from
σοῦ ἐξῆλθον, καὶ ἐπίστευσαν ὅτι σύ
thee I came forth, and they believed that thou
με ἀπέστειλας. **9** ἐγὼ περὶ αὐτῶν ἐρωτῶ·
me didst send. I concerning them make request;
οὐ περὶ τοῦ κόσμου ἐρωτῶ, ἀλλὰ περὶ
not concerning the world do I make request, but concerning
ὧν δέδωκάς μοι, ὅτι σοί εἰσιν,
[those] whom thou hast given to me, because to thee[c] they are,
=thine
10 καὶ τὰ ἐμὰ πάντα σά ἐστιν καὶ
and [2]*the* [3]my things [1]all [5]thine [4]is(are) and
τὰ σὰ ἐμά, καὶ δεδόξασμαι ἐν αὐτοῖς.
the thy things mine, and I have been glorified in them.
11 καὶ οὐκέτι εἰμὶ ἐν τῷ κόσμῳ, καὶ
And no longer am I in the world, and
αὐτοὶ ἐν τῷ κόσμῳ εἰσίν, κἀγὼ πρὸς
they in the world are, and I to
σὲ ἔρχομαι. πάτερ ἅγιε, τήρησον αὐτοὺς
thee come. Father holy, keep them
ἐν τῷ ὀνόματί σου ᾧ δέδωκάς μοι,
in the name of thee which thou hast given to me,
ἵνα ὦσιν ἓν καθὼς ἡμεῖς. **12** ὅτε ἤμην
that they may be one as we. When I was
μετ' αὐτῶν, ἐγὼ ἐτήρουν αὐτοὺς ἐν
with them, I kept them in
τῷ ὀνόματί σου ᾧ δέδωκάς μοι, καὶ
the name of thee which thou hast given to me, and

Son, that your Son may
glorify you. 2For you
granted him authority
over all people that he
might give eternal life to
all those you have given
him. 3Now this is eter-
nal life: that they may
know you, the only true
God, and Jesus Christ,
whom you have sent. 4I
have brought you glory
on earth by completing
the work you gave me
to do. 5And now, Fa-
ther, glorify me in your
presence with the glory
I had with you before
the world began.

Jesus Prays for His Disciples

6"I have revealed
you[x] to those whom
you gave me out of the
world. They were
yours; you gave them to
me and they have
obeyed your word.
7Now they know that
everything you have
given me comes from
you. 8For I gave them
the words you gave me
and they accepted
them. They knew with
certainty that I came
from you, and they be-
lieved that you sent me.
9I pray for them. I am
not praying for the
world, but for those you
have given me, for they
are yours. 10All I have is
yours, and all you have
is mine. And glory has
come to me through
them. 11I will remain in
the world no longer, but
they are still in the
world, and I am coming
to you. Holy Father,
protect them by the
power of your name—
the name you gave me
—so that they may be
one as we are one.
12While I was with
them, I protected them
and kept them safe by

[x] 6 Greek *your name*; also in verse 26

ed them, and not one of them was lost except the one destined to be lost,[w] so that the scripture might be fulfilled.
13 But now I am coming to you, and I speak these things in the world so that they may have my joy made complete in themselves.[x]
14 I have given them your word, and the world has hated them because they do not belong to the world, just as I do not belong to the world.
15 I am not asking you to take them out of the world, but I ask you to protect them from the evil one.[y]
16 They do not belong to the world, just as I do not belong to the world.
17 Sanctify them in the truth; your word is truth.
18 As you have sent me into the world, so I have sent them into the world.
19 And for their sakes I sanctify myself, so that they also may be sanctified in truth.

20 "I ask not only on behalf of these, but also on behalf of those who will believe in me through their word,
21 that they may all be one. As you, Father, are in me and I am in you, may they also be in us,[z] so that the world may believe that you have sent me.
22 The glory that you have given me I have given them, so that they may be one, as we are one,
23 I in them and you in me, that they may become completely one, so that the world may know that you have sent me and have loved them even as you have loved me.
24 Father, I desire that those also, whom you have given me, may be with me where

[w] Gk *except the son of destruction*
[x] Or *among themselves*
[y] Or *from evil*
[z] Other ancient authorities read *be one in us*

ἐφύλαξα, καὶ οὐδεὶς ἐξ αὐτῶν ἀπώλετο
I guarded, and not one of them perished
εἰ μὴ ὁ υἱὸς τῆς ἀπωλείας, ἵνα ἡ
except the son – perdition, that the
γραφὴ πληρωθῇ. **13** νῦν δὲ πρὸς σὲ
scripture might be fulfilled. But now to thee
ἔρχομαι, καὶ ταῦτα λαλῶ ἐν τῷ κόσμῳ
I come, and these things I speak in the world
ἵνα ἔχωσιν τὴν χαρὰν τὴν ἐμὴν
that they may have *the* [2]joy – [1]my
πεπληρωμένην ἐν ἑαυτοῖς. **14** ἐγὼ δέδωκα
having been fulfilled in themselves. I have given
αὐτοῖς τὸν λόγον σου, καὶ ὁ κόσμος
to them the word of thee, and the world
ἐμίσησεν αὐτούς, ὅτι οὐκ εἰσὶν ἐκ τοῦ
hated them, because they are not of the
κόσμου καθὼς ἐγὼ οὐκ εἰμὶ ἐκ τοῦ
world as I am not of the
κόσμου. **15** οὐκ ἐρωτῶ ἵνα ἄρῃς αὐτοὺς
world. I do not request that thou shouldest take them
ἐκ τοῦ κόσμου, ἀλλ' ἵνα τηρήσῃς αὐτοὺς
out of the world, but that thou shouldest keep them
ἐκ τοῦ πονηροῦ. **16** ἐκ τοῦ κόσμου
out of the evil [?one]. Of the world
οὐκ εἰσὶν καθὼς ἐγὼ οὐκ εἰμὶ ἐκ τοῦ
they are not as I am not of the
κόσμου. **17** ἁγίασον αὐτοὺς ἐν τῇ
world. Sanctify them in(?by) the
ἀληθείᾳ· ὁ λόγος ὁ σὸς ἀλήθειά ἐστιν.
truth; *the* [2]word – [1]thy truth is.
18 καθὼς ἐμὲ ἀπέστειλας εἰς τὸν κόσμον,
As me thou didst send into the world,
κἀγὼ ἀπέστειλα αὐτοὺς εἰς τὸν κόσμον·
I also sent them into the world;
19 καὶ ὑπὲρ αὐτῶν [ἐγὼ] ἁγιάζω ἐμαυτόν,
and on behalf of them I sanctify myself,
ἵνα ὦσιν καὶ αὐτοὶ ἡγιασμένοι ἐν ἀληθείᾳ.
that [3]may be [2]also [1]they *having been* sanctified in truth.
20 Οὐ περὶ τούτων δὲ ἐρωτῶ μόνον,
[2]Not [3]concerning [4]these [1]but I make request only,
ἀλλὰ καὶ περὶ τῶν πιστευόντων διὰ
but also concerning the [ones] believing through
τοῦ λόγου αὐτῶν εἰς ἐμέ, **21** ἵνα πάντες
the word of them in me, that all
ἓν ὦσιν, καθὼς σύ, πατήρ, ἐν ἐμοὶ
one may be, as thou, Father, in me
κἀγὼ ἐν σοί, ἵνα καὶ αὐτοὶ ἐν ἡμῖν
and I in thee, that also they in us
ὦσιν, ἵνα ὁ κόσμος πιστεύῃ ὅτι σύ
may be, that the world may believe that thou
με ἀπέστειλας. **22** κἀγὼ τὴν δόξαν ἣν
me didst send. And I the glory which
δέδωκάς μοι δέδωκα αὐτοῖς, ἵνα ὦσιν
thou hast given to me have given to them, that they may be
ἓν καθὼς ἡμεῖς ἕν· **23** ἐγὼ ἐν αὐτοῖς
one as we [are] one; I in them
καὶ σὺ ἐν ἐμοί, ἵνα ὦσιν τετελειωμένοι
and thou in me, that they may be *having been* perfected
εἰς ἕν, ἵνα γινώσκῃ ὁ κόσμος ὅτι σύ
in one, that may know the world that thou
με ἀπέστειλας καὶ ἠγάπησας αὐτοὺς
me didst send and didst love them
καθὼς ἐμὲ ἠγάπησας. **24** Πατήρ, ὃ
as me thou didst love. Father, what
δέδωκάς μοι, θέλω ἵνα ὅπου εἰμὶ ἐγὼ
thou hast given to me, I wish that where am I

that name you gave me. None has been lost except the one doomed to destruction so that Scripture would be fulfilled.
13 "I am coming to you now, but I say these things while I am still in the world, so that they may have the full measure of my joy within them.
14 I have given them your word and the world has hated them, for they are not of the world any more than I am of the world.
15 My prayer is not that you take them out of the world but that you protect them from the evil one.
16 They are not of the world, even as I am not of it.
17 Sanctify[y] them by the truth; your word is truth.
18 As you sent me into the world, I have sent them into the world.
19 For them I sanctify myself, that they too may be truly sanctified.

Jesus Prays for All Believers

20 "My prayer is not for them alone. I pray also for those who will believe in me through their message,
21 that all of them may be one, Father, just as you are in me and I am in you. May they also be in us so that the world may believe that you have sent me.
22 I have given them the glory that you gave me, that they may be one as we are one:
23 I in them and you in me. May they be brought to complete unity to let the world know that you sent me and have loved them even as you have loved me.

24 "Father, I want those you have given me to be with me where

[y] 17 Greek *hagiazo (set apart for sacred use* or *make holy)*; also in verse 19

I am, to see my glory,
which you have given me
because you loved me be-
fore the foundation of the
world.
25 "Righteous Father,
the world does not know
you, but I know you; and
these know that you have
sent me. 26 I made your
name known to them, and I
will make it known, so that
the love with which you
have loved me may be in
them, and I in them."

κἀκεῖνοι ὦσιν μετ' ἐμοῦ, ἵνα θεωρῶσιν
those also may be with me, that they may behold
τὴν δόξαν τὴν ἐμήν, ἣν δέδωκάς μοι
the [2]glory – [1]my, which thou hast given to me
ὅτι ἠγάπησάς με πρὸ καταβολῆς κόσμου.
because thou didst love me before [the] foundation of [the] world.
25 πατὴρ δίκαιε, καὶ ὁ κόσμος σε
Father righteous, indeed the world thee
οὐκ ἔγνω, ἐγὼ δέ σε ἔγνων, καὶ οὗτοι
knew not, but I thee knew, and these
ἔγνωσαν ὅτι σύ με ἀπέστειλας· 26 καὶ
knew that thou me didst send; and
ἐγνώρισα αὐτοῖς τὸ ὄνομά σου καὶ
I made known to them the name of thee and
γνωρίσω, ἵνα ἡ ἀγάπη ἣν ἠγάπησάς
will make known, that the love [with] which thou lovedst
με ἐν αὐτοῖς ᾖ κἀγὼ ἐν αὐτοῖς.
me in them may be and I in them.

I am, and to see my glo-
ry, the glory you have
given me because you
loved me before the cre-
ation of the world.
25 "Righteous Father,
though the world does
not know you, I know
you, and they know that
you have sent me. 26 I
have made you known
to them, and will con-
tinue to make you
known in order that the
love you have for me
may be in them and that
I myself may be in
them."

Chapter 18

The Betrayal and Arrest of Jesus

AFTER Jesus had spo-
ken these words, he
went out with his disciples
across the Kidron valley to
a place where there was a
garden, which he and his
disciples entered. 2 Now
Judas, who betrayed him,
also knew the place, be-
cause Jesus often met there
with his disciples. 3 So Judas brought a detachment
of soldiers together with
police from the chief
priests and the Pharisees,
and they came there with
lanterns and torches and
weapons. 4 Then Jesus,
knowing all that was to
happen to him, came for-
ward and asked them,
"Whom are you looking
for?" 5 They answered,
"Jesus of Nazareth."[a]
Jesus replied, "I am he."[b]
Judas, who betrayed him,
was standing with them.
6 When Jesus[c] said to
them, "I am he,"[b] they
stepped back and fell to the
ground. 7 Again he asked
them, "Whom are you
looking for?" And they
said, "Jesus of Naza-
reth."[a] 8 Jesus answered,
"I told you that I am he.[b]
So if you are looking for
me, let these men go."

18 Ταῦτα εἰπὼν Ἰησοῦς ἐξῆλθεν σὺν
These things having said Jesus went forth with
τοῖς μαθηταῖς αὐτοῦ πέραν τοῦ χειμάρρου
the disciples of him across the torrent
τοῦ Κεδρών, ὅπου ἦν κῆπος, εἰς ὃν
– Kedron, where there was a garden, into which
εἰσῆλθεν αὐτὸς καὶ οἱ μαθηταὶ αὐτοῦ.
entered he and the disciples of him.
2 ᾔδει δὲ καὶ Ἰούδας ὁ παραδιδοὺς
[1]Now [7]knew [3]also [2]Judas [4]the [one] [5]betraying
αὐτὸν τὸν τόπον, ὅτι πολλάκις συνήχθη
[6]him [8]the [9]place, because often assembled
Ἰησοῦς ἐκεῖ μετὰ τῶν μαθητῶν αὐτοῦ.
Jesus there with the disciples of him.
3 ὁ οὖν Ἰούδας λαβὼν τὴν σπεῖραν
– Therefore Judas taking the band
καὶ ἐκ τῶν ἀρχιερέων καὶ [ἐκ] τῶν
and [2]from [3]the [4]chief priests [5]and [6]from [7]the
Φαρισαίων ὑπηρέτας ἔρχεται ἐκεῖ μετὰ
[8]Pharisees [1]attendants comes there with
φανῶν καὶ λαμπάδων καὶ ὅπλων. 4 Ἰησοῦς
lanterns and lamps and weapons. Jesus
οὖν εἰδὼς πάντα τὰ ἐρχόμενα ἐπ' αὐτὸν
therefore knowing all the things coming on him
ἐξῆλθεν καὶ λέγει αὐτοῖς· τίνα ζητεῖτε;
went forth and says to them: Whom seek ye?
5 ἀπεκρίθησαν αὐτῷ· Ἰησοῦν τὸν
They answered him: Jesus the
Ναζωραῖον. λέγει αὐτοῖς· ἐγώ εἰμι.
Nazarene. He tells them: I am.
εἱστήκει δὲ καὶ Ἰούδας ὁ παραδιδοὺς
Now stood also Judas the [one] betraying
αὐτὸν μετ' αὐτῶν. 6 ὡς οὖν εἶπεν
him with them. When therefore he told
αὐτοῖς· ἐγώ εἰμι, ἀπῆλθαν εἰς τὰ ὀπίσω
them: I am, they went away back †
καὶ ἔπεσαν χαμαί. 7 πάλιν οὖν
and fell on the ground. Again therefore
ἐπηρώτησεν αὐτούς· τίνα ζητεῖτε; οἱ δὲ
he questioned them: Whom seek ye? And they
εἶπαν· Ἰησοῦν τὸν Ναζωραῖον. 8 ἀπεκρίθη
said: Jesus the Nazarene. Answered
Ἰησοῦς· εἶπον ὑμῖν ὅτι ἐγώ εἰμι· εἰ
Jesus: I told you that I am; if
οὖν ἐμὲ ζητεῖτε, ἄφετε τούτους ὑπάγειν·
therefore me ye seek, allow these to go;

Chapter 18

Jesus Arrested

WHEN he had finished
praying, Jesus left
with his disciples and
crossed the Kidron Valley.
On the other side there was
an olive grove, and he and
his disciples went into it.
2 Now Judas, who be-
trayed him, knew the
place, because Jesus had
often met there with his disciples. 3 So Judas came to
the grove, guiding a detachment of soldiers and some
officials from the chief
priests and Pharisees. They
were carrying torches, lanterns and weapons.
4 Jesus, knowing all that
was going to happen to
him, went out and asked
them, "Who is it you
want?"
5 "Jesus of Nazareth,"
they replied.
"I am he," Jesus said.
(And Judas the traitor was
standing there with them.)
6 When Jesus said, "I am
he," they drew back and
fell to the ground.
7 Again he asked them,
"Who is it you want?"
And they said, "Jesus of
Nazareth."
8 "I told you that I am
he," Jesus answered. "If
you are looking for me,
then let these men go."

[a] Gk *the Nazorean*
[b] Gk *I am*
[c] Gk *he*

9This was to fulfill the word
that he had spoken, "I did
not lose a single one of
those whom you gave me."
10Then Simon Peter, who
had a sword, drew it,
struck the high priest's
slave, and cut off his right
ear. The slave's name was
Malchus. 11Jesus said to
Peter, "Put your sword
back into its sheath. Am I
not to drink the cup that the
Father has given me?"

Jesus before the High Priest

12 So the soldiers, their
officer, and the Jewish police arrested Jesus and
bound him. 13First they
took him to Annas, who
was the father-in-law of Caiaphas, the high priest that
year. 14Caiaphas was the
one who had advised the
Jews that it was better to
have one person die for the
people.

Peter Denies Jesus

15 Simon Peter and an-
other disciple followed
Jesus. Since that disciple
was known to the high
priest, he went with Jesus
into the courtyard of the
high priest, 16but Peter was
standing outside at the
gate. So the other disciple,
who was known to the high
priest, went out, spoke to
the woman who guarded
the gate, and brought Peter
in. 17The woman said to
Peter, "You are not also
one of this man's disciples,
are you?" He said, "I am
not." 18Now the slaves and
the police had made a charcoal fire because it was
cold, and they were standing around it and warming
themselves. Peter also was

9 ἵνα πληρωθῇ ὁ λόγος ὃν εἶπεν, ὅτι
that might be fulfilled the word which he said, –
οὓς δέδωκάς μοι, οὐκ ἀπώλεσα ἐξ
[Those] whom thou hast given to me, I lost not of
αὐτῶν οὐδένα. **10** Σίμων οὖν Πέτρος
them no(any)one. [1]Simon [3]therefore [2]Peter
ἔχων μάχαιραν εἵλκυσεν αὐτὴν καὶ ἔπαισεν
having a sword drew it and smote
τὸν τοῦ ἀρχιερέως δοῦλον καὶ ἀπέκοψεν
[1]the [3]of the [4]high priest [2]slave and cut off
αὐτοῦ τὸ ὠτάριον τὸ δεξιόν· ἦν δὲ
of him the [2]ear – [1]right; and was
ὄνομα τῷ δούλῳ Μάλχος. **11** εἶπεν οὖν
name to the slave[c] Malchus. Said therefore
ὁ Ἰησοῦς τῷ Πέτρῳ· βάλε τὴν μάχαιραν
– Jesus – to Peter: Put the sword
εἰς τὴν θήκην· τὸ ποτήριον ὃ δέδωκέν
into the sheath; the cup which has given
μοι ὁ πατήρ, οὐ μὴ πίω αὐτό;
to me the Father, by no means shall I drink it?
12 Ἡ οὖν σπεῖρα καὶ ὁ χιλίαρχος
Therefore the band and the chiliarch
καὶ οἱ ὑπηρέται τῶν Ἰουδαίων συνέλαβον
and the attendants of the Jews took
τὸν Ἰησοῦν καὶ ἔδησαν αὐτόν, **13** καὶ
– Jesus and bound him, and
ἤγαγον πρὸς Ἄνναν πρῶτον· ἦν γὰρ
led to Annas first; for he was
πενθερὸς τοῦ Καϊάφα, ὃς ἦν ἀρχιερεὺς
father-in-law – of Caiaphas, who was high priest
τοῦ ἐνιαυτοῦ ἐκείνου· **14** ἦν δὲ Καϊάφας
– year of that; now it was Caiaphas
ὁ συμβουλεύσας τοῖς Ἰουδαίοις ὅτι
the [one] having advised the Jews that
συμφέρει ἕνα ἄνθρωπον ἀποθανεῖν ὑπὲρ
it is(was) expedient one man to die on behalf of
τοῦ λαοῦ. **15** Ἠκολούθει δὲ τῷ Ἰησοῦ
the people. And followed – Jesus
Σίμων Πέτρος καὶ ἄλλος μαθητής. ὁ δὲ
Simon Peter and another disciple. – And
μαθητὴς ἐκεῖνος ἦν γνωστὸς τῷ ἀρχιερεῖ,
disciple that was known to the high priest,
καὶ συνεισῆλθεν τῷ Ἰησοῦ εἰς τὴν αὐλὴν
and entered with – Jesus into the court
τοῦ ἀρχιερέως, **16** ὁ δὲ Πέτρος εἱστήκει
of the high priest, – but Peter stood
πρὸς τῇ θύρᾳ ἔξω. ἐξῆλθεν οὖν ὁ
at the door outside. Went out therefore the
μαθητὴς ὁ ἄλλος ὁ γνωστὸς τοῦ ἀρχιερέως
[2]disciple – [1]other – known of(to) the high priest
καὶ εἶπεν τῇ θυρωρῷ, καὶ εἰσήγαγεν
and told the portress, and brought in
τὸν Πέτρον. **17** λέγει οὖν τῷ Πέτρῳ ἡ
– Peter. Says therefore – to Peter the
παιδίσκη ἡ θυρωρός· μὴ καὶ σὺ ἐκ
maidservant the portress: *Not* also thou of
τῶν μαθητῶν εἶ τοῦ ἀνθρώπου τούτου;
the disciples art – man of this?
λέγει ἐκεῖνος· οὐκ εἰμί. **18** εἱστήκεισαν δὲ
Says that one: I am not. And stood
οἱ δοῦλοι καὶ οἱ ὑπηρέται ἀνθρακιὰν
the slaves and the attendants a fire
πεποιηκότες, ὅτι ψῦχος ἦν, καὶ
having made, because cold it was, and
ἐθερμαίνοντο· ἦν δὲ καὶ ὁ Πέτρος μετ'
were warming themselves; and was also – Peter with

9This happened so that the
words he had spoken
would be fulfilled: "I have
not lost one of those you
gave me."[z]
10Then Simon Peter, who
had a sword, drew it and
struck the high priest's servant, cutting off his right
ear. (The servant's name
was Malchus.)
11Jesus commanded Pe-
ter, "Put your sword away!
Shall I not drink the cup the
Father has given me?"

Jesus Taken to Annas

12Then the detachment of
soldiers with its commander and the Jewish officials
arrested Jesus. They bound
him 13and brought him first
to Annas, who was the fa-
ther-in-law of Caiaphas,
the high priest that year.
14Caiaphas was the one
who had advised the Jews
that it would be good if one
man died for the people.

Peter's First Denial

15Simon Peter and anoth-
er disciple were following
Jesus. Because this disciple
was known to the high
priest, he went with Jesus
into the high priest's courtyard, 16but Peter had to
wait outside at the door.
The other disciple, who
was known to the high
priest, came back, spoke to
the girl on duty there and
brought Peter in.
17"You are not one of his
disciples, are you?" the girl
at the door asked Peter.
He replied, "I am not."
18It was cold, and the servants and officials stood
around a fire they had made
to keep warm. Peter also

[z]9 John 6:39

standing with them and
warming himself.

The High Priest Questions Jesus

19 Then the high priest
questioned Jesus about his
disciples and about his
teaching. 20 Jesus an-
swered, "I have spoken
openly to the world; I have
always taught in syna-
gogues and in the temple,
where all the Jews come together. I have said nothing
in secret. 21 Why do you
ask me? Ask those who
heard what I said to them;
they know what I said."
22 When he had said this,
one of the police standing
nearby struck Jesus on the
face, saying, "Is that how
you answer the high
priest?" 23 Jesus answered,
"If I have spoken wrongly,
testify to the wrong. But if
I have spoken rightly, why
do you strike me?" 24 Then
Annas sent him bound to
Caiaphas the high priest.

Peter Denies Jesus Again

25 Now Simon Peter
was standing and warming
himself. They asked him,
"You are not also one of his
disciples, are you?" He denied it and said, "I am not."
26 One of the slaves of the
high priest, a relative of the
man whose ear Peter had
cut off, asked, "Did I not
see you in the garden with
him?" 27 Again Peter denied
it, and at that moment the
cock crowed.

Jesus before Pilate

28 Then they took Jesus
from Caiaphas to Pilate's
headquarters.[d] It was early in the morning. They
themselves did not enter
the headquarters,[d] so as to
avoid ritual defilement and
to be able to eat the Passover. 29 So Pilate went out
to them and said, "What accusation do you bring
against this man?" 30 They
answered, "If this man
were not a criminal, we
would not have handed him
over to you." 31 Pilate said

[d] Gk *the praetorium*

αὐτῶν ἑστὼς καὶ θερμαινόμενος. 19 Ὁ
them standing and warming himself. – [1]The
οὖν ἀρχιερεὺς ἠρώτησεν τὸν Ἰησοῦν
[2]therefore [3]high priest questioned – Jesus
περὶ τῶν μαθητῶν αὐτοῦ καὶ περὶ τῆς
about the disciples of him and about the
διδαχῆς αὐτοῦ. 20 ἀπεκρίθη αὐτῷ Ἰησοῦς·
teaching of him. Answered him Jesus:
ἐγὼ παρρησίᾳ λελάληκα τῷ κόσμῳ· ἐγὼ
I with plainness have spoken to the world; I
πάντοτε ἐδίδαξα ἐν συναγωγῇ καὶ ἐν
always taught in a synagogue and in
τῷ ἱερῷ, ὅπου πάντες οἱ Ἰουδαῖοι
the temple, where all the Jews
συνέρχονται, καὶ ἐν κρυπτῷ ἐλάλησα
come together, and in secret I spoke
οὐδέν. 21 τί με ἐρωτᾷς; ἐρώτησον
nothing. Why me questionest thou? question
τοὺς ἀκηκοότας τί ἐλάλησα αὐτοῖς· ἴδε
the [ones] having heard what I spoke to them; behold[,]
οὗτοι οἴδασιν ἃ εἶπον ἐγώ. 22 ταῦτα
these know what things said I. These things
δὲ αὐτοῦ εἰπόντος εἷς παρεστηκὼς τῶν
and him saying[a] one standing by of the
[a] =And as he said this
ὑπηρετῶν ἔδωκεν ῥάπισμα τῷ Ἰησοῦ
attendants gave a blow – to Jesus
εἰπών· οὕτως ἀποκρίνῃ τῷ ἀρχιερεῖ;
saying: Thus answerest thou the high priest?
23 ἀπεκρίθη αὐτῷ Ἰησοῦς· εἰ κακῶς
Answered him Jesus: If ill
ἐλάλησα, μαρτύρησον περὶ τοῦ κακοῦ·
I spoke, witness concerning the evil;
εἰ δὲ καλῶς, τί με δέρεις; 24 ἀπέστειλεν
but if well, why me beatest thou? [3]Sent
οὖν αὐτὸν ὁ Ἅννας δεδεμένον πρὸς
[2]therefore [4]him – [1]Annas *having been* bound to
Καϊαφᾶν τὸν ἀρχιερέα. 25 Ἦν δὲ Σίμων
Caiaphas the high priest. Now was Simon
Πέτρος ἑστὼς καὶ θερμαινόμενος. εἶπον
Peter standing and warming himself. They said
οὖν αὐτῷ· μὴ καὶ σὺ ἐκ τῶν μαθητῶν
therefore to him: *Not* also thou of the disciples
αὐτοῦ εἶ; ἠρνήσατο ἐκεῖνος καὶ εἶπεν·
of him art? Denied that one and said:
οὐκ εἰμί. 26 λέγει εἷς ἐκ τῶν δούλων τοῦ
I am not. Says one of the slaves of the
ἀρχιερέως, συγγενὴς ὢν οὗ ἀπέκοψεν
high priest, [2]a relative [1]being [3][of him] of whom [6]cut off
Πέτρος τὸ ὠτίον· οὐκ ἐγώ σε εἶδον
[4]Peter [5]the [7]ear: [2]Not [3]I [4]thee [1]saw
ἐν τῷ κήπῳ μετ' αὐτοῦ; 27 πάλιν οὖν
in the garden with him? Again therefore
ἠρνήσατο Πέτρος, καὶ εὐθέως ἀλέκτωρ
denied Peter, and immediately a cock
ἐφώνησεν.
sounded(crew).

28 Ἄγουσιν οὖν τὸν Ἰησοῦν ἀπὸ τοῦ
They lead therefore – Jesus from –
Καϊαφᾶ εἰς τὸ πραιτώριον· ἦν δὲ πρωΐ·
Caiaphas to the prætorium; and it was early;
καὶ αὐτοὶ οὐκ εἰσῆλθον εἰς τὸ πραιτώριον,
and they entered not into the prætorium,
ἵνα μὴ μιανθῶσιν ἀλλὰ φάγωσιν τὸ
lest they should be defiled but might eat the
πάσχα. 29 ἐξῆλθεν οὖν ὁ Πιλᾶτος ἔξω
passover. Went forth therefore – Pilate outside

was standing with them,
warming himself.

The High Priest Questions Jesus

19 Meanwhile, the high
priest questioned Jesus
about his disciples and his
teaching.
20 "I have spoken openly
to the world," Jesus re-
plied. "I always taught in
synagogues or at the tem-
ple, where all the Jews
come together. I said nothing in secret. 21 Why question me? Ask those who
heard me. Surely they
know what I said."
22 When Jesus said this,
one of the officials nearby
struck him in the face. "Is
this the way you answer the
high priest?" he demanded.
23 "If I said something
wrong," Jesus replied,
"testify as to what is
wrong. But if I spoke the
truth, why did you strike
me?" 24 Then Annas sent
him, still bound, to Caiaphas the high priest.[a]

Peter's Second and Third Denials

25 As Simon Peter stood
warming himself, he was
asked, "You are not one of
his disciples, are you?"
He denied it, saying, "I
am not."
26 One of the high priest's
servants, a relative of the
man whose ear Peter had
cut off, challenged him,
"Didn't I see you with him
in the olive grove?"
27 Again Peter denied it, and
at that moment a rooster
began to crow.

Jesus Before Pilate

28 Then the Jews led Jesus
from Caiaphas to the pal-
ace of the Roman gover-
nor. By now it was early
morning, and to avoid ceremonial uncleanness the
Jews did not enter the palace; they wanted to be able
to eat the Passover. 29 So
Pilate came out to them and
asked, "What charges are
you bringing against this
man?"
30 "If he were not a criminal," they replied, "we
would not have handed him
over to you."
31 Pilate said, "Take him

[a] 24 Or *(Now Annas had sent him, still bound, to Caiaphas the high priest.)*

to them, "Take him your-
selves and judge him ac-
cording to your law." The
Jews replied, "We are not
permitted to put anyone to
death." 32(This was to fulfill what Jesus had said
when he indicated the kind
of death he was to die.)

33 Then Pilate entered
the headquarters[d] again,
summoned Jesus, and
asked him, "Are you the
King of the Jews?" 34Jesus
answered, "Do you ask this
on your own, or did others
tell you about me?" 35Pi-
late replied, "I am not a
Jew, am I? Your own na-
tion and the chief priests
have handed you over to
me. What have you done?"
36Jesus answered, "My
kingdom is not from this
world. If my kingdom were
from this world, my followers would be fighting to
keep me from being handed
over to the Jews. But as it
is, my kingdom is not from
here." 37Pilate asked him,
"So you are a king?" Jesus
answered, "You say that I
am a king. For this I was
born, and for this I came
into the world, to testify to
the truth. Everyone who
belongs to the truth listens
to my voice." 38Pilate
asked him, "What is
truth?"

πρὸς αὐτοὺς καὶ φησίν· τίνα κατηγορίαν
to them and says: What accusation

φέρετε τοῦ ἀνθρώπου τούτου; 30 ἀπεκρίθησαν
bring ye – man of this? They answered

καὶ εἶπαν αὐτῷ· εἰ μὴ ἦν
and said to him: Unless was

οὗτος κακὸν ποιῶν, οὐκ ἄν σοι
this man evil doing, [2]would [3]not [7]to thee

παρεδώκαμεν αὐτόν. 31 εἶπεν οὖν αὐτοῖς
[1]we [4]have [5]delivered [6]him. Said therefore to them

ὁ Πιλᾶτος· λάβετε αὐτὸν ὑμεῖς, καὶ
– Pilate: Take him ye, and

κατὰ τὸν νόμον ὑμῶν κρίνατε αὐτόν.
according to the law of you judge ye him.

εἶπον αὐτῷ οἱ Ἰουδαῖοι· ἡμῖν οὐκ ἔξεστιν
Said to him the Jews: For us it is not lawful

ἀποκτεῖναι οὐδένα· 32 ἵνα ὁ λόγος τοῦ
to kill no(any)one; that the word –

Ἰησοῦ πληρωθῇ ὃν εἶπεν σημαίνων ποίῳ
of Jesus might be fulfilled which he said signifying by what

θανάτῳ ἤμελλεν ἀποθνῄσκειν. 33 Εἰσῆλθεν
death he was about to die. Entered

οὖν πάλιν εἰς τὸ πραιτώριον ὁ Πιλᾶτος
therefore again into the prætorium – Pilate

καὶ ἐφώνησεν τὸν Ἰησοῦν καὶ εἶπεν
and called – Jesus and said

αὐτῷ· σὺ εἶ ὁ βασιλεὺς τῶν Ἰουδαίων;
to him: Thou art the king of the Jews?

34 ἀπεκρίθη Ἰησοῦς· ἀφ' ἑαυτοῦ σὺ τοῦτο
Answered Jesus: From [thy]self [2]thou [3]this

λέγεις, ἢ ἄλλοι εἶπόν σοι περὶ ἐμοῦ;
[1]sayest, or others told thee about me?

35 ἀπεκρίθη ὁ Πιλᾶτος· μήτι ἐγὼ
Answered – Pilate: *not* I

Ἰουδαῖός εἰμι; τὸ ἔθνος τὸ σὸν καὶ
a Jew am? *the* [2]nation – [1]thy and

οἱ ἀρχιερεῖς παρέδωκάν σε ἐμοί· τί
the chief priests delivered thee to me; what

ἐποίησας; 36 ἀπεκρίθη Ἰησοῦς· ἡ βασιλεία
didst thou? Answered Jesus: *The* [2]kingdom

ἡ ἐμὴ οὐκ ἔστιν ἐκ τοῦ κόσμου τούτου·
– [1]my is not of – world this;

εἰ ἐκ τοῦ κόσμου τούτου ἦν ἡ βασιλεία
if of – world this was *the* [2]kingdom

ἡ ἐμή, οἱ ὑπηρέται ἂν οἱ ἐμοὶ ἠγωνίζοντο,
– [1]my, *the* [2]attendants [3]would – [1]my [4]have struggled,

ἵνα μὴ παραδοθῶ τοῖς Ἰουδαίοις· νῦν
that I should not be delivered to the Jews; [2]now

δὲ ἡ βασιλεία ἡ ἐμὴ οὐκ ἔστιν ἐντεῦθεν.
[1]but *the* [3]kingdom – [2]my is not hence.

37 εἶπεν οὖν αὐτῷ ὁ Πιλᾶτος· οὐκοῦν
Said therefore to him – Pilate: Not really

βασιλεὺς εἶ σύ; ἀπεκρίθη [ὁ] Ἰησοῦς·
a king art thou? Answered – Jesus:

σὺ λέγεις ὅτι βασιλεύς εἰμι. ἐγὼ εἰς
Thou sayest that a king I am. I for

τοῦτο γεγέννημαι καὶ εἰς τοῦτο ἐλήλυθα
this have been born and for this I have come

εἰς τὸν κόσμον, ἵνα μαρτυρήσω τῇ
into the world, that I might witness to the

ἀληθείᾳ· πᾶς ὁ ὢν ἐκ τῆς ἀληθείας
truth; everyone being of the truth

ἀκούει μου τῆς φωνῆς. 38 λέγει αὐτῷ
hears of me the voice. Says to him

ὁ Πιλᾶτος· τί ἐστιν ἀλήθεια; Καὶ
– Pilate: What is truth? And

yourselves and judge him
by your own law."

"But we have no right to
execute anyone," the Jews
objected. 32This happened
so that the words Jesus had
spoken indicating the kind
of death he was going to die
would be fulfilled.

33Pilate then went back
inside the palace, sum-
moned Jesus and asked
him, "Are you the king of
the Jews?"

34"Is that your own
idea," Jesus asked, "or did
others talk to you about
me?"

35"Am I a Jew?" Pilate
replied. "It was your people and your chief priests
who handed you over to
me. What is it you have
done?"

36Jesus said, "My king-
dom is not of this world. If
it were, my servants would
fight to prevent my arrest
by the Jews. But now my
kingdom is from another
place."

37"You are a king, then!"
said Pilate.

Jesus answered, "You
are right in saying I am a
king. In fact, for this reason
I was born, and for this I
came into the world, to testify to the truth. Everyone
on the side of truth listens
to me."

38"What is truth?" Pilate
asked. With this he went

Jesus Sentenced to Death

After he had said this, he
went out to the Jews again
and told them, "I find no
case against him. 39 But you
have a custom that I release
someone for you at the
Passover. Do you want me
to release for you the King
of the Jews?" 40 They
shouted in reply, "Not this
man, but Barabbas!" Now
Barabbas was a bandit.

τοῦτο εἰπὼν πάλιν ἐξῆλθεν πρὸς τοὺς
this having said again he went forth to the

Ἰουδαίους, καὶ λέγει αὐτοῖς· ἐγὼ οὐδεμίαν
Jews, and tells them : [1]I [2]no

εὑρίσκω ἐν αὐτῷ αἰτίαν. 39 ἔστιν δὲ
[3]find [5]in [6]him [4]crime. But there is

συνήθεια ὑμῖν ἵνα ἕνα ἀπολύσω ὑμῖν
a custom to you[e] that one I should release to you

ἐν τῷ πάσχα· βούλεσθε οὖν ἀπολύσω
at the Passover; will ye therefore [that] I release

ὑμῖν τὸν βασιλέα τῶν Ἰουδαίων; 40 ἐκραύ-
to you the king of the Jews? They cried

γασαν οὖν πάλιν λέγοντες· μὴ τοῦτον,
out therefore again saying : Not this man,

ἀλλὰ τὸν Βαραββᾶν. ἦν δὲ ὁ Βαραββᾶς
but – Barabbas [1]But [3]was – [2]Barabbas

λῃστής.
[4]a robber.

out again to the Jews and
said, "I find no basis for a
charge against him. 39 But it
is your custom for me to
release to you one prisoner
at the time of the Passover.
Do you want me to release
'the king of the Jews'?"
40 They shouted back,
"No, not him! Give us Barabbas!" Now Barabbas
had taken part in a rebellion.

Chapter 19

THEN Pilate took Jesus
and had him flogged.
2 And the soldiers wove a
crown of thorns and put it
on his head, and they
dressed him in a purple
robe. 3 They kept coming
up to him, saying, "Hail,
King of the Jews!" and
striking him on the face.
4 Pilate went out again and
said to them, "Look, I am
bringing him out to you to
let you know that I find no
case against him." 5 So
Jesus came out, wearing
the crown of thorns and the
purple robe. Pilate said to
them, "Here is the man!"
6 When the chief priests and
the police saw him, they
shouted, "Crucify him!
Crucify him!" Pilate said to
them, "Take him your-
selves and crucify him; I
find no case against him."
7 The Jews answered him,
"We have a law, and ac-
cording to that law he ought
to die because he has
claimed to be the Son of
God."
8 Now when Pilate
heard this, he was more
afraid than ever. 9 He en-

19 Τότε οὖν ἔλαβεν ὁ Πιλᾶτος
Then therefore [2]took – [1]Pilate

τὸν Ἰησοῦν καὶ ἐμαστίγωσεν. 2 καὶ οἱ
– [3]Jesus and scourged [him]. And the

στρατιῶται πλέξαντες στέφανον ἐξ ἀκανθῶν
soldiers having plaited a wreath out of thorns

ἐπέθηκαν αὐτοῦ τῇ κεφαλῇ, καὶ ἱμάτιον
put [it] on of him the head, and [4]garment

πορφυροῦν περιέβαλον αὐτόν, 3 καὶ ἤρχοντο
[3]a purple [1]threw round [2]him, and came

πρὸς αὐτὸν καὶ ἔλεγον· χαῖρε ὁ βασιλεὺς
to him and said : Hail[,] – king

τῶν Ἰουδαίων· καὶ ἐδίδοσαν αὐτῷ
of the Jews; and they gave him

ῥαπίσματα. 4 Καὶ ἐξῆλθεν πάλιν ἔξω
blows. And went forth again outside

ὁ Πιλᾶτος καὶ λέγει αὐτοῖς· ἴδε ἄγω
– Pilate and says to them : Behold [1]I bring

ὑμῖν αὐτὸν ἔξω, ἵνα γνῶτε ὅτι οὐδεμίαν
[4]to you [2]him [3]out, that ye may know that no

αἰτίαν εὑρίσκω ἐν αὐτῷ. 5 ἐξῆλθεν
crime I find in him. Came forth

οὖν ὁ Ἰησοῦς ἔξω, φορῶν τὸν ἀκάνθινον
therefore – Jesus outside, wearing the thorny

στέφανον καὶ τὸ πορφυροῦν ἱμάτιον. καὶ
wreath and the purple garment. And

λέγει αὐτοῖς· ἰδοὺ ὁ ἄνθρωπος. 6 ὅτε
he says to them : Behold[,] the man. When

οὖν εἶδον αὐτὸν οἱ ἀρχιερεῖς καὶ οἱ
therefore saw him the chief priests and the

ὑπηρέται, ἐκραύγασαν λέγοντες· σταύρωσον
attendants, they shouted saying : Crucify[,]

σταύρωσον. λέγει αὐτοῖς ὁ Πιλᾶτος·
crucify. Says to them – Pilate :

λάβετε αὐτὸν ὑμεῖς καὶ σταυρώσατε·
[1]Take [3]him [2]ye and crucify;

ἐγὼ γὰρ οὐχ εὑρίσκω ἐν αὐτῷ αἰτίαν.
for I find not in him crime.

7 ἀπεκρίθησαν αὐτῷ οἱ Ἰουδαῖοι· ἡμεῖς
Answered him the Jews : We

νόμον ἔχομεν, καὶ κατὰ τὸν νόμον
a law have, and according to the law

ὀφείλει ἀποθανεῖν, ὅτι υἱὸν θεοῦ ἑαυτὸν
he ought to die, because Son of God himself

ἐποίησεν. 8 Ὅτε οὖν ἤκουσεν ὁ Πιλᾶτος
he made. When therefore heard – Pilate

τοῦτον τὸν λόγον, μᾶλλον ἐφοβήθη, 9 καὶ
this – word, more he was afraid, and

Chapter 19

Jesus Sentenced to be Crucified

THEN Pilate took Jesus
and had him flogged.
2 The soldiers twisted together a crown of thorns
and put it on his head. They
clothed him in a purple
robe 3 and went up to him
again and again, saying,
"Hail, king of the Jews!"
And they struck him in the
face.
4 Once more Pilate came
out and said to the Jews,
"Look, I am bringing him
out to you to let you know
that I find no basis for a
charge against him."
5 When Jesus came out
wearing the crown of
thorns and the purple robe,
Pilate said to them, "Here
is the man!"
6 As soon as the chief
priests and their officials
saw him, they shouted,
"Crucify! Crucify!"
But Pilate answered,
"You take him and crucify
him. As for me, I find no
basis for a charge against
him."
7 The Jews insisted, "We
have a law, and according
to that law he must die, because he claimed to be the
Son of God."
8 When Pilate heard this,
he was even more afraid,

tered his headquarters[d]
again and asked Jesus,
"Where are you from?" But
Jesus gave him no answer.
10Pilate therefore said to
him, "Do you refuse to
speak to me? Do you not
know that I have power to
release you, and power to
crucify you?" 11Jesus an-
swered him, "You would
have no power over me un-
less it had been given you
from above; therefore the
one who handed me over to
you is guilty of a greater
sin." 12From then on Pilate
tried to release him, but the
Jews cried out, "If you release this man, you are no
friend of the emperor. Everyone who claims to be a
king sets himself against
the emperor."
13 When Pilate heard
these words, he brought
Jesus outside and sat[e] on
the judge's bench at a place
called The Stone Pave-
ment, or in Hebrew[f] Gabbatha. 14Now it was the
day of Preparation for the
Passover; and it was about
noon. He said to the Jews,
"Here is your King!"
15They cried out, "Away
with him! Away with him!
Crucify him!" Pilate asked
them, "Shall I crucify your
King?" The chief priests
answered, "We have no
king but the emperor."
16Then he handed him over
to them to be crucified.

The Crucifixion of Jesus

So they took Jesus;
17and carrying the cross by
himself, he went out to
what is called The Place of
the Skull, which in He-
brew[f] is called Golgotha.
18There they crucified him,
and with him two others,
one on either side, with
Jesus between them. 19Pi-
late also had an inscription

εἰσῆλθεν εἰς τὸ πραιτώριον πάλιν καὶ
entered into the prætorium again and
λέγει τῷ Ἰησοῦ· πόθεν εἶ σύ; ὁ δὲ
says – to Jesus : Whence art thou? – But
Ἰησοῦς ἀπόκρισιν οὐκ ἔδωκεν αὐτῷ.
Jesus answer did not give him.
10 λέγει οὖν αὐτῷ ὁ Πιλᾶτος· ἐμοὶ
Says therefore to him – Pilate : To me
οὐ λαλεῖς; οὐκ οἶδας ὅτι ἐξουσίαν ἔχω
speakest thou not? knowest thou not that authority I have
ἀπολῦσαί σε καὶ ἐξουσίαν ἔχω σταυρῶσαί
to release thee and authority I have to crucify
σε; **11** ἀπεκρίθη Ἰησοῦς· οὐκ εἶχες
thee? Answered Jesus : Thou hadst not
ἐξουσίαν κατ' ἐμοῦ οὐδεμίαν εἰ μὴ ἦν
[2]authority [3]against [4]me [1]no(any) unless it was
δεδομένον σοι ἄνωθεν· διὰ τοῦτο ὁ
having been given thee from above; therefore the [one]
παραδούς μέ σοι μείζονα ἁμαρτίαν ἔχει.
having delivered me to thee a greater sin has.
12 ἐκ τούτου ὁ Πιλᾶτος ἐζήτει ἀπολῦσαι
From this – Pilate sought to release
αὐτόν· οἱ δὲ Ἰουδαῖοι ἐκραύγασαν λέγοντες·
him; but the Jews shouted saying :
ἐὰν τοῦτον ἀπολύσῃς, οὐκ εἶ φίλος τοῦ
If this man thou releasest, thou art not a friend –
Καίσαρος· πᾶς ὁ βασιλέα ἑαυτὸν ποιῶν
of Cæsar; everyone a king himself making
ἀντιλέγει τῷ Καίσαρι. **13** Ὁ οὖν Πιλᾶτος
speaks against – Cæsar. – Therefore Pilate
ἀκούσας τῶν λόγων τούτων ἤγαγεν ἔξω
hearing – words these brought outside
τὸν Ἰησοῦν, καὶ ἐκάθισεν ἐπὶ βήματος
– Jesus, and sat on a tribunal
εἰς τόπον λεγόμενον Λιθόστρωτον, Ἑβραϊστὶ δὲ
in a place *being* called Pavement, but in Hebrew
Γαββαθά. **14** ἦν δὲ παρασκευὴ τοῦ
Gabbatha. Now it was preparation of the
πάσχα, ὥρα ἦν ὡς ἕκτη· καὶ λέγει
Passover, hour it was about sixth; and he says
τοῖς Ἰουδαίοις· ἴδε ὁ βασιλεὺς ὑμῶν.
to the Jews; Behold[,] the king of you.
15 ἐκραύγασαν οὖν ἐκεῖνοι· ἆρον ἆρον,
Shouted therefore those : Take[,] take,
σταύρωσον αὐτόν. λέγει αὐτοῖς ὁ Πιλᾶτος·
crucify him. Says to them – Pilate :
τὸν βασιλέα ὑμῶν σταυρώσω; ἀπεκρίθησαν
The king of you shall I crucify? Answered
οἱ ἀρχιερεῖς· οὐκ ἔχομεν βασιλέα εἰ
the chief priests : We have not a king ex-
μὴ Καίσαρα. **16** τότε οὖν παρέδωκεν
cept Cæsar. Then therefore he delivered
αὐτὸν αὐτοῖς ἵνα σταυρωθῇ.
him to them that he should be crucified.

Παρέλαβον οὖν τὸν Ἰησοῦν· **17** καὶ
They took therefore – Jesus; and
βαστάζων ἑαυτῷ τὸν σταυρὸν ἐξῆλθεν
carrying [3]to himself [c] [1]the [2]cross he went forth
εἰς τὸν λεγόμενον κρανίου τόπον, ὃ
to [1]the [3]*being* called [4]of a skull [2]place, which
λέγεται Ἑβραϊστὶ Γολγοθά, **18** ὅπου αὐτὸν
is called in Hebrew Golgotha, where him
ἐσταύρωσαν, καὶ μετ' αὐτοῦ ἄλλους δύο
they crucified, and with him others two
ἐντεῦθεν καὶ ἐντεῦθεν, μέσον δὲ τὸν
on this side and on that, † and in the middle –

9and he went back inside
the palace. "Where do you
come from?" he asked
Jesus, but Jesus gave him
no answer. 10"Do you re-
fuse to speak to me?" Pi-
late said. "Don't you realize I have power either to
free you or to crucify
you?"
11Jesus answered, "You
would have no power over
me if it were not given to
you from above. Therefore
the one who handed me
over to you is guilty of a
greater sin."
12From then on, Pilate
tried to set Jesus free, but
the Jews kept shouting, "If
you let this man go, you are
no friend of Caesar. Any-
one who claims to be a king
opposes Caesar."
13When Pilate heard this,
he brought Jesus out and
sat down on the judge's
seat at a place known as the
Stone Pavement (which in
Aramaic is Gabbatha). 14It
was the day of Preparation
of Passover Week, about
the sixth hour.
"Here is your king," Pi-
late said to the Jews.
15But they shouted,
"Take him away! Take him
away! Crucify him!"
"Shall I crucify your
king?" Pilate asked.
"We have no king but
Caesar," the chief priests
answered.
16Finally Pilate handed
him over to them to be crucified.

The Crucifixion

So the soldiers took
charge of Jesus. 17Carrying
his own cross, he went out
to the place of the Skull
(which in Aramaic is called
Golgotha). 18Here they crucified him, and with him
two others—one on each
side and Jesus in the middle.

[e] Or *seated him*
[f] That is, *Aramaic*

written and put on the
cross. It read, "Jesus of
Nazareth,[g] the King of the
Jews." 20 Many of the Jews
read this inscription, because the place where
Jesus was crucified was
near the city; and it was
written in Hebrew,[h] in
Latin, and in Greek.
21 Then the chief priests of
the Jews said to Pilate, "Do
not write, 'The King of the
Jews,' but, 'This man said,
I am King of the Jews.'"
22 Pilate answered, "What I
have written I have writ-
ten." 23 When the soldiers
had crucified Jesus, they
took his clothes and divided them into four parts, one
for each soldier. They also
took his tunic; now the tunic was seamless, woven in
one piece from the top.
24 So they said to one another, "Let us not tear it,
but cast lots for it to see
who will get it." This was to
fulfill what the scripture
says,

"They divided my
clothes among
themselves,
and for my clothing
they cast lots."

25 And that is what the soldiers did.
Meanwhile, standing
near the cross of Jesus
were his mother, and his
mother's sister, Mary the
wife of Clopas, and Mary
Magdalene. 26 When Jesus
saw his mother and the disciple whom he loved standing beside her, he said to
his mother, "Woman, here
is your son." 27 Then he
said to the disciple, "Here
is your mother." And from
that hour the disciple took

[g] Gk *the Nazorean*
[h] That is, *Aramaic*

Ἰησοῦν. **19** ἔγραψεν δὲ καὶ τίτλον ὁ
Jesus. And wrote also a title –
Πιλᾶτος καὶ ἔθηκεν ἐπὶ τοῦ σταυροῦ·
Pilate and put [it] on the cross;
ἦν δὲ γεγραμμένον· ΙΗΣΟΥΣ Ο
and it was *having been* written : JESUS THE
ΝΑΖΩΡΑΙΟΣ Ο ΒΑΣΙΛΕΥΣ ΤΩΝ
NAZARENE THE KING OF THE
ΙΟΥΔΑΙΩΝ. **20** τοῦτον οὖν τὸν τίτλον
JEWS. [1]This [3]therefore – [2]title
πολλοὶ ἀνέγνωσαν τῶν Ἰουδαίων, ὅτι
[1]many [4]read [2]of the [3]Jews, because
ἐγγὺς ἦν ὁ τόπος τῆς πόλεως ὅπου
[7]near [6]was [1]the [2]place [4]the [5]city [3]where
ἐσταυρώθη ὁ Ἰησοῦς· καὶ ἦν γεγραμμένον
[6]was crucified – [4]Jesus; and it was *having been* written
Ἑβραϊστί, Ῥωμαϊστί, Ἑλληνιστί. **21** ἔλεγον
in Hebrew, in Latin, in Greek. Said
οὖν τῷ Πιλάτῳ οἱ ἀρχιερεῖς τῶν Ἰουδαίων·
therefore – to Pilate the chief priests of the Jews :
μὴ γράφε· ὁ βασιλεὺς τῶν Ἰουδαίων,
Write not : The king of the Jews,
ἀλλ' ὅτι ἐκεῖνος εἶπεν· βασιλεύς εἰμι
but that that man said : King I am
τῶν Ἰουδαίων. **22** ἀπεκρίθη ὁ Πιλᾶτος·
of the Jews. Answered – Pilate :
ὃ γέγραφα, γέγραφα. **23** Οἱ οὖν
What I have written, I have written. Therefore the
στρατιῶται, ὅτε ἐσταύρωσαν τὸν Ἰησοῦν,
soldiers. when they crucified – Jesus,
ἔλαβον τὰ ἱμάτια αὐτοῦ καὶ ἐποίησαν
took the garments of him and made
τέσσερα μέρη, ἑκάστῳ στρατιώτῃ μέρος,
four parts, to each soldier a part,
καὶ τὸν χιτῶνα. ἦν δὲ ὁ χιτὼν ἄρραφος,
and the tunic. Now was the tunic seamless,
ἐκ τῶν ἄνωθεν ὑφαντὸς δι' ὅλου. **24** εἶπαν
from the top woven throughout. They said
οὖν πρὸς ἀλλήλους· μὴ σχίσωμεν αὐτόν,
therefore to one another : Let us not tear it,
ἀλλὰ λάχωμεν περὶ αὐτοῦ τίνος ἔσται·
but let us cast lots about it of whom it shall be;
ἵνα ἡ γραφὴ πληρωθῇ· διεμερίσαντο τὰ
that the scripture might be fulfilled : They parted the
ἱμάτιά μου ἑαυτοῖς καὶ ἐπὶ τὸν ἱματισμόν
garments of me to themselves and over the raiment
μου ἔβαλον κλῆρον. Οἱ μὲν οὖν στρατιῶται
of me they cast a lot. [3]The –* [2]therefore [4]soldiers
ταῦτα ἐποίησαν. **25** εἱστήκεισαν δὲ παρὰ
[5]these things did. [2]there stood [1]But by
τῷ σταυρῷ τοῦ Ἰησοῦ ἡ μήτηρ αὐτοῦ
the cross – of Jesus the mother of him
καὶ ἡ ἀδελφὴ τῆς μητρὸς αὐτοῦ, Μαρία
and the sister of the mother of him, Mary
ἡ τοῦ Κλωπᾶ καὶ Μαρία ἡ Μαγδαληνή.
the [?wife] – of Clopas and Mary the Magdalene.
26 Ἰησοῦς οὖν ἰδὼν τὴν μητέρα καὶ
Jesus therefore seeing the(his) mother and
τὸν μαθητὴν παρεστῶτα ὃν ἠγάπα, λέγει
the disciple standing by whom he loved, says
τῇ μητρί· γύναι, ἴδε ὁ υἱός σου.
to the(his) mother : Woman, behold[,] the son of thee.
27 εἶτα λέγει τῷ μαθητῇ· ἴδε ἡ μήτηρ
Then he says to the disciple : Behold[,] the mother

* μέν is scarcely translatable. But note the δέ in ver. 25 : John contrasts two groups—the soldiers and the women.

19 Pilate had a notice prepared and fastened to the
cross. It read: JESUS OF NAZ-
ARETH, THE KING OF THE
JEWS. 20 Many of the Jews
read this sign, for the place
where Jesus was crucified
was near the city, and the
sign was written in Aramaic, Latin and Greek. 21 The
chief priests of the Jews
protested to Pilate, "Do
not write 'The King of the
Jews,' but that this man
claimed to be king of the
Jews."
22 Pilate answered, "What
I have written, I have written."
23 When the soldiers cru-
cified Jesus, they took his
clothes, dividing them into
four shares, one for each of
them, with the undergar-
ment remaining. This gar-
ment was seamless, woven
in one piece from top to
bottom.
24 "Let's not tear it," they
said to one another. "Let's
decide by lot who will get
it."
This happened that the
scripture might be fulfilled
which said,

"They divided my
garments among
them
and cast lots for my
clothing."[b]

So this is what the soldiers
did.
25 Near the cross of Jesus
stood his mother, his mother's sister, Mary the wife of
Clopas, and Mary Magda-
lene. 26 When Jesus saw his
mother there, and the disciple whom he loved stand-
ing nearby, he said to his
mother, "Dear woman,
here is your son," 27 and to
the disciple, "Here is your
mother." From that time

[b] 24 Psalm 22:18

her into his own home.
28 After this, when
Jesus knew that all was
now finished, he said (in order to fulfill the scripture),
"I am thirsty." 29 A jar full
of sour wine was standing
there. So they put a sponge
full of the wine on a branch
of hyssop and held it to his
mouth. 30 When Jesus had
received the wine, he said,
"It is finished." Then he
bowed his head and gave
up his spirit.

Jesus' Side Is Pierced

31 Since it was the day
of Preparation, the Jews
did not want the bodies left
on the cross during the sabbath, especially because
that sabbath was a day of
great solemnity. So they
asked Pilate to have the
legs of the crucified men
broken and the bodies re-
moved. 32 Then the soldiers
came and broke the legs of
the first and of the other
who had been crucified
with him. 33 But when they
came to Jesus and saw that
he was already dead, they
did not break his legs. 34 Instead, one of the soldiers
pierced his side with a
spear, and at once blood
and water came out. 35 (He
who saw this has testified
so that you also may be-
lieve. His testimony is true,
and he knows[i] that he tells
the truth.) 36 These things
occurred so that the scripture might be fulfilled,
"None of his bones shall be
broken." 37 And again an-
other passage of scripture
says, "They will look on
the one whom they have
pierced."

The Burial of Jesus

38 After these things,
Joseph of Arimathea, who

[i] Or *there is one who knows*

σου. καὶ ἀπ᾽ ἐκείνης τῆς ὥρας ἔλαβεν
of thee. And from that – hour took
ὁ μαθητὴς αὐτὴν εἰς τὰ ἴδια. 28 Μετὰ
the disciple her to his own [home]. † After
τοῦτο εἰδὼς ὁ Ἰησοῦς ὅτι ἤδη πάντα
this knowing – Jesus that now all things
τετέλεσται, ἵνα τελειωθῇ ἡ γραφή, λέγει·
have been finished, that might be fulfilled the scripture, says:
διψῶ. 29 σκεῦος ἔκειτο ὄξους μεστόν·
I thirst. A vessel was set of vinegar full;
σπόγγον οὖν μεστὸν τοῦ ὄξους ὑσσώπῳ
[3]a sponge therefore [4]full [5]of the [6]vinegar [8]a hyssop §
περιθέντες προσήνεγκαν αὐτοῦ τῷ στόματι.
[2]putting [7]round they brought [it] to of him the mouth.
30 ὅτε οὖν ἔλαβεν τὸ ὄξος [ὁ] Ἰησοῦς
When therefore took the vinegar – Jesus
εἶπεν· τετέλεσται, καὶ κλίνας τὴν κεφαλὴν
he said: It has been finished, and inclining the(his) head
παρέδωκεν τὸ πνεῦμα.
delivered up the(his) spirit.
31 Οἱ οὖν Ἰουδαῖοι, ἐπεὶ παρασκευὴ
The [2]therefore [1]Jews, since preparation
ἦν, ἵνα μὴ μείνῃ ἐπὶ τοῦ σταυροῦ τὰ
it was, that might not remain on the cross the
σώματα ἐν τῷ σαββάτῳ, ἦν γὰρ μεγάλη
bodies on the sabbath, for was great
ἡ ἡμέρα ἐκείνου τοῦ σαββάτου, ἠρώτησαν
the day of that – sabbath, they asked
τὸν Πιλᾶτον ἵνα κατεαγῶσιν αὐτῶν τὰ
– Pilate that might be broken of them the
σκέλη καὶ ἀρθῶσιν. 32 ἦλθον οὖν οἱ
legs and they might be taken. Came therefore the
στρατιῶται, καὶ τοῦ μὲν πρώτου κατέαξαν
soldiers, and of the –* first broke
τὰ σκέλη καὶ τοῦ ἄλλου τοῦ
the legs and of the other –
συσταυρωθέντος αὐτῷ· 33 ἐπὶ δὲ τὸν
crucified with him; [3]on [1]but –
Ἰησοῦν ἐλθόντες, ὡς εἶδον ἤδη αὐτὸν
[4]Jesus [2]coming, when they saw already him
τεθνηκότα, οὐ κατέαξαν αὐτοῦ τὰ σκέλη,
to have died, they did not break of him the legs,
34 ἀλλ᾽ εἷς τῶν στρατιωτῶν λόγχῃ αὐτοῦ
but one of the soldiers with a lance of him
τὴν πλευρὰν ἔνυξεν, καὶ ἐξῆλθεν εὐθὺς αἷμα
the side pricked, and there came out immediately blood
καὶ ὕδωρ. 35 καὶ ὁ ἑωρακὼς μεμαρτύρηκεν,
and water. And the [one] having seen has witnessed,
καὶ ἀληθινὴ αὐτοῦ ἐστιν ἡ μαρτυρία,
and true of him is the witness,
καὶ ἐκεῖνος οἶδεν ὅτι ἀληθῆ λέγει, ἵνα
and that one knows that truly he says, that
καὶ ὑμεῖς πιστεύητε. 36 ἐγένετο γὰρ
also ye may believe. For happened
ταῦτα ἵνα ἡ γραφὴ πληρωθῇ· ὀστοῦν
these things that the scripture might be fulfilled: A bone
οὐ συντριβήσεται αὐτοῦ. 37 καὶ πάλιν
shall not be broken of him. And again
ἑτέρα γραφὴ λέγει· ὄψονται εἰς ὃν
another scripture says: They shall look at [him] whom
ἐξεκέντησαν. 38 Μετὰ δὲ ταῦτα ἠρώτησεν
they pierced. Now after these things [14]asked
τὸν Πιλᾶτον Ἰωσὴφ ἀπὸ Ἁριμαθαίας,
– [15]Pilate [1]Joseph [2]from [3]Arimathæa,

§ It has been suggested that ὑσσώπῳ is a graphic error for ὑσσῷ (*pilum*), pike; but *cf.* Mat. 27. 48.

* See note on 19. 24. Here see ver. 33—two actions contrasted.

on, this disciple took her
into his home.

The Death of Jesus

28 Later, knowing that all
was now completed, and so
that the Scripture would be
fulfilled, Jesus said, "I am
thirsty." 29 A jar of wine
vinegar was there, so they
soaked a sponge in it, put
the sponge on a stalk of the
hyssop plant, and lifted it to
Jesus' lips. 30 When he had
received the drink, Jesus
said, "It is finished." With
that, he bowed his head and
gave up his spirit.
31 Now it was the day of
Preparation, and the next
day was to be a special Sabbath. Because the Jews did
not want the bodies left on
the crosses during the Sabbath, they asked Pilate to
have the legs broken and
the bodies taken down.
32 The soldiers therefore
came and broke the legs of
the first man who had been
crucified with Jesus, and
then those of the other.
33 But when they came to
Jesus and found that he was
already dead, they did not
break his legs. 34 Instead,
one of the soldiers pierced
Jesus' side with a spear,
bringing a sudden flow of
blood and water. 35 The
man who saw it has given
testimony, and his testimony is true. He knows that
he tells the truth, and he
testifies so that you also
may believe. 36 These
things happened so that the
scripture would be fulfilled:
"Not one of his bones will
be broken,"[c] 37 and, as another scripture says,
"They will look on the one
they have pierced."[d]

The Burial of Jesus

38 Later, Joseph of Arimathea asked Pilate for the

[c] 36 Exodus 12:46; Num. 9:12; Psalm 34:20
[d] 37 Zech. 12:10

was a disciple of Jesus, though a secret one because of his fear of the Jews, asked Pilate to let him take away the body of Jesus. Pilate gave him permission; so he came and removed his body. 39 Nicodemus, who had at first come to Jesus by night, also came, bringing a mixture of myrrh and aloes, weighing about a hundred pounds. 40 They took the body of Jesus and wrapped it with the spices in linen cloths, according to the burial custom of the Jews. 41 Now there was a garden in the place where he was crucified, and in the garden there was a new tomb in which no one had ever been laid. 42 And so, because it was the Jewish day of Preparation, and the tomb was nearby, they laid Jesus there.

ὢν μαθητὴς [τοῦ] Ἰησοῦ κεκρυμμένος
[4]being [5]a disciple – [6]of Jesus [8]*having been* hidden

δὲ διὰ τὸν φόβον τῶν Ἰουδαίων, ἵνα
[7]but [9]because of [10]the [11]fear [12]of the [13]Jews, that

ἄρῃ τὸ σῶμα τοῦ Ἰησοῦ· καὶ
he might take the body – of Jesus; and

ἐπέτρεψεν ὁ Πιλᾶτος. ἦλθεν οὖν καὶ ἦρεν
allowed – Pilate. He came therefore and took

τὸ σῶμα αὐτοῦ. 39 ἦλθεν δὲ καὶ Νικόδημος,
the body of him. And came also Nicodemus,

ὁ ἐλθὼν πρὸς αὐτὸν νυκτὸς τὸ πρῶτον,
the [one] having come to him of (by) night at first,†

φέρων μίγμα σμύρνης καὶ ἀλόης ὡς
bearing a mixture of myrrh and aloes about

λίτρας ἑκατόν. 40 ἔλαβον οὖν τὸ σῶμα
pounds a hundred. They took therefore the body

τοῦ Ἰησοῦ καὶ ἔδησαν αὐτὸ ὀθονίοις
– of Jesus and bound it in sheets

μετὰ τῶν ἀρωμάτων, καθὼς ἔθος ἐστὶν
with the spices, as custom is

τοῖς Ἰουδαίοις ἐνταφιάζειν. 41 ἦν δὲ
with the Jews to bury. Now there was

ἐν τῷ τόπῳ ὅπου ἐσταυρώθη κῆπος,
in the place where he was crucified a garden,

καὶ ἐν τῷ κήπῳ μνημεῖον καινόν, ἐν
and in the garden tomb a new, in

ᾧ οὐδέπω οὐδεὶς ἦν τεθειμένος· 42 ἐκεῖ
which never yet no(any) one was *having been* put; there

οὖν διὰ τὴν παρασκευὴν τῶν Ἰουδαίων,
therefore because of the preparation of the Jews,

ὅτι ἐγγὺς ἦν τὸ μνημεῖον, ἔθηκαν τὸν
because near was the tomb, they put –

Ἰησοῦν.
Jesus.

body of Jesus. Now Joseph was a disciple of Jesus, but secretly because he feared the Jews. With Pilate's permission, he came and took the body away. 39 He was accompanied by Nicodemus, the man who earlier had visited Jesus at night. Nicodemus brought a mixture of myrrh and aloes, about seventy-five pounds.[e] 40 Taking Jesus' body, the two of them wrapped it, with the spices, in strips of linen. This was in accordance with Jewish burial customs. 41 At the place where Jesus was crucified, there was a garden, and in the garden a new tomb, in which no one had ever been laid. 42 Because it was the Jewish day of Preparation and since the tomb was nearby, they laid Jesus there.

Chapter 20

The Resurrection of Jesus

EARLY on the first day of the week, while it was still dark, Mary Magdalene came to the tomb and saw that the stone had been removed from the tomb. 2 So she ran and went to Simon Peter and the other disciple, the one whom Jesus loved, and said to them, "They have taken the Lord out of the tomb, and we do not know where they have laid him." 3 Then Peter and the other disciple set out and went toward the tomb. 4 The two were running together, but the other disciple outran Peter and reached the tomb first. 5 He bent down to look in and

20 Τῇ δὲ μιᾷ τῶν σαββάτων Μαρία
Now on the one(first) [day] of the week Mary

ἡ Μαγδαληνὴ ἔρχεται πρωῒ σκοτίας ἔτι
the Magdalene comes early darkness yet
=while it was yet dark

οὔσης εἰς τὸ μνημεῖον, καὶ βλέπει τὸν
being[a] to the tomb, and sees the

λίθον ἠρμένον ἐκ τοῦ μνημείου.
stone having been taken out of the tomb.

2 τρέχει οὖν καὶ ἔρχεται πρὸς Σίμωνα
She runs therefore and comes to Simon

Πέτρον καὶ πρὸς τὸν ἄλλον μαθητὴν ὃν
Peter and to the other disciple whom

ἐφίλει ὁ Ἰησοῦς, καὶ λέγει αὐτοῖς· Ἦραν
[2]loved — [1]Jesus, and says to them: They took

τὸν κύριον ἐκ τοῦ μνημείου, καὶ οὐκ οἴδαμεν
the Lord out of the tomb, and we do not know

ποῦ ἔθηκαν αὐτόν. 3 Ἐξῆλθεν οὖν ὁ
where they put him. Went forth therefore –

Πέτρος καὶ ὁ ἄλλος μαθητής, καὶ ἤρχοντο
Peter and the other disciple, and came

εἰς τὸ μνημεῖον. 4 ἔτρεχον δὲ οἱ δύο
to the tomb. And ran the two

ὁμοῦ· καὶ ὁ ἄλλος μαθητὴς προέδραμεν
together; and the other disciple ran before

τάχιον τοῦ Πέτρου καὶ ἦλθεν πρῶτος
more quickly [than] – Peter and came first

εἰς τὸ μνημεῖον, 5 καὶ παρακύψας βλέπει
to the tomb, and stooping sees

Chapter 20

The Empty Tomb

EARLY on the first day of the week, while it was still dark, Mary Magdalene went to the tomb and saw that the stone had been removed from the entrance. 2 So she came running to Simon Peter and the other disciple, the one Jesus loved, and said, "They have taken the Lord out of the tomb, and we don't know where they have put him!"

3 So Peter and the other disciple started for the tomb. 4 Both were running, but the other disciple outran Peter and reached the tomb first. 5 He bent over and looked in at the strips

[j] Gk lacks *to look*
[k] That is, *Aramaic*

[e] 39 Greek *a hundred litrai* (about 34 kilograms)

saw the linen wrappings lying there, but he did not go
in. [6]Then Simon Peter
came, following him, and
went into the tomb. He saw
the linen wrappings lying
there, [7]and the cloth that
had been on Jesus' head,
not lying with the linen
wrappings but rolled up in a
place by itself. [8]Then the
other disciple, who reached
the tomb first, also went in,
and he saw and believed;
[9]for as yet they did not understand the scripture, that
he must rise from the dead.
[10]Then the disciples returned to their homes.

Jesus Appears to Mary Magdalene

11 But Mary stood
weeping outside the tomb.
As she wept, she bent over
to look[j] into the tomb;
[12]and she saw two angels in
white, sitting where the
body of Jesus had been lying, one at the head and the
other at the feet. [13]They
said to her, "Woman, why
are you weeping?" She said
to them, "They have taken
away my Lord, and I do not
know where they have laid
him." [14]When she had said
this, she turned around and
saw Jesus standing there,
but she did not know that it
was Jesus. [15]Jesus said to
her, "Woman, why are you
weeping? Whom are you
looking for?" Supposing
him to be the gardener, she
said to him, "Sir, if you
have carried him away, tell
me where you have laid
him, and I will take him
away." [16]Jesus said to her,
"Mary!" She turned and
said to him in Hebrew,[k]
"Rabbouni!" (which means
Teacher). [17]Jesus said to
her, "Do not hold on to me,

[j] Gk lacks *to look*
[k] That is, *Aramaic*

κείμενα τὰ ὀθόνια, οὐ μέντοι εἰσῆλθεν.
lying the sheets, not however he entered.

6 ἔρχεται οὖν καὶ Σίμων Πέτρος ἀκο-
Comes therefore also Simon Peter follow-

λουθῶν αὐτῷ, καὶ εἰσῆλθεν εἰς τὸ
ing him, and entered into the

μνημεῖον· καὶ θεωρεῖ τὰ ὀθόνια κείμενα,
tomb; and he beholds the sheets lying,

7 καὶ τὸ σουδάριον, ὃ ἦν ἐπὶ τῆς
and the kerchief, which was on the

κεφαλῆς αὐτοῦ, οὐ μετὰ τῶν ὀθονίων
head of him, not with the sheets

κείμενον ἀλλὰ χωρὶς ἐντετυλιγμένον εἰς
lying but apart having been wrapped up in

ἕνα τόπον. **8** τότε οὖν εἰσῆλθεν καὶ
one place. Then therefore entered also

ὁ ἄλλος μαθητὴς ὁ ἐλθὼν πρῶτος εἰς
the other disciple – having come first to

τὸ μνημεῖον, καὶ εἶδεν καὶ ἐπίστευσεν·
the tomb, and he saw and believed;

9 οὐδέπω γὰρ ᾔδεισαν τὴν γραφήν, ὅτι
for not yet they knew the scripture, that

δεῖ αὐτὸν ἐκ νεκρῶν ἀναστῆναι.
it behoves him from [the] dead to rise again.

10 ἀπῆλθον οὖν πάλιν πρὸς αὐτοὺς οἱ
Went away therefore again to themselves* the

μαθηταί. **11** Μαρία δὲ εἱστήκει πρὸς
disciples. But Mary stood at

τῷ μνημείῳ ἔξω κλαίουσα. ὡς οὖν
the tomb outside weeping. As therefore

ἔκλαιεν, παρέκυψεν εἰς τὸ μνημεῖον,
she was weeping, she stooped into the tomb,

12 καὶ θεωρεῖ δύο ἀγγέλους ἐν λευκοῖς
and beholds two angels in white

καθεζομένους, ἕνα πρὸς τῇ κεφαλῇ καὶ
sitting, one at the head and

ἕνα πρὸς τοῖς ποσίν, ὅπου ἔκειτο τὸ
one at the feet, where lay the

σῶμα τοῦ Ἰησοῦ. **13** καὶ λέγουσιν αὐτῇ
body – of Jesus. And say to her

ἐκεῖνοι· γύναι, τί κλαίεις; λέγει αὐτοῖς
those: Woman, why weepest thou? She says to them[,]

ὅτι ἦραν τὸν κύριόν μου, καὶ οὐκ οἶδα
– They took the Lord of me, and I know not

ποῦ ἔθηκαν αὐτόν. **14** ταῦτα εἰποῦσα
where they put him. These things saying

ἐστράφη εἰς τὰ ὀπίσω, καὶ θεωρεῖ τὸν
she turned back,† and beholds –

Ἰησοῦν ἑστῶτα, καὶ οὐκ ᾔδει ὅτι Ἰησοῦς
Jesus standing, and knew not that Jesus

ἐστιν. **15** λέγει αὐτῇ Ἰησοῦς· γύναι,
it is(was). Says to her Jesus: Woman,

τί κλαίεις; τίνα ζητεῖς; ἐκείνη δοκοῦσα
why weepest thou? whom seekest thou? That one thinking

ὅτι ὁ κηπουρός ἐστιν, λέγει αὐτῷ· κύριε,
that the gardener it is(was), says to him: Sir,

εἰ σὺ ἐβάστασας αὐτόν, εἰπέ μοι ποῦ
if thou didst carry him, tell me where

ἔθηκας αὐτόν, κἀγὼ αὐτὸν ἀρῶ. **16** λέγει
thou didst put him, and I him will take. Says

αὐτῇ Ἰησοῦς· Μαριάμ. στραφεῖσα ἐκείνη
to her Jesus: Mary. Turning that one

λέγει αὐτῷ Ἑβραϊστί· ῥαββουνί (ὃ λέγεται
says to him in Hebrew: Rabboni (which is said

διδάσκαλε). **17** λέγει αὐτῇ Ἰησοῦς· μή
Teacher). Says to her Jesus: Not

* That is, to their own home; *cf.* 19. 27.

of linen lying there but did
not go in. [6]Then Simon Peter, who was behind him,
arrived and went into the
tomb. He saw the strips of
linen lying there, [7]as well as
the burial cloth that had
been around Jesus' head.
The cloth was folded up by
itself, separate from the lin-
en. [8]Finally the other disciple, who had reached the
tomb first, also went in-
side. He saw and believed.
[9](They still did not understand from Scripture that
Jesus had to rise from the
dead.)

Jesus Appears to Mary Magdalene

[10]Then the disciples went
back to their homes, [11]but
Mary stood outside the
tomb crying. As she wept,
she bent over to look into
the tomb [12]and saw two angels in white, seated where
Jesus' body had been, one
at the head and the other at
the foot.

[13]They asked her,
"Woman, why are you cry-
ing?"

"They have taken my
Lord away," she said,
"and I don't know where
they have put him." [14]At
this, she turned around and
saw Jesus standing there,
but she did not realize that
it was Jesus.

[15]"Woman," he said,
"why are you crying? Who
is it you are looking for?"

Thinking he was the gar-
dener, she said, "Sir, if you
have carried him away, tell
me where you have put
him, and I will get him."

[16]Jesus said to her,
"Mary."

She turned toward him
and cried out in Aramaic,
"Rabboni!" (which means
Teacher).

[17]Jesus said, "Do not

because I have not yet ascended to the Father. But go to my brothers and say to them, 'I am ascending to my Father and your Father, to my God and your God.' " 18 Mary Magdalene went and announced to the disciples, "I have seen the Lord"; and she told them that he had said these things to her.

Jesus Appears to the Disciples

19 When it was evening on that day, the first day of the week, and the doors of the house where the disciples had met were locked for fear of the Jews, Jesus came and stood among them and said, "Peace be with you." 20 After he said this, he showed them his hands and his side. Then the disciples rejoiced when they saw the Lord. 21 Jesus said to them again, "Peace be with you. As the Father has sent me, so I send you." 22 When he had said this, he breathed on them and said to them, "Receive the Holy Spirit. 23 If you forgive the sins of any, they are forgiven them; if you retain the sins of any, they are retained."

Jesus and Thomas

24 But Thomas (who was called the Twin[j]), one of the twelve, was not with them when Jesus came. 25 So the other disciples told him, "We have seen the Lord." But he said to them, "Unless I see the mark of the nails in his hands, and put my finger in the mark of the nails and my hand in his side, I will not believe."

[j] Gk *Didymus*

μου ἅπτου, οὔπω γὰρ ἀναβέβηκα πρὸς
me touch, for not yet have I ascended to
τὸν πατέρα· πορεύου δὲ πρὸς τοὺς
the Father; but go thou to the
ἀδελφούς μου καὶ εἰπὲ αὐτοῖς· ἀναβαίνω
brothers of me and tell them: I ascend
πρὸς τὸν πατέρα μου καὶ πατέρα ὑμῶν
to the Father of me and Father of you
καὶ θεόν μου καὶ θεὸν ὑμῶν. 18 ἔρχεται
and God of me and God of you. Comes
Μαριὰμ ἡ Μαγδαληνὴ ἀγγέλλουσα τοῖς
Mary the Magdalene announcing to the
μαθηταῖς ὅτι ἑώρακα τὸν κύριον, καὶ
disciples[,] – I have seen the Lord, and
ταῦτα εἶπεν αὐτῇ.
these things he said to her.
19 Οὔσης οὖν ὀψίας τῇ ἡμέρᾳ ἐκείνῃ
Being therefore early evening[a] – day on that
=Therefore when it was early evening
τῇ μιᾷ σαββάτων, καὶ τῶν θυρῶν
the one(first) of the week, and the doors
κεκλεισμένων ὅπου ἦσαν οἱ μαθηταὶ διὰ
having been shut[a] where were the disciples because of
τὸν φόβον τῶν Ἰουδαίων, ἦλθεν ὁ Ἰησοῦς
the fear of the Jews, came – Jesus
καὶ ἔστη εἰς τὸ μέσον, καὶ λέγει αὐτοῖς·
and stood in the midst, and says to them:
εἰρήνη ὑμῖν. 20 καὶ τοῦτο εἰπὼν ἔδειξεν
Peace to you. And this saying he showed
καὶ τὰς χεῖρας καὶ τὴν πλευρὰν αὐτοῖς.
both the(his) hands and the(his) side to them.
ἐχάρησαν οὖν οἱ μαθηταὶ ἰδόντες τὸν
Rejoiced therefore the disciples seeing the
κύριον. 21 εἶπεν οὖν αὐτοῖς [ὁ Ἰησοῦς]
Lord. Said therefore to them – Jesus
πάλιν· εἰρήνη ὑμῖν· καθὼς ἀπέσταλκέν
again: Peace to you; as has sent
με ὁ πατήρ, κἀγὼ πέμπω ὑμᾶς. 22 καὶ
me the Father, I also send you. And
τοῦτο εἰπὼν ἐνεφύσησεν καὶ λέγει αὐτοῖς·
this saying he breathed in and says to them:
λάβετε πνεῦμα ἅγιον. 23 ἄν τινων
Receive ye Spirit Holy. Of whomever
ἀφῆτε τὰς ἁμαρτίας, ἀφέωνται αὐτοῖς·
ye forgive the sins, they have been forgiven to them;
ἄν τινων κρατῆτε, κεκράτηνται.
of whomever ye hold, they have been held.
24 Θωμᾶς δὲ εἷς ἐκ τῶν δώδεκα,
But Thomas one of the twelve,
ὁ λεγόμενος Δίδυμος, οὐκ ἦν μετ' αὐτῶν
– *being* called Twin, was not with them
ὅτε ἦλθεν Ἰησοῦς. 25 ἔλεγον οὖν αὐτῷ
when came Jesus. Said therefore to him
οἱ ἄλλοι μαθηταί· ἑωράκαμεν τὸν κύριον.
the other disciples: We have seen the Lord.
ὁ δὲ εἶπεν αὐτοῖς· ἐὰν μὴ ἴδω ἐν
But he said to them: Unless I see in
ταῖς χερσὶν αὐτοῦ τὸν τύπον τῶν ἥλων
the hands of him the mark of the nails
καὶ βάλω τὸν δάκτυλόν μου εἰς τὸν
and put the finger of me into the
τόπον τῶν ἥλων καὶ βάλω μου τὴν
place of the nails and put of me the
χεῖρα εἰς τὴν πλευρὰν αὐτοῦ, οὐ μὴ
hand into the side of him, by no means

hold on to me, for I have not yet returned to the Father. Go instead to my brothers and tell them, 'I am returning to my Father and your Father, to my God and your God.' "

18 Mary Magdalene went to the disciples with the news: "I have seen the Lord!" And she told them that he had said these things to her.

Jesus Appears to His Disciples

19 On the evening of that first day of the week, when the disciples were together, with the doors locked for fear of the Jews, Jesus came and stood among them and said, "Peace be with you!" 20 After he said this, he showed them his hands and side. The disciples were overjoyed when they saw the Lord.

21 Again Jesus said, "Peace be with you! As the Father has sent me, I am sending you." 22 And with that he breathed on them and said, "Receive the Holy Spirit. 23 If you forgive anyone his sins, they are forgiven; if you do not forgive them, they are not forgiven."

Jesus Appears to Thomas

24 Now Thomas (called Didymus), one of the Twelve, was not with the disciples when Jesus came. 25 So the other disciples told him, "We have seen the Lord!"

But he said to them, "Unless I see the nail marks in his hands and put my finger where the nails were, and put my hand into his side, I will not believe it."

26 A week later his dis-
ciples were again in the
house, and Thomas was
with them. Although the
doors were shut, Jesus
came and stood among
them and said, "Peace be
with you." 27 Then he said
to Thomas, "Put your fin-
ger here and see my hands.
Reach out your hand and
put it in my side. Do not
doubt but believe."
28 Thomas answered him,
"My Lord and my God!"
29 Jesus said to him, "Have
you believed because you
have seen me? Blessed are
those who have not seen
and yet have come to be-
lieve."

The Purpose of This Book

30 Now Jesus did many
other signs in the presence
of his disciples, which are
not written in this book.
31 But these are written so
that you may come to be-
lieve[m] that Jesus is the
Messiah,[n] the Son of God,
and that through believing
you may have life in his
name.

πιστεύσω. **26** Καὶ μεθ' ἡμέρας ὀκτὼ
will I believe. And after days eight
πάλιν ἦσαν ἔσω οἱ μαθηταὶ αὐτοῦ, καὶ
again were within the disciples of him, and
Θωμᾶς μετ' αὐτῶν. ἔρχεται ὁ Ἰησοῦς
Thomas with them. Comes – Jesus
τῶν θυρῶν κεκλεισμένων, καὶ ἔστη εἰς
the doors having been shut*, and stood in
τὸ μέσον καὶ εἶπεν· εἰρήνη ὑμῖν. **27** εἶτα
the midst and said: Peace to you. Then
λέγει τῷ Θωμᾷ· φέρε τὸν δάκτυλόν
he says – to Thomas: Bring the finger
σου ὧδε καὶ ἴδε τὰς χεῖράς μου, καὶ
of thee here and see the hands of me, and
φέρε τὴν χεῖρά σου καὶ βάλε εἰς τὴν
bring the hand of thee and put into the
πλευράν μου, καὶ μὴ γίνου ἄπιστος
side of me, and be not faithless
ἀλλὰ πιστός. **28** ἀπεκρίθη Θωμᾶς καὶ
but faithful. Answered Thomas and
εἶπεν αὐτῷ· ὁ κύριός μου καὶ ὁ θεός
said to him: The Lord of me and the God
μου. **29** λέγει αὐτῷ ὁ Ἰησοῦς· ὅτι
of me. Says to him – Jesus: Because
ἑώρακάς με, πεπίστευκας; μακάριοι οἱ
thou hast seen me, hast thou believed? blessed the [ones]
μὴ ἰδόντες καὶ πιστεύσαντες.
not seeing and§ believing.
30 Πολλὰ μὲν οὖν καὶ ἄλλα σημεῖα
Many –* therefore and other signs
ἐποίησεν ὁ Ἰησοῦς ἐνώπιον τῶν μαθητῶν,
did – Jesus before the disciples,
ἃ οὐκ ἔστιν γεγραμμένα ἐν τῷ βιβλίῳ
which is(are) not *having been* written in – roll
τούτῳ· **31** ταῦτα δὲ γέγραπται ἵνα
this; but these* has(ve) been written that
πιστεύητε ὅτι Ἰησοῦς ἐστιν ὁ χριστὸς ὁ
ye may believe that Jesus is the Christ the
υἱὸς τοῦ θεοῦ, καὶ ἵνα πιστεύοντες ζωὴν
Son – of God, and that believing life
ἔχητε ἐν τῷ ὀνόματι αὐτοῦ.
ye may have in the name of him.

26A week later his disci-
ples were in the house
again, and Thomas was
with them. Though the
doors were locked, Jesus
came and stood among
them and said, "Peace be
with you!" 27Then he said
to Thomas, "Put your fin-
ger here; see my hands.
Reach out your hand and
put it into my side. Stop
doubting and believe."
28Thomas said to him,
"My Lord and my God!"
29Then Jesus told him,
"Because you have seen
me, you have believed;
blessed are those who have
not seen and yet have be-
lieved."
30Jesus did many other
miraculous signs in the
presence of his disciples,
which are not recorded in
this book. 31But these are
written that you may[f] believe that Jesus is the
Christ, the Son of God, and
that by believing you may
have life in his name.

Chapter 21

Jesus Appears to Seven Disciples

AFTER these things
Jesus showed himself
again to the disciples by the
Sea of Tiberias; and he
showed himself in this way.
2 Gathered there together
were Simon Peter, Thomas
called the Twin,[l] Nathanael of Cana in Galilee, the
sons of Zebedee, and two
others of his disciples. 3 Simon Peter said to them, "I
am going fishing." They
said to him, "We will go
with you." They went out
and got into the boat, but
that night they caught nothing.

21 Μετὰ ταῦτα ἐφανέρωσεν ἑαυτὸν πάλιν
After these things manifested himself again
Ἰησοῦς τοῖς μαθηταῖς ἐπὶ τῆς θαλάσσης
Jesus to the disciples on the sea
τῆς Τιβεριάδος· ἐφανέρωσεν δὲ οὕτως.
– of Tiberias; and he manifested [himself] thus.
2 ἦσαν ὁμοῦ Σίμων Πέτρος καὶ Θωμᾶς
There were together Simon Peter and Thomas
ὁ λεγόμενος Δίδυμος καὶ Ναθαναὴλ ὁ
– *being* called Twin and Nathanael –
ἀπὸ Κανὰ τῆς Γαλιλαίας καὶ οἱ τοῦ
from Cana – of Galilee and the [sons] –
Ζεβεδαίου καὶ ἄλλοι ἐκ τῶν μαθητῶν
of Zebedee and others of the disciples
αὐτοῦ δύο. **3** λέγει αὐτοῖς Σίμων Πέτρος·
of him two. Says to them Simon Peter:
ὑπάγω ἁλιεύειν. λέγουσιν αὐτῷ· ἐρχόμεθα
I am going to fish. They say to him: Are coming
καὶ ἡμεῖς σὺν σοί. ἐξῆλθον καὶ ἐνέβησαν
also we with thee. They went forth and embarked
εἰς τὸ πλοῖον, καὶ ἐν ἐκείνῃ τῇ νυκτὶ
in the boat, and in that – night

Chapter 21

Jesus and the Miraculous Catch of Fish

AFTERWARD Jesus ap-
peared again to his
disciples, by the Sea of Tiberias.[g] It happened this
way: 2Simon Peter, Thom-
as (called Didymus), Na-
thanael from Cana in Galilee, the sons of Zebedee,
and two other disciples
were together. 3"I'm going
out to fish," Simon Peter
told them, and they said,
"We'll go with you." So
they went out and got into
the boat, but that night they

[m] Other ancient authorities read *may continue to believe*
[n] Or *the Christ*

* See note on 19. 24 and 32.
§ καί sometimes = and yet; see 5. 40; 8. 55; 9. 30; 16. 32; 17. 11.

[f] 31 Some manuscripts *may continue to*
[g] 1 That is, Sea of Galilee

4 Just after daybreak,
Jesus stood on the beach;
but the disciples did not
know that it was Jesus.
5 Jesus said to them, "Children, you have no fish,
have you?" They answered
him, "No." 6 He said to
them, "Cast the net to the
right side of the boat, and
you will find some." So
they cast it, and now they
were not able to haul it in
because there were so
many fish. 7 That disciple
whom Jesus loved said to
Peter, "It is the Lord!"
When Simon Peter heard
that it was the Lord, he put
on some clothes, for he was
naked, and jumped into the
sea. 8 But the other disciples came in the boat, dragging the net full of fish, for
they were not far from the
land, only about a hundred
yards[o] off.
9 When they had gone
ashore, they saw a charcoal
fire there, with fish on it,
and bread. 10 Jesus said to
them, "Bring some of the
fish that you have just
caught." 11 So Simon Peter
went aboard and hauled the
net ashore, full of large
fish, a hundred fifty-three
of them; and though there
were so many, the net was
not torn. 12 Jesus said to
them, "Come and have
breakfast." Now none of
the disciples dared to ask
him, "Who are you?" be-
cause they knew it was the
Lord. 13 Jesus came and
took the bread and gave it
to them, and did the same
with the fish. 14 This was
now the third time that
Jesus appeared to the disciples after he was raised
from the dead.

[o] Gk *two hundred cubits*

ἐπίασαν οὐδέν. **4** πρωΐας δὲ ἤδη γινομένης
they caught nothing. Early morning but now becoming[a]
=But when it became early morning
ἔστη Ἰησοῦς εἰς τὸν αἰγιαλόν· οὐ μέντοι
stood Jesus in(on) the shore; not however
ᾔδεισαν οἱ μαθηταὶ ὅτι Ἰησοῦς ἐστιν.
knew the disciples that Jesus it is(was).
5 λέγει οὖν αὐτοῖς Ἰησοῦς· παιδία, μή
Says therefore to them Jesus: Children, *not*
τι προσφάγιον ἔχετε; ἀπεκρίθησαν αὐτῷ·
any fish have ye? They answered him:
οὔ. **6** ὁ δὲ εἶπεν αὐτοῖς· βάλετε εἰς τὰ
No. So he said to them: Cast in the
δεξιὰ μέρη τοῦ πλοίου τὸ δίκτυον, καὶ
right parts of the boat the net, and
εὑρήσετε. ἔβαλον οὖν, καὶ οὐκέτι αὐτὸ
ye will find. They cast therefore, and [1]no longer [4]it
ἑλκύσαι ἴσχυον ἀπὸ τοῦ πλήθους τῶν
[3]to drag [2]were they able from the multitude of the
ἰχθύων. **7** λέγει οὖν ὁ μαθητὴς ἐκεῖνος
fishes. Says therefore – disciple that
ὃν ἠγάπα ὁ Ἰησοῦς τῷ Πέτρῳ· ὁ κύριός
whom [2]loved – [1]Jesus – to Peter: The Lord
ἐστιν. Σίμων οὖν Πέτρος, ἀκούσας ὅτι
it is. [2]Simon [1]therefore [3]Peter, hearing that
ὁ κύριός ἐστιν, τὸν ἐπενδύτην διεζώσατο,
the Lord it is(was), [2][with]the [3]coat [1]girded himself,
ἦν γὰρ γυμνός, καὶ ἔβαλεν ἑαυτὸν εἰς
for he was naked, and threw himself into
τὴν θάλασσαν· **8** οἱ δὲ ἄλλοι μαθηταὶ
the sea; but the other disciples
τῷ πλοιαρίῳ ἦλθον, οὐ γὰρ ἦσαν μακρὰν
in the little boat came, for not they were far
ἀπὸ τῆς γῆς ἀλλὰ ὡς ἀπὸ πηχῶν
from the land but about from cubits
διακοσίων, σύροντες τὸ δίκτυον τῶν ἰχθύων.
two hundred dragging the net of the fishes.
9 ὡς οὖν ἀπέβησαν εἰς τὴν γῆν, βλέπουσιν
When therefore they disembarked onto the land, they see
ἀνθρακιὰν κειμένην καὶ ὀψάριον ἐπικείμενον
a coal fire lying and a fish lying on
καὶ ἄρτον. **10** λέγει αὐτοῖς ὁ Ἰησοῦς·
and bread. Says to them – Jesus:
ἐνέγκατε ἀπὸ τῶν ὀψαρίων ὧν ἐπιάσατε
Bring from the fishes which ye caught
νῦν. **11** ἀνέβη Σίμων Πέτρος καὶ εἵλκυσεν
now. Went up Simon Peter and dragged
τὸ δίκτυον εἰς τὴν γῆν μεστὸν ἰχθύων
the net to the land full fishes
μεγάλων ἑκατὸν πεντήκοντα τριῶν· καὶ
of great a hundred fifty three; and
τοσούτων ὄντων οὐκ ἐσχίσθη τὸ δίκτυον.
so many being[a] was not torn the net.
12 λέγει αὐτοῖς ὁ Ἰησοῦς· δεῦτε ἀριστήσατε.
Says to them – Jesus: Come breakfast ye.
οὐδεὶς ἐτόλμα τῶν μαθητῶν ἐξετάσαι
No one dared of the disciples to question
αὐτόν· σὺ τίς εἶ; εἰδότες ὅτι ὁ κύριός
him: Thou who art? knowing that the Lord
ἐστιν. **13** ἔρχεται Ἰησοῦς καὶ λαμβάνει
it is(was). Comes Jesus and takes
τὸν ἄρτον καὶ δίδωσιν αὐτοῖς, καὶ τὸ
the bread and gives to them, and the
ὀψάριον ὁμοίως. **14** τοῦτο ἤδη τρίτον
fish likewise. This [was] now [the] third [time] [that]
ἐφανερώθη Ἰησοῦς τοῖς μαθηταῖς ἐγερθεὶς
[2]was manifested [1]Jesus to the disciples raised

caught nothing.
4Early in the morning,
Jesus stood on the shore,
but the disciples did not realize that it was Jesus.
5He called out to them,
"Friends, haven't you any
fish?"
"No," they answered.
6He said, "Throw your
net on the right side of the
boat and you will find
some." When they did,
they were unable to haul
the net in because of the
large number of fish.
7Then the disciple whom
Jesus loved said to Peter,
"It is the Lord!" As soon
as Simon Peter heard him
say, "It is the Lord," he
wrapped his outer garment
around him (for he had tak-
en it off) and jumped into
the water. 8The other disciples followed in the boat,
towing the net full of fish,
for they were not far from
shore, about a hundred
yards.[h] 9When they landed, they saw a fire of burning coals there with fish on
it, and some bread.
10Jesus said to them,
"Bring some of the fish you
have just caught."
11Simon Peter climbed
aboard and dragged the net
ashore. It was full of large
fish, 153, but even with so
many the net was not torn.
12Jesus said to them,
"Come and have break-
fast." None of the disciples
dared ask him, "Who are
you?" They knew it was
the Lord. 13Jesus came,
took the bread and gave it
to them, and did the same
with the fish. 14This was
now the third time Jesus
appeared to his disciples after he was raised from the
dead.

[h]8 Greek *about two hundred cubits* (about 90 meters)

Jesus and Peter

15 When they had fin-
ished breakfast, Jesus said
to Simon Peter, "Simon
son of John, do you love me
more than these?" He said
to him, "Yes, Lord; you
know that I love you."
Jesus said to him, "Feed
my lambs." 16 A second
time he said to him, "Simon
son of John, do you love
me?" He said to him, "Yes,
Lord; you know that I love
you." Jesus said to him,
"Tend my sheep." 17 He
said to him the third time,
"Simon son of John, do you
love me?" Peter felt hurt
because he said to him the
third time, "Do you love
me?" And he said to him,
"Lord, you know every-
thing; you know that I love
you." Jesus said to him,
"Feed my sheep. 18 Very
truly, I tell you, when you
were younger, you used to
fasten your own belt and to
go wherever you wished.
But when you grow old,
you will stretch out your
hands, and someone else
will fasten a belt around
you and take you where
you do not wish to go."
19 (He said this to indicate
the kind of death by which
he would glorify God.) After this he said to him, "Follow me."

Jesus and the Beloved Disciple

20 Peter turned and saw
the disciple whom Jesus
loved following them; he
was the one who had re-
clined next to Jesus at the
supper and had said,
"Lord, who is it that is going to betray you?" 21 When
Peter saw him, he said to
Jesus, "Lord, what about
him?" 22 Jesus said to him,
"If it is my will that he remain until I come, what is
that to you? Follow me!"
23 So the rumor spread in
the community[p] that this
disciple would not die. Yet

[p] Gk *among the brothers*

ἐκ νεκρῶν.
from [the] dead.
15 Ὅτε οὖν ἠρίστησαν, λέγει τῷ
When therefore they breakfasted, says –
Σίμωνι Πέτρῳ ὁ Ἰησοῦς· Σίμων Ἰωάννου,
to Simon Peter – Jesus: Simon [son] of John,
ἀγαπᾷς με πλέον τούτων; λέγει αὐτῷ·
lovest thou me more [than] these? He says to him:
ναί, κύριε, σὺ οἶδας ὅτι φιλῶ σε. λέγει
Yes, Lord, thou knowest that I love thee. He says
αὐτῷ· βόσκε τὰ ἀρνία μου. **16** λέγει
to him: Feed the lambs of me. He says
αὐτῷ πάλιν δεύτερον· Σίμων Ἰωάννου,
to him again secondly: Simon [son] of John,
ἀγαπᾷς με; λέγει αὐτῷ· ναί, κύριε,
lovest thou me? He says to him: Yes, Lord,
σὺ οἶδας ὅτι φιλῶ σε. λέγει αὐτῷ·
thou knowest that I love thee. He says to him:
ποίμαινε τὰ προβάτιά μου. **17** λέγει
Shepherd the little sheep of me. He says
αὐτῷ τὸ τρίτον· Σίμων Ἰωάννου, φιλεῖς
to him the third [time]: Simon [son] of John, lovest thou
με; ἐλυπήθη ὁ Πέτρος ὅτι εἶπεν αὐτῷ
me? Was grieved – Peter that he said to him
τὸ τρίτον· φιλεῖς με; καὶ εἶπεν αὐτῷ·
the third [time]: Lovest thou me? and said to him:
κύριε, πάντα σὺ οἶδας, σὺ γινώσκεις
Lord, all things thou knowest, thou knowest
ὅτι φιλῶ σε· λέγει αὐτῷ Ἰησοῦς· βόσκε
that I love thee; says to him Jesus: Feed
τὰ προβάτιά μου. **18** ἀμὴν ἀμὴν λέγω
the little sheep of me. Truly truly I tell
σοι, ὅτε ἦς νεώτερος, ἐζώννυες σεαυτὸν
thee, when thou wast younger, thou girdedst thyself
καὶ περιεπάτεις ὅπου ἤθελες· ὅταν δὲ
and walkedst where thou wishedst; but when
γηράσῃς, ἐκτενεῖς τὰς χεῖράς σου, καὶ
thou growest old, thou wilt stretch out the hands of thee, and
ἄλλος ζώσει σε καὶ οἴσει ὅπου οὐ θέλεις.
another will gird thee and will carry where thou wishest not.
19 τοῦτο δὲ εἶπεν σημαίνων ποίῳ θανάτῳ
And this he said signifying by what death
δοξάσει τὸν θεόν. καὶ τοῦτο εἰπὼν λέγει
he will glorify – God. And this saying he tells
αὐτῷ· ἀκολούθει μοι. **20** ἐπιστραφεὶς ὁ
him: Follow me. Turning –
Πέτρος βλέπει τὸν μαθητὴν ὃν ἠγάπα ὁ
Peter sees the disciple whom [2]loved –
Ἰησοῦς ἀκολουθοῦντα, ὃς καὶ ἀνέπεσεν
[1]Jesus following, who also leaned
ἐν τῷ δείπνῳ ἐπὶ τὸ στῆθος αὐτοῦ καὶ
at the supper on the breast of him and
εἶπεν· κύριε, τίς ἐστιν ὁ παραδιδούς σε;
said: Lord, who is the[one] betraying thee?
21 τοῦτον οὖν ἰδὼν ὁ Πέτρος λέγει τῷ
[4]This one [2]therefore [3]seeing – [1]Peter says –
Ἰησοῦ· κύριε, οὗτος δὲ τί; **22** λέγει
to Jesus: Lord, and this one what? Says
αὐτῷ ὁ Ἰησοῦς· ἐὰν αὐτὸν θέλω μένειν
to him – Jesus: If him I wish to remain
ἕως ἔρχομαι, τί πρὸς σέ; σύ μοι
until I come, what to thee? [2]thou [3]me
ἀκολούθει. **23** ἐξῆλθεν οὖν οὗτος ὁ λόγος
[1]follow. Went forth therefore this – word
εἰς τοὺς ἀδελφοὺς ὅτι ὁ μαθητὴς ἐκεῖνος
to the brothers that – disciple that

Jesus Reinstates Peter

15 When they had finished
eating, Jesus said to Simon
Peter, "Simon son of John,
do you truly love me more
than these?"
"Yes, Lord," he said,
"you know that I love
you."
Jesus said, "Feed my
lambs."
16 Again Jesus said, "Si-
mon son of John, do you
truly love me?"
He answered, "Yes,
Lord, you know that I love
you."
Jesus said, "Take care of
my sheep."
17 The third time he said to
him, "Simon son of John,
do you love me?"
Peter was hurt because
Jesus asked him the third
time, "Do you love me?"
He said, "Lord, you know
all things; you know that I
love you."
Jesus said, "Feed my
sheep. 18 I tell you the truth,
when you were younger
you dressed yourself and
went where you wanted;
but when you are old you
will stretch out your hands,
and someone else will dress
you and lead you where
you do not want to go."
19 Jesus said this to indicate
the kind of death by which
Peter would glorify God.
Then he said to him, "Follow me!"
20 Peter turned and saw
that the disciple whom
Jesus loved was following
them. (This was the one
who had leaned back
against Jesus at the supper
and had said, "Lord, who
is going to betray you?")
21 When Peter saw him, he
asked, "Lord, what about
him?"
22 Jesus answered, "If I
want him to remain alive
until I return, what is that
to you? You must follow
me." 23 Because of this, the
rumor spread among the
brothers that this disciple

Jesus did not say to him that he would not die, but, "If it is my will that he remain until I come, what is that to you?"[q]
24 This is the disciple who is testifying to these things and has written them, and we know that his testimony is true. [25]But there are also many other things that Jesus did; if every one of them were written down, I suppose that the world itself could not contain the books that would be written.

οὐκ ἀποθνῄσκει· οὐκ εἶπεν δὲ αὐτῷ ὁ
does not die; but said not to him –
Ἰησοῦς ὅτι οὐκ ἀποθνῄσκει, ἀλλ'· ἐὰν
Jesus that he does not die, but: If
αὐτὸν θέλω μένειν ἕως ἔρχομαι, τί πρὸς
him I wish to remain until I come, what to
σέ;
thee?
24 Οὗτός ἐστιν ὁ μαθητὴς ὁ μαρτυρῶν
This is the disciple – witnessing
περὶ τούτων καὶ ὁ γράψας ταῦτα,
concerning these things and – having written these things,
καὶ οἴδαμεν ὅτι ἀληθὴς αὐτοῦ ἡ μαρτυρία
and we know that true of him the witness
ἐστίν. **25** Ἔστιν δὲ καὶ ἄλλα πολλὰ ἃ
is. And there are also other things many which
ἐποίησεν ὁ Ἰησοῦς, ἅτινα ἐὰν γράφηται
did – Jesus, which if they were written
καθ' ἕν, οὐδ' αὐτὸν οἶμαι τὸν κόσμον
singly,† [5]not [4][it]self [1]I think [2]the [3]world
χωρήσειν τὰ γραφόμενα βιβλία.
[6]to contain [7]the [8]being written [9]rolls.

would not die. But Jesus did not say that he would not die; he only said, "If I want him to remain alive until I return, what is that to you?"
[24]This is the disciple who testifies to these things and who wrote them down. We know that his testimony is true.
[25]Jesus did many other things as well. If every one of them were written down, I suppose that even the whole world would not have room for the books that would be written.

[q] Other ancient authorities lack *what is that to you*

The
Acts
of the Apostles

Chapter 1

The Promise of the Holy Spirit

IN the first book, The-
ophilus, I wrote about
all that Jesus did and taught
from the beginning 2until
the day when he was taken
up to heaven, after giving
instructions through the
Holy Spirit to the apostles
whom he had chosen. 3Af-
ter his suffering he presented himself alive to them by
many convincing proofs,
appearing to them during
forty days and speaking
about the kingdom of God.
4While staying[a] with
them, he ordered them not
to leave Jerusalem, but to
wait there for the promise
of the Father. "This," he
said, "is what you have
heard from me; 5for John
baptized with water, but
you will be baptized with[b]
the Holy Spirit not many
days from now."

The Ascension of Jesus

6 So when they had
come together, they asked
him, "Lord, is this the time
when you will restore the
kingdom to Israel?" 7He
replied, "It is not for you to
know the times or periods
that the Father has set by
his own authority. 8But
you will receive power
when the Holy Spirit has
come upon you; and you
will be my witnesses in Jerusalem, in all Judea and
Samaria, and to the ends of
the earth." 9When he had
said this, as they were
watching, he was lifted up,
and a cloud took him out of
their sight. 10While he was
going and they were gazing
up toward heaven, sudden-
ly two men in white robes
stood by them. 11They

[a] Or *eating*
[b] Or *by*

ΠΡΑΞΕΙΣ ΑΠΟΣΤΟΛΩΝ
Acts of Apostles

1 Τὸν μὲν πρῶτον λόγον ἐποιησάμην
The – first account I made

περὶ πάντων, ὦ Θεόφιλε, ὧν ἤρξατο
concerning all things, O Theophilus, which began

ὁ Ἰησοῦς ποιεῖν τε καὶ διδάσκειν,
– Jesus both to do and to teach,

2 ἄχρι ἧς ἡμέρας ἐντειλάμενος τοῖς
until which day [3]having given injunctions [6]to the
=the day on which

ἀποστόλοις διὰ πνεύματος ἁγίου οὓς
[7]apostles [2]through [5]Spirit [4]Holy [8]whom

ἐξελέξατο ἀνελήμφθη· **3** οἷς καὶ παρέστησεν
[9]he chose [1]he was taken up; to whom also he presented

ἑαυτὸν ζῶντα μετὰ τὸ παθεῖν αὐτὸν ἐν
himself living after the to suffer him[b] by
=he suffered

πολλοῖς τεκμηρίοις, δι' ἡμερῶν τεσσεράκοντα
many infallible proofs, through days forty

ὀπτανόμενος αὐτοῖς καὶ λέγων τὰ περὶ
being seen by them and speaking the things concerning

τῆς βασιλείας τοῦ θεοῦ· **4** καὶ συναλιζόμενος
the kingdom – of God; and meeting with [them]

παρήγγειλεν αὐτοῖς ἀπὸ Ἱεροσολύμων μὴ
he charged them from Jerusalem not

χωρίζεσθαι, ἀλλὰ περιμένειν τὴν ἐπαγγελίαν
to depart, but to await the promise

τοῦ πατρὸς ἣν ἠκούσατέ μου· **5** ὅτι
of the Father which ye heard of me: because

Ἰωάννης μὲν ἐβάπτισεν ὕδατι, ὑμεῖς δὲ
John indeed baptized in water, but ye

ἐν πνεύματι βαπτισθήσεσθε ἁγίῳ οὐ μετὰ
in [3]Spirit [1]will be baptized [2]Holy not after

πολλὰς ταύτας ἡμέρας. **6** Οἱ μὲν οὖν
many *these* days. [2]the [ones] [1]So then

συνελθόντες ἠρώτων αὐτὸν λέγοντες· κύριε,
[3]coming together questioned him saying: Lord,

εἰ ἐν τῷ χρόνῳ τούτῳ ἀποκαθιστάνεις
if at this time restorest thou

τὴν βασιλείαν τῷ Ἰσραήλ; **7** εἶπεν πρὸς
the kingdom – to Israel? He said to

αὐτούς· οὐχ ὑμῶν ἐστιν γνῶναι χρόνους
them: Not of you it is to know times

ἢ καιροὺς οὓς ὁ πατὴρ ἔθετο ἐν τῇ
or seasons which the Father placed in the(his)

ἰδίᾳ ἐξουσίᾳ, **8** ἀλλὰ λήμψεσθε δύναμιν
own authority, but ye will receive power

ἐπελθόντος τοῦ ἁγίου πνεύματος ἐφ' ὑμᾶς,
coming *upon* the Holy Spirit[a] upon you,
=when the Holy Spirit comes

καὶ ἔσεσθέ μου μάρτυρες ἔν τε Ἰερουσαλὴμ
and ye will be of me witnesses both in Jerusalem

καὶ ἐν πάσῃ τῇ Ἰουδαίᾳ καὶ Σαμαρείᾳ
and in all – Judæa and Samaria

καὶ ἕως ἐσχάτου τῆς γῆς. **9** καὶ ταῦτα
and unto [the] extremity of the earth. And these things

εἰπὼν βλεπόντων αὐτῶν ἐπήρθη, καὶ
saying looking them[a] he was taken up, and
=as they looked

νεφέλη ὑπέλαβεν αὐτὸν ἀπὸ τῶν ὀφθαλμῶν
a cloud received him from the eyes

αὐτῶν. **10** καὶ ὡς ἀτενίζοντες ἦσαν εἰς
of them. And as gazing they were to

τὸν οὐρανὸν πορευομένου αὐτοῦ, καὶ ἰδοὺ
– heaven going him,[a] – behold[,]
=as he went,

ἄνδρες δύο παρειστήκεισαν αὐτοῖς ἐν ἐσθήσεσι
men two stood by them in garments

Acts

Chapter 1

Jesus Taken Up Into Heaven

IN my former book, The-
ophilus, I wrote about
all that Jesus began to do
and to teach 2until the day
he was taken up to heaven,
after giving instructions
through the Holy Spirit to
the apostles he had chosen.
3After his suffering, he
showed himself to these
men and gave many con-
vincing proofs that he was
alive. He appeared to them
over a period of forty days
and spoke about the king-
dom of God. 4On one occa-
sion, while he was eating
with them, he gave them
this command: "Do not
leave Jerusalem, but wait
for the gift my Father
promised, which you have
heard me speak about. 5For
John baptized with[a] water,
but in a few days you will
be baptized with the Holy
Spirit."

6So when they met to-
gether, they asked him,
"Lord, are you at this time
going to restore the kingdom to Israel?"

7He said to them: "It is
not for you to know the
times or dates the Father
has set by his own authority. 8But you will receive
power when the Holy Spirit
comes on you; and you will
be my witnesses in Jerusalem, and in all Judea and
Samaria, and to the ends of
the earth."

9After he said this, he was
taken up before their very
eyes, and a cloud hid him
from their sight.

10They were looking in-
tently up into the sky as he
was going, when suddenly
two men dressed in white
stood beside them. 11"Men

[a]5 Or *in*

said, "Men of Galilee, why
do you stand looking up toward heaven? This Jesus,
who has been taken up
from you into heaven, will
come in the same way as
you saw him go into heav-
en."

Matthias Chosen to Replace Judas

12 Then they returned
to Jerusalem from the
mount called Olivet, which
is near Jerusalem, a sab-
bath day's journey away.
13 When they had entered
the city, they went to the
room upstairs where they
were staying, Peter, and
John, and James, and An-
drew, Philip and Thomas,
Bartholomew and Mat-
thew, James son of Alphaeus, and Simon the Zealot,
and Judas son of[c] James.
14 All these were constantly
devoting themselves to
prayer, together with certain women, including
Mary the mother of Jesus,
as well as his brothers.
15 In those days Peter
stood up among the believers[d] (together the crowd
numbered about one hun-
dred twenty persons) and
said, 16 "Friends,[e] the
scripture had to be fulfilled,
which the Holy Spirit
through David foretold
concerning Judas, who be-
came a guide for those who
arrested Jesus— 17 for he
was numbered among us
and was allotted his share
in this ministry." 18 (Now
this man acquired a field
with the reward of his wickedness; and falling head-
long,[f] he burst open in the
middle and all his bowels
gushed out. 19 This became

λευκαῖς, **11** οἳ καὶ εἶπαν· ἄνδρες Γαλιλαῖοι,
white, who also said : *Men* Galilæans,
τί ἑστήκατε βλέποντες εἰς τὸν οὐρανόν;
why stand ye looking to – heaven ?
οὗτος ὁ Ἰησοῦς ὁ ἀναλημφθεὶς
This – Jesus the [one] having been taken up
ἀφ᾽ ὑμῶν εἰς τὸν οὐρανὸν οὕτως ἐλεύσεται
from you to – heaven thus will come
ὃν τρόπον ἐθεάσασθε αὐτὸν πορευόμενον
in the way† ye beheld him going
εἰς τὸν οὐρανόν. **12** Τότε ὑπέστρεψαν
to – heaven. Then they returned
εἰς Ἰερουσαλὴμ ἀπὸ ὄρους τοῦ καλου-
to Jerusalem from [the] mount the [one] *being*
μένου ἐλαιῶνος, ὅ ἐστιν ἐγγὺς Ἰερουσαλὴμ
called of [the] olive grove, which is near Jerusalem
σαββάτου ἔχον ὁδόν. **13** καὶ ὅτε εἰσῆλθον,
of a sabbath having a way. And when they entered,
=a sabbath's journey off.
εἰς τὸ ὑπερῷον ἀνέβησαν οὗ ἦσαν
into the upper room they went up where they were
καταμένοντες, ὅ τε Πέτρος καὶ Ἰωάννης
waiting, – both Peter and John
καὶ Ἰάκωβος καὶ Ἀνδρέας, Φίλιππος καὶ
and James and Andrew, Philip and
Θωμᾶς, Βαρθολομαῖος καὶ Μαθθαῖος,
Thomas, Bartholomew and Matthew,
Ἰάκωβος Ἁλφαίου καὶ Σίμων ὁ ζηλωτὴς
James [son] of Alphæus and Simon the zealot
καὶ Ἰούδας Ἰακώβου. **14** οὗτοι πάντες
and Judas [brother] of James. These all
ἦσαν προσκαρτεροῦντες ὁμοθυμαδὸν τῇ
were continuing steadfastly with one mind –
προσευχῇ σὺν γυναιξὶν καὶ Μαριὰμ τῇ
in prayer with [the] women and Mary the
μητρὶ [τοῦ] Ἰησοῦ καὶ σὺν τοῖς ἀδελφοῖς
mother – of Jesus and with the brothers
αὐτοῦ.
of him.

15 Καὶ ἐν ταῖς ἡμέραις ταύταις ἀναστὰς
And in these days standing up
Πέτρος ἐν μέσῳ τῶν ἀδελφῶν εἶπεν·
Peter in [the] midst of the brothers said :
ἦν τε ὄχλος ὀνομάτων ἐπὶ τὸ αὐτὸ
[6]was [1]and [2][the] [3]crowd [4]of names [5]together
ὡσεὶ ἑκατὸν εἴκοσι· **16** ἄνδρες ἀδελφοί,
about a hundred twenty : *Men* brothers,
ἔδει πληρωθῆναι τὴν γραφὴν ἣν
it behoved to be fulfilled the scripture which
προεῖπεν τὸ πνεῦμα τὸ ἅγιον διὰ στόματος
spoke before the Spirit – Holy through [the] mouth
Δαυὶδ περὶ Ἰούδα τοῦ γενομένου ὁδηγοῦ
of David concerning Judas the [one] having become guide
τοῖς συλλαβοῦσιν Ἰησοῦν, **17** ὅτι κατ-
to the [ones] taking Jesus, because *having*
ηριθμημένος ἦν ἐν ἡμῖν καὶ ἔλαχεν τὸν
been numbered he was among us and obtained the
κλῆρον τῆς διακονίας ταύτης. **18** οὗτος μὲν οὖν
portion of this ministry. This one therefore
ἐκτήσατο χωρίον ἐκ μισθοῦ τῆς
bought a field out of [the] reward –
ἀδικίας, καὶ πρηνὴς γενόμενος ἐλάκησεν
of unrighteousness, and swollen up having become he burst asunder
μέσος, καὶ ἐξεχύθη πάντα τὰ σπλάγχνα
in the middle, and were poured out all the bowels

of Galilee," they said,
"why do you stand here
looking into the sky? This
same Jesus, who has been
taken from you into heav-
en, will come back in the
same way you have seen
him go into heaven."

Matthias Chosen to Replace Judas

12 Then they returned to
Jerusalem from the hill
called the Mount of Olives,
a Sabbath day's walk[b]
from the city. 13 When they
arrived, they went upstairs
to the room where they
were staying. Those pre-
sent were Peter, John,
James and Andrew; Philip
and Thomas, Bartholomew
and Matthew; James son of
Alphaeus and Simon the
Zealot, and Judas son of
James. 14 They all joined together constantly in prayer,
along with the women and
Mary the mother of Jesus,
and with his brothers.
15 In those days Peter
stood up among the believers[c] (a group numbering
about a hundred and twen-
ty) 16 and said, "Brothers,
the Scripture had to be fulfilled which the Holy Spirit
spoke long ago through the
mouth of David concerning
Judas, who served as guide
for those who arrested
Jesus— 17 he was one of our
number and shared in this
ministry."
18 (With the reward he got
for his wickedness, Judas
bought a field; there he fell
headlong, his body burst
open and all his intestines

[c] Or *the brother of*
[d] Gk *brothers*
[e] Gk *Men, brothers*
[f] Or *swelling up*

[b] *12* That is, about 3/4 mile (about 1,100 meters)
[c] *15* Greek *brothers*

known to all the residents
of Jerusalem, so that the
field was called in their language Hakeldama, that is,
Field of Blood.) 20 "For it is
written in the book of
Psalms,
'Let his homestead
become
desolate,
and let there be no
one to live
in it';
and
'Let another take his
position of
overseer.'
21 So one of the men who
have accompanied us dur-
ing all the time that the
Lord Jesus went in and out
among us, 22 beginning
from the baptism of John
until the day when he was
taken up from us—one of
these must become a wit-
ness with us to his resurrection." 23 So they proposed
two, Joseph called Barsabbas, who was also known
as Justus, and Matthias.
24 Then they prayed and
said, "Lord, you know ev-
eryone's heart. Show us
which one of these two you
have chosen 25 to take the
place[g] in this ministry and
apostleship from which Judas turned aside to go to his
own place." 26 And they
cast lots for them, and the
lot fell on Matthias; and he
was added to the eleven
apostles.

αὐτοῦ· **19** καὶ γνωστὸν ἐγένετο πᾶσι τοῖς
of him; and known it became to all the
κατοικοῦσιν Ἰερουσαλήμ, ὥστε κληθῆναι
[ones] inhabiting Jerusalem, so as to be called
τὸ χωρίον ἐκεῖνο τῇ ἰδίᾳ διαλέκτῳ αὐτῶν
that field in their own language
Ἀκελδαμάχ, τοῦτ' ἔστιν χωρίον
Aceldamach, this is Field
αἵματος. **20** γέγραπται γὰρ ἐν βίβλῳ
of blood. For it has been written in [the] roll
ψαλμῶν· γενηθήτω ἡ ἔπαυλις αὐτοῦ ἔρημος
of Psalms: Let become the estate of him deserted
καὶ μὴ ἔστω ὁ κατοικῶν ἐν αὐτῇ, καί·
and let not be the [one] dwelling in it, and:
τὴν ἐπισκοπὴν αὐτοῦ λαβέτω ἕτερος.
The office of him let take another.
21 δεῖ οὖν τῶν συνελθόντων ἡμῖν ἀνδρῶν
It behoves* therefore ¹of the ³accompanying ⁴us ²men
ἐν παντὶ χρόνῳ ᾧ εἰσῆλθεν καὶ
in all [the] time in which went in and
ἐξῆλθεν ἐφ' ἡμᾶς ὁ κύριος Ἰησοῦς,
went out among us the Lord Jesus,
22 ἀρξάμενος ἀπὸ τοῦ βαπτίσματος
beginning from the baptism
Ἰωάννου ἕως τῆς ἡμέρας ἧς ἀνελήμφθη
of John until the day when he was taken up
ἀφ' ἡμῶν, μάρτυρα τῆς ἀναστάσεως
from us, ⁶a witness* ⁷of the ⁸resurrection
αὐτοῦ σὺν ἡμῖν γενέσθαι ἕνα τούτων.
⁹of him ⁵with ⁴us ³to become ¹one* ²of these.
23 Καὶ ἔστησαν δύο, Ἰωσὴφ τὸν καλού-
And they set two, Joseph the [one] *being*
μενον Βαρσαββᾶν, ὃς ἐπεκλήθη Ἰοῦστος,
called Barsabbas, who was surnamed Justus,
καὶ Μαθθίαν. **24** καὶ προσευξάμενοι εἶπαν·
and Matthias. And praying they said:
σὺ κύριε καρδιογνῶστα πάντων, ἀνάδειξον
Thou Lord Heart-knower of all men, show
ὃν ἐξελέξω ἐκ τούτων τῶν δύο ἕνα
whom thou didst choose of these – two one
25 λαβεῖν τὸν τόπον τῆς διακονίας ταύτης
to take the place of this ministry
καὶ ἀποστολῆς, ἀφ' ἧς παρέβη Ἰούδας
and apostleship, from which fell Judas
πορευθῆναι εἰς τὸν τόπον τὸν ἴδιον.
to go to the(his) place – own.
26 καὶ ἔδωκαν κλήρους αὐτοῖς, καὶ ἔπεσεν
And they gave lots for them, and fell
ὁ κλῆρος ἐπὶ Μαθθίαν, καὶ συγκατεψηφίσθη
the lot on Matthias, and he was reckoned along *with*
μετὰ τῶν ἕνδεκα ἀποστόλων.
with the eleven apostles.

spilled out. 19 Everyone in
Jerusalem heard about this,
so they called that field in
their language Akeldama,
that is, Field of Blood.)
20 "For," said Peter, "it is
written in the book of
Psalms,
" 'May his place be
deserted;
let there be no one to
dwell in it,'[d]
and,
" 'May another take his
place of
leadership.'[e]
21 Therefore it is necessary
to choose one of the men
who have been with us the
whole time the Lord Jesus
went in and out among us,
22 beginning from John's
baptism to the time when
Jesus was taken up from
us. For one of these must
become a witness with us
of his resurrection."
23 So they proposed two
men: Joseph called Barsabbas (also known as Justus)
and Matthias. 24 Then they
prayed, "Lord, you know
everyone's heart. Show us
which of these two you
have chosen 25 to take over
this apostolic ministry,
which Judas left to go
where he belongs." 26 Then
they cast lots, and the lot
fell to Matthias; so he was
added to the eleven apos-
tles.

Chapter 2

The Coming of the Holy Spirit

WHEN the day of Pen-
tecost had come,
they were all together in
one place. 2 And suddenly
from heaven there came a
sound like the rush of a violent wind, and it filled the

2 Καὶ ἐν τῷ συμπληροῦσθαι τὴν ἡμέραν
And in the to be completed the day
=when the day of Pentecost was completed
τῆς πεντηκοστῆς ἦσαν πάντες ὁμοῦ ἐπὶ
– of Pentecost° they were all *together* to-
τὸ αὐτό· **2** καὶ ἐγένετο ἄφνω ἐκ τοῦ
gether;† and there was suddenly out of –
οὐρανοῦ ἦχος ὥσπερ φερομένης πνοῆς
heaven a sound as ⁶being borne ¹of ²a ⁴wind

Chapter 2

The Holy Spirit Comes at Pentecost

WHEN the day of Pen-
tecost came, they
were all together in one
place. 2 Suddenly a sound
like the blowing of a violent

[g] Other ancient authorities read *the share*

* The object (according to the Greek construction) of the verb δεῖ is ἕνα, with μάρτυρα as its complement after γενέσθαι.

[d] 20 Psalm 69:25
[e] 20 Psalm 109:8

entire house where they were sitting. 3 Divided tongues, as of fire, appeared among them, and a tongue rested on each of them. 4 All of them were filled with the Holy Spirit and began to speak in other languages, as the Spirit gave them ability.

5 Now there were devout Jews from every nation under heaven living in Jerusalem. 6 And at this sound the crowd gathered and was bewildered, because each one heard them speaking in the native language of each. 7 Amazed and astonished, they asked, "Are not all these who are speaking Galileans? 8 And how is it that we hear, each of us, in our own native language? 9 Parthians, Medes, Elamites, and residents of Mesopotamia, Judea and Cappadocia, Pontus and Asia, 10 Phrygia and Pamphylia, Egypt and the parts of Libya belonging to Cyrene, and visitors from Rome, both Jews and proselytes, 11 Cretans and Arabs—in our own languages we hear them speaking about God's deeds of power." 12 All were amazed and perplexed, saying to one another, "What does this mean?" 13 But others sneered and said, "They are filled with new wine."

Peter Addresses the Crowd

14 But Peter, standing with the eleven, raised his voice and addressed them,

βιαίας καὶ ἐπλήρωσεν ὅλον τὸν οἶκον
3violent and it filled all the house
οὗ ἦσαν καθήμενοι, 3 καὶ ὤφθησαν αὐτοῖς
where they were sitting, and there appeared to them
διαμεριζόμεναι γλῶσσαι ὡσεὶ πυρός, καὶ
being distributed tongues as of fire, and
ἐκάθισεν ἐφ' ἕνα ἕκαστον αὐτῶν, 4 καὶ
it sat on 2one 1each of them, and
ἐπλήσθησαν πάντες πνεύματος ἁγίου, καὶ
they were filled all of(with) Spirit Holy, and
ἤρξαντο λαλεῖν ἑτέραις γλώσσαις καθὼς
began to speak in other tongues as
τὸ πνεῦμα ἐδίδου ἀποφθέγγεσθαι αὐτοῖς.
the Spirit gave 2to speak out 1them.
5 Ἦσαν δὲ εἰς Ἰερουσαλὴμ κατοικοῦντες
Now there were in Jerusalem dwelling
Ἰουδαῖοι, ἄνδρες εὐλαβεῖς ἀπὸ παντὸς ἔθνους
Jews, men devout from every nation
τῶν ὑπὸ τὸν οὐρανόν· 6 γενομένης
of the [ones] under – heaven; happening
δὲ τῆς φωνῆς ταύτης συνῆλθεν τὸ πλῆθος
and this sound* came together the multitude
=when this sound happened
καὶ συνεχύθη, ὅτι ἤκουον εἷς ἕκαστος
and were confounded, because they heard 4one 3each
τῇ ἰδίᾳ διαλέκτῳ λαλούντων αὐτῶν.
5in his own language 2speaking 1them.
7 ἐξίσταντο δὲ καὶ ἐθαύμαζον λέγοντες·
And they were amazed and marvelled saying:
οὐχὶ ἰδοὺ πάντες οὗτοί εἰσιν οἱ λαλοῦντες
3not 1behold 4all 5these 2are 6the [ones] 7speaking
Γαλιλαῖοι; 8 καὶ πῶς ἡμεῖς ἀκούομεν
8Galilæans? and how 2we 1hear
ἕκαστος τῇ ἰδίᾳ διαλέκτῳ ἡμῶν ἐν ᾗ
3each 5in his own language 4of us in which
ἐγεννήθημεν, 9 Πάρθοι καὶ Μῆδοι καὶ
we were born, Parthians and Medes and
Ἐλαμῖται, καὶ οἱ κατοικοῦντες τὴν
Elamites, and the [ones] inhabiting –
Μεσοποταμίαν, Ἰουδαίαν τε καὶ Καππα-
Mesopotamia, both Judæa and Cappa-
δοκίαν, Πόντον καὶ τὴν Ἀσίαν, 10 Φρυγίαν
docia, Pontus and – Asia, Phrygia
τε καὶ Παμφυλίαν, Αἴγυπτον καὶ τὰ
both and Pamphylia, Egypt and the
μέρη τῆς Λιβύης τῆς κατὰ Κυρήνην,
regions – of Libya – over against Cyrene,
καὶ οἱ ἐπιδημοῦντες Ῥωμαῖοι, 11 Ἰουδαῖοί
and the temporarily residing Romans, 2Jews
τε καὶ προσήλυτοι, Κρῆτες καὶ Ἄραβες,
1both and proselytes, Cretans and Arabians,
ἀκούομεν λαλούντων αὐτῶν ταῖς ἡμετέραις
we hear 2speaking 1them in *the* our
γλώσσαις τὰ μεγαλεῖα τοῦ θεοῦ;
tongues the great deeds – of God?
12 ἐξίσταντο δὲ πάντες καὶ διηποροῦντο,
And were amazed all and were troubled,
ἄλλος πρὸς ἄλλον λέγοντες· τί θέλει
other to other saying: What wishes
τοῦτο εἶναι; 13 ἕτεροι δὲ διαχλευάζοντες
this to be? But others mocking
ἔλεγον ὅτι γλεύκους μεμεστωμένοι εἰσίν.
said[,] – Of(with) sweet wine *having been* filled they are.
14 Σταθεὶς δὲ ὁ Πέτρος σὺν τοῖς ἕνδεκα
But standing – Peter with the eleven
ἐπῆρεν τὴν φωνὴν αὐτοῦ καὶ ἀπεφθέγξατο
lifted up the voice of him and spoke out

wind came from heaven and filled the whole house where they were sitting. 3 They saw what seemed to be tongues of fire that separated and came to rest on each of them. 4 All of them were filled with the Holy Spirit and began to speak in other tongues[f] as the Spirit enabled them.

5 Now there were staying in Jerusalem God-fearing Jews from every nation under heaven. 6 When they heard this sound, a crowd came together in bewilderment, because each one heard them speaking in his own language. 7 Utterly amazed, they asked: "Are not all these men who are speaking Galileans? 8 Then how is it that each of us hears them in his own native language? 9 Parthians, Medes and Elamites; residents of Mesopotamia, Judea and Cappadocia, Pontus and Asia, 10 Phrygia and Pamphylia, Egypt and the parts of Libya near Cyrene; visitors from Rome 11 (both Jews and converts to Judaism); Cretans and Arabs—we hear them declaring the wonders of God in our own tongues!" 12 Amazed and perplexed, they asked one another, "What does this mean?"

13 Some, however, made fun of them and said, "They have had too much wine.[g]"

Peter Addresses the Crowd

14 Then Peter stood up with the Eleven, raised his voice and addressed the

f4 Or *languages*; also in verse 11
g13 Or *sweet wine*

"Men of Judea and all who live in Jerusalem, let this be known to you, and listen to what I say. [15]Indeed, these are not drunk, as you suppose, for it is only nine o'clock in the morning.
[16]No, this is what was spoken through the prophet Joel:
17 'In the last days it
will be, God
declares,
that I will pour out
my Spirit upon
all flesh,
and your sons and
your daughters
shall prophesy,
and your young men
shall
see visions,
and your old men
shall
dream dreams.
18 Even upon my slaves,
both men and
women,
in those days I will
pour out
my Spirit;
and they shall
prophesy.
19 And I will show
portents in the
heaven above
and signs on the
earth below,
blood, and fire,
and smoky mist.
20 The sun shall be
turned to
darkness
and the moon to
blood,
before the coming
of the Lord's
great and
glorious day.
21 Then everyone who
calls on the
name of the
Lord shall
be saved.'

22 "You that are Israelites,[h] listen to what I have to say: Jesus of Nazareth,[i] a man attested to you by God with deeds of power, wonders, and signs that God did through him among you, as you yourselves know— [23]this man, handed over to you according to the definite plan and foreknowledge of God, you crucified and killed by the

αὐτοῖς·
to them :
Ἄνδρες Ἰουδαῖοι καὶ οἱ κατοικοῦντες
Men Jews and the [ones] inhabiting
Ἰερουσαλὴμ πάντες, τοῦτο ὑμῖν γνωστὸν
Jerusalem all, this to you known
ἔστω, καὶ ἐνωτίσασθε τὰ ῥήματά μου.
let be, and give ear to the words of me.
15 οὐ γὰρ ὡς ὑμεῖς ὑπολαμβάνετε οὗτοι
For not as ye imagine these men
μεθύουσιν, ἔστιν γὰρ ὥρα τρίτη τῆς
are drunk, for it is hour third of the
ἡμέρας, **16** ἀλλὰ τοῦτό ἐστιν τὸ εἰρημένον
day, but this is the thing having been spoken
διὰ τοῦ προφήτου Ἰωήλ· **17** καὶ ἔσται
through the prophet Joel : And it shall be
ἐν ταῖς ἐσχάταις ἡμέραις, λέγει ὁ θεός,
in the last days, says – God,
ἐκχεῶ ἀπὸ τοῦ πνεύματός μου ἐπὶ
I will pour out from the Spirit of me on
πᾶσαν σάρκα, καὶ προφητεύσουσιν οἱ υἱοὶ
all flesh, and will prophesy the sons
ὑμῶν καὶ αἱ θυγατέρες ὑμῶν, καὶ οἱ
of you and the daughters of you, and the
νεανίσκοι ὑμῶν ὁράσεις ὄψονται, καὶ οἱ
young men of you visions will see, and the
πρεσβύτεροι ὑμῶν ἐνυπνίοις ἐνυπνιασθήσονται·
old men of you dreams will dream;
18 καὶ γε ἐπὶ τοὺς δούλους μου καὶ ἐπὶ
and – on the male slaves of me and on
τὰς δούλας μου ἐν ταῖς ἡμέραις ἐκείναις
the female slaves of me in those days
ἐκχεῶ ἀπὸ τοῦ πνεύματός μου, καὶ
I will pour out from the Spirit of me, and
προφητεύσουσιν. **19** καὶ δώσω τέρατα ἐν
they will prophesy. And I will give wonders in
τῷ οὐρανῷ ἄνω καὶ σημεῖα ἐπὶ τῆς
the heaven above and signs on the
γῆς κάτω, αἷμα καὶ πῦρ καὶ ἀτμίδα
earth below, blood and fire and vapour
καπνοῦ. **20** ὁ ἥλιος μεταστραφήσεται εἰς
of smoke. The sun will be turned into
σκότος καὶ ἡ σελήνη εἰς αἷμα, πρὶν
darkness and the moon into blood, before
ἐλθεῖν ἡμέραν κυρίου τὴν μεγάλην καὶ
⁷to come(comes) ⁵day ⁶of [the] Lord ¹the ²great ³and
ἐπιφανῆ. **21** καὶ ἔσται πᾶς ὃς ἐὰν
⁴notable.[b] And it will be everyone whoever
ἐπικαλέσηται τὸ ὄνομα κυρίου σωθήσεται.
invokes the name of [the] Lord will be saved.
22 Ἄνδρες Ἰσραηλῖται, ἀκούσατε τοὺς
Men Israelites, hear ye –
λόγους τούτους· Ἰησοῦν τὸν Ναζωραῖον,
words these: Jesus the Nazarene,
ἄνδρα ἀποδεδειγμένον ἀπὸ τοῦ θεοῦ εἰς
a man *having been* approved from – God among
ὑμᾶς δυνάμεσι καὶ τέρασι καὶ σημείοις,
you by powerful deeds and wonders and signs,
οἷς ἐποίησεν δι' αὐτοῦ ὁ θεὸς ἐν μέσῳ
which did through him – God in [the] midst
ὑμῶν, καθὼς αὐτοὶ οἴδατε, **23** τοῦτον
of you, as [your]selves ye know, this man
τῇ ὡρισμένῃ βουλῇ καὶ προγνώσει τοῦ
³by the ⁴*having been* fixed ⁵counsel ⁶and ⁷foreknowledge –
θεοῦ ἔκδοτον διὰ χειρὸς ἀνόμων
⁸of God ¹given up ⁹through ¹⁰[the] hand ¹¹of lawless men

crowd: "Fellow Jews and all of you who live in Jerusalem, let me explain this to you; listen carefully to what I say. [15]These men are not drunk, as you suppose. It's only nine in the morning! [16]No, this is what was spoken by the prophet Joel:

17" 'In the last days, God
says,
I will pour out my
Spirit on all people.
Your sons and daughters
will prophesy,
your young men will
see visions,
your old men will
dream dreams.
18Even on my servants,
both men and
women,
I will pour out my
Spirit in those days,
and they will prophesy.
19I will show wonders in
the heaven above
and signs on the earth
below,
blood and fire and
billows of smoke.
20The sun will be turned to
darkness
and the moon to blood
before the coming of
the great and
glorious day of the
Lord.
21And everyone who calls
on the name of the
Lord will be
saved.'[h]

22"Men of Israel, listen to this: Jesus of Nazareth was a man accredited by God to you by miracles, wonders and signs, which God did among you through him, as you yourselves know. [23]This man was handed over to you by God's set purpose and foreknowledge; and you, with the help of wicked men,[i] put him to death by nailing him

[h] Gk *Men, Israelites*
[i] Gk *the Nazorean*

[h] 21 Joel 2:28-32
[i] 23 Or *of those not having the law* (that is, Gentiles)

hands of those outside the
law. 24 But God raised him
up, having freed him from
death,[j] because it was impossible for him to be held
in its power. 25 For David
says concerning him,
'I saw the Lord
always before
me,
for he is at my right
hand so that I
will not be
shaken;
26 therefore my heart
was glad, and
my tongue
rejoiced;
moreover my flesh
will live in hope.
27 For you will not
abandon my
soul to Hades,
or let your Holy
One experience
corruption.
28 You have made
known to me
the ways of life;
you will make me
full of gladness
with your
presence.'
29 "Fellow Israelites,[k]
I may say to you confidently of our ancestor David
that he both died and was
buried, and his tomb is with
us to this day. 30 Since he
was a prophet, he knew
that God had sworn with an
oath to him that he would
put one of his descendants
on his throne. 31 Foreseeing
this, David[l] spoke of the
resurrection of the Messiah,[m] saying,
'He was not
abandoned to
Hades,
nor did his flesh
experience
corruption.'
32 This Jesus God raised up,
and of that all of us are wit
nesses. 33 Being therefore
exalted at[n] the right hand
of God, and having re-
ceived from the Father the
promise of the Holy Spirit,
he has poured out this that
you both see and hear.
34 For David did not ascend

[j] Gk *the pains of death*
[k] Gk *Men, brothers*
[l] Gk *he*
[m] Or *the Christ*
[n] Or *by*

προσπήξαντες ἀνείλατε, **24** ὃν ὁ θεὸς
[8]fastening* [12]ye killed, whom – God
ἀνέστησεν λύσας τὰς ὠδῖνας τοῦ θανάτου,
raised up loosening the pangs – of death,
καθότι οὐκ ἦν δυνατὸν κρατεῖσθαι αὐτὸν
because it was not possible [2]to be held [1]him
ὑπ' αὐτοῦ. **25** Δαυὶδ γὰρ λέγει εἰς
by it. For David says [as] to
αὐτόν· προορώμην τὸν κύριον ἐνώπιόν
him: I foresaw the Lord before
μου διὰ παντός, ὅτι ἐκ δεξιῶν μού
me always, because on right of me
ἐστιν, ἵνα μὴ σαλευθῶ. **26** διὰ τοῦτο
he is, lest I be moved. Therefore
ηὐφράνθη μου ἡ καρδία καὶ ἠγαλλιάσατο
was glad of me the heart and exulted
ἡ γλῶσσά μου, ἔτι δὲ καὶ ἡ σάρξ
the tongue of me, and now also the flesh
μου κατασκηνώσει ἐπ' ἐλπίδι, **27** ὅτι οὐκ
of me will dwell on(in) hope, because not
ἐγκαταλείψεις τὴν ψυχήν μου εἰς ᾅδην
thou wilt abandon the soul of me in hades
οὐδὲ δώσεις τὸν ὅσιόν σου ἰδεῖν
nor wilt thou give the holy one of thee to see
διαφθοράν. **28** ἐγνώρισάς μοι ὁδοὺς ζωῆς,
corruption. Thou madest known to me ways of life,
πληρώσεις με εὐφροσύνης μετὰ τοῦ προσώ-
thou wilt fill me of(with) gladness with the pres-
που σου. **29** Ἄνδρες ἀδελφοί, ἐξὸν εἰπεῖν
ence of thee. *Men* brothers, it is permitted to speak
μετὰ παρρησίας πρὸς ὑμᾶς περὶ τοῦ
with plainness to you concerning the
πατριάρχου Δαυίδ, ὅτι καὶ ἐτελεύτησεν
patriarch David, that both he died
καὶ ἐτάφη, καὶ τὸ μνῆμα αὐτοῦ ἔστιν
and was buried, and the tomb of him is
ἐν ἡμῖν ἄχρι τῆς ἡμέρας ταύτης.
among us until this day.
30 προφήτης οὖν ὑπάρχων καὶ εἰδὼς ὅτι
A prophet therefore being and knowing that
ὅρκῳ ὤμοσεν αὐτῷ ὁ θεὸς ἐκ καρποῦ
with an oath swore to him – God of [the] fruit
τῆς ὀσφύος αὐτοῦ καθίσαι ἐπὶ τὸν θρόνον
of the loin[s] of him to sit on the throne
αὐτοῦ, **31** προϊδὼν ἐλάλησεν περὶ τῆς
of him, foreseeing he spoke concerning the
ἀναστάσεως τοῦ Χριστοῦ, ὅτι οὔτε
resurrection of the Christ, that neither
ἐγκατελείφθη εἰς ᾅδην οὔτε ἡ σὰρξ
he was abandoned in hades nor the flesh
αὐτοῦ εἶδεν διαφθοράν. **32** τοῦτον τὸν
of him saw corruption. This –
Ἰησοῦν ἀνέστησεν ὁ θεός, οὗ πάντες
Jesus [2]raised up – [1]God, of which all
ἡμεῖς ἐσμεν μάρτυρες· **33** τῇ δεξιᾷ οὖν
we are witnesses; to the right [hand] therefore
τοῦ θεοῦ ὑψωθεὶς τήν τε ἐπαγγελίαν
– of God having been exalted [6]the [1]and [7]promise
τοῦ πνεύματος τοῦ ἁγίου λαβὼν παρὰ
[8]of the [10]Spirit – [9]Holy [2]receiving [3]from
τοῦ πατρὸς ἐξέχεεν τοῦτο ὃ ὑμεῖς καὶ
[4]the [5]Father he poured out this which ye both
βλέπετε καὶ ἀκούετε. **34** οὐ γὰρ Δαυὶδ
see and hear. For not David

* That is, to a tree; see ch. 5. 30.

to the cross. 24 But God
raised him from the dead,
freeing him from the agony
of death, because it was impossible for death to keep
its hold on him. 25 David
said about him:

"'I saw the Lord always
before me.
Because he is at my
right hand,
I will not be shaken.
26 Therefore my heart is
glad and my tongue
rejoices;
my body also will live
in hope,
27 because you will not
abandon me to the
grave,
nor will you let your
Holy One see
decay.
28 You have made known
to me the paths of
life;
you will fill me with joy
in your presence.'[j]

29 "Brothers, I can tell
you confidently that the patriarch David died and was
buried, and his tomb is here
to this day. 30 But he was a
prophet and knew that God
had promised him on oath
that he would place one of
his descendants on his
throne. 31 Seeing what was
ahead, he spoke of the resurrection of the Christ,[k]
that he was not abandoned
to the grave, nor did his
body see decay. 32 God has
raised this Jesus to life, and
we are all witnesses of the
fact. 33 Exalted to the right
hand of God, he has re-
ceived from the Father the
promised Holy Spirit and
has poured out what you
now see and hear. 34 For
David did not ascend to

[j] *28* Psalm 16:8-11
[k] *31* Or *Messiah.* "The Christ" (Greek) and "the Messiah" (Hebrew) both mean "the Anointed One"; also in verse 36.

into the heavens, but he
himself says,
'The Lord said to my
Lord,
"Sit at my right hand,
35 until I make your
enemies your
footstool." '
36Therefore let the entire
house of Israel know with
certainty that God has
made him both Lord and
Messiah,[o] this Jesus whom
you crucified."

The First Converts

37 Now when they
heard this, they were cut to
the heart and said to Peter
and to the other apostles,
"Brothers,[p] what should
we do?" 38Peter said to
them, "Repent, and be baptized every one of you in
the name of Jesus Christ so
that your sins may be forgiven; and you will receive
the gift of the Holy Spirit.
39For the promise is for
you, for your children, and
for all who are far away,
everyone whom the Lord
our God calls to him."
40And he testified with
many other arguments and
exhorted them, saying,
"Save yourselves from this
corrupt generation." 41So
those who welcomed his
message were baptized,
and that day about three
thousand persons were
added. 42They devoted
themselves to the apostles'
teaching and fellowship, to
the breaking of bread and
the prayers.

Life among the Believers

43 Awe came upon ev-
eryone, because many
wonders and signs were being done by the apostles.
44All who believed were together and had all things in
common; 45they would sell
their possessions and

[o] Or *Christ*
[p] Gk *Men, brothers*

ἀνέβη εἰς τοὺς οὐρανούς, λέγει δὲ αὐτός·
ascended to the heavens, but says he:
εἶπεν κύριος τῷ κυρίῳ μου· κάθου ἐκ
Said [the] LORD to the Lord of me: Sit at
δεξιῶν μου, 35 ἕως ἂν θῶ τοὺς ἐχθρούς
right of me, until I put the enemies
σου ὑποπόδιον τῶν ποδῶν σου. 36 ἀσφαλῶς
of thee a footstool of the feet of thee. Assuredly
οὖν γινωσκέτω πᾶς οἶκος Ἰσραὴλ ὅτι
therefore [1]let [6]know [2]all [3][the] [4]house [5]of Israel that
καὶ κύριον αὐτὸν καὶ χριστὸν ἐποίησεν
[4]both [5]Lord [3]him [6]and [7]Christ [2]made
ὁ θεος, τοῦτον τὸν Ἰησοῦν ὃν ὑμεῖς
– [1]God, this – Jesus whom ye
ἐσταυρώσατε. 37 Ἀκούσαντες δὲ κατενύγ-
crucified. And hearing they were
ησαν τὴν καρδίαν, εἶπόν τε πρὸς τὸν
stung [in] the heart, and said to –
Πέτρον καὶ τοὺς λοιποὺς ἀποστόλους·
Peter and the remaining apostles:
τί ποιήσωμεν, ἄνδρες ἀδελφοί; 38 Πέτρος
What may we do, *men* brothers? Peter
δὲ πρὸς αὐτούς· μετανοήσατε, καὶ
And to them: Repent ye, and
βαπτισθήτω ἕκαστος ὑμῶν ἐπὶ τῷ ὀνόματι
let be baptized each of you on the name
Ἰησοῦ Χριστοῦ εἰς ἄφεσιν τῶν
of Jesus Christ [with a view] to forgiveness of the
ἁμαρτιῶν ὑμῶν, καὶ λήμψεσθε τὴν δωρεὰν
sins of you, and ye will receive the gift
τοῦ ἁγίου πνεύματος. 39 ὑμῖν γάρ ἐστιν
of the Holy Spirit. For to you is
ἡ ἐπαγγελία καὶ τοῖς τέκνοις ὑμῶν καὶ
the promise and to the children of you and
πᾶσιν τοῖς εἰς μακράν, ὅσους ἂν
to all the [ones] far away, as many as
προσκαλέσηται κύριος ὁ θεὸς ἡμῶν.
may call to [him] [the] Lord the God of us.
40 ἑτέροις τε λόγοις πλείοσιν διεμαρτύρατο,
And with other words many he solemnly witnessed,
καὶ παρεκάλει αὐτοὺς λέγων· σώθητε
and exhorted them saying: Be ye saved
ἀπὸ τῆς γενεᾶς τῆς σκολιᾶς ταύτης. 41 οἱ
from – [3]generation – [2]perverse [1]this. The [ones]
μὲν οὖν ἀποδεξάμενοι τὸν λόγον αὐτοῦ
– therefore welcoming the word of him
ἐβαπτίσθησαν, καὶ προσετέθησαν ἐν
were baptized, and there were added in
τῇ ἡμέρᾳ ἐκείνῃ ψυχαὶ ὡσεὶ τρισχίλιαι·
that day souls about three thousand;
42 ἦσαν δὲ προσκαρτεροῦντες τῇ διδαχῇ
and they were continuing steadfastly in the teaching
τῶν ἀποστόλων καὶ τῇ κοινωνίᾳ, τῇ
of the apostles and in the fellowship, in the
κλάσει τοῦ ἄρτου καὶ ταῖς προσευχαῖς.
breaking of the loaf and in the prayers.
43 Ἐγίνετο δὲ πάσῃ ψυχῇ φόβος· πολλὰ δὲ
And came to every soul fear; and many
τέρατα καὶ σημεῖα διὰ τῶν ἀποστόλων
wonders and signs through the apostles
ἐγίνετο. 44 πάντες δὲ οἱ πιστεύσαντες
happened. And all the believing [ones]
ἐπὶ τὸ αὐτὸ εἶχον ἅπαντα κοινά, 45 καὶ
together had all things common, and
τὰ κτήματα καὶ τὰς ὑπάρξεις ἐπίπρασκον
the properties and the possessions they sold

heaven, and yet he said,
" 'The Lord said to my
Lord:
"Sit at my right hand
35until I make your
enemies
a footstool for your
feet." '[l]
36"Therefore let all Israel
be assured of this: God has
made this Jesus, whom you
crucified, both Lord and
Christ."
37When the people heard
this, they were cut to the
heart and said to Peter and
the other apostles, "Brothers, what shall we do?"
38Peter replied, "Repent
and be baptized, every one
of you, in the name of Jesus
Christ for the forgiveness
of your sins. And you will
receive the gift of the Holy
Spirit. 39The promise is for
you and your children and
for all who are far off—for
all whom the Lord our God
will call."
40With many other words
he warned them; and he
pleaded with them, "Save
yourselves from this cor-
rupt generation." 41Those
who accepted his message
were baptized, and about
three thousand were added
to their number that day.

The Fellowship of the Believers

42They devoted them-
selves to the apostles'
teaching and to the fellowship, to the breaking of
bread and to prayer. 43Ev-
eryone was filled with awe,
and many wonders and mi-
raculous signs were done
by the apostles. 44All the
believers were together and
had everything in common.
45Selling their possessions

[l] *35* Psalm 110:1

goods and distribute the
proceeds[q] to all, as any
had need. 46 Day by day, as
they spent much time to-
gether in the temple, they
broke bread at home[r] and
ate their food with glad and
generous[s] hearts, 47 praising God and having the
goodwill of all the people.
And day by day the Lord
added to their number
those who were being
saved.

Chapter 3

Peter Heals a Crippled Beggar

One day Peter and
John were going up to
the temple at the hour of
prayer, at three o'clock in
the afternoon. 2 And a man
lame from birth was being
carried in. People would
lay him daily at the gate of
the temple called the Beautiful Gate so that he could
ask for alms from those entering the temple. 3 When
he saw Peter and John
about to go into the temple,
he asked them for alms.
4 Peter looked intently at
him, as did John, and said,
"Look at us." 5 And he
fixed his attention on them,
expecting to receive something from them. 6 But Peter said, "I have no silver or
gold, but what I have I give
you; in the name of Jesus
Christ of Nazareth,[t] stand
up and walk." 7 And he
took him by the right hand
and raised him up; and immediately his feet and ankles were made strong.
8 Jumping up, he stood and
began to walk, and he en-
tered the temple with them,
walking and leaping and
praising God. 9 All the peo-

[q] Gk *them*
[r] Or *from house to house*
[s] Or *sincere*
[t] Gk *the Nazorean*

καὶ διεμέριζον αὐτὰ πᾶσιν, καθότι ἄν
and distributed them to all, according as
τις χρείαν εἶχεν. **46** καθ' ἡμέραν τε
anyone need had. And from day to day†
προσκαρτεροῦντες ὁμοθυμαδὸν ἐν τῷ ἱερῷ,
continuing steadfastly with one mind in the temple,
κλῶντές τε κατ' οἶκον ἄρτον, μετε-
and [1]breaking [3]from house to house† [2]bread, they
λάμβανον τροφῆς ἐν ἀγαλλιάσει καὶ
shared food in gladness and
ἀφελότητι καρδίας, **47** αἰνοῦντες τὸν θεὸν
simplicity of heart, praising – God
καὶ ἔχοντες χάριν πρὸς ὅλον τὸν λαόν.
and having favour with all the people.
ὁ δὲ κύριος προσετίθει τοὺς σῳζομένους
And the Lord added the [ones] being saved
καθ' ἡμέραν ἐπὶ τὸ αὐτό.
from day to day† together.†

3 Πέτρος δὲ καὶ Ἰωάννης ἀνέβαινον
Now Peter and John were going up
εἰς τὸ ἱερὸν ἐπὶ τὴν ὥραν τῆς προσευχῆς
to the temple at the hour of the prayer
τὴν ἐνάτην. **2** καί τις ἀνὴρ χωλὸς ἐκ
the ninth. And a certain man [2]lame [3]from
κοιλίας μητρὸς αὐτοῦ ὑπάρχων ἐβαστάζετο,
[4][the] womb [5]of [the] mother [6]of him [1]being was being carried,
ὃν ἐτίθουν καθ' ἡμέραν πρὸς τὴν θύραν
whom they used to put from day to day† at the door
τοῦ ἱεροῦ τὴν λεγομένην ὡραίαν τοῦ
of the temple – *being* called Beautiful –
αἰτεῖν ἐλεημοσύνην παρὰ τῶν εἰσπορευομέ-
to ask[d] alms from the [ones] enter-
νων εἰς τὸ ἱερόν· **3** ὃς ἰδὼν Πέτρον καὶ
ing into the temple; who seeing Peter and
Ἰωάννην μέλλοντας εἰσιέναι εἰς τὸ ἱερὸν
John being about to go *in* into the temple
ἠρώτα ἐλεημοσύνην λαβεῖν. **4** ἀτενίσας δὲ
asked alms to receive. And [2]gazing
Πέτρος εἰς αὐτὸν σὺν τῷ Ἰωάννῃ εἶπεν·
[1]Peter at him with – John said:
βλέψον εἰς ἡμᾶς. **5** ὁ δὲ ἐπεῖχεν αὐτοῖς
Look at us. And he paid heed to them
προσδοκῶν τι παρ' αὐτῶν λαβεῖν. **6** εἶπεν
expecting something from them to receive. said
δὲ Πέτρος· ἀργύριον καὶ χρυσίον οὐχ
And Peter: Silver and gold not
ὑπάρχει μοι· ὃ δὲ ἔχω, τοῦτό σοι δίδωμι·
is to me[c]; but what I have, this to thee I give;
=I have not;
ἐν τῷ ὀνόματι Ἰησοῦ Χριστοῦ τοῦ
in the name of Jesus Christ the
Ναζωραίου περιπάτει. **7** καὶ πιάσας αὐτὸν τῆς
Nazarene walk. And seizing him of(by)
δεξιᾶς χειρὸς ἤγειρεν αὐτόν· παραχρῆμα
the right hand he raised him; [2]at once
δὲ ἐστερεώθησαν αἱ βάσεις αὐτοῦ καὶ τὰ
[1]and were made firm the feet of him and the
σφυδρά, **8** καὶ ἐξαλλόμενος ἔστη, καὶ
ankle-bones, and leaping up he stood, and
περιεπάτει, καὶ εἰσῆλθεν σὺν αὐτοῖς εἰς
walked, and entered with them into
τὸ ἱερὸν περιπατῶν καὶ ἀλλόμενος καὶ
the temple walking and leaping and

and goods, they gave to
anyone as he had need.
46 Every day they continued
to meet together in the temple courts. They broke
bread in their homes and
ate together with glad and
sincere hearts, 47 praising
God and enjoying the favor
of all the people. And the
Lord added to their number
daily those who were being
saved.

Chapter 3

Peter Heals the Crippled Beggar

One day Peter and John
were going up to the
temple at the time of prayer
—at three in the afternoon.
2 Now a man crippled from
birth was being carried to
the temple gate called
Beautiful, where he was
put every day to beg from
those going into the temple
courts. 3 When he saw Peter
and John about to enter, he
asked them for money. 4 Peter looked straight at him,
as did John. Then Peter
said, "Look at us!" 5 So the
man gave them his atten-
tion, expecting to get something from them.
6 Then Peter said, "Silver
or gold I do not have, but
what I have I give you. In
the name of Jesus Christ of
Nazareth, walk." 7 Taking
him by the right hand, he
helped him up, and instantly the man's feet and ankles
became strong. 8 He
jumped to his feet and began to walk. Then he went
with them into the temple
courts, walking and jump-

ple saw him walking and praising God, [10]and they recognized him as the one who used to sit and ask for alms at the Beautiful Gate of the temple; and they were filled with wonder and amazement at what had happened to him.

Peter Speaks in Solomon's Portico

11 While he clung to Peter and John, all the people ran together to them in the portico called Solomon's Portico, utterly astonished. [12]When Peter saw it, he addressed the people, "You Israelites,[u] why do you wonder at this, or why do you stare at us, as though by our own power or piety we had made him walk? [13]The God of Abraham, the God of Isaac, and the God of Jacob, the God of our ancestors has glorified his servant[v] Jesus, whom you handed over and rejected in the presence of Pilate, though he had decided to release him. [14]But you rejected the Holy and Righteous One and asked to have a murderer given to you, [15]and you killed the Author of life, whom God raised from the dead. To this we are witnesses. [16]And by faith in his name, his name itself has made this man strong, whom you see and know; and the faith that is through Jesus[w] has given him this perfect health in the presence of all of you.

17 "And now, friends,[x] I know that you acted in ignorance, as did also your rulers. [18]In this way God

αἰνῶν τὸν θεόν. 9 καὶ εἶδεν πᾶς ὁ
praising – God. And [4]saw [1]all [2]the

λαὸς αὐτὸν περιπατοῦντα καὶ αἰνοῦντα
[3]people him walking and praising

τὸν θεόν· 10 ἐπεγίνωσκον δὲ αὐτόν, ὅτι
– God; and they recognized him, that

οὗτος ἦν ὁ πρὸς τὴν ἐλεημοσύνην
this was the [one] for – alms

καθήμενος ἐπὶ τῇ ὡραίᾳ πύλῃ τοῦ ἱεροῦ,
sitting at the Beautiful gate of the temple,

καὶ ἐπλήσθησαν θάμβους καὶ ἐκστάσεως
and they were filled of(with) amazement and bewilderment

ἐπὶ τῷ συμβεβηκότι αὐτῷ. 11 Κρατοῦντος δὲ
at the thing having happened to him. And holding =as he held

αὐτοῦ τὸν Πέτρον καὶ τὸν Ἰωάννην
him[a] – Peter and – John

συνέδραμεν πᾶς ὁ λαὸς πρὸς αὐτοὺς
ran together all the people to them

ἐπὶ τῇ στοᾷ τῇ καλουμένῃ Σολομῶντος
at the porch – *being* called of Solomon

ἔκθαμβοι. 12 ἰδὼν δὲ ὁ Πέτρος ἀπεκρίνατο
greatly amazed. And [2]seeing – [1]Peter answered

πρὸς τὸν λαόν· ἄνδρες Ἰσραηλῖται, τί
to the people: *Men* Israelites, why

θαυμάζετε ἐπὶ τούτῳ, ἢ ἡμῖν τί ἀτενίζετε
marvel ye at this man, or at us why gaze ye

ὡς ἰδίᾳ δυνάμει ἢ εὐσεβείᾳ πεποιηκόσιν
as by [our] own power or piety having made

τοῦ περιπατεῖν αὐτόν; 13 ὁ θεὸς Ἀβραὰμ
– to walk[d] him? The God of Abraham

καὶ Ἰσαὰκ καὶ Ἰακώβ, ὁ θεὸς τῶν
and Isaac and Jacob, the God of the

πατέρων ἡμῶν, ἐδόξασεν τὸν παῖδα αὐτοῦ
fathers of us, glorified the servant of him

Ἰησοῦν, ὃν ὑμεῖς μὲν παρεδώκατε καὶ
Jesus, whom ye – delivered and

ἠρνήσασθε κατὰ πρόσωπον Πιλάτου,
denied in [the] presence of Pilate,

κρίναντος ἐκείνου ἀπολύειν· 14 ὑμεῖς δὲ
having decided that one[a] to release [him]; but ye
=when he had decided

τὸν ἅγιον καὶ δίκαιον ἠρνήσασθε, καὶ
the holy and just one denied, and

ᾐτήσασθε ἄνδρα φονέα χαρισθῆναι ὑμῖν,
asked *a man* a murderer to be granted you,

15 τὸν δὲ ἀρχηγὸν τῆς ζωῆς ἀπεκτείνατε,
and the Author – of life ye killed,

ὃν ὁ θεὸς ἤγειρεν ἐκ νεκρῶν, οὗ ἡμεῖς
whom – God raised from [the] dead, of which we

μάρτυρές ἐσμεν. 16 καὶ ἐπὶ τῇ πίστει
witnesses are. And on the faith

τοῦ ὀνόματος αὐτοῦ τοῦτον, ὃν θεωρεῖτε
of(in) the name* of him [5]this man, [6]whom [7]ye behold

καὶ οἴδατε, ἐστερέωσεν τὸ ὄνομα αὐτοῦ,
[8]and [9]know, [4]made firm [1]the [2]name [3]of him,

καὶ ἡ πίστις ἡ δι' αὐτοῦ ἔδωκεν αὐτῷ
and the faith – through him gave him

τὴν ὁλοκληρίαν ταύτην ἀπέναντι πάντων
this soundness before all

ὑμῶν. 17 καὶ νῦν, ἀδελφοί, οἶδα ὅτι
you. And now, brothers, I know that

κατὰ ἄγνοιαν ἐπράξατε, ὥσπερ καὶ οἱ
by way of ignorance ye acted, as also the

* Objective genitive; *cf.* "the fear of God" = the fear which has God for its object; and see Gal. 2. 20, etc.

ing, and praising God. [9]When all the people saw him walking and praising God, [10]they recognized him as the same man who used to sit begging at the temple gate called Beautiful, and they were filled with wonder and amazement at what had happened to him.

Peter Speaks to the Onlookers

[11]While the beggar held on to Peter and John, all the people were astonished and came running to them in the place called Solomon's Colonnade. [12]When Peter saw this, he said to them: "Men of Israel, why does this surprise you? Why do you stare at us as if by our own power or godliness we had made this man walk? [13]The God of Abraham, Isaac and Jacob, the God of our fathers, has glorified his servant Jesus. You handed him over to be killed, and you disowned him before Pilate, though he had decided to let him go. [14]You disowned the Holy and Righteous One and asked that a murderer be released to you. [15]You killed the author of life, but God raised him from the dead. We are witnesses of this. [16]By faith in the name of Jesus, this man whom you see and know was made strong. It is Jesus' name and the faith that comes through him that has given this complete healing to him, as you can all see.

[17]"Now, brothers, I know that you acted in ignorance, as did your lead-

[u] Gk *Men, Israelites*
[v] Or *child*
[w] Gk *him*
[x] Gk *brothers*

fulfilled what he had foretold through all the prophets, that his Messiah[y]
would suffer. 19 Repent
therefore, and turn to God
so that your sins may be
wiped out, 20 so that times
of refreshing may come
from the presence of the
Lord, and that he may send
the Messiah[z] appointed for
you, that is, Jesus, 21 who
must remain in heaven until
the time of universal resto-
ration that God announced
long ago through his holy
prophets. 22 Moses said,
'The Lord your God will
raise up for you from your
own people[a] a prophet like
me. You must listen to
whatever he tells you.
23 And it will be that everyone who does not listen to
that prophet will be utterly
rooted out of the people.'
24 And all the prophets, as
many as have spoken, from
Samuel and those after
him, also predicted these
days. 25 You are the de-
scendants of the prophets
and of the covenant that
God gave to your ances-
tors, saying to Abraham,
'And in your descendants
all the families of the earth
shall be blessed.' 26 When
God raised up his servant,[b]
he sent him first to you, to
bless you by turning each
of you from your wicked
ways."

Chapter 4

Peter and John before the Council

WHILE Peter and John[c] were speaking to the people, the priests, the captain of the temple, and the Sadducees

[y] Or *his Christ*
[z] Or *the Christ*
[a] Gk *brothers*
[b] Or *child*
[c] Gk *While they*

ἄρχοντες ὑμῶν· 18 ὁ δὲ θεὸς ἃ
rulers of you; – but God the things which
προκατήγγειλεν διὰ στόματος πάντων
he foreannounced through [the] mouth of all
τῶν προφητῶν, παθεῖν τὸν χριστὸν αὐτοῦ,
the prophets, to suffer the Christ of him[b],
=that his Christ was to suffer,
ἐπλήρωσεν οὕτως. 19 μετανοήσατε οὖν
fulfilled thus. Repent ye therefore
καὶ ἐπιστρέψατε πρὸς τὸ ἐξαλειφθῆναι
and turn for the to be wiped away
=that your sins may be wiped away,
ὑμῶν τὰς ἁμαρτίας, 20 ὅπως ἂν ἔλθωσιν
of you the sins, so as may come
καιροὶ ἀναψύξεως ἀπὸ προσώπου τοῦ
times of refreshing from [the] presence of the
κυρίου καὶ ἀποστείλῃ τὸν προκεχειρισμένον
Lord and he may send [1]the [3]*having been* foreappointed
ὑμῖν χριστὸν Ἰησοῦν, 21 ὃν δεῖ οὐρανὸν
[4]for you [2]Christ [5]Jesus, whom it behoves heaven
μὲν δέξασθαι ἄχρι χρόνων ἀποκαταστάσεως
– to receive until [the] times of restitution
πάντων ὧν ἐλάλησεν ὁ θεὸς διὰ στόματος
of all things which [2]spoke – [1]God [3]through [4][the] mouth
τῶν ἁγίων ἀπ' αἰῶνος αὐτοῦ προφητῶν.
[5]of the [6]holy [8]from [10][the] age [9]of him [7]prophets.
22 Μωϋσῆς μὲν εἶπεν ὅτι προφήτην ὑμῖν
Moses indeed said[,] – [4]A prophet [5]for you
ἀναστήσει κύριος ὁ θεὸς ἐκ τῶν ἀδελφῶν
[3]will raise up [1](the) Lord – [2]God of the brothers
ὑμῶν ὡς ἐμέ· αὐτοῦ ἀκούσεσθε κατὰ
of you as me; him shall ye hear according to
πάντα ὅσα ἂν λαλήσῃ πρὸς ὑμᾶς.
all things whatever he may speak to you.
23 ἔσται δὲ πᾶσα ψυχὴ ἥτις ἐὰν μὴ ἀκούσῃ
And it shall be every soul whoever hears not
τοῦ προφήτου ἐκείνου ἐξολεθρευθήσεται
that prophet will be utterly destroyed
ἐκ τοῦ λαοῦ. 24 καὶ πάντες δὲ οἱ
out of the people. [2]also [3]all [1]And the
προφῆται ἀπὸ Σαμουὴλ καὶ τῶν καθεξῆς
prophets from Samuel and the [ones] in order
ὅσοι ἐλάλησαν καὶ κατήγγειλαν τὰς ἡμέρας
as many as spoke also announced – days
ταύτας. 25 ὑμεῖς ἐστε οἱ υἱοὶ τῶν
these. Ye are the sons of the
προφητῶν καὶ τῆς διαθήκης ἧς ὁ θεὸς
prophets and of the covenant which – God
διέθετο πρὸς τοὺς πατέρας ὑμῶν, λέγων
made with the fathers of us, saying
πρὸς Ἀβραάμ· καὶ ἐν τῷ σπέρματί
to Abraham: And in the seed
σου ἐνευλογηθήσονται πᾶσαι αἱ πατριαὶ
of thee shall be blessed all the families
τῆς γῆς. 26 ὑμῖν πρῶτον ἀναστήσας ὁ
of the earth. To you first [2]having raised up –
θεὸς τὸν παῖδα αὐτοῦ ἀπέστειλεν αὐτὸν
[1]God the servant of him sent him
εὐλογοῦντα ὑμᾶς ἐν τῷ ἀποστρέφειν
blessing you in the to turn away
=in turning away
ἕκαστον ἀπὸ τῶν πονηριῶν ὑμῶν.
each one from the iniquities of you.
4 Λαλούντων δὲ αὐτῶν πρὸς τὸν λαόν,
And speaking them[a] to the people,
=while they were speaking
ἐπέστησαν αὐτοῖς οἱ ἱερεῖς καὶ ὁ στρατηγὸς
came upon them the priests and the commandant

ers. 18 But this is how God
fulfilled what he had foretold through all the prophets, saying that his Christ[m]
would suffer. 19 Repent,
then, and turn to God, so
that your sins may be
wiped out, that times of refreshing may come from
the Lord, 20 and that he may
send the Christ, who has
been appointed for you—
even Jesus. 21 He must remain in heaven until the
time comes for God to re-
store everything, as he
promised long ago through
his holy prophets. 22 For
Moses said, 'The Lord
your God will raise up for
you a prophet like me from
among your own people;
you must listen to every-
thing he tells you. 23 Anyone who does not listen to
him will be completely cut
off from among his peo-
ple.'[n]
24 "Indeed, all the prophets from Samuel on, as
many as have spoken, have
foretold these days. 25 And
you are heirs of the prophets and of the covenant
God made with your fa-
thers. He said to Abraham,
'Through your offspring all
peoples on earth will be
blessed.'[o] 26 When God
raised up his servant, he
sent him first to you to
bless you by turning each
of you from your wicked
ways."

Chapter 4

Peter and John Before the Sanhedrin

THE priests and the captain of the temple guard and the Sadducees

[m] *18* Or *Messiah*; also in verse 20
[n] *23* Deut. 18:15,18,19
[o] *25* Gen. 22:18; 26:4

came to them, 2 much annoyed because they were teaching the people and proclaiming that in Jesus there is the resurrection of the dead. 3 So they arrested them and put them in custody until the next day, for it was already evening. 4 But many of those who heard the word believed; and they numbered about five thousand.

5 The next day their rulers, elders, and scribes assembled in Jerusalem, 6 with Annas the high priest, Caiaphas, John,[d] and Alexander, and all who were of the high-priestly family. 7 When they had made the prisoners[e] stand in their midst, they inquired, "By what power or by what name did you do this?" 8 Then Peter, filled with the Holy Spirit, said to them, "Rulers of the people and elders, 9 if we are questioned today because of a good deed done to someone who was sick and are asked how this man has been healed, 10 let it be known to all of you, and to all the people of Israel, that this man is standing before you in good health by the name of Jesus Christ of Nazareth,[f] whom you crucified, whom God raised from the dead. 11 This Jesus[g] is

'the stone that was
rejected by you,
the builders;
it has become the
cornerstone.'[h]

12 There is salvation in no one else, for there is no other name under heaven giv-

[d] Other ancient authorities read *Jonathan*
[e] Gk *them*
[f] Gk *the Nazorean*
[g] Gk *This*
[h] Or *keystone*

τοῦ ἱεροῦ καὶ οἱ Σαδδουκαῖοι, **2** διαπονούμενοι
of the temple and the Sadducees, being greatly troubled

διὰ τὸ διδάσκειν αὐτοὺς τὸν λαὸν καὶ
because of the to teach them[b] the people and
=because they taught . . . announced

καταγγέλλειν ἐν τῷ Ἰησοῦ τὴν ἀνάστασιν
to announce[b] by – Jesus the resurrection

τὴν ἐκ νεκρῶν, **3** καὶ ἐπέβαλον αὐτοῖς
– from [the] dead, and laid on them

τὰς χεῖρας καὶ ἔθεντο εἰς τήρησιν εἰς
the(ir) hands and put in guard till

τὴν αὔριον· ἦν γὰρ ἑσπέρα ἤδη. **4** πολλοὶ
the morrow; for it was evening now. many

δὲ τῶν ἀκουσάντων τὸν λόγον ἐπίστευσαν,
But of the [ones] hearing the word believed,

καὶ ἐγενήθη ἀριθμὸς τῶν ἀνδρῶν ὡς
and became [the] number of the men about

χιλιάδες πέντε.
thousand*s* five.

5 Ἐγένετο δὲ ἐπὶ τὴν αὔριον
Now it came to pass on the morrow

συναχθῆναι αὐτῶν τοὺς ἄρχοντας καὶ τοὺς
to be assembled of them the rulers and the

πρεσβυτέρους καὶ τοὺς γραμματεῖς ἐν
elders and the scribes in

Ἰερουσαλήμ, **6** καὶ Ἅννας ὁ ἀρχιερεὺς
Jerusalem, and Annas* the high priest

καὶ Καϊαφᾶς καὶ Ἰωάννης καὶ Ἀλέξανδρος
and Caiaphas and John and Alexander

καὶ ὅσοι ἦσαν ἐκ γένους ἀρχιερατικοῦ,
and as many as were of [the] race high-priestly,

7 καὶ στήσαντες αὐτοὺς ἐν τῷ μέσῳ
and having stood them in the midst

ἐπυνθάνοντο· ἐν ποίᾳ δυνάμει ἢ ἐν ποίῳ
inquired : By what power or in what

ὀνόματι ἐποιήσατε τοῦτο ὑμεῖς; **8** τότε
name did this ye? Then

Πέτρος πλησθεὶς πνεύματος ἁγίου εἶπεν
Peter filled of(with) [the] Spirit Holy said

πρὸς αὐτούς· ἄρχοντες τοῦ λαοῦ καὶ
to them : Rulers of the people and

πρεσβύτεροι, **9** εἰ ἡμεῖς σήμερον ἀνα-
elders, if we to-day are be-

κρινόμεθα ἐπὶ εὐεργεσίᾳ ἀνθρώπου ἀσθενοῦς,
ing examined on a good deed man of an infirm,
=[done to] an infirm man,

ἐν τίνι οὗτος σέσωσται, **10** γνωστὸν ἔστω
by what this man has been healed, known let it be

πᾶσιν ὑμῖν καὶ παντὶ τῷ λαῷ Ἰσραήλ,
to all you and to all the people of Israel,

ὅτι ἐν τῷ ὀνόματι Ἰησοῦ Χριστοῦ τοῦ
that in the name of Jesus Christ the

Ναζωραίου, ὃν ὑμεῖς ἐσταυρώσατε, ὃν ὁ
Nazarene, whom ye crucified, whom –

θεὸς ἤγειρεν ἐκ νεκρῶν, ἐν τούτῳ οὗτος
God raised from [the] dead, in this [name] this man

παρέστηκεν ἐνώπιον ὑμῶν ὑγιής. **11** οὗτός
stands before you whole. This

ἐστιν ὁ λίθος ὁ ἐξουθενηθεὶς ὑφ᾽ ὑμῶν
is the stone – despised by you

τῶν οἰκοδόμων, ὁ γενόμενος εἰς κεφαλὴν
the [ones] building, the [one] become *to* head

γωνίας. **12** καὶ οὐκ ἔστιν ἐν ἄλλῳ οὐδενὶ
of [the] corner. And there is not [1]in [3]other [2]no(any)

ἡ σωτηρία· οὐδὲ γὰρ ὄνομά ἐστιν ἕτερον
the salvation: for neither [3]name [1]is there [2]other

*** The rough breathing in the Greek is ignored in the transliteration of some familiar proper names.**

came up to Peter and John while they were speaking to the people. 2 They were greatly disturbed because the apostles were teaching the people and proclaiming in Jesus the resurrection of the dead. 3 They seized Peter and John, and because it was evening, they put them in jail until the next day. 4 But many who heard the message believed, and the number of men grew to about five thousand.

5 The next day the rulers, elders and teachers of the law met in Jerusalem. 6 Annas the high priest was there, and so were Caiaphas, John, Alexander and the other men of the high priest's family. 7 They had Peter and John brought before them and began to question them: "By what power or what name did you do this?"

8 Then Peter, filled with the Holy Spirit, said to them: "Rulers and elders of the people! 9 If we are being called to account today for an act of kindness shown to a cripple and are asked how he was healed, 10 then know this, you and all the people of Israel: It is by the name of Jesus Christ of Nazareth, whom you crucified but whom God raised from the dead, that this man stands before you healed. 11 He is

" 'the stone you builders
rejected,
which has become the
capstone.'[p][q]

12 Salvation is found in no one else, for there is no other name under heaven giv-

[p] 11 Or *cornerstone*
[q] 11 Psalm 118:22

en among mortals by which
we must be saved."
13 Now when they saw
the boldness of Peter and
John and realized that they
were uneducated and ordi-
nary men, they were
amazed and recognized
them as companions of
Jesus. 14 When they saw
the man who had been
cured standing beside
them, they had nothing to
say in opposition. 15 So
they ordered them to leave
the council while they discussed the matter with one
another. 16 They said,
"What will we do with
them? For it is obvious to
all who live in Jerusalem
that a notable sign has been
done through them; we
cannot deny it. 17 But to
keep it from spreading further among the people, let
us warn them to speak no
more to anyone in this
name." 18 So they called
them and ordered them not
to speak or teach at all in
the name of Jesus. 19 But
Peter and John answered
them, "Whether it is right
in God's sight to listen to
you rather than to God, you
must judge; 20 for we cannot keep from speaking
about what we have seen
and heard." 21 After threatening them again, they let
them go, finding no way to
punish them because of the
people, for all of them
praised God for what had
happened. 22 For the man
on whom this sign of healing had been performed

ὑπὸ τὸν οὐρανὸν τὸ δεδομένον ἐν
under – heaven – having been given among
ἀνθρώποις ἐν ᾧ δεῖ σωθῆναι ἡμᾶς.
men by which it behoves [2]to be saved [1]us.
13 Θεωροῦντες δὲ τὴν τοῦ Πέτρου
And beholding the – of Peter
παρρησίαν καὶ Ἰωάννου, καὶ καταλαβόμενοι
boldness and of John, and perceiving
ὅτι ἄνθρωποι ἀγράμματοί εἰσιν καὶ
that men unlettered they are(were) and
ἰδιῶται, ἐθαύμαζον, ἐπεγίνωσκόν τε αὐτοὺς
laymen, they marvelled, and recognized them
ὅτι σὺν τῷ Ἰησοῦ ἦσαν, 14 τόν τε
that with – Jesus they were(had been), [3]the [1]and
ἄνθρωπον βλέποντες σὺν αὐτοῖς ἑστῶτα τὸν
[4]man [2]seeing [7]with [8]them [6]standing –
τεθεραπευμένον, οὐδὲν εἶχον ἀντειπεῖν.
[5]having been healed, nothing they had to say against.
15 κελεύσαντες δὲ αὐτοὺς ἔξω τοῦ συνεδρίου
So having commanded them outside the council
ἀπελθεῖν, συνέβαλλον πρὸς ἀλλήλους
to go, they discussed *with* with one another
16 λέγοντες· τί ποιήσωμεν τοῖς ἀνθρώποις
saying: What may we do – men
τούτοις; ὅτι μὲν γὰρ γνωστὸν σημεῖον
to these? for that indeed a notable sign
γέγονεν δι' αὐτῶν, πᾶσιν τοῖς κατοικοῦσιν
has happened through them, to all the [ones] inhabiting
Ἰερουσαλὴμ φανερόν, καὶ οὐ δυνάμεθα
Jerusalem [is] manifest, and we cannot
ἀρνεῖσθαι· 17 ἀλλ' ἵνα μὴ ἐπὶ πλεῖον
to deny [it]; but [1]lest [3]more†
διανεμηθῇ εἰς τὸν λαόν, ἀπειλησώμεθα
[2]it is spread abroad [4]to the people, let us threaten
αὐτοῖς μηκέτι λαλεῖν ἐπὶ τῷ ὀνόματι
them no longer to speak on – name
τούτῳ μηδενὶ ἀνθρώπων. 18 καὶ καλέσαντες
this to no(any)one of men. And calling
αὐτοὺς παρήγγειλαν καθόλου μὴ φθέγγεσθαι
them they charged at all not to utter
μηδὲ διδάσκειν ἐπὶ τῷ ὀνόματι τοῦ
nor to teach on the name –
Ἰησοῦ. 19 ὁ δὲ Πέτρος καὶ Ἰωάννης
of Jesus. – But Peter and John
ἀποκριθέντες εἶπον πρὸς αὐτούς· εἰ
answering said to them: If
δίκαιόν ἐστιν ἐνώπιον τοῦ θεοῦ, ὑμῶν
right it is before – God, you
ἀκούειν μᾶλλον ἢ τοῦ θεοῦ, κρίνατε·
to hear rather than – God, decide ye;
20 οὐ δυνάμεθα γὰρ ἡμεῖς ἃ εἴδαμεν
for cannot we [the] things which we saw
καὶ ἠκούσαμεν μὴ λαλεῖν. 21 οἱ δὲ
and heard not *to* speak. And they
προσαπειλησάμενοι ἀπέλυσαν αὐτούς, μηδὲν
having added threats released them, nothing
εὑρίσκοντες τὸ πῶς κολάσωνται αὐτούς,
finding – how they might punish them,
διὰ τὸν λαόν, ὅτι πάντες ἐδόξαζον τὸν
because of the people, because all men glorified –
θεὸν ἐπὶ τῷ γεγονότι· 22 ἐτῶν γὰρ
God on the thing having happened; for of years
ἦν πλειόνων τεσσεράκοντα ὁ ἄνθρωπος
was more [than] forty the man
ἐφ' ὃν γεγόνει τὸ σημεῖον τοῦτο τῆς
on whom had happened this sign –

en to men by which we
must be saved."
13 When they saw the
courage of Peter and John
and realized that they were
unschooled, ordinary men,
they were astonished and
they took note that these
men had been with Jesus.
14 But since they could see
the man who had been
healed standing there with
them, there was nothing
they could say. 15 So they
ordered them to withdraw
from the Sanhedrin and
then conferred together.
16 "What are we going to do
with these men?" they
asked. "Everybody living
in Jerusalem knows they
have done an outstanding
miracle, and we cannot
deny it. 17 But to stop this
thing from spreading any
further among the people,
we must warn these men to
speak no longer to anyone
in this name."
18 Then they called them
in again and commanded
them not to speak or teach
at all in the name of Jesus.
19 But Peter and John re-
plied, "Judge for your-
selves whether it is right in
God's sight to obey you
rather than God. 20 For we
cannot help speaking about
what we have seen and
heard."
21 After further threats
they let them go. They
could not decide how to
punish them, because all
the people were praising
God for what had hap-
pened. 22 For the man who
was miraculously healed
was over forty years old.

was more than forty years
old.

The Believers Pray for Boldness

23 After they were re-
leased, they went to their
friends[i] and reported what
the chief priests and the elders had said to them.
24When they heard it, they
raised their voices together
to God and said, "Sover-
eign Lord, who made the
heaven and the earth, the
sea, and everything in
them, 25it is you who said
by the Holy Spirit through
our ancestor David, your
servant:[b]

'Why did the Gentiles
rage,
and the peoples
imagine vain
things?
26 The kings of the earth
took their stand,
and the rulers have
gathered
together
against the Lord
and against his
Messiah.'[j]

27For in this city, in fact,
both Herod and Pontius Pilate, with the Gentiles and
the peoples of Israel, gathered together against your
holy servant[k] Jesus, whom
you anointed, 28to do whatever your hand and your
plan had predestined to
take place. 29And now,
Lord, look at their threats,
and grant to your servants[l]
to speak your word with all
boldness, 30while you
stretch out your hand to
heal, and signs and won-
ders are performed through
the name of your holy servant[k] Jesus." 31When they
had prayed, the place in
which they were gathered
together was shaken; and
they were all filled with the
Holy Spirit and spoke the
word of God with boldness.

The Believers Share Their Possessions

32 Now the whole
group of those who be-
lieved were of one heart

[i] Gk *their own*
[j] Or *his Christ*
[k] Or *child*
[l] Gk *slaves*

ἰάσεως. 23 Ἀπολυθέντες δὲ ἦλθον πρὸς
of cure. And being released they went to

τοὺς ἰδίους καὶ ἀπήγγειλαν ὅσα πρὸς
the(ir) own [people] and reported what things to

αὐτοὺς οἱ ἀρχιερεῖς καὶ οἱ πρεσβύτεροι
them the chief priests and the elders

εἶπαν. 24 οἱ δὲ ἀκούσαντες ὁμοθυμαδὸν
said. And they having heard with one mind

ἦραν φωνὴν πρὸς τὸν θεὸν καὶ εἶπαν·
lifted voice to – God and said:

δέσποτα, σὺ ὁ ποιήσας τὸν οὐρανὸν καὶ
Master, thou the [one] having made the heaven and

τὴν γῆν καὶ τὴν θάλασσαν καὶ πάντα
the earth and the sea and all things

τὰ ἐν αὐτοῖς, 25 ὁ τοῦ πατρὸς ἡμῶν
– in them, [1]the [one] [8]the [9]father [10]of us

διὰ πνεύματος ἁγίου στόματος Δαυὶδ
[3]through [5][the] Spirit [4]Holy [6][by] mouth [7]of David

παιδός σου εἰπών· ἱνατί ἐφρύαξαν ἔθνη
[11]servant [12]of thee [2]saying :* Why raged nations

καὶ λαοὶ ἐμελέτησαν κενά; 26 παρέστησαν
and peoples devised vain things? came

οἱ βασιλεῖς τῆς γῆς καὶ οἱ ἄρχοντες
the kings of the earth and the rulers

συνήχθησαν ἐπὶ τὸ αὐτὸ κατὰ τοῦ κυρίου
assembled together against the Lord

καὶ κατὰ τοῦ χριστοῦ αὐτοῦ.
and against the Christ of him.

27 συνήχθησαν γὰρ ἐπ' ἀληθείας ἐν τῇ
For assembled in truth in –

πόλει ταύτῃ ἐπὶ τὸν ἅγιον παῖδά σου
city this against the holy servant of thee

Ἰησοῦν, ὃν ἔχρισας, Ἡρῴδης τε καὶ
Jesus, whom thou didst anoint, both Herod and

Πόντιος Πιλᾶτος σὺν ἔθνεσιν καὶ λαοῖς
Pontius Pilate with nations and peoples

Ἰσραήλ, 28 ποιῆσαι ὅσα ἡ χείρ σου καὶ
of Israel, to do what things the hand of thee and

ἡ βουλὴ προώρισεν γενέσθαι. 29 καὶ τὰ
the counsel foreordained to happen. And –

νῦν, κύριε, ἔπιδε ἐπὶ τὰς ἀπειλὰς αὐτῶν,
now, Lord, look *on* on the threatenings of them,

καὶ δὸς τοῖς δούλοις σου μετὰ παρρησίας
and give to the slaves of thee with [2]boldness

πάσης λαλεῖν τὸν λόγον σου, 30 ἐν τῷ
[1]all to speak the word of thee, by the

τὴν χεῖρα ἐκτείνειν σε εἰς ἴασιν καὶ
the hand to stretch forth thee[b] for cure and
=by stretching forth thy hand

σημεῖα καὶ τέρατα γίνεσθαι διὰ τοῦ
signs and wonders to happen through the

ὀνόματος τοῦ ἁγίου παιδός σου Ἰησοῦ.
name of the holy servant of thee Jesus.

31 καὶ δεηθέντων αὐτῶν ἐσαλεύθη ὁ τόπος
And requesting them[a] was shaken the place
=as they were making request

ἐν ᾧ ἦσαν συνηγμένοι, καὶ ἐπλήσθησαν
in which they were *having been* assembled, and they were filled

ἅπαντες τοῦ ἁγίου πνεύματος, καὶ ἐλάλουν
all of(with) the Holy Spirit, and spoke

τὸν λόγον τοῦ θεοῦ μετὰ παρρησίας.
the word – of God with boldness.

32 Τοῦ δὲ πλήθους τῶν πιστευσάντων
[1]Now [6]of [7]the [2]multitude [8]of the [ones] [10]having believed

* It is recognized that there is a primitive error in the text in the first half of ver. 25; it is impossible to construe it as it stands. See ch. 1. 16.

The Believers' Prayer

23On their release, Peter
and John went back to their
own people and reported
all that the chief priests and
elders had said to them.
24When they heard this,
they raised their voices together in prayer to God.
"Sovereign Lord," they
said, "you made the heav-
en and the earth and the
sea, and everything in
them. 25You spoke by the
Holy Spirit through the
mouth of your servant, our
father David:

" 'Why do the nations
rage
and the peoples plot in
vain?
26The kings of the earth
take their stand
and the rulers gather
together
against the Lord
and against his
Anointed One.'[r s]

27Indeed Herod and Pon-
tius Pilate met together
with the Gentiles and the
people[t] of Israel in this city
to conspire against your
holy servant Jesus, whom
you anointed. 28They did
what your power and will
had decided beforehand
should happen. 29Now,
Lord, consider their threats
and enable your servants to
speak your word with great
boldness. 30Stretch out
your hand to heal and perform miraculous signs and
wonders through the name
of your holy servant
Jesus."

31After they prayed, the
place where they were
meeting was shaken. And
they were all filled with the
Holy Spirit and spoke the
word of God boldly.

The Believers Share Their Possessions

32All the believers were
one in heart and mind. No

[r]26 That is, Christ or Messiah
[s]26 Psalm 2:1,2
[t]27 The Greek is plural.

and soul, and no one
claimed private ownership
of any possessions, but everything they owned was
held in common. 33 With
great power the apostles
gave their testimony to the
resurrection of the Lord
Jesus, and great grace was
upon them all. 34 There was
not a needy person among
them, for as many as
owned lands or houses sold
them and brought the pro-
ceeds of what was sold.
35 They laid it at the apostles' feet, and it was distributed to each as any had
need. 36 There was a Le-
vite, a native of Cyprus, Joseph, to whom the apostles
gave the name Barnabas
(which means "son of en-
couragement"). 37 He sold a
field that belonged to him,
then brought the money,
and laid it at the apostles'
feet.

ἦν καρδία καὶ ψυχὴ μία, καὶ οὐδὲ
[11]was [2][the] [3]heart [4]and [5]soul [12]one, and [1]not
εἷς τι τῶν ὑπαρχόντων αὐτῷ ἔλεγεν
[2]one [4]anything [5]of the [6]possessions [belonging] [7]to him[c] [3]said
ἴδιον εἶναι, ἀλλʼ ἦν αὐτοῖς πάντα κοινά.
[8][his] own [9]to be, but were to them[c] all things common.
33 καὶ δυνάμει μεγάλῃ ἀπεδίδουν τὸ
And [1]with [3]power [2]great [6]gave [7]the
μαρτύριον οἱ ἀπόστολοι τοῦ κυρίου Ἰησοῦ
[8]testimony [4]the [5]apostles [11]of the [12]Lord [13]Jesus
τῆς ἀναστάσεως, χάρις τε μεγάλη ἦν
[9]of the [10]resurrection, and [2]grace [1]great was
ἐπὶ πάντας αὐτούς. 34 οὐδὲ γὰρ ἐνδεής
upon all them. [1]For [2]neither [5]needy
τις ἦν ἐν αὐτοῖς· ὅσοι γὰρ κτήτορες
[4]anyone [3]was among them; for as many as owners
χωρίων ἢ οἰκιῶν ὑπῆρχον, πωλοῦντες
of lands or of houses were, selling
ἔφερον τὰς τιμὰς τῶν πιπρασκομένων
brought the prices of the things being sold
35 καὶ ἐτίθουν παρὰ τοὺς πόδας τῶν
and placed at the feet of the
ἀποστόλων· διεδίδοτο δὲ ἑκάστῳ καθότι ἄν
apostles; and it was distributed to each according as
τις χρείαν εἶχεν. 36 Ἰωσὴφ δὲ ὁ
anyone need had. And Joseph the [one]
ἐπικληθεὶς Βαρναβᾶς ἀπὸ τῶν ἀποστόλων,
surnamed Barnabas from(by) the apostles,
ὅ ἐστιν μεθερμηνευόμενον υἱὸς παρακλήσεως,
which is being translated Son of consolation,
Λευίτης, Κύπριος τῷ γένει, 37 ὑπάρχοντος
a Levite, a Cypriote – by race, being
αὐτῷ ἀγροῦ, πωλήσας ἤνεγκεν τὸ χρῆμα
to him[c] a field,[a] having sold [it] brought the proceeds
=as he had a field,
καὶ ἔθηκεν πρὸς τοὺς πόδας τῶν ἀποστόλων.
and placed at the feet of the apostles.

one claimed that any of his
possessions was his own,
but they shared everything
they had. 33 With great power the apostles continued to
testify to the resurrection
of the Lord Jesus, and
much grace was upon them
all. 34 There were no needy
persons among them. For
from time to time those
who owned lands or houses
sold them, brought the
money from the sales 35 and
put it at the apostles' feet,
and it was distributed to
anyone as he had need.
36 Joseph, a Levite from
Cyprus, whom the apostles
called Barnabas (which
means Son of Encourage-
ment), 37 sold a field he
owned and brought the
money and put it at the
apostles' feet.

Chapter 5

Ananias and Sapphira

BUT a man named Ana-
nias, with the consent
of his wife Sapphira, sold a
piece of property, 2 with his
wife's knowledge, he kept
back some of the proceeds,
and brought only a part and
laid it at the apostles' feet.
3 "Ananias," Peter asked,
"why has Satan filled your
heart to lie to the Holy Spirit and to keep back part of
the proceeds of the land?
4 While it remained unsold,
did it not remain your own?
And after it was sold, were
not the proceeds at your
disposal? How is it that you
have contrived this deed in

5 Ἀνὴρ δέ τις Ἁνανίας ὀνόματι σὺν
And a certain man Ananias* by name with
Σαπφίρῃ τῇ γυναικὶ αὐτοῦ ἐπώλησεν
Sapphira the wife of him sold
κτῆμα, 2 καὶ ἐνοσφίσατο ἀπὸ τῆς τιμῆς,
a property, and appropriated from the price,
συνειδυίης καὶ τῆς γυναικός, καὶ ἐνέγκας
aware of [it] also the(his) wife,[a] and bringing
=his wife also being aware of it,
μέρος τι παρὰ τοὺς πόδας τῶν ἀποστόλων
a certain part at the feet of the apostles
ἔθηκεν. 3 εἶπεν δὲ ὁ Πέτρος· Ἁνανία,
placed [it]. But said – Peter : Ananias,
διὰ τί ἐπλήρωσεν ὁ σατανᾶς τὴν καρδίαν
why filled – Satan the heart
σου, ψεύσασθαί σε τὸ πνεῦμα τὸ ἅγιον
of thee, to deceive thee[b] the Spirit – Holy
=that thou shouldest deceive
καὶ νοσφίσασθαι ἀπὸ τῆς τιμῆς τοῦ
and to appropriate from the price of the
χωρίου; 4 οὐχὶ μένον σοὶ ἔμενεν καὶ
land? Not remaining to thee it remained and
πραθὲν ἐν τῇ σῇ ἐξουσίᾳ ὑπῆρχεν; τί ὅτι
sold in – thy authority it was? Why
ἔθου ἐν τῇ καρδίᾳ σου τὸ πρᾶγμα
was put in the heart of thee – action

* See note to 4. 6.

Chapter 5

Ananias and Sapphira

NOW a man named An-
anias, together with
his wife Sapphira, also sold
a piece of property. 2 With
his wife's full knowledge he
kept back part of the money for himself, but brought
the rest and put it at the
apostles' feet.
3 Then Peter said, "Ana-
nias, how is it that Satan
has so filled your heart that
you have lied to the Holy
Spirit and have kept for
yourself some of the money
you received for the land?
4 Didn't it belong to you before it was sold? And after
it was sold, wasn't the
money at your disposal?
What made you think of doing such a thing? You have

your heart? You did not lie
to us[m] but to God!" 5Now
when Ananias heard these
words, he fell down and
died. And great fear seized
all who heard of it. 6The
young men came and
wrapped up his body,[n]
then carried him out and
buried him.
7 After an interval of
about three hours his wife
came in, not knowing what
had happened. 8Peter said
to her, "Tell me whether
you and your husband sold
the land for such and such
a price." And she said,
"Yes, that was the price."
9Then Peter said to her,
"How is it that you have
agreed together to put the
Spirit of the Lord to the
test? Look, the feet of
those who have buried
your husband are at the
door, and they will carry
you out." 10Immediately
she fell down at his feet and
died. When the young men
came in they found her
dead, so they carried her
out and buried her beside
her husband. 11And great
fear seized the whole
church and all who heard of
these things.

The Apostles Heal Many

12 Now many signs and
wonders were done among
the people through the
apostles. And they were all
together in Solomon's Portico. 13None of the rest
dared to join them, but the
people held them in high es-
teem. 14Yet more than ever
believers were added to the
Lord, great numbers of
both men and women, 15so
that they even carried out
the sick into the streets,
and laid them on cots and
mats, in order that Peter's

[m] Gk *to men*
[n] Meaning of Gk uncertain

τοῦτο; οὐκ ἐψεύσω ἀνθρώποις ἀλλὰ
this? thou didst not lie to men but
τῷ θεῷ. 5 ἀκούων δὲ ὁ Ἀνανίας
– to God. And hearing – Ananias
τοὺς λόγους τούτους πεσὼν ἐξέψυξεν· καὶ
these words falling expired; and
ἐγένετο φόβος μέγας ἐπὶ πάντας τοὺς
came fear great on all the [ones]
ἀκούοντας. 6 ἀναστάντες δὲ οἱ νεώτεροι
hearing. And rising up the young men
συνέστειλαν αὐτὸν καὶ ἐξενέγκαντες ἔθαψαν.
wrapped him and carrying out buried [him].
7 Ἐγένετο δὲ ὡς ὡρῶν τριῶν διάστημα
¹And there was ³of about ⁵hours ⁴three ²an interval
καὶ ἡ γυνὴ αὐτοῦ μὴ εἰδυῖα τὸ γεγονὸς
and the wife of him not knowing the thing having happened
εἰσῆλθεν. 8 ἀπεκρίθη δὲ πρὸς αὐτὴν
entered. And answered *to* her
Πέτρος· εἰπέ μοι, εἰ τοσούτου τὸ χωρίον
Peter: Tell me, if of(for) so much the land
ἀπέδοσθε; ἡ δὲ εἶπεν· ναί, τοσούτου.
ye sold? And she said: Yes, of(for) so much.
9 ὁ δὲ Πέτρος πρὸς αὐτήν· τί ὅτι
– And Peter to her: Why
συνεφωνήθη ὑμῖν πειράσαι τὸ πνεῦμα
was it agreed with you to tempt the Spirit
κυρίου; ἰδοὺ οἱ πόδες τῶν θαψάντων τὸν
of [the] Lord? behold[,] the feet of the [ones] having buried the
ἄνδρα σου ἐπὶ τῇ θύρᾳ καὶ ἐξοίσουσίν
husband of thee at the door and they will carry out
σε. 10 ἔπεσεν δὲ παραχρῆμα πρὸς τοὺς
thee. And she fell at once at the
πόδας αὐτοῦ καὶ ἐξέψυξεν· εἰσελθόντες δὲ
feet of him and expired; and entering
οἱ νεανίσκοι εὗρον αὐτὴν νεκράν, καὶ
the young men found her dead, and
ἐξενέγκαντες ἔθαψαν πρὸς τὸν ἄνδρα
carrying out buried [her] beside the husband
αὐτῆς. 11 Καὶ ἐγένετο φόβος μέγας
of her. And came fear great
ἐφ᾽ ὅλην τὴν ἐκκλησίαν καὶ ἐπὶ πάντας
on all the church and on all
τοὺς ἀκούοντας ταῦτα.
the [ones] hearing these things.
12 Διὰ δὲ τῶν χειρῶν τῶν ἀποστόλων
And through the hands of the apostles
ἐγίνετο σημεῖα καὶ τέρατα πολλὰ ἐν
⁵happened ²signs ³and ⁴wonders ¹many among
τῷ λαῷ· καὶ ἦσαν ὁμοθυμαδὸν πάντες
the people; and were with one mind all
ἐν τῇ στοᾷ Σολομῶντος· 13 τῶν δὲ
in the porch of Solomon; and of the
λοιπῶν οὐδεὶς ἐτόλμα κολλᾶσθαι αὐτοῖς,
rest no one dared to be joined to them,
ἀλλ᾽ ἐμεγάλυνεν αὐτοὺς ὁ λαός· 14 μᾶλλον
but magnified them the people; ²more
δὲ προσετίθεντο πιστεύοντες τῷ κυρίῳ,
¹and were added believing [ones] to the Lord,
πλήθη ἀνδρῶν τε καὶ γυναικῶν· 15 ὥστε
multitudes both of men and of women; so as
καὶ εἰς τὰς πλατείας ἐκφέρειν τοὺς
even into the streets to bring out =they brought out the
ἀσθενεῖς καὶ τιθέναι ἐπὶ κλιναρίων καὶ
ailing and to place on pallets and

not lied to men but to
God."
5When Ananias heard
this, he fell down and died.
And great fear seized all
who heard what had hap-
pened. 6Then the young
men came forward,
wrapped up his body, and
carried him out and buried
him.
7About three hours later
his wife came in, not knowing what had happened.
8Peter asked her, "Tell me,
is this the price you and Ananias got for the land?"
"Yes," she said, "that is
the price."
9Peter said to her, "How
could you agree to test the
Spirit of the Lord? Look!
The feet of the men who
buried your husband are at
the door, and they will carry you out also."
10At that moment she fell
down at his feet and died.
Then the young men came
in and, finding her dead,
carried her out and buried
her beside her husband.
11Great fear seized the
whole church and all who
heard about these events.

The Apostles Heal Many

12The apostles performed
many miraculous signs and
wonders among the people.
And all the believers used
to meet together in Solo-
mon's Colonnade. 13No
one else dared join them,
even though they were
highly regarded by the people. 14Nevertheless, more
and more men and women
believed in the Lord and
were added to their num-
ber. 15As a result, people
brought the sick into the
streets and laid them on
beds and mats so that at

shadow might fall on some of them as he came by. 16 A great number of people would also gather from the towns around Jerusalem, bringing the sick and those tormented by unclean spirits, and they were all cured.

The Apostles Are Persecuted

17 Then the high priest took action; he and all who were with him (that is, the sect of the Sadducees), being filled with jealousy, 18 arrested the apostles and put them in the public prison. 19 But during the night an angel of the Lord opened the prison doors, brought them out, and said, 20 "Go, stand in the temple and tell the people the whole message about this life." 21 When they heard this, they entered the temple at daybreak and went on with their teaching.

When the high priest and those with him arrived, they called together the council and the whole body of the elders of Israel, and sent to the prison to have them brought. 22 But when the temple police went there, they did not find them in the prison; so they returned and reported, 23 "We found the prison securely locked and the guards standing at the doors, but when we opened them, we found no one inside." 24 Now when the captain of the temple and the chief priests heard these words, they were perplexed about them, wondering what might be going on. 25 Then someone arrived and announced, "Look, the men whom you put in prison are standing in

κραβάτων, ἵνα ἐρχομένου Πέτρου κἂν ἡ σκιὰ
mattresses, that [5]coming [4]of Peter [1]if even [2]the [3]shadow
ἐπισκιάσῃ τινὶ αὐτῶν. **16** συνήρχετο δὲ
might overshadow some one of them. And came together
καὶ τὸ πλῆθος τῶν πέριξ πόλεων
also the multitude of the [2]round about [1]cities
Ἰερουσαλήμ, φέροντες ἀσθενεῖς καὶ
Jerusalem, carrying ailing [ones] and
ὀχλουμένους ὑπὸ πνευμάτων ἀκαθάρτων,
being tormented by spirits unclean,
οἵτινες ἐθεραπεύοντο ἅπαντες.
who were healed all.
17 Ἀναστὰς δὲ ὁ ἀρχιερεὺς καὶ πάντες
And rising up the high priest and all
οἱ σὺν αὐτῷ, ἡ οὖσα αἵρεσις τῶν
the[ones] with him, the existing sect of the
Σαδδουκαίων, ἐπλήσθησαν ζήλου **18** καὶ
Sadducees, were filled of(with) jealousy and
ἐπέβαλον τὰς χεῖρας ἐπὶ τοὺς ἀποστόλους
laid *on* the(ir) hands on the apostles
καὶ ἔθεντο αὐτοὺς ἐν τηρήσει δημοσίᾳ.
and put them in custody publicly.
19 Ἄγγελος δὲ κυρίου διὰ νυκτὸς
But an angel of [the] Lord through(during) [the] night
ἤνοιξε τὰς θύρας τῆς φυλακῆς ἐξαγαγών τε
opened the doors of the prison and leading out
αὐτοὺς εἶπεν· **20** πορεύεσθε καὶ σταθέντες
them said : Go ye and standing
λαλεῖτε ἐν τῷ ἱερῷ τῷ λαῷ πάντα
speak in the temple to the people all
τὰ ῥήματα τῆς ζωῆς ταύτης.
the words of this life.
21 ἀκούσαντες δὲ εἰσῆλθον ὑπὸ τὸν ὄρθρον
And having heard they entered about the dawn
εἰς τὸ ἱερὸν καὶ ἐδίδασκον. Παραγενόμενος δὲ
into the temple and taught. And having come
ὁ ἀρχιερεὺς καὶ οἱ σὺν αὐτῷ
the high priest and the [ones] with him
συνεκάλεσαν τὸ συνέδριον καὶ πᾶσαν τὴν
called together the council and all the
γερουσίαν τῶν υἱῶν Ἰσραήλ, καὶ ἀπέστειλαν
senate of the sons of Israel, and sent
εἰς τὸ δεσμωτήριον ἀχθῆναι αὐτούς.
to the jail to be brought them.[b]
22 οἱ δὲ παραγενόμενοι ὑπηρέται οὐχ εὗρον
[1]But [2]the [4]having come [3]attendants found not
αὐτοὺς ἐν τῇ φυλακῇ· ἀναστρέψαντες δὲ
them in the prison; and having returned
ἀπήγγειλαν **23** λέγοντες ὅτι τὸ δεσμωτήριον
they reported saying[,] – The jail
εὕρομεν κεκλεισμένον ἐν πάσῃ ἀσφαλείᾳ
we found *having been* shut in all security
καὶ τοὺς φύλακας ἑστῶτας ἐπὶ τῶν
and the guards standing at the
θυρῶν, ἀνοίξαντες δὲ ἔσω οὐδένα εὕρομεν.
doors, but having opened [3]inside [2]no one [1]we found.
24 ὡς δὲ ἤκουσαν τοὺς λόγους τούτους
And as [9]heard [10]these [11]words
ὅ τε στρατηγὸς τοῦ ἱεροῦ καὶ οἱ ἀρχιερεῖς,
[2]the [1]both [3]commandant [4]of the [5]temple [6]and [7]the [8]chief priests,
διηπόρουν περὶ αὐτῶν τί ἂν γένοιτο
they were in doubt about them what [2]might become
τοῦτο. **25** παραγενόμενος δέ τις ἀπήγγειλεν
[1]this thing. And having come someone reported
αὐτοῖς ὅτι ἰδοὺ οἱ ἄνδρες, οὓς
to them[,] – Behold[,] the men, whom

least Peter's shadow might fall on some of them as he passed by. 16 Crowds gathered also from the towns around Jerusalem, bringing their sick and those tormented by evil[u] spirits, and all of them were healed.

The Apostles Persecuted

17 Then the high priest and all his associates, who were members of the party of the Sadducees, were filled with jealousy. 18 They arrested the apostles and put them in the public jail. 19 But during the night an angel of the Lord opened the doors of the jail and brought them out. 20 "Go, stand in the temple courts," he said, "and tell the people the full message of this new life."

21 At daybreak they entered the temple courts, as they had been told, and began to teach the people.

When the high priest and his associates arrived, they called together the Sanhedrin—the full assembly of the elders of Israel—and sent to the jail for the apostles. 22 But on arriving at the jail, the officers did not find them there. So they went back and reported, 23 "We found the jail securely locked, with the guards standing at the doors; but when we opened them, we found no one inside." 24 On hearing this report, the captain of the temple guard and the chief priests were puzzled, wondering what would come of this.

25 Then someone came and said, "Look! The men you put in jail are standing

[u]16 Greek *unclean*

the temple and teaching the
people!" 26Then the cap-
tain went with the temple
police and brought them,
but without violence, for
they were afraid of being
stoned by the people.
27 When they had
brought them, they had
them stand before the
council. The high priest
questioned them, 28saying,
"We gave you strict orders
not to teach in this name,[o]
yet here you have filled Jerusalem with your teaching
and you are determined to
bring this man's blood on
us." 29But Peter and the
apostles answered, "We
must obey God rather than
any human authority.[p]
30The God of our ancestors
raised up Jesus, whom you
had killed by hanging him
on a tree. 31God exalted
him at his right hand as
Leader and Savior that he
might give repentance to
Israel and forgiveness of
sins. 32And we are wit-
nesses to these things, and
so is the Holy Spirit whom
God has given to those who
obey him."
33 When they heard
this, they were enraged and
wanted to kill them. 34But a
Pharisee in the council
named Gamaliel, a teacher
of the law, respected by all
the people, stood up and
ordered the men to be put
outside for a short time.
35Then he said to them,
"Fellow Israelites,[q] consider carefully what you
propose to do to these men.

ἔθεσθε ἐν τῇ φυλακῇ, εἰσὶν ἐν τῷ ἱερῷ
ye put in the prison, are in the temple

ἑστῶτες καὶ διδάσκοντες τὸν λαόν.
standing and teaching the people.

26 Τότε ἀπελθὼν ὁ στρατηγὸς σὺν τοῖς
Then going the commandant with the

ὑπηρέταις ἦγεν αὐτούς, οὐ μετὰ βίας,
attendants brought them, not with force,

ἐφοβοῦντο γὰρ τὸν λαόν, μὴ λιθασθῶσιν·
for they feared the people, lest they should be stoned;

27 ἀγαγόντες δὲ αὐτοὺς ἔστησαν ἐν τῷ
and bringing them they stood in the

συνεδρίῳ. καὶ ἐπηρώτησεν αὐτοὺς ὁ
council. And questioned them the

ἀρχιερεὺς **28** λέγων· παραγγελίᾳ παρηγ-
high priest saying: With charge we
=We strictly

γείλαμεν ὑμῖν μὴ διδάσκειν ἐπὶ
charged you not to teach on(in)

τῷ ὀνόματι τούτῳ, καὶ ἰδοὺ πεπληρώκατε
this name, and behold ye have filled

τὴν Ἰερουσαλὴμ τῆς διδαχῆς ὑμῶν, καὶ
– Jerusalem of(with) the teaching of you, and

βούλεσθε ἐπαγαγεῖν ἐφ' ἡμᾶς τὸ αἷμα
intend to bring *on* on us the blood

τοῦ ἀνθρώπου τούτου. **29** ἀποκριθεὶς δὲ
of this man. And answering

Πέτρος καὶ οἱ ἀπόστολοι εἶπαν· πειθαρχεῖν
Peter and the apostles said: [2]to obey

δεῖ θεῷ μᾶλλον ἢ ἀνθρώποις. **30** ὁ
[1]It behoves God rather than men. The

θεὸς τῶν πατέρων ἡμῶν ἤγειρεν Ἰησοῦν,
God of the fathers of us raised Jesus,

ὃν ὑμεῖς διεχειρίσασθε κρεμάσαντες ἐπὶ
whom ye killed hanging on

ξύλου· **31** τοῦτον ὁ θεὸς ἀρχηγὸν καὶ
a tree; this man – God a Ruler and

σωτῆρα ὕψωσεν τῇ δεξιᾷ αὐτοῦ τοῦ
a Saviour exalted to the right [hand] of him –

δοῦναι μετάνοιαν τῷ Ἰσραὴλ καὶ ἄφεσιν
to give[d] repentance – to Israel and forgiveness

ἁμαρτιῶν. **32** καὶ ἡμεῖς ἐσμεν μάρτυρες
of sins. And we are witnesses

τῶν ῥημάτων τούτων, καὶ τὸ πνεῦμα
of these words(things), and the Spirit

τὸ ἅγιον ὃ ἔδωκεν ὁ θεὸς τοῖς
– Holy which [2]gave – [1]God to the

πειθαρχοῦσιν αὐτῷ. **33** οἱ δὲ ἀκούσαντες
[ones] obeying him. And the [ones] hearing

διεπρίοντο καὶ ἐβούλοντο ἀνελεῖν αὐτούς.
were cut* and intended to kill them.

34 Ἀναστὰς δέ τις ἐν τῷ συνεδριῳ
[1]But [4]standing up [2]a certain [5]in [6]the [7]council

Φαρισαῖος ὀνόματι Γαμαλιήλ, νομοδιδάσκαλος
[3]Pharisee by name Gamaliel, a teacher of the law

τίμιος παντὶ τῷ λαῷ, ἐκέλευσεν ἔξω
honoured by all the people, commanded [4]outside

βραχὺ τοὺς ἀνθρώπους ποιῆσαι, **35** εἶπέν
[5]a little [2]the [3]men [1]to make(put), [2]said

τε πρὸς αὐτούς· ἄνδρες Ἰσραηλῖται,
[1]and to them: *Men* Israelites,

προσέχετε ἑαυτοῖς ἐπὶ τοῖς ἀνθρώποις τούτοις
take heed to yourselves [4]on(to) [5]these [6]men

in the temple courts teaching the people." 26At that,
the captain went with his
officers and brought the
apostles. They did not use
force, because they feared
that the people would stone
them.
27Having brought the
apostles, they made them
appear before the Sanhe-
drin to be questioned by the
high priest. 28"We gave
you strict orders not to
teach in this name," he
said. "Yet you have filled
Jerusalem with your teaching and are determined to
make us guilty of this man's
blood."
29Peter and the other
apostles replied: "We must
obey God rather than men!
30The God of our fathers
raised Jesus from the dead
—whom you had killed by
hanging him on a tree.
31God exalted him to his
own right hand as Prince
and Savior that he might
give repentance and for-
giveness of sins to Israel.
32We are witnesses of these
things, and so is the Holy
Spirit, whom God has giv-
en to those who obey him."
33When they heard this,
they were furious and
wanted to put them to
death. 34But a Pharisee
named Gamaliel, a teacher
of the law, who was hon-
ored by all the people,
stood up in the Sanhedrin
and ordered that the men
be put outside for a little
while. 35Then he addressed
them: "Men of Israel, consider carefully what you in-

[o] Other ancient authorities read *Did we not give you strict orders not to teach in this name?*
[p] Gk *than men*
[q] Gk *Men, Israelites*

* **That is, to the heart; *cf.* 7. 54.**

36 For some time ago Theudas rose up, claiming to be
somebody, and a number
of men, about four hun-
dred, joined him; but he
was killed, and all who followed him were dispersed
and disappeared. 37 After
him Judas the Galilean rose
up at the time of the census
and got people to follow
him; he also perished, and
all who followed him were
scattered. 38 So in the
present case, I tell you,
keep away from these men
and let them alone; because
if this plan or this undertaking is of human origin, it
will fail; 39 but if it is of
God, you will not be able to
overthrow them—in that
case you may even be
found fighting against
God!"
They were convinced by
him, 40 and when they had
called in the apostles, they
had them flogged. Then
they ordered them not to
speak in the name of Jesus,
and let them go. 41 As they
left the council, they rejoiced that they were considered worthy to suffer
dishonor for the sake of the
name. 42 And every day in
the temple and at home[r]
they did not cease to teach
and proclaim Jesus as the
Messiah.[s]

τί μέλλετε πράσσειν. **36** πρὸ γὰρ
[1]what [2]ye intend [3]to do. For before
τούτων τῶν ἡμερῶν ἀνέστη Θευδᾶς, λέγων
these – days stood up Theudas, saying
εἶναί τινα ἑαυτόν, ᾧ προσεκλίθη ἀνδρῶν
to be someone himself, [1]to whom [6]were attached [3]of men
ἀριθμὸς ὡς τετρακοσίων· ὃς ἀνῃρέθη, καὶ
[2]a number [4]about [5]four hundreds; who was killed, and
πάντες ὅσοι ἐπείθοντο αὐτῷ διελύθησαν
all as many as obeyed him were dispersed
καὶ ἐγένοντο εἰς οὐδέν. **37** μετὰ τοῦτον
and came to nothing. After this
ἀνέστη Ἰούδας ὁ Γαλιλαῖος ἐν ταῖς
stood up Judas the Galilæan in the
ἡμέραις τῆς ἀπογραφῆς καὶ ἀπέστησεν
days of the enrolment and drew away
λαὸν ὀπίσω αὐτοῦ· κἀκεῖνος ἀπώλετο,
people after him; and that man perished,
καὶ πάντες ὅσοι ἐπείθοντο αὐτῷ
and all as many as obeyed him
διεσκορπίσθησαν. **38** καὶ τὰ νῦν λέγω
were scattered. And – now I say
ὑμῖν, ἀπόστητε ἀπὸ τῶν ἀνθρώπων τούτων
to you, stand away from these men
καὶ ἄφετε αὐτούς· ὅτι ἐὰν ᾖ ἐξ ἀνθρώπων
and leave them; because if be of men
ἡ βουλὴ αὕτη ἢ τὸ ἔργον τοῦτο,
this counsel or this work,
καταλυθήσεται· **39** εἰ δὲ ἐκ θεοῦ ἐστιν,
it will be destroyed; but if of God it is,
οὐ δυνήσεσθε καταλῦσαι αὐτούς, μήποτε
ye will not be able to destroy them, lest
καὶ θεομάχοι εὑρεθῆτε. ἐπείσθησαν δὲ
even fighters against God ye be found. And they obeyed
αὐτῷ, **40** καὶ προσκαλεσάμενοι τοὺς
him, and having called to [them] the
ἀποστόλους δείραντες παρήγγειλαν μὴ
apostles beating charged not
λαλεῖν ἐπὶ τῷ ὀνόματι τοῦ Ἰησοῦ καὶ
to speak on(in) the name – of Jesus and
ἀπέλυσαν. **41** Οἱ μὲν οὖν ἐπορεύοντο
released [them]. They – therefore went
χαίροντες ἀπὸ προσώπου τοῦ συνεδρίου,
rejoicing from [the] presence of the council,
ὅτι κατηξιώθησαν ὑπὲρ τοῦ ὀνόματος
because they were deemed worthy on behalf of the name
ἀτιμασθῆναι· **42** πᾶσάν τε ἡμέραν ἐν τῷ
to be dishonoured; and every day in the
ἱερῷ καὶ κατ' οἶκον οὐκ ἐπαύοντο
temple and from house to house† they ceased not
διδάσκοντες καὶ εὐαγγελιζόμενοι τὸν χριστὸν
teaching and preaching the Christ
Ἰησοῦν.
Jesus.

tend to do to these men.
36 Some time ago Theudas
appeared, claiming to be
somebody, and about four
hundred men rallied to him.
He was killed, all his followers were dispersed, and
it all came to nothing. 37 After him, Judas the Galilean
appeared in the days of the
census and led a band of
people in revolt. He too
was killed, and all his followers were scattered.
38 Therefore, in the present
case I advise you: Leave
these men alone! Let them
go! For if their purpose or
activity is of human origin,
it will fail. 39 But if it is from
God, you will not be able to
stop these men; you will
only find yourselves fighting against God."
40 His speech persuaded
them. They called the apostles in and had them
flogged. Then they ordered
them not to speak in the
name of Jesus, and let them
go.
41 The apostles left the
Sanhedrin, rejoicing be-
cause they had been counted worthy of suffering disgrace for the Name. 42 Day
after day, in the temple
courts and from house to
house, they never stopped
teaching and proclaiming
the good news that Jesus is
the Christ.[v]

Chapter 6

Seven Chosen to Serve

NOW during those
days, when the disci-
ples were increasing in
number, the Hellenists
complained against the Hebrews because their wid-
ows were being neglected
in the daily distribution of
food. 2 And the twelve

6 Ἐν δὲ ταῖς ἡμέραις ταύταις
Now in these days
πληθυνόντων τῶν μαθητῶν ἐγένετο
being multiplied the disciples[a] there was
=as the disciples were multiplied
γογγυσμὸς τῶν Ἑλληνιστῶν πρὸς τοὺς
a murmuring of the Hellenists against the
Ἑβραίους, ὅτι παρεθεωροῦντο ἐν τῇ
Hebrews, because [4]were overlooked [5]in [6]the
διακονίᾳ τῇ καθημερινῇ αἱ χῆραι αὐτῶν.
[8]service – [7]daily [1]the [2]widows [3]of them.

Chapter 6

The Choosing of the Seven

IN those days when the
number of disciples was
increasing, the Grecian
Jews among them com-
plained against the Hebraic
Jews because their widows
were being overlooked in
the daily distribution of

[r] Or *from house to house*
[s] Or *the Christ*

[v] 42 Or *Messiah*

called together the whole
community of the disciples
and said, "It is not right that
we should neglect the word
of God in order to wait on
tables.[t] 3 Therefore,
friends,[u] select from
among yourselves seven
men of good standing, full
of the Spirit and of wisdom,
whom we may appoint to
this task, 4 while we, for our
part, will devote ourselves
to prayer and to serving the
word." 5 What they said
pleased the whole commu-
nity, and they chose Ste-
phen, a man full of faith and
the Holy Spirit, together
with Philip, Prochorus, Nicanor, Timon, Parmenas,
and Nicolaus, a proselyte
of Antioch. 6 They had
these men stand before the
apostles, who prayed and
laid their hands on them.
7 The word of God con-
tinued to spread; the number of the disciples in-
creased greatly in Jerusalem, and a great many of
the priests became obedi-
ent to the faith.

The Arrest of Stephen

8 Stephen, full of grace
and power, did great won-
ders and signs among the
people. 9 Then some of
those who belonged to the
synagogue of the Freedmen
(as it was called), Cyre-
nians, Alexandrians, and
others of those from Cilicia
and Asia, stood up and argued with Stephen. 10 But
they could not withstand
the wisdom and the Spirit[v]
with which he spoke.
11 Then they secretly insti-
gated some men to say,
"We have heard him speak
blasphemous words against
Moses and God." 12 They
stirred up the people as

[t] Or *keep accounts*
[u] Gk *brothers*
[v] Or *spirit*

2 προσκαλεσάμενοι δὲ οἱ δώδεκα τὸ
[4]having called to [them] [1]And [2]the [3]twelve the
πλῆθος τῶν μαθητῶν εἶπαν· οὐκ ἀρεστόν
multitude of the disciples said : not pleasing
ἐστιν ἡμᾶς καταλείψαντας τὸν λόγον τοῦ
It is us leaving the word –
θεοῦ διακονεῖν τραπέζαις. **3** ἐπισκέψασθε
of God to serve tables. look ye out
δέ, ἀδελφοί, ἄνδρας ἐξ ὑμῶν μαρτυρουμένους
But, brothers, [2]men [3]of [4]you [5]being witnessed to
ἑπτὰ πλήρεις πνεύματος καὶ σοφίας, οὓς
[1]seven [as] full of Spirit and of wisdom, whom
καταστήσομεν ἐπὶ τῆς χρείας ταύτης·
we will appoint over this office;
4 ἡμεῖς δὲ τῇ προσευχῇ καὶ τῇ διακονίᾳ
but we to the prayer and to the service
τοῦ λόγου προσκαρτερήσομεν. **5** καὶ ἤρεσεν
of the word will keep. And [3]pleased
ὁ λόγος ἐνώπιον παντὸς τοῦ πλήθους,
[1]the [2]word before all the multitude,
καὶ ἐξελέξαντο Στέφανον, ἄνδρα πλήρη
and they chose Stephen, a man full
πίστεως καὶ πνεύματος ἁγίου, καὶ Φίλιππον
of faith and Spirit of Holy, and Philip
καὶ Πρόχορον καὶ Νικάνορα καὶ Τίμωνα
and Prochorus and Nicanor and Timon
καὶ Παρμενᾶν καὶ Νικόλαον προσήλυτον
and Parmenas and Nicolaus a proselyte
Ἀντιοχέα, **6** οὓς ἔστησαν ἐνώπιον τῶν
of Antioch, whom they set before the
ἀποστόλων, καὶ προσευξάμενοι ἐπέθηκαν
apostles, and having prayed they placed on
αὐτοῖς τὰς χεῖρας.
them the(ir) hands.
7 Καὶ ὁ λόγος τοῦ θεοῦ ηὔξανεν, καὶ
And the word – of God grew, and
ἐπληθύνετο ὁ ἀριθμὸς τῶν μαθητῶν ἐν
was multiplied the number of the disciples in
Ἰερουσαλὴμ σφόδρα, πολύς τε ὄχλος τῶν
Jerusalem greatly, and a much(great) crowd of the
ἱερέων ὑπήκουον τῇ πίστει.
priests obeyed the faith.
8 Στέφανος δὲ πλήρης χάριτος καὶ
And Stephen full of grace and
δυνάμεως ἐποίει τέρατα καὶ σημεῖα μεγάλα
of power did wonders and signs great
ἐν τῷ λαῷ. **9** ἀνέστησαν δέ τινες τῶν
among the people. But rose up some of the [ones]
ἐκ τῆς συναγωγῆς τῆς λεγομένης
of the synagogue – *being* called
Λιβερτίνων καὶ Κυρηναίων καὶ Ἀλεξ-
of Freedmen and of Cyrenians and of
ανδρέων καὶ τῶν ἀπὸ Κιλικίας καὶ
Alexandrians and of the [ones] from Cilicia and
Ἀσίας συζητοῦντες τῷ Στεφάνῳ, **10** καὶ
Asia discussing – with Stephen, and
οὐκ ἴσχυον ἀντιστῆναι τῇ σοφίᾳ καὶ
were not able to withstand the wisdom and
τῷ πνεύματι ᾧ ἐλάλει. **11** τότε ὑπέβαλον
the spirit with which he spoke. Then they suborned
ἄνδρας λέγοντας ὅτι ἀκηκόαμεν αὐτοῦ
men saying[,] – We have heard him
λαλοῦντος ῥήματα βλάσφημα εἰς Μωϋσῆν
speaking words blasphemous against Moses
καὶ τὸν θεόν· **12** συνεκίνησάν τε τὸν
and – God; and they stirred up the

food. 2 So the Twelve gathered all the disciples together and said, "It would
not be right for us to neglect
the ministry of the word of
God in order to wait on tables. 3 Brothers, choose
seven men from among you
who are known to be full of
the Spirit and wisdom. We
will turn this responsibility
over to them 4 and will give
our attention to prayer and
the ministry of the word."
5 This proposal pleased
the whole group. They
chose Stephen, a man full
of faith and of the Holy
Spirit; also Philip, Proco-
rus, Nicanor, Timon, Par-
menas, and Nicolas from
Antioch, a convert to Judaism. 6 They presented these
men to the apostles, who
prayed and laid their hands
on them.
7 So the word of God
spread. The number of disciples in Jerusalem in-
creased rapidly, and a large
number of priests became
obedient to the faith.

Stephen Seized

8 Now Stephen, a man full
of God's grace and power,
did great wonders and mi-
raculous signs among the
people. 9 Opposition arose,
however, from members of
the Synagogue of the
Freedmen (as it was called)
—Jews of Cyrene and Al-
exandria as well as the
provinces of Cilicia and
Asia. These men began to
argue with Stephen, 10 but
they could not stand up
against his wisdom or the
Spirit by whom he spoke.
11 Then they secretly persuaded some men to say,
"We have heard Stephen
speak words of blasphemy
against Moses and against
God."
12 So they stirred up the

well as the elders and the
scribes; then they suddenly
confronted him, seized
him, and brought him be-
fore the council. 13 They set
up false witnesses who
said, "This man never
stops saying things against
this holy place and the law;
14 for we have heard him
say that this Jesus of Nazareth[w] will destroy this
place and will change the
customs that Moses hand-
ed on to us." 15 And all who
sat in the council looked intently at him, and they saw
that his face was like the
face of an angel.

λαὸν καὶ τοὺς πρεσβυτέρους καὶ τοὺς
people and the elders and the
γραμματεῖς, καὶ ἐπιστάντες συνήρπασαν
scribes, and coming on they seized
αὐτὸν καὶ ἤγαγον εἰς τὸ συνέδριον,
him and led to the council,
13 ἔστησάν τε μάρτυρας ψευδεῖς λέγοντας·
and stood witnesses false saying :
ὁ ἄνθρωπος οὗτος οὐ παύεται λαλῶν
This man ceases not speaking
ῥήματα κατὰ τοῦ τόπου τοῦ ἁγίου [τούτου]
words against – [3]place – [2]holy [1]this
καὶ τοῦ νόμου· 14 ἀκηκόαμεν γὰρ αὐτοῦ
and the law; for we have heard him
λέγοντος ὅτι Ἰησοῦς ὁ Ναζωραῖος οὗτος
saying that [2]Jesus [3]the [4]Nazarene [1]this
καταλύσει τὸν τόπον τοῦτον καὶ ἀλλάξει
will destroy this place and will change
τὰ ἔθη ἃ παρέδωκεν ἡμῖν Μωϋσῆς.
the customs which delivered to us Moses.
15 καὶ ἀτενίσαντες εἰς αὐτὸν πάντες οἱ
And gazing at him all the
καθεζόμενοι ἐν τῷ συνεδρίῳ εἶδον τὸ
[ones] sitting in the council saw the
πρόσωπον αὐτοῦ ὡσεὶ πρόσωπον ἀγγέλου.
face of him as a face of an angel.

people and the elders and
the teachers of the law.
They seized Stephen and
brought him before the
Sanhedrin. 13 They pro-
duced false witnesses, who
testified, "This fellow never stops speaking against
this holy place and against
the law. 14 For we have
heard him say that this
Jesus of Nazareth will destroy this place and change
the customs Moses handed
down to us."
15 All who were sitting in
the Sanhedrin looked in-
tently at Stephen, and they
saw that his face was like
the face of an angel.

Chapter 7

Stephen's Speech to the Council

THEN the high priest
asked him, "Are these
things so?" 2 And Stephen
replied:
"Brothers[x] and fathers,
listen to me. The God of
glory appeared to our an-
cestor Abraham when he
was in Mesopotamia, be-
fore he lived in Haran, 3 and
said to him, 'Leave your
country and your relatives
and go to the land that I will
show you.' 4 Then he left
the country of the Chaldeans and settled in Haran.
After his father died, God
had him move from there to
this country in which you
are now living. 5 He did not
give him any of it as a heritage, not even a foot's
length, but promised to
give it to him as his possession and to his descendants
after him, even though he

7 Εἶπεν δὲ ὁ ἀρχιερεύς· εἰ ταῦτα
And said the high priest : If these things
οὕτως ἔχει; 2 ὁ δὲ ἔφη·
thus have(are)? And he said:
Ἄνδρες ἀδελφοὶ καὶ πατέρες, ἀκούσατε.
Men brothers and fathers, hear ye.
Ὁ θεὸς τῆς δόξης ὤφθη τῷ πατρὶ
The God – of glory appeared to the father
ἡμῶν Ἀβραὰμ ὄντι ἐν τῇ Μεσοποταμίᾳ
of us Abraham being in – Mesopotamia
πρὶν ἢ κατοικῆσαι αὐτὸν ἐν Χαρράν,
before to dwell him[b] in Charran,
=he dwelt
3 καὶ εἶπεν πρὸς αὐτόν· ἔξελθε ἐκ τῆς
and said to him : Go forth out of the
γῆς σου καὶ τῆς συγγενείας σου, καὶ
land of thee and the kindred of thee, and
δεῦρο εἰς τὴν γῆν ἣν ἂν σοι δείξω.
come into the land whichever to thee I may show.
4 τότε ἐξελθὼν ἐκ γῆς Χαλδαίων
Then going forth out of [the] land of [the] Chaldæans
κατῴκησεν ἐν Χαρράν. κἀκεῖθεν μετὰ
he dwelt in Charran. And thence after
τὸ ἀποθανεῖν τὸν πατέρα αὐτοῦ μετῴκισεν
the to die the father of him[b] [God] removed
=his father died
αὐτὸν εἰς τὴν γῆν ταύτην εἰς ἣν ὑμεῖς
him into this land in which ye
νῦν κατοικεῖτε, 5 καὶ οὐκ ἔδωκεν αὐτῷ
now dwell, and gave not to him
κληρονομίαν ἐν αὐτῇ οὐδὲ βῆμα ποδός,
an inheritance in it nor a foot's space,
καὶ ἐπηγγείλατο δοῦναι αὐτῷ εἰς
and promised to give him for
κατάσχεσιν αὐτὴν καὶ τῷ σπέρματι αὐτοῦ
a possession it and to the seed of him
μετ' αὐτόν, οὐκ ὄντος αὐτῷ τέκνου.
after him, not being to him[c] a child.[a]
=while he had no child.

Chapter 7

Stephen's Speech to the Sanhedrin

THEN the high priest
asked him, "Are these
charges true?"
2 To this he replied:
"Brothers and fathers, listen to me! The God of glory
appeared to our father
Abraham while he was still
in Mesopotamia, before he
lived in Haran. 3 'Leave
your country and your people,' God said, 'and go to
the land I will show you.'[w]
4 "So he left the land of
the Chaldeans and settled
in Haran. After the death of
his father, God sent him to
this land where you are
now living. 5 He gave him
no inheritance here, not
even a foot of ground. But
God promised him that he
and his descendants after
him would possess the
land, even though at that
time Abraham had no

[w] Gk *the Nazorean*
[x] Gk *Men, brothers*

[w] 3 Gen. 12:1

had no child. 6 And God spoke in these terms, that his descendants would be resident aliens in a country belonging to others, who would enslave them and mistreat them during four hundred years. 7 'But I will judge the nation that they serve,' said God, 'and after that they shall come out and worship me in this place.' 8 Then he gave him the covenant of circumcision. And so Abraham[y] became the father of Isaac and circumcised him on the eighth day; and Isaac became the father of Jacob, and Jacob of the twelve patriarchs.

9 "The patriarchs, jealous of Joseph, sold him into Egypt; but God was with him, 10 and rescued him from all his afflictions, and enabled him to win favor and to show wisdom when he stood before Pharaoh, king of Egypt, who appointed him ruler over Egypt and over all his household. 11 Now there came a famine throughout Egypt and Canaan, and great suffering, and our ancestors could find no food. 12 But when Jacob heard that there was grain in Egypt, he sent our ancestors there on their first visit. 13 On the second visit Joseph made himself known to his brothers, and Joseph's family became known to Pharaoh. 14 Then Joseph sent and invited his father Jacob and all his relatives to come to him, seventy-five in all; 15 so Jacob went down to Egypt. He himself died there as

[y] Gk *he*

6 ἐλάλησεν δὲ οὕτως ὁ θεός, ὅτι ἔσται
And spoke thus – God, that will be
τὸ σπέρμα αὐτοῦ πάροικον ἐν γῇ ἀλλοτρίᾳ,
the seed of him a sojourner in a land belonging to others,
καὶ δουλώσουσιν αὐτὸ καὶ κακώσουσιν
and they will enslave it and will ill-treat
ἔτη τετρακόσια· **7** καὶ τὸ ἔθνος ᾧ ἐὰν
years four hundred; and the nation whichever
δουλεύσουσιν κρινῶ ἐγώ, ὁ θεὸς εἶπεν,
they will serve will judge I, – God said,
καὶ μετὰ ταῦτα ἐξελεύσονται καὶ
and after these things they will come forth and
λατρεύσουσίν μοι ἐν τῷ τόπῳ τούτῳ.
will worship me in this place.
8 καὶ ἔδωκεν αὐτῷ διαθήκην περιτομῆς·
And he gave him a covenant of circumcision;
καὶ οὕτως ἐγέννησεν τὸν Ἰσαὰκ καὶ
and thus he begat – Isaac and
περιέτεμεν αὐτὸν τῇ ἡμέρᾳ τῇ ὀγδόῃ,
circumcised him on the day – eighth,
καὶ Ἰσαὰκ τὸν Ἰακώβ, καὶ Ἰακὼβ
and Isaac [begat] – Jacob, and Jacob [begat]
τοὺς δώδεκα πατριάρχας. **9** Καὶ οἱ
the twelve patriarchs. And the
πατριάρχαι ζηλώσαντες τὸν Ἰωσὴφ
patriarchs becoming jealous – [2]Joseph
ἀπέδοντο εἰς Αἴγυπτον· καὶ ἦν ὁ θεὸς
[1]sold into Egypt; and was – God
μετ' αὐτοῦ, **10** καὶ ἐξείλατο αὐτὸν ἐκ
with him, and rescued him out of
πασῶν τῶν θλίψεων αὐτοῦ, καὶ ἔδωκεν
all the afflictions of him, and gave
αὐτῷ χάριν καὶ σοφίαν ἐναντίον Φαραὼ
him favour and wisdom before Pharaoh
βασιλέως Αἰγύπτου, καὶ κατέστησεν αὐτὸν
king of Egypt, and he appointed him
ἡγούμενον ἐπ' Αἴγυπτον καὶ ὅλον τὸν
governor over Egypt and all the
οἶκον αὐτοῦ. **11** ἦλθεν δὲ λιμὸς ἐφ'
household of him. But came a famine over
ὅλην τὴν Αἴγυπτον καὶ Χανάαν καὶ
all – Egypt and Canaan and
θλῖψις μεγάλη, καὶ οὐχ ηὕρισκον
affliction great, and found not
χορτάσματα οἱ πατέρες ἡμῶν. **12** ἀκούσας
sustenance the fathers of us. [3]having heard
δὲ Ἰακὼβ ὄντα σιτία εἰς Αἴγυπτον
[1]But [2]Jacob [5]being [4]corn in Egypt
ἐξαπέστειλεν τοὺς πατέρας ἡμῶν πρῶτον·
sent forth the fathers of us first;
13 καὶ ἐν τῷ δευτέρῳ ἐγνωρίσθη Ἰωσὴφ
and at the second [time] was made known Joseph
τοῖς ἀδελφοῖς αὐτοῦ, καὶ φανερὸν ἐγένετο τῷ
to the brothers of him, and [5]manifest [4]became –
Φαραὼ τὸ γένος Ἰωσήφ. **14** ἀποστείλας δὲ
[6]to Pharaoh [1]the [2]race [3]of Joseph. And sending
Ἰωσὴφ μετεκαλέσατο Ἰακὼβ τὸν πατέρα
Joseph called Jacob the father
αὐτοῦ καὶ πᾶσαν τὴν συγγένειαν ἐν
of him and all the(his) kindred in
ψυχαῖς ἑβδομήκοντα πέντε. **15** καὶ κατέβη
souls seventy-five. And went down
Ἰακὼβ εἰς Αἴγυπτον, καὶ ἐτελεύτησεν
Jacob to Egypt, and died
αὐτὸς καὶ οἱ πατέρες ἡμῶν, **16** καὶ
he and the fathers of us, and

child. 6 God spoke to him in this way: 'Your descendants will be strangers in a country not their own, and they will be enslaved and mistreated four hundred years. 7 But I will punish the nation they serve as slaves,' God said, 'and afterward they will come out of that country and worship me in this place.'[x] 8 Then he gave Abraham the covenant of circumcision. And Abraham became the father of Isaac and circumcised him eight days after his birth. Later Isaac became the father of Jacob, and Jacob became the father of the twelve patriarchs.

9 "Because the patriarchs were jealous of Joseph, they sold him as a slave into Egypt. But God was with him 10 and rescued him from all his troubles. He gave Joseph wisdom and enabled him to gain the goodwill of Pharaoh king of Egypt; so he made him ruler over Egypt and all his palace.

11 "Then a famine struck all Egypt and Canaan, bringing great suffering, and our fathers could not find food. 12 When Jacob heard that there was grain in Egypt, he sent our fathers on their first visit. 13 On their second visit, Joseph told his brothers who he was, and Pharaoh learned about Joseph's family. 14 After this, Joseph sent for his father Jacob and his whole family, seventy-five in all. 15 Then Jacob went down to Egypt, where he and our fathers

[x] 7 Gen. 15:13,14

well as our ancestors,
16and their bodies[z] were
brought back to Shechem
and laid in the tomb that
Abraham had bought for a
sum of silver from the sons
of Hamor in Shechem.
17 "But as the time
drew near for the fulfillment of the promise that
God had made to Abraham,
our people in Egypt in-
creased and multiplied
18until another king who
had not known Joseph
ruled over Egypt. 19He
dealt craftily with our race
and forced our ancestors to
abandon their infants so
that they would die. 20At
this time Moses was born,
and he was beautiful before
God. For three months he
was brought up in his fa-
ther's house; 21and when
he was abandoned, Phar-
aoh's daughter adopted
him and brought him up as
her own son. 22So Moses
was instructed in all the
wisdom of the Egyptians
and was powerful in his
words and deeds.
23 "When he was forty
years old, it came into his
heart to visit his relatives,
the Israelites.[a] 24When he
saw one of them being
wronged, he defended the
oppressed man and
avenged him by striking
down the Egyptian. 25He
supposed that his kinsfolk
would understand that God
through him was rescuing
them, but they did not understand. 26The next day
he came to some of them as
they were quarreling and
tried to reconcile them,
saying, 'Men, you are
brothers; why do you
wrong each other?' 27But

[z]Gk *they*
[a]Gk *his brothers, the sons of Israel*

μετετέθησαν εἰς Συχὲμ καὶ ἐτέθησαν ἐν
were transferred to Sychem and were put in
τῷ μνήματι ᾧ ὠνήσατο Ἀβραὰμ τιμῆς
the tomb which ²bought ¹Abraham of(for) a price
ἀργυρίου παρὰ τῶν υἱῶν Ἑμμὼρ ἐν
of silver from the sons of Emmor in
Συχέμ. **17** Καθὼς δὲ ἤγγιζεν ὁ χρόνος
Sychem. And as drew near the time
τῆς ἐπαγγελίας ἧς ὡμολόγησεν ὁ θεὸς
of the promise which ²declared – ¹God
τῷ Ἀβραάμ, ηὔξησεν ὁ λαὸς καὶ
to Abraham, ³grew ¹the ²people and
ἐπληθύνθη ἐν Αἰγύπτῳ, **18** ἄχρι οὗ ἀνέστη
were multiplied in Egypt, until ³rose up
βασιλεὺς ἕτερος ἐπ' Αἴγυπτον, ὃς οὐκ ᾔδει
²king ¹another over Egypt, who did not know
τὸν Ἰωσήφ. **19** οὗτος κατασοφισάμενος
– Joseph. This man dealing craftily with
τὸ γένος ἡμῶν ἐκάκωσεν τοὺς πατέρας
the race of us ill-treated the fathers
τοῦ ποιεῖν τὰ βρέφη ἔκθετα αὐτῶν
– to make[d] ¹the ²babes ⁴exposed ³of them
εἰς τὸ μὴ ζῳογονεῖσθαι. **20** Ἐν ᾧ
to the not to be preserved alive. At which
=so that they should not be . . .
καιρῷ ἐγεννήθη Μωϋσῆς, καὶ ἦν ἀστεῖος
time was born Moses, and was fair
τῷ θεῷ· ὃς ἀνετράφη μῆνας τρεῖς ἐν
– to God; who was reared months three in
τῷ οἴκῳ τοῦ πατρός· **21** ἐκτεθέντος δὲ
the house of the(his) father; being exposed and
=and when he was exposed
αὐτοῦ ἀνείλατο αὐτὸν ἡ θυγάτηρ Φαραὼ
him[a] took up him the daughter of Pharaoh
καὶ ἀνεθρέψατο αὐτὸν ἑαυτῇ εἰς υἱόν.
and reared him to herself for a son.
=as her own son.
22 καὶ ἐπαιδεύθη Μωϋσῆς πάσῃ σοφίᾳ
And was trained Moses in all [the] wisdom
Αἰγυπτίων, ἦν δὲ δυνατὸς ἐν λόγοις
of [the] Egyptians, and was powerful in words
καὶ ἔργοις αὐτοῦ. **23** Ὡς δὲ ἐπληροῦτο
and works of him. But when ³was fulfilled
αὐτῷ τεσσερακονταέτης χρόνος, ἀνέβη ἐπὶ
⁴to him ²of forty years ¹a time, it came up upon
τὴν καρδίαν αὐτοῦ ἐπισκέψασθαι τοὺς
the heart of him to visit the
ἀδελφοὺς αὐτοῦ τοὺς υἱοὺς Ἰσραήλ. **24** καὶ
brothers of him the sons of Israel. And
ἰδών τινα ἀδικούμενον ἠμύνατο, καὶ
seeing one being injured he defended [him], and
ἐποίησεν ἐκδίκησιν τῷ καταπονουμένῳ
he wrought vengeance for the [one] getting the worse
πατάξας τὸν Αἰγύπτιον. **25** ἐνόμιζεν δὲ
striking the Egyptian. Now he supposed
συνιέναι τοὺς ἀδελφοὺς ὅτι ὁ θεὸς διὰ
to understand the(his) brothers[b] that – God through
=that his brothers would understand
χειρὸς αὐτοῦ δίδωσιν σωτηρίαν αὐτοῖς·
hand of him would give salvation to them;
οἱ δὲ οὐ συνῆκαν. **26** τῇ τε ἐπιούσῃ
but they understood not. And on the coming
ἡμέρᾳ ὤφθη αὐτοῖς μαχομένοις, καὶ
day he appeared to them fighting, and
συνήλλασσεν αὐτοὺς εἰς εἰρήνην εἰπών·
attempted to reconcile them in peace saying:
ἄνδρες, ἀδελφοί ἐστε· ἱνατί ἀδικεῖτε
Men, brothers ye are; why injure ye

died. 16Their bodies were
brought back to Shechem
and placed in the tomb that
Abraham had bought from
the sons of Hamor at She-
chem for a certain sum of
money.
17"As the time drew near
for God to fulfill his promise to Abraham, the num-
ber of our people in Egypt
greatly increased. 18Then
another king, who knew
nothing about Joseph, be-
came ruler of Egypt. 19He
dealt treacherously with
our people and oppressed
our forefathers by forcing
them to throw out their
newborn babies so that
they would die.
20"At that time Moses
was born, and he was no
ordinary child.[y] For three
months he was cared for in
his father's house. 21When
he was placed outside,
Pharaoh's daughter took
him and brought him up as
her own son. 22Moses was
educated in all the wisdom
of the Egyptians and was
powerful in speech and action.
23"When Moses was for-
ty years old, he decided to
visit his fellow Israelites.
24He saw one of them being
mistreated by an Egyptian,
so he went to his defense
and avenged him by killing
the Egyptian. 25Moses
thought that his own people
would realize that God was
using him to rescue them,
but they did not. 26The next
day Moses came upon two
Israelites who were fighting. He tried to reconcile
them by saying, 'Men, you
are brothers; why do you
want to hurt each other?'

[y]20 Or *was fair in the sight of God*

the man who was wronging
his neighbor pushed Mo-
ses[b] aside, saying, 'Who
made you a ruler and a
judge over us? 28 Do you
want to kill me as you killed
the Egyptian yesterday?'
29 When he heard this, Moses fled and became a resident alien in the land of
Midian. There he became
the father of two sons.
30 "Now when forty
years had passed, an angel
appeared to him in the wilderness of Mount Sinai, in
the flame of a burning bush.
31 When Moses saw it, he
was amazed at the sight;
and as he approached to
look, there came the voice
of the Lord: 32 'I am the
God of your ancestors, the
God of Abraham, Isaac,
and Jacob.' Moses began to
tremble and did not dare to
look. 33 Then the Lord said
to him, 'Take off the sandals from your feet, for the
place where you are standing is holy ground. 34 I have
surely seen the mistreat-
ment of my people who are
in Egypt and have heard
their groaning, and I have
come down to rescue them.
Come now, I will send you
to Egypt.'
35 "It was this Moses
whom they rejected when
they said, 'Who made you a
ruler and a judge?' and
whom God now sent as
both ruler and liberator
through the angel who ap-
peared to him in the bush.
36 He led them out, having
performed wonders and
signs in Egypt, at the Red
Sea, and in the wilderness
for forty years. 37 This is
the Moses who said to the

[b] Gk *him*

ἀλλήλους; 27 ὁ δὲ ἀδικῶν τὸν πλησίον
each other? But the [one] injuring the(his) neighbour

ἀπώσατο αὐτὸν εἰπών· τίς σε κατέστησεν
thrust away him saying: Who thee appointed

ἄρχοντα καὶ δικαστὴν ἐφ' ἡμῶν; 28 μὴ
a ruler and a judge over us? *not*

ἀνελεῖν με σὺ θέλεις ὃν τρόπον ἀνεῖλες
to kill me thou wishest in the same way as† thou killedst

ἐχθὲς τὸν Αἰγύπτιον; 29 ἔφυγεν δὲ
yesterday the Egyptian? So fled

Μωϋσῆς ἐν τῷ λόγῳ τούτῳ, καὶ ἐγένετο
Moses at this word, and became

πάροικος ἐν γῇ Μαδιάμ, οὗ ἐγέννησεν
a sojourner in [the] land Midian, where he begat

υἱοὺς δύο. 30 Καὶ πληρωθέντων ἐτῶν
sons two. And being fulfilled years
=when forty years were fulfilled

τεσσεράκοντα ὤφθη αὐτῷ ἐν τῇ ἐρήμῳ
forty[a] appeared to him in the desert

τοῦ ὄρους Σινὰ ἄγγελος ἐν φλογὶ πυρὸς
of the mount Sinai an angel in a flame of fire

βάτου. 31 ὁ δὲ Μωϋσῆς ἰδὼν ἐθαύμαζεν
of a thorn bush. – And Moses seeing marvelled at

τὸ ὅραμα· προσερχομένου δὲ αὐτοῦ κατα-
the vision; and approaching him[a] to take
=as he approached

νοῆσαι ἐγένετο φωνὴ κυρίου· 32 ἐγὼ ὁ
notice there was a voice of [the] Lord: I the

θεὸς τῶν πατέρων σου, ὁ θεὸς Ἀβραὰμ
God of the fathers of thee, the God of Abraham

καὶ Ἰσαὰκ καὶ Ἰακώβ. ἔντρομος δὲ
and of Isaac and of Jacob. But trembling

γενόμενος Μωϋσῆς οὐκ ἐτόλμα κατανοῆσαι.
becoming Moses dared not *to* take notice.

33 εἶπεν δὲ αὐτῷ ὁ κύριος· λῦσον τὸ
And said to him the Lord: Loosen the

ὑπόδημα τῶν ποδῶν σου· ὁ γὰρ τόπος
sandal of the feet of thee; for the place

ἐφ' ᾧ ἕστηκας γῆ ἁγία ἐστίν. 34 ἰδὼν
on which thou standest ground holy is. Seeing

εἶδον τὴν κάκωσιν τοῦ λαοῦ μου τοῦ
I saw the ill-treatment of the people of me –

ἐν Αἰγύπτῳ, καὶ τοῦ στεναγμοῦ αὐτοῦ
in Egypt, and the groan of it

ἤκουσα, καὶ κατέβην ἐξελέσθαι αὐτούς·
I heard, and I came down to rescue them;

καὶ νῦν δεῦρο ἀποστείλω σε εἰς Αἴγυπτον.
and now come I will send thee to Egypt.

35 Τοῦτον τὸν Μωϋσῆν, ὃν ἠρνήσαντο
This – Moses, whom they denied

εἰπόντες· τίς σε κατέστησεν ἄρχοντα καὶ
saying: Who thee appointed a ruler and

δικαστήν; τοῦτον ὁ θεὸς καὶ ἄρχοντα
a judge? this man – God both a ruler

καὶ λυτρωτὴν ἀπέσταλκεν σὺν χειρὶ
and a redeemer has sent with [the] hand

ἀγγέλου τοῦ ὀφθέντος αὐτῷ ἐν τῇ βάτῳ.
of [the] angel – appearing to him in the bush.

36 οὗτος ἐξήγαγεν αὐτοὺς ποιήσας τέρατα
This man led forth them doing wonders

καὶ σημεῖα ἐν γῇ Αἰγύπτῳ καὶ ἐν
and signs in [the] land Egypt and in

ἐρυθρᾷ θαλάσσῃ καὶ ἐν τῇ ἐρήμῳ ἔτη
[the] Red Sea and in the desert years

τεσσεράκοντα. 37 οὗτός ἐστιν ὁ Μωϋσῆς
forty. This is the Moses

27 "But the man who was
mistreating the other
pushed Moses aside and
said, 'Who made you ruler
and judge over us? 28 Do
you want to kill me as you
killed the Egyptian yesterday?'[z] 29 When Moses
heard this, he fled to Midian, where he settled as a
foreigner and had two sons.
30 "After forty years had
passed, an angel appeared
to Moses in the flames of a
burning bush in the desert
near Mount Sinai. 31 When
he saw this, he was amazed
at the sight. As he went
over to look more closely,
he heard the Lord's voice:
32 'I am the God of your fathers, the God of Abraham,
Isaac and Jacob.'[a] Moses
trembled with fear and did
not dare to look.
33 "Then the Lord said to
him, 'Take off your san-
dals; the place where you
are standing is holy ground.
34 I have indeed seen the op-
pression of my people in
Egypt. I have heard their
groaning and have come
down to set them free. Now
come, I will send you back
to Egypt.'[b]
35 "This is the same Mo-
ses whom they had rejected
with the words, 'Who made
you ruler and judge?' He
was sent to be their ruler
and deliverer by God him-
self, through the angel who
appeared to him in the
bush. 36 He led them out of
Egypt and did wonders and
miraculous signs in Egypt,
at the Red Sea[c] and for forty years in the desert.
37 "This is that Moses

[z] *28* Exodus 2:14
[a] *32* Exodus 3:6
[b] *34* Exodus 3:5,7,8,10
[c] *36* That is, Sea of Reeds

Israelites, 'God will raise
up a prophet for you from
your own people[c] as he
raised me up.' 38He is the
one who was in the congregation in the wilderness
with the angel who spoke to
him at Mount Sinai, and
with our ancestors; and he
received living oracles to
give to us. 39Our ancestors
were unwilling to obey
him; instead, they pushed
him aside, and in their
hearts they turned back to
Egypt, 40saying to Aaron,
'Make gods for us who will
lead the way for us; as for
this Moses who led us out
from the land of Egypt, we
do not know what has hap-
pened to him.' 41At that
time they made a calf, offered a sacrifice to the idol,
and reveled in the works of
their hands. 42But God
turned away from them and
handed them over to wor-
ship the host of heaven, as
it is written in the book of
the prophets:
'Did you offer to me
slain victims and
sacrifices
forty years in the
wilderness,
O house of
Israel?
43 No; you took along
the tent
of Moloch,
and the star of your
god Rephan,
the images that
you made
to worship;
so I will remove you
beyond
Babylon.'
44 "Our ancestors had
the tent of testimony in the
wilderness, as God[d] di-
rected when he spoke to
Moses, ordering him to
make it according to the
pattern he had seen. 45Our
ancestors in turn brought it
in with Joshua when they
dispossessed the nations
that God drove out before

[c] Gk *your brothers*
[d] Gk *he*

ὁ εἴπας τοῖς υἱοῖς Ἰσραήλ· προφήτην
– saying to the sons of Israel : A prophet
ὑμῖν ἀναστήσει ὁ θεὸς ἐκ τῶν ἀδελφῶν
for you will raise up – God of the brothers
ὑμῶν ὡς ἐμέ. 38 οὗτός ἐστιν ὁ γενόμενος
of you as me. This is the [one] having been
ἐν τῇ ἐκκλησίᾳ ἐν τῇ ἐρήμῳ μετὰ τοῦ
in the church in the desert with the
ἀγγέλου τοῦ λαλοῦντος αὐτῷ ἐν τῷ
angel – speaking to him in the
ὄρει Σινὰ καὶ τῶν πατέρων ἡμῶν, ὃς
mount Sinai and [with] the fathers of us, who
ἐδέξατο λόγια ζῶντα δοῦναι ὑμῖν, 39 ᾧ
received oracles living to give to you, [1]to whom
οὐκ ἠθέλησαν ὑπήκοοι γενέσθαι οἱ πατέρες
[5]wished [6]not [8]obedient [7]to become [2]the [3]fathers
ἡμῶν, ἀλλὰ ἀπώσαντο καὶ ἐστράφησαν
[4]of us, but thrust away and turned
ἐν ταῖς καρδίαις αὐτῶν εἰς Αἴγυπτον,
in the hearts of them to Egypt,
40 εἰπόντες τῷ Ἀαρών· ποίησον ἡμῖν
saying – to Aaron : Make for us
θεοὺς οἳ προπορεύσονται ἡμῶν· ὁ γὰρ
gods which will go before us; – for
Μωϋσῆς οὗτος, ὃς ἐξήγαγεν ἡμᾶς ἐκ
this Moses, who led forth us out of
γῆς Αἰγύπτου, οὐκ οἴδαμεν τί ἐγένετο
[the] land Egypt, we know not what happened
αὐτῷ. 41 καὶ ἐμοσχοποίησαν ἐν
to him. And they made [a model of] a calf in
ταῖς ἡμέραις ἐκείναις καὶ ἀνήγαγον θυσίαν τῷ
those days and brought up a sacrifice to the
εἰδώλῳ, καὶ εὐφραίνοντο ἐν τοῖς ἔργοις
idol, and made merry in the works
τῶν χειρῶν αὐτῶν. 42 ἔστρεψεν δὲ ὁ
of the hands of them. And [2]turned –
θεὸς καὶ παρέδωκεν αὐτοὺς λατρεύειν
[1]God and delivered them to worship
τῇ στρατιᾷ τοῦ οὐρανοῦ, καθὼς γέγραπται
the host – of heaven, as it has been written
ἐν βίβλῳ τῶν προφητῶν· μὴ σφάγια
in [the] roll of the prophets : *Not* victims
καὶ θυσίας προσηνέγκατέ μοι ἔτη
and sacrifices ye offered to me years
τεσσεράκοντα ἐν τῇ ἐρήμῳ, οἶκος Ἰσραήλ,
forty in the desert, [O] house of Israel,
43 καὶ ἀνελάβετε τὴν σκηνὴν τοῦ Μόλοχ
and ye took up the tent – of Moloch
καὶ τὸ ἄστρον τοῦ θεοῦ Ῥομφά, τοὺς
and the star of the god Rompha, the
τύπους οὓς ἐποιήσατε προσκυνεῖν αὐτοῖς;
models which ye made to worship them?
καὶ μετοικιῶ ὑμᾶς ἐπέκεινα Βαβυλῶνος.
and I will deport you beyond Babylon.
44 Ἡ σκηνὴ τοῦ μαρτυρίου ἦν τοῖς
The tent – of witness was to the
=Our fathers had the tent of witness
πατράσιν ἡμῶν ἐν τῇ ἐρήμῳ, καθὼς
fathers of us° in the desert, as
διετάξατο ὁ λαλῶν τῷ Μωϋσῇ ποιῆσαι
commanded the [one] speaking – to Moses to make
αὐτὴν κατὰ τὸν τύπον ὃν ἑωράκει·
it according to the model which he had seen;
45 ἣν καὶ εἰσήγαγον διαδεξάμενοι οἱ
which also [5]brought in [4]having received [1]the
πατέρες ἡμῶν μετὰ Ἰησοῦ ἐν τῇ κατα-
[2]fathers [3]of us with Jesus in the pos-

who told the Israelites,
'God will send you a prophet like me from your own
people.'[d] 38He was in the
assembly in the desert,
with the angel who spoke to
him on Mount Sinai, and
with our fathers; and he received living words to pass
on to us.
39"But our fathers re-
fused to obey him. Instead,
they rejected him and in
their hearts turned back to
Egypt. 40They told Aaron,
'Make us gods who will go
before us. As for this fellow
Moses who led us out of
Egypt—we don't know
what has happened to
him!'[e] 41That was the time
they made an idol in the
form of a calf. They
brought sacrifices to it and
held a celebration in honor
of what their hands had
made. 42But God turned
away and gave them over
to the worship of the heavenly bodies. This agrees
with what is written in the
book of the prophets:

" 'Did you bring me
sacrifices and
offerings
forty years in the
desert, O house of
Israel?
43You have lifted up the
shrine of Molech
and the star of your
god Rephan,
the idols you made to
worship.
Therefore I will send you
into exile'[f] beyond
Babylon.

44"Our forefathers had
the tabernacle of the Testimony with them in the desert. It had been made as
God directed Moses, ac-
cording to the pattern he
had seen. 45Having re-
ceived the tabernacle, our
fathers under Joshua
brought it with them when
they took the land from the
nations God drove out be-
fore them. It remained in

[d] *37* Deut. 18:15
[e] *40* Exodus 32:1
[f] *43* Amos 5:25-27

our ancestors. And it was
there until the time of David, 46 who found favor
with God and asked that he
might find a dwelling place
for the house of Jacob.[e]
47 But it was Solomon who
built a house for him. 48 Yet
the Most High does not
dwell in houses made with
human hands;[f] as the
prophet says,
49 'Heaven is my throne,
and the earth is my
footstool.
What kind of house
will you build
for me, says the
Lord,
or what is the place
of my rest?
50 Did not my hand
make all these
things?'
51 "You stiff-necked
people, uncircumcised in
heart and ears, you are forever opposing the Holy
Spirit, just as your ancestors used to do. 52 Which of
the prophets did your an-
cestors not persecute?
They killed those who foretold the coming of the Righteous One, and now you
have become his betrayers
and murderers. 53 You are
the ones that received the
law as ordained by angels,
and yet you have not kept
it."

The Stoning of Stephen

54 When they heard
these things, they became
enraged and ground their
teeth at Stephen.[g] 55 But
filled with the Holy Spirit,
he gazed into heaven and
saw the glory of God and
Jesus standing at the right
hand of God. 56 "Look," he
said, "I see the heavens
opened and the Son of Man
standing at the right hand of
God!" 57 But they covered
their ears, and with a loud
shout all rushed together
against him. 58 Then they

σχέσει τῶν ἐθνῶν, ὧν ἐξῶσεν ὁ θεὸς
session of the nations, whom put out - God
ἀπὸ προσώπου τῶν πατέρων ἡμῶν, ἕως
from [the] face of the fathers of us, until
τῶν ἡμερῶν Δαυίδ· **46** ὃς εὗρεν χάριν
the days of David; who found favour
ἐνώπιον τοῦ θεοῦ καὶ ᾐτήσατο εὑρεῖν
before - God and asked to find
σκήνωμα τῷ οἴκῳ Ἰακώβ. **47** Σολομὼν δὲ
a tent for the house of Jacob. But Solomon
οἰκοδόμησεν αὐτῷ οἶκον. **48** ἀλλ'
built for him a house. But
οὐχ ὁ ὕψιστος ἐν χειροποιήτοις κατοικεῖ·
4not 1the 2Most High 5in 6[places] made by hand 3dwells;
καθὼς ὁ προφήτης λέγει· **49** ὁ οὐρανός
as the prophet says: The heaven
μοι θρόνος, ἡ δὲ γῆ ὑποπόδιον τῶν
to me a throne, and the earth a footstool of the
ποδῶν μου· ποῖον οἶκον οἰκοδομήσετέ μοι,
feet of me; what house will ye build for me,
λέγει κύριος, ἢ τίς τόπος τῆς καταπαύσεώς
says [the] Lord, or what place of the rest
μου; **50** οὐχὶ ἡ χείρ μου ἐποίησεν ταῦτα
of me? not the hand of me made these things
πάντα; **51** Σκληροτράχηλοι καὶ ἀπερίτμητοι
all? Hard-necked and uncircumcised
καρδίαις καὶ τοῖς ὠσίν, ὑμεῖς ἀεὶ τῷ
in hearts and - ears, ye always the
πνεύματι τῷ ἁγίῳ ἀντιπίπτετε, ὡς οἱ
Spirit - Holy oppose, as the
πατέρες ὑμῶν καὶ ὑμεῖς. **52** τίνα τῶν
fathers of you also ye. Which of the
προφητῶν οὐκ ἐδίωξαν οἱ πατέρες ὑμῶν;
prophets persecuted not the fathers of you?
καὶ ἀπέκτειναν τοὺς προκαταγγείλαντας
and they killed the [ones] announcing beforehand
περὶ τῆς ἐλεύσεως τοῦ δικαίου, οὗ
concerning the coming of the righteous one, of whom
νῦν ὑμεῖς προδόται καὶ φονεῖς ἐγένεσθε,
now ye betrayers and murderers became,
53 οἵτινες ἐλάβετε τὸν νόμον εἰς διαταγὰς
who received the law in(by) dispositions
ἀγγέλων, καὶ οὐκ ἐφυλάξατε.
of angels, and did not keep [it].
54 Ἀκούοντες δὲ ταῦτα διεπρίοντο ταῖς
And hearing these things they were cut to the
καρδίαις αὐτῶν καὶ ἔβρυχον τοὺς ὀδόντας
hearts of them and gnashed the teeth
ἐπ' αὐτόν. **55** ὑπάρχων δὲ πλήρης
at him. But being full
πνεύματος ἁγίου ἀτενίσας εἰς τὸν οὐρανὸν
of [the] Spirit Holy gazing into - heaven
εἶδεν δόξαν θεοῦ καὶ Ἰησοῦν ἑστῶτα ἐκ
he saw [the] glory of God and Jesus standing at
δεξιῶν τοῦ θεοῦ, **56** καὶ εἶπεν· ἰδοὺ
[the] right [hand] - of God, and said: Behold
θεωρῶ τοὺς οὐρανοὺς διηνοιγμένους καὶ
I see the heavens *having been* opened up and
τὸν υἱὸν τοῦ ἀνθρώπου ἐκ δεξιῶν ἑστῶτα
the Son - of man at [the] right [hand] standing
τοῦ θεοῦ. **57** κράξαντες δὲ φωνῇ μεγάλῃ
- of God. And crying out voice with a great
συνέσχον τὰ ὦτα αὐτῶν, καὶ ὥρμησαν
they closed the ears of them, and rushed
ὁμοθυμαδὸν ἐπ' αὐτόν, **58** καὶ ἐκβαλόντες
with one mind on him, and casting *out*

the land until the time of
David, 46 who enjoyed
God's favor and asked that
he might provide a dwelling
place for the God of Ja-
cob.[g] 47 But it was Solomon
who built the house for
him.
48 "However, the Most
High does not live in
houses made by men. As
the prophet says:

49 " 'Heaven is my throne,
and the earth is my
footstool.
What kind of house will
you build for me?
says the Lord.
Or where will my
resting place be?
50 Has not my hand made
all these things?'[h]

51 "You stiff-necked peo-
ple, with uncircumcised
hearts and ears! You are
just like your fathers: You
always resist the Holy Spirit! 52 Was there ever a
prophet your fathers did
not persecute? They even
killed those who predicted
the coming of the Right-
eous One. And now you
have betrayed and mur-
dered him— 53 you who
have received the law that
was put into effect through
angels but have not obeyed
it."

The Stoning of Stephen

54 When they heard this,
they were furious and
gnashed their teeth at him.
55 But Stephen, full of the
Holy Spirit, looked up to
heaven and saw the glory of
God, and Jesus standing at
the right hand of God.
56 "Look," he said, "I see
heaven open and the Son of
Man standing at the right
hand of God."
57 At this they covered

[e] Other ancient authorities read *for the God of Jacob*
[f] Gk *with hands*
[g] Gk *him*

[g] *46* Some early manuscripts *the house of Jacob*
[h] *50* Isaiah 66:1,2

dragged him out of the city
and began to stone him;
and the witnesses laid their
coats at the feet of a young
man named Saul. 59While
they were stoning Stephen,
he prayed, "Lord Jesus, receive my spirit." 60Then he
knelt down and cried out in
a loud voice, "Lord, do not
hold this sin against them."
When he had said this, he
died.[h] 1And Saul approved
of their killing him.

Saul Persecutes the Church

That day a severe perse-
cution began against the
church in Jerusalem, and
all except the apostles were
scattered throughout the
countryside of Judea and
Samaria. 2Devout men bur-
ied Stephen and made loud
lamentation over him. 3But
Saul was ravaging the
church by entering house
after house; dragging off
both men and women, he
committed them to prison.

Philip Preaches in Samaria

4 Now those who were
scattered went from place
to place, proclaiming the
word. 5Philip went down to
the city[i] of Samaria and
proclaimed the Messiah[j]
to them. 6The crowds with
one accord listened eagerly
to what was said by Philip,
hearing and seeing the
signs that he did, 7for unclean spirits, crying with
loud shrieks, came out of
many who were possessed;
and many others who were
paralyzed or lame were
cured. 8So there was great

[h] Gk *fell asleep*
[i] Other ancient authorities read *a city*
[j] Or *the Christ*

ἔξω τῆς πόλεως ἐλιθοβόλουν. καὶ οἱ
outside the city they stoned [him]. And the
μάρτυρες ἀπέθεντο τὰ ἱμάτια αὐτῶν παρὰ
witnesses put off the garments of them at
τοὺς πόδας νεανίου καλουμένου Σαύλου.
the feet of a young man *being* called Saul.
59 καὶ ἐλιθοβόλουν τὸν Στέφανον, ἐπικαλ-
And they stoned – Stephen, invok-
ούμενον καὶ λέγοντα· κύριε Ἰησοῦ, δέξαι
ing [God] and saying: Lord Jesus, receive
τὸ πνεῦμά μου. 60 θεὶς δὲ τὰ γόνατα
the spirit of me. And placing the knees
=kneeling down
ἔκραξεν φωνῇ μεγάλῃ· κύριε, μὴ στήσῃς
he cried voice with a great: Lord, place not
αὐτοῖς ταύτην τὴν ἁμαρτίαν. καὶ τοῦτο
to them this – sin. And ²this
εἰπὼν ἐκοιμήθη. 8 Σαῦλος δὲ ἦν συνευδοκῶν
¹saying he fell asleep. And Saul was consenting
τῇ ἀναιρέσει αὐτοῦ.
to the killing of him.
Ἐγένετο δὲ ἐν ἐκείνῃ τῇ ἡμέρᾳ
And there was in that – day
διωγμὸς μέγας ἐπὶ τὴν ἐκκλησίαν τὴν
persecution a great on(against) the church –
ἐν Ἱεροσολύμοις· πάντες [δὲ] διεσπάρησαν
in Jerusalem; and all were scattered
κατὰ τὰς χώρας τῆς Ἰουδαίας καὶ
throughout the countries – of Judæa and
Σαμαρείας πλὴν τῶν ἀποστόλων.
Samaria except the apostles.
2 συνεκόμισαν δὲ τὸν Στέφανον ἄνδρες
And ³recovered – ⁴Stephen ²men
εὐλαβεῖς καὶ ἐποίησαν κοπετὸν μέγαν
¹devout and made lamentation great
ἐπ᾽ αὐτῷ. 3 Σαῦλος δὲ ἐλυμαίνετο τὴν
over him. But Saul ravaged the
ἐκκλησίαν κατὰ τοὺς οἴκους εἰσπορευόμενος,
church house by house† entering,
σύρων τε ἄνδρας καὶ γυναῖκας παρεδίδου
dragging both men and women delivered
εἰς φυλακήν.
to prison.
4 Οἱ μὲν οὖν διασπαρέντες διῆλθον
The [ones] –* therefore being scattered passed through
εὐαγγελιζόμενοι τὸν λόγον. 5 Φίλιππος δὲ
preaching the word. But Philip
κατελθὼν εἰς τὴν πόλιν τῆς
going down to the city –
Σαμαρείας ἐκήρυσσεν αὐτοῖς τὸν Χριστόν.
of Samaria proclaimed to them the Christ.
6 προσεῖχον δὲ οἱ ὄχλοι τοῖς
And gave heed the crowds to the things
λεγομένοις ὑπὸ τοῦ Φιλίππου ὁμοθυμαδὸν
being said by – Philip with one mind
ἐν τῷ ἀκούειν αὐτοὺς καὶ βλέπειν τὰ
in the to hear them and to see[be] the
=as they heard and saw
σημεῖα ἃ ἐποίει. 7 πολλοὶ γὰρ τῶν
signs which he was doing. For many of the
ἐχόντων πνεύματα ἀκάθαρτα βοῶντα φωνῇ
[ones] having spirits unclean crying ²voice
μεγάλῃ ἐξήρχοντο· πολλοὶ δὲ παραλελυμένοι
¹with a great came out; and many *having been* paralysed
καὶ χωλοὶ ἐθεραπεύθησαν· 8 ἐγένετο δὲ
and lame were healed; and there was

* See note on John 19. 24.

their ears and, yelling at the
top of their voices, they all
rushed at him, 58dragged
him out of the city and began to stone him. Mean-
while, the witnesses laid
their clothes at the feet of a
young man named Saul.
59While they were stoning
him, Stephen prayed,
"Lord Jesus, receive my
spirit." 60Then he fell on
his knees and cried out,
"Lord, do not hold this sin
against them." When he
had said this, he fell asleep.

Chapter 8

AND Saul was there, giv-
ing approval to his
death.

The Church Persecuted and Scattered

On that day a great persecution broke out against
the church at Jerusalem,
and all except the apostles
were scattered throughout
Judea and Samaria. 2Godly
men buried Stephen and
mourned deeply for him.
3But Saul began to destroy
the church. Going from
house to house, he dragged
off men and women and put
them in prison.

Philip in Samaria

4Those who had been
scattered preached the
word wherever they went.
5Philip went down to a city
in Samaria and proclaimed
the Christ[i] there. 6When
the crowds heard Philip
and saw the miraculous
signs he did, they all paid
close attention to what he
said. 7With shrieks, evil[j]
spirits came out of many,
and many paralytics and
cripples were healed. 8So

[i] 5 Or *Messiah*
[j] 7 Greek *unclean*

joy in that city.
9 Now a certain man
named Simon had previ-
ously practiced magic in
the city and amazed the
people of Samaria, saying
that he was someone great.
10All of them, from the
least to the greatest, listened to him eagerly, saying, "This man is the power
of God that is called
Great." 11And they lis-
tened eagerly to him be-
cause for a long time he had
amazed them with his mag-
ic. 12But when they be-
lieved Philip, who was proclaiming the good news
about the kingdom of God
and the name of Jesus
Christ, they were baptized,
both men and women.
13Even Simon himself be-
lieved. After being bap-
tized, he stayed constantly
with Philip and was amazed
when he saw the signs and
great miracles that took
place.
14 Now when the apos-
tles at Jerusalem heard that
Samaria had accepted the
word of God, they sent Peter and John to them. 15The
two went down and prayed
for them that they might receive the Holy Spirit 16(for
as yet the Spirit had not
come[k] upon any of them;
they had only been bap-
tized in the name of the
Lord Jesus). 17Then Peter
and John[l] laid their hands
on them, and they received
the Holy Spirit. 18Now
when Simon saw that the
Spirit was given through
the laying on of the apostles' hands, he offered
them money, 19saying,
"Give me also this power
so that anyone on whom I
lay my hands may receive

[k] Gk *fallen*
[l] Gk *they*

πολλὴ χαρὰ ἐν τῇ πόλει ἐκείνῃ. 9 Ἀνὴρ δέ τις
much joy in that city. And a certain man

ὀνόματι Σίμων προϋπῆρχεν ἐν τῇ
by name Simon was previously in the

πόλει μαγεύων καὶ ἐξιστάνων τὸ
city practising sorcery and astonishing the

ἔθνος τῆς Σαμαρείας, λέγων εἶναί τινα
nation – of Samaria, saying [2]to be [3]someone

ἑαυτὸν μέγαν, 10 ᾧ προσεῖχον πάντες
[1]himself [4]great, to whom gave heed all

ἀπὸ μικροῦ ἕως μεγάλου λέγοντες· οὗτός
from small to great saying : This man

ἐστιν ἡ δύναμις τοῦ θεοῦ ἡ καλουμένη
is the power – of God – *being* called

μεγάλη. 11 προσεῖχον δὲ αὐτῷ διὰ τὸ
great. And they gave heed to him because of the

ἱκανῷ χρόνῳ ταῖς μαγείαις ἐξεστακέναι
for a considerable time by the sorceries to have astonished
=because for a considerable time he had astonished them by his sorceries.

αὐτούς. 12 ὅτε δὲ ἐπίστευσαν τῷ Φιλίππῳ
them. But when they believed – Philip

εὐαγγελιζομένῳ περὶ τῆς βασιλείας τοῦ
preaching about the kingdom –

θεοῦ καὶ τοῦ ὀνόματος Ἰησοῦ Χριστοῦ,
of God and the name of Jesus Christ,

ἐβαπτίζοντο ἄνδρες τε καὶ γυναῖκες.
they were baptized both men and women.

13 ὁ δὲ Σίμων καὶ αὐτὸς ἐπίστευσεν,
– And Simon also [him]self believed,

καὶ βαπτισθεὶς ἦν προσκαρτερῶν τῷ
and having been baptized was attaching himself –

Φιλίππῳ, θεωρῶν τε σημεῖα καὶ δυνάμεις
to Philip, and beholding signs and powerful deeds

μεγάλας γινομένας ἐξίστατο. 14 Ἀκούσαντες
great happening he was amazed. [4]hearing

δὲ οἱ ἐν Ἱεροσολύμοις ἀπόστολοι ὅτι
[1]And [2]the [5]in [6]Jerusalem [3]apostles that

δέδεκται ἡ Σαμάρεια τὸν λόγον τοῦ
[2]has received – [1]Samaria the word –

θεοῦ, ἀπέστειλαν πρὸς αὐτοὺς Πέτρον
of God, they sent to them Peter

καὶ Ἰωάννην, 15 οἵτινες καταβάντες
and John, who going down

προσηύξαντο περὶ αὐτῶν ὅπως λάβωσιν
prayed concerning them so as they might receive

πνεῦμα ἅγιον· 16 οὐδέπω γὰρ ἦν ἐπ'
Spirit Holy; for [2]not yet [1]he was [4]on

οὐδενὶ αὐτῶν ἐπιπεπτωκός, μόνον δὲ
[5]no(any)one [6]of them [3]having fallen *on*, but only

βεβαπτισμένοι ὑπῆρχον εἰς τὸ ὄνομα τοῦ
having been baptized they were in the name of the

κυρίου Ἰησοῦ. 17 τότε ἐπετίθεσαν τὰς
Lord Jesus. Then they laid *on* the(ir)

χεῖρας ἐπ' αὐτούς, καὶ ἐλάμβανον πνεῦμα
hands on them, and they received [2]Spirit

ἅγιον. 18 ἰδὼν δὲ ὁ Σίμων ὅτι διὰ
[1]Holy. And [2]seeing – [1]Simon that through

τῆς ἐπιθέσεως τῶν χειρῶν τῶν ἀποστόλων
the laying on of the hands of the apostles

δίδοται τὸ πνεῦμα, προσήνεγκεν αὐτοῖς
is(was) given the Spirit, he offered them

χρήματα λέγων· 19 δότε κἀμοὶ τὴν
money saying : Give me also –

ἐξουσίαν ταύτην ἵνα ᾧ ἐὰν ἐπιθῶ τὰς
authority this that whomever I lay on the(my)

there was great joy in that
city.

Simon the Sorcerer

9Now for some time a
man named Simon had
practiced sorcery in the
city and amazed all the people of Samaria. He boasted
that he was someone great,
10and all the people, both
high and low, gave him
their attention and ex-
claimed, "This man is the
divine power known as the
Great Power." 11They fol-
lowed him because he had
amazed them for a long
time with his magic. 12But
when they believed Philip
as he preached the good
news of the kingdom of
God and the name of Jesus
Christ, they were baptized,
both men and women. 13Si-
mon himself believed and
was baptized. And he fol-
lowed Philip everywhere,
astonished by the great
signs and miracles he saw.
14When the apostles in Jerusalem heard that Samaria
had accepted the word of
God, they sent Peter and
John to them. 15When they
arrived, they prayed for
them that they might re-
ceive the Holy Spirit, 16be-
cause the Holy Spirit had
not yet come upon any of
them; they had simply been
baptized into[k] the name of
the Lord Jesus. 17Then Peter and John placed their
hands on them, and they received the Holy Spirit.
18When Simon saw that
the Spirit was given at the
laying on of the apostles'
hands, he offered them
money 19and said, "Give
me also this ability so that
everyone on whom I lay my
hands may receive the
Holy Spirit."

[k] *16* Or *in*

the Holy Spirit." 20 But Peter said to him, "May your
silver perish with you, because you thought you
could obtain God's gift
with money! 21 You have
no part or share in this, for
your heart is not right before God. 22 Repent therefore of this wickedness of
yours, and pray to the Lord
that, if possible, the intent
of your heart may be for-
given you. 23 For I see that
you are in the gall of bitterness and the chains of
wickedness." 24 Simon an-
swered, "Pray for me to the
Lord, that nothing of what
you[m] have said may hap-
pen to me."
25 Now after Peter and
John[n] had testified and
spoken the word of the
Lord, they returned to Jerusalem, proclaiming the
good news to many villages
of the Samaritans.

Philip and the Ethiopian Eunuch

26 Then an angel of the
Lord said to Philip, "Get up
and go toward the south[o]
to the road that goes down
from Jerusalem to Gaza."
(This is a wilderness road.)
27 So he got up and went.
Now there was an Ethiopi-
an eunuch, a court official
of the Candace, queen of
the Ethiopians, in charge of
her entire treasury. He had
come to Jerusalem to wor-
ship 28 and was returning
home; seated in his chariot,
he was reading the prophet
Isaiah. 29 Then the Spirit
said to Philip, "Go over to
this chariot and join it."

[m] The Greek word for *you* and the verb *pray* are plural
[n] Gk *after they*
[o] Or *go at noon*

χεῖρας λαμβάνῃ πνεῦμα ἅγιον. **20** Πέτρος δὲ
hands he may receive Spirit Holy. But Peter

εἶπεν πρὸς αὐτόν· τὸ ἀργύριόν σου
said to him: The silver of thee

σὺν σοὶ εἴη εἰς ἀπώλειαν, ὅτι τὴν δωρεὰν
with thee may it be into perdition, because the gift

τοῦ θεοῦ ἐνόμισας διὰ χρημάτων κτᾶσθαι.
– of God thou didst suppose through money to get.

21 οὐκ ἔστιν σοι μερὶς οὐδὲ κλῆρος
There is not to thee[c] part nor lot
=Thou hast no

ἐν τῷ λόγῳ τούτῳ· ἡ γὰρ καρδία σου
in this matter; for the heart of thee

οὐκ ἔστιν εὐθεῖα ἔναντι τοῦ θεοῦ.
is not right before – God.

22 μετανόησον οὖν ἀπὸ τῆς κακίας σου
Repent thou therefore from – [2]wickedness [3]of thee

ταύτης, καὶ δεήθητι τοῦ κυρίου εἰ ἄρα
[1]this, and petition the Lord if perhaps

ἀφεθήσεταί σοι ἡ ἐπίνοια τῆς καρδίας
will be forgiven thee the thought of the heart

σου· **23** εἰς γὰρ χολὴν πικρίας καὶ
of thee; for in gall of bitterness and

σύνδεσμον ἀδικίας ὁρῶ σε ὄντα.
bond of unrighteousness I see thee being.

24 ἀποκριθεὶς δὲ ὁ Σίμων εἶπεν· δεήθητε
And answering – Simon said: Petition

ὑμεῖς ὑπὲρ ἐμοῦ πρὸς τὸν κύριον, ὅπως
ye for me to the Lord, so as

μηδὲν ἐπέλθῃ ἐπ' ἐμὲ ὧν εἰρήκατε.
[1]not one [4]may come *on* [5]on [6]me [2]of the things which [3]ye have spoken.

25 Οἱ μὲν οὖν διαμαρτυράμενοι καὶ λαλή-
They – therefore having solemnly witnessed and having

σαντες τὸν λόγον τοῦ κυρίου ὑπέστρεφον
spoken the word of the Lord returned

εἰς Ἱεροσόλυμα, πολλάς τε κώμας τῶν
to Jerusalem, and [2]many [3]villages [4]of the

Σαμαριτῶν εὐηγγελίζοντο.
[5]Samaritans [1]evangelized.

26 Ἄγγελος δὲ κυρίου ἐλάλησεν πρὸς
But an angel of [the] Lord spoke to

Φίλιππον λέγων· ἀνάστηθι καὶ πορεύου
Philip saying: Rise up and go

κατὰ μεσημβρίαν ἐπὶ τὴν ὁδὸν τὴν
along south on the way –

καταβαίνουσαν ἀπὸ Ἰερουσαλὴμ εἰς Γάζαν·
going down from Jerusalem to Gaza;

αὕτη ἐστὶν ἔρημος. **27** καὶ ἀναστὰς
this is desert. And rising up

ἐπορεύθη. καὶ ἰδοὺ ἀνὴρ Αἰθίοψ εὐνοῦχος
he went. And behold[,] *a man* Ethiopian a eunuch

δυνάστης Κανδάκης βασιλίσσης Αἰθιόπων,
a courtier of Candace queen of [the] Ethiopians,

ὃς ἦν ἐπὶ πάσης τῆς γάζης αὐτῆς,
who was over all the treasure of her,

[ὃς] ἐληλύθει προσκυνήσων εἰς Ἰερουσαλήμ,
who had come worshipping in Jerusalem,

28 ἦν δὲ ὑποστρέφων καὶ καθήμενος ἐπὶ
and was returning and sitting on

τοῦ ἅρματος αὐτοῦ καὶ ἀνεγίνωσκεν τὸν
the chariot of him and was reading the

προφήτην Ἠσαΐαν. **29** εἶπεν δὲ τὸ πνεῦμα
prophet Esaias. And said the Spirit

τῷ Φιλίππῳ· πρόσελθε καὶ κολλήθητι
– to Philip: Approach and keep company with

20 Peter answered: "May
your money perish with
you, because you thought
you could buy the gift of
God with money! 21 You
have no part or share in this
ministry, because your
heart is not right before
God. 22 Repent of this wickedness and pray to the
Lord. Perhaps he will forgive you for having such a
thought in your heart. 23 For
I see that you are full of bitterness and captive to sin."
24 Then Simon answered,
"Pray to the Lord for me so
that nothing you have said
may happen to me."
25 When they had testified
and proclaimed the word of
the Lord, Peter and John
returned to Jerusalem,
preaching the gospel in
many Samaritan villages.

Philip and the Ethiopian

26 Now an angel of the
Lord said to Philip, "Go
south to the road—the desert road—that goes down
from Jerusalem to Gaza."
27 So he started out, and on
his way he met an Ethiopian[l] eunuch, an important
official in charge of all the
treasury of Candace, queen
of the Ethiopians. This man
had gone to Jerusalem to
worship, 28 and on his way
home was sitting in his
chariot reading the book of
Isaiah the prophet. 29 The
Spirit told Philip, "Go to

[l] 27 That is, from the upper Nile region

30 So Philip ran up to it and
heard him reading the
prophet Isaiah. He asked,
"Do you understand what
you are reading?" 31 He replied, "How can I, unless
someone guides me?" And
he invited Philip to get in
and sit beside him. 32 Now
the passage of the scripture
that he was reading was
this:

"Like a sheep he was
led to the
slaughter,
and like a lamb
silent before
its shearer,
so he does not
open his mouth.
33 In his humiliation
justice was
denied him.
Who can describe
his generation?
For his life is
taken away from
the earth."

34 The eunuch asked Philip,
"About whom, may I ask
you, does the prophet say
this, about himself or about
someone else?" 35 Then
Philip began to speak, and
starting with this scripture,
he proclaimed to him the
good news about Jesus.
36 As they were going along
the road, they came to
some water; and the eu-
nuch said, "Look, here is
water! What is to prevent
me from being baptized?"[p]
38 He commanded the char-
iot to stop, and both of
them, Philip and the eu-
nuch, went down into the
water, and Philip[q] bap-
tized him. 39 When they
came up out of the water,
the Spirit of the Lord
snatched Philip away; the
eunuch saw him no more,
and went on his way rejoicing. 40 But Philip found
himself at Azotus, and as
he was passing through the

[p] Other ancient authorities add all or most of verse 37, *And Philip said, "If you believe with all your heart, you may." And he replied, "I believe that Jesus Christ is the Son of God."*

[q] Gk *he*

τῷ ἅρματι τούτῳ. **30** προσδραμὼν δὲ
this chariot. And running up
ὁ Φίλιππος ἤκουσεν αὐτοῦ ἀναγινώσκοντος
– Philip heard him reading
Ἠσαΐαν τὸν προφήτην, καὶ εἶπεν· ἆρά γε
Esaias the prophet, and said: Then
γινώσκεις ἃ ἀναγινώσκεις; **31** ὁ δὲ
knowest thou what things thou art reading? And he
εἶπεν· πῶς γὰρ ἂν δυναίμην ἐὰν μή
said: How indeed should I be able unless
τις ὁδηγήσει με; παρεκάλεσέν τε τὸν
someone shall guide me? And he besought –
Φίλιππον ἀναβάντα καθίσαι σὺν αὐτῷ.
Philip coming up to sit with him.
32 ἡ δὲ περιοχὴ τῆς γραφῆς ἣν ἀνεγίνω-
Now the passage of the scripture which he was
σκεν ἦν αὕτη· ὡς πρόβατον ἐπὶ σφαγὴν
reading was this: As a sheep to slaughter
ἤχθη, καὶ ὡς ἀμνὸς ἐναντίον τοῦ κείροντος
he was led, and as a lamb before the [one] shearing
αὐτὸν ἄφωνος, οὕτως οὐκ ἀνοίγει τὸ
it [is] dumb, so he opens not the
στόμα αὐτοῦ. **33** Ἐν τῇ ταπεινώσει
mouth of him. In the humiliation
ἡ κρίσις αὐτοῦ ἤρθη· τὴν γενεὰν αὐτοῦ
the judgment of him was taken away; the generation of him
τίς διηγήσεται; ὅτι αἴρεται ἀπὸ τῆς
who will relate? because is taken from the
γῆς ἡ ζωὴ αὐτοῦ. **34** ἀποκριθεὶς δὲ ὁ
earth the life of him. And answering the
εὐνοῦχος τῷ Φιλίππῳ εἶπεν· δέομαί σου,
eunuch – to Philip said: I ask thee,
περὶ τίνος ὁ προφήτης λέγει τοῦτο;
about whom the prophet says this?
περὶ ἑαυτοῦ ἢ περὶ ἑτέρου τινός;
about himself or about other someone?
35 ἀνοίξας δὲ ὁ Φίλιππος τὸ στόμα
And opening – Philip the mouth
αὐτοῦ καὶ ἀρξάμενος ἀπὸ τῆς γραφῆς ταύτης
of him and beginning from this scripture
εὐηγγελίσατο αὐτῷ τὸν Ἰησοῦν.
preached to him – Jesus.
36 ὡς δὲ ἐπορεύοντο κατὰ τὴν ὁδόν,
And as they were going along the way,
ἦλθον ἐπί τι ὕδωρ, καί φησιν ὁ εὐνοῦχος·
they came upon certain water, and says the eunuch:
ἰδοὺ ὕδωρ· τί κωλύει με βαπτισθῆναι;‡
Behold[,] water; what prevents me to be baptized?
38 καὶ ἐκέλευσεν στῆναι τὸ ἅρμα, καὶ
And he commanded to stand the chariot, and
κατέβησαν ἀμφότεροι εἰς τὸ ὕδωρ, ὅ
went down both into the water, –
τε Φίλιππος καὶ ὁ εὐνοῦχος, καὶ ἐβάπτισεν
both Philip and the eunuch, and he baptized
αὐτόν. **39** ὅτε δὲ ἀνέβησαν ἐκ τοῦ ὕδατος,
him. And when they came up out of the water,
πνεῦμα κυρίου ἥρπασεν τὸν Φίλιππον,
[the] Spirit of [the] Lord seized – Philip,
καὶ οὐκ εἶδεν αὐτὸν οὐκέτι ὁ εὐνοῦχος,
and saw not him no(any) more the eunuch,
ἐπορεύετο γὰρ τὴν ὁδὸν αὐτοῦ χαίρων.
for he went the way of him rejoicing.
40 Φίλιππος δὲ εὑρέθη εἰς Ἄζωτον, καὶ
But Philip was found in – Azotus, and

‡ Verse 37 omitted by Nestle; *cf.* NIV footnote.

that chariot and stay near
it."
30 Then Philip ran up to
the chariot and heard the
man reading Isaiah the
prophet. "Do you under-
stand what you are read-
ing?" Philip asked.
31 "How can I," he said,
"unless someone explains
it to me?" So he invited
Philip to come up and sit
with him.
32 The eunuch was reading
this passage of Scripture:

"He was led like a sheep
to the slaughter,
and as a lamb before
the shearer is silent,
so he did not open his
mouth.
33 In his humiliation he was
deprived of justice.
Who can speak of his
descendants?
For his life was taken
from the earth."[m]

34 The eunuch asked Phil-
ip, "Tell me, please, who is
the prophet talking about,
himself or someone else?"
35 Then Philip began with
that very passage of Scripture and told him the good
news about Jesus.
36 As they traveled along
the road, they came to
some water and the eunuch
said, "Look, here is water.
Why shouldn't I be bap-
tized?"[n] 38 And he gave orders to stop the chariot.
Then both Philip and the
eunuch went down into the
water and Philip baptized
him. 39 When they came up
out of the water, the Spirit
of the Lord suddenly took
Philip away, and the eu-
nuch did not see him again,
but went on his way rejoicing. 40 Philip, however, appeared at Azotus and trav-

[m] *33* Isaiah 53:7,8

[n] *36* Some late manuscripts *baptized?" 37 Philip said, "If you believe with all your heart, you may." The eunuch answered, "I believe that Jesus Christ is the Son of God."*

region, he proclaimed the
good news to all the towns
until he came to Caesarea.

Chapter 9

The Conversion of Saul

MEANWHILE Saul,
still breathing
threats and murder against
the disciples of the Lord,
went to the high priest 2and
asked him for letters to the
synagogues at Damascus,
so that if he found any who
belonged to the Way, men
or women, he might bring
them bound to Jerusalem.
3Now as he was going
along and approaching Da-
mascus, suddenly a light
from heaven flashed
around him. 4He fell to the
ground and heard a voice
saying to him, "Saul, Saul,
why do you persecute
me?" 5He asked, "Who are
you, Lord?" The reply
came, "I am Jesus, whom
you are persecuting. 6But
get up and enter the city,
and you will be told what
you are to do." 7The men
who were traveling with
him stood speechless be-
cause they heard the voice
but saw no one. 8Saul got
up from the ground, and
though his eyes were open,
he could see nothing; so
they led him by the hand
and brought him into Da-
mascus. 9For three days he
was without sight, and neither ate nor drank.
10 Now there was a dis-
ciple in Damascus named
Ananias. The Lord said to
him in a vision, "Ananias."
He answered, "Here I am,
Lord." 11The Lord said to
him, "Get up and go to the

διερχόμενος εὐηγγελίζετο τὰς πόλεις πάσας
passing through he evangelized the cities all
ἕως τοῦ ἐλθεῖν αὐτὸν εἰς Καισάρειαν.
until the to come him[b] to Cæsarea.
=he came

9 Ὁ δὲ Σαῦλος ἔτι ἐμπνέων ἀπειλῆς
– But Saul still breathing threatening
καὶ φόνου εἰς τοὺς μαθητὰς τοῦ κυρίου,
and murder against the disciples of the Lord,
προσελθὼν τῷ ἀρχιερεῖ 2 ᾐτήσατο παρ'
approaching *to* the high priest asked from
αὐτοῦ ἐπιστολὰς εἰς Δαμασκὸν πρὸς τὰς
him letters to Damascus for the
συναγωγάς, ὅπως ἐάν τινας εὕρῃ τῆς
synagogues, so as if [2]any [1]he found [4]of the
ὁδοῦ ὄντας, ἄνδρας τε καὶ γυναῖκας, δεδεμένους
[5]way [3]being, both men and women, [2]*having been* bound
ἀγάγῃ εἰς Ἰερουσαλήμ. 3 Ἐν
[1]he might bring [them] to Jerusalem. in
δὲ τῷ πορεύεσθαι ἐγένετο αὐτὸν ἐγγίζειν
Now the to go[e] it came to pass him to draw near[b]
=as he went =he drew near
τῇ Δαμασκῷ, ἐξαίφνης τε αὐτὸν περιήστ-
– to Damascus, and suddenly [5]him [4]shone
ραψεν φῶς ἐκ τοῦ οὐρανοῦ, 4 καὶ πεσὼν
round [1]a light [2]out of – [3]heaven, and falling
ἐπὶ τὴν γῆν ἤκουσεν φωνὴν λέγουσαν
on the earth he heard a voice saying
αὐτῷ· Σαοὺλ Σαούλ, τί με διώκεις;
to him: Saul[,] Saul, why me persecutest thou?
5 εἶπεν δέ· τίς εἶ, κύριε; ὁ δέ· ἐγώ
And he said: Who art thou, Lord? And he [said]: I
εἰμι Ἰησοῦς ὃν σὺ διώκεις· 6 ἀλλὰ
am Jesus whom thou persecutest; but
ἀνάστηθι καὶ εἴσελθε εἰς τὴν πόλιν,
rise thou up, and enter into the city,
καὶ λαληθήσεταί σοι ὅ τί σε δεῖ ποιεῖν.
and it shall be told thee what thee it behoves to do.
7 οἱ δὲ ἄνδρες οἱ συνοδεύοντες αὐτῷ
Now the men – journeying with him
εἱστήκεισαν ἐνεοί, ἀκούοντες μὲν τῆς
stood speechless, hearing indeed the
φωνῆς, μηδένα δὲ θεωροῦντες. 8 ἠγέρθη δὲ
sound, but no man beholding. And was raised
Σαῦλος ἀπὸ τῆς γῆς, ἀνεῳγμένων δὲ
Saul from the ground, and having been opened
=when his eyes were opened
τῶν ὀφθαλμῶν αὐτοῦ οὐδὲν ἔβλεπεν·
the eyes of him[a] nothing he saw;
χειραγωγοῦντες δὲ αὐτὸν εἰσήγαγον εἰς
and leading by the hand him they brought *in* into
Δαμασκόν. 9 καὶ ἦν ἡμέρας τρεῖς μὴ
Damascus. And he was days three not
βλέπων, καὶ οὐκ ἔφαγεν οὐδὲ ἔπιεν.
seeing, and ate not nor drank.
10 Ἦν δέ τις μαθητὴς ἐν Δαμασκῷ
Now there was a certain disciple in Damascus
ὀνόματι Ἁνανίας, καὶ εἶπεν πρὸς αὐτὸν
by name Ananias, and said to him
ἐν ὁράματι ὁ κύριος· Ἁνανία. ὁ δὲ
in a vision the Lord: Ananias. And he
εἶπεν· ἰδοὺ ἐγώ, κύριε. 11 ὁ δὲ κύριος
said: Behold[,] I, Lord. And the Lord
πρὸς αὐτόν· ἀναστὰς πορεύθητι ἐπὶ τὴν
[said] to him: Rising up go thou to the

eled about, preaching the
gospel in all the towns until
he reached Caesarea.

Chapter 9

Saul's Conversion

MEANWHILE, Saul
was still breathing
out murderous threats
against the Lord's disci-
ples. He went to the high
priest 2and asked him for
letters to the synagogues in
Damascus, so that if he
found any there who be-
longed to the Way, whether
men or women, he might
take them as prisoners to
Jerusalem. 3As he neared
Damascus on his journey,
suddenly a light from heav-
en flashed around him. 4He
fell to the ground and heard
a voice say to him, "Saul,
Saul, why do you persecute
me?"
5"Who are you, Lord?"
Saul asked.
"I am Jesus, whom you
are persecuting," he re-
plied. 6"Now get up and go
into the city, and you will
be told what you must do."
7The men traveling with
Saul stood there speech-
less; they heard the sound
but did not see anyone.
8Saul got up from the
ground, but when he
opened his eyes he could
see nothing. So they led
him by the hand into Da-
mascus. 9For three days he
was blind, and did not eat
or drink anything.
10In Damascus there was
a disciple named Ananias.
The Lord called to him in a
vision, "Ananias!"
"Yes, Lord," he an-
swered.
11The Lord told him, "Go
to the house of Judas on

street called Straight, and
at the house of Judas look
for a man of Tarsus named
Saul. At this moment he is
praying, 12and he has seen
in a vision[r] a man named
Ananias come in and lay his
hands on him so that he
might regain his sight."
13But Ananias answered,
"Lord, I have heard from
many about this man, how
much evil he has done to
your saints in Jerusalem;
14and here he has authority
from the chief priests to
bind all who invoke your
name." 15But the Lord said
to him, "Go, for he is an
instrument whom I have
chosen to bring my name
before Gentiles and kings
and before the people of Israel; 16I myself will show
him how much he must suf-
fer for the sake of my
name." 17So Ananias went
and entered the house. He
laid his hands on Saul[s] and
said, "Brother Saul, the
Lord Jesus, who appeared
to you on your way here,
has sent me so that you
may regain your sight and
be filled with the Holy Spirit." 18And immediately
something like scales fell
from his eyes, and his sight
was restored. Then he got
up and was baptized, 19and
after taking some food, he
regained his strength.

Saul Preaches in Damascus

For several days he was
with the disciples in Da-
mascus, 20and immediately
he began to proclaim Jesus
in the synagogues, saying,
"He is the Son of God."
21All who heard him were
amazed and said, "Is not
this the man who made
havoc in Jerusalem among
those who invoked this
name? And has he not

[r] Other ancient authorities lack *in a vision*
[s] Gk *him*

ῥύμην τὴν καλουμένην εὐθεῖαν καὶ ζήτησον
street – *being* called Straight and seek
ἐν οἰκίᾳ Ἰούδα Σαῦλον ὀνόματι Ταρσέα·
in [the] house of Judas [3]Saul [2]by name [1]a Tarsian;
ἰδοὺ γὰρ προσεύχεται, 12 καὶ εἶδεν ἄνδρα
for behold he is praying, and saw [3]a man
[ἐν ὁράματι] Ἁνανίαν ὀνόματι εἰσελθόντα
[1]in [2]a vision Ananias by name coming in
καὶ ἐπιθέντα αὐτῷ χεῖρας, ὅπως ἀναβλέψῃ.
and putting on him hands, so as he may see again.
13 ἀπεκρίθη δὲ Ἁνανίας· κύριε, ἤκουσα
And answered Ananias: Lord, I heard
ἀπὸ πολλῶν περὶ τοῦ ἀνδρὸς τούτου,
from many about this man,
ὅσα κακὰ τοῖς ἁγίοις σου ἐποίησεν
how many evil things to the saints of thee he did
ἐν Ἰερουσαλήμ· 14 καὶ ὧδε ἔχει ἐξουσίαν
in Jerusalem; and here he has authority
παρὰ τῶν ἀρχιερέων δῆσαι πάντας τοὺς
from the chief priests to bind all the
ἐπικαλουμένους τὸ ὄνομά σου. 15 εἶπεν
[ones] invoking the name of thee. said
δὲ πρὸς αὐτὸν ὁ κύριος· πορεύου, ὅτι
But to him the Lord: Go thou, because
σκεῦος ἐκλογῆς ἐστίν μοι οὗτος τοῦ
[3]a vessel [4]of choice [2]is [5]to me [1]this man –
βαστάσαι τὸ ὄνομά μου ἐνώπιον [τῶν]
to bear[d] the name of me [1]before [3]the
ἐθνῶν τε καὶ βασιλέων υἱῶν τε Ἰσραήλ·
[4]nations [1]both [5]and [6]kings [8]sons [7]and [9]of Israel;
16 ἐγὼ γὰρ ὑποδείξω αὐτῷ ὅσα δεῖ
for I will show him how many things it behoves
αὐτὸν ὑπὲρ τοῦ ὀνόματός μου παθεῖν.
him on behalf of the name of me to suffer.
17 Ἀπῆλθεν δὲ Ἁνανίας καὶ εἰσῆλθεν
And went away Ananias and entered
εἰς τὴν οἰκίαν, καὶ ἐπιθεὶς ἐπ' αὐτὸν
into the house, and putting *on* on him
τὰς χεῖρας εἶπεν· Σαοὺλ ἀδελφέ, ὁ
the(his) hands said: Saul brother, the
κύριος ἀπέσταλκέν με, Ἰησοῦς ὁ ὀφθείς σοι
Lord has sent me, Jesus the [one] appearing to thee
ἐν τῇ ὁδῷ ᾗ ἤρχου, ὅπως ἀναβλέψῃς
in the way which thou camest, so as thou mayest see again
καὶ πλησθῇς πνεύματος ἁγίου. 18 καὶ
and be filled of(with) Spirit Holy. And
εὐθέως ἀπέπεσαν αὐτοῦ ἀπὸ τῶν ὀφθαλμῶν
immediately fell away of him from the eyes
ὡς λεπίδες, ἀνέβλεψέν τε, καὶ ἀναστὰς
as scales, and he saw again, and rising up
ἐβαπτίσθη, 19 καὶ λαβὼν τροφὴν ἐνίσχυσεν.
was baptized, and taking food was strengthened.
Ἐγένετο δὲ μετὰ τῶν ἐν Δαμασκῷ
Now he was with the in Damascus
μαθητῶν ἡμέρας τινάς, 20 καὶ εὐθέως
disciples days some, and immediately
ἐν ταῖς συναγωγαῖς ἐκήρυσσεν τὸν Ἰησοῦν,
in the synagogues he proclaimed – Jesus,
ὅτι οὗτός ἐστιν ὁ υἱὸς τοῦ θεοῦ.
that this one is the Son – of God.
21 ἐξίσταντο δὲ πάντες οἱ ἀκούοντες καὶ
And were amazed all the [ones] hearing and
ἔλεγον· οὐχ οὗτός ἐστιν ὁ πορθήσας
said: Not this man is the [one] having destroyed
εἰς Ἰερουσαλὴμ τοὺς ἐπικαλουμένους
in Jerusalem the [ones] invoking

Straight Street and ask for a
man from Tarsus named
Saul, for he is praying. 12In
a vision he has seen a man
named Ananias come and
place his hands on him to
restore his sight."
13"Lord," Ananias an-
swered, "I have heard
many reports about this
man and all the harm he has
done to your saints in Jerusalem. 14And he has come
here with authority from
the chief priests to arrest all
who call on your name."
15But the Lord said to Ananias, "Go! This man is my
chosen instrument to carry
my name before the Gen-
tiles and their kings and before the people of Israel. 16I
will show him how much he
must suffer for my name."
17Then Ananias went to
the house and entered it.
Placing his hands on Saul,
he said, "Brother Saul, the
Lord—Jesus, who ap-
peared to you on the road
as you were coming here—
has sent me so that you
may see again and be filled
with the Holy Spirit."
18Immediately, something
like scales fell from Saul's
eyes, and he could see
again. He got up and was
baptized, 19and after taking
some food, he regained his
strength.

Saul in Damascus and Jerusalem

Saul spent several days
with the disciples in Da-
mascus. 20At once he began
to preach in the synagogues
that Jesus is the Son of
God. 21All those who heard
him were astonished and
asked, "Isn't he the man
who raised havoc in Jerusalem among those who call
on this name? And hasn't

come here for the purpose of bringing them bound before the chief priests?" 22 Saul became increasingly more powerful and confounded the Jews who lived in Damascus by proving that Jesus[t] was the Messiah.[u]

Saul Escapes from the Jews

23 After some time had passed, the Jews plotted to kill him, 24 but their plot became known to Saul. They were watching the gates day and night so that they might kill him; 25 but his disciples took him by night and let him down through an opening in the wall,[v] lowering him in a basket.

Saul in Jerusalem

26 When he had come to Jerusalem, he attempted to join the disciples; and they were all afraid of him, for they did not believe that he was a disciple. 27 But Barnabas took him, brought him to the apostles, and described for them how on the road he had seen the Lord, who had spoken to him, and how in Damascus he had spoken boldly in the name of Jesus. 28 So he went in and out among them in Jerusalem, speaking boldly in the name of the Lord. 29 He spoke and argued with the Hellenists; but they were attempting to kill him. 30 When the believers[w] learned of it, they brought him down to Caesarea and sent him off to Tarsus.

31 Meanwhile the church throughout Judea, Galilee, and Samaria had peace and was built up.

[t] Gk *that this*
[u] Or *the Christ*
[v] Gk *through the wall*
[w] Gk *brothers*

τὸ ὄνομα τοῦτο, καὶ ὧδε εἰς τοῦτο ἐληλύθει,
this name, and here for this he had come,

ἵνα δεδεμένους αὐτοὺς ἀγάγῃ ἐπὶ τοὺς
that *having been* bound them he might bring before the

ἀρχιερεῖς; 22 Σαῦλος δὲ μᾶλλον ἐνε-
chief priests? But Saul more was filled

δυναμοῦτο καὶ συνέχυννεν Ἰουδαίους τοὺς κατ-
with power and confounded Jews the [ones]

οικοῦντας ἐν Δαμασκῷ, συμβιβάζων ὅτι οὗτός
dwelling in Damascus, proving that this one

ἐστιν ὁ χριστός. 23 Ὡς δὲ ἐπληροῦντο
is the Christ. And when were fulfilled

ἡμέραι ἱκαναί, 24 συνεβουλεύσαντο
days considerable(many), consulted together

οἱ Ἰουδαῖοι ἀνελεῖν αὐτόν· ἐγνώσθη δὲ
the Jews to kill him; but was known

τῷ Σαύλῳ ἡ ἐπιβουλὴ αὐτῶν. παρετη-
– to Saul the plot of them. And they

ροῦντο δὲ καὶ τὰς πύλας ἡμέρας τε καὶ
carefully watched also the gates both by day and

νυκτὸς ὅπως αὐτὸν ἀνέλωσιν· 25 λαβόντες δὲ
by night so as him they might destroy; but [4]taking

οἱ μαθηταὶ αὐτοῦ νυκτὸς διὰ τοῦ
[1]the [2]disciples [3]of him by night through the

τείχους καθῆκαν αὐτὸν χαλάσαντες ἐν
wall let down him lowering in

σπυρίδι. 26 Παραγενόμενος δὲ εἰς
a basket. And arriving at

Ἰερουσαλὴμ ἐπείραζεν κολλᾶσθαι τοῖς
Jerusalem he tried to be joined to the

μαθηταῖς· καὶ πάντες ἐφοβοῦντο αὐτόν,
disciples; and all feared him,

μὴ πιστεύοντες ὅτι ἐστὶν μαθητής.
not believing that he is(was) a disciple.

27 Βαρναβᾶς δὲ ἐπιλαβόμενος αὐτὸν ἤγαγεν
But Barnabas taking hold of him led

πρὸς τοὺς ἀποστόλους, καὶ διηγήσατο
to the apostles, and narrated

αὐτοῖς πῶς ἐν τῇ ὁδῷ εἶδεν τὸν κύριον
to them how in the way he saw the Lord

καὶ ὅτι ἐλάλησεν αὐτῷ, καὶ πῶς ἐν
and that he spoke to him, and how in

Δαμασκῷ ἐπαρρησιάσατο ἐν τῷ ὀνόματι
Damascus he spoke boldly in the name

Ἰησοῦ. 28 καὶ ἦν μετ' αὐτῶν εἰσπορευόμενος
of Jesus. And he was with them going in

καὶ ἐκπορευόμενος εἰς Ἰερουσαλήμ,
and going out in Jerusalem,

παρρησιαζόμενος ἐν τῷ ὀνόματι τοῦ
speaking boldly in the name of the

κυρίου, 29 ἐλάλει τε καὶ συνεζήτει πρὸς
Lord, [2]spoke [1]both [3]and [4]discussed with

τοὺς Ἑλληνιστάς· οἱ δὲ ἐπεχείρουν ἀνελεῖν
the Hellenists; and they attempted to kill

αὐτόν. 30 ἐπιγνόντες δὲ οἱ ἀδελφοὶ
him. But [3]knowing [1]the [2]brothers

κατήγαγον αὐτὸν εἰς Καισάρειαν καὶ
brought down him to Cæsarea and

ἐξαπέστειλαν αὐτὸν εἰς Ταρσόν.
sent forth him to Tarsus.

31 Ἡ μὲν οὖν ἐκκλησία καθ' ὅλης
[2]The – [1]therefore [3]church throughout all

τῆς Ἰουδαίας καὶ Γαλιλαίας καὶ Σαμαρείας
– Judæa and Galilee and Samaria

εἶχεν εἰρήνην οἰκοδομουμένη καὶ πορευομένη
had peace being built and going

he come here to take them as prisoners to the chief priests?" 22 Yet Saul grew more and more powerful and baffled the Jews living in Damascus by proving that Jesus is the Christ.[o]

23 After many days had gone by, the Jews conspired to kill him, 24 but Saul learned of their plan. Day and night they kept close watch on the city gates in order to kill him. 25 But his followers took him by night and lowered him in a basket through an opening in the wall.

26 When he came to Jerusalem, he tried to join the disciples, but they were all afraid of him, not believing that he really was a disciple. 27 But Barnabas took him and brought him to the apostles. He told them how Saul on his journey had seen the Lord and that the Lord had spoken to him, and how in Damascus he had preached fearlessly in the name of Jesus. 28 So Saul stayed with them and moved about freely in Jerusalem, speaking boldly in the name of the Lord. 29 He talked and debated with the Grecian Jews, but they tried to kill him. 30 When the brothers learned of this, they took him down to Caesarea and sent him off to Tarsus.

31 Then the church throughout Judea, Galilee and Samaria enjoyed a time of peace. It was strengthened; and encouraged by

[o] 22 Or *Messiah*

Living in the fear of the Lord and in the comfort of the Holy Spirit, it increased in numbers.

The Healing of Aeneas

32 Now as Peter went here and there among all the believers,[x] he came down also to the saints living in Lydda. 33 There he found a man named Aeneas, who had been bedridden for eight years, for he was paralyzed. 34 Peter said to him, "Aeneas, Jesus Christ heals you; get up and make your bed!" And immediately he got up. 35 And all the residents of Lydda and Sharon saw him and turned to the Lord.

Peter in Lydda and Joppa

36 Now in Joppa there was a disciple whose name was Tabitha, which in Greek is Dorcas.[y] She was devoted to good works and acts of charity. 37 At that time she became ill and died. When they had washed her, they laid her in a room upstairs. 38 Since Lydda was near Joppa, the disciples, who heard that Peter was there, sent two men to him with the request, "Please come to us without delay." 39 So Peter got up and went with them; and when he arrived, they took him to the room upstairs. All the widows stood beside him, weeping and showing tunics and other clothing that Dorcas had made while she was with them. 40 Peter put all of them outside, and then he knelt down and prayed. He turned to the body and said, "Tabitha, get up."

[x] Gk *all of them*

τῷ φόβῳ τοῦ κυρίου, καὶ τῇ παρακλήσει
in the fear of the Lord, and in the comfort
τοῦ ἁγίου πνεύματος ἐπληθύνετο.
of the Holy Spirit was multiplied.
32 Ἐγένετο δὲ Πέτρον διερχόμενον διὰ
Now it came to pass Peter passing *through* through
πάντων κατελθεῖν καὶ πρὸς τοὺς ἁγίους
all [quarters] to come down[b] also to the saints
τοὺς κατοικοῦντας Λύδδα. **33** εὗρεν δὲ
– inhabiting Lydda. And he found
ἐκεῖ ἄνθρωπόν τινα ὀνόματι Αἰνέαν ἐξ
there a certain man by name Aeneas of
ἐτῶν ὀκτὼ κατακείμενον ἐπὶ κραβάτου,
years eight lying on a mattress,
ὃς ἦν παραλελυμένος. **34** καὶ εἶπεν αὐτῷ
who was *having been* paralysed. And said to him
ὁ Πέτρος· Αἰνέα, ἰᾶταί σε Ἰησοῦς Χριστός·
– Peter: Aeneas, cures thee Jesus Christ;
ἀνάστηθι καὶ στρῶσον σεαυτῷ. καὶ
rise up and gird thyself. And
εὐθέως ἀνέστη. **35** καὶ εἶδαν αὐτὸν
immediately he rose up. And saw him
πάντες οἱ κατοικοῦντες Λύδδα καὶ τὸν
all the [ones] inhabiting Lydda and –
Σαρῶνα, οἵτινες ἐπέστρεψαν ἐπὶ τὸν κύριον.
Saron, who turned to the Lord.
Ἐν Ἰόππῃ δέ τις ἦν μαθήτρια ὀνόματι
[2]in [3]Joppa [1]Now [5]a certain [4]was [6]disciple by name
Ταβιθά, **36** ἣ διερμηνευομένη λέγεται
Tabitha, who being translated is called
Δορκάς· αὕτη ἦν πλήρης ἔργων ἀγαθῶν
Dorcas; this woman was full works of good
καὶ ἐλεημοσυνῶν ὧν ἐποίει. **37** ἐγένετο δὲ
and of alms which she did. And it happened
ἐν ταῖς ἡμέραις ἐκείναις ἀσθενήσασαν
in those days ailing
αὐτὴν ἀποθανεῖν· λούσαντες δὲ ἔθηκαν
she to die[b]; and having washed they put [her]
=being ill she died;
ἐν ὑπερῴῳ. **38** ἐγγὺς δὲ οὔσης Λύδδας
in an upper room. Now [3]near [2]being [1]Lydda[a]
τῇ Ἰόππῃ οἱ μαθηταὶ ἀκούσαντες ὅτι
– to Joppa the disciples having heard that
Πέτρος ἐστὶν ἐν αὐτῇ ἀπέστειλαν δύο
Peter is(was) in it sent two
ἄνδρας πρὸς αὐτὸν παρακαλοῦντες· μὴ
men to him beseeching: [2]not
ὀκνήσῃς διελθεῖν ἕως ἡμῶν. **39** ἀναστὰς δὲ
[1]hesitate to come to us. And rising up
Πέτρος συνῆλθεν αὐτοῖς· ὃν παραγενόμενον
Peter went with them; whom arriving
ἀνήγαγον εἰς τὸ ὑπερῷον, καὶ παρέστησαν
they led up into the upper room, and stood by
αὐτῷ πᾶσαι αἱ χῆραι κλαίουσαι καὶ
him all the widows weeping and
ἐπιδεικνύμεναι χιτῶνας καὶ ἱμάτια, ὅσα
showing tunics and garments, which
ἐποίει μετ' αὐτῶν οὖσα ἡ Δορκάς.
[3]made [4]with [5]them [2]being – [1]Dorcas.
40 ἐκβαλὼν δὲ ἔξω πάντας ὁ Πέτρος
And [2]putting *out* [4]outside [3]all – [1]Peter
καὶ θεὶς τὰ γόνατα προσηύξατο, καὶ
and placing the knees he prayed, and
=kneeling down
ἐπιστρέψας πρὸς τὸ σῶμα εἶπεν· Ταβιθά,
turning to the body said: Tabitha,

the Holy Spirit, it grew in numbers, living in the fear of the Lord.

Aeneas and Dorcas

32 As Peter traveled about the country, he went to visit the saints in Lydda. 33 There he found a man named Aeneas, a paralytic who had been bedridden for eight years. 34 "Aeneas," Peter said to him, "Jesus Christ heals you. Get up and take care of your mat." Immediately Aeneas got up. 35 All those who lived in Lydda and Sharon saw him and turned to the Lord.

36 In Joppa there was a disciple named Tabitha (which, when translated, is Dorcas[p]), who was always doing good and helping the poor. 37 About that time she became sick and died, and her body was washed and placed in an upstairs room. 38 Lydda was near Joppa; so when the disciples heard that Peter was in Lydda, they sent two men to him and urged him, "Please come at once!"

39 Peter went with them, and when he arrived he was taken upstairs to the room. All the widows stood around him, crying and showing him the robes and other clothing that Dorcas had made while she was still with them.

40 Peter sent them all out of the room; then he got down on his knees and prayed. Turning toward the dead woman, he said,

[p]36 Both *Tabitha* (Aramaic) and *Dorcas* (Greek) mean *gazelle*.

Then she opened her eyes,
and seeing Peter, she sat
up. 41 He gave her his hand
and helped her up. Then
calling the saints and widows, he showed her to be
alive. 42 This became
known throughout Joppa,
and many believed in the
Lord. 43 Meanwhile he
stayed in Joppa for some
time with a certain Simon,
a tanner.

Chapter 10

Peter and Cornelius

IN Caesarea there was a
man named Cornelius, a
centurion of the Italian Cohort, as it was called. 2 He
was a devout man who
feared God with all his
household; he gave alms
generously to the people
and prayed constantly to
God. 3 One afternoon at
about three o'clock he had
a vision in which he clearly
saw an angel of God com-
ing in and saying to him,
"Cornelius." 4 He stared at
him in terror and said,
"What is it, Lord?" He answered, "Your prayers and
your alms have ascended
as a memorial before God.
5 Now send men to Joppa
for a certain Simon who is
called Peter; 6 he is lodging
with Simon, a tanner,
whose house is by the seaside." 7 When the angel
who spoke to him had left,
he called two of his slaves
and a devout soldier from
the ranks of those who
served him, 8 and after telling them everything, he

[y] The name Tabitha in Aramaic and the name Dorcas in Greek mean *a gazelle*

ἀνάστηθι. ἡ δὲ ἤνοιξεν τοὺς ὀφθαλμοὺς
rise up. And she opened the eyes

αὐτῆς, καὶ ἰδοῦσα τὸν Πέτρον ἀνεκάθισεν.
of her, and seeing – Peter sat up.

41 δοὺς δὲ αὐτῇ χεῖρα ἀνέστησεν αὐτήν·
And giving her a hand he raised up her;

φωνήσας δὲ τοὺς ἁγίους καὶ τὰς χήρας
and calling the saints and the widows

παρέστησεν αὐτὴν ζῶσαν. **42** γνωστὸν δὲ
he presented her living. And known

ἐγένετο καθ' ὅλης τῆς Ἰόππης, καὶ
it became throughout all – Joppa, and

ἐπίστευσαν πολλοὶ ἐπὶ τὸν κύριον.
believed many on the Lord.

43 Ἐγένετο δὲ ἡμέρας ἱκανὰς μεῖναι ἐν
And it came to pass days several to remain in
=he remained many days

Ἰόππῃ παρά τινι Σίμωνι βυρσεῖ.
Joppa with one Simon a tanner.

10 Ἀνὴρ δέ τις ἐν Καισαρείᾳ ὀνόματι
Now a certain man in Cæsarea by name

Κορνήλιος, ἑκατοντάρχης ἐκ σπείρης τῆς
Cornelius, a centurion of a cohort –

καλουμένης Ἰταλικῆς, **2** εὐσεβὴς καὶ
being called Italian, devout and

φοβούμενος τὸν θεὸν σὺν παντὶ τῷ οἴκῳ
fearing – God with all the household

αὐτοῦ, ποιῶν ἐλεημοσύνας πολλὰς τῷ
of him, doing alms many to the

λαῷ καὶ δεόμενος τοῦ θεοῦ διὰ παντός,
people and petitioning – God continually,

3 εἶδεν ἐν ὁράματι φανερῶς, ὡσεὶ περὶ
saw in a vision clearly, as it were around

ὥραν ἐνάτην τῆς ἡμέρας, ἄγγελον τοῦ
hour ninth of the day, an angel –

θεοῦ εἰσελθόντα πρὸς αὐτὸν καὶ εἰπόντα
of God entering to him and saying

αὐτῷ· Κορνήλιε. **4** ὁ δὲ ἀτενίσας αὐτῷ
to him: Cornelius. And he gazing at him

καὶ ἔμφοβος γενόμενος εἶπεν· τί ἐστιν,
and terrified becoming said: What is it,

κύριε; εἶπεν δὲ αὐτῷ· αἱ προσευχαί
lord? And he said to him: The prayers

σου καὶ αἱ ἐλεημοσύναι σου ἀνέβησαν
of thee and the alms of thee went up

εἰς μνημόσυνον ἔμπροσθεν τοῦ θεοῦ. **5** καὶ
for a memorial before – God. And

νῦν πέμψον ἄνδρας εἰς Ἰόππην καὶ
now send men to Joppa and

μετάπεμψαι Σίμωνά τινα ὃς ἐπικαλεῖται
[summon ²Simon ¹one who is surnamed

Πέτρος· **6** οὗτος ξενίζεται παρά τινι
Peter; this man is lodged with one

Σίμωνι βυρσεῖ, ᾧ ἐστιν οἰκία παρὰ
Simon a tanner, to whom is a house[c] by
=who has a house

θάλασσαν. **7** ὡς δὲ ἀπῆλθεν ὁ ἄγγελος ὁ
[the] sea. And as went away the angel –

λαλῶν αὐτῷ, φωνήσας δύο τῶν οἰκετῶν
speaking to him, calling two of the household slaves

καὶ στρατιώτην εὐσεβῆ τῶν προσκαρτερούν-
and soldier a devout of the [ones] waiting

των αὐτῷ, **8** καὶ ἐξηγησάμενος ἅπαντα
on him, and explaining all things

"Tabitha, get up." She
opened her eyes, and see-
ing Peter she sat up. 41 He
took her by the hand and
helped her to her feet. Then
he called the believers and
the widows and presented
her to them alive. 42 This
became known all over
Joppa, and many people
believed in the Lord. 43 Peter stayed in Joppa for
some time with a tanner
named Simon.

Chapter 10

Cornelius Calls for Peter

AT Caesarea there was a
man named Corneli-
us, a centurion in what was
known as the Italian Regi-
ment. 2 He and all his family
were devout and God-fear-
ing; he gave generously to
those in need and prayed to
God regularly. 3 One day at
about three in the after-
noon he had a vision. He
distinctly saw an angel of
God, who came to him and
said, "Cornelius!"
4 Cornelius stared at him
in fear. "What is it, Lord?"
he asked.
The angel answered,
"Your prayers and gifts to
the poor have come up as a
memorial offering before
God. 5 Now send men to
Joppa to bring back a man
named Simon who is called
Peter. 6 He is staying with
Simon the tanner, whose
house is by the sea."
7 When the angel who
spoke to him had gone,
Cornelius called two of his
servants and a devout soldier who was one of his attendants. 8 He told them ev-

sent them to Joppa.
9 About noon the next
day, as they were on their
journey and approaching
the city, Peter went up on
the roof to pray. 10 He became hungry and wanted
something to eat; and while
it was being prepared, he
fell into a trance. 11 He saw
the heaven opened and
something like a large sheet
coming down, being low-
ered to the ground by its
four corners. 12 In it were
all kinds of four-footed
creatures and reptiles and
birds of the air. 13 Then he
heard a voice saying, "Get
up, Peter; kill and eat."
14 But Peter said, "By no
means, Lord; for I have
never eaten anything that is
profane or unclean." 15 The
voice said to him again, a
second time, "What God
has made clean, you must
not call profane." 16 This
happened three times, and
the thing was suddenly tak-
en up to heaven.
17 Now while Peter was
greatly puzzled about what
to make of the vision that
he had seen, suddenly the
men sent by Cornelius ap-
peared. They were asking
for Simon's house and
were standing by the gate.
18 They called out to ask
whether Simon, who was
called Peter, was staying
there. 19 While Peter was
still thinking about the vision, the Spirit said to him,
"Look, three[z] men are
searching for you. 20 Now
get up, go down, and go
with them without hesita-
tion; for I have sent them."

[z] One ancient authority reads *two*; others lack the word

αὐτοῖς ἀπέστειλεν αὐτοὺς εἰς τὴν Ἰόππην.
to them sent them to – Joppa.
9 Τῇ δὲ ἐπαύριον ὁδοιπορούντων ἐκείνων
And on the morrow journeying those
καὶ τῇ πόλει ἐγγιζόντων ἀνέβη Πέτρος
and to the city drawing near[a] went up Peter
=as they journeyed and drew near to the city
ἐπὶ τὸ δῶμα προσεύξασθαι περὶ ὥραν
onto the roof to pray about hour
ἕκτην. 10 ἐγένετο δὲ πρόσπεινος καὶ
sixth. And he became hungry and
ἤθελεν γεύσασθαι· παρασκευαζόντων δὲ
wished to taste(eat); and preparing
=while they prepared
αὐτῶν ἐγένετο ἐπ' αὐτὸν ἔκστασις, 11 καὶ
them[a] there came on him an ecstasy, and
θεωρεῖ τὸν οὐρανὸν ἀνεῳγμένον καὶ
he beholds the heaven having been opened and
καταβαῖνον σκεῦός τι ὡς ὀθόνην μεγάλην,
coming down a certain vessel like sheet a great,
τέσσαρσιν ἀρχαῖς καθιέμενον ἐπὶ τῆς γῆς,
by four corners being let down onto the earth,
12 ἐν ᾧ ὑπῆρχεν πάντα τὰ τετράποδα
in which were all the quadrupeds
καὶ ἑρπετὰ τῆς γῆς καὶ πετεινὰ τοῦ
and reptiles of the earth and birds of the
οὐρανοῦ. 13 καὶ ἐγένετο φωνὴ πρὸς
heaven(air). And there came a voice to
αὐτόν· ἀναστάς, Πέτρε, θῦσον καὶ φάγε.
him: Rise up, Peter, slay and eat.
14 ὁ δὲ Πέτρος εἶπεν· μηδαμῶς, κύριε,
– But Peter said: Not at all, Lord,
ὅτι οὐδέποτε ἔφαγον πᾶν κοινὸν καὶ
because never did I eat every(any)thing common and
ἀκάθαρτον. 15 καὶ φωνὴ πάλιν ἐκ δευτέρου
unclean. And a voice again a second [time]
πρὸς αὐτόν· ἃ ὁ θεὸς ἐκαθάρισεν σὺ
[came] to him: What things – God cleansed [3]thou
μὴ κοίνου. 16 τοῦτο δὲ ἐγένετο ἐπὶ
[2]not [1]treat [4]as [5]unclean. And this occurred on
τρίς, καὶ εὐθὺς ἀνελήμφθη τὸ σκεῦος
three [occasions], and immediately was taken up the vessel
εἰς τὸν οὐρανόν. 17 Ὡς δὲ ἐν ἑαυτῷ
into – heaven. Now as in himself
διηπόρει ὁ Πέτρος τί ἂν εἴη τὸ ὅραμα
was doubting – Peter what might be the vision
ὃ εἶδεν, ἰδοὺ οἱ ἄνδρες οἱ ἀπεσταλμένοι
which he saw, behold[,] the men – *having been* sent
ὑπὸ τοῦ Κορνηλίου διερωτήσαντες τὴν
by – Cornelius asking for the
οἰκίαν τοῦ Σίμωνος ἐπέστησαν ἐπὶ τὸν
house – of Simon stood *at* at the
πυλῶνα, 18 καὶ φωνήσαντες ἐπυνθάνοντο
porch, and calling inquired
εἰ Σίμων ὁ ἐπικαλούμενος Πέτρος ἐνθάδε
if Simon – *being* surnamed Peter here
ξενίζεται. 19 Τοῦ δὲ Πέτρου διενθυμουμένου
is lodged. – And Peter pondering[a]
=while Peter pondered
περὶ τοῦ ὁράματος εἶπεν τὸ πνεῦμα·
about the vision [3]said [1]the [2]Spirit:
ἰδοὺ ἄνδρες δύο ζητοῦντές σε· 20 ἀλλὰ
Behold[,] men two seeking thee: but
ἀναστὰς κατάβηθι, καὶ πορεύου σὺν αὐτοῖς
rising up go down, and go with them
μηδὲν διακρινόμενος, ὅτι ἐγὼ ἀπέσταλκα
nothing doubting, because I have sent

erything that had happened
and sent them to Joppa.

Peter's Vision

9 About noon the follow-
ing day as they were on
their journey and ap-
proaching the city, Peter
went up on the roof to pray.
10 He became hungry and
wanted something to eat,
and while the meal was being prepared, he fell into a
trance. 11 He saw heaven
opened and something like
a large sheet being let down
to earth by its four corners.
12 It contained all kinds of
four-footed animals, as
well as reptiles of the earth
and birds of the air. 13 Then
a voice told him, "Get up,
Peter. Kill and eat."
14 "Surely not, Lord!"
Peter replied. "I have never eaten anything impure or
unclean."
15 The voice spoke to him
a second time, "Do not call
anything impure that God
has made clean."
16 This happened three
times, and immediately the
sheet was taken back to
heaven.
17 While Peter was won-
dering about the meaning
of the vision, the men sent
by Cornelius found out
where Simon's house was
and stopped at the gate.
18 They called out, asking if
Simon who was known as
Peter was staying there.
19 While Peter was still
thinking about the vision,
the Spirit said to him, "Simon, three[q] men are looking for you. 20 So get up and
go downstairs. Do not hesitate to go with them, for I
have sent them."

[q] *19* One early manuscript *two*; other manuscripts do not have the number.

21So Peter went down to
the men and said, "I am the
one you are looking for;
what is the reason for your
coming?" 22They an-
swered, "Cornelius, a centurion, an upright and God-
fearing man, who is well
spoken of by the whole
Jewish nation, was directed
by a holy angel to send for
you to come to his house
and to hear what you have
to say." 23So Peter[a] invited them in and gave them
lodging.
The next day he got up
and went with them, and
some of the believers[b]
from Joppa accompanied
him. 24The following day
they came to Caesarea.
Cornelius was expecting
them and had called together his relatives and close
friends. 25On Peter's arrival Cornelius met him, and
falling at his feet, wor-
shiped him. 26But Peter
made him get up, saying,
"Stand up; I am only a mortal." 27And as he talked
with him, he went in and
found that many had as-
sembled; 28and he said to
them, "You yourselves
know that it is unlawful for
a Jew to associate with or
to visit a Gentile; but God
has shown me that I should
not call anyone profane or
unclean. 29So when I was
sent for, I came without objection. Now may I ask
why you sent for me?"
30 Cornelius replied,
"Four days ago at this very
hour, at three o'clock, I
was praying in my house

[a] Gk *he*
[b] Gk *brothers*

αὐτούς. **21** καταβὰς δὲ Πέτρος πρὸς
them. And going down Peter to

τοὺς ἄνδρας εἶπεν· ἰδοὺ ἐγώ εἰμι ὅν
the men said: Behold[,] I am [he] whom

ζητεῖτε· τίς ἡ αἰτία δι' ἣν πάρεστε;
ye seek; what [is] the cause for which ye are here?

22 οἱ δὲ εἶπαν· Κορνήλιος ἑκατοντάρχης,
And they said: Cornelius a centurion,

ἀνὴρ δίκαιος καὶ φοβούμενος τὸν θεόν,
a man just and fearing – God,

μαρτυρούμενός τε ὑπὸ ὅλου τοῦ ἔθνους
and being witnessed to by all the nation

τῶν Ἰουδαίων, ἐχρηματίσθη ὑπὸ ἀγγέλου
of the Jews, was warned by angel

ἁγίου μεταπέμψασθαί σε εἰς τὸν οἶκον
a holy to summon thee to the house

αὐτοῦ καὶ ἀκοῦσαι ῥήματα παρὰ σοῦ.
of him and to hear words from thee.

23 εἰσκαλεσάμενος οὖν αὐτοὺς ἐξένισεν.
Calling in therefore them he lodged.

Τῇ δὲ ἐπαύριον ἀναστὰς ἐξῆλθεν σὺν
And on the morrow rising up he went forth with

αὐτοῖς, καί τινες τῶν ἀδελφῶν τῶν
them, and some of the brothers –

ἀπὸ Ἰόππης συνῆλθον αὐτῷ. **24** τῇ δὲ
from Joppa accompanied him. And on the

ἐπαύριον εἰσῆλθεν εἰς τὴν Καισάρειαν·
morrow he entered into – Cæsarea;

ὁ δὲ Κορνήλιος ἦν προσδοκῶν αὐτούς,
– and Cornelius was awaiting them,

συγκαλεσάμενος τοὺς συγγενεῖς αὐτοῦ καὶ
having called together the relatives of him and

τοὺς ἀναγκαίους φίλους. **25** Ὡς δὲ
the intimate friends. Now when

ἐγένετο τοῦ εἰσελθεῖν τὸν Πέτρον,
it came to pass the to enter – Peter,[b]
= Now it came to pass when Peter entered,

συναντήσας αὐτῷ ὁ Κορνήλιος πεσὼν
[2]meeting [3]him – [1]Cornelius falling

ἐπὶ τοὺς πόδας προσεκύνησεν. **26** ὁ δὲ
at the(his) feet worshipped. – But

Πέτρος ἤγειρεν αὐτὸν λέγων· ἀνάστηθι·
Peter raised him saying: Stand up;

καὶ ἐγὼ αὐτὸς ἄνθρωπός εἰμι. **27** καὶ
also I [my]self a man am. And

συνομιλῶν αὐτῷ εἰσῆλθεν, καὶ εὑρίσκει
talking with him he entered, and finds

συνεληλυθότας πολλούς, **28** ἔφη τε πρὸς
having come together many, and said to

αὐτούς· ὑμεῖς ἐπίστασθε ὡς ἀθέμιτόν ἐστιν
them: Ye understand how unlawful it is

ἀνδρὶ Ἰουδαίῳ κολλᾶσθαι ἢ προσέρχεσθαι
for *a man* a Jew to adhere or to approach

ἀλλοφύλῳ· κἀμοὶ ὁ θεὸς ἔδειξεν μηδένα
a foreigner; and to me – God showed [2]not any

κοινὸν ἢ ἀκάθαρτον λέγειν ἄνθρωπον·
[4]common [5]or [6]unclean [1]to call [3]man;

29 διὸ καὶ ἀναντιρρήτως ἦλθον μετα-
wherefore indeed [3]unquestioningly [2]I came [1]being

πεμφθείς. πυνθάνομαι οὖν, τίνι λόγῳ
summoned. I inquire therefore, for what reason

μετεπέμψασθέ με; **30** καὶ ὁ Κορνήλιος
ye summoned me? And – Cornelius

ἔφη· ἀπὸ τετάρτης ἡμέρας μέχρι ταύτης τῆς
said: From fourth day until this –
= Four days ago

ὥρας ἤμην τὴν ἐνάτην προσευχόμενος
hour I was [at] the ninth praying

21Peter went down and
said to the men, "I'm the
one you're looking for.
Why have you come?"
22The men replied, "We
have come from Cornelius
the centurion. He is a righteous and God-fearing man,
who is respected by all the
Jewish people. A holy an-
gel told him to have you
come to his house so that
he could hear what you
have to say." 23Then Peter
invited the men into the
house to be his guests.

Peter at Cornelius' House

The next day Peter start-
ed out with them, and some
of the brothers from Joppa
went along. 24The follow-
ing day he arrived in Caesarea. Cornelius was expecting them and had called together his relatives and
close friends. 25As Peter
entered the house, Cornelius met him and fell at his
feet in reverence. 26But Peter made him get up.
"Stand up," he said, "I am
only a man myself."
27Talking with him, Peter
went inside and found a
large gathering of people.
28He said to them: "You
are well aware that it is
against our law for a Jew to
associate with a Gentile or
visit him. But God has
shown me that I should not
call any man impure or unclean. 29So when I was sent
for, I came without raising
any objection. May I ask
why you sent for me?"
30Cornelius answered:
"Four days ago I was in my
house praying at this hour,
at three in the afternoon.

when suddenly a man in
dazzling clothes stood before me. 31 He said, 'Cornelius, your prayer has
been heard and your alms
have been remembered be-
fore God. 32 Send therefore
to Joppa and ask for Simon,
who is called Peter; he is
staying in the home of Simon, a tanner, by the sea.'
33 Therefore I sent for you
immediately, and you have
been kind enough to come.
So now all of us are here in
the presence of God to listen to all that the Lord has
commanded you to say."

Gentiles Hear the Good News

34 Then Peter began to
speak to them: "I truly understand that God shows
no partiality, 35 but in every
nation anyone who fears
him and does what is right
is acceptable to him. 36 You
know the message he sent
to the people of Israel,
preaching peace by Jesus
Christ—he is Lord of all.
37 That message spread
throughout Judea, begin-
ning in Galilee after the
baptism that John an-
nounced: 38 how God
anointed Jesus of Nazareth
with the Holy Spirit and
with power; how he went
about doing good and healing all who were oppressed
by the devil, for God was
with him. 39 We are wit-
nesses to all that he did
both in Judea and in Jerusalem. They put him to death
by hanging him on a tree;
40 but God raised him on the
third day and allowed him

ἐν τῷ οἴκῳ μου, καὶ ἰδοὺ ἀνὴρ ἔστη
in the house of me, and behold[,] a man stood

ἐνώπιόν μου ἐν ἐσθῆτι λαμπρᾷ, **31** καὶ
before me in clothing bright, and

φησίν· Κορνήλιε, εἰσηκούσθη σου ἡ
says: Cornelius, was heard of thee the

προσευχὴ καὶ αἱ ἐλεημοσύναι σου ἐμνήσθησαν
prayer and the alms of thee were remembered

ἐνώπιον τοῦ θεοῦ. **32** πέμψον οὖν εἰς
before – God. Send thou therefore to

Ἰόππην καὶ μετακάλεσαι Σίμωνα ὃς ἐπι-
Joppa and send for Simon who is

καλεῖται Πέτρος· οὗτος ξενίζεται ἐν οἰκίᾳ
surnamed Peter; this man is lodged in [the] house

Σίμωνος βυρσέως παρὰ θάλασσαν. **33** ἐξαυτῆς
of Simon a tanner by [the] sea. At once

οὖν ἔπεμψα πρὸς σέ, σύ τε καλῶς
therefore I sent to thee, and thou well

ἐποίησας παραγενόμενος. νῦν οὖν πάντες
didst arriving. Now therefore all

ἡμεῖς ἐνώπιον τοῦ θεοῦ πάρεσμεν ἀκοῦσαι
we before – God are present to hear

πάντα τὰ προστεταγμένα σοι ὑπὸ τοῦ
all the things having been commanded thee by the

κυρίου. **34** Ἀνοίξας δὲ Πέτρος τὸ στόμα
Lord. And opening Peter the(his) mouth

εἶπεν· ἐπ' ἀληθείας καταλαμβάνομαι ὅτι
said: On(in) truth I perceive that

οὐκ ἔστιν προσωπολήμπτης ὁ θεός, **35** ἀλλ'
³not ²is ⁴a respecter of persons – ¹God, but

ἐν παντὶ ἔθνει ὁ φοβούμενος αὐτὸν καὶ
in every nation the [one] fearing him and

ἐργαζόμενος δικαιοσύνην δεκτὸς αὐτῷ ἐστιν·
working righteousness acceptable to him is;

36 τὸν λόγον ὃν ἀπέστειλεν τοῖς υἱοῖς
the word which he sent to the sons

Ἰσραὴλ εὐαγγελιζόμενος εἰρήνην διὰ Ἰησοῦ
of Israel preaching peace through Jesus

Χριστοῦ· οὗτός ἐστιν πάντων κύριος.
Christ: this one is of all Lord.

37 ὑμεῖς οἴδατε τὸ γενόμενον ῥῆμα καθ'
Ye know the having become thing throughout
=that which took place

ὅλης τῆς Ἰουδαίας, ἀρξάμενος ἀπὸ τῆς
all – Judæa, beginning from –

Γαλιλαίας μετὰ τὸ βάπτισμα ὃ ἐκήρυξεν
Galilee after the baptism which ²proclaimed

Ἰωάννης, **38** Ἰησοῦν τὸν ἀπὸ Ναζαρέθ,
¹John, Jesus the one from Nazareth,

ὡς ἔχρισεν αὐτὸν ὁ θεὸς πνεύματι ἁγίῳ
how anointed him – God with Spirit Holy

καὶ δυνάμει, ὃς διῆλθεν εὐεργετῶν καὶ
and power, who went about doing good and

ἰώμενος πάντας τοὺς καταδυναστευομένους
curing all the [ones] being oppressed

ὑπὸ τοῦ διαβόλου, ὅτι ὁ θεὸς ἦν μετ'
by the devil, because – God was with

αὐτοῦ· **39** καὶ ἡμεῖς μάρτυρες πάντων
him; and we [are] witnesses of all things

ὧν ἐποίησεν ἔν τε τῇ χώρᾳ τῶν Ἰουδαίων
which he did both in the country of the Jews

καὶ Ἰερουσαλήμ· ὃν καὶ ἀνεῖλαν
and Jerusalem; whom indeed they killed

κρεμάσαντες ἐπὶ ξύλου. **40** τοῦτον ὁ
hanging on a tree. This one -

θεὸς ἤγειρεν ἐν τῇ τρίτῃ ἡμέρᾳ καὶ
God raised on the third day and

Suddenly a man in shining
clothes stood before me
31 and said, 'Cornelius, God
has heard your prayer and
remembered your gifts to
the poor. 32 Send to Joppa
for Simon who is called Peter. He is a guest in the
home of Simon the tanner,
who lives by the sea.' 33 So I
sent for you immediately,
and it was good of you to
come. Now we are all here
in the presence of God to
listen to everything the
Lord has commanded you
to tell us."
34 Then Peter began to
speak: "I now realize how
true it is that God does not
show favoritism 35 but accepts men from every na-
tion who fear him and do
what is right. 36 You know
the message God sent to
the people of Israel, telling
the good news of peace
through Jesus Christ, who
is Lord of all. 37 You know
what has happened
throughout Judea, begin-
ning in Galilee after the
baptism that John preached
—38 how God anointed
Jesus of Nazareth with the
Holy Spirit and power, and
how he went around doing
good and healing all who
were under the power of
the devil, because God was
with him.
39 "We are witnesses of
everything he did in the
country of the Jews and in
Jerusalem. They killed him
by hanging him on a tree,
40 but God raised him from
the dead on the third day

to appear, [41] not to all the
people but to us who were
chosen by God as wit-
nesses, and who ate and
drank with him after he
rose from the dead. [42] He
commanded us to preach to
the people and to testify
that he is the one ordained
by God as judge of the living and the dead. [43] All the
prophets testify about him
that everyone who believes
in him receives forgiveness
of sins through his name."

Gentiles Receive the Holy Spirit

44 While Peter was still
speaking, the Holy Spirit
fell upon all who heard the
word. [45] The circumcised
believers who had come
with Peter were astounded
that the gift of the Holy
Spirit had been poured out
even on the Gentiles, [46] for
they heard them speaking
in tongues and extolling
God. Then Peter said,
[47] "Can anyone withhold
the water for baptizing
these people who have re-
ceived the Holy Spirit just
as we have?" [48] So he ordered them to be baptized
in the name of Jesus Christ.
Then they invited him to
stay for several days.

ἔδωκεν αὐτὸν ἐμφανῆ γενέσθαι, **41** οὐ
gave him visible to become, not

παντὶ τῷ λαῷ, ἀλλὰ μάρτυσιν τοῖς
to all the people, but to witnesses –

προκεχειροτονημένοις ὑπὸ τοῦ θεοῦ, ἡμῖν,
having been previously appointed by – God, to us,

οἵτινες συνεφάγομεν καὶ συνεπίομεν αὐτῷ
who ate with and drank with him

μετὰ τὸ ἀναστῆναι αὐτὸν ἐκ νεκρῶν·
after the to rise again him[b] out of [the] dead;
=he rose again

42 καὶ παρήγγειλεν ἡμῖν κηρῦξαι τῷ λαῷ
and he commanded us to proclaim to the people

καὶ διαμαρτύρασθαι ὅτι οὗτός ἐστιν ὁ
and solemnly to witness that this man is the [one]

ὡρισμένος ὑπὸ τοῦ θεοῦ κριτὴς ζώντων
having been designated by – God judge of living

καὶ νεκρῶν. **43** τούτῳ πάντες οἱ προφῆται
and of dead. To this man all the prophets

μαρτυροῦσιν, ἄφεσιν ἁμαρτιῶν λαβεῖν διὰ
witness, [6]forgiveness [7]of sins [5]to receive [8]through

τοῦ ὀνόματος αὐτοῦ πάντα τὸν πιστεύοντα
[9]the [10]name [11]of him [1]everyone [2]believing

εἰς αὐτόν. **44** Ἔτι λαλοῦντος τοῦ Πέτρου
[3]in [4]him. Yet speaking – Peter[a]
=While Peter was still speaking

τὰ ῥήματα ταῦτα ἐπέπεσεν τὸ πνεῦμα
these words [4]fell *on* [1]the [3]Spirit

τὸ ἅγιον ἐπὶ πάντας τοὺς ἀκούοντας
– [2]Holy on all the [ones] hearing

τὸν λόγον. **45** καὶ ἐξέστησαν οἱ ἐκ
the discourse. And [6]were amazed [1]the [3]of [the]

περιτομῆς πιστοὶ ὅσοι συνῆλθαν τῷ Πέτρῳ,
[4]circumcision [2]faithful as many as accompanied – Peter,

ὅτι καὶ ἐπὶ τὰ ἔθνη ἡ δωρεὰ τοῦ ἁγίου
because also on the nations the gift of the Holy

πνεύματος ἐκκέχυται· **46** ἤκουον γὰρ
Spirit has been poured out; for they heard

αὐτῶν λαλούντων γλώσσαις καὶ μεγαλυνόν-
them speaking in tongues and magnify-

των τὸν θεόν. τότε ἀπεκρίθη Πέτρος·
ing – God. Then answered Peter:

47 μήτι τὸ ὕδωρ δύναται κωλῦσαί τις
Not [4]the [5]water [1]can [3]*to* forbid [2]anyone

τοῦ μὴ βαπτισθῆναι τούτους, οἵτινες τὸ
– [7]not [8]to be baptized[d] [6]these, who the

πνεῦμα τὸ ἅγιον ἔλαβον ὡς καὶ ἡμεῖς;
Spirit – Holy received as also we?

48 προσέταξεν δὲ αὐτοὺς ἐν τῷ ὀνόματι
And he commanded them in the name

Ἰησοῦ Χριστοῦ βαπτισθῆναι. τότε ἠρώτησαν
of Jesus Christ to be baptized. Then they asked

αὐτὸν ἐπιμεῖναι ἡμέρας τινάς.
him to remain days some.

and caused him to be seen.
[41] He was not seen by all the
people, but by witnesses
whom God had already
chosen—by us who ate and
drank with him after he
rose from the dead. [42] He
commanded us to preach to
the people and to testify
that he is the one whom
God appointed as judge of
the living and the dead.
[43] All the prophets testify
about him that everyone
who believes in him re-
ceives forgiveness of sins
through his name."
[44] While Peter was still
speaking these words, the
Holy Spirit came on all who
heard the message. [45] The
circumcised believers who
had come with Peter were
astonished that the gift of
the Holy Spirit had been
poured out even on the
Gentiles. [46] For they heard
them speaking in tongues[r]
and praising God.
Then Peter said, [47] "Can
anyone keep these people
from being baptized with
water? They have received
the Holy Spirit just as we
have." [48] So he ordered that
they be baptized in the
name of Jesus Christ. Then
they asked Peter to stay
with them for a few days.

Chapter 11

Peter's Report to the Church at Jerusalem

NOW the apostles and
the believers[c] who
were in Judea heard that
the Gentiles had also ac-
cepted the word of God.
[2] So when Peter went up to
Jerusalem, the circumcised

11 Ἤκουσαν δὲ οἱ ἀπόστολοι καὶ οἱ
Now heard the apostles and the

ἀδελφοὶ οἱ ὄντες κατὰ τὴν Ἰουδαίαν
brothers – being throughout – Judæa

ὅτι καὶ τὰ ἔθνη ἐδέξαντο τὸν λόγον
that also the nations received the word

τοῦ θεοῦ. **2** Ὅτε δὲ ἀνέβη Πέτρος εἰς
– of God. And when went up Peter to

Ἰερουσαλήμ, διεκρίνοντο πρὸς αὐτὸν οἱ
Jerusalem, disputed with him the [ones]

Chapter 11

Peter Explains His Actions

THE apostles and the
brothers throughout
Judea heard that the Gen-
tiles also had received the
word of God. [2] So when Peter went up to Jerusalem,

[c] Gk *brothers*

[r] 46 Or *other languages*

believers[d] criticized him,
3saying, "Why did you go
to uncircumcised men and
eat with them?" 4Then Pe-
ter began to explain it to
them, step by step, saying,
5"I was in the city of Joppa
praying, and in a trance I
saw a vision. There was
something like a large sheet
coming down from heaven,
being lowered by its four
corners; and it came close
to me. 6As I looked at it
closely I saw four-footed
animals, beasts of prey,
reptiles, and birds of the
air. 7I also heard a voice
saying to me, 'Get up, Peter; kill and eat.' 8But I replied, 'By no means, Lord;
for nothing profane or unclean has ever entered my
mouth.' 9But a second time
the voice answered from
heaven, 'What God has
made clean, you must not
call profane.' 10This happened three times; then everything was pulled up
again to heaven. 11At that
very moment three men,
sent to me from Caesarea,
arrived at the house where
we were. 12The Spirit told
me to go with them and not
to make a distinction be-
tween them and us.[e] These
six brothers also accompanied me, and we entered
the man's house. 13He told
us how he had seen the angel standing in his house
and saying, 'Send to Joppa
and bring Simon, who is
called Peter; 14he will give
you a message by which
you and your entire household will be saved.' 15And

[d] Gk lacks *believers*
[e] Or *not to hesitate*

ἐκ περιτομῆς **3** λέγοντες ὅτι εἰσῆλθες
of [the] circumcision saying[,] – Thou enteredst

πρὸς ἄνδρας ἀκροβυστίαν ἔχοντας καὶ
to men uncircumcision having and

συνέφαγες αὐτοῖς. **4** ἀρξάμενος δὲ Πέτρος
didst eat with them. And beginning Peter

ἐξετίθετο αὐτοῖς καθεξῆς λέγων· **5** ἐγὼ
explained to them in order saying: I

ἤμην ἐν πόλει Ἰόππῃ προσευχόμενος, καὶ
was in [the] city Joppa praying, and

εἶδον ἐν ἐκστάσει ὅραμα, καταβαῖνον
I saw in an ecstasy a vision, coming down

σκεῦός τι ὡς ὀθόνην μεγάλην τέσσαρσιν
a certain vessel as sheet a great by four

ἀρχαῖς καθιεμένην ἐκ τοῦ οὐρανοῦ, καὶ
corners having been let down out of – heaven, and

ἦλθεν ἄχρι ἐμοῦ· **6** εἰς ἣν ἀτενίσας
it came up to me; into which gazing

κατενόουν, καὶ εἶδον τὰ τετράποδα τῆς
I perceived, and I saw the quadrupeds of the

γῆς καὶ τὰ θηρία καὶ τὰ ἑρπετὰ καὶ τὰ
earth and the wild beasts and the reptiles and the

πετεινὰ τοῦ οὐρανοῦ. **7** ἤκουσα δὲ καὶ
birds of the heaven(air). And I heard also

φωνῆς λεγούσης μοι· ἀναστάς, Πέτρε,
a voice saying to me: Rise up, Peter,

θῦσον καὶ φάγε. **8** εἶπον δέ· μηδαμῶς,
slay and eat. And I said : Not at all,

κύριε, ὅτι κοινὸν ἢ ἀκάθαρτον οὐδέποτε
Lord, because a common or unclean thing never

εἰσῆλθεν εἰς τὸ στόμα μου. **9** ἀπεκρίθη δὲ
entered into the mouth of me. And answered

ἐκ δευτέρου φωνὴ ἐκ τοῦ οὐρανοῦ·
a second [time] a voice out of – heaven:

ἃ ὁ θεὸς ἐκαθάρισεν σὺ μὴ κοίνου.
What things – God cleansed thou regard not common.

10 τοῦτο δὲ ἐγένετο ἐπὶ τρίς, καὶ
And this happened on three [occasions], and

ἀνεσπάσθη πάλιν ἅπαντα εἰς τὸν οὐρανόν.
was pulled up again all things to – heaven.

11 καὶ ἰδοὺ ἐξαυτῆς τρεῖς ἄνδρες ἐπέστησαν
And behold at once three men stood *at*

ἐπὶ τὴν οἰκίαν ἐν ᾗ ἦμεν, ἀπεσταλμένοι
at the house in which I was, having been sent

ἀπὸ Καισαρείας πρός με. **12** εἶπεν δὲ
from Cæsarea to me. And [3]told

τὸ πνεῦμά μοι συνελθεῖν αὐτοῖς μηδὲν
[1]the [2]Spirit [4]me to go with them nothing

διακρίναντα. ἦλθον δὲ σὺν ἐμοὶ καὶ
doubting. And came with me also

οἱ ἓξ ἀδελφοὶ οὗτοι, καὶ εἰσήλθομεν εἰς
– six brothers these, and we entered into

τὸν οἶκον τοῦ ἀνδρός. **13** ἀπήγγειλεν δὲ
the house of the man. And he reported

ἡμῖν πῶς εἶδεν τὸν ἄγγελον ἐν τῷ
to us how he saw the angel in the

οἴκῳ αὐτοῦ σταθέντα καὶ εἰπόντα·
house of him standing and saying:

ἀπόστειλον εἰς Ἰόππην καὶ μετάπεμψαι
Send to Joppa and summon

Σίμωνα τὸν ἐπικαλούμενον Πέτρον, **14** ὃς
Simon – *being* surnamed Peter, who

λαλήσει ῥήματα πρὸς σὲ ἐν οἷς σωθήσῃ
will speak words to thee by which mayest be saved

σὺ καὶ πᾶς ὁ οἶκός σου. **15** ἐν δὲ
thou and all the household of thee. And in

the circumcised believers
criticized him 3and said,
"You went into the house
of uncircumcised men and
ate with them."
4Peter began and ex-
plained everything to them
precisely as it had hap-
pened: 5"I was in the city of
Joppa praying, and in a
trance I saw a vision. I saw
something like a large sheet
being let down from heaven
by its four corners, and it
came down to where I was.
6I looked into it and saw
four-footed animals of the
earth, wild beasts, reptiles,
and birds of the air. 7Then I
heard a voice telling me,
'Get up, Peter. Kill and
eat.'
8"I replied, 'Surely not,
Lord! Nothing impure or
unclean has ever entered
my mouth.'
9"The voice spoke from
heaven a second time, 'Do
not call anything impure
that God has made clean.'
10This happened three
times, and then it was all
pulled up to heaven again.
11"Right then three men
who had been sent to me
from Caesarea stopped at
the house where I was staying. 12The Spirit told me to
have no hesitation about
going with them. These six
brothers also went with
me, and we entered the
man's house. 13He told us
how he had seen an angel
appear in his house and
say, 'Send to Joppa for Simon who is called Peter.
14He will bring you a message through which you
and all your household will
be saved.'

as I began to speak, the Holy Spirit fell upon them just as it had upon us at the beginning. 16 And I remembered the word of the Lord, how he had said, 'John baptized with water, but you will be baptized with the Holy Spirit.' 17 If then God gave them the same gift that he gave us when we believed in the Lord Jesus Christ, who was I that I could hinder God?" 18 When they heard this, they were silenced. And they praised God, saying, "Then God has given even to the Gentiles the repentance that leads to life."

The Church in Antioch

19 Now those who were scattered because of the persecution that took place over Stephen traveled as far as Phoenicia, Cyprus, and Antioch, and they spoke the word to no one except Jews. 20 But among them were some men of Cyprus and Cyrene who, on coming to Antioch, spoke to the Hellenists[f] also, proclaiming the Lord Jesus. 21 The hand of the Lord was with them, and a great number became believers and turned to the Lord. 22 News of this came to the ears of the church in Jerusalem, and they sent Barnabas to Antioch. 23 When he came and saw the grace of God, he rejoiced, and he exhorted them all to remain faithful to the Lord with steadfast devotion; 24 for he was a good man, full of the Holy Spirit and of faith. And a

[f] Other ancient authorities read *Greeks*

τῷ ἄρξασθαί με λαλεῖν ἐπέπεσεν τὸ
the to begin me[be] to speak [4]fell *on* [1]the
=as I began

πνεῦμα τὸ ἅγιον ἐπ' αὐτοὺς ὥσπερ καὶ
[3]Spirit – [2]Holy on them as also

ἐφ' ἡμᾶς ἐν ἀρχῇ. **16** ἐμνήσθην δὲ τοῦ
on us at [the] beginning. And I remembered the

ῥήματος τοῦ κυρίου, ὡς ἔλεγεν· Ἰωάννης
word of the Lord, how he said: John

μὲν ἐβάπτισεν ὕδατι, ὑμεῖς δὲ βαπτισθήσεσθε
indeed baptized with water, but ye will be baptized

ἐν πνεύματι ἁγίῳ. **17** εἰ οὖν τὴν ἴσην
in Spirit Holy. If therefore [4]the [5]equal

δωρεὰν ἔδωκεν αὐτοῖς ὁ θεὸς ὡς καὶ
[6]gift [2]gave [3]them – [1]God as also

ἡμῖν, πιστεύσασιν ἐπὶ τὸν κύριον Ἰησοῦν
to us, having believed on the Lord Jesus

Χριστόν, ἐγὼ τίς ἤμην δυνατὸς κωλῦσαι
Christ, [2]I [1]who [3]was [to be] able to hinder

τὸν θεόν; **18** ἀκούσαντες δὲ ταῦτα ἡσύχασαν,
– God? And hearing these things they kept silence

καὶ ἐδόξασαν τὸν θεὸν λέγοντες· ἄρα καὶ
and glorified – God saying: Then also

τοῖς ἔθνεσιν ὁ θεὸς τὴν μετάνοιαν εἰς
to the nations – God – repentance to

ζωὴν ἔδωκεν.
life gave.

19 Οἱ μὲν οὖν διασπαρέντες ἀπὸ τῆς
The [ones] – therefore being scattered from the

θλίψεως τῆς γενομένης ἐπὶ Στεφάνῳ
affliction – occurring over Stephen

διῆλθον ἕως Φοινίκης καὶ Κύπρου καὶ
passed through to Phœnicia and Cyprus and

Ἀντιοχείας, μηδενὶ λαλοῦντες τὸν λόγον
Antioch, to no one speaking the word

εἰ μὴ μόνον Ἰουδαίοις. **20** Ἦσαν δέ
except only to Jews. But [4]were

τινες ἐξ αὐτῶν ἄνδρες Κύπριοι καὶ
[1]some [2]of [3]them *men* Cypriotes and

Κυρηναῖοι, οἵτινες ἐλθόντες εἰς Ἀντιόχειαν
Cyrenians, who coming to Antioch

ἐλάλουν καὶ πρὸς τοὺς Ἕλληνας,
spoke also to the Greeks,

εὐαγγελιζόμενοι τὸν κύριον Ἰησοῦν. **21** καὶ ἦν
preaching the Lord Jesus. And was

χεὶρ κυρίου μετ' αὐτῶν, πολύς τε
[the] hand of [the] Lord with them, and a much(great)

ἀριθμὸς ὁ πιστεύσας ἐπέστρεψεν ἐπὶ τὸν
number – believing turned to the

κύριον. **22** Ἠκούσθη δὲ ὁ λόγος εἰς
Lord. And was heard the account in

τὰ ὦτα τῆς ἐκκλησίας τῆς οὔσης ἐν
the ears of the church – being in

Ἰερουσαλὴμ περὶ αὐτῶν, καὶ ἐξαπέστειλαν
Jerusalem about them, and they sent out

Βαρναβᾶν ἕως Ἀντιοχείας· **23** ὃς παραγεν-
Barnabas to Antioch; who arriv-

όμενος καὶ ἰδὼν τὴν χάριν τὴν τοῦ
ing and seeing the grace – –

θεοῦ ἐχάρη, καὶ παρεκάλει πάντας τῇ
of God rejoiced, and exhorted all –

προθέσει τῆς καρδίας προσμένειν τῷ
with purpose – of heart to remain with the

κυρίῳ, **24** ὅτι ἦν ἀνὴρ ἀγαθὸς καὶ
Lord, because he was man a good and

πλήρης πνεύματος ἁγίου καὶ πίστεως.
full of [the] Spirit Holy and of faith.

15 "As I began to speak, the Holy Spirit came on them as he had come on us at the beginning. 16 Then I remembered what the Lord had said: 'John baptized with[s] water, but you will be baptized with the Holy Spirit.' 17 So if God gave them the same gift as he gave us, who believed in the Lord Jesus Christ, who was I to think that I could oppose God?"

18 When they heard this, they had no further objections and praised God, saying, "So then, God has granted even the Gentiles repentance unto life."

The Church in Antioch

19 Now those who had been scattered by the persecution in connection with Stephen traveled as far as Phoenicia, Cyprus and Antioch, telling the message only to Jews. 20 Some of them, however, men from Cyprus and Cyrene, went to Antioch and began to speak to Greeks also, telling them the good news about the Lord Jesus. 21 The Lord's hand was with them, and a great number of people believed and turned to the Lord.

22 News of this reached the ears of the church at Jerusalem, and they sent Barnabas to Antioch. 23 When he arrived and saw the evidence of the grace of God, he was glad and encouraged them all to remain true to the Lord with all their hearts. 24 He was a good man, full of the Holy Spirit and faith, and a great num-

[s] 16 Or *in*

great many people were
brought to the Lord.
25 Then Barnabas went to
Tarsus to look for Saul,
26 and when he had found
him, he brought him to Antioch. So it was that for an
entire year they met with[g]
the church and taught a
great many people, and it
was in Antioch that the disciples were first called
"Christians."

27 At that time prophets
came down from Jerusalem
to Antioch. 28 One of them
named Agabus stood up
and predicted by the Spirit
that there would be a severe famine over all the
world; and this took place
during the reign of Claudius. 29 The disciples determined that according to
their ability, each would
send relief to the believers[h] living in Judea; 30 this
they did, sending it to the
elders by Barnabas and
Saul.

καὶ προσετέθη ὄχλος ἱκανὸς τῷ κυρίῳ.
And was added a crowd considerable to the Lord.

25 ἐξῆλθεν δὲ εἰς Ταρσὸν ἀναζητῆσαι
And he went forth to Tarsus to seek

Σαῦλον, 26 καὶ εὑρὼν ἤγαγεν εἰς Ἀντιόχειαν.
Saul, and finding brought to Antioch.

ἐγένετο δὲ αὐτοῖς καὶ ἐνιαυτὸν ὅλον
And it happened to them also year a whole

συναχθῆναι ἐν τῇ ἐκκλησίᾳ καὶ διδάξαι
to be assembled in the church and to teach

ὄχλον ἱκανόν, χρηματίσαι τε πρώτως ἐν
a crowd considerable, and to call firstly in

Ἀντιοχείᾳ τοὺς μαθητὰς Χριστιανούς.
Antioch the disciples Christians.

27 Ἐν ταύταις δὲ ταῖς ἡμέραις κατῆλθον
And in these – days came down

ἀπὸ Ἱεροσολύμων προφῆται εἰς Ἀντιόχειαν·
from Jerusalem prophets to Antioch;

28 ἀναστὰς δὲ εἷς ἐξ αὐτῶν ὀνόματι
and rising up one of them by name

Ἅγαβος ἐσήμαινεν διὰ τοῦ πνεύματος
Agabus signified through the Spirit

λιμὸν μεγάλην μέλλειν ἔσεσθαι ἐφ' ὅλην τὴν
famine a great to be about to be over all the

οἰκουμένην· ἥτις ἐγένετο ἐπὶ Κλαυδίου.
inhabited earth; which happened in the time of Claudius.

29 τῶν δὲ μαθητῶν καθὼς εὐπορεῖτό
So [3]of the [4]disciples [1]as [6]was prosperous

τις, ὥρισαν ἕκαστος αὐτῶν εἰς διακονίαν
[2]anyone, they determined each of them for ministration

πέμψαι τοῖς κατοικοῦσιν ἐν τῇ Ἰουδαίᾳ
to send [1]to the [3]dwelling [4]in – [5]Judæa

ἀδελφοῖς· 30 ὃ καὶ ἐποίησαν ἀποστείλαντες
[2]brothers; which indeed they did sending

πρὸς τοὺς πρεσβυτέρους διὰ χειρὸς
to the elders through [the] hand

Βαρναβᾶ καὶ Σαύλου.
of Barnabas and of Saul.

ber of people were brought
to the Lord.

25 Then Barnabas went to
Tarsus to look for Saul,
26 and when he found him,
he brought him to Antioch.
So for a whole year Barnabas and Saul met with the
church and taught great
numbers of people. The
disciples were called Christians first at Antioch.

27 During this time some
prophets came down from
Jerusalem to Antioch.
28 One of them, named Agabus, stood up and through
the Spirit predicted that a
severe famine would
spread over the entire Roman world. (This happened
during the reign of Claudius.) 29 The disciples, each
according to his ability, decided to provide help for
the brothers living in Judea. 30 This they did, sending their gift to the elders by
Barnabas and Saul.

Chapter 12

James Killed and Peter Imprisoned

ABOUT that time King
Herod laid violent
hands upon some who belonged to the church. 2 He
had James, the brother of
John, killed with the
sword. 3 After he saw that it
pleased the Jews, he proceeded to arrest Peter also.
(This was during the festival of Unleavened Bread.)
4 When he had seized him,
he put him in prison and
handed him over to four
squads of soldiers to guard
him, intending to bring him
out to the people after the
Passover. 5 While Peter
was kept in prison, the
church prayed fervently to

12 Κατ' ἐκεῖνον δὲ τὸν καιρὸν ἐπέβαλεν
Now at that – time laid on

Ἡρῴδης ὁ βασιλεὺς τὰς χεῖρας κακῶσαί
Herod the king the(his) hands to ill-treat

τινας τῶν ἀπὸ τῆς ἐκκλησίας. 2 ἀνεῖλεν δὲ
some of the [ones] from the church. And he killed

Ἰάκωβον τὸν ἀδελφὸν Ἰωάννου μαχαίρῃ.
James the brother of John with a sword.

3 ἰδὼν δὲ ὅτι ἀρεστόν ἐστιν τοῖς Ἰουδαίοις
And seeing that pleasing it is(was) to the Jews

προσέθετο συλλαβεῖν καὶ Πέτρον, ἦσαν δὲ
he added to arrest also Peter, and they were

ἡμέραι τῶν ἀζύμων, 4 ὃν καὶ πιάσας
days – of unleavened bread, whom also seizing

ἔθετο εἰς φυλακήν, παραδοὺς τέσσαρσιν
he put in prison, delivering to four

τετραδίοις στρατιωτῶν φυλάσσειν αὐτόν,
quaternions of soldiers to guard him,

βουλόμενος μετὰ τὸ πάσχα ἀναγαγεῖν
intending after the Passover to bring up

αὐτὸν τῷ λαῷ. 5 ὁ μὲν οὖν Πέτρος
him to the people. – –* therefore Peter

ἐτηρεῖτο ἐν τῇ φυλακῇ· προσευχὴ δὲ ἦν
was kept in the prison; but prayer was

* μέν and δέ are in contrast : "on one hand . . ."—"on the other . . ."

Chapter 12

Peter's Miraculous Escape From Prison

IT was about this time
that King Herod arrested some who belonged to
the church, intending to
persecute them. 2 He had
James, the brother of John,
put to death with the
sword. 3 When he saw that
this pleased the Jews, he
proceeded to seize Peter
also. This happened during
the Feast of Unleavened
Bread. 4 After arresting
him, he put him in prison,
handing him over to be
guarded by four squads of
four soldiers each. Herod
intended to bring him out
for public trial after the
Passover.

5 So Peter was kept in
prison, but the church was

[g] Or *were guests of*
[h] Gk *brothers*

God for him.

Peter Delivered from Prison

6 The very night before Herod was going to bring him out, Peter, bound with two chains, was sleeping between two soldiers, while guards in front of the door were keeping watch over the prison. 7 Suddenly an angel of the Lord appeared and a light shone in the cell. He tapped Peter on the side and woke him, saying, "Get up quickly." And the chains fell off his wrists. 8 The angel said to him, "Fasten your belt and put on your sandals." He did so. Then he said to him, "Wrap your cloak around you and follow me." 9 Peter[i] went out and followed him; he did not realize that what was happening with the angel's help was real; he thought he was seeing a vision. 10 After they had passed the first and the second guard, they came before the iron gate leading into the city. It opened for them of its own accord, and they went outside and walked along a lane, when suddenly the angel left him. 11 Then Peter came to himself and said, "Now I am sure that the Lord has sent his angel and rescued me from the hands of Herod and from all that the Jewish people were expecting."

12 As soon as he realized this, he went to the house of Mary, the mother of John whose other name was Mark, where many had gathered and were praying.

[i] Gk *He*

ἐκτενῶς γινομένη ὑπὸ τῆς ἐκκλησίας πρὸς
earnestly being made by the church to

τὸν θεὸν περὶ αὐτοῦ. **6** Ὅτε δὲ ἤμελλεν
– God concerning him. And when ²was about

προαγαγεῖν αὐτὸν ὁ Ἡρῴδης, τῇ νυκτὶ
³to bring forward ⁴him – ¹Herod, – ²night

ἐκείνῃ ἦν ὁ Πέτρος κοιμώμενος μεταξὺ
¹in that was – Peter sleeping between

δύο στρατιωτῶν δεδεμένος ἁλύσεσιν δυσίν,
two soldiers having been bound with chains two,

φύλακές τε πρὸ τῆς θύρας ἐτήρουν τὴν
and guards before the door were keeping the

φυλακήν. **7** καὶ ἰδοὺ ἄγγελος κυρίου
prison. And behold[,] an angel of [the] Lord

ἐπέστη, καὶ φῶς ἔλαμψεν ἐν τῷ οἰκήματι·
came upon, and a light shone in the building;

πατάξας δὲ τὴν πλευρὰν τοῦ Πέτρου
and striking the side – of Peter

ἤγειρεν αὐτὸν λέγων· ἀνάστα ἐν τάχει.
he raised him saying: Rise up in haste.

καὶ ἐξέπεσαν αὐτοῦ αἱ ἁλύσεις ἐκ τῶν
And fell *off* of him the chains off the(his)

χειρῶν. **8** εἶπεν δὲ ὁ ἄγγελος πρὸς
hands. And said the angel to

αὐτόν· ζῶσαι καὶ ὑπόδησαι τὰ σανδάλιά
him: Gird thyself and put on the sandals

σου. ἐποίησεν δὲ οὕτως. καὶ λέγει
of thee. And he did so. And he tells

αὐτῷ· περιβαλοῦ τὸ ἱμάτιόν σου καὶ
him: Cast round the garment of thee and

ἀκολούθει μοι. **9** καὶ ἐξελθὼν ἠκολούθει,
follow me. And going forth he followed,

καὶ οὐκ ᾔδει ὅτι ἀληθές ἐστιν τὸ
and knew not that ³true ²is(was) ¹the thing

γινόμενον διὰ τοῦ ἀγγέλου, ἐδόκει δὲ
happening through the angel, but he thought

ὅραμα βλέπειν. **10** διελθόντες δὲ πρώτην
a vision to see. And going through [the] first

φυλακὴν καὶ δευτέραν ἦλθαν ἐπὶ τὴν
prison and [the] second they came on the

πύλην τὴν σιδηρᾶν τὴν φέρουσαν εἰς τὴν
gate – iron – leading to the

πόλιν, ἥτις αὐτομάτη ἠνοίγη αὐτοῖς, καὶ
city, which of itself was opened to them, and

ἐξελθόντες προῆλθον ῥύμην μίαν, καὶ
going out they went forward street one, and

εὐθέως ἀπέστη ὁ ἄγγελος ἀπ' αὐτοῦ.
immediately departed the angel from him.

11 καὶ ὁ Πέτρος ἐν ἑαυτῷ γενόμενος
And – Peter in himself having become

εἶπεν· νῦν οἶδα ἀληθῶς ὅτι ἐξαπέστειλεν
said: Now I know truly that sent forth

ὁ κύριος τὸν ἄγγελον αὐτοῦ καὶ ἐξείλατό
the Lord the angel of him and delivered

με ἐκ χειρὸς Ἡρῴδου καὶ πάσης τῆς
me out of [the] hand of Herod and of all the

προσδοκίας τοῦ λαοῦ τῶν Ἰουδαίων.
expectation of the people of the Jews.

12 συνιδών τε ἦλθεν ἐπὶ τὴν οἰκίαν τῆς
And realizing he came on the house –

Μαρίας τῆς μητρὸς Ἰωάννου τοῦ
of Mary the mother of John –

ἐπικαλουμένου Μάρκου, οὗ ἦσαν ἱκανοὶ
being surnamed Mark, where were many

συνηθροισμένοι καὶ προσευχόμενοι. **13** κρού-
having been assembled and praying. And

earnestly praying to God for him.

6The night before Herod was to bring him to trial, Peter was sleeping between two soldiers, bound with two chains, and sentries stood guard at the entrance. 7Suddenly an angel of the Lord appeared and a light shone in the cell. He struck Peter on the side and woke him up. "Quick, get up!" he said, and the chains fell off Peter's wrists.

8Then the angel said to him, "Put on your clothes and sandals." And Peter did so. "Wrap your cloak around you and follow me," the angel told him. 9Peter followed him out of the prison, but he had no idea that what the angel was doing was really happening; he thought he was seeing a vision. 10They passed the first and second guards and came to the iron gate leading to the city. It opened for them by itself, and they went through it. When they had walked the length of one street, suddenly the angel left him.

11Then Peter came to himself and said, "Now I know without a doubt that the Lord sent his angel and rescued me from Herod's clutches and from everything the Jewish people were anticipating."

12When this had dawned on him, he went to the house of Mary the mother of John, also called Mark, where many people had gathered and were praying.

[13]When he knocked at the outer gate, a maid named Rhoda came to answer. [14]On recognizing Peter's voice, she was so overjoyed that, instead of opening the gate, she ran in and announced that Peter was standing at the gate. [15]They said to her, "You are out of your mind!" But she insisted that it was so. They said, "It is his angel." [16]Meanwhile Peter continued knocking; and when they opened the gate, they saw him and were amazed. [17]He motioned to them with his hand to be silent, and described for them how the Lord had brought him out of the prison. And he added, "Tell this to James and to the believers."[h] Then he left and went to another place.

18 When morning came, there was no small commotion among the soldiers over what had become of Peter. [19]When Herod had searched for him and could not find him, he examined the guards and ordered them to be put to death. Then Peter[j] went down from Judea to Caesarea and stayed there.

The Death of Herod

20 Now Herod was angry with the people of Tyre and Sidon. So they came to him in a body; and after winning over Blastus, the king's chamberlain, they asked for a reconciliation, because their country depended on the king's country for food. [21]On an appointed day Herod put on his royal robes, took his seat on the platform, and delivered a public address to them. [22]The people kept shouting, "The voice of a

[j] Gk *he*

σαντος δὲ αὐτοῦ τὴν θύραν τοῦ πυλῶνος
knocking him[a] the door of the porch
=as he knocked

προσῆλθεν παιδίσκη ὑπακοῦσαι ὀνόματι
approached a maidservant to listen by name

Ῥόδη, **14** καὶ ἐπιγνοῦσα τὴν φωνὴν τοῦ
Rhoda, and recognizing the voice –

Πέτρου ἀπὸ τῆς χαρᾶς οὐκ ἤνοιξεν τὸν
of Peter from – joy she did not open the

πυλῶνα, εἰσδραμοῦσα δὲ ἀπήγγειλεν ἑστάναι
porch, but running in announced [1]to stand

τὸν Πέτρον πρὸ τοῦ πυλῶνος. **15** οἱ δὲ
– [1]Peter before the porch. But they

πρὸς αὐτὴν εἶπαν· μαίνῃ. ἡ δὲ διϊσχυρίζετο
to her said: Thou ravest. But she emphatically asserted

οὕτως ἔχειν. οἱ δὲ ἔλεγον· ὁ ἄγγελός
so to have(be). So they said: The angel

ἐστιν αὐτοῦ. **16** ὁ δὲ Πέτρος ἐπέμενεν
it is of him. – But Peter continued

κρούων· ἀνοίξαντες δὲ εἶδαν αὐτὸν καὶ
knocking; and having opened they saw him and

ἐξέστησαν. **17** κατασείσας δὲ αὐτοῖς τῇ
were amazed. And beckoning to them with the

χειρὶ σιγᾶν διηγήσατο αὐτοῖς πῶς ὁ
hand to be quiet he related to them how the

κύριος αὐτὸν ἐξήγαγεν ἐκ τῆς φυλακῆς,
Lord him led *out* out of the prison,

εἶπέν τε· ἀπαγγείλατε Ἰακώβῳ καὶ τοῖς
and said: Report to James and to the

ἀδελφοῖς ταῦτα. καὶ ἐξελθὼν ἐπορεύθη εἰς
brothers these things. And going out he went to

ἕτερον τόπον. **18** Γενομένης δὲ ἡμέρας ἦν
another place. And becoming day[a] there was
=when it became day

τάραχος οὐκ ὀλίγος ἐν τοῖς στρατιώταις,
disturbance not a little among the soldiers,

τί ἄρα ὁ Πέτρος ἐγένετο. **19** Ἡρῴδης δὲ
what then – [of] Peter became. And Herod

ἐπιζητήσας αὐτὸν καὶ μὴ εὑρών,
searching for him and not finding,

ἀνακρίνας τοὺς φύλακας ἐκέλευσεν ἀπ-
examining the guards commanded to

αχθῆναι, καὶ κατελθὼν ἀπὸ τῆς Ἰουδαίας
be led away,* and going down from – Judæa

εἰς Καισάρειαν διέτριβεν. **20** Ἦν δὲ
to Cæsarea stayed. Now he was

θυμομαχῶν Τυρίοις καὶ Σιδωνίοις·
being furiously angry with Tyrians and Sidonians;

ὁμοθυμαδὸν δὲ παρῆσαν πρὸς αὐτόν, καὶ
and with one mind they came to him, and

πείσαντες Βλάστον τὸν ἐπὶ τοῦ κοιτῶνος
having persuaded Blastus the one over the bedchamber

τοῦ βασιλέως ᾐτοῦντο εἰρήνην, διὰ τὸ
of the king they asked peace, because the

τρέφεσθαι αὐτῶν τὴν χώραν ἀπὸ τῆς
to be fed of them the country[b] from the
=their country was fed

βασιλικῆς. **21** τακτῇ δὲ ἡμέρᾳ ὁ Ἡρῴδης
royal. And on an appointed day – Herod

ἐνδυσάμενος ἐσθῆτα βασιλικὴν καθίσας ἐπὶ
having been arrayed with clothing regal sitting on

τοῦ βήματος ἐδημηγόρει πρὸς αὐτούς·
the tribunal made a public speech to them;

22 ὁ δὲ δῆμος ἐπεφώνει· θεοῦ φωνὴ
and the mob cried out: Of a god a voice

* That is, to execution.

[13]Peter knocked at the outer entrance, and a servant girl named Rhoda came to answer the door. [14]When she recognized Peter's voice, she was so overjoyed she ran back without opening it and exclaimed, "Peter is at the door!"

[15]"You're out of your mind," they told her. When she kept insisting that it was so, they said, "It must be his angel."

[16]But Peter kept on knocking, and when they opened the door and saw him, they were astonished. [17]Peter motioned with his hand for them to be quiet and described how the Lord had brought him out of prison. "Tell James and the brothers about this," he said, and then he left for another place.

[18]In the morning, there was no small commotion among the soldiers as to what had become of Peter. [19]After Herod had a thorough search made for him and did not find him, he cross-examined the guards and ordered that they be executed.

Herod's Death

Then Herod went from Judea to Caesarea and stayed there a while. [20]He had been quarreling with the people of Tyre and Sidon; they now joined together and sought an audience with him. Having secured the support of Blastus, a trusted personal servant of the king, they asked for peace, because they depended on the king's country for their food supply.

[21]On the appointed day Herod, wearing his royal robes, sat on his throne and delivered a public address to the people. [22]They shouted, "This is the voice

god, and not of a mortal!"
23And immediately, be-
cause he had not given the
glory to God, an angel of
the Lord struck him down,
and he was eaten by worms
and died.
24 But the word of God
continued to advance and
gain adherents. 25Then after completing their mis-
sion Barnabas and Saul returned to[k] Jerusalem and
brought with them John,
whose other name was
Mark.

καὶ οὐκ ἀνθρώπου. 23 παραχρῆμα δὲ
and not of a man. And at once
ἐπάταξεν αὐτὸν ἄγγελος κυρίου ἀνθ' ὧν
smote him an angel of [the] Lord because
οὐκ ἔδωκεν τὴν δόξαν τῷ θεῷ, καὶ
he gave not the glory – to God, and
γενόμενος σκωληκόβρωτος ἐξέψυξεν.
becoming eaten by worms he expired.
24 Ὁ δὲ λόγος τοῦ κυρίου ηὔξανεν
But the word of the Lord grew
καὶ ἐπληθύνετο. 25 Βαρναβᾶς δὲ καὶ
and increased. And Barnabas and
Σαῦλος ὑπέστρεψαν ἐξ Ἰερουσαλήμ,
Saul returned out of Jerusalem,
πληρώσαντες τὴν διακονίαν, συμπαρα-
having completed the ministration, taking
λαβόντες Ἰωάννην τὸν ἐπικληθέντα Μᾶρκον.
with [them] John – surnamed Mark.

of a god, not of a man."
23Immediately, because
Herod did not give praise to
God, an angel of the Lord
struck him down, and he
was eaten by worms and
died.
24But the word of God
continued to increase and
spread.
25When Barnabas and
Saul had finished their mission, they returned from[l]
Jerusalem, taking with
them John, also called
Mark.

Chapter 13

Barnabas and Saul Commissioned

NOW in the church at
Antioch there were
prophets and teachers:
Barnabas, Simeon who was
called Niger, Lucius of Cyrene, Manaen a member of
the court of Herod the ruler,[l] and Saul. 2While they
were worshiping the Lord
and fasting, the Holy Spirit
said, "Set apart for me Barnabas and Saul for the work
to which I have called
them." 3Then after fasting
and praying they laid their
hands on them and sent
them off.

The Apostles Preach in Cyprus

4 So, being sent out by
the Holy Spirit, they went
down to Seleucia; and from
there they sailed to Cyprus.
5When they arrived at Salamis, they proclaimed the
word of God in the syna-
gogues of the Jews. And
they had John also to assist
them. 6When they had
gone through the whole island as far as Paphos, they
met a certain magician, a
Jewish false prophet,
named Bar-Jesus. 7He was
with the proconsul, Sergius
Paulus, an intelligent man,

13 Ἦσαν δὲ ἐν Ἀντιοχείᾳ κατὰ τὴν
Now there were in Antioch among the
οὖσαν ἐκκλησίαν προφῆται καὶ διδάσκαλοι
existing church prophets and teachers
ὅ τε Βαρναβᾶς καὶ Συμεὼν ὁ καλούμενος
– both Barnabas and Simeon – *being* called
Νίγερ, καὶ Λούκιος ὁ Κυρηναῖος, Μαναήν τε
Niger, and Lucius the Cyrenian, and Manaen
Ἡρῴδου τοῦ τετραάρχου σύντροφος
[2]of Herod [3]the [4]tetrarch [1]foster brother
καὶ Σαῦλος. 2 Λειτουργούντων δὲ αὐτῶν
and Saul. And ministering them[a]
=as they ministered
τῷ κυρίῳ καὶ νηστευόντων εἶπεν τὸ
to the Lord and fasting[a] said the
πνεῦμα τὸ ἅγιον· ἀφορίσατε δή μοι
Spirit – Holy: [2]Separate ye [1]so then [3]to me
τὸν Βαρναβᾶν καὶ Σαῦλον εἰς τὸ ἔργον
– Barnabas and Saul for the work
ὃ προσκέκλημαι αὐτούς· 3 τότε νηστεύ-
[to] which I have called them; then having
σαντες καὶ προσευξάμενοι καὶ ἐπιθέντες
fasted and *having* prayed and [1]laying [4]on
τὰς χεῖρας αὐτοῖς ἀπέλυσαν.
[2]the(ir) [3]hands [4]them they dismissed [them].
4 Αὐτοὶ μὲν οὖν ἐκπεμφθέντες ὑπὸ τοῦ
They – therefore sent out by the
ἁγίου πνεύματος κατῆλθον εἰς Σελεύκειαν,
Holy Spirit went down to Seleucia,
ἐκεῖθέν τε ἀπέπλευσαν εἰς Κύπρον, 5 καὶ
and thence sailed away to Cyprus, and
γενόμενοι ἐν Σαλαμῖνι κατήγγελλον τὸν
being in Salamis they announced the
λόγον τοῦ θεοῦ ἐν ταῖς συναγωγαῖς τῶν
word – of God in the synagogues of the
Ἰουδαίων· εἶχον δὲ καὶ Ἰωάννην ὑπηρέτην.
Jews; and they had also John [as] attendant.
6 Διελθόντες δὲ ὅλην τὴν νῆσον ἄχρι
And passing through all the island unto
Πάφου εὗρον ἄνδρα τινὰ μάγον ψευδο-
Paphos they found a certain man a sorcerer a [2]false
προφήτην Ἰουδαῖον, ᾧ ὄνομα Βαριησοῦς,
[3]prophet [1]Jewish, to whom name[c] Barjesus,
=whose name was
7 ὃς ἦν σὺν τῷ ἀνθυπάτῳ Σεργίῳ
who was with the proconsul Sergius

Chapter 13

Barnabas and Saul Sent Off

IN the church at Antioch
there were prophets and
teachers: Barnabas, Sime-
on called Niger, Lucius of
Cyrene, Manaen (who had
been brought up with Her-
od the tetrarch) and Saul.
2While they were worship-
ing the Lord and fasting,
the Holy Spirit said, "Set
apart for me Barnabas and
Saul for the work to which I
have called them." 3So after they had fasted and
prayed, they placed their
hands on them and sent
them off.

On Cyprus

4The two of them, sent on
their way by the Holy Spirit, went down to Seleucia
and sailed from there to Cyprus. 5When they arrived at
Salamis, they proclaimed
the word of God in the Jewish synagogues. John was
with them as their helper.
6They traveled through
the whole island until they
came to Paphos. There
they met a Jewish sorcerer
and false prophet named
Bar-Jesus, 7who was an attendant of the proconsul,

[k]Other ancient authorities read *from*
[l]Gk *tetrarch*

[l]25 Some manuscripts *to*

who summoned Barnabas
and Saul and wanted to
hear the word of God. 8 But
the magician Elymas (for
that is the translation of his
name) opposed them and
tried to turn the proconsul
away from the faith. 9 But
Saul, also known as Paul,
filled with the Holy Spirit,
looked intently at him
10 and said, "You son of the
devil, you enemy of all
righteousness, full of all deceit and villainy, will you
not stop making crooked
the straight paths of the
Lord? 11 And now listen—
the hand of the Lord is
against you, and you will be
blind for a while, unable to
see the sun." Immediately
mist and darkness came
over him, and he went
about groping for someone
to lead him by the hand.
12 When the proconsul saw
what had happened, he be-
lieved, for he was aston-
ished at the teaching about
the Lord.

Paul and Barnabas in Antioch of Pisidia

13 Then Paul and his
companions set sail from
Paphos and came to Perga
in Pamphylia. John, how-
ever, left them and re-
turned to Jerusalem; 14 but
they went on from Perga
and came to Antioch in Pisidia. And on the sabbath
day they went into the synagogue and sat down. 15 After the reading of the law
and the prophets, the officials of the synagogue sent
them a message, saying,
"Brothers, if you have any
word of exhortation for the
people, give it." 16 So Paul
stood up and with a gesture
began to speak:

Παύλῳ, ἀνδρὶ συνετῷ. οὗτος προσ-
Paulus, man an intelligent. This man calling
καλεσάμενος Βαρναβᾶν καὶ Σαῦλον ἐπεζήτησεν
to [him] Barnabas and Saul sought
ἀκοῦσαι τὸν λόγον τοῦ θεοῦ· 8 ἀνθίστατο δὲ
to hear the word – of God; but opposed
αὐτοῖς Ἐλύμας ὁ μάγος, οὕτως γὰρ
them Elymas the sorcerer, for so
μεθερμηνεύεται τὸ ὄνομα αὐτοῦ, ζητῶν
is translated the name of him, seeking
διαστρέψαι τὸν ἀνθύπατον ἀπὸ τῆς
to divert the proconsul from the
πίστεως. 9 Σαῦλος δέ, ὁ καὶ Παῦλος,
faith. But Saul, the [one] also Paul,
πλησθεὶς πνεύματος ἁγίου ἀτενίσας εἰς
filled of(with) Spirit Holy gazing at
αὐτὸν εἶπεν· 10 Ὦ πλήρης παντὸς δόλου
him said: O full of all deceit
καὶ πάσης ῥᾳδιουργίας, υἱὲ διαβόλου,
and of all fraud, son of [the] devil,
ἐχθρὲ πάσης δικαιοσύνης, οὐ παύσῃ
enemy of all righteousness, wilt thou not cease
διαστρέφων τὰς ὁδοὺς τοῦ κυρίου τὰς
perverting the ways of the Lord –
εὐθείας; 11 καὶ νῦν ἰδοὺ χεὶρ κυρίου
right? And now behold[,] [the] hand of [the] Lord
ἐπὶ σέ, καὶ ἔσῃ τυφλὸς μὴ βλέπων
[is] on thee, and thou wilt be blind not seeing
τὸν ἥλιον ἄχρι καιροῦ. παραχρῆμα δὲ
the sun until [such] a time. And at once
ἔπεσεν ἐπ' αὐτὸν ἀχλὺς καὶ σκότος, καὶ
fell on him a mist and darkness, and
περιάγων ἐζήτει χειραγωγούς. 12 τότε
going about he sought leaders by the hand Then
ἰδὼν ὁ ἀνθύπατος τὸ γεγονὸς
[3]seeing [1]the [2]proconsul the thing having occurred
ἐπίστευσεν, ἐκπλησσόμενος ἐπὶ τῇ διδαχῇ
believed, being astounded at the teaching
τοῦ κυρίου.
of the Lord.
13 Ἀναχθέντες δὲ ἀπὸ τῆς Πάφου οἱ
And setting sail from – Paphos the ones
περὶ Παῦλον ἦλθον εἰς Πέργην τῆς
around(with) Paul came to Perga –
Παμφυλίας· Ἰωάννης δὲ ἀποχωρήσας ἀπ'
of Pamphylia; and John departing from
αὐτῶν ὑπέστρεψεν εἰς Ἱεροσόλυμα.
them returned to Jerusalem.
14 Αὐτοὶ δὲ διελθόντες ἀπὸ τῆς Πέργης
And they going through from – Perga
παρεγένοντο εἰς Ἀντιόχειαν τὴν Πισιδίαν,
arrived in Antioch the Pisidian,
καὶ ἐλθόντες εἰς τὴν συναγωγὴν τῇ
and going into the synagogue on the
ἡμέρᾳ τῶν σαββάτων ἐκάθισαν. 15 μετὰ δὲ
day of the sabbaths sat down. And after
τὴν ἀνάγνωσιν τοῦ νόμου καὶ τῶν
the reading of the law and of the
προφητῶν ἀπέστειλαν οἱ ἀρχισυνάγωγοι
prophets sent the synagogue rulers
πρὸς αὐτοὺς λέγοντες· ἄνδρες ἀδελφοί,
to them saying: *Men* brothers,
εἴ τίς ἐστιν ἐν ὑμῖν λόγος παρακλήσεως
[1]if [5]any [2]there is [3]among [4]you [6]word of exhortation
πρὸς τὸν λαόν, λέγετε. 16 ἀναστὰς δὲ
to the people, say ye. And [1]rising up

Sergius Paulus. The pro-
consul, an intelligent man,
sent for Barnabas and Saul
because he wanted to hear
the word of God. 8But Elymas the sorcerer (for that is
what his name means) op-
posed them and tried to
turn the proconsul from the
faith. 9Then Saul, who was
also called Paul, filled with
the Holy Spirit, looked
straight at Elymas and said,
10"You are a child of the
devil and an enemy of ev-
erything that is right! You
are full of all kinds of deceit
and trickery. Will you never stop perverting the right
ways of the Lord? 11Now
the hand of the Lord is
against you. You are going
to be blind, and for a time
you will be unable to see
the light of the sun."
Immediately mist and
darkness came over him,
and he groped about, seeking someone to lead him by
the hand. 12When the pro-
consul saw what had hap-
pened, he believed, for he
was amazed at the teaching
about the Lord.

In Pisidian Antioch

13From Paphos, Paul and
his companions sailed to
Perga in Pamphylia, where
John left them to return to
Jerusalem. 14From Perga
they went on to Pisidian
Antioch. On the Sabbath
they entered the synagogue
and sat down. 15After the
reading of the Law and
the Prophets, the syna-
gogue rulers sent word to
them, saying, "Brothers, if
you have a message of en-
couragement for the peo-
ple, please speak."
16Standing up, Paul mo-

"You Israelites,[m] and
others who fear God, lis-
ten. 17 The God of this people Israel chose our ancestors and made the people
great during their stay in
the land of Egypt, and with
uplifted arm he led them
out of it. 18 For about forty
years he put up with[n] them
in the wilderness. 19 After
he had destroyed seven nations in the land of Canaan,
he gave them their land as
an inheritance 20 for about
four hundred fifty years.
After that he gave them
judges until the time of the
prophet Samuel. 21 Then
they asked for a king; and
God gave them Saul son of
Kish, a man of the tribe of
Benjamin, who reigned for
forty years. 22 When he had
removed him, he made Da-
vid their king. In his testimony about him he said, 'I
have found David, son of
Jesse, to be a man after my
heart, who will carry out all
my wishes.' 23 Of this
man's posterity God has
brought to Israel a Savior,
Jesus, as he promised;
24 before his coming John
had already proclaimed a
baptism of repentance to all
the people of Israel. 25 And
as John was finishing his
work, he said, 'What do
you suppose that I am? I
am not he. No, but one is
coming after me; I am not
worthy to untie the thong of
the sandals[o] on his feet.'
26 "My brothers, you
descendants of Abraham's
family, and others who fear
God, to us[p] the message of

Παῦλος καὶ κατασείσας τῇ χειρὶ εἶπεν·
[4]Paul [2]and [3]beckoning [4]with the(his) [5]hand said:
ἄνδρες Ἰσραηλῖται καὶ οἱ φοβούμενοι τὸν
Men Israelites and the [ones] fearing –
θεόν, ἀκούσατε. 17 ὁ θεὸς τοῦ λαοῦ
God, hear ye. The God – people
τούτου Ἰσραὴλ ἐξελέξατο τοὺς πατέρας
of this Israel chose the fathers
ἡμῶν, καὶ τὸν λαὸν ὕψωσεν ἐν τῇ
of us, and [2]the [3]people [1]exalted in the
παροικίᾳ ἐν γῇ Αἰγύπτου, καὶ μετὰ
sojourn in [the] land of Egypt, and with
βραχίονος ὑψηλοῦ ἐξήγαγεν αὐτοὺς ἐξ
arm a high he led forth them out of
αὐτῆς, 18 καὶ ὡς τεσσερακονταέτη χρόνον
it, and about forty years time
ἐτροποφόρησεν αὐτοὺς ἐν τῇ ἐρήμῳ, 19 καὶ
endured them in the desert, and
καθελὼν ἔθνη ἑπτὰ ἐν γῇ Χανάαν
having destroyed nations seven in [the] land Canaan
κατεκληρονόμησεν τὴν γῆν αὐτῶν 20 ὡς
gave as an inheritance the land of them about
ἔτεσιν τετρακοσίοις καὶ πεντήκοντα. καὶ
years four hundred*s* and fifty. And
μετὰ ταῦτα ἔδωκεν κριτὰς ἕως Σαμουὴλ
after these things he gave judges until Samuel
προφήτου. 21 κἀκεῖθεν ᾐτήσαντο βασιλέα,
a prophet. And thence they asked a king,
καὶ ἔδωκεν αὐτοῖς ὁ θεὸς τὸν Σαοὺλ
and gave them – God – Saul
υἱὸν Κίς, ἄνδρα ἐκ φυλῆς Βενιαμίν,
son of Cis, a man of [the] tribe of Benjamin,
ἔτη τεσσεράκοντα· 22 καὶ μεταστήσας
years forty; and removing
αὐτὸν ἤγειρεν τὸν Δαυὶδ αὐτοῖς εἰς
him he raised – David to them for
βασιλέα, ᾧ καὶ εἶπεν μαρτυρήσας·
a king, to whom also he said giving witness:
εὗρον Δαυὶδ τὸν τοῦ Ἰεσσαί, ἄνδρα
I found David the [son] – of Jesse, a man
κατὰ τὴν καρδίαν μου, ὃς ποιήσει πάντα
according to the heart of me, who will do all
τὰ θελήματά μου. 23 τούτου ὁ θεὸς
the wishes of me. [4]Of this man – [5]God
ἀπὸ τοῦ σπέρματος κατ' ἐπαγγελίαν
[1]from [2]the [3]seed according to promise
ἤγαγεν τῷ Ἰσραὴλ σωτῆρα Ἰησοῦν,
brought – to Israel a Saviour Jesus,
24 προκηρύξαντος Ἰωάννου πρὸ προσώπου
previously proclaiming John[a] before *face*
=when John had previously proclaimed
τῆς εἰσόδου αὐτοῦ βάπτισμα μετανοίας
of the entrance of him a baptism of repentance
παντὶ τῷ λαῷ Ἰσραήλ. 25 ὡς δὲ
to all the people of Israel. Now as
ἐπλήρου Ἰωάννης τὸν δρόμον, ἔλεγεν·
completed John the(his) course, he said:
τί ἐμὲ ὑπονοεῖτε εἶναι; οὐκ εἰμὶ ἐγώ·
What me suppose ye to be? [3]Not [2]am [1]I;
ἀλλ' ἰδοὺ ἔρχεται μετ' ἐμὲ οὗ οὐκ εἰμὶ
but behold he comes after me of whom I am not
ἄξιος τὸ ὑπόδημα τῶν ποδῶν λῦσαι.
worthy the sandal of the feet to loosen.
26 Ἄνδρες ἀδελφοί, υἱοὶ γένους Ἀβραὰμ
Men brothers, sons of [the] race of Abraham
καὶ οἱ ἐν ὑμῖν φοβούμενοι τὸν θεόν,
and the [ones] among you fearing – God,

tioned with his hand and
said: "Men of Israel and
you Gentiles who worship
God, listen to me! 17 The
God of the people of Israel
chose our fathers; he made
the people prosper during
their stay in Egypt, with
mighty power he led them
out of that country, 18 he endured their conduct[u] for
about forty years in the
desert, 19 he overthrew sev-
en nations in Canaan and
gave their land to his people as their inheritance.
20 All this took about 450
years.
"After this, God gave
them judges until the time
of Samuel the prophet.
21 Then the people asked for
a king, and he gave them
Saul son of Kish, of the
tribe of Benjamin, who
ruled forty years. 22 After
removing Saul, he made
David their king. He testified concerning him: 'I
have found David son of
Jesse a man after my own
heart; he will do everything
I want him to do.'
23 "From this man's de-
scendants God has brought
to Israel the Savior Jesus,
as he promised. 24 Before
the coming of Jesus, John
preached repentance and
baptism to all the people of
Israel. 25 As John was
completing his work, he
said: 'Who do you think I
am? I am not that one. No,
but he is coming after me,
whose sandals I am not
worthy to untie.'
26 "Brothers, children of
Abraham, and you God-
fearing Gentiles, it is to us

[m] Gk *Men, Israelites*
[n] Other ancient authorities read *cared for*
[o] Gk *untie the sandals*
[p] Other ancient authorities read *you*

[u] *18* Some manuscripts *and cared for them*

this salvation has been
sent. 27 Because the residents of Jerusalem and
their leaders did not recognize him or understand the
words of the prophets that
are read every sabbath,
they fulfilled those words
by condemning him.
28 Even though they found
no cause for a sentence of
death, they asked Pilate to
have him killed. 29 When
they had carried out everything that was written
about him, they took him
down from the tree and laid
him in a tomb. 30 But God
raised him from the dead;
31 and for many days he appeared to those who came
up with him from Galilee to
Jerusalem, and they are
now his witnesses to the
people. 32 And we bring
you the good news that
what God promised to our
ancestors 33 he has fulfilled
for us, their children, by
raising Jesus; as also it is
written in the second
psalm,

'You are my Son;
today I have
begotten you.'

34 As to his raising him from
the dead, no more to return
to corruption, he has spoken in this way,

'I will give you the
holy promises
made to David.'

35 Therefore he has also
said in another psalm,

'You will not let your
Holy One
experience
corruption.'

36 For David, after he had
served the purpose of God
in his own generation,
died,[q] was laid beside his
ancestors, and experienced
corruption; 37 but he whom
God raised up experienced
no corruption. 38 Let it be
known to you therefore,
my brothers, that through
this man forgiveness of sins

[q] Gk *fell asleep*

ἡμῖν ὁ λόγος τῆς σωτηρίας ταύτης
to us the word of this salvation
ἐξαπεστάλη. 27 οἱ γὰρ κατοικοῦντες ἐν
was sent forth. For the [ones] dwelling in
Ἰερουσαλὴμ καὶ οἱ ἄρχοντες αὐτῶν τοῦτον
Jerusalem and the rulers of them 2this man
ἀγνοήσαντες καὶ τὰς φωνὰς τῶν προφητῶν τὰς
1not knowing and the voices of the prophets –
κατὰ πᾶν σάββατον ἀναγινωσκομένας
2throughout(on) 3every 4sabbath 1being read
κρίναντες ἐπλήρωσαν, 28 καὶ μηδεμίαν
judging they fulfilled, and no
αἰτίαν θανάτου εὑρόντες ᾐτήσαντο Πιλᾶτον
cause of death finding they asked Pilate
ἀναιρεθῆναι αὐτόν· 29 ὡς δὲ ἐτέλεσαν πάντα
to be destroyed him; and when they finished all
τὰ περὶ αὐτοῦ γεγραμμένα, καθελόντες
the things concerning him having been written, taking down
ἀπὸ τοῦ ξύλου ἔθηκαν εἰς μνημεῖον.
from the tree they laid in a tomb.
30 ὁ δὲ θεὸς ἤγειρεν αὐτὸν ἐκ νεκρῶν·
– But God raised him out of [the] dead;
31 ὃς ὤφθη ἐπὶ ἡμέρας πλείους τοῖς
who appeared over days many to the [ones]
συναναβᾶσιν αὐτῷ ἀπὸ τῆς Γαλιλαίας εἰς
having come up with him from – Galilee to
Ἰερουσαλήμ, οἵτινες [νῦν] εἰσιν μάρτυρες
Jerusalem, who now are witnesses
αὐτοῦ πρὸς τὸν λαόν. 32 καὶ ἡμεῖς
of him to the people. And we
ὑμᾶς εὐαγγελιζόμεθα τὴν πρὸς τοὺς
[to] you preach 1the 4to 5the
πατέρας ἐπαγγελίαν γενομένην, 33 ὅτι
6fathers 2promise 3having come, that
ταύτην ὁ θεὸς ἐκπεπλήρωκεν τοῖς τέκνοις
this [promise] – God has fulfilled 2*to* the 3children
ἡμῖν ἀναστήσας Ἰησοῦν, ὡς καὶ ἐν τῷ
1to us raising up Jesus, as also in the
ψαλμῷ γέγραπται τῷ δευτέρῳ· υἱός μου
2psalm 3it has been written – 1second: Son of me
εἶ σύ, ἐγὼ σήμερον γεγέννηκά σε. 34 ὅτι δὲ
art thou, I to-day have begotten thee. And that
ἀνέστησεν αὐτὸν ἐκ νεκρῶν μηκέτι
he raised up him out of [the] dead no more
μέλλοντα ὑποστρέφειν εἰς διαφθοράν, οὕτως
being about to return to corruption, thus
εἴρηκεν ὅτι δώσω ὑμῖν τὰ ὅσια Δαυὶδ τὰ
he has said[,] – I will give you the 2holy things 3of David *the*
πιστά. 35 διότι καὶ ἐν ἑτέρῳ λέγει·
1faithful. Wherefore also in another [psalm] he says:
οὐ δώσεις τὸν ὅσιόν σου ἰδεῖν διαφθοράν.
Thou wilt not give the holy one of thee to see corruption.
36 Δαυὶδ μὲν γὰρ ἰδίᾳ γενεᾷ ὑπηρετήσας
For David indeed [his] own generation having served
τῇ τοῦ θεοῦ βουλῇ ἐκοιμήθη καὶ προσετέθη
by the – of God counsel fell asleep and was added
πρὸς τοὺς πατέρας αὐτοῦ καὶ εἶδεν
to the fathers of him and saw
διαφθοράν· 37 ὃν δὲ ὁ θεὸς ἤγειρεν,
corruption; but [he] whom – God raised,
οὐκ εἶδεν διαφθοράν. 38 γνωστὸν οὖν
did not see corruption. Known therefore
ἔστω ὑμῖν, ἄνδρες ἀδελφοί, ὅτι διὰ
let it be to you, *men* brothers, that through

that this message of salvation has been sent. 27 The
people of Jerusalem and
their rulers did not recognize Jesus, yet in condemning him they fulfilled the
words of the prophets that
are read every Sabbath.
28 Though they found no
proper ground for a death
sentence, they asked Pilate
to have him executed.
29 When they had carried
out all that was written
about him, they took him
down from the tree and laid
him in a tomb. 30 But God
raised him from the dead,
31 and for many days he was
seen by those who had
traveled with him from Galilee to Jerusalem. They are
now his witnesses to our
people.

32 "We tell you the good
news: What God promised
our fathers 33 he has fulfilled
for us, their children, by
raising up Jesus. As it is
written in the second
Psalm:

" 'You are my Son;
today I have become
your Father.'[v][w]

34 The fact that God raised
him from the dead, never to
decay, is stated in these
words:

" 'I will give you the
holy and sure
blessings promised
to David.'[x]

35 So it is stated elsewhere:

" 'You will not let your
Holy One see
decay.'[y]

36 "For when David had
served God's purpose in
his own generation, he fell
asleep; he was buried with
his fathers and his body de-
cayed. 37 But the one whom
God raised from the dead
did not see decay.

38 "Therefore, my broth-
ers, I want you to know
that through Jesus the for-

[v] *33* Or *have begotten you*
[w] *33* Psalm 2:7
[x] *34* Isaiah 55:3
[y] *35* Psalm 16:10

is proclaimed to you; 39by
this Jesus[r] everyone who
believes is set free from all
those sins[s] from which you
could not be freed by the
law of Moses. 40Beware,
therefore, that what the
prophets said does not happen to you:
41 'Look, you scoffers!
Be amazed and
perish,
for in your days I am
doing a work,
a work that you will
never believe,
even if someone
tells you.' "
42 As Paul and Barna-
bas[t] were going out, the
people urged them to speak
about these things again the
next sabbath. 43When the
meeting of the synagogue
broke up, many Jews and
devout converts to Judaism
followed Paul and Barna-
bas, who spoke to them and
urged them to continue in
the grace of God.
44 The next sabbath al-
most the whole city gath-
ered to hear the word of the
Lord.[u] 45But when the
Jews saw the crowds, they
were filled with jealousy;
and blaspheming, they contradicted what was spoken
by Paul. 46Then both Paul
and Barnabas spoke out
boldly, saying, "It was necessary that the word of God
should be spoken first to
you. Since you reject it and
judge yourselves to be unworthy of eternal life, we
are now turning to the Gentiles. 47For so the Lord has
commanded us, saying,
'I have set you to be
a light for
the Gentiles,
so that you may
bring salvation
to the ends of
the earth.' "
48 When the Gentiles
heard this, they were glad
and praised the word of the
Lord; and as many as had

[r] Gk *this*
[s] Gk *all*
[t] Gk *they*
[u] Other ancient authorities read *God*

τούτου ὑμῖν ἄφεσις ἁμαρτιῶν καταγγέλ-
this man to you forgiveness of sins is an-
λεται, καὶ ἀπὸ πάντων ὧν οὐκ ἠδυνήθητε
nounced, and from all things from which ye could not
ἐν νόμῳ Μωϋσέως δικαιωθῆναι, **39** ἐν
by [the] law of Moses *to* be justified, by
τούτῳ πᾶς ὁ πιστεύων δικαιοῦται. **40** βλέπετε
this man everyone believing is justified. Look ye
οὖν μὴ ἐπέλθῃ τὸ εἰρημένον
therefore lest come on [you] the thing having been said
ἐν τοῖς προφήταις· **41** ἴδετε, οἱ κατα-
in the prophets: See, the des-
φρονηταί, καὶ θαυμάσατε καὶ ἀφανίσθητε,
pisers, and marvel ye and perish,
ὅτι ἔργον ἐργάζομαι ἐγὼ ἐν ταῖς ἡμέραις
because a work work I in the days
ὑμῶν, ἔργον ὃ οὐ μὴ πιστεύσητε ἐάν
of you, a work which by no means ye believe if
τις ἐκδιηγῆται ὑμῖν. **42** Ἐξιόντων δὲ
anyone declares to you. And going out
=as they went out
αὐτῶν παρεκάλουν εἰς τὸ μεταξὺ σάββατον
them[a] they besought in the intervening sabbath(week)
λαληθῆναι αὐτοῖς τὰ ῥήματα ταῦτα.
to be spoken to them these words.
43 λυθείσης δὲ τῆς συναγωγῆς ἠκολούθησαν
And being broken up the assembly[a] [8]followed
=when the assembly was broken up
πολλοὶ τῶν Ἰουδαίων καὶ τῶν σεβομένων
[1]many [2]of the [3]Jews [4]and [5]of the [6]worshipping
προσηλύτων τῷ Παύλῳ καὶ τῷ Βαρναβᾷ,
[7]proselytes – [9]Paul and – Barnabas,
οἵτινες προσλαλοῦντες αὐτοῖς ἔπειθον αὐτοὺς
who speaking to them persuaded them
προσμένειν τῇ χάριτι τοῦ θεοῦ. **44** Τῷ δὲ
to continue in the grace – of God. And on the
ἐρχομένῳ σαββάτῳ σχεδὸν πᾶσα ἡ
coming sabbath almost all the
πόλις συνήχθη ἀκοῦσαι τὸν λόγον τοῦ
city was assembled to hear the word –
θεοῦ. **45** ἰδόντες δὲ οἱ Ἰουδαῖοι τοὺς
of God. But [3]seeing [1]the [2]Jews the
ὄχλους ἐπλήσθησαν ζήλου, καὶ ἀντέλεγον
crowds were filled of(with) jealousy, and contradicted
τοῖς ὑπὸ Παύλου λαλουμένοις βλασφημοῦντες.
the things by Paul being spoken blaspheming.
46 παρρησιασάμενοί τε ὁ Παῦλος καὶ ὁ
And speaking boldly – Paul and –
Βαρναβᾶς εἶπαν· ὑμῖν ἦν ἀναγκαῖον πρῶτον
Barnabas said: To you it was necessary firstly
λαληθῆναι τὸν λόγον τοῦ θεοῦ· ἐπειδὴ
to be spoken the word – of God; since
ἀπωθεῖσθε αὐτὸν καὶ οὐκ ἀξίους κρίνετε
ye put away it and not worthy judge
ἑαυτοὺς τῆς αἰωνίου ζωῆς, ἰδοὺ στρεφόμεθα
yourselves of the eternal life, behold we turn
εἰς τὰ ἔθνη. **47** οὕτως γὰρ ἐντέταλται
to the nations. For thus has commanded
ἡμῖν ὁ κύριος· τέθεικά σε εἰς φῶς
us the Lord: I have set thee for a light
ἐθνῶν τοῦ εἶναί σε εἰς σωτηρίαν ἕως
of nations – to be thee[b] for salvation to
ἐσχάτου τῆς γῆς. **48** ἀκούοντα δὲ τὰ ἔθνη
[the] end of the earth. And [3]hearing [1]the [2]nations
ἔχαιρον καὶ ἐδόξαζον τὸν λόγον τοῦ κυρίου, καὶ
rejoiced and glorified the word of the Lord, and

giveness of sins is pro-
claimed to you. 39Through
him everyone who believes
is justified from everything
you could not be justified
from by the law of Moses.
40Take care that what the
prophets have said does
not happen to you:

41" 'Look, you scoffers,
wonder and perish,
for I am going to do
something in your
days
that you would never
believe,
even if someone told
you.'[z]"

42As Paul and Barnabas
were leaving the syna-
gogue, the people invited
them to speak further about
these things on the next
Sabbath. 43When the con-
gregation was dismissed,
many of the Jews and de-
vout converts to Judaism
followed Paul and Barna-
bas, who talked with them
and urged them to continue
in the grace of God.
44On the next Sabbath al-
most the whole city gath-
ered to hear the word of the
Lord. 45When the Jews saw
the crowds, they were
filled with jealousy and
talked abusively against
what Paul was saying.
46Then Paul and Barna-
bas answered them boldly:
"We had to speak the word
of God to you first. Since
you reject it and do not consider yourselves worthy of
eternal life, we now turn to
the Gentiles. 47For this is
what the Lord has com-
manded us:

" 'I have made you[a] a
light for the
Gentiles,
that you[a] may bring
salvation to the ends
of the earth.'[b]"

48When the Gentiles
heard this, they were glad
and honored the word of

[z]*41* Hab. 1:5
[a]*47* The Greek is singular.
[b]*47* Isaiah 49:6

been destined for eternal
life became believers.
49Thus the word of the
Lord spread throughout the
region. 50But the Jews in-
cited the devout women of
high standing and the leading men of the city, and
stirred up persecution
against Paul and Barnabas,
and drove them out of their
region. 51So they shook the
dust off their feet in protest
against them, and went to
Iconium. 52And the disci-
ples were filled with joy
and with the Holy Spirit.

Chapter 14

Paul and Barnabas in Iconium

THE same thing oc-
curred in Iconium,
where Paul and Barnabas[r]
went into the Jewish synagogue and spoke in such a
way that a great number of
both Jews and Greeks be-
came believers. 2But the
unbelieving Jews stirred up
the Gentiles and poisoned
their minds against the
brothers. 3So they re-
mained for a long time,
speaking boldly for the
Lord, who testified to the
word of his grace by grant-
ing signs and wonders to be
done through them. 4But
the residents of the city
were divided; some sided
with the Jews, and some
with the apostles. 5And
when an attempt was made
by both Gentiles and Jews,
with their rulers, to mistreat them and to stone
them, 6the apostles[r]
learned of it and fled to
Lystra and Derbe, cities of
Lycaonia, and to the sur-
rounding country; 7and
there they continued pro-
claiming the good news.

Paul and Barnabas in Lystra and Derbe

8 In Lystra there was a
man sitting who could not

ἐπίστευσαν ὅσοι ἦσαν τεταγμένοι εἰς
[7]believed [1]as many as [2]were [3]*having been* disposed [4]to
ζωὴν αἰώνιον· **49** διεφέρετο δὲ ὁ λόγος τοῦ
[6]life [5]eternal; and was carried *through* the word of the
κυρίου δι' ὅλης τῆς χώρας. **50** οἱ δὲ
Lord through all the country. But the
Ἰουδαῖοι παρώτρυναν τὰς σεβομένας γυναῖκας
Jews urged on the [3]worshipping [2]women
τὰς εὐσχήμονας καὶ τοὺς πρώτους τῆς
– [1]honourable and the chief men of the
πόλεως, καὶ ἐπήγειραν διωγμὸν ἐπὶ τὸν
city, and raised up persecution against –
Παῦλον καὶ Βαρναβᾶν, καὶ ἐξέβαλον αὐτοὺς
Paul and Barnabas, and expelled them
ἀπὸ τῶν ὁρίων αὐτῶν. **51** οἱ δὲ ἐκτιναξάμενοι
from the borders of them. But they shaking off
τὸν κονιορτὸν τῶν ποδῶν ἐπ' αὐτοὺς ἦλθον
the dust of the(ir) feet on them came
εἰς Ἰκόνιον, **52** οἵ τε μαθηταὶ ἐπλη-
to Iconium, and the disciples were
ροῦντο χαρᾶς καὶ πνεύματος ἁγίου.
filled of(with) joy and of(with) Spirit Holy.

14 Ἐγένετο δὲ ἐν Ἰκονίῳ κατὰ τὸ αὐτὸ
Now it happened in Iconium [a]together†
εἰσελθεῖν αὐτοὺς εἰς τὴν συναγωγὴν
[1]to enter them[b] into the synagogue
=they entered
τῶν Ἰουδαίων καὶ λαλῆσαι οὕτως ὥστε
of the Jews and to speak[b] so as
πιστεῦσαι Ἰουδαίων τε καὶ Ἑλλήνων
to believe both of Jews and of Greeks
πολὺ πλῆθος. **2** οἱ δὲ ἀπειθήσαντες
a much(great) multitude. But the disobeying
Ἰουδαῖοι ἐπήγειραν καὶ ἐκάκωσαν τὰς
Jews excited and embittered the
ψυχὰς τῶν ἐθνῶν κατὰ τῶν ἀδελφῶν.
minds of the nations against the brothers.
3 ἱκανὸν μὲν οὖν χρόνον διέτριψαν
A considerable – [a]therefore [1]time they continued
παρρησιαζόμενοι ἐπὶ τῷ κυρίῳ τῷ μαρ-
speaking boldly on the Lord – wit-
τυροῦντι ἐπὶ τῷ λόγῳ τῆς χάριτος αὐτοῦ,
nessing to the word of the grace of him,
διδόντι σημεῖα καὶ τέρατα γίνεσθαι διὰ
giving signs and wonders to happen through
τῶν χειρῶν αὐτῶν. **4** ἐσχίσθη δὲ τὸ
the hands of them. But was divided the
πλῆθος τῆς πόλεως, καὶ οἱ μὲν ἦσαν
multitude of the city, and some were
σὺν τοῖς Ἰουδαίοις, οἱ δὲ σὺν τοῖς
with the Jews, but others with the
ἀποστόλοις. **5** ὡς δὲ ἐγένετο ὁρμὴ τῶν
apostles. And when there was a rush [3]of the
ἐθνῶν τε καὶ Ἰουδαίων σὺν τοῖς ἄρχουσιν
[a]nations [1]both [4]and of Jews with the rulers
αὐτῶν ὑβρίσαι καὶ λιθοβολῆσαι αὐτούς,
of them to insult and to stone them,
6 συνιδόντες κατέφυγον εἰς τὰς πόλεις
perceiving they escaped to the cities
τῆς Λυκαονίας Λύστραν καὶ Δέρβην καὶ
– of Lycaonia Lystra and Derbe and
τὴν περίχωρον· **7** κἀκεῖ εὐαγγελιζόμενοι
the neighbourhood; and there evangelizing
ἦσαν. **8** Καί τις ἀνὴρ ἀδύνατος ἐν
they were. And a certain man impotent in

the Lord; and all who were
appointed for eternal life
believed.
49The word of the Lord
spread through the whole
region. 50But the Jews in-
cited the God-fearing wom-
en of high standing and the
leading men of the city.
They stirred up persecution
against Paul and Barnabas,
and expelled them from
their region. 51So they
shook the dust from their
feet in protest against them
and went to Iconium.
52And the disciples were
filled with joy and with the
Holy Spirit.

Chapter 14

In Iconium

AT Iconium Paul and
Barnabas went as
usual into the Jewish synagogue. There they spoke so
effectively that a great
number of Jews and Gen-
tiles believed. 2But the
Jews who refused to be-
lieve stirred up the Gentiles
and poisoned their minds
against the brothers. 3So
Paul and Barnabas spent
considerable time there,
speaking boldly for the
Lord, who confirmed the
message of his grace by enabling them to do miracu-
lous signs and wonders.
4The people of the city
were divided; some sided
with the Jews, others with
the apostles. 5There was a
plot afoot among the Gen-
tiles and Jews, together
with their leaders, to mistreat them and stone them.
6But they found out about it
and fled to the Lycaonian
cities of Lystra and Derbe
and to the surrounding
country, 7where they con-
tinued to preach the good
news.

In Lystra and Derbe

8In Lystra there sat a man
crippled in his feet, who

use his feet and had never walked, for he had been crippled from birth. 9 He listened to Paul as he was speaking. And Paul, looking at him intently and seeing that he had faith to be healed, 10 said in a loud voice, "Stand upright on your feet." And the man[v] sprang up and began to walk. 11 When the crowds saw what Paul had done, they shouted in the Lycaonian language, "The gods have come down to us in human form!" 12 Barnabas they called Zeus, and Paul they called Hermes, because he was the chief speaker. 13 The priest of Zeus, whose temple was just outside the city,[w] brought oxen and garlands to the gates; he and the crowds wanted to offer sacrifice. 14 When the apostles Barnabas and Paul heard of it, they tore their clothes and rushed out into the crowd, shouting, 15 "Friends,[x] why are you doing this? We are mortals just like you, and we bring you good news, that you should turn from these worthless things to the living God, who made the heaven and the earth and the sea and all that is in them. 16 In past generations he allowed all the nations to follow their own ways; 17 yet he has not left himself without a witness in doing good—giving you rains from heaven and fruitful seasons, and filling you with food and your hearts with joy." 18 Even with

[v] Gk *he*
[w] Or *The priest of Zeus-Outside-the-City*
[x] Gk *Men*

Λύστροις τοῖς ποσὶν ἐκάθητο, χωλὸς ἐκ
Lystra in the feet sat, lame from

κοιλίας μητρὸς αὐτοῦ ὃς οὐδέποτε
[the] womb of [the] mother of him who never

περιεπάτησεν. 9 οὗτος ἤκουεν τοῦ Παύλου
walked. This man heard – Paul

λαλοῦντος· ὃς ἀτενίσας αὐτῷ καὶ ἰδὼν
speaking; who gazing at him and seeing

ὅτι ἔχει πίστιν τοῦ σωθῆναι, 10 εἶπεν
that he has(had) faith – to be healed,[d] said

μεγάλῃ φωνῇ· ἀνάστηθι ἐπὶ τοὺς πόδας
with a great(loud) voice: Stand up on the feet

σου ὀρθός. καὶ ἥλατο καὶ περιεπάτει.
of thee erect. And he leaped up and walked.

11 οἵ τε ὄχλοι ἰδόντες ὃ ἐποίησεν Παῦλος
And the crowds seeing what did Paul

ἐπῆραν τὴν φωνὴν αὐτῶν Λυκαονιστὶ
lifted up the voice of them in Lycaonian

λέγοντες· οἱ θεοὶ ὁμοιωθέντες ἀνθρώποις
saying: The gods made like men

κατέβησαν πρὸς ἡμᾶς, 12 ἐκάλουν τε τὸν
came down to us, and they called –

Βαρναβᾶν Δία, τὸν δὲ Παῦλον Ἑρμῆν,
Barnabas Zeus, – and Paul Hermes,

ἐπειδὴ αὐτὸς ἦν ὁ ἡγούμενος τοῦ λόγου.
since he was the leader of the discourse.

13 ὅ τε ἱερεὺς τοῦ Διὸς τοῦ ὄντος πρὸ
And the priest – of Zeus – being before

τῆς πόλεως, ταύρους καὶ στέμματα ἐπὶ
the city, bulls and garlands to

τοὺς πυλῶνας ἐνέγκας, σὺν τοῖς ὄχλοις
the gates bringing, with the crowds

ἤθελεν θύειν. 14 ἀκούσαντες δὲ οἱ
wished to sacrifice. But [6]hearing [1]the

ἀπόστολοι Βαρναβᾶς καὶ Παῦλος, διαρ-
[2]apostles [3]Barnabas [4]and [5]Paul, rend-

ρήξαντες τὰ ἱμάτια ἑαυτῶν ἐξεπήδησαν εἰς
ing the garments of them*selves* rushed out into

τὸν ὄχλον, κράζοντες 15 καὶ λέγοντες·
the crowd, crying out and saying:

ἄνδρες, τί ταῦτα ποιεῖτε; καὶ ἡμεῖς
Men, why these things do ye? [2]also [1]we

ὁμοιοπαθεῖς ἐσμεν ὑμῖν ἄνθρωποι, εὐαγ-
[5]of like nature [3]are [6]to you [4]men, preach-

γελιζόμενοι ὑμᾶς ἀπὸ τούτων τῶν ματαίων
ing [to] you from these – vanities

ἐπιστρέφειν ἐπὶ θεὸν ζῶντα, ὃς ἐποίησεν
to turn to God a living, who made

τὸν οὐρανὸν καὶ τὴν γῆν καὶ τὴν
the heaven and the earth and the

θάλασσαν καὶ πάντα τὰ ἐν αὐτοῖς· 16 ὃς
sea and all the things in them; who

ἐν ταῖς παρῳχημέναις γενεαῖς εἴασεν πάντα
in the having passed generations allowed all

τὰ ἔθνη πορεύεσθαι ταῖς ὁδοῖς αὐτῶν·
the nations to go in the ways of them;

17 καίτοι οὐκ ἀμάρτυρον αὐτὸν ἀφῆκεν
and yet [2]not [4]unwitnessed [3]himself [1]left

ἀγαθουργῶν, οὐρανόθεν ὑμῖν ὑετοὺς διδοὺς
doing good, [4]from heaven [3]us [2]rain [1]giving

καὶ καιροὺς καρποφόρους, ἐμπιπλῶν τροφῆς
and times fruit-bearing, filling of(with) food

καὶ εὐφροσύνης τὰς καρδίας ὑμῶν. 18 καὶ
and of(with) gladness the hearts of us. And

was lame from birth and had never walked. 9 He listened to Paul as he was speaking. Paul looked directly at him, saw that he had faith to be healed 10 and called out, "Stand up on your feet!" At that, the man jumped up and began to walk.

11 When the crowd saw what Paul had done, they shouted in the Lycaonian language, "The gods have come down to us in human form!" 12 Barnabas they called Zeus, and Paul they called Hermes because he was the chief speaker. 13 The priest of Zeus, whose temple was just outside the city, brought bulls and wreaths to the city gates because he and the crowd wanted to offer sacrifices to them.

14 But when the apostles Barnabas and Paul heard of this, they tore their clothes and rushed out into the crowd, shouting: 15 "Men, why are you doing this? We too are only men, human like you. We are bringing you good news, telling you to turn from these worthless things to the living God, who made heaven and earth and sea and everything in them. 16 In the past, he let all nations go their own way. 17 Yet he has not left himself without testimony: He has shown kindness by giving you rain from heaven and crops in their seasons; he provides you with plenty of food and fills your hearts with joy."

these words, they scarcely restrained the crowds from offering sacrifice to them.

19 But Jews came there from Antioch and Iconium and won over the crowds. Then they stoned Paul and dragged him out of the city, supposing that he was dead. 20 But when the disciples surrounded him, he got up and went into the city. The next day he went on with Barnabas to Derbe.

The Return to Antioch in Syria

21 After they had proclaimed the good news to that city and had made many disciples, they returned to Lystra, then on to Iconium and Antioch. 22 There they strengthened the souls of the disciples and encouraged them to continue in the faith, saying, "It is through many persecutions that we must enter the kingdom of God." 23 And after they had appointed elders for them in each church, with prayer and fasting they entrusted them to the Lord in whom they had come to believe. 24 Then they passed through Pisidia and came to Pamphylia. 25 When they had spoken the word in Perga, they went down to Attalia. 26 From there they sailed back to Antioch, where they had been commended to the grace of God for the work[y] that they had completed. 27 When they arrived, they called the church together and related all that God had done with them, and how he had opened a door of faith for the Gentiles. 28 And they stayed there with the disciples for some time.

ταῦτα λέγοντες μόλις κατέπαυσαν τοὺς
these things saying scarcely they restrained the
ὄχλους τοῦ μὴ θύειν αὐτοῖς. 19 Ἐπῆλθαν
crowds – not to sacrifice[d] to them. [6]came upon [the scene]
δὲ ἀπὸ Ἀντιοχείας καὶ Ἰκονίου Ἰουδαῖοι,
And [2]from [3]Antioch [4]and [5]Iconium [1]Jews,
καὶ πείσαντες τοὺς ὄχλους καὶ λιθάσαντες
and persuading the crowds and stoning
τὸν Παῦλον ἔσυρον ἔξω τῆς πόλεως,
– Paul dragged outside the city,
νομίζοντες αὐτὸν τεθνηκέναι. 20 κυκλω-
supposing him to have died. But sur-
σάντων δὲ τῶν μαθητῶν αὐτὸν ἀναστὰς
rounding the disciples[a] him rising up
=as the disciples surrounded
εἰσῆλθεν εἰς τὴν πόλιν. Καὶ τῇ ἐπαύριον
he entered into the city. And on the morrow
ἐξῆλθεν σὺν τῷ Βαρναβᾷ εἰς Δέρβην.
he went forth with – Barnabas to Derbe.
21 εὐαγγελιζόμενοί τε τὴν πόλιν ἐκείνην
And evangelizing that city
καὶ μαθητεύσαντες ἱκανοὺς ὑπέστρεψαν εἰς
and having made disciples many they returned to
τὴν Λύστραν καὶ εἰς Ἰκόνιον καὶ [εἰς]
– Lystra and to Iconium and to
Ἀντιόχειαν, 22 ἐπιστηρίζοντες τὰς ψυχὰς
Antioch, confirming the minds
τῶν μαθητῶν, παρακαλοῦντες ἐμμένειν τῇ
of the disciples, exhorting to continue in the
πίστει, καὶ ὅτι διὰ πολλῶν θλίψεων
faith, and that through many afflictions
δεῖ ἡμᾶς εἰσελθεῖν εἰς τὴν βασιλείαν τοῦ
it behoves us to enter into the kingdom –
θεοῦ. 23 χειροτονήσαντες δὲ αὐτοῖς κατ᾽
of God. And having appointed for them in
ἐκκλησίαν πρεσβυτέρους, προσευξάμενοι
every church elders, praying
μετὰ νηστειῶν παρέθεντο αὐτοὺς τῷ κυρίῳ
with fastings they committed them to the Lord
εἰς ὃν πεπιστεύκεισαν. 24 καὶ διελθόντες
in whom they had believed. And passing through
τὴν Πισιδίαν ἦλθον εἰς τὴν Παμφυλίαν,
– Pisidia they came to – Pamphylia,
25 καὶ λαλήσαντες εἰς τὴν Πέργην τὸν
and speaking in – Perga the
λόγον κατέβησαν εἰς Ἀττάλειαν, κἀκεῖθεν
word they came down to Attalia, and thence
ἀπέπλευσαν εἰς Ἀντιόχειαν, 26 ὅθεν ἦσαν
sailed away to Antioch, whence they were
παραδεδομένοι τῇ χάριτι τοῦ θεοῦ εἰς
having been commended to the grace – of God for
τὸ ἔργον ὃ ἐπλήρωσαν. 27 Παραγεν-
the work which they accomplished. And having
όμενοι δὲ καὶ συναγαγόντες τὴν ἐκκλησίαν,
arrived and assembling the church,
ἀνήγγελλον ὅσα ἐποίησεν ὁ θεὸς μετ᾽
they reported what things did – God with
αὐτῶν, καὶ ὅτι ἤνοιξεν τοῖς ἔθνεσιν
them, and that he opened to the nations
θύραν πίστεως. 28 διέτριβον δὲ χρόνον
a door of faith. And they continued time
οὐκ ὀλίγον σὺν τοῖς μαθηταῖς.
not a little with the disciples.

18 Even with these words, they had difficulty keeping the crowd from sacrificing to them.

19 Then some Jews came from Antioch and Iconium and won the crowd over. They stoned Paul and dragged him outside the city, thinking he was dead. 20 But after the disciples had gathered around him, he got up and went back into the city. The next day he and Barnabas left for Derbe.

The Return to Antioch in Syria

21 They preached the good news in that city and won a large number of disciples. Then they returned to Lystra, Iconium and Antioch, 22 strengthening the disciples and encouraging them to remain true to the faith. "We must go through many hardships to enter the kingdom of God," they said. 23 Paul and Barnabas appointed elders[c] for them in each church and, with prayer and fasting, committed them to the Lord, in whom they had put their trust. 24 After going through Pisidia, they came into Pamphylia, 25 and when they had preached the word in Perga, they went down to Attalia.

26 From Attalia they sailed back to Antioch, where they had been committed to the grace of God for the work they had now completed. 27 On arriving there, they gathered the church together and reported all that God had done through them and how he had opened the door of faith to the Gentiles. 28 And they stayed there a long time with the disciples.

[y] Or *committed in the grace of God to the work*

[c] 23 Or *Barnabas ordained elders*; or *Barnabas had elders elected*

Chapter 15

The Council at Jerusalem

THEN certain individu-
als came down from
Judea and were teaching
the brothers, "Unless you
are circumcised according
to the custom of Moses,
you cannot be saved."
2 And after Paul and Barnabas had no small dissension
and debate with them, Paul
and Barnabas and some of
the others were appointed
to go up to Jerusalem to discuss this question with the
apostles and the elders.
3 So they were sent on their
way by the church, and as
they passed through both
Phoenicia and Samaria,
they reported the conver-
sion of the Gentiles, and
brought great joy to all the
believers.[z] 4 When they
came to Jerusalem, they
were welcomed by the
church and the apostles
and the elders, and they reported all that God had
done with them. 5 But some
believers who belonged to
the sect of the Pharisees
stood up and said, "It is
necessary for them to be
circumcised and ordered to
keep the law of Moses."
6 The apostles and the
elders met together to consider this matter. 7 After
there had been much de-
bate, Peter stood up and
said to them, "My broth-
ers,[a] you know that in the
early days God made a
choice among you, that I
should be the one through
whom the Gentiles would
hear the message of the
good news and become be-
lievers. 8 And God, who
knows the human heart,
testified to them by giving

[z] Gk *brothers*
[a] Gk *Men, brothers*

15 Καὶ τινες κατελθόντες ἀπὸ τῆς
And some going down from –
Ἰουδαίας ἐδίδασκον τοὺς ἀδελφοὺς ὅτι
Judæa taught the brothers[,] –
ἐὰν μὴ περιτμηθῆτε τῷ ἔθει τῷ Μωϋσέως,
Unless ye are circumcised by the custom – of Moses,
οὐ δύνασθε σωθῆναι. **2** γενομένης δὲ
ye cannot *to* be saved. And taking place
στάσεως καὶ ζητήσεως οὐκ ὀλίγης τῷ
discord and questioning not a little[a] –
=when there took place not a little . . .
Παύλῳ καὶ τῷ Βαρναβᾷ πρὸς αὐτούς,
by Paul and – Barnabas with them,
ἔταξαν ἀναβαίνειν Παῦλον καὶ Βαρναβᾶν
they assigned to go up Paul and Barnabas
καί τινας ἄλλους ἐξ αὐτῶν πρὸς τοὺς
and some others of them to the
ἀποστόλους καὶ πρεσβυτέρους εἰς Ἰερουσαλὴμ
apostles and elders in Jerusalem
περὶ τοῦ ζητήματος τούτου. **3** Οἱ μὲν
about this question. They –
οὖν προπεμφθέντες ὑπὸ τῆς ἐκκλησίας
therefore being set forward by the church
διήρχοντο τήν τε Φοινίκην καὶ Σαμάρειαν
passed through – both Phœnicia and Samaria
ἐκδιηγούμενοι τὴν ἐπιστροφὴν τῶν ἐθνῶν,
telling in detail the conversion of the nations,
καὶ ἐποίουν χαρὰν μεγάλην πᾶσιν τοῖς
and caused joy great to all the
ἀδελφοῖς. **4** παραγενόμενοι δὲ εἰς Ἰεροσόλυμα
brothers. And having arrived in Jerusalem
παρεδέχθησαν ἀπὸ τῆς ἐκκλησίας καὶ τῶν
they were welcomed from the church and the
ἀποστόλων καὶ τῶν πρεσβυτέρων, ἀνήγ-
apostles and the elders, and
γειλάν τε ὅσα ὁ θεὸς ἐποίησεν μετ'
reported what things – God did with
αὐτῶν. **5** Ἐξανέστησαν δέ τινες τῶν
them. But stood forth some of the [ones]
ἀπὸ τῆς αἱρέσεως τῶν Φαρισαίων
from the sect of the Pharisees
πεπιστευκότες, λέγοντες ὅτι δεῖ περιτέμνειν
having believed, saying[,] – It behoves to circumcise
αὐτοὺς παραγγέλλειν τε τηρεῖν τὸν νόμον
them and to charge to keep the law
Μωϋσέως.
of Moses.
6 Συνήχθησάν τε οἱ ἀπόστολοι καὶ οἱ
And were assembled the apostles and the
πρεσβύτεροι ἰδεῖν περὶ τοῦ λόγου τούτου.
elders to see about this matter.
7 Πολλῆς δὲ ζητήσεως γενομένης ἀναστὰς
And much questioning having taken place[a] rising up
=When much questioning had . . .
Πέτρος εἶπεν πρὸς αὐτούς· ἄνδρες ἀδελφοί,
Peter said to them: *Men* brothers,
ὑμεῖς ἐπίστασθε ὅτι ἀφ' ἡμερῶν ἀρχαίων
ye understand that from days olden
ἐν ὑμῖν ἐξελέξατο ὁ θεὸς διὰ τοῦ στόματός
[3]among [4]you [2]chose – [1]God through the mouth
μου ἀκοῦσαι τὰ ἔθνη τὸν λόγον τοῦ
of me [3]to hear [1]the [2]nations the word of the
εὐαγγελίου καὶ πιστεῦσαι. **8** καὶ ὁ
gospel and to believe. And [2]the
καρδιογνώστης θεὸς ἐμαρτύρησεν αὐτοῖς
[3]Heart-knower [1]God witnessed to them

Chapter 15

The Council at Jerusalem

SOME men came down
from Judea to Antioch
and were teaching the
brothers: "Unless you are
circumcised, according to
the custom taught by Mo-
ses, you cannot be saved."
2 This brought Paul and
Barnabas into sharp dis-
pute and debate with them.
So Paul and Barnabas were
appointed, along with some
other believers, to go up to
Jerusalem to see the apostles and elders about this
question. 3 The church sent
them on their way, and as
they traveled through
Phoenicia and Samaria,
they told how the Gentiles
had been converted. This
news made all the brothers
very glad. 4 When they
came to Jerusalem, they
were welcomed by the
church and the apostles
and elders, to whom they
reported everything God
had done through them.
5 Then some of the believers who belonged to the
party of the Pharisees
stood up and said, "The
Gentiles must be circum-
cised and required to obey
the law of Moses."
6 The apostles and elders
met to consider this question. 7 After much discussion, Peter got up and addressed them: "Brothers,
you know that some time
ago God made a choice
among you that the Gen-
tiles might hear from my
lips the message of the gospel and believe. 8 God, who
knows the heart, showed

them the Holy Spirit, just
as he did to us; 9and in
cleansing their hearts by
faith he has made no dis-
tinction between them and
us. 10Now therefore why
are you putting God to the
test by placing on the neck
of the disciples a yoke that
neither our ancestors nor
we have been able to bear?
11On the contrary, we be-
lieve that we will be saved
through the grace of the
Lord Jesus, just as they
will."
12 The whole assembly
kept silence, and listened
to Barnabas and Paul as
they told of all the signs and
wonders that God had done
through them among the
Gentiles. 13After they finished speaking, James re-
plied, "My brothers,[a] listen to me. 14Simeon has related how God first looked
favorably on the Gentiles,
to take from among them a
people for his name. 15This
agrees with the words of
the prophets, as it is written,

16 'After this I will
return,
and I will rebuild the
dwelling of
David, which
has fallen;
from its ruins I will
rebuild it,
and I will set it
up,
17 so that all other
peoples may
seek the Lord—
even all the Gentiles
over whom my
name has been
called.
Thus says the
Lord, who has
been making
these things
18known from
long ago.'[b]

19Therefore I have reached
the decision that we should
not trouble those Gentiles
who are turning to God,
20but we should write to

δοὺς τὸ πνεῦμα τὸ ἅγιον καθὼς καὶ
giving the Spirit – Holy as also

ἡμῖν, 9 καὶ οὐθὲν διέκρινεν μεταξὺ ἡμῶν
to us, and nothing distinguished between [2]us

τε καὶ αὐτῶν, τῇ πίστει καθαρίσας τὰς
[1]both and them, – by faith cleansing the

καρδίας αὐτῶν. 10 νῦν οὖν τί πειράζετε
hearts of them. Now therefore why test ye

τὸν θεόν, ἐπιθεῖναι ζυγὸν ἐπὶ τὸν
– God, to put *on* a yoke on the

τράχηλον τῶν μαθητῶν, ὃν οὔτε οἱ
neck of the disciples, which neither the

πατέρες ἡμῶν οὔτε ἡμεῖς ἰσχύσαμεν
fathers of us nor we were able

βαστάσαι; 11 ἀλλὰ διὰ τῆς χάριτος τοῦ
to bear? but through the grace of the

κυρίου Ἰησοῦ πιστεύομεν σωθῆναι καθ'
Lord Jesus we believe to be saved in

ὃν τρόπον κἀκεῖνοι. 12 Ἐσίγησεν δὲ
the same way as† those also. And was silent

πᾶν τὸ πλῆθος, καὶ ἤκουον Βαρναβᾶ
all the multitude, and heard Barnabas

καὶ Παύλου ἐξηγουμένων ὅσα ἐποίησεν
and Paul relating [1]what [6]did

ὁ θεὸς σημεῖα καὶ τέρατα ἐν τοῖς
– [5]God [2]signs [3]and [4]wonders among the

ἔθνεσιν δι' αὐτῶν. 13 Μετὰ δὲ τὸ σιγῆσαι
nations through them. And after the to keep silence
=they kept silence

αὐτοὺς ἀπεκρίθη Ἰάκωβος λέγων· 14 ἄνδρες
them[b] answered James saying: *Men*

ἀδελφοί, ἀκούσατέ μου. Συμεὼν ἐξηγήσατο
brothers, hear ye me. Simeon declared

καθὼς πρῶτον ὁ θεὸς ἐπεσκέψατο λαβεῖν ἐξ
even as firstly – God visited to take out of

ἐθνῶν λαὸν τῷ ὀνόματι αὐτοῦ. 15 καὶ
[the] nations a people for the name of him. And

τούτῳ συμφωνοῦσιν οἱ λόγοι τῶν προφητῶν,
to this agree the words of the prophets,

καθὼς γέγραπται· 16 μετὰ ταῦτα
even as it has been written: After these things

ἀναστρέψω καὶ ἀνοικοδομήσω τὴν σκηνὴν
I will return and I will rebuild the tent

Δαυὶδ τὴν πεπτωκυῖαν, καὶ τὰ κατεστραμ-
of David – having fallen, and the things having been

μένα αὐτῆς ἀνοικοδομήσω καὶ ἀνορθώσω
overturned of it I will rebuild and I will rear again
=its ruins

αὐτήν, 17 ὅπως ἂν ἐκζητήσωσιν οἱ
it, so as – [4]may seek [1]the

κατάλοιποι τῶν ἀνθρώπων τὸν κύριον,
[2]rest – [3]of men [5]the [6]Lord,

καὶ πάντα τὰ ἔθνη ἐφ' οὓς ἐπικέκληται
even all the nations on whom has been invoked

τὸ ὄνομά μου ἐπ' αὐτούς, λέγει κύριος
the name of me *on* *them,* says [the] Lord

ποιῶν ταῦτα 18 γνωστὰ ἀπ' αἰῶνος.
doing these things known from [the] age.

19 διὸ ἐγὼ κρίνω μὴ παρενοχλεῖν τοῖς
Wherefore I decide not to trouble the [ones]

ἀπὸ τῶν ἐθνῶν ἐπιστρέφουσιν ἐπὶ τὸν
from the nations turning to –

θεόν, 20 ἀλλὰ ἐπιστεῖλαι αὐτοῖς τοῦ
God, but to write word to them –

that he accepted them by
giving the Holy Spirit to
them, just as he did to us.
9He made no distinction
between us and them, for
he purified their hearts by
faith. 10Now then, why do
you try to test God by putting on the necks of the disciples a yoke that neither
we nor our fathers have
been able to bear? 11No!
We believe it is through the
grace of our Lord Jesus
that we are saved, just as
they are."
12The whole assembly be-
came silent as they listened
to Barnabas and Paul telling about the miraculous
signs and wonders God had
done among the Gentiles
through them. 13When they
finished, James spoke up:
"Brothers, listen to me.
14Simon[d] has described to
us how God at first showed
his concern by taking from
the Gentiles a people for
himself. 15The words of the
prophets are in agreement
with this, as it is written:

16" 'After this I will return
and rebuild David's
fallen tent.
Its ruins I will rebuild,
and I will restore it,
17that the remnant of men
may seek the Lord,
and all the Gentiles
who bear my name,
says the Lord, who does
these things'[e]
18 that have been known
for ages.[f]

19"It is my judgment,
therefore, that we should
not make it difficult for the
Gentiles who are turning to
God. 20Instead we should
write to them, telling them

[b]Other ancient authorities read *things. 18Known to God from of old are all his works.'*

[d]14 Greek *Simeon,* a variant of *Simon;* that is, Peter
[e]17 Amos 9:11,12
[f]17,18 Some manuscripts *things'— / 18known to the Lord for ages is his work*

them to abstain only from
things polluted by idols and
from fornication and from
whatever has been stran-
gled[c] and from blood.
21 For in every city, for generations past, Moses has
had those who proclaim
him, for he has been read
aloud every sabbath in the
synagogues."

The Council's Letter to Gentile Believers

22 Then the apostles
and the elders, with the
consent of the whole
church, decided to choose
men from among their
members[d] and to send
them to Antioch with Paul
and Barnabas. They sent
Judas called Barsabbas,
and Silas, leaders among
the brothers, 23 with the following letter: "The brothers, both the apostles and
the elders, to the believers[e] of Gentile origin in
Antioch and Syria and Cilicia, greetings. 24 Since we
have heard that certain persons who have gone out
from us, though with no instructions from us, have
said things to disturb you
and have unsettled your
minds,[f] 25 we have decided
unanimously to choose representatives[g] and send
them to you, along with our
beloved Barnabas and
Paul, 26 who have risked
their lives for the sake of
our Lord Jesus Christ.
27 We have therefore sent
Judas and Silas, who themselves will tell you the same
things by word of mouth.
28 For it has seemed good to
the Holy Spirit and to us to
impose on you no further
burden than these essen-
tials: 29 that you abstain
from what has been sacri-
ficed to idols and from
blood and from what is
strangled[h] and from fornication. If you keep your-
selves from these, you will

[c] Other ancient authorities lack *and from whatever has been strangled*
[d] Gk *from among them*
[e] Gk *brothers*
[f] Other ancient authorities add *saying, 'You must be circumcised and keep the law,'*
[g] Gk *men*
[h] Other ancient authorities lack *and from what is strangled*

ἀπέχεσθαι τῶν ἀλισγημάτων τῶν εἰδώλων
to abstain from[d] the pollutions – of idols

καὶ τῆς πορνείας καὶ πνικτοῦ καὶ τοῦ
and – fornication and a thing strangled and –

αἵματος. 21 Μωϋσῆς γὰρ ἐκ γενεῶν
blood. For 1Moses 2from 4generations

ἀρχαίων κατὰ πόλιν τοὺς κηρύσσοντας
3ancient 6in every city 7the [ones] 8proclaiming

αὐτὸν ἔχει ἐν ταῖς συναγωγαῖς κατὰ
9him 5has 11in 12the 13synagogues 14on

πᾶν σάββατον ἀναγινωσκόμενος. 22 Τότε
15every 16sabbath 10being read. Then

ἔδοξε τοῖς ἀποστόλοις καὶ τοῖς πρεσ-
it seemed [good] to the apostles and to the el-

βυτέροις σὺν ὅλῃ τῇ ἐκκλησίᾳ ἐκλεξαμένους
ders with all the church chosen

ἄνδρας ἐξ αὐτῶν πέμψαι εἰς Ἀντιόχειαν
men of them to send to Antioch

σὺν τῷ Παύλῳ καὶ Βαρναβᾷ, Ἰούδαν
with – Paul and Barnabas, Judas

τὸν καλούμενον Βαρσαββᾶν καὶ Σιλᾶν,
– *being* called Barsabbas and Silas,

ἄνδρας ἡγουμένους ἐν τοῖς ἀδελφοῖς,
men leading among the brothers,

23 γράψαντες διὰ χειρὸς αὐτῶν· Οἱ
writing through [the] hand of them: The

ἀπόστολοι καὶ οἱ πρεσβύτεροι ἀδελφοὶ
apostles and the elder brothers

τοῖς κατὰ τὴν Ἀντιόχειαν καὶ Συρίαν
1to the 5throughout – 6Antioch 7and 8Syria

καὶ Κιλικίαν ἀδελφοῖς τοῖς ἐξ ἐθνῶν
9and 10Cilicia 2brothers – 3of [the] 4nations

χαίρειν. 24 Ἐπειδὴ ἠκούσαμεν ὅτι τινὲς
11greeting. Since we heard that some

ἐξ ἡμῶν ἐτάραξαν ὑμᾶς λόγοις ἀνασκευάζ-
of us troubled you with words unsettl-

οντες τὰς ψυχὰς ὑμῶν, οἷς οὐ διεστειλάμεθα,
ing the minds of you, to whom we did not give commission,

25 ἔδοξεν ἡμῖν γενομένοις ὁμοθυμαδόν,
it seemed [good] to us becoming of one mind,

ἐκλεξαμένους ἄνδρας πέμψαι πρὸς ὑμᾶς
chosen men to send to you

σὺν τοῖς ἀγαπητοῖς ἡμῶν Βαρναβᾷ καὶ
with the beloved of us Barnabas and

Παύλῳ, 26 ἀνθρώποις παραδεδωκόσι τὰς
Paul, men having given up the

ψυχὰς αὐτῶν ὑπὲρ τοῦ ὀνόματος τοῦ
lives of them on behalf of the name of the

κυρίου ἡμῶν Ἰησοῦ Χριστοῦ. 27 ἀπεστάλ-
Lord of us Jesus Christ. We have

καμεν οὖν Ἰούδαν καὶ Σιλᾶν, καὶ αὐτοὺς
sent therefore Judas and Silas, and they

διὰ λόγου ἀπαγγέλλοντας τὰ αὐτά.
through (by) speech announcing the same things.

28 ἔδοξεν γὰρ τῷ πνεύματι τῷ ἁγίῳ
For it seemed [good] to the Spirit – Holy

καὶ ἡμῖν μηδὲν πλέον ἐπιτίθεσθαι ὑμῖν
and to us 3*no*thing 5more 1to be put on 2you

βάρος πλὴν τούτων τῶν ἐπάναγκες,
4burden than these – necessary things,

29 ἀπέχεσθαι εἰδωλοθύτων καὶ αἵματος καὶ
to abstain from idol sacrifices and blood and

πνικτῶν καὶ πορνείας· ἐξ ὧν διατηροῦντες
things strangled and fornication; from which keeping

to abstain from food polluted by idols, from sexual immorality, from the meat of
strangled animals and from
blood. 21 For Moses has
been preached in every city
from the earliest times and
is read in the synagogues
on every Sabbath."

The Council's Letter to Gentile Believers

22 Then the apostles and
elders, with the whole
church, decided to choose
some of their own men and
send them to Antioch with
Paul and Barnabas. They
chose Judas (called Barsabbas) and Silas, two men
who were leaders among
the brothers. 23 With them
they sent the following letter:

The apostles and elders,
your brothers,

To the Gentile believers
in Antioch, Syria and
Cilicia:

Greetings.

24 We have heard that
some went out from us
without our authoriza-
tion and disturbed you,
troubling your minds by
what they said. 25 So we
all agreed to choose
some men and send
them to you with our
dear friends Barnabas
and Paul— 26 men who
have risked their lives
for the name of our
Lord Jesus Christ.
27 Therefore we are
sending Judas and Silas
to confirm by word of
mouth what we are
writing. 28 It seemed
good to the Holy Spirit
and to us not to burden
you with anything be-
yond the following re-
quirements: 29 You are
to abstain from food
sacrificed to idols, from
blood, from the meat of
strangled animals and
from sexual immorality.

do well. Farewell."
30 So they were sent off
and went down to Antioch.
When they gathered the
congregation together,
they delivered the letter.
31 When its members[i] read
it, they rejoiced at the exhortation. 32 Judas and Silas, who were themselves
prophets, said much to encourage and strengthen the
believers.[e] 33 After they
had been there for some
time, they were sent off in
peace by the believers[e] to
those who had sent them.[j]
35 But Paul and Barnabas
remained in Antioch, and
there, with many others,
they taught and proclaimed
the word of the Lord.

Paul and Barnabas Separate

36 After some days Paul
said to Barnabas, "Come,
let us return and visit the
believers[e] in every city
where we proclaimed the
word of the Lord and see
how they are doing."
37 Barnabas wanted to take
with them John called
Mark. 38 But Paul decided
not to take with them one
who had deserted them in
Pamphylia and had not ac-
companied them in the
work. 39 The disagreement
became so sharp that they
parted company; Barnabas
took Mark with him and
sailed away to Cyprus.
40 But Paul chose Silas and
set out, the believers[e]
commending him to the
grace of the Lord. 41 He
went through Syria and Cilicia, strengthening the
churches.

[i] Gk *When they*
[j] Other ancient authorities add verse 34, *But it seemed good to Silas to remain there*

ἑαυτοὺς εὖ πράξετε. Ἔρρωσθε.
yourselves well ye will do. Farewell.
30 Οἱ μὲν οὖν ἀπολυθέντες κατῆλθον εἰς
They – therefore being dismissed went down to
Ἀντιόχειαν, καὶ συναγαγόντες τὸ πλῆθος
Antioch, and assembling the multitude
ἐπέδωκαν τὴν ἐπιστολήν. 31 ἀναγνόντες δὲ
handed in the letter. And having read
ἐχάρησαν ἐπὶ τῇ παρακλήσει. 32 Ἰούδας τε
they rejoiced at the exhortation. And Judas
καὶ Σιλᾶς, καὶ αὐτοὶ προφῆται ὄντες,
and Silas, also [them]selves prophets being,
διὰ λόγου πολλοῦ παρεκάλεσαν τοὺς
through (by) speech much exhorted the
ἀδελφοὺς καὶ ἐπεστήριξαν· 33 ποιήσαντες δὲ
brothers and confirmed; and having continued
χρόνον ἀπελύθησαν μετ' εἰρήνης ἀπὸ
a time they were dismissed with peace from
τῶν ἀδελφῶν πρὸς τοὺς ἀποστείλαντας
the brothers to the [ones] having sent
αὐτούς. ‡ 35 Παῦλος δὲ καὶ Βαρναβᾶς
them. But Paul and Barnabas
διέτριβον ἐν Ἀντιοχείᾳ, διδάσκοντες καὶ
stayed in Antioch, teaching and
εὐαγγελιζόμενοι μετὰ καὶ ἑτέρων πολλῶν
preaching [1]with [4]also [3]others [2]many
τὸν λόγον τοῦ κυρίου.
the word of the Lord.
36 Μετὰ δέ τινας ἡμέρας εἶπεν πρὸς
Now after some days [2]said [3]to
Βαρναβᾶν Παῦλος· ἐπιστρέψαντες δὴ
[4]Barnabas [1]Paul: Returning then
ἐπισκεψώμεθα τοὺς ἀδελφοὺς κατὰ πόλιν
let us visit the brothers throughout [2]city
πᾶσαν ἐν αἷς κατηγγείλαμεν τὸν λόγον
[1]every in which we announced the word
τοῦ κυρίου, πῶς ἔχουσιν. 37 Βαρναβᾶς
of the Lord, how they have(are). Barnabas
δὲ ἐβούλετο συμπαραλαβεῖν καὶ τὸν
And wished to take with [them] also –
Ἰωάννην τὸν καλούμενον Μᾶρκον· 38 Παῦλος
John – *being* called Mark; [2]Paul
δὲ ἠξίου, τὸν ἀποστάντα ἀπ' αὐτῶν
[1]but [3]thought fit, – [7]withdrawing [8]from [9]them
ἀπὸ Παμφυλίας καὶ μὴ συνελθόντα αὐτοῖς
[10]from [11]Pamphylia [12]and [13]not [14]going with [15]them
εἰς τὸ ἔργον, μὴ συμπαραλαμβάνειν τοῦτον.
[16]to [17]the [18]work, [4]not [6]to take with [them] [5]this one.
39 ἐγένετο δὲ παροξυσμός, ὥστε ἀποχωρισ-
And there was sharp feeling, so as to separ-
θῆναι αὐτοὺς ἀπ' ἀλλήλων, τόν τε
ate them from each other, – and
Βαρναβᾶν παραλαβόντα τὸν Μᾶρκον
Barnabas taking – Mark
ἐκπλεῦσαι εἰς Κύπρον. 40 Παῦλος δὲ
to sail away to Cyprus. But Paul
ἐπιλεξάμενος Σιλᾶν ἐξῆλθεν, παραδοθεὶς
having chosen Silas went forth, being commended
τῇ χάριτι τοῦ κυρίου ὑπὸ τῶν
to the grace of the Lord by the
ἀδελφῶν· 41 διήρχετο δὲ τὴν Συρίαν
brothers; and he went through – Syria
καὶ Κιλικίαν ἐπιστηρίζων τὰς ἐκκλησίας.
and Cilicia confirming the churches.

‡ Verse 34 omitted by Nestle; *cf.* NIV

You will do well to
avoid these things.

Farewell.

30 The men were sent off
and went down to Antioch,
where they gathered the
church together and delivered the letter. 31 The people read it and were glad for
its encouraging message.
32 Judas and Silas, who
themselves were prophets,
said much to encourage
and strengthen the broth-
ers. 33 After spending some
time there, they were sent
off by the brothers with the
blessing of peace to return
to those who had sent
them.[g] 35 But Paul and Barnabas remained in Antioch,
where they and many oth-
ers taught and preached the
word of the Lord.

Disagreement Between Paul and Barnabas

36 Some time later Paul
said to Barnabas, "Let us
go back and visit the brothers in all the towns where
we preached the word of
the Lord and see how they
are doing." 37 Barnabas
wanted to take John, also
called Mark, with them,
38 but Paul did not think it
wise to take him, because
he had deserted them in
Pamphylia and had not
continued with them in the
work. 39 They had such a
sharp disagreement that
they parted company. Bar-
nabas took Mark and sailed
for Cyprus, 40 but Paul
chose Silas and left, commended by the brothers to
the grace of the Lord. 41 He
went through Syria and Cilicia, strengthening the
churches.

[g] 33 Some manuscripts *them, 34 but Silas decided to remain there*

Chapter 16

Timothy Joins Paul and Silas

PAUL[k] went on also to Derbe and to Lystra, where there was a disciple named Timothy, the son of a Jewish woman who was a believer; but his father was a Greek. 2 He was well spoken of by the believers[e] in Lystra and Iconium. 3 Paul wanted Timothy to accompany him; and he took him and had him circumcised because of the Jews who were in those places, for they all knew that his father was a Greek. 4 As they went from town to town, they delivered to them for observance the decisions that had been reached by the apostles and elders who were in Jerusalem. 5 So the churches were strengthened in the faith and increased in numbers daily.

Paul's Vision of the Man of Macedonia

6 They went through the region of Phrygia and Galatia, having been forbidden by the Holy Spirit to speak the word in Asia. 7 When they had come opposite Mysia, they attempted to go into Bithynia, but the Spirit of Jesus did not allow them; 8 so, passing by Mysia, they went down to Troas. 9 During the night Paul had a vision: there stood a man of Macedonia pleading with him and saying, "Come over to Macedonia and help us." 10 When he had seen the vision, we immediately tried to cross over to Macedonia, being convinced that God had called us to proclaim the good news to

[k]Gk *He*

16 Κατήντησεν δὲ καὶ εἰς Δέρβην καὶ
And he came down also to Derbe and

εἰς Λύστραν. καὶ ἰδοὺ μαθητής τις ἦν
to Lystra. And behold[,] a certain disciple was

ἐκεῖ ὀνόματι Τιμόθεος, υἱὸς γυναικὸς
there by name Timothy, son [3]woman

Ἰουδαίας πιστῆς πατρὸς δὲ Ἕλληνος,
[2]Jewish [1]of a faithful [4]but [5]father [6]of a Greek,

2 ὃς ἐμαρτυρεῖτο ὑπὸ τῶν ἐν Λύστροις
who was witnessed to by [1]the [5]in [6]Lystra

καὶ Ἰκονίῳ ἀδελφῶν. **3** τοῦτον ἠθέλησεν
[7]and [8]Iconium [2]brothers. [3]This one [2]wished

ὁ Παῦλος σὺν αὐτῷ ἐξελθεῖν, καὶ λαβὼν
– [1]Paul with him to go forth, and taking

περιέτεμεν αὐτὸν διὰ τοὺς Ἰουδαίους τοὺς
circumcised him on account of the Jews –

ὄντας ἐν τοῖς τόποις ἐκείνοις· ᾔδεισαν
being in those places; [2]they knew

γὰρ ἅπαντες ὅτι Ἕλλην ὁ πατὴρ αὐτοῦ
[1]for all that a Greek the father of him

ὑπῆρχεν. **4** Ὡς δὲ διεπορεύοντο τὰς
was. Now as they went through the

πόλεις, παρεδίδοσαν αὐτοῖς φυλάσσειν τὰ
cities, they delivered to them* to keep the

δόγματα τὰ κεκριμένα ὑπὸ τῶν ἀποστόλων
decrees – having been decided [on] by the apostles

καὶ πρεσβυτέρων τῶν ἐν Ἱεροσολύμοις.
and elders – in Jerusalem.

5 Αἱ μὲν οὖν ἐκκλησίαι ἐστερεοῦντο
[2]The – [1]therefore [3]churches were strengthened

τῇ πίστει καὶ ἐπερίσσευον τῷ ἀριθμῷ
in the faith and increased – in number

καθ' ἡμέραν.
daily.

6 Διῆλθον δὲ τὴν Φρυγίαν καὶ Γαλατικὴν
And they went through the Phrygian and Galatian

χώραν, κωλυθέντες ὑπὸ τοῦ ἁγίου
country, being prevented by the Holy

πνεύματος λαλῆσαι τὸν λόγον ἐν τῇ
Spirit to speak =from speaking the word in –

Ἀσίᾳ· **7** ἐλθόντες δὲ κατὰ τὴν Μυσίαν
Asia; but coming against – Mysia

ἐπείραζον εἰς τὴν Βιθυνίαν πορευθῆναι,
they attempted into – Bithynia to go,

καὶ οὐκ εἴασεν αὐτοὺς τὸ πνεῦμα Ἰησοῦ·
and [5]not [6]allowed [7]them [1]the [2]Spirit [3]of Jesus;

8 παρελθόντες δὲ τὴν Μυσίαν κατέβησαν
so passing by – Mysia they came down

εἰς Τρῳάδα. **9** καὶ ὅραμα διὰ νυκτὸς
to Troas. And a vision through (during) [the] night

τῷ Παύλῳ ὤφθη, ἀνήρ Μακεδών τις
– to Paul appeared, a *man* Macedonian certain

ἦν ἑστὼς καὶ παρακαλῶν αὐτὸν καὶ
was standing and beseeching him and

λέγων· διαβὰς εἰς Μακεδονίαν βοήθησον
saying: Crossing into Macedonia help

ἡμῖν. **10** ὡς δὲ τὸ ὅραμα εἶδεν, εὐθέως
us. So when the vision he saw, immediately

ἐζητήσαμεν ἐξελθεῖν εἰς Μακεδονίαν,
we sought to go forth to Macedonia,

συμβιβάζοντες ὅτι προσκέκληται ἡμᾶς ὁ
concluding that [2]has(had) called [3]us –

* Note the gender: πόλις is feminine.

Chapter 16

Timothy Joins Paul and Silas

HE came to Derbe and then to Lystra, where a disciple named Timothy lived, whose mother was a Jewess and a believer, but whose father was a Greek. 2The brothers at Lystra and Iconium spoke well of him. 3Paul wanted to take him along on the journey, so he circumcised him because of the Jews who lived in that area, for they all knew that his father was a Greek. 4As they traveled from town to town, they delivered the decisions reached by the apostles and elders in Jerusalem for the people to obey. 5So the churches were strengthened in the faith and grew daily in numbers.

Paul's Vision of the Man of Macedonia

6Paul and his companions traveled throughout the region of Phrygia and Galatia, having been kept by the Holy Spirit from preaching the word in the province of Asia. 7When they came to the border of Mysia, they tried to enter Bithynia, but the Spirit of Jesus would not allow them to. 8So they passed by Mysia and went down to Troas. 9During the night Paul had a vision of a man of Macedonia standing and begging him, "Come over to Macedonia and help us." 10After Paul had seen the vision, we got ready at once to leave for Macedonia, concluding that God had called us to them.

The Conversion of Lydia

11 We set sail from Tro-
as and took a straight
course to Samothrace, the
following day to Neapolis,
12 and from there to Philippi, which is a leading city of
the district[l] of Macedonia
and a Roman colony. We
remained in this city for
some days. 13 On the sab-
bath day we went outside
the gate by the river, where
we supposed there was a
place of prayer; and we sat
down and spoke to the
women who had gathered
there. 14 A certain woman
named Lydia, a worshiper
of God, was listening to us;
she was from the city of
Thyatira and a dealer in
purple cloth. The Lord
opened her heart to listen
eagerly to what was said by
Paul. 15 When she and her
household were baptized,
she urged us, saying, "If
you have judged me to be
faithful to the Lord, come
and stay at my home." And
she prevailed upon us.

Paul and Silas in Prison

16 One day, as we were
going to the place of
prayer, we met a slave girl
who had a spirit of divina-
tion and brought her own-
ers a great deal of money by
fortune-telling. 17 While she
followed Paul and us, she
would cry out, "These men
are slaves of the Most High
God, who proclaim to you[m]
a way of salvation." 18 She
kept doing this for many
days. But Paul, very much
annoyed, turned and said
to the spirit, "I order you in
the name of Jesus Christ to
come out of her." And it
came out that very hour.

[l] Other authorities read *a city of the first district*
[m] Other ancient authorities read *to us*

θεὸς εὐαγγελίσασθαι αὐτούς.
[1]God to evangelize them.

11 Ἀναχθέντες δὲ ἀπὸ Τρῳάδος εὐθυδρο-
And setting sail from Troas we ran a

μήσαμεν εἰς Σαμοθρᾴκην, τῇ δὲ ἐπιούσῃ
straight course to Samothracia, and on the next day

εἰς Νέαν πόλιν, 12 κἀκεῖθεν εἰς Φιλίππους,
to Neapolis, and thence to Philippi,

ἥτις ἐστὶν πρώτη τῆς μερίδος Μακεδονίας
which is [1][the] [3]first [4]of the [5]part [6]of Macedonia

πόλις, κολωνία. Ἦμεν δὲ ἐν ταύτῃ τῇ
[2]city, a colony. And we were in this –

πόλει διατρίβοντες ἡμέρας τινάς. 13 τῇ τε
city staying days some. And on the

ἡμέρᾳ τῶν σαββάτων ἐξήλθομεν ἔξω τῆς
day of the sabbaths we went forth outside the

πύλης παρὰ ποταμὸν οὗ ἐνομίζομεν
gate by a river where we supposed

προσευχὴν εἶναι, καὶ καθίσαντες ἐλαλοῦμεν
a place of prayer to be, and sitting we spoke

ταῖς συνελθούσαις γυναιξίν. 14 καί τις
to the [2]coming together [1]women. And a certain

γυνὴ ὀνόματι Λυδία, πορφυρόπωλις
woman by name Lydia, a dealer in purple-dyed [garments]

πόλεως Θυατίρων, σεβομένη τὸν θεόν,
of [the] city of Thyatira, worshipping – God,

ἤκουεν, ἧς ὁ κύριος διήνοιξεν τὴν καρδίαν
heard, of whom the Lord opened up the heart

προσέχειν τοῖς λαλουμένοις ὑπὸ Παύλου.
to take heed to the things being spoken by Paul.

15 ὡς δὲ ἐβαπτίσθη καὶ ὁ οἶκος αὐτῆς,
And when she was baptized and the household of her,

παρεκάλεσεν λέγουσα· εἰ κεκρίκατέ με
she besought saying: If ye have decided me

πιστὴν τῷ κυρίῳ εἶναι, εἰσελθόντες εἰς
faithful to the Lord to be, entering into

τὸν οἶκόν μου μένετε· καὶ παρεβιάσατο
the house of me remain; and she urged

ἡμᾶς. 16 Ἐγένετο δὲ πορευομένων ἡμῶν
us. And it happened going us* =as we went

εἰς τὴν προσευχήν, παιδίσκην τινὰ ἔχουσαν
to the place of prayer, a certain maid having

πνεῦμα πύθωνα ὑπαντῆσαι ἡμῖν, ἥτις
a spirit of a python to meet us, who

ἐργασίαν πολλὴν παρεῖχεν τοῖς κυρίοις
[3]gain [2]much [1]brought to the masters

αὐτῆς μαντευομένη. 17 αὕτη κατακολουθοῦσα
of her practising soothsaying. This one following after

τῷ Παύλῳ καὶ ἡμῖν ἔκραζεν λέγουσα·
– Paul and us cried out saying:

οὗτοι οἱ ἄνθρωποι δοῦλοι τοῦ θεοῦ τοῦ
These – men slaves of the God –

ὑψίστου εἰσίν, οἵτινες καταγγέλλουσιν ὑμῖν
most high are, who announce to you

ὁδὸν σωτηρίας. 18 τοῦτο δὲ ἐποίει ἐπὶ
a way of salvation. And this she did over

πολλὰς ἡμέρας. διαπονηθεὶς δὲ Παῦλος
many days. But becoming greatly troubled Paul

καὶ ἐπιστρέψας τῷ πνεύματι εἶπεν· παραγ-
and turning [2]to the [3]spirit [1]he said: I

γέλλω σοι ἐν ὀνόματι Ἰησοῦ Χριστοῦ
charge thee in [the] name of Jesus Christ

ἐξελθεῖν ἀπ' αὐτῆς· καὶ ἐξῆλθεν αὐτῇ
to come out from her; and it came out in the

preach the gospel to them.

Lydia's Conversion in Philippi

11 From Troas we put out
to sea and sailed straight
for Samothrace, and the
next day on to Neapolis.
12 From there we traveled to
Philippi, a Roman colony
and the leading city of that
district of Macedonia. And
we stayed there several
days.
13 On the Sabbath we
went outside the city gate
to the river, where we expected to find a place of
prayer. We sat down and
began to speak to the wom-
en who had gathered there.
14 One of those listening
was a woman named Lyd-
ia, a dealer in purple cloth
from the city of Thyatira,
who was a worshiper of
God. The Lord opened her
heart to respond to Paul's
message. 15 When she and
the members of her house-
hold were baptized, she invited us to her home. "If
you consider me a believer
in the Lord," she said,
"come and stay at my
house." And she persuad-
ed us.

Paul and Silas in Prison

16 Once when we were go-
ing to the place of prayer,
we were met by a slave girl
who had a spirit by which
she predicted the future.
She earned a great deal of
money for her owners by
fortune-telling. 17 This girl
followed Paul and the rest
of us, shouting, "These
men are servants of the
Most High God, who are
telling you the way to be
saved." 18 She kept this up
for many days. Finally Paul
became so troubled that he
turned around and said to
the spirit, "In the name of
Jesus Christ I command
you to come out of her!" At
that moment the spirit left
her.

19 But when her owners
saw that their hope of making money was gone, they
seized Paul and Silas and
dragged them into the marketplace before the authorities. 20 When they had
brought them before the
magistrates, they said,
"These men are disturbing
our city; they are Jews
21 and are advocating customs that are not lawful for
us as Romans to adopt or
observe." 22 The crowd
joined in attacking them,
and the magistrates had
them stripped of their
clothing and ordered them
to be beaten with rods.
23 After they had given
them a severe flogging,
they threw them into prison
and ordered the jailer to
keep them securely. 24 Following these instructions,
he put them in the inner-
most cell and fastened their
feet in the stocks.
25 About midnight Paul
and Silas were praying and
singing hymns to God, and
the prisoners were listening
to them. 26 Suddenly there
was an earthquake, so violent that the foundations of
the prison were shaken;
and immediately all the
doors were opened and ev-
eryone's chains were un-
fastened. 27 When the jailer
woke up and saw the prison
doors wide open, he drew
his sword and was about to
kill himself, since he supposed that the prisoners
had escaped. 28 But Paul
shouted in a loud voice,
"Do not harm yourself, for
we are all here." 29 The jailer[n] called for lights, and

[n] Gk *He*

τῇ ὥρᾳ. **19** Ἰδόντες δὲ οἱ κύριοι αὐτῆς
same hour.* And [4]seeing [1]the [2]masters [3]of her

ὅτι ἐξῆλθεν ἡ ἐλπὶς τῆς ἐργασίας αὐτῶν,
[5]that [11]went out [6]the [7]hope [8]of the [9]gain [10]of them,

ἐπιλαβόμενοι τὸν Παῦλον καὶ τὸν Σιλᾶν
having seized – Paul and – Silas

εἵλκυσαν εἰς τὴν ἀγορὰν ἐπὶ τοὺς ἄρχοντας,
dragged to the marketplace before the rulers,

20 καὶ προσαγαγόντες αὐτοὺς τοῖς στρατηγοῖς
and [1]bringing [3]to [2]them the prætors

εἶπαν· οὗτοι οἱ ἄνθρωποι ἐκταράσσουσιν
said: These – men are greatly troubling

ἡμῶν τὴν πόλιν, Ἰουδαῖοι ὑπάρχοντες,
of us the city, [2]Jews [1]being,

21 καὶ καταγγέλλουσιν ἔθη ἃ οὐκ ἔξεστιν
and they announce customs which it is not lawful

ἡμῖν παραδέχεσθαι οὐδὲ ποιεῖν Ῥωμαίοις
for us to receive nor to do [2]Romans

οὖσιν. **22** καὶ συνεπέστη ὁ ὄχλος κατ'
[1]being. And rose up together the crowd against

αὐτῶν, καὶ οἱ στρατηγοὶ περιρήξαντες
them, and the prætors tearing off

αὐτῶν τὰ ἱμάτια ἐκέλευον ῥαβδίζειν,
of them the garments commanded to flog,

23 πολλάς δὲ ἐπιθέντες αὐτοῖς πληγὰς
and [2]many [1]laying on [3]them [4]stripes

ἔβαλον εἰς φυλακήν, παραγγείλαντες τῷ
threw into prison, charging the

δεσμοφύλακι ἀσφαλῶς τηρεῖν αὐτούς· **24** ὃς
jailer securely to keep them; who

παραγγελίαν τοιαύτην λαβὼν ἔβαλεν αὐτοὺς
[3]a charge [2]such [1]having received threw them

εἰς τὴν ἐσωτέραν φυλακὴν καὶ τοὺς
into the inner prison and [2]the

πόδας ἠσφαλίσατο αὐτῶν εἰς τὸ ξύλον.
[3]feet [1]secured [4]of them in the stocks.

25 Κατὰ δὲ τὸ μεσονύκτιον Παῦλος καὶ
And about – midnight Paul and

Σιλᾶς προσευχόμενοι ὕμνουν τὸν θεόν,
Silas praying [1]praised [2]in a hymn – [3]God,

ἐπηκροῶντο δὲ αὐτῶν οἱ δέσμιοι· **26** ἄφνω δὲ
and [3]listened to [4]them [1]the [2]prisoners; and suddenly

σεισμὸς ἐγένετο μέγας, ὥστε σαλευ-
[3]earthquake [1]there was [2]a great, so as to be

θῆναι τὰ θεμέλια τοῦ δεσμωτηρίου·
shaken the foundations of the jail;

ἠνεῴχθησαν δὲ παραχρῆμα αἱ θύραι πᾶσαι,
and [5]were opened [1]at once [2]the [4]doors [3]all,

καὶ πάντων τὰ δεσμὰ ἀνέθη. **27** ἔξυπνος δὲ
and [3]of all [1]the [2]bonds were loosened. And [4]awake

γενόμενος ὁ δεσμοφύλαξ καὶ ἰδὼν
[3]having become [1]the [2]jailer and seeing

ἀνεῳγμένας τὰς θύρας τῆς φυλακῆς,
having been opened the doors of the prison,

σπασάμενος τὴν μάχαιραν ἤμελλεν ἑαυτὸν
having drawn the sword was about himself

ἀναιρεῖν, νομίζων ἐκπεφευγέναι τοὺς
to kill, supposing to have escaped the

δεσμίους. **28** ἐφώνησεν δὲ Παῦλος μεγάλῃ
prisoners. But called Paul with a great(loud)

φωνῇ λέγων· μηδὲν πράξῃς σεαυτῷ κακόν,
voice saying: [1]*Nothing* [3]do [4]thyself [2]harm,

ἅπαντες γάρ ἐσμεν ἐνθάδε. **29** αἰτήσας
for [2]all [1]we are [3]here. asking

* See Luke 2. 38.

19When the owners of the
slave girl realized that their
hope of making money was
gone, they seized Paul and
Silas and dragged them into
the marketplace to face the
authorities. 20They brought
them before the magis-
trates and said, "These
men are Jews, and are
throwing our city into an
uproar 21by advocating
customs unlawful for us
Romans to accept or prac-
tice."
22The crowd joined in the
attack against Paul and Silas, and the magistrates ordered them to be stripped
and beaten. 23After they
had been severely flogged,
they were thrown into prison, and the jailer was commanded to guard them
carefully. 24Upon receiving
such orders, he put them in
the inner cell and fastened
their feet in the stocks.
25About midnight Paul
and Silas were praying and
singing hymns to God, and
the other prisoners were
listening to them. 26Sud-
denly there was such a violent earthquake that the
foundations of the prison
were shaken. At once all
the prison doors flew open,
and everybody's chains
came loose. 27The jailer
woke up, and when he saw
the prison doors open, he
drew his sword and was
about to kill himself be-
cause he thought the prisoners had escaped. 28But
Paul shouted, "Don't harm
yourself! We are all here!"
29The jailer called for

rushing in, he fell down trembling before Paul and Silas. 30 Then he brought them outside and said, "Sirs, what must I do to be saved?" 31 They answered, "Believe on the Lord Jesus, and you will be saved, you and your household." 32 They spoke the word of the Lord[o] to him and to all who were in his house. 33 At the same hour of the night he took them and washed their wounds; then he and his entire family were baptized without delay. 34 He brought them up into the house and set food before them; and he and his entire household rejoiced that he had become a believer in God.

35 When morning came, the magistrates sent the police, saying, "Let those men go." 36 And the jailer reported the message to Paul, saying, "The magistrates sent word to let you go; therefore come out now and go in peace." 37 But Paul replied, "They have beaten us in public, uncondemned, men who are Roman citizens, and have thrown us into prison; and now are they going to discharge us in secret? Certainly not! Let them come and take us out themselves." 38 The police reported these words to the magistrates, and they were afraid when they heard that they were Roman citizens; 39 so they came and apologized to them. And they took them out and asked

δὲ φῶτα εἰσεπήδησεν, καὶ ἔντρομος
And lights he rushed in, and trembling

γενόμενος προσέπεσεν τῷ Παύλῳ καὶ
becoming he fell before – Paul and

Σιλᾷ, 30 καὶ προαγαγὼν αὐτοὺς ἔξω ἔφη·
Silas, and [1]leading [3]forward [2]them outside said:

κύριοι, τί με δεῖ ποιεῖν ἵνα σωθῶ;
Sirs, what [2]me [1]behoves it to do that I may be saved?

31 οἱ δὲ εἶπαν· πίστευσον ἐπὶ τὸν κύριον
And they said: Believe on the Lord

Ἰησοῦν, καὶ σωθήσῃ σὺ καὶ ὁ οἶκός
Jesus, and shalt be saved thou and the household

σου. 32 καὶ ἐλάλησαν αὐτῷ τὸν λόγον
of thee. And they spoke to him the word

τοῦ θεοῦ σὺν πᾶσιν τοῖς ἐν τῇ οἰκίᾳ
– of God with all the [ones] in the house

αὐτοῦ. 33 καὶ παραλαβὼν αὐτοὺς ἐν
of him. And taking them in

ἐκείνῃ τῇ ὥρᾳ τῆς νυκτὸς ἔλουσεν ἀπὸ
that – hour of the night he washed *from*

τῶν πληγῶν, καὶ ἐβαπτίσθη αὐτὸς καὶ
the stripes, and was baptized he and

οἱ αὐτοῦ ἅπαντες παραχρῆμα, 34 ἀναγαγών
the of him =all his all at once, [2]bringing up

τε αὐτοὺς εἰς τὸν οἶκον παρέθηκεν
[1]and them to the house he set before [them]

τράπεζαν, καὶ ἠγαλλιάσατο πανοικεὶ πεπι-
a table, and exulted with all the household having

στευκὼς τῷ θεῷ. 35 Ἡμέρας δὲ γενομένης
believed – God. And day coming[a] =when day came

ἀπέστειλαν οἱ στρατηγοὶ τοὺς ῥαβδούχους
[3]sent [1]the [2]prætors the tipstaffs

λέγοντες· ἀπόλυσον τοὺς ἀνθρώπους
saying: Release – men

ἐκείνους. 36 ἀπήγγειλεν δὲ ὁ δεσμοφύλαξ
those. And announced the jailer

τοὺς λόγους τούτους πρὸς τὸν Παῦλον,
these words to – Paul,

ὅτι ἀπέσταλκαν οἱ στρατηγοὶ ἵνα ἀπολυθῆτε.
– [3]have sent [1]The [2]prætors that ye may be released.

νῦν οὖν ἐξελθόντες πορεύεσθε ἐν εἰρήνῃ.
Now therefore going forth proceed in peace.

37 ὁ δὲ Παῦλος ἔφη πρὸς αὐτούς·
– But Paul said to them:

δείραντες ἡμᾶς δημοσίᾳ ἀκατακρίτους,
Having beaten us publicly uncondemned,

ἀνθρώπους Ῥωμαίους ὑπάρχοντας, ἔβαλαν
men [2]Romans [1]being, they threw [us]

εἰς φυλακήν· καὶ νῦν λάθρα ἡμᾶς ἐκβάλ-
into prison; and now secretly us they

λουσιν; οὐ γάρ, ἀλλὰ ἐλθόντες αὐτοὶ
expel? No indeed, but coming [them]selves

ἡμᾶς ἐξαγαγέτωσαν. 38 ἀπήγγειλαν δὲ τοῖς
us let them bring out. And [3]reported [4]to the

στρατηγοῖς οἱ ῥαβδοῦχοι τὰ ῥήματα ταῦτα.
[5]prætors [1]the [2]tipstaffs these words.

ἐφοβήθησαν δὲ ἀκούσαντες ὅτι Ῥωμαῖοί
And they were afraid hearing that Romans

εἰσιν, 39 καὶ ἐλθόντες παρεκάλεσαν
they are(were), and coming besought

αὐτούς, καὶ ἐξαγαγόντες ἠρώτων ἀπελθεῖν
them, and bringing out asked to go away

lights, rushed in and fell trembling before Paul and Silas. 30 He then brought them out and asked, "Sirs, what must I do to be saved?"

31 They replied, "Believe in the Lord Jesus, and you will be saved—you and your household." 32 Then they spoke the word of the Lord to him and to all the others in his house. 33 At that hour of the night the jailer took them and washed their wounds; then immediately he and all his family were baptized. 34 The jailer brought them into his house and set a meal before them; he was filled with joy because he had come to believe in God—he and his whole family.

35 When it was daylight, the magistrates sent their officers to the jailer with the order: "Release those men." 36 The jailer told Paul, "The magistrates have ordered that you and Silas be released. Now you can leave. Go in peace."

37 But Paul said to the officers: "They beat us publicly without a trial, even though we are Roman citizens, and threw us into prison. And now do they want to get rid of us quietly? No! Let them come themselves and escort us out."

38 The officers reported this to the magistrates, and when they heard that Paul and Silas were Roman citizens, they were alarmed. 39 They came to appease them and escorted them from the prison, requesting

[o] Other ancient authorities read *word of God*

them to leave the city.
40 After leaving the prison
they went to Lydia's home;
and when they had seen
and encouraged the broth-
ers and sisters[p] there, they
departed.

Chapter 17

The Uproar in Thessalonica

AFTER Paul and Silas[q]
had passed through
Amphipolis and Apollonia,
they came to Thessalonica,
where there was a syna-
gogue of the Jews. 2 And
Paul went in, as was his
custom, and on three sab-
bath days argued with them
from the scriptures, 3 explaining and proving that it
was necessary for the Messiah[r] to suffer and to rise
from the dead, and saying,
"This is the Messiah,[r]
Jesus whom I am proclaim-
ing to you." 4 Some of them
were persuaded and joined
Paul and Silas, as did a
great many of the devout
Greeks and not a few of the
leading women. 5 But the
Jews became jealous, and
with the help of some ruffi-
ans in the marketplaces
they formed a mob and set
the city in an uproar. While
they were searching for
Paul and Silas to bring them
out to the assembly, they
attacked Jason's house.
6 When they could not find
them, they dragged Jason
and some believers[p] be-
fore the city authorities,[s]
shouting, "These people
who have been turning the
world upside down have
come here also, 7 and Jason
has entertained them as
guests. They are all acting
contrary to the decrees of
the emperor, saying that
there is another king named
Jesus." 8 The people and
the city officials were dis-

[p] Gk *brothers*
[q] Gk *they*
[r] Or *the Christ*
[s] Gk *politarchs*

ἀπὸ τῆς πόλεως. 40 ἐξελθόντες δὲ ἀπὸ
from the city. And going out from
τῆς φυλακῆς εἰσῆλθον πρὸς τὴν Λυδίαν,
the prison they entered to [the house of] – Lydia,
καὶ ἰδόντες παρεκάλεσαν τοὺς ἀδελφοὺς
and seeing they exhorted the brothers
καὶ ἐξῆλθαν.
and went forth.

17 Διοδεύσαντες δὲ τὴν Ἀμφίπολιν καὶ
And travelling through – Amphipolis and
τὴν Ἀπολλωνίαν ἦλθον εἰς Θεσσαλονίκην,
– Apollonia they came to Thessalonica,
ὅπου ἦν συναγωγὴ τῶν Ἰουδαίων. 2 κατὰ
where was a synagogue of the Jews. according to
δὲ τὸ εἰωθὸς τῷ Παύλῳ εἰσῆλθεν πρὸς
And the custom – with Paul° he entered to
αὐτούς, καὶ ἐπὶ σάββατα τρία διελέξατο
them, and on sabbaths three lectured
αὐτοῖς ἀπὸ τῶν γραφῶν, 3 διανοίγων
to them from the scriptures, opening up
καὶ παρατιθέμενος ὅτι τὸν χριστὸν ἔδει
and setting before [them] that [2]the [3]Christ [1]it behoved
παθεῖν καὶ ἀναστῆναι ἐκ νεκρῶν, καὶ
to suffer and to rise again out of [the] dead, and
ὅτι οὗτός ἐστιν ὁ χριστός, ὁ Ἰησοῦς,
that this is(was) the Christ, – Jesus,
ὃν ἐγὼ καταγγέλλω ὑμῖν. 4 καί τινες
whom I announce to you. And some
ἐξ αὐτῶν ἐπείσθησαν καὶ προσεκληρώθησαν
of them were persuaded and threw in their lot
τῷ Παύλῳ καὶ τῷ Σιλᾷ, τῶν τε
– with Paul and – Silas, both of the
σεβομένων Ἑλλήνων πλῆθος πολύ, γυναικῶν τε
worshipping Greeks [2]multitude [1]a much (great), and of [3]women
τῶν πρώτων οὐκ ὀλίγαι. 5 Ζηλώσαντες δὲ
[1]the [2]chief not a few. But becoming jealous
οἱ Ἰουδαῖοι καὶ προσλαβόμενοι τῶν
the Jews and taking aside of the
ἀγοραίων ἄνδρας τινὰς πονηροὺς καὶ
loungers in the marketplace men some wicked and
ὀχλοποιήσαντες ἐθορύβουν τὴν πόλιν, καὶ
having gathered a crowd disturbed the city, and
ἐπιστάντες τῇ οἰκίᾳ Ἰάσονος ἐζήτουν
coming on the house of Jason sought
αὐτοὺς προαγαγεῖν εἰς τὸν δῆμον· 6 μὴ
them to bring forward to the mob; [2]not
εὑρόντες δὲ αὐτοὺς ἔσυρον Ἰάσονα καί
[3]finding [1]but them they dragged Jason and
τινας ἀδελφοὺς ἐπὶ τοὺς πολιτάρχας,
some brothers to the politarchs,
βοῶντες ὅτι οἱ τὴν οἰκουμένην ἀναστατώ-
crying[,] – [2]the [ones] [4]the [5]inhabited earth [3]having turned
σαντες οὗτοι καὶ ἐνθάδε πάρεισιν, 7 οὓς
upside down [1]these men also here have arrived, whom
ὑποδέδεκται Ἰάσων· καὶ οὗτοι πάντες
[2]has received [1]Jason; and these all
ἀπέναντι τῶν δογμάτων Καίσαρος
[2]contrary to [3]the [4]decrees [5]of Cæsar
πράσσουσιν, βασιλέα ἕτερον λέγοντες εἶναι
[1]act, [4]king [3]another [1]saying [2]to be
Ἰησοῦν. 8 ἐτάραξαν δὲ τὸν ὄχλον καὶ
[5]Jesus. And they troubled the crowd and

them to leave the city. 40 After Paul and Silas came out
of the prison, they went to
Lydia's house, where they
met with the brothers and
encouraged them. Then
they left.

Chapter 17

In Thessalonica

WHEN they had passed
through Amphipolis
and Apollonia, they came
to Thessalonica, where
there was a Jewish syna-
gogue. 2 As his custom was,
Paul went into the syna-
gogue, and on three Sab-
bath days he reasoned with
them from the Scriptures,
3 explaining and proving
that the Christ[h] had to suffer and rise from the dead.
"This Jesus I am proclaiming to you is the Christ,[h]"
he said. 4 Some of the Jews
were persuaded and joined
Paul and Silas, as did a
large number of God-fear-
ing Greeks and not a few
prominent women.
5 But the Jews were jeal-
ous; so they rounded up
some bad characters from
the marketplace, formed a
mob and started a riot in the
city. They rushed to Ja-
son's house in search of
Paul and Silas in order to
bring them out to the
crowd.[i] 6 But when they
did not find them, they
dragged Jason and some
other brothers before the
city officials, shouting:
"These men who have
caused trouble all over the
world have now come here,
7 and Jason has welcomed
them into his house. They
are all defying Caesar's decrees, saying that there is
another king, one called
Jesus." 8 When they heard
this, the crowd and the city

[h] 3 Or *Messiah*
[i] 5 Or *the assembly of the people*

turbed when they heard
this, 9and after they had
taken bail from Jason and
the others, they let them
go.

Paul and Silas in Beroea

10 That very night the
believers[p] sent Paul and
Silas off to Beroea; and
when they arrived, they
went to the Jewish syna-
gogue. 11These Jews were
more receptive than those
in Thessalonica, for they
welcomed the message
very eagerly and examined
the scriptures every day to
see whether these things
were so. 12Many of them
therefore believed, including not a few Greek women
and men of high standing.
13But when the Jews of
Thessalonica learned that
the word of God had been
proclaimed by Paul in Be-
roea as well, they came
there too, to stir up and in-
cite the crowds. 14Then the
believers[p] immediately
sent Paul away to the coast,
but Silas and Timothy re-
mained behind. 15Those
who conducted Paul
brought him as far as Athens; and after receiving instructions to have Silas and
Timothy join him as soon
as possible, they left him.

Paul in Athens

16 While Paul was wait-
ing for them in Athens, he
was deeply distressed to
see that the city was full of
idols. 17So he argued in the
synagogue with the Jews
and the devout persons,
and also in the market-

τοὺς πολιτάρχας ἀκούοντας ταῦτα, 9 καὶ
the politarchs hearing these things, and
λαβόντες τὸ ἱκανὸν παρὰ τοῦ Ἰάσονος
taking the surety from – Jason
καὶ τῶν λοιπῶν ἀπέλυσαν αὐτούς. 10 Οἱ δὲ
and the rest released them. And the
ἀδελφοὶ εὐθέως διὰ νυκτὸς ἐξέπεμψαν
brothers immediately through (during) [the] night sent forth
τόν τε Παῦλον καὶ τὸν Σιλᾶν εἰς Βέροιαν,
– both Paul and – Silas to Berœa,
οἵτινες παραγενόμενοι εἰς τὴν συναγωγὴν
who having arrived [2]into [3]the synagogue
τῶν Ἰουδαίων ἀπῄεσαν· 11 οὗτοι δὲ ἦσαν
[4]of the [5]Jews [1]went; and these were
εὐγενέστεροι τῶν ἐν Θεσσαλονίκῃ, οἵτινες
more noble [than] the [ones] in Thessalonica, who
ἐδέξαντο τὸν λόγον μετὰ πάσης προθυμίας,
received the word with all eagerness,
[τὸ] καθ' ἡμέραν ἀνακρίνοντες τὰς γραφὰς
– daily examining the scriptures
εἰ ἔχοι ταῦτα οὕτως. 12 πολλοὶ μὲν
if [2]have(are) [1]these things [3]so. Many –
οὖν ἐξ αὐτῶν ἐπίστευσαν, καὶ τῶν
therefore of them believed, and of the
Ἑλληνίδων γυναικῶν τῶν εὐσχημόνων καὶ
[3]Greek [3]women – [1]honourable and
ἀνδρῶν οὐκ ὀλίγοι. 13 Ὡς δὲ ἔγνωσαν
of men not a few. But when [5]knew
οἱ ἀπὸ τῆς Θεσσαλονίκης Ἰουδαῖοι ὅτι
[1]the [3]from – [4]Thessalonica [2]Jews that
καὶ ἐν τῇ Βεροίᾳ κατηγγέλη ὑπὸ τοῦ
also in – Berœa was announced by –
Παύλου ὁ λόγος τοῦ θεοῦ, ἦλθον κἀκεῖ
Paul the word – of God, they came there also
σαλεύοντες καὶ ταράσσοντες τοὺς ὄχλους.
shaking and troubling the crowds.
14 εὐθέως δὲ τότε τὸν Παῦλον ἐξαπέστειλαν
So immediately then – [4]Paul [3]sent away
οἱ ἀδελφοὶ πορεύεσθαι ἕως ἐπὶ τὴν
[1]the [2]brothers to go as far as to the
θάλασσαν· ὑπέμεινάν τε ὅ τε Σιλᾶς καὶ
sea; [1]but [6]remained – [2]both [3]Silas [4]and
ὁ Τιμόθεος ἐκεῖ. 15 οἱ δὲ καθιστάνοντες
– [5]Timothy [7]there. And the [ones] conducting
τὸν Παῦλον ἤγαγον ἕως Ἀθηνῶν, καὶ
– Paul brought [him] as far as Athens, and
λαβόντες ἐντολὴν πρὸς τὸν Σιλᾶν καὶ τὸν
receiving a command to – Silas and –
Τιμόθεον ἵνα ὡς τάχιστα ἔλθωσιν πρὸς
Timothy that as quickly [as possible] they should come to
αὐτὸν ἐξῄεσαν.
him they departed.

16 Ἐν δὲ ταῖς Ἀθήναις ἐκδεχομένου
And in – Athens awaiting
=while Paul awaited them,
αὐτοὺς τοῦ Παύλου, παρωξύνετο τὸ πνεῦμα
them – Paul,[a] [4]was provoked [1]the [2]spirit
αὐτοῦ ἐν αὐτῷ θεωροῦντος κατείδωλον
[3]of him in him beholding [4]full of images
οὖσαν τὴν πόλιν. 17 διελέγετο μὲν οὖν
[3]being [1]the [2]city. He addressed –* therefore
ἐν τῇ συναγωγῇ τοῖς Ἰουδαίοις καὶ
in the synagogue the Jews and

* See note on ch. 12. 5.

officials were thrown into
turmoil. 9Then they made
Jason and the others post
bond and let them go.

In Berea

10As soon as it was night,
the brothers sent Paul and
Silas away to Berea. On arriving there, they went to
the Jewish synagogue.
11Now the Bereans were of
more noble character than
the Thessalonians, for they
received the message with
great eagerness and exam-
ined the Scriptures every
day to see if what Paul said
was true. 12Many of the
Jews believed, as did also a
number of prominent
Greek women and many
Greek men.
13When the Jews in Thes-
salonica learned that Paul
was preaching the word of
God at Berea, they went
there too, agitating the
crowds and stirring them
up. 14The brothers immediately sent Paul to the coast,
but Silas and Timothy
stayed at Berea. 15The men
who escorted Paul brought
him to Athens and then left
with instructions for Silas
and Timothy to join him as
soon as possible.

In Athens

16While Paul was waiting
for them in Athens, he was
greatly distressed to see
that the city was full of
idols. 17So he reasoned in
the synagogue with the
Jews and the God-fearing

place[t] every day with
those who happened to be
there. 18 Also some Epicurean and Stoic philoso-
phers debated with him.
Some said, "What does this
babbler want to say?" Others said, "He seems to be a
proclaimer of foreign divin-
ities." (This was because
he was telling the good
news about Jesus and the
resurrection.) 19 So they
took him and brought him
to the Areopagus and asked
him, "May we know what
this new teaching is that
you are presenting? 20 It
sounds rather strange to us,
so we would like to know
what it means." 21 Now all
the Athenians and the foreigners living there would
spend their time in nothing
but telling or hearing something new.
22 Then Paul stood in
front of the Areopagus and
said, "Athenians, I see how
extremely religious you are
in every way. 23 For as I
went through the city and
looked carefully at the objects of your worship, I
found among them an altar
with the inscription, 'To an
unknown god.' What there-
fore you worship as un-
known, this I proclaim to
you. 24 The God who made
the world and everything in
it, he who is Lord of heaven
and earth, does not live in
shrines made by human
hands, 25 nor is he served
by human hands, as though
he needed anything, since
he himself gives to all mortals life and breath and all
things. 26 From one ancestor[u] he made all nations to
inhabit the whole earth,
and he allotted the times of

[t] Or *civic center*; Gk *agora*
[u] Gk *From one*; other ancient authorities read *From one blood*

τοῖς σεβομένοις καὶ ἐν τῇ ἀγορᾷ κατὰ
the [ones] worshipping and in the marketplace –
πᾶσαν ἡμέραν πρὸς τοὺς παρατυγχάνοντας.
every day to the [ones] chancing to be [there].
18 τινὲς δὲ καὶ τῶν Ἐπικουρείων καὶ
But some also of the Epicurean and
Στωϊκῶν φιλοσόφων συνέβαλλον αὐτῷ, καί
Stoic philosophers fell in with him, and
τινες ἔλεγον· τί ἂν θέλοι ὁ σπερμολόγος
some said: What may wish – [2]ignorant plagiarist
οὗτος λέγειν; οἱ δέ· ξένων δαιμονίων
[1]this to say? And others [said]: Of foreign demons
δοκεῖ καταγγελεὺς εἶναι· ὅτι τὸν Ἰησοῦν
he seems an announcer to be; because – Jesus
καὶ τὴν ἀνάστασιν εὐηγγελίζετο. 19 ἐπιλα-
and the resurrection he preached. taking
βόμενοι δὲ αὐτοῦ ἐπὶ τὸν Ἄρειον πάγον
hold And of him to the Areopagus
ἤγαγον, λέγοντες· δυνάμεθα γνῶναι τίς
they led [him], saying: Can we *to* know what
ἡ καινὴ αὕτη ἡ ὑπὸ σοῦ λαλουμένη
[1]this [2]new – [5]by [6]thee [4]being spoken
διδαχή; 20 ξενίζοντα γάρ τινα εἰσφέρεις
[3]teaching [is]? for [2]startling things [1]some thou bringest *in*
εἰς τὰς ἀκοὰς ἡμῶν· βουλόμεθα οὖν
to the ears of us; we are minded therefore
γνῶναι τίνα θέλει ταῦτα εἶναι. 21 Ἀθηναῖοι
to know what wish*es* these things to be. [2]Athenians
δὲ πάντες καὶ οἱ ἐπιδημοῦντες ξένοι εἰς
Now [1]all [3]and [4]the [6]dwelling [5]strangers [8]for
οὐδὲν ἕτερον ηὐκαίρουν ἢ λέγειν τι ἢ
[9]nothing [10]different [7]have leisure either to say something or
ἀκούειν τι καινότερον. 22 Σταθεὶς δὲ
to hear something newer. And standing
Παῦλος ἐν μέσῳ τοῦ Ἀρείου πάγου
[5]Paul [1]in [2][the] midst [3]of the [4]Areopagus
ἔφη· ἄνδρες Ἀθηναῖοι, κατὰ πάντα ὡς
said: *Men* Athenians, in everything how
δεισιδαιμονεστέρους ὑμᾶς θεωρῶ. 23 διερχόμενος
very religious [2]you [1]I behold. passing along
γὰρ καὶ ἀναθεωρῶν τὰ σεβάσματα ὑμῶν
For and looking up at the objects of worship of you
εὗρον καὶ βωμὸν ἐν ᾧ ἐπεγέγραπτο·
I found also an altar in which had been inscribed:
ΑΓΝΩΣΤΩ ΘΕΩ. ὃ οὖν ἀγνοοῦντες
TO AN UNKNOWN GOD. What therefore being ignorant
εὐσεβεῖτε, τοῦτο ἐγὼ καταγγέλλω ὑμῖν.
ye reverence, this I announce to you.
24 ὁ θεὸς ὁ ποιήσας τὸν κόσμον καὶ
The God the [one] having made the world and
πάντα τὰ ἐν αὐτῷ, οὗτος οὐρανοῦ καὶ
all the things in it, this one [3]of heaven [4]and
γῆς ὑπάρχων κύριος οὐκ ἐν χειροποιήτοις
[5]of earth [1]being [2]lord [2]not [3]in [4]hand-made
ναοῖς κατοικεῖ, 25 οὐδὲ ὑπὸ χειρῶν
[5]shrines [1]dwells, nor [2]by [4]hands
ἀνθρωπίνων θεραπεύεται προσδεόμενός
[3]human [1]is served having need
τινος, αὐτὸς διδοὺς πᾶσι ζωὴν καὶ πνοὴν
of anything, he giving to all life and breath
καὶ τὰ πάντα· 26 ἐποίησέν τε ἐξ ἑνὸς
and – all things; and he made of one
πᾶν ἔθνος ἀνθρώπων κατοικεῖν ἐπὶ παντὸς
every nation of men to dwell on all
προσώπου τῆς γῆς, ὁρίσας προστεταγμένους
[the] face of the earth, fixing *having been* appointed

Greeks, as well as in the
marketplace day by day
with those who happened
to be there. 18 A group of
Epicurean and Stoic philosophers began to dispute
with him. Some of them
asked, "What is this bab-
bler trying to say?" Others
remarked, "He seems to be
advocating foreign gods."
They said this because Paul
was preaching the good
news about Jesus and the
resurrection. 19 Then they
took him and brought him
to a meeting of the Areopagus, where they said to
him, "May we know what
this new teaching is that
you are presenting? 20 You
are bringing some strange
ideas to our ears, and we
want to know what they
mean." 21 (All the Athenians and the foreigners who
lived there spent their time
doing nothing but talking
about and listening to the
latest ideas.)
22 Paul then stood up in
the meeting of the Areopagus and said: "Men of Athens! I see that in every way
you are very religious.
23 For as I walked around
and looked carefully at
your objects of worship, I
even found an altar with
this inscription: TO AN UN-
KNOWN GOD. Now what you
worship as something un-
known I am going to pro-
claim to you.
24 "The God who made
the world and everything in
it is the Lord of heaven and
earth and does not live in
temples built by hands.
25 And he is not served by
human hands, as if he need
ed anything, because he
himself gives all men life
and breath and everything
else. 26 From one man he
made every nation of men,
that they should inhabit the
whole earth; and he determined the times set for

their existence and the
boundaries of the places
where they would live, 27 so
that they would search for
God[v] and perhaps grope
for him and find him—
though indeed he is not far
from each one of us. 28 For
'In him we live and move
and have our being'; as
even some of your own po-
ets have said,
'For we too are his
offspring.'
29 Since we are God's offspring, we ought not to
think that the deity is like
gold, or silver, or stone, an
image formed by the art
and imagination of mortals.
30 While God has over-
looked the times of human
ignorance, now he com-
mands all people every-
where to repent, 31 because
he has fixed a day on which
he will have the world
judged in righteousness by
a man whom he has ap-
pointed, and of this he has
given assurance to all by
raising him from the dead."
32 When they heard of
the resurrection of the
dead, some scoffed; but
others said, "We will hear
you again about this." 33 At
that point Paul left them.
34 But some of them joined
him and became believers,
including Dionysius the Areopagite and a woman
named Damaris, and others
with them.

καιροὺς καὶ τὰς ὁροθεσίας τῆς κατοικίας
seasons and the boundaries of the dwelling
αὐτῶν, 27 ζητεῖν τὸν θεόν, εἰ ἄρα γε
of them, to seek – God, if perchance
ψηλαφήσειαν αὐτὸν καὶ εὕροιεν, καί γε
they might feel after him and might find, though
οὐ μακρὰν ἀπὸ ἑνὸς ἑκάστου ἡμῶν
[2]not [3]far [4]from [5]one [6]each [7]of us
ὑπάρχοντα. 28 ἐν αὐτῷ γὰρ ζῶμεν καὶ
[1]being. [2]in [3]him [1]For we live and
κινούμεθα καὶ ἐσμέν, ὡς καί τινες τῶν
move and are, as indeed some of the
καθ' ὑμᾶς ποιητῶν εἰρήκασιν· τοῦ γὰρ
[3]among [4]you [2]poets have said: [2]of him [1]For
καὶ γένος ἐσμέν. 29 γένος οὖν ὑπάρχοντες
[3]also [5]offspring [4]we are. Offspring therefore being
τοῦ θεοῦ οὐκ ὀφείλομεν νομίζειν, χρυσῷ
– of God we ought not to suppose, [5]*to* gold
ἢ ἀργύρῳ ἢ λίθῳ, χαράγματι τέχνης
[6]or [7]*to* silver [8]or [9]*to* stone, [10]*to* an engraved work [11]of art
καὶ ἐνθυμήσεως ἀνθρώπου, τὸ θεῖον εἶναι
[12]and [13]of meditation [14]of man, [1]the [2]divine nature [3]to be
ὅμοιον. 30 τοὺς μὲν οὖν χρόνους τῆς
[4]like. [5]The [1]so [2]then [6]times –
ἀγνοίας ὑπεριδὼν ὁ θεὸς τὰ νῦν
[7]of ignorance [4]having overlooked – [3]God – now
ἀπαγγέλλει τοῖς ἀνθρώποις πάντας πανταχοῦ
declares – to men all men everywhere
μετανοεῖν, 31 καθότι ἔστησεν ἡμέραν ἐν
to repent, because he set a day in
ᾗ μέλλει κρίνειν τὴν οἰκουμένην ἐν
which he is about to judge the inhabited earth in
δικαιοσύνῃ, ἐν ἀνδρὶ ᾧ ὥρισεν, πίστιν
righteousness, by a man whom he designated, [2]a guarantee
παρασχὼν πᾶσιν ἀναστήσας αὐτὸν ἐκ
[1]offering to all having raised up him out of
νεκρῶν. 32 ἀκούσαντες δὲ ἀνάστασιν
[the] dead. And hearing [of] a resurrection
νεκρῶν, οἱ μὲν ἐχλεύαζον, οἱ δὲ εἶπαν·
of dead persons, some scoffed, others said:
ἀκουσόμεθά σου περὶ τούτου καὶ πάλιν.
We will hear thee concerning this also **again.**
33 οὕτως ὁ Παῦλος ἐξῆλθεν ἐκ μέσου
Thus – Paul went forth from [the] midst
αὐτῶν. 34 τινὲς δὲ ἄνδρες κολληθέντες
of them. But some men adhering
αὐτῷ ἐπίστευσαν, ἐν οἷς καὶ Διονύσιος
to him believed, among whom both Dionysius
ὁ Ἀρεοπαγίτης καὶ γυνὴ ὀνόματι Δάμαρις
the Areopagite and a woman by name Damaris
καὶ ἕτεροι σὺν αὐτοῖς.
and others with them.

them and the exact places
where they should live.
27God did this so that men
would seek him and per-
haps reach out for him and
find him, though he is not
far from each one of us.
28'For in him we live and
move and have our being.'
As some of your own poets
have said, 'We are his offspring.'
29"Therefore since we
are God's offspring, we
should not think that the divine being is like gold or silver or stone—an image
made by man's design and
skill. 30In the past God
overlooked such igno-
rance, but now he com-
mands all people every-
where to repent. 31For he
has set a day when he will
judge the world with justice
by the man he has appointed. He has given proof of
this to all men by raising
him from the dead."
32When they heard about
the resurrection of the
dead, some of them
sneered, but others said,
"We want to hear you
again on this subject." 33At
that, Paul left the Council.
34A few men became fol-
lowers of Paul and be-
lieved. Among them was
Dionysius, a member of the
Areopagus, also a woman
named Damaris, and a
number of others.

Chapter 18

Paul in Corinth

AFTER this Paul[w] left
Athens and went to
Corinth. 2 There he found a
Jew named Aquila, a native
of Pontus, who had recently come from Italy with his
wife Priscilla, because

18 Μετὰ ταῦτα χωρισθεὶς ἐκ τῶν
After these things departing out of –
Ἀθηνῶν ἦλθεν εἰς Κόρινθον. 2 καὶ
Athens he came to Corinth. And
εὑρών τινα Ἰουδαῖον ὀνόματι Ἀκύλαν,
finding a certain Jew by name Aquila,
Ποντικὸν τῷ γένει, προσφάτως ἐληλυθότα
belonging to Pontus – by race, recently having come
ἀπὸ τῆς Ἰταλίας, καὶ Πρίσκιλλαν γυναῖκα
from – Italy, and Priscilla wife

Chapter 18

In Corinth

AFTER this, Paul left
Athens and went to
Corinth. 2There he met a
Jew named Aquila, a native
of Pontus, who had recently come from Italy with his
wife Priscilla, because

[v] Other ancient authorities read *the Lord*
[w] Gk *he*

Claudius had ordered all
Jews to leave Rome. Paul[x]
went to see them, 3 and, because he was of the same
trade, he stayed with them,
and they worked
together—by trade they
were tentmakers. 4 Every
sabbath he would argue in
the synagogue and would
try to convince Jews and
Greeks.
5 When Silas and Timo-
thy arrived from Macedo-
nia, Paul was occupied
with proclaiming the
word,[y] testifying to the
Jews that the Messiah[z]
was Jesus. 6 When they opposed and reviled him, in
protest he shook the dust
from his clothes[a] and said
to them, "Your blood be on
your own heads! I am innocent. From now on I will go
to the Gentiles." 7 Then he
left the synagogue[b] and
went to the house of a man
named Titius[c] Justus, a
worshiper of God; his
house was next door to the
synagogue. 8 Crispus, the
official of the synagogue,
became a believer in the
Lord, together with all his
household; and many of the
Corinthians who heard
Paul became believers and
were baptized. 9 One night
the Lord said to Paul in a
vision, "Do not be afraid,
but speak and do not be silent; 10 for I am with you,
and no one will lay a hand
on you to harm you, for
there are many in this city
who are my people." 11 He
stayed there a year and six
months, teaching the word
of God among them.
12 But when Gallio was
proconsul of Achaia, the

αὐτοῦ, διὰ τὸ διατεταχέναι Κλαύδιον
of him, because of the to have commanded Claudius[b]
=because Claudius had commanded

χωρίζεσθαι πάντας τοὺς Ἰουδαίους ἀπὸ
to depart all the Jews from

τῆς Ῥώμης, προσῆλθεν αὐτοῖς, 3 καὶ
– Rome, he came to them, and

διὰ τὸ ὁμότεχνον εἶναι ἔμενεν παρ'
because of the of the same trade to be[b] he remained with
=because [he] was of the same trade

αὐτοῖς, καὶ ἠργάζοντο· ἦσαν γὰρ σκηνοποιοὶ
them, and they wrought; for they were tentmakers

τῇ τέχνῃ. 4 διελέγετο δὲ ἐν τῇ συναγωγῇ
– by trade. And he lectured in the synagogue

κατὰ πᾶν σάββατον, ἔπειθέν τε Ἰουδαίους
on every sabbath, he persuaded both Jews

καὶ Ἕλληνας. 5 Ὡς δὲ κατῆλθον ἀπὸ
and Greeks. And when came down from

τῆς Μακεδονίας ὅ τε Σιλᾶς καὶ ὁ
– Macedonia – both Silas and –

Τιμόθεος, συνείχετο τῷ λόγῳ ὁ Παῦλος,
Timothy, was pressed by the word – Paul,

διαμαρτυρόμενος τοῖς Ἰουδαίοις εἶναι τὸν
solemnly witnessing to the Jews to be the
=that Jesus was the Christ.

χριστὸν Ἰησοῦν. 6 ἀντιτασσομένων δὲ αὐτῶν
Christ Jesus. But resisting them
=when they resisted and blasphemed

καὶ βλασφημούντων ἐκτιναξάμενος τὰ ἱμάτια
and blaspheming[a] shaking off the(his) garments

εἶπεν πρὸς αὐτούς· τὸ αἷμα ὑμῶν ἐπὶ
he said to them: The blood of you on

τὴν κεφαλὴν ὑμῶν· καθαρὸς ἐγὼ ἀπὸ
the head of you; clean I from

τοῦ νῦν εἰς τὰ ἔθνη πορεύσομαι. 7 καὶ
– now to the nations will go. And

μεταβὰς ἐκεῖθεν ἦλθεν εἰς οἰκίαν τινὸς
removing thence he went into [the] house of one

ὀνόματι Τιτίου Ἰούστου σεβομένου τὸν
by name Titius Justus worshipping –

θεόν, οὗ ἡ οἰκία ἦν συνομοροῦσα τῇ
God, of whom the house was being next door to the

συναγωγῇ. 8 Κρίσπος δὲ ὁ ἀρχισυνάγωγος
synagogue. Now Crispus the synagogue ruler

ἐπίστευσεν τῷ κυρίῳ σὺν ὅλῳ τῷ οἴκῳ
believed the Lord with all the household

αὐτοῦ, καὶ πολλοὶ τῶν Κορινθίων ἀκούοντες
of him, and many of the Corinthians hearing

ἐπίστευον καὶ ἐβαπτίζοντο. 9 Εἶπεν δὲ
believed and were baptized. And said

ὁ κύριος ἐν νυκτὶ δι' ὁράματος τῷ
the Lord in [the] night through a vision –

Παύλῳ· μὴ φοβοῦ, ἀλλὰ λάλει καὶ
to Paul: Do not fear, but speak and

μὴ σιωπήσῃς, 10 διότι ἐγώ εἰμι μετὰ σοῦ
keep not silence, because I am with thee

καὶ οὐδεὶς ἐπιθήσεταί σοι τοῦ κακῶσαί
and no one shall set on thee – to illtreat[d]

σε, διότι λαός ἐστί μοι πολὺς ἐν
thee, because people is to me much[e] in
=I have a great people

τῇ πόλει ταύτῃ. 11 Ἐκάθισεν δὲ ἐνιαυτὸν
this city. And he sat a year

καὶ μῆνας ἓξ διδάσκων ἐν αὐτοῖς τὸν
and months six teaching among them the

λόγον τοῦ θεοῦ. 12 Γαλλίωνος δὲ
word – of God. And Gallio
=when Gallio

Claudius had ordered all
the Jews to leave Rome.
Paul went to see them, 3 and
because he was a tentmak-
er as they were, he stayed
and worked with them.
4 Every Sabbath he rea-
soned in the synagogue,
trying to persuade Jews
and Greeks.
5 When Silas and Timothy
came from Macedonia,
Paul devoted himself exclu-
sively to preaching, testifying to the Jews that Jesus
was the Christ.[j] 6 But when
the Jews opposed Paul and
became abusive, he shook
out his clothes in protest
and said to them, "Your
blood be on your own
heads! I am clear of my responsibility. From now on
I will go to the Gentiles."
7 Then Paul left the synagogue and went next door
to the house of Titius Justus, a worshiper of God.
8 Crispus, the synagogue
ruler, and his entire household believed in the Lord;
and many of the Corinthi-
ans who heard him be-
lieved and were baptized.
9 One night the Lord
spoke to Paul in a vision:
"Do not be afraid; keep on
speaking, do not be silent.
10 For I am with you, and no
one is going to attack and
harm you, because I have
many people in this city."
11 So Paul stayed for a year
and a half, teaching them
the word of God.
12 While Gallio was pro-

[x] Gk *He*
[y] Gk *with the word*
[z] Or *the Christ*
[a] Gk *reviled him, he shook out his clothes*
[b] Gk *left there*
[c] Other ancient authorities read *Titus*

[j] Or *Messiah;* also in verse 28

Jews made a united attack on Paul and brought him before the tribunal. 13 They said, "This man is persuading people to worship God in ways that are contrary to the law." 14 Just as Paul was about to speak, Gallio said to the Jews, "If it were a matter of crime or serious villainy, I would be justified in accepting the complaint of you Jews; 15 but since it is a matter of questions about words and names and your own law, see to it yourselves; I do not wish to be a judge of these matters." 16 And he dismissed them from the tribunal. 17 Then all of them[d] seized Sosthenes, the official of the synagogue, and beat him in front of the tribunal. But Gallio paid no attention to any of these things.

Paul's Return to Antioch

18 After staying there for a considerable time, Paul said farewell to the believers[e] and sailed for Syria, accompanied by Priscilla and Aquila. At Cenchreae he had his hair cut, for he was under a vow. 19 When they reached Ephesus, he left them there, but first he himself went into the synagogue and had a discussion with the Jews. 20 When they asked him to stay longer, he declined; 21 but on taking leave of them, he said, "I[f] will return to you, if God wills." Then he set sail from Ephesus.

22 When he had landed at Caesarea, he went up to Jerusalem[g] and greeted the church, and then went

[d] Other ancient authorities read *all the Greeks*
[e] Gk *brothers*
[f] Other ancient authorities read *I must at all costs keep the approaching festival in Jerusalem, but I*
[g] Gk *went up*

ἀνθυπάτου ὄντος τῆς Ἀχαΐας κατεπέστησαν
proconsul being[a] – of Achaia [4]set on
was proconsul

ὁμοθυμαδὸν οἱ Ἰουδαῖοι τῷ Παύλῳ καὶ
[3]with one mind [1]the [2]Jews – Paul and

ἤγαγον αὐτὸν ἐπὶ τὸ βῆμα, 13 λέγοντες
brought him to the tribunal, saying[,]

ὅτι παρὰ τὸν νόμον ἀναπείθει οὗτος
– [6][differently] from [7]the [8]law [2]urges [1]This man

τοὺς ἀνθρώπους σέβεσθαι τὸν θεόν.
– [3]men [4]to worship – [5]God.

14 μέλλοντος δὲ τοῦ Παύλου ἀνοίγειν τὸ
And being about – Paul[a] to open the(his)
=when Paul was about

στόμα εἶπεν ὁ Γαλλίων πρὸς τοὺς
mouth said – Gallio to the

Ἰουδαίους· εἰ μὲν ἦν ἀδίκημά τι
Jews: If indeed it was crime some

ἢ ῥᾳδιούργημα πονηρόν, ὦ Ἰουδαῖοι,
or villainy evil, O Jews,

κατὰ λόγον ἂν ἀνεσχόμην ὑμῶν· 15 εἰ δὲ ζητή-
rightly I would endure you; but if ques-

ματά ἐστιν περὶ λόγου καὶ ὀνομάτων καὶ
tions it is concerning a word and names and

νόμου τοῦ καθ' ὑμᾶς, ὄψεσθε αὐτοί·
law the according to you, ye will see [your]selves;
=your law,

κριτὴς ἐγὼ τούτων οὐ βούλομαι εἶναι.
a judge [1]I [4]of these things [2]do not intend [3]to be.

16 καὶ ἀπήλασεν αὐτοὺς ἀπὸ τοῦ βήματος.
And he drove away them from the tribunal.

17 ἐπιλαβόμενοι δὲ πάντες Σωσθένην τὸν
But [2]seizing [1]all Sosthenes the

ἀρχισυνάγωγον ἔτυπτον ἔμπροσθεν τοῦ
synagogue ruler they struck [him] in front of the

βήματος· καὶ οὐδὲν τούτων τῷ Γαλλίωνι
tribunal; and not one of these things – [2]to Gallio

ἔμελεν. 18 Ὁ δὲ Παῦλος ἔτι προσμείνας
[1]mattered. – But Paul yet having remained

ἡμέρας ἱκανάς, τοῖς ἀδελφοῖς ἀποταξάμενος
days many, to the brothers bidding farewell

ἐξέπλει εἰς τὴν Συρίαν, καὶ σὺν αὐτῷ
he sailed away to – Syria, and with him

Πρίσκιλλα καὶ Ἀκύλας, κειράμενος ἐν
Priscilla and Aquila, having shorn in

Κεγχρεαῖς τὴν κεφαλήν· εἶχεν γὰρ εὐχήν.
Cenchrea the(his) head; for he had a vow.

19 κατήντησαν δὲ εἰς Ἔφεσον, κἀκείνους
And they came down to Ephesus, and those

κατέλιπεν αὐτοῦ, αὐτὸς δὲ εἰσελθὼν εἰς
he left there, but he entering into

τὴν συναγωγὴν διελέξατο τοῖς Ἰουδαίοις.
the synagogue lectured to the Jews.

20 ἐρωτώντων δὲ αὐτῶν ἐπὶ πλείονα
And asking them[a] over a more(longer)
=as they asked

χρόνον μεῖναι οὐκ ἐπένευσεν, 21 ἀλλὰ
time to remain he consented not, but

ἀποταξάμενος καὶ εἰπών· πάλιν ἀνακάμψω
bidding farewell and saying: Again I will return

πρὸς ὑμᾶς τοῦ θεοῦ θέλοντος, ἀνήχθη
to you – God willing,[a] he set sail
=if God wills,

ἀπὸ τῆς Ἐφέσου, 22 καὶ κατελθὼν εἰς
from – Ephesus, and coming down to

Καισάρειαν, ἀναβὰς καὶ ἀσπασάμενος τὴν
Cæsarea, going up and greeting the

consul of Achaia, the Jews made a united attack on Paul and brought him into court. 13 "This man," they charged, "is persuading the people to worship God in ways contrary to the law."

14 Just as Paul was about to speak, Gallio said to the Jews, "If you Jews were making a complaint about some misdemeanor or serious crime, it would be reasonable for me to listen to you. 15 But since it involves questions about words and names and your own law—settle the matter yourselves. I will not be a judge of such things." 16 So he had them ejected from the court. 17 Then they all turned on Sosthenes the synagogue ruler and beat him in front of the court. But Gallio showed no concern whatever.

Priscilla, Aquila and Apollos

18 Paul stayed on in Corinth for some time. Then he left the brothers and sailed for Syria, accompanied by Priscilla and Aquila. Before he sailed, he had his hair cut off at Cenchrea because of a vow he had taken. 19 They arrived at Ephesus, where Paul left Priscilla and Aquila. He himself went into the synagogue and reasoned with the Jews. 20 When they asked him to spend more time with them, he declined. 21 But as he left, he promised, "I will come back if it is God's will." Then he set sail from Ephesus. 22 When he landed at Caesarea, he went up and greeted the

down to Antioch. 23 After spending some time there he departed and went from place to place through the region of Galatia[h] and Phrygia, strengthening all the disciples.

Ministry of Apollos

24 Now there came to Ephesus a Jew named Apollos, a native of Alexandria. He was an eloquent man, well-versed in the scriptures. 25 He had been instructed in the Way of the Lord; and he spoke with burning enthusiasm and taught accurately the things concerning Jesus, though he knew only the baptism of John. 26 He began to speak boldly in the synagogue; but when Priscilla and Aquila heard him, they took him aside and explained the Way of God to him more accurately. 27 And when he wished to cross over to Achaia, the believers[i] encouraged him and wrote to the disciples to welcome him. On his arrival he greatly helped those who through grace had become believers, 28 for he powerfully refuted the Jews in public, showing by the scriptures that the Messiah[j] is Jesus.

ἐκκλησίαν, κατέβη εἰς Ἀντιόχειαν, 23 καὶ
church, he went down to Antioch, and

ποιήσας χρόνον τινὰ ἐξῆλθεν, διερχόμενος
having spent time some he went forth, passing through

καθεξῆς τὴν Γαλατικὴν χώραν καὶ Φρυγίαν,
in order the Galatian country and Phrygia,

στηρίζων πάντας τοὺς μαθητάς.
confirming all the disciples.

24 Ἰουδαῖος δέ τις Ἀπολλῶς ὀνόματι,
And a certain Jew Apollos by name,

Ἀλεξανδρεὺς τῷ γένει, ἀνὴρ λόγιος,
an Alexandrian – by race, a man eloquent,

κατήντησεν εἰς Ἔφεσον, δυνατὸς ὢν ἐν
came to Ephesus, powerful being in

ταῖς γραφαῖς. 25 οὗτος ἦν κατηχημένος
the scriptures. This man was orally instructed [in]

τὴν ὁδὸν τοῦ κυρίου, καὶ ζέων τῷ
the way of the Lord, and burning –

πνεύματι ἐλάλει καὶ ἐδίδασκεν ἀκριβῶς
in spirit he spoke and taught accurately

τὰ περὶ τοῦ Ἰησοῦ, ἐπιστάμενος
the things concerning – Jesus, understanding

μόνον τὸ βάπτισμα Ἰωάννου· 26 οὗτός τε
only the baptism of John; and this man

ἤρξατο παρρησιάζεσθαι ἐν τῇ συναγωγῇ.
began to speak boldly in the synagogue.

ἀκούσαντες δὲ αὐτοῦ Πρίσκιλλα καὶ
And hearing him Priscilla and

Ἀκύλας προσελάβοντο αὐτὸν καὶ ἀκριβέστε-
Aquila took him and more accurate-

ρον αὐτῷ ἐξέθεντο τὴν ὁδὸν τοῦ θεοῦ.
ly to him explained the way – of God.

27 βουλομένου δὲ αὐτοῦ διελθεῖν εἰς τὴν
And intending him[a] to go through into –
=when he intended

Ἀχαΐαν, προτρεψάμενοι οἱ ἀδελφοὶ ἔγραψαν
Achaia, being encouraged the brothers wrote

τοῖς μαθηταῖς ἀποδέξασθαι αὐτόν· ὃς
to the disciples to welcome him; who

παραγενόμενος συνεβάλετο πολὺ τοῖς
arriving contributed much to the [ones]

πεπιστευκόσιν διὰ τῆς χάριτος· 28 εὐτόνως
having believed through – grace, [2]vehemently

γὰρ τοῖς Ἰουδαίοις διακατηλέγχετο δημοσίᾳ
[1]for [4]the [5]Jews [3]he confuted publicly

ἐπιδεικνὺς διὰ τῶν γραφῶν εἶναι τὸν
proving through the scriptures [2]to be [3]the

χριστὸν Ἰησοῦν.
[4]Christ [1]Jesus.

church and then went down to Antioch.

23 After spending some time in Antioch, Paul set out from there and traveled from place to place throughout the region of Galatia and Phrygia, strengthening all the disciples.

24 Meanwhile a Jew named Apollos, a native of Alexandria, came to Ephesus. He was a learned man, with a thorough knowledge of the Scriptures. 25 He had been instructed in the way of the Lord, and he spoke with great fervor[k] and taught about Jesus accurately, though he knew only the baptism of John. 26 He began to speak boldly in the synagogue. When Priscilla and Aquila heard him, they invited him to their home and explained to him the way of God more adequately.

27 When Apollos wanted to go to Achaia, the brothers encouraged him and wrote to the disciples there to welcome him. On arriving, he was a great help to those who by grace had believed. 28 For he vigorously refuted the Jews in public debate, proving from the Scriptures that Jesus was the Christ.

Chapter 19

Paul in Ephesus

WHILE Apollos was in Corinth, Paul passed through the interior regions and came to Ephesus, where he found some disciples. 2 He said to them, "Did you receive the Holy Spirit when you became believers?" They replied, "No, we have not even heard that there is a Holy Spirit." 3 Then he said, "Into what then were you

19 Ἐγένετο δὲ ἐν τῷ τὸν Ἀπολλῶ
Now it came to pass in the – Apollos
=while Apollos was

εἶναι ἐν Κορίνθῳ Παῦλον διελθόντα τὰ
to be[be] in Corinth Paul having passed through the

ἀνωτερικὰ μέρη ἐλθεῖν εἰς Ἔφεσον καὶ
higher parts to come[b] to Ephesus and

εὑρεῖν τινας μαθητάς, 2 εἶπέν τε πρὸς
to find[b] some disciples, and said to

αὐτούς· εἰ πνεῦμα ἅγιον ἐλάβετε πιστεύσαν-
them: If Spirit Holy ye received believ-

τες; οἱ δὲ πρὸς αὐτόν· ἀλλ' οὐδ' εἰ
ing? And they [said] to him: But [2]not [3]if

πνεῦμα ἅγιον ἔστιν ἠκούσαμεν. 3 εἶπέν τε·
[6]Spirit [5]Holy [4]there is [1]we heard. And he said:

Chapter 19

Paul in Ephesus

WHILE Apollos was at Corinth, Paul took the road through the interior and arrived at Ephesus. There he found some disciples 2 and asked them, "Did you receive the Holy Spirit when[l] you believed?"

They answered, "No, we have not even heard that there is a Holy Spirit."

3 So Paul asked, "Then

[h] Gk *the Galatian region*
[i] Gk *brothers*
[j] Or *the Christ*

[k] 25 Or *with fervor in the Spirit*
[l] 2 Or *after*

baptized?" They answered,
"Into John's baptism."
4 Paul said, "John baptized
with the baptism of repentance, telling the people to
believe in the one who was
to come after him, that is,
in Jesus." 5 On hearing this,
they were baptized in the
name of the Lord Jesus.
6 When Paul had laid his
hands on them, the Holy
Spirit came upon them, and
they spoke in tongues and
prophesied— 7 altogether
there were about twelve of
them.
8 He entered the syna-
gogue and for three months
spoke out boldly, and ar-
gued persuasively about
the kingdom of God.
9 When some stubbornly refused to believe and spoke
evil of the Way before the
congregation, he left them,
taking the disciples with
him, and argued daily in the
lecture hall of Tyrannus.[k]
10 This continued for two
years, so that all the residents of Asia, both Jews
and Greeks, heard the
word of the Lord.

The Sons of Sceva

11 God did extraordi-
nary miracles through Paul,
12 so that when the hand-
kerchiefs or aprons that
had touched his skin were
brought to the sick, their
diseases left them, and the
evil spirits came out of
them. 13 Then some itiner-
ant Jewish exorcists tried
to use the name of the Lord
Jesus over those who had
evil spirits, saying, "I ad-

εἰς τί οὖν ἐβαπτίσθητε; οἱ δὲ εἶπαν·
To what therefore were ye baptized? And they said:

εἰς τὸ Ἰωάννου βάπτισμα. **4** εἶπεν δὲ
To the of John baptism. And said

Παῦλος· Ἰωάννης ἐβάπτισεν βάπτισμα μετα-
Paul: John baptized [with] a baptism of repent-

νοίας, τῷ λαῷ λέγων εἰς τὸν ἐρχόμενον
ance, [2]to the [3]people [1]saying [6]in [7]the [one] [8]coming

μετ' αὐτὸν ἵνα πιστεύσωσιν, τοῦτ' ἔστιν
[9]after [10]him [4]that [5]they should believe, this is

εἰς τὸν Ἰησοῦν. **5** ἀκούσαντες δὲ ἐβαπτίσ-
in – Jesus. And hearing they were

θησαν εἰς τὸ ὄνομα τοῦ κυρίου Ἰησοῦ.
baptized in the name of the Lord Jesus.

6 καὶ ἐπιθέντος αὐτοῖς τοῦ Παύλου χεῖρας
And laying on them – Paul hands[a]
=as Paul laid [his] hands on them

ἦλθε τὸ πνεῦμα τὸ ἅγιον ἐπ' αὐτούς,
came the Spirit – Holy on them,

ἐλάλουν τε γλώσσαις καὶ ἐπροφήτευον.
and they spoke in tongues and prophesied.

7 ἦσαν δὲ οἱ πάντες ἄνδρες ὡσεὶ δώδεκα.
And [4]were [2]the [1]all [3]men about twelve.

8 Εἰσελθὼν δὲ εἰς τὴν συναγωγὴν
And entering into the synagogue

ἐπαρρησιάζετο ἐπὶ μῆνας τρεῖς διαλεγόμενος
he spoke boldly over months three lecturing

καὶ πείθων περὶ τῆς βασιλείας τοῦ θεοῦ.
and persuading concerning the kingdom – of God.

9 ὡς δέ τινες ἐσκληρύνοντο καὶ ἠπείθουν
But as some were hardened and disobeyed

κακολογοῦντες τὴν ὁδὸν ἐνώπιον τοῦ
speaking ill [of] the way before the

πλήθους, ἀποστὰς ἀπ' αὐτῶν ἀφώρισεν
multitude, withdrawing from them he separated

τοὺς μαθητάς, καθ' ἡμέραν διαλεγόμενος
the disciples, daily lecturing

ἐν τῇ σχολῇ Τυράννου. **10** τοῦτο δὲ
in the school of Tyrannus. And this

ἐγένετο ἐπὶ ἔτη δύο, ὥστε πάντας τοὺς
happened over years two, so as all the
=so that all who inhabited

κατοικοῦντας τὴν Ἀσίαν ἀκοῦσαι τὸν
[ones] inhabiting – Asia to hear[b] the
Asia heard

λόγον τοῦ κυρίου, Ἰουδαίους τε καὶ
word of the Lord, [3]Jews [1]both and

Ἕλληνας. **11** Δυνάμεις τε οὐ τὰς τυχούσας
Greeks. And powerful deeds not the ordinary

ὁ θεὸς ἐποίει διὰ τῶν χειρῶν Παύλου,
– God did through the hands of Paul,

12 ὥστε καὶ ἐπὶ τοὺς ἀσθενοῦντας
so as even onto the [ones] ailing
=so that there were even brought away from his skin hand-

ἀποφέρεσθαι ἀπὸ τοῦ χρωτὸς αὐτοῦ
to be brought away from the skin of him
kerchiefs or aprons onto those who ailed and the diseases were rid

σουδάρια ἢ σιμικίνθια καὶ ἀπαλλάσσεσθαι
handkerchiefs or aprons and to be rid
from them, and the evil spirits went out.

ἀπ' αὐτῶν τὰς νόσους, τά τε πνεύματα
from them the diseases, and the spirits

τὰ πονηρὰ ἐκπορεύεσθαι. **13** Ἐπεχείρησαν δέ
evil to go out. But [7]attempted

τινες καὶ τῶν περιερχομένων Ἰουδαίων
[1]some [2]also [3]of the [4]strolling [5]Jews

ἐξορκιστῶν ὀνομάζειν ἐπὶ τοὺς ἔχοντας
[6]exorcists to name over the [ones] having

what baptism did you re-
ceive?"
"John's baptism," they
replied.
4 Paul said, "John's bap-
tism was a baptism of re-
pentance. He told the people to believe in the one
coming after him, that is, in
Jesus." 5 On hearing this,
they were baptized into[m]
the name of the Lord Jesus.
6 When Paul placed his
hands on them, the Holy
Spirit came on them, and
they spoke in tongues[n] and
prophesied. 7 There were
about twelve men in all.
8 Paul entered the syna-
gogue and spoke boldly
there for three months, arguing persuasively about
the kingdom of God. 9 But
some of them became ob-
stinate; they refused to believe and publicly maligned
the Way. So Paul left them.
He took the disciples with
him and had discussions
daily in the lecture hall of
Tyrannus. 10 This went on
for two years, so that all the
Jews and Greeks who lived
in the province of Asia
heard the word of the Lord.
11 God did extraordinary
miracles through Paul, 12 so
that even handkerchiefs
and aprons that had
touched him were taken to
the sick, and their illnesses
were cured and the evil
spirits left them.
13 Some Jews who went
around driving out evil
spirits tried to invoke the
name of the Lord Jesus
over those who were de-

[k] Other ancient authorities read *of a certain Tyrannus, from eleven o'clock in the morning to four in the afternoon*

[m] 5 Or *in*
[n] 6 Or *other languages*

jure you by the Jesus whom
Paul proclaims." 14 Seven
sons of a Jewish high priest
named Sceva were doing
this. 15 But the evil spirit
said to them in reply,
"Jesus I know, and Paul I
know; but who are you?"
16 Then the man with the
evil spirit leaped on them,
mastered them all, and so
overpowered them that
they fled out of the house
naked and wounded.
17 When this became
known to all residents of
Ephesus, both Jews and
Greeks, everyone was awe-
struck; and the name of the
Lord Jesus was praised.
18 Also many of those who
became believers con-
fessed and disclosed their
practices. 19 A number of
those who practiced magic
collected their books and
burned them publicly;
when the value of these
books[l] was calculated, it
was found to come to fifty
thousand silver coins. 20 So
the word of the Lord grew
mightily and prevailed.

The Riot in Ephesus

21 Now after these
things had been accom-
plished, Paul resolved in
the Spirit to go through
Macedonia and Achaia,
and then to go on to Jerusalem. He said, "After I have
gone there, I must also see
Rome." 22 So he sent two of
his helpers, Timothy and

τὰ πνεύματα τὰ πονηρὰ τὸ ὄνομα τοῦ
the spirits – evil the name of the

κυρίου Ἰησοῦ λέγοντες· ὁρκίζω ὑμᾶς τὸν
Lord Jesus saying: I exorcise you [by] –

Ἰησοῦν ὃν Παῦλος κηρύσσει. **14** ἦσαν δέ
Jesus whom Paul proclaims. And there were

τινος Σκευᾶ Ἰουδαίου ἀρχιερέως ἑπτὰ
[3]of one [4]Sceva [5]a Jewish [6]chief priest [1]seven

υἱοὶ τοῦτο ποιοῦντες. **15** ἀποκριθὲν δὲ
[2]sons [8]this [7]doing. And answering

τὸ πνεῦμα τὸ πονηρὸν εἶπεν αὐτοῖς·
the spirit – evil said to them:

τὸν [μὲν] Ἰησοῦν γινώσκω καὶ τὸν
– [2]indeed [1]Jesus I know and –

Παῦλον ἐπίσταμαι· ὑμεῖς δὲ τίνες ἐστέ;
Paul I understand; but ye who are?

16 καὶ ἐφαλόμενος ὁ ἄνθρωπος ἐπ' αὐτούς,
And [9]leaping on [1]the [2]man [10]on [11]them,

ἐν ᾧ ἦν τὸ πνεῦμα τὸ πονηρόν,
[3]in [4]whom [5]was [6]the [8]spirit – [7]evil,

κατακυριεύσας ἀμφοτέρων ἴσχυσεν κατ'
overmastering both was strong against

αὐτῶν, ὥστε γυμνοὺς καὶ τετραυματισμένους
them, so as naked and *having been* wounded
=so that they escaped out of that house naked and wounded.

ἐκφυγεῖν ἐκ τοῦ οἴκου ἐκείνου. **17** τοῦτο
to escape out of that house. this

δὲ ἐγένετο γνωστὸν πᾶσιν Ἰουδαίοις τε
And became known to all [2]Jews [1]both

καὶ Ἕλλησιν τοῖς κατοικοῦσιν τὴν Ἔφεσον,
and Greeks – inhabiting – Ephesus,

καὶ ἐπέπεσεν φόβος ἐπὶ πάντας αὐτούς,
and [2]fell *on* [1]fear [3]on [5]all [4]them,

καὶ ἐμεγαλύνετο τὸ ὄνομα τοῦ κυρίου
and was magnified the name of the Lord

Ἰησοῦ· **18** πολλοί τε τῶν πεπιστευκότων
Jesus; and many of the [ones] having believed

ἤρχοντο ἐξομολογούμενοι καὶ ἀναγγέλλοντες
came confessing and telling

τὰς πράξεις αὐτῶν. **19** ἱκανοὶ δὲ τῶν τὰ
the doings of them. And a considerable number of the [ones] the

περίεργα πραξάντων συνενέγκαντες τὰς βίβλους
curious things doing bringing together the rolls

κατέκαιον ἐνώπιον πάντων· καὶ συνεψήφισαν
burnt before all; and they reckoned up

τὰς τιμὰς αὐτῶν καὶ εὗρον ἀργυρίου μυριάδας
the prices of them and found [pieces] [3]of silver [2]thousand

πέντε. **20** Οὕτως κατὰ κράτος τοῦ κυρίου
[1]five. Thus by might [3]of the [4]Lord

ὁ λόγος ηὔξανεν καὶ ἴσχυεν.
[1]the [2]word increased and was strong.

21 Ὡς δὲ ἐπληρώθη ταῦτα, ἔθετο ὁ
And when were fulfilled these things, purposed –

Παῦλος ἐν τῷ πνεύματι διελθὼν τὴν
Paul in the(his) spirit passing through –

Μακεδονίαν καὶ Ἀχαΐαν πορεύεσθαι εἰς
Macedonia and Achaia to go to

Ἱεροσόλυμα, εἰπὼν ὅτι μετὰ τὸ γενέσθαι
Jerusalem, saying[,] – After the to become
=After I am

με ἐκεῖ δεῖ με καὶ Ῥώμην ἰδεῖν.
me[b] there it behoves me [2]also [3]Rome [1]to see.

22 ἀποστείλας δὲ εἰς Μακεδονίαν δύο
And sending into Macedonia two

mon-possessed. They
would say, "In the name of
Jesus, whom Paul
preaches, I command you
to come out." 14 Seven sons
of Sceva, a Jewish chief
priest, were doing this.
15 ⌞One day⌟ the evil spirit
answered them, "Jesus I
know, and I know about
Paul, but who are you?"
16 Then the man who had
the evil spirit jumped on
them and overpowered
them all. He gave them
such a beating that they ran
out of the house naked and
bleeding.
17 When this became
known to the Jews and
Greeks living in Ephesus,
they were all seized with
fear, and the name of the
Lord Jesus was held in high
honor. 18 Many of those
who believed now came
and openly confessed their
evil deeds. 19 A number
who had practiced sorcery
brought their scrolls to-
gether and burned them
publicly. When they calculated the value of the
scrolls, the total came to
fifty thousand drachmas.[o]
20 In this way the word of
the Lord spread widely and
grew in power.
21 After all this had happened, Paul decided to go
to Jerusalem, passing
through Macedonia and
Achaia. "After I have been
there," he said, "I must
visit Rome also." 22 He sent
two of his helpers, Timothy

[o] *19* A drachma was a silver coin worth about a day's wages.

Erastus, to Macedonia,
while he himself stayed for
some time longer in Asia.
23 About that time no
little disturbance broke out
concerning the Way. 24 A
man named Demetrius, a
silversmith who made sil-
ver shrines of Artemis,
brought no little business to
the artisans. 25 These he
gathered together, with the
workers of the same trade,
and said, "Men, you know
that we get our wealth from
this business. 26 You also
see and hear that not only
in Ephesus but in almost
the whole of Asia this Paul
has persuaded and drawn
away a considerable num-
ber of people by saying that
gods made with hands are
not gods. 27 And there is
danger not only that this
trade of ours may come
into disrepute but also that
the temple of the great goddess Artemis will be
scorned, and she will be deprived of her majesty that
brought all Asia and the
world to worship her."
28 When they heard
this, they were enraged and
shouted, "Great is Artemis
of the Ephesians!" 29 The
city was filled with the confusion; and people[m] rushed
together to the theater,
dragging with them Gaius
and Aristarchus, Macedo-
nians who were Paul's travel companions. 30 Paul
wished to go into the
crowd, but the disciples
would not let him; 31 even
some officials of the province of Asia,[n] who were

[l] Gk *them*
[m] Gk *they*
[n] Gk *some of the Asiarchs*

τῶν διακονούντων αὐτῷ, Τιμόθεον καὶ
of the [ones] ministering to him, Timothy and

Ἔραστον, αὐτὸς ἐπέσχεν χρόνον εἰς τὴν
Erastus, he delayed a time in –

Ἀσίαν. 23 Ἐγένετο δὲ κατὰ τὸν καιρὸν
Asia. Now there was about – time

ἐκεῖνον τάραχος οὐκ ὀλίγος περὶ τῆς
that [3]trouble [1]no [2]little concerning the

ὁδοῦ. 24 Δημήτριος γάρ τις ὀνόματι,
way. For [2]Demetrius [1]one by name,

ἀργυροκόπος, ποιῶν ναοὺς ἀργυροῦς
a silversmith, making shrines silver

Ἀρτέμιδος παρείχετο τοῖς τεχνίταις οὐκ
of Artemis provided the artisans no

ὀλίγην ἐργασίαν, 25 οὓς συναθροίσας καὶ
little trade, [2]whom [1]assembling also

τοὺς περὶ τὰ τοιαῦτα ἐργάτας εἶπεν·
[1]the [3]about(in) – [4]such things [2]workmen said:

ἄνδρες, ἐπίστασθε ὅτι ἐκ ταύτης τῆς
Men, ye understand that from this –

ἐργασίας ἡ εὐπορία ἡμῖν ἐστιν, 26 καὶ
trade the gain to us is,[e] and
=we have [our] gain,

θεωρεῖτε καὶ ἀκούετε ὅτι οὐ μόνον
ye behold and hear that [7]not [8]only

Ἐφέσου ἀλλὰ σχεδὸν πάσης τῆς Ἀσίας
[9]of Ephesus [10]but [11]almost [12]of all – [13]Asia

ὁ Παῦλος οὗτος πείσας μετέστησεν ἱκανὸν
– [2]Paul [1]this [3]having persuaded [4]perverted [5]a considerable

ὄχλον, λέγων ὅτι οὐκ εἰσὶν θεοὶ οἱ διὰ
[6]crowd, saying that they are not gods [1]the [ones] [3]through

χειρῶν γινόμενοι. 27 οὐ μόνον δὲ τοῦτο
[4]hands [2]coming into being. [2]not [3]only [1]Now [4]this

κινδυνεύει ἡμῖν τὸ μέρος εἰς ἀπελεγμὸν
[5]is in danger to us the share[c] [6]into [8]disrepute
=[5]our share

ἐλθεῖν, ἀλλὰ καὶ τὸ τῆς μεγάλης θεᾶς
[7]to come, but also [1]the [3]of the [4]great [5]goddess

Ἀρτέμιδος ἱερὸν εἰς οὐθὲν λογισθῆναι,
[6]Artemis [2]temple [8]for(as) [9]nothing [7]to be reckoned,

μέλλειν τε καὶ καθαιρεῖσθαι τῆς μεγα-
[3]to be about [1]and [2]also [4]to be diminished the great-

λειότητος αὐτῆς, ἣν ὅλη ἡ Ἀσία καὶ
ness of her, whom all – Asia and

ἡ οἰκουμένη σέβεται. 28 ἀκούσαντες δὲ
the inhabited earth worships. And hearing

καὶ γενόμενοι πλήρεις θυμοῦ ἔκραζον
and becoming full of anger they cried out

λέγοντες· μεγάλη ἡ Ἄρτεμις Ἐφεσίων.
saying: Great [is] – Artemis of [the] Ephesians.

29 καὶ ἐπλήσθη ἡ πόλις τῆς συγχύσεως,
And was filled the city of(with) the confusion,

ὥρμησάν τε ὁμοθυμαδὸν εἰς τὸ θέατρον,
and they rushed with one mind into the theatre,

συναρπάσαντες Γάϊον καὶ Ἀρίσταρχον
keeping a firm grip on Gaius and Aristarchus[,]

Μακεδόνας, συνεκδήμους Παύλου. 30 Παύλου
Macedonians, travelling companions of Paul. Paul

δὲ βουλομένου εἰσελθεῖν εἰς τὸν δῆμον
And intending[a] to enter into the mob
=as Paul intended

οὐκ εἴων αὐτὸν οἱ μαθηταί· 31 τινὲς
[5]not [6]allowed [4]him [1]the [2]disciples; some

δὲ καὶ τῶν Ἀσιαρχῶν, ὄντες αὐτῷ
and also of the Asiarchs, being to him

and Erastus, to Macedonia,
while he stayed in the province of Asia a little longer.

The Riot in Ephesus

23 About that time there
arose a great disturbance
about the Way. 24 A silversmith named Demetrius,
who made silver shrines of
Artemis, brought in no little business for the craftsmen. 25 He called them together, along with the
workmen in related trades,
and said: "Men, you know
we receive a good income
from this business. 26 And
you see and hear how this
fellow Paul has convinced
and led astray large num-
bers of people here in Ephesus and in practically the
whole province of Asia. He
says that man-made gods
are no gods at all. 27 There is
danger not only that our
trade will lose its good
name, but also that the temple of the great goddess Artemis will be discredited,
and the goddess herself,
who is worshiped through-
out the province of Asia
and the world, will be
robbed of her divine majesty."
28 When they heard this,
they were furious and be-
gan shouting: "Great is Artemis of the Ephesians!"
29 Soon the whole city was
in an uproar. The people
seized Gaius and Aristar-
chus, Paul's traveling companions from Macedonia,
and rushed as one man into
the theater. 30 Paul wanted
to appear before the crowd,
but the disciples would not
let him. 31 Even some of the
officials of the province,

friendly to him, sent him a
message urging him not to
venture into the theater.
32 Meanwhile, some were
shouting one thing, some
another; for the assembly
was in confusion, and most
of them did not know why
they had come together.
33 Some of the crowd gave
instructions to Alexander,
whom the Jews had pushed
forward. And Alexander
motioned for silence and
tried to make a defense before the people. 34 But
when they recognized that
he was a Jew, for about two
hours all of them shouted in
unison, "Great is Artemis
of the Ephesians!" 35 But
when the town clerk had
quieted the crowd, he said,
"Citizens of Ephesus, who
is there that does not know
that the city of the Ephesians is the temple keeper of
the great Artemis and of the
statue that fell from heav-
en?[o] 36 Since these things
cannot be denied, you
ought to be quiet and do
nothing rash. 37 You have
brought these men here
who are neither temple robbers nor blasphemers of
our[p] goddess. 38 If therefore Demetrius and the artisans with him have a com-
plaint against anyone, the
courts are open, and there
are proconsuls; let them
bring charges there against
one another. 39 If there is
anything further[q] you want
to know, it must be settled
in the regular assembly.
40 For we are in danger of
being charged with rioting
today, since there is no
cause that we can give to
justify this commotion."

[o] Meaning of Gk uncertain
[p] Other ancient authorities read *your*
[q] Other ancient authorities read *about other matters*

φίλοι, πέμψαντες πρὸς αὐτὸν παρεκάλουν
friends, sending to him besought

μὴ δοῦναι ἑαυτὸν εἰς τὸ θέατρον. 32 ἄλλοι
not to give himself in the theatre. Others

μὲν οὖν ἄλλο τι ἔκραζον· ἦν γὰρ
indeed therefore [2]different [1]something cried out; for [3]was

ἡ ἐκκλησία συγκεχυμένη, καὶ οἱ πλείους
[1]the [2]assembly *having been* confounded, and the majority

οὐκ ᾔδεισαν τίνος ἕνεκα συνεληλύθεισαν.
knew not [2]of what [1]on account they had come together.

33 ἐκ δὲ τοῦ ὄχλου συνεβίβασαν Ἀλέξανδρον,
But [some] of the crowd instructed Alexander,

προβαλόντων αὐτὸν τῶν Ἰουδαίων· ὁ δὲ
putting forward him the Jews[a]; – and
=as the Jews put him forward;

Ἀλέξανδρος κατασείσας τὴν χεῖρα ἤθελεν
Alexander waving the(his) hand wished

ἀπολογεῖσθαι τῷ δήμῳ. 34 ἐπιγνόντες δὲ
to defend himself to the mob. But knowing

ὅτι Ἰουδαῖός ἐστιν, φωνὴ ἐγένετο μία
that a Jew he is(was), [3]voice [1]there was [2]one

ἐκ πάντων, ὡς ἐπὶ ὥρας δύο κράζοντες·
from all, about over hours two crying out:

μεγάλη ἡ Ἄρτεμις Ἐφεσίων. 35 κατα-
Great [is] – Artemis of [the] Ephesians. [4]having

στείλας δὲ ὁ γραμματεὺς τὸν ὄχλον
quietened [1]And [2]the [3]town clerk the crowd

φησίν· ἄνδρες Ἐφέσιοι, τίς γάρ ἐστιν
says: *Men* Ephesians, who indeed is there

ἀνθρώπων ὃς οὐ γινώσκει τὴν Ἐφεσίων
of men who does not know [1]the [3]of [the] Ephesians

πόλιν νεωκόρον οὖσαν τῆς μεγάλης
[2]city [5]temple warden [4]being of the great

Ἀρτέμιδος καὶ τοῦ διοπετοῦς; 36 ἀναντιρ-
Artemis and of the [image] fallen from the sky? undeni-

ρήτων οὖν ὄντων τούτων δέον ἐστὶν
able therefore being these things[a] necessary it is
=as these things are undeniable

ὑμᾶς κατεσταλμένους ὑπάρχειν καὶ μηδὲν
you [2]*having been* quietened [1]to be and [4]nothing

προπετὲς πράσσειν. 37 ἠγάγετε γὰρ τοὺς
[5]rash [1]to do. For ye brought –

ἄνδρας τούτους οὔτε ἱεροσύλους οὔτε
men these neither temple robbers nor

βλασφημοῦντας τὴν θεὸν ἡμῶν. 38 εἰ
blaspheming the goddess of you. If

μὲν οὖν Δημήτριος καὶ οἱ σὺν αὐτῷ
indeed therefore Demetrius and [1]the [3]with [4]him

τεχνῖται ἔχουσι πρός τινα λόγον, ἀγοραῖοι
[2]artisans have against anyone an account, assizes

ἄγονται καὶ ἀνθύπατοί εἰσιν, ἐγκαλείτωσαν
are being(held) and proconsuls there are, let them bring a charge against

ἀλλήλοις. 39 εἰ δέ τι περαιτέρω ἐπιζητεῖτε,
one another. But if [2]anything [3]further [1]ye seek,

ἐν τῇ ἐννόμῳ ἐκκλησίᾳ ἐπιλυθήσεται.
in the lawful assembly it will be settled.

40 καὶ γὰρ κινδυνεύομεν ἐγκαλεῖσθαι
For indeed we are in danger to be charged with

στάσεως περὶ τῆς σήμερον, μηδενὸς
insurrection concerning to-day, *nothing*

αἰτίου ὑπάρχοντος, περὶ οὗ οὐ δυνησόμεθα
cause being[a], concerning which we shall *not* be able
=there being no cause,

ἀποδοῦναι λόγον περὶ τῆς συστροφῆς
to give account concerning – [2]crowding together

friends of Paul, sent him a
message begging him not to
venture into the theater.
32 The assembly was in
confusion: Some were
shouting one thing, some
another. Most of the people
did not even know why
they were there. 33 The
Jews pushed Alexander to
the front, and some of the
crowd shouted instructions
to him. He motioned for silence in order to make a defense before the people.
34 But when they realized he
was a Jew, they all shouted
in unison for about two
hours: "Great is Artemis of
the Ephesians!"
35 The city clerk quieted
the crowd and said: "Men
of Ephesus, doesn't all the
world know that the city of
Ephesus is the guardian of
the temple of the great Artemis and of her image,
which fell from heaven?
36 Therefore, since these
facts are undeniable, you
ought to be quiet and not do
anything rash. 37 You have
brought these men here,
though they have neither
robbed temples nor blas-
phemed our goddess. 38 If,
then, Demetrius and his fellow craftsmen have a grievance against anybody, the
courts are open and there
are proconsuls. They can
press charges. 39 If there is
anything further you want
to bring up, it must be settled in a legal assembly.
40 As it is, we are in danger
of being charged with rioting because of today's
events. In that case we
would not be able to ac-
count for this commotion,
since there is no reason for

41 When he had said this, he
dismissed the assembly.

Chapter 20

Paul Goes to Macedonia and Greece

AFTER the uproar had
ceased, Paul sent for
the disciples; and after encouraging them and saying
farewell, he left for Macedonia. 2 When he had gone
through those regions and
had given the believers[r]
much encouragement, he
came to Greece, 3 where he
stayed for three months.
He was about to set sail for
Syria when a plot was made
against him by the Jews,
and so he decided to return
through Macedonia. 4 He
was accompanied by Sopa-
ter son of Pyrrhus from Beroea, by Aristarchus and
Secundus from Thessaloni-
ca, by Gaius from Derbe,
and by Timothy, as well as
by Tychicus and Trophi-
mus from Asia. 5 They went
ahead and were waiting for
us in Troas; 6 but we sailed
from Philippi after the days
of Unleavened Bread, and
in five days we joined them
in Troas, where we stayed
for seven days.

Paul's Farewell Visit to Troas

7 On the first day of the
week, when we met to
break bread, Paul was
holding a discussion with
them; since he intended to
leave the next day, he continued speaking until midnight. 8 There were many
lamps in the room upstairs
where we were meeting.
9 A young man named Eu-
tychus, who was sitting in
the window, began to sink
off into a deep sleep while
Paul talked still longer.

[r] Gk *given them*

ταύτης. 41 καὶ ταῦτα εἰπὼν ἀπέλυσεν τὴν
[1]this. And these things saying he dismissed the

ἐκκλησίαν.
assembly.

Chapter 20

20 Μετὰ δὲ τὸ παύσασθαι τὸν θόρυβον
And after the to cease the uproar[b]
=after the uproar ceased

μεταπεμψάμενος ὁ Παῦλος τοὺς μαθητὰς
[3]summoning – [1]Paul [5]the [6]disciples

καὶ παρακαλέσας, ἀσπασάμενος ἐξῆλθεν
[2]and [4]exhorting, taking leave he went forth

πορεύεσθαι εἰς Μακεδονίαν. 2 διελθὼν δὲ
to go to Macedonia. And having gone through

τὰ μέρη ἐκεῖνα καὶ παρακαλέσας αὐτοὺς
those parts and having exhorted them

λόγῳ πολλῷ ἦλθεν εἰς τὴν Ἑλλάδα,
[1]with [3]speech [2]much he came into – Greece,

3 ποιήσας τε μῆνας τρεῖς, γενομένης
and spending months three, there being

ἐπιβουλῆς αὐτῷ ὑπὸ τῶν Ἰουδαίων
a plot[a] [against] him by the Jews

μέλλοντι ἀνάγεσθαι εἰς τὴν Συρίαν, ἐγένετο
being about to set sail to(for) – Syria, he was
=as he was about

γνώμης τοῦ ὑποστρέφειν διὰ Μακεδονίας.
of a mind – to return[d] through Macedonia.

4 συνείπετο δὲ αὐτῷ Σώπατρος Πύρρου
And there accompanied him Sopater [son] of Pyrrhus

Βεροιαῖος, Θεσσαλονικέων δὲ Ἀρίσταρχος
a Berœan, and of Thessalonians Aristarchus

καὶ Σέκουνδος, καὶ Γάϊος Δερβαῖος καὶ
and Secundus, and Gaius a Derbæan and

Τιμόθεος, Ἀσιανοὶ δὲ Τύχικος καὶ
Timothy, and Asians Tychicus and

Τρόφιμος. 5 οὗτοι δὲ προελθόντες ἔμενον
Trophimus. And these men going forward awaited

ἡμᾶς ἐν Τρῳάδι· 6 ἡμεῖς δὲ ἐξεπλεύσαμεν
us in Troas; and we sailed away

μετὰ τὰς ἡμέρας τῶν ἀζύμων ἀπὸ
after the days – of unleavened bread from

Φιλίππων, καὶ ἤλθομεν πρὸς αὐτοὺς εἰς
Philippi, and came to them in

τὴν Τρῳάδα ἄχρι ἡμερῶν πέντε, ὅπου
– Troas until days five, where

διετρίψαμεν ἡμέρας ἑπτά. 7 Ἐν δὲ τῇ
we stayed days seven. And on the

μιᾷ τῶν σαββάτων συνηγμένων ἡμῶν
one(first) of the [day] sabbaths(week) having been assembled us[a]
=as we were assembled

κλάσαι ἄρτον ὁ Παῦλος διελέγετο αὐτοῖς,
to break bread – Paul lectured to them,

μέλλων ἐξιέναι τῇ ἐπαύριον, παρέτεινέν τε
being about to depart on the morrow, and continued

τὸν λόγον μέχρι μεσονυκτίου. 8 ἦσαν δὲ
the speech until midnight. Now there were

λαμπάδες ἱκαναὶ ἐν τῷ ὑπερῴῳ οὗ
lamps a considerable number of in the upper room where

ἦμεν συνηγμένοι. 9 καθεζόμενος δέ τις
we were *having been* assembled. And sitting a certain

νεανίας ὀνόματι Εὔτυχος ἐπὶ τῆς θυρίδος,
young man by name Eutychus on the window sill,

καταφερόμενος ὕπνῳ βαθεῖ, διαλεγομένου
being overborne sleep by a deep, lecturing

it." 41 After he had said
this, he dismissed the assembly.

Chapter 20

Through Macedonia and Greece

WHEN the uproar had
ended, Paul sent for
the disciples and, after encouraging them, said good-
by and set out for Macedonia. 2 He traveled through
that area, speaking many
words of encouragement to
the people, and finally arrived in Greece, 3 where he
stayed three months. Be-
cause the Jews made a plot
against him just as he was
about to sail for Syria, he
decided to go back through
Macedonia. 4 He was ac-
companied by Sopater son
of Pyrrhus from Berea, Aristarchus and Secundus
from Thessalonica, Gaius
from Derbe, Timothy also,
and Tychicus and Trophi-
mus from the province of
Asia. 5 These men went on
ahead and waited for us at
Troas. 6 But we sailed from
Philippi after the Feast of
Unleavened Bread, and
five days later joined the
others at Troas, where we
stayed seven days.

Eutychus Raised From the Dead at Troas

7 On the first day of the
week we came together to
break bread. Paul spoke to
the people and, because he
intended to leave the next
day, kept on talking until
midnight. 8 There were
many lamps in the upstairs
room where we were meet-
ing. 9 Seated in a window
was a young man named
Eutychus, who was sinking
into a deep sleep as Paul
talked on and on. When he

Overcome by sleep, he fell
to the ground three floors
below and was picked up
dead. 10 But Paul went
down, and bending over
him took him in his arms,
and said, "Do not be
alarmed, for his life is in
him." 11 Then Paul went upstairs, and after he had broken bread and eaten, he
continued to converse with
them until dawn; then he
left. 12 Meanwhile they had
taken the boy away alive
and were not a little comforted.

The Voyage from Troas to Miletus

13 We went ahead to the
ship and set sail for Assos,
intending to take Paul on
board there; for he had
made this arrangement, intending to go by land himself. 14 When he met us in
Assos, we took him on
board and went to Mityle-
ne. 15 We sailed from there,
and on the following day
we arrived opposite Chios.
The next day we touched at
Samos, and[s] the day after
that we came to Miletus.
16 For Paul had decided to
sail past Ephesus, so that
he might not have to spend
time in Asia, he was eager
to be in Jerusalem, if possible, on the day of Pente-
cost.

Paul Speaks to the Ephesian Elders

17 From Miletus he sent
a message to Ephesus, asking the elders of the church
to meet him. 18 When they
came to him, he said to
them:
"You yourselves know
how I lived among you the
entire time from the first

[s] Other ancient authorities add *after remaining at Trogyllium*

τοῦ Παύλου ἐπὶ πλεῖον, κατενεχθεὶς ἀπὸ
– Paul* for a longer time, having been overborne from
=while Paul lectured

τοῦ ὕπνου ἔπεσεν ἀπὸ τοῦ τριστέγου
the sleep he fell from the third floor*

κάτω καὶ ἤρθη νεκρός. 10 καταβὰς δὲ
down and was taken up dead. But going down

ὁ Παῦλος ἐπέπεσεν αὐτῷ καὶ συμπεριλαβὼν
– Paul fell on him and closely embracing [him]

εἶπεν· μὴ θορυβεῖσθε· ἡ γὰρ ψυχὴ αὐτοῦ
said: Be ye not terrified; for the life of him

ἐν αὐτῷ ἐστιν. 11 ἀναβὰς δὲ καὶ κλάσας
in him is. And going up and breaking

τὸν ἄρτον καὶ γευσάμενος, ἐφ' ἱκανόν τε
the bread and tasting, and over a considerable [time]

ὁμιλήσας ἄχρι αὐγῆς, οὕτως ἐξῆλθεν.
conversing until light [of day], thus he went forth.

12 ἤγαγον δὲ τὸν παῖδα ζῶντα, καὶ
And they brought the lad living, and

παρεκλήθησαν οὐ μετρίως. 13 Ἡμεῖς δὲ
were comforted not moderately. And we

προελθόντες ἐπὶ τὸ πλοῖον ἀνήχθημεν
going before onto the ship set sail

ἐπὶ τὴν Ἆσσον, ἐκεῖθεν μέλλοντες ἀνα-
to(for) – Assos, thence intending to

λαμβάνειν τὸν Παῦλον· οὕτως γὰρ
take up – Paul; for thus

διατεταγμένος ἦν, μέλλων αὐτὸς πεζεύειν.
having been arranged it was, ²intending ¹he to go afoot.

14 ὡς δὲ συνέβαλλεν ἡμῖν εἰς τὴν Ἆσσον,
Now when he met with us in – Assos,

ἀναλαβόντες αὐτὸν ἤλθομεν εἰς Μιτυλήνην·
taking up him we came to Mitylene;

15 κἀκεῖθεν ἀποπλεύσαντες τῇ ἐπιούσῃ
and thence sailing away on the next [day]

κατηντήσαμεν ἄντικρυς Χίου, τῇ δὲ ἑτέρᾳ
we arrived off Chios, and on the other(next)

παρεβάλομεν εἰς Σάμον, τῇ δὲ ἐχομένῃ
we crossed over to Samos, and on the next

ἤλθομεν εἰς Μίλητον. 16 κεκρίκει γὰρ ὁ
we came to Miletus. For had decided –

Παῦλος παραπλεῦσαι τὴν Ἔφεσον, ὅπως
Paul to sail past – Ephesus, so as

μὴ γένηται αὐτῷ χρονοτριβῆσαι ἐν τῇ
not be to him to spend time in –
=so that he should not . . .

Ἀσίᾳ· ἔσπευδεν γάρ, εἰ δυνατὸν εἴη
Asia; for he hasted, if possible it might be

αὐτῷ, τὴν ἡμέραν τῆς πεντηκοστῆς
to him, the day – of Pentecost

γενέσθαι εἰς Ἱεροσόλυμα.
to be in Jerusalem.

17 Ἀπὸ δὲ τῆς Μιλήτου πέμψας εἰς
And from – Miletus sending to

Ἔφεσον μετεκαλέσατο τοὺς πρεσβυτέρους
Ephesus he summoned the elders

τῆς ἐκκλησίας. 18 ὡς δὲ παρεγένοντο
of the church. And when they came

πρὸς αὐτόν, εἶπεν αὐτοῖς· ὑμεῖς ἐπίστασθε,
to him, he said to them: Ye understand,

ἀπὸ πρώτης ἡμέρας ἀφ' ἧς ἐπέβην εἰς
from [the] first day from which I set foot *on* in

* Souter remarks that it is uncertain whether the ground floor was counted or not in the enunciation; "if so, we should have to translate 'the second floor'."

was sound asleep, he fell to
the ground from the third
story and was picked up
dead. 10 Paul went down,
threw himself on the young
man and put his arms
around him. "Don't be
alarmed," he said. "He's
alive!" 11 Then he went upstairs again and broke
bread and ate. After talking
until daylight, he left. 12 The
people took the young man
home alive and were greatly comforted.

Paul's Farewell to the Ephesian Elders

13 We went on ahead to
the ship and sailed for Assos, where we were going
to take Paul aboard. He had
made this arrangement be-
cause he was going there on
foot. 14 When he met us at
Assos, we took him aboard
and went on to Mitylene.
15 The next day we set sail
from there and arrived off
Kios. The day after that we
crossed over to Samos, and
on the following day ar-
rived at Miletus. 16 Paul had
decided to sail past Ephesus to avoid spending time
in the province of Asia, for
he was in a hurry to reach
Jerusalem, if possible, by
the day of Pentecost.
17 From Miletus, Paul sent
to Ephesus for the elders of
the church. 18 When they
arrived, he said to them:
"You know how I lived the
whole time I was with you,

day that I set foot in Asia,
19 serving the Lord with all
humility and with tears, enduring the trials that came
to me through the plots of
the Jews. 20 I did not shrink
from doing anything help-
ful, proclaiming the mes-
sage to you and teaching
you publicly and from
house to house, 21 as I testified to both Jews and
Greeks about repentance
toward God and faith to-
ward our Lord Jesus.
22 And now, as a captive to
the Spirit,[t] I am on my
way to Jerusalem, not
knowing what will happen
to me there, 23 except that
the Holy Spirit testifies to
me in every city that im-
prisonment and persecu-
tions are waiting for me.
24 But I do not count my life
of any value to myself, if
only I may finish my course
and the ministry that I received from the Lord
Jesus, to testify to the good
news of God's grace.
25 "And now I know
that none of you, among
whom I have gone about
proclaiming the kingdom,
will ever see my face again.
26 Therefore I declare to
you this day that I am not
responsible for the blood of
any of you, 27 for I did not
shrink from declaring to
you the whole purpose of
God. 28 Keep watch over
yourselves and over all the
flock, of which the Holy
Spirit has made you over-
seers, to shepherd the
church of God[u] that he obtained with the blood of his
own Son.[v] 29 I know that

[t] Or *And now, bound in the spirit*
[u] Other ancient authorities read *of the Lord*
[v] Or *with his own blood*; Gk *with the blood of his Own*

τὴν Ἀσίαν, πῶς μεθ' ὑμῶν τὸν πάντα
– Asia, how with you the whole
χρόνον ἐγενόμην, 19 δουλεύων τῷ κυρίῳ
time I was, serving the Lord
μετὰ πάσης ταπεινοφροσύνης καὶ δακρύων
with all humility and tears
καὶ πειρασμῶν τῶν συμβάντων μοι ἐν
and trials – happening to me by
ταῖς ἐπιβουλαῖς τῶν Ἰουδαίων, 20 ὡς
the plots of the Jews, as
οὐδὲν ὑπεστειλάμην τῶν συμφερόντων τοῦ
[2]nothing [1]I kept back of the things beneficial –
μὴ ἀναγγεῖλαι ὑμῖν καὶ διδάξαι ὑμᾶς
not to declare[d] to you and to teach[d] you
δημοσίᾳ καὶ κατ' οἴκους, 21 διαμαρτυρόμενος
publicly and from house to house,† solemnly witnessing
Ἰουδαίοις τε καὶ Ἕλλησιν τὴν εἰς θεὸν
[2]to Jews [1]both and to Greeks – toward God
μετάνοιαν καὶ πίστιν εἰς τὸν κύριον
repentance and faith toward(?in) the Lord
ἡμῶν Ἰησοῦν. 22 καὶ νῦν ἰδοὺ δεδεμένος
of us Jesus. And now behold having been bound
ἐγὼ τῷ πνεύματι πορεύομαι εἰς Ἰερουσαλήμ,
I by the Spirit am going to Jerusalem,
τὰ ἐν αὐτῇ συναντήσοντα ἐμοὶ
[3]the things [6]in [7]it [4]going to meet [5]me
μὴ εἰδώς, 23 πλὴν ὅτι τὸ πνεῦμα τὸ
[1]not [2]knowing, except that the Spirit –
ἅγιον κατὰ πόλιν διαμαρτύρεταί μοι λέγον
Holy in every city† solemnly witnesses to me saying
ὅτι δεσμὰ καὶ θλίψεις με μένουσιν.
that bonds and afflictions me await.
24 ἀλλ' οὐδενὸς λόγου ποιοῦμαι τὴν ψυχὴν
But [4]of nothing [5]account [1]I make [2]the(my) [3]life
τιμίαν ἐμαυτῷ ὡς τελειώσω τὸν δρόμον
precious to myself so as I may finish the course
μου καὶ τὴν διακονίαν ἣν ἔλαβον παρὰ
of me and the ministry which I received from
τοῦ κυρίου Ἰησοῦ, διαμαρτύρασθαι τὸ
the Lord Jesus, to witness solemnly the
εὐαγγέλιον τῆς χάριτος τοῦ θεοῦ. 25 καὶ
gospel of the grace – of God. And
νῦν ἰδοὺ ἐγὼ οἶδα ὅτι οὐκέτι ὄψεσθε
now behold I know that [4]no more [3]will see
τὸ πρόσωπόν μου ὑμεῖς πάντες ἐν οἷς
[5]the [6]face [7]of me [1]ye [2]all among whom
διῆλθον κηρύσσων τὴν βασιλείαν. 26 διότι
I went about proclaiming the kingdom. Wherefore
μαρτύρομαι ὑμῖν ἐν τῇ σήμερον ἡμέρᾳ
I witness to you on this day
ὅτι καθαρός εἰμι ἀπὸ τοῦ αἵματος πάντων·
that clean I am from the blood of all men;
27 οὐ γὰρ ὑπεστειλάμην τοῦ μὴ ἀναγγεῖλαι
for I kept not back – not to declare[d]
πᾶσαν τὴν βουλὴν τοῦ θεοῦ ὑμῖν.
all the counsel – of God to you.
28 προσέχετε ἑαυτοῖς καὶ παντὶ τῷ
Take heed to yourselves and to all the
ποιμνίῳ, ἐν ᾧ ὑμᾶς τὸ πνεῦμα τὸ
flock, in which [5]you [1]the [3]Spirit –
ἅγιον ἔθετο ἐπισκόπους, ποιμαίνειν τὴν
[2]Holy [4]placed overseers, to shepherd the
ἐκκλησίαν τοῦ θεοῦ, ἣν περιεποιήσατο
church – of God, which he acquired
διὰ τοῦ αἵματος τοῦ ἰδίου. 29 ἐγὼ
through the blood of the(his) own.* I

* This = his own blood *or* the blood of his own [?Son].

from the first day I came
into the province of Asia.
19 I served the Lord with
great humility and with
tears, although I was se-
verely tested by the plots of
the Jews. 20 You know that
I have not hesitated to
preach anything that would
be helpful to you but have
taught you publicly and
from house to house. 21 I
have declared to both Jews
and Greeks that they must
turn to God in repentance
and have faith in our Lord
Jesus.
22 "And now, compelled
by the Spirit, I am going to
Jerusalem, not knowing
what will happen to me
there. 23 I only know that in
every city the Holy Spirit
warns me that prison and
hardships are facing me.
24 However, I consider my
life worth nothing to me, if
only I may finish the race
and complete the task the
Lord Jesus has given me—
the task of testifying to the
gospel of God's grace.
25 "Now I know that none
of you among whom I have
gone about preaching the
kingdom will ever see me
again. 26 Therefore, I declare to you today that I am
innocent of the blood of all
men. 27 For I have not hesitated to proclaim to you the
whole will of God. 28 Keep
watch over yourselves and
all the flock of which the
Holy Spirit has made you
overseers.[p] Be shepherds
of the church of God,[q]
which he bought with his
own blood. 29 I know that

[p] 28 Traditionally *bishops*
[q] 28 Many manuscripts *of the Lord*

after I have gone, savage
wolves will come in among
you, not sparing the flock.
30 Some even from your
own group will come dis-
torting the truth in order to
entice the disciples to follow them. 31 Therefore be
alert, remembering that for
three years I did not cease
night or day to warn everyone with tears. 32 And now
I commend you to God and
to the message of his grace,
a message that is able to
build you up and to give
you the inheritance among
all who are sanctified. 33 I
coveted no one's silver or
gold or clothing. 34 You
know for yourselves that I
worked with my own hands
to support myself and my
companions. 35 In all this I
have given you an example
that by such work we must
support the weak, remem-
bering the words of the
Lord Jesus, for he himself
said, 'It is more blessed to
give than to receive.' "
36 When he had fin-
ished speaking, he knelt
down with them all and
prayed. 37 There was much
weeping among them all;
they embraced Paul and
kissed him, 38 grieving especially because of what he
had said, that they would
not see him again. Then
they brought him to the
ship.

Chapter 21

Paul's Journey to Jerusalem

WHEN we had parted
from them and set
sail, we came by a straight
course to Cos, and the next
day to Rhodes, and from

οἶδα ὅτι εἰσελεύσονται μετὰ τὴν ἄφιξίν
know that [7]will come in [1]after [2]the [3]departure

μου λύκοι βαρεῖς εἰς ὑμᾶς μὴ φειδόμενοι
[4]of me [6]wolves [5]grievous [8]*in*to you not sparing

τοῦ ποιμνίου, 30 καὶ ἐξ ὑμῶν αὐτῶν
the flock, and of you [your]selves

ἀναστήσονται ἄνδρες λαλοῦντες διεστραμμένα
will rise up men speaking *having been* perverted things

τοῦ ἀποσπᾶν τοὺς μαθητὰς ὀπίσω ἑαυτῶν.
– to drag away[d] the disciples after themselves.

31 διὸ γρηγορεῖτε, μνημονεύοντες ὅτι
Wherefore watch ye, remembering that

τριετίαν νύκτα καὶ ἡμέραν οὐκ ἐπαυσάμην
for three years night and day I ceased not

μετὰ δακρύων νουθετῶν ἕνα ἕκαστον.
with tears admonishing [2]one [1]each.

32 καὶ τὰ νῦν παρατίθεμαι ὑμᾶς τῷ
And – now I commend you to the

κυρίῳ καὶ τῷ λόγῳ τῆς χάριτος αὐτοῦ
Lord and to the word of the grace of him

τῷ δυναμένῳ οἰκοδομῆσαι καὶ δοῦναι τὴν
– being able to build and to give the

κληρονομίαν ἐν τοῖς ἡγιασμένοις πᾶσιν.
inheritance among [2]the [ones] [3]having been sanctified [1]all.

33 ἀργυρίου ἢ χρυσίου ἢ ἱματισμοῦ οὐδενὸς
Silver or gold or raiment of no one

ἐπεθύμησα· 34 αὐτοὶ γινώσκετε ὅτι ταῖς
I coveted; [your]selves ye know that [4]to the

χρείαις μου καὶ τοῖς οὖσιν μετ' ἐμοῦ
[5]needs [6]of me [7]and [8]to the [ones] [9]being [10]with [11]me

ὑπηρέτησαν αἱ χεῖρες αὗται. 35 πάντα
[3]ministered [1]these [2]hands. All things

ὑπέδειξα ὑμῖν, ὅτι οὕτως κοπιῶντας δεῖ
I showed you, that thus labouring it behoves

ἀντιλαμβάνεσθαι τῶν ἀσθενούντων, μνημονεύειν
to succour the ailing [ones], [2]to remember

τε τῶν λόγων τοῦ κυρίου Ἰησοῦ, ὅτι
[1]and the words of the Lord Jesus, that

αὐτὸς εἶπεν· μακάριόν ἐστιν μᾶλλον διδόναι
he said: Blessed it is rather to give

ἢ λαμβάνειν. 36 καὶ ταῦτα εἰπών,
than to receive. And [2]these things [1]having said,

θεὶς τὰ γόνατα αὐτοῦ σὺν πᾶσιν αὐτοῖς
placing the knees of him with [2]all [1]them
=kneeling down

προσηύξατο. 37 ἱκανὸς δὲ κλαυθμὸς ἐγένετο
he prayed. And [2]considerable [3]weeping [1]there was

πάντων, καὶ ἐπιπεσόντες ἐπὶ τὸν τράχηλον
of all, and falling *on* on the neck

τοῦ Παύλου κατεφίλουν αὐτόν, 38 ὀδυνώ-
– of Paul they kissed fervently him, suffer-

μενοι μάλιστα ἐπὶ τῷ λόγῳ ᾧ εἰρήκει,
ing most over the word which he had said,

ὅτι οὐκέτι μέλλουσιν τὸ πρόσωπον αὐτοῦ
that no more they are(were) the face of him

θεωρεῖν. προέπεμπον δὲ αὐτὸν εἰς τὸ
to behold. And they escorted him to the

πλοῖον.
ship.

21 Ὡς δὲ ἐγένετο ἀναχθῆναι ἡμᾶς
Now when it came to pass to set sail we

ἀποσπασθέντας ἀπ' αὐτῶν, εὐθυδρομήσαντες
having been withdrawn from them, taking a straight course

ἤλθομεν εἰς τὴν Κῶ, τῇ δὲ ἑξῆς εἰς
we came to – Cos, and on the next [day] to

after I leave, savage wolves
will come in among you and
will not spare the flock.
30 Even from your own
number men will arise and
distort the truth in order to
draw away disciples after
them. 31 So be on your
guard! Remember that for
three years I never stopped
warning each of you night
and day with tears.
32 "Now I commit you to
God and to the word of his
grace, which can build you
up and give you an inheritance among all those who
are sanctified. 33 I have not
coveted anyone's silver or
gold or clothing. 34 You
yourselves know that these
hands of mine have sup-
plied my own needs and the
needs of my companions.
35 In everything I did, I
showed you that by this
kind of hard work we must
help the weak, remember-
ing the words the Lord
Jesus himself said: 'It is
more blessed to give than
to receive.' "
36 When he had said this,
he knelt down with all of
them and prayed. 37 They
all wept as they embraced
him and kissed him. 38 What
grieved them most was his
statement that they would
never see his face again.
Then they accompanied
him to the ship.

Chapter 21

On to Jerusalem

AFTER we had torn our-
selves away from
them, we put out to sea and
sailed straight to Cos. The

there to Patara.[w] 2 When
we found a ship bound for
Phoenicia, we went on
board and set sail. 3 We
came in sight of Cyprus;
and leaving it on our left,
we sailed to Syria and landed at Tyre, because the
ship was to unload its cargo
there. 4 We looked up the
disciples and stayed there
for seven days. Through
the Spirit they told Paul not
to go on to Jerusalem.
5 When our days there were
ended, we left and proceeded on our journey; and all
of them, with wives and
children, escorted us outside the city. There we
knelt down on the beach
and prayed 6 and said farewell to one another. Then
we went on board the ship,
and they returned home.
7 When we had fin-
ished[x] the voyage from
Tyre, we arrived at Ptolemais; and we greeted the
believers[y] and stayed with
them for one day. 8 The
next day we left and came
to Caesarea; and we went
into the house of Philip the
evangelist, one of the sev-
en, and stayed with him.
9 He had four unmarried
daughters[z] who had the
gift of prophecy. 10 While
we were staying there for
several days, a prophet
named Agabus came down
from Judea. 11 He came to
us and took Paul's belt,
bound his own feet and

[w] Other ancient authorities add *and Myra*
[x] Or *continued*
[y] Gk *brothers*
[z] Gk *four daughters, virgins,*

τὴν Ῥόδον κἀκεῖθεν εἰς Πάταρα· 2 καὶ
– Rhodes and thence to Patara; and

εὑρόντες πλοῖον διαπερῶν εἰς Φοινίκην,
having found a ship crossing over to Phœnice,

ἐπιβάντες ἀνήχθημεν. 3 ἀναφάναντες δὲ
embarking we set sail. And sighting

τὴν Κύπρον καὶ καταλιπόντες αὐτὴν
– Cyprus and leaving it

εὐώνυμον ἐπλέομεν εἰς Συρίαν, καὶ κατήλ-
on the left we sailed to Syria, and came

θομεν εἰς Τύρον· ἐκεῖσε γὰρ τὸ πλοῖον
down to Tyre; for there the ship

ἦν ἀποφορτιζόμενον τὸν γόμον. 4 ἀνευρ-
was unloading the cargo. find-

όντες δὲ τοὺς μαθητὰς ἐπεμείναμεν αὐτοῦ
ing And the disciples we remained there

ἡμέρας ἑπτά· οἵτινες τῷ Παύλῳ ἔλεγον
days seven; who – 2Paul 1told

διὰ τοῦ πνεύματος μὴ ἐπιβαίνειν εἰς
through the Spirit not to go up to

Ἱεροσόλυμα. 5 ὅτε δὲ ἐγένετο ἐξαρτίσαι
Jerusalem. But when it came to pass to accomplish
= we accomplished

ἡμᾶς τὰς ἡμέρας, ἐξελθόντες ἐπορευόμεθα
us[b] the days, going forth we journeyed

προπεμπόντων ἡμᾶς πάντων σὺν γυναιξὶ
2escorting 3us 1all[a] with women

καὶ τέκνοις ἕως ἔξω τῆς πόλεως, καὶ
and children as far as outside the city, and

θέντες τὰ γόνατα ἐπὶ τὸν αἰγιαλὸν
placing the knees on the shore
= kneeling

προσευξάμενοι 6 ἀπησπασάμεθα ἀλλήλους,
praying we gave parting greetings to one another,

καὶ ἐνέβημεν εἰς τὸ πλοῖον, ἐκεῖνοι δὲ
and embarked in the ship, and those

ὑπέστρεψαν εἰς τὰ ἴδια. 7 Ἡμεῖς δὲ
returned to 1the(ir) 3things 2own. But we
= home.

τὸν πλοῦν διανύσαντες ἀπὸ Τύρου κατηντή-
2the 3voyage 1finishing from Tyre ar-

σαμεν εἰς Πτολεμαΐδα, καὶ ἀσπασάμενοι
rived at Ptolemais, and greeting

τοὺς ἀδελφοὺς ἐμείναμεν ἡμέραν μίαν
the brothers we remained day one

παρ' αὐτοῖς. 8 τῇ δὲ ἐπαύριον ἐξελθόντες
with them. And on the morrow going forth

ἤλθομεν εἰς Καισάρειαν, καὶ εἰσελθόντες
we came to Cæsarea, and entering

εἰς τὸν οἶκον Φιλίππου τοῦ εὐαγγελιστοῦ
into the house of Philip the evangelist

ὄντος ἐκ τῶν ἑπτά, ἐμείναμεν παρ'
being of the seven, we remained with

αὐτῷ. 9 τούτῳ δὲ ἦσαν θυγατέρες
him. Now to this man were daughters
= this man had four daughters

τέσσαρες παρθένοι προφητεύουσαι. 10 Ἐπιμεν-
four[c] virgins prophesying. remain-

όντων δὲ ἡμέρας πλείους κατῆλθέν τις
ing[a] And days more(many) 5came down 1a certain

ἀπὸ τῆς Ἰουδαίας προφήτης ὀνόματι
6from – 7Judæa 2prophet 3by name

Ἅγαβος, 11 καὶ ἐλθὼν πρὸς ἡμᾶς καὶ
4Agabus, and coming to us and

ἄρας τὴν ζώνην τοῦ Παύλου, δήσας
taking the girdle – of Paul, having bound

next day we went to
Rhodes and from there to
Patara. 2 We found a ship
crossing over to Phoenicia,
went on board and set sail.
3 After sighting Cyprus and
passing to the south of it,
we sailed on to Syria. We
landed at Tyre, where our
ship was to unload its cargo. 4 Finding the disciples
there, we stayed with them
seven days. Through the
Spirit they urged Paul not
to go on to Jerusalem. 5 But
when our time was up, we
left and continued on our
way. All the disciples and
their wives and children accompanied us out of the
city, and there on the beach
we knelt to pray. 6 After
saying good-by to each other, we went aboard the
ship, and they returned
home.
7 We continued our voy-
age from Tyre and landed
at Ptolemais, where we
greeted the brothers and
stayed with them for a day.
8 Leaving the next day, we
reached Caesarea and
stayed at the house of Philip the evangelist, one of the
Seven. 9 He had four un-
married daughters who
prophesied.
10 After we had been there
a number of days, a prophet named Agabus came
down from Judea. 11 Com-
ing over to us, he took
Paul's belt, tied his own

hands with it, and said,
"Thus says the Holy Spirit,
'This is the way the Jews in
Jerusalem will bind the
man who owns this belt and
will hand him over to the
Gentiles.' " 12 When we
heard this, we and the people there urged him not to
go up to Jerusalem. 13 Then
Paul answered, "What are
you doing, weeping and
breaking my heart? For I
am ready not only to be
bound but even to die in Jerusalem for the name of the
Lord Jesus." 14 Since he
would not be persuaded,
we remained silent except
to say, "The Lord's will be
done."
15 After these days we
got ready and started to go
up to Jerusalem. 16 Some of
the disciples from Caesarea
also came along and
brought us to the house of
Mnason of Cyprus, an ear-
ly disciple, with whom we
were to stay.

Paul Visits James at Jerusalem

17 When we arrived in
Jerusalem, the brothers
welcomed us warmly.
18 The next day Paul went
with us to visit James; and
all the elders were present.
19 After greeting them, he
related one by one the
things that God had done
among the Gentiles through
his ministry. 20 When they
heard it, they praised God.
Then they said to him,
"You see, brother, how
many thousands of believ-
ers there are among the

ἑαυτοῦ τοὺς πόδας καὶ τὰς χεῖρας εἶπεν·
of himself the feet and the hands said:
τάδε λέγει τὸ πνεῦμα τὸ ἅγιον· τὸν
These things says the Spirit – Holy: [7]The
ἄνδρα οὗ ἐστιν ἡ ζώνη αὕτη οὕτως
[8]man [9]of whom [10]is [11]this [12]girdle [1]thus
δήσουσιν ἐν Ἰερουσαλὴμ οἱ Ἰουδαῖοι καὶ
[4]will bind [5]in [6]Jerusalem [2]the [3]Jews and
παραδώσουσιν εἰς χεῖρας ἐθνῶν. 12 ὡς
will deliver into [the] hands of [the] nations. when
δὲ ἠκούσαμεν ταῦτα, παρεκαλοῦμεν ἡμεῖς
And we heard these things, [6]besought [2]we
τε καὶ οἱ ἐντόπιοι τοῦ μὴ ἀναβαίνειν
[1]both [3]and [4]the [5]residents – [8]not [9]to go up[d]
αὐτὸν εἰς Ἰερουσαλήμ. 13 τότε ἀπεκρίθη
[7]him to Jerusalem. Then answered
ὁ Παῦλος τί ποιεῖτε κλαίοντες καὶ
– Paul: What are ye doing weeping and
συνθρύπτοντές μου τὴν καρδίαν; ἐγὼ γὰρ
weakening of me the heart? For I
οὐ μόνον δεθῆναι ἀλλὰ καὶ ἀποθανεῖν
not only to be bound but also to die
εἰς Ἰερουσαλὴμ ἑτοίμως ἔχω ὑπὲρ τοῦ
in Jerusalem readily have on behalf of the
= am ready
ὀνόματος τοῦ κυρίου Ἰησοῦ. 14 μὴ
name of the Lord Jesus. Not
πειθομένου δὲ αὐτοῦ ἡσυχάσαμεν εἰπόντες·
being persuaded and him[a] we kept silence having said:
= And when he was not persuaded
τοῦ κυρίου τὸ θέλημα γινέσθω.
[4]Of the [5]Lord [2]the [3]will [1]let [6]be [done].
15 Μετὰ δὲ τὰς ἡμέρας ταύτας
And after these days
ἐπισκευασάμενοι ἀνεβαίνομεν εἰς Ἱεροσόλυμα·
having made ready we went up to Jerusalem;
16 συνῆλθον δὲ καὶ τῶν μαθητῶν ἀπὸ
and went *with* also [some] of the disciples from
Καισαρείας σὺν ἡμῖν, ἄγοντες παρ' ᾧ
Cæsarea with us, bringing [one] with whom
ξενισθῶμεν Μνάσωνί τινι Κυπρίῳ,
we might be lodged Mnason a certain Cypriote,
ἀρχαίῳ μαθητῇ. 17 Γενομένων δὲ ἡμῶν εἰς
an ancient (early) disciple. And being us[a] in
= when we were
Ἱεροσόλυμα ἀσμένως ἀπεδέξαντο ἡμᾶς οἱ
Jerusalem [5]joyfully [3]received [4]us [1]the
ἀδελφοί. 18 τῇ δὲ ἐπιούσῃ εἰσῄει ὁ
[2]brothers. And on the next day went in –
Παῦλος σὺν ἡμῖν πρὸς Ἰάκωβον, πάντες
Paul with us to James, [2]all
τε παρεγένοντο οἱ πρεσβύτεροι. 19 καὶ
[1]and [5]came [3]the [4]elders. And
ἀσπασάμενος αὐτοὺς ἐξηγεῖτο καθ' ἓν
having greeted them he related according to one
= singly
ἕκαστον ὧν ἐποίησεν ὁ θεὸς ἐν τοῖς
each of [the things] which did – God among the
ἔθνεσιν διὰ τῆς διακονίας αὐτοῦ. 20 οἱ
nations through the ministry of him. they
δὲ ἀκούσαντες ἐδόξαζον τὸν θεόν, εἶπάν τε
And hearing glorified – God, and said
αὐτῷ· θεωρεῖς, ἀδελφέ, πόσαι μυριάδες
to him: Thou beholdest, brother, how many *ten* thousands
εἰσὶν ἐν τοῖς Ἰουδαίοις τῶν πεπιστευκότων,
there are among the Jews – having believed,

hands and feet with it and
said, "The Holy Spirit
says, 'In this way the Jews
of Jerusalem will bind the
owner of this belt and will
hand him over to the Gen-
tiles.' "
12 When we heard this, we
and the people there pleaded with Paul not to go up to
Jerusalem. 13 Then Paul answered, "Why are you
weeping and breaking my
heart? I am ready not only
to be bound, but also to die
in Jerusalem for the name
of the Lord Jesus." 14 When
he would not be dissuaded,
we gave up and said, "The
Lord's will be done."
15 After this, we got ready
and went up to Jerusalem.
16 Some of the disciples
from Caesarea accompa-
nied us and brought us to
the home of Mnason,
where we were to stay. He
was a man from Cyprus and
one of the early disciples.

Paul's Arrival at Jerusalem

17 When we arrived at Je-
rusalem, the brothers re-
ceived us warmly. 18 The
next day Paul and the rest
of us went to see James,
and all the elders were present. 19 Paul greeted them
and reported in detail what
God had done among the
Gentiles through his ministry.
20 When they heard this,
they praised God. Then
they said to Paul: "You
see, brother, how many
thousands of Jews have be-

Jews, and they are all zealous for the law. 21 They
have been told about you
that you teach all the Jews
living among the Gentiles
to forsake Moses, and that
you tell them not to circumcise their children or observe the customs. 22 What
then is to be done? They
will certainly hear that you
have come. 23 So do what
we tell you. We have four
men who are under a vow.
24 Join these men, go
through the rite of purification with them, and pay for
the shaving of their heads.
Thus all will know that
there is nothing in what
they have been told about
you, but that you yourself
observe and guard the law.
25 But as for the Gentiles
who have become believ-
ers, we have sent a letter
with our judgment that they
should abstain from what
has been sacrificed to idols
and from blood and from
what is strangled[a] and
from fornication." 26 Then
Paul took the men, and the
next day, having purified
himself, he entered the
temple with them, making
public the completion of
the days of purification
when the sacrifice would
be made for each of them.

Paul Arrested in the Temple

27 When the seven days
were almost completed, the
Jews from Asia, who had
seen him in the temple,
stirred up the whole crowd.
They seized him, 28 shouting, "Fellow Israelites,
help! This is the man who is
teaching everyone every-
where against our people,

[a] Other ancient authorities lack *and from what is strangled*

καὶ πάντες ζηλωταὶ τοῦ νόμου ὑπάρχουσιν·
and all zealots of the law are;

21 κατηχήθησαν δὲ περὶ σοῦ ὅτι ἀποστα-
and they were informed about thee that [8]apo-

σίαν διδάσκεις ἀπὸ Μωϋσέως τοὺς κατὰ
stasy [1]thou teachest [9]from [10]Moses [3]the [5]throughout

τὰ ἔθνη πάντας Ἰουδαίους, λέγων μὴ
[6]the [7]nations [2]all [4]Jews, [1]telling [3]not

περιτέμνειν αὐτοὺς τὰ τέκνα μηδὲ τοῖς
[4]to circumcise [2]them the children nor in the

ἔθεσιν περιπατεῖν. **22** τί οὖν ἐστιν;
customs to walk. What therefore is it?

πάντως ἀκούσονται ὅτι ἐλήλυθας. **23** τοῦτο
At all events they will hear that thou hast come. This

οὖν ποίησον ὅ σοι λέγομεν· εἰσὶν ἡμῖν
therefore do thou which thee we tell: There are to us[e] =We have

ἄνδρες τέσσαρες εὐχὴν ἔχοντες ἐφ' ἑαυτῶν·
men four a vow having on themselves;

24 τούτους παραλαβὼν ἁγνίσθητι σὺν αὐτοῖς,
these taking be thou purified with them,

καὶ δαπάνησον ἐπ' αὐτοῖς ἵνα ξυρήσονται
and spend on them that they will shave

τὴν κεφαλήν, καὶ γνώσονται πάντες ὅτι
the head, and will know all men that

ὧν κατήχηνται περὶ σοῦ οὐδέν
[3][of the things] of which [4]they have been informed [5]about [6]thee [2]nothing

ἐστιν, ἀλλὰ στοιχεῖς καὶ αὐτὸς φυλάσσων τὸν
[1]there is, but thou walkest also [thy]self keeping the

νόμον. **25** περὶ δὲ τῶν πεπιστευκότων
law. And concerning [1]the [3]having believed

ἐθνῶν ἡμεῖς ἐπεστείλαμεν κρίναντες φυλάσ-
[2]nations we joined in writing [1]judging [3]to keep

σεσθαι αὐτοὺς τό τε εἰδωλόθυτον καὶ
themselves [2]them [4][from] [6]the [5]both idol sacrifice and

αἷμα καὶ πνικτὸν καὶ πορνείαν. **26** τότε
blood and a thing strangled and fornication. Then

ὁ Παῦλος παραλαβὼν τοὺς ἄνδρας τῇ
– Paul taking the men on the

ἐχομένῃ ἡμέρᾳ σὺν αὐτοῖς ἁγνισθεὶς εἰσῄει
next day with them having been purified went in

εἰς τὸ ἱερόν, διαγγέλλων τὴν ἐκπλήρωσιν
to the temple, announcing the completion

τῶν ἡμερῶν τοῦ ἁγνισμοῦ, ἕως οὗ
of the days of the purification, until

προσηνέχθη ὑπὲρ ἑνὸς ἑκάστου αὐτῶν ἡ
should be offered on behalf of [2]one [1]each of them the

προσφορά.
offering.

27 Ὡς δὲ ἔμελλον αἱ ἑπτὰ ἡμέραι
Now when were about the seven days

συντελεῖσθαι, οἱ ἀπὸ τῆς Ἀσίας Ἰουδαῖοι
to be fulfilled, [1]the [3]from – [4]Asia [2]Jews

θεασάμενοι αὐτὸν ἐν τῷ ἱερῷ συνέχεον
seeing him in the temple stirred up

πάντα τὸν ὄχλον, καὶ ἐπέβαλαν ἐπ'
all the crowd, and laid *on* on

αὐτὸν τὰς χεῖρας, **28** κράζοντες· ἄνδρες
him the(ir) hands, crying out: *Men*

Ἰσραηλῖται, βοηθεῖτε· οὗτός ἐστιν ὁ
Israelites, help: this is the

ἄνθρωπος ὁ κατὰ τοῦ λαοῦ καὶ τοῦ
man [1]the [one] [5]against [6]the [7]people [8]and [9]the

νόμου καὶ τοῦ τόπου τούτου πάντας
[10]law [11]and [12]this [13]place [3]all men

lieved, and all of them are
zealous for the law. 21 They
have been informed that
you teach all the Jews who
live among the Gentiles to
turn away from Moses, telling them not to circumcise
their children or live according to our customs.
22 What shall we do? They
will certainly hear that you
have come, 23 so do what
we tell you. There are four
men with us who have
made a vow. 24 Take these
men, join in their purification rites and pay their expenses, so that they can
have their heads shaved.
Then everybody will know
there is no truth in these reports about you, but that
you yourself are living in
obedience to the law. 25 As
for the Gentile believers,
we have written to them
our decision that they
should abstain from food
sacrificed to idols, from
blood, from the meat of
strangled animals and from
sexual immorality."
26 The next day Paul took
the men and purified him-
self along with them. Then
he went to the temple to
give notice of the date
when the days of purification would end and the offering would be made for
each of them.

Paul Arrested

27 When the seven days
were nearly over, some
Jews from the province of
Asia saw Paul at the tem-
ple. They stirred up the
whole crowd and seized
him, 28 shouting, "Men of
Israel, help us! This is the
man who teaches all men
everywhere against our

our law, and this place;
more than that, he has actually brought Greeks into
the temple and has defiled
this holy place." 29 For they
had previously seen Trophimus the Ephesian with him
in the city, and they supposed that Paul had
brought him into the tem-
ple. 30 Then all the city was
aroused, and the people
rushed together. They
seized Paul and dragged
him out of the temple, and
immediately the doors
were shut. 31 While they
were trying to kill him,
word came to the tribune of
the cohort that all Jerusalem was in an uproar. 32 Immediately he took soldiers
and centurions and ran
down to them. When they
saw the tribune and the soldiers, they stopped beating
Paul. 33 Then the tribune
came, arrested him, and ordered him to be bound with
two chains; he inquired
who he was and what he
had done. 34 Some in the
crowd shouted one thing,
some another; and as he
could not learn the facts because of the uproar, he ordered him to be brought
into the barracks. 35 When
Paul[b] came to the steps,
the violence of the mob was
so great that he had to be
carried by the soldiers.
36 The crowd that followed
kept shouting, "Away with
him!"

Paul Defends Himself

37 Just as Paul was
about to be brought into the
barracks, he said to the tribune, "May I say some-
thing to you?" The tri-

[b] Gk *he*

πανταχῇ διδάσκων, ἔτι τε καὶ Ἕλληνας
[4]everywhere [3]teaching, and even also Greeks
εἰσήγαγεν εἰς τὸ ἱερὸν καὶ κεκοίνωκεν
brought *in* into the temple and has profaned
τὸν ἅγιον τόπον τοῦτον. 29 ἦσαν γὰρ
– [2]holy [3]place [1]this. For they were
προεωρακότες Τρόφιμον τὸν Ἐφέσιον ἐν
having previously seen Trophimus the Ephesian in
τῇ πόλει σὺν αὐτῷ, ὃν ἐνόμιζον ὅτι
the city with him, whom they supposed that
εἰς τὸ ἱερὸν εἰσήγαγεν ὁ Παῦλος. 30 ἐκινήθη
[3]into [4]the [5]temple [2]brought *in* – [1]Paul. [5]was moved
τε ἡ πόλις ὅλη καὶ ἐγένετο συνδρομὴ
[1]And [2]the [4]city [3]whole and there was a running together
τοῦ λαοῦ, καὶ ἐπιλαβόμενοι τοῦ Παύλου
of the people, and laying hold – of Paul
εἷλκον αὐτὸν ἔξω τοῦ ἱεροῦ, καὶ εὐθέως
they dragged him outside the temple, and immediately
ἐκλείσθησαν αἱ θύραι. 31 Ζητούντων τε
were shut the doors. And [while they were] seeking[a]
αὐτὸν ἀποκτεῖναι ἀνέβη φάσις τῷ
[2]him [1]to kill [4]came up [3]information to the
χιλιάρχῳ τῆς σπείρης ὅτι ὅλη συγχύν-
chiliarch of the cohort that [1]all [3]is(was) in
νεται Ἰερουσαλήμ· 32 ὃς ἐξαυτῆς παρα-
confusion [2]Jerusalem; who at once tak-
λαβὼν στρατιώτας καὶ ἑκατοντάρχας
ing soldiers and centurions
κατέδραμεν ἐπ᾽ αὐτούς· οἱ δὲ ἰδόντες
ran down on them; and they seeing
τὸν χιλίαρχον καὶ τοὺς στρατιώτας
the chiliarch and the soldiers
ἐπαύσαντο τύπτοντες τὸν Παῦλον. 33 τότε
ceased beating – Paul. Then
ἐγγίσας ὁ χιλίαρχος ἐπελάβετο αὐτοῦ
drawing near the chiliarch laid hold of him
καὶ ἐκέλευσεν δεθῆναι ἁλύσεσι δυσί, καὶ
and commanded to be bound chains with two, and
ἐπυνθάνετο τίς εἴη καὶ τί ἐστιν πεποιηκώς.
inquired who he might be and what he is having done.
34 ἄλλοι δὲ ἄλλο τι ἐπεφώνουν ἐν τῷ
And [1]others [2]different [3]something [4]called out [5]among [6]the
ὄχλῳ· μὴ δυναμένου δὲ αὐτοῦ γνῶναι
[7]crowd; and not being able =as he was not able him[a] to know
τὸ ἀσφαλὲς διὰ τὸν θόρυβον, ἐκέλευσεν
the certain thing because of the uproar, he commanded
ἄγεσθαι αὐτὸν εἰς τὴν παρεμβολήν. 35 ὅτε
to be brought him into the fort. when
δὲ ἐγένετο ἐπὶ τοὺς ἀναβαθμούς, συνέβη
And he was on the steps, it happened
βαστάζεσθαι αὐτὸν ὑπὸ τῶν στρατιωτῶν
to be carried him[b] by he soldiers =he was carried
διὰ τὴν βίαν τοῦ ὄχλου· 36 ἠκολούθει
because of the violence of the crowd; [6]followed
γὰρ τὸ πλῆθος τοῦ λαοῦ κράζοντες·
[1]for [2]the [3]multitude [4]of the [5]people crying out:
αἶρε αὐτόν. 37 Μέλλων τε εἰσάγεσθαι
Take away him. And being about to be brought *in*
εἰς τὴν παρεμβολὴν ὁ Παῦλος λέγει τῷ
into the fort – Paul says to the
χιλιάρχῳ· εἰ ἔξεστίν μοι εἰπεῖν τι πρὸς
chiliarch: If it is lawful for me to say something to

people and our law and this
place. And besides, he has
brought Greeks into the
temple area and defiled this
holy place." 29(They had
previously seen Trophimus
the Ephesian in the city
with Paul and assumed that
Paul had brought him into
the temple area.)
30The whole city was
aroused, and the people
came running from all di-
rections. Seizing Paul, they
dragged him from the tem-
ple, and immediately the
gates were shut. 31While
they were trying to kill him,
news reached the com-
mander of the Roman
troops that the whole city
of Jerusalem was in an uproar. 32He at once took
some officers and soldiers
and ran down to the crowd.
When the rioters saw the
commander and his sol-
diers, they stopped beating
Paul.
33The commander came
up and arrested him and ordered him to be bound with
two chains. Then he asked
who he was and what he
had done. 34Some in the
crowd shouted one thing
and some another, and
since the commander could
not get at the truth because
of the uproar, he ordered
that Paul be taken into the
barracks. 35When Paul
reached the steps, the violence of the mob was so
great he had to be carried
by the soldiers. 36The
crowd that followed kept
shouting, "Away with
him!"

Paul Speaks to the Crowd

37As the soldiers were
about to take Paul into the
barracks, he asked the
commander, "May I say
something to you?"

bune[c] replied, "Do you
know Greek? 38Then you
are not the Egyptian who
recently stirred up a revolt
and led the four thousand
assassins out into the wilderness?" 39Paul replied,
"I am a Jew, from Tarsus in
Cilicia, a citizen of an important city; I beg you, let
me speak to the people."
40When he had given him
permission, Paul stood on
the steps and motioned to
the people for silence; and
when there was a great
hush, he addressed them in
the Hebrew[d] language,
saying:

Chapter 22

"BROTHERS and fa-
thers, listen to the
defense that I now make
before you."
2 When they heard him
addressing them in He-
brew,[d] they became even
more quiet. Then he said:
3 "I am a Jew, born in
Tarsus in Cilicia, but
brought up in this city at the
feet of Gamaliel, educated
strictly according to our ancestral law, being zealous
for God, just as all of you
are today. 4I persecuted
this Way up to the point of
death by binding both men
and women and putting
them in prison, 5as the high
priest and the whole council of elders can testify
about me. From them I also
received letters to the
brothers in Damascus, and
I went there in order to bind

[c]Gk *He*
[d]That is, *Aramaic*

σέ; ὁ δὲ ἔφη· Ἑλληνιστὶ γινώσκεις;
thee? And he said: in Greek Knowest thou [to speak]?*

38 οὐκ ἄρα σὺ εἶ ὁ Αἰγύπτιος ὁ πρὸ
[2]Not [4]then [3]thou [1]art the Egyptian the [one] before

τούτων τῶν ἡμερῶν ἀναστατώσας καὶ
these – days unsettling and

ἐξαγαγὼν εἰς τὴν ἔρημον τοὺς τετρα-
leading out into the desert the four

κισχιλίους ἄνδρας τῶν σικαρίων; 39 εἶπεν
thousand men of the Sicarii? said

δὲ ὁ Παῦλος· ἐγὼ ἄνθρωπος μέν εἰμι
And – Paul: I *a man* indeed am

Ἰουδαῖος, Ταρσεύς, τῆς Κιλικίας οὐκ
a Jew, a Tarsian, – of Cilicia not

ἀσήμου πόλεως πολίτης· δέομαι δέ σου,
of a mean city a citizen; and I beg of thee,

ἐπίτρεψόν μοι λαλῆσαι πρὸς τὸν λαόν.
permit me to speak to the people.

40 ἐπιτρέψαντος δὲ αὐτοῦ ὁ Παῦλος ἑστὼς
And permitting him[a] – Paul standing
=when he gave permission

ἐπὶ τῶν ἀναβαθμῶν κατέσεισεν τῇ χειρὶ
on the steps beckoned with the(his) hand

τῷ λαῷ· πολλῆς δὲ σιγῆς γενομένης
to the people; and much silence becoming[a]
=when there was great silence

προσεφώνησεν τῇ Ἑβραΐδι διαλέκτῳ λέγων·
he addressed in the Hebrew language saying:

22 Ἄνδρες ἀδελφοὶ καὶ πατέρες, ἀκούσατέ
Men brothers and fathers, hear ye

μου τῆς πρὸς ὑμᾶς νυνὶ ἀπολογίας.
[3]of me [1]the [5]to [6]you [4]now [2]defence.

— 2 ἀκούσαντες δὲ ὅτι τῇ Ἑβραΐδι
(And hearing that in the Hebrew

διαλέκτῳ προσεφώνει αὐτοῖς μᾶλλον
language he addressed them more

παρέσχον ἡσυχίαν. καὶ φησίν· — 3 ἐγώ εἰμι
they showed quietness. And he says:) I am

ἀνὴρ Ἰουδαῖος, γεγεννημένος ἐν Ταρσῷ
a man a Jew, having been born in Tarsus

τῆς Κιλικίας, ἀνατεθραμμένος δὲ ἐν τῇ
– of Cilicia, and having been brought up in –

πόλει ταύτῃ, παρὰ τοὺς πόδας Γαμαλιὴλ
city this, at the feet of Gamaliel

πεπαιδευμένος κατὰ ἀκρίβειαν τοῦ πατρῴου
having been trained according to [the] exactness of the ancestral

νόμου, ζηλωτὴς ὑπάρχων τοῦ θεοῦ καθὼς
law a zealot being – of God even as

πάντες ὑμεῖς ἐστε σήμερον· 4 ὃς ταύτην
all ye are to-day; who this

τὴν ὁδὸν ἐδίωξα ἄχρι θανάτου, δεσμεύων
– way persecuted as far as to death, binding

καὶ παραδιδοὺς εἰς φυλακὰς ἄνδρας τε
and delivering to prisons both men

καὶ γυναῖκας. 5 ὡς καὶ ὁ ἀρχιερεὺς
and women. As even the high priest

μαρτυρεῖ μοι καὶ πᾶν τὸ πρεσβυτέριον·
witnesses to me and all the senate;

παρ' ὧν καὶ ἐπιστολὰς δεξάμενος πρὸς
from whom also letters having received to

τοὺς ἀδελφοὺς εἰς Δαμασκὸν ἐπορευόμην,
the brothers in Damascus I journeyed,

* See note on page xviii.

"Do you speak Greek?"
he replied. 38"Aren't you
the Egyptian who started a
revolt and led four thou-
sand terrorists out into the
desert some time ago?"
39Paul answered, "I am a
Jew, from Tarsus in Cilicia,
a citizen of no ordinary
city. Please let me speak to
the people."
40Having received the
commander's permission,
Paul stood on the steps and
motioned to the crowd.
When they were all silent,
he said to them in Arama-
ic[r]: 1"Brothers and fa-
thers, listen now to my defense."
2When they heard him
speak to them in Aramaic,
they became very quiet.
Then Paul said: 3"I am a
Jew, born in Tarsus of Cilicia, but brought up in this
city. Under Gamaliel I was
thoroughly trained in the
law of our fathers and was
just as zealous for God as
any of you are today. 4I
persecuted the followers of
this Way to their death, arresting both men and wom-
en and throwing them into
prison, 5as also the high
priest and all the Council
can testify. I even obtained
letters from them to their
brothers in Damascus, and

[r]40 Or possibly *Hebrew*; also in 22:2

those who were there and to bring them back to Jerusalem for punishment.

Paul Tells of His Conversion

6 "While I was on my way and approaching Damascus, about noon a great light from heaven suddenly shone about me. 7 I fell to the ground and heard a voice saying to me, 'Saul, Saul, why are you persecuting me?' 8 I answered, 'Who are you, Lord?' Then he said to me, 'I am Jesus of Nazareth[e] whom you are persecuting.' 9 Now those who were with me saw the light but did not hear the voice of the one who was speaking to me. 10 I asked, 'What am I to do, Lord?' The Lord said to me, 'Get up and go to Damascus; there you will be told everything that has been assigned to you to do.' 11 Since I could not see because of the brightness of that light, those who were with me took my hand and led me to Damascus.

12 "A certain Ananias, who was a devout man according to the law and well spoken of by all the Jews living there, 13 came to me; and standing beside me, he said, 'Brother Saul, regain your sight!' In that very hour I regained my sight and saw him. 14 Then he said, 'The God of our ancestors has chosen you to know his will, to see the Righteous One and to hear his own voice; 15 for you will be his witness to all the world of what you have seen and heard. 16 And now why do you delay? Get up, be baptized, and have your sins washed away, calling

ἄξων καὶ τοὺς ἐκεῖσε ὄντας δεδεμένους
leading also the [ones] ²there ¹being *having been* bound

εἰς Ἰερουσαλὴμ ἵνα τιμωρηθῶσιν.
to Jerusalem that they might be punished.

6 Ἐγένετο δέ μοι πορευομένῳ καὶ ἐγγίζοντι
Now it happened to me journeying and drawing near

τῇ Δαμασκῷ περὶ μεσημβρίαν ἐξαίφνης ἐκ
– to Damascus about midday suddenly out of

τοῦ οὐρανοῦ περιαστράψαι φῶς ἱκανὸν
– heaven ⁴to shine *round* ¹a ³light ²considerable

περὶ ἐμέ, **7** ἔπεσά τε εἰς τὸ ἔδαφος
round me, and I fell to the ground

καὶ ἤκουσα φωνῆς λεγούσης μοι· Σαοὺλ
and heard a voice saying to me: Saul[,]

Σαούλ, τί με διώκεις; **8** ἐγὼ δὲ ἀπεκρίθην·
Saul, why me persecutest thou? And I answered:

τίς εἶ, κύριε; εἶπέν τε πρὸς ἐμέ· ἐγώ
Who art thou, Lord? And he said to me: I

εἰμι Ἰησοῦς ὁ Ναζωραῖος, ὃν σὺ διώκεις.
am Jesus the Nazarene, whom thou persecutest.

9 οἱ δὲ σὺν ἐμοὶ ὄντες τὸ μὲν φῶς
Now ¹the [ones] ³with ⁴me ²being ⁷the ⁶indeed ⁸light

ἐθεάσαντο, τὴν δὲ φωνὴν οὐκ ἤκουσαν
⁵beheld, but the voice they heard not

τοῦ λαλοῦντός μοι. **10** εἶπον δέ· τί
of the [one] speaking to me. And I said: What

ποιήσω, κύριε; ὁ δὲ κύριος εἶπεν πρός
may I do, Lord? And the Lord said to

με· ἀναστὰς πορεύου εἰς Δαμασκόν, κἀκεῖ σοι
me: Rising up go into Damascus, and there to thee

λαληθήσεται περὶ πάντων ὧν τέτακταί
it will be told concerning all things which has(ve) been arranged

σοι ποιῆσαι. **11** ὡς δὲ οὐκ ἐνέβλεπον
for thee to do. And as I saw not

ἀπὸ τῆς δόξης τοῦ φωτὸς ἐκείνου,
from the glory of that light,

χειραγωγούμενος ὑπὸ τῶν συνόντων μοι
being led by the hand by the [ones] being with me

ἦλθον εἰς Δαμασκόν. **12** Ἁνανίας δέ τις,
I went into Damascus. And a certain Ananias,

ἀνὴρ εὐλαβὴς κατὰ τὸν νόμον, μαρτυρού-
a man devout according to the law, being witnessed

μενος ὑπὸ πάντων τῶν κατοικούντων
[to] by all ¹the ³dwelling ⁴[there]

Ἰουδαίων, **13** ἐλθὼν πρὸς ἐμὲ καὶ ἐπιστὰς
²Jews, coming to me and standing by

εἶπέν μοι· Σαοὺλ ἀδελφέ, ἀνάβλεψον.
said to me: Saul brother, look up.

κἀγὼ αὐτῇ τῇ ὥρᾳ ἀνέβλεψα εἰς αὐτόν.
And I in that hour* looked up at him.

14 ὁ δὲ εἶπεν· ὁ θεὸς τῶν πατέρων
And he said: The God of the fathers

ἡμῶν προεχειρίσατό σε γνῶναι τὸ θέλημα
of us previously appointed thee to know the will

αὐτοῦ καὶ ἰδεῖν τὸν δίκαιον καὶ ἀκοῦσαι
of him and to see the Just One and to hear

φωνὴν ἐκ τοῦ στόματος αὐτοῦ, **15** ὅτι
a voice out of the mouth of him, because

ἔσῃ μάρτυς αὐτῷ πρὸς πάντας ἀνθρώπους
thou wilt be a witness to him[c] to all men

ὧν ἑώρακας καὶ ἤκουσας. **16** καὶ νῦν
of things which thou hast seen and didst hear. And now

τί μέλλεις; ἀναστὰς βάπτισαι καὶ ἀπόλου-
what intendest thou? Rising up be baptized and wash

went there to bring these people as prisoners to Jerusalem to be punished.

6 "About noon as I came near Damascus, suddenly a bright light from heaven flashed around me. 7 I fell to the ground and heard a voice say to me, 'Saul! Saul! Why do you persecute me?'

8 " 'Who are you, Lord?' I asked.

" 'I am Jesus of Nazareth, whom you are persecuting,' he replied. 9 My companions saw the light, but they did not understand the voice of him who was speaking to me.

10 " 'What shall I do, Lord?' I asked.

" 'Get up,' the Lord said, 'and go into Damascus. There you will be told all that you have been assigned to do.' 11 My companions led me by the hand into Damascus, because the brilliance of the light had blinded me.

12 "A man named Ananias came to see me. He was a devout observer of the law and highly respected by all the Jews living there. 13 He stood beside me and said, 'Brother Saul, receive your sight!' And at that very moment I was able to see him.

14 "Then he said: 'The God of our fathers has chosen you to know his will and to see the Righteous One and to hear words from his mouth. 15 You will be his witness to all men of what you have seen and heard. 16 And now what are you waiting for? Get up, be baptized and wash your

[e] Gk *the Nazorean*

* See Luke 2. 38.

on his name.'

Paul Sent to the Gentiles

17 "After I had returned
to Jerusalem and while I
was praying in the temple,
I fell into a trance 18and
saw Jesus[f] saying to me,
'Hurry and get out of Jerusalem quickly, because
they will not accept your
testimony about me.'
19And I said, 'Lord, they
themselves know that in
every synagogue I impris-
oned and beat those who
believed in you. 20And
while the blood of your witness Stephen was shed, I
myself was standing by, ap-
proving and keeping the
coats of those who killed
him.' 21Then he said to me,
'Go, for I will send you far
away to the Gentiles.'"

Paul and the Roman Tribune

22 Up to this point they
listened to him, but then
they shouted, "Away with
such a fellow from the
earth! For he should not be
allowed to live." 23And
while they were shouting,
throwing off their cloaks,
and tossing dust into the
air, 24the tribune directed
that he was to be brought
into the barracks, and ordered him to be examined
by flogging, to find out the
reason for this outcry
against him. 25But when
they had tied him up with
thongs,[g] Paul said to the
centurion who was stand-
ing by, "Is it legal for you to
flog a Roman citizen who is
uncondemned?" 26When
the centurion heard that, he
went to the tribune and said
to him, "What are you

σαι τὰς ἁμαρτίας σου, ἐπικαλεσάμενος τὸ
away the sins of thee, invoking the

ὄνομα αὐτοῦ. 17 Ἐγένετο δέ μοι ὑποστρέ-
name of him. And it happened to me having

ψαντι εἰς Ἰερουσαλὴμ καὶ προσευχομένου
returned to Jerusalem and praying
=as I was praying

μου ἐν τῷ ἱερῷ γενέσθαι με ἐν ἐκστάσει,
me[a] in the temple to become me[b] in an ecstasy,
=I became

18 καὶ ἰδεῖν αὐτὸν λέγοντά μοι· σπεῦσον
and to see[b] him saying to me; Haste
=I saw

καὶ ἔξελθε ἐν τάχει ἐξ Ἰερουσαλήμ,
and go forth quickly out of Jerusalem,

διότι οὐ παραδέξονταί σου μαρτυρίαν
because they will not receive of thee witness

περὶ ἐμοῦ. 19 κἀγὼ εἶπον· κύριε, αὐτοὶ
concerning me. And I said: Lord, they

ἐπίστανται ὅτι ἐγὼ ἤμην φυλακίζων καὶ
understand that I was imprisoning and

δέρων κατὰ τὰς συναγωγὰς τοὺς πιστεύον-
beating throughout the synagogues the [ones] believ-

τας ἐπὶ σέ· 20 καὶ ὅτε ἐξεχύννετο τὸ αἷμα
ing on thee; and when was being shed the blood

Στεφάνου τοῦ μάρτυρός σου, καὶ αὐτὸς
of Stephen the witness of thee, even [my]self

ἤμην ἐφεστὼς καὶ συνευδοκῶν καὶ
I was standing by and consenting and

φυλάσσων τὰ ἱμάτια τῶν ἀναιρούντων
keeping the garments of the [ones] killing

αὐτόν. 21 καὶ εἶπεν πρός με· πορεύου,
him. And he said to me: Go,

ὅτι ἐγὼ εἰς ἔθνη μακρὰν ἐξαποστελῶ σε.
because I to nations afar will send forth thee.

22 Ἤκουον δὲ αὐτοῦ ἄχρι τούτου τοῦ
And they heard him as far as to this –

λόγου, καὶ ἐπῆραν τὴν φωνὴν αὐτῶν
word, and lifted up the voice of them

λέγοντες· αἶρε ἀπὸ τῆς γῆς τὸν τοιοῦτον·
saying: Take from the earth such a man;

οὐ γὰρ καθῆκεν αὐτὸν ζῆν. 23 κραυγαζόν-
for not it is fitting him to live. And shout-

των τε αὐτῶν καὶ ῥιπτούντων τὰ ἱμάτια
ing them and tearing[a] the(ir) garments
=as they shouted and tore . . .

καὶ κονιορτὸν βαλλόντων εἰς τὸν ἀέρα,
and [2]dust [1]throwing[a] in the air,
=threw dust

24 ἐκέλευσεν ὁ χιλίαρχος εἰσάγεσθαι αὐτὸν
commanded the chiliarch to be brought *in* him

εἰς τὴν παρεμβολήν, εἴπας μάστιξιν
into the fort, bidding [3]with scourges

ἀνετάζεσθαι αὐτόν, ἵνα ἐπιγνῷ δι' ἣν
[2]to be examined [1]him, that he might fully know for what

αἰτίαν οὕτως ἐπεφώνουν αὐτῷ. 25 ὡς δὲ
crime thus they were calling against him. But as

προέτειναν αὐτὸν τοῖς ἱμᾶσιν, εἶπεν πρὸς
they stretched forward him with the thongs, [2]said [3]to

τὸν ἑστῶτα ἑκατόνταρχον ὁ Παῦλος· εἰ
[4]the [6]standing [by] [5]centurion – [1]Paul: [1]If

ἄνθρωπον Ῥωμαῖον καὶ ἀκατάκριτον ἔξεστιν
a man [6]a Roman [6]and [7]uncondemned [2]it is lawful

ὑμῖν μαστίζειν; 26 ἀκούσας δὲ ὁ ἑκατον-
[3]for you [4]to scourge? And [3]hearing [1]the [2]cen-

τάρχης προσελθὼν τῷ χιλιάρχῳ ἀπήγγειλεν
turion approaching *to* the chiliarch reported

sins away, calling on his
name.'
17"When I returned to Je-
rusalem and was praying at
the temple, I fell into a
trance 18and saw the Lord
speaking. 'Quick!' he said
to me. 'Leave Jerusalem
immediately, because they
will not accept your testimony about me.'
19"'Lord,' I replied,
'these men know that I
went from one synagogue
to another to imprison and
beat those who believe in
you. 20And when the blood
of your martyr[s] Stephen
was shed, I stood there giving my approval and guarding the clothes of those who
were killing him.'
21"Then the Lord said to
me, 'Go; I will send you far
away to the Gentiles.'"

Paul the Roman Citizen

22The crowd listened to
Paul until he said this. Then
they raised their voices and
shouted, "Rid the earth of
him! He's not fit to live!"
23As they were shouting
and throwing off their
cloaks and flinging dust
into the air, 24the com-
mander ordered Paul to be
taken into the barracks. He
directed that he be flogged
and questioned in order to
find out why the people
were shouting at him like
this. 25As they stretched
him out to flog him, Paul
said to the centurion standing there, "Is it legal for
you to flog a Roman citizen
who hasn't even been
found guilty?"
26When the centurion
heard this, he went to the
commander and reported

[f] Gk *him*
[g] Or *up for the lashes*

[s] 20 Or *witness*

about to do? This man is a Roman citizen." 27 The tribune came and asked Paul,[f] "Tell me, are you a Roman citizen?" And he said, "Yes." 28 The tribune answered, "It cost me a large sum of money to get my citizenship." Paul said, "But I was born a citizen."
29 Immediately those who were about to examine him drew back from him; and the tribune also was afraid, for he realized that Paul was a Roman citizen and that he had bound him.

Paul before the Council

30 Since he wanted to find out what Paul[h] was being accused of by the Jews, the next day he released him and ordered the chief priests and the entire council to meet. He brought Paul down and had him stand before them.

Chapter 23

WHILE Paul was looking intently at the council he said, "Brothers,[i] up to this day I have lived my life with a clear conscience before God."
2 Then the high priest Ananias ordered those standing near him to strike him on the mouth. 3 At this Paul said to him, "God will strike you, you whitewashed wall! Are you sitting there to judge me according to the law, and yet in violation of the law you order me to be struck?"
4 Those standing nearby said, "Do you dare to insult God's high priest?" 5 And Paul said, "I did not realize, brothers, that he was high priest; for it is written, 'You shall not speak evil of a leader of your people.'"
6 When Paul noticed that some were Sadducees

[h] Gk *he*
[i] Gk *Men, brothers*

λέγων· τί μέλλεις ποιεῖν; ὁ γὰρ ἄνθρωπος
saying: What art thou about to do? – for [2]man
οὗτος Ῥωμαῖός ἐστιν. 27 προσελθὼν δὲ
[1]this [4]a Roman [3]is. And approaching
ὁ χιλίαρχος εἶπεν αὐτῷ· λέγε μοι, σὺ
the chiliarch said to him: Tell me, thou
Ῥωμαῖος εἶ; ὁ δὲ ἔφη· ναί. 28 ἀπεκρίθη
a Roman art? And he said: Yes. answered
δὲ ὁ χιλίαρχος· ἐγὼ πολλοῦ κεφαλαίου
And the chiliarch: [1]I [5]of(for) much(great) [6]sum [of money]
τὴν πολιτείαν ταύτην ἐκτησάμην. ὁ δὲ
[3]this [4]citizenship [2]acquired. – So
Παῦλος ἔφη· ἐγὼ δὲ καὶ γεγέννημαι.
Paul said: But I indeed have been born.
29 εὐθέως οὖν ἀπέστησαν ἀπ' αὐτοῦ οἱ
Immediately therefore [5]stood away [6]from [7]him [1]the [ones]
μέλλοντες αὐτὸν ἀνετάζειν· καὶ ὁ χιλίαρχος
[2]being about [4]him [3]to examine; [4]also [2]the [3]chiliarch
δὲ ἐφοβήθη ἐπιγνοὺς ὅτι Ῥωμαῖός ἐστιν
[1]and feared fully knowing that a Roman he is(was)
καὶ ὅτι αὐτὸν ἦν δεδεκώς.
and that [3]him [1]he was [2]having bound.
30 Τῇ δὲ ἐπαύριον βουλόμενος γνῶναι τὸ
And on the morrow being minded to know the
ἀσφαλές, τὸ τί κατηγορεῖται ὑπὸ τῶν
certain thing, – why he was accused by the
Ἰουδαίων, ἔλυσεν αὐτόν, καὶ ἐκέλευσεν
Jews, he released him, and commanded
συνελθεῖν τοὺς ἀρχιερεῖς καὶ πᾶν τὸ
to come together the chief priests and all the
συνέδριον, καὶ καταγαγὼν τὸν Παῦλον
council, and having brought down – Paul
ἔστησεν εἰς αὐτούς. 23 ἀτενίσας δὲ
set [him] among them. And [2]gazing
ὁ Παῦλος τῷ συνεδρίῳ εἶπεν· ἄνδρες
– [1]Paul at the council said: *Men*
ἀδελφοί, ἐγὼ πάσῃ συνειδήσει ἀγαθῇ
brothers, I in all conscience good
πεπολίτευμαι τῷ θεῷ ἄχρι ταύτης τῆς
have lived – to God until this –
ἡμέρας. 2 ὁ δὲ ἀρχιερεὺς Ἁνανίας
day. And the high priest Ananias
ἐπέταξεν τοῖς παρεστῶσιν αὐτῷ τύπτειν
gave order to the [ones] standing by him to strike
αὐτοῦ τὸ στόμα. 3 τότε ὁ Παῦλος πρὸς
of him the mouth. Then – Paul to
αὐτὸν εἶπεν· τύπτειν σε μέλλει ὁ θεός,
him said: [3]To strike [4]thee [2]is about – [1]God,
τοῖχε κεκονιαμένε· καὶ σὺ κάθῃ κρίνων
wall *having been* whitened; and thou sittest judging
με κατὰ τὸν νόμον, καὶ παρανομῶν
me according to the law, and contravening law
κελεύεις με τύπτεσθαι; 4 οἱ δὲ παρεστῶτες
commandest me to be struck? And the [ones] standing by
εἶπαν· τὸν ἀρχιερέα τοῦ θεοῦ λοιδορεῖς;
said: The high priest – of God revilest thou?
5 ἔφη τε ὁ Παῦλος· οὐκ ᾔδειν, ἀδελφοί,
And said – Paul: I did not know, brothers,
ὅτι ἐστὶν ἀρχιερεύς· γέγραπται γὰρ ὅτι
that he is high priest; for it has been written[,] –
ἄρχοντα τοῦ λαοῦ σου οὐκ ἐρεῖς κακῶς.
A ruler of the people of thee thou shalt not speak evilly.
6 γνοὺς δὲ ὁ Παῦλος ὅτι τὸ ἓν μέρος
And knowing – Paul that the one part

it. "What are you going to do?" he asked. "This man is a Roman citizen."
27 The commander went to Paul and asked, "Tell me, are you a Roman citizen?"
"Yes, I am," he answered.
28 Then the commander said, "I had to pay a big price for my citizenship."
"But I was born a citizen," Paul replied.
29 Those who were about to question him withdrew immediately. The commander himself was alarmed when he realized that he had put Paul, a Roman citizen, in chains.

Before the Sanhedrin

30 The next day, since the commander wanted to find out exactly why Paul was being accused by the Jews, he released him and ordered the chief priests and all the Sanhedrin to assemble. Then he brought Paul and had him stand before them.

Chapter 23

PAUL looked straight at the Sanhedrin and said, "My brothers, I have fulfilled my duty to God in all good conscience to this day." 2 At this the high priest Ananias ordered those standing near Paul to strike him on the mouth.
3 Then Paul said to him, "God will strike you, you whitewashed wall! You sit there to judge me according to the law, yet you yourself violate the law by commanding that I be struck!"
4 Those who were standing near Paul said, "You dare to insult God's high priest?"
5 Paul replied, "Brothers, I did not realize that he was the high priest; for it is written: 'Do not speak evil about the ruler of your people.'[r]"
6 Then Paul, knowing that some of them were Saddu-

[r] 5 Exodus 22:28

and others were Pharisees, he called out in the council, "Brothers, I am a Pharisee, a son of Pharisees. I am on trial concerning the hope of the resurrection[j] of the dead." 7 When he said this, a dissension began between the Pharisees and the Sadducees, and the assembly was divided. 8 (The Sadducees say that there is no resurrection, or angel, or spirit; but the Pharisees acknowledge all three.) 9 Then a great clamor arose, and certain scribes of the Pharisees' group stood up and contended, "We find nothing wrong with this man. What if a spirit or an angel has spoken to him?" 10 When the dissension became violent, the tribune, fearing that they would tear Paul to pieces, ordered the soldiers to go down, take him by force, and bring him into the barracks.

11 That night the Lord stood near him and said, "Keep up your courage! For just as you have testified for me in Jerusalem, so you must bear witness also in Rome."

The Plot to Kill Paul

12 In the morning the Jews joined in a conspiracy and bound themselves by an oath neither to eat nor drink until they had killed Paul. 13 There were more than forty who joined in this conspiracy. 14 They went to the chief priests and elders and said, "We have strictly bound ourselves by an oath to taste

[j] Gk *concerning hope and resurrection*

ἐστὶν Σαδδουκαίων τὸ δὲ ἕτερον Φαρισαίων
is(was) of Sadducees but the other of Pharisees
ἔκραζεν ἐν τῷ συνεδρίῳ· ἄνδρες ἀδελφοί,
cried out in the council: *Men* brothers,
ἐγὼ Φαρισαῖός εἰμι, υἱὸς Φαρισαίων· περὶ
I a Pharisee am, a son of Pharisees; concerning
ἐλπίδος καὶ ἀναστάσεως νεκρῶν κρίνομαι.
hope and resurrection of dead ones I am being judged.
7 τοῦτο δὲ αὐτοῦ λαλοῦντος ἐγένετο
And this him saying[a] there was
=as he said this
στάσις τῶν Φαρισαίων καὶ Σαδδουκαίων,
a discord of the Pharisees and Sadducees,
καὶ ἐσχίσθη τὸ πλῆθος. 8 Σαδδουκαῖοι
and was divided the multitude. Sadducees
γὰρ λέγουσιν μὴ εἶναι ἀνάστασιν μήτε
For say not to be a resurrection nor
ἄγγελον μήτε πνεῦμα, Φαρισαῖοι δὲ
angel nor spirit, but Pharisees
ὁμολογοῦσιν τὰ ἀμφότερα. 9 ἐγένετο δὲ
confess – both. And there was
κραυγὴ μεγάλη, καὶ ἀναστάντες τινὲς
cry a great, and rising up some
τῶν γραμματέων τοῦ μέρους τῶν Φαρισαίων
of the scribes of the part of the Pharisees
διεμάχοντο λέγοντες· οὐδὲν κακὸν εὑρίσκομεν
strove saying: Nothing evil we find
ἐν τῷ ἀνθρώπῳ τούτῳ· εἰ δὲ πνεῦμα
in this man; and if [1]a spirit
ἐλάλησεν αὐτῷ ἢ ἄγγελος —. 10 Πολλῆς δὲ
[4]spoke [5]to him [2]or [3]an angel —. And much
γινομένης στάσεως φοβηθεὶς ὁ χιλίαρχος
arising discord[a] [3]fearing [1]the [2]chiliarch
=when much discord arose
μὴ διασπασθῇ ὁ Παῦλος ὑπ' αὐτῶν,
[4]lest [6]should be torn asunder – [5]Paul by them,
ἐκέλευσεν τὸ στράτευμα καταβὰν ἁρπάσαι
commanded the soldiery coming down to seize
αὐτὸν ἐκ μέσου αὐτῶν ἄγειν τε εἰς
him out of [the] midst of them and to bring [him] into
τὴν παρεμβολήν. 11 Τῇ δὲ ἐπιούσῃ
the fort. And in the following
νυκτὶ ἐπιστὰς αὐτῷ ὁ κύριος εἶπεν·
night [3]coming *on* [4]to him [1]the [2]Lord said:
θάρσει· ὡς γὰρ διεμαρτύρω τὰ περὶ
Be of good courage; for as thou didst solemnly witness the concerning things
ἐμοῦ εἰς Ἰερουσαλήμ, οὕτω σε δεῖ καὶ
me in Jerusalem, so thee it behoves also
εἰς Ῥώμην μαρτυρῆσαι. 12 Γενομένης δὲ
in Rome to witness. And becoming
ἡμέρας ποιήσαντες συστροφὴν οἱ Ἰουδαῖοι
day[a] [3]making [4]a conspiracy [1]the [2]Jews
=when it became day
ἀνεθεμάτισαν ἑαυτούς, λέγοντες μήτε φαγεῖν
cursed themselves, saying neither to eat
μήτε πεῖν ἕως οὗ ἀποκτείνωσιν τὸν
nor to drink until they should kill –
Παῦλον. 13 ἦσαν δὲ πλείους τεσσεράκοντα
Paul. And there were more [than] forty
οἱ ταύτην τὴν συνωμοσίαν ποιησάμενοι·
the [ones] this – plot making;
14 οἵτινες προσελθόντες τοῖς ἀρχιερεῦσιν
who approaching *to* the chief priests
καὶ τοῖς πρεσβυτέροις εἶπαν· ἀναθέματι
and *to* the elders said: With a curse

cees and the others Pharisees, called out in the Sanhedrin, "My brothers, I am a Pharisee, the son of a Pharisee. I stand on trial because of my hope in the resurrection of the dead." 7 When he said this, a dispute broke out between the Pharisees and the Sadducees, and the assembly was divided. 8 (The Sadducees say that there is no resurrection, and that there are neither angels nor spirits, but the Pharisees acknowledge them all.)

9 There was a great uproar, and some of the teachers of the law who were Pharisees stood up and argued vigorously. "We find nothing wrong with this man," they said. "What if a spirit or an angel has spoken to him?" 10 The dispute became so violent that the commander was afraid Paul would be torn to pieces by them. He ordered the troops to go down and take him away from them by force and bring him into the barracks.

11 The following night the Lord stood near Paul and said, "Take courage! As you have testified about me in Jerusalem, so you must also testify in Rome."

The Plot to Kill Paul

12 The next morning the Jews formed a conspiracy and bound themselves with an oath not to eat or drink until they had killed Paul. 13 More than forty men were involved in this plot. 14 They went to the chief priests and elders and said, "We have taken a solemn oath not to eat anything un-

no food until we have killed
Paul. 15 Now then, you and
the council must notify the
tribune to bring him down
to you, on the pretext that
you want to make a more
thorough examination of
his case. And we are ready
to do away with him before
he arrives."
16 Now the son of
Paul's sister heard about
the ambush; so he went and
gained entrance to the barracks and told Paul. 17 Paul
called one of the centurions
and said, "Take this young
man to the tribune, for he
has something to report to
him." 18 So he took him,
brought him to the tribune,
and said, "The prisoner
Paul called me and asked
me to bring this young man
to you; he has something to
tell you." 19 The tribune
took him by the hand, drew
him aside privately, and
asked, "What is it that you
have to report to me?"
20 He answered, "The Jews
have agreed to ask you to
bring Paul down to the
council tomorrow, as
though they were going to
inquire more thoroughly
into his case. 21 But do not
be persuaded by them, for
more than forty of their
men are lying in ambush for
him. They have bound
themselves by an oath neither to eat nor drink until
they kill him. They are
ready now and are waiting
for your consent." 22 So the
tribune dismissed the

ἀνεθεματίσαμεν ἑαυτοὺς μηδενὸς γεύσασθαι
we cursed ourselves *of* nothing to taste
ἕως οὗ ἀποκτείνωμεν τὸν Παῦλον. 15 νῦν
until we may kill – Paul. Now
οὖν ὑμεῖς ἐμφανίσατε τῷ χιλιάρχῳ σὺν
therefore [2]ye [1]inform the chiliarch with
τῷ συνεδρίῳ ὅπως καταγάγῃ αὐτὸν εἰς
the council so as he may bring down him to
ὑμᾶς ὡς μέλλοντας διαγινώσκειν ἀκριβέστε-
you as intending to ascertain *exactly* more accurate-
ρον τὰ περὶ αὐτοῦ· ἡμεῖς δὲ πρὸ τοῦ
ly the things concerning him; and we before –
ἐγγίσαι αὐτὸν ἕτοιμοί ἐσμεν τοῦ ἀνελεῖν
to draw near him[b] ready are – to kill[a]
=he draws near
αὐτόν. 16 Ἀκούσας δὲ ὁ υἱὸς τῆς ἀδελφῆς
him. And [6]hearing [1]the [2]son [3]of the [4]sister
Παύλου τὴν ἐνέδραν, παραγενόμενος καὶ
[5]of Paul the treachery, coming and
εἰσελθὼν εἰς τὴν παρεμβολὴν ἀπήγγειλεν
entering into the fort reported
τῷ Παύλῳ. 17 προσκαλεσάμενος δὲ ὁ
– to Paul. And [2]calling to [him] –
Παῦλος ἕνα τῶν ἑκατονταρχῶν ἔφη· τὸν
[1]Paul one of the centurions said: –
νεανίαν τοῦτον ἄπαγε πρὸς τὸν χιλίαρχον,
[3]youth [2]this [1]Bring up to the chiliarch,
ἔχει γὰρ ἀπαγγεῖλαί τι αὐτῷ. 18 ὁ
for [1]he has [3]to report [2]something [4]to him. He
μὲν οὖν παραλαβὼν αὐτὸν ἤγαγεν πρὸς
– therefore taking [2]him [1]brought to
τὸν χιλίαρχον καὶ φησίν· ὁ δέσμιος
the chiliarch and says: The prisoner
Παῦλος προσκαλεσάμενός με ἠρώτησεν
Paul calling to [him] me asked
τοῦτον τὸν νεανίσκον ἀγαγεῖν πρὸς σέ,
[2]this – [3]young man [1]to bring to thee,
ἔχοντά τι λαλῆσαί σοι. 19 ἐπιλαβόμενος
having something to tell thee. [3]laying hold
δὲ τῆς χειρὸς αὐτοῦ ὁ χιλίαρχος καὶ
And [4]of the [5]hand [6]of him [1]the [2]chiliarch and
ἀναχωρήσας κατ᾽ ἰδίαν ἐπυνθάνετο· τί
retiring [2]privately [1]inquired: What
ἐστιν ὃ ἔχεις ἀπαγγεῖλαί μοι; 20 εἶπεν
is it which thou hast to report to me? he said[,]
δὲ ὅτι οἱ Ἰουδαῖοι συνέθεντο τοῦ ἐρωτῆσαί
And – The Jews agreed – to ask[d]
σε ὅπως αὔριον τὸν Παῦλον καταγάγῃς
thee so as to-morrow – [2]Paul [1]thou shouldest bring down
εἰς τὸ συνέδριον ὡς μέλλον τι ἀκριβέστερον
to the council as intending something more accurately
πυνθάνεσθαι περὶ αὐτοῦ. 21 σὺ οὖν μὴ
to inquire concerning him. Thou therefore not
πεισθῇς αὐτοῖς· ἐνεδρεύουσιν γὰρ αὐτὸν
be persuaded by them; for there lie in wait for him
ἐξ αὐτῶν ἄνδρες πλείους τεσσεράκοντα,
of them [4]men [1]more [2][than] [3]forty,
οἵτινες ἀνεθεμάτισαν ἑαυτοὺς μήτε φαγεῖν
who cursed themselves neither to eat
μήτε πεῖν ἕως οὗ ἀνέλωσιν αὐτόν, καὶ νῦν
nor to drink until they kill him, and now
εἰσιν ἕτοιμοι προσδεχόμενοι τὴν ἀπὸ σοῦ
they are ready awaiting [1]the [3]from [4]thee
ἐπαγγελίαν. 22 ὁ μὲν οὖν χιλίαρχος
[2]promise. the – Therefore chiliarch

til we have killed Paul.
15 Now then, you and the
Sanhedrin petition the
commander to bring him
before you on the pretext of
wanting more accurate in-
formation about his case.
We are ready to kill him before he gets here."
16 But when the son of
Paul's sister heard of this
plot, he went into the barracks and told Paul.
17 Then Paul called one of
the centurions and said,
"Take this young man to
the commander; he has
something to tell him."
18 So he took him to the
commander.
The centurion said,
"Paul, the prisoner, sent
for me and asked me to
bring this young man to you
because he has something
to tell you."
19 The commander took
the young man by the hand,
drew him aside and asked,
"What is it you want to tell
me?"
20 He said: "The Jews
have agreed to ask you to
bring Paul before the Sanhedrin tomorrow on the
pretext of wanting more accurate information about
him. 21 Don't give in to
them, because more than
forty of them are waiting in
ambush for him. They have
taken an oath not to eat or
drink until they have killed
him. They are ready now,
waiting for your consent to
their request."
22 The commander dis-

young man, ordering him,
"Tell no one that you have
informed me of this."

Paul Sent to Felix the Governor

23 Then he summoned
two of the centurions and
said, "Get ready to leave by
nine o'clock tonight for
Caesarea with two hundred
soldiers, seventy horse-
men, and two hundred
spearmen. 24 Also provide
mounts for Paul to ride, and
take him safely to Felix the
governor." 25 He wrote a
letter to this effect:
26 "Claudius Lysias to
his Excellency the gover-
nor Felix, greetings. 27 This
man was seized by the Jews
and was about to be killed
by them, but when I had
learned that he was a Ro-
man citizen, I came with
the guard and rescued him.
28 Since I wanted to know
the charge for which they
accused him, I had him
brought to their council. 29 I
found that he was accused
concerning questions of
their law, but was charged
with nothing deserving
death or imprisonment.
30 When I was informed
that there would be a plot
against the man, I sent him
to you at once, ordering his
accusers also to state before you what they have
against him.[k]"
31 So the soldiers, ac-
cording to their instruc-
tions, took Paul and
brought him during the
night to Antipatris. 32 The
next day they let the horsemen go on with him, while
they returned to the bar-
racks. 33 When they came
to Caesarea and delivered

[k] Other ancient authorities add *Farewell*

ἀπέλυσε τὸν νεανίσκον, παραγγείλας μηδενὶ
dismissed the young man, charging [him] to no one

ἐκλαλῆσαι ὅτι ταῦτα ἐνεφάνισας πρὸς ἐμέ.
to divulge that these things thou reportedst to me.

23 Καὶ προσκαλεσάμενός τινας δύο τῶν
And calling to [him] a certain two of the

ἑκατονταρχῶν εἶπεν· ἑτοιμάσατε στρατιώτας
centurions he said: Prepare ye soldiers

διακοσίους ὅπως πορευθῶσιν ἕως Καισαρείας,
two hundred so as they may go as far as Cæsarea,

καὶ ἱππεῖς ἑβδομήκοντα καὶ δεξιολάβους
and horsemen seventy and spearmen

διακοσίους, ἀπὸ τρίτης ὥρας τῆς νυκτός,
two hundred, from third hour of the night,

24 κτήνη τε παραστῆσαι, ἵνα ἐπιβιβάσαντες
and beasts to stand by, that putting on

τὸν Παῦλον διασώσωσι πρὸς Φήλικα τὸν
– Paul they may bring [him] safely to Felix the

ἡγεμόνα, 25 γράψας ἐπιστολὴν ἔχουσαν
governor, writing a letter having

τὸν τύπον τοῦτον· 26 Κλαύδιος Λυσίας τῷ
this pattern: Claudius Lysias to the

κρατίστῳ ἡγεμόνι Φήλικι χαίρειν. 27 Τὸν
most excellent governor Felix greeting. –

ἄνδρα τοῦτον συλλημφθέντα ὑπὸ τῶν
man This having been arrested by the

Ἰουδαίων καὶ μέλλοντα ἀναιρεῖσθαι ὑπ’
Jews and being about to be killed by

αὐτῶν ἐπιστὰς σὺν τῷ στρατεύματι
them coming on [the scene] with the soldiery

ἐξειλάμην, μαθὼν ὅτι Ῥωμαῖός ἐστιν·
I rescued, having learned that a Roman he is;

28 βουλόμενός τε ἐπιγνῶναι τὴν αἰτίαν
and being minded to know fully the cause

δι’ ἣν ἐνεκάλουν αὐτῷ, κατήγαγον εἰς
on account of which they were accusing him, I brought [him] down to

τὸ συνέδριον αὐτῶν· 29 ὃν εὗρον ἐγκαλούμενον
the council of them; whom I found being accused

περὶ ζητημάτων τοῦ νόμου αὐτῶν, μηδὲν
about questions of the law of them, [3]*nothing*

δὲ ἄξιον θανάτου ἢ δεσμῶν ἔχοντα
[1]but [4]worthy [5]of death [7]or [8]of bonds [2]having

ἔγκλημα. 30 μηνυθείσης δέ μοι ἐπιβουλῆς
[6]charge. And being revealed to me a plot[a]
=when it was revealed to me that there was a plot

εἰς τὸν ἄνδρα ἔσεσθαι, ἐξαυτῆς ἔπεμψα
against the man to be, at once I sent

πρὸς σέ, παραγγείλας καὶ τοῖς κατηγόροις
to thee, commanding also the accusers

λέγειν πρὸς αὐτὸν ἐπὶ σοῦ. 31 Οἱ μὲν
to say to him before thee. the –

οὖν στρατιῶται κατὰ τὸ διατεταγμένον
Therefore soldiers according to the thing *having been* appointed

αὐτοῖς ἀναλαβόντες τὸν Παῦλον ἤγαγον
them taking up – Paul brought

διὰ νυκτὸς εἰς τὴν Ἀντιπατρίδα· 32 τῇ δὲ
through (during) [the] night to – Antipatris; and on the

ἐπαύριον ἐάσαντες τοὺς ἱππεῖς ἀπέρχεσθαι
morrow allowing the horsemen to depart

σὺν αὐτῷ, ὑπέστρεψαν εἰς τὴν παρεμβολήν·
with him, they returned to the fort;

33 οἵτινες εἰσελθόντες εἰς τὴν Καισάρειαν
who entering into – Cæsarea

missed the young man and
cautioned him, "Don't tell
anyone that you have re-
ported this to me."

Paul Transferred to Caesarea

23 Then he called two of
his centurions and ordered
them, "Get ready a detachment of two hundred sol-
diers, seventy horsemen
and two hundred spear-
men[u] to go to Caesarea at
nine tonight. 24 Provide
mounts for Paul so that he
may be taken safely to
Governor Felix."
25 He wrote a letter as follows:

26 Claudius Lysias,

To His Excellency,
Governor Felix:

Greetings.

27 This man was seized
by the Jews and they
were about to kill him,
but I came with my
troops and rescued him,
for I had learned that he
is a Roman citizen. 28 I
wanted to know why
they were accusing him,
so I brought him to their
Sanhedrin. 29 I found
that the accusation had
to do with questions
about their law, but
there was no charge
against him that de-
served death or impris-
onment. 30 When I was
informed of a plot to be
carried out against the
man, I sent him to you
at once. I also ordered
his accusers to present
to you their case against
him.

31 So the soldiers, carrying out their orders, took
Paul with them during the
night and brought him as
far as Antipatris. 32 The
next day they let the cavalry go on with him, while
they returned to the bar-
racks. 33 When the cavalry
arrived in Caesarea, they

[u] *23* The meaning of the Greek for this word is uncertain.

the letter to the governor,
they presented Paul also
before him. 34 On reading
the letter, he asked what
province he belonged to,
and when he learned that
he was from Cilicia, 35 he
said, "I will give you a hearing when your accusers arrive." Then he ordered that
he be kept under guard in
Herod's headquarters.[l]

καὶ ἀναδόντες τὴν ἐπιστολὴν τῷ ἡγεμόνι,
and handing over the letter to the governor,

παρέστησαν καὶ τὸν Παῦλον αὐτῷ.
presented also – Paul to him.

34 ἀναγνοὺς δὲ καὶ ἐπερωτήσας ἐκ ποίας
And having read and asking of what

ἐπαρχείας ἐστίν, καὶ πυθόμενος ὅτι ἀπὸ
province he is(was), and learning[,] – From

Κιλικίας, 35 διακούσομαί σου, ἔφη, ὅταν
Cilicia, I will hear thee, he said, when

καὶ οἱ κατήγοροί σου παραγένωνται·
also the accusers of thee arrive;

κελεύσας ἐν τῷ πραιτωρίῳ τοῦ Ἡρῴδου
commanding in the prætorium – of Herod
=that he be kept in Herod's prætorium.

φυλάσσεσθαι αὐτόν.
to be kept him.

delivered the letter to the
governor and handed Paul
over to him. 34 The governor read the letter and
asked what province he
was from. Learning that he
was from Cilicia, 35 he said,
"I will hear your case when
your accusers get here."
Then he ordered that Paul
be kept under guard in Herod's palace.

Chapter 24

Paul before Felix at Caesarea

FIVE days later the high
priest Ananias came
down with some elders and
an attorney, a certain Tertullus, and they reported
their case against Paul to
the governor. 2 When
Paul[m] had been sum-
moned, Tertullus began to
accuse him, saying:
"Your Excellency,[n] be-
cause of you we have long
enjoyed peace, and reforms
have been made for this
people because of your
foresight. 3 We welcome
this in every way and ev-
erywhere with utmost gratitude. 4 But, to detain you
no further, I beg you to
hear us briefly with your
customary graciousness.
5 We have, in fact, found
this man a pestilent fellow,
an agitator among all the
Jews throughout the world,
and a ringleader of the sect
of the Nazarenes.[o] 6 He
even tried to profane the
temple, and so we seized
him.[p] 8 By examining him
yourself you will be able to
learn from him concerning
everything of which we accuse him."
9 The Jews also joined
in the charge by asserting
that all this was true.

24 Μετὰ δὲ πέντε ἡμέρας κατέβη ὁ
And after five days came down the

ἀρχιερεὺς Ἁνανίας μετὰ πρεσβυτέρων τινῶν
high priest Ananias with elders some

καὶ ῥήτορος Τερτύλλου τινός, οἵτινες
and an orator Tertullus one, who

ἐνεφάνισαν τῷ ἡγεμόνι κατὰ τοῦ Παύλου.
informed the governor against – Paul.

2 κληθέντος δὲ [αὐτοῦ] ἤρξατο κατηγορεῖν
And being called him [2]began [3]to accuse
=when he was called

ὁ Τέρτυλλος λέγων· πολλῆς εἰρήνης
– [1]Tertullus saying: Much peace

τυγχάνοντες διὰ σοῦ καὶ διορθωμάτων
obtaining through thee and reforms

γινομένων τῷ ἔθνει τούτῳ διὰ τῆς σῆς
coming to this nation through – thy

προνοίας, 3 πάντῃ τε καὶ πανταχοῦ
forethought, both in everything and everywhere

ἀποδεχόμεθα, κράτιστε Φῆλιξ, μετὰ πάσης
we welcome, most excellent Felix, with all

εὐχαριστίας. 4 ἵνα δὲ μὴ ἐπὶ πλεῖόν
thankfulness. But that [2]not [4]more

σε ἐγκόπτω, παρακαλῶ ἀκοῦσαί σε ἡμῶν
[3]thee [1]I hinder, I beseech [2]to hear [1]thee us

συντόμως τῇ σῇ ἐπιεικείᾳ. 5 εὑρόντες γὰρ
briefly – in thy forbearance. For having found

τὸν ἄνδρα τοῦτον λοιμὸν καὶ κινοῦντα
this man pestilent and moving

στάσεις πᾶσιν τοῖς Ἰουδαίοις τοῖς κατὰ
seditions [among] all the Jews – throughout

τὴν οἰκουμένην πρωτοστάτην τε τῆς τῶν
the inhabited [earth] and a ringleader of the [2]of the

Ναζωραίων αἱρέσεως, 6 ὃς καὶ τὸ ἱερὸν
[3]Nazarenes [1]sect, who also [3]the [4]temple

ἐπείρασεν βεβηλῶσαι, ὃν καὶ ἐκρατήσαμεν,
[1]attempted [2]to profane, whom also we laid hold of,‡

8 παρ' οὗ δυνήσῃ αὐτὸς ἀνακρίνας
from whom thou wilt be able [thy]self [2]having examined

περὶ πάντων τούτων ἐπιγνῶναι ὧν ἡμεῖς
[3]concerning [4]all [5]these things [1]to know fully of which we

κατηγοροῦμεν αὐτοῦ. 9 συνεπέθεντο δὲ
accuse him. And [4]joined in

καὶ οἱ Ἰουδαῖοι φάσκοντες ταῦτα οὕτως
[3]also [1]the [2]Jews alleging these things thus

‡ Verse 7 omitted by Nestle; *cf.* NIV footnote.

Chapter 24

The Trial Before Felix

FIVE days later the high
priest Ananias went
down to Caesarea with
some of the elders and a
lawyer named Tertullus,
and they brought their
charges against Paul before
the governor. 2 When Paul
was called in, Tertullus
presented his case before
Felix: "We have enjoyed a
long period of peace under
you, and your foresight has
brought about reforms in
this nation. 3 Everywhere
and in every way, most excellent Felix, we acknowledge this with profound
gratitude. 4 But in order not
to weary you further, I
would request that you be
kind enough to hear us
briefly.
5 "We have found this
man to be a troublemaker,
stirring up riots among the
Jews all over the world. He
is a ringleader of the Nazarene sect 6 and even tried to
desecrate the temple; so we
seized him. 8 By[v] examining him yourself you will be
able to learn the truth about
all these charges we are
bringing against him."
9 The Jews joined in the
accusation, asserting that
these things were true.

[l] Gk *praetorium*
[m] Gk *he*
[n] Gk lacks *Your Excellency*
[o] Gk *Nazoreans*
[p] Other ancient authorities add *and we would have judged him according to our law. 7But the chief captain Lysias came and with great violence took him out of our hands, 8commanding his accusers to come before you.*

[v] 6-8 Some manuscripts *him and wanted to judge him according to our law. 7But the commander, Lysias, came and with the use of much force snatched him from our hands 8and ordered his accusers to come before you. By*

Paul's Defense before Felix

10 When the governor
motioned to him to speak,
Paul replied:
"I cheerfully make my
defense, knowing that for
many years you have been
a judge over this nation.
11 As you can find out, it is
not more than twelve days
since I went up to worship
in Jerusalem. 12 They did
not find me disputing with
anyone in the temple or
stirring up a crowd either in
the synagogues or throughout the city. 13 Neither can
they prove to you the
charge that they now bring
against me. 14 But this I admit to you, that according
to the Way, which they call
a sect, I worship the God of
our ancestors, believing everything laid down according to the law or written in
the prophets. 15 I have a
hope in God—a hope that
they themselves also
accept—that there will be a
resurrection of both[q] the
righteous and the unrigh-
teous. 16 Therefore I do my
best always to have a clear
conscience toward God
and all people. 17 Now after
some years I came to bring
alms to my nation and to
offer sacrifices. 18 While I
was doing this, they found
me in the temple, completing the rite of purification,
without any crowd or dis-
turbance. 19 But there were
some Jews from Asia—
they ought to be here be-
fore you to make an accu-
sation, if they have any-
thing against me. 20 Or let
these men here tell what

[q] Other ancient authorities read *of the dead, both of*

ἔχειν. 10 Ἀπεκρίθη τε ὁ Παῦλος,
to have(be). And answered – Paul,

νεύσαντος αὐτῷ τοῦ ἡγεμόνος λέγειν· ἐκ
[3]having beckoned [4]to him [1]the [2]governor* to speak: [4]of (for)

πολλῶν ἐτῶν ὄντα σε κριτὴν τῷ ἔθνει τούτῳ
[5]many [6]years [3]being (to be) [2]thee [7]a judge [8]to [9]this [10]nation

ἐπιστάμενος εὐθύμως τὰ περὶ
[1]understanding [12]cheerfully [13][as to] [14]the things [15]concerning

ἐμαυτοῦ ἀπολογοῦμαι, 11 δυναμένου σου
[16]myself [11]I defend myself, being able thee* =as thou art able

ἐπιγνῶναι ὅτι οὐ πλείους εἰσίν μοι ἡμέραι
to know fully that [3]not [4]more [1]there are [2]to [5][than] [7]days me

δώδεκα ἀφ' ἧς ἀνέβην προσκυνήσων εἰς
[6]twelve from =since which I went up worshipping in

Ἰερουσαλήμ. 12 καὶ οὔτε ἐν τῷ ἱερῷ
Jerusalem. And neither in the temple

εὗρόν με πρός τινα διαλεγόμενον ἢ
they found me [2]with [3]anyone [1]discoursing or

ἐπίστασιν ποιοῦντα ὄχλου, οὔτε ἐν ταῖς
[2]collection [1]making of a crowd, neither in the

συναγωγαῖς οὔτε κατὰ τὴν πόλιν, 13 οὐδὲ
synagogues nor throughout the city, nor

παραστῆσαι δύνανταί σοι περὶ ὧν νυνὶ
[2]to prove [1]are they able to thee con- cerning [the] things of which now

κατηγοροῦσίν μου. 14 ὁμολογῶ δὲ τοῦτό
they accuse me. But I confess this

σοι, ὅτι κατὰ τὴν ὁδὸν ἣν λέγουσιν
to thee, that according to the way which they say(call)

αἵρεσιν οὕτως λατρεύω τῷ πατρῴῳ θεῷ,
a sect thus I worship the ancestral God,

πιστεύων πᾶσι τοῖς κατὰ τὸν νόμον καὶ
believing all the things according to the law and

τοῖς ἐν τοῖς προφήταις γεγραμμένοις,
the things in the prophets *having been* written,

15 ἐλπίδα ἔχων εἰς τὸν θεόν, ἣν καὶ
hope having toward – God, which [3]also

αὐτοὶ οὗτοι προσδέχονται, ἀνάστασιν μέλ-
[2][them]selves [1]these expect, a resurrection to be

λειν ἔσεσθαι δικαίων τε καὶ ἀδίκων.
about to be both of just and of unjust.

16 ἐν τούτῳ καὶ αὐτὸς ἀσκῶ ἀπρόσκοπον
By this also [2][my]self [1]I exercise [4]a blameless

συνείδησιν ἔχειν πρὸς τὸν θεὸν καὶ τοὺς
[5]conscience [3]to have toward – God and –

ἀνθρώπους διὰ παντός. 17 δι' ἐτῶν δὲ
men always. And after years

πλειόνων ἐλεημοσύνας ποιήσων εἰς τὸ
many [2]alms [1]making(bringing) [3]to [4]the

ἔθνος μου παρεγενόμην καὶ προσφοράς,
[5]nation [6]of me [9]I arrived [7]and [8]offerings,

18 ἐν αἷς εὗρόν με ἡγνισμένον ἐν τῷ
among which they found me *having been* purified in the

ἱερῷ, οὐ μετὰ ὄχλου οὐδὲ μετὰ θορύβου,
temple, not with a crowd nor with uproar,

19 τινὲς δὲ ἀπὸ τῆς Ἀσίας Ἰουδαῖοι,
but some [2]from – [3]Asia [1]Jews,

οὓς ἔδει ἐπὶ σοῦ παρεῖναι καὶ κατηγορεῖν
whom it behoved before thee to be present and to accuse

εἴ τι ἔχοιεν πρὸς ἐμέ. 20 ἢ αὐτοὶ
if anything they have against me. Or [3][them]selves

10When the governor mo-
tioned for him to speak,
Paul replied: "I know that
for a number of years you
have been a judge over this
nation; so I gladly make my
defense. 11You can easily
verify that no more than
twelve days ago I went up
to Jerusalem to worship.
12My accusers did not find
me arguing with anyone at
the temple, or stirring up a
crowd in the synagogues or
anywhere else in the city.
13And they cannot prove to
you the charges they are
now making against me.
14However, I admit that I
worship the God of our fathers as a follower of the
Way, which they call a
sect. I believe everything
that agrees with the Law
and that is written in the
Prophets, 15and I have the
same hope in God as these
men, that there will be a
resurrection of both the
righteous and the wicked.
16So I strive always to keep
my conscience clear before
God and man.
17"After an absence of
several years, I came to Jerusalem to bring my people
gifts for the poor and to present offerings. 18I was cere-
monially clean when they
found me in the temple
courts doing this. There
was no crowd with me, nor
was I involved in any disturbance. 19But there are
some Jews from the prov-
ince of Asia, who ought to
be here before you and
bring charges if they have
anything against me. 20Or
these who are here should

crime they had found when
I stood before the council,
21 unless it was this one sentence that I called out while
standing before them, 'It is
about the resurrection of
the dead that I am on trial
before you today.' "
22 But Felix, who was
rather well informed about
the Way, adjourned the
hearing with the comment,
"When Lysias the tribune
comes down, I will decide
your case." 23 Then he ordered the centurion to keep
him in custody, but to let
him have some liberty and
not to prevent any of his
friends from taking care of
his needs.

Paul Held in Custody

24 Some days later
when Felix came with his
wife Drusilla, who was
Jewish, he sent for Paul and
heard him speak concern-
ing faith in Christ Jesus.
25 And as he discussed justice, self-control, and the
coming judgment, Felix became frightened and said,
"Go away for the present;
when I have an opportuni-
ty, I will send for you."
26 At the same time he
hoped that money would be
given him by Paul, and for
that reason he used to send
for him very often and converse with him.
27 After two years had
passed, Felix was succeed-
ed by Porcius Festus; and
since he wanted to grant
the Jews a favor, Felix left
Paul in prison.

Chapter 25

Paul Appeals to Caesar

THREE days after Fes-
tus had arrived in the
province, he went up from
Caesarea to Jerusalem

οὗτοι εἰπάτωσαν τί εὗρον ἀδίκημα στάντος
[3]these [1]let [4]say [1]what [3]they found [2]misdeed standing

μου ἐπὶ τοῦ συνεδρίου, 21 ἢ περὶ μιᾶς
me[a] before the council, unless concerning [2]one
=while I stood

ταύτης φωνῆς ἧς ἐκέκραξα ἐν αὐτοῖς
[1]this voice which I have cried out [2]among [3]them

ἑστὼς ὅτι περὶ ἀναστάσεως νεκρῶν ἐγὼ
[1]standing[,] – Concerning a resurrection of dead persons I

κρίνομαι σήμερον ἐφ' ὑμῶν. 22 Ἀνεβάλετο
am being judged to-day before you. [2]postponed

δὲ αὐτοὺς ὁ Φῆλιξ, ἀκριβέστερον εἰδὼς
And [3]them – [1]Felix, more exactly knowing

τὰ περὶ τῆς ὁδοῦ, εἴπας· ὅταν Λυσίας ὁ
the things con-cerning the way, saying: When Lysias the

χιλίαρχος καταβῇ, διαγνώσομαι τὰ καθ'
chiliarch comes down, I will determine the things as to

ὑμᾶς· 23 διαταξάμενος τῷ ἑκατοντάρχῃ
you; commanding the centurion

τηρεῖσθαι αὐτὸν ἔχειν τε ἄνεσιν καὶ
to keep him and to have indulgence and

μηδένα κωλύειν τῶν ἰδίων αὐτοῦ ὑπηρετεῖν
[2]no one [1]to forbid of his own [people] to attend

αὐτῷ. 24 Μετὰ δὲ ἡμέρας τινὰς παραγενό-
him. And after days some [2]arriv-

μενος ὁ Φῆλιξ σὺν Δρουσίλλῃ τῇ ἰδίᾳ
ing – [1]Felix with Drusilla the(his) own

γυναικὶ οὔσῃ Ἰουδαίᾳ μετεπέμψατο τὸν
wife being a Jewess he sent for –

Παῦλον, καὶ ἤκουσεν αὐτοῦ περὶ τῆς
Paul, and heard him about [1]the(?his)

εἰς Χριστὸν Ἰησοῦν πίστεως. 25 διαλεγομέ-
[3]in [4]Christ [5]Jesus [2]faith. discours-
=And as he discoursed

νου δὲ αὐτοῦ περὶ δικαιοσύνης καὶ
ing And him[a] concerning righteousness and

ἐγκρατείας καὶ τοῦ κρίματος τοῦ μέλλοντος
self-control and the [2]judgment – [1]coming

ἔμφοβος γενόμενος ὁ Φῆλιξ ἀπεκρίθη·
afraid becoming – Felix answered:

τὸ νῦν ἔχον πορεύου, καιρὸν δὲ μεταλαβὼν
For the present† go thou, but [2]time [1]taking [3]later

μετακαλέσομαί σε· 26 ἅμα καὶ ἐλπίζων
I will send for thee; at the same time also hoping

ὅτι χρήματα δοθήσεται αὐτῷ ὑπὸ τοῦ
that money will be given him by –

Παύλου· διὸ καὶ πυκνότερον αὐτὸν
Paul: wherefore also more frequently him

μεταπεμπόμενος ὡμίλει αὐτῷ. 27 Διετίας δὲ
sending for he conversed with him. And two years

πληρωθείσης ἔλαβεν διάδοχον ὁ Φῆλιξ
being completed[a] [2]received [3]a successor – [1]Felix

Πόρκιον Φῆστον· θέλων τε χάριτα κατα-
Porcius Festus; and wishing a favour to

θέσθαι τοῖς Ἰουδαίοις ὁ Φῆλιξ κατέλιπε
show to the Jews – Felix left

τὸν Παῦλον δεδεμένον.
– Paul *having been* bound.

25 Φῆστος οὖν ἐπιβὰς τῇ ἐπαρχείῳ
Festus therefore having entered the province

μετὰ τρεῖς ἡμέρας ἀνέβη εἰς Ἱεροσόλυμα
after three days went up to Jerusalem

state what crime they
found in me when I stood
before the Sanhedrin—
21unless it was this one
thing I shouted as I stood in
their presence: 'It is concerning the resurrection of
the dead that I am on trial
before you today.' "
22Then Felix, who was
well acquainted with the
Way, adjourned the pro-
ceedings. "When Lysias
the commander comes,"
he said, "I will decide your
case." 23He ordered the
centurion to keep Paul under guard but to give him
some freedom and permit
his friends to take care of
his needs.
24Several days later Felix
came with his wife Drusilla, who was a Jewess. He
sent for Paul and listened to
him as he spoke about faith
in Christ Jesus. 25As Paul
discoursed on righteous-
ness, self-control and the
judgment to come, Felix
was afraid and said,
"That's enough for now!
You may leave. When I
find it convenient, I will
send for you." 26At the
same time he was hoping
that Paul would offer him a
bribe, so he sent for him
frequently and talked with
him.
27When two years had
passed, Felix was succeed-
ed by Porcius Festus, but
because Felix wanted to
grant a favor to the Jews,
he left Paul in prison.

Chapter 25

The Trial Before Festus

THREE days after arriv-
ing in the province,
Festus went up from Caes-
area to Jerusalem, 2where

2where the chief priests
and the leaders of the Jews
gave him a report against
Paul. They appealed to him
3and requested, as a favor
to them against Paul,[r] to
have him transferred to Jerusalem. They were, in
fact, planning an ambush to
kill him along the way.
4Festus replied that Paul
was being kept at Caesa-
rea, and that he himself intended to go there shortly.
5"So," he said, "let those of
you who have the authority
come down with me, and if
there is anything wrong
about the man, let them accuse him."
6 After he had stayed
among them not more than
eight or ten days, he went
down to Caesarea; the next
day he took his seat on the
tribunal and ordered Paul
to be brought. 7When he
arrived, the Jews who had
gone down from Jerusalem
surrounded him, bringing
many serious charges
against him, which they
could not prove. 8Paul said
in his defense, "I have in no
way committed an offense
against the law of the Jews,
or against the temple, or
against the emperor." 9But
Festus, wishing to do the
Jews a favor, asked Paul,
"Do you wish to go up to
Jerusalem and be tried
there before me on these
charges?" 10Paul said, "I
am appealing to the emper-
or's tribunal; this is where I
should be tried. I have done
no wrong to the Jews, as
you very well know.
11Now if I am in the wrong
and have committed some-
thing for which I deserve to
die, I am not trying to escape death; but if there is

[r] Gk *him*

ἐν ὑμῖν, φησίν, δυνατοὶ συγκαταβάντες,
[4]among [5]you, [6]he says, [3]able men going down with [me],

ἀπὸ Καισαρείας, **2** ἐνεφάνισάν τε αὐτῷ
from Cæsarea, and [8]informed [9]him

οἱ ἀρχιερεῖς καὶ οἱ πρῶτοι τῶν Ἰουδαίων
[1]the [2]chief priests [3]and [4]the [5]chiefs [6]of the [7]Jews

κατὰ τοῦ Παύλου, καὶ παρεκάλουν αὐτὸν
against – Paul, and they besought him

3 αἰτούμενοι χάριν κατ' αὐτοῦ, ὅπως μετα-
asking a favour against him, so as he might

πέμψηται αὐτὸν εἰς Ἰερουσαλήμ, ἐνέδραν
summon him to Jerusalem, a plot

ποιοῦντες ἀνελεῖν αὐτὸν κατὰ τὴν ὁδόν.
making to kill him by the way.

4 ὁ μὲν οὖν Φῆστος ἀπεκρίθη τηρεῖσθαι
– – Therefore Festus answered [2]to be kept

τὸν Παῦλον εἰς Καισάρειαν, ἑαυτὸν δὲ
– [1]Paul in Cæsarea, and [2]himself

μέλλειν ἐν τάχει ἐκπορεύεσθαι· **5** οἱ οὖν
[1]to intend shortly to go forth; [2]the [1]therefore

εἴ τί ἐστιν ἐν τῷ ἀνδρὶ ἄτοπον,
if anything there is in the man amiss,

κατηγορείτωσαν αὐτοῦ. **6** Διατρίψας δὲ ἐν
let them accuse him. And having stayed among

αὐτοῖς ἡμέρας οὐ πλείους ὀκτὼ ἢ δέκα,
them days not more [than] eight or ten,

καταβὰς εἰς Καισάρειαν, τῇ ἐπαύριον
going down to Cæsarea, on the morrow

καθίσας ἐπὶ τοῦ βήματος ἐκέλευσεν τὸν
sitting on the tribunal he commanded –

Παῦλον ἀχθῆναι. **7** παραγενομένου δὲ
Paul to be brought. And arriving
=when he arrived

αὐτοῦ περιέστησαν αὐτὸν οἱ ἀπὸ Ἱεροσο-
him[a] [6]stood round [7]him [1]the [4]from [5]Jeru-

λύμων καταβεβηκότες Ἰουδαῖοι, πολλὰ καὶ
salem [3]having come down [2]Jews, many and

βαρέα αἰτιώματα καταφέροντες, ἃ οὐκ
heavy charges bringing against [him], which not

ἴσχυον ἀποδεῖξαι, **8** τοῦ Παύλου ἀπολογου-
they were able to prove, – Paul defending him-

μένου ὅτι οὔτε εἰς τὸν νόμον τῶν
self[,][a] – Neither against the law of the
=while Paul defended himself,

Ἰουδαίων οὔτε εἰς τὸ ἱερὸν οὔτε εἰς
Jews nor against the temple nor against

Καίσαρά τι ἥμαρτον. **9** ὁ Φῆστος δὲ,
Cæsar anything I sinned. – But Festus,

θέλων τοῖς Ἰουδαίοις χάριν καταθέσθαι,
wishing the Jews a favour to show,

ἀποκριθεὶς τῷ Παύλῳ εἶπεν· Θέλεις εἰς
answering – Paul said: Dost thou wish [2]to

Ἱεροσόλυμα ἀναβὰς ἐκεῖ περὶ τούτων
[3]Jerusalem [1]going up [4]there [8]concerning [9]these things

κριθῆναι ἐπ' ἐμοῦ; **10** εἶπεν δὲ ὁ Παῦλος·
[5]to be judged [6]before [7]me? And said – Paul:

ἑστὼς ἐπὶ τοῦ βήματος Καίσαρός εἰμι,
Standing before the tribunal of Cæsar I am,

οὗ με δεῖ κρίνεσθαι. Ἰουδαίους οὐδὲν
where me it behoves to be judged. Jews nothing

ἠδίκηκα, ὡς καὶ σὺ κάλλιον ἐπιγινώσκεις.
I have wronged, as indeed thou very well knowest.

11 εἰ μὲν οὖν ἀδικῶ καὶ ἄξιον θανάτου
If – therefore I do wrong and worthy of death

πέπραχά τι, οὐ παραιτοῦμαι τὸ ἀποθανεῖν·
I have done anything, I do not refuse *the* to die;

the chief priests and Jewish
leaders appeared before
him and presented the
charges against Paul. 3They
urgently requested Festus,
as a favor to them, to have
Paul transferred to Jerusalem, for they were preparing an ambush to kill him
along the way. 4Festus answered, "Paul is being held
at Caesarea, and I myself
am going there soon. 5Let
some of your leaders come
with me and press charges
against the man there, if he
has done anything wrong."
6After spending eight or
ten days with them, he
went down to Caesarea,
and the next day he con-
vened the court and or-
dered that Paul be brought
before him. 7When Paul appeared, the Jews who had
come down from Jerusalem
stood around him, bringing
many serious charges
against him, which they
could not prove.
8Then Paul made his de-
fense: "I have done noth-
ing wrong against the law of
the Jews or against the temple or against Caesar."
9Festus, wishing to do the
Jews a favor, said to Paul,
"Are you willing to go up to
Jerusalem and stand trial
before me there on these
charges?"
10Paul answered: "I am
now standing before Cae-
sar's court, where I ought
to be tried. I have not done
any wrong to the Jews, as
you yourself know very
well. 11If, however, I am
guilty of doing anything deserving death, I do not refuse to die. But if the

nothing to their charges
against me, no one can turn
me over to them. I appeal
to the emperor." 12 Then
Festus, after he had con-
ferred with his council, replied, "You have appealed
to the emperor; to the emperor you will go."

Festus Consults King Agrippa

13 After several days
had passed, King Agrippa
and Bernice arrived at
Caesarea to welcome Fes-
tus. 14 Since they were
staying there several days,
Festus laid Paul's case before the king, saying,
"There is a man here who
was left in prison by Felix.
15 When I was in Jerusalem,
the chief priests and the elders of the Jews informed
me about him and asked for
a sentence against him. 16 I
told them that it was not the
custom of the Romans to
hand over anyone before
the accused had met the accusers face to face and had
been given an opportunity
to make a defense against
the charge. 17 So when they
met here, I lost no time, but
on the next day took my
seat on the tribunal and ordered the man to be
brought. 18 When the ac-
cusers stood up, they did
not charge him with any of
the crimes[s] that I was expecting. 19 Instead they had
certain points of disagreement with him about their
own religion and about a
certain Jesus, who had
died, but whom Paul as-
serted to be alive. 20 Since I
was at a loss how to investigate these questions, I
asked whether he wished to
go to Jerusalem and be

s Other ancient authorities read *with anything*

εἰ δὲ οὐδέν ἐστιν ὧν οὗτοι κατηγοροῦσίν
but if not one there is of [the things] which these accuse

μου, οὐδείς με δύναται αὐτοῖς χαρίσασθαι·
me, no one 3me 1can 4to them 2to grant;

Καίσαρα ἐπικαλοῦμαι. 12 τότε ὁ Φῆστος
2Cæsar 1I appeal to. Then – Festus

συλλαλήσας μετὰ τοῦ συμβουλίου ἀπεκρίθη·
having talked *with* with the council answered:

Καίσαρα ἐπικέκλησαι, ἐπὶ Καίσαρα πορεύσῃ.
2Cæsar 1thou hast appealed to, before Cæsar thou shalt go.

13 Ἡμερῶν δὲ διαγενομένων τινῶν
And days passing some[a]
=when some days had passed

Ἀγρίππας ὁ βασιλεὺς καὶ Βερνίκη
Agrippa the king and Bernice

κατήντησαν εἰς Καισάρειαν ἀσπασάμενοι
arrived at Cæsarea greeting

τὸν Φῆστον. 14 ὡς δὲ πλείους ἡμέρας
– Festus. And as more days

διέτριβον ἐκεῖ, ὁ Φῆστος τῷ βασιλεῖ
they stayed there, – Festus 2to the 3king

ἀνέθετο τὰ κατὰ τὸν Παῦλον λέγων·
1set forth the matters regarding – Paul saying:

ἀνήρ τίς ἐστιν καταλελειμμένος ὑπὸ
A certain man there is having been left behind by

Φήλικος δέσμιος, 15 περὶ οὗ γενομένου
Felix prisoner, about whom being
=when I was

μου εἰς Ἱεροσόλυμα ἐνεφάνισαν οἱ ἀρχιερεῖς
me[a] in Jerusalem 8informed 1the 2chief priests

καὶ οἱ πρεσβύτεροι τῶν Ἰουδαίων,
3and 4the 5elders 6of the 7Jews,

αἰτούμενοι κατ᾽ αὐτοῦ καταδίκην· 16 πρὸς
asking against him sentence; to

οὓς ἀπεκρίθην ὅτι οὐκ ἔστιν ἔθος Ῥωμαίοις
whom I answered that it is not a custom with Romans

χαρίζεσθαί τινα ἄνθρωπον πρὶν ἢ ὁ
to grant any man before the

κατηγορούμενος κατὰ πρόσωπον ἔχοι τοὺς
[one] being accused face to face† should have the

κατηγόρους τόπον τε ἀπολογίας λάβοι
accusers 3place* 1and 4of defence 2receive

περὶ τοῦ ἐγκλήματος. 17 συνελθόντων
concerning the charge. Coming together[a]

οὖν ἐνθάδε ἀναβολὴν μηδεμίαν ποιησάμενος
therefore thither 3delay 2no 1making

τῇ ἑξῆς καθίσας ἐπὶ τοῦ βήματος ἐκέλευσα
on the next [day] sitting on the tribunal I commanded

ἀχθῆναι τὸν ἄνδρα· 18 περὶ οὗ σταθέντες
to be brought the man; concerning whom standing

οἱ κατήγοροι οὐδεμίαν αἰτίαν ἔφερον ὧν
the accusers 3no 2charge 1brought 4of 6things 7which

ἐγὼ ὑπενόουν πονηρῶν, 19 ζητήματα δέ
8I 9suspected 5evil, but 2questions

τινα περὶ τῆς ἰδίας δεισιδαιμονίας εἶχον
3certain 4about 5the(ir) own 6religion 1they had

πρὸς αὐτὸν καὶ περί τινος Ἰησοῦ
with him and about one Jesus

τεθνηκότος, ὃν ἔφασκεν ὁ Παῦλος ζῆν.
having died, whom 2asserted – 1Paul to live.

20 ἀπορούμενος δὲ ἐγὼ τὴν περὶ τούτων
And 2being perplexed at 1I 3the 5about 6these things

ζήτησιν ἔλεγον εἰ βούλοιτο πορεύεσθαι εἰς
4debate said if he wished to go to

* That is, opportunity.

charges brought against me
by these Jews are not true,
no one has the right to hand
me over to them. I appeal
to Caesar!"
12 After Festus had con-
ferred with his council, he
declared: "You have ap-
pealed to Caesar. To Cae-
sar you will go!"

Festus Consults King Agrippa

13 A few days later King
Agrippa and Bernice ar-
rived at Caesarea to pay
their respects to Festus.
14 Since they were spending
many days there, Festus
discussed Paul's case with
the king. He said: "There is
a man here whom Felix left
as a prisoner. 15 When I
went to Jerusalem, the
chief priests and elders of
the Jews brought charges
against him and asked that
he be condemned.
16 "I told them that it is
not the Roman custom to
hand over any man before
he has faced his accusers
and has had an opportunity
to defend himself against
their charges. 17 When they
came here with me, I did
not delay the case, but con-
vened the court the next
day and ordered the man to
be brought in. 18 When his
accusers got up to speak,
they did not charge him
with any of the crimes I had
expected. 19 Instead, they
had some points of dispute
with him about their own
religion and about a dead
man named Jesus who Paul
claimed was alive. 20 I was
at a loss how to investigate
such matters; so I asked if
he would be willing to go to

tried there on these
charges.[r] 21 But when Paul
had appealed to be kept in
custody for the decision of
his Imperial Majesty, I ordered him to be held until I
could send him to the em-
peror." 22 Agrippa said to
Festus, "I would like to
hear the man myself." "Tomorrow," he said, "you
will hear him."

Paul Brought before Agrippa

23 So on the next day
Agrippa and Bernice came
with great pomp, and they
entered the audience hall
with the military tribunes
and the prominent men of
the city. Then Festus gave
the order and Paul was
brought in. 24 And Festus
said, "King Agrippa and all
here present with us, you
see this man about whom
the whole Jewish commu-
nity petitioned me, both in
Jerusalem and here, shouting that he ought not to live
any longer. 25 But I found
that he had done nothing
deserving death; and when
he appealed to his Imperial
Majesty, I decided to send
him. 26 But I have nothing
definite to write to our sovereign about him. There-
fore I have brought him before all of you, and especially before you, King
Agrippa, so that, after we
have examined him, I may
have something to write—
27 for it seems to me unreasonable to send a prisoner
without indicating the
charges against him."

Chapter 26

Paul Defends Himself before Agrippa

AGRIPPA said to Paul, "You have permission to speak for yourself."

[r] Gk *on them*

Ἱεροσόλυμα κἀκεῖ κρίνεσθαι περὶ τούτων.
Jerusalem and there to be judged about these things.

21 τοῦ δὲ Παύλου ἐπικαλεσαμένου τηρηθῆναι
– But Paul having appealed[a] to be kept
=when Paul appealed

αὐτὸν εἰς τὴν τοῦ Σεβαστοῦ διάγνωσιν,
him to the – [2]of Augustus [1]decision,

ἐκέλευσα τηρεῖσθαι αὐτὸν ἕως οὗ ἀναπέμψω
I commanded to be kept him until I may send up

αὐτὸν πρὸς Καίσαρα. 22 Ἀγρίππας δὲ
him to Cæsar. And Agrippa

πρὸς τὸν Φῆστον· ἐβουλόμην καὶ αὐτὸς
[said] to – Festus: I was minded also [my]self

τοῦ ἀνθρώπου ἀκοῦσαι. αὔριον, φησίν,
the man to hear. Tomorrow, he says,

ἀκούσῃ αὐτοῦ. 23 Τῇ οὖν ἐπαύριον
thou shalt hear him. [2]On the [1]therefore [3]morrow

ἐλθόντος τοῦ Ἀγρίππα καὶ τῆς Βερνίκης
coming – Agrippa and – Bernice[a]
=when Agrippa and Bernice came

μετὰ πολλῆς φαντασίας καὶ εἰσελθόντων
with much display and entering[a]

εἰς τὸ ἀκροατήριον σύν τε χιλιάρχοις
into the place of audience with both chiliarchs

καὶ ἀνδράσιν τοῖς κατ' ἐξοχὴν τῆς πόλεως,
and [3]men [1]the [2]chief † of the city,

καὶ κελεύσαντος τοῦ Φήστου ἤχθη ὁ
and having commanded – Festus[a] [2]was brought –
=when Festus commanded

Παῦλος. 24 καί φησιν ὁ Φῆστος· Ἀγρίππα
[1]Paul. And says – Festus: Agrippa

βασιλεῦ καὶ πάντες οἱ συμπαρόντες ἡμῖν
king and all the [2]present together with [3]us

ἄνδρες, θεωρεῖτε τοῦτον περὶ οὗ ἅπαν τὸ
[1]men, ye behold this man about whom all the

πλῆθος τῶν Ἰουδαίων ἐνέτυχόν μοι ἔν τε
multitude of the Jews petitioned me [2]in [1]both

Ἱεροσολύμοις καὶ ἐνθάδε, βοῶντες μὴ
Jerusalem and here, crying not

δεῖν αὐτὸν ζῆν μηκέτι. 25 ἐγὼ δὲ κατε-
ought him to live *no* longer. But I dis-
=that he ought not to live any longer.

λαβόμην μηδὲν ἄξιον αὐτὸν θανάτου
covered [3]nothing [4]worthy [1]him [5]of death

πεπραχέναι, αὐτοῦ δὲ τούτου ἐπικαλεσαμένου
[2]to have done, but [him]self this man appealing to[a]
=when he himself appealed to

τὸν Σεβαστὸν ἔκρινα πέμπειν. 26 περὶ
– Augustus I decided to send. Concerning

οὗ ἀσφαλές τι γράψαι τῷ κυρίῳ οὐκ
whom [4]certain [3]anything [5]to write [6]to the [7]lord [2]not

ἔχω· διὸ προήγαγον αὐτὸν ἐφ' ὑμῶν καὶ
[1]I have; wherefore I brought forth him before you and

μάλιστα ἐπὶ σοῦ, βασιλεῦ Ἀγρίππα, ὅπως
most of all before thee, king Agrippa, so as
=when

τῆς ἀνακρίσεως γενομένης σχῶ τί γράψω·
the examination being[a] I may have what I may write;
there has been an examination

27 ἄλογον γάρ μοι δοκεῖ πέμποντα δέσμιον
for [2]unreasonable [3]to me [1]it seems sending a prisoner

μὴ καὶ τὰς κατ' αὐτοῦ αἰτίας σημᾶναι.
not also [2]the [4]against [5]him [3]charges [1]to signify.

26 Ἀγρίππας δὲ πρὸς τὸν Παῦλον ἔφη·
And Agrippa to – Paul said:

ἐπιτρέπεταί σοι ὑπὲρ σεαυτοῦ λέγειν.
It is permitted to thee on behalf of thyself to speak.

Jerusalem and stand trial
there on these charges.
21 When Paul made his ap-
peal to be held over for the
Emperor's decision, I or-
dered him held until I could
send him to Caesar."
22 Then Agrippa said to
Festus, "I would like to
hear this man myself."
He replied, "Tomorrow
you will hear him."

Paul Before Agrippa

23 The next day Agrippa
and Bernice came with
great pomp and entered the
audience room with the
high ranking officers and
the leading men of the city.
At the command of Festus,
Paul was brought in. 24 Festus said: "King Agrippa,
and all who are present
with us, you see this man!
The whole Jewish commu-
nity has petitioned me
about him in Jerusalem and
here in Caesarea, shouting
that he ought not to live any
longer. 25 I found he had
done nothing deserving of
death, but because he made
his appeal to the Emperor I
decided to send him to
Rome. 26 But I have nothing
definite to write to His Majesty about him. Therefore I
have brought him before all
of you, and especially before you, King Agrippa, so
that as a result of this investigation I may have some-
thing to write. 27 For I think
it is unreasonable to send
on a prisoner without spec-
ifying the charges against
him."

Chapter 26

THEN Agrippa said to Paul, "You have permission to speak for yourself."

Then Paul stretched out his
hand and began to defend
himself:
2 "I consider myself for-
tunate that it is before you,
King Agrippa, I am to make
my defense today against
all the accusations of the
Jews, 3 because you are especially familiar with all the
customs and controversies
of the Jews; therefore I beg
of you to listen to me patiently.
4 "All the Jews know
my way of life from my
youth, a life spent from the
beginning among my own
people and in Jerusalem.
5 They have known for a
long time, if they are willing
to testify, that I have belonged to the strictest sect
of our religion and lived as
a Pharisee. 6 And now I
stand here on trial on account of my hope in the
promise made by God to
our ancestors, 7 a promise
that our twelve tribes hope
to attain, as they earnestly
worship day and night. It is
for this hope, your Excellency,[u] that I am accused
by Jews! 8 Why is it thought
incredible by any of you
that God raises the dead?
9 "Indeed, I myself was
convinced that I ought to
do many things against the
name of Jesus of Naza-
reth.[v] 10 And that is what I
did in Jerusalem; with authority received from the
chief priests, I not only
locked up many of the
saints in prison, but I also
cast my vote against them
when they were being con-
demned to death. 11 By
punishing them often in all
the synagogues I tried to
force them to blaspheme;
and since I was so furiously
enraged at them, I pursued

τότε ὁ Παῦλος ἐκτείνας τὴν χεῖρα
Then – Paul stretching out the(his) hand

ἀπελογεῖτο· 2 Περὶ πάντων ὧν ἐγκαλοῦμαι
defended himself: Concerning all things of which I am being accused

ὑπὸ Ἰουδαίων, βασιλεῦ Ἀγρίππα, ἥγημαι
by Jews, king Agrippa, I consider

ἐμαυτὸν μακάριον ἐπὶ σοῦ μέλλων σήμερον
myself happy [2]before [4]thee [1]being about [5]to-day

ἀπολογεῖσθαι, 3 μάλιστα γνώστην ὄντα σε
[3]to defend myself, most of all [3]an expert [2]being [1]thee

πάντων τῶν κατὰ Ἰουδαίους ἐθῶν τε
[5]of all [6]the [8]among [9]Jews [7]customs [4]both

καὶ ζητημάτων· διὸ δέομαι μακροθύμως
[10]and [11]questions; wherefore I beg patiently

ἀκοῦσαί μου. 4 Τὴν μὲν οὖν βίωσίν
to hear me. [3]the [1]So [2]then [4]manner of life

μου ἐκ νεότητος τὴν ἀπ' ἀρχῆς γενομένην
of me from youth – [2]from [4]beginning [1]having been [3][the]

ἐν τῷ ἔθνει μου ἔν τε Ἱεροσολύμοις
in the nation of me [2]in [1]and Jerusalem

ἴσασι πάντες Ἰουδαῖοι, 5 προγινώσκοντές
know all Jews, previously knowing

με ἄνωθεν, ἐὰν θέλωσι μαρτυρεῖν, ὅτι
me from the first, if they are willing to testify, that

κατὰ τὴν ἀκριβεστάτην αἵρεσιν τῆς
according to the most exact sect –

ἡμετέρας θρησκείας ἔζησα Φαρισαῖος. 6 καὶ
of our religion I lived a Pharisee. And

νῦν ἐπ' ἐλπίδι τῆς εἰς τοὺς πατέρας
now on(in) hope of the [5]to [6]the [7]fathers

ἡμῶν ἐπαγγελίας γενομένης ὑπὸ τοῦ θεοῦ
[8]of us [1]promise [2]having been [made] [3]by – [4]God

ἕστηκα κρινόμενος, 7 εἰς ἣν τὸ δωδεκά-
I stand being judged, to which the twelve

φυλον ἡμῶν ἐν ἐκτενείᾳ νύκτα καὶ
tribes of us with earnestness night and

ἡμέραν λατρεῦον ἐλπίζει καταντῆσαι· περὶ
day worshipping hopes to arrive; concerning

ἧς ἐλπίδος ἐγκαλοῦμαι ὑπὸ Ἰουδαίων,
which hope I am accused by Jews,

βασιλεῦ. 8 τί ἄπιστον κρίνεται παρ'
[O] king. Why incredible is it judged by

ὑμῖν εἰ ὁ θεὸς νεκροὺς ἐγείρει; 9 ἐγὼ
you if – God [2]dead persons [1]raises? [3]I

μὲν οὖν ἔδοξα ἐμαυτῷ πρὸς τὸ ὄνομα
[1]indeed [2]then [4]thought [5]to myself [10]to [11]the [12]name

Ἰησοῦ τοῦ Ναζωραίου δεῖν πολλὰ ἐναντία
[13]of Jesus [14]the [15]Nazarene [6]ought [8]many things [9]contrary

πρᾶξαι· 10 ὃ καὶ ἐποίησα ἐν Ἱεροσολύμοις,
[7]to do; which indeed I did in Jerusalem,

καὶ πολλούς τε τῶν ἁγίων ἐγὼ ἐν
and many – of the saints [1]I [3]in

φυλακαῖς κατέκλεισα τὴν παρὰ τῶν
[4]prisons [2]shut up [6]the [8]from [9]the

ἀρχιερέων ἐξουσίαν λαβών, ἀναιρουμένων τε
[10]chief priests [7]authority [5]having received, being killed and
=and when they were killed

αὐτῶν κατήνεγκα ψῆφον, 11 καὶ κατὰ
them[a] I cast a vote, and throughout

πάσας τὰς συναγωγὰς πολλάκις τιμωρῶν
all the synagogues often punishing

αὐτοὺς ἠνάγκαζον βλασφημεῖν, περισσῶς τε
them I compelled [them] to blaspheme, and excessively

ἐμμαινόμενος αὐτοῖς ἐδίωκον ἕως καὶ εἰς
raging against them I persecuted as far as even to

So Paul motioned with his
hand and began his de-
fense: 2 "King Agrippa, I
consider myself fortunate
to stand before you today
as I make my defense
against all the accusations
of the Jews, 3 and especially
so because you are well acquainted with all the Jewish
customs and controversies.
Therefore, I beg you to listen to me patiently.
4 "The Jews all know the
way I have lived ever since
I was a child, from the beginning of my life in my
own country, and also in
Jerusalem. 5 They have
known me for a long time
and can testify, if they are
willing, that according to
the strictest sect of our religion, I lived as a Pharisee.
6 And now it is because of
my hope in what God has
promised our fathers that I
am on trial today. 7 This is
the promise our twelve
tribes are hoping to see fulfilled as they earnestly
serve God day and night. O
king, it is because of this
hope that the Jews are accusing me. 8 Why should
any of you consider it incredible that God raises the
dead?
9 "I too was convinced
that I ought to do all that
was possible to oppose the
name of Jesus of Nazareth.
10 And that is just what I did
in Jerusalem. On the au-
thority of the chief priests I
put many of the saints in
prison, and when they were
put to death, I cast my vote
against them. 11 Many a
time I went from one synagogue to another to have
them punished, and I tried
to force them to blas-
pheme. In my obsession
against them, I even went

[u] Gk *O king*
[v] Gk *the Nazorean*

them even to foreign cities.

Paul Tells of His Conversion

12 "With this in mind, I
was traveling to Damascus
with the authority and commission of the chief priests,
13 when at midday along the
road, your Excellency,[v] I
saw a light from heaven,
brighter than the sun, shining around me and my com-
panions. 14 When we had all
fallen to the ground, I heard
a voice saying to me in the
Hebrew[w] language, 'Saul,
Saul, why are you perse-
cuting me? It hurts you to
kick against the goads.' 15 I
asked, 'Who are you,
Lord?' The Lord an-
swered, 'I am Jesus whom
you are persecuting. 16 But
get up and stand on your
feet; for I have appeared to
you for this purpose, to appoint you to serve and testify to the things in which
you have seen me[x] and to
those in which I will appear
to you. 17 I will rescue you
from your people and from
the Gentiles—to whom I
am sending you 18 to open
their eyes so that they may
turn from darkness to light
and from the power of Sa-
tan to God, so that they
may receive forgiveness of
sins and a place among
those who are sanctified by
faith in me.'

Paul Tells of His Preaching

19 "After that, King
Agrippa, I was not disobedient to the heavenly vi-
sion, 20 but declared first to
those in Damascus, then in
Jerusalem and throughout
the countryside of Judea,
and also to the Gentiles,
that they should repent and
turn to God and do deeds
consistent with repen-
tance. 21 For this reason the
Jews seized me in the tem-

[w] That is, *Aramaic*
[x] Other ancient authorities read *the things that you have seen*

τὰς ἔξω πόλεις. 12 Ἐν οἷς πορευόμενος
the outside cities. In which journeying
εἰς τὴν Δαμασκὸν μετ' ἐξουσίας καὶ
to – Damascus with authority and
ἐπιτροπῆς τῆς τῶν ἀρχιερέων, 13 ἡμέρας
power to decide – of the chief priests, at [2]day
μέσης κατὰ τὴν ὁδὸν εἶδον, βασιλεῦ,
[1]mid along the way I saw, [O] king,
οὐρανόθεν ὑπὲρ τὴν λαμπρότητα τοῦ ἡλίου
[3]from heaven [2]above [4]the [5]brightness [6]of the [7]sun
περιλάμψαν με φῶς καὶ τοὺς σὺν ἐμοὶ
[8]shining round [9]me [1]a light [10]and [11]the [ones] [13]with [14]me
πορευομένους· 14 πάντων τε καταπεσόντων
[12]journeying; and all having fallen down
=when we had all fallen
ἡμῶν εἰς τὴν γῆν ἤκουσα φωνὴν λέγουσαν
us[a] to the earth I heard a voice saying
πρός με τῇ Ἑβραΐδι διαλέκτῳ· Σαοὺλ
to me in the Hebrew language: Saul[,]
Σαούλ, τί με διώκεις; σκληρόν σοι
Saul, why me persecutest thou? hard for thee
πρὸς κέντρα λακτίζειν. 15 ἐγὼ δὲ εἶπα·
against goads to kick. And I said:
τίς εἶ, κύριε; ὁ δὲ κύριος εἶπεν· ἐγώ
Who art thou, Lord? And the Lord said: I
εἰμι Ἰησοῦς ὃν σὺ διώκεις. 16 ἀλλὰ
am Jesus whom thou persecutest. But
ἀνάστηθι καὶ στῆθι ἐπὶ τοὺς πόδας σου·
rise thou up and stand on the feet of thee;
εἰς τοῦτο γὰρ ὤφθην σοι, προχειρίσασθαί
[2]for [3]this [purpose] [1]for I appeared to thee, to appoint
σε ὑπηρέτην καὶ μάρτυρα ὧν τε
thee an attendant and a witness [2]of the things which [1]both
εἶδές με ὧν τε ὀφθήσομαί σοι,
[3]thou sawest [4]me [6]of the things which [5]and I will appear to thee,
17 ἐξαιρούμενός σε ἐκ τοῦ λαοῦ καὶ ἐκ
delivering thee from the people and from
τῶν ἐθνῶν, εἰς οὓς ἐγὼ ἀποστέλλω σε,
the nations, to whom I send thee,
18 ἀνοῖξαι ὀφθαλμοὺς αὐτῶν, τοῦ ἐπιστρέψαι
to open eyes of them, – to turn[b]
ἀπὸ σκότους εἰς φῶς καὶ τῆς ἐξουσίας
from darkness to light and [from] the authority
τοῦ σατανᾶ ἐπὶ τὸν θεόν, τοῦ λαβεῖν
– of Satan to – God, – to receive
=that they may receive
αὐτοὺς ἄφεσιν ἁμαρτιῶν καὶ κλῆρον ἐν
them[bd] forgiveness of sins and a lot among
τοῖς ἡγιασμένοις πίστει τῇ εἰς ἐμέ.
the [ones] *having been* sanctified by faith – in me.
19 Ὅθεν, βασιλεῦ Ἀγρίππα, οὐκ ἐγενόμην
Whence, king Agrippa, I was not
ἀπειθὴς τῇ οὐρανίῳ ὀπτασίᾳ, 20 ἀλλὰ
disobedient to the heavenly vision, but
τοῖς ἐν Δαμασκῷ πρῶτόν τε καὶ
to the [ones] in Damascus first*ly* and also
Ἱεροσολύμοις, πᾶσάν τε τὴν χώραν τῆς
[in] Jerusalem, and all the country –
Ἰουδαίας καὶ τοῖς ἔθνεσιν ἀπήγγελλον
of Judæa and to the nations I announced
μετανοεῖν καὶ ἐπιστρέφειν ἐπὶ τὸν θεόν,
to repent and to turn to – God,
ἄξια τῆς μετανοίας ἔργα πράσσοντας.
[3]worthy [4]of the [5]repentance [2]works [1]doing.
21 ἕνεκα τούτων με Ἰουδαῖοι συλλαβόμενοι
On account of these things [3]me [1]Jews [2]having seized

to foreign cities to persecute them.
12 "On one of these jour-
neys I was going to Damascus with the authority and
commission of the chief
priests. 13 About noon, O
king, as I was on the road, I
saw a light from heaven,
brighter than the sun, blazing around me and my com-
panions. 14 We all fell to the
ground, and I heard a voice
saying to me in Aramaic,[w]
'Saul, Saul, why do you
persecute me? It is hard for
you to kick against the
goads.'
15 "Then I asked, 'Who
are you, Lord?'
" 'I am Jesus, whom you
are persecuting,' the Lord
replied. 16 'Now get up and
stand on your feet. I have
appeared to you to appoint
you as a servant and as a
witness of what you have
seen of me and what I will
show you. 17 I will rescue
you from your own people
and from the Gentiles. I am
sending you to them 18 to
open their eyes and turn
them from darkness to
light, and from the power of
Satan to God, so that they
may receive forgiveness of
sins and a place among
those who are sanctified by
faith in me.'
19 "So then, King Agrip-
pa, I was not disobedient to
the vision from heaven.
20 First to those in Damascus, then to those in Jerusalem and in all Judea, and to
the Gentiles also, I
preached that they should
repent and turn to God and
prove their repentance by
their deeds. 21 That is why
the Jews seized me in the

[w] 14 Or *Hebrew*

ple and tried to kill me.
22To this day I have had
help from God, and so I
stand here, testifying to
both small and great, saying nothing but what the
prophets and Moses said
would take place: 23that
the Messiah[y] must suffer,
and that, by being the first
to rise from the dead, he
would proclaim light both
to our people and to the
Gentiles."

Paul Appeals to Agrippa to Believe

24 While he was making
this defense, Festus ex-
claimed, "You are out of
your mind, Paul! Too much
learning is driving you insane!" 25But Paul said, "I
am not out of my mind,
most excellent Festus, but
I am speaking the sober
truth. 26Indeed the king
knows about these things,
and to him I speak freely;
for I am certain that none of
these things has escaped
his notice, for this was not
done in a corner. 27King
Agrippa, do you believe the
prophets? I know that you
believe." 28Agrippa said to
Paul, "Are you so quickly
persuading me to become a
Christian?"[z] 29Paul re-
plied, "Whether quickly or
not, I pray to God that not
only you but also all who
are listening to me today
might become such as I
am—except for these
chains."
30 Then the king got up,
and with him the governor
and Bernice and those who
had been seated with them;
31and as they were leaving,
they said to one another,
"This man is doing nothing

ἐν τῷ ἱερῷ ἐπειρῶντο διαχειρίσασθαι.
in the temple tried to kill [me].

22 ἐπικουρίας οὖν τυχὼν τῆς ἀπὸ τοῦ
Succour therefore having obtained – from –

θεοῦ ἄχρι τῆς ἡμέρας ταύτης ἕστηκα
God until this day I stand

μαρτυρόμενος μικρῷ τε καὶ μεγάλῳ, οὐδὲν
witnessing [2]to small [1]both and to great, [3]nothing

ἐκτὸς λέγων ὧν τε οἱ προφῆται
[2]apart from [1]saying [4]the things which [5]both [6]the [7]prophets

ἐλάλησαν μελλόντων γίνεσθαι καὶ Μωϋσῆς,
[10]said [11]being about [12]to happen [8]and [9]Moses,

23 εἰ παθητὸς ὁ χριστός, εἰ πρῶτος
if subject to suffering the Christ, if first

ἐξ ἀναστάσεως νεκρῶν φῶς μέλλει
by a resurrection of dead persons [3]a light [1]he is about

καταγγέλλειν τῷ τε λαῷ καὶ τοῖς ἔθνεσιν.
[2]to announce [3]to the [4]both people and to the nations.

24 Ταῦτα δὲ αὐτοῦ ἀπολογουμένου ὁ Φῆστος
And these things him defending himself* – Festus
*=as he defended himself with these things

μεγάλῃ τῇ φωνῇ φησιν· μαίνῃ, Παῦλε·
[2]great [1]with the(his) [3]voice says: Thou ravest, Paul:

τὰ πολλά σε γράμματα εἰς μανίαν
[1]the [2]many [5]thee [3]letters [6]to [7]madness

περιτρέπει. 25 ὁ δὲ Παῦλος· οὐ μαίνομαι,
[4]turn[s]. – But Paul: I do not rave,

φησίν, κράτιστε Φῆστε, ἀλλὰ ἀληθείας
he says, most excellent Festus, but [3]of truth

καὶ σωφροσύνης ῥήματα ἀποφθέγγομαι.
[4]and [5]of good sense [2]words [1]speak forth.

26 ἐπίσταται γὰρ περὶ τούτων ὁ βασιλεύς,
For [3]understands [4]about [5]these things [1]the [2]king,

πρὸς ὃν καὶ παρρησιαζόμενος λαλῶ·
to whom indeed being bold of speech I speak;

λανθάνειν γὰρ αὐτὸν τούτων οὐ πείθομαι
for [4]to be hidden [from] [5]him [3]of these things *not* [1]I am persuaded

οὐθέν· οὐ γάρ ἐστιν ἐν γωνίᾳ πεπραγμένον
[2]nothing; for [3]not [2]is [5]in [6]a corner [4]having been done

τοῦτο. 27 πιστεύεις, βασιλεῦ Ἀγρίππα,
[1]this. Believest thou, king Agrippa,

τοῖς προφήταις; οἶδα ὅτι πιστεύεις. 28 ὁ
the prophets? I know that thou believest. –

δὲ Ἀγρίππας πρὸς τὸν Παῦλον· ἐν
And Agrippa [said] to – Paul: In

ὀλίγῳ με πείθεις Χριστιανὸν ποιῆσαι.
a little [2]me [1]thou persuadest [4]a Christian [3]to make(act).

29 ὁ δὲ Παῦλος· εὐξαίμην ἂν τῷ θεῷ
– And Paul [said]: I would pray – God

καὶ ἐν ὀλίγῳ καὶ ἐν μεγάλῳ οὐ μόνον
both in a little and in great not only

σὲ ἀλλὰ καὶ πάντας τοὺς ἀκούοντάς
thee but also all the [ones] hearing

μου σήμερον γενέσθαι τοιούτους ὁποῖος
me to-day [2]to become [1]such of what kind

καὶ ἐγώ εἰμι, παρεκτὸς τῶν δεσμῶν
indeed I am, except – bonds

τούτων. 30 Ἀνέστη τε ὁ βασιλεὺς καὶ
these. Rose up both the king and

ὁ ἡγεμὼν ἥ τε Βερνίκη καὶ οἱ συγ-
the governor – and Bernice and the [ones] sit-

καθήμενοι αὐτοῖς, 31 καὶ ἀναχωρήσαντες
ting with them, and having left

ἐλάλουν πρὸς ἀλλήλους λέγοντες ὅτι οὐδὲν
spoke to one another saying [,] – [4]nothing

temple courts and tried to
kill me. 22But I have had
God's help to this very day,
and so I stand here and testify to small and great alike.
I am saying nothing beyond
what the prophets and Mo-
ses said would happen—
23that the Christ[x] would
suffer and, as the first to
rise from the dead, would
proclaim light to his own
people and to the Gen-
tiles."
24At this point Festus in-
terrupted Paul's defense.
"You are out of your mind,
Paul!" he shouted. "Your
great learning is driving
you insane."
25"I am not insane, most
excellent Festus," Paul replied. "What I am saying is
true and reasonable. 26The
king is familiar with these
things, and I can speak
freely to him. I am con-
vinced that none of this has
escaped his notice, because
it was not done in a corner.
27King Agrippa, do you believe the prophets? I know
you do."
28Then Agrippa said to
Paul, "Do you think that in
such a short time you can
persuade me to be a Christian?"
29Paul replied, "Short
time or long—I pray God
that not only you but all
who are listening to me to-
day may become what I
am, except for these
chains."
30The king rose, and with
him the governor and Ber-
nice and those sitting with
them. 31They left the room,
and while talking with one
another, they said, "This

[y] Or *the Christ*
[z] Or *Quickly you will persuade me to play the Christian*

[x] 23 Or *Messiah*

to deserve death or imprisonment." 32 Agrippa said to
Festus, "This man could
have been set free if he had
not appealed to the emper-
or."

Chapter 27

Paul Sails for Rome

WHEN it was decided
that we were to sail
for Italy, they transferred
Paul and some other pris-
oners to a centurion of the
Augustan Cohort, named
Julius. 2 Embarking on a
ship of Adramyttium that
was about to set sail to the
ports along the coast of
Asia, we put to sea, accompanied by Aristarchus, a
Macedonian from Thessa-
lonica. 3 The next day we
put in at Sidon; and Julius
treated Paul kindly, and allowed him to go to his
friends to be cared for.
4 Putting out to sea from
there, we sailed under the
lee of Cyprus, because the
winds were against us. 5 After we had sailed across the
sea that is off Cilicia and
Pamphylia, we came to
Myra in Lycia. 6 There the
centurion found an Alexandrian ship bound for Italy
and put us on board. 7 We
sailed slowly for a number
of days and arrived with
difficulty off Cnidus, and as
the wind was against us, we
sailed under the lee of
Crete off Salmone. 8 Sailing
past it with difficulty, we
came to a place called Fair
Havens, near the city of
Lasea.
9 Since much time had

θανάτου ἢ δεσμῶν ἄξιον πράσσει ὁ
[6]of death [7]or [8]of bonds [5]worthy [3]does –

ἄνθρωπος οὗτος. 32 Ἀγρίππας δὲ τῷ
[2]man [1]This. And Agrippa –

Φήστῳ ἔφη· ἀπολελύσθαι ἐδύνατο
to Festus said: [3]*to* have been released [2]was able(could)

ὁ ἄνθρωπος οὗτος εἰ μὴ ἐπεκέκλητο Καίσαρα.
[1]This man if he had not appealed to Cæsar.

27 Ὡς δὲ ἐκρίθη τοῦ ἀποπλεῖν ἡμᾶς
And when it was decided – to sail us[bd]
=that we should sail

εἰς τὴν Ἰταλίαν, παρεδίδουν τόν τε
to – Italy, they delivered – both

Παῦλον καί τινας ἑτέρους δεσμώτας
Paul and some other prisoners

ἑκατοντάρχῃ ὀνόματι Ἰουλίῳ σπείρης
to a centurion by name Julius of a cohort

Σεβαστῆς. 2 ἐπιβάντες δὲ πλοίῳ Ἀδρα-
Augustan. And embarking in a ship belonging to

μυττηνῷ μέλλοντι πλεῖν εἰς τοὺς κατὰ
Adramyttium being about to sail [1]for [2]the [4]along [the coast of]

τὴν Ἀσίαν τόπους ἀνήχθημεν, ὄντος σὺν
– [5]Asia [3]places we set sail, being with

ἡμῖν Ἀριστάρχου Μακεδόνος Θεσσαλονικέως·
us Aristarchus a Macedonian[a] of Thessalonica;

3 τῇ τε ἑτέρᾳ κατήχθημεν εἰς Σιδῶνα,
and on the next [day] we were brought to land at Sidon,

φιλανθρώπως τε ὁ Ἰούλιος τῷ Παύλῳ
and [3]kindly – [1]Julius – [5]Paul

χρησάμενος ἐπέτρεψεν πρὸς τοὺς φίλους
[2]treating [him] [4]allowed [7]to [8]the [9]friends

πορευθέντι ἐπιμελείας τυχεῖν. 4 κἀκεῖθεν
[6]going [11]attention [10]to obtain. And thence

ἀναχθέντες ὑπεπλεύσαμεν τὴν Κύπρον διὰ
putting to sea we sailed close to – Cyprus because of

τὸ τοὺς ἀνέμους εἶναι ἐναντίους, 5 τό τε
– the winds to be(being) contrary, and [1]the

πέλαγος τὸ κατὰ τὴν Κιλικίαν καὶ
[2]sea – [4]against – [5]Cilicia [6]and

Παμφυλίαν διαπλεύσαντες κατήλθαμεν εἰς
[7]Pamphylia [1]sailing over we came down to

Μύρα τῆς Λυκίας. 6 Κἀκεῖ εὑρὼν ὁ
Myra – of Lycia. And there [3]having found [1]the

ἑκατοντάρχης πλοῖον Ἀλεξανδρῖνον πλέον
[2]centurion ship an Alexandrian sailing

εἰς τὴν Ἰταλίαν ἐνεβίβασεν ἡμᾶς εἰς
to – Italy he embarked us in

αὐτό. 7 ἐν ἱκαναῖς δὲ ἡμέραις βραδυπλο-
it. And in a number of days sailing

οῦντες καὶ μόλις γενόμενοι κατὰ τὴν
slowly and hardly coming against –

Κνίδον, μὴ προσεῶντος ἡμᾶς τοῦ ἀνέμου,
Cnidus, not allowing us the wind,[a]
=as the wind did not allow us,

ὑπεπλεύσαμεν τὴν Κρήτην κατὰ Σαλμώνην,
we sailed close to – Crete against Salmone,

8 μόλις τε παραλεγόμενοι αὐτὴν ἤλθομεν
and hardly sailing along it we came

εἰς τόπον τινὰ καλούμενον Καλοὺς λιμένας,
to place a certain *being* called Fair Havens,

ᾧ ἐγγὺς ἦν πόλις Λασαία. 9 Ἱκανοῦ δὲ
[2]to which [1]near was a city Lasæa. And much
=when

man is not doing anything
that deserves death or imprisonment."
32 Agrippa said to Festus,
"This man could have been
set free if he had not appealed to Caesar."

Chapter 27

Paul Sails for Rome

WHEN it was decided
that we would sail
for Italy, Paul and some
other prisoners were handed over to a centurion
named Julius, who be-
longed to the Imperial Reg-
iment. 2 We boarded a ship
from Adramyttium about to
sail for ports along the
coast of the province of
Asia, and we put out to sea.
Aristarchus, a Macedonian
from Thessalonica, was
with us.
3 The next day we landed
at Sidon; and Julius, in
kindness to Paul, allowed
him to go to his friends so
they might provide for his
needs. 4 From there we put
out to sea again and passed
to the lee of Cyprus be-
cause the winds were
against us. 5 When we had
sailed across the open sea
off the coast of Cilicia and
Pamphylia, we landed at
Myra in Lycia. 6 There the
centurion found an Alexandrian ship sailing for Italy
and put us on board. 7 We
made slow headway for
many days and had difficulty arriving off Cnidus.
When the wind did not al-
low us to hold our course,
we sailed to the lee of
Crete, opposite Salmone.
8 We moved along the coast
with difficulty and came to
a place called Fair Havens,
near the town of Lasea.
9 Much time had been

been lost and sailing was
now dangerous, because
even the Fast had already
gone by, Paul advised
them, 10 saying, "Sirs, I can
see that the voyage will be
with danger and much
heavy loss, not only of the
cargo and the ship, but also
of our lives." 11 But the centurion paid more attention
to the pilot and to the owner of the ship than to what
Paul said. 12 Since the harbor was not suitable for
spending the winter, the
majority was in favor of
putting to sea from there,
on the chance that some-
how they could reach
Phoenix, where they could
spend the winter. It was a
harbor of Crete, facing
southwest and northwest.

The Storm at Sea

13 When a moderate
south wind began to blow,
they thought they could
achieve their purpose; so
they weighed anchor and
began to sail past Crete,
close to the shore. 14 But
soon a violent wind, called
the northeaster, rushed
down from Crete.[a] 15 Since
the ship was caught and
could not be turned head-
on into the wind, we gave
way to it and were driven.
16 By running under the lee
of a small island called Cauda[b] we were scarcely able
to get the ship's boat under
control. 17 After hoisting it
up they took measures[c] to
undergird the ship; then,
fearing that they would run
on the Syrtis, they lowered
the sea anchor and so were

[a] Gk *it*
[b] Other ancient authorities read *Clauda*
[c] Gk *helps*

χρόνου διαγενομένου καὶ ὄντος ἤδη
time having passed[a] and being now
much time had passed =as the voyage

ἐπισφαλοῦς τοῦ πλοὸς διὰ τὸ καὶ τὴν
dangerous the voyage[a] on account of – also the
was now dangerous =because also the fast had now

νηστείαν ἤδη παρεληλυθέναι, παρῄνει ὁ
fast now to have gone by, [2]advised –
gone by,

Παῦλος 10 λέγων αὐτοῖς· ἄνδρες, θεωρῶ
[1]Paul saying to them: Men, I see

ὅτι μετὰ ὕβρεως καὶ πολλῆς ζημίας οὐ
that with injury and much loss not

μόνον τοῦ φορτίου καὶ τοῦ πλοίου ἀλλὰ
only of the cargo and of the ship but

καὶ τῶν ψυχῶν ἡμῶν μέλλειν ἔσεσθαι
also of the lives of us [3]to be about [4]to be
=will be

τὸν πλοῦν. 11 ὁ δὲ ἑκατοντάρχης τῷ
[1]the [2]voyage. But the centurion [2]the

κυβερνήτῃ καὶ τῷ ναυκλήρῳ μᾶλλον
[3]steersman [4]and [5]the [6]shipmaster [7]rather

ἐπείθετο ἢ τοῖς ὑπὸ Παύλου λεγομένοις.
[1]was persuaded by [8]than [9]the [11]by [12]Paul [10]things said.

12 ἀνευθέτου δὲ τοῦ λιμένος ὑπάρχοντος
But unsuitable the port being[a]
=as the port was unsuitable

πρὸς παραχειμασίαν οἱ πλείονες ἔθεντο
for wintering the majority placed
=decided

βουλὴν ἀναχθῆναι ἐκεῖθεν, εἴ πως δύναιντο
counsel to set sail thence, if some-how they might be able

καταντήσαντες εἰς Φοίνικα παραχειμάσαι,
having arrived at Phœnix to pass the winter,

λιμένα τῆς Κρήτης βλέποντα κατὰ λίβα
a port – of Crete looking toward south-west

καὶ κατὰ χῶρον. 13 Ὑποπνεύσαντος δὲ
and toward north-west. And blowing gently
=when a south wind

νότου δόξαντες τῆς προθέσεως κεκρατηκέναι,
a south wind[a] thinking [2]the(ir) [3]purpose [1]to have obtained,
blew gently

ἄραντες ἆσσον παρελέγοντο τὴν Κρήτην.
raising [anchor] [3]close in-shore [1]they coasted by – [2]Crete.

14 μετ᾿ οὐ πολὺ δὲ ἔβαλεν κατ᾿ αὐτῆς
And after not much there beat down it

ἄνεμος τυφωνικὸς ὁ καλούμενος εὐρακύλων·
wind a tempestuous – *being* called Euraquilo;

15 συναρπασθέντος δὲ τοῦ πλοίου καὶ μὴ
and [3]being seized [1]the [2]ship[a] and not

δυναμένου ἀντοφθαλμεῖν τῷ ἀνέμῳ ἐπιδόντες
being able[a] to beat up against the wind giving way

ἐφερόμεθα. 16 νησίον δέ τι ὑποδραμόντες
we were borne. And [3]islet [2]a certain [1]running under the lee of

καλούμενον Κλαῦδα ἰσχύσαμεν μόλις
being called Clauda we were able hardly

περικρατεῖς γενέσθαι τῆς σκάφης, 17 ἣν
control to get of the boat, which

ἄραντες βοηθείαις ἐχρῶντο, ὑποζωννύντες
taking [2]helps [1]they used, undergirding

τὸ πλοῖον· φοβούμενοί τε μὴ εἰς τὴν
the ship; and fearing lest into

Σύρτιν ἐκπέσωσιν, χαλάσαντες τὸ σκεῦος,
Syrtis they might fall off,* lowering the tackle,

* This is the classical Greek word for a ship being driven out of her course on to shoals, rocks, etc. (Page). See also vers 26 and 29.

lost, and sailing had al-
ready become dangerous
because by now it was after
the Fast.[y] So Paul warned
them, 10 "Men, I can see
that our voyage is going to
be disastrous and bring
great loss to ship and cargo,
and to our own lives also."
11 But the centurion, in-
stead of listening to what
Paul said, followed the advice of the pilot and of the
owner of the ship. 12 Since
the harbor was unsuitable
to winter in, the majority
decided that we should sail
on, hoping to reach Phoe-
nix and winter there. This
was a harbor in Crete, facing both southwest and
northwest.

The Storm

13 When a gentle south
wind began to blow, they
thought they had obtained
what they wanted; so they
weighed anchor and sailed
along the shore of Crete.
14 Before very long, a wind
of hurricane force, called
the "northeaster," swept
down from the island.
15 The ship was caught by
the storm and could not
head into the wind; so we
gave way to it and were
driven along. 16 As we
passed to the lee of a small
island called Cauda, we
were hardly able to make
the lifeboat secure. 17 When
the men had hoisted it
aboard, they passed ropes
under the ship itself to hold
it together. Fearing that
they would run aground on
the sandbars of Syrtis, they
lowered the sea anchor and

[y] 9 That is, the Day of Atonement (Yom Kippur)

driven. 18We were being
pounded by the storm so violently that on the next day
they began to throw the
cargo overboard, 19and on
the third day with their own
hands they threw the ship's
tackle overboard. 20When
neither sun nor stars ap-
peared for many days, and
no small tempest raged, all
hope of our being saved
was at last abandoned.
21 Since they had been
without food for a long
time, Paul then stood up
among them and said,
"Men, you should have listened to me and not have
set sail from Crete and
thereby avoided this dam-
age and loss. 22I urge you
now to keep up your cour-
age, for there will be no loss
of life among you, but only
of the ship. 23For last night
there stood by me an angel
of the God to whom I be-
long and whom I worship,
24and he said, 'Do not be
afraid, Paul; you must
stand before the emperor;
and indeed, God has granted safety to all those who
are sailing with you.' 25So
keep up your courage,
men, for I have faith in God
that it will be exactly as I
have been told. 26But we
will have to run aground on
some island."
27 When the fourteenth
night had come, as we were
drifting across the sea of
Adria, about midnight the
sailors suspected that they
were nearing land. 28So
they took soundings and
found twenty fathoms; a little farther on they took

οὕτως ἐφέροντο. 18 σφοδρῶς δὲ χειμαζ-
thus they were borne. But exceedingly being in
=as we were exceedingly in . . .

ομένων ἡμῶν τῇ ἑξῆς ἐκβολὴν ἐποιοῦντο,
the grip of a storm us[a] on the next [day] a jettisoning they made,

19 καὶ τῇ τρίτῃ αὐτόχειρες τὴν σκευὴν
and on the third [day] with their own hands the tackle

τοῦ πλοίου ἔρριψαν. 20 μήτε δὲ ἡλίου
of the ship they threw [out]. And neither sun
=when neither . . .

μήτε ἄστρων ἐπιφαινόντων ἐπὶ πλείονας
nor appeared stars appearing[a] over many

ἡμέρας, χειμῶνός τε οὐκ ὀλίγου ἐπικειμένου,
days, and stormy weather no little pressing hard,[a]

λοιπὸν περιῃρεῖτο ἐλπὶς πᾶσα τοῦ σῴζεσθαι
now was taken away 2hope 1all – to be saved
=that we might

ἡμᾶς. 21 Πολλῆς τε ἀσιτίας ὑπαρχούσης
us.[bd] be saved. And much abstinence being[a]
=when there was long abstinence

τότε σταθεὶς ὁ Παῦλος ἐν μέσῳ αὐτῶν εἶπεν·
then 2standing – 1Paul in [the] midst of them said:

ἔδει μέν, ὦ ἄνδρες, πειθαρχήσαντάς
It behoved [you], – O men, obeying

μοι μὴ ἀνάγεσθαι ἀπὸ τῆς Κρήτης
me not to set sail from – Crete

κερδῆσαί τε τὴν ὕβριν ταύτην καὶ τὴν
and to come by – injury this and –

ζημίαν. 22 καὶ τὰ νῦν παραινῶ ὑμᾶς
loss. And – now I advise you

εὐθυμεῖν· ἀποβολὴ γὰρ ψυχῆς οὐδεμία
to be of good cheer; for 3throwing away 4of life 2no

ἔσται ἐξ ὑμῶν πλὴν τοῦ πλοίου.
1there will be of you but of the ship.

23 παρέστη γάρ μοι ταύτῃ τῇ νυκτὶ
For there stood by me *in* this – night

τοῦ θεοῦ οὗ εἰμι, ᾧ καὶ λατρεύω,
– 2of God 3of whom 4I am, 5whom 6also 7I serve,

ἄγγελος 24 λέγων· μὴ φοβοῦ, Παῦλε·
1an angel saying: Fear not, Paul;

Καίσαρί σε δεῖ παραστῆναι, καὶ ἰδοὺ
4Cæsar 2thee 1it behoves 3to stand before, and behold

κεχάρισταί σοι ὁ θεὸς πάντας τοὺς
3has given 2thee – 1God all the [ones]

πλέοντας μετὰ σοῦ. 25 διὸ εὐθυμεῖτε,
sailing with thee. Wherefore be ye of good cheer,

ἄνδρες· πιστεύω γὰρ τῷ θεῷ ὅτι οὕτως
men; for I believe – God that thus

ἔσται καθ᾽ ὃν τρόπον λελάληταί μοι.
it will be in the way in which† it has been spoken to me.

26 εἰς νῆσον δέ τινα δεῖ ἡμᾶς ἐκπεσεῖν.
6Onto 7island 1but 8a certain 2it behoves 3us 4to fall off.

27 Ὡς δὲ τεσσαρεσκαιδεκάτη νὺξ ἐγένετο
Now when [the] fourteenth night came

διαφερομένων ἡμῶν ἐν τῷ Ἀδρίᾳ, κατὰ
being carried about us[a] in the Adria, about
=while we were being carried about

μέσον τῆς νυκτὸς ὑπενόουν οἱ ναῦται
[the] middle of the night 3supposed 1the 2sailors

προσάγειν τινὰ αὐτοῖς χώραν. 28 καὶ
4to approach 5some 6to them 7country. And

βολίσαντες εὗρον ὀργυιὰς εἴκοσι, βραχὺ δὲ
sounding they found fathoms twenty, and 2a little

let the ship be driven along.
18We took such a violent
battering from the storm
that the next day they began to throw the cargo
overboard. 19On the third
day, they threw the ship's
tackle overboard with their
own hands. 20When neither
sun nor stars appeared for
many days and the storm
continued raging, we finally gave up all hope of being
saved.
21After the men had gone
a long time without food,
Paul stood up before them
and said: "Men, you
should have taken my ad-
vice not to sail from Crete;
then you would have
spared yourselves this
damage and loss. 22But
now I urge you to keep up
your courage, because not
one of you will be lost; only
the ship will be destroyed.
23Last night an angel of the
God whose I am and whom
I serve stood beside me
24and said, 'Do not be
afraid, Paul. You must
stand trial before Caesar;
and God has graciously giv-
en you the lives of all who
sail with you.' 25So keep up
your courage, men, for I
have faith in God that it will
happen just as he told me.
26Nevertheless, we must
run aground on some is-
land."

The Shipwreck

27On the fourteenth night
we were still being driven
across the Adriatic[z] Sea,
when about midnight the
sailors sensed they were
approaching land. 28They
took soundings and found
that the water was a hun-
dred and twenty feet[a]
deep. A short time later

[z]27 In ancient times the name referred to an area extending well south of Italy.

[a]28 Greek *twenty orguias* (about 37 meters)

soundings again and found
fifteen fathoms. 29 Fearing
that we might run on the
rocks, they let down four
anchors from the stern and
prayed for day to come.
30 But when the sailors tried
to escape from the ship and
had lowered the boat into
the sea, on the pretext of
putting out anchors from
the bow, 31 Paul said to the
centurion and the soldiers,
"Unless these men stay in
the ship, you cannot be
saved." 32 Then the soldiers
cut away the ropes of the
boat and set it adrift.
33 Just before day-
break, Paul urged all of
them to take some food,
saying, "Today is the fourteenth day that you have
been in suspense and re-
maining without food, having eaten nothing. 34 Therefore I urge you to take some
food, for it will help you
survive; for none of you
will lose a hair from your
heads." 35 After he had said
this, he took bread; and
giving thanks to God in the
presence of all, he broke it
and began to eat. 36 Then all
of them were encouraged
and took food for them-
selves. 37 (We were in all
two hundred seventy-six[d]
persons in the ship.) 38 After they had satisfied their
hunger, they lightened the
ship by throwing the wheat
into the sea.

The Shipwreck

39 In the morning they
did not recognize the land,
but they noticed a bay with

διαστήσαντες καὶ πάλιν βολίσαντες εὗρον
1having moved also again sounding they found

ὀργυιὰς δεκαπέντε· 29 φοβούμενοί τε μή
fathoms fifteen; and fearing lest

που κατὰ τραχεῖς τόπους ἐκπέσωμεν,
2somewhere 3against 4rough 5places 1we might fall off,

ἐκ πρύμνης ῥίψαντες ἀγκύρας τέσσαρας
out of [the] stern throwing anchors four

ηὔχοντο ἡμέραν γενέσθαι. 30 Τῶν δὲ
they prayed day to become. And the

ναυτῶν ζητούντων φυγεῖν ἐκ τοῦ πλοίου
sailors seeking[a] to flee out of the ship
=when the sailors sought

καὶ χαλασάντων τὴν σκάφην εἰς τὴν
and lowering[a] the boat into the
=lowered

θάλασσαν προφάσει ὡς ἐκ πρῴρης ἀγκύρας
sea under pretence as 4out of 5[the] prow 3anchors

μελλόντων ἐκτείνειν, 31 εἶπεν ὁ Παῦλος
1intending 2to cast *out*, said – Paul

τῷ ἑκατοντάρχῃ καὶ τοῖς στρατιώταις·
to the centurion and to the soldiers:

ἐὰν μὴ οὗτοι μείνωσιν ἐν τῷ πλοίῳ,
Unless these remain in the ship,

ὑμεῖς σωθῆναι οὐ δύνασθε. 32 τότε
ye 2*to* be saved 1cannot. Then

ἀπέκοψαν οἱ στρατιῶται τὰ σχοινία τῆς
cut away the soldiers the ropes of the

σκάφης καὶ εἴασαν αὐτὴν ἐκπεσεῖν.
boat and let it *to* fall off.

33 Ἄχρι δὲ οὗ ἡμέρα ἤμελλεν γίνεσθαι,
And until day was about to come,

παρεκάλει ὁ Παῦλος ἅπαντας μεταλαβεῖν
besought – Paul all to partake

τροφῆς λέγων· τεσσαρεσκαιδεκάτην σήμερον
of food saying: 2[the] fourteenth 1To-day [is]

ἡμέραν προσδοκῶντες ἄσιτοι διατελεῖτε,
3day 5waiting 6without food 4ye continued,

μηθὲν προσλαβόμενοι. 34 διὸ παρακαλῶ
nothing taking. Wherefore I beseech

ὑμᾶς μεταλαβεῖν τροφῆς· τοῦτο γὰρ πρὸς
you to partake of food; for this to

τῆς ὑμετέρας σωτηρίας ὑπάρχει· οὐδενὸς
– your salvation is; 2of no one

γὰρ ὑμῶν θρὶξ ἀπὸ τῆς κεφαλῆς ἀπολεῖται.
1for of you a hair from the head shall perish.

35 εἴπας δὲ ταῦτα καὶ λαβὼν ἄρτον
And saying these things and taking bread

εὐχαρίστησεν τῷ θεῷ ἐνώπιον πάντων
he gave thanks – to God before all

καὶ κλάσας ἤρξατο ἐσθίειν. 36 εὔθυμοι δὲ
and breaking began to eat. And 4in good spirits

γενόμενοι πάντες καὶ αὐτοὶ προσελάβοντο
3becoming 1all 2also they took

τροφῆς. 37 ἤμεθα δὲ αἱ πᾶσαι ψυχαὶ
food. Now we were 2the 1all souls

ἐν τῷ πλοίῳ διακόσιαι ἑβδομήκοντα ἕξ.
in the ship two hundreds [and] seventy six.

38 κορεσθέντες δὲ τροφῆς ἐκούφιζον τὸ
And having been satisfied of(with) food they lightened the

πλοῖον ἐκβαλλόμενοι τὸν σῖτον εἰς τὴν
ship throwing out the wheat into the

θάλασσαν. 39 Ὅτε δὲ ἡμέρα ἐγένετο,
sea. And when day came,

τὴν γῆν οὐκ ἐπεγίνωσκον, κόλπον δέ
2the 3land 1they did not recognize, but 2bay

they took soundings again
and found it was ninety
feet[b] deep. 29Fearing that
we would be dashed
against the rocks, they
dropped four anchors from
the stern and prayed for
daylight. 30In an attempt to
escape from the ship, the
sailors let the lifeboat down
into the sea, pretending
they were going to lower
some anchors from the
bow. 31Then Paul said to
the centurion and the soldiers, "Unless these men
stay with the ship, you cannot be saved." 32So the soldiers cut the ropes that held
the lifeboat and let it fall
away.
33Just before dawn Paul
urged them all to eat. "For
the last fourteen days," he
said, "you have been in
constant suspense and
have gone without food—
you haven't eaten any-
thing. 34Now I urge you to
take some food. You need
it to survive. Not one of
you will lose a single hair
from his head." 35After he
said this, he took some
bread and gave thanks to
God in front of them all.
Then he broke it and began
to eat. 36They were all encouraged and ate some
food themselves. 37Alto-
gether there were 276 of us
on board. 38When they had
eaten as much as they
wanted, they lightened the
ship by throwing the grain
into the sea.
39When daylight came,
they did not recognize the
land, but they saw a bay

[d] Other ancient authorities read *seventy-six*; others, *about seventy-six*

[b] 28 Greek *fifteen orguias* (about 27 meters)

a beach, on which they planned to run the ship ashore, if they could. [40]So they cast off the anchors and left them in the sea. At the same time they loosened the ropes that tied the steering-oars; then hoisting the foresail to the wind, they made for the beach. [41]But striking a reef,[e] they ran the ship aground; the bow stuck and remained immovable, but the stern was being broken up by the force of the waves. [42]The soldiers' plan was to kill the prisoners, so that none might swim away and escape; [43]but the centurion, wishing to save Paul, kept them from carrying out their plan. He ordered those who could swim to jump overboard first and make for the land, [44]and the rest to follow, some on planks and others on pieces of the ship. And so it was that all were brought safely to land.

τινα κατενόουν ἔχοντα αἰγιαλόν, εἰς ὃν
[2]a certain [1]they noticed having a shore, into which
ἐβουλεύοντο εἰ δύναιντο ἐξῶσαι τὸ πλοῖον.
they were minded if they were able to drive the ship.
40 καὶ τὰς ἀγκύρας περιελόντες εἴων
And [2]the [3]anchors [1]having cast off they left [them]
εἰς τὴν θάλασσαν, ἅμα ἀνέντες τὰς
in the sea, at the same time loosening the
ζευκτηρίας τῶν πηδαλίων, καὶ ἐπάραντες
fastenings of the rudders, and raising
τὸν ἀρτέμωνα τῇ πνεούσῃ κατεῖχον εἰς
the foresail to the breeze they held [the ship] to
τὸν αἰγιαλόν. **41** περιπεσόντες δὲ εἰς
the shore. And coming upon *to*
τόπον διθάλασσον ἐπέκειλαν τὴν ναῦν,
a place between two seas they drove the vessel,
καὶ ἡ μὲν πρῷρα ἐρείσασα ἔμεινεν
and [2]the [1]while prow having run aground remained
ἀσάλευτος, ἡ δὲ πρύμνα ἐλύετο ὑπὸ
immovable, [2]the [1]yet stern was broken by
τῆς βίας. **42** Τῶν δὲ στρατιωτῶν βουλὴ
the force.* Now [2]of the [3]soldiers [1][the] mind
ἐγένετο ἵνα τοὺς δεσμώτας ἀποκτείνωσιν,
was that [2]the [3]prisoners [1]they should kill,
μή τις ἐκκολυμβήσας διαφύγῃ· **43** ὁ δὲ
lest anyone swimming out should escape; but the
ἑκατοντάρχης βουλόμενος διασῶσαι τὸν
centurion being minded to save –
Παῦλον ἐκώλυσεν αὐτοὺς τοῦ βουλήματος,
Paul forbade them the(ir) intention,
ἐκέλευσέν τε τοὺς δυναμένους κολυμβᾶν
and commanded the [ones] being able to swim
ἀπορίψαντας πρώτους ἐπὶ τὴν γῆν
casting [themselves] overboard first onto the land
ἐξιέναι, **44** καὶ τοὺς λοιποὺς οὓς μὲν ἐπὶ
to go out, and the rest some on
σανίσιν, οὓς δὲ ἐπί τινων τῶν ἀπὸ τοῦ
planks, others on some of the things from the
πλοίου. καὶ οὕτως ἐγένετο πάντας
ship. And thus it came to pass all
διασωθῆναι ἐπὶ τὴν γῆν.
to be saved on the land.

with a sandy beach, where they decided to run the ship aground if they could. [40]Cutting loose the anchors, they left them in the sea and at the same time untied the ropes that held the rudders. Then they hoisted the foresail to the wind and made for the beach. [41]But the ship struck a sandbar and ran aground. The bow stuck fast and would not move, and the stern was broken to pieces by the pounding of the surf.

[42]The soldiers planned to kill the prisoners to prevent any of them from swimming away and escaping. [43]But the centurion wanted to spare Paul's life and kept them from carrying out their plan. He ordered those who could swim to jump overboard first and get to land. [44]The rest were to get there on planks or on pieces of the ship. In this way everyone reached land in safety.

Chapter 28

Paul on the Island of Malta

AFTER we had reached safety, we then learned that the island was called Malta. [2]The natives showed us unusual kindness. Since it had begun to rain and was cold, they kindled a fire and welcomed all of us around it. [3]Paul had gathered a bundle of brushwood and was putting it on the fire, when a viper, driven out by the heat, fastened itself on his hand. [4]When the natives saw the crea-

28 Καὶ διασωθέντες τότε ἐπέγνωμεν ὅτι
And having been saved then we found out that
Μελίτη ἡ νῆσος καλεῖται. **2** οἵ τε
Melita the island is(was) called. And the
βάρβαροι παρεῖχον οὐ τὴν τυχοῦσαν
foreigners [1]showed [2]not [4]the [5]ordinary
φιλανθρωπίαν ἡμῖν· ἅψαντες γὰρ πυρὰν
[6]kindness [3]us; for having lit a fire
προσελάβοντο πάντας ἡμᾶς διὰ τὸν ὑετὸν
they welcomed [2]all [1]us because of the rain
τὸν ἐφεστῶτα καὶ διὰ τὸ ψῦχος. **3** συστρέ-
– coming on and because of the cold. col-
ψαντος δὲ τοῦ Παύλου φρυγάνων τι
lecting And – Paul[a] [3]of sticks [1]a
=when Paul collected
πλῆθος καὶ ἐπιθέντος ἐπὶ τὴν πυράν,
[2]quantity and putting *on*[a] on the fire,
=put them
ἔχιδνα ἀπὸ τῆς θέρμης ἐξελθοῦσα καθῆψεν
a snake from the heat coming out fastened on
τῆς χειρὸς αὐτοῦ. **4** ὡς δὲ εἶδον οἱ
the hand of him. And when [3]saw [1]the

Chapter 28

Ashore on Malta

ONCE safely on shore, we found out that the island was called Malta. [2]The islanders showed us unusual kindness. They built a fire and welcomed us all because it was raining and cold. [3]Paul gathered a pile of brushwood and, as he put it on the fire, a viper, driven out by the heat, fastened itself on his hand. [4]When the islanders saw

[e] Gk *place of two seas*

* That is, of the waves, as indeed some MSS have.

ture hanging from his hand,
they said to one another,
"This man must be a mur-
derer; though he has es-
caped from the sea, justice
has not allowed him to
live." 5 He, however, shook
off the creature into the fire
and suffered no harm.
6 They were expecting him
to swell up or drop dead,
but after they had waited a
long time and saw that
nothing unusual had hap-
pened to him, they changed
their minds and began to
say that he was a god.
7 Now in the neighbor-
hood of that place were
lands belonging to the leading man of the island,
named Publius, who re-
ceived us and entertained
us hospitably for three
days. 8 It so happened that
the father of Publius lay
sick in bed with fever and
dysentery. Paul visited him
and cured him by praying
and putting his hands on
him. 9 After this happened,
the rest of the people on the
island who had diseases
also came and were cured.
10 They bestowed many
honors on us, and when we
were about to sail, they put
on board all the provisions
we needed.

Paul Arrives at Rome

11 Three months later
we set sail on a ship that
had wintered at the island,
an Alexandrian ship with
the Twin Brothers as its figurehead. 12 We put in at
Syracuse and stayed there
for three days; 13 then we
weighed anchor and came
to Rhegium. After one day

βάρβαροι κρεμάμενον τὸ θηρίον ἐκ τῆς
[2]foreigners [6]hanging [4]the [5]beast from the
χειρὸς αὐτοῦ, πρὸς ἀλλήλους ἔλεγον·
hand of him, to one another they said:
πάντως φονεύς ἐστιν ὁ ἄνθρωπος οὗτος,
To be sure [4]a murderer [3]is [1]this man,
ὃν διασωθέντα ἐκ τῆς θαλάσσης ἡ δίκη
whom having been saved out of the sea – justice
ζῆν οὐκ εἴασεν. 5 ὁ μὲν οὖν ἀποτινάξας
[2]to live [1]did not allow. He – then shaking off
τὸ θηρίον εἰς τὸ πῦρ ἔπαθεν οὐδὲν
the beast into the fire suffered no
κακόν· 6 οἱ δὲ προσεδόκων αὐτὸν μέλλειν
harm; but they expected him to be about
πίμπρασθαι ἢ καταπίπτειν ἄφνω νεκρόν.
to swell or to fall down suddenly dead.
ἐπὶ πολὺ δὲ αὐτῶν προσδοκώντων καὶ
But over much [time] they expecting and
= while they expected and beheld
θεωρούντων μηδὲν ἄτοπον εἰς αὐτὸν
beholding[a] nothing amiss [2]to [3]him
γινόμενον, μεταβαλόμενοι ἔλεγον αὐτὸν εἶναι
[1]happening, changing their minds they said him to be
θεόν. 7 Ἐν δὲ τοῖς περὶ τὸν τόπον
a god. Now in the [parts] about – place
ἐκεῖνον ὑπῆρχεν χωρία τῷ πρώτῳ τῆς
that were lands to the chief man[c] of the
= the chief man . . . had lands
νήσου ὀνόματι Ποπλίῳ, ὃς ἀναδεξάμενος
island by name Publius, who welcoming
ἡμᾶς ἡμέρας τρεῖς φιλοφρόνως ἐξένισεν.
us [4]days [3]three [2]friendlily [1]lodged [us].
8 ἐγένετο δὲ τὸν πατέρα τοῦ Ποπλίου
Now it happened the father – of Publius
πυρετοῖς καὶ δυσεντερίῳ συνεχόμενον
[3]feverish attacks [4]and [5]dysentery [2]suffering from
κατακεῖσθαι, πρὸς ὃν ὁ Παῦλος εἰσελθὼν
[1]to be lying down, to whom – Paul entering
καὶ προσευξάμενος, ἐπιθεὶς τὰς χεῖρας
and praying, [1]putting [4]on [2]the(his) [3]hands
αὐτῷ ἰάσατο αὐτόν. 9 τούτου δὲ γενομένου
[5]him cured him. And this happening[a]
= when this happened
καὶ οἱ λοιποὶ οἱ ἐν τῇ νήσῳ ἔχοντες
[3]also [1]the [2]rest – in the island having
ἀσθενείας προσήρχοντο καὶ ἐθεραπεύοντο,
ailments came up and were healed,
10 οἳ καὶ πολλαῖς τιμαῖς ἐτίμησαν ἡμᾶς
who also with many honours honoured us
καὶ ἀναγομένοις ἐπέθεντο τὰ πρὸς τὰς
and on our putting to sea placed on [us] the things for the(our)
χρείας.
needs.
11 Μετὰ δὲ τρεῖς μῆνας ἀνήχθημεν ἐν
And after three months we embarked in
πλοίῳ παρακεχειμακότι ἐν τῇ νήσῳ,
a ship having passed the winter in the island,
Ἀλεξανδρίνῳ, παρασήμῳ Διοσκούροις. 12 καὶ
an Alexandrian, with a sign Dioscuri. And
καταχθέντες εἰς Συρακούσας ἐπεμείναμεν
being brought to land to(at) Syracuse we remained
ἡμέρας τρεῖς, 13 ὅθεν περιελθόντες κατην-
days three, whence tacking we ar-
τήσαμεν εἰς Ῥήγιον. καὶ μετὰ μίαν
rived at Rhegium. And after one

the snake hanging from his
hand, they said to each other, "This man must be a
murderer; for though he escaped from the sea, Justice
has not allowed him to
live." 5 But Paul shook the
snake off into the fire and
suffered no ill effects. 6 The
people expected him to
swell up or suddenly fall
dead, but after waiting a
long time and seeing nothing unusual happen to him,
they changed their minds
and said he was a god.
7 There was an estate
nearby that belonged to
Publius, the chief official of
the island. He welcomed us
to his home and for three
days entertained us hospitably. 8 His father was sick
in bed, suffering from fever
and dysentery. Paul went
in to see him and, after
prayer, placed his hands on
him and healed him. 9 When
this had happened, the rest
of the sick on the island
came and were cured.
10 They honored us in many
ways and when we were
ready to sail, they fur-
nished us with the supplies
we needed.

Arrival at Rome

11 After three months we
put out to sea in a ship that
had wintered in the island.
It was an Alexandrian ship
with the figurehead of the
twin gods Castor and Pol-
lux. 12 We put in at Syracuse and stayed there three
days. 13 From there we set
sail and arrived at Rhegi-

there a south wind sprang
up, and on the second day
we came to Puteoli.
14 There we found believ-
ers[f] and were invited to
stay with them for seven
days. And so we came to
Rome. 15 The believers[f]
from there, when they
heard of us, came as far as
the Forum of Appius and
Three Taverns to meet us.
On seeing them, Paul
thanked God and took
courage.
16 When we came into
Rome, Paul was allowed to
live by himself, with the
soldier who was guarding
him.

Paul and Jewish Leaders in Rome

17 Three days later he
called together the local
leaders of the Jews. When
they had assembled, he
said to them, "Brothers,
though I had done nothing
against our people or the
customs of our ancestors,
yet I was arrested in Jerusalem and handed over to
the Romans. 18 When they
had examined me, the Ro-
mans[g] wanted to release
me, because there was no
reason for the death penalty in my case. 19 But when
the Jews objected, I was
compelled to appeal to the
emperor—even though I
had no charge to bring
against my nation. 20 For
this reason therefore I have
asked to see you and speak
with you,[h] since it is for
the sake of the hope of Israel that I am bound with this
chain." 21 They replied,
"We have received no let-
ters from Judea about you,

ἡμέραν ἐπιγενομένου νότου δευτεραῖοι
day coming on a south wind[a] on the second day
=as a south wind came on

ἤλθομεν εἰς Ποτιόλους, 14 οὗ εὑρόντες
we came to Puteoli, where having found

ἀδελφοὺς παρεκλήθημεν παρ' αὐτοῖς ἐπιμεῖναι
brothers we were besought with them to remain

ἡμέρας ἑπτά· καὶ οὕτως εἰς τὴν Ῥώμην
days seven; and thus to – Rome

ἤλθαμεν. 15 κἀκεῖθεν οἱ ἀδελφοὶ ἀκούσαντες
we went. And thence the brothers having heard

τὰ περὶ ἡμῶν ἦλθαν εἰς ἀπάντησιν ἡμῖν
the things con- cerning us came to a meeting with us

ἄχρι Ἀππίου φόρου καὶ Τριῶν ταβερνῶν,
as far as Appii Forum and Three Taverns,

οὓς ἰδὼν ὁ Παῦλος εὐχαριστήσας τῷ
whom seeing – Paul thanking –

θεῷ ἔλαβε θάρσος. 16 Ὅτε δὲ εἰσήλθομεν
God he took courage. And when we entered

εἰς Ῥώμην, ἐπετράπη τῷ Παύλῳ μένειν
into Rome, he* permitted – Paul to remain

καθ' ἑαυτὸν σὺν τῷ φυλάσσοντι αὐτὸν
by himself with [1]the [3]guarding [4]him

στρατιώτῃ.
[2]soldier.

17 Ἐγένετο δὲ μετὰ ἡμέρας τρεῖς
And it came to pass after days three

συγκαλέσασθαι αὐτὸν τοὺς ὄντας τῶν
to call together him[b] the [ones] being of the
=he called together

Ἰουδαίων πρώτους· συνελθόντων δὲ αὐτῶν
Jews first(chief); and coming together them[a]
=and when they came together

ἔλεγεν πρὸς αὐτούς· ἐγώ, ἄνδρες ἀδελφοί,
he said to them: I, *men* brothers,

οὐδὲν ἐναντίον ποιήσας τῷ λαῷ ἢ τοῖς
[2]nothing [3]contrary [1]having done to the people or to the

ἔθεσι τοῖς πατρῴοις, δέσμιος ἐξ Ἱεροσο-
customs – ancestral, a prisoner from Jeru-

λύμων παρεδόθην εἰς τὰς χεῖρας τῶν
salem I was delivered into the hands of the

Ῥωμαίων, 18 οἵτινες ἀνακρίναντές με ἐβούλοντο
Romans, who having examined me were minded

ἀπολῦσαι διὰ τὸ μηδεμίαν αἰτίαν θανάτου
to release on account of – no cause of death

ὑπάρχειν ἐν ἐμοί· 19 ἀντιλεγόντων δὲ
to be in me; but speaking against [this]
=when the Jews spoke

τῶν Ἰουδαίων ἠναγκάσθην ἐπικαλέσασθαι
the Jews[a] I was compelled to appeal to
against this

Καίσαρα, οὐχ ὡς τοῦ ἔθνους μου ἔχων
Cæsar, not as [4]the [5]nation [6]of me [1]having

τι κατηγορεῖν. 20 διὰ ταύτην οὖν τὴν
[2]anything [3]to accuse. [1]On account of [3]this [4]therefore –

αἰτίαν παρεκάλεσα ὑμᾶς ἰδεῖν καὶ προσ-
[2]cause I called you to see and to

λαλῆσαι· εἵνεκεν γὰρ τῆς ἐλπίδος τοῦ
speak to; for for the sake of the hope –

Ἰσραὴλ τὴν ἅλυσιν ταύτην περίκειμαι.
of Israel [2]this [3]chain [1]I have round [me].

21 οἱ δὲ πρὸς αὐτὸν εἶπαν· ἡμεῖς οὔτε
And they to him said: We neither

γράμματα περὶ σοῦ ἐδεξάμεθα ἀπὸ τῆς
[2]letters [3]about [4]thee [1]received from –

um. The next day the south
wind came up, and on the
following day we reached
Puteoli. 14 There we found
some brothers who invited
us to spend a week with
them. And so we came to
Rome. 15 The brothers there
had heard that we were
coming, and they traveled
as far as the Forum of Appius and the Three Taverns
to meet us. At the sight of
these men Paul thanked
God and was encouraged.
16 When we got to Rome,
Paul was allowed to live by
himself, with a soldier to
guard him.

Paul Preaches at Rome Under Guard

17 Three days later he
called together the leaders
of the Jews. When they had
assembled, Paul said to
them: "My brothers, al-
though I have done nothing
against our people or
against the customs of our
ancestors, I was arrested in
Jerusalem and handed over
to the Romans. 18 They examined me and wanted to
release me, because I was
not guilty of any crime deserving death. 19 But when
the Jews objected, I was
compelled to appeal to
Caesar—not that I had any
charge to bring against my
own people. 20 For this reason I have asked to see you
and talk with you. It is because of the hope of Israel
that I am bound with this
chain."
21 They replied, "We have
not received any letters
from Judea concerning

[f] Gk *brothers*
[g] Gk *they*
[h] Or *I have asked you to see me and speak with me*

* That is, the officer to whom Paul was handed over by the centurion Julius.

and none of the brothers
coming here has reported
or spoken anything evil
about you. 22 But we would
like to hear from you what
you think, for with regard
to this sect we know that
everywhere it is spoken
against."

Paul Preaches in Rome

23 After they had set a
day to meet with him, they
came to him at his lodgings
in great numbers. From
morning until evening he
explained the matter to
them, testifying to the kingdom of God and trying to
convince them about Jesus
both from the law of Moses
and from the prophets.
24 Some were convinced by
what he had said, while
others refused to believe.
25 So they disagreed with
each other; and as they
were leaving, Paul made
one further statement:
"The Holy Spirit was right
in saying to your ancestors
through the prophet Isaiah,
26 'Go to this people and
say,
You will indeed listen,
but never
understand,
and you will indeed
look, but never
perceive.
27 For this people's
heart has
grown dull,
and their ears are
hard of hearing,
and they have
shut their eyes;
so that they might
not look with
their eyes,
and listen with their
ears,
and understand with
their heart and
turn—
and I would heal
them.'
28 Let it be known to you
then that this salvation of
God has been sent to the
Gentiles; they will lis-
ten."[i]
30 He lived there two
whole years at his own expense[j] and welcomed all

[i]Other ancient authorities add verse 29, *And when he had said these words, the Jews departed, arguing vigorously among themselves*
[j]Or *in his own hired dwelling*

Ἰουδαίας, οὔτε παραγενόμενός τις τῶν
Judæa, nor arriving anyone of the
ἀδελφῶν ἀπήγγειλεν ἢ ἐλάλησέν τι περὶ
brothers told or spoke anything [2]about
σοῦ πονηρόν. 22 ἀξιοῦμεν δὲ παρὰ σοῦ
[3]thee [1]evil. But we think fit from thee
ἀκοῦσαι ἃ φρονεῖς· περὶ μὲν γὰρ τῆς
to hear what things thou thinkest; [5]concerning [2]indeed [1]for –
αἱρέσεως ταύτης γνωστὸν ἡμῖν ἐστιν ὅτι
[6]sect [4]this [7]known [8]to us [3]it is that
πανταχοῦ ἀντιλέγεται. 23 Ταξάμενοι δὲ
everywhere it is spoken against. And arranging
αὐτῷ ἡμέραν ἦλθον πρὸς αὐτὸν εἰς τὴν
with him a day [2]came [3]to [4]him [5]in [6]the(his)
ξενίαν πλείονες, οἷς ἐξετίθετο διαμαρτυρ-
[7]lodging [1]more, to whom he set forth solemnly
όμενος τὴν βασιλείαν τοῦ θεοῦ, πείθων
witnessing the kingdom – of God, [2]persuading
τε αὐτοὺς περὶ τοῦ Ἰησοῦ ἀπό τε τοῦ
[1]and them concerning – Jesus from both the
νόμου Μωϋσέως καὶ τῶν προφητῶν, ἀπὸ
law of Moses and the prophets, from
πρωῒ ἕως ἑσπέρας. 24 καὶ οἱ μὲν
morning until evening. And some
ἐπείθοντο τοῖς λεγομένοις, 25 οἱ δὲ
were persuaded by the things being said, others
ἠπίστουν· ἀσύμφωνοι δὲ ὄντες πρὸς ἀλλή-
disbelieved; and [2]disagreed [1]being with one an-
λους ἀπελύοντο, εἰπόντος τοῦ Παύλου
other they were dismissed, having said – Paul[a]
=after Paul had said
ῥῆμα ἕν, ὅτι καλῶς τὸ πνεῦμα τὸ ἅγιον
word one, – Well the Spirit – Holy
ἐλάλησεν διὰ Ἠσαΐου τοῦ προφήτου πρὸς
spoke through Esaias the prophet to
τοὺς πατέρας ὑμῶν 26 λέγων· πορεύθητι
the fathers of you saying: Go thou
πρὸς τὸν λαὸν τοῦτον καὶ εἰπόν· ἀκοῇ
to this people and say: In hearing
ἀκούσετε καὶ οὐ μὴ συνῆτε, καὶ βλέποντες
ye will hear and by no means understand, and looking
βλέψετε καὶ οὐ μὴ ἴδητε· 27 ἐπαχύνθη
ye will look and by no means see; [2]was thickened
γὰρ ἡ καρδία τοῦ λαοῦ τούτου, καὶ
[1]for the heart of this people, and
τοῖς ὠσὶν βαρέως ἤκουσαν, καὶ τοὺς
with the(ir) ears heavily they heard, and the
ὀφθαλμοὺς αὐτῶν ἐκάμμυσαν· μήποτε ἴδωσιν
eyes of them they closed; lest at any time they see
τοῖς ὀφθαλμοῖς καὶ τοῖς ὠσὶν ἀκούσωσιν
with the eyes and with the ears hear
καὶ τῇ καρδίᾳ συνῶσιν καὶ ἐπιστρέψωσιν,
and with the heart understand and turn,
καὶ ἰάσομαι αὐτούς. 28 γνωστὸν οὖν
and I shall cure them. Known therefore
ἔστω ὑμῖν ὅτι τοῖς ἔθνεσιν ἀπεστάλη
let it be to you that to the nations was sent
τοῦτο τὸ σωτήριον τοῦ θεοῦ· αὐτοὶ καὶ
this – salvation – of God; and they
ἀκούσονται.‡
will hear.
30 Ἐνέμεινεν δὲ διετίαν ὅλην ἐν ἰδίῳ
And he remained a whole two years in [his] own
μισθώματι, καὶ ἀπεδέχετο πάντας τοὺς
hired apartment, and welcomed all the

‡ Verse 29 omitted by Nestle; *cf.* NIV footnote.

you, and none of the brothers who have come from
there has reported or said
anything bad about you.
22 But we want to hear what
your views are, for we
know that people every-
where are talking against
this sect."
23 They arranged to meet
Paul on a certain day, and
came in even larger num-
bers to the place where he
was staying. From morning
till evening he explained
and declared to them the
kingdom of God and tried
to convince them about
Jesus from the Law of Mo-
ses and from the Prophets.
24 Some were convinced by
what he said, but others
would not believe. 25 They
disagreed among them-
selves and began to leave
after Paul had made this final statement: "The Holy
Spirit spoke the truth to
your forefathers when he
said through Isaiah the
prophet:

26 " 'Go to this people and
say,
"You will be ever
hearing but never
understanding;
you will be ever seeing
but never
perceiving."
27 For this people's heart
has become
calloused;
they hardly hear with
their ears,
and they have closed
their eyes.
Otherwise they might
see with their eyes,
hear with their ears,
understand with their
hearts
and turn, and I would
heal them.'[c]

28 "Therefore I want you
to know that God's salva-
tion has been sent to the
Gentiles, and they will listen!"[d]
30 For two whole years
Paul stayed there in his
own rented house and wel-

[c]27 Isaiah 6:9,10
[d]28 Some manuscripts *listen!"*
29 *After he said this, the Jews left, arguing vigorously among themselves.*

who came to him, [31]proclaiming the kingdom of
God and teaching about the
Lord Jesus Christ with all
boldness and without hindrance.

εἰσπορευομένους πρὸς αὐτόν, 31 κηρύσσων
[ones] coming in to him, proclaiming
τὴν βασιλείαν τοῦ θεοῦ καὶ διδάσκων
the kingdom – of God and teaching
τὰ περὶ τοῦ κυρίου Ἰησοῦ Χριστοῦ
the things concerning the Lord Jesus Christ
μετὰ πάσης παρρησίας ἀκωλύτως.
with all boldness unhinderedly.

comed all who came to see
him. [31]Boldly and without
hindrance he preached the
kingdom of God and taught
about the Lord Jesus
Christ.

The Letter of Paul to
the
Romans

Chapter 1

Salutation

PAUL, a servant[a] of
Jesus Christ, called to
be an apostle, set apart for
the gospel of God, 2 which
he promised beforehand
through his prophets in the
holy scriptures, 3 the gospel
concerning his Son, who
was descended from David
according to the flesh 4 and
was declared to be Son of
God with power according
to the spirit[b] of holiness by
resurrection from the dead,
Jesus Christ our Lord,
5 through whom we have
received grace and apostleship to bring about the obedience of faith among all
the Gentiles for the sake of
his name, 6 including yourselves who are called to belong to Jesus Christ,
7 To all God's beloved
in Rome, who are called to
be saints:
Grace to you and peace
from God our Father and
the Lord Jesus Christ.

Prayer of Thanksgiving

8 First, I thank my God
through Jesus Christ for all
of you, because your faith
is proclaimed throughout
the world. 9 For God,
whom I serve with my spirit by announcing the gos-
pel[c] of his Son, is my witness that without ceasing I
remember you always in
my prayers, 10 asking that
by God's will I may some-
how at last succeed in coming to you. 11 For I am longing to see you so that I may
share with you some spiritual gift to strengthen
you— 12 or rather so that
we may be mutually en-
couraged by each other's
faith, both yours and mine.

[a] Gk *slave*
[b] Or *Spirit*
[c] Gk *my spirit in the gospel*

ΠΡΟΣ ΡΩΜΑΙΟΥΣ
To Romans

1 Παῦλος δοῦλος Χριστοῦ Ἰησοῦ, κλητὸς
Paul a slave of Christ Jesus, called

ἀπόστολος ἀφωρισμένος εἰς εὐαγγέλιον
an apostle *having been* separated to [the] gospel

θεοῦ, **2** ὃ προεπηγγείλατο διὰ τῶν
of God, which he promised beforehand through the

προφητῶν αὐτοῦ ἐν γραφαῖς ἁγίαις **3** περὶ
prophets of him in writings holy concerning

τοῦ υἱοῦ αὐτοῦ τοῦ γενομένου ἐκ
the Son of him – come of

σπέρματος Δαυὶδ κατὰ σάρκα, **4** τοῦ
[the] seed of David according to [the] flesh, –

ὁρισθέντος υἱοῦ θεοῦ ἐν δυνάμει
designated Son of God in power

κατὰ πνεῦμα ἁγιωσύνης ἐξ ἀναστάσεως
according to [the] Spirit of holiness by a resurrection

νεκρῶν, Ἰησοῦ Χριστοῦ τοῦ κυρίου ἡμῶν,
of dead persons, Jesus Christ the Lord of us,

5 δι᾽ οὗ ἐλάβομεν χάριν καὶ ἀποστολὴν
through whom we received grace and apostleship

εἰς ὑπακοὴν πίστεως ἐν πᾶσιν τοῖς
for obedience of faith among all the

ἔθνεσιν ὑπὲρ τοῦ ὀνόματος αὐτοῦ, **6** ἐν
nations on behalf of the name of him, among

οἷς ἐστε καὶ ὑμεῖς κλητοὶ Ἰησοῦ Χριστοῦ,
whom are also ye called of Jesus Christ,

7 πᾶσιν τοῖς οὖσιν ἐν Ῥώμῃ ἀγαπητοῖς
to all the [ones] being in Rome beloved

θεοῦ, κλητοῖς ἁγίοις· χάρις ὑμῖν καὶ
of God, called holy: Grace to you and

εἰρήνη ἀπὸ θεοῦ πατρὸς ἡμῶν καὶ κυρίου
peace from God [the] Father of us and Lord

Ἰησοῦ Χριστοῦ.
Jesus Christ.

8 Πρῶτον μὲν εὐχαριστῶ τῷ θεῷ μου
Firstly – I thank the God of me

διὰ Ἰησοῦ Χριστοῦ περὶ πάντων ὑμῶν,
through Jesus Christ concerning all you,

ὅτι ἡ πίστις ὑμῶν καταγγέλλεται ἐν
because the faith of you is being announced in

ὅλῳ τῷ κόσμῳ. **9** μάρτυς γάρ μού
all the world. For witness of me

ἐστιν ὁ θεός, ᾧ λατρεύω ἐν τῷ πνεύματί
is – God, whom I serve in the spirit

μου ἐν τῷ εὐαγγελίῳ τοῦ υἱοῦ αὐτοῦ,
of me in the gospel of the Son of him,

ὡς ἀδιαλείπτως μνείαν ὑμῶν ποιοῦμαι
how unceasingly mention of you I make

10 πάντοτε ἐπὶ τῶν προσευχῶν μου,
always on(in) the prayers of me,

δεόμενος εἴ πως ἤδη ποτὲ εὐοδω-
requesting if somehow now at some time I shall have

θήσομαι ἐν τῷ θελήματι τοῦ θεοῦ ἐλθεῖν
a happy journey in the will – of God to come

πρὸς ὑμᾶς. **11** ἐπιποθῶ γὰρ ἰδεῖν ὑμᾶς,
unto you. For I long to see you,

ἵνα τι μεταδῶ χάρισμα ὑμῖν πνευματικὸν
that [3]some [1]I may impart [4]gift [5]to you [2]spiritual

εἰς τὸ στηριχθῆναι ὑμᾶς, **12** τοῦτο δέ
for the to be established you,[b] and this
=that ye may be established,

ἐστιν συμπαρακληθῆναι ἐν ὑμῖν διὰ τῆς
is to be encouraged *with* among you through [1]the

ἐν ἀλλήλοις πίστεως ὑμῶν τε καὶ ἐμοῦ.
[3]in [4]one another [2]faith [6]of you [5]both [7]and [8]of me.

Romans

Chapter 1

PAUL, a servant of
Christ Jesus, called to
be an apostle and set apart
for the gospel of God—
2 the gospel he promised beforehand through his
prophets in the Holy Scriptures 3 regarding his Son,
who as to his human nature
was a descendant of David,
4 and who through the Spirit[a] of holiness was declared
with power to be the Son of
God[b] by his resurrection
from the dead: Jesus Christ
our Lord. 5 Through him
and for his name's sake, we
received grace and apostleship to call people from
among all the Gentiles to
the obedience that comes
from faith. 6 And you also
are among those who are
called to belong to Jesus
Christ.

7 To all in Rome who are
loved by God and called to
be saints:

Grace and peace to you
from God our Father and
from the Lord Jesus Christ.

Paul's Longing to Visit Rome

8 First, I thank my God
through Jesus Christ for all
of you, because your faith
is being reported all over
the world. 9 God, whom I
serve with my whole heart
in preaching the gospel of
his Son, is my witness how
constantly I remember you
10 in my prayers at all times;
and I pray that now at last
by God's will the way may
be opened for me to come
to you.
11 I long to see you so that
I may impart to you some
spiritual gift to make you
strong— 12 that is, that you
and I may be mutually en-
couraged by each other's

[a] 4 Or *who as to his spirit*
[b] 4 Or *was appointed to be the Son of God with power*

13 I want you to know, brothers and sisters,[d] that I have often intended to come to you (but thus far have been prevented), in order that I may reap some harvest among you as I have among the rest of the Gentiles. 14 I am a debtor both to Greeks and to barbarians, both to the wise and to the foolish 15—hence my eagerness to proclaim the gospel to you also who are in Rome.

The Power of the Gospel

16 For I am not ashamed of the gospel; it is the power of God for salvation to everyone who has faith, to the Jew first and also to the Greek. 17 For in it the righteousness of God is revealed through faith for faith; as it is written, "The one who is righteous will live by faith."[e]

The Guilt of Humankind

18 For the wrath of God is revealed from heaven against all ungodliness and wickedness of those who by their wickedness suppress the truth. 19 For what can be known about God is plain to them, because God has shown it to them. 20 Ever since the creation of the world his eternal power and divine nature, invisible though they are, have been understood and seen through the things he has made. So they are without excuse; 21 for though they knew God, they did not honor him as God or give thanks to him, but they became futile in their thinking, and their senseless minds were darkened. 22 Claiming to be wise, they became fools; 23 and they exchanged the glory of the immortal God for images resembling a mortal human being or birds or four-footed animals or reptiles.

13 οὐ θέλω δὲ ὑμᾶς ἀγνοεῖν, ἀδελφοί,
[3]not [2]I wish [1]But you to be ignorant, brothers,
ὅτι πολλάκις προεθέμην ἐλθεῖν πρὸς ὑμᾶς,
that often I purposed to come unto you,
καὶ ἐκωλύθην ἄχρι τοῦ δεῦρο, ἵνα τινὰ
and was hindered until the present, that some
καρπὸν σχῶ καὶ ἐν ὑμῖν καθὼς καὶ
fruit I may have also among you as indeed
ἐν τοῖς λοιποῖς ἔθνεσιν. **14** Ἕλλησίν
among the remaining nations. [2]to Greeks
τε καὶ βαρβάροις, σοφοῖς τε καὶ ἀνοήτοις
[1]Both [3]and [4]to foreigners, [6]to wise men [5]both [7]and [8]to foolish
ὀφειλέτης εἰμί· **15** οὕτως τὸ κατ' ἐμὲ
[10]a debtor [9]I am; so as far as in me lies†
πρόθυμον καὶ ὑμῖν τοῖς ἐν Ῥώμῃ
[I am] eager [2]also [3]to you [4]*the [ones]* [5]in [6]Rome
εὐαγγελίσασθαι. **16** οὐ γὰρ ἐπαισχύνομαι
[1]to preach. For I am not ashamed of
τὸ εὐαγγέλιον· δύναμις γὰρ θεοῦ ἐστιν
the gospel; [2]power [1]for of God it is
εἰς σωτηρίαν παντὶ τῷ πιστεύοντι, Ἰουδαίῳ
to salvation to everyone believing, [2]to Jew
τε πρῶτον καὶ Ἕλληνι. **17** δικαιοσύνη
[1]both firstly and to Greek. a righteousness
γὰρ θεοῦ ἐν αὐτῷ ἀποκαλύπτεται ἐκ
For of God in it is revealed from
πίστεως εἰς πίστιν, καθὼς γέγραπται·
faith to faith, as it has been written:
ὁ δὲ δίκαιος ἐκ πίστεως ζήσεται.
Now the just man by faith will live.
18 Ἀποκαλύπτεται γὰρ ὀργὴ θεοῦ ἀπ'
For [4]is revealed [1][the] [2]wrath [3]of God from
οὐρανοῦ ἐπὶ πᾶσαν ἀσέβειαν καὶ ἀδικίαν
heaven against all impiety and unrighteousness
ἀνθρώπων τῶν τὴν ἀλήθειαν ἐν ἀδικίᾳ
of men – [2]the [3]truth [4]in [5]unrighteousness
κατεχόντων, **19** διότι τὸ γνωστὸν τοῦ θεοῦ
[1]holding fast, because the thing known – of God
φανερόν ἐστιν ἐν αὐτοῖς· ὁ θεὸς γὰρ αὐτοῖς
manifest is among them; – for God to them
ἐφανέρωσεν. **20** τὰ γὰρ ἀόρατα αὐτοῦ
manifested [it]. For the invisible things of him
ἀπὸ κτίσεως κόσμου τοῖς ποιήμασιν
[2]from [3][the] [4]creation [5]of [the] world [7]by the [8]things made
νοούμενα καθορᾶται, ἥ τε
[6]being understood [1]is(are) clearly seen, [10]the [9]both
ἀΐδιος αὐτοῦ δύναμις καὶ θειότης, εἰς
[11]everlasting [15]of him [12]power [13]and [14]divinity, for
τὸ εἶναι αὐτοὺς ἀναπολογήτους, **21** διότι
the to be them[b] without excuse, because
=so that they are
γνόντες τὸν θεὸν οὐχ ὡς θεὸν ἐδόξασαν
knowing – God [2]not [3]as [4]God [1]they glorified [him]
ἢ ηὐχαρίστησαν, ἀλλὰ ἐματαιώθησαν ἐν
[5]or [6]thanked [him], but became vain in
τοῖς διαλογισμοῖς αὐτῶν, καὶ ἐσκοτίσθη
the reasonings of them, and [5]was darkened
ἡ ἀσύνετος αὐτῶν καρδία. **22** φάσκοντες
[1]the [2]undiscerning [4]of them [3]heart. Asserting
εἶναι σοφοὶ ἐμωράνθησαν, **23** καὶ ἤλλαξαν
to be wise they became foolish, and changed
τὴν δόξαν τοῦ ἀφθάρτου θεοῦ ἐν ὁμοιώματι
the glory of the incorruptible God in[to] a likeness
εἰκόνος φθαρτοῦ ἀνθρώπου καὶ πετεινῶν
of an image of corruptible man and birds
καὶ τετραπόδων καὶ ἑρπετῶν· **24** διὸ
and quadrupeds and reptiles; wherefore

faith. 13 I do not want you to be unaware, brothers, that I planned many times to come to you (but have been prevented from doing so until now) in order that I might have a harvest among you, just as I have had among the other Gentiles.

14 I am obligated both to Greeks and non-Greeks, both to the wise and the foolish. 15 That is why I am so eager to preach the gospel also to you who are at Rome.

16 I am not ashamed of the gospel, because it is the power of God for the salvation of everyone who believes: first for the Jew, then for the Gentile. 17 For in the gospel a righteousness from God is revealed, a righteousness that is by faith from first to last,[c] just as it is written: "The righteous will live by faith."[d]

God's Wrath Against Mankind

18 The wrath of God is being revealed from heaven against all the godlessness and wickedness of men who suppress the truth by their wickedness, 19 since what may be known about God is plain to them, because God has made it plain to them. 20 For since the creation of the world God's invisible qualities—his eternal power and divine nature—have been clearly seen, being understood from what has been made, so that men are without excuse.

21 For although they knew God, they neither glorified him as God nor gave thanks to him, but their thinking became futile and their foolish hearts were darkened. 22 Although they claimed to be wise, they became fools 23 and exchanged the glory of the immortal God for images made to look like mortal man and birds and animals and reptiles.

[d] Gk *brothers*
[e] Or *The one who is righteous through faith will live*

[c] 17 Or *is from faith to faith*
[d] 17 Hab. 2:4

24 Therefore God gave
them up in the lusts of their
hearts to impurity, to the
degrading of their bodies
among themselves, 25 be-
cause they exchanged the
truth about God for a lie
and worshiped and served
the creature rather than the
Creator, who is blessed forever! Amen.
26 For this reason God
gave them up to degrading
passions. Their women ex-
changed natural inter-
course for unnatural, 27 and
in the same way also the
men, giving up natural intercourse with women,
were consumed with pas-
sion for one another. Men
committed shameless acts
with men and received in
their own persons the due
penalty for their error.
28 And since they did
not see fit to acknowledge
God, God gave them up to
a debased mind and to
things that should not be
done. 29 They were filled
with every kind of wickedness, evil, covetousness,
malice. Full of envy, murder, strife, deceit, craftiness, they are gossips,
30 slanderers, God-haters,[f]
insolent, haughty, boastful,
inventors of evil, rebellious
toward parents, 31 foolish,
faithless, heartless, ruthless. 32 They know God's
decree, that those who
practice such things de-
serve to die—yet they not
only do them but even ap-
plaud others who practice
them.

παρέδωκεν αὐτοὺς ὁ θεὸς ἐν ταῖς
[2]gave up [3]them – [1]God in the

ἐπιθυμίαις τῶν καρδιῶν αὐτῶν εἰς ἀκαθαρ-
desires of the hearts of them to unclean-

σίαν τοῦ ἀτιμάζεσθαι τὰ σώματα αὐτῶν
ness – to be dishonoured[d] the bodies of them

ἐν αὐτοῖς. 25 Οἵτινες μετήλλαξαν τὴν
among them[selves]. Who changed the

ἀλήθειαν τοῦ θεοῦ ἐν τῷ ψεύδει, καὶ
truth – of God in[to] the lie, and

ἐσεβάσθησαν καὶ ἐλάτρευσαν τῇ κτίσει
worshipped and served the creature

παρὰ τὸν κτίσαντα, ὅς ἐστιν εὐλογητὸς
rather than the [one] having created, who is blessed

εἰς τοὺς αἰῶνας· ἀμήν. 26 διὰ τοῦτο
unto the ages: Amen. Therefore

παρέδωκεν αὐτοὺς ὁ θεὸς εἰς πάθη
[2]gave up [3]them – [1]God to passions

ἀτιμίας· αἵ τε γὰρ θήλειαι αὐτῶν
of dishonour; [3]the [2]even [1]for females of them

μετήλλαξαν τὴν φυσικὴν χρῆσιν εἰς τὴν
changed the natural use to the [use]

παρὰ φύσιν, 27 ὁμοίως τε καὶ οἱ ἄρσενες
against nature, [2]likewise [1]and also the males

ἀφέντες τὴν φυσικὴν χρῆσιν τῆς θηλείας
leaving the natural use of the female

ἐξεκαύθησαν ἐν τῇ ὀρέξει αὐτῶν εἰς
burned in the desire of them toward

ἀλλήλους, ἄρσενες ἐν ἄρσεσιν τὴν
one another, males among males [2]the

ἀσχημοσύνην κατεργαζόμενοι καὶ τὴν
[3]unseemliness [1]working and [4]the

ἀντιμισθίαν ἣν ἔδει τῆς πλάνης αὐτῶν
[5]requital [9]which [10]behoved [6]of the [7]error [8]of them

ἐν ἑαυτοῖς ἀπολαμβάνοντες. 28 Καὶ
[2]in [3]themselves [1]receiving back. And

καθὼς οὐκ ἐδοκίμασαν τὸν θεὸν ἔχειν
as they thought not fit – God to have

ἐν ἐπιγνώσει, παρέδωκεν αὐτοὺς ὁ θεὸς
in knowledge, [2]gave up [3]them [1]God

εἰς ἀδόκιμον νοῦν, ποιεῖν τὰ μὴ καθήκοντα,
to a reprobate mind, to do the things not *being* proper,

29 πεπληρωμένους πάσῃ ἀδικίᾳ πονηρίᾳ
having been filled with all unrighteousness wickedness

πλεονεξίᾳ κακίᾳ, μεστοὺς φθόνου φόνου
covetousness evil, full of envy *of* murder

ἔριδος δόλου κακοηθείας, ψιθυριστάς,
of strife *of* guile *of* malignity, whisperers,*

30 καταλάλους, θεοστυγεῖς, ὑβριστάς, ὑπερ-
railers, God-haters, insolent, arro-

ηφάνους, ἀλαζόνας, ἐφευρετὰς κακῶν,
gant, boasters, inventors of evil things,

γονεῦσιν ἀπειθεῖς, 31 ἀσυνέτους, ἀσυνθέτους,
to parents disobedient, undiscerning, faithless,

ἀστόργους, ἀνελεήμονας· 32 οἵτινες τὸ
without natural affection, unmerciful; who [2]the

δικαίωμα τοῦ θεοῦ ἐπιγνόντες, ὅτι οἱ
[3]ordinance – [4]of God [1]knowing, that the

τὰ τοιαῦτα πράσσοντες ἄξιοι θανάτου
the [2]such things [1][ones] practising worthy of death

εἰσίν, οὐ μόνον αὐτὰ ποιοῦσιν, ἀλλὰ
are, not only them do, but

καὶ συνευδοκοῦσιν τοῖς πράσσουσιν.
also consent to the [ones] practising.

* "In a bad sense" (Abbott-Smith).

24Therefore God gave
them over in the sinful desires of their hearts to sexual impurity for the degrading of their bodies with one
another. 25They exchanged
the truth of God for a lie,
and worshiped and served
created things rather than
the Creator—who is forev-
er praised. Amen.
26Because of this, God
gave them over to shameful
lusts. Even their women
exchanged natural rela-
tions for unnatural ones.
27In the same way the men
also abandoned natural relations with women and
were inflamed with lust for
one another. Men commit-
ted indecent acts with other
men, and received in themselves the due penalty for
their perversion.
28Furthermore, since
they did not think it worth-
while to retain the knowledge of God, he gave them
over to a depraved mind, to
do what ought not to be
done. 29They have become
filled with every kind of
wickedness, evil, greed and
depravity. They are full of
envy, murder, strife, deceit
and malice. They are gos-
sips, 30slanderers, God-
haters, insolent, arrogant
and boastful; they invent
ways of doing evil; they disobey their parents; 31they
are senseless, faithless,
heartless, ruthless. 32Al-
though they know God's
righteous decree that those
who do such things deserve
death, they not only continue to do these very things
but also approve of those
who practice them.

[f] Or *God-hated*

Chapter 2

The Righteous Judgment of God

THEREFORE you have no excuse, whoever you are, when you judge others; for in passing judgment on another you condemn yourself, because you, the judge, are doing the very same things. 2 You say,[g] "We know that God's judgment on those who do such things is in accordance with truth." 3 Do you imagine, whoever you are, that when you judge those who do such things and yet do them yourself, you will escape the judgment of God? 4 Or do you despise the riches of his kindness and forbearance and patience? Do you not realize that God's kindness is meant to lead you to repentance? 5 But by your hard and impenitent heart you are storing up wrath for yourself on the day of wrath, when God's righteous judgment will be revealed. 6 For he will repay according to each one's deeds: 7 to those who by patiently doing good seek for glory and honor and immortality, he will give eternal life; 8 while for those who are self-seeking and who obey not the truth but wickedness, there will be wrath and fury. 9 There will be anguish and distress for everyone who does evil, the Jew first and also the Greek, 10 but glory and honor and peace for everyone who does good, the Jew first and also the Greek. 11 For God shows no partiality.

12 All who have sinned apart from the law will also

[g] Gk lacks *You say*

2 Διὸ ἀναπολόγητος εἶ, ὦ ἄνθρωπε
Wherefore inexcusable thou art, O man

πᾶς ὁ κρίνων· ἐν ᾧ γὰρ κρίνεις τὸν
everyone judging; ^{2}in ^{3}what ^{1}for thou judgest the

ἕτερον, σεαυτὸν κατακρίνεις· τὰ γὰρ αὐτὰ
other, thyself thou condemnest; for the same things

πράσσεις ὁ κρίνων. 2 οἴδαμεν δὲ ὅτι τὸ
thou practisest the [one] judging. But we know that the

κρίμα τοῦ θεοῦ ἐστιν κατὰ ἀλήθειαν ἐπὶ
judgment – of God is according to truth on

τοὺς τὰ τοιαῦτα πράσσοντας. 3 λογίζῃ
the *the* ^{2}such things ^{1}[ones] practising. reckonest thou

δὲ τοῦτο, ὦ ἄνθρωπε ὁ κρίνων τοὺς
And this, O man the [one] judging the [ones]

τὰ τοιαῦτα πράσσοντας καὶ ποιῶν αὐτά,
the such things practising and doing them,

ὅτι σὺ ἐκφεύξῃ τὸ κρίμα τοῦ θεοῦ;
that thou wilt escape the judgment – of God?

4 ἢ τοῦ πλούτου τῆς χρηστότητος αὐτοῦ
or the riches of the kindness of him

καὶ τῆς ἀνοχῆς καὶ τῆς μακροθυμίας
and the forbearance and the longsuffering

καταφρονεῖς, ἀγνοῶν ὅτι τὸ χρηστὸν τοῦ
despisest thou, not knowing that the kindness –

θεοῦ εἰς μετάνοιάν σε ἄγει; 5 κατὰ δὲ
of God to repentance thee leads? but according to

τὴν σκληρότητά σου καὶ ἀμετανόητον
the hardness of thee and impenitent

καρδίαν θησαυρίζεις σεαυτῷ ὀργὴν ἐν
heart treasurest for thyself wrath in

ἡμέρᾳ ὀργῆς καὶ ἀποκαλύψεως δικαιοκρισίας
a day of wrath and *of* revelation of a righteous judgment

τοῦ θεοῦ, 6 ὃς ἀποδώσει ἑκάστῳ κατὰ τὰ
– of God, who will requite to each man according to the

ἔργα αὐτοῦ· 7 τοῖς μὲν καθ' ὑπομονὴν
works of him: to the [ones] on one hand ^{2}by ^{3}endurance

ἔργου ἀγαθοῦ δόξαν καὶ τιμὴν καὶ
^{5}work ^{4}of(in) good ^{6}glory ^{7}and ^{8}honour ^{9}and

ἀφθαρσίαν ζητοῦσιν ζωὴν αἰώνιον·
^{10}incorruption ^{1}seeking ^{12}life ^{11}eternal;

8 τοῖς δὲ ἐξ ἐριθείας καὶ ἀπειθοῦσι τῇ
to the [ones] on the other of self-seeking and disobeying the

ἀληθείᾳ πειθομένοις δὲ τῇ ἀδικίᾳ, ὀργὴ
truth ^{2}obeying ^{1}but – unrighteousness, wrath

καὶ θυμός. 9 θλῖψις καὶ στενοχωρία ἐπὶ
and anger. Affliction and anguish on

πᾶσαν ψυχὴν ἀνθρώπου τοῦ κατεργαζομένου
every soul of man – working

τὸ κακόν, Ἰουδαίου τε πρῶτον καὶ
the evil, both of Jew firstly and

Ἕλληνος· 10 δόξα δὲ καὶ τιμὴ καὶ
of Greek; but glory and honour and

εἰρήνη παντὶ τῷ ἐργαζομένῳ τὸ ἀγαθόν,
peace to everyone working the good,

Ἰουδαίῳ τε πρῶτον καὶ Ἕλληνι. 11 οὐ
both to Jew firstly and to Greek. not

γάρ ἐστιν προσωπολημψία παρὰ τῷ θεῷ.
For is respect of persons with – God.

12 Ὅσοι γὰρ ἀνόμως ἥμαρτον, ἀνόμως
For as many as without law sinned, without law

Chapter 2

God's Righteous Judgment

YOU, therefore, have no excuse, you who pass judgment on someone else, for at whatever point you judge the other, you are condemning yourself, because you who pass judgment do the same things. 2 Now we know that God's judgment against those who do such things is based on truth. 3 So when you, a mere man, pass judgment on them and yet do the same things, do you think you will escape God's judgment? 4 Or do you show contempt for the riches of his kindness, tolerance and patience, not realizing that God's kindness leads you toward repentance?

5 But because of your stubbornness and your unrepentant heart, you are storing up wrath against yourself for the day of God's wrath, when his righteous judgment will be revealed. 6 God "will give to each person according to what he has done."[e] 7 To those who by persistence in doing good seek glory, honor and immortality, he will give eternal life. 8 But for those who are self-seeking and who reject the truth and follow evil, there will be wrath and anger. 9 There will be trouble and distress for every human being who does evil: first for the Jew, then for the Gentile; 10 but glory, honor and peace for everyone who does good: first for the Jew, then for the Gentile. 11 For God does not show favoritism.

12 All who sin apart from the law will also perish

[e] 6 Psalm 62:12; Prov. 24:12

perish apart from the law,
and all who have sinned under the law will be judged
by the law. 13 For it is not
the hearers of the law who
are righteous in God's
sight, but the doers of the
law who will be justified.
14 When Gentiles, who do
not possess the law, do in-
stinctively what the law requires, these, though not
having the law, are a law to
themselves. 15 They show
that what the law requires
is written on their hearts, to
which their own con-
science also bears witness;
and their conflicting
thoughts will accuse or perhaps excuse them 16 on the
day when, according to my
gospel, God, through Jesus
Christ, will judge the secret
thoughts of all.

The Jews and the Law

17 But if you call your-
self a Jew and rely on the
law and boast of your relation to God 18 and know his
will and determine what is
best because you are in-
structed in the law, 19 and if
you are sure that you are a
guide to the blind, a light to
those who are in darkness,
20 a corrector of the foolish,
a teacher of children, having in the law the embodiment of knowledge and
truth, 21 you, then, that
teach others, will you not
teach yourself? While you
preach against stealing, do
you steal? 22 You that forbid adultery, do you com-
mit adultery? You that abhor idols, do you rob temples? 23 You that boast in
the law, do you dishonor
God by breaking the law?
24 For, as it is written, "The
name of God is blasphemed
among the Gentiles be-
cause of you."

καὶ ἀπολοῦνται· καὶ ὅσοι ἐν νόμῳ
also will perish; and as many as in (under) law

ἥμαρτον, διὰ νόμου κριθήσονται· 13 οὐ
sinned, through law will be judged; [2]not

γὰρ οἱ ἀκροαταὶ νόμου δίκαιοι παρὰ
[1]for the hearers of law [are] just with

[τῷ] θεῷ, ἀλλ' οἱ ποιηταὶ νόμου
– God, but the doers of law

δικαιωθήσονται. 14 ὅταν γὰρ ἔθνη τὰ
will be justified. For whenever nations –

μὴ νόμον ἔχοντα φύσει τὰ τοῦ νόμου
[1]not [3]law [2]having by nature the things of the law

ποιῶσιν, οὗτοι νόμον μὴ ἔχοντες ἑαυτοῖς
do, these [3]law [1]not [2]having to themselves

εἰσιν νόμος· 15 οἵτινες ἐνδείκνυνται τὸ
are a law; who show the

ἔργον τοῦ νόμου γραπτὸν ἐν ταῖς καρδίαις
work of the law written in the hearts

αὐτῶν, συμμαρτυρούσης αὐτῶν τῆς συνει-
of them, witnessing with of them the con-
=while their conscience witnesses with and their

δήσεως καὶ μεταξὺ ἀλλήλων τῶν λογισμῶν
science and between one another the thoughts
thoughts among themselves accuse or even excuse,

κατηγορούντων ἢ καὶ ἀπολογουμένων, 16 ἐν
accusing or even excusing,[a] in

ᾗ ἡμέρᾳ κρίνει ὁ θεὸς τὰ κρυπτὰ τῶν
what day judges – God the hidden things –

ἀνθρώπων κατὰ τὸ εὐαγγέλιόν μου διὰ
of men according to the gospel of me through

Χριστοῦ Ἰησοῦ. 17 Εἰ δὲ σὺ Ἰουδαῖος
Christ Jesus. But if thou [2]a Jew

ἐπονομάζῃ καὶ ἐπαναπαύῃ νόμῳ καὶ
[1]art named and restest on law and

καυχᾶσαι ἐν θεῷ 18 καὶ γινώσκεις τὸ
boastest in God and knowest the

θέλημα καὶ δοκιμάζεις τὰ διαφέροντα
will and approvest the things excelling

κατηχούμενος ἐκ τοῦ νόμου, 19 πέποιθάς τε
being instructed out of the law, and having persuaded

σεαυτὸν ὁδηγὸν εἶναι τυφλῶν, φῶς
thyself a guide to be of blind [persons], a light

τῶν ἐν σκότει, 20 παιδευτὴν ἀφρόνων,
of the [ones] in darkness, an instructor of foolish [persons],

διδάσκαλον νηπίων, ἔχοντα τὴν μόρφωσιν
a teacher of infants, having the form

τῆς γνώσεως καὶ τῆς ἀληθείας ἐν τῷ
– of knowledge and of the truth in the

νόμῳ· 21 ὁ οὖν διδάσκων ἕτερον σεαυτὸν
law: the [one] therefore teaching another thyself

οὐ διδάσκεις; ὁ κηρύσσων μὴ κλέπτειν
teachest thou not? the [one] proclaiming not to steal

κλέπτεις; 22 ὁ λέγων μὴ μοιχεύειν
stealest thou? the [one] saying not to commit adultery

μοιχεύεις; ὁ βδελυσσόμενος τὰ εἴδωλα
dost thou commit adultery? the [one] detesting the idols

ἱεροσυλεῖς; 23 ὃς ἐν νόμῳ καυχᾶσαι, διὰ
dost thou rob temples? who in law boastest, through

τῆς παραβάσεως τοῦ νόμου τὸν θεὸν
– transgression of the law – [2]God

ἀτιμάζεις; 24 τὸ γὰρ ὄνομα τοῦ θεοῦ
[1]dishonourest thou? for the name – of God

δι' ὑμᾶς βλασφημεῖται ἐν τοῖς ἔθνεσιν,
because of you is blasphemed among the nations,

apart from the law, and all
who sin under the law will
be judged by the law. 13 For
it is not those who hear the
law who are righteous in
God's sight, but it is those
who obey the law who will
be declared righteous.
14 (Indeed, when Gentiles,
who do not have the law,
do by nature things re-
quired by the law, they are
a law for themselves, even
though they do not have the
law, 15 since they show that
the requirements of the law
are written on their hearts,
their consciences also bearing witness, and their
thoughts now accusing,
now even defending them.)
16 This will take place on the
day when God will judge
men's secrets through
Jesus Christ, as my gospel
declares.

The Jews and the Law

17 Now you, if you call
yourself a Jew; if you rely
on the law and brag about
your relationship to God;
18 if you know his will and
approve of what is superior
because you are instructed
by the law; 19 if you are convinced that you are a guide
for the blind, a light for
those who are in the dark,
20 an instructor of the foolish, a teacher of infants, because you have in the law
the embodiment of knowl-
edge and truth— 21 you,
then, who teach others, do
you not teach yourself?
You who preach against
stealing, do you steal?
22 You who say that people
should not commit adul-
tery, do you commit adul-
tery? You who abhor idols,
do you rob temples? 23 You
who brag about the law, do
you dishonor God by
breaking the law? 24 As it is
written: "God's name is
blasphemed among the
Gentiles because of you."[f]

[f]24 Isaiah 52:5; Ezek. 36:22

25 Circumcision indeed
is of value if you obey the
law; but if you break the
law, your circumcision has
become uncircumcision.
26 So, if those who are uncircumcised keep the re-
quirements of the law, will
not their uncircumcision be
regarded as circumcision?
27 Then those who are
physically uncircumcised
but keep the law will condemn you that have the
written code and circumcision but break the law.
28 For a person is not a Jew
who is one outwardly, nor
is true circumcision something external and physical.
29 Rather, a person is a Jew
who is one inwardly, and
real circumcision is a matter of the heart—it is spiritual and not literal. Such a
person receives praise not
from others but from God.

Chapter 3

THEN what advantage
has the Jew? Or what
is the value of circumci-
sion? 2 Much, in every way.
For in the first place the
Jews[h] were entrusted with
the oracles of God. 3 What
if some were unfaithful?
Will their faithlessness nullify the faithfulness of God?
4 By no means! Although
everyone is a liar, let God
be proved true, as it is written,

"So that you may be justified in your words,
and prevail in your judging."[i]

5 But if our injustice serves
to confirm the justice of
God, what should we say?
That God is unjust to inflict
wrath on us? (I speak in a
human way.) 6 By no
means! For then how could
God judge the world? 7 But
if through my falsehood
God's truthfulness
abounds to his glory, why

[h] Gk *they*
[i] Gk *when you are being judged*

καθὼς γέγραπται. **25** περιτομὴ μὲν γὰρ
as it has been written. circumcision indeed For
ὠφελεῖ ἐὰν νόμον πράσσῃς· ἐὰν δὲ
profits if law thou practisest; but if
παραβάτης νόμου ᾖς, ἡ περιτομή σου
a transgressor of law thou art, the circumcision of thee
ἀκροβυστία γέγονεν. **26** ἐὰν οὖν ἡ ἀκρο-
uncircumcision has become. If therefore the uncir-
βυστία τὰ δικαιώματα τοῦ νόμου φυλάσσῃ,
cumcision the ordinances of the law keeps,
οὐχ ἡ ἀκροβυστία αὐτοῦ εἰς περιτομὴν
not the uncircumcision of him for circumcision
λογισθήσεται; **27** καὶ κρινεῖ ἡ ἐκ φύσεως
will be reckoned? and [8]will judge [1]the [3]by [4]nature
ἀκροβυστία τὸν νόμον τελοῦσα σὲ τὸν
[2]uncircumcision [6]the [7]law [5]keeping [9]thee [10]the
διὰ γράμματος καὶ περιτομῆς παραβάτην
[13]through [14]letter [15]and [16]circumcision [11]transgressor
νόμου. **28** οὐ γὰρ ὁ ἐν τῷ φανερῷ
[12]of law. For [2]not [3]the [5]in [6]the [7]open
Ἰουδαῖός ἐστιν, οὐδὲ ἡ ἐν τῷ φανερῷ
[4]Jew [1]he is, nor [1]the [3]in [4]the [5]open
ἐν σαρκὶ περιτομή· **29** ἀλλ' ὁ ἐν τῷ
[6]in [7]flesh [2]circumcision; but [1]the [3]in [4]the
κρυπτῷ Ἰουδαῖος, καὶ περιτομὴ καρδίας
[5]secret [2]Jew [is], and circumcision [is] of heart
ἐν πνεύματι οὐ γράμματι, οὗ ὁ ἔπαινος
in spirit not letter, of whom the praise [is]
οὐκ ἐξ ἀνθρώπων ἀλλ' ἐκ τοῦ θεοῦ.
not from men but from – God.
3 Τί οὖν τὸ περισσὸν τοῦ Ἰουδαίου,
What therefore the advantage of the Jew,
ἢ τίς ἡ ὠφέλεια τῆς περιτομῆς; **2** πολὺ
or what the profit – of circumcision? Much
κατὰ πάντα τρόπον. πρῶτον μὲν [γὰρ]
by every way. [3]Firstly [2]indeed [1]for
ὅτι ἐπιστεύθησαν τὰ λόγια τοῦ θεοῦ.
because they were entrusted [with] the oracles - of God.
3 τί γάρ; εἰ ἠπίστησάν τινες, μὴ ἡ
For what? If [2]disbelieved [1]some, *not* the
ἀπιστία αὐτῶν τὴν πίστιν τοῦ θεοῦ
unbelief of them the faith - of God
καταργήσει; **4** μὴ γένοιτο· γινέσθω δὲ
will destroy? May it not be; but let be
ὁ θεὸς ἀληθής, πᾶς δὲ ἄνθρωπος ψεύστης,
– God true, and every man a liar,
καθάπερ γέγραπται· ὅπως ἂν δικαιωθῇς
as it has been written: So as – thou mayest be justified
ἐν τοῖς λόγοις σου καὶ νικήσεις ἐν
in the sayings of thee and wilt overcome in
τῷ κρίνεσθαί σε. **5** εἰ δὲ ἡ ἀδικία
the to be judged thee.[be] Now if the unrighteousness
=when thou art judged.
ἡμῶν θεοῦ δικαιοσύνην συνίστησιν, τί
of us [3]of God [2]a righteousness [1]commends, what
ἐροῦμεν; μὴ ἄδικος ὁ θεὸς ὁ ἐπιφέρων
shall we say? *not* unrighteous – God the [one] inflicting
τὴν ὀργήν; κατὰ ἄνθρωπον λέγω. **6** μὴ
– wrath? according to man I say. not
γένοιτο· ἐπεὶ πῶς κρινεῖ ὁ θεὸς τὸν
May it be; otherwise how will judge – God the
κόσμον; **7** εἰ δὲ ἡ ἀλήθεια τοῦ θεοῦ
world? But if the truth – of God

25 Circumcision has value
if you observe the law, but
if you break the law, you
have become as though you
had not been circumcised.
26 If those who are not circumcised keep the law's requirements, will they not
be regarded as though they
were circumcised? 27 The
one who is not circumcised
physically and yet obeys
the law will condemn you
who, even though you have
the[g] written code and circumcision, are a lawbreaker.

28 A man is not a Jew if he
is only one outwardly, nor
is circumcision merely outward and physical. 29 No, a
man is a Jew if he is one
inwardly; and circumcision
is circumcision of the
heart, by the Spirit, not by
the written code. Such a
man's praise is not from
men, but from God.

Chapter 3

God's Faithfulness

WHAT advantage,
then, is there in be-
ing a Jew, or what value is
there in circumcision?
2 Much in every way! First
of all, they have been entrusted with the very words
of God.

3 What if some did not
have faith? Will their lack
of faith nullify God's faithfulness? 4 Not at all! Let
God be true, and every man
a liar. As it is written:

"So that you may be proved right when you speak
and prevail when you judge."[h]

5 But if our unrighteous-
ness brings out God's righteousness more clearly,
what shall we say? That
God is unjust in bringing his
wrath on us? (I am using a
human argument.) 6 Cer-
tainly not! If that were so,
how could God judge the
world? 7 Someone might argue, "If my falsehood en-

[g] 27 *Or who, by means of a*
[h] 4 Psalm 51:4

am I still being condemned as a sinner? 8 And why not say (as some people slander us by saying that we say), "Let us do evil so that good may come"? Their condemnation is deserved!

None Is Righteous

9 What then? Are we any better off?[j] No, not at all; for we have already charged that all, both Jews and Greeks, are under the power of sin, 10 as it is written:

"There is no one who
is righteous, not
even one;
11 there is no one who
has
understanding,
there is no one
who seeks God.
12 All have turned aside,
together they
have become
worthless;
there is no one who
shows kindness,
there is not even
one."
13 "Their throats are
opened graves;
they use their
tongues to
deceive."
"The venom of vipers
is under
their lips."
14 "Their mouths are
full of cursing
and bitterness."
15 "Their feet are swift
to shed blood;
16 ruin and misery are
in their paths,
17 and the way of peace
they have
not known."
18 "There is no fear of
God before their
eyes."

19 Now we know that whatever the law says, it speaks to those who are under the law, so that every mouth may be silenced, and the whole world may be held accountable to God. 20 For "no human being will be justified in his sight" by deeds prescribed by the law, for through the law comes the knowledge of sin.

Righteousness through Faith

21 But now, apart from law, the righteousness of God has been disclosed, and is attested by the law

[j] Or *at any disadvantage?*

ἐν τῷ ἐμῷ ψεύσματι ἐπερίσσευσεν εἰς
by – my lie abounded to
τὴν δόξαν αὐτοῦ, τί ἔτι κἀγὼ ὡς
the glory of him, why still I also as
ἁμαρτωλὸς κρίνομαι; **8** καὶ μὴ καθὼς
a sinner am judged? and not as
βλασφημούμεθα καὶ καθώς φασίν τινες
we are blasphemed and as [2]say [1]some
ἡμᾶς λέγειν ὅτι ποιήσωμεν τὰ κακὰ
us to say[,] – Let us do – evil things
=that we say,
ἵνα ἔλθῃ τὰ ἀγαθά; ὧν τὸ κρίμα
that may come – good things? of whom the judgment
ἔνδικόν ἐστιν. **9** Τί οὖν; προεχόμεθα;
just is. What therefore? Do we excel?
οὐ πάντως· προῃτιασάμεθα γὰρ Ἰουδαίους
not at all; for we previously accused [2]Jews
τε καὶ Ἕλληνας πάντας ὑφ' ἁμαρτίαν
[1]both and Greeks all under sin
εἶναι, **10** καθὼς γέγραπται ὅτι οὐκ ἔστιν
to be, as it has been written[,] – There is not
δίκαιος οὐδὲ εἷς, οὐκ ἔστιν ὁ
a righteous man not one, there is not the [one]
συνίων, **11** οὐκ ἔστιν ὁ ἐκζητῶν τὸν θεόν·
under-standing, there is not the [one] seeking – God;
12 πάντες ἐξέκλιναν, ἅμα ἠχρεώθησαν·
all turned away, together became unprofitable;
οὐκ ἔστιν ὁ ποιῶν χρηστότητα, οὐκ
there is not the [one] doing kindness, not
ἔστιν ἕως ἑνός. **13** τάφος ἀνεῳγμένος
there is so much as one. A grave *having been* opened
ὁ λάρυγξ αὐτῶν, ταῖς γλώσσαις αὐτῶν
the throat of them, with the tongues of them
ἐδολιοῦσαν, ἰὸς ἀσπίδων ὑπὸ τὰ χείλη
they acted deceitfully, poison of asps under the lips
αὐτῶν· **14** ὧν τὸ στόμα ἀρᾶς καὶ πικρίας
of them; of whom the mouth [2]of cursing [3]and [4]bitterness
γέμει· **15** ὀξεῖς οἱ πόδες αὐτῶν ἐκχέαι
[1]is full; swift the feet of them to shed
αἷμα, **16** σύντριμμα καὶ ταλαιπωρία ἐν
blood, ruin and misery in
ταῖς ὁδοῖς αὐτῶν, **17** καὶ ὁδὸν εἰρήνης
the ways of them, and a way of peace
οὐκ ἔγνωσαν. **18** οὐκ ἔστιν φόβος θεοῦ
they knew not. There is not fear of God
ἀπέναντι τῶν ὀφθαλμῶν αὐτῶν. **19** οἴδαμεν
before the eyes of them. we know
δὲ ὅτι ὅσα ὁ νόμος λέγει τοῖς ἐν τῷ
But that whatever things the law says to the [ones] in the
νόμῳ λαλεῖ, ἵνα πᾶν στόμα φραγῇ καὶ
law it speaks, in order that every mouth may be stopped and
ὑπόδικος γένηται πᾶς ὁ κόσμος τῷ
[5]under judgment [4]may become [1]all [2]the [3]world –
θεῷ· **20** διότι ἐξ ἔργων νόμου οὐ
to God; because by works of law not
δικαιωθήσεται πᾶσα σὰρξ ἐνώπιον αὐτοῦ·
will be justified all flesh* before him;
διὰ γὰρ νόμου ἐπίγνωσις ἁμαρτίας.
for through law [is] full knowledge of sin.
21 Νυνὶ δὲ χωρὶς νόμου δικαιοσύνη
But now without law a righteousness
θεοῦ πεφανέρωται, μαρτυρουμένη ὑπὸ τοῦ
of God has been manifested, being witnessed by the

* That is, no flesh will be justified . . .

hances God's truthfulness and so increases his glory, why am I still condemned as a sinner?" 8 Why not say—as we are being slanderously reported as saying and as some claim that we say—"Let us do evil that good may result"? Their condemnation is deserved.

No One Is Righteous

9 What shall we conclude then? Are we any better[i]? Not at all! We have already made the charge that Jews and Gentiles alike are all under sin. 10 As it is written:

"There is no one
righteous, not even
one;
11 there is no one who
understands,
no one who seeks God.
12 All have turned away,
they have together
become worthless;
there is no one who does
good,
not even one."[j]
13 "Their throats are open
graves;
their tongues practice
deceit."[k]
"The poison of vipers is
on their lips."[l]
14 "Their mouths are full
of cursing and
bitterness."[m]
15 "Their feet are swift to
shed blood;
16 ruin and misery mark
their ways,
17 and the way of peace
they do not
know."[n]
18 "There is no fear of
God before their
eyes."[o]

19 Now we know that whatever the law says, it says to those who are under the law, so that every mouth may be silenced and the whole world held accountable to God. 20 Therefore no one will be declared righteous in his sight by observing the law; rather, through the law we become conscious of sin.

Righteousness Through Faith

21 But now a righteousness from God, apart from law, has been made known,

[i] 9 Or *worse*
[j] 12 Psalms 14:1-3; 53:1-3; Eccles. 7:20
[k] 13 Psalm 5:9
[l] 13 Psalm 140:3
[m] 14 Psalm 10:7
[n] 17 Isaiah 59:7,8
[o] 18 Psalm 36:1

and the prophets, 22the
righteousness of God
through faith in Jesus
Christ[k] for all who believe.
For there is no distinction,
23since all have sinned and
fall short of the glory of
God; 24they are now justified by his grace as a gift,
through the redemption
that is in Christ Jesus,
25whom God put forward
as a sacrifice of atone-
ment[l] by his blood, effective through faith. He did
this to show his righteousness, because in his divine
forbearance he had passed
over the sins previously
committed; 26it was to
prove at the present time
that he himself is righteous
and that he justifies the one
who has faith in Jesus.[m]
27 Then what becomes
of boasting? It is excluded.
By what law? By that of
works? No, but by the law
of faith. 28For we hold that
a person is justified by faith
apart from works pre-
scribed by the law. 29Or is
God the God of Jews only?
Is he not the God of Gen-
tiles also? Yes, of Gentiles
also, 30since God is one;
and he will justify the circumcised on the ground of
faith and the uncircumcised
through that same faith.
31Do we then overthrow
the law by this faith? By no
means! On the contrary,
we uphold the law.

Chapter 4

The Example of Abraham

WHAT then are we to
say was gained by[n]
Abraham, our ancestor ac-
cording to the flesh? 2For if
Abraham was justified by
works, he has something to
boast about, but not before
God. 3For what does the
scripture say? "Abraham
believed God, and it was
reckoned to him as righ-

[k] Or *through the faith of Jesus Christ*
[l] Or *a place of atonement*
[m] Or *who has the faith of Jesus*
[n] Other ancient authorities read *say about*

νόμου καὶ τῶν προφητῶν, 22 δικαιοσύνη
law and the prophets, [2]a righteousness
δὲ θεοῦ διὰ πίστεως ['Ιησοῦ] Χριστοῦ,
[1]and of God through faith of(in) Jesus Christ,
εἰς πάντας τοὺς πιστεύοντας· οὐ γάρ
to all the [ones] believing; for not
ἐστιν διαστολή· 23 πάντες γὰρ ἥμαρτον
there is difference; for all sinned
καὶ ὑστεροῦνται τῆς δόξης τοῦ θεοῦ,
and come short of the glory – of God,
24 δικαιούμενοι δωρεὰν τῇ αὐτοῦ χάριτι
being justified freely by the of him grace
διὰ τῆς ἀπολυτρώσεως τῆς ἐν Χριστῷ
through the redemption – in Christ
'Ιησοῦ· 25 ὃν προέθετο ὁ θεὸς ἱλαστήριον
Jesus; whom set forth – God a propitiation
διὰ πίστεως ἐν τῷ αὐτοῦ αἵματι, εἰς
through faith by the of him blood, for
ἔνδειξιν τῆς δικαιοσύνης αὐτοῦ διὰ τὴν
a showing forth of the righteousness of him because of the
πάρεσιν τῶν προγεγονότων ἁμαρτημάτων
passing by of the [2]having previously occurred [1]sins
26 ἐν τῇ ἀνοχῇ τοῦ θεοῦ, πρὸς τὴν
in the forbearance – of God, for the
ἔνδειξιν τῆς δικαιοσύνης αὐτοῦ ἐν τῷ
showing forth of the righteousness of him in the
νῦν καιρῷ, εἰς τὸ εἶναι αὐτὸν δίκαιον
present time, for the to be him[b] just
=that he should be
καὶ δικαιοῦντα τὸν ἐκ πίστεως 'Ιησοῦ.
and justifying the [one] of faith of(in) Jesus.
27 Ποῦ οὖν ἡ καύχησις; ἐξεκλείσθη. διὰ
Where therefore the boasting? It was shut out. Through
ποίου νόμου; τῶν ἔργων; οὐχί, ἀλλὰ
what law? – of works? no, but
διὰ νόμου πίστεως. 28 λογιζόμεθα γὰρ
through a law of faith. For we reckon
δικαιοῦσθαι πίστει ἄνθρωπον χωρὶς ἔργων
[3]to be justified [2]by faith [1]a man without works
νόμου. 29 ἢ 'Ιουδαίων ὁ θεὸς μόνον;
of law. Or of Jews [is he] the God only?
οὐχὶ καὶ ἐθνῶν; ναὶ καὶ ἐθνῶν, 30 εἴπερ
not also of nations? Yes[,] also of nations, since [there is]
εἷς ὁ θεὸς ὃς δικαιώσει περιτομὴν ἐκ
one – God who will justify circumcision by
πίστεως καὶ ἀκροβυστίαν διὰ τῆς πίστεως.
faith and uncircumcision through the faith.
31 νόμον οὖν καταργοῦμεν διὰ τῆς
[3]Law [2]therefore [1]do we destroy through the
πίστεως; μὴ γένοιτο, ἀλλὰ νόμον ἱστάνομεν.
faith? May it not be, but [2]law [1]we establish.

4 Τί οὖν ἐροῦμεν εὑρηκέναι 'Αβραὰμ
What therefore shall we say to have found Abraham
τὸν προπάτορα ἡμῶν κατὰ σάρκα; 2 εἰ
the forefather of us according to flesh? if
γὰρ 'Αβραὰμ ἐξ ἔργων ἐδικαιώθη, ἔχει
For Abraham by works was justified, he has
καύχημα· ἀλλ' οὐ πρὸς θεόν. 3 τί γὰρ
a boast; but not with God. For what
ἡ γραφὴ λέγει; ἐπίστευσεν δὲ 'Αβραὰμ
the scripture says? And [2]believed [1]Abraham
τῷ θεῷ, καὶ ἐλογίσθη αὐτῷ εἰς
– God, and it was reckoned to him for

to which the Law and the
Prophets testify. 22This
righteousness from God
comes through faith in
Jesus Christ to all who believe. There is no difference, 23for all have sinned
and fall short of the glory of
God, 24and are justified
freely by his grace through
the redemption that came
by Christ Jesus. 25God presented him as a sacrifice of
atonement,[p] through faith
in his blood. He did this to
demonstrate his justice, because in his forbearance he
had left the sins committed
beforehand unpunished—
26he did it to demonstrate
his justice at the present
time, so as to be just and
the one who justifies those
who have faith in Jesus.
27Where, then, is boast-
ing? It is excluded. On what
principle? On that of ob-
serving the law? No, but on
that of faith. 28For we
maintain that a man is justified by faith apart from observing the law. 29Is God
the God of Jews only? Is he
not the God of Gentiles
too? Yes, of Gentiles too,
30since there is only one
God, who will justify the
circumcised by faith and
the uncircumcised through
that same faith. 31Do we,
then, nullify the law by this
faith? Not at all! Rather, we
uphold the law.

Chapter 4

Abraham Justified by Faith

WHAT then shall we
say that Abraham,
our forefather, discovered
in this matter? 2If, in fact,
Abraham was justified by
works, he had something to
boast about—but not be-
fore God. 3What does the
Scripture say? "Abraham
believed God, and it was
credited to him as right-
eousness."[q]

[p] 25 Or *as the one who would turn aside his wrath, taking away sin*
[q] 3 Gen. 15:6; also in verse 22

teousness." 4 Now to one
who works, wages are not
reckoned as a gift but as
something due. 5 But to one
who without works trusts
him who justifies the un-
godly, such faith is reckoned as righteousness. 6 So
also David speaks of the
blessedness of those to
whom God reckons righ-
teousness apart from
works:
7 "Blessed are those
whose iniquities
are forgiven,
and whose sins are
covered;
8 blessed is the one
against whom
the Lord will
not reckon sin."
9 Is this blessedness,
then, pronounced only on
the circumcised, or also on
the uncircumcised? We
say, "Faith was reckoned
to Abraham as righteous-
ness." 10 How then was it
reckoned to him? Was it
before or after he had been
circumcised? It was not after, but before he was circumcised. 11 He received
the sign of circumcision as
a seal of the righteousness
that he had by faith while
he was still uncircumcised.
The purpose was to make
him the ancestor of all who
believe without being circumcised and who thus
have righteousness reck-
oned to them, 12 and likewise the ancestor of the circumcised who are not only
circumcised but who also
follow the example of the
faith that our ancestor
Abraham had before he
was circumcised.

God's Promise Realized through Faith

13 For the promise that
he would inherit the world
did not come to Abraham
or to his descendants
through the law but
through the righteousness
of faith. 14 If it is the adherents of the law who are to
be the heirs, faith is null

δικαιοσύνην. 4 τῷ δὲ ἐργαζομένῳ ὁ
righteousness. Now to the [one] working the

μισθὸς οὐ λογίζεται κατὰ χάριν ἀλλὰ
reward is not reckoned according to grace but

κατὰ ὀφείλημα· 5 τῷ δὲ μὴ ἐργαζομένῳ,
according to debt; but to the [one] not working,

πιστεύοντι δὲ ἐπὶ τὸν δικαιοῦντα τὸν
but believing on the [one] justifying the

ἀσεβῆ, λογίζεται ἡ πίστις αὐτοῦ εἰς
impious man, is reckoned the faith of him for

δικαιοσύνην, 6 καθάπερ καὶ Δαυὶδ λέγει
righteousness, even as also David says

τὸν μακαρισμὸν τοῦ ἀνθρώπου ᾧ ὁ
the blessedness of the man to whom –

θεὸς λογίζεται δικαιοσύνην χωρὶς ἔργων·
God reckons righteousness without works:

7 μακάριοι ὧν ἀφέθησαν αἱ ἀνομίαι
Blessed [are they] of whom were forgiven the lawlessnesses

καὶ ὧν ἐπεκαλύφθησαν αἱ ἁμαρτίαι·
and of whom were covered over the sins;

8 μακάριος ἀνὴρ οὗ οὐ μὴ λογίσηται
blessed [is] a man of whom by no means [3]may reckon

κύριος ἁμαρτίαν 9 ὁ μακαρισμὸς οὖν
[1][the] Lord sin. – [2]blessedness [3]then

οὗτος ἐπὶ τὴν περιτομὴν ἢ καὶ ἐπὶ
[1]This on the circumcision or also on

τὴν ἀκροβυστίαν; λέγομεν γάρ· ἐλογίσθη
the uncircumcision? for we say: [3]was reckoned

τῷ Ἀβραὰμ ἡ πίστις εἰς δικαιοσύνην.
– [4]to Abraham [1]The(his) [2]faith for righteousness.

10 πῶς οὖν ἐλογίσθη; ἐν περιτομῇ ὄντι
How then was it reckoned? in circumcision being

ἢ ἐν ἀκροβυστίᾳ; οὐκ ἐν περιτομῇ ἀλλ᾽
or in uncircumcision? not in circumcision but

ἐν ἀκροβυστίᾳ· 11 καὶ σημεῖον ἔλαβεν
in uncircumcision; and [2]a sign [1]he received

περιτομῆς σφραγῖδα τῆς δικαιοσύνης τῆς
of circumcision a seal of the righteousness of the

πίστεως τῆς ἐν τῇ ἀκροβυστίᾳ, εἰς
faith – [while] in – uncircumcision, for =so

τὸ εἶναι αὐτὸν πατέρα πάντων τῶν
the to be him[b] a father of all the
that he should be

πιστευόντων δι᾽ ἀκροβυστίας, εἰς τὸ
[ones] believing through uncircumcision, for the =that right-

λογισθῆναι αὐτοῖς [τὴν] δικαιοσύνην, 12 καὶ
to be reckoned to them – righteousness,[b] and
eousness should be reckoned to them,

πατέρα περιτομῆς τοῖς οὐκ ἐκ περιτομῆς
a father of circumcision to the [ones] not of circumcision

μόνον ἀλλὰ καὶ τοῖς στοιχοῦσιν τοῖς
only but also to the [ones] walking in the

ἴχνεσιν τῆς ἐν ἀκροβυστίᾳ πίστεως τοῦ
steps [1]of the [7]in [8]uncircumcision [2]faith [3]of the

πατρὸς ἡμῶν Ἀβραάμ. 13 Οὐ γὰρ διὰ
[4]father [5]of us [6]Abraham. For not through

νόμου ἡ ἐπαγγελία τῷ Ἀβραὰμ ἢ τῷ
law the promise – to Abraham or to the

σπέρματι αὐτοῦ, τὸ κληρονόμον αὐτὸν
seed of him, the heir him
=that he should be heir

εἶναι κόσμου, ἀλλὰ διὰ δικαιοσύνης πίστεως.
to be[b] of [the] world, but through a righteousness of faith.

14 εἰ γὰρ οἱ ἐκ νόμου κληρονόμοι,
For if [1]the [3][are] [4]of [5]law [2]heirs,

4 Now when a man works,
his wages are not credited
to him as a gift, but as an
obligation. 5 However, to
the man who does not work
but trusts God who justifies
the wicked, his faith is
credited as righteousness.
6 David says the same thing
when he speaks of the
blessedness of the man to
whom God credits right-
eousness apart from works:

7 "Blessed are they
whose transgressions
are forgiven,
whose sins are
covered.
8 Blessed is the man
whose sin the Lord will
never count against
him."[r]

9 Is this blessedness only
for the circumcised, or also
for the uncircumcised? We
have been saying that
Abraham's faith was cred-
ited to him as righteous-
ness. 10 Under what circumstances was it credited?
Was it after he was circumcised, or before? It was not
after, but before! 11 And he
received the sign of circumcision, a seal of the righteousness that he had by
faith while he was still uncircumcised. So then, he is
the father of all who believe
but have not been circum-
cised, in order that righteousness might be credited
to them. 12 And he is also
the father of the circum-
cised who not only are circumcised but who also
walk in the footsteps of the
faith that our father Abraham had before he was circumcised.
13 It was not through law
that Abraham and his off-
spring received the promise
that he would be heir of the
world, but through the
righteousness that comes
by faith. 14 For if those who
live by law are heirs, faith

[r]8 Psalm 32:1,2

and the promise is void.
15 For the law brings wrath;
but where there is no law,
neither is there violation.
16 For this reason it de-
pends on faith, in order that
the promise may rest on
grace and be guaranteed to
all his descendants, not
only to the adherents of the
law but also to those who
share the faith of Abraham
(for he is the father of all of
us, 17 as it is written, "I
have made you the father of
many nations")—in the
presence of the God in
whom he believed, who
gives life to the dead and
calls into existence the
things that do not exist.
18 Hoping against hope, he
believed that he would become "the father of many
nations," according to what
was said, "So numerous
shall your descendants be."
19 He did not weaken in
faith when he considered
his own body, which was
already[o] as good as dead
(for he was about a hundred
years old), or when he considered the barrenness of
Sarah's womb. 20 No dis-
trust made him waver con-
cerning the promise of
God, but he grew strong in
his faith as he gave glory to
God, 21 being fully con-
vinced that God was able to
do what he had promised.
22 Therefore his faith[p]
"was reckoned to him as
righteousness." 23 Now the
words, "it was reckoned to
him," were written not for
his sake alone, 24 but for
ours also. It will be reckoned to us who believe in
him who raised Jesus our
Lord from the dead, 25 who

κεκένωται ἡ πίστις καὶ κατήργηται
[2]has been emptied – [1]faith and [3]has been destroyed

ἡ ἐπαγγελία· **15** ὁ γὰρ νόμος ὀργὴν
[1]the [2]promise; for the law [2]wrath

κατεργάζεται· οὗ δὲ οὐκ ἔστιν νόμος,
[1]works; and where there is not law,

οὐδὲ παράβασις. **16** Διὰ τοῦτο ἐκ πίστεως,
neither [is there] transgression. Therefore [it is] of faith,

ἵνα κατὰ χάριν, εἰς τὸ εἶναι βεβαίαν
in order that [it may be] according to grace, for the to be firm =so that the promise shall be firm

τὴν ἐπαγγελίαν παντὶ τῷ σπέρματι, οὐ
the promise[b] to all the seed, not

τῷ ἐκ τοῦ νόμου μόνον ἀλλὰ καὶ τῷ
to the [seed] of the law only but also to the [seed]

ἐκ πίστεως Ἀβραάμ, ὅς ἐστιν πατὴρ
of [the] faith of Abraham, who is father

πάντων ἡμῶν, **17** καθὼς γέγραπται ὅτι
of all us, as it has been written[,] –

πατέρα πολλῶν ἐθνῶν τέθεικά σε,
A father of many nations I have appointed thee,

κατέναντι οὗ ἐπίστευσεν θεοῦ τοῦ ζωο-
before [2]whom [3]he believed [1]God the [one] quick-

ποιοῦντος τοὺς νεκροὺς καὶ καλοῦντος
ening the dead [ones] and calling

τὰ μὴ ὄντα ὡς ὄντα· **18** ὃς παρ' ἐλπίδα
the things not being as being; who beyond hope

ἐπ' ἐλπίδι ἐπίστευσεν, εἰς τὸ γενέσθαι
on hope believed, for the to become =so that he should become

αὐτὸν πατέρα πολλῶν ἐθνῶν κατὰ τὸ
him[b] a father of many nations according to the thing

εἰρημένον· οὕτως ἔσται τὸ σπέρμα σου·
having been said: So shall be the seed of thee;

19 καὶ μὴ ἀσθενήσας τῇ πίστει κατενόησεν
and not weakening – in faith he considered

τὸ ἑαυτοῦ σῶμα νενεκρωμένον, ἑκατονταέτης
[1]the [3]of himself [2]body to have died, a hundred years

που ὑπάρχων, καὶ τὴν νέκρωσιν τῆς
about being, and the death of the

μήτρας Σάρρας· **20** εἰς δὲ τὴν ἐπαγγελίαν
womb of Sarah; but [2]against [3]the [4]promise

τοῦ θεοῦ οὐ διεκρίθη τῇ ἀπιστίᾳ, ἀλλὰ
– [5]of God [1]he did not decide – [6]by unbelief, but

ἐνεδυναμώθη τῇ πίστει, δοὺς δόξαν τῷ
was empowered – by faith, giving glory –

θεῷ **21** καὶ πληροφορηθεὶς ὅτι ὃ ἐπήγγελται
to God and being fully persuaded that what he has promised

δυνατός ἐστιν καὶ ποιῆσαι. **22** διὸ [καὶ]
able he is also to do. Wherefore also

ἐλογίσθη αὐτῷ εἰς δικαιοσύνην. **23** Οὐκ
it was reckoned to him for righteousness. not

ἐγράφη δὲ δι' αὐτὸν μόνον ὅτι ἐλογίσθη
it was written Now because of him only that it was reckoned

αὐτῷ, **24** ἀλλὰ καὶ δι' ἡμᾶς, οἷς μέλλει
to him, but also because of us, to whom it is about

λογίζεσθαι, τοῖς πιστεύουσιν ἐπὶ τὸν
to be reckoned, to the [ones] believing on the [one]

ἐγείραντα Ἰησοῦν τὸν κύριον ἡμῶν ἐκ
having raised Jesus the Lord of us out of

has no value and the promise is worthless, 15 because
law brings wrath. And
where there is no law there
is no transgression.
16 Therefore, the promise
comes by faith, so that it
may be by grace and may
be guaranteed to all Abraham's offspring—not only
to those who are of the law
but also to those who are of
the faith of Abraham. He is
the father of us all. 17 As it is
written: "I have made you
a father of many na-
tions."[s] He is our father in
the sight of God, in whom
he believed—the God who
gives life to the dead and
calls things that are not as
though they were.
18 Against all hope, Abraham in hope believed and
so became the father of
many nations, just as it had
been said to him, "So shall
your offspring be."[t]
19 Without weakening in his
faith, he faced the fact that
his body was as good as
dead—since he was about
a hundred years old—and
that Sarah's womb was
also dead. 20 Yet he did not
waver through unbelief regarding the promise of
God, but was strengthened
in his faith and gave glory
to God, 21 being fully persuaded that God had power
to do what he had prom-
ised. 22 This is why "it was
credited to him as right-
eousness." 23 The words
"it was credited to him"
were written not for him
alone, 24 but also for us, to
whom God will credit righteousness—for us who be-
lieve in him who raised
Jesus our Lord from the

[o] Other ancient authorities lack *already*
[p] Gk *Therefore it*

[s] *17* Gen. 17:5
[t] *18* Gen. 15:5

was handed over to death
for our trespasses and was
raised for our justification.

Chapter 5

Results of Justification

THEREFORE, since we
are justified by faith,
we[q] have peace with God
through our Lord Jesus
Christ, 2 through whom we
have obtained access[r] to
this grace in which we
stand; and we[s] boast in our
hope of sharing the glory of
God. 3 And not only that,
but we[s] also boast in our
sufferings, knowing that
suffering produces endur-
ance, 4 and endurance produces character, and character produces hope, 5 and
hope does not disappoint
us, because God's love has
been poured into our hearts
through the Holy Spirit that
has been given to us.
6 For while we were still
weak, at the right time
Christ died for the ungodly.
7 Indeed, rarely will anyone
die for a righteous
person—though perhaps
for a good person someone
might actually dare to die.
8 But God proves his love
for us in that while we still
were sinners Christ died for
us. 9 Much more surely
then, now that we have
been justified by his blood,
will we be saved through
him from the wrath of
God.[t] 10 For if while we
were enemies, we were
reconciled to God through
the death of his Son, much
more surely, having been
reconciled, will we be
saved by his life. 11 But
more than that, we even

[q] Other ancient authorities read *let us*
[r] Other ancient authorities add *by faith*
[s] Or *let us*
[t] Gk *the wrath*

νεκρῶν, **25** ὃς παρεδόθη διὰ τὰ παραπ-
[the] dead, who was delivered because of the of-
τώματα ἡμῶν καὶ ἠγέρθη διὰ τὴν
fences of us and was raised because of the
δικαίωσιν ἡμῶν.
justification of us.

5 Δικαιωθέντες οὖν ἐκ πίστεως εἰρήνην
Having been justified therefore by faith peace
ἔχομεν πρὸς τὸν θεὸν διὰ τοῦ κυρίου
we have with – God through the Lord
ἡμῶν Ἰησοῦ Χριστοῦ, **2** δι' οὗ καὶ τὴν
of us Jesus Christ, through whom also the
προσαγωγὴν ἐσχήκαμεν [τῇ πίστει] εἰς
access we have had – by faith into
τὴν χάριν ταύτην ἐν ᾗ ἑστήκαμεν, καὶ
this grace in which we stand, and
καυχώμεθα ἐπ' ἐλπίδι τῆς δόξης τοῦ
boast on hope of the glory –
θεοῦ. **3** οὐ μόνον δέ, ἀλλὰ καὶ καυχώμεθα
of God. And not only [so], but also we boast
ἐν ταῖς θλίψεσιν, εἰδότες ὅτι ἡ θλῖψις
in – afflictions, knowing that – affliction
ὑπομονὴν κατεργάζεται, **4** ἡ δὲ ὑπομονὴ
patience works, – and patience
δοκιμήν, ἡ δὲ δοκιμὴ ἐλπίδα· **5** ἡ δὲ
proof, – and proof hope; – and
ἐλπὶς οὐ καταισχύνει, ὅτι ἡ ἀγάπη
hope does not put to shame, because the love
τοῦ θεοῦ ἐκκέχυται ἐν ταῖς καρδίαις
– of God has been poured out in the hearts
ἡμῶν διὰ πνεύματος ἁγίου τοῦ δοθέντος
of us through Spirit Holy – given
ἡμῖν· **6** εἴ γε Χριστὸς ὄντων ἡμῶν
to us; indeed [7]Christ [2]being [1]us
=when we were weak
ἀσθενῶν ἔτι κατὰ καιρὸν ὑπὲρ ἀσεβῶν
[4]weak[a] [3]yet [5]according to [6]time [9]on behalf of [10]impious ones
ἀπέθανεν. **7** μόλις γὰρ ὑπὲρ δικαίου
[8]died. For hardly on behalf of a just man
τις ἀποθανεῖται· ὑπὲρ γὰρ τοῦ ἀγαθοῦ
anyone will die; for on behalf of the good man
τάχα τις καὶ τολμᾷ ἀποθανεῖν· **8** συνίστησιν
perhaps someone even dares to die; [2]commends
δὲ τὴν ἑαυτοῦ ἀγάπην εἰς ἡμᾶς ὁ θεὸς
but [3]the [5]of himself [4]love [6]to [7]us – [1]God
ὅτι ἔτι ἁμαρτωλῶν ὄντων ἡμῶν Χριστὸς
that yet sinners being us[a] Christ
=while we were yet sinners
ὑπὲρ ἡμῶν ἀπέθανεν. **9** πολλῷ οὖν μᾶλλον
on behalf of us died. By much therefore rather
δικαιωθέντες νῦν ἐν τῷ αἵματι αὐτοῦ
having been justified now by the blood of him
σωθησόμεθα δι' αὐτοῦ ἀπὸ τῆς ὀργῆς.
we shall be saved through him from the wrath.
10 εἰ γὰρ ἐχθροὶ ὄντες κατηλλάγημεν
For if enemies being we were reconciled
τῷ θεῷ διὰ τοῦ θανάτου τοῦ υἱοῦ αὐτοῦ,
– to God through the death of the Son of him,
πολλῷ μᾶλλον καταλλαγέντες σωθησόμεθα
by much rather having been reconciled we shall be saved
ἐν τῇ ζωῇ αὐτοῦ· **11** οὐ μόνον δέ, ἀλλὰ
by the life of him; and not only [so], but

dead. 25 He was delivered
over to death for our sins
and was raised to life for
our justification.

Chapter 5

Peace and Joy

THEREFORE, since we
have been justified
through faith, we[u] have
peace with God through
our Lord Jesus Christ,
2 through whom we have
gained access by faith into
this grace in which we now
stand. And we[u] rejoice in
the hope of the glory of
God. 3 Not only so, but we[u]
also rejoice in our sufferings, because we know that
suffering produces perse-
verance; 4 perseverance,
character; and character,
hope. 5 And hope does not
disappoint us, because God
has poured out his love into
our hearts by the Holy
Spirit, whom he has given
us.
6 You see, at just the right
time, when we were still
powerless, Christ died for
the ungodly. 7 Very rarely
will anyone die for a righteous man, though for a
good man someone might
possibly dare to die. 8 But
God demonstrates his own
love for us in this: While we
were still sinners, Christ
died for us.
9 Since we have now been
justified by his blood, how
much more shall we be
saved from God's wrath
through him! 10 For if, when
we were God's enemies,
we were reconciled to him
through the death of his
Son, how much more, hav-
ing been reconciled, shall
we be saved through his
life! 11 Not only is this so,

[u] *1,2,3* Or *let us*

boast in God through our
Lord Jesus Christ, through
whom we have now re-
ceived reconciliation.

Adam and Christ

12 Therefore, just as sin
came into the world
through one man, and
death came through sin,
and so death spread to all
because all have sinned—
13 sin was indeed in the
world before the law, but
sin is not reckoned when
there is no law. 14 Yet death
exercised dominion from
Adam to Moses, even over
those whose sins were not
like the transgression of
Adam, who is a type of the
one who was to come.
15 But the free gift is not
like the trespass. For if the
many died through the one
man's trespass, much more
surely have the grace of
God and the free gift in the
grace of the one man, Jesus
Christ, abounded for the
many. 16 And the free gift is
not like the effect of the one
man's sin. For the judg-
ment following one tres-
pass brought condemna-
tion, but the free gift following many trespasses
brings justification. 17 If,
because of the one man's
trespass, death exercised
dominion through that one,
much more surely will
those who receive the
abundance of grace and the
free gift of righteousness
exercise dominion in life
through the one man, Jesus
Christ.
18 Therefore just as one
man's trespass led to condemnation for all, so one

καὶ καυχώμενοι ἐν τῷ θεῷ διὰ τοῦ
also boasting in – God through the

κυρίου ἡμῶν Ἰησοῦ [Χριστοῦ], δι' οὗ
Lord of us Jesus Christ, through whom

νῦν τὴν καταλλαγὴν ἐλάβομεν.
now the reconciliation we received.

12 Διὰ τοῦτο ὥσπερ δι' ἑνὸς ἀνθρώπου
Therefore as through one man

ἡ ἁμαρτία εἰς τὸν κόσμον εἰσῆλθεν,
– sin into the world entered,

καὶ διὰ τῆς ἁμαρτίας ὁ θάνατος, καὶ
and through – sin – death, [2]also

οὕτως εἰς πάντας ἀνθρώπους ὁ θάνατος
[1]so to all men – death

διῆλθεν, ἐφ' ᾧ πάντες ἥμαρτον· 13 ἄχρι
passed, inasmuch as all sinned; until

γὰρ νόμου ἁμαρτία ἦν ἐν κόσμῳ, ἁμαρτία
for law sin was in [the] world, sin

δὲ οὐκ ἐλλογεῖται μὴ ὄντος νόμου·
but is not reckoned not being law[a];
=when there is no law;

14 ἀλλὰ ἐβασίλευσεν ὁ θάνατος ἀπὸ Ἀδὰμ
but [2]reigned – [1]death from Adam

μέχρι Μωϋσέως καὶ ἐπὶ τοὺς μὴ
until Moses even over the [ones] not

ἁμαρτήσαντας ἐπὶ τῷ ὁμοιώματι τῆς
sinning on the likeness of the

παραβάσεως Ἀδάμ, ὅς ἐστιν τύπος τοῦ
transgression of Adam, who is a type of the

μέλλοντος. 15 Ἀλλ' οὐχ ὡς τὸ παράπτωμα,
[one] coming. But not as the offence,

οὕτως [καὶ] τὸ χάρισμα· εἰ γὰρ τῷ
so also the free gift; for if [1]by the

τοῦ ἑνὸς παραπτώματι οἱ πολλοὶ
[3]of the [4]one [man] [2]offence the many

ἀπέθανον, πολλῷ μᾶλλον ἡ χάρις τοῦ θεοῦ
died, by much rather the grace – of God

καὶ ἡ δωρεὰ ἐν χάριτι τῇ τοῦ ἑνὸς
and the gift in grace – of the one

ἀνθρώπου Ἰησοῦ Χριστοῦ εἰς τοὺς πολλοὺς
man Jesus Christ to the many

ἐπερίσσευσεν. 16 καὶ οὐχ ὡς δι' ἑνὸς
abounded. And not as through one [man]

ἁμαρτήσαντος τὸ δώρημα· τὸ μὲν γὰρ
sinning the gift; [3]the [2]on one hand [1]for

κρίμα ἐξ ἑνὸς εἰς κατάκριμα, τὸ δὲ
judgment [is] of one [offence] to condemnation, on the other the

χάρισμα ἐκ πολλῶν παραπτωμάτων εἰς
free gift [is] of many offences to

δικαίωμα. 17 εἰ γὰρ τῷ τοῦ ἑνὸς
justification. For if [1]by the [3]of the [4]one [man]

παραπτώματι ὁ θάνατος ἐβασίλευσεν διὰ
[2]offence – death reigned through

τοῦ ἑνός, πολλῷ μᾶλλον οἱ τὴν περισσείαν
the one [man], by much rather [1]the [ones] [3]the [4]abundance

τῆς χάριτος καὶ τῆς δωρεᾶς τῆς
[5]of the [6]grace [7]and [8]of the [9]gift –

δικαιοσύνης λαμβάνοντες ἐν ζωῇ βασιλεύ-
[10]of righteousness [2]receiving [12]in [13]life [11]will

σουσιν διὰ τοῦ ἑνὸς Ἰησοῦ Χριστοῦ.
reign through the one [man] Jesus Christ.

18 Ἄρα οὖν ὡς δι' ἑνὸς παραπτώματος
So therefore as through one offence

εἰς πάντας ἀνθρώπους εἰς κατάκριμα,
to all men to condemnation,

but we also rejoice in God
through our Lord Jesus
Christ, through whom we
have now received recon-
ciliation.

Death Through Adam,
Life Through Christ

12Therefore, just as sin
entered the world through
one man, and death
through sin, and in this way
death came to all men, because all sinned— 13for before the law was given, sin
was in the world. But sin is
not taken into account
when there is no law.
14Nevertheless, death
reigned from the time of
Adam to the time of Moses,
even over those who did
not sin by breaking a command, as did Adam, who
was a pattern of the one to
come.
15But the gift is not like
the trespass. For if the
many died by the trespass
of the one man, how much
more did God's grace and
the gift that came by the
grace of the one man, Jesus
Christ, overflow to the
many! 16Again, the gift of
God is not like the result of
the one man's sin: The
judgment followed one sin
and brought condemna-
tion, but the gift followed
many trespasses and
brought justification. 17For
if, by the trespass of the
one man, death reigned
through that one man, how
much more will those who
receive God's abundant
provision of grace and of
the gift of righteousness
reign in life through the one
man, Jesus Christ.
18Consequently, just as
the result of one trespass
was condemnation for all

man's act of righteousness
leads to justification and
life for all. 19 For just as by
the one man's disobedience
the many were made sin-
ners, so by the one man's
obedience the many will be
made righteous. 20 But law
came in, with the result that
the trespass multiplied; but
where sin increased, grace
abounded all the more,
21 so that, just as sin exercised dominion in death, so
grace might also exercise
dominion through justification[u] leading to eternal life
through Jesus Christ our
Lord.

οὕτως καὶ δι' ἑνὸς δικαιώματος εἰς
so also through one righteous act to
πάντας ἀνθρώπους εἰς δικαίωσιν ζωῆς·
all men to justification of life;
19 ὥσπερ γὰρ διὰ τῆς παρακοῆς τοῦ
for as through the disobedience of the
ἑνὸς ἀνθρώπου ἁμαρτωλοὶ κατεστάθησαν
one man 4sinners 3were constituted
οἱ πολλοί, οὕτως καὶ διὰ τῆς ὑπακοῆς
1the 2many, so also through the obedience
τοῦ ἑνὸς δίκαιοι κατασταθήσονται οἱ
of the one [man] 4righteous 3will be constituted 1the
πολλοί. 20 νόμος δὲ παρεισῆλθεν ἵνα
2many. But law entered in order that
πλεονάσῃ τὸ παράπτωμα· οὗ δὲ ἐπλεόνασεν
might abound the offence; but where abounded
ἡ ἁμαρτία, ὑπερεπερίσσευσεν ἡ χάρις,
– sin, more abounded – grace,
21 ἵνα ὥσπερ ἐβασίλευσεν ἡ ἁμαρτία ἐν
in order that as reigned – sin by
τῷ θανάτῳ, οὕτως καὶ ἡ χάρις βασιλεύσῃ
– death, so also – grace might reign
διὰ δικαιοσύνης εἰς ζωὴν αἰώνιον διὰ
through righteousness to life eternal through
Ἰησοῦ Χριστοῦ τοῦ κυρίου ἡμῶν.
Jesus Christ the Lord of us.

one act of righteousness
was justification that brings
life for all men. 19 For just as
through the disobedience
of the one man the many
were made sinners, so also
through the obedience of
the one man the many will
be made righteous.
20 The law was added so
that the trespass might increase. But where sin in-
creased, grace increased all
the more, 21 so that, just as
sin reigned in death, so also
grace might reign through
righteousness to bring eternal life through Jesus
Christ our Lord.

Chapter 6

Dying and Rising with Christ

WHAT then are we to
say? Should we con-
tinue in sin in order that
grace may abound? 2 By no
means! How can we who
died to sin go on living in it?
3 Do you not know that all
of us who have been bap-
tized into Christ Jesus were
baptized into his death?
4 Therefore we have been
buried with him by baptism
into death, so that, just as
Christ was raised from the
dead by the glory of the Father, so we too might walk
in newness of life.
5 For if we have been
united with him in a death
like his, we will certainly be
united with him in a resurrection like his. 6 We know
that our old self was crucified with him so that the
body of sin might be de-
stroyed, and we might no
longer be enslaved to sin.
7 For whoever has died is
freed from sin. 8 But if we

6 Τί οὖν ἐροῦμεν; ἐπιμένωμεν τῇ
What therefore shall we say? May we continue –
ἁμαρτίᾳ, ἵνα ἡ χάρις πλεονάσῃ; 2 μὴ
in sin, in order that – grace may abound? not
γένοιτο. οἵτινες ἀπεθάνομεν τῇ ἁμαρτίᾳ,
May it be. Who *we* died – to sin,
πῶς ἔτι ζήσομεν ἐν αὐτῇ; 3 ἢ ἀγνοεῖτε
how yet shall we live in it? or are ye ignorant
ὅτι ὅσοι ἐβαπτίσθημεν εἰς Χριστὸν
that as many as *we* were baptized into Christ
Ἰησοῦν, εἰς τὸν θάνατον αὐτοῦ ἐβαπτίσ-
Jesus, into the death of him we were
θημεν; 4 συνετάφημεν οὖν αὐτῷ διὰ τοῦ
baptized? 2We were buried with 1therefore him through –
βαπτίσματος εἰς τὸν θάνατον, ἵνα ὥσπερ
baptism into – death, in order that as
ἠγέρθη Χριστὸς ἐκ νεκρῶν διὰ τῆς
was raised Christ from [the] dead through the
δόξης τοῦ πατρός, οὕτως καὶ ἡμεῖς ἐν
glory of the Father, so also we in
καινότητι ζωῆς περιπατήσωμεν. 5 εἰ γὰρ
newness of life might walk. For if
σύμφυτοι γεγόναμεν τῷ ὁμοιώματι τοῦ
united with we have become in the likeness of the
θανάτου αὐτοῦ, ἀλλὰ καὶ τῆς ἀναστάσεως
death of him, but(so) also of the(his) resurrection
ἐσόμεθα· 6 τοῦτο γινώσκοντες, ὅτι ὁ
we shall be; this knowing, that the
παλαιὸς ἡμῶν ἄνθρωπος συνεσταυρώθη, ἵνα
1old 3of us 2man was crucified with [him], in order that
καταργηθῇ τὸ σῶμα τῆς ἁμαρτίας, τοῦ
might be destroyed the body – of sin, –
μηκέτι δουλεύειν ἡμᾶς τῇ ἁμαρτίᾳ· 7 ὁ
no longer to serve us[bd] – sin; 2the (one)
=that we should no longer serve
γὰρ ἀποθανὼν δεδικαίωται ἀπὸ τῆς
1for having died has been justified from –

Chapter 6

Dead to Sin, Alive in Christ

WHAT shall we say,
then? Shall we go on
sinning so that grace may
increase? 2 By no means!
We died to sin; how can we
live in it any longer? 3 Or
don't you know that all of
us who were baptized into
Christ Jesus were baptized
into his death? 4 We were
therefore buried with him
through baptism into death
in order that, just as Christ
was raised from the dead
through the glory of the Father, we too may live a new
life.
5 If we have been united
with him like this in his
death, we will certainly
also be united with him in
his resurrection. 6 For we
know that our old self was
crucified with him so that
the body of sin might be
done away with,[v] that we
should no longer be slaves
to sin— 7 because anyone
who has died has been
freed from sin.

[u] Or *righteousness*

[v] 6 Or *be rendered powerless*

have died with Christ, we
believe that we will also
live with him. 9We know
that Christ, being raised
from the dead, will never
die again; death no longer
has dominion over him.
10The death he died, he
died to sin, once for all; but
the life he lives, he lives to
God. 11So you also must
consider yourselves dead
to sin and alive to God in
Christ Jesus.
12 Therefore, do not let
sin exercise dominion in
your mortal bodies, to
make you obey their pas-
sions. 13No longer present
your members to sin as instruments[v] of wickedness,
but present yourselves to
God as those who have
been brought from death to
life, and present your members to God as instru-
ments[v] of righteousness.
14For sin will have no dominion over you, since you
are not under law but under
grace.

Slaves of Righteousness

15 What then? Should
we sin because we are not
under law but under grace?
By no means! 16Do you not
know that if you present
yourselves to anyone as
obedient slaves, you are
slaves of the one whom you
obey, either of sin, which
leads to death, or of obedience, which leads to righteousness? 17But thanks be
to God that you, having
once been slaves of sin,
have become obedient
from the heart to the form
of teaching to which you
were entrusted, 18and that
you, having been set free
from sin, have become
slaves of righteousness. 19I
am speaking in human
terms because of your natural limitations.[w] For just
as you once presented your
members as slaves to impurity and to greater and
greater iniquity, so now

[v] Or *weapons*
[w] Gk *the weakness of your flesh*

ἁμαρτίας. **8** εἰ δὲ ἀπεθάνομεν σὺν Χριστῷ,
sin. But if we died with Christ

πιστεύομεν ὅτι καὶ συζήσομεν αὐτῷ,
we believe that also we shall live with him,

9 εἰδότες ὅτι Χριστὸς ἐγερθεὶς ἐκ νεκρῶν
knowing that Christ having been raised from [the] dead

οὐκέτι ἀποθνήσκει, θάνατος αὐτοῦ οὐκέτι
no more dies, death [3]*of* him [1]no more

κυριεύει. **10** ὃ γὰρ ἀπέθανεν, τῇ ἁμαρτίᾳ
[2]lords it over. For in that† he died, – to sin

ἀπέθανεν ἐφάπαξ· ὃ δὲ ζῇ, ζῇ τῷ θεῷ.
he died once; but in that† he lives, he lives – to God.

11 οὕτως καὶ ὑμεῖς λογίζεσθε ἑαυτοὺς
So also [2]ye [1]reckon yourselves

εἶναι νεκροὺς μὲν τῇ ἁμαρτίᾳ ζῶντας
to be dead indeed – to sin [2]living

δὲ τῷ θεῷ ἐν Χριστῷ Ἰησοῦ. **12** μὴ
[1]but – to God in Christ Jesus. [3]not

οὖν βασιλευέτω ἡ ἁμαρτία ἐν τῷ θνητῷ
[1]There-fore [2]let [5]reign – [4]sin [6]in [7]the [8]mortal

ὑμῶν σώματι εἰς τὸ ὑπακούειν ταῖς
[10]of you [9]body for the to obey the
=to obey its lusts,

ἐπιθυμίαις αὐτοῦ, **13** μηδὲ παριστάνετε τὰ
lusts of it, neither present ye the

μέλη ὑμῶν ὅπλα ἀδικίας τῇ ἁμαρτίᾳ,
members of you weapons of unrighteousness – to sin,

ἀλλὰ παραστήσατε ἑαυτοὺς τῷ θεῷ ὡσεὶ
but present ye yourselves – to God as

ἐκ νεκρῶν ζῶντας καὶ τὰ μέλη ὑμῶν
from [the] dead living and the members of you

ὅπλα δικαιοσύνης τῷ θεῷ, **14** ἁμαρτία
weapons of righteousness – to God, [2]sin

γὰρ ὑμῶν οὐ κυριεύσει· οὐ γάρ ἐστε
[1]for [4]*of* you [3]shall not lord it over; for ye are not

ὑπὸ νόμον ἀλλὰ ὑπὸ χάριν. **15** Τί οὖν;
under law but under grace. What therefore?

ἁμαρτήσωμεν, ὅτι οὐκ ἐσμὲν ὑπὸ νόμον
may we sin, because we are not under law

ἀλλὰ ὑπὸ χάριν; μὴ γένοιτο. **16** οὐκ
but under grace? May it not be. not

οἴδατε ὅτι ᾧ παριστάνετε ἑαυτοὺς δούλους
Know ye that to whom ye present yourselves slaves

εἰς ὑπακοήν, δοῦλοί ἐστε ᾧ ὑπακούετε,
for obedience, slaves ye are whom ye obey,

ἤτοι ἁμαρτίας εἰς θάνατον ἢ ὑπακοῆς
whether of sin to death or of obedience

εἰς δικαιοσύνην, **17** χάρις δὲ τῷ θεῷ
to righteousness? But thanks – to God

ὅτι ἦτε δοῦλοι τῆς ἁμαρτίας, ὑπηκούσατε
that ye were slaves – of sin, [2]ye obeyed

δὲ ἐκ καρδίας εἰς ὃν παρεδόθητε τύπον
[1]but out of [the] heart [3]to [4]which [5]ye were delivered [1]a form

διδαχῆς, **18** ἐλευθερωθέντες δὲ ἀπὸ τῆς
[2]of teaching, and having been freed from –

ἁμαρτίας ἐδουλώθητε τῇ δικαιοσύνῃ.
sin ye were enslaved – to righteousness.

19 ἀνθρώπινον λέγω διὰ τὴν ἀσθένειαν
Humanly I say because of the weakness

τῆς σαρκὸς ὑμῶν. ὥσπερ γὰρ παρεστήσατε
of the flesh of you. For as ye presented

τὰ μέλη ὑμῶν δοῦλα τῇ ἀκαθαρσίᾳ καὶ
the members of you slaves – to uncleanness and

8Now if we died with
Christ, we believe that we
will also live with him. 9For
we know that since Christ
was raised from the dead,
he cannot die again; death
no longer has mastery over
him. 10The death he died,
he died to sin once for all;
but the life he lives, he lives
to God.
11In the same way, count
yourselves dead to sin but
alive to God in Christ
Jesus. 12Therefore do not
let sin reign in your mortal
body so that you obey its
evil desires. 13Do not offer
the parts of your body to
sin, as instruments of wickedness, but rather offer
yourselves to God, as those
who have been brought
from death to life; and offer
the parts of your body to
him as instruments of righteousness. 14For sin shall
not be your master, be-
cause you are not under
law, but under grace.

Slaves to Righteousness

15What then? Shall we sin
because we are not under
law but under grace? By no
means! 16Don't you know
that when you offer your-
selves to someone to obey
him as slaves, you are
slaves to the one whom you
obey—whether you are
slaves to sin, which leads to
death, or to obedience,
which leads to righteous-
ness? 17But thanks be to
God that, though you used
to be slaves to sin, you
wholeheartedly obeyed the
form of teaching to which
you were entrusted. 18You
have been set free from sin
and have become slaves to
righteousness.
19I put this in human
terms because you are
weak in your natural
selves. Just as you used to
offer the parts of your body
in slavery to impurity and

present your members as
slaves to righteousness for
sanctification.
20 When you were
slaves of sin, you were free
in regard to righteousness.
21 So what advantage did
you then get from the
things of which you now
are ashamed? The end of
those things is death. 22 But
now that you have been
freed from sin and enslaved
to God, the advantage you
get is sanctification. The
end is eternal life. 23 For the
wages of sin is death, but
the free gift of God is eternal life in Christ Jesus our
Lord.

Chapter 7

An Analogy from Marriage

DO you not know,
brothers and
sisters[x]—for I am speaking to those who know the
law—that the law is bind-
ing on a person only during
that person's lifetime?
2 Thus a married woman is
bound by the law to her
husband as long as he lives;
but if her husband dies, she
is discharged from the law
concerning the husband.
3 Accordingly, she will be
called an adulteress if she
lives with another man
while her husband is alive.
But if her husband dies, she
is free from that law, and if
she marries another man,
she is not an adulteress.
4 In the same way, my
friends,[x] you have died to
the law through the body of
Christ, so that you may belong to another, to him who
has been raised from the
dead in order that we may
bear fruit for God. 5 While
we were living in the flesh,
our sinful passions,
aroused by the law, were at

[x] Gk *brothers*

τῇ ἀνομίᾳ εἰς τὴν ἀνομίαν, οὕτως νῦν
– to iniquity unto – iniquity, so now
παραστήσατε τὰ μέλη ὑμῶν δοῦλα τῇ
present ye the members of you slaves –
δικαιοσύνῃ εἰς ἁγιασμόν. 20 ὅτε γὰρ
to righteousness unto sanctification. For when
δοῦλοι ἦτε τῆς ἁμαρτίας, ἐλεύθεροι ἦτε
slaves ye were – of sin, free ye were
τῇ δικαιοσύνῃ. 21 τίνα οὖν καρπὸν εἴχετε
– to righteousness. What ²therefore ¹fruit had ye
τότε; ἐφ' οἷς νῦν ἐπαισχύνεσθε· τὸ γὰρ
then? Over which things now ye are ashamed; for the
τέλος ἐκείνων θάνατος. 22 νυνὶ δὲ ἐλευ-
end of those things [is] death. But now having
θερωθέντες ἀπὸ τῆς ἁμαρτίας δουλωθέντες
been freed from – sin ²having been enslaved
δὲ τῷ θεῷ, ἔχετε τὸν καρπὸν ὑμῶν εἰς
¹and – to God, ye have the fruit of you to
ἁγιασμόν, τὸ δὲ τέλος ζωὴν αἰώνιον.
sanctification, and the end life eternal.
23 τὰ γὰρ ὀψώνια τῆς ἁμαρτίας θάνατος,
For the wages – of sin [is] death,
τὸ δὲ χάρισμα τοῦ θεοῦ ζωὴ αἰώνιος
but the free gift – of God life eternal
ἐν Χριστῷ Ἰησοῦ τῷ κυρίῳ ἡμῶν.
in Christ Jesus the Lord of us.

7 Ἢ ἀγνοεῖτε, ἀδελφοί, γινώσκουσιν γὰρ
Or are ye ignorant, brothers, for to [ones] knowing
νόμον λαλῶ, ὅτι ὁ νόμος κυριεύει τοῦ
law I speak, that the law lords it over the
ἀνθρώπου ἐφ' ὅσον χρόνον ζῇ; 2 ἡ γὰρ
man over such time [as] he lives? For the
ὕπανδρος γυνὴ τῷ ζῶντι ἀνδρὶ δέδεται
²married ¹woman to the living husband has been bound
νόμῳ· ἐὰν δὲ ἀποθάνῃ ὁ ἀνήρ, κατήργηται
by law; but if dies the husband, she has been discharged
ἀπὸ τοῦ νόμου τοῦ ἀνδρός. 3 ἄρα οὖν
from the law of the husband. Therefore
ζῶντος τοῦ ἀνδρὸς μοιχαλὶς χρηματίσει
living the husband[a] an adulteress she will be called
= while the husband lives
ἐὰν γένηται ἀνδρὶ ἑτέρῳ· ἐὰν δὲ ἀποθάνῃ
if she becomes ²husband ¹to a different; but if dies
ὁ ἀνήρ, ἐλευθέρα ἐστὶν ἀπὸ τοῦ νόμου,
the husband, free she is from the law,
τοῦ μὴ εἶναι αὐτὴν μοιχαλίδα γενομένην
– not to be her[d] an adulteress having become
=so that she is not
ἀνδρὶ ἑτέρῳ. 4 ὥστε, ἀδελφοί μου, καὶ
²husband ¹to a different. So, brothers of me, also
ὑμεῖς ἐθανατώθητε τῷ νόμῳ διὰ τοῦ
ye were put to death to the law through the
σώματος τοῦ Χριστοῦ, εἰς τὸ γενέσθαι
body – of Christ, for *the* to become
=that ye might belong
ὑμᾶς ἑτέρῳ, τῷ ἐκ νεκρῶν ἐγερθέντι,
you[b] to a different, to the [one] from [the] dead having been raised,
ἵνα καρποφορήσωμεν τῷ θεῷ. 5 ὅτε
in order that we may bear fruit – to God. when
γὰρ ἤμεν ἐν τῇ σαρκί, τὰ παθήματα
For we were in the flesh, the passions

to ever-increasing wickedness, so now offer them in
slavery to righteousness
leading to holiness. 20 When
you were slaves to sin, you
were free from the control
of righteousness. 21 What
benefit did you reap at that
time from the things you
are now ashamed of? Those
things result in death! 22 But
now that you have been set
free from sin and have become slaves to God, the
benefit you reap leads to
holiness, and the result is
eternal life. 23 For the wages
of sin is death, but the gift
of God is eternal life in[w]
Christ Jesus our Lord.

Chapter 7

An Illustration From Marriage

DO you not know,
brothers—for I am
speaking to men who know
the law—that the law has
authority over a man only
as long as he lives? 2 For example, by law a married
woman is bound to her husband as long as he is alive,
but if her husband dies, she
is released from the law of
marriage. 3 So then, if she
marries another man while
her husband is still alive,
she is called an adulteress.
But if her husband dies, she
is released from that law
and is not an adulteress,
even though she marries
another man.
4 So, my brothers, you
also died to the law through
the body of Christ, that you
might belong to another, to
him who was raised from
the dead, in order that we
might bear fruit to God.
5 For when we were con-
trolled by the sinful na-
ture,[x] the sinful passions

[w] 23 Or *through*
[x] 5 Or *the flesh*; also in verse 25

work in our members to bear fruit for death. [6]But now we are discharged from the law, dead to that which held us captive, so that we are slaves not under the old written code but in the new life of the Spirit.

The Law and Sin

7 What then should we say? That the law is sin? By no means! Yet, if it had not been for the law, I would not have known sin. I would not have known what it is to covet if the law had not said, "You shall not covet." [8]But sin, seizing an opportunity in the commandment, produced in me all kinds of covetousness. Apart from the law sin lies dead. [9]I was once alive apart from the law, but when the commandment came, sin revived [10]and I died, and the very commandment that promised life proved to be death to me. [11]For sin, seizing an opportunity in the commandment, deceived me and through it killed me. [12]So the law is holy, and the commandment is holy and just and good.

13 Did what is good, then, bring death to me? By no means! It was sin, working death in me through what is good, in order that sin might be shown to be sin, and through the commandment might become sinful beyond measure.

The Inner Conflict

14 For we know that the law is spiritual; but I am of the flesh, sold into slavery under sin.[y] [15]I do not understand my own actions. For I do not do what I

τῶν ἁμαρτιῶν τὰ διὰ τοῦ νόμου ἐνηργεῖτο
– of sins – through the law operated

ἐν τοῖς μέλεσιν ἡμῶν εἰς τὸ καρποφορῆσαι
in the members of us *for the* to bear fruit

τῷ θανάτῳ· **6** νυνὶ δὲ κατηργήθημεν ἀπὸ
– to death; but now we were discharged from

τοῦ νόμου, ἀποθανόντες ἐν ᾧ κατειχόμεθα,
the law, having died [to that] in which we were held fast,

ὥστε δουλεύειν [ἡμᾶς] ἐν καινότητι
so as to serve us[b] in newness

πνεύματος καὶ οὐ παλαιότητι γράμματος.
of spirit and not [in] oldness of letter.

7 Τί οὖν ἐροῦμεν; ὁ νόμος ἁμαρτία;
What therefore shall we say? the law sin?

μὴ γένοιτο· ἀλλὰ τὴν ἁμαρτίαν οὐκ
May it not be; yet – sin not

ἔγνων εἰ μὴ διὰ νόμου· τήν τε γὰρ
I knew except through law; – [2]also [1]for

ἐπιθυμίαν οὐκ ᾔδειν εἰ μὴ ὁ νόμος
lust I knew not except the law

ἔλεγεν· οὐκ ἐπιθυμήσεις· **8** ἀφορμὴν δὲ
said : Thou shalt not lust; but [3]occasion

λαβοῦσα ἡ ἁμαρτία διὰ τῆς ἐντολῆς
[2]taking – [1]sin through the commandment

κατειργάσατο ἐν ἐμοὶ πᾶσαν ἐπιθυμίαν·
wrought in me every lust;

χωρὶς γὰρ νόμου ἁμαρτία νεκρά. **9** ἐγὼ
for without law sin [is] dead. I

δὲ ἔζων χωρὶς νόμου ποτέ· ἐλθούσης δὲ
And was living without law then; but coming =when the

τῆς ἐντολῆς ἡ ἁμαρτία ἀνέζησεν, **10** ἐγὼ
the commandment[a] – sin revived, [2]I
commandment came

δὲ ἀπέθανον, καὶ εὑρέθη μοι ἡ ἐντολὴ
[1]and died, and [6]was found [7]to me [1]the [2]commandment

ἡ εἰς ζωήν, αὕτη εἰς θάνατον· **11** ἡ γὰρ
– [3]for [4]life, [5]this to death; – for

ἁμαρτία ἀφορμὴν λαβοῦσα διὰ τῆς
sin [2]occasion [1]taking through the

ἐντολῆς ἐξηπάτησέν με καὶ δι' αὐτῆς
commandment deceived me and through it

ἀπέκτεινεν. **12** ὥστε ὁ μὲν νόμος ἅγιος,
killed [me]. So the – law [is] holy,

καὶ ἡ ἐντολὴ ἁγία καὶ δικαία καὶ ἀγαθή.
and the commandment holy and just and good.

13 Τὸ οὖν ἀγαθὸν ἐμοὶ ἐγένετο θάνατος;
[2]The [1]therefore good to me became death?

μὴ γένοιτο· ἀλλὰ ἡ ἁμαρτία, ἵνα φανῇ
May it not be; yet – sin, in order that it might appear

ἁμαρτία, διὰ τοῦ ἀγαθοῦ μοι κατεργαζομένη
sin, through the good [3]to me [1]working

θάνατον, ἵνα γένηται καθ' ὑπερβολὴν
[2]death, in order that [5]might become [6]excessively†

ἁμαρτωλὸς ἡ ἁμαρτία διὰ τῆς ἐντολῆς.
[7]sinful – [1]sin [2]through [3]the [4]commandment.

14 οἴδαμεν γὰρ ὅτι ὁ νόμος πνευματικός
For we know that the law spiritual

ἐστιν· ἐγὼ δὲ σάρκινός εἰμι, πεπραμένος
is; but I fleshy am, *having been* sold

ὑπὸ τὴν ἁμαρτίαν. **15** ὃ γὰρ κατεργάζομαι
under – sin. For what I work

οὐ γινώσκω· οὐ γὰρ ὃ θέλω τοῦτο
I know not; for not what I wish this

aroused by the law were at work in our bodies, so that we bore fruit for death. [6]But now, by dying to what once bound us, we have been released from the law so that we serve in the new way of the Spirit, and not in the old way of the written code.

Struggling With Sin

[7]What shall we say, then? Is the law sin? Certainly not! Indeed I would not have known what sin was except through the law. For I would not have known what coveting really was if the law had not said, "Do not covet."[y] [8]But sin, seizing the opportunity afforded by the commandment, produced in me every kind of covetous desire. For apart from law, sin is dead. [9]Once I was alive apart from law; but when the commandment came, sin sprang to life and I died. [10]I found that the very commandment that was intended to bring life actually brought death. [11]For sin, seizing the opportunity afforded by the commandment, deceived me, and through the commandment put me to death. [12]So then, the law is holy, and the commandment is holy, righteous and good.

[13]Did that which is good, then, become death to me? By no means! But in order that sin might be recognized as sin, it produced death in me through what was good, so that through the commandment sin might become utterly sinful.

[14]We know that the law is spiritual; but I am unspiritual, sold as a slave to sin. [15]I do not understand what I do. For what I want to do

[y] Gk *sold under sin*

[y]7 Exodus 20:17; Deut. 5:21

want, but I do the very
thing I hate. 16 Now if I do
what I do not want, I agree
that the law is good. 17 But
in fact it is no longer I that
do it, but sin that dwells
within me. 18 For I know
that nothing good dwells
within me, that is, in my
flesh. I can will what is
right, but I cannot do it.
19 For I do not do the good
I want, but the evil I do not
want is what I do. 20 Now if
I do what I do not want, it
is no longer I that do it, but
sin that dwells within me.
21 So I find it to be a law
that when I want to do what
is good, evil lies close at
hand. 22 For I delight in the
law of God in my inmost
self, 23 but I see in my members another law at war
with the law of my mind,
making me captive to the
law of sin that dwells in my
members. 24 Wretched man
that I am! Who will rescue
me from this body of
death? 25 Thanks be to God
through Jesus Christ our
Lord!
So then, with my mind I
am a slave to the law of
God, but with my flesh I am
a slave to the law of sin.

Chapter 8

Life in the Spirit

THERE is therefore
now no condemnation
for those who are in Christ
Jesus. 2 For the law of the
Spirit[z] of life in Christ
Jesus has set you[a] free
from the law of sin and of

[z] Or *spirit*
[a] Here the Greek word *you* is singular number; other ancient authorities read *me* or *us*

πράσσω, ἀλλ᾽ ὃ μισῶ τοῦτο ποιῶ. 16 εἰ
I practise, but what I hate this I do. if

δὲ ὃ οὐ θέλω τοῦτο ποιῶ, σύμφημι
But what I wish not this I do, I agree with

τῷ νόμῳ ὅτι καλός. 17 νυνὶ δὲ οὐκέτι
the law that [it is] good. But now no longer

ἐγὼ κατεργάζομαι αὐτὸ ἀλλὰ ἡ ἐνοικοῦσα
I work it but 1the 3indwelling

ἐν ἐμοὶ ἁμαρτία. 18 οἶδα γὰρ ὅτι οὐκ
4in 5me 2sin. For I know that not

οἰκεῖ ἐν ἐμοί, τοῦτ᾽ ἔστιν ἐν τῇ σαρκί
dwells in me, this is in the flesh

μου, ἀγαθόν· τὸ γὰρ θέλειν παράκειταί
of me, [that which is] good; – for to wish is present

μοι, τὸ δὲ κατεργάζεσθαι τὸ καλὸν
to me, – but 2to work 3the 4good

οὔ· 19 οὐ γὰρ ὃ θέλω ποιῶ ἀγαθόν,
1not; for not what 3I wish 2I do 1good,

ἀλλὰ ὃ οὐ θέλω κακὸν τοῦτο πράσσω.
but what 2I wish not 1evil this I practise.

20 εἰ δὲ ὃ οὐ θέλω ἐγὼ τοῦτο ποιῶ,
But if what 2wish not 1I this I do,

οὐκέτι ἐγὼ κατεργάζομαι αὐτὸ ἀλλὰ ἡ
no longer I work it but 1the

οἰκοῦσα ἐν ἐμοὶ ἁμαρτία. 21 εὑρίσκω
3dwelling 4in 5me 2sin. I find

ἄρα τὸν νόμον τῷ θέλοντι ἐμοὶ ποιεῖν
then the law 2the [one] 3wishing 1to me to do

τὸ καλόν, ὅτι ἐμοὶ τὸ κακὸν παράκειται·
the good, that to me the evil is present;

22 συνήδομαι γὰρ τῷ νόμῳ τοῦ θεοῦ κατὰ
for I delight in the law – of God according to

τὸν ἔσω ἄνθρωπον, 23 βλέπω δὲ ἕτερον
the inner man, but I see a different

νόμον ἐν τοῖς μέλεσίν μου ἀντιστρατευόμενον
law in the members of me warring against

τῷ νόμῳ τοῦ νοός μου καὶ αἰχμαλωτίζοντά
the law of the mind of me and taking captive

με ἐν τῷ νόμῳ τῆς ἁμαρτίας τῷ ὄντι
me by the law – of sin the [one] being

ἐν τοῖς μέλεσίν μου. 24 Ταλαίπωρος
in the members of me. 1Wretched

ἐγὼ ἄνθρωπος· τίς με ῥύσεται ἐκ τοῦ
3I 2man; who me will deliver from the

σώματος τοῦ θανάτου τούτου; 25 χάρις
body of this death? Thanks

τῷ θεῷ διὰ Ἰησοῦ Χριστοῦ τοῦ κυρίου
– to God through Jesus Christ the Lord

ἡμῶν. Ἄρα οὖν αὐτὸς ἐγὼ τῷ μὲν
of us. So then 2[my]self 1I 4with the 3on one hand

νοῒ δουλεύω νόμῳ θεοῦ, τῇ δὲ σαρκὶ
5mind serve [the] law of God, on the other with the flesh

νόμῳ ἁμαρτίας. 8 οὐδὲν ἄρα νῦν κατάκριμα
[the] law of sin. 4No 1then 3now 5condemnation 2[there is]

τοῖς ἐν Χριστῷ Ἰησοῦ. 2 ὁ γὰρ νόμος τοῦ
to the [ones] in Christ Jesus. For the law of the

πνεύματος τῆς ζωῆς ἐν Χριστῷ Ἰησοῦ
spirit – of life in Christ Jesus

ἠλευθέρωσέν σε ἀπὸ τοῦ νόμου τῆς
freed thee from the law –

I do not do, but what I hate
I do. 16 And if I do what I do
not want to do, I agree that
the law is good. 17 As it is, it
is no longer I myself who
do it, but it is sin living in
me. 18 I know that nothing
good lives in me, that is, in
my sinful nature.[z] For I
have the desire to do what
is good, but I cannot carry
it out. 19 For what I do is not
the good I want to do; no,
the evil I do not want to
do—this I keep on doing.
20 Now if I do what I do not
want to do, it is no longer I
who do it, but it is sin living
in me that does it.
21 So I find this law at
work: When I want to do
good, evil is right there
with me. 22 For in my inner
being I delight in God's
law; 23 but I see another law
at work in the members of
my body, waging war
against the law of my mind
and making me a prisoner
of the law of sin at work
within my members.
24 What a wretched man I
am! Who will rescue me
from this body of death?
25 Thanks be to God—
through Jesus Christ our
Lord!
So then, I myself in my
mind am a slave to God's
law, but in the sinful nature
a slave to the law of sin.

Chapter 8

Life Through the Spirit

THEREFORE, there is
now no condemnation
for those who are in Christ
Jesus,[a] 2 because through
Christ Jesus the law of the
Spirit of life set me free

[z] *18* Or *my flesh*
[a] *1* Some later manuscripts *Jesus, who do not live according to the sinful nature but according to the Spirit.*

death. 3 For God has done
what the law, weakened by
the flesh, could not do: by
sending his own Son in the
likeness of sinful flesh, and
to deal with sin,[b] he condemned sin in the flesh, 4 so
that the just requirement of
the law might be fulfilled in
us, who walk not according
to the flesh but according to
the Spirit.[z] 5 For those who
live according to the flesh
set their minds on the
things of the flesh, but
those who live according to
the Spirit[z] set their minds
on the things of the Spirit.[z]
6 To set the mind on the
flesh is death, but to set the
mind on the Spirit[z] is life
and peace. 7 For this reason
the mind that is set on the
flesh is hostile to God; it
does not submit to God's
law—indeed it cannot,
8 and those who are in the
flesh cannot please God.
9 But you are not in the
flesh; you are in the Spirit,[z] since the Spirit of God
dwells in you. Anyone who
does not have the Spirit of
Christ does not belong to
him. 10 But if Christ is in
you, though the body is
dead because of sin, the
Spirit[z] is life because of
righteousness. 11 If the
Spirit of him who raised
Jesus from the dead dwells
in you, he who raised
Christ[c] from the dead will
give life to your mortal bodies also through[d] his Spirit
that dwells in you.
12 So then, brothers
and sisters,[e] we are debtors, not to the flesh, to live

[b] Or *and as a sin offering*
[c] Other ancient authorities read *the Christ* or *Christ Jesus* or *Jesus Christ*
[d] Other ancient authorities read *on account of*
[e] Gk *brothers*

ἁμαρτίας καὶ τοῦ θανάτου. 3 τὸ γὰρ
of sin and – of death. For the
ἀδύνατον τοῦ νόμου, ἐν ᾧ ἠσθένει διὰ
impossible thing of the law, in which it was weak through
τῆς σαρκός, ὁ θεὸς τὸν ἑαυτοῦ υἱὸν
the flesh, – [1]God [3]the [5]of himself [4]Son
πέμψας ἐν ὁμοιώματι σαρκὸς ἁμαρτίας
[2]sending in likeness of flesh of sin
καὶ περὶ ἁμαρτίας κατέκρινεν τὴν ἁμαρτίαν
and concerning sin condemned – sin
ἐν τῇ σαρκί, 4 ἵνα τὸ δικαίωμα τοῦ
in the flesh, in order that the ordinance of the
νόμου πληρωθῇ ἐν ἡμῖν τοῖς μὴ κατὰ
law may be fulfilled in us the [ones] not according to
σάρκα περιπατοῦσιν ἀλλὰ κατὰ πνεῦμα.
flesh walking but according to spirit.
5 οἱ γὰρ κατὰ σάρκα ὄντες τὰ τῆς
For the [ones] according to flesh being the things of the
σαρκὸς φρονοῦσιν, οἱ δὲ κατὰ πνεῦμα
flesh mind, but the [ones] according to spirit
τὰ τοῦ πνεύματος. 6 τὸ γὰρ φρόνημα
the things of the Spirit. For the mind
τῆς σαρκὸς θάνατος, τὸ δὲ φρόνημα
of the flesh [is] death, but the mind
τοῦ πνεύματος ζωὴ καὶ εἰρήνη. 7 διότι
of the Spirit life and peace. Wherefore
τὸ φρόνημα τῆς σαρκὸς ἔχθρα εἰς θεόν·
the mind of the flesh [is] enmity against God;
τῷ γὰρ νόμῳ τοῦ θεοῦ οὐχ ὑποτάσσεται,
for to the law – of God it is not subject,
οὐδὲ γὰρ δύναται· 8 οἱ δὲ ἐν σαρκὶ
neither indeed can it; and the [ones] [2]in [3]flesh
ὄντες θεῷ ἀρέσαι οὐ δύνανται. 9 ὑμεῖς
[1]being [6]God [5]to please [4]cannot. ye
δὲ οὐκ ἐστὲ ἐν σαρκὶ ἀλλὰ ἐν πνεύματι,
But are not in flesh but in Spirit,
εἴπερ πνεῦμα θεοῦ οἰκεῖ ἐν ὑμῖν. εἰ
since [the] Spirit of God dwells in you. if
δέ τις πνεῦμα Χριστοῦ οὐκ ἔχει, οὗτος
But anyone [the] Spirit of Christ has not, this one
οὐκ ἔστιν αὐτοῦ. 10 εἰ δὲ Χριστὸς
is not of him. But if Christ
ἐν ὑμῖν, τὸ μὲν σῶμα νεκρὸν διὰ
[is] in you, [2]the [1]on one hand [3]body [is] dead because of
ἁμαρτίαν, τὸ δὲ πνεῦμα ζωὴ διὰ
sin, [2]the [1]on the other [3]spirit [is] life because of
δικαιοσύνην. 11 εἰ δὲ τὸ πνεῦμα τοῦ
righteousness. But if the Spirit of the [one]
ἐγείραντος τὸν Ἰησοῦν ἐκ νεκρῶν οἰκεῖ ἐν
having raised – Jesus from [the] dead dwells in
ὑμῖν, ὁ ἐγείρας ἐκ νεκρῶν Χριστὸν
you, the [one] having raised from [the] dead Christ
Ἰησοῦν ζωοποιήσει καὶ τὰ θνητὰ σώματα
Jesus will quicken also the mortal bodies
ὑμῶν διὰ τοῦ ἐνοικοῦντος αὐτοῦ πνεύματος
of you through the [3]indwelling [2]of him [1]Spirit
ἐν ὑμῖν.
[4]in [5]you.
12 Ἄρα οὖν, ἀδελφοί, ὀφειλέται ἐσμέν,
So then, brothers, debtors we are,

from the law of sin and
death. 3 For what the law
was powerless to do in that
it was weakened by the sinful nature,[b] God did by
sending his own Son in the
likeness of sinful man to be
a sin offering.[c] And so he
condemned sin in sinful
man,[d] 4 in order that the
righteous requirements of
the law might be fully met
in us, who do not live according to the sinful nature
but according to the Spirit.
5 Those who live accord-
ing to the sinful nature have
their minds set on what that
nature desires; but those
who live in accordance
with the Spirit have their
minds set on what the Spirit
desires. 6 The mind of sinful
man[e] is death, but the mind
controlled by the Spirit is
life and peace; 7 the sinful
mind[f] is hostile to God. It
does not submit to God's
law, nor can it do so.
8 Those controlled by the
sinful nature cannot please
God.
9 You, however, are con-
trolled not by the sinful nature but by the Spirit, if the
Spirit of God lives in you.
And if anyone does not
have the Spirit of Christ, he
does not belong to Christ.
10 But if Christ is in you,
your body is dead because
of sin, yet your spirit is
alive because of righteousness. 11 And if the Spirit of
him who raised Jesus from
the dead is living in you, he
who raised Christ from the
dead will also give life to
your mortal bodies through
his Spirit, who lives in you.
12 Therefore, brothers, we
have an obligation—but it

[b]3 Or *the flesh*; also in verses 4, 5, 8, 9, 12 and 13
[c]3 Or *man, for sin*
[d]3 Or *in the flesh*
[e]6 Or *mind set on the flesh*
[f]7 Or *the mind set on the flesh*

according to the flesh—
[13]for if you live according
to the flesh, you will die;
but if by the Spirit you put
to death the deeds of the
body, you will live. [14]For
all who are led by the Spirit
of God are children of God.
[15]For you did not receive a
spirit of slavery to fall back
into fear, but you have received a spirit of adoption.
When we cry, "Abba![f] Father!" [16]it is that very Spirit
bearing witness[g] with our
spirit that we are children
of God, [17]and if children,
then heirs, heirs of God and
joint heirs with Christ—if,
in fact, we suffer with him
so that we may also be glorified with him.

Future Glory

18 I consider that the
sufferings of this present
time are not worth comparing with the glory about to
be revealed to us. [19]For the
creation waits with eager
longing for the revealing of
the children of God; [20]for
the creation was subjected
to futility, not of its own
will but by the will of the
one who subjected it, in
hope [21]that the creation itself will be set free from its
bondage to decay and will
obtain the freedom of the
glory of the children of
God. [22]We know that the
whole creation has been
groaning in labor pains until now; [23]and not only the
creation, but we ourselves,
who have the first fruits of
the Spirit, groan inwardly
while we wait for adoption,
the redemption of our bodies. [24]For in[h] hope we
were saved. Now hope that

[f] Aramaic for *Father*
[g] Or [15]*a spirit of adoption, by which we cry, "Abba! Father!"* [16]*The Spirit itself bears witness*
[h] Or *by*

οὐ τῇ σαρκὶ τοῦ κατὰ σάρκα ζῆν. 13 εἰ
not to the flesh – according to flesh to live[d]. if

γὰρ κατὰ σάρκα ζῆτε, μέλλετε ἀποθνῄσκειν·
For according to flesh ye live, ye are about to die:

εἰ δὲ πνεύματι τὰς πράξεις τοῦ σώματος
but if by [the] Spirit the practices of the body

θανατοῦτε, ζήσεσθε. 14 ὅσοι γὰρ πνεύματι
ye put to death, ye will live. For as many as by [the] Spirit

θεοῦ ἄγονται, οὗτοι υἱοί εἰσιν θεοῦ.
of God are led, these sons are of God.

15 οὐ γὰρ ἐλάβετε πνεῦμα δουλείας πάλιν
For ye received not a spirit of slavery again

εἰς φόβον, ἀλλὰ ἐλάβετε πνεῦμα υἱοθεσίας,
for fear, but ye received a spirit of adoption,

ἐν ᾧ κράζομεν· ἀββὰ ὁ πατήρ. 16 αὐτὸ
by which we cry: Abba – Father. [3]it(him)self

τὸ πνεῦμα συμμαρτυρεῖ τῷ πνεύματι ἡμῶν
[1]The [2]Spirit witnesses with the spirit of us

ὅτι ἐσμὲν τέκνα θεοῦ. 17 εἰ δὲ τέκνα,
that we are children of God. And if children,

καὶ κληρονόμοι· κληρονόμοι μὲν θεοῦ,
also heirs; heirs on one hand of God,

συγκληρονόμοι δὲ Χριστοῦ, εἴπερ συμπάσ-
joint heirs on the other of Christ, since we suffer

χομεν ἵνα καὶ συνδοξασθῶμεν. 18 Λογίζομαι
with[him] in order that also we may be glorified with [him]. I reckon

γὰρ ὅτι οὐκ ἄξια τὰ παθήματα τοῦ
For that [6][are] [7]not [8]worthy [1]the [2]sufferings [3]of the

νῦν καιροῦ πρὸς τὴν μέλλουσαν δόξαν
[4]now [5]time [to (present) be compared] with the coming glory

ἀποκαλυφθῆναι εἰς ἡμᾶς. 19 ἡ γὰρ
to be revealed to us. For the

ἀποκαραδοκία τῆς κτίσεως τὴν ἀποκάλυψιν
anxious watching of the creation [2]the [3]revelation

τῶν υἱῶν τοῦ θεοῦ ἀπεκδέχεται. 20 τῇ
[4]of the [5]sons – [6]of God [1]is eagerly expecting. –

γὰρ ματαιότητι ἡ κτίσις ὑπετάγη, οὐχ
For to vanity the creation was subjected, not

ἑκοῦσα, ἀλλὰ διὰ τὸν ὑποτάξαντα, ἐφ'
willing[ly], but because of the [one] subjecting, in

ἐλπίδι 21 διότι καὶ αὐτὴ ἡ κτίσις
hope because even itself the creation

ἐλευθερωθήσεται ἀπὸ τῆς δουλείας τῆς
will be freed from the slavery –

φθορᾶς εἰς τὴν ἐλευθερίαν τῆς δόξης
of corruption to the freedom of the glory

τῶν τέκνων τοῦ θεοῦ. 22 οἴδαμεν γὰρ
of the children – of God. For we know

ὅτι πᾶσα ἡ κτίσις συστενάζει καὶ
that all the creation groans together and

συνωδίνει ἄχρι τοῦ νῦν· 23 οὐ μόνον δέ,
travails together until – now; and not only [so],

ἀλλὰ καὶ αὐτοὶ τὴν ἀπαρχὴν τοῦ πνεύματος
but also [our]selves [2]the [3]firstfruit [4]of the [5]Spirit

ἔχοντες [ἡμεῖς] καὶ αὐτοὶ ἐν ἑαυτοῖς
[1]having we also [our]selves in ourselves

στενάζομεν υἱοθεσίαν ἀπεκδεχόμενοι, τὴν
groan adoption eagerly expecting, the

ἀπολύτρωσιν τοῦ σώματος ἡμῶν. 24 τῇ
redemption of the body of us. –

γὰρ ἐλπίδι ἐσώθημεν· ἐλπὶς δὲ βλεπομένη
For by hope we were saved; but hope being seen

is not to the sinful nature,
to live according to it. [13]For
if you live according to the
sinful nature, you will die;
but if by the Spirit you put
to death the misdeeds of
the body, you will live,
[14]because those who are
led by the Spirit of God are
sons of God. [15]For you did
not receive a spirit that
makes you a slave again to
fear, but you received the
Spirit of sonship.[g] And by
him we cry, "*Abba*,[h] Father." [16]The Spirit himself
testifies with our spirit that
we are God's children.
[17]Now if we are children,
then we are heirs—heirs of
God and co-heirs with
Christ, if indeed we share
in his sufferings in order
that we may also share in
his glory.

Future Glory

[18]I consider that our present sufferings are not
worth comparing with the
glory that will be revealed
in us. [19]The creation waits
in eager expectation for the
sons of God to be revealed.
[20]For the creation was subjected to frustration, not by
its own choice, but by the
will of the one who subjected it, in hope [21]that[i] the
creation itself will be liber-
ated from its bondage to decay and brought into the
glorious freedom of the
children of God.

[22]We know that the whole
creation has been groaning
as in the pains of childbirth
right up to the present time.
[23]Not only so, but we ourselves, who have the firstfruits of the Spirit, groan inwardly as we wait eagerly
for our adoption as sons,
the redemption of our bodies. [24]For in this hope we
were saved. But hope that

[g] *15* Or *adoption*
[h] *15* Aramaic for *Father*
[i] *20,21* Or *subjected it in hope.* [21]*For*

is seen is not hope. For who
hopes[i] for what is seen?
25 But if we hope for what
we do not see, we wait for
it with patience.
26 Likewise the Spirit
helps us in our weakness;
for we do not know how to
pray as we ought, but that
very Spirit intercedes[j]
with sighs too deep for
words. 27 And God,[k] who
searches the heart, knows
what is the mind of the
Spirit, because the Spirit[l]
intercedes for the saints according to the will of God.[m]
28 We know that all
things work together for
good[n] for those who love
God, who are called ac-
cording to his purpose.
29 For those whom he foreknew he also predestined
to be conformed to the image of his Son, in order that
he might be the firstborn
within a large family.[o]
30 And those whom he pre-
destined he also called; and
those whom he called he
also justified; and those
whom he justified he also
glorified.

God's Love in Christ Jesus

31 What then are we to
say about these things? If
God is for us, who is
against us? 32 He who did
not withhold his own Son,
but gave him up for all of
us, will he not with him also
give us everything else?
33 Who will bring any
charge against God's elect?
It is God who justifies.
34 Who is to condemn? It is
Christ Jesus, who died,
yes, who was raised, who is
at the right hand of God,
who indeed intercedes for
us.[p] 35 Who will separate
us from the love of Christ?
Will hardship, or distress,
or persecution, or famine,

[i] Other ancient authorities read *awaits*
[j] Other ancient authorities add *for us*
[k] Gk *the one*
[l] Gk *he* or *it*
[m] Gk *according to God*
[n] Other ancient authorities read *God makes all things work together for good,* or *in all things God works for good*
[o] Gk *among many brothers*
[p] Or *Is it Christ Jesus . . . for us?*

οὐκ ἔστιν ἐλπίς· ὃ γὰρ βλέπει τις,
is not hope; for what sees anyone,
τί καὶ ἐλπίζει; 25 εἰ δὲ ὃ οὐ βλέπομεν
why also he hopes? but if what we do not see
ἐλπίζομεν, δι' ὑπομονῆς ἀπεκδεχόμεθα.
we hope [for], through patience we eagerly expect.
26 ὡσαύτως δὲ καὶ τὸ πνεῦμα συναντιλαμ-
And similarly also the Spirit takes
βάνεται τῇ ἀσθενείᾳ ἡμῶν· τὸ γὰρ τί
share in the weakness of us; – for what
προσευξώμεθα καθὸ δεῖ οὐκ οἴδαμεν, ἀλλὰ
we may pray as it behoves we know not, but
αὐτὸ τὸ πνεῦμα ὑπερεντυγχάνει στεναγμοῖς
it(him)self the Spirit supplicates on [our] behalf with groanings
ἀλαλήτοις· 27 ὁ δὲ ἐρευνῶν τὰς καρδίας
unutterable; and the [one] searching the hearts
οἶδεν τί τὸ φρόνημα τοῦ πνεύματος,
knows what [is] the mind of the Spirit,
ὅτι κατὰ θεὸν ἐντυγχάνει ὑπὲρ ἁγίων.
because according to God he supplicates on behalf of saints.
28 οἴδαμεν δὲ ὅτι τοῖς ἀγαπῶσιν τὸν
And we know that to the [ones] loving –
θεὸν πάντα συνεργεῖ [ὁ θεὸς] εἰς ἀγαθόν,
God ³all things ²works together – ¹God for good,
τοῖς κατὰ πρόθεσιν κλητοῖς οὖσιν. 29 ὅτι
to the [ones] ³according to ⁴purpose ²called ¹being. Because
οὓς προέγνω, καὶ προώρισεν συμμόρφους
whom he foreknew, also he foreordained conformed to
τῆς εἰκόνος τοῦ υἱοῦ αὐτοῦ, εἰς τὸ
of the image of the Son of him, for *the* =that he should be
εἶναι αὐτὸν πρωτότοκον ἐν πολλοῖς
to be him[b] firstborn among many
ἀδελφοῖς· 30 οὓς δὲ προώρισεν, τούτους
brothers; but whom he foreordained, these
καὶ ἐκάλεσεν· καὶ οὓς ἐκάλεσεν, τούτους
also he called; and whom he called, these
καὶ ἐδικαίωσεν· οὓς δὲ ἐδικαίωσεν, τούτους
also he justified; but whom he justified, these
καὶ ἐδόξασεν. 31 Τί οὖν ἐροῦμεν πρὸς
also he glorified. What therefore shall we say to
ταῦτα; εἰ ὁ θεὸς ὑπὲρ ἡμῶν, τίς καθ'
these things? If – God on behalf of us, who against
ἡμῶν; ὅς γε τοῦ ἰδίου υἱοῦ οὐκ ἐφείσατο,
us? Who indeed the(his) own Son spared not,
32 ἀλλὰ ὑπὲρ ἡμῶν πάντων παρέδωκεν
but on behalf of us all delivered
αὐτόν, πῶς οὐχὶ καὶ σὺν αὐτῷ τὰ πάντα
him, how not also with him – all things
ἡμῖν χαρίσεται; 33 τίς ἐγκαλέσει κατὰ
to us will he freely give? Who will bring a charge *against* against
ἐκλεκτῶν θεοῦ; θεὸς ὁ δικαιῶν· 34 τίς
chosen ones of God? God [is] the [one] justifying; who
ὁ κατακρινῶν; Χριστὸς Ἰησοῦς ὁ ἀποθανών,
the [one] condemning? Christ Jesus [is] the [one] having died,
μᾶλλον δὲ ἐγερθείς, ὅς ἐστιν ἐν δεξιᾷ
but rather having been raised, who is at [the] right [hand]
τοῦ θεοῦ, ὃς καὶ ἐντυγχάνει ὑπὲρ ἡμῶν.
– of God, who also supplicates on behalf of us.
35 τίς ἡμᾶς χωρίσει ἀπὸ τῆς ἀγάπης
Who us will separate from the love
τοῦ Χριστοῦ; θλῖψις ἢ στενοχωρία ἢ
– of Christ? affliction or distress or

is seen is no hope at all.
Who hopes for what he al-
ready has? 25 But if we hope
for what we do not yet
have, we wait for it patiently.
26 In the same way, the
Spirit helps us in our weakness. We do not know what
we ought to pray for, but
the Spirit himself inter-
cedes for us with groans
that words cannot express.
27 And he who searches our
hearts knows the mind of
the Spirit, because the
Spirit intercedes for the
saints in accordance with
God's will.

More Than Conquerors

28 And we know that in all
things God works for the
good of those who love
him,[j] who[k] have been
called according to his purpose. 29 For those God foreknew he also predestined
to be conformed to the likeness of his Son, that he
might be the firstborn
among many brothers.
30 And those he predes-
tined, he also called; those
he called, he also justified;
those he justified, he also
glorified.
31 What, then, shall we
say in response to this? If
God is for us, who can be
against us? 32 He who did
not spare his own Son, but
gave him up for us all—
how will he not also, along
with him, graciously give
us all things? 33 Who will
bring any charge against
those whom God has cho-
sen? It is God who justifies.
34 Who is he that con-
demns? Christ Jesus, who
died—more than that, who
was raised to life—is at the
right hand of God and is
also interceding for us.
35 Who shall separate us
from the love of Christ?
Shall trouble or hardship or
persecution or famine or

[j] 28 Some manuscripts *And we know that all things work together for good to those who love God*
[k] 28 Or *works together with those who love him to bring about what is good—with those who*

or nakedness, or peril, or
sword? 36 As it is written,
"For your sake we are
being killed all
day long;
we are accounted as
sheep to be
slaughtered."
37 No, in all these things we
are more than conquerors
through him who loved us.
38 For I am convinced that
neither death, nor life, nor
angels, nor rulers, nor
things present, nor things
to come, nor powers, 39 nor
height, nor depth, nor anything else in all creation,
will be able to separate us
from the love of God in
Christ Jesus our Lord.

διωγμὸς ἢ λιμὸς ἢ γυμνότης ἢ κίνδυνος
persecution or famine or nakedness or peril
ἢ μάχαιρα; 36 καθὼς γέγραπται ὅτι ἕνεκεν
or sword? As it has been written[,] – For the sake
σοῦ θανατούμεθα ὅλην τὴν ἡμέραν,
of thee we are being put to death all the day,
ἐλογίσθημεν ὡς πρόβατα σφαγῆς. 37 ἀλλ'
we were reckoned as sheep of(for) slaughter. But
ἐν τούτοις πᾶσιν ὑπερνικῶμεν διὰ τοῦ
in these things all we overconquer through the
ἀγαπήσαντος ἡμᾶς. 38 πέπεισμαι γὰρ
[one] having loved us. For I have been persuaded
ὅτι οὔτε θάνατος οὔτε ζωὴ οὔτε ἄγγελοι
that not death nor life nor angels
οὔτε ἀρχαὶ οὔτε ἐνεστῶτα οὔτε μέλλοντα
nor rulers nor things present nor things coming
οὔτε δυνάμεις 39 οὔτε ὕψωμα οὔτε βάθος
nor powers nor height nor depth
οὔτε τις κτίσις ἑτέρα δυνήσεται ἡμᾶς
nor any creature other will be able us
χωρίσαι ἀπὸ τῆς ἀγάπης τοῦ θεοῦ τῆς
to separate from the love – of God –
ἐν Χριστῷ Ἰησοῦ τῷ κυρίῳ ἡμῶν.
in Christ Jesus the Lord of us.

nakedness or danger or
sword? 36 As it is written:

"For your sake we face
death all day long;
we are considered as
sheep to be
slaughtered."[l]

37 No, in all these things we
are more than conquerors
through him who loved us.
38 For I am convinced that
neither death nor life, neither angels nor demons,[m]
neither the present nor the
future, nor any powers,
39 neither height nor depth,
nor anything else in all creation, will be able to separate us from the love of God
that is in Christ Jesus our
Lord.

Chapter 9

God's Election of Israel

I am speaking the truth in
Christ—I am not lying;
my conscience confirms it
by the Holy Spirit— 2 I
have great sorrow and un-
ceasing anguish in my
heart. 3 For I could wish
that I myself were accursed
and cut off from Christ for
the sake of my own peo-
ple,[q] my kindred according to the flesh. 4 They are
Israelites, and to them belong the adoption, the glory, the covenants, the giving of the law, the worship,
and the promises; 5 to them
belong the patriarchs, and
from them, according to
the flesh, comes the Messiah,[r] who is over all, God
blessed forever.[s] Amen.
6 It is not as though the
word of God had failed. For
not all Israelites truly belong to Israel, 7 and not all
of Abraham's children are
his true descendants; but
"It is through Isaac that descendants shall be named
for you." 8 This means that
it is not the children of the
flesh who are the children

9 Ἀλήθειαν λέγω ἐν Χριστῷ, οὐ
Truth I say in Christ, not
ψεύδομαι, συμμαρτυρούσης μοι τῆς
I lie, witnessing with me the
συνειδήσεώς μου ἐν πνεύματι ἁγίῳ, 2 ὅτι
conscience[a] of me in [the] Spirit Holy, that
λύπη μοί ἐστιν μεγάλη καὶ ἀδιάλειπτος
grief to me is great and incessant
=I have great grief and . . .
ὀδύνη τῇ καρδίᾳ μου. 3 ηὐχόμην γὰρ
pain[c] in the heart of me. For I was praying
ἀνάθεμα εἶναι αὐτὸς ἐγὼ ἀπὸ τοῦ Χριστοῦ
[4]a curse [3]to be [2][my]self [1]I from – Christ
ὑπὲρ τῶν ἀδελφῶν μου τῶν συγγενῶν
on behalf of the brothers of me the kinsmen
μου κατὰ σάρκα, 4 οἵτινές εἰσιν Ἰσραη-
of me according to flesh, who are Israel-
λῖται, ὧν ἡ υἱοθεσία καὶ ἡ δόξα καὶ
ites, of whom the adoption and the glory and
αἱ διαθῆκαι καὶ ἡ νομοθεσία καὶ ἡ
the covenants and the giving of [the] law and the
λατρεία καὶ αἱ ἐπαγγελίαι, 5 ὧν οἱ
service and the promises, of whom the
πατέρες, καὶ ἐξ ὧν ὁ Χριστὸς τὸ κατὰ
fathers, and from whom the Christ – according to
σάρκα· ὁ ὢν ἐπὶ πάντων θεὸς εὐλογητὸς
flesh; the [one] being over all God blessed
εἰς τοὺς αἰῶνας, ἀμήν. 6 Οὐχ οἷον δὲ
unto the ages, amen. Not of course
ὅτι ἐκπέπτωκεν ὁ λόγος τοῦ θεοῦ. οὐ
that has failed the word – of God. not
γὰρ πάντες οἱ ἐξ Ἰσραήλ, οὗτοι Ἰσραήλ·
For all the [ones] of Israel, these [are of] Israel;
7 οὐδ' ὅτι εἰσὶν σπέρμα Ἀβραάμ, πάντες
neither because they are seed of Abraham, [are they] all
τέκνα, ἀλλ'· ἐν Ἰσαὰκ κληθήσεταί σοι
children, but: In Isaac will be called to thee
σπέρμα. 8 τοῦτ' ἔστιν, οὐ τὰ τέκνα τῆς
seed.[c] This is, not the children of the
=thy seed.

Chapter 9

God's Sovereign Choice

I SPEAK the truth in
Christ—I am not lying,
my conscience confirms it
in the Holy Spirit— 2 I have
great sorrow and unceasing
anguish in my heart. 3 For I
could wish that I myself
were cursed and cut off
from Christ for the sake of
my brothers, those of my
own race, 4 the people of Israel. Theirs is the adoption
as sons; theirs the divine
glory, the covenants, the
receiving of the law, the
temple worship and the
promises. 5 Theirs are the
patriarchs, and from them
is traced the human ancestry of Christ, who is God
over all, forever praised![n]
Amen.
6 It is not as though God's
word had failed. For not all
who are descended from Israel are Israel. 7 Nor because they are his descendants are they all Abraham's
children. On the contrary,
"It is through Isaac that
your offspring will be reckoned."[o] 8 In other words, it
is not the natural children

[q] Gk *my brothers*
[r] Or *the Christ*
[s] Or *Messiah, who is God over all, blessed forever*; or *Messiah. May he who is God over all be blessed forever*

[l] 36 Psalm 44:22
[m] 38 Or *nor heavenly rulers*
[n] 5 Or *Christ, who is over all. God be forever praised!* Or *Christ. God who is over all be forever praised!*
[o] 7 Gen. 21:12

of God, but the children of the promise are counted as descendants. 9 For this is what the promise said, "About this time I will return and Sarah shall have a son." 10 Nor is that all; something similar happened to Rebecca when she had conceived children by one husband, our ancestor Isaac. 11 Even before they had been born or had done anything good or bad (so that God's purpose of election might continue, 12 not by works but by his call) she was told, "The elder shall serve the younger." 13 As it is written,

"I have loved Jacob,
but I have hated
Esau."

14 What then are we to say? Is there injustice on God's part? By no means! 15 For he says to Moses,

"I will have mercy on
whom I
have mercy,
and I will have
compassion on
whom I have
compassion."

16 So it depends not on human will or exertion, but on God who shows mercy. 17 For the scripture says to Pharaoh, "I have raised you up for the very purpose of showing my power in you, so that my name may be proclaimed in all the earth." 18 So then he has mercy on whomever he chooses, and he hardens the heart of whomever he chooses.

God's Wrath and Mercy

19 You will say to me then, "Why then does he still find fault? For who can resist his will?" 20 But who indeed are you, a human being, to argue with God? Will what is molded say to the one who molds it, "Why have you made me like this?" 21 Has the potter

σαρκὸς ταῦτα τέκνα τοῦ θεοῦ, ἀλλὰ
flesh these children of God, but
τὰ τέκνα τῆς ἐπαγγελίας λογίζεται εἰς
the children of the promise is(are) reckoned for
σπέρμα. 9 ἐπαγγελίας γὰρ ὁ λόγος οὗτος·
a seed. For [5]of promise [3]the [4]word [1]this [2][is]:
κατὰ τὸν καιρὸν τοῦτον ἐλεύσομαι καὶ
According to this time I will come and
ἔσται τῇ Σάρρᾳ υἱός. 10 οὐ μόνον δέ,
will be – to Sara a son.[c] And not only [so],
=Sarah will have a son.
ἀλλὰ καὶ Ῥεβεκκὰ ἐξ ἑνὸς κοίτην ἔχουσα,
but also Rebecca [2]from [3]one [1]conceiving,†
Ἰσαὰκ τοῦ πατρὸς ἡμῶν· 11 μήπω γὰρ
Isaac the father of us; for not yet
γεννηθέντων μηδὲ πραξάντων τι ἀγαθὸν
being born* nor practising* anything good
ἢ φαῦλον, ἵνα ἡ κατ' ἐκλογὴν πρόθεσις
or bad, in order that [1]the [4]according to [5]choice [3]purpose
τοῦ θεοῦ μένῃ, 12 οὐκ ἐξ ἔργων ἀλλ'
– [2]of God might remain, not of works but
ἐκ τοῦ καλοῦντος, ἐρρέθη αὐτῇ ὅτι ὁ
of the [one] calling, it was said to her[,] – The
μείζων δουλεύσει τῷ ἐλάσσονι· 13 καθάπερ
greater will serve the lesser; even as
γέγραπται· τὸν Ἰακὼβ ἠγάπησα, τὸν δὲ
it has been written: – Jacob I loved, – but
Ἠσαῦ ἐμίσησα.
Esau I hated.
14 Τί οὖν ἐροῦμεν; μὴ ἀδικία παρὰ
What therefore shall we say? *not* unrighteousness with
τῷ θεῷ; μὴ γένοιτο. 15 τῷ Μωϋσεῖ
– God? May it not be. – [2]to Moses
γὰρ λέγει· ἐλεήσω ὃν ἂν ἐλεῶ, καὶ
[1]For he says: I will have mercy on whomever I have mercy, and
οἰκτιρήσω ὃν ἂν οἰκτίρω. 16 ἄρα οὖν
I will pity whomever I pity. So therefore [it is]
οὐ τοῦ θέλοντος οὐδὲ τοῦ τρέχοντος,
not of the [one] wishing nor of the [one] running,
ἀλλὰ τοῦ ἐλεῶντος θεοῦ. 17 λέγει γὰρ
but of the [one] having mercy God. For says
ἡ γραφὴ τῷ Φαραὼ ὅτι εἰς αὐτὸ τοῦτο
the scripture – to Pharaoh[,] – For this very thing
ἐξήγειρά σε, ὅπως ἐνδείξωμαι ἐν σοὶ
I raised up thee, so as I may show forth in thee
τὴν δύναμίν μου, καὶ ὅπως διαγγελῇ τὸ
the power of me, and so as might be published abroad the
ὄνομά μου ἐν πάσῃ τῇ γῇ. 18 ἄρα οὖν
name of me in all the earth. So therefore
ὃν θέλει ἐλεεῖ, ὃν δὲ θέλει σκληρύνει.
whom he wishes he has mercy, but whom he wishes he hardens.
19 Ἐρεῖς μοι οὖν· τί ἔτι μέμφεται;
Thou wilt say to me therefore: Why still finds he fault?
τῷ γὰρ βουλήματι αὐτοῦ τίς ἀνθέστηκεν;
for [3]the [4]counsel [5]of him [1]who [2]resisted?
20 ὦ ἄνθρωπε, μενοῦν γε σὺ τίς εἶ ὁ
O man, nay rather [3]thou [1]who [2]art the
ἀνταποκρινόμενος τῷ θεῷ; μὴ ἐρεῖ τὸ
[one] replying against – God? *not* [3]Will say [1]the
πλάσμα τῷ πλάσαντι· τί με ἐποίησας
[2]thing formed to the [one] having formed: Why [2]me [1]madest thou

who are God's children, but it is the children of the promise who are regarded as Abraham's offspring. 9 For this was how the promise was stated: "At the appointed time I will return, and Sarah will have a son."[p]

10 Not only that, but Rebekah's children had one and the same father, our father Isaac. 11 Yet, before the twins were born or had done anything good or bad —in order that God's purpose in election might stand: 12 not by works but by him who calls—she was told, "The older will serve the younger."[q] 13 Just as it is written: "Jacob I loved, but Esau I hated."[r]

14 What then shall we say? Is God unjust? Not at all! 15 For he says to Moses,

"I will have mercy on
whom I have mercy,
and I will have
compassion on
whom I have
compassion."[s]

16 It does not, therefore, depend on man's desire or effort, but on God's mercy. 17 For the Scripture says to Pharaoh: "I raised you up for this very purpose, that I might display my power in you and that my name might be proclaimed in all the earth."[t] 18 Therefore God has mercy on whom he wants to have mercy, and he hardens whom he wants to harden.

19 One of you will say to me: "Then why does God still blame us? For who resists his will?" 20 But who are you, O man, to talk back to God? "Shall what is formed say to him who formed it, 'Why did you make me like this?' "[u]

[p] 9 Gen. 18:10,14
[q] 12 Gen. 25:23
[r] 13 Mal. 1:2,3
[s] 15 Exodus 33:19
[t] 17 Exodus 9:16
[u] 20 Isaiah 29:16; 45:9

no right over the clay, to
make out of the same lump
one object for special use
and another for ordinary
use? 22What if God, desiring to show his wrath and to
make known his power,
has endured with much pa-
tience the objects of wrath
that are made for destruction; 23and what if he has
done so in order to make
known the riches of his glory for the objects of mercy,
which he has prepared be-
forehand for glory— 24in-
cluding us whom he has
called, not from the Jews
only but also from the Gentiles? 25As indeed he says
in Hosea,

"Those who were not
my people I will
call 'my people,'
and her who was
not beloved I
will call
'beloved.' "
26 "And in the very
place where it
was said to
them, 'You are
not my people,'
there they shall be
called children
of the living
God."

27 And Isaiah cries out
concerning Israel, "Though
the number of the children
of Israel were like the sand
of the sea, only a remnant
of them will be saved; 28for
the Lord will execute his
sentence on the earth
quickly and decisively."[t]
29And as Isaiah predicted,

"If the Lord of hosts
had not left
survivors[u] to
us,
we would have
fared like
Sodom
and been made like
Gomorrah."

Israel's Unbelief

30 What then are we to
say? Gentiles, who did not
strive for righteousness,
have attained it, that is,
righteousness through
faith; 31but Israel, who did
strive for the righteousness
that is based on the law, did
not succeed in fulfilling that
law. 32Why not? Because
they did not strive for it on
the basis of faith, but as if it
were based on works. They
have stumbled over the
stumbling stone, 33as it is

[t] Other ancient authorities read *for he will finish his work and cut it short in righteousness, because the Lord will make the sentence shortened on the earth*
[u] Or *descendants*; Gk *seed*

οὕτως; **21** ἢ οὐκ ἔχει ἐξουσίαν ὁ κεραμεὺς
thus? or has not [3]authority [1]the [2]potter
τοῦ πηλοῦ ἐκ τοῦ αὐτοῦ φυράματος
of the clay out of the same lump
ποιῆσαι ὃ μὲν εἰς τιμὴν σκεῦος, ὃ δὲ
to make [1]this [3]to [4]honour [2]vessel, that
εἰς ἀτιμίαν; **22** εἰ δὲ θέλων ὁ θεὸς
to dishonour? But if wishing – God
ἐνδείξασθαι τὴν ὀργὴν καὶ γνωρίσαι τὸ
to show forth the(his) wrath and to make known the
δυνατὸν αὐτοῦ ἤνεγκεν ἐν πολλῇ μακρο-
ability of him bore in much long-
θυμίᾳ σκεύη ὀργῆς κατηρτισμένα εἰς
suffering vessels of wrath *having been* fitted for
ἀπώλειαν, **23** καὶ ἵνα γνωρίσῃ τὸν πλοῦτον
destruction, and in order that he might make known the riches
τῆς δόξης αὐτοῦ ἐπὶ σκεύη ἐλέους, ἃ
of the glory of him on vessels of mercy, which
προητοίμασεν εἰς δόξαν, **24** οὓς καὶ
he previously prepared for glory, whom also
ἐκάλεσεν ἡμᾶς οὐ μόνον ἐξ Ἰουδαίων
he called[,] us not only of Jews
ἀλλὰ καὶ ἐξ ἐθνῶν; **25** ὡς καὶ ἐν τῷ
but also of nations? As also in –
Ὡσηὲ λέγει· καλέσω τὸν οὐ λαόν μου
Osee he says: I will call the [2]not [1]people of me
λαόν μου καὶ τὴν οὐκ ἠγαπημένην
a people of me and the not having been loved
ἠγαπημένην· **26** καὶ ἔσται ἐν τῷ τόπῳ
having been loved; and it shall be in the place
οὗ ἐρρέθη [αὐτοῖς]· οὐ λαός μου ὑμεῖς,
where it was said to them: not a people of me ye [are],
ἐκεῖ κληθήσονται υἱοὶ θεοῦ ζῶντος.
there they will be called sons [2]God [1]of a living.
27 Ἠσαΐας δὲ κράζει ὑπὲρ τοῦ Ἰσραήλ·
But Esaias cries on behalf of – Israel:
ἐὰν ᾖ ὁ ἀριθμὸς τῶν υἱῶν Ἰσραὴλ
If be the number of the sons of Israel
ὡς ἡ ἄμμος τῆς θαλάσσης, τὸ ὑπόλειμμα
as the sand of the sea, the remnant
σωθήσεται· **28** λόγον γὰρ συντελῶν καὶ
will be saved; for [6]an account [1]accomplishing [2]and
συντέμνων ποιήσει κύριος ἐπὶ τῆς γῆς.
[3]cutting short [5]will make [4][the] Lord on the earth.
29 καὶ καθὼς προείρηκεν Ἠσαΐας· εἰ μὴ
And as [2]has previously said [1]Esaias: Except
κύριος σαβαὼθ ἐγκατέλιπεν ἡμῖν σπέρμα,
[the] Lord of hosts left to us a seed,
ὡς Σόδομα ἂν ἐγενήθημεν καὶ ὡς Γόμορρα
as Sodom we would have become and as Gomorra
ἂν ὡμοιώθημεν.
we would have been likened.

30 Τί οὖν ἐροῦμεν; ὅτι ἔθνη τὰ μὴ
What therefore shall we say? that nations – not
διώκοντα δικαιοσύνην κατέλαβεν δικαιοσύνην,
pursuing righteousness apprehended righteousness,
δικαιοσύνην δὲ τὴν ἐκ πίστεως· **31** Ἰσραὴλ
but a righteousness – of faith; [2]Israel
δὲ διώκων νόμον δικαιοσύνης εἰς νόμον
[1]but pursuing a law of righteousness [2]to(at) [3]a law
οὐκ ἔφθασεν. **32** διὰ τί; ὅτι οὐκ ἐκ
[1]did not arrive. Why? Because not of
πίστεως ἀλλ' ὡς ἐξ ἔργων· προσέκοψαν
faith but as of works; they stumbled
τῷ λίθῳ τοῦ προσκόμματος, **33** καθὼς
at the stone – of stumbling, as

21Does not the potter have
the right to make out of the
same lump of clay some
pottery for noble purposes
and some for common use?
22What if God, choosing
to show his wrath and make
his power known, bore
with great patience the objects of his wrath—pre-
pared for destruction?
23What if he did this to
make the riches of his glory
known to the objects of his
mercy, whom he prepared
in advance for glory—
24even us, whom he also
called, not only from the
Jews but also from the Gentiles? 25As he says in Hosea:

"I will call them 'my
people' who are not
my people;
and I will call her 'my
loved one' who is
not my loved
one,"[v]

26and,

"It will happen that in
the very place
where it was said to
them,
'You are not my
people,'
they will be called 'sons
of the living
God.' "[w]

27Isaiah cries out con-
cerning Israel:

"Though the number of
the Israelites be like
the sand by the sea,
only the remnant will
be saved.
28For the Lord will carry
out
his sentence on earth
with speed and
finality."[x]

29It is just as Isaiah said
previously:

"Unless the Lord
Almighty
had left us
descendants,
we would have become
like Sodom,
we would have been
like Gomorrah."[y]

Israel's Unbelief

30What then shall we say?
That the Gentiles, who did
not pursue righteousness,
have obtained it, a righteousness that is by faith;
31but Israel, who pursued a
law of righteousness, has
not attained it. 32Why not?
Because they pursued it
not by faith but as if it were
by works. They stumbled
over the "stumbling

[v] 25 Hosea 2:23
[w] 26 Hosea 1:10
[x] 28 Isaiah 10:22,23
[y] 29 Isaiah 1:9

written,
"See, I am laying in
Zion a stone
that will make
people stumble,
a rock that will
make them fall,
and whoever
believes in him[v]
will not be put
to shame."

Chapter 10

BROTHERS and sis-
ters,[w] my heart's de-
sire and prayer to God for
them is that they may be
saved. 2 I can testify that
they have a zeal for God,
but it is not enlightened.
3 For, being ignorant of the
righteousness that comes
from God, and seeking to
establish their own, they
have not submitted to
God's righteousness. 4 For
Christ is the end of the law
so that there may be righteousness for everyone
who believes.

Salvation Is for All

5 Moses writes con-
cerning the righteousness
that comes from the law,
that "the person who does
these things will live by
them." 6 But the righteousness that comes from faith
says, "Do not say in your
heart, 'Who will ascend
into heaven?' " (that is, to
bring Christ down) 7 "or
'Who will descend into the
abyss?' " (that is, to bring
Christ up from the dead).
8 But what does it say?
"The word is near
you,
on your lips and in
your heart"
(that is, the word of faith
that we proclaim); 9 be-
cause[x] if you confess with
your lips that Jesus is Lord
and believe in your heart
that God raised him from
the dead, you will be saved.
10 For one believes with the
heart and so is justified,
and one confesses with the
mouth and so is saved.
11 The scripture says, "No
one who believes in him

v Or *trusts in it*
w Gk *Brothers*
x Or *namely, that*

γέγραπται· ἰδοὺ τίθημι ἐν Σιὼν λίθον
it has been written: Behold I place in Sion a stone

προσκόμματος καὶ πέτραν σκανδάλου, καὶ
of stumbling and a rock of offence, and

ὁ πιστεύων ἐπ' αὐτῷ οὐ καταισχυνθήσεται.
the [one] believing on him will not be put to shame.

10 Ἀδελφοί, ἡ μὲν εὐδοκία τῆς ἐμῆς
Brothers, the – good pleasure – of my

καρδίας καὶ ἡ δέησις πρὸς τὸν θεὸν
heart and the request to – God

ὑπὲρ αὐτῶν εἰς σωτηρίαν. **2** μαρτυρῶ
on behalf of them [is] for salvation. I witness

γὰρ αὐτοῖς ὅτι ζῆλον θεοῦ ἔχουσιν, ἀλλ'
For to them that a zeal of God they have, but

οὐ κατ' ἐπίγνωσιν· **3** ἀγνοοῦντες γὰρ τὴν
not according to knowledge; for not knowing the

τοῦ θεοῦ δικαιοσύνην, καὶ τὴν ἰδίαν
– [2]of God [1]righteousness, and the(ir) own

ζητοῦντες στῆσαι, τῇ δικαιοσύνῃ τοῦ θεοῦ
seeking to establish, to the righteousness – of God

οὐχ ὑπετάγησαν. **4** τέλος γὰρ νόμου
they did not submit. For end of law

Χριστὸς εἰς δικαιοσύνην παντὶ τῷ
Christ [is] for righteousness to everyone

πιστεύοντι. **5** Μωϋσῆς γὰρ γράφει ὅτι
believing. For Moses writes[,] –

τὴν δικαιοσύνην τὴν ἐκ νόμου ὁ ποιήσας
[4]the [5]righteousness – [6]of [7]law [1]The [2]doing

ἄνθρωπος ζήσεται ἐν αὐτῇ. **6** ἡ δὲ
[3]man will live by it. But the

ἐκ πίστεως δικαιοσύνη οὕτως λέγει· μὴ
[2]of [3]faith [1]righteousness thus says: not

εἴπῃς ἐν τῇ καρδίᾳ σου· τίς ἀναβήσεται
Say in the heart of thee: Who will ascend

εἰς τὸν οὐρανόν; τοῦτ' ἔστιν Χριστὸν
into – heaven? this is Christ

καταγαγεῖν· **7** ἤ· τίς καταβήσεται εἰς
to bring down; or: Who will descend into

τὴν ἄβυσσον; τοῦτ' ἔστιν Χριστὸν ἐκ
the abyss? this is Christ from

νεκρῶν ἀναγαγεῖν. **8** ἀλλὰ τί λέγει;
[the] dead to bring up. But what says it?

ἐγγύς σου τὸ ῥῆμά ἐστιν, ἐν τῷ στόματί
Near thee the word is, in the mouth

σου καὶ ἐν τῇ καρδίᾳ σου· τοῦτ' ἔστιν
of thee and in the heart of thee; this is

τὸ ῥῆμα τῆς πίστεως ὃ κηρύσσομεν.
the word – of faith which we proclaim.

9 ὅτι ἐὰν ὁμολογήσῃς ἐν τῷ στόματί
Because if thou confessest with the mouth

σου κύριον Ἰησοῦν, καὶ πιστεύσῃς ἐν
of thee Lord Jesus, and believest in

τῇ καρδίᾳ σου ὅτι ὁ θεὸς αὐτὸν ἤγειρεν
the heart of thee that – God him raised

ἐκ νεκρῶν, σωθήσῃ· **10** καρδίᾳ γὰρ
from [the] dead, thou wilt be saved; for with heart

πιστεύεται εἰς δικαιοσύνην, στόματι δὲ
[one] believes to righteousness, and with mouth

ὁμολογεῖται εἰς σωτηρίαν. **11** λέγει γὰρ
[one] confesses to salvation. For says

ἡ γραφή· πᾶς ὁ πιστεύων ἐπ' αὐτῷ
the scripture: Everyone believing on him

stone." 33 As it is written:

"See, I lay in Zion a
stone that causes
men to stumble
and a rock that makes
them fall,
and the one who trusts in
him will never be
put to shame."[z]

Chapter 10

BROTHERS, my
heart's desire and
prayer to God for the Israelites is that they may be
saved. 2 For I can testify
about them that they are
zealous for God, but their
zeal is not based on knowledge. 3 Since they did not
know the righteousness
that comes from God and
sought to establish their
own, they did not submit to
God's righteousness.
4 Christ is the end of the law
so that there may be righteousness for everyone who
believes.
5 Moses describes in this
way the righteousness that
is by the law: "The man
who does these things will
live by them."[a] 6 But the
righteousness that is by
faith says: "Do not say in
your heart, 'Who will as-
cend into heaven?'[b]" (that
is, to bring Christ down)
7 "or 'Who will descend
into the deep?'[c]" (that is,
to bring Christ up from the
dead). 8 But what does it
say? "The word is near
you; it is in your mouth and
in your heart,"[d] that is, the
word of faith we are pro-
claiming: 9 That if you confess with your mouth,
"Jesus is Lord," and be-
lieve in your heart that God
raised him from the dead,
you will be saved. 10 For it
is with your heart that you
believe and are justified,
and it is with your mouth
that you confess and are
saved. 11 As the Scripture
says, "Anyone who trusts

z33 Isaiah 8:14; 28:16
a5 Lev. 18:5
b6 Deut. 30:12
c7 Deut. 30:13
d8 Deut. 30:14

will be put to shame."
12 For there is no distinction between Jew and
Greek; the same Lord is
Lord of all and is generous
to all who call on him.
13 For, "Everyone who
calls on the name of the
Lord shall be saved."
14 But how are they to
call on one in whom they
have not believed? And
how are they to believe in
one of whom they have
never heard? And how are
they to hear without someone to proclaim him?
15 And how are they to proclaim him unless they are
sent? As it is written, "How
beautiful are the feet of
those who bring good
news!" 16 But not all have
obeyed the good news;[y]
for Isaiah says, "Lord, who
has believed our message?"
17 So faith comes from what
is heard, and what is heard
comes through the word of
Christ.[z]
18 But I ask, have they
not heard? Indeed they
have; for

"Their voice has gone
out to all
the earth,
and their words to
the ends of the
world."

19 Again I ask, did Israel not
understand? First Moses
says,

"I will make you
jealous of those
who are not a
nation;
with a foolish nation
I will make you
angry."

20 Then Isaiah is so bold as
to say,

"I have been found by
those who did
not seek me;
I have shown
myself to those
who did not ask
for me."

21 But of Israel he says, "All
day long I have held out my
hands to a disobedient and
contrary people."

οὐ καταισχυνθήσεται. 12 οὐ γάρ ἐστιν
will not be put to shame. For there is no
διαστολὴ Ἰουδαίου τε καὶ Ἕλληνος. ὁ
difference [2]of Jew [1]both [3]and [4]of Greek.* the
γὰρ αὐτὸς κύριος πάντων, πλουτῶν εἰς
For same Lord of all, is rich to
πάντας τοὺς ἐπικαλουμένους αὐτόν· 13 πᾶς
all the [ones] calling on him; [2]everyone
γὰρ ὃς ἂν ἐπικαλέσηται τὸ ὄνομα κυρίου
[1]for whoever calls on the name of [the] Lord
σωθήσεται. 14 Πῶς οὖν ἐπικαλέσωνται εἰς
will be saved. How therefore may they call on in [one]
ὃν οὐκ ἐπίστευσαν; πῶς δὲ πιστεύσωσιν
whom they believed not? And how may they believe
οὗ οὐκ ἤκουσαν; πῶς δὲ ἀκούσωσιν
of whom they heard not? And how may they hear
χωρὶς κηρύσσοντος; 15 πῶς δὲ κηρύξωσιν
without [one] heralding? And how may they herald
ἐὰν μὴ ἀποσταλῶσιν; καθάπερ γέγραπται·
if they are not sent? As it has been written:
ὡς ὡραῖοι οἱ πόδες τῶν εὐαγγελιζομένων
How beautiful the feet of the [ones] announcing *good*
ἀγαθά. 16 ἀλλ' οὐ πάντες ὑπήκουσαν τῷ
good things. But not all obeyed the
εὐαγγελίῳ. Ἠσαΐας γὰρ λέγει· κύριε,
gospel. For Esaias says: Lord,
τίς ἐπίστευσεν τῇ ἀκοῇ ἡμῶν; 17 ἄρα
who believed the hearing of us? Then
ἡ πίστις ἐξ ἀκοῆς, ἡ δὲ ἀκοὴ διὰ
– faith [is] from hearing, and the hearing through
ῥήματος Χριστοῦ. 18 ἀλλὰ λέγω, μὴ
a word of Christ. But I say, *not*
οὐκ ἤκουσαν; μενοῦνγε· εἰς πᾶσαν
did they not hear? Nay rather: To all
τὴν γῆν ἐξῆλθεν ὁ φθόγγος αὐτῶν,
the earth went out the utterance of them,
καὶ εἰς τὰ πέρατα τῆς οἰκουμένης τὰ
and to the ends of the inhabited earth the
ῥήματα αὐτῶν. 19 ἀλλὰ λέγω, μὴ Ἰσραὴλ
words of them. But I say, *not* Israel
οὐκ ἔγνω; πρῶτος Μωϋσῆς λέγει· ἐγὼ
did not know? First Moses says: I
παραζηλώσω ὑμᾶς ἐπ' οὐκ ἔθνει, ἐπ'
will provoke to jealousy you on(by) not a nation, on(by)
ἔθνει ἀσυνέτῳ παροργιῶ ὑμᾶς. 20 Ἠσαΐας
a nation unintelligent I will anger you. Esaias
δὲ ἀποτολμᾷ καὶ λέγει· εὑρέθην τοῖς
But is quite bold and says: I was found by the [ones]
ἐμὲ μὴ ζητοῦσιν, ἐμφανὴς ἐγενόμην τοῖς
[3]me [1]not [2]seeking, manifest I became to the [ones]
ἐμὲ μὴ ἐπερωτῶσιν. 21 πρὸς δὲ τὸν
[3]me [1]not [2]inquiring [for]. But to –
Ἰσραὴλ λέγει· ὅλην τὴν ἡμέραν ἐξεπέτασα
Israel he says: All the day I stretched out
τὰς χεῖράς μου πρὸς λαὸν ἀπειθοῦντα
the hands of me to a people disobeying
καὶ ἀντιλέγοντα.
and contradicting.

in him will never be put to
shame."[e] 12 For there is no
difference between Jew
and Gentile—the same
Lord is Lord of all and richly blesses all who call on
him, 13 for, "Everyone who
calls on the name of the
Lord will be saved."[f]
14 How, then, can they
call on the one they have
not believed in? And how
can they believe in the one
of whom they have not
heard? And how can they
hear without someone
preaching to them? 15 And
how can they preach unless
they are sent? As it is written, "How beautiful are the
feet of those who bring
good news!"[g]
16 But not all the Israelites
accepted the good news.
For Isaiah says, "Lord,
who has believed our mes-
sage?"[h] 17 Consequently,
faith comes from hearing
the message, and the mes-
sage is heard through the
word of Christ. 18 But I ask:
Did they not hear? Of
course they did:

"Their voice has gone
out into all the
earth,
their words to the ends
of the world."[i]

19 Again I ask: Did Israel
not understand? First, Moses says,

"I will make you
envious by those
who are not a
nation;
I will make you angry
by a nation that has
no
understanding."[j]

20 And Isaiah boldly says,

"I was found by those
who did not seek
me;
I revealed myself to
those who did not
ask for me."[k]

21 But concerning Israel he
says,

"All day long I have
held out my hands
to a disobedient and
obstinate people."[l]

[y] Or *gospel*
[z] Or *about Christ*; other ancient authorities read *of God*

* That is, between these two classes.

[e] *11* Isaiah 28:16
[f] *13* Joel 2:32
[g] *15* Isaiah 52:7
[h] *16* Isaiah 53:1
[i] *18* Psalm 19:4
[j] *19* Deut. 32:21
[k] *20* Isaiah 65:1
[l] *21* Isaiah 65:2

Chapter 11

Israel's Rejection Is Not Final

I ask, then, has God rejected his people? By no means! I myself am an Israelite, a descendant of Abraham, a member of the tribe of Benjamin. 2 God has not rejected his people whom he foreknew. Do you not know what the scripture says of Elijah, how he pleads with God against Israel? 3 "Lord, they have killed your prophets, they have demolished your altars; I alone am left, and they are seeking my life." 4 But what is the divine reply to him? "I have kept for myself seven thousand who have not bowed the knee to Baal." 5 So too at the present time there is a remnant, chosen by grace. 6 But if it is by grace, it is no longer on the basis of works, otherwise grace would no longer be grace.[a]

7 What then? Israel failed to obtain what it was seeking. The elect obtained it, but the rest were hardened, 8 as it is written,

"God gave them a sluggish spirit,
eyes that would not see
and ears that would not hear,
down to this very day."

9 And David says,

"Let their table become a snare and a trap,
a stumbling block and a retribution for them;
10 let their eyes be darkened so that they cannot see,
and keep their backs forever bent."

The Salvation of the Gentiles

11 So I ask, have they stumbled so as to fall? By no means! But through their stumbling[b] salvation has come to the Gentiles, so as to make Israel[c] jealous. 12 Now if their stum-

[a] Other ancient authorities add *But if it is by works, it is no longer on the basis of grace, otherwise work would no longer be work*
[b] Gk *transgression*
[c] Gk *them*

11 Λέγω οὖν, μὴ ἀπώσατο ὁ θεὸς
I say therefore, ²did *not* put away – ¹God

τὸν λαὸν αὐτοῦ; μὴ γένοιτο· καὶ γὰρ
the people of him? May it not be; for even

ἐγὼ Ἰσραηλίτης εἰμί, ἐκ σπέρματος
I an Israelite am, of [the] seed

Ἀβραάμ, φυλῆς Βενιαμίν. **2** οὐκ ἀπώσατο
of Abraham, of [the] tribe of Benjamin. did not put away

ὁ θεὸς τὸν λαὸν αὐτοῦ ὃν προέγνω.
– God the people of him whom he foreknew.

ἢ οὐκ οἴδατε ἐν Ἠλίᾳ τί λέγει ἡ
Or know ye not in Elias what says the

γραφή, ὡς ἐντυγχάνει τῷ θεῷ κατὰ τοῦ
scripture, how he supplicates – God against –

Ἰσραήλ; **3** κύριε, τοὺς προφήτας σου
Israel? Lord, the prophets of thee

ἀπέκτειναν, τὰ θυσιαστήριά σου κατέσκαψαν,
they killed, the altars of thee they dug down,

κἀγὼ ὑπελείφθην μόνος καὶ ζητοῦσιν τὴν
and I was left behind alone and they seek the

ψυχήν μου. **4** ἀλλὰ τί λέγει αὐτῷ ὁ
life of me. But what says to him the

χρηματισμός; κατέλιπον ἐμαυτῷ ἑπτακισ-
[divine] response? I reserved to myself seven

χιλίους ἄνδρας, οἵτινες οὐκ ἔκαμψαν γόνυ
thousands men, who bowed not knee

τῇ Βάαλ. **5** οὕτως οὖν καὶ ἐν τῷ νῦν
– to Baal. So therefore also in the present

καιρῷ λεῖμμα κατ' ἐκλογὴν χάριτος
time a remnant according to a choice of grace

γέγονεν· **6** εἰ δὲ χάριτι, οὐκέτι ἐξ ἔργων,
has become; and if by grace, no more of works,

ἐπεὶ ἡ χάρις οὐκέτι γίνεται χάρις. **7** Τί
since – grace no more becomes grace. What

οὖν; ὃ ἐπιζητεῖ Ἰσραήλ, τοῦτο οὐκ
therefore? What ²seeks after ¹Israel, this not

ἐπέτυχεν, ἡ δὲ ἐκλογὴ ἐπέτυχεν· οἱ δὲ
he obtained, but the choice obtained [it]; and the

λοιποὶ ἐπωρώθησαν, **8** καθάπερ γέγραπται·
rest were hardened, as it has been written:

ἔδωκεν αὐτοῖς ὁ θεὸς πνεῦμα κατανύξεως,
Gave to them – God a spirit of torpor,

ὀφθαλμοὺς τοῦ μὴ βλέπειν καὶ ὦτα
eyes – not to see[d] and ears

τοῦ μὴ ἀκούειν, ἕως τῆς σήμερον ἡμέρας
– not to hear,[d] until the present† day.

9 καὶ Δαυὶδ λέγει· γενηθήτω ἡ τράπεζα
And David says: Let become the table

αὐτῶν εἰς παγίδα καὶ εἰς θήραν καὶ
of them for a snare and for a net and

εἰς σκάνδαλον καὶ εἰς ἀνταπόδομα αὐτοῖς,
for an offence and for a recompence to them,

10 σκοτισθήτωσαν οἱ ὀφθαλμοὶ αὐτῶν τοῦ
let be darkened the eyes of them –

μὴ βλέπειν, καὶ τὸν νῶτον αὐτῶν διὰ
not to see,[d] and the back of them al-

παντὸς σύγκαμψον.
ways bending.

11 Λέγω οὖν, μὴ ἔπταισαν ἵνα πέσωσιν;
I say therefore, did they *not* stumble in order that they might fall?

μὴ γένοιτο· ἀλλὰ τῷ αὐτῶν παραπτώματι
May it not be; but by the ²of them ¹trespass

ἡ σωτηρία τοῖς ἔθνεσιν, εἰς τὸ παραζηλῶσαι
– salvation [came] to the nations, *for the* to provoke to jealousy

Chapter 11

The Remnant of Israel

I ASK then: Did God reject his people? By no means! I am an Israelite myself, a descendant of Abraham, from the tribe of Benjamin. 2 God did not reject his people, whom he foreknew. Don't you know what the Scripture says in the passage about Elijah—how he appealed to God against Israel: 3 "Lord, they have killed your prophets and torn down your altars; I am the only one left, and they are trying to kill me"[m]? 4 And what was God's answer to him? "I have reserved for myself seven thousand who have not bowed the knee to Baal."[n] 5 So too, at the present time there is a remnant chosen by grace. 6 And if by grace, then it is no longer by works; if it were, grace would no longer be grace.[o]

7 What then? What Israel sought so earnestly it did not obtain, but the elect did. The others were hardened, 8 as it is written:

"God gave them a spirit of stupor,
eyes so that they could not see
and ears so that they could not hear,
to this very day."[p]

9 And David says:

"May their table become a snare and a trap,
a stumbling block and a retribution for them.
10 May their eyes be darkened so they cannot see,
and their backs be bent forever."[q]

Ingrafted Branches

11 Again I ask: Did they stumble so as to fall beyond recovery? Not at all! Rather, because of their transgression, salvation has come to the Gentiles to make Israel envious. 12 But

[m] *3* 1 Kings 19:10,14
[n] *4* 1 Kings 19:18
[o] *6* Some manuscripts *by grace. But if by works, then it is no longer grace; if it were, work would no longer be work.*
[p] *8* Deut. 29:4; Isaiah 29:10
[q] *10* Psalm 69:22,23

bling[b] means riches for the
world, and if their defeat
means riches for Gentiles,
how much more will their
full inclusion mean!
13 Now I am speaking
to you Gentiles. Inasmuch
then as I am an apostle to
the Gentiles, I glorify my
ministry 14 in order to make
my own people[d] jealous,
and thus save some of
them. 15 For if their rejection is the reconciliation of
the world, what will their
acceptance be but life from
the dead! 16 If the part of the
dough offered as first fruits
is holy, then the whole
batch is holy; and if the root
is holy, then the branches
also are holy.
17 But if some of the
branches were broken off,
and you, a wild olive shoot,
were grafted in their place
to share the rich root[e] of
the olive tree, 18 do not
boast over the branches. If
you do boast, remember
that it is not you that support the root, but the root
that supports you. 19 You
will say, "Branches were
broken off so that I might
be grafted in." 20 That is
true. They were broken off
because of their unbelief,
but you stand only through
faith. So do not become
proud, but stand in awe.
21 For if God did not spare
the natural branches, perhaps he will not spare
you.[f] 22 Note then the
kindness and the severity
of God: severity toward
those who have fallen, but
God's kindness toward
you, provided you continue
in his kindness; otherwise
you also will be cut off.
23 And even those of Israel,[g] if they do not persist in
unbelief, will be grafted in,
for God has the power to

[d] Gk *my flesh*
[e] Other ancient authorities read *the richness*
[f] Other ancient authorities read *neither will he spare you*
[g] Gk lacks *of Israel*

αὐτούς. 12 εἰ δὲ τὸ παράπτωμα αὐτῶν
them. But if the trespass of them
πλοῦτος κόσμου καὶ τὸ ἥττημα αὐτῶν
[is] [the] riches of [the] world and the defect of them
πλοῦτος ἐθνῶν, πόσῳ μᾶλλον τὸ πλήρωμα
[is] [the] riches of [the] nations, by how much more the fulness
αὐτῶν. 13 Ὑμῖν δὲ λέγω τοῖς ἔθνεσιν.
of them. But to you 3I say[,] 1the 2nations.
ἐφ' ὅσον μὲν οὖν εἰμι ἐγὼ ἐθνῶν ἀπόστο-
Forasmuch as in-deed there-fore 2am 1I 4of nations 3an apos-
λος, τὴν διακονίαν μου δοξάζω, 14 εἴ πως
tle, the ministry of me I glorify, if somehow
παραζηλώσω μου τὴν σάρκα καὶ σώσω
I may provoke to jealousy of me the flesh and may save
τινὰς ἐξ αὐτῶν. 15 εἰ γὰρ ἡ ἀποβολὴ
some of them. For if the casting away
αὐτῶν καταλλαγὴ κόσμου, τίς ἡ πρόσλημψις
of them [is] [the] reconciliation of [the] world, what the reception
εἰ μὴ ζωὴ ἐκ νεκρῶν; 16 εἰ δὲ ἡ
if not life from [the] dead? And if the
ἀπαρχὴ ἁγία, καὶ τὸ φύραμα· καὶ εἰ
firstfruit [is] holy, also the lump; and if
ἡ ῥίζα ἁγία, καὶ οἱ κλάδοι. 17 Εἰ δέ
the root [is] holy, also the branches. But if
τινες τῶν κλάδων ἐξεκλάσθησαν, σὺ δὲ
some of the branches were broken off, and thou
ἀγριέλαιος ὢν ἐνεκεντρίσθης ἐν αὐτοῖς
2a wild olive 1being wast grafted in among them
καὶ συγκοινωνὸς τῆς ῥίζης τῆς πιότητος
and 2a partaker 3of the 4root* 5of the 6fatness
τῆς ἐλαίας ἐγένου, 18 μὴ κατακαυχῶ
7of the 8olive-tree 1didst become, boast not against
τῶν κλάδων· εἰ δὲ κατακαυχᾶσαι, οὐ
of the branches; but if thou boastest, not
σὺ τὴν ῥίζαν βαστάζεις ἀλλὰ ἡ ῥίζα σέ.
thou the root bearest but the root thee.
19 ἐρεῖς οὖν· ἐξεκλάσθησαν κλάδοι ἵνα
Thou wilt say therefore: 2Were broken off 1branches in order that
ἐγὼ ἐγκεντρισθῶ. 20 καλῶς· τῇ ἀπιστίᾳ
I might be grafted in. Well. – for unbelief
ἐξεκλάσθησαν, σὺ δὲ τῇ πίστει ἕστηκας.
they were broken off, and thou – by faith standest.
μὴ ὑψηλὰ φρόνει, ἀλλὰ φοβοῦ· 21 εἰ
2Not 3high things 1mind, but fear; 2if
γὰρ ὁ θεὸς τῶν κατὰ φύσιν κλάδων
1for – 3God 5the 7according to 8nature 6branches
οὐκ ἐφείσατο, οὐδὲ σοῦ φείσεται. 22 ἴδε
4spared not. neither thee will he spare. See
οὖν χρηστότητα καὶ ἀποτομίαν θεοῦ· ἐπὶ
therefore [the] kindness and [the] severity of God: 2on
μὲν τοὺς πεσόντας ἀποτομία, ἐπὶ δὲ
1on one hand, the [ones] having fallen severity, 2on 1on the other
σὲ χρηστότης θεοῦ, ἐὰν ἐπιμένῃς τῇ
thee [the] kindness of God, if thou continuest in the (his)
χρηστότητι, ἐπεὶ καὶ σὺ ἐκκοπήσῃ.
kindness, since also thou wilt be cut off.
23 κἀκεῖνοι δέ, ἐὰν μὴ ἐπιμένωσιν τῇ
And those also, if they continue not –
ἀπιστίᾳ, ἐγκεντρισθήσονται· δυνατὸς γάρ
in unbelief, will be grafted in; for 3able

* Some MSS insert *καὶ* (and) here; as it is, the two nouns in the genitive must be in apposition; *cf.* Col. 1. 18, 2. 2; John 8. 44.

if their transgression means
riches for the world, and
their loss means riches for
the Gentiles, how much
greater riches will their fullness bring!
13 I am talking to you Gentiles. Inasmuch as I am the
apostle to the Gentiles, I
make much of my ministry
14 in the hope that I may
somehow arouse my own
people to envy and save
some of them. 15 For if their
rejection is the reconciliation of the world, what will
their acceptance be but life
from the dead? 16 If the part
of the dough offered as
firstfruits is holy, then the
whole batch is holy; if the
root is holy, so are the
branches.
17 If some of the branches
have been broken off, and
you, though a wild olive
shoot, have been grafted in
among the others and now
share in the nourishing sap
from the olive root, 18 do
not boast over those
branches. If you do, con-
sider this: You do not support the root, but the root
supports you. 19 You will
say then, "Branches were
broken off so that I could
be grafted in." 20 Granted.
But they were broken off
because of unbelief, and
you stand by faith. Do not
be arrogant, but be afraid.
21 For if God did not spare
the natural branches, he
will not spare you either.
22 Consider therefore the
kindness and sternness of
God: sternness to those
who fell, but kindness to
you, provided that you
continue in his kindness.
Otherwise, you also will be
cut off. 23 And if they do not
persist in unbelief, they will

graft them in again. 24 For if
you have been cut from
what is by nature a wild olive tree and grafted, contrary to nature, into a cultivated olive tree, how much
more will these natural
branches be grafted back
into their own olive tree.

All Israel Will Be Saved

25 So that you may not
claim to be wiser than you
are, brothers and sisters,[h]
I want you to understand
this mystery: a hardening
has come upon part of Israel, until the full number of
the Gentiles has come in.
26 And so all Israel will be
saved; as it is written,

"Out of Zion will
come the
Deliverer;
he will banish
ungodliness
from Jacob."
27 "And this is my
covenant
with them,
when I take away
their sins."

28 As regards the gospel
they are enemies of God[i]
for your sake; but as re-
gards election they are beloved, for the sake of their
ancestors; 29 for the gifts
and the calling of God are
irrevocable. 30 Just as you
were once disobedient to
God but have now received
mercy because of their disobedience, 31 so they have
now been disobedient in order that, by the mercy
shown to you, they too may
now[j] receive mercy. 32 For
God has imprisoned all in
disobedience so that he
may be merciful to all.
33 O the depth of the
riches and wisdom and
knowledge of God! How
unsearchable are his judgments and how inscrutable
his ways!
34 "For who has known
the mind of the
Lord?
Or who has been his

[h] Gk *brothers*
[i] Gk lacks *of God*
[j] Other ancient authorities lack *now*

ἐστιν ὁ θεὸς πάλιν ἐγκεντρίσαι αὐτούς.
[2]is – [1]God [7]again [4]to graft [6]in [5]them.
24 εἰ γὰρ σὺ ἐκ τῆς κατὰ φύσιν ἐξεκόπης
For if thou [2]out of [3]the [5]according to [6]nature [1]wast cut *out*
ἀγριελαίου καὶ παρὰ φύσιν ἐνεκεντρίσθης
[4]wild olive and against nature wast grafted *in*
εἰς καλλιέλαιον, πόσῳ μᾶλλον οὗτοι οἱ
into a cultivated olive, by how much more these the [ones]
κατὰ φύσιν ἐγκεντρισθήσονται τῇ ἰδίᾳ
according to nature will be grafted in the(ir) own
ἐλαίᾳ. 25 Οὐ γὰρ θέλω ὑμᾶς ἀγνοεῖν,
olive-tree. For I wish not you to be ignorant,
ἀδελφοί, τὸ μυστήριον τοῦτο, ἵνα μὴ
brothers, [of] this mystery, lest
ἦτε ἐν ἑαυτοῖς φρόνιμοι, ὅτι πώρωσις
ye be in yourselves wise, that hardness
ἀπὸ μέρους τῷ Ἰσραὴλ γέγονεν ἄχρι οὗ
from(in) part – to Israel has happened until
τὸ πλήρωμα τῶν ἐθνῶν εἰσέλθῃ, 26 καὶ
the fulness of the nations comes in, and
οὕτως πᾶς Ἰσραὴλ σωθήσεται, καθὼς
so all Israel will be saved, as
γέγραπται· ἥξει ἐκ Σιὼν ὁ ῥυόμενος,
it has been written: [3]will come [4]out of [5]Sion [1]The [one] [2]delivering,
ἀποστρέψει ἀσεβείας ἀπὸ Ἰακώβ. 27 καὶ
he will turn away impiety from Jacob. And
αὕτη αὐτοῖς ἡ παρ' ἐμοῦ διαθήκη, ὅταν
this [is] [5]with them [1]the [3]from [4]me [2]covenant, when
ἀφέλωμαι τὰς ἁμαρτίας αὐτῶν. 28 κατὰ
I take away the sins of them. [2]According to
μὲν τὸ εὐαγγέλιον ἐχθροὶ δι' ὑμᾶς,
[1]on one hand the gospel enemies because of you,
κατὰ δὲ τὴν ἐκλογὴν ἀγαπητοὶ διὰ
[2]according to [1]on the other the choice beloved because of
τοὺς πατέρας· 29 ἀμεταμέλητα γὰρ τὰ
the fathers; for unrepented the
χαρίσματα καὶ ἡ κλῆσις τοῦ θεοῦ.
free gifts and the calling – of God.
30 ὥσπερ γὰρ ὑμεῖς ποτε ἠπειθήσατε
For as ye then disobeyed
τῷ θεῷ, νῦν δὲ ἠλεήθητε τῇ τούτων
– God, but now ye obtained mercy [1]by the [3]of these
ἀπειθείᾳ, 31 οὕτως καὶ οὗτοι νῦν ἠπείθησαν
[2]disobedience, so also these now disobeyed
τῷ ὑμετέρῳ ἐλέει ἵνα καὶ αὐτοὶ νῦν
– [2]by your [3]mercy [1]in order that also they now
ἐλεηθῶσιν. 32 συνέκλεισεν γὰρ ὁ θεὸς
may obtain mercy. For [2]shut up – [1]God
τοὺς πάντας εἰς ἀπείθειαν ἵνα τοὺς
– all in disobedience in order that –
πάντας ἐλεήσῃ.
to all he may show mercy.
33 Ὦ βάθος πλούτου καὶ σοφίας καὶ
O [the] depth of [the] riches and of [the] wisdom and
γνώσεως θεοῦ· ὡς ἀνεξερεύνητα τὰ κρίματα
of [the] knowledge of God; how inscrutable the judgments
αὐτοῦ καὶ ἀνεξιχνίαστοι αἱ ὁδοὶ αὐτοῦ.
of him and unsearchable the ways of him.
34 τίς γὰρ ἔγνω νοῦν κυρίου; ἢ τίς
.For who knew [the] mind of [the] Lord? or who

be grafted in, for God is
able to graft them in again.
24 After all, if you were cut
out of an olive tree that is
wild by nature, and con-
trary to nature were grafted
into a cultivated olive tree,
how much more readily
will these, the natural
branches, be grafted into
their own olive tree!

All Israel Will Be Saved

25 I do not want you to be
ignorant of this mystery,
brothers, so that you may
not be conceited: Israel has
experienced a hardening in
part until the full number of
the Gentiles has come in.
26 And so all Israel will be
saved, as it is written:

"The deliverer will come
from Zion;
he will turn
godlessness away
from Jacob.
27 And this is[r] my
covenant with them
when I take away their
sins."[s]

28 As far as the gospel is
concerned, they are ene-
mies on your account; but
as far as election is concerned, they are loved on
account of the patriarchs,
29 for God's gifts and his call
are irrevocable. 30 Just as
you who were at one time
disobedient to God have
now received mercy as a
result of their disobedi-
ence, 31 so they too have
now become disobedient in
order that they too may
now[t] receive mercy as a
result of God's mercy to
you. 32 For God has bound
all men over to disobedi-
ence so that he may have
mercy on them all.

Doxology

33 Oh, the depth of the
riches of the wisdom
and[u] knowledge of
God!
How unsearchable his
judgments,
and his paths beyond
tracing out!
34 "Who has known the
mind of the Lord?
Or who has been his
counselor?"[v]
35 "Who has ever given to
God,

[r] *27* Or *will be*
[s] *27* Isaiah 59:20,21; 27:9; Jer. 31:33,34
[t] *31* Some manuscripts do not have *now*.
[u] *33* Or *riches and the wisdom and the*
[v] *34* Isaiah 40:13

counselor?"
35 "Or who has given a
gift to him,
to receive a gift in
return?"
36 For from him and
through him and to him are
all things. To him be the
glory forever. Amen.

Chapter 12

The New Life in Christ

I appeal to you therefore,
brothers and sisters,[k]
by the mercies of God, to
present your bodies as a
living sacrifice, holy and
acceptable to God, which is
your spiritual[l] worship.
2 Do not be conformed to
this world,[m] but be transformed by the renewing of
your minds, so that you
may discern what is the will
of God—what is good and
acceptable and perfect.[n]
3 For by the grace given
to me I say to everyone
among you not to think of
yourself more highly than
you ought to think, but to
think with sober judgment,
each according to the measure of faith that God has
assigned. 4 For as in one
body we have many mem-
bers, and not all the members have the same func-
tion, 5 so we, who are
many, are one body in
Christ, and individually we
are members one of anoth-
er. 6 We have gifts that differ according to the grace
given to us: prophecy, in
proportion to faith; 7 ministry, in ministering; the
teacher, in teaching; 8 the
exhorter, in exhortation;
the giver, in generosity; the
leader, in diligence; the

[k] Gk *brothers*
[l] Or *reasonable*
[m] Gk *age*
[n] Or *what is the good and acceptable and perfect will of God*

σύμβουλος αὐτοῦ ἐγένετο; 35 ἢ τίς
counsellor of him became? or who

προέδωκεν αὐτῷ, καὶ ἀνταποδοθήσεται
previously gave to him, and it will be repaid

αὐτῷ; 36 ὅτι ἐξ αὐτοῦ καὶ δι' αὐτοῦ
to him? Because of him and through him

καὶ εἰς αὐτὸν τὰ πάντα· αὐτῷ ἡ δόξα
and to him – all things; to him the glory

εἰς τοὺς αἰῶνας· ἀμήν.
unto the ages: Amen.

12 Παρακαλῶ οὖν ὑμᾶς, ἀδελφοί, διὰ
I beseech therefore you, brothers, through

τῶν οἰκτιρμῶν τοῦ θεοῦ, παραστῆσαι τὰ
the compassions – of God, to present the

σώματα ὑμῶν θυσίαν ζῶσαν ἁγίαν τῷ
bodies of you sacrifice a living holy –

θεῷ εὐάρεστον, τὴν λογικὴν λατρείαν
2to God 1well-pleasing, the reasonable service

ὑμῶν· 2 καὶ μὴ συσχηματίζεσθε τῷ αἰῶνι
of you; and be ye not conformed – age

τούτῳ, ἀλλὰ μεταμορφοῦσθε τῇ ἀνακαινώσει
to this, but be ye transformed by the renewing

τοῦ νοός, εἰς τὸ δοκιμάζειν ὑμᾶς τί τὸ
of the mind, *for the* to prove you[b] what the
=so that ye may prove

θέλημα τοῦ θεοῦ, τὸ ἀγαθὸν καὶ εὐάρεστον
will – of God, the good and well-pleasing

καὶ τέλειον.
and perfect.

3 Λέγω γὰρ διὰ τῆς χάριτος τῆς
For I say through the grace –

δοθείσης μοι παντὶ τῷ ὄντι ἐν ὑμῖν,
given to me to everyone being among you,

μὴ ὑπερφρονεῖν παρ' ὃ δεῖ φρονεῖν,
not to have high thoughts beyond what it behoves to think,

ἀλλὰ φρονεῖν εἰς τὸ σωφρονεῖν, ἑκάστῳ
but to think *to the* to be sober-minded, 4to each

ὡς ὁ θεὸς ἐμέρισεν μέτρον πίστεως.
1as – 2God 3divided a measure of faith.

4 καθάπερ γὰρ ἐν ἑνὶ σώματι πολλὰ
For as in one body many

μέλη ἔχομεν, τὰ δὲ μέλη πάντα οὐ τὴν
members we have, but 2the 3members 1all 5not 6the

αὐτὴν ἔχει πρᾶξιν, 5 οὕτως οἱ πολλοὶ
7same 4has(ve) 8action, so the many

ἓν σῶμά ἐσμεν ἐν Χριστῷ, τὸ δὲ καθ'
one body we are in Christ, – and each

εἷς ἀλλήλων μέλη. 6 ἔχοντες δὲ χαρίσματα
one 2of one another 1members. And having gifts

κατὰ τὴν χάριν τὴν δοθεῖσαν ἡμῖν διάφορα,
2according to 3the 4grace – 5given 6to us 1differing,

εἴτε προφητείαν, κατὰ τὴν ἀναλογίαν τῆς
whether prophecy, according to the proportion of the

πίστεως· 7 εἴτε διακονίαν, ἐν τῇ διακονίᾳ·
faith; or ministry, in the ministry;

εἴτε ὁ διδάσκων, ἐν τῇ διδασκαλίᾳ·
or the [one] teaching, in the teaching;

8 εἴτε ὁ παρακαλῶν, ἐν τῇ παρακλήσει·
or the [one] exhorting, in the exhortation;

ὁ μεταδιδοὺς ἐν ἁπλότητι, ὁ προϊστάμενος
the [one] sharing in simplicity, the [one] taking the lead

that God should repay
him?"[w]
36 For from him and
through him and to
him are all things.
To him be the glory
forever! Amen.

Chapter 12

Living Sacrifices

THEREFORE, I urge
you, brothers, in view
of God's mercy, to offer
your bodies as living sacrifices, holy and pleasing to
God—this is your spiritu-
al[x] act of worship. 2 Do not
conform any longer to the
pattern of this world, but be
transformed by the renew-
ing of your mind. Then you
will be able to test and approve what God's will is—
his good, pleasing and perfect will.
3 For by the grace given
me I say to every one of
you: Do not think of yourself more highly than you
ought, but rather think of
yourself with sober judg-
ment, in accordance with
the measure of faith God
has given you. 4 Just as each
of us has one body with
many members, and these
members do not all have
the same function, 5 so in
Christ we who are many
form one body, and each
member belongs to all the
others. 6 We have different
gifts, according to the grace
given us. If a man's gift is
prophesying, let him use it
in proportion to his[y] faith.
7 If it is serving, let him
serve; if it is teaching, let
him teach; 8 if it is encouraging, let him encourage; if it
is contributing to the needs
of others, let him give generously; if it is leadership,
let him govern diligently; if

[w] *35* Job 41:11
[x] *1* Or *reasonable*
[y] *6* Or *in agreement with the*

compassionate, in cheerfulness.

Marks of the True Christian

9 Let love be genuine; hate what is evil, hold fast to what is good; 10 love one another with mutual affection; outdo one another in showing honor. 11 Do not lag in zeal, be ardent in spirit, serve the Lord.[o] 12 Rejoice in hope, be patient in suffering, persevere in prayer. 13 Contribute to the needs of the saints; extend hospitality to strangers.

14 Bless those who persecute you; bless and do not curse them. 15 Rejoice with those who rejoice, weep with those who weep. 16 Live in harmony with one another; do not be haughty, but associate with the lowly;[p] do not claim to be wiser than you are. 17 Do not repay anyone evil for evil, but take thought for what is noble in the sight of all. 18 If it is possible, so far as it depends on you, live peaceably with all. 19 Beloved, never avenge yourselves, but leave room for the wrath of God;[q] for it is written, "Vengeance is mine, I will repay, says the Lord." 20 No, "if your enemies are hungry, feed them; if they are thirsty, give them something to drink; for by doing this you will heap burning coals on their heads." 21 Do not be overcome by evil, but overcome evil with good.

Chapter 13

Being Subject to Authorities

LET every person be subject to the governing authorities; for there is no authority except from God, and those authorities that

[o] Other ancient authorities read *serve the opportune time*
[p] Or *give yourselves to humble tasks*
[q] Gk *the wrath*

ἐν σπουδῇ, ὁ ἐλεῶν ἐν ἱλαρότητι. 9 ἡ
in diligence, the [one] showing mercy in cheerfulness. –

ἀγάπη ἀνυπόκριτος. ἀποστυγοῦντες τὸ
[Let] love [be] unassumed. Shrinking from the

πονηρόν, κολλώμενοι τῷ ἀγαθῷ· 10 τῇ
evil, cleaving to the good; –

φιλαδελφίᾳ εἰς ἀλλήλους φιλόστοργοι, τῇ
in brotherly love to one another loving warmly, –

τιμῇ ἀλλήλους προηγούμενοι, 11 τῇ σπουδῇ
in honour one another preferring, – in zeal

μὴ ὀκνηροί, τῷ πνεύματι ζέοντες, τῷ
not slothful, – in spirit burning, the

κυρίῳ δουλεύοντες, 12 τῇ ἐλπίδι χαίροντες,
Lord serving, – in hope rejoicing,

τῇ θλίψει ὑπομένοντες, τῇ προσευχῇ
– in affliction showing endurance, – in prayer

προσκαρτεροῦντες, 13 ταῖς χρείαις τῶν
steadfastly continuing, to the needs of the

ἁγίων κοινωνοῦντες, τὴν φιλοξενίαν
saints imparting, – hospitality

διώκοντες. 14 εὐλογεῖτε τοὺς διώκοντας,
pursuing. Bless ye the [ones] persecuting,

εὐλογεῖτε καὶ μὴ καταρᾶσθε. 15 χαίρειν
bless and do not curse. To rejoice

μετὰ χαιρόντων, κλαίειν μετὰ κλαιόντων.
with rejoicing [ones], to weep with weeping [ones].

16 τὸ αὐτὸ εἰς ἀλλήλους φρονοῦντες· μὴ
The same thing toward one another minding; not

τὰ ὑψηλὰ φρονοῦντες ἀλλὰ τοῖς ταπεινοῖς
[2]the [3]high things [1]minding but to the humble

συναπαγόμενοι. μὴ γίνεσθε φρόνιμοι παρ'
condescending. Become not wise with

ἑαυτοῖς. 17 μηδενὶ κακὸν ἀντὶ κακοῦ
yourselves. To no one evil instead of evil

ἀποδιδόντες· προνοούμενοι καλὰ ἐνώπιον
returning; providing for good things before

πάντων ἀνθρώπων· 18 εἰ δυνατόν, τὸ ἐξ
all men; if possible, as far as it

ὑμῶν, μετὰ πάντων ἀνθρώπων εἰρηνεύοντες·
rests with you,† with all men seeking peace;

19 μὴ ἑαυτοὺς ἐκδικοῦντες, ἀγαπητοί, ἀλλὰ
not [2]yourselves [1]avenging, beloved, but

δότε τόπον τῇ ὀργῇ· γέγραπται γάρ·
give place – to wrath; for it has been written:

ἐμοὶ ἐκδίκησις, ἐγὼ ἀνταποδώσω, λέγει
To me vengeance,[c] I will repay, says
=Vengeance is mine,

κύριος. 20 ἀλλὰ ἐὰν πεινᾷ ὁ ἐχθρός
[the] Lord. But if hungers the enemy

σου, ψώμιζε αὐτόν· ἐὰν διψᾷ, πότιζε
of thee, feed him; if he thirsts, give [2]drink

αὐτόν· τοῦτο γὰρ ποιῶν ἄνθρακας πυρὸς
[1]him; for this doing coals of fire

σωρεύσεις ἐπὶ τὴν κεφαλὴν αὐτοῦ. 21 μὴ
thou wilt heap on the head of him. not

νικῶ ὑπὸ τοῦ κακοῦ, ἀλλὰ νίκα
Be conquered by the evil, but conquer

ἐν τῷ ἀγαθῷ τὸ κακόν. 13 Πᾶσα
[3]by [4]the [5]good [1]the [2]evil. [2]Every

ψυχὴ ἐξουσίαις ὑπερεχούσαις ὑποτασσέσθω.
[3]soul [7]authorities [6]to superior [1]let [4]be [5]subject.

οὐ γὰρ ἔστιν ἐξουσία εἰ μὴ
For there is no authority except

ὑπὸ θεοῦ, αἱ δὲ οὖσαι ὑπὸ θεοῦ
by God, and the existing [ones] by God

it is showing mercy, let him do it cheerfully.

Love

9 Love must be sincere. Hate what is evil; cling to what is good. 10 Be devoted to one another in brotherly love. Honor one another above yourselves. 11 Never be lacking in zeal, but keep your spiritual fervor, serving the Lord. 12 Be joyful in hope, patient in affliction, faithful in prayer. 13 Share with God's people who are in need. Practice hospitality.

14 Bless those who persecute you; bless and do not curse. 15 Rejoice with those who rejoice; mourn with those who mourn. 16 Live in harmony with one another. Do not be proud, but be willing to associate with people of low position.[z] Do not be conceited.

17 Do not repay anyone evil for evil. Be careful to do what is right in the eyes of everybody. 18 If it is possible, as far as it depends on you, live at peace with everyone. 19 Do not take revenge, my friends, but leave room for God's wrath, for it is written: "It is mine to avenge; I will repay,"[a] says the Lord. 20 On the contrary:

"If your enemy is
hungry, feed him;
if he is thirsty, give him
something to drink.
In doing this, you will
heap burning coals
on his head."[b]

21 Do not be overcome by evil, but overcome evil with good.

Chapter 13

Submission to the Authorities

EVERYONE must submit himself to the governing authorities, for there is no authority except that which God has established.

[z] 16 Or *willing to do menial work*
[a] 19 Deut. 32:35
[b] 20 Prov. 25:21,22

exist have been instituted by God. 2Therefore whoever resists authority resists what God has appointed, and those who resist will incur judgment. 3For rulers are not a terror to good conduct, but to bad. Do you wish to have no fear of the authority? Then do what is good, and you will receive its approval; 4for it is God's servant for your good. But if you do what is wrong, you should be afraid, for the authority[r] does not bear the sword in vain! It is the servant of God to execute wrath on the wrongdoer. 5Therefore one must be subject, not only because of wrath but also because of conscience. 6For the same reason you also pay taxes, for the authorities are God's servants, busy with this very thing. 7Pay to all what is due them—taxes to whom taxes are due, revenue to whom revenue is due, respect to whom respect is due, honor to whom honor is due.

Love for One Another

8 Owe no one anything, except to love one another; for the one who loves another has fulfilled the law. 9The commandments, "You shall not commit adultery; You shall not murder; You shall not steal; You shall not covet"; and any other commandment, are summed up in this word, "Love your neighbor as yourself." 10Love does no wrong to a neighbor; therefore, love is the fulfilling of the law.

τεταγμέναι εἰσίν. 2 ὥστε ὁ ἀντιτασσόμενος
having been ordained are. So the [one] resisting

τῇ ἐξουσίᾳ τῇ τοῦ θεοῦ διαταγῇ ἀνθέστη-
the authority [2]the – [4]of God [3]ordinance [1]has op-

κεν· οἱ δὲ ἀνθεστηκότες ἑαυτοῖς κρίμα
posed; and the [ones] having opposed to themselves judgment

λήμψονται. 3 οἱ γὰρ ἄρχοντες οὐκ εἰσὶν
will receive. For the rulers are not

φόβος τῷ ἀγαθῷ ἔργῳ ἀλλὰ τῷ κακῷ.
a fear to the good work but to the evil.

θέλεις δὲ μὴ φοβεῖσθαι τὴν ἐξουσίαν;
And wishest thou not to fear the authority?

τὸ ἀγαθὸν ποίει, καὶ ἕξεις ἔπαινον ἐξ
[2]the [3]good [1]do, and thou wilt have praise from

αὐτῆς· 4 θεοῦ γὰρ διάκονός ἐστιν σοὶ
it; for of God a minister he is to thee

εἰς τὸ ἀγαθόν. ἐὰν δὲ τὸ κακὸν ποιῇς,
for the good. But if the evil thou doest,

φοβοῦ· οὐ γὰρ εἰκῇ τὴν μάχαιραν φορεῖ·
fear; for not in vain the sword he bears;

θεοῦ γὰρ διάκονός ἐστιν ἔκδικος εἰς
for of God a minister he is an avenger for

ὀργὴν τῷ τὸ κακὸν πράσσοντι. 5 διὸ
wrath to the [one] [2]the [3]evil [1]practising. Wherefore

ἀνάγκη ὑποτάσσεσθαι, οὐ μόνον διὰ τὴν
it is necessary to be subject, not only because of –

ὀργὴν ἀλλὰ καὶ διὰ τὴν συνείδησιν.
wrath but also because of – conscience.

6 διὰ τοῦτο γὰρ καὶ φόρους τελεῖτε·
For therefore also taxes pay ye;

λειτουργοὶ γὰρ θεοῦ εἰσιν εἰς αὐτὸ τοῦτο
for ministers of God they are for this very thing

προσκαρτεροῦντες. 7 ἀπόδοτε πᾶσιν τὰς
attending constantly. Render to all men the

ὀφειλάς, τῷ τὸν φόρον τὸν φόρον,
dues, to the [one] the tax the tax,*

τῷ τὸ τέλος τὸ τέλος, τῷ τὸν φόβον
to the [one] the tribute the tribute, to the [one] *the* fear

τὸν φόβον, τῷ τὴν τιμὴν τὴν τιμήν.
the fear, to the [one] *the* honour *the* honour.

8 Μηδενὶ μηδὲν ὀφείλετε, εἰ μὴ τὸ
To no one no(any)thing owe ye, except –

ἀλλήλους ἀγαπᾶν· ὁ γὰρ ἀγαπῶν τὸν
one another to love; for the [one] loving the

ἕτερον νόμον πεπλήρωκεν. 9 τὸ γὰρ
other law has fulfilled. For

οὐ μοιχεύσεις, οὐ φονεύσεις, οὐ κλέψεις,
Thou shalt not commit adultery, Thou shalt not kill, Thou shalt not steal,

οὐκ ἐπιθυμήσεις, καὶ εἴ τις ἑτέρα ἐντολή,
Thou shalt not covet, and if any [there is] other commandment,

ἐν τῷ λόγῳ τούτῳ ἀνακεφαλαιοῦται, [ἐν
[2]in [3]this [4]word [1]it is summed up, in

τῷ]· ἀγαπήσεις τὸν πλησίον σου ὡς
– : Thou shalt love the neighbour of thee as

σεαυτόν. 10 ἡ ἀγάπη τῷ πλησίον κακὸν
thyself. – Love [3]to the (one's) [4]neighbour [2]evil

οὐκ ἐργάζεται· πλήρωμα οὖν νόμου ἡ
[1]works not; [3][is] [4]fulfilment [1]therefore [5]of law –

The authorities that exist have been established by God. 2Consequently, he who rebels against the authority is rebelling against what God has instituted, and those who do so will bring judgment on themselves. 3For rulers hold no terror for those who do right, but for those who do wrong. Do you want to be free from fear of the one in authority? Then do what is right and he will commend you. 4For he is God's servant to do you good. But if you do wrong, be afraid, for he does not bear the sword for nothing. He is God's servant, an agent of wrath to bring punishment on the wrongdoer. 5Therefore, it is necessary to submit to the authorities, not only because of possible punishment but also because of conscience.

6This is also why you pay taxes, for the authorities are God's servants, who give their full time to governing. 7Give everyone what you owe him: If you owe taxes, pay taxes; if revenue, then revenue; if respect, then respect; if honor, then honor.

Love, for the Day Is Near

8Let no debt remain outstanding, except the continuing debt to love one another, for he who loves his fellowman has fulfilled the law. 9The commandments, "Do not commit adultery," "Do not murder," "Do not steal," "Do not covet,"[c] and whatever other commandment there may be, are summed up in this one rule: "Love your neighbor as yourself."[d] 10Love does no harm to its neighbor. Therefore love is the fulfillment of the law.

* The phrase between the commas is elliptical; understand—to the [one demanding] the tax [render] the tax. So of the following phrases.

[r] Gk *it*

[c] 9 Exodus 20:13-15,17; Deut. 5:17-19,21
[d] 9 Lev. 19:18

An Urgent Appeal

11 Besides this, you
know what time it is, how it
is now the moment for you
to wake from sleep. For
salvation is nearer to us
now than when we became
believers; 12 the night is far
gone, the day is near. Let
us then lay aside the works
of darkness and put on the
armor of light; 13 let us live
honorably as in the day, not
in reveling and drunken-
ness, not in debauchery
and licentiousness, not in
quarreling and jealousy.
14 Instead, put on the Lord
Jesus Christ, and make no
provision for the flesh, to
gratify its desires.

ἀγάπη. 11 Καὶ τοῦτο εἰδότες τὸν καιρόν,
[2]love. And this[,] knowing the time,

ὅτι ὥρα ἤδη ὑμᾶς ἐξ ὕπνου ἐγερθῆναι·
that hour now you out of sleep to be raised;[b]
=it is now an hour for you to be raised out of sleep;

νῦν γὰρ ἐγγύτερον ἡμῶν ἡ σωτηρία
for now nearer [is] of us the salvation

ἢ ὅτε ἐπιστεύσαμεν. 12 ἡ νὺξ προέκοψεν,
than when we believed. The night advanced,

ἡ δὲ ἡμέρα ἤγγικεν. ἀποθώμεθα οὖν
and the day has drawn near. Let us cast off therefore

τὰ ἔργα τοῦ σκότους, ἐνδυσώμεθα δὲ
the works of the darkness, and let us put on

τὰ ὅπλα τοῦ φωτός. 13 ὡς ἐν ἡμέρᾳ
the weapons of the light. As in [the] day

εὐσχημόνως περιπατήσωμεν, μὴ κώμοις καὶ
becomingly let us walk, not in revellings and

μέθαις, μὴ κοίταις καὶ ἀσελγείαις, μὴ
in drunken bouts, not in beds* and excesses, not

ἔριδι καὶ ζήλῳ· 14 ἀλλὰ ἐνδύσασθε τὸν
in strife and *in* jealousy; but put ye on the

κύριον Ἰησοῦν Χριστόν, καὶ τῆς σαρκὸς
Lord Jesus Christ, and of the flesh

πρόνοιαν μὴ ποιεῖσθε εἰς ἐπιθυμίας.
forethought make not for [its] lusts.

11 And do this, under-
standing the present time.
The hour has come for you
to wake up from your slumber, because our salvation
is nearer now than when we
first believed. 12 The night is
nearly over; the day is almost here. So let us put
aside the deeds of darkness
and put on the armor of
light. 13 Let us behave decently, as in the daytime,
not in orgies and drunkenness, not in sexual immo-
rality and debauchery, not
in dissension and jealousy.
14 Rather, clothe yourselves
with the Lord Jesus Christ,
and do not think about how
to gratify the desires of the
sinful nature.[e]

Chapter 14

Do Not Judge Another

WELCOME those who
are weak in faith,[s]
but not for the purpose of
quarreling over opinions.
2 Some believe in eating
anything, while the weak
eat only vegetables.
3 Those who eat must not
despise those who abstain,
and those who abstain must
not pass judgment on those
who eat; for God has wel-
comed them. 4 Who are you
to pass judgment on ser-
vants of another? It is before their own lord that
they stand or fall. And they
will be upheld, for the
Lord[t] is able to make them
stand.
5 Some judge one day to
be better than another,
while others judge all days
to be alike. Let all be fully
convinced in their own
minds. 6 Those who ob-
serve the day, observe it in
honor of the Lord. Also
those who eat, eat in honor
of the Lord, since they give
thanks to God; while those
who abstain, abstain in

14 Τὸν δὲ ἀσθενοῦντα τῇ πίστει
Now the [one] being weak in the faith

προσλαμβάνεσθε, μὴ εἰς διακρίσεις διαλογισ-
receive ye, not to judgments of

μῶν. 2 ὃς μὲν πιστεύει φαγεῖν πάντα,
thoughts. One man† indeed believes to eat all things,

ὁ δὲ ἀσθενῶν λάχανα ἐσθίει. 3 ὁ ἐσθίων
but the [one] being weak herbs eats. [2]The [one] [3]eating

τὸν μὴ ἐσθίοντα μὴ ἐξουθενείτω, ὁ δὲ
[6]the [one] [7]not [8]eating [4]not [1]let [5]despise, and [2]the [one]

μὴ ἐσθίων τὸν ἐσθίοντα μὴ κρινέτω,
[4]not [5]eating [7]the [one] [8]eating [3]not [1]let [6]judge,

ὁ θεὸς· γὰρ αὐτὸν προσελάβετο. 4 σὺ
– for God him received. [2]Thou

τίς εἶ ὁ κρίνων ἀλλότριον οἰκέτην; τῷ
[1]who [3]art [4]the [one] [5]judging [7]belonging to another [6]a *household* servant? to the(his)

ἰδίῳ κυρίῳ στήκει ἢ πίπτει· σταθήσεται
own lord he stands or falls; [2]he will stand

δέ, δυνατεῖ γὰρ ὁ κύριος στῆσαι αὐτόν.
[1]but, for is able the Lord to stand him.

5 ὃς μὲν [γὰρ] κρίνει ἡμέραν παρ'
one man† indeed judges a day above

ἡμέραν, ὃς δὲ κρίνει πᾶσαν ἡμέραν·
a day, another† judges every day;

ἕκαστος ἐν τῷ ἰδίῳ νοῒ πληροφορείσθω.
each man in the(his) own mind let him be fully persuaded.

6 ὁ φρονῶν τὴν ἡμέραν κυρίῳ φρονεῖ.
The [one] minding the day to [the] Lord he minds [it].

καὶ ὁ ἐσθίων κυρίῳ ἐσθίει, εὐχαριστεῖ γὰρ
And the [one] eating to [the] Lord he eats, for he gives thanks

τῷ θεῷ· καὶ ὁ μὴ ἐσθίων κυρίῳ
– to God; and the [one] not eating to [the] Lord

Chapter 14

The Weak and the Strong

ACCEPT him whose faith
is weak, without pass-
ing judgment on disputable
matters. 2 One man's faith
allows him to eat every-
thing, but another man,
whose faith is weak, eats
only vegetables. 3 The man
who eats everything must
not look down on him who
does not, and the man who
does not eat everything
must not condemn the man
who does, for God has ac-
cepted him. 4 Who are you
to judge someone else's
servant? To his own master
he stands or falls. And he
will stand, for the Lord is
able to make him stand.
5 One man considers one
day more sacred than an-
other; another man considers every day alike. Each
one should be fully con-
vinced in his own mind.
6 He who regards one day as
special, does so to the
Lord. He who eats meat,
eats to the Lord, for he
gives thanks to God; and he
who abstains, does so to

[s] Or *conviction*
[t] Other ancient authorities read *for God*

* That is, illicit sexual intercourse.

[e] 14 Or *the flesh*

honor of the Lord and give
thanks to God.
7 We do not live to our-
selves, and we do not die to
ourselves. 8 If we live, we
live to the Lord, and if we
die, we die to the Lord; so
then, whether we live or
whether we die, we are the
Lord's. 9 For to this end
Christ died and lived again,
so that he might be Lord of
both the dead and the living.
10 Why do you pass
judgment on your brother
or sister?[u] Or you, why do
you despise your brother or
sister?[u] For we will all
stand before the judgment
seat of God.[v] 11 For it is
written,

"As I live, says the
Lord, every
knee shall bow
to me,
and every tongue
shall give praise
to[w] God."

12 So then, each of us will
be accountable to God.[x]

Do Not Make Another Stumble

13 Let us therefore no
longer pass judgment on
one another, but resolve instead never to put a stumbling block or hindrance in
the way of another.[y] 14 I
know and am persuaded in
the Lord Jesus that nothing
is unclean in itself; but it is
unclean for anyone who
thinks it unclean. 15 If your
brother or sister[u] is being
injured by what you eat,
you are no longer walking
in love. Do not let what you
eat cause the ruin of one for
whom Christ died. 16 So do
not let your good be spoken
of as evil. 17 For the kingdom of God is not food and
drink but righteousness and
peace and joy in the Holy
Spirit. 18 The one who thus
serves Christ is acceptable
to God and has human ap-

[u] Gk *brother*
[v] Other ancient authorities read *of Christ*
[w] Or *confess*
[x] Other ancient authorities lack *to God*
[y] Gk *of a brother*

οὐκ ἐσθίει, καὶ εὐχαριστεῖ τῷ θεῷ.
he eats not, and gives thanks – to God.
7 οὐδεὶς γὰρ ἡμῶν ἑαυτῷ ζῇ, καὶ οὐδεὶς
For no one of us to himself lives, and no one
ἑαυτῷ ἀποθνῄσκει· 8 ἐάν τε γὰρ ζῶμεν,
to himself dies; for whether we live,
τῷ κυρίῳ ζῶμεν, ἐάν τε ἀποθνῄσκωμεν,
to the Lord we live, or if we die,
τῷ κυρίῳ ἀποθνῄσκομεν. ἐάν τε οὖν
to the Lord we die. Whether therefore
ζῶμεν ἐάν τε ἀποθνῄσκωμεν, τοῦ κυρίου
we live or if we die, of the Lord
ἐσμέν. 9 εἰς τοῦτο γὰρ Χριστὸς ἀπέθανεν
we are. for this For Christ died
καὶ ἔζησεν, ἵνα καὶ νεκρῶν καὶ ζώντων
and lived [again], in order that both of dead and of living [ones]
κυριεύσῃ. 10 σὺ δὲ τί κρίνεις τὸν ἀδελφόν
he might be Lord. ³thou And ¹why ²judgest the brother
σου; ἢ καὶ σὺ τί ἐξουθενεῖς τὸν ἀδελφόν
of thee? or ²indeed ⁴thou ¹why ³despisest the brother
σου; πάντες γὰρ παραστησόμεθα τῷ
of thee? for all we shall stand before the
βήματι τοῦ θεοῦ. 11 γέγραπται γάρ·
tribunal – of God. For it has been written:
ζῶ ἐγώ, λέγει κύριος, ὅτι ἐμοὶ κάμψει
Live I, says [the] Lord, that to me will bend
πᾶν γόνυ, καὶ πᾶσα γλῶσσα ἐξομολογήσεται
every knee, and every tongue will confess
τῷ θεῷ. 12 ἄρα [οὖν] ἕκαστος ἡμῶν
– to God. So therefore each one of us
περὶ ἑαυτοῦ λόγον δώσει [τῷ θεῷ].
concerning himself account will give – to God.
13 Μηκέτι οὖν ἀλλήλους κρίνωμεν· ἀλλὰ
No longer therefore one another let us judge; but
τοῦτο κρίνατε μᾶλλον, τὸ μὴ τιθέναι
this judge ye rather, – not to put
πρόσκομμα τῷ ἀδελφῷ ἢ σκάνδαλον.
a stumbling-block to the brother or an offence.
14 οἶδα καὶ πέπεισμαι ἐν κυρίῳ Ἰησοῦ
I know and have been persuaded by [the] Lord Jesus
ὅτι οὐδὲν κοινὸν δι' ἑαυτοῦ· εἰ μὴ
that nothing [is] common through itself; except
τῷ λογιζομένῳ τι κοινὸν εἶναι, ἐκείνῳ
to the [one] reckoning anything common to be, to that man [it is]
κοινόν. 15 εἰ γὰρ διὰ βρῶμα ὁ ἀδελφός
common. For if because of food the brother
σου λυπεῖται, οὐκέτι κατὰ ἀγάπην
of thee is grieved, no longer according to love
περιπατεῖς. μὴ τῷ βρώματί σου ἐκεῖνον
thou walkest. ²Not ³by the ⁴food ⁵of thee ⁶that man
ἀπόλλυε, ὑπὲρ οὗ Χριστὸς ἀπέθανεν.
¹destroy, on behalf of whom Christ died.
16 μὴ βλασφημείσθω οὖν ὑμῶν τὸ ἀγαθόν.
Let not be blasphemed therefore of you the good.
17 οὐ γάρ ἐστιν ἡ βασιλεία τοῦ θεοῦ
For not is the kingdom – of God
βρῶσις καὶ πόσις, ἀλλὰ δικαιοσύνη καὶ
eating and drinking, but righteousness and
εἰρήνη καὶ χαρὰ ἐν πνεύματι ἁγίῳ·
peace and joy in [the] Spirit Holy;
18 ὁ γὰρ ἐν τούτῳ δουλεύων τῷ Χριστῷ
for the [one] in this serving – Christ

the Lord and gives thanks
to God. 7 For none of us
lives to himself alone and
none of us dies to himself
alone. 8 If we live, we live to
the Lord; and if we die, we
die to the Lord. So, whether we live or die, we belong
to the Lord.
9 For this very reason,
Christ died and returned to
life so that he might be the
Lord of both the dead and
the living. 10 You, then,
why do you judge your
brother? Or why do you
look down on your broth-
er? For we will all stand before God's judgment seat.
11 It is written:

" 'As surely as I live,'
says the Lord,
'every knee will bow
before me;
every tongue will
confess to God.' "[f]

12 So then, each of us will
give an account of himself
to God.
13 Therefore let us stop
passing judgment on one
another. Instead, make up
your mind not to put any
stumbling block or obstacle
in your brother's way. 14 As
one who is in the Lord
Jesus, I am fully convinced
that no food[g] is unclean in
itself. But if anyone regards
something as unclean, then
for him it is unclean. 15 If
your brother is distressed
because of what you eat,
you are no longer acting in
love. Do not by your eating
destroy your brother for
whom Christ died. 16 Do not
allow what you consider
good to be spoken of as
evil. 17 For the kingdom of
God is not a matter of eating and drinking, but of
righteousness, peace and
joy in the Holy Spirit, 18 because anyone who serves

[f] *11* Isaiah 45:23
[g] *14* Or *that nothing*

proval. 19 Let us then pursue what makes for peace
and for mutual upbuilding.
20 Do not, for the sake of
food, destroy the work of
God. Everything is indeed
clean, but it is wrong for
you to make others fall by
what you eat; 21 it is good
not to eat meat or drink
wine or do anything that
makes your brother or sister[u] stumble.[z] 22 The faith
that you have, have as your
own conviction before
God. Blessed are those
who have no reason to condemn themselves because
of what they approve.
23 But those who have
doubts are condemned if
they eat, because they do
not act from faith;[s] for
whatever does not proceed
from faith[s] is sin.[a]

Chapter 15

Please Others, Not Yourselves

WE who are strong
ought to put up with
the failings of the weak,
and not to please our-
selves. 2 Each of us must
please our neighbor for the
good purpose of building
up the neighbor. 3 For
Christ did not please himself; but, as it is written,
"The insults of those who
insult you have fallen on
me." 4 For whatever was
written in former days was
written for our instruction,
so that by steadfastness
and by the encouragement
of the scriptures we might
have hope. 5 May the God
of steadfastness and en-
couragement grant you to
live in harmony with one
another, in accordance
with Christ Jesus, 6 so that
together you may with one
voice glorify the God and

[z] Other ancient authorities add *or be upset or be weakened*
[a] Other authorities, some ancient, add here 16.25-27

εὐάρεστος τῷ θεῷ καὶ δόκιμος τοῖς
[is] well-pleasing – to God and approved –
ἀνθρώποις. **19** ἄρα οὖν τὰ τῆς εἰρήνης
by men. So therefore the things – of peace
διώκωμεν καὶ τὰ τῆς οἰκοδομῆς τῆς
let us pursue and the things – of building [up] –
εἰς ἀλλήλους. **20** μὴ ἕνεκεν βρώματος
for one another. Not for the sake of food
κατάλυε τὸ ἔργον τοῦ θεοῦ. πάντα
undo thou the work – of God. All things
μὲν καθαρά, ἀλλὰ κακὸν τῷ ἀνθρώπῳ
indeed [are] clean, but evil to the man
τῷ διὰ προσκόμματος ἐσθίοντι. **21** καλὸν
– [3]through [3]a stumbling-block [1]eating. Good [it is]
τὸ μὴ φαγεῖν κρέα μηδὲ πιεῖν οἶνον
– not to eat flesh nor to drink wine
μηδὲ ἐν ᾧ ὁ ἀδελφός σου προσκόπτει.
nor [anything] by which the brother of thee stumbles.
22 σὺ πίστιν ἣν ἔχεις κατὰ σεαυτὸν
[3]Thou [1]faith [2]which [4]hast [6]by [7]thyself
ἔχε ἐνώπιον τοῦ θεοῦ. μακάριος ὁ
[5]have before – God. Blessed the [one]
μὴ κρίνων ἑαυτὸν ἐν ᾧ δοκιμάζει·
not judging himself in what he approves;
23 ὁ δὲ διακρινόμενος ἐὰν φάγῃ κατα-
but the [one] doubting if he eats has been
κέκριται, ὅτι οὐκ ἐκ πίστεως· πᾶν
condemned, because not of faith; [2]all
δὲ ὃ οὐκ ἐκ πίστεως ἁμαρτία ἐστίν.
[1]and which [is] not of faith sin is.
15 Ὀφείλομεν δὲ ἡμεῖς οἱ δυνατοὶ τὰ
[5]Ought [1]so [2]we [3]the [4]strong [7]the
ἀσθενήματα τῶν ἀδυνάτων βαστάζειν, καὶ
[8]weaknesses [9]of the [10]not strong [6]to bear, and
μὴ ἑαυτοῖς ἀρέσκειν. **2** ἕκαστος ἡμῶν
not [our]selves to please. Each one of us
τῷ πλησίον ἀρεσκέτω εἰς τὸ ἀγαθὸν
the(his) neighbour let him please for – good
πρὸς οἰκοδομήν· **3** καὶ γὰρ ὁ Χριστὸς
to building [up]; for even – Christ
οὐχ ἑαυτῷ ἤρεσεν· ἀλλὰ καθὼς γέ-
[2]not [3]himself [1]pleased; but as it has
γραπται· οἱ ὀνειδισμοὶ τῶν ὀνειδιζόντων
been written: The reproaches of the [ones] reproaching
σε ἐπέπεσαν ἐπ' ἐμέ. **4** ὅσα γὰρ
thee fell *on* on me. For whatever things
προεγράφη, εἰς τὴν ἡμετέραν διδασκαλίαν
were previously written, for – our teaching
ἐγράφη, ἵνα διὰ τῆς ὑπομονῆς καὶ
were written, in order that through – patience and
διὰ τῆς παρακλήσεως τῶν γραφῶν τὴν
through the comfort of the writings –
ἐλπίδα ἔχωμεν. **5** ὁ δὲ θεὸς τῆς ὑπομονῆς
hope we may have. And the God – of patience
καὶ τῆς παρακλήσεως δῴη ὑμῖν τὸ
and – of comfort give to you [2]the
αὐτὸ φρονεῖν ἐν ἀλλήλοις κατὰ Χριστὸν
[3]same thing [1]to mind among one another according to Christ
Ἰησοῦν, **6** ἵνα ὁμοθυμαδὸν ἐν ἑνὶ στόματι
Jesus, in order that with one accord with one mouth

Christ in this way is pleasing to God and approved by
men.
19 Let us therefore make
every effort to do what
leads to peace and to mutual edification. 20 Do not destroy the work of God for
the sake of food. All food is
clean, but it is wrong for a
man to eat anything that
causes someone else to
stumble. 21 It is better not to
eat meat or drink wine or to
do anything else that will
cause your brother to fall.
22 So whatever you be-
lieve about these things
keep between yourself and
God. Blessed is the man
who does not condemn
himself by what he ap-
proves. 23 But the man who
has doubts is condemned if
he eats, because his eating
is not from faith; and everything that does not come
from faith is sin.

Chapter 15

WE who are strong
ought to bear with
the failings of the weak and
not to please ourselves.
2 Each of us should please
his neighbor for his good,
to build him up. 3 For even
Christ did not please himself but, as it is written:
"The insults of those who
insult you have fallen on
me."[h] 4 For everything that
was written in the past was
written to teach us, so that
through endurance and the
encouragement of the
Scriptures we might have
hope.
5 May the God who gives
endurance and encourage-
ment give you a spirit of
unity among yourselves as
you follow Christ Jesus,
6 so that with one heart and
mouth you may glorify the

[h] 3 Psalm 69:9

Father of our Lord Jesus
Christ.

The Gospel for Jews and Gentiles Alike

7 Welcome one anoth-
er, therefore, just as Christ
has welcomed you, for the
glory of God. 8For I tell
you that Christ has become
a servant of the circum-
cised on behalf of the truth
of God in order that he
might confirm the promises
given to the patriarchs,
9and in order that the Gentiles might glorify God for
his mercy. As it is written,
"Therefore I will
confess[b] you
among the
Gentiles,
and sing praises to
your name";
10and again he says,
"Rejoice, O Gentiles,
with his
people";
11and again,
"Praise the Lord, all
you Gentiles,
and let all the
peoples
praise him";
12and again Isaiah says,
"The root of Jesse
shall come,
the one who rises to
rule
the Gentiles;
in him the Gentiles
shall hope."
13May the God of hope fill
you with all joy and peace
in believing, so that you
may abound in hope by the
power of the Holy Spirit.

Paul's Reason for Writing So Boldly

14 I myself feel confi-
dent about you, my broth-
ers and sisters,[c] that you
yourselves are full of goodness, filled with all knowledge, and able to instruct
one another. 15Neverthe-
less on some points I have
written to you rather boldly
by way of reminder, be-
cause of the grace given me
by God 16to be a minister of

[b] Or *thank*
[c] Gk *brothers*

δοξάζητε τὸν θεὸν καὶ πατέρα τοῦ
ye may glorify the God and Father of the
κυρίου ἡμῶν Ἰησοῦ Χριστοῦ.
Lord of us Jesus Christ.
7 Διὸ προσλαμβάνεσθε ἀλλήλους, καθὼς
Wherefore receive ye one another, as
καὶ ὁ Χριστὸς προσελάβετο ἡμᾶς εἰς
also – Christ received us to
δόξαν τοῦ θεοῦ. 8 λέγω γὰρ Χριστὸν
[the] glory – of God. For I say Christ
διάκονον γεγενῆσθαι περιτομῆς ὑπὲρ
a minister to have become of [the] circumcision on behalf of
ἀληθείας θεοῦ, εἰς τὸ βεβαιῶσαι τὰς
[the] truth of God, – – to confirm the
ἐπαγγελίας τῶν πατέρων, 9 τὰ δὲ ἔθνη
promises of the fathers, and [1]the [2]nations
ὑπὲρ ἐλέους δοξάσαι τὸν θεόν, καθὼς
[5]on behalf of [6]mercy [3]to glorify – [4]God, as
γέγραπται· διὰ τοῦτο ἐξομολογήσομαί σοι
it has been written: Therefore I will confess to thee
ἐν ἔθνεσιν καὶ τῷ ὀνόματί σου ψαλῶ.
among nations and to the name of thee I will sing praise.
10 καὶ πάλιν λέγει· εὐφράνθητε, ἔθνη,
And again he says: Be glad, nations,
μετὰ τοῦ λαοῦ αὐτοῦ. 11 καὶ πάλιν·
with the people of him. And again:
αἰνεῖτε, πάντα τὰ ἔθνη, τὸν κύριον,
Praise, all the nations, the Lord,
καὶ ἐπαινεσάτωσαν αὐτὸν πάντες οἱ λαοί.
and let praise him all the peoples.
12 καὶ πάλιν Ἠσαΐας λέγει· ἔσται
And again Esaias says: There shall be
ἡ ῥίζα τοῦ Ἰεσσαί, καὶ ὁ ἀνιστάμενος
the root – of Jesse, and the [one] rising up
ἄρχειν ἐθνῶν· ἐπ' αὐτῷ ἔθνη ἐλπιοῦσιν.
to rule nations; on him nations will hope.
13 Ὁ δὲ θεὸς τῆς ἐλπίδος πληρώσαι
Now the God – of hope fill
ὑμᾶς πάσης χαρᾶς καὶ εἰρήνης ἐν τῷ
you of(with) all joy and peace in –
πιστεύειν, εἰς τὸ περισσεύειν ὑμᾶς ἐν
to believe (believing), for – to abound you[b] in
τῇ ἐλπίδι ἐν δυνάμει πνεύματος ἁγίου.
– hope by [the] power of [the] Spirit Holy.
14 Πέπεισμαι δέ, ἀδελφοί μου, καὶ
But I have been persuaded, brothers of me, even
αὐτὸς ἐγὼ περὶ ὑμῶν, ὅτι καὶ αὐτοὶ
[2][my]self [1]I concerning you, that also [your]selves
μεστοί ἐστε ἀγαθωσύνης, πεπληρωμένοι
full ye are of goodness, having been filled
πάσης τῆς γνώσεως, δυνάμενοι καὶ
of(with) all – knowledge, being able also
ἀλλήλους νουθετεῖν. 15 τολμηροτέρως δὲ
one another to admonish. And more daringly
ἔγραψα ὑμῖν ἀπὸ μέρους, ὡς ἐπαναμιμνή-
I wrote to you in part, as remind-
σκων ὑμᾶς διὰ τὴν χάριν τὴν δοθεῖσάν
ing you by the grace – given
μοι ἀπὸ τοῦ θεοῦ 16 εἰς τὸ εἶναί με
to me from – God *for the* to be me[b] =that I should be

God and Father of our Lord
Jesus Christ.
7Accept one another,
then, just as Christ accepted you, in order to bring
praise to God. 8For I tell
you that Christ has become
a servant of the Jews[i] on
behalf of God's truth, to
confirm the promises made
to the patriarchs 9so that
the Gentiles may glorify
God for his mercy, as it is
written:
"Therefore I will praise
you among the
Gentiles;
I will sing hymns to
your name."[j]
10Again, it says,
"Rejoice, O Gentiles,
with his people."[k]
11And again,
"Praise the Lord, all you
Gentiles,
and sing praises to him,
all you peoples."[l]
12And again, Isaiah says,
"The Root of Jesse will
spring up,
one who will arise to
rule over the
nations;
the Gentiles will hope in
him."[m]
13May the God of hope fill
you with all joy and peace
as you trust in him, so that
you may overflow with
hope by the power of the
Holy Spirit.

Paul the Minister to the Gentiles

14I myself am convinced,
my brothers, that you yourselves are full of goodness,
complete in knowledge and
competent to instruct one
another. 15I have written
you quite boldly on some
points, as if to remind you
of them again, because of
the grace God gave me 16to
be a minister of Christ

[i] *8* Greek *circumcision*
[j] *9* 2 Samuel 22:50; Psalm 18:49
[k] *10* Deut. 32:43
[l] *11* Psalm 117:1
[m] *12* Isaiah 11:10

Christ Jesus to the Gentiles
in the priestly service of the
gospel of God, so that the
offering of the Gentiles
may be acceptable, sanctified by the Holy Spirit. 17 In
Christ Jesus, then, I have
reason to boast of my work
for God. 18 For I will not
venture to speak of any-
thing except what Christ
has accomplished[d]
through me to win obedi-
ence from the Gentiles, by
word and deed, 19 by the
power of signs and won-
ders, by the power of the
Spirit of God,[e] so that
from Jerusalem and as far
around as Illyricum I have
fully proclaimed the good
news[f] of Christ. 20 Thus I
make it my ambition to proclaim the good news,[f] not
where Christ has already
been named, so that I do
not build on someone else's
foundation, 21 but as it is
written,

"Those who have never been told of him shall see,
and those who have never heard of him shall understand."

Paul's Plan to Visit Rome

22 This is the reason
that I have so often been
hindered from coming to
you. 23 But now, with no
further place for me in
these regions, I desire, as I
have for many years, to
come to you 24 when I go to
Spain. For I do hope to see
you on my journey and to
be sent on by you, once I
have enjoyed your compa-
ny for a little while. 25 At
present, however, I am going to Jerusalem in a ministry to the saints; 26 for Macedonia and Achaia have
been pleased to share their
resources with the poor

[d] Gk *speak of those things that Christ has not accomplished*
[e] Other ancient authorities read *of the Spirit* or *of the Holy Spirit*
[f] Or *gospel*

λειτουργὸν Χριστοῦ Ἰησοῦ εἰς τὰ ἔθνη,
a minister of Christ Jesus to the nations,
ἱερουργοῦντα τὸ εὐαγγέλιον τοῦ θεοῦ,
sacrificing the gospel – of God,
ἵνα γένηται ἡ προσφορὰ τῶν ἐθνῶν
in order that [6]may be [1]the [2]offering [3]of the [4]nations
εὐπρόσδεκτος, ἡγιασμένη ἐν πνεύματι
acceptable, having been sanctified by [the] Spirit
ἁγίῳ. 17 ἔχω οὖν τὴν καύχησιν ἐν
Holy. I have therefore the boasting in
Χριστῷ Ἰησοῦ τὰ πρὸς τὸν θεόν· 18 οὐ
Christ Jesus the things with* – God; [4]not
γὰρ τολμήσω τι λαλεῖν ὧν οὐ
[1]for [2]I [3]will [5]dare [7]anything [6]to speak of [the] things which [3]not
κατειργάσατο Χριστὸς δι' ἐμοῦ εἰς ὑπακοὴν
[2]did [4]work [5]out [1]Christ through me for obedience
ἐθνῶν, λόγῳ καὶ ἔργῳ, 19 ἐν δυνάμει
of [the] nations, in word and work, by power
σημείων καὶ τεράτων, ἐν δυνάμει πνεύματος·
of signs and wonders, by power of [the] Spirit;
ὥστε με ἀπὸ Ἰερουσαλὴμ καὶ κύκλῳ
so as me from Jerusalem and around
=I should fulfil the gospel . . . from . . . Illyricum.
μέχρι τοῦ Ἰλλυρικοῦ πεπληρωκέναι τὸ
unto – Illyricum to have fulfilled[b] the
εὐαγγέλιον τοῦ Χριστοῦ. 20 οὕτως δὲ
gospel – of Christ. And so
φιλοτιμούμενον εὐαγγελίζεσθαι οὐχ ὅπου
eagerly striving to evangelize not where
ὠνομάσθη Χριστός, ἵνα μὴ ἐπ' ἀλλότριον
[2]was named [1]Christ, in order that not on [3]belonging to another
θεμέλιον οἰκοδομῶ, 21 ἀλλὰ καθὼς
[1]a foundation I should build, but as
γέγραπται· ὄψονται οἷς οὐκ ἀνηγγέλη
it has been written: They shall see to whom it was not announced
περὶ αὐτοῦ, καὶ οἳ οὐκ ἀκηκόασιν
concerning him, and [those] who have not heard
συνήσουσιν. 22 διὸ καὶ ἐνεκοπτόμην τὰ
will understand. Wherefore also I was hindered –
πολλὰ τοῦ ἐλθεῖν πρὸς ὑμᾶς· 23 νυνὶ
many(much) – to come[d] to you; [2]now
δὲ μηκέτι τόπον ἔχων ἐν τοῖς κλίμασι
[1]but no longer [2]place [1]having in – [3]regions
τούτοις, ἐπιποθίαν δὲ ἔχων τοῦ ἐλθεῖν
[1]these, and [2]a desire [1]having – to come[d]
πρὸς ὑμᾶς ἀπὸ ἱκανῶν ἐτῶν, 24 ὡς ἂν
to you from several years, whenever
πορεύωμαι εἰς τὴν Σπανίαν· ἐλπίζω γὰρ
I journey to – Spain; for I hope
διαπορευόμενος θεάσασθαι ὑμᾶς καὶ ὑφ'
journeying through to behold you and by
ὑμῶν προπεμφθῆναι ἐκεῖ, ἐὰν ὑμῶν πρῶτον
you to be set forward there, if of(with) you firstly
ἀπὸ μέρους ἐμπλησθῶ, 25 — νυνὶ δὲ
in part I may be filled, — but now
πορεύομαι εἰς Ἰερουσαλὴμ διακονῶν τοῖς
I am going to Jerusalem ministering to the
ἁγίοις. 26 ηὐδόκησαν γὰρ Μακεδονία καὶ
saints. For thought it good Macedonia and
Ἀχαΐα κοινωνίαν τινὰ ποιήσασθαι εἰς
Achaia [3]contribution [2]some [1]to make for

* That is, the things that have to do with . . .

Jesus to the Gentiles with
the priestly duty of pro-
claiming the gospel of God,
so that the Gentiles might
become an offering acceptable to God, sanctified by
the Holy Spirit.
17 Therefore I glory in
Christ Jesus in my service
to God. 18 I will not venture
to speak of anything except
what Christ has accom-
plished through me in leading the Gentiles to obey
God by what I have said
and done— 19 by the power
of signs and miracles,
through the power of the
Spirit. So from Jerusalem
all the way around to Illyricum, I have fully pro-
claimed the gospel of
Christ. 20 It has always been
my ambition to preach the
gospel where Christ was
not known, so that I would
not be building on someone
else's foundation. 21 Rather, as it is written:

"Those who were not told about him will see,
and those who have not heard will understand."[n]

22 This is why I have often
been hindered from coming
to you.

Paul's Plan to Visit Rome

23 But now that there is no
more place for me to work
in these regions, and since I
have been longing for many
years to see you, 24 I plan to
do so when I go to Spain. I
hope to visit you while
passing through and to
have you assist me on my
journey there, after I have
enjoyed your company for
a while. 25 Now, however, I
am on my way to Jerusalem
in the service of the saints
there. 26 For Macedonia
and Achaia were pleased to
make a contribution for the

[n] *21* Isaiah 52:15

among the saints at Jerusalem. 27 They were pleased
to do this, and indeed they
owe it to them; for if the
Gentiles have come to
share in their spiritual
blessings, they ought also
to be of service to them in
material things. 28 So, when
I have completed this, and
have delivered to them
what has been collected,[g] I
will set out by way of you
to Spain; 29 and I know that
when I come to you, I will
come in the fullness of the
blessing[h] of Christ.
30 I appeal to you,
brothers and sisters,[c] by
our Lord Jesus Christ and
by the love of the Spirit, to
join me in earnest prayer to
God on my behalf, 31 that I
may be rescued from the
unbelievers in Judea, and
that my ministry[i] to Jerusalem may be acceptable to
the saints, 32 so that by
God's will I may come to
you with joy and be re-
freshed in your company.
33 The God of peace be with
all of you.[j] Amen.

τοὺς πτωχοὺς τῶν ἁγίων τῶν ἐν Ἰερου-
the poor of the saints – in Jeru-
σαλήμ. 27 ηὐδόκησαν γάρ, καὶ ὀφειλέται
salem. For they thought it good, and debtors
εἰσὶν αὐτῶν· εἰ γὰρ τοῖς πνευματικοῖς
they are of them; for if in the spiritual things
αὐτῶν ἐκοινώνησαν τὰ ἔθνη, ὀφείλουσιν
of them [3]shared [1]the [2]nations, they ought
καὶ ἐν τοῖς σαρκικοῖς λειτουργῆσαι αὐτοῖς.
also in the fleshly things to minister to them.
28 τοῦτο οὖν ἐπιτελέσας, καὶ σφραγισάμενος
This therefore having completed, and having sealed
αὐτοῖς τὸν καρπὸν τοῦτον, 29 ἀπελεύσομαι
to them this fruit, I will go away
δι' ὑμῶν εἰς Σπανίαν· οἶδα δὲ ὅτι
through you to Spain; and I know that
ἐρχόμενος πρὸς ὑμᾶς ἐν πληρώματι
coming to you in [the] fulness
εὐλογίας Χριστοῦ ἐλεύσομαι. 30 Παρακαλῶ
of [the] blessing of Christ I will come. I beseech
δὲ ὑμᾶς, [ἀδελφοί], διὰ τοῦ κυρίου
Now you, brothers, through the Lord
ἡμῶν Ἰησοῦ Χριστοῦ καὶ διὰ τῆς ἀγάπης
of us Jesus Christ and through the love
τοῦ πνεύματος, συναγωνίσασθαί μοι ἐν
of the Spirit, to strive with me in
ταῖς προσευχαῖς ὑπὲρ ἐμοῦ πρὸς τὸν
the prayers on behalf of me to –
θεόν, 31 ἵνα ῥυσθῶ ἀπὸ τῶν ἀπειθούντων
God, in order that I may be delivered from the [ones] disobeying
ἐν τῇ Ἰουδαίᾳ καὶ ἡ διακονία μου
in – Judæa and the ministry of me
ἡ εἰς Ἰερουσαλὴμ εὐπρόσδεκτος τοῖς
– to Jerusalem [2]acceptable [3]to the
ἁγίοις γένηται, 32 ἵνα ἐν χαρᾷ ἐλθὼν
[4]saints [1]may be, in order that in joy coming
πρὸς ὑμᾶς διὰ θελήματος θεοῦ συνανα-
to you through [the] will of God I may
παύσωμαι ὑμῖν. 33 ὁ δὲ θεὸς τῆς
rest with you. And the God –
εἰρήνης μετὰ πάντων ὑμῶν· ἀμήν.
of peace [be] with all you: Amen.

poor among the saints in
Jerusalem. 27 They were
pleased to do it, and indeed
they owe it to them. For if
the Gentiles have shared in
the Jews' spiritual blessings, they owe it to the
Jews to share with them
their material blessings.
28 So after I have completed
this task and have made
sure that they have re-
ceived this fruit, I will go to
Spain and visit you on the
way. 29 I know that when I
come to you, I will come in
the full measure of the
blessing of Christ.
30 I urge you, brothers, by
our Lord Jesus Christ and
by the love of the Spirit, to
join me in my struggle by
praying to God for me.
31 Pray that I may be rescued from the unbelievers
in Judea and that my ser-
vice in Jerusalem may be
acceptable to the saints
there, 32 so that by God's
will I may come to you with
joy and together with you
be refreshed. 33 The God of
peace be with you all.
Amen.

Chapter 16

Personal Greetings

I commend to you our
sister Phoebe, a dea-
con[k] of the church at Cenchreae, 2 so that you may
welcome her in the Lord as
is fitting for the saints, and
help her in whatever she
may require from you, for
she has been a benefactor
of many and of myself as
well.
3 Greet Prisca and Aq-
uila, who work with me in
Christ Jesus, 4 and who

16 Συνίστημι δὲ ὑμῖν Φοίβην τὴν
Now I commend to you Phœbe the
ἀδελφὴν ἡμῶν, οὖσαν [καὶ] διάκονον τῆς
sister of us, being also a minister of the
ἐκκλησίας τῆς ἐν Κεγχρεαῖς, 2 ἵνα
church – in Cenchrea, in order that
αὐτὴν προσδέξησθε ἐν κυρίῳ ἀξίως τῶν
[2]her [1]ye may receive in [the] Lord worthily of the
ἁγίων, καὶ παραστῆτε αὐτῇ ἐν ᾧ ἂν
saints, and may stand by her in [1]whatever
ὑμῶν χρῄζῃ πράγματι· καὶ γὰρ αὐτὴ
[4]of you [3]she may have need [2]thing; for indeed she
προστάτις πολλῶν ἐγενήθη καὶ ἐμοῦ αὐτοῦ.
a protectress of many became and of myself.
3 Ἀσπάσασθε Πρίσκαν καὶ Ἀκύλαν τοὺς
Greet ye Prisca and Aquila the
συνεργούς μου ἐν Χριστῷ Ἰησοῦ, 4 οἵτινες
fellow-workers of me in Christ Jesus, who

Chapter 16

Personal Greetings

I COMMEND to you our
sister Phoebe, a ser-
vant[o] of the church in Cenchrea. 2 I ask you to receive
her in the Lord in a way
worthy of the saints and to
give her any help she may
need from you, for she has
been a great help to many
people, including me.
3 Greet Priscilla[p] and Aquila, my fellow workers
in Christ Jesus. 4 They

[g] Gk *have sealed to them this fruit*
[h] Other ancient authorities add *of the gospel*
[i] Other ancient authorities read *my bringing of a gift*
[j] One ancient authority adds 16.25-27 here
[k] Or *minister*

[o] *1* Or *deaconess*
[p] *3* Greek *Prisca*, a variant of *Priscilla*

risked their necks for my
life, to whom not only I
give thanks, but also all the
churches of the Gentiles.
5 Greet also the church in
their house. Greet my be-
loved Epaenetus, who was
the first convert[l] in Asia
for Christ. 6 Greet Mary,
who has worked very hard
among you. 7 Greet Andro-
nicus and Junia,[m] my relatives[n] who were in prison
with me; they are promi-
nent among the apostles,
and they were in Christ before I was. 8 Greet Ampliatus, my beloved in the
Lord. 9 Greet Urbanus, our
co-worker in Christ, and
my beloved Stachys.
10 Greet Apelles, who is approved in Christ. Greet
those who belong to the
family of Aristobulus.
11 Greet my relative[o] Herodion. Greet those in the
Lord who belong to the
family of Narcissus.
12 Greet those workers in
the Lord, Tryphaena and
Tryphosa. Greet the be-
loved Persis, who has
worked hard in the Lord.
13 Greet Rufus, chosen in
the Lord; and greet his
mother—a mother to me
also. 14 Greet Asyncritus,
Phlegon, Hermes, Patro-
bas, Hermas, and the
brothers and sisters[p] who
are with them. 15 Greet Philologus, Julia, Nereus and
his sister, and Olympas,
and all the saints who are
with them. 16 Greet one another with a holy kiss. All
the churches of Christ greet
you.

[l] Gk *first fruits*
[m] Or *Junias*; other ancient authorities read *Julia*
[n] Or *compatriots*
[o] Or *compatriot*
[p] Gk *brothers*

ὑπὲρ τῆς ψυχῆς μου τὸν ἑαυτῶν τράχηλον
on behalf of the life of me [2]the [4]of themselves [3]neck

ὑπέθηκαν, οἷς οὐκ ἐγὼ μόνος εὐχαριστῶ
[1]risked, to whom not I only give thanks

ἀλλὰ καὶ πᾶσαι αἱ ἐκκλησίαι τῶν ἐθνῶν,
but also all the churches of the nations,

5 καὶ τὴν κατ᾽ οἶκον αὐτῶν ἐκκλησίαν.
and [1]the [3]in [4]house [5]of them [2]church.

ἀσπάσασθε Ἐπαίνετον τὸν ἀγαπητόν μου,
Greet Epænetus the beloved of me,

ὅς ἐστιν ἀπαρχὴ τῆς Ἀσίας εἰς Χριστόν.
who is firstfruit – of Asia for Christ.

6 ἀσπάσασθε Μαρίαν, ἥτις πολλὰ ἐκοπίασεν
Greet Mary, who many things (much) laboured

εἰς ὑμᾶς. 7 ἀσπάσασθε Ἀνδρόνικον καὶ
for you. Greet Andronicus and

Ἰουνιᾶν τοὺς συγγενεῖς μου καὶ συναιχμα-
Junius the kinsmen of me and fellow-

λώτους μου, οἵτινές εἰσιν ἐπίσημοι ἐν
captives of me, who are notable among

τοῖς ἀποστόλοις, οἳ καὶ πρὸ ἐμοῦ γέγοναν
the apostles, who indeed before me have been

ἐν Χριστῷ. 8 ἀσπάσασθε Ἀμπλιᾶτον τὸν
in Christ. Greet Ampliatus the

ἀγαπητόν μου ἐν κυρίῳ. 9 ἀσπάσασθε
beloved of me in [the] Lord. Greet

Οὐρβανὸν τὸν συνεργὸν ἡμῶν ἐν Χριστῷ
Urbanus the fellow-worker of us in Christ

καὶ Στάχυν τὸν ἀγαπητόν μου. 10 ἀσπάσ-
and Stachys the beloved of me. Greet

ασθε Ἀπελλῆν τὸν δόκιμον ἐν Χριστῷ.
Apelles the approved in Christ.

ἀσπάσασθε τοὺς ἐκ τῶν Ἀριστοβούλου.
Greet the [ones] of the [family] of Aristobulus.

11 ἀσπάσασθε Ἡρῳδίωνα τὸν συγγενῆ μου.
Greet Herodion the kinsman of me.

ἀσπάσασθε τοὺς ἐκ τῶν Ναρκίσσου τοὺς
Greet the [ones] of the [family] of Narcissus –

ὄντας ἐν κυρίῳ. 12 ἀσπάσασθε Τρύφαιναν
being in [the] Lord. Greet Tryphæna

καὶ Τρυφῶσαν τὰς κοπιώσας ἐν κυρίῳ.
and Tryphosa the [ones] labouring in [the] Lord.

ἀσπάσασθε Περσίδα τὴν ἀγαπητήν, ἥτις
Greet Persis the beloved, who

πολλὰ ἐκοπίασεν ἐν κυρίῳ. 13 ἀσπάσασθε
many things (much) laboured in [the] Lord. Greet

Ῥοῦφον τὸν ἐκλεκτὸν ἐν κυρίῳ καὶ
Rufus the chosen in [the] Lord and

τὴν μητέρα αὐτοῦ καὶ ἐμοῦ. 14 ἀσπάσασθε
the mother of him and of me. Greet

Ἀσύγκριτον, Φλέγοντα, Ἑρμῆν, Πατροβᾶν,
Asyncritus, Phlegon, Hermes, Patrobas,

Ἑρμᾶν, καὶ τοὺς σὺν αὐτοῖς ἀδελφούς.
Hermas, and the [2]with [3]them [1]brothers.

15 ἀσπάσασθε Φιλόλογον καὶ Ἰουλίαν,
Greet Philologus and Julia,

Νηρέα καὶ τὴν ἀδελφὴν αὐτοῦ, καὶ
Nereus and the sister of him, and

Ὀλυμπᾶν, καὶ τοὺς σὺν αὐτοῖς πάντας
Olympas, and [2]the [4]with [5]them [1]all

ἁγίους. 16 ἀσπάσασθε ἀλλήλους ἐν φιλήματι
[3]saints. Greet one another with kiss

ἁγίῳ. ἀσπάζονται ὑμᾶς αἱ ἐκκλησίαι
a holy. [5]greet [6]you [2]the [3]churches

risked their lives for
me. Not only I but all
the churches of the
Gentiles are grateful to
them.
5 Greet also the church
that meets at their
house.
Greet my dear friend
Epenetus, who was the
first convert to Christ
in the province of Asia.
6 Greet Mary, who
worked very hard for
you.
7 Greet Andronicus and
Junias, my relatives
who have been in pris-
on with me. They are
outstanding among the
apostles, and they were
in Christ before I was.
8 Greet Ampliatus, whom
I love in the Lord.
9 Greet Urbanus, our fel-
low worker in Christ,
and my dear friend Sta-
chys.
10 Greet Apelles, tested
and approved in Christ.
Greet those who belong
to the household of
Aristobulus.
11 Greet Herodion, my relative.
Greet those in the house-
hold of Narcissus who
are in the Lord.
12 Greet Tryphena and
Tryphosa, those wom-
en who work hard in
the Lord.
Greet my dear friend
Persis, another woman
who has worked very
hard in the Lord.
13 Greet Rufus, chosen in
the Lord, and his moth-
er, who has been a
mother to me, too.
14 Greet Asyncritus, Phlegon, Hermes, Patro-
bas, Hermas and the
brothers with them.
15 Greet Philologus, Julia,
Nereus and his sister,
and Olympas and all
the saints with them.
16 Greet one another with a
holy kiss.
All the churches of
Christ send greetings.

Final Instructions

17 I urge you, brothers
and sisters,[p] to keep an
eye on those who cause dissensions and offenses, in
opposition to the teaching
that you have learned;
avoid them. 18For such
people do not serve our
Lord Christ, but their own
appetites,[q] and by smooth
talk and flattery they deceive the hearts of the
simple-minded. 19For
while your obedience is
known to all, so that I rejoice over you, I want you
to be wise in what is good
and guileless in what is evil.
20The God of peace will
shortly crush Satan under
your feet. The grace of our
Lord Jesus Christ be with
you.[r]
21 Timothy, my co-
worker, greets you; so do
Lucius and Jason and So-
sipater, my relatives.[n]
22 I Tertius, the writer
of this letter, greet you in
the Lord.[s]
23 Gaius, who is host to
me and to the whole
church, greets you. Eras-
tus, the city treasurer, and
our brother Quartus, greet
you.[t]

Final Doxology

25 Now to God[u] who is
able to strengthen you according to my gospel and
the proclamation of Jesus
Christ, according to the
revelation of the mystery
that was kept secret for
long ages 26but is now disclosed, and through the
prophetic writings is made
known to all the Gentiles,
according to the command

πᾶσαι τοῦ Χριστοῦ.
[1]All – [4]of Christ.
17 Παρακαλῶ δὲ ὑμᾶς, ἀδελφοί, σκοπεῖν
Now I beseech you, brothers, to watch
τοὺς τὰς διχοστασίας καὶ τὰ σκάνδαλα
[1]the [ones] [3]the [4]divisions [5]and [6]the [7]offences
παρὰ τὴν διδαχὴν ἣν ὑμεῖς ἐμάθετε
[8]beside [9]the [10]teaching [11]which [12]ye [13]learned
ποιοῦντας, καὶ ἐκκλίνετε ἀπ' αὐτῶν· **18** οἱ
[2]making, and turn away from them; –
γὰρ τοιοῦτοι τῷ κυρίῳ ἡμῶν Χριστῷ
for such men [3]the [4]Lord [5]of us [2]Christ
οὐ δουλεύουσιν ἀλλὰ τῇ ἑαυτῶν κοιλίᾳ,
[1]serve not but the of themselves belly,
καὶ διὰ τῆς χρηστολογίας καὶ εὐλογίας
and through – fair speech and flattering speech
ἐξαπατῶσιν τὰς καρδίας τῶν ἀκάκων.
deceive the hearts of the guileless.
19 ἡ γὰρ ὑμῶν ὑπακοὴ εἰς πάντας
[2]the [1]For [4]of you [3]obedience [6]to [7]all men
ἀφίκετο· ἐφ' ὑμῖν οὖν χαίρω, θέλω
[5]came; over you therefore I rejoice, [2]I wish
δὲ ὑμᾶς σοφοὺς εἶναι εἰς τὸ ἀγαθόν,
[1]and you wise to be to the good,
ἀκεραίους δὲ εἰς τὸ κακόν. **20** ὁ δὲ
but simple to the evil. And the
θεὸς τῆς εἰρήνης συντρίψει τὸν σατανᾶν
God – of peace will crush – Satan
ὑπὸ τοὺς πόδας ὑμῶν ἐν τάχει.
under the feet of you soon.
Ἡ χάρις τοῦ κυρίου ἡμῶν Ἰησοῦ
The grace of the Lord of us Jesus [be]
μεθ' ὑμῶν.
with you.
21 Ἀσπάζεται ὑμᾶς Τιμόθεος ὁ συνεργός
[5]greets [6]you [1]Timothy [2]the [3]fellow-worker
μου, καὶ Λούκιος καὶ Ἰάσων καὶ
[4]of me, and Lucius and Jason and
Σωσίπατρος οἱ συγγενεῖς μου. **22** ἀσπάζ-
Sosipater the kinsmen of me. [7]greet
ομαι ὑμᾶς ἐγὼ Τέρτιος ὁ γράψας τὴν
[8]you [1]I [2]Tertius [3]the [one] [4]writing [5]the
ἐπιστολὴν ἐν κυρίῳ. **23** ἀσπάζεται ὑμᾶς
[6]epistle in [the] Lord. [9]greets [10]you
Γάϊος ὁ ξένος μου καὶ ὅλης τῆς
[1]Gaius [2]the [3]host [4]of me [5]and [6]of all [7]the
ἐκκλησίας. ἀσπάζεται ὑμᾶς Ἔραστος ὁ
[8]church. [6]greets [7]you [1]Erastus [2]the
οἰκονόμος τῆς πόλεως καὶ Κούαρτος ὁ
[3]treasurer [4]of the [5]city and Quartus the (?his)
ἀδελφός.‡
brother.
25 Τῷ δὲ δυναμένῳ ὑμᾶς στηρίξαι κατὰ
Now to the [one] *being* able [2]you [1]to establish according to
τὸ εὐαγγέλιόν μου καὶ τὸ κήρυγμα
the gospel of me and the proclamation
Ἰησοῦ Χριστοῦ, κατὰ ἀποκάλυψιν μυστηρίου
of Jesus Christ, according to [the] revelation of [the] mystery
χρόνοις αἰωνίοις σεσιγημένου, **26** φανερω-
[2]in times [3]eternal [1]having been kept silent, [2]mani-
θέντος δὲ νῦν διά τε γραφῶν προφητικῶν
fested [1]but now and through writings prophetic

17I urge you, brothers, to
watch out for those who
cause divisions and put ob-
stacles in your way that are
contrary to the teaching
you have learned. Keep
away from them. 18For
such people are not serving
our Lord Christ, but their
own appetites. By smooth
talk and flattery they deceive the minds of naive
people. 19Everyone has
heard about your obedi-
ence, so I am full of joy
over you; but I want you to
be wise about what is good,
and innocent about what is
evil.
20The God of peace will
soon crush Satan under
your feet.
The grace of our Lord
Jesus be with you.
21Timothy, my fellow
worker, sends his greetings
to you, as do Lucius, Jason
and Sosipater, my rela-
tives.
22I, Tertius, who wrote
down this letter, greet you
in the Lord.
23Gaius, whose hospitali-
ty I and the whole church
here enjoy, sends you his
greetings.
Erastus, who is the city's
director of public works,
and our brother Quartus
send you their greetings.[q]
25Now to him who is able
to establish you by my gospel and the proclamation of
Jesus Christ, according to
the revelation of the mystery hidden for long ages
past, 26but now revealed
and made known through

[q] Gk *their own belly*
[r] Other ancient authorities lack this sentence
[s] Or *I Tertius, writing this letter in the Lord, greet you*
[t] Other ancient authorities add verse 24, *The grace of our Lord Jesus Christ be with all of you. Amen.*
[u] Gk *the one*

‡ Verse 24 omitted by Nestle; *cf.* NIV footnote.

[q] 23 Some manuscripts *their greetings.* 24*May the grace of our Lord Jesus Christ be with all of you. Amen.*

of the eternal God, to bring
about the obedience of
faith— 27 to the only wise
God, through Jesus Christ,
to whom[v] be the glory forever! Amen.[w]

κατ᾽ ἐπιταγὴν τοῦ αἰωνίου θεοῦ εἰς
according to [the] command of the eternal God [6]for

ὑπακοὴν πίστεως εἰς πάντα τὰ ἔθνη
[7]obedience [8]of faith [2]to [3]all [4]the [5]nations

γνωρισθέντος, 27 μόνῳ σοφῷ θεῷ, διὰ
[1]made known, [2]only [3]wise [1]to God, through

᾽Ιησοῦ Χριστοῦ, ᾧ ἡ δόξα εἰς τοὺς
Jesus Christ, to whom (him)[c] the glory unto the

αἰῶνας τῶν αἰώνων· ἀμήν.
ages of the ages: Amen.

the prophetic writings by
the command of the eternal
God, so that all nations
might believe and obey him
—27to the only wise God be
glory forever through Jesus
Christ! Amen.

[v]Other ancient authorities lack *to whom*. The verse then reads, *to the only wise God be the glory through Jesus Christ forever. Amen.*

[w]Other ancient authorities lack 16.25-27 or include it after 14.23 or 15.33; others put verse 24 after verse 27

The First Letter of Paul
to the
Corinthians

Chapter 1

Salutation

PAUL, called to be an
apostle of Christ Jesus
by the will of God, and our
brother Sosthenes,
2 To the church of God
that is in Corinth, to those
who are sanctified in Christ
Jesus, called to be saints,
together with all those who
in every place call on the
name of our Lord Jesus
Christ, both their Lord[a]
and ours:
3 Grace to you and
peace from God our Father
and the Lord Jesus Christ.

4 I give thanks to my[b]
God always for you be-
cause of the grace of God
that has been given you in
Christ Jesus, 5for in every
way you have been en-
riched in him, in speech
and knowledge of every
kind— 6just as the testimony of[c] Christ has been
strengthened among you—
7so that you are not lacking
in any spiritual gift as you
wait for the revealing of our
Lord Jesus Christ. 8He will
also strengthen you to the
end, so that you may be
blameless on the day of our
Lord Jesus Christ. 9God is
faithful; by him you were
called into the fellowship of
his Son, Jesus Christ our
Lord.

Divisions in the Church

10 Now I appeal to you,
brothers and sisters,[d] by
the name of our Lord Jesus
Christ, that all of you be in
agreement and that there
be no divisions among you,
but that you be united in the
same mind and the same
purpose. 11For it has been
reported to me by Chloe's

[a] Gk *theirs*
[b] Other ancient authorities lack *my*
[c] Or *to*
[d] Gk *brothers*

ΠΡΟΣ ΚΟΡΙΝΘΙΟΥΣ Α
To Corinthians 1

1 Παῦλος κλητὸς ἀπόστολος Χριστοῦ
Paul a called apostle of Christ
Ἰησοῦ διὰ θελήματος θεοῦ καὶ Σωσθένης
Jesus through [the] will of God and Sosthenes
ὁ ἀδελφὸς **2** τῇ ἐκκλησίᾳ τοῦ θεοῦ
the(?his) brother to the church – of God
τῇ οὔσῃ ἐν Κορίνθῳ, ἡγιασμένοις ἐν
– existing in Corinth, to [ones] having been sanctified in
Χριστῷ Ἰησοῦ, κλητοῖς ἁγίοις, σὺν πᾶσιν
Christ Jesus, called saints, with all
τοῖς ἐπικαλουμένοις τὸ ὄνομα τοῦ κυρίου
the [ones] calling on the name of the Lord
ἡμῶν Ἰησοῦ Χριστοῦ ἐν παντὶ τόπῳ,
of us Jesus Christ in every place,
αὐτῶν καὶ ἡμῶν· **3** χάρις ὑμῖν καὶ
of them and of us: Grace to you and
εἰρήνη ἀπὸ θεοῦ πατρὸς ἡμῶν καὶ κυρίου
peace from God Father of us and Lord
Ἰησοῦ Χριστοῦ.
Jesus Christ.

4 Εὐχαριστῶ τῷ θεῷ πάντοτε περὶ
I gave thanks – to God always concerning
ὑμῶν ἐπὶ τῇ χάριτι τοῦ θεοῦ τῇ δοθείσῃ
you on the grace – of God – given
ὑμῖν ἐν Χριστῷ Ἰησοῦ, **5** ὅτι ἐν παντὶ
to you in Christ Jesus, because in everything
ἐπλουτίσθητε ἐν αὐτῷ, ἐν παντὶ λόγῳ
ye were enriched in him, in all speech
καὶ πάσῃ γνώσει, **6** καθὼς τὸ μαρτύριον
and all knowledge, as the testimony
τοῦ Χριστοῦ ἐβεβαιώθη ἐν ὑμῖν, **7** ὥστε
– of Christ was confirmed in you, so as
ὑμᾶς μὴ ὑστερεῖσθαι ἐν μηδενὶ χαρίσματι,
you not to be wanting[b] in no(any) gift,
ἀπεκδεχομένους τὴν ἀποκάλυψιν τοῦ κυρίου
awaiting the revelation of the Lord
ἡμῶν Ἰησοῦ Χριστοῦ· **8** ὃς καὶ βεβαιώσει
of us Jesus Christ; who also will confirm
ὑμᾶς ἕως τέλους ἀνεγκλήτους ἐν τῇ
you till [the] end blameless in the
ἡμέρᾳ τοῦ κυρίου ἡμῶν Ἰησοῦ [Χριστοῦ].
day of the Lord of us Jesus Christ.
9 πιστὸς ὁ θεός, δι' οὗ ἐκλήθητε εἰς
Faithful [is] – God, through whom ye were called to
κοινωνίαν τοῦ υἱοῦ αὐτοῦ Ἰησοῦ Χριστοῦ
[the] fellowship of the Son of him Jesus Christ
τοῦ κυρίου ἡμῶν.
the Lord of us.

10 Παρακαλῶ δὲ ὑμᾶς, ἀδελφοί, διὰ
Now I beseech you, brothers, through
τοῦ ὀνόματος τοῦ κυρίου ἡμῶν Ἰησοῦ
the name of the Lord of us Jesus
Χριστοῦ, ἵνα τὸ αὐτὸ λέγητε πάντες,
Christ, *in order* that the same thing ye say all,
καὶ μὴ ᾖ ἐν ὑμῖν σχίσματα, ἦτε δὲ
and not be among you divisions, but ye may be
κατηρτισμένοι ἐν τῷ αὐτῷ νοῒ καὶ
***having been* joined together in the same mind and**
ἐν τῇ αὐτῇ γνώμῃ. **11** ἐδηλώθη γάρ μοι
in the same opinion. For it was shown to me

1 Corinthians

Chapter 1

PAUL, called to be an
apostle of Christ Jesus
by the will of God, and our
brother Sosthenes,

2To the church of God in
Corinth, to those sanctified
in Christ Jesus and called to
be holy, together with all
those everywhere who call
on the name of our Lord
Jesus Christ—their Lord
and ours:

3Grace and peace to you
from God our Father and
the Lord Jesus Christ.

Thanksgiving

4I always thank God for
you because of his grace
given you in Christ Jesus.
5For in him you have been
enriched in every way—in
all your speaking and in all
your knowledge— 6be-
cause our testimony about
Christ was confirmed in
you. 7Therefore you do not
lack any spiritual gift as
you eagerly wait for our
Lord Jesus Christ to be revealed. 8He will keep you
strong to the end, so that
you will be blameless on
the day of our Lord Jesus
Christ. 9God, who has
called you into fellowship
with his Son Jesus Christ
our Lord, is faithful.

Divisions in the Church

10I appeal to you, broth-
ers, in the name of our Lord
Jesus Christ, that all of you
agree with one another so
that there may be no divisions among you and that
you may be perfectly united in mind and thought.
11My brothers, some from

people that there are quarrels among you, my broth-
ers and sisters.[e] 12 What I
mean is that each of you
says, "I belong to Paul," or
"I belong to Apollos," or "I
belong to Cephas," or "I
belong to Christ." 13 Has
Christ been divided? Was
Paul crucified for you? Or
were you baptized in the
name of Paul? 14 I thank
God[f] that I baptized none
of you except Crispus and
Gaius, 15 so that no one can
say that you were baptized
in my name. 16 (I did baptize also the household of
Stephanas; beyond that, I
do not know whether I baptized anyone else.) 17 For
Christ did not send me to
baptize but to proclaim the
gospel, and not with elo-
quent wisdom, so that the
cross of Christ might not be
emptied of its power.

Christ the Power and Wisdom of God

18 For the message
about the cross is foolishness to those who are perishing, but to us who are
being saved it is the power
of God. 19 For it is written,
"I will destroy the
wisdom of
the wise,
and the discernment
of the discerning
I will thwart."
20 Where is the one who is
wise? Where is the scribe?
Where is the debater of this
age? Has not God made
foolish the wisdom of the
world? 21 For since, in the
wisdom of God, the world
did not know God through
wisdom, God decided,
through the foolishness of
our proclamation, to save
those who believe. 22 For
Jews demand signs and
Greeks desire wisdom,
23 but we proclaim Christ
crucified, a stumbling
block to Jews and foolish-

[e] Gk *my brothers*
[f] Other ancient authorities read *I am thankful*

περὶ ὑμῶν, ἀδελφοί μου, ὑπὸ τῶν
concerning you, brothers of me, by the [ones]
Χλόης, ὅτι ἔριδες ἐν ὑμῖν εἰσιν. **12** λέγω
of Chloe, that strifes among you there are. I say
δὲ τοῦτο, ὅτι ἕκαστος ὑμῶν λέγει· ἐγὼ
Now this, because each of you says: I
μέν εἰμι Παύλου, ἐγὼ δὲ Ἀπολλῶ,
indeed am of Paul, but I of Apollos,
ἐγὼ δὲ Κηφᾶ, ἐγὼ δὲ Χριστοῦ.
but I of Cephas, but I of Christ.
13 μεμέρισται ὁ Χριστός; μὴ Παῦλος
Has been divided – Christ? *Not* Paul
ἐσταυρώθη ὑπὲρ ὑμῶν, ἢ εἰς τὸ ὄνομα
was crucified on behalf of you, or in the name
Παύλου ἐβαπτίσθητε; **14** εὐχαριστῶ ὅτι
of Paul were ye baptized? I give thanks that
οὐδένα ὑμῶν ἐβάπτισα εἰ μὴ Κρίσπον
not one of you I baptized except Crispus
καὶ Γάϊον· **15** ἵνα μή τις εἴπῃ ὅτι
and Gaius; lest anyone should say that
εἰς τὸ ἐμὸν ὄνομα ἐβαπτίσθητε. **16** ἐβάπτισα δὲ
in – my name ye were baptized. But I baptized
καὶ τὸν Στεφανᾶ οἶκον· λοιπὸν οὐκ οἶδα
also the of Stephanas household; for the rest I know not
εἴ τινα ἄλλον ἐβάπτισα. **17** οὐ
if any other I baptized. [5]not
γὰρ ἀπέστειλέν με Χριστὸς βαπτίζειν
[1]For [3]sent [4]me [2]Christ to baptize
ἀλλὰ εὐαγγελίζεσθαι, οὐκ ἐν σοφίᾳ λόγου,
but to evangelize, not in wisdom of speech,
ἵνα μὴ κενωθῇ ὁ σταυρὸς τοῦ Χριστοῦ.
lest [4]be made vain [1]the [2]cross – [3]of Christ.
18 Ὁ λόγος γὰρ ὁ τοῦ σταυροῦ τοῖς
For the word – of the cross [2]to the [ones]
μὲν ἀπολλυμένοις μωρία ἐστίν, τοῖς
[1]on one hand [3]perishing [5]folly [4]is, [2]*to* the [ones]
δὲ σῳζομένοις ἡμῖν δύναμις θεοῦ ἐστιν.
[1]on the other [4]being saved [3]to us [6][the] [7]power [8]of God [5]it is.
19 γέγραπται γάρ· ἀπολῶ τὴν σοφίαν
For it has been written: I will destroy the wisdom
τῶν σοφῶν, καὶ τὴν σύνεσιν τῶν συνετῶν
of the wise ones, and the understanding of the prudent
ἀθετήσω. **20** ποῦ σοφός; ποῦ γραμματεύς;
I will set aside. Where [is the] wise man? where [is the] scribe?
ποῦ συζητητὴς τοῦ αἰῶνος τούτου; οὐχὶ
where [is the] disputant of this age? [2]Not
ἐμώρανεν ὁ θεὸς τὴν σοφίαν τοῦ κόσμου;
[1]made [8]foolish – [3]God [4]the [5]wisdom [6]of the [7]world?
21 ἐπειδὴ γὰρ ἐν τῇ σοφίᾳ τοῦ θεοῦ
for since in the wisdom – of God
οὐκ ἔγνω ὁ κόσμος διὰ τῆς σοφίας
[6]knew [7]not [1]the [2]world [3]through [4]the(its) [5]wisdom
τὸν θεόν, εὐδόκησεν ὁ θεὸς διὰ τῆς
– [8]God, [2]thought well – [1]God through the
μωρίας τοῦ κηρύγματος σῶσαι τοὺς
folly of the proclamation to save the
πιστεύοντας. **22** ἐπειδὴ καὶ Ἰουδαῖοι σημεῖα
[ones] believing. Seeing that both Jews [2]signs
αἰτοῦσιν καὶ Ἕλληνες σοφίαν ζητοῦσιν,
[1]ask and Greeks [2]wisdom [1]seek,
23 ἡμεῖς δὲ κηρύσσομεν Χριστὸν ἐσταυρωμένον,
[2]we [1]yet proclaim Christ *having been* crucified,

Chloe's household have informed me that there are
quarrels among you.
12 What I mean is this: One
of you says, "I follow
Paul"; another, "I follow
Apollos"; another, "I follow Cephas[a]"; still another, "I follow Christ."
13 Is Christ divided? Was
Paul crucified for you?
Were you baptized into[b]
the name of Paul? 14 I am
thankful that I did not baptize any of you except Crispus and Gaius, 15 so no one
can say that you were baptized into my name. 16 (Yes,
I also baptized the household of Stephanas; beyond
that, I don't remember if I
baptized anyone else.)
17 For Christ did not send
me to baptize, but to
preach the gospel—not
with words of human wis-
dom, lest the cross of
Christ be emptied of its
power.

Christ the Wisdom and Power of God

18 For the message of the
cross is foolishness to
those who are perishing,
but to us who are being
saved it is the power of
God. 19 For it is written:

"I will destroy the
wisdom of the wise;
the intelligence of the
intelligent I will
frustrate."[c]

20 Where is the wise man?
Where is the scholar?
Where is the philosopher of
this age? Has not God made
foolish the wisdom of the
world? 21 For since in the
wisdom of God the world
through its wisdom did not
know him, God was
pleased through the fool-
ishness of what was
preached to save those who
believe. 22 Jews demand miraculous signs and Greeks
look for wisdom, 23 but we
preach Christ crucified: a
stumbling block to Jews

[a] 12 That is, Peter
[b] 13 Or *in*; also in verse 15
[c] 19 Isaiah 29:14

ness to Gentiles, 24 but to
those who are the called,
both Jews and Greeks,
Christ the power of God
and the wisdom of God.
25 For God's foolishness is
wiser than human wisdom,
and God's weakness is
stronger than human
strength.
26 Consider your own
call, brothers and sisters:[d]
not many of you were wise
by human standards,[g] not
many were powerful, not
many were of noble birth.
27 But God chose what is
foolish in the world to
shame the wise; God chose
what is weak in the world to
shame the strong; 28 God
chose what is low and de-
spised in the world, things
that are not, to reduce to
nothing things that are,
29 so that no one[h] might
boast in the presence of
God. 30 He is the source of
your life in Christ Jesus,
who became for us wisdom
from God, and righteous-
ness and sanctification and
redemption, 31 in order
that, as it is written, "Let
the one who boasts, boast
in[i] the Lord."

Chapter 2

Proclaiming Christ Crucified

WHEN I came to you,
brothers and sis-
ters,[d] I did not come proclaiming the mystery[j] of
God to you in lofty words
or wisdom. 2 For I decided
to know nothing among
you except Jesus Christ,
and him crucified. 3 And I
came to you in weakness
and in fear and in much

[g] Gk *according to the flesh*
[h] Gk *no flesh*
[i] Or *of*
[j] Other ancient authorities read *testimony*

Ἰουδαίοις μὲν σκάνδαλον, ἔθνεσιν δὲ
to Jews on one hand an offence, to nations on the other

μωρίαν, 24 αὐτοῖς δὲ τοῖς κλητοῖς,
folly, but to them the called ones,

Ἰουδαίοις τε καὶ Ἕλλησιν, Χριστὸν θεοῦ
²to Jews ¹both and to Greeks, Christ of God

δύναμιν καὶ θεοῦ σοφίαν. 25 ὅτι τὸ
power and of God wisdom. Because the

μωρὸν τοῦ θεοῦ σοφώτερον τῶν ἀνθρώπων
foolish thing – of God wiser [than] – men

ἐστίν, καὶ τὸ ἀσθενὲς τοῦ θεοῦ ἰσχυρότερον
is, and the weak thing – of God stronger [than]

τῶν ἀνθρώπων. 26 Βλέπετε γὰρ τὴν
– men. For ye see the

κλῆσιν ὑμῶν, ἀδελφοί, ὅτι οὐ πολλοὶ
calling of you, brothers, that not many

σοφοὶ κατὰ σάρκα, οὐ πολλοὶ δυνατοί,
wise men according to flesh, not many powerful,

οὐ πολλοὶ εὐγενεῖς· 27 ἀλλὰ τὰ μωρὰ
not many well born; but the foolish things

τοῦ κόσμου ἐξελέξατο ὁ θεὸς ἵνα καται-
of the world ²chose – ¹God in order he might that

σχύνῃ τοὺς σοφούς, καὶ τὰ ἀσθενῆ τοῦ
shame the wise men, and the weak things of the

κόσμου ἐξελέξατο ὁ θεὸς ἵνα καταισχύνῃ
world ²chose – ¹God in order that he might shame

τὰ ἰσχυρά, 28 καὶ τὰ ἀγενῆ τοῦ κόσμου
the strong things, and the base things of the world

καὶ τὰ ἐξουθενημένα ἐξελέξατο ὁ θεός,
and the things being despised ²chose – ¹God,

τὰ μὴ ὄντα, ἵνα τὰ ὄντα καταργήσῃ,
the things not being, in order that ³the things ⁴being ¹he might abolish,

29 ὅπως μὴ καυχήσηται πᾶσα σάρξ
so as not might boast all flesh*

ἐνώπιον τοῦ θεοῦ. 30 ἐξ αὐτοῦ δὲ ὑμεῖς
before – God. And of him ye

ἐστε ἐν Χριστῷ Ἰησοῦ, ὃς ἐγενήθη
are in Christ Jesus, who became

σοφία ἡμῖν ἀπὸ θεοῦ, δικαιοσύνη τε
wisdom to us from God, ²righteousness ¹both

καὶ ἁγιασμὸς καὶ ἀπολύτρωσις, 31 ἵνα καθὼς
and sanctification and redemption, in order that as

γέγραπται· ὁ καυχώμενος ἐν κυρίῳ καυχάσθω.
it has been written: The [one] boasting ²in ³[the] Lord ¹let him boast.

2 Κἀγὼ ἐλθὼν πρὸς ὑμᾶς, ἀδελφοί,
And I coming to you, brothers,

ἦλθον οὐ καθ' ὑπεροχὴν λόγου ἢ σοφίας
came not according to excellence of speech or of wisdom

καταγγέλλων ὑμῖν τὸ μαρτύριον τοῦ θεοῦ.
announcing to you the testimony – of God.

2 οὐ γὰρ ἔκρινά τι εἰδέναι ἐν ὑμῖν
For I decided not anything to know among you

εἰ μὴ Ἰησοῦν Χριστὸν καὶ τοῦτον
except Jesus Christ and this one

ἐσταυρωμένον. 3 κἀγὼ ἐν ἀσθενείᾳ καὶ
having been crucified. And I in weakness and

* That is, so that no flesh might boast. *Cf.* Mat. 24. 22.

and foolishness to Gentiles,
24 but to those whom God
has called, both Jews and
Greeks, Christ the power
of God and the wisdom of
God. 25 For the foolishness
of God is wiser than man's
wisdom, and the weakness
of God is stronger than
man's strength.
26 Brothers, think of what
you were when you were
called. Not many of you
were wise by human stan-
dards; not many were influ-
ential; not many were of
noble birth. 27 But God
chose the foolish things of
the world to shame the
wise; God chose the weak
things of the world to
shame the strong. 28 He
chose the lowly things of
this world and the despised
things—and the things that
are not—to nullify the
things that are, 29 so that no
one may boast before him.
30 It is because of him that
you are in Christ Jesus,
who has become for us wisdom from God—that is,
our righteousness, holiness
and redemption. 31 There-
fore, as it is written: "Let
him who boasts boast in the
Lord."[d]

Chapter 2

WHEN I came to you,
brothers, I did not
come with eloquence or superior wisdom as I pro-
claimed to you the testimony about God.[e] 2 For I resolved to know nothing
while I was with you except
Jesus Christ and him crucified. 3 I came to you in
weakness and fear, and

[d] *31* Jer. 9:24
[e] *1* Some manuscripts *as I proclaimed to you God's mystery*

trembling. 4My speech and
my proclamation were not
with plausible words of
wisdom,[k] but with a demonstration of the Spirit and
of power, 5so that your
faith might rest not on human wisdom but on the
power of God.

The True Wisdom of God

6 Yet among the mature
we do speak wisdom,
though it is not a wisdom of
this age or of the rulers of
this age, who are doomed
to perish. 7But we speak
God's wisdom, secret and
hidden, which God decreed
before the ages for our glory. 8None of the rulers of
this age understood this;
for if they had, they would
not have crucified the Lord
of glory. 9But, as it is written,

"What no eye has
seen, nor
ear heard,
nor the human heart
conceived,
what God has
prepared for
those who love
him"—

10these things God has revealed to us through the
Spirit; for the Spirit
searches everything, even
the depths of God. 11For
what human being knows
what is truly human except
the human spirit that is
within? So also no one
comprehends what is truly
God's except the Spirit of
God. 12Now we have re-
ceived not the spirit of the
world, but the Spirit that is
from God, so that we may
understand the gifts be-
stowed on us by God.
13And we speak of these
things in words not taught

ἐν φόβῳ καὶ ἐν τρόμῳ πολλῷ ἐγενόμην
in fear and in trembling much was
πρὸς ὑμᾶς, 4 καὶ ὁ λόγος μου καὶ τὸ
with you, and the speech of me and the
κήρυγμά μου οὐκ ἐν πειθοῖς σοφίας
proclamation of me not in [1]persuasive [3]of wisdom
λόγοις, ἀλλ' ἐν ἀποδείξει πνεύματος καὶ
[2]words, but in demonstration of spirit and
δυνάμεως, 5 ἵνα ἡ πίστις ὑμῶν μὴ ᾖ
of power, in order that the faith of you may not be
ἐν σοφίᾳ ἀνθρώπων ἀλλ' ἐν δυνάμει
in [the] wisdom of men but in [the] power
θεοῦ.
of God.
6 Σοφίαν δὲ λαλοῦμεν ἐν τοῖς τελείοις,
But [2]wisdom [1]we speak among the perfect ones,
σοφίαν δὲ οὐ τοῦ αἰῶνος τούτου οὐδὲ
yet wisdom not of this age neither
τῶν ἀρχόντων τοῦ αἰῶνος τούτου τῶν
of the leaders of this age of the [ones]
καταργουμένων· 7 ἀλλὰ λαλοῦμεν θεοῦ
being brought to naught; but we speak [2]of God
σοφίαν ἐν μυστηρίῳ, τὴν ἀποκεκρυμμένην,
[1]a wisdom in mystery, – having been hidden,
ἣν προώρισεν ὁ θεὸς πρὸ τῶν αἰώνων
which [2]foreordained – [1]God before the ages
εἰς δόξαν ἡμῶν· 8 ἣν οὐδεὶς τῶν ἀρχόντων
for glory of us; which not one of the leaders
τοῦ αἰῶνος τούτου ἔγνωκεν· εἰ γὰρ
of this age has known; for if
ἔγνωσαν, οὐκ ἂν τὸν κύριον τῆς δόξης
they knew, not – the Lord – of glory
ἐσταύρωσαν· 9 ἀλλὰ καθὼς γέγραπται· ἃ
they would have crucified;* but as it has been written: Things which
ὀφθαλμὸς οὐκ εἶδεν καὶ οὖς οὐκ ἤκουσεν
eye saw not and ear heard not
καὶ ἐπὶ καρδίαν ἀνθρώπου οὐκ ἀνέβη,
and on heart of man came not up,
ὅσα ἡτοίμασεν ὁ θεὸς τοῖς ἀγαπῶσιν
how many [2]prepared – [1]God for the [ones] loving
αὐτόν. 10 ἡμῖν γὰρ ἀπεκάλυψεν ὁ θεὸς
him. [1]For [4]to us [3]revealed – [2]God
διὰ τοῦ πνεύματος· τὸ γὰρ πνεῦμα πάντα
through the Spirit; for the Spirit all things
ἐρευνᾷ, καὶ τὰ βάθη τοῦ θεοῦ. 11 τίς
searches, even the deep things – of God. [2]who
γὰρ οἶδεν ἀνθρώπων τὰ τοῦ ἀνθρώπου
[1]For [4]knows [3]of men the things – of a man
εἰ μὴ τὸ πνεῦμα τοῦ ἀνθρώπου τὸ
except the spirit – of a man –
ἐν αὐτῷ; οὕτως καὶ τὰ τοῦ θεοῦ οὐδεὶς
in him? so also the things – of God no one
ἔγνωκεν εἰ μὴ τὸ πνεῦμα τοῦ θεοῦ.
has known except the Spirit – of God.
12 ἡμεῖς δὲ οὐ τὸ πνεῦμα τοῦ κόσμου
And we not the spirit of the world
ἐλάβομεν ἀλλὰ τὸ πνεῦμα τὸ ἐκ τοῦ θεοῦ,
received but the Spirit – from – God,
ἵνα εἰδῶμεν τὰ ὑπὸ τοῦ θεοῦ
in order that we may know the things by – God
χαρισθέντα ἡμῖν· 13 ἃ καὶ λαλοῦμεν οὐκ
freely given to us; which things also we speak not

with much trembling. 4My
message and my preaching
were not with wise and persuasive words, but with a
demonstration of the Spirit's power, 5so that your
faith might not rest on
men's wisdom, but on
God's power.

Wisdom From the Spirit

6We do, however, speak
a message of wisdom
among the mature, but not
the wisdom of this age or of
the rulers of this age, who
are coming to nothing.
7No, we speak of God's secret wisdom, a wisdom that
has been hidden and that
God destined for our glory
before time began. 8None
of the rulers of this age understood it, for if they had,
they would not have crucified the Lord of glory.
9However, as it is written:

"No eye has seen,
no ear has heard,
no mind has conceived
what God has prepared
for those who love
him"[f]—

10but God has revealed it to
us by his Spirit.
The Spirit searches all
things, even the deep
things of God. 11For who
among men knows the
thoughts of a man except
the man's spirit within him?
In the same way no one
knows the thoughts of God
except the Spirit of God.
12We have not received the
spirit of the world but the
Spirit who is from God,
that we may understand
what God has freely given
us. 13This is what we
speak, not in words taught

[k] Other ancient authorities read *the persuasiveness of wisdom*

* This rendering is demanded by the preceding ἄν.

[f] 9 Isaiah 64:4

by human wisdom but taught by the Spirit, interpreting spiritual things to those who are spiritual.[l]

14 Those who are unspiritual[m] do not receive the gifts of God's Spirit, for they are foolishness to them, and they are unable to understand them because they are spiritually discerned. 15 Those who are spiritual discern all things, and they are themselves subject to no one else's scrutiny.

16 "For who has known
the mind
of the Lord
so as to instruct
him?"

But we have the mind of Christ.

Chapter 3

On Divisions in the Corinthian Church

AND so, brothers and sisters,[n] I could not speak to you as spiritual people, but rather as people of the flesh, as infants in Christ. 2 I fed you with milk, not solid food, for you were not ready for solid food. Even now you are still not ready, 3 for you are still of the flesh. For as long as there is jealousy and quarreling among you, are you not of the flesh, and behaving according to human inclinations? 4 For when one says, "I belong to Paul," and another, "I belong to Apollos," are you not merely human?

5 What then is Apollos? What is Paul? Servants through whom you came to believe, as the Lord assigned to each. 6 I planted, Apollos watered, but God gave the growth. 7 So neither the one who plants nor the one who waters is anything, but only God who gives the growth. 8 The one who plants and the one who waters have a common purpose, and each will receive wages according to the labor of each. 9 For we are God's servants, working together; you are God's field, God's building.

10 According to the grace of God given to me, like a skilled master builder

[l] Or *interpreting spiritual things in spiritual language*, or *comparing spiritual things with spiritual*
[m] Or *natural*
[n] Gk *brothers*

ἐν διδακτοῖς ἀνθρωπίνης σοφίας λόγοις,
in [2]taught [3]of human [4]wisdom [1]words,

ἀλλ' ἐν διδακτοῖς πνεύματος, πνευματικοῖς
but in [words] taught of [the] Spirit, [3]with spiritual things

πνευματικὰ συγκρίνοντες. **14** ψυχικὸς δὲ
[2]spiritual things [1]comparing. But a natural

ἄνθρωπος οὐ δέχεται τὰ τοῦ πνεύματος
man receives not the things of the Spirit

τοῦ θεοῦ· μωρία γὰρ αὐτῷ ἐστιν, καὶ
– of God; for folly to him they are, and

οὐ δύναται γνῶναι, ὅτι πνευματικῶς
he cannot *to* know, because [2]spiritually

ἀνακρίνεται. **15** ὁ δὲ πνευματικὸς ἀνακρίνει
[1]they are [3]discerned. But the spiritual man [2]discerns

μὲν πάντα, αὐτὸς δὲ ὑπ' οὐδενὸς
[1]on one hand all things, [2]he [1]on the other [4]by [5]no one

ἀνακρίνεται. **16** τίς γὰρ ἔγνω νοῦν
[3]is discerned. For who knew [the] mind

κυρίου, ὃς συμβιβάσει αὐτόν; ἡμεῖς δὲ
of [the] Lord, who will instruct him? But we

νοῦν Χριστοῦ ἔχομεν.
[the] mind of Christ have.

3 Κἀγώ, ἀδελφοί, οὐκ ἠδυνήθην λαλῆσαι
And I, brothers, was not able to speak

ὑμῖν ὡς πνευματικοῖς ἀλλ' ὡς σαρκίνοις,
to you as to spiritual men but as to fleshy,

ὡς νηπίοις ἐν Χριστῷ. **2** γάλα ὑμᾶς
as to infants in Christ. [3]Milk [2]you

ἐπότισα, οὐ βρῶμα· οὔπω γὰρ ἐδύνασθε.
[1]I gave [4]to drink, not food; for ye were not then able.

ἀλλ' οὐδὲ [ἔτι] νῦν δύνασθε, **3** ἔτι γὰρ
But neither yet now are ye able, for still

σαρκικοί ἐστε. ὅπου γὰρ ἐν ὑμῖν ζῆλος
fleshly ye are. For whereas among you [there is] jealousy

καὶ ἔρις, οὐχὶ σαρκικοί ἐστε καὶ κατὰ
and strife, [2]not [3]fleshly [1]are ye [4]and [6]according to

ἄνθρωπον περιπατεῖτε; **4** ὅταν γὰρ λέγῃ
[7]man [5]walk? For whenever says

τις· ἐγὼ μέν εἰμι Παύλου, ἕτερος δέ·
anyone: I – am of Paul, and another:

ἐγὼ Ἀπολλῶ, οὐκ ἄνθρωποί ἐστε; **5** Τί
I of Apollos, [2]not [3]men [1]are ye? What

οὖν ἐστιν Ἀπολλῶς; τί δέ ἐστιν Παῦλος;
therefore is Apollos? and what is Paul?

διάκονοι δι' ὧν ἐπιστεύσατε, καὶ ἑκάστῳ
Ministers through whom ye believed, even [2]to each one

ὡς ὁ κύριος ἔδωκεν. **6** ἐγὼ ἐφύτευσα,
[1]as the Lord gave. I planted,

Ἀπολλῶς ἐπότισεν, ἀλλὰ ὁ θεὸς ηὔξανεν·
Apollos watered, but – God made to grow;

7 ὥστε οὔτε ὁ φυτεύων ἐστίν τι οὔτε
so as neither the [one] planting is anything nor

ὁ ποτίζων, ἀλλ' ὁ αὐξάνων θεός. **8** ὁ
the [one] watering, but [2]the [one] [3]making to grow [1]God. [2]The [one]

φυτεύων δὲ καὶ ὁ ποτίζων ἕν εἰσιν,
[3]planting [1]so and the [one] watering one* are,

ἕκαστος δὲ τὸν ἴδιον μισθὸν λήμψεται
and each one the(his) own reward will receive

* Notice the neuter gender, though "thing" cannot very well be expressed; *cf.* John 10. 30.

us by human wisdom but in words taught by the Spirit, expressing spiritual truths in spiritual words.[g] 14 The man without the Spirit does not accept the things that come from the Spirit of God, for they are foolishness to him, and he cannot understand them, because they are spiritually discerned. 15 The spiritual man makes judgments about all things, but he himself is not subject to any man's judgment:

16 "For who has known the
mind of the Lord
that he may instruct
him?"[h]

But we have the mind of Christ.

Chapter 3

On Divisions in the Church

BROTHERS, I could not address you as spiritual but as worldly—mere infants in Christ. 2 I gave you milk, not solid food, for you were not yet ready for it. Indeed, you are still not ready. 3 You are still worldly. For since there is jealousy and quarreling among you, are you not worldly? Are you not acting like mere men? 4 For when one says, "I follow Paul," and another, "I follow Apollos," are you not mere men?

5 What, after all, is Apollos? And what is Paul? Only servants, through whom you came to believe—as the Lord has assigned to each his task. 6 I planted the seed, Apollos watered it, but God made it grow. 7 So neither he who plants nor he who waters is anything, but only God, who makes things grow. 8 The man who plants and the man who waters have one purpose, and each will be rewarded according to his own labor. 9 For we are God's fellow workers; you are God's field, God's building.

10 By the grace God has

[g] 13 Or *Spirit, interpreting spiritual truths to spiritual men*
[h] 16 Isaiah 40:13

I laid a foundation, and
someone else is building on
it. Each builder must
choose with care how to
build on it. 11 For no one
can lay any foundation other than the one that has
been laid; that foundation
is Jesus Christ. 12 Now if
anyone builds on the foundation with gold, silver,
precious stones, wood,
hay, straw— 13 the work of
each builder will become
visible, for the Day will dis-
close it, because it will be
revealed with fire, and the
fire will test what sort of
work each has done. 14 If
what has been built on the
foundation survives, the
builder will receive a reward. 15 If the work is
burned up, the builder will
suffer loss; the builder will
be saved, but only as
through fire.

16 Do you not know
that you are God's temple
and that God's Spirit
dwells in you?[o] 17 If anyone destroys God's temple,
God will destroy that person. For God's temple is
holy, and you are that temple.

18 Do not deceive your-
selves. If you think that
you are wise in this age,
you should become fools so
that you may become wise.
19 For the wisdom of this
world is foolishness with
God. For it is written,

"He catches the wise
in their
craftiness,"

20 and again,

"The Lord knows the
thoughts of the
wise,
that they are futile."

21 So let no one boast about

[o] In verses 16 and 17 the Greek word for *you* is plural

κατὰ τὸν ἴδιον κόπον. 9 θεοῦ γάρ ἐσμεν
according to his own labour. For of God we are

συνεργοί· θεοῦ γεώργιον, θεοῦ οἰκοδομή
fellow-workers; [3]of God [2]a tillage, [5]of God [4]a building

ἐστε. 10 Κατὰ τὴν χάριν τοῦ θεοῦ τὴν
[1]ye are. According to the grace – of God –

δοθεῖσάν μοι ὡς σοφὸς ἀρχιτέκτων
given to me as a wise master builder

θεμέλιον ἔθηκα, ἄλλος δὲ ἐποικοδομεῖ.
a foundation I laid, but another builds on [it].

ἕκαστος δὲ βλεπέτω πῶς ἐποικοδομεῖ.
But each one let him look how he builds on [it].

11 θεμέλιον γὰρ ἄλλον οὐδεὶς δύναται θεῖναι
For foundation other no one is able to lay

παρὰ τὸν κείμενον, ὅς ἐστιν Ἰησοῦς
beside the [one] being laid, who is Jesus

Χριστός. 12 εἰ δέ τις ἐποικοδομεῖ ἐπὶ
Christ. Now if anyone builds *on* on

τὸν θεμέλιον χρυσίον, ἀργύριον, λίθους
the foundation gold, silver, stones

τιμίους, ξύλα, χόρτον, καλάμην, 13 ἑκάστου
precious, woods, hay, stubble, of each one

τὸ ἔργον φανερὸν γενήσεται· ἡ γὰρ ἡμέρα
the work manifest will become; for the day

δηλώσει, ὅτι ἐν πυρὶ ἀποκαλύπτεται,
will declare [it], because by fire it is revealed,

καὶ ἑκάστου τὸ ἔργον ὁποῖόν ἐστιν
and [3]of each one [1]the [2]work [8]of what sort [9]it is

τὸ πῦρ αὐτὸ δοκιμάσει. 14 εἴ τινος
[4]the [5]fire [7]it [6]will prove. If of anyone

τὸ ἔργον μενεῖ ὃ ἐποικοδόμησεν, μισθὸν
the work remains which he built *on*, a reward

λήμψεται· 15 εἴ τινος τὸ ἔργον κατακαήσεται,
he will receive; if of anyone the work will be consumed,

ζημιωθήσεται, αὐτὸς δὲ σωθήσεται,
he will suffer loss, but he will be saved,

οὕτως δὲ ὡς διὰ πυρός. 16 Οὐκ οἴδατε
yet so as through fire. Know ye not

ὅτι ναὸς θεοῦ ἐστε καὶ τὸ πνεῦμα τοῦ
that a shrine of God ye are and the Spirit –

θεοῦ ἐν ὑμῖν οἰκεῖ; 17 εἴ τις τὸν ναὸν
of God in you dwells? If anyone the shrine

τοῦ θεοῦ φθείρει, φθερεῖ τοῦτον ὁ θεός·
– of God defiles, [2]will defile [3]this man – [1]God;

ὁ γὰρ ναὸς τοῦ θεοῦ ἅγιός ἐστιν, οἵτινές
for the shrine – of God holy is, who(which)

ἐστε ὑμεῖς.
are ye.

18 Μηδεὶς ἑαυτὸν ἐξαπατάτω· εἴ τις
No one himself let deceive; if anyone

δοκεῖ σοφὸς εἶναι ἐν ὑμῖν ἐν τῷ αἰῶνι
thinks wise to be among you in – age

τούτῳ, μωρὸς γενέσθω, ἵνα γένηται
this, foolish let him become, in order that he may become

σοφός. 19 ἡ γὰρ σοφία τοῦ κόυμοι
wise. For the wisdom – world

τούτου μωρία παρὰ τῷ θεῷ ἐστιν.
of this folly with – God is.

γέγραπται γάρ· ὁ δρασσόμενος τοὺς σοφοὺς
For it has been written: The [one] grasping the wise

ἐν τῇ πανουργίᾳ αὐτῶν· 20 καὶ πάλιν·
in the craftiness of them; and again:

κύριος γινώσκει τοὺς διαλογισμοὺς τῶν
[The] Lord knows the reasonings of the

σοφῶν, ὅτι εἰσὶν μάταιοι. 21 ὥστε μηδεὶς
wise, that they are vain. So as no one

given me, I laid a foundation as an expert builder,
and someone else is building on it. But each one
should be careful how he
builds. 11 For no one can lay
any foundation other than
the one already laid, which
is Jesus Christ. 12 If any
man builds on this foundation using gold, silver, costly stones, wood, hay or
straw, 13 his work will be
shown for what it is, be-
cause the Day will bring it
to light. It will be revealed
with fire, and the fire will
test the quality of each
man's work. 14 If what he
has built survives, he will
receive his reward. 15 If it is
burned up, he will suffer
loss; he himself will be
saved, but only as one escaping through the flames.

16 Don't you know that
you yourselves are God's
temple and that God's Spirit lives in you? 17 If anyone
destroys God's temple,
God will destroy him; for
God's temple is sacred, and
you are that temple.

18 Do not deceive your-
selves. If any one of you
thinks he is wise by the
standards of this age, he
should become a "fool" so
that he may become wise.
19 For the wisdom of this
world is foolishness in
God's sight. As it is written: "He catches the wise
in their craftiness"[i]; 20 and
again, "The Lord knows
that the thoughts of the
wise are futile."[j] 21 So
then, no more boasting

[i] 19 Job 5:13
[j] 20 Psalm 94:11

human leaders. For all
things are yours, 22 whether
Paul or Apollos or Cephas
or the world or life or death
or the present or the
future—all belong to you,
23 and you belong to Christ,
and Christ belongs to God.

Chapter 4

The Ministry of the Apostles

THINK of us in this
way, as servants of
Christ and stewards of
God's mysteries. 2 More-
over, it is required of stewards that they be found
trustworthy. 3 But with me
it is a very small thing that
I should be judged by you
or by any human court. I do
not even judge myself. 4 I
am not aware of anything
against myself, but I am not
thereby acquitted. It is the
Lord who judges me.
5 Therefore do not pro-
nounce judgment before
the time, before the Lord
comes, who will bring to
light the things now hidden
in darkness and will dis-
close the purposes of the
heart. Then each one will
receive commendation
from God.
6 I have applied all this
to Apollos and myself for
your benefit, brothers and
sisters,[p] so that you may
learn through us the meaning of the saying, "Nothing
beyond what is written," so
that none of you will be
puffed up in favor of one
against another. 7 For who
sees anything different in
you?[q] What do you have
that you did not receive?
And if you received it, why
do you boast as if it were
not a gift?
8 Already you have all
you want! Already you
have become rich! Quite
apart from us you have become kings! Indeed, I wish
that you had become kings,
so that we might be kings
with you! 9 For I think that

καυχάσθω ἐν ἀνθρώποις· πάντα γὰρ ὑμῶν
let boast in men; for all things of you
ἐστιν, 22 εἴτε Παῦλος εἴτε Ἀπολλῶς
is(are), whether Paul or Apollos
εἴτε Κηφᾶς, εἴτε κόσμος εἴτε ζωὴ εἴτε
or Cephas, or [the] world or life or
θάνατος, εἴτε ἐνεστῶτα εἴτε μέλλοντα,
death, or things present or things coming,
πάντα ὑμῶν, 23 ὑμεῖς δὲ Χριστοῦ, Χριστὸς δὲ
all things of you, and ye of Christ, and Christ
θεοῦ. 4 Οὕτως ἡμᾶς λογιζέσθω ἄνθρωπος ὡς
of God. So [4]us [1]let [3]reckon [2]a man as
ὑπηρέτας Χριστοῦ καὶ οἰκονόμους μυστηρίων
attendants of Christ and stewards of mysteries
θεοῦ. 2 ὧδε λοιπὸν ζητεῖται ἐν τοῖς
of God. Here for the rest it is sought among –
οἰκονόμοις ἵνα πιστός τις εὑρεθῇ. 3 ἐμοὶ
stewards *in order that* [3]faithful [1]*any*one [2]be found. to me
δὲ εἰς ἐλάχιστόν ἐστιν ἵνα ὑφ᾽ ὑμῶν
And for a very little thing it is *in order* that by you
ἀνακριθῶ ἢ ὑπὸ ἀνθρωπίνης ἡμέρας· ἀλλ᾽
I am judged or by a human day;* but
οὐδὲ ἐμαυτὸν ἀνακρίνω· 4 οὐδὲν γὰρ
not myself I judge; for nothing
ἐμαυτῷ σύνοιδα, ἀλλ᾽ οὐκ ἐν τούτῳ
against myself I know, but not by this
δεδικαίωμαι· ὁ δὲ ἀνακρίνων με κύριός
have I been justified; but the [one] judging me [the] Lord
ἐστιν. 5 ὥστε μὴ πρὸ καιροῦ τι κρίνετε,
is. So as not before time anything judge ye,
ἕως ἂν ἔλθῃ ὁ κύριος, ὃς καὶ φωτίσει
until comes the Lord, who both will shed light on
τὰ κρυπτὰ τοῦ σκότους καὶ φανερώσει
the hidden things of the darkness and will manifest
τὰς βουλὰς τῶν καρδιῶν· καὶ τότε ὁ
the counsels of the hearts; and then the
ἔπαινος γενήσεται ἑκάστῳ ἀπὸ τοῦ θεοῦ.
praise will be to each one[c] from – God.
6 Ταῦτα δέ, ἀδελφοί, μετεσχημάτισα εἰς
Now these things, brothers, I adapted to
ἐμαυτὸν καὶ Ἀπολλῶν δι᾽ ὑμᾶς, ἵνα
myself and Apollos because of you, in order that
ἐν ἡμῖν μάθητε τὸ μὴ ὑπὲρ ἃ
among us ye may learn – not [to think] above what things
γέγραπται, ἵνα μὴ εἷς ὑπὲρ τοῦ ἑνὸς
has(ve) been written, lest [2]one [3]on behalf of [4]the [5]one
φυσιοῦσθε κατὰ τοῦ ἑτέρου. 7 τίς γάρ σε
[1]ye are puffed up against the other. For who thee
διακρίνει; τί δὲ ἔχεις ὃ οὐκ ἔλαβες;
distinguishes? and what hast thou which thou didst not receive?
εἰ δὲ καὶ ἔλαβες, τί καυχᾶσαι ὡς μὴ
and if indeed thou didst receive, why boastest thou as not
λαβών; 8 ἤδη κεκορεσμένοι ἐστέ· ἤδη
receiving? Now *having been* glutted ye are; now
ἐπλουτήσατε· χωρὶς ἡμῶν ἐβασιλεύσατε· καὶ
ye became rich; without us ye reigned; and
ὄφελόν γε ἐβασιλεύσατε, ἵνα
[2]an advantage [3]really [1][it is] [that] ye reigned, in order that
καὶ ἡμεῖς ὑμῖν συμβασιλεύσωμεν. 9 δοκῶ
also we [2]you [1]might reign with. I think

about men! All things are
yours, 22 whether Paul or
Apollos or Cephas[k] or the
world or life or death or the
present or the future—all
are yours, 23 and you are of
Christ, and Christ is of
God.

Chapter 4

Apostles of Christ

SO then, men ought to
regard us as servants
of Christ and as those entrusted with the secret
things of God. 2 Now it is
required that those who
have been given a trust
must prove faithful. 3 I care
very little if I am judged by
you or by any human court;
indeed, I do not even judge
myself. 4 My conscience is
clear, but that does not
make me innocent. It is the
Lord who judges me.
5 Therefore judge nothing
before the appointed time;
wait till the Lord comes.
He will bring to light what
is hidden in darkness and
will expose the motives of
men's hearts. At that time
each will receive his praise
from God.
6 Now, brothers, I have
applied these things to myself and Apollos for your
benefit, so that you may
learn from us the meaning
of the saying, "Do not go
beyond what is written."
Then you will not take
pride in one man over
against another. 7 For who
makes you different from
anyone else? What do you
have that you did not re-
ceive? And if you did re-
ceive it, why do you boast
as though you did not?
8 Already you have all you
want! Already you have become rich! You have be-
come kings—and that
without us! How I wish that
you really had become
kings so that we might be
kings with you! 9 For it

[p] Gk *brothers*
[q] Or *Who makes you different from another?*

* ? of judgment.

[k] 22 That is, Peter

God has exhibited us apostles as last of all, as though
sentenced to death, be-
cause we have become a
spectacle to the world, to
angels and to mortals.
10 We are fools for the sake
of Christ, but you are wise
in Christ. We are weak, but
you are strong. You are
held in honor, but we in disrepute. 11 To the present
hour we are hungry and
thirsty, we are poorly
clothed and beaten and
homeless, 12 and we grow
weary from the work of our
own hands. When reviled,
we bless; when persecuted,
we endure; 13 when slan-
dered, we speak kindly.
We have become like the
rubbish of the world, the
dregs of all things, to this
very day.

Fatherly Admonition

14 I am not writing this
to make you ashamed, but
to admonish you as my be-
loved children. 15 For
though you might have ten
thousand guardians in
Christ, you do not have
many fathers. Indeed, in
Christ Jesus I became your
father through the gospel.
16 I appeal to you, then, be
imitators of me. 17 For this
reason I sent[r] you Timothy, who is my beloved and
faithful child in the Lord, to
remind you of my ways in
Christ Jesus, as I teach
them everywhere in every
church. 18 But some of you,
thinking that I am not coming to you, have become arrogant. 19 But I will come to
you soon, if the Lord wills,
and I will find out not the
talk of these arrogant people but their power. 20 For
the kingdom of God de-

[r] Or *am sending*

γάρ, ὁ θεὸς ἡμᾶς τοὺς ἀποστόλους
For, – God us the apostles
ἐσχάτους ἀπέδειξεν ὡς ἐπιθανατίους, ὅτι
last showed forth as doomed to death, because
θέατρον ἐγενήθημεν τῷ κόσμῳ καὶ ἀγγέλοις
a spectacle we became to the world both to angels
καὶ ἀνθρώποις. 10 ἡμεῖς μωροὶ διὰ
and to men. We [are] fools because of
Χριστόν, ὑμεῖς δὲ φρόνιμοι ἐν Χριστῷ·
Christ, but ye [are] prudent in Christ;
ἡμεῖς ἀσθενεῖς, ὑμεῖς δὲ ἰσχυροί· ὑμεῖς
we [are] weak, but ye [are] strong; ye [are]
ἔνδοξοι, ἡμεῖς δὲ ἄτιμοι. 11 ἄχρι τῆς
held in honour, but we [are] unhonoured. Until the
ἄρτι ὥρας καὶ πεινῶμεν καὶ διψῶμεν
present hour [2]both [1]we [3]hunger and thirst
καὶ γυμνιτεύομεν καὶ κολαφιζόμεθα καὶ
and are naked and are buffeted and
ἀστατοῦμεν 12 καὶ κοπιῶμεν ἐργαζόμενοι
are unsettled and labour working
ταῖς ἰδίαις χερσίν· λοιδορούμενοι εὐλο-
with the(our) own hands; being reviled we
γοῦμεν, διωκόμενοι ἀνεχόμεθα, 13 δυσφημού-
bless, being persecuted we endure, being de-
μενοι παρακαλοῦμεν· ὡς περικαθάρματα τοῦ
famed we beseech; as refuse of the
κόσμου ἐγενήθημεν, πάντων περίψημα ἕως
world we became, [2]of all things [1]offscouring until
ἄρτι.
now.

14 Οὐκ ἐντρέπων ὑμᾶς γράφω ταῦτα,
Not shaming you I write these things,
ἀλλ' ὡς τέκνα μου ἀγαπητὰ νουθετῶν.
but as children of me beloved admonishing.
15 ἐὰν γὰρ μυρίους παιδαγωγοὺς ἔχητε
For if ten thousand trainers ye have
ἐν Χριστῷ, ἀλλ' οὐ πολλοὺς πατέρας·
in Christ, yet not many fathers;
ἐν γὰρ Χριστῷ Ἰησοῦ διὰ τοῦ εὐαγγελίου
for in Christ Jesus through the gospel
ἐγὼ ὑμᾶς ἐγέννησα. 16 παρακαλῶ οὖν
I [2]you [1]begat. I beseech therefore
ὑμᾶς, μιμηταί μου γίνεσθε. 17 Διὰ τοῦτο
you, imitators of me become ye. Because of this
αὐτὸ ἔπεμψα ὑμῖν Τιμόθεον, ὅς ἐστίν
very thing I sent to you Timothy, who is
μου τέκνον ἀγαπητὸν καὶ πιστὸν ἐν
of me a child beloved and faithful in
κυρίῳ, ὃς ὑμᾶς ἀναμνήσει τὰς ὁδούς
[the] Lord, who [2]you [1]will remind [of] the ways
μου τὰς ἐν Χριστῷ [Ἰησοῦ], καθὼς
of me – in Christ Jesus, as
πανταχοῦ ἐν πάσῃ ἐκκλησίᾳ διδάσκω.
everywhere in every church I teach.
18 ὡς μὴ ἐρχομένου δέ μου πρὸς ὑμᾶς
When not coming now me* to you
=Now when I did not come
ἐφυσιώθησάν τινες· 19 ἐλεύσομαι δὲ ταχέως
[2]were puffed up [1]some; but I will come shortly
πρὸς ὑμᾶς, ἐὰν ὁ κύριος θελήσῃ, καὶ
to you, if the Lord wills, and
γνώσομαι οὐ τὸν λόγον τῶν πεφυσιωμένων
I will know not the speech of the [ones] having been puffed up
ἀλλὰ τὴν δύναμιν· 20 οὐ γὰρ ἐν λόγῳ
but the power; for [4][is] [5]not [6]in [7]speech

seems to me that God has
put us apostles on display
at the end of the proces-
sion, like men condemned
to die in the arena. We have
been made a spectacle to
the whole universe, to angels as well as to men. 10 We
are fools for Christ, but you
are so wise in Christ! We
are weak, but you are
strong! You are honored,
we are dishonored! 11 To
this very hour we go hun-
gry and thirsty, we are in
rags, we are brutally treated, we are homeless. 12 We
work hard with our own
hands. When we are
cursed, we bless; when we
are persecuted, we endure
it; 13 when we are slan-
dered, we answer kindly.
Up to this moment we have
become the scum of the
earth, the refuse of the
world.
14 I am not writing this to
shame you, but to warn
you, as my dear children.
15 Even though you have
ten thousand guardians in
Christ, you do not have
many fathers, for in Christ
Jesus I became your father
through the gospel.
16 Therefore I urge you to
imitate me. 17 For this reason I am sending to you
Timothy, my son whom I
love, who is faithful in the
Lord. He will remind you
of my way of life in Christ
Jesus, which agrees with
what I teach everywhere in
every church.
18 Some of you have be-
come arrogant, as if I were
not coming to you. 19 But I
will come to you very soon,
if the Lord is willing, and
then I will find out not only
how these arrogant people
are talking, but what power
they have. 20 For the kingdom of God is not a matter

pends not on talk but on
power. 21 What would you
prefer? Am I to come to
you with a stick, or with
love in a spirit of gentleness?

Chapter 5

Sexual Immorality Defiles the Church

IT is actually reported
that there is sexual im-
morality among you, and of
a kind that is not found
even among pagans; for a
man is living with his father's wife. 2 And you are
arrogant! Should you not
rather have mourned, so
that he who has done this
would have been removed
from among you?
3 For though absent in
body, I am present in spirit;
and as if present I have already pronounced judg-
ment 4 in the name of the
Lord Jesus on the man who
has done such a thing.[s]
When you are assembled,
and my spirit is present
with the power of our Lord
Jesus, 5 you are to hand this
man over to Satan for the
destruction of the flesh, so
that his spirit may be saved
in the day of the Lord.[t]
6 Your boasting is not a
good thing. Do you not
know that a little yeast
leavens the whole batch of
dough? 7 Clean out the old
yeast so that you may be a
new batch, as you really
are unleavened. For our
paschal lamb, Christ, has
been sacrificed. 8 There-
fore, let us celebrate the
festival, not with the old
yeast, the yeast of malice
and evil, but with the unleavened bread of sincerity
and truth.

Sexual Immorality Must Be Judged

9 I wrote to you in my
letter not to associate with
sexually immoral
persons— 10 not at all
meaning the immoral of
this world, or the greedy
and robbers, or idolaters,

[s] Or *on the man who has done such a thing in the name of the Lord Jesus*

[t] Other ancient authorities add *Jesus*

ἡ βασιλεία τοῦ θεοῦ, ἀλλ' ἐν δυνάμει.
[1]the [2]kingdom – [3]of God, but in power.

21 τί θέλετε; ἐν ῥάβδῳ ἔλθω πρὸς ὑμᾶς,
What will ye? with a rod I come to you,

ἢ ἐν ἀγάπῃ πνεύματί τε πραΰτητος;
or in love and a spirit of meekness?

5 Ὅλως ἀκούεται ἐν ὑμῖν πορνεία,
Actually is heard among you fornication,

καὶ τοιαύτη πορνεία ἥτις οὐδὲ ἐν τοῖς
and such fornication which [is] not among the

ἔθνεσιν, ὥστε γυναῖκά τινα τοῦ πατρὸς
nations, so as [3]wife [1]one [4]of the [5]father

ἔχειν. 2 καὶ ὑμεῖς πεφυσιωμένοι ἐστέ,
[2]to have.[b] And ye *having been* puffed up are,

καὶ οὐχὶ μᾶλλον ἐπενθήσατε, ἵνα ἀρθῇ
and not rather mourned, in order that [8]might be removed

ἐκ μέσου ὑμῶν ὁ τὸ ἔργον τοῦτο πράξας;
[6]from [7][the] [8]midst [9]of you [1]the [one] [3]this [4]deed [2]having done?

3 ἐγὼ μὲν γάρ, ἀπὼν τῷ σώματι,
For I indeed, being absent in the body,

παρὼν δὲ τῷ πνεύματι, ἤδη κέκρικα
but being present in the spirit, already have judged

ὡς παρὼν τὸν οὕτως τοῦτο κατεργα-
as being present [1]the [one] [3]thus [4]this thing [2]having

σάμενον 4 ἐν τῷ ὀνόματι τοῦ κυρίου
wrought in the name of the Lord

Ἰησοῦ συναχθέντων ὑμῶν καὶ τοῦ ἐμοῦ
Jesus being assembled you and – my
=when you are assembled . . .

πνεύματος σὺν τῇ δυνάμει τοῦ κυρίου
spirit[a] with the power of the Lord

ἡμῶν Ἰησοῦ 5 παραδοῦναι τὸν τοιοῦτον
of us Jesus to deliver such a person

τῷ σατανᾷ εἰς ὄλεθρον τῆς σαρκός,
– to Satan for destruction of the flesh,

ἵνα τὸ πνεῦμα σωθῇ ἐν τῇ ἡμέρᾳ τοῦ
in order that the spirit may be saved in the day of the

κυρίου. 6 Οὐ καλὸν τὸ καύχημα ὑμῶν.
Lord. Not good [is] the boast of you.

οὐκ οἴδατε ὅτι μικρὰ ζύμη ὅλον τὸ
Know ye not that a little leaven all the

φύραμα ζυμοῖ; 7 ἐκκαθάρατε τὴν παλαιὰν
lump leavens? Purge out the old

ζύμην, ἵνα ἦτε νέον φύραμα, καθώς
leaven, in order that ye may be a new lump, as

ἐστε ἄζυμοι. καὶ γὰρ τὸ πάσχα ἡμῶν
ye are unleavened. For indeed the passover of us

ἐτύθη Χριστός. 8 ὥστε ἑορτάζωμεν μὴ
was sacrificed[,] Christ. So as let us keep feast not

ἐν ζύμῃ παλαιᾷ μηδὲ ἐν ζύμῃ κακίας
with leaven old nor with leaven of malice

καὶ πονηρίας, ἀλλ' ἐν ἀζύμοις εἰλικρινείας
and *of* evil, but with unleavened [loaves] of sincerity

καὶ ἀληθείας. 9 Ἔγραψα ὑμῖν ἐν τῇ
and *of* truth. I wrote to you in the

ἐπιστολῇ μὴ συναναμίγνυσθαι πόρνοις,
epistle not to associate intimately *with* with fornicators,

10 οὐ πάντως τοῖς πόρνοις τοῦ κόσμου
not altogether with the fornicators – world

τούτου ἢ τοῖς πλεονέκταις καὶ ἅρπαξιν
of this or with the covetous and rapacious

of talk but of power.
21 What do you prefer? Shall
I come to you with a whip,
or in love and with a gentle
spirit?

Chapter 5

Expel the Immoral Brother!

IT is actually reported
that there is sexual im-
morality among you, and of
a kind that does not occur
even among pagans: A man
has his father's wife. 2 And
you are proud! Shouldn't
you rather have been filled
with grief and have put out
of your fellowship the man
who did this? 3 Even though
I am not physically pre-
sent, I am with you in spirit. And I have already
passed judgment on the one
who did this, just as if I
were present. 4 When you
are assembled in the name
of our Lord Jesus and I am
with you in spirit, and the
power of our Lord Jesus is
present, 5 hand this man
over to Satan, so that the
sinful nature[l] may be destroyed and his spirit saved
on the day of the Lord.
6 Your boasting is not
good. Don't you know that
a little yeast works through
the whole batch of dough?
7 Get rid of the old yeast
that you may be a new
batch without yeast—as
you really are. For Christ,
our Passover lamb, has
been sacrificed. 8 Therefore
let us keep the Festival, not
with the old yeast, the
yeast of malice and wickedness, but with bread without yeast, the bread of sincerity and truth.
9 I have written you in my
letter not to associate with
sexually immoral people—
10 not at all meaning the
people of this world who
are immoral, or the greedy
and swindlers, or idolaters.

[l] 5 Or *that his body*; or *that the flesh*

since you would then need
to go out of the world.
11 But now I am writing to
you not to associate with
anyone who bears the
name of brother or sister[u]
who is sexually immoral or
greedy, or is an idolater, re-
viler, drunkard, or robber.
Do not even eat with such a
one. 12 For what have I to
do with judging those outside? Is it not those who are
inside that you are to
judge? 13 God will judge
those outside. "Drive out
the wicked person from
among you."

Chapter 6

Lawsuits among Believers

WHEN any of you has
a grievance against
another, do you dare to
take it to court before the
unrighteous, instead of taking it before the saints? 2 Do
you not know that the
saints will judge the world?
And if the world is to be
judged by you, are you in-
competent to try trivial
cases? 3 Do you not know
that we are to judge
angels—to say nothing of
ordinary matters? 4 If you
have ordinary cases, then,
do you appoint as judges
those who have no standing
in the church? 5 I say this to
your shame. Can it be that
there is no one among you
wise enough to decide be-
tween one believer[u] and
another, 6 but a believer[u]
goes to court against a
believer[u]—and before unbelievers at that?
7 In fact, to have law-
suits at all with one another
is already a defeat for you.
Why not rather be
wronged? Why not rather
be defrauded? 8 But you
yourselves wrong and
defraud—and believers[v]
at that.
9 Do you not know that
wrongdoers will not inherit
the kingdom of God? Do
not be deceived! Fornica-

[u] Gk *brother*
[v] Gk *brothers*

ἢ εἰδωλολάτραις, ἐπεὶ ὠφείλετε ἄρα ἐκ
or idolaters, since ye ought then out of

τοῦ κόσμου ἐξελθεῖν. 11 νῦν δὲ ἔγραψα
the world to go *out*. But now I wrote

ὑμῖν μὴ συναναμίγνυσθαι ἐάν τις ἀδελφὸς
to you not to associate intimately with if anyone a brother

ὀνομαζόμενος ᾖ πόρνος ἢ πλεονέκτης ἢ
being named is a fornicator or a covetous man or

εἰδωλολάτρης ἢ λοίδορος ἢ μέθυσος ἢ
an idolater or a railer or a drunkard or

ἅρπαξ, τῷ τοιούτῳ μηδὲ συνεσθίειν. 12 τί
a rapacious man, with such a man not to eat *with*. what

γάρ μοι τοὺς ἔξω κρίνειν; οὐχὶ τοὺς
For [is it] to me [2]the ones [3]without [1]to judge? [1]Not [4]the ones

ἔσω ὑμεῖς κρίνετε; 13 τοὺς δὲ ἔξω
[5]within [2]ye [3]judge? But the ones without

ὁ θεὸς κρινεῖ. ἐξάρατε τὸν πονηρὸν ἐξ
– God will judge. Remove the evil man out of

ὑμῶν αὐτῶν.
yourselves.

6 Τολμᾷ τις ὑμῶν πρᾶγμα ἔχων πρὸς
Dares anyone of you [2]a matter [1]having against

τὸν ἕτερον κρίνεσθαι ἐπὶ τῶν ἀδίκων,
the(an) other to be judged before the unjust,

καὶ οὐχὶ ἐπὶ τῶν ἁγίων; 2 ἢ οὐκ οἴδατε
and not before the saints? or know ye not

ὅτι οἱ ἅγιοι τὸν κόσμον κρινοῦσιν; καὶ
that the saints the world will judge? and

εἰ ἐν ὑμῖν κρίνεται ὁ κόσμος, ἀνάξιοί
if [4]by [5]you [3]is judged [1]the [2]world, [6]unworthy

ἐστε κριτηρίων ἐλαχίστων; 3 οὐκ οἴδατε
[7]are ye [9]judgments? [8]of very little? Know ye not

ὅτι ἀγγέλους κρινοῦμεν, μήτι γε βιωτικά;
that angels we will judge, not to speak of things of this life?

4 βιωτικὰ μὲν οὖν κριτήρια ἐὰν ἔχητε,
[6]Of this life [4]indeed [2]therefore [5]judgments [1]if [3]ye have,

τοὺς ἐξουθενημένους ἐν τῇ ἐκκλησίᾳ,
the ones *being* despised in the church,

τούτους καθίζετε; 5 πρὸς ἐντροπὴν ὑμῖν
these sit ye? For shame to you

λέγω. οὕτως οὐκ ἔνι ἐν ὑμῖν οὐδεὶς
I say. Thus there is no room among you [for] *no* one

σοφός, ὃς δυνήσεται διακρῖναι ἀνὰ μέσον
wise man, who will be able to discern in your midst

τοῦ ἀδελφοῦ αὐτοῦ; 6 ἀλλὰ ἀδελφὸς μετὰ
the brother of him? But brother with

ἀδελφοῦ κρίνεται, καὶ τοῦτο ἐπὶ ἀπίστων;
brother is judged, and this before unbelievers?

7 ἤδη μὲν οὖν ὅλως ἥττημα ὑμῖν ἐστιν
Now indeed therefore [2]altogether [3]a failure [4]with you [1]there is

ὅτι κρίματα ἔχετε μεθ' ἑαυτῶν. διὰ τί
[5]that [7]lawsuits [6]ye have with yourselves. Why

οὐχὶ μᾶλλον ἀδικεῖσθε; διὰ τί οὐχὶ
not rather be wronged? Why not

μᾶλλον ἀποστερεῖσθε; 8 ἀλλὰ ὑμεῖς ἀδικεῖτε
rather be deprived? But ye do wrong

καὶ ἀποστερεῖτε, καὶ τοῦτο ἀδελφούς.
and deprive, and this brothers.

9 ἢ οὐκ οἴδατε ὅτι ἄδικοι θεοῦ βασιλείαν
Or know ye not that unrighteous men [3]of God [2][the] kingdom

οὐ κληρονομήσουσιν; μὴ πλανᾶσθε· οὔτε
[1]will not inherit? Be not led astray; not

In that case you would
have to leave this world.
11 But now I am writing you
that you must not associate
with anyone who calls himself a brother but is sexually immoral or greedy, an
idolater or a slanderer, a
drunkard or a swindler.
With such a man do not
even eat.
12 What business is it of
mine to judge those outside
the church? Are you not to
judge those inside? 13 God
will judge those outside.
"Expel the wicked man
from among you."[m]

Chapter 6

Lawsuits Among Believers

IF any of you has a dis-
pute with another, dare
he take it before the ungodly for judgment instead of
before the saints? 2 Do you
not know that the saints
will judge the world? And if
you are to judge the world,
are you not competent to
judge trivial cases? 3 Do you
not know that we will judge
angels? How much more
the things of this life!
4 Therefore, if you have disputes about such matters,
appoint as judges even men
of little account in the
church![n] 5 I say this to
shame you. Is it possible
that there is nobody among
you wise enough to judge a
dispute between believers?
6 But instead, one brother
goes to law against another
—and this in front of unbelievers!
7 The very fact that you
have lawsuits among you
means you have been com-
pletely defeated already.
Why not rather be
wronged? Why not rather
be cheated? 8 Instead, you
yourselves cheat and do
wrong, and you do this to
your brothers.
9 Do you not know that
the wicked will not inherit
the kingdom of God? Do

[m] *13* Deut. 17:7; 19:19; 21:21; 22:21,24; 24:7
[n] *4* Or *matters, do you appoint as judges men of little account in the church?*

tors, idolaters, adulterers,
male prostitutes, sodom-
ites, 10 thieves, the greedy,
drunkards, revilers,
robbers—none of these
will inherit the kingdom of
God. 11 And this is what
some of you used to be. But
you were washed, you
were sanctified, you were
justified in the name of the
Lord Jesus Christ and in
the Spirit of our God.

Glorify God in Body and Spirit

12 "All things are lawful
for me," but not all things
are beneficial. "All things
are lawful for me," but I
will not be dominated by
anything. 13 "Food is meant
for the stomach and the
stomach for food,"[w] and
God will destroy both one
and the other. The body is
meant not for fornication
but for the Lord, and the
Lord for the body. 14 And
God raised the Lord and
will also raise us by his
power. 15 Do you not know
that your bodies are mem-
bers of Christ? Should I
therefore take the members
of Christ and make them
members of a prostitute?
Never! 16 Do you not know
that whoever is united to a
prostitute becomes one
body with her? For it is
said, "The two shall be one
flesh." 17 But anyone united
to the Lord becomes one
spirit with him. 18 Shun fornication! Every sin that a
person commits is outside
the body; but the fornicator
sins against the body itself.
19 Or do you not know that
your body is a temple[x] of

[w] The quotation may extend to the word *other*

[x] Or *sanctuary*

πόρνοι οὔτε εἰδωλολάτραι οὔτε μοιχοὶ
fornicators nor idolaters nor adulterers

οὔτε μαλακοὶ οὔτε ἀρσενοκοῖται **10** οὔτε
nor voluptuous persons nor sodomites nor

κλέπται οὔτε πλεονέκται, οὐ μέθυσοι,
thieves nor covetous persons, not drunkards,

οὐ λοίδοροι, οὐχ ἅρπαγες βασιλείαν θεοῦ
not revilers, not rapacious persons 2[the] kingdom 3of God

κληρονομήσουσιν. **11** καὶ ταῦτά τινες ἦτε·
1will inherit. And these things 2some [of you] 1*ye* were;

ἀλλὰ ἀπελούσασθε, ἀλλὰ ἡγιάσθητε, ἀλλὰ
but ye were washed, but ye were sanctified, but

ἐδικαιώθητε ἐν τῷ ὀνόματι τοῦ κυρίου
ye were justified in the name of the Lord

Ἰησοῦ Χριστοῦ καὶ ἐν τῷ πνεύματι
Jesus Christ and by the Spirit

τοῦ θεοῦ ἡμῶν.
of the God of us.

12 Πάντα μοι ἔξεστιν, ἀλλ' οὐ πάντα
All things to me [are] lawful, but not all things

συμφέρει. πάντα μοι ἔξεστιν, ἀλλ' οὐκ
expedient. All things to me [are] lawful, but not

ἐγὼ ἐξουσιασθήσομαι ὑπό τινος. **13** τὰ
I will be ruled by anyone. –

βρώματα τῇ κοιλίᾳ, καὶ ἡ κοιλία τοῖς
Foods for the belly, and the belly –

βρώμασιν· ὁ δὲ θεὸς καὶ ταύτην καὶ
for foods; – but God both this and

ταῦτα καταργήσει. τὸ δὲ σῶμα οὐ τῇ
these will destroy. But the body [is] not –

πορνείᾳ ἀλλὰ τῷ κυρίῳ, καὶ ὁ κύριος
for fornication but for the Lord, and the Lord

τῷ σώματι· **14** ὁ δὲ θεὸς καὶ τὸν κύριον
for the body; – and God both the Lord

ἤγειρεν καὶ ἡμᾶς ἐξεγερεῖ διὰ τῆς
raised and us will raise up through the

δυνάμεως αὐτοῦ. **15** οὐκ οἴδατε ὅτι τὰ
power of him. Know ye not that the

σώματα ὑμῶν μέλη Χριστοῦ ἐστιν; ἄρας
bodies of you members of Christ (is)are? Taking

οὖν τὰ μέλη τοῦ Χριστοῦ ποιήσω πόρνης
therefore the members – of Christ shall I make [them] 2of a harlot

μέλη; μὴ γένοιτο. **16** ἢ οὐκ οἴδατε ὅτι
1members? May it not be. Or know ye not that

ὁ κολλώμενος τῇ πόρνῃ ἓν σῶμά ἐστιν;
the [one] *being* joined – to a harlot one body is?

ἔσονται γάρ, φησίν, οἱ δύο εἰς σάρκα
For 4will be, 3he says, 1the 2two 5into 7flesh

μίαν. **17** ὁ δὲ κολλώμενος τῷ κυρίῳ
6one. But the [one] *being* joined to the Lord

ἓν πνεῦμά ἐστιν. **18** φεύγετε τὴν πορνείαν.
one spirit is. Flee ye – fornication.

πᾶν ἁμάρτημα ὃ ἐὰν ποιήσῃ ἄνθρωπος
Every sin whichever 2may do 1a man

ἐκτὸς τοῦ σώματός ἐστιν· ὁ δὲ πορνεύων
outside the body is; but the [one] committing fornication

εἰς τὸ ἴδιον σῶμα ἁμαρτάνει. **19** ἢ
against the(his) own body sins. Or

οὐκ οἴδατε ὅτι τὸ σῶμα ὑμῶν ναὸς
know ye not that the body of you 2a shrine

τοῦ ἐν ὑμῖν ἁγίου πνεύματός ἐστιν,
3of the 6in 7you 4Holy 5Spirit 1is,

not be deceived: Neither
the sexually immoral nor
idolaters nor adulterers nor
male prostitutes nor homo-
sexual offenders 10 nor
thieves nor the greedy nor
drunkards nor slanderers
nor swindlers will inherit
the kingdom of God. 11 And
that is what some of you
were. But you were
washed, you were sancti-
fied, you were justified in
the name of the Lord Jesus
Christ and by the Spirit of
our God.

Sexual Immorality

12 "Everything is permis-
sible for me"—but not ev-
erything is beneficial. "Everything is permissible for
me"—but I will not be
mastered by anything.
13 "Food for the stomach
and the stomach for food"
—but God will destroy
them both. The body is not
meant for sexual immorality, but for the Lord, and the
Lord for the body. 14 By his
power God raised the Lord
from the dead, and he will
raise us also. 15 Do you not
know that your bodies are
members of Christ himself?
Shall I then take the members of Christ and unite
them with a prostitute?
Never! 16 Do you not know
that he who unites himself
with a prostitute is one with
her in body? For it is said,
"The two will become one
flesh."[o] 17 But he who
unites himself with the
Lord is one with him in
spirit.
18 Flee from sexual immo-
rality. All other sins a man
commits are outside his
body, but he who sins sexually sins against his own
body. 19 Do you not know
that your body is a temple
of the Holy Spirit, who is in

[o] *16* Gen. 2:24

the Holy Spirit within you, which you have from God, and that you are not your own? 20 For you were bought with a price; therefore glorify God in your body.

Chapter 7

Directions concerning Marriage

NOW concerning the matters about which you wrote: "It is well for a man not to touch a woman." 2 But because of cases of sexual immorality, each man should have his own wife and each woman her own husband. 3 The husband should give to his wife her conjugal rights, and likewise the wife to her husband. 4 For the wife does not have authority over her own body, but the husband does; likewise the husband does not have authority over his own body, but the wife does. 5 Do not deprive one another except perhaps by agreement for a set time, to devote yourselves to prayer, and then come together again, so that Satan may not tempt you because of your lack of self-control. 6 This I say by way of concession, not of command. 7 I wish that all were as I myself am. But each has a particular gift from God, one having one kind and another a different kind.

8 To the unmarried and the widows I say that it is well for them to remain unmarried as I am. 9 But if they are not practicing self-control, they should marry. For it is better to marry than to be aflame with passion.

10 To the married I give this command—not I but the Lord—that the wife should not separate from her husband 11 (but if she does separate, let her re-

οὗ ἔχετε ἀπὸ θεοῦ, καὶ οὐκ ἐστὲ ἑαυτῶν;
which ye have from God, and ye are not of yourselves?

20 ἠγοράσθητε γὰρ τιμῆς· δοξάσατε δὴ
For ye were bought of(with) a price; glorify ye then

τὸν θεὸν ἐν τῷ σώματι ὑμῶν.
– God in the body of you.

7 Περὶ δὲ ὧν ἐγράψατε, καλὸν ἀνθρώπῳ
Now about things of which ye wrote, [it is] good for a man

γυναικὸς μὴ ἅπτεσθαι· 2 διὰ δὲ τὰς
[3]a woman* [1]not [2]to touch; but because of the

πορνείας ἕκαστος τὴν ἑαυτοῦ γυναῖκα
fornications each man [2]the [4]of himself [3]wife

ἐχέτω, καὶ ἑκάστη τὸν ἴδιον ἄνδρα
[1]let him have, and each woman the(her) own husband

ἐχέτω. 3 τῇ γυναικὶ ὁ ἀνὴρ τὴν ὀφειλὴν
let her have. To the wife [2]the [3]husband [4]the [5]debt

ἀποδιδότω, ὁμοίως δὲ καὶ ἡ γυνὴ τῷ
[1]let *him* pay, and likewise also the wife to the

ἀνδρί. 4 ἡ γυνὴ τοῦ ἰδίου σώματος
husband. The wife of the(her) own body

οὐκ ἐξουσιάζει ἀλλὰ ὁ ἀνήρ· ὁμοίως
has not authority but the husband; [2]likewise

δὲ καὶ ὁ ἀνὴρ τοῦ ἰδίου σώματος οὐκ
[1]and also the husband of the(his) own body not

ἐξουσιάζει ἀλλὰ ἡ γυνή. 5 μὴ ἀποστερεῖτε
has authority but the wife. Deprive not ye

ἀλλήλους, εἰ μήτι ἂν ἐκ συμφώνου πρὸς
each other, unless by agreement for

καιρὸν ἵνα σχολάσητε τῇ προσευχῇ καὶ
a time in order that ye may have leisure – for prayer and

πάλιν ἐπὶ τὸ αὐτὸ ἦτε, ἵνα μὴ πειράζῃ
[2]again [3]together [1]*ye* may be, lest [2]tempt

ὑμᾶς ὁ σατανᾶς διὰ τὴν ἀκρασίαν [ὑμῶν].
[3]you – [1]Satan because of the want of self-control of you.

6 τοῦτο δὲ λέγω κατὰ συγγνώμην, οὐ
Now this I say by allowance, not

κατ' ἐπιταγήν. 7 θέλω δὲ πάντας
by command. And I wish all

ἀνθρώπους εἶναι ὡς καὶ ἐμαυτόν· ἀλλὰ
men to be as even myself; but

ἕκαστος ἴδιον ἔχει χάρισμα ἐκ θεοῦ,
each man [2][his] own [1]has gift of God,

ὁ μὲν οὕτως, ὁ δὲ οὕτως.
one thus, another thus.

8 Λέγω δὲ τοῖς ἀγάμοις καὶ ταῖς χήραις,
Now I say to the unmarried men and to the widows,

καλὸν αὐτοῖς ἐὰν μείνωσιν ὡς κἀγώ· 9 εἰ δὲ
[it is] good for them if they remain as I also; but if

οὐκ ἐγκρατεύονται, γαμησάτωσαν· κρεῖττον
they do not exercise self-control, let them marry; better

γάρ ἐστιν γαμεῖν ἢ πυροῦσθαι. 10 τοῖς
for it is to marry than to burn. to the [ones]

δὲ γεγαμηκόσιν παραγγέλλω, οὐκ ἐγὼ
But having married I enjoin, not I

ἀλλὰ ὁ κύριος, γυναῖκα ἀπὸ ἀνδρὸς μὴ
but the Lord, a woman from [her] husband not

χωρισθῆναι, 11 — ἐὰν δὲ καὶ χωρισθῇ,
to be separated,[b] but if indeed she is separated,

you, whom you have received from God? You are not your own; 20 you were bought at a price. Therefore honor God with your body.

Chapter 7

Marriage

NOW for the matters you wrote about: It is good for a man not to marry.[p] 2 But since there is so much immorality, each man should have his own wife, and each woman her own husband. 3 The husband should fulfill his marital duty to his wife, and likewise the wife to her husband. 4 The wife's body does not belong to her alone but also to her husband. In the same way, the husband's body does not belong to him alone but also to his wife. 5 Do not deprive each other except by mutual consent and for a time, so that you may devote yourselves to prayer. Then come together again so that Satan will not tempt you because of your lack of self-control. 6 I say this as a concession, not as a command. 7 I wish that all men were as I am. But each man has his own gift from God; one has this gift, another has that.

8 Now to the unmarried and the widows I say: It is good for them to stay unmarried, as I am. 9 But if they cannot control themselves, they should marry, for it is better to marry than to burn with passion.

10 To the married I give this command (not I, but the Lord): A wife must not separate from her husband. 11 But if she does, she must

* As the same Greek word γυνή means "wife" or "(?married) woman" it is not always easy to differentiate in translating. So also the one Greek word ἀνήρ means "man" or "husband"

p1 Or "*It is good for a man not to have sexual relations with a woman.*"

main unmarried or else be
reconciled to her husband),
and that the husband
should not divorce his wife.
12 To the rest I say—I
and not the Lord—that if
any believer[y] has a wife
who is an unbeliever, and
she consents to live with
him, he should not divorce
her. 13 And if any woman
has a husband who is an unbeliever, and he consents
to live with her, she should
not divorce him. 14 For the
unbelieving husband is
made holy through his
wife, and the unbelieving
wife is made holy through
her husband. Otherwise,
your children would be unclean, but as it is, they are
holy. 15 But if the unbelieving partner separates, let it
be so; in such a case the
brother or sister is not
bound. It is to peace that
God has called you.[z]
16 Wife, for all you know,
you might save your hus-
band. Husband, for all you
know, you might save your
wife.

The Life That the Lord Has Assigned

17 However that may
be, let each of you lead the
life that the Lord has assigned, to which God called
you. This is my rule in all
the churches. 18 Was any-
one at the time of his call
already circumcised? Let
him not seek to remove the
marks of circumcision.
Was anyone at the time of
his call uncircumcised? Let
him not seek circumcision.
19 Circumcision is nothing,
and uncircumcision is nothing; but obeying the com-
mandments of God is ev-
erything. 20 Let each of you
remain in the condition in
which you were called.
21 Were you a slave
when called? Do not be
concerned about it. Even if
you can gain your freedom,
make use of your present
condition now more than
ever.[a] 22 For whoever was

[y] Gk *brother*
[z] Other ancient authorities read *us*
[a] Or *avail yourself of the opportunity*

μενέτω ἄγαμος ἢ τῷ ἀνδρὶ καταλλαγήτω,
let her remain unmarried or to the(her) husband be reconciled,

— καὶ ἄνδρα γυναῖκα μὴ ἀφιέναι. 12 Τοῖς
and a husband [his] wife not to leave.[b] to the

δὲ λοιποῖς λέγω ἐγώ, οὐχ ὁ κύριος·
And rest say I, not the Lord:

εἴ τις ἀδελφὸς γυναῖκα ἔχει ἄπιστον, καὶ
If any brother [2]a wife [1]has unbelieving, and

αὕτη συνευδοκεῖ οἰκεῖν μετ' αὐτοῦ, μὴ
this one consents to dwell with him, not

ἀφιέτω αὐτήν· 13 καὶ γυνὴ ἥτις ἔχει
let him leave her; and a woman who has

ἄνδρα ἄπιστον, καὶ οὗτος συνευδοκεῖ οἰκεῖν
a husband unbelieving, and this one consents to dwell

μετ' αὐτῆς, μὴ ἀφιέτω τὸν ἄνδρα.
with her, let her not leave the(her) husband.

14 ἡγίασται γὰρ ὁ ἀνὴρ ὁ ἄπιστος ἐν
For [4]has been sanctified [1]the [3]husband – [2]unbelieving by

τῇ γυναικί, καὶ ἡγίασται ἡ γυνὴ ἡ
the wife, and [4]has been sanctified [1]the [3]wife –

ἄπιστος ἐν τῷ ἀδελφῷ· ἐπεὶ ἄρα τὰ
[2]unbelieving by the brother; since then the

τέκνα ὑμῶν ἀκάθαρτά ἐστιν, νῦν δὲ
children of you [2]unclean [1]is(are), but now

ἅγιά ἐστιν. 15 εἰ δὲ ὁ ἄπιστος χωρίζ-
[2]holy [1]they are. But if the unbelieving one separates

εται, χωριζέσθω· οὐ δεδούλωται ὁ
him/herself, let him/her be separated; [6]has not been enslaved [1]the

ἀδελφὸς ἢ ἡ ἀδελφὴ ἐν τοῖς τοιούτοις·
[2]brother [3]or [4]the [5]sister in such matters;

ἐν δὲ εἰρήνῃ κέκληκεν ὑμᾶς ὁ θεός.
but [4]in [5]peace [2]has called [3]you – [1]God.

16 τί γὰρ οἶδας, γύναι, εἰ τὸν ἄνδρα
For what knowest thou, wife, if the(thy) husband

σώσεις; ἢ τί οἶδας, ἄνερ, εἰ τὴν
thou wilt save? or what knowest thou, husband, if the(thy)

γυναῖκα σώσεις; 17 Εἰ μὴ ἑκάστῳ ὡς
wife thou wilt save? Only [5]to each [1]as

μεμέρικεν ὁ κύριος, ἕκαστον ὡς κέκληκεν
[4]has divided [2]the [3]Lord, [4]each [1]as [3]has called

ὁ θεός, οὕτως περιπατείτω. καὶ οὕτως
– [2]God, so let him walk. And so

ἐν ταῖς ἐκκλησίαις πάσαις διατάσσομαι.
[2]in [4]the [5]churches [3]all [1]I command.

18 περιτετμημένος τις ἐκλήθη; μὴ
[4]Having been circumcised [2]anyone [1]was [3]called? not

ἐπισπάσθω· ἐν ἀκροβυστίᾳ κέκληταί τις;
let him be uncircumcised; in uncircumcision has been called anyone?

μὴ περιτεμνέσθω. 19 ἡ περιτομὴ οὐδέν
let him not be circumcised. – Circumcision nothing

ἐστιν, καὶ ἡ ἀκροβυστία οὐδέν ἐστιν,
is, and – uncircumcision nothing is,

ἀλλὰ τήρησις ἐντολῶν θεοῦ. 20 ἕκαστος
but [the] keeping of commandments of God. Each one

ἐν τῇ κλήσει ᾗ ἐκλήθη, ἐν ταύτῃ
in the calling in which he was called, in this

μενέτω. 21 δοῦλος ἐκλήθης; μή σοι
let him remain. A slave wast thou called? not to thee

μελέτω· ἀλλ' εἰ καὶ δύνασαι ἐλεύθερος
let it matter; but if indeed thou art able [2]free

γενέσθαι, μᾶλλον χρῆσαι. 22 ὁ γὰρ ἐν
[1]to become, [2]rather [1]use [it]. For [1]the [one] [4]in

remain unmarried or else
be reconciled to her hus-
band. And a husband must
not divorce his wife.
12 To the rest I say this (I,
not the Lord): If any brother has a wife who is not a
believer and she is willing
to live with him, he must
not divorce her. 13 And if a
woman has a husband who
is not a believer and he is
willing to live with her, she
must not divorce him.
14 For the unbelieving husband has been sanctified
through his wife, and the
unbelieving wife has been
sanctified through her believing husband. Otherwise
your children would be unclean, but as it is, they are
holy.
15 But if the unbeliever
leaves, let him do so. A believing man or woman is
not bound in such circum-
stances; God has called us
to live in peace. 16 How do
you know, wife, whether
you will save your hus-
band? Or, how do you
know, husband, whether
you will save your wife?
17 Nevertheless, each one
should retain the place in
life that the Lord assigned
to him and to which God
has called him. This is the
rule I lay down in all the
churches. 18 Was a man already circumcised when he
was called? He should not
become uncircumcised.
Was a man uncircumcised
when he was called? He
should not be circumcised.
19 Circumcision is nothing
and uncircumcision is nothing. Keeping God's com-
mands is what counts.
20 Each one should remain
in the situation which he
was in when God called
him. 21 Were you a slave
when you were called?
Don't let it trouble you—
although if you can gain
your freedom, do so. 22 For

called in the Lord as a slave
is a freed person belonging
to the Lord, just as whoever was free when called is a
slave of Christ. 23 You were
bought with a price; do not
become slaves of human
masters. 24 In whatever
condition you were called,
brothers and sisters,[b]
there remain with God.

The Unmarried and the Widows

25 Now concerning vir-
gins, I have no command of
the Lord, but I give my
opinion as one who by the
Lord's mercy is trustwor-
thy. 26 I think that, in view
of the impending[c] crisis, it
is well for you to remain as
you are. 27 Are you bound
to a wife? Do not seek to be
free. Are you free from a
wife? Do not seek a wife.
28 But if you marry, you do
not sin, and if a virgin marries, she does not sin. Yet
those who marry will experience distress in this life,[d]
and I would spare you that.
29 I mean, brothers and sisters,[b] the appointed time
has grown short; from now
on, let even those who have
wives be as though they
had none, 30 and those who
mourn as though they were
not mourning, and those
who rejoice as though they
were not rejoicing, and
those who buy as though
they had no possessions,
31 and those who deal with
the world as though they
had no dealings with it. For
the present form of this
world is passing away.
32 I want you to be free
from anxieties. The unmarried man is anxious about
the affairs of the Lord, how
to please the Lord; 33 but
the married man is anxious
about the affairs of the

κυρίῳ κληθεὶς δοῦλος ἀπελεύθερος κυρίου
[5][the] Lord [1]called [3]a slave [7]a freed man [8]of [the] Lord
ἐστίν· ὁμοίως ὁ ἐλεύθερος κληθεὶς δοῦλός
[6]is; likewise [1]the [one] [3]a free man [2]called [5]a slave
ἐστιν Χριστοῦ. 23 τιμῆς ἠγοράσθητε· μὴ
[4]is [6]of Christ. Of(with) a price ye were bought; not
γίνεσθε δοῦλοι ἀνθρώπων. 24 ἕκαστος ἐν
become ye slaves of men. Each one in
ᾧ ἐκλήθη, ἀδελφοί, ἐν τούτῳ μενέτω
what [state] he was called, brothers, in this let him remain
παρὰ θεῷ.
with God.
25 Περὶ δὲ τῶν παρθένων ἐπιταγὴν
Now about the virgins a command
κυρίου οὐκ ἔχω, γνώμην δὲ δίδωμι ὡς
of [the] Lord I have not, but an opinion I give as
ἠλεημένος ὑπὸ κυρίου πιστὸς εἶναι.
having had mercy by [the] Lord faithful to be.
26 Νομίζω οὖν τοῦτο καλὸν ὑπάρχειν
I suppose therefore this good to be
διὰ τὴν ἐνεστῶσαν ἀνάγκην, ὅτι καλὸν
because of the present necessity, that [it is] good
ἀνθρώπῳ τὸ οὕτως εἶναι. 27 δέδεσαι
for a man – so to be. Hast thou been bound
γυναικί; μὴ ζήτει λύσιν· λέλυσαι ἀπὸ
to a woman? do not seek release; hast thou been released from
γυναικός; μὴ ζήτει γυναῖκα. 28 ἐὰν
a woman? do not seek a woman. if
δὲ καὶ γαμήσῃς, οὐχ ἥμαρτες, καὶ ἐὰν
But indeed thou marriest, thou sinnedst not, and if
γήμῃ ἡ παρθένος, οὐχ ἥμαρτεν· θλῖψιν
[3]marries [1]the [2]virgin, she sinned not; [3]affliction
δὲ τῇ σαρκὶ ἕξουσιν οἱ τοιοῦτοι, ἐγὼ
but [4]in the [5]flesh [2]will have – [1]such, [2]I
δὲ ὑμῶν φείδομαι. 29 Τοῦτο δέ φημι,
[1]and [4]you [3]am sparing. But this I say,
ἀδελφοί, ὁ καιρὸς συνεσταλμένος ἐστίν·
brothers, the time *having been* shortened is;
τὸ λοιπὸν ἵνα καὶ οἱ ἔχοντες γυναῖκας
for the rest in order that both the [ones] having wives
ὡς μὴ ἔχοντες ὦσιν, 30 καὶ οἱ κλαίοντες
as not having may be, and the [ones] weeping
ὡς μὴ κλαίοντες, καὶ οἱ χαίροντες ὡς
as not weeping, and the [ones] rejoicing as
μὴ χαίροντες, καὶ οἱ ἀγοράζοντες ὡς
not rejoicing, and the [ones] buying as
μὴ κατέχοντες, 31 καὶ οἱ χρώμενοι τὸν
not holding, and the [ones] using the
κόσμον ὡς μὴ καταχρώμενοι· παράγει
world as not abusing [it]; [4]is passing away
γὰρ τὸ σχῆμα τοῦ κόσμου τούτου.
for [1]the [2]fashion [3]of this world.
32 Θέλω δὲ ὑμᾶς ἀμερίμνους εἶναι. ὁ
But I wish you without care to be. The
ἄγαμος μεριμνᾷ τὰ τοῦ κυρίου, 33 πῶς
unmarried man cares for the things of the Lord, how
ἀρέσῃ τῷ κυρίῳ· ὁ δὲ γαμήσας μεριμνᾷ
he may please the Lord; but the [one] having married cares for

he who was a slave when he
was called by the Lord is
the Lord's freedman; similarly, he who was a free
man when he was called is
Christ's slave. 23 You were
bought at a price; do not become slaves of men.
24 Brothers, each man, as
responsible to God, should
remain in the situation God
called him to.
25 Now about virgins: I
have no command from the
Lord, but I give a judgment
as one who by the Lord's
mercy is trustworthy. 26 Because of the present crisis,
I think that it is good for
you to remain as you are.
27 Are you married? Do not
seek a divorce. Are you unmarried? Do not look for a
wife. 28 But if you do marry,
you have not sinned; and if
a virgin marries, she has
not sinned. But those who
marry will face many troubles in this life, and I want
to spare you this.
29 What I mean, brothers,
is that the time is short.
From now on those who
have wives should live as if
they had none; 30 those who
mourn, as if they did not;
those who are happy, as if
they were not; those who
buy something, as if it were
not theirs to keep; 31 those
who use the things of the
world, as if not engrossed
in them. For this world in
its present form is passing
away.
32 I would like you to be
free from concern. An un-
married man is concerned
about the Lord's affairs—
how he can please the
Lord. 33 But a married man
is concerned about the af-

[b] Gk *brothers*
[c] Or *present*
[d] Gk *in the flesh*

world, how to please his wife, [34]and his interests are divided. And the unmarried woman and the virgin are anxious about the affairs of the Lord, so that they may be holy in body and spirit; but the married woman is anxious about the affairs of the world, how to please her husband. [35]I say this for your own benefit, not to put any restraint upon you, but to promote good order and unhindered devotion to the Lord.

36 If anyone thinks that he is not behaving properly toward his fiancée,[e] if his passions are strong, and so it has to be, let him marry as he wishes; it is no sin. Let them marry. [37]But if someone stands firm in his resolve, being under no necessity but having his own desire under control, and has determined in his own mind to keep her as his fiancée,[e] he will do well. [38]So then, he who marries his fiancée[e] does well; and he who refrains from marriage will do better.

39 A wife is bound as long as her husband lives. But if the husband dies,[f] she is free to marry anyone she wishes, only in the Lord. [40]But in my judgment she is more blessed if she remains as she is. And I think that I too have the Spirit of God.

Chapter 8

Food Offered to Idols

NOW concerning food sacrificed to idols: we know that "all of us pos-

[e] Gk *virgin*
[f] Gk *falls asleep*

τὰ τοῦ κόσμου, πῶς ἀρέσῃ τῇ γυναικί,
the things of the world, how he may please the(his) wife,

34 καὶ μεμέρισται. καὶ ἡ γυνὴ ἡ ἄγαμος
and has been divided. And the [2]woman – [1]unmarried

καὶ ἡ παρθένος μεριμνᾷ τὰ τοῦ κυρίου,
and the virgin cares for the things of the Lord,

ἵνα ᾖ ἁγία καὶ τῷ σώματι καὶ τῷ
in order that she may be holy both in the body and in the

πνεύματι· ἡ δὲ γαμήσασα μεριμνᾷ τὰ
spirit; but the [one] having married cares for the things

τοῦ κόσμου, πῶς ἀρέσῃ τῷ ἀνδρί.
of the world, how she may please the(her) husband.

35 τοῦτο δὲ πρὸς τὸ ὑμῶν αὐτῶν σύμφορον
And [2]this [3]for [4]the [6]of yourselves [5]advantage

λέγω, οὐχ ἵνα βρόχον ὑμῖν ἐπιβάλω,
[1]I say, not in order that [3]a restraint [2]you [1]I may put on,

ἀλλὰ πρὸς τὸ εὔσχημον καὶ εὐπάρεδρον
but for the thing comely and waiting on

τῷ κυρίῳ ἀπερισπάστως. **36** Εἰ δέ τις
the Lord undistractedly. But if anyone

ἀσχημονεῖν ἐπὶ τὴν παρθένον αὐτοῦ
[2]to behave dishonourably [3]toward [4]the [5]virgin [6]of him

νομίζει, ἐὰν ᾖ ὑπέρακμος, καὶ οὕτως
[1]thinks, if he/she is past the bloom of youth, and so

ὀφείλει γίνεσθαι, ὃ θέλει ποιείτω· οὐχ
ought to be, what he wishes let him do; not

ἁμαρτάνει· γαμείτωσαν. **37** ὃς δὲ ἕστηκεν
he sins; let them marry. But [he] who stands

ἐν τῇ καρδίᾳ αὐτοῦ ἑδραῖος, μὴ
in the heart of him firm, not

ἔχων ἀνάγκην, ἐξουσίαν δὲ ἔχει περὶ
having necessity, but authority has concerning

τοῦ ἰδίου θελήματος, καὶ τοῦτο κέκρικεν
the(his) own will, and this has decided

ἐν τῇ ἰδίᾳ καρδίᾳ, τηρεῖν τὴν ἑαυτοῦ
in the(his) own heart, to keep the of himself

παρθένον, καλῶς ποιήσει. **38** ὥστε καὶ
virgin, [2]well [1]he will do. So as both

ὁ γαμίζων τὴν ἑαυτοῦ παρθένον καλῶς
the [one] marrying the of himself virgin [2]well

ποιεῖ, καὶ ὁ μὴ γαμίζων κρεῖσσον ποιήσει.
[1]does, and the [one] not marrying [2]better [1]will do.

39 Γυνὴ δέδεται ἐφ' ὅσον χρόνον ζῇ
A wife has been bound for so long a time as lives

ὁ ἀνὴρ αὐτῆς· ἐὰν δὲ κοιμηθῇ ὁ ἀνήρ,
the husband of her; but if sleeps the husband,

ἐλευθέρα ἐστὶν ᾧ θέλει γαμηθῆναι, μόνον
[2]free [1]she is [4]to whom [5]she wishes [3]to be married, only

ἐν κυρίῳ. **40** μακαριωτέρα δέ ἐστιν
in [the] Lord. But happier she is

ἐὰν οὕτως μείνῃ, κατὰ τὴν ἐμὴν γνώμην·
if so she remains, according to – my opinion;

δοκῶ δὲ κἀγὼ πνεῦμα θεοῦ ἔχειν.
and I think I also [the] Spirit of God *to* have.

8 Περὶ δὲ τῶν εἰδωλοθύτων, οἴδαμεν
Now about *the* idolatrous sacrifices, we know

fairs of this world—how he can please his wife— [34]and his interests are divided. An unmarried woman or virgin is concerned about the Lord's affairs: Her aim is to be devoted to the Lord in both body and spirit. But a married woman is concerned about the affairs of this world—how she can please her husband. [35]I am saying this for your own good, not to restrict you, but that you may live in a right way in undivided devotion to the Lord.

[36]If anyone thinks he is acting improperly toward the virgin he is engaged to, and if she is getting along in years and he feels he ought to marry, he should do as he wants. He is not sinning. They should get married. [37]But the man who has settled the matter in his own mind, who is under no compulsion but has control over his own will, and who has made up his mind not to marry the virgin—this man also does the right thing. [38]So then, he who marries the virgin does right, but he who does not marry her does even better.[q]

[39]A woman is bound to her husband as long as he lives. But if her husband dies, she is free to marry anyone she wishes, but he must belong to the Lord. [40]In my judgment, she is happier if she stays as she is—and I think that I too have the Spirit of God.

Chapter 8

Food Sacrificed to Idols

NOW about food sacrificed to idols: We

[q] 36-38 Or [36]*If anyone thinks he is not treating his daughter properly, and if she is getting along in years, and he feels she ought to marry, he should do as he wants. He is not sinning. He should let her get married.* [37]*But the man who has settled the matter in his own mind, who is under no compulsion but has control over his own will, and who has made up his mind to keep the virgin unmarried—this man also does the right thing.* [38]*So then, he who gives his virgin in marriage does right, but he who does not give her in marriage does even better.*

sess knowledge." Knowl-
edge puffs up, but love
builds up. 2 Anyone who
claims to know something
does not yet have the necessary knowledge; 3 but
anyone who loves God is
known by him.
4 Hence, as to the eat-
ing of food offered to idols,
we know that "no idol in
the world really exists,"
and that "there is no God
but one." 5 Indeed, even
though there may be so-
called gods in heaven or on
earth—as in fact there are
many gods and many
lords— 6 yet for us there is
one God, the Father, from
whom are all things and for
whom we exist, and one
Lord, Jesus Christ, through
whom are all things and
through whom we exist.
7 It is not everyone,
however, who has this
knowledge. Since some
have become so accus-
tomed to idols until now,
they still think of the food
they eat as food offered to
an idol; and their con-
science, being weak, is defiled. 8 "Food will not bring
us close to God."[g] We are
no worse off if we do not
eat, and no better off if we
do. 9 But take care that this
liberty of yours does not
somehow become a stum-
bling block to the weak.
10 For if others see you,
who possess knowledge,
eating in the temple of an
idol, might they not, since
their conscience is weak,
be encouraged to the point
of eating food sacrificed to
idols? 11 So by your knowledge those weak believers
for whom Christ died are
destroyed.[h] 12 But when
you thus sin against mem-
bers of your family,[i] and
wound their conscience
when it is weak, you sin

[g] The quotation may extend to the end of the verse
[h] Gk *the weak brother . . . is destroyed*
[i] Gk *against the brothers*

ὅτι πάντες γνῶσιν ἔχομεν. ἡ γνῶσις
that [2]all [4]knowledge [1]we [3]have. – Knowledge
φυσιοῖ, ἡ δὲ ἀγάπη οἰκοδομεῖ· εἴ τις
puffs up, – but love builds up; if anyone
δοκεῖ ἐγνωκέναι τι, 2 οὔπω ἔγνω καθὼς
thinks to have known anything, not yet he knew as
δεῖ γνῶναι· 3 εἰ δέ τις ἀγαπᾷ τὸν
it behoves [him] to know; but if anyone loves –
θεόν, οὗτος ἔγνωσται ὑπ' αὐτοῦ. 4 Περὶ
God, this one has been known by him. About
τῆς βρώσεως οὖν τῶν εἰδωλοθύτων
the eating therefore – of idolatrous sacrifices
οἴδαμεν ὅτι οὐδὲν εἴδωλον ἐν κόσμῳ,
we know that [there is] no idol in [the] world,
καὶ ὅτι οὐδεὶς θεὸς εἰ μὴ εἷς. 5 καὶ
and that [there is] no God except one. even
γὰρ εἴπερ εἰσὶν λεγόμενοι θεοὶ εἴτε ἐν
For if there are *being* called gods either in
οὐρανῷ εἴτε ἐπὶ γῆς, ὥσπερ εἰσὶν θεοὶ
heaven or on earth, even as there are gods
πολλοὶ καὶ κύριοι πολλοί, 6 ἀλλ' ἡμῖν
many and lords many, yet to us
εἷς θεὸς ὁ πατήρ, ἐξ οὗ τὰ πάντα καὶ
[there is] one God the Father, of whom – [are] all things and
ἡμεῖς εἰς αὐτόν, καὶ εἷς κύριος Ἰησοῦς
we in him, and one Lord Jesus
Χριστός, δι' οὗ τὰ πάντα καὶ ἡμεῖς
Christ, through whom – [are] all things and we
δι' αὐτοῦ. 7 Ἀλλ' οὐκ ἐν πᾶσιν ἡ
through him. But [there is] not in all men the (this)
γνῶσις· τινὲς δὲ τῇ συνηθείᾳ ἕως ἄρτι
knowledge; and some by *the* habit until now
τοῦ εἰδώλου ὡς εἰδωλόθυτον ἐσθίουσιν,
[2]of the [3]idol [4]as [5]an idolatrous sacrifice [1]eat,
καὶ ἡ συνείδησις αὐτῶν ἀσθενὴς οὖσα
and the conscience of them [2]weak [1]being
μολύνεται. 8 βρῶμα δὲ ἡμᾶς οὐ παραστήσει
is defiled. But food [2]us [1]will not commend
τῷ θεῷ· οὔτε ἐὰν μὴ φάγωμεν ὑστερούμεθα,
– to God; neither if we eat not are we behind,
οὔτε ἐὰν φάγωμεν περισσεύομεν. 9 βλέπετε
nor if we eat do we excel. look ye
δὲ μή πως ἡ ἐξουσία ὑμῶν αὕτη
But lest somehow *the* [2]authority [3]of you [1]this
πρόσκομμα γένηται τοῖς ἀσθενέσιν. 10 ἐὰν
a stumbling-block becomes to the weak ones. if
γάρ τις ἴδῃ σὲ τὸν ἔχοντα γνῶσιν ἐν
For anyone sees thee the [one] having knowledge [2]in
εἰδωλείῳ κατακείμενον, οὐχὶ ἡ συνείδησις
[3]an idol's temple [1]sitting, [2]not [3]the [4]conscience
αὐτοῦ ἀσθενοῦς ὄντος οἰκοδομηθήσεται εἰς
[5]of him [7]weak [6][he] being[a] [1]will [8]be emboldened –
τὸ τὰ εἰδωλόθυτα ἐσθίειν; 11 ἀπόλλυται
– [10]the [11]idolatrous sacrifices [9]to eat? [3]is destroyed
γὰρ ὁ ἀσθενῶν ἐν τῇ σῇ γνώσει, ὁ
For [1]the [one] [2]being weak by – thy knowledge, the
ἀδελφὸς δι' ὃν Χριστὸς ἀπέθανεν. 12 οὕτως
brother because of whom Christ died. so
δὲ ἁμαρτάνοντες εἰς τοὺς ἀδελφοὺς καὶ
And sinning against the brothers and
τύπτοντες αὐτῶν τὴν συνείδησιν ἀσθενοῦσαν
wounding of them the conscience being weak

know that we all possess
knowledge.[r] Knowledge
puffs up, but love builds
up. 2 The man who thinks
he knows something does
not yet know as he ought to
know. 3 But the man who
loves God is known by
God.
4 So then, about eating
food sacrificed to idols: We
know that an idol is nothing
at all in the world and that
there is no God but one.
5 For even if there are so-
called gods, whether in
heaven or on earth (as indeed there are many
"gods" and many
"lords"), 6 yet for us there
is but one God, the Father,
from whom all things came
and for whom we live; and
there is but one Lord, Jesus
Christ, through whom all
things came and through
whom we live.
7 But not everyone knows
this. Some people are still
so accustomed to idols that
when they eat such food
they think of it as having
been sacrificed to an idol,
and since their conscience
is weak, it is defiled. 8 But
food does not bring us near
to God; we are no worse if
we do not eat, and no better
if we do.
9 Be careful, however,
that the exercise of your
freedom does not become a
stumbling block to the
weak. 10 For if anyone with
a weak conscience sees
you who have this knowl-
edge eating in an idol's temple, won't he be embold-
ened to eat what has been
sacrificed to idols? 11 So this
weak brother, for whom
Christ died, is destroyed by
your knowledge. 12 When
you sin against your brothers in this way and wound
their weak conscience, you
sin against Christ. 13 There-

[r] 1 Or *"We all possess knowledge," as you say*

against Christ. [13]Therefore, if food is a cause of their falling,[j] I will never eat meat, so that I may not cause one of them[k] to fall.

εἰς Χριστὸν ἁμαρτάνετε. 13 διόπερ εἰ
[2]against [3]Christ [1]ye sin. Wherefore if
βρῶμα σκανδαλίζει τὸν ἀδελφόν μου, οὐ
food offends the brother of me, by no
μὴ φάγω κρέα εἰς τὸν αἰῶνα, ἵνα μὴ
means I eat flesh unto the age, lest
τὸν ἀδελφόν μου σκανδαλίσω.
[2]the [3]brother [4]of me [1]I offend.

fore, if what I eat causes my brother to fall into sin, I will never eat meat again, so that I will not cause him to fall.

Chapter 9

The Rights of an Apostle

AM I not free? Am I not an apostle? Have I not seen Jesus our Lord? Are you not my work in the Lord? [2]If I am not an apostle to others, at least I am to you; for you are the seal of my apostleship in the Lord.
3 This is my defense to those who would examine me. [4]Do we not have the right to our food and drink? [5]Do we not have the right to be accompanied by a believing wife,[l] as do the other apostles and the brothers of the Lord and Cephas? [6]Or is it only Barnabas and I who have no right to refrain from working for a living? [7]Who at any time pays the expenses for doing military service? Who plants a vineyard and does not eat any of its fruit? Or who tends a flock and does not get any of its milk?
8 Do I say this on human authority? Does not the law also say the same? [9]For it is written in the law of Moses, "You shall not muzzle an ox while it is treading out the grain." Is it for oxen that God is concerned? [10]Or does he not speak entirely for our sake? It was indeed written for our sake, for whoever plows should plow in hope and whoever threshes should thresh in hope of a share in the crop. [11]If we have sown spiritual good among you, is it too much if we reap your material ben-

9 Οὐκ εἰμὶ ἐλεύθερος; οὐκ εἰμὶ ἀπόστολος;
Am I not free? am I not an apostle?
οὐχὶ Ἰησοῦν τὸν κύριον ἡμῶν ἑόρακα;
not Jesus the Lord of us I have seen?
οὐ τὸ ἔργον μου ὑμεῖς ἐστε ἐν κυρίῳ;
not the work of me ye are in [the] Lord?
2 εἰ ἄλλοις οὐκ εἰμὶ ἀπόστολος, ἀλλά
If to others I am not an apostle, yet
γε ὑμῖν εἰμι· ἡ γὰρ σφραγίς μου τῆς
indeed to you I am; for the seal [2]of me [1]of the
ἀποστολῆς ὑμεῖς ἐστε ἐν κυρίῳ. 3 Ἡ
[3]apostleship ye are in [the] Lord. –
ἐμὴ ἀπολογία τοῖς ἐμὲ ἀνακρίνουσίν ἐστιν
My defence to the [ones] [2]me [1]examining is
αὕτη. 4 μὴ οὐκ ἔχομεν ἐξουσίαν φαγεῖν
this. *not* Have we not authority to eat
καὶ πεῖν; 5 μὴ οὐκ ἔχομεν ἐξουσίαν
and to drink? *not* have we not authority
ἀδελφὴν γυναῖκα περιάγειν, ὡς καὶ οἱ
a sister a wife to lead about, as also the
λοιποὶ ἀπόστολοι καὶ οἱ ἀδελφοὶ τοῦ
remaining apostles and the brothers of the
κυρίου καὶ Κηφᾶς; 6 ἢ μόνος ἐγὼ καὶ
Lord and Cephas? or only I and
Βαρναβᾶς οὐκ ἔχομεν ἐξουσίαν μὴ
Barnabas have we not authority not
ἐργάζεσθαι; 7 Τίς στρατεύεται ἰδίοις
to work? Who soldiers at [his] own
ὀψωνίοις ποτέ; τίς φυτεύει ἀμπελῶνα καὶ
wages at any time? who plants a vineyard and
τὸν καρπὸν αὐτοῦ οὐκ ἐσθίει; ἢ τίς
the fruit of it eats not? or who
ποιμαίνει ποίμνην καὶ ἐκ τοῦ γάλακτος
shepherds a flock and of the milk
τῆς ποίμνης οὐκ ἐσθίει; 8 μὴ κατὰ
of the flock eats not? *Not* according to
ἄνθρωπον ταῦτα λαλῶ, ἢ καὶ ὁ νόμος
man these things I speak, or also the law
ταῦτα οὐ λέγει; 9 ἐν γὰρ τῷ Μωϋσέως
these things says not? for in the of Moses
νόμῳ γέγραπται· οὐ κημώσεις βοῦν
law it has been written: Thou shalt not muzzle an ox
ἀλοῶντα. μὴ τῶν βοῶν μέλει τῷ θεῷ;
threshing. *not* – of oxen matters it – to God?
10 ἢ δι' ἡμᾶς πάντως λέγει; δι' ἡμᾶς
or because of us altogether he says? because of us
γὰρ ἐγράφη, ὅτι ὀφείλει ἐπ' ἐλπίδι
for it was written, because [3]ought [4]on(in) [5]hope
ὁ ἀροτριῶν ἀροτριᾶν, καὶ ὁ ἀλοῶν ἐπ'
[1]the [one] [2]ploughing [6]to plough, and the [one] threshing on(in)
ἐλπίδι τοῦ μετέχειν. 11 εἰ ἡμεῖς ὑμῖν
hope of the to partake. =of partaking. If we to you
τὰ πνευματικὰ ἐσπείραμεν, μέγα εἰ ἡμεῖς
– spiritual things sowed, [is it] a great thing if we

Chapter 9

The Rights of an Apostle

AM I not free? Am I not an apostle? Have I not seen Jesus our Lord? Are you not the result of my work in the Lord? [2]Even though I may not be an apostle to others, surely I am to you! For you are the seal of my apostleship in the Lord.
[3]This is my defense to those who sit in judgment on me. [4]Don't we have the right to food and drink? [5]Don't we have the right to take a believing wife along with us, as do the other apostles and the Lord's brothers and Cephas[s]? [6]Or is it only I and Barnabas who must work for a living?
[7]Who serves as a soldier at his own expense? Who plants a vineyard and does not eat of its grapes? Who tends a flock and does not drink of the milk? [8]Do I say this merely from a human point of view? Doesn't the Law say the same thing? [9]For it is written in the Law of Moses: "Do not muzzle an ox while it is treading out the grain."[t] Is it about oxen that God is concerned? [10]Surely he says this for us, doesn't he? Yes, this was written for us, because when the plowman plows and the thresher threshes, they ought to do so in the hope of sharing in the harvest. [11]If we have sown spiritual seed among

[j] Gk *my brother's falling*
[k] Gk *cause my brother*
[l] Gk *a sister as wife*

[s] 5 That is, Peter
[t] 9 Deut. 25:4

efits? 12If others share this
rightful claim on you, do
not we still more?
Nevertheless, we have
not made use of this right,
but we endure anything
rather than put an obstacle
in the way of the gospel of
Christ. 13Do you not know
that those who are em-
ployed in the temple ser-
vice get their food from the
temple, and those who
serve at the altar share in
what is sacrificed on the altar? 14In the same way, the
Lord commanded that
those who proclaim the
gospel should get their living by the gospel.
15 But I have made no
use of any of these rights,
nor am I writing this so that
they may be applied in my
case. Indeed, I would rather die than that—no one
will deprive me of my
ground for boasting! 16If I
proclaim the gospel, this
gives me no ground for
boasting, for an obligation
is laid on me, and woe to
me if I do not proclaim the
gospel! 17For if I do this of
my own will, I have a re-
ward; but if not of my own
will, I am entrusted with a
commission. 18What then
is my reward? Just this:
that in my proclamation I
may make the gospel free
of charge, so as not to make
full use of my rights in the
gospel.
19 For though I am free
with respect to all, I have
made myself a slave to all,
so that I might win more of
them. 20To the Jews I be-
came as a Jew, in order to
win Jews. To those under
the law I became as one under the law (though I my-
self am not under the law)
so that I might win those
under the law. 21To those

ὑμῶν τὰ σαρκικὰ θερίσομεν; 12 εἰ ἄλλοι
of you – fleshly things shall reap? If others

τῆς ὑμῶν ἐξουσίας μετέχουσιν, οὐ
[3]of the [4]of you [5]authority [1]have a share *of*, not

μᾶλλον ἡμεῖς; ἀλλ' οὐκ ἐχρησάμεθα
rather we? But we did not use

τῇ ἐξουσίᾳ ταύτῃ, ἀλλὰ πάντα στέγομεν
this authority, but [2]all things [1]we put up with

ἵνα μή τινα ἐγκοπὴν δῶμεν τῷ εὐαγγελίῳ
lest [2]anyone [3]an obstacle [1]we should give to the gospel

τοῦ Χριστοῦ. 13 Οὐκ οἴδατε ὅτι οἱ
– of Christ. Know ye not that the [ones]

τὰ ἱερὰ ἐργαζόμενοι τὰ ἐκ τοῦ ἱεροῦ
– [2]sacred things [1]working [at] [4]the things [5]of [6]the [7]temple

ἐσθίουσιν, οἱ τῷ θυσιαστηρίῳ παρεδρεύοντες
[3]eat, the [ones] [2]the [3]altar [1]attending [on]

τῷ θυσιαστηρίῳ συμμερίζονται; 14 οὕτως
[5]the [6]altar [4]partake with? So

καὶ ὁ κύριος διέταξεν τοῖς τὸ εὐαγγέλιον
also the Lord ordained the [ones] [2]the [3]gospel

καταγγέλλουσιν ἐκ τοῦ εὐαγγελίου ζῆν.
[1]announcing [5]of [6]the [7]gospel [4]to live.

15 ἐγὼ δὲ οὐ κέχρημαι οὐδενὶ τούτων.
But I have not used *not* one of these things.

Οὐκ ἔγραψα δὲ ταῦτα ἵνα οὕτως γένηται
And I did not write these things in order that so it might be

ἐν ἐμοί· καλὸν γάρ μοι μᾶλλον ἀποθανεῖν
in me; for good [it is] to me rather to die

ἢ — τὸ καύχημά μου οὐδεὶς κενώσει.
than — the boast of me no man shall empty.

16 ἐὰν γὰρ εὐαγγελίζωμαι, οὐκ ἔστιν
For if I preach good news, there is not =I have no boast;

μοι καύχημα· ἀνάγκη γάρ μοι ἐπίκειται·
to me boast;[c] for necessity [2]me [1]is laid on;

οὐαὶ γάρ μοί ἐστιν ἐὰν μὴ εὐαγγελίσωμαι.
for woe [2]to me [1]is if I do not preach good tidings.

17 εἰ γὰρ ἑκὼν τοῦτο πράσσω, μισθὸν
For if willingly [2]this [1]I do, [2]a reward

ἔχω· εἰ δὲ ἄκων, οἰκονομίαν πεπίστευμαι.
[1]I have; but if unwillingly, [2]a stewardship [1]I have been entrusted [with].

18 τίς οὖν μού ἐστιν ὁ μισθός; ἵνα
What therefore [4]of me [1]is [2]the [3]reward? *in order that*

εὐαγγελιζόμενος ἀδάπανον θήσω τὸ
preaching good tidings [4]without charge [1]I may place [2]the

εὐαγγέλιον, εἰς τὸ μὴ καταχρήσασθαι
[3]good tidings, so as† not to use to the full

τῇ ἐξουσίᾳ μου ἐν τῷ εὐαγγελίῳ.
the authority of me in the good tidings.

19 Ἐλεύθερος γὰρ ὢν ἐκ πάντων πᾶσιν
For [2]free [1]being of all men [3]to all men

ἐμαυτὸν ἐδούλωσα, ἵνα τοὺς πλείονας
[2]myself [1]I enslaved, in order that the more

κερδήσω· 20 καὶ ἐγενόμην τοῖς Ἰουδαίοις
I might gain; and I became to the Jews

ὡς Ἰουδαῖος, ἵνα Ἰουδαίους κερδήσω·
as a Jew, in order that Jews I might gain;

τοῖς ὑπὸ νόμον ὡς ὑπὸ νόμον, μὴ ὢν
to the ones under law as under law, not being

αὐτὸς ὑπὸ νόμον, ἵνα τοὺς ὑπὸ νόμον
[my]self under law, in order that the ones under law

you, is it too much if we
reap a material harvest
from you? 12If others have
this right of support from
you, shouldn't we have it
all the more?
But we did not use this
right. On the contrary, we
put up with anything rather
than hinder the gospel of
Christ. 13Don't you know
that those who work in the
temple get their food from
the temple, and those who
serve at the altar share in
what is offered on the altar?
14In the same way, the
Lord has commanded that
those who preach the gos-
pel should receive their living from the gospel.
15But I have not used any
of these rights. And I am
not writing this in the hope
that you will do such things
for me. I would rather die
than have anyone deprive
me of this boast. 16Yet
when I preach the gospel, I
cannot boast, for I am compelled to preach. Woe to
me if I do not preach the
gospel! 17If I preach voluntarily, I have a reward; if
not voluntarily, I am simply discharging the trust
committed to me. 18What
then is my reward? Just
this: that in preaching the
gospel I may offer it free of
charge, and so not make
use of my rights in preaching it.
19Though I am free and
belong to no man, I make
myself a slave to everyone,
to win as many as possible.
20To the Jews I became like
a Jew, to win the Jews. To
those under the law I be-
came like one under the law
(though I myself am not under the law), so as to win
those under the law. 21To

outside the law I became as one outside the law (though I am not free from God's law but am under Christ's law) so that I might win those outside the law. 22 To the weak I became weak, so that I might win the weak. I have become all things to all people, that I might by all means save some. 23 I do it all for the sake of the gospel, so that I may share in its blessings.
24 Do you not know that in a race the runners all compete, but only one receives the prize? Run in such a way that you may win it. 25 Athletes exercise self-control in all things; they do it to receive a perishable wreath, but we an imperishable one. 26 So I do not run aimlessly, nor do I box as though beating the air; 27 but I punish my body and enslave it, so that after proclaiming to others I myself should not be disqualified.

κερδήσω· **21** τοῖς ἀνόμοις ὡς ἄνομος,
I might gain; to the ones without law as without law,
μὴ ὢν ἄνομος θεοῦ ἀλλ' ἔννομος Χριστοῦ,
not being without [the] law of God but under [the] law of Christ,
ἵνα κερδάνω τοὺς ἀνόμους· **22** ἐγενόμην
in order that I may gain the ones without law; I became
τοῖς ἀσθενέσιν ἀσθενής, ἵνα τοὺς ἀσθενεῖς
[2]to the [3]weak [1]weak, in order that the weak
κερδήσω· τοῖς πᾶσιν γέγονα πάντα, ἵνα
I might gain; – to all men I have become all things, in order that
πάντως τινὰς σώσω. **23** πάντα δὲ ποιῶ
in any case [2]some [1]I might save. But all things I do
διὰ τὸ εὐαγγέλιον, ἵνα συγκοινωνὸς αὐτοῦ
because of the good tidings, in order that [2]a joint partaker [3]of it
γένωμαι. **24** Οὐκ οἴδατε ὅτι οἱ ἐν
[1]I may become. Know ye not that the [ones] [2]in
σταδίῳ τρέχοντες πάντες μὲν τρέχουσιν,
[3]a racecourse [1]running all indeed run,
εἷς δὲ λαμβάνει τὸ βραβεῖον; οὕτως
but one receives the prize? So
τρέχετε ἵνα καταλάβητε. **25** πᾶς δὲ ὁ
run in order that ye may obtain. And everyone
ἀγωνιζόμενος πάντα ἐγκρατεύεται, ἐκεῖνοι
struggling [in] all things exercises self-control, those
μὲν οὖν ἵνα φθαρτὸν στέφανον λάβωσιν,
indeed therefore in order that [2]a corruptible [3]crown [1]they may receive,
ἡμεῖς δὲ ἄφθαρτον. **26** ἐγὼ τοίνυν οὕτως
but we an incorruptible. I accordingly so
τρέχω ὡς οὐκ ἀδήλως, οὕτως πυκτεύω
run as not unclearly, so I box
ὡς οὐκ ἀέρα δέρων· **27** ἀλλὰ ὑπωπιάζω
as not [2]air [1]beating; but I treat severely
μου τὸ σῶμα καὶ δουλαγωγῶ, μή πως
of me the body and lead [it] as a slave, lest
ἄλλοις κηρύξας αὐτὸς ἀδόκιμος γένωμαι.
to others having proclaimed [2][my]self [5]disapproved [1]I [3]may [4]become.

those not having the law I became like one not having the law (though I am not free from God's law but am under Christ's law), so as to win those not having the law. 22 To the weak I became weak, to win the weak. I have become all things to all men so that by all possible means I might save some. 23 I do all this for the sake of the gospel, that I may share in its blessings.
24 Do you not know that in a race all the runners run, but only one gets the prize? Run in such a way as to get the prize. 25 Everyone who competes in the games goes into strict training. They do it to get a crown that will not last; but we do it to get a crown that will last forever. 26 Therefore I do not run like a man running aimlessly; I do not fight like a man beating the air. 27 No, I beat my body and make it my slave so that after I have preached to others, I myself will not be disqualified for the prize.

Chapter 10

Warnings from Israel's History

I do not want you to be unaware, brothers and sisters,[m] that our ancestors were all under the cloud, and all passed through the sea, 2 and all were baptized into Moses in the cloud and in the sea, 3 and all ate the same spiritual food, 4 and all drank the same spiritual drink. For they drank from the spiritual rock that followed them, and the rock was Christ. 5 Nevertheless, God was not pleased with most of them, and they were struck down in the wilderness.

10 Οὐ θέλω γὰρ ὑμᾶς ἀγνοεῖν, ἀδελφοί,
For I wish not you to be ignorant, brothers,
ὅτι οἱ πατέρες ἡμῶν πάντες ὑπὸ τὴν
that the fathers of us all under the
νεφέλην ἦσαν καὶ πάντες διὰ τῆς θαλάσσης
cloud were and all through the sea
διῆλθον, **2** καὶ πάντες εἰς τὸν Μωϋσῆν
passed *through*, and all [2]to – [3]Moses
ἐβαπτίσαντο ἐν τῇ νεφέλῃ καὶ ἐν τῇ
[1]were baptized in the cloud and in the
θαλάσσῃ, **3** καὶ πάντες τὸ αὐτὸ πνευματικὸν
sea, and all [2]the [3]same [4]spiritual
βρῶμα ἔφαγον, **4** καὶ πάντες τὸ αὐτὸ
[5]food [1]ate, and all [2]the [3]same
πνευματικὸν ἔπιον πόμα· ἔπινον γὰρ ἐκ
[4]spiritual [1]drank [5]drink; for they drank of
πνευματικῆς ἀκολουθούσης πέτρας, ἡ πέτρα
a spiritual [2]following [1]rock, [2]the [3]rock
δὲ ἦν ὁ Χριστός. **5** 'Αλλ' οὐκ ἐν τοῖς
[1]and was *the* Christ. But [7]not [1]in(with) [2]the
πλείοσιν αὐτῶν εὐδόκησεν ὁ θεός·
[3]majority [4]of them [6]was [8]well [9]pleased – [5]God;
κατεστρώθησαν γὰρ ἐν τῇ ἐρήμῳ.
for they were scattered in the desert.

Chapter 10

Warnings From Israel's History

FOR I do not want you to be ignorant of the fact, brothers, that our forefathers were all under the cloud and that they all passed through the sea. 2 They were all baptized into Moses in the cloud and in the sea. 3 They all ate the same spiritual food 4 and drank the same spiritual drink; for they drank from the spiritual rock that accompanied them, and that rock was Christ. 5 Nevertheless, God was not pleased with most of them; their bodies were scattered over the desert.

[m] Gk *brothers*

6 Now these things oc-
curred as examples for us,
so that we might not desire
evil as they did. 7Do not
become idolaters as some
of them did; as it is written,
"The people sat down to
eat and drink, and they rose
up to play." 8We must not
indulge in sexual immorality as some of them did, and
twenty-three thousand fell
in a single day. 9We must
not put Christ[n] to the test,
as some of them did, and
were destroyed by ser-
pents. 10And do not com-
plain as some of them did,
and were destroyed by the
destroyer. 11These things
happened to them to serve
as an example, and they
were written down to in-
struct us, on whom the
ends of the ages have
come. 12So if you think you
are standing, watch out
that you do not fall. 13No
testing has overtaken you
that is not common to ev-
eryone. God is faithful, and
he will not let you be tested
beyond your strength, but
with the testing he will also
provide the way out so that
you may be able to endure
it.
14 Therefore, my dear
friends,[o] flee from the worship of idols. 15I speak as to
sensible people; judge for
yourselves what I say.
16The cup of blessing that
we bless, is it not a sharing
in the blood of Christ? The
bread that we break, is it
not a sharing in the body of
Christ? 17Because there is
one bread, we who are
many are one body, for we

[n] Other ancient authorities read *the Lord*
[o] Gk *my beloved*

6 ταῦτα δὲ τύποι ἡμῶν ἐγενήθησαν, εἰς
Now these things types of us were, for
τὸ μὴ εἶναι ἡμᾶς ἐπιθυμητὰς κακῶν,
the not to be us[b] longers after evil things,
=so that we should not be . . .
καθὼς κἀκεῖνοι ἐπεθύμησαν. 7 μηδὲ
as those indeed longed. Neither
εἰδωλολάτραι γίνεσθε, καθώς τινες αὐτῶν·
idolaters be ye, as some of them;
ὥσπερ γέγραπται· ἐκάθισεν ὁ λαὸς φαγεῖν
as it has been written: Sat the people to eat
καὶ πεῖν, καὶ ἀνέστησαν παίζειν. 8 μηδὲ
and to drink, and stood up to play. Neither
πορνεύωμεν, καθώς τινες αὐτῶν ἐπόρνευσαν
let us commit fornication, as some of them committed fornication
καὶ ἔπεσαν μιᾷ ἡμέρᾳ εἴκοσι τρεῖς
and fell in one day twenty-three
χιλιάδες. 9 μηδὲ ἐκπειράζωμεν τὸν κύριον,
thousands. Neither let us overtempt the Lord,
καθώς τινες αὐτῶν ἐπείρασαν καὶ ὑπὸ
as some of them tempted and by
τῶν ὄφεων ἀπώλλυντο. 10 μηδὲ γογγύζετε,
the serpents were destroyed. Neither murmur ye,
καθάπερ τινὲς αὐτῶν ἐγόγγυσαν, καὶ
even as some of them murmured, and
ἀπώλοντο ὑπὸ τοῦ ὀλεθρευτοῦ. 11 ταῦτα δὲ
were destroyed by the destroyer. Now these things
τυπικῶς συνέβαινεν ἐκείνοις, ἐγράφη δὲ
[2]typically [1]happened [3]to those men, and was(were) written
πρὸς νουθεσίαν ἡμῶν, εἰς οὓς τὰ
for admonition of us, to whom the
τέλη τῶν αἰώνων κατήντηκεν. 12 Ὥστε
ends of the ages has(ve) arrived. So as
ὁ δοκῶν ἑστάναι βλεπέτω μὴ πέσῃ.
the [one] thinking to stand let him look lest he falls.

13 πειρασμὸς ὑμᾶς οὐκ εἴληφεν εἰ μὴ
Temptation you has not taken except
ἀνθρώπινος· πιστὸς δὲ ὁ θεός, ὃς οὐκ
[what is] human; but faithful [is] – God, who not
ἐάσει ὑμᾶς πειρασθῆναι ὑπὲρ ὃ δύνασθε,
will allow you to be tempted beyond what you are able [to bear],
ἀλλὰ ποιήσει σὺν τῷ πειρασμῷ καὶ τὴν
but will make with the temptation also the
ἔκβασιν τοῦ δύνασθαι ὑπενεγκεῖν.
way out – to be able to endure.[d]
=so that ye may be able . . .

14 Διόπερ, ἀγαπητοί μου, φεύγετε ἀπὸ
Wherefore, beloved of me, flee ye from
τῆς εἰδωλολατρίας. 15 ὡς φρονίμοις λέγω·
– idolatry. [2]As [3]to prudent men [1]I say;
κρίνατε ὑμεῖς ὅ φημι. 16 Τὸ ποτήριον
judge ye what I say. The cup
τῆς εὐλογίας ὃ εὐλογοῦμεν, οὐχὶ κοινωνία
– of blessing which we bless, [2]not [3]a communion
ἐστὶν τοῦ αἵματος τοῦ Χριστοῦ; τὸν
[1]is it of the blood – of Christ? the
ἄρτον ὃν κλῶμεν, οὐχὶ κοινωνία τοῦ
bread which we break, [2]not [3]a communion [4]of the
σώματος τοῦ Χριστοῦ ἐστιν; 17 ὅτι εἷς
[5]body – [6]of Christ [1]is it? Because [4]one
ἄρτος, ἓν σῶμα οἱ πολλοί ἐσμεν· οἱ γὰρ
[5]bread, [6]one [7]body [2]the [3]many [1]we are; – for

6Now these things oc-
curred as examples[u] to
keep us from setting our
hearts on evil things as they
did. 7Do not be idolaters, as
some of them were; as it is
written: "The people sat
down to eat and drink and
got up to indulge in pagan
revelry."[v] 8We should not
commit sexual immorality,
as some of them did—and
in one day twenty-three
thousand of them died.
9We should not test the
Lord, as some of them did
—and were killed by
snakes. 10And do not grumble, as some of them did—
and were killed by the destroying angel.
11These things happened
to them as examples and
were written down as
warnings for us, on whom
the fulfillment of the ages
has come. 12So, if you think
you are standing firm, be
careful that you don't fall!
13No temptation has seized
you except what is com-
mon to man. And God is
faithful; he will not let you
be tempted beyond what
you can bear. But when
you are tempted, he will
also provide a way out so
that you can stand up under
it.

Idol Feasts and the Lord's Supper

14Therefore, my dear
friends, flee from idolatry.
15I speak to sensible people; judge for yourselves
what I say. 16Is not the cup
of thanksgiving for which
we give thanks a participation in the blood of Christ?
And is not the bread that
we break a participation in
the body of Christ? 17Be-
cause there is one loaf, we,
who are many, are one

[u]6 Or *types*; also in verse 11
[v]7 Exodus 32:6

all partake of the one bread. 18 Consider the people of Israel;[p] are not those who eat the sacrifices partners in the altar? 19 What do I imply then? That food sacrificed to idols is anything, or that an idol is anything? 20 No, I imply that what pagans sacrifice, they sacrifice to demons and not to God. I do not want you to be partners with demons. 21 You cannot drink the cup of the Lord and the cup of demons. You cannot partake of the table of the Lord and the table of demons. 22 Or are we provoking the Lord to jealousy? Are we stronger than he?

Do All to the Glory of God

23 "All things are lawful," but not all things are beneficial. "All things are lawful," but not all things build up. 24 Do not seek your own advantage, but that of the other. 25 Eat whatever is sold in the meat market without raising any question on the ground of conscience, 26 for "the earth and its fullness are the Lord's." 27 If an unbeliever invites you to a meal and you are disposed to go, eat whatever is set before you without raising any question on the ground of conscience. 28 But if someone says to you, "This has been offered in sacrifice," then do not eat it, out of consideration for the one who informed you, and for the sake of conscience— 29 I mean the other's conscience, not your own. For why should my liberty be subject to the judgment of someone else's conscience? 30 If I partake with thankfulness, why should I

[p] Gk *Israel according to the flesh*

πάντες ἐκ τοῦ ἑνὸς ἄρτου μετέχομεν.
all of the one bread we partake.

18 βλέπετε τὸν Ἰσραὴλ κατὰ σάρκα·
See ye – Israel according to [the] flesh;

οὐχ οἱ ἐσθίοντες τὰς θυσίας κοινωνοὶ
[2]not [3]the [ones] [4]eating [5]the [6]sacrifices [7]sharers

τοῦ θυσιαστηρίου εἰσίν; 19 τί οὖν φημι;
[8]of the [9]altar [1]are? What therefore do I say?

ὅτι εἰδωλόθυτόν τί ἐστιν; ἢ ὅτι εἴδωλόν
that an idolatrous sacrifice [2]anything [1]is? or that an idol

τί ἐστιν; 20 ἀλλ' ὅτι ἃ θύουσιν,
[2]anything [1]is? but that [the] things which they sacrifice,

δαιμονίοις καὶ οὐ θεῷ θύουσιν· οὐ θέλω
to demons and not to God they sacrifice; [2]not [3]I wish

δὲ ὑμᾶς κοινωνοὺς τῶν δαιμονίων γίνεσθαι.
[1]and you sharers of the demons to become.

21 οὐ δύνασθε ποτήριον κυρίου πίνειν
Ye cannot [2]a cup [3]of [the] Lord [1]*to* drink

καὶ ποτήριον δαιμονίων· οὐ δύνασθε
and a cup of demons; ye cannot

τραπέζης κυρίου μετέχειν καὶ τραπέζης
[2]of a table [3]of [the] Lord [1]*to* partake and of a table

δαιμονίων. 22 ἢ παραζηλοῦμεν τὸν κύριον;
of demons. Or do we make jealous the Lord?

μὴ ἰσχυρότεροι αὐτοῦ ἐσμεν;
Not [2]stronger [than] [3]he [1]are we?

23 Πάντα ἔξεστιν, ἀλλ' οὐ πάντα
All things [are] lawful, but not all things

συμφέρει· πάντα ἔξεστιν, ἀλλ' οὐ πάντα
are] expedient; all things [are] lawful, but not all things

οἰκοδομεῖ. 24 μηδεὶς τὸ ἑαυτοῦ ζητείτω
edifies(fy). No one the thing of himself let him seek

ἀλλὰ τὸ τοῦ ἑτέρου. 25 Πᾶν τὸ ἐν
but the thing of the other. Everything [2]in

μακέλλῳ πωλούμενον ἐσθίετε μηδὲν
[3]a meat market [1]*being* sold eat ye [2]nothing

ἀνακρίνοντες διὰ τὴν συνείδησιν· 26 τοῦ
[1]examining because of – conscience; [2]of the

κυρίου γὰρ ἡ γῆ καὶ τὸ πλήρωμα
[3]Lord [1]for the earth and the fulness

αὐτῆς. 27 εἴ τις καλεῖ ὑμᾶς τῶν ἀπίστων
of it. If anyone invites you of the unbelievers

καὶ θέλετε πορεύεσθαι, πᾶν τὸ παρατι-
and ye wish to go, [2]everything [3]*being* set

θέμενον ὑμῖν ἐσθίετε μηδὲν ἀνακρίνοντες
before [4]you [1]eat [6]nothing [5]examining

διὰ τὴν συνείδησιν. 28 ἐὰν δέ τις ὑμῖν
because of – conscience. But if anyone [2]to you

εἴπῃ· τοῦτο ἱερόθυτόν ἐστιν, μὴ ἐσθίετε
[1]says: This [2]slain in sacrifice [1]is, do not eat

δι' ἐκεῖνον τὸν μηνύσαντα καὶ τὴν
because of that man the [one] pointing out and –

συνείδησιν· 29 συνείδησιν δὲ λέγω οὐχὶ
conscience: [3]conscience [1]but [2]I say not

τὴν ἑαυτοῦ ἀλλὰ τὴν τοῦ ἑτέρου. ἱνατί
the one of himself but the one of the other.* why

γὰρ ἡ ἐλευθερία μου κρίνεται ὑπὸ ἄλλης
For the freedom of me is judged by [2]of another

συνειδήσεως; 30 εἰ ἐγὼ χάριτι μετέχω,
[1]conscience? If I by grace partake,

* That is, not the conscience of the person invited, to whom the apostle's words are addressed, but the conscience of the person "pointing out."

body, for we all partake of the one loaf.

18 Consider the people of Israel: Do not those who eat the sacrifices participate in the altar? 19 Do I mean then that a sacrifice offered to an idol is anything, or that an idol is anything? 20 No, but the sacrifices of pagans are offered to demons, not to God, and I do not want you to be participants with demons. 21 You cannot drink the cup of the Lord and the cup of demons too; you cannot have a part in both the Lord's table and the table of demons. 22 Are we trying to arouse the Lord's jealousy? Are we stronger than he?

The Believer's Freedom

23 "Everything is permissible"—but not everything is beneficial. "Everything is permissible"—but not everything is constructive. 24 Nobody should seek his own good, but the good of others.

25 Eat anything sold in the meat market without raising questions of conscience, 26 for, "The earth is the Lord's, and everything in it."[w]

27 If some unbeliever invites you to a meal and you want to go, eat whatever is put before you without raising questions of conscience. 28 But if anyone says to you, "This has been offered in sacrifice," then do not eat it, both for the sake of the man who told you and for conscience' sake[x]—29 the other man's conscience, I mean, not yours. For why should my freedom be judged by another's conscience? 30 If I take part in the meal with

[w] 26 Psalm 24:1

[x] 28 Some manuscripts *conscience' sake, for "the earth is the Lord's and everything in it"*

be denounced because of
that for which I give
thanks?
31 So, whether you eat
or drink, or whatever you
do, do everything for the
glory of God. 32 Give no offense to Jews or to Greeks
or to the church of God,
33 just as I try to please everyone in everything I do,
not seeking my own advan-
tage, but that of many, so
that they may be saved.
1 Be imitators of me, as I am
of Christ.

Head Coverings

2 I commend you be-
cause you remember me in
everything and maintain
the traditions just as I handed them on to you. 3 But I
want you to understand
that Christ is the head of
every man, and the hus-
band[q] is the head of his
wife,[r] and God is the head
of Christ. 4 Any man who
prays or prophesies with
something on his head disgraces his head, 5 but any
woman who prays or
prophesies with her head
unveiled disgraces her
head—it is one and the
same thing as having her
head shaved. 6 For if a
woman will not veil herself,
then she should cut off her
hair; but if it is disgraceful
for a woman to have her
hair cut off or to be shaved,
she should wear a veil.
7 For a man ought not to
have his head veiled, since
he is the image and reflection[s] of God; but woman is
the reflection[s] of man. 8 Indeed, man was not made
from woman, but woman
from man. 9 Neither was
man created for the sake of

[q] The same Greek word means *man* or *husband*
[r] Or *head of the woman*
[s] Or *glory*

τί βλασφημοῦμαι ὑπὲρ οὗ ἐγὼ εὐχαριστῶ;
why am I evil spoken of because of what I give thanks [for]?

31 Εἴτε οὖν ἐσθίετε εἴτε πίνετε εἴτε
Whether therefore ye eat or *ye* drink or

τι ποιεῖτε, πάντα εἰς δόξαν θεοῦ ποιεῖτε.
what[ever] ye do, all things to [the] glory of God do *ye*.

32 ἀπρόσκοποι καὶ Ἰουδαίοις γίνεσθε καὶ
²Without offence ³both ⁴to Jews ¹be ye ⁵and

Ἕλλησιν καὶ τῇ ἐκκλησίᾳ τοῦ θεοῦ,
⁶to Greeks and to the church – of God,

33 καθὼς κἀγὼ πάντα πᾶσιν ἀρέσκω,
as I also [in] all things all men please,

μὴ ζητῶν τὸ ἐμαυτοῦ σύμφορον ἀλλὰ
not seeking the of myself advantage but

τὸ τῶν πολλῶν, ἵνα σωθῶσιν. 11 μιμηταί
the (that) of the many, in order that they may be saved. Imitators

μου γίνεσθε, καθὼς κἀγὼ Χριστοῦ.
of me be ye, as I also [am] of Christ.

2 Ἐπαινῶ δὲ ὑμᾶς ὅτι πάντα μου
But I praise you because ²all things ³of me

μέμνησθε καὶ καθὼς παρέδωκα ὑμῖν τὰς
¹ye have remembered and ⁴as ⁵I delivered ⁶to you ²the

παραδόσεις κατέχετε. 3 Θέλω δὲ ὑμᾶς
³traditions ¹ye hold fast. But I wish you

εἰδέναι ὅτι παντὸς ἀνδρὸς ἡ κεφαλὴ ὁ
to know that ⁵of every ⁶man ³the ⁴head –

Χριστός ἐστιν, κεφαλὴ δὲ γυναικὸς ὁ
¹Christ ²is, and [the] head of a woman the

ἀνήρ, κεφαλὴ δὲ τοῦ Χριστοῦ ὁ θεός.
man, and [the] head – of Christ – God.

4 πᾶς ἀνὴρ προσευχόμενος ἢ προφητεύων
Every man praying or prophesying

κατὰ κεφαλῆς ἔχων καταισχύνει τὴν
³down over ⁴[his] head ¹having ²[anything] shames the

κεφαλὴν αὐτοῦ. 5 πᾶσα δὲ γυνὴ προσ-
head of him. But every woman pray-

ευχομένη ἢ προφητεύουσα ἀκατακαλύπτῳ
ing or prophesying ²unveiled

τῇ κεφαλῇ καταισχύνει τὴν κεφαλὴν αὐτῆς·
¹with the(her) ³head shames the head of her;

ἓν γάρ ἐστιν καὶ τὸ αὐτὸ τῇ ἐξυρημένῃ.
for ²one ¹it is and the same thing with the woman having been shaved.

6 εἰ γὰρ οὐ κατακαλύπτεται γυνή, καὶ
For if ²is not veiled ¹a woman, also

κειράσθω· εἰ δὲ αἰσχρὸν γυναικὶ τὸ
let her be shorn; but if shameful for a woman –

κείρασθαι ἢ ξυρᾶσθαι, κατακαλυπτέσθω.
to be shorn or *to be* shaved, let her be veiled.

7 ἀνὴρ μὲν γὰρ οὐκ ὀφείλει κατα-
For a man indeed ought not to be

καλύπτεσθαι τὴν κεφαλήν, εἰκὼν καὶ δόξα
veiled the head,[b] ²[the] image ³and ⁴glory

θεοῦ ὑπάρχων· ἡ γυνὴ δὲ δόξα ἀνδρός
⁵of God ¹being; but the woman ²[the] glory ³of a man

ἐστιν. 8 οὐ γάρ ἐστιν ἀνὴρ ἐκ γυναικός,
¹is. For ³not ²is ¹man of woman,

ἀλλὰ γυνὴ ἐξ ἀνδρός· 9 καὶ γὰρ οὐκ
but woman of man; for indeed ³not

thankfulness, why am I denounced because of some-
thing I thank God for?
31 So whether you eat or
drink or whatever you do,
do it all for the glory of
God. 32 Do not cause any-
one to stumble, whether
Jews, Greeks or the church
of God— 33 even as I try to
please everybody in every
way. For I am not seeking
my own good but the good
of many, so that they may
be saved. 1 Follow my ex-
ample, as I follow the example of Christ.

Propriety in Worship

2 I praise you for remem-
bering me in everything
and for holding to the
teachings,[y] just as I passed
them on to you.
3 Now I want you to real-
ize that the head of every
man is Christ, and the head
of the woman is man, and
the head of Christ is God.
4 Every man who prays or
prophesies with his head
covered dishonors his
head. 5 And every woman
who prays or prophesies
with her head uncovered
dishonors her head—it is
just as though her head
were shaved. 6 If a woman
does not cover her head,
she should have her hair
cut off; and if it is a disgrace
for a woman to have her
hair cut or shaved off, she
should cover her head. 7 A
man ought not to cover his
head,[z] since he is the image and glory of God; but
the woman is the glory of
man. 8 For man did not
come from woman, but
woman from man; 9 neither
was man created for wom-

[y] 2 Or *traditions*
[z] 4-7 Or *⁴Every man who prays or prophesies with long hair dishonors his head. ⁵And every woman who prays or prophesies with no covering of hair on her head dishonors her head—she is just like one of the "shorn women." ⁶If a woman has no covering, let her be for now with short hair, but since it is a disgrace for a woman to have her hair shorn or shaved, she should grow it again. ⁷A man ought not to have long hair*

woman, but woman for the
sake of man. 10 For this reason a woman ought to have
a symbol of[t] authority on
her head,[u] because of the
angels. 11 Nevertheless, in
the Lord woman is not in-
dependent of man or man
independent of woman.
12 For just as woman came
from man, so man comes
through woman; but all
things come from God.
13 Judge for yourselves: is it
proper for a woman to pray
to God with her head un-
veiled? 14 Does not nature
itself teach you that if a
man wears long hair, it is
degrading to him, 15 but if a
woman has long hair, it is
her glory? For her hair is
given to her for a covering.
16 But if anyone is disposed
to be contentious—we
have no such custom, nor
do the churches of God.

Abuses at the Lord's Supper

17 Now in the following
instructions I do not commend you, because when
you come together it is not
for the better but for the
worse. 18 For, to begin
with, when you come to-
gether as a church, I hear
that there are divisions
among you; and to some
extent I believe it. 19 Indeed, there have to be factions among you, for only
so will it become clear who
among you are genuine.
20 When you come togeth-
er, it is not really to eat the
Lord's supper. 21 For when
the time comes to eat, each
of you goes ahead with
your own supper, and one
goes hungry and another

ἐκτίσθη ἀνὴρ διὰ τὴν γυναῖκα, ἀλλὰ
[2]was [4]created [1]man because of the woman, but

γυνὴ διὰ τὸν ἄνδρα. **10** διὰ τοῦτο
woman because of the man. Therefore

ὀφείλει ἡ γυνὴ ἐξουσίαν ἔχειν ἐπὶ τῆς
ought the woman authority to have on the

κεφαλῆς διὰ τοὺς ἀγγέλους. **11** πλὴν
head because of the angels. Nevertheless

οὔτε γυνὴ χωρὶς ἀνδρὸς οὔτε ἀνὴρ χωρὶς
neither woman without man nor man without

γυναικὸς ἐν κυρίῳ· **12** ὥσπερ γὰρ ἡ
woman in [the] Lord; for as the

γυνὴ ἐκ τοῦ ἀνδρός, οὕτως καὶ ὁ ἀνὴρ
woman of the man, so also the man

διὰ τῆς γυναικός· τὰ δὲ πάντα ἐκ τοῦ
through the woman; – but all things of –

θεοῦ. **13** Ἐν ὑμῖν αὐτοῖς κρίνατε· πρέπον
God. Among you [your]selves judge: [2]fitting

ἐστὶν γυναῖκα ἀκατακάλυπτον τῷ θεῷ
[1]is it [3][for] [4]a woman [7]unveiled – [6]to God

προσεύχεσθαι; **14** οὐδὲ ἡ φύσις αὐτὴ
[5]to pray? Not – nature [her]self

διδάσκει ὑμᾶς ὅτι ἀνὴρ μὲν ἐὰν κομᾷ,
teaches you that a man indeed if he wears his hair long,

ἀτιμία αὐτῷ ἐστιν, **15** γυνὴ δὲ ἐὰν
[2]a dishonour [3]to him [1]it is, but a woman if

κομᾷ, δόξα αὐτῇ ἐστιν; ὅτι ἡ κόμη
she wears her hair long, [2]a glory [3]to her [1]it is? because the long hair

ἀντὶ περιβολαίου δέδοται αὐτῇ. **16** Εἰ
instead of a veil has been given to her. if

δέ τις δοκεῖ φιλόνεικος εἶναι, ἡμεῖς
But anyone thinks [2]contentious [1]to be, we

τοιαύτην συνήθειαν οὐκ ἔχομεν, οὐδὲ αἱ
[2]such [3]a custom [1]have not, neither the

ἐκκλησίαι τοῦ θεοῦ.
churches – of God.

17 Τοῦτο δὲ παραγγέλλων οὐκ ἐπαινῶ
But this charging I do not praise

ὅτι οὐκ εἰς τὸ κρεῖσσον ἀλλὰ εἰς τὸ
because not for the better but for the

ἧσσον συνέρχεσθε. **18** πρῶτον μὲν γὰρ
worse ye come together. For firstly indeed

συνερχομένων ὑμῶν ἐν ἐκκλησίᾳ ἀκούω
coming together you[a] in church I hear
=when ye come together

σχίσματα ἐν ὑμῖν ὑπάρχειν, καὶ μέρος
divisions among you to be, and [2]part

τι πιστεύω. **19** δεῖ γὰρ καὶ αἱρέσεις
[1]some I believe. For it behoves indeed sects

ἐν ὑμῖν εἶναι, ἵνα [καὶ] οἱ δόκιμοι
among you to be, in order that also the approved ones

φανεροὶ γένωνται ἐν ὑμῖν. **20** Συν-
manifest may become among you. Coming

ερχομένων οὖν ὑμῶν ἐπὶ τὸ αὐτὸ οὐκ
together therefore you[a] together not
=When therefore ye come

ἔστιν κυριακὸν δεῖπνον φαγεῖν· **21** ἕκαστος
it is of the Lord* a supper to eat; [2]each one

γὰρ τὸ ἴδιον δεῖπνον προλαμβάνει ἐν
[1]for the(his) own supper takes before in

τῷ φαγεῖν, καὶ ὃς μὲν πεινᾷ, ὃς δὲ
– to eat(eating), and one† hungers, another†

an, but woman for man.
10 For this reason, and because of the angels, the
woman ought to have a sign
of authority on her head.
11 In the Lord, however,
woman is not independent
of man, nor is man independent of woman. 12 For as
woman came from man, so
also man is born of woman.
But everything comes from
God. 13 Judge for your-
selves: Is it proper for a
woman to pray to God with
her head uncovered?
14 Does not the very nature
of things teach you that if a
man has long hair, it is a
disgrace to him, 15 but that
if a woman has long hair, it
is her glory? For long hair is
given to her as a covering.
16 If anyone wants to be
contentious about this, we
have no other practice—
nor do the churches of
God.

The Lord's Supper

17 In the following direc-
tives I have no praise for
you, for your meetings do
more harm than good. 18 In
the first place, I hear that
when you come together as
a church, there are divi-
sions among you, and to
some extent I believe it.
19 No doubt there have to be
differences among you to
show which of you have
God's approval. 20 When
you come together, it is not
the Lord's Supper you eat,
21 for as you eat, each of
you goes ahead without
waiting for anybody else.
One remains hungry, an-

[t] Gk lacks *a symbol of*
[u] Or *have freedom of choice regarding her head*

* Note that κυριακός is an adjective, for which no exact English equivalent is available. Only other occurrence in N.T., Rev. 1. 10.

becomes drunk. 22 What!
Do you not have homes to
eat and drink in? Or do you
show contempt for the
church of God and humili-
ate those who have noth-
ing? What should I say to
you? Should I commend
you? In this matter I do not
commend you!

The Institution of the Lord's Supper

23 For I received from
the Lord what I also handed on to you, that the Lord
Jesus on the night when he
was betrayed took a loaf of
bread, 24 and when he had
given thanks, he broke it
and said, "This is my body
that is for[v] you. Do this in
remembrance of me." 25 In
the same way he took the
cup also, after supper, saying, "This cup is the new
covenant in my blood. Do
this, as often as you drink
it, in remembrance of me."
26 For as often as you eat
this bread and drink the
cup, you proclaim the
Lord's death until he
comes.

Partaking of the Supper Unworthily

27 Whoever, therefore,
eats the bread or drinks the
cup of the Lord in an un-
worthy manner will be an-
swerable for the body and
blood of the Lord. 28 Examine yourselves, and only
then eat of the bread and
drink of the cup. 29 For all
who eat and drink[w] without
discerning the body,[x] eat
and drink judgment against
themselves. 30 For this reason many of you are weak
and ill, and some have
died.[y] 31 But if we judged
ourselves, we would not be
judged. 32 But when we are
judged by the Lord, we are
disciplined[z] so that we
may not be condemned

[v] Other ancient authorities read *is broken for*
[w] Other ancient authorities add *in an unworthy manner,*
[x] Other ancient authorities read *the Lord's body*
[y] Gk *fallen asleep*
[z] Or *When we are judged, we are being disciplined by the Lord*

μεθύει. 22 μὴ γὰρ οἰκίας οὐκ ἔχετε
is drunken. Not indeed [2]houses [1]have ye not
εἰς τὸ ἐσθίειν καὶ πίνειν; ἢ τῆς ἐκκλησίας
– – to eat and to drink? or the church
τοῦ θεοῦ καταφρονεῖτε, καὶ καταισχύνετε
– of God despise ye, and shame
τοὺς μὴ ἔχοντας; τί εἴπω ὑμῖν; ἐπαινέσω
the [ones] not having? What may I say to you? shall I praise
ὑμᾶς; ἐν τούτῳ οὐκ ἐπαινῶ. 23 Ἐγὼ
you? In this I praise not. I
γὰρ παρέλαβον ἀπὸ τοῦ κυρίου, ὃ καὶ
For received from the Lord, what also
παρέδωκα ὑμῖν, ὅτι ὁ κύριος Ἰησοῦς
I delivered to you, that the Lord Jesus
ἐν τῇ νυκτὶ ᾗ παρεδίδοτο ἔλαβεν ἄρτον
in the night in which he was betrayed took bread
24 καὶ εὐχαριστήσας ἔκλασεν καὶ εἶπεν·
and having given thanks broke and said:
τοῦτό μού ἐστιν τὸ σῶμα τὸ ὑπὲρ
This of me is the body – on behalf of
ὑμῶν· τοῦτο ποιεῖτε εἰς τὴν ἐμὴν
you; this do ye for – my
ἀνάμνησιν. 25 ὡσαύτως καὶ τὸ ποτήριον
remembrance. Similarly also the cup
μετὰ τὸ δειπνῆσαι, λέγων· τοῦτο τὸ
after the to sup, saying: This –
ποτήριον ἡ καινὴ διαθήκη ἐστὶν ἐν τῷ
cup [2]the [3]new [4]covenant [1]is in –
ἐμῷ αἵματι· τοῦτο ποιεῖτε, ὁσάκις ἐὰν
my blood; this do ye, as often as
πίνητε, εἰς τὴν ἐμὴν ἀνάμνησιν. 26 ὁσάκις
ye drink, for – my remembrance. as often
γὰρ ἐὰν ἐσθίητε τὸν ἄρτον τοῦτον καὶ
For as ye eat this bread and
τὸ ποτήριον πίνητε, τὸν θάνατον τοῦ
[2]the [3]cup [1]drink, the death of the
κυρίου καταγγέλλετε, ἄχρι οὗ ἔλθῃ.
Lord ye declare, until he comes.
27 Ὥστε ὃς ἂν ἐσθίῃ τὸν ἄρτον ἢ
So as whoever eats the bread or
πίνῃ τὸ ποτήριον τοῦ κυρίου ἀναξίως,
drinks the cup of the Lord unworthily,
ἔνοχος ἔσται τοῦ σώματος καὶ τοῦ
guilty will be of the body and of the
αἵματος τοῦ κυρίου. 28 δοκιμαζέτω δὲ
blood of the Lord. But [1]let [3]prove
ἄνθρωπος ἑαυτόν, καὶ οὕτως ἐκ τοῦ
[2]a man [4]himself, and so of the
ἄρτου ἐσθιέτω καὶ ἐκ τοῦ ποτηρίου
bread let him eat and of the cup
πινέτω· 29 ὁ γὰρ ἐσθίων καὶ πίνων
let him drink; for the [one] eating and drinking
κρίμα ἑαυτῷ ἐσθίει καὶ πίνει μὴ διακρίνων
[4]judgment [5]to himself [1]eats [2]and [3]drinks not discerning
τὸ σῶμα. 30 διὰ τοῦτο ἐν ὑμῖν πολλοὶ
the body. Therefore among you many
ἀσθενεῖς καὶ ἄρρωστοι καὶ κοιμῶνται
[are] weak and feeble and [2]sleep
ἱκανοί. 31 εἰ δὲ ἑαυτοὺς διεκρίνομεν,
[1]a number. But if ourselves we discerned,
οὐκ ἂν ἐκρινόμεθα· 32 κρινόμενοι δὲ ὑπὸ
we should not be judged; but being judged by
τοῦ κυρίου παιδευόμεθα, ἵνα μὴ σὺν
the Lord we are chastened, lest with

other gets drunk. 22 Don't
you have homes to eat and
drink in? Or do you despise
the church of God and hu-
miliate those who have
nothing? What shall I say to
you? Shall I praise you for
this? Certainly not!
23 For I received from the
Lord what I also passed on
to you: The Lord Jesus, on
the night he was betrayed,
took bread, 24 and when he
had given thanks, he broke
it and said, "This is my
body, which is for you; do
this in remembrance of
me." 25 In the same way, after supper he took the cup,
saying, "This cup is the
new covenant in my blood;
do this, whenever you
drink it, in remembrance of
me." 26 For whenever you
eat this bread and drink this
cup, you proclaim the
Lord's death until he
comes.
27 Therefore, whoever
eats the bread or drinks the
cup of the Lord in an un-
worthy manner will be
guilty of sinning against the
body and blood of the
Lord. 28 A man ought to examine himself before he
eats of the bread and drinks
of the cup. 29 For anyone
who eats and drinks with-
out recognizing the body of
the Lord eats and drinks
judgment on himself.
30 That is why many among
you are weak and sick, and
a number of you have fallen
asleep. 31 But if we judged
ourselves, we would not
come under judgment.
32 When we are judged by
the Lord, we are being disciplined so that we will not

along with the world.
33 So then, my brothers
and sisters,[a] when you
come together to eat, wait
for one another. 34 If you
are hungry, eat at home, so
that when you come to-
gether, it will not be for
your condemnation. About
the other things I will give
instructions when I come.

Chapter 12

Spiritual Gifts

NOW concerning spiri-
tual gifts,[b] brothers
and sisters,[a] I do not want
you to be uninformed.
2 You know that when you
were pagans, you were en-
ticed and led astray to idols
that could not speak.
3 Therefore I want you to
understand that no one
speaking by the Spirit of
God ever says "Let Jesus
be cursed!" and no one can
say "Jesus is Lord" except
by the Holy Spirit.
4 Now there are variet-
ies of gifts, but the same
Spirit; 5 and there are varieties of services, but the
same Lord; 6 and there are
varieties of activities, but it
is the same God who acti-
vates all of them in everyone. 7 To each is given the
manifestation of the Spirit
for the common good. 8 To
one is given through the
Spirit the utterance of wisdom, and to another the utterance of knowledge ac-
cording to the same Spirit,
9 to another faith by the
same Spirit, to another gifts
of healing by the one Spirit,
10 to another the working of
miracles, to another prophecy, to another the discern
ment of spirits, to another
various kinds of tongues, to
another the interpretation
of tongues. 11 All these are
activated by one and the
same Spirit, who allots to
each one individually just

[a] Gk *brothers*
[b] Or *spiritual persons*

τῷ κόσμῳ κατακριθῶμεν. **33** Ὥστε,
the world we are condemned. So as,
ἀδελφοί μου, συνερχόμενοι εἰς τὸ φαγεῖν
brothers of me, coming together *for* *the* to eat
ἀλλήλους ἐκδέχεσθε. **34** εἴ τις πεινᾷ,
one another await ye. If anyone hungers,
ἐν οἴκῳ ἐσθιέτω, ἵνα μὴ εἰς κρίμα
at home let him eat, lest to judgment
συνέρχησθε. τὰ δὲ λοιπὰ ὡς ἂν ἔλθω
ye come together. And the remaining matters whenever I come
διατάξομαι.
I will arrange.

12 Περὶ δὲ τῶν πνευματικῶν, ἀδελφοί,
Now about the spiritual matters, brothers,
οὐ θέλω ὑμᾶς ἀγνοεῖν. **2** Οἴδατε ὅτι
I do not wish you to be ignorant. Ye know that
ὅτε ἔθνη ἦτε πρὸς τὰ εἴδωλα τὰ ἄφωνα
when [2]nations [1]ye were [4]to [5]the [7]idols – [6]voiceless
ὡς ἂν ἤγεσθε ἀπαγόμενοι. **3** διὸ γνωρίζω
[8]however [3]ye were led [9][ye were] [10]being led away.* Wherefore I make known
ὑμῖν ὅτι οὐδεὶς ἐν πνεύματι θεοῦ λαλῶν
to you that no one [2]by [3][the] Spirit [4]of God [1]speaking
λέγει· ΑΝΑΘΕΜΑ ΙΗΣΟΥΣ, καὶ οὐδεὶς
says: A CURSE [IS] JESUS, and no one
δύναται εἰπεῖν· ΚΥΡΙΟΣ ΙΗΣΟΥΣ, εἰ μὴ
can *to* say: LORD JESUS, except
ἐν πνεύματι ἁγίῳ.
by [the] [2]Spirit [1]Holy.
4 Διαιρέσεις δὲ χαρισμάτων εἰσίν, τὸ δὲ αὐτὸ
Now differences of gifts there are, but the same
πνεῦμα· **5** καὶ διαιρέσεις διακονιῶν εἰσιν, καὶ
Spirit; and differences of ministries there are, and
ὁ αὐτὸς κύριος· **6** καὶ διαιρέσεις ἐνεργημάτων
the same Lord; and differences of operations
εἰσίν, ὁ δὲ αὐτὸς θεὸς ὁ ἐνεργῶν τὰ
there are, but the same God – operating –
πάντα ἐν πᾶσιν. **7** ἑκάστῳ δὲ δίδοται
all things in all. But to each one is given
ἡ φανέρωσις τοῦ πνεύματος πρὸς τὸ
the manifestation of the Spirit to *the*
συμφέρον. **8** ᾧ μὲν γὰρ διὰ τοῦ πνεύματος
profit*ing*. For to one through the Spirit
δίδοται λόγος σοφίας, ἄλλῳ δὲ λόγος
is given a word of wisdom, and to another a word
γνώσεως κατὰ τὸ αὐτὸ πνεῦμα, **9** ἑτέρῳ
of knowledge according to the same Spirit, to another
πίστις ἐν τῷ αὐτῷ πνεύματι, ἄλλῳ δὲ
faith by the same Spirit, and to another
χαρίσματα ἰαμάτων ἐν τῷ ἑνὶ πνεύματι,
gifts of cures by the one Spirit,
10 ἄλλῳ δὲ ἐνεργήματα δυνάμεων, ἄλλῳ
and to another operations of powers, to another
[δὲ] προφητεία, ἄλλῳ δὲ διακρίσεις πνευ-
and prophecy, and to another discernings of
μάτων, ἑτέρῳ γένη γλωσσῶν, ἄλλῳ δὲ
spirits, to another kinds of tongues, and to another
ἑρμηνεία γλωσσῶν· **11** πάντα δὲ ταῦτα
interpretation of tongues: and [8]all [9]these things
ἐνεργεῖ τὸ ἓν καὶ τὸ αὐτὸ πνεῦμα,
[7]operates [1]the [2]one [3]and [4]the [5]same [6]Spirit,

* It is thought that there is a scribal error in this verse; see commentaries on the Greek text. We have been guided by G. G. Findlay, *The Expositor's Greek Testament*.

be condemned with the
world.
33 So then, my brothers,
when you come together to
eat, wait for each other. 34 If
anyone is hungry, he
should eat at home, so that
when you meet together it
may not result in judgment.
And when I come I will
give further directions.

Chapter 12

Spiritual Gifts

NOW about spiritual
gifts, brothers, I do
not want you to be igno-
rant. 2 You know that when
you were pagans, somehow
or other you were influ-
enced and led astray to
mute idols. 3 Therefore I tell
you that no one who is
speaking by the Spirit of
God says, "Jesus be
cursed," and no one can
say, "Jesus is Lord," ex-
cept by the Holy Spirit.
4 There are different kinds
of gifts, but the same Spirit.
5 There are different kinds
of service, but the same
Lord. 6 There are different
kinds of working, but the
same God works all of them
in all men.
7 Now to each one the
manifestation of the Spirit
is given for the common
good. 8 To one there is giv-
en through the Spirit the
message of wisdom, to an-
other the message of
knowledge by means of the
same Spirit, 9 to another
faith by the same Spirit, to
another gifts of healing by
that one Spirit, 10 to another
miraculous powers, to an-
other prophecy, to another
distinguishing between
spirits, to another speaking
in different kinds of
tongues,[a] and to still another the interpretation of
tongues.[a] 11 All these are
the work of one and the
same Spirit, and he gives

[a] *10* Or *languages*; also in verse 28

as the Spirit chooses.

One Body with Many Members

12 For just as the body
is one and has many mem-
bers, and all the members
of the body, though many,
are one body, so it is with
Christ. 13 For in the one
Spirit we were all baptized
into one body—Jews or
Greeks, slaves or free—
and we were all made to
drink of one Spirit.
14 Indeed, the body
does not consist of one
member but of many. 15 If
the foot would say, "Be-
cause I am not a hand, I do
not belong to the body,"
that would not make it any
less a part of the body.
16 And if the ear would say,
"Because I am not an eye,
I do not belong to the
body," that would not
make it any less a part of
the body. 17 If the whole
body were an eye, where
would the hearing be? If the
whole body were hearing,
where would the sense of
smell be? 18 But as it is, God
arranged the members in
the body, each one of them,
as he chose. 19 If all were a
single member, where
would the body be? 20 As it
is, there are many mem-
bers, yet one body. 21 The
eye cannot say to the hand,
"I have no need of you,"
nor again the head to the
feet, "I have no need of
you." 22 On the contrary,
the members of the body
that seem to be weaker are
indispensable, 23 and those
members of the body that
we think less honorable we
clothe with greater honor,
and our less respectable
members are treated with
greater respect; 24 whereas

διαιροῦν ἰδίᾳ ἑκάστῳ καθὼς βούλεται.
distributing [2]separately† [1]to each one as he purposes.

12 Καθάπερ γὰρ τὸ σῶμα ἕν ἐστιν
For as the body [2]one [1]is

καὶ μέλη πολλὰ ἔχει, πάντα δὲ τὰ
and [3]members [2]many [1]has, but all the

μέλη τοῦ σώματος πολλὰ ὄντα ἕν ἐστιν
members of the body [2]many [1]being [4]one [3]is(are)

σῶμα, οὕτως καὶ ὁ Χριστός· 13 καὶ γὰρ
body, so also *the* Christ; for indeed

ἐν ἑνὶ πνεύματι ἡμεῖς πάντες εἰς ἓν
[4]by [5]one [6]Spirit [1]we [2]all [7]into [8]one

σῶμα ἐβαπτίσθημεν, εἴτε Ἰουδαῖοι εἴτε
[9]body [3]were baptized, whether Jews or

Ἕλληνες, εἴτε δοῦλοι εἴτε ἐλεύθεροι, καὶ
Greeks, whether slaves or free, and

πάντες ἓν πνεῦμα ἐποτίσθημεν. 14 καὶ
all one Spirit *we* were given to drink. indeed

γὰρ τὸ σῶμα οὐκ ἔστιν ἓν μέλος ἀλλὰ
For the body is not one member but

πολλά. 15 ἐὰν εἴπῃ ὁ πούς· ὅτι οὐκ
many. If [3]says [1]the [2]foot: Because not

εἰμὶ χείρ, οὐκ εἰμὶ ἐκ τοῦ σώματος,
I am a hand, I am not of the body,

οὐ παρὰ τοῦτο οὐκ ἔστιν ἐκ τοῦ σώματος.
not for this it is not of the body.

16 καὶ ἐὰν εἴπῃ τὸ οὖς· ὅτι οὐκ εἰμὶ
And if says the ear: Because I am not

ὀφθαλμός, οὐκ εἰμὶ ἐκ τοῦ σώματος,
an eye, I am not of the body,

οὐ παρὰ τοῦτο οὐκ ἔστιν ἐκ τοῦ σώματος.
not for this it is not of the body.

17 εἰ ὅλον τὸ σῶμα ὀφθαλμός, ποῦ
If all the body [was] an eye, where

ἡ ἀκοή; εἰ ὅλον ἀκοή, ποῦ ἡ ὄσφρησις;
[would be] the hearing? if all hearing, where the smelling?

18 νῦν δὲ ὁ θεὸς ἔθετο τὰ μέλη, ἓν
But now – God set the members, [2]one

ἕκαστον αὐτῶν ἐν τῷ σώματι καθὼς
[1]each of them in the body as

ἠθέλησεν. 19 εἰ δὲ ἦν τὰ πάντα ἓν
he wished. And if [3]was – [1]all [4]one

μέλος, ποῦ τὸ σῶμα; 20 νῦν δὲ πολλὰ
member, where the body? But now many

μὲν μέλη, ἓν δὲ σῶμα. 21 οὐ δύναται
[2]indeed [1]members, but one body. [3]cannot

δὲ ὁ ὀφθαλμὸς εἰπεῖν τῇ χειρί· χρείαν
And [1]the* [2]eye *to* say to the hand: Need

σου οὐκ ἔχω, ἢ πάλιν ἡ κεφαλὴ τοῖς
of thee I have not, or again the head to the

ποσίν· χρείαν ὑμῶν οὐκ ἔχω· 22 ἀλλὰ
feet: Need of you I have not; but

πολλῷ μᾶλλον τὰ δοκοῦντα μέλη τοῦ
by much more [1]the [5]seeming [2]members [3]of the

σώματος ἀσθενέστερα ὑπάρχειν ἀναγκαῖά ἐστιν,
[4]body [7]weaker [6]to be [9]necessary [8]is(are),

23 καὶ ἃ δοκοῦμεν ἀτιμότερα εἶναι
and [1][members] [4]which [5]we think [7]less honourable [6]to be

τοῦ σώματος, τούτοις τιμὴν περισσοτέραν
[2]of the [3]body, to these honour more abundant

περιτίθεμεν, καὶ τὰ ἀσχήμονα ἡμῶν
we put round, and the uncomely [members] of us

εὐσχημοσύνην περισσοτέραν ἔχει, 24 τὰ δὲ
[3]comeliness [2]more abundant [1]has(ve), but th

them to each one, just as he
determines.

One Body, Many Parts

12 The body is a unit,
though it is made up of
many parts; and though all
its parts are many, they
form one body. So it is with
Christ. 13 For we were all
baptized by[b] one Spirit
into one body—whether
Jews or Greeks, slave or
free—and we were all giv-
en the one Spirit to drink.
14 Now the body is not
made up of one part but of
many. 15 If the foot should
say, "Because I am not a
hand, I do not belong to the
body," it would not for that
reason cease to be part of
the body. 16 And if the ear
should say, "Because I am
not an eye, I do not belong
to the body," it would not
for that reason cease to be
part of the body. 17 If the
whole body were an eye,
where would the sense of
hearing be? If the whole
body were an ear, where
would the sense of smell
be? 18 But in fact God has
arranged the parts in the
body, every one of them,
just as he wanted them to
be. 19 If they were all one
part, where would the body
be? 20 As it is, there are
many parts, but one body.
21 The eye cannot say to
the hand, "I don't need
you!" And the head cannot
say to the feet, "I don't
need you!" 22 On the con-
trary, those parts of the
body that seem to be weaker are indispensable, 23 and
the parts that we think are
less honorable we treat
with special honor. And the
parts that are unpresent-
able are treated with special modesty, 24 while our

[b]13 Or *with*; or *in*

our more respectable mem-
bers do not need this. But
God has so arranged the
body, giving the greater
honor to the inferior member, 25 that there may be no
dissension within the body,
but the members may have
the same care for one an-
other. 26 If one member suffers, all suffer together with
it; if one member is hon-
ored, all rejoice together
with it.
27 Now you are the
body of Christ and individually members of it. 28 And
God has appointed in the
church first apostles, second prophets, third teachers; then deeds of power,
then gifts of healing, forms
of assistance, forms of
leadership, various kinds of
tongues. 29 Are all apos-
tles? Are all prophets? Are
all teachers? Do all work
miracles? 30 Do all possess
gifts of healing? Do all
speak in tongues? Do all interpret? 31 But strive for the
greater gifts. And I will
show you a still more excellent way.

Chapter 13

The Gift of Love

IF I speak in the tongues
of mortals and of an-
gels, but do not have love,
I am a noisy gong or a
clanging cymbal. 2 And if I
have prophetic powers,
and understand all mysteries and all knowledge, and
if I have all faith, so as to
remove mountains, but do
not have love, I am noth-
ing. 3 If I give away all my
possessions, and if I hand
over my body so that I may
boast,[c] but do not have
love, I gain nothing.

[c] Other ancient authorities read *body to be burned*

εὐσχήμονα ἡμῶν οὐ χρείαν ἔχει. ἀλλὰ ὁ
comely [members] of us [2]no [3]need [1]has(ve). But –

θεὸς συνεκέρασεν τὸ σῶμα, τῷ ὑστερουμένῳ
God blended together the body, [4]to the [member] [5]lacking

περισσοτέραν δοὺς τιμήν, 25 ἵνα μὴ ᾖ
[3]more abundant [1]giving [2]honour, lest there be

σχίσμα ἐν τῷ σώματι, ἀλλὰ τὸ αὐτὸ
division in the body, but [4]the [5]same

ὑπὲρ ἀλλήλων μεριμνῶσιν τὰ μέλη.
[6]on behalf of [7]one another [3]should care [1]the [2]members.

26 καὶ εἴτε πάσχει ἓν μέλος, συμπάσχει
And whether [3]suffers [1]one [2]member, [7]suffers with [it]

πάντα τὰ μέλη· εἴτε δοξάζεται μέλος,
[4]all [5]the [6]members; or [2]is glorified [1]a member,

συγχαίρει πάντα τὰ μέλη. 27 ὑμεῖς
[6]rejoices with [it] [3]all [4]the [5]members. ye

δέ ἐστε σῶμα Χριστοῦ καὶ μέλη ἐκ
And are a body of Christ and members in

μέρους. 28 Καὶ οὓς μὲν ἔθετο ὁ θεὸς
part. And [3]some† [2]placed – [1]God

ἐν τῇ ἐκκλησίᾳ πρῶτον ἀποστόλους, δεύτε-
in the church firstly apostles, second-

ρον προφήτας, τρίτον διδασκάλους, ἔπειτα
ly prophets, thirdly teachers, then

δυνάμεις, ἔπειτα χαρίσματα ἰαμάτων,
powers, then gifts of cures,

ἀντιλήμψεις, κυβερνήσεις, γένη γλωσσῶν.
helps, governings, kinds of tongues.

29 μὴ πάντες ἀπόστολοι; μὴ πάντες
Not all [are] apostles? *not* all

προφῆται; μὴ πάντες διδάσκαλοι; μὴ
prophets? *not* all teachers? *not*

πάντες δυνάμεις; 30 μὴ πάντες χαρίσματα
all powers? *not* all [2]gifts

ἔχουσιν ἰαμάτων; μὴ πάντες γλώσσαις
[1]have of cures? *not* all [2]with tongues

λαλοῦσιν; μὴ πάντες διερμηνεύουσιν;
[1]speak? *not* all interpret?

31 ζηλοῦτε δὲ τὰ χαρίσματα τὰ μείζονα.
but desire ye eagerly the [2]gifts – [1]greater.

Καὶ ἔτι καθ' ὑπερβολὴν ὁδὸν ὑμῖν
And yet [4]according to [5]excellence [3]a way [2]to you

δείκνυμι. 13 Ἐὰν ταῖς γλώσσαις τῶν ἀνθρώπων
[1]I show. If in the tongues – of men

λαλῶ καὶ τῶν ἀγγέλων, ἀγάπην δὲ
I speak and – of angels, but love

μὴ ἔχω, γέγονα χαλκὸς ἠχῶν ἢ
I have not, I have become [2]brass [1]sounding or

κύμβαλον ἀλαλάζον. 2 καὶ ἐὰν ἔχω
cymbal a tinkling. And if I have

προφητείαν καὶ εἰδῶ τὰ μυστήρια πάντα
prophecy and know [2]the [3]mysteries [1]all

καὶ πᾶσαν τὴν γνῶσιν, κἂν ἔχω πᾶσαν
and all – knowledge, and if I have all

τὴν πίστιν ὥστε ὄρη μεθιστάναι, ἀγάπην
– faith so as mountains to remove, [2]love

δὲ μὴ ἔχω, οὐθέν εἰμι. 3 κἂν ψωμίσω
[1]but I have not, nothing I am. And if I dole out

πάντα τὰ ὑπάρχοντά μου, καὶ ἐὰν παραδῶ
all the goods of me, and if I deliver

τὸ σῶμά μου ἵνα καυθήσομαι, ἀγάπην
the body of me in order that I shall be burned, [2]love

δὲ μὴ ἔχω, οὐδὲν ὠφελοῦμαι. 4 Ἡ
[1]but I have not, nothing I am profited. –

presentable parts need no
special treatment. But God
has combined the members
of the body and has given
greater honor to the parts
that lacked it, 25 so that
there should be no division
in the body, but that its
parts should have equal
concern for each other. 26 If
one part suffers, every part
suffers with it; if one part is
honored, every part re-
joices with it.
27 Now you are the body
of Christ, and each one of
you is a part of it. 28 And in
the church God has ap-
pointed first of all apostles,
second prophets, third
teachers, then workers of
miracles, also those having
gifts of healing, those able
to help others, those with
gifts of administration, and
those speaking in different
kinds of tongues. 29 Are all
apostles? Are all prophets?
Are all teachers? Do all
work miracles? 30 Do all
have gifts of healing? Do all
speak in tongues[c]? Do all
interpret? 31 But eagerly desire[d] the greater gifts.

Love

And now I will show you
the most excellent way.

Chapter 13

IF I speak in the tongues[e]
of men and of angels,
but have not love, I am only
a resounding gong or a
clanging cymbal. 2 If I have
the gift of prophecy and can
fathom all mysteries and all
knowledge, and if I have a
faith that can move moun-
tains, but have not love, I
am nothing. 3 If I give all I
possess to the poor and sur-
render my body to the
flames,[f] but have not love,
I gain nothing.

[c] 30 Or *other languages*
[d] 31 Or *But you are eagerly desiring*
[e] 1 Or *languages*
[f] 3 Some early manuscripts *body that I may boast*

4 Love is patient; love is
kind; love is not envious or
boastful or arrogant 5 or
rude. It does not insist on
its own way; it is not irrita-
ble or resentful; 6 it does
not rejoice in wrongdoing,
but rejoices in the truth. 7 It
bears all things, believes all
things, hopes all things, endures all things.
8 Love never ends. But
as for prophecies, they will
come to an end; as for
tongues, they will cease; as
for knowledge, it will come
to an end. 9 For we know
only in part, and we prophesy only in part; 10 but
when the complete comes,
the partial will come to an
end. 11 When I was a child,
I spoke like a child, I
thought like a child, I reasoned like a child; when I
became an adult, I put an
end to childish ways. 12 For
now we see in a mirror,
dimly,[d] but then we will
see face to face. Now I
know only in part; then I
will know fully, even as I
have been fully known.
13 And now faith, hope, and
love abide, these three; and
the greatest of these is love.

ἀγάπη μακροθυμεῖ, χρηστεύεται ἡ ἀγάπη,
Love suffers long, is kind – love,
οὐ ζηλοῖ, ἡ ἀγάπη οὐ περπερεύεται,
is not jealous, – love does not vaunt itself,
οὐ φυσιοῦται, 5 οὐκ ἀσχημονεῖ, οὐ ζητεῖ
is not puffed up, does not act unbecomingly, does not seek
τὰ ἑαυτῆς, οὐ παροξύνεται, οὐ λογίζεται
the things of her(it)self, is not provoked, does not reckon
τὸ κακόν, 6 οὐ χαίρει ἐπὶ τῇ ἀδικίᾳ,
the evil, rejoices not over the wrong,
συγχαίρει δὲ τῇ ἀληθείᾳ· 7 πάντα στέγει,
but rejoices with the truth; all things covers,
πάντα πιστεύει, πάντα ἐλπίζει, πάντα
all things believes, all things hopes, all things
ὑπομένει. 8 Ἡ ἀγάπη οὐδέποτε πίπτει·
endures. – Love never falls;
εἴτε δὲ προφητεῖαι, καταργηθήσονται· εἴτε
but whether prophecies, they will be abolished; or
γλῶσσαι, παύσονται· εἴτε γνῶσις, κατ-
tongues, they will cease; or knowledge, it will
αργηθήσεται. 9 ἐκ μέρους γὰρ γινώσκομεν
be abolished. For in part we know
καὶ ἐκ μέρους προφητεύομεν· 10 ὅταν
and in part we prophesy; [2]when
δὲ ἔλθῃ τὸ τέλειον, τὸ ἐκ μέρους
[1]but [5]comes [3]the [4]perfect thing, the thing in part
καταργηθήσεται. 11 ὅτε ἤμην νήπιος,
will be abolished. When I was an infant,
ἐλάλουν ὡς νήπιος, ἐφρόνουν ὡς νήπιος,
I spoke as an infant, I thought as an infant,
ἐλογιζόμην ὡς νήπιος· ὅτε γέγονα ἀνήρ,
I reckoned as an infant; when I have become a man,
κατήργηκα τὰ τοῦ νηπίου. 12 βλέπομεν
I have abolished the things of the infant. we see
γὰρ ἄρτι δι' ἐσόπτρου ἐν αἰνίγματι,
For yet through a mirror in a riddle,
τότε δὲ πρόσωπον πρὸς πρόσωπον· ἄρτι
but then face to face; yet
γινώσκω ἐκ μέρους, τότε δὲ ἐπιγνώσομαι
I know in part, but then I shall fully know
καθὼς καὶ ἐπεγνώσθην. 13 νυνὶ δὲ μένει
as also I was fully known. But now remains
πίστις, ἐλπίς, ἀγάπη, τὰ τρία ταῦτα·
faith, hope, love, these three;
μείζων δὲ τούτων ἡ ἀγάπη.
and [the] greater of these [is] – love.

4 Love is patient, love is
kind. It does not envy, it
does not boast, it is not
proud. 5 It is not rude, it is
not self-seeking, it is not
easily angered, it keeps no
record of wrongs. 6 Love
does not delight in evil but
rejoices with the truth. 7 It
always protects, always
trusts, always hopes, al-
ways perseveres.
8 Love never fails. But
where there are prophe-
cies, they will cease; where
there are tongues, they will
be stilled; where there is
knowledge, it will pass
away. 9 For we know in part
and we prophesy in part,
10 but when perfection
comes, the imperfect disap-
pears. 11 When I was a
child, I talked like a child, I
thought like a child, I reasoned like a child. When I
became a man, I put childish ways behind me. 12 Now
we see but a poor reflection
as in a mirror; then we shall
see face to face. Now I
know in part; then I shall
know fully, even as I am
fully known.
13 And now these three remain: faith, hope and love.
But the greatest of these is
love.

Chapter 14

Gifts of Prophecy and Tongues

PURSUE love and strive
for the spiritual gifts,
and especially that you
may prophesy. 2 For those
who speak in a tongue do
not speak to other people
but to God; for nobody understands them, since they
are speaking mysteries in
the Spirit. 3 On the other
hand, those who prophesy
speak to other people for
their upbuilding and en-
couragement and consola-
tion. 4 Those who speak in a
tongue build up them-
selves, but those who
prophesy build up the

14 Διώκετε τὴν ἀγάπην, ζηλοῦτε δὲ
Pursue ye – love, but desire eagerly
τὰ πνευματικά, μᾶλλον δὲ ἵνα προφητεύητε.
the spiritual [gifts], and rather in order that ye may prophesy.
2 ὁ γὰρ λαλῶν γλώσσῃ οὐκ ἀνθρώποις
For the [one] speaking in a tongue [2]not to men
λαλεῖ ἀλλὰ θεῷ· οὐδεὶς γὰρ ἀκούει,
[1]speaks but to God; for no one hears,
πνεύματι δὲ λαλεῖ μυστήρια· 3 ὁ δὲ
but in spirit he speaks mysteries; but the [one]
προφητεύων ἀνθρώποις λαλεῖ οἰκοδομὴν καὶ
prophesying to men speaks edification and
παράκλησιν καὶ παραμυθίαν. 4 ὁ λαλῶν
encouragement and consolation. The [one] speaking
γλώσσῃ ἑαυτὸν οἰκοδομεῖ· ὁ δὲ προφητεύων
in a tongue himself edifies; but the [one] prophesying

Chapter 14

Gifts of Prophecy and Tongues

FOLLOW the way of
love and eagerly desire
spiritual gifts, especially
the gift of prophecy. 2 For
anyone who speaks in a
tongue[g] does not speak to
men but to God. Indeed, no
one understands him; he ut-
ters mysteries with his spirit.[h] 3 But everyone who
prophesies speaks to men
for their strengthening, encouragement and comfort.
4 He who speaks in a tongue
edifies himself, but he who
prophesies edifies the

[d] Gk *in a riddle*

[g] 2 Or *another language*; also in verses 4, 13, 14, 19, 26 and 27
[h] 2 Or *by the Spirit*

church. 5 Now I would like
all of you to speak in
tongues, but even more to
prophesy. One who proph-
esies is greater than one
who speaks in tongues, unless someone interprets, so
that the church may be
built up.
6 Now, brothers and
sisters,[e] if I come to you
speaking in tongues, how
will I benefit you unless I
speak to you in some revelation or knowledge or
prophecy or teaching? 7 It
is the same way with lifeless instruments that produce sound, such as the
flute or the harp. If they do
not give distinct notes, how
will anyone know what is
being played? 8 And if the
bugle gives an indistinct
sound, who will get ready
for battle? 9 So with yourselves; if in a tongue you
utter speech that is not intelligible, how will anyone
know what is being said?
For you will be speaking
into the air. 10 There are
doubtless many different
kinds of sounds in the
world, and nothing is without sound. 11 If then I do
not know the meaning of a
sound, I will be a foreigner
to the speaker and the
speaker a foreigner to me.
12 So with yourselves; since
you are eager for spiritual
gifts, strive to excel in them
for building up the church.
13 Therefore, one who
speaks in a tongue should
pray for the power to interpret. 14 For if I pray in a
tongue, my spirit prays but
my mind is unproductive.
15 What should I do then? I
will pray with the spirit, but

[e] Gk *brothers*

ἐκκλησίαν οἰκοδομεῖ. **5** θέλω δὲ πάντας
a church edifies. Now I wish all

ὑμᾶς λαλεῖν γλώσσαις, μᾶλλον δὲ ἵνα
you to speak in tongues, but rather *in order* that

προφητεύητε· μείζων δὲ ὁ προφητεύων ἢ
ye may prophesy; and greater the [one] prophesying than

ὁ λαλῶν γλώσσαις, ἐκτὸς εἰ μὴ διερμηνεύῃ,
the speaking [one] in tongues, *except* unless he interprets,

ἵνα ἡ ἐκκλησία οἰκοδομὴν λάβῃ. **6** νῦν δέ,
in order that the church edification may receive. But now,

ἀδελφοί, ἐὰν ἔλθω πρὸς ὑμᾶς γλώσσαις
brothers, if I come to you in tongues

λαλῶν, τί ὑμᾶς ὠφελήσω, ἐὰν μὴ ὑμῖν
speaking, what [2]you [1]shall I profit, except [3]to you

λαλήσω ἢ ἐν ἀποκαλύψει ἢ ἐν γνώσει
[1]I speak either in a revelation or in knowledge

ἢ ἐν προφητείᾳ ἢ διδαχῇ; **7** ὅμως τὰ
or in prophecy or *in* teaching? Yet –

ἄψυχα φωνὴν διδόντα, εἴτε αὐλὸς εἴτε
lifeless things [2]a sound [1]giving, whether pipe or

κιθάρα, ἐὰν διαστολὴν τοῖς φθόγγοις μὴ
harp, if [2]a distinction [4]in the [5]sounds [3]not

δῷ, πῶς γνωσθήσεται τὸ αὐλούμενον ἢ
[1]they give, how will it be known the thing being piped or

τὸ κιθαριζόμενον; **8** καὶ γὰρ ἐὰν ἄδηλον
the thing being harped? For indeed if [2]an uncertain

σάλπιγξ φωνὴν δῷ, τίς παρασκευάσεται
[1]a trumpet [3]sound [4]gives, who will prepare himself

εἰς πόλεμον; **9** οὕτως καὶ ὑμεῖς διὰ
for war? so also [2]ye [6]through

τῆς γλώσσης ἐὰν μὴ εὔσημον λόγον
[7]the [8]tongue [1]unless [4]a clear [5]word

δῶτε, πῶς γνωσθήσεται τὸ λαλούμενον;
[3]give, how will it be known the thing being said?

ἔσεσθε γὰρ εἰς ἀέρα λαλοῦντες. **10** τοσαῦτα
for [1]ye will be [3]into [4]air [2]speaking. [2]So many

εἰ τύχοι γένη φωνῶν εἰσιν ἐν κόσμῳ,
[3]it may be† [4]kinds [5]of sounds [1]there are in [the] world,

καὶ οὐδὲν ἄφωνον· **11** ἐὰν οὖν μὴ εἰδῶ
and not one [is] voiceless; if therefore I know not

τὴν δύναμιν τῆς φωνῆς, ἔσομαι τῷ
the power of the sound, I shall be to the

λαλοῦντι βάρβαρος καὶ ὁ λαλῶν ἐν ἐμοὶ
[one] speaking a foreigner and the speaking [one] in(to) me

βάρβαρος. **12** οὕτως καὶ ὑμεῖς, ἐπεὶ
a foreigner. So also ye, since

ζηλωταί ἐστε πνευμάτων, πρὸς τὴν
zealots ye are of spirit[ual thing]s, [2]to [3]the

οἰκοδομὴν τῆς ἐκκλησίας ζητεῖτε ἵνα περισ-
[4]edification [5]of the [6]church [1]seek ye in order that ye may

σεύητε. **13** Διὸ ὁ λαλῶν γλώσσῃ προσευχ-
abound. Wherefore the speaking [one] in a tongue let him

έσθω ἵνα διερμηνεύῃ. **14** ἐὰν γὰρ προσεύχωμαι
pray *in order* that he may interpret. For if I pray

γλώσσῃ, τὸ πνεῦμά μου προσεύχεται,
in a tongue, the spirit of me prays,

ὁ δὲ νοῦς μου ἄκαρπός ἐστιν. **15** τί
but the mind of me unfruitful is. What

οὖν ἐστιν; προσεύξομαι τῷ πνεύματι,
therefore is it? I will pray with the spirit,

church. 5 I would like every
one of you to speak in
tongues,[i] but I would rather have you prophesy. He
who prophesies is greater
than one who speaks in
tongues,[i] unless he interprets, so that the church
may be edified.
6 Now, brothers, if I come
to you and speak in
tongues, what good will I
be to you, unless I bring
you some revelation or
knowledge or prophecy or
word of instruction? 7 Even
in the case of lifeless things
that make sounds, such as
the flute or harp, how will
anyone know what tune is
being played unless there is
a distinction in the notes?
8 Again, if the trumpet does
not sound a clear call, who
will get ready for battle?
9 So it is with you. Unless
you speak intelligible
words with your tongue,
how will anyone know
what you are saying? You
will just be speaking into
the air. 10 Undoubtedly
there are all sorts of languages in the world, yet
none of them is without
meaning. 11 If then I do not
grasp the meaning of what
someone is saying, I am a
foreigner to the speaker,
and he is a foreigner to me.
12 So it is with you. Since
you are eager to have spiritual gifts, try to excel in
gifts that build up the
church.
13 For this reason anyone
who speaks in a tongue
should pray that he may interpret what he says. 14 For
if I pray in a tongue, my
spirit prays, but my mind is
unfruitful. 15 So what shall I
do? I will pray with my spir-

[i] 5 Or *other languages*; also in verses 6, 18, 22, 23 and 39

I will pray with the mind
also; I will sing praise with
the spirit, but I will sing
praise with the mind also.
16 Otherwise, if you say a
blessing with the spirit,
how can anyone in the position of an outsider say the
"Amen" to your thanksgiv-
ing, since the outsider does
not know what you are saying? 17 For you may give
thanks well enough, but the
other person is not built up.
18 I thank God that I speak
in tongues more than all of
you; 19 nevertheless, in
church I would rather
speak five words with my
mind, in order to instruct
others also, than ten thousand words in a tongue.
20 Brothers and sis-
ters,[e] do not be children in
your thinking; rather, be infants in evil, but in thinking
be adults. 21 In the law it is
written,

"By people of strange
tongues
and by the lips of
foreigners
I will speak to this
people;
yet even then they
will not listen to
me,"

says the Lord. 22 Tongues,
then, are a sign not for believers but for unbelievers,
while prophecy is not for
unbelievers but for believers. 23 If, therefore, the
whole church comes to-
gether and all speak in
tongues, and outsiders or
unbelievers enter, will they
not say that you are out of
your mind? 24 But if all
prophesy, an unbeliever or
outsider who enters is reproved by all and called to
account by all. 25 After the
secrets of the unbeliever's
heart are disclosed, that
person will bow down be-
fore God and worship him,
declaring, "God is really
among you."

Orderly Worship

26 What should be done

προσεύξομαι δὲ καὶ τῷ νοΐ· ψαλῶ τῷ
[2]I will pray [1]and [3]also with the mind; I will sing with the

πνεύματι, ψαλῶ δὲ καὶ τῷ νοΐ. 16 ἐπεὶ
spirit, . [2]I will sing [1]and [3]also with the mind. Otherwise

ἐὰν εὐλογῇς [ἐν] πνεύματι, ὁ ἀναπληρῶν
if thou blessest in spirit, the [one] occupying

τὸν τόπον τοῦ ἰδιώτου πῶς ἐρεῖ τὸ
the place of the uninstructed how will he say the

ἀμὴν ἐπὶ τῇ σῇ εὐχαριστίᾳ; ἐπειδὴ τί
"amen" at – thy giving thanks? Since what

λέγεις οὐκ οἶδεν· 17 σὺ μὲν γὰρ καλῶς
thou sayest he knows not; [2]thou [3]indeed [1]for [5]well

εὐχαριστεῖς, ἀλλ' ὁ ἕτερος οὐκ οἰκοδομεῖται.
[4]givest thanks, but the other is not edified.

18 εὐχαριστῶ τῷ θεῷ, πάντων ὑμῶν μᾶλ-
I give thanks – to God, [5]all [4]you [3]more

λον γλώσσαις λαλῶ· 19 ἀλλὰ ἐν ἐκκλησίᾳ
than [2]in tongues [1]I speak; but in a church

θέλω πέντε λόγους τῷ νοΐ μου λαλῆσαι,
[1]I wish [3]five [4]words [5]with the [6]mind [7]of me [2]to speak,

ἵνα καὶ ἄλλους κατηχήσω, ἢ μυρίους
in order that also others I may instruct, than ten thousands

λόγους ἐν γλώσσῃ. 20 Ἀδελφοί, μὴ
words in a tongue. Brothers, [2]not

παιδία γίνεσθε ταῖς φρεσίν, ἀλλὰ τῇ
[3]children [1]be ye in the(your) minds, but –

κακίᾳ νηπιάζετε, ταῖς δὲ φρεσὶν τέλειοι
in malice be ye infantlike, and in the(your) minds mature

γίνεσθε. 21 ἐν τῷ νόμῳ γέγραπται ὅτι
be ye. In the law it has been written that

ἐν ἑτερογλώσσοις καὶ ἐν χείλεσιν ἑτέρων
in other tongues and in lips of others

λαλήσω τῷ λαῷ τούτῳ, καὶ οὐδ' οὕτως
I will speak to this people, and not so

εἰσακούσονταί μου, λέγει κύριος. 22 ὥστε
will they hear me, says [the] Lord. So as

αἱ γλῶσσαι εἰς σημεῖόν εἰσιν οὐ τοῖς
the tongues [2]for [3]a sign [1]are not to the

πιστεύουσιν ἀλλὰ τοῖς ἀπίστοις, ἡ δὲ
[ones] believing but to the unbelievers, and *the*

προφητεία οὐ τοῖς ἀπίστοις ἀλλὰ τοῖς
prophecy [is] not to the unbelievers but to the

πιστεύουσιν. 23 Ἐὰν οὖν συνέλθῃ ἡ
[ones] believing. If therefore [4]comes *together* [1]the

ἐκκλησία ὅλη ἐπὶ τὸ αὐτὸ καὶ πάντες
[3]church [2]whole together and all

λαλῶσιν γλώσσαις, εἰσέλθωσιν δὲ ἰδιῶται
speak in tongues, and [4]enter [1]uninstructed

ἢ ἄπιστοι, οὐκ ἐροῦσιν ὅτι μαίνεσθε;
[2]or [3]unbelievers, will they not say that ye rave?

24 ἐὰν δὲ πάντες προφητεύωσιν, εἰσέλθῃ δέ
but if all prophesy, and [5]enters

τις ἄπιστος ἢ ἰδιώτης, ἐλέγχεται ὑπὸ
[1]some [2]unbeliever [3]or [4]uninstructed, he is convicted by

πάντων, ἀνακρίνεται ὑπὸ πάντων, 25 τὰ
all, he is judged by all, the

κρυπτὰ τῆς καρδίας αὐτοῦ φανερὰ γίνεται,
hidden things of the heart of him [2]manifest [1]becomes,

καὶ οὕτως πεσὼν ἐπὶ πρόσωπον προσκυνή-
and so falling on [his] face he will wor-

σει τῷ θεῷ, ἀπαγγέλλων ὅτι ὄντως
ship – God, declaring that really

ὁ θεὸς ἐν ὑμῖν ἐστιν. 26 Τί οὖν ἐστιν,
– God [2]among [3]you [1]is. What therefore is it,

it, but I will also pray with
my mind; I will sing with
my spirit, but I will also
sing with my mind. 16 If you
are praising God with your
spirit, how can one who
finds himself among those
who do not understand[j]
say "Amen" to your
thanksgiving, since he does
not know what you are saying? 17 You may be giving
thanks well enough, but the
other man is not edified.
18 I thank God that I speak
in tongues more than all of
you. 19 But in the church I
would rather speak five intelligible words to instruct
others than ten thousand
words in a tongue.
20 Brothers, stop thinking
like children. In regard to
evil be infants, but in your
thinking be adults. 21 In the
Law it is written:

"Through men of
strange tongues
and through the lips of
foreigners
I will speak to this
people,
but even then they will
not listen to me,"[k]

says the Lord.
22 Tongues, then, are a
sign, not for believers but
for unbelievers; prophecy,
however, is for believers,
not for unbelievers. 23 So if
the whole church comes together and everyone
speaks in tongues, and
some who do not under-
stand[l] or some unbelievers
come in, will they not say
that you are out of your
mind? 24 But if an unbeliever or someone who does
not understand[m] comes in
while everybody is prophesying, he will be convinced
by all that he is a sinner and
will be judged by all, 25 and
the secrets of his heart will
be laid bare. So he will fall
down and worship God, ex-
claiming, "God is really
among you!"

Orderly Worship

26 What then shall we say,

j16 Or *among the inquirers*
k21 Isaiah 28:11,12
l23 Or *some inquirers*
m24 Or *or some inquirer*

then, my friends?[e] When
you come together, each
one has a hymn, a lesson, a
revelation, a tongue, or an
interpretation. Let all
things be done for building
up. 27 If anyone speaks in a
tongue, let there be only
two or at most three, and
each in turn; and let one interpret. 28 But if there is no
one to interpret, let them be
silent in church and speak
to themselves and to God.
29 Let two or three prophets
speak, and let the others
weigh what is said. 30 If a
revelation is made to someone else sitting nearby, let
the first person be silent.
31 For you can all prophesy
one by one, so that all may
learn and all be encour-
aged. 32 And the spirits of
prophets are subject to the
prophets, 33 for God is a
God not of disorder but of
peace.
(As in all the churches of
the saints, 34 women should
be silent in the churches.
For they are not permitted
to speak, but should be
subordinate, as the law also
says. 35 If there is anything
they desire to know, let
them ask their husbands at
home. For it is shameful for
a woman to speak in
church.[f] 36 Or did the word
of God originate with you?
Or are you the only ones it
has reached?)
37 Anyone who claims
to be a prophet, or to have
spiritual powers, must acknowledge that what I am
writing to you is a com-
mand of the Lord. 38 Any-
one who does not recog-
nize this is not to be recognized. 39 So, my friends,[g]
be eager to prophesy, and
do not forbid speaking in
tongues; 40 but all things
should be done decently
and in order.

ἀδελφοί; ὅταν συνέρχησθε, ἕκαστος ψαλμὸν
brothers? whenever ye come together, each one a psalm
ἔχει, διδαχὴν ἔχει, ἀποκάλυψιν ἔχει, γλῶσ-
has, a teaching he has, a revelation he has, a
σαν ἔχει, ἑρμηνείαν ἔχει· πάντα πρὸς
tongue he has, an interpretation he has; [2]all things [4]for
οἰκοδομὴν γινέσθω. **27** εἴτε γλώσσῃ τις
[5]edification [1]let [3]be. If in a tongue anyone
λαλεῖ, κατὰ δύο ἢ τὸ πλεῖστον τρεῖς,
speaks, by two or the most three,
καὶ ἀνὰ μέρος, **28** καὶ εἷς διερμηνευέτω·
and in turn,† and [2]one [1]let [3]interpret;
ἐὰν δὲ μὴ ᾖ διερμηνευτής, σιγάτω ἐν
but if there is not an interpreter, let him be silent in
ἐκκλησίᾳ, ἑαυτῷ δὲ λαλείτω καὶ τῷ
church, and to himself let him speak and –
θεῷ. **29** προφῆται δὲ δύο ἢ τρεῖς λαλεί-
to God. And prophets two or three let them
τωσαν, καὶ οἱ ἄλλοι διακρινέτωσαν·
speak, and the others let discern;
30 ἐὰν δὲ ἄλλῳ ἀποκαλυφθῇ καθημένῳ, ὁ
but if [1]to another [3][something] [4]is revealed [2]sitting, the
πρῶτος σιγάτω. **31** δύνασθε γὰρ καθ'
first let be silent. For ye can [3]sin-
ἕνα πάντες προφητεύειν, ἵνα πάντες
gly† [1]all [2]to prophesy, in order that all
μανθάνωσιν καὶ πάντες παρακαλῶνται.
may learn and all may be encouraged.
32 καὶ πνεύματα προφητῶν προφήταις
And [the] spirits of prophets to prophets
ὑποτάσσεται· **33** οὐ γάρ ἐστιν ἀκαταστασίας
is(are) subject; for [3]not [2]is [4]of tumult
ὁ θεὸς ἀλλὰ εἰρήνης. Ὡς ἐν πάσαις
– [1]God but of peace. As in all
ταῖς ἐκκλησίαις τῶν ἁγίων, **34** αἱ γυναῖκες
the churches of the saints, [2]the [3]women
ἐν ταῖς ἐκκλησίαις σιγάτωσαν· οὐ γὰρ
[5]in [6]the [7]churches [1]let [4]be silent; [2]not [1]for
ἐπιτρέπεται αὐταῖς λαλεῖν, ἀλλὰ ὑποτασ-
[3]it is [4]permitted to them to speak, but let them
σέσθωσαν, καθὼς καὶ ὁ νόμος λέγει.
be subject, as also the law says.
35 εἰ δέ τι μαθεῖν θέλουσιν, ἐν οἴκῳ
But if [2]anything [3]to learn [1]they wish, [6]at home
τοὺς ἰδίους ἄνδρας ἐπερωτάτωσαν· αἰσχρὸν
[2]the(ir) [3]own [4]husbands [1]let them question; [3]a shame
γάρ ἐστιν γυναικὶ λαλεῖν ἐν ἐκκλησίᾳ.
[1]for [2]it is for a woman to speak in a church.
36 ἢ ἀφ' ὑμῶν ὁ λόγος τοῦ θεοῦ ἐξῆλθεν,
Or from you [2]the [3]word – [4]of God [1]went forth,
ἢ εἰς ὑμᾶς μόνους κατήντησεν; **37** Εἴ
or to you only did it reach? If
τις δοκεῖ προφήτης εἶναι ἢ πνευματικός,
anyone thinks [2]a prophet [1]to be or a spiritual man,
ἐπιγινωσκέτω ἃ γράφω ὑμῖν ὅτι
let him clearly know [the] things which I write to you that
κυρίου ἐστὶν ἐντολή· **38** εἰ δέ τις
of [the] Lord they are a commandment; but if anyone
ἀγνοεῖ, ἀγνοεῖται. **39** Ὥστε, ἀδελφοί
is ignorant, let him be ignorant. So as, brothers
μου, ζηλοῦτε τὸ προφητεύειν, καὶ τὸ
of me, be ye eager – to prophesy, and –
λαλεῖν μὴ κωλύετε γλώσσαις· **40** πάντα
[2]to speak [1]forbid not in tongues; [2]all things
δὲ εὐσχημόνως καὶ κατὰ τάξιν γινέσθω.
and [4]becomingly [5]and [6]according to [7]order [1]let [3]be done.

brothers? When you come
together, everyone has a
hymn, or a word of instruction, a revelation, a tongue
or an interpretation. All of
these must be done for the
strengthening of the
church. 27 If anyone speaks
in a tongue, two—or at the
most three—should speak,
one at a time, and someone
must interpret. 28 If there is
no interpreter, the speaker
should keep quiet in the
church and speak to him-
self and God.
29 Two or three prophets
should speak, and the others should weigh carefully
what is said. 30 And if a revelation comes to someone
who is sitting down, the
first speaker should stop.
31 For you can all prophesy
in turn so that everyone
may be instructed and en-
couraged. 32 The spirits of
prophets are subject to the
control of prophets. 33 For
God is not a God of disorder but of peace.
As in all the congrega-
tions of the saints, 34 wom-
en should remain silent in
the churches. They are not
allowed to speak, but must
be in submission, as the
Law says. 35 If they want to
inquire about something,
they should ask their own
husbands at home; for it is
disgraceful for a woman to
speak in the church.
36 Did the word of God
originate with you? Or are
you the only people it has
reached? 37 If anybody
thinks he is a prophet or
spiritually gifted, let him
acknowledge that what I
am writing to you is the
Lord's command. 38 If he
ignores this, he himself will
be ignored.[n]
39 Therefore, my broth-
ers, be eager to prophesy,
and do not forbid speaking
in tongues. 40 But every-
thing should be done in a
fitting and orderly way.

[f] Other ancient authorities put verses 34-35 after verse 40
[g] Gk *my brothers*

[n] 38 Some manuscripts *If he is ignorant of this, let him be ignorant*

Chapter 15

The Resurrection of Christ

NOW I would remind
you, brothers and sis-
ters,[g] of the good news[h]
that I proclaimed to you,
which you in turn received,
in which also you stand,
2through which also you
are being saved, if you hold
firmly to the message that I
proclaimed to you—unless
you have come to believe in
vain.
3 For I handed on to
you as of first importance
what I in turn had received:
that Christ died for our sins
in accordance with the
scriptures, 4and that he
was buried, and that he was
raised on the third day in
accordance with the scriptures, 5and that he ap-
peared to Cephas, then to
the twelve. 6Then he ap-
peared to more than five
hundred brothers and sis-
ters[i] at one time, most of
whom are still alive, though
some have died.[j] 7Then he
appeared to James, then to
all the apostles. 8Last of
all, as to one untimely
born, he appeared also to
me. 9For I am the least of
the apostles, unfit to be
called an apostle, because I
persecuted the church of
God. 10But by the grace of
God I am what I am, and
his grace toward me has not
been in vain. On the con-
trary, I worked harder than
any of them—though it was
not I, but the grace of God
that is with me. 11Whether
then it was I or they, so we
proclaim and so you have
come to believe.

The Resurrection of the Dead

12 Now if Christ is pro-
claimed as raised from the
dead, how can some of you
say there is no resurrection
of the dead? 13If there is no
resurrection of the dead,
then Christ has not been
raised; 14and if Christ has
not been raised, then our

[h] Or *gospel*
[i] Gk *brothers*
[j] Gk *fallen asleep*

15 Γνωρίζω δὲ ὑμῖν, ἀδελφοί, τὸ
Now I make known to you, brothers, the
εὐαγγέλιον ὃ εὐηγγελισάμην ὑμῖν, ὃ καὶ
good tidings which I preached to you, which also
παρελάβετε, ἐν ᾧ καὶ ἑστήκατε, **2** δι'
ye received, in which also ye stand, through
οὗ καὶ σῴζεσθε, τίνι λόγῳ εὐηγγελισάμην
which also ye are saved, ³to what ⁴word ⁵I preached
ὑμῖν εἰ κατέχετε, ἐκτὸς εἰ μὴ εἰκῇ
⁶to you ¹if ²ye hold fast, *except* unless in vain
ἐπιστεύσατε. **3** παρέδωκα γὰρ ὑμῖν ἐν
ye believed. For I delivered to you among
πρώτοις, ὃ καὶ παρέλαβον, ὅτι Χριστὸς
[the] first things, what also I received, that Christ
ἀπέθανεν ὑπὲρ τῶν ἁμαρτιῶν ἡμῶν κατὰ
died on behalf of the sins of us according to
τὰς γραφάς, **4** καὶ ὅτι ἐτάφη, καὶ ὅτι
the scriptures, and that he was buried, and that
ἐγήγερται τῇ ἡμέρᾳ τῇ τρίτῃ κατὰ
he has been raised on the ³day – ¹third according to
τὰς γραφάς, **5** καὶ ὅτι ὤφθη Κηφᾷ,
the scriptures, and that he was seen by Cephas,
εἶτα τοῖς δώδεκα· **6** ἔπειτα ὤφθη ἐπάνω
then by the twelve; afterward he was seen ²over
πεντακοσίοις ἀδελφοῖς ἐφάπαξ, ἐξ ὧν οἱ
¹by ³five hundreds brothers at one time, of whom the
πλείονες μένουσιν ἕως ἄρτι, τινὲς δὲ
majority remain until now, though some
ἐκοιμήθησαν· **7** ἔπειτα ὤφθη Ἰακώβῳ, εἶτα
fell asleep; afterward he was seen by James, then
τοῖς ἀποστόλοις πᾶσιν· **8** ἔσχατον δὲ
by the apostles all; and lastly
πάντων ὡσπερεὶ τῷ ἐκτρώματι ὤφθη
of all even as if to the(an) abortion he was seen
κἀμοί. **9** Ἐγὼ γάρ εἰμι ὁ ἐλάχιστος
by me also. For I am the least
τῶν ἀποστόλων, ὃς οὐκ εἰμὶ ἱκανὸς
of the apostles, who am not sufficient
καλεῖσθαι ἀπόστολος, διότι ἐδίωξα τὴν
to be called an apostle, because I persecuted the
ἐκκλησίαν τοῦ θεοῦ· **10** χάριτι δὲ θεοῦ
church – of God; but by [the] grace of God
εἰμι ὅ εἰμι, καὶ ἡ χάρις αὐτοῦ ἡ εἰς
I am what I am, and the grace of him – to
ἐμὲ οὐ κενὴ ἐγενήθη, ἀλλὰ περισσότερον
me not empty was, but ²more abundantly [than]
αὐτῶν πάντων ἐκοπίασα, οὐκ ἐγὼ δὲ
³them ⁴all ¹I laboured, ²not ³I ¹yet
ἀλλὰ ἡ χάρις τοῦ θεοῦ σὺν ἐμοί. **11** εἴτε
but the grace – of God with me. Whether
οὖν ἐγὼ εἴτε ἐκεῖνοι, οὕτως κηρύσσομεν
therefore I or those, so we proclaim
καὶ οὕτως ἐπιστεύσατε.
and so ye believed.

12 Εἰ δὲ Χριστὸς κηρύσσεται ὅτι ἐκ
But if Christ is proclaimed that from
νεκρῶν ἐγήγερται, πῶς λέγουσιν ἐν ὑμῖν
[the] dead he has been raised, how say ²among ³you
τινες ὅτι ἀνάστασις νεκρῶν οὐκ ἔστιν;
¹some that a resurrection of dead persons there is not?
13 εἰ δὲ ἀνάστασις νεκρῶν οὐκ ἔστιν,
Now if a resurrection of dead persons there is not,
οὐδὲ Χριστὸς ἐγήγερται· **14** εἰ δὲ Χριστὸς
neither Christ has been raised; and if Christ

Chapter 15

The Resurrection of Christ

NOW, brothers, I want
to remind you of the
gospel I preached to you,
which you received and on
which you have taken your
stand. 2By this gospel you
are saved, if you hold firmly to the word I preached to
you. Otherwise, you have
believed in vain.
3For what I received I
passed on to you as of first
importance[o]: that Christ
died for our sins according
to the Scriptures, 4that he
was buried, that he was
raised on the third day according to the Scriptures,
5and that he appeared to
Peter,[p] and then to the
Twelve. 6After that, he appeared to more than five
hundred of the brothers at
the same time, most of
whom are still living,
though some have fallen
asleep. 7Then he appeared
to James, then to all the
apostles, 8and last of all he
appeared to me also, as to
one abnormally born.
9For I am the least of the
apostles and do not even
deserve to be called an
apostle, because I perse-
cuted the church of God.
10But by the grace of God I
am what I am, and his grace
to me was not without ef-
fect. No, I worked harder
than all of them—yet not I,
but the grace of God that
was with me. 11Whether,
then, it was I or they, this is
what we preach, and this is
what you believed.

The Resurrection of the Dead

12But if it is preached that
Christ has been raised from
the dead, how can some of
you say that there is no resurrection of the dead? 13If
there is no resurrection of
the dead, then not even
Christ has been raised.
14And if Christ has not been

[o] 3 Or *you at the first*
[p] 5 Greek *Cephas*

proclamation has been in
vain and your faith has
been in vain. 15 We are even
found to be misrepre-
senting God, because we
testified of God that he
raised Christ—whom he
did not raise if it is true that
the dead are not raised.
16 For if the dead are not
raised, then Christ has not
been raised. 17 If Christ has
not been raised, your faith
is futile and you are still in
your sins. 18 Then those
also who have died[j] in
Christ have perished. 19 If
for this life only we have
hoped in Christ, we are of
all people most to be pitied.
20 But in fact Christ has
been raised from the dead,
the first fruits of those who
have died.[j] 21 For since
death came through a hu-
man being, the resurrection
of the dead has also come
through a human being;
22 for as all die in Adam, so
all will be made alive in
Christ. 23 But each in his
own order: Christ the first
fruits, then at his coming
those who belong to Christ.
24 Then comes the end,[k]
when he hands over the
kingdom to God the Fa-
ther, after he has destroyed
every ruler and every au-
thority and power. 25 For
he must reign until he has
put all his enemies under
his feet. 26 The last enemy
to be destroyed is death.
27 For "God[l] has put all
things in subjection under
his feet." But when it says,
"All things are put in subjection," it is plain that this

οὐκ ἐγήγερται, κενὸν ἄρα τὸ κήρυγμα
has not been raised, empty then the proclamation

ἡμῶν, κενὴ καὶ ἡ πίστις ὑμῶν· **15** εὑρισκ-
of us, empty also the faith of you; [2]we are

όμεθα δὲ καὶ ψευδομάρτυρες τοῦ θεοῦ,
found [1]and also false witnesses – of God,

ὅτι ἐμαρτυρήσαμεν κατὰ τοῦ θεοῦ ὅτι
because we witnessed as to – God that

ἤγειρεν τὸν Χριστόν, ὃν οὐκ ἤγειρεν
he raised – Christ, whom he raised not

εἴπερ ἄρα νεκροὶ οὐκ ἐγείρονται. **16** εἰ
if then dead persons are not raised. if

γὰρ νεκροὶ οὐκ ἐγείρονται, οὐδὲ Χριστὸς
For dead persons are not raised, neither Christ

ἐγήγερται· **17** εἰ δὲ Χριστὸς οὐκ ἐγήγερται,
has been raised; and if Christ has not been raised,

ματαία ἡ πίστις ὑμῶν [ἐστιν], ἔτι ἐστὲ
[5]useless [1]the [2]faith [3]of you [4]is, [2]still [1]ye are

ἐν ταῖς ἁμαρτίαις ὑμῶν. **18** ἄρα καὶ οἱ
in the sins of you. Then also the [ones]

κοιμηθέντες ἐν Χριστῷ ἀπώλοντο. **19** εἰ
having fallen asleep in Christ perished. If

ἐν τῇ ζωῇ ταύτῃ ἐν Χριστῷ ἠλπικότες
in this life [3]in [4]Christ [2]having hoped

ἐσμὲν μόνον, ἐλεεινότεροι πάντων ἀνθρώπων
[1]we are [5]only, more pitiful [than] all men

ἐσμέν. **20** Νυνὶ δὲ Χριστὸς ἐγήγερται
we are. But now Christ has been raised

ἐκ νεκρῶν, ἀπαρχὴ τῶν κεκοιμημένων.
from [the] dead, firstfruit of the [ones] having fallen asleep.

21 ἐπειδὴ γὰρ δι' ἀνθρώπου θάνατος, καὶ
For since through a man death [came], also

δι' ἀνθρώπου ἀνάστασις νεκρῶν. **22** ὥσπερ
through a man a resurrection of dead persons [came]. as

γὰρ ἐν τῷ Ἀδὰμ πάντες ἀποθνῄσκουσιν,
For in – Adam all die,

οὕτως καὶ ἐν τῷ Χριστῷ πάντες ζωοποιη-
so also in – Christ all will be

θήσονται. **23** Ἕκαστος δὲ ἐν τῷ ἰδίῳ
made alive. But each one in the(his) own

τάγματι· ἀπαρχὴ Χριστός, ἔπειτα οἱ τοῦ
order: [the] firstfruit Christ, afterward the [ones] –

Χριστοῦ ἐν τῇ παρουσίᾳ αὐτοῦ, **24** εἶτα
of Christ in the presence of him, then

τὸ τέλος, ὅταν παραδιδοῖ τὴν βασιλείαν
the end, when*ever* he delivers the kingdom

τῷ θεῷ καὶ πατρί, ὅταν καταργήσῃ
– to God even [the] Father, when*ever* he abolishes

πᾶσαν ἀρχὴν καὶ πᾶσαν ἐξουσίαν καὶ
all rule and all authority and

δύναμιν. **25** δεῖ γὰρ αὐτὸν βασιλεύειν
power. For it behoves him to reign

ἄχρι οὗ θῇ πάντας τοὺς ἐχθροὺς ὑπὸ
until he puts all the(his) enemies under

τοὺς πόδας αὐτοῦ. **26** ἔσχατος ἐχθρὸς
the feet of him. [The] last enemy

καταργεῖται ὁ θάνατος· πάντα γὰρ ὑπέταξεν
is abolished – death; for all things he subjected

ὑπὸ τοὺς πόδας αὐτοῦ. **27** ὅταν δὲ
under the feet of him. But when*ever*

εἴπῃ ὅτι πάντα ὑποτέτακται, δῆλον ὅτι
he says that all things have been subjected, [it is] clear that

raised, our preaching is
useless and so is your faith.
15 More than that, we are
then found to be false witnesses about God, for we
have testified about God
that he raised Christ from
the dead. But he did not
raise him if in fact the dead
are not raised. 16 For if the
dead are not raised, then
Christ has not been raised
either. 17 And if Christ has
not been raised, your faith
is futile; you are still in your
sins. 18 Then those also who
have fallen asleep in Christ
are lost. 19 If only for this
life we have hope in Christ,
we are to be pitied more
than all men.
20 But Christ has indeed
been raised from the dead,
the firstfruits of those who
have fallen asleep. 21 For
since death came through a
man, the resurrection of
the dead comes also
through a man. 22 For as in
Adam all die, so in Christ
all will be made alive. 23 But
each in his own turn:
Christ, the firstfruits; then,
when he comes, those who
belong to him. 24 Then the
end will come, when he
hands over the kingdom to
God the Father after he has
destroyed all dominion, authority and power. 25 For he
must reign until he has put
all his enemies under his
feet. 26 The last enemy to be
destroyed is death. 27 For
he "has put everything under his feet."[q] Now when
it says that "everything"
has been put under him, it
is clear that this does not

[k] Or *Then come the rest*
[l] Gk *he*

[q] 27 Psalm 8:6

does not include the one
who put all things in subjection under him. 28 When all
things are subjected to him,
then the Son himself will
also be subjected to the one
who put all things in subjection under him, so that God
may be all in all.
29 Otherwise, what will
those people do who re-
ceive baptism on behalf of
the dead? If the dead are
not raised at all, why are
people baptized on their
behalf?
30 And why are we put-
ting ourselves in danger every hour? 31 I die every day!
That is as certain, brothers
and sisters,[i] as my boasting of you—a boast that I
make in Christ Jesus our
Lord. 32 If with merely human hopes I fought with
wild animals at Ephesus,
what would I have gained
by it? If the dead are not
raised,

"Let us eat and drink,
for tomorrow we
die."

33 Do not be deceived:
"Bad company ruins
good morals."
34 Come to a sober and right
mind, and sin no more; for
some people have no
knowledge of God. I say
this to your shame.

The Resurrection Body

35 But someone will
ask, "How are the dead
raised? With what kind of
body do they come?"
36 Fool! What you sow does
not come to life unless it
dies. 37 And as for what you
sow, you do not sow the
body that is to be, but a
bare seed, perhaps of
wheat or of some other
grain. 38 But God gives it a
body as he has chosen, and
to each kind of seed its own
body. 39 Not all flesh is
alike, but there is one flesh
for human beings, another
for animals, another for
birds, and another for fish.

ἐκτὸς τοῦ ὑποτάξαντος αὐτῷ τὰ πάντα.
[it is] apart from [one] the having subjected to him – all things.

28 ὅταν δὲ ὑποταγῇ αὐτῷ τὰ πάντα,
But when*ever* is(are) subjected to him – all things,

τότε καὶ αὐτὸς ὁ υἱὸς ὑποταγήσεται
then also [3][him]self [1]the [2]Son will be subjected

τῷ ὑποτάξαντι αὐτῷ τὰ πάντα, ἵνα
to the [one] having subjected to him – all things, in order that

ᾖ ὁ θεὸς πάντα ἐν πᾶσιν. 29 Ἐπεὶ
[2]may be – [1]God all things in all. Otherwise

τί ποιήσουσιν οἱ βαπτιζόμενοι ὑπὲρ τῶν
what will they do the [ones] being baptized on behalf of the

νεκρῶν; εἰ ὅλως νεκροὶ οὐκ ἐγείρονται,
dead? if actually dead persons are not raised,

τί καὶ βαπτίζονται ὑπὲρ αὐτῶν; 30 τί
why indeed are they baptized on behalf of them? why

καὶ ἡμεῖς κινδυνεύομεν πᾶσαν ὥραν;
also [2]we [1]are [3]in danger every hour?

31 καθ' ἡμέραν ἀποθνήσκω, νὴ τὴν
Daily I die, by –

ὑμετέραν καύχησιν, ἀδελφοί, ἣν ἔχω ἐν
your boasting, brothers, which I have in

Χριστῷ Ἰησοῦ τῷ κυρίῳ ἡμῶν. 32 εἰ
Christ Jesus the Lord of us. If

κατὰ ἄνθρωπον ἐθηριομάχησα ἐν Ἐφέσῳ,
according to man I fought with wild beasts in Ephesus,

τί μοι τὸ ὄφελος; εἰ νεκροὶ οὐκ ἐγείρονται,
what to me the profit?[c] If dead persons are not raised,
=what profit have I?

φάγωμεν καὶ πίωμεν, αὔριον γὰρ ἀποθνή-
let us eat and *let us* drink, for to-morrow we

σκομεν. 33 μὴ πλανᾶσθε· φθείρουσιν ἤθη
die. Be ye not led astray: [3]Corrupt [5]customs

χρηστὰ ὁμιλίαι κακαί. 34 ἐκνήψατε δικαίως
[4]good [2]associations [1]bad. Become ye sober righteously

καὶ μὴ ἁμαρτάνετε· ἀγνωσίαν γὰρ θεοῦ
and do not sin; for [3]ignorance [4]of God

τινες ἔχουσιν· πρὸς ἐντροπὴν ὑμῖν λαλῶ.
[1]some [2]have: [3]for [4]shame [2]to you [1]I speak.

35 Ἀλλὰ ἐρεῖ τις· πῶς ἐγείρονται οἱ
But [2]will say [1]someone: How are raised the

νεκροί; ποίῳ δὲ σώματι ἔρχονται; 36 ἄφρων,
dead? and with what sort [of] body do they come? Foolish man,

σὺ ὃ σπείρεις, οὐ ζωοποιεῖται ἐὰν μὴ
[2]thou [1]what sowest, is not made alive unless

ἀποθάνῃ· 37 καὶ ὃ σπείρεις, οὐ τὸ σῶμα
it dies; and what thou sowest, not the body

τὸ γενησόμενον σπείρεις, ἀλλὰ γυμνὸν
– going to become thou sowest, but a naked

κόκκον εἰ τύχοι σίτου ἤ τινος τῶν
grain it may be† of wheat or some one of the

λοιπῶν· 38 ὁ δὲ θεὸς δίδωσιν αὐτῷ
rest; – but God gives to it

σῶμα καθὼς ἠθέλησεν, καὶ ἑκάστῳ τῶν
a body as he wished, and to each of the

σπερμάτων ἴδιον σῶμα. 39 οὐ πᾶσα
seeds [its] own body. [3][is] not [1]All

σὰρξ ἡ αὐτὴ σάρξ, ἀλλὰ ἄλλη μὲν
[2]flesh the same flesh, but other(one) indeed

ἀνθρώπων, ἄλλη δὲ σὰρξ κτηνῶν, ἄλλη δὲ
of men, and another flesh of animals, and another

σὰρξ πτηνῶν, ἄλλη δὲ ἰχθύων. 40 καὶ
flesh of birds, and another of fishes. And [there

include God himself, who
put everything under
Christ. 28 When he has done
this, then the Son himself
will be made subject to him
who put everything under
him, so that God may be all
in all.
29 Now if there is no resurrection, what will those do
who are baptized for the
dead? If the dead are not
raised at all, why are people baptized for them?
30 And as for us, why do we
endanger ourselves every
hour? 31 I die every day—I
mean that, brothers—just
as surely as I glory over
you in Christ Jesus our
Lord. 32 If I fought wild
beasts in Ephesus for merely human reasons, what
have I gained? If the dead
are not raised,

"Let us eat and drink,
for tomorrow we
die."[r]

33 Do not be misled: "Bad
company corrupts good
character." 34 Come back
to your senses as you
ought, and stop sinning; for
there are some who are ignorant of God—I say this
to your shame.

The Resurrection Body

35 But someone may ask,
"How are the dead raised?
With what kind of body will
they come?" 36 How fool-
ish! What you sow does not
come to life unless it dies.
37 When you sow, you do
not plant the body that will
be, but just a seed, perhaps
of wheat or of something
else. 38 But God gives it a
body as he has determined,
and to each kind of seed he
gives its own body. 39 All
flesh is not the same: Men
have one kind of flesh, animals have another, birds
another and fish another.

[r] 32 Isaiah 22:13

40There are both heavenly
bodies and earthly bodies,
but the glory of the heavenly is one thing, and that of
the earthly is another.
41There is one glory of the
sun, and another glory of
the moon, and another glory of the stars; indeed, star
differs from star in glory.
42 So it is with the res-
urrection of the dead. What
is sown is perishable, what
is raised is imperishable.
43It is sown in dishonor, it
is raised in glory. It is sown
in weakness, it is raised in
power. 44It is sown a physical body, it is raised a spiritual body. If there is a physical body, there is also a
spiritual body. 45Thus it is
written, "The first man,
Adam, became a living be-
ing"; the last Adam became
a life-giving spirit. 46But it
is not the spiritual that is
first, but the physical, and
then the spiritual. 47The
first man was from the
earth, a man of dust; the
second man is[m] from heav-
en. 48As was the man of
dust, so are those who are
of the dust; and as is the
man of heaven, so are those
who are of heaven. 49Just
as we have borne the image
of the man of dust, we will[n]
also bear the image of the
man of heaven.
50 What I am saying,
brothers and sisters,[o] is
this: flesh and blood cannot
inherit the kingdom of God,
nor does the perishable inherit the imperishable.
51Listen, I will tell you a
mystery! We will not all
die,[p] but we will all be
changed, 52in a moment, in
the twinkling of an eye, at
the last trumpet. For the
trumpet will sound, and the
dead will be raised imper-

[m] Other ancient authorities add *the Lord*
[n] Other ancient authorities read *let us*
[o] Gk *brothers*
[p] Gk *fall asleep*

σώματα ἐπουράνια, καὶ σώματα ἐπίγεια·
are] bodies heavenly, and bodies earthly;
ἀλλὰ ἑτέρα μὲν ἡ τῶν ἐπουρανίων δόξα,
but [7]other (one) [6][is] [5]indeed [1]the [3]of the [4]heavenly [bodies] [2]glory,
ἑτέρα δὲ ἡ τῶν ἐπιγείων. 41 ἄλλη
and other the [glory] of the earthly [bodies]. Other(one)
δόξα ἡλίου, καὶ ἄλλη δόξα σελήνης,
glory of [the] sun, and another glory of [the] moon,
καὶ ἄλλη δόξα ἀστέρων· ἀστὴρ γὰρ
and another glory of [the] stars; for star
ἀστέρος διαφέρει ἐν δόξῃ. 42 οὕτως καὶ
from star differs in glory. So also
ἡ ἀνάστασις τῶν νεκρῶν. σπείρεται ἐν
the resurrection of the dead. It is sown in
φθορᾷ, ἐγείρεται ἐν ἀφθαρσίᾳ· 43 σπείρεται
corruption, it is raised in incorruption; it is sown
ἐν ἀτιμίᾳ, ἐγείρεται ἐν δόξῃ· σπείρεται
in dishonour, it is raised in glory; it is sown
ἐν ἀσθενείᾳ, ἐγείρεται ἐν δυνάμει· 44 σπείρ-
in weakness, it is raised in power; it is
εται σῶμα ψυχικόν, ἐγείρεται σῶμα
sown body a natural, it is raised body
πνευματικόν. Εἰ ἔστιν σῶμα ψυχικόν,
a spiritual. If there is body a natural,
ἔστιν καὶ πνευματικόν. 45 οὕτως καὶ
there is also a spiritual [body]. So also
γέγραπται· ἐγένετο ὁ πρῶτος ἄνθρωπος
it has been written: [5]became [1]The [2]first [3]man
Ἀδὰμ εἰς ψυχὴν ζῶσαν· ὁ ἔσχατος
[4]Adam – soul a living; the last
Ἀδὰμ εἰς πνεῦμα ζωοποιοῦν. 46 ἀλλ᾽
Adam – spirit a life-giving. But
οὐ πρῶτον τὸ πνευματικὸν ἀλλὰ τὸ
not firstly the spiritual [body] but the
ψυχικόν, ἔπειτα τὸ πνευματικόν. 47 ὁ
natural, afterward the spiritual. The
πρῶτος ἄνθρωπος ἐκ γῆς χοϊκός, ὁ
first man [was] out of earth earthy, the
δεύτερος ἄνθρωπος ἐξ οὐρανοῦ. 48 οἷος ὁ
second man [is] out of heaven. Such the
χοϊκός, τοιοῦτοι καὶ οἱ χοϊκοί, καὶ οἷος
earthy man, such also the earthy ones, and such
ὁ ἐπουράνιος, τοιοῦτοι καὶ οἱ ἐπουράνιοι·
the heavenly man, such also the heavenly ones;
49 καὶ καθὼς ἐφορέσαμεν τὴν εἰκόνα τοῦ
and as we bore the image of the
χοϊκοῦ, φορέσομεν καὶ τὴν εἰκόνα τοῦ
earthy man, we shall bear also the image of the
ἐπουρανίου. 50 Τοῦτο δέ φημι, ἀδελφοί,
heavenly man. And this I say, brothers,
ὅτι σὰρξ καὶ αἷμα βασιλείαν θεοῦ κληρο-
that flesh and blood [3][the] kingdom [4]of God [2]*to*
νομῆσαι οὐ δύναται, οὐδὲ ἡ φθορὰ τὴν
inherit [1]cannot, neither – [1]corruption –
ἀφθαρσίαν κληρονομεῖ. 51 ἰδοὺ μυστήριον
[3]incorruption [2]inherits. Behold[,] a mystery
ὑμῖν λέγω· πάντες οὐ κοιμηθησόμεθα,
to you I tell: all We shall not fall asleep,
πάντες δὲ ἀλλαγησόμεθα, 52 ἐν ἀτόμῳ,
but all . we shall be changed, in a moment,
ἐν ῥιπῇ ὀφθαλμοῦ, ἐν τῇ ἐσχάτῃ σάλπιγγι·
in a glance of an eye, at the last trumpet;
σαλπίσει γάρ, καὶ οἱ νεκροὶ ἐγερθήσονται
for a trumpet will sound, and the dead will be raised

40There are also heavenly
bodies and there are earthly bodies; but the splendor
of the heavenly bodies is
one kind, and the splendor
of the earthly bodies is another. 41The sun has one
kind of splendor, the moon
another and the stars an-
other; and star differs from
star in splendor.
42So will it be with the
resurrection of the dead.
The body that is sown is
perishable, it is raised imperishable; 43it is sown in
dishonor, it is raised in glory; it is sown in weakness,
it is raised in power; 44it is
sown a natural body, it is
raised a spiritual body.
If there is a natural body,
there is also a spiritual
body. 45So it is written:
"The first man Adam be-
came a living being"[s]; the
last Adam, a life-giving
spirit. 46The spiritual did
not come first, but the natural, and after that the spiritual. 47The first man was of
the dust of the earth, the
second man from heaven.
48As was the earthly man,
so are those who are of the
earth; and as is the man
from heaven, so also are
those who are of heaven.
49And just as we have
borne the likeness of the
earthly man, so shall we[t]
bear the likeness of the man
from heaven.
50I declare to you, brothers, that flesh and blood
cannot inherit the kingdom
of God, nor does the per-
ishable inherit the imperishable. 51Listen, I tell you
a mystery: We will not all
sleep, but we will all be
changed—52in a flash, in
the twinkling of an eye, at
the last trumpet. For the
trumpet will sound, the
dead will be raised imper-

[s] 45 Gen. 2:7
[t] 49 Some early manuscripts *so let us*

ishable, and we will be
changed. 53 For this perishable body must put on im-
perishability, and this mortal body must put on im-
mortality. 54 When this
perishable body puts on im-
perishability, and this mortal body puts on immortality, then the saying that is
written will be fulfilled:

"Death has been
swallowed up
in victory."
55 "Where, O death, is
your victory?
Where, O death, is
your sting?"

56 The sting of death is sin,
and the power of sin is the
law. 57 But thanks be to
God, who gives us the victory through our Lord
Jesus Christ.
58 Therefore, my be-
loved,[q] be steadfast, immovable, always excelling
in the work of the Lord, because you know that in the
Lord your labor is not in
vain.

Chapter 16

The Collection for the Saints

NOW concerning the
collection for the
saints: you should follow
the directions I gave to the
churches of Galatia. 2 On
the first day of every week,
each of you is to put aside
and save whatever extra
you earn, so that collec-
tions need not be taken
when I come. 3 And when I
arrive, I will send any
whom you approve with
letters to take your gift to
Jerusalem. 4 If it seems ad-
visable that I should go
also, they will accompany
me.

Plans for Travel

5 I will visit you after
passing through
Macedonia—for I intend to
pass through Macedonia—

[q] Gk *beloved brothers*

ἄφθαρτοι, καὶ ἡμεῖς ἀλλαγησόμεθα. **53** Δεῖ
incorruptible, and we shall be changed. it behoves
γὰρ τὸ φθαρτὸν τοῦτο ἐνδύσασθαι
For – corruptible this to put on
ἀφθαρσίαν καὶ τὸ θνητὸν τοῦτο ἐνδύσασθαι
incorruption and – mortal this to put on
ἀθανασίαν. **54** ὅταν δὲ τὸ φθαρτὸν τοῦτο
immortality. And when*ever* this [that is] corruptible
ἐνδύσηται ἀφθαρσίαν καὶ τὸ θνητὸν τοῦτο
shall put on incorruption and this [that is] mortal
ἐνδύσηται ἀθανασίαν, τότε γενήσεται ὁ
shall put on immortality, then will be the
λόγος ὁ γεγραμμένος· κατεπόθη ὁ θάνατος
word – having been written: ²was swallowed up – ¹Death
εἰς νῖκος. **55** ποῦ σου, θάνατε, τὸ νῖκος;
in victory. Where of thee, [O] death, the victory?
ποῦ σου, θάνατε, τὸ κέντρον; **56** τὸ δὲ
where of thee, [O] death, the sting? Now the
κέντρον τοῦ θανάτου ἡ ἁμαρτία, ἡ δὲ
sting – of death – [is] sin, and the
δύναμις τῆς ἁμαρτίας ὁ νόμος· **57** τῷ
power – of sin [is] the law; –
δὲ θεῷ χάρις τῷ διδόντι ἡμῖν τὸ νῖκος
but to God thanks the [one] giving to us the victory
διὰ τοῦ κυρίου ἡμῶν Ἰησοῦ Χριστοῦ.
through the Lord of us Jesus Christ.
58 Ὥστε, ἀδελφοί μου ἀγαπητοί, ἑδραῖοι
So as, brothers of me beloved, firm
γίνεσθε, ἀμετακίνητοι, περισσεύοντες ἐν τῷ
be ye, unmovable, abounding in the
ἔργῳ τοῦ κυρίου πάντοτε, εἰδότες ὅτι
work of the Lord always, knowing that
ὁ κόπος ὑμῶν οὐκ ἔστιν κενὸς ἐν κυρίῳ.
the labour of you is not empty in [the] Lord.

16 Περὶ δὲ τῆς λογείας τῆς εἰς τοὺς
Now about the collection – for the
ἁγίους, ὥσπερ διέταξα ταῖς ἐκκλησίαις
saints, as I charged the churches
τῆς Γαλατίας, οὕτως καὶ ὑμεῖς ποιήσατε.
– of Galatia, so also ²ye ¹do.
2 κατὰ μίαν σαββάτου ἕκαστος ὑμῶν
Every one of a week each of you
=On the first day of every week
παρ' ἑαυτῷ τιθέτω θησαυρίζων ὅ τι ἐὰν
by himself let him put storing up whatever
εὐοδῶται, ἵνα μὴ ὅταν ἔλθω τότε λογεῖαι
he is prospered, lest when*ever* I come then ²collections
γίνωνται. **3** ὅταν δὲ παραγένωμαι, οὓς
¹there are. And when*ever* I arrive, whom-
ἐὰν δοκιμάσητε, δι' ἐπιστολῶν τούτους
ever ye approve, through epistles these
πέμψω ἀπενεγκεῖν τὴν χάριν ὑμῶν εἰς
I will send to carry the grace(gift) of you to
Ἰερουσαλήμ· **4** ἐὰν δὲ ἄξιον ᾖ τοῦ κἀμὲ
Jerusalem; and if ²fitting ¹it is – me also
πορεύεσθαι, σὺν ἐμοὶ πορεύσονται.
to go,[d] with me they shall go.
5 Ἐλεύσομαι δὲ πρὸς ὑμᾶς ὅταν Μακε-
And I will come to you when*ever* ²Mace-
δονίαν διέλθω· Μακεδονίαν γὰρ διέρχομαι,
donia ¹I pass through; for ²Macedonia ¹I am passing through,*

* "Futuristic present"; *cf.* John 14. 3 and ch. 15. 32.

ishable, and we will be
changed. 53 For the perishable must clothe itself with
the imperishable, and the
mortal with immortality.
54 When the perishable has
been clothed with the im-
perishable, and the mortal
with immortality, then the
saying that is written will
come true: "Death has
been swallowed up in vic-
tory."[u]

55 "Where, O death, is
your victory?
Where, O death, is
your sting?"[v]

56 The sting of death is sin,
and the power of sin is the
law. 57 But thanks be to
God! He gives us the victory through our Lord Jesus
Christ.
58 Therefore, my dear
brothers, stand firm. Let
nothing move you. Always
give yourselves fully to the
work of the Lord, because
you know that your labor in
the Lord is not in vain.

Chapter 16

The Collection for God's People

NOW about the collec-
tion for God's people:
Do what I told the Galatian
churches to do. 2 On the
first day of every week,
each one of you should set
aside a sum of money in
keeping with his income,
saving it up, so that when I
come no collections will
have to be made. 3 Then,
when I arrive, I will give
letters of introduction to
the men you approve and
send them with your gift to
Jerusalem. 4 If it seems ad-
visable for me to go also,
they will accompany me.

Personal Requests

5 After I go through Macedonia, I will come to you—
for I will be going through

[u] *54* Isaiah 25:8
[v] *55* Hosea 13:14

6and perhaps I will stay
with you or even spend the
winter, so that you may
send me on my way, wher-
ever I go. 7I do not want to
see you now just in passing,
for I hope to spend some
time with you, if the Lord
permits. 8But I will stay in
Ephesus until Pentecost,
9for a wide door for effective work has opened to
me, and there are many adversaries.
10 If Timothy comes,
see that he has nothing to
fear among you, for he is
doing the work of the Lord
just as I am; 11therefore let
no one despise him. Send
him on his way in peace, so
that he may come to me; for
I am expecting him with the
brothers.
12 Now concerning our
brother Apollos, I strongly
urged him to visit you with
the other brothers, but he
was not at all willing[r] to
come now. He will come
when he has the opportunity.

Final Messages and Greetings

13 Keep alert, stand
firm in your faith, be courageous, be strong. 14Let all
that you do be done in love.
15 Now, brothers and
sisters,[o] you know that
members of the household
of Stephanas were the first
converts in Achaia, and
they have devoted them-
selves to the service of the
saints; 16I urge you to put
yourselves at the service of
such people, and of everyone who works and toils
with them. 17I rejoice at the
coming of Stephanas and
Fortunatus and Achaicus,
because they have made up
for your absence; 18for
they refreshed my spirit as

[r] *Or it was not at all God's will for him*

6 πρὸς ὑμᾶς δὲ τυχὸν καταμενῶ ἢ
7with 8you 1and 2possibly 3I will remain 4or
καὶ παραχειμάσω, ἵνα ὑμεῖς με προπέμ-
5even 6spend the winter, in order that 2ye 1me may set
ψητε οὗ ἐὰν πορεύωμαι. 7 οὐ θέλω γὰρ
forward wherever I may go. For I do not wish
ὑμᾶς ἄρτι ἐν παρόδῳ ἰδεῖν· ἐλπίζω γὰρ
2you 3yet 4in 5passage 1to see; for I am hoping
χρόνον τινὰ ἐπιμεῖναι πρὸς ὑμᾶς, ἐὰν
3time 2some 1to remain with you, if
ὁ κύριος ἐπιτρέψῃ. 8 ἐπιμενῶ δὲ ἐν
the Lord permits. But I will remain in
Ἐφέσῳ ἕως τῆς πεντηκοστῆς· 9 θύρα
Ephesus until – Pentecost; 5door
γάρ μοι ἀνέῳγεν μεγάλη καὶ ἐνεργής,
1for 7to me 6opened 2a great 3and 4effective,
καὶ ἀντικείμενοι πολλοί. 10 Ἐὰν δὲ
and [there are] 2opposing 1many. Now if
ἔλθῃ Τιμόθεος, βλέπετε ἵνα ἀφόβως
2comes 1Timothy, see in order that fearlessly
γένηται πρὸς ὑμᾶς· τὸ γὰρ ἔργον κυρίου
he is with you; for the work of [the] Lord
ἐργάζεται ὡς κἀγώ· 11 μή τις οὖν αὐτὸν
he works as I also; 3not 5any-one 4there-fore 2him
ἐξουθενήσῃ. προπέμψατε δὲ αὐτὸν ἐν
1despise. But set ye forward him in
εἰρήνῃ, ἵνα ἔλθῃ πρός με· ἐκδέχομαι γὰρ
peace, in order that he may come to me; for I am awaiting
αὐτὸν μετὰ τῶν ἀδελφῶν. 12 Περὶ δὲ
him with the brothers. Now about
Ἀπολλῶ τοῦ ἀδελφοῦ, πολλὰ παρεκάλεσα
2Apollos *the* 1brother, 3much 1I besought
αὐτὸν ἵνα ἔλθῃ πρὸς ὑμᾶς μετὰ τῶν
2him in order that he would come to you with the
ἀδελφῶν· καὶ πάντως οὐκ ἦν θέλημα
brothers; and altogether it was not [his] will
ἵνα νῦν ἔλθῃ, ἐλεύσεται δὲ ὅταν εὐκαιρήσῃ.
in order that 2now 1he should come, but he will come whenever he has opportunity.
13 Γρηγορεῖτε, στήκετε ἐν τῇ πίστει,
Watch ye, stand in the faith,
ἀνδρίζεσθε, κραταιοῦσθε. 14 πάντα ὑμῶν
play the man, be strong. 2All things 3of you
ἐν ἀγάπῃ γινέσθω.
4in 5love 1let be.
15 Παρακαλῶ δὲ ὑμᾶς, ἀδελφοί· οἴδατε
Now I beseech you, brothers: Know ye
τὴν οἰκίαν Στεφανᾶ, ὅτι ἐστὶν ἀπαρχὴ
the household of Stephanas, that it is firstfruit
τῆς Ἀχαΐας καὶ εἰς διακονίαν τοῖς
– of Achaia and to ministry to the
ἁγίοις ἔταξαν ἑαυτούς· 16 ἵνα καὶ ὑμεῖς
saints they appointed themselves; in order that also ye
ὑποτάσσησθε τοῖς τοιούτοις καὶ παντὶ τῷ
may submit – to such ones and to everyone
συνεργοῦντι καὶ κοπιῶντι. 17 χαίρω δὲ
working with [?me] and labouring. Now I rejoice
ἐπὶ τῇ παρουσίᾳ Στεφανᾶ καὶ Φορτουνάτου
at the presence of Stephanas and of Fortunatus
καὶ Ἀχαϊκοῦ, ὅτι τὸ ὑμέτερον ὑστέρημα
and of Achaicus, that – 3your 4lack
οὗτοι ἀνεπλήρωσαν· 18 ἀνέπαυσαν γὰρ τὸ
1these 2supplied; for they refreshed –

Macedonia. 6Perhaps I will
stay with you awhile, or
even spend the winter, so
that you can help me on my
journey, wherever I go. 7I
do not want to see you now
and make only a passing
visit; I hope to spend some
time with you, if the Lord
permits. 8But I will stay on
at Ephesus until Pentecost,
9because a great door for
effective work has opened
to me, and there are many
who oppose me.
10If Timothy comes, see
to it that he has nothing to
fear while he is with you,
for he is carrying on the
work of the Lord, just as I
am. 11No one, then, should
refuse to accept him. Send
him on his way in peace so
that he may return to me. I
am expecting him along
with the brothers.
12Now about our brother
Apollos: I strongly urged
him to go to you with the
brothers. He was quite unwilling to go now, but he
will go when he has the opportunity.
13Be on your guard; stand
firm in the faith; be men of
courage; be strong. 14Do
everything in love.
15You know that the
household of Stephanas
were the first converts in
Achaia, and they have de-
voted themselves to the
service of the saints. I urge
you, brothers, 16to submit
to such as these and to everyone who joins in the
work, and labors at it. 17I
was glad when Stephanas,
Fortunatus and Achaicus
arrived, because they have
supplied what was lacking
from you. 18For they re-

well as yours. So give recognition to such persons.
19 The churches of Asia send greetings. Aquila and Prisca, together with the church in their house, greet you warmly in the Lord.
20 All the brothers and sisters[o] send greetings. Greet one another with a holy kiss.

21 I, Paul, write this greeting with my own hand.
22 Let anyone be accursed who has no love for the Lord. Our Lord, come![s]
23 The grace of the Lord Jesus be with you.
24 My love be with all of you in Christ Jesus.[t]

ἐμὸν πνεῦμα καὶ τὸ ὑμῶν. ἐπιγινώσκετε
my spirit and – of you(yours). Recognize ye
οὖν τοὺς τοιούτους.
therefore – such ones.
19 Ἀσπάζονται ὑμᾶς αἱ ἐκκλησίαι τῆς
[4]Greet [5]you [1]the [2]churches –
Ἀσίας. ἀσπάζεται ὑμᾶς ἐν κυρίῳ πολλὰ
[3]of Asia. [4]Greets [5]you [7]in [8][the] Lord [6]much
Ἀκύλας καὶ Πρίσκα σὺν τῇ κατ' οἶκον
[1]Aquila [2]and [3]Prisca [9]with [10]the [12]in [the] house
αὐτῶν ἐκκλησίᾳ. 20 ἀσπάζονται ὑμᾶς οἱ
[13]of them [11]church. [4]Greet [5]you [2]the
ἀδελφοὶ πάντες. Ἀσπάσασθε ἀλλήλους ἐν
[3]brothers [1]all. Greet ye one another with
φιλήματι ἁγίῳ. 21 Ὁ ἀσπασμὸς τῇ
kiss a holy. [1]The [2]greeting –
ἐμῇ χειρὶ Παύλου. 22 εἴ τις οὐ φιλεῖ
[4]with my [5]hand [3]of Paul. If anyone loves not
τὸν κύριον, ἤτω ἀνάθεμα. μαράνα θά.
the Lord, let him be a curse. Marana tha.
23 ἡ χάρις τοῦ κυρίου Ἰησοῦ μεθ' ὑμῶν.
The grace of the Lord Jesus [be] with you.
24 ἡ ἀγάπη μου μετὰ πάντων ὑμῶν ἐν
The love of me [be] with [2]all [1]you in
Χριστῷ Ἰησοῦ.
Christ Jesus.

freshed my spirit and yours also. Such men deserve recognition.

Final Greetings

19The churches in the province of Asia send you greetings. Aquila and Priscilla[w] greet you warmly in the Lord, and so does the church that meets at their house. 20All the brothers here send you greetings. Greet one another with a holy kiss.
21I, Paul, write this greeting in my own hand.
22If anyone does not love the Lord—a curse be on him. Come, O Lord[x]!
23The grace of the Lord Jesus be with you.
24My love to all of you in Christ Jesus. Amen.[y]

[s] Gk *Marana tha*. These Aramaic words can also be read *Maran atha*, meaning *Our Lord has come*
[t] Other ancient authorities add *Amen*

[w] *19* Greek *Prisca*, a variant of *Priscilla*
[x] *22* In Aramaic the expression *Come, O Lord* is *Marana tha*.
[y] *24* Some manuscripts do not have *Amen*.

The Second Letter of Paul to the

Corinthians

Chapter 1

Salutation

PAUL, an apostle of
Christ Jesus by the will
of God, and Timothy our
brother,
To the church of God
that is in Corinth, including
all the saints throughout
Achaia:
2 Grace to you and
peace from God our Father
and the Lord Jesus Christ.

Paul's Thanksgiving after Affliction

3 Blessed be the God
and Father of our Lord
Jesus Christ, the Father of
mercies and the God of all
consolation, 4who con-
soles us in all our affliction,
so that we may be able to
console those who are in
any affliction with the consolation with which we ourselves are consoled by
God. 5For just as the sufferings of Christ are abundant for us, so also our consolation is abundant
through Christ. 6If we are
being afflicted, it is for your
consolation and salvation;
if we are being consoled, it
is for your consolation,
which you experience
when you patiently endure
the same sufferings that we
are also suffering. 7Our
hope for you is unshaken;
for we know that as you
share in our sufferings, so
also you share in our consolation.
8 We do not want you to
be unaware, brothers and
sisters,[a] of the affliction
we experienced in Asia; for
we were so utterly, unbear-
ably crushed that we de-
spaired of life itself. 9In-
deed, we felt that we had
received the sentence of
death so that we would rely

[a] Gk *brothers*

ΠΡΟΣ ΚΟΡΙΝΘΙΟΥΣ Β

To Corinthians 2

1 Παῦλος ἀπόστολος Χριστοῦ Ἰησοῦ
Paul an apostle of Christ Jesus

διὰ θελήματος θεοῦ καὶ Τιμόθεος ὁ
through [the] will of God and Timothy the

ἀδελφὸς τῇ ἐκκλησίᾳ τοῦ θεοῦ τῇ οὔσῃ
brother to the church – of God – being

ἐν Κορίνθῳ σὺν τοῖς ἁγίοις πᾶσιν τοῖς
in Corinth with [2]the [3]saints [1]all –

οὖσιν ἐν ὅλῃ τῇ Ἀχαΐᾳ· 2 χάρις ὑμῖν καὶ
being in all – Achaia: Grace to you and

εἰρήνη ἀπὸ θεοῦ πατρὸς ἡμῶν καὶ κυρίου
peace from God [the] Father of us and [the] Lord

Ἰησοῦ Χριστοῦ.
Jesus Christ.

3 Εὐλογητὸς ὁ θεὸς καὶ πατὴρ τοῦ
Blessed [be] the God and Father of the

κυρίου ἡμῶν Ἰησοῦ Χριστοῦ, ὁ πατὴρ
Lord of us Jesus Christ, the Father

τῶν οἰκτιρμῶν καὶ θεὸς πάσης παρακλήσ-
– of compassions and God of all com-

εως, 4 ὁ παρακαλῶν ἡμᾶς ἐπὶ πάσῃ
fort, the [one] comforting us on(in) all

τῇ θλίψει ἡμῶν, εἰς τὸ δύνασθαι ἡμᾶς
the affliction of us, [with a view] to – to be able us[b] =our being able

παρακαλεῖν τοὺς ἐν πάσῃ θλίψει διὰ
to comfort the ones in every affliction through

τῆς παρακλήσεως ἧς παρακαλούμεθα αὐτοὶ
the comfort of(with) which we are comforted [our-]selves

ὑπὸ τοῦ θεοῦ. 5 ὅτι καθὼς περισσεύει τὰ
by – God. Because as abounds the

παθήματα τοῦ Χριστοῦ εἰς ἡμᾶς, οὕτως
sufferings – of Christ in us, so

διὰ τοῦ Χριστοῦ περισσεύει καὶ ἡ παρά-
through – Christ abounds also the com-

κλησις ἡμῶν. 6 εἴτε δὲ θλιβόμεθα, ὑπὲρ
fort of us. Now whether we are afflicted, on behalf of

τῆς ὑμῶν παρακλήσεως καὶ σωτηρίας· εἴτε
the [4]of you [1]comfort [2]and [3]salvation; or

παρακαλούμεθα, ὑπὲρ τῆς ὑμῶν παρακλή-
we are comforted, on behalf of the [2]of you [1]com-

σεως τῆς ἐνεργουμένης ἐν ὑπομονῇ τῶν
fort – operating in endurance of the

αὐτῶν παθημάτων ὧν καὶ ἡμεῖς πάσχομεν,
same sufferings which also we suffer,

7 καὶ ἡ ἐλπὶς ἡμῶν βεβαία ὑπὲρ ὑμῶν
and the hope of us [is] firm on behalf of you

εἰδότες ὅτι ὡς κοινωνοί ἐστε τῶν παθημά-
knowing that as partakers ye are of the suffer-

των, οὕτως καὶ τῆς παρακλήσεως. 8 Οὐ
ings, so also of the comfort. not

γὰρ θέλομεν ὑμᾶς ἀγνοεῖν, ἀδελφοί, ὑπὲρ
For we wish you to be ignorant, brothers, as to

τῆς θλίψεως ἡμῶν τῆς γενομένης ἐν
the affliction of us – having been in

τῇ Ἀσίᾳ, ὅτι καθ' ὑπερβολὴν ὑπὲρ
– Asia, that excessively† beyond

δύναμιν ἐβαρήθημεν, ὥστε ἐξαπορηθῆναι
power we were burdened, so as to despair =so that we despaired even

ἡμᾶς καὶ τοῦ ζῆν· 9 ἀλλὰ αὐτοὶ ἐν
us[b] even – to live; but [our]selves in
of life;

ἑαυτοῖς τὸ ἀπόκριμα τοῦ θανάτου ἐσχήκα-
ourselves the sentence – of death we have

2 Corinthians

Chapter 1

PAUL, an apostle of
Christ Jesus by the will
of God, and Timothy our
brother,

To the church of God in
Corinth, together with all
the saints throughout
Achaia:

2Grace and peace to you
from God our Father and
the Lord Jesus Christ.

The God of All Comfort

3Praise be to the God and
Father of our Lord Jesus
Christ, the Father of compassion and the God of all
comfort, 4who comforts us
in all our troubles, so that
we can comfort those in
any trouble with the com-
fort we ourselves have received from God. 5For just
as the sufferings of Christ
flow over into our lives, so
also through Christ our
comfort overflows. 6If we
are distressed, it is for your
comfort and salvation; if
we are comforted, it is for
your comfort, which pro-
duces in you patient endurance of the same sufferings
we suffer. 7And our hope
for you is firm, because we
know that just as you share
in our sufferings, so also
you share in our comfort.
8We do not want you to
be uninformed, brothers,
about the hardships we suffered in the province of
Asia. We were under great
pressure, far beyond our
ability to endure, so that we
despaired even of life. 9In-
deed, in our hearts we felt

not on ourselves but on
God who raises the dead.
10 He who rescued us from
so deadly a peril will continue to rescue us; on him
we have set our hope that
he will rescue us again, 11 as
you also join in helping us
by your prayers, so that
many will give thanks on
our[b] behalf for the blessing
granted us through the
prayers of many.

The Postponement of Paul's Visit

12 Indeed, this is our
boast, the testimony of our
conscience: we have be-
haved in the world with
frankness[c] and godly sincerity, not by earthly wisdom but by the grace of
God—and all the more to-
ward you. 13 For we write
you nothing other than
what you can read and also
understand; I hope you will
understand until the end—
14 as you have already understood us in part—that
on the day of the Lord
Jesus we are your boast
even as you are our boast.
15 Since I was sure of
this, I wanted to come to
you first, so that you might
have a double favor;[d] 16 I
wanted to visit you on my
way to Macedonia, and to
come back to you from
Macedonia and have you
send me on to Judea.
17 Was I vacillating when I
wanted to do this? Do I
make my plans according
to ordinary human stan-
dards,[e] ready to say "Yes,

[b] Other ancient authorities read *your*
[c] Other ancient authorities read *holiness*
[d] Other ancient authorities read *pleasure*
[e] Gk *according to the flesh*

μεν, ἵνα μὴ πεποιθότες ὦμεν ἐφ' ἑαυτοῖς
had, in order that [2]not [3]having trusted [1]we might be on ourselves

ἀλλ' ἐπὶ τῷ θεῷ τῷ ἐγείροντι τοὺς
but on – God the [one] raising the

νεκρούς· 10 ὃς ἐκ τηλικούτου θανάτου
dead; who out of so great a death

ἐρρύσατο ἡμᾶς καὶ ῥύσεται, εἰς ὃν
delivered us and will deliver, in whom

ἠλπίκαμεν [ὅτι] καὶ ἔτι ῥύσεται, 11 συν-
we have hoped that indeed yet he will deliver, co-

υπουργούντων καὶ ὑμῶν ὑπὲρ ἡμῶν τῇ
operating also you[a] on behalf of us –
=while ye also coöperate

δεήσει, ἵνα ἐκ πολλῶν προσώπων τὸ
in petition, in order that [4]by [5]many [6]persons [7][for] [8]the

εἰς ἡμᾶς χάρισμα διὰ πολλῶν εὐχαριστηθῇ
[10]to [11]us [9]gift [12]through [13]many [1]thanks may be given

ὑπὲρ ἡμῶν.
[2]on behalf of [3]us.

12 Ἡ γὰρ καύχησις ἡμῶν αὕτη ἐστίν,
For the boasting of us [2]this [1]is,

τὸ μαρτύριον τῆς συνειδήσεως ἡμῶν, ὅτι
the testimony of the conscience of us, because

ἐν ἁγιότητι καὶ εἰλικρινείᾳ τοῦ θεοῦ,
in sanctity and sincerity – of God,

οὐκ ἐν σοφίᾳ σαρκικῇ ἀλλ' ἐν χάριτι
not in wisdom fleshly but in [the] grace

θεοῦ, ἀνεστράφημεν ἐν τῷ κόσμῳ, περισ-
of God, we behaved in the world, [2]more

σοτέρως δὲ πρὸς ὑμᾶς. 13 οὐ γὰρ ἄλλα
[3]especially [1]and with you. [2]Not [1]for [4]other things

γράφομεν ὑμῖν ἀλλ' ἢ ἃ ἀναγινώσκετε
[3]we write to you *other* than what ye read

ἢ καὶ ἐπιγινώσκετε, ἐλπίζω δὲ ὅτι
or even perceive, and I hope that

ἕως τέλους ἐπιγνώσεσθε, 14 καθὼς καὶ
to [the] end ye will perceive, as also

ἐπέγνωτε ἡμᾶς ἀπὸ μέρους, ὅτι καύχημα
ye perceived us from(in) part, because [2]boast

ὑμῶν ἐσμεν καθάπερ καὶ ὑμεῖς ἡμῶν
[3]of you [1]we are even as also ye of us

ἐν τῇ ἡμέρᾳ τοῦ κυρίου ἡμῶν Ἰησοῦ.
in the day of the Lord of us Jesus.

15 Καὶ ταύτῃ τῇ πεποιθήσει ἐβουλόμην
And in this – persuasion I determined

πρότερον πρὸς ὑμᾶς ἐλθεῖν ἵνα δευτέραν
formerly to you to come in order that a second

χάριν σχῆτε, 16 καὶ δι' ὑμῶν διελθεῖν
grace ye might have, and through you to pass *through*

εἰς Μακεδονίαν, καὶ πάλιν ἀπὸ Μακεδονίας
into Macedonia, and again from Macedonia

ἐλθεῖν πρὸς ὑμᾶς καὶ ὑφ' ὑμῶν
to come to you and by you

προπεμφθῆναι εἰς τὴν Ἰουδαίαν. 17 τοῦτο
to be set forward to – Judæa. This

οὖν βουλόμενος μήτι ἄρα τῇ ἐλαφρίᾳ
therefore determining *not* [3]then – [4]fickleness

ἐχρησάμην; ἢ ἃ βουλεύομαι κατὰ σάρκα
[1]did I use? or [the] things which I determine according to [the] flesh

βουλεύομαι, ἵνα ᾖ παρ' ἐμοὶ τὸ ναὶ
do I determine, in order that there may be with me the Yes

the sentence of death. But
this happened that we
might not rely on ourselves
but on God, who raises the
dead. 10 He has delivered us
from such a deadly peril,
and he will deliver us. On
him we have set our hope
that he will continue to deliver us, 11 as you help us by
your prayers. Then many
will give thanks on our[a] behalf for the gracious favor
granted us in answer to the
prayers of many.

Paul's Change of Plans

12 Now this is our boast:
Our conscience testifies
that we have conducted
ourselves in the world, and
especially in our relations
with you, in the holiness
and sincerity that are from
God. We have done so not
according to worldly wis-
dom but according to
God's grace. 13 For we do
not write you anything you
cannot read or understand.
And I hope that, 14 as you
have understood us in part,
you will come to under-
stand fully that you can
boast of us just as we will
boast of you in the day of
the Lord Jesus.
15 Because I was confi-
dent of this, I planned to
visit you first so that you
might benefit twice. 16 I
planned to visit you on my
way to Macedonia and to
come back to you from
Macedonia, and then to
have you send me on my
way to Judea. 17 When I
planned this, did I do it
lightly? Or do I make my
plans in a worldly manner
so that in the same breath I

[a] *11* Many manuscripts *your*

yes" and "No, no" at the
same time? 18 As surely as
God is faithful, our word to
you has not been "Yes and
No." 19 For the Son of God,
Jesus Christ, whom we
proclaimed among you, Silvanus and Timothy and I,
was not "Yes and No"; but
in him it is always "Yes."
20 For in him every one of
God's promises is a "Yes."
For this reason it is through
him that we say the
"Amen," to the glory of
God. 21 But it is God who
establishes us with you in
Christ and has anointed us,
22 by putting his seal on us
and giving us his Spirit in
our hearts as a first install-
ment.
23 But I call on God as
witness against me: it was
to spare you that I did not
come again to Corinth. 24 I
do not mean to imply that
we lord it over your faith;
rather, we are workers with
you for your joy, because
you stand firm in the faith.
1 So I made up my mind not
to make you another pain-
ful visit. 2 For if I cause you
pain, who is there to make
me glad but the one whom
I have pained? 3 And I
wrote as I did, so that when
I came, I might not suffer
pain from those who should
have made me rejoice; for I
am confident about all of
you, that my joy would be
the joy of all of you. 4 For I
wrote you out of much distress and anguish of heart
and with many tears, not to
cause you pain, but to let
you know the abundant
love that I have for you.

ναὶ καὶ τὸ οὒ οὔ; 18 πιστὸς δὲ ὁ
yes and the No no? But faithful [is] –
θεὸς ὅτι ὁ λόγος ἡμῶν ὁ πρὸς ὑμᾶς
God that the word of us – to you
οὐκ ἔστιν ναὶ καὶ οὔ. 19 ὁ τοῦ θεοῦ
is not yes and no. [3]the – [4]of God
γὰρ υἱὸς Χριστὸς Ἰησοῦς ὁ ἐν ὑμῖν
[1]For [5]Son Christ Jesus [1]the [3]among [4]you [one]
δι' ἡμῶν κηρυχθείς, δι' ἐμοῦ καὶ Σιλουανοῦ
[5]through [6]us [2]proclaimed, through me and Silvanus
καὶ Τιμοθέου, οὐκ ἐγένετο ναὶ καὶ οὔ,
and Timothy, was not yes and no,
ἀλλὰ ναὶ ἐν αὐτῷ γέγονεν. 20 ὅσαι γὰρ
but [2]Yes [3]in [4]him [1]has been. For as many
ἐπαγγελίαι θεοῦ, ἐν αὐτῷ τὸ ναί· διὸ
[as are] promises of God, in him [is] the Yes; wherefore
καὶ δι' αὐτοῦ τὸ ἀμὴν τῷ θεῷ πρὸς
also through him the Amen – [3]to God [1]unto
δόξαν δι' ἡμῶν. 21 ὁ δὲ βεβαιῶν ἡμᾶς
[2]glory through us. But the [one] making firm us
σὺν ὑμῖν εἰς Χριστὸν καὶ χρίσας ἡμᾶς
with you in Christ and having anointed us [is]
θεός, 22 ὁ καὶ σφραγισάμενος ἡμᾶς καὶ
God, the [one] both having sealed us and
δοὺς τὸν ἀρραβῶνα τοῦ πνεύματος ἐν
having given the earnest of the Spirit in
ταῖς καρδίαις ἡμῶν.
the hearts of us.
23 Ἐγὼ δὲ μάρτυρα τὸν θεὸν ἐπικαλοῦμαι
Now [4]I [7][as] witness – [6]God [5]invoke
ἐπὶ τὴν ἐμὴν ψυχήν, ὅτι φειδόμενος
[1]on – [2]my [3]life, that sparing
ὑμῶν οὐκέτι ἦλθον εἰς Κόρινθον. 24 οὐχ ὅτι
you [2]no more [1]I came to Corinth. Not that
κυριεύομεν ὑμῶν τῆς πίστεως, ἀλλὰ συνεργοί
we rule over [3]of you [1]the [2]faith, but [2]fellow-workers
ἐσμεν τῆς χαρᾶς ὑμῶν· τῇ γὰρ πίστει
[1]we are of the joy of you; – for by faith
ἑστήκατε. 2 ἔκρινα δὲ ἐμαυτῷ τοῦτο, τὸ μὴ
ye stand. But I decided in myself this, – not
πάλιν ἐν λύπῃ πρὸς ὑμᾶς ἐλθεῖν. 2 εἰ
again [4]in [5]grief [2]to [3]you [1]to come. if
γὰρ ἐγὼ λυπῶ ὑμᾶς, καὶ τίς ὁ εὐφραίνων
For I grieve you, then who the [one] making glad
με εἰ μὴ ὁ λυπούμενος ἐξ ἐμοῦ; 3 καὶ
me except the [one] being grieved by me? And
ἔγραψα τοῦτο αὐτὸ ἵνα μὴ ἐλθὼν λύπην
I wrote this very thing lest coming grief
σχῶ ἀφ' ὧν ἔδει με χαίρειν, πεποιθὼς
I should have from [those] whom it behoved me to rejoice, having confidence
ἐπὶ πάντας ὑμᾶς ὅτι ἡ ἐμὴ χαρὰ πάντων
in [2]all [1]you that – my joy [3]all
ὑμῶν ἐστιν. 4 ἐκ γὰρ πολλῆς θλίψεως
[2]of you [1]is. For out of much affliction
καὶ συνοχῆς καρδίας ἔγραψα ὑμῖν διὰ
and anxiety of heart I wrote to you through
πολλῶν δακρύων, οὐχ ἵνα λυπηθῆτε, ἀλλὰ
many tears, not in order that ye should be grieved, but
τὴν ἀγάπην ἵνα γνῶτε ἣν ἔχω περισ-
[2]the [3]love [1]in order that [2]ye should know [5]which I have more

say, "Yes, yes" and "No,
no"?
18 But as surely as God is
faithful, our message to
you is not "Yes" and
"No." 19 For the Son of
God, Jesus Christ, who
was preached among you
by me and Silas[b] and Timothy, was not "Yes" and
"No," but in him it has always been "Yes." 20 For no
matter how many promises
God has made, they are
"Yes" in Christ. And so
through him the "Amen" is
spoken by us to the glory of
God. 21 Now it is God who
makes both us and you
stand firm in Christ. He
anointed us, 22 set his seal
of ownership on us, and put
his Spirit in our hearts as a
deposit, guaranteeing what
is to come.
23 I call God as my witness
that it was in order to spare
you that I did not return to
Corinth. 24 Not that we lord
it over your faith, but we
work with you for your joy,
because it is by faith you
stand firm.

1 So I made up
my mind that I would not
make another painful visit
to you. 2 For if I grieve you,
who is left to make me glad
but you whom I have
grieved? 3 I wrote as I did so
that when I came I should
not be distressed by those
who ought to make me re-
joice. I had confidence in
all of you, that you would
all share my joy. 4 For I
wrote you out of great distress and anguish of heart
and with many tears, not to

[b]19 Greek *Silvanus*, a variant of *Silas*

Forgiveness for the Offender

5 But if anyone has caused pain, he has caused it not to me, but to some extent—not to exaggerate it—to all of you. 6 This punishment by the majority is enough for such a person; 7 so now instead you should forgive and console him, so that he may not be overwhelmed by excessive sorrow. 8 So I urge you to reaffirm your love for him. 9 I wrote for this reason: to test you and to know whether you are obedient in everything. 10 Anyone whom you forgive, I also forgive. What I have forgiven, if I have forgiven anything, has been for your sake in the presence of Christ. 11 And we do this so that we may not be outwitted by Satan; for we are not ignorant of his designs.

Paul's Anxiety in Troas

12 When I came to Troas to proclaim the good news of Christ, a door was opened for me in the Lord; 13 but my mind could not rest because I did not find my brother Titus there. So I said farewell to them and went on to Macedonia.

14 But thanks be to God, who in Christ always leads us in triumphal procession, and through us spreads in every place the fragrance that comes from knowing him. 15 For we are the aroma of Christ to God among those who are being saved and among those who are perishing; 16 to the one a fragrance from death to death, to the other a fragrance from life to life. Who is sufficient for these things? 17 For we are not peddlers of God's word like

σοτέρως εἰς ὑμᾶς. 5 Εἰ δέ τις λελύπηκεν,
abundantly to you. But if anyone has grieved,
οὐκ ἐμὲ λελύπηκεν, ἀλλὰ ἀπὸ μέρους,
not me he has grieved, but from(in) part,
ἵνα μὴ ἐπιβαρῶ, πάντας ὑμᾶς. 6 ἱκανὸν
lest I am burdensome, [2]all [1]you. Enough
τῷ τοιούτῳ ἡ ἐπιτιμία αὕτη ἡ ὑπὸ
for such a one this punishment – by
τῶν πλειόνων, 7 ὥστε τοὐναντίον μᾶλλον
the majority, so as on the contrary rather
ὑμᾶς χαρίσασθαι καὶ παρακαλέσαι, μή πως
you to forgive and to comfort,[b] lest
=ye should rather forgive and comfort,
τῇ περισσοτέρᾳ λύπῃ καταποθῇ ὁ τοιοῦτος.
[3]by the [4]more abundant [5]grief [2]should be swallowed up [1]such a one.
8 διὸ παρακαλῶ ὑμᾶς κυρῶσαι εἰς αὐτὸν
Wherefore I beseech you to confirm to him
ἀγάπην· 9 εἰς τοῦτο γὰρ καὶ ἔγραψα,
[your] love; [2]to [3]this [end] [1]for indeed I wrote,
ἵνα γνῶ τὴν δοκιμὴν ὑμῶν, εἰ εἰς πάντα
in order that I might know the proof of you, if in all things
ὑπήκοοί ἐστε. 10 ᾧ δέ τι χαρίζεσθε,
obedient ye are. Now to whom anything ye forgive,
κἀγώ· καὶ γὰρ ἐγὼ ὃ κεχάρισμαι, εἴ
I also; for indeed [2]I [1]what [3]have forgiven, if
τι κεχάρισμαι, δι' ὑμᾶς ἐν προσώπῳ
[2]anything [1]I have forgiven, [it is] on account of you in [the] person
Χριστοῦ, 11 ἵνα μὴ πλεονεκτηθῶμεν ὑπὸ
of Christ, lest we are taken advantage of by
τοῦ σατανᾶ· οὐ γὰρ αὐτοῦ τὰ νοήματα
– Satan; for [3]not [7]of him [5]the [6]designs
ἀγνοοῦμεν. 12 Ἐλθὼν δὲ εἰς τὴν Τρῳάδα εἰς
[1]we [2]are [4]ignorant [of]. But coming to – Troas in
τὸ εὐαγγέλιον τοῦ Χριστοῦ, καὶ θύρας
the gospel – of Christ, and a door
μοι ἀνεῳγμένης ἐν κυρίῳ, 13 οὐκ ἔσχηκα
to me having been opened[a] by [the] Lord, I *have* had no
ἄνεσιν τῷ πνεύματί μου τῷ μὴ εὑρεῖν
rest to the spirit of me in the not to find
=when I did not find . . .
με Τίτον τὸν ἀδελφόν μου, ἀλλὰ ἀποτα-
me[be] Titus the brother of me, but saying
ξάμενος αὐτοῖς ἐξῆλθον εἰς Μακεδονίαν.
farewell to them I went forth into Macedonia.
14 Τῷ δὲ θεῷ χάρις τῷ πάντοτε
– But [2]to God [1]thanks the [one] always
θριαμβεύοντι ἡμᾶς ἐν τῷ Χριστῷ καὶ
leading in triumph us in – Christ and
τὴν ὀσμὴν τῆς γνώσεως αὐτοῦ φανεροῦντι
[4]the [5]odour [6]of the [7]knowledge [8]of him [1]manifesting
δι' ἡμῶν ἐν παντὶ τόπῳ· 15 ὅτι Χριστοῦ
[3]through [2]us in every place; because of Christ
εὐωδία ἐσμὲν τῷ θεῷ ἐν τοῖς σῳζομένοις
a sweet smell we are – to God in the [ones] being saved
καὶ ἐν τοῖς ἀπολλυμένοις, 16 οἷς μὲν
and in the [ones] perishing, to the [latter]†
ὀσμὴ ἐκ θανάτου εἰς θάνατον, οἷς δὲ
an odour out of death unto death, to the [former]†
ὀσμὴ ἐκ ζωῆς εἰς ζωήν. καὶ πρὸς
an odour out of life unto life. And for
ταῦτα τίς ἱκανός; 17 οὐ γάρ ἐσμεν
these things who [is] competent? For we are not
ὡς οἱ πολλοὶ καπηλεύοντες τὸν λόγον
as the many hawking the word

grieve you but to let you know the depth of my love for you.

Forgiveness for the Sinner

5If anyone has caused grief, he has not so much grieved me as he has grieved all of you, to some extent—not to put it too severely. 6The punishment inflicted on him by the majority is sufficient for him. 7Now instead, you ought to forgive and comfort him, so that he will not be overwhelmed by excessive sorrow. 8I urge you, therefore, to reaffirm your love for him. 9The reason I wrote you was to see if you would stand the test and be obedient in everything. 10If you forgive anyone, I also forgive him. And what I have forgiven—if there was anything to forgive—I have forgiven in the sight of Christ for your sake, 11in order that Satan might not outwit us. For we are not unaware of his schemes.

Ministers of the New Covenant

12Now when I went to Troas to preach the gospel of Christ and found that the Lord had opened a door for me, 13I still had no peace of mind, because I did not find my brother Titus there. So I said good-by to them and went on to Macedonia.

14But thanks be to God, who always leads us in triumphal procession in Christ and through us spreads everywhere the fragrance of the knowledge of him. 15For we are to God the aroma of Christ among those who are being saved and those who are perishing. 16To the one we are the smell of death; to the other, the fragrance of life. And who is equal to such a task? 17Unlike so many, we do not peddle the word of God

so many;[f] but in Christ we
speak as persons of sincerity, as persons sent from
God and standing in his
presence.

Chapter 3

Ministers of the New Covenant

ARE we beginning to
commend ourselves
again? Surely we do not
need, as some do, letters of
recommendation to you or
from you, do we? 2 You
yourselves are our letter,
written on our[g] hearts, to
be known and read by all;
3 and you show that you are
a letter of Christ, prepared
by us, written not with ink
but with the Spirit of the
living God, not on tablets of
stone but on tablets of human hearts.
4 Such is the confidence
that we have through
Christ toward God. 5 Not
that we are competent of
ourselves to claim anything
as coming from us; our
competence is from God,
6 who has made us compe-
tent to be ministers of a
new covenant, not of letter
but of spirit; for the letter
kills, but the Spirit gives
life.
7 Now if the ministry of
death, chiseled in letters on
stone tablets,[h] came in glory so that the people of Israel could not gaze at Moses' face because of the glory of his face, a glory now
set aside, 8 how much more
will the ministry of the
Spirit come in glory? 9 For
if there was glory in the
ministry of condemnation,
much more does the minis-
try of justification abound
in glory! 10 Indeed, what
once had glory has lost its

[f] Other ancient authorities read *like the others*
[g] Other ancient authorities read *your*
[h] Gk *on stones*

τοῦ θεοῦ, ἀλλ' ὡς ἐξ εἰλικρινείας, ἀλλ'
– of God, but as of sincerity, but
ὡς ἐκ θεοῦ κατέναντι θεοῦ ἐν Χριστῷ
as of God before God in Christ
λαλοῦμεν.
we speak.

3 Ἀρχόμεθα πάλιν ἑαυτοὺς συνιστάνειν;
Do we begin again ourselves to commend?
ἢ μὴ χρῄζομεν ὥς τινες συστατικῶν
or *not* need we as some commendatory
ἐπιστολῶν πρὸς ὑμᾶς ἢ ἐξ ὑμῶν; 2 ἡ
epistles to you or from you? The
ἐπιστολὴ ἡμῶν ὑμεῖς ἐστε, ἐγγεγραμμένη
epistle of us ye are, *having been* inscribed
ἐν ταῖς καρδίαις ἡμῶν, γινωσκομένη καὶ
in the hearts of us, *being* known and
ἀναγινωσκομένη ὑπὸ πάντων ἀνθρώπων,
being read by all men,
3 φανερούμενοι ὅτι ἐστὲ ἐπιστολὴ Χριστοῦ
being manifested that ye are an epistle of Christ
διακονηθεῖσα ὑφ' ἡμῶν, ἐγγεγραμμένη οὐ
ministered by us, *having been* inscribed not
μέλανι ἀλλὰ πνεύματι θεοῦ ζῶντος, οὐκ
by ink but by [the] Spirit of ²God ¹a living, not
ἐν πλαξὶν λιθίναις ἀλλ' ἐν πλαξὶν καρδίαις
in ²tablets ¹stony but in tablets [which are] ²hearts
σαρκίναις.
¹fleshy.
4 Πεποίθησιν δὲ τοιαύτην ἔχομεν διὰ
³confidence ¹And ²such we have through
τοῦ Χριστοῦ πρὸς τὸν θεόν. 5 οὐχ
– Christ toward – God. Not
ὅτι ἀφ' ἑαυτῶν ἱκανοί ἐσμεν λογίσασθαί
that ³from ⁴ourselves ²competent ¹we are to reckon
τι ὡς ἐξ ἑαυτῶν, ἀλλ' ἡ ἱκανότης
any-thing as of ourselves, but the competence
ἡμῶν ἐκ τοῦ θεοῦ, 6 ὃς καὶ ἱκάνωσεν
of us [is] of – God, who also made competent
ἡμᾶς διακόνους καινῆς διαθήκης, οὐ
us [as] ministers of a new covenant, not
γράμματος ἀλλὰ πνεύματος· τὸ γὰρ γράμμα
of letter but of spirit; for the letter
ἀποκτείνει, τὸ δὲ πνεῦμα ζωοποιεῖ. 7 Εἰ
kills, but the spirit makes alive. if
δὲ ἡ διακονία τοῦ θανάτου ἐν γράμμασιν
Now the ministry – of death in letters
ἐντετυπωμένη λίθοις ἐγενήθη ἐν δόξῃ,
having been engraved in stones was in glory,
ὥστε μὴ δύνασθαι ἀτενίσαι τοὺς υἱοὺς
so as not to be able to gaze the sons
=so that the sons of Israel were not able to gaze
Ἰσραὴλ εἰς τὸ πρόσωπον Μωϋσέως διὰ
of Israel[b] at the face of Moses on account of
τὴν δόξαν τοῦ προσώπου αὐτοῦ τὴν
the glory of the face of him –
καταργουμένην, 8 πῶς οὐχὶ μᾶλλον ἡ
being done away, how ²not ³rather ⁴the
διακονία τοῦ πνεύματος ἔσται ἐν δόξῃ;
⁵ministry ⁶of the ⁷Spirit ¹will ⁸be in glory?
9 εἰ γὰρ ἡ διακονία τῆς κατακρίσεως
For if the ministry – of condemnation
δόξα, πολλῷ μᾶλλον περισσεύει ἡ διακονία
[was] glory, by much rather ⁴abounds ¹the ²ministry
τῆς δικαιοσύνης δόξῃ. 10 καὶ γὰρ οὐ
– ³of righteousness in glory. For indeed ²not

for profit. On the contrary,
in Christ we speak before
God with sincerity, like
men sent from God.

Chapter 3

ARE we beginning to
commend ourselves
again? Or do we need, like
some people, letters of recommendation to you or
from you? 2 You yourselves
are our letter, written on
our hearts, known and read
by everybody. 3 You show
that you are a letter from
Christ, the result of our
ministry, written not with
ink but with the Spirit of the
living God, not on tablets of
stone but on tablets of human hearts.
4 Such confidence as this
is ours through Christ before God. 5 Not that we are
competent in ourselves to
claim anything for our-
selves, but our competence
comes from God. 6 He has
made us competent as min-
isters of a new covenant—
not of the letter but of the
Spirit; for the letter kills,
but the Spirit gives life.

The Glory of the New Covenant

7 Now if the ministry that
brought death, which was
engraved in letters on
stone, came with glory, so
that the Israelites could not
look steadily at the face of
Moses because of its glory,
fading though it was, 8 will
not the ministry of the Spirit be even more glorious?
9 If the ministry that con-
demns men is glorious,
how much more glorious is
the ministry that brings
righteousness! 10 For what
was glorious has no glory

glory because of the greater
glory; 11 for if what was set
aside came through glory,
much more has the perma-
nent come in glory!
12 Since, then, we have
such a hope, we act with
great boldness, 13 not like
Moses, who put a veil over
his face to keep the people
of Israel from gazing at the
end of the glory that[i] was
being set aside. 14 But their
minds were hardened. In-
deed, to this very day,
when they hear the reading
of the old covenant, that
same veil is still there,
since only in Christ is it set
aside. 15 Indeed, to this
very day whenever Moses
is read, a veil lies over their
minds; 16 but when one
turns to the Lord, the veil is
removed. 17 Now the Lord
is the Spirit, and where the
Spirit of the Lord is, there
is freedom. 18 And all of us,
with unveiled faces, seeing
the glory of the Lord as
though reflected in a mirror, are being transformed
into the same image from
one degree of glory to another; for this comes from
the Lord, the Spirit.

δεδόξασται τὸ δεδοξασμένον ἐν τούτῳ
[4]has been glorified [1]the [thing] [2]having been glorified in this

τῷ μέρει εἵνεκεν τῆς ὑπερβαλλούσης δόξης.
– respect for the sake of the excelling glory.

11 εἰ γὰρ τὸ καταργούμενον διὰ δόξης,
For if the [thing] being done away [was] through glory,

πολλῷ μᾶλλον τὸ μένον ἐν δόξῃ.
by much more the [thing] remaining [is] in glory.

12 Ἔχοντες οὖν τοιαύτην ἐλπίδα πολλῇ
Having therefore such hope [2]much

παρρησίᾳ χρώμεθα, 13 καὶ οὐ καθάπερ
[3]boldness [1]we use, and not as

Μωϋσῆς ἐτίθει κάλυμμα ἐπὶ τὸ πρόσωπον
Moses put a veil on the face

αὐτοῦ, πρὸς τὸ μὴ ἀτενίσαι τοὺς υἱοὺς
of him, for *the* [4]not [5]to gaze [1]the [2]sons

Ἰσραὴλ εἰς τὸ τέλος τοῦ καταργουμένου.
[3]of Israel[b] at the end of the [thing] being done away.

14 ἀλλὰ ἐπωρώθη τὰ νοήματα αὐτῶν.
But were hardened the thoughts of them.

ἄχρι γὰρ τῆς σήμερον ἡμέρας τὸ αὐτὸ
For until the present day the same

κάλυμμα ἐπὶ τῇ ἀναγνώσει τῆς παλαιᾶς
veil [2]on(at) [3]the [4]reading [5]of the [6]old

διαθήκης μένει, μὴ ἀνακαλυπτόμενον ὅτι
[7]covenant [1]remains, not being unveiled* that

ἐν Χριστῷ καταργεῖται. 15 ἀλλʼ ἕως
in Christ it is being done away. But until

σήμερον ἡνίκα ἂν ἀναγινώσκηται Μωϋσῆς
to-day whenever [2]is being read [1]Moses

κάλυμμα ἐπὶ τὴν καρδίαν αὐτῶν κεῖται·
a veil [2]on [3]the [4]heart [5]of them [1]lies;

16 ἡνίκα δὲ ἐὰν ἐπιστρέψῃ πρὸς κύριον,
but whenever it§ turns to [the] Lord,

περιαιρεῖται τὸ κάλυμμα. 17 ὁ δὲ κύριος
[3]is taken away [1]the [2]veil. Now the Lord

τὸ πνεῦμά ἐστιν· οὗ δὲ τὸ πνεῦμα
[2]the [3]Spirit [1]is; and where the Spirit

κυρίου, ἐλευθερία. 18 ἡμεῖς δὲ πάντες
of [the] Lord [is], [there is] freedom. But we all

ἀνακεκαλυμμένῳ προσώπῳ τὴν δόξαν
[2]*having been* unveiled [1]with face [3]the [4]glory

κυρίου κατοπτριζόμενοι τὴν αὐτὴν εἰκόνα
[5]of [the] Lord [1]beholding in a mirror [6]the [7]same [8]image

μεταμορφούμεθα ἀπὸ δόξης εἰς δόξαν,
[1]are being changed [into] from glory to glory,

καθάπερ ἀπὸ κυρίου πνεύματος.
even as from [the] Lord Spirit.

now in comparison with the
surpassing glory. 11And if
what was fading away
came with glory, how much
greater is the glory of that
which lasts!
12Therefore, since we
have such a hope, we are
very bold. 13We are not like
Moses, who would put a
veil over his face to keep
the Israelites from gazing at
it while the radiance was
fading away. 14But their
minds were made dull, for
to this day the same veil remains when the old cove-
nant is read. It has not been
removed, because only in
Christ is it taken away.
15Even to this day when
Moses is read, a veil covers
their hearts. 16But whenever anyone turns to the
Lord, the veil is taken
away. 17Now the Lord is
the Spirit, and where the
Spirit of the Lord is, there
is freedom. 18And we, who
with unveiled faces all reflect[c] the Lord's glory, are
being transformed into his
likeness with ever-increasing glory, which comes
from the Lord, who is the
Spirit.

Chapter 4

Treasure in Clay Jars

THEREFORE, since it
is by God's mercy that
we are engaged in this ministry, we do not lose heart.
2We have renounced the
shameful things that one
hides; we refuse to practice
cunning or to falsify God's
word; but by the open
statement of the truth we
commend ourselves to the

4 Διὰ τοῦτο, ἔχοντες τὴν διακονίαν
Therefore, having – ministry

ταύτην, καθὼς ἠλεήθημεν, οὐκ ἐγκακοῦμεν,
this, as we obtained mercy, we faint not,

2 ἀλλὰ ἀπειπάμεθα τὰ κρυπτὰ τῆς αἰσχύνης,
but we have renounced the hidden things – of shame,

μὴ περιπατοῦντες ἐν πανουργίᾳ μηδὲ
not walking in craftiness nor

δολοῦντες τὸν λόγον τοῦ θεοῦ, ἀλλὰ
adulterating the word – of God, but

τῇ φανερώσει τῆς ἀληθείας συνιστάνοντες
by the manifestation of the truth commending

Chapter 4

Treasures in Jars of Clay

THEREFORE, since
through God's mercy
we have this ministry, we
do not lose heart. 2Rather,
we have renounced secret
and shameful ways; we do
not use deception, nor do
we distort the word of God.
On the contrary, by setting
forth the truth plainly we

[i] Gk *of what*

* That is, revealed (Conybeare and Howson). § ? their heart.

[c] 18 Or *contemplate*

conscience of everyone in the sight of God. [3]And even if our gospel is veiled, it is veiled to those who are perishing. [4]In their case the god of this world has blinded the minds of the unbelievers, to keep them from seeing the light of the gospel of the glory of Christ, who is the image of God. [5]For we do not proclaim ourselves; we proclaim Jesus Christ as Lord and ourselves as your slaves for Jesus' sake. [6]For it is the God who said, "Let light shine out of darkness," who has shone in our hearts to give the light of the knowledge of the glory of God in the face of Jesus Christ.

7 But we have this treasure in clay jars, so that it may be made clear that this extraordinary power belongs to God and does not come from us. [8]We are afflicted in every way, but not crushed; perplexed, but not driven to despair; [9]persecuted, but not forsaken; struck down, but not destroyed; [10]always carrying in the body the death of Jesus, so that the life of Jesus may also be made visible in our bodies. [11]For while we live, we are always being given up to death for Jesus' sake, so that the life of Jesus may be made visible in our mortal flesh. [12]So death is at work in us, but life in you.

13 But just as we have the same spirit of faith that

ἑαυτοὺς πρὸς πᾶσαν συνείδησιν ἀνθρώπων
ourselves to every conscience of men

ἐνώπιον τοῦ θεοῦ. **3** εἰ δὲ καὶ ἔστιν
before – God. But if indeed [4]is

κεκαλυμμένον τὸ εὐαγγέλιον ἡμῶν, ἐν
[5]*having been* hidden [1]the [2]gospel [3]of us, in

τοῖς ἀπολλυμένοις ἐστὶν κεκαλυμμένον, **4** ἐν
the [ones] perishing it is *having been* hidden, in

οἷς ὁ θεὸς τοῦ αἰῶνος τούτου ἐτύφλωσεν
whom the god of this age blinded

τὰ νοήματα τῶν ἀπίστων εἰς τὸ μὴ
the thoughts of the [ones] unbelieving [with a view] to *the* not

=so that the enlightenment . . . should not shine forth,

αὐγάσαι τὸν φωτισμὸν τοῦ εὐαγγελίου
to shine forth the enlightenment of the gospel

τῆς δόξης τοῦ Χριστοῦ, ὅς ἐστιν εἰκὼν
of the glory – of Christ, who is [the] image

τοῦ θεοῦ. **5** οὐ γὰρ ἑαυτοὺς κηρύσσομεν
– of God. For [2]not [3]ourselves [1]we proclaim

ἀλλὰ Χριστὸν Ἰησοῦν κύριον, ἑαυτοὺς δὲ
but Christ Jesus [as] Lord, and ourselves

δούλους ὑμῶν διὰ Ἰησοῦν. **6** ὅτι ὁ
slaves of you on account of Jesus. Because –

θεὸς ὁ εἰπών· ἐκ σκότους φῶς λάμψει,
God the [one] saying: Out of darkness light shall shine,

ὃς ἔλαμψεν ἐν ταῖς καρδίαις ἡμῶν πρὸς
[is] [he] who shone in the hearts of us for

φωτισμὸν τῆς γνώσεως τῆς δόξης τοῦ
enlightenment of the knowledge of the glory –

θεοῦ ἐν προσώπῳ Χριστοῦ.
of God in [the] face of Christ.

7 Ἔχομεν δὲ τὸν θησαυρὸν τοῦτον ἐν
And we have this treasure in

ὀστρακίνοις σκεύεσιν, ἵνα ἡ ὑπερβολὴ
earthenware vessels, in order that the excellence

τῆς δυνάμεως ᾖ τοῦ θεοῦ καὶ μὴ ἐξ
of the power may be – of God and not of

ἡμῶν· **8** ἐν παντὶ θλιβόμενοι ἀλλ' οὐ
us; in every [way] *being* afflicted but not

στενοχωρούμενοι, ἀπορούμενοι ἀλλ' οὐκ
being restrained, *being* in difficulties but not

ἐξαπορούμενοι, **9** διωκόμενοι ἀλλ' οὐκ
despairing, *being* persecuted but not

ἐγκαταλειπόμενοι, καταβαλλόμενοι ἀλλ' οὐκ
being deserted, *being* cast down but not

ἀπολλύμενοι, **10** πάντοτε τὴν νέκρωσιν τοῦ
perishing, always [5]the [6]dying –

Ἰησοῦ ἐν τῷ σώματι περιφέροντες, ἵνα
[7]of Jesus [2]in [3]the [4]body [1]bearing about, in order that

καὶ ἡ ζωὴ τοῦ Ἰησοῦ ἐν τῷ σώματι
also the life – of Jesus in the body

ἡμῶν φανερωθῇ. **11** ἀεὶ γὰρ ἡμεῖς οἱ
of us might be manifested. For always we the

ζῶντες εἰς θάνατον παραδιδόμεθα διὰ
[ones] living to death are being delivered on account of

Ἰησοῦν, ἵνα καὶ ἡ ζωὴ τοῦ Ἰησοῦ
Jesus, in order that also the life – of Jesus

φανερωθῇ ἐν τῇ θνητῇ σαρκὶ ἡμῶν.
might be manifested in the mortal flesh of us.

12 ὥστε ὁ θάνατος ἐν ἡμῖν ἐνεργεῖται,
So as – death in us operates,

ἡ δὲ ζωὴ ἐν ὑμῖν. **13** ἔχοντες δὲ τὸ
– but life in you. And having the

commend ourselves to every man's conscience in the sight of God. [3]And even if our gospel is veiled, it is veiled to those who are perishing. [4]The god of this age has blinded the minds of unbelievers, so that they cannot see the light of the gospel of the glory of Christ, who is the image of God. [5]For we do not preach ourselves, but Jesus Christ as Lord, and ourselves as your servants for Jesus' sake. [6]For God, who said, "Let light shine out of darkness,"[d] made his light shine in our hearts to give us the light of the knowledge of the glory of God in the face of Christ.

[7]But we have this treasure in jars of clay to show that this all-surpassing power is from God and not from us. [8]We are hard pressed on every side, but not crushed; perplexed, but not in despair; [9]persecuted, but not abandoned; struck down, but not destroyed. [10]We always carry around in our body the death of Jesus, so that the life of Jesus may also be revealed in our body. [11]For we who are alive are always being given over to death for Jesus' sake, so that his life may be revealed in our mortal body. [12]So then, death is at work in us, but life is at work in you.

[13]It is written: "I be-

is in accordance with
scripture—"I believed, and
so I spoke"—we also be-
lieve, and so we speak,
14 because we know that
the one who raised the
Lord Jesus will raise us
also with Jesus, and will
bring us with you into his
presence. 15 Yes, every-
thing is for your sake, so
that grace, as it extends to
more and more people,
may increase thanksgiving,
to the glory of God.

Living by Faith

16 So we do not lose
heart. Even though our
outer nature is wasting
away, our inner nature is
being renewed day by day.
17 For this slight momen-
tary affliction is preparing
us for an eternal weight of
glory beyond all measure,
18 because we look not at
what can be seen but at
what cannot be seen; for
what can be seen is temporary, but what cannot be
seen is eternal.

Chapter 5

FOR we know that if the
earthly tent we live in
is destroyed, we have a
building from God, a house
not made with hands, eternal in the heavens. 2 For in
this tent we groan, longing
to be clothed with our
heavenly dwelling— 3 if indeed, when we have taken
it off[j] we will not be found
naked. 4 For while we are
still in this tent, we groan
under our burden, because
we wish not to be un-
clothed but to be further
clothed, so that what is
mortal may be swallowed
up by life. 5 He who has
prepared us for this very

[j] Other ancient authorities read *put it on*

αὐτὸ πνεῦμα τῆς πίστεως, κατὰ τὸ
same spirit – of faith, according to the thing

γεγραμμένον· ἐπίστευσα, διὸ ἐλάλησα, καὶ
having been written: I believed, therefore I spoke, both

ἡμεῖς πιστεύομεν, διὸ καὶ λαλοῦμεν, **14** εἰδότες
we believe, and therefore we speak, knowing

ὅτι ὁ ἐγείρας τὸν κύριον Ἰησοῦν καὶ
that the [one] having raised the Lord Jesus [3]also

ἡμᾶς σὺν Ἰησοῦ ἐγερεῖ καὶ παραστήσει
[2]us [4]with [5]Jesus [1]will raise and will present [us]

σὺν ὑμῖν. **15** τὰ γὰρ πάντα δι' ὑμᾶς,
with you. – For all things [are] on account of you,

ἵνα ἡ χάρις πλεονάσασα διὰ τῶν πλειόνων
in order that – grace increased through the majority

τὴν εὐχαριστίαν περισσεύσῃ εἰς τὴν δόξαν
[2]the [3]thanksgiving [1]may cause to abound to the glory

τοῦ θεοῦ. **16** Διὸ οὐκ ἐγκακοῦμεν, ἀλλ'
– of God. Wherefore we faint not, but

εἰ καὶ ὁ ἔξω ἡμῶν ἄνθρωπος διαφθείρεται,
if indeed the outward [2]of us [1]man is being disabled,

ἀλλ' ὁ ἔσω ἡμῶν ἀνακαινοῦται ἡμέρᾳ
yet the inward [man] of us is being renewed day

καὶ ἡμέρᾳ. **17** τὸ γὰρ παραυτίκα ἐλαφρὸν
and(by) day. For the present lightness

τῆς θλίψεως καθ' ὑπερβολὴν εἰς ὑπερβολὴν
of the affliction [3]excessively [4]to [5]excess

αἰώνιον βάρος δόξης κατεργάζεται ἡμῖν,
[6]an eternal [7]weight [8]of glory [1]works [2]for us,

18 μὴ σκοπούντων ἡμῶν τὰ βλεπόμενα
not considering us* the things *being* seen
=while we do not consider

ἀλλὰ τὰ μὴ βλεπόμενα· τὰ γὰρ βλεπόμενα
but the things not *being* seen; for the things *being* seen

πρόσκαιρα, τὰ δὲ μὴ βλεπόμενα αἰώνια.
[are] temporary, but the things not *being* seen [are] eternal.

5 Οἴδαμεν γὰρ ὅτι ἐὰν ἡ ἐπίγειος
For we know that if the earthly

ἡμῶν οἰκία τοῦ σκήνους καταλυθῇ,
[4]of us [1]house [2]of the [3]tabernacle is destroyed,

οἰκοδομὴν ἐκ θεοῦ ἔχομεν, οἰκίαν ἀχειρο-
a building of God we have, a house not made

ποίητον αἰώνιον ἐν τοῖς οὐρανοῖς. **2** καὶ
by hands eternal in *the* heavens. indeed

γὰρ ἐν τούτῳ στενάζομεν, τὸ οἰκητήριον
For in this* we groan, [3]the [4]dwelling-place

ἡμῶν τὸ ἐξ οὐρανοῦ ἐπενδύσασθαι ἐπιπο-
[5]of us – [6]out of [7]heaven [2]to put on [1]greatly

θοῦντες, **3** εἴ γε καὶ ἐνδυσάμενοι οὐ
desiring, if indeed being clothed not

γυμνοὶ εὑρεθησόμεθα. **4** καὶ γὰρ οἱ
naked we shall be found. For indeed [2]the [ones]

ὄντες ἐν τῷ σκήνει στενάζομεν βαρούμενοι,
[3]being [4]in [5]the [6]tabernacle [1]we groan being burdened,

ἐφ' ᾧ οὐ θέλομεν ἐκδύσασθαι ἀλλ'
inasmuch as we do not wish to put off but

ἐπενδύσασθαι, ἵνα καταποθῇ τὸ θνητὸν
to put on, in order that [3]may be swallowed up [1]the [2]mortal

ὑπὸ τῆς ζωῆς. **5** ὁ δὲ κατεργασάμενος
by *the* life. Now the [one] having wrought

* Neuter, going back to σκῆνος in the preceding verse.

lieved; therefore I have
spoken."[e] With that same
spirit of faith we also believe and therefore speak,
14 because we know that the
one who raised the Lord
Jesus from the dead will
also raise us with Jesus and
present us with you in his
presence. 15 All this is for
your benefit, so that the
grace that is reaching more
and more people may cause
thanksgiving to overflow to
the glory of God.

16 Therefore we do not
lose heart. Though out-
wardly we are wasting
away, yet inwardly we are
being renewed day by day.
17 For our light and momentary troubles are achieving
for us an eternal glory that
far outweighs them all. 18 So
we fix our eyes not on what
is seen, but on what is unseen. For what is seen is
temporary, but what is unseen is eternal.

Chapter 5

Our Heavenly Dwelling

NOW we know that if
the earthly tent we
live in is destroyed, we
have a building from God,
an eternal house in heaven,
not built by human hands.
2 Meanwhile we groan,
longing to be clothed with
our heavenly dwelling, 3 because when we are clothed,
we will not be found naked.
4 For while we are in this
tent, we groan and are burdened, because we do not
wish to be unclothed but to
be clothed with our heav-
enly dwelling, so that what
is mortal may be swallowed
up by life. 5 Now it is God

[e] 13 Psalm 116:10

thing is God, who has given
us the Spirit as a guarantee.
6 So we are always con-
fident; even though we
know that while we are at
home in the body we are
away from the Lord— 7 for
we walk by faith, not by
sight. 8 Yes, we do have
confidence, and we would
rather be away from the
body and at home with the
Lord. 9 So whether we are
at home or away, we make
it our aim to please him.
10 For all of us must appear
before the judgment seat of
Christ, so that each may receive recompense for what
has been done in the body,
whether good or evil.

The Ministry of Reconciliation

11 Therefore, knowing
the fear of the Lord, we try
to persuade others; but we
ourselves are well known
to God, and I hope that we
are also well known to your
consciences. 12 We are not
commending ourselves to
you again, but giving you
an opportunity to boast
about us, so that you may
be able to answer those
who boast in outward ap-
pearance and not in the
heart. 13 For if we are beside ourselves, it is for
God; if we are in our right
mind, it is for you. 14 For
the love of Christ urges us
on, because we are con-
vinced that one has died for
all; therefore all have died.
15 And he died for all, so
that those who live might

ἡμᾶς εἰς αὐτὸ τοῦτο θεός, ὁ δοὺς
us for this very thing [is] God, the [one] having given

ἡμῖν τὸν ἀρραβῶνα τοῦ πνεύματος. 6 Θαρ-
to us the earnest of the Spirit. Being

ροῦντες οὖν πάντοτε καὶ εἰδότες ὅτι
of good cheer therefore always and knowing that

ἐνδημοῦντες ἐν τῷ σώματι ἐκδημοῦμεν
being at home in the body we are away from home

ἀπὸ τοῦ κυρίου· 7 διὰ πίστεως γὰρ
from the Lord; ²through ³faith ¹for

περιπατοῦμεν, οὐ διὰ εἴδους· 8 θαρροῦμεν
we walk, not through appearance; we are of good cheer

δὲ καὶ εὐδοκοῦμεν μᾶλλον ἐκδημῆσαι ἐκ
then and think it good rather to go away from home out of

τοῦ σώματος καὶ ἐνδημῆσαι πρὸς τὸν
the body and to come home to the

κύριον. 9 διὸ καὶ φιλοτιμούμεθα, εἴτε
Lord. Wherefore also we are ambitious, whether

ἐνδημοῦντες εἴτε ἐκδημοῦντες, εὐάρεστοι
being at home or being away from home, wellpleasing

αὐτῷ εἶναι. 10 τοὺς γὰρ πάντας ἡμᾶς
to him to be. – For ³all ²us

φανερωθῆναι δεῖ ἔμπροσθεν τοῦ βήματος
⁴to be manifested ¹it behoves before the tribunal

τοῦ Χριστοῦ, ἵνα κομίσηται ἕκαστος τὰ
– of Christ, in order that ²may receive ¹each one the things

διὰ τοῦ σώματος πρὸς ἃ ἔπραξεν, εἴτε
through the body according to what things he practised, either

ἀγαθὸν εἴτε φαῦλον.
good or worthless.

11 Εἰδότες οὖν τὸν φόβον τοῦ κυρίου
Knowing therefore the fear of the Lord

ἀνθρώπους πείθομεν, θεῷ δὲ πεφανερώμεθα·
²men ¹we persuade, and to God we have been made manifest;

ἐλπίζω δὲ καὶ ἐν ταῖς συνειδήσεσιν
and I hope also in the consciences

ὑμῶν πεφανερῶσθαι. 12 οὐ πάλιν ἑαυτοὺς
of you to have been made manifest. Not again ²ourselves

συνιστάνομεν ὑμῖν, ἀλλὰ ἀφορμὴν διδόντες
¹we commend to you, but ³an occasion ¹giving

ὑμῖν καυχήματος ὑπὲρ ἡμῶν, ἵνα ἔχητε
²to you of a boast on behalf of us, in order that ye may have [it]

πρὸς τοὺς ἐν προσώπῳ καυχωμένους καὶ
in reference to the [ones] ²in ³face ¹boasting and

μὴ ἐν καρδίᾳ. 13 εἴτε γὰρ ἐξέστημεν,
not in heart. For whether we are mad,

θεῷ· εἴτε σωφρονοῦμεν, ὑμῖν. 14 ἡ γὰρ
[it is] to God; or we are in our senses, [it is] for you. For the

ἀγάπη τοῦ Χριστοῦ συνέχει ἡμᾶς, κρίναντας
love – of Christ constrains us, judging

τοῦτο, ὅτι εἷς ὑπὲρ πάντων ἀπέθανεν·
this, that one on behalf of all men died;

ἄρα οἱ πάντες ἀπέθανον· 15 καὶ ὑπὲρ
then the all died; and ²on behalf of

πάντων ἀπέθανεν ἵνα οἱ ζῶντες μηκέτι
³all ¹he died in order that the [ones] living no more

who has made us for this
very purpose and has given
us the Spirit as a deposit,
guaranteeing what is to
come.
6 Therefore we are always
confident and know that as
long as we are at home in
the body we are away from
the Lord. 7 We live by faith,
not by sight. 8 We are confident, I say, and would prefer to be away from the
body and at home with the
Lord. 9 So we make it our
goal to please him, whether
we are at home in the body
or away from it. 10 For we
must all appear before the
judgment seat of Christ,
that each one may receive
what is due him for the
things done while in the
body, whether good or bad.

The Ministry of Reconciliation

11 Since, then, we know
what it is to fear the Lord,
we try to persuade men.
What we are is plain to
God, and I hope it is also
plain to your conscience.
12 We are not trying to commend ourselves to you
again, but are giving you an
opportunity to take pride in
us, so that you can answer
those who take pride in
what is seen rather than in
what is in the heart. 13 If we
are out of our mind, it is for
the sake of God; if we are in
our right mind, it is for you.
14 For Christ's love compels
us, because we are con-
vinced that one died for all,
and therefore all died.
15 And he died for all, that
those who live should no

live no longer for them-
selves, but for him who
died and was raised for
them.
16 From now on, there-
fore, we regard no one from
a human point of view;[k]
even though we once knew
Christ from a human point
of view,[k] we know him no
longer in that way. 17 So if
anyone is in Christ, there is
a new creation: everything
old has passed away; see,
everything has become
new! 18 All this is from God,
who reconciled us to him-
self through Christ, and has
given us the ministry of reconciliation; 19 that is, in
Christ God was reconciling
the world to himself,[l] not
counting their trespasses
against them, and entrust-
ing the message of reconciliation to us. 20 So we are
ambassadors for Christ,
since God is making his appeal through us; we entreat
you on behalf of Christ, be
reconciled to God. 21 For
our sake he made him to be
sin who knew no sin, so
that in him we might be-
come the righteousness of
God.

ἑαυτοῖς ζῶσιν ἀλλὰ τῷ ὑπὲρ αὐτῶν
to themselves may live but to the [one] on behalf of them

ἀποθανόντι καὶ ἐγερθέντι. 16 Ὥστε ἡμεῖς
having died and having been raised. So as [3]we

ἀπὸ τοῦ νῦν οὐδένα οἴδαμεν κατὰ σάρκα·
[1]from – [2]now [5]no man [4]know according to flesh;

εἰ καὶ ἐγνώκαμεν κατὰ σάρκα Χριστόν,
if indeed [1]we have known [3]according to [4]flesh [2]Christ,

ἀλλὰ νῦν οὐκέτι γινώσκομεν. 17 ὥστε
yet now no more we know [him]. So as

εἴ τις ἐν Χριστῷ, καινὴ κτίσις· τὰ
if anyone [is] in Christ, [he is] a new creation; the

ἀρχαῖα παρῆλθεν, ἰδοὺ γέγονεν καινά.
old things passed away, behold they have become new.

18 τὰ δὲ πάντα ἐκ τοῦ θεοῦ τοῦ καταλ-
– And all things [are] of – God the [one] having

λάξαντος ἡμᾶς ἑαυτῷ διὰ Χριστοῦ καὶ
reconciled us to himself through Christ and

δόντος ἡμῖν τὴν διακονίαν τῆς καταλλαγῆς,
having given to us the ministry – of reconciliation,

19 ὡς ὅτι θεὸς ἦν ἐν Χριστῷ κόσμον
as that God was in Christ [2][the] world

καταλλάσσων ἑαυτῷ, μὴ λογιζόμενος αὐτοῖς
[1]reconciling to himself, not reckoning to them

τὰ παραπτώματα αὐτῶν, καὶ θέμενος
the trespasses of them, and placing

ἐν ἡμῖν τὸν λόγον τῆς καταλλαγῆς.
in us the word – of reconciliation.

20 Ὑπὲρ Χριστοῦ οὖν πρεσβεύομεν ὡς
On behalf of Christ therefore we are ambassadors as

τοῦ θεοῦ παρακαλοῦντος δι' ἡμῶν· δεόμεθα
– God beseeching[a] through us; we beg

ὑπὲρ Χριστοῦ, καταλλάγητε τῷ θεῷ.
on behalf of Christ, Be ye reconciled – to God.

21 τὸν μὴ γνόντα ἁμαρτίαν ὑπὲρ ἡμῶν
[2]The [one] [3]not [4]knowing [5]sin [7]on behalf of [8]us

ἁμαρτίαν ἐποίησεν, ἵνα ἡμεῖς γενώμεθα
[6]sin [1]he made, in order that we might become

δικαιοσύνη θεοῦ ἐν αὐτῷ.
[the] righteousness of God in him.

longer live for themselves
but for him who died for
them and was raised again.
16So from now on we re-
gard no one from a worldly
point of view. Though we
once regarded Christ in this
way, we do so no longer.
17Therefore, if anyone is in
Christ, he is a new creation;
the old has gone, the new
has come! 18All this is from
God, who reconciled us to
himself through Christ and
gave us the ministry of reconciliation: 19that God was
reconciling the world to
himself in Christ, not
counting men's sins against
them. And he has commit-
ted to us the message of
reconciliation. 20We are
therefore Christ's ambas-
sadors, as though God
were making his appeal
through us. We implore
you on Christ's behalf: Be
reconciled to God. 21God
made him who had no sin to
be sin[f] for us, so that in
him we might become the
righteousness of God.

Chapter 6

AS we work together
with him,[m] we urge
you also not to accept the
grace of God in vain. 2 For
he says,
"At an acceptable
time I have
listened to you,
and on a day of
salvation I have
helped you."
See, now is the acceptable
time; see, now is the day of
salvation! 3 We are putting
no obstacle in anyone's
way, so that no fault may
be found with our ministry,
4 but as servants of God we
have commended our-
selves in every way:
through great endurance, in
afflictions, hardships, calamities, 5 beatings, impris-

[k] Gk *according to the flesh*
[l] Or *God was in Christ reconciling the world to himself*
[m] Gk *As we work together*

6 Συνεργοῦντες δὲ καὶ παρακαλοῦμεν μὴ
And working together also we beseech [2]not

εἰς κενὸν τὴν χάριν τοῦ θεοῦ δέξασθαι
[7]to no purpose [4]the [5]grace – [6]of God [3]to receive

ὑμᾶς· 2 λέγει γάρ· καιρῷ δεκτῷ ἐπήκουσά
[1]you; for he says: In a time acceptable I heard

σου καὶ ἐν ἡμέρᾳ σωτηρίας ἐβοήθησά
thee and in a day of salvation I helped

σοι· ἰδοὺ νῦν καιρὸς εὐπρόσδεκτος, ἰδοὺ
thee; behold now a time acceptable, behold

νῦν ἡμέρα σωτηρίας· 3 — μηδεμίαν ἐν
now a day of salvation; [2]no [4]in

μηδενὶ διδόντες προσκοπήν, ἵνα μὴ
[5]no(any)thing [1]giving [3]cause of stumbling, lest

μωμηθῇ ἡ διακονία, 4 ἀλλ' ἐν παντὶ
[3]be blamed [1]the [2]ministry, but in everything

συνιστάνοντες ἑαυτοὺς ὡς θεοῦ διάκονοι,
commending ourselves as [2]of God [1]ministers,

ἐν ὑπομονῇ πολλῇ, ἐν θλίψεσιν, ἐν
in [2]endurance [1]much, in afflictions, in

ἀνάγκαις, ἐν στενοχωρίαις, ἐν πληγαῖς,
necessities, in straits, in stripes,

Chapter 6

AS God's fellow workers
we urge you not to re-
ceive God's grace in vain.
2For he says,
"In the time of my favor
I heard you,
and in the day of
salvation I helped
you."[g]
I tell you, now is the time of
God's favor, now is the day
of salvation.

Paul's Hardships

3We put no stumbling
block in anyone's path, so
that our ministry will not be
discredited. 4Rather, as
servants of God we com-
mend ourselves in every
way: in great endurance; in
troubles, hardships and dis-

[f]21 Or *be a sin offering*
[g]2 Isaiah 49:8

onments, riots, labors,
sleepless nights, hunger;
6 by purity, knowledge, patience, kindness, holiness
of spirit, genuine love,
7 truthful speech, and the
power of God; with the
weapons of righteousness
for the right hand and for
the left; 8 in honor and dishonor, in ill repute and
good repute. We are treated as impostors, and yet
are true; 9 as unknown, and
yet are well known; as dying, and see—we are alive;
as punished, and yet not
killed; 10 as sorrowful, yet
always rejoicing; as poor,
yet making many rich; as
having nothing, and yet
possessing everything.
11 We have spoken
frankly to you Corinthians;
our heart is wide open to
you. 12 There is no restric-
tion in our affections, but
only in yours. 13 In return—
I speak as to children—
open wide your hearts also.

The Temple of the Living God

14 Do not be mis-
matched with unbelievers.
For what partnership is
there between righteous-
ness and lawlessness? Or
what fellowship is there between light and darkness?
15 What agreement does
Christ have with Beliar? Or
what does a believer share
with an unbeliever? 16 What
agreement has the temple
of God with idols? For we[n]
are the temple of the living
God; as God said,

"I will live in them
and walk among
them,
and I will be their
God,
and they shall be
my people.

[n] Other ancient authorities read *you*

5 ἐν φυλακαῖς, ἐν ἀκαταστασίαις, ἐν κόποις,
in prisons, in commotions, in labours,
ἐν ἀγρυπνίαις, ἐν νηστείαις, 6 ἐν ἁγνότητι,
in watchings, in fastings, in purity,
ἐν γνώσει, ἐν μακροθυμίᾳ, ἐν χρηστότητι,
in knowledge, in long-suffering, in kindness,
ἐν πνεύματι ἁγίῳ, ἐν ἀγάπῃ ἀνυποκρίτῳ,
in spirit a holy, in love unfeigned,
7 ἐν λόγῳ ἀληθείας, ἐν δυνάμει θεοῦ·
in a word of truth, in power of God;
διὰ τῶν ὅπλων τῆς δικαιοσύνης τῶν
through the weapons – of righteousness of the
δεξιῶν καὶ ἀριστερῶν, 8 διὰ δόξης καὶ
right [hand] and of left, through glory and
ἀτιμίας, διὰ δυσφημίας καὶ εὐφημίας·
dishonour, through ill report and good report;
ὡς πλάνοι καὶ ἀληθεῖς, 9 ὡς ἀγνοούμενοι
as deceivers and* true men, as being unknown
καὶ ἐπιγινωσκόμενοι, ὡς ἀποθνῄσκοντες καὶ
and* being well known, as dying and
ἰδοὺ ζῶμεν, ὡς παιδευόμενοι καὶ μὴ
behold we live, as being chastened and not
θανατούμενοι, 10 ὡς λυπούμενοι ἀεὶ δὲ
being put to death, as being grieved ²always ¹but
χαίροντες, ὡς πτωχοὶ πολλοὺς δὲ πλουτίζ-
rejoicing, as poor ²many ¹but ³en-
οντες, ὡς μηδὲν ἔχοντες καὶ πάντα
riching, as ²nothing ¹having ³and* ⁵all things
κατέχοντες.
⁴possessing.

11 Τὸ στόμα ἡμῶν ἀνέῳγεν πρὸς ὑμᾶς,
The mouth of us has opened to you,
Κορίνθιοι, ἡ καρδία ἡμῶν πεπλάτυνται·
Corinthians, the heart of us has been enlarged;
12 οὐ στενοχωρεῖσθε ἐν ἡμῖν, στενοχωρεῖσθε
ye are not restrained in us, ²ye are restrained
δὲ ἐν τοῖς σπλάγχνοις ὑμῶν· 13 τὴν δὲ
¹but in the bowels of you; but [for] the
αὐτὴν ἀντιμισθίαν, ὡς τέκνοις λέγω,
same recompence, as to children I say,
πλατύνθητε καὶ ὑμεῖς.
be enlarged also ye.

14 Μὴ γίνεσθε ἑτεροζυγοῦντες ἀπίστοις·
Do not ye become unequally yoked [with] unbelievers;
τίς γὰρ μετοχὴ δικαιοσύνῃ καὶ ἀνομίᾳ,
for what share righteousness[c] and lawlessness,[c]
=have righteousness and lawlessness,
ἢ τίς κοινωνία φωτὶ πρὸς σκότος; 15 τίς
or what fellowship light[c] with darkness? what
=has light
δὲ συμφώνησις Χριστοῦ πρὸς Βελιάρ,
and agreement of Christ with Beliar,
ἢ τίς μερὶς πιστῷ μετὰ ἀπίστου; 16 τίς
or what part a believer[c] with an unbeliever? what
=has a believer
δὲ συγκατάθεσις ναῷ θεοῦ μετὰ εἰδώλων;
and union a shrine[c] of God with idols?
=has a shrine
ἡμεῖς γὰρ ναὸς θεοῦ ἐσμεν ζῶντος·
For ¹we ³a shrine ⁵God ²are ⁴of a living;
καθὼς εἶπεν ὁ θεὸς ὅτι ἐνοικήσω ἐν
as said – God[,] – I will dwell among
αὐτοῖς καὶ ἐμπεριπατήσω, καὶ ἔσομαι
them and I will walk among [them], and I will be
αὐτῶν θεός, καὶ αὐτοὶ ἔσονταί μου λαός.
of them God, and they shall be of me a people.

* Evidently = and yet, as in some other places; *cf.* John 20. 29.

tresses; 5 in beatings, im-
prisonments and riots; in
hard work, sleepless nights
and hunger; 6 in purity, understanding, patience and
kindness; in the Holy Spirit
and in sincere love; 7 in
truthful speech and in the
power of God; with weap-
ons of righteousness in the
right hand and in the left;
8 through glory and dishon-
or, bad report and good report; genuine, yet regarded
as impostors; 9 known, yet
regarded as unknown; dy-
ing, and yet we live on;
beaten, and yet not killed;
10 sorrowful, yet always rejoicing; poor, yet making
many rich; having nothing,
and yet possessing every-
thing.
11 We have spoken freely
to you, Corinthians, and
opened wide our hearts to
you. 12 We are not with-
holding our affection from
you, but you are withhold-
ing yours from us. 13 As a
fair exchange—I speak as
to my children—open wide
your hearts also.

Do Not Be Yoked With Unbelievers

14 Do not be yoked together with unbelievers. For
what do righteousness and
wickedness have in com-
mon? Or what fellowship
can light have with dark-
ness? 15 What harmony is
there between Christ and
Belial[h]? What does a believer have in common with
an unbeliever? 16 What
agreement is there between
the temple of God and
idols? For we are the temple of the living God. As
God has said: "I will live
with them and walk among
them, and I will be their
God, and they will be my
people."[i]

[h] *15* Greek *Beliar*, a variant of *Belial*

[i] *16* Lev. 26:12; Jer. 32:38; Ezek. 37:27

17 Therefore come out
from them,
and be separate
from them, says
the Lord,
and touch nothing
unclean;
then I will welcome
you,
18 and I will be your
father,
and you shall be my
sons and
daughters,
says the Lord
Almighty."

Chapter 7

SINCE we have these
promises, beloved, let
us cleanse ourselves from
every defilement of body
and of spirit, making holiness perfect in the fear of
God.

Paul's Joy at the Church's Repentance

2 Make room in your
hearts[o] for us; we have
wronged no one, we have
corrupted no one, we have
taken advantage of no one.
3I do not say this to condemn you, for I said before
that you are in our hearts,
to die together and to live
together. 4I often boast
about you; I have great
pride in you; I am filled
with consolation; I am
overjoyed in all our affliction.
5 For even when we
came into Macedonia, our
bodies had no rest, but we
were afflicted in every
way—disputes without and
fears within. 6But God,
who consoles the down-
cast, consoled us by the arrival of Titus, 7and not only
by his coming, but also by
the consolation with which
he was consoled about you,
as he told us of your longing, your mourning, your
zeal for me, so that I rejoiced still more. 8For even
if I made you sorry with my
letter, I do not regret it
(though I did regret it, for I
see that I grieved you with

[o]Gk lacks *in your hearts*

17 διὸ ἐξέλθατε ἐκ μέσου αὐτῶν καὶ
Wherefore come ye out from [the] midst of them and
ἀφορίσθητε, λέγει κύριος, καὶ ἀκαθάρτου
be ye separated, says [the] Lord, and an unclean thing
μὴ ἅπτεσθε· **18** κἀγὼ εἰσδέξομαι ὑμᾶς, καὶ
do not touch; and I will welcome in you, and
ἔσομαι ὑμῖν εἰς πατέρα, καὶ ὑμεῖς ἔσεσθέ
I will be to you *for* a father, and ye shall be
μοι εἰς υἱοὺς καὶ θυγατέρας, λέγει κύριος
to me *for* sons and daughters, says [the] Lord
παντοκράτωρ. **7** ταύτας οὖν ἔχοντες τὰς ἐπ-
[the] Almighty. [3]These [2]therefore [1]having – [4]pro-
αγγελίας, ἀγαπητοί, καθαρίσωμεν ἑαυτοὺς ἀπὸ
mises, beloved, let us cleanse ourselves from
παντὸς μολυσμοῦ σαρκὸς καὶ πνεύματος,
all pollution of flesh and of spirit,
ἐπιτελοῦντες ἁγιωσύνην ἐν φόβῳ θεοῦ.
perfecting holiness in [the] fear of God.
2 Χωρήσατε ἡμᾶς· οὐδένα ἠδικήσαμεν,
Make room for us; no one we wronged,
οὐδένα ἐφθείραμεν, οὐδένα ἐπλεονεκτήσαμεν.
no one we injured, no one we defrauded.
3 πρὸς κατάκρισιν οὐ λέγω· προείρηκα
For condemnation I say not; [1]I have previously said
γὰρ ὅτι ἐν ταῖς καρδίαις ἡμῶν ἐστε
[1]for that in the hearts of us ye are
εἰς τὸ συναποθανεῖν καὶ συζῆν. **4** πολλή
***for* – to die with [you] and to live with [you]. Much**
μοι παρρησία πρὸς ὑμᾶς, πολλή μοι
to me[c] boldness toward you, much to me[c]
=I have much =I have much
καύχησις ὑπὲρ ὑμῶν· πεπλήρωμαι τῇ
boasting on behalf of you; I have been filled –
παρακλήσει, ὑπερπερισσεύομαι τῇ χαρᾷ ἐπὶ
with comfort, I overflow – with joy on(in)
πάσῃ τῇ θλίψει ἡμῶν. **5** Καὶ γὰρ
all the affliction of us. For indeed
ἐλθόντων ἡμῶν εἰς Μακεδονίαν οὐδεμίαν
coming us[a] into Macedonia [5]no
=when we came
ἔσχηκεν ἄνεσιν ἡ σὰρξ ἡμῶν, ἀλλ᾽ ἐν
[4]*has* had [6]rest [1]the [2]flesh [3]of us, but in
παντὶ θλιβόμενοι· ἔξωθεν μάχαι, ἔσωθεν
every way being afflicted; without [were] fightings, within
φόβοι. **6** ἀλλ᾽ ὁ παρακαλῶν τοὺς ταπεινοὺς
[were] fears. But [2]the [one] [3]comforting [4]the [5]humble
παρεκάλεσεν ἡμᾶς ὁ θεὸς ἐν τῇ παρουσίᾳ
[6]comforted [7]us – [1]God by the presence
Τίτου· **7** οὐ μόνον δὲ ἐν τῇ παρουσίᾳ
of Titus; and not only by the presence
αὐτοῦ, ἀλλὰ καὶ ἐν τῇ παρακλήσει ᾗ
of him, but also by the comfort with which
παρεκλήθη ἐφ᾽ ὑμῖν, ἀναγγέλλων ἡμῖν
he was comforted over you, reporting to us
τὴν ὑμῶν ἐπιπόθησιν, τὸν ὑμῶν ὀδυρμόν,
[1]the [2]of you [3]eager longing, [1]the [2]of you [3]mourning,
τὸν ὑμῶν ζῆλον ὑπὲρ ἐμοῦ, ὥστε με
[1]the [2]of you [3]zeal on behalf of me, so as me
μᾶλλον χαρῆναι. **8** Ὅτι εἰ καὶ ἐλύπησα
more to rejoice.[b] Because if indeed I grieved
=so that I rejoiced more.
ὑμᾶς ἐν τῇ ἐπιστολῇ, οὐ μεταμέλομαι·
you by the epistle, I do not regret;
εἰ καὶ μετεμελόμην, βλέπω ὅτι ἡ ἐπιστολὴ
if indeed I regretted, I see that – epistle

17"Therefore come out
from them
and be separate,
says the Lord.
Touch no unclean thing,
and I will receive
you."[j]
18"I will be a Father to
you,
and you will be my
sons and daughters,
says the Lord
Almighty."[k]

Chapter 7

SINCE we have these
promises, dear friends,
let us purify ourselves from
everything that contami-
nates body and spirit, perfecting holiness out of reverence for God.

Paul's Joy

2Make room for us in
your hearts. We have
wronged no one, we have
corrupted no one, we have
exploited no one. 3I do not
say this to condemn you; I
have said before that you
have such a place in our
hearts that we would live or
die with you. 4I have great
confidence in you; I take
great pride in you. I am
greatly encouraged; in all
our troubles my joy knows
no bounds.
5For when we came into
Macedonia, this body of
ours had no rest, but we
were harassed at every turn
—conflicts on the outside,
fears within. 6But God,
who comforts the down-
cast, comforted us by the
coming of Titus, 7and not
only by his coming but also
by the comfort you had giv-
en him. He told us about
your longing for me, your
deep sorrow, your ardent
concern for me, so that my
joy was greater than ever.
8Even if I caused you sorrow by my letter, I do not
regret it. Though I did re-

[j]*17* Isaiah 52:11; Ezek. 20:34,41
[k]*18* 2 Samuel 7:14; 7:8

that letter, though only
briefly). 9 Now I rejoice,
not because you were
grieved, but because your
grief led to repentance; for
you felt a godly grief, so
that you were not harmed
in any way by us. 10 For
godly grief produces a repentance that leads to salvation and brings no regret,
but worldly grief produces
death. 11 For see what earnestness this godly grief
has produced in you, what
eagerness to clear your-
selves, what indignation,
what alarm, what longing,
what zeal, what punish-
ment! At every point you
have proved yourselves
guiltless in the matter. 12 So
although I wrote to you, it
was not on account of the
one who did the wrong, nor
on account of the one who
was wronged, but in order
that your zeal for us might
be made known to you be-
fore God. 13 In this we find
comfort.

In addition to our own
consolation, we rejoiced
still more at the joy of Titus, because his mind has
been set at rest by all of
you. 14 For if I have been
somewhat boastful about
you to him, I was not dis-
graced; but just as everything we said to you was
true, so our boasting to Titus has proved true as well.
15 And his heart goes out all
the more to you, as he remembers the obedience of
all of you, and how you
welcomed him with fear
and trembling. 16 I rejoice,
because I have complete
confidence in you.

ἐκείνη εἰ καὶ πρὸς ὥραν ἐλύπησεν ὑμᾶς,
that if indeed for an hour it grieved you,
9 νῦν χαίρω, οὐχ ὅτι ἐλυπήθητε, ἀλλ'
now I rejoice, not that ye were grieved, but
ὅτι ἐλυπήθητε εἰς μετάνοιαν· ἐλυπήθητε
that ye were grieved to repentance; [2]ye were grieved
γὰρ κατὰ θεόν, ἵνα ἐν μηδενὶ ζημιωθῆτε
[1]for according to God, in order that in nothing ye might suffer loss
ἐξ ἡμῶν. 10 ἡ γὰρ κατὰ θεὸν λύπη
by us. For [1]the [3]according to [4]God [2]grief
μετάνοιαν εἰς σωτηρίαν ἀμεταμέλητον
[7]repentance [8]to [9]salvation [6]unregrettable
ἐργάζεται· ἡ δὲ τοῦ κόσμου λύπη θάνατον
[5]works; but [1]the [3]of the [4]world [2]grief [6]death
κατεργάζεται. 11 ἰδοὺ γὰρ αὐτὸ τοῦτο
[5]works out. For behold this very thing[,]
τὸ κατὰ θεὸν λυπηθῆναι πόσην κατειργά-
– [2]according to [3]God [1]to be grieved[,] [1]what [3]it worked
σατο ὑμῖν σπουδήν, ἀλλὰ ἀπολογίαν, ἀλλὰ
out [4]in you [2]earnestness, but [what] defence, but
ἀγανάκτησιν, ἀλλὰ φόβον, ἀλλὰ ἐπιπόθησιν,
vexation, but fear, but eager desire,
ἀλλὰ ζῆλον, ἀλλὰ ἐκδίκησιν. ἐν παντὶ
but zeal, but vengeance. In everything
συνεστήσατε ἑαυτοὺς ἁγνοὺς εἶναι τῷ
ye commended yourselves pure to be in the
πράγματι. 12 ἄρα εἰ καὶ ἔγραψα ὑμῖν,
affair. Then if indeed I wrote to you,
οὐχ ἕνεκεν τοῦ ἀδικήσαντος οὐδὲ ἕνεκεν
not for the sake of the [one] having done wrong nor for the sake of
τοῦ ἀδικηθέντος, ἀλλ' ἕνεκεν τοῦ φανερω-
the [one] having been wronged, but for the sake of – to be mani-
θῆναι τὴν σπουδὴν ὑμῶν τὴν ὑπὲρ ἡμῶν
fested the earnestness[bd] of you – on behalf of us
πρὸς ὑμᾶς ἐνώπιον τοῦ θεοῦ. 13 διὰ
toward you before – God. There-
τοῦτο παρακεκλήμεθα. Ἐπὶ δὲ τῇ
fore we have been comforted. But as to the
παρακλήσει ἡμῶν περισσοτέρως μᾶλλον
comfort of us abundantly more
ἐχάρημεν ἐπὶ τῇ χαρᾷ Τίτου, ὅτι ἀναπέ-
we rejoiced over the joy of Titus, because has been
παυται τὸ πνεῦμα αὐτοῦ ἀπὸ πάντων
rested the spirit of him from(by) all
ὑμῶν· 14 ὅτι εἴ τι αὐτῷ ὑπὲρ ὑμῶν
you; because if [2]anything [3]to him [4]on behalf of [5]you
κεκαύχημαι, οὐ κατῃσχύνθην, ἀλλ' ὡς
[1]I have boasted, I was not shamed, but as
πάντα ἐν ἀληθείᾳ ἐλαλήσαμεν ὑμῖν, οὕτως
[2]all things [3]in [4]truth [1]we spoke [5]to you, so
καὶ ἡ καύχησις ἡμῶν ἐπὶ Τίτου ἀλήθεια
also the boasting of us over Titus [2]truth
ἐγενήθη. 15 καὶ τὰ σπλάγχνα αὐτοῦ
[1]became. And the bowels of him
περισσοτέρως εἰς ὑμᾶς ἐστιν ἀναμιμνῃσκομέ-
[2]abundantly [3]toward [4]you [1]is(are) [he] remember-
νου τὴν πάντων ὑμῶν ὑπακοήν, ὡς μετὰ
ing[a] [1]the [3]of all [4]you [2]obedience, as with
φόβου καὶ τρόμου ἐδέξασθε αὐτόν.
fear and trembling ye received him.
16 χαίρω ὅτι ἐν παντὶ θαρρῶ ἐν ὑμῖν.
I rejoice that in everything I am confident in you.

gret it—I see that my letter
hurt you, but only for a little while— 9 yet now I am
happy, not because you
were made sorry, but be-
cause your sorrow led you
to repentance. For you became sorrowful as God in-
tended and so were not
harmed in any way by us.
10 Godly sorrow brings repentance that leads to salvation and leaves no regret,
but worldly sorrow brings
death. 11 See what this godly sorrow has produced in
you: what earnestness,
what eagerness to clear
yourselves, what indigna-
tion, what alarm, what
longing, what concern,
what readiness to see justice done. At every point
you have proved your-
selves to be innocent in this
matter. 12 So even though I
wrote to you, it was not on
account of the one who did
the wrong or of the injured
party, but rather that before God you could see for
yourselves how devoted to
us you are. 13 By all this we
are encouraged.

In addition to our own encouragement, we were es-
pecially delighted to see
how happy Titus was, be-
cause his spirit has been refreshed by all of you. 14 I
had boasted to him about
you, and you have not em-
barrassed me. But just as
everything we said to you
was true, so our boasting
about you to Titus has
proved to be true as well.
15 And his affection for you
is all the greater when he
remembers that you were
all obedient, receiving him
with fear and trembling. 16 I
am glad I can have com-
plete confidence in you.

Chapter 8

Encouragement to Be Generous

WE want you to know,
brothers and sis-
ters,[p] about the grace of
God that has been granted
to the churches of Macedonia; 2for during a severe ordeal of affliction, their
abundant joy and their extreme poverty have over-
flowed in a wealth of generosity on their part. 3For, as
I can testify, they voluntarily gave according to their
means, and even beyond
their means, 4begging us
earnestly for the privilege[q]
of sharing in this ministry
to the saints— 5and this,
not merely as we expected;
they gave themselves first
to the Lord and, by the will
of God, to us, 6so that we
might urge Titus that, as he
had already made a begin-
ning, so he should also
complete this generous undertaking[r] among you.
7Now as you excel in
everything—in faith, in
speech, in knowledge, in
utmost eagerness, and in
our love for you[s]—so we
want you to excel also in
this generous undertak-
ing.[r]
8 I do not say this as a
command, but I am testing
the genuineness of your
love against the earnest-
ness of others. 9For you
know the generous act[t] of
our Lord Jesus Christ, that
though he was rich, yet for
your sakes he became
poor, so that by his poverty
you might become rich.
10And in this matter I am
giving my advice: it is appropriate for you who be-
gan last year not only to do
something but even to de-
sire to do something—
11now finish doing it, so

[p] Gk *brothers*
[q] Gk *grace*
[r] Gk *this grace*
[s] Other ancient authorities read *your love for us*
[t] Gk *the grace*

8 Γνωρίζομεν δὲ ὑμῖν, ἀδελφοί, τὴν
Now we make known to you, brothers, the

χάριν τοῦ θεοῦ τὴν δεδομένην ἐν ταῖς
grace – of God – *having been* given among the

ἐκκλησίαις τῆς Μακεδονίας, **2** ὅτι ἐν πολλῇ
churches – of Macedonia, that in much

δοκιμῇ θλίψεως ἡ περισσεία τῆς χαρᾶς
proving of affliction the abundance of the joy

αὐτῶν καὶ ἡ κατὰ βάθους πτωχεία
of them and [1]the [3]according to [4]depth [2]poverty
=their extreme poverty

αὐτῶν ἐπερίσσευσεν εἰς τὸ πλοῦτος τῆς
of them abounded to the riches of the

ἁπλότητος αὐτῶν· **3** ὅτι κατὰ δύναμιν,
liberality of them; that according to [their] power,

μαρτυρῶ, καὶ παρὰ δύναμιν, αὐθαίρετοι
I witness, and beyond [their] power, of their own accord

4 μετὰ πολλῆς παρακλήσεως δεόμενοι ἡμῶν
with much beseeching requesting of us

τὴν χάριν καὶ τὴν κοινωνίαν τῆς διακονίας
the grace and the fellowship of the ministry

τῆς εἰς τοὺς ἁγίους, **5** καὶ οὐ καθὼς
– to the saints, and not as

ἠλπίσαμεν, ἀλλὰ ἑαυτοὺς ἔδωκαν πρῶτον
we hoped, but themselves gave first*ly*

τῷ κυρίῳ καὶ ἡμῖν διὰ θελήματος θεοῦ,
to the Lord and to us through [the] will of God,

6 εἰς τὸ παρακαλέσαι ἡμᾶς Τίτον, ἵνα
for – to beseech us[b] Titus, in order that
=that we should beseech

καθὼς προενήρξατο οὕτως καὶ ἐπιτελέσῃ
as previously he began so also he should complete

εἰς ὑμᾶς καὶ τὴν χάριν ταύτην. **7** ἀλλ'
in you also this grace. But

ὥσπερ ἐν παντὶ περισσεύετε, πίστει καὶ
as in everything ye abound, in faith and

λόγῳ καὶ γνώσει καὶ πάσῃ σπουδῇ
in word and in knowledge and in all diligence

καὶ τῇ ἐξ ἡμῶν ἐν ὑμῖν ἀγάπῃ, ἵνα
and – [2]from [3]us [4]in(to) [5]you [1]in love, [see] that

καὶ ἐν ταύτῃ τῇ χάριτι περισσεύητε.
[5]also [2]in [3]this – [4]grace [1]ye may abound.

8 Οὐ κατ' ἐπιταγὴν λέγω, ἀλλὰ διὰ
[2]Not [3]by way of [4]command [1]I say,* but through

τῆς ἑτέρων σπουδῆς καὶ τὸ τῆς ὑμετέρας
[1]the [3]of others [2]diligence also [3]the – [4]of your

ἀγάπης γνήσιον δοκιμάζων· **9** γινώσκετε
[5]love [2]reality [1]proving; [2]ye know

γὰρ τὴν χάριν τοῦ κυρίου ἡμῶν Ἰησοῦ
[1]for the grace of the Lord of us Jesus

[Χριστοῦ], ὅτι δι' ὑμᾶς ἐπτώχευσεν
Christ, that on account of you [3]he impoverished [himself]

πλούσιος ὤν, ἵνα ὑμεῖς τῇ ἐκείνου πτωχείᾳ
[2]rich [1]being, in order that ye [1]by the [3]of that one [2]poverty

πλουτήσητε. **10** καὶ γνώμην ἐν τούτῳ
might become rich. And [4]an opinion [1]in [2]this

δίδωμι· τοῦτο γὰρ ὑμῖν συμφέρει, οἵτινες
[3]I give: for this [2]for you [1]is expedient, who

οὐ μόνον τὸ ποιῆσαι ἀλλὰ καὶ τὸ θέλειν
not only the to do but also the to will

προενήρξασθε ἀπὸ πέρυσι· **11** νυνὶ δὲ καὶ
previously *ye* began from last year; but now also
=a year ago;

* That is, Paul is not issuing a command. *Cf.* I. Cor. 7. 6.

Chapter 8

Generosity Encouraged

AND now, brothers, we
want you to know
about the grace that God
has given the Macedonian
churches. 2Out of the most
severe trial, their overflowing joy and their extreme
poverty welled up in rich
generosity. 3For I testify
that they gave as much as
they were able, and even
beyond their ability. En-
tirely on their own, 4they
urgently pleaded with us
for the privilege of sharing
in this service to the saints.
5And they did not do as we
expected, but they gave
themselves first to the Lord
and then to us in keeping
with God's will. 6So we
urged Titus, since he had
earlier made a beginning, to
bring also to completion
this act of grace on your
part. 7But just as you excel
in everything—in faith, in
speech, in knowledge, in
complete earnestness and
in your love for us[l]—see
that you also excel in this
grace of giving.
8I am not commanding
you, but I want to test the
sincerity of your love by
comparing it with the earnestness of others. 9For
you know the grace of our
Lord Jesus Christ, that
though he was rich, yet for
your sakes he became
poor, so that you through
his poverty might become
rich.
10And here is my advice
about what is best for you
in this matter: Last year
you were the first not only
to give but also to have the
desire to do so. 11Now fin-

[l]7 Some manuscripts *in our love for you*

that your eagerness may be
matched by completing it
according to your means.
[12]For if the eagerness is
there, the gift is acceptable
according to what one
has—not according to
what one does not have. [13]I
do not mean that there
should be relief for others
and pressure on you, but it
is a question of a fair balance between [14]your
present abundance and
their need, so that their
abundance may be for your
need, in order that there
may be a fair balance. [15]As
it is written,

"The one who had
much did not
have too much,
and the one who
had little did not
have too little."

Commendation of Titus

16 But thanks be to God
who put in the heart of Titus the same eagerness for
you that I myself have.
[17]For he not only accepted
our appeal, but since he is
more eager than ever, he is
going to you of his own accord. [18]With him we are
sending the brother who is
famous among all the
churches for his proclaiming the good news;[u] [19]and
not only that, but he has
also been appointed by the
churches to travel with us
while we are administering
this generous undertaking
for the glory of the Lord
himself[v] and to show our
goodwill. [20]We intend that
no one should blame us
about this generous gift
that we are administering,
[21]for we intend to do what
is right not only in the
Lord's sight but also in the
sight of others. [22]And with
them we are sending our

τὸ ποιῆσαι ἐπιτελέσατε, ὅπως καθάπερ ἡ
[2]the [3]to do [1]complete ye, so as as the
προθυμία τοῦ θέλειν, οὕτως καὶ τὸ
eagerness of the to will, so also the
ἐπιτελέσαι ἐκ τοῦ ἔχειν. 12 εἰ γὰρ ἡ
to complete out of the to have. =what ye have. For if the
προθυμία πρόκειται, καθὸ ἐὰν ἔχῃ
eagerness is already there, according to whatever one has
εὐπρόσδεκτος, οὐ καθὸ οὐκ ἔχει. 13 οὐ
it is acceptable, not according to [what] one has not. not
γὰρ ἵνα ἄλλοις ἄνεσις, ὑμῖν θλῖψις,
For in order that to others [there may be] relief, to you distress,
ἀλλ' ἐξ ἰσότητος 14 ἐν τῷ νῦν καιρῷ
but by equality at the present time
τὸ ὑμῶν περίσσευμα εἰς τὸ ἐκείνων
the [2]of you [1]abundance [may be] for the [2]of those
ὑστέρημα, ἵνα καὶ τὸ ἐκείνων περίσσευμα
[1]lack, in order that also the [2]of those [1]abundance
γένηται εἰς τὸ ὑμῶν ὑστέρημα, ὅπως
may be for the [2]of you [1]lack, so as
γένηται ἰσότης, 15 καθὼς γέγραπται· ὁ
there may be equality, as it has been written: He
τὸ πολὺ οὐκ ἐπλεόνασεν, καὶ ὁ τὸ
the much did not abound, and he the
ὀλίγον οὐκ ἠλαττόνησεν. 16 Χάρις δὲ
little had not less. But thanks [be]
τῷ θεῷ τῷ διδόντι τὴν αὐτὴν σπουδὴν
– to God – giving the same diligence
ὑπὲρ ὑμῶν ἐν τῇ καρδίᾳ Τίτου, 17 ὅτι
on behalf of you in the heart of Titus, because
τὴν μὲν παράκλησιν ἐδέξατο, σπουδαιότερος
[3]the [1]indeed [4]beseeching [2]he received, [3]more diligent
δὲ ὑπάρχων αὐθαίρετος ἐξῆλθεν πρὸς ὑμᾶς.
[1]and [2]being of his own accord he went forth to you.
18 συνεπέμψαμεν δὲ μετ' αὐτοῦ τὸν
And we sent *with* with him the
ἀδελφὸν οὗ ὁ ἔπαινος ἐν τῷ εὐαγγελίῳ
brother of whom the praise in the gospel
διὰ πασῶν τῶν ἐκκλησιῶν, 19 οὐ μόνον δὲ
[is] through[out] all the churches, and not only [this]
ἀλλὰ καὶ χειροτονηθεὶς ὑπὸ τῶν ἐκκλησιῶν
but also [3]having been elected [4]by [5]the [6]churches
συνέκδημος ἡμῶν ἐν τῇ χάριτι ταύτῃ
[1]a travelling companion [2]of us in this grace
τῇ διακονουμένῃ ὑφ' ἡμῶν πρὸς τὴν
– being ministered by us to [1]the
αὐτοῦ τοῦ κυρίου δόξαν καὶ προθυμίαν
[5][him]self [3]of the [4]Lord [2]glory and eagerness
ἡμῶν, 20 στελλόμενοι τοῦτο, μή τις ἡμᾶς
of us, avoiding this, lest anyone [2]us
μωμήσηται ἐν τῇ ἁδρότητι ταύτῃ τῇ
[1]should blame in this bounty –
διακονουμένῃ ὑφ' ἡμῶν· 21 προνοοῦμεν γὰρ
being ministered by us; for we provide
καλὰ οὐ μόνον ἐνώπιον κυρίου ἀλλὰ καὶ
good things not only before [the] Lord but also
ἐνώπιον ἀνθρώπων. 22 συνεπέμψαμεν δὲ
before men. And we sent with

ish the work, so that your
eager willingness to do it
may be matched by your
completion of it, according
to your means. [12]For if the
willingness is there, the gift
is acceptable according to
what one has, not accord-
ing to what he does not
have.
[13]Our desire is not that
others might be relieved
while you are hard pressed,
but that there might be
equality. [14]At the present
time your plenty will supply what they need, so that
in turn their plenty will supply what you need. Then
there will be equality, [15]as
it is written: "He who gathered much did not have too
much, and he who gathered
little did not have too little."[m]

Titus Sent to Corinth

[16]I thank God, who put
into the heart of Titus the
same concern I have for
you. [17]For Titus not only
welcomed our appeal, but
he is coming to you with
much enthusiasm and on
his own initiative. [18]And
we are sending along with
him the brother who is
praised by all the churches
for his service to the gospel. [19]What is more, he was
chosen by the churches to
accompany us as we carry
the offering, which we administer in order to honor
the Lord himself and to
show our eagerness to
help. [20]We want to avoid
any criticism of the way we
administer this liberal gift.
[21]For we are taking pains to
do what is right, not only in
the eyes of the Lord but
also in the eyes of men.
[22]In addition, we are

[u]Or *the gospel*
[v]Other ancient authorities lack *himself*

[m]*15* Exodus 16:18

brother whom we have often tested and found eager in many matters, but who is now more eager than ever because of his great confidence in you. 23 As for Titus, he is my partner and co-worker in your service; as for our brothers, they are messengers[w] of the churches, the glory of Christ. 24 Therefore openly before the churches, show them the proof of your love and of our reason for boasting about you.

αὐτοῖς τὸν ἀδελφὸν ἡμῶν, ὃν ἐδοκιμάσαμεν
them the brother of us, whom [1]we proved
ἐν πολλοῖς πολλάκις σπουδαῖον ὄντα, νυνὶ
[5]in [6]many things [4]many times [3]diligent [2]being, [2]now
δὲ πολὺ σπουδαιότερον πεποιθήσει πολλῇ
[1]and much more diligent [1]in [3]confidence [2]much
τῇ εἰς ὑμᾶς. 23 εἴτε ὑπὲρ Τίτου, κοινωνὸς
– toward you. Whether as to Titus, [2]partner
ἐμὸς καὶ εἰς ὑμᾶς συνεργός· εἴτε ἀδελφοὶ
[1]my [3]and [5]for [6]you [4]fellow-worker; or brothers
ἡμῶν, ἀπόστολοι ἐκκλησιῶν, δόξα Χριστοῦ.
of us, apostles of churches, [the] glory of Christ.
24 τὴν οὖν ἔνδειξιν τῆς ἀγάπης ὑμῶν
[7]The [1]therefore [8]demonstration [9]of the [10]love [11]of you
καὶ ἡμῶν καυχήσεως ὑπὲρ ὑμῶν εἰς
[12]and [14]of us [13]boasting [15]on behalf of [16]you [17]to
αὐτοὺς ἐνδεικνύμενοι εἰς πρόσωπον τῶν
[18]them [2]showing forth [3]in [4][the] presence [5]of the
ἐκκλησιῶν.
[6]churches.

sending with them our brother who has often proved to us in many ways that he is zealous, and now even more so because of his great confidence in you. 23 As for Titus, he is my partner and fellow worker among you; as for our brothers, they are representatives of the churches and an honor to Christ. 24 Therefore show these men the proof of your love and the reason for our pride in you, so that the churches can see it.

Chapter 9

The Collection for Christians at Jerusalem

NOW it is not necessary for me to write you about the ministry to the saints, 2 for I know your eagerness, which is the subject of my boasting about you to the people of Macedonia, saying that Achaia has been ready since last year; and your zeal has stirred up most of them. 3 But I am sending the brothers in order that our boasting about you may not prove to have been empty in this case, so that you may be ready, as I said you would be; 4 otherwise, if some Macedonians come with me and find that you are not ready, we would be humiliated—to say nothing of you—in this undertaking.[x] 5 So I thought it necessary to urge the brothers to go on ahead to you, and arrange in advance for this bountiful gift that you have promised, so that it may be ready as a voluntary gift and not as an extortion.

6 The point is this: the one who sows sparingly will also reap sparingly,

9 Περὶ μὲν γὰρ τῆς διακονίας τῆς
[3]Concerning [2]indeed [1]for the ministry –
εἰς τοὺς ἁγίους περισσόν μοί ἐστιν τὸ
to the saints [3]superfluous [2]for me [1]it is –
γράφειν ὑμῖν· 2 οἶδα γὰρ τὴν προθυμίαν
to write to you; for I know the eagerness
ὑμῶν ἣν ὑπὲρ ὑμῶν καυχῶμαι Μακε-
of you which on behalf of you I boast to Mace-
δόσιν ὅτι Ἀχαΐα παρεσκεύασται ἀπὸ
donians that Achaia has made preparations from
πέρυσι, καὶ τὸ ὑμῶν ζῆλος ἠρέθισεν
last year, =a year ago, and the [2]of you [1]zeal stirred up
τοὺς πλείονας. 3 ἔπεμψα δὲ τοὺς ἀδελφούς,
the greater number. And I sent the brothers,
ἵνα μὴ τὸ καύχημα ἡμῶν τὸ ὑπὲρ
lest the boast of us – on behalf
ὑμῶν κενωθῇ ἐν τῷ μέρει τούτῳ, ἵνα
of you should be emptied in this respect, in order that
καθὼς ἔλεγον παρεσκευασμένοι ἦτε, 4 μή
as I said *having been* prepared ye were,
πως ἐὰν ἔλθωσιν σὺν ἐμοὶ Μακεδόνες
lest if [2]come [3]with [4]me [1]Macedonians
καὶ εὕρωσιν ὑμᾶς ἀπαρασκευάστους
and find you unprepared
καταισχυνθῶμεν ἡμεῖς, ἵνα μὴ λέγωμεν
[2]should be shamed [1]we, *in order that* we say not
ὑμεῖς, ἐν τῇ ὑποστάσει ταύτῃ. 5 ἀναγκαῖον
ye, in this confidence. [2]Necessary
οὖν ἡγησάμην παρακαλέσαι τοὺς ἀδελφοὺς
[3]therefore [1]I thought [it] to beseech the brothers
ἵνα προέλθωσιν εἰς ὑμᾶς καὶ προκαταρτί-
in order that they go forward to you and arrange before-
σωσιν τὴν προεπηγγελμένην εὐλογίαν ὑμῶν,
hand [1]the [4]having been promised [2]blessing [3]of you,
ταύτην ἑτοίμην εἶναι οὕτως ὡς εὐλογίαν
this ready to be thus as a blessing
καὶ μὴ ὡς πλεονεξίαν. 6 Τοῦτο δέ,
and not as greediness. And this,
ὁ σπείρων φειδομένως φειδομένως καὶ
the [one] sowing sparingly [2]sparingly [1]also

Chapter 9

THERE is no need for me to write to you about this service to the saints. 2 For I know your eagerness to help, and I have been boasting about it to the Macedonians, telling them that since last year you in Achaia were ready to give; and your enthusiasm has stirred most of them to action. 3 But I am sending the brothers in order that our boasting about you in this matter should not prove hollow, but that you may be ready, as I said you would be. 4 For if any Macedonians come with me and find you unprepared, we—not to say anything about you—would be ashamed of having been so confident. 5 So I thought it necessary to urge the brothers to visit you in advance and finish the arrangements for the generous gift you had promised. Then it will be ready as a generous gift, not as one grudgingly given.

Sowing Generously

6 Remember this: Whoever sows sparingly will also

[w] Gk *apostles*
[x] Other ancient authorities add *of boasting*

and the one who sows bountifully will also reap bountifully. 7 Each of you must give as you have made up your mind, not reluctantly or under compulsion, for God loves a cheerful giver. 8 And God is able to provide you with every blessing in abundance, so that by always having enough of everything, you may share abundantly in every good work. 9 As it is written,

"He scatters abroad,
he gives to the poor;
his righteousness[y] endures forever."

10 He who supplies seed to the sower and bread for food will supply and multiply your seed for sowing and increase the harvest of your righteousness.[y] 11 You will be enriched in every way for your great generosity, which will produce thanksgiving to God through us; 12 for the rendering of this ministry not only supplies the needs of the saints but also overflows with many thanksgivings to God. 13 Through the testing of this ministry you glorify God by your obedience to the confession of the gospel of Christ and by the generosity of your sharing with them and with all others, 14 while they long for you and pray for you because of the surpassing grace of God that he has given you. 15 Thanks be to God for his indescribable gift!

Chapter 10

Paul Defends His Ministry

I myself, Paul, appeal to you by the meekness and gentleness of Christ—I who am humble when face to face with you, but bold

[y] Or *benevolence*

θερίσει, καὶ ὁ σπείρων ἐπ' εὐλογίαις ἐπ'
[1]will reap, and the [one] sowing on(for) blessings [3]on(for)
εὐλογίαις καὶ θερίσει. 7 ἕκαστος καθὼς
[4]blessings [2]also [1]will reap. Each one as
προῄρηται τῇ καρδίᾳ, μὴ ἐκ λύπης ἢ
he chose in the(his) heart, not of grief or
ἐξ ἀνάγκης· ἱλαρὸν γὰρ δότην ἀγαπᾷ ὁ
of necessity; for [3]a cheerful [4]giver [2]loves –
θεός. 8 δυνατεῖ δὲ ὁ θεὸς πᾶσαν χάριν
[1]God. And [2]is able – [1]God [4]all [5]grace
περισσεῦσαι εἰς ὑμᾶς, ἵνα ἐν παντὶ
[3]to cause to abound toward you, in order that [5]in [6]everything
πάντοτε πᾶσαν αὐτάρκειαν ἔχοντες περισ-
[1]always [3]all [4]self-sufficiency [2]having ye may
σεύητε εἰς πᾶν ἔργον ἀγαθόν, 9 καθὼς
abound to every work good, as
γέγραπται· ἐσκόρπισεν, ἔδωκεν τοῖς πένησιν,
it has been written: He scattered, he gave to the poor,
ἡ δικαιοσύνη αὐτοῦ μένει εἰς τὸν αἰῶνα.
the righteousness of him remains unto the age.
10 ὁ δὲ ἐπιχορηγῶν σπέρμα τῷ σπείροντι
Now the [one] providing seed for the [one] sowing
καὶ ἄρτον εἰς βρῶσιν χορηγήσει καὶ
[1]both [2]bread [4]for [5]food [3]will supply and
πληθυνεῖ τὸν σπόρον ὑμῶν καὶ αὐξήσει
will multiply the seed of you and will increase
τὰ γενήματα τῆς δικαιοσύνης ὑμῶν· 11 ἐν
the fruits of the righteousness of you; in
παντὶ πλουτιζόμενοι εἰς πᾶσαν ἁπλότητα,
everything being enriched to all liberality,
ἥτις κατεργάζεται δι' ἡμῶν εὐχαριστίαν
which works out through us thanksgiving
τῷ θεῷ· 12 ὅτι ἡ διακονία τῆς λειτουργίας
– to God; because the ministry – service
ταύτης οὐ μόνον ἐστὶν προσαναπληροῦσα
of this not only is making up
τὰ ὑστερήματα τῶν ἁγίων, ἀλλὰ καὶ
the things lacking of the saints, but [is] also
περισσεύουσα διὰ πολλῶν εὐχαριστιῶν τῷ
abounding through many thanksgivings –
θεῷ· 13 διὰ τῆς δοκιμῆς τῆς διακονίας
to God; through the proof – ministry
ταύτης δοξάζοντες τὸν θεὸν ἐπὶ τῇ
of this glorifying – God on the
ὑποταγῇ τῆς ὁμολογίας ὑμῶν εἰς τὸ
submission of the confession of you to the
εὐαγγέλιον τοῦ Χριστοῦ καὶ ἁπλότητι
gospel – of Christ and [on the] liberality
τῆς κοινωνίας εἰς αὐτοὺς καὶ εἰς πάντας,
of the fellowship toward them and toward all men,
14 καὶ αὐτῶν δεήσει ὑπὲρ ὑμῶν ἐπιποθούν-
and [1]them [4]with request [5]on behalf of [6]you [2]longing
των ὑμᾶς διὰ τὴν ὑπερβάλλουσαν χάριν
after[a] [3]you on account of the excelling grace
τοῦ θεοῦ ἐφ' ὑμῖν. 15 Χάρις τῷ θεῷ
– of God upon you. Thanks – to God
ἐπὶ τῇ ἀνεκδιηγήτῳ αὐτοῦ δωρεᾷ.
for the indescribable of him gift.

10 Αὐτὸς δὲ ἐγὼ Παῦλος παρακαλῶ
[my]self Now I Paul beseech
ὑμᾶς διὰ τῆς πραΰτητος καὶ ἐπιεικείας
you through the meekness and forbearance
τοῦ Χριστοῦ, ὃς κατὰ πρόσωπον μὲν
– of Christ, who according to face indeed

reap sparingly, and whoever sows generously will also reap generously. 7 Each man should give what he has decided in his heart to give, not reluctantly or under compulsion, for God loves a cheerful giver. 8 And God is able to make all grace abound to you, so that in all things at all times, having all that you need, you will abound in every good work. 9 As it is written:

"He has scattered
abroad his gifts to the poor;
his righteousness
endures forever."[n]

10 Now he who supplies seed to the sower and bread for food will also supply and increase your store of seed and will enlarge the harvest of your righteousness. 11 You will be made rich in every way so that you can be generous on every occasion, and through us your generosity will result in thanksgiving to God.

12 This service that you perform is not only supplying the needs of God's people but is also overflowing in many expressions of thanks to God. 13 Because of the service by which you have proved yourselves, men will praise God for the obedience that accompanies your confession of the gospel of Christ, and for your generosity in sharing with them and with everyone else. 14 And in their prayers for you their hearts will go out to you, because of the surpassing grace God has given you. 15 Thanks be to God for his indescribable gift!

Chapter 10

Paul's Defense of His Ministry

BY the meekness and gentleness of Christ, I appeal to you—I, Paul, who am "timid" when face to face with you, but

[n] 9 Psalm 112:9

toward you when I am
away!— 2I ask that when I
am present I need not show
boldness by daring to op-
pose those who think we
are acting according to human standards.[z] 3Indeed,
we live as human beings,[a]
but we do not wage war according to human stan-
dards;[z] 4for the weapons
of our warfare are not
merely human,[b] but they
have divine power to de-
stroy strongholds. We de-
stroy arguments 5and ev-
ery proud obstacle raised
up against the knowledge
of God, and we take every
thought captive to obey
Christ. 6We are ready to
punish every disobedience
when your obedience is
complete.
7 Look at what is before
your eyes. If you are confident that you belong to
Christ, remind yourself of
this, that just as you belong
to Christ, so also do we.
8Now, even if I boast a little too much of our authority, which the Lord gave for
building you up and not for
tearing you down, I will not
be ashamed of it. 9I do not
want to seem as though I
am trying to frighten you
with my letters. 10For they
say, "His letters are
weighty and strong, but his
bodily presence is weak,
and his speech contempt-
ible." 11Let such people
understand that what we
say by letter when absent,
we will also do when
present.
12 We do not dare to
classify or compare our-
selves with some of those
who commend themselves.
But when they measure

ταπεινὸς ἐν ὑμῖν, ἀπὼν δὲ θαρρῶ εἰς
[am] humble among you, but being absent am bold toward

ὑμᾶς· 2 δέομαι δὲ τὸ μὴ παρὼν θαρρῆσαι
you: now I request – not being present to be bold

τῇ πεποιθήσει ᾗ λογίζομαι τολμῆσαι ἐπί
in the confidence which I reckon to be daring toward

τινας τοὺς λογιζομένους ἡμᾶς ὡς κατὰ
some the [ones] reckoning us as [2]according to

σάρκα περιπατοῦντας. 3 Ἐν σαρκὶ γὰρ
[3]flesh [1]walking. in flesh For

περιπατοῦντες οὐ κατὰ σάρκα στρατευόμεθα,
walking not according to flesh we war,

4 τὰ γὰρ ὅπλα τῆς στρατείας ἡμῶν
for the weapons of the warfare of us [are]

οὐ σαρκικὰ ἀλλὰ δυνατὰ τῷ θεῷ πρὸς
not fleshly but powerful – to God to

καθαίρεσιν ὀχυρωμάτων, λογισμοὺς καθαιροῦν-
overthrow of strongholds, [2]reasonings [1]overthrow-

τες 5 καὶ πᾶν ὕψωμα ἐπαιρόμενον κατὰ
ing and every high thing rising up against

τῆς γνώσεως τοῦ θεοῦ, καὶ αἰχμαλωτίζοντες
the knowledge – of God, and taking captive

πᾶν νόημα εἰς τὴν ὑπακοὴν τοῦ Χριστοῦ,
every design to the obedience – of Christ,

6 καὶ ἐν ἑτοίμῳ ἔχοντες ἐκδικῆσαι πᾶσαν
and in readiness having to avenge all
=being ready

παρακοήν, ὅταν πληρωθῇ ὑμῶν ἡ ὑπακοή.
disobedience, whenever [4]is fulfilled [3]of you [1]the [2]obedience.

7 Τὰ κατὰ πρόσωπον βλέπετε. εἴ τις
[2]The things [3]according to [4]face (appearance) [1]ye look [at]. If anyone

πέποιθεν ἑαυτῷ Χριστοῦ εἶναι, τοῦτο
has persuaded himself [2]of Christ [1]to be, this

λογιζέσθω πάλιν ἐφ' ἑαυτοῦ, ὅτι καθὼς
let him reckon again as to himself, that as

αὐτὸς Χριστοῦ, οὕτως καὶ ἡμεῖς. 8 ἐάν
he [is] of Christ, so also [are] we. [2]if

τε γὰρ περισσότερόν τι καυχήσωμαι περὶ
[3]even [1]For [6]more abundantly [5]somewhat [4]I should boast concerning

τῆς ἐξουσίας ἡμῶν, ἧς ἔδωκεν ὁ κύριος
the authority of us, which [3]gave [1]the [2]Lord

εἰς οἰκοδομὴν καὶ οὐκ εἰς καθαίρεσιν
for edification and not for overthrow

ὑμῶν, οὐκ αἰσχυνθήσομαι, 9 ἵνα μὴ δόξω
of you, I shall not be shamed, in order that I may not seem

ὡσὰν ἐκφοβεῖν ὑμᾶς διὰ τῶν ἐπιστολῶν.
as though to frighten you through the epistles.

10 ὅτι αἱ ἐπιστολαὶ μέν, φησίν, βαρεῖαι
Because the(his) epistles indeed, he says, [are] weighty

καὶ ἰσχυραί, ἡ δὲ παρουσία τοῦ σώματος
and strong, but the presence of the(his) body [is]

ἀσθενὴς καὶ ὁ λόγος ἐξουθενημένος.
weak and the(his) speech *being* despised.

11 τοῦτο λογιζέσθω ὁ τοιοῦτος, ὅτι οἷοί
This let reckon such a one, that such as

ἐσμεν τῷ λόγῳ δι' ἐπιστολῶν ἀπόντες,
we are – in word through epistles being absent,

τοιοῦτοι καὶ παρόντες τῷ ἔργῳ. 12 Οὐ
such also being present – in work. [3]not

γὰρ τολμῶμεν ἐγκρῖναι ἢ συγκρῖναι
[1]For [2]we dare *to* class with or *to* compare

ἑαυτούς τισιν τῶν ἑαυτοὺς συνιστανόντων·
ourselves with some of the [ones] [2]themselves [1]commending;

"bold" when away! 2I beg
you that when I come I may
not have to be as bold as I
expect to be toward some
people who think that we
live by the standards of this
world. 3For though we live
in the world, we do not
wage war as the world
does. 4The weapons we
fight with are not the weapons of the world. On the
contrary, they have divine
power to demolish strong-
holds. 5We demolish argu-
ments and every pretension
that sets itself up against
the knowledge of God, and
we take captive every
thought to make it obedient
to Christ. 6And we will be
ready to punish every act of
disobedience, once your
obedience is complete.
7You are looking only on
the surface of things.[o] If
anyone is confident that he
belongs to Christ, he
should consider again that
we belong to Christ just as
much as he. 8For even if I
boast somewhat freely
about the authority the
Lord gave us for building
you up rather than pulling
you down, I will not be
ashamed of it. 9I do not
want to seem to be trying to
frighten you with my let-
ters. 10For some say, "His
letters are weighty and
forceful, but in person he is
unimpressive and his
speaking amounts to noth-
ing." 11Such people should
realize that what we are in
our letters when we are absent, we will be in our actions when we are present.
12We do not dare to clas-
sify or compare ourselves
with some who commend
themselves. When they

[z] Gk *according to the flesh*
[a] Gk *in the flesh*
[b] Gk *fleshly*

[o] 7 Or *Look at the obvious facts*

themselves by one another,
and compare themselves
with one another, they do
not show good sense.
13 We, however, will not
boast beyond limits, but
will keep within the field
that God has assigned to
us, to reach out even as far
as you. 14 For we were not
overstepping our limits
when we reached you; we
were the first to come all
the way to you with the
good news[c] of Christ.
15 We do not boast beyond
limits, that is, in the labors
of others; but our hope is
that, as your faith in-
creases, our sphere of action among you may be
greatly enlarged, 16 so that
we may proclaim the good
news[c] in lands beyond
you, without boasting of
work already done in someone else's sphere of action.
17 "Let the one who boasts,
boast in the Lord." 18 For it
is not those who commend
themselves that are ap-
proved, but those whom
the Lord commends.

Chapter 11

Paul and the False Apostles

I wish you would bear
with me in a little fool-
ishness. Do bear with me!
2 I feel a divine jealousy for
you, for I promised you in
marriage to one husband,
to present you as a chaste
virgin to Christ. 3 But I am
afraid that as the serpent
deceived Eve by its cun-
ning, your thoughts will be
led astray from a sincere
and pure[d] devotion to
Christ. 4 For if someone
comes and proclaims an-
other Jesus than the one we
proclaimed, or if you re-
ceive a different spirit from

[c] Or *the gospel*
[d] Other ancient authorities lack *and pure*

ἀλλὰ αὐτοὶ ἐν ἑαυτοῖς ἑαυτοὺς μετροῦντες
but they [3]among [4]themselves [2]themselves [1]measuring

καὶ συγκρίνοντες ἑαυτοὺς ἑαυτοῖς οὐ
and comparing themselves with themselves not

συνιᾶσιν. 13 ἡμεῖς δὲ οὐκ εἰς τὰ ἄμετρα
do understand. But we [3]not [4]immeasurably†

καυχησόμεθα, ἀλλὰ κατὰ τὸ μέτρον τοῦ
[1]will [2]boast, but according to the measure of the

κανόνος οὗ ἐμέρισεν ἡμῖν ὁ θεὸς μέτρου,
rule which [2]divided [3]to us – [1]God of(in) measure,

ἐφικέσθαι ἄχρι καὶ ὑμῶν. 14 οὐ γὰρ
to reach as far as even you. For not

ὡς μὴ ἐφικνούμενοι εἰς ὑμᾶς ὑπερεκτείνομεν
as not reaching to you do we overstretch

ἑαυτούς, ἄχρι γὰρ καὶ ὑμῶν ἐφθάσαμεν
ourselves, for as far as even you we came

ἐν τῷ εὐαγγελίῳ τοῦ Χριστοῦ, 15 οὐκ
in the gospel – of Christ, not

εἰς τὰ ἄμετρα καυχώμενοι ἐν ἀλλοτρίοις
immeasurably† boasting in others'†

κόποις, ἐλπίδα δὲ ἔχοντες αὐξανομένης
labours, but [2]hope [1]having growing
=as your faith grows

τῆς πίστεως ὑμῶν ἐν ὑμῖν μεγαλυνθῆναι
the faith of you[a] [2]among [3]you [1]to be magnified

κατὰ τὸν κανόνα ἡμῶν εἰς περισσείαν,
according to the rule of us in abundance,

16 εἰς τὰ ὑπερέκεινα ὑμῶν εὐαγγελίσασθαι,
in the [parts] beyond you to preach good tidings,

οὐκ ἐν ἀλλοτρίῳ κανόνι εἰς τὰ ἕτοιμα
not [2]in [3]another's† [4]rule [5]in – [6]things ready

καυχήσασθαι. 17 Ὁ δὲ καυχώμενος ἐν
[1]to boast. But the [one] boasting [2]in

κυρίῳ καυχάσθω· 18 οὐ γὰρ ὁ ἑαυτὸν
[3][the] Lord [1]let him boast; for not the [one] himself

συνιστάνων, ἐκεῖνός ἐστιν δόκιμος, ἀλλὰ
commending, that one is approved, but

ὃν ὁ κύριος συνίστησιν.
whom the Lord commends.

11 Ὄφελον ἀνείχεσθέ μου μικρόν τι
I would that ye endured me a little [bit]

ἀφροσύνης· ἀλλὰ καὶ ἀνέχεσθέ μου.
of foolishness; but indeed ye do endure me.

2 ζηλῶ γὰρ ὑμᾶς θεοῦ ζήλῳ, ἡρμοσάμην
For I am jealous [of] you [2]of God [1]with a jealousy, [2]I betrothed

γὰρ ὑμᾶς ἑνὶ ἀνδρὶ παρθένον ἁγνὴν
[1]for you to one husband [4]virgin [3]a pure

παραστῆσαι τῷ Χριστῷ· 3 φοβοῦμαι δὲ
[1]to present – to Christ; and I fear

μή πως, ὡς ὁ ὄφις ἐξηπάτησεν Εὕαν
lest somehow, as the serpent deceived Eve

ἐν τῇ πανουργίᾳ αὐτοῦ, φθαρῇ τὰ νοήματα
by the cleverness of him, [4]should be seduced [1]the [2]thoughts

ὑμῶν ἀπὸ τῆς ἁπλότητος [καὶ τῆς
of you from the simplicity and the

ἁγνότητος] τῆς εἰς Χριστόν. 4 εἰ μὲν
purity – in Christ. [2]if [3]indeed

γὰρ ὁ ἐρχόμενος ἄλλον Ἰησοῦν κηρύσσει
[1]For the [one] coming [2]another [3]Jesus [1]proclaims

ὃν οὐκ ἐκηρύξαμεν, ἢ πνεῦμα ἕτερον
whom we did not proclaim, or [3]spirit [2]a different

measure themselves by
themselves and compare
themselves with them-
selves, they are not wise.
13 We, however, will not
boast beyond proper limits,
but will confine our boasting to the field God has assigned to us, a field that
reaches even to you. 14 We
are not going too far in our
boasting, as would be the
case if we had not come to
you, for we did get as far as
you with the gospel of
Christ. 15 Neither do we go
beyond our limits by boasting of work done by oth-
ers.[p] Our hope is that, as
your faith continues to
grow, our area of activity
among you will greatly ex-
pand, 16 so that we can
preach the gospel in the regions beyond you. For we
do not want to boast about
work already done in an-
other man's territory.
17 But, "Let him who
boasts boast in the
Lord."[q] 18 For it is not the
one who commends him-
self who is approved, but
the one whom the Lord
commends.

Chapter 11

Paul and the False Apostles

I HOPE you will put up
with a little of my fool-
ishness; but you are al-
ready doing that. 2 I am jealous for you with a godly
jealousy. I promised you to
one husband, to Christ, so
that I might present you as
a pure virgin to him. 3 But I
am afraid that just as Eve
was deceived by the ser-
pent's cunning, your minds
may somehow be led astray
from your sincere and pure
devotion to Christ. 4 For if
someone comes to you and
preaches a Jesus other than
the Jesus we preached, or if
you receive a different spir-

[p] 13-15 Or *[13] We, however, will not boast about things that cannot be measured, but we will boast according to the standard of measurement that the God of measure has assigned us—a measurement that relates even to you. [14] . . . . [15] Neither do we boast about things that cannot be measured in regard to the work done by others.*
[q] 17 Jer. 9:24

the one you received, or a
different gospel from the
one you accepted, you submit to it readily enough. 5 I
think that I am not in the
least inferior to these
super-apostles. 6 I may be
untrained in speech, but
not in knowledge; certainly
in every way and in all
things we have made this
evident to you.
7 Did I commit a sin by
humbling myself so that
you might be exalted, be-
cause I proclaimed God's
good news[e] to you free of
charge? 8 I robbed other
churches by accepting support from them in order to
serve you. 9 And when I
was with you and was in
need, I did not burden anyone, for my needs were
supplied by the friends[f]
who came from Macedo-
nia. So I refrained and will
continue to refrain from
burdening you in any way.
10 As the truth of Christ is in
me, this boast of mine will
not be silenced in the regions of Achaia. 11 And
why? Because I do not love
you? God knows I do!
12 And what I do I will
also continue to do, in order to deny an opportunity
to those who want an op-
portunity to be recognized
as our equals in what they
boast about. 13 For such
boasters are false apostles,
deceitful workers, disguis-
ing themselves as apostles
of Christ. 14 And no won-
der! Even Satan disguises
himself as an angel of light.
15 So it is not strange if his
ministers also disguise
themselves as ministers of
righteousness. Their end
will match their deeds.

λαμβάνετε ὃ οὐκ ἐλάβετε, ἢ εὐαγγέλιον
[1]ye receive which ye did not receive, or [2]gospel

ἕτερον ὃ οὐκ ἐδέξασθε, καλῶς ἀνέχεσθε.
[1]a different which ye did not receive, [3][him] [2]well [1]ye endure.

5 λογίζομαι γὰρ μηδὲν ὑστερηκέναι τῶν
For I reckon nothing to have come behind *of* the

ὑπερλίαν ἀποστόλων. 6 εἰ δὲ καὶ ἰδιώτης
super- apostles. But if indeed [I am] unskilled

τῷ λόγῳ, ἀλλ' οὐ τῇ γνώσει, ἀλλ' ἐν
– in speech, yet not – in knowledge, but in

παντὶ φανερώσαντες ἐν πᾶσιν εἰς ὑμᾶς.
every [way] having manifested [ourselves] in all things to you.

7 Ἢ ἁμαρτίαν ἐποίησα ἐμαυτὸν ταπεινῶν
Or [2]sin [1]did I commit [4]myself [3]humbling

ἵνα ὑμεῖς ὑψωθῆτε, ὅτι δωρεὰν τὸ τοῦ
in order that ye might be exalted, because [5]freely [2]the –

θεοῦ εὐαγγέλιον εὐηγγελισάμην ὑμῖν;
[4]of God [3]gospel [1]I preached *good tidings* to you?

8 ἄλλας ἐκκλησίας ἐσύλησα λαβὼν ὀψώνιον
Other churches I robbed taking wages

πρὸς τὴν ὑμῶν διακονίαν, 9 καὶ παρὼν
for [1]the [3]of you [2]ministry, and being present

πρὸς ὑμᾶς καὶ ὑστερηθεὶς οὐ κατενάρκησα
with you and lacking I was *not* an encumbrance

οὐθενός· τὸ γὰρ ὑστέρημά μου προσανε-
of no man; for the lack of me [6]made

πλήρωσαν οἱ ἀδελφοὶ ἐλθόντες ἀπὸ Μακε-
up [1]the [2]brothers [3]coming [4]from [5]Mace-

δονίας· καὶ ἐν παντὶ ἀβαρῆ ἐμαυτὸν
donia; and in every [way] [3]unburdensome [2]myself

ὑμῖν ἐτήρησα καὶ τηρήσω. 10 ἔστιν
[4]to you [1]I kept and I will keep. [3]is

ἀλήθεια Χριστοῦ ἐν ἐμοί, ὅτι ἡ καύχησις
[1][The] truth [2]of Christ in me, that – boasting

αὕτη οὐ φραγήσεται εἰς ἐμὲ ἐν τοῖς
this shall not be stopped in me in the

κλίμασιν τῆς Ἀχαΐας. 11 διὰ τί; ὅτι
regions – of Achaia. Why? because

οὐκ ἀγαπῶ ὑμᾶς; ὁ θεὸς οἶδεν. 12 Ὃ
I love not you? – God knows. what

δὲ ποιῶ, καὶ ποιήσω, ἵνα ἐκκόψω τὴν
But I do, also I will do, in order that I may cut off the

ἀφορμὴν τῶν θελόντων ἀφορμήν, ἵνα ἐν
occasion of the [ones] desiring an occasion, in order that where-

ᾧ καυχῶνται εὑρεθῶσιν καθὼς καὶ ἡμεῖς.
in they boast they may be found as also we.

13 οἱ γὰρ τοιοῦτοι ψευδαπόστολοι, ἐργάται
– For such [are] false apostles, [2]workmen

δόλιοι, μετασχηματιζόμενοι εἰς ἀποστόλους
[1]deceitful, transforming themselves into apostles

Χριστοῦ. 14 καὶ οὐ θαῦμα· αὐτὸς γὰρ
of Christ. And no wonder; [3][him]self [1]for

ὁ σατανᾶς μετασχηματίζεται εἰς ἄγγελον
– [2]Satan transforms himself into an angel

φωτός. 15 οὐ μέγα οὖν εἰ καὶ οἱ
of light. No great thing therefore if also the

διάκονοι αὐτοῦ μετασχηματίζονται ὡς
ministers of him transform themselves as

διάκονοι δικαιοσύνης· ὧν τὸ τέλος ἔσται
ministers of righteousness; of whom the end will be

κατὰ τὰ ἔργα αὐτῶν.
according to the works of them.

it from the one you re-
ceived, or a different gospel from the one you ac-
cepted, you put up with it
easily enough. 5 But I do not
think I am in the least inferior to those "super-apostles." 6 I may not be a
trained speaker, but I do
have knowledge. We have
made this perfectly clear to
you in every way.
7 Was it a sin for me to
lower myself in order to el-
evate you by preaching the
gospel of God to you free of
charge? 8 I robbed other
churches by receiving support from them so as to
serve you. 9 And when I
was with you and needed
something, I was not a burden to anyone, for the
brothers who came from
Macedonia supplied what I
needed. I have kept myself
from being a burden to you
in any way, and will continue to do so. 10 As surely as
the truth of Christ is in me,
nobody in the regions of
Achaia will stop this boasting of mine. 11 Why? Be-
cause I do not love you?
God knows I do! 12 And I
will keep on doing what I
am doing in order to cut the
ground from under those
who want an opportunity to
be considered equal with us
in the things they boast
about.
13 For such men are false
apostles, deceitful work-
men, masquerading as
apostles of Christ. 14 And
no wonder, for Satan him-
self masquerades as an angel of light. 15 It is not surprising, then, if his servants
masquerade as servants of
righteousness. Their end
will be what their actions
deserve.

[e] Gk *the gospel of God*
[f] Gk *brothers*

Paul's Sufferings as an Apostle

16 I repeat, let no one
think that I am a fool; but if
you do, then accept me as a
fool, so that I too may boast
a little. 17 What I am saying
in regard to this boastful
confidence, I am saying not
with the Lord's authority,
but as a fool; 18 since many
boast according to human
standards,[g] I will also
boast. 19 For you gladly put
up with fools, being wise
yourselves! 20 For you put
up with it when someone
makes slaves of you, or
preys upon you, or takes
advantage of you, or puts
on airs, or gives you a slap
in the face. 21 To my shame,
I must say, we were too
weak for that!

But whatever anyone
dares to boast of—I am
speaking as a fool—I also
dare to boast of that. 22 Are
they Hebrews? So am I.
Are they Israelites? So am
I. Are they descendants of
Abraham? So am I. 23 Are
they ministers of Christ? I
am talking like a
madman—I am a better
one: with far greater la-
bors, far more imprison-
ments, with countless flog-
gings, and often near death.
24 Five times I have re-
ceived from the Jews the
forty lashes minus one.
25 Three times I was beaten
with rods. Once I received
a stoning. Three times I
was shipwrecked; for a
night and a day I was adrift
at sea; 26 on frequent jour-
neys, in danger from rivers,
danger from bandits, dan-
ger from my own people,
danger from Gentiles, danger in the city, danger in the
wilderness, danger at sea,
danger from false brothers
and sisters;[f] 27 in toil and
hardship, through many a
sleepless night, hungry and
thirsty, often without food,
cold and naked. 28 And, be-

[g] Gk *according to the flesh*

16 Πάλιν λέγω, μή τίς με δόξῃ ἄφρονα
Again I say, [3]not [2]anyone [4]me [1]think [6]foolish
εἶναι· εἰ δὲ μή γε, κἂν ὡς ἄφρονα
[5]to be; otherwise, even if as foolish
δέξασθέ με, ἵνα κἀγὼ μικρόν τι καυχήσ-
receive ye me, in order that I also a little [bit] may
ωμαι. 17 ὃ λαλῶ, οὐ κατὰ κύριον λαλῶ,
boast. What I speak, not according to [the] Lord I speak,
ἀλλ' ὡς ἐν ἀφροσύνῃ, ἐν ταύτῃ τῇ
but as in folly, in this –
ὑποστάσει τῆς καυχήσεως. 18 ἐπεὶ πολλοὶ
confidence – of boasting. Since many
καυχῶνται κατὰ [τὴν] σάρκα, κἀγὼ
boast according to the flesh, I also
καυχήσομαι. 19 ἡδέως γὰρ ἀνέχεσθε τῶν
will boast. For gladly ye endure –
ἀφρόνων φρόνιμοι ὄντες· 20 ἀνέχεσθε γὰρ
fools [2]prudent [1]being; for ye endure
εἴ τις ὑμᾶς καταδουλοῖ, εἴ τις κατεσθίει,
if anyone [2]you [1]enslaves, if anyone devours [you],
εἴ τις λαμβάνει, εἴ τις ἐπαίρεται, εἴ
if anyone receives [you],* if anyone lifts himself up, if
τις εἰς πρόσωπον ὑμᾶς δέρει. 21 κατὰ
anyone [3]in [4][the] face [2]you [1]beats(hits). According to
ἀτιμίαν λέγω, ὡς ὅτι ἡμεῖς ἠσθενήκαμεν·
dishonour I say, as that we have been weak;
ἐν ᾧ δ' ἄν τις τολμᾷ, ἐν ἀφροσύνῃ
but in whatever [respect] anyone dares, in folly
λέγω, τολμῶ κἀγώ. 22 Ἑβραῖοί εἰσιν;
I say, [2]dare [1]I [3]also. Hebrews are they?
κἀγώ. Ἰσραηλῖταί εἰσιν; κἀγώ. σπέρμα
I also. Israelites are they? I also. Seed
Ἀβραάμ εἰσιν; κἀγώ. 23 διάκονοι Χριστοῦ
of Abraham are they? I also. Ministers of Christ
εἰσιν; παραφρονῶν λαλῶ, ὑπὲρ ἐγώ· ἐν
are they? being out of my mind I speak, [2]beyond (more) [1]I: in
κόποις περισσοτέρως, ἐν φυλακαῖς περισ-
labours more abundantly, in prisons more
σοτέρως, ἐν πληγαῖς ὑπερβαλλόντως, ἐν
abundantly, in stripes excessively, in
θανάτοις πολλάκις. 24 ὑπὸ Ἰουδαίων
deaths many times. By Jews
πεντάκις τεσσεράκοντα παρὰ μίαν ἔλαβον,
five times forty [stripes] less one I received,
25 τρὶς ἐρραβδίσθην, ἅπαξ ἐλιθάσθην, τρὶς
thrice I was beaten with rods, once I was stoned, thrice
ἐναυάγησα, 26 νυχθήμερον ἐν τῷ βυθῷ
I was shipwrecked, a night and a day in the deep
πεποίηκα· ὁδοιπορίαις πολλάκις, κινδύνοις
I have done(been); in travels many times, in perils
ποταμῶν, κινδύνοις λῃστῶν, κινδύνοις ἐκ
of rivers, in perils of robbers, in perils of
γένους, κινδύνοις ἐξ ἐθνῶν, κινδύνοις ἐν
[my] kind, in perils of nations, in perils in
πόλει, κινδύνοις ἐν ἐρημίᾳ, κινδύνοις ἐν
a city, in perils in a desert, in perils in(at)
θαλάσσῃ, κινδύνοις ἐν ψευδαδέλφοις, 27 κόπῳ
sea, in perils among false brothers, in labour
καὶ μόχθῳ, ἐν ἀγρυπνίαις πολλάκις, ἐν
and hardship, in watchings many times, in
λιμῷ καὶ δίψει, ἐν νηστείαις πολλάκις,
famine and thirst, in fastings many times,

* ? takes [you in].

Paul Boasts About His Sufferings

16 I repeat: Let no one
take me for a fool. But if
you do, then receive me
just as you would a fool, so
that I may do a little boasting. 17 In this self-confident
boasting I am not talking as
the Lord would, but as a
fool. 18 Since many are
boasting in the way the
world does, I too will
boast. 19 You gladly put up
with fools since you are so
wise! 20 In fact, you even
put up with anyone who en-
slaves you or exploits you
or takes advantage of you
or pushes himself forward
or slaps you in the face.
21 To my shame I admit that
we were too weak for that!

What anyone else dares
to boast about—I am
speaking as a fool—I also
dare to boast about. 22 Are
they Hebrews? So am I.
Are they Israelites? So am
I. Are they Abraham's de-
scendants? So am I. 23 Are
they servants of Christ? (I
am out of my mind to talk
like this.) I am more. I have
worked much harder, been
in prison more frequently,
been flogged more severe-
ly, and been exposed to
death again and again.
24 Five times I received
from the Jews the forty
lashes minus one. 25 Three
times I was beaten with
rods, once I was stoned,
three times I was ship-
wrecked, I spent a night
and a day in the open sea,
26 I have been constantly on
the move. I have been in
danger from rivers, in danger from bandits, in danger
from my own countrymen,
in danger from Gentiles; in
danger in the city, in danger
in the country, in danger at
sea; and in danger from
false brothers. 27 I have labored and toiled and have
often gone without sleep; I
have known hunger and
thirst and have often gone

sides other things, I am under daily pressure because of my anxiety for all the churches. 29 Who is weak, and I am not weak? Who is made to stumble, and I am not indignant?

30 If I must boast, I will boast of the things that show my weakness. 31 The God and Father of the Lord Jesus (blessed be he forever!) knows that I do not lie. 32 In Damascus, the governor[h] under King Aretas guarded the city of Damascus in order to[i] seize me, 33 but I was let down in a basket through a window in the wall,[j] and escaped from his hands.

Chapter 12

Paul's Visions and Revelations

IT is necessary to boast; nothing is to be gained by it, but I will go on to visions and revelations of the Lord. 2 I know a person in Christ who fourteen years ago was caught up to the third heaven—whether in the body or out of the body I do not know; God knows. 3 And I know that such a person—whether in the body or out of the body I do not know; God knows— 4 was caught up into Paradise and heard things that are not to be told, that no mortal is permitted to repeat. 5 On behalf of such a one I will boast, but on my own behalf I will not boast, except of my weaknesses. 6 But if I wish to boast, I will not be a fool, for I will be speaking the truth. But I refrain from it, so that no one may think better of me than what is seen in me or heard from me, 7 even considering the

[h] Gk *ethnarch*

[i] Other ancient authorities read *and wanted to*

[j] Gk *through the wall*

ἐν ψύχει καὶ γυμνότητι· **28** χωρὶς τῶν
in cold and nakedness; apart from the things

παρεκτὸς ἡ ἐπίστασίς μοι ἡ καθ' ἡμέραν,
without[,] the conspiring against me – daily,

ἡ μέριμνα πασῶν τῶν ἐκκλησιῶν. **29** τίς
the care of all the churches. Who

ἀσθενεῖ, καὶ οὐκ ἀσθενῶ; τίς σκανδαλίζεται,
is weak, and I am not weak? who is offended,

καὶ οὐκ ἐγὼ πυροῦμαι; **30** εἰ καυχᾶσθαι
and ²not ¹I ³burn? If to boast

δεῖ, τὰ τῆς ἀσθενείας μου καυχήσομαι.
it behoves [me], the things of the weakness of me I will boast.

31 ὁ θεὸς καὶ πατὴρ τοῦ κυρίου Ἰησοῦ
The God and Father of the Lord Jesus

οἶδεν, ὁ ὢν εὐλογητὸς εἰς τοὺς αἰῶνας,
knows, the [one] being blessed unto the ages,

ὅτι οὐ ψεύδομαι. **32** ἐν Δαμασκῷ ὁ
that I am not lying. In Damascus the

ἐθνάρχης Ἁρέτα τοῦ βασιλέως ἐφρούρει
ethnarch of Aretas *of* the king guarded

τὴν πόλιν Δαμασκηνῶν πιάσαι με, **33** καὶ
the city of [the] Damascenes to seize me, and

διὰ θυρίδος ἐν σαργάνῃ ἐχαλάσθην διὰ
through a window in a basket I was lowered through

τοῦ τείχους καὶ ἐξέφυγον τὰς χεῖρας αὐτοῦ.
the wall and escaped the hands of him.

12 Καυχᾶσθαι δεῖ, οὐ συμφέρον μέν,
To boast it behoves [me], not expedient indeed,

ἐλεύσομαι δὲ εἰς ὀπτασίας καὶ ἀποκαλύψεις
so I will come to visions and revelations

κυρίου. **2** οἶδα ἄνθρωπον ἐν Χριστῷ
of [the] Lord. I know a man in Christ

πρὸ ἐτῶν δεκατεσσάρων, — εἴτε ἐν
before years fourteen, (whether in

σώματι οὐκ οἶδα, εἴτε ἐκτὸς τοῦ σώματος
[the] body I know not, or outside the body

οὐκ οἶδα, ὁ θεὸς οἶδεν, — ἁρπαγέντα
I know not, – God knows,) ²caught

τὸν τοιοῦτον ἕως τρίτου οὐρανοῦ. **3** καὶ
– ¹such a one to [the] third heaven. And

οἶδα τὸν τοιοῦτον ἄνθρωπον — εἴτε
I know – such a man (whether

ἐν σώματι εἴτε χωρὶς τοῦ σώματος
in [the] body or apart from the body

[οὐκ οἶδα], ὁ θεὸς οἶδεν, — **4** ὅτι
I know not, – God knows,) that

ἡρπάγη εἰς τὸν παράδεισον καὶ ἤκουσεν
he was caught into the paradise and heard

ἄρρητα ῥήματα, ἃ οὐκ ἐξὸν ἀνθρώπῳ
unspeakable words, which it is not permissible for a man

λαλῆσαι. **5** ὑπὲρ τοῦ τοιούτου καυχήσομαι,
to speak. On behalf of – such a one I will boast,

ὑπὲρ δὲ ἐμαυτοῦ οὐ καυχήσομαι εἰ
but on behalf of myself I will not boast ex-

μὴ ἐν ταῖς ἀσθενείαις. **6** ἐὰν γὰρ θελήσω
cept in the(my) weaknesses. For if I shall wish

καυχήσασθαι, οὐκ ἔσομαι ἄφρων, ἀλήθειαν
to boast, I shall not be foolish, ²truth

γὰρ ἐρῶ· φείδομαι δέ, μή τις εἰς ἐμὲ
¹for ³I will speak; but I spare, lest anyone to me

λογίσηται ὑπὲρ ὃ βλέπει με ἢ ἀκούει
reckons beyond what he sees me or hears

without food; I have been cold and naked. 28 Besides everything else, I face daily the pressure of my concern for all the churches. 29 Who is weak, and I do not feel weak? Who is led into sin, and I do not inwardly burn?

30 If I must boast, I will boast of the things that show my weakness. 31 The God and Father of the Lord Jesus, who is to be praised forever, knows that I am not lying. 32 In Damascus the governor under King Aretas had the city of the Damascenes guarded in order to arrest me. 33 But I was lowered in a basket from a window in the wall and slipped through his hands.

Chapter 12

Paul's Vision and His Thorn

I MUST go on boasting. Although there is nothing to be gained, I will go on to visions and revelations from the Lord. 2 I know a man in Christ who fourteen years ago was caught up to the third heaven. Whether it was in the body or out of the body I do not know—God knows. 3 And I know that this man—whether in the body or apart from the body I do not know, but God knows— 4 was caught up to paradise. He heard inexpressible things, things that man is not permitted to tell. 5 I will boast about a man like that, but I will not boast about myself, except about my weaknesses. 6 Even if I should choose to boast, I would not be a fool, because I would be speaking the truth. But I refrain, so no one will think more of me than is warranted by what I do or say.

exceptional character of
the revelations. Therefore,
to keep[k] me from being too
elated, a thorn was given
me in the flesh, a messenger of Satan to torment me,
to keep me from being too
elated.[l] 8Three times I appealed to the Lord about
this, that it would leave me,
9but he said to me, "My
grace is sufficient for you,
for power[m] is made perfect
in weakness." So, I will
boast all the more gladly of
my weaknesses, so that the
power of Christ may dwell
in me. 10Therefore I am
content with weaknesses,
insults, hardships, persecutions, and calamities for the
sake of Christ; for whenever I am weak, then I am
strong.

Paul's Concern for the Corinthian Church

11 I have been a fool!
You forced me to it. Indeed
you should have been the
ones commending me, for I
am not at all inferior to
these super-apostles, even
though I am nothing. 12The
signs of a true apostle were
performed among you with
utmost patience, signs and
wonders and mighty
works. 13How have you
been worse off than the
other churches, except that
I myself did not burden
you? Forgive me this
wrong!
14 Here I am, ready to
come to you this third time.
And I will not be a burden,
because I do not want what
is yours but you; for children ought not to lay up for
their parents, but parents
for their children. 15I will
most gladly spend and be
spent for you. If I love you

[k] Other ancient authorities read *To keep*
[l] Other ancient authorities lack *to keep me from being too elated*
[m] Other ancient authorities read *my power*

ἐξ ἐμοῦ **7** καὶ τῇ ὑπερβολῇ τῶν ἀποκα-
of me and by the excess of the revela-
λύψεων. διὸ ἵνα μὴ ὑπεραίρωμαι, ἐδόθη
tions. Wherefore lest I should be exceedingly uplifted, there was given
μοι σκόλοψ τῇ σαρκί, ἄγγελος σατανᾶ,
to me a thorn in the flesh, a messenger of Satan,
ἵνα με κολαφίζῃ, ἵνα μὴ ὑπεραίρωμαι.
in order that [2]me [1]he might buffet, lest I should be exceedingly uplifted.
8 ὑπὲρ τούτου τρὶς τὸν κύριον παρεκάλεσα,
As to this thrice the Lord I besought,
ἵνα ἀποστῇ ἀπ' ἐμοῦ. **9** καὶ εἴρηκέν
in order that it might depart from me. And he *has* said
μοι· ἀρκεῖ σοι ἡ χάρις μου· ἡ γὰρ
to me: [4]Suffices [5]thee [1]the [2]grace [3]of me; for the(my)
δύναμις ἐν ἀσθενείᾳ τελεῖται. Ἥδιστα
power in weakness is perfected. Most gladly
οὖν μᾶλλον καυχήσομαι ἐν ταῖς ἀσθενείαις,
therefore rather I will boast in the(my) weaknesses,
ἵνα ἐπισκηνώσῃ ἐπ' ἐμὲ ἡ δύναμις τοῦ
in order that [4]might overshadow *over* [5]me [1]the [2]power –
Χριστοῦ. **10** διὸ εὐδοκῶ ἐν ἀσθενείαις,
[3]of Christ. Wherefore I am well pleased in weaknesses,
ἐν ὕβρεσιν, ἐν ἀνάγκαις, ἐν διωγμοῖς
in insults, in necessities, in persecutions
καὶ στενοχωρίαις, ὑπὲρ Χριστοῦ· ὅταν
and difficulties, on behalf of Christ; [2]whenever
γὰρ ἀσθενῶ, τότε δυνατός εἰμι.
[1]for I am weak, then [2]powerful [1]I am.
11 Γέγονα ἄφρων· ὑμεῖς με ἠναγκάσατε.
I have become foolish; ye me compelled.
ἐγὼ γὰρ ὤφειλον ὑφ' ὑμῶν συνίστασθαι.
For I ought by you to be commended.
οὐδὲν γὰρ ὑστέρησα τῶν ὑπερλίαν
For nothing I lacked of the super-
ἀποστόλων, εἰ καὶ οὐδέν εἰμι. **12** τὰ
apostles, [2]if [1]even [4]nothing [3]I am. [2]The
μὲν σημεῖα τοῦ ἀποστόλου κατειργάσθη
[1]indeed signs of the apostle were wrought
ἐν ὑμῖν ἐν πάσῃ ὑπομονῇ, σημείοις τε
among you in all endurance, [2]by signs [1]both
καὶ τέρασιν καὶ δυνάμεσιν. **13** τί γάρ
and by wonders and by powerful deeds. For what
ἐστιν ὃ ἡσσώθητε ὑπὲρ τὰς λοιπὰς
is it which ye were less than the remaining
ἐκκλησίας, εἰ μὴ ὅτι αὐτὸς ἐγὼ οὐ
churches, except that [2][my]self [1]I [5]not
κατενάρκησα ὑμῶν; χαρίσασθέ μοι τὴν
[3]encumbered [4]*of* you? Forgive ye me –
ἀδικίαν ταύτην. **14** Ἰδοὺ τρίτον τοῦτο
wrong this. Behold [2][the] third [time] [1]this [is]
ἑτοίμως ἔχω ἐλθεῖν πρὸς ὑμᾶς, καὶ
I am ready† to come to you, and
οὐ καταναρκήσω· οὐ γὰρ ζητῶ τὰ ὑμῶν
I will not encumber [you]; [3]not [1]for [2]I seek the things of you
ἀλλὰ ὑμᾶς. οὐ γὰρ ὀφείλει τὰ τέκνα
but you. For [4]not [3]ought [1]the [2]children
τοῖς γονεῦσιν θησαυρίζειν, ἀλλὰ οἱ γονεῖς
for the parents to lay up treasure, but the parents
τοῖς τέκνοις. **15** ἐγὼ δὲ ἥδιστα δαπανήσω
for the children. But I most gladly will spend
καὶ ἐκδαπανηθήσομαι ὑπὲρ τῶν ψυχῶν
and will be spent out on behalf of the souls

7To keep me from becom-
ing conceited because of
these surpassingly great
revelations, there was giv-
en me a thorn in my flesh, a
messenger of Satan, to torment me. 8Three times I
pleaded with the Lord to
take it away from me. 9But
he said to me, "My grace is
sufficient for you, for my
power is made perfect in
weakness." Therefore I
will boast all the more gladly about my weaknesses,
so that Christ's power may
rest on me. 10That is why,
for Christ's sake, I delight
in weaknesses, in insults,
in hardships, in persecu-
tions, in difficulties. For
when I am weak, then I am
strong.

Paul's Concern for the Corinthians

11I have made a fool of
myself, but you drove me
to it. I ought to have been
commended by you, for I
am not in the least inferior
to the "super-apostles,"
even though I am nothing.
12The things that mark an
apostle—signs, wonders
and miracles—were done
among you with great per-
severance. 13How were
you inferior to the other
churches, except that I was
never a burden to you? Forgive me this wrong!
14Now I am ready to visit
you for the third time, and I
will not be a burden to you,
because what I want is not
your possessions but you.
After all, children should
not have to save up for their
parents, but parents for
their children. 15So I will
very gladly spend for you

more, am I to be loved less?
16 Let it be assumed that I
did not burden you. Nevertheless (you say) since I
was crafty, I took you in by
deceit. 17 Did I take advantage of you through any of
those whom I sent to you?
18 I urged Titus to go, and
sent the brother with him.
Titus did not take advan-
tage of you, did he? Did we
not conduct ourselves with
the same spirit? Did we not
take the same steps?
19 Have you been
thinking all along that we
have been defending our-
selves before you? We are
speaking in Christ before
God. Everything we do,
beloved, is for the sake of
building you up. 20 For I
fear that when I come, I
may find you not as I wish,
and that you may find me
not as you wish; I fear that
there may perhaps be quarreling, jealousy, anger,
selfishness, slander, gos-
sip, conceit, and disorder.
21 I fear that when I come
again, my God may humble
me before you, and that I
may have to mourn over
many who previously
sinned and have not repented of the impurity, sexual
immorality, and licentiousness that they have prac-
ticed.

Chapter 13

Further Warning

THIS is the third time I
am coming to you.
"Any charge must be sus-
tained by the evidence of
two or three witnesses." 2 I
warned those who sinned
previously and all the others, and I warn them now
while absent, as I did when
present on my second visit,
that if I come again, I will
not be lenient— 3 since you
desire proof that Christ is

ὑμῶν. εἰ περισσοτέρως ὑμᾶς ἀγαπῶ,
of you. If more abundantly [2]you [1]I love,

ἧσσον ἀγαπῶμαι; 16 Ἔστω δέ, ἐγὼ οὐ
[the] less am I loved? But let it be, I not

κατεβάρησα ὑμᾶς· ἀλλὰ ὑπάρχων πανοῦργος
burdened you; but being crafty

δόλῳ ὑμᾶς ἔλαβον. 17 μή τινα ὧν
[3]with guile [2]you [1]I took. *Not* anyone of whom

ἀπέσταλκα πρὸς ὑμᾶς, 18 δι' αὐτοῦ
I have sent to you, through him

ἐπλεονέκτησα ὑμᾶς; παρεκάλεσα Τίτον καὶ
did I defraud you? I besought Titus and

συναπέστειλα τὸν ἀδελφόν· μήτι ἐπλεο-
sent with [him] the brother; *not* [2]de-

νέκτησεν ὑμᾶς Τίτος; οὐ τῷ αὐτῷ
frauded [3]you [1]Titus? [2]not [3]by the [4]same

πνεύματι περιεπατήσαμεν; οὐ τοῖς αὐτοῖς
[5]spirit [1]walked we? not in the same

ἴχνεσιν;
steps?

19 Πάλαι δοκεῖτε ὅτι ὑμῖν ἀπολογούμεθα.
Already ye think that to you we are making a defence.

κατέναντι θεοῦ ἐν Χριστῷ λαλοῦμεν· τὰ
Before God in Christ we speak; –

δὲ πάντα, ἀγαπητοί, ὑπὲρ τῆς ὑμῶν
but all things, beloved, [are] on behalf of [1]the [3]of you

οἰκοδομῆς. 20 φοβοῦμαι γὰρ μή πως ἐλθὼν
[2]edification. For I fear lest coming

οὐχ οἵους θέλω εὕρω ὑμᾶς, κἀγὼ εὑρεθῶ
[3]not [4]such as [5]I wish [1]I may find [2]you, and I am found

ὑμῖν οἷον οὐ θέλετε, μή πως ἔρις,
by you such as ye wish not, lest strife,

ζῆλος, θυμοί, ἐριθεῖαι, καταλαλιαί, ψιθυρισ-
jealousy, angers, rivalries, detractions, whisper-

μοί, φυσιώσεις, ἀκαταστασίαι· 21 μὴ πάλιν
ings, puffings up, disturbances; lest again

ἐλθόντος μου ταπεινώσῃ με ὁ θεός μου
coming me[a] [4]may humble [5]me [1]the [2]God [3]of me
=when I come

πρὸς ὑμᾶς, καὶ πενθήσω πολλοὺς τῶν
with you, and I shall mourn many of the [ones]

προημαρτηκότων καὶ μὴ μετανοησάντων
having previously sinned and not repenting

ἐπὶ τῇ ἀκαθαρσίᾳ καὶ πορνείᾳ καὶ
over the uncleanness and fornication and

ἀσελγείᾳ ᾗ ἔπραξαν. 13 Τρίτον τοῦτο
lewdness which they practised. [2][The] third [time] [1]this [is]

ἔρχομαι πρὸς ὑμᾶς· ἐπὶ στόματος
I am coming to you; at [the] mouth

δύο μαρτύρων καὶ τριῶν σταθήσεται
of two witnesses and of three shall be established

πᾶν ῥῆμα. 2 προείρηκα καὶ προλέγω,
every word. I have previously said and I say beforehand,

ὡς παρὼν τὸ δεύτερον καὶ ἀπὼν
as being present the second [time] and being absent

νῦν, τοῖς προημαρτηκόσιν καὶ τοῖς
now, to the [ones] having previously sinned and [1]to [3]the

λοιποῖς πᾶσιν, ὅτι ἐὰν ἔλθω εἰς τὸ
[4]remaining [ones] [2]all, that if I come *in the*

πάλιν οὐ φείσομαι, 3 ἐπεὶ δοκιμὴν ζητεῖτε
again I will not spare, since [2]a proof [1]ye seek

everything I have and ex-
pend myself as well. If I
love you more, will you
love me less? 16 Be that as it
may, I have not been a burden to you. Yet, crafty fellow that I am, I caught you
by trickery! 17 Did I exploit
you through any of the men
I sent you? 18 I urged Titus
to go to you and I sent our
brother with him. Titus did
not exploit you, did he? Did
we not act in the same spirit
and follow the same
course?
19 Have you been thinking
all along that we have been
defending ourselves to
you? We have been speak-
ing in the sight of God as
those in Christ; and everything we do, dear friends, is
for your strengthening.
20 For I am afraid that when
I come I may not find you
as I want you to be, and
you may not find me as you
want me to be. I fear that
there may be quarreling,
jealousy, outbursts of anger, factions, slander, gos-
sip, arrogance and disor-
der. 21 I am afraid that when
I come again my God will
humble me before you, and
I will be grieved over many
who have sinned earlier
and have not repented of
the impurity, sexual sin and
debauchery in which they
have indulged.

Chapter 13

Final Warnings

THIS will be my third
visit to you. "Every
matter must be established
by the testimony of two or
three witnesses."[r] 2 I already gave you a warning
when I was with you the
second time. I now repeat it
while absent: On my return
I will not spare those who
sinned earlier or any of the
others, 3 since you are demanding proof that Christ

[r] 1 Deut. 19:15

speaking in me. He is not
weak in dealing with you,
but is powerful in you. 4 For
he was crucified in weak-
ness, but lives by the power
of God. For we are weak in
him,[n] but in dealing with
you we will live with him by
the power of God.
5 Examine yourselves
to see whether you are living in the faith. Test yourselves. Do you not realize
that Jesus Christ is in
you?—unless, indeed, you
fail to meet the test! 6 I hope
you will find out that we
have not failed. 7 But we
pray to God that you may
not do anything wrong—
not that we may appear to
have met the test, but that
you may do what is right,
though we may seem to
have failed. 8 For we cannot do anything against the
truth, but only for the truth.
9 For we rejoice when we
are weak and you are
strong. This is what we
pray for, that you may become perfect. 10 So I write
these things while I am
away from you, so that
when I come, I may not
have to be severe in using
the authority that the Lord
has given me for building
up and not for tearing
down.

Final Greetings and Benediction

11 Finally, brothers and
sisters,[o] farewell.[p] Put
things in order, listen to my
appeal,[q] agree with one another, live in peace; and the
God of love and peace will
be with you. 12 Greet one
another with a holy kiss.
All the saints greet you.
13 The grace of the
Lord Jesus Christ, the love

[n] Other ancient authorities read *with him*
[o] Gk *brothers*
[p] Or *rejoice*
[q] Or *encourage one another*

τοῦ ἐν ἐμοὶ λαλοῦντος Χριστοῦ, ὃς εἰς
– [5]in [6]me [4]speaking [3]of Christ, who toward
ὑμᾶς οὐκ ἀσθενεῖ ἀλλὰ δυνατεῖ ἐν ὑμῖν.
you is not weak but is powerful in you.
4 καὶ γὰρ ἐσταυρώθη ἐξ ἀσθενείας, ἀλλὰ
For indeed he was crucified out of weakness, but
ζῇ ἐκ δυνάμεως θεοῦ. καὶ γὰρ ἡμεῖς
he lives by [the] power of God. For indeed we
ἀσθενοῦμεν ἐν αὐτῷ, ἀλλὰ ζήσομεν σὺν
are weak in him, but we shall live with
αὐτῷ ἐκ δυνάμεως θεοῦ εἰς ὑμᾶς.
him by [the] power of God toward you.
5 Ἑαυτοὺς πειράζετε εἰ ἐστὲ ἐν τῇ
[2]Yourselves [1]test if ye are in the
πίστει, ἑαυτοὺς δοκιμάζετε· ἢ οὐκ
faith, [2]yourselves [1]prove; or not
ἐπιγινώσκετε ἑαυτοὺς ὅτι Ἰησοῦς Χριστὸς
perceive ye yourselves that Jesus Christ [is]
ἐν ὑμῖν, εἰ μήτι ἀδόκιμοί ἐστε. 6 ἐλπίζω
in you, unless [2]counterfeits [1]ye are. I hope
δὲ ὅτι γνώσεσθε ὅτι ἡμεῖς οὐκ ἐσμὲν
But that ye will know that we are not
ἀδόκιμοι. 7 εὐχόμεθα δὲ πρὸς τὸν θεὸν
counterfeits. Now we pray to – God
μὴ ποιῆσαι ὑμᾶς κακὸν μηδέν, οὐχ
not to do you[b] evil *none*, not
=that ye do no . . .
ἵνα ἡμεῖς δόκιμοι φανῶμεν, ἀλλ' ἵνα
in order that we [2]approved [1]may appear, but in order that
ὑμεῖς τὸ καλὸν ποιῆτε, ἡμεῖς δὲ ὡς
ye [2]the [3]good [1]may do, and we [2]as
ἀδόκιμοι ὦμεν. 8 οὐ γὰρ δυνάμεθά
[3]counterfeits [1]may be. For we cannot [do]
τι κατὰ τῆς ἀληθείας, ἀλλὰ ὑπὲρ τῆς
any-thing against the truth, but on behalf of the
ἀληθείας. 9 χαίρομεν γὰρ ὅταν ἡμεῖς
truth. For we rejoice when*ever* we
ἀσθενῶμεν, ὑμεῖς δὲ δυνατοὶ ἦτε· τοῦτο
are weak, and ye powerful are; this
καὶ εὐχόμεθα, τὴν ὑμῶν κατάρτισιν. 10 Διὰ
also we pray, the [2]of you [1]restoration. There-
τοῦτο ταῦτα ἀπὼν γράφω, ἵνα παρὼν
fore [2]these things [3]being absent [1]I write, in order that being present
μὴ ἀποτόμως χρήσωμαι κατὰ τὴν ἐξουσίαν
[2]not [3]sharply [1]I may deal according to the authority
ἣν ὁ κύριος ἔδωκέν μοι εἰς οἰκοδομὴν
which the Lord gave me for edification
καὶ οὐκ εἰς καθαίρεσιν.
and not for overthrow.
11 Λοιπόν, ἀδελφοί, χαίρετε, καταρτίζεσθε,
For the rest,† brothers, rejoice, restore yourselves,
παρακαλεῖσθε, τὸ αὐτὸ φρονεῖτε, εἰρηνεύετε,
admonish yourselves, the same thing think, be at peace,
καὶ ὁ θεὸς τῆς ἀγάπης καὶ εἰρήνης
and the God – of love and of peace
ἔσται μεθ' ὑμῶν. 12 Ἀσπάσασθε ἀλλήλους
will be with you. Greet ye one another
ἐν ἁγίῳ φιλήματι. Ἀσπάζονται ὑμᾶς οἱ
with a holy kiss. [4]greet [5]you [1]the
ἅγιοι πάντες.
[3]saints [2]All.
13 Ἡ χάρις τοῦ κυρίου Ἰησοῦ Χριστοῦ
The grace of the Lord Jesus Christ

is speaking through me. He
is not weak in dealing with
you, but is powerful among
you. 4For to be sure, he
was crucified in weakness,
yet he lives by God's power. Likewise, we are weak
in him, yet by God's power
we will live with him to
serve you.
5Examine yourselves to
see whether you are in the
faith; test yourselves. Do
you not realize that Christ
Jesus is in you—unless, of
course, you fail the test?
6And I trust that you will
discover that we have not
failed the test. 7Now we
pray to God that you will
not do anything wrong. Not
that people will see that we
have stood the test but that
you will do what is right
even though we may seem
to have failed. 8For we cannot do anything against the
truth, but only for the truth.
9We are glad whenever we
are weak but you are
strong; and our prayer is for
your perfection. 10This is
why I write these things
when I am absent, that
when I come I may not
have to be harsh in my use
of authority—the authority
the Lord gave me for building you up, not for tearing
you down.

Final Greetings

11Finally, brothers, good-
by. Aim for perfection, listen to my appeal, be of one
mind, live in peace. And
the God of love and peace
will be with you.
12Greet one another with
a holy kiss. 13All the saints
send their greetings.
14May the grace of the

of God, and the commu-
nion of[r] the Holy Spirit be
with all of you.

καὶ ἡ ἀγάπη τοῦ θεοῦ καὶ ἡ κοινωνία
and the love – of God and the fellowship
τοῦ ἁγίου πνεύματος μετὰ πάντων ὑμῶν.
of the Holy Spirit [be] with ²all ¹you.

Lord Jesus Christ, and the
love of God, and the fellowship of the Holy Spirit be
with you all.

The Letter of Paul to the

Galatians

Chapter 1

Salutation

PAUL an apostle—sent
neither by human
commission nor from hu-
man authorities, but
through Jesus Christ and
God the Father, who raised
him from the dead— 2 and
all the members of God's
family[a] who are with me,
To the churches of Gala-
tia:
3 Grace to you and
peace from God our Father
and the Lord Jesus Christ,
4 who gave himself for our
sins to set us free from the
present evil age, according
to the will of our God and
Father, 5 to whom be the
glory forever and ever.
Amen.

There Is No Other Gospel

6 I am astonished that
you are so quickly deserting the one who called you
in the grace of Christ and
are turning to a different
gospel— 7 not that there is
another gospel, but there
are some who are confus-
ing you and want to pervert
the gospel of Christ. 8 But
even if we or an angel[b]
from heaven should pro-
claim to you a gospel contrary to what we pro-
claimed to you, let that one
be accursed! 9 As we have
said before, so now I re-
peat, if anyone proclaims
to you a gospel contrary to
what you received, let that
one be accursed!

[r] Or *and the sharing in*
[a] Gk *all the brothers*
[b] Or *a messenger*

ΠΡΟΣ ΓΑΛΑΤΑΣ
To Galatians

1 Παῦλος ἀπόστολος, οὐκ ἀπ' ἀνθρώπων
Paul an apostle, not from men
οὐδὲ δι' ἀνθρώπου ἀλλὰ διὰ Ἰησοῦ
nor through man but through Jesus
Χριστοῦ καὶ θεοῦ πατρὸς τοῦ ἐγείραντος
Christ and God [the] Father the [one] having raised
αὐτὸν ἐκ νεκρῶν, 2 καὶ οἱ σὺν ἐμοὶ
him out of [the] dead, and ²the ⁴with ⁵me
πάντες ἀδελφοί, ταῖς ἐκκλησίαις τῆς
¹all ³brothers, to the churches –
Γαλατίας· 3 χάρις ὑμῖν καὶ εἰρήνη ἀπὸ
of Galatia: Grace to you and peace from
θεοῦ πατρὸς ἡμῶν καὶ κυρίου Ἰησοῦ
God Father of us and Lord Jesus
Χριστοῦ, 4 τοῦ δόντος ἑαυτὸν ὑπὲρ τῶν
Christ, the [one] having given himself on behalf of the
ἁμαρτιῶν ἡμῶν, ὅπως ἐξέληται ἡμᾶς ἐκ
sins of us, so as he might deliver us out of
τοῦ αἰῶνος τοῦ ἐνεστῶτος πονηροῦ κατὰ
the ³age – ¹present ²evil according to
τὸ θέλημα τοῦ θεοῦ καὶ πατρὸς ἡμῶν,
the will of the God and Father of us,
5 ᾧ ἡ δόξα εἰς τοὺς αἰῶνας τῶν
to whom the [be] glory unto the ages of the
αἰώνων· ἀμήν.
ages: Amen.
6 Θαυμάζω ὅτι οὕτως ταχέως μετατίθεσθε
I wonder that thus quickly ye are removing
ἀπὸ τοῦ καλέσαντος ὑμᾶς ἐν χάριτι
from the [one] having called you by [the] grace
Χριστοῦ εἰς ἕτερον εὐαγγέλιον, 7 ὃ οὐκ
of Christ to another gospel, which not
ἔστιν ἄλλο· εἰ μή τινές εἰσιν οἱ ταράσ-
is another; only ²some ¹there are – troubl-
σοντες ὑμᾶς καὶ θέλοντες μεταστρέψαι
ing you and wishing to pervert
τὸ εὐαγγέλιον τοῦ Χριστοῦ. 8 ἀλλὰ
the gospel – of Christ. But
καὶ ἐὰν ἡμεῖς ἢ ἄγγελος ἐξ οὐρανοῦ
even if we or an angel out of heaven
εὐαγγελίσηται [ὑμῖν] παρ' ὃ εὐηγγελισάμεθα
should preach a gospel to you beside what we preached
ὑμῖν, ἀνάθεμα ἔστω. 9 ὡς προειρήκαμεν,
to you, ²a curse ¹let him be. As we have previously said,
καὶ ἄρτι πάλιν λέγω, εἴ τις ὑμᾶς εὐαγ-
also now again I say, if anyone ²you ¹preaches
γελίζεται παρ' ὃ παρελάβετε, ἀνάθεμα
³a gospel beside what ye received, ²a curse
ἔστω.
¹let him be.

Galatians

Chapter 1

PAUL, an apostle—sent
not from men nor by
man, but by Jesus Christ
and God the Father, who
raised him from the dead—
2 and all the brothers with
me,

To the churches in Gala-
tia:

3 Grace and peace to you
from God our Father and
the Lord Jesus Christ,
4 who gave himself for our
sins to rescue us from the
present evil age, according
to the will of our God and
Father, 5 to whom be glory
for ever and ever. Amen.

No Other Gospel

6 I am astonished that you
are so quickly deserting the
one who called you by the
grace of Christ and are
turning to a different gospel
—7 which is really no gospel at all. Evidently some
people are throwing you
into confusion and are trying to pervert the gospel of
Christ. 8 But even if we or
an angel from heaven
should preach a gospel other than the one we
preached to you, let him be
eternally condemned! 9 As
we have already said, so
now I say again: If anybody
is preaching to you a gospel
other than what you ac-
cepted, let him be eternally
condemned!

10 Am I now seeking
human approval, or God's
approval? Or am I trying to
please people? If I were
still pleasing people, I
would not be a servant[c] of
Christ.

Paul's Vindication of His Apostleship

11 For I want you to
know, brothers and sis-
ters,[d] that the gospel that
was proclaimed by me is
not of human origin; 12 for I
did not receive it from a human source, nor was I
taught it, but I received it
through a revelation of
Jesus Christ.
13 You have heard, no
doubt, of my earlier life in
Judaism. I was violently
persecuting the church of
God and was trying to de-
stroy it. 14 I advanced in Judaism beyond many among
my people of the same age,
for I was far more zealous
for the traditions of my ancestors. 15 But when God,
who had set me apart be-
fore I was born and called
me through his grace, was
pleased 16 to reveal his Son
to me,[e] so that I might proclaim him among the Gen-
tiles, I did not confer with
any human being, 17 nor did
I go up to Jerusalem to
those who were already
apostles before me, but I
went away at once into
Arabia, and afterwards I
returned to Damascus.
18 Then after three
years I did go up to Jerusalem to visit Cephas and
stayed with him fifteen
days; 19 but I did not see
any other apostle except
James the Lord's brother.
20 In what I am writing to
you, before God, I do not
lie! 21 Then I went into the

[c] Gk *slave*
[d] Gk *brothers*
[e] Gk *in me*

10 Ἄρτι γὰρ ἀνθρώπους πείθω ἢ τὸν
For now men do I persuade or –

θεόν; ἢ ζητῶ ἀνθρώποις ἀρέσκειν; εἰ
God? or do I seek men to please? If

ἔτι ἀνθρώποις ἤρεσκον, Χριστοῦ δοῦλος
still men I pleased, [2]of Christ [3]a slave

οὐκ ἂν ἤμην. **11** γνωρίζω γὰρ ὑμῖν,
[1]I would not have been. For I make known to you,

ἀδελφοί, τὸ εὐαγγέλιον τὸ εὐαγγελισθὲν
brothers, the gospel – preached

ὑπ᾿ ἐμοῦ ὅτι οὐκ ἔστιν κατὰ ἄνθρωπον
by me that it is not according to man;

12 οὐδὲ γὰρ ἐγὼ παρὰ ἀνθρώπου παρέλαβον
for [4]not [1]I [5]from [6]man [3]received

αὐτὸ οὔτε ἐδιδάχθην, ἀλλὰ δι᾿ ἀποκαλύψεως
[2]it nor was I taught [by man], but through a revelation

Ἰησοῦ Χριστοῦ. **13** Ἠκούσατε γὰρ τὴν
of Jesus Christ. For ye heard –

ἐμὴν ἀναστροφήν ποτε ἐν τῷ Ἰουδαϊσμῷ,
my conduct then in – Judaism,

ὅτι καθ᾿ ὑπερβολὴν ἐδίωκον τὴν ἐκκλησίαν
that excessively† I persecuted the church

τοῦ θεοῦ καὶ ἐπόρθουν αὐτήν, **14** καὶ
– of God and wasted it, and

προέκοπτον ἐν τῷ Ἰουδαϊσμῷ ὑπὲρ πολλοὺς
progressed in – Judaism beyond many

συνηλικιώτας ἐν τῷ γένει μου, περισ-
contemporaries in the race of me, [2]abun-

σοτέρως ζηλωτὴς ὑπάρχων τῶν πατρικῶν
dantly [3]a zealot [1]being [4]of the [5]ancestral

μου παραδόσεων. **15** Ὅτε δὲ εὐδόκησεν
[7]of me [6]traditions. But when [14]was pleased

ὁ ἀφορίσας με ἐκ κοιλίας μητρός μου
[1]the [one] [2]having separated [3]me [4]from [5][the] womb [6]of mother [7]of me

καὶ καλέσας διὰ τῆς χάριτος αὐτοῦ
[8]and [9]having called [10]through [11]the [12]grace [13]of him

16 ἀποκαλύψαι τὸν υἱὸν αὐτοῦ ἐν ἐμοί,
to reveal the Son of him in me,

ἵνα εὐαγγελίζωμαι αὐτὸν ἐν τοῖς ἔθνεσιν,
in order that I might preach him among the nations,

εὐθέως οὐ προσανεθέμην σαρκὶ καὶ αἵματι,
immediately I conferred not with flesh and blood,

17 οὐδὲ ἀνῆλθον εἰς Ἱεροσόλυμα πρὸς
neither did I go up to Jerusalem to

τοὺς πρὸ ἐμοῦ ἀποστόλους, ἀλλὰ ἀπῆλθον
[1]the [3]before [4]me [2]apostles, but I went away

εἰς Ἀραβίαν, καὶ πάλιν ὑπέστρεψα εἰς
into Arabia, and again returned to

Δαμασκόν. **18** Ἔπειτα μετὰ τρία ἔτη
Damascus. Then after three years

ἀνῆλθον εἰς Ἱεροσόλυμα ἱστορῆσαι Κηφᾶν,
I went up to Jerusalem to visit Cephas,

καὶ ἐπέμεινα πρὸς αὐτὸν ἡμέρας δεκαπέντε·
and remained with him days fifteen;

19 ἕτερον δὲ τῶν ἀποστόλων οὐκ εἶδον,
but other of the apostles I saw not,

εἰ μὴ Ἰάκωβον τὸν ἀδελφὸν τοῦ κυρίου.
except James the brother of the Lord.

20 ἃ δὲ γράφω ὑμῖν, ἰδοὺ ἐνώπιον τοῦ
Now what things I write to you, behold before –

θεοῦ ὅτι οὐ ψεύδομαι. **21** ἔπειτα ἦλθον
God – I lie not. Then I went

10 Am I now trying to win
the approval of men, or of
God? Or am I trying to
please men? If I were still
trying to please men, I
would not be a servant of
Christ.

Paul Called by God

11 I want you to know,
brothers, that the gospel I
preached is not something
that man made up. 12 I did
not receive it from any
man, nor was I taught it;
rather, I received it by revelation from Jesus Christ.
13 For you have heard of
my previous way of life in
Judaism, how intensely I
persecuted the church of
God and tried to destroy it.
14 I was advancing in Judaism beyond many Jews of
my own age and was ex-
tremely zealous for the traditions of my fathers. 15 But
when God, who set me
apart from birth[a] and
called me by his grace, was
pleased 16 to reveal his Son
in me so that I might preach
him among the Gentiles, I
did not consult any man,
17 nor did I go up to Jerusalem to see those who were
apostles before I was, but I
went immediately into Arabia and later returned to
Damascus.
18 Then after three years, I
went up to Jerusalem to get
acquainted with Peter[b] and
stayed with him fifteen
days. 19 I saw none of the
other apostles—only
James, the Lord's brother.
20 I assure you before God
that what I am writing you
is no lie. 21 Later I went to
Syria and Cilicia. 22 I was
personally unknown to the

[a] 15 Or *from my mother's womb*
[b] 18 Greek *Cephas*

regions of Syria and Cilicia,
22and I was still unknown
by sight to the churches of
Judea that are in Christ;
23they only heard it said,
"The one who formerly
was persecuting us is now
proclaiming the faith he
once tried to destroy."
24And they glorified God
because of me.

Chapter 2

Paul and the Other Apostles

THEN after fourteen
years I went up again
to Jerusalem with Barna-
bas, taking Titus along with
me. 2I went up in response
to a revelation. Then I laid
before them (though only in
a private meeting with the
acknowledged leaders) the
gospel that I proclaim
among the Gentiles, in order to make sure that I was
not running, or had not run,
in vain. 3But even Titus,
who was with me, was not
compelled to be circum-
cised, though he was a
Greek. 4But because of
false believers[f] secretly
brought in, who slipped in
to spy on the freedom we
have in Christ Jesus, so
that they might enslave
us— 5we did not submit to
them even for a moment, so
that the truth of the gospel
might always remain with
you. 6And from those who
were supposed to be ac-
knowledged leaders (what
they actually were makes
no difference to me; God
shows no partiality)—
those leaders contributed
nothing to me. 7On the contrary, when they saw that I
had been entrusted with the
gospel for the uncircum-
cised, just as Peter had
been entrusted with the
gospel for the circumcised
8(for he who worked
through Peter making him
an apostle to the circum-
cised also worked through
me in sending me to the
Gentiles), 9and when

[f]Gk *false brothers*

εἰς τὰ κλίματα τῆς Συρίας καὶ τῆς
into the regions - of Syria and -

Κιλικίας. **22** ἤμην δὲ ἀγνοούμενος τῷ
of Cilicia. And I was *being* unknown -

προσώπῳ ταῖς ἐκκλησίαις τῆς Ἰουδαίας
by face to the churches - of Judæa

ταῖς ἐν Χριστῷ. **23** μόνον δὲ ἀκούοντες
- in Christ. But only hearing

ἦσαν ὅτι ὁ διώκων ἡμᾶς ποτε νῦν
they were that the [one] [2]persecuting [3]us [1]then now

εὐαγγελίζεται τὴν πίστιν ἥν ποτε ἐπόρθει,
preaches the faith which then he was destroying,

24 καὶ ἐδόξαζον ἐν ἐμοὶ τὸν θεόν.
and they glorified [2]in [3]me - [1]God.

2 Ἔπειτα διὰ δεκατεσσάρων ἐτῶν πάλιν
Then through fourteen years again

ἀνέβην εἰς Ἱεροσόλυμα μετὰ Βαρναβᾶ,
I went up to Jerusalem with Barnabas,

συμπαραλαβὼν καὶ Τίτον· **2** ἀνέβην δὲ
taking with [me] also Titus; and I went up

κατὰ ἀποκάλυψιν· καὶ ἀνεθέμην αὐτοῖς
according to a revelation; and I put before them

τὸ εὐαγγέλιον ὃ κηρύσσω ἐν τοῖς ἔθνεσιν,
the gospel which I proclaim among the nations,

κατ' ἰδίαν δὲ τοῖς δοκοῦσιν, μή πως
[2]privately [1]but to the [ones] seeming,• lest

εἰς κενὸν τρέχω ἢ ἔδραμον. **3** ἀλλ'
in vain I run or I ran. But

οὐδὲ Τίτος ὁ σὺν ἐμοί, Ἕλλην ὤν,
not Titus the [one] with me, a Greek being,

ἠναγκάσθη περιτμηθῆναι· **4** διὰ δὲ τοὺς
was compelled to be circumcised; but on account of [1]the

παρεισάκτους ψευδαδέλφους, οἵτινες παρεισ-
[3]brought in secretly [2]false brothers, who stole

ῆλθον κατασκοπῆσαι τὴν ἐλευθερίαν ἡμῶν
in to spy on the freedom of us

ἣν ἔχομεν ἐν Χριστῷ Ἰησοῦ, ἵνα ἡμᾶς
which we have in Christ Jesus, in order that [2]us

καταδουλώσουσιν· **5** οἷς οὐδὲ πρὸς ὥραν
[1]they will(might) enslave; to whom not for an hour

εἴξαμεν τῇ ὑποταγῇ, ἵνα ἡ ἀλήθεια
yielded we - in subjection, in order that the truth

τοῦ εὐαγγελίου διαμείνῃ πρὸς ὑμᾶς. **6** ἀπὸ
of the gospel might continue with you. from

δὲ τῶν δοκούντων εἶναί τι, — ὁποῖοί
But the [ones] seeming to be something, (of what kind

ποτε ἦσαν οὐδέν μοι διαφέρει· πρόσωπον
[2]then [1]they were [4]nothing [5]to me [3]matters: [8][the] face

[ὁ] θεὸς ἀνθρώπου οὐ λαμβάνει — ἐμοὶ
- [6]God [9]of a man [7]receives not,) [2]to me

γὰρ οἱ δοκοῦντες οὐδὲν προσανέθεντο,
[1]for the [ones] seeming• nothing added,

7 ἀλλὰ τοὐναντίον ἰδόντες ὅτι πεπίστευμαι
but on the contrary seeing that I have been entrusted [with]

τὸ εὐαγγέλιον τῆς ἀκροβυστίας καθὼς
the gospel of the uncircumcision as

Πέτρος τῆς περιτομῆς, **8** ὁ γὰρ ἐνεργήσας
Peter [that] of the circumcision, for the [one] operating

Πέτρῳ εἰς ἀποστολὴν τῆς περιτομῆς
in Peter to an apostleship of the circumcision

ἐνήργησεν καὶ ἐμοὶ εἰς τὰ ἔθνη, **9** καὶ
operated also in me to the nations, and

• *Cf.* the full expressions in vers. 6 (earlier) and 9.

churches of Judea that are
in Christ. 23They only
heard the report: "The man
who formerly persecuted
us is now preaching the
faith he once tried to destroy." 24And they praised
God because of me.

Chapter 2

Paul Accepted by the Apostles

FOURTEEN years later
I went up again to Je-
rusalem, this time with
Barnabas. I took Titus
along also. 2I went in response to a revelation and
set before them the gospel
that I preach among the
Gentiles. But I did this privately to those who seemed
to be leaders, for fear that I
was running or had run my
race in vain. 3Yet not even
Titus, who was with me,
was compelled to be cir-
cumcised, even though he
was a Greek. 4⌊This matter
arose⌋ because some false
brothers had infiltrated our
ranks to spy on the freedom
we have in Christ Jesus and
to make us slaves. 5We did
not give in to them for a
moment, so that the truth
of the gospel might remain
with you.

6As for those who seemed
to be important—whatever
they were makes no difference to me; God does not
judge by external appear-
ance—those men added
nothing to my message.
7On the contrary, they saw
that I had been entrusted
with the task of preaching
the gospel to the Gentiles,[c]
just as Peter had been to the
Jews.[d] 8For God, who was
at work in the ministry of
Peter as an apostle to the
Jews, was also at work in
my ministry as an apostle
to the Gentiles. 9James, Pe-

[c]7 Greek *uncircumcised*
[d]7 Greek *circumcised*; also in verses 8 and 9

James and Cephas and
John, who were acknowl-
edged pillars, recognized
the grace that had been giv-
en to me, they gave to Barnabas and me the right
hand of fellowship, agreeing that we should go to the
Gentiles and they to the circumcised. 10They asked
only one thing, that we remember the poor, which
was actually what I was[g]
eager to do.

Paul Rebukes Peter at Antioch

11 But when Cephas
came to Antioch, I opposed
him to his face, because he
stood self-condemned;
12for until certain people
came from James, he used
to eat with the Gentiles.
But after they came, he
drew back and kept himself
separate for fear of the circumcision faction. 13And
the other Jews joined him
in this hypocrisy, so that
even Barnabas was led
astray by their hypocrisy.
14But when I saw that they
were not acting consistently with the truth of the gospel, I said to Cephas before
them all, "If you, though a
Jew, live like a Gentile and
not like a Jew, how can you
compel the Gentiles to live
like Jews?"[h]

Jews and Gentiles Are Saved by Faith

15 We ourselves are
Jews by birth and not Gentile sinners; 16yet we know
that a person is justified[i]
not by the works of the law
but through faith in Jesus
Christ.[j] And we have
come to believe in Christ
Jesus, so that we might be
justified by faith in Christ,[k]
and not by doing the works
of the law, because no one
will be justified by the
works of the law. 17But if,
in our effort to be justified
in Christ, we ourselves

[g] Or *had been*
[h] Some interpreters hold that the quotation extends into the following paragraph
[i] Or *reckoned as righteous;* and so elsewhere
[j] Or *the faith of Jesus Christ*
[k] Or *the faith of Christ*

γνόντες τὴν χάριν τὴν δοθεῖσάν μοι,
knowing the grace – given to me,
Ἰάκωβος καὶ Κηφᾶς καὶ Ἰωάννης, οἱ
James and Cephas and John, the
δοκοῦντες στῦλοι εἶναι, δεξιὰς ἔδωκαν
[ones] seeming [2]pillars [1]to be, [5]right [hands] [1]gave
ἐμοὶ καὶ Βαρναβᾷ κοινωνίας, ἵνα ἡμεῖς
[2]to me [3]and [4]to Barnabas [6]of fellowship, in order that we [should
εἰς τὰ ἔθνη, αὐτοὶ δὲ εἰς τὴν περιτομήν·
go] to the nations, but they to the circumcision;
10 μόνον τῶν πτωχῶν ἵνα μνημονεύωμεν,
only [3]the [4]poor *in order* [1]that [2]we might remember,
ὃ καὶ ἐσπούδασα αὐτὸ τοῦτο ποιῆσαι.
which indeed [2]I was eager [1]this very thing to do.
11 Ὅτε δὲ ἦλθεν Κηφᾶς εἰς Ἀντιόχειαν,
But when [2]came [1]Cephas to Antioch,
κατὰ πρόσωπον αὐτῷ ἀντέστην, ὅτι
against [his] face *to* him I opposed, because
κατεγνωσμένος ἦν. 12 πρὸ τοῦ γὰρ
[2]having been condemned [1]he was. Before the for
=For before some came . . .
ἐλθεῖν τινας ἀπὸ Ἰακώβου μετὰ τῶν
to come some[b] from James [2]with [3]the
ἐθνῶν συνήσθιεν· ὅτε δὲ ἦλθον, ὑπέστελλεν
[4]nations [1]he ate *with*; but when they came, he withdrew
καὶ ἀφώριζεν ἑαυτόν, φοβούμενος τοὺς
and separated himself, fearing the [ones]
ἐκ περιτομῆς· 13 καὶ συνυπεκρίθησαν αὐτῷ
of [the] circumcision; and dissembled along with him
[καὶ] οἱ λοιποὶ Ἰουδαῖοι, ὥστε καὶ
also the remaining Jews, so as even
Βαρναβᾶς συναπήχθη αὐτῶν τῇ ὑποκρίσει.
Barnabas was led away with [3]of them [1]the [2]dissembling.
14 ἀλλ' ὅτε εἶδον ὅτι οὐκ ὀρθοποδοῦσιν
But when I saw that they walk[ed] not straight
πρὸς τὴν ἀλήθειαν τοῦ εὐαγγελίου, εἶπον
with the truth of the gospel, I said
τῷ Κηφᾷ ἔμπροσθεν πάντων· εἰ σὺ
– to Cephas in front of all: If thou
Ἰουδαῖος ὑπάρχων ἐθνικῶς καὶ οὐκ
[2]a Jew [1]being as a Gentile and not
Ἰουδαϊκῶς ζῇς, πῶς τὰ ἔθνη ἀναγκάζεις
as a Jew livest, how [2]the [3]nations [1]compellest thou
ἰουδαΐζειν; 15 Ἡμεῖς φύσει Ἰουδαῖοι καὶ
to judaize? We by nature Jews and
οὐκ ἐξ ἐθνῶν ἁμαρτωλοί, 16 εἰδότες δὲ
not [2]of [3]nations [1]sinners, and knowing
ὅτι οὐ δικαιοῦται ἄνθρωπος ἐξ ἔργων
that [2]is not justified [1]a man by works
νόμου ἐὰν μὴ διὰ πίστεως Χριστοῦ
of law except(but) through faith of(in) Christ
Ἰησοῦ, καὶ ἡμεῖς εἰς Χριστὸν Ἰησοῦν
Jesus,* even we [2]in [3]Christ [4]Jesus
ἐπιστεύσαμεν, ἵνα δικαιωθῶμεν ἐκ πίστεως
[1]believed, in order that we might be justified by faith
Χριστοῦ καὶ οὐκ ἐξ ἔργων νόμου, ὅτι
of(in) Christ* and not by works of law, because
ἐξ ἔργων νόμου οὐ δικαιωθήσεται πᾶσα
by works of law not will be justified all
=no flesh will be justified.
σάρξ. 17 εἰ δὲ ζητοῦντες δικαιωθῆναι
flesh. But if seeking to be justified

* Objective genitive, as is shown by the intervening sentence see also 3. 22, 26). *Cf.* "fear of God".

ter[e] and John, those reput-
ed to be pillars, gave me
and Barnabas the right
hand of fellowship when
they recognized the grace
given to me. They agreed
that we should go to the
Gentiles, and they to the
Jews. 10All they asked was
that we should continue to
remember the poor, the
very thing I was eager to
do.

Paul Opposes Peter

11When Peter came to
Antioch, I opposed him to
his face, because he was
clearly in the wrong. 12Be-
fore certain men came from
James, he used to eat with
the Gentiles. But when
they arrived, he began to
draw back and separate
himself from the Gentiles
because he was afraid of
those who belonged to the
circumcision group. 13The
other Jews joined him in his
hypocrisy, so that by their
hypocrisy even Barnabas
was led astray.
14When I saw that they
were not acting in line with
the truth of the gospel, I
said to Peter in front of
them all, "You are a Jew,
yet you live like a Gentile
and not like a Jew. How is
it, then, that you force Gentiles to follow Jewish customs?
15"We who are Jews by
birth and not 'Gentile sinners' 16know that a man is
not justified by observing
the law, but by faith in
Jesus Christ. So we, too,
have put our faith in Christ
Jesus that we may be justified by faith in Christ and
not by observing the law,
because by observing the
law no one will be justified
17"If, while we seek to be
justified in Christ, it be-

[e] 9 Greek *Cephas;* also in verses 11 and 14

have been found to be sinners, is Christ then a servant of sin? Certainly not!
18 But if I build up again the
very things that I once tore
down, then I demonstrate
that I am a transgressor.
19 For through the law I
died to the law, so that I
might live to God. I have
been crucified with Christ;
20 and it is no longer I who
live, but it is Christ who
lives in me. And the life I
now live in the flesh I live
by faith in the Son of God,[l]
who loved me and gave
himself for me. 21 I do not
nullify the grace of God; for
if justification[m] comes
through the law, then
Christ died for nothing.

Chapter 3

Law or Faith

YOU foolish Galatians!
Who has bewitched
you? It was before your
eyes that Jesus Christ was
publicly exhibited as crucified! 2 The only thing I want
to learn from you is this:
Did you receive the Spirit
by doing the works of the
law or by believing what
you heard? 3 Are you so
foolish? Having started
with the Spirit, are you now
ending with the flesh? 4 Did
you experience so much for
nothing?—if it really was
for nothing. 5 Well then,
does God[n] supply you with
the Spirit and work mira-
cles among you by your doing the works of the law, or
by your believing what you
heard?
6 Just as Abraham "be-
lieved God, and it was
reckoned to him as righ-
teousness," 7 so, you see,
those who believe are the
descendants of Abraham.
8 And the scripture, foreseeing that God would justify the Gentiles by faith,
declared the gospel beforehand to Abraham, saying,
"All the Gentiles shall be

[l] Or *by the faith of the Son of God*
[m] Or *righteousness*
[n] Gk *he*

ἐν Χριστῷ εὑρέθημεν καὶ αὐτοὶ ἁμαρτωλοί,
in Christ we were found also [our]selves sinners,
ἆρα Χριστὸς ἁμαρτίας διάκονος; μὴ
then [is] Christ [2]of sin [1]a minister? not
γένοιτο. 18 εἰ γὰρ ἃ κατέλυσα ταῦτα
May it be. For if what things I destroyed these things
πάλιν οἰκοδομῶ, παραβάτην ἐμαυτὸν συνισ-
again I build, [3]a transgressor [2]myself [1]I con-
τάνω. 19 ἐγὼ γὰρ διὰ νόμου νόμῳ
stitute. For I through law [2]to law
ἀπέθανον ἵνα θεῷ ζήσω. 20 Χριστῷ συνεσ-
[1]died in order that to God I might live. With Christ I have
ταύρωμαι· ζῶ δὲ οὐκέτι ἐγώ, ζῇ δὲ
been co-crucified; and [2]live [3]no more [1]I, but [2]lives
ἐν ἐμοὶ Χριστός· ὃ δὲ νῦν ζῶ ἐν σαρκί,
[3]in [4]me [1]Christ; and what now I live in [the] flesh,
ἐν πίστει ζῶ τῇ τοῦ υἱοῦ τοῦ θεοῦ
[2]by [3]faith [1]I live – of(in) the Son – of God
τοῦ ἀγαπήσαντός με καὶ παραδόντος ἑαυτὸν
– loving me and giving up himself
ὑπὲρ ἐμοῦ. 21 Οὐκ ἀθετῶ τὴν χάριν
on behalf of me. I do not set aside the grace
τοῦ θεοῦ· εἰ γὰρ διὰ νόμου δικαιοσύνη,
– of God; for if through law righteousness [comes],
ἄρα Χριστὸς δωρεὰν ἀπέθανεν.
then Christ without cause died.

3 Ὦ ἀνόητοι Γαλάται, τίς ὑμᾶς
O foolish Galatians, who you
ἐβάσκανεν, οἷς κατ' ὀφθαλμοὺς Ἰησοῦς
bewitched, to whom before [the] eyes Jesus
Χριστὸς προεγράφη ἐσταυρωμένος; 2 τοῦτο
Christ was portrayed having been crucified? This
μόνον θέλω μαθεῖν ἀφ' ὑμῶν, ἐξ ἔργων
only I wish to learn from you, by works
νόμου τὸ πνεῦμα ἐλάβετε ἢ ἐξ ἀκοῆς
of law the Spirit received ye or by hearing
πίστεως; 3 οὕτως ἀνόητοί ἐστε; ἐναρξάμενοι
of faith? thus foolish are ye? having begun
πνεύματι νῦν σαρκὶ ἐπιτελεῖσθε; 4 τοσαῦτα
in [the] Spirit now in [the] flesh are ye being perfected? so many things
ἐπάθετε εἰκῇ; 5 εἴ γε καὶ εἰκῇ. ὁ
suffered ye in vain? if indeed in vain. The [one]
οὖν ἐπιχορηγῶν ὑμῖν τὸ πνεῦμα καὶ
therefore supplying to you the Spirit and
ἐνεργῶν δυνάμεις ἐν ὑμῖν ἐξ ἔργων
working powerful deeds among you [is it] by works
νόμου ἢ ἐξ ἀκοῆς πίστεως; 6 Καθὼς
of law or by hearing of faith? As
Ἀβραὰμ ἐπίστευσεν τῷ θεῷ, καὶ ἐλογίσθη
Abraham believed – God, and it was reckoned
αὐτῷ εἰς δικαιοσύνην. 7 γινώσκετε ἄρα
to him for righteousness. Know ye then
ὅτι οἱ ἐκ πίστεως, οὗτοι υἱοί εἰσιν
that the [ones] of faith, [1]these [3]sons [2]are
Ἀβραάμ. 8 προϊδοῦσα δὲ ἡ γραφὴ ὅτι
[4]of Abraham. And [3]foreseeing [1]the [2]scripture [4]that
ἐκ πίστεως δικαιοῖ τὰ ἔθνη ὁ θεός,
[9]by [10]faith [6]would justify [7]the [8]nations – [5]God,
προευηγγελίσατο τῷ Ἀβραὰμ ὅτι ἐνευλογη-
preached good tidings before – to Abraham that [4]will be

comes evident that we ourselves are sinners, does
that mean that Christ promotes sin? Absolutely not!
18 If I rebuild what I destroyed, I prove that I am a
lawbreaker. 19 For through
the law I died to the law so
that I might live for God. 20 I
have been crucified with
Christ and I no longer live,
but Christ lives in me. The
life I live in the body, I live
by faith in the Son of God,
who loved me and gave
himself for me. 21 I do not
set aside the grace of God,
for if righteousness could
be gained through the law,
Christ died for nothing!"[f]

Chapter 3

Faith or Observance of the Law

YOU foolish Galatians!
Who has bewitched
you? Before your very eyes
Jesus Christ was clearly
portrayed as crucified. 2 I
would like to learn just one
thing from you: Did you receive the Spirit by observing the law, or by believing
what you heard? 3 Are you
so foolish? After beginning
with the Spirit, are you now
trying to attain your goal by
human effort? 4 Have you
suffered so much for nothing—if it really was for
nothing? 5 Does God give
you his Spirit and work
miracles among you be-
cause you observe the law,
or because you believe
what you heard?
6 Consider Abraham: "He
believed God, and it was
credited to him as right-
eousness."[g] 7 Understand,
then, that those who be-
lieve are children of Abraham. 8 The Scripture foresaw that God would justify
the Gentiles by faith, and
announced the gospel in
advance to Abraham: "All
nations will be blessed

[f] *21* Some interpreters end the quotation after verse 14.
[g] *6* Gen. 15:6

blessed in you." 9 For this reason, those who believe are blessed with Abraham who believed.

10 For all who rely on the works of the law are under a curse; for it is written, "Cursed is everyone who does not observe and obey all the things written in the book of the law." 11 Now it is evident that no one is justified before God by the law; for "The one who is righteous will live by faith."[o] 12 But the law does not rest on faith; on the contrary, "Whoever does the works of the law[p] will live by them." 13 Christ redeemed us from the curse of the law by becoming a curse for us—for it is written, "Cursed is everyone who hangs on a tree"— 14 in order that in Christ Jesus the blessing of Abraham might come to the Gentiles, so that we might receive the promise of the Spirit through faith.

The Promise to Abraham

15 Brothers and sisters,[q] I give an example from daily life: once a person's will[r] has been ratified, no one adds to it or annuls it. 16 Now the promises were made to Abraham and to his offspring;[s] it does not say, "And to offsprings,"[t] as of many; but it says, "And to your offspring,"[s] that is, to one person, who is Christ. 17 My point is this: the law, which came four hundred thirty years later, does not annul a covenant previously ratified by God, so as to nullify the promise. 18 For if the inheritance comes from the law, it no longer comes from the promise; but God granted it to Abraham

[o] Or *The one who is righteous through faith will live*
[p] Gk *does them*
[q] Gk *Brothers*
[r] Or *covenant* (as in verse 17)
[s] Gk *seed*
[t] Gk *seeds*

θήσονται ἐν σοὶ πάντα τὰ ἔθνη. 9 ὥστε
blessed ¹in ²thee ³all ⁴the ⁵nations. So as
οἱ ἐκ πίστεως εὐλογοῦνται σὺν τῷ πιστῷ
the[ones]of faith are blessed with the believing
Ἀβραάμ. 10 Ὅσοι γὰρ ἐξ ἔργων νόμου
Abraham. For as many as ²of ³works ⁴of law
εἰσίν, ὑπὸ κατάραν εἰσίν· γέγραπται γὰρ
¹are, ⁶under ⁷a curse ⁵are; for it has been written[,]
ὅτι ἐπικατάρατος πᾶς ὃς οὐκ ἐμμένει
– Accursed everyone who continues not
πᾶσιν τοῖς γεγραμμένοις ἐν τῷ βιβλίῳ
in all the things having been written in the roll
τοῦ νόμου τοῦ ποιῆσαι αὐτά. 11 ὅτι
of the law – to do[d] them. that
δὲ ἐν νόμῳ οὐδεὶς δικαιοῦται παρὰ τῷ
Now by law no man is justified before –
θεῷ δῆλον, ὅτι ὁ δίκαιος ἐκ πίστεως
God [is] clear, because the just man by faith
ζήσεται· 12 ὁ δὲ νόμος οὐκ ἔστιν ἐκ
will live; and the law is not of
πίστεως, ἀλλ' ὁ ποιήσας αὐτὰ ζήσεται
faith, but the [one] doing them will live
ἐν αὐτοῖς. 13 Χριστὸς ἡμᾶς ἐξηγόρασεν
by them. Christ ²us ¹redeemed
ἐκ τῆς κατάρας τοῦ νόμου γενόμενος
out of the curse of the law becoming
ὑπὲρ ἡμῶν κατάρα, ὅτι γέγραπται·
³on behalf of ⁴us ¹a curse, because it has been written:
ἐπικατάρατος πᾶς ὁ κρεμάμενος ἐπὶ
Accursed everyone hanging on
ξύλου, 14 ἵνα εἰς τὰ ἔθνη ἡ εὐλογία
a tree, in order that ⁵to ⁶the ⁷nations ¹the ²blessing
τοῦ Ἀβραὰμ γένηται ἐν Ἰησοῦ Χριστῷ,
– ³of Abraham ⁴might be in Jesus Christ,
ἵνα τὴν ἐπαγγελίαν τοῦ πνεύματος λάβωμεν
in order that ²the ³promise ⁴of the ⁵Spirit ¹we might receive
διὰ τῆς πίστεως. 15 Ἀδελφοί, κατὰ
through *the* faith. Brothers, according to
ἄνθρωπον λέγω. ὅμως ἀνθρώπου κεκυρω-
man I say. Nevertheless ⁶of man ⁷having been
μένην διαθήκην οὐδεὶς ἀθετεῖ ἢ ἐπιδια-
ratified ⁵a covenant ¹no one ²sets aside ³or ⁴makes
τάσσεται. 16 τῷ δὲ Ἀβραὰμ ἐρρέθησαν
additions [to]. – Now to Abraham were said
αἱ ἐπαγγελίαι καὶ τῷ σπέρματι αὐτοῦ.
the promises and to the seed of him.
οὐ λέγει· καὶ τοῖς σπέρμασιν, ὡς ἐπὶ
It says not: And to the seeds, as concerning
πολλῶν, ἀλλ' ὡς ἐφ' ἑνός· καὶ τῷ
many, but as concerning one: And to the
σπέρματί σου, ὅς ἐστιν Χριστός. 17 τοῦτο δὲ
seed of thee, who is Christ. And this
λέγω· διαθήκην προκεκυρωμένην ὑπὸ
I say: ¹⁰A covenant ¹¹having been previously ratified ¹²by
τοῦ θεοῦ ὁ μετὰ τετρακόσια καὶ τριάκοντα
– ¹³God ¹the ⁴after ⁵four hundred ⁶and ⁷thirty
ἔτη γεγονὼς νόμος οὐκ ἀκυροῖ, εἰς τὸ
⁸years ³having come into being ²law ⁹does not annul, so as†
καταργῆσαι τὴν ἐπαγγελίαν. 18 εἰ γὰρ
to abolish the promise. For if
ἐκ νόμου ἡ κληρονομία, οὐκέτι ἐξ
⁴of ⁵law ¹the ²inheritance ³[is], no more [is it] of
ἐπαγγελίας· τῷ δὲ Ἀβραὰμ δι' ἐπαγγελίας
promise; – but ⁴to Abraham ⁵through ⁶promise

through you."[h] 9 So those who have faith are blessed along with Abraham, the man of faith.

10 All who rely on observing the law are under a curse, for it is written: "Cursed is everyone who does not continue to do everything written in the Book of the Law."[i] 11 Clearly no one is justified before God by the law, because, "The righteous will live by faith."[j] 12 The law is not based on faith; on the contrary, "The man who does these things will live by them."[k] 13 Christ redeemed us from the curse of the law by becoming a curse for us, for it is written: "Cursed is everyone who is hung on a tree."[l] 14 He redeemed us in order that the blessing given to Abraham might come to the Gentiles through Christ Jesus, so that by faith we might receive the promise of the Spirit.

The Law and the Promise

15 Brothers, let me take an example from everyday life. Just as no one can set aside or add to a human covenant that has been duly established, so it is in this case. 16 The promises were spoken to Abraham and to his seed. The Scripture does not say "and to seeds," meaning many people, but "and to your seed,"[m] meaning one person, who is Christ. 17 What I mean is this: The law, introduced 430 years later, does not set aside the covenant previously established by God and thus do away with the promise. 18 For if the inheritance depends on the law, then it no longer depends on a promise; but God in his grace gave it to

[h] *8* Gen. 12:3; 18:18; 22:18
[i] *10* Deut. 27:26
[j] *11* Hab. 2:4
[k] *12* Lev. 18:5
[l] *13* Deut. 21:23
[m] *16* Gen. 12:7; 13:15; 24:7

through the promise.

The Purpose of the Law

19 Why then the law? It
was added because of
transgressions, until the
offspring[u] would come to
whom the promise had
been made; and it was or-
dained through angels by a
mediator. 20 Now a media-
tor involves more than one
party; but God is one.
21 Is the law then op-
posed to the promises of
God? Certainly not! For if a
law had been given that
could make alive, then
righteousness would in-
deed come through the law.
22 But the scripture has imprisoned all things under
the power of sin, so that
what was promised through
faith in Jesus Christ[v] might
be given to those who be-
lieve.
23 Now before faith
came, we were imprisoned
and guarded under the law
until faith would be re-
vealed. 24 Therefore the law
was our disciplinarian until
Christ came, so that we
might be justified by faith.
25 But now that faith has
come, we are no longer
subject to a disciplinarian,
26 for in Christ Jesus you
are all children of God
through faith. 27 As many of
you as were baptized into
Christ have clothed your-
selves with Christ. 28 There
is no longer Jew or Greek,
there is no longer slave or
free, there is no longer male
and female; for all of you
are one in Christ Jesus.
29 And if you belong to
Christ, then you are Abraham's offspring,[u] heirs according to the promise.

Chapter 4

My point is this: heirs,
as long as they are
minors, are no better than
slaves, though they are the
owners of all the property;
2 but they remain under
guardians and trustees until
the date set by the father.

[u] Gk *seed*
[v] Or *through the faith of Jesus Christ*

κεχάρισται ὁ θεός. 19 Τί οὖν ὁ νόμος;
[2]has given [3][it] – [1]God. Why therefore the law?

τῶν παραβάσεων χάριν προσετέθη, ἄχρις
[3]the [4]transgressions [2]by reason of [1]it was added, until

ἂν ἔλθῃ τὸ σπέρμα ᾧ ἐπήγγελται,
[3]should come [1]the [2]seed to whom it has been promised,

διαταγεὶς δι' ἀγγέλων, ἐν χειρὶ μεσίτου.
being ordained through angels, by [the] hand of a mediator.

20 ὁ δὲ μεσίτης ἑνὸς οὐκ ἔστιν, ὁ
Now the mediator [2]of one [1]is not, –

δὲ θεὸς εἷς ἐστιν. 21 ὁ οὖν νόμος κατὰ
but God [2]one [1]is. [Is] the [2]therefore [1]law against

τῶν ἐπαγγελιῶν [τοῦ θεοῦ]; μὴ γένοιτο.
the promises – of God? May it not be.

εἰ γὰρ ἐδόθη νόμος ὁ δυνάμενος ζωοποι-
For if [2]was given [1]a law – being able to make

ῆσαι, ὄντως ἐκ νόμου ἂν ἦν ἡ δικαιοσύνη·
alive, really [3]by [4]law [2]would have been – [1]righteousness;

22 ἀλλὰ συνέκλεισεν ἡ γραφὴ τὰ πάντα
but [3]shut up [1]the [2]scripture all mankind†

ὑπὸ ἁμαρτίαν ἵνα ἡ ἐπαγγελία ἐκ πίστεως
under sin in order that the promise by faith

Ἰησοῦ Χριστοῦ δοθῇ τοῖς πιστεύουσιν.
of(in) Jesus Christ might be given to the [ones] believing.

23 Πρὸ τοῦ δὲ ἐλθεῖν τὴν πίστιν ὑπὸ
before *the* But to come *the* faith[b] under
=But before faith came

νόμον ἐφρουρούμεθα συγκλειόμενοι εἰς τὴν
law we were guarded being shut up to the

μέλλουσαν πίστιν ἀποκαλυφθῆναι. 24 ὥστε
[2]being about [1]faith to be revealed. So as

ὁ νόμος παιδαγωγὸς ἡμῶν γέγονεν εἰς
the law [3]a trainer [2]of us [1]has become [up] to

Χριστόν, ἵνα ἐκ πίστεως δικαιωθῶμεν·
Christ, in order that by faith we might be justified;

25 ἐλθούσης δὲ τῆς πίστεως οὐκέτι ὑπὸ
but [3]having come [1]*the* [2]faith[a] [5]no more [6]under

παιδαγωγόν ἐσμεν. 26 Πάντες γὰρ υἱοὶ
[7]a trainer [4]we are. For all sons

θεοῦ ἐστε διὰ τῆς πίστεως ἐν Χριστῷ
of God ye are through *the* faith in Christ

Ἰησοῦ· 27 ὅσοι γὰρ εἰς Χριστὸν ἐβαπτίσ-
Jesus; for as many as [2]into [3]Christ [1]*ye* were

θητε, Χριστὸν ἐνεδύσασθε. 28 οὐκ ἔνι
baptized, [2]Christ [1]ye put on. There cannot be

Ἰουδαῖος οὐδὲ Ἕλλην, οὐκ ἔνι δοῦλος
Jew nor Greek, there cannot be slave

οὐδὲ ἐλεύθερος, οὐκ ἔνι ἄρσεν καὶ θῆλυ·
nor freeman, there cannot be male and female;

πάντες γὰρ ὑμεῖς εἷς ἐστε ἐν Χριστῷ
for [2]all [1]ye [4]one [3]are in Christ

Ἰησοῦ. 29 εἰ δὲ ὑμεῖς Χριστοῦ, ἄρα
Jesus. But if ye [are] of Christ, then

τοῦ Ἀβραὰμ σπέρμα ἐστέ, κατ' ἐπαγγελίαν
– [3]of Abraham [2]a seed [1]are ye, according to promise

κληρονόμοι. 4 Λέγω δέ, ἐφ' ὅσον χρόνον ὁ
heirs. But I say, over so long a time as the

κληρονόμος νήπιός ἐστιν, οὐδὲν διαφέρει
heir [2]an infant [1]is, [3]nothing [1]he differs [2][from]

δούλου κύριος πάντων ὤν, 2 ἀλλὰ ὑπὸ
[4]a slave [6]lord [7]of all [5]being, but [2]under

ἐπιτρόπους ἐστὶν καὶ οἰκονόμους ἄχρι τῆς
[3]guardians [1]is and stewards until the

Abraham through a prom-
ise.
19 What, then, was the
purpose of the law? It was
added because of trans-
gressions until the Seed to
whom the promise referred
had come. The law was put
into effect through angels
by a mediator. 20 A mediator, however, does not represent just one party; but
God is one.
21 Is the law, therefore,
opposed to the promises of
God? Absolutely not! For if
a law had been given that
could impart life, then
righteousness would cer-
tainly have come by the
law. 22 But the Scripture declares that the whole world
is a prisoner of sin, so that
what was promised, being
given through faith in Jesus
Christ, might be given to
those who believe.
23 Before this faith came,
we were held prisoners by
the law, locked up until
faith should be revealed.
24 So the law was put in
charge to lead us to Christ[n]
that we might be justified
by faith. 25 Now that faith
has come, we are no longer
under the supervision of
the law.

Sons of God

26 You are all sons of God
through faith in Christ
Jesus, 27 for all of you who
were baptized into Christ
have clothed yourselves
with Christ. 28 There is neither Jew nor Greek, slave
nor free, male nor female,
for you are all one in Christ
Jesus. 29 If you belong to
Christ, then you are Abraham's seed, and heirs ac-
cording to the promise.

Chapter 4

What I am saying is
that as long as the
heir is a child, he is no different from a slave, al-
though he owns the whole
estate. 2 He is subject to
guardians and trustees until
the time set by his father.
3 So also, when we were

[n]24 Or *charge until Christ came*

3So with us; while we were
minors, we were enslaved
to the elemental spirits[w] of
the world. 4But when the
fullness of time had come,
God sent his Son, born of a
woman, born under the
law, 5in order to redeem
those who were under the
law, so that we might re-
ceive adoption as children.
6And because you are children, God has sent the
Spirit of his Son into our[x]
hearts, crying, "Abba![y]
Father!" 7So you are no
longer a slave but a child,
and if a child then also an
heir, through God.[z]

Paul Reproves the Galatians

8 Formerly, when you
did not know God, you
were enslaved to beings
that by nature are not gods.
9Now, however, that you
have come to know God, or
rather to be known by God,
how can you turn back
again to the weak and beggarly elemental spirits?[a]
How can you want to be
enslaved to them again?
10You are observing spe-
cial days, and months, and
seasons, and years. 11I am
afraid that my work for you
may have been wasted.
12 Friends,[b] I beg you,
become as I am, for I also
have become as you are.
You have done me no
wrong. 13You know that it
was because of a physical
infirmity that I first announced the gospel to you;
14though my condition put
you to the test, you did not
scorn or despise me, but
welcomed me as an angel of
God, as Christ Jesus.
15What has become of the
good will you felt? For I
testify that, had it been possible, you would have torn
out your eyes and given

[w] Or *the rudiments*
[x] Other ancient authorities read *your*
[y] Aramaic for *Father*
[z] Other ancient authorities read *an heir of God through Christ*
[a] Or *beggarly rudiments*
[b] Gk *Brothers*

προθεσμίας τοῦ πατρός. 3 οὕτως καὶ
term previously appointed of the father. So also
ἡμεῖς, ὅτε ἦμεν νήπιοι, ὑπὸ τὰ στοιχεῖα
we, when we were infants, under the elements
τοῦ κόσμου ἤμεθα δεδουλωμένοι· 4 ὅτε
of the world we were *having been* enslaved; when
δὲ ἦλθεν τὸ πλήρωμα τοῦ χρόνου,
but came the fulness of the time,
ἐξαπέστειλεν ὁ θεὸς τὸν υἱὸν αὐτοῦ,
sent forth – God the Son of him,
γενόμενον ἐκ γυναικός, γενόμενον ὑπὸ
becoming of a woman, becoming under
νόμον, 5 ἵνα τοὺς ὑπὸ νόμον ἐξαγοράσῃ,
law, in order that 2the ones 3under 4law 1he might redeem,
ἵνα τὴν υἱοθεσίαν ἀπολάβωμεν. 6 Ὅτι δέ
in order that 2the 3adoption of sons 1we might receive. And because
ἐστε υἱοί, ἐξαπέστειλεν ὁ θεὸς τὸ
ye are sons, 2sent forth – 1God the
πνεῦμα τοῦ υἱοῦ αὐτοῦ εἰς τὰς καρδίας
Spirit of the Son of him into the hearts
ἡμῶν, κρᾶζον· ἀββὰ ὁ πατήρ. 7 ὥστε
of us, crying: Abba – Father. So as
οὐκέτι εἶ δοῦλος ἀλλὰ υἱός· εἰ δὲ υἱός,
no more art thou a slave but a son; and if a son,
καὶ κληρονόμος διὰ θεοῦ.
also an heir through God.

8 Ἀλλὰ τότε μὲν οὐκ εἰδότες θεὸν
But then indeed not knowing God
ἐδουλεύσατε τοῖς φύσει μὴ οὖσιν θεοῖς·
ye served as slaves 1the 5by nature 4not 3being 2gods;
9 νῦν δὲ γνόντες θεόν, μᾶλλον δὲ
but now knowing God, but rather
γνωσθέντες ὑπὸ θεοῦ, πῶς ἐπιστρέφετε
being known by God, how turn ye
πάλιν ἐπὶ τὰ ἀσθενῆ καὶ πτωχὰ στοιχεῖα,
again to the weak and poor elements,
οἷς πάλιν ἄνωθεν δουλεῦσαι θέλετε;
to which again 2anew 3to serve 1ye wish?
10 ἡμέρας παρατηρεῖσθε καὶ μῆνας καὶ
2days 1Ye observe and months and
καιροὺς καὶ ἐνιαυτούς. 11 φοβοῦμαι ὑμᾶς
seasons and years. I fear [for] you
μή πως εἰκῇ κεκοπίακα εἰς ὑμᾶς.
lest in vain I have laboured among you.

12 Γίνεσθε ὡς ἐγώ, ὅτι κἀγὼ ὡς
Be ye as I [am], because I also [am] as
ὑμεῖς, ἀδελφοί, δέομαι ὑμῶν. οὐδέν με
ye [are], brothers, I beg of you. Nothing me
ἠδικήσατε· 13 οἴδατε δὲ ὅτι δι' ἀσθένειαν
ye wronged; and ye know that on account of weakness
τῆς σαρκὸς εὐηγγελισάμην ὑμῖν τὸ
of the flesh I preached good tidings to you –
πρότερον, 14 καὶ τὸν πειρασμὸν ὑμῶν
formerly, and the trial of you
ἐν τῇ σαρκί μου οὐκ ἐξουθενήσατε οὐδὲ
in the flesh of me ye despised not nor
ἐξεπτύσατε, ἀλλὰ ὡς ἄγγελον θεοῦ ἐδέξασθέ
disdained *ye*, but as a messenger of God ye received
με, ὡς Χριστὸν Ἰησοῦν. 15 ποῦ οὖν
me, as Christ Jesus. Where therefore
ὁ μακαρισμὸς ὑμῶν; μαρτυρῶ γὰρ ὑμῖν
the felicitation of you?* for I witness to you
ὅτι εἰ δυνατὸν τοὺς ὀφθαλμοὺς ὑμῶν
that if possible 2the 3eyes 4of you

* That is, "your felicitation [of me]".

children, we were in slavery under the basic principles of the world. 4But
when the time had fully
come, God sent his Son,
born of a woman, born un-
der law, 5to redeem those
under law, that we might
receive the full rights of
sons. 6Because you are
sons, God sent the Spirit of
his Son into our hearts, the
Spirit who calls out,
"*Abba*,[o] Father." 7So you
are no longer a slave, but a
son; and since you are a
son, God has made you
also an heir.

Paul's Concern for the Galatians

8Formerly, when you did
not know God, you were
slaves to those who by nature are not gods. 9But now
that you know God—or
rather are known by God—
how is it that you are turning back to those weak and
miserable principles? Do
you wish to be enslaved by
them all over again? 10You
are observing special days
and months and seasons
and years! 11I fear for you,
that somehow I have wast-
ed my efforts on you.
12I plead with you, brothers, become like me, for I
became like you. You have
done me no wrong. 13As
you know, it was because
of an illness that I first
preached the gospel to you.
14Even though my illness
was a trial to you, you did
not treat me with contempt
or scorn. Instead, you welcomed me as if I were an
angel of God, as if I were
Christ Jesus himself.
15What has happened to all
your joy? I can testify that,
if you could have done so,
you would have torn out
your eyes and given them

[o]6 Aramaic for *Father*

them to me. 16Have I now
become your enemy by
telling you the truth?
17They make much of you,
but for no good purpose;
they want to exclude you,
so that you may make
much of them. 18It is good
to be made much of for a
good purpose at all times,
and not only when I am
present with you. 19My little children, for whom I am
again in the pain of childbirth until Christ is formed
in you, 20I wish I were
present with you now and
could change my tone, for I
am perplexed about you.

The Allegory of Hagar and Sarah

21 Tell me, you who de-
sire to be subject to the law,
will you not listen to the
law? 22For it is written that
Abraham had two sons,
one by a slave woman and
the other by a free woman.
23One, the child of the
slave, was born according
to the flesh; the other, the
child of the free woman,
was born through the
promise. 24Now this is an
allegory: these women are
two covenants. One wom-
an, in fact, is Hagar, from
Mount Sinai, bearing children for slavery. 25Now
Hagar is Mount Sinai in
Arabia[c] and corresponds
to the present Jerusalem,
for she is in slavery with
her children. 26But the other woman corresponds to
the Jerusalem above; she is
free, and she is our mother.
27For it is written,

"Rejoice, you
childless one,
you who bear
no children,
burst into song and
shout, you who
endure no
birthpangs;
for the children of the
desolate woman
are more
numerous
than the children of
the one who is
married."

28Now you,[d] my friends,[e]
are children of the promise,
like Isaac. 29But just as at
that time the child who was
born according to the flesh

[c] Other ancient authorities read *For Sinai is a mountain in Arabia*
[d] Other ancient authorities read *we*
[e] Gk *brothers*

ἐξορύξαντες ἐδώκατέ μοι. **16** ὥστε ἐχθρὸς
[1]gouging out ye gave [them] to me. So that [2]an enemy

ὑμῶν γέγονα ἀληθεύων ὑμῖν; **17** ζηλοῦσιν
[3]of you [1]have I become speaking truth to you? They are zealous of

ὑμᾶς οὐ καλῶς, ἀλλὰ ἐκκλεῖσαι ὑμᾶς
you not well, but [2]to exclude [3]you

θέλουσιν, **18** ἵνα αὐτοὺς ζηλοῦτε. καλὸν δὲ
[1]wish, in order that them ye may be zealous of. But [it is] good

ζηλοῦσθαι ἐν καλῷ πάντοτε, καὶ μὴ
to be zealous in a good thing always, and not

μόνον ἐν τῷ παρεῖναί με πρὸς ὑμᾶς,
only in the to be present me[be] with you,
=when I am present

19 τέκνα μου, οὓς πάλιν ὠδίνω μέχρις οὗ
children of me,[for] whom again I travail in birth until

μορφωθῇ Χριστὸς ἐν ὑμῖν· **20** ἤθελον δὲ
[2]is formed [1]Christ in you; and I wished

παρεῖναι πρὸς ὑμᾶς ἄρτι καὶ ἀλλάξαι
to be present with you just now and to change

τὴν φωνήν μου, ὅτι ἀποροῦμαι ἐν ὑμῖν.
the voice of me, because I am perplexed in(about) you.

21 Λέγετέ μοι, οἱ ὑπὸ νόμον θέλοντες
Tell me, the [ones] [3]under [4]law [1]wishing

εἶναι, τὸν νόμον οὐκ ἀκούετε; **22** γέγραπται
[2]to be, [2]the [3]law [1]hear ye not? [2]it has been written

γὰρ ὅτι Ἀβραὰμ δύο υἱοὺς ἔσχεν, ἕνα
[1]for that Abraham two sons had, one

ἐκ τῆς παιδίσκης καὶ ἕνα ἐκ τῆς ἐλευ-
of the maidservant and one of the free

θέρας. **23** ἀλλ᾽ ὁ [μὲν] ἐκ τῆς παιδίσκης
woman. But the [one] indeed of the maidservant

κατὰ σάρκα γεγέννηται, ὁ δὲ ἐκ τῆς
according to flesh has been born, and the [one] of the

ἐλευθέρας διὰ τῆς ἐπαγγελίας. **24** ἅτινά
free woman through the promise. Which things

ἐστιν ἀλληγορούμενα· αὗται γάρ εἰσιν
is(are) being allegorized; for these are

δύο διαθῆκαι, μία μὲν ἀπὸ ὄρους Σινά,
two covenants, one indeed from mount Sina,

εἰς δουλείαν γεννῶσα, ἥτις ἐστὶν Ἁγάρ.
to slavery bringing forth, which is Hagar.

25 τὸ δὲ Ἁγὰρ Σινὰ ὄρος ἐστὶν ἐν
[4]The [1]now [3]Hagar [6]Sina [5]mount [2]is in

τῇ Ἀραβίᾳ· συστοιχεῖ δὲ τῇ νῦν
– Arabia; and corresponds to the now

Ἰερουσαλήμ, δουλεύει γὰρ μετὰ τῶν
Jerusalem, for she serves as a slave with the

τέκνων αὐτῆς. **26** ἡ δὲ ἄνω Ἰερουσαλὴμ
children of her. But the above Jerusalem

ἐλευθέρα ἐστίν, ἥτις ἐστὶν μήτηρ ἡμῶν·
free is, who is mother of us;

27 γέγραπται γάρ· εὐφράνθητι, στεῖρα ἡ
for it has been written: Be thou glad, barren[,] the [one]

οὐ τίκτουσα, ῥῆξον καὶ βόησον, ἡ οὐκ
not bearing, break forth and shout, the [one] not

ὠδίνουσα· ὅτι πολλὰ τὰ τέκνα τῆς ἐρήμου
travailing; because many [are] the children of the desolate

μᾶλλον ἢ τῆς ἐχούσης τὸν ἄνδρα. **28** ὑμεῖς
rather than of the [one] having the husband. ye

δέ, ἀδελφοί, κατὰ Ἰσαὰκ ἐπαγγελίας τέκνα
But, brothers, [4]according to [5]Isaac [3]of promise [2]children

ἐστέ. **29** ἀλλ᾽ ὥσπερ τότε ὁ κατὰ σάρκα
[1]are. But even as then the [one] according to flesh

to me. 16Have I now be-
come your enemy by telling
you the truth?
17Those people are zeal-
ous to win you over, but for
no good. What they want is
to alienate you ⌊from us⌋, so
that you may be zealous for
them. 18It is fine to be zealous, provided the purpose
is good, and to be so always
and not just when I am with
you. 19My dear children,
for whom I am again in the
pains of childbirth until
Christ is formed in you,
20how I wish I could be
with you now and change
my tone, because I am perplexed about you!

Hagar and Sarah

21Tell me, you who want
to be under the law, are you
not aware of what the law
says? 22For it is written that
Abraham had two sons,
one by the slave woman
and the other by the free
woman. 23His son by the
slave woman was born in
the ordinary way; but his
son by the free woman was
born as the result of a
promise.
24These things may be
taken figuratively, for the
women represent two cov-
enants. One covenant is
from Mount Sinai and
bears children who are to
be slaves: This is Hagar.
25Now Hagar stands for
Mount Sinai in Arabia and
corresponds to the present
city of Jerusalem, because
she is in slavery with her
children. 26But the Jerusalem that is above is free,
and she is our mother.
27For it is written:

"Be glad, O barren
woman,
who bears no children;
break forth and cry
aloud,
you who have no labor
pains;
because more are the
children of the
desolate woman
than of her who has a
husband."[p]

28Now you, brothers, like
Isaac, are children of promise. 29At that time the son
born in the ordinary way

[p] 27 Isaiah 54:1

persecuted the child who
was born according to the
Spirit, so it is now also.
30 But what does the scripture say? "Drive out the
slave and her child; for the
child of the slave will not
share the inheritance with
the child of the free woman." 31 So then, friends,[e]
we are children, not of the
slave but of the free woman. 1 For freedom Christ
has set us free. Stand firm,
therefore, and do not submit again to a yoke of slavery.

The Nature of Christian Freedom

2 Listen! I, Paul, am
telling you that if you let
yourselves be circumcised,
Christ will be of no benefit
to you. 3 Once again I testify to every man who lets
himself be circumcised that
he is obliged to obey the entire law. 4 You who want to
be justified by the law have
cut yourselves off from
Christ; you have fallen
away from grace. 5 For
through the Spirit, by faith,
we eagerly wait for the
hope of righteousness.
6 For in Christ Jesus neither
circumcision nor uncir-
cumcision counts for any-
thing; the only thing that
counts is faith working[f]
through love.
7 You were running
well; who prevented you
from obeying the truth?
8 Such persuasion does not
come from the one who
calls you. 9 A little yeast
leavens the whole batch of
dough. 10 I am confident
about you in the Lord that
you will not think other-
wise. But whoever it is that
is confusing you will pay
the penalty. 11 But my
friends,[e] why am I still being persecuted if I am still
preaching circumcision? In
that case the offense of the
cross has been removed.
12 I wish those who unsettle
you would castrate them-
selves!

[f] Or *made effective*

γεννηθεὶς ἐδίωκεν τὸν κατὰ πνεῦμα, οὕτως
born persecuted the [one] [born] according to spirit, so
καὶ νῦν. 30 ἀλλὰ τί λέγει ἡ γραφή;
also now. But what says the scripture?
ἔκβαλε τὴν παιδίσκην καὶ τὸν υἱὸν αὐτῆς·
Cast out the maidservant and the son of her;
οὐ γὰρ μὴ κληρονομήσει ὁ υἱὸς τῆς
for by no means [5]shall inherit [1]the [2]son [3]of the
παιδίσκης μετὰ τοῦ υἱοῦ τῆς ἐλευθέρας.
[4]maidservant with the son of the free woman.
31 διό, ἀδελφοί, οὐκ ἐσμὲν παιδίσκης
Wherefore, brothers, we are not [2]of a maidservant
τέκνα ἀλλὰ τῆς ἐλευθέρας.
[1]children but of the free woman.

5 Τῇ ἐλευθερίᾳ ἡμᾶς Χριστὸς ἠλευθέρωσεν·
For *the* freedom [2]us [1]Christ [3]freed;
στήκετε οὖν καὶ μὴ πάλιν ζυγῷ δουλείας
stand firm therefore and not again with a yoke of slavery
ἐνέχεσθε.
be entangled.
2 Ἴδε ἐγὼ Παῦλος λέγω ὑμῖν ὅτι
Behold[,] I Paul tell you that
ἐὰν περιτέμνησθε Χριστὸς ὑμᾶς οὐδὲν
if ye are circumcised Christ [3]you [2]nothing
ὠφελήσει. 3 μαρτύρομαι δὲ πάλιν παντὶ
[1]will profit. And I testify again to every
ἀνθρώπῳ περιτεμνομένῳ ὅτι ὀφειλέτης ἐστὶν
man being circumcised that [2]a debtor [1]he is
ὅλον τὸν νόμον ποιῆσαι. 4 κατηργήθητε
[4]all [5]the [6]law [3]to do. Ye were discharged
ἀπὸ Χριστοῦ οἵτινες ἐν νόμῳ δικαιοῦσθε,
from Christ who by law are justified,
τῆς χάριτος ἐξεπέσατε. 5 ἡμεῖς γὰρ
***the* [2]grace [1]ye fell from. For we**
πνεύματι ἐκ πίστεως ἐλπίδα δικαιοσύνης
in spirit by faith [the] hope of righteousness
ἀπεκδεχόμεθα. 6 ἐν γὰρ Χριστῷ Ἰησοῦ
eagerly expect. For in Christ Jesus
οὔτε περιτομή τι ἰσχύει οὔτε ἀκροβυστία,
neither circumcision [2]anything [1]avails nor uncircumcision,
ἀλλὰ πίστις δι' ἀγάπης ἐνεργουμένη.
but faith [2]through [3]love [1]operating.
7 Ἐτρέχετε καλῶς· τίς ὑμᾶς ἐνέκοψεν
Ye were running well: who [2]you [1]hindered
ἀληθείᾳ μὴ πείθεσθαι; 8 ἡ πεισμονὴ οὐκ
[5]by truth [3]not [4]to be persuaded? the(this) persuasion not
ἐκ τοῦ καλοῦντος ὑμᾶς. 9 μικρὰ ζύμη
of the [one] calling you. A little leaven
ὅλον τὸ φύραμα ζυμοῖ. 10 ἐγὼ πέποιθα
all the lump leavens. I trust
εἰς ὑμᾶς ἐν κυρίῳ ὅτι οὐδὲν ἄλλο φρο-
as to† you in [the] Lord that [2]nothing [3]other [1]ye
νήσετε· ὁ δὲ ταράσσων ὑμᾶς βαστάσει
will think; but the [one] troubling you shall bear
τὸ κρίμα, ὅστις ἐὰν ᾖ. 11 Ἐγὼ δέ,
the judgment, whoever he may be. [1]But [4]I,
ἀδελφοί, εἰ περιτομὴν ἔτι κηρύσσω, τί
[2]brothers, [3]if [7]circumcision [5]still [6]proclaim, why
ἔτι διώκομαι; ἄρα κατήργηται τὸ
still am I being persecuted? then has been annulled the
σκάνδαλον τοῦ σταυροῦ. 12 Ὄφελον καὶ
offence of the cross. I would that indeed
ἀποκόψονται οἱ ἀναστατοῦντες ὑμᾶς.
[4]will(might) cut themselves off [1]the [ones] [2]unsettling [3]you.

persecuted the son born by
the power of the Spirit. It is
the same now. 30 But what
does the Scripture say?
"Get rid of the slave woman and her son, for the
slave woman's son will
never share in the inheritance with the free wom-
an's son."[q] 31 Therefore,
brothers, we are not children of the slave woman,
but of the free woman.

Chapter 5

Freedom in Christ

IT is for freedom that
Christ has set us free.
Stand firm, then, and do
not let yourselves be burdened again by a yoke of
slavery.
2 Mark my words! I, Paul,
tell you that if you let yourselves be circumcised,
Christ will be of no value to
you at all. 3 Again I declare
to every man who lets himself be circumcised that he
is obligated to obey the
whole law. 4 You who are
trying to be justified by law
have been alienated from
Christ; you have fallen
away from grace. 5 But by
faith we eagerly await
through the Spirit the righteousness for which we
hope. 6 For in Christ Jesus
neither circumcision nor
uncircumcision has any
value. The only thing that
counts is faith expressing
itself through love.
7 You were running a good
race. Who cut in on you
and kept you from obeying
the truth? 8 That kind of persuasion does not come
from the one who calls you.
9 "A little yeast works
through the whole batch of
dough." 10 I am confident in
the Lord that you will take
no other view. The one
who is throwing you into
confusion will pay the penalty, whoever he may be.
11 Brothers, if I am still
preaching circumcision,
why am I still being persecuted? In that case the offense of the cross has been
abolished. 12 As for those
agitators, I wish they
would go the whole way
and emasculate them-
selves!

[q] 30 Gen. 21:10

13 For you were called to freedom, brothers and sisters;[e] only do not use your freedom as an opportunity for self-indulgence,[g] but through love become slaves to one another. 14 For the whole law is summed up in a single commandment, "You shall love your neighbor as yourself." 15 If, however, you bite and devour one another, take care that you are not consumed by one another.

The Works of the Flesh

16 Live by the Spirit, I say, and do not gratify the desires of the flesh. 17 For what the flesh desires is opposed to the Spirit, and what the Spirit desires is opposed to the flesh; for these are opposed to each other, to prevent you from doing what you want. 18 But if you are led by the Spirit, you are not subject to the law. 19 Now the works of the flesh are obvious: fornication, impurity, licentiousness, 20 idolatry, sorcery, enmities, strife, jealousy, anger, quarrels, dissensions, factions, 21 envy,[h] drunkenness, carousing, and things like these. I am warning you, as I warned you before: those who do such things will not inherit the kingdom of God.

The Fruit of the Spirit

22 By contrast, the fruit of the Spirit is love, joy, peace, patience, kindness, generosity, faithfulness, 23 gentleness, and self-control. There is no law against such things. 24 And those who belong to Christ Jesus have crucified the flesh with its passions and desires. 25 If we live by the Spirit, let us also be guided by the Spirit. 26 Let us not become conceited, competing against one another, envying one another.

[g] Gk *the flesh*
[h] Other ancient authorities add *murder*

13 Ὑμεῖς γὰρ ἐπ' ἐλευθερίᾳ ἐκλήθητε,
For ye for freedom were called,

ἀδελφοί· μόνον μὴ τὴν ἐλευθερίαν εἰς
brothers; only [use] not the freedom for

ἀφορμὴν τῇ σαρκί, ἀλλὰ διὰ τῆς ἀγάπης
advantage to the flesh, but through – love

δουλεύετε ἀλλήλοις. **14** ὁ γὰρ πᾶς νόμος
serve ye as slaves one another. For the whole law

ἐν ἑνὶ λόγῳ πεπλήρωται, ἐν τῷ· ἀγα-
in one word has been summed up, in the [word]: Thou

πήσεις τὸν πλησίον σου ὡς σεαυτόν.
shalt love the neighbour of thee as thyself.

15 εἰ δὲ ἀλλήλους δάκνετε καὶ κατεσθίετε,
But if [4]one another [1]ye bite [2]and [3]*ye* devour,

βλέπετε μὴ ὑπ' ἀλλήλων ἀναλωθῆτε.
see lest by one another ye are destroyed.

16 Λέγω δέ, πνεύματι περιπατεῖτε καὶ
Now I say, in spirit walk ye and

ἐπιθυμίαν σαρκὸς οὐ μὴ τελέσητε. **17** ἡ
[the] lust of [the] flesh by no means ye will perform. the

γὰρ σὰρξ ἐπιθυμεῖ κατὰ τοῦ πνεύματος,
For flesh lusts against the spirit,

τὸ δὲ πνεῦμα κατὰ τῆς σαρκός, ταῦτα
and the spirit against the flesh, [2]these

γὰρ ἀλλήλοις ἀντίκειται, ἵνα μὴ ἃ ἐὰν
[1]for [4]each other [3]oppose*s*, lest whatever things

θέλητε ταῦτα ποιῆτε. **18** εἰ δὲ πνεύματι
ye wish these ye do. But if by [the] Spirit

ἄγεσθε, οὐκ ἐστὲ ὑπὸ νόμον. **19** φανερὰ δέ
ye are led, ye are not under law. Now [6]manifest

ἐστιν τὰ ἔργα τῆς σαρκός, ἅτινά ἐστιν
[5]is(are) [1]the [2]works [3]of the [4]flesh, which is(are)

πορνεία, ἀκαθαρσία, ἀσέλγεια, **20** εἰδωλο-
fornication, uncleanness, lewdness, idola-

λατρία, φαρμακεία, ἔχθραι, ἔρις, ζῆλος,
try, sorcery, enmities, strife, jealousy,

θυμοί, ἐριθεῖαι, διχοστασίαι, αἱρέσεις,
angers, rivalries, divisions, sects,

21 φθόνοι, μέθαι, κῶμοι, καὶ τὰ ὅμοια
envyings, drunkennesses, revellings, and – like things

τούτοις, ἃ προλέγω ὑμῖν καθὼς προεῖπον,
to these, which I tell [2]beforehand [1]you as I previously said,

ὅτι οἱ τὰ τοιαῦτα πράσσοντες βασιλείαν
that the [ones] – [2]such things [1]practising [4][the] kingdom

θεοῦ οὐ κληρονομήσουσιν. **22** ὁ δὲ καρπὸς
[5]of God [3]will not inherit. But the fruit

τοῦ πνεύματός ἐστιν ἀγάπη, χαρά, εἰρήνη,
of the Spirit is love, joy, peace,

μακροθυμία, χρηστότης, ἀγαθωσύνη, πίστις,
longsuffering, kindness, goodness, faithfulness,

23 πραΰτης, ἐγκράτεια· κατὰ τῶν τοιούτων
meekness, self-control; against – such things

οὐκ ἔστιν νόμος. **24** οἱ δὲ τοῦ Χριστοῦ
there is no law. Now the ones – of Christ

Ἰησοῦ τὴν σάρκα ἐσταύρωσαν σὺν τοῖς
Jesus [2]the [3]flesh [1]crucified with the(its)

παθήμασιν καὶ ταῖς ἐπιθυμίαις. **25** Εἰ
passions and the(its) lusts. If

ζῶμεν πνεύματι, πνεύματι καὶ στοιχῶμεν.
we live in [the] Spirit, in [the] Spirit also let us walk.

26 μὴ γινώμεθα κενόδοξοι, ἀλλήλους
Let us not become vainglorious, one another

προκαλούμενοι, ἀλλήλοις φθονοῦντες.
provoking, one another envying.

13 You, my brothers, were called to be free. But do not use your freedom to indulge the sinful nature[r]; rather, serve one another in love. 14 The entire law is summed up in a single command: "Love your neighbor as yourself."[s] 15 If you keep on biting and devouring each other, watch out or you will be destroyed by each other.

Life by the Spirit

16 So I say, live by the Spirit, and you will not gratify the desires of the sinful nature. 17 For the sinful nature desires what is contrary to the Spirit, and the Spirit what is contrary to the sinful nature. They are in conflict with each other, so that you do not do what you want. 18 But if you are led by the Spirit, you are not under law.

19 The acts of the sinful nature are obvious: sexual immorality, impurity and debauchery; 20 idolatry and witchcraft; hatred, discord, jealousy, fits of rage, selfish ambition, dissensions, factions 21 and envy; drunkenness, orgies, and the like. I warn you, as I did before, that those who live like this will not inherit the kingdom of God.

22 But the fruit of the Spirit is love, joy, peace, patience, kindness, goodness, faithfulness, 23 gentleness and self-control. Against such things there is no law. 24 Those who belong to Christ Jesus have crucified the sinful nature with its passions and desires. 25 Since we live by the Spirit, let us keep in step with the Spirit. 26 Let us not become conceited, provoking and envying each other.

[r] *13* Or *the flesh*; also in verses 16, 17, 19 and 24
[s] *14* Lev. 19:18

Chapter 6

Bear One Another's Burdens

MY friends,[i] if anyone is detected in a transgression, you who have received the Spirit should restore such a one in a spirit of gentleness. Take care that you yourselves are not tempted. 2 Bear one another's burdens, and in this way you will fulfill[j] the law of Christ. 3 For if those who are nothing think they are something, they deceive themselves. 4 All must test their own work; then that work, rather than their neighbor's work, will become a cause for pride. 5 For all must carry their own loads.

6 Those who are taught the word must share in all good things with their teacher.

7 Do not be deceived; God is not mocked, for you reap whatever you sow. 8 If you sow to your own flesh, you will reap corruption from the flesh; but if you sow to the Spirit, you will reap eternal life from the Spirit. 9 So let us not grow weary in doing what is right, for we will reap at harvest-time, if we do not give up. 10 So then, whenever we have an opportunity, let us work for the good of all, and especially for those of the family of faith.

Final Admonitions and Benediction

11 See what large letters I make when I am writing in my own hand! 12 It is those who want to make a good showing in the flesh that try to compel you to be circumcised—only that they may not be persecuted for the cross of Christ. 13 Even the circumcised do not themselves obey the law, but they want you to

[i] Gk *Brothers*
[j] Other ancient authorities read *in this way fulfill*

6 Ἀδελφοί, ἐὰν καὶ προλημφθῇ ἄνθρω-
Brothers, if indeed [2]is overtaken [1]a
πος ἔν τινι παραπτώματι, ὑμεῖς οἱ
man in some trespass, ye the
πνευματικοὶ καταρτίζετε τὸν τοιοῦτον ἐν
spiritual [ones] restore – such a one in
πνεύματι πραΰτητος, σκοπῶν σεαυτόν, μὴ
a spirit of meekness, considering thyself, lest
καὶ σὺ πειρασθῇς. **2** Ἀλλήλων τὰ βάρη
also thou art tempted. Of one another the loads
βαστάζετε, καὶ οὕτως ἀναπληρώσετε τὸν
bear ye, and so ye will fulfil the
νόμον τοῦ Χριστοῦ. **3** εἰ γὰρ δοκεῖ
law – of Christ. For if [2]thinks
τις εἶναί τι μηδὲν ὤν, φρεναπατᾷ ἑαυτόν.
[1]anyone [3]to be [4]something [5]nothing [6]being, he deceives himself.
4 τὸ δὲ ἔργον ἑαυτοῦ δοκιμαζέτω ἕκαστος,
But the work of himself [1]let [3]prove [2]each man,
καὶ τότε εἰς ἑαυτὸν μόνον τὸ καύχημα
and then in himself alone the boast
ἕξει καὶ οὐκ εἰς τὸν ἕτερον· **5** ἕκαστος
he will have and not in the other man; [2]each man
γὰρ τὸ ἴδιον φορτίον βαστάσει. **6** Κοινωνείτω δὲ
[1]for the(his) own burden will bear. And [5]let him share
ὁ κατηχούμενος τὸν λόγον τῷ κατη-
[1]the [2]being instructed [in] [3]the [4]word [6]with the [one] in- [one]
χοῦντι ἐν πᾶσιν ἀγαθοῖς. **7** Μὴ πλανᾶσθε,
structing in all good things. Be ye not led astray,
θεὸς οὐ μυκτηρίζεται. ὃ γὰρ ἐὰν σπείρῃ
God is not mocked. For whatever [2]may sow
ἄνθρωπος, τοῦτο καὶ θερίσει· **8** ὅτι ὁ
[1]a man, this also he will reap; because the
σπείρων εἰς τὴν σάρκα ἑαυτοῦ ἐκ τῆς
[one] sowing to the flesh of himself of the
σαρκὸς θερίσει φθοράν, ὁ δὲ σπείρων
flesh will reap corruption, but the [one] sowing
εἰς τὸ πνεῦμα ἐκ τοῦ πνεύματος θερίσει
to the spirit of the Spirit will reap
ζωὴν αἰώνιον. **9** τὸ δὲ καλὸν ποιοῦντες
life eternal. And [3]the [4]good [1]doing
μὴ ἐγκακῶμεν· καιρῷ γὰρ ἰδίῳ
let us not lose heart; for in its own time
θερίσομεν μὴ ἐκλυόμενοι. **10** Ἄρα οὖν
we shall reap not failing. Then therefore
ὡς καιρὸν ἔχομεν, ἐργαζώμεθα τὸ ἀγαθὸν
as [2]time [1]we have, let us do the good
πρὸς πάντας, μάλιστα δὲ πρὸς τοὺς
to all men, and most of all to the
οἰκείους τῆς πίστεως.
members of the family of the faith.

11 Ἴδετε πηλίκοις ὑμῖν γράμμασιν
Ye see in how large [2]to you [1]letters
ἔγραψα τῇ ἐμῇ χειρί. **12** Ὅσοι θέλουσιν
[3]I wrote – with my hand. As many as wish
εὐπροσωπῆσαι ἐν σαρκί, οὗτοι ἀναγκάζουσιν
to look well in [the] flesh, these compel
ὑμᾶς περιτέμνεσθαι, μόνον ἵνα τῷ
you to be circumcised, only in order that [3]for the
σταυρῷ τοῦ Χριστοῦ [Ἰησοῦ] μὴ
[4]cross – [5]of Christ [6]Jesus [1]not
διώκωνται. **13** οὐδὲ γὰρ οἱ περιτεμνόμενοι
[2]they are persecuted. For [3]not [1]the [ones] [2]being circumcised
αὐτοὶ νόμον φυλάσσουσιν, ἀλλὰ θέλουσιν
[4]themselves [6]law [5]keep, but they wish

Chapter 6

Doing Good to All

BROTHERS, if someone is caught in a sin, you who are spiritual should restore him gently. But watch yourself, or you also may be tempted. 2 Carry each other's burdens, and in this way you will fulfill the law of Christ. 3 If anyone thinks he is something when he is nothing, he deceives himself. 4 Each one should test his own actions. Then he can take pride in himself, without comparing himself to somebody else, 5 for each one should carry his own load.

6 Anyone who receives instruction in the word must share all good things with his instructor.

7 Do not be deceived: God cannot be mocked. A man reaps what he sows. 8 The one who sows to please his sinful nature, from that nature[t] will reap destruction; the one who sows to please the Spirit, from the Spirit will reap eternal life. 9 Let us not become weary in doing good, for at the proper time we will reap a harvest if we do not give up. 10 Therefore, as we have opportunity, let us do good to all people, especially to those who belong to the family of believers.

Not Circumcision but a New Creation

11 See what large letters I use as I write to you with my own hand!

12 Those who want to make a good impression outwardly are trying to compel you to be circumcised. The only reason they do this is to avoid being persecuted for the cross of Christ. 13 Not even those who are circumcised obey the law, yet they want you

[t] 8 Or *his flesh, from the flesh*

be circumcised so that they
may boast about your
flesh. 14 May I never boast
of anything except the
cross of our Lord Jesus
Christ, by which[k] the
world has been crucified to
me, and I to the world.
15 For[l] neither circumcision nor uncircumcision is
anything; but a new cre-
ation is everything! 16 As
for those who will follow
this rule—peace be upon
them, and mercy, and upon
the Israel of God.
17 From now on, let no
one make trouble for me;
for I carry the marks of
Jesus branded on my body.
18 May the grace of our
Lord Jesus Christ be with
your spirit, brothers and
sisters.[m] Amen.

ὑμᾶς περιτέμνεσθαι ἵνα ἐν τῇ ὑμετέρᾳ
you to be circumcised in order that [2]in – [3]your

σαρκὶ καυχήσωνται. **14** ἐμοὶ δὲ μὴ γένοιτο
[4]flesh [1]they may boast. But to me may it not be

καυχᾶσθαι εἰ μὴ ἐν τῷ σταυρῷ τοῦ
to boast except in the cross of the

κυρίου ἡμῶν Ἰησοῦ Χριστοῦ, δι' οὗ
Lord of us Jesus Christ, through whom

ἐμοὶ κόσμος ἐσταύρωται κἀγὼ κόσμῳ.
to me [the] world has been crucified and I to [the] world.

15 οὔτε γὰρ περιτομή τί ἐστιν οὔτε
For neither circumcision [2]anything [1]is nor

ἀκροβυστία, ἀλλὰ καινὴ κτίσις. **16** καὶ
uncircumcision, but a new creation. And

ὅσοι τῷ κανόνι τούτῳ στοιχήσουσιν,
as many as by this rule will walk,

εἰρήνη ἐπ' αὐτοὺς καὶ ἔλεος, καὶ ἐπὶ τὸν
peace on them and mercy, and on the

Ἰσραὴλ τοῦ θεοῦ.
Israel – of God.

17 Τοῦ λοιποῦ κόπους μοι μηδεὶς
For the rest [5]troubles [4]me [2]no one

παρεχέτω· ἐγὼ γὰρ τὰ στίγματα τοῦ
[1]let [3]cause; for [1]I [3]the [4]brands –

Ἰησοῦ ἐν τῷ σώματί μου βαστάζω.
[5]of Jesus [6]in [7]the [8]body [9]of me [2]bear.

18 Ἡ χάρις τοῦ κυρίου ἡμῶν Ἰησοῦ
The grace of the Lord of us Jesus

Χριστοῦ μετὰ τοῦ πνεύματος ὑμῶν,
Christ with the spirit of you,

ἀδελφοί· ἀμήν.
brothers: Amen.

to be circumcised that they
may boast about your
flesh. 14May I never boast
except in the cross of our
Lord Jesus Christ, through
which[u] the world has been
crucified to me, and I to the
world. 15Neither circumcision nor uncircumcision
means anything; what
counts is a new creation.
16Peace and mercy to all
who follow this rule, even
to the Israel of God.
17Finally, let no one
cause me trouble, for I bear
on my body the marks of
Jesus.
18The grace of our Lord
Jesus Christ be with your
spirit, brothers. Amen.

The Letter of Paul to the

Ephesians

Chapter 1

Salutation

PAUL, an apostle of
Christ Jesus by the will
of God,
To the saints who are in
Ephesus and are faithful[a]
in Christ Jesus:
2 Grace to you and
peace from God our Father
and the Lord Jesus Christ.

Spiritual Blessings in Christ

3 Blessed be the God
and Father of our Lord
Jesus Christ, who has
blessed us in Christ with
every spiritual blessing in
the heavenly places, 4 just
as he chose us in Christ[b]
before the foundation of
the world to be holy and
blameless before him in
love. 5 He destined us for

ΠΡΟΣ ΕΦΕΣΙΟΥΣ

To Ephesians

1 Παῦλος ἀπόστολος Χριστοῦ Ἰησοῦ διὰ
Paul an apostle of Christ Jesus through

θελήματος θεοῦ τοῖς ἁγίοις τοῖς οὖσιν
[the] will of God to the saints – being

[ἐν Ἐφέσῳ] καὶ πιστοῖς ἐν Χριστῷ
in Ephesus and faithful in Christ

Ἰησοῦ· **2** χάρις ὑμῖν καὶ εἰρήνη ἀπὸ
Jesus: Grace to you and peace from

θεοῦ πατρὸς ἡμῶν καὶ κυρίου Ἰησοῦ
God Father of us and Lord Jesus

Χριστοῦ.
Christ.

3 Εὐλογητὸς ὁ θεὸς καὶ πατὴρ τοῦ
Blessed the God and Father of the

κυρίου ἡμῶν Ἰησοῦ Χριστοῦ, ὁ εὐλογήσας
Lord of us Jesus Christ, the [one] having blessed

ἡμᾶς ἐν πάσῃ εὐλογίᾳ πνευματικῇ ἐν
us with every blessing spiritual in

τοῖς ἐπουρανίοις ἐν Χριστῷ, **4** καθὼς
the heavenlies in Christ, as

ἐξελέξατο ἡμᾶς ἐν αὐτῷ πρὸ καταβολῆς
he chose us in him before [the] foundation

κόσμου, εἶναι ἡμᾶς ἁγίους καὶ ἀμώμους
of [the] world, to be us holy and unblemished[b]

=that we should be . . .

κατενώπιον αὐτοῦ, ἐν ἀγάπῃ **5** προορίσας
before him, in love predestinating

Ephesians

Chapter 1

PAUL, an apostle of
Christ Jesus by the will
of God,
To the saints in Ephe-
sus,[a] the faithful[b] in Christ
Jesus:
2Grace and peace to you
from God our Father and
the Lord Jesus Christ.

Spiritual Blessings in Christ

3Praise be to the God and
Father of our Lord Jesus
Christ, who has blessed us
in the heavenly realms with
every spiritual blessing in
Christ. 4For he chose us in
him before the creation of
the world to be holy and
blameless in his sight. In
love 5he[c] predestined us to

[k] Or *through whom*
[l] Other ancient authorities add *in Christ Jesus*
[m] Gk *brothers*
[a] Other ancient authorities lack *in Ephesus*, reading *saints who are also faithful*
[b] Gk *in him*

[u] *14* Or *whom*
[a] *1* Some early manuscripts do not have *in Ephesus*.
[b] *1* Or *believers who are*
[c] *4,5* Or *sight in love. 5He*

adoption as his children
through Jesus Christ, ac-
cording to the good plea-
sure of his will, 6to the
praise of his glorious grace
that he freely bestowed on
us in the Beloved. 7In him
we have redemption
through his blood, the forgiveness of our trespasses,
according to the riches of
his grace 8that he lavished
on us. With all wisdom and
insight 9he has made
known to us the mystery of
his will, according to his
good pleasure that he set
forth in Christ, 10as a plan
for the fullness of time, to
gather up all things in him,
things in heaven and things
on earth. 11In Christ we
have also obtained an in-
heritance,[c] having been
destined according to the
purpose of him who accom-
plishes all things according
to his counsel and will, 12so
that we, who were the first
to set our hope on Christ,
might live for the praise of
his glory. 13In him you
also, when you had heard
the word of truth, the gospel of your salvation, and
had believed in him, were
marked with the seal of the
promised Holy Spirit;
14this[d] is the pledge of our
inheritance toward re-
demption as God's own
people, to the praise of his
glory.

Paul's Prayer

15 I have heard of your
faith in the Lord Jesus and
your love[e] toward all the
saints, and for this reason

[c] Or *been made a heritage*
[d] Other ancient authorities read *who*
[e] Other ancient authorities lack *and your love*

ἡμᾶς εἰς υἱοθεσίαν διὰ Ἰησοῦ Χριστοῦ
us to adoption of sons through Jesus Christ

εἰς αὐτόν, κατὰ τὴν εὐδοκίαν τοῦ
to him[self], according to the good pleasure of the

θελήματος αὐτοῦ, **6** εἰς ἔπαινον δόξης
will of him, to [the] praise of [the] glory

τῆς χάριτος αὐτοῦ, ἧς ἐχαρίτωσεν ἡμᾶς
of the grace of him, of(with) which he favoured us

ἐν τῷ ἠγαπημένῳ, **7** ἐν ᾧ ἔχομεν τὴν
in the [one] *having been* loved, in whom we have the

ἀπολύτρωσιν διὰ τοῦ αἵματος αὐτοῦ, τὴν
redemption through the blood of him, the

ἄφεσιν τῶν παραπτωμάτων, κατὰ τὸ
forgiveness – of trespasses, according to the

πλοῦτος τῆς χάριτος αὐτοῦ, **8** ἧς ἐπερίσ-
riches of the grace of him, which he made to

σευσεν εἰς ἡμᾶς ἐν πάσῃ σοφίᾳ καὶ
abound to us in all wisdom and

φρονήσει **9** γνωρίσας ἡμῖν τὸ μυστήριον
intelligence making known to us the mystery

τοῦ θελήματος αὐτοῦ, κατὰ τὴν εὐδοκίαν
of the will of him, according to the good pleasure

αὐτοῦ, ἣν προέθετο ἐν αὐτῷ **10** εἰς
of him, which he purposed in him[self] for

οἰκονομίαν τοῦ πληρώματος τῶν καιρῶν,
a stewardship of the fulness of the times,

ἀνακεφαλαιώσασθαι τὰ πάντα ἐν τῷ
to head up – all things in –

Χριστῷ, τὰ ἐπὶ τοῖς οὐρανοῖς καὶ τὰ
Christ, the things on(in) *the* heavens and the things

ἐπὶ τῆς γῆς· ἐν αὐτῷ, **11** ἐν ᾧ καὶ
on the earth; in him, in whom also

ἐκληρώθημεν προορισθέντες κατὰ πρόθεσιν
we were chosen as [his] inheritance being predestinated according to [the] purpose

τοῦ τὰ πάντα ἐνεργοῦντος κατὰ τὴν
of the [one] – [2]all things [1]operating according to the

βουλὴν τοῦ θελήματος αὐτοῦ, **12** εἰς τὸ
counsel of the will of him, for *the*

εἶναι ἡμᾶς εἰς ἔπαινον δόξης αὐτοῦ
to be us[b] to [the] praise of [the] glory of him
=that we should be

τοὺς προηλπικότας ἐν τῷ Χριστῷ· **13** ἐν
the [ones] having previously hoped in – Christ; in

ᾧ καὶ ὑμεῖς, ἀκούσαντες τὸν λόγον
whom also ye, hearing the word

τῆς ἀληθείας, τὸ εὐαγγέλιον τῆς σωτηρίας
– of truth, the gospel of the salvation

ὑμῶν, ἐν ᾧ καὶ πιστεύσαντες ἐσφραγίσθητε
of you, in whom also believing ye were sealed

τῷ πνεύματι τῆς ἐπαγγελίας τῷ ἁγίῳ,
with [1]the [3]Spirit – [4]of promise – [2]holy,

14 ὅς ἐστιν ἀρραβὼν τῆς κληρονομίας
who is an earnest of the inheritance

ἡμῶν, εἰς ἀπολύτρωσιν τῆς περιποιήσεως,
of us, till [the] redemption of the possession,

εἰς ἔπαινον τῆς δόξης αὐτοῦ.
to [the] praise of the glory of him.

15 Διὰ τοῦτο κἀγώ, ἀκούσας τὴν καθ'
Therefore I also, hearing the [2]among

ὑμᾶς πίστιν ἐν τῷ κυρίῳ Ἰησοῦ καὶ
[3]you [1]faith in the Lord Jesus and

τὴν ἀγάπην τὴν εἰς πάντας τοὺς ἁγίους,
the love – to all the saints,

be adopted as his sons
through Jesus Christ, in accordance with his pleasure
and will— 6to the praise of
his glorious grace, which
he has freely given us in the
One he loves. 7In him we
have redemption through
his blood, the forgiveness
of sins, in accordance with
the riches of God's grace
8that he lavished on us with
all wisdom and understanding. 9And he[d] made known
to us the mystery of his will
according to his good pleasure, which he purposed in
Christ, 10to be put into effect when the times will
have reached their fulfillment—to bring all things in
heaven and on earth to-
gether under one head,
even Christ.
11In him we were also
chosen,[e] having been predestined according to the
plan of him who works out
everything in conformity
with the purpose of his will,
12in order that we, who
were the first to hope in
Christ, might be for the
praise of his glory. 13And
you also were included in
Christ when you heard the
word of truth, the gospel of
your salvation. Having believed, you were marked in
him with a seal, the promised Holy Spirit, 14who is a
deposit guaranteeing our
inheritance until the re-
demption of those who are
God's possession—to the
praise of his glory.

Thanksgiving and Prayer

15For this reason, ever
since I heard about your
faith in the Lord Jesus and
your love for all the saints,

[d] 8,9 Or *us. With all wisdom and understanding, 9he*
[e] 11 Or *were made heirs*

16 I do not cease to give
thanks for you as I remember you in my prayers. 17 I
pray that the God of our
Lord Jesus Christ, the Father of glory, may give you
a spirit of wisdom and revelation as you come to know
him, 18 so that, with the
eyes of your heart enlightened, you may know what
is the hope to which he has
called you, what are the
riches of his glorious inheritance among the saints,
19 and what is the immea-
surable greatness of his
power for us who believe,
according to the working of
his great power. 20 God[f]
put this power to work in
Christ when he raised him
from the dead and seated
him at his right hand in the
heavenly places, 21 far
above all rule and authority
and power and dominion,
and above every name that
is named, not only in this
age but also in the age to
come. 22 And he has put all
things under his feet and
has made him the head over
all things for the church,
23 which is his body, the
fullness of him who fills all
in all.

16 οὐ παύομαι εὐχαριστῶν ὑπὲρ ὑμῶν
do not cease giving thanks on behalf of you
μνείαν ποιούμενος ἐπὶ τῶν προσευχῶν
mention making on(in) the prayers
μου, **17** ἵνα ὁ θεὸς τοῦ κυρίου ἡμῶν
of me, *in order* that the God of the Lord of us
Ἰησοῦ Χριστοῦ, ὁ πατὴρ τῆς δόξης,
Jesus Christ, the Father – of glory,
δῴη ὑμῖν πνεῦμα σοφίας καὶ ἀποκαλύψεως
may give to you a spirit of wisdom and of revelation
ἐν ἐπιγνώσει αὐτοῦ, **18** πεφωτισμένους τοὺς
in a full knowledge of him, having been enlightened the
ὀφθαλμοὺς τῆς καρδίας [ὑμῶν,] εἰς τὸ
eyes of the heart of you, for *the*
εἰδέναι ὑμᾶς τίς ἐστιν ἡ ἐλπὶς τῆς
to know you[b] what is the hope of the
=that ye should know
κλήσεως αὐτοῦ, τίς ὁ πλοῦτος τῆς δόξης
calling of him, what the riches of the glory
τῆς κληρονομίας αὐτοῦ ἐν τοῖς ἁγίοις,
of the inheritance of him in the saints,
19 καὶ τί τὸ ὑπερβάλλον μέγεθος τῆς
and what the excelling greatness of the
δυνάμεως αὐτοῦ εἰς ἡμᾶς τοὺς πιστεύοντας
power of him toward us the [ones] believing
κατὰ τὴν ἐνέργειαν τοῦ κράτους τῆς
according to the operation of the might of the
ἰσχύος αὐτοῦ, **20** ἣν ἐνήργηκεν ἐν τῷ
strength of him, which he has operated in –
Χριστῷ ἐγείρας αὐτὸν ἐκ νεκρῶν, καὶ
Christ raising him from [the] dead, and
καθίσας ἐν δεξιᾷ αὐτοῦ ἐν τοῖς ἐπου-
seating [him] at [the] right [hand] of him in the heaven-
ρανίοις **21** ὑπεράνω πάσης ἀρχῆς καὶ
lies far above all rule and
ἐξουσίας καὶ δυνάμεως καὶ κυριότητος
authority and power and lordship
καὶ παντὸς ὀνόματος ὀνομαζομένου οὐ
and every name being named not
μόνον ἐν τῷ αἰῶνι τούτῳ ἀλλὰ καὶ
only in this age but also
ἐν τῷ μέλλοντι· **22** καὶ πάντα ὑπέταξεν
in the coming; and all things subjected
ὑπὸ τοὺς πόδας αὐτοῦ, καὶ αὐτὸν ἔδωκεν
under the feet of him, and [2]him [1]gave
κεφαλὴν ὑπὲρ πάντα τῇ ἐκκλησίᾳ, **23** ἥτις
[to be] head over all things to the church, which
ἐστὶν τὸ σῶμα αὐτοῦ, τὸ πλήρωμα
is the body of him, the fulness
τοῦ τὰ πάντα ἐν πᾶσιν πληρουμένου.
of the [one] – [2]all things [3]with [4]all things [1]filling.

16 I have not stopped giving
thanks for you, remember-
ing you in my prayers. 17 I
keep asking that the God of
our Lord Jesus Christ, the
glorious Father, may give
you the Spirit[f] of wisdom
and revelation, so that you
may know him better. 18 I
pray also that the eyes of
your heart may be enlightened in order that you may
know the hope to which he
has called you, the riches of
his glorious inheritance in
the saints, 19 and his incom-
parably great power for us
who believe. That power is
like the working of his
mighty strength, 20 which
he exerted in Christ when
he raised him from the dead
and seated him at his right
hand in the heavenly
realms, 21 far above all rule
and authority, power and
dominion, and every title
that can be given, not only
in the present age but also
in the one to come. 22 And
God placed all things under
his feet and appointed him
to be head over everything
for the church, 23 which is
his body, the fullness of
him who fills everything in
every way.

Chapter 2

From Death to Life

YOU were dead through
the trespasses and
sins 2 in which you once
lived, following the course
of this world, following the
ruler of the power of the
air, the spirit that is now at
work among those who are
disobedient. 3 All of us

2 Καὶ ὑμᾶς ὄντας νεκροὺς τοῖς παραπτώ-
And you being dead in the tres-
μασιν καὶ ταῖς ἁμαρτίαις ὑμῶν, **2** ἐν
passes and in the sins of you, in
αἷς ποτε περιεπατήσατε κατὰ τὸν αἰῶνα
which then ye walked according to the age
τοῦ κόσμου τούτου, κατὰ τὸν ἄρχοντα
of this world, according to the ruler
τῆς ἐξουσίας τοῦ ἀέρος, τοῦ πνεύματος
of the authority of the air, of the spirit
τοῦ νῦν ἐνεργοῦντος ἐν τοῖς υἱοῖς τῆς
– now operating in the sons –
ἀπειθείας· **3** ἐν οἷς καὶ ἡμεῖς πάντες
of disobedience; among whom also we all

Chapter 2

Made Alive in Christ

AS for you, you were
dead in your trans-
gressions and sins, 2 in
which you used to live
when you followed the
ways of this world and of
the ruler of the kingdom of
the air, the spirit who is
now at work in those who
are disobedient. 3 All of us

[f] Gk *He*

[f] 17 Or *a spirit*

once lived among them in
the passions of our flesh,
following the desires of
flesh and senses, and we
were by nature children of
wrath, like everyone else.
4But God, who is rich in
mercy, out of the great love
with which he loved us
5even when we were dead
through our trespasses,
made us alive together with
Christ[g]—by grace you
have been saved— 6and
raised us up with him and
seated us with him in the
heavenly places in Christ
Jesus, 7so that in the ages
to come he might show the
immeasurable riches of his
grace in kindness toward us
in Christ Jesus. 8For by
grace you have been saved
through faith, and this is
not your own doing; it is the
gift of God— 9not the re-
sult of works, so that no
one may boast. 10For we
are what he has made us,
created in Christ Jesus for
good works, which God
prepared beforehand to be
our way of life.

One in Christ

11 So then, remember
that at one time you Gen-
tiles by birth,[h] called "the
uncircumcision" by those
who are called "the
circumcision"—a physical
circumcision made in the
flesh by human hands—
12remember that you were
at that time without Christ,
being aliens from the commonwealth of Israel, and
strangers to the covenants
of promise, having no hope
and without God in the
world. 13But now in Christ
Jesus you who once were
far off have been brought
near by the blood of Christ.

ἀνεστράφημέν ποτε ἐν ταῖς ἐπιθυμίαις
conducted ourselves then in the lusts

τῆς σαρκὸς ἡμῶν, ποιοῦντες τὰ θελήματα
of the flesh of us, doing the wishes

τῆς σαρκὸς καὶ τῶν διανοιῶν, καὶ
of the flesh and of the understandings, and

ἤμεθα τέκνα φύσει ὀργῆς ὡς καὶ οἱ
were ²children ¹by nature of wrath as also the

λοιποί· **4** ὁ δὲ θεὸς πλούσιος ὢν ἐν
rest; – but God ²rich ¹being in

ἐλέει, διὰ τὴν πολλὴν ἀγάπην αὐτοῦ
mercy, because of the much love of his

ἣν ἠγάπησεν ἡμᾶς, **5** καὶ ὄντας ἡμᾶς
[with] which he loved us, even being =when we were us

νεκροὺς τοῖς παραπτώμασιν συνεζωοποίησεν
dead – in trespasses quickened [us] with

τῷ Χριστῷ, — χάριτί ἐστε σεσῳσμένοι,
– Christ, (by grace ye are *having been* saved,)

— **6** καὶ συνήγειρεν καὶ συνεκάθισεν ἐν
and raised [us] with and seated [us] with in

τοῖς ἐπουρανίοις ἐν Χριστῷ Ἰησοῦ, **7** ἵνα
the heavenlies in Christ Jesus, in order that

ἐνδείξηται ἐν τοῖς αἰῶσιν τοῖς ἐπερχομένοις
he might show forth in the ages – coming on

τὸ ὑπερβάλλον πλοῦτος τῆς χάριτος αὐτοῦ
the excelling riches of the grace of him

ἐν χρηστότητι ἐφ' ἡμᾶς ἐν Χριστῷ
in kindness toward us in Christ

Ἰησοῦ. **8** τῇ γὰρ χάριτί ἐστε σεσῳσμένοι
Jesus. – For by grace ye are *having been* saved

διὰ πίστεως· καὶ τοῦτο οὐκ ἐξ ὑμῶν,
through faith; and this not of you,

θεοῦ τὸ δῶρον· **9** οὐκ ἐξ ἔργων, ἵνα μή
of God [is] the gift; not of works, lest

τις καυχήσηται. **10** αὐτοῦ γάρ ἐσμεν
anyone should boast. For of him we are

ποίημα, κτισθέντες ἐν Χριστῷ Ἰησοῦ
a product, created in Christ Jesus

ἐπὶ ἔργοις ἀγαθοῖς, οἷς προητοίμασεν
unto works good, which ²previously prepared

ὁ θεὸς ἵνα ἐν αὐτοῖς περιπατήσωμεν.
– ¹God in order that in them we might walk.

11 Διὸ μνημονεύετε ὅτι ποτὲ ὑμεῖς τὰ
Wherefore remember ye that when ye the

ἔθνη ἐν σαρκί, οἱ λεγόμενοι ἀκροβυστία
nations in [the] flesh, the [ones] *being* called uncircumcision

ὑπὸ τῆς λεγομένης περιτομῆς ἐν σαρκὶ
by the *being* called circumcision in [the] flesh

χειροποιήτου, **12** ὅτι ἦτε τῷ καιρῷ ἐκείνῳ
made by hand, that ye were at that time

χωρὶς Χριστοῦ, ἀπηλλοτριωμένοι τῆς
without Christ, having been alienated from the

πολιτείας τοῦ Ἰσραὴλ καὶ ξένοι τῶν
commonwealth – of Israel and strangers of(from) the

διαθηκῶν τῆς ἐπαγγελίας, ἐλπίδα μὴ
covenants – of promise, hope not

ἔχοντες καὶ ἄθεοι ἐν τῷ κόσμῳ. **13** νυνὶ
having and godless in the world. now

δὲ ἐν Χριστῷ Ἰησοῦ ὑμεῖς οἵ ποτε
But in Christ Jesus ye the [ones] then

ὄντες μακρὰν ἐγενήθητε ἐγγὺς ἐν τῷ
being afar became near by the

also lived among them at
one time, gratifying the
cravings of our sinful nature[g] and following its desires and thoughts. Like
the rest, we were by nature
objects of wrath. 4But because of his great love for
us, God, who is rich in mercy, 5made us alive with
Christ even when we were
dead in transgressions—it
is by grace you have been
saved. 6And God raised us
up with Christ and seated
us with him in the heavenly
realms in Christ Jesus, 7in
order that in the coming
ages he might show the in-
comparable riches of his
grace, expressed in his
kindness to us in Christ
Jesus. 8For it is by grace
you have been saved,
through faith—and this not
from yourselves, it is the
gift of God— 9not by
works, so that no one can
boast. 10For we are God's
workmanship, created in
Christ Jesus to do good
works, which God pre-
pared in advance for us to
do.

One in Christ

11Therefore, remember
that formerly you who are
Gentiles by birth and called
"uncircumcised" by those
who call themselves "the
circumcision" (that done in
the body by the hands of
men)— 12remember that at
that time you were separate
from Christ, excluded from
citizenship in Israel and
foreigners to the covenants
of the promise, without
hope and without God in
the world. 13But now in
Christ Jesus you who once
were far away have been

[g] Other ancient authorities read *in Christ*
[h] Gk *in the flesh*

[g] 3 Or *our flesh*

14 For he is our peace; in his flesh he has made both groups into one and has broken down the dividing wall, that is, the hostility between us. 15 He has abolished the law with its commandments and ordinances, that he might create in himself one new humanity in place of the two, thus making peace, 16 and might reconcile both groups to God in one body[i] through the cross, thus putting to death that hostility through it.[j] 17 So he came and proclaimed peace to you who were far off and peace to those who were near; 18 for through him both of us have access in one Spirit to the Father. 19 So then you are no longer strangers and aliens, but you are citizens with the saints and also members of the household of God, 20 built upon the foundation of the apostles and prophets, with Christ Jesus himself as the cornerstone.[k] 21 In him the whole structure is joined together and grows into a holy temple in the Lord; 22 in whom you also are built together spiritually[l] into a dwelling place for God.

αἵματι τοῦ Χριστοῦ. 14 Αὐτὸς γάρ
blood – of Christ. For he

ἐστιν ἡ εἰρήνη ἡμῶν, ὁ ποιήσας τὰ
is the peace of us, the [one] having made –

ἀμφότερα ἓν καὶ τὸ μεσότοιχον τοῦ
both one and 2the 3middle wall –

φραγμοῦ λύσας, τὴν ἔχθραν, ἐν τῇ σαρκὶ
4of partition 1having broken, the enmity, 2in 3the 4flesh

αὐτοῦ 15 τὸν νόμον τῶν ἐντολῶν ἐν
5of him 6the 7law 8of the 9commandments 10in

δόγμασιν καταργήσας, ἵνα τοὺς δύο κτίσῃ
11decrees 1having abolished, in order that 4the 5two 2he might create

ἐν αὐτῷ εἰς ἕνα καινὸν ἄνθρωπον ποιῶν
6in 7him[self] 8into 9one 10new 11man 1making

εἰρήνην, 16 καὶ ἀποκαταλλάξῃ τοὺς
2peace, and might reconcile –

ἀμφοτέρους ἐν ἑνὶ σώματι τῷ θεῷ διὰ
both in one body – to God through

τοῦ σταυροῦ, ἀποκτείνας τὴν ἔχθραν ἐν
the cross, killing the enmity in

αὐτῷ· 17 καὶ ἐλθὼν εὐηγγελίσατο εἰρήνην
him[self]; and coming preached peace

ὑμῖν τοῖς μακρὰν καὶ εἰρήνην τοῖς ἐγγύς·
to you the ones afar and peace to the ones near;

18 ὅτι δι' αὐτοῦ ἔχομεν τὴν προσαγωγὴν
because through him 1we 3have – 4access

οἱ ἀμφότεροι ἐν ἑνὶ πνεύματι πρὸς τὸν
– 2both by one Spirit unto the

πατέρα. 19 ἄρα οὖν οὐκέτι ἐστὲ ξένοι
Father. Then therefore no more are ye strangers

καὶ πάροικοι, ἀλλὰ ἐστὲ συμπολῖται τῶν
and sojourners, but ye are fellow-citizens of the

ἁγίων καὶ οἰκεῖοι τοῦ θεοῦ, 20 ἐποικοδομη-
saints and members of the family – of God, having been

θέντες ἐπὶ τῷ θεμελίῳ τῶν ἀποστόλων
built *on* on the foundation of the apostles

καὶ προφητῶν, ὄντος ἀκρογωνιαίου αὐτοῦ
and prophets, 4being 5cornerstone 3[him]self

Χριστοῦ Ἰησοῦ, 21 ἐν ᾧ πᾶσα οἰκοδομὴ
1Christ 2Jesus,[a] in whom all [the] building

συναρμολογουμένη αὔξει εἰς ναὸν ἅγιον
being fitted together grows into shrine a holy

ἐν κυρίῳ, 22 ἐν ᾧ καὶ ὑμεῖς συνοικοδομεῖσθε
in [the] Lord, in whom also ye are being built together

εἰς κατοικητήριον τοῦ θεοῦ ἐν πνεύματι.
into a dwelling-place – of God in spirit.

brought near through the blood of Christ.

14 For he himself is our peace, who has made the two one and has destroyed the barrier, the dividing wall of hostility, 15 by abolishing in his flesh the law with its commandments and regulations. His purpose was to create in himself one new man out of the two, thus making peace, 16 and in this one body to reconcile both of them to God through the cross, by which he put to death their hostility. 17 He came and preached peace to you who were far away and peace to those who were near. 18 For through him we both have access to the Father by one Spirit.

19 Consequently, you are no longer foreigners and aliens, but fellow citizens with God's people and members of God's household, 20 built on the foundation of the apostles and prophets, with Christ Jesus himself as the chief cornerstone. 21 In him the whole building is joined together and rises to become a holy temple in the Lord. 22 And in him you too are being built together to become a dwelling in which God lives by his Spirit.

Chapter 3

Paul's Ministry to the Gentiles

THIS is the reason that I Paul am a prisoner for[m] Christ Jesus for the sake of you Gentiles— 2 for surely you have already heard of the commission of God's grace that was given me for you, 3 and how the mystery was made known to me by revelation, as I wrote above in a few words, 4 a reading of which will enable you to perceive my understanding of the mystery of Christ. 5 In for-

3 Τούτου χάριν ἐγὼ Παῦλος ὁ δέσμιος
2*of* this 1By reason of I Paul the prisoner

τοῦ Χριστοῦ Ἰησοῦ ὑπὲρ ὑμῶν τῶν
– of Christ Jesus on behalf of you the

ἐθνῶν 2 — εἴ γε ἠκούσατε τὴν οἰκονομίαν
nations — if indeed ye heard the stewardship

τῆς χάριτος τοῦ θεοῦ τῆς δοθείσης μοι
of the grace – of God – given to me

εἰς ὑμᾶς, 3 ὅτι κατὰ ἀποκάλυψιν ἐγνωρίσθη
for you, that by way of revelation was made known

μοι τὸ μυστήριον, καθὼς προέγραψα ἐν
to me the mystery, as I previously wrote in

ὀλίγῳ, 4 πρὸς ὃ δύνασθε ἀναγινώσκοντες
brief, as to which 2ye can 1reading

νοῆσαι τὴν σύνεσίν μου ἐν τῷ μυστηρίῳ
to realize the understanding of me in the mystery

Chapter 3

Paul the Preacher to the Gentiles

FOR this reason I, Paul, the prisoner of Christ Jesus for the sake of you Gentiles—

2 Surely you have heard about the administration of God's grace that was given to me for you, 3 that is, the mystery made known to me by revelation, as I have already written briefly. 4 In reading this, then, you will be able to understand my insight into the mystery of

[i] Or *reconcile both of us in one body for God*
[j] Or *in him*, or *in himself*
[k] Or *keystone*
[l] Gk *in the Spirit*
[m] Or *of*

mer generations this mys-
tery[n] was not made known
to humankind, as it has
now been revealed to his
holy apostles and prophets
by the Spirit: 6 that is, the
Gentiles have become fel-
low heirs, members of the
same body, and sharers in
the promise in Christ Jesus
through the gospel.
7 Of this gospel I have
become a servant accord-
ing to the gift of God's
grace that was given me by
the working of his power.
8 Although I am the very
least of all the saints, this
grace was given to me to
bring to the Gentiles the
news of the boundless
riches of Christ, 9 and to
make everyone see[o] what
is the plan of the mystery
hidden for ages in[p] God
who created all things; 10 so
that through the church the
wisdom of God in its rich
variety might now be made
known to the rulers and authorities in the heavenly
places. 11 This was in accordance with the eternal
purpose that he has carried
out in Christ Jesus our
Lord, 12 in whom we have
access to God in boldness
and confidence through
faith in him.[q] 13 I pray
therefore that you[r] may
not lose heart over my sufferings for you; they are
your glory.

Prayer for the Readers

14 For this reason I bow
my knees before the Fa-
ther,[s] 15 from whom every
family[t] in heaven and on
earth takes its name. 16 I
pray that, according to the
riches of his glory, he may
grant that you may be
strengthened in your inner
being with power through

[n] Gk *it*
[o] Other ancient authorities read *to bring to light*
[p] Or *by*
[q] Or *the faith of him*
[r] Or *I*
[s] Other ancient authorities add *of our Lord Jesus Christ*
[t] Gk *fatherhood*

τοῦ Χριστοῦ, **5** ὃ ἑτέραις γενεαῖς οὐκ
– of Christ, which in other generations not
ἐγνωρίσθη τοῖς υἱοῖς τῶν ἀνθρώπων ὡς
was made known to the sons – of men as
νῦν ἀπεκαλύφθη τοῖς ἁγίοις ἀποστόλοις
now it was revealed to the holy apostles
αὐτοῦ καὶ προφήταις ἐν πνεύματι, **6** εἶναι
of him and prophets in spirit, ³to be
τὰ ἔθνη συγκληρονόμα καὶ σύσσωμα καὶ
¹the ²nations joint-heirs and a joint-body and
συμμέτοχα τῆς ἐπαγγελίας ἐν Χριστῷ
joint-sharers of the promise in Christ
Ἰησοῦ διὰ τοῦ εὐαγγελίου, **7** οὗ ἐγενήθην
Jesus through the gospel, of which I became
διάκονος κατὰ τὴν δωρεὰν τῆς χάριτος
a minister according to the gift of the grace
τοῦ θεοῦ τῆς δοθείσης μοι κατὰ τὴν
– of God – given to me according to the
ἐνέργειαν τῆς δυνάμεως αὐτοῦ. **8** ἐμοὶ
operation of the power of him. To me
τῷ ἐλαχιστοτέρῳ πάντων ἁγίων ἐδόθη
the leaster* of all saints was given
ἡ χάρις αὕτη, τοῖς ἔθνεσιν εὐαγγελίσασθαι
this grace, to the nations to preach
τὸ ἀνεξιχνίαστον πλοῦτος τοῦ Χριστοῦ,
the unsearchable riches – of Christ,
9 καὶ φωτίσαι τίς ἡ οἰκονομία τοῦ
and to bring to light what [is] the stewardship of the
μυστηρίου τοῦ ἀποκεκρυμμένου ἀπὸ τῶν
mystery – *having been* hidden from the
αἰώνων ἐν τῷ θεῷ τῷ τὰ πάντα κτίσαντι,
ages in – God ¹the [one] – ³all things ²having created,
10 ἵνα γνωρισθῇ νῦν ταῖς ἀρχαῖς καὶ
in order that might be made known now to the rulers and
ταῖς ἐξουσίαις ἐν τοῖς ἐπουρανίοις διὰ
to the authorities in the heavenlies through
τῆς ἐκκλησίας ἡ πολυποίκιλος σοφία τοῦ
the church the manifold wisdom –
θεοῦ, **11** κατὰ πρόθεσιν τῶν αἰώνων ἣν
of God, according to [the] purpose of the ages which
ἐποίησεν ἐν τῷ Χριστῷ Ἰησοῦ τῷ κυρίῳ
he made in – Christ Jesus the Lord
ἡμῶν, **12** ἐν ᾧ ἔχομεν τὴν παρρησίαν
of us, in whom we have – boldness
καὶ προσαγωγὴν ἐν πεποιθήσει διὰ τῆς
and access in confidence through *the*
πίστεως αὐτοῦ. **13** διὸ αἰτοῦμαι μὴ
faith of(in) him.* Wherefore I ask [you] not
ἐγκακεῖν ἐν ταῖς θλίψεσίν μου ὑπὲρ
to faint in the afflictions of me on behalf
ὑμῶν, ἥτις ἐστὶν δόξα ὑμῶν. **14** Τούτου
of you, which is glory of you. ²*of* this
χάριν κάμπτω τὰ γόνατά μου πρὸς
¹By reason of I bend the knees of me unto
τὸν πατέρα, **15** ἐξ οὗ πᾶσα πατριὰ
the Father, of whom every fatherhood
ἐν οὐρανοῖς καὶ ἐπὶ γῆς ὀνομάζεται,
in heavens and on earth is named,
16 ἵνα δῷ ὑμῖν κατὰ τὸ πλοῦτος τῆς
in order that he may give you according to the riches of the
δόξης αὐτοῦ δυνάμει κραταιωθῆναι διὰ
glory of him by power to become mighty through

* This is quite literal!—the apostle coins a word.
* See Gal. 2. 16.

Christ, 5 which was not
made known to men in oth-
er generations as it has now
been revealed by the Spirit
to God's holy apostles and
prophets. 6 This mystery is
that through the gospel the
Gentiles are heirs together
with Israel, members to-
gether of one body, and
sharers together in the
promise in Christ Jesus.
7 I became a servant of
this gospel by the gift of
God's grace given me
through the working of his
power. 8 Although I am less
than the least of all God's
people, this grace was giv-
en me: to preach to the
Gentiles the unsearchable
riches of Christ, 9 and to
make plain to everyone the
administration of this mystery, which for ages past
was kept hidden in God,
who created all things.
10 His intent was that now,
through the church, the
manifold wisdom of God
should be made known to
the rulers and authorities in
the heavenly realms, 11 according to his eternal purpose which he accom-
plished in Christ Jesus our
Lord. 12 In him and through
faith in him we may ap-
proach God with freedom
and confidence. 13 I ask
you, therefore, not to be
discouraged because of my
sufferings for you, which
are your glory.

A Prayer for the Ephesians

14 For this reason I kneel
before the Father, 15 from
whom his whole family[h] in
heaven and on earth de-
rives its name. 16 I pray that
out of his glorious riches he
may strengthen you with

[h] 15 Or *whom all fatherhood*

his Spirit, 17 and that Christ
may dwell in your hearts
through faith, as you are
being rooted and grounded
in love, 18 I pray that you
may have the power to
comprehend, with all the
saints, what is the breadth
and length and height and
depth, 19 and to know the
love of Christ that sur-
passes knowledge, so that
you may be filled with all
the fullness of God.
20 Now to him who by
the power at work within us
is able to accomplish abundantly far more than all we
can ask or imagine, 21 to
him be glory in the church
and in Christ Jesus to all
generations, forever and
ever. Amen.

Chapter 4

Unity in the Body of Christ

I therefore, the prisoner
in the Lord, beg you to
lead a life worthy of the
calling to which you have
been called, 2 with all humility and gentleness, with
patience, bearing with one
another in love, 3 making
every effort to maintain the
unity of the Spirit in the
bond of peace. 4 There is
one body and one Spirit,
just as you were called to
the one hope of your calling, 5 one Lord, one faith,
one baptism, 6 one God and
Father of all, who is above
all and through all and in
all.
7 But each of us was
given grace according to
the measure of Christ's
gift. 8 Therefore it is said,
"When he ascended
on high he made
captivity itself

τοῦ πνεύματος αὐτοῦ εἰς τὸν ἔσω ἄνθρω-
the Spirit of him in the inward man,
πον, 17 κατοικῆσαι τὸν Χριστὸν διὰ τῆς
to dwell – Christ[b] through –
=that Christ may dwell
πίστεως ἐν ταῖς καρδίαις ὑμῶν, ἐν
faith in the hearts of you, in
ἀγάπῃ ἐρριζωμένοι καὶ τεθεμελιωμένοι,
love *having been* rooted and *having been* founded,
18 ἵνα ἐξισχύσητε καταλαβέσθαι σὺν πᾶσιν
in order that ye may have strength to apprehend with all
τοῖς ἁγίοις τί τὸ πλάτος καὶ μῆκος
the saints what [is] the breadth and length
καὶ ὕψος καὶ βάθος, 19 γνῶναί τε τὴν
and height and depth, and to know [1]the
ὑπερβάλλουσαν τῆς γνώσεως ἀγάπην τοῦ
[4]excelling – [5]knowledge [2]love –
Χριστοῦ, ἵνα πληρωθῆτε εἰς πᾶν τὸ
[3]of Christ, *in order* that ye may be filled to all the
πλήρωμα τοῦ θεοῦ.
fulness – of God.

20 Τῷ δὲ δυναμένῳ ὑπὲρ πάντα ποιῆσαι
Now to the [one] being able beyond all things to do
ὑπερεκπερισσοῦ ὧν αἰτούμεθα ἢ νοοῦμεν
superabundantly *of* which we ask or *we* think
κατὰ τὴν δύναμιν τὴν ἐνεργουμένην ἐν
according to the power – operating in
ἡμῖν, 21 αὐτῷ ἡ δόξα ἐν τῇ ἐκκλησίᾳ
us, to him [be] the glory in the church
καὶ ἐν Χριστῷ Ἰησοῦ εἰς πάσας τὰς
and in Christ Jesus unto all the
γενεὰς τοῦ αἰῶνος τῶν αἰώνων· ἀμήν.
generations of the age of the ages: Amen.

4 Παρακαλῶ οὖν ὑμᾶς ἐγὼ ὁ δέσμιος
[7]beseech [6]therefore [8]you [1]I [2]the [3]prisoner
ἐν κυρίῳ ἀξίως περιπατῆσαι τῆς κλήσεως
[4]in [5][the] Lord [10]worthily [9]to walk of the calling
ἧς ἐκλήθητε, 2 μετὰ πάσης ταπεινοφροσύνης
of(with) which ye were called, with all humility
καὶ πραΰτητος, μετὰ μακροθυμίας,
and meekness, with longsuffering,
ἀνεχόμενοι ἀλλήλων ἐν ἀγάπῃ, 3 σπου-
forbearing one another in love, being
δάζοντες τηρεῖν τὴν ἑνότητα τοῦ πνεύματος
eager to keep the unity of the Spirit
ἐν τῷ συνδέσμῳ τῆς εἰρήνης· ἓν σῶμα
in the bond – of peace; [there is] one body
καὶ ἓν πνεῦμα, 4 καθὼς καὶ ἐκλήθητε
and one Spirit, as also ye were called
ἐν μιᾷ ἐλπίδι τῆς κλήσεως ὑμῶν· 5 εἷς
in one hope of the calling of you; one
κύριος, μία πίστις, ἓν βάπτισμα· 6 εἷς
Lord, one faith, one baptism; one
θεὸς καὶ πατὴρ πάντων, ὁ ἐπὶ πάντων
God and Father of all, the [one] over all
καὶ διὰ πάντων καὶ ἐν πᾶσιν. 7 Ἑνὶ
and through all and in all. [2]to [4]one
δὲ ἑκάστῳ ἡμῶν ἐδόθη ἡ χάρις κατὰ
[1]But [3]each of us was given – grace according to
τὸ μέτρον τῆς δωρεᾶς τοῦ Χριστοῦ.
the measure of the gift – of Christ.
8 διὸ λέγει· ἀναβὰς εἰς ὕψος ᾐχμαλώτευσεν
Wherefore he says: Having ascended to height he led captive

power through his Spirit in
your inner being, 17 so that
Christ may dwell in your
hearts through faith. And I
pray that you, being rooted
and established in love,
18 may have power, together with all the saints, to
grasp how wide and long
and high and deep is the
love of Christ, 19 and to
know this love that sur-
passes knowledge—that
you may be filled to the
measure of all the fullness
of God.
20 Now to him who is able
to do immeasurably more
than all we ask or imagine,
according to his power that
is at work within us, 21 to
him be glory in the church
and in Christ Jesus
throughout all generations,
for ever and ever! Amen.

Chapter 4

Unity in the Body of Christ

As a prisoner for the
Lord, then, I urge you
to live a life worthy of the
calling you have received.
2 Be completely humble and
gentle; be patient, bearing
with one another in love.
3 Make every effort to keep
the unity of the Spirit
through the bond of peace.
4 There is one body and one
Spirit—just as you were
called to one hope when
you were called— 5 one
Lord, one faith, one bap-
tism; 6 one God and Father
of all, who is over all and
through all and in all.
7 But to each one of us
grace has been given as
Christ apportioned it. 8 This
is why it[i] says:

"When he ascended on
high,
he led captives in his

[i]8 Or *God*

a captive;
he gave gifts to his
people."

9(When it says, "He ascended," what does it mean but that he had also descended[u] into the lower parts of the earth? 10He who descended is the same one who ascended far above all the heavens, so that he might fill all things.) 11The gifts he gave were that some would be apostles, some prophets, some evangelists, some pastors and teachers, 12to equip the saints for the work of ministry, for building up the body of Christ, 13until all of us come to the unity of the faith and of the knowledge of the Son of God, to maturity, to the measure of the full stature of Christ. 14We must no longer be children, tossed to and fro and blown about by every wind of doctrine, by people's trickery, by their craftiness in deceitful scheming. 15But speaking the truth in love, we must grow up in every way into him who is the head, into Christ, 16from whom the whole body, joined and knit together by every ligament with which it is equipped, as each part is working properly, promotes the body's growth in building itself up in love.

The Old Life and the New

17 Now this I affirm and insist on in the Lord: you must no longer live as the Gentiles live, in the futility of their minds. 18They are darkened in their under-

[u] Other ancient authorities add *first*

αἰχμαλωσίαν, ἔδωκεν δόματα τοῖς ἀνθρώποις.
captivity, he gave gifts – to men.
9 τὸ δὲ ἀνέβη τί ἐστιν εἰ μὴ ὅτι καὶ
Now the "he ascended" what is it except that also
κατέβη εἰς τὰ κατώτερα μέρη τῆς γῆς;
he descended into the lower parts of the earth?
10 ὁ καταβὰς αὐτός ἐστιν καὶ ὁ ἀναβὰς
The descending [one] himself is also the ascending [one]
ὑπεράνω πάντων τῶν οὐρανῶν, ἵνα
far above all the heavens, in order that
πληρώσῃ τὰ πάντα. **11** καὶ αὐτὸς ἔδωκεν
he might fill – all things. And he gave
τοὺς μὲν ἀποστόλους, τοὺς δὲ προφήτας,
some† apostles, some† prophets,
τοὺς δὲ εὐαγγελιστάς, τοὺς δὲ ποιμένας
some† evangelists, some† shepherds
καὶ διδασκάλους, **12** πρὸς τὸν καταρτισμὸν
and teachers, for the perfecting
τῶν ἁγίων εἰς ἔργον διακονίας, εἰς
of the saints to [the] work of ministry, to
οἰκοδομὴν τοῦ σώματος τοῦ Χριστοῦ,
building of the body – of Christ,
13 μέχρι καταντήσωμεν οἱ πάντες εἰς
until [1]we [3]arrive – [2]all at
τὴν ἑνότητα τῆς πίστεως καὶ τῆς ἐπιγνώ-
the unity of the faith and of the full know-
σεως τοῦ υἱοῦ τοῦ θεοῦ, εἰς ἄνδρα τέλειον,
ledge of the Son – of God, at [2]man [1]a complete,
εἰς μέτρον ἡλικίας τοῦ πληρώματος τοῦ
at [the] measure of [the] stature of the fulness –
Χριστοῦ, **14** ἵνα μηκέτι ὦμεν νήπιοι,
of Christ, in order that no more we may be infants,
κλυδωνιζόμενοι καὶ περιφερόμενοι παντὶ ἀνέμῳ
being blown and *being* carried round by every wind
τῆς διδασκαλίας ἐν τῇ κυβείᾳ τῶν ἀνθρώ-
– of teaching in the sleight – of
πων, ἐν πανουργίᾳ πρὸς τὴν μεθοδείαν
men, in cleverness unto the craftiness
τῆς πλάνης, **15** ἀληθεύοντες δὲ ἐν ἀγάπῃ
– of error, but speaking truth in love
αὐξήσωμεν εἰς αὐτὸν τὰ πάντα, ὅς ἐστιν
we may grow into him in all respects,† who is
ἡ κεφαλή, Χριστός, **16** ἐξ οὗ πᾶν τὸ
the head, Christ, of whom all the
σῶμα συναρμολογούμενον καὶ συμβιβαζόμενον
body being fitted together and *being* brought together
διὰ πάσης ἁφῆς τῆς ἐπιχορηγίας κατ᾽
through every band – of supply according to
ἐνέργειαν ἐν μέτρῳ ἑνὸς ἑκάστου μέρους
[the] operation in measure of [2]one [1]each part
τὴν αὔξησιν τοῦ σώματος ποιεῖται εἰς
[2]the [3]growth [4]of the [5]body [1]makes for
οἰκοδομὴν ἑαυτοῦ ἐν ἀγάπῃ.
building of itself in love.
17 Τοῦτο οὖν λέγω καὶ μαρτύρομαι ἐν
This therefore I say and witness in
κυρίῳ, μηκέτι ὑμᾶς περιπατεῖν καθὼς
[the] Lord, no more you to walk as
καὶ τὰ ἔθνη περιπατεῖ ἐν ματαιότητι
also the nations walks in vanity
τοῦ νοὸς αὐτῶν, **18** ἐσκοτωμένοι τῇ
of the mind of them, [2]*having been* darkened [3]in the (their)

train
and gave gifts to
men."[j]

9(What does "he ascended" mean except that he also descended to the lower, earthly regions[k]? 10He who descended is the very one who ascended higher than all the heavens, in order to fill the whole universe.) 11It was he who gave some to be apostles, some to be prophets, some to be evangelists, and some to be pastors and teachers, 12to prepare God's people for works of service, so that the body of Christ may be built up 13until we all reach unity in the faith and in the knowledge of the Son of God and become mature, attaining to the whole measure of the fullness of Christ.

14Then we will no longer be infants, tossed back and forth by the waves, and blown here and there by every wind of teaching and by the cunning and craftiness of men in their deceitful scheming. 15Instead, speaking the truth in love, we will in all things grow up into him who is the Head, that is, Christ. 16From him the whole body, joined and held together by every supporting ligament, grows and builds itself up in love, as each part does its work.

Living as Children of Light

17So I tell you this, and insist on it in the Lord, that you must no longer live as the Gentiles do, in the futility of their thinking. 18They are darkened in their un-

[j]8 Psalm 68:18
[k]9 Or *the depths of the earth*

standing, alienated from the life of God because of their ignorance and hardness of heart. 19 They have lost all sensitivity and have abandoned themselves to licentiousness, greedy to practice every kind of impurity. 20 That is not the way you learned Christ! 21 For surely you have heard about him and were taught in him, as truth is in Jesus. 22 You were taught to put away your former way of life, your old self, corrupt and deluded by its lusts, 23 and to be renewed in the spirit of your minds, 24 and to clothe yourselves with the new self, created according to the likeness of God in true righteousness and holiness.

Rules for the New Life

25 So then, putting away falsehood, let all of us speak the truth to our neighbors, for we are members of one another. 26 Be angry but do not sin; do not let the sun go down on your anger, 27 and do not make room for the devil. 28 Thieves must give up stealing; rather let them labor and work honestly with their own hands, so as to have something to share with the needy. 29 Let no evil talk come out of your mouths, but only what is useful for building up,[v] as there is need, so that your words may give grace to those who hear. 30 And do not grieve the Holy Spirit of God, with which you were marked with a seal for

διανοίᾳ ὄντες, ἀπηλλοτριωμένοι τῆς ζωῆς
[2]intellect [1]being, having been alienated [from] the life

τοῦ θεοῦ, διὰ τὴν ἄγνοιαν τὴν οὖσαν
– of God, through the ignorance – being

ἐν αὐτοῖς, διὰ τὴν πώρωσιν τῆς καρδίας
in them, on account of the hardness of the heart

αὐτῶν, **19** οἵτινες ἀπηλγηκότες ἑαυτοὺς
of them, who having ceased to care [2]themselves

παρέδωκαν τῇ ἀσελγείᾳ εἰς ἐργασίαν
[1]gave up – to lewdness for work

ἀκαθαρσίας πάσης ἐν πλεονεξίᾳ. **20** ὑμεῖς
[2]uncleanness [1]of all in greediness. ye

δὲ οὐχ οὕτως ἐμάθετε τὸν Χριστόν,
But not so learned – Christ,

21 εἴ γε αὐτὸν ἠκούσατε καὶ ἐν αὐτῷ
if indeed [2]him [1]ye heard and [3]by [4]him

ἐδιδάχθητε καθώς ἐστιν ἀλήθεια ἐν τῷ
[5]were taught as [2]is [1]truth in –

Ἰησοῦ, **22** ἀποθέσθαι ὑμᾶς κατὰ τὴν
Jesus, to put off = that ye put off you[b] as regards the(your)

προτέραν ἀναστροφὴν τὸν παλαιὸν ἄνθρωπον
former conduct the old man

τὸν φθειρόμενον κατὰ τὰς ἐπιθυμίας τῆς
– being corrupted according to the lusts –

ἀπάτης, **23** ἀνανεοῦσθαι δὲ τῷ πνεύματι
of deceit, and *to* be renewed in the spirit

τοῦ νοὸς ὑμῶν **24** καὶ ἐνδύσασθαι τὸν
of the mind of you and *to* put on the

καινὸν ἄνθρωπον τὸν κατὰ θεὸν κτισθέντα
new man – [2]according to [3]God [1]created

ἐν δικαιοσύνῃ καὶ ὁσιότητι τῆς ἀληθείας.
in righteousness and holiness – of truth.

25 Διὸ ἀποθέμενοι τὸ ψεῦδος λαλεῖτε
Wherefore putting off the lie speak ye

ἀλήθειαν ἕκαστος μετὰ τοῦ πλησίον αὐτοῦ,
truth each man with the neighbour of him,

ὅτι ἐσμὲν ἀλλήλων μέλη. **26** ὀργίζεσθε
because we are of one another members. Be ye wrathful

καὶ μὴ ἁμαρτάνετε· ὁ ἥλιος μὴ
and do not sin; [3]the [4]sun [2]not

ἐπιδυέτω ἐπὶ παροργισμῷ ὑμῶν, **27** μηδὲ
[1]let [5]set *on* on provocation of you, nor

δίδοτε τόπον τῷ διαβόλῳ. **28** ὁ κλέπτων
give ye place to the devil. The [one] stealing

μηκέτι κλεπτέτω, μᾶλλον δὲ κοπιάτω
no more let him steal, but rather let him labour

ἐργαζόμενος ταῖς ἰδίαις χερσὶν τὸ ἀγαθόν,
working with the(his) own hands the good thing,

ἵνα ἔχῃ μεταδιδόναι τῷ χρείαν ἔχοντι.
in order that he may have to share [with] the [one] [2]need [1]having

29 πᾶς λόγος σαπρὸς ἐκ τοῦ στόματος
Every [2]word [1]corrupt out of the mouth

ὑμῶν μὴ ἐκπορευέσθω, ἀλλὰ εἴ τις
of you let not proceed*, but if any

ἀγαθὸς πρὸς οἰκοδομὴν τῆς χρείας, ἵνα
[is] good to improvement of the need, in order that

δῷ χάριν τοῖς ἀκούουσιν. **30** καὶ μὴ λυπεῖτε
it may give grace to the [ones] hearing. And do not grieve

τὸ πνεῦμα τὸ ἅγιον τοῦ θεοῦ, ἐν ᾧ
the Spirit – Holy – of God, by whom

ἐσφραγίσθητε εἰς ἡμέραν ἀπολυτρώσεως.
ye were sealed for a day of redemption.

derstanding and separated from the life of God because of the ignorance that is in them due to the hardening of their hearts. 19 Having lost all sensitivity, they have given themselves over to sensuality so as to indulge in every kind of impurity, with a continual lust for more.

20 You, however, did not come to know Christ that way. 21 Surely you heard of him and were taught in him in accordance with the truth that is in Jesus. 22 You were taught, with regard to your former way of life, to put off your old self, which is being corrupted by its deceitful desires; 23 to be made new in the attitude of your minds; 24 and to put on the new self, created to be like God in true righteousness and holiness.

25 Therefore each of you must put off falsehood and speak truthfully to his neighbor, for we are all members of one body. 26 "In your anger do not sin"[l]: Do not let the sun go down while you are still angry, 27 and do not give the devil a foothold. 28 He who has been stealing must steal no longer, but must work, doing something useful with his own hands, that he may have something to share with those in need.

29 Do not let any unwholesome talk come out of your mouths, but only what is helpful for building others up according to their needs, that it may benefit those who listen. 30 And do not grieve the Holy Spirit of God, with whom you were sealed for the day of

[v] Other ancient authorities read *building up faith*

* That is, " let no corrupt word proceed . . . "

[l] 26 Psalm 4:4

the day of redemption.
31 Put away from you all bitterness and wrath and an-
ger and wrangling and slander, together with all malice, 32 and be kind to one
another, tenderhearted,
forgiving one another, as
God in Christ has forgiven
you.[w] 1 Therefore be imitators of God, as beloved
children, 2 and live in love,
as Christ loved us[x] and
gave himself up for us, a
fragrant offering and sacrifice to God.

Renounce Pagan Ways

3 But fornication and
impurity of any kind, or
greed, must not even be
mentioned among you, as
is proper among saints.
4 Entirely out of place is ob-
scene, silly, and vulgar
talk; but instead, let there
be thanksgiving. 5 Be sure
of this, that no fornicator or
impure person, or one who
is greedy (that is, an idolater), has any inheritance in
the kingdom of Christ and
of God.
6 Let no one deceive
you with empty words, for
because of these things the
wrath of God comes on
those who are disobedient.
7 Therefore do not be associated with them. 8 For
once you were darkness,
but now in the Lord you are
light. Live as children of
light— 9 for the fruit of the
light is found in all that is
good and right and true.
10 Try to find out what is
pleasing to the Lord.
11 Take no part in the unfruitful works of darkness,
but instead expose them.
12 For it is shameful even to
mention what such people
do secretly; 13 but everything exposed by the light

[w] Other ancient authorities read *us*
[x] Other ancient authorities read *you*

31 πᾶσα πικρία καὶ θυμὸς καὶ
All bitterness and anger and
ὀργὴ καὶ κραυγὴ καὶ βλασφημία ἀρθήτω
wrath and clamour and blasphemy let it be removed
ἀφ' ὑμῶν σὺν πάσῃ κακίᾳ. **32** γίνεσθε
from you with all evil. be ye
δὲ εἰς ἀλλήλους χρηστοί, εὔσπλαγχνοι,
And to one another kind, tenderhearted,
χαριζόμενοι ἑαυτοῖς καθὼς καὶ ὁ θεὸς
forgiving yourselves as also – God
ἐν Χριστῷ ἐχαρίσατο ὑμῖν. **5** Γίνεσθε
in Christ forgave you. Be ye
οὖν μιμηταὶ τοῦ θεοῦ, ὡς τέκνα
therefore imitators – of God, as children
ἀγαπητά, **2** καὶ περιπατεῖτε ἐν ἀγάπῃ,
beloved, and walk ye in love,
καθὼς καὶ ὁ Χριστὸς ἠγάπησεν ὑμᾶς
as also – Christ loved you
καὶ παρέδωκεν ἑαυτὸν ὑπὲρ ἡμῶν
and gave up himself on behalf of us
προσφορὰν καὶ θυσίαν τῷ θεῷ εἰς ὀσμὴν
an offering and a sacrifice – to God for an odour
εὐωδίας. **3** Πορνεία δὲ καὶ ἀκαθαρσία
of sweet smell. But fornication and [2]uncleanness
πᾶσα ἢ πλεονεξία μηδὲ ὀνομαζέσθω ἐν
[1]all or greediness not let it be named among
ὑμῖν, καθὼς πρέπει ἁγίοις, **4** καὶ αἰσχρότης
you, as is fitting for saints, and baseness
καὶ μωρολογία ἢ εὐτραπελία, ἃ οὐκ
and foolish talking or raillery, which things not
ἀνῆκεν, ἀλλὰ μᾶλλον εὐχαριστία. **5** τοῦτο
are becoming, but rather thanksgiving. this
γὰρ ἴστε γινώσκοντες, ὅτι πᾶς πόρνος
For be ye knowing, that every fornicator
ἢ ἀκάθαρτος ἢ πλεονέκτης, ὅ ἐστιν
or unclean man or greedy, who is
εἰδωλολάτρης, οὐκ ἔχει κληρονομίαν ἐν τῇ
an idolater, not has inheritance in the
βασιλείᾳ τοῦ Χριστοῦ καὶ θεοῦ. **6** Μηδεὶς
kingdom – of Christ and of God. [3]No man
ὑμᾶς ἀπατάτω κενοῖς λόγοις· διὰ ταῦτα
[4]you [1]let [2]deceive with empty words; because of these things
γὰρ ἔρχεται ἡ ὀργὴ τοῦ θεοῦ ἐπὶ τοὺς
for is coming the wrath – of God on the
υἱοὺς τῆς ἀπειθείας. **7** μὴ οὖν γίνεσθε
sons – of disobedience. Not therefore be ye
συμμέτοχοι αὐτῶν· **8** ἦτε γάρ ποτε σκότος,
partakers of them; for ye were then darkness,
νῦν δὲ φῶς ἐν κυρίῳ· ὡς τέκνα φωτὸς
but now light in [the] Lord; as children of light
περιπατεῖτε, **9** — ὁ γὰρ καρπὸς τοῦ
walk ye, (for the fruit of the
φωτὸς ἐν πάσῃ ἀγαθωσύνῃ καὶ δικαιοσύνῃ
light [is] in all goodness and righteousness
καὶ ἀληθείᾳ, — **10** δοκιμάζοντες τί ἐστιν
and truth,) proving what is
εὐάρεστον τῷ κυρίῳ, **11** καὶ μὴ συγκοι-
well-pleasing to the Lord, and do not have fellow-
νωνεῖτε τοῖς ἔργοις τοῖς ἀκάρποις τοῦ
ship with the [2]works – [1]unfruitful –
σκότους, μᾶλλον δὲ καὶ ἐλέγχετε, **12** τὰ
of darkness, but rather even reprove [them], [5]the
γὰρ κρυφῇ γινόμενα ὑπ' αὐτῶν αἰσχρόν
for [6]hidden things [7]being done [8]by [9]them [2]shameful
ἐστιν καὶ λέγειν· **13** τὰ δὲ πάντα ἐλεγχόμενα
[1]it is [3]even [4]to speak [of]; – but all things being reproved

redemption. 31 Get rid of all
bitterness, rage and anger,
brawling and slander, along
with every form of malice.
32 Be kind and compassionate to one another, forgiving each other, just as in
Christ God forgave you.

Chapter 5

BE imitators of God,
therefore, as dearly
loved children 2 and live a
life of love, just as Christ
loved us and gave himself
up for us as a fragrant offering and sacrifice to God.
3 But among you there
must not be even a hint of
sexual immorality, or of
any kind of impurity, or of
greed, because these are
improper for God's holy
people. 4 Nor should there
be obscenity, foolish talk
or coarse joking, which are
out of place, but rather
thanksgiving. 5 For of this
you can be sure: No immoral, impure or greedy person
—such a man is an idola-
ter—has any inheritance in
the kingdom of Christ and
of God.[m] 6 Let no one deceive you with empty
words, for because of such
things God's wrath comes
on those who are disobedient. 7 Therefore do not be
partners with them.
8 For you were once dark-
ness, but now you are light
in the Lord. Live as children of light 9 (for the fruit
of the light consists in all
goodness, righteousness
and truth) 10 and find out
what pleases the Lord.
11 Have nothing to do with
the fruitless deeds of darkness, but rather expose
them. 12 For it is shameful
even to mention what the
disobedient do in secret.
13 But everything exposed

[m] 5 Or *kingdom of the Christ and God*

becomes visible, 14 for everything that becomes visible is light. Therefore it says,

"Sleeper, awake!
Rise from the dead,
and Christ will shine on you."

15 Be careful then how you live, not as unwise people but as wise, 16 making the most of the time, because the days are evil. 17 So do not be foolish, but understand what the will of the Lord is. 18 Do not get drunk with wine, for that is debauchery; but be filled with the Spirit, 19 as you sing psalms and hymns and spiritual songs among yourselves, singing and making melody to the Lord in your hearts, 20 giving thanks to God the Father at all times and for everything in the name of our Lord Jesus Christ.

The Christian Household

21 Be subject to one another out of reverence for Christ.

22 Wives, be subject to your husbands as you are to the Lord. 23 For the husband is the head of the wife just as Christ is the head of the church, the body of which he is the Savior. 24 Just as the church is subject to Christ, so also wives ought to be, in everything, to their husbands.

25 Husbands, love your wives, just as Christ loved the church and gave himself up for her, 26 in order to make her holy by cleansing her with the washing of water by the word, 27 so as to present the church to himself in splendor, without a spot or wrinkle or anything of the kind—yes, so that

ὑπὸ τοῦ φωτὸς φανεροῦται· **14** πᾶν γὰρ
by the light is(are) manifested; for everything

τὸ φανερούμενον φῶς ἐστιν. διὸ λέγει·
– being manifested [2]light [1]is. Wherefore he says:

ἔγειρε, ὁ καθεύδων, καὶ ἀνάστα ἐκ τῶν
Rise, the sleeping [one], and stand up out of the

νεκρῶν, καὶ ἐπιφαύσει σοι ὁ Χριστός.
dead [ones], and will shine on thee – Christ.

15 Βλέπετε οὖν ἀκριβῶς πῶς περιπατεῖτε,
See ye therefore carefully how ye walk,

μὴ ὡς ἄσοφοι ἀλλ' ὡς σοφοί, **16** ἐξαγοραζ-
not as unwise but as wise, redeem-

όμενοι τὸν καιρόν, ὅτι αἱ ἡμέραι πονηραί
ing the time, because the days evil

εἰσιν. **17** διὰ τοῦτο μὴ γίνεσθε ἄφρονες,
are. Therefore be ye not foolish,

ἀλλὰ συνίετε τί τὸ θέλημα τοῦ κυρίου.
but understand what the will of the Lord [is].

18 καὶ μὴ μεθύσκεσθε οἴνῳ, ἐν ᾧ ἐστιν
And be ye not drunk with wine, in which is

ἀσωτία, ἀλλὰ πληροῦσθε ἐν πνεύματι,
wantonness, but be filled by [the] Spirit,

19 λαλοῦντες ἑαυτοῖς ψαλμοῖς καὶ ὕμνοις
speaking to yourselves in psalms and hymns

καὶ ᾠδαῖς πνευματικαῖς, ᾄδοντες καὶ
and songs spiritual, singing and

ψάλλοντες τῇ καρδίᾳ ὑμῶν τῷ κυρίῳ,
psalming with the heart of you to the Lord,

20 εὐχαριστοῦντες πάντοτε ὑπὲρ πάντων
giving thanks always for all things

ἐν ὀνόματι τοῦ κυρίου ἡμῶν Ἰησοῦ
in [the] name of the Lord of us Jesus

Χριστοῦ τῷ θεῷ καὶ πατρί, **21** ὑποτασ-
Christ – to God even [the] Father, being

σόμενοι ἀλλήλοις ἐν φόβῳ Χριστοῦ. **22** Αἱ
subject to one another in [the] fear of Christ. The

γυναῖκες τοῖς ἰδίοις ἀνδράσιν ὡς τῷ
wives to the(ir) own husbands as to the

κυρίῳ, **23** ὅτι ἀνήρ ἐστιν κεφαλὴ τῆς
Lord, because a man is head of the

γυναικὸς ὡς καὶ ὁ Χριστὸς κεφαλὴ
woman as also – Christ [is] head

τῆς ἐκκλησίας, αὐτὸς σωτὴρ τοῦ σώματος.
of the church, [him]self Saviour of the body.

24 ἀλλὰ ὡς ἡ ἐκκλησία ὑποτάσσεται τῷ
But as the church is subject –

Χριστῷ, οὕτως καὶ αἱ γυναῖκες τοῖς
to Christ, so also the wives to the(ir)

ἀνδράσιν ἐν παντί. **25** Οἱ ἄνδρες, ἀγαπᾶτε
husbands in everything. The husbands, love ye

τὰς γυναῖκας, καθὼς καὶ ὁ Χριστὸς
the(your) wives, as also – Christ

ἠγάπησεν τὴν ἐκκλησίαν καὶ ἑαυτὸν
loved the church and himself

παρέδωκεν ὑπὲρ αὐτῆς, **26** ἵνα αὐτὴν
gave up on behalf of it, in order that it

ἁγιάσῃ καθαρίσας τῷ λουτρῷ τοῦ
he might sanctify cleansing by the washing of the

ὕδατος ἐν ῥήματι, **27** ἵνα παραστήσῃ αὐτὸς
water by word, in order that [2]might present [1]he

ἑαυτῷ ἔνδοξον τὴν ἐκκλησίαν, μὴ ἔχουσαν
[6]to himself [5]glorious [3]the [4]church, not having

σπίλον ἢ ῥυτίδα ἤ τι τῶν τοιούτων,
spot or wrinkle or any of *the* such things,

by the light becomes visible, 14 for it is light that makes everything visible. This is why it is said:

"Wake up, O sleeper,
rise from the dead,
and Christ will shine on you."

15 Be very careful, then, how you live—not as unwise but as wise, 16 making the most of every opportunity, because the days are evil. 17 Therefore do not be foolish, but understand what the Lord's will is. 18 Do not get drunk on wine, which leads to debauchery. Instead, be filled with the Spirit. 19 Speak to one another with psalms, hymns and spiritual songs. Sing and make music in your heart to the Lord, 20 always giving thanks to God the Father for everything, in the name of our Lord Jesus Christ.

21 Submit to one another out of reverence for Christ.

Wives and Husbands

22 Wives, submit to your husbands as to the Lord. 23 For the husband is the head of the wife as Christ is the head of the church, his body, of which he is the Savior. 24 Now as the church submits to Christ, so also wives should submit to their husbands in everything.

25 Husbands, love your wives, just as Christ loved the church and gave himself up for her 26 to make her holy, cleansing[n] her by the washing with water through the word, 27 and to present her to himself as a radiant church, without stain or wrinkle or any oth-

[n]26 Or *having cleansed*

she may be holy and with-
out blemish. 28 In the same
way, husbands should love
their wives as they do their
own bodies. He who loves
his wife loves himself.
29 For no one ever hates his
own body, but he nourishes
and tenderly cares for it,
just as Christ does for the
church, 30 because we are
members of his body.[y]
31 "For this reason a man
will leave his father and
mother and be joined to his
wife, and the two will become one flesh." 32 This is a
great mystery, and I am applying it to Christ and the
church. 33 Each of you,
however, should love his
wife as himself, and a wife
should respect her hus-
band.

Chapter 6

Children and Parents

CHILDREN, obey your
parents in the Lord,[z]
for this is right. 2 "Honor
your father and mother"—
this is the first commandment with a promise. 3 "so
that it may be well with you
and you may live long on
the earth."
4 And, fathers, do not
provoke your children to
anger, but bring them up in
the discipline and instruction of the Lord.

Slaves and Masters

5 Slaves, obey your
earthly masters with fear
and trembling, in single-
ness of heart, as you obey
Christ; 6 not only while being watched, and in order
to please them, but as
slaves of Christ, doing the
will of God from the heart.

[y] Other ancient authorities add *of his flesh and of his bones*
[z] Other ancient authorities lack *in the Lord*

ἀλλ' ἵνα ᾖ ἁγία καὶ ἄμωμος. **28** οὕτως
but *in order that* it might be holy and unblemished. So

ὀφείλουσιν [καὶ] οἱ ἄνδρες ἀγαπᾶν τὰς
ought also the husbands to love the

ἑαυτῶν γυναῖκας ὡς τὰ ἑαυτῶν σώματα.
of themselves wives as the of themselves bodies.

ὁ ἀγαπῶν τὴν ἑαυτοῦ γυναῖκα ἑαυτὸν
The [one] loving the of himself wife himself

ἀγαπᾷ· **29** οὐδεὶς γάρ ποτε τὴν ἑαυτοῦ
loves; for no man ever the of himself

σάρκα ἐμίσησεν, ἀλλὰ ἐκτρέφει καὶ θάλπει
flesh hated, but nourishes and cherishes

αὐτήν, καθὼς καὶ ὁ Χριστὸς τὴν ἐκ-
it, as also – Christ the

κλησίαν, **30** ὅτι μέλη ἐσμὲν τοῦ σώματος
church, because members we are of the body

αὐτοῦ. **31** ἀντὶ τούτου καταλείψει ἄνθρωπος
of him. For this ²shall leave ¹a man

[τὸν] πατέρα καὶ [τὴν] μητέρα καὶ
the(his) father and the(his) mother and

προσκολληθήσεται πρὸς τὴν γυναῖκα αὐτοῦ,
shall cleave to the wife of him,

καὶ ἔσονται οἱ δύο εἰς σάρκα μίαν.
and ³shall be ¹the ²two ⁴for ⁶flesh ⁵one.

32 τὸ μυστήριον τοῦτο μέγα ἐστίν, ἐγὼ
This mystery great is, ²I

δὲ λέγω εἰς Χριστὸν καὶ [εἰς] τὴν
¹but say as to Christ and as to the

ἐκκλησίαν. **33** πλὴν καὶ ὑμεῖς οἱ
church. Nevertheless also ye *the*

καθ' ἕνα ἕκαστος τὴν ἑαυτοῦ γυναῖκα
one by one† each ¹the ³of himself ²wife

οὕτως ἀγαπάτω ὡς ἑαυτόν, ἡ δὲ
so let him love as himself, and the

γυνὴ ἵνα φοβῆται τὸν ἄνδρα. **6** Τὰ
wife *in order* that she fears the(her) husband. The

τέκνα, ὑπακούετε τοῖς γονεῦσιν ὑμῶν
children, obey ye the parents of you

ἐν κυρίῳ· τοῦτο γάρ ἐστιν δίκαιον.
in [the] Lord; for this is right.

2 τίμα τὸν πατέρα σου καὶ τὴν μητέρα,
Honour the father of thee and the mother,

ἥτις ἐστὶν ἐντολὴ πρώτη ἐν ἐπαγγελίᾳ,
which is ³commandment ¹[the] ²first with a promise,

3 ἵνα εὖ σοι γένηται καὶ ἔσῃ μακρο-
in order that well with thee it may be and thou mayest be long-

χρόνιος ἐπὶ τῆς γῆς. **4** Καὶ οἱ πατέρες,
timed(lived) on the earth. And the fathers,

μὴ παροργίζετε τὰ τέκνα ὑμῶν, ἀλλὰ
do not ye provoke to wrath the children of you, but

ἐκτρέφετε αὐτὰ ἐν παιδείᾳ καὶ νουθεσίᾳ
nurture them in [the] discipline and admonition

κυρίου. **5** Οἱ δοῦλοι, ὑπακούετε τοῖς
of [the] Lord. The slaves, obey ye ¹the(your)

κατὰ σάρκα κυρίοις μετὰ φόβου καὶ
³according to ⁴flesh ²lords with fear and

τρόμου ἐν ἁπλότητι τῆς καρδίας ὑμῶν
trembling in singleness of the heart of you

ὡς τῷ Χριστῷ, **6** μὴ κατ' ὀφθαλμοδουλίαν
as – to Christ, not by way of eye-service

ὡς ἀνθρωπάρεσκοι, ἀλλ' ὡς δοῦλοι Χριστοῦ
as men-pleasers, but as slaves of Christ

ποιοῦντες τὸ θέλημα τοῦ θεοῦ ἐκ ψυχῆς,
doing the will – of God from [the] soul,

er blemish, but holy and
blameless. 28 In this same
way, husbands ought to
love their wives as their
own bodies. He who loves
his wife loves himself. 29 After all, no one ever hated
his own body, but he feeds
and cares for it, just as
Christ does the church—
30 for we are members of his
body. 31 "For this reason a
man will leave his father
and mother and be united
to his wife, and the two will
become one flesh."[o]
32 This is a profound mystery—but I am talking
about Christ and the
church. 33 However, each
one of you also must love
his wife as he loves himself,
and the wife must respect
her husband.

Chapter 6

Children and Parents

CHILDREN, obey your
parents in the Lord,
for this is right. 2 "Honor
your father and mother"—
which is the first commandment with a promise—
3 "that it may go well with
you and that you may enjoy
long life on the earth."[p]
4 Fathers, do not exasper-
ate your children; instead,
bring them up in the training and instruction of the
Lord.

Slaves and Masters

5 Slaves, obey your earthly masters with respect and
fear, and with sincerity of
heart, just as you would
obey Christ. 6 Obey them
not only to win their favor
when their eye is on you,
but like slaves of Christ,
doing the will of God from

[o] *31* Gen. 2:24
[p] *3* Deut. 5:16

7Render service with en-
thusiasm, as to the Lord
and not to men and women,
8knowing that whatever
good we do, we will receive
the same again from the
Lord, whether we are
slaves or free.
9 And, masters, do the
same to them. Stop threatening them, for you know
that both of you have the
same Master in heaven,
and with him there is no
partiality.

The Whole Armor of God

10 Finally, be strong in
the Lord and in the strength
of his power. 11Put on the
whole armor of God, so
that you may be able to
stand against the wiles of
the devil. 12For our[a] struggle is not against enemies of
blood and flesh, but against
the rulers, against the authorities, against the cos-
mic powers of this present
darkness, against the spiritual forces of evil in the
heavenly places. 13There-
fore take up the whole armor of God, so that you
may be able to withstand
on that evil day, and having
done everything, to stand
firm. 14Stand therefore,
and fasten the belt of truth
around your waist, and put
on the breastplate of righteousness. 15As shoes for
your feet put on whatever
will make you ready to proclaim the gospel of peace.
16With all of these,[b] take
the shield of faith, with
which you will be able to
quench all the flaming arrows of the evil one.
17Take the helmet of salvation, and the sword of the

[a]Other ancient authorities read *your*
[b]Or *In all circumstances*

7 μετ' εὐνοίας δουλεύοντες ὡς τῷ κυρίῳ
with goodwill serving as slaves as to the Lord

καὶ οὐκ ἀνθρώποις, 8 εἰδότες ὅτι ἕκαστος
and not to men, knowing that each man

ἐάν τι ποιήσῃ ἀγαθόν, τοῦτο κομίσεται
whatever ²he does ¹good thing, this he will get

παρὰ κυρίου, εἴτε δοῦλος εἴτε ἐλεύθερος.
from [the] Lord, whether a slave or a freeman.

9 Καὶ οἱ κύριοι, τὰ αὐτὰ ποιεῖτε πρὸς
And the lords, the same things do ye toward

αὐτούς, ἀνιέντες τὴν ἀπειλήν, εἰδότες ὅτι
them, forbearing *the* threatening, knowing that

καὶ αὐτῶν καὶ ὑμῶν ὁ κύριός ἐστιν
both of them and of you the Lord is

ἐν οὐρανοῖς, καὶ προσωπολημψία οὐκ
in heavens, and respect of persons not

ἔστιν παρ' αὐτῷ.
is with him.

10 Τοῦ λοιποῦ, ἐνδυναμοῦσθε ἐν κυρίῳ
For the rest,† be ye empowered in [the] Lord

καὶ ἐν τῷ κράτει τῆς ἰσχύος αὐτοῦ.
and in the might of the strength of him.

11 ἐνδύσασθε τὴν πανοπλίαν τοῦ θεοῦ
Put ye on the whole armour – of God

πρὸς τὸ δύνασθαι ὑμᾶς στῆναι πρὸς
for the to be able you[b] to stand against
=so that ye are able . . .

τὰς μεθοδείας τοῦ διαβόλου· 12 ὅτι οὐκ
the craftinesses of the devil; because not

ἔστιν ἡμῖν ἡ πάλη πρὸς αἷμα καὶ σάρκα,
is to us the conflict[c] against blood and flesh,
=our conflict is not

ἀλλὰ πρὸς τὰς ἀρχάς, πρὸς τὰς ἐξουσίας,
but against the rulers, against the authorities,

πρὸς τοὺς κοσμοκράτορας τοῦ σκότους
against the world rulers – darkness

τούτου, πρὸς τὰ πνευματικὰ τῆς πονηρίας
of this, against the spiritual [hosts] – of evil

ἐν τοῖς ἐπουρανίοις. 13 διὰ τοῦτο
in the heavenlies. Therefore

ἀναλάβετε τὴν πανοπλίαν τοῦ θεοῦ, ἵνα
take ye up the whole armour – of God, in order that

δυνηθῆτε ἀντιστῆναι ἐν τῇ ἡμέρᾳ τῇ
ye may be able to resist in the day –

πονηρᾷ καὶ ἅπαντα κατεργασάμενοι στῆναι.
evil and all things having wrought to stand.

14 στῆτε οὖν περιζωσάμενοι τὴν ὀσφὺν
Stand ye therefore girding round the loin[s]

ὑμῶν ἐν ἀληθείᾳ, καὶ ἐνδυσάμενοι τὸν
of you with truth, and putting on the

θώρακα τῆς δικαιοσύνης, 15 καὶ ὑπο-
breastplate – of righteousness, and shoe-

δησάμενοι τοὺς πόδας ἐν ἑτοιμασίᾳ τοῦ
ing the feet with readiness of the

εὐαγγελίου τῆς εἰρήνης, 16 ἐν πᾶσιν
gospel – of peace, in all

ἀναλαβόντες τὸν θυρεὸν τῆς πίστεως, ἐν
taking up the shield – of faith, by

ᾧ δυνήσεσθε πάντα τὰ βέλη τοῦ πονηροῦ
which ye will be able ²all ³the ⁴darts ⁶of the ⁷evil one

τὰ πεπυρωμένα σβέσαι· 17 καὶ τὴν
– ⁵having been equipped with fire ¹to quench; and the

περικεφαλαίαν τοῦ σωτηρίου δέξασθε, καὶ
helmet – of salvation take ye, and

your heart. 7Serve whole-
heartedly, as if you were
serving the Lord, not men,
8because you know that the
Lord will reward everyone
for whatever good he does,
whether he is slave or free.
9And masters, treat your
slaves in the same way. Do
not threaten them, since
you know that he who is
both their Master and
yours is in heaven, and
there is no favoritism with
him.

The Armor of God

10Finally, be strong in the
Lord and in his mighty
power. 11Put on the full armor of God so that you can
take your stand against the
devil's schemes. 12For our
struggle is not against flesh
and blood, but against the
rulers, against the authorities, against the powers of
this dark world and against
the spiritual forces of evil in
the heavenly realms.
13Therefore put on the full
armor of God, so that when
the day of evil comes, you
may be able to stand your
ground, and after you have
done everything, to stand.
14Stand firm then, with the
belt of truth buckled
around your waist, with the
breastplate of righteous-
ness in place, 15and with
your feet fitted with the
readiness that comes from
the gospel of peace. 16In
addition to all this, take up
the shield of faith, with
which you can extinguish
all the flaming arrows of the
evil one. 17Take the helmet
of salvation and the sword

Spirit, which is the word of God.
18 Pray in the Spirit at all times in every prayer and supplication. To that end keep alert and always persevere in supplication for all the saints. 19 Pray also for me, so that when I speak, a message may be given to me to make known with boldness the mystery of the gospel,[c] 20 for which I am an ambassador in chains. Pray that I may declare it boldly, as I must speak.

Personal Matters and Benediction

21 So that you also may know how I am and what I am doing, Tychicus will tell you everything. He is a dear brother and a faithful minister in the Lord. 22 I am sending him to you for this very purpose, to let you know how we are, and to encourage your hearts.
23 Peace be to the whole community,[d] and love with faith, from God the Father and the Lord Jesus Christ. 24 Grace be with all who have an undying love for our Lord Jesus Christ.[e]

τὴν μάχαιραν τοῦ πνεύματος, ὅ ἐστιν
the sword of the Spirit, which* is

ῥῆμα θεοῦ, 18 διὰ πάσης προσευχῆς καὶ
[the] word of God, by means of all prayer and

δεήσεως, προσευχόμενοι ἐν παντὶ καιρῷ
petition, praying at every time

ἐν πνεύματι, καὶ εἰς αὐτὸ ἀγρυπνοῦντες
in spirit, and [3]to [3]it [1]watching

ἐν πάσῃ προσκαρτερήσει καὶ δεήσει περὶ
in all perseverance and petition concerning

πάντων τῶν ἁγίων, 19 καὶ ὑπὲρ ἐμοῦ,
all the saints, and on behalf of me,

ἵνα μοι δοθῇ λόγος ἐν ἀνοίξει τοῦ
in order that to me may be given speech in opening of the

στόματός μου, ἐν παρρησίᾳ γνωρίσαι τὸ
mouth of me, in boldness to make known the

μυστήριον τοῦ εὐαγγελίου, 20 ὑπὲρ οὗ
mystery of the gospel, on behalf of which

πρεσβεύω ἐν ἁλύσει, ἵνα ἐν αὐτῷ παρ-
I am an ambassador in a chain, in order that in it I may

ρησιάσωμαι ὡς δεῖ με λαλῆσαι.
speak boldly as it behoves me to speak.

21 Ἵνα δὲ εἰδῆτε καὶ ὑμεῖς τὰ κατ'
Now in order that [3]may know [2]also [1]ye the things about

ἐμέ, τί πράσσω, πάντα γνωρίσει ὑμῖν
me, what I am doing, all things [10]will make known [11]to you

Τύχικος ὁ ἀγαπητὸς ἀδελφὸς καὶ πιστὸς
[1]Tychicus [2]the [3]beloved [4]brother [5]and [6]faithful

διάκονος ἐν κυρίῳ, 22 ὃν ἔπεμψα πρὸς
[7]minister [8]in [9][the] Lord, whom I sent to

ὑμᾶς εἰς αὐτὸ τοῦτο, ἵνα γνῶτε τὰ
you for this very thing, in order that ye may know the things

περὶ ἡμῶν καὶ παρακαλέσῃ τὰς καρδίας
concerning us and may comfort the hearts

ὑμῶν.
of you.

23 Εἰρήνη τοῖς ἀδελφοῖς καὶ ἀγάπη
Peace to the brothers and love

μετὰ πίστεως ἀπὸ θεοῦ πατρὸς καὶ
with faith from God [the] Father and

κυρίου Ἰησοῦ Χριστοῦ. 24 ἡ χάρις μετὰ
[the] Lord Jesus Christ. – Grace [be] with

πάντων τῶν ἀγαπώντων τὸν κύριον ἡμῶν
all the [ones] loving the Lord of us

Ἰησοῦν Χριστὸν ἐν ἀφθαρσίᾳ.
Jesus Christ in incorruptibility.

of the Spirit, which is the word of God. 18 And pray in the Spirit on all occasions with all kinds of prayers and requests. With this in mind, be alert and always keep on praying for all the saints.
19 Pray also for me, that whenever I open my mouth, words may be given me so that I will fearlessly make known the mystery of the gospel, 20 for which I am an ambassador in chains. Pray that I may declare it fearlessly, as I should.

Final Greetings

21 Tychicus, the dear brother and faithful servant in the Lord, will tell you everything, so that you also may know how I am and what I am doing. 22 I am sending him to you for this very purpose, that you may know how we are, and that he may encourage you.
23 Peace to the brothers, and love with faith from God the Father and the Lord Jesus Christ. 24 Grace to all who love our Lord Jesus Christ with an undying love.

The Letter of Paul to the

Philippians

Chapter 1

Salutation

PAUL and Timothy, servants[a] of Christ Jesus,
To all the saints in Christ Jesus who are in Philippi,

[c] Other ancient authorities lack *of the gospel*
[d] Gk *to the brothers*
[e] Other ancient authorities add *Amen*
[a] Gk *slaves*

ΠΡΟΣ ΦΙΛΙΠΠΗΣΙΟΥΣ

To Philippians

1 Παῦλος καὶ Τιμόθεος δοῦλοι Χριστοῦ
Paul and Timothy slaves of Christ

Ἰησοῦ πᾶσιν τοῖς ἁγίοις ἐν Χριστῷ
Jesus to all the saints in Christ

Ἰησοῦ τοῖς οὖσιν ἐν Φιλίπποις σὺν
Jesus – being in Philippi with

*** Neuter, agreeing with πνεῦμα, not feminine to agree with μάχαιρα.**

Philippians

Chapter 1

PAUL and Timothy, servants of Christ Jesus,
To all the saints in Christ Jesus at Philippi, together

with the bishops[b] and deacons:[c]
2 Grace to you and
peace from God our Father
and the Lord Jesus Christ.

Paul's Prayer for the Philippians

3 I thank my God every
time I remember you,
4 constantly praying with
joy in every one of my
prayers for all of you, 5 because of your sharing in the
gospel from the first day
until now. 6 I am confident
of this, that the one who began a good work among
you will bring it to completion by the day of Jesus
Christ. 7 It is right for me to
think this way about all of
you, because you hold me
in your heart,[d] for all of
you share in God's grace[e]
with me, both in my imprisonment and in the defense
and confirmation of the
gospel. 8 For God is my witness, how I long for all of
you with the compassion of
Christ Jesus. 9 And this is
my prayer, that your love
may overflow more and
more with knowledge and
full insight 10 to help you to
determine what is best, so
that in the day of Christ you
may be pure and blameless,
11 having produced the harvest of righteousness that
comes through Jesus Christ
for the glory and praise of
God.

Paul's Present Circumstances

12 I want you to know,
beloved[f] that what has
happened to me has actually helped to spread the gospel, 13 so that it has become
known throughout the

[b] *Or overseers*
[c] *Or overseers and helpers*
[d] *Or because I hold you in my heart*
[e] Gk *in grace*
[f] Gk *brothers*

ἐπισκόποις καὶ διακόνοις· **2** χάρις ὑμῖν
bishops and ministers: Grace to you

καὶ εἰρήνη ἀπὸ θεοῦ πατρὸς ἡμῶν καὶ
and peace from God Father of us and

κυρίου Ἰησοῦ Χριστοῦ.
[the] Lord Jesus Christ.

3 Εὐχαριστῶ τῷ θεῷ μου ἐπὶ πάσῃ
I thank the God of me at all

τῇ μνείᾳ ὑμῶν, **4** πάντοτε ἐν πάσῃ
the remembrance of you, always in every

δεήσει μου ὑπὲρ πάντων ὑμῶν μετὰ
petition of me on behalf of all you with

χαρᾶς τὴν δέησιν ποιούμενος, **5** ἐπὶ τῇ
joy the petition making, over the

κοινωνίᾳ ὑμῶν εἰς τὸ εὐαγγέλιον ἀπὸ
fellowship of you in the gospel from

τῆς πρώτης ἡμέρας ἄχρι τοῦ νῦν,
the first day until *the* now,

6 πεποιθὼς αὐτὸ τοῦτο, ὅτι ὁ ἐναρξάμενος
being confident [of] this very thing, that the [one] having begun

ἐν ὑμῖν ἔργον ἀγαθὸν ἐπιτελέσει ἄχρι
in you work a good will complete [it] until

ἡμέρας Χριστοῦ Ἰησοῦ· **7** καθώς ἐστιν
[the] day of Christ Jesus; as it is

δίκαιον ἐμοὶ τοῦτο φρονεῖν ὑπὲρ πάντων
right for me this to think *on behalf* of all

ὑμῶν, διὰ τὸ ἔχειν με ἐν τῇ καρδίᾳ
you, because of the to have me[b] in the heart
=because I have you in the(my) heart,

ὑμᾶς, ἔν τε τοῖς δεσμοῖς μου καὶ ἐν
you, both in the bonds of me and in

τῇ ἀπολογίᾳ καὶ βεβαιώσει τοῦ εὐαγγελίου
the defence and confirmation of the gospel

συγκοινωνούς μου τῆς χάριτος πάντας
[4]partakers [7]of me [5]of the [6]grace [3]all

ὑμᾶς ὄντας. **8** μάρτυς γάρ μου ὁ θεός,
[1]you [2]being. [4]witness [1]For [5]of me – [2]God [3][is],

ὡς ἐπιποθῶ πάντας ὑμᾶς ἐν σπλάγχνοις
how I long after all you in [the] bowels

Χριστοῦ Ἰησοῦ. **9** Καὶ τοῦτο προσεύχομαι,
of Christ Jesus. And this I pray,

ἵνα ἡ ἀγάπη ὑμῶν ἔτι μᾶλλον καὶ
in order that the love of you yet more and

μᾶλλον περισσεύῃ ἐν ἐπιγνώσει καὶ πάσῃ
more may abound in full knowledge and all

αἰσθήσει, **10** εἰς τὸ δοκιμάζειν ὑμᾶς τὰ
perception, for the to prove you[b] the things
=that ye may prove

διαφέροντα, ἵνα ἦτε εἰλικρινεῖς καὶ
differing, in order that ye may be sincere and

ἀπρόσκοποι εἰς ἡμέραν Χριστοῦ, **11** πεπληρω-
unoffending in [the] day of Christ, having been

μένοι καρπὸν δικαιοσύνης τὸν διὰ Ἰησοῦ
filled [with] [the] fruit of righteousness – through Jesus

Χριστοῦ, εἰς δόξαν καὶ ἔπαινον θεοῦ.
Christ, to [the] glory and praise of God.

12 Γινώσκειν δὲ ὑμᾶς βούλομαι, ἀδελφοί,
Now [3]to know [2]you [1]I wish, brothers,

ὅτι τὰ κατ' ἐμὲ μᾶλλον εἰς προκοπὴν
that the things about me* [2]rather [3]to [4][the] advance
= my affairs

τοῦ εὐαγγελίου ἐλήλυθεν, **13** ὥστε τοὺς
[5]of the [6]gospel [1]has(ve) come, so as the

* *Cf.* ver. 27; ch. 2. 19, 20, 23; Eph. 6. 21, 22; Col. 4. 7, 8.

with the overseers[a] and
deacons:

2 Grace and peace to you
from God our Father and
the Lord Jesus Christ.

Thanksgiving and Prayer

3 I thank my God every
time I remember you. 4 In
all my prayers for all of
you, I always pray with joy
5 because of your partnership in the gospel from the
first day until now, 6 being
confident of this, that he
who began a good work in
you will carry it on to completion until the day of
Christ Jesus.
7 It is right for me to feel
this way about all of you,
since I have you in my
heart; for whether I am in
chains or defending and
confirming the gospel, all
of you share in God's grace
with me. 8 God can testify
how I long for all of you
with the affection of Christ
Jesus.
9 And this is my prayer:
that your love may abound
more and more in knowl-
edge and depth of insight,
10 so that you may be able to
discern what is best and
may be pure and blameless
until the day of Christ,
11 filled with the fruit of
righteousness that comes
through Jesus Christ—to
the glory and praise of God.

Paul's Chains Advance the Gospel

12 Now I want you to
know, brothers, that what
has happened to me has really served to advance the
gospel. 13 As a result, it has

[a] 1 Traditionally *bishops*

whole imperial guard[g] and
to everyone else that my
imprisonment is for Christ;
14 and most of the brothers
and sisters,[f] having been
made confident in the Lord
by my imprisonment, dare
to speak the word[h] with
greater boldness and without fear.
15 Some proclaim
Christ from envy and rivalry, but others from good-
will. 16 These proclaim
Christ out of love, knowing
that I have been put here
for the defense of the gospel; 17 the others proclaim
Christ out of selfish ambition, not sincerely but intending to increase my suffering in my imprisonment.
18 What does it matter? Just
this, that Christ is pro-
claimed in every way,
whether out of false mo-
tives or true; and in that I
rejoice.
Yes, and I will continue
to rejoice, 19 for I know that
through your prayers and
the help of the Spirit of
Jesus Christ this will turn
out for my deliverance. 20 It
is my eager expectation
and hope that I will not be
put to shame in any way,
but that by my speaking
with all boldness, Christ
will be exalted now as always in my body, whether
by life or by death. 21 For to
me, living is Christ and dying is gain. 22 If I am to live
in the flesh, that means
fruitful labor for me; and I
do not know which I prefer.
23 I am hard pressed be-
tween the two: my desire is
to depart and be with
Christ, for that is far better;
24 but to remain in the flesh
is more necessary for you.
25 Since I am convinced of
this, I know that I will re-

[g] Gk *whole praetorium*
[h] Other ancient authorities read *word of God*

δεσμούς μου φανεροὺς ἐν Χριστῷ γενέσθαι
bonds of me [2]manifest [3]in [4]Christ [1]*to* become
ἐν ὅλῳ τῷ πραιτωρίῳ καὶ τοῖς λοιποῖς
in all the prætorium and to [2]the [3]rest
πᾶσιν, 14 καὶ τοὺς πλείονας τῶν ἀδελφῶν
[1]all, and the majority of the brothers
ἐν κυρίῳ πεποιθότας τοῖς δεσμοῖς μου
in [the] Lord being confident in the bonds of me
περισσοτέρως τολμᾶν ἀφόβως τὸν λόγον
[2]more exceedingly [1]*to* dare [3]fearlessly [5]the [6]word
τοῦ θεοῦ λαλεῖν. 15 τινὲς μὲν καὶ διὰ
- [7]of God [4]to speak. Some indeed even because of
φθόνον καὶ ἔριν, τινὲς δὲ καὶ δι' εὐδοκίαν
envy and strife, but some also because of good-will
τὸν Χριστὸν κηρύσσουσιν· 16 οἱ μὲν ἐξ
– Christ proclaim; these† from
ἀγάπης, εἰδότες ὅτι εἰς ἀπολογίαν τοῦ
love, knowing that for defence of the
εὐαγγελίου κεῖμαι, 17 οἱ δὲ ἐξ ἐριθείας
gospel I am set, those† from rivalry
τὸν Χριστὸν καταγγέλλουσιν, οὐχ ἁγνῶς,
– [2]Christ [1]announce, not purely,
οἰόμενοι θλῖψιν ἐγείρειν τοῖς δεσμοῖς μου.
thinking [2]affliction [1]to raise to the bonds of me.
18 Τί γάρ; πλὴν ὅτι παντὶ τρόπῳ,
What then? nevertheless that in every way,
εἴτε προφάσει εἴτε ἀληθείᾳ, Χριστὸς
whether in pretence or in truth, Christ
καταγγέλλεται, καὶ ἐν τούτῳ χαίρω· ἀλλὰ
is announced, and in this I rejoice; yet
καὶ χαρήσομαι· 19 οἶδα γὰρ ὅτι τοῦτό
also I will rejoice; for I know that this
μοι ἀποβήσεται εἰς σωτηρίαν διὰ τῆς
to me will result in salvation through the
ὑμῶν δεήσεως καὶ ἐπιχορηγίας τοῦ
[2]of you [1]petition and supply of the
πνεύματος Ἰησοῦ Χριστοῦ, 20 κατὰ τὴν
spirit of Jesus Christ, according to the
ἀποκαραδοκίαν καὶ ἐλπίδα μου ὅτι ἐν
eager expectation and hope of me that in
οὐδενὶ αἰσχυνθήσομαι, ἀλλ' ἐν πάσῃ παρ-
nothing I shall be shamed, but with all bold-
ρησίᾳ ὡς πάντοτε καὶ νῦν μεγαλυνθήσεται
ness as always also now shall be magnified
Χριστὸς ἐν τῷ σώματί μου, εἴτε διὰ
Christ in the body of me, whether through
ζωῆς εἴτε διὰ θανάτου. 21 ἐμοὶ γὰρ
life or through death. For to me
τὸ ζῆν Χριστὸς καὶ τὸ ἀποθανεῖν κέρδος.
– to live [is] Christ and – to die [is] gain.
22 εἰ δὲ τὸ ζῆν ἐν σαρκί, τοῦτό μοι
But if – to live in [the] flesh, this to me
καρπὸς ἔργου, καὶ τί αἱρήσομαι οὐ
[is] fruit of [?my] work, and what I shall choose not
γνωρίζω. 23 συνέχομαι δὲ ἐκ τῶν δύο,
I perceive. But I am constrained by the two,
τὴν ἐπιθυμίαν ἔχων εἰς τὸ ἀναλῦσαι καὶ
[2]the [3]desire [1]having *for the* to depart and
σὺν Χριστῷ εἶναι, πολλῷ γὰρ μᾶλλον
[2]with [3]Christ [1]to be, for by much [this is] rather
κρεῖσσον· 24 τὸ δὲ ἐπιμένειν τῇ σαρκὶ
better; – but to remain in the flesh [is]
ἀναγκαιότερον δι' ὑμᾶς. 25 καὶ τοῦτο
more necessary on account of you. And this

become clear throughout
the whole palace guard[b]
and to everyone else that I
am in chains for Christ.
14 Because of my chains,
most of the brothers in the
Lord have been encour-
aged to speak the word of
God more courageously
and fearlessly.
15 It is true that some
preach Christ out of envy
and rivalry, but others out
of goodwill. 16 The latter do
so in love, knowing that I
am put here for the defense
of the gospel. 17 The former
preach Christ out of selfish
ambition, not sincerely,
supposing that they can stir
up trouble for me while I
am in chains.[c] 18 But what
does it matter? The important thing is that in every
way, whether from false
motives or true, Christ is
preached. And because of
this I rejoice.
Yes, and I will continue
to rejoice, 19 for I know that
through your prayers and
the help given by the Spirit
of Jesus Christ, what has
happened to me will turn
out for my deliverance.[d]
20 I eagerly expect and hope
that I will in no way be
ashamed, but will have sufficient courage so that now
as always Christ will be exalted in my body, whether
by life or by death. 21 For to
me, to live is Christ and to
die is gain. 22 If I am to go on
living in the body, this will
mean fruitful labor for me.
Yet what shall I choose? I
do not know! 23 I am torn
between the two: I desire to
depart and be with Christ,
which is better by far; 24 but
it is more necessary for you
that I remain in the body.
25 Convinced of this, I know

[b] 13 Or *whole palace*
[c] 16,17 Some late manuscripts have verses 16 and 17 in reverse order.
[d] 19 Or *salvation*

main and continue with all
of you for your progress
and joy in faith, 26 so that I
may share abundantly in
your boasting in Christ
Jesus when I come to you
again.
27 Only, live your life in
a manner worthy of the
gospel of Christ, so that,
whether I come and see
you or am absent and hear
about you, I will know that
you are standing firm in one
spirit, striving side by side
with one mind for the faith
of the gospel, 28 and are in
no way intimidated by your
opponents. For them this is
evidence of their destruction, but of your salvation.
And this is God's doing.
29 For he has graciously
granted you the privilege
not only of believing in
Christ, but of suffering for
him as well— 30 since you
are having the same struggle that you saw I had and
now hear that I still have.

Chapter 2

Imitating Christ's Humility

IF then there is any encouragement in Christ,
any consolation from love,
any sharing in the Spirit,
any compassion and sympathy, 2 make my joy complete: be of the same mind,
having the same love, being
in full accord and of one
mind. 3 Do nothing from
selfish ambition or conceit,
but in humility regard others as better than yourselves. 4 Let each of you
look not to your own interests, but to the interests of
others. 5 Let the same mind

πεποιθὼς οἶδα, ὅτι μενῶ καὶ παραμενῶ
being confident I know, that I shall remain and continue

πᾶσιν ὑμῖν εἰς τὴν ὑμῶν προκοπὴν καὶ
with all you for the 5of you 1advance 2and

χαρὰν τῆς πίστεως, 26 ἵνα τὸ καύχημα
3joy 4of the 6faith, in order that the boast

ὑμῶν περισσεύῃ ἐν Χριστῷ Ἰησοῦ ἐν
of you may abound in Christ Jesus in

ἐμοὶ διὰ τῆς ἐμῆς παρουσίας πάλιν
me through – my presence again

πρὸς ὑμᾶς.
with you.

27 Μόνον ἀξίως τοῦ εὐαγγελίου τοῦ
Only 2worthily 3of the 4gospel –

Χριστοῦ πολιτεύεσθε, ἵνα εἴτε ἐλθὼν καὶ
5of Christ 1conduct yourselves, in order that whether coming and

ἰδὼν ὑμᾶς εἴτε ἀπὼν ἀκούω τὰ περὶ
seeing you or being absent I hear the things concerning

ὑμῶν, ὅτι στήκετε ἐν ἑνὶ πνεύματι,
you, that ye stand in one spirit,

μιᾷ ψυχῇ συναθλοῦντες τῇ πίστει τοῦ
with one soul striving together in the faith of the

εὐαγγελίου, 28 καὶ μὴ πτυρόμενοι ἐν
gospel, and not being terrified in

μηδενὶ ὑπὸ τῶν ἀντικειμένων, ἥτις ἐστὶν
no(any) thing by the [ones] opposing, which is

αὐτοῖς ἔνδειξις ἀπωλείας, ὑμῶν δὲ
to them a proof of destruction, but of you

σωτηρίας, καὶ τοῦτο ἀπὸ θεοῦ· 29 ὅτι
of salvation, and this from God; because

ὑμῖν ἐχαρίσθη τὸ ὑπὲρ Χριστοῦ, οὐ
to you it was given – on behalf of Christ, not

μόνον τὸ εἰς αὐτὸν πιστεύειν ἀλλὰ καὶ
only – in him to believe but also

τὸ ὑπὲρ αὐτοῦ πάσχειν, 30 τὸν αὐτὸν
– on behalf of him to suffer, the same

ἀγῶνα ἔχοντες οἷον εἴδετε ἐν ἐμοὶ
struggle having which ye saw in me

καὶ νῦν ἀκούετε ἐν ἐμοί. 2 Εἴ τις
and now hear in me. 1If [there is] 3any

οὖν παράκλησις ἐν Χριστῷ, εἴ τι
2therefore comfort in Christ, if any

παραμύθιον ἀγάπης, εἴ τις κοινωνία
consolation of love, if any fellowship

πνεύματος, εἴ τις σπλάγχνα καὶ οἰκτιρμοί,
of spirit, if any compassions and pities,

2 πληρώσατέ μου τὴν χαρὰν ἵνα τὸ
fulfil ye of me the joy *in order* that the

αὐτὸ φρονῆτε, τὴν αὐτὴν ἀγάπην ἔχοντες,
same thing ye think, the same love having,

σύμψυχοι, τὸ ἓν φρονοῦντες, 3 μηδὲν κατ'
one in soul, the one thing thinking, [doing] nothing by way of

ἐριθείαν μηδὲ κατὰ κενοδοξίαν, ἀλλὰ τῇ
rivalry nor by way of vainglory, but –

ταπεινοφροσύνῃ ἀλλήλους ἡγούμενοι ὑπερ-
in humility 2one another 1deeming sur-

έχοντας ἑαυτῶν, 4 μὴ τὰ ἑαυτῶν ἕκαστοι
passing themselves, not 3the things 4of themselves 1each *ones*

σκοποῦντες, ἀλλὰ καὶ τὰ ἑτέρων ἕκαστοι.
2looking at, but 2also 3the things 4of others 1each *ones*.

that I will remain, and I will
continue with all of you for
your progress and joy in the
faith, 26 so that through my
being with you again your
joy in Christ Jesus will
overflow on account of me.
27 Whatever happens,
conduct yourselves in a
manner worthy of the gospel of Christ. Then, whether I come and see you or
only hear about you in my
absence, I will know that
you stand firm in one spirit,
contending as one man for
the faith of the gospel
28 without being frightened
in any way by those who
oppose you. This is a sign
to them that they will be destroyed, but that you will
be saved—and that by
God. 29 For it has been
granted to you on behalf of
Christ not only to believe
on him, but also to suffer
for him, 30 since you are going through the same struggle you saw I had, and now
hear that I still have.

Chapter 2

Imitating Christ's Humility

IF you have any encouragement from being
united with Christ, if any
comfort from his love, if
any fellowship with the
Spirit, if any tenderness
and compassion, 2 then
make my joy complete by
being like-minded, having
the same love, being one in
spirit and purpose. 3 Do
nothing out of selfish ambition or vain conceit, but in
humility consider others
better than yourselves.
4 Each of you should look
not only to your own interests, but also to the interests of others.

be in you that was[i] in Christ Jesus,
6 who, though he was in the form of God,
did not regard equality with God
as something to be exploited,
7 but emptied himself,
taking the form of a slave,
being born in human likeness.
And being found in human form,
8 he humbled himself
and became obedient to the point of death—
even death on a cross.

9 Therefore God also highly exalted him
and gave him the name
that is above every name,
10 so that at the name of Jesus
every knee should bend,
in heaven and on earth and under the earth,
11 and every tongue should confess
that Jesus Christ is Lord,
to the glory of God the Father.

Shining as Lights in the World

12 Therefore, my beloved, just as you have always obeyed me, not only in my presence, but much more now in my absence, work out your own salvation with fear and trembling; 13 for it is God who is
at work in you, enabling you both to will and to work for his good pleasure.
14 Do all things without murmuring and arguing,
15 so that you may be blameless and innocent, children of God without blemish in the midst of a crooked and perverse generation, in which you shine
like stars in the world. 16 It
is by your holding fast to the word of life that I can boast on the day of Christ that I did not run in vain or
labor in vain. 17 But even if
I am being poured out as a libation over the sacrifice and the offering of your faith, I am glad and rejoice

[i] Or *that you have*

5 τοῦτο φρονεῖτε ἐν ὑμῖν ὃ καὶ ἐν
This think ye among you which also [was] in

Χριστῷ Ἰησοῦ, 6 ὃς ἐν μορφῇ θεοῦ
Christ Jesus, who in [the] form of God

ὑπάρχων οὐχ ἁρπαγμὸν ἡγήσατο τὸ εἶναι
subsisting [2]not [3]robbery [1]deemed [it] *the* to be

ἴσα θεῷ, 7 ἀλλὰ ἑαυτὸν ἐκένωσεν μορφὴν
equal *things* with God, but himself emptied [2][the] form

δούλου λαβών, ἐν ὁμοιώματι ἀνθρώπων
[3]of a slave [1]taking, [2]in [3]likeness [4]of men

γενόμενος· καὶ σχήματι εὑρεθεὶς ὡς
[1]becoming; and [2]in fashion [1]being found as

ἄνθρωπος 8 ἐταπείνωσεν ἑαυτὸν γενόμενος
a man he humbled himself becoming

ὑπήκοος μέχρι θανάτου, θανάτου δὲ σταυροῦ.
obedient until death, and death of a cross.

9 διὸ καὶ ὁ θεὸς αὐτὸν ὑπερύψωσεν
Wherefore also – God [2]him [1]highly exalted

καὶ ἐχαρίσατο αὐτῷ τὸ ὄνομα τὸ ὑπὲρ
and gave to him the name – above

πᾶν ὄνομα, 10 ἵνα ἐν τῷ ὀνόματι Ἰησοῦ
every name, in order that in the name of Jesus

πᾶν γόνυ κάμψῃ ἐπουρανίων καὶ ἐπιγείων
every knee should bend of heavenly [beings] and earthly [beings]

καὶ καταχθονίων, 11 καὶ πᾶσα γλῶσσα
and [beings] under the earth, and every tongue

ἐξομολογήσηται ὅτι κύριος Ἰησοῦς
should acknowledge that [3]Lord [1]Jesus

Χριστὸς εἰς δόξαν θεοῦ πατρός.
[2]Christ [is] to [the] glory of God [the] Father.

12 Ὥστε, ἀγαπητοί μου, καθὼς πάντοτε
So as, beloved of me, as always

ὑπηκούσατε, μὴ ὡς ἐν τῇ παρουσίᾳ
ye obeyed, not as in the presence

μου μόνον ἀλλὰ νῦν πολλῷ μᾶλλον ἐν
of me only but now by more rather in

τῇ ἀπουσίᾳ μου, μετὰ φόβου καὶ τρόμου
the absence of me, with fear and trembling

τὴν ἑαυτῶν σωτηρίαν κατεργάζεσθε· 13 θεὸς
[1]the [3]of yourselves [2]salvation work out; [2]God

γάρ ἐστιν ὁ ἐνεργῶν ἐν ὑμῖν καὶ τὸ
[1]for is the [one] operating in you both *the*

θέλειν καὶ τὸ ἐνεργεῖν ὑπὲρ τῆς εὐδοκίας.
to will and *the* to operate on behalf of the(his) goodwill.

14 πάντα ποιεῖτε χωρὶς γογγυσμῶν καὶ
All things do ye without murmurings and

διαλογισμῶν, 15 ἵνα γένησθε ἄμεμπτοι καὶ
disputings, in order that ye may be blameless and

ἀκέραιοι, τέκνα θεοῦ ἄμωμα μέσον
harmless, children of God faultless in the midst of

γενεᾶς σκολιᾶς καὶ διεστραμμένης, ἐν
a generation crooked and *having been* perverted, among

οἷς φαίνεσθε ὡς φωστῆρες ἐν κόσμῳ,
whom ye shine as luminaries in [the] world,

16 λόγον ζωῆς ἐπέχοντες, εἰς καύχημα
a word of life holding up, for a boast

ἐμοὶ εἰς ἡμέραν Χριστοῦ, ὅτι οὐκ εἰς
to me[c] in [the] day of Christ, that not in

κενὸν ἔδραμον οὐδὲ εἰς κενὸν ἐκοπίασα.
vain I ran nor in vain laboured.

17 Ἀλλὰ εἰ καὶ σπένδομαι ἐπὶ τῇ θυσίᾳ
But if indeed I am poured out on the sacrifice

καὶ λειτουργίᾳ τῆς πίστεως ὑμῶν, χαίρω
and service of the faith of you, I rejoice

5 Your attitude should be the same as that of Christ Jesus:

6 Who, being in very nature[e] God,
did not consider equality with God
something to be grasped,
7 but made himself nothing,
taking the very nature[f] of a servant,
being made in human likeness.
8 And being found in appearance as a man,
he humbled himself
and became obedient to death—
even death on a cross!
9 Therefore God exalted him to the highest place
and gave him the name that is above every name,
10 that at the name of Jesus every knee should bow,
in heaven and on earth and under the earth,
11 and every tongue confess that Jesus Christ is Lord,
to the glory of God the Father.

Shining as Stars

12 Therefore, my dear
friends, as you have always obeyed—not only in my presence, but now much more in my absence—continue to work out your salvation with fear and trembling, 13 for it is God who works in you to will and to act according to his good purpose.
14 Do everything without complaining or arguing,
15 so that you may become blameless and pure, children of God without fault in a crooked and depraved generation, in which you shine like stars in the universe
16 as you hold out[g] the word of life—in order that I may boast on the day of Christ that I did not run or labor for nothing.
17 But
even if I am being poured out like a drink offering on the sacrifice and service coming from your faith, I

[e] 6 Or *in the form of*
[f] 7 Or *the form*
[g] 16 Or *hold on to*

with all of you— 18 and in
the same way you also
must be glad and rejoice
with me.

Timothy and Epaphroditus

19 I hope in the Lord
Jesus to send Timothy to
you soon, so that I may be
cheered by news of you. 20 I
have no one like him who
will be genuinely con-
cerned for your welfare.
21 All of them are seeking
their own interests, not
those of Jesus Christ. 22 But
Timothy's[j] worth you
know, how like a son with
a father he has served with
me in the work of the gospel. 23 I hope therefore to
send him as soon as I see
how things go with me;
24 and I trust in the Lord
that I will also come soon.
25 Still, I think it necessary to send to you
Epaphroditus—my brother
and co-worker and fellow
soldier, your messenger[k]
and minister to my need;
26 for he has been longing
for[l] all of you, and has
been distressed because
you heard that he was ill.
27 He was indeed so ill that
he nearly died. But God
had mercy on him, and not
only on him but on me also,
so that I would not have
one sorrow after another.
28 I am the more eager to
send him, therefore, in order that you may rejoice at
seeing him again, and that I
may be less anxious.
29 Welcome him then in the
Lord with all joy, and hon-
or such people, 30 because
he came close to death for
the work of Christ,[m] risking his life to make up for

καὶ συγχαίρω πᾶσιν ὑμῖν· 18 τὸ δὲ αὐτὸ
and rejoice with [2]all [1]you; and the same

καὶ ὑμεῖς χαίρετε καὶ συγχαίρετέ μοι.
also ye rejoice and rejoice with me.

19 Ἐλπίζω δὲ ἐν κυρίῳ Ἰησοῦ Τιμόθεον
But I hope in [the] Lord Jesus [3]Timothy

ταχέως πέμψαι ὑμῖν, ἵνα κἀγὼ εὐψυχῶ
[4]shortly [1]to send [2]to you, in order that I also may be of good cheer

γνοὺς τὰ περὶ ὑμῶν. 20 οὐδένα γὰρ
knowing the things concerning you. For no one

ἔχω ἰσόψυχον, ὅστις γνησίως τὰ περὶ
I have likeminded, who genuinely [2]the things [3]concerning

ὑμῶν μεριμνήσει· 21 οἱ πάντες γὰρ τὰ
[4]you [1]will care for; *the* for all [3]the things

ἑαυτῶν ζητοῦσιν, οὐ τὰ Χριστοῦ Ἰησοῦ.
[2]of themselves [1]seek, not the things of Christ Jesus.

22 τὴν δὲ δοκιμὴν αὐτοῦ γινώσκετε, ὅτι
But the character of him ye know, that

ὡς πατρὶ τέκνον σὺν ἐμοὶ ἐδούλευσεν
as [3]a father [1]a child[2][serves] [5]with [6]me [4]he served

εἰς τὸ εὐαγγέλιον. 23 τοῦτον μὲν οὖν
in the gospel. This one – therefore

ἐλπίζω πέμψαι ὡς ἂν ἀφίδω τὰ περὶ
I hope to send [2]whenever [3]I see [4]the things [5]concerning

ἐμὲ ἐξαυτῆς· 24 πέποιθα δὲ ἐν κυρίῳ
[6]me [1]immediately; but I trust in [the] Lord

ὅτι καὶ αὐτὸς ταχέως ἐλεύσομαι. 25 Ἀναγ-
that [2]also [3][my]self [4]shortly [1]I will come. [5]neces-

καῖον δὲ ἡγησάμην Ἐπαφρόδιτον τὸν
sary But [1]I deemed [it] [6]Epaphroditus [7]the

ἀδελφὸν καὶ συνεργὸν καὶ συστρατιώτην
[8]brother [9]and [10]fellow-worker [11]and [12]fellow-soldier

μου, ὑμῶν δὲ ἀπόστολον καὶ λειτουργὸν
[13]of me, [14]and [16]of you [15]apostle [17]and [18]minister

τῆς χρείας μου, πέμψαι πρὸς ὑμᾶς,
[19]of the [20]need [21]of me, [2]to send [4]to [5]you,

26 ἐπειδὴ ἐπιποθῶν ἦν πάντας ὑμᾶς, καὶ
since [2]longing after [1]he was [4]all [3]you, and

ἀδημονῶν, διότι ἠκούσατε ὅτι ἠσθένησεν.
[was] being troubled, because ye heard that he ailed.

27 καὶ γὰρ ἠσθένησεν παραπλήσιον θανάτῳ·
For indeed he ailed coming near to death;

ἀλλὰ ὁ θεὸς ἠλέησεν αὐτόν, οὐκ αὐτὸν
but – God had mercy on him, [2]not [3]him

δὲ μόνον ἀλλὰ καὶ ἐμέ, ἵνα μὴ λύπην
[1]and only but also me, lest grief

ἐπὶ λύπην σχῶ. 28 σπουδαιοτέρως οὖν
on grief I should have. More eagerly therefore

ἔπεμψα αὐτόν, ἵνα ἰδόντες αὐτὸν πάλιν
I sent him, in order that seeing him again

χαρῆτε κἀγὼ ἀλυπότερος ὦ. 29 προσδέχεσθε
ye may rejoice and [1]I [3]less grieved [2]may be. Receive ye

οὖν αὐτὸν ἐν κυρίῳ μετὰ πάσης χαρᾶς,
therefore him in [the] Lord with all joy,

καὶ τοὺς τοιούτους ἐντίμους ἔχετε, 30 ὅτι
and – [2]such *ones* [3]honoured [1]hold ye, because

διὰ τὸ ἔργον Χριστοῦ μέχρι θανάτου
on account of the work of Christ [2]as far as [3]death

ἤγγισεν παραβολευσάμενος τῇ ψυχῇ, ἵνα
[1]he drew near exposing the(his) life, in order that

am glad and rejoice with all
of you. 18 So you too should
be glad and rejoice with
me.

Timothy and Epaphroditus

19 I hope in the Lord Jesus
to send Timothy to you
soon, that I also may be
cheered when I receive
news about you. 20 I have
no one else like him, who
takes a genuine interest in
your welfare. 21 For everyone looks out for his own
interests, not those of Jesus
Christ. 22 But you know that
Timothy has proved him-
self, because as a son with
his father he has served
with me in the work of the
gospel. 23 I hope, therefore,
to send him as soon as I see
how things go with me.
24 And I am confident in the
Lord that I myself will
come soon.
25 But I think it is necessary to send back to you
Epaphroditus, my brother,
fellow worker and fellow
soldier, who is also your
messenger, whom you sent
to take care of my needs.
26 For he longs for all of you
and is distressed because
you heard he was ill. 27 Indeed he was ill, and almost
died. But God had mercy
on him, and not on him only
but also on me, to spare me
sorrow upon sorrow.
28 Therefore I am all the
more eager to send him, so
that when you see him
again you may be glad and I
may have less anxiety.
29 Welcome him in the Lord
with great joy, and honor
men like him, 30 because he
almost died for the work of

[j] Gk *his*
[k] Gk *apostle*
[l] Other ancient authorities read *longing to see*
[m] Other ancient authorities read *of the Lord*

those services that you
could not give me.

Chapter 3

FINALLY, my brothers
and sisters,[n] rejoice[o]
in the Lord.

Breaking with the Past

To write the same things
to you is not troublesome
to me, and for you it is a
safeguard.
2 Beware of the dogs,
beware of the evil workers,
beware of those who muti-
late the flesh![p] 3 For it is we
who are the circumcision,
who worship in the Spirit of
God[q] and boast in Christ
Jesus and have no confi-
dence in the flesh— 4 even
though I, too, have reason
for confidence in the flesh.
If anyone else has reason
to be confident in the flesh,
I have more: 5 circumcised
on the eighth day, a mem-
ber of the people of Israel,
of the tribe of Benjamin, a
Hebrew born of Hebrews;
as to the law, a Pharisee;
6 as to zeal, a persecutor of
the church; as to righteousness under the law, blameless.
7 Yet whatever gains I
had, these I have come to
regard as loss because of
Christ. 8 More than that, I
regard everything as loss
because of the surpassing
value of knowing Christ
Jesus my Lord. For his
sake I have suffered the
loss of all things, and I regard them as rubbish, in order that I may gain Christ
9 and be found in him, not
having a righteousness of
my own that comes from
the law, but one that comes
through faith in Christ,[r]
the righteousness from God

[n] Gk *my brothers*
[o] Or *farewell*
[p] Gk *the mutilation*
[q] Other ancient authorities read *worship God in spirit*
[r] Or *through the faith of Christ*

ἀναπληρώσῃ τὸ ὑμῶν ὑστέρημα τῆς πρός
he might fill up [1]the [3]of you [2]lack – [5]toward
με λειτουργίας.
[6]me [4]of service.

3 Τὸ λοιπόν, ἀδελφοί μου, χαίρετε ἐν
For the rest, brothers of me, rejoice ye in
κυρίῳ. τὰ αὐτὰ γράφειν ὑμῖν ἐμοὶ μὲν
[the] Lord. [2]The [3]same things [1]to write to you for me indeed
οὐκ ὀκνηρόν, ὑμῖν δὲ ἀσφαλές.
[is] not irksome, but for you safe.
2 Βλέπετε τοὺς κύνας, βλέπετε τοὺς
Look [to] the dogs, look [to] the
κακοὺς ἐργάτας, βλέπετε τὴν κατατομήν.
evil workmen, look [to] the concision.*
3 ἡμεῖς γάρ ἐσμεν ἡ περιτομή, οἱ
For we are the circumcision, the [ones]
πνεύματι θεοῦ λατρεύοντες καὶ καυχώμενοι
[3]by [the] Spirit [2]of God [1]worshipping and boasting
ἐν Χριστῷ Ἰησοῦ καὶ οὐκ ἐν σαρκὶ
in Christ Jesus and [2]not [3]in [the] [4]flesh
πεποιθότες, **4** καίπερ ἐγὼ ἔχων πεποίθησιν
[1]trusting, even though I having trust
καὶ ἐν σαρκί. Εἴ τις δοκεῖ ἄλλος
also in [the] flesh. If any [2]thinks [1]other man
πεποιθέναι ἐν σαρκί, ἐγὼ μᾶλλον·
to trust in [the] flesh, I more:
5 περιτομῇ ὀκταήμερος, ἐκ γένους Ἰσραήλ,
in circumcision eighth day, of [the] race of Israel,
φυλῆς Βενιαμίν, Ἑβραῖος ἐξ Ἑβραίων,
[the] tribe of Benjamin, a Hebrew of Hebrew [parents],
κατὰ νόμον Φαρισαῖος, **6** κατὰ ζῆλος
according to [the] law a Pharisee, by way of zeal
διώκων τὴν ἐκκλησίαν, κατὰ δικαιοσύνην
persecuting the church, according to [the] righteousness
τὴν ἐν νόμῳ γενόμενος ἄμεμπτος. **7** ἀλλὰ
– in [the] law being blameless. But
ἅτινα ἦν μοι κέρδη, ταῦτα ἥγημαι διὰ
what things were to me gain, these I have deemed [2]on account of
τὸν Χριστὸν ζημίαν. **8** ἀλλὰ μενοῦν γε
– [3]Christ [1]loss. *But* nay rather
καὶ ἡγοῦμαι πάντα ζημίαν εἶναι διὰ
[2]also [1]I deem [3]all things [5]loss [4]to be on account of
τὸ ὑπερέχον τῆς γνώσεως Χριστοῦ Ἰησοῦ
the excellency of the knowledge of Christ Jesus
τοῦ κυρίου μου, δι' ὃν τὰ πάντα
the Lord of me, on account of whom – all things
ἐζημιώθην, καὶ ἡγοῦμαι σκύβαλα ἵνα
I suffered loss, and deem [them] refuse in order that
Χριστὸν κερδήσω **9** καὶ εὑρεθῶ ἐν αὐτῷ,
Christ I might gain and be found in him,
μὴ ἔχων ἐμὴν δικαιοσύνην τὴν ἐκ νόμου,
not having my righteousness the [one] of law,
ἀλλὰ τὴν διὰ πίστεως Χριστοῦ, τὴν
but the [one] through faith of(in) Christ,* [1]the

* The apostle uses a "studiously contemptuous paronomasia" (Ellicott). He does not use περιτομή, the proper word for "circumcision", "as this, though now abrogated in Christ, had still its spiritual aspects."

* See Gal. 2. 20.

Christ, risking his life to
make up for the help you
could not give me.

Chapter 3

No Confidence in the Flesh

FINALLY, my broth-
ers, rejoice in the
Lord! It is no trouble for me
to write the same things to
you again, and it is a safeguard for you.
2 Watch out for those
dogs, those men who do
evil, those mutilators of the
flesh. 3 For it is we who are
the circumcision, we who
worship by the Spirit of
God, who glory in Christ
Jesus, and who put no confidence in the flesh—
4 though I myself have reasons for such confidence.
If anyone else thinks he
has reasons to put confi-
dence in the flesh, I have
more: 5 circumcised on the
eighth day, of the people of
Israel, of the tribe of Benjamin, a Hebrew of Hebrews;
in regard to the law, a Pharisee; 6 as for zeal, persecuting the church; as for legal-
istic righteousness, faultless.
7 But whatever was to my
profit I now consider loss
for the sake of Christ.
8 What is more, I consider
everything a loss compared
to the surpassing greatness
of knowing Christ Jesus my
Lord, for whose sake I
have lost all things. I consider them rubbish, that I
may gain Christ 9 and be
found in him, not having a
righteousness of my own
that comes from the law,
but that which is through
faith in Christ—the right-

based on faith. 10 I want to
know Christ[s] and the power of his resurrection and
the sharing of his sufferings
by becoming like him in his
death, 11 if somehow I may
attain the resurrection from
the dead.

Pressing toward the Goal

12 Not that I have al-
ready obtained this or have
already reached the goal;[t]
but I press on to make it my
own, because Christ Jesus
has made me his own.
13 Beloved,[u] I do not consider that I have made it my
own;[v] but this one thing I
do: forgetting what lies behind and straining forward
to what lies ahead, 14 I
press on toward the goal for
the prize of the heavenly[w]
call of God in Christ Jesus.
15 Let those of us then who
are mature be of the same
mind; and if you think differently about anything,
this too God will reveal to
you. 16 Only let us hold fast
to what we have attained.
17 Brothers and sis-
ters,[u] join in imitating me,
and observe those who live
according to the example
you have in us. 18 For many
live as enemies of the cross
of Christ; I have often told
you of them, and now I tell
you even with tears.
19 Their end is destruction;
their god is the belly; and
their glory is in their
shame; their minds are set
on earthly things. 20 But our
citizenship[x] is in heaven,
and it is from there that we
are expecting a Savior, the
Lord Jesus Christ. 21 He
will transform the body of
our humiliation[y] that it
may be conformed to the
body of his glory,[z] by the

[s] Gk *him*
[t] Or *have already been made perfect*
[u] Gk *Brothers*
[v] Other ancient authorities read *my own yet*
[w] Gk *upward*
[x] Or *commonwealth*
[y] Or *our humble bodies*
[z] Or *his glorious body*

ἐκ θεοῦ δικαιοσύνην ἐπὶ τῇ πίστει,
[5]of [4]God [3]righteousness [based] on – faith,
10 τοῦ γνῶναι αὐτὸν καὶ τὴν δύναμιν
– to know[d] him and the power
τῆς ἀναστάσεως αὐτοῦ καὶ κοινωνίαν
of the resurrection of him and [the] fellowship
παθημάτων αὐτοῦ, συμμορφιζόμενος τῷ
of sufferings of him, being conformed to the
θανάτῳ αὐτοῦ, 11 εἴ πως καταντήσω εἰς
death of him, if [some]how I may attain *to* to
τὴν ἐξανάστασιν τὴν ἐκ νεκρῶν. 12 Οὐχ
the out-resurrection – from [the] dead. Not
ὅτι ἤδη ἔλαβον ἢ ἤδη τετελείωμαι,
that already I received or already have been perfected,
διώκω δὲ εἰ καὶ καταλάβω, ἐφ' ᾧ
but I follow if indeed I may lay hold, inasmuch as
καὶ κατελήμφθην ὑπὸ Χριστοῦ Ἰησοῦ.
also I was laid hold of by Christ Jesus.
13 ἀδελφοί, ἐγὼ ἐμαυτὸν οὔπω λογίζομαι
Brothers, [3]I [4]myself [1]not yet [2]reckon
κατειληφέναι· ἓν δέ, τὰ μὲν ὀπίσω
to have laid hold; but one thing [I do], [3]the things [2]on one hand [4]behind
ἐπιλανθανόμενος τοῖς δὲ ἔμπροσθεν ἐπεκ-
[1]forgetting [3]the things [1]on the other [4]before [2]stretching
τεινόμενος, 14 κατὰ σκοπὸν διώκω εἰς
forward to, according to a mark I follow for
τὸ βραβεῖον τῆς ἄνω κλήσεως τοῦ θεοῦ
the prize of the above calling – of God
ἐν Χριστῷ Ἰησοῦ. 15 Ὅσοι οὖν τέλειοι,
in Christ Jesus. [2]As many as [1]therefore [are] perfect,
τοῦτο φρονῶμεν· καὶ εἴ τι ἑτέρως
[2]this [1]let us think; and if anything otherwise
φρονεῖτε, καὶ τοῦτο ὁ θεὸς ὑμῖν ἀποκα-
ye think, even this – God to you will
λύψει· 16 πλὴν εἰς ὃ ἐφθάσαμεν, τῷ
reveal; nevertheless to what we arrived, by the
αὐτῷ στοιχεῖν. 17 Συμμιμηταί μου
same to walk. Fellow-imitators of me
γίνεσθε, ἀδελφοί, καὶ σκοπεῖτε τοὺς οὕτω
be ye, brothers, and mark the [ones] thus
περιπατοῦντας καθὼς ἔχετε τύπον ἡμᾶς.
walking as ye have [2]an example [1]us.
18 πολλοὶ γὰρ περιπατοῦσιν οὓς πολλάκις
For many walk [of] whom often
ἔλεγον ὑμῖν, νῦν δὲ καὶ κλαίων λέγω,
I said to you, and now also weeping I say,
τοὺς ἐχθροὺς τοῦ σταυροῦ τοῦ Χριστοῦ,
the enemies of the cross – of Christ,
19 ὧν τὸ τέλος ἀπώλεια, ὧν ὁ θεὸς
of whom the end [is] destruction, of whom the god [is]
ἡ κοιλία καὶ ἡ δόξα ἐν τῇ αἰσχύνῃ
the belly and the glory in the shame
αὐτῶν, οἱ τὰ ἐπίγεια φρονοῦντες. 20 ἡμῶν
of them, the [ones] the earthly things thinking. of us
γὰρ τὸ πολίτευμα ἐν οὐρανοῖς ὑπάρχει,
For the citizenship in heavens is,
ἐξ οὗ καὶ σωτῆρα ἀπεκδεχόμεθα κύριον
from where also [2]a Saviour [1]we await Lord
Ἰησοῦν Χριστόν, 21 ὃς μετασχηματίσει τὸ
Jesus Christ, who will change the
σῶμα τῆς ταπεινώσεως ἡμῶν σύμμορφον
body of the humiliation of us [making it] conformed
τῷ σώματι τῆς δόξης αὐτοῦ, κατὰ τὴν
to the body of the glory of him, according to the

eousness that comes from
God and is by faith. 10 I
want to know Christ and
the power of his resurrection and the fellowship of
sharing in his sufferings,
becoming like him in his
death, 11 and so, somehow,
to attain to the resurrection
from the dead.

Pressing on Toward the Goal

12 Not that I have already
obtained all this, or have already been made perfect,
but I press on to take hold
of that for which Christ
Jesus took hold of me.
13 Brothers, I do not consider myself yet to have taken
hold of it. But one thing I
do: Forgetting what is behind and straining toward
what is ahead, 14 I press on
toward the goal to win the
prize for which God has
called me heavenward in
Christ Jesus.
15 All of us who are ma-
ture should take such a
view of things. And if on
some point you think dif-
ferently, that too God will
make clear to you. 16 Only
let us live up to what we
have already attained.
17 Join with others in following my example, broth-
ers, and take note of those
who live according to the
pattern we gave you. 18 For,
as I have often told you before and now say again
even with tears, many live
as enemies of the cross of
Christ. 19 Their destiny is
destruction, their god is
their stomach, and their
glory is in their shame.
Their mind is on earthly
things. 20 But our citizenship is in heaven. And we
eagerly await a Savior from
there, the Lord Jesus
Christ, 21 who, by the power that enables him to bring
everything under his con-
trol, will transform our

power that also enables
him to make all things subject to himself. 1 Therefore,
my brothers and sisters,[a]
whom I love and long for,
my joy and crown, stand
firm in the Lord in this way,
my beloved.

Exhortations

2 I urge Euodia and I
urge Syntyche to be of the
same mind in the Lord.
3 Yes, and I ask you also,
my loyal companion,[b] help
these women, for they have
struggled beside me in the
work of the gospel, together with Clement and the
rest of my co-workers,
whose names are in the
book of life.
4 Rejoice[c] in the Lord
always; again I will say,
Rejoice.[c] 5 Let your gentleness be known to everyone. The Lord is near. 6 Do
not worry about anything,
but in everything by prayer
and supplication with
thanksgiving let your re-
quests be made known to
God. 7 And the peace of
God, which surpasses all
understanding, will guard
your hearts and your minds
in Christ Jesus.

8 Finally, beloved,[d]
whatever is true, whatever
is honorable, whatever is
just, whatever is pure,
whatever is pleasing, whatever is commendable, if
there is any excellence and
if there is anything worthy
of praise, think about[e]
these things. 9 Keep on doing the things that you have
learned and received and
heard and seen in me, and
the God of peace will be
with you.

Acknowledgment of the Philippians' Gift

10 I rejoice[f] in the Lord
greatly that now at last you
have revived your concern
for me; indeed, you were

[a] Gk *my brothers*
[b] Or *loyal Syzygus*
[c] Or *Farewell*
[d] Gk *brothers*
[e] Gk *take account of*
[f] Gk *I rejoiced*

ἐνέργειαν τοῦ δύνασθαι αὐτὸν καὶ ὑποτάξαι
operation of the to be able him[b] even to subject
=of his ability

αὐτῷ τὰ πάντα. **4** °Ὥστε, ἀδελφοί μου
to him[self] – all things. So as, brothers of me

ἀγαπητοὶ καὶ ἐπιπόθητοι, χαρὰ καὶ
beloved and longed for, joy and

στέφανός μου, οὕτως στήκετε ἐν κυρίῳ, ἀγαπητοί.
crown of me, so stand in [the] Lord, beloved.

2 Εὐοδίαν παρακαλῶ καὶ Συντύχην
[2]Euodia [1]I beseech and [2]Syntyche

παρακαλῶ τὸ αὐτὸ φρονεῖν ἐν κυρίῳ.
[1]I beseech [4]the [5]same thing [3]to think in [the] Lord.

3 ναὶ ἐρωτῶ καὶ σέ, γνήσιε σύζυγε,
Yes[,] I ask also thee, genuine yoke-fellow,

συλλαμβάνου αὐταῖς, αἵτινες ἐν τῷ εὐαγ-
help them, who [3]in [4]the [5]gos-

γελίῳ συνήθλησάν μοι μετὰ καὶ Κλήμεντος
pel [1]struggled with [2]me with both Clement

καὶ τῶν λοιπῶν συνεργῶν μου, ὧν
and the remaining fellow-workers of me, of whom

τὰ ὀνόματα ἐν βίβλῳ ζωῆς. **4** Χαίρετε
the names [are] in [the] book of life. Rejoice ye

ἐν κυρίῳ πάντοτε· πάλιν ἐρῶ, χαίρετε.
in [the] Lord always; again I will say, rejoice.

5 τὸ ἐπιεικὲς ὑμῶν γνωσθήτω πᾶσιν
The forbearance of you let it be known to all

ἀνθρώποις. ὁ κύριος ἐγγύς. **6** μηδὲν
men. The Lord [is] near. [2]Nothing

μεριμνᾶτε, ἀλλ' ἐν παντὶ τῇ προσευχῇ
[1]be ye anxious about, but in everything – by prayer

καὶ τῇ δεήσει μετὰ εὐχαριστίας τὰ
and – *by* petition with thanksgivings the

αἰτήματα ὑμῶν γνωριζέσθω πρὸς τὸν
requests of you let be made known to –

θεόν. **7** καὶ ἡ εἰρήνη τοῦ θεοῦ ἡ
God. And the peace – of God –

ὑπερέχουσα πάντα νοῦν φρουρήσει τὰς
surpassing all understanding will guard the

καρδίας ὑμῶν καὶ τὰ νοήματα ὑμῶν
hearts of you and the thoughts of you

ἐν Χριστῷ Ἰησοῦ. **8** Τὸ λοιπόν, ἀδελφοί,
in Christ Jesus. For the rest, brothers,

ὅσα ἐστὶν ἀληθῆ, ὅσα σεμνά, ὅσα δίκαια,
whatever things are true, whatever things grave, whatever things just,

ὅσα ἁγνά, ὅσα προσφιλῆ, ὅσα εὔφημα,
whatever things pure, whatever things lovable, • whatever things well-spoken of,

εἴ τις ἀρετὴ καὶ εἴ τις ἔπαινος, **9** ταῦτα
if any virtue and if any praise, these things

λογίζεσθε· ἃ καὶ ἐμάθετε καὶ παρελάβετε
consider ye; which [2]both things [1]ye [3]learned and *ye* received

καὶ ἠκούσατε καὶ εἴδετε ἐν ἐμοί, ταῦτα
and *ye* heard and *ye* saw in me, these

πράσσετε· καὶ ὁ θεὸς τῆς εἰρήνης ἔσται
practise; and the God – of peace will be

μεθ' ὑμῶν.
with you.

10 Ἐχάρην δὲ ἐν κυρίῳ μεγάλως ὅτι
Now I rejoiced in [the] Lord greatly that

ἤδη ποτὲ ἀνεθάλετε τὸ ὑπὲρ ἐμοῦ φρονεῖν·
already at one time ye revived the on behalf of me to think;
=now at length =your thought for me;

lowly bodies so that they
will be like his glorious
body.

Chapter 4

THEREFORE, my
brothers, you whom I
love and long for, my joy
and crown, that is how you
should stand firm in the
Lord, dear friends!

Exhortations

2 I plead with Euodia and I
plead with Syntyche to
agree with each other in the
Lord. 3 Yes, and I ask you,
loyal yokefellow,[h] help
these women who have
contended at my side in the
cause of the gospel, along
with Clement and the rest
of my fellow workers,
whose names are in the
book of life.
4 Rejoice in the Lord al-
ways. I will say it again: Rejoice! 5 Let your gentleness
be evident to all. The Lord
is near. 6 Do not be anxious
about anything, but in everything, by prayer and petition, with thanksgiving,
present your requests to
God. 7 And the peace of
God, which transcends all
understanding, will guard
your hearts and your minds
in Christ Jesus.
8 Finally, brothers, whatever is true, whatever is noble, whatever is right,
whatever is pure, whatever
is lovely, whatever is admi-
rable—if anything is excellent or praiseworthy—
think about such things.
9 Whatever you have
learned or received or
heard from me, or seen in
me—put it into practice.
And the God of peace will
be with you.

Thanks for Their Gifts

10 I rejoice greatly in the
Lord that at last you have
renewed your concern for
me. Indeed, you have been

[h] 3 Or *loyal Syzygus*

concerned for me, but had
no opportunity to show it.[g]
11 Not that I am referring to
being in need; for I have
learned to be content with
whatever I have. 12 I know
what it is to have little, and
I know what it is to have
plenty. In any and all circumstances I have learned
the secret of being well-fed
and of going hungry, of
having plenty and of being
in need. 13 I can do all
things through him who
strengthens me. 14 In any
case, it was kind of you to
share my distress.
15 You Philippians in-
deed know that in the early
days of the gospel, when I
left Macedonia, no church
shared with me in the matter of giving and receiving,
except you alone. 16 For
even when I was in Thessalonica, you sent me help for
my needs more than once.
17 Not that I seek the gift,
but I seek the profit that ac-
cumulates to your account.
18 I have been paid in full
and have more than
enough; I am fully satis-
fied, now that I have re-
ceived from Epaphroditus
the gifts you sent, a fragrant offering, a sacrifice
acceptable and pleasing to
God. 19 And my God will
fully satisfy every need of
yours according to his
riches in glory in Christ
Jesus. 20 To our God and
Father be glory forever and
ever. Amen.

Final Greetings and Benediction

21 Greet every saint in
Christ Jesus. The friends[h]
who are with me greet you.
22 All the saints greet you,
especially those of the emperor's household.

[g] Gk lacks *to show it*
[h] Gk *brothers*

ἐφ' ᾧ καὶ ἐφρονεῖτε, ἠκαιρεῖσθε δέ.
as to which indeed ye thought, but ye had no opportunity.

11 οὐχ ὅτι καθ' ὑστέρησιν λέγω· ἐγὼ
Not that 2by way of 3lack 1I say; 2I

γὰρ ἔμαθον ἐν οἷς εἰμι αὐτάρκης εἶναι.
1for learned in what conditions I am 2self-sufficient 1to be.

12 οἶδα καὶ ταπεινοῦσθαι, οἶδα καὶ περισ-
I know both to be humbled, and I know to

σεύειν· ἐν παντὶ καὶ ἐν πᾶσιν μεμύημαι,
abound; in everything and in all things I have been initiated,

καὶ χορτάζεσθαι καὶ πεινᾶν, καὶ περισ-
both to be filled and to hunger, both to

σεύειν καὶ ὑστερεῖσθαι. 13 πάντα ἰσχύω
abound and to lack. 2All things 1I can do

ἐν τῷ ἐνδυναμοῦντί με. 14 πλὴν καλῶς
in the [one] empowering me. Nevertheless 2well

ἐποιήσατε συγκοινωνήσαντές μου τῇ θλίψει.
1ye did having partnership in 3of me 1the 2affliction.

15 οἴδατε δὲ καὶ ὑμεῖς, Φιλιππήσιοι, ὅτι
And 2know 3also 1ye, Philippians, that

ἐν ἀρχῇ τοῦ εὐαγγελίου, ὅτε ἐξῆλθον
in [the] beginning of the gospel, when I went out

ἀπὸ Μακεδονίας, οὐδεμία μοι ἐκκλησία
from Macedonia, not one 3me 1church

ἐκοινώνησεν εἰς λόγον δόσεως καὶ λήμψεως
2shared with in matter of giving and receiving

εἰ μὴ ὑμεῖς μόνοι, 16 ὅτι καὶ ἐν
except ye only, because indeed in

Θεσσαλονίκῃ καὶ ἅπαξ καὶ δὶς εἰς τὴν
Thessalonica both once and twice to the =to my need

χρείαν μοι ἐπέμψατε. 17 οὐχ ὅτι ἐπιζητῶ
need to me[c] ye sent. Not that I seek

τὸ δόμα, ἀλλὰ ἐπιζητῶ τὸν καρπὸν
the gift, but I seek the fruit

τὸν πλεονάζοντα εἰς λόγον ὑμῶν. 18 ἀπέχω
– increasing to account of you. I have

δὲ πάντα καὶ περισσεύω· πεπλήρωμαι
But all things and abound; I have been filled

δεξάμενος παρὰ Ἐπαφροδίτου τὰ παρ'
receiving from Epaphroditus the things from

ὑμῶν, ὀσμὴν εὐωδίας, θυσίαν δεκτήν,
you, an odour of sweet smell, a sacrifice acceptable,

εὐάρεστον τῷ θεῷ. 19 ὁ δὲ θεός μου
well-pleasing – to God. And the God of me

πληρώσει πᾶσαν χρείαν ὑμῶν κατὰ τὸ
will fill every need of you according to the

πλοῦτος αὐτοῦ ἐν δόξῃ ἐν Χριστῷ Ἰησοῦ.
riches of him in glory in Christ Jesus.

20 τῷ δὲ θεῷ καὶ πατρὶ ἡμῶν ἡ δόξα
to the Now God and Father of us [be] the glory

εἰς τοὺς αἰῶνας τῶν αἰώνων· ἀμήν.
unto the ages of the ages: Amen.

21 Ἀσπάσασθε πάντα ἅγιον ἐν Χριστῷ
Greet ye every saint in Christ

Ἰησοῦ. ἀσπάζονται ὑμᾶς οἱ σὺν ἐμοὶ
Jesus. 5greet 6you 1The 2with 3me

ἀδελφοί. 22 ἀσπάζονται ὑμᾶς πάντες οἱ
4brothers. 4greet 5you 1All 2the

ἅγιοι, μάλιστα δὲ οἱ ἐκ τῆς Καίσαρος
3saints, but most of all the ones of 1the 2of Cæsar

οἰκίας.
3household.

concerned, but you had no
opportunity to show it. 11 I
am not saying this because
I am in need, for I have
learned to be content whatever the circumstances. 12 I
know what it is to be in
need, and I know what it is
to have plenty. I have
learned the secret of being
content in any and every
situation, whether well fed
or hungry, whether living
in plenty or in want. 13 I can
do everything through him
who gives me strength.
14 Yet it was good of you
to share in my troubles.
15 Moreover, as you Philippians know, in the early
days of your acquaintance
with the gospel, when I set
out from Macedonia, not
one church shared with me
in the matter of giving and
receiving, except you only;
16 for even when I was in
Thessalonica, you sent me
aid again and again when I
was in need. 17 Not that I
am looking for a gift, but I
am looking for what may be
credited to your account.
18 I have received full payment and even more; I am
amply supplied, now that I
have received from Epaph-
roditus the gifts you sent.
They are a fragrant offering, an acceptable sacri-
fice, pleasing to God.
19 And my God will meet all
your needs according to his
glorious riches in Christ
Jesus.
20 To our God and Father
be glory for ever and ever.
Amen.

Final Greetings

21 Greet all the saints in
Christ Jesus. The brothers
who are with me send
greetings. 22 All the saints
send you greetings, espe-
cially those who belong to
Caesar's household.

23 The grace of the
Lord Jesus Christ be with
your spirit.[i]

23 Ἡ χάρις τοῦ κυρίου Ἰησοῦ Χριστοῦ
The grace of the Lord Jesus Christ
μετὰ τοῦ πνεύματος ὑμῶν.
[be] with the spirit of you.

23The grace of the Lord
Jesus Christ be with your
spirit. Amen.[i]

The Letter of Paul to
the

Colossians

Chapter 1

Salutation

PAUL, an apostle of
Christ Jesus by the will
of God, and Timothy our
brother,
2 To the saints and
faithful brothers and sisters[a] in Christ in Colossae:
Grace to you and peace
from God our Father.

Paul Thanks God for the Colossians

3 In our prayers for you
we always thank God, the
Father of our Lord Jesus
Christ, 4for we have heard
of your faith in Christ Jesus
and of the love that you
have for all the saints, 5be-
cause of the hope laid up
for you in heaven. You
have heard of this hope before in the word of the
truth, the gospel 6that has
come to you. Just as it is
bearing fruit and growing in
the whole world, so it has
been bearing fruit among
yourselves from the day
you heard it and truly com-
prehended the grace of
God. 7This you learned
from Epaphras, our be-
loved fellow servant.[b] He
is a faithful minister of
Christ on your[c] behalf,
8and he has made known to
us your love in the Spirit.
9 For this reason, since
the day we heard it, we
have not ceased praying for

ΠΡΟΣ ΚΟΛΟΣΣΑΕΙΣ

To Colossians

1 Παῦλος ἀπόστολος Χριστοῦ Ἰησοῦ διὰ
Paul an apostle of Christ Jesus through
θελήματος θεοῦ καὶ Τιμόθεος ὁ ἀδελφὸς
[the] will of God and Timothy the brother
2 τοῖς ἐν Κολοσσαῖς ἁγίοις καὶ πιστοῖς
to the in Colossae saints and faithful
ἀδελφοῖς ἐν Χριστῷ· χάρις ὑμῖν καὶ
brothers in Christ: Grace to you and
εἰρήνη ἀπὸ θεοῦ πατρὸς ἡμῶν.
peace from God Father of us.
3 Εὐχαριστοῦμεν τῷ θεῷ πατρὶ τοῦ
We give thanks – to God Father of the
κυρίου ἡμῶν Ἰησοῦ [Χριστοῦ] πάντοτε
Lord of us Jesus Christ always
περὶ ὑμῶν προσευχόμενοι, **4** ἀκούσαντες
²concerning ³you ¹praying, having heard
τὴν πίστιν ὑμῶν ἐν Χριστῷ Ἰησοῦ
the faith of you in Christ Jesus
καὶ τὴν ἀγάπην ἣν ἔχετε εἰς πάντας
and the love which ye have toward all
τοὺς ἁγίους **5** διὰ τὴν ἐλπίδα τὴν
the saints because of the hope –
ἀποκειμένην ὑμῖν ἐν τοῖς οὐρανοῖς, ἣν
being laid up for you in *the* heavens, which
προηκούσατε ἐν τῷ λόγῳ τῆς ἀληθείας
ye previously heard in the word of the truth
τοῦ εὐαγγελίου **6** τοῦ παρόντος εἰς ὑμᾶς,
of the gospel – coming to you,
καθὼς καὶ ἐν παντὶ τῷ κόσμῳ ἐστὶν
as also in all the world it is
καρποφορούμενον καὶ αὐξανόμενον καθὼς
bearing fruit and growing as
καὶ ἐν ὑμῖν, ἀφ' ἧς ἡμέρας ἠκούσατε
also in you, from which day ye heard
=the day on which
καὶ ἐπέγνωτε τὴν χάριν τοῦ θεοῦ ἐν
and fully knew the grace – of God in
ἀληθείᾳ· **7** καθὼς ἐμάθετε ἀπὸ Ἐπαφρᾶ
truth; as ye learned from Epaphras
τοῦ ἀγαπητοῦ συνδούλου ἡμῶν, ὅς ἐστιν
the beloved fellow-slave of us, who is
πιστὸς ὑπὲρ ὑμῶν διάκονος τοῦ Χριστοῦ,
¹a faithful ⁴on behalf of ⁵you ²minister – ³of Christ,
8 ὁ καὶ δηλώσας ἡμῖν τὴν ὑμῶν ἀγάπην
the [one] also having shown to us ¹the ²of you ³love
ἐν πνεύματι.
in spirit.
9 Διὰ τοῦτο καὶ ἡμεῖς, ἀφ' ἧς ἡμέρας
Therefore also we, from which day
=the day on which
ἠκούσαμεν, οὐ παυόμεθα ὑπὲρ ὑμῶν
we heard, do not cease on behalf of you

Colossians

Chapter 1

PAUL, an apostle of
Christ Jesus by the will
of God, and Timothy our
brother,
2To the holy and faithful[a]
brothers in Christ at Colos-
se:
Grace and peace to you
from God our Father.[b]

Thanksgiving and Prayer

3We always thank God,
the Father of our Lord
Jesus Christ, when we pray
for you, 4because we have
heard of your faith in Christ
Jesus and of the love you
have for all the saints—
5the faith and love that
spring from the hope that is
stored up for you in heaven
and that you have already
heard about in the word of
truth, the gospel 6that has
come to you. All over the
world this gospel is bearing
fruit and growing, just as it
has been doing among you
since the day you heard it
and understood God's
grace in all its truth. 7You
learned it from Epaphras,
our dear fellow servant,
who is a faithful minister of
Christ on our[c] behalf, 8and
who also told us of your
love in the Spirit.
9For this reason, since
the day we heard about
you, we have not stopped

[i] Other ancient authorities add *Amen*
[a] Gk *brothers*
[b] Gk *slave*
[c] Other ancient authorities read *our*

[i] 23 Some manuscripts do not have *Amen.*
[a] 2 Or *believing*
[b] 2 Some manuscripts *Father and the Lord Jesus Christ*
[c] 7 Some manuscripts *your*

you and asking that you
may be filled with the
knowledge of God's[d] will
in all spiritual wisdom and
understanding, 10 so that
you may lead lives worthy
of the Lord, fully pleasing
to him, as you bear fruit in
every good work and as
you grow in the knowledge
of God. 11 May you be
made strong with all the
strength that comes from
his glorious power, and
may you be prepared to endure everything with pa-
tience, while joyfully 12 giving thanks to the Father,
who has enabled[e] you[f] to
share in the inheritance of
the saints in the light. 13 He
has rescued us from the
power of darkness and
transferred us into the kingdom of his beloved Son,
14 in whom we have re-
demption, the forgiveness
of sins.[g]

The Supremacy of Christ

15 He is the image of the
invisible God, the firstborn
of all creation; 16 for in[h]
him all things in heaven and
on earth were created,
things visible and invisible,
whether thrones or domin-
ions or rulers or powers—
all things have been created
through him and for him.
17 He himself is before all
things, and in[h] him all
things hold together. 18 He
is the head of the body, the
church; he is the beginning,
the firstborn from the dead,
so that he might come to
have first place in everything. 19 For in him all the
fullness of God was pleased
to dwell, 20 and through him
God was pleased to recon-
cile to himself all things,

[d] Gk *his*
[e] Other ancient authorities read *called*
[f] Other ancient authorities read *us*
[g] Other ancient authorities add *through his blood*
[h] Or *by*

προσευχόμενοι καὶ αἰτούμενοι ἵνα πληρω-
praying and asking *in order* that ye may be

θῆτε τὴν ἐπίγνωσιν τοῦ θελήματος αὐτοῦ
filled [with] the full knowledge of the will of him

ἐν πάσῃ σοφίᾳ καὶ συνέσει πνευματικῇ,
in all wisdom and understanding spiritual,

10 περιπατῆσαι ἀξίως τοῦ κυρίου εἰς
to walk worthily of the Lord to

πᾶσαν ἀρεσκείαν, ἐν παντὶ ἔργῳ ἀγαθῷ
all pleasing, in every work good

καρποφοροῦντες καὶ αὐξανόμενοι τῇ
bearing fruit and growing in the

ἐπιγνώσει τοῦ θεοῦ, 11 ἐν πάσῃ δυνάμει
full knowledge – of God, with all power

δυναμούμενοι κατὰ τὸ κράτος τῆς δόξης
being empowered according to the might of the glory

αὐτοῦ εἰς πᾶσαν ὑπομονὴν καὶ μακρο-
of him to all endurance and long-

θυμίαν, μετὰ χαρᾶς 12 εὐχαριστοῦντες τῷ
suffering, with joy giving thanks to the

πατρὶ τῷ ἱκανώσαντι ὑμᾶς εἰς τὴν μερίδα
Father – having made [2]fit [1]you for the part

τοῦ κλήρου τῶν ἁγίων ἐν τῷ φωτί·
of the lot of the saints in *the* light;

13 ὃς ἐρρύσατο ἡμᾶς ἐκ τῆς ἐξουσίας
who delivered us out of the authority

τοῦ σκότους καὶ μετέστησεν εἰς τὴν
of *the* darkness and transferred into the

βασιλείαν τοῦ υἱοῦ τῆς ἀγάπης αὐτοῦ,
kingdom of the Son of the love of him,

14 ἐν ᾧ ἔχομεν τὴν ἀπολύτρωσιν, τὴν
in whom we have *the* redemption, the

ἄφεσιν τῶν ἁμαρτιῶν· 15 ὅς ἐστιν εἰκὼν
forgiveness of the (our) sins; who is an image

τοῦ θεοῦ τοῦ ἀοράτου, πρωτότοκος πάσης
of the God – invisible, firstborn of all

κτίσεως, 16 ὅτι ἐν αὐτῷ ἐκτίσθη τὰ
creation, because in him were created –

πάντα ἐν τοῖς οὐρανοῖς καὶ ἐπὶ τῆς
all things in *the* heavens and on the

γῆς, τὰ ὁρατὰ καὶ τὰ ἀόρατα, εἴτε
earth, the visible and the invisible, whether

θρόνοι εἴτε κυριότητες εἴτε ἀρχαὶ εἴτε
thrones or lordships or rulers or

ἐξουσίαι· τὰ πάντα δι' αὐτοῦ καὶ εἰς
authorities; – all things through him and for

αὐτὸν ἔκτισται· 17 καὶ αὐτός ἐστιν πρὸ
him have been created; and he is before

πάντων καὶ τὰ πάντα ἐν αὐτῷ συνέστηκεν,
all things and – all things in him consisted,

18 καὶ αὐτός ἐστιν ἡ κεφαλὴ τοῦ σώματος,
and he is the head of the body,

τῆς ἐκκλησίας· ὅς ἐστιν ἀρχή, πρωτότοκος
of the church; who is [the] beginning, firstborn

ἐκ τῶν νεκρῶν, ἵνα γένηται ἐν πᾶσιν
from the dead, in order that [4]may be [2]in [3]all things

αὐτὸς πρωτεύων, 19 ὅτι ἐν αὐτῷ εὐδόκησεν
[1]he [5]holding the first place, because in him [4]was well pleased

πᾶν τὸ πλήρωμα κατοικῆσαι 20 καὶ δι'
[1]all [2]the [3]fulness to dwell and through

αὐτοῦ ἀποκαταλλάξαι τὰ πάντα εἰς αὐτόν,
him to reconcile – all things to him[?self],

praying for you and asking
God to fill you with the
knowledge of his will
through all spiritual wisdom and understanding.
10 And we pray this in order
that you may live a life worthy of the Lord and may
please him in every way:
bearing fruit in every good
work, growing in the
knowledge of God, 11 being
strengthened with all power according to his glorious
might so that you may have
great endurance and pa-
tience, and joyfully 12 giving
thanks to the Father, who
has qualified you[d] to share
in the inheritance of the
saints in the kingdom of
light. 13 For he has rescued
us from the dominion of
darkness and brought us
into the kingdom of the Son
he loves, 14 in whom we
have redemption,[e] the forgiveness of sins.

The Supremacy of Christ

15 He is the image of the
invisible God, the firstborn
over all creation. 16 For by
him all things were created:
things in heaven and on
earth, visible and invisible,
whether thrones or powers
or rulers or authorities; all
things were created by him
and for him. 17 He is before
all things, and in him all
things hold together. 18 And
he is the head of the body,
the church; he is the beginning and the firstborn from
among the dead, so that in
everything he might have
the supremacy. 19 For God
was pleased to have all his
fullness dwell in him, 20 and
through him to reconcile to
himself all things, whether

[d] 12 Some manuscripts *us*
[e] 14 A few late manuscripts *redemption through his blood*

whether on earth or in
heaven, by making peace
through the blood of his
cross.
21 And you who were
once estranged and hostile
in mind, doing evil deeds,
22 he has now reconciled[i]
in his fleshly body[j]
through death, so as to
present you holy and
blameless and irreproach-
able before him— 23 pro-
vided that you continue securely established and
steadfast in the faith, without shifting from the hope
promised by the gospel that
you heard, which has been
proclaimed to every crea-
ture under heaven. I, Paul,
became a servant of this
gospel.

Paul's Interest in the Colossians

24 I am now rejoicing in
my sufferings for your
sake, and in my flesh I am
completing what is lacking
in Christ's afflictions for
the sake of his body, that is,
the church. 25 I became its
servant according to God's
commission that was given
to me for you, to make the
word of God fully known,
26 the mystery that has been
hidden throughout the ages
and generations but has
now been revealed to his
saints. 27 To them God
chose to make known how
great among the Gentiles
are the riches of the glory of
this mystery, which is
Christ in you, the hope of
glory. 28 It is he whom we
proclaim, warning every-
one and teaching everyone

[i] Other ancient authorities read *you have now been reconciled*
[j] Gk *in the body of his flesh*

εἰρηνοποιήσας διὰ τοῦ αἵματος τοῦ σταυροῦ
making peace through the blood of the cross

αὐτοῦ, δι' αὐτοῦ εἴτε τὰ ἐπὶ τῆς γῆς
of him, through him whether the things on the earth

εἴτε τὰ ἐν τοῖς οὐρανοῖς. 21 Καὶ ὑμᾶς
or the things in *the* heavens. And you

ποτε ὄντας ἀπηλλοτριωμένους καὶ ἐχθροὺς
then being *having been* alienated and enemies

τῇ διανοίᾳ ἐν τοῖς ἔργοις τοῖς πονηροῖς,
in *the* mind by the(your) works – evil,

22 νυνὶ δὲ ἀποκατήλλαξεν ἐν τῷ σώματι
but now he reconciled in the body

τῆς σαρκὸς αὐτοῦ διὰ τοῦ θανάτου,
of the flesh of him through the(his) death,

παραστῆσαι ὑμᾶς ἁγίους καὶ ἀμώμους
to present you holy and blameless

καὶ ἀνεγκλήτους κατενώπιον αὐτοῦ, 23 εἴ
and irreproachable before him, if

γε ἐπιμένετε τῇ πίστει τεθεμελιωμένοι
indeed ye continue in the faith having been founded

καὶ ἑδραῖοι καὶ μὴ μετακινούμενοι ἀπὸ
and steadfast and not being moved away from

τῆς ἐλπίδος τοῦ εὐαγγελίου οὗ ἠκούσατε,
the hope of the gospel which ye heard,

τοῦ κηρυχθέντος ἐν πάσῃ κτίσει τῇ
– proclaimed in all creation –

ὑπὸ τὸν οὐρανόν, οὗ ἐγενόμην ἐγὼ
under *the* heaven, of which ³became ¹I

Παῦλος διάκονος.
²Paul a minister.

24 Νῦν χαίρω ἐν τοῖς παθήμασιν ὑπὲρ
Now I rejoice in the(my) sufferings on behalf of

ὑμῶν, καὶ ἀνταναπληρῶ τὰ ὑστερήματα
you, and fill up the things lacking

τῶν θλίψεων τοῦ Χριστοῦ ἐν τῇ σαρκί
of the afflictions – of Christ in the flesh

μου ὑπὲρ τοῦ σώματος αὐτοῦ, ὅ ἐστιν
of me on behalf of the body of him, which is

ἡ ἐκκλησία, 25 ἧς ἐγενόμην ἐγὼ διάκονος
the church, of which became I a minister

κατὰ τὴν οἰκονομίαν τοῦ θεοῦ τὴν
according to the stewardship – of God –

δοθεῖσάν μοι εἰς ὑμᾶς πληρῶσαι τὸν
given to me for you to fulfil the

λόγον τοῦ θεοῦ, 26 τὸ μυστήριον τὸ
word – of God, the mystery –

ἀποκεκρυμμένον ἀπὸ τῶν αἰώνων καὶ
having been hidden from the ages and

ἀπὸ τῶν γενεῶν — νῦν δὲ ἐφανερώθη
from the generations — but now was manifested

τοῖς ἁγίοις αὐτοῦ, 27 οἷς ἠθέλησεν ὁ
to the saints of him, to whom ²wished –

θεὸς γνωρίσαι τί τὸ πλοῦτος τῆς δόξης
¹God to make known what [is] the riches of the glory

τοῦ μυστηρίου τούτου ἐν τοῖς ἔθνεσιν,
– mystery of this among the nations,

ὅς ἐστιν Χριστὸς ἐν ὑμῖν, ἡ ἐλπὶς τῆς
who is Christ in you, the hope of the

δόξης· 28 ὃν ἡμεῖς καταγγέλλομεν νου-
glory; whom we announce warn-

θετοῦντες πάντα ἄνθρωπον καὶ διδάσκοντες
ing every man and teaching

things on earth or things in
heaven, by making peace
through his blood, shed on
the cross.
21 Once you were alienat-
ed from God and were ene-
mies in your minds because
of[f] your evil behavior.
22 But now he has recon-
ciled you by Christ's physical body through death to
present you holy in his
sight, without blemish and
free from accusation— 23 if
you continue in your faith,
established and firm, not
moved from the hope held
out in the gospel. This is the
gospel that you heard and
that has been proclaimed to
every creature under heav-
en, and of which I, Paul,
have become a servant.

Paul's Labor for the Church

24 Now I rejoice in what
was suffered for you, and I
fill up in my flesh what is
still lacking in regard to
Christ's afflictions, for the
sake of his body, which is
the church. 25 I have be-
come its servant by the
commission God gave me
to present to you the word
of God in its fullness—
26 the mystery that has been
kept hidden for ages and
generations, but is now disclosed to the saints. 27 To
them God has chosen to
make known among the
Gentiles the glorious riches
of this mystery, which is
Christ in you, the hope of
glory.
28 We proclaim him, ad-
monishing and teaching everyone with all wisdom, so

[f] 21 Or *minds, as shown by*

in all wisdom, so that we
may present everyone ma-
ture in Christ. 29 For this I
toil and struggle with all the
energy that he powerfully
inspires within me.

Chapter 2

FOR I want you to know
how much I am strug-
gling for you, and for those
in Laodicea, and for all
who have not seen me face
to face. 2 I want their hearts
to be encouraged and united in love, so that they may
have all the riches of assured understanding and
have the knowledge of
God's mystery, that is,
Christ himself,[k] 3 in whom
are hidden all the treasures
of wisdom and knowledge.
4 I am saying this so that no
one may deceive you with
plausible arguments. 5 For
though I am absent in body,
yet I am with you in spirit,
and I rejoice to see your
morale and the firmness of
your faith in Christ.

Fullness of Life in Christ

6 As you therefore have
received Christ Jesus the
Lord, continue to live your
lives[l] in him, 7 rooted and
built up in him and established in the faith, just as
you were taught, abound-
ing in thanksgiving.

8 See to it that no one
takes you captive through
philosophy and empty de-
ceit, according to human
tradition, according to the
elemental spirits of the universe,[m] and not according
to Christ. 9 For in him the
whole fullness of deity

[k] Other ancient authorities read *of the mystery of God, both of the Father and of Christ*
[l] Gk *to walk*
[m] Or *the rudiments of the world*

πάντα ἄνθρωπον ἐν πάσῃ σοφίᾳ,
every man in all wisdom,
ἵνα παραστήσωμεν πάντα ἄνθρωπον
in order that we may present every man
τέλειον ἐν Χριστῷ· 29 εἰς ὃ καὶ κοπιῶ
mature in Christ; for which also I labour
ἀγωνιζόμενος κατὰ τὴν ἐνέργειαν αὐτοῦ
struggling according to the operation of him
τὴν ἐνεργουμένην ἐν ἐμοὶ ἐν δυνάμει.
– operating in me in power.
2 Θέλω γὰρ ὑμᾶς εἰδέναι ἡλίκον ἀγῶνα
For I wish you to know how great a struggle
ἔχω ὑπὲρ ὑμῶν καὶ τῶν ἐν Λαοδικείᾳ
I have on behalf of you and the [ones] in Laodicea
καὶ ὅσοι οὐχ ἑόρακαν τὸ πρόσωπόν μου
and as many as have not seen the face of me
ἐν σαρκί, 2 ἵνα παρακληθῶσιν αἱ καρδίαι
in flesh, in order that [4]may be comforted [1]the [2]hearts
αὐτῶν, συμβιβασθέντες ἐν ἀγάπῃ καὶ εἰς
[3]of them, being joined together in love and for
πᾶν πλοῦτος τῆς πληροφορίας τῆς
all riches of the full assurance –
συνέσεως, εἰς ἐπίγνωσιν τοῦ μυστηρίου
of understanding, for full knowledge of the mystery
τοῦ θεοῦ, Χριστοῦ, 3 ἐν ᾧ εἰσιν πάντες
– of God, of Christ, in whom [1]are [3]all
οἱ θησαυροὶ τῆς σοφίας καὶ γνώσεως
[4]the [5]treasures – [6]of wisdom [7]and [8]of knowledge
ἀπόκρυφοι. 4 Τοῦτο λέγω ἵνα μηδεὶς
[2]hidden. This I say in order that no one
ὑμᾶς παραλογίζηται ἐν πιθανολογίᾳ. 5 εἰ
[2]you [1]may beguile with persuasive speech. if
γὰρ καὶ τῇ σαρκὶ ἄπειμι, ἀλλὰ τῷ
For indeed in the flesh I am absent, yet in the
πνεύματι σὺν ὑμῖν εἰμι, χαίρων καὶ
spirit [2]with [3]you [1]I am, rejoicing and
βλέπων ὑμῶν τὴν τάξιν καὶ τὸ στερέωμα
seeing [3]of you [1]the [2]order and the firmness
τῆς εἰς Χριστὸν πίστεως ὑμῶν.
of the [3]in [4]Christ [1]faith [2]of you.
6 Ὡς οὖν παρελάβετε τὸν Χριστὸν
As therefore ye received – Christ
Ἰησοῦν τὸν κύριον, ἐν αὐτῷ περιπατεῖτε,
Jesus the Lord, in him walk ye,
7 ἐρριζωμένοι καὶ ἐποικοδομούμενοι ἐν αὐτῷ
having been rooted and being built up in him
καὶ βεβαιούμενοι τῇ πίστει καθὼς ἐδιδάχ-
and being confirmed in the faith as ye were
θητε, περισσεύοντες ἐν εὐχαριστίᾳ.
taught, abounding in thanksgiving.
8 Βλέπετε μή τις ὑμᾶς ἔσται ὁ συλαγωγῶν
Look ye lest [3]anyone [4]you [1]there shall be – [2]robbing
διὰ τῆς φιλοσοφίας καὶ κενῆς ἀπάτης
through – philosophy and empty deceit
κατὰ τὴν παράδοσιν τῶν ἀνθρώπων, κατὰ
according to the tradition – of men, according to
τὰ στοιχεῖα τοῦ κόσμου καὶ οὐ κατὰ
the elements of the world and not according to
Χριστόν· 9 ὅτι ἐν αὐτῷ κατοικεῖ πᾶν
Christ; because in him dwells all

that we may present everyone perfect in Christ. 29 To
this end I labor, struggling
with all his energy, which
so powerfully works in me.

Chapter 2

I WANT you to know
how much I am strug-
gling for you and for those
at Laodicea, and for all
who have not met me per-
sonally. 2 My purpose is
that they may be encour-
aged in heart and united in
love, so that they may have
the full riches of complete
understanding, in order
that they may know the
mystery of God, namely,
Christ, 3 in whom are hidden all the treasures of wisdom and knowledge. 4 I tell
you this so that no one may
deceive you by fine-sound-
ing arguments. 5 For though
I am absent from you in
body, I am present with
you in spirit and delight to
see how orderly you are
and how firm your faith in
Christ is.

Freedom From Human Regulations Through Life With Christ

6 So then, just as you received Christ Jesus as
Lord, continue to live in
him, 7 rooted and built up in
him, strengthened in the
faith as you were taught,
and overflowing with
thankfulness.
8 See to it that no one
takes you captive through
hollow and deceptive phi-
losophy, which depends on
human tradition and the basic principles of this world
rather than on Christ.
9 For in Christ all the full-

dwells bodily, 10and you
have come to fullness in
him, who is the head of every ruler and authority.
11In him also you were circumcised with a spiritual
circumcision,[n] by putting
off the body of the flesh in
the circumcision of Christ;
12when you were buried
with him in baptism, you
were also raised with him
through faith in the power
of God, who raised him
from the dead. 13And when
you were dead in tres-
passes and the uncircumcision of your flesh, God[o]
made you[p] alive together
with him, when he forgave
us all our trespasses,
14erasing the record that
stood against us with its legal demands. He set this
aside, nailing it to the
cross. 15He disarmed[q] the
rulers and authorities and
made a public example of
them, triumphing over
them in it.
16 Therefore do not let
anyone condemn you in
matters of food and drink
or of observing festivals,
new moons, or sabbaths.
17These are only a shadow
of what is to come, but the
substance belongs to
Christ. 18Do not let anyone
disqualify you, insisting on
self-abasement and wor-
ship of angels, dwelling[r]
on visions,[s] puffed up
without cause by a human
way of thinking,[t] 19and
not holding fast to the head,
from whom the whole
body, nourished and held
together by its ligaments

[n] Gk *a circumcision made without hands*
[o] Gk *he*
[p] Other ancient authorities read *made us*; others, *made*
[q] Or *divested himself of*
[r] Other ancient authorities read *not dwelling*
[s] Meaning of Gk uncertain
[t] Gk *by the mind of his flesh*

τὸ πλήρωμα τῆς θεότητος σωματικῶς,
the fulness of the Godhead bodily,

10 καὶ ἐστὲ ἐν αὐτῷ πεπληρωμένοι, ὅς
and ye are in him *having been* filled, who

ἐστιν ἡ κεφαλὴ πάσης ἀρχῆς καὶ ἐξουσίας,
is the head of all rule and authority,

11 ἐν ᾧ καὶ περιετμήθητε περιτομῇ
in whom also ye were circumcised with a circumcision

ἀχειροποιήτῳ ἐν τῇ ἀπεκδύσει τοῦ σώματος
not handwrought by the putting off of the body

τῆς σαρκός, ἐν τῇ περιτομῇ τοῦ Χριστοῦ,
of the flesh, by the circumcision – of Christ,

12 συνταφέντες αὐτῷ ἐν τῷ βαπτίσματι,
co-buried with him in the baptism,

ἐν ᾧ καὶ συνηγέρθητε διὰ τῆς πίστεως
in whom also ye were co-raised through the faith

τῆς ἐνεργείας τοῦ θεοῦ τοῦ ἐγείραντος
of(in) the operation – of God – raising

αὐτὸν ἐκ νεκρῶν· 13 καὶ ὑμᾶς νεκροὺς
him from [the] dead; and you dead

ὄντας τοῖς παραπτώμασιν καὶ τῇ ἀκρο-
being in the trespasses and in the uncir-

βυστίᾳ τῆς σαρκὸς ὑμῶν, συνεζωοποίησεν
cumcision of the flesh of you, he co-quickened

ὑμᾶς σὺν αὐτῷ, χαρισάμενος ἡμῖν πάντα
you with him, forgiving us all

τὰ παραπτώματα· 14 ἐξαλείψας τὸ καθ'
the trespasses; wiping out [1]the [3]against

ἡμῶν χειρόγραφον τοῖς δόγμασιν ὃ ἦν
[4]us [2]handwriting – in ordinances which was

ὑπεναντίον ἡμῖν, καὶ αὐτὸ ἦρκεν ἐκ
contrary to us, and [2]it [1]has taken out of

τοῦ μέσου, προσηλώσας αὐτὸ τῷ σταυρῷ·
the midst(way), nailing it to the cross;

15 ἀπεκδυσάμενος τὰς ἀρχὰς καὶ τὰς
putting off the rulers and the

ἐξουσίας ἐδειγμάτισεν ἐν παρρησίᾳ,
authorities he exposed [them] with openness,

θριαμβεύσας αὐτοὺς ἐν αὐτῷ.
triumphing [over] them in it.

16 Μὴ οὖν τις ὑμᾶς κρινέτω ἐν βρώσει
[2]Not [3]there-fore [4]any-one [6]you [1]let [5]judge in eating

καὶ ἐν πόσει ἢ ἐν μέρει ἑορτῆς ἢ
and in drinking or in respect of a feast or

νεομηνίας ἢ σαββάτων, 17 ἅ ἐστιν σκιὰ
of a new moon or of sabbaths, which things is(are) a shadow

τῶν μελλόντων, τὸ δὲ σῶμα τοῦ Χριστοῦ.
of things coming, but the body [is] – of Christ.

18 μηδεὶς ὑμᾶς καταβραβευέτω θέλων ἐν
[2]No one [4]you [1]let [3]give judgment against wishing [to do so] in

ταπεινοφροσύνῃ καὶ θρησκείᾳ τῶν ἀγγέλων,
humility* and worship of the angels,

ἃ ἑόρακεν ἐμβατεύων, εἰκῇ φυσιούμενος
[4]things which [3]he has seen [1]intruding into, in vain being puffed up

ὑπὸ τοῦ νοὸς τῆς σαρκὸς αὐτοῦ, 19 καὶ
by the mind of the flesh of him, and

οὐ κρατῶν τὴν κεφαλήν, ἐξ οὗ πᾶν
not holding the head, from whom all

τὸ σῶμα διὰ τῶν ἁφῶν καὶ συνδέσμων
the body [4]by means of [5]the (its) [6]joints [7]and [8]bands

* Ellicott supplies " false ". *Cf.* ver. 23.

ness of the Deity lives in
bodily form, 10and you
have been given fullness in
Christ, who is the head
over every power and au-
thority. 11In him you were
also circumcised, in the
putting off of the sinful nature,[g] not with a circumcision done by the hands of
men but with the circumcision done by Christ, 12hav-
ing been buried with him in
baptism and raised with
him through your faith in
the power of God, who
raised him from the dead.
13When you were dead in
your sins and in the uncircumcision of your sinful
nature,[h] God made you[i]
alive with Christ. He forgave us all our sins, 14hav-
ing canceled the written
code, with its regulations,
that was against us and that
stood opposed to us; he
took it away, nailing it to
the cross. 15And having disarmed the powers and au-
thorities, he made a public
spectacle of them, triumphing over them by the
cross.[j]
16Therefore do not let
anyone judge you by what
you eat or drink, or with
regard to a religious festival, a New Moon celebra-
tion or a Sabbath day.
17These are a shadow of the
things that were to come;
the reality, however, is
found in Christ. 18Do not
let anyone who delights in
false humility and the worship of angels disqualify
you for the prize. Such a
person goes into great detail about what he has seen,
and his unspiritual mind
puffs him up with idle no-
tions. 19He has lost connection with the Head, from
whom the whole body, sup-
ported and held together by

[g] *11* Or *the flesh*
[h] *13* Or *your flesh*
[i] *13* Some manuscripts *us*
[j] *15* Or *them in him*

and sinews, grows with a
growth that is from God.

Warnings against False Teachers

20 If with Christ you
died to the elemental spirits
of the universe,[m] why do
you live as if you still belonged to the world? Why
do you submit to regula-
tions, 21 "Do not handle,
Do not taste, Do not
touch"? 22 All these regulations refer to things that
perish with use; they are
simply human commands
and teachings. 23 These
have indeed an appearance
of wisdom in promoting
self-imposed piety, humility, and severe treatment of
the body, but they are of no
value in checking self-
indulgence.[u]

Chapter 3

The New Life in Christ

So if you have been
raised with Christ,
seek the things that are
above, where Christ is,
seated at the right hand of
God. 2 Set your minds on
things that are above, not
on things that are on earth,
3 for you have died, and
your life is hidden with
Christ in God. 4 When
Christ who is your[v] life is
revealed, then you also will
be revealed with him in glory.
5 Put to death, there-
fore, whatever in you is
earthly: fornication, impurity, passion, evil desire,
and greed (which is idolatry). 6 On account of these
the wrath of God is coming
on those who are disobedient.[w] 7 These are the ways
you also once followed,
when you were living that
life.[x] 8 But now you must
get rid of all such things—
anger, wrath, malice, slander, and abusive[y] language
from your mouth. 9 Do not
lie to one another, seeing
that you have stripped off
the old self with its prac-

[u] Or *are of no value, serving only to indulge the flesh*
[v] Other authorities read *our*
[w] Other ancient authorities lack *on those who are disobedient* (Gk *the children of disobedience*)
[x] Or *living among such people*
[y] Or *filthy*

ἐπιχορηγούμενον καὶ συμβιβαζόμενον αὔξει
being supplied and being joined together will grow
τὴν αὔξησιν τοῦ θεοῦ.
[with] the growth – of God.
20 Εἰ ἀπεθάνετε σὺν Χριστῷ ἀπὸ τῶν στοι-
If ye died with Christ from the ele-
χείων τοῦ κόσμου, τί ὡς ζῶντες ἐν κόσμῳ
ments of the world, why as living in [the] world
δογματίζεσθε· **21** μὴ ἅψῃ μηδὲ γεύσῃ μηδὲ
are ye subject to [its] decrees: Do not touch nor taste nor
θίγῃς, **22** ἅ ἐστιν πάντα εἰς φθορὰν
handle, which things is(are) all for corruption
τῇ ἀποχρήσει, κατὰ τὰ ἐντάλματα καὶ
in the using, according to the injunctions and
διδασκαλίας τῶν ἀνθρώπων; **23** ἅτινά ἐστιν
teachings – of men? which things is(are)
λόγον μὲν ἔχοντα σοφίας ἐν ἐθελοθρησκίᾳ
a repute indeed having of wisdom in self-imposed worship
καὶ ταπεινοφροσύνῃ καὶ ἀφειδίᾳ σώματος, οὐκ
and humility and severity of [the] body, not
ἐν τιμῇ τινι πρὸς πλησμονὴν τῆς σαρκός.
in honour any for satisfaction of the flesh.
3 Εἰ οὖν συνηγέρθητε τῷ Χριστῷ, τὰ
If therefore ye were co-raised – with Christ, the things
ἄνω ζητεῖτε, οὗ ὁ Χριστός ἐστιν ἐν
above seek, where – Christ is at
δεξιᾷ τοῦ θεοῦ καθήμενος· **2** τὰ ἄνω
[the] right [hand] – of God sitting; the things above
φρονεῖτε, μὴ τὰ ἐπὶ τῆς γῆς. **3** ἀπεθάνετε
mind ye, not the things on the earth. ye died
γάρ, καὶ ἡ ζωὴ ὑμῶν κέκρυπται σὺν
For, and the life of you has been hidden with
τῷ Χριστῷ ἐν τῷ θεῷ· **4** ὅταν ὁ Χριστὸς
– Christ in – God; whenever – Christ
φανερωθῇ, ἡ ζωὴ ἡμῶν, τότε καὶ ὑμεῖς
is manifested, the life of us, then also ye
σὺν αὐτῷ φανερωθήσεσθε ἐν δόξῃ.
with him will be manifested in glory.
5 Νεκρώσατε οὖν τὰ μέλη τὰ ἐπὶ
Put ye to death therefore the (your) members – on
τῆς γῆς, πορνείαν, ἀκαθαρσίαν, πάθος,
the earth, fornication, uncleanness, passion,
ἐπιθυμίαν κακήν, καὶ τὴν πλεονεξίαν ἥτις
desire bad, and – covetousness which
ἐστὶν εἰδωλολατρία, **6** δι' ἃ ἔρχεται ἡ
is idolatry, because of which things is coming the
ὀργὴ τοῦ θεοῦ· **7** ἐν οἷς καὶ ὑμεῖς
wrath – of God; in which indeed ye
περιεπατήσατέ ποτε, ὅτε ἐζῆτε ἐν τούτοις·
walked then, when ye lived in these things;
8 νυνὶ δὲ ἀπόθεσθε καὶ ὑμεῖς τὰ πάντα,
but now put away also ye – all things,
ὀργήν, θυμόν, κακίαν, βλασφημίαν, αἰσχρο-
wrath, anger, malice, blasphemy, a-
λογίαν ἐκ τοῦ στόματος ὑμῶν· **9** μὴ
buse out of the mouth of you; not
ψεύδεσθε εἰς ἀλλήλους, ἀπεκδυσάμενοι τὸν
lie ye to one another, having put off the
παλαιὸν ἄνθρωπον σὺν ταῖς πράξεσιν
old man with the practices

its ligaments and sinews,
grows as God causes it to
grow.
20 Since you died with
Christ to the basic principles of this world, why, as
though you still belonged to
it, do you submit to its
rules: 21 "Do not handle! Do
not taste! Do not touch!"?
22 These are all destined to
perish with use, because
they are based on human
commands and teachings.
23 Such regulations indeed
have an appearance of wisdom, with their self-im-
posed worship, their false
humility and their harsh
treatment of the body, but
they lack any value in restraining sensual indul-
gence.

Chapter 3

Rules for Holy Living

Since, then, you have
been raised with
Christ, set your hearts on
things above, where Christ
is seated at the right hand of
God. 2 Set your minds on
things above, not on earthly things. 3 For you died,
and your life is now hidden
with Christ in God. 4 When
Christ, who is your[k] life,
appears, then you also will
appear with him in glory.
5 Put to death, therefore,
whatever belongs to your
earthly nature: sexual immorality, impurity, lust,
evil desires and greed,
which is idolatry. 6 Because
of these, the wrath of God
is coming.[l] 7 You used to
walk in these ways, in the
life you once lived. 8 But
now you must rid your-
selves of all such things as
these: anger, rage, malice,
slander, and filthy language
from your lips. 9 Do not lie
to each other, since you
have taken off your old self
with its practices 10 and

[k] 4 Some manuscripts *our*
[l] 6 Some early manuscripts *coming on those who are disobedient*

tices 10 and have clothed
yourselves with the new
self, which is being re-
newed in knowledge ac-
cording to the image of its
creator. 11 In that renewal[z]
there is no longer Greek
and Jew, circumcised and
uncircumcised, barbarian,
Scythian, slave and free;
but Christ is all and in all!
12 As God's chosen
ones, holy and beloved,
clothe yourselves with
compassion, kindness, hu-
mility, meekness, and pa-
tience. 13 Bear with one another and, if anyone has a
complaint against another,
forgive each other; just as
the Lord[a] has forgiven
you, so you also must forgive. 14 Above all, clothe
yourselves with love,
which binds everything together in perfect harmony.
15 And let the peace of
Christ rule in your hearts,
to which indeed you were
called in the one body. And
be thankful. 16 Let the word
of Christ[b] dwell in you
richly; teach and admonish
one another in all wisdom;
and with gratitude in your
hearts sing psalms, hymns,
and spiritual songs to
God.[c] 17 And whatever
you do, in word or deed, do
everything in the name of
the Lord Jesus, giving
thanks to God the Father
through him.

Rules for Christian Households

18 Wives, be subject to
your husbands, as is fitting
in the Lord. 19 Husbands,
love your wives and never
treat them harshly.
20 Children, obey your
parents in everything, for

[z] Gk *its creator,* 11 *where*
[a] Other ancient authorities read *just as Christ*
[b] Other ancient authorities read *of God,* or *of the Lord*
[c] Other ancient authorities read *to the Lord*

αὐτοῦ, 10 καὶ ἐνδυσάμενοι τὸν νέον τὸν
of him, and having put on the new man –
ἀνακαινούμενον εἰς ἐπίγνωσιν κατ' εἰκόνα
being renewed in full knowledge according to [the] image
τοῦ κτίσαντος αὐτόν, 11 ὅπου οὐκ ἔνι
of the [one] creating him, where [4]have no place
Ἕλλην καὶ Ἰουδαῖος, περιτομὴ καὶ
[1]Greek [2]and [3]Jew, circumcision and
ἀκροβυστία, βάρβαρος, Σκύθης, δοῦλος,
uncircumcision, barbarian, Scythian, slave,
ἐλεύθερος, ἀλλὰ πάντα καὶ ἐν πᾶσιν
freeman, but [3]all things [4]and [5]in [6]all
Χριστός. 12 Ἐνδύσασθε οὖν, ὡς ἐκλεκτοὶ
[1]Christ [2][is]. Put ye on therefore, as chosen ones
τοῦ θεοῦ ἅγιοι καὶ ἠγαπημένοι, σπλάγχνα
– of God holy and having been loved, bowels
οἰκτιρμοῦ, χρηστότητα, ταπεινοφροσύνην,
of compassion, kindness, humility,
πραΰτητα, μακροθυμίαν, 13 ἀνεχόμενοι ἀλ-
meekness, long-suffering, forbearing one
λήλων καὶ χαριζόμενοι ἑαυτοῖς, ἐάν τις
another and forgiving yourselves, if anyone
πρός τινα ἔχῃ μομφήν· καθὼς καὶ ὁ
[3]against [4]anyone [1]has [2]a complaint; as indeed the
κύριος ἐχαρίσατο ὑμῖν οὕτως καὶ ὑμεῖς·
Lord forgave you so also ye;
14 ἐπὶ πᾶσιν δὲ τούτοις τὴν ἀγάπην,
[2]over [3]all [1]and these things – love,
ὅ ἐστιν σύνδεσμος τῆς τελειότητος. 15 καὶ
which is [the] bond – of completeness. And
ἡ εἰρήνη τοῦ Χριστοῦ βραβευέτω ἐν ταῖς
[2]the [3]peace – [4]of Christ [1]let [5]rule in the
καρδίαις ὑμῶν, εἰς ἣν καὶ ἐκλήθητε
hearts of you, to which indeed ye were called
ἐν ἑνὶ σώματι· καὶ εὐχάριστοι γίνεσθε.
in one body; and thankful be ye.
16 ὁ λόγος τοῦ Χριστοῦ ἐνοικείτω ἐν
[2]The [3]word – [4]of Christ [1]let [5]indwell in
ὑμῖν πλουσίως, ἐν πάσῃ σοφίᾳ διδάσκοντες
you richly, in all wisdom teaching
καὶ νουθετοῦντες ἑαυτούς, ψαλμοῖς ὕμνοις
and admonishing yourselves, in psalms[,] hymns[,]
ᾠδαῖς πνευματικαῖς ἐν τῇ χάριτι ᾄδοντες
[and] [2]songs [1]spiritual with – grace singing
ἐν ταῖς καρδίαις ὑμῶν τῷ θεῷ· 17 καὶ
in the hearts of you – to God; and
πᾶν ὅ τι ἐὰν ποιῆτε ἐν λόγῳ ἢ ἐν
everything whatever ye do in word or in
ἔργῳ, πάντα ἐν ὀνόματι κυρίου Ἰησοῦ,
work, all things [do] in [the] name of [the] Lord Jesus,
εὐχαριστοῦντες τῷ θεῷ πατρὶ δι' αὐτοῦ.
giving thanks – to God [the] Father through him.
18 Αἱ γυναῖκες, ὑποτάσσεσθε τοῖς
The wives, be ye subject to the(your)
ἀνδράσιν, ὡς ἀνῆκεν ἐν κυρίῳ. 19 Οἱ
husbands, as is befitting in [the] Lord. The
ἄνδρες, ἀγαπᾶτε τὰς γυναῖκας καὶ μὴ
husbands, love ye the(your) wives and not
πικραίνεσθε πρὸς αὐτάς. 20 Τὰ τέκνα,
be bitter toward them. The children,
ὑπακούετε τοῖς γονεῦσιν κατὰ πάντα,
obey ye the(your) parents in all respects,

have put on the new self,
which is being renewed in
knowledge in the image of
its Creator. 11 Here there is
no Greek or Jew, circum-
cised or uncircumcised,
barbarian, Scythian, slave
or free, but Christ is all, and
is in all.
12 Therefore, as God's
chosen people, holy and
dearly loved, clothe yourselves with compassion,
kindness, humility, gentleness and patience. 13 Bear
with each other and forgive
whatever grievances you
may have against one an-
other. Forgive as the Lord
forgave you. 14 And over all
these virtues put on love,
which binds them all to-
gether in perfect unity.
15 Let the peace of Christ
rule in your hearts, since as
members of one body you
were called to peace. And
be thankful. 16 Let the word
of Christ dwell in you richly
as you teach and admonish
one another with all wis-
dom, and as you sing
psalms, hymns and spiritual songs with gratitude in
your hearts to God. 17 And
whatever you do, whether
in word or deed, do it all in
the name of the Lord Jesus,
giving thanks to God the
Father through him.

Rules for Christian Households

18 Wives, submit to your
husbands, as is fitting in the
Lord.
19 Husbands, love your
wives and do not be harsh
with them.
20 Children, obey your
parents in everything, for

this is your acceptable duty
in the Lord. 21 Fathers, do
not provoke your children,
or they may lose heart.
22 Slaves, obey your earthly
masters[d] in everything,
not only while being
watched and in order to
please them, but whole-
heartedly, fearing the
Lord.[d] 23 Whatever your
task, put yourselves into it,
as done for the Lord and
not for your masters,[e]
24 since you know that from
the Lord you will receive
the inheritance as your reward; you serve[f] the Lord
Christ. 25 For the wrongdoer will be paid back for
whatever wrong has been
done, and there is no partiality. 1 Masters, treat your
slaves justly and fairly, for
you know that you also
have a Master in heaven.

Further Instructions

2 Devote yourselves to
prayer, keeping alert in it
with thanksgiving. 3 At the
same time pray for us as
well that God will open to
us a door for the word, that
we may declare the mys-
tery of Christ, for which I
am in prison, 4 so that I may
reveal it clearly, as I
should.
5 Conduct yourselves
wisely toward outsiders,
making the most of the
time.[g] 6 Let your speech always be gracious, seasoned
with salt, so that you may
know how you ought to an-
swer everyone.

Final Greetings and Benediction

7 Tychicus will tell you
all the news about me; he is
a beloved brother, a faithful minister, and a fellow

[d] In Greek the same word is used for *master* and *Lord*
[e] Gk *not for men*
[f] Or *you are slaves of*, or *be slaves of*
[g] Or *opportunity*

τοῦτο γὰρ εὐάρεστόν ἐστιν ἐν κυρίῳ.
for this well-pleasing is in [the] Lord.

21 Οἱ πατέρες, μὴ ἐρεθίζετε τὰ τέκνα
The fathers, do not ye provoke the children

ὑμῶν, ἵνα μὴ ἀθυμῶσιν. 22 Οἱ δοῦλοι,
of you, lest they be disheartened. The slaves,

ὑπακούετε κατὰ πάντα τοῖς κατὰ σάρκα
obey ye in all respects [1]the (your) [3]according to [4][the] flesh

κυρίοις, μὴ ἐν ὀφθαλμοδουλίαις ὡς
[2]lords, not with eyeservice as

ἀνθρωπάρεσκοι, ἀλλ' ἐν ἁπλότητι καρδίας
men-pleasers, but in singleness of heart

φοβούμενοι τὸν κύριον. 23 ὃ ἐὰν ποιῆτε,
fearing the Lord. Whatever ye do,

ἐκ ψυχῆς ἐργάζεσθε ὡς τῷ κυρίῳ καὶ
from [the] soul work ye as to the Lord and

οὐκ ἀνθρώποις, 24 εἰδότες ὅτι ἀπὸ κυρίου
not to men, knowing that from [the] Lord

ἀπολήμψεσθε τὴν ἀνταπόδοσιν τῆς κλη-
ye will receive the reward of the in-

ρονομίας. τῷ κυρίῳ Χριστῷ δουλεύετε·
heritance. The Lord Christ ye serve;

25 ὁ γὰρ ἀδικῶν κομίσεται ὃ ἠδίκησεν,
for the [one] doing wrong will receive what he did wrong,

καὶ οὐκ ἔστιν προσωπολημψία. 4 Οἱ κύριοι,
and there is no respect of persons. The lords,

τὸ δίκαιον καὶ τὴν ἰσότητα τοῖς δούλοις
[2]the [3]just thing [4]and [5]the [6]equality [7]to the(your) [8]slaves

παρέχεσθε, εἰδότες ὅτι καὶ ὑμεῖς ἔχετε
[1]supply ye, knowing that also ye have

κύριον ἐν οὐρανῷ.
a Lord in heaven.

2 Τῇ προσευχῇ προσκαρτερεῖτε, γρηγο-
In *the* prayer continue ye, watch-

ροῦντες ἐν αὐτῇ ἐν εὐχαριστίᾳ, 3 προσευ-
ing in it with thanksgiving, pray-

χόμενοι ἅμα καὶ περὶ ἡμῶν, ἵνα ὁ
ing together also concerning us, *in order* that –

θεὸς ἀνοίξῃ ἡμῖν θύραν τοῦ λόγου,
God may open to us a door of the word,

λαλῆσαι τὸ μυστήριον τοῦ Χριστοῦ, δι'
to speak the mystery – of Christ, because of

ὃ καὶ δέδεμαι, 4 ἵνα φανερώσω αὐτὸ
which indeed I have been bound, in order that I may manifest it

ὡς δεῖ με λαλῆσαι. 5 Ἐν σοφίᾳ
as it behoves me to speak. In wisdom

περιπατεῖτε πρὸς τοὺς ἔξω, τὸν καιρὸν
walk ye toward the ones outside, [2]the [3]time

ἐξαγοραζόμενοι. 6 ὁ λόγος ὑμῶν πάντοτε
[1]redeeming. The speech of you [let it be] always

ἐν χάριτι, ἅλατι ἠρτυμένος, εἰδέναι πῶς
in grace, with salt *having been* seasoned, to know how

δεῖ ὑμᾶς ἑνὶ ἑκάστῳ ἀποκρίνεσθαι.
it behoves you [3]one [2]each [1]to answer.

7 Τὰ κατ' ἐμὲ πάντα γνωρίσει ὑμῖν Τύχικος
[2]The [3]about things [4]me [1]all [6]will make known [7]to you [5]Tychicus

ὁ ἀγαπητὸς ἀδελφὸς καὶ πιστὸς διάκονος
the beloved brother and faithful minister

this pleases the Lord.
21 Fathers, do not embit-
ter your children, or they
will become discouraged.
22 Slaves, obey your
earthly masters in every-
thing; and do it, not only
when their eye is on you
and to win their favor, but
with sincerity of heart and
reverence for the Lord.
23 Whatever you do, work
at it with all your heart, as
working for the Lord, not
for men, 24 since you know
that you will receive an inheritance from the Lord as
a reward. It is the Lord
Christ you are serving.
25 Anyone who does wrong
will be repaid for his
wrong, and there is no favoritism.

Chapter 4

MASTERS, provide your slaves with what is right and fair, because you know that you also have a Master in heaven.

Further Instructions

2 Devote yourselves to
prayer, being watchful and
thankful. 3 And pray for us,
too, that God may open a
door for our message, so
that we may proclaim the
mystery of Christ, for
which I am in chains. 4 Pray
that I may proclaim it clearly, as I should. 5 Be wise in
the way you act toward
outsiders; make the most of
every opportunity. 6 Let
your conversation be al-
ways full of grace, sea-
soned with salt, so that you
may know how to answer
everyone.

Final Greetings

7 Tychicus will tell you all
the news about me. He is a
dear brother, a faithful min-

servant[h] in the Lord. 8I
have sent him to you for
this very purpose, so that
you may know how we
are[i] and that he may encourage your hearts; 9he is
coming with Onesimus, the
faithful and beloved brother, who is one of you. They
will tell you about everything here.
10 Aristarchus my fel-
low prisoner greets you, as
does Mark the cousin of
Barnabas, concerning
whom you have received
instructions—if he comes
to you, welcome him.
11And Jesus who is called
Justus greets you. These
are the only ones of the circumcision among my co-
workers for the kingdom of
God, and they have been a
comfort to me. 12Epa-
phras, who is one of you, a
servant[h] of Christ Jesus,
greets you. He is always
wrestling in his prayers on
your behalf, so that you
may stand mature and fully
assured in everything that
God wills. 13For I testify
for him that he has worked
hard for you and for those
in Laodicea and in Hierapolis. 14Luke, the beloved
physician, and Demas greet
you. 15Give my greetings
to the brothers and sisters[j]
in Laodicea, and to Nym-
pha and the church in her
house. 16And when this letter has been read among
you, have it read also in the
church of the Laodiceans;
and see that you read also
the letter from Laodicea.
17And say to Archippus,
"See that you complete the

[h] Gk *slave*
[i] Other authorities read *that I may know how you are*
[j] Gk *brothers*

καὶ σύνδουλος ἐν κυρίῳ, 8 ὃν ἔπεμψα
and fellow-slave in [the] Lord, whom I sent

πρὸς ὑμᾶς εἰς αὐτὸ τοῦτο, ἵνα γνῶτε
to you for this very thing, in order that ye might know

τὰ περὶ ἡμῶν καὶ παρακαλέσῃ τὰς
the things concerning us and he might comfort the

καρδίας ὑμῶν, 9 σὺν Ὀνησίμῳ τῷ πιστῷ
hearts of you, with Onesimus the faithful

καὶ ἀγαπητῷ ἀδελφῷ, ὅς ἐστιν ἐξ ὑμῶν·
and beloved brother, who is of you;

πάντα ὑμῖν γνωρίσουσιν τὰ ὧδε.
[1]all [3]to you [2]they will make known [4]the things [5]here.

10 Ἀσπάζεται ὑμᾶς Ἀρίσταρχος ὁ
[5]greets [6]you [1]Aristarchus [2]the

συναιχμάλωτός μου, καὶ Μᾶρκος ὁ ἀνεψιὸς
[3]fellow-captive [4]of me, and Mark the cousin

Βαρναβᾶ, (περὶ οὗ ἐλάβετε ἐντολάς, ἐὰν
of Barnabas, (concerning whom ye received commandments, if

ἔλθῃ πρὸς ὑμᾶς, δέξασθε αὐτόν,) 11 καὶ
he comes to you, receive ye him,) and

Ἰησοῦς ὁ λεγόμενος Ἰοῦστος, οἱ ὄντες
Jesus the [one] *being* named Justus, the [ones] being

ἐκ περιτομῆς οὗτοι μόνοι συνεργοὶ εἰς
of [the] circumcision these only fellow-workers for

τὴν βασιλείαν τοῦ θεοῦ, οἵτινες ἐγενή-
the kingdom – of God, who be-

θησάν μοι παρηγορία. 12 ἀσπάζεται ὑμᾶς
came to me a comfort. [2]greets [3]you

Ἐπαφρᾶς ὁ ἐξ ὑμῶν, δοῦλος Χριστοῦ
[1]Epaphras the [one] of you, a slave of Christ

Ἰησοῦ, πάντοτε ἀγωνιζόμενος ὑπὲρ ὑμῶν
Jesus, always struggling on behalf of you

ἐν ταῖς προσευχαῖς, ἵνα σταθῆτε τέλειοι
in the prayers, in order that ye may stand complete

καὶ πεπληροφορημένοι ἐν παντὶ θελήματι
and having been fully assured in all [the] will

τοῦ θεοῦ. 13 μαρτυρῶ γὰρ αὐτῷ ὅτι
– of God. For I bear witness to him that

ἔχει πολὺν πόνον ὑπὲρ ὑμῶν καὶ τῶν
he has much distress on behalf of you and the ones

ἐν Λαοδικείᾳ καὶ τῶν ἐν Ἱεραπόλει.
in Laodicea and the ones in Hierapolis.

14 ἀσπάζεται ὑμᾶς Λουκᾶς ὁ ἰατρὸς ὁ
[7]greets [8]you [1]Luke [2]the [4]physician –

ἀγαπητὸς καὶ Δημᾶς. 15 Ἀσπάσασθε
[3]beloved [5]and [6]Demas. Greet ye

τοὺς ἐν Λαοδικείᾳ ἀδελφοὺς καὶ Νύμφαν
[1]the [3]in [4]Laodicea [2]brothers and Nymphas

καὶ τὴν κατ' οἶκον αὐτῆς ἐκκλησίαν.
and [1]the [3]at [4][the] house [5]of her [2]church.

16 καὶ ὅταν ἀναγνωσθῇ παρ' ὑμῖν ἡ
And whenever is read before you the(this)

ἐπιστολή, ποιήσατε ἵνα καὶ ἐν τῇ
epistle, cause *in order* that [2]also [3]in [4]the

Λαοδικέων ἐκκλησίᾳ ἀναγνωσθῇ, καὶ τὴν
[6]of [the] Laodiceans [5]church [1]it is read, and [5]the [one]

ἐκ Λαοδικείας ἵνα καὶ ὑμεῖς ἀναγνῶτε.
[6]of [7]Laodicea [1]*in order* that [2]also [3]ye [4]read.

17 καὶ εἴπατε Ἀρχίππῳ· βλέπε τὴν
And tell Archippus: Look [to] the

ister and fellow servant in
the Lord. 8I am sending
him to you for the express
purpose that you may
know about our[m] circum-
stances and that he may encourage your hearts. 9He is
coming with Onesimus, our
faithful and dear brother,
who is one of you. They
will tell you everything that
is happening here.
10My fellow prisoner Ar-
istarchus sends you his
greetings, as does Mark,
the cousin of Barnabas.
(You have received in-
structions about him; if he
comes to you, welcome
him.) 11Jesus, who is called
Justus, also sends greet-
ings. These are the only
Jews among my fellow
workers for the kingdom of
God, and they have proved
a comfort to me. 12Epa-
phras, who is one of you
and a servant of Christ
Jesus, sends greetings. He
is always wrestling in
prayer for you, that you
may stand firm in all the
will of God, mature and fully assured. 13I vouch for
him that he is working hard
for you and for those at Laodicea and Hierapolis.
14Our dear friend Luke, the
doctor, and Demas send
greetings. 15Give my greetings to the brothers at Laodicea, and to Nympha and
the church in her house.
16After this letter has
been read to you, see that it
is also read in the church of
the Laodiceans and that
you in turn read the letter
from Laodicea.
17Tell Archippus: "See to
it that you complete the

[m]8 Some manuscripts *that he may know about your*

task that you have received in the Lord."

18 I, Paul, write this greeting with my own hand. Remember my chains. Grace be with you.[k]

διακονίαν ἣν παρέλαβες ἐν κυρίῳ, ἵνα
ministry which thou receivedst in [the] Lord, in order that
αὐτὴν πληροῖς.
²it ¹thou mayest fulfil.
18 Ὁ ἀσπασμὸς τῇ ἐμῇ χειρὶ Παύλου.
The greeting – by my hand[,] of Paul.
μνημονεύετέ μου τῶν δεσμῶν. ἡ χάρις
Remember ye of me the bonds. – Grace [be]
μεθ' ὑμῶν.
with you.

work you have received in the Lord."
18I, Paul, write this greeting in my own hand. Remember my chains. Grace be with you.

The First Letter of Paul to the

Thessalonians

Chapter 1

Salutation

PAUL, Silvanus, and Timothy,
To the church of the Thessalonians in God the Father and the Lord Jesus Christ:
Grace to you and peace.

The Thessalonians' Faith and Example

2 We always give thanks to God for all of you and mention you in our prayers, constantly 3 remembering before our God and Father your work of faith and labor of love and steadfastness of hope in our Lord Jesus Christ. 4 For we know, brothers and sisters[a] beloved by God, that he has chosen you, 5 because our message of the gospel came to you not in word only, but also in power and in the Holy Spirit and with full conviction; just as you know what kind of persons we proved to be among you for your sake. 6 And you became imitators of us and of the Lord, for in spite of persecution you received the word with joy inspired by the Holy Spirit, 7 so that you became an example to all the believers in Macedonia and in Achaia.

[k] Other ancient authorities add *Amen*

[a] Gk *brothers*

ΠΡΟΣ ΘΕΣΣΑΛΟΝΙΚΕΙΣ Α
To Thessalonians 1

1 Παῦλος καὶ Σιλουανὸς καὶ Τιμόθεος
Paul and Silvanus and Timothy
τῇ ἐκκλησίᾳ Θεσσαλονικέων ἐν θεῷ πατρὶ
to the church of [the] Thessalonians in God [the] Father
καὶ κυρίῳ Ἰησοῦ Χριστῷ· χάρις ὑμῖν
and [the] Lord Jesus Christ: Grace [be] to you
καὶ εἰρήνη.
and peace.
2 Εὐχαριστοῦμεν τῷ θεῷ πάντοτε περὶ
We give thanks – to God always concerning
πάντων ὑμῶν, μνείαν ποιούμενοι ἐπὶ τῶν
²all ¹you, mention making on(in) the
προσευχῶν ἡμῶν, ἀδιαλείπτως 3 μνημονεύοντες
prayers of us, unceasingly remembering
ὑμῶν τοῦ ἔργου τῆς πίστεως
of you the work – of faith
καὶ τοῦ κόπου τῆς ἀγάπης καὶ τῆς
and the labour – of love and the
ὑπομονῆς τῆς ἐλπίδος τοῦ κυρίου ἡμῶν
endurance – of hope of(in) the Lord of us
Ἰησοῦ Χριστοῦ ἔμπροσθεν τοῦ θεοῦ καὶ
Jesus Christ before the God and
πατρὸς ἡμῶν, 4 εἰδότες, ἀδελφοὶ ἠγαπημένοι
Father of us, knowing, brothers having been loved
ὑπὸ [τοῦ] θεοῦ, τὴν ἐκλογὴν ὑμῶν,
by – God, the choice of you,
5 ὅτι τὸ εὐαγγέλιον ἡμῶν οὐκ ἐγενήθη
because the gospel of us became not
εἰς ὑμᾶς ἐν λόγῳ μόνον, ἀλλὰ καὶ ἐν
to you in word only, but also in
δυνάμει καὶ ἐν πνεύματι ἁγίῳ καὶ
power and in Spirit Holy and
πληροφορίᾳ πολλῇ, καθὼς οἴδατε οἷοι
²assurance ¹much, as ye know what sort
ἐγενήθημεν ἐν ὑμῖν δι' ὑμᾶς. 6 καὶ
we were among you because of you. And
ὑμεῖς μιμηταὶ ἡμῶν ἐγενήθητε καὶ τοῦ
¹ye ³imitators ⁴of us ²became and of the
κυρίου, δεξάμενοι τὸν λόγον ἐν θλίψει
Lord, welcoming the word in ²affliction
πολλῇ μετὰ χαρᾶς πνεύματος ἁγίου, 7 ὥστε
¹much with joy of ²Spirit ¹[the] Holy, so as
γενέσθαι ὑμᾶς τύπον πᾶσιν τοῖς πιστεύουσιν
to become you[b] a pattern to all the [ones] believing
=so that ye became
ἐν τῇ Μακεδονίᾳ καὶ ἐν τῇ Ἀχαΐᾳ.
in – Macedonia and in – Achaia.

1 Thessalonians

Chapter 1

PAUL, Silas[a] and Timothy,
To the church of the Thessalonians in God the Father and the Lord Jesus Christ:
Grace and peace to you.[b]

Thanksgiving for the Thessalonians' Faith

2We always thank God for all of you, mentioning you in our prayers. 3We continually remember before our God and Father your work produced by faith, your labor prompted by love, and your endurance inspired by hope in our Lord Jesus Christ.
4For we know, brothers loved by God, that he has chosen you, 5because our gospel came to you not simply with words, but also with power, with the Holy Spirit and with deep conviction. You know how we lived among you for your sake. 6You became imitators of us and of the Lord; in spite of severe suffering, you welcomed the message with the joy given by the Holy Spirit. 7And so you became a model to all the believers in Macedonia and

[a] 1 Greek *Silvanus*, a variant of *Silas*
[b] 1 Some early manuscripts *you from God our Father and the Lord Jesus Christ*

[8] For the word of the Lord has sounded forth from you not only in Macedonia and Achaia, but in every place your faith in God has become known, so that we have no need to speak about it. [9] For the people of those regions[b] report about us what kind of welcome we had among you, and how you turned to God from idols, to serve a living and true God, [10] and to wait for his Son from heaven, whom he raised from the dead—Jesus, who rescues us from the wrath that is coming.

8 ἀφ' ὑμῶν γὰρ ἐξήχηται ὁ λόγος τοῦ
[2]from [3]you [1]For sounded the word of the

κυρίου οὐ μόνον ἐν τῇ Μακεδονίᾳ καὶ
Lord not only in – Macedonia and

Ἀχαΐᾳ, ἀλλ' ἐν παντὶ τόπῳ ἡ πίστις
Achaia, but in every place the faith

ὑμῶν ἡ πρὸς τὸν θεὸν ἐξελήλυθεν, ὥστε
of you – toward – God has gone out, so as

μὴ χρείαν ἔχειν ἡμᾶς λαλεῖν τι· **9** αὐτοὶ
not need to have us[b] to speak anything; [2][them]selves
=so that we have no need

γὰρ περὶ ἡμῶν ἀπαγγέλλουσιν ὁποίαν
[1]for [4]concerning [5]us [3]they relate what sort of

εἴσοδον ἔσχομεν πρὸς ὑμᾶς, καὶ πῶς
entrance we had to you, and how

ἐπεστρέψατε πρὸς τὸν θεὸν ἀπὸ τῶν
ye turned to – God from *the*

εἰδώλων δουλεύειν θεῷ ζῶντι καὶ ἀληθινῷ,
idols to serve a God living and true,

10 καὶ ἀναμένειν τὸν υἱὸν αὐτοῦ ἐκ
and to await the Son of him from

τῶν οὐρανῶν, ὃν ἤγειρεν ἐκ τῶν νεκρῶν,
the heavens, whom he raised from the dead,

Ἰησοῦν τὸν ῥυόμενον ἡμᾶς ἐκ τῆς ὀργῆς
Jesus the [one] delivering us from the wrath

τῆς ἐρχομένης.
– coming.

Achaia. [8] The Lord's message rang out from you not only in Macedonia and Achaia—your faith in God has become known everywhere. Therefore we do not need to say anything about it, [9] for they themselves report what kind of reception you gave us. They tell how you turned to God from idols to serve the living and true God, [10] and to wait for his Son from heaven, whom he raised from the dead—Jesus, who rescues us from the coming wrath.

Chapter 2

Paul's Ministry in Thessalonica

YOU yourselves know, brothers and sisters,[a] that our coming to you was not in vain, [2] but though we had already suffered and been shamefully mistreated at Philippi, as you know, we had courage in our God to declare to you the gospel of God in spite of great opposition. [3] For our appeal does not spring from deceit or impure motives or trickery, [4] but just as we have been approved by God to be entrusted with the message of the gospel, even so we speak, not to please mortals, but to please God who tests our hearts. [5] As you know and as God is our witness, we never came with words of flattery or with a pretext for greed; [6] nor did we seek praise from mortals, whether from you or from

2 Αὐτοὶ γὰρ οἴδατε, ἀδελφοί, τὴν
For [your]selves ye know, brothers, the

εἴσοδον ἡμῶν τὴν πρὸς ὑμᾶς, ὅτι οὐ
entrance of us – to you, that not

κενὴ γέγονεν, **2** ἀλλὰ προπαθόντες καὶ
in vain it has been, but having previously suffered and

ὑβρισθέντες καθὼς οἴδατε ἐν Φιλίπποις
having been insulted as ye know in Philippi

ἐπαρρησιασάμεθα ἐν τῷ θεῷ ἡμῶν λαλῆσαι
we were bold in the God of us to speak

πρὸς ὑμᾶς τὸ εὐαγγέλιον τοῦ θεοῦ ἐν
to you the gospel – of God in

πολλῷ ἀγῶνι. **3** ἡ γὰρ παράκλησις
much struggle. For the exhortation

ἡμῶν οὐκ ἐκ πλάνης οὐδὲ ἐξ ἀκαθαρσίας
of us not of error nor of uncleanness

οὐδὲ ἐν δόλῳ, **4** ἀλλὰ καθὼς δεδοκιμάσμεθα
nor in guile, but as we have been approved

ὑπὸ τοῦ θεοῦ πιστευθῆναι τὸ εὐαγγέλιον
by – God to be entrusted [with] the gospel

οὕτως λαλοῦμεν, οὐχ ὡς ἀνθρώποις ἀρέ-
so we speak, not as [2]men [1]pleas-

σκοντες, ἀλλὰ θεῷ τῷ δοκιμάζοντι τὰς
ing, but God the [one] proving the

καρδίας ἡμῶν. **5** οὔτε γάρ ποτε ἐν
hearts of us. For neither then with

λόγῳ κολακείας ἐγενήθημεν, καθὼς οἴδατε,
word of flattery were we, as ye know,

οὔτε ἐν προφάσει πλεονεξίας, θεὸς μάρτυς,
nor with pretext of covetousness, God [is] witness,

6 οὔτε ζητοῦντες ἐξ ἀνθρώπων δόξαν,
nor seeking from men glory,

οὔτε ἀφ' ὑμῶν οὔτε ἀπ' ἄλλων, **7** δυνάμε-
neither from you nor from others, being

Chapter 2

Paul's Ministry in Thessalonica

YOU know, brothers, that our visit to you was not a failure. [2] We had previously suffered and been insulted in Philippi, as you know, but with the help of our God we dared to tell you his gospel in spite of strong opposition. [3] For the appeal we make does not spring from error or impure motives, nor are we trying to trick you. [4] On the contrary, we speak as men approved by God to be entrusted with the gospel. We are not trying to please men but God, who tests our hearts. [5] You know we never used flattery, nor did we put on a mask to cover up greed—God is our witness. [6] We were not looking for praise from men, not from you or anyone else.

[b] Gk *For they*

others, 7though we might
have made demands as
apostles of Christ. But we
were gentle[c] among you,
like a nurse tenderly caring
for her own children. 8So
deeply do we care for you
that we are determined to
share with you not only the
gospel of God but also our
own selves, because you
have become very dear to
us.
9 You remember our la-
bor and toil, brothers and
sisters;[a] we worked night
and day, so that we might
not burden any of you
while we proclaimed to you
the gospel of God. 10You
are witnesses, and God
also, how pure, upright,
and blameless our conduct
was toward you believers.
11As you know, we dealt
with each one of you like a
father with his children,
12urging and encouraging
you and pleading that you
lead a life worthy of God,
who calls you into his own
kingdom and glory.
13 We also constantly
give thanks to God for this,
that when you received the
word of God that you heard
from us, you accepted it
not as a human word but as
what it really is, God's
word, which is also at work
in you believers. 14For
you, brothers and sisters,[a]
became imitators of the
churches of God in Christ
Jesus that are in Judea, for
you suffered the same

νοι ἐν βάρει εἶναι ὡς Χριστοῦ ἀπόστολοι·
able [2]with [3]weight* [1]to be as [2]of Christ [1]apostles;

ἀλλὰ ἐγενήθημεν ἤπιοι ἐν μέσῳ ὑμῶν,
but we were gentle in [the] midst of you,

ὡς ἐὰν τροφὸς θάλπῃ τὰ ἑαυτῆς τέκνα·
as if a nurse should cherish [1]the [2]of herself [3]children;

8 οὕτως ὁμειρόμενοι ὑμῶν ηὐδοκοῦμεν
so longing for you we were well pleased

μεταδοῦναι ὑμῖν οὐ μόνον τὸ εὐαγγέλιον
to impart to you not only the gospel

τοῦ θεοῦ ἀλλὰ καὶ τὰς ἑαυτῶν ψυχάς,
– of God but also [1]the [2]of ourselves [3]souls,

διότι ἀγαπητοὶ ἡμῖν ἐγενήθητε. 9 μνημο-
because [2]beloved [3]to us [1]ye became. ye re-

νεύετε γάρ, ἀδελφοί, τὸν κόπον ἡμῶν
member For, brothers, the labour of us

καὶ τὸν μόχθον· νυκτὸς καὶ ἡμέρας
and the toil; night and day

ἐργαζόμενοι πρὸς τὸ μὴ ἐπιβαρῆσαί τινα
working for *the* not to put a burden on any-one

ὑμῶν ἐκηρύξαμεν εἰς ὑμᾶς τὸ εὐαγγέλιον
of you we proclaimed to you the gospel

τοῦ θεοῦ. 10 ὑμεῖς μάρτυρες καὶ ὁ
– of God. Ye [are] witnesses and –

θεός, ὡς ὁσίως καὶ δικαίως καὶ ἀμέμπτως
God, how holily and righteously and blamelessly

ὑμῖν τοῖς πιστεύουσιν ἐγενήθημεν, 11 καθά-
[2]to you [3]the [ones] [4]believing [1]we were, even

περ οἴδατε ὡς ἕνα ἕκαστον ὑμῶν ὡς
as ye know how [2]one [1]each of you as

πατὴρ τέκνα ἑαυτοῦ παρακαλοῦντες ὑμᾶς
a father children of himself exhorting you

καὶ παραμυθούμενοι 12 καὶ μαρτυρόμενοι εἰς
and consoling and witnessing for

τὸ περιπατεῖν ὑμᾶς ἀξίως τοῦ θεοῦ
the to walk you[b] worthily – of God
=that ye should walk

τοῦ καλοῦντος ὑμᾶς εἰς τὴν ἑαυτοῦ
the [one] calling you to [1]the [2]of himself

βασιλείαν καὶ δόξαν.
[3]kingdom [4]and [5]glory.

13 Καὶ διὰ τοῦτο καὶ ἡμεῖς εὐχαρισ-
And therefore also we give

τοῦμεν τῷ θεῷ ἀδιαλείπτως, ὅτι παρα-
thanks – to God unceasingly, that having

λαβόντες λόγον ἀκοῆς παρ' ἡμῶν τοῦ
received [1][the] word [2]of hearing [4]from [5]us –

θεοῦ ἐδέξασθε οὐ λόγον ἀνθρώπων ἀλλὰ
[3]of God ye welcomed [it] not [as] a word of men but

καθὼς ἀληθῶς ἐστιν λόγον θεοῦ, ὃς
as truly it is a word of God, which

καὶ ἐνεργεῖται ἐν ὑμῖν τοῖς πιστεύουσιν.
also operates in you the [ones] believing.

14 ὑμεῖς γὰρ μιμηταὶ ἐγενήθητε, ἀδελφοί,
For ye [2]imitators [1]became, brothers,

τῶν ἐκκλησιῶν τοῦ θεοῦ τῶν οὐσῶν ἐν
of the churches – of God – being in

τῇ Ἰουδαίᾳ ἐν Χριστῷ Ἰησοῦ, ὅτι τὰ
– Judæa in Christ Jesus, because [4]the

As apostles of Christ we
could have been a burden
to you, 7but we were gentle
among you, like a mother
caring for her little children. 8We loved you so
much that we were delighted to share with you not
only the gospel of God but
our lives as well, because
you had become so dear to
us. 9Surely you remember,
brothers, our toil and hardship; we worked night and
day in order not to be a burden to anyone while we
preached the gospel of God
to you.
10You are witnesses, and
so is God, of how holy,
righteous and blameless we
were among you who be-
lieved. 11For you know that
we dealt with each of you
as a father deals with his
own children, 12encourag-
ing, comforting and urging
you to live lives worthy of
God, who calls you into his
kingdom and glory.
13And we also thank God
continually because, when
you received the word of
God, which you heard from
us, you accepted it not as
the word of men, but as it
actually is, the word of
God, which is at work in
you who believe. 14For
you, brothers, became imitators of God's churches in
Judea, which are in Christ
Jesus: You suffered from

[c] Other ancient authorities read *infants*

* ? dignity, authority.

things from your own com-
patriots as they did from
the Jews, 15 who killed both
the Lord Jesus and the
prophets,[d] and drove us
out; they displease God
and oppose everyone 16 by
hindering us from speaking
to the Gentiles so that they
may be saved. Thus they
have constantly been filling
up the measure of their
sins; but God's wrath has
overtaken them at last.[e]

Paul's Desire to Visit the Thessalonians Again

17 As for us, brothers
and sisters,[a] when, for a
short time, we were made
orphans by being separated
from you—in person, not
in heart—we longed with
great eagerness to see you
face to face. 18 For we
wanted to come to you—
certainly I, Paul, wanted to
again and again—but Satan
blocked our way. 19 For
what is our hope or joy or
crown of boasting before
our Lord Jesus at his coming? Is it not you? 20 Yes,
you are our glory and joy!

Chapter 3

THEREFORE when we
could bear it no lon-
ger, we decided to be left
alone in Athens; 2 and we
sent Timothy, our brother
and co-worker for God in
proclaiming[f] the gospel of
Christ, to strengthen and
encourage you for the sake
of your faith, 3 so that no
one would be shaken by
these persecutions. In-
deed, you yourselves know
that this is what we are destined for. 4 In fact, when we

αὐτὰ ἐπάθετε καὶ ὑμεῖς ὑπὸ τῶν ἰδίων
[5]same things [4]suffered [3]also [1]ye by the(your) own

συμφυλετῶν, καθὼς καὶ αὐτοὶ ὑπὸ τῶν
fellow-tribesmen, as also they by the

Ἰουδαίων, 15 τῶν καὶ τὸν κύριον
Jews, the [ones] [1]both [3]the [4]Lord

ἀποκτεινάντων Ἰησοῦν καὶ τοὺς προφήτας,
[2]killing [5]Jesus and the prophets,

καὶ ἡμᾶς ἐκδιωξάντων, καὶ θεῷ μὴ
and [2]us [1]chasing [3]out, and [3]God [1]not

ἀρεσκόντων, καὶ πᾶσιν ἀνθρώποις ἐναντίων,
[2]pleasing, and to all men contrary,

16 κωλυόντων ἡμᾶς τοῖς ἔθνεσιν λαλῆσαι
hindering us [2]to the [3]nations [1]to speak
=from speaking . . .

ἵνα σωθῶσιν, εἰς τὸ ἀναπληρῶσαι αὐτῶν
in order that they may be saved, *for the* to fill up [2]of them

τὰς ἁμαρτίας πάντοτε. ἔφθασεν δὲ ἐπ᾽
[1]the [3]sins always. But [3]came [4]on

αὐτοὺς ἡ ὀργὴ εἰς τέλος.
[5]them [1]the [2]wrath to [the] end.

17 Ἡμεῖς δέ, ἀδελφοί, ἀπορφανισθέντες
But we brothers, being bereaved

ἀφ᾽ ὑμῶν πρὸς καιρὸν ὥρας προσώπῳ
from you for time of an hour in face (presence)

οὐ καρδίᾳ, περισσοτέρως ἐσπουδάσαμεν τὸ
not in heart, more abundantly were eager [2]the

πρόσωπον ὑμῶν ἰδεῖν ἐν πολλῇ ἐπιθυμίᾳ.
[3]face [4]of you [1]to see with much desire.

18 διότι ἠθελήσαμεν ἐλθεῖν πρὸς ὑμᾶς,
Wherefore we wished to come to you,

ἐγὼ μὲν Παῦλος καὶ ἅπαξ καὶ δίς,
I [2]indeed [1]Paul both once and twice (again),

καὶ ἐνέκοψεν ἡμᾶς ὁ σατανᾶς. 19 τίς
and [2]hindered [3]us – [1]Satan. what

γὰρ ἡμῶν ἐλπὶς ἢ χαρὰ ἢ στέφανος
For [is] [2]of us [1]hope or joy or crown

καυχήσεως — ἢ οὐχὶ καὶ ὑμεῖς —
of boasting — – not even ye —

ἔμπροσθεν τοῦ κυρίου ἡμῶν Ἰησοῦ
before the Lord of us Jesus

ἐν τῇ αὐτοῦ παρουσίᾳ; 20 ὑμεῖς γάρ
in(at) the [2]of him [1]presence? for ye

ἐστε ἡ δόξα ἡμῶν καὶ ἡ χαρά.
are [1]the [2]glory [6]of us [3]and [4]the [5]joy.

3 Διὸ μηκέτι στέγοντες ηὐδοκήσαμεν
Wherefore no longer bearing up we were well pleased

καταλειφθῆναι ἐν Ἀθήναις μόνοι 2 καὶ
to be left in Athens alone, and

ἐπέμψαμεν Τιμόθεον, τὸν ἀδελφὸν ἡμῶν
we sent Timothy, the brother of us

καὶ συνεργὸν τοῦ θεοῦ ἐν τῷ εὐαγγελίῳ
and fellow-worker – of God in the gospel

τοῦ Χριστοῦ, εἰς τὸ στηρίξαι ὑμᾶς καὶ
– of Christ, *for the* to establish you and

παρακαλέσαι ὑπὲρ τῆς πίστεως ὑμῶν 3 τὸ
to exhort on behalf of the faith of you –

μηδένα σαίνεσθαι ἐν ταῖς θλίψεσιν ταύταις.
no one to be drawn aside[b] by these afflictions.

αὐτοὶ γὰρ οἴδατε ὅτι εἰς τοῦτο κείμεθα·
For [your]selves ye know that to this we are appointed;

your own countrymen the
same things those churches
suffered from the Jews,
15 who killed the Lord Jesus
and the prophets and also
drove us out. They dis-
please God and are hostile
to all men 16 in their effort to
keep us from speaking to
the Gentiles so that they
may be saved. In this way
they always heap up their
sins to the limit. The wrath
of God has come upon
them at last.[c]

Paul's Longing to See the Thessalonians

17 But, brothers, when we
were torn away from you
for a short time (in person,
not in thought), out of our
intense longing we made
every effort to see you.
18 For we wanted to come to
you—certainly I, Paul, did,
again and again—but Satan
stopped us. 19 For what is
our hope, our joy, or the
crown in which we will glory in the presence of our
Lord Jesus when he
comes? Is it not you? 20 Indeed, you are our glory and
joy.

Chapter 3

SO when we could stand
it no longer, we
thought it best to be left by
ourselves in Athens. 2 We
sent Timothy, who is our
brother and God's fellow
worker[d] in spreading the
gospel of Christ, to
strengthen and encourage
you in your faith, 3 so that
no one would be unsettled
by these trials. You know
quite well that we were destined for them. 4 In fact,

[d] Other ancient authorities read *their own prophets*
[e] Or *completely* or *forever*
[f] Gk lacks *proclaiming*

[c] 16 Or *them fully*
[d] 2 Some manuscripts *brother and fellow worker*; other manuscripts *brother and God's servant*

were with you, we told you
beforehand that we were to
suffer persecution; so it
turned out, as you know.
5 For this reason, when I
could bear it no longer, I
sent to find out about your
faith; I was afraid that
somehow the tempter had
tempted you and that our
labor had been in vain.

Timothy's Encouraging Report

6 But Timothy has just
now come to us from you,
and has brought us the
good news of your faith and
love. He has told us also
that you always remember
us kindly and long to see
us—just as we long to see
you. 7 For this reason,
brothers and sisters,[g] during all our distress and persecution we have been en-
couraged about you
through your faith. 8 For we
now live, if you continue to
stand firm in the Lord.
9 How can we thank God
enough for you in return for
all the joy that we feel before our God because of
you? 10 Night and day we
pray most earnestly that we
may see you face to face
and restore whatever is
lacking in your faith.
11 Now may our God
and Father himself and our
Lord Jesus direct our way
to you. 12 And may the
Lord make you increase
and abound in love for one
another and for all, just as
we abound in love for you.
13 And may he so strength-
en your hearts in holiness
that you may be blameless
before our God and Father
at the coming of our Lord

[g] Gk *brothers*

4 καὶ γὰρ ὅτε πρὸς ὑμᾶς ἦμεν,
for even when with you we were,
προελέγομεν ὑμῖν ὅτι μέλλομεν θλίβεσθαι,
we said before to you that we are about to be afflicted,
καθὼς καὶ ἐγένετο καὶ οἴδατε. **5** διὰ
as indeed it happened and ye know. There-
τοῦτο κἀγὼ μηκέτι στέγων ἔπεμψα εἰς
fore I also no longer bearing up sent *for*
τὸ γνῶναι τὴν πίστιν ὑμῶν, μή πως
the to know the faith of you, lest [some]how
ἐπείρασεν ὑμᾶς ὁ πειράζων καὶ εἰς
[3]tempted [4]you [1]the [one] [2]tempting and in
=the tempter
κενὸν γένηται ὁ κόπος ἡμῶν. **6** Ἄρτι
vain became the labour of us. now
δὲ ἐλθόντος Τιμοθέου πρὸς ἡμᾶς ἀφ'
But coming Timothy[a] to us from
=when Timothy came
ὑμῶν καὶ εὐαγγελισαμένου ἡμῖν τὴν πίστιν
you and announcing good news[a] to us [of] the faith
καὶ τὴν ἀγάπην ὑμῶν, καὶ ὅτι ἔχετε
and the love of you, and that ye have
μνείαν ἡμῶν ἀγαθὴν πάντοτε, ἐπιποθοῦντες
[3]remembrance [2]of us [1]good always, longing
ἡμᾶς ἰδεῖν καθάπερ καὶ ἡμεῖς ὑμᾶς,
[2]us [1]to see even as also we you,
7 διὰ τοῦτο παρεκλήθημεν, ἀδελφοί, ἐφ'
therefore we were comforted, brothers, over
ὑμῖν ἐπὶ πάσῃ τῇ ἀνάγκῃ καὶ θλίψει
you on all the distress and affliction
ἡμῶν διὰ τῆς ὑμῶν πίστεως, **8** ὅτι
of us through the [2]of you [1]faith, because
νῦν ζῶμεν ἐὰν ὑμεῖς στήκετε ἐν κυρίῳ.
now we live if ye stand in [the] Lord.
9 τίνα γὰρ εὐχαριστίαν δυνάμεθα τῷ θεῷ
For what thanks are we able – to God
ἀνταποδοῦναι περὶ ὑμῶν ἐπὶ πάσῃ τῇ
to return concerning you over all the
χαρᾷ ᾗ χαίρομεν δι' ὑμᾶς ἔμπροσθεν
joy [with] which we rejoice because of you before
τοῦ θεοῦ ἡμῶν, **10** νυκτὸς καὶ ἡμέρας
the God of us, night and day
ὑπερεκπερισσοῦ δεόμενοι εἰς τὸ ἰδεῖν ὑμῶν
exceedingly petitioning *for the* to see of you
τὸ πρόσωπον καὶ καταρτίσαι τὰ ὑστερήματα
the face and to adjust the shortcomings
τῆς πίστεως ὑμῶν; **11** Αὐτὸς δὲ ὁ θεὸς
of the faith of you? Now [him]self the God
καὶ πατὴρ ἡμῶν καὶ ὁ κύριος ἡμῶν
and Father of us and the Lord of us
Ἰησοῦς κατευθύναι τὴν ὁδὸν ἡμῶν πρὸς
Jesus may he direct the way of us to
ὑμᾶς· **12** ὑμᾶς δὲ ὁ κύριος πλεονάσαι
you; and [4]you [1]the [2]Lord [3]make [5]to abound
καὶ περισσεύσαι τῇ ἀγάπῃ εἰς ἀλλήλους
and to exceed – in love to one another
καὶ εἰς πάντας, καθάπερ καὶ ἡμεῖς
and to all men, even as also we
εἰς ὑμᾶς, **13** εἰς τὸ στηρίξαι ὑμῶν τὰς
to you, *for the* to establish of you the
καρδίας ἀμέμπτους ἐν ἁγιωσύνῃ ἔμπροσθεν
hearts blameless in holiness before
τοῦ θεοῦ καὶ πατρὸς ἡμῶν ἐν τῇ παρουσίᾳ
the God and Father of us in(at) the presence

when we were with you, we
kept telling you that we
would be persecuted. And
it turned out that way, as
you well know. 5For this
reason, when I could stand
it no longer, I sent to find
out about your faith. I was
afraid that in some way the
tempter might have tempt-
ed you and our efforts
might have been useless.

Timothy's Encouraging Report

6But Timothy has just
now come to us from you
and has brought good news
about your faith and love.
He has told us that you always have pleasant memo-
ries of us and that you long
to see us, just as we also
long to see you. 7There-
fore, brothers, in all our
distress and persecution we
were encouraged about you
because of your faith. 8For
now we really live, since
you are standing firm in the
Lord. 9How can we thank
God enough for you in re-
turn for all the joy we have
in the presence of our God
because of you? 10Night
and day we pray most ear-
nestly that we may see you
again and supply what is
lacking in your faith.
11Now may our God and
Father himself and our
Lord Jesus clear the way
for us to come to you.
12May the Lord make your
love increase and overflow
for each other and for everyone else, just as ours
does for you. 13May he
strengthen your hearts so
that you will be blameless
and holy in the presence of
our God and Father when

Jesus with all his saints.

Chapter 4

A Life Pleasing to God

FINALLY, brothers and sisters,[g] we ask and urge you in the Lord Jesus that, as you learned from us how you ought to live and to please God (as, in fact, you are doing), you should do so more and more. [2]For you know what instructions we gave you through the Lord Jesus. [3]For this is the will of God, your sanctification: that you abstain from fornication; [4]that each one of you know how to control your own body[h] in holiness and honor, [5]not with lustful passion, like the Gentiles who do not know God; [6]that no one wrong or exploit a brother or sister[i] in this matter, because the Lord is an avenger in all these things, just as we have already told you beforehand and solemnly warned you. [7]For God did not call us to impurity but in holiness. [8]Therefore whoever rejects this rejects not human authority but God, who also gives his Holy Spirit to you.

9 Now concerning love of the brothers and sisters,[g] you do not need to have anyone write to you, for you yourselves have been taught by God to love one another; [10]and indeed you do love all the brothers and sisters[g] throughout

[h] Or *how to take a wife for himself*
[i] Gk *brother*

τοῦ κυρίου ἡμῶν Ἰησοῦ μετὰ πάντων
of the Lord of us Jesus with all

τῶν ἁγίων αὐτοῦ.
the saints of him.

4 Λοιπὸν οὖν, ἀδελφοί, ἐρωτῶμεν ὑμᾶς
For the rest therefore, brothers, we ask you

καὶ παρακαλοῦμεν ἐν κυρίῳ Ἰησοῦ, ἵνα
and *we* beseech in [the] Lord Jesus, *in order* that

καθὼς παρελάβετε παρ' ἡμῶν τὸ πῶς
as ye received from us *the* how

δεῖ ὑμᾶς περιπατεῖν καὶ ἀρέσκειν θεῷ,
it behoves you to walk and to please God,

καθὼς καὶ περιπατεῖτε, ἵνα περισσεύητε
as indeed ye do walk, *in order* that ye abound

μᾶλλον. 2 οἴδατε γὰρ τίνας παραγγελίας
more. For ye know what injunctions

ἐδώκαμεν ὑμῖν διὰ τοῦ κυρίου Ἰησοῦ.
we gave you through the Lord Jesus.

3 Τοῦτο γάρ ἐστιν θέλημα τοῦ θεοῦ,
For this is [the] will – of God,

ὁ ἁγιασμὸς ὑμῶν, ἀπέχεσθαι ὑμᾶς ἀπὸ
the sanctification of you, to abstain you[b] from

τῆς πορνείας, 4 εἰδέναι ἕκαστον ὑμῶν
– fornication, [3]to know* [1]each one[b] [2]of you

τὸ ἑαυτοῦ σκεῦος κτᾶσθαι ἐν ἁγιασμῷ
[5]the [7]of himself [6]vessel [4]to possess in sanctification

καὶ τιμῇ, 5 μὴ ἐν πάθει ἐπιθυμίας
and honour, not in passion of lust

καθάπερ καὶ τὰ ἔθνη τὰ μὴ εἰδότα
even as indeed the nations – not knowing

τὸν θεόν, 6 τὸ μὴ ὑπερβαίνειν καὶ
God, – not to go beyond and

πλεονεκτεῖν ἐν τῷ πράγματι τὸν ἀδελφὸν
to defraud in the matter the brother

αὐτοῦ, διότι ἔκδικος κύριος περὶ πάντων
of him, because [2][the] avenger [1][the] Lord [is] concerning all

τούτων, καθὼς καὶ προείπαμεν ὑμῖν καὶ
these, as indeed we previously told you and

διεμαρτυράμεθα. 7 οὐ γὰρ ἐκάλεσεν ἡμᾶς
solemnly witnessed. For [4]not [2]called [3]us

ὁ θεὸς ἐπὶ ἀκαθαρσίᾳ ἀλλ' ἐν ἁγιασμῷ.
– [1]God to uncleanness but in sanctification.

8 τοιγαροῦν ὁ ἀθετῶν οὐκ ἄνθρωπον
Wherefore the [one] rejecting [2]not [3]man

ἀθετεῖ ἀλλὰ τὸν θεὸν τὸν καὶ διδόντα
[1]rejects but – God the [one] indeed giving

τὸ πνεῦμα αὐτοῦ τὸ ἅγιον εἰς ὑμᾶς.
the [2]Spirit [3]of him – [1]Holy to you.

9 Περὶ δὲ τῆς φιλαδελφίας οὐ χρείαν
Now concerning – brotherly love not need

ἔχετε γράφειν ὑμῖν· αὐτοὶ γὰρ ὑμεῖς
ye have [for me] to write to you; for [2][your]selves [1]ye

θεοδίδακτοί ἐστε εἰς τὸ ἀγαπᾶν ἀλλήλους·
[4]taught by God [3]are *for the* to love one another;

10 καὶ γὰρ ποιεῖτε αὐτὸ εἰς πάντας
for indeed ye do it toward all

τοὺς ἀδελφοὺς [τοὺς] ἐν ὅλῃ τῇ Μακεδο-
the brothers – in all – Macedo-

* That is, "to be able": see note on page xvi.

our Lord Jesus comes with all his holy ones.

Chapter 4

Living to Please God

FINALLY, brothers, we instructed you how to live in order to please God, as in fact you are living. Now we ask you and urge you in the Lord Jesus to do this more and more. [2]For you know what instructions we gave you by the authority of the Lord Jesus.

[3]It is God's will that you should be sanctified: that you should avoid sexual immorality; [4]that each of you should learn to control his own body[e] in a way that is holy and honorable, [5]not in passionate lust like the heathen, who do not know God; [6]and that in this matter no one should wrong his brother or take advantage of him. The Lord will punish men for all such sins, as we have already told you and warned you. [7]For God did not call us to be impure, but to live a holy life. [8]Therefore, he who rejects this instruction does not reject man but God, who gives you his Holy Spirit.

[9]Now about brotherly love we do not need to write to you, for you yourselves have been taught by God to love each other. [10]And in fact, you do love all the brothers throughout

[e]4 Or *learn to live with his own wife*; or *learn to acquire a wife*

Macedonia. But we urge
you, beloved,[g] to do so
more and more, 11to aspire
to live quietly, to mind your
own affairs, and to work
with your hands, as we directed you, 12so that you
may behave properly to-
ward outsiders and be de-
pendent on no one.

The Coming of the Lord

13 But we do not want
you to be uninformed,
brothers and sisters,[g]
about those who have
died,[j] so that you may not
grieve as others do who
have no hope. 14For since
we believe that Jesus died
and rose again, even so,
through Jesus, God will
bring with him those who
have died.[j] 15For this we
declare to you by the word
of the Lord, that we who
are alive, who are left until
the coming of the Lord, will
by no means precede those
who have died.[j] 16For the
Lord himself, with a cry of
command, with the archan-
gel's call and with the
sound of God's trumpet,
will descend from heaven,
and the dead in Christ will
rise first. 17Then we who
are alive, who are left, will
be caught up in the clouds
together with them to meet
the Lord in the air; and so
we will be with the Lord
forever. 18Therefore en-
courage one another with
these words.

νία. Παρακαλοῦμεν δὲ ὑμᾶς, ἀδελφοί,
nia. But we exhort you, brothers,

περισσεύειν μᾶλλον, 11 καὶ φιλοτιμεῖσθαι
to abound more, and to strive eagerly

ἡσυχάζειν καὶ πράσσειν τὰ ἴδια καὶ
to be quiet and to practise the (your) own things and

ἐργάζεσθαι ταῖς χερσὶν ὑμῶν, καθὼς ὑμῖν
to work with the hands of you, as ^{2}you

παρηγγείλαμεν, 12 ἵνα περιπατῆτε εὐσχη-
^{1}we enjoined, in order that ye may walk becom-

μόνως πρὸς τοὺς ἔξω καὶ μηδενὸς
ingly toward the [ones] outside and ^{3}of nothing

χρείαν ἔχητε.
^{2}need ^{1}*ye* may have.

13 Οὐ θέλομεν δὲ ὑμᾶς ἀγνοεῖν, ἀδελφοί,
Now we do not wish you to be ignorant, brothers,

περὶ τῶν κοιμωμένων, ἵνα μὴ λυπῆσθε
concerning the [ones] sleeping, lest ye grieve

καθὼς καὶ οἱ λοιποὶ οἱ μὴ ἔχοντες
as indeed the rest – not having

ἐλπίδα. 14 εἰ γὰρ πιστεύομεν ὅτι Ἰησοῦς
hope. For if we believe that Jesus

ἀπέθανεν καὶ ἀνέστη, οὕτως καὶ ὁ θεὸς
died and rose again, so also – ^{5}God

τοὺς κοιμηθέντας διὰ τοῦ Ἰησοῦ ἄξει
^{1}the [ones] ^{2}having slept ^{3}through – ^{4}Jesus will bring

σὺν αὐτῷ. 15 Τοῦτο γὰρ ὑμῖν λέγομεν
with him. For this to you we say

ἐν λόγῳ κυρίου, ὅτι ἡμεῖς οἱ ζῶντες
by a word of [the] Lord, that we the [ones] living

οἱ περιλειπόμενοι εἰς τὴν παρουσίαν τοῦ
– remaining to the presence of the

κυρίου οὐ μὴ φθάσωμεν τοὺς κοιμηθέντας·
Lord by no means may precede the [ones] having slept;

16 ὅτι αὐτὸς ὁ κύριος ἐν κελεύσματι,
because ^{3}[him]self ^{1}the ^{2}Lord with a word of command,

ἐν φωνῇ ἀρχαγγέλου καὶ ἐν σάλπιγγι
with a voice of an archangel and with a trumpet

θεοῦ, καταβήσεται ἀπ' οὐρανοῦ, καὶ οἱ
of God, will descend from heaven, and the

νεκροὶ ἐν Χριστῷ ἀναστήσονται πρῶτον,
dead in Christ will rise again first*ly*,

17 ἔπειτα ἡμεῖς οἱ ζῶντες οἱ περιλειπόμενοι
then we the [ones] living – remaining

ἅμα σὺν αὐτοῖς ἁρπαγησόμεθα ἐν νεφέλαις
together with them shall be seized in clouds

εἰς ἀπάντησιν τοῦ κυρίου εἰς ἀέρα·
to a meeting of the Lord in air;

καὶ οὕτως πάντοτε σὺν κυρίῳ ἐσόμεθα.
and so always with [the] Lord we shall be.

18 Ὥστε παρακαλεῖτε ἀλλήλους ἐν τοῖς λόγοις
Therefore comfort ye one another with – words

τούτοις.
these.

Macedonia. Yet we urge
you, brothers, to do so
more and more.
11Make it your ambition
to lead a quiet life, to mind
your own business and to
work with your hands, just
as we told you, 12so that
your daily life may win the
respect of outsiders and so
that you will not be dependent on anybody.

The Coming of the Lord

13Brothers, we do not
want you to be ignorant
about those who fall
asleep, or to grieve like the
rest of men, who have no
hope. 14We believe that
Jesus died and rose again
and so we believe that God
will bring with Jesus those
who have fallen asleep in
him. 15According to the
Lord's own word, we tell
you that we who are still
alive, who are left till the
coming of the Lord, will
certainly not precede those
who have fallen asleep.
16For the Lord himself will
come down from heaven,
with a loud command, with
the voice of the archangel
and with the trumpet call of
God, and the dead in Christ
will rise first. 17After that,
we who are still alive and
are left will be caught up
together with them in the
clouds to meet the Lord in
the air. And so we will be
with the Lord forever.
18Therefore encourage
each other with these
words.

[j] Gk *fallen asleep*

Chapter 5

NOW concerning the
times and the sea-
sons, brothers and sis-
ters,[g] you do not need to
have anything written to
you. 2For you yourselves
know very well that the day
of the Lord will come like a
thief in the night. 3When
they say, "There is peace
and security," then sudden
destruction will come upon
them, as labor pains come
upon a pregnant woman,
and there will be no escape!
4But you, beloved,[k] are
not in darkness, for that
day to surprise you like a
thief; 5for you are all children of light and children of
the day; we are not of the
night or of darkness. 6So
then let us not fall asleep as
others do, but let us keep
awake and be sober; 7for
those who sleep sleep at
night, and those who are
drunk get drunk at night.
8But since we belong to the
day, let us be sober, and
put on the breastplate of
faith and love, and for a helmet the hope of salvation.
9For God has destined us
not for wrath but for ob-
taining salvation through
our Lord Jesus Christ,
10who died for us, so that
whether we are awake or
asleep we may live with
him. 11Therefore encour-
age one another and build
up each other, as indeed
you are doing.

Final Exhortations, Greetings, and Benediction

12 But we appeal to
you, brothers and sisters,[k]
to respect those who labor
among you, and have
charge of you in the Lord
and admonish you; 13es-
teem them very highly in
love because of their work.

[k] Gk *brothers*

5 Περὶ δὲ τῶν χρόνων καὶ τῶν καιρῶν,
But concerning the times and the seasons,
ἀδελφοί, οὐ χρείαν ἔχετε ὑμῖν γράφεσθαι·
brothers, [2]not [3]need [1]ye have [5]to you [4]to be written;
2 αὐτοὶ γὰρ ἀκριβῶς οἴδατε ὅτι ἡμέρα
for [2][your]selves [3]accurately [1]ye know that [the] day
κυρίου ὡς κλέπτης ἐν νυκτὶ οὕτως
of [the] Lord as a thief at night so
ἔρχεται. 3 ὅταν λέγωσιν· εἰρήνη καὶ
it comes. Whenever they say : Peace and
ἀσφάλεια, τότε αἰφνίδιος αὐτοῖς ἐφίσταται
safety, then [1]sudden [4]them [3]comes on
ὄλεθρος ὥσπερ ἡ ὠδὶν τῇ ἐν γαστρὶ
[2]destruction as the birth pang to the pregnant
ἐχούσῃ, καὶ οὐ μὴ ἐκφύγωσιν. 4 ὑμεῖς
woman,† and by no means may they escape. ye
δέ, ἀδελφοί, οὐκ ἐστὲ ἐν σκότει, ἵνα
But, brothers, are not in darkness, in order that
ἡ ἡμέρα ὑμᾶς ὡς κλέπτης καταλάβῃ·
the day you as a thief should overtake;
5 πάντες γὰρ ὑμεῖς υἱοὶ φωτός ἐστε
for all ye [2]sons [3]of light [1]are
καὶ υἱοὶ ἡμέρας. Οὐκ ἐσμὲν νυκτὸς
and sons of [the] day. We are not of [the] night
οὐδὲ σκότους· 6 ἄρα οὖν μὴ καθεύδωμεν
nor of darkness; therefore let us not sleep
ὡς οἱ λοιποί, ἀλλὰ γρηγορῶμεν καὶ
as the rest, but let us watch and
νήφωμεν. 7 οἱ γὰρ καθεύδοντες νυκτὸς
be sober. For the [ones] sleeping by night
καθεύδουσιν, καὶ οἱ μεθυσκόμενοι νυκτὸς
sleep, and the [ones] being drunk by night
μεθύουσιν· 8 ἡμεῖς δὲ ἡμέρας ὄντες
are drunk; but we of [the] day being
νήφωμεν, ἐνδυσάμενοι θώρακα πίστεως καὶ
let us be sober, putting on a breastplate of faith and
ἀγάπης καὶ περικεφαλαίαν ἐλπίδα σωτηρίας·
of love and a helmet hope of salvation;
9 ὅτι οὐκ ἔθετο ἡμᾶς ὁ θεὸς εἰς ὀργὴν
because [2]did not appoint [3]us – [1]God to wrath
ἀλλὰ εἰς περιποίησιν σωτηρίας διὰ τοῦ
but to obtainment of salvation through the
κυρίου ἡμῶν Ἰησοῦ Χριστοῦ, 10 τοῦ
Lord of us Jesus Christ, the
ἀποθανόντος περὶ ἡμῶν, ἵνα εἴτε γρηγορ-
[one] having died concerning us, in order whether we
ῶμεν εἴτε καθεύδωμεν ἅμα σὺν αὐτῷ
watch or *we* sleep [2]together [3]with [4]him
ζήσωμεν. 11 Διὸ παρακαλεῖτε ἀλλήλους
[1]we may live. Therefore comfort ye one another
καὶ οἰκοδομεῖτε εἷς τὸν ἕνα, καθὼς καὶ
and edify ye one the one(other), as indeed
ποιεῖτε.
ye do.
12 Ἐρωτῶμεν δὲ ὑμᾶς, ἀδελφοί, εἰδέναι
Now we ask you, brothers, to know
τοὺς κοπιῶντας ἐν ὑμῖν καὶ προϊσταμένους
the [ones] labouring among you and taking the lead
ὑμῶν ἐν κυρίῳ καὶ νουθετοῦντας ὑμᾶς,
of you in [the] Lord and admonishing you,
13 καὶ ἡγεῖσθαι αὐτοὺς ὑπερεκπερισσῶς
and consider them most exceedingly

Chapter 5

NOW, brothers, about
times and dates we do
not need to write to you,
2for you know very well
that the day of the Lord will
come like a thief in the
night. 3While people are
saying, "Peace and safe-
ty," destruction will come
on them suddenly, as labor
pains on a pregnant wom-
an, and they will not es-
cape.
4But you, brothers, are
not in darkness so that this
day should surprise you
like a thief. 5You are all
sons of the light and sons of
the day. We do not belong
to the night or to the darkness. 6So then, let us not be
like others, who are asleep,
but let us be alert and self-
controlled. 7For those who
sleep, sleep at night, and
those who get drunk, get
drunk at night. 8But since
we belong to the day, let us
be self-controlled, putting
on faith and love as a
breastplate, and the hope
of salvation as a helmet.
9For God did not appoint us
to suffer wrath but to receive salvation through our
Lord Jesus Christ. 10He
died for us so that, whether
we are awake or asleep, we
may live together with him.
11Therefore encourage one
another and build each other up, just as in fact you are
doing.

Final Instructions

12Now we ask you, broth-
ers, to respect those who
work hard among you, who
are over you in the Lord
and who admonish you.
13Hold them in the highest
regard in love because of

Be at peace among your-
selves. 14 And we urge you,
beloved[k] to admonish the
idlers, encourage the faint
hearted, help the weak, be
patient with all of them.
15 See that none of you re-
pays evil for evil, but always seek to do good to
one another and to all.
16 Rejoice always, 17 pray
without ceasing, 18 give
thanks in all circum-
stances; for this is the will
of God in Christ Jesus for
you. 19 Do not quench the
Spirit. 20 Do not despise the
words of prophets,[l] 21 but
test everything; hold fast to
what is good; 22 abstain
from every form of evil.
23 May the God of
peace himself sanctify you
entirely; and may your
spirit and soul and body be
kept sound[m] and blameless
at the coming of our Lord
Jesus Christ. 24 The one
who calls you is faithful,
and he will do this.
25 Beloved,[n] pray for
us.
26 Greet all the brothers
and sisters[k] with a holy
kiss. 27 I solemnly com-
mand you by the Lord that
this letter be read to all of
them.[o]
28 The grace of our
Lord Jesus Christ be with
you.[p]

ἐν ἀγάπῃ διὰ τὸ ἔργον αὐτῶν. εἰρηνεύετε ἐν ἑαυτοῖς.
in love because of the work of them. Be at peace among yourselves.

14 Παρακαλοῦμεν δὲ ὑμᾶς, ἀδελφοί, νουθετεῖτε τοὺς ἀτάκτους, παραμυθεῖσθε τοὺς ὀλιγοψύχους, ἀντέχεσθε τῶν ἀσθενῶν, μακροθυμεῖτε πρὸς πάντας.
And we exhort you, brothers, admonish the idle, console the faint-hearted, hold on to the [ones] being weak, be longsuffering with all men.

15 ὁρᾶτε μή τις κακὸν ἀντὶ κακοῦ τινι ἀποδῷ, ἀλλὰ πάντοτε τὸ ἀγαθὸν διώκετε εἰς ἀλλήλους καὶ εἰς πάντας.
See lest anyone [3]evil [4]instead of [5]evil [2]to anyone [1]returns, but always [2]the [3]good [1]follow ye in regard to one another and in regard to all men.

16 Πάντοτε χαίρετε,
Always rejoice ye,

17 ἀδιαλείπτως προσεύχεσθε,
unceasingly pray,

18 ἐν παντὶ εὐχαριστεῖτε· τοῦτο γὰρ θέλημα θεοῦ ἐν Χριστῷ Ἰησοῦ εἰς ὑμᾶς.
in everything give thanks; for this [is] [the] will of God in Christ Jesus in regard to you.

19 Τὸ πνεῦμα μὴ σβέννυτε,
The Spirit do not quench,

20 προφητείας μὴ ἐξουθενεῖτε·
prophecies not despise;

21 πάντα δὲ δοκιμάζετε, τὸ καλὸν κατέχετε·
and [2]all things [1]prove, the good hold fast;

22 ἀπὸ παντὸς εἴδους πονηροῦ ἀπέχεσθε.
from every form of evil abstain.

23 Αὐτὸς δὲ ὁ θεὸς τῆς εἰρήνης ἁγιάσαι ὑμᾶς ὁλοτελεῖς, καὶ ὁλόκληρον ὑμῶν τὸ πνεῦμα καὶ ἡ ψυχὴ καὶ τὸ σῶμα ἀμέμπτως ἐν τῇ παρουσίᾳ τοῦ κυρίου ἡμῶν Ἰησοῦ Χριστοῦ τηρηθείη.
And [4][him]self [1]the [2]God – [3]of peace may he sanctify you complete, and entire of you the spirit and the soul and the body blamelessly in(at) the presence of the Lord of us Jesus Christ may be kept.

24 πιστὸς ὁ καλῶν ὑμᾶς, ὃς καὶ ποιήσει.
Faithful [is] the [one] calling you, who indeed will do [it].

25 Ἀδελφοί, προσεύχεσθε [καὶ] περὶ ἡμῶν.
Brothers, pray ye also concerning us.

26 Ἀσπάσασθε τοὺς ἀδελφοὺς πάντας ἐν φιλήματι ἁγίῳ.
Greet ye [2]the [3]brothers [1]all with kiss a holy.

27 Ἐνορκίζω ὑμᾶς τὸν κύριον ἀναγνωσθῆναι τὴν ἐπιστολὴν πᾶσιν τοῖς ἀδελφοῖς.
I adjure you [by] the Lord [3]to be read [1]the(this) [2]epistle to all the brothers.

28 Ἡ χάρις τοῦ κυρίου ἡμῶν Ἰησοῦ Χριστοῦ μεθ' ὑμῶν.
The grace of the Lord of us Jesus Christ [be] with you.

their work. Live in peace
with each other. 14 And we
urge you, brothers, warn
those who are idle, encourage the timid, help the
weak, be patient with ev-
eryone. 15 Make sure that
nobody pays back wrong
for wrong, but always try to
be kind to each other and to
everyone else.
16 Be joyful always; 17 pray
continually; 18 give thanks
in all circumstances, for
this is God's will for you in
Christ Jesus.
19 Do not put out the Spirit's fire; 20 do not treat
prophecies with contempt.
21 Test everything. Hold on
to the good. 22 Avoid every
kind of evil.
23 May God himself, the
God of peace, sanctify you
through and through. May
your whole spirit, soul and
body be kept blameless at
the coming of our Lord
Jesus Christ. 24 The one
who calls you is faithful and
he will do it.
25 Brothers, pray for us.
26 Greet all the brothers
with a holy kiss. 27 I charge
you before the Lord to
have this letter read to all
the brothers.
28 The grace of our Lord
Jesus Christ be with you.

[l] Gk *despise prophecies*
[m] Or *complete*
[n] Gk *Brothers*
[o] Gk *to all the brothers*
[p] Other ancient authorities add *Amen*

The Second Letter of
Paul to the
Thessalonians
Chapter 1
Salutation

PAUL, Silvanus, and
Timothy,
To the church of the Thessalonians in God our Fa-
ther and the Lord Jesus
Christ:
2 Grace to you and
peace from God our[a] Fa-
ther and the Lord Jesus
Christ.

Thanksgiving

3 We must always give
thanks to God for you,
brothers and sisters,[b] as is
right, because your faith is
growing abundantly, and
the love of everyone of you
for one another is increasing. 4 Therefore we our-
selves boast of you among
the churches of God for
your steadfastness and
faith during all your persecutions and the afflictions
that you are enduring.

The Judgment at Christ's Coming

5 This is evidence of the
righteous judgment of God,
and is intended to make
you worthy of the kingdom
of God, for which you are
also suffering. 6 For it is indeed just of God to repay
with affliction those who
afflict you, 7 and to give relief to the afflicted as well
as to us, when the Lord
Jesus is revealed from
heaven with his mighty angels 8 in flaming fire, inflicting vengeance on those
who do not know God and
on those who do not obey
the gospel of our Lord
Jesus. 9 These will suffer
the punishment of eternal
destruction, separated
from the presence of the
Lord and from the glory of
his might, 10 when he
comes to be glorified by his

[a] Other ancient authorities read *the*
[b] Gk *brothers*

ΠΡΟΣ ΘΕΣΣΑΛΟΝΙΚΕΙΣ Β
To Thessalonians 2

1 Παῦλος καὶ Σιλουανὸς καὶ Τιμόθεος
Paul and Silvanus and Timothy

τῇ ἐκκλησίᾳ Θεσσαλονικέων ἐν θεῷ πατρὶ
to the church of [the] Thessalonians in God Father

ἡμῶν καὶ κυρίῳ Ἰησοῦ Χριστῷ· **2** χάρις
of us and [the] Lord Jesus Christ: Grace [be]

ὑμῖν καὶ εἰρήνη ἀπὸ θεοῦ πατρὸς καὶ
to you and peace from God [the] Father and

κυρίου Ἰησοῦ Χριστοῦ.
[the] Lord Jesus Christ.

3 Εὐχαριστεῖν ὀφείλομεν τῷ θεῷ πάντοτε
To give thanks we ought – to God always

περὶ ὑμῶν, ἀδελφοί, καθὼς ἄξιόν ἐστιν,
concerning you, brothers, as [2]meet [1]it is,

ὅτι ὑπεραυξάνει ἡ πίστις ὑμῶν καὶ
because [4]grows exceedingly [1]the [2]faith [3]of you and

πλεονάζει ἡ ἀγάπη ἑνὸς ἑκάστου πάντων
[9]increases [1]the [2]love [4]one [3]of each [5]all

ὑμῶν εἰς ἀλλήλους, **4** ὥστε αὐτοὺς ἡμᾶς
[6]of you [7]to [8]one another, so as [our]selves us
=so that we ourselves boast

ἐν ὑμῖν ἐγκαυχᾶσθαι ἐν ταῖς ἐκκλησίαις
in you to boast[b] in the churches
in you

τοῦ θεοῦ ὑπὲρ τῆς ὑπομονῆς ὑμῶν καὶ
– of God for the [1]endurance [4]of you [2]and

πίστεως ἐν πᾶσιν τοῖς διωγμοῖς ὑμῶν
[3]faith in all the persecutions of you

καὶ ταῖς θλίψεσιν αἷς ἀνέχεσθε, **5** ἔνδειγμα
and the afflictions which ye endure, a plain token

τῆς δικαίας κρίσεως τοῦ θεοῦ, εἰς τὸ
of the just judgment – of God, for the

καταξιωθῆναι ὑμᾶς τῆς βασιλείας τοῦ
to be accounted worthy you[b] of the kingdom –
=so that ye may be accounted worthy

θεοῦ, ὑπὲρ ἧς καὶ πάσχετε, **6** εἴπερ
of God, on behalf of which indeed ye suffer, since

δίκαιον παρὰ θεῷ ἀνταποδοῦναι τοῖς
[it is] a just thing with God to repay [2]to the [ones]

θλίβουσιν ὑμᾶς θλῖψιν **7** καὶ ὑμῖν τοῖς
[3]afflicting [4]you [1]affliction and [4]to you [5]the [ones]

θλιβομένοις ἄνεσιν μεθ' ἡμῶν, ἐν τῇ
[6]being afflicted [1]rest [2]with [3]us, at the

ἀποκαλύψει τοῦ κυρίου Ἰησοῦ ἀπ'
revelation of the Lord Jesus from

οὐρανοῦ μετ' ἀγγέλων δυνάμεως αὐτοῦ
heaven with angels of power of him

8 ἐν πυρὶ φλογός, διδόντος ἐκδίκησιν τοῖς
in fire of flame, giving full vengeance to the [ones]

μὴ εἰδόσιν θεὸν καὶ τοῖς μὴ ὑπακούουσιν
not knowing God and to the [ones] not obeying

τῷ εὐαγγελίῳ τοῦ κυρίου ἡμῶν Ἰησοῦ,
the gospel of the Lord of us Jesus,

9 οἵτινες δίκην τίσουσιν ὄλεθρον αἰώνιον
who [3][the] penalty [1]will pay [4]destruction [2]eternal

ἀπὸ προσώπου τοῦ κυρίου καὶ ἀπὸ
from [the] face of the Lord and from

τῆς δόξης τῆς ἰσχύος αὐτοῦ, **10** ὅταν
the glory of the strength of him, whenever

2 Thessalonians
Chapter 1

PAUL, Silas[a] and Timo-
thy,

To the church of the
Thessalonians in God our
Father and the Lord Jesus
Christ:

2Grace and peace to you
from God the Father and
the Lord Jesus Christ.

Thanksgiving and Prayer

3We ought always to
thank God for you, broth-
ers, and rightly so, because
your faith is growing more
and more, and the love every one of you has for each
other is increasing. 4There-
fore, among God's
churches we boast about
your perseverance and
faith in all the persecutions
and trials you are enduring.
5All this is evidence that
God's judgment is right,
and as a result you will be
counted worthy of the kingdom of God, for which you
are suffering. 6God is just:
He will pay back trouble to
those who trouble you 7and
give relief to you who are
troubled, and to us as well.
This will happen when the
Lord Jesus is revealed from
heaven in blazing fire with
his powerful angels. 8He
will punish those who do
not know God and do not
obey the gospel of our Lord
Jesus. 9They will be pun-
ished with everlasting destruction and shut out from
the presence of the Lord
and from the majesty of his
power 10on the day he

[a] *1* Greek *Silvanus,* a variant of *Silas*

saints and to be marveled at
on that day among all who
have believed, because our
testimony to you was be-
lieved. 11 To this end we always pray for you, asking
that our God will make you
worthy of his call and will
fulfill by his power every
good resolve and work of
faith, 12 so that the name of
our Lord Jesus may be glorified in you, and you in
him, according to the grace
of our God and the Lord
Jesus Christ.

ἔλθῃ ἐνδοξασθῆναι ἐν τοῖς ἁγίοις αὐτοῦ
he comes to be glorified in the saints of him

καὶ θαυμασθῆναι ἐν πᾶσιν τοῖς πιστεύσασιν,
and to be admired in all the [ones] having believed,

ὅτι ἐπιστεύθη τὸ μαρτύριον ἡμῶν ἐφ'
because [2]was believed [1]the [2]testimony [3]of us [4]to

ὑμᾶς, ἐν τῇ ἡμέρᾳ ἐκείνῃ. 11 Εἰς ὃ
[5]you, in that day. For which

καὶ προσευχόμεθα πάντοτε περὶ ὑμῶν,
indeed we pray always concerning you,

ἵνα ὑμᾶς ἀξιώσῃ τῆς κλήσεως ὁ θεὸς
in order that [3]you [4]may [5]deem [7]worthy [8]of the [9]calling [1]the [2]God

ἡμῶν καὶ πληρώσῃ πᾶσαν εὐδοκίαν
[3]of us and may fulfil every good pleasure

ἀγαθωσύνης καὶ ἔργον πίστεως ἐν δυνάμει,
of goodness and work of faith in power,

12 ὅπως ἐνδοξασθῇ τὸ ὄνομα τοῦ κυρίου
so as [7]may be glorified [1]the [2]name [3]of the [4]Lord

ἡμῶν Ἰησοῦ ἐν ὑμῖν, καὶ ὑμεῖς ἐν
[5]of us [6]Jesus in you, and ye in

αὐτῷ, κατὰ τὴν χάριν τοῦ θεοῦ ἡμῶν
him, according to the grace of the [1]God [4]of us

καὶ κυρίου Ἰησοῦ Χριστοῦ.
[2]and [3]Lord Jesus Christ.

comes to be glorified in his
holy people and to be marveled at among all those
who have believed. This in-
cludes you, because you
believed our testimony to
you.
11With this in mind, we
constantly pray for you,
that our God may count
you worthy of his calling,
and that by his power he
may fulfill every good purpose of yours and every act
prompted by your faith.
12We pray this so that the
name of our Lord Jesus
may be glorified in you, and
you in him, according to
the grace of our God and
the Lord Jesus Christ.[b]

Chapter 2

The Man of Lawlessness

As to the coming of our
Lord Jesus Christ and
our being gathered together
to him, we beg you, brothers and sisters,[b] 2 not to be
quickly shaken in mind or
alarmed, either by spirit or
by word or by letter, as
though from us, to the effect that the day of the Lord
is already here. 3 Let no one
deceive you in any way; for
that day will not come unless the rebellion comes
first and the lawless one[c] is
revealed, the one destined
for destruction.[d] 4 He opposes and exalts himself
above every so-called god
or object of worship, so
that he takes his seat in the
temple of God, declaring
himself to be God. 5 Do you
not remember that I told
you these things when I
was still with you? 6 And
you know what is now re-
straining him, so that he

2 Ἐρωτῶμεν δὲ ὑμᾶς, ἀδελφοί, ὑπὲρ
Now we request you, brothers, by

τῆς παρουσίας τοῦ κυρίου [ἡμῶν] Ἰησοῦ
the presence of the Lord of us Jesus

Χριστοῦ καὶ ἡμῶν ἐπισυναγωγῆς ἐπ' αὐτόν,
Christ and [2]of us [1]gathering together to him,

2 εἰς τὸ μὴ ταχέως σαλευθῆναι ὑμᾶς
– – not quickly to be shaken you[b]

ἀπὸ τοῦ νοὸς μηδὲ θροεῖσθαι, μήτε
from the(your) mind nor to be disturbed, neither

διὰ πνεύματος μήτε διὰ λόγου μήτε
through a spirit nor through speech nor

δι' ἐπιστολῆς ὡς δι' ἡμῶν, ὡς ὅτι
through an epistle as through us, as that

ἐνέστηκεν ἡ ἡμέρα τοῦ κυρίου. 3 μή
[5]is come [1]the [2]day [3]of the [4]Lord. Not

τις ὑμᾶς ἐξαπατήσῃ κατὰ μηδένα τρόπον·
anyone [2]you [1]may deceive by(in) no(any) way;

ὅτι ἐὰν μὴ ἔλθῃ ἡ ἀποστασία πρῶτον
because unless [3]comes [1]the [2]apostasy [4]first*ly*

καὶ ἀποκαλυφθῇ ὁ ἄνθρωπος τῆς ἀνομίας,
and [4]is revealed [1]the [2]man – [3]of lawlessness,

ὁ υἱὸς τῆς ἀπωλείας, 4 ὁ ἀντικείμενος
the son – of perdition, the [one] setting against

καὶ ὑπεραιρόμενος ἐπὶ πάντα λεγόμενον
and exalting himself over everything *being* called

θεὸν ἢ σέβασμα, ὥστε αὐτὸν εἰς τὸν
God or object of worship, so as him in the

ναὸν τοῦ θεοῦ καθίσαι, ἀποδεικνύντα ἑαυ-
shrine – of God to sit,[b] showing him-

τὸν ὅτι ἐστὶν θεός. 5 Οὐ μνημονεύετε
self that he is a god. Do ye not remember

ὅτι ἔτι ὢν πρὸς ὑμᾶς ταῦτα ἔλεγον
that yet being with you [2]these things [1]I used to tell

ὑμῖν; 6 καὶ νῦν τὸ κατέχον οἴδατε,
[3]you? and now the [thing] restraining ye know,

Chapter 2

The Man of Lawlessness

CONCERNING the
coming of our Lord
Jesus Christ and our being
gathered to him, we ask
you, brothers, 2not to become easily unsettled or
alarmed by some prophe-
cy, report or letter sup-
posed to have come from
us, saying that the day of
the Lord has already come.
3Don't let anyone deceive
you in any way, for that
day will not come until the
rebellion occurs and the
man of lawlessness[c] is revealed, the man doomed to
destruction. 4He will op-
pose and will exalt himself
over everything that is
called God or is worshiped,
so that he sets himself up in
God's temple, proclaiming
himself to be God.
5Don't you remember
that when I was with you I
used to tell you these
things? 6And now you
know what is holding him

[c] Gk *the man of lawlessness*; other ancient authorities read *the man of sin*
[d] Gk *the son of destruction*

[b] 12 Or *God and Lord, Jesus Christ*
[c] 3 Some manuscripts *sin*

may be revealed when his
time comes. 7 For the mystery of lawlessness is already at work, but only until the one who now re-
strains it is removed. 8 And
then the lawless one will be
revealed, whom the Lord
Jesus[e] will destroy[f] with
the breath of his mouth, an-
nihilating him by the manifestation of his coming.
9 The coming of the lawless
one is apparent in the working of Satan, who uses all
power, signs, lying won-
ders, 10 and every kind of
wicked deception for those
who are perishing, because
they refused to love the
truth and so be saved.
11 For this reason God
sends them a powerful de-
lusion, leading them to believe what is false, 12 so that
all who have not believed
the truth but took pleasure
in unrighteousness will be
condemned.

Chosen for Salvation

13 But we must always
give thanks to God for you,
brothers and sisters[b] beloved by the Lord, because
God chose you as the first
fruits[g] for salvation
through sanctification by
the Spirit and through belief in the truth. 14 For this
purpose he called you
through our proclamation
of the good news,[h] so that
you may obtain the glory of
our Lord Jesus Christ. 15 So
then, brothers and sis-
ters,[b] stand firm and hold
fast to the traditions that
you were taught by us, either by word of mouth or
by our letter.
16 Now may our Lord
Jesus Christ himself and
God our Father, who loved
us and through grace gave
us eternal comfort and

[e] Other ancient authorities lack *Jesus*
[f] Other ancient authorities read *consume*
[g] Other ancient authorities read *from the beginning*
[h] Or *through our gospel*

εἰς τὸ ἀποκαλυφθῆναι αὐτὸν ἐν τῷ
for *the* [2]to be revealed [1]him[b] in the
αὐτοῦ καιρῷ. **7** τὸ γὰρ μυστήριον ἤδη
[3]of him [1]time. For the mystery [2]already
ἐνεργεῖται τῆς ἀνομίας· μόνον ὁ κατέχων
[3]operates – [1]of lawlessness; only [there is] the restraining [one]
ἄρτι ἕως ἐκ μέσου γένηται. **8** καὶ τότε
just now until [2]out of [3][the] midst [1]it comes. And then
ἀποκαλυφθήσεται ὁ ἄνομος, ὃν ὁ κύριος
will be revealed the lawless one, whom the Lord
[Ἰησοῦς] ἀνελεῖ τῷ πνεύματι τοῦ στό-
Jesus will destroy by the spirit of the mouth
ματος αὐτοῦ καὶ καταργήσει τῇ ἐπιφανείᾳ
of him and bring to nothing by the outshining
τῆς παρουσίας αὐτοῦ, **9** οὗ ἐστιν ἡ
of the presence of him, of whom [3]is [1]the
παρουσία κατ' ἐνέργειαν τοῦ σατανᾶ ἐν
[2]presence according to [the] operation – of Satan with
πάσῃ δυνάμει καὶ σημείοις καὶ τέρασιν
all power and signs and wonders
ψεύδους **10** καὶ ἐν πάσῃ ἀπάτῃ ἀδικίας
of a lie and with all deceit of unrighteousness
τοῖς ἀπολλυμένοις, ἀνθ' ὧν τὴν ἀγάπην
in the [ones] perishing, because the love
τῆς ἀληθείας οὐκ ἐδέξαντο εἰς τὸ σωθῆναι
of the truth they received not for *the* [2]to be saved
αὐτούς. **11** καὶ διὰ τοῦτο πέμπει αὐτοῖς
[1]them.[b] And therefore [2]sends [3]to them
ὁ θεὸς ἐνέργειαν πλάνης εἰς τὸ πιστεῦσαι
– [1]God an operation of error for *the* [2]to believe
αὐτοὺς τῷ ψεύδει, **12** ἵνα κριθῶσιν πάντες
[1]them[b] the lie, in order that [10]may be judged [1]all
οἱ μὴ πιστεύσαντες τῇ ἀληθείᾳ ἀλλὰ
[2]the [ones] [3]not [4]having believed [5]the [6]truth [7]but
εὐδοκήσαντες τῇ ἀδικίᾳ.
[8]having had pleasure – [9]in unrighteousness.
13 Ἡμεῖς δὲ ὀφείλομεν εὐχαριστεῖν τῷ
But we ought to thank –
θεῷ πάντοτε περὶ ὑμῶν, ἀδελφοὶ ἠγαπη-
God always concerning you, brothers having been
μένοι ὑπὸ κυρίου, ὅτι εἵλατο ὑμᾶς ὁ
loved by [the] Lord, because [2]chose [3]you –
θεὸς ἀπαρχὴν εἰς σωτηρίαν ἐν ἁγιασμῷ
[1]God firstfruit to salvation by sanctification
πνεύματος καὶ πίστει ἀληθείας, **14** εἰς
of spirit and faith of(in) [the] truth, to
ὃ καὶ ἐκάλεσεν ὑμᾶς διὰ τοῦ εὐαγγελίου
which also he called you through the gospel
ἡμῶν, εἰς περιποίησιν δόξης τοῦ κυρίου
of us, to obtainment of [the] glory of the Lord
ἡμῶν Ἰησοῦ Χριστοῦ. **15** Ἄρα οὖν,
of us Jesus Christ. So then,
ἀδελφοί, στήκετε, καὶ κρατεῖτε τὰς
brothers, stand, and hold the
παραδόσεις ἃς ἐδιδάχθητε εἴτε διὰ λόγου
traditions which ye were taught either through speech
εἴτε δι' ἐπιστολῆς ἡμῶν. **16** Αὐτὸς δὲ
or through an epistle of us. And [6][him]self
ὁ κύριος ἡμῶν Ἰησοῦς Χριστὸς καὶ
[1]the [2]Lord [3]of us [4]Jesus [5]Christ and
ὁ θεὸς ὁ πατὴρ ἡμῶν, ὁ ἀγαπήσας
the God the Father of us, the [one] having loved

back, so that he may be revealed at the proper time.
7For the secret power of
lawlessness is already at
work; but the one who now
holds it back will continue
to do so till he is taken out
of the way. 8And then the
lawless one will be re-
vealed, whom the Lord
Jesus will overthrow with
the breath of his mouth and
destroy by the splendor of
his coming. 9The coming of
the lawless one will be in
accordance with the work
of Satan displayed in all
kinds of counterfeit miracles, signs and wonders,
10and in every sort of evil
that deceives those who are
perishing. They perish because they refused to love
the truth and so be saved.
11For this reason God
sends them a powerful de-
lusion so that they will believe the lie 12and so that all
will be condemned who
have not believed the truth
but have delighted in wickedness.

Stand Firm

13But we ought always to
thank God for you, broth-
ers loved by the Lord, because from the beginning
God chose you[d] to be
saved through the sanctifying work of the Spirit and
through belief in the truth.
14He called you to this
through our gospel, that
you might share in the glory
of our Lord Jesus Christ.
15So then, brothers, stand
firm and hold to the teachings[e] we passed on to you,
whether by word of mouth
or by letter.
16May our Lord Jesus
Christ himself and God our
Father, who loved us and
by his grace gave us eternal

[d] *13* Some manuscripts *because God chose you as his firstfruits*
[e] *15* Or *traditions*

good hope, 17comfort your hearts and strengthen them in every good work and word.

ἡμᾶς καὶ δοὺς παράκλησιν αἰωνίαν καὶ
us and having given [2]comfort [1]eternal [3]and
ἐλπίδα ἀγαθὴν ἐν χάριτι, 17 παρακαλέσαι
[5]hope [4]a good by grace, may he comfort
ὑμῶν τὰς καρδίας καὶ στηρίξαι ἐν παντὶ
of you the hearts and *may he confirm* in every
ἔργῳ καὶ λόγῳ ἀγαθῷ.
[2]work [3]and [4]word [1]good.

encouragement and good hope, 17encourage your hearts and strengthen you in every good deed and word.

Chapter 3

Request for Prayer

FINALLY, brothers and sisters,[i] pray for us, so that the word of the Lord may spread rapidly and be glorified everywhere, just as it is among you, 2and that we may be rescued from wicked and evil people; for not all have faith. 3But the Lord is faithful; he will strengthen you and guard you from the evil one.[j] 4And we have confidence in the Lord concerning you, that you are doing and will go on doing the things that we command. 5May the Lord direct your hearts to the love of God and to the steadfastness of Christ.

Warning against Idleness

6 Now we command you, beloved,[i] in the name of our Lord Jesus Christ, to keep away from believers who are[k] living in idleness and not according to the tradition that they[l] received from us. 7For you yourselves know how you ought to imitate us; we were not idle when we were with you, 8and we did not eat anyone's bread without paying for it; but with toil and labor we worked night and day, so that we might not burden any of you. 9This was not because we do not have that right, but

[i] Gk *brothers*
[j] Or *from evil*
[k] Gk *from every brother who is*
[l] Other ancient authorities read *you*

3 Τὸ λοιπὸν προσεύχεσθε, ἀδελφοί, περὶ
For the rest pray ye, brothers, concerning
ἡμῶν, ἵνα ὁ λόγος τοῦ κυρίου τρέχῃ
us, in order that the word of the Lord may run
καὶ δοξάζηται καθὼς καὶ πρὸς ὑμᾶς,
and be glorified as indeed with you,
2 καὶ ἵνα ῥυσθῶμεν ἀπὸ τῶν ἀτόπων
and *in order* that we may be delivered from – perverse
καὶ πονηρῶν ἀνθρώπων· οὐ γὰρ πάντων
and evil men; for [3][is] not [4]of all men
ἡ πίστις. 3 Πιστὸς δέ ἐστιν ὁ κύριος,
[1]the [2]faith. But faithful is the Lord,
ὃς στηρίξει ὑμᾶς καὶ φυλάξει ἀπὸ τοῦ
who will confirm you and will guard from the
πονηροῦ. 4 πεποίθαμεν δὲ ἐν κυρίῳ
evil [?one]. And we are persuaded in [the] Lord
ἐφ' ὑμᾶς, ὅτι ἃ παραγγέλλομεν [καὶ]
as to you, that what things we charge both
ποιεῖτε καὶ ποιήσετε. 5 Ὁ δὲ κύριος
ye do and will do. And [2]the [3]Lord
κατευθύναι ὑμῶν τὰς καρδίας εἰς τὴν
[1]may [4]direct [7]of you [5]the [6]hearts into the
ἀγάπην τοῦ θεοῦ καὶ εἰς τὴν ὑπομονὴν
love – of God and into the patience
τοῦ Χριστοῦ.
– of Christ.
6 Παραγγέλλομεν δὲ ὑμῖν, ἀδελφοί, ἐν
Now we charge you, brothers, in
ὀνόματι τοῦ κυρίου Ἰησοῦ Χριστοῦ,
[the] name of the Lord Jesus Christ,
στέλλεσθαι ὑμᾶς ἀπὸ παντὸς ἀδελφοῦ
to draw back you[b] from every brother
ἀτάκτως περιπατοῦντος καὶ μὴ κατὰ τὴν
[2]idly [1]walking and not according to the
παράδοσιν ἣν παρελάβετε παρ' ἡμῶν.
tradition which ye received from us.
7 αὐτοὶ γὰρ οἴδατε πῶς δεῖ μιμεῖσθαι
For [your]selves ye know how it behoves to imitate
ἡμᾶς, ὅτι οὐκ ἠτακτήσαμεν ἐν ὑμῖν,
us, because we were not idle among you,
8 οὐδὲ δωρεὰν ἄρτον ἐφάγομεν παρά τινος,
nor [5][as] a gift [2]bread [1]ate [3]from [4]anyone,
ἀλλ' ἐν κόπῳ καὶ μόχθῳ νυκτὸς καὶ
but by labour and struggle by night and
ἡμέρας ἐργαζόμενοι πρὸς τὸ μὴ ἐπιβαρῆσαί
by day working for *the* not to emburden
τινα ὑμῶν· 9 οὐχ ὅτι οὐκ ἔχομεν
anyone of you; not that we have not
ἐξουσίαν, ἀλλ' ἵνα ἑαυτοὺς τύπον δῶμεν
authority, but in order that [2]ourselves [3]an example [1]we might give

Chapter 3

Request for Prayer

FINALLY, brothers, pray for us that the message of the Lord may spread rapidly and be honored, just as it was with you. 2And pray that we may be delivered from wicked and evil men, for not everyone has faith. 3But the Lord is faithful, and he will strengthen and protect you from the evil one. 4We have confidence in the Lord that you are doing and will continue to do the things we command. 5May the Lord direct your hearts into God's love and Christ's perseverance.

Warning Against Idleness

6In the name of the Lord Jesus Christ, we command you, brothers, to keep away from every brother who is idle and does not live according to the teaching[f] you received from us. 7For you yourselves know how you ought to follow our example. We were not idle when we were with you, 8nor did we eat anyone's food without paying for it. On the contrary, we worked night and day, laboring and toiling so that we would not be a burden to any of you. 9We did this, not because we do not have the right to such help, but in order to make ourselves a

f6 Or *tradition*

in order to give you an example to imitate. [10]For
even when we were with
you, we gave you this command: Anyone unwilling to
work should not eat. [11]For
we hear that some of you
are living in idleness, mere
busybodies, not doing any
work. [12]Now such persons
we command and exhort in
the Lord Jesus Christ to do
their work quietly and to
earn their own living.
[13]Brothers and sisters,[m] do
not be weary in doing what
is right.
14 Take note of those
who do not obey what we
say in this letter; have nothing to do with them, so that
they may be ashamed.
[15]Do not regard them as enemies, but warn them as
believers.[n]

Final Greetings and Benediction

16 Now may the Lord of
peace himself give you
peace at all times in all
ways. The Lord be with all
of you.
17 I, Paul, write this
greeting with my own
hand. This is the mark in
every letter of mine; it is
the way I write. [18]The
grace of our Lord Jesus
Christ be with all of you.[o]

ὑμῖν εἰς τὸ μιμεῖσθαι ἡμᾶς. **10** καὶ
to you for *the* to imitate us. even
γὰρ ὅτε ἦμεν πρὸς ὑμᾶς, τοῦτο παρηγ-
For when we were with you, this we
γέλλομεν ὑμῖν, ὅτι εἴ τις οὐ θέλει
charged you, that if anyone does not wish
ἐργάζεσθαι, μηδὲ ἐσθιέτω. **11** ἀκούομεν
to work, neither let him eat. we hear [of]
γάρ τινας περιπατοῦντας ἐν ὑμῖν ἀτάκτως,
For some walking among you idly,
μηδὲν ἐργαζομένους ἀλλὰ περιεργαζομένους·
nothing working but working round;
12 τοῖς δὲ τοιούτοις παραγγέλλομεν καὶ
– and *to* such we charge and
παρακαλοῦμεν ἐν κυρίῳ Ἰησοῦ Χριστῷ
exhort in [the] Lord Jesus Christ
ἵνα μετὰ ἡσυχίας ἐργαζόμενοι τὸν
in order that ²with ³quietness ¹working ⁵the
ἑαυτῶν ἄρτον ἐσθίωσιν. **13** Ὑμεῖς δέ,
⁷of themselves ⁶bread ⁴they may eat. And ye,
ἀδελφοί, μὴ ἐγκακήσητε καλοποιοῦντες
brothers, do not lose heart doing good.
14 εἰ δέ τις οὐχ ὑπακούει τῷ λόγῳ
And if anyone obeys not the word
ἡμῶν διὰ τῆς ἐπιστολῆς, τοῦτον σημειοῦσθε,
of us through the epistle, this man mark,
μὴ συναναμίγνυσθαι αὐτῷ, ἵνα ἐντραπῇ·
not to mix with* him, in order that he may be put to shame;
15 καὶ μὴ ὡς ἐχθρὸν ἡγεῖσθε, ἀλλὰ
and yet not as an enemy deem ye [him], but
νουθετεῖτε ὡς ἀδελφόν. **16** Αὐτὸς δὲ
admonish as a brother. And ⁴[him]self
ὁ κύριος τῆς εἰρήνης δῴη ὑμῖν τὴν
¹the ²Lord – ³of peace may he give to you the (?his)
εἰρήνην διὰ παντὸς ἐν παντὶ τρόπῳ.
peace always in every way.
ὁ κύριος μετὰ πάντων ὑμῶν.
The Lord [be] with ²all ¹you.
17 Ὁ ἀσπασμὸς τῇ ἐμῇ χειρὶ Παύλου,
The greeting – by my hand[,] of Paul,
ὅ ἐστιν σημεῖον ἐν πάσῃ ἐπιστολῇ·
which is a sign in every epistle:
οὕτως γράφω. **18** ἡ χάρις τοῦ κυρίου
thus I write. The grace of the Lord
ἡμῶν Ἰησοῦ Χριστοῦ μετὰ πάντων ὑμῶν.
of us Jesus Christ [be] with ²all ¹you.

model for you to follow.
[10]For even when we were
with you, we gave you this
rule: "If a man will not
work, he shall not eat."
[11]We hear that some
among you are idle. They
are not busy; they are busybodies. [12]Such people we
command and urge in the
Lord Jesus Christ to settle
down and earn the bread
they eat. [13]And as for you,
brothers, never tire of doing what is right.
[14]If anyone does not obey
our instruction in this letter, take special note of
him. Do not associate with
him, in order that he may
feel ashamed. [15]Yet do not
regard him as an enemy,
but warn him as a brother.

Final Greetings

[16]Now may the Lord of
peace himself give you
peace at all times and in every way. The Lord be with
all of you.
[17]I, Paul, write this greeting in my own hand, which
is the distinguishing mark
in all my letters. This is
how I write.
[18]The grace of our Lord
Jesus Christ be with you
all.

The First Letter of Paul to

Timothy

Chapter 1

Salutation

PAUL, an apostle of
Christ Jesus by the
command of God our Sav-
ior and of Christ Jesus our
hope,
2 To Timothy, my loyal
child in the faith:
Grace, mercy, and peace

ΠΡΟΣ ΤΙΜΟΘΕΟΝ Α

To Timothy 1

1 Παῦλος ἀπόστολος Χριστοῦ Ἰησοῦ κατ'
Paul an apostle of Christ Jesus according to
ἐπιταγὴν θεοῦ σωτῆρος ἡμῶν καὶ Χριστοῦ
a command of God Saviour of us and of Christ
Ἰησοῦ τῆς ἐλπίδος ἡμῶν **2** Τιμοθέῳ
Jesus the hope of us to Timothy
γνησίῳ τέκνῳ ἐν πίστει· χάρις, ἔλεος,
a true child in [the] faith: Grace, mercy,

1 Timothy

Chapter 1

PAUL, an apostle of
Christ Jesus by the
command of God our Sav-
ior and of Christ Jesus our
hope,
[2]To Timothy my true son
in the faith:

[m] Gk *Brothers*
[n] Gk *a brother*
[o] Other ancient authorities add *Amen*

* Imperatival infinitive, as elsewhere (Phil. 3. 16, etc.).

from God the Father and Christ Jesus our Lord.

Warning against False Teachers

3 I urge you, as I did when I was on my way to Macedonia, to remain in Ephesus so that you may instruct certain people not to teach any different doctrine, 4and not to occupy themselves with myths and endless genealogies that promote speculations rather than the divine training[a] that is known by faith. 5But the aim of such instruction is love that comes from a pure heart, a good conscience, and sincere faith. 6Some people have deviated from these and turned to meaningless talk, 7desiring to be teachers of the law, without understanding either what they are saying or the things about which they make assertions.

8 Now we know that the law is good, if one uses it legitimately. 9This means understanding that the law is laid down not for the innocent but for the lawless and disobedient, for the godless and sinful, for the unholy and profane, for those who kill their father or mother, for murderers, 10fornicators, sodomites, slave traders, liars, perjurers, and whatever else is contrary to the sound teaching 11that conforms to the glorious gospel of the blessed God, which he entrusted to me.

Gratitude for Mercy

12 I am grateful to Christ Jesus our Lord, who has strengthened me, because he judged me faithful and appointed me to his service, 13even though I was formerly a blasphemer, a persecutor, and a man of violence. But I received mercy because I had acted ignorantly in unbelief,

[a] Or *plan*

εἰρήνη ἀπὸ θεοῦ πατρὸς καὶ Χριστοῦ
peace from God [the] Father and Christ

Ἰησοῦ τοῦ κυρίου ἡμῶν.
Jesus the Lord of us.

3 Καθὼς παρεκάλεσά σε προσμεῖναι ἐν
As I besought thee to remain in

Ἐφέσῳ, πορευόμενος εἰς Μακεδονίαν, ἵνα
Ephesus, [I] going into Macedonia, in order that

παραγγείλῃς τισὶν μὴ ἑτεροδιδασκαλεῖν
thou mightest charge certain persons not to teach differently

4 μηδὲ προσέχειν μύθοις καὶ γενεαλογίαις
nor to pay attention to tales and to [2]genealogies

ἀπεράντοις, αἵτινες ἐκζητήσεις παρέχουσιν
[1]unending, which [2]questionings [1]provide

μᾶλλον ἢ οἰκονομίαν θεοῦ τὴν ἐν πίστει·
rather than a stewardship of God – in faith:

5 τὸ δὲ τέλος τῆς παραγγελίας ἐστὶν
now the end of the charge is

ἀγάπη ἐκ καθαρᾶς καρδίας καὶ συνειδήσεως
love out of a clean heart and conscience

ἀγαθῆς καὶ πίστεως ἀνυποκρίτου, **6** ὧν
a good and faith unfeigned, from which things

τινες ἀστοχήσαντες ἐξετράπησαν εἰς
some missing aim turned aside to

ματαιολογίαν, **7** θέλοντες εἶναι νομοδιδάσ-
vain talking, wishing to be law-

καλοι, μὴ νοοῦντες μήτε ἃ λέγουσιν
teachers, not understanding either what things they say

μήτε περὶ τίνων διαβεβαιοῦνται. **8** οἴδαμεν
nor concerning what things they emphatically assert. we know

δὲ ὅτι καλὸς ὁ νόμος, ἐάν τις αὐτῷ
Now that [3][is] [4]good [1]the [2]law, if anyone [2]it

νομίμως χρῆται, **9** εἰδὼς τοῦτο, ὅτι
[3]lawfully [1]uses, knowing this, that

δικαίῳ νόμος οὐ κεῖται, ἀνόμοις δὲ
[3]for a just man [1]law [2]is not laid down, but for lawless men

καὶ ἀνυποτάκτοις, ἀσεβέσι καὶ ἁμαρτωλοῖς,
and for unruly, for impious and for sinners,

ἀνοσίοις καὶ βεβήλοις, πατρολῴαις καὶ
for unholy and for profane, for parricides and

μητρολῴαις, ἀνδροφόνοις, **10** πόρνοις, ἀρ-
for matricides, for menkillers, for fornicators, for

σενοκοίταις, ἀνδραποδισταῖς, ψεύσταις, ἐπιόρ-
paederasts, for menstealers, for liars, for per-

κοις, καὶ εἴ τι ἕτερον τῇ ὑγιαινούσῃ
jurers, and if any other thing [2]*to* the [3]*being* healthful

διδασκαλίᾳ ἀντίκειται, **11** κατὰ τὸ εὐαγ-
[4]teaching [1]opposes, according to the gos-

γέλιον τῆς δόξης τοῦ μακαρίου θεοῦ,
pel of the glory of the blessed God,

ὃ ἐπιστεύθην ἐγώ. **12** Χάριν ἔχω τῷ
which [2]was entrusted [with] [1]I. Thanks I have to the

ἐνδυναμώσαντί με Χριστῷ Ἰησοῦ τῷ κυρίῳ
[one] empowering me Christ Jesus the Lord

ἡμῶν, ὅτι πιστόν με ἡγήσατο θέμενος
of us, because [3]faithful [2]me [1]he deemed putting [me]

εἰς διακονίαν, **13** τὸ πρότερον ὄντα
into [the] ministry, formerly being

βλάσφημον καὶ διώκτην καὶ ὑβριστήν·
a blasphemer and a persecutor and insolent;

ἀλλὰ ἠλεήθην, ὅτι ἀγνοῶν ἐποίησα ἐν
but I obtained mercy, because being ignorant I acted in

Grace, mercy and peace from God the Father and Chrst Jesus our Lord.

Warning Against False Teachers of the Law

3As I urged you when I went into Macedonia, stay there in Ephesus so that you may command certain men not to teach false doctrines any longer 4nor to devote themselves to myths and endless genealogies. These promote controversies rather than God's work —which is by faith. 5The goal of this command is love, which comes from a pure heart and a good conscience and a sincere faith. 6Some have wandered away from these and turned to meaningless talk. 7They want to be teachers of the law, but they do not know what they are talking about or what they so confidently affirm.

8We know that the law is good if one uses it properly. 9We also know that law[a] is made not for the righteous but for lawbreakers and rebels, the ungodly and sinful, the unholy and irreligious; for those who kill their fathers or mothers, for murderers, 10for adulterers and perverts, for slave traders and liars and perjurers—and for whatever else is contrary to the sound doctrine 11that conforms to the glorious gospel of the blessed God, which he entrusted to me.

The Lord's Grace to Paul

12I thank Christ Jesus our Lord, who has given me strength, that he considered me faithful, appointing me to his service. 13Even though I was once a blasphemer and a persecutor and a violent man, I was shown mercy because I acted in ignorance and un-

[a] 9 Or *that the law*

14 and the grace of our Lord overflowed for me with the faith and love that are in Christ Jesus. 15 The saying is sure and worthy of full acceptance, that Christ Jesus came into the world to save sinners—of whom I am the foremost. 16 But for that very reason I received mercy, so that in me, as the foremost, Jesus Christ might display the utmost patience, making me an example to those who would come to believe in him for eternal life. 17 To the King of the ages, immortal, invisible, the only God, be honor and glory forever and ever.[b] Amen.

18 I am giving you these instructions, Timothy, my child, in accordance with the prophecies made earlier about you, so that by following them you may fight the good fight, 19 having faith and a good conscience. By rejecting conscience, certain persons have suffered shipwreck in the faith; 20 among them are Hymenaeus and Alexander, whom I have turned over to Satan, so that they may learn not to blaspheme.

ἀπιστίᾳ, **14** ὑπερεπλεόνασεν δὲ ἡ χάρις
unbelief, and superabounded the grace

τοῦ κυρίου ἡμῶν μετὰ πίστεως καὶ
of the Lord of us with faith and

ἀγάπης τῆς ἐν Χριστῷ Ἰησοῦ. **15** πιστὸς
love – in Christ Jesus. Faithful [is]

ὁ λόγος καὶ πάσης ἀποδοχῆς ἄξιος,
the word and [2]of all [3]acceptance [1]worthy,

ὅτι Χριστὸς Ἰησοῦς ἦλθεν εἰς τὸν κόσμον
that Christ Jesus came into the world

ἁμαρτωλοὺς σῶσαι· ὧν πρῶτός εἰμι ἐγώ·
sinners to save; of whom first(chief) am I;

16 ἀλλὰ διὰ τοῦτο ἠλεήθην, ἵνα ἐν
but because of this I obtained mercy, in order that in

ἐμοὶ πρώτῳ ἐνδείξηται Ἰησοῦς Χριστὸς
me first might show forth Jesus Christ

τὴν ἅπασαν μακροθυμίαν, πρὸς ὑποτύπωσιν
– all longsuffering, for a pattern

τῶν μελλόντων πιστεύειν ἐπ' αὐτῷ εἰς
of the [ones] coming to believe on him to

ζωὴν αἰώνιον. **17** Τῷ δὲ βασιλεῖ τῶν
life eternal. Now to the King of the

αἰώνων, ἀφθάρτῳ ἀοράτῳ μόνῳ θεῷ, τιμὴ
ages, incorruptible invisible only God, [be] honour

καὶ δόξα εἰς τοὺς αἰῶνας τῶν αἰώνων·
and glory unto the ages of the ages:

ἀμήν. **18** Ταύτην τὴν παραγγελίαν παρα-
Amen. This – charge I com-

τίθεμαί σοι, τέκνον Τιμόθεε, κατὰ τὰς
mit to thee, child Timothy, according to the

προαγούσας ἐπὶ σὲ προφητείας, ἵνα
preceding [2]respecting [3]thee [1]prophecies, in order that

στρατεύῃ ἐν αὐταῖς τὴν καλὴν στρατείαν,
thou mightest war by them the good warfare,

19 ἔχων πίστιν καὶ ἀγαθὴν συνείδησιν,
having faith and a good conscience,

ἥν τινες ἀπωσάμενοι περὶ τὴν πίστιν
which some thrusting away [2]concerning [3]the [4]faith

ἐναυάγησαν· **20** ὧν ἐστιν Ὑμέναιος καὶ
[1]made shipwreck; of whom is Hymenæus and

Ἀλέξανδρος, οὓς παρέδωκα τῷ σατανᾷ,
Alexander, whom I delivered – to Satan,

ἵνα παιδευθῶσιν μὴ βλασφημεῖν.
in order that they may be taught not to blaspheme.

belief. 14 The grace of our Lord was poured out on me abundantly, along with the faith and love that are in Christ Jesus.

15 Here is a trustworthy saying that deserves full acceptance: Christ Jesus came into the world to save sinners—of whom I am the worst. 16 But for that very reason I was shown mercy so that in me, the worst of sinners, Christ Jesus might display his unlimited patience as an example for those who would believe on him and receive eternal life. 17 Now to the King eternal, immortal, invisible, the only God, be honor and glory for ever and ever. Amen.

18 Timothy, my son, I give you this instruction in keeping with the prophecies once made about you, so that by following them you may fight the good fight, 19 holding on to faith and a good conscience. Some have rejected these and so have shipwrecked their faith. 20 Among them are Hymenaeus and Alexander, whom I have handed over to Satan to be taught not to blaspheme.

Chapter 2

Instructions concerning Prayer

FIRST of all, then, I urge that supplications, prayers, intercessions, and thanksgivings be made for everyone, 2 for kings and all who are in high positions, so that we may lead a quiet and peaceable life in all godliness and dignity. 3 This is right and is accept-

2 Παρακαλῶ οὖν πρῶτον πάντων
I exhort therefore first*ly* of all

ποιεῖσθαι δεήσεις, προσευχάς, ἐντεύξεις,
to be made petitions, prayers, intercessions,

εὐχαριστίας, ὑπὲρ πάντων ἀνθρώπων,
thanksgivings, on behalf of all men,

2 ὑπὲρ βασιλέων καὶ πάντων τῶν ἐν
on behalf of kings and all the [ones] [2]in

ὑπεροχῇ ὄντων, ἵνα ἤρεμον καὶ ἡσύχιον
[3]eminence [1]being, in order that [2]a tranquil [3]and [4]quiet

βίον διάγωμεν ἐν πάσῃ εὐσεβείᾳ καὶ
[5]life [1]we may lead in all piety and

σεμνότητι. **3** τοῦτο καλὸν καὶ ἀπόδεκτον
gravity. This [is] good and acceptable

Chapter 2

Instructions on Worship

I URGE, then, first of all, that requests, prayers, intercession and thanksgiving be made for everyone —2 for kings and all those in authority, that we may live peaceful and quiet lives in all godliness and holiness. 3 This is good, and pleases

[b] Gk *to the ages of the ages*

able in the sight of God our
Savior, 4who desires ev-
eryone to be saved and to
come to the knowledge of
the truth. 5For

there is one God;
there is also one mediator between God and humankind,
Christ Jesus, himself human,
6 who gave himself a ransom for all

—this was attested at the
right time. 7For this I was
appointed a herald and an
apostle (I am telling the
truth,[c] I am not lying), a
teacher of the Gentiles in
faith and truth.
8 I desire, then, that in
every place the men should
pray, lifting up holy hands
without anger or argument;
9also that the women
should dress themselves
modestly and decently in
suitable clothing, not with
their hair braided, or with
gold, pearls, or expensive
clothes, 10but with good
works, as is proper for
women who profess rever-
ence for God. 11Let a woman[d] learn in silence with
full submission. 12I permit
no woman[d] to teach or to
have authority over a
man;[e] she is to keep silent.
13For Adam was formed
first, then Eve; 14and
Adam was not deceived,
but the woman was de-
ceived and became a transgressor. 15Yet she will be
saved through childbear-
ing, provided they continue
in faith and love and holiness, with modesty.

Chapter 3

Qualifications of Bishops

THE saying is sure:[f]
whoever aspires to the
office of bishop[g] desires a
noble task. 2Now a bish-
op[h] must be above re-
proach, married only

[c] Other ancient authorities add *in Christ*
[d] Or *wife*
[e] Or *her husband*
[f] Some interpreters place these words at the end of the previous paragraph. Other ancient authorities read *The saying is commonly accepted*
[g] Or *overseer*
[h] Or *an overseer*

ἐνώπιον τοῦ σωτῆρος ἡμῶν θεοῦ, **4** ὃς
before the Saviour of us God, who

πάντας ἀνθρώπους θέλει σωθῆναι καὶ εἰς
[2]all [3]men [1]wishes to be saved and [2]to

ἐπίγνωσιν ἀληθείας ἐλθεῖν. **5** εἷς γὰρ
[3]a full knowledge [4]of truth [1]to come. For [2]one

θεός, εἷς καὶ μεσίτης θεοῦ καὶ ἀνθρώπων,
[1][there is] [3]God, one also mediator of God and of men,

ἄνθρωπος Χριστὸς Ἰησοῦς, **6** ὁ δοὺς
a man Christ Jesus, the [one] having given

ἑαυτὸν ἀντίλυτρον ὑπὲρ πάντων, τὸ
himself a ransom on behalf of all, the

μαρτύριον καιροῖς ἰδίοις· **7** εἰς ὃ ἐτέθην
testimony in its own times; for which [2]was appointed

ἐγὼ κῆρυξ καὶ ἀπόστολος, ἀλήθειαν λέγω,
[1]I a herald and an apostle, [2]truth [1]I say,

οὐ ψεύδομαι, διδάσκαλος ἐθνῶν ἐν πίστει
I do not lie, a teacher of nations in faith

καὶ ἀληθείᾳ. **8** Βούλομαι οὖν προσεύχεσθαι
and truth. I desire therefore [3]to pray

τοὺς ἄνδρας ἐν παντὶ τόπῳ ἐπαίροντας
[1]the [2]men in every place lifting up

ὁσίους χεῖρας χωρὶς ὀργῆς καὶ διαλογισμοῦ.
holy hands without wrath and doubting.

9 Ὡσαύτως γυναῖκας ἐν καταστολῇ κοσμίῳ,
Similarly women in clothing orderly,

μετὰ αἰδοῦς καὶ σωφροσύνης κοσμεῖν
[3]with [4]modesty [5]and [6]sobriety [1]to adorn

ἑαυτάς, μὴ ἐν πλέγμασιν καὶ χρυσίῳ
[2]themselves, not with plaiting and gold

ἢ μαργαρίταις ἢ ἱματισμῷ πολυτελεῖ,
or pearls or raiment costly,

10 ἀλλ᾽ ὃ πρέπει γυναιξὶν ἐπαγγελλομέναις
but what suits women professing

θεοσέβειαν, δι᾽ ἔργων ἀγαθῶν. **11** γυνὴ
reverence, by means of [2]works [1]good. A woman

ἐν ἡσυχίᾳ μανθανέτω ἐν πάσῃ ὑποταγῇ·
in silence let learn in all subjection;

12 διδάσκειν δὲ γυναικὶ οὐκ ἐπιτρέπω,
but [3]to teach [2]a woman [1]I do not permit,

οὐδὲ αὐθεντεῖν ἀνδρός, ἀλλ᾽ εἶναι ἐν
nor to exercise authority of(over) a man, but to be in

ἡσυχίᾳ. **13** Ἀδὰμ γὰρ πρῶτος ἐπλάσθη,
silence. For Adam first was formed,

εἶτα Εὕα. **14** καὶ Ἀδὰμ οὐκ ἠπατήθη,
then Eve. And Adam was not deceived,

ἡ δὲ γυνὴ ἐξαπατηθεῖσα ἐν παραβάσει
but the woman being deceived [2]in [3]transgression

γέγονεν· **15** σωθήσεται δὲ διὰ τῆς
[1]has become; but she will be saved through the(her)

τεκνογονίας, ἐὰν μείνωσιν ἐν πίστει καὶ
childbearing, if they remain in faith and

ἀγάπῃ καὶ ἁγιασμῷ μετὰ σωφροσύνης.
love and sanctification with sobriety.

3 Πιστὸς ὁ λόγος· εἴ τις ἐπισκοπῆς
Faithful [is] the word: If anyone [2]oversight

ὀρέγεται, καλοῦ ἔργου ἐπιθυμεῖ. **2** δεῖ
[1]aspires to, [2]a good [3]work [1]he desires. It behoves

οὖν τὸν ἐπίσκοπον ἀνεπίλημπτον εἶναι,
therefore the bishop without reproach to be,

God our Savior, 4who
wants all men to be saved
and to come to a knowledge
of the truth. 5For there is
one God and one mediator
between God and men, the
man Christ Jesus, 6who
gave himself as a ransom
for all men—the testimony
given in its proper time.
7And for this purpose I was
appointed a herald and an
apostle—I am telling the
truth, I am not lying—and a
teacher of the true faith to
the Gentiles.
8I want men everywhere
to lift up holy hands in
prayer, without anger or
disputing.
9I also want women to
dress modestly, with de-
cency and propriety, not
with braided hair or gold or
pearls or expensive
clothes, 10but with good
deeds, appropriate for
women who profess to
worship God.
11A woman should learn
in quietness and full submission. 12I do not permit a
woman to teach or to have
authority over a man; she
must be silent. 13For Adam
was formed first, then Eve.
14And Adam was not the
one deceived; it was the
woman who was deceived
and became a sinner. 15But
women[b] will be saved[c]
through childbearing—if
they continue in faith, love
and holiness with propri-
ety.

Chapter 3

Overseers and Deacons

HERE is a trustworthy
saying: If anyone sets
his heart on being an overseer,[d] he desires a noble
task. 2Now the overseer
must be above reproach,

[b] 15 Greek *she*
[c] 15 Or *restored*
[d] 1 Traditionally *bishop*; also in verse 2

once,[i] temperate, sensible, respectable, hospitable, an apt teacher, 3 not a drunkard, not violent but gentle, not quarrelsome, and not a lover of money. 4 He must manage his own household well, keeping his children submissive and respectful in every way— 5 for if someone does not know how to manage his own household, how can he take care of God's church? 6 He must not be a recent convert, or he may be puffed up with conceit and fall into the condemnation of the devil. 7 Moreover, he must be well thought of by outsiders, so that he may not fall into disgrace and the snare of the devil.

Qualifications of Deacons

8 Deacons likewise must be serious, not double-tongued, not indulging in much wine, not greedy for money; 9 they must hold fast to the mystery of the faith with a clear conscience. 10 And let them first be tested; then, if they prove themselves blameless, let them serve as deacons. 11 Women[j] likewise must be serious, not slanderers, but temperate, faithful in all things. 12 Let deacons be married only once,[k] and let them manage their children and their households well; 13 for those who serve well as deacons gain a good standing for themselves and great boldness in the faith that is in Christ Jesus.

The Mystery of Our Religion

14 I hope to come to you soon, but I am writing these instructions to you so that, 15 if I am delayed, you may know how one ought to behave in the household of God, which is the church

[i] Gk *the husband of one wife*
[j] Or *Their wives*, or *Women deacons*
[k] Gk *be husbands of one wife*

μιᾶς γυναικὸς ἄνδρα, νηφάλιον, σώφρονα,
of one wife husband, temperate, sensible,
κόσμιον, φιλόξενον, διδακτικόν, **3** μὴ
orderly, hospitable, apt at teaching, not
πάροινον, μὴ πλήκτην, ἀλλὰ ἐπιεικῆ,
an excessive drinker, not a striker, but forbearing,
ἄμαχον, ἀφιλάργυρον, **4** τοῦ ἰδίου οἴκου
uncontentious, not avaricious, [3]the(his) [4]own [5]household
καλῶς προϊστάμενον, τέκνα ἔχοντα ἐν
[2]well [1]ruling, children having in
ὑποταγῇ μετὰ πάσης σεμνότητος, **5** (εἰ
subjection with all gravity, [2](if
δέ τις τοῦ ἰδίου οἴκου προστῆναι οὐκ
[1]but [3]anyone [7]the(his) [8]own [9]household [6]to rule [5]not*
οἶδεν, πῶς ἐκκλησίας θεοῦ ἐπιμελήσεται;)
[4]knows, how [2]a church [3]of God [1]will he care for ?)
6 μὴ νεόφυτον, ἵνα μὴ τυφωθεὶς εἰς
not a neophyte(recent convert), lest being puffed up [2]into
κρίμα ἐμπέσῃ τοῦ διαβόλου. **7** δεῖ δὲ
[3]judgment [1]he fall *in* of the devil. And it behoves
καὶ μαρτυρίαν καλὴν ἔχειν ἀπὸ τῶν
also [3]witness [2]a good [1]to have from the [ones]
ἔξωθεν, ἵνα μὴ εἰς ὀνειδισμὸν ἐμπέσῃ
outside, lest [2]into [3]reproach [1]he fall *in*
καὶ παγίδα τοῦ διαβόλου. **8** Διακόνους
and a snare of the devil. [It behoves] deacons
ὡσαύτως σεμνούς, μὴ διλόγους, μὴ οἴνῳ
similarly [to be] grave, not double-tongued, not [3]wine
πολλῷ προσέχοντας, μὴ αἰσχροκερδεῖς,
[2]to much [1]*being* addicted, not fond of base gain,
9 ἔχοντας τὸ μυστήριον τῆς πίστεως ἐν
having the mystery of the faith with
καθαρᾷ συνειδήσει. **10** καὶ οὗτοι δὲ
a clean conscience. [4]Also [3]these [1]and
δοκιμαζέσθωσαν πρῶτον, εἶτα διακονείτωσαν
[2]let [5]be proved first*ly*, then let them minister
ἀνέγκλητοι ὄντες. **11** γυναῖκας ὡσαύτως
[2]irreproachable [1]being. [It behoves]* wives similarly
σεμνάς, μὴ διαβόλους, νηφαλίους, πιστὰς
[to be] grave, not slanderers, sober, faithful
ἐν πᾶσιν. **12** διάκονοι ἔστωσαν μιᾶς
in all things. [2]Deacons [1]let [3]be [5]of one
γυναικὸς ἄνδρες, τέκνων καλῶς προϊστάμενοι
[6]wife [4]husbands, [2]children [7]well [1]ruling
καὶ τῶν ἰδίων οἴκων. **13** οἱ γὰρ καλῶς
[3]and [4]the(ir) [5]own [6]households. For the [ones] [2]well
διακονήσαντες βαθμὸν ἑαυτοῖς καλὸν
[1]having ministered [6]position [4]for themselves [5]a good
περιποιοῦνται καὶ πολλὴν παρρησίαν ἐν
[3]acquire and much boldness in
πίστει τῇ ἐν Χριστῷ Ἰησοῦ. **14** Ταῦτά
faith the [one] in Christ Jesus. These things
σοι γράφω ἐλπίζων ἐλθεῖν πρὸς σὲ
to thee I write hoping to come to thee
τάχιον· **15** ἐὰν δὲ βραδύνω, ἵνα εἰδῇς
shortly; but if I delay, in order that thou mayest know
πῶς δεῖ ἐν οἴκῳ θεοῦ ἀναστρέφεσθαι,
how it behoves in [the] household of God to behave,

* That is, "cannot"; see note on page xvi.

* See verses 7 and 8.

the husband of but one wife, temperate, self-controlled, respectable, hospitable, able to teach, 3 not given to drunkenness, not violent but gentle, not quarrelsome, not a lover of money. 4 He must manage his own family well and see that his children obey him with proper respect. 5 (If anyone does not know how to manage his own family, how can he take care of God's church?) 6 He must not be a recent convert, or he may become conceited and fall under the same judgment as the devil. 7 He must also have a good reputation with outsiders, so that he will not fall into disgrace and into the devil's trap.

8 Deacons, likewise, are to be men worthy of respect, sincere, not indulging in much wine, and not pursuing dishonest gain. 9 They must keep hold of the deep truths of the faith with a clear conscience. 10 They must first be tested; and then if there is nothing against them, let them serve as deacons.

11 In the same way, their wives[e] are to be women worthy of respect, not malicious talkers but temperate and trustworthy in everything.

12 A deacon must be the husband of but one wife and must manage his children and his household well. 13 Those who have served well gain an excellent standing and great assurance in their faith in Christ Jesus.

14 Although I hope to come to you soon, I am writing you these instructions so that, 15 if I am delayed, you will know how people ought to conduct themselves in God's house-

[e] *11* Or *way, deaconesses*

of the living God, the pillar
and bulwark of the truth.
16Without any doubt, the
mystery of our religion is
great:

He[l] was revealed in
flesh,
vindicated[m] in
spirit,[n]
seen by angels,
proclaimed among
Gentiles,
believed in
throughout the
world,
taken up in glory.

Chapter 4

False Asceticism

NOW the Spirit ex-
pressly says that in
later[o] times some will renounce the faith by paying
attention to deceitful spirits
and teachings of demons,
2through the hypocrisy of
liars whose consciences are
seared with a hot iron.
3They forbid marriage and
demand abstinence from
foods, which God created
to be received with thanksgiving by those who believe
and know the truth. 4For
everything created by God
is good, and nothing is to be
rejected, provided it is received with thanksgiving;
5for it is sanctified by
God's word and by prayer.

A Good Minister of Jesus Christ

6 If you put these in-
structions before the brothers and sisters,[p] you will
be a good servant[q] of
Christ Jesus, nourished on
the words of the faith and of
the sound teaching that you
have followed. 7Have
nothing to do with profane
myths and old wives' tales.
Train yourself in godliness,
8for, while physical training is of some value, godliness is valuable in every
way, holding promise for
both the present life and the
life to come. 9The saying is
sure and worthy of full ac-

[l]Gk *Who*; other ancient authorities read *God*; others, *Which*
[m]Or *justified*
[n]Or *by the Spirit*
[o]Or *the last*
[p]Gk *brothers*
[q]Or *deacon*

ἥτις ἐστὶν ἐκκλησία θεοῦ ζῶντος, στῦλος
which is [the] church 2God 1of [the] living, pillar
καὶ ἑδραίωμα τῆς ἀληθείας. 16 καὶ
and bulwark of the truth. And
ὁμολογουμένως μέγα ἐστὶν τὸ τῆς εὐσεβείας
confessedly great is the – 2of piety
μυστήριον· ὃς ἐφανερώθη ἐν σαρκί,
1mystery: Who was manifested in flesh,
ἐδικαιώθη ἐν πνεύματι, ὤφθη ἀγγέλοις,
was justified in spirit, *was* seen by angels,
ἐκηρύχθη ἐν ἔθνεσιν, ἐπιστεύθη ἐν κόσμῳ,
was proclaimed among nations, *was* believed in [the] world,
ἀνελήμφθη ἐν δόξῃ.
was taken up in glory.

4 Τὸ δὲ πνεῦμα ῥητῶς λέγει ὅτι
Now the Spirit 2in words† 1says that
ἐν ὑστέροις καιροῖς ἀποστήσονταί τινες
in later times 2will depart from 1some
τῆς πίστεως, προσέχοντες πνεύμασιν
the faith, attending to 2spirits
πλάνοις καὶ διδασκαλίαις δαιμονίων, 2 ἐν
1misleading and teachings of demons, 2in
ὑποκρίσει ψευδολόγων, κεκαυστηριασμένων
3hypocrisy 1of men who speak lies, having been branded on
τὴν ἰδίαν συνείδησιν, 3 κωλυόντων γαμεῖν,
the(ir) own conscience, forbidding to marry,
ἀπέχεσθαι βρωμάτων, ἃ ὁ θεὸς ἔκτισεν
[bidding] to abstain from foods, which – God created
εἰς μετάλημψιν μετὰ εὐχαριστίας τοῖς
for partaking with thanksgiving by the
πιστοῖς καὶ ἐπεγνωκόσι τὴν ἀλήθειαν.
believers and [those] having fully known the truth.
4 ὅτι πᾶν κτίσμα θεοῦ καλόν, καὶ
Because every creature of God [is] good, and
οὐδὲν ἀπόβλητον μετὰ εὐχαριστίας λαμβαν-
nothing [is] to be put away 2with 3thanksgiving 1being
όμενον· 5 ἁγιάζεται γὰρ διὰ λόγου θεοῦ
received; for it is *being* sanctified through a word of God
καὶ ἐντεύξεως. 6 Ταῦτα ὑποτιθέμενος
and petition. 2These things 1suggesting
τοῖς ἀδελφοῖς καλὸς ἔσῃ διάκονος Χριστοῦ
3to the 4brothers 6a good 5thou wilt be 7minister of Christ
Ἰησοῦ, ἐντρεφόμενος τοῖς λόγοις τῆς
Jesus, being nourished by the words of the
πίστεως καὶ τῆς καλῆς διδασκαλίας ᾗ
faith and of the good teaching which
παρηκολούθηκας· 7 τοὺς δὲ βεβήλους καὶ
thou hast followed; but the profane and
γραώδεις μύθους παραιτοῦ. γύμναζε δὲ
old-womanish tales refuse. And exercise
σεαυτὸν πρὸς εὐσέβειαν. 8 ἡ γὰρ σωματικὴ
thyself to piety. – For bodily
γυμνασία πρὸς ὀλίγον ἐστὶν ὠφέλιμος·
exercise 3for 4a little 1is 2profitable;
ἡ δὲ εὐσέβεια πρὸς πάντα ὠφέλιμός
– but piety 3for 4all things 2profitable
ἐστιν, ἐπαγγελίαν ἔχουσα ζωῆς τῆς νῦν
1is, promise having 3life 1of the 2now (present)
καὶ τῆς μελλούσης. 9 πιστὸς ὁ λόγος
and of the coming. Faithful [is] the word

hold, which is the church of
the living God, the pillar
and foundation of the truth.
16Beyond all question, the
mystery of godliness is
great:

He[f] appeared in a
body,[g]
was vindicated by the
Spirit,
was seen by angels,
was preached among
the nations,
was believed on in the
world,
was taken up in glory.

Chapter 4

Instructions to Timothy

THE Spirit clearly says
that in later times
some will abandon the faith
and follow deceiving spirits
and things taught by de-
mons. 2Such teachings
come through hypocritical
liars, whose consciences
have been seared as with a
hot iron. 3They forbid people to marry and order
them to abstain from cer-
tain foods, which God created to be received with
thanksgiving by those who
believe and who know the
truth. 4For everything God
created is good, and nothing is to be rejected if it is
received with thanksgiv-
ing, 5because it is consecrated by the word of God
and prayer.
6If you point these things
out to the brothers, you will
be a good minister of Christ
Jesus, brought up in the
truths of the faith and of the
good teaching that you
have followed. 7Have nothing to do with godless
myths and old wives' tales;
rather, train yourself to be
godly. 8For physical training is of some value, but
godliness has value for all
things, holding promise for
both the present life and the
life to come.
9This is a trustworthy

[f]16 Some manuscripts *God*
[g]16 Or *in the flesh*

ceptance. 10For to this end
we toil and struggle,[r] because we have our hope set
on the living God, who is
the Savior of all people, especially of those who be-
lieve.
11 These are the things
you must insist on and
teach. 12Let no one despise
your youth, but set the believers an example in
speech and conduct, in
love, in faith, in purity.
13Until I arrive, give attention to the public reading of
scripture,[s] to exhorting, to
teaching. 14Do not neglect
the gift that is in you, which
was given to you through
prophecy with the laying
on of hands by the council
of elders.[t] 15Put these
things into practice, devote
yourself to them, so that all
may see your progress.
16Pay close attention to
yourself and to your teaching; continue in these
things, for in doing this you
will save both yourself and
your hearers.

καὶ πάσης ἀποδοχῆς ἄξιος· **10** εἰς τοῦτο
and [2]of all [3]acceptance [1]worthy; [1]to [2]this

γὰρ κοπιῶμεν καὶ ἀγωνιζόμεθα, ὅτι
[1]for we labour and struggle, because

ἠλπίκαμεν ἐπὶ θεῷ ζῶντι, ὅς ἐστιν
we have set [our] hope on [2]God [1]a living, who is

σωτὴρ πάντων ἀνθρώπων, μάλιστα πιστῶν.
[the] Saviour of all men, especially of believers.

11 Παράγγελλε ταῦτα καὶ δίδασκε.
Charge thou these things and teach.

12 μηδείς σου τῆς νεότητος καταφρονείτω,
[2]No one [5]of thee [3]the [4]youth [1]let despise,

ἀλλὰ τύπος γίνου τῶν πιστῶν ἐν λόγῳ,
but [2]a pattern [1]become thou of the believers in speech,

ἐν ἀναστροφῇ, ἐν ἀγάπῃ, ἐν πίστει,
in behaviour, in love, in faith,

ἐν ἁγνείᾳ. **13** ἕως ἔρχομαι πρόσεχε
in purity. Until I come attend

τῇ ἀναγνώσει, τῇ παρακλήσει, τῇ διδασ-
to the reading,* to the exhortation, to the teach-

καλίᾳ. **14** μὴ ἀμέλει τοῦ ἐν σοὶ
ing. Do not be neglectful [1]of the [3]in [4]thee

χαρίσματος, ὃ ἐδόθη σοι διὰ προφητείας
[2]gift, which was given to thee by means of prophecy

μετὰ ἐπιθέσεως τῶν χειρῶν τοῦ πρε-
with laying on of the hands of the body

σβυτερίου. **15** ταῦτα μελέτα, ἐν τούτοις
of elders. [2]These things [1]attend to, [1]in [2]these things

ἴσθι, ἵνα σου ἡ προκοπὴ φανερὰ ᾖ
[1]be thou, in order that of thee the advance clear may be

πᾶσιν. **16** ἔπεχε σεαυτῷ καὶ τῇ διδασκαλίᾳ,
to all men. Take heed to thyself and to the teaching,

ἐπίμενε αὐτοῖς· τοῦτο γὰρ ποιῶν καὶ
continue in them; for this doing both

σεαυτὸν σώσεις καὶ τοὺς ἀκούοντάς σου.
thyself thou wilt save and the [ones] hearing thee.

saying that deserves full acceptance 10(and for this we
labor and strive), that we
have put our hope in the living God, who is the Savior
of all men, and especially of
those who believe.
11Command and teach
these things. 12Don't let
anyone look down on you
because you are young, but
set an example for the believers in speech, in life, in
love, in faith and in purity.
13Until I come, devote
yourself to the public reading of Scripture, to preaching and to teaching. 14Do
not neglect your gift, which
was given you through a
prophetic message when
the body of elders laid their
hands on you.
15Be diligent in these matters; give yourself wholly
to them, so that everyone
may see your progress.
16Watch your life and doctrine closely. Persevere in
them, because if you do,
you will save both yourself
and your hearers.

Chapter 5

Duties toward Believers

DO not speak harshly to
an older man,[u] but
speak to him as to a father,
to younger men as broth-
ers, 2to older women as
mothers, to younger wom-
en as sisters—with abso-
lute purity.
3 Honor widows who
are really widows. 4If a
widow has children or
grandchildren, they should
first learn their religious
duty to their own family
and make some repayment
to their parents; for this is
pleasing in God's sight.
5The real widow, left
alone, has set her hope on

5 Πρεσβυτέρῳ μὴ ἐπιπλήξῃς, ἀλλὰ
An older man do not rebuke, but

παρακάλει ὡς πατέρα, νεωτέρους ὡς
exhort as a father, younger men as

ἀδελφούς, **2** πρεσβυτέρας ὡς μητέρας,
brothers, older women as mothers,

νεωτέρας ὡς ἀδελφὰς ἐν πάσῃ ἁγνείᾳ.
younger women as sisters with all purity.

3 Χήρας τίμα τὰς ὄντως χήρας. **4** εἰ δέ
[2]Widows [1]honour [3]the [4]real*ly* [5]widows. But if

τις χήρα τέκνα ἢ ἔκγονα ἔχει, μαν-
any widow [2]children [3]or [4]grandchildren [1]has, let

θανέτωσαν πρῶτον τὸν ἴδιον οἶκον εὐσεβεῖν
them learn firstly [2]the(ir) [3]own [4]household [1]to show piety to

καὶ ἀμοιβὰς ἀποδιδόναι τοῖς προγόνοις·
and [2]requitals [1]to return to the(ir) forebears;

τοῦτο γάρ ἐστιν ἀπόδεκτον ἐνώπιον τοῦ
for this is acceptable before

θεοῦ. **5** ἡ δὲ ὄντως χήρα καὶ μεμονωμένη
God. But the real*ly* widow and *having been* left alone

* That is, the reading aloud in public worship of the Scriptures (as nearly always in the N.T.).

Chapter 5

Advice About Widows, Elders and Slaves

DO not rebuke an older
man harshly, but ex-
hort him as if he were your
father. Treat younger men
as brothers, 2older women
as mothers, and younger
women as sisters, with absolute purity.
3Give proper recognition
to those widows who are
really in need. 4But if a widow has children or grand-
children, these should learn
first of all to put their religion into practice by caring
for their own family and so
repaying their parents and
grandparents, for this is
pleasing to God. 5The widow who is really in need
and left all alone puts her

[r] Other ancient authorities read *suffer reproach*
[s] Gk *to the reading*
[t] Gk *by the presbytery*
[u] Or *an elder*, or *a presbyter*

God and continues in sup-
plications and prayers night
and day; 6but the widow[v]
who lives for pleasure is
dead even while she lives.
7Give these commands as
well, so that they may be
above reproach. 8And
whoever does not provide
for relatives, and especially
for family members, has
denied the faith and is
worse than an unbeliever.
9 Let a widow be put on
the list if she is not less than
sixty years old and has
been married only once;[w]
10she must be well attested
for her good works, as one
who has brought up chil-
dren, shown hospitality,
washed the saints' feet,
helped the afflicted, and
devoted herself to doing
good in every way. 11But
refuse to put younger widows on the list; for when
their sensual desires alienate them from Christ, they
want to marry, 12and so
they incur condemnation
for having violated their
first pledge. 13Besides that,
they learn to be idle, gad-
ding about from house to
house; and they are not
merely idle, but also gossips and busybodies, say-
ing what they should not
say. 14So I would have
younger widows marry,
bear children, and manage
their households, so as to
give the adversary no occasion to revile us. 15For
some have already turned
away to follow Satan. 16If
any believing woman[x] has
relatives who are really
widows, let her assist
them; let the church not be
burdened, so that it can assist those who are real widows.
17 Let the elders who
rule well be considered
worthy of double honor,[y]
especially those who labor

[v] Gk *she*
[w] Gk *the wife of one husband*
[x] Other ancient authorities read *believing man or woman*; others, *believing man*
[y] Or *compensation*

ἤλπικεν ἐπὶ θεὸν καὶ προσμένει ταῖς
has set [her] hope on God and continues in the
δεήσεσιν καὶ ταῖς προσευχαῖς νυκτὸς καὶ
petitions and the prayers night and
ἡμέρας· 6 ἡ δὲ σπαταλῶσα ζῶσα τέθνηκεν.
day; but the [one] living wantonly 2living 1has died.
7 καὶ ταῦτα παράγγελλε, ἵνα ἀνεπίλημπτοι
And these things charge thou, in order that 2without reproach
ὦσιν. 8 εἰ δέ τις τῶν ἰδίων καὶ μάλιστα
1they may be. But if anyone 2the(his) 3own [people] 4and 5especially
οἰκείων οὐ προνοεῖ, τὴν πίστιν ἤρνηται
[his] 6family 1provides not [for], 2the 3faith 1he has denied
καὶ ἔστιν ἀπίστου χείρων. 9 χήρα
and is 2an unbeliever 1worse [than]. A widow
καταλεγέσθω μὴ ἔλαττον ἐτῶν ἑξήκοντα
let be enrolled 2not 3less [than] 5*of* years 4sixty
γεγονυῖα, ἑνὸς ἀνδρὸς γυνή, 10 ἐν ἔργοις
1having become, of one man wife, 2by 4works
καλοῖς μαρτυρουμένη, εἰ ἐτεκνοτρόφησεν,
3good 1being witnessed, if she brought up children,
εἰ ἐξενοδόχησεν, εἰ ἁγίων πόδας ἔνιψεν,
if she entertained strangers, if 3of saints 2feet 1she washed,
εἰ θλιβομένοις ἐπήρκεσεν, εἰ παντὶ ἔργῳ
if 2*being* afflicted [ones], 1she relieved, if 2every 4work
ἀγαθῷ ἐπηκολούθησεν. 11 νεωτέρας δὲ
3good 1she followed after. But younger
χήρας παραιτοῦ· ὅταν γὰρ καταστρηνιάσωσιν
widows refuse; for whenever they grow wanton against
τοῦ Χριστοῦ, γαμεῖν θέλουσιν, 12 ἔχουσαι
– Christ, 2to marry 1they wish, having
κρίμα ὅτι τὴν πρώτην πίστιν ἠθέτησαν·
judgment because 2the(ir) 3first 4faith 1they set aside;
13 ἅμα δὲ καὶ ἀργαὶ μανθάνουσιν
and at the same time also 2idle 1they learn [to be]
περιερχόμεναι τὰς οἰκίας, οὐ μόνον δὲ
going round the houses, 2not 3only 1and
ἀργαὶ ἀλλὰ καὶ φλύαροι καὶ περίεργοι,
idle but also gossips and busybodies,
λαλοῦσαι τὰ μὴ δέοντα. 14 βούλομαι
speaking the things not proper. I will
οὖν νεωτέρας γαμεῖν, τεκνογονεῖν,
therefore younger women to marry, to bear children,
οἰκοδεσποτεῖν, μηδεμίαν ἀφορμὴν διδόναι
to be mistress of a house, 2no 3occasion 1to give
τῷ ἀντικειμένῳ λοιδορίας χάριν· 15 ἤδη
to the [one] opposing 2reproach 1on account of; 2already
γάρ τινες ἐξετράπησαν ὀπίσω τοῦ σατανᾶ.
1for some turned aside behind – Satan.
16 εἴ τις πιστὴ ἔχει χήρας, ἐπαρκείτω
If any believing woman has widows, let her relieve
αὐταῖς, καὶ μὴ βαρείσθω ἡ ἐκκλησία,
them, and not let be burdened the church,
ἵνα ταῖς ὄντως χήραις ἐπαρκέσῃ. 17 Οἱ
in order that 2the 3real*ly* 4widows 1it may relieve. 2The
καλῶς προεστῶτες πρεσβύτεροι διπλῆς
5well 4ruling 3elders 9of double

hope in God and continues
night and day to pray and to
ask God for help. 6But the
widow who lives for plea-
sure is dead even while she
lives. 7Give the people
these instructions, too, so
that no one may be open to
blame. 8If anyone does not
provide for his relatives,
and especially for his im-
mediate family, he has denied the faith and is worse
than an unbeliever.
9No widow may be put on
the list of widows unless
she is over sixty, has been
faithful to her husband,[h]
10and is well known for her
good deeds, such as bringing up children, showing
hospitality, washing the
feet of the saints, helping
those in trouble and devoting herself to all kinds of
good deeds.
11As for younger widows,
do not put them on such a
list. For when their sensual
desires overcome their
dedication to Christ, they
want to marry. 12Thus they
bring judgment on them-
selves, because they have
broken their first pledge.
13Besides, they get into the
habit of being idle and going about from house to
house. And not only do
they become idlers, but
also gossips and busybod-
ies, saying things they
ought not to. 14So I counsel
younger widows to marry,
to have children, to manage
their homes and to give the
enemy no opportunity for
slander. 15Some have in
fact already turned away to
follow Satan.
16If any woman who is a
believer has widows in her
family, she should help
them and not let the church
be burdened with them, so
that the church can help
those widows who are really in need.
17The elders who direct
the affairs of the church
well are worthy of double
honor, especially those

[h] 9 Or *has had but one husband*

in preaching and teaching;
18 for the scripture says,
"You shall not muzzle an
ox while it is treading out
the grain," and, "The laborer deserves to be paid."
19 Never accept any accu-
sation against an elder except on the evidence of two
or three witnesses. 20 As for
those who persist in sin, rebuke them in the presence
of all, so that the rest also
may stand in fear. 21 In the
presence of God and of
Christ Jesus and of the
elect angels, I warn you to
keep these instructions
without prejudice, doing
nothing on the basis of partiality. 22 Do not ordain[z]
anyone hastily, and do not
participate in the sins of
others; keep yourself pure.
23 No longer drink only
water, but take a little wine
for the sake of your stomach and your frequent ailments.
24 The sins of some
people are conspicuous and
precede them to judgment,
while the sins of others follow them there. 25 So also
good works are conspicu-
ous; and even when they
are not, they cannot remain
hidden.

Chapter 6

LET all who are under the
yoke of slavery regard
their masters as worthy of
all honor, so that the name
of God and the teaching
may not be blasphemed.
2 Those who have believing
masters must not be disre-
spectful to them on the
ground that they are mem-
bers of the church;[a] rather
they must serve them all
the more, since those who
benefit by their service are
believers and beloved.[b]

False Teaching and True Riches

Teach and urge these du-

[z] Gk *Do not lay hands on*
[a] Gk *are brothers*
[b] Or *since they are believers and beloved, who devote themselves to good deeds*

τιμῆς ἀξιούσθωσαν, μάλιστα οἱ κοπιῶντες
[10]honour [1]let [6]be [7]deemed [8]worthy, especially the labouring [ones]

ἐν λόγῳ καὶ διδασκαλίᾳ. **18** λέγει γὰρ
in speech and teaching. For says

ἡ γραφή· βοῦν ἀλοῶντα οὐ φιμώσεις,
the scripture: An ox threshing thou shalt not muzzle,

καί· ἄξιος ὁ ἐργάτης τοῦ μισθοῦ αὐτοῦ.
and: Worthy [is] the workman of the pay of him.

19 κατὰ πρεσβυτέρου κατηγορίαν μὴ παρα-
Against an elder accusation do not re-

δέχου, ἐκτὸς εἰ μὴ ἐπὶ δύο ἢ τριῶν
ceive, *except* unless on [the word of] two or three

μαρτύρων. **20** Τοὺς ἁμαρτάνοντας ἐνώπιον
witnesses. The [ones] sinning [2]before

πάντων ἔλεγχε, ἵνα καὶ οἱ λοιποὶ φόβον
[3]all [1]reprove thou, in order that [3]also [1]the [2]rest [5]fear

ἔχωσιν. **21** Διαμαρτύρομαι ἐνώπιον τοῦ
[4]may have. I solemnly witness before –

θεοῦ καὶ Χριστοῦ Ἰησοῦ καὶ τῶν
God and Christ Jesus and the

ἐκλεκτῶν ἀγγέλων ἵνα ταῦτα φυλάξῃς
chosen angels *in order* that these things thou guard

χωρὶς προκρίματος, μηδὲν ποιῶν κατὰ
without prejudgment, [2]nothing [1]doing by way of

πρόσκλισιν. **22** χεῖρας ταχέως μηδενὶ
inclination. [3]Hands [2]quickly [4]no man

ἐπιτίθει, μηδὲ κοινώνει ἁμαρτίαις ἀλ-
[1]lay [5]on, nor share [2]sins [1]in

λοτρίαις· σεαυτὸν ἁγνὸν τήρει. **23** Μηκέτι
others'†; [3]thyself [2]pure [1]keep. No longer

ὑδροπότει, ἀλλὰ οἴνῳ ὀλίγῳ χρῶ διὰ
drink water, but [3]wine [2]a little [1]use on account of

τὸν στόμαχον καὶ τὰς πυκνάς σου
the(thy) stomach and the frequent [2]of thee

ἀσθενείας. **24** Τινῶν ἀνθρώπων αἱ ἁμαρτίαι
[1]weaknesses. [3]of some [4]men [1]The [2]sins

πρόδηλοί εἰσιν προάγουσαι εἰς κρίσιν,
[6]clear beforehand [5]are going before to judgment,

τισὶν δὲ καὶ ἐπακολουθοῦσιν· **25** ὡσαύτως
but some indeed they follow on; similarly

καὶ τὰ ἔργα τὰ καλὰ πρόδηλα, καὶ
also the [2]works – [1]good [are] clear beforehand, and

τὰ ἄλλως ἔχοντα κρυβῆναι οὐ δύνανται.
the [ones] [2]otherwise [1]having (being) [4]*to* be hidden [3]cannot.

6 Ὅσοι εἰσὶν ὑπὸ ζυγὸν δοῦλοι, τοὺς
As many as are under a yoke [being] slaves, [2]the(ir)

ἰδίους δεσπότας πάσης τιμῆς ἀξίους ἡγείσ-
[3]own [4]masters [6]of all [7]honour [5]worthy [1]let them

θωσαν, ἵνα μὴ τὸ ὄνομα τοῦ θεοῦ καὶ
deem, lest the name – of God and

ἡ διδασκαλία βλασφημῆται. **2** οἱ δὲ
the teaching be blasphemed. And [1]the [ones]

πιστοὺς ἔχοντες δεσπότας μὴ καταφρο-
[3]believing [2]having [4]masters not let them

νείτωσαν, ὅτι ἀδελφοί εἰσιν, ἀλλὰ μᾶλλον
despise [them], because brothers they are, but rather

δουλευέτωσαν, ὅτι πιστοί εἰσιν καὶ
let them serve as slaves, because [6]believing [5]are [7]and

ἀγαπητοὶ οἱ τῆς εὐεργεσίας ἀντιλαμ-
[8]beloved [1]the [ones] [3]*of* the [4]good service [2]receiving in

βανόμενοι.
return.

whose work is preaching
and teaching. 18 For the
Scripture says, "Do not
muzzle the ox while it is
treading out the grain,"[i]
and "The worker deserves
his wages."[j] 19 Do not entertain an accusation
against an elder unless it is
brought by two or three
witnesses. 20 Those who sin
are to be rebuked publicly,
so that the others may take
warning.
21 I charge you, in the
sight of God and Christ
Jesus and the elect angels,
to keep these instructions
without partiality, and to
do nothing out of favoritism.
22 Do not be hasty in the
laying on of hands, and do
not share in the sins of others. Keep yourself pure.
23 Stop drinking only wa-
ter, and use a little wine because of your stomach and
your frequent illnesses.
24 The sins of some men
are obvious, reaching the
place of judgment ahead of
them; the sins of others trail
behind them. 25 In the same
way, good deeds are obvi-
ous, and even those that
are not cannot be hidden.

Chapter 6

ALL who are under the
yoke of slavery
should consider their masters worthy of full respect,
so that God's name and our
teaching may not be slan-
dered. 2 Those who have
believing masters are not to
show less respect for them
because they are brothers.
Instead, they are to serve
them even better, because
those who benefit from
their service are believers,
and dear to them. These are
the things you are to teach
and urge on them.

[i] *18* Deut. 25:4
[j] *18* Luke 10:7

ties. 3 Whoever teaches
otherwise and does not
agree with the sound words
of our Lord Jesus Christ
and the teaching that is in
accordance with godliness,
4 is conceited, understanding nothing, and has a mor-
bid craving for controversy
and for disputes about
words. From these come
envy, dissension, slander,
base suspicions, 5 and
wrangling among those
who are depraved in mind
and bereft of the truth,
imagining that godliness is
a means of gain.[c] 6 Of
course, there is great gain
in godliness combined with
contentment; 7 for we
brought nothing into the
world, so that[d] we can take
nothing out of it; 8 but if we
have food and clothing, we
will be content with these.
9 But those who want to be
rich fall into temptation and
are trapped by many senseless and harmful desires
that plunge people into ruin
and destruction. 10 For the
love of money is a root of
all kinds of evil, and in their
eagerness to be rich some
have wandered away from
the faith and pierced themselves with many pains.

The Good Fight of Faith

11 But as for you, man
of God, shun all this; pursue righteousness, godli-
ness, faith, love, endur-
ance, gentleness. 12 Fight
the good fight of the faith;
take hold of the eternal life,
to which you were called
and for which you made[e]
the good confession in the

[c] Other ancient authorities add *Withdraw yourself from such people*
[d] Other ancient authorities read *world—it is certain that*
[e] Gk *confessed*

Ταῦτα δίδασκε καὶ παρακάλει. **3** εἴ
These things teach thou and exhort. If

τις ἑτεροδιδασκαλεῖ καὶ μὴ προσέρχεται
anyone teaches differently and consents not

ὑγιαίνουσιν λόγοις τοῖς τοῦ κυρίου ἡμῶν
to *being* healthy words the [words] of the Lord of us

Ἰησοῦ Χριστοῦ, καὶ τῇ κατ' εὐσέβειαν
Jesus Christ, and [1]to the [3]according to [4]piety

διδασκαλίᾳ, **4** τετύφωται, μηδὲν ἐπιστά-
[2]teaching, he has been puffed up, [2]nothing [1]under-

μενος, ἀλλὰ νοσῶν περὶ ζητήσεις καὶ
standing, but being diseased about questionings and

λογομαχίας, ἐξ ὧν γίνεται φθόνος, ἔρις,
battles of words, out of which comes envy, strife,

βλασφημίαι, ὑπόνοιαι πονηραί, **5** διαπαρα-
blasphemies, [2]suspicions [1]evil, perpetual

τριβαὶ διεφθαρμένων ἀνθρώπων τὸν νοῦν
wranglings [2]having been corrupted [1]of men the mind
=of men with corrupted mind

καὶ ἀπεστερημένων τῆς ἀληθείας, νομιζ-
and *having been* deprived of the truth, sup-

όντων πορισμὸν εἶναι τὴν εὐσέβειαν.
posing [3]gain [2]to be *the* [1]piety.*

6 ἔστιν δὲ πορισμὸς μέγας ἡ εὐσέβεια
But [4]is [6]gain [5]great *the* [1]piety

μετὰ αὐταρκείας· **7** οὐδὲν γὰρ εἰσηνέγκαμεν
[2]with [3]self-sufficiency;* for nothing we have brought *in*

εἰς τὸν κόσμον, ὅτι οὐδὲ ἐξενεγκεῖν
into the world, because neither [2]*to* carry out

τι δυνάμεθα· **8** ἔχοντες δὲ διατροφὰς καὶ
[3]anything [1]can we; but having foods and

σκεπάσματα, τούτοις ἀρκεσθησόμεθα. **9** οἱ
clothings, with these things we will be satisfied. the

δὲ βουλόμενοι πλουτεῖν ἐμπίπτουσιν εἰς
But [ones] resolving to be rich fall *in* into

πειρασμὸν καὶ παγίδα καὶ ἐπιθυμίας πολλὰς
temptation and a snare and [5]lusts [1]many

ἀνοήτους καὶ βλαβεράς, αἵτινες βυθίζουσιν
[2]foolish [3]and [4]injurious, which [1]cause [3]to sink

τοὺς ἀνθρώπους εἰς ὄλεθρον καὶ ἀπώλειαν.
– [2]men into ruin and destruction.

10 ῥίζα γὰρ πάντων τῶν κακῶν ἐστιν
For [4]a root [5]of all – [6]evils [3]is

ἡ φιλαργυρία, ἧς τινες ὀρεγόμενοι
[1]the [2]love of money,* of which some hankering after

ἀπεπλανήθησαν ἀπὸ τῆς πίστεως καὶ
wandered away from the faith and

ἑαυτοὺς περιέπειραν ὀδύναις πολλαῖς. **11** Σὺ
themselves pierced round [2]pains [1]by many. thou

δέ, ὦ ἄνθρωπε θεοῦ, ταῦτα φεῦγε· δίωκε
But, O man of God, these things flee; [2]pursue

δὲ δικαιοσύνην, εὐσέβειαν, πίστιν, ἀγάπην,
[1]and righteousness, piety, faith, love,

ὑπομονήν, πραϋπαθίαν. **12** ἀγωνίζου τὸν
endurance, meekness. Struggle the

καλὸν ἀγῶνα τῆς πίστεως, ἐπιλαβοῦ τῆς
good struggle of the faith, lay hold on *the*

αἰωνίου ζωῆς, εἰς ἣν ἐκλήθης καὶ ὡμολό-
eternal life, to which thou wast called and didst con-

γησας τὴν καλὴν ὁμολογίαν ἐνώπιον
fess the good confession before

* For order of words see note on John 1. 1.

Love of Money

3 If anyone teaches false
doctrines and does not
agree to the sound instruction of our Lord Jesus
Christ and to godly teaching, 4 he is conceited and
understands nothing. He
has an unhealthy interest in
controversies and quarrels
about words that result in
envy, strife, malicious talk,
evil suspicions 5 and constant friction between men
of corrupt mind, who have
been robbed of the truth
and who think that godli-
ness is a means to financial
gain.
6 But godliness with con-
tentment is great gain. 7 For
we brought nothing into the
world, and we can take
nothing out of it. 8 But if we
have food and clothing, we
will be content with that.
9 People who want to get
rich fall into temptation and
a trap and into many foolish
and harmful desires that
plunge men into ruin and
destruction. 10 For the love
of money is a root of all
kinds of evil. Some people,
eager for money, have
wandered from the faith
and pierced themselves
with many griefs.

Paul's Charge to Timothy

11 But you, man of God,
flee from all this, and pursue righteousness, godli-
ness, faith, love, endurance
and gentleness. 12 Fight the
good fight of the faith. Take
hold of the eternal life to
which you were called
when you made your good

presence of many wit-
nesses. 13 In the presence
of God, who gives life to all
things, and of Christ Jesus,
who in his testimony before
Pontius Pilate made the
good confession, I charge
you 14 to keep the com-
mandment without spot or
blame until the manifestation of our Lord Jesus
Christ, 15 which he will
bring about at the right
time—he who is the
blessed and only Sover-
eign, the King of kings and
Lord of lords. 16 It is he
alone who has immortality
and dwells in unapproach-
able light, whom no one has
ever seen or can see; to him
be honor and eternal do-
minion. Amen.
17 As for those who in
the present age are rich,
command them not to be
haughty, or to set their
hopes on the uncertainty of
riches, but rather on God
who richly provides us with
everything for our enjoy-
ment. 18 They are to do
good, to be rich in good
works, generous, and
ready to share, 19 thus storing up for themselves the
treasure of a good foundation for the future, so that
they may take hold of the
life that really is life.

Personal Instructions and Benediction

20 Timothy, guard what
has been entrusted to you.
Avoid the profane chatter
and contradictions of what
is falsely called knowledge;
21 by professing it some
have missed the mark as regards the faith.
Grace be with you.[f]

πολλῶν μαρτύρων. 13 παραγγέλλω ἐνώπιον
many witnesses. I charge before
τοῦ θεοῦ τοῦ ζῳογονοῦντος τὰ πάντα
– God the [one] quickening – all things
καὶ Χριστοῦ Ἰησοῦ τοῦ μαρτυρήσαντος
and Christ Jesus the [one] having witnessed
ἐπὶ Ποντίου Πιλάτου τὴν καλὴν ὁμολογίαν,
in the time of Pontius Pilate the good confession,
14 τηρῆσαί σε τὴν ἐντολὴν ἄσπιλον
2to keep 1thee* the(this) commandment unspotted
ἀνεπίλημπτον μέχρι τῆς ἐπιφανείας τοῦ
without reproach until the appearance of the
κυρίου ἡμῶν Ἰησοῦ Χριστοῦ, 15 ἣν
Lord of us Jesus Christ, which§
καιροῖς ἰδίοις δείξει ὁ μακάριος καὶ
7in its/his own times 6will show 1the 2blessed 3and
μόνος δυνάστης, ὁ βασιλεὺς τῶν βασιλευ-
4only 5Potentate, the King of the [ones] reign-
όντων καὶ κύριος τῶν κυριευόντων, 16 ὁ
ing and Lord of the [ones] ruling, the
μόνος ἔχων ἀθανασίαν, φῶς οἰκῶν
only [one] having immortality, 2light 1inhabiting
ἀπρόσιτον, ὃν εἶδεν οὐδεὶς ἀνθρώπων οὐδὲ
unapproachable, whom 3saw 1no one 2of men nor
ἰδεῖν δύναται· ᾧ τιμὴ καὶ κράτος αἰώνιον·
2*to* see 1can; to whom [be] honour and might eternal:
ἀμήν. 17 Τοῖς πλουσίοις ἐν τῷ νῦν
Amen. 2the 3rich 4in 5the 6now (present)
αἰῶνι παράγγελλε μὴ ὑψηλοφρονεῖν, μηδὲ
7age 1Charge thou not to be highminded, nor
ἠλπικέναι ἐπὶ πλούτου ἀδηλότητι, ἀλλ’
to have set [their] hope on 2of riches 1[the] uncertainty, but
ἐπὶ θεῷ τῷ παρέχοντι ἡμῖν πάντα
on God the [one] offering to us all things
πλουσίως εἰς ἀπόλαυσιν, 18 ἀγαθοεργεῖν,
richly for enjoyment, to work good,
πλουτεῖν ἐν ἔργοις καλοῖς, εὐμεταδότους
to be rich in 2works 1good, 2ready to impart
εἶναι, κοινωνικούς, 19 ἀποθησαυρίζοντας
1to be, generous, treasuring away
ἑαυτοῖς θεμέλιον καλὸν εἰς τὸ μέλλον,
for themselves 2foundation 1a good for the future,
ἵνα ἐπιλάβωνται τῆς ὄντως ζωῆς. 20 Ὦ
in order that they may lay hold on the real*ly* life. O
Τιμόθεε, τὴν παραθήκην φύλαξον, ἐκτρεπ-
Timothy, 2the 3deposit 1guard, turning
όμενος τὰς βεβήλους κενοφωνίας καὶ
aside from *the* profane empty utterances and
ἀντιθέσεις τῆς ψευδωνύμου γνώσεως, 21 ἥν
opposing tenets of *the* falsely named knowledge, which
τινες ἐπαγγελλόμενοι περὶ τὴν πίστιν
some promising concerning the faith
ἠστόχησαν.
missed aim.
Ἡ χάρις μεθ’ ὑμῶν.
– Grace [be] with you.

confession in the presence
of many witnesses. 13 In the
sight of God, who gives life
to everything, and of Christ
Jesus, who while testifying
before Pontius Pilate made
the good confession, I
charge you 14 to keep this
command without spot or
blame until the appearing
of our Lord Jesus Christ,
15 which God will bring
about in his own time—
God, the blessed and only
Ruler, the King of kings
and Lord of lords, 16 who
alone is immortal and who
lives in unapproachable
light, whom no one has
seen or can see. To him be
honor and might forever.
Amen.

17 Command those who
are rich in this present
world not to be arrogant
nor to put their hope in
wealth, which is so uncertain, but to put their hope in
God, who richly provides
us with everything for our
enjoyment. 18 Command
them to do good, to be rich
in good deeds, and to be
generous and willing to
share. 19 In this way they
will lay up treasure for
themselves as a firm foundation for the coming age,
so that they may take hold
of the life that is truly life.
20 Timothy, guard what
has been entrusted to your
care. Turn away from god-
less chatter and the opposing ideas of what is falsely
called knowledge, 21 which
some have professed and in
so doing have wandered
from the faith.

Grace be with you.

[f] The Greek word for *you* here is plural; in other ancient authorities it is singular. Other ancient authorities add *Amen*

* "thee" is the direct object of the verb "charge" in ver. 13: "I charge . . . thee to keep . . ."

§ The antecedent to this relative pronoun is "appearance", not "Jesus Christ".

The Second Letter of
Paul to

Timothy

Chapter 1

Salutation

PAUL, an apostle of Christ Jesus by the will of God, for the sake of the promise of life that is in Christ Jesus,

2 To Timothy, my beloved child:

Grace, mercy, and peace from God the Father and Christ Jesus our Lord.

Thanksgiving and Encouragement

3 I am grateful to God—
whom I worship with a
clear conscience, as my ancestors did—when I re-
member you constantly in
my prayers night and day.
4 Recalling your tears, I
long to see you so that I
may be filled with joy. 5 I
am reminded of your sin-
cere faith, a faith that lived
first in your grandmother
Lois and your mother Eu-
nice and now, I am sure,
lives in you. 6 For this reason I remind you to rekin-
dle the gift of God that is
within you through the laying on of my hands; 7 for
God did not give us a spirit
of cowardice, but rather a
spirit of power and of love
and of self-discipline.
8 Do not be ashamed,
then, of the testimony
about our Lord or of me his
prisoner, but join with me
in suffering for the gospel,
relying on the power of
God, 9 who saved us and
called us with a holy calling, not according to our
works but according to his
own purpose and grace.
This grace was given to us
in Christ Jesus before the
ages began, 10 but it has
now been revealed through

ΠΡΟΣ ΤΙΜΟΘΕΟΝ Β
To Timothy 2

1 Παῦλος ἀπόστολος Χριστοῦ Ἰησοῦ διὰ
Paul an apostle of Christ Jesus through
θελήματος θεοῦ κατ' ἐπαγγελίαν ζωῆς
[the] will of God by way of a promise of life
τῆς ἐν Χριστῷ Ἰησοῦ 2 Τιμοθέῳ ἀγαπητῷ
– in Christ Jesus to Timothy beloved
τέκνῳ· χάρις, ἔλεος, εἰρήνη ἀπὸ θεοῦ
child: Grace, mercy, peace from God
πατρὸς καὶ Χριστοῦ Ἰησοῦ τοῦ κυρίου
[our] Father and Christ Jesus the Lord
ἡμῶν.
of us.
3 Χάριν ἔχω τῷ θεῷ, ᾧ λατρεύω
Thanks I have – to God, whom I worship
ἀπὸ προγόνων ἐν καθαρᾷ συνειδήσει, ὡς
from [my] forebears in a clean conscience, as
ἀδιάλειπτον ἔχω τὴν περὶ σοῦ μνείαν
unceasingly I have 1the 3concerning 4thee 2remembrance
ἐν ταῖς δεήσεσίν μου νυκτὸς καὶ ἡμέρας,
in the petitions of me night and day,
4 ἐπιποθῶν σε ἰδεῖν, μεμνημένος σου
longing 2thee 1to see, having been reminded 3of thee
τῶν δακρύων, ἵνα χαρᾶς πληρωθῶ,
1of the 2tears, in order that of(with) joy I may be filled,
5 ὑπόμνησιν λαβὼν τῆς ἐν σοὶ ἀνυποκρίτου
2recollection 1taking 3of the 5in 7thee 4unfeigned
πίστεως, ἥτις ἐνῴκησεν πρῶτον ἐν τῇ
6faith, which *in*dwelt firstly in the
μάμμῃ σου Λωΐδι καὶ τῇ μητρί σου
grandmother of thee Lois and [in] the mother of thee
Εὐνίκῃ, πέπεισμαι δὲ ὅτι καὶ ἐν σοί.
Eunice, and I have been persuaded that [it dwells] also in thee.
6 Δι' ἣν αἰτίαν ἀναμιμνῄσκω σε ἀνα-
For which cause I remind thee to fan
ζωπυρεῖν τὸ χάρισμα τοῦ θεοῦ, ὅ ἐστιν
the flame [of] the gift – of God, which is
ἐν σοὶ διὰ τῆς ἐπιθέσεως τῶν χειρῶν
in thee through the laying on of the hands
μου. 7 οὐ γὰρ ἔδωκεν ἡμῖν ὁ θεὸς
of me. 3not For 2gave 4to us – 1God
πνεῦμα δειλίας, ἀλλὰ δυνάμεως καὶ ἀγάπης
a spirit of cowardice, but of power and of love
καὶ σωφρονισμοῦ. 8 μὴ οὖν ἐπαισχυνθῇς
and of self-control. 2not 1Therefore 3be 4thou ashamed [of]
τὸ μαρτύριον τοῦ κυρίου ἡμῶν μηδὲ
the testimony of the Lord of us nor
ἐμὲ τὸν δέσμιον αὐτοῦ, ἀλλὰ συγ-
[of] me the prisoner of him, but suffer
κακοπάθησον τῷ εὐαγγελίῳ κατὰ δύναμιν
ill with the gospel according to [the] power
θεοῦ, 9 τοῦ σώσαντος ἡμᾶς καὶ καλέσαντος
of God, of the [one] having saved us and having called
κλήσει ἁγίᾳ, οὐ κατὰ τὰ ἔργα ἡμῶν
2calling 1with a holy, not according to the works of us
ἀλλὰ κατὰ ἰδίαν πρόθεσιν καὶ χάριν,
but according to [his] own purpose and grace,
τὴν δοθεῖσαν ἡμῖν ἐν Χριστῷ Ἰησοῦ
– given to us in Christ Jesus
πρὸ χρόνων αἰωνίων, 10 φανερωθεῖσαν δὲ
before times eternal, but manifested

2 Timothy

Chapter 1

PAUL, an apostle of Christ Jesus by the will of God, according to the promise of life that is in Christ Jesus,

2 To Timothy, my dear son:

Grace, mercy and peace from God the Father and Christ Jesus our Lord.

Encouragement to Be Faithful

3 I thank God, whom I
serve, as my forefathers
did, with a clear con-
science, as night and day I
constantly remember you
in my prayers. 4 Recalling
your tears, I long to see
you, so that I may be filled
with joy. 5 I have been reminded of your sincere
faith, which first lived in
your grandmother Lois and
in your mother Eunice and,
I am persuaded, now lives
in you also. 6 For this reason I remind you to fan into
flame the gift of God, which
is in you through the laying
on of my hands. 7 For God
did not give us a spirit of
timidity, but a spirit of
power, of love and of self-
discipline.
8 So do not be ashamed to
testify about our Lord, or
ashamed of me his prison-
er. But join with me in suffering for the gospel, by the
power of God, 9 who has
saved us and called us to a
holy life—not because of
anything we have done but
because of his own purpose
and grace. This grace was
given us in Christ Jesus before the beginning of time,
10 but it has now been re-

the appearing of our Savior
Christ Jesus, who abol-
ished death and brought life
and immortality to light
through the gospel. 11For
this gospel I was appointed
a herald and an apostle and
a teacher,[a] 12and for this
reason I suffer as I do. But
I am not ashamed, for I
know the one in whom I
have put my trust, and I am
sure that he is able to guard
until that day what I have
entrusted to him.[b] 13Hold
to the standard of sound
teaching that you have
heard from me, in the faith
and love that are in Christ
Jesus. 14Guard the good
treasure entrusted to you,
with the help of the Holy
Spirit living in us.
15 You are aware that
all who are in Asia have
turned away from me, in-
cluding Phygelus and Her-
mogenes. 16May the Lord
grant mercy to the house-
hold of Onesiphorus, be-
cause he often refreshed
me and was not ashamed of
my chain; 17when he ar-
rived in Rome, he eagerly[c]
searched for me and found
me 18—may the Lord grant
that he will find mercy from
the Lord on that day! And
you know very well how
much service he rendered
in Ephesus.

νῦν διὰ τῆς ἐπιφανείας τοῦ σωτῆρος
now through the appearance of the Saviour
ἡμῶν Χριστοῦ Ἰησοῦ, καταργήσαντος μὲν
of us Christ Jesus, [2]abrogating [1]on one hand
τὸν θάνατον φωτίσαντος δὲ ζωὴν καὶ
– death [2]bringing to light [1]on the other life and
ἀφθαρσίαν διὰ τοῦ εὐαγγελίου, 11 εἰς ὃ
incorruption through the gospel, for which
ἐτέθην ἐγὼ κῆρυξ καὶ ἀπόστολος καὶ
[2]was appointed [1]I a herald and an apostle and
διδάσκαλος· 12 δι' ἣν αἰτίαν καὶ ταῦτα
a teacher; for which cause also these things
πάσχω, ἀλλ' οὐκ ἐπαισχύνομαι, οἶδα γὰρ
I suffer, but I am not ashamed, for I know
ᾧ πεπίστευκα, καὶ πέπεισμαι ὅτι δυνατός
whom I have believed, and I have been persuaded that [2]able
ἐστιν τὴν παραθήκην μου φυλάξαι εἰς
[1]he is [4]the [5]deposit [6]of me [3]to guard to
ἐκείνην τὴν ἡμέραν. 13 ὑποτύπωσιν ἔχε
that – day. [2]a pattern [1]Have thou
ὑγιαινόντων λόγων ὧν παρ' ἐμοῦ ἤκουσας
of *being* healthy words which [2]from [3]me [1]thou heardest
ἐν πίστει καὶ ἀγάπῃ τῇ ἐν Χριστῷ
in faith and love – in Christ
Ἰησοῦ· 14 τὴν καλὴν παραθήκην φύλαξον
Jesus; the good deposit guard
διὰ πνεύματος ἁγίου τοῦ ἐνοικοῦντος ἐν
through Spirit [the] Holy – *in*dwelling in
ἡμῖν. 15 Οἶδας τοῦτο, ὅτι ἀπεστράφησάν
us. Thou knowest this, that turned away from
με πάντες οἱ ἐν τῇ Ἀσίᾳ, ὧν ἐστιν
me all the ones in – Asia, of whom is
Φύγελος καὶ Ἑρμογένης. 16 δῴη ἔλεος
Phygelus and Hermogenes. [1]May [4]give [5]mercy
ὁ κύριος τῷ Ὀνησιφόρου οἴκῳ, ὅτι
[2]the [3]Lord [6]to the [8]of Onesiphorus [7]house hold, because
πολλάκις με ἀνέψυξεν καὶ τὴν ἅλυσίν
often me he refreshed and the chain
μου οὐκ ἐπαισχύνθη, 17 ἀλλὰ γενόμενος
of me was not ashamed [of], but coming to be
ἐν Ῥώμῃ σπουδαίως ἐζήτησέν με καὶ
in Rome [2]diligently [1]he [3]sought [6]me [4]and
εὗρεν· — 18 δῴη αὐτῷ ὁ κύριος εὑρεῖν
[5]found; ([1]May [4]give [5]to him [2]the [3]Lord to find
ἔλεος παρὰ κυρίου ἐν ἐκείνῃ τῇ ἡμέρᾳ·
mercy from [the] Lord in that – day;)
— καὶ ὅσα ἐν Ἐφέσῳ διηκόνησεν,
and what things in Ephesus he served,
βέλτιον σὺ γινώσκεις.
very well thou knowest.

vealed through the appearing of our Savior, Christ
Jesus, who has destroyed
death and has brought life
and immortality to light
through the gospel. 11And
of this gospel I was ap-
pointed a herald and an
apostle and a teacher.
12That is why I am suffering
as I am. Yet I am not
ashamed, because I know
whom I have believed, and
am convinced that he is
able to guard what I have
entrusted to him for that
day.
13What you heard from
me, keep as the pattern of
sound teaching, with faith
and love in Christ Jesus.
14Guard the good deposit
that was entrusted to you
—guard it with the help of
the Holy Spirit who lives in
us.
15You know that every-
one in the province of Asia
has deserted me, including
Phygelus and Hermogenes.
16May the Lord show
mercy to the household of
Onesiphorus, because he
often refreshed me and was
not ashamed of my chains.
17On the contrary, when he
was in Rome, he searched
hard for me until he found
me. 18May the Lord grant
that he will find mercy from
the Lord on that day! You
know very well in how
many ways he helped me in
Ephesus.

Chapter 2

A Good Soldier of Christ Jesus

YOU then, my child, be
strong in the grace
that is in Christ Jesus; 2and
what you have heard from
me through many wit-
nesses entrust to faithful
people who will be able to

[a] Other ancient authorities add *of the Gentiles*
[b] Or *what has been entrusted to me*
[c] Or *promptly*

2 Σὺ οὖν, τέκνον μου, ἐνδυναμοῦ ἐν
Thou therefore, child of me, be empowered by
τῇ χάριτι τῇ ἐν Χριστῷ Ἰησοῦ, 2 καὶ
the grace – in Christ Jesus, and
ἃ ἤκουσας παρ' ἐμοῦ διὰ πολλῶν
what things thou heardest from me through many
μαρτύρων, ταῦτα παράθου πιστοῖς ἀνθρώ-
witnesses, these commit to faithful men,

Chapter 2

YOU then, my son, be
strong in the grace
that is in Christ Jesus. 2And
the things you have heard
me say in the presence of
many witnesses entrust to
reliable men who will also

teach others as well. 3 Share in suffering like a good soldier of Christ Jesus. 4 No one serving in the army gets entangled in everyday affairs; the soldier's aim is to please the enlisting officer. 5 And in the case of an athlete, no one is crowned without competing according to the rules. 6 It is the farmer who does the work who ought to have the first share of the crops. 7 Think over what I say, for the Lord will give you understanding in all things.

8 Remember Jesus Christ, raised from the dead, a descendant of David—that is my gospel, 9 for which I suffer hardship, even to the point of being chained like a criminal. But the word of God is not chained. 10 Therefore I endure everything for the sake of the elect, so that they may also obtain the salvation that is in Christ Jesus, with eternal glory. 11 The saying is sure:

If we have died with him, we will also live with him;
12 if we endure, we will also reign with him;
if we deny him, he will also deny us;
13 if we are faithless, he remains faithful—
for he cannot deny himself.

A Worker Approved by God

14 Remind them of this, and warn them before God[d] that they are to avoid wrangling over words, which does no good but only ruins those who are listening. 15 Do your best to present yourself to God as one approved by him, a worker who has no need to be ashamed, rightly explaining the word of truth.

[d] Other ancient authorities read *the Lord*

ποις, οἵτινες ἱκανοὶ ἔσονται καὶ ἑτέρους
who [2]competent [1]will be [3]also [4]others

διδάξαι. 3 Συγκακοπάθησον ὡς καλὸς
[5]to teach. Suffer ill with* as a good

στρατιώτης Χριστοῦ Ἰησοῦ. 4 οὐδεὶς
soldier of Christ Jesus. No one

στρατευόμενος ἐμπλέκεται ταῖς τοῦ βίου
soldiering is involved [1]with the – [3]of life

πραγματείαις, ἵνα τῷ στρατολογήσαντι
[2]affairs, in order that [2]the [one] [3]having enlisted [him]

ἀρέσῃ. 5 ἐὰν δὲ καὶ ἀθλῇ τις, οὐ
[1]he may please. And if also [2]wrestles [1]any-one, not

στεφανοῦται ἐὰν μὴ νομίμως ἀθλήσῃ.
he is crowned unless [2]lawfully [1]he wrestles.

6 τὸν κοπιῶντα γεωργὸν δεῖ πρῶτον τῶν
[2]the [3]labouring [4]husbandman [1]It behoves [6]firstly [7]of the

καρπῶν μεταλαμβάνειν. 7 νόει ὃ λέγω·
[8]fruits [5]to partake. Consider what I say;

δώσει γάρ σοι ὁ κύριος σύνεσιν ἐν
for [3]will give [4]thee [1]the [2]Lord understanding in

πᾶσιν. 8 μνημόνευε Ἰησοῦν Χριστὸν
all things. Remember Jesus Christ

ἐγηγερμένον ἐκ νεκρῶν, ἐκ σπέρματος
having been raised from [the] dead, of [the] seed

Δαυίδ, κατὰ τὸ εὐαγγέλιόν μου· 9 ἐν
of David, according to the gospel of me; in

ᾧ κακοπαθῶ μέχρι δεσμῶν ὡς κακοῦργος,
which I suffer ill unto bonds as an evildoer,

ἀλλὰ ὁ λόγος τοῦ θεοῦ οὐ δέδεται.
but the word – of God has not been bound.

10 διὰ τοῦτο πάντα ὑπομένω διὰ τοὺς
Therefore all things I endure on account of the

ἐκλεκτούς, ἵνα καὶ αὐτοὶ σωτηρίας τύχωσιν
chosen ones, in order that [2]also [1]they [4]salvation [3]may obtain

τῆς ἐν Χριστῷ Ἰησοῦ μετὰ δόξης
– in Christ Jesus with glory

αἰωνίου. 11 πιστὸς ὁ λόγος· εἰ γὰρ
eternal. Faithful [is] the word: for if

συναπεθάνομεν, καὶ συζήσομεν· 12 εἰ
we died with [him], also we shall live with [him]; if

ὑπομένομεν, καὶ συμβασιλεύσομεν· εἰ
we endure, also we shall reign with [him]; if

ἀρνησόμεθα, κἀκεῖνος ἀρνήσεται ἡμᾶς· 13 εἰ
we *shall* deny, that one also will deny us; if

ἀπιστοῦμεν, ἐκεῖνος πιστὸς μένει, ἀρνή-
we disbelieve, that one [2]faithful [1]remains, [3]to

σασθαι γὰρ ἑαυτὸν οὐ δύναται. 14 Ταῦτα
deny [1]for [4]himself [2]he cannot. These things

ὑπομίμνῃσκε, διαμαρτυρόμενος ἐνώπιον τοῦ
remind thou [them] [of], solemnly witnessing before –

θεοῦ μὴ λογομαχεῖν, ἐπ' οὐδὲν χρήσιμον,
God not to fight with words, [2]for [3]nothing [1]useful,

ἐπὶ καταστροφῇ τῶν ἀκουόντων. 15 σπού-
for overthrowing of the [ones] hearing. [1]Be

δασον σεαυτὸν δόκιμον παραστῆσαι τῷ
eager [3]thyself [4]approved [2]to present –

θεῷ, ἐργάτην ἀνεπαίσχυντον, ὀρθοτομοῦντα
to God, a workman unashamed, cutting straight

τὸν λόγον τῆς ἀληθείας. 16 τὰς δὲ
the word – of truth. – But

* See 1. 8.

be qualified to teach others. 3 Endure hardship with us like a good soldier of Christ Jesus. 4 No one serving as a soldier gets involved in civilian affairs—he wants to please his commanding officer. 5 Similarly, if anyone competes as an athlete, he does not receive the victor's crown unless he competes according to the rules. 6 The hardworking farmer should be the first to receive a share of the crops. 7 Reflect on what I am saying, for the Lord will give you insight into all this.

8 Remember Jesus Christ, raised from the dead, descended from David. This is my gospel, 9 for which I am suffering even to the point of being chained like a criminal. But God's word is not chained. 10 Therefore I endure everything for the sake of the elect, that they too may obtain the salvation that is in Christ Jesus, with eternal glory.

11 Here is a trustworthy saying:

If we died with him,
we will also live with him;
12 if we endure,
we will also reign with him.
If we disown him,
he will also disown us;
13 if we are faithless,
he will remain faithful,
for he cannot disown himself.

A Workman Approved by God

14 Keep reminding them of these things. Warn them before God against quarreling about words; it is of no value, and only ruins those who listen. 15 Do your best to present yourself to God as one approved, a workman who does not need to be ashamed and who correctly handles the word of truth. 16 Avoid godless

16Avoid profane chatter,
for it will lead people into
more and more impiety,
17and their talk will spread
like gangrene. Among them
are Hymenaeus and Phile-
tus, 18who have swerved
from the truth by claiming
that the resurrection has already taken place. They
are upsetting the faith of
some. 19But God's firm
foundation stands, bearing
this inscription: "The Lord
knows those who are his,"
and, "Let everyone who
calls on the name of the
Lord turn away from wick-
edness."
20 In a large house there
are utensils not only of gold
and silver but also of wood
and clay, some for special
use, some for ordinary.
21All who cleanse them-
selves of the things I have
mentioned[e] will become
special utensils, dedicated
and useful to the owner of
the house, ready for every
good work. 22Shun youth-
ful passions and pursue
righteousness, faith, love,
and peace, along with those
who call on the Lord from
a pure heart. 23Have nothing to do with stupid and
senseless controversies;
you know that they breed
quarrels. 24And the Lord's
servant[f] must not be quarrelsome but kindly to ev-
eryone, an apt teacher, patient, 25correcting oppo-
nents with gentleness. God
may perhaps grant that
they will repent and come
to know the truth, 26and
that they may escape from
the snare of the devil, hav-

βεβήλους κενοφωνίας περιΐστασο· ἐπὶ πλεῖον
profane empty utterances shun; [2]to [4]more

γὰρ προκόψουσιν ἀσεβείας, 17 καὶ ὁ λόγος
[1]for [3]they will advance of impiety, and the word

αὐτῶν ὡς γάγγραινα νομὴν ἕξει· ὧν
of them as a canker feeding will have; of whom

ἐστιν Ὑμέναιος καὶ Φίλητος, 18 οἵτινες
is(are) Hymenæus and Philetus, who

περὶ τὴν ἀλήθειαν ἠστόχησαν, λέγοντες
concerning the truth missed aim, saying

ἀνάστασιν ἤδη γεγονέναι, καὶ ἀνατρέπουσιν
[the] resurrection already to have become, and overturn

τήν τινων πίστιν. 19 ὁ μέντοι στερεὸς
the [2]of some [1]faith. [3]the [1]However firm

θεμέλιος τοῦ θεοῦ ἕστηκεν, ἔχων τὴν
foundation – of God stands, having –

σφραγῖδα ταύτην· ἔγνω κύριος τοὺς ὄντας
seal this: [2]knew [1][The] Lord the [ones] being

αὐτοῦ, καί· ἀποστήτω ἀπὸ ἀδικίας πᾶς
of him, and: Let stand away from iniquity every-

ὁ ὀνομάζων τὸ ὄνομα κυρίου. 20 ἐν
one naming the name of [the] Lord. [2]in

μεγάλῃ δὲ οἰκίᾳ οὐκ ἔστιν μόνον σκεύη
[3]a great [1]Now [4]house there is(are) not only vessels

χρυσᾶ καὶ ἀργυρᾶ, ἀλλὰ καὶ ξύλινα
golden and silvern, but also wooden

καὶ ὀστράκινα, καὶ ἃ μὲν εἰς τιμὴν ἃ δὲ
and earthen, and some to honour others

εἰς ἀτιμίαν· 21 ἐὰν οὖν τις ἐκκαθάρῃ
to dishonour; if therefore anyone cleanses

ἑαυτὸν ἀπὸ τούτων, ἔσται σκεῦος εἰς
himself from these [latter], he will be a vessel to

τιμήν, ἡγιασμένον, εὔχρηστον τῷ δεσπότῃ,
honour, *having been* sanctified, suitable for the master,

εἰς πᾶν ἔργον ἀγαθὸν ἡτοιμασμένον.
to every work good *having been* prepared.

22 τὰς δὲ νεωτερικὰς ἐπιθυμίας φεῦγε,
Now *the* [2]youthful [3]lusts [1]flee,

δίωκε δὲ δικαιοσύνην, πίστιν, ἀγάπην,
but pursue righteousness, faith, love,

εἰρήνην μετὰ τῶν ἐπικαλουμένων τὸν
peace with the [ones] calling on the

κύριον ἐκ καθαρᾶς καρδίας. 23 τὰς δὲ
Lord out of a clean heart. – But

μωρὰς καὶ ἀπαιδεύτους ζητήσεις παραιτοῦ,
foolish and uninstructed questionings refuse,

εἰδὼς ὅτι γεννῶσιν μάχας· 24 δοῦλον δὲ
knowing that they beget fights; and [2]a slave

κυρίου οὐ δεῖ μάχεσθαι ἀλλὰ ἤπιον
[3]of [the] Lord [1]it behoves not to fight but gentle

εἶναι πρὸς πάντας, διδακτικόν, ἀνεξίκακον,
to be toward all men, apt to teach, forbearing,

25 ἐν πραΰτητι παιδεύοντα τοὺς ἀντιδιατι-
in meekness instructing the [ones] oppos-

θεμένους, μήποτε δώῃ αὐτοῖς ὁ θεὸς
ing, [if] perhaps [2]may give [3]them – [1]God

μετάνοιαν εἰς ἐπίγνωσιν ἀληθείας, 26 καὶ
repentance for a full knowledge of truth, and

ἀνανήψωσιν ἐκ τῆς τοῦ διαβόλου παγίδος,
they may return to soberness out of [1]the [3]of the [4]devil [2]snare,

chatter, because those who
indulge in it will become
more and more ungodly.
17Their teaching will spread
like gangrene. Among them
are Hymenaeus and Phile-
tus, 18who have wandered
away from the truth. They
say that the resurrection
has already taken place,
and they destroy the faith
of some. 19Nevertheless,
God's solid foundation
stands firm, sealed with
this inscription: "The Lord
knows those who are
his,"[a] and, "Everyone
who confesses the name of
the Lord must turn away
from wickedness."
20In a large house there
are articles not only of gold
and silver, but also of wood
and clay; some are for noble purposes and some for
ignoble. 21If a man cleanses
himself from the latter, he
will be an instrument for
noble purposes, made holy,
useful to the Master and
prepared to do any good
work.
22Flee the evil desires of
youth, and pursue right-
eousness, faith, love and
peace, along with those
who call on the Lord out of
a pure heart. 23Don't have
anything to do with foolish
and stupid arguments, be-
cause you know they pro-
duce quarrels. 24And the
Lord's servant must not
quarrel; instead, he must be
kind to everyone, able to
teach, not resentful.
25Those who oppose him he
must gently instruct, in the
hope that God will grant
them repentance leading
them to a knowledge of the
truth, 26and that they will
come to their senses and
escape from the trap of the

[e] Gk *of these things*
[f] Gk *slave*

[a] *19* Num. 16:5 (see Septuagint)

ing been held captive by
him to do his will.[g]

Chapter 3

Godlessness in the Last Days

YOU must understand
this, that in the last
days distressing times will
come. 2 For people will be
lovers of themselves, lovers of money, boasters, arrogant, abusive, disobedient to their parents, un-
grateful, unholy,
3 inhuman, implacable,
slanderers, profligates,
brutes, haters of good,
4 treacherous, reckless,
swollen with conceit, lovers of pleasure rather than
lovers of God, 5 holding to
the outward form of godliness but denying its power.
Avoid them! 6 For among
them are those who make
their way into households
and captivate silly women,
overwhelmed by their sins
and swayed by all kinds of
desires, 7 who are always
being instructed and can
never arrive at a knowledge
of the truth. 8 As Jannes
and Jambres opposed Mo-
ses, so these people, of corrupt mind and counterfeit
faith, also oppose the truth.
9 But they will not make
much progress, because, as
in the case of those two
men,[h] their folly will become plain to everyone.

Paul's Charge to Timothy

10 Now you have ob-
served my teaching, my
conduct, my aim in life, my
faith, my patience, my
love, my steadfastness,
11 my persecutions and suffering the things that happened to me in Antioch,

[g] Or *by him, to do his* (that is, God's) *will*

[h] Gk lacks *two men*

ἐζωγρημένοι ὑπ' αὐτοῦ εἰς τὸ ἐκείνου θέλημα.
having been caught by him[,] to 1the 3of that one* 2will.

Chapter 3

3 Τοῦτο δὲ γίνωσκε, ὅτι ἐν ἐσχάταις
And this know thou, that in [the] last

ἡμέραις ἐνστήσονται καιροὶ χαλεποί·
days 3will be at hand 2times 1grievous;

2 ἔσονται γὰρ οἱ ἄνθρωποι φίλαυτοι,
for 2will be – 1men self-lovers,

φιλάργυροι, ἀλαζόνες, ὑπερήφανοι, βλάσφημοι,
money-lovers, boasters, arrogant, blasphemers,

γονεῦσιν ἀπειθεῖς, ἀχάριστοι, ἀνόσιοι,
2to parents 1disobedient, unthankful, unholy,

3 ἄστοργοι, ἄσπονδοι, διάβολοι, ἀκρατεῖς,
without natural affection, implacable, slanderers, incontinent,

ἀνήμεροι, ἀφιλάγαθοι, **4** προδόται, προπετεῖς,
untamed, haters of good [things/men], betrayers, reckless,

τετυφωμένοι, φιλήδονοι μᾶλλον ἢ φιλόθεοι,
having been puffed up, pleasure-lovers rather than God-lovers,

5 ἔχοντες μόρφωσιν εὐσεβείας τὴν δὲ
having a form of piety but the

δύναμιν αὐτῆς ἠρνημένοι· καὶ τούτους
power of it having denied: and 2these

ἀποτρέπου. **6** ἐκ τούτων γάρ εἰσιν οἱ
3turn away 1from. 2of 3these 1For are the

ἐνδύνοντες εἰς τὰς οἰκίας καὶ αἰχμαλωτίζ-
[ones] creeping into – houses and captur-

οντες γυναικάρια σεσωρευμένα ἁμαρτίαις,
ing silly women *having been* heaped* with sins,

ἀγόμενα ἐπιθυμίαις ποικίλαις, **7** πάντοτε
being led* lusts by various, always

μανθάνοντα καὶ μηδέποτε εἰς ἐπίγνωσιν
learning* and never 3to 4a full knowledge

ἀληθείας ἐλθεῖν δυνάμενα. **8** ὃν τρόπον
5of truth 2to come 1being able.* by what way

δὲ Ἰάννης καὶ Ἰαμβρῆς ἀντέστησαν
Now Jannes and Jambres opposed

Μωϋσεῖ, οὕτως καὶ οὗτοι ἀνθίστανται τῇ
Moses, so also these oppose the

ἀληθείᾳ, ἄνθρωποι κατεφθαρμένοι τὸν νοῦν,
truth, men having been corrupted the mind, =with corrupted mind,

ἀδόκιμοι περὶ τὴν πίστιν. **9** ἀλλ' οὐ
reprobate as to the faith. But not

προκόψουσιν ἐπὶ πλεῖον· ἡ γὰρ ἄνοια
they will advance to more; =farther; for the folly

αὐτῶν ἔκδηλος ἔσται πᾶσιν, ὡς καὶ
of them very clear will be to all men, as also

ἡ ἐκείνων ἐγένετο. **10** Σὺ δὲ παρηκολού-
the [folly] of those became. But thou hast closely

θησάς μου τῇ διδασκαλίᾳ, τῇ ἀγωγῇ,
followed of me the teaching, the conduct,

τῇ προθέσει, τῇ πίστει, τῇ μακροθυμίᾳ,
the purpose, the faith, the longsuffering,

τῇ ἀγάπῃ, τῇ ὑπομονῇ, **11** τοῖς διωγμοῖς,
the love, the endurance, the persecutions,

τοῖς παθήμασιν, οἷά μοι ἐγένετο ἐν
the sufferings, which 2to me 1happened in

* That is, of God (the remoter antecedent).

* Agreeing with "silly women" (neut. pl.).

devil, who has taken them
captive to do his will.

Chapter 3

Godlessness in the Last Days

BUT mark this: There
will be terrible times
in the last days. 2 People
will be lovers of them-
selves, lovers of money,
boastful, proud, abusive,
disobedient to their par-
ents, ungrateful, unholy,
3 without love, unforgiving,
slanderous, without self-
control, brutal, not lovers
of the good, 4 treacherous,
rash, conceited, lovers of
pleasure rather than lovers
of God— 5 having a form of
godliness but denying its
power. Have nothing to do
with them.
6 They are the kind who
worm their way into homes
and gain control over
weak-willed women, who
are loaded down with sins
and are swayed by all kinds
of evil desires, 7 always
learning but never able to
acknowledge the truth.
8 Just as Jannes and Jam-
bres opposed Moses, so
also these men oppose the
truth—men of depraved
minds, who, as far as the
faith is concerned, are rejected. 9 But they will not
get very far because, as in
the case of those men, their
folly will be clear to everyone.

Paul's Charge to Timothy

10 You, however, know all
about my teaching, my way
of life, my purpose, faith,
patience, love, endurance,
11 persecutions, sufferings
—what kinds of things hap-

Iconium, and Lystra. What persecutions I endured! Yet the Lord rescued me from all of them. 12 Indeed, all who want to live a godly life in Christ Jesus will be persecuted. 13 But wicked people and impostors will go from bad to worse, deceiving others and being deceived. 14 But as for you, continue in what you have learned and firmly believed, knowing from whom you learned it, 15 and how from childhood you have known the sacred writings that are able to instruct you for salvation through faith in Christ Jesus. 16 All scripture is inspired by God and is[i] useful for teaching, for reproof, for correction, and for training in righteousness, 17 so that everyone who belongs to God may be proficient, equipped for every good work.

Chapter 4

In the presence of God and of Christ Jesus, who is to judge the living and the dead, and in view of his appearing and his kingdom, I solemnly urge you: 2 proclaim the message; be persistent whether the time is favorable or unfavorable; convince, rebuke, and encourage, with the utmost patience in teaching. 3 For the time is coming when people will not put up with sound doctrine, but having itching ears, they will accumulate for themselves teachers to suit their own desires, 4 and will turn away from listening to the truth and wander away to myths. 5 As for you, always

[i] Or *Every scripture inspired by God is also*

Ἀντιοχείᾳ, ἐν Ἰκονίῳ, ἐν Λύστροις· οἵους
Antioch, in Iconium, in Lystra: what

διωγμοὺς ὑπήνεγκα, καὶ ἐκ πάντων με
persecutions I bore, and out of all [4]me

ἐρρύσατο ὁ κύριος. **12** καὶ πάντες δὲ
[3]delivered [1]the [2]Lord. [3]indeed [2]all [1]And

οἱ θέλοντες ζῆν εὐσεβῶς ἐν Χριστῷ
the [ones] wishing to live piously in Christ

Ἰησοῦ διωχθήσονται. **13** πονηροὶ δὲ ἄν-
Jesus will be persecuted. But evil men

θρωποι καὶ γόητες προκόψουσιν ἐπὶ τὸ
and impostors will advance to the

χεῖρον, πλανῶντες καὶ πλανώμενοι. **14** σὺ
worse, deceiving and being deceived. [2]thou

δὲ μένε ἐν οἷς ἔμαθες καὶ ἐπιστώθης,
But [1]continue in what things thou didst learn and wast assured of,

εἰδὼς παρὰ τίνων ἔμαθες, **15** καὶ ὅτι
knowing from whom* thou didst learn, and that

ἀπὸ βρέφους ἱερὰ γράμματα οἶδας, τὰ
from a babe [2]sacred [3]letters [1]thou knowest, the [ones]

δυνάμενά σε σοφίσαι εἰς σωτηρίαν διὰ
being able thee to make wise to salvation through

πίστεως τῆς ἐν Χριστῷ Ἰησοῦ. **16** πᾶσα
faith – in Christ Jesus. Every

γραφὴ θεόπνευστος καὶ ὠφέλιμος πρὸς
scripture [is] God-breathed and profitable for

διδασκαλίαν, πρὸς ἐλεγμόν, πρὸς ἐπανόρ-
teaching, for reproof, for cor-

θωσιν, πρὸς παιδείαν τὴν ἐν δικαιοσύνῃ,
rection, for instruction – in righteousness,

17 ἵνα ἄρτιος ᾖ ὁ τοῦ θεοῦ ἄνθρωπος,
in order that [5]fitted [4]may be [1]the – [3]of God [2]man,

πρὸς πᾶν ἔργον ἀγαθὸν ἐξηρτισμένος.
for every work good *having been* furnished.

4 Διαμαρτύρομαι ἐνώπιον τοῦ θεοῦ καὶ
I solemnly witness before – God and

Χριστοῦ Ἰησοῦ, τοῦ μέλλοντος κρίνειν
Christ Jesus, the [one] being about to judge

ζῶντας καὶ νεκρούς, καὶ τὴν ἐπιφάνειαν
living [ones] and dead, both [by] the appearance

αὐτοῦ καὶ τὴν βασιλείαν αὐτοῦ· **2** κήρυξον
of him and [by] the kingdom of him: proclaim

τὸν λόγον, ἐπίστηθι εὐκαίρως ἀκαίρως,
the word, be attentive seasonably[,] unseasonably,

ἔλεγξον, ἐπιτίμησον, παρακάλεσον, ἐν πάσῃ
reprove, admonish, exhort, with all

μακροθυμίᾳ καὶ διδαχῇ. **3** Ἔσται γὰρ
longsuffering and teaching. For there will be

καιρὸς ὅτε τῆς ὑγιαινούσης διδασκαλίας
a time when [2]the [3]*being* healthy [4]teaching

οὐκ ἀνέξονται, ἀλλὰ κατὰ τὰς ἰδίας
[1]they will not bear with, but according to the(ir) own

ἐπιθυμίας ἑαυτοῖς ἐπισωρεύσουσιν διδασ-
lusts [2]to themselves [1]they will heap up [3]teach-

κάλους κνηθόμενοι τὴν ἀκοήν, **4** καὶ ἀπὸ
ers tickling the ear, and [6]from

μὲν τῆς ἀληθείας τὴν ἀκοὴν ἀποστρέψουσιν,
[1]on one hand [6]the [7]truth [3]the [4]ear [2]will turn away,

ἐπὶ δὲ τοὺς μύθους ἐκτραπήσονται. **5** σὺ
[3]to [1]on the other *the* [4]tales [2]will be turned aside. [2]thou

* Plural.

pened to me in Antioch, Iconium and Lystra, the persecutions I endured. Yet the Lord rescued me from all of them. 12 In fact, everyone who wants to live a godly life in Christ Jesus will be persecuted, 13 while evil men and impostors will go from bad to worse, deceiving and being deceived. 14 But as for you, continue in what you have learned and have become convinced of, because you know those from whom you learned it, 15 and how from infancy you have known the holy Scriptures, which are able to make you wise for salvation through faith in Christ Jesus. 16 All Scripture is God-breathed and is useful for teaching, rebuking, correcting and training in righteousness, 17 so that the man of God may be thoroughly equipped for every good work.

Chapter 4

In the presence of God and of Christ Jesus, who will judge the living and the dead, and in view of his appearing and his kingdom, I give you this charge: 2 Preach the Word; be prepared in season and out of season; correct, rebuke and encourage—with great patience and careful instruction. 3 For the time will come when men will not put up with sound doctrine. Instead, to suit their own desires, they will gather around them a great number of teachers to say what their itching ears want to hear. 4 They will turn their ears away from the truth and turn aside to myths.

be sober, endure suffering,
do the work of an evange-
list, carry out your ministry
fully.
6 As for me, I am al-
ready being poured out as a
libation, and the time of my
departure has come. 7 I
have fought the good fight,
I have finished the race, I
have kept the faith. 8 From
now on there is reserved
for me the crown of righ-
teousness, which the Lord,
the righteous judge, will
give me on that day, and
not only to me but also to
all who have longed for his
appearing.

Personal Instructions

9 Do your best to come
to me soon, 10 for Demas, in
love with this present
world, has deserted me and
gone to Thessalonica;
Crescens has gone to Galatia,[j] Titus to Dalmatia.
11 Only Luke is with me.
Get Mark and bring him
with you, for he is useful in
my ministry. 12 I have sent
Tychicus to Ephesus.
13 When you come, bring
the cloak that I left with
Carpus at Troas, also the
books, and above all the
parchments. 14 Alexander
the coppersmith did me
great harm; the Lord will
pay him back for his deeds.
15 You also must beware of
him, for he strongly op-
posed our message.
16 At my first defense
no one came to my support,
but all deserted me. May it
not be counted against
them! 17 But the Lord stood
by me and gave me
strength, so that through
me the message might be
fully proclaimed and all the

δὲ νῆφε ἐν πᾶσιν, κακοπάθησον, ἔργον
But [1]be sober in all things, suffer evil, [3][the] work

ποίησον εὐαγγελιστοῦ, τὴν διακονίαν σου
[1]do of an evangelist, [2]the [3]ministry [4]of thee

πληροφόρησον. 6 Ἐγὼ γὰρ ἤδη σπένδομαι,
[1]fulfil. For I already am being poured out,

καὶ ὁ καιρὸς τῆς ἀναλύσεώς μου ἐφέστη-
and the time of the departure of me has

κεν. 7 τὸν καλὸν ἀγῶνα ἠγώνισμαι,
arrived. The good struggle I have struggled,

τὸν δρόμον τετέλεκα, τὴν πίστιν τετήρηκα·
the course I have finished, the faith I have kept:

8 λοιπὸν ἀπόκειταί μοι ὁ τῆς δικαιοσύνης
for the rest there is laid up for me [1]the – [3]of righteousness

στέφανος, ὃν ἀποδώσει μοι ὁ κύριος
[2]crown, which [6]will render [7]to me [1]the [2]Lord

ἐν ἐκείνῃ τῇ ἡμέρᾳ, ὁ δίκαιος κριτής,
[8]in [9]that – [10]day, [3]the [4]righteous [5]judge,

οὐ μόνον δὲ ἐμοὶ ἀλλὰ καὶ πᾶσι τοῖς
[2]not [3]only [1]and to me but also to all the [ones]

ἠγαπηκόσι τὴν ἐπιφάνειαν αὐτοῦ.
having loved the appearance of him.

9 Σπούδασον ἐλθεῖν πρός με ταχέως·
Hasten to come to me shortly;

10 Δημᾶς γάρ με ἐγκατέλιπεν ἀγαπήσας
[2]Demas [1]For [4]me [3]forsook loving

τὸν νῦν αἰῶνα, καὶ ἐπορεύθη εἰς Θεσσαλο-
the now (present) age, and went to Thessalo-

νίκην, Κρήσκης εἰς Γαλατίαν, Τίτος εἰς
nica, Crescens to Galatia, Titus to

Δαλματίαν· 11 Λουκᾶς ἐστιν μόνος μετ᾽
Dalmatia; Luke is alone with

ἐμοῦ. Μᾶρκον ἀναλαβὼν ἄγε μετὰ σεαυτοῦ·
me. Mark taking bring with thyself;

ἔστιν γάρ μοι εὔχρηστος εἰς διακονίαν.
[2]he is [1]for [4]to me [3]useful for ministry.

12 Τύχικον δὲ ἀπέστειλα εἰς Ἔφεσον.
And Tychicus I sent to Ephesus.

13 τὸν φαιλόνην, ὃν ἀπέλιπον ἐν Τρῳάδι
The cloak, which I left in Troas

παρὰ Κάρπῳ, ἐρχόμενος φέρε, καὶ τὰ
with Carpus, coming bring thou, and the

βιβλία, μάλιστα τὰς μεμβράνας. 14 Ἀλέξ-
scrolls, especially the parchments. Alex-

ανδρος ὁ χαλκεὺς πολλά μοι κακὰ
ander the coppersmith [3]many [2]*to* me [4]evils

ἐνεδείξατο· ἀποδώσει αὐτῷ ὁ κύριος κατὰ
[1]showed; [3]will render [4]to him [1]the [2]Lord according to

τὰ ἔργα αὐτοῦ· 15 ὃν καὶ σὺ φυλάσσου·
the works of him; whom also [2]thou [1]guard [3][against];

λίαν γὰρ ἀντέστη τοῖς ἡμετέροις λόγοις.
for greatly he opposed – our words.

16 Ἐν τῇ πρώτῃ μου ἀπολογίᾳ οὐδείς
At the first [2]of me [1]defence no one

μοι παρεγένετο, ἀλλὰ πάντες με ἐγκατέ-
[2]me [1]was beside, but all men [2]me [1]for-

λιπον· μὴ αὐτοῖς λογισθείη· 17 ὁ δὲ
sook; not to them may it be reckoned; but the

κύριός μοι παρέστη καὶ ἐνεδυνάμωσέν με,
Lord [2]me [1]stood with and empowered me,

ἵνα δι᾽ ἐμοῦ τὸ κήρυγμα πληροφορηθῇ
in order that through me the proclamation might be accomplished

5 But you, keep your head
in all situations, endure
hardship, do the work of an
evangelist, discharge all the
duties of your ministry.
6 For I am already being
poured out like a drink offering, and the time has
come for my departure. 7 I
have fought the good fight,
I have finished the race, I
have kept the faith. 8 Now
there is in store for me the
crown of righteousness,
which the Lord, the righteous Judge, will award to
me on that day—and not
only to me, but also to all
who have longed for his appearing.

Personal Remarks

9 Do your best to come to
me quickly, 10 for Demas,
because he loved this
world, has deserted me and
has gone to Thessalonica.
Crescens has gone to Galatia, and Titus to Dalmatia.
11 Only Luke is with me.
Get Mark and bring him
with you, because he is
helpful to me in my ministry. 12 I sent Tychicus to
Ephesus. 13 When you
come, bring the cloak that I
left with Carpus at Troas,
and my scrolls, especially
the parchments.
14 Alexander the metal-
worker did me a great deal
of harm. The Lord will repay him for what he has
done. 15 You too should be
on your guard against him,
because he strongly op-
posed our message.
16 At my first defense, no
one came to my support,
but everyone deserted me.
May it not be held against
them. 17 But the Lord stood
at my side and gave me
strength, so that through
me the message might be
fully proclaimed and all the

[j] Other ancient authorities read *Gaul*

Gentiles might hear it. So I
was rescued from the lion's
mouth. 18 The Lord will
rescue me from every evil
attack and save me for his
heavenly kingdom. To him
be the glory forever and
ever. Amen.

Final Greetings and Benediction

19 Greet Prisca and Aq-
uila, and the household of
Onesiphorus. 20 Erastus remained in Corinth; Trophimus I left ill in Miletus.
21 Do your best to come before winter. Eubulus sends
greetings to you, as do Pudens and Linus and Claudia
and all the brothers and sisters.[k]
22 The Lord be with
your spirit. Grace be with
you.[l]

καὶ ἀκούσωσιν πάντα τὰ ἔθνη, καὶ
and [4]might hear [1]all [2]the [3]nations, and
ἐρρύσθην ἐκ στόματος λέοντος. 18 ῥύσεταί
I was delivered out of [the] mouth of [the] lion. [2]will deliver
με ὁ κύριος ἀπὸ παντὸς ἔργου πονηροῦ
[3]me [1]The [2]Lord from every work wicked
καὶ σώσει εἰς τὴν βασιλείαν αὐτοῦ τὴν
and will save to the [2]kingdom [3]of him –
ἐπουράνιον· ᾧ ἡ δόξα εἰς τοὺς αἰῶνας
[1]heavenly: to whom [be] the glory unto the ages
τῶν αἰώνων, ἀμήν.
of the ages, Amen.
19 Ἄσπασαι Πρίσκαν καὶ Ἀκύλαν καὶ
Greet Prisca and Aquila and
τὸν Ὀνησιφόρου οἶκον. 20 Ἔραστος
the [2]of Onesiphorus [1]household. Erastus
ἔμεινεν ἐν Κορίνθῳ, Τρόφιμον δὲ ἀπέλιπον
remained in Corinth, but Trophimus I left
ἐν Μιλήτῳ ἀσθενοῦντα. 21 Σπούδασον
in Miletus ailing. Hasten
πρὸ χειμῶνος ἐλθεῖν. Ἀσπάζεταί σε
before winter to come. Greets thee
Εὔβουλος καὶ Πούδης καὶ Λίνος καὶ
Eubulus and Pudens and Linus and
Κλαυδία καὶ οἱ ἀδελφοὶ πάντες.
Claudia and [2]the [3]brothers [1]all.
22 Ὁ κύριος μετὰ τοῦ πνεύματός σου.
The Lord [be] with the spirit of thee.
ἡ χάρις μεθ' ὑμῶν.
– Grace [be] with you.

Gentiles might hear it. And
I was delivered from the
lion's mouth. 18The Lord
will rescue me from every
evil attack and will bring
me safely to his heavenly
kingdom. To him be glory
for ever and ever. Amen.

Final Greetings

19Greet Priscilla[b] and
Aquila and the household
of Onesiphorus. 20Erastus
stayed in Corinth, and I left
Trophimus sick in Miletus.
21Do your best to get here
before winter. Eubulus
greets you, and so do Pu-
dens, Linus, Claudia and
all the brothers.
22The Lord be with your
spirit. Grace be with you.

The Letter of Paul to

Titus

Chapter 1

Salutation

PAUL, a servant[a] of
God and an apostle of
Jesus Christ, for the sake of
the faith of God's elect and
the knowledge of the truth
that is in accordance with
godliness, 2 in the hope of
eternal life that God, who
never lies, promised before
the ages began— 3 in due
time he revealed his word
through the proclamation
with which I have been entrusted by the command of
God our Savior,
4 To Titus, my loyal
child in the faith we share:
Grace[b] and peace from
God the Father and Christ
Jesus our Savior.

ΠΡΟΣ ΤΙΤΟΝ
To Titus

1 Παῦλος δοῦλος θεοῦ, ἀπόστολος δὲ
Paul a slave of God, and an apostle
Ἰησοῦ Χριστοῦ κατὰ πίστιν ἐκλεκτῶν
of Jesus Christ according to [the] faith of chosen ones
θεοῦ καὶ ἐπίγνωσιν ἀληθείας τῆς κατ'
of God and full knowledge of [the] truth – according to
εὐσέβειαν 2 ἐπ' ἐλπίδι ζωῆς αἰωνίου,
piety on(in) hope life of eternal,
ἣν ἐπηγγείλατο ὁ ἀψευδὴς θεὸς πρὸ
which [4]promised [1]the [2]unlying [3]God before
χρόνων αἰωνίων, 3 ἐφανέρωσεν δὲ καιροῖς
times eternal, but [3]manifested [2]times
ἰδίοις τὸν λόγον αὐτοῦ ἐν κηρύγματι
[1]in [its] own the word of him in a proclamation
ὃ ἐπιστεύθην ἐγὼ κατ' ἐπιταγὴν τοῦ
which [2]was entrusted [with] [1]I according to [the] command of the
σωτῆρος ἡμῶν θεοῦ, 4 Τίτῳ γνησίῳ τέκνῳ
Saviour of us God, to Titus a true child
κατὰ κοινὴν πίστιν· χάρις καὶ εἰρήνη
according to a common faith: Grace and peace
ἀπὸ θεοῦ πατρὸς καὶ Χριστοῦ Ἰησοῦ
from God [the] Father and Christ Jesus
τοῦ σωτῆρος ἡμῶν.
the Saviour of us.

Titus

Chapter 1

PAUL, a servant of God
and an apostle of Jesus
Christ for the faith of God's
elect and the knowledge of
the truth that leads to godliness—2a faith and knowl-
edge resting on the hope of
eternal life, which God,
who does not lie, promised
before the beginning of
time, 3and at his appointed
season he brought his word
to light through the preaching entrusted to me by the
command of God our Sav-
ior,

4To Titus, my true son in
our common faith:

Grace and peace from
God the Father and Christ
Jesus our Savior.

[k] Gk *all the brothers*
[l] The Greek word for *you* here is plural. Other ancient authorities add *Amen*
[a] Gk *slave*
[b] Other ancient authorities read *Grace, mercy,*

[b] 19 Greek *Prisca*, a variant of *Priscilla*

Titus in Crete

5 I left you behind in Crete for this reason, so that you should put in order what remained to be done, and should appoint elders in every town, as I directed you: 6 someone who is blameless, married only once,[c] whose children are believers, not accused of debauchery and not rebellious. 7 For a bishop,[d] as God's steward, must be blameless; he must not be arrogant or quick-tempered or addicted to wine or violent or greedy for gain; 8 but he must be hospitable, a lover of goodness, prudent, upright, devout, and self-controlled. 9 He must have a firm grasp of the word that is trustworthy in accordance with the teaching, so that he may be able both to preach with sound doctrine and to refute those who contradict it.

10 There are also many rebellious people, idle talkers and deceivers, especially those of the circumcision; 11 they must be silenced, since they are upsetting whole families by teaching for sordid gain what it is not right to teach. 12 It was one of them, their very own prophet, who said,

"Cretans are always
liars, vicious
brutes, lazy
gluttons."

13 That testimony is true. For this reason rebuke them sharply, so that they may become sound in the faith, 14 not paying attention to Jewish myths or to commandments of those who reject the truth. 15 To the pure all things are pure, but to the corrupt and unbelieving nothing is pure.

[c] Gk *husband of one wife*
[d] Or *an overseer*

5 Τούτου χάριν ἀπέλιπόν σε ἐν Κρήτῃ,
For this reason† I left thee in Crete,

ἵνα τὰ λείποντα ἐπιδιορθώσῃ, καὶ
in order that the things wanting thou shouldest set in order, and

καταστήσῃς κατὰ πόλιν πρεσβυτέρους, ὡς ἐγώ
shouldest appoint in each city elders, as I

σοι διεταξάμην, 6 εἴ τίς ἐστιν ἀνέγκλητος,
[2]thee [1]charged, if anyone is unreprovable,

μιᾶς γυναικὸς ἀνήρ, τέκνα ἔχων πιστά,
[3]of one [4]wife [1]husband, [3]children [1]having [2]believing,

μὴ ἐν κατηγορίᾳ ἀσωτίας ἢ ἀνυπότακτα.
not in accusation of profligacy or unruly.*

7 δεῖ γὰρ τὸν ἐπίσκοπον ἀνέγκλητον εἶναι
For it behoves the bishop [2]unreprovable [1]to be

ὡς θεοῦ οἰκονόμον, μὴ αὐθάδη, μὴ
as of God a steward, not self-pleasing, not

ὀργίλον, μὴ πάροινον, μὴ πλήκτην, μὴ
passionate, not given to wine, not a striker, not

αἰσχροκερδῆ, 8 ἀλλὰ φιλόξενον, φιλάγαθον,
greedy of base gain, but hospitable, a lover of good [men/things],

σώφρονα, δίκαιον, ὅσιον, ἐγκρατῆ, 9 ἀντεχ-
sensible, just, holy, self-controlled, holding

όμενον τοῦ κατὰ τὴν διδαχὴν πιστοῦ
to [1]the [4]according to [5]the [6]teaching [2]faithful

λόγου, ἵνα δυνατὸς ᾖ καὶ παρακαλεῖν
[3]word, in order that [2]able [1]he may be both to exhort

ἐν τῇ διδασκαλίᾳ τῇ ὑγιαινούσῃ καὶ
by the [2]teaching – [1]*being* healthy and

τοὺς ἀντιλέγοντας ἐλέγχειν. 10 Εἰσὶν γὰρ
[2]the [ones] [3]contradicting [1]to convince. For there are

πολλοὶ ἀνυπότακτοι, ματαιολόγοι καὶ
many unruly men, vain talkers and

φρεναπάται, μάλιστα οἱ ἐκ τῆς περιτομῆς,
deceivers, specially the ones of the circumcision,

11 οὓς δεῖ ἐπιστομίζειν, οἵτινες ὅλους
whom it behoves to stop the mouth, who [2]whole

οἴκους ἀνατρέπουσιν διδάσκοντες ἃ μὴ
[3]households [1]overturn teaching things which [3]not

δεῖ αἰσχροῦ κέρδους χάριν. 12 εἶπέν
[1]it behoves [4]base [5]gain [6]for the sake of. [7]Said

τις ἐξ αὐτῶν ἴδιος αὐτῶν προφήτης·
[1]a certain one [2]of [3]them [4]an own [6]of them [5]prophet:

Κρῆτες ἀεὶ ψεῦσται, κακὰ θηρία, γαστέρες
Cretans [are] always liars, evil beasts, [2]gluttons

ἀργαί. 13 ἡ μαρτυρία αὕτη ἐστὶν ἀληθής.
[1]idle. This witness is true.

δι' ἣν αἰτίαν ἔλεγχε αὐτοὺς ἀποτόμως,
For which cause reprove them severely,

ἵνα ὑγιαίνωσιν ἐν τῇ πίστει, 14 μὴ
in order that they may be healthy in the faith, not

προσέχοντες Ἰουδαϊκοῖς μύθοις καὶ
giving heed to Jewish tales and

ἐντολαῖς ἀνθρώπων ἀποστρεφομένων τὴν
commandments of men perverting the

ἀλήθειαν. 15 πάντα καθαρὰ τοῖς καθαροῖς·
truth. All things [are] clean to the clean;

τοῖς δὲ μεμιαμμένοις καὶ ἀπίστοις οὐδὲν
but to the [ones] *having been* defiled and unfaithful nothing

* In agreement with "children" (neut. pl.).

Titus' Task on Crete

5 The reason I left you in Crete was that you might straighten out what was left unfinished and appoint[a] elders in every town, as I directed you. 6 An elder must be blameless, the husband of but one wife, a man whose children believe and are not open to the charge of being wild and disobedient. 7 Since an overseer[b] is entrusted with God's work, he must be blameless—not overbearing, not quick-tempered, not given to drunkenness, not violent, not pursuing dishonest gain. 8 Rather he must be hospitable, one who loves what is good, who is self-controlled, upright, holy and disciplined. 9 He must hold firmly to the trustworthy message as it has been taught, so that he can encourage others by sound doctrine and refute those who oppose it.

10 For there are many rebellious people, mere talkers and deceivers, especially those of the circumcision group. 11 They must be silenced, because they are ruining whole households by teaching things they ought not to teach—and that for the sake of dishonest gain. 12 Even one of their own prophets has said, "Cretans are always liars, evil brutes, lazy gluttons." 13 This testimony is true. Therefore, rebuke them sharply, so that they will be sound in the faith 14 and will pay no attention to Jewish myths or to the commands of those who reject the truth. 15 To the pure, all things are pure, but to those who are corrupted and do not believe,

[a] 5 Or *ordain*
[b] 7 Traditionally *bishop*

Their very minds and consciences are corrupted. 16They profess to know God, but they deny him by their actions. They are detestable, disobedient, unfit for any good work.

Chapter 2

Teach Sound Doctrine

BUT as for you, teach what is consistent with sound doctrine. 2Tell the older men to be temperate, serious, prudent, and sound in faith, in love, and in endurance.

3 Likewise, tell the older women to be reverent in behavior, not to be slanderers or slaves to drink; they are to teach what is good, 4so that they may encourage the young women to love their husbands, to love their children, 5to be self-controlled, chaste, good managers of the household, kind, being submissive to their husbands, so that the word of God may not be discredited.

6 Likewise, urge the younger men to be self-controlled. 7Show yourself in all respects a model of good works, and in your teaching show integrity, gravity, 8and sound speech that cannot be censured; then any opponent will be put to shame, having nothing evil to say of us.

9 Tell slaves to be submissive to their masters and to give satisfaction in every respect; they are not to talk back, 10not to pilfer, but to show complete and perfect fidelity, so that in everything they may be an ornament to the doctrine of God our Savior.

11 For the grace of God has appeared, bringing salvation to all,[e] 12training us

[e] Or *has appeared to all, bringing salvation*

καθαρόν, ἀλλὰ μεμίανται αὐτῶν καὶ ὁ
[is] clean, but 6has(ve) been defiled 7of them 1both 2the

νοῦς καὶ ἡ συνείδησις. 16 θεὸν ὁμολο-
3mind 4and 5the 6conscience. 3God 1they pro-

γοῦσιν εἰδέναι, τοῖς δὲ ἔργοις ἀρνοῦνται,
fess 2to know, but by the(ir) works they deny [him],

βδελυκτοὶ ὄντες καὶ ἀπειθεῖς καὶ πρὸς
2abominable 1being and disobedient and to

πᾶν ἔργον ἀγαθὸν ἀδόκιμοι.
every 2work 1good reprobate.

2 Σὺ δὲ λάλει ἃ πρέπει τῇ ὑγιαινούσῃ
But 2thou 1speak things which becomes the *being* healthy

διδασκαλίᾳ. 2 Πρεσβύτας νηφαλίους εἶναι,
teaching. Aged men 2sober 1to be,

σεμνούς, σώφρονας, ὑγιαίνοντας τῇ πίστει,
grave, sensible, *being* healthy in the faith,

τῇ ἀγάπῃ, τῇ ὑπομονῇ· 3 πρεσβύτιδας
– in love, – in endurance; aged women

ὡσαύτως ἐν καταστήματι ἱεροπρεπεῖς, μὴ
similarly in demeanour reverent, not

διαβόλους, μηδὲ οἴνῳ πολλῷ δεδουλωμένας,
slanderers, nor 3wine 2by much 1*having been* enslaved,

καλοδιδασκάλους, 4 ἵνα σωφρονίζωσιν τὰς
teachers of what is good, in order that they may train the

νέας φιλάνδρους εἶναι, φιλοτέκνους,
young women 2lovers of [their] husbands 1to be, child-lovers,

5 σώφρονας, ἁγνάς, οἰκουργούς, ἀγαθάς,
sensible, pure, home-workers, good,

ὑποτασσομένας τοῖς ἰδίοις ἀνδράσιν,
being subject to the(ir) own husbands,

ἵνα μὴ ὁ λόγος τοῦ θεοῦ βλασφημῆται.
lest the word – of God be blasphemed.

6 Τοὺς νεωτέρους ὡσαύτως παρακάλει
The younger men similarly exhort

σωφρονεῖν 7 περὶ πάντα, σεαυτὸν παρ-
to be sensible about all things, 2thyself 1show-

εχόμενος τύπον καλῶν ἔργων, ἐν τῇ
ing a pattern of good works, in the

διδασκαλίᾳ ἀφθορίαν, σεμνότητα, 8 λόγον
teaching uncorruptness, gravity, 2speech

ὑγιῆ ἀκατάγνωστον, ἵνα ὁ ἐξ ἐναντίας
1healthy 3irreprehensible, in order that the man of [the] contrary [side]

ἐντραπῇ μηδὲν ἔχων λέγειν περὶ ἡμῶν
may be put to shame 3nothing 1having 4to say 5about 6us

φαῦλον. 9 Δούλους ἰδίοις δεσπόταις
2bad. Slaves to [their] own masters

ὑποτάσσεσθαι ἐν πᾶσιν, εὐαρέστους εἶναι,
to be subject in all things, well-pleasing to be,

μὴ ἀντιλέγοντας, 10 μὴ νοσφιζομένους, ἀλλὰ
not contradicting, not peculating, but

πᾶσαν πίστιν ἐνδεικνυμένους ἀγαθήν, ἵνα
2all 4faith 1showing 3good, in order that

τὴν διδασκαλίαν τὴν τοῦ σωτῆρος ἡμῶν
2the 3teaching – 4of the 5Saviour 6of us

θεοῦ κοσμῶσιν ἐν πᾶσιν. 11 Ἐπεφάνη
7God 1they may adorn in all things. 5appeared

γὰρ ἡ χάρις τοῦ θεοῦ σωτήριος πᾶσιν
For 1the 2grace – 3of God 4saving to all

nothing is pure. In fact, both their minds and consciences are corrupted. 16They claim to know God, but by their actions they deny him. They are detestable, disobedient and unfit for doing anything good.

Chapter 2

What Must Be Taught to Various Groups

YOU must teach what is in accord with sound doctrine. 2Teach the older men to be temperate, worthy of respect, self-controlled, and sound in faith, in love and in endurance.

3Likewise, teach the older women to be reverent in the way they live, not to be slanderers or addicted to much wine, but to teach what is good. 4Then they can train the younger women to love their husbands and children, 5to be self-controlled and pure, to be busy at home, to be kind, and to be subject to their husbands, so that no one will malign the word of God.

6Similarly, encourage the young men to be self-controlled. 7In everything set them an example by doing what is good. In your teaching show integrity, seriousness 8and soundness of speech that cannot be condemned, so that those who oppose you may be ashamed because they have nothing bad to say about us.

9Teach slaves to be subject to their masters in everything, to try to please them, not to talk back to them, 10and not to steal from them, but to show that they can be fully trusted, so that in every way they will make the teaching about God our Savior attractive.

11For the grace of God that brings salvation has appeared to all men. 12It

to renounce impiety and
worldly passions, and in
the present age to live lives
that are self-controlled, upright, and godly, 13 while
we wait for the blessed
hope and the manifestation
of the glory of our great
God and Savior,[f] Jesus
Christ. 14 He it is who gave
himself for us that he might
redeem us from all iniquity
and purify for himself a
people of his own who are
zealous for good deeds.
15 Declare these things;
exhort and reprove with all
authority.[g] Let no one
look down on you.

Chapter 3

Maintain Good Deeds

REMIND them to be
subject to rulers and
authorities, to be obedient,
to be ready for every good
work, 2 to speak evil of no
one, to avoid quarreling, to
be gentle, and to show every courtesy to everyone.
3 For we ourselves were
once foolish, disobedient,
led astray, slaves to various passions and pleasures,
passing our days in malice
and envy, despicable, hating one another. 4 But when
the goodness and loving
kindness of God our Savior
appeared, 5 he saved us,
not because of any works
of righteousness that we
had done, but according to
his mercy, through the water[h] of rebirth and renewal
by the Holy Spirit. 6 This
Spirit he poured out on us
richly through Jesus Christ
our Savior, 7 so that, having
been justified by his grace,
we might become heirs ac-
cording to the hope of eternal life. 8 The saying is sure.

[f] Or *of the great God and our Savior*
[g] Gk *commandment*
[h] Gk *washing*

ἀνθρώποις, **12** παιδεύουσα ἡμᾶς, ἵνα
men, instructing us, *in order* that

ἀρνησάμενοι τὴν ἀσέβειαν καὶ τὰς κοσμικὰς
denying – impiety and – worldly

ἐπιθυμίας σωφρόνως καὶ δικαίως καὶ
lusts [2]sensibly [3]and [4]righteously [5]and

εὐσεβῶς ζήσωμεν ἐν τῷ νῦν αἰῶνι,
[6]piously [1]we might live in the now(present) age,

13 προσδεχόμενοι τὴν μακαρίαν ἐλπίδα καὶ
expecting the blessed hope and

ἐπιφάνειαν τῆς δόξης τοῦ μεγάλου θεοῦ
appearance of the glory of the great God

καὶ σωτῆρος ἡμῶν Χριστοῦ Ἰησοῦ, **14** ὃς
and Saviour of us Christ Jesus, who

ἔδωκεν ἑαυτὸν ὑπὲρ ἡμῶν ἵνα λυτρώσηται
gave himself on behalf of us in order that he might ransom

ἡμᾶς ἀπὸ πάσης ἀνομίας καὶ καθαρίσῃ
us from all iniquity and *might* cleanse

ἑαυτῷ λαὸν περιούσιον, ζηλωτὴν καλῶν ἔργων.
for himself a people [his] own possession, zealous of good works.

15 Ταῦτα λάλει καὶ παρακάλει καὶ ἔλεγχε
These things speak thou and exhort and reprove

μετὰ πάσης ἐπιταγῆς· μηδείς σου περιφρονείτω.
with all command; [2]no one [4]*of* thee [1]let [3]despise.

3 Ὑπομίμνῃσκε αὐτοὺς ἀρχαῖς ἐξουσίαις
Remind thou them [2]to rulers [3][and] [4]authorities

ὑποτάσσεσθαι, πειθαρχεῖν, πρὸς πᾶν ἔργον
[1]to be subject, to be obedient, [3]to [4]every [6]work

ἀγαθὸν ἑτοίμους εἶναι, **2** μηδένα βλασ-
[5]good [2]ready [1]to be, no one to

φημεῖν, ἀμάχους εἶναι, ἐπιεικεῖς, πᾶσαν
rail at, uncontentious to be, forbearing, [2]all

ἐνδεικνυμένους πραΰτητα πρὸς πάντας
[1]showing forth meekness to all

ἀνθρώπους. **3** Ἦμεν γάρ ποτε καὶ ἡμεῖς
men. For [3]were [4]then [2]also [1]we

ἀνόητοι, ἀπειθεῖς, πλανώμενοι, δουλεύοντες
senseless, disobedient, being deceived, serving [as slaves]

ἐπιθυμίαις καὶ ἡδοναῖς ποικίλαις, ἐν κακίᾳ
[4]lusts [5]and [6]pleasures [1]various, [2]in [3]evil

καὶ φθόνῳ διάγοντες, στυγητοί, μισοῦντες
[4]and [5]envy [1]living, hateful, hating

ἀλλήλους. **4** ὅτε δὲ ἡ χρηστότης καὶ
one another. But when the kindness and

ἡ φιλανθρωπία ἐπεφάνη τοῦ σωτῆρος ἡμῶν
the love to man [4]appeared [1]of the [2]Saviour [3]of us

θεοῦ, **5** οὐκ ἐξ ἔργων τῶν ἐν δικαιοσύνῃ
[4]God, not by works – [4]in [5]righteousness

ἃ ἐποιήσαμεν ἡμεῖς, ἀλλὰ κατὰ τὸ
[1]which [3]did [2]we, but according to the

αὐτοῦ ἔλεος ἔσωσεν ἡμᾶς διὰ λουτροῦ
of him mercy he saved us through [the] washing

παλιγγενεσίας καὶ ἀνακαινώσεως πνεύματος
of regeneration and renewal [3]Spirit

ἁγίου, **6** οὗ ἐξέχεεν ἐφ' ἡμᾶς πλουσίως
[1]of [the] Holy, which he shed on us richly

διὰ Ἰησοῦ Χριστοῦ τοῦ σωτῆρος ἡμῶν,
through Jesus Christ the Saviour of us,

7 ἵνα δικαιωθέντες τῇ ἐκείνου χάριτι
in order that being justified [1]by the [2]of that one [3]grace

κληρονόμοι γενηθῶμεν κατ' ἐλπίδα ζωῆς
heirs we might become according to a hope of life

teaches us to say "No" to
ungodliness and worldly
passions, and to live self-
controlled, upright and
godly lives in this present
age, 13 while we wait for the
blessed hope—the glorious
appearing of our great God
and Savior, Jesus Christ,
14 who gave himself for us
to redeem us from all wickedness and to purify for
himself a people that are his
very own, eager to do what
is good.
15 These, then, are the
things you should teach.
Encourage and rebuke with
all authority. Do not let
anyone despise you.

Chapter 3

Doing What Is Good

REMIND the people to
be subject to rulers
and authorities, to be obedient, to be ready to do
whatever is good, 2 to slander no one, to be peaceable
and considerate, and to
show true humility toward
all men.
3 At one time we too were
foolish, disobedient, de-
ceived and enslaved by all
kinds of passions and pleasures. We lived in malice
and envy, being hated and
hating one another. 4 But
when the kindness and love
of God our Savior ap-
peared, 5 he saved us, not
because of righteous things
we had done, but because
of his mercy. He saved us
through the washing of rebirth and renewal by the
Holy Spirit, 6 whom he
poured out on us generously through Jesus Christ our
Savior, 7 so that, having
been justified by his grace,
we might become heirs
having the hope of eternal

I desire that you insist on these things, so that those who have come to believe in God may be careful to devote themselves to good works; these things are excellent and profitable to everyone. 9 But avoid stupid controversies, genealogies, dissensions, and quarrels about the law, for they are unprofitable and worthless. 10 After a first and second admonition, have nothing more to do with anyone who causes divisions, 11 since you know that such a person is perverted and sinful, being self-condemned.

Final Messages and Benediction

12 When I send Artemas to you, or Tychicus, do your best to come to me at Nicopolis, for I have decided to spend the winter there. 13 Make every effort to send Zenas the lawyer and Apollos on their way, and see that they lack nothing. 14 And let people learn to devote themselves to good works in order to meet urgent needs, so that they may not be unproductive.

15 All who are with me send greetings to you. Greet those who love us in the faith.

Grace be with all of you.[i]

αἰωνίου. 8 Πιστὸς ὁ λόγος, καὶ περὶ
eternal. Faithful [is] the word, and as to

τούτων βούλομαί σε διαβεβαιοῦσθαι, ἵνα
these things I wish thee to affirm confidently, in order that

φροντίζωσιν καλῶν ἔργων προΐστασθαι οἱ
⁴may take thought ⁶of good ⁷works ⁵to maintain ¹the [ones]

πεπιστευκότες θεῷ. ταῦτά ἐστιν καλὰ
²having believed ³God. These things is(are) good

καὶ ὠφέλιμα τοῖς ἀνθρώποις· 9 μωρὰς
and profitable – to men; ²foolish

δὲ ζητήσεις καὶ γενεαλογίας καὶ ἔριν
¹but questionings and genealogies and strife

καὶ μάχας νομικὰς περιΐστασο· εἰσὶν γὰρ
and ²fights ¹legal shun thou; for they are

ἀνωφελεῖς καὶ μάταιοι. 10 αἱρετικὸν
unprofitable and vain. A factious

ἄνθρωπον μετὰ μίαν καὶ δευτέραν
man after one and a second

νουθεσίαν παραιτοῦ, 11 εἰδὼς ὅτι ἐξέστραπ-
admonition avoid, knowing that ²has been per-

ται ὁ τοιοῦτος καὶ ἁμαρτάνει ὢν αὐτο-
verted ¹such a man and sins being self-

κατάκριτος.
condemned.

12 Ὅταν πέμψω Ἀρτεμᾶν πρὸς σὲ
Whenever I send Artemas to thee

ἢ Τύχικον, σπούδασον ἐλθεῖν πρός με
or Tychicus, hasten to come to me

εἰς Νικόπολιν· ἐκεῖ γὰρ κέκρικα παραχειμά-
in Nicopolis; for there I have decided to spend [the]

σαι. 13 Ζηνᾶν τὸν νομικὸν καὶ Ἀπολλῶν
winter. Zenas the lawyer and Apollos

σπουδαίως πρόπεμψον, ἵνα μηδὲν αὐτοῖς
urgently send forward, in order that nothing to them

λείπῃ. 14 μανθανέτωσαν δὲ καὶ οἱ ἡμέτεροι
may be lacking. And ¹let ⁴learn ³also – ²our [people]

καλῶν ἔργων προΐστασθαι εἰς τὰς ἀναγ-
⁶of good ⁷works ⁵to maintain for – neces-

καίας χρείας, ἵνα μὴ ὦσιν ἄκαρποι.
sary wants, lest they be unfruitful.

15 Ἀσπάζονταί σε οἱ μετ᾽ ἐμοῦ πάντες.
⁵greet ⁶thee ²the [ones] ³with ⁴me ¹All.

ἄσπασαι τοὺς φιλοῦντας ἡμᾶς ἐν πίστει.
Greet thou the [ones] loving us in [the] faith.

Ἡ χάρις μετὰ πάντων ὑμῶν.
– Grace [be] with ²all ¹you.

life. 8This is a trustworthy saying. And I want you to stress these things, so that those who have trusted in God may be careful to devote themselves to doing what is good. These things are excellent and profitable for everyone.

9But avoid foolish controversies and genealogies and arguments and quarrels about the law, because these are unprofitable and useless. 10Warn a divisive person once, and then warn him a second time. After that, have nothing to do with him. 11You may be sure that such a man is warped and sinful; he is self-condemned.

Final Remarks

12As soon as I send Artemas or Tychicus to you, do your best to come to me at Nicopolis, because I have decided to winter there. 13Do everything you can to help Zenas the lawyer and Apollos on their way and see that they have everything they need. 14Our people must learn to devote themselves to doing what is good, in order that they may provide for daily necessities and not live unproductive lives.

15Everyone with me sends you greetings. Greet those who love us in the faith.

Grace be with you all.

The Letter of Paul to

Philemon

Salutation

PAUL, a prisoner of Christ Jesus, and Timothy our brother,[a]

To Philemon our dear friend and co-worker, 2 to Apphia our sister,[b] to Archippus our fellow soldier,

[i] Other ancient authorities add *Amen*

[a] Gk *the brother*

[b] Gk *the sister*

ΠΡΟΣ ΦΙΛΗΜΟΝΑ

To Philemon

1 Παῦλος δέσμιος Χριστοῦ Ἰησοῦ καὶ
Paul a prisoner of Christ Jesus and

Τιμόθεος ὁ ἀδελφὸς Φιλήμονι τῷ ἀγαπητῷ
Timothy the brother to Philemon the beloved

καὶ συνεργῷ ἡμῶν 2 καὶ Ἀπφίᾳ τῇ
and a fellow-worker of us and to Apphia the

ἀδελφῇ καὶ Ἀρχίππῳ τῷ συστρατιώτῃ
sister and to Archippus the fellow-soldier

Philemon

PAUL, a prisoner of Christ Jesus, and Timothy our brother,

To Philemon our dear friend and fellow worker, 2to Apphia our sister, to Archippus our fellow sol-

and to the church in your
house:
3 Grace to you and
peace from God our Father
and the Lord Jesus Christ.

Philemon's Love and Faith

4 When I remember
you[c] in my prayers, I always thank my God 5be-
cause I hear of your love
for all the saints and your
faith toward the Lord
Jesus. 6I pray that the sharing of your faith may be-
come effective when you
perceive all the good that
we[d] may do for Christ. 7I
have indeed received much
joy and encouragement
from your love, because
the hearts of the saints have
been refreshed through
you, my brother.

Paul's Plea for Onesimus

8 For this reason,
though I am bold enough in
Christ to command you to
do your duty, 9yet I would
rather appeal to you on the
basis of love—and I, Paul,
do this as an old man, and
now also as a prisoner of
Christ Jesus.[e] 10I am appealing to you for my child,
Onesimus, whose father I
have become during my im-
prisonment. 11Formerly he
was useless to you, but
now he is indeed useful[f]
both to you and to me. 12I
am sending him, that is, my
own heart, back to you. 13I
wanted to keep him with
me, so that he might be of
service to me in your place
during my imprisonment
for the gospel; 14but I preferred to do nothing without your consent, in order
that your good deed might
be voluntary and not some-

[c] From verse 4 through verse 21, *you* is singular
[d] Other ancient authorities read *you* (plural)
[e] Or *as an ambassador of Christ Jesus, and now also his prisoner*
[f] The name Onesimus means *useful* or (compare verse 20) *beneficial*

ἡμῶν καὶ τῇ κατ' οἶκόν σου ἐκκλησίᾳ·
of us and [1]to the [3]at [4]house [5]of thee [2]church:
3 χάρις ὑμῖν καὶ εἰρήνη ἀπὸ θεοῦ πατρὸς
Grace to you and peace from God Father
ἡμῶν καὶ κυρίου Ἰησοῦ Χριστοῦ.
of us and Lord Jesus Christ.
4 Εὐχαριστῶ τῷ θεῷ μου πάντοτε μνείαν
I give thanks to the God of me always [2]mention
σου ποιούμενος ἐπὶ τῶν προσευχῶν μου,
[3]of thee [1]making at the prayers of me,
5 ἀκούων σου τὴν ἀγάπην καὶ τὴν
hearing of thee the love and the
πίστιν ἣν ἔχεις πρὸς τὸν κύριον Ἰησοῦν
faith which thou hast toward the Lord Jesus
καὶ εἰς πάντας τοὺς ἁγίους, 6 ὅπως
and to all the saints, so as
ἡ κοινωνία τῆς πίστεώς σου ἐνεργὴς
the fellowship of the faith of thee [2]operative
γένηται ἐν ἐπιγνώσει παντὸς ἀγαθοῦ τοῦ
[1]may become in a full knowledge of every good thing –
ἐν ἡμῖν εἰς Χριστόν. 7 χαρὰν γὰρ
in us for Christ. [4]joy [1]For
πολλὴν ἔσχον καὶ παράκλησιν ἐπὶ τῇ
[3]much [2]I had and consolation over the
ἀγάπῃ σου, ὅτι τὰ σπλάγχνα τῶν ἁγίων
love of thee, because the bowels of the saints
ἀναπέπαυται διὰ σοῦ, ἀδελφέ. 8 Διό,
has(ve) been refreshed through thee, brother. Wherefore,
πολλὴν ἐν Χριστῷ παρρησίαν ἔχων ἐπιτάσ-
[3]much [4]in [5]Christ [2]boldness [1]having to
σειν σοι τὸ ἀνῆκον, 9 διὰ τὴν ἀγάπην
charge thee the befitting thing, because of – love
μᾶλλον παρακαλῶ· τοιοῦτος ὢν ὡς Παῦλος
rather I beseech; such a one being as Paul
πρεσβύτης, νυνὶ δὲ καὶ δέσμιος Χριστοῦ
an old man, and now also a prisoner of Christ
Ἰησοῦ, 10 παρακαλῶ σε περὶ τοῦ ἐμοῦ
Jesus, I beseech thee concerning – my
τέκνου, ὃν ἐγέννησα ἐν τοῖς δεσμοῖς,
child, whom I begat in the(my) bonds,
Ὀνήσιμον, 11 τόν ποτέ σοι ἄχρηστον
Onesimus, the [one] then (formerly) [2]to thee [1]useless
νυνὶ δὲ καὶ σοὶ καὶ ἐμοὶ εὔχρηστον,
but now [2]both [3]to thee [4]and [5]to me [1]useful,
12 ὃν ἀνέπεμψά σοι, αὐτόν, τοῦτ' ἔστιν
whom I sent back to thee, him, this is
τὰ ἐμὰ σπλάγχνα· 13 ὃν ἐγὼ ἐβουλόμην
– my bowels; whom I resolved
πρὸς ἐμαυτὸν κατέχειν, ἵνα ὑπὲρ σοῦ
with myself to retain, in order that on behalf of thee
μοι διακονῇ ἐν τοῖς δεσμοῖς τοῦ εὐαγ-
to me he might minister in the bonds of the gos-
γελίου, 14 χωρὶς δὲ τῆς σῆς γνώμης
pel, but without – thy opinion
οὐδὲν ἠθέλησα ποιῆσαι, ἵνα μὴ ὡς κατὰ
[2]nothing [1]I was willing [3]to do, in order that not [5]as [6]by way of
ἀνάγκην τὸ ἀγαθόν σου ᾖ ἀλλὰ κατὰ
[7]necessity [1]the [2]good [3]of thee [4]might be but by way of

dier and to the church that
meets in your home:

3Grace to you and peace
from God our Father and
the Lord Jesus Christ.

Thanksgiving and Prayer

4I always thank my God
as I remember you in my
prayers, 5because I hear
about your faith in the Lord
Jesus and your love for all
the saints. 6I pray that you
may be active in sharing
your faith, so that you will
have a full understanding of
every good thing we have
in Christ. 7Your love has
given me great joy and encouragement, because you,
brother, have refreshed the
hearts of the saints.

Paul's Plea for Onesimus

8Therefore, although in
Christ I could be bold and
order you to do what you
ought to do, 9yet I appeal to
you on the basis of love. I
then, as Paul—an old man
and now also a prisoner of
Christ Jesus— 10I appeal to
you for my son Onesimus,[a]
who became my son while I
was in chains. 11Formerly
he was useless to you, but
now he has become useful
both to you and to me.
12I am sending him—who
is my very heart—back to
you. 13I would have liked to
keep him with me so that he
could take your place in
helping me while I am in
chains for the gospel. 14But
I did not want to do any-
thing without your consent,
so that any favor you do
will be spontaneous and

[a] 10 *Onesimus* means *useful.*

thing forced. 15 Perhaps this
is the reason he was separated from you for a while,
so that you might have him
back forever, 16 no longer
as a slave but more than a
slave, a beloved brother—
especially to me but how
much more to you, both in
the flesh and in the Lord.
17 So if you consider me
your partner, welcome him
as you would welcome me.
18 If he has wronged you in
any way, or owes you any-
thing, charge that to my account. 19 I, Paul, am writing
this with my own hand: I
will repay it. I say nothing
about your owing me even
your own self. 20 Yes,
brother, let me have this
benefit from you in the
Lord! Refresh my heart in
Christ. 21 Confident of your
obedience, I am writing to
you, knowing that you will
do even more than I say.
22 One thing more—
prepare a guest room for
me, for I am hoping
through your prayers to be
restored to you.

Final Greetings and Benediction

23 Epaphras, my fellow
prisoner in Christ Jesus,
sends greetings to you,[g]
24 and so do Mark, Aristarchus, Demas, and Luke,
my fellow workers.
25 The grace of the
Lord Jesus Christ be with
your spirit.[h]

ἑκούσιον. **15** τάχα γὰρ διὰ τοῦτο ἐχωρίσθη
[being] voluntary. For perhaps therefore he departed

πρὸς ὥραν, ἵνα αἰώνιον αὐτὸν ἀπέχῃς,
for an hour, in order that [3]eternally [2]him [1]thou mightest receive,

16 οὐκέτι ὡς δοῦλον ἀλλὰ ὑπὲρ δοῦλον,
no longer as a slave but beyond a slave,

ἀδελφὸν ἀγαπητόν, μάλιστα ἐμοί, πόσῳ
a brother beloved, specially to me, [2]by how much

δὲ μᾶλλον σοὶ καὶ ἐν σαρκὶ καὶ ἐν
[1]and more to thee both in [the] flesh and in

κυρίῳ. **17** εἰ οὖν με ἔχεις κοινωνόν,
[the] Lord. If therefore me thou hast [as] a partner,

προσλαβοῦ αὐτὸν ὡς ἐμέ. **18** εἰ δέ
receive him as me. And if

τι ἠδίκησέν σε ἢ ὀφείλει, τοῦτο ἐμοὶ
anything he wronged thee or owes, [3]this [2]to me

ἐλλόγα· **19** ἐγὼ Παῦλος ἔγραψα τῇ ἐμῇ
[1]reckon: I Paul wrote – with my

χειρί, ἐγὼ ἀποτίσω· ἵνα μὴ λέγω σοι
hand, I will repay; lest I say to thee

ὅτι καὶ σεαυτόν μοι προσοφείλεις. **20** ναί,
that indeed [3]thyself [2]to me [1]thou owest besides. Yes,

ἀδελφέ, ἐγώ σου ὀναίμην ἐν κυρίῳ·
brother, [1]I [5]of thee [2]may [3]have [4]help in [the] Lord;

ἀνάπαυσόν μου τὰ σπλάγχνα ἐν Χριστῷ.
refresh of me the bowels in Christ.

21 Πεποιθὼς τῇ ὑπακοῇ σου ἔγραψά
Having trusted to the obedience of thee I wrote

σοι, εἰδὼς ὅτι καὶ ὑπὲρ ἃ λέγω ποιήσεις.
to thee, knowing that indeed beyond what things I say thou wilt do.

22 ἅμα δὲ καὶ ἑτοίμαζέ μοι ξενίαν·
And at the same time also prepare for me lodging;

ἐλπίζω γὰρ ὅτι διὰ τῶν προσευχῶν
for I hope that through the prayers

ὑμῶν χαρισθήσομαι ὑμῖν.
of you I shall be given to you.

23 Ἀσπάζεταί σε Ἐπαφρᾶς ὁ συναιχμά-
[6]greets [9]thee [1]Epaphras [2]the [3]fellow-

λωτός μου ἐν Χριστῷ Ἰησοῦ, **24** Μᾶρκος,
captive [4]of me [5]in [6]Christ [7]Jesus, [also] Mark,

Ἀρίσταρχος, Δημᾶς, Λουκᾶς, οἱ συνεργοί
Aristarchus, Demas, Luke, the fellow-workers

μου.
of me.

25 Ἡ χάρις τοῦ κυρίου Ἰησοῦ Χριστοῦ
The grace of the Lord Jesus Christ

μετὰ τοῦ πνεύματος ὑμῶν.
[be] with the spirit of you.

not forced. 15 Perhaps the
reason he was separated
from you for a little while
was that you might have
him back for good— 16 no
longer as a slave, but better
than a slave, as a dear
brother. He is very dear to
me but even dearer to you,
both as a man and as a
brother in the Lord.
17 So if you consider me a
partner, welcome him as
you would welcome me.
18 If he has done you any
wrong or owes you any
thing, charge it to me. 19 I,
Paul, am writing this with
my own hand. I will pay it
back—not to mention that
you owe me your very self.
20 I do wish, brother, that I
may have some benefit
from you in the Lord; re-
fresh my heart in Christ.
21 Confident of your obedience, I write to you, knowing that you will do even
more than I ask.
22 And one thing more:
Prepare a guest room for
me, because I hope to be
restored to you in answer
to your prayers.

23 Epaphras, my fellow
prisoner in Christ Jesus,
sends you greetings. 24 And
so do Mark, Aristarchus,
Demas and Luke, my fel-
low workers.
25 The grace of the Lord
Jesus Christ be with your
spirit.

The Letter to the

Hebrews

Chapter 1

God Has Spoken by His Son

LONG ago God spoke to
our ancestors in many
and various ways by the
prophets, 2 but in these last

[g] Here *you* is singular
[h] Other ancient authorities add *Amen*

ΠΡΟΣ ΕΒΡΑΙΟΥΣ
To Hebrews

1 Πολυμερῶς καὶ πολυτρόπως πάλαι ὁ
[1]In many portions [2]and [3]in many ways [4]of old –

θεὸς λαλήσας τοῖς πατράσιν ἐν τοῖς
God [5]having spoken [6]to the [7]fathers by the

Hebrews

Chapter 1

The Son Superior to Angels

IN the past God spoke to
our forefathers through
the prophets at many times
and in various ways, 2 but in

days he has spoken to us by
a Son,[a] whom he appointed heir of all things,
through whom he also cre-
ated the worlds. 3 He is the
reflection of God's glory
and the exact imprint of
God's very being, and he
sustains[b] all things by his
powerful word. When he
had made purification for
sins, he sat down at the
right hand of the Majesty
on high, 4 having become as
much superior to angels as
the name he has inherited is
more excellent than theirs.

The Son Is Superior to Angels

5 For to which of the an-
gels did God ever say,
"You are my Son;
today I have
begotten you"?
Or again,
"I will be his Father,
and he will be my
Son"?
6 And again, when he brings
the firstborn into the world,
he says,
"Let all God's angels
worship him."
7 Of the angels he says,
"He makes his angels
winds,
and his servants
flames of fire."
8 But of the Son he says,
"Your throne,
O God,[c] is
forever and
ever,
and the righteous
scepter is the
scepter of your[d]
kingdom.
9 You have loved
righteousness
and hated
wickedness;
therefore God, your
God, has
anointed you
with the oil of
gladness beyond
your
companions."
10 And,
"In the beginning,
Lord, you
founded the
earth,

[a] Or *the Son*
[b] Or *bears along*
[c] Or *God is your throne*
[d] Other ancient authorities read *his*

προφήταις 2 ἐπ' ἐσχάτου τῶν ἡμερῶν
prophets in [the] last – days
τούτων ἐλάλησεν ἡμῖν ἐν υἱῷ, ὃν ἔθηκεν
of these spoke to us in a Son, whom he appointed
κληρονόμον πάντων, δι' οὗ καὶ ἐποίησεν
heir of all things, through whom indeed he made
τοὺς αἰῶνας· 3 ὃς ὢν ἀπαύγασμα τῆς
the ages; who being [the] radiance of the (his)
δόξης καὶ χαρακτὴρ τῆς ὑποστάσεως αὐτοῦ,
glory and [the] representation of the reality of him,
φέρων τε τὰ πάντα τῷ ῥήματι τῆς
and bearing – all things by the word of the
δυνάμεως αὐτοῦ, καθαρισμὸν τῶν ἁμαρτιῶν
power of him, [2]cleansing – [3]of sins
ποιησάμενος ἐκάθισεν ἐν δεξιᾷ τῆς
[1]having made sat on [the] right [hand] of the
μεγαλωσύνης ἐν ὑψηλοῖς, 4 τοσούτῳ
greatness in high places, [2]by so much
κρείττων γενόμενος τῶν ἀγγέλων ὅσῳ
[3]better [1]becoming [4][than] the angels as
διαφορώτερον παρ' αὐτοὺς κεκληρονόμηκεν
[2]a more excellent [4]than [5]them [1]he has inherited
ὄνομα. 5 Τίνι γὰρ εἶπέν ποτε τῶν
[3]name. For to which [3]said he [4]ever [1]of the
ἀγγέλων· υἱός μου εἶ σύ, ἐγὼ σήμερον
[2]angels: Son of me art thou, I to-day
γεγέννηκά σε; καὶ πάλιν· ἐγὼ ἔσομαι
have begotten thee? and again: I will be
αὐτῷ εἰς πατέρα, καὶ αὐτὸς ἔσται μοι
to him for a father, and he shall be to me
εἰς υἱόν; 6 ὅταν δὲ πάλιν εἰσαγάγῃ
for a son? and whenever again he brings in
τὸν πρωτότοκον εἰς τὴν οἰκουμένην, λέγει·
the firstborn into the inhabited [earth], he says:
καὶ προσκυνησάτωσαν αὐτῷ πάντες ἄγγελοι
And let worship him all angels
θεοῦ. 7 καὶ πρὸς μὲν τοὺς ἀγγέλους
of God. And with regard to – the angels
λέγει· ὁ ποιῶν τοὺς ἀγγέλους αὐτοῦ
he says: The [one] making the angels of him
πνεύματα, καὶ τοὺς λειτουργοὺς αὐτοῦ
spirits, and the ministers of him
πυρὸς φλόγα· 8 πρὸς δὲ τὸν υἱόν· ὁ
[2]of fire [1]a flame; but with regard to the Son: The
θρόνος σου ὁ θεὸς εἰς τὸν αἰῶνα τοῦ
throne of thee[,] – God[,]* [is] unto the age of the
αἰῶνος, καὶ ἡ ῥάβδος τῆς εὐθύτητος
age, and the rod – of uprightness [is]
ῥάβδος τῆς βασιλείας αὐτοῦ. 9 ἠγάπησας
[the] rod of the kingdom of him. Thou lovedst
δικαιοσύνην καὶ ἐμίσησας ἀνομίαν· διὰ
righteousness and hatedst lawlessness; there-
τοῦτο ἔχρισέν σε, ὁ θεός, ὁ θεός σου
fore [4]anointed [5]thee, – [6]God,* [1]the [2]God [3]of thee
ἔλαιον ἀγαλλιάσεως παρὰ τοὺς μετόχους
[with] oil of gladness above the partners
σου. 10 καί· σὺ κατ' ἀρχάς, κύριε,
of thee. And: Thou at [the] beginnings, Lord,
τὴν γῆν ἐθεμελίωσας, καὶ ἔργα τῶν
[2]the [3]earth [1]didst found, and [4]works [5]of the

* Articular vocative; see ver. 10.

these last days he has spoken to us by his Son, whom
he appointed heir of all
things, and through whom
he made the universe. 3The
Son is the radiance of
God's glory and the exact
representation of his being,
sustaining all things by his
powerful word. After he
had provided purification
for sins, he sat down at the
right hand of the Majesty in
heaven. 4So he became as
much superior to the angels
as the name he has inherited is superior to theirs.
5For to which of the an-
gels did God ever say,

"You are my Son;
today I have become
your Father"[a][b]?

Or again,

"I will be his Father,
and he will be my
Son"[c]?

6And again, when God
brings his firstborn into the
world, he says,

"Let all God's angels
worship him."[d]

7In speaking of the angels
he says,

"He makes his angels
winds,
his servants flames of
fire."[e]

8But about the Son he says,

"Your throne, O God,
will last for ever and
ever,
and righteousness will
be the scepter of
your kingdom.
9You have loved
righteousness and
hated wickedness;
therefore God, your
God, has set you
above your
companions
by anointing you with
the oil of joy."[f]

10He also says,

"In the beginning, O
Lord, you laid the
foundations of the
earth,

[a]5 Or *have begotten you*
[b]5 Psalm 2:7
[c]5 2 Samuel 7:14; 1 Chron. 17:13
[d]6 Deut. 32:43 (see Dead Sea Scrolls and Septuagint)
[e]7 Psalm 104:4
[f]9 Psalm 45:6,7

and the heavens are
the work of
your hands;
11 they will perish, but
you remain;
they will all wear
out like
clothing;
12 like a cloak you will
roll them up,
and like clothing[e]
they will be
changed.
But you are the same,
and your years will
never end."
13 But to which of the angels has he ever said,
"Sit at my right hand
until I make your
enemies a
footstool for
your feet"?
14 Are not all angels[f] spirits
in the divine service, sent
to serve for the sake of
those who are to inherit salvation?

Chapter 2

Warning to Pay Attention

THEREFORE we must
pay greater attention
to what we have heard, so
that we do not drift away
from it. 2 For if the message
declared through angels
was valid, and every transgression or disobedience
received a just penalty,
3 how can we escape if we
neglect so great a salva-
tion? It was declared at first
through the Lord, and it
was attested to us by those
who heard him, 4 while God
added his testimony by
signs and wonders and various miracles, and by gifts
of the Holy Spirit, distributed according to his will.

Exaltation through Abasement

5 Now God[g] did not
subject the coming world,
about which we are speak-
ing, to angels. 6 But someone has testified some-
where,
"What are human
beings that you
are mindful of
them,[h]
or mortals, that you
care for them?[i]
7 You have made them
for a little while
lower[j] than the
angels;

[e] Other ancient authorities lack *like clothing*
[f] Gk *all of them*
[g] Gk *he*
[h] Gk *What is man that you are mindful of him?*
[i] Gk *or the son of man that you care for him?* In the Hebrew of Psalm 8.4-6 both *man* and *son of man* refer to all humankind
[j] Or *them only a little lower*

χειρῶν σού εἰσιν οἱ οὐρανοί· **11** αὐτοὶ
[6]hands [7]of thee [5]are [1]the [2]heavens; they

ἀπολοῦνται, σὺ δὲ διαμένεις· καὶ πάντες
will perish, but thou remainest; and all

ὡς ἱμάτιον παλαιωθήσονται, **12** καὶ ὡσεὶ
as a garment will become old, and as

περιβόλαιον ἑλίξεις αὐτούς, ὡς ἱμάτιον
a mantle thou wilt roll up them, as a garment

καὶ ἀλλαγήσονται· σὺ δὲ ὁ αὐτὸς εἶ
also they will be changed; but thou the same art

καὶ τὰ ἔτη σου οὐκ ἐκλείψουσιν. **13** πρὸς
and the years of thee will not fail. [2]to

τίνα δὲ τῶν ἀγγέλων εἴρηκέν ποτε·
[3]which [1]But of the angels has he said at any time:

κάθου ἐκ δεξιῶν μου ἕως ἂν θῶ τοὺς
Sit at [the] right of me until I put the

ἐχθρούς σου ὑποπόδιον τῶν ποδῶν σου;
enemies of thee a footstool of the feet of thee?

14 οὐχὶ πάντες εἰσὶν λειτουργικὰ πνεύματα
[2]not [3]all [1]are they [4]ministering [5]spirits

εἰς διακονίαν ἀποστελλόμενα διὰ τοὺς
[7]for [8]service [6]being sent forth because of the [ones]

μέλλοντας κληρονομεῖν σωτηρίαν; **2** Διὰ
being about to inherit salvation? There-

τοῦτο δεῖ περισσοτέρως προσέχειν ἡμᾶς
fore [1]it behoves [4]more abundantly [3]to give heed [2]us

τοῖς ἀκουσθεῖσιν, μήποτε παραρυῶμεν.
to the things heard, lest we drift away.

2 εἰ γὰρ ὁ δι' ἀγγέλων λαληθεὶς λόγος
For if [1]the [4]through [5]angels [3]spoken [2]word

ἐγένετο βέβαιος, καὶ πᾶσα παράβασις
was firm, and every transgression

καὶ παρακοὴ ἔλαβεν ἔνδικον μισθαποδοσίαν,
and disobedience received a just recompence,

3 πῶς ἡμεῖς ἐκφευξόμεθα τηλικαύτης
how [2]we [1]shall [3]escape [5]so great

ἀμελήσαντες σωτηρίας; ἥτις ἀρχὴν λαβοῦσα
[4]neglecting [6]a salvation? which [2]a beginning [1]having received

λαλεῖσθαι διὰ τοῦ κυρίου, ὑπὸ τῶν
to be spoken through the Lord, by the

ἀκουσάντων εἰς ἡμᾶς ἐβεβαιώθη, **4** συνεπι-
[ones] hearing to us was confirmed, [2]bearing

μαρτυροῦντος τοῦ θεοῦ σημείοις τε καὶ
witness with – [1]God[a] [4]by signs [3]both and

τέρασιν καὶ ποικίλαις δυνάμεσιν καὶ
by wonders and *by* various powerful deeds and

πνεύματος ἁγίου μερισμοῖς κατὰ τὴν αὐτοῦ
[3]Spirit [2]of [the] Holy [1]*by* distributions according to the [3]of him

θέλησιν.
[1]will.

5 Οὐ γὰρ ἀγγέλοις ὑπέταξεν τὴν
For not to angels subjected he the

οἰκουμένην τὴν μέλλουσαν, περὶ ἧς
[2]inhabited [earth] – [1]coming, about which

λαλοῦμεν. **6** διεμαρτύρατο δέ πού τις
we speak. But [2]solemnly witnessed [3]somewhere [1]one

λέγων· τί ἐστιν ἄνθρωπος ὅτι μιμνήσκῃ
saying: What is man that thou rememberest

αὐτοῦ; ἢ υἱὸς ἀνθρώπου ὅτι ἐπισκέπτῃ
him? or a son of man that thou observest

αὐτόν; **7** ἠλάττωσας αὐτὸν βραχύ τι παρ'
him? Thou madest [3]less [1]him [2]a little than

and the heavens are the
work of your hands.
11 They will perish, but you
remain;
they will all wear out
like a garment.
12 You will roll them up
like a robe;
like a garment they will
be changed.
But you remain the
same,
and your years will
never end."[g]
13 To which of the angels
did God ever say,

"Sit at my right hand
until I make your
enemies
a footstool for your
feet"[h]?

14 Are not all angels ministering spirits sent to serve
those who will inherit salvation?

Chapter 2

Warning to Pay Attention

WE must pay more
careful attention,
therefore, to what we have
heard, so that we do not
drift away. 2 For if the message spoken by angels was
binding, and every viola-
tion and disobedience re-
ceived its just punishment,
3 how shall we escape if we
ignore such a great salvation? This salvation, which
was first announced by the
Lord, was confirmed to us
by those who heard him.
4 God also testified to it by
signs, wonders and various
miracles, and gifts of the
Holy Spirit distributed according to his will.

Jesus Made Like His Brothers

5 It is not to angels that he
has subjected the world to
come, about which we are
speaking. 6 But there is a
place where someone has
testified:

"What is man that you
are mindful of him,
the son of man that you
care for him?
7 You made him a little[i]
lower than the
angels;

[g] *12* Psalm 102:25-27
[h] *13* Psalm 110:1
[i] *7* Or *him for a little while*; also in verse 9

you have crowned
them with glory
and honor,[k]
8 subjecting all things
under
their feet."
Now in subjecting all things
to them, God[g] left nothing
outside their control. As it
is, we do not yet see everything in subjection to them,
9 but we do see Jesus, who
for a little while was made
lower[l] than the angels,
now crowned with glory
and honor because of the
suffering of death, so that
by the grace of God[m] he
might taste death for everyone.
10 It was fitting that
God,[n] for whom and
through whom all things
exist, in bringing many
children to glory, should
make the pioneer of their
salvation perfect through
sufferings. 11 For the one
who sanctifies and those
who are sanctified all have
one Father.[o] For this reason Jesus[n] is not ashamed
to call them brothers and
sisters,[p] 12 saying,
"I will proclaim your
name to my
brothers and
sisters,[p]
in the midst of the
congregation I
will praise you."
13 And again,
"I will put my trust in
him."
And again,
"Here am I and the
children whom
God has given
me."
14 Since, therefore, the
children share flesh and
blood, he himself likewise
shared the same things, so
that through death he might
destroy the one who has
the power of death, that is,
the devil, 15 and free those
who all their lives were
held in slavery by the fear
of death. 16 For it is clear

[k] Other ancient authorities add *and set them over the works of your hands*
[l] Or *who was made a little lower*
[m] Other ancient authorities read *apart from God*
[n] Gk *he*
[o] Gk *are all of one*
[p] Gk *brothers*

ἀγγέλους, δόξῃ καὶ τιμῇ ἐστεφάνωσας
angels, with glory and *with* honour thou crownedst
αὐτόν, 8 πάντα ὑπέταξας ὑποκάτω τῶν
him, all things thou subjectedst underneath the
ποδῶν αὐτοῦ. ἐν τῷ γὰρ ὑποτάξαι
feet of him. [1]in *the* For [2]*to* subject[ing]
[αὐτῷ] τὰ πάντα οὐδὲν ἀφῆκεν αὐτῷ
[4]to him – [3]all things [6]nothing [5]he left [8]to him
ἀνυπότακτον. Νῦν δὲ οὔπω ὁρῶμεν
[7]unsubjected. But now not yet we see
αὐτῷ τὰ πάντα ὑποτεταγμένα· 9 τὸν δὲ
[3]to him – [1]all things [2]having been subjected; [3]the [one] [1]but
βραχύ τι παρ' ἀγγέλους ἠλαττωμένον
[5]a little [6]than [7]angels [4]having been made less
βλέπομεν Ἰησοῦν διὰ τὸ πάθημα τοῦ
[2]we see [8]Jesus because of the suffering –
θανάτου δόξῃ καὶ τιμῇ ἐστεφανωμένον,
of death with glory and *with* honour having been crowned,
ὅπως χάριτι θεοῦ ὑπὲρ παντὸς γεύσηται
so as by [the] grace of God [3]on behalf of [4]every man [1]he might taste
θανάτου. 10 Ἔπρεπεν γὰρ αὐτῷ, δι'
of [2]death. For it was fitting for him, because of
ὃν τὰ πάντα καὶ δι' οὗ τὰ πάντα,
whom – all things and through whom – all things,
πολλοὺς υἱοὺς εἰς δόξαν ἀγαγόντα τὸν
[10]many [11]sons [12]to [13]glory [9]leading [4]the
ἀρχηγὸν τῆς σωτηρίας αὐτῶν διὰ
[5]author [6]of the [7]salvation [8]of them [2]through
παθημάτων τελειῶσαι. 11 ὅ τε γὰρ
[3]sufferings [1]to perfect. [2]the [one] [3]both [1]For
ἁγιάζων καὶ οἱ ἁγιαζόμενοι ἐξ ἑνὸς
sanctifying and the [ones] being sanctified [are] [2]of [3]one
πάντες· δι' ἣν αἰτίαν οὐκ ἐπαισχύνεται
[1]all; for which cause he is not ashamed
ἀδελφοὺς αὐτοὺς καλεῖν, 12 λέγων· ἀπαγ-
[3]brothers [2]them [1]to call, saying: I will
γελῶ τὸ ὄνομά σου τοῖς ἀδελφοῖς μου,
announce the name of thee to the brothers of me,
ἐν μέσῳ ἐκκλησίας ὑμνήσω σε· 13 καὶ
in [the] midst of [the] church I will hymn thee; and
πάλιν· ἐγὼ ἔσομαι πεποιθὼς ἐπ' αὐτῷ·
again: I will be having trusted on(in) him;
καὶ πάλιν· ἰδοὺ ἐγὼ καὶ τὰ παιδία
and again: Behold[,] I and the children
ἅ μοι ἔδωκεν ὁ θεός. 14 Ἐπεὶ οὖν
whom [3]to me [2]gave – [1]God. Since therefore
τὰ παιδία κεκοινώνηκεν αἵματος καὶ
the children has(ve) partaken of blood and
σαρκός, καὶ αὐτὸς παραπλησίως μετέσχεν
of flesh, [2]also [3][him]self [4]in like manner [1]he shared
τῶν αὐτῶν, ἵνα διὰ τοῦ θανάτου
the same things, in order that through the(?his) death
καταργήσῃ τὸν τὸ κράτος ἔχοντα τοῦ
he might destroy [1]the [one] [3]the [4]might [2]having –
θανάτου, τοῦτ' ἔστιν τὸν διάβολον, 15 καὶ
of death, this is the devil, and
ἀπαλλάξῃ τούτους, ὅσοι φόβῳ θανάτου
release these, as many as by fear of death
διὰ παντὸς τοῦ ζῆν ἔνοχοι ἦσαν δουλείας.
through all the(ir) [time] to live [2]involved in [1]were slavery.

you crowned him with
glory and honor
8 and put everything
under his feet."[j]
In putting everything under
him, God left nothing that
is not subject to him. Yet at
present we do not see ev-
erything subject to him.
9 But we see Jesus, who was
made a little lower than the
angels, now crowned with
glory and honor because he
suffered death, so that by
the grace of God he might
taste death for everyone.
10 In bringing many sons
to glory, it was fitting that
God, for whom and
through whom everything
exists, should make the author of their salvation perfect through suffering.
11 Both the one who makes
men holy and those who
are made holy are of the
same family. So Jesus is
not ashamed to call them
brothers. 12 He says,
"I will declare your
name to my
brothers;
in the presence of the
congregation I will
sing your praises."[k]
13 And again,
"I will put my trust in
him."[l]
And again he says,
"Here am I, and the
children God has
given me."[m]
14 Since the children have
flesh and blood, he too
shared in their humanity so
that by his death he might
destroy him who holds the
power of death—that is,
the devil— 15 and free those
who all their lives were
held in slavery by their fear

[j] *8* Psalm 8:4-6
[k] *12* Psalm 22:22
[l] *13* Isaiah 8:17
[m] *13* Isaiah 8:18

that he did not come to help
angels, but the descendants
of Abraham. 17 Therefore
he had to become like his
brothers and sisters[p] in every respect, so that he
might be a merciful and
faithful high priest in the
service of God, to make a
sacrifice of atonement for
the sins of the people.
18 Because he himself was
tested by what he suffered,
he is able to help those who
are being tested.

Chapter 3

Moses a Servant, Christ a Son

THEREFORE, brothers
and sisters,[p] holy
partners in a heavenly calling, consider that Jesus,
the apostle and high priest
of our confession, 2 was
faithful to the one who appointed him, just as Moses
also "was faithful in all[q]
God's[r] house." 3 Yet
Jesus[s] is worthy of more
glory than Moses, just as
the builder of a house has
more honor than the house
itself. 4 (For every house is
built by someone, but the
builder of all things is God.)
5 Now Moses was faithful
in all God's[r] house as a
servant, to testify to the
things that would be spo-
ken later. 6 Christ, however, was faithful over
God's[r] house as a son, and
we are his house if we hold
firm[t] the confidence and
the pride that belong to
hope.

Warning against Unbelief

7 Therefore, as the
Holy Spirit says,
"Today, if you hear
his voice,
8 do not harden your
hearts as in
the rebellion,

[q] Other ancient authorities lack *all*
[r] Gk *his*
[s] Gk *this one*
[t] Other ancient authorities add *to the end*

16 οὐ γὰρ δήπου ἀγγέλων ἐπιλαμβάνεται,
[4]not [1]For [2]of course [5]of angels [3]he takes hold,

ἀλλὰ σπέρματος Ἀβραὰμ ἐπιλαμβάνεται.
but of [the] seed of Abraham he takes hold.

17 ὅθεν ὤφειλεν κατὰ πάντα τοῖς ἀδελφοῖς
Whence he owed (ought) by all means† [2]*to* the (his) [3]brothers

ὁμοιωθῆναι, ἵνα ἐλεήμων γένηται καὶ
[1]to become like, in order that [2]a merciful [1]he might become and

πιστὸς ἀρχιερεὺς τὰ πρὸς τὸν θεόν,
faithful high priest [in] the things in regard to – God,

εἰς τὸ ἱλάσκεσθαι τὰς ἁμαρτίας τοῦ
for the to make propitiation for the sins of the

λαοῦ. 18 ἐν ᾧ γὰρ πέπονθεν αὐτὸς
people. [2]in [3]what [way] [1]For [5]has suffered [4]he

πειρασθείς, δύναται τοῖς πειραζομένοις
being tempted, he is able [2]the [ones] [3]being tempted

βοηθῆσαι.
[1]to help.

3 Ὅθεν, ἀδελφοὶ ἅγιοι, κλήσεως
Whence, brothers holy, [3]calling

ἐπουρανίου μέτοχοι, κατανοήσατε τὸν
[2]of a heavenly [1]sharers, consider the

ἀπόστολον καὶ ἀρχιερέα τῆς ὁμολογίας
apostle and high priest of the confession

ἡμῶν Ἰησοῦν, 2 πιστὸν ὄντα τῷ ποιήσαντι
of us[,] Jesus, faithful being to the [one] making

αὐτόν, ὡς καὶ Μωϋσῆς ἐν [ὅλῳ] τῷ
him, as also Moses in all the

οἴκῳ αὐτοῦ. 3 πλείονος γὰρ οὗτος δόξης
household of him. For [3]of more [1]this one [4]glory

παρὰ Μωϋσῆν ἠξίωται καθ' ὅσον πλείονα
[5]than [6]Moses [2]has been counted worthy by so much as [8]more

τιμὴν ἔχει τοῦ οἴκου ὁ κατασκευάσας
[9]honour [4]has [7][than] [8]the [9]house [1]the [one] [2]having prepared

αὐτόν. 4 πᾶς γὰρ οἶκος κατασκευάζεται
[3]it. For every house is prepared

ὑπό τινος, ὁ δὲ πάντα κατασκευάσας
by someone, but [1]the [one] [3]all things [2]having prepared

θεός. 5 καὶ Μωϋσῆς μὲν πιστὸς ἐν
[is] God. And Moses on one hand faithful [was] in

ὅλῳ τῷ οἴκῳ αὐτοῦ ὡς θεράπων εἰς
all the household of him as a servant for

μαρτύριον τῶν λαληθησομένων, 6 Χριστὸς
a testimony of the things being spoken [in the future], Christ

δὲ ὡς υἱὸς ἐπὶ τὸν οἶκον αὐτοῦ· οὗ
on the other as a Son over the household of him; of whom

οἶκός ἐσμεν ἡμεῖς, ἐὰν τὴν παρρησίαν
a household are we, if [2]the [3]confidence

καὶ τὸ καύχημα τῆς ἐλπίδος [μέχρι
[4]and [5]the [6]boast [7]of the [8]hope [10]until

τέλους βεβαίαν] κατάσχωμεν. 7 Διό,
[11][the] end [9]firm [1]we hold fast. Wherefore,

καθὼς λέγει τὸ πνεῦμα τὸ ἅγιον· σήμερον
as says the Spirit – Holy: To-day

ἐὰν τῆς φωνῆς αὐτοῦ ἀκούσητε, 8 μὴ
if the voice of him ye hear, not

σκληρύνητε τὰς καρδίας ὑμῶν ὡς ἐν
harden ye the hearts of you as in

of death. 16 For surely it is
not angels he helps, but
Abraham's descendants.
17 For this reason he had to
be made like his brothers in
every way, in order that he
might become a merciful
and faithful high priest in
service to God, and that he
might make atonement
for[n] the sins of the people.
18 Because he himself suffered when he was tempt-
ed, he is able to help those
who are being tempted.

Chapter 3

Jesus Greater Than Moses

THEREFORE, holy
brothers, who share in
the heavenly calling, fix
your thoughts on Jesus, the
apostle and high priest
whom we confess. 2 He was
faithful to the one who appointed him, just as Moses
was faithful in all God's
house. 3 Jesus has been
found worthy of greater
honor than Moses, just as
the builder of a house has
greater honor than the
house itself. 4 For every
house is built by someone,
but God is the builder of everything. 5 Moses was faithful as a servant in all God's
house, testifying to what
would be said in the future.
6 But Christ is faithful as a
son over God's house. And
we are his house, if we hold
on to our courage and the
hope of which we boast.

Warning Against Unbelief

7 So, as the Holy Spirit
says:

"Today, if you hear his
voice,
8 do not harden your
hearts
as you did in the
rebellion,

[n] 17 Or *and that he might turn aside God's wrath, taking away*

as on the day of
testing in the
wilderness,
9 where your ancestors
put me to
the test,
though they had
seen my works
10for forty
years.
Therefore I was angry
with that
generation,
and I said, 'They
always go astray
in their hearts,
and they have not
known
my ways.'
11 As in my anger I
swore,
'They will not enter
my rest.' "
12Take care, brothers and
sisters,[p] that none of you
may have an evil, unbelieving heart that turns away
from the living God. 13But
exhort one another every
day, as long as it is called
"today," so that none of
you may be hardened by
the deceitfulness of sin.
14For we have become
partners of Christ, if only
we hold our first confi-
dence firm to the end. 15As
it is said,

"Today, if you hear
his voice,
do not harden your
hearts as in
the rebellion."

16Now who were they who
heard and yet were rebel-
lious? Was it not all those
who left Egypt under the
leadership of Moses? 17But
with whom was he angry
forty years? Was it not
those who sinned, whose
bodies fell in the wilderness? 18And to whom did
he swear that they would
not enter his rest, if not to
those who were disobedi-
ent? 19So we see that they
were unable to enter be-
cause of unbelief.

τῷ παραπικρασμῷ κατὰ τὴν ἡμέραν τοῦ
the provocation in the day of the
πειρασμοῦ ἐν τῇ ἐρήμῳ, **9** οὗ ἐπείρασαν
temptation in the desert, when [4]tempted
οἱ πατέρες ὑμῶν ἐν δοκιμασίᾳ καὶ εἶδον
[1]the [2]fathers [3]of you in proving and saw
τὰ ἔργα μου τεσσεράκοντα ἔτη· **10** διὸ
the works of me forty years; wherefore
προσώχθισα τῇ γενεᾷ ταύτῃ καὶ εἶπον·
I was angry with this generation and I said:
ἀεὶ πλανῶνται τῇ καρδίᾳ· αὐτοὶ δὲ
Always they err in the heart; and they
οὐκ ἔγνωσαν τὰς ὁδούς μου, **11** ὡς
knew not the ways of me, as
ὤμοσα ἐν τῇ ὀργῇ μου· εἰ εἰσελεύσονται
I swore in the wrath of me: If they shall enter
εἰς τὴν κατάπαυσίν μου. **12** Βλέπετε,
into the rest of me. Look ye,
ἀδελφοί, μήποτε ἔσται ἔν τινι ὑμῶν
brothers, lest there shall be in anyone of you
καρδία πονηρὰ ἀπιστίας ἐν τῷ ἀποστῆναι
[2]heart [1]an evil of unbelief in *the* *to* depart[ing]
ἀπὸ θεοῦ ζῶντος, **13** ἀλλὰ παρακαλεῖτε
from God a living, but exhort
ἑαυτοὺς καθ' ἑκάστην ἡμέραν, ἄχρις οὗ
yourselves – each day, while
τὸ σήμερον καλεῖται, ἵνα μὴ σκληρυνθῇ
the to-day it is being called, lest [4]be hardened
τις ἐξ ὑμῶν ἀπάτῃ τῆς ἁμαρτίας· **14** μέτ-
[1]anyone [2]of [3]you by [the] deceit – of sin; [2]shar-
οχοι γὰρ τοῦ Χριστοῦ γεγόναμεν, ἐάνπερ
ers [1]for [4]of the [5]Christ [3]we have become, if indeed
τὴν ἀρχὴν τῆς ὑποστάσεως μέχρι τέλους
[3]the [4]beginning [5]of the [6]assurance [7]until [8][the] end
βεβαίαν κατάσχωμεν. **15** ἐν τῷ λέγεσθαι·
[2]firm [1]we hold fast. In the to be said•: =While it is said:
σήμερον ἐὰν τῆς φωνῆς αὐτοῦ ἀκούσητε,
To-day if the voice of him ye hear,
μὴ σκληρύνητε τὰς καρδίας ὑμῶν ὡς
do not harden the hearts of you as
ἐν τῷ παραπικρασμῷ. **16** τίνες γὰρ
in the provocation. For some
ἀκούσαντες παρεπίκραναν; ἀλλ' οὐ πάντες
hearing provoked? yet not all
οἱ ἐξελθόντες ἐξ Αἰγύπτου διὰ
the [ones] coming *out* out of Egypt through
Μωϋσέως; **17** τίσιν δὲ προσώχθισεν τεσ-
Moses? but with whom was he angry for-
σεράκοντα ἔτη; οὐχὶ τοῖς ἁμαρτήσασιν,
ty years? [was it] not with the [ones] sinning,
ὧν τὰ κῶλα ἔπεσεν ἐν τῇ ἐρήμῳ;
of whom the corpses fell in the desert?
18 τίσιν δὲ ὤμοσεν μὴ εἰσελεύσεσθαι εἰς
and to whom swore he not to enter into
τὴν κατάπαυσιν αὐτοῦ εἰ μὴ τοῖς
the rest of him except to the
ἀπειθήσασιν; **19** καὶ βλέπομεν ὅτι οὐκ
[ones] disobeying? and we see that not
ἠδυνήθησαν εἰσελθεῖν δι' ἀπιστίαν.
they were able to enter because of disbelief.

during the time of
testing in the desert,
9where your fathers
tested and tried me
and for forty years saw
what I did.
10That is why I was angry
with that generation,
and I said, 'Their
hearts are always
going astray,
and they have not
known my ways.'
11So I declared on oath in
my anger,
'They shall never enter
my rest.' "[o]

12See to it, brothers, that
none of you has a sinful,
unbelieving heart that turns
away from the living God.
13But encourage one another daily, as long as it is
called Today, so that none
of you may be hardened by
sin's deceitfulness. 14We
have come to share in
Christ if we hold firmly till
the end the confidence we
had at first. 15As has just
been said:

"Today, if you hear his
voice,
do not harden your
hearts
as you did in the
rebellion."[p]

16Who were they who
heard and rebelled? Were
they not all those Moses led
out of Egypt? 17And with
whom was he angry for forty years? Was it not with
those who sinned, whose
bodies fell in the desert?
18And to whom did God
swear that they would never enter his rest if not to
those who disobeyed[q]?
19So we see that they were
not able to enter, because
of their unbelief.

[o] *11* Psalm 95:7-11
[p] *15,7* Psalm 95:7,8
[q] *18* Or *disbelieved*

Chapter 4

The Rest That God Promised

THEREFORE, while
the promise of enter-
ing his rest is still open, let
us take care that none of
you should seem to have
failed to reach it. 2 For indeed the good news came
to us just as to them; but
the message they heard did
not benefit them, because
they were not united by
faith with those who lis-
tened.[u] 3 For we who have
believed enter that rest,
just as God[v] has said,

"As in my anger I
swore,
'They shall not enter
my rest,'"

though his works were finished at the foundation of
the world. 4 For in one
place it speaks about the
seventh day as follows,
"And God rested on the
seventh day from all his
works." 5 And again in this
place it says, "They shall
not enter my rest." 6 Since
therefore it remains open
for some to enter it, and
those who formerly re-
ceived the good news failed
to enter because of disobedience, 7 again he sets a certain day—"today"—
saying through David much
later, in the words already
quoted,

"Today, if you hear
his voice,
do not harden your
hearts."

8 For if Joshua had given
them rest, God[v] would not
speak later about another
day. 9 So then, a sabbath
rest still remains for the
people of God; 10 for those
who enter God's rest also
cease from their labors as
God did from his. 11 Let us

[u] Other ancient authorities read *it did not meet with faith in those who listened*
[v] Gk *he*

---

4 Φοβηθῶμεν οὖν μήποτε καταλειπομένης
Let us fear therefore lest 2being left
ἐπαγγελίας εἰσελθεῖν εἰς τὴν κατάπαυσιν
1a promise to enter into the rest
αὐτοῦ δοκῇ τις ἐξ ὑμῶν ὑστερηκέναι.
of him 4seems 1anyone 2of 3you to have come short.
2 καὶ γὰρ ἐσμεν εὐηγγελισμένοι καθάπερ
For indeed we are having had good news preached [to us] even as
κἀκεῖνοι· ἀλλ' οὐκ ὠφέλησεν ὁ λόγος
those also; but 4did not profit 1the 2word
τῆς ἀκοῆς ἐκείνους μὴ συγκεκερασμένος
– 3of hearing those not having been mixed together
τῇ πίστει τοῖς ἀκούσασιν. **3** Εἰσερχόμεθα
– with faith in the [ones] hearing. we enter
γὰρ εἰς [τὴν] κατάπαυσιν οἱ πιστεύσαντες,
For into the rest the [ones] believing,
καθὼς εἴρηκεν· ὡς ὤμοσα ἐν τῇ ὀργῇ
as he has said: As I swore in the wrath
μου· εἰ εἰσελεύσονται εἰς τὴν κατάπαυσίν
of me: If they shall enter into the rest
μου, καίτοι τῶν ἔργων ἀπὸ καταβολῆς
of me, though the works 2from 3[the] foundation
κόσμου γενηθέντων. **4** εἴρηκεν γάρ που
4of [the] world 1having come into being. For he has said somewhere
περὶ τῆς ἑβδόμης οὕτως· καὶ κατέπαυσεν
concerning the seventh [day] thus: And 2rested
ὁ θεὸς ἐν τῇ ἡμέρᾳ τῇ ἑβδόμῃ ἀπὸ
– 1God in the 2day – 1seventh from
πάντων τῶν ἔργων αὐτοῦ· **5** καὶ ἐν
all the works of him; and in
τούτῳ πάλιν· εἰ εἰσελεύσονται εἰς τὴν
this [place] again: If they shall enter into the
κατάπαυσίν μου. **6** ἐπεὶ οὖν ἀπολείπεται
rest of me. Since therefore it remains
τινὰς εἰσελθεῖν εἰς αὐτήν, καὶ οἱ πρότερον
[for] some to enter into it, and the [ones] formerly
εὐαγγελισθέντες οὐκ εἰσῆλθον δι' ἀπείθειαν,
having good news preached [to them] did not enter because of disobedience,
7 πάλιν τινὰ ὁρίζει ἡμέραν, σήμερον, ἐν
again 2a certain 1he defines day, to-day, 3in
Δαυὶδ λέγων μετὰ τοσοῦτον χρόνον, καθὼς
4David 1saying after such a time, as
προείρηται· σήμερον ἐὰν τῆς φωνῆς αὐτοῦ
he has previously said: To-day if the voice of him
ἀκούσητε, μὴ σκληρύνητε τὰς καρδίας
ye hear, do not harden the hearts
ὑμῶν. **8** εἰ γὰρ αὐτοὺς Ἰησοῦς κατέπαυσεν,
of you. For if 3them 1Jesus(Joshua) 2rested,
οὐκ ἂν περὶ ἄλλης ἐλάλει μετὰ ταῦτα
3not – 5concerning 6another 1he 2would 4have spoken 8after 9these things
ἡμέρας. **9** ἄρα ἀπολείπεται σαββατισμὸς
7day. Then 2remains 1a sabbath rest
τῷ λαῷ τοῦ θεοῦ. **10** ὁ γὰρ εἰσελθὼν
to the people – of God. For the [one] having entered
εἰς τὴν κατάπαυσιν αὐτοῦ καὶ αὐτὸς
into the rest of him also [him]self
κατέπαυσεν ἀπὸ τῶν ἔργων αὐτοῦ,
rested from the works of him,
ὥσπερ ἀπὸ τῶν ἰδίων ὁ θεός. **11** Σπου-
as from the(his) own – God [did]. Let us

Chapter 4

A Sabbath-Rest for the People of God

THEREFORE, since the
promise of entering his
rest still stands, let us be
careful that none of you be
found to have fallen short
of it. 2 For we also have had
the gospel preached to us,
just as they did; but the
message they heard was of
no value to them, because
those who heard did not
combine it with faith.[r]
3 Now we who have be-
lieved enter that rest, just
as God has said,

"So I declared on oath
in my anger,
'They shall never enter
my rest.'"[s]

And yet his work has been
finished since the creation
of the world. 4 For some-
where he has spoken about
the seventh day in these
words: "And on the sev-
enth day God rested from
all his work."[t] 5 And again
in the passage above he
says, "They shall never enter my rest."
6 It still remains that some
will enter that rest, and
those who formerly had the
gospel preached to them
did not go in, because of
their disobedience. 7 Therefore God again set a certain
day, calling it Today, when
a long time later he spoke
through David, as was said
before:

"Today, if you hear his
voice,
do not harden your
hearts."[p]

8 For if Joshua had given
them rest, God would not
have spoken later about another day. 9 There remains,
then, a Sabbath-rest for the
people of God; 10 for anyone
who enters God's rest also
rests from his own work,
just as God did from his.

[r] 2 Many manuscripts *because they did not share in the faith of those who obeyed*
[s] 3 Psalm 95:11; also in verse 5
[t] 4 Gen. 2:2

therefore make every effort to enter that rest, so that no one may fall through such disobedience as theirs.

12 Indeed, the word of God is living and active, sharper than any two-edged sword, piercing until it divides soul from spirit, joints from marrow; it is able to judge the thoughts and intentions of the heart. 13 And before him no creature is hidden, but all are naked and laid bare to the eyes of the one to whom we must render an account.

Jesus the Great High Priest

14 Since, then, we have a great high priest who has passed through the heavens, Jesus, the Son of God, let us hold fast to our confession. 15 For we do not have a high priest who is unable to sympathize with our weaknesses, but we have one who in every respect has been tested[w] as we are, yet without sin. 16 Let us therefore approach the throne of grace with boldness, so that we may receive mercy and find grace to help in time of need.

δάσωμεν οὖν εἰσελθεῖν εἰς ἐκείνην τὴν
be eager therefore to enter into that –

κατάπαυσιν, ἵνα μή ἐν τῷ αὐτῷ τις
rest, lest [3]in [4]the [5]same [1]anyone

ὑποδείγματι πέσῃ τῆς ἀπειθείας. **12** Ζῶν
[6]example [2]falls – of disobedience. [[4]is] [5]living

γὰρ ὁ λόγος τοῦ θεοῦ καὶ ἐνεργὴς
For [1]the [2]word – [3]of God and operative

καὶ τομώτερος ὑπὲρ πᾶσαν μάχαιραν
and sharper beyond every [2]sword

δίστομον καὶ διϊκνούμενος ἄχρι μερισμοῦ
[1]two-mouthed (edged) and passing through as far as division

ψυχῆς καὶ πνεύματος, ἁρμῶν τε καὶ
of soul and of spirit, [2]of joints [1]both and

μυελῶν, καὶ κριτικὸς ἐνθυμήσεων καὶ
of marrows, and able to judge of thoughts and

ἐννοιῶν καρδίας· **13** καὶ οὐκ ἔστιν κτίσις
intentions of a heart; and there is no creature

ἀφανὴς ἐνώπιον αὐτοῦ, πάντα δὲ γυμνὰ
unmanifest before him, but all things [are] naked

καὶ τετραχηλισμένα τοῖς ὀφθαλμοῖς αὐτοῦ,
and *having been* laid open to the eyes of him,

πρὸς ὃν ἡμῖν ὁ λόγος.
with whom to us [is] the word(account).° =is our account.

14 Ἔχοντες οὖν ἀρχιερέα μέγαν διεληλυ-
Having therefore high priest a great having gone

θότα τοὺς οὐρανούς, Ἰησοῦν τὸν υἱὸν
through the heavens, Jesus the Son

τοῦ θεοῦ, κρατῶμεν τῆς ὁμολογίας. **15** οὐ
– of God, let us hold the confession. [2]not

γὰρ ἔχομεν ἀρχιερέα μὴ δυνάμενον
[1]For [3]we have a high priest not being able

συμπαθῆσαι ταῖς ἀσθενείαις ἡμῶν, πεπει-
to suffer with the weaknesses of us, [2]having

ρασμένον δὲ κατὰ πάντα καθ' ὁμοιότητα
been tempted [1]but in all respects† according to [our] likeness

χωρὶς ἁμαρτίας. **16** προσερχώμεθα οὖν
apart from sin. Let us approach therefore

μετὰ παρρησίας τῷ θρόνῳ τῆς χάριτος,
with confidence *to* the throne – of grace,

ἵνα λάβωμεν ἔλεος καὶ χάριν εὕρωμεν
in order that we may receive mercy and [2]grace *we* [1]may find

εἰς εὔκαιρον βοήθειαν.
for timely help.

11 Let us, therefore, make every effort to enter that rest, so that no one will fall by following their example of disobedience.

12 For the word of God is living and active. Sharper than any double-edged sword, it penetrates even to dividing soul and spirit, joints and marrow; it judges the thoughts and attitudes of the heart. 13 Nothing in all creation is hidden from God's sight Everything is uncovered and laid bare before the eyes of him to whom we must give account.

Jesus the Great High Priest

14 Therefore, since we have a great high priest who has gone through the heavens,[u] Jesus the Son of God, let us hold firmly to the faith we profess. 15 For we do not have a high priest who is unable to sympathize with our weaknesses, but we have one who has been tempted in every way, just as we are—yet was without sin. 16 Let us then approach the throne of grace with confidence, so that we may receive mercy and find grace to help us in our time of need.

Chapter 5

EVERY high priest chosen from among mortals is put in charge of things pertaining to God on their behalf, to offer gifts and sacrifices for sins. 2 He is able to deal gently with the ignorant and wayward, since he himself is subject to weakness; 3 and because

5 Πᾶς γὰρ ἀρχιερεὺς ἐξ ἀνθρώπων
For every high priest [2]out of [3]men

λαμβανόμενος ὑπὲρ ἀνθρώπων καθίσταται
[1]being taken on behalf of men is appointed [in]

τὰ πρὸς τὸν θεόν, ἵνα προσφέρῃ δῶρά
the things in regard to – God, in order that he may offer [2]gifts

τε καὶ θυσίας ὑπὲρ ἁμαρτιῶν, **2** μετριο-
[1]both and sacrifices on behalf of sins, [2]to feel in

παθεῖν δυνάμενος τοῖς ἀγνοοῦσιν καὶ
due measure [1]being able for the [ones] not knowing and

πλανωμένοις, ἐπεὶ καὶ αὐτὸς περίκειται
being led astray, since also he is set round [with]

Chapter 5

EVERY high priest is selected from among men and is appointed to represent them in matters related to God, to offer gifts and sacrifices for sins. 2 He is able to deal gently with those who are ignorant and are going astray, since he himself is subject to weak-

[w] Or *tempted*

[u] 14 Or *gone into heaven*

of this he must offer sacrifice for his own sins as well
as for those of the people.
4And one does not pre-
sume to take this honor,
but takes it only when
called by God, just as Aaron was.
5 So also Christ did not
glorify himself in becoming
a high priest, but was appointed by the one who
said to him,
"You are my Son,
today I have
begotten you";
6as he says also in another
place,
"You are a priest
forever,
according to the
order of
Melchizedek."
7 In the days of his
flesh, Jesus[y] offered up
prayers and supplications,
with loud cries and tears, to
the one who was able to
save him from death, and
he was heard because of his
reverent submission. 8Al-
though he was a Son, he
learned obedience through
what he suffered; 9and having been made perfect, he
became the source of eternal salvation for all who
obey him, 10having been
designated by God a high
priest according to the order of Melchizedek.

Warning against Falling Away

11 About this[x] we have
much to say that is hard to
explain, since you have become dull in understand-
ing. 12For though by this
time you ought to be teachers, you need someone to
teach you again the basic
elements of the oracles of
God. You need milk, not
solid food; 13for everyone

[x] Or *him*

ἀσθένειαν, 3 καὶ δι' αὐτὴν ὀφείλει, καθὼς
weakness, and because of it he ought, as

περὶ τοῦ λαοῦ, οὕτως καὶ περὶ ἑαυτοῦ
concerning the people, so also concerning himself

προσφέρειν περὶ ἁμαρτιῶν. 4 καὶ οὐχ
to offer concerning sins. And [2]not

ἑαυτῷ τις λαμβάνει τὴν τιμήν, ἀλλὰ
[4]to himself [1]anyone [3]takes the honour, but

καλούμενος ὑπὸ τοῦ θεοῦ, καθώσπερ καὶ
being called by – God, even as indeed

Ἀαρών. 5 Οὕτως καὶ ὁ Χριστὸς οὐχ
Aaron. So also – Christ [2]not

ἑαυτὸν ἐδόξασεν γενηθῆναι ἀρχιερέα, ἀλλ'
[3]himself [1]glorified to become a high priest, but

ὁ λαλήσας πρὸς αὐτόν· υἱός μου εἶ
the [one] speaking to him: Son of me art

σύ, ἐγὼ σήμερον γεγέννηκά σε· 6 καθὼς
thou, I to-day have begotten thee; as

καὶ ἐν ἑτέρῳ λέγει· σὺ ἱερεὺς εἰς τὸν
also in another [psalm] he says: Thou [art] a priest unto the

αἰῶνα κατὰ τὴν τάξιν Μελχισέδεκ. 7 ὃς
age according to the order of Melchisedec. Who

ἐν ταῖς ἡμέραις τῆς σαρκὸς αὐτοῦ δεήσεις
in the days of the flesh of him [3]petitions

τε καὶ ἱκετηρίας πρὸς τὸν δυνάμενον
[2]both [4]and [5]entreaties [11]to [12]the [one] [13]*being* able

σώζειν αὐτὸν ἐκ θανάτου μετὰ κραυγῆς
[14]to save [15]him [16]out of [17]death [6]with [8]crying

ἰσχυρᾶς καὶ δακρύων προσενέγκας καὶ
[7]strong [9]and [10]tears [1]offering and

εἰσακουσθεὶς ἀπὸ τῆς εὐλαβείας, 8 καίπερ
being heard from(for) the(his) devoutness, though

ὢν υἱός, ἔμαθεν ἀφ' ὧν ἔπαθεν τὴν
being a Son, he learned [2]from [3][the] things which [4]he suffered –

ὑπακοήν, 9 καὶ τελειωθεὶς ἐγένετο πᾶσιν
[1]obedience, and being perfected he became to all

τοῖς ὑπακούουσιν αὐτῷ αἴτιος σωτηρίας
the [ones] obeying him [the] cause [2]salvation

αἰωνίου, 10 προσαγορευθεὶς ὑπὸ τοῦ θεοῦ
[1]of eternal, being designated by – God

ἀρχιερεὺς κατὰ τὴν τάξιν Μελχισέδεκ.
a high priest according to the order of Melchisedec.

11 Περὶ οὗ πολὺς ἡμῖν ὁ λόγος καὶ
Concerning whom much to us the [1]word[c] [2]and
=we have much to say and hard . . .

δυσερμήνευτος λέγειν, ἐπεὶ νωθροὶ γεγόνατε
[4]hard to interpret [3]to say, since dull ye have become

ταῖς ἀκοαῖς. 12 καὶ γὰρ ὀφείλοντες
in *the* hearings. For indeed owing*

εἶναι διδάσκαλοι διὰ τὸν χρόνον, πάλιν
to be teachers because of the time, [3]again

χρείαν ἔχετε τοῦ διδάσκειν ὑμᾶς τινα
[2]need [1]ye have – [5]to teach[d] [6]you [4]someone

τὰ στοιχεῖα τῆς ἀρχῆς τῶν λογίων
the rudiments of the beginning of the oracles

τοῦ θεοῦ, καὶ γεγόνατε χρείαν ἔχοντες
– of God, and ye have become [2]need [1]having

γάλακτος, οὐ στερεᾶς τροφῆς. 13 πᾶς
of milk, not of solid food. every

* That is, " ye ought . . . "

God's word all over again.
You need milk, not solid
ness. 3This is why he has to
offer sacrifices for his own
sins, as well as for the sins
of the people.
4No one takes this honor
upon himself; he must be
called by God, just as Aaron was. 5So Christ also did
not take upon himself the
glory of becoming a high
priest. But God said to him,

"You are my Son;
today I have become
your Father."[v][w]

6And he says in another
place,

"You are a priest
forever,
in the order of
Melchizedek."[x]

7During the days of Jesus'
life on earth, he offered up
prayers and petitions with
loud cries and tears to the
one who could save him
from death, and he was
heard because of his reverent submission. 8Although
he was a son, he learned
obedience from what he
suffered 9and, once made
perfect, he became the
source of eternal salvation
for all who obey him 10and
was designated by God to
be high priest in the order
of Melchizedek.

Warning Against Falling Away

11We have much to say
about this, but it is hard to
explain because you are
slow to learn. 12In fact,
though by this time you
ought to be teachers, you
need someone to teach you
the elementary truths of

[v]5 Or *have begotten you*
[w]5 Psalm 2:7
[x]6 Psalm 110:4

who lives on milk, being
still an infant, is unskilled
in the word of righteous-
ness. 14 But solid food is for
the mature, for those
whose faculties have been
trained by practice to distinguish good from evil.

Chapter 6

The Peril of Falling Away

THEREFORE let us go
on toward perfec-
tion,[y] leaving behind the
basic teaching about
Christ, and not laying again
the foundation: repentance
from dead works and faith
toward God, 2 instruction
about baptisms, laying on
of hands, resurrection of
the dead, and eternal judgment. 3 And we will do[z]
this, if God permits. 4 For it
is impossible to restore
again to repentance those
who have once been en-
lightened, and have tasted
the heavenly gift, and have
shared in the Holy Spirit,
5 and have tasted the goodness of the word of God and
the powers of the age to
come, 6 and then have fall-
en away, since on their own
they are crucifying again
the Son of God and are
holding him up to con-
tempt. 7 Ground that drinks
up the rain falling on it repeatedly, and that pro-
duces a crop useful to those
for whom it is cultivated,
receives a blessing from
God. 8 But if it produces
thorns and thistles, it is
worthless and on the verge
of being cursed; its end is to
be burned over.
9 Even though we speak
in this way, beloved, we
are confident of better
things in your case, things
that belong to salvation.
10 For God is not unjust; he

[y] Or *toward maturity*
[z] Other ancient authorities read *let us do*

γὰρ ὁ μετέχων γάλακτος ἄπειρος λόγου
For one partaking of milk [is] without experience of [the] word

δικαιοσύνης, νήπιος γάρ ἐστιν· 14 τελείων δέ
of righteousness, for [2]an infant [1]he is; but [4]of mature men

ἐστιν ἡ στερεὰ τροφή, τῶν διὰ τὴν
[3]is *the* [1]solid [2]food, of the [ones] because of the(ir)

ἕξιν τὰ αἰσθητήρια γεγυμνασμένα ἐχόντων
condition [2]the(ir) [3]faculties *having been* [4]exercised [1]having

πρὸς διάκρισιν καλοῦ τε καὶ κακοῦ.
for distinction [2]of good [1]both and of bad.

6 Διὸ ἀφέντες τὸν τῆς ἀρχῆς τοῦ Χριστοῦ
Wherefore leaving [1]the [3]of the [4]beginning – [5]of Christ

λόγον ἐπὶ τὴν τελειότητα φερώμεθα, μὴ
[2]word [7]on to – [8]maturity [6]let us be borne, not

πάλιν θεμέλιον καταβαλλόμενοι μετανοίας
again [2]a foundation [1]laying down of repentance

ἀπὸ νεκρῶν ἔργων, καὶ πίστεως ἐπὶ
from dead works, and of faith toward

θεόν, 2 βαπτισμῶν διδαχῆς, ἐπιθέσεώς τε
God, [2]of baptisms [1]of teaching, and of laying on

χειρῶν, ἀναστάσεως νεκρῶν, καὶ κρίματος
of hands, of resurrection of dead persons, and [2]judgment

αἰωνίου. 3 καὶ τοῦτο ποιήσομεν, ἐάνπερ
[1]of eternal. And this will we do, if indeed

ἐπιτρέπῃ ὁ θεός. 4 Ἀδύνατον γὰρ τοὺς
[2]permits – [1]God. For [it is] impossible [for] the [ones]

ἅπαξ φωτισθέντας γευσαμένους τε τῆς
once being enlightened and tasting of the

δωρεᾶς τῆς ἐπουρανίου καὶ μετόχους
[2]gift – [1]heavenly and sharers

γενηθέντας πνεύματος ἁγίου 5 καὶ καλὸν
becoming Spirit of [the] Holy and [3][the] good

γευσαμένους θεοῦ ῥῆμα δυνάμεις τε
[1]tasting [4]of God [2]word and powerful deeds

μέλλοντος αἰῶνος, 6 καὶ παραπεσόντας, πάλιν
of a coming age, and falling away, again

ἀνακαινίζειν εἰς μετάνοιαν, ἀνασταυροῦντας
to renew to repentance, crucifying again

ἑαυτοῖς τὸν υἱὸν τοῦ θεοῦ καὶ παρα-
for themselves the Son – of God and putting

δειγματίζοντας. 7 γῆ γὰρ ἡ πιοῦσα
[him] to open shame. For earth – drinking

τὸν ἐπ᾽ αὐτῆς ἐρχόμενον πολλάκις ὑετὸν
[1]the [5]upon [6]it [3]coming [4]often [2]rain

καὶ τίκτουσα βοτάνην εὔθετον ἐκείνοις
and bearing fodder suitable for those

δι᾽ οὓς καὶ γεωργεῖται, μεταλαμβάνει
on account of whom indeed it is farmed, receives

εὐλογίας ἀπὸ τοῦ θεοῦ· 8 ἐκφέρουσα δὲ
blessing from – God; but bringing forth

ἀκάνθας καὶ τριβόλους ἀδόκιμος καὶ
thorns and thistles [it is] disapproved and

κατάρας ἐγγύς, ἧς τὸ τέλος εἰς καῦσιν.
[2]a curse [1]near, of which the end [is] for burning.

9 Πεπείσμεθα δὲ περὶ ὑμῶν, ἀγαπητοί,
But we have been persuaded concerning you, beloved,

τὰ κρείσσονα καὶ ἐχόμενα σωτηρίας, εἰ
the better things and having salvation, if

καὶ οὕτως λαλοῦμεν. 10 οὐ γὰρ ἄδικος
indeed [2]so [1]we speak. For [2]not [3]unjust

food! 13 Anyone who lives
on milk, being still an infant, is not acquainted with
the teaching about right-
eousness. 14 But solid food
is for the mature, who by
constant use have trained
themselves to distinguish
good from evil.

Chapter 6

THEREFORE let us
leave the elementary
teachings about Christ and
go on to maturity, not laying again the foundation of
repentance from acts that
lead to death,[y] and of faith
in God, 2 instruction about
baptisms, the laying on of
hands, the resurrection of
the dead, and eternal judgment. 3 And God permit-
ting, we will do so.
4 It is impossible for those
who have once been en-
lightened, who have tasted
the heavenly gift, who have
shared in the Holy Spirit,
5 who have tasted the goodness of the word of God and
the powers of the coming
age, 6 if they fall away, to be
brought back to repen-
tance, because[z] to their
loss they are crucifying the
Son of God all over again
and subjecting him to public disgrace.
7 Land that drinks in the
rain often falling on it and
that produces a crop useful
to those for whom it is
farmed receives the blessing of God. 8 But land that
produces thorns and this-
tles is worthless and is in
danger of being cursed. In
the end it will be burned.
9 Even though we speak
like this, dear friends, we
are confident of better
things in your case—things
that accompany salvation.
10 God is not unjust; he will

[y] 1 Or *from useless rituals*
[z] 6 Or *repentance while*

will not overlook your
work and the love that you
showed for his sake[a] in
serving the saints, as you
still do. 11 And we want
each one of you to show the
same diligence so as to realize the full assurance of
hope to the very end, 12 so
that you may not become
sluggish, but imitators of
those who through faith
and patience inherit the
promises.

The Certainty of God's Promise

13 When God made a
promise to Abraham, be-
cause he had no one greater
by whom to swear, he
swore by himself, 14 saying,
"I will surely bless you and
multiply you." 15 And thus
Abraham,[b] having patiently endured, obtained the
promise. 16 Human beings,
of course, swear by some-
one greater than them-
selves, and an oath given as
confirmation puts an end to
all dispute. 17 In the same
way, when God desired to
show even more clearly to
the heirs of the promise the
unchangeable character of
his purpose, he guaranteed
it by an oath, 18 so that
through two unchangeable
things, in which it is impossible that God would prove
false, we who have taken
refuge might be strongly
encouraged to seize the
hope set before us. 19 We
have this hope, a sure and
steadfast anchor of the
soul, a hope that enters the
inner shrine behind the curtain, 20 where Jesus, a forerunner on our behalf, has
entered, having become a
high priest forever according to the order of Melchizedek.

[a] Gk *for his name*
[b] Gk *he*

ὁ θεὸς ἐπιλαθέσθαι τοῦ ἔργου ὑμῶν
– [1]God [is] to be forgetful of the work of you
καὶ τῆς ἀγάπης ἧς ἐνεδείξασθε εἰς τὸ
and of the love which ye showed to the
ὄνομα αὐτοῦ, διακονήσαντες τοῖς ἁγίοις
name of him, having ministered to the saints
καὶ διακονοῦντες. 11 ἐπιθυμοῦμεν δὲ
and ministering. But we desire
ἕκαστον ὑμῶν τὴν αὐτὴν ἐνδείκνυσθαι
each one of you [2]the [3]same [1]to show
σπουδὴν πρὸς τὴν πληροφορίαν τῆς ἐλπίδος
eagerness to the full assurance of *the* hope
ἄχρι τέλους, 12 ἵνα μὴ νωθροὶ γένησθε,
unto [the] end, lest dull ye become,
μιμηταὶ δὲ τῶν διὰ πίστεως καὶ μακρο-
but imitators of the [ones] through faith and long-
θυμίας κληρονομούντων τὰς ἐπαγγελίας.
suffering inheriting the promises.
13 Τῷ γὰρ Ἀβραὰμ ἐπαγγειλάμενος ὁ
– For [3]to Abraham [2]making promise –
θεός, ἐπεὶ κατ᾽ οὐδενὸς εἶχεν μείζονος
[1]God, since [2]by [3]no one [1]he had [4]greater
ὀμόσαι, ὤμοσεν καθ᾽ ἑαυτοῦ, 14 λέγων·
to swear, swore by himself, saying:
εἰ μὴν εὐλογῶν εὐλογήσω σε καὶ πληθύνων
If surely blessing I will bless thee and multiplying
πληθυνῶ σε· 15 καὶ οὕτως μακροθυμήσας
I will multiply thee; and so being longsuffering
ἐπέτυχεν τῆς ἐπαγγελίας. 16 ἄνθρωποι γὰρ
he obtained the promise. For men
κατὰ τοῦ μείζονος ὀμνύουσιν, καὶ πάσης
by the greater swear, and [6]of all
αὐτοῖς ἀντιλογίας πέρας εἰς βεβαίωσιν ὁ
[3][is] [4]to them [7]contradiction [5]an end [8]for [9]confirmation [1]the
ὅρκος· 17 ἐν ᾧ περισσότερον βουλόμενος
[2]oath; wherein [3]more abundantly [2]resolving
ὁ θεὸς ἐπιδεῖξαι τοῖς κληρονόμοις τῆς
– [1]God to show to the heirs of the
ἐπαγγελίας τὸ ἀμετάθετον τῆς βουλῆς
promise the unchangeableness of the resolve
αὐτοῦ ἐμεσίτευσεν ὅρκῳ, 18 ἵνα διὰ
of him interposed by an oath, in order that through
δύο πραγμάτων ἀμεταθέτων, ἐν οἷς ἀδύνατον
two [2]things [1]unchangeable, in which [it was] impossible
ψεύσασθαι θεόν, ἰσχυρὰν παράκλησιν ἔχωμεν
[2]to lie [1]God,[b] [2]a strong [3]consolation [1]we may have[,]
οἱ καταφυγόντες κρατῆσαι τῆς προκειμένης
the [ones] having fled to lay hold of the [2]set before [us]
ἐλπίδος· 19 ἣν ὡς ἄγκυραν ἔχομεν τῆς
[1]hope; which as an anchor we have of the
ψυχῆς ἀσφαλῆ τε καὶ βεβαίαν καὶ
soul [2]safe [1]both and firm and
εἰσερχομένην εἰς τὸ ἐσώτερον τοῦ κατα-
entering into the inner [side] of the veil,
πετάσματος, 20 ὅπου πρόδρομος ὑπὲρ ἡμῶν
where a forerunner on behalf of us
εἰσῆλθεν Ἰησοῦς, κατὰ τὴν τάξιν Μελχισέ-
entered[,] Jesus, [6]according to [7]the [8]order [9]of Melchise-
δεκ ἀρχιερεὺς γενόμενος εἰς τὸν αἰῶνα.
dec [5]a high priest [1]becoming [2]unto [3]the [4]age.

not forget your work and
the love you have shown
him as you have helped his
people and continue to help
them. 11 We want each of
you to show this same diligence to the very end, in
order to make your hope
sure. 12 We do not want you
to become lazy, but to imitate those who through
faith and patience inherit
what has been promised.

The Certainty of God's Promise

13 When God made his
promise to Abraham, since
there was no one greater
for him to swear by, he
swore by himself, 14 saying,
"I will surely bless you and
give you many descend-
ants."[a] 15 And so after
waiting patiently, Abraham
received what was prom-
ised.

16 Men swear by someone
greater than themselves,
and the oath confirms what
is said and puts an end to all
argument. 17 Because God
wanted to make the un-
changing nature of his purpose very clear to the heirs
of what was promised, he
confirmed it with an oath.
18 God did this so that, by
two unchangeable things in
which it is impossible for
God to lie, we who have
fled to take hold of the hope
offered to us may be greatly
encouraged. 19 We have this
hope as an anchor for the
soul, firm and secure. It enters the inner sanctuary behind the curtain, 20 where
Jesus, who went before us,
has entered on our behalf.
He has become a high
priest forever, in the order
of Melchizedek.

[a] *14* Gen. 22:17

Chapter 7

The Priestly Order of Melchizedek

THIS "King Melchize-
dek of Salem, priest of
the Most High God, met
Abraham as he was return-
ing from defeating the kings
and blessed him"; 2and to
him Abraham apportioned
"one-tenth of everything."
His name, in the first place,
means "king of righteous-
ness"; next he is also king
of Salem, that is, "king of
peace." 3Without father,
without mother, without
genealogy, having neither
beginning of days nor end
of life, but resembling the
Son of God, he remains a
priest forever.
4 See how great he is!
Even[c] Abraham the patriarch gave him a tenth of the
spoils. 5And those descendants of Levi who receive
the priestly office have a
commandment in the law to
collect tithes[d] from the
people, that is, from their
kindred,[e] though these
also are descended from
Abraham. 6But this man,
who does not belong to
their ancestry, collected
tithes[d] from Abraham and
blessed him who had re-
ceived the promises. 7It is
beyond dispute that the inferior is blessed by the superior. 8In the one case,
tithes are received by those
who are mortal; in the other, by one of whom it is testified that he lives. 9One
might even say that Levi
himself, who receives
tithes, paid tithes through
Abraham, 10for he was still
in the loins of his ancestor

[c] Other ancient authorities lack *Even*
[d] Or *a tenth*
[e] Gk *brothers*

7 Οὗτος γὰρ ὁ Μελχισέδεκ, βασιλεὺς
For this – Melchisedec, king
Σαλήμ, ἱερεὺς τοῦ θεοῦ τοῦ ὑψίστου,
of Salem, priest – 2God 1of the 3most high,
ὁ συναντήσας Ἀβραὰμ ὑποστρέφοντι ἀπὸ
the [one] meeting Abraham returning from
τῆς κοπῆς τῶν βασιλέων καὶ εὐλογήσας
the slaughter of the kings and blessing
αὐτόν, 2 ᾧ καὶ δεκάτην ἀπὸ πάντων
him, to whom indeed 3a tenth 4from 5all
ἐμέρισεν Ἀβραάμ, πρῶτον μὲν ἑρμηνευ-
2divided 1Abraham, firstly on one hand being inter-
όμενος βασιλεὺς δικαιοσύνης, ἔπειτα δὲ καὶ
preted King of righteousness, then on the other also
βασιλεὺς Σαλήμ, ὅ ἐστιν βασιλεὺς εἰρήνης,
King of Salem, which is King of peace,
3 ἀπάτωρ, ἀμήτωρ, ἀγενεαλόγητος, μήτε
without father, without mother, without pedigree, 2neither
ἀρχὴν ἡμερῶν μήτε ζωῆς τέλος ἔχων,
3beginning 4of days 5nor 7of life 6end 1having,
ἀφωμοιωμένος δὲ τῷ υἱῷ τοῦ θεοῦ, μένει
but *having been* made like *to* the Son – of God, remains
ἱερεὺς εἰς τὸ διηνεκές. 4 Θεωρεῖτε δὲ
a priest in *the* perpetuity. Now behold ye
πηλίκος οὗτος, ᾧ δεκάτην Ἀβραὰμ
how great this man [was], to whom 5a tenth 3Abraham
ἔδωκεν ἐκ τῶν ἀκροθινίων ὁ πατριάρχης.
4gave 6of 7the 8spoils 1the 2patriarch.
5 καὶ οἱ μὲν ἐκ τῶν υἱῶν Λευὶ τὴν
And 2the [ones] 1on one hand 3of 4the 5sons 6of Levi 8the
ἱερατείαν λαμβάνοντες ἐντολὴν ἔχουσιν
9priesthood 7receiving 11a commandment 10have
ἀποδεκατοῦν τὸν λαὸν κατὰ τὸν νόμον,
to take tithes from the people according to the law,
τοῦτ' ἔστιν τοὺς ἀδελφοὺς αὐτῶν, καίπερ
this is the brothers of them, though
ἐξεληλυθότας ἐκ τῆς ὀσφύος Ἀβραάμ·
having come forth out of the loin[s] of Abraham;
6 ὁ δὲ μὴ γενεαλογούμενος ἐξ αὐτῶν
2the [one] 1on the other not counting [his] pedigree from them
δεδεκάτωκεν Ἀβραάμ, καὶ τὸν ἔχοντα
has tithed Abraham, and 2the [one] 3having
τὰς ἐπαγγελίας εὐλόγηκεν. 7 χωρὶς δὲ
4the 5promises 1has blessed. And without
πάσης ἀντιλογίας τὸ ἔλαττον ὑπὸ τοῦ
all(any) contradiction the less 2by 3the
κρείττονος εὐλογεῖται. 8 καὶ ὧδε μὲν
4better 1is blessed. And here on one hand
δεκάτας ἀποθνήσκοντες ἄνθρωποι λαμβά-
4tithes 1dying 2men 3re-
νουσιν, ἐκεῖ δὲ μαρτυρούμενος ὅτι ζῇ.
ceive, there on the other being witnessed that he lives.
9 καὶ ὡς ἔπος εἰπεῖν, δι' Ἀβραὰμ
And as a word =so to speak, to say, through Abraham
καὶ Λευὶς ὁ δεκάτας λαμβάνων δεδε-
indeed Levi 1the [one] 3tithes 2receiving has
κάτωται· 10 ἔτι γὰρ ἐν τῇ ὀσφύϊ τοῦ
been tithed; for 2yet 3in 4the 5loin[s] 6of the(his)

Chapter 7

Melchizedek the Priest

THIS Melchizedek was
king of Salem and
priest of God Most High.
He met Abraham returning
from the defeat of the kings
and blessed him, 2and
Abraham gave him a tenth
of everything. First, his
name means "king of righteousness"; then also,
"king of Salem" means
"king of peace." 3Without
father or mother, without
genealogy, without begin-
ning of days or end of life,
like the Son of God he remains a priest forever.
4Just think how great he
was: Even the patriarch
Abraham gave him a tenth
of the plunder! 5Now the
law requires the descend-
ants of Levi who become
priests to collect a tenth
from the people—that is,
their brothers—even
though their brothers are
descended from Abraham.
6This man, however, did
not trace his descent from
Levi, yet he collected a
tenth from Abraham and
blessed him who had the
promises. 7And without
doubt the lesser person is
blessed by the greater. 8In
the one case, the tenth is
collected by men who die;
but in the other case, by
him who is declared to be
living. 9One might even say
that Levi, who collects the
tenth, paid the tenth
through Abraham, 10be-
cause when Melchizedek

when Melchizedek met
him.

Another Priest, Like Melchizedek

11 Now if perfection
had been attainable
through the levitical
priesthood—for the people
received the law under this
priesthood—what further
need would there have
been to speak of another
priest arising according to
the order of Melchizedek,
rather than one according
to the order of Aaron?
12For when there is a
change in the priesthood,
there is necessarily a
change in the law as well.
13Now the one of whom
these things are spoken belonged to another tribe,
from which no one has ever
served at the altar. 14For it
is evident that our Lord
was descended from Judah,
and in connection with that
tribe Moses said nothing
about priests.
15 It is even more obvi-
ous when another priest
arises, resembling Melchizedek, 16one who has be-
come a priest, not through
a legal requirement con-
cerning physical descent,
but through the power of an
indestructible life. 17For it
is attested of him,

"You are a priest
forever,
according to the
order of
Melchizedek."

18There is, on the one
hand, the abrogation of an
earlier commandment be-
cause it was weak and inef-
fectual 19(for the law made
nothing perfect); there is,
on the other hand, the introduction of a better hope,
through which we ap-
proach God.
20 This was confirmed
with an oath; for others
who became priests took
their office without an
oath, 21but this one became
a priest with an oath, be-

πατρὸς ἦν ὅτε συνήντησεν αὐτῷ Μελχισέ-
7father 1he was 8when 10met 11him 9Melchise-

δεκ. 11 Εἰ μὲν οὖν τελείωσις διὰ τῆς
dec. If – therefore perfection 2through 3the

Λευιτικῆς ἱερωσύνης ἦν, ὁ λαὸς γὰρ
4Levitical 5priestly office 1was, 4the 5people 1for

ἐπ' αὐτῆς νενομοθέτηται, τίς ἔτι χρεία
2under* 3it has been furnished with law, why yet need

κατὰ τὴν τάξιν Μελχισέδεκ ἕτερον
[was there for] 4according to 5the 6order 7of Melchisedec 1another

ἀνίστασθαι ἱερέα καὶ οὐ κατὰ τὴν τάξιν
3to arise 2priest and not 2according to 3the 4order

Ἀαρὼν λέγεσθαι; 12 μετατιθεμένης γὰρ
5of Aaron 1to be said(named)? for 3being changed

τῆς ἱερωσύνης ἐξ ἀνάγκης καὶ νόμου
1the 2priestly office3 6of 7necessity 5also 9of law

μετάθεσις γίνεται. 13 ἐφ' ὃν γὰρ λέγεται
8a change 4there occurs. 2[he] 3with respect to 4whom 1For 5is(are) said

ταῦτα, φυλῆς ἑτέρας μετέσχηκεν, ἀφ'
6these things, 3tribe 2of another 1has partaken, from

ἧς οὐδεὶς προσέσχηκεν τῷ θυσιαστηρίῳ·
which no one has devoted himself to the altar;

14 πρόδηλον γὰρ ὅτι ἐξ Ἰούδα ἀνατέταλκεν
for it is perfectly clear that out of Juda has risen

ὁ κύριος ἡμῶν, εἰς ἣν φυλὴν περὶ ἱερέων
the Lord of us, as to which tribe concerning priests

οὐδὲν Μωϋσῆς ἐλάλησεν. 15 καὶ περισ-
3nothing 1Moses 2spoke. And more

σότερον ἔτι κατάδηλόν ἐστιν, εἰ κατὰ
abundantly still quite clear is it, if according to

τὴν ὁμοιότητα Μελχισέδεκ ἀνίσταται ἱερεὺς
the likeness of Melchisedec arises priest

ἕτερος, 16 ὃς οὐ κατὰ νόμον ἐντολῆς
another, who not according to [the] law 2commandment

σαρκίνης γέγονεν ἀλλὰ κατὰ δύναμιν ζωῆς
1of a fleshy has become but according to [the] power life

ἀκαταλύτου. 17 μαρτυρεῖται γὰρ ὅτι σὺ
of an indissoluble. For it is witnessed that Thou

ἱερεὺς εἰς τὸν αἰῶνα κατὰ τὴν τάξιν
a priest unto the age according to the order

Μελχισέδεκ. 18 ἀθέτησις μὲν γὰρ γίνεται
of Melchisedec. 4an annulment 2on one hand 1For 3there comes about

προαγούσης ἐντολῆς διὰ τὸ αὐτῆς ἀσθενὲς
of [the] preceding commandment because of 1the 5of it 2weak[ness]

καὶ ἀνωφελές, 19 οὐδὲν γὰρ ἐτελείωσεν
3and 4unprofitable[ness], for 4nothing 3perfected

ὁ νόμος, ἐπεισαγωγὴ δὲ κρείττονος ἐλπίδος,
1the 2law, 2a bringing in 1on the other of a better hope,

δι' ἧς ἐγγίζομεν τῷ θεῷ. 20 καὶ καθ'
through which we draw near – to God. And in pro-

ὅσον οὐ χωρὶς ὁρκωμοσίας, — οἱ μὲν
portion as not without oath-taking, 3the (they) 2on one hand

γὰρ χωρὶς ὁρκωμοσίας εἰσὶν ἱερεῖς
1for 7without 8oath-taking 4are 6priests

* See note on ch. 9. 15.

met Abraham, Levi was
still in the body of his ancestor.

Jesus Like Melchizedek

11If perfection could have
been attained through the
Levitical priesthood (for on
the basis of it the law was
given to the people), why
was there still need for another priest to come—one
in the order of Melchize-
dek, not in the order of Aaron? 12For when there is a
change of the priesthood,
there must also be a change
of the law. 13He of whom
these things are said be-
longed to a different tribe,
and no one from that tribe
has ever served at the altar.
14For it is clear that our
Lord descended from Ju-
dah, and in regard to that
tribe Moses said nothing
about priests. 15And what
we have said is even more
clear if another priest like
Melchizedek appears,
16one who has become a
priest not on the basis of a
regulation as to his ancestry but on the basis of the
power of an indestructible
life. 17For it is declared:

"You are a priest
forever,
in the order of
Melchizedek."[b]

18The former regulation is
set aside because it was
weak and useless 19(for the
law made nothing perfect),
and a better hope is introduced, by which we draw
near to God.
20And it was not without
an oath! Others became
priests without any oath,

[b] 17,21 Psalm 110:4

cause of the one who said
to him,
"The Lord has sworn
and will not change
his mind,
'You are a priest
forever' "—
22accordingly Jesus has
also become the guarantee
of a better covenant.
23 Furthermore, the
former priests were many
in number, because they
were prevented by death
from continuing in office;
24but he holds his priesthood permanently, be-
cause he continues forever.
25Consequently he is able
for all time to save[f] those
who approach God through
him, since he always lives
to make intercession for
them.
26 For it was fitting that
we should have such a high
priest, holy, blameless, undefiled, separated from sinners, and exalted above the
heavens. 27Unlike the other[g] high priests, he has no
need to offer sacrifices day
after day, first for his own
sins, and then for those of
the people; this he did once
for all when he offered himself. 28For the law appoints
as high priests those who
are subject to weakness,
but the word of the oath,
which came later than the
law, appoints a Son who
has been made perfect forever.

γεγονότες, 21 ὁ δὲ μετὰ ὁρκωμοσίας διὰ
[5]having become, the (he) on the other with oath-taking through

τοῦ λέγοντος πρὸς αὐτόν· ὤμοσεν κύριος,
the [one] saying to him: swore [The] Lord,

καὶ οὐ μεταμεληθήσεται· σὺ ἱερεὺς εἰς
and will not change [his] mind: Thou [art] a priest unto

τὸν αἰῶνα· — 22 κατὰ τοσοῦτο καὶ
the age;) by so much indeed

κρείττονος διαθήκης γέγονεν ἔγγυος Ἰησοῦς.
[4]of a better [5]covenant [2]has become [3]surety [1]Jesus.

23 καὶ οἱ μὲν πλείονές εἰσιν γεγονότες
And the (they) on one hand [3]many [1]are [2]having become

ἱερεῖς διὰ τὸ θανάτῳ κωλύεσθαι παραμέ-
[4]priests because of *the* [2]by death [1]to be prevented [3]to con-
=being prevented by death from continuing;

νειν· 24 ὁ δὲ διὰ τὸ μένειν αὐτὸν εἰς
tinue; the (he) on the other because *the* to remain him[b] unto
=because he remains

τὸν αἰῶνα ἀπαράβατον ἔχει τὴν ἱερωσύνην·
the age [4]intransmissible [1]has [2]the [3]priestly office;

25 ὅθεν καὶ σῴζειν εἰς τὸ παντελὲς
whence indeed [2]to save [3]to [4]the [5]entire
= entirely

δύναται τοὺς προσερχομένους δι' αὐτοῦ
[1]he is able the [ones] [1]approaching [3]through [4]him

τῷ θεῷ, πάντοτε ζῶν εἰς τὸ ἐντυγχάνειν
– [2]*to* God, always living *for* *the* to intercede

ὑπὲρ αὐτῶν. 26 τοιοῦτος γὰρ ἡμῖν καὶ
on behalf of them. For [1]such [4]to us [3]indeed

ἔπρεπεν ἀρχιερεύς, ὅσιος, ἄκακος, ἀμίαντος,
[4]was suitable [2]a high priest, holy, harmless, undefiled,

κεχωρισμένος ἀπὸ τῶν ἁμαρτωλῶν, καὶ
having been separated from – sinners, and

ὑψηλότερος τῶν οὐρανῶν γενόμενος· 27 ὃς
higher [than] the heavens becoming; who

οὐκ ἔχει καθ' ἡμέραν ἀνάγκην, ὥσπερ
has not [2]daily [1]necessity, as

οἱ ἀρχιερεῖς, πρότερον ὑπὲρ τῶν ἰδίων
the high priests, firstly on behalf of the(his) own

ἁμαρτιῶν θυσίας ἀναφέρειν, ἔπειτα τῶν
sins sacrifices to offer up, then the [sins]

τοῦ λαοῦ· τοῦτο γὰρ ἐποίησεν ἐφάπαξ
of the people; for this he did once for all

ἑαυτὸν ἀνενέγκας. 28 ὁ νόμος γὰρ
himself offering up. For the law

ἀνθρώπους καθίστησιν ἀρχιερεῖς ἔχοντας
[2]men [1]appoints [5]high priests [3]having

ἀσθένειαν, ὁ λόγος δὲ τῆς ὁρκωμοσίας
[4]weakness, but the word of the oath-taking

τῆς μετὰ τὸν νόμον υἱὸν εἰς τὸν αἰῶνα
– after the law [appoints] a Son [2]unto [3]the [4]age

τετελειωμένον.
[1]having been perfected.

21but he became a priest
with an oath when God said
to him:
"The Lord has sworn
and will not change his
mind:
'You are a priest
forever.' "[b]
22Because of this oath,
Jesus has become the guarantee of a better covenant.
23Now there have been
many of those priests,
since death prevented them
from continuing in office;
24but because Jesus lives
forever, he has a perma-
nent priesthood. 25There-
fore he is able to save completely[c] those who come to
God through him, because
he always lives to intercede
for them.
26Such a high priest meets
our need—one who is holy,
blameless, pure, set apart
from sinners, exalted
above the heavens. 27Un-
like the other high priests,
he does not need to offer
sacrifices day after day,
first for his own sins, and
then for the sins of the people. He sacrificed for their
sins once for all when he
offered himself. 28For the
law appoints as high priests
men who are weak; but the
oath, which came after the
law, appointed the Son,
who has been made perfect
forever.

Chapter 8

Mediator of a Better Covenant

NOW the main point in what we are saying is this: we have such a high priest, one who is seated at the right hand of the throne of the Majesty in the heav-

8 Κεφάλαιον δὲ ἐπὶ τοῖς λεγομένοις,
Now a summary over(of) the things being said,

τοιοῦτον ἔχομεν ἀρχιερέα, ὃς ἐκάθισεν
[2]such [1]we have a high priest, who sat

ἐν δεξιᾷ τοῦ θρόνου τῆς μεγαλωσύνης
at [the] right of the throne of the greatness

Chapter 8

The High Priest of a New Covenant

THE point of what we are saying is this: We do have such a high priest, who sat down at the right hand of the throne of the Majesty in heaven,
2and

[f] Or *able to save completely*
[g] Gk lacks *other*

[c] 25 Or *forever*

ens, 2a minister in the sanctuary and the true tent[h]
that the Lord, and not any
mortal, has set up. 3For every high priest is appointed
to offer gifts and sacrifices;
hence it is necessary for
this priest also to have
something to offer. 4Now if
he were on earth, he would
not be a priest at all, since
there are priests who offer
gifts according to the law.
5They offer worship in a
sanctuary that is a sketch
and shadow of the heaven-
ly one; for Moses, when he
was about to erect the
tent,[h] was warned, "See
that you make everything
according to the pattern
that was shown you on the
mountain." 6But Jesus[i]
has now obtained a more
excellent ministry, and to
that degree he is the mediator of a better covenant,
which has been enacted
through better promises.
7For if that first covenant
had been faultless, there
would have been no need to
look for a second one.
8 God[j] finds fault with
them when he says:

"The days are surely
coming, says the
Lord,
when I will establish
a new covenant
with the house
of Israel
and with the house
of Judah;
9 not like the covenant
that I made with
their ancestors,
on the day when I
took them by
the hand to lead
them out of the
land of Egypt;
for they did not
continue in
my covenant,
and so I had no
concern for
them, says the
Lord.

[h] Or *tabernacle*
[i] Gk *he*
[j] Gk *He*

ἐν τοῖς οὐρανοῖς, 2 τῶν ἁγίων λειτουργὸς
in *the* heavens, [3]of the [4]holy things [1]a minister

καὶ τῆς σκηνῆς τῆς ἀληθινῆς, ἣν ἔπηξεν
and of the [2]tabernacle – [1]true, which [2]erected

ὁ κύριος, οὐκ ἄνθρωπος. 3 Πᾶς γὰρ
[1]the [2]Lord, not man. For every

ἀρχιερεὺς εἰς τὸ προσφέρειν δῶρά τε
high priest *for* *the* [2]to offer [4]gifts [3]both

καὶ θυσίας καθίσταται· ὅθεν ἀναγκαῖον
[5]and [6]sacrifices [1]is appointed; whence [it is] necessary

ἔχειν τι καὶ τοῦτον ὃ προσενέγκῃ. 4 εἰ
[3]to have [4]something [2]also [1]this [priest] which he may offer. If

μὲν οὖν ἦν ἐπὶ γῆς, οὐδ' ἂν ἦν ἱερεύς,
– therefore he were on earth, he would not be a priest,

ὄντων τῶν προσφερόντων κατὰ νόμον
[there] being the [ones] offering[a] [3]according to [4]law

τὰ δῶρα· 5 οἵτινες ὑποδείγματι καὶ σκιᾷ
[1]the [2]gifts; who [2]an example [3]and [4]a shadow

λατρεύουσιν τῶν ἐπουρανίων, καθὼς
[1]serve of the heavenly things, as

κεχρημάτισται Μωϋσῆς μέλλων ἐπιτελεῖν
[2]has been warned [1]Moses being about to complete

τὴν σκηνήν· ὅρα γάρ φησιν, ποιήσεις
the tabernacle; for See[,] he says, thou shalt make

πάντα κατὰ τὸν τύπον τὸν δειχθέντα
all things according to the pattern – shown

σοι ἐν τῷ ὄρει· 6 νῦν δὲ διαφορωτέρας
to thee in the mount; but now [2]a more excellent

τέτυχεν λειτουργίας, ὅσῳ καὶ κρείττονός
[1]he has obtained ministry, by so much indeed [4]of a better

ἐστιν διαθήκης μεσίτης, ἥτις ἐπὶ κρείττοσιν
[1][as] [2]he is [5]covenant [3]mediator, which [2]on [3]better

ἐπαγγελίαις νενομοθέτηται. 7 εἰ γὰρ ἡ
[4]promises [1]has been enacted. For if –

πρώτη ἐκείνη ἦν ἄμεμπτος, οὐκ ἂν
[2]first [covenant] [1]that was faultless, [2]would not

δευτέρας ἐζητεῖτο τόπος. 8 μεμφόμενος
[4]of(for) a second [3]have been sought [1]place. finding fault [with]

γὰρ αὐτοὺς λέγει· ἰδοὺ ἡμέραι ἔρχονται,
For them he says: Behold[,] days are coming,

λέγει κύριος, καὶ συντελέσω ἐπὶ τὸν
says [the] Lord, and I will effect over the

οἶκον Ἰσραὴλ καὶ ἐπὶ τὸν οἶκον Ἰούδα
household of Israel and over the household of Juda

διαθήκην καινήν, 9 οὐ κατὰ τὴν διαθήκην
covenant a new, not according to the covenant

ἣν ἐποίησα τοῖς πατράσιν αὐτῶν ἐν
which I made with the fathers of them in

ἡμέρᾳ ἐπιλαβομένου μου τῆς χειρὸς αὐτῶν
[the] day taking me[a] =when I took the hand of them

ἐξαγαγεῖν αὐτοὺς ἐκ γῆς Αἰγύπτου, ὅτι
to lead forth them out of [the] land of Egypt, because

αὐτοὶ οὐκ ἐνέμειναν ἐν τῇ διαθήκῃ μου,
they continued not *in* in the covenant of me,

κἀγὼ ἠμέλησα αὐτῶν, λέγει κύριος. 10 ὅτι
and I disregarded them, says [the] Lord. Because

who serves in the sanctu-
ary, the true tabernacle set
up by the Lord, not by
man.
3Every high priest is ap-
pointed to offer both gifts
and sacrifices, and so it was
necessary for this one also
to have something to offer.
4If he were on earth, he
would not be a priest, for
there are already men who
offer the gifts prescribed by
the law. 5They serve at a
sanctuary that is a copy and
shadow of what is in heav-
en. This is why Moses was
warned when he was about
to build the tabernacle:
"See to it that you make
everything according to the
pattern shown you on the
mountain."[d] 6But the ministry Jesus has received is
as superior to theirs as the
covenant of which he is mediator is superior to the old
one, and it is founded on
better promises.
7For if there had been
nothing wrong with that
first covenant, no place
would have been sought for
another. 8But God found
fault with the people and
said[e]:

"The time is coming,
declares the Lord,
when I will make a new
covenant
with the house of Israel
and with the house of
Judah.
9It will not be like the
covenant
I made with their
forefathers
when I took them by the
hand
to lead them out of
Egypt,
because they did not
remain faithful to
my covenant,
and I turned away from
them,
declares the Lord.

[d] 5 Exodus 25:40
[e] 8 Some manuscripts may be translated *fault and said to the people.*

10 This is the covenant that I will make with the house of Israel
after those days, says the Lord:
I will put my laws in their minds,
and write them on their hearts,
and I will be their God,
and they shall be my people.
11 And they shall not teach one another
or say to each other, 'Know the Lord,'
for they shall all know me,
from the least of them to the greatest.
12 For I will be merciful toward their iniquities,
and I will remember their sins no more."
13 In speaking of "a new covenant," he has made the first one obsolete. And what is obsolete and growing old will soon disappear.

αὕτη ἡ διαθήκη ἣν διαθήσομαι τῷ οἴκῳ
this [is] the covenant which I will covenant with the household

Ἰσραὴλ μετὰ τὰς ἡμέρας ἐκείνας, λέγει
of Israel after those days, says

κύριος, διδοὺς νόμους μου εἰς τὴν διάνοιαν
[the] Lord, giving laws of me into the mind

αὐτῶν, καὶ ἐπὶ καρδίας αὐτῶν ἐπιγράψω
of them, and on hearts of them I will inscribe

αὐτούς, καὶ ἔσομαι αὐτοῖς εἰς θεὸν
them, and I will be to them *for* God

καὶ αὐτοὶ ἔσονταί μοι εἰς λαόν. 11 καὶ
and they shall be to me *for* a people. And

οὐ μὴ διδάξωσιν ἕκαστος τὸν πολίτην
by no means may they teach each man the citizen

αὐτοῦ καὶ ἕκαστος τὸν ἀδελφὸν αὐτοῦ,
of him and each man the brother of him,

λέγων· γνῶθι τὸν κύριον, ὅτι πάντες
saying: Know thou the Lord, because all

εἰδήσουσίν με ἀπὸ μικροῦ ἕως μεγάλου
will know me from little to great

αὐτῶν. 12 ὅτι ἵλεως ἔσομαι ταῖς ἀδικίαις
of them. Because merciful I will be to the unrighteousnesses

αὐτῶν, καὶ τῶν ἁμαρτιῶν αὐτῶν οὐ μὴ
of them, and the sins of them by no means

μνησθῶ ἔτι. 13 ἐν τῷ λέγειν καινὴν
I may remember more. In the to say° 'new'
=When he says

πεπαλαίωκεν τὴν πρώτην· τὸ δὲ παλαι-
he has made old the first; and the thing being

ούμενον καὶ γηράσκον ἐγγὺς ἀφανισμοῦ.
made old and growing aged [is] near vanishing.

10 This is the covenant I will make with the house of Israel
after that time, declares the Lord.
I will put my laws in their minds
and write them on their hearts.
I will be their God,
and they will be my people.
11 No longer will a man teach his neighbor,
or a man his brother, saying, 'Know the Lord,'
because they will all know me,
from the least of them to the greatest.
12 For I will forgive their wickedness
and will remember their sins no more."[f]

13 By calling this covenant "new," he has made the first one obsolete; and what is obsolete and aging will soon disappear.

Chapter 9

The Earthly and the Heavenly Sanctuaries

NOW even the first covenant had regulations for worship and an earthly sanctuary. 2 For a tent[h] was constructed, the first one, in which were the lampstand, the table, and the bread of the Presence;[k] this is called the Holy Place. 3 Behind the second curtain was a tent[l] called the Holy of Holies. 4 In it stood the golden altar of incense and the ark of the covenant overlaid on all sides with gold, in which there were a golden urn holding the manna, and Aaron's rod that budded, and the tablets of the covenant; 5 above it were the cherubim of glory overshadowing the mercy seat.[m] Of these things we cannot speak now in detail.

9 Εἶχε μὲν οὖν καὶ ἡ πρώτη δικαι-
[5]had [1]So then [6]both [2]the [3]first [4][covenant] ordin-

ώματα λατρείας τό τε ἅγιον κοσμικόν.
ances of service [9]the [1]and [4]holy place [8]worldly.

2 σκηνὴ γὰρ κατεσκευάσθη ἡ πρώτη,
For a tabernacle was prepared[,] the first,

ἐν ᾗ ἥ τε λυχνία καὶ ἡ τράπεζα καὶ
in which [were] [2]the [1]both lampstand and the table and

ἡ πρόθεσις τῶν ἄρτων, ἥτις λέγεται
the setting forth of the loaves, which is called

Ἅγια· 3 μετὰ δὲ τὸ δεύτερον καταπέτασμα
Holy; and after the second veil

σκηνὴ ἡ λεγομένη Ἅγια Ἁγίων, 4 χρυσοῦν
a tabernacle the [one] *being* called Holy of Holies, [2]a golden

ἔχουσα θυμιατήριον καὶ τὴν κιβωτὸν τῆς
[1]having altar and the ark of the

διαθήκης περικεκαλυμμένην πάντοθεν χρυσίῳ,
covenant *having been* covered round on all sides with gold,

ἐν ᾗ στάμνος χρυσῆ ἔχουσα τὸ μάννα
in which [were] pot a golden having the manna

καὶ ἡ ῥάβδος Ἀαρὼν ἡ βλαστήσασα
and the rod of Aaron – budded

καὶ αἱ πλάκες τῆς διαθήκης, 5 ὑπεράνω
and the tablets of the covenant, [2]above

δὲ αὐτῆς Χερουβὶν δόξης κατασκιάζοντα
[1]and it cherubim of glory overshadowing

τὸ ἱλαστήριον· περὶ ὧν οὐκ ἔστιν νῦν
the mercy-seat; concerning which things there is not [?time] now

Chapter 9

Worship in the Earthly Tabernacle

NOW the first covenant had regulations for worship and also an earthly sanctuary. 2 A tabernacle was set up. In its first room were the lampstand, the table and the consecrated bread; this was called the Holy Place. 3 Behind the second curtain was a room called the Most Holy Place, 4 which had the golden altar of incense and the gold-covered ark of the covenant. This ark contained the gold jar of manna, Aaron's staff that had budded, and the stone tablets of the covenant. 5 Above the ark were the cherubim of the Glory, overshadowing the atonement cover.[g] But we

[k] Gk *the presentation of the loaves*
[l] Or *tabernacle*
[m] Or *the place of atonement*

[f] 12 Jer. 31:31-34
[g] 5 Traditionally *the mercy seat*

6 Such preparations
having been made, the
priests go continually into
the first tent[l] to carry out
their ritual duties; 7 but
only the high priest goes
into the second, and he but
once a year, and not without taking the blood that he
offers for himself and for
the sins committed unin-
tentionally by the people.
8 By this the Holy Spirit indicates that the way into
the sanctuary has not yet
been disclosed as long as
the first tent[l] is still standing. 9 This is a symbol[n] of
the present time, during
which gifts and sacrifices
are offered that cannot perfect the conscience of the
worshiper, 10 but deal only
with food and drink and
various baptisms, regula-
tions for the body imposed
until the time comes to set
things right.
11 But when Christ
came as a high priest of the
good things that have
come,[o] then through the
greater and perfect[p] tent[l]
(not made with hands, that
is, not of this creation),
12 he entered once for all
into the Holy Place, not
with the blood of goats and
calves, but with his own
blood, thus obtaining eternal redemption. 13 For if the
blood of goats and bulls,
with the sprinkling of the
ashes of a heifer, sanctifies
those who have been de-
filed so that their flesh is
purified, 14 how much more
will the blood of Christ,
who through the eternal
Spirit[q] offered himself

[n] Gk *parable*
[o] Other ancient authorities read *good things to come*
[p] Gk *more perfect*
[q] Other ancient authorities read *Holy Spirit*

λέγειν κατὰ μέρος. **6** τούτων δὲ οὕτως
to speak in detail. These things now thus
=Now when these things had

κατεσκευασμένων εἰς μὲν τὴν πρώτην
having been prepared* 8into 1on one 7the 9first
been thus prepared hand

σκηνὴν διὰ παντὸς εἰσίασιν οἱ ἱερεῖς
6tabernacle 4at all times 5go in 2the 3priests

τὰς λατρείας ἐπιτελοῦντες, **7** εἰς δὲ τὴν
11the 12services 10accomplishing, 3into 1on the 5the
other

δευτέραν ἅπαξ τοῦ ἐνιαυτοῦ μόνος ὁ
4second 8once 9of(in) the 10year [goes] 5the
7alone

ἀρχιερεύς, οὐ χωρὶς αἵματος ὃ προσφέρει
6high priest, not without blood which he offers

ὑπὲρ ἑαυτοῦ καὶ τῶν τοῦ λαοῦ ἀγνοημά-
on be- himself and 1the 3of the 4people 2ignor-
half of

των, **8** τοῦτο δηλοῦντος τοῦ πνεύματος
ances, 5this 4showing 1the 3Spirit

τοῦ ἁγίου, μήπω πεφανερῶσθαι τὴν τῶν
– 2Holy,* 5not yet 6to have been 1the 3of the
manifested

ἁγίων ὁδὸν ἔτι τῆς πρώτης σκηνῆς
4holies 2way 10still 7the 8first 9tabernacle

ἐχούσης στάσιν, **9** ἥτις παραβολὴ εἰς τὸν
11having* 12standing, which [was] a parable for the

καιρὸν τὸν ἐνεστηκότα, καθ' ἣν δῶρά
time – present, accord- which 2gifts
ing to

τε καὶ θυσίαι προσφέρονται μὴ δυνάμεναι
1both and sacrifices are being offered not being able

κατὰ συνείδησιν τελειῶσαι τὸν λατρεύοντα,
in respect conscience to perfect the [one] serving,
of

10 μόνον ἐπὶ βρώμασιν καὶ πόμασιν καὶ
only on foods and drinks and

διαφόροις βαπτισμοῖς, δικαιώματα σαρκὸς
various washings, ordinances of flesh

μέχρι καιροῦ διορθώσεως ἐπικείμενα.
2until 3a time 4of amendment 1*being* imposed.

11 Χριστὸς δὲ παραγενόμενος ἀρχιερεὺς
But Christ having appeared a high priest

τῶν γενομένων ἀγαθῶν, διὰ τῆς μείζονος
1of the 3having come 2good things, through the greater
about

καὶ τελειοτέρας σκηνῆς οὐ χειροποιήτου,
and more perfect tabernacle not made by hand,

τοῦτ' ἔστιν οὐ ταύτης τῆς κτίσεως,
this is not of this – creation,

12 οὐδὲ δι' αἵματος τράγων καὶ μόσχων,
nor through blood of goats and *of* calves,

διὰ δὲ τοῦ ἰδίου αἵματος εἰσῆλθεν ἐφάπαξ
but the own blood entered once for
through (his) all

εἰς τὰ ἅγια, αἰωνίαν λύτρωσιν εὑράμενος.
into the holies, eternal redemption having found.

13 εἰ γὰρ τὸ αἷμα τράγων καὶ ταύρων
For if the blood of goats and *of* bulls

καὶ σποδὸς δαμάλεως ῥαντίζουσα τοὺς
and ashes of a heifer sprinkling the [ones]

κεκοινωμένους ἁγιάζει πρὸς τὴν τῆς
having been polluted sanctifies to 1the 3of the

σαρκὸς καθαρότητα, **14** πόσῳ μᾶλλον τὸ
4flesh 2cleanness, by how much more the

αἷμα τοῦ Χριστοῦ, ὃς διὰ πνεύματος
blood – of Christ, who through 3Spirit

cannot discuss these things
in detail now.
6When everything had
been arranged like this, the
priests entered regularly
into the outer room to carry
on their ministry. 7But only
the high priest entered the
inner room, and that only
once a year, and never
without blood, which he offered for himself and for the
sins the people had com-
mitted in ignorance. 8The
Holy Spirit was showing by
this that the way into the
Most Holy Place had not
yet been disclosed as long
as the first tabernacle was
still standing. 9This is an il-
lustration for the present
time, indicating that the
gifts and sacrifices being
offered were not able to
clear the conscience of the
worshiper. 10They are only
a matter of food and drink
and various ceremonial
washings—external regu-
lations applying until the
time of the new order.

The Blood of Christ

11When Christ came as
high priest of the good
things that are already
here,[h] he went through the
greater and more perfect
tabernacle that is not man-
made, that is to say, not a
part of this creation. 12He
did not enter by means of
the blood of goats and
calves; but he entered the
Most Holy Place once for
all by his own blood, having obtained eternal re-
demption. 13The blood of
goats and bulls and the
ashes of a heifer sprinkled
on those who are ceremoni-
ally unclean sanctify them
so that they are outwardly
clean. 14How much more,
then, will the blood of
Christ, who through the
eternal Spirit offered him-

[h] 11 Some early manuscripts *are to come*

without blemish to God,
purify our[r] conscience
from dead works to wor-
ship the living God!
15 For this reason he is
the mediator of a new covenant, so that those who are
called may receive the
promised eternal inheri-
tance, because a death has
occurred that redeems
them from the transgres-
sions under the first covenant.[s] 16 Where a will[s] is
involved, the death of the
one who made it must be
established. 17 For a will[s]
takes effect only at death,
since it is not in force as
long as the one who made it
is alive. 18 Hence not even
the first covenant was inau-
gurated without blood.
19 For when every com-
mandment had been told to
all the people by Moses in
accordance with the law,
he took the blood of calves
and goats,[t] with water and
scarlet wool and hyssop,
and sprinkled both the
scroll itself and all the people, 20 saying, "This is the
blood of the covenant that
God has ordained for you."
21 And in the same way he
sprinkled with the blood
both the tent[u] and all the
vessels used in worship.
22 Indeed, under the law almost everything is purified
with blood, and without the
shedding of blood there is
no forgiveness of sins.

Christ's Sacrifice Takes Away Sin

23 Thus it was neces-
sary for the sketches of the
heavenly things to be purified with these rites, but the

αἰωνίου ἑαυτὸν προσήνεγκεν ἄμωμον τῷ
1[the] eternal 4himself 3offered unblemished –
θεῷ, καθαριεῖ τὴν συνείδησιν ἡμῶν ἀπὸ
to God, will cleanse the conscience of us from
νεκρῶν ἔργων εἰς τὸ λατρεύειν θεῷ
dead works *for* *the* to serve 2God
ζῶντι. 15 Καὶ διὰ τοῦτο διαθήκης καινῆς
1[the] living. And therefore 4covenant 3of a new
μεσίτης ἐστίν, ὅπως θανάτου γενομένου
2mediator 1he is, so as death having occurred[a]
εἰς ἀπολύτρωσιν τῶν ἐπὶ τῇ πρώτῃ
for redemption 1of the 3under* 4the 5first
διαθήκῃ παραβάσεων τὴν ἐπαγγελίαν
6covenant 2transgressions 10the 11promise
λάβωσιν οἱ κεκλημένοι τῆς αἰωνίου
9may receive 7the [ones] 8having been called 12of the 13eternal
κληρονομίας. 16 Ὅπου γὰρ διαθήκη,
14inheritance. For where [there is] a covenant,
θάνατον ἀνάγκη φέρεσθαι τοῦ διαθεμένου·
3[the] death 1[there is] necessity 2to be offered 4of the [one] 5making covenant;
17 διαθήκη γὰρ ἐπὶ νεκροῖς βεβαία, ἐπεὶ
for a covenant over dead [? bodies] [is] firm, since
μήποτε ἰσχύει ὅτε ζῇ ὁ διαθέμενος.
never has it strength when 3lives 1the [one] 2making covenant.
18 ὅθεν οὐδὲ ἡ πρώτη χωρὶς αἵματος
Whence neither the first [covenant] 2without 3blood
ἐγκεκαίνισται. 19 λαληθείσης γὰρ πάσης
1has been dedicated. For 3having been spoken 1every
ἐντολῆς κατὰ τὸν νόμον ὑπὸ Μωϋσέως
2commandment[a] 9according to 10the 11law 4by 5Moses
παντὶ τῷ λαῷ, λαβὼν τὸ αἷμα τῶν
6to all 7the 8people, taking the blood of the
μόσχων καὶ τῶν τράγων μετὰ ὕδατος
calves and of the goats with water
καὶ ἐρίου κοκκίνου καὶ ὑσσώπου, αὐτό
and 2wool 1scarlet and hyssop, 4it[self]
τε τὸ βιβλίον καὶ πάντα τὸν λαὸν
2both 3the 4scroll 6and 7all 8the 9people
ἐρράντισεν, 20 λέγων· τοῦτο τὸ αἷμα τῆς
1he sprinkled, saying: This [is] the blood of the
διαθήκης ἧς ἐνετείλατο πρὸς ὑμᾶς ὁ
covenant which 2enjoined 3to 4you –
θεός. 21 καὶ τὴν σκηνὴν δὲ καὶ πάντα
1God. 2both 3the 4tabernacle 1And and all
τὰ σκεύη τῆς λειτουργίας τῷ αἵματι
the vessels of the service with the blood
ὁμοίως ἐρράντισεν. 22 καὶ σχεδὸν ἐν
likewise he sprinkled. And 4almost 7by
αἵματι πάντα καθαρίζεται κατὰ τὸν νόμον,
8blood 5all things 6is(are) cleansed 1according to 2the 3law,
καὶ χωρὶς αἱματεκχυσίας οὐ γίνεται
and without bloodshedding there becomes no
ἄφεσις. 23 Ἀνάγκη οὖν τὰ μὲν ὑπο-
remission. [There was] necessity therefore 2[for] 3the 1on one hand 4ex-
δείγματα τῶν ἐν τοῖς οὐρανοῖς τούτοις
amples of the things in *the* heavens 2by these

self unblemished to God,
cleanse our consciences
from acts that lead to
death,[i] so that we may
serve the living God!
15 For this reason Christ is
the mediator of a new covenant, that those who are
called may receive the
promised eternal inheri-
tance—now that he has
died as a ransom to set
them free from the sins
committed under the first
covenant.
16 In the case of a will,[j] it
is necessary to prove the
death of the one who made
it, 17 because a will is in
force only when somebody
has died; it never takes effect while the one who
made it is living. 18 This is
why even the first covenant
was not put into effect
without blood. 19 When Moses had proclaimed every
commandment of the law
to all the people, he took
the blood of calves, together with water, scarlet wool
and branches of hyssop,
and sprinkled the scroll and
all the people. 20 He said,
"This is the blood of the
covenant, which God has
commanded you to
keep."[k] 21 In the same
way, he sprinkled with the
blood both the tabernacle
and everything used in its
ceremonies. 22 In fact, the
law requires that nearly everything be cleansed with
blood, and without the
shedding of blood there is
no forgiveness.
23 It was necessary, then,
for the copies of the heavenly things to be purified
with these sacrifices, but

[r] Other ancient authorities read *your*
[s] The Greek word used here means both *covenant* and *will*
[t] Other ancient authorities lack *and goats*

* It may seem strange to translate a preposition which means "on" or "over" by "under"; but ἐπί has the meaning of "during the time of" (see Mark 2. 26; I. Tim. 6. 13).

[i] *14* Or *from useless rituals*
[j] *16* Same Greek word as *covenant*; also in verse 17
[k] *20* Exodus 24:8

heavenly things themselves need better sacrifices than these. 24 For Christ did not enter a sanctuary made by human hands, a mere copy of the true one, but he entered into heaven itself, now to appear in the presence of God on our behalf. 25 Nor was it to offer himself again and again, as the high priest enters the Holy Place year after year with blood that is not his own; 26 for then he would have had to suffer again and again since the foundation of the world. But as it is, he has appeared once for all at the end of the age to remove sin by the sacrifice of himself. 27 And just as it is appointed for mortals to die once, and after that the judgment, 28 so Christ, having been offered once to bear the sins of many, will appear a second time, not to deal with sin, but to save those who are eagerly waiting for him.

καθαρίζεσθαι, αὐτὰ δὲ τὰ ἐπουράνια
[1]to be cleansed, [5][them]-selves [1]on the other [2][for] [3]the [4]heavenly things

κρείττοσιν θυσίαις παρὰ ταύτας. **24** οὐ
by better sacrifices than these. not

γὰρ εἰς χειροποίητα εἰσῆλθεν ἅγια Χριστός,
For into [2]made by hand [4]entered [1]holies [3]Christ,

ἀντίτυπα τῶν ἀληθινῶν, ἀλλ' εἰς αὐτὸν
figures of the true things, but into [3][it]self

τὸν οὐρανόν, νῦν ἐμφανισθῆναι τῷ προσώπῳ
[1]*the* [2]heaven, now to appear in the presence

τοῦ θεοῦ ὑπὲρ ἡμῶν· **25** οὐδ' ἵνα πολ-
– of God on behalf of us; nor *in order* that often

λάκις προσφέρῃ ἑαυτόν, ὥσπερ ὁ ἀρχιερεὺς
he should offer himself, even as the high priest

εἰσέρχεται εἰς τὰ ἅγια κατ' ἐνιαυτὸν
enters into the holies year by year†

ἐν αἵματι ἀλλοτρίῳ, **26** ἐπεὶ ἔδει αὐτὸν
with blood belonging to others, since it behoved him

πολλάκις παθεῖν ἀπὸ καταβολῆς κόσμου·
often to suffer from [the] foundation of [the] world;

νυνὶ δὲ ἅπαξ ἐπὶ συντελείᾳ τῶν αἰώνων
but now once at [the] completion of the ages

εἰς ἀθέτησιν τῆς ἁμαρτίας διὰ τῆς θυσίας
for annulment – of sin through the sacrifice

αὐτοῦ πεφανέρωται. **27** καὶ καθ' ὅσον
of him he has been manifested. And as

ἀπόκειται τοῖς ἀνθρώποις ἅπαξ ἀποθανεῖν,
it is reserved – to men once to die,

μετὰ δὲ τοῦτο κρίσις, **28** οὕτως καὶ
and after this judgment, so also

ὁ Χριστός, ἅπαξ προσενεχθεὶς εἰς τὸ
– Christ, once having been offered *for the*

πολλῶν ἀνενεγκεῖν ἁμαρτίας, ἐκ δευτέρου
[3]of many [1]to bear [2]sins, [2]a second [time]

χωρὶς ἁμαρτίας ὀφθήσεται τοῖς αὐτὸν
[3]without [4]sin [1]will appear [5]to the [ones] [7]him

ἀπεκδεχομένοις εἰς σωτηρίαν.
[6]expecting for salvation.

the heavenly things themselves with better sacrifices than these. 24For Christ did not enter a man-made sanctuary that was only a copy of the true one; he entered heaven itself, now to appear for us in God's presence. 25Nor did he enter heaven to offer himself again and again, the way the high priest enters the Most Holy Place every year with blood that is not his own. 26Then Christ would have had to suffer many times since the creation of the world. But now he has appeared once for all at the end of the ages to do away with sin by the sacrifice of himself. 27Just as man is destined to die once, and after that to face judgment, 28so Christ was sacrificed once to take away the sins of many people; and he will appear a second time, not to bear sin, but to bring salvation to those who are waiting for him.

Chapter 10

Christ's Sacrifice Once for All

Since the law has only a shadow of the good things to come and not the true form of these realities, it[u] can never, by the same sacrifices that are continually offered year after year, make perfect those who approach. 2 Otherwise, would they not have ceased being offered, since the worshipers, cleansed once for all, would no longer have any consciousness of sin? 3 But in these sacrifices there is a reminder of sin year after year. 4 For it is impossible for the blood of bulls and goats to take away sins. 5 Consequently, when Christ[v] came into the world, he said,

[u] Other ancient authorities read *they*
[v] Gk *he*

10 Σκιὰν γὰρ ἔχων ὁ νόμος τῶν
For [4]a shadow [3]having [1]the [2]law of the

μελλόντων ἀγαθῶν, οὐκ αὐτὴν τὴν εἰκόνα
coming good things, not [3][it]self [1]the [2]image

τῶν πραγμάτων, κατ' ἐνιαυτὸν ταῖς αὐταῖς
of the matters, [8]every [9]year† [3]by the [4]same

θυσίαις ἃς προσφέρουσιν εἰς τὸ διηνεκὲς
[5]sacrifices [6]which [7]they offer [10]continually†

οὐδέποτε δύναται τοὺς προσερχομένους
[2]never [1]can [12]the [ones] [13]approaching

τελειῶσαι· **2** ἐπεὶ οὐκ ἂν ἐπαύσαντο
[11]*to* perfect; since would not they have ceased

προσφερόμεναι, διὰ τὸ μηδεμίαν ἔχειν
being offered, because of *the* [7]no [5]to have

ἔτι συνείδησιν ἁμαρτιῶν τοὺς λατρεύοντας
[6]still [8]conscience [9]of sins [1]the [ones] [2]serving

ἅπαξ κεκαθαρισμένους; **3** ἀλλ' ἐν αὐταῖς
[3]once [4]having been cleansed ? But in them [there

ἀνάμνησις ἁμαρτιῶν κατ' ἐνιαυτόν·
is] a remembrance of sins yearly†;

4 ἀδύνατον γὰρ αἷμα ταύρων καὶ τράγων
for [it is] impossible blood of bulls and *of* goats

ἀφαιρεῖν ἁμαρτίας. **5** Διὸ εἰσερχόμενος εἰς
to take away sins. Wherefore entering into

Chapter 10

Christ's Sacrifice Once for All

The law is only a shadow of the good things that are coming—not the realities themselves. For this reason it can never, by the same sacrifices repeated endlessly year after year, make perfect those who draw near to worship. 2If it could, would they not have stopped being offered? For the worshipers would have been cleansed once for all, and would no longer have felt guilty for their sins. 3But those sacrifices are an annual reminder of sins, 4because it is impossible for the blood of bulls and goats to take away sins.

5Therefore, when Christ came into the world, he

"Sacrifices and
offerings you
have not
desired,
but a body you have
prepared for me;
6 in burnt offerings and
sin offerings
you have taken no
pleasure.
7 Then I said, 'See,
God, I have
come to do your
will, O God'
(in the scroll of the
book[w] it is
written of me)."
8 When he said above,
"You have neither desired
nor taken pleasure in sacrifices and offerings and
burnt offerings and sin offerings" (these are offered
according to the law),
9 then he added, "See, I
have come to do your will."
He abolishes the first in order to establish the second.
10 And it is by God's will[x]
that we have been sancti-
fied through the offering of
the body of Jesus Christ
once for all.
11 And every priest
stands day after day at his
service, offering again and
again the same sacrifices
that can never take away
sins. 12 But when Christ[y]
had offered for all time a
single sacrifice for sins, "he
sat down at the right hand
of God," 13 and since then
has been waiting "until his
enemies would be made a
footstool for his feet."
14 For by a single offering
he has perfected for all time
those who are sanctified.
15 And the Holy Spirit also
testifies to us, for after saying,
16 "This is the covenant
that I will make
with them

[w] Meaning of Gk uncertain
[x] Gk *by that will*
[y] Gk *this one*

τὸν κόσμον λέγει· θυσίαν καὶ προσφορὰν
the world he says: Sacrifice and offering

οὐκ ἠθέλησας, σῶμα δὲ κατηρτίσω μοι·
thou didst not wish, but a body thou didst prepare for me;

6 ὁλοκαυτώματα καὶ περὶ ἁμαρτίας οὐκ
burnt offerings and [sacrifices] concerning sins not

εὐδόκησας. **7** τότε εἶπον· ἰδοὺ ἥκω,
thou wast well pleased [with]. Then I said: Behold I have come,

ἐν κεφαλίδι βιβλίου γέγραπται περὶ ἐμοῦ,
in a heading of a scroll it has been written concerning me,

τοῦ ποιῆσαι ὁ θεὸς τὸ θέλημά σου.
– to do[,][d] – God[,]* the will of thee.

8 ἀνώτερον λέγων ὅτι θυσίας καὶ προσ-
Above saying that sacrifices and offer-

φορὰς καὶ ὁλοκαυτώματα καὶ περὶ ἁμαρτίας
ings and burnt offerings and [sacrifices] concerning sins

οὐκ ἠθέλησας οὐδὲ εὐδόκησας, αἵτινες
thou didst not wish nor *thou* wast well pleased [with], which

κατὰ νόμον προσφέρονται, **9** τότε εἴρηκεν·
according to law are offered, then he *has* said:

ἰδοὺ ἥκω τοῦ ποιῆσαι τὸ θέλημά σου.
Behold I have come – to do[d] the will of thee.

ἀναιρεῖ τὸ πρῶτον ἵνα τὸ δεύτερον
He takes away the first in order that the second

στήσῃ· **10** ἐν ᾧ θελήματι ἡγιασμένοι ἐσμὲν
he may set up; by which will [2]*having been* sanctified [1]we are

διὰ τῆς προσφορᾶς τοῦ σώματος Ἰησοῦ
through the offering of the body of Jesus

Χριστοῦ ἐφάπαξ. **11** Καὶ πᾶς μὲν ἱερεὺς
Christ once for all. And [2]every [1]on one hand [3]priest

ἕστηκεν καθ' ἡμέραν λειτουργῶν καὶ τὰς
stands daily† ministering and [3]the

αὐτὰς πολλάκις προσφέρων θυσίας, αἵτινες
[4]same [1]often [2]offering [5]sacrifices, which

οὐδέποτε δύνανται περιελεῖν ἁμαρτίας· **12** οὗτος
never can *to* take away sins; [2]this [priest]

δὲ μίαν ὑπὲρ ἁμαρτιῶν προσενέγκας
[1]on the other [4]one [6]on behalf of [7]sins [3]having offered

θυσίαν εἰς τὸ διηνεκὲς ἐκάθισεν ἐν δεξιᾷ
[5]sacrifice [9]in – [10]perpetuity [8]sat at [the] right [hand]

τοῦ θεοῦ, **13** τὸ λοιπὸν ἐκδεχόμενος ἕως
– of God, henceforth expecting till

τεθῶσιν οἱ ἐχθροὶ αὐτοῦ ὑποπόδιον τῶν
[4]are put [1]the [2]enemies [3]of him a footstool of the

ποδῶν αὐτοῦ. **14** μιᾷ γὰρ προσφορᾷ
feet of him. For by one offering

τετελείωκεν εἰς τὸ διηνεκὲς τοὺς ἁγιαζ-
he has perfected in – perpetuity the [ones] being

ομένους. **15** Μαρτυρεῖ δὲ ἡμῖν καὶ
sanctified. And [5]witnesses [6]to us [4]indeed

τὸ πνεῦμα τὸ ἅγιον· μετὰ γὰρ τὸ
[1]the [3]Spirit – [2]Holy; for after *the*

εἰρηκέναι· **16** αὕτη ἡ διαθήκη ἣν δια-
to have said: = having said: This [is] the covenant which I will

* The "articular vocative"; *cf.* 1. 8, 9.

said:

"Sacrifice and offering
you did not desire,
but a body you
prepared for me;
6 with burnt offerings and
sin offerings
you were not pleased.
7 Then I said, 'Here I
am—it is written
about me in the
scroll—
I have come to do your
will, O God.' "[l]

8 First he said, "Sacrifices
and offerings, burnt offerings and sin offerings you
did not desire, nor were
you pleased with them"
(although the law required
them to be made). 9 Then he
said, "Here I am, I have
come to do your will." He
sets aside the first to establish the second. 10 And by
that will, we have been
made holy through the sacrifice of the body of Jesus
Christ once for all.
11 Day after day every
priest stands and performs
his religious duties; again
and again he offers the
same sacrifices, which can
never take away sins. 12 But
when this priest had of-
fered for all time one sacrifice for sins, he sat down at
the right hand of God.
13 Since that time he waits
for his enemies to be made
his footstool, 14 because by
one sacrifice he has made
perfect forever those who
are being made holy.
15 The Holy Spirit also
testifies to us about this.
First he says:

16 "This is the covenant I
will make with them

[l]7 Psalm 40:6-8 (see Septuagint)

after those days,
says the Lord:
I will put my laws in
their hearts,
and I will write
them on
their minds,"
17he also adds,
"I will remember[z]
their sins and
their lawless
deeds no more."
18Where there is forgive-
ness of these, there is no
longer any offering for sin.

A Call to Persevere

19 Therefore, my
friends,[a] since we have
confidence to enter the
sanctuary by the blood of
Jesus, 20by the new and living way that he opened for
us through the curtain (that
is, through his flesh), 21and
since we have a great priest
over the house of God,
22let us approach with a
true heart in full assurance
of faith, with our hearts
sprinkled clean from an evil
conscience and our bodies
washed with pure water.
23Let us hold fast to the
confession of our hope
without wavering, for he
who has promised is faithful. 24And let us consider
how to provoke one anoth-
er to love and good deeds,
25not neglecting to meet together, as is the habit of
some, but encouraging one
another, and all the more as
you see the Day approach-
ing.
26 For if we willfully
persist in sin after having
received the knowledge of
the truth, there no longer
remains a sacrifice for sins,
27but a fearful prospect of
judgment, and a fury of fire
that will consume the ad-
versaries. 28Anyone who

[z] Gk *on their minds and I will remember*
[a] Gk *Therefore, brothers*

θήσομαι πρὸς αὐτοὺς μετὰ τὰς ἡμέρας
covenant to them after – days
ἐκείνας, λέγει κύριος· διδοὺς νόμους μου
those, says [the] Lord: Giving laws of me
ἐπὶ καρδίας αὐτῶν, καὶ ἐπὶ τὴν διάνοιαν
on hearts of them, also on the mind
αὐτῶν ἐπιγράψω αὐτούς, **17** καὶ τῶν
of them I will inscribe them, and the
ἁμαρτιῶν αὐτῶν καὶ τῶν ἀνομιῶν αὐτῶν
sins of them and the iniquities of them
οὐ μὴ μνησθήσομαι ἔτι. **18** ὅπου δὲ
by no means I will remember still. Now where
ἄφεσις τούτων, οὐκέτι προσφορὰ περὶ
forgiveness of these [is], no longer [there is] offering concerning
ἁμαρτίας.
sins.
19 Ἔχοντες οὖν, ἀδελφοί, παρρησίαν εἰς
Having therefore, brothers, confidence for
τὴν εἴσοδον τῶν ἁγίων ἐν τῷ αἵματι
the entering of the holies by the blood
Ἰησοῦ, **20** ἣν ἐνεκαίνισεν ἡμῖν ὁδὸν
of Jesus, which he dedicated for us[,] a way
πρόσφατον καὶ ζῶσαν διὰ τοῦ κατα-
fresh and living through the veil,
πετάσματος, τοῦτ' ἔστιν τῆς σαρκὸς αὐτοῦ,
this is the flesh of him,
21 καὶ ἱερέα μέγαν ἐπὶ τὸν οἶκον τοῦ
and priest a great over the household –
θεοῦ, **22** προσερχώμεθα μετὰ ἀληθινῆς
of God, let us approach with a true
καρδίας ἐν πληροφορίᾳ πίστεως, ῥεραν-
heart in full assurance of faith, having been
τισμένοι τὰς καρδίας ἀπὸ συνειδήσεως
sprinkled [as to] the hearts from [3]conscience
πονηρᾶς καὶ λελουσμένοι τὸ σῶμα ὕδατι
[2]an evil and having been bathed [as to] the body [2]water
καθαρῷ· **23** κατέχωμεν τὴν ὁμολογίαν τῆς
[1]in clean; let us hold fast the confession of the (our)
ἐλπίδος ἀκλινῆ, πιστὸς γὰρ ὁ ἐπαγ-
hope unyieldingly, for faithful [is] the [one] pro-
γειλάμενος, **24** καὶ κατανοῶμεν ἀλλήλους
mising, and let us consider one another
εἰς παροξυσμὸν ἀγάπης καὶ καλῶν ἔργων,
to incitement of love and of good works,
25 μὴ ἐγκαταλείποντες τὴν ἐπισυναγωγὴν
not forsaking the coming together
ἑαυτῶν, καθὼς ἔθος τισίν, ἀλλὰ παρα-
of [our]selves, as custom with some [is], but ex-
καλοῦντες, καὶ τοσούτῳ μᾶλλον ὅσῳ
horting, and by so much more as
βλέπετε ἐγγίζουσαν τὴν ἡμέραν. **26** Ἑκουσίως
ye see [3]drawing near [1]the [2]day. wilfully
γὰρ ἁμαρτανόντων ἡμῶν μετὰ τὸ λαβεῖν
For sinning us[a] after *the* to receive
=when we sin wilfully =receiving
τὴν ἐπίγνωσιν τῆς ἀληθείας, οὐκέτι περὶ
the full knowledge of the truth, [5]no more [2]concerning
ἁμαρτιῶν ἀπολείπεται θυσία, **27** φοβερὰ
[3]sins [4]remains [1]a sacrifice, [3]fearful
δέ τις ἐκδοχὴ κρίσεως καὶ πυρὸς ζῆλος
[1]but [2]some expectation of judgment and [2]of fire [1]zeal
ἐσθίειν μέλλοντος τοὺς ὑπεναντίους.
[4]to consume [3]being about the adversaries.

after that time, says the
Lord.
I will put my laws in
their hearts,
and I will write them
on their minds."[m]
17Then he adds:
"Their sins and lawless
acts
I will remember no
more."[n]
18And where these have
been forgiven, there is no
longer any sacrifice for sin.

A Call to Persevere

19Therefore, brothers,
since we have confidence
to enter the Most Holy
Place by the blood of Jesus,
20by a new and living way
opened for us through the
curtain, that is, his body,
21and since we have a great
priest over the house of
God, 22let us draw near to
God with a sincere heart in
full assurance of faith, having our hearts sprinkled to
cleanse us from a guilty
conscience and having our
bodies washed with pure
water. 23Let us hold un-
swervingly to the hope we
profess, for he who prom-
ised is faithful. 24And let us
consider how we may spur
one another on toward love
and good deeds. 25Let us
not give up meeting together, as some are in the habit
of doing, but let us encourage one another—and all
the more as you see the
Day approaching.
26If we deliberately keep
on sinning after we have received the knowledge of
the truth, no sacrifice for
sins is left, 27but only a
fearful expectation of judgment and of raging fire that
will consume the enemies

[m] *16* Jer. 31:33
[n] *17* Jer. 31:34

has violated the law of Moses dies without mercy "on the testimony of two or three witnesses." 29 How much worse punishment do you think will be deserved by those who have spurned the Son of God, profaned the blood of the covenant by which they were sanctified, and outraged the Spirit of grace? 30 For we know the one who said, "Vengeance is mine, I will repay." And again, "The Lord will judge his people." 31 It is a fearful thing to fall into the hands of the living God.

32 But recall those earlier days when, after you had been enlightened, you endured a hard struggle with sufferings, 33 sometimes being publicly exposed to abuse and persecution, and sometimes being partners with those so treated. 34 For you had compassion for those who were in prison, and you cheerfully accepted the plundering of your possessions, knowing that you yourselves possessed something better and more lasting. 35 Do not, therefore, abandon that confidence of yours; it brings a great reward. 36 For you need endurance, so that when you have done the will of God, you may receive what was promised.

37 For yet "in a very
little while,
the one who is
coming will
come and will
not delay;
38 but my righteous one
will live
by faith.
My soul takes no
pleasure in
anyone who
shrinks back."

28 ἀθετήσας τις νόμον Μωϋσέως χωρὶς
[2]Disregarding [1]anyone [3]law [4]of Moses [6]without

οἰκτιρμῶν ἐπὶ δυσὶν ἢ τρισὶν μάρτυσιν
[7]compassions [8]on [the word of] [9]two [10]or [11]three [12]witnesses

ἀποθνῄσκει· **29** πόσῳ δοκεῖτε χείρονος
[5]dies; by how much think ye [2]of worse

ἀξιωθήσεται τιμωρίας ὁ τὸν υἱὸν τοῦ
[1]will be thought worthy [3]punishment [4]the [one] [6]the [7]Son –

θεοῦ καταπατήσας καὶ τὸ αἷμα τῆς
[8]of God [5]having trampled [on] and [3]the [4]blood [5]of the

διαθήκης κοινὸν ἡγησάμενος, ἐν ᾧ ἡγιάσθη,
[6]covenant [2]common [1]having deemed, by which he was sanctified,

καὶ τὸ πνεῦμα τῆς χάριτος ἐνυβρίσας.
and [2]the [3]Spirit – [4]of grace [1]having insulted.

30 οἴδαμεν γὰρ τὸν εἰπόντα· ἐμοὶ
For we know the [one] having said: To me =Vengeance

ἐκδίκησις, ἐγὼ ἀνταποδώσω· καὶ πάλιν·
vengeance,° is mine, I will repay; and again:

κρινεῖ κύριος τὸν λαὸν αὐτοῦ. **31** φοβερὸν
[2]will judge [[1]The] Lord the people of him. A fearful thing [it is]

τὸ ἐμπεσεῖν εἰς χεῖρας θεοῦ ζῶντος.
the to fall *in* into [the] hands [2]God [1]of a living.

32 Ἀναμιμνῄσκεσθε δὲ τὰς πρότερον ἡμέρας,
But remember ye the [2]formerly [1]days,

ἐν αἷς φωτισθέντες πολλὴν ἄθλησιν
in which being enlightened [2]a much(great) [3]struggle

ὑπεμείνατε παθημάτων, **33** τοῦτο μὲν
[1]ye endured [4]of sufferings, *this* on one hand

ὀνειδισμοῖς τε καὶ θλίψεσιν θεατριζόμενοι,
[2]to reproaches [3]both [4]and [5]to afflictions [1]being exposed,

τοῦτο δὲ κοινωνοὶ τῶν οὕτως ἀναστρεφ-
this on the other [3]sharers [2]of the [ones] [5]thus [4]liv-

ομένων γενηθέντες. **34** καὶ γὰρ τοῖς
ing [1]having become. For indeed in *the*

δεσμίοις συνεπαθήσατε, καὶ τὴν ἁρπαγὴν
bonds ye suffered together, and [4]the [5]seizure

τῶν ὑπαρχόντων ὑμῶν μετὰ χαρᾶς
[6]of the [7]possessions [8]of you [2]with [3]joy

προσεδέξασθε, γινώσκοντες ἔχειν ἑαυτοὺς
[1]ye accepted, knowing [2]to have [1][your]selves

κρείσσονα ὕπαρξιν καὶ μένουσαν. **35** Μὴ
[3]a better [6]possession [4]and [5]remaining. not

ἀποβάλητε οὖν τὴν παρρησίαν ὑμῶν, ἥτις
Cast ye away therefore the confidence of you, which

ἔχει μεγάλην μισθαποδοσίαν. **36** ὑπομονῆς
has a great recompence. [3]of endurance

γὰρ ἔχετε χρείαν ἵνα τὸ θέλημα τοῦ
For [1]ye have [2]need in order that [5]the [6]will –

θεοῦ ποιήσαντες κομίσησθε τὴν ἐπαγγελίαν.
[7]of God [1]having done ye may obtain the promise.

37 ἔτι γὰρ μικρὸν ὅσον ὅσον, ὁ ἐρχόμενος
For yet [2]little [1]a very,* the coming [one]

ἥξει καὶ οὐ χρονίσει· **38** ὁ δὲ δίκαιός
will come and will not delay; but the just man

μου ἐκ πίστεως ζήσεται, καὶ ἐὰν ὑπο-
of me by faith will live, and if he

* *Cf.* our "so so".

of God. 28 Anyone who rejected the law of Moses died without mercy on the testimony of two or three witnesses. 29 How much more severely do you think a man deserves to be punished who has trampled the Son of God under foot, who has treated as an unholy thing the blood of the covenant that sanctified him, and who has insulted the Spirit of grace? 30 For we know him who said, "It is mine to avenge; I will repay,"[o] and again, "The Lord will judge his people."[p] 31 It is a dreadful thing to fall into the hands of the living God.

32 Remember those earlier days after you had received the light, when you stood your ground in a great contest in the face of suffering. 33 Sometimes you were publicly exposed to insult and persecution; at other times you stood side by side with those who were so treated. 34 You sympathized with those in prison and joyfully accepted the confiscation of your property, because you knew that you yourselves had better and lasting possessions.

35 So do not throw away your confidence; it will be richly rewarded. 36 You need to persevere so that when you have done the will of God, you will receive what he has promised. 37 For in just a very little while,

"He who is coming will
come and will not
delay.
38 But my righteous one[q]
will live by faith.
And if he shrinks back,

[o] *30* Deut. 32:35
[p] *30* Deut. 32:36; Psalm 135:14
[q] *38* One early manuscript *But the righteous*

39But we are not among
those who shrink back and
so are lost, but among
those who have faith and so
are saved.

στείληται, οὐκ εὐδοκεῖ ἡ ψυχή μου
withdraws, [4]is not well pleased [1]the [2]soul [3]of me

ἐν αὐτῷ. 39 ἡμεῖς δὲ οὐκ ἐσμὲν ὑποστολῆς
in him. But we are not of withdrawal

εἰς ἀπώλειαν, ἀλλὰ πίστεως εἰς περιποίησιν
to destruction, but of faith to possession

ψυχῆς.
of soul.

I will not be pleased
with him."[r]

39But we are not of those
who shrink back and are
destroyed, but of those
who believe and are saved.

Chapter 11

The Meaning of Faith

NOW faith is the assur-
ance of things hoped
for, the conviction of things
not seen. 2Indeed, by
faith[b] our ancestors received approval. 3By faith
we understand that the
worlds were prepared by
the word of God, so that
what is seen was made
from things that are not visible.[c]

The Examples of Abel, Enoch, and Noah

4 By faith Abel offered
to God a more acceptable[d]
sacrifice than Cain's.
Through this he received
approval as righteous, God
himself giving approval to
his gifts; he died, but
through his faith[e] he still
speaks. 5By faith Enoch
was taken so that he did not
experience death; and "he
was not found, because
God had taken him." For it
was attested before he was
taken away that "he had
pleased God." 6And with-
out faith it is impossible to
please God, for whoever
would approach him must
believe that he exists and
that he rewards those who
seek him. 7By faith Noah,
warned by God about
events as yet unseen, re-
spected the warning and
built an ark to save his
household; by this he condemned the world and be-
came an heir to the righ-
teousness that is in accordance with faith.

11 Ἔστιν δὲ πίστις ἐλπιζομένων ὑπό-
Now [2]is [1]faith [4]of things being hoped [3][the]

στασις, πραγμάτων ἔλεγχος οὐ βλεπομένων.
reality, [2]of things [1][the] proof not being seen.

2 ἐν ταύτῃ γὰρ ἐμαρτυρήθησαν οἱ
by this For [2]obtained witness [1]the

πρεσβύτεροι. 3 Πίστει νοοῦμεν κατηρτίσθαι
[2]elders. By faith we understand [4]to have been adjusted

τοὺς αἰῶνας ῥήματι θεοῦ, εἰς τὸ μὴ
[1]the [2]ages by a word of God, so as† [3]not

ἐκ φαινομένων τὸ βλεπόμενον γεγονέναι.
[5]out of [6]things appearing [1]the thing [2]being seen [4]to have become.

4 Πίστει πλείονα θυσίαν Ἄβελ παρὰ
By faith [4]a greater(? better) [5]sacrifice [1]Abel [6]than

Κάϊν προσήνεγκεν τῷ θεῷ, δι' ἧς
[7]Cain [2]offered – [3]to God, through which

ἐμαρτυρήθη εἶναι δίκαιος, μαρτυροῦντος ἐπὶ
he obtained witness to be just, [2]witnessing [3]over

τοῖς δώροις αὐτοῦ τοῦ θεοῦ, καὶ δι'
[4]the [5]gifts [6]of him – [1]God,[a] and through

αὐτῆς ἀποθανὼν ἔτι λαλεῖ. 5 Πίστει
it having died still he speaks. By faith

Ἑνὼχ μετετέθη τοῦ μὴ ἰδεῖν θάνατον,
Enoch was removed – not to see[d] death,

καὶ οὐχ ηὑρίσκετο διότι μετέθηκεν αὐτὸν
and was not found because [2]removed [3]him

ὁ θεός. 6 πρὸ γὰρ τῆς μεταθέσεως
[1]God. For before the(his) removal

μεμαρτύρηται εὐαρεστηκέναι τῷ θεῷ· χωρὶς
he has obtained witness to have been well-pleasing – to God; [2]without

δὲ πίστεως ἀδύνατον εὐαρεστῆσαι· πιστεῦσαι
[1]but faith [it is] impossible to be well-pleasing [to God]; [6]to believe

γὰρ δεῖ τὸν προσερχόμενον [τῷ] θεῷ,
[1]for [5]it behoves [2]the [one] [4]approaching – [3]to God,

ὅτι ἔστιν καὶ τοῖς ἐκζητοῦσιν αὐτὸν
that he is and [3]to the [ones] [4]seeking [6]out [5]him

μισθαποδότης γίνεται. 7 Πίστει χρηματισ-
[2]a rewarder [1]becomes. By faith [2]having been warned [by

θεὶς Νῶε περὶ τῶν μηδέπω βλεπομένων,
God*] [1]Noah concerning the things not yet being seen,

εὐλαβηθεὶς κατεσκεύασεν κιβωτὸν εἰς
being devout prepared an ark for

σωτηρίαν τοῦ οἴκου αὐτοῦ, δι' ἧς
[the] salvation of the household of him, through which

κατέκρινεν τὸν κόσμον, καὶ τῆς κατὰ
he condemned the world, and [4]of the [5]according to

πίστιν δικαιοσύνης ἐγένετο κληρονόμος.
[6]faith [3]righteousness [1]became [2]heir.

Chapter 11

By Faith

NOW faith is being sure
of what we hope for
and certain of what we do
not see. 2This is what the
ancients were commended
for.
3By faith we understand
that the universe was
formed at God's command,
so that what is seen was not
made out of what was visible.
4By faith Abel offered
God a better sacrifice than
Cain did. By faith he was
commended as a righteous
man, when God spoke well
of his offerings. And by
faith he still speaks, even
though he is dead.
5By faith Enoch was tak-
en from this life, so that he
did not experience death;
he could not be found, because God had taken him
away. For before he was
taken, he was commended
as one who pleased God.
6And without faith it is impossible to please God, because anyone who comes
to him must believe that he
exists and that he rewards
those who earnestly seek
him.
7By faith Noah, when
warned about things not
yet seen, in holy fear built
an ark to save his family.
By his faith he condemned
the world and became heir
of the righteousness that
comes by faith.

[b] Gk *by this*
[c] Or *was not made out of visible things*
[d] Gk *greater*
[e] Gk *through it*

* This must be understood, as the word always (or at least generally) has reference to a divine communication.

[r] 38 Hab. 2:3,4

The Faith of Abraham

8 By faith Abraham obeyed when he was called to set out for a place that he was to receive as an inheritance; and he set out, not knowing where he was going. 9 By faith he stayed for a time in the land he had been promised, as in a foreign land, living in tents, as did Isaac and Jacob, who were heirs with him of the same promise. 10 For he looked forward to the city that has foundations, whose architect and builder is God. 11 By faith he received power of procreation, even though he was too old—and Sarah herself was barren—because he considered him faithful who had promised.[f] 12 Therefore from one person, and this one as good as dead, descendants were born, "as many as the stars of heaven and as the innumerable grains of sand by the seashore."

13 All of these died in faith without having received the promises, but from a distance they saw and greeted them. They confessed that they were strangers and foreigners on the earth, 14 for people who speak in this way make it clear that they are seeking a homeland. 15 If they had been thinking of the land that they had left behind, they would have had opportunity to return. 16 But as it is, they desire a better country, that is, a heavenly one. Therefore God is not ashamed to be called their God; indeed, he has prepared a city for them.

17 By faith Abraham, when put to the test, offered up Isaac. He who had

8 Πίστει καλούμενος Ἀβραὰμ ὑπήκουσεν
By faith [2]being called [1]Abraham [11]obeyed
ἐξελθεῖν εἰς τόπον ὃν ἤμελλεν λαμβάνειν
[3]to go forth [4]to [5]a place [6]which [7]he was about [8]to receive
εἰς κληρονομίαν, καὶ ἐξῆλθεν μὴ ἐπιστάμε-
[9]for [10]an inheritance, and went forth not understand-
νος ποῦ ἔρχεται. 9 Πίστει παρῴκησεν
ing where he goes(went). By faith he sojourned
εἰς γῆν τῆς ἐπαγγελίας ὡς ἀλλοτρίαν,
in a land – of promise as a foreigner,
ἐν σκηναῖς κατοικήσας, μετὰ Ἰσαὰκ καὶ
in tents dwelling, with Isaac and
Ἰακὼβ τῶν συγκληρονόμων τῆς ἐπαγ-
Jacob the co-heirs of the [2]pro-
γελίας τῆς αὐτῆς· 10 ἐξεδέχετο γὰρ τὴν
mise – [1]same; for he expected the
τοὺς θεμελίους ἔχουσαν πόλιν, ἧς τεχνίτης
[3]the [4]foundations [2]having [1]city, of which [1]artificer
καὶ δημιουργὸς ὁ θεός. 11 Πίστει καὶ
[4]and [5]maker – [1]God [2][is]. By faith also
αὐτὴ Σάρρα δύναμιν εἰς καταβολὴν
[2][her]self [1]Sara [4]power [5]for [6]conception
σπέρματος ἔλαβεν καὶ παρὰ καιρὸν ἡλικίας,
[7]of seed [3]received even beyond time of age,
ἐπεὶ πιστὸν ἡγήσατο τὸν ἐπαγγειλάμενον.
since [2]faithful [1]she deemed the [one] having promised.
12 διὸ καὶ ἀφ᾽ ἑνὸς ἐγενήθησαν, καὶ
Wherefore indeed from one there became, and
ταῦτα νενεκρωμένου, καθὼς τὰ ἄστρα
that too† [he] having died,* as the stars
τοῦ οὐρανοῦ τῷ πλήθει καὶ ὡς ἡ ἄμμος
of *the* heaven – in multitude and as the [1]sand
ἡ παρὰ τὸ χεῖλος τῆς θαλάσσης ἡ
– [3]by [4]the [5]lip [6]of the [7]sea –
ἀναρίθμητος. 13 Κατὰ πίστιν ἀπέθανον
[1]innumerable. [4]By way of [5]faith [3]died
οὗτοι πάντες, μὴ κομισάμενοι τὰς ἐπαγ-
[1]these [2]all, not having obtained the pro-
γελίας, ἀλλὰ πόρρωθεν αὐτὰς ἰδόντες καὶ
mises, but [5]from afar [4]them [1]seeing [2]and
ἀσπασάμενοι, καὶ ὁμολογήσαντες ὅτι ξένοι
[3]greeting, and confessing that [2]strangers
καὶ παρεπίδημοί εἰσιν ἐπὶ τῆς γῆς.
[3]and [4]sojourners [1]they are on the earth (? land).
14 οἱ γὰρ τοιαῦτα λέγοντες ἐμφανίζουσιν
For the [ones] [2]such things [1]saying make manifest
ὅτι πατρίδα ἐπιζητοῦσιν. 15 καὶ εἰ μὲν
that [2]a fatherland [1]they seek. And if on one hand
ἐκείνης ἐμνημόνευον ἀφ᾽ ἧς ἐξέβησαν,
[2]that [1]they remembered from which they came out,
εἶχον ἂν καιρὸν ἀνακάμψαι· 16 νῦν
they might have had time(opportunity) to return; now
δὲ κρείττονος ὀρέγονται, τοῦτ᾽ ἔστιν
on the other [2]a better [1]they aspire to, this is
ἐπουρανίου. διὸ οὐκ ἐπαισχύνεται αὐτοὺς
a heavenly. Wherefore [2]is not ashamed [of] [3]them
ὁ θεὸς θεὸς ἐπικαλεῖσθαι αὐτῶν· ἡτοίμασεν
– [1]God [5]God [4]to be called [6]of them; [2]he prepared
γὰρ αὐτοῖς πόλιν. 17 Πίστει προσενήνοχεν
[1]for for them a city. By faith [3]*has* offered up
Ἀβραὰμ τὸν Ἰσαὰκ πειραζόμενος, καὶ
[1]Abraham – [4]Isaac [2]being tested, and

8 By faith Abraham, when called to go to a place he would later receive as his inheritance, obeyed and went, even though he did not know where he was going. 9 By faith he made his home in the promised land like a stranger in a foreign country; he lived in tents, as did Isaac and Jacob, who were heirs with him of the same promise. 10 For he was looking forward to the city with foundations, whose architect and builder is God.

11 By faith Abraham, even though he was past age—and Sarah herself was barren—was enabled to become a father because he[s] considered him faithful who had made the promise. 12 And so from this one man, and he as good as dead, came descendants as numerous as the stars in the sky and as countless as the sand on the seashore.

13 All these people were still living by faith when they died. They did not receive the things promised; they only saw them and welcomed them from a distance. And they admitted that they were aliens and strangers on earth. 14 People who say such things show that they are looking for a country of their own. 15 If they had been thinking of the country they had left, they would have had opportunity to return. 16 Instead, they were longing for a better country—a heavenly one. Therefore God is not ashamed to be called their God, for he has prepared a city for them.

17 By faith Abraham, when God tested him, offered Isaac as a sacrifice.

[f] Other ancient authorities read *By faith Sarah herself, though barren, received power to conceive, even when she was too old, because she considered him faithful who had promised.*

[s] 11 Or *By faith even Sarah, who was past age, was enabled to bear children because she*

received the promises was
ready to offer up his only
son, [18]of whom he had
been told, "It is through
Isaac that descendants
shall be named for you."
[19]He considered the fact
that God is able even to
raise someone from the
dead—and figuratively
speaking, he did receive
him back. [20]By faith Isaac
invoked blessings for the
future on Jacob and Esau.
[21]By faith Jacob, when dying, blessed each of the
sons of Joseph, "bowing in
worship over the top of his
staff." [22]By faith Joseph, at
the end of his life, made
mention of the exodus of
the Israelites and gave instructions about his burial.[g]

The Faith of Moses

23 By faith Moses was
hidden by his parents for
three months after his
birth, because they saw
that the child was beautiful;
and they were not afraid of
the king's edict.[h] [24]By
faith Moses, when he was
grown up, refused to be
called a son of Pharaoh's
daughter, [25]choosing rather to share ill-treatment
with the people of God than
to enjoy the fleeting pleasures of sin. [26]He considered abuse suffered for the
Christ[i] to be greater
wealth than the treasures of
Egypt, for he was looking
ahead to the reward. [27]By
faith he left Egypt, unafraid
of the king's anger; for he
persevered as though[j] he
saw him who is invisible.
[28]By faith he kept the Passover and the sprinkling of
blood, so that the destroyer

τὸν μονογενῆ προσέφερεν ὁ τὰς ἐπαγγελίας
[6]the [7]only begotten (his) [5]was offering up [1]the [3]the [one] [4]promises

ἀναδεξάμενος, 18 πρὸς ὃν ἐλαλήθη ὅτι
[2]having undertaken, as to whom it was spoken[,] –

ἐν Ἰσαὰκ κληθήσεταί σοι σπέρμα,
In Isaac shall be called to thee a seed,° =thy seed,

19 λογισάμενος ὅτι καὶ ἐκ νεκρῶν ἐγείρειν
reckoning that [4]even [6]from [7]dead [5]to raise

δυνατὸς ὁ θεός· ὅθεν αὐτὸν καὶ ἐν
[3][was] [2]able – [1]God; whence [5]him [1]indeed [2]in

παραβολῇ ἐκομίσατο. 20 Πίστει καὶ περὶ
[3]a parable [4]he obtained. By faith also [6]concerning

μελλόντων εὐλόγησεν Ἰσαὰκ τὸν Ἰακὼβ
[7]coming things [2]blessed [1]Isaac – [3]Jacob

καὶ τὸν Ἠσαῦ. 21 Πίστει Ἰακὼβ
[4]and – [5]Esau. By faith Jacob

ἀποθνῄσκων ἕκαστον τῶν υἱῶν Ἰωσὴφ
dying [2]each [3]of the [4]sons [5]of Joseph

εὐλόγησεν, καὶ προσεκύνησεν ἐπὶ τὸ ἄκρον
[1]blessed, and worshipped on the tip

τῆς ῥάβδου αὐτοῦ. 22 Πίστει Ἰωσὴφ
of the rod of him. By faith Joseph

τελευτῶν περὶ τῆς ἐξόδου τῶν υἱῶν
dying [2]concerning [3]the [4]exodus [5]of the [6]sons

Ἰσραὴλ ἐμνημόνευσεν καὶ περὶ τῶν
[7]of Israel [1]remembered and [2]concerning [3]the

ὀστέων αὐτοῦ ἐνετείλατο. 23 Πίστει
[4]bones [5]of him [1]gave orders. By faith

Μωϋσῆς γεννηθεὶς ἐκρύβη τρίμηνον ὑπὸ
Moses having been born was hidden three months by

τῶν πατέρων αὐτοῦ, διότι εἶδον ἀστεῖον
the parents of him, because they saw [3][to be] fine

τὸ παιδίον, καὶ οὐκ ἐφοβήθησαν τὸ
[1]the [2]child, and they did not fear the

διάταγμα τοῦ βασιλέως. 24 Πίστει Μωϋσῆς
decree of the king. By faith Moses

μέγας γενόμενος ἠρνήσατο λέγεσθαι υἱὸς
[2]great [1]having become denied to be said(called) son

θυγατρὸς Φαραώ, 25 μᾶλλον ἑλόμενος
of [the] daughter of Pharaoh, rather choosing

συγκακουχεῖσθαι τῷ λαῷ τοῦ θεοῦ ἢ
to be ill treated with the people – of God than

πρόσκαιρον ἔχειν ἁμαρτίας ἀπόλαυσιν,
for a time to have [2]of sin [1]enjoyment,

26 μείζονα πλοῦτον ἡγησάμενος τῶν
[5]greater [6]riches [1]deeming [7][than] [8]the

Αἰγύπτου θησαυρῶν τὸν ὀνειδισμὸν τοῦ
[10]of Egypt [9]treasures [2]the [3]reproach –

Χριστοῦ· ἀπέβλεπεν γὰρ εἰς τὴν μισθ-
[4]of Christ; for he was looking away to the recom-

αποδοσίαν. 27 Πίστει κατέλιπεν Αἴγυπτον,
pence. By faith he left Egypt,

μὴ φοβηθεὶς τὸν θυμὸν τοῦ βασιλέως·
not fearing the anger of the king;

τὸν γὰρ ἀόρατον ὡς ὁρῶν ἐκαρτέρησεν.
for [4]the [5]unseen [one] [2]as [3]seeing [1]he endured.

28 Πίστει πεποίηκεν τὸ πάσχα καὶ τὴν
By faith he *has* made the passover and the

πρόσχυσιν τοῦ αἵματος, ἵνα μὴ ὁ
affusion of the blood, lest the

ὀλεθρεύων τὰ πρωτότοκα θίγῃ αὐτῶν.
[one] destroying [2]the [3]firstborns [1]should touch [4]of them.

He who had received the
promises was about to sacrifice his one and only son,
[18]even though God had said
to him, "It is through Isaac
that your offspring[t] will be
reckoned."[u] [19]Abraham
reasoned that God could
raise the dead, and figuratively speaking, he did receive Isaac back from
death.

[20]By faith Isaac blessed
Jacob and Esau in regard to
their future.

[21]By faith Jacob, when he
was dying, blessed each of
Joseph's sons, and wor-
shiped as he leaned on the
top of his staff.

[22]By faith Joseph, when
his end was near, spoke
about the exodus of the Israelites from Egypt and
gave instructions about his
bones.

[23]By faith Moses' parents
hid him for three months after he was born, because
they saw he was no ordi-
nary child, and they were
not afraid of the king's
edict.

[24]By faith Moses, when
he had grown up, refused to
be known as the son of
Pharaoh's daughter. [25]He
chose to be mistreated
along with the people of
God rather than to enjoy
the pleasures of sin for a
short time. [26]He regarded
disgrace for the sake of
Christ as of greater value
than the treasures of
Egypt, because he was
looking ahead to his re-
ward. [27]By faith he left
Egypt, not fearing the
king's anger; he persevered
because he saw him who is
invisible. [28]By faith he kept
the Passover and the sprinkling of blood, so that the

[g] Gk *his bones*
[h] Other ancient authorities add *By faith Moses, when he was grown up, killed the Egyptian, because he observed the humiliation of his people* (Gk *brothers*)
[i] Or *the Messiah*
[j] Or *because*

[t] *18* Greek *seed*
[u] *18* Gen. 21:12

of the firstborn would not
touch the firstborn of Israel.[k]

The Faith of Other
Israelite Heroes

29 By faith the people
passed through the Red Sea
as if it were dry land, but
when the Egyptians at-
tempted to do so they were
drowned. 30 By faith the
walls of Jericho fell after
they had been encircled for
seven days. 31 By faith Rahab the prostitute did not
perish with those who were
disobedient,[l] because she
had received the spies in
peace.
32 And what more
should I say? For time
would fail me to tell of Gideon, Barak, Samson, Jeph-
thah, of David and Samuel
and the prophets— 33 who
through faith conquered
kingdoms, administered
justice, obtained promises,
shut the mouths of lions,
34 quenched raging fire, escaped the edge of the
sword, won strength out of
weakness, became mighty
in war, put foreign armies
to flight. 35 Women re-
ceived their dead by resurrection. Others were tor-
tured, refusing to accept release, in order to obtain a
better resurrection. 36 Others suffered mocking and
flogging, and even chains
and imprisonment. 37 They
were stoned to death, they
were sawn in two,[m] they
were killed by the sword;
they went about in skins of
sheep and goats, destitute,
persecuted, tormented—
38 of whom the world was
not worthy. They wan-
dered in deserts and mountains, and in caves and
holes in the ground.
39 Yet all these, though
they were commended for

29 Πίστει διέβησαν τὴν ἐρυθρὰν θάλασσαν
By faith they went through the Red Sea

ὡς διὰ ξηρᾶς γῆς, ἧς πεῖραν λαβόντες
as through dry land, which [4]trial [3]taking

οἱ Αἰγύπτιοι κατεπόθησαν. **30** Πίστει
[1]the [2]Egyptians were swallowed up. By faith

τὰ τείχη Ἰεριχὼ ἔπεσαν κυκλωθέντα ἐπὶ
the walls of Jericho fell having been encircled during

ἑπτὰ ἡμέρας. **31** Πίστει Ῥαὰβ ἡ πόρνη
seven days. By faith Rahab the prostitute

οὐ συναπώλετο τοῖς ἀπειθήσασιν, δεξαμένη
did not perish with the [ones] disobeying, having received

τοὺς κατασκόπους μετ᾽ εἰρήνης. **32** Καὶ
the spies with peace. And

τί ἔτι λέγω; ἐπιλείψει με γὰρ διηγούμενον
what more may I say? [4]will fail [5]me [1]for [6]recounting

ὁ χρόνος περὶ Γεδεών, Βαράκ, Σαμψών,
[2]the [3]time concerning Gedeon, Barak, Samson,

Ἰεφθάε, Δαυὶδ τε καὶ Σαμουὴλ καὶ
Jephthae, [2]David [1]both and Samuel and

τῶν προφητῶν, **33** οἳ διὰ πίστεως
the prophets, who through faith

κατηγωνίσαντο βασιλείας, ἠργάσαντο δι-
overcame kingdoms, wrought right-

καιοσύνην, ἐπέτυχον ἐπαγγελιῶν, ἔφραξαν
eousness, obtained promises, stopped

στόματα λεόντων, **34** ἔσβεσαν δύναμιν
mouths of lions, quenched [the] power

πυρός, ἔφυγον στόματα μαχαίρης, ἐδυναμώ-
of fire, escaped mouths(edges) of [the] sword, were em-

θησαν ἀπὸ ἀσθενείας, ἐγενήθησαν ἰσχυροὶ
powered from weakness, became strong

ἐν πολέμῳ, παρεμβολὰς ἔκλιναν ἀλλοτρίων.
in battle, [1]armies [3]made to yield [2]of foreigners.

35 ἔλαβον γυναῖκες ἐξ ἀναστάσεως τοὺς
[2]received [1]women [6]by [7]resurrection [3]the

νεκροὺς αὐτῶν· ἄλλοι δὲ ἐτυμπανίσθησαν,
[4]dead [5]of them; but others were beaten to death,

οὐ προσδεξάμενοι τὴν ἀπολύτρωσιν, ἵνα
not accepting – deliverance, in order that

κρείττονος ἀναστάσεως τύχωσιν· **36** ἕτεροι
[2]a better [3]resurrection [1]they might obtain; others

δὲ ἐμπαιγμῶν καὶ μαστίγων πεῖραν ἔλαβον,
and [3]of mockings [4]and [5]*of* scourgings [2]trial [1]took,

ἔτι δὲ δεσμῶν καὶ φυλακῆς· **37** ἐλιθάσ-
and more of bonds and of prison; they were

θησαν, ἐπειράσθησαν, ἐπρίσθησαν, ἐν φόνῳ
stoned, they were tried, they were sawn asunder, [2]by [3]murder

μαχαίρης ἀπέθανον, περιῆλθον ἐν μηλωταῖς,
[4]of sword [1]they died, they went about in sheepskins,

ἐν αἰγείοις δέρμασιν, ὑστερούμενοι,
in goatskins, being in want,

θλιβόμενοι, κακουχούμενοι, **38** ὧν οὐκ ἦν
being afflicted, *being* ill treated, of whom was not

ἄξιος ὁ κόσμος, ἐπὶ ἐρημίαις πλανώμενοι
worthy the world, [2]over [3]deserts [1]wandering

καὶ ὄρεσιν καὶ σπηλαίοις καὶ ταῖς ὀπαῖς
and mountains and caves and the holes

τῆς γῆς. **39** Καὶ οὗτοι πάντες μαρτυρη-
of the earth. And these all having obtained

destroyer of the firstborn
would not touch the firstborn of Israel.
29By faith the people
passed through the Red
Sea[v] as on dry land; but
when the Egyptians tried to
do so, they were drowned.
30By faith the walls of Jericho fell, after the people
had marched around them
for seven days.
31By faith the prostitute
Rahab, because she wel-
comed the spies, was not
killed with those who were
disobedient.[w]
32And what more shall I
say? I do not have time to
tell about Gideon, Barak,
Samson, Jephthah, David,
Samuel and the prophets,
33who through faith con-
quered kingdoms, adminis-
tered justice, and gained
what was promised; who
shut the mouths of lions,
34quenched the fury of the
flames, and escaped the
edge of the sword; whose
weakness was turned to
strength; and who became
powerful in battle and rout-
ed foreign armies. 35Wom-
en received back their
dead, raised to life again.
Others were tortured and
refused to be released, so
that they might gain a better resurrection. 36Some
faced jeers and flogging,
while still others were
chained and put in prison.
37They were stoned[x]; they
were sawed in two; they
were put to death by the
sword. They went about in
sheepskins and goatskins,
destitute, persecuted and
mistreated—38the world
was not worthy of them.
They wandered in deserts
and mountains, and in
caves and holes in the
ground.
39These were all com-
mended for their faith, yet

[k] Gk *would not touch them*
[l] Or *unbelieving*
[m] Other ancient authorities add *they were tempted*

[v] 29 That is, Sea of Reeds
[w] 31 Or *unbelieving*
[x] 37 Some early manuscripts *stoned; they were put to the test;*

their faith, did not receive
what was promised,
40 since God had provided
something better so that
they would not, apart from
us, be made perfect.

Chapter 12

The Example of Jesus

THEREFORE, since we
are surrounded by so
great a cloud of witnesses,
let us also lay aside every
weight and the sin that
clings so closely,[n] and let
us run with perseverance
the race that is set before
us, 2 looking to Jesus the pioneer and perfecter of our
faith, who for the sake of[o]
the joy that was set before
him endured the cross, dis-
regarding its shame, and
has taken his seat at the
right hand of the throne of
God.
3 Consider him who en-
dured such hostility against
himself from sinners,[p] so
that you may not grow weary or lose heart. 4 In your
struggle against sin you
have not yet resisted to the
point of shedding your
blood. 5 And you have forgotten the exhortation that
addresses you as
children—

"My child, do not
regard lightly
the discipline of
the Lord,
or lose heart when
you are
punished by
him;
6 for the Lord
disciplines those
whom he loves,
and chastises every
child whom he
accepts."

7 Endure trials for the sake
of discipline. God is treating you as children; for
what child is there whom a
parent does not discipline?
8 If you do not have that discipline in which all children
share, then you are illegitimate and not his children.
9 Moreover, we had human

[n] Other ancient authorities read *sin that easily distracts*
[o] Or *who instead of*
[p] Other ancient authorities read *such hostility from sinners against themselves*

θέντες διὰ τῆς πίστεως οὐκ ἐκομίσαντο
witness through the(ir) faith obtained not
τὴν ἐπαγγελίαν, 40 τοῦ θεοῦ περὶ ἡμῶν
the promise, – God [4]concerning [5]us
κρεῖττόν τι προβλεψαμένου, ἵνα μὴ χωρὶς
[3]better [2]something [1]having foreseen,[a] in order that not without
ἡμῶν τελειωθῶσιν.
us they should be perfected.

12 Τοιγαροῦν καὶ ἡμεῖς, τοσοῦτον ἔχοντες
So therefore [2]also [1]we, [3]such [1]having
περικείμενον ἡμῖν νέφος μαρτύρων, ὄγκον
[5]lying around [6]us [2]a cloud [4]of witnesses, [3]encumbrance
ἀποθέμενοι πάντα καὶ τὴν εὐπερίστατον
[1]putting away [2]every [4]and [5]the [7]most besetting
ἁμαρτίαν, δι' ὑπομονῆς τρέχωμεν τὸν
[6]sin, through endurance let us run [1]the
προκείμενον ἡμῖν ἀγῶνα, 2 ἀφορῶντες εἰς
[3]set before [4]us [2]contest(race), looking away to
τὸν τῆς πίστεως ἀρχηγὸν καὶ τελειωτὴν
[1]the [5]of the [6]faith [2]author [3]and [4]finisher
Ἰησοῦν, ὃς ἀντὶ τῆς προκειμένης αὐτῷ
Jesus, who against [1]the [3]set before [4]him
χαρᾶς ὑπέμεινεν σταυρὸν αἰσχύνης κατα-
[2]joy endured a cross [2]shame [1]de-
φρονήσας, ἐν δεξιᾷ τε τοῦ θρόνου τοῦ
spising, [3]at [4][the] right [hand] [1]and [5]of the [6]throne –
θεοῦ κεκάθικεν. 3 ἀναλογίσασθε γὰρ τὸν
[7]of God [2]has taken [his] seat. For consider ye [1]the [one]
τοιαύτην ὑπομεμενηκότα ὑπὸ τῶν ἁμαρτω-
[3]such [2]having endured [5]by – [6]of sin-
λῶν εἰς ἑαυτὸν ἀντιλογίαν, ἵνα μὴ κάμητε
ners [7]against [8]himself [4]contradiction, lest ye grow weary
ταῖς ψυχαῖς ὑμῶν ἐκλυόμενοι. 4 Οὔπω
[2]in the [3]souls [4]of you [1]fainting. Not yet
μέχρις αἵματος ἀντικατέστητε πρὸς τὴν
[2]until [3]blood [1]ye resisted [5]against –
ἁμαρτίαν ἀνταγωνιζόμενοι, 5 καὶ ἐκλέλησθε
[6]sin [4]struggling against, and ye have forgotten
τῆς παρακλήσεως, ἥτις ὑμῖν ὡς υἱοῖς
the exhortation, which [2]with you [3]as [4]with sons
διαλέγεται· υἱέ μου, μὴ ὀλιγώρει παιδείας
[1]discourses: Son of me, do not make light of [the] discipline
κυρίου, μηδὲ ἐκλύου ὑπ' αὐτοῦ ἐλεγχόμενος·
of [the] Lord, nor faint [2]by [3]him [1]being reproved;
6 ὃν γὰρ ἀγαπᾷ κύριος παιδεύει, μαστιγοῖ
for whom [2]loves [1][the] Lord he disciplines, [2]scourges
δὲ πάντα υἱὸν ὃν παραδέχεται. 7 εἰς
[1]and every son whom he receives. For
παιδείαν ὑπομένετε· ὡς υἱοῖς ὑμῖν
discipline endure ye; [4]as [5]with sons [3]with you
προσφέρεται ὁ θεός· τίς γὰρ υἱὸς ὃν
[2]is dealing – [1]God; for what son whom [is there]
οὐ παιδεύει πατήρ; 8 εἰ δὲ χωρίς ἐστε
[2]disciplines not [1]a father? But if [2]without [1]ye are
παιδείας, ἧς μέτοχοι γεγόνασιν πάντες,
discipline, of which [3]sharers [2]have become [1]all,
ἄρα νόθοι καὶ οὐχ υἱοί ἐστε. 9 εἶτα
then bastards and not sons ye are. Furthermore

none of them received what
had been promised. 40 God
had planned something better for us so that only together with us would they
be made perfect.

Chapter 12

God Disciplines His Sons

THEREFORE, since we
are surrounded by
such a great cloud of witnesses, let us throw off everything that hinders and
the sin that so easily entan-
gles, and let us run with
perseverance the race
marked out for us. 2 Let us
fix our eyes on Jesus, the
author and perfecter of our
faith, who for the joy set
before him endured the
cross, scorning its shame,
and sat down at the right
hand of the throne of God.
3 Consider him who en-
dured such opposition from
sinful men, so that you will
not grow weary and lose
heart.
4 In your struggle against
sin, you have not yet resisted to the point of shedding
your blood. 5 And you have
forgotten that word of encouragement that ad-
dresses you as sons:

"My son, do not make
light of the Lord's
discipline,
and do not lose heart
when he rebukes
you,
6 because the Lord
disciplines those he
loves,
and he punishes
everyone he accepts
as a son."[y]

7 Endure hardship as dis-
cipline; God is treating you
as sons. For what son is not
disciplined by his father?
8 If you are not disciplined
(and everyone undergoes
discipline), then you are illegitimate children and not
true sons. 9 Moreover, we

[y] 6 Prov. 3:11,12

parents to discipline us,
and we respected them.
Should we not be even
more willing to be subject
to the Father of spirits and
live? 10 For they disciplined
us for a short time as
seemed best to them, but
he disciplines us for our
good, in order that we may
share his holiness. 11 Now,
discipline always seems
painful rather than pleasant
at the time, but later it
yields the peaceful fruit of
righteousness to those who
have been trained by it.
12 Therefore lift your
drooping hands and
strengthen your weak
knees, 13 and make straight
paths for your feet, so that
what is lame may not be put
out of joint, but rather be
healed.

Warnings against Rejecting God's Grace

14 Pursue peace with
everyone, and the holiness
without which no one will
see the Lord. 15 See to it
that no one fails to obtain
the grace of God; that no
root of bitterness springs
up and causes trouble, and
through it many become
defiled. 16 See to it that no
one becomes like Esau, an
immoral and godless person,
son, who sold his birthright
for a single meal. 17 You
know that later, when he
wanted to inherit the blessing,
ing, he was rejected, for he
found no chance to repent,[q]
pent,[q] even though he
sought the blessing[r] with
tears.
18 You have not come
to something[s] that can be
touched, a blazing fire, and
darkness, and gloom, and a
tempest, 19 and the sound

τοὺς μὲν τῆς σαρκὸς ἡμῶν πατέρας
the – ³of the ⁴flesh ⁵of us ²fathers

εἴχομεν παιδευτὰς καὶ ἐνετρεπόμεθα· οὐ
¹we had ⁶correctors and we respected [them]: ⁸not

πολὺ μᾶλλον ὑποταγησόμεθα τῷ πατρὶ
⁹much ⁷more ¹shall ²we ⁴be ⁵subject to the Father

τῶν πνευμάτων καὶ ζήσομεν; 10 οἱ μὲν
– of spirits and we shall live? ²they ³indeed

γὰρ πρὸς ὀλίγας ἡμέρας κατὰ τὸ δοκοῦν
¹for for a few days according to the thing seeming [good]

αὐτοῖς ἐπαίδευον, ὁ δὲ ἐπὶ τὸ συμφέρον
to them disciplined [us], but he for the(our) profit

εἰς τὸ μεταλαβεῖν τῆς ἁγιότητος αὐτοῦ.
for the to partake of the sanctity of him.

11 πᾶσα μὲν παιδεία πρὸς μὲν τὸ παρὸν
²All ¹on one hand ³discipline ⁴for ⁷indeed ⁵the ⁶present

οὐ δοκεῖ χαρᾶς εἶναι ἀλλὰ λύπης, ὕστερον
seems not ²of joy ¹to be but of grief, ²later

δὲ καρπὸν εἰρηνικὸν τοῖς δι' αὐτῆς
¹on the other ⁸fruit ⁴peaceable ⁷to the ⁹through [ones] ¹⁰it

γεγυμνασμένοις ἀποδίδωσιν δικαιοσύνης.
⁸having been exercised ³it gives back ⁶of righteousness.

12 Διὸ τὰς παρειμένας χεῖρας καὶ τὰ
Wherefore ²the ³*having been* wearied ⁴hands ⁵and ⁶the

παραλελυμένα γόνατα ἀνορθώσατε, 13 καὶ
⁷*having been* paralysed ⁸knees ¹straighten ye, and

τροχιὰς ὀρθὰς ποιεῖτε τοῖς ποσὶν ὑμῶν,
tracks straight make for the feet of you,

ἵνα μὴ τὸ χωλὸν ἐκτραπῇ, ἰαθῇ δὲ
lest the lame be turned aside, ³may be cured ¹but

μᾶλλον. 14 Εἰρήνην διώκετε μετὰ πάντων,
²rather. Peace follow with all men,

καὶ τὸν ἁγιασμόν, οὗ χωρὶς οὐδεὶς
and – sanctification, ²which ¹without no one

ὄψεται τὸν κύριον, 15 ἐπισκοποῦντες μή
will see the Lord, observing not(lest)

τις ὑστερῶν ἀπὸ τῆς χάριτος τοῦ θεοῦ,
anyone fail*ing* from the grace – of God,

μή τις ῥίζα πικρίας ἄνω φύουσα ἐνοχλῇ
not (lest) any root of bitterness ²up ¹growing disturb

καὶ διὰ ταύτης μιανθῶσιν οἱ πολλοί,
and through this ²be defiled *the* ¹many,

16 μή τις πόρνος ἢ βέβηλος ὡς Ἠσαῦ,
not(lest) any fornicator or profane man as Esau,

ὃς ἀντὶ βρώσεως μιᾶς ἀπέδοτο τὰ
who against ²eating ¹one gave up the

πρωτοτόκια ἑαυτοῦ. 17 ἴστε γὰρ ὅτι
rights of the firstborn of himself. For ye know that

καὶ μετέπειτα θέλων κληρονομῆσαι τὴν
indeed afterwards wishing to inherit the

εὐλογίαν ἀπεδοκιμάσθη, μετανοίας γὰρ
blessing he was rejected, for ⁴of repentance

τόπον οὐχ εὗρεν, καίπερ μετὰ δακρύων
³place ²not ¹he found, though with tears

ἐκζητήσας αὐτήν. 18 Οὐ γὰρ προσεληλύθατε
seeking out it. For ²not ¹ye ³have ⁴approached

ψηλαφωμένῳ καὶ κεκαυμένῳ πυρὶ καὶ
to [a mountain] being felt and having been ignited with fire and

γνόφῳ καὶ ζόφῳ καὶ θυέλλῃ 19 καὶ
to darkness and *to* deep gloom and *to* whirlwind and

have all had human fathers
who disciplined us and we
respected them for it. How
much more should we submit
mit to the Father of our
spirits and live! 10 Our fathers
thers disciplined us for a little
tle while as they thought
best; but God disciplines us
for our good, that we may
share in his holiness. 11 No
discipline seems pleasant at
the time, but painful. Later
on, however, it produces a
harvest of righteousness
and peace for those who
have been trained by it.
12 Therefore, strengthen
your feeble arms and weak
knees. 13 "Make level paths
for your feet,"[z] so that the
lame may not be disabled,
but rather healed.

Warning Against Refusing God

14 Make every effort to
live in peace with all men
and to be holy; without holiness
liness no one will see the
Lord. 15 See to it that no one
misses the grace of God
and that no bitter root
grows up to cause trouble
and defile many. 16 See that
no one is sexually immoral,
or is godless like Esau, who
for a single meal sold his
inheritance rights as the
oldest son. 17 Afterward, as
you know, when he wanted
to inherit this blessing, he
was rejected. He could
bring about no change of
mind, though he sought the
blessing with tears.
18 You have not come to a
mountain that can be
touched and that is burning
with fire; to darkness,
gloom and storm; 19 to a

[q] Or *no chance to change his father's mind*
[r] Gk *it*
[s] Other ancient authorities read *a mountain*

[z] *13* Prov. 4:26

of a trumpet, and a voice whose words made the hearers beg that not another word be spoken to them. 20 (For they could not endure the order that was given, "If even an animal touches the mountain, it shall be stoned to death." 21 Indeed, so terrifying was the sight that Moses said, "I tremble with fear.") 22 But you have come to Mount Zion and to the city of the living God, the heavenly Jerusalem, and to innumerable angels in festal gathering, 23 and to the assembly[t] of the firstborn who are enrolled in heaven, and to God the judge of all, and to the spirits of the righteous made perfect, 24 and to Jesus, the mediator of a new covenant, and to the sprinkled blood that speaks a better word than the blood of Abel.

25 See that you do not refuse the one who is speaking; for if they did not escape when they refused the one who warned them on earth, how much less will we escape if we reject the one who warns from heaven! 26 At that time his voice shook the earth; but now he has promised, "Yet once more I will shake not only the earth but also the heaven." 27 This phrase, "Yet once more," indicates the removal of what is shaken—that is, created things—so that what cannot be shaken may remain. 28 Therefore, since we are receiving a kingdom that cannot be shaken, let us give thanks, by which we offer to God an acceptable worship with reverence and awe; 29 for indeed our God is a consuming fire.

[t] Or *angels, and to the festal gathering* [23]*and assembly*

σάλπιγγος ἤχῳ καὶ φωνῇ ῥημάτων, ἧς
[2]of trumpet [1]*to* a sound and *to* a voice of words, which

οἱ ἀκούσαντες παρῃτήσαντο μὴ προστεθῆναι
the [ones] hearing entreated not to be added

αὐτοῖς λόγον· **20** οὐκ ἔφερον γὰρ τὸ
to them a word; [3]not [2]they bore [1]for the thing

διαστελλόμενον· κἂν θηρίον θίγῃ τοῦ ὄρους,
being charged: If even a beast touches the mountain,

λιθοβοληθήσεται· **21** καί, οὕτω φοβερὸν ἦν
it shall be stoned; and, so fearful was

τὸ φανταζόμενον, Μωϋσῆς εἶπεν· ἔκφοβός
the thing appearing, Moses said: [2]Terrified

εἰμι καὶ ἔντρομος· **22** ἀλλὰ προσεληλύθατε
[1]I am and trembling; but ye have approached

Σιὼν ὄρει καὶ πόλει θεοῦ ζῶντος,
[2]Zion [1]*to* mount and *to* a city [2]God [1]of [the] living,

Ἰερουσαλὴμ ἐπουρανίῳ, καὶ μυριάσιν
[2]Jerusalem [1]*to* a heavenly, and *to* myriads

ἀγγέλων, **23** πανηγύρει καὶ ἐκκλησίᾳ
of angels, *to* an assembly and a church

πρωτοτόκων ἀπογεγραμμένων ἐν οὐρανοῖς,
of firstborn [ones] *having been* enrolled in heavens,

καὶ κριτῇ θεῷ πάντων, καὶ πνεύμασι
and [2]judge [1]*to* God of all men, and *to* spirits

δικαίων τετελειωμένων, **24** καὶ διαθήκης
of just men *having been* made perfect, and [4]covenant

νέας μεσίτῃ Ἰησοῦ, καὶ αἵματι ῥαντισμοῦ
[3]of a new [2]mediator [1]*to* Jesus, and *to* blood of sprinkling

κρεῖττον λαλοῦντι παρὰ τὸν Ἄβελ.
[2]a better thing [1]speaking than – Abel.

25 Βλέπετε μὴ παραιτήσησθε τὸν λαλοῦντα·
Look ye [that] [2]not [1]ye refuse the [one] speaking;

εἰ γὰρ ἐκεῖνοι οὐκ ἐξέφυγον ἐπὶ γῆς
for if those escaped not [4]on [5]earth

παραιτησάμενοι τὸν χρηματίζοντα, πολὺ
[1]refusing [2]the [one] [3]warning, much

μᾶλλον ἡμεῖς οἱ τὸν ἀπ' οὐρανῶν
more we* [1]the [ones] [3]the [one] [4][warning] [5]from [6]heavens

ἀποστρεφόμενοι· **26** οὗ ἡ φωνὴ τὴν γῆν
[2]turning from; of whom the voice [3]the [4]earth

ἐσάλευσεν τότε, νῦν δὲ ἐπήγγελται λέγων·
[2]shook [1]then, but now he has promised saying:

ἔτι ἅπαξ ἐγὼ σείσω οὐ μόνον τὴν
Yet once I will shake not only the

γῆν ἀλλὰ καὶ τὸν οὐρανόν. **27** τὸ δὲ
earth but also *the* heaven. Now the [phrase]

ἔτι ἅπαξ δηλοῖ τὴν τῶν σαλευομένων
'Yet once' declares [1]the [3]of the things [4]being shaken

μετάθεσιν ὡς πεποιημένων, ἵνα μείνῃ τὰ
[2]removal as of things having been made, in order that [4]may remain [1]the things

μὴ σαλευόμενα. **28** Διὸ βασιλείαν ἀσάλευτος
[2]not [3]being shaken. Wherefore [3]kingdom [2]an unshakable

παραλαμβάνοντες ἔχωμεν χάριν, δι' ἧς
[1]receiving let us have grace, through which

λατρεύωμεν εὐαρέστως τῷ θεῷ, μετὰ
we may serve [2]well-pleasingly – [1]God, with

εὐλαβείας καὶ δέους· **29** καὶ γὰρ ὁ θεὸς
devoutness and awe; for indeed the God

ἡμῶν πῦρ καταναλίσκον.
of us [is] fire a consuming.

* That is, "much more [shall] we [not escape]"; or, putting it in another way, "much less shall we escape."

trumpet blast or to such a voice speaking words that those who heard it begged that no further word be spoken to them, 20 because they could not bear what was commanded: "If even an animal touches the mountain, it must be stoned."[a] 21 The sight was so terrifying that Moses said, "I am trembling with fear."[b]

22 But you have come to Mount Zion, to the heavenly Jerusalem, the city of the living God. You have come to thousands upon thousands of angels in joyful assembly, 23 to the church of the firstborn, whose names are written in heaven. You have come to God, the judge of all men, to the spirits of righteous men made perfect, 24 to Jesus the mediator of a new covenant, and to the sprinkled blood that speaks a better word than the blood of Abel.

25 See to it that you do not refuse him who speaks. If they did not escape when they refused him who warned them on earth, how much less will we, if we turn away from him who warns us from heaven? 26 At that time his voice shook the earth, but now he has promised, "Once more I will shake not only the earth but also the heavens."[c] 27 The words "once more" indicate the removing of what can be shaken—that is, created things—so that what cannot be shaken may remain.

28 Therefore, since we are receiving a kingdom that cannot be shaken, let us be thankful, and so worship God acceptably with reverence and awe, 29 for our "God is a consuming fire."[d]

[a] *20* Exodus 19:12,13
[b] *21* Deut. 9:19
[c] *26* Haggai 2:6
[d] *29* Deut. 4:24

Chapter 13

Service Well-Pleasing to God

LET mutual love contin-
ue. 2 Do not neglect to
show hospitality to strangers, for by doing that some
have entertained angels
without knowing it. 3 Re-
member those who are in
prison, as though you were
in prison with them; those
who are being tortured, as
though you yourselves
were being tortured.[u] 4 Let
marriage be held in honor
by all, and let the marriage
bed be kept undefiled; for
God will judge fornicators
and adulterers. 5 Keep your
lives free from the love of
money, and be content
with what you have; for he
has said, "I will never leave
you or forsake you." 6 So
we can say with confi-
dence,

"The Lord is my helper;
I will not be afraid.
What can anyone do to me?"

7 Remember your lead-
ers, those who spoke the
word of God to you; con-
sider the outcome of their
way of life, and imitate
their faith. 8 Jesus Christ is
the same yesterday and to-
day and forever. 9 Do not
be carried away by all kinds
of strange teachings; for it
is well for the heart to be
strengthened by grace, not
by regulations about
food,[v] which have not benefited those who observe
them. 10 We have an altar
from which those who offi-
ciate in the tent[w] have no
right to eat. 11 For the bodies of those animals whose
blood is brought into the
sanctuary by the high priest
as a sacrifice for sin are
burned outside the camp.
12 Therefore Jesus also suffered outside the city gate
in order to sanctify the peo-

[u] Gk *were in the body*
[v] Gk *not by foods*
[w] Or *tabernacle*

13 Ἡ φιλαδελφία μενέτω. 2 τῆς
– [2]brotherly love [1]Let *it* [3]remain. –

φιλοξενίας μὴ ἐπιλανθάνεσθε· διὰ ταύτης
of hospitality Be ye not forgetful; [2]through [3]this

γὰρ ἔλαθόν τινες ξενίσαντες ἀγγέλους.
[1]for [5]unconsciously† [4]some [6]entertaining(ed) [7]angels.

3 μιμνήσκεσθε τῶν δεσμίων ὡς συνδεδεμένοι,
Be ye mindful of the prisoners as *having been* bound with [them],

τῶν κακουχουμένων ὡς καὶ αὐτοὶ ὄντες
of the [ones] *being* ill treated as also [your]selves being

ἐν σώματι. 4 Τίμιος ὁ γάμος ἐν πᾶσιν
in [the] body. [4]honourable [1][Let] – [2]marriage [3][be] in all

καὶ ἡ κοίτη ἀμίαντος· πόρνους γὰρ
and the bed undefiled; for fornicators

καὶ μοιχοὺς κρινεῖ ὁ θεός. 5 Ἀφιλάργυρος
and adulterers [2]will judge – [1]God. [5]without love of money

ὁ τρόπος, ἀρκούμενοι τοῖς παροῦσιν·
[1][Let] [2]the (your) [3]way of life [4][be], being satisfied with the things present;

αὐτὸς γὰρ εἴρηκεν· οὐ μή σε ἀνῶ οὐδ'
for he has said: By no means thee will I leave nor

οὐ μή σε ἐγκαταλίπω· 6 ὥστε θαρροῦντας
by no(any) means thee I forsake; so as being of good cheer

ἡμᾶς λέγειν· κύριος ἐμοὶ βοηθός, οὐ
us to say[b]: [The] Lord to me[o] [is] a helper, not

φοβηθήσομαι· τί ποιήσει μοι ἄνθρωπος;
I will fear; what [1]will [3]do [4]to me [2]man ?

7 Μνημονεύετε τῶν ἡγουμένων ὑμῶν,
Remember the [ones] leading of you,

οἵτινες ἐλάλησαν ὑμῖν τὸν λόγον τοῦ
who spoke to you the word –

θεοῦ, ὧν ἀναθεωροῦντες τὴν ἔκβασιν τῆς
of God, [6]of whom [1]looking at [2]the [3]result [4]of the

ἀναστροφῆς μιμεῖσθε τὴν πίστιν. 8 Ἰησοῦς
[5]conduct imitate ye the(ir) faith. Jesus

Χριστὸς ἐχθὲς καὶ σήμερον ὁ αὐτὸς
Christ [4]yesterday [5]and [6]to-day [1][is] [2]the [3]same

καὶ εἰς τοὺς αἰῶνας. 9 Διδαχαῖς ποικίλαις
and unto the ages. [5]teachings [2]by various

καὶ ξέναις μὴ παραφέρεσθε· καλὸν γὰρ
[3]and [4]strange [1]Do not be carried away; for [it is] good

χάριτι βεβαιοῦσθαι τὴν καρδίαν, οὐ
[4]by grace [3]to be confirmed [1]the [2]heart,[b] not

βρώμασιν, ἐν οἷς οὐκ ὠφελήθησαν οἱ
by foods, by which [3]were not profited [1]the

περιπατοῦντες. 10 ἔχομεν θυσιαστήριον ἐξ
[2][ones] walking. We have an altar of

οὗ φαγεῖν οὐκ ἔχουσιν ἐξουσίαν οἱ τῇ
which [7]to eat [5]have not [6]authority [1]the [ones] [3]the

σκηνῇ λατρεύοντες. 11 ὧν γὰρ εἰσφέρεται
[4]tabernacle [2]serving. For [3]of what [7]is brought *in*

ζῴων τὸ αἷμα περὶ ἁμαρτίας εἰς τὰ
[4]animals [1]the [2]blood [5]concerning [6]sins into the

ἅγια διὰ τοῦ ἀρχιερέως, τούτων τὰ
holies through the high priest, of these the

σώματα κατακαίεται ἔξω τῆς παρεμβολῆς.
bodies is(are) burned outside the camp.

12 διὸ καὶ Ἰησοῦς, ἵνα ἁγιάσῃ διὰ
Wherefore indeed Jesus, in order that he might sanctify [3]through

Chapter 13

Concluding Exhortations

KEEP on loving each
other as brothers.
2 Do not forget to entertain
strangers, for by so doing
some people have enter-
tained angels without
knowing it. 3 Remember
those in prison as if you
were their fellow prisoners,
and those who are mistreated as if you yourselves
were suffering.
4 Marriage should be hon-
ored by all, and the mar-
riage bed kept pure, for
God will judge the adulter-
er and all the sexually immoral. 5 Keep your lives
free from the love of money
and be content with what
you have, because God has
said,

"Never will I leave you;
never will I forsake
you."[e]

6 So we say with confi-
dence,

"The Lord is my helper;
I will not be afraid.
What can man do to
me?"[f]

7 Remember your leaders,
who spoke the word of God
to you. Consider the out-
come of their way of life
and imitate their faith.
8 Jesus Christ is the same
yesterday and today and
forever.
9 Do not be carried away
by all kinds of strange
teachings. It is good for our
hearts to be strengthened
by grace, not by ceremonial foods, which are of no
value to those who eat
them. 10 We have an altar
from which those who min-
ister at the tabernacle have
no right to eat.
11 The high priest carries
the blood of animals into
the Most Holy Place as a
sin offering, but the bodies
are burned outside the
camp. 12 And so Jesus also
suffered outside the city

[e]5 Deut. 31:6
[f]6 Psalm 118:6,7

ple by his own blood. 13 Let
us then go to him outside
the camp and bear the
abuse he endured. 14 For
here we have no lasting
city, but we are looking for
the city that is to come.
15 Through him, then, let us
continually offer a sacrifice
of praise to God, that is, the
fruit of lips that confess his
name. 16 Do not neglect to
do good and to share what
you have, for such sacri-
fices are pleasing to God.
17 Obey your leaders
and submit to them, for
they are keeping watch
over your souls and will
give an account. Let them
do this with joy and not
with sighing—for that
would be harmful to you.
18 Pray for us; we are
sure that we have a clear
conscience, desiring to act
honorably in all things. 19 I
urge you all the more to do
this, so that I may be restored to you very soon.

Benediction

20 Now may the God of
peace, who brought back
from the dead our Lord
Jesus, the great shepherd
of the sheep, by the blood
of the eternal covenant,
21 make you complete in everything good so that you
may do his will, working
among us[x] that which is
pleasing in his sight,
through Jesus Christ, to
whom be the glory forever
and ever. Amen.

[x] Other ancient authorities read *you*

τοῦ ἰδίου αἵματος τὸν λαόν, ἔξω τῆς
[4]the(his) [5]own [6]blood [1]the [2]people, outside the
πύλης ἔπαθεν. 13 τοίνυν ἐξερχώμεθα πρὸς
gate suffered. So let us go forth to
αὐτὸν ἔξω τῆς παρεμβολῆς τὸν ὀνειδισμὸν
him outside the camp the reproach
αὐτοῦ φέροντες· 14 οὐ γὰρ ἔχομεν ὧδε
of him bearing; for [2]not [1]we have here
μένουσαν πόλιν, ἀλλὰ τὴν μέλλουσαν
a continuing city, but the [one] coming
ἐπιζητοῦμεν. 15 Δι' αὐτοῦ οὖν ἀναφέρωμεν
we seek. Through him therefore let us offer up
θυσίαν αἰνέσεως διὰ παντὸς τῷ θεῷ,
a sacrifice of praise always – to God,
τοῦτ' ἔστιν καρπὸν χειλέων ὁμολογούντων
this is fruit of lips confessing
τῷ ὀνόματι αὐτοῦ. 16 τῆς δὲ εὐποιΐας
to the name of him. But of the doing good
καὶ κοινωνίας μὴ ἐπιλανθάνεσθε· τοιαύταις
and sharing be ye not forgetful; [2]with such
γὰρ θυσίαις εὐαρεστεῖται ὁ θεός. 17 Πεί-
[1]for sacrifices [3]is well pleased – [1]God. Obey
θεσθε τοῖς ἡγουμένοις ὑμῶν καὶ ὑπείκετε·
ye the [ones] leading of you and submit to [them];
αὐτοὶ γὰρ ἀγρυπνοῦσιν ὑπὲρ τῶν ψυχῶν
for they watch on behalf of the souls
ὑμῶν ὡς λόγον ἀποδώσοντες· ἵνα μετὰ
of you as [2]account [1]rendering*; in order that with
χαρᾶς τοῦτο ποιῶσιν καὶ μὴ στενάζ-
joy [2]this [1]they may do and not groan-
οντες· ἀλυσιτελὲς γὰρ ὑμῖν τοῦτο.
ing; for profitless to you this [would be].
18 Προσεύχεσθε περὶ ἡμῶν· πειθόμεθα
Pray ye concerning us; [3]we are persuaded
γὰρ ὅτι καλὴν συνείδησιν ἔχομεν, ἐν
[1]for that a good conscience we have, [4]in
πᾶσιν καλῶς θέλοντες ἀναστρέφεσθαι.
[6]all [respects] [8]well [1]wishing [2]to behave.
19 περισσοτέρως δὲ παρακαλῶ τοῦτο
And more abundantly I beseech [you] this
ποιῆσαι, ἵνα τάχιον ἀποκατασταθῶ ὑμῖν.
to do, in order that sooner I may be restored to you.
20 Ὁ δὲ θεὸς τῆς εἰρήνης, ὁ ἀναγαγὼν
Now the God – of peace, the [one] having led up
ἐκ νεκρῶν τὸν ποιμένα τῶν προβάτων
out of [the] dead the [2]shepherd [3]of the [4]sheep
τὸν μέγαν ἐν αἵματι διαθήκης αἰωνίου,
the [1]great in (? with) blood [2]covenant [1]of an eternal,
τὸν κύριον ἡμῶν Ἰησοῦν, 21 καταρτίσαι
the Lord of us Jesus, *may he* adjust
ὑμᾶς ἐν παντὶ ἀγαθῷ εἰς τὸ ποιῆσαι
you in every good thing *for the* to do
τὸ θέλημα αὐτοῦ, ποιῶν ἐν ἡμῖν τὸ
the will of him, doing in us the [thing]
εὐάρεστον ἐνώπιον αὐτοῦ διὰ Ἰησοῦ
wellpleasing before him through Jesus
Χριστοῦ, ᾧ ἡ δόξα εἰς τοὺς αἰῶνας
Christ, to whom [be] the glory unto the ages

* **In the future.**

gate to make the people
holy through his own
blood. 13 Let us, then, go to
him outside the camp,
bearing the disgrace he
bore. 14 For here we do not
have an enduring city, but
we are looking for the city
that is to come.
15 Through Jesus, there-
fore, let us continually offer to God a sacrifice of
praise—the fruit of lips that
confess his name. 16 And do
not forget to do good and to
share with others, for with
such sacrifices God is
pleased.
17 Obey your leaders and
submit to their authority.
They keep watch over you
as men who must give an
account. Obey them so that
their work will be a joy, not
a burden, for that would be
of no advantage to you.
18 Pray for us. We are sure
that we have a clear con-
science and desire to live
honorably in every way. 19 I
particularly urge you to
pray so that I may be re-
stored to you soon.
20 May the God of peace,
who through the blood of
the eternal covenant
brought back from the dead
our Lord Jesus, that great
Shepherd of the sheep,
21 equip you with every-
thing good for doing his
will, and may he work in us
what is pleasing to him,
through Jesus Christ, to
whom be glory for ever and

Final Exhortation and Greetings

22 I appeal to you,
brothers and sisters,[y] bear
with my word of exhorta-
tion, for I have written to
you briefly. 23 I want you to
know that our brother Timothy has been set free; and
if he comes in time, he will
be with me when I see you.
24 Greet all your leaders
and all the saints. Those
from Italy send you greetings. 25 Grace be with all of
you.[z]

τῶν αἰώνων· ἀμήν. **22** Παρακαλῶ δὲ
of the ages: Amen. And I beseech

ὑμᾶς, ἀδελφοί, ἀνέχεσθε τοῦ λόγου τῆς
you, brothers, endure the word –

παρακλήσεως· καὶ γὰρ διὰ βραχέων
of beseeching; for indeed through few [words]

ἐπέστειλα ὑμῖν. **23** Γινώσκετε τὸν ἀδελφὸν
I wrote to you. Know ye the brother

ἡμῶν Τιμόθεον ἀπολελυμένον, μεθ' οὗ
of us Timothy having been released, with whom

ἐὰν τάχιον ἔρχηται ὄψομαι ὑμᾶς.
if sooner I come I will see you.

24 Ἀσπάσασθε πάντας τοὺς ἡγουμένους
Greet ye all the [ones] leading

ὑμῶν καὶ πάντας τοὺς ἁγίους. Ἀσπάζονται
of you and all the saints. [4]greet

ὑμᾶς οἱ ἀπὸ τῆς Ἰταλίας.
[5]you [1]The [ones] [2]from – [3]Italy.

25 Ἡ χάρις μετὰ πάντων ὑμῶν.
– Grace [be] with all you.

ever. Amen.

22Brothers, I urge you to
bear with my word of ex-
hortation, for I have written you only a short letter.
23I want you to know that
our brother Timothy has
been released. If he arrives
soon, I will come with him
to see you.
24Greet all your leaders
and all God's people.
Those from Italy send you
their greetings.
25Grace be with you all.

The Letter of

JAMES

Chapter 1

Salutation

JAMES, a servant[a] of
God and of the Lord
Jesus Christ,
To the twelve tribes in
the Dispersion:
Greetings.

Faith and Wisdom

2 My brothers and sis-
ters,[b] whenever you face
trials of any kind, consider
it nothing but joy, 3 because
you know that the testing of
your faith produces endurance; 4 and let endurance
have its full effect, so that
you may be mature and
complete, lacking in nothing.
5 If any of you is lacking
in wisdom, ask God, who
gives to all generously and
ungrudgingly, and it will be
given you. 6 But ask in
faith, never doubting, for
the one who doubts is like a
wave of the sea, driven and
tossed by the wind; 7, 8 for
the doubter, being double-

ΙΑΚΩΒΟΥ ΕΠΙΣΤΟΛΗ

[2]Of James [1]Epistle

1 Ἰάκωβος θεοῦ καὶ κυρίου Ἰησοῦ
James [2]of God [3]and [4]of [the] Lord [5]Jesus

Χριστοῦ δοῦλος ταῖς δώδεκα φυλαῖς ταῖς
[6]Christ [1]a slave to the twelve tribes –

ἐν τῇ διασπορᾷ χαίρειν.
in the dispersion greeting.*

2 Πᾶσαν χαρὰν ἡγήσασθε, ἀδελφοί μου,
All joy deem [it], brothers of me,

ὅταν πειρασμοῖς περιπέσητε ποικίλοις,
whenever [3]trials [1]ye fall [2]into various,

3 γινώσκοντες ὅτι τὸ δοκίμιον ὑμῶν τῆς
knowing that the approved part [3]of you [1]of the
=that which is approved in your faith

πίστεως κατεργάζεται ὑπομονήν. **4** ἡ δὲ
[2]faith works endurance. – And

ὑπομονὴ ἔργον τέλειον ἐχέτω, ἵνα ἦτε
endurance [3]work [2]perfect [1]let it have, in order that ye may be

τέλειοι καὶ ὁλόκληροι, ἐν μηδενὶ λειπόμενοι.
perfect and entire, in nothing wanting.

5 Εἰ δέ τις ὑμῶν λείπεται σοφίας, αἰτείτω
if But anyone of you wants wisdom, let him ask

παρὰ τοῦ διδόντος θεοῦ πᾶσιν ἁπλῶς
from [2]the [one] [3]giving [1]God to all men unreservedly

καὶ μὴ ὀνειδίζοντος, καὶ δοθήσεται αὐτῷ.
and not reproaching, and it will be given to him.

6 αἰτείτω δὲ ἐν πίστει, μηδὲν διακριν-
But let him ask in faith, nothing doubt-

όμενος· ὁ γὰρ διακρινόμενος ἔοικεν κλύδωνι
ing; for the [one] doubting is like a wave

θαλάσσης ἀνεμιζομένῳ καὶ ῥιπιζομένῳ.
of [the] sea *being* driven by wind and *being* tossed.

7 μὴ γὰρ οἰέσθω ὁ ἄνθρωπος ἐκεῖνος
For let not [3]suppose [1]that [2]man

ὅτι λήμψεταί τι παρὰ τοῦ κυρίου, **8** ἀνὴρ
that he will receive anything from the Lord, a man

James

Chapter 1

JAMES, a servant of God
and of the Lord Jesus
Christ,

To the twelve tribes scattered among the nations:

Greetings.

Trials and Temptations

2Consider it pure joy, my
brothers, whenever you
face trials of many kinds,
3because you know that the
testing of your faith devel-
ops perseverance. 4Perse-
verance must finish its
work so that you may be
mature and complete, not
lacking anything. 5If any of
you lacks wisdom, he
should ask God, who gives
generously to all without
finding fault, and it will be
given to him. 6But when he
asks, he must believe and
not doubt, because he who
doubts is like a wave of the
sea, blown and tossed by
the wind. 7That man should
not think he will receive
anything from the Lord;

[y] Gk *brothers*
[z] Other ancient authorities add *Amen*
[a] Gk *slave*
[b] Gk *brothers*

* See note on Phil. 3.16 in Introduction.

minded and unstable in every way, must not expect to
receive anything from the
Lord.

Poverty and Riches

9 Let the believer[c] who
is lowly boast in being
raised up, 10 and the rich in
being brought low, because
the rich will disappear like
a flower in the field. 11 For
the sun rises with its
scorching heat and withers
the field; its flower falls,
and its beauty perishes. It
is the same way with the
rich; in the midst of a busy
life, they will wither away.

Trial and Temptation

12 Blessed is anyone
who endures temptation.
Such a one has stood the
test and will receive the
crown of life that the
Lord[d] has promised to
those who love him. 13 No
one, when tempted, should
say, "I am being tempted
by God"; for God cannot be
tempted by evil and he himself tempts no one. 14 But
one is tempted by one's
own desire, being lured and
enticed by it; 15 then, when
that desire has conceived,
it gives birth to sin, and that
sin, when it is fully grown,
gives birth to death. 16 Do
not be deceived, my be-
loved.[e]
17 Every generous act
of giving, with every perfect gift, is from above,
coming down from the Fa-
ther of lights, with whom
there is no variation or
shadow due to change.[f]
18 In fulfillment of his own
purpose he gave us birth by
the word of truth, so that
we would become a kind of
first fruits of his creatures.

Hearing and Doing the Word

19 You must under-
stand this, my beloved:[e]
let everyone be quick to lis-

[c] Gk *brother*
[d] Gk *he*; other ancient authorities read *God*
[e] Gk *my beloved brothers*
[f] Other ancient authorities read *variation due to a shadow of turning*

δίψυχος, ἀκατάστατος ἐν πάσαις ταῖς
two-souled, unsettled in all the
ὁδοῖς αὐτοῦ. **9** Καυχάσθω δὲ ὁ ἀδελφὸς
ways of him. But let [4]boast [1]the [3]brother
ὁ ταπεινὸς ἐν τῷ ὕψει αὐτοῦ, **10** ὁ δὲ
– [2]humble in the height of him, and the
πλούσιος ἐν τῇ ταπεινώσει αὐτοῦ, ὅτι
rich one in the humiliation of him, because
ὡς ἄνθος χόρτου παρελεύσεται. **11** ἀνέτειλεν
as a flower of grass he will pass away. [4]rose
γὰρ ὁ ἥλιος σὺν τῷ καύσωνι καὶ ἐξήρανεν
[1]For [2]the [3]sun with the hot wind and dried
τὸν χόρτον, καὶ τὸ ἄνθος αὐτοῦ ἐξέπεσεν
the grass, and the flower of it fell out
καὶ ἡ εὐπρέπεια τοῦ προσώπου αὐτοῦ
and the comeliness of the appearance of it
ἀπώλετο· οὕτως καὶ ὁ πλούσιος ἐν ταῖς
perished; thus also the rich man in the
πορείαις αὐτοῦ μαρανθήσεται. **12** Μακάριος
goings of him will fade away. Blessed
ἀνὴρ ὃς ὑπομένει πειρασμόν, ὅτι δόκιμος
[the] man who endures trial, because [2]approved
γενόμενος λήμψεται τὸν στέφανον τῆς
[1]having become he will receive the crown –
ζωῆς, ὃν ἐπηγγείλατο τοῖς ἀγαπῶσιν αὐτόν.
of life, which he promised to the [ones] loving him.
13 Μηδεὶς πειραζόμενος λεγέτω ὅτι ἀπὸ
[2]no man [3]being tempted [1]Let [4]say[,] – From
θεοῦ πειράζομαι· ὁ γὰρ θεὸς ἀπείραστός
God I am tempted; – for God [2]untempted
ἐστιν κακῶν, πειράζει δὲ αὐτὸς οὐδένα.
[1]is of(with) evil things, and [2]tempts [1]he no man.
14 ἕκαστος δὲ πειράζεται ὑπὸ τῆς ἰδίας
But each man is tempted by the(his) own
ἐπιθυμίας ἐξελκόμενος καὶ δελεαζόμενος·
lusts being drawn out and *being* enticed;
15 εἶτα ἡ ἐπιθυμία συλλαβοῦσα τίκτει
then – lust having conceived bears
ἁμαρτίαν, ἡ δὲ ἁμαρτία ἀποτελεσθεῖσα
sin, – and sin having been fully formed
ἀποκύει θάνατον. **16** Μὴ πλανᾶσθε, ἀδελφοί
brings forth death. Do not err, [2]brothers
μου ἀγαπητοί.
[3]of me [1]beloved.

17 Πᾶσα δόσις ἀγαθὴ καὶ πᾶν δώρημα
Every [2]giving [1]good and every [2]gift
τέλειον ἄνωθέν ἐστιν καταβαῖνον ἀπὸ τοῦ
[1]perfect [4]from above [3]is coming down from the
πατρὸς τῶν φώτων, παρ' ᾧ οὐκ ἔνι
Father of the lights, with whom [5]has no place
παραλλαγὴ ἢ τροπῆς ἀποσκίασμα. **18** βου-
[1]change [2]or [4]of turning [3]shadow. Having
ληθεὶς ἀπεκύησεν ἡμᾶς λόγῳ ἀληθείας,
purposed he brought forth us by a word of truth,
εἰς τὸ εἶναι ἡμᾶς ἀπαρχήν τινα τῶν
for the to be =that we should be us[b] [2]firstfruit [1]a certain [3]of the
αὐτοῦ κτισμάτων.
[5]of him [4]creatures.

19 Ἴστε, ἀδελφοί μου ἀγαπητοί. ἔστω
Know ye, [2]brothers [3]of me [1]beloved. [2]let be

8he is a double-minded
man, unstable in all he
does.
9The brother in humble
circumstances ought to
take pride in his high position. 10But the one who is
rich should take pride in his
low position, because he
will pass away like a wild
flower. 11For the sun rises
with scorching heat and
withers the plant; its blos-
som falls and its beauty is
destroyed. In the same
way, the rich man will fade
away even while he goes
about his business.
12Blessed is the man who
perseveres under trial, because when he has stood
the test, he will receive the
crown of life that God has
promised to those who love
him.
13When tempted, no one
should say, "God is tempting me." For God cannot
be tempted by evil, nor
does he tempt anyone;
14but each one is tempted
when, by his own evil de-
sire, he is dragged away
and enticed. 15Then, after
desire has conceived, it
gives birth to sin; and sin,
when it is full-grown, gives
birth to death.
16Don't be deceived, my
dear brothers. 17Every
good and perfect gift is
from above, coming down
from the Father of the
heavenly lights, who does
not change like shifting
shadows. 18He chose to
give us birth through the
word of truth, that we
might be a kind of firstfruits
of all he created.

Listening and Doing

19My dear brothers, take
note of this: Everyone

ten, slow to speak, slow to
anger; 20 for your anger
does not produce God's
righteousness. 21 Therefore
rid yourselves of all sordid-
ness and rank growth of
wickedness, and welcome
with meekness the implanted word that has the power
to save your souls.
22 But be doers of the
word, and not merely hearers who deceive them-
selves. 23 For if any are
hearers of the word and not
doers, they are like those
who look at themselves[g] in
a mirror; 24 for they look at
themselves and, on going
away, immediately forget
what they were like. 25 But
those who look into the
perfect law, the law of liberty, and persevere, being
not hearers who forget but
doers who act—they will
be blessed in their doing.
26 If any think they are
religious, and do not bridle
their tongues but deceive
their hearts, their religion is
worthless. 27 Religion that
is pure and undefiled be-
fore God, the Father, is
this: to care for orphans
and widows in their dis-
tress, and to keep oneself
unstained by the world.

δὲ πᾶς ἄνθρωπος ταχὺς εἰς τὸ ἀκοῦσαι,
1But every man swift *for the* to hear,
βραδὺς εἰς τὸ λαλῆσαι, βραδὺς εἰς ὀργήν·
slow *for the* to speak, slow to wrath;
20 ὀργὴ γὰρ ἀνδρὸς δικαιοσύνην θεοῦ
for [the] wrath of a man 2[the] righteousness 3of God
οὐκ ἐργάζεται. **21** διὸ ἀποθέμενοι πᾶσαν
1works not. Wherefore putting away all
ῥυπαρίαν καὶ περισσείαν κακίας ἐν πραΰ-
filthiness and superfluity of evil in meek-
τητι δέξασθε τὸν ἔμφυτον λόγον τὸν
ness receive ye the implanted word –
δυνάμενον σῶσαι τὰς ψυχὰς ὑμῶν. **22** γίν-
being able to save the souls of you. be-
εσθε δὲ ποιηταὶ λόγου, καὶ μὴ ἀκροαταὶ
come ye And doers of [the] word, and not hearers
μόνον παραλογιζόμενοι ἑαυτούς. **23** ὅτι
only misleading yourselves. Because
εἴ τις ἀκροατὴς λόγου ἐστὶν καὶ οὐ
if anyone 2a hearer 3of [the] word 1is and not
ποιητής, οὗτος ἔοικεν ἀνδρὶ κατανοοῦντι
a doer, this one is like a man perceiving
τὸ πρόσωπον τῆς γενέσεως αὐτοῦ ἐν
the face of the birth of him in
ἐσόπτρῳ· **24** κατενόησεν γὰρ ἑαυτὸν καὶ
a mirror; for he perceived himself and
ἀπελήλυθεν, καὶ εὐθέως ἐπελάθετο ὁποῖος
has gone away, and straightway forgot what sort
ἦν. **25** ὁ δὲ παρακύψας εἰς νόμον
he was. But the [one] having looked *into* into 3law
τέλειον τὸν τῆς ἐλευθερίας καὶ παραμείνας,
2perfect 1the – of freedom and remaining,
οὐκ ἀκροατὴς ἐπιλησμονῆς γενόμενος ἀλλὰ
not 2a hearer 3of forgetfulness* 1becoming but
ποιητὴς ἔργου, οὗτος μακάριος ἐν τῇ
a doer of [the] work, this one 2blessed 3in 4the
ποιήσει αὐτοῦ ἔσται. **26** Εἴ τις δοκεῖ
5doing 6of him 1will be. If anyone thinks
θρησκὸς εἶναι, μὴ χαλιναγωγῶν γλῶσσαν
2religious 1to be, not bridling tongue
ἑαυτοῦ ἀλλὰ ἀπατῶν καρδίαν ἑαυτοῦ,
of himself but deceiving heart of himself,
τούτου μάταιος ἡ θρησκεία. **27** θρησκεία
of this one vain the religion. Religion
καθαρὰ καὶ ἀμίαντος παρὰ τῷ θεῷ
clean and undefiled before the God
καὶ πατρὶ αὕτη ἐστίν, ἐπισκέπτεσθαι
and Father 2this 1is, to visit
ὀρφανοὺς καὶ χήρας ἐν τῇ θλίψει αὐτῶν,
orphans and widows in the affliction of them,
ἄσπιλον ἑαυτὸν τηρεῖν ἀπὸ τοῦ κόσμου.
unspotted himself to keep from the world.

should be quick to listen,
slow to speak and slow to
become angry, 20 for man's
anger does not bring about
the righteous life that God
desires. 21 Therefore, get
rid of all moral filth and the
evil that is so prevalent and
humbly accept the word
planted in you, which can
save you.
22 Do not merely listen to
the word, and so deceive
yourselves. Do what it
says. 23 Anyone who listens
to the word but does not do
what it says is like a man
who looks at his face in a
mirror 24 and, after looking
at himself, goes away and
immediately forgets what
he looks like. 25 But the man
who looks intently into the
perfect law that gives freedom, and continues to do
this, not forgetting what he
has heard, but doing it—he
will be blessed in what he
does.
26 If anyone considers
himself religious and yet
does not keep a tight rein
on his tongue, he deceives
himself and his religion is
worthless. 27 Religion that
God our Father accepts as
pure and faultless is this: to
look after orphans and widows in their distress and to
keep oneself from being
polluted by the world.

Chapter 2

Warning against Partiality

MY brothers and sis-
ters,[h] do you with
your acts of favoritism really believe in our glorious
Lord Jesus Christ?[i] 2 For if
a person with gold rings
and in fine clothes comes
into your assembly, and if a

[g] Gk *at the face of his birth*
[h] Gk *My brothers*
[i] Or *hold the faith of our glorious Lord Jesus Christ without acts of favoritism*

2 Ἀδελφοί μου, μὴ ἐν προσωπολημψίαις
Brothers of me, not in respects of persons
ἔχετε τὴν πίστιν τοῦ κυρίου ἡμῶν Ἰησοῦ
have ye the faith of the Lord of us Jesus
Χριστοῦ τῆς δόξης. **2** ἐὰν γὰρ εἰσέλθῃ
Christ[,] *of* the glory.* For if [there] enters
εἰς συναγωγὴν ὑμῶν ἀνὴρ χρυσοδακτύλιος
into a synagogue of you a man gold-fingered

* Genitive of quality: "a forgetful hearer."

* That is, taking "the glory" as in apposition to "Jesus Christ"; see Luke 2. 32*b*.

Chapter 2

Favoritism Forbidden

MY brothers, as believ-
ers in our glorious
Lord Jesus Christ, don't
show favoritism. 2 Suppose
a man comes into your
meeting wearing a gold ring

poor person in dirty clothes also comes in, 3and if you take notice of the one wearing the fine clothes and say, “Have a seat here, please,” while to the one who is poor you say, “Stand there,” or, “Sit at my feet,”[j] 4have you not made distinctions among yourselves, and become judges with evil thoughts? 5Listen, my beloved brothers and sisters.[b] Has not God chosen the poor in the world to be rich in faith and to be heirs of the kingdom that he has promised to those who love him? 6But you have dishonored the poor. Is it not the rich who oppress you? Is it not they who drag you into court? 7Is it not they who blaspheme the excellent name that was invoked over you?

8 You do well if you really fulfill the royal law according to the scripture, “You shall love your neighbor as yourself.” 9But if you show partiality, you commit sin and are convicted by the law as transgressors. 10For whoever keeps the whole law but fails in one point has become accountable for all of it. 11For the one who said, “You shall not commit adultery,” also said, “You shall not murder.” Now if you do not commit adultery but if you murder, you have become a transgressor of the law. 12So speak and so act as those who are to be judged by the law of liberty. 13For judgment will be without mercy to anyone who has shown no mercy; mercy triumphs over judgment.

Faith without Works Is Dead

14 What good is it, my

[j] Gk *Sit under my footstool*

ἐν ἐσθῆτι λαμπρᾷ, εἰσέλθῃ δὲ καὶ πτωχὸς
in [2]clothing [1]splendid, and [there] enters also a poor man

ἐν ῥυπαρᾷ ἐσθῆτι, 3 ἐπιβλέψητε δὲ ἐπὶ
in shabby clothing, and ye look *on* on

τὸν φοροῦντα τὴν ἐσθῆτα τὴν λαμπρὰν
the [one] wearing the clothing – splendid

καὶ εἴπητε· σὺ κάθου ὧδε καλῶς, καὶ
and say: [2]thou [1]Sit here well, and

τῷ πτωχῷ εἴπητε· σὺ στῆθι ἐκεῖ ἢ
to the poor man ye say: [2]thou [1]Stand there or

κάθου ὑπὸ τὸ ὑποπόδιόν μου, 4 οὐ
sit under the footstool of me, not

διεκρίθητε ἐν ἑαυτοῖς καὶ ἐγένεσθε κριταὶ
did ye discriminate among yourselves and became judges

διαλογισμῶν πονηρῶν; 5 Ἀκούσατε, ἀδελφοί
[2]thoughts [1]of evil ?§ Hear ye, brothers

μου ἀγαπητοί. οὐχ ὁ θεὸς ἐξελέξατο
of me beloved. [2]not – [3]God [1]Chose

τοὺς πτωχοὺς τῷ κόσμῳ πλουσίους ἐν
the poor in the world rich in

πίστει καὶ κληρονόμους τῆς βασιλείας
faith and heirs of the kingdom

ἧς ἐπηγγείλατο τοῖς ἀγαπῶσιν αὐτόν;
which he promised to the [ones] loving him?

6 ὑμεῖς δὲ ἠτιμάσατε τὸν πτωχόν. οὐχ
But ye dishonoured the poor man. [Do] not

οἱ πλούσιοι καταδυναστεύουσιν ὑμῶν, καὶ
the rich men oppress you, and

αὐτοὶ ἕλκουσιν ὑμᾶς εἰς κριτήρια; 7 οὐκ
they drag you to tribunals ? [Do] not

αὐτοὶ βλασφημοῦσιν τὸ καλὸν ὄνομα τὸ
they blaspheme the good name –

ἐπικληθὲν ἐφ᾽ ὑμᾶς; 8 εἰ μέντοι νόμον
called *on* on you ? If indeed [3]law

τελεῖτε βασιλικὸν κατὰ τὴν γραφήν·
[1]ye fulfil [2]a royal according to the scripture:

ἀγαπήσεις τὸν πλησίον σου ὡς σεαυτόν,
Thou shalt love the neighbour of thee as thyself,

καλῶς ποιεῖτε· 9 εἰ δὲ προσωπολημπτεῖτε,
[2]well [1]ye do; but if ye respect persons,

ἁμαρτίαν ἐργάζεσθε, ἐλεγχόμενοι ὑπὸ τοῦ
[2]sin [1]ye work, being reproved by the

νόμου ὡς παραβάται. 10 ὅστις γὰρ
law as transgressors. For [1][he] who

ὅλον τὸν νόμον τηρήσῃ, πταίσῃ δὲ ἐν
[3]all [4]the [5]law [2]keeps, yet stumbles in

ἑνί, γέγονεν πάντων ἔνοχος. 11 ὁ γὰρ
one thing, he has become [2]of all [1]guilty. For the [one]

εἰπών· μὴ μοιχεύσῃς, εἶπεν καί· μὴ
saying: Do not commit adultery, said also: not

φονεύσῃς· εἰ δὲ οὐ μοιχεύεις, φονεύεις
Do murder; now if thou dost not commit adultery, [2]murderest

δέ, γέγονας παραβάτης νόμου. 12 οὕτως
[1]but, thou hast become a transgressor of [the] law. So

λαλεῖτε καὶ οὕτως ποιεῖτε ὡς διὰ νόμου
speak ye and so do ye as [3]through [4]a law

ἐλευθερίας μέλλοντες κρίνεσθαι. 13 ἡ γὰρ
[5]of freedom [1]being about [2]to be judged. For the

κρίσις ἀνέλεος τῷ μὴ ποιήσαντι ἔλεος·
judgment [will be] unmerciful to the [one] not do(show)ing mercy;

κατακαυχᾶται ἔλεος κρίσεως. 14 Τί τὸ
[2]exults over [1]mercy *of* judgment. What [is] the

§ Genitive of quality: “ evil-thinking judges.”

and fine clothes, and a poor man in shabby clothes also comes in. 3If you show special attention to the man wearing fine clothes and say, “Here's a good seat for you,” but say to the poor man, “You stand there” or “Sit on the floor by my feet,” 4have you not discriminated among yourselves and become judges with evil thoughts?

5Listen, my dear brothers: Has not God chosen those who are poor in the eyes of the world to be rich in faith and to inherit the kingdom he promised those who love him? 6But you have insulted the poor. Is it not the rich who are exploiting you? Are they not the ones who are dragging you into court? 7Are they not the ones who are slandering the noble name of him to whom you belong?

8If you really keep the royal law found in Scripture, “Love your neighbor as yourself,”[a] you are doing right. 9But if you show favoritism, you sin and are convicted by the law as lawbreakers. 10For whoever keeps the whole law and yet stumbles at just one point is guilty of breaking all of it. 11For he who said, “Do not commit adultery,”[b] also said, “Do not murder.”[c] If you do not commit adultery but do commit murder, you have become a lawbreaker.

12Speak and act as those who are going to be judged by the law that gives freedom, 13because judgment without mercy will be shown to anyone who has not been merciful. Mercy triumphs over judgment!

Faith and Deeds

14What good is it, my

[a] *8* Lev. 19:18
[b] *11* Exodus 20:14; Deut. 5:18
[c] *11* Exodus 20:13; Deut. 5:17

brothers and sisters,[k] if
you say you have faith but
do not have works? Can
faith save you? 15 If a brother or sister is naked and
lacks daily food, 16 and one
of you says to them, "Go in
peace; keep warm and eat
your fill," and yet you do
not supply their bodily
needs, what is the good of
that? 17 So faith by itself, if
it has no works, is dead.
18 But someone will
say, "You have faith and I
have works." Show me
your faith apart from your
works, and I by my works
will show you my faith.
19 You believe that God is
one; you do well. Even the
demons believe—and
shudder. 20 Do you want to
be shown, you senseless
person, that faith apart
from works is barren?
21 Was not our ancestor
Abraham justified by
works when he offered his
son Isaac on the altar?
22 You see that faith was active along with his works,
and faith was brought to
completion by the works.
23 Thus the scripture was
fulfilled that says, "Abraham believed God, and it
was reckoned to him as
righteousness," and he was
called the friend of God.
24 You see that a person is
justified by works and not
by faith alone. 25 Likewise,
was not Rahab the prosti-
tute also justified by works
when she welcomed the
messengers and sent them
out by another road? 26 For

[k] Gk *brothers*

ὄφελος, ἀδελφοί μου, ἐὰν πίστιν λέγῃ
profit, brothers of me, if [4]faith [2]says

τις ἔχειν ἔργα δὲ μὴ ἔχῃ; μὴ δύναται
[1]anyone [3]to have [6]works [5]but [7]not [8]has ? *not* can

ἡ πίστις σῶσαι αὐτόν; 15 ἐὰν ἀδελφὸς
the faith *to* save him ? If a brother

ἢ ἀδελφὴ γυμνοὶ ὑπάρχωσιν καὶ λειπόμενοι
or a sister [2]naked [1]are and lacking

τῆς ἐφημέρου τροφῆς, 16 εἴπῃ δέ τις
of the daily food, and [4]says [1]anyone

αὐτοῖς ἐξ ὑμῶν· ὑπάγετε ἐν εἰρήνῃ,
[5]to them [2]of [3]you: Go ye in peace,

θερμαίνεσθε καὶ χορτάζεσθε, μὴ δῶτε
be warmed and filled, [4]not [3]ye give

δὲ αὐτοῖς τὰ ἐπιτήδεια τοῦ σώματος,
[1]but [2]them the necessaries of the body,

τί τὸ ὄφελος; 17 οὕτως καὶ ἡ πίστις,
what [is] the profit ? So indeed – faith,

ἐὰν μὴ ἔχῃ ἔργα, νεκρά ἐστιν καθ'
if it has not works, [2]dead [1]is by

ἑαυτήν. 18 ἀλλ' ἐρεῖ τις· σὺ πίστιν
itself. But [2]will say [1]someone: Thou [2]faith

ἔχεις, κἀγὼ ἔργα ἔχω· δεῖξόν μοι τὴν
[1]hast, and I [2]works [1]have; show me the

πίστιν σου χωρὶς τῶν ἔργων, κἀγώ
faith of thee without the works, and I

σοι δείξω ἐκ τῶν ἔργων μου τὴν πίστιν.
thee will show [4]by [5]the [6]works [3]of me [1]the [2]faith.

19 σὺ πιστεύεις ὅτι εἷς ἐστιν ὁ θεός;
Thou believest that [3]one [2]is – [1]God ?

καλῶς ποιεῖς· καὶ τὰ δαιμόνια πιστεύουσιν
[2]well [1]thou doest; also the demons believe

καὶ φρίσσουσιν. 20 θέλεις δὲ γνῶναι,
and shudder. But art thou willing to know,

ὦ ἄνθρωπε κενέ, ὅτι ἡ πίστις χωρὶς
O [2]man [1]vain, that – faith without

τῶν ἔργων ἀργή ἐστιν; 21 Ἀβραὰμ ὁ
– works barren is ? Abraham the

πατὴρ ἡμῶν οὐκ ἐξ ἔργων ἐδικαιώθη,
father of us not by works was justified,

ἀνενέγκας Ἰσαὰκ τὸν υἱὸν αὐτοῦ ἐπὶ
offering up Isaac the son of him on

τὸ θυσιαστήριον; 22 βλέπεις ὅτι ἡ πίστις
the altar ? Thou seest that – faith

συνήργει τοῖς ἔργοις αὐτοῦ, καὶ ἐκ
worked with the works of him, and by

τῶν ἔργων ἡ πίστις ἐτελειώθη, 23 καὶ
the works the faith was perfected, and

ἐπληρώθη ἡ γραφὴ ἡ λέγουσα· ἐπίστευσεν
was fulfilled the scripture – saying: believed

δὲ Ἀβραὰμ τῷ θεῷ, καὶ ἐλογίσθη αὐτῷ
And Abraham – God, and it was reckoned to him

εἰς δικαιοσύνην, καὶ φίλος θεοῦ ἐκλήθη.
for righteousness, and [2]friend [3]of God [1]he was called.

24 ὁρᾶτε ὅτι ἐξ ἔργων δικαιοῦται ἄνθρωπος
Ye see that by works [2]is justified [1]a man

καὶ οὐκ ἐκ πίστεως μόνον. 25 ὁμοίως
and not by faith only. likewise

δὲ καὶ Ῥαὰβ ἡ πόρνη οὐκ ἐξ ἔργων
And also Rahab the prostitute not by works

ἐδικαιώθη, ὑποδεξαμένη τοὺς ἀγγέλους καὶ
was justified, entertaining the messengers and

brothers, if a man claims to
have faith but has no
deeds? Can such faith save
him? 15 Suppose a brother
or sister is without clothes
and daily food. 16 If one of
you says to him, "Go, I
wish you well; keep warm
and well fed," but does
nothing about his physical
needs, what good is it? 17 In
the same way, faith by itself, if it is not accompanied by action, is dead.
18 But someone will say,
"You have faith; I have
deeds."
Show me your faith with-
out deeds, and I will show
you my faith by what I do.
19 You believe that there is
one God. Good! Even the
demons believe that—and
shudder.
20 You foolish man, do
you want evidence that
faith without deeds is useless[d]? 21 Was not our ancestor Abraham considered
righteous for what he did
when he offered his son
Isaac on the altar? 22 You
see that his faith and his actions were working together, and his faith was made
complete by what he did.
23 And the scripture was fulfilled that says, "Abraham
believed God, and it was
credited to him as right-
eousness,"[e] and he was
called God's friend. 24 You
see that a person is justified
by what he does and not by
faith alone.
25 In the same way, was
not even Rahab the prostitute considered righteous
for what she did when she
gave lodging to the spies
and sent them off in a dif-

[d] 20 Some early manuscripts *dead*
[e] 23 Gen. 15:6

just as the body without the
spirit is dead, so faith without works is also dead.

Chapter 3

Taming the Tongue

NOT many of you
should become
teachers, my brothers and
sisters,[k] for you know that
we who teach will be
judged with greater strict-
ness. 2 For all of us make
many mistakes. Anyone
who makes no mistakes in
speaking is perfect, able to
keep the whole body in
check with a bridle. 3 If we
put bits into the mouths of
horses to make them obey
us, we guide their whole
bodies. 4 Or look at ships:
though they are so large
that it takes strong winds to
drive them, yet they are
guided by a very small rudder wherever the will of the
pilot directs. 5 So also the
tongue is a small member,
yet it boasts of great exploits.
How great a forest is set
ablaze by a small fire! 6 And
the tongue is a fire. The
tongue is placed among our
members as a world of iniquity; it stains the whole
body, sets on fire the cycle
of nature,[l] and is itself set
on fire by hell.[m] 7 For every
species of beast and bird, of
reptile and sea creature,
can be tamed and has been
tamed by the human spe-
cies, 8 but no one can tame
the tongue—a restless evil,
full of deadly poison. 9 With
it we bless the Lord and Father, and with it we curse
those who are made in the
likeness of God. 10 From

[l] Or *wheel of birth*
[m] Gk *Gehenna*

ἑτέρᾳ ὁδῷ ἐκβαλοῦσα; **26** ὥσπερ γὰρ τὸ
by a different way sending [them] forth? For as the

σῶμα χωρὶς πνεύματος νεκρόν ἐστιν, οὕτως
body without spirit [2]dead [1]is, so

καὶ ἡ πίστις χωρὶς ἔργων νεκρά ἐστιν.
also – faith without works [2]dead [1]is.

3 Μὴ πολλοὶ διδάσκαλοι γίνεσθε, ἀδελφοί
[2]not [3]many [4]teachers [1]Become ye, brothers

μου, εἰδότες ὅτι μεῖζον κρίμα λημψόμεθα.
of me, knowing that greater judgment we shall receive.

2 πολλὰ γὰρ πταίομεν ἅπαντες· εἴ τις
For [in] many [respects] we stumble all; if anyone

ἐν λόγῳ οὐ πταίει, οὗτος τέλειος ἀνήρ,
[3]in [4]word [1]stumbles not, this [is] a perfect man,

δυνατὸς χαλιναγωγῆσαι καὶ ὅλον τὸ σῶμα.
able [2]to bridle [1]indeed all the body.

3 εἰ δὲ τῶν ἵππων τοὺς χαλινοὺς εἰς
Now if – [6]of horses – [2]bridles [3]into

τὰ στόματα βάλλομεν εἰς τὸ πείθεσθαι
[4]the [5]mouths [1]we put for the to obey
=to make them obey us,

αὐτοὺς ἡμῖν, καὶ ὅλον τὸ σῶμα αὐτῶν
them[b] *to* us, and [2]all [3]the [4]body [5]of them

μετάγομεν. **4** ἰδοὺ καὶ τὰ πλοῖα, τηλικαῦτα
[1]we direct. Behold also the ships, [2]so great

ὄντα καὶ ὑπὸ ἀνέμων σκληρῶν ἐλαυνόμενα,
[1]being [3]and [5]by [7]winds [6]hard(strong) [4]*being* driven,

μετάγεται ὑπὸ ἐλαχίστου πηδαλίου ὅπου
is(are) directed by a very little helm where

ἡ ὁρμὴ τοῦ εὐθύνοντος βούλεται· **5** οὕτως
the impulse of the [one] steering resolves; so

καὶ ἡ γλῶσσα μικρὸν μέλος ἐστὶν καὶ
also the tongue [2]a little [3]member [1]is and

μεγάλα αὐχεῖ. ἰδοὺ ἡλίκον πῦρ ἡλίκον
great things boasts. Behold how little a fire [2]how great

ὕλην ἀνάπτει· **6** καὶ ἡ γλῶσσα πῦρ,
[3]wood [1]kindles; and the tongue [is] a fire,

ὁ κόσμος τῆς ἀδικίας, ἡ γλῶσσα καθίστα-
the world – of iniquity, the tongue is

ται ἐν τοῖς μέλεσιν ἡμῶν, ἡ σπιλοῦσα
set among the members of us, spotting

ὅλον τὸ σῶμα καὶ φλογίζουσα τὸν
all the body and inflaming the

τροχὸν τῆς γενέσεως καὶ φλογιζομένη
course – of nature and being inflamed

ὑπὸ τῆς γεέννης. **7** πᾶσα γὰρ φύσις
by gehenna. For every nature

θηρίων τε καὶ πετεινῶν, ἑρπετῶν τε
[2]of beasts [1]both and of birds, [2]of reptiles [1]both

καὶ ἐναλίων δαμάζεται καὶ δεδάμασται
and of marine creatures is tamed and has been tamed

τῇ φύσει τῇ ἀνθρωπίνῃ, **8** τὴν δὲ
by *the* [2]nature – [1]human, but the

γλῶσσαν οὐδεὶς δαμάσαι δύναται ἀνθρώπων·
tongue [1]no one [4]to tame [3]is able [2]of men;

ἀκατάστατον κακόν, μεστὴ ἰοῦ θανατηφόρου.
an unruly evil, full [2]poison [1]of death-dealing.

9 ἐν αὐτῇ εὐλογοῦμεν τὸν κύριον καὶ
By this we bless the Lord and

πατέρα, καὶ ἐν αὐτῇ καταρώμεθα τοὺς
Father, and by this we curse –

ἀνθρώπους τοὺς καθ' ὁμοίωσιν θεοῦ
men – [2]according to [3]likeness [4]of God

ferent direction? 26As the
body without the spirit is
dead, so faith without
deeds is dead.

Chapter 3

Taming the Tongue

NOT many of you
should presume to be
teachers, my brothers, because you know that we
who teach will be judged
more strictly. 2We all stumble in many ways. If any-
one is never at fault in what
he says, he is a perfect
man, able to keep his whole
body in check.
3When we put bits into
the mouths of horses to
make them obey us, we can
turn the whole animal. 4Or
take ships as an example.
Although they are so large
and are driven by strong
winds, they are steered by
a very small rudder
wherever the pilot wants to
go. 5Likewise the tongue is
a small part of the body, but
it makes great boasts. Consider what a great forest is
set on fire by a small spark.
6The tongue also is a fire, a
world of evil among the
parts of the body. It corrupts the whole person,
sets the whole course of his
life on fire, and is itself set
on fire by hell.
7All kinds of animals,
birds, reptiles and crea-
tures of the sea are being
tamed and have been
tamed by man, 8but no man
can tame the tongue. It is a
restless evil, full of deadly
poison.
9With the tongue we
praise our Lord and Fa-
ther, and with it we curse
men, who have been made

the same mouth come
blessing and cursing. My
brothers and sisters,[n] this
ought not to be so. 11 Does
a spring pour forth from the
same opening both fresh
and brackish water? 12 Can
a fig tree, my brothers and
sisters,[o] yield olives, or a
grapevine figs? No more
can salt water yield fresh.

Two Kinds of Wisdom

13 Who is wise and un-
derstanding among you?
Show by your good life that
your works are done with
gentleness born of wisdom.
14 But if you have bitter
envy and selfish ambition
in your hearts, do not be
boastful and false to the
truth. 15 Such wisdom does
not come down from
above, but is earthly, unspiritual, devilish. 16 For
where there is envy and
selfish ambition, there will
also be disorder and wickedness of every kind. 17 But
the wisdom from above is
first pure, then peaceable,
gentle, willing to yield, full
of mercy and good fruits,
without a trace of partiality
or hypocrisy. 18 And a harvest of righteousness is
sown in peace for[p] those
who make peace.

Chapter 4

Friendship with the World

THOSE conflicts and
disputes among you,
where do they come from?
Do they not come from
your cravings that are at
war within you? 2 You want
something and do not have
it; so you commit murder.
And you covet[q] something
and cannot obtain it; so you
engage in disputes and conflicts. You do not have, because you do not ask. 3 You
ask and do not receive, because you ask wrongly, in

[n] Gk *My brothers*
[o] Gk *my brothers*
[p] Or *by*
[q] Or *you murder and you covet*

γεγονότας· **10** ἐκ τοῦ αὐτοῦ στόματος ἐξέρχεται
[1]having become; out of the same mouth comes forth
εὐλογία καὶ κατάρα. οὐ χρή, ἀδελφοί
blessing and cursing. It is not fitting, brothers
μου, ταῦτα οὕτως γίνεσθαι. **11** μήτι
of me, these things so to be. *Not*
ἡ πηγὴ ἐκ τῆς αὐτῆς ὀπῆς βρύει τὸ
the fountain out of the same hole sends forth the
γλυκὺ καὶ τὸ πικρόν; **12** μὴ δύναται,
sweet and the bitter ? *Not* can,
ἀδελφοί μου, συκῆ ἐλαίας ποιῆσαι ἢ
brothers of me, a fig-tree [2]olives [1]*to* produce or
ἄμπελος σῦκα; οὔτε ἁλυκὸν γλυκὺ
a vine figs ? neither [1]salt [4]sweet
ποιῆσαι ὕδωρ. **13** Τίς σοφὸς καὶ ἐπιστήμων
[3]*to* make [2]water. Who [is] wise and knowing
ἐν ὑμῖν; δειξάτω ἐκ τῆς καλῆς ἀναστροφῆς
among you ? let him show by the(his) good conduct
τὰ ἔργα αὐτοῦ ἐν πραΰτητι σοφίας.
the works of him in meekness of wisdom.*
14 εἰ δὲ ζῆλον πικρὸν ἔχετε καὶ ἐριθείαν
But if [3]jealousy [2]bitter [1]ye have and rivalry
ἐν τῇ καρδίᾳ ὑμῶν, μὴ κατακαυχᾶσθε
in the heart of you, do not exult over
καὶ ψεύδεσθε κατὰ τῆς ἀληθείας. **15** οὐκ
and lie against the truth. [4]not
ἔστιν αὕτη ἡ σοφία ἄνωθεν κατερχομένη,
[3]is [1]This – [2]wisdom [6]from above [5]coming down,
ἀλλὰ ἐπίγειος, ψυχική, δαιμονιώδης· **16** ὅπου
but [is] earthly, natural, demon-like; [2]where
γὰρ ζῆλος καὶ ἐριθεία, ἐκεῖ ἀκαταστασία
[1]for jealousy and rivalry [are], there [is] tumult
καὶ πᾶν φαῦλον πρᾶγμα. **17** ἡ δὲ ἄνωθεν
and every worthless practice. But [1]the [3]from above
σοφία πρῶτον μὲν ἁγνή ἐστιν, ἔπειτα
[2]wisdom [5]firstly – [6]pure [4]is, then
εἰρηνική, ἐπιεικής, εὐπειθής, μεστὴ ἐλέους
peaceable, forbearing, compliant, full of mercy
καὶ καρπῶν ἀγαθῶν, ἀδιάκριτος, ἀνυπό-
and [2]fruits [1]of good, without uncertainty, un-
κριτος. **18** καρπὸς δὲ δικαιοσύνης ἐν
feigned. And [the] fruit of righteousness [2]in
εἰρήνῃ σπείρεται τοῖς ποιοῦσιν εἰρήνην.
[3]peace [1]is sown for the [ones] making peace.

4 Πόθεν πόλεμοι καὶ πόθεν μάχαι ἐν
Whence wars and whence fights among
ὑμῖν; οὐκ ἐντεῦθεν, ἐκ τῶν ἡδονῶν
you ? not thence, out of the pleasures
ὑμῶν τῶν στρατευομένων ἐν τοῖς μέλεσιν
of you – soldiering in the members
ὑμῶν; **2** ἐπιθυμεῖτε, καὶ οὐκ ἔχετε·
of you ? Ye desire, and have not;
φονεύετε καὶ ζηλοῦτε, καὶ οὐ δύνασθε
ye murder and are jealous, and are not able
ἐπιτυχεῖν· μάχεσθε καὶ πολεμεῖτε. οὐκ
to obtain; ye fight and ye war. not
ἔχετε διὰ τὸ μὴ αἰτεῖσθαι ὑμᾶς· **3** αἰτεῖτε
Ye have be-cause of *the* not to ask you[b]; ye ask
=because ye ask not;
καὶ οὐ λαμβάνετε, διότι κακῶς αἰτεῖσθε,
and receive not, because [2]ill [1]ye ask,

*** Genitive of quality : " a wise meekness."**

in God's likeness. 10 Out of
the same mouth come
praise and cursing. My
brothers, this should not
be. 11 Can both fresh water
and salt[f] water flow from
the same spring? 12 My
brothers, can a fig tree bear
olives, or a grapevine bear
figs? Neither can a salt
spring produce fresh water.

Two Kinds of Wisdom

13 Who is wise and under-
standing among you? Let
him show it by his good life,
by deeds done in the humility that comes from wis-
dom. 14 But if you harbor
bitter envy and selfish ambition in your hearts, do not
boast about it or deny the
truth. 15 Such "wisdom"
does not come down from
heaven but is earthly, unspiritual, of the devil. 16 For
where you have envy and
selfish ambition, there you
find disorder and every evil
practice.
17 But the wisdom that
comes from heaven is first
of all pure; then peace-lov-
ing, considerate, submis-
sive, full of mercy and good
fruit, impartial and sincere.
18 Peacemakers who sow in
peace raise a harvest of
righteousness.

Chapter 4

Submit Yourselves to God

WHAT causes fights
and quarrels among
you? Don't they come from
your desires that battle
within you? 2 You want
something but don't get it.
You kill and covet, but you
cannot have what you
want. You quarrel and
fight. You do not have, because you do not ask God.
3 When you ask, you do not
receive, because you ask
with wrong motives, that

[f] 11 Greek *bitter* (see also verse 14)

order to spend what you get
on your pleasures. 4 Adulterers! Do you not know
that friendship with the
world is enmity with God?
Therefore whoever wishes
to be a friend of the world
becomes an enemy of God.
5 Or do you suppose that it
is for nothing that the scripture says, "God[r] yearns
jealously for the spirit that
he has made to dwell in
us"? 6 But he gives all the
more grace; therefore it
says,

"God opposes the
proud,
but gives grace to
the humble."

7 Submit yourselves therefore to God. Resist the
devil, and he will flee from
you. 8 Draw near to God,
and he will draw near to
you. Cleanse your hands,
you sinners, and purify
your hearts, you double-
minded. 9 Lament and
mourn and weep. Let your
laughter be turned into
mourning and your joy into
dejection. 10 Humble yourselves before the Lord, and
he will exalt you.

Warning against Judging Another

11 Do not speak evil
against one another, brothers and sisters.[s] Whoever
speaks evil against another
or judges another, speaks
evil against the law and
judges the law; but if you
judge the law, you are not a
doer of the law but a judge.
12 There is one lawgiver and
judge who is able to save
and to destroy. So who,
then, are you to judge your
neighbor?

Boasting about Tomorrow

13 Come now, you who
say, "Today or tomorrow
we will go to such and such
a town and spend a year
there, doing business and
making money." 14 Yet you
do not even know what to-

[r] Gk *He*
[s] Gk *brothers*

ἵνα ἐν ταῖς ἡδοναῖς ὑμῶν δαπανήσητε.
in order that in the pleasures of you ye may spend.

4 μοιχαλίδες, οὐκ οἴδατε ὅτι ἡ φιλία
Adulteresses, know ye not that the friendship

τοῦ κόσμου ἔχθρα τοῦ θεοῦ ἐστιν; ὃς
of the world [2]enmity – [3]of God [1]is ? Who-

ἐὰν οὖν βουληθῇ φίλος εἶναι τοῦ κόσμου,
ever therefore [1]resolves [3]a friend [2]to be of the world,

ἐχθρὸς τοῦ θεοῦ καθίσταται. 5 ἢ δοκεῖτε
[2]an enemy – [3]of God [1]is constituted. Or think ye

ὅτι κενῶς ἡ γραφὴ λέγει· πρὸς φθόνον
that vainly the scripture says: [8]to [9]envy

ἐπιποθεῖ τὸ πνεῦμα ὃ κατῴκισεν ἐν
[7]yearns [1]The [2]Spirit [3]which [4]dwelt [5]in

ἡμῖν; 6 μείζονα δὲ δίδωσιν χάριν· διὸ
[6]you ? But [2]greater [1]he gives [3]grace; wherefore

λέγει· ὁ θεὸς ὑπερηφάνοις ἀντιτάσσεται,
it* says: – God [2]arrogant men [1]resists,

ταπεινοῖς δὲ δίδωσιν χάριν. 7 ὑποτάγητε
but to humble men he gives grace. Be ye subject

οὖν τῷ θεῷ· ἀντίστητε δὲ τῷ διαβόλῳ,
therefore – to God; but oppose the devil,

καὶ φεύξεται ἀφ' ὑμῶν· 8 ἐγγίσατε τῷ
and he will flee from you; draw near –

θεῷ, καὶ ἐγγίσει ὑμῖν. καθαρίσατε
to God, and he will draw near to you. Cleanse ye

χεῖρας, ἁμαρτωλοί, καὶ ἁγνίσατε καρδίας,
hands, sinners, and purify hearts,

δίψυχοι. 9 ταλαιπωρήσατε καὶ πενθήσατε
two-souled (double-minded). Be ye distressed and mourn

καὶ κλαύσατε· ὁ γέλως ὑμῶν εἰς πένθος
and weep; the laughter of you to mourning

μετατραπήτω καὶ ἡ χαρὰ εἰς κατήφειαν.
let it be turned and the joy to dejection.

10 ταπεινώθητε ἐνώπιον κυρίου, καὶ ὑψώσει
Be ye humbled before [the] Lord, and he will exalt

ὑμᾶς. 11 Μὴ καταλαλεῖτε ἀλλήλων, ἀδελφοί.
you. Speak not against one another, brothers.

ὁ καταλαλῶν ἀδελφοῦ ἢ κρίνων τὸν
The [one] speaking against a brother or judging the

ἀδελφὸν αὐτοῦ καταλαλεῖ νόμου καὶ κρίνει
brother of him speaks against law and judges

νόμον· εἰ δὲ νόμον κρίνεις, οὐκ εἶ
law; and if law thou judgest, thou art not

ποιητὴς νόμου ἀλλὰ κριτής. 12 εἷς ἐστιν
a doer of law but a judge. One is

νομοθέτης καὶ κριτής, ὁ δυνάμενος
lawgiver and judge, the [one] being able

σῶσαι καὶ ἀπολέσαι· σὺ δὲ τίς εἶ, ὁ
to save and to destroy; [4]thou [1]and [2]who [3]art, the

κρίνων τὸν πλησίον;
[one] judging the(thy) neighbour ?

13 Ἄγε νῦν οἱ λέγοντες· σήμερον ἢ
Come now the [ones] saying: To-day or

αὔριον πορευσόμεθα εἰς τήνδε τὴν πόλιν
to-morrow we will go into this city

καὶ ποιήσομεν ἐκεῖ ἐνιαυτὸν καὶ ἐμπορευ-
and we will do there a year and *we will*

σόμεθα καὶ κερδήσομεν· 14 οἵτινες οὐκ
trade and *we will* make a profit; who not

* That is, " the scripture " (as ver. 5).

you may spend what you
get on your pleasures.
4 You adulterous people,
don't you know that friendship with the world is hatred toward God? Anyone
who chooses to be a friend
of the world becomes an
enemy of God. 5 Or do you
think Scripture says without reason that the spirit he
caused to live in us envies
intensely?[g] 6 But he gives
us more grace. That is why
Scripture says:

"God opposes the proud
but gives grace to the
humble."[h]

7 Submit yourselves,
then, to God. Resist the
devil, and he will flee from
you. 8 Come near to God
and he will come near to
you. Wash your hands, you
sinners, and purify your
hearts, you double-mind-
ed. 9 Grieve, mourn and
wail. Change your laughter
to mourning and your joy to
gloom. 10 Humble your-
selves before the Lord, and
he will lift you up.
11 Brothers, do not slan-
der one another. Anyone
who speaks against his
brother or judges him
speaks against the law and
judges it. When you judge
the law, you are not keeping it, but sitting in judgment on it. 12 There is only
one Lawgiver and Judge,
the one who is able to save
and destroy. But you—
who are you to judge your
neighbor?

Boasting About Tomorrow

13 Now listen, you who
say, "Today or tomorrow
we will go to this or that
city, spend a year there,
carry on business and make
money." 14 Why, you do

[g] 5 Or *that God jealously longs for the spirit that he made to live in us; or that the Spirit he caused to live in us longs jealously*
[h] 6 Prov. 3:34

morrow will bring. What is
your life? For you are a
mist that appears for a little
while and then vanishes.
15 Instead you ought to say,
"If the Lord wishes, we will
live and do this or that."
16 As it is, you boast in your
arrogance; all such boasting is evil. 17 Anyone, then,
who knows the right thing
to do and fails to do it, commits sin.

Chapter 5

Warning to Rich Oppressors

COME now, you rich
people, weep and wail
for the miseries that are
coming to you. 2 Your
riches have rotted, and
your clothes are moth-
eaten. 3 Your gold and silver have rusted, and their
rust will be evidence
against you, and it will eat
your flesh like fire. You
have laid up treasure[r] for
the last days. 4 Listen! The
wages of the laborers who
mowed your fields, which
you kept back by fraud, cry
out, and the cries of the
harvesters have reached
the ears of the Lord of
hosts. 5 You have lived on
the earth in luxury and in
pleasure; you have fattened
your hearts in a day of
slaughter. 6 You have condemned and murdered the
righteous one, who does
not resist you.

Patience in Suffering

7 Be patient, therefore,
beloved,[s] until the coming
of the Lord. The farmer
waits for the precious crop
from the earth, being pa-
tient with it until it receives
the early and the late rains.

[r] Or *will eat your flesh, since you have stored up fire*

ἐπίστασθε τῆς αὔριον ποία ἡ ζωὴ ὑμῶν.
ye know 5of the 6morrow 1what 2the 3life 4of you [will be].

ἀτμὶς γάρ ἐστε ἡ πρὸς ὀλίγον φαινομένη,
For 2a vapour 1ye are – 4for 5a little while 3appearing,

ἔπειτα καὶ ἀφανιζομένη· **15** ἀντὶ τοῦ
thereafter indeed disappearing; instead of *the*

λέγειν ὑμᾶς· ἐὰν ὁ κύριος θελήσῃ, καὶ
to say you[b]: If the Lord wills, both
=your saying:

ζήσομεν καὶ ποιήσομεν τοῦτο ἢ ἐκεῖνο.
we will live and *we will* do this or that.

16 νῦν δὲ καυχᾶσθε ἐν ταῖς ἀλαζονείαις
But now ye boast in the vauntings

ὑμῶν· πᾶσα καύχησις τοιαύτη πονηρά
of you; all 2boasting 1such 4evil

ἐστιν. **17** εἰδότι οὖν καλὸν ποιεῖν καὶ
3is. 2to [one] knowing* 1Therefore 4good 3to do and

μὴ ποιοῦντι, ἁμαρτία αὐτῷ ἐστιν.
not doing, 3sin 1to him 2it is.

5 Ἄγε νῦν οἱ πλούσιοι, κλαύσατε
Come now *the* rich men, weep ye

ὀλολύζοντες ἐπὶ ταῖς ταλαιπωρίαις ὑμῶν
crying aloud over the hardships of you

ταῖς ἐπερχομέναις. **2** ὁ πλοῦτος ὑμῶν
– coming upon. The riches of you

σέσηπεν, καὶ τὰ ἱμάτια ὑμῶν σητόβρωτα
have become corrupted, and the garments of you moth-eaten

γέγονεν, **3** ὁ χρυσὸς ὑμῶν καὶ ὁ ἄργυρος
have become, the gold of you and the silver

κατίωται, καὶ ὁ ἰὸς αὐτῶν εἰς μαρτύριον
has become rusted over, and the poison of them for a testimony

ὑμῖν ἔσται καὶ φάγεται τὰς σάρκας
to(against) you will be and will eat the fleshes

ὑμῶν ὡς πῦρ. ἐθησαυρίσατε ἐν ἐσχάταις
of you as fire. Ye treasured in [the] last

ἡμέραις. **4** ἰδοὺ ὁ μισθὸς τῶν ἐργατῶν
days. Behold[,] the wages of the workmen

τῶν ἀμησάντων τὰς χώρας ὑμῶν ὁ
– having reaped the lands of you –

ἀφυστερημένος ἀφ᾽ ὑμῶν κράζει, καὶ αἱ
being kept back from(by) you cries, and the

βοαὶ τῶν θερισάντων εἰς τὰ ὦτα κυρίου
cries of the having reaped [ones] 1into 2the 4ears 5of [the] Lord

σαβαὼθ εἰσελήλυθαν. **5** ἐτρυφήσατε ἐπὶ
6of hosts 1have entered. Ye lived daintily on

τῆς γῆς καὶ ἐσπαταλήσατε, ἐθρέψατε τὰς
the earth and lived riotously, ye nourished the

καρδίας ὑμῶν ἐν ἡμέρᾳ σφαγῆς. **6** κατε-
hearts of you in a day of slaughter. Ye

δικάσατε, ἐφονεύσατε τὸν δίκαιον· οὐκ
condemned, ye murdered the righteous man; not

ἀντιτάσσεται ὑμῖν.
he resists you.

7 Μακροθυμήσατε οὖν, ἀδελφοί, ἕως τῆς
Be ye longsuffering therefore, brothers, until the

παρουσίας τοῦ κυρίου. ἰδοὺ ὁ γεωργὸς
presence of the Lord. Behold[,] the farmer

ἐκδέχεται τὸν τίμιον καρπὸν τῆς γῆς,
awaits the precious fruit of the earth,

μακροθυμῶν ἐπ᾽ αὐτῷ ἕως λάβῃ πρόϊμον
being longsuffering over it until he receives early

*See note on page xvi.

not even know what will
happen tomorrow. What is
your life? You are a mist
that appears for a little
while and then vanishes.
15 Instead, you ought to say,
"If it is the Lord's will, we
will live and do this or
that." 16 As it is, you boast
and brag. All such boasting
is evil. 17 Anyone, then,
who knows the good he
ought to do and doesn't do
it, sins.

Chapter 5

Warning to Rich Oppressors

NOW listen, you rich
people, weep and
wail because of the misery
that is coming upon you.
2 Your wealth has rotted,
and moths have eaten your
clothes. 3 Your gold and silver are corroded. Their
corrosion will testify
against you and eat your
flesh like fire. You have
hoarded wealth in the last
days. 4 Look! The wages
you failed to pay the workmen who mowed your
fields are crying out against
you. The cries of the harvesters have reached the
ears of the Lord Almighty.
5 You have lived on earth in
luxury and self-indulgence.
You have fattened your-
selves in the day of slaughter.[i] 6 You have con-
demned and murdered in-
nocent men, who were not
opposing you.

Patience in Suffering

7 Be patient, then, brothers, until the Lord's coming. See how the farmer
waits for the land to yield
its valuable crop and how
patient he is for the autumn

[i] 5 Or *yourselves as in a day of feasting*

8 You also must be patient.
Strengthen your hearts, for
the coming of the Lord is
near.[u] 9 Beloved,[v] do not
grumble against one another, so that you may not be
judged. See, the Judge is
standing at the doors! 10 As
an example of suffering and
patience, beloved,[s] take
the prophets who spoke in
the name of the Lord. 11 Indeed we call blessed those
who showed endurance.
You have heard of the en-
durance of Job, and you
have seen the purpose of
the Lord, how the Lord is
compassionate and merci-
ful.
12 Above all, my be-
loved,[s] do not swear, either by heaven or by earth
or by any other oath, but let
your "Yes" be yes and your
"No" be no, so that you
may not fall under condemnation.

The Prayer of Faith

13 Are any among you
suffering? They should
pray. Are any cheerful?
They should sing songs of
praise. 14 Are any among
you sick? They should call
for the elders of the church
and have them pray over
them, anointing them with
oil in the name of the Lord.
15 The prayer of faith will
save the sick, and the Lord
will raise them up; and anyone who has committed
sins will be forgiven.
16 Therefore confess your
sins to one another, and
pray for one another, so
that you may be healed.
The prayer of the righteous
is powerful and effective.
17 Elijah was a human being
like us, and he prayed fervently that it might not
rain, and for three years
and six months it did not

[u] Or *is at hand*
[v] Gk *Brothers*

καὶ ὄψιμον. 8 μακροθυμήσατε καὶ ὑμεῖς,
and latter [rain]. Be [3]longsuffering [2]also [1]ye,

στηρίξατε τὰς καρδίας ὑμῶν, ὅτι ἡ
establish the hearts of you, because the

παρουσία τοῦ κυρίου ἤγγικεν. 9 μὴ
presence of the Lord has drawn near. not

στενάζετε, ἀδελφοί, κατ᾽ ἀλλήλων ἵνα μὴ
Murmur ye, brothers, against one another lest

κριθῆτε· ἰδοὺ ὁ κριτὴς πρὸ τῶν θυρῶν
ye be judged; behold[,] the judge [2]before [3]the [4]doors

ἕστηκεν. 10 ὑπόδειγμα λάβετε, ἀδελφοί,
[1]stands. [5]an example [1]Take ye, [2]brothers,

τῆς κακοπαθίας καὶ τῆς μακροθυμίας
– [6]of suffering ill [7]and – [8]of longsuffering

τοὺς προφήτας, οἳ ἐλάλησαν ἐν τῷ
[3]the [4]prophets, who spoke in the

ὀνόματι κυρίου. 11 ἰδοὺ μακαρίζομεν τοὺς
name of [the] Lord. Behold we count blessed the

ὑπομείναντας· τὴν ὑπομονὴν Ἰὼβ ἠκούσατε,
[ones] enduring; [2]the [3]endurance [4]of Job [1]ye heard [of],

καὶ τὸ τέλος κυρίου εἴδετε, ὅτι πολύ-
and [2]the [3]end [4]of [the] Lord [1]ye saw, that [4]very

σπλαγχνός ἐστιν ὁ κύριος καὶ οἰκτίρμων.
compassionate [3]is [1]the [2]Lord and pitiful.

12 Πρὸ πάντων δέ, ἀδελφοί μου, μὴ
[2]before [3]all things [1]But, brothers of me, not

ὀμνύετε, μήτε τὸν οὐρανὸν μήτε τὴν
swear ye, neither by *the* heaven nor by the

γῆν μήτε ἄλλον τινὰ ὅρκον· ἤτω δὲ
earth nor [2]other [1]any oath; but let be

ὑμῶν τὸ ναὶ ναί, καὶ τὸ οὒ οὔ, ἵνα μὴ
of you the Yes yes, and the No no, lest

ὑπὸ κρίσιν πέσητε. 13 Κακοπαθεῖ τις
[2]under [3]judgment [1]ye fall. Suffers ill anyone

ἐν ὑμῖν; προσευχέσθω· εὐθυμεῖ τις;
among you ? let him pray; is cheerful anyone ?

ψαλλέτω. 14 ἀσθενεῖ τις ἐν ὑμῖν;
let him sing a psalm. Is weak anyone among you ?

προσκαλεσάσθω τοὺς πρεσβυτέρους τῆς
let him summon the elders of the

ἐκκλησίας, καὶ προσευξάσθωσαν ἐπ᾽ αὐτὸν
church, and let them pray over him

ἀλείψαντες ἐλαίῳ ἐν τῷ ὀνόματι τοῦ
having anointed [him] with oil in the name of the

κυρίου. 15 καὶ ἡ εὐχὴ τῆς πίστεως
Lord. And the prayer – of faith

σώσει τὸν κάμνοντα, καὶ ἐγερεῖ αὐτὸν
will heal the [one] being sick, and [3]will raise [4]him

ὁ κύριος· κἂν ἁμαρτίας ᾖ πεποιηκώς,
[1]the [2]Lord; and if [3]sins [1]he may be [2]having done,

ἀφεθήσεται αὐτῷ. 16 ἐξομολογεῖσθε οὖν
it will be forgiven him. Confess ye therefore

ἀλλήλοις τὰς ἁμαρτίας, καὶ προσεύχεσθε
to one another the(your) sins, and pray ye

ὑπὲρ ἀλλήλων, ὅπως ἰαθῆτε. πολὺ
on behalf of one another, so as ye may be cured. [5]much(very)

ἰσχύει δέησις δικαίου ἐνεργουμένη.
[4]is [6]strong [1]*a* petition [2]of a righteous man [3]being made effective.

17 Ἠλίας ἄνθρωπος ἦν ὁμοιοπαθὴς ἡμῖν,
Elias [2]a man [1]was of like feeling to us,

and spring rains. 8 You too,
be patient and stand firm,
because the Lord's coming
is near. 9 Don't grumble
against each other, brothers, or you will be judged.
The Judge is standing at the
door!
10 Brothers, as an example
of patience in the face of
suffering, take the prophets
who spoke in the name of
the Lord. 11 As you know,
we consider blessed those
who have persevered. You
have heard of Job's perseverance and have seen
what the Lord finally
brought about. The Lord is
full of compassion and mercy.
12 Above all, my brothers,
do not swear—not by
heaven or by earth or by
anything else. Let your
"Yes" be yes, and your
"No," no, or you will be
condemned.

The Prayer of Faith

13 Is any one of you in
trouble? He should pray. Is
anyone happy? Let him
sing songs of praise. 14 Is
any one of you sick? He
should call the elders of the
church to pray over him
and anoint him with oil in
the name of the Lord.
15 And the prayer offered in
faith will make the sick person well; the Lord will raise
him up. If he has sinned, he
will be forgiven. 16 Therefore confess your sins to
each other and pray for
each other so that you may
be healed. The prayer of a
righteous man is powerful
and effective.
17 Elijah was a man just
like us. He prayed earnestly that it would not rain,

rain on the earth. 18 Then he
prayed again, and the heav-
en gave rain and the earth
yielded its harvest.
19 My brothers and sis-
ters,[w] if anyone among you
wanders from the truth and
is brought back by another,
20 you should know that
whoever brings back a sinner from wandering will
save the sinner's[x] soul
from death and will cover a
multitude of sins.

καὶ προσευχῇ προσηύξατο τοῦ μὴ βρέξαι,
and [2]in prayer [1]he prayed – not to rain,[d]
=that it should not rain,
καὶ οὐκ ἔβρεξεν ἐπὶ τῆς γῆς ἐνιαυτοὺς
and it rained not on the earth [2]years
τρεῖς καὶ μῆνας ἕξ· 18 καὶ πάλιν προσ-
[1]three and [2]months [1]six; and again he
ηύξατο, καὶ ὁ οὐρανὸς ὑετὸν ἔδωκεν καὶ
prayed, and the heaven [2]rain [1]gave and
ἡ γῆ ἐβλάστησεν τὸν καρπὸν αὐτῆς.
the earth brought forth the fruit of it.
19 Ἀδελφοί μου, ἐάν τις ἐν ὑμῖν πλανηθῇ
Brothers of me, if anyone among you errs
ἀπὸ τῆς ἀληθείας καὶ ἐπιστρέψῃ τις
from the truth and [2]turns [1]anyone
αὐτόν, 20 γινώσκετε ὅτι ὁ ἐπιστρέψας
him, know ye that the [one] turning
ἁμαρτωλὸν ἐκ πλάνης ὁδοῦ αὐτοῦ σώσει
a sinner out of [the] error of way of him will save
ψυχὴν αὐτοῦ ἐκ θανάτου καὶ καλύψει
soul of him out of death and will hide
πλῆθος ἁμαρτιῶν.
a multitude of sins.

and it did not rain on the
land for three and a half
years. 18 Again he prayed,
and the heavens gave rain,
and the earth produced its
crops.
19 My brothers, if one of
you should wander from
the truth and someone
should bring him back,
20 remember this: Whoever
turns a sinner from the error of his way will save him
from death and cover over
a multitude of sins.

The First Letter of

Peter

Chapter 1

Salutation

PETER, an apostle of
Jesus Christ,
To the exiles of the Dis-
persion in Pontus, Galatia,
Cappadocia, Asia, and Bi-
thynia, 2 who have been
chosen and destined by
God the Father and sanctified by the Spirit to be obedient to Jesus Christ and to
be sprinkled with his blood:
May grace and peace be
yours in abundance.

A Living Hope

3 Blessed be the God
and Father of our Lord
Jesus Christ! By his great
mercy he has given us a
new birth into a living hope
through the resurrection of
Jesus Christ from the dead,
4 and into an inheritance
that is imperishable, undefiled, and unfading, kept in
heaven for you, 5 who are
being protected by the
power of God through faith
for a salvation ready to be
revealed in the last time.

ΠΕΤΡΟΥ Α

Of Peter 1

1 Πέτρος ἀπόστολος Ἰησοῦ Χριστοῦ
Peter an apostle of Jesus Christ
ἐκλεκτοῖς παρεπιδήμοις διασπορᾶς Πόντου,
to [the] chosen sojourners of [the] dispersion of Pontus,
Γαλατίας, Καππαδοκίας, Ἀσίας καὶ
of Galatia, *of* Cappadocia, *of* Asia and
Βιθυνίας, 2 κατὰ πρόγνωσιν θεοῦ πατρός,
of Bithynia, according to [the] foreknowledge of God Father,
ἐν ἁγιασμῷ πνεύματος, εἰς ὑπακοὴν καὶ
in sanctification of spirit, to obedience and
ῥαντισμὸν αἵματος Ἰησοῦ Χριστοῦ· χάρις
sprinkling of [the] blood of Jesus Christ: Grace
ὑμῖν καὶ εἰρήνη πληθυνθείη.
to you and peace *may it* be multiplied.
3 Εὐλογητὸς ὁ θεὸς καὶ πατὴρ τοῦ
Blessed [be] the God and Father of the
κυρίου ἡμῶν Ἰησοῦ Χριστοῦ, ὁ κατὰ τὸ
Lord of us Jesus Christ, the [one] according to the
πολὺ αὐτοῦ ἔλεος ἀναγεννήσας ἡμᾶς εἰς
much (great) of him mercy having regenerated us to
ἐλπίδα ζῶσαν δι' ἀναστάσεως Ἰησοῦ
[2]hope [1]a living through [the] resurrection of Jesus
Χριστοῦ ἐκ νεκρῶν, 4 εἰς κληρονομίαν
Christ from [the] dead, to an inheritance
ἄφθαρτον καὶ ἀμίαντον καὶ ἀμάραντον,
incorruptible and undefiled and unfading,
τετηρημένην ἐν οὐρανοῖς εἰς ὑμᾶς 5 τοὺς
having been kept in heavens for you the [ones]
ἐν δυνάμει θεοῦ φρουρουμένους διὰ πίστεως
[2]by [3][the] power [4]of God [1]being guarded through faith
εἰς σωτηρίαν ἑτοίμην ἀποκαλυφθῆναι ἐν
to a salvation ready to be revealed at

1 Peter

Chapter 1

PETER, an apostle of
Jesus Christ,
To God's elect, strangers
in the world, scattered
throughout Pontus, Gala-
tia, Cappadocia, Asia and
Bithynia, 2 who have been
chosen according to the
foreknowledge of God the
Father, through the sanctifying work of the Spirit, for
obedience to Jesus Christ
and sprinkling by his blood:
Grace and peace be yours
in abundance.

Praise to God for a Living Hope

3 Praise be to the God and
Father of our Lord Jesus
Christ! In his great mercy
he has given us new birth
into a living hope through
the resurrection of Jesus
Christ from the dead, 4 and
into an inheritance that can
never perish, spoil or fade
—kept in heaven for you,
5 who through faith are
shielded by God's power
until the coming of the salvation that is ready to be
revealed in the last time.

[w] Gk *My brothers*
[x] Gk *his*

6In this you rejoice,[a] even
if now for a little while you
have had to suffer various
trials, 7so that the genuineness of your faith—being
more precious than gold
that, though perishable, is
tested by fire—may be
found to result in praise and
glory and honor when
Jesus Christ is revealed.
8Although you have not
seen[b] him, you love him;
and even though you do not
see him now, you believe in
him and rejoice with an indescribable and glorious
joy, 9for you are receiving
the outcome of your faith,
the salvation of your souls.
10 Concerning this sal-
vation, the prophets who
prophesied of the grace
that was to be yours made
careful search and inquiry,
11inquiring about the person or time that the Spirit of
Christ within them indicated when it testified in advance to the sufferings destined for Christ and the
subsequent glory. 12It was
revealed to them that they
were serving not them-
selves but you, in regard to
the things that have now
been announced to you
through those who brought
you good news by the Holy
Spirit sent from heaven—
things into which angels
long to look!

A Call to Holy Living

13 Therefore prepare
your minds for action;[c]
discipline yourselves; set
all your hope on the grace
that Jesus Christ will bring
you when he is revealed.
14Like obedient children,
do not be conformed to the
desires that you formerly
had in ignorance. 15In-
stead, as he who called you
is holy, be holy yourselves

[a] Or *Rejoice in this*
[b] Other ancient authorities read *known*
[c] Gk *gird up the loins of your mind*

καιρῷ ἐσχάτῳ. **6** ἐν ᾧ ἀγαλλιᾶσθε,
[2]time [1][the] last. In which ye exult,

ὀλίγον ἄρτι εἰ δέον λυπηθέντες ἐν
a little [while] yet if necessary grieving by

ποικίλοις πειρασμοῖς, **7** ἵνα τὸ δοκίμιον
manifold trials, in order that the proving

ὑμῶν τῆς πίστεως πολυτιμότερον χρυσίου
[3]of you [1]of the [2]faith[,] much more precious [than] [2]gold

τοῦ ἀπολλυμένου, διὰ πυρὸς δὲ δοκιμαζ-
– [1]of perishing, [3]through [4]fire [1]yet [2]being

ομένου, εὑρεθῇ εἰς ἔπαινον καὶ δόξαν
proved, may be found to praise and glory

καὶ τιμὴν ἐν ἀποκαλύψει Ἰησοῦ Χριστοῦ·
and honour at [the] revelation of Jesus Christ;

8 ὃν οὐκ ἰδόντες ἀγαπᾶτε, εἰς ὃν ἄρτι
whom not having seen ye love, in whom yet

μὴ ὁρῶντες πιστεύοντες δὲ ἀγαλλιᾶσθε
not seeing [2]believing [1]but ye exult

χαρᾷ ἀνεκλαλήτῳ καὶ δεδοξασμένῃ,
with joy unspeakable and *having been* glorified,

9 κομιζόμενοι τὸ τέλος τῆς πίστεως
obtaining the end of the(your) faith

σωτηρίαν ψυχῶν. **10** περὶ ἧς σωτηρίας
[the] salvation of [your] souls. Concerning which salvation

ἐξεζήτησαν καὶ ἐξηρεύνησαν προφῆται οἱ
[9]sought out [10]and [11]searched out [1]prophets [2]the

περὶ τῆς εἰς ὑμᾶς χάριτος προφητεύσαντες,
[4]con-cerning [5]the [7]for [8]you [6]grace [3][ones] prophesying,

11 ἐρευνῶντες εἰς τίνα ἢ ποῖον καιρὸν
searching for what or what sort of time

ἐδήλου τὸ ἐν αὐτοῖς πνεῦμα Χριστοῦ
[6]made clear [1]the [4]in [5]them [2]Spirit [3]of Christ

προμαρτυρόμενον τὰ εἰς Χριστὸν παθήματα
[7]forewitnessing [8]the [10]for [11]Christ [9]sufferings

καὶ τὰς μετὰ ταῦτα δόξας. **12** οἷς
[12]and [13]the [15]after [16]these [14]glories. To whom

ἀπεκαλύφθη ὅτι οὐχ ἑαυτοῖς ὑμῖν δὲ
it was revealed that not to themselves [2]to you [1]but

διηκόνουν αὐτά, ἃ νῦν ἀνηγγέλη ὑμῖν
they ministered the same things, which now were announced to you

διὰ τῶν εὐαγγελισαμένων ὑμᾶς ἐν
through the [ones] having evangelized you by

πνεύματι ἁγίῳ ἀποσταλέντι ἀπ᾽ οὐρανοῦ,
[2]Spirit [1][the] Holy sent forth from heaven,

εἰς ἃ ἐπιθυμοῦσιν ἄγγελοι παρακῦψαι.
into [1]which things [3]long [2]angels [4]to look into.

13 Διὸ ἀναζωσάμενοι τὰς ὀσφύας τῆς
Wherefore girding up the loins of the

διανοίας ὑμῶν, νήφοντες, τελείως ἐλπίσατε
mind of you, being sober, perfectly hope

ἐπὶ τὴν φερομένην ὑμῖν χάριν ἐν
on [1]the [3]being brought [4]to you [2]grace at

ἀποκαλύψει Ἰησοῦ Χριστοῦ. **14** ὡς τέκνα
[the] revelation of Jesus Christ. As children

ὑπακοῆς, μὴ συσχηματιζόμενοι ταῖς πρότε-
of obedience,* not fashioning yourselves to the [6]form-

ρον ἐν τῇ ἀγνοίᾳ ὑμῶν ἐπιθυμίαις, **15** ἀλλὰ
erly [2]in [3]the [4]ignorance [5]of you [1]longings, but

κατὰ τὸν καλέσαντα ὑμᾶς ἅγιον καὶ
accord-ing to [1]the [3]having called [4]you [2]holy [one] [7]also

* Genitive of quality: " obedient children."

6In this you greatly rejoice,
though now for a little
while you may have had to
suffer grief in all kinds of
trials. 7These have come so
that your faith—of greater
worth than gold, which perishes even though refined
by fire—may be proved
genuine and may result in
praise, glory and honor
when Jesus Christ is re-
vealed. 8Though you have
not seen him, you love him;
and even though you do not
see him now, you believe in
him and are filled with an
inexpressible and glorious
joy, 9for you are receiving
the goal of your faith, the
salvation of your souls.
10Concerning this salva-
tion, the prophets, who
spoke of the grace that was
to come to you, searched
intently and with the greatest care, 11trying to find out
the time and circumstances
to which the Spirit of Christ
in them was pointing when
he predicted the sufferings
of Christ and the glories
that would follow. 12It was
revealed to them that they
were not serving them-
selves but you, when they
spoke of the things that
have now been told you by
those who have preached
the gospel to you by the
Holy Spirit sent from heav-
en. Even angels long to
look into these things.

Be Holy

13Therefore, prepare
your minds for action; be
self-controlled; set your
hope fully on the grace to
be given you when Jesus
Christ is revealed. 14As
obedient children, do not
conform to the evil desires
you had when you lived in
ignorance. 15But just as he
who called you is holy, so

in all your conduct; 16for it
is written, "You shall be
holy, for I am holy."
17 If you invoke as Fa-
ther the one who judges all
people impartially according to their deeds, live in
reverent fear during the
time of your exile. 18You
know that you were ran-
somed from the futile ways
inherited from your ancestors, not with perishable
things like silver or gold,
19but with the precious
blood of Christ, like that of
a lamb without defect or
blemish. 20He was destined
before the foundation of
the world, but was revealed
at the end of the ages for
your sake. 21Through him
you have come to trust in
God, who raised him from
the dead and gave him glory, so that your faith and
hope are set on God.
22 Now that you have
purified your souls by your
obedience to the truth[d] so
that you have genuine mu-
tual love, love one another
deeply[e] from the heart.[f]
23You have been born
anew, not of perishable but
of imperishable seed,
through the living and enduring word of God.[g]
24For

"All flesh is like grass
and all its glory like
the flower
of grass.
The grass withers,
and the flower falls,
25 but the word of the
Lord endures
forever."

That word is the good news
that was announced to you.

Chapter 2

The Living Stone and a Chosen People

RID yourselves, there-
fore, of all malice, and
all guile, insincerity, envy,
and all slander. 2Like newborn infants, long for the
pure, spiritual milk. so that

[d] Other ancient authorities add *through the Spirit*

[e] Or *constantly*

[f] Other ancient authorities read *a pure heart*

[g] Or *through the word of the living and enduring God*

αὐτοὶ ἅγιοι ἐν πάσῃ ἀναστροφῇ γενήθητε,
[7][your]-selves [8]holy [9]in [10]all [11]conduct [6]become ye,

16 διότι γέγραπται· [ὅτι] ἅγιοι ἔσεσθε,
because it has been written: – Holy ye shall be,

ὅτι ἐγὼ ἅγιος. **17** καὶ εἰ πατέρα
because I [am] holy. And if [2]Father

ἐπικαλεῖσθε τὸν ἀπροσωπολήμπτως κρίνοντα
[1]ye invoke [as] [3]the [one] [5]without respect to persons [4]judging

κατὰ τὸ ἑκάστου ἔργον, ἐν φόβῳ τὸν
according to the [2]of each man [1]work, [2]in [3]fear [4]the

τῆς παροικίας ὑμῶν χρόνον ἀναστράφητε,
[6]of the [7]sojourning [8]of you [5]time [1]pass,

18 εἰδότες ὅτι οὐ φθαρτοῖς, ἀργυρίῳ ἢ
knowing that not with corruptible things, silver or

χρυσίῳ, ἐλυτρώθητε ἐκ τῆς ματαίας ὑμῶν
gold, ye were redeemed from the vain [3]of you

ἀναστροφῆς πατροπαραδότου, **19** ἀλλὰ τιμίῳ
[1]conduct delivered from [your] fathers, but with precious

αἵματι ὡς ἀμνοῦ ἀμώμου καὶ ἀσπίλου
blood[,] as of a lamb unblemished and unspotted[,]

Χριστοῦ, **20** προεγνωσμένου μὲν πρὸ κατα-
of Christ, *having been* foreknown on one hand from [the]

βολῆς κόσμου, φανερωθέντος δὲ ἐπ᾽ ἐσχάτου
foundation of [the] world, manifested on the other in [the] last

τῶν χρόνων δι᾽ ὑμᾶς **21** τοὺς δι᾽ αὐτοῦ
of the times because of you the ones through him

πιστοὺς εἰς θεὸν τὸν ἐγείραντα αὐτὸν
believing in God the [one] having raised him

ἐκ νεκρῶν καὶ δόξαν αὐτῷ δόντα, ὥστε
from [the] dead and [2]glory [3]to him [1]having given, so as

τὴν πίστιν ὑμῶν καὶ ἐλπίδα εἶναι εἰς
the [1]faith [4]of you [2]and [3]hope to be in

θεόν. **22** Τὰς ψυχὰς ὑμῶν ἡγνικότες
God. [2]The [3]souls [4]of you [1]having purified

ἐν τῇ ὑπακοῇ τῆς ἀληθείας εἰς φιλαδελφίαν
by – obedience of(to) the truth to [2]brotherly love

ἀνυπόκριτον, ἐκ καρδίας ἀλλήλους ἀγαπήσατε
[1]unfeigned, [4]from [5][the] heart [2]one another [1]love ye

ἐκτενῶς, **23** ἀναγεγεννημένοι οὐκ ἐκ σπορᾶς
[3]earnestly, having been regenerated not by [2]seed

φθαρτῆς ἀλλὰ ἀφθάρτου, διὰ λόγου ζῶντος
[1]corruptible but incorruptible, through [4]word [1][the] living

θεοῦ καὶ μένοντος. **24** διότι πᾶσα σὰρξ
[5]of God [2]and [3]remaining. Because all flesh [is]

ὡς χόρτος, καὶ πᾶσα δόξα αὐτῆς ὡς
as grass, and all [the] glory of it as

ἄνθος χόρτου· ἐξηράνθη ὁ χόρτος, καὶ
a flower of grass; was dried the grass, and

τὸ ἄνθος ἐξέπεσεν· **25** τὸ δὲ ῥῆμα κυρίου
the flower fell out; but the word of [the] Lord

μένει εἰς τὸν αἰῶνα. τοῦτο δέ ἐστιν
remains unto the age. And this is

τὸ ῥῆμα τὸ εὐαγγελισθὲν εἰς ὑμᾶς.
the word – preached [as good news] to you.

2 Ἀποθέμενοι οὖν πᾶσαν κακίαν καὶ
Putting away therefore all malice and

πάντα δόλον καὶ ὑποκρίσεις καὶ φθόνους
all guile and hypocrisies and envies

καὶ πάσας καταλαλιάς, **2** ὡς ἀρτιγέννητα
and all detractions, as newborn

βρέφη τὸ λογικὸν ἄδολον γάλα ἐπιποθήσατε,
babes [2]the [3]spiritual [4]pure [5]milk [1]desire ye,

be holy in all you do; 16for it
is written: "Be holy, be-
cause I am holy."[a]
17Since you call on a Fa-
ther who judges each man's
work impartially, live your
lives as strangers here in
reverent fear. 18For you
know that it was not with
perishable things such as
silver or gold that you were
redeemed from the empty
way of life handed down to
you from your forefathers,
19but with the precious
blood of Christ, a lamb
without blemish or defect.
20He was chosen before the
creation of the world, but
was revealed in these last
times for your sake.
21Through him you believe
in God, who raised him
from the dead and glorified
him, and so your faith and
hope are in God.
22Now that you have pu-
rified yourselves by obeying the truth so that you
have sincere love for your
brothers, love one another
deeply, from the heart.[b]
23For you have been born
again, not of perishable
seed, but of imperishable,
through the living and enduring word of God. 24For,

"All men are like grass,
and all their glory is
like the flowers of
the field;
the grass withers and the
flowers fall,
25 but the word of the
Lord stands
forever."[c]

And this is the word that
was preached to you.

Chapter 2

THEREFORE, rid your-
selves of all malice and
all deceit, hypocrisy, envy,
and slander of every kind.
2Like newborn babies,
crave pure spiritual milk,

[a] *16* Lev. 11:44,45; 19:2; 20:7

[b] *22* Some early manuscripts *from a pure heart*

[c] *25* Isaiah 40:6-8

by it you may grow into salvation— 3if indeed you have tasted that the Lord is good.

4 Come to him, a living stone, though rejected by mortals yet chosen and precious in God's sight, and 5like living stones, let yourselves be built[h] into a spiritual house, to be a holy priesthood, to offer spiritual sacrifices acceptable to God through Jesus Christ. 6For it stands in scripture:

"See, I am laying in Zion a stone,
a cornerstone chosen and precious;
and whoever believes in him[i] will not be put to shame."

7To you then who believe, he is precious; but for those who do not believe,

"The stone that the builders rejected
has become the very head of the corner,"

8and

"A stone that makes them stumble,
and a rock that makes them fall."

They stumble because they disobey the word, as they were destined to do.

9 But you are a chosen race, a royal priesthood, a holy nation, God's own people,[j] in order that you may proclaim the mighty acts of him who called you out of darkness into his marvelous light.

10 Once you were not a people,
but now you are God's people;
once you had not received mercy,
but now you have received mercy.

Live as Servants of God

11 Beloved, I urge you as aliens and exiles to abstain from the desires of the flesh that wage war against the soul. 12Conduct yourselves honorably among the Gentiles, so that, though they malign you as

[h] Or *you yourselves are being built*
[i] Or *it*
[j] Gk *a people for his possession*

ἵνα ἐν αὐτῷ αὐξηθῆτε εἰς σωτηρίαν,
in order that by it ye may grow to salvation,

3 εἰ ἐγεύσασθε ὅτι χρηστὸς ὁ κύριος.
if ye tasted that [3]good [1]the [2]Lord [is].

4 πρὸς ὃν προσερχόμενοι, λίθον ζῶντα,
to whom approaching, [2]stone [1]a living,

ὑπὸ ἀνθρώπων μὲν ἀποδεδοκιμασμένον παρὰ
by men on one hand *having been* rejected [3]by

δὲ θεῷ ἐκλεκτὸν ἔντιμον, 5 καὶ
[1]on the other [4]God [2]chosen[,] precious, [2]also

αὐτοὶ ὡς λίθοι ζῶντες οἰκοδομεῖσθε οἶκος
[1][your]selves [3]as [5]stones [4]living are being built [2]house

πνευματικὸς εἰς ἱεράτευμα ἅγιον, ἀνενέγκαι
[1]a spiritual for [2]priesthood [1]a holy, to offer

πνευματικὰς θυσίας εὐπροσδέκτους θεῷ διὰ
spiritual sacrifices acceptable to God through

Ἰησοῦ Χριστοῦ· 6 διότι περιέχει ἐν γραφῇ·
Jesus Christ; because it is contained in scripture:

ἰδοὺ τίθημι ἐν Σιὼν λίθον ἐκλεκτὸν
Behold I lay in Sion [4]stone [1]a chosen

ἀκρογωνιαῖον ἔντιμον, καὶ ὁ πιστεύων
[3]corner foundation [2]precious, and the [one] believing

ἐπ' αὐτῷ οὐ μὴ καταισχυνθῇ. 7 ὑμῖν
on it(him) by no means will be shamed. To you =Yours

οὖν ἡ τιμὴ τοῖς πιστεύουσιν· ἀπιστοῦσιν
therefore [3][is] [4]the [5]honour [1]the [ones] [2]believing[c]; [2]to unbelieving [ones]
therefore who believe is the honour;

δὲ λίθος ὃν ἀπεδοκίμασαν οἱ οἰκοδομοῦντες,
[1]but a stone which [3]rejected [1]the [ones] [2]building,

οὗτος ἐγενήθη εἰς κεφαλὴν γωνίας 8 καὶ
this came to be for head of [the] corner and

λίθος προσκόμματος καὶ πέτρα σκανδάλου·
a stone of stumbling and a rock of offence;

οἳ προσκόπτουσιν τῷ λόγῳ ἀπειθοῦντες,
who stumble at the word disobeying,

9 εἰς ὃ καὶ ἐτέθησαν· ὑμεῖς δὲ γένος
to which indeed they were appointed; but ye [are] [2]race

ἐκλεκτόν, βασίλειον ἱεράτευμα, ἔθνος ἅγιον,
[1]a chosen, a royal priesthood, nation a holy,

λαὸς εἰς περιποίησιν, ὅπως τὰς ἀρετὰς
a people for possession, so as [2]the [3]virtues

ἐξαγγείλητε τοῦ ἐκ σκότους ὑμᾶς καλέ-
[1]ye may tell out [4]of the [one] [7]out of [8]darkness [6]you [5]having

σαντος εἰς τὸ θαυμαστὸν αὐτοῦ φῶς·
called into the marvellous [2]of him [1]light;

10 οἵ ποτε οὐ λαός, νῦν δὲ λαὸς θεοῦ,
who then [were] not a people, but [are] now a people of God,

οἱ οὐκ ἠλεημένοι, νῦν δὲ ἐλεηθέντες.
the [ones] not having been pitied, but now pitied.

11 Ἀγαπητοί, παρακαλῶ ὡς παροίκους
Beloved, I exhort [you] as sojourners

καὶ παρεπιδήμους ἀπέχεσθαι τῶν σαρκικῶν
and aliens to abstain from – fleshly

ἐπιθυμιῶν, αἵτινες στρατεύονται κατὰ τῆς
lusts, which war against the

ψυχῆς· 12 τὴν ἀναστροφὴν ὑμῶν ἐν τοῖς
soul; [2]the [3]conduct [4]of you [5]among [6]the

ἔθνεσιν ἔχοντες καλήν, ἵνα ἐν ᾧ κατα-
[7]nations [1]having [8]good, in order that while they

so that by it you may grow up in your salvation, 3now that you have tasted that the Lord is good.

The Living Stone and a Chosen People

4As you come to him, the living Stone—rejected by men but chosen by God and precious to him— 5you also, like living stones, are being built into a spiritual house to be a holy priesthood, offering spiritual sacrifices acceptable to God through Jesus Christ. 6For in Scripture it says:

"See, I lay a stone in Zion,
a chosen and precious cornerstone,
and the one who trusts in him
will never be put to shame."[d]

7Now to you who believe, this stone is precious. But to those who do not believe,

"The stone the builders rejected
has become the capstone,"[e][f]

8and,

"A stone that causes men to stumble
and a rock that makes them fall."[g]

They stumble because they disobey the message—which is also what they were destined for.

9But you are a chosen people, a royal priesthood, a holy nation, a people belonging to God, that you may declare the praises of him who called you out of darkness into his wonderful light. 10Once you were not a people, but now you are the people of God; once you had not received mercy, but now you have received mercy.

11Dear friends, I urge you, as aliens and strangers in the world, to abstain from sinful desires, which war against your soul. 12Live such good lives among the pagans that, though they accuse you of

[d]6 Isaiah 28:16
[e]7 Or *cornerstone*
[f]7 Psalm 118:22
[g]8 Isaiah 8:14

evildoers, they may see
your honorable deeds and
glorify God when he comes
to judge.[k]
13 For the Lord's sake
accept the authority of every human institution,[l]
whether of the emperor as
supreme, 14 or of gover-
nors, as sent by him to punish those who do wrong and
to praise those who do
right. 15 For it is God's will
that by doing right you
should silence the igno-
rance of the foolish. 16 As
servants[m] of God, live as
free people, yet do not use
your freedom as a pretext
for evil. 17 Honor everyone.
Love the family of believers.[n] Fear God. Honor the
emperor.

The Example of Christ's Suffering

18 Slaves, accept the
authority of your masters
with all deference, not only
those who are kind and
gentle but also those who
are harsh. 19 For it is a credit to you if, being aware of
God, you endure pain while
suffering unjustly. 20 If you
endure when you are beat-
en for doing wrong, what
credit is that? But if you endure when you do right and
suffer for it, you have
God's approval. 21 For to
this you have been called,
because Christ also suf-
fered for you, leaving you
an example, so that you
should follow in his steps.
22 "He committed no
sin,
and no deceit was
found in
his mouth."
23 When he was abused, he
did not return abuse; when
he suffered, he did not
threaten; but he entrusted
himself to the one who
judges justly. 24 He himself

[k] Gk *God on the day of visitation*
[l] Or *every institution ordained for human beings*
[m] Gk *slaves*
[n] Gk *Love the brotherhood*

λαλοῦσιν ὑμῶν ὡς κακοποιῶν, ἐκ τῶν
speak against you as evildoers, by the (your)

καλῶν ἔργων ἐποπτεύοντες δοξάσωσιν τὸν
good works observing they may glorify –

θεὸν ἐν ἡμέρᾳ ἐπισκοπῆς.
God in a day of visitation.

13 Ὑποτάγητε πάσῃ ἀνθρωπίνῃ κτίσει
Submit to every human ordinance

διὰ τὸν κύριον· εἴτε βασιλεῖ ὡς ὑπερέχοντι,
because of the Lord: whether to a king as being supreme,

14 εἴτε ἡγεμόσιν ὡς δι' αὐτοῦ πεμπομένοις
or to governors as through him being sent

εἰς ἐκδίκησιν κακοποιῶν ἔπαινον δὲ
for vengeance of(on) evildoers [2]praise [1]but

ἀγαθοποιῶν· 15 ὅτι οὕτως ἐστὶν τὸ
of welldoers; because so is the

θέλημα τοῦ θεοῦ, ἀγαθοποιοῦντας φιμοῦν
will – of God, doing good to silence

τὴν τῶν ἀφρόνων ἀνθρώπων ἀγνωσίαν·
[1]the – [3]of foolish [4]men [2]ignorance;

16 ὡς ἐλεύθεροι, καὶ μὴ ὡς ἐπικάλυμμα
as free, and not [3]as [4]a cloak

ἔχοντες τῆς κακίας τὴν ἐλευθερίαν, ἀλλ'
[1]having *the* [5]of evil *the* [2]freedom, but

ὡς θεοῦ δοῦλοι. 17 πάντας τιμήσατε,
as of God slaves. [2]All men [1]honour ye,

τὴν ἀδελφότητα ἀγαπᾶτε, τὸν θεὸν
[2]the [3]brotherhood [1]love, – [2]God

φοβεῖσθε, τὸν βασιλέα τιμᾶτε. 18 Οἱ
[1]fear, [2]the [3]king [1]honour. –

οἰκέται, ὑποτασσόμενοι ἐν παντὶ φόβῳ
House servants, submitting yourselves in all fear

τοῖς δεσπόταις, οὐ μόνον τοῖς ἀγαθοῖς
to the(your) masters, not only to the good

καὶ ἐπιεικέσιν ἀλλὰ καὶ τοῖς σκολιοῖς.
and forbearing but also to the perverse.

19 τοῦτο γὰρ χάρις εἰ διὰ συνείδησιν
For this [is] a favour if because of conscience

θεοῦ ὑποφέρει τις λύπας πάσχων ἀδίκως.
of God [2]bears [1]anyone griefs suffering unjustly.

20 ποῖον γὰρ κλέος εἰ ἁμαρτάνοντες καὶ
For what glory [is it] if sinning and

κολαφιζόμενοι ὑπομενεῖτε; ἀλλ' εἰ ἀγαθο-
being buffeted ye endure? but if doing

ποιοῦντες καὶ πάσχοντες ὑπομενεῖτε, τοῦτο
good and suffering ye endure, this [is]

χάρις παρὰ θεῷ. 21 εἰς τοῦτο γὰρ
a favour with God. [2]to [3]this [1]For

ἐκλήθητε, ὅτι καὶ Χριστὸς ἔπαθεν ὑπὲρ
ye were called, because indeed Christ suffered on behalf of

ὑμῶν, ὑμῖν ὑπολιμπάνων ὑπογραμμὸν ἵνα
you, [2]to you [1]leaving behind an example in order that

ἐπακολουθήσητε τοῖς ἴχνεσιν αὐτοῦ· 22 ὃς
ye should follow the steps of him; who

ἁμαρτίαν οὐκ ἐποίησεν οὐδὲ εὑρέθη δόλος
[3]sin [2]not [1]did nor was [2]found [1]guile

ἐν τῷ στόματι αὐτοῦ· 23 ὃς λοιδορούμενος
in the mouth of him; who being reviled

οὐκ ἀντελοιδόρει, πάσχων οὐκ ἠπείλει,
reviled not in return, suffering he threatened not,

παρεδίδου δὲ τῷ κρίνοντι δικαίως· 24 ὃς
but delivered [himself] to the [one] judging righteously; who

doing wrong, they may see
your good deeds and glorify God on the day he visits
us.

Submission to Rulers and Masters

13 Submit yourselves for
the Lord's sake to every
authority instituted among
men: whether to the king,
as the supreme authority,
14 or to governors, who are
sent by him to punish those
who do wrong and to com-
mend those who do right.
15 For it is God's will that by
doing good you should si-
lence the ignorant talk of
foolish men. 16 Live as free
men, but do not use your
freedom as a cover-up for
evil; live as servants of
God. 17 Show proper re-
spect to everyone: Love
the brotherhood of believers, fear God, honor the
king.
18 Slaves, submit your-
selves to your masters with
all respect, not only to
those who are good and
considerate, but also to
those who are harsh. 19 For
it is commendable if a man
bears up under the pain of
unjust suffering because he
is conscious of God. 20 But
how is it to your credit if
you receive a beating for
doing wrong and endure it?
But if you suffer for doing
good and you endure it, this
is commendable before
God. 21 To this you were
called, because Christ suffered for you, leaving you
an example, that you
should follow in his steps.

22 "He committed no sin,
and no deceit was
found in his
mouth."[h]

23 When they hurled their
insults at him, he did not
retaliate; when he suffered,
he made no threats. In-
stead, he entrusted himself
to him who judges justly.

[h] 22 Isaiah 53:9

bore our sins in his body on
the cross,[o] so that, free
from sins, we might live for
righteousness; by his
wounds[p] you have been
healed. 25 For you were going astray like sheep, but
now you have returned to
the shepherd and guardian
of your souls.

Chapter 3

Wives and Husbands

WIVES, in the same
way, accept the au-
thority of your husbands,
so that, even if some of
them do not obey the word,
they may be won over without a word by their wives'
conduct, 2 when they see
the purity and reverence of
your lives. 3 Do not adorn
yourselves outwardly by
braiding your hair, and by
wearing gold ornaments or
fine clothing; 4 rather, let
your adornment be the in-
ner self with the lasting
beauty of a gentle and quiet
spirit, which is very precious in God's sight. 5 It
was in this way long ago
that the holy women who
hoped in God used to adorn
themselves by accepting
the authority of their husbands. 6 Thus Sarah obeyed
Abraham and called him
lord. You have become her
daughters as long as you do
what is good and never let
fears alarm you.
7 Husbands, in the
same way, show consider-
ation for your wives in your
life together, paying honor
to the woman as the weaker
sex,[q] since they too are
also heirs of the gracious
gift of life—so that nothing
may hinder your prayers.

Suffering for Doing Right

8 Finally, all of you,
have unity of spirit, sympathy, love for one another, a

τὰς ἁμαρτίας ἡμῶν αὐτὸς ἀνήνεγκεν ἐν
[3]the [4]sins [5]of us [1][him]self [2]carried up in

τῷ σώματι αὐτοῦ ἐπὶ τὸ ξύλον, ἵνα
the body of him onto the tree, in order that

ταῖς ἁμαρτίαις ἀπογενόμενοι τῇ δικαιοσύνῃ
– [2]to sins [1]dying – [4]to righteousness

ζήσωμεν· οὗ τῷ μώλωπι ἰάθητε.
[3]we might live; [3]of whom [1]by the [2]bruise ye were cured.

25 ἦτε γὰρ ὡς πρόβατα πλανώμενοι,
[2]ye were [1]For [4]as [5]sheep [3]wandering,

ἀλλὰ ἐπεστράφητε νῦν ἐπὶ τὸν ποιμένα
but ye turned now to the shepherd

καὶ ἐπίσκοπον τῶν ψυχῶν ὑμῶν.
and bishop of the souls of you.

3 Ὁμοίως γυναῖκες, ὑποτασσόμεναι τοῖς
Likewise wives, submitting yourselves to the (your)

ἰδίοις ἀνδράσιν, ἵνα καὶ εἴ τινες ἀπειθοῦσιν
own husbands, in order that even if any disobey

τῷ λόγῳ, διὰ τῆς τῶν γυναικῶν ἀναστροφῆς
the word, through [1]the [3]of the(ir) [4]wives [2]conduct

ἄνευ λόγου κερδηθήσονται, 2 ἐποπτεύσαντες
without a word they will(may) be gained, observing

τὴν ἐν φόβῳ ἁγνὴν ἀναστροφὴν ὑμῶν.
[1]the [5]in [6]fear [2]pure [3]conduct [4]of you.

3 ὧν ἔστω οὐχ ὁ ἔξωθεν ἐμπλοκῆς
Of whom let it be not [1]the [2]outward [4]of plaiting

τριχῶν καὶ περιθέσεως χρυσίων ἢ ἐνδύσεως
[5]of hairs [6]and [7]of putting round(on) [8]of gold [ornaments] [9]or [10]of clothing

ἱματίων κόσμος, 4 ἀλλ᾽ ὁ κρυπτὸς τῆς
[11]of(with) garments [3]adorning, but [1]the [2]hidden [4]of the

καρδίας ἄνθρωπος ἐν τῷ ἀφθάρτῳ τοῦ
[5]heart [3]man in(?by) the incorruptible [adorning] of the

πραέος καὶ ἡσυχίου πνεύματος, ὅ ἐστιν
meek and quiet spirit, which is

ἐνώπιον τοῦ θεοῦ πολυτελές. 5 οὕτως
before – God of great value. so

γάρ ποτε καὶ αἱ ἅγιαι γυναῖκες αἱ
For then indeed the holy women –

ἐλπίζουσαι εἰς θεὸν ἐκόσμουν ἑαυτάς,
hoping in God adorned themselves,

ὑποτασσόμεναι τοῖς ἰδίοις ἀνδράσιν, 6 ὡς
submitting themselves to the(ir) own husbands, as

Σάρρα ὑπήκουσεν τῷ Ἀβραάμ, κύριον
Sara obeyed – Abraham, [3]lord

αὐτὸν καλοῦσα· ἧς ἐγενήθητε τέκνα
[2]him [1]calling; of whom ye became children

ἀγαθοποιοῦσαι καὶ μὴ φοβούμεναι μηδεμίαν
doing good and not fearing no(any)

πτόησιν. 7 Οἱ ἄνδρες ὁμοίως, συνοικοῦντες
terror. – Husbands likewise, dwelling together

κατὰ γνῶσιν ὡς ἀσθενεστέρῳ σκεύει τῷ
according to knowledge as with a weaker vessel the

γυναικείῳ, ἀπονέμοντες τιμὴν ὡς καὶ
female, assigning honour as indeed

συγκληρονόμοις χάριτος ζωῆς, εἰς τὸ μὴ
co-heirs of [the] grace of life, *for the* not

ἐγκόπτεσθαι τὰς προσευχὰς ὑμῶν. 8 Τὸ δὲ
to be hindered the prayers of you.[b] Now the

τέλος πάντες ὁμόφρονες, συμπαθεῖς,
end[,] [be ye] all of one mind, sympathetic,

24 He himself bore our sins
in his body on the tree, so
that we might die to sins
and live for righteousness;
by his wounds you have
been healed. 25 For you
were like sheep going
astray, but now you have
returned to the Shepherd
and Overseer of your souls.

Chapter 3

Wives and Husbands

WIVES, in the same
way be submissive
to your husbands so that, if
any of them do not believe
the word, they may be won
over without words by the
behavior of their wives,
2 when they see the purity
and reverence of your
lives. 3 Your beauty should
not come from outward
adornment, such as braided
hair and the wearing of gold
jewelry and fine clothes.
4 Instead, it should be that
of your inner self, the unfading beauty of a gentle
and quiet spirit, which is of
great worth in God's sight.
5 For this is the way the holy
women of the past who put
their hope in God used to
make themselves beautiful.
They were submissive to
their own husbands, 6 like
Sarah, who obeyed Abra-
ham and called him her
master. You are her daughters if you do what is right
and do not give way to fear.
7 Husbands, in the same
way be considerate as you
live with your wives, and
treat them with respect as
the weaker partner and as
heirs with you of the gracious gift of life, so that
nothing will hinder your
prayers.

Suffering for Doing Good

8 Finally, all of you, live in
harmony with one another;
be sympathetic, love as

[o] Or *carried up our sins in his body to the tree*
[p] Gk *bruise*
[q] Gk *vessel*

tender heart, and a humble
mind. 9 Do not repay evil
for evil or abuse for abuse;
but, on the contrary, repay
with a blessing. It is for this
that you were called—that
you might inherit a blessing. 10 For
"Those who desire life
and desire to see
good days,
let them keep their
tongues
from evil
and their lips from
speaking deceit;
11 let them turn away
from evil and do
good;
let them seek peace
and pursue it.
12 For the eyes of the
Lord are on
the righteous,
and his ears are
open to
their prayer.
But the face of the
Lord is against
those who do
evil."
13 Now who will harm
you if you are eager to do
what is good? 14 But even if
you do suffer for doing
what is right, you are
blessed. Do not fear what
they fear,[r] and do not be
intimidated, 15 but in your
hearts sanctify Christ as
Lord. Always be ready to
make your defense to any-
one who demands from you
an accounting for the hope
that is in you; 16 yet do it
with gentleness and reverence.[s] Keep your con-
science clear, so that, when
you are maligned, those
who abuse you for your
good conduct in Christ may
be put to shame. 17 For it is
better to suffer for doing
good, if suffering should be
God's will, than to suffer
for doing evil. 18 For Christ
also suffered[t] for sins once
for all, the righteous for the
unrighteous, in order to
bring you[u] to God. He was

[r] Gk *their fear*
[s] Or *respect*
[t] Other ancient authorities read *died*
[u] Other ancient authorities read *us*

φιλάδελφοι, εὔσπλαγχνοι, ταπεινόφρονες,
loving [the] brothers, compassionate, humble-minded,
9 μὴ ἀποδιδόντες κακὸν ἀντὶ κακοῦ ἢ
not giving back evil instead of evil or
λοιδορίαν ἀντὶ λοιδορίας, τοὐναντίον δὲ
reviling instead of reviling, but on the contrary
εὐλογοῦντες, ὅτι εἰς τοῦτο ἐκλήθητε ἵνα
blessing, because to this ye were called in order that
εὐλογίαν κληρονομήσητε. **10** ὁ γὰρ θέλων
blessing ye might inherit. For the [one] wishing
ζωὴν ἀγαπᾶν καὶ ἰδεῖν ἡμέρας ἀγαθάς,
[2]life [1]to love and to see [2]days [1]good,
παυσάτω τὴν γλῶσσαν ἀπὸ κακοῦ καὶ
let him restrain the(his) tongue from evil and
χείλη τοῦ μὴ λαλῆσαι δόλον, **11** ἐκκλινάτω
[his] lips – not to speak[d] guile, [2]let him turn aside
δὲ ἀπὸ κακοῦ καὶ ποιησάτω ἀγαθόν,
[1]and from evil and let him do good,
ζητησάτω εἰρήνην καὶ διωξάτω αὐτήν·
let him seek peace and pursue it;
12 ὅτι ὀφθαλμοὶ κυρίου ἐπὶ δικαίους καὶ
because [the] eyes of [the] Lord [are] on [the] righteous and
ὦτα αὐτοῦ εἰς δέησιν αὐτῶν, πρόσωπον
[the] ears of him [open] to [the] petition of them, [2][the] face
δὲ κυρίου ἐπὶ ποιοῦντας κακά.
[1]but of [the] Lord [is] against [ones] doing evil things.
13 Καὶ τίς ὁ κακώσων ὑμᾶς ἐὰν τοῦ
And who [is] the [one] harming you if [3]of the
ἀγαθοῦ ζηλωταὶ γένησθε; **14** ἀλλ' εἰ καὶ
[4]good [2]zealots [1]ye become ? but if indeed
πάσχοιτε διὰ δικαιοσύνην, μακάριοι. τὸν
ye suffer because of righteousness, blessed [are ye]. [3]the
δὲ φόβον αὐτῶν μὴ φοβηθῆτε μηδὲ
[1]But [4]fear [5]of them [2]fear ye not nor
ταραχθῆτε, **15** κύριον δὲ τὸν Χριστὸν
be ye troubled, [1]but [4][as] [5]Lord – [3]Christ
ἁγιάσατε ἐν ταῖς καρδίαις ὑμῶν, ἕτοιμοι
[2]sanctify in the hearts of you, ready
ἀεὶ πρὸς ἀπολογίαν παντὶ τῷ αἰτοῦντι
always for defence to every one asking
ὑμᾶς λόγον περὶ τῆς ἐν ὑμῖν ἐλπίδος,
you a word concerning [1]the [3]in [4]you [2]hope,
16 ἀλλὰ μετὰ πραΰτητος καὶ φόβου,
but with meekness and fear,
συνείδησιν ἔχοντες ἀγαθήν, ἵνα ἐν ᾧ
[3]conscience [1]having [2]a good, in order that while
καταλαλεῖσθε καταισχυνθῶσιν οἱ ἐπηρεάζον-
ye are spoken against [3]may be shamed [by] [1]the [ones] [2]abusing
τες ὑμῶν τὴν ἀγαθὴν ἐν Χριστῷ
[you] [7]of you [4]the [5]good [8]in [9]Christ
ἀναστροφήν. **17** κρεῖττον γὰρ ἀγαθοποι-
[6]conduct. For [it is] better doing
οῦντας, εἰ θέλοι τὸ θέλημα τοῦ θεοῦ,
good, if [4]wills [1]the [2]will – [3]of God,
πάσχειν ἢ κακοποιοῦντας. **18** ὅτι καὶ
to suffer than doing evil. Because indeed
Χριστὸς ἅπαξ περὶ ἁμαρτιῶν ἀπέθανεν,
Christ once [2]concerning [3]sins [1]died,
δίκαιος ὑπὲρ ἀδίκων, ἵνα ὑμᾶς προσαγάγῃ
a righteous man on behalf of unrighteous ones, in order that [2]you [1]he might bring

brothers, be compassion-
ate and humble. 9 Do not repay evil with evil or insult
with insult, but with blessing, because to this you
were called so that you may
inherit a blessing. 10 For,

"Whoever would love
life
and see good days
must keep his tongue
from evil
and his lips from
deceitful speech.
11 He must turn from evil
and do good;
he must seek peace and
pursue it.
12 For the eyes of the Lord
are on the righteous
and his ears are
attentive to their
prayer,
but the face of the Lord
is against those who
do evil."[i]

13 Who is going to harm
you if you are eager to do
good? 14 But even if you
should suffer for what is
right, you are blessed. "Do
not fear what they fear[j]; do
not be frightened."[k] 15 But
in your hearts set apart
Christ as Lord. Always be
prepared to give an answer
to everyone who asks you
to give the reason for the
hope that you have. But do
this with gentleness and respect, 16 keeping a clear
conscience, so that those
who speak maliciously
against your good behavior
in Christ may be ashamed
of their slander. 17 It is better, if it is God's will, to
suffer for doing good than
for doing evil. 18 For Christ
died for sins once for all,
the righteous for the un-
righteous, to bring you to

[i] *12* Psalm 34:12-16
[j] *14* Or *not fear their threats*
[k] *14* Isaiah 8:12

put to death in the flesh, but
made alive in the spirit, 19in
which also he went and
made a proclamation to the
spirits in prison, 20who in
former times did not obey,
when God waited patiently
in the days of Noah, during
the building of the ark, in
which a few, that is, eight
persons, were saved
through water. 21And bap-
tism, which this prefigured,
now saves you—not as a
removal of dirt from the
body, but as an appeal to
God for[v] a good con-
science, through the resurrection of Jesus Christ,
22who has gone into heav-
en and is at the right hand
of God, with angels, au-
thorities, and powers made
subject to him.

Chapter 4

Good Stewards of God's Grace

SINCE therefore Christ
suffered in the flesh,[w]
arm yourselves also with
the same intention (for
whoever has suffered in the
flesh has finished with sin),
2so as to live for the rest of
your earthly life[x] no longer
by human desires but by
the will of God. 3You have
already spent enough time
in doing what the Gentiles
like to do, living in licentiousness, passions, drunkenness, revels, carousing,
and lawless idolatry. 4They
are surprised that you no
longer join them in the
same excesses of dissipa-
tion, and so they blas-
pheme.[y] 5But they will
have to give an accounting
to him who stands ready to
judge the living and the
dead. 6For this is the reason the gospel was pro-
claimed even to the dead,
so that, though they had

[v] Or *a pledge to God from*
[w] Other ancient authorities add *for us*; others, *for you*
[x] Gk *rest of the time in the flesh*
[y] Or *they malign you*

τῷ θεῷ, θανατωθεὶς μὲν σαρκὶ ζωοποιηθεὶς
– to God, being put to death on one hand in [the] flesh[,] quickened

δὲ πνεύματι· **19** ἐν ᾧ καὶ τοῖς ἐν
on the other in [the] spirit; in which indeed [5]to the [6]in

φυλακῇ πνεύμασιν πορευθεὶς ἐκήρυξεν,
[8]prison [3]spirits [1]going he proclaimed,

20 ἀπειθήσασίν ποτε ὅτε ἀπεξεδέχετο ἡ
to disobeying ones then when [4]waited [1]the

τοῦ θεοῦ μακροθυμία ἐν ἡμέραις Νῶε
– [3]of God [2]longsuffering in [the] days of Noe

κατασκευαζομένης κιβωτοῦ, εἰς ἣν ὀλίγοι,
[2]being prepared [1]an ark,[a] in which a few,

τοῦτ' ἔστιν ὀκτὼ ψυχαί, διεσώθησαν δι'
this is eight souls, were quite saved through

ὕδατος. **21** ὃ καὶ ὑμᾶς ἀντίτυπον νῦν
water. [1]Which [3]also [6]us [2]figure [4]now

σῴζει βάπτισμα, οὐ σαρκὸς ἀπόθεσις
[5]saves [even] baptism, not [3]of [the] flesh [1]a putting away

ῥύπου ἀλλὰ συνειδήσεως ἀγαθῆς ἐπερώτημα
[2]of [the] filth but [3]conscience [2]of a good [1]an answer

εἰς θεόν, δι' ἀναστάσεως Ἰησοῦ Χριστοῦ,
toward God, through [the] resurrection of Jesus Christ,

22 ὅς ἐστιν ἐν δεξιᾷ θεοῦ, πορευθεὶς
who is at [the] right [hand] of God, having gone

εἰς οὐρανόν, ὑποταγέντων αὐτῷ ἀγγέλων
into heaven, [6]being subjected [7]to him [1]angels

καὶ ἐξουσιῶν καὶ δυνάμεων.
[2]and [3]authorities [4]and [5]powers[a].

4 Χριστοῦ οὖν παθόντος σαρκὶ καὶ ὑμεῖς
[2]Christ [1]therefore having suffered[a] in [the] flesh [2]also [1]ye

τὴν αὐτὴν ἔννοιαν ὁπλίσασθε, ὅτι ὁ
[4]the [5]same [6]mind [3]arm yourselves [with], because the [one]

παθὼν σαρκὶ πέπαυται ἁμαρτίας, **2** εἰς
having suffered in [the] flesh has ceased from sin, for

τὸ μηκέτι ἀνθρώπων ἐπιθυμίαις ἀλλὰ
the [1]no longer [9]of men [8]in [the] lusts [10]but

θελήματι θεοῦ τὸν ἐπίλοιπον ἐν σαρκὶ
[11]in [the] will [12]of God [3]the [4]remaining [6]in [7][the] flesh

βιῶσαι χρόνον. **3** ἀρκετὸς γὰρ ὁ παρεληλυ-
[2]to live [5]time. For [6]sufficient [1]the [3]having passed

θὼς χρόνος τὸ βούλημα τῶν ἐθνῶν
away [2]time [4][is] [7]the [8]purpose [9]of the [10]nations

κατειργάσθαι, πεπορευμένους ἐν ἀσελγείαις,
[5]to have worked out, having gone [on] in licentiousnesses,

ἐπιθυμίαις, οἰνοφλυγίαις, κώμοις, πότοις
lusts, debaucheries, carousals, drinking bouts

καὶ ἀθεμίτοις εἰδωλολατρίαις. **4** ἐν ᾧ
and unlawful idolatries. While

ξενίζονται μὴ συντρεχόντων ὑμῶν εἰς
they are surprised [2]not [3]running with [1]you[a] to

τὴν αὐτὴν τῆς ἀσωτίας ἀνάχυσιν, βλασ-
the same – [2]of profligacy [1]excess, blas-

φημοῦντες· **5** οἳ ἀποδώσουσιν λόγον τῷ
pheming; who will render account to the [one]

ἑτοίμως ἔχοντι κρῖναι ζῶντας καὶ νεκρούς.
readily having to judge living and dead.
=who is ready

6 εἰς τοῦτο γὰρ καὶ νεκροῖς εὐηγγελίσθη,
[2]for [3]this [1]For indeed [2]to dead men [1]good news was preached,

God. He was put to death in
the body but made alive by
the Spirit, 19through
whom[l] also he went and
preached to the spirits in
prison 20who disobeyed
long ago when God waited
patiently in the days of
Noah while the ark was being built. In it only a few
people, eight in all, were
saved through water, 21and
this water symbolizes baptism that now saves you
also—not the removal of
dirt from the body but the
pledge[m] of a good con-
science toward God. It
saves you by the resurrection of Jesus Christ, 22who
has gone into heaven and is
at God's right hand—with
angels, authorities and
powers in submission to
him.

Chapter 4

Living for God

THEREFORE, since
Christ suffered in his
body, arm yourselves also
with the same attitude, because he who has suffered
in his body is done with sin.
2As a result, he does not
live the rest of his earthly
life for evil human desires,
but rather for the will of
God. 3For you have spent
enough time in the past doing what pagans choose to
do—living in debauchery,
lust, drunkenness, orgies,
carousing and detestable
idolatry. 4They think it
strange that you do not
plunge with them into the
same flood of dissipation,
and they heap abuse on
you. 5But they will have to
give account to him who is
ready to judge the living
and the dead. 6For this is
the reason the gospel was
preached even to those
who are now dead, so that

[l] *18,19* Or *alive in the spirit, 19through which*
[m] *21* Or *response*

been judged in the flesh as everyone is judged, they might live in the spirit as God does.

7 The end of all things is near;[c] therefore be serious and discipline yourselves for the sake of your prayers. 8 Above all, maintain constant love for one another, for love covers a multitude of sins. 9 Be hospitable to one another without complaining. 10 Like good stewards of the manifold grace of God, serve one another with whatever gift each of you has received. 11 Whoever speaks must do so as one speaking the very words of God; whoever serves must do so with the strength that God supplies, so that God may be glorified in all things through Jesus Christ. To him belong the glory and the power forever and ever. Amen.

Suffering as a Christian

12 Beloved, do not be surprised at the fiery ordeal that is taking place among you to test you, as though something strange were happening to you. 13 But rejoice insofar as you are sharing Christ's sufferings, so that you may also be glad and shout for joy when his glory is revealed. 14 If you are reviled for the name of Christ, you are blessed, because the spirit of glory,[a] which is the Spirit of God, is resting on you.[b] 15 But let none of you suffer as a murderer, a thief, a criminal, or even as a mischief maker. 16 Yet if any of you suffers as a Christian, do not consider it a disgrace, but glorify God because you bear this name. 17 For the time has

ἵνα κριθῶσι μὲν κατὰ ἀνθρώπους
in order that ²they might be judged ¹on one hand according to men

σαρκί, ζῶσι δὲ κατὰ θεὸν πνεύματι.
in [the] flesh, ²might live ¹on the other according to God in [the] spirit.

7 Πάντων δὲ τὸ τέλος ἤγγικεν.
Now of all things the end has drawn near.

σωφρονήσατε οὖν καὶ νήψατε εἰς
Be ye soberminded therefore and be *ye* sober unto

προσευχάς· 8 πρὸ πάντων τὴν εἰς ἑαυτοὺς
prayers; before all things – ⁴to ⁵yourselves

ἀγάπην ἐκτενῆ ἔχοντες, ὅτι ἀγάπη
³love ²fervent ¹having, because love

καλύπτει πλῆθος ἁμαρτιῶν· 9 φιλόξενοι εἰς
covers a multitude of sins; [be] hospitable to

ἀλλήλους ἄνευ γογγυσμοῦ· 10 ἕκαστος καθὼς
one another without murmuring; each one as

ἔλαβεν χάρισμα, εἰς ἑαυτοὺς αὐτὸ διακον-
he received a gift, ³to ⁴yourselves ²it ¹minister-

οῦντες ὡς καλοὶ οἰκονόμοι ποικίλης χάριτος
ing as good stewards of [the] manifold grace

θεοῦ· 11 εἴ τις λαλεῖ, ὡς λόγια θεοῦ·
of God; if anyone speaks, as [the] oracles of God;

εἴ τις διακονεῖ, ὡς ἐξ ἰσχύος ἧς χορηγεῖ
if anyone ministers, as by strength which ²supplies

ὁ θεός· ἵνα ἐν πᾶσιν δοξάζηται ὁ θεὸς
– ¹God; in order that in all things ²may be glorified – ¹God

διὰ Ἰησοῦ Χριστοῦ, ᾧ ἐστιν ἡ δόξα
through Jesus Christ, to whom = whose is[c] the glory

καὶ τὸ κράτος εἰς τοὺς αἰῶνας τῶν
and the might unto the ages of the

αἰώνων· ἀμήν.
ages: Amen.

12 Ἀγαπητοί, μὴ ξενίζεσθε τῇ ἐν ὑμῖν
Beloved, be not surprised [at] ¹the ⁴among ⁵you

πυρώσει πρὸς πειρασμὸν ὑμῖν γινομένῃ,
²fiery trial ⁶for ⁷trial ⁸to you ³happening,

ὡς ξένου ὑμῖν συμβαίνοντος, 13 ἀλλὰ
as a surprising thing ²to you ¹occurring[a], but

καθὸ κοινωνεῖτε τοῖς τοῦ Χριστοῦ
²as ³ye share ⁴the – ⁶of Christ

παθήμασιν χαίρετε, ἵνα καὶ ἐν τῇ ἀπο-
⁵sufferings ¹rejoice, in order that also at the reve-

καλύψει τῆς δόξης αὐτοῦ χαρῆτε ἀγαλ-
lation of the glory of him ye may rejoice exult-

λιώμενοι. 14 εἰ ὀνειδίζεσθε ἐν ὀνόματι
ing. If ye are reproached in [the] name

Χριστοῦ, μακάριοι, ὅτι τὸ τῆς δόξης
of Christ, blessed [are ye], because ¹the – ²of glory

καὶ τὸ τοῦ θεοῦ πνεῦμα ἐφ' ὑμᾶς
³and ⁵*the*(?that) – ⁶of God ⁴spirit ⁸on ⁹you

ἀναπαύεται. 15 μὴ γάρ τις ὑμῶν πασχέτω
⁷rests. ³Not ¹for ⁴anyone ⁵of you ²let ⁶suffer

ὡς φονεὺς ἢ κλέπτης ἢ κακοποιὸς ἢ
as a murderer or a thief or an evildoer or

ὡς ἀλλοτριεπίσκοπος· 16 εἰ δὲ ὡς
as a pryer into other men's affairs; but if as

Χριστιανός, μὴ αἰσχυνέσθω, δοξαζέτω δὲ
a Christian, let him not be shamed, but let him glorify

τὸν θεὸν ἐν τῷ ὀνόματι τούτῳ. 17 ὅτι
– God by this name. Because

they might be judged according to men in regard to the body, but live according to God in regard to the spirit.

7 The end of all things is near. Therefore be clear minded and self-controlled so that you can pray. 8 Above all, love each other deeply, because love covers over a multitude of sins. 9 Offer hospitality to one another without grumbling. 10 Each one should use whatever gift he has received to serve others, faithfully administering God's grace in its various forms. 11 If anyone speaks, he should do it as one speaking the very words of God. If anyone serves, he should do it with the strength God provides, so that in all things God may be praised through Jesus Christ. To him be the glory and the power for ever and ever. Amen.

Suffering for Being a Christian

12 Dear friends, do not be surprised at the painful trial you are suffering, as though something strange were happening to you. 13 But rejoice that you participate in the sufferings of Christ, so that you may be overjoyed when his glory is revealed. 14 If you are insulted because of the name of Christ, you are blessed, for the Spirit of glory and of God rests on you. 15 If you suffer, it should not be as a murderer or thief or any other kind of criminal, or even as a meddler. 16 However, if you suffer as a Christian, do not be ashamed, but praise God that you bear that name.

[c] Or *is at hand*
[a] Other ancient authorities add *and of power*
[b] Other ancient authorities add *On their part he is blasphemed, but on your part he is glorified*

come for judgment to begin
with the household of God;
if it begins with us, what
will be the end for those
who do not obey the gospel
of God? 18 And

"If it is hard for the
righteous
to be saved,
what will become of
the ungodly and
the sinners?"

19 Therefore, let those suffering in accordance with
God's will entrust them-
selves to a faithful Creator,
while continuing to do
good.

[ὁ] καιρὸς τοῦ ἄρξασθαι τὸ κρίμα ἀπὸ
the time [?has come] – to begin[d] the judgment from

τοῦ οἴκου τοῦ θεοῦ· εἰ δὲ πρῶτον ἀφ'
the household – of God; and if firstly from

ἡμῶν, τί τὸ τέλος τῶν ἀπειθούντων
us, what [will be] the end of the [ones] disobeying

τῷ τοῦ θεοῦ εὐαγγελίῳ; 18 καὶ εἰ ὁ
the – [2]of God [1]gospel? and if the

δίκαιος μόλις σῴζεται, ὁ [δὲ] ἀσεβὴς
righteous man scarcely is saved, [3]the – [4]impious

καὶ ἁμαρτωλὸς ποῦ φανεῖται; 19 ὥστε
[5]and [6]sinner [1]where [2]will [7]appear ? so as

καὶ οἱ πάσχοντες κατὰ τὸ θέλημα τοῦ
indeed the [ones] suffering according to the will –

θεοῦ πιστῷ κτίστῃ παρατιθέσθωσαν τὰς
of God [5]to a faithful [6]Creator [1]let them commit [2]the

ψυχὰς αὐτῶν ἐν ἀγαθοποιΐᾳ.
[3]souls [4]of them in welldoing.

17 For it is time for judgment
to begin with the family of
God; and if it begins with
us, what will the outcome
be for those who do not
obey the gospel of God?
18 And,

"If it is hard for the
righteous to be
saved,
what will become of
the ungodly and the
sinner?"[n]

19 So then, those who suffer according to God's will
should commit themselves
to their faithful Creator and
continue to do good.

Chapter 5

Tending the Flock of God

NOW as an elder myself
and a witness of the
sufferings of Christ, as well
as one who shares in the
glory to be revealed, I exhort the elders among you
2 to tend the flock of God
that is in your charge, exercising the oversight,[c] not
under compulsion but willingly, as God would have
you do it[d]—not for sordid
gain but eagerly. 3 Do not
lord it over those in your
charge, but be examples to
the flock. 4 And when the
chief shepherd appears,
you will win the crown of
glory that never fades
away. 5 In the same way,
you who are younger must
accept the authority of the
elders.[e] And all of you
must clothe yourselves
with humility in your dealings with one another, for

"God opposes the
proud,
but gives grace to
the humble."

6 Humble yourselves
therefore under the mighty
hand of God, so that he
may exalt you in due time.
7 Cast all your anxiety on
him, because he cares for

5 Πρεσβυτέρους οὖν ἐν ὑμῖν παρακαλῶ
Elders therefore among you I exhort

ὁ συμπρεσβύτερος καὶ μάρτυς τῶν τοῦ
the co-elder and witness [1]of the –

Χριστοῦ παθημάτων, ὁ καὶ τῆς μελλούσης
[3]of Christ [2]sufferings, [1]the [3]also [4]of the [6]*being* about

ἀποκαλύπτεσθαι δόξης κοινωνός· 2 ποιμάνατε
[7]to be revealed [5]glory [2]sharer : shepherd

τὸ ἐν ὑμῖν ποίμνιον τοῦ θεοῦ, μὴ
[1]the [4]among [5]you [2]flock – [3]of God, not

ἀναγκαστῶς ἀλλὰ ἑκουσίως κατὰ θεόν,
by way of compulsion but willingly according to God,

μηδὲ αἰσχροκερδῶς ἀλλὰ προθύμως, 3 μηδ'
nor from eagerness for base gain but eagerly, nor

ὡς κατακυριεύοντες τῶν κλήρων ἀλλὰ
as exercising lordship over the lots* but

τύποι γινόμενοι τοῦ ποιμνίου· 4 καὶ
[2]examples [1]becoming of the flock; and

φανερωθέντος τοῦ ἀρχιποίμενος κομιεῖσθε
appearing the chief shepherd[a] ye will receive
=when the chief shepherd appears

τὸν ἀμαράντινον τῆς δόξης στέφανον.
the unfading – [2]of glory [1]crown.

5 Ὁμοίως, νεώτεροι, ὑποτάγητε πρεσβυτέ-
Likewise, younger men, submit yourselves to older

ροις· πάντες δὲ ἀλλήλοις τὴν ταπεινοφρο-
men; and all [3]to one another – [2]humil-

σύνην ἐγκομβώσασθε, ὅτι ὁ θεὸς ὑπερηφάνοις
ity [1]gird ye on, because – God [2]arrogant men

ἀντιτάσσεται, ταπεινοῖς δὲ δίδωσιν χάριν.
[1]resists, but to humble men he gives grace.

6 Ταπεινώθητε οὖν ὑπὸ τὴν κραταιὰν
Be ye humbled therefore under the mighty

χεῖρα τοῦ θεοῦ, ἵνα ὑμᾶς ὑψώσῃ ἐν
hand – of God, in order that [2]you [1]he may exalt in

καιρῷ, 7 πᾶσαν τὴν μέριμναν ὑμῶν
time, [2]all [3]the [4]anxiety [5]of you

ἐπιρίψαντες ἐπ' αὐτόν, ὅτι αὐτῷ μέλει
[1]casting on him, because [2]to him [1]it matters

Chapter 5

To Elders and Young Men

TO the elders among
you, I appeal as a fel-
low elder, a witness of
Christ's sufferings and one
who also will share in the
glory to be revealed: 2 Be
shepherds of God's flock
that is under your care,
serving as overseers—not
because you must, but be-
cause you are willing, as
God wants you to be; not
greedy for money, but ea-
ger to serve; 3 not lording it
over those entrusted to
you, but being examples to
the flock. 4 And when the
Chief Shepherd appears,
you will receive the crown
of glory that will never fade
away.
5 Young men, in the same
way be submissive to those
who are older. All of you,
clothe yourselves with humility toward one another,
because,

"God opposes the proud
but gives grace to the
humble."[o]

6 Humble yourselves,
therefore, under God's
mighty hand, that he may
lift you up in due time.
7 Cast all your anxiety on
him because he cares for
you.

[c] Other ancient authorities lack *exercising the oversight*
[d] Other ancient authorities lack *as God would have you do it*
[e] Or *of those who are older*

* That is, the various spheres assigned to the elders.

[n] *18* Prov. 11:31
[o] *5* Prov. 3:34

you. 8 Discipline your-
selves, keep alert.[f] Like a
roaring lion your adversary
the devil prowls around,
looking for someone to devour. 9 Resist him, steadfast in your faith, for you
know that your brothers
and sisters[g] in all the world
are undergoing the same
kinds of suffering. 10 And
after you have suffered for
a little while, the God of all
grace, who has called you
to his eternal glory in
Christ, will himself restore,
support, strengthen, and
establish you. 11 To him be
the power forever and
ever. Amen.

Final Greetings and Benediction

12 Through Silvanus,
whom I consider a faithful
brother, I have written this
short letter to encourage
you and to testify that this
is the true grace of God.
Stand fast in it. 13 Your sister church[h] in Babylon,
chosen together with you,
sends you greetings; and so
does my son Mark. 14 Greet
one another with a kiss of
love.
Peace to all of you who
are in Christ.[i]

περὶ ὑμῶν. 8 Νήψατε, γρηγορήσατε. ὁ
concerning you. Be ye sober, watch ye. The

ἀντίδικος ὑμῶν διάβολος ὡς λέων ὠρυόμενος
adversary of you [the] devil as a lion roaring

περιπατεῖ ζητῶν τινα καταπιεῖν· 9 ᾧ
walks about seeking whom to devour; whom

ἀντίστητε στερεοὶ τῇ πίστει, εἰδότες τὰ
oppose firm in the faith, knowing the

αὐτὰ τῶν παθημάτων τῇ ἐν τῷ κόσμῳ
same things *of the* sufferings [2]in the [5]in [6]the [7]world

ὑμῶν ἀδελφότητι ἐπιτελεῖσθαι. 10 Ὁ δὲ
[4]of you [3]brotherhood [1]to be accomplished. [2]the [1]Now

θεὸς πάσης χάριτος, ὁ καλέσας ὑμᾶς
God of all grace, the [one] having called you

εἰς τὴν αἰώνιον αὐτοῦ δόξαν ἐν Χριστῷ,
to the [1]eternal [3]of him [2]glory in Christ,

ὀλίγον παθόντας αὐτὸς καταρτίσει, στηρίξει,
[1][you] [3]a little [2]having suffered [him]self will adjust, confirm,

σθενώσει, θεμελιώσει. 11 αὐτῷ τὸ κράτος
strengthen, found. To him [is][c] the might =His is*

εἰς τοὺς αἰῶνας τῶν αἰώνων· ἀμήν.
unto the ages of the ages: Amen.

12 Διὰ Σιλουανοῦ ὑμῖν τοῦ πιστοῦ
Through Silvanus to you the faithful

ἀδελφοῦ, ὡς λογίζομαι, δι' ὀλίγων ἔγραψα,
brother, as I reckon, by means of a few [words] I wrote,

παρακαλῶν καὶ ἐπιμαρτυρῶν ταύτην εἶναι
exhorting and witnessing this to be

ἀληθῆ χάριν τοῦ θεοῦ, εἰς ἣν στῆτε.
[the] true grace – of God, in which ye stand.

13 Ἀσπάζεται ὑμᾶς ἡ ἐν Βαβυλῶνι
[10]greets [11]you [1]The [3]in [4]Babylon

συνεκλεκτὴ καὶ Μᾶρκος ὁ υἱός μου.
[2]co-chosen [? church] [5]and [6]Mark [7]the [8]son [9]of me.

14 ἀσπάσασθε ἀλλήλους ἐν φιλήματι ἀγάπης.
Greet ye one another with a kiss of love.

Εἰρήνη ὑμῖν πᾶσιν τοῖς ἐν Χριστῷ.
Peace to you all the ones in Christ.

8 Be self-controlled and
alert. Your enemy the devil
prowls around like a roaring lion looking for someone to devour. 9 Resist him,
standing firm in the faith,
because you know that
your brothers throughout
the world are undergoing
the same kind of sufferings.
10 And the God of all
grace, who called you to his
eternal glory in Christ, after you have suffered a little while, will himself restore you and make you
strong, firm and steadfast.
11 To him be the power for
ever and ever. Amen.

Final Greetings

12 With the help of Silas,[p]
whom I regard as a faithful
brother, I have written to
you briefly, encouraging
you and testifying that this
is the true grace of God.
Stand fast in it.
13 She who is in Babylon,
chosen together with you,
sends you her greetings,
and so does my son Mark.
14 Greet one another with a
kiss of love.
Peace to all of you who
are in Christ.

The Second Letter of

Peter

Chapter 1

Salutation

SIMEON[a] Peter, a ser-
vant[b] and apostle of
Jesus Christ,
To those who have re-
ceived a faith as precious as
ours through the righteousness of our God and Savior
Jesus Christ:[c]
2 May grace and peace
be yours in abundance in
the knowledge of God and
of Jesus our Lord.

The Christian's Call and Election

3 His divine power has
given us everything needed

ΠΕΤΡΟΥ Β

Of Peter 2

1 Συμεὼν Πέτρος δοῦλος καὶ ἀπόστολος
Symeon Peter a slave and an apostle

Ἰησοῦ Χριστοῦ τοῖς ἰσότιμον ἡμῖν
of Jesus Christ [1]to the [ones] [3]equally precious [5]with us

λαχοῦσιν πίστιν ἐν δικαιοσύνῃ τοῦ θεοῦ
[2]having obtained [4]faith in [the] righteousness of the God

ἡμῶν καὶ σωτῆρος Ἰησοῦ Χριστοῦ·
of us and Saviour Jesus Christ:

2 χάρις ὑμῖν καὶ εἰρήνη πληθυνθείη ἐν
Grace to you and peace *may it* be multiplied by

ἐπιγνώσει τοῦ θεοῦ καὶ Ἰησοῦ τοῦ
a full knowledge – of God and of Jesus the

κυρίου ἡμῶν.
Lord of us.

3 Ὡς τὰ πάντα ἡμῖν τῆς θείας δυνάμεως
As – all things to us the divine power
=his divine power has given us all things . . .

2 Peter

Chapter 1

SIMON Peter, a servant
and apostle of Jesus
Christ,

To those who through the
righteousness of our God
and Savior Jesus Christ
have received a faith as
precious as ours:

2 Grace and peace be
yours in abundance
through the knowledge of
God and of Jesus our Lord.

Making One's Calling and Election Sure

3 His divine power has
given us everything we

[f] Or *be vigilant*
[g] Gk *your brotherhood*
[h] Gk *She who is*
[i] Other ancient authorities add *Amen*
[a] Other ancient authorities read *Simon*
[b] Gk *slave*
[c] Or *of our God and the Savior Jesus Christ*

* *Cf.* 4. 11 (a statement of fact, not a wish).

[p] 12 Greek *Silvanus*, a variant of *Silas*

for life and godliness,
through the knowledge of
him who called us by[d] his
own glory and goodness.
4 Thus he has given us,
through these things, his
precious and very great
promises, so that through
them you may escape from
the corruption that is in the
world because of lust, and
may become participants of
the divine nature. 5 For this
very reason, you must
make every effort to sup-
port your faith with goodness, and goodness with
knowledge, 6 and knowl-
edge with self-control, and
self-control with endur-
ance, and endurance with
godliness, 7 and godliness
with mutual[e] affection,
and mutual[e] affection with
love. 8 For if these things
are yours and are increasing among you, they keep
you from being ineffective
and unfruitful in the knowledge of our Lord Jesus
Christ. 9 For anyone who
lacks these things is nearsighted and blind, and is
forgetful of the cleansing of
past sins. 10 Therefore,
brothers and sisters,[f] be
all the more eager to confirm your call and election,
for if you do this, you will
never stumble. 11 For in
this way, entry into the
eternal kingdom of our
Lord and Savior Jesus
Christ will be richly provided for you.
12 Therefore I intend to
keep on reminding you of
these things, though you
know them already and are
established in the truth that
has come to you. 13 I think

αὐτοῦ τὰ πρὸς ζωὴν καὶ εὐσέβειαν δεδωρημένης
of him – [belonging] to life and piety having given[a]

διὰ τῆς ἐπιγνώσεως τοῦ καλέσαντος ἡμᾶς
through the full knowledge of the [one] having called us

ἰδίᾳ δόξῃ καὶ ἀρετῇ, 4 δι' ὧν τὰ τίμια
to [his] own glory and virtue, through which *the* [3]precious things

καὶ μέγιστα ἡμῖν ἐπαγγέλματα δεδώρηται,
[4]and [5]very great [2]to us [6]promises [1]he has given,

ἵνα διὰ τούτων γένησθε θείας κοινωνοὶ
in order that through these ye might become [2]of a divine [1]sharers

φύσεως, ἀποφυγόντες τῆς ἐν τῷ κόσμῳ
[3]nature, escaping from [1]the [3]in [4]the [5]world

ἐν ἐπιθυμίᾳ φθορᾶς. 5 καὶ αὐτὸ τοῦτο
[6]by [7]lust [2]corruption. [2]also [3]for this very thing (reason)

δὲ σπουδὴν πᾶσαν παρεισενέγκαντες
[1]But [6]diligence [5]all [4]bringing in

ἐπιχορηγήσατε ἐν τῇ πίστει ὑμῶν τὴν
supply in the faith of you –

ἀρετήν, ἐν δὲ τῇ ἀρετῇ τὴν γνῶσιν,
virtue, and in – virtue – knowledge,

6 ἐν δὲ τῇ γνώσει τὴν ἐγκράτειαν,
and in – knowledge – self-control,

ἐν δὲ τῇ ἐγκρατείᾳ τὴν ὑπομονήν, ἐν
and in – self-control – endurance, [2]in

δὲ τῇ ὑπομονῇ τὴν εὐσέβειαν, 7 ἐν δὲ
[1]and – endurance – piety, and in

τῇ εὐσεβείᾳ τὴν φιλαδελφίαν, ἐν δὲ
– piety – brotherly friendship, and in

τῇ φιλαδελφίᾳ τὴν ἀγάπην. 8 ταῦτα
– brotherly friendship – love. these things

γὰρ ὑμῖν ὑπάρχοντα καὶ πλεονάζοντα
For [2]in you [1]being and abounding

οὐκ ἀργοὺς οὐδὲ ἀκάρπους καθίστησιν
[3]not [4]barren [5]nor [6]unfruitful [1]makes [2][you]

εἰς τὴν τοῦ κυρίου ἡμῶν Ἰησοῦ Χριστοῦ
in [1]the [3]of the [4]Lord [5]of us [6]Jesus [7]Christ

ἐπίγνωσιν· 9 ᾧ γὰρ μὴ πάρεστιν ταῦτα,
[2]full knowledge; for [he] in whom [3]not [2]is(are) [4]present [1]these things,

τυφλός ἐστιν μυωπάζων, λήθην λαβὼν
[2]blind [1]is being short-sighted, forgetfulness taking – being forgetful

τοῦ καθαρισμοῦ τῶν πάλαι αὐτοῦ ἁμαρτιῶν.
of the cleansing of the [3]in time past [2]of him [1]sins.

10 διὸ μᾶλλον, ἀδελφοί, σπουδάσατε
Wherefore rather, brothers, be ye diligent

βεβαίαν ὑμῶν τὴν κλῆσιν καὶ ἐκλογὴν
[8]firm [7]of you [3]the [4]calling [5]and [6]choice

ποιεῖσθαι· ταῦτα γὰρ ποιοῦντες οὐ μὴ
[1]to make; for these things doing by no means

πταίσητέ ποτε. 11 οὕτως γὰρ πλουσίως
ye will fail ever. For so [3]richly

ἐπιχορηγηθήσεται ὑμῖν ἡ εἴσοδος εἰς τὴν
[1]will be supplied [2]to you the entrance into the

αἰώνιον βασιλείαν τοῦ κυρίου ἡμῶν καὶ
eternal kingdom of the Lord of us and

σωτῆρος Ἰησοῦ Χριστοῦ.
Saviour Jesus Christ.

12 Διὸ μελλήσω ἀεὶ ὑμᾶς ὑπομιμνήσκειν
Wherefore I *will* intend always you to remind

περὶ τούτων, καίπερ εἰδότας καὶ
concerning these things, though knowing and

ἐστηριγμένους ἐν τῇ παρούσῃ ἀληθείᾳ.
having been confirmed in the present truth.

need for life and godliness
through our knowledge of
him who called us by his
own glory and goodness.
4 Through these he has giv-
en us his very great and
precious promises, so that
through them you may par-
ticipate in the divine nature
and escape the corruption
in the world caused by evil
desires.
5 For this very reason,
make every effort to add to
your faith goodness; and to
goodness, knowledge; 6 and
to knowledge, self-control;
and to self-control, perseverance; and to persever-
ance, godliness; 7 and to
godliness, brotherly kindness; and to brotherly kindness, love. 8 For if you possess these qualities in increasing measure, they will
keep you from being inef-
fective and unproductive in
your knowledge of our
Lord Jesus Christ. 9 But if
anyone does not have
them, he is nearsighted and
blind, and has forgotten
that he has been cleansed
from his past sins.
10 Therefore, my broth-
ers, be all the more eager to
make your calling and election sure. For if you do
these things, you will never
fall, 11 and you will receive
a rich welcome into the
eternal kingdom of our
Lord and Savior Jesus
Christ.

Prophecy of Scripture

12 So I will always remind
you of these things, even
though you know them and
are firmly established in the
truth you now have. 13 I

[d] Other ancient authorities read *through*
[e] Gk *brotherly*
[f] Gk *brothers*

it right, as long as I am in
this body,[g] to refresh your
memory, 14 since I know
that my death[h] will come
soon, as indeed our Lord
Jesus Christ has made clear
to me. 15 And I will make
every effort so that after
my departure you may be
able at any time to recall
these things.

Eyewitnesses of Christ's Glory

16 For we did not follow
cleverly devised myths
when we made known to
you the power and coming
of our Lord Jesus Christ,
but we had been eyewit-
nesses of his majesty.
17 For he received honor
and glory from God the Father when that voice was
conveyed to him by the
Majestic Glory, saying,
"This is my Son, my Be-
loved,[i] with whom I am
well pleased." 18 We our-
selves heard this voice
come from heaven, while
we were with him on the
holy mountain.
19 So we have the pro-
phetic message more fully
confirmed. You will do
well to be attentive to this
as to a lamp shining in a
dark place, until the day
dawns and the morning star
rises in your hearts. 20 First
of all you must understand
this, that no prophecy of
scripture is a matter of
one's own interpretation,
21 because no prophecy
ever came by human will,
but men and women moved
by the Holy Spirit spoke
from God.[j]

13 δίκαιον δὲ ἡγοῦμαι, ἐφ᾽ ὅσον εἰμι
And [2]right [1]I deem [it], so long as† I am
ἐν τούτῳ τῷ σκηνώματι, διεγείρειν ὑμᾶς
in this – tabernacle, to rouse you
ἐν ὑπομνήσει, **14** εἰδὼς ὅτι ταχινή ἐστιν
by a reminder, knowing that soon is
ἡ ἀπόθεσις τοῦ σκηνώματός μου, καθὼς
the putting off of the tabernacle of me, as
καὶ ὁ κύριος ἡμῶν Ἰησοῦς Χριστὸς
indeed the Lord of us Jesus Christ
ἐδήλωσέν μοι· **15** σπουδάσω δὲ καὶ
made clear to me; and I will be diligent also
ἑκάστοτε ἔχειν ὑμᾶς μετὰ τὴν ἐμὴν
[6]always [7]to have [2]you [3]after – [4]my
ἔξοδον τὴν τούτων μνήμην ποιεῖσθαι.
[5]exodus [8]the [10]of these things [9]memory [1]to cause.
16 οὐ γὰρ σεσοφισμένοις μύθοις ἐξακολου-
For not [3]having been cleverly devised [2]fables [1]follow-
θήσαντες ἐγνωρίσαμεν ὑμῖν τὴν τοῦ κυρίου
ing we made known to you [1]the [5]of the [6]Lord
ἡμῶν Ἰησοῦ Χριστοῦ δύναμιν καὶ
[7]of us [8]Jesus [9]Christ [2]power [3]and
παρουσίαν, ἀλλ᾽ ἐπόπται γενηθέντες τῆς
[4]presence, but [2]eyewitnesses [1]having become [3]of the
ἐκείνου μεγαλειότητος. **17** λαβὼν γὰρ
[5]of that one [4]majesty. For receiving
παρὰ θεοῦ πατρὸς τιμὴν καὶ δόξαν
from God [the] Father honour and glory
φωνῆς ἐνεχθείσης αὐτῷ τοιᾶσδε ὑπὸ τῆς
[3]a voice [5]being borne[a] [4]to him [1]such by the
μεγαλοπρεποῦς δόξης· ὁ υἱός μου ὁ
magnificent glory: The Son of me the
ἀγαπητός μου οὗτός ἐστιν, εἰς ὃν ἐγὼ
beloved of me this is, in whom I
εὐδόκησα, — **18** καὶ ταύτην τὴν φωνὴν
was wellpleased,— and this – voice
ἡμεῖς ἠκούσαμεν ἐξ οὐρανοῦ ἐνεχθεῖσαν
we heard [2]out of [3]heaven [1]being borne
σὺν αὐτῷ ὄντες ἐν τῷ ἁγίῳ ὄρει. **19** καὶ
[5]with [6]him [4]being in the holy mountain. And
ἔχομεν βεβαιότερον τὸν προφητικὸν λόγον,
we have more firm the prophetic word,
ᾧ καλῶς ποιεῖτε προσέχοντες ὡς λύχνῳ
to which [2]well [1]ye do taking heed as to a lamp
φαίνοντι ἐν αὐχμηρῷ τόπῳ, ἕως οὗ
shining in a murky place, until
ἡμέρα διαυγάσῃ καὶ φωσφόρος ἀνατείλῃ
day dawns and [the] daystar rises
ἐν ταῖς καρδίαις ὑμῶν· **20** τοῦτο πρῶτον
in the hearts of you; [2]this [3]firstly
γινώσκοντες, ὅτι πᾶσα προφητεία γραφῆς
[1]knowing, that every =no . . . is . . . prophecy of scripture
ἰδίας ἐπιλύσεως οὐ γίνεται· **21** οὐ γὰρ
of [its] own solution not becomes; for not
θελήματι ἀνθρώπου ἠνέχθη προφητεία
by will of man [2]was borne [1]prophecy
ποτέ, ἀλλὰ ὑπὸ πνεύματος ἁγίου φερόμενοι
at any time, but [6]by [8]Spirit [7][the] Holy [5]being borne
ἐλάλησαν ἀπὸ θεοῦ ἄνθρωποι.
[2]spoke [3]from [4]God [1]men.

think it is right to refresh
your memory as long as I
live in the tent of this body,
14 because I know that I will
soon put it aside, as our
Lord Jesus Christ has made
clear to me. 15 And I will
make every effort to see
that after my departure you
will always be able to remember these things.
16 We did not follow cleverly invented stories when
we told you about the power and coming of our Lord
Jesus Christ, but we were
eyewitnesses of his majesty. 17 For he received honor
and glory from God the Father when the voice came
to him from the Majestic
Glory, saying, "This is my
Son, whom I love; with him
I am well pleased."[a] 18 We
ourselves heard this voice
that came from heaven
when we were with him on
the sacred mountain.
19 And we have the word
of the prophets made more
certain, and you will do
well to pay attention to it,
as to a light shining in a
dark place, until the day
dawns and the morning star
rises in your hearts.
20 Above all, you must understand that no prophecy
of Scripture came about by
the prophet's own interpretation. 21 For prophecy never had its origin in the will
of man, but men spoke
from God as they were carried along by the Holy Spirit.

[g] Gk *tent*
[h] Gk *the putting off of my tent*
[i] Other ancient authorities read *my beloved Son*
[j] Other ancient authorities read *but moved by the Holy Spirit saints of God spoke*

[a] *17* Matt. 17:5; Mark 9:7; Luke 9:35

Chapter 2

False Prophets and Their Punishment

BUT false prophets also
arose among the peo-
ple, just as there will be
false teachers among you,
who will secretly bring in
destructive opinions. They
will even deny the Master
who bought them—
bringing swift destruction
on themselves. 2 Even so,
many will follow their licentious ways, and be-
cause of these teachers[k]
the way of truth will be maligned. 3 And in their greed
they will exploit you with
deceptive words. Their
condemnation, pro-
nounced against them long
ago, has not been idle, and
their destruction is not
asleep.
4 For if God did not
spare the angels when they
sinned, but cast them into
hell[l] and committed them
to chains[m] of deepest darkness to be kept until the
judgment; 5 and if he did not
spare the ancient world,
even though he saved
Noah, a herald of righ-
teousness, with seven others, when he brought a
flood on a world of the ungodly; 6 and if by turning
the cities of Sodom and Gomorrah to ashes he con-
demned them to extinc-
tion[n] and made them an
example of what is coming
to the ungodly;[o] 7 and if he
rescued Lot, a righteous
man greatly distressed by
the licentiousness of the
lawless 8 (for that righteous
man, living among them
day after day, was tormented in his righteous soul by
their lawless deeds that he
saw and heard), 9 then the
Lord knows how to rescue
the godly from trial, and to
keep the unrighteous under
punishment until the day of
judgment 10—especially
those who indulge their

[k] Gk *because of them*
[l] Gk *Tartaros*
[m] Other ancient authorities read *pits*
[n] Other ancient authorities lack *to extinction*
[o] Other ancient authorities read *an example to those who were to be ungodly*

2 Ἐγένοντο δὲ καὶ ψευδοπροφῆται ἐν
But there were also false prophets among

τῷ λαῷ, ὡς καὶ ἐν ὑμῖν ἔσονται
the people, as indeed among you there will be

ψευδοδιδάσκαλοι, οἵτινες παρεισάξουσιν
false teachers, who will secretly bring in

αἱρέσεις ἀπωλείας, καὶ τὸν ἀγοράσαντα
opinions of destruction,* and [3]the [4]having bought

αὐτοὺς δεσπότην ἀρνούμενοι, ἐπάγοντες
[5]them [2]Master [1]denying, bringing on

ἑαυτοῖς ταχινὴν ἀπώλειαν· 2 καὶ πολλοὶ
themselves swift destruction; and many

ἐξακολουθήσουσιν αὐτῶν ταῖς ἀσελγείαις,
will follow [3]of them [1]the [2]licentiousness*es*,

δι' οὓς ἡ ὁδὸς τῆς ἀληθείας βλασφημη-
be- cause of whom the way of *the* truth will be

θήσεται· 3 καὶ ἐν πλεονεξίᾳ πλαστοῖς
blasphemed; and by covetousness with fabricated

λόγοις ὑμᾶς ἐμπορεύσονται· οἷς τὸ κρίμα
words [2]you [1]they will make merchandise of; for whom the judg- ment

ἔκπαλαι οὐκ ἀργεῖ, καὶ ἡ ἀπώλεια
of old lingers not, and the destruction

αὐτῶν οὐ νυστάζει. 4 εἰ γὰρ ὁ θεὸς
of them slumbers not. For if – God

ἀγγέλων ἁμαρτησάντων οὐκ ἐφείσατο, ἀλλὰ
[2]angels [3]sinning [1]spared not, but

σιροῖς ζόφου ταρταρώσας παρέδωκεν
[2]in pits [3]of gloom [1]consigning to Tartarus [4]delivered [them]

εἰς κρίσιν τηρουμένους, 5 καὶ ἀρχαίου
[5]to [7]judgment [6]being kept, and [2][the] ancient

κόσμου οὐκ ἐφείσατο, ἀλλὰ ὄγδοον Νῶε
[3]world [1]spared not, but [2][the] eighth man [3]Noe

δικαιοσύνης κήρυκα ἐφύλαξεν, κατακλυσμὸν
[5]of righteousness [4]a herald [1]guarded, [2]a flood

κόσμῳ ἀσεβῶν ἐπάξας, 6 καὶ πόλεις
[4]a world [5]of impious men [1]bringing [3]on, and [2][the] cities

Σοδόμων καὶ Γομόρρας τεφρώσας
[4]of Sodom [5]and [6]Gomorra [1]covering [them] with ashes

καταστροφῇ κατέκρινεν, ὑπόδειγμα μελ-
[7]by an overthrow [2]condemned, [3]an example [5]of men

λόντων ἀσεβεῖν τεθεικώς, 7 καὶ δίκαιον
intending [4]to live impiously [1]having set(made), and [2]righteous

Λὼτ καταπονούμενον ὑπὸ τῆς τῶν ἀθέσμων
[3]Lot [4]*being* oppressed [5]by [6]the [10]of the [11]lawless

ἐν ἀσελγείᾳ ἀναστροφῆς ἐρρύσατο· 8 βλέμ-
[8]in [9]licentiousness [7]conduct [1]delivered; [2]in

ματι γὰρ καὶ ἀκοῇ ὁ δίκαιος ἐγκατοικῶν
seeing [1]for and in hear- ing the (that) righteous man dwelling

ἐν αὐτοῖς ἡμέραν ἐξ ἡμέρας ψυχὴν
among them day after† day [3][his] [4]soul

δικαίαν ἀνόμοις ἔργοις ἐβασάνιζεν·
[2]righteous [5]with [their] lawless [6]works [1]tormented;

9 οἶδεν κύριος εὐσεβεῖς ἐκ πειρασμοῦ
[2]knows* [1][the] Lord [4]pious men [5]out of [6]trial

ῥύεσθαι, ἀδίκους δὲ εἰς ἡμέραν κρίσεως
[3]to deliver, [2]unjust men [1]but [5]for [6]a day [7]of judgment

κολαζομένους τηρεῖν, 10 μάλιστα δὲ τοὺς
[4]being punished [3]to keep, and most of all [1]the

* Genitive of quality : " destructive opinions."

* That is, " the Lord can deliver "; see note on page xviii.

Chapter 2

False Teachers and Their Destruction

BUT there were also
false prophets among
the people, just as there
will be false teachers
among you. They will se-
cretly introduce destruc-
tive heresies, even denying
the sovereign Lord who
bought them—bringing
swift destruction on themselves. 2 Many will follow
their shameful ways and
will bring the way of truth
into disrepute. 3 In their
greed these teachers will
exploit you with stories
they have made up. Their
condemnation has long
been hanging over them,
and their destruction has
not been sleeping.
4 For if God did not spare
angels when they sinned,
but sent them to hell,[b] putting them into gloomy dun-
geons[c] to be held for judgment; 5 if he did not spare
the ancient world when he
brought the flood on its ungodly people, but protected
Noah, a preacher of righteousness, and seven oth-
ers; 6 if he condemned the
cities of Sodom and Go-
morrah by burning them to
ashes, and made them an
example of what is going to
happen to the ungodly;
7 and if he rescued Lot, a
righteous man, who was
distressed by the filthy
lives of lawless men 8 (for
that righteous man, living
among them day after day,
was tormented in his righteous soul by the lawless
deeds he saw and heard)—
9 if this is so, then the Lord
knows how to rescue godly
men from trials and to hold
the unrighteous for the day
of judgment, while continuing their punishment.[d]
10 This is especially true of

[b]4 Greek *Tartarus*
[c]4 Some manuscripts *into chains of darkness*
[d]9 Or *unrighteous for punishment until the day of judgment*

flesh in depraved lust, and
who despise authority.
Bold and willful, they are
not afraid to slander the
glorious ones,[p] 11 whereas
angels, though greater in
might and power, do not
bring against them a slanderous judgment from the
Lord.[q] 12 These people,
however, are like irrational
animals, mere creatures of
instinct, born to be caught
and killed. They slander
what they do not under-
stand, and when those
creatures are destroyed,[r]
they also will be destroyed,
13 suffering[s] the penalty for
doing wrong. They count it
a pleasure to revel in the
daytime. They are blots
and blemishes, reveling in
their dissipation[t] while
they feast with you. 14 They
have eyes full of adultery,
insatiable for sin. They entice unsteady souls. They
have hearts trained in
greed. Accursed children!
15 They have left the
straight road and have gone
astray, following the road
of Balaam son of Bosor,[u]
who loved the wages of doing wrong, 16 but was re-
buked for his own trans-
gression; a speechless donkey spoke with a human
voice and restrained the
prophet's madness.
17 These are waterless
springs and mists driven by
a storm; for them the deepest darkness has been re-
served. 18 For they speak
bombastic nonsense, and
with licentious desires of
the flesh they entice people
who have just[v] escaped
from those who live in error. 19 They promise them
freedom, but they them-

ὀπίσω σαρκὸς ἐν ἐπιθυμίᾳ μιασμοῦ
[3]after [4]flesh [5]in [6]lust [7]of defilement*
πορευομένους καὶ κυριότητος καταφρονοῦντας.
[2][ones] going [8]and [10]dominion [9]despising.
τολμηταὶ αὐθάδεις, δόξας οὐ τρέμουσιν
[2]darers [1]Self-satisfied, glories they do not tremble [at]
βλασφημοῦντες, 11 ὅπου ἄγγελοι ἰσχύϊ καὶ
blaspheming, where angels [3]in strength [4]and
δυνάμει μείζονες ὄντες οὐ φέρουσιν κατ'
[5]in power [2]greater [1]being do not bring against
αὐτῶν παρὰ κυρίῳ βλάσφημον κρίσιν.
them before [the] Lord railing judgment.
12 οὗτοι δέ, ὡς ἄλογα ζῷα γεγεννημένα
But these men, [1]as [4]without reason [5]animals [6]having been born
φυσικὰ εἰς ἅλωσιν καὶ φθοράν, ἐν οἷς
[3]natural for capture and corruption, [5]in [3]things which
ἀγνοοῦσιν βλασφημοῦντες, ἐν τῇ φθορᾷ
[4]they are ignorant [of] [1]railing, in the corruption
αὐτῶν καὶ φθαρήσονται, 13 ἀδικούμενοι
of them indeed they will be corrupted, suffering wrong
μισθὸν ἀδικίας· ἡδονὴν ἡγούμενοι τὴν
[as] wages of wrong; [3][to be] pleasure [1]deeming –
ἐν ἡμέρᾳ τρυφήν, σπίλοι καὶ μῶμοι
[5]in [6][the] day [2]luxury, spots and blemishes
ἐντρυφῶντες ἐν ταῖς ἀπάταις αὐτῶν
revelling in the deceits of them
συνευωχούμενοι ὑμῖν, 14 ὀφθαλμοὺς ἔχοντες
feasting along with you, [2]eyes [1]having
μεστοὺς μοιχαλίδος καὶ ἀκαταπαύστους
full of an adulteress and not ceasing from
ἁμαρτίας, δελεάζοντες ψυχὰς ἀστηρίκτους,
sin, alluring [2]souls [1]unsteady,
καρδίαν γεγυμνασμένην πλεονεξίας ἔχοντες,
[2]a heart [3]*having been* exercised [4]of(in) covetousness [1]having,
κατάρας τέκνα· 15 καταλείποντες εὐθεῖαν
[2]of curse [1]children; forsaking a straight
ὁδὸν ἐπλανήθησαν, ἐξακολουθήσαντες τῇ
way they erred, following the
ὁδῷ τοῦ Βαλαὰμ τοῦ Βεώρ, ὃς μισθὸν
way – of Balaam the [son] of Beor, who [3][the] wages
ἀδικίας ἠγάπησεν, 16 ἔλεγξιν δὲ ἔσχεν
[3]of wrong [1]loved, and [2]reproof [1]had
ἰδίας παρανομίας· ὑποζύγιον ἄφωνον ἐν
of [his] own transgression; [2]ass [1]a dumb [4]with
ἀνθρώπου φωνῇ φθεγξάμενον ἐκώλυσεν
[6]of a man [5]voice [3]speaking restrained
τὴν τοῦ προφήτου παραφρονίαν. 17 οὗτοί
[1]the [3]of the [4]prophet [2]madness. These men
εἰσιν πηγαὶ ἄνυδροι καὶ ὁμίχλαι ὑπὸ
are [2]springs [1]waterless and mists [2]by
λαίλαπος ἐλαυνόμεναι, οἷς ὁ ζόφος τοῦ
[3]storm [1]being driven, for whom the gloom of *the*
σκότους τετήρηται. 18 ὑπέρογκα γὰρ
darkness has been kept. For [2]immoderate [words]
ματαιότητος φθεγγόμενοι δελεάζουσιν ἐν
[3]of vanity [1]speaking they allure by
ἐπιθυμίαις σαρκὸς ἀσελγείαις τοὺς ὀλίγως
[the] lusts of [the] flesh in excesses the [ones] almost
ἀποφεύγοντας τοὺς ἐν πλάνῃ ἀναστρε-
escaping [1]the [ones] [3]in [4]error [2]liv-
φομένους, 19 ἐλευθερίαν αὐτοῖς ἐπαγγελ-
ing, [3]freedom [2]*to* them [1]promis-

* Genitive of quality: "defiling lust."

those who follow the cor-
rupt desire of the sinful nature[e] and despise authority.
Bold and arrogant, these
men are not afraid to slander celestial beings; 11 yet
even angels, although they
are stronger and more powerful, do not bring slanderous accusations against
such beings in the presence
of the Lord. 12 But these
men blaspheme in matters
they do not understand.
They are like brute beasts,
creatures of instinct, born
only to be caught and de-
stroyed, and like beasts
they too will perish.
13 They will be paid back
with harm for the harm
they have done. Their idea
of pleasure is to carouse in
broad daylight. They are
blots and blemishes, reveling in their pleasures while
they feast with you.[f]
14 With eyes full of adultery,
they never stop sinning;
they seduce the unstable;
they are experts in greed—
an accursed brood! 15 They
have left the straight way
and wandered off to follow
the way of Balaam son of
Beor, who loved the wages
of wickedness. 16 But he
was rebuked for his wrongdoing by a donkey—a
beast without speech—
who spoke with a man's
voice and restrained the
prophet's madness.
17 These men are springs
without water and mists
driven by a storm. Blackest
darkness is reserved for
them. 18 For they mouth
empty, boastful words and,
by appealing to the lustful
desires of sinful human nature, they entice people
who are just escaping from
those who live in error.
19 They promise them free-

[p] Or *angels*; Gk *glories*
[q] Other ancient authorities read *before the Lord*; others lack the phrase
[r] Gk *in their destruction*
[s] Other ancient authorities read *receiving*
[t] Other ancient authorities read *love feasts*
[u] Other ancient authorities read *Beor*
[v] Other ancient authorities read *actually*

[e] *10* Or *the flesh*
[f] *13* Some manuscripts *in their love feasts*

selves are slaves of corruption; for people are slaves
to whatever masters them.
20 For if, after they have escaped the defilements of
the world through the
knowledge of our Lord and
Savior Jesus Christ, they
are again entangled in them
and overpowered, the last
state has become worse for
them than the first. 21 For it
would have been better for
them never to have known
the way of righteousness
than, after knowing it, to
turn back from the holy
commandment that was
passed on to them. 22 It has
happened to them accord-
ing to the true proverb,

"The dog turns back
to its
own vomit,"

and,

"The sow is washed
only to wallow
in the mud."

Chapter 3

The Promise of the Lord's Coming

THIS is now, beloved,
the second letter I am
writing to you; in them I am
trying to arouse your sincere intention by reminding
you 2 that you should re-
member the words spoken
in the past by the holy
prophets, and the com-
mandment of the Lord and
Savior spoken through
your apostles. 3 First of all
you must understand this,
that in the last days scoffers
will come, scoffing and indulging their own lusts
4 and saying, "Where is the
promise of his coming? For
ever since our ancestors
died,[w] all things continue
as they were from the be-
ginning of creation!" 5 They
deliberately ignore this
fact, that by the word of
God heavens existed long
ago and an earth was

[w] Gk *our fathers fell asleep*

λόμενοι, αὐτοὶ δοῦλοι ὑπάρχοντες τῆς
ing, [them]selves 2slaves 1being –

φθορᾶς· ᾧ γάρ τις ἥττηται, τούτῳ
of corruption; for by whom anyone has been defeated, to this man

δεδούλωται. 20 εἰ γὰρ ἀποφυγόντες τὰ
he has been enslaved. For if having escaped the

μιάσματα τοῦ κόσμου ἐν ἐπιγνώσει τοῦ
defilements of the world by a full knowledge of the

κυρίου καὶ σωτῆρος Ἰησοῦ Χριστοῦ,
Lord and Saviour Jesus Christ,

τούτοις δὲ πάλιν ἐμπλακέντες ἡττῶνται,
yet by these again having been entangled have been defeated,

γέγονεν αὐτοῖς τὰ ἔσχατα χείρονα τῶν
3have become 4to them 1the 2last things worse [than] the

πρώτων. 21 κρεῖττον γὰρ ἦν αὐτοῖς
first. For better it was for them

μὴ ἐπεγνωκέναι τὴν ὁδὸν τῆς δικαιοσύνης,
not to have fully known the way – of righteousness,

ἢ ἐπιγνοῦσιν ὑποστρέψαι ἐκ τῆς παρα-
than fully knowing to turn from 1the 4de-

δοθείσης αὐτοῖς ἁγίας ἐντολῆς. 22 συμβέ-
livered 5to them 2holy 3commandment. 5has

βηκεν αὐτοῖς τὸ τῆς ἀληθοῦς παροιμίας·
happened 6to them 1The thing 2of the 3true 4proverb:

κύων ἐπιστρέψας ἐπὶ τὸ ἴδιον ἐξέραμα,
[The] dog turning upon the(its) own vomit,

καί· ὗς λουσαμένη εἰς κυλισμὸν βορβόρου.
and: [The] sow washed to wallowing of mud.

3 Ταύτην ἤδη, ἀγαπητοί, δευτέραν ὑμῖν
1This 4now, 6beloved, 2second 7to you

γράφω ἐπιστολήν, ἐν αἷς διεγείρω ὑμῶν
5I write 3epistle, in [both] which I rouse 4of you

ἐν ὑπομνήσει τὴν εἰλικρινῆ διάνοιαν,
5by 6reminder 1the 2sincere 3mind,

2 μνησθῆναι τῶν προειρημένων ῥημάτων
to remember the 2having been previously spoken 1words

ὑπὸ τῶν ἁγίων προφητῶν καὶ τῆς τῶν
by the holy prophets and 1the 3of the

ἀποστόλων ὑμῶν ἐντολῆς τοῦ κυρίου καὶ
4apostles 5of you 2commandment of the Lord and

σωτῆρος, 3 τοῦτο πρῶτον γινώσκοντες, ὅτι
Saviour, 2this 3first*ly* 1knowing, that

ἐλεύσονται ἐπ' ἐσχάτων τῶν ἡμερῶν ἐν
there will come during [the] last of the days 3in

ἐμπαιγμονῇ ἐμπαῖκται κατὰ τὰς ἰδίας
4mocking 1mockers 5according to 6the(ir) 7own

ἐπιθυμίας αὐτῶν πορευόμενοι 4 καὶ λέγοντες·
8lusts *of them* 2going and saying:

ποῦ ἐστιν ἡ ἐπαγγελία τῆς παρουσίας
Where is the promise of the presence

αὐτοῦ; ἀφ' ἧς γὰρ οἱ πατέρες ἐκοι-
of him? 2from 3which [day] 1for the fathers fell
=for from the day when . . .

μήθησαν, πάντα οὕτως διαμένει ἀπ'
asleep, all things so remains from

ἀρχῆς κτίσεως. 5 λανθάνει γὰρ αὐτοὺς
[the] beginning of creation. For 2is concealed [from] 3them

τοῦτο θέλοντας ὅτι οὐρανοὶ ἦσαν ἔκπαλαι
1this wishing* that heavens were of old

* That is, they wish it to be so.

dom, while they them-
selves are slaves of depravity—for a man is a slave to
whatever has mastered
him. 20 If they have escaped
the corruption of the world
by knowing our Lord and
Savior Jesus Christ and are
again entangled in it and
overcome, they are worse
off at the end than they
were at the beginning. 21 It
would have been better for
them not to have known the
way of righteousness, than
to have known it and then
to turn their backs on the
sacred command that was
passed on to them. 22 Of
them the proverbs are true:
"A dog returns to its vomit,"[g] and, "A sow that is
washed goes back to her
wallowing in the mud."

Chapter 3

The Day of the Lord

DEAR friends, this is
now my second letter
to you. I have written both
of them as reminders to
stimulate you to whole-
some thinking. 2 I want you
to recall the words spoken
in the past by the holy
prophets and the command
given by our Lord and Savior through your apostles.
3 First of all, you must understand that in the last
days scoffers will come,
scoffing and following their
own evil desires. 4 They will
say, "Where is this 'com-
ing' he promised? Ever
since our fathers died, ev
erything goes on as it has
since the beginning of creation." 5 But they deliberately forget that long ago by
God's word the heavens
existed and the earth was

[g] 22 Prov. 26:11

formed out of water and by means of water, 6through which the world of that time was deluged with water and perished. 7But by the same word the present heavens and earth have been reserved for fire, being kept until the day of judgment and destruction of the godless.

8 But do not ignore this one fact, beloved, that with the Lord one day is like a thousand years, and a thousand years are like one day. 9The Lord is not slow about his promise, as some think of slowness, but is patient with you,[x] not wanting any to perish, but all to come to repentance. 10But the day of the Lord will come like a thief, and then the heavens will pass away with a loud noise, and the elements will be dissolved with fire, and the earth and everything that is done on it will be disclosed.[y]

11 Since all these things are to be dissolved in this way, what sort of persons ought you to be in leading lives of holiness and godliness, 12waiting for and hastening[z] the coming of the day of God, because of which the heavens will be set ablaze and dissolved, and the elements will melt with fire? 13But, in accordance with his promise, we wait for new heavens and a new earth, where righteousness is at home.

Final Exhortation and Doxology

14 Therefore, beloved, while you are waiting for

καὶ γῆ ἐξ ὕδατος καὶ δι' ὕδατος
and earth by water and through water
συνεστῶσα τῷ τοῦ θεοῦ λόγῳ, 6 δι'
[1]having been held together [2]by the – [4]of God [3]word, through
ὧν ὁ τότε κόσμος ὕδατι κατακλυσθεὶς
which things the then§ world [2]by water [1]being inundated
ἀπώλετο· 7 οἱ δὲ νῦν οὐρανοὶ καὶ ἡ
perished; but the now heavens and the
γῆ τῷ αὐτῷ λόγῳ τεθησαυρισμένοι εἰσὶν
earth by the same word [2]*having been* stored up [1]are
πυρὶ τηρούμενοι εἰς ἡμέραν κρίσεως καὶ
[3]for fire [1]being kept in a day of judgment and
ἀπωλείας τῶν ἀσεβῶν ἀνθρώπων. 8 Ἓν
destruction of *the* impious men. [2]one
δὲ τοῦτο μὴ λανθανέτω ὑμᾶς, ἀγαπητοί,
But [1]this [3]thing let not be concealed [from] you, beloved,
ὅτι μία ἡμέρα παρὰ κυρίῳ ὡς χίλια
that one day with [the] Lord [is] as a thousand
ἔτη καὶ χίλια ἔτη ὡς ἡμέρα μία. 9 οὐ
years and a thousand years as [2]day [1]one. [3]not
βραδύνει κύριος τῆς ἐπαγγελίας, ὥς τινες
[2]is [4]slow [1][The] Lord of the (his) promise, as some
βραδύτητα ἡγοῦνται, ἀλλὰ μακροθυμεῖ εἰς
[2]slowness [1]deem, but is longsuffering toward
ὑμᾶς, μὴ βουλόμενός τινας ἀπολέσθαι
you, not purposing any to perish
ἀλλὰ πάντας εἰς μετάνοιαν χωρῆσαι.
but all men [2]to [3]repentance [1]to come.
10 Ἥξει δὲ ἡμέρα κυρίου ὡς κλέπτης,
But will come [the] day of [the] Lord as a thief,
ἐν ᾗ οἱ οὐρανοὶ ῥοιζηδὸν παρελεύσονται,
in which the heavens [2]with rushing sound [1]will pass away,
στοιχεῖα δὲ καυσούμενα λυθήσεται, καὶ
and [the] elements burning will be dissolved, and
γῆ καὶ τὰ ἐν αὐτῇ ἔργα εὑρεθήσεται.
[the] earth and [1]the [3]in [4]it [2]works will be discovered.
11 Τούτων οὕτως πάντων λυομένων
[2]these things [3]thus [1]All [4]being dissolved•
ποταποὺς δεῖ ὑπάρχειν [ὑμᾶς] ἐν ἁγίαις
what sort of men it behoves [2]to be [1]you in holy
ἀναστροφαῖς καὶ εὐσεβείαις, 12 προσδοκῶντας
conduct• and piety,• awaiting
καὶ σπεύδοντας τὴν παρουσίαν τῆς τοῦ
and hastening the presence [1]of the –
θεοῦ ἡμέρας, δι' ἣν οὐρανοὶ πυρούμενοι
[2]of God [1]day, on account of which [the] heavens being set on fire
λυθήσονται καὶ στοιχεῖα καυσούμενα
will be dissolved and [the] elements burning
τήκεται. 13 καινοὺς δὲ οὐρανοὺς καὶ
melts. But new heavens and
γῆν καινὴν κατὰ τὸ ἐπάγγελμα αὐτοῦ
[2]earth [1]a new according to the promise of him
προσδοκῶμεν, ἐν οἷς δικαιοσύνη κατοικεῖ.
we await, in which righteousness dwells.
14 Διό, ἀγαπητοί, ταῦτα προσδοκῶντες
Wherefore, beloved, [2]these things [1]awaiting

formed out of water and by water. 6By these waters also the world of that time was deluged and destroyed. 7By the same word the present heavens and earth are reserved for fire, being kept for the day of judgment and destruction of ungodly men.

8But do not forget this one thing, dear friends: With the Lord a day is like a thousand years, and a thousand years are like a day. 9The Lord is not slow in keeping his promise, as some understand slowness. He is patient with you, not wanting anyone to perish, but everyone to come to repentance.

10But the day of the Lord will come like a thief. The heavens will disappear with a roar; the elements will be destroyed by fire, and the earth and everything in it will be laid bare.[h]

11Since everything will be destroyed in this way, what kind of people ought you to be? You ought to live holy and godly lives 12as you look forward to the day of God and speed its coming.[i] That day will bring about the destruction of the heavens by fire, and the elements will melt in the heat. 13But in keeping with his promise we are looking forward to a new heaven and a new earth, the home of righteousness.

14So then, dear friends, since you are looking for-

[x] Other ancient authorities read *on your account*
[y] Other ancient authorities read *will be burned up*
[z] Or *earnestly desiring*

§ This is allowable English : *cf.* "the then Prime Minister."
• The Greek plurals cannot be literally reproduced in English.

[h] 10 Some manuscripts *be burned up*
[i] 12 Or *as you wait eagerly for the day of God to come*

these things, strive to be
found by him at peace,
without spot or blemish;
15 and regard the patience
of our Lord as salvation. So
also our beloved brother
Paul wrote to you accord-
ing to the wisdom given
him, 16 speaking of this as
he does in all his letters.
There are some things in
them hard to understand,
which the ignorant and unstable twist to their own destruction, as they do the
other scriptures. 17 You
therefore, beloved, since
you are forewarned, be-
ware that you are not carried away with the error of
the lawless and lose your
own stability. 18 But grow
in the grace and knowledge
of our Lord and Savior
Jesus Christ. To him be the
glory both now and to the
day of eternity. Amen.[a]

σπουδάσατε ἄσπιλοι καὶ ἀμώμητοι αὐτῷ
be diligent [8]spotless [9]and [7]unblemished [2]by him
εὑρεθῆναι ἐν εἰρήνῃ, 15 καὶ τὴν τοῦ
[1]to be found [3]in [4]peace, and [2]the [4]of the
κυρίου ἡμῶν μακροθυμίαν σωτηρίαν ἡγεῖσθε,
[5]Lord [6]of us [3]longsuffering [7]salvation [1]deem,
καθὼς καὶ ὁ ἀγαπητὸς ἡμῶν ἀδελφὸς
as indeed the beloved [2]of us [1]brother
Παῦλος κατὰ τὴν δοθεῖσαν αὐτῷ σοφίαν
Paul according to [1]the [3]given [4]to him [2]wisdom
ἔγραψεν ὑμῖν, 16 ὡς καὶ ἐν πάσαις
wrote to you, as also in all [his]
ἐπιστολαῖς λαλῶν ἐν αὐταῖς περὶ τούτων,
epistles speaking in them concerning these things,
ἐν αἷς ἐστιν δυσνόητά τινα, ἃ οἱ
in which is(are) [2]hard to understand [1]some things, which the
ἀμαθεῖς καὶ ἀστήρικτοι στρεβλοῦσιν ὡς
unlearned and unsteady twist as
καὶ τὰς λοιπὰς γραφὰς πρὸς τὴν ἰδίαν
also the remaining scriptures to the(ir) own
αὐτῶν ἀπώλειαν. 17 Ὑμεῖς οὖν, ἀγαπητοί,
of them destruction. Ye therefore, beloved,
προγινώσκοντες φυλάσσεσθε ἵνα μὴ τῇ
knowing before guard lest [2]by the
τῶν ἀθέσμων πλάνῃ συναπαχθέντες ἐκπέ-
[4]of the [5]lawless [3]error [1]being led away *with* ye fall
σητε τοῦ ἰδίου στηριγμοῦ, 18 αὐξάνετε
from the(your) own stability, [2]grow ye
δὲ ἐν χάριτι καὶ γνώσει τοῦ κυρίου
[1]but in grace and knowledge of the Lord
ἡμῶν καὶ σωτῆρος Ἰησοῦ Χριστοῦ.
of us and Saviour Jesus Christ.
αὐτῷ ἡ δόξα καὶ νῦν καὶ εἰς
To him[c] [is] the glory both now and unto
=His is* =for ever.
ἡμέραν αἰῶνος.
a day of age.§

ward to this, make every
effort to be found spotless,
blameless and at peace
with him. 15 Bear in mind
that our Lord's patience
means salvation, just as our
dear brother Paul also
wrote you with the wisdom
that God gave him. 16 He
writes the same way in all
his letters, speaking in
them of these matters. His
letters contain some things
that are hard to under-
stand, which ignorant and
unstable people distort, as
they do the other Scrip-
tures, to their own destruction.
17 Therefore, dear friends,
since you already know
this, be on your guard so
that you may not be carried
away by the error of law-
less men and fall from your
secure position. 18 But grow
in the grace and knowledge
of our Lord and Savior
Jesus Christ. To him be glory both now and forever!
Amen.

The First Letter of
John

Chapter 1

The Word of Life

WE declare to you
what was from the
beginning, what we have
heard, what we have seen
with our eyes, what we
have looked at and touched
with our hands, concerning
the word of life— 2 this life
was revealed, and we have
seen it and testify to it, and
declare to you the eternal
life that was with the Father and was revealed to
us— 3 we declare to you
what we have seen and

ΙΩΑΝΝΟΥ Α
Of John 1

1 Ὃ ἦν ἀπ' ἀρχῆς, ὃ ἀκηκόαμεν,
What was from [the] beginning, what we have heard,
ὃ ἑωράκαμεν τοῖς ὀφθαλμοῖς ἡμῶν, ὃ
what we have seen with the eyes of us, what
ἐθεασάμεθα καὶ αἱ χεῖρες ἡμῶν ἐψηλάφησαν,
we beheld and the hands of us touched,
περὶ τοῦ λόγου τῆς ζωῆς, — 2 καὶ
concerning the word – of life, — and
ἡ ζωὴ ἐφανερώθη, καὶ ἑωράκαμεν καὶ
the life was manifested, and we have seen and
μαρτυροῦμεν καὶ ἀπαγγέλλομεν ὑμῖν τὴν
we bear witness and *we* announce to you the
ζωὴν τὴν αἰώνιον, ἥτις ἦν πρὸς τὸν
life – eternal, which was with the
πατέρα καὶ ἐφανερώθη ἡμῖν, — 3 ὃ
Father and was manifested to us, — what
ἑωράκαμεν καὶ ἀκηκόαμεν, ἀπαγγέλλομεν
we have seen and *we* have heard, we announce

1 John

Chapter 1

The Word of Life

THAT which was from
the beginning, which
we have heard, which we
have seen with our eyes,
which we have looked at
and our hands have
touched—this we proclaim
concerning the Word of
life. 2 The life appeared; we
have seen it and testify to
it, and we proclaim to you
the eternal life, which was
with the Father and has appeared to us. 3 We proclaim
to you what we have seen

[a] Other ancient authorities lack *Amen*

* See note on I. Pet. 5. 11. § ? "An age-lasting (*i.e.* eternal) day."

heard so that you also may have fellowship with us; and truly our fellowship is with the Father and with his Son Jesus Christ. 4 We are writing these things so that our[a] joy may be complete.

God Is Light

5 This is the message we have heard from him and proclaim to you, that God is light and in him there is no darkness at all. 6 If we say that we have fellowship with him while we are walking in darkness, we lie and do not do what is true; 7 but if we walk in the light as he himself is in the light, we have fellowship with one another, and the blood of Jesus his Son cleanses us from all sin. 8 If we say that we have no sin, we deceive ourselves, and the truth is not in us. 9 If we confess our sins, he who is faithful and just will forgive us our sins and cleanse us from all unrighteousness. 10 If we say that we have not sinned, we make him a liar, and his word is not in us.

Chapter 2

Christ Our Advocate

MY little children, I am writing these things to you so that you may not sin. But if anyone does sin, we have an advocate with the Father, Jesus Christ the righteous; 2 and he is the atoning sacrifice for our sins, and not for ours only but also for the sins of the

[a] Other ancient authorities read *your*

καὶ ὑμῖν, ἵνα καὶ ὑμεῖς κοινωνίαν ἔχητε
also to you, in order that [2]also [1]ye [4]fellowship [3]may have

μεθ' ἡμῶν. καὶ ἡ κοινωνία δὲ ἡ ἡμετέρα
with us. [2]indeed *the* [4]fellowship [1]And – [3]our

μετὰ τοῦ πατρὸς καὶ μετὰ τοῦ υἱοῦ
[is] with the Father and with the Son

αὐτοῦ Ἰησοῦ Χριστοῦ. 4 καὶ ταῦτα
of him Jesus Christ. And these things

γράφομεν ἡμεῖς ἵνα ἡ χαρὰ ἡμῶν ᾖ
write we in order that the joy of us may be

πεπληρωμένη.
having been fulfilled.

5 Καὶ ἔστιν αὕτη ἡ ἀγγελία ἣν
And [2]is [1]this the message which

ἀκηκόαμεν ἀπ' αὐτοῦ καὶ ἀναγγέλλομεν
we have heard from him and *we* announce

ὑμῖν, ὅτι ὁ θεὸς φῶς ἐστιν καὶ σκοτία
to you, that – God [2]light [1]is and [5]darkness

ἐν αὐτῷ οὐκ ἔστιν οὐδεμία. 6 Ἐὰν
[1]in [2]him [4]not [3]is *none.* If

εἴπωμεν ὅτι κοινωνίαν ἔχομεν μετ' αὐτοῦ
we say that [2]fellowship [1]we have with him

καὶ ἐν τῷ σκότει περιπατῶμεν, ψευδόμεθα
and [2]in [3]the [4]darkness [1]*we* walk, we lie

καὶ οὐ ποιοῦμεν τὴν ἀλήθειαν· 7 ἐὰν
and are not doing the truth; [2]if

δὲ ἐν τῷ φωτὶ περιπατῶμεν ὡς αὐτός
[1]but [4]in [5]the [6]light [3]we walk as he

ἐστιν ἐν τῷ φωτί, κοινωνίαν ἔχομεν
is in the light, [2]fellowship [1]we have

μετ' ἀλλήλων καὶ τὸ αἷμα Ἰησοῦ τοῦ
with each other and the blood of Jesus the

υἱοῦ αὐτοῦ καθαρίζει ἡμᾶς ἀπὸ πάσης
Son of him cleanses us from all

ἁμαρτίας. 8 ἐὰν εἴπωμεν ὅτι ἁμαρτίαν
sin. If we say that sin

οὐκ ἔχομεν, ἑαυτοὺς πλανῶμεν καὶ ἡ
we have not, [2]ourselves [1]we deceive and the

ἀλήθεια οὐκ ἔστιν ἐν ἡμῖν. 9 ἐὰν
truth is not in us. If

ὁμολογῶμεν τὰς ἁμαρτίας ἡμῶν, πιστός
we confess the sins of us, faithful

ἐστιν καὶ δίκαιος, ἵνα ἀφῇ ἡμῖν τὰς
he is and righteous, in order that he may forgive us the

ἁμαρτίας καὶ καθαρίσῃ ἡμᾶς ἀπὸ πάσης
sins and *he* may cleanse us from all

ἀδικίας. 10 ἐὰν εἴπωμεν ὅτι οὐχ
iniquity. If we say that not

ἡμαρτήκαμεν, ψεύστην ποιοῦμεν αὐτὸν
we have sinned, a liar we make him

καὶ ὁ λόγος αὐτοῦ οὐκ ἔστιν ἐν ἡμῖν.
and the word of him is not in us.

2 Τεκνία μου, ταῦτα γράφω ὑμῖν ἵνα
Little children of me, these things I write to you in order that

μὴ ἁμάρτητε. καὶ ἐάν τις ἁμάρτῃ,
ye sin not. And if anyone sins,

παράκλητον ἔχομεν πρὸς τὸν πατέρα,
an advocate we have with the Father,

Ἰησοῦν Χριστὸν δίκαιον· 2 καὶ αὐτὸς
Jesus Christ [the] righteous; and he

ἱλασμός ἐστιν περὶ τῶν ἁμαρτιῶν ἡμῶν,
[2]a propitiation [1]is concerning the sins of us,

οὐ περὶ τῶν ἡμετέρων δὲ μόνον ἀλλὰ
[2]not [3]concerning – [4]ours [1]but only but

and heard, so that you also may have fellowship with us. And our fellowship is with the Father and with his Son, Jesus Christ. 4We write this to make our[a] joy complete.

Walking in the Light

5This is the message we have heard from him and declare to you: God is light; in him there is no darkness at all. 6If we claim to have fellowship with him yet walk in the darkness, we lie and do not live by the truth. 7But if we walk in the light, as he is in the light, we have fellowship with one another, and the blood of Jesus, his Son, purifies us from all[b] sin.

8If we claim to be without sin, we deceive ourselves and the truth is not in us. 9If we confess our sins, he is faithful and just and will forgive us our sins and purify us from all unrighteousness. 10If we claim we have not sinned, we make him out to be a liar and his word has no place in our lives.

Chapter 2

MY dear children, I write this to you so that you will not sin. But if anybody does sin, we have one who speaks to the Father in our defense—Jesus Christ, the Righteous One. 2He is the atoning sacrifice for our sins, and not only for ours but also for[c] the

[a]4 Some manuscripts *your*
[b]7 Or *every*
[c]2 Or *He is the one who turns aside God's wrath, taking away our sins, and not only ours but also*

whole world.
3 Now by this we may
be sure that we know him,
if we obey his command-
ments. 4 Whoever says, "I
have come to know him,"
but does not obey his commandments, is a liar, and in
such a person the truth
does not exist; 5 but whoever obeys his word, truly in
this person the love of God
has reached perfection. By
this we may be sure that we
are in him: 6 whoever says,
"I abide in him," ought to
walk just as he walked.

A New Commandment

7 Beloved, I am writing
you no new command-
ment, but an old command-
ment that you have had
from the beginning; the old
commandment is the word
that you have heard. 8 Yet I
am writing you a new com-
mandment that is true in
him and in you, because[b]
the darkness is passing
away and the true light is
already shining. 9 Whoever
says, "I am in the light,"
while hating a brother or
sister,[c] is still in the darkness. 10 Whoever loves a
brother or sister[d] lives in
the light, and in such a person[e] there is no cause for
stumbling. 11 But whoever
hates another believer[f] is
in the darkness, walks in
the darkness, and does not
know the way to go, be-
cause the darkness has
brought on blindness.
12 I am writing to you,
little children,
because your sins
are forgiven on

[b] Or *that*
[c] Gk *hating a brother*
[d] Gk *loves a brother*
[e] Or *in it*
[f] Gk *hates a brother*

καὶ περὶ ὅλου τοῦ κόσμου. 3 καὶ ἐν
also concerning all the world. And by

τούτῳ γινώσκομεν ὅτι ἐγνώκαμεν αὐτόν,
this we know that we have known him,

ἐὰν τὰς ἐντολὰς αὐτοῦ τηρῶμεν. 4 ὁ
if [2]the [3]commandments [4]of him [1]we keep. The [one]

λέγων ὅτι Ἔγνωκα αὐτόν, καὶ τὰς ἐντολὰς
saying[,] – I have known him, and [3]the [4]commandments

αὐτοῦ μὴ τηρῶν, ψεύστης ἐστίν, καὶ
[5]of him [1]not [2]keeping, [2]a liar [1]is, and

ἐν τούτῳ ἡ ἀλήθεια οὐκ ἔστιν· 5 ὃς δ'
in this man the truth is not; but who-

ἂν τηρῇ αὐτοῦ τὸν λόγον, ἀληθῶς ἐν
ever keeps [3]of him [1]the [2]word, truly in

τούτῳ ἡ ἀγάπη τοῦ θεοῦ τετελείωται.
this man the love – of God has been perfected.

ἐν τούτῳ γινώσκομεν ὅτι ἐν αὐτῷ ἐσμεν.
By this we know that [2]in [3]him [1]we are.

6 ὁ λέγων ἐν αὐτῷ μένειν ὀφείλει καθὼς
The [one] saying in him to remain ought as

ἐκεῖνος περιεπάτησεν καὶ αὐτὸς οὕτως
that [one]* walked also [him]self so

περιπατεῖν.
to walk.

7 Ἀγαπητοί, οὐκ ἐντολὴν καινὴν γράφω
Beloved, [2]not [4]commandment [3]a new [1]I write

ὑμῖν, ἀλλ' ἐντολὴν παλαιὰν ἣν εἴχετε
to you, but [2]commandment [1]an old which ye had

ἀπ' ἀρχῆς· ἡ ἐντολὴ ἡ παλαιά ἐστιν
from [the] beginning; the [2]commandment – [1]old is

ὁ λόγος ὃν ἠκούσατε. 8 πάλιν ἐντολὴν
the word which ye heard. Again [2]commandment

καινὴν γράφω ὑμῖν, ὅ ἐστιν ἀληθὲς
[1]a new I write to you, what is true

ἐν αὐτῷ καὶ ἐν ὑμῖν, ὅτι ἡ σκοτία
in him and in you, because the darkness

παράγεται καὶ τὸ φῶς τὸ ἀληθινὸν
is passing and the [2]light – [1]true

ἤδη φαίνει. 9 ὁ λέγων ἐν τῷ φωτὶ
already shines. The [one] saying in the light

εἶναι καὶ τὸν ἀδελφὸν αὐτοῦ μισῶν
to be and the brother of him hating

ἐν τῇ σκοτίᾳ ἐστὶν ἕως ἄρτι. 10 ὁ
in the darkness is until now. The

ἀγαπῶν τὸν ἀδελφὸν αὐτοῦ ἐν τῷ φωτὶ
[one] loving the brother of him in the light

μένει, καὶ σκάνδαλον ἐν αὐτῷ οὐκ ἔστιν·
remains, and offence in him is not;

11 ὁ δὲ μισῶν τὸν ἀδελφὸν αὐτοῦ ἐν
but the [one] hating the brother of him in

τῇ σκοτίᾳ ἐστὶν καὶ ἐν τῇ σκοτίᾳ
the darkness is and in the darkness

περιπατεῖ, καὶ οὐκ οἶδεν ποῦ ὑπάγει,
walks, and knows not where he is going,

ὅτι ἡ σκοτία ἐτύφλωσεν τοὺς ὀφθαλμοὺς
because the darkness blinded the eyes

αὐτοῦ. 12 Γράφω ὑμῖν, τεκνία, ὅτι
of him. I write to you, little children, because

ἀφέωνται ὑμῖν αἱ ἁμαρτίαι διὰ τὸ ὄνομα
have been forgiven *to* you the (your) sins on account of the name

* **In a number of places John uses this demonstrative adjective as a substitute for " Christ " : " the remoter antecedent." See also John 2. 21.**

sins of the whole world.
3 We know that we have
come to know him if we
obey his commands. 4 The
man who says, "I know
him," but does not do what
he commands is a liar, and
the truth is not in him. 5 But
if anyone obeys his word,
God's love[d] is truly made
complete in him. This is
how we know we are in
him: 6 Whoever claims to
live in him must walk as
Jesus did.
7 Dear friends, I am not
writing you a new com-
mand but an old one, which
you have had since the beginning. This old command
is the message you have
heard. 8 Yet I am writing
you a new command; its
truth is seen in him and
you, because the darkness
is passing and the true light
is already shining.
9 Anyone who claims to
be in the light but hates his
brother is still in the darkness. 10 Whoever loves his
brother lives in the light,
and there is nothing in him[e]
to make him stumble. 11 But
whoever hates his brother
is in the darkness and walks
around in the darkness; he
does not know where he is
going, because the dark-
ness has blinded him.

12 I write to you, dear
children,
because your sins have
been forgiven on

[d] 5 Or *word, love for God*
[e] 10 Or *it*

account of his
name.
13 I am writing to you,
fathers,
because you know
him who is from
the beginning.
I am writing to you,
young people,
because you have
conquered
the evil one.
14 I write to you,
children,
because you know
the Father.
I write to you,
fathers,
because you know
him who is from
the beginning.
I write to you, young
people,
because you are
strong
and the word of
God abides
in you,
and you have
overcome the
evil one.

15 Do not love the
world or the things in the
world. The love of the Father is not in those who
love the world; 16 for all
that is in the world—the
desire of the flesh, the desire of the eyes, the pride in
riches—comes not from
the Father but from the
world. 17 And the world and
its desire[g] are passing
away, but those who do the
will of God live forever.

Warning against Antichrists

18 Children, it is the last
hour! As you have heard
that antichrist is coming, so
now many antichrists have
come. From this we know
that it is the last hour.
19 They went out from us,
but they did not belong to
us; for if they had belonged
to us, they would have remained with us. But by going out they made it plain
that none of them belongs
to us. 20 But you have been
anointed by the Holy One,
and all of you have knowledge.[h] 21 I write to you, not
because you do not know
the truth, but because you
know it, and you know that
no lie comes from the truth.

[g] Or *the desire for it*
[h] Other ancient authorities read *you know all things*

αὐτοῦ. 13 γράφω ὑμῖν, πατέρες, ὅτι
of him. I write to you, fathers, because
ἐγνώκατε τὸν ἀπ' ἀρχῆς. γράφω ὑμῖν,
ye have known the [one] from [the] beginning. I write to you,
νεανίσκοι, ὅτι νενικήκατε τὸν πονηρόν.
young men, because ye have overcome the evil one.
14 ἔγραψα ὑμῖν, παιδία, ὅτι ἐγνώκατε
I wrote to you, young children, because ye have known
τὸν πατέρα. ἔγραψα ὑμῖν, πατέρες,
the Father. I wrote to you, fathers,
ὅτι ἐγνώκατε τὸν ἀπ' ἀρχῆς. ἔγραψα
because ye have known the [one] from [the] beginning. I wrote
ὑμῖν, νεανίσκοι, ὅτι ἰσχυροί ἐστε καὶ
to you, young men, because strong ye are and
ὁ λόγος τοῦ θεοῦ ἐν ὑμῖν μένει καὶ
the word – of God in you remains and
νενικήκατε τὸν πονηρόν. 15 Μὴ ἀγαπᾶτε
ye have overcome the evil one. Love ye not
τὸν κόσμον μηδὲ τὰ ἐν τῷ κόσμῳ.
the world nor the things in the world.
ἐάν τις ἀγαπᾷ τὸν κόσμον, οὐκ ἔστιν
If anyone loves the world, [5]not [6]is
ἡ ἀγάπη τοῦ πατρὸς ἐν αὐτῷ· 16 ὅτι
[1]the [2]love [3]of the [4]Father in him; because
πᾶν τὸ ἐν τῷ κόσμῳ, ἡ ἐπιθυμία τῆς
all that which† [is] in the world, the lust of the
σαρκὸς καὶ ἡ ἐπιθυμία τῶν ὀφθαλμῶν
flesh and the lust of the eyes
καὶ ἡ ἀλαζονεία τοῦ βίου, οὐκ ἔστιν
and the vainglory – of life, is not
ἐκ τοῦ πατρός, ἀλλὰ ἐκ τοῦ κόσμου
of the Father, but of the world
ἐστίν. 17 καὶ ὁ κόσμος παράγεται καὶ
is. And the world is passing away and
ἡ ἐπιθυμία αὐτοῦ· ὁ δὲ ποιῶν τὸ θέλημα
the lust of it; but the [one] doing the will
τοῦ θεοῦ μένει εἰς τὸν αἰῶνα.
– of God remains unto the age.
18 Παιδία, ἐσχάτη ὥρα ἐστίν, καὶ
Young children, a last hour it is, and
καθὼς ἠκούσατε ὅτι ἀντίχριστος ἔρχεται,
as ye heard that antichrist is coming,
καὶ νῦν ἀντίχριστοι πολλοὶ γεγόνασιν·
even now [2]antichrists [1]many have arisen;
ὅθεν γινώσκομεν ὅτι ἐσχάτη ὥρα ἐστίν.
whence we know that a last hour it is.
19 ἐξ ἡμῶν ἐξῆλθαν, ἀλλ' οὐκ ἦσαν
From us they went out, but they were not
ἐξ ἡμῶν· εἰ γὰρ ἐξ ἡμῶν ἦσαν, μεμενή-
of us; for if of us they were, they would
κεισαν ἂν μεθ' ἡμῶν· ἀλλ' ἵνα φανερω-
have remained with us; but in order that it might be
θῶσιν ὅτι οὐκ εἰσὶν πάντες ἐξ ἡμῶν.
manifested that they are not all of us.
20 καὶ ὑμεῖς χρῖσμα ἔχετε ἀπὸ τοῦ
And ye an anointing have from the
ἁγίου, καὶ οἴδατε πάντες. 21 οὐκ ἔγραψα
Holy One, and [1]ye [3]know [2]all. I wrote not
ὑμῖν ὅτι οὐκ οἴδατε τὴν ἀλήθειαν, ἀλλ'
to you because ye know not the truth, but
ὅτι οἴδατε αὐτήν, καὶ ὅτι πᾶν ψεῦδος
because ye know it, and because every lie
=no lie is . . .

account of his name.
13 I write to you, fathers,
because you have
known him who is
from the beginning.
I write to you, young
men,
because you have
overcome the evil
one.
I write to you, dear
children,
because you have
known the Father.
14 I write to you, fathers,
because you have
known him who is
from the beginning.
I write to you, young
men,
because you are
strong,
and the word of God
lives in you,
and you have
overcome the evil
one.

Do Not Love the World

15 Do not love the world or
anything in the world. If
anyone loves the world, the
love of the Father is not in
him. 16 For everything in
the world—the cravings of
sinful man, the lust of his
eyes and the boasting of
what he has and does—
comes not from the Father
but from the world. 17 The
world and its desires pass
away, but the man who
does the will of God lives
forever.

Warning Against Antichrists

18 Dear children, this is
the last hour; and as you
have heard that the anti-
christ is coming, even now
many antichrists have
come. This is how we know
it is the last hour. 19 They
went out from us, but they
did not really belong to us.
For if they had belonged to
us, they would have re-
mained with us; but their
going showed that none of
them belonged to us.
20 But you have an anointing from the Holy One, and
all of you know the truth.[f]
21 I do not write to you because you do not know the
truth, but because you do
know it and because no lie
comes from the truth.

[f] 20 Some manuscripts *and you know all things*

22Who is the liar but the
one who denies that Jesus
is the Christ?[i] This is the
antichrist, the one who denies the Father and the
Son. 23No one who denies
the Son has the Father; everyone who confesses the
Son has the Father also.
24Let what you heard from
the beginning abide in you.
If what you heard from the
beginning abides in you,
then you will abide in the
Son and in the Father.
25And this is what he has
promised us,[j] eternal life.
26 I write these things to
you concerning those who
would deceive you. 27As
for you, the anointing that
you received from him
abides in you, and so you
do not need anyone to
teach you. But as his
anointing teaches you
about all things, and is true
and is not a lie, and just as
it has taught you, abide in
him.[k]
28 And now, little chil-
dren, abide in him, so that
when he is revealed we
may have confidence and
not be put to shame before
him at his coming.

Children of God

29 If you know that he is
righteous, you may be sure
that everyone who does
right has been born of him.
1See what love the Father
has given us, that we
should be called children of
God; and that is what we
are. The reason the world
does not know us is that it

[i] Or *the Messiah*
[j] Other ancient authorities read *you*
[k] Or *it*

ἐκ τῆς ἀληθείας οὐκ ἔστιν. 22 Τίς
of the truth is not. Who

ἐστιν ὁ ψεύστης εἰ μὴ ὁ ἀρνούμενος
is the liar except the [one] denying

ὅτι Ἰησοῦς οὐκ ἔστιν ὁ χριστός; οὗτός
that Jesus *not* is the Christ ? this

ἐστιν ὁ ἀντίχριστος, ὁ ἀρνούμενος τὸν
is the antichrist, the [one] denying the

πατέρα καὶ τὸν υἱόν. 23 πᾶς ὁ ἀρνούμενος
Father and the Son. Everyone denying

τὸν υἱὸν οὐδὲ τὸν πατέρα ἔχει· ὁ
the Son [2]neither [3]the [4]Father [1]has; the

ὁμολογῶν τὸν υἱὸν καὶ τὸν πατέρα ἔχει.
[one] confessing the Son [2]also [3]the [4]Father [1]has.

24 ὑμεῖς ὃ ἠκούσατε ἀπ' ἀρχῆς, ἐν
[2]Ye [1]what heard from [the] beginning, in

ὑμῖν μενέτω. ἐὰν ἐν ὑμῖν μείνῃ ὃ ἀπ'
you let it remain. If [6]in [7]you [5]remains [1]what [2]from

ἀρχῆς ἠκούσατε, καὶ ὑμεῖς ἐν τῷ υἱῷ
[3][the] beginning [4]ye heard, [2]both [1]ye [4]in [5]the [6]Son

καὶ [ἐν] τῷ πατρὶ μενεῖτε. 25 καὶ
[7]and [8]in [9]the [10]Father [3]will remain. And

αὕτη ἐστὶν ἡ ἐπαγγελία ἣν αὐτὸς ἐπηγ-
this is the promise which he pro-

γείλατο ἡμῖν, τὴν ζωὴν τὴν αἰώνιον.
mised us, the life – eternal.

26 Ταῦτα ἔγραψα ὑμῖν περὶ τῶν πλανών-
These things I wrote to you concerning the [ones] leading

των ὑμᾶς. 27 καὶ ὑμεῖς τὸ χρῖσμα
[2]astray [1]you. And [4]ye [1]the [2]anointing

ὃ ἐλάβετε ἀπ' αὐτοῦ μένει ἐν ὑμῖν,
[3]which received from him remains in you,

καὶ οὐ χρείαν ἔχετε ἵνα τις διδάσκῃ
and [2]no [3]need [1]ye have *in order that* anyone should teach

ὑμᾶς· ἀλλ' ὡς τὸ αὐτοῦ χρῖσμα διδάσκει
you; but as the [2]of him [1]anointing teaches

ὑμᾶς περὶ πάντων, καὶ ἀληθές ἐστιν
you concerning all things, and [2]true [1]is

καὶ οὐκ ἔστιν ψεῦδος, καὶ καθὼς ἐδίδαξεν
and is not a lie, and as he/it taught

ὑμᾶς, μένετε ἐν αὐτῷ.
you, remain ye in him.

28 Καὶ νῦν, τεκνία, μένετε ἐν αὐτῷ,
And now, little children, remain ye in him,

ἵνα ἐὰν φανερωθῇ σχῶμεν παρρησίαν καὶ
in order that if he is manifested we may have confidence and

μὴ αἰσχυνθῶμεν ἀπ' αὐτοῦ ἐν τῇ παρουσίᾳ
not be shamed from him in the presence

αὐτοῦ. 29 ἐὰν εἰδῆτε ὅτι δίκαιός ἐστιν,
of him. If ye know that [2]righteous [1]he is,

γινώσκετε ὅτι καὶ πᾶς ὁ ποιῶν τὴν
know ye that also every one doing –

δικαιοσύνην ἐξ αὐτοῦ γεγέννηται.
righteousness [2]of [3]him [1]has been born.

3 Ἴδετε ποταπὴν ἀγάπην δέδωκεν ἡμῖν
See ye what manner of love [3]has given [4]to us

ὁ πατὴρ ἵνα τέκνα θεοῦ κληθῶμεν,
[1]the [2]Father in order that [2]children [3]of God [1]we may be called,

καὶ ἐσμέν. διὰ τοῦτο ὁ κόσμος οὐ
and we are. Therefore the world [2]not

22Who is the liar? It is the
man who denies that Jesus
is the Christ. Such a man is
the antichrist—he denies
the Father and the Son.
23No one who denies the
Son has the Father; whoever acknowledges the Son
has the Father also.
24See that what you have
heard from the beginning
remains in you. If it does,
you also will remain in the
Son and in the Father.
25And this is what he promised us—even eternal life.
26I am writing these
things to you about those
who are trying to lead you
astray. 27As for you, the
anointing you received
from him remains in you,
and you do not need any-
one to teach you. But as his
anointing teaches you
about all things and as that
anointing is real, not counterfeit—just as it has taught
you, remain in him.

Children of God

28And now, dear chil-
dren, continue in him, so
that when he appears we
may be confident and un-
ashamed before him at his
coming.
29If you know that he is
righteous, you know that
everyone who does what is
right has been born of him.

Chapter 3

How great is the love
the Father has lav-
ished on us, that we should
be called children of God!
And that is what we are!
The reason the world does

did not know him. 2Be-
loved, we are God's chil-
dren now; what we will be
has not yet been revealed.
What we do know is this:
when he[k] is revealed, we
will be like him, for we will
see him as he is. 3And all
who have this hope in him
purify themselves, just as
he is pure.
4 Everyone who com-
mits sin is guilty of lawlessness; sin is lawlessness.
5You know that he was re-
vealed to take away sins,
and in him there is no sin.
6No one who abides in him
sins; no one who sins has
either seen him or known
him. 7Little children, let no
one deceive you. Everyone
who does what is right is
righteous, just as he is righteous. 8Everyone who
commits sin is a child of the
devil; for the devil has been
sinning from the beginning.
The Son of God was re-
vealed for this purpose, to
destroy the works of the
devil. 9Those who have
been born of God do not
sin, because God's seed
abides in them;[l] they cannot sin, because they have
been born of God. 10The
children of God and the
children of the devil are revealed in this way: all who
do not do what is right are
not from God, nor are those
who do not love their
brothers and sisters.[m]

Love One Another

11 For this is the mes-
sage you have heard from

[l] *Or because the children of God abide in him*
[m] Gk *his brother*

γινώσκει ἡμᾶς, ὅτι οὐκ ἔγνω αὐτόν.
[1]knows [2]us, because it knew not him.

2 ἀγαπητοί, νῦν τέκνα θεοῦ ἐσμεν, καὶ
Beloved, [2]now [3]children [4]of God [1]we are, and

οὔπω ἐφανερώθη τί ἐσόμεθα. οἴδαμεν
not yet was it manifested what we shall be. We know

ὅτι ἐὰν φανερωθῇ ὅμοιοι αὐτῷ ἐσόμεθα,
that if he(?it) is manifested like him we shall be,

ὅτι ὀψόμεθα αὐτὸν καθώς ἐστιν. **3** καὶ
because we shall see him as he is. And

πᾶς ὁ ἔχων τὴν ἐλπίδα ταύτην ἐπ'
everyone having this hope on

αὐτῷ ἁγνίζει ἑαυτὸν καθὼς ἐκεῖνος ἁγνός
him purifies himself as that one* [2]pure

ἐστιν. **4** πᾶς ὁ ποιῶν τὴν ἁμαρτίαν
[1]is. Everyone doing – sin

καὶ τὴν ἀνομίαν ποιεῖ, καὶ ἡ ἁμαρτία
[2]also – [3]lawlessness [1]does, and – sin

ἐστὶν ἡ ἀνομία. **5** καὶ οἴδατε ὅτι ἐκεῖνος
is – lawlessness. And ye know that that one*

ἐφανερώθη ἵνα τὰς ἁμαρτίας ἄρῃ, καὶ
was manifested in order that – sins he might bear, and

ἁμαρτία ἐν αὐτῷ οὐκ ἔστιν. **6** πᾶς ὁ
sin [2]in [3]him [1]is not. Everyone

ἐν αὐτῷ μένων οὐχ ἁμαρτάνει· πᾶς ὁ
[2]in [3]him [1]remaining sins not; everyone

ἁμαρτάνων οὐχ ἑώρακεν αὐτὸν οὐδὲ
sinning has not seen him nor

ἔγνωκεν αὐτόν. **7** Τεκνία, μηδεὶς πλανάτω
has known him. Little children, [2]no man [1]let [3]lead [5]astray

ὑμᾶς· ὁ ποιῶν τὴν δικαιοσύνην δίκαιός
[4]you; the [one] doing – righteousness [2]righteous

ἐστιν, καθὼς ἐκεῖνος δίκαιός ἐστιν· **8** ὁ
[1]is, as that one* [2]righteous [1]is; the

ποιῶν τὴν ἁμαρτίαν ἐκ τοῦ διαβόλου
[one] doing – sin [2]of [3]the [4]devil

ἐστίν, ὅτι ἀπ' ἀρχῆς ὁ διάβολος ἁμαρτάνει.
[1]is, because [4]from [5][the] beginning [1]the [2]devil [3]sins.

εἰς τοῦτο ἐφανερώθη ὁ υἱὸς τοῦ θεοῦ,
For this was manifested the Son – of God,

ἵνα λύσῃ τὰ ἔργα τοῦ διαβόλου.
in order that he might undo the works of the devil.

9 Πᾶς ὁ γεγεννημένος ἐκ τοῦ θεοῦ
Everyone having been begotten of – God

ἁμαρτίαν οὐ ποιεῖ, ὅτι σπέρμα αὐτοῦ
[3]sin [2]not [1]does, because seed of him

ἐν αὐτῷ μένει· καὶ οὐ δύναται ἁμαρτάνειν,
in him remains; and he cannot *to* sin,

ὅτι ἐκ τοῦ θεοῦ γεγέννηται. **10** ἐν
because of – God he has been begotten. By

τούτῳ φανερά ἐστιν τὰ τέκνα τοῦ θεοῦ
this [2]manifest [1]is(are) the children – of God

καὶ τὰ τέκνα τοῦ διαβόλου· πᾶς ὁ
and the children of the devil; everyone

μὴ ποιῶν δικαιοσύνην οὐκ ἔστιν ἐκ
not doing righteousness is not of

τοῦ θεοῦ, καὶ ὁ μὴ ἀγαπῶν τὸν ἀδελφὸν
– God, and the [one] not loving the brother

αὐτοῦ. **11** ὅτι αὕτη ἐστὶν ἡ ἀγγελία
of him. Because this is the message

* See ch. 2. 6.

not know us is that it did
not know him. 2Dear
friends, now we are chil-
dren of God, and what we
will be has not yet been
made known. But we know
that when he appears,[g] we
shall be like him, for we
shall see him as he is. 3Ev-
eryone who has this hope in
him purifies himself, just as
he is pure.
4Everyone who sins
breaks the law; in fact, sin
is lawlessness. 5But you
know that he appeared so
that he might take away our
sins. And in him is no sin.
6No one who lives in him
keeps on sinning. No one
who continues to sin has either seen him or known
him.
7Dear children, do not let
anyone lead you astray. He
who does what is right is
righteous, just as he is
righteous. 8He who does
what is sinful is of the devil,
because the devil has been
sinning from the beginning.
The reason the Son of God
appeared was to destroy
the devil's work. 9No one
who is born of God will
continue to sin, because
God's seed remains in him;
he cannot go on sinning,
because he has been born
of God. 10This is how we
know who the children of
God are and who the chil-
dren of the devil are: Anyone who does not do what
is right is not a child of God;
nor is anyone who does not
love his brother.

Love One Another

11This is the message you

[g]2 Or *when it is made known*

the beginning, that we
should love one another.
12 We must not be like Cain
who was from the evil one
and murdered his brother.
And why did he murder
him? Because his own
deeds were evil and his
brother's righteous. 13 Do
not be astonished, brothers
and sisters,[n] that the world
hates you. 14 We know that
we have passed from death
to life because we love one
another. Whoever does not
love abides in death. 15 All
who hate a brother or sister[m] are murderers, and
you know that murderers
do not have eternal life
abiding in them. 16 We
know love by this, that he
laid down his life for us—
and we ought to lay down
our lives for one another.
17 How does God's love
abide in anyone who has
the world's goods and sees
a brother or sister[o] in need
and yet refuses help?
18 Little children, let us
love, not in word or
speech, but in truth and action. 19 And by this we will
know that we are from the
truth and will reassure our
hearts before him 20 whenever our hearts condemn
us; for God is greater than
our hearts, and he knows
everything. 21 Beloved, if
our hearts do not condemn

ἣν ἠκούσατε ἀπ' ἀρχῆς, ἵνα ἀγαπῶμεν
which ye heard from [the] beginning, *in order* that we should love

ἀλλήλους· 12 οὐ καθὼς Κάϊν ἐκ τοῦ
one another; not as Cain [3]of [4]the

πονηροῦ ἦν καὶ ἔσφαξεν τὸν ἀδελφὸν
[4]evil one [1]was and slew the brother

αὐτοῦ· καὶ χάριν τίνος ἔσφαξεν αὐτόν;
of him; and for the sake of what slew he him?

ὅτι τὰ ἔργα αὐτοῦ πονηρὰ ἦν, τὰ δὲ
because the works of him [2]evil [1]was(were), but the [works]

τοῦ ἀδελφοῦ αὐτοῦ δίκαια. 13 μὴ
of the brother of him righteous. not

θαυμάζετε, ἀδελφοί, εἰ μισεῖ ὑμᾶς ὁ
Marvel ye, brothers, if [3]hates [4]you [1]the

κόσμος. 14 ἡμεῖς οἴδαμεν ὅτι μεταβεβή-
[2]world. We know that we have re-

καμεν ἐκ τοῦ θανάτου εἰς τὴν ζωήν,
moved out of *the* death into *the* life,

ὅτι ἀγαπῶμεν τοὺς ἀδελφούς· ὁ μὴ
because we love the brothers; the [one] not

ἀγαπῶν μένει ἐν τῷ θανάτῳ. 15 πᾶς
loving remains in – death. Every-

ὁ μισῶν τὸν ἀδελφὸν αὐτοῦ ἀνθρωποκτόνος
one hating the brother of him [2]a murderer

ἐστίν, καὶ οἴδατε ὅτι πᾶς ἀνθρωποκτόνος
[1]is, and ye know that every murderer
=no murderer has . . .

οὐκ ἔχει ζωὴν αἰώνιον ἐν αὐτῷ μένουσαν.
has not life eternal in him remaining.

16 ἐν τούτῳ ἐγνώκαμεν τὴν ἀγάπην, ὅτι
By this we have known – love, because

ἐκεῖνος ὑπὲρ ἡμῶν τὴν ψυχὴν αὐτοῦ
that one* on behalf of us the life of him

ἔθηκεν· καὶ ἡμεῖς ὀφείλομεν ὑπὲρ τῶν
laid down; and we ought on behalf of the

ἀδελφῶν τὰς ψυχὰς θεῖναι. 17 ὃς δ'
brothers the(our) lives to lay down. Who-

ἂν ἔχῃ τὸν βίον τοῦ κόσμου καὶ θεωρῇ
ever has the means of life of the world and beholds

τὸν ἀδελφὸν αὐτοῦ χρείαν ἔχοντα καὶ
the brother of him [2]need [1]having and

κλείσῃ τὰ σπλάγχνα αὐτοῦ ἀπ' αὐτοῦ,
shuts the bowels of him from him,

πῶς ἡ ἀγάπη τοῦ θεοῦ μένει ἐν αὐτῷ;
how [2]the [3]love – [4]of God [1]remains in him?

18 Τεκνία, μὴ ἀγαπῶμεν λόγῳ μηδὲ τῇ
Little children, let us not love in word nor in *the*

γλώσσῃ, ἀλλὰ ἐν ἔργῳ καὶ ἀληθείᾳ.
tongue, but in work and truth.

19 ἐν τούτῳ γνωσόμεθα ὅτι ἐκ τῆς ἀληθείας
By this we shall know that [2]of [3]the [4]truth

ἐσμέν, καὶ ἔμπροσθεν αὐτοῦ πείσομεν
[1]we are, and before him shall persuade

τὴν καρδίαν ἡμῶν 20 ὅτι ἐὰν καταγινώσκῃ
the heart of us that if [4]blames [us]

ἡμῶν ἡ καρδία, ὅτι μείζων ἐστὶν ὁ
[3]of us [1]the [2]heart, that greater is –

θεὸς τῆς καρδίας ἡμῶν καὶ γινώσκει
God [than] the heart of us and knows

πάντα. 21 Ἀγαπητοί, ἐὰν ἡ καρδία
all things. Beloved, if the(our) heart

heard from the beginning:
We should love one anoth-
er. 12 Do not be like Cain,
who belonged to the evil
one and murdered his
brother. And why did he
murder him? Because his
own actions were evil and
his brother's were right-
eous. 13 Do not be sur-
prised, my brothers, if the
world hates you. 14 We
know that we have passed
from death to life, because
we love our brothers. Anyone who does not love re-
mains in death. 15 Anyone
who hates his brother is a
murderer, and you know
that no murderer has eternal life in him.
16 This is how we know
what love is: Jesus Christ
laid down his life for us.
And we ought to lay down
our lives for our brothers.
17 If anyone has material
possessions and sees his
brother in need but has no
pity on him, how can the
love of God be in him?
18 Dear children, let us not
love with words or tongue
but with actions and in
truth. 19 This then is how we
know that we belong to the
truth, and how we set our
hearts at rest in his presence 20 whenever our hearts
condemn us. For God is
greater than our hearts, and
he knows everything.
21 Dear friends, if our

[n] Gk *brothers*
[o] Gk *brother*

* See ch. 2. 6, 3. 3, 5, 7.

us, we have boldness before God; [22]and we receive from him whatever we ask, because we obey his commandments and do what pleases him.

23 And this is his commandment, that we should believe in the name of his Son Jesus Christ and love one another, just as he has commanded us. [24]All who obey his commandments abide in him, and he abides in them. And by this we know that he abides in us, by the Spirit that he has given us.

μὴ καταγινώσκῃ, παρρησίαν ἔχομεν πρὸς
does not blame [us], confidence we have with

τὸν θεόν, 22 καὶ ὃ ἐὰν αἰτῶμεν λαμβάν-
– God, and whatever we ask we re-

ομεν ἀπ' αὐτοῦ, ὅτι τὰς ἐντολὰς αὐτοῦ
ceive from him, because [3]the [3]commandments [4]of him

τηροῦμεν καὶ τὰ ἀρεστὰ ἐνώπιον αὐτοῦ
[1]we keep and [3]the things [3]pleasing [4]before [5]him

ποιοῦμεν. 23 καὶ αὕτη ἐστὶν ἡ ἐντολὴ
[1]*we* do. And this is the commandment

αὐτοῦ, ἵνα πιστεύσωμεν τῷ ὀνόματι τοῦ
of him, *in order that* we should believe the name of the

υἱοῦ αὐτοῦ Ἰησοῦ Χριστοῦ καὶ ἀγαπῶμεν
Son of him Jesus Christ and love

ἀλλήλους καθὼς ἔδωκεν ἐντολὴν ἡμῖν.
one another as he gave commandment to us.

24 καὶ ὁ τηρῶν τὰς ἐντολὰς αὐτοῦ ἐν
And the [one] keeping the commandments of him in

αὐτῷ μένει καὶ αὐτὸς ἐν αὐτῷ· καὶ
him remains and he in him; and

ἐν τούτῳ γινώσκομεν ὅτι μένει ἐν ἡμῖν,
by this we know that he remains in us,

ἐκ τοῦ πνεύματος οὗ ἡμῖν ἔδωκεν.
by the Spirit whom to us he gave.

hearts do not condemn us, we have confidence before God [22]and receive from him anything we ask, because we obey his commands and do what pleases him. [23]And this is his command: to believe in the name of his Son, Jesus Christ, and to love one another as he commanded us. [24]Those who obey his commands live in him, and he in them. And this is how we know that he lives in us: We know it by the Spirit he gave us.

Chapter 4

Testing the Spirits

BELOVED, do not believe every spirit, but test the spirits to see whether they are from God; for many false prophets have gone out into the world. [2]By this you know the Spirit of God: every spirit that confesses that Jesus Christ has come in the flesh is from God, [3]and every spirit that does not confess Jesus[p] is not from God. And this is the spirit of the antichrist, of which you have heard that it is coming; and now it is already in the world. [4]Little children, you are from God, and have conquered them; for the one who is in you is greater than the one who is in the world. [5]They are from the world; therefore what they say is from the world, and the world listens to them. [6]We are

[p]Other ancient authorities read *does away with Jesus* (Gk *dissolves Jesus*)

4 Ἀγαπητοί, μὴ παντὶ πνεύματι
Beloved, [2]not [3]every [4]spirit

πιστεύετε, ἀλλὰ δοκιμάζετε τὰ πνεύματα
[1]believe ye, but prove the spirits

εἰ ἐκ τοῦ θεοῦ ἐστιν, ὅτι πολλοὶ
if of – God they are, because many

ψευδοπροφῆται ἐξεληλύθασιν εἰς τὸν
false prophets have gone forth into the

κόσμον. 2 ἐν τούτῳ γινώσκετε τὸ πνεῦμα
world. By this know ye the Spirit

τοῦ θεοῦ· πᾶν πνεῦμα ὃ ὁμολογεῖ Ἰησοῦν
– of God: every spirit which confesses Jesus

Χριστὸν ἐν σαρκὶ ἐληλυθότα ἐκ τοῦ
Christ [2]in [3][the] flesh [1]having come [4]of –

θεοῦ ἐστιν, 3 καὶ πᾶν πνεῦμα ὃ μὴ
[5]God [4]is, and every spirit which not

ὁμολογεῖ τὸν Ἰησοῦν ἐκ τοῦ θεοῦ οὐκ
confesses – Jesus [3]of – [4]God [2]not

ἔστιν· καὶ τοῦτό ἐστιν τὸ τοῦ ἀντιχρίστου,
[1]is; and this is the [spirit] of the antichrist,

ὃ ἀκηκόατε ὅτι ἔρχεται, καὶ νῦν ἐν
which ye have heard that it is coming, and [2]now [4]in

τῷ κόσμῳ ἐστὶν ἤδη. 4 ὑμεῖς ἐκ τοῦ
[5]the [6]world [1]is [3]already. Ye of –

θεοῦ ἐστε, τεκνία, καὶ νενικήκατε αὐτούς,
God are, little children, and have overcome them,

ὅτι μείζων ἐστὶν ὁ ἐν ὑμῖν ἢ ὁ ἐν
because greater is the [one] in you than the [one] in

τῷ κόσμῳ. 5 αὐτοὶ ἐκ τοῦ κόσμου
the world. [1]They [3]of [4]the [5]world

εἰσίν· διὰ τοῦτο ἐκ τοῦ κόσμου λαλοῦσιν
[2]are; therefore [2]of [3]the [4]world [1]they speak

καὶ ὁ κόσμος αὐτῶν ἀκούει. 6 ἡμεῖς
and the world them hears. [1]We

Chapter 4

Test the Spirits

DEAR friends, do not believe every spirit, but test the spirits to see whether they are from God, because many false prophets have gone out into the world. [2]This is how you can recognize the Spirit of God: Every spirit that acknowledges that Jesus Christ has come in the flesh is from God, [3]but every spirit that does not acknowledge Jesus is not from God. This is the spirit of the antichrist, which you have heard is coming and even now is already in the world.

[4]You, dear children, are from God and have overcome them, because the one who is in you is greater than the one who is in the world. [5]They are from the world and therefore speak from the viewpoint of the world, and the world listens to them. [6]We are from

from God. Whoever knows
God listens to us, and whoever is not from God does
not listen to us. From this
we know the spirit of truth
and the spirit of error.

God Is Love

7 Beloved, let us love
one another, because love
is from God; everyone who
loves is born of God and
knows God. 8 Whoever
does not love does not
know God, for God is love.
9 God's love was revealed
among us in this way: God
sent his only Son into the
world so that we might live
through him. 10 In this is
love, not that we loved God
but that he loved us and
sent his Son to be the atoning sacrifice for our sins.
11 Beloved, since God
loved us so much, we also
ought to love one another.
12 No one has ever seen
God; if we love one another, God lives in us, and his
love is perfected in us.

13 By this we know that
we abide in him and he in
us, because he has given us
of his Spirit. 14 And we
have seen and do testify
that the Father has sent his
Son as the Savior of the
world. 15 God abides in
those who confess that
Jesus is the Son of God,
and they abide in God. 16 So
we have known and believe
the love that God has for

ἐκ τοῦ θεοῦ ἐσμεν· ὁ γινώσκων τὸν
[3]of – [4]God [2]are; the [one] knowing –
θεὸν ἀκούει ἡμῶν, ὃς οὐκ ἔστιν ἐκ
God hears us, [he] who is not of
τοῦ θεοῦ οὐκ ἀκούει ἡμῶν. ἐκ τούτου
– God hears not us. From this
γινώσκομεν τὸ πνεῦμα τῆς ἀληθείας καὶ
we know the spirit – of truth and
τὸ πνεῦμα τῆς πλάνης.
the spirit – of error.
7 Ἀγαπητοί, ἀγαπῶμεν ἀλλήλους, ὅτι
Beloved, let us love one another, because
ἡ ἀγάπη ἐκ τοῦ θεοῦ ἐστιν, καὶ πᾶς ὁ
– love [2]of – [3]God [1]is, and everyone
ἀγαπῶν ἐκ τοῦ θεοῦ γεγέννηται καὶ
loving [2]of – [3]God [1]has been begotten and
γινώσκει τὸν θεόν. **8** ὁ μὴ ἀγαπῶν
knows – God. The [one] not loving
οὐκ ἔγνω τὸν θεόν, ὅτι ὁ θεὸς ἀγάπη
knew not – God, because – God [2]love
ἐστίν. **9** ἐν τούτῳ ἐφανερώθη ἡ ἀγάπη
[1]is. By this was manifested the love
τοῦ θεοῦ ἐν ἡμῖν, ὅτι τὸν υἱὸν αὐτοῦ
– of God in(to) us, because [3]the [5]Son [6]of him
τὸν μονογενῆ ἀπέσταλκεν ὁ θεὸς εἰς
– [4]only begotten [2]has sent – [1]God into
τὸν κόσμον ἵνα ζήσωμεν δι' αὐτοῦ.
the world in order that we might live through him.
10 ἐν τούτῳ ἐστὶν ἡ ἀγάπη, οὐχ ὅτι
In this is – love, not that
ἡμεῖς ἠγαπήκαμεν τὸν θεόν, ἀλλ' ὅτι
we have loved – God, but that
αὐτὸς ἠγάπησεν ἡμᾶς καὶ ἀπέστειλεν τὸν
he loved us and sent the
υἱὸν αὐτοῦ ἱλασμὸν περὶ τῶν ἁμαρτιῶν
Son of him a propitiation concerning the sins
ἡμῶν. **11** ἀγαπητοί, εἰ οὕτως ὁ θεὸς
of us. Beloved, if so – God
ἠγάπησεν ἡμᾶς, καὶ ἡμεῖς ὀφείλομεν
loved us, [2]also [1]we [3]ought
ἀλλήλους ἀγαπᾶν. **12** θεὸν οὐδεὶς πώποτε
[5]one another [4]to love. [4]God [1]no man [2]ever
τεθέαται· ἐὰν ἀγαπῶμεν ἀλλήλους, ὁ θεὸς
[3]has beheld; if we love one another, – God
ἐν ἡμῖν μένει καὶ ἡ ἀγάπη αὐτοῦ
in us remains and the love of him
τετελειωμένη ἐν ἡμῖν ἐστιν. **13** Ἐν
[2]*having been* perfected [3]in [4]us [1]is. By
τούτῳ γινώσκομεν ὅτι ἐν αὐτῷ μένομεν
this we know that in him we remain
καὶ αὐτὸς ἐν ἡμῖν, ὅτι ἐκ τοῦ πνεύματος
and he in us, because [2]of [4]the [5]Spirit
αὐτοῦ δέδωκεν ἡμῖν. **14** καὶ ἡμεῖς
[6]of him [1]he has given [3]us. And we
τεθεάμεθα καὶ μαρτυροῦμεν ὅτι ὁ πατὴρ
have beheld and bear witness that the Father
ἀπέσταλκεν τὸν υἱὸν σωτῆρα τοῦ κόσμου.
has sent the Son [as] Saviour of the world.
15 ὃς ἐὰν ὁμολογήσῃ ὅτι Ἰησοῦς ἐστιν
Whoever confesses that Jesus is
ὁ υἱὸς τοῦ θεοῦ, ὁ θεὸς ἐν αὐτῷ μένει
the Son – of God, – God in him remains
καὶ αὐτὸς ἐν τῷ θεῷ. **16** καὶ ἡμεῖς
and he in – God. And we
ἐγνώκαμεν καὶ πεπιστεύκαμεν τὴν ἀγάπην
have known and have believed the love

God, and whoever knows
God listens to us; but whoever is not from God does
not listen to us. This is how
we recognize the Spirit[h] of
truth and the spirit of falsehood.

God's Love and Ours

7 Dear friends, let us love
one another, for love
comes from God. Every-
one who loves has been
born of God and knows
God. 8 Whoever does not
love does not know God,
because God is love. 9 This
is how God showed his love
among us: He sent his one
and only Son[i] into the
world that we might live
through him. 10 This is love:
not that we loved God, but
that he loved us and sent
his Son as an atoning sacrifice for[j] our sins. 11 Dear
friends, since God so loved
us, we also ought to love
one another. 12 No one has
ever seen God; but if we
love one another, God lives
in us and his love is made
complete in us.

13 We know that we live in
him and he in us, because
he has given us of his Spirit.
14 And we have seen and
testify that the Father has
sent his Son to be the Savior of the world. 15 If anyone acknowledges that
Jesus is the Son of God,
God lives in him and he in
God. 16 And so we know
and rely on the love God
has for us.

[h]6 Or *spirit*
[i]9 Or *his only begotten Son*
[j]10 Or *as the one who would turn aside his wrath, taking away*

us.
God is love, and those
who abide in love abide in
God, and God abides in
them. 17 Love has been perfected among us in this:
that we may have boldness
on the day of judgment, because as he is, so are we in
this world. 18 There is no
fear in love, but perfect
love casts out fear; for fear
has to do with punishment,
and whoever fears has not
reached perfection in love.
19 We love[q] because he
first loved us. 20 Those who
say, "I love God," and hate
their brothers or sisters,[r]
are liars; for those who do
not love a brother or sister[s] whom they have seen,
cannot love God whom
they have not seen. 21 The
commandment we have
from him is this: those who
love God must love their
brothers and sisters[r] also.

ἣν ἔχει ὁ θεὸς ἐν ἡμῖν. Ὁ θεὸς ἀγάπη
which [2]has – [1]God in(to) us. – God [2]love

ἐστίν, καὶ ὁ μένων ἐν τῇ ἀγάπῃ ἐν
[1]is, and the remaining [one] in – love [2]in

τῷ θεῷ μένει καὶ ὁ θεὸς ἐν αὐτῷ
– [3]God [1]remains and – God [2]in [3]him

μένει. 17 Ἐν τούτῳ τετελείωται ἡ ἀγάπη
[1]remains. By this [2]has been perfected – [1]love

μεθ' ἡμῶν, ἵνα παρρησίαν ἔχωμεν ἐν
with us, in order that [2]confidence [1]we may have in

τῇ ἡμέρᾳ τῆς κρίσεως, ὅτι καθὼς ἐκεῖνός•
the day – of judgment, because as that one•

ἐστιν καὶ ἡμεῖς ἐσμεν ἐν τῷ κόσμῳ
is [3]also [1]we [2]are in – world

τούτῳ. 18 φόβος οὐκ ἔστιν ἐν τῇ ἀγάπῃ,
this. Fear is not in – love,

ἀλλ' ἡ τελεία ἀγάπη ἔξω βάλλει τὸν
but – perfect love [2]out [1]casts *the*

φόβον, ὅτι ὁ φόβος κόλασιν ἔχει, ὁ δὲ
fear, because – fear [2]punishment [1]has, and the

φοβούμενος οὐ τετελείωται ἐν τῇ ἀγάπῃ.
[one] fearing has not been perfected in – love.

19 ἡμεῖς ἀγαπῶμεν, ὅτι αὐτὸς πρῶτος
We love, because he first

ἠγάπησεν ἡμᾶς. 20 ἐάν τις εἴπῃ ὅτι
loved us. If anyone says[,] –

ἀγαπῶ τὸν θεόν, καὶ τὸν ἀδελφὸν αὐτοῦ
I love – God, and [2]the [3]brother [4]of him

μισῇ, ψεύστης ἐστίν· ὁ γὰρ μὴ ἀγαπῶν
[1]hates, [2]a liar [1]he is; for the [one] not loving

τὸν ἀδελφὸν αὐτοῦ ὃν ἑώρακεν, τὸν
the brother of him whom he has seen, –

θεὸν ὃν οὐχ ἑώρακεν οὐ δύναται ἀγαπᾶν.
[3]God [4]whom [5]he has not seen [1]*he* cannot [2]*to* love.

21 καὶ ταύτην τὴν ἐντολὴν ἔχομεν ἀπ'
And this – commandment we have from

αὐτοῦ, ἵνα ὁ ἀγαπῶν τὸν θεὸν ἀγαπᾷ
him, in order that the [one] loving – God loves

καὶ τὸν ἀδελφὸν αὐτοῦ.
also the brother of him.

God is love. Whoever
lives in love lives in God,
and God in him. 17In this
way, love is made complete
among us so that we will
have confidence on the day
of judgment, because in
this world we are like him.
18There is no fear in love.
But perfect love drives out
fear, because fear has to do
with punishment. The one
who fears is not made perfect in love.
19We love because he
first loved us. 20If anyone
says, "I love God," yet
hates his brother, he is a
liar. For anyone who does
not love his brother, whom
he has seen, cannot love
God, whom he has not
seen. 21And he has given us
this command: Whoever
loves God must also love
his brother.

Chapter 5

Faith Conquers the World

EVERYONE who be-
lieves that Jesus is the
Christ[t] has been born of
God, and everyone who
loves the parent loves the
child. 2 By this we know
that we love the children of
God, when we love God
and obey his command-
ments. 3 For the love of
God is this, that we obey
his commandments. And
his commandments are not

5 Πᾶς ὁ πιστεύων ὅτι Ἰησοῦς ἐστιν
Everyone believing that Jesus is

ὁ χριστὸς ἐκ τοῦ θεοῦ γεγέννηται, καὶ
the Christ [2]of – [3]God [1]has been begotten, and

πᾶς ὁ ἀγαπῶν τὸν γεννήσαντα ἀγαπᾷ
everyone loving the [one] begetting loves

τὸν γεγεννημένον ἐξ αὐτοῦ. 2 ἐν τούτῳ
the [one] having been begotten of him. By this

γινώσκομεν ὅτι ἀγαπῶμεν τὰ τέκνα τοῦ
we know that we love the children –

θεοῦ, ὅταν τὸν θεὸν ἀγαπῶμεν καὶ τὰς
of God, when*ever* – [2]God [1]we love and [2]the

ἐντολὰς αὐτοῦ ποιῶμεν. 3 αὕτη γάρ
[3]commandments [4]of him [1]*we* do. For this

ἐστιν ἡ ἀγάπη τοῦ θεοῦ, ἵνα τὰς ἐντολὰς
is the love – of God, *in order* that [2]the [3]commandments

αὐτοῦ τηρῶμεν· καὶ αἱ ἐντολαὶ αὐτοῦ
[4]of him [1]we keep; and the commandments of him

Chapter 5

Faith in the Son of God

EVERYONE who be-
lieves that Jesus is the
Christ is born of God, and
everyone who loves the father loves his child as well.
2This is how we know that
we love the children of
God: by loving God and
carrying out his com-
mands. 3This is love for
God: to obey his com-
mands. And his commands

[q] Other ancient authorities add *him*; others add *God*
[r] Gk *brothers*
[s] Gk *brother*
[t] Or *the Messiah*

• See ch. 2. 6, 3. 3, 5, 7, 16.

burdensome, 4 for whatever is born of God conquers the world. And this is the victory that conquers the world, our faith. 5 Who is it that conquers the world but the one who believes that Jesus is the Son of God?

Testimony concerning the Son of God

6 This is the one who came by water and blood, Jesus Christ, not with the water only but with the water and the blood. And the Spirit is the one that testifies, for the Spirit is the truth. 7 There are three that testify:[u] 8 the Spirit and the water and the blood, and these three agree. 9 If we receive human testimony, the testimony of God is greater; for this is the testimony of God that he has testified to his Son. 10 Those who believe in the Son of God have the testimony in their hearts. Those who do not believe in God[v] have made him a liar by not believing in the testimony that God has given concerning his Son. 11 And this is the testimony: God gave us eternal life, and this life is in his Son. 12 Whoever has the Son has life; whoever does not have the Son of God does not have life.

Epilogue

13 I write these things to you who believe in the

βαρεῖαι οὐκ εἰσίν, **4** ὅτι πᾶν τὸ γεγεν-
heavy are not, because everything having

νημένον ἐκ τοῦ θεοῦ νικᾷ τὸν κόσμον·
been begotten of – God overcomes the world;

καὶ αὕτη ἐστὶν ἡ νίκη ἡ νικήσασα τὸν
and this is the victory – overcoming the

κόσμον, ἡ πίστις ἡμῶν. **5** Τίς ἐστιν
world, the faith of us. ²Who ³is

[δὲ] ὁ νικῶν τὸν κόσμον εἰ μὴ ὁ
¹and the [one] overcoming the world except the

πιστεύων ὅτι Ἰησοῦς ἐστιν ὁ υἱὸς τοῦ
[one] believing that Jesus is the Son –

θεοῦ; **6** οὗτός ἐστιν ὁ ἐλθὼν δι' ὕδατος
of God? This is the [one] coming through water

καὶ αἵματος, Ἰησοῦς Χριστός· οὐκ ἐν
and blood, Jesus Christ; not by

τῷ ὕδατι μόνον, ἀλλ' ἐν τῷ ὕδατι καὶ
the water only, but by the water and

ἐν τῷ αἵματι· καὶ τὸ πνεῦμά ἐστιν τὸ
by the blood; and the Spirit is the

μαρτυροῦν, ὅτι τὸ πνεῦμά ἐστιν ἡ ἀλήθεια.
[one] bearing witness, because the Spirit is the truth.

7 ὅτι τρεῖς εἰσιν οἱ μαρτυροῦντες, **8** τὸ
Because three there are the [ones] bearing witness, the

πνεῦμα καὶ τὸ ὕδωρ καὶ τὸ αἷμα, καὶ
Spirit and the water and the blood, and

οἱ τρεῖς εἰς τὸ ἕν εἰσιν. **9** εἰ τὴν
the three ²in *the* ³one ¹are. If ³the

μαρτυρίαν τῶν ἀνθρώπων λαμβάνομεν, ἡ
²witness – ⁴of men ¹we receive, the

μαρτυρία τοῦ θεοῦ μείζων ἐστίν, ὅτι
witness – of God ²greater ¹is, because

αὕτη ἐστὶν ἡ μαρτυρία τοῦ θεοῦ, ὅτι
this is the witness – of God, because

μεμαρτύρηκεν περὶ τοῦ υἱοῦ αὐτοῦ. **10** ὁ
he has borne witness concerning the Son of him. The

πιστεύων εἰς τὸν υἱὸν τοῦ θεοῦ ἔχει
[one] believing in the Son – of God has

τὴν μαρτυρίαν ἐν αὐτῷ. ὁ μὴ πιστεύων
the witness in him. The [one] not believing

τῷ θεῷ ψεύστην πεποίηκεν αὐτόν, ὅτι
– God ³a liar ¹has made ²him, because

οὐ πεπίστευκεν εἰς τὴν μαρτυρίαν ἣν
he has not believed in the witness which

μεμαρτύρηκεν ὁ θεὸς περὶ τοῦ υἱοῦ
²has borne witness – ¹God concerning the Son

αὐτοῦ. **11** καὶ αὕτη ἐστὶν ἡ μαρτυρία,
of him. And this is the witness,

ὅτι ζωὴν αἰώνιον ἔδωκεν ὁ θεὸς ἡμῖν,
that ⁵life ⁴eternal ²gave – ¹God ³to us,

καὶ αὕτη ἡ ζωὴ ἐν τῷ υἱῷ αὐτοῦ
and this – life ²in ³the ⁴Son ⁵of him

ἐστιν. **12** ὁ ἔχων τὸν υἱὸν ἔχει τὴν
¹is. The [one] having the Son has *the*

ζωήν· ὁ μὴ ἔχων τὸν υἱὸν τοῦ θεοῦ
life; the [one] not having the Son – of God

τὴν ζωὴν οὐκ ἔχει.
the life has not.

13 Ταῦτα ἔγραψα ὑμῖν ἵνα εἰδῆτε ὅτι
These things I wrote to you in order that ye may know that

are not burdensome, 4 for everyone born of God overcomes the world. This is the victory that has overcome the world, even our faith. 5 Who is it that overcomes the world? Only he who believes that Jesus is the Son of God.

6 This is the one who came by water and blood—Jesus Christ. He did not come by water only, but by water and blood. And it is the Spirit who testifies, because the Spirit is the truth. 7 For there are three that testify: 8 the[k] Spirit, the water and the blood; and the three are in agreement. 9 We accept man's testimony, but God's testimony is greater because it is the testimony of God, which he has given about his Son. 10 Anyone who believes in the Son of God has this testimony in his heart. Anyone who does not believe God has made him out to be a liar, because he has not believed the testimony God has given about his Son. 11 And this is the testimony: God has given us eternal life, and this life is in his Son. 12 He who has the Son has life; he who does not have the Son of God does not have life.

Concluding Remarks

13 I write these things to you who believe in the

[u] A few other authorities read (with variations) 7 *There are three that testify in heaven, the Father, the Word, and the Holy Spirit, and these three are one.* 8 *And there are three that testify on earth:*
[v] Other ancient authorities read *in the Son*

[k] 7,8 Late manuscripts of the Vulgate *testify in heaven: the Father, the Word and the Holy Spirit, and these three are one.* 8 *And there are three that testify on earth: the* (not found in any Greek manuscript before the sixteenth century)

name of the Son of God, so
that you may know that
you have eternal life.
14 And this is the bold-
ness we have in him, that if
we ask anything according
to his will, he hears us.
15 And if we know that he
hears us in whatever we
ask, we know that we have
obtained the requests made
of him. 16 If you see your
brother or sister[w] committing what is not a mortal
sin, you will ask, and God[x]
will give life to such a
one—to those whose sin is
not mortal. There is sin that
is mortal; I do not say that
you should pray about that.
17 All wrongdoing is sin, but
there is sin that is not mortal.
18 We know that those
who are born of God do not
sin, but the one who was
born of God protects them,
and the evil one does not
touch them. 19 We know
that we are God's children,
and that the whole world
lies under the power of the
evil one. 20 And we know
that the Son of God has
come and has given us un-
derstanding so that we may
know him who is true;[y]
and we are in him who is
true, in his Son Jesus
Christ. He is the true God
and eternal life.
21 Little children, keep
yourselves from idols.[z]

ζωὴν ἔχετε αἰώνιον, τοῖς πιστεύουσιν
[2]life [1]ye have [3]eternal, to the [ones] believing

εἰς τὸ ὄνομα τοῦ υἱοῦ τοῦ θεοῦ. 14 Καὶ
in the name of the Son – of God. And

αὕτη ἐστὶν ἡ παρρησία ἣν ἔχομεν πρὸς
this is the confidence which we have toward

αὐτόν, ὅτι ἐάν τι αἰτώμεθα κατὰ τὸ
him, that if [2]anything [1]we ask according to the

θέλημα αὐτοῦ ἀκούει ἡμῶν. 15 καὶ
will of him he hears us. And

ἐὰν οἴδαμεν ὅτι ἀκούει ἡμῶν ὃ ἐὰν
if we know that he hears us whatever

αἰτώμεθα, οἴδαμεν ὅτι ἔχομεν τὰ αἰτήματα
we ask, we know that we have the requests

ἃ ᾐτήκαμεν ἀπ' αὐτοῦ. 16 Ἐάν τις
which we have asked from him. If anyone

ἴδῃ τὸν ἀδελφὸν αὐτοῦ ἁμαρτάνοντα
sees the brother of him sinning

ἁμαρτίαν μὴ πρὸς θάνατον, αἰτήσει, καὶ
a sin not unto death, he shall ask, and

δώσει αὐτῷ ζωήν, τοῖς ἁμαρτάνουσιν
he will give to him life, to the [ones] sinning

μὴ πρὸς θάνατον. ἔστιν ἁμαρτία πρὸς
not unto death. There is a sin unto

θάνατον· οὐ περὶ ἐκείνης λέγω ἵνα
death; not concerning that do I say *in order that*

ἐρωτήσῃ. 17 πᾶσα ἀδικία ἁμαρτία ἐστίν,
he should inquire. All iniquity [2]sin [1]is,

καὶ ἔστιν ἁμαρτία οὐ πρὸς θάνατον.
and there is a sin not unto death.

18 Οἴδαμεν ὅτι πᾶς ὁ γεγεννημένος ἐκ
We know that everyone having been begotten of

τοῦ θεοῦ οὐχ ἁμαρτάνει, ἀλλ' ὁ γεννηθεὶς
– God sins not, but the [one] begotten

ἐκ τοῦ θεοῦ τηρεῖ αὐτόν, καὶ ὁ πονηρὸς
of – God keeps him, and the evil one

οὐχ ἅπτεται αὐτοῦ. 19 οἴδαμεν ὅτι ἐκ
does not touch him. We know that of

τοῦ θεοῦ ἐσμεν, καὶ ὁ κόσμος ὅλος ἐν
– God we are, and the [2]world [1]whole in

τῷ πονηρῷ κεῖται. 20 οἴδαμεν δὲ ὅτι
the evil one lies. [2]we know [1]And that

ὁ υἱὸς τοῦ θεοῦ ἥκει, καὶ δέδωκεν
the Son – of God is come, and has given

ἡμῖν διάνοιαν ἵνα γινώσκωμεν τὸν
to us an understanding in order that we might know the

ἀληθινόν· καὶ ἐσμὲν ἐν τῷ ἀληθινῷ,
true [one]; and we are in the true [one],

ἐν τῷ υἱῷ αὐτοῦ Ἰησοῦ Χριστῷ. οὗτός
in the Son of him Jesus Christ. This

ἐστιν ὁ ἀληθινὸς θεὸς καὶ ζωὴ αἰώνιος.
is the true God and life eternal.

21 Τεκνία, φυλάξατε ἑαυτὰ ἀπὸ τῶν
Little children, guard yourselves from *the*

εἰδώλων.
idols.

name of the Son of God so
that you may know that
you have eternal life. 14 This
is the confidence we have
in approaching God: that if
we ask anything according
to his will, he hears us.
15 And if we know that he
hears us—whatever we ask
—we know that we have
what we asked of him.
16 If anyone sees his
brother commit a sin that
does not lead to death, he
should pray and God will
give him life. I refer to
those whose sin does not
lead to death. There is a sin
that leads to death. I am not
saying that he should pray
about that. 17 All wrongdoing is sin, and there is sin
that does not lead to death.
18 We know that anyone
born of God does not con-
tinue to sin; the one who
was born of God keeps him
safe, and the evil one cannot harm him. 19 We know
that we are children of
God, and that the whole
world is under the control
of the evil one. 20 We know
also that the Son of God has
come and has given us un-
derstanding, so that we
may know him who is true.
And we are in him who is
true—even in his Son Jesus
Christ. He is the true God
and eternal life.
21 Dear children, keep
yourselves from idols.

[w] Gk *your brother*
[x] Gk *he*
[y] Other ancient authorities read *know the true God*
[z] Other ancient authorities add *Amen*

The Second Letter of
John

Salutation

THE elder to the elect lady and her children, whom I love in the truth, and not only I but also all who know the truth, 2 because of the truth that abides in us and will be with us forever:

3 Grace, mercy, and peace will be with us from God the Father and from[a] Jesus Christ, the Father's Son, in truth and love.

Truth and Love

4 I was overjoyed to find some of your children walking in the truth, just as we have been commanded by the Father. 5 But now, dear lady, I ask you, not as though I were writing you a new commandment, but one we have had from the beginning, let us love one another. 6 And this is love, that we walk according to his commandments; this is the commandment just as you have heard it from the beginning—you must walk in it.

7 Many deceivers have gone out into the world, those who do not confess that Jesus Christ has come in the flesh; any such person is the deceiver and the antichrist! 8 Be on your guard, so that you do not lose what we[b] have worked for, but may receive a full reward. 9 Everyone who does not abide in the teaching of Christ, but goes beyond it, does not have God; whoever abides in the teaching has

[a] Other ancient authorities add *the Lord*

[b] Other ancient authorities read *you*

ΙΩΑΝΝΟΥ Β
Of John 2

1 Ὁ πρεσβύτερος ἐκλεκτῇ κυρίᾳ καὶ
The elder to [the] chosen lady and

τοῖς τέκνοις αὐτῆς, οὓς ἐγὼ ἀγαπῶ ἐν
to the children of her, whom I love in

ἀληθείᾳ, καὶ οὐκ ἐγὼ μόνος ἀλλὰ καὶ
truth, and not I alone but also

πάντες οἱ ἐγνωκότες τὴν ἀλήθειαν, 2 διὰ
all the [ones] having known the truth, because of

τὴν ἀλήθειαν τὴν μένουσαν ἐν ἡμῖν,
the truth – remaining among us,

καὶ μεθ' ἡμῶν ἔσται εἰς τὸν αἰῶνα.
and with us will be unto the age.

3 ἔσται μεθ' ἡμῶν χάρις ἔλεος εἰρήνη
[4]will be [5]with [6]us [1]Grace[,] [2]mercy[,] [3]peace

παρὰ θεοῦ πατρός, καὶ παρὰ Ἰησοῦ
from God [the] Father, and from Jesus

Χριστοῦ τοῦ υἱοῦ τοῦ πατρός, ἐν ἀληθείᾳ
Christ the Son of the Father, in truth

καὶ ἀγάπῃ.
and love.

4 Ἐχάρην λίαν ὅτι εὕρηκα ἐκ τῶν
I rejoiced greatly because I have found [some] of the

τέκνων σου περιπατοῦντας ἐν ἀληθείᾳ,
children of thee walking in truth,

καθὼς ἐντολὴν ἐλάβομεν παρὰ τοῦ πατρός.
as commandment we received from the Father.

5 καὶ νῦν ἐρωτῶ σε, κυρία, οὐχ ὡς
And now I request thee, lady, not as

ἐντολὴν γράφων σοι καινήν, ἀλλὰ ἣν
[3]commandment [1]writing [4]to thee [2]a new, but which

εἴχομεν ἀπ' ἀρχῆς, ἵνα ἀγαπῶμεν
we had from [the] beginning, *in order that* we should love

ἀλλήλους. 6 καὶ αὕτη ἐστὶν ἡ ἀγάπη,
one another. And this is – love,

ἵνα περιπατῶμεν κατὰ τὰς ἐντολὰς
in order that we should walk according to the commandments

αὐτοῦ· αὕτη ἡ ἐντολή ἐστιν, καθὼς
of him; this [2]the [3]commandment [1]is, as

ἠκούσατε ἀπ' ἀρχῆς, ἵνα ἐν αὐτῇ
ye heard from [the] beginning, *in order that* [2]in [3]it

περιπατῆτε. 7 ὅτι πολλοὶ πλάνοι ἐξῆλθον
[1]ye should walk. Because many deceivers went forth

εἰς τὸν κόσμον, οἱ μὴ ὁμολογοῦντες
into the world, the [ones] not confessing

Ἰησοῦν Χριστὸν ἐρχόμενον ἐν σαρκί·
Jesus Christ coming in [the] flesh;

οὗτός ἐστιν ὁ πλάνος καὶ ὁ ἀντίχριστος.
this is the deceiver and the antichrist.

8 βλέπετε ἑαυτούς, ἵνα μὴ ἀπολέσητε
See yourselves, lest ye lose

ἃ ἠργασάμεθα, ἀλλὰ μισθὸν πλήρη
[the] things which we wrought, but [3]reward [2]a full

ἀπολάβητε. 9 πᾶς ὁ προάγων καὶ μὴ
[1]ye may receive. Everyone going forward and not

μένων ἐν τῇ διδαχῇ τοῦ Χριστοῦ θεὸν
remaining in the teaching – of Christ [3]God

οὐκ ἔχει· ὁ μένων ἐν τῇ διδαχῇ, οὗτος
[2]not [1]has; the [one] remaining in the teaching, this one

2 John

THE elder,

To the chosen lady and her children, whom I love in the truth—and not I only, but also all who know the truth— 2 because of the truth, which lives in us and will be with us forever:

3 Grace, mercy and peace from God the Father and from Jesus Christ, the Father's Son, will be with us in truth and love.

4 It has given me great joy to find some of your children walking in the truth, just as the Father commanded us. 5 And now, dear lady, I am not writing you a new command but one we have had from the beginning. I ask that we love one another. 6 And this is love: that we walk in obedience to his commands. As you have heard from the beginning, his command is that you walk in love.

7 Many deceivers, who do not acknowledge Jesus Christ as coming in the flesh, have gone out into the world. Any such person is the deceiver and the antichrist. 8 Watch out that you do not lose what you have worked for, but that you may be rewarded fully. 9 Anyone who runs ahead and does not continue in the teaching of Christ does not have God; whoever continues in the teaching

both the Father and the
Son. [10]Do not receive into
the house or welcome any-
one who comes to you and
does not bring this teaching; [11]for to welcome is to
participate in the evil deeds
of such a person.

Final Greetings

12 Although I have
much to write to you, I
would rather not use paper
and ink; instead I hope to
come to you and talk with
you face to face, so that our
joy may be complete.
13 The children of your
elect sister send you their
greetings.[c]

καὶ τὸν πατέρα καὶ τὸν υἱὸν ἔχει.
[2]both [3]the [4]Father [5]and [6]the [7]Son [1]has.

10 εἴ τις ἔρχεται πρὸς ὑμᾶς καὶ ταύτην
If anyone comes to you and this

τὴν διδαχὴν οὐ φέρει, μὴ λαμβάνετε
– teaching brings not, do not ye receive

αὐτὸν εἰς οἰκίαν, καὶ χαίρειν αὐτῷ μὴ
him into [your] house, and [4]to rejoice [3]him [2]not

λέγετε· 11 ὁ λέγων γὰρ αὐτῷ χαίρειν
[1]tell ye*; [2]the [one] [3]telling [1]for him to rejoice

κοινωνεῖ τοῖς ἔργοις αὐτοῦ τοῖς πονηροῖς.
shares in the [3]works [3]of him – [1]evil.

12 Πολλὰ ἔχων ὑμῖν γράφειν οὐκ
[2]Many things [1]having [4]to you [3]to write [6]not

ἐβουλήθην διὰ χάρτου καὶ μέλανος, ἀλλὰ
[5]I purpose by means of paper and ink, but

ἐλπίζω γενέσθαι πρὸς ὑμᾶς καὶ στόμα
I am hoping to be with you and [2]mouth

πρὸς στόμα λαλῆσαι, ἵνα ἡ χαρὰ ἡμῶν
[3]to [4]mouth [1]to speak, in order that the joy of us

πεπληρωμένη ᾖ. 13 Ἀσπάζεταί σε τὰ
having been fulfilled may be. [7]greets [8]thee [1]The

τέκνα τῆς ἀδελφῆς σου τῆς ἐκλεκτῆς.
[2]children [3]of the [5]sister [6]of thee – [4]chosen.

has both the Father and the
Son. [10]If anyone comes to
you and does not bring this
teaching, do not take him
into your house or wel-
come him. [11]Anyone who
welcomes him shares in his
wicked work.
[12]I have much to write to
you, but I do not want to
use paper and ink. Instead,
I hope to visit you and talk
with you face to face, so
that our joy may be com-
plete.

[13]The children of your
chosen sister send their
greetings.

The Third Letter of

John

Salutation

THE elder to the be-
loved Gaius, whom I
love in truth.

Gaius Commended for His Hospitality

2 Beloved, I pray that
all may go well with you
and that you may be in
good health, just as it is
well with your soul. [3]I was
overjoyed when some of
the friends[a] arrived and
testified to your faithfulness to the truth, namely
how you walk in the truth.
[4]I have no greater joy than
this, to hear that my children are walking in the
truth.
5 Beloved, you do faith-
fully whatever you do for
the friends,[a] even though
they are strangers to you;
[6]they have testified to your

ΙΩΑΝΝΟΥ Γ

Of John 3

1 Ὁ πρεσβύτερος Γαΐῳ τῷ ἀγαπητῷ,
The elder to Gaius the beloved,

ὃν ἐγὼ ἀγαπῶ ἐν ἀληθείᾳ.
whom I love in truth.

2 Ἀγαπητέ, περὶ πάντων εὔχομαί σε
Beloved, concerning all things I pray thee =that

εὐοδοῦσθαι καὶ ὑγιαίνειν, καθὼς εὐοδοῦταί
to prosper thou mayest prosper . . . and to be in health, as [4]prospers

σου ἡ ψυχή. 3 ἐχάρην γὰρ λίαν ἐρχομένων
[3]of thee [1]the [2]soul. For I rejoiced greatly coming =when [some]

ἀδελφῶν καὶ μαρτυρούντων σου τῇ
brothers and bearing witness[a] of thee in the
brothers came and bore witness

ἀληθείᾳ, καθὼς σὺ ἐν ἀληθείᾳ περιπατεῖς.
truth, as thou in truth walkest.

4 μειζοτέραν τούτων οὐκ ἔχω χαράν, ἵνα
[3]greater [4][than] [5]these things [1]I have no [2]joy, *in order* that

ἀκούω τὰ ἐμὰ τέκνα ἐν τῇ ἀληθείᾳ
I hear – my children [2]in [3]the [4]truth

περιπατοῦντα. 5 Ἀγαπητέ, πιστὸν ποιεῖς
[1]walking. Beloved, faithfully thou doest

ὃ ἐὰν ἐργάσῃ εἰς τοὺς ἀδελφοὺς καὶ
whatever thou workest for the brothers and

τοῦτο ξένους, 6 οἳ ἐμαρτύρησάν σου τῇ
this strangers, who bore witness of thee –

3 John

THE elder,
To my dear friend Ga-
ius, whom I love in the
truth.

[2]Dear friend, I pray that
you may enjoy good health
and that all may go well
with you, even as your soul
is getting along well. [3]It
gave me great joy to have
some brothers come and
tell about your faithfulness
to the truth and how you
continue to walk in the
truth. [4]I have no greater joy
than to hear that my children are walking in the
truth.
[5]Dear friend, you are
faithful in what you are doing for the brothers, even
though they are strangers
to you. [6]They have told the

[c] Other ancient authorities add *Amen*

[a] Gk *brothers*

* That is, "do not greet him."

love before the church.
You will do well to send
them on in a manner wor-
thy of God; 7 for they began
their journey for the sake of
Christ,[b] accepting no support from non-believers.[c]
8 Therefore we ought to
support such people, so
that we may become co-
workers with the truth.

Diotrephes and Demetrius

9 I have written some-
thing to the church; but Diotrephes, who likes to put
himself first, does not acknowledge our authority.
10 So if I come, I will call
attention to what he is doing in spreading false
charges against us. And not
content with those charges,
he refuses to welcome the
friends,[a] and even pre-
vents those who want to do
so and expels them from
the church.
11 Beloved, do not imi-
tate what is evil but imitate
what is good. Whoever
does good is from God;
whoever does evil has not
seen God. 12 Everyone has
testified favorably about
Demetrius, and so has the
truth itself. We also testify
for him,[d] and you know
that our testimony is true.

Final Greetings

13 I have much to write
to you, but I would rather
not write with pen and ink;
14 instead I hope to see you
soon, and we will talk together face to face.
15 Peace to you. The
friends send you their
greetings. Greet the friends
there, each by name.

[b] Gk *for the sake of the name*
[c] Gk *the Gentiles*
[d] Gk lacks *for him*

ἀγάπῃ ἐνώπιον ἐκκλησίας, οὓς καλῶς
in love before [the] church, whom well
ποιήσεις προπέμψας ἀξίως τοῦ θεοῦ·
thou wilt do sending forward worthily – of God;
7 ὑπὲρ γὰρ τοῦ ὀνόματος ἐξῆλθαν μηδὲν
for on behalf of the name they went forth [2]nothing
λαμβάνοντες ἀπὸ τῶν ἐθνικῶν. **8** ἡμεῖς
[1]taking from the Gentiles. We
οὖν ὀφείλομεν ὑπολαμβάνειν τοὺς τοιούτους,
therefore ought to entertain – such men,
ἵνα συνεργοὶ γινώμεθα τῇ ἀληθείᾳ.
in order that [2]co-workers [1]we may become in the truth.

9 Ἔγραψά τι τῇ ἐκκλησίᾳ· ἀλλ' ὁ
I wrote something to the church; but the [one]
φιλοπρωτεύων αὐτῶν Διοτρέφης οὐκ
loving to be first of them Diotrephes not
ἐπιδέχεται ἡμᾶς. **10** διὰ τοῦτο, ἐὰν
receives us. Therefore, if
ἔλθω, ὑπομνήσω αὐτοῦ τὰ ἔργα ἃ ποιεῖ
I come, I will remember [3]of him [1]the [2]works which he does
λόγοις πονηροῖς φλυαρῶν ἡμᾶς, καὶ μὴ
[4]words [3]with evil [1]prating against [2]us, and not
ἀρκούμενος ἐπὶ τούτοις οὔτε αὐτὸς
being satisfied on(with) these [2]neither [1]he
ἐπιδέχεται τοὺς ἀδελφοὺς καὶ τοὺς
[3]receives the brothers and the
βουλομένους κωλύει καὶ ἐκ τῆς ἐκκλησίας
[ones] purposing he prevents and [2]out of [3]the [4]church
ἐκβάλλει.
[1]puts *out*.

11 Ἀγαπητέ, μὴ μιμοῦ τὸ κακὸν ἀλλὰ
Beloved, imitate not the bad but
τὸ ἀγαθόν. ὁ ἀγαθοποιῶν ἐκ τοῦ θεοῦ
the good. The [one] doing good [2]of – [3]God
ἐστιν· ὁ κακοποιῶν οὐχ ἑώρακεν τὸν
[1]is; the [one] doing ill has not seen –
θεόν. **12** Δημητρίῳ μεμαρτύρηται ὑπὸ
God. To Demetrius witness has been borne by
πάντων καὶ ὑπὸ αὐτῆς τῆς ἀληθείας·
all and by [3][it]self [1]the [2]truth;
καὶ ἡμεῖς δὲ μαρτυροῦμεν, καὶ οἶδας
[3]also [2]we [1]and bear witness, and thou knowest
ὅτι ἡ μαρτυρία ἡμῶν ἀληθής ἐστιν.
that the witness of us [2]true [1]is.
13 Πολλὰ εἶχον γράψαι σοι, ἀλλ' οὐ
[2]Many things [1]I had to write to thee, but not
θέλω διὰ μέλανος καὶ καλάμου σοι
I wish [3]by means of [4]ink [5]and [6]pen [2]to thee
γράφειν· **14** ἐλπίζω δὲ εὐθέως σε ἰδεῖν,
[1]to write; but I am hoping [3]immediately [2]thee [1]to see,
καὶ στόμα πρὸς στόμα λαλήσομεν.
and [2]mouth [3]to [4]mouth [1]we will speak.
15 Εἰρήνη σοι. ἀσπάζονταί σε οἱ φίλοι.
Peace to thee. [3]greet [4]thee [1]The [2]friends.
ἀσπάζου τοὺς φίλους κατ' ὄνομα.
Greet thou the friends by name.

church about your love.
You will do well to send
them on their way in a manner worthy of God. 7 It was
for the sake of the Name
that they went out, receiving no help from the pa-
gans. 8 We ought therefore
to show hospitality to such
men so that we may work
together for the truth.
9 I wrote to the church,
but Diotrephes, who loves
to be first, will have nothing to do with us. 10 So if I
come, I will call attention
to what he is doing, gossip-
ing maliciously about us.
Not satisfied with that, he
refuses to welcome the
brothers. He also stops
those who want to do so
and puts them out of the
church.
11 Dear friend, do not imitate what is evil but what is
good. Anyone who does
what is good is from God.
Anyone who does what is
evil has not seen God.
12 Demetrius is well spoken
of by everyone—and even
by the truth itself. We also
speak well of him, and you
know that our testimony is
true.
13 I have much to write
you, but I do not want to do
so with pen and ink. 14 I
hope to see you soon, and
we will talk face to face.

Peace to you. The friends
here send their greetings.
Greet the friends there by
name.

The Letter of

Jude

Salutation

JUDE,[a] a servant[b] of
Jesus Christ and broth-
er of James,
To those who are called,
who are beloved[c] in[d] God
the Father and kept safe
for[d] Jesus Christ:
2 May mercy, peace,
and love be yours in abundance.

Occasion of the Letter

3 Beloved, while eager-
ly preparing to write to you
about the salvation we
share, I find it necessary to
write and appeal to you to
contend for the faith that
was once for all entrusted
to the saints. 4 For certain
intruders have stolen in
among you, people who
long ago were designated
for this condemnation as
ungodly, who pervert the
grace of our God into licentiousness and deny our
only Master and Lord,
Jesus Christ.[e]

Judgment on False Teachers

5 Now I desire to re-
mind you, though you are
fully informed, that the
Lord, who once for all
saved[f] a people out of the
land of Egypt, afterward
destroyed those who did
not believe. 6 And the angels who did not keep their
own position, but left their
proper dwelling, he has
kept in eternal chains in
deepest darkness for the
judgment of the great Day.
7 Likewise, Sodom and Go-
morrah and the surround-
ing cities, which, in the
same manner as they, in-
dulged in sexual immorality
and pursued unnatural
lust,[g] serve as an example
by undergoing a punish-
ment of eternal fire.
8 Yet in the same way
these dreamers also defile
the flesh, reject authority,
and slander the glorious
ones.[h] 9 But when the arch-

[a] Gk *Judas*
[b] Gk *slave*
[c] Other ancient authorities read *sanctified*
[d] Or *by*
[e] Or *the only Master and our Lord Jesus Christ*
[f] Other ancient authorities read *though you were once for all fully informed, that Jesus* (or *Joshua*) *who saved*
[g] Gk *went after other flesh*
[h] Or *angels*; Gk *glories*

ΙΟΥΔΑ

Of Jude

1 Ἰούδας Ἰησοῦ Χριστοῦ δοῦλος, ἀδελφὸς
Jude of Jesus Christ a slave, [2]brother
δὲ Ἰακώβου, τοῖς ἐν θεῷ πατρὶ
[1]and of James, [1]to the [ones] [4]by [5]God [6][the] Father
ἠγαπημένοις καὶ Ἰησοῦ Χριστῷ
[3]having been loved [7]and [9]for Jesus [10]Christ
τετηρημένοις κλητοῖς. 2 ἔλεος ὑμῖν καὶ
[8]having been kept [2]called. Mercy to you and
εἰρήνη καὶ ἀγάπη πληθυνθείη.
peace and love may *it* be multiplied.
3 Ἀγαπητοί, πᾶσαν σπουδὴν ποιούμενος
Beloved, [2]all [3]haste [1]making
γράφειν ὑμῖν περὶ τῆς κοινῆς ἡμῶν
to write to you concerning the common [2]of us
σωτηρίας, ἀνάγκην ἔσχον γράψαι ὑμῖν
[1]salvation, necessity I had to write to you
παρακαλῶν ἐπαγωνίζεσθαι τῇ ἅπαξ
exhorting to contend for [1]the [3]once
παραδοθείσῃ τοῖς ἁγίοις πίστει. 4 παρεισε-
[4]delivered [5]to the [6]saints [2]faith. [3]crept
δύησαν γάρ τινες ἄνθρωποι, οἱ πάλαι
in For [1]certain [2]men, the [ones] of old
προγεγραμμένοι εἰς τοῦτο τὸ κρίμα,
having been previously written for this – judgment,
ἀσεβεῖς, τὴν τοῦ θεοῦ ἡμῶν χάριτα
impious men, [2]the [4]of the [5]God [6]of us [3]grace
μετατιθέντες εἰς ἀσέλγειαν καὶ τὸν μόνον
[1]making [7]a pretext for wantonness and [2]the [3]only
δεσπότην καὶ κύριον ἡμῶν Ἰησοῦν Χριστὸν
[4]Master [5]and [6]Lord [7]of us [8]Jesus [9]Christ
ἀρνούμενοι. 5 Ὑπομνῆσαι δὲ ὑμᾶς βούλομαι,
[1]denying. But [2]to remind [3]you [1]I purpose,
εἰδότας ἅπαξ πάντα, ὅτι κύριος λαὸν
[2]knowing [1]once all things, that [the] Lord [2][the] people
ἐκ γῆς Αἰγύπτου σώσας τὸ δεύτερον
[3]out of [4][the] land [5]of Egypt [1]having saved in the second place
τοὺς μὴ πιστεύσαντας ἀπώλεσεν, 6 ἀγγέλους
[2]the [ones] [3]not [4]believing [1]destroyed, [2]angels
τε τοὺς μὴ τηρήσαντας τὴν ἑαυτῶν
[1]and – not having kept the [2]of themselves
ἀρχὴν ἀλλὰ ἀπολιπόντας τὸ ἴδιον
[1]rule but having deserted the(ir) own
οἰκητήριον εἰς κρίσιν μεγάλης ἡμέρας
habitation [6]for [7][the] judgment [8]of [the] great [9]day
δεσμοῖς ἀϊδίοις ὑπὸ ζόφον τετήρηκεν·
[3]bonds [2]in everlasting [4]under [5]gloom [1]he has kept;
7 ὡς Σόδομα καὶ Γόμορρα καὶ αἱ περὶ
as Sodom and Gomorra and [1]the [3]round
αὐτὰς πόλεις, τὸν ὅμοιον τρόπον τούτοις
[4]them [2]cities, in the like manner to these
ἐκπορνεύσασαι καὶ ἀπελθοῦσαι ὀπίσω σαρκὸς
committing fornication and going away after [2]flesh
ἑτέρας, πρόκεινται δεῖγμα πυρὸς αἰωνίου
[1]different, are set forth an example [4]fire [3]of eternal
δίκην ὑπέχουσαι. 8 Ὁμοίως μέντοι καὶ
[2]vengeance [1]undergoing. Likewise indeed also
οὗτοι ἐνυπνιαζόμενοι σάρκα μὲν μιαίνουσιν,
these dreaming [ones] [3]flesh [1]on one hand [2]defile,
κυριότητα δὲ ἀθετοῦσιν, δόξας δὲ
[3]lordship [1]on the other [2]despise, and [2]glories

Jude

JUDE, a servant of Jesus
Christ and a brother of
James,
To those who have been
called, who are loved by
God the Father and kept
by[a] Jesus Christ:
2 Mercy, peace and love
be yours in abundance.

The Sin and Doom of Godless Men

3 Dear friends, although I
was very eager to write to
you about the salvation we
share, I felt I had to write
and urge you to contend for
the faith that was once for
all entrusted to the saints.
4 For certain men whose
condemnation was written
about[b] long ago have secretly slipped in among
you. They are godless men,
who change the grace of
our God into a license for
immorality and deny Jesus
Christ our only Sovereign
and Lord.
5 Though you already
know all this, I want to remind you that the Lord[c]
delivered his people out of
Egypt, but later destroyed
those who did not believe.
6 And the angels who did
not keep their positions of
authority but abandoned
their own home—these he
has kept in darkness,
bound with everlasting
chains for judgment on the
great Day. 7 In a similar
way, Sodom and Gomorrah
and the surrounding towns
gave themselves up to sexual immorality and perversion. They serve as an example of those who suffer
the punishment of eternal
fire.
8 In the very same way,
these dreamers pollute
their own bodies, reject authority and slander celestial

[a] 1 Or *for*; or *in*
[b] 4 Or *men who were marked out for condemnation*
[c] 5 Some early manuscripts *Jesus*

angel Michael contended
with the devil and disputed
about the body of Moses,
he did not dare to bring a
condemnation of slander[i]
against him, but said, "The
Lord rebuke you!" 10But
these people slander whatever they do not under-
stand, and they are de-
stroyed by those things
that, like irrational animals,
they know by instinct.
11Woe to them! For they go
the way of Cain, and abandon themselves to Ba-
laam's error for the sake of
gain, and perish in Korah's
rebellion. 12These are
blemishes[j] on your love-
feasts, while they feast
with you without fear,
feeding themselves.[k] They
are waterless clouds car-
ried along by the winds; autumn trees without fruit,
twice dead, uprooted;
13wild waves of the sea,
casting up the foam of their
own shame; wandering
stars, for whom the deepest
darkness has been reserved
forever.
14 It was also about
these that Enoch, in the
seventh generation from
Adam, prophesied, saying,
"See, the Lord is coming[l]
with ten thousands of his
holy ones, 15to execute
judgment on all, and to convict everyone of all the
deeds of ungodliness that
they have committed in
such an ungodly way, and
of all the harsh things that
ungodly sinners have spo-
ken against him." 16These
are grumblers and malcon-
tents; they indulge their
own lusts; they are bom-
bastic in speech, flattering
people to their own advantage.

βλασφημοῦσιν. 9 Ὁ δὲ Μιχαὴλ ὁ ἀρχάγ-
[1]rail at. – But Michael the arch-

γελος, ὅτε τῷ διαβόλῳ διακρινόμενος
angel, when [2]with the [3]devil [1]contending

διελέγετο περὶ τοῦ Μωϋσέως σώματος,
he argued about [1]the [3]of Moses [2]body,

οὐκ ἐτόλμησεν κρίσιν ἐπενεγκεῖν βλασφημίας,
durst not [2]a judgment [1]*to* bring *on* of railing,

ἀλλὰ εἶπεν· ἐπιτιμήσαι σοι κύριος. 10 οὗτοι
but said: [2]rebuke [3]thee [1][The] Lord. these men

δὲ ὅσα μὲν οὐκ οἴδασιν βλασφημοῦσιν,
But what things on one hand they know not they rail at,

ὅσα δὲ φυσικῶς ὡς τὰ ἄλογα ζῷα
what things on the other [2]naturally [3]as [4]the [5]without reason [6]animals

ἐπίστανται, ἐν τούτοις φθείρονται. 11 οὐαὶ
[1]they understand, by these they are corrupted. Woe

αὐτοῖς, ὅτι τῇ ὁδῷ τοῦ Κάϊν ἐπορεύθησαν,
to them, because in the way – of Cain they went,

καὶ τῇ πλάνῃ τοῦ Βαλαὰμ μισθοῦ
and [2]to the [3]error – [4]of Balaam [5]of(for) reward

ἐξεχύθησαν, καὶ τῇ ἀντιλογίᾳ τοῦ Κόρε
[1]gave themselves up, and [2]in the [3]dispute – [4]of Korah

ἀπώλοντο. 12 Οὗτοί εἰσιν οἱ ἐν ταῖς
[1]perished. These men are [1]the [3]in [4]the

ἀγάπαις ὑμῶν σπιλάδες συνευωχούμενοι
[5]love feasts [6]of you [2]rocks feasting together

ἀφόβως, ἑαυτοὺς ποιμαίνοντες, νεφέλαι
without fear, [2]themselves [1]feeding, [2]clouds

ἄνυδροι ὑπὸ ἀνέμων παραφερόμεναι, δένδρα
[1]waterless [4]by [5]winds [3]*being* carried away, [2]trees

φθινοπωρινὰ ἄκαρπα δὶς ἀποθανόντα
[1]autumn without fruit twice dying

ἐκριζωθέντα, 13 κύματα ἄγρια θαλάσσης
having been uprooted, [2]waves [1]fierce [3]of [the] sea

ἐπαφρίζοντα τὰς ἑαυτῶν αἰσχύνας, ἀστέρες
[4]foaming up [5]the [7]of themselves [6]shames, [2]stars

πλανῆται, οἷς ὁ ζόφος τοῦ σκότους
[1]wandering, for whom the gloom – of darkness

εἰς αἰῶνα τετήρηται. 14 Ἐπροφήτευσεν
unto [the] age has been kept. [7]prophesied

δὲ καὶ τούτοις ἕβδομος ἀπὸ Ἀδὰμ
[1]And [3]also [8]to these men [4][the] seventh [5]from [6]Adam

Ἑνὼχ λέγων· ἰδοὺ ἦλθεν κύριος ἐν
[2]Enoch saying: Behold came [the] Lord with

ἁγίαις μυριάσιν αὐτοῦ, 15 ποιῆσαι κρίσιν
saints ten thousands of him, to do judgment

κατὰ πάντων καὶ ἐλέγξαι πάντας τοὺς
against all men and to rebuke all the

ἀσεβεῖς περὶ πάντων τῶν ἔργων ἀσεβείας
impious concerning all the works of impiety

αὐτῶν ὧν ἠσέβησαν καὶ περὶ πάντων
of them which they impiously did and concerning all

τῶν σκληρῶν ὧν ἐλάλησαν κατ' αὐτοῦ
the hard things which [3]spoke [4]against [5]him

ἁμαρτωλοὶ ἀσεβεῖς. 16 Οὗτοί εἰσιν γογ-
[2]sinners [1]impious. These men are [1]mur-

γυσταί μεμψίμοιροι, κατὰ τὰς ἐπιθυμίας
murers [1]querulous, [2]according to [3]the [4]lusts

αὐτῶν πορευόμενοι, καὶ τὸ στόμα αὐτῶν
[5]of them [1]going, and the mouth of them

λαλεῖ ὑπέρογκα, θαυμάζοντες πρόσωπα
speaks arrogant things, admiring faces

beings. 9But even the archangel Michael, when he
was disputing with the devil about the body of Moses,
did not dare to bring a slanderous accusation against
him, but said, "The Lord
rebuke you!" 10Yet these
men speak abusively
against whatever they do
not understand; and what
things they do understand
by instinct, like unreason-
ing animals—these are the
very things that destroy
them.
11Woe to them! They
have taken the way of Cain;
they have rushed for profit
into Balaam's error; they
have been destroyed in Korah's rebellion.
12These men are blemish-
es at your love feasts, eating with you without the
slightest qualm—shep-
herds who feed only them-
selves. They are clouds
without rain, blown along
by the wind; autumn trees,
without fruit and uprooted
—twice dead. 13They are
wild waves of the sea,
foaming up their shame;
wandering stars, for whom
blackest darkness has been
reserved forever.
14Enoch, the seventh
from Adam, prophesied
about these men: "See, the
Lord is coming with thou-
sands upon thousands of
his holy ones 15to judge everyone, and to convict all
the ungodly of all the ungodly acts they have done
in the ungodly way, and of
all the harsh words ungodly
sinners have spoken
against him." 16These men
are grumblers and fault-
finders; they follow their
own evil desires; they boast
about themselves and flat-

[i] Or *condemnation for blasphemy*
[j] Or *reefs*
[k] Or *without fear. They are shepherds who care only for themselves*
[l] Gk *came*

Warnings and Exhortations

17 But you, beloved,
must remember the predic-
tions of the apostles of our
Lord Jesus Christ; 18 for
they said to you, "In the
last time there will be scoffers, indulging their own ungodly lusts." 19 It is these
worldly people, devoid of
the Spirit, who are causing
divisions. 20 But you, beloved, build yourselves up
on your most holy faith;
pray in the Holy Spirit;
21 keep yourselves in the
love of God; look forward
to the mercy of our Lord
Jesus Christ that leads to[m]
eternal life. 22 And have
mercy on some who are
wavering; 23 save others by
snatching them out of the
fire; and have mercy on still
others with fear, hating
even the tunic defiled by
their bodies.[n]

Benediction

24 Now to him who is
able to keep you from falling, and to make you stand
without blemish in the
presence of his glory with
rejoicing, 25 to the only God
our Savior, through Jesus
Christ our Lord, be glory,
majesty, power, and au-
thority, before all time and
now and forever. Amen.

[m] Gk *Christ to*
[n] Gk *by the flesh*. The Greek text of verses 22-23 is uncertain at several points

ὠφελείας χάριν.
[2]advantage [1]for the sake of.

17 Ὑμεῖς δέ, ἀγαπητοί, μνήσθητε τῶν
But ye, beloved, be mindful of the
ῥημάτων τῶν προειρημένων ὑπὸ τῶν
words – previously spoken by the
ἀποστόλων τοῦ κυρίου ἡμῶν Ἰησοῦ
apostles of the Lord of us Jesus
Χριστοῦ, **18** ὅτι ἔλεγον ὑμῖν· ἐπ' ἐσχάτου
Christ, because they told you: At [the] last
τοῦ χρόνου ἔσονται ἐμπαῖκται κατὰ τὰς
of the time will be mockers [2]according to [3]the
ἑαυτῶν ἐπιθυμίας πορευόμενοι τῶν ἀσεβειῶν.
[6]of themselves [4]lusts [1]going – [5]of impious things.
19 Οὗτοί εἰσιν οἱ ἀποδιορίζοντες, ψυχικοί,
These men are the [ones] making separations, natural,
πνεῦμα μὴ ἔχοντες. **20** ὑμεῖς δέ, ἀγαπητοί,
[3]spirit [1]not [2]having. But ye, beloved,
ἐποικοδομοῦντες ἑαυτοὺς τῇ ἁγιωτάτῃ ὑμῶν
building up yourselves in the most holy [2]of you
πίστει, ἐν πνεύματι ἁγίῳ προσευχόμενοι,
[1]faith, [2]in [4]Spirit [3][the] Holy [1]praying.
21 ἑαυτοὺς ἐν ἀγάπῃ θεοῦ τηρήσατε,
[2]yourselves [3]in [4][the] love [5]of God [1]keep,
προσδεχόμενοι τὸ ἔλεος τοῦ κυρίου ἡμῶν
awaiting the mercy of the Lord of us
Ἰησοῦ Χριστοῦ εἰς ζωὴν αἰώνιον. **22** καὶ
Jesus Christ to life eternal. And
οὓς μὲν ἐλεᾶτε διακρινομένους **23** σῴζετε
some [2]pity ye [1][who are] wavering [2]save
ἐκ πυρὸς ἁρπάζοντες, οὓς δὲ ἐλεᾶτε
[3]out of [4]fire [1]seizing, others pity
ἐν φόβῳ, μισοῦντες καὶ τὸν ἀπὸ τῆς
with fear, hating even [1]the [4]from [5]the
σαρκὸς ἐσπιλωμένον χιτῶνα.
[6]flesh [3]*having been* spotted [2]tunic.

24 Τῷ δὲ δυναμένῳ φυλάξαι ὑμᾶς
Now to the [one] *being* able to guard you
ἀπταίστους καὶ στῆσαι κατενώπιον τῆς
without stumbling and to set [you] before the
δόξης αὐτοῦ ἀμώμους ἐν ἀγαλλιάσει,
glory of him unblemished with exultation,
25 μόνῳ θεῷ σωτῆρι ἡμῶν διὰ Ἰησοῦ
to [the] only God Saviour of us through Jesus
Χριστοῦ τοῦ κυρίου ἡμῶν δόξα μεγαλωσύνη
Christ the Lord of us [be] glory[,] greatness[,]
κράτος καὶ ἐξουσία πρὸ παντὸς τοῦ
might[,] and authority before all the
αἰῶνος καὶ νῦν καὶ εἰς πάντας τοὺς
age and now and unto all the
αἰῶνας· ἀμήν.
ages: Amen.

ter others for their own advantage.

A Call to Persevere

17 But, dear friends, re-
member what the apostles
of our Lord Jesus Christ
foretold. 18 They said to
you, "In the last times
there will be scoffers who
will follow their own un-
godly desires." 19 These are
the men who divide you,
who follow mere natural in-
stincts and do not have the
Spirit.

20 But you, dear friends,
build yourselves up in your
most holy faith and pray in
the Holy Spirit. 21 Keep
yourselves in God's love as
you wait for the mercy of
our Lord Jesus Christ to
bring you to eternal life.

22 Be merciful to those
who doubt; 23 snatch others
from the fire and save
them; to others show mer-
cy, mixed with fear—hat-
ing even the clothing
stained by corrupted flesh.

Doxology

24 To him who is able to
keep you from falling and
to present you before his
glorious presence without
fault and with great joy—
25 to the only God our Savior be glory, majesty, power and authority, through
Jesus Christ our Lord, before all ages, now and for-
evermore! Amen.

The
Revelation
to John

Chapter 1

Introduction and Salutation

THE revelation of Jesus
Christ, which God
gave him to show his ser-
vants[a] what must soon
take place; he made[b] it
known by sending his angel
to his servant[c] John, 2who
testified to the word of God
and to the testimony of
Jesus Christ, even to all
that he saw.
3 Blessed is the one who
reads aloud the words of
the prophecy, and blessed
are those who hear and
who keep what is written in
it; for the time is near.

4 John to the seven
churches that are in Asia:
Grace to you and peace
from him who is and who
was and who is to come,
and from the seven spirits
who are before his throne,
5and from Jesus Christ, the
faithful witness, the firstborn of the dead, and the
ruler of the kings of the
earth.
To him who loves us and
freed[d] us from our sins by
his blood, 6and made[b] us
to be a kingdom, priests
serving[e] his God and Father, to him be glory and
dominion forever and ever.
Amen.
7 Look! He is coming
with the clouds;
every eye will see
him,
even those who
pierced him;
and on his account
all the tribes of
the earth will
wail.
So it is to be. Amen.
8 "I am the Alpha and
the Omega," says the Lord

[a] Gk *slaves*
[b] Gk *and he made*
[c] Gk *slave*
[d] Other ancient authorities read *washed*
[e] Gk *priests to*

ΑΠΟΚΑΛΥΨΙΣ ΙΩΑΝΝΟΥ
A Revelation of John

1 Ἀποκάλυψις Ἰησοῦ Χριστοῦ, ἣν
A revelation of Jesus Christ, which
ἔδωκεν αὐτῷ ὁ θεός, δεῖξαι τοῖς δούλοις
[2]gave [3]to him – [1]God, to show to the slaves
αὐτοῦ ἃ δεῖ γενέσθαι ἐν τάχει, καὶ
of him things which it behoves to occur with speed, and
ἐσήμανεν ἀποστείλας διὰ τοῦ ἀγγέλου
he signified sending through the angel
αὐτοῦ τῷ δούλῳ αὐτοῦ Ἰωάννῃ, 2 ὃς
of him to the slave of him John, who
ἐμαρτύρησεν τὸν λόγον τοῦ θεοῦ καὶ
bore witness [of] the word – of God and
τὴν μαρτυρίαν Ἰησοῦ Χριστοῦ, ὅσα εἶδεν.
the witness of Jesus Christ, as many things as he saw.
3 Μακάριος ὁ ἀναγινώσκων καὶ οἱ
Blessed [is] the [one] reading and the
ἀκούοντες τοὺς λόγους τῆς προφητείας
[ones] hearing the words of the prophecy
καὶ τηροῦντες τὰ ἐν αὐτῇ γεγραμμένα·
and keeping the things [3]in [4]it [1]having been written;
ὁ γὰρ καιρὸς ἐγγύς.
[2]the [1]for time [is] near.
4 Ἰωάννης ταῖς ἑπτὰ ἐκκλησίαις ταῖς
John to the seven churches –
ἐν τῇ Ἀσίᾳ· χάρις ὑμῖν καὶ εἰρήνη
in – Asia: Grace to you and peace
ἀπὸ ὁ ὢν καὶ ὁ ἦν καὶ ὁ ἐρχόμενος,
from the [one] being =the one who is and the [one who] was and the [one] coming,
καὶ ἀπὸ τῶν ἑπτὰ πνευμάτων ἃ ἐνώπιον
and from the seven spirits which [are] before
τοῦ θρόνου αὐτοῦ, 5 καὶ ἀπὸ Ἰησοῦ
the throne of him, and from Jesus
Χριστοῦ, ὁ μάρτυς ὁ πιστός, ὁ πρωτότοκος
Christ, the [2]witness – [1]faithful, the firstborn
τῶν νεκρῶν καὶ ὁ ἄρχων τῶν βασιλέων
of the dead and the ruler of the kings
τῆς γῆς. Τῷ ἀγαπῶντι ἡμᾶς καὶ λύσαντι
of the earth. To the [one] loving us and having loosed
ἡμᾶς ἐκ τῶν ἁμαρτιῶν ἡμῶν ἐν τῷ
us out of the sins of us by the
αἵματι αὐτοῦ, 6 καὶ ἐποίησεν ἡμᾶς
blood of him, and made us
βασιλείαν, ἱερεῖς τῷ θεῷ καὶ πατρὶ
a kingdom, priests to the God and Father
αὐτοῦ, αὐτῷ ἡ δόξα καὶ τὸ κράτος
of him, to him [is] = his is the glory and the might
εἰς τοὺς αἰῶνας τῶν αἰώνων· ἀμήν.
unto the ages of the ages: Amen.
7 Ἰδοὺ ἔρχεται μετὰ τῶν νεφελῶν,
Behold he comes with the clouds,
καὶ ὄψεται αὐτὸν πᾶς ὀφθαλμὸς καὶ
and [3]will see [4]him [1]every [2]eye and
οἵτινες αὐτὸν ἐξεκέντησαν, καὶ κόψονται
[those] who [2]him [1]pierced, and [6]will wail
ἐπ᾽ αὐτὸν πᾶσαι αἱ φυλαὶ τῆς γῆς.
[7]over [8]him [1]all [2]the [3]tribes [4]of the [5]land.
ναί, ἀμήν.
Yes, amen.
8 Ἐγώ εἰμι τὸ ἄλφα καὶ τὸ ὦ, λέγει
I am the alpha and the omega, says

Revelation

Chapter 1

Prologue

THE revelation of Jesus
Christ, which God
gave him to show his ser-
vants what must soon take
place. He made it known
by sending his angel to his
servant John, 2who testifies
to everything he saw—that
is, the word of God and the
testimony of Jesus Christ.
3Blessed is the one who
reads the words of this
prophecy, and blessed are
those who hear it and take
to heart what is written in
it, because the time is near.

Greetings and Doxology

4John,

To the seven churches in
the province of Asia:

Grace and peace to you
from him who is, and who
was, and who is to come,
and from the seven spirits[a]
before his throne, 5and
from Jesus Christ, who is
the faithful witness, the
firstborn from the dead,
and the ruler of the kings of
the earth.

To him who loves us and
has freed us from our sins
by his blood, 6and has
made us to be a kingdom
and priests to serve his God
and Father—to him be glo-
ry and power for ever and
ever! Amen.

7Look, he is coming with
the clouds,
and every eye will see
him,
even those who pierced
him;
and all the peoples of
the earth will mourn
because of him.
So shall it be!
Amen

8"I am the Alpha and the
Omega," says the Lord

[a] 4 Or *the sevenfold Spirit*

God, who is and who was
and who is to come, the Almighty.

A Vision of Christ

9 I, John, your brother
who share with you in
Jesus the persecution and
the kingdom and the pa-
tient endurance, was on the
island called Patmos be-
cause of the word of God
and the testimony of
Jesus.[f] 10 I was in the spirit[g] on the Lord's day, and
I heard behind me a loud
voice like a trumpet 11 saying, "Write in a book what
you see and send it to the
seven churches, to Ephe-
sus, to Smyrna, to Perga-
mum, to Thyatira, to Sar-
dis, to Philadelphia, and to
Laodicea."
12 Then I turned to see
whose voice it was that
spoke to me, and on turning
I saw seven golden lamp-
stands, 13 and in the midst
of the lampstands I saw one
like the Son of Man,
clothed with a long robe
and with a golden sash
across his chest. 14 His
head and his hair were
white as white wool, white
as snow; his eyes were like
a flame of fire, 15 his feet
were like burnished
bronze, refined as in a furnace, and his voice was like
the sound of many waters.
16 In his right hand he held
seven stars, and from his
mouth came a sharp, two-
edged sword, and his face
was like the sun shining
with full force.

κύριος ὁ θεός, ὁ ὢν καὶ ὁ ἦν
[the] Lord – God, the [one] being =the one who is and the [one who] was

καὶ ὁ ἐρχόμενος, ὁ παντοκράτωρ.
and the [one] coming, the Almighty.

9 Ἐγὼ Ἰωάννης, ὁ ἀδελφὸς ὑμῶν καὶ
I John, the brother of you and

συγκοινωνὸς ἐν τῇ θλίψει καὶ βασιλείᾳ
co-sharer in the affliction and kingdom

καὶ ὑπομονῇ ἐν Ἰησοῦ, ἐγενόμην ἐν
and endurance in Jesus, came to be in

τῇ νήσῳ τῇ καλουμένῃ Πάτμῳ διὰ
the island – *being* called Patmos on account of

τὸν λόγον τοῦ θεοῦ καὶ τὴν μαρτυρίαν
the word – of God and the witness

Ἰησοῦ. 10 ἐγενόμην ἐν πνεύματι ἐν
of Jesus. I came to be in [the] spirit on

τῇ κυριακῇ ἡμέρᾳ, καὶ ἤκουσα ὀπίσω
the imperial* day, and heard behind

μου φωνὴν μεγάλην ὡς σάλπιγγος
me [2]voice [1]a great(loud) as of a trumpet

11 λεγούσης· ὃ βλέπεις γράψον εἰς βιβλίον
saying: What thou seest write in a scroll

καὶ πέμψον ταῖς ἑπτὰ ἐκκλησίαις, εἰς
and send to the seven churches, to

Ἔφεσον καὶ εἰς Σμύρναν καὶ εἰς Πέργαμον
Ephesus and to Smyrna and to Pergamum

καὶ εἰς Θυάτιρα καὶ εἰς Σάρδεις καὶ
and to Thyatira and to Sardis and

εἰς Φιλαδέλφειαν καὶ εἰς Λαοδίκειαν.
to Philadelphia and to Laodicea.

12 Καὶ ἐπέστρεψα βλέπειν τὴν φωνὴν
And I turned to see the voice

ἥτις ἐλάλει μετ' ἐμοῦ· καὶ ἐπιστρέψας
which spoke with me; and having turned

εἶδον ἑπτὰ λυχνίας χρυσᾶς, 13 καὶ ἐν
I saw seven [2]lampstands [1]golden, and in

μέσῳ τῶν λυχνιῶν ὅμοιον υἱὸν ἀνθρώπου,
[the] midst of the lampstands [one] like a son of man,*

ἐνδεδυμένον ποδήρη καὶ περιεζωσμένον
having been clothed to the feet and *having been* girdled round

πρὸς τοῖς μαστοῖς ζώνην χρυσᾶν· 14 ἡ
at the breasts [2]girdle [1][with] a golden; [3]the

δὲ κεφαλὴ αὐτοῦ καὶ αἱ τρίχες λευκαὶ
[1]and head of him and the hairs white

ὡς ἔριον λευκὸν ὡς χιών, καὶ οἱ ὀφθαλμοὶ
as wool white as snow, and the eyes

αὐτοῦ ὡς φλὸξ πυρός, 15 καὶ οἱ πόδες
of him as a flame of fire, and the feet

αὐτοῦ ὅμοιοι χαλκολιβάνῳ ὡς ἐν καμίνῳ
of him like *to* burnished brass as [3]in [2]a furnace

πεπυρωμένης, καὶ ἡ φωνὴ αὐτοῦ ὡς
[1]having been fired, and the voice of him as

φωνὴ ὑδάτων πολλῶν, 16 καὶ ἔχων ἐν
a sound waters of many, and having in

τῇ δεξιᾷ χειρὶ αὐτοῦ ἀστέρας ἑπτά,
the right hand of him [2]stars [1]seven,

καὶ ἐκ τοῦ στόματος αὐτοῦ ῥομφαία
and out of the mouth of him [4]sword

δίστομος ὀξεῖα ἐκπορευομένη, καὶ ἡ ὄψις
[3]two-mouthed(edged) [2]a sharp [1]proceeding, and the face

God, "who is, and who
was, and who is to come,
the Almighty."

One Like a Son of Man

9 I, John, your brother and
companion in the suffering
and kingdom and patient
endurance that are ours in
Jesus, was on the island of
Patmos because of the
word of God and the testimony of Jesus. 10 On the
Lord's Day I was in the
Spirit, and I heard behind
me a loud voice like a trumpet, 11 which said: "Write
on a scroll what you see
and send it to the seven
churches: to Ephesus,
Smyrna, Pergamum, Thya-
tira, Sardis, Philadelphia
and Laodicea."
12 I turned around to see
the voice that was speaking
to me. And when I turned I
saw seven golden lamp-
stands, 13 and among the
lampstands was someone
"like a son of man,"[b]
dressed in a robe reaching
down to his feet and with a
golden sash around his
chest. 14 His head and hair
were white like wool, as
white as snow, and his eyes
were like blazing fire. 15 His
feet were like bronze glow-
ing in a furnace, and his
voice was like the sound of
rushing waters. 16 In his
right hand he held seven
stars, and out of his mouth
came a sharp double-edged
sword. His face was like

[f] Or *testimony to Jesus*
[g] Or *in the Spirit*

* See I. Cor. 11. 20.
* Anarthrous; see also ch. 14. 14 and John 5. 27, and *cf.* Heb. 2. 6.

[b] 13 Daniel 7:13

17 When I saw him, I fell at his feet as though dead. But he placed his right hand on me, saying, "Do not be afraid; I am the first and the last, [18]and the living one. I was dead, and see, I am alive forever and ever; and I have the keys of Death and of Hades. [19]Now write what you have seen, what is, and what is to take place after this. [20]As for the mystery of the seven stars that you saw in my right hand, and the seven golden lampstands: the seven stars are the angels of the seven churches, and the seven lampstands are the seven churches.

αὐτοῦ ὡς ὁ ἥλιος φαίνει ἐν τῇ δυνάμει
of him as the sun shines in the power

αὐτοῦ. **17** Καὶ ὅτε εἶδον αὐτόν, ἔπεσα
of it. And when I saw him, I fell

πρὸς τοὺς πόδας αὐτοῦ ὡς νεκρός· καὶ
at the feet of him as dead; and

ἔθηκεν τὴν δεξιὰν αὐτοῦ ἐπ' ἐμὲ λέγων·
he placed the right [hand] of him on me saying:

μὴ φοβοῦ· ἐγώ εἰμι ὁ πρῶτος καὶ
Fear not: I am the first and

ὁ ἔσχατος **18** καὶ ὁ ζῶν, καὶ ἐγενόμην
the last and the living [one], and I became

νεκρὸς καὶ ἰδοὺ ζῶν εἰμι εἰς τοὺς
dead and behold [2]living [1]I am unto the

αἰῶνας τῶν αἰώνων, καὶ ἔχω τὰς κλεῖς
ages of the ages, and I have the keys

τοῦ θανάτου καὶ τοῦ ᾅδου. **19** γράψον
– of death and – of hades. Write thou

οὖν ἃ εἶδες καὶ ἃ εἰσὶν καὶ ἃ
therefore [the] things which thou sawest and [the] things which are and [the] things which

μέλλει γενέσθαι μετὰ ταῦτα. **20** τὸ
(is)are *about* to occur after these things. The

μυστήριον τῶν ἑπτὰ ἀστέρων οὓς εἶδες
mystery of the seven stars which thou sawest

ἐπὶ τῆς δεξιᾶς μου, καὶ τὰς ἑπτὰ
on the right [hand] of me, and the seven

λυχνίας τὰς χρυσᾶς· οἱ ἑπτὰ ἀστέρες
[2]lampstands – [1]golden: the seven stars

ἄγγελοι τῶν ἑπτὰ ἐκκλησιῶν εἰσιν, καὶ
messengers* of the seven churches are, and

αἱ λυχνίαι αἱ ἑπτὰ ἑπτὰ ἐκκλησίαι εἰσίν.
the [2]lampstands – [1]seven [4]seven [5]churches [3]are.

the sun shining in all its brilliance.
[17]When I saw him, I fell at his feet as though dead. Then he placed his right hand on me and said: "Do not be afraid. I am the First and the Last. [18]I am the Living One; I was dead, and behold I am alive for ever and ever! And I hold the keys of death and Hades.
[19]"Write, therefore, what you have seen, what is now and what will take place later. [20]The mystery of the seven stars that you saw in my right hand and of the seven golden lampstands is this: The seven stars are the angels[c] of the seven churches, and the seven lampstands are the seven churches.

Chapter 2

The Message to Ephesus

"TO the angel of the church in Ephesus write: These are the words of him who holds the seven stars in his right hand, who walks among the seven golden lampstands:
2 "I know your works, your toil and your patient endurance. I know that you cannot tolerate evildoers; you have tested those who claim to be apostles but are not, and have found them to be false. [3]I also know that you are enduring patiently and bearing up for the sake of my name, and that you have not grown weary. [4]But I have this against you, that you have abandoned the love you

2 Τῷ ἀγγέλῳ τῆς ἐν Ἐφέσῳ ἐκκλησίας
To the messenger [1]of the [3]in [4]Ephesus [2]church

γράψον·
write thou:

Τάδε λέγει ὁ κρατῶν τοὺς ἑπτὰ
These things says the [one] holding the seven

ἀστέρας ἐν τῇ δεξιᾷ αὐτοῦ, ὁ περιπατῶν
stars in the right [hand] of him, the [one] walking

ἐν μέσῳ τῶν ἑπτὰ λυχνιῶν τῶν
in [the] midst of the seven [2]lampstands –

χρυσῶν· **2** οἶδα τὰ ἔργα σου καὶ τὸν
[1]golden: I know the works of thee and the

κόπον καὶ τὴν ὑπομονήν σου, καὶ ὅτι
labour and the endurance of thee, and that

οὐ δύνῃ βαστάσαι κακούς, καὶ ἐπείρασας
thou canst not *to* bear bad men, and didst try

τοὺς λέγοντας ἑαυτοὺς ἀποστόλους καὶ
the [ones] say(call)ing themselves apostles and

οὐκ εἰσίν, καὶ εὗρες αὐτοὺς ψευδεῖς·
are not, and didst find them liars;

3 καὶ ὑπομονὴν ἔχεις, καὶ ἐβάστασας
and [2]endurance [1]thou hast, and didst bear

διὰ τὸ ὄνομά μου, καὶ οὐ κεκοπίακας.
because of the name of me, and hast not grown weary.

4 ἀλλὰ ἔχω κατὰ σοῦ ὅτι τὴν ἀγάπην
But I have against thee that [3]the [4]love

Chapter 2

To the Church in Ephesus

"TO the angel[d] of the church in Ephesus write:

These are the words of him who holds the seven stars in his right hand and walks among the seven golden lampstands: [2]I know your deeds, your hard work and your perseverance. I know that you cannot tolerate wicked men, that you have tested those who claim to be apostles but are not, and have found them false. [3]You have persevered and have endured hardships for my name, and have not grown weary.
[4]Yet I hold this against you: You have

* This, of course, is the prime meaning of the word: whether these beings were "messengers" from the churches, or supernatural beings, "angels" as usually understood, is a matter of exegesis.

[c]20 Or *messengers*
[d]1 Or *messenger*; also in verses 8, 12 and 18

had at first. [5]Remember
then from what you have
fallen; repent, and do the
works you did at first. If
not, I will come to you and
remove your lampstand
from its place, unless you
repent. [6]Yet this is to your
credit: you hate the works
of the Nicolaitans, which I
also hate. [7]Let anyone who
has an ear listen to what the
Spirit is saying to the
churches. To everyone
who conquers, I will give
permission to eat from the
tree of life that is in the paradise of God.

The Message to Smyrna

8 "And to the angel of
the church in Smyrna
write: These are the words
of the first and the last, who
was dead and came to life:
9 "I know your afflic-
tion and your poverty,
even though you are rich. I
know the slander on the
part of those who say that
they are Jews and are not,
but are a synagogue of Satan. [10]Do not fear what you
are about to suffer. Be-
ware, the devil is about to
throw some of you into
prison so that you may be
tested, and for ten days you
will have affliction. Be
faithful until death, and I
will give you the crown of
life. [11]Let anyone who has
an ear listen to what the
Spirit is saying to the
churches. Whoever con-
quers will not be harmed by
the second death.

The Message to Pergamum

12 "And to the angel of
the church in Pergamum
write: These are the words

σου τὴν πρώτην ἀφῆκας. **5** μνημόνευε
[2]of thee – [3]first [1]thou didst leave. Remember

οὖν πόθεν πέπτωκας, καὶ μετανόησον
therefore whence thou hast fallen, and repent

καὶ τὰ πρῶτα ἔργα ποίησον· εἰ δὲ
and [2]the [3]first [4]works [1]do; and if

μή, ἔρχομαί σοι καὶ κινήσω τὴν λυχνίαν
not, I am coming to thee and will move the lampstand

σου ἐκ τοῦ τόπου αὐτῆς, ἐὰν μὴ
of thee out of the place of it, unless

μετανοήσῃς. **6** ἀλλὰ τοῦτο ἔχεις, ὅτι
thou repentest. But this thou hast, that

μισεῖς τὰ ἔργα τῶν Νικολαϊτῶν, ἃ
thou hatest the works of the Nicolaitans, which

κἀγὼ μισῶ. **7** Ὁ ἔχων οὖς ἀκουσάτω
I also hate. The [one] having an ear let him hear

τί τὸ πνεῦμα λέγει ταῖς ἐκκλησίαις.
what the Spirit says to the churches.

Τῷ νικῶντι δώσω αὐτῷ φαγεῖν ἐκ
To the [one] overcoming I will give *to him* to eat of

τοῦ ξύλου τῆς ζωῆς, ὅ ἐστιν ἐν τῷ
the tree – of life, which is in the

παραδείσῳ τοῦ θεοῦ.
paradise – of God.

8 Καὶ τῷ ἀγγέλῳ τῆς ἐν Σμύρνῃ
And to the messenger [1]of the [3]in [4]Smyrna

ἐκκλησίας γράψον·
[2]church write thou:

Τάδε λέγει ὁ πρῶτος καὶ ὁ ἔσχατος,
These things says the first and the last,

ὃς ἐγένετο νεκρὸς καὶ ἔζησεν· **9** οἶδά
who became dead and lived [again]: I know

σου τὴν θλῖψιν καὶ τὴν πτωχείαν, ἀλλὰ
[6]of thee [1]the [2]affliction [3]and [4]the [5]poverty, but

πλούσιος εἶ, καὶ τὴν βλασφημίαν ἐκ
rich thou art, and the railing of

τῶν λεγόντων Ἰουδαίους εἶναι ἑαυτούς,
the [ones] say(call)ing [3]Jews [2]to be [1]themselves,

καὶ οὐκ εἰσὶν ἀλλὰ συναγωγὴ τοῦ σατανᾶ.
and they are not but a synagogue – of Satan.

10 μὴ φοβοῦ ἃ μέλλεις πάσχειν. ἰδοὺ
Do not fear [the] things which thou art about to suffer. Behold[,]

μέλλει βάλλειν ὁ διάβολος ἐξ ὑμῶν
[3]is about [4]to cast [1]the [2]devil [some] of you

εἰς φυλακὴν ἵνα πειρασθῆτε, καὶ ἕξετε
into prison in order that ye may be tried, and ye will have

θλῖψιν ἡμερῶν δέκα. γίνου πιστὸς ἄχρι
affliction [2]days [1]ten. Be thou faithful until

θανάτου, καὶ δώσω σοι τὸν στέφανον
death, and I will give thee the crown

τῆς ζωῆς. **11** Ὁ ἔχων οὖς ἀκουσάτω
– of life. The [one] having an ear let him hear

τί τὸ πνεῦμα λέγει ταῖς ἐκκλησίαις.
what the Spirit says to the churches.

Ὁ νικῶν οὐ μὴ ἀδικηθῇ ἐκ τοῦ θανάτου
The [one] overcoming by no means will be hurt by the [2]death

τοῦ δευτέρου.
– [1]second.

12 Καὶ τῷ ἀγγέλῳ τῆς ἐν Περγάμῳ
And to the messenger [1]of the [3]in [4]Pergamum

ἐκκλησίας γράψον·
[2]church write thou:

forsaken your first love.
[5]Remember the height
from which you have
fallen! Repent and do
the things you did at
first. If you do not re-
pent, I will come to you
and remove your lamp-
stand from its place.
[6]But you have this in
your favor: You hate
the practices of the Nic-
olaitans, which I also
hate.
[7]He who has an ear,
let him hear what the
Spirit says to the
churches. To him who
overcomes, I will give
the right to eat from the
tree of life, which is in
the paradise of God.

To the Church in Smyrna

[8]"To the angel of the
church in Smyrna write:

These are the words
of him who is the First
and the Last, who died
and came to life again.
[9]I know your afflictions
and your poverty—yet
you are rich! I know the
slander of those who
say they are Jews and
are not, but are a syna-
gogue of Satan. [10]Do
not be afraid of what
you are about to suffer.
I tell you, the devil will
put some of you in pris-
on to test you, and you
will suffer persecution
for ten days. Be faith-
ful, even to the point of
death, and I will give
you the crown of life.
[11]He who has an ear,
let him hear what the
Spirit says to the
churches. He who over-
comes will not be hurt
at all by the second
death.

To the Church in Pergamum

[12]"To the angel of the
church in Pergamum write:

of him who has the sharp
two-edged sword:
13 "I know where you
are living, where Satan's
throne is. Yet you are holding fast to my name, and
you did not deny your faith
in me[h] even in the days of
Antipas my witness, my
faithful one, who was killed
among you, where Satan
lives. 14 But I have a few
things against you: you
have some there who hold
to the teaching of Balaam,
who taught Balak to put a
stumbling block before the
people of Israel, so that
they would eat food sacrificed to idols and practice
fornication. 15 So you also
have some who hold to the
teaching of the Nicolaitans.
16 Repent then. If not, I will
come to you soon and make
war against them with the
sword of my mouth. 17 Let
anyone who has an ear listen to what the Spirit is saying to the churches. To everyone who conquers I will
give some of the hidden
manna, and I will give a
white stone, and on the
white stone is written a new
name that no one knows
except the one who re-
ceives it.

The Message to Thyatira

18 "And to the angel of
the church in Thyatira
write: These are the words
of the Son of God, who has
eyes like a flame of fire, and
whose feet are like bur-
nished bronze:
19 "I know your
works—your love, faith,
service, and patient endurance. I know that your last
works are greater than the
first. 20 But I have this

[h] Or *deny my faith*

Τάδε λέγει ὁ ἔχων τὴν ῥομφαίαν τὴν
These things says the having [one] the [3]sword –

δίστομον τὴν ὀξεῖαν· **13** οἶδα ποῦ κατοικεῖς·
[1]two-mouthed (edged) – [2]sharp: I know where thou dwellest;

ὅπου ὁ θρόνος τοῦ σατανᾶ· καὶ κρατεῖς
where the throne – of Satan [is]; and thou holdest

τὸ ὄνομά μου, καὶ οὐκ ἠρνήσω τὴν
the name of me, and didst not deny the

πίστιν μου καὶ ἐν ταῖς ἡμέραις Ἀντιπᾶς
faith of me even in the days of Antipas

ὁ μάρτυς μου ὁ πιστός μου, ὃς
[1]the [3]witness [2]of me *the* [5]faithful *of me,* who

ἀπεκτάνθη παρ' ὑμῖν, ὅπου ὁ σατανᾶς
was killed among you, where – Satan

κατοικεῖ. **14** ἀλλ' ἔχω κατὰ σοῦ ὀλίγα,
dwells. But I have against thee a few things,

ὅτι ἔχεις ἐκεῖ κρατοῦντας τὴν διδαχὴν
because thou hast there [ones] holding the teaching

Βαλαάμ, ὃς ἐδίδασκεν τῷ Βαλὰκ βαλεῖν
of Balaam, who taught – Balak to cast

σκάνδαλον ἐνώπιον τῶν υἱῶν Ἰσραήλ,
a stumbling-block before the sons of Israel,

φαγεῖν εἰδωλόθυτα καὶ πορνεῦσαι. **15** οὕτως
to eat idol sacrifices and to commit fornication. So

ἔχεις καὶ σὺ κρατοῦντας τὴν διδαχὴν
[2]hast [3]also [1]thou [ones] holding the teaching

τῶν Νικολαϊτῶν ὁμοίως. **16** μετανόησον
of the Nicolaitans likewise. Repent thou

οὖν· εἰ δὲ μή, ἔρχομαί σοι ταχὺ καὶ
therefore; otherwise, I am coming to thee quickly and

πολεμήσω μετ' αὐτῶν ἐν τῇ ῥομφαίᾳ
will fight with them with the sword

τοῦ στόματός μου. **17** Ὁ ἔχων οὖς
of the mouth of me. The [one] having an ear

ἀκουσάτω τί τὸ πνεῦμα λέγει ταῖς
let him hear what the Spirit says to the

ἐκκλησίαις. Τῷ νικῶντι δώσω αὐτῷ
churches. To the [one] overcoming I will give *to him*

τοῦ μάννα τοῦ κεκρυμμένου, καὶ δώσω
of the [2]manna – [1]*having been* hidden, and I will give

αὐτῷ ψῆφον λευκήν, καὶ ἐπὶ τὴν ψῆφον
him [2]stone [1]a white, and on the stone

ὄνομα καινὸν γεγραμμένον, ὃ οὐδεὶς οἶδεν
[2]name [1]a new *having been* written, which no man knows

εἰ μὴ ὁ λαμβάνων.
except the [one] receiving [it].

18 Καὶ τῷ ἀγγέλῳ τῆς ἐν Θυατίροις
And to the messenger [1]of the [3]in [4]Thyatira

ἐκκλησίας γράψον·
[2]church write thou:

Τάδε λέγει ὁ υἱὸς τοῦ θεοῦ, ὁ ἔχων
These things says the Son – of God, the having [one]

τοὺς ὀφθαλμοὺς [αὐτοῦ] ὡς φλόγα πυρός,
the eyes of him as a flame of fire,

καὶ οἱ πόδες αὐτοῦ ὅμοιοι χαλκολιβάνῳ·
and the feet of him like *to* burnished brass:

19 οἶδά σου τὰ ἔργα καὶ τὴν ἀγάπην
I know of thee the works and the love

καὶ τὴν πίστιν καὶ τὴν διακονίαν καὶ
and the faith and the ministry and

τὴν ὑπομονήν σου, καὶ τὰ ἔργα σου
the endurance *of thee,* and the [2]works [3]of thee

τὰ ἔσχατα πλείονα τῶν πρώτων. **20** ἀλλὰ
the [1]last more [than] the first. But

These are the words
of him who has the
sharp, double-edged
sword. 13 I know where
you live—where Satan
has his throne. Yet you
remain true to my
name. You did not re-
nounce your faith in
me, even in the days of
Antipas, my faithful
witness, who was put to
death in your city—
where Satan lives.
14 Nevertheless, I
have a few things
against you: You have
people there who hold
to the teaching of Ba-
laam, who taught Balak
to entice the Israelites
to sin by eating food
sacrificed to idols and
by committing sexual
immorality. 15 Likewise
you also have those
who hold to the teach-
ing of the Nicolaitans.
16 Repent therefore!
Otherwise, I will soon
come to you and will
fight against them with
the sword of my mouth.
17 He who has an ear,
let him hear what the
Spirit says to the
churches. To him who
overcomes, I will give
some of the hidden
manna. I will also give
him a white stone with a
new name written on it,
known only to him who
receives it.

To the Church in Thyatira

18 "To the angel of the
church in Thyatira write:

These are the words
of the Son of God,
whose eyes are like
blazing fire and whose
feet are like burnished
bronze. 19 I know your
deeds, your love and
faith, your service and
perseverance, and that
you are now doing more
than you did at first.

against you: you tolerate
that woman Jezebel, who
calls herself a prophet and
is teaching and beguiling
my servants[i] to practice
fornication and to eat food
sacrificed to idols. 21 I gave
her time to repent, but she
refuses to repent of her fornication. 22 Beware, I am
throwing her on a bed, and
those who commit adultery
with her I am throwing into
great distress, unless they
repent of her doings; 23 and
I will strike her children
dead. And all the churches
will know that I am the one
who searches minds and
hearts, and I will give to
each of you as your works
deserve. 24 But to the rest
of you in Thyatira, who do
not hold this teaching, who
have not learned what
some call 'the deep things
of Satan,' to you I say, I do
not lay on you any other
burden; 25 only hold fast to
what you have until I come.
26 To everyone who con-
quers and continues to do
my works to the end,
I will give authority over the nations;
27 to rule[j] them with an iron rod,
as when clay pots are shattered—
28 even as I also received
authority from my Father.
To the one who conquers I
will also give the morning
star. 29 Let anyone who has
an ear listen to what the
Spirit is saying to the
churches.

ἔχω κατὰ σοῦ ὅτι ἀφεῖς τὴν γυναῖκα
I have against thee that thou permittest the woman
Ἰεζάβελ, ἡ λέγουσα ἑαυτὴν προφῆτιν,
Jezabel, the [one] say(call)ing herself a prophetess,
καὶ διδάσκει καὶ πλανᾷ τοὺς ἐμοὺς
and she teaches and deceives – my
δούλους πορνεῦσαι καὶ φαγεῖν εἰδωλόθυτα·
slaves to commit fornication and to eat idol sacrifices;
21 καὶ ἔδωκα αὐτῇ χρόνον ἵνα μετανοήσῃ,
and I gave her time in order that she might repent,
καὶ οὐ θέλει μετανοῆσαι ἐκ τῆς πορνείας
and she wishes not to repent of the fornication
αὐτῆς. 22 ἰδοὺ βάλλω αὐτὴν εἰς κλίνην,
of her. Behold[,] I am casting her into a bed,
καὶ τοὺς μοιχεύοντας μετ' αὐτῆς εἰς
and the [ones] committing adultery with her into
θλῖψιν μεγάλην, ἐὰν μὴ μετανοήσουσιν
[2]affliction [1]great, unless they shall repent
ἐκ τῶν ἔργων αὐτῆς· 23 καὶ τὰ τέκνα
of the works of her; and the children
αὐτῆς ἀποκτενῶ ἐν θανάτῳ· καὶ γνώσονται
of her I will kill with death; and [4]will know
πᾶσαι αἱ ἐκκλησίαι ὅτι ἐγώ εἰμι ὁ
[1]all [2]the [3]churches that I am the [one]
ἐρευνῶν νεφροὺς καὶ καρδίας, καὶ δώσω
searching kidneys and hearts, and I will give
ὑμῖν ἑκάστῳ κατὰ τὰ ἔργα ὑμῶν.
to you each one according to the works of you.
24 ὑμῖν δὲ λέγω τοῖς λοιποῖς τοῖς ἐν
But to you I say *to* the rest – in
Θυατίροις, ὅσοι οὐκ ἔχουσιν τὴν διδαχὴν
Thyatira, as many as have not – teaching
ταύτην, οἵτινες οὐκ ἔγνωσαν τὰ βαθέα
this, who knew not the deep things
τοῦ σατανᾶ, ὡς λέγουσιν· οὐ βάλλω
– of Satan, as they say: I am not casting
ἐφ' ὑμᾶς ἄλλο βάρος· 25 πλὴν ὃ ἔχετε
on you another burden; nevertheless what ye have
κρατήσατε ἄχρι οὗ ἂν ἥξω. 26 Καὶ
hold until I shall come. And
ὁ νικῶν καὶ ὁ τηρῶν ἄχρι τέλους τὰ
the [one] over-coming and the [one] keeping until [the] end the
ἔργα μου, δώσω αὐτῷ ἐξουσίαν ἐπὶ
works of me, I will give him authority over
τῶν ἐθνῶν, 27 καὶ ποιμανεῖ αὐτοὺς ἐν
the nations, and he will shepherd them with
ῥάβδῳ σιδηρᾷ, ὡς τὰ σκεύη τὰ κεραμικὰ
[2]staff [1]an iron, as *the* [2]vessels – [1]clay
συντρίβεται, ὡς κἀγὼ εἴληφα παρὰ
is(are) broken, as I also have received from
τοῦ πατρός μου, 28 καὶ δώσω αὐτῷ τὸν
the Father of me, and I will give him the
ἀστέρα τὸν πρωϊνόν. 29 Ὁ ἔχων οὖς
[2]star – [1]morning. The [one] having an ear
ἀκουσάτω τί τὸ πνεῦμα λέγει ταῖς
let him hear what the Spirit says to the
ἐκκλησίαις
churches.

20 Nevertheless, I
have this against you:
You tolerate that wom-
an Jezebel, who calls
herself a prophetess. By
her teaching she mis-
leads my servants into
sexual immorality and
the eating of food sacri-
ficed to idols. 21 I have
given her time to repent
of her immorality, but
she is unwilling. 22 So I
will cast her on a bed of
suffering, and I will
make those who com-
mit adultery with her
suffer intensely, unless
they repent of her ways.
23 I will strike her children dead. Then all the
churches will know that
I am he who searches
hearts and minds, and I
will repay each of you
according to your
deeds. 24 Now I say to
the rest of you in Thya-
tira, to you who do not
hold to her teaching and
have not learned Sa-
tan's so-called deep se-
crets (I will not impose
any other burden on
you): 25 Only hold on to
what you have until I
come.
26 To him who over-
comes and does my will
to the end, I will give
authority over the na-
tions—

27 'He will rule them with an iron scepter;
he will dash them to pieces like pottery'[e]—

just as I have received
authority from my Fa-
ther. 28 I will also give
him the morning star.
29 He who has an ear, let
him hear what the Spirit
says to the churches.

[i] Gk *slaves*
[j] Or *to shepherd*

[e] *27* Psalm 2:9

Chapter 3

The Message to Sardis

"AND to the angel of
the church in Sar-
dis write: These are the
words of him who has the
seven spirits of God and the
seven stars:
"I know your works; you
have a name of being alive,
but you are dead. 2 Wake
up, and strengthen what remains and is on the point of
death, for I have not found
your works perfect in the
sight of my God. 3 Remem-
ber then what you received
and heard; obey it, and repent. If you do not wake
up, I will come like a thief,
and you will not know at
what hour I will come to
you. 4 Yet you have still a
few persons in Sardis who
have not soiled their
clothes; they will walk with
me, dressed in white, for
they are worthy. 5 If you
conquer, you will be
clothed like them in white
robes, and I will not blot
your name out of the book
of life; I will confess your
name before my Father and
before his angels. 6 Let anyone who has an ear listen to
what the Spirit is saying to
the churches.

The Message to Philadelphia

7 "And to the angel of
the church in Philadelphia
write:

These are the words
of the holy one,
the true one,
who has the key of
David,
who opens and no
one will shut,
who shuts and no
one opens:

8 "I know your works.
Look, I have set before you
an open door, which no one
is able to shut. I know that
you have but little power,
and yet you have kept my
word and have not denied
my name. 9 I will make
those of the synagogue of

3 Καὶ τῷ ἀγγέλῳ τῆς ἐν Σάρδεσιν
And to the messenger [1]of the [3]in [4]Sardis

ἐκκλησίας γράψον·
[2]church write thou:

Τάδε λέγει ὁ ἔχων τὰ ἑπτὰ πνεύματα
These things says the [one] having the seven Spirits

τοῦ θεοῦ καὶ τοὺς ἑπτὰ ἀστέρας· οἶδά
– of God and the seven stars: I know

σου τὰ ἔργα, ὅτι ὄνομα ἔχεις ὅτι ζῇς,
[3]of thee [1]the [2]works, that a name thou hast that thou livest,

καὶ νεκρὸς εἶ. **2** γίνου γρηγορῶν, καὶ
and [yet] [2]dead [1]thou art. Be thou watching, and

στήρισον τὰ λοιπὰ ἃ ἔμελλον ἀποθανεῖν·
establish the things remaining which were about to die;

οὐ γὰρ εὕρηκά σου ἔργα πεπληρωμένα
for I have not found of thee works *having been* fulfilled

ἐνώπιον τοῦ θεοῦ μου· **3** μνημόνευε οὖν
before the God of me; remember therefore

πῶς εἴληφας καὶ ἤκουσας, καὶ τήρει
how thou hast received and didst hear, and keep

καὶ μετανόησον. ἐὰν οὖν μὴ γρηγορήσῃς,
and repent. If therefore thou dost not watch,

ἥξω ὡς κλέπτης, καὶ οὐ μὴ γνῷς ποίαν
I will come as a thief, and by no means thou knowest at what

ὥραν ἥξω ἐπὶ σέ. **4** ἀλλὰ ἔχεις ὀλίγα
hour I will come on thee. But thou hast a few

ὀνόματα ἐν Σάρδεσιν ἃ οὐκ ἐμόλυναν τὰ
names in Sardis which did not defile the

ἱμάτια αὐτῶν, καὶ περιπατήσουσιν μετ'
garments of them, and they shall walk with

ἐμοῦ ἐν λευκοῖς, ὅτι ἄξιοί εἰσιν. **5** Ὁ
me in white [garments], because [2]worthy [1]they are. The [one]

νικῶν οὕτως περιβαλεῖται ἐν ἱματίοις
overcoming [2]thus [1]shall be clothed in [2]garments

λευκοῖς, καὶ οὐ μὴ ἐξαλείψω τὸ ὄνομα
[1]white, and by no means will I blot *out* the name

αὐτοῦ ἐκ τῆς βίβλου τῆς ζωῆς, καὶ
of him out of the scroll – of life, and

ὁμολογήσω τὸ ὄνομα αὐτοῦ ἐνώπιον τοῦ
I will confess the name of him before the

πατρός μου καὶ ἐνώπιον τῶν ἀγγέλων
Father of me and before the angels

αὐτοῦ. **6** Ὁ ἔχων οὖς ἀκουσάτω τί τὸ
of him. The [one] having an ear let him hear what the

πνεῦμα λέγει ταῖς ἐκκλησίαις.
Spirit says to the churches.

7 Καὶ τῷ ἀγγέλῳ τῆς ἐν Φιλαδελφείᾳ
And to the messenger [1]of the [3]in [4]Philadelphia

ἐκκλησίας γράψον·
[2]church write thou:

Τάδε λέγει ὁ ἅγιος, ὁ ἀληθινός, ὁ
These things says the holy [one], the true [one], the [one]

ἔχων τὴν κλεῖν Δαυίδ, ὁ ἀνοίγων καὶ
having the key of David, the [one] opening and

οὐδεὶς κλείσει, καὶ κλείων καὶ οὐδεὶς
no one shall shut, and shutting and no one

ἀνοίγει· **8** οἶδά σου τὰ ἔργα· ἰδοὺ
opens: I know of thee the works; behold[,]

δέδωκα ἐνώπιόν σου θύραν ἠνεῳγμένην,
I have given before thee a door *having been* opened,

Chapter 3

To the Church in Sardis

"TO the angel[f] of the
church in Sardis
write:

These are the words
of him who holds the
seven spirits[g] of God
and the seven stars. I
know your deeds; you
have a reputation of be-
ing alive, but you are
dead. 2 Wake up!
Strengthen what re-
mains and is about to
die, for I have not found
your deeds complete in
the sight of my God.
3 Remember, therefore,
what you have received
and heard; obey it, and
repent. But if you do
not wake up, I will
come like a thief, and
you will not know at
what time I will come to
you.
4 Yet you have a few
people in Sardis who
have not soiled their
clothes. They will walk
with me, dressed in
white, for they are wor-
thy. 5 He who over-
comes will, like them,
be dressed in white. I
will never blot out his
name from the book of
life, but will acknowl-
edge his name before
my Father and his an-
gels. 6 He who has an
ear, let him hear what
the Spirit says to the
churches.

To the Church in Philadelphia

7 "To the angel of the
church in Philadelphia
write:

These are the words
of him who is holy and
true, who holds the key
of David. What he
opens no one can shut,
and what he shuts no
one can open. 8 I know
your deeds. See, I have
placed before you an
open door that no one
can shut. I know that
you have little strength,
yet you have kept my
word and have not de-
nied my name. 9 I will
make those who are of
the synagogue of Satan,

[f] 1 Or *messenger*; also in verses 7 and 14
[g] 1 Or *the sevenfold Spirit*

Satan who say that they are Jews and are not, but are lying—I will make them come and bow down before your feet, and they will learn that I have loved you. 10Because you have kept my word of patient endurance, I will keep you from the hour of trial that is coming on the whole world to test the inhabitants of the earth. 11I am coming soon; hold fast to what you have, so that no one may seize your crown. 12If you conquer, I will make you a pillar in the temple of my God; you will never go out of it. I will write on you the name of my God, and the name of the city of my God, the new Jerusalem that comes down from my God out of heaven, and my own new name. 13Let anyone who has an ear listen to what the Spirit is saying to the churches.

The Message to Laodicea

14 "And to the angel of the church in Laodicea write: The words of the Amen, the faithful and true witness, the origin[k] of God's creation:

15 "I know your works;

[k] *Or beginning*

ἣν οὐδεὶς δύναται κλεῖσαι αὐτήν· ὅτι
which no one can *to* shut *it;* because

μικρὰν ἔχεις δύναμιν, καὶ ἐτήρησάς μου
[2]a little [1]thou hast power, and didst keep of me

τὸν λόγον καὶ οὐκ ἠρνήσω τὸ ὄνομά
the word and didst not deny the name

μου. 9 ἰδοὺ διδῶ ἐκ τῆς συναγωγῆς
of me. Behold[,] I may (will) give [some] of the synagogue

τοῦ σατανᾶ, τῶν λεγόντων ἑαυτοὺς
– of Satan, the [ones] say(call)ing themselves

Ἰουδαίους εἶναι, καὶ οὐκ εἰσὶν ἀλλὰ
Jews to be, and they are not but

ψεύδονται· ἰδοὺ ποιήσω αὐτοὺς ἵνα
they lie; behold[,] I will make them *in order* that

ἥξουσιν καὶ προσκυνήσουσιν ἐνώπιον τῶν
they shall come and *they* shall worship before the

ποδῶν σου, καὶ γνῶσιν ὅτι ἐγὼ ἠγάπησά
feet of thee, and *they* shall know that I loved

σε. 10 ὅτι ἐτήρησας τὸν λόγον τῆς
thee. Because thou didst keep the word of the

ὑπομονῆς μου, κἀγώ σε τηρήσω ἐκ
endurance of me, I also [2]thee [1]will keep out of

τῆς ὥρας τοῦ πειρασμοῦ τῆς μελλούσης
the hour – of trial – *being* about

ἔρχεσθαι ἐπὶ τῆς οἰκουμένης ὅλης, πειράσαι
to come on [2]the [3]inhabited [earth] [1]all, to try

τοὺς κατοικοῦντας ἐπὶ τῆς γῆς. 11 ἔρχομαι
the [ones] dwelling on the earth. I am coming

ταχύ· κράτει ὃ ἔχεις, ἵνα μηδεὶς λάβῃ
quickly; hold what thou hast, in order that no one takes

τὸν στέφανόν σου. 12 Ὁ νικῶν, ποιήσω
the crown of thee. The [one] overcoming, I will make

αὐτὸν στῦλον ἐν τῷ ναῷ τοῦ θεοῦ
him a pillar in the shrine of the God

μου, καὶ ἔξω οὐ μὴ ἐξέλθῃ ἔτι, καὶ
of me, and out by no means he will go forth [any] longer, and

γράψω ἐπ' αὐτὸν τὸ ὄνομα τοῦ θεοῦ
I will write on him the name of the God

μου καὶ τὸ ὄνομα τῆς πόλεως τοῦ
of me and the name of the city of the

θεοῦ μου, τῆς καινῆς Ἰερουσαλὴμ ἡ
God of me, *of* the new Jerusalem –

καταβαίνουσα ἐκ τοῦ οὐρανοῦ ἀπὸ τοῦ
descending out of – heaven from the

θεοῦ μου, καὶ τὸ ὄνομά μου τὸ καινόν.
God of me, and [1]the [3]name [4]of me – [2]new.

13 Ὁ ἔχων οὖς ἀκουσάτω τί τὸ πνεῦμα
The [one] having an ear let him hear what the Spirit

λέγει ταῖς ἐκκλησίαις.
says to the churches.

14 Καὶ τῷ ἀγγέλῳ τῆς ἐν Λαοδικείᾳ
And to the messenger [1]of the [3]in [4]Laodicea

ἐκκλησίας γράψον·
[2]church write thou:

Τάδε λέγει ὁ ἀμήν, ὁ μάρτυς ὁ
These things says the Amen, the [4]witness –

πιστὸς καὶ ἀληθινός, ἡ ἀρχὴ τῆς κτίσεως
[1]faithful [2]and [3]true, the chief of the creation

τοῦ θεοῦ· 15 οἶδά σου τὰ ἔργα, ὅτι
– of God: I know of thee the works, that

who claim to be Jews though they are not, but are liars—I will make them come and fall down at your feet and acknowledge that I have loved you. 10Since you have kept my command to endure patiently, I will also keep you from the hour of trial that is going to come upon the whole world to test those who live on the earth.

11I am coming soon. Hold on to what you have, so that no one will take your crown. 12Him who overcomes I will make a pillar in the temple of my God. Never again will he leave it. I will write on him the name of my God and the name of the city of my God, the new Jerusalem, which is coming down out of heaven from my God; and I will also write on him my new name. 13He who has an ear, let him hear what the Spirit says to the churches.

To the Church in Laodicea

14"To the angel of the church in Laodicea write:

These are the words of the Amen, the faithful and true witness, the ruler of God's creation. 15I know your deeds,

you are neither cold nor
hot. I wish that you were
either cold or hot. 16 So, because you are lukewarm,
and neither cold nor hot, I
am about to spit you out of
my mouth. 17 For you say,
'I am rich, I have pros-
pered, and I need nothing.'
You do not realize that you
are wretched, pitiable,
poor, blind, and naked.
18 Therefore I counsel you
to buy from me gold refined
by fire so that you may be
rich; and white robes to
clothe you and to keep the
shame of your nakedness
from being seen; and salve
to anoint your eyes so that
you may see. 19 I reprove
and discipline those whom
I love. Be earnest, therefore, and repent. 20 Listen!
I am standing at the door,
knocking; if you hear my
voice and open the door, I
will come in to you and eat
with you, and you with me.
21 To the one who conquers
I will give a place with me
on my throne, just as I myself conquered and sat
down with my Father on
his throne. 22 Let anyone
who has an ear listen to
what the Spirit is saying to
the churches."

οὔτε ψυχρὸς εἶ οὔτε ζεστός. ὄφελον
neither cold art thou nor hot. I would that†

ψυχρὸς ἦς ἢ ζεστός. 16 οὕτως ὅτι
cold thou wast or hot. So because

χλιαρὸς εἶ, καὶ οὔτε ζεστὸς οὔτε ψυχρός,
lukewarm thou art, and neither hot nor cold,

μέλλω σε ἐμέσαι ἐκ τοῦ στόματός μου.
I am about* ²thee ¹to vomit out of the mouth of me.

17 ὅτι λέγεις ὅτι πλούσιός εἰμι καὶ
Because thou sayest[,] – ²rich ¹I am and

πεπλούτηκα καὶ οὐδὲν χρείαν ἔχω, καὶ
I have become rich and ²no ³need ¹*I* have, and

οὐκ οἶδας ὅτι σὺ εἶ ὁ ταλαίπωρος
knowest not that thou art the [one] wretched

καὶ ἐλεεινὸς καὶ πτωχὸς καὶ τυφλὸς
and pitiable and poor and blind

καὶ γυμνός, 18 συμβουλεύω σοι ἀγοράσαι
and naked, I counsel thee to buy

παρ' ἐμοῦ χρυσίον πεπυρωμένον ἐκ πυρὸς
from me gold *having been* refined *by fire* by fire

ἵνα πλουτήσῃς, καὶ ἱμάτια λευκὰ ἵνα
in order that thou mayest be rich, and ²garments ¹white in order that

περιβάλῃ καὶ μὴ φανερωθῇ ἡ αἰσχύνη
thou mayest be clothed and ⁶may not be manifested ¹the ²shame

τῆς γυμνότητός σου, καὶ κολλύριον
³of the ⁴nakedness ⁵of thee, and eyesalve

ἐγχρῖσαι τοὺς ὀφθαλμούς σου ἵνα βλέπῃς.
to anoint the eyes of thee in order that thou mayest see.

19 ἐγὼ ὅσους ἐὰν φιλῶ ἐλέγχω καὶ
²I ¹as many as love I rebuke and

παιδεύω· ζήλευε οὖν καὶ μετανόησον.
I chasten; be hot therefore and repent thou.

20 Ἰδοὺ ἕστηκα ἐπὶ τὴν θύραν καὶ
Behold[,] I stand at the door and

κρούω· ἐάν τις ἀκούσῃ τῆς φωνῆς μου
I knock; if anyone hears the voice of me

καὶ ἀνοίξῃ τὴν θύραν, εἰσελεύσομαι πρὸς
and opens the door, I will enter to

αὐτὸν καὶ δειπνήσω μετ' αὐτοῦ καὶ
him and *I* will dine with him and

αὐτὸς μετ' ἐμοῦ. 21 Ὁ νικῶν, δώσω
he with me. The [one] overcoming, I will give

αὐτῷ καθίσαι μετ' ἐμοῦ ἐν τῷ θρόνῳ
him to sit with me in the throne

μου, ὡς κἀγὼ ἐνίκησα καὶ ἐκάθισα
of me, as I also overcame and sat

μετὰ τοῦ πατρός μου ἐν τῷ θρόνῳ
with the Father of me in the throne

αὐτοῦ. 22 Ὁ ἔχων οὖς ἀκουσάτω τί
of him. The [one] having an ear let him hear what

τὸ πνεῦμα λέγει ταῖς ἐκκλησίαις.
the Spirit says to the churches.

that you are neither
cold nor hot. I wish you
were either one or the
other! 16So, because
you are lukewarm—
neither hot nor cold—I
am about to spit you out
of my mouth. 17You
say, 'I am rich; I have
acquired wealth and do
not need a thing.' But
you do not realize that
you are wretched, piti-
ful, poor, blind and na-
ked. 18I counsel you to
buy from me gold re-
fined in the fire, so you
can become rich; and
white clothes to wear,
so you can cover your
shameful nakedness;
and salve to put on your
eyes, so you can see.
19Those whom I love I
rebuke and discipline.
So be earnest, and re-
pent. 20Here I am! I
stand at the door and
knock. If anyone hears
my voice and opens the
door, I will come in and
eat with him, and he
with me.
21To him who over-
comes, I will give the
right to sit with me on
my throne, just as I
overcame and sat down
with my Father on his
throne. 22He who has an
ear, let him hear what
the Spirit says to the
churches."

Chapter 4

The Heavenly Worship

AFTER this I looked, and there in heaven a door stood open! And the first voice, which I had heard speaking to me like a trumpet, said, "Come up

4 Μετὰ ταῦτα εἶδον, καὶ ἰδοὺ θύρα
After these things I saw, and behold[,] a door

ἠνεῳγμένη ἐν τῷ οὐρανῷ, καὶ ἡ φωνὴ
having been opened in – heaven, and the ²voice

ἡ πρώτη ἣν ἤκουσα ὡς σάλπιγγος
– ¹first which I heard as of a trumpet

Chapter 4

The Throne in Heaven

AFTER this I looked, and there before me was a door standing open in heaven. And the voice I had first heard speaking to me like a

* As so often (see also ch. 1. 19, 2. 10), this verb does not necessarily connote imminence, but only simple futurity.

here, and I will show you
what must take place after
this." 2 At once I was in the
spirit,[i] and there in heaven
stood a throne, with one
seated on the throne! 3 And
the one seated there looks
like jasper and carnelian,
and around the throne is a
rainbow that looks like an
emerald. 4 Around the
throne are twenty-four
thrones, and seated on the
thrones are twenty-four elders, dressed in white
robes, with golden crowns
on their heads. 5 Coming
from the throne are flashes
of lightning, and rumblings
and peals of thunder, and in
front of the throne burn
seven flaming torches,
which are the seven spirits
of God; 6 and in front of the
throne there is something
like a sea of glass, like crystal.

Around the throne, and
on each side of the throne,
are four living creatures,
full of eyes in front and behind: 7 the first living creature like a lion, the second
living creature like an ox,
the third living creature
with a face like a human
face, and the fourth living
creature like a flying eagle.
8 And the four living creatures, each of them with six
wings, are full of eyes all
around and inside. Day and
night without ceasing they
sing,

[i] Or *in the Spirit*

λαλούσης μετ' ἐμοῦ, λέγων· ἀνάβα ὧδε,
speaking with me, saying: Come up here,

καὶ δείξω σοι ἃ δεῖ γενέσθαι μετὰ
and I will show thee things which it behoves to occur after

ταῦτα. εὐθέως ἐγενόμην ἐν πνεύματι·
these things. Immediately I became in spirit;

2 καὶ ἰδοὺ θρόνος ἔκειτο ἐν τῷ οὐρανῷ,
and behold[,] a throne was set in – heaven,

καὶ ἐπὶ τὸν θρόνον καθήμενος, 3 καὶ
and on the throne a sitting [one], and

ὁ καθήμενος ὅμοιος ὁράσει λίθῳ ἰάσπιδι
the [one] sitting [was] like in appearance [2]stone [1]*to* a jasper

καὶ σαρδίῳ, καὶ ἶρις κυκλόθεν τοῦ
[2]and [3]a sardius, and [there was] a rainbow round the

θρόνου ὅμοιος ὁράσει σμαραγδίνῳ. 4 καὶ
throne like in appearance *to* an emerald. And

κυκλόθεν τοῦ θρόνου θρόνους εἴκοσι
round the throne [I saw] [2]thrones [1]twenty-

τέσσαρας, καὶ ἐπὶ τοὺς θρόνους εἴκοσι
four, and on the thrones twenty-

τέσσαρας πρεσβυτέρους καθημένους περι-
four elders sitting *having been*

βεβλημένους ἐν ἱματίοις λευκοῖς, καὶ ἐπὶ
clothed in garments white, and on

τὰς κεφαλὰς αὐτῶν στεφάνους χρυσοῦς
the heads of them [2]crowns [1]golden.

5 καὶ ἐκ τοῦ θρόνου ἐκπορεύονται ἀστραπαὶ
And out of the throne come forth lightnings

καὶ φωναὶ καὶ βρονταί· καὶ ἑπτὰ λαμπάδες
and voices* and thunders; and seven lamps

πυρὸς καιόμεναι ἐνώπιον τοῦ θρόνου, ἅ
of fire [are] burning before the throne, which

εἰσιν τὰ ἑπτὰ πνεύματα τοῦ θεοῦ· 6 καὶ
are the seven Spirits – of God; and

ἐνώπιον τοῦ θρόνου ὡς θάλασσα ὑαλίνη
before the throne as [2]sea [1]a glassy

ὁμοία κρυστάλλῳ· καὶ ἐν μέσῳ τοῦ
like *to* crystal; and in [the] midst of the

θρόνου καὶ κύκλῳ τοῦ θρόνου τέσσερα
throne and round the throne four

ζῷα γέμοντα ὀφθαλμῶν ἔμπροσθεν καὶ
living creatures filling(full) of eyes before and

ὄπισθεν. 7 καὶ τὸ ζῷον τὸ πρῶτον
behind. And the [2]living creature – [1]first

ὅμοιον λέοντι, καὶ τὸ δεύτερον ζῷον
[was] like *to* a lion, and the second living creature

ὅμοιον μόσχῳ, καὶ τὸ τρίτον ζῷον ἔχων
like *to* a calf, and the third living creature having

τὸ πρόσωπον ὡς ἀνθρώπου, καὶ τὸ
the(its) face as of a man, and the

τέταρτον ζῷον ὅμοιον ἀετῷ πετομένῳ.
fourth living creature like eagle *to* a flying.

8 καὶ τὰ τέσσερα ζῷα, ἓν καθ' ἓν
And the four living creatures, one by one

αὐτῶν ἔχων ἀνὰ πτέρυγας ἕξ, κυκλόθεν
of them having each [2]wings [1]six, around

καὶ ἔσωθεν γέμουσιν ὀφθαλμῶν· καὶ
and within are full of eyes; and

ἀνάπαυσιν οὐκ ἔχουσιν ἡμέρας καὶ νυκτὸς
respite they have not day and night

* Or "sounds"; and so elsewhere.

trumpet said, "Come up
here, and I will show you
what must take place after
this." 2 At once I was in the
Spirit, and there before me
was a throne in heaven with
someone sitting on it. 3 And
the one who sat there had
the appearance of jasper
and carnelian. A rainbow,
resembling an emerald, encircled the throne. 4 Surrounding the throne were
twenty-four other thrones,
and seated on them were
twenty-four elders. They
were dressed in white and
had crowns of gold on their
heads. 5 From the throne
came flashes of lightning,
rumblings and peals of
thunder. Before the throne,
seven lamps were blazing.
These are the seven spir-
its[h] of God. 6 Also before
the throne there was what
looked like a sea of glass,
clear as crystal.

In the center, around the
throne, were four living
creatures, and they were
covered with eyes, in front
and in back. 7 The first living creature was like a lion,
the second was like an ox,
the third had a face like a
man, the fourth was like a
flying eagle. 8 Each of the
four living creatures had
six wings and was covered
with eyes all around, even
under his wings. Day and
night they never stop saying:

[h] 5 Or *the sevenfold Spirit*

"Holy, holy, holy,
the Lord God the
Almighty,
who was and is and
is to come."
9 And whenever the living
creatures give glory and
honor and thanks to the one
who is seated on the
throne, who lives forever
and ever, 10 the twenty-four
elders fall before the one
who is seated on the throne
and worship the one who
lives forever and ever; they
cast their crowns before
the throne, singing,
11 "You are worthy, our
Lord and God,
to receive glory and
honor
and power,
for you created all
things,
and by your will
they existed and
were created."

Chapter 5

The Scroll and the Lamb

THEN I saw in the right
hand of the one seated
on the throne a scroll written on the inside and on the
back, sealed[m] with seven
seals; 2 and I saw a mighty
angel proclaiming with a
loud voice, "Who is worthy
to open the scroll and break
its seals?" 3 And no one in
heaven or on earth or under
the earth was able to open
the scroll or to look into it.
4 And I began to weep bitterly because no one was
found worthy to open the
scroll or to look into it.
5 Then one of the elders
said to me, "Do not weep.
See, the Lion of the tribe of

[m] Or *written on the inside, and sealed on the back*

λέγοντες· ἅγιος ἅγιος ἅγιος κύριος ὁ
saying: Holy[,] holy[,] holy[,] Lord –
θεὸς ὁ παντοκράτωρ, ὁ ἦν καὶ ὁ ὢν
God the Almighty, the [one who] was and the being [one] = the one who is
καὶ ὁ ἐρχόμενος. 9 Καὶ ὅταν δώσουσιν
and the coming [one]. And whenever ³shall give
τὰ ζῷα δόξαν καὶ τιμὴν καὶ εὐχαριστίαν
¹the ²living creatures glory and honour and thanks
τῷ καθημένῳ ἐπὶ τῷ θρόνῳ τῷ ζῶντι
to the [one] sitting on the throne[,] to the living [one]
εἰς τοὺς αἰῶνας τῶν αἰώνων, 10 πεσοῦνται
unto the ages of the ages, ⁴will fall
οἱ εἴκοσι τέσσαρες πρεσβύτεροι ἐνώπιον
¹the ²twenty-four ³elders before
τοῦ καθημένου ἐπὶ τοῦ θρόνου, καὶ
the [one] sitting on the throne, and
προσκυνήσουσιν τῷ ζῶντι εἰς τοὺς αἰῶνας
they will worship the [one] living unto the ages
τῶν αἰώνων, καὶ βαλοῦσιν τοὺς στεφάνους
of the ages, and will cast the crowns
αὐτῶν ἐνώπιον τοῦ θρόνου, λέγοντες·
of them before the throne, saying:
11 ἄξιος εἶ, ὁ κύριος καὶ ὁ θεὸς ἡμῶν,
Worthy art thou, the Lord and the God of us,
λαβεῖν τὴν δόξαν καὶ τὴν τιμὴν καὶ
to receive the glory and the honour and
τὴν δύναμιν, ὅτι σὺ ἔκτισας τὰ πάντα,
the power, because thou createdst – all things,*
καὶ διὰ τὸ θέλημά σου ἦσαν καὶ
and on account of the will of thee they were and
ἐκτίσθησαν.
they were created.

5 Καὶ εἶδον ἐπὶ τὴν δεξιὰν τοῦ
And I saw on the right [hand] of the [one]
καθημένου ἐπὶ τοῦ θρόνου βιβλίον
sitting on the throne a scroll
γεγραμμένον ἔσωθεν καὶ ὄπισθεν,
having been written within and on the reverse side,
κατεσφραγισμένον σφραγῖσιν ἑπτά. 2 καὶ
having been sealed with ²seals ¹seven. And
εἶδον ἄγγελον ἰσχυρὸν κηρύσσοντα ἐν
I saw angel a strong proclaiming in
φωνῇ μεγάλῃ· τίς ἄξιος ἀνοῖξαι τὸ
²voice ¹a great(loud): Who [is] worthy to open the
βιβλίον καὶ λῦσαι τὰς σφραγῖδας αὐτοῦ;
scroll and to loosen the seals of it ?
3 καὶ οὐδεὶς ἐδύνατο ἐν τῷ οὐρανῷ
And no one was able in – heaven
οὐδὲ ἐπὶ τῆς γῆς οὐδὲ ὑποκάτω τῆς
nor on the earth nor underneath the
γῆς ἀνοῖξαι τὸ βιβλίον οὔτε βλέπειν
earth to open the scroll nor to see(look at)
αὐτό. 4 καὶ ἔκλαιον πολύ, ὅτι οὐδεὶς
it. And I wept much, because no one
ἄξιος εὑρέθη ἀνοῖξαι τὸ βιβλίον οὔτε
worthy was found to open the scroll nor
βλέπειν αὐτό. 5 καὶ εἷς ἐκ τῶν πρεσ-
to look at it. And one of the el-
βυτέρων λέγει μοι· μὴ κλαῖε· ἰδοὺ
ders says to me: Weep not; behold[,]

* τὰ πάντα = the universe.

"Holy, holy, holy
is the Lord God Almighty,
who was, and is, and is to
come."

9 Whenever the living creatures give glory, honor and
thanks to him who sits on
the throne and who lives
for ever and ever, 10 the
twenty-four elders fall
down before him who sits
on the throne, and worship
him who lives for ever and
ever. They lay their crowns
before the throne and say:

11 "You are worthy, our
Lord and God,
to receive glory and
honor and power,
for you created all
things,
and by your will they
were created
and have their being."

Chapter 5

The Scroll and the Lamb

THEN I saw in the right
hand of him who sat on
the throne a scroll with
writing on both sides and
sealed with seven seals.
2 And I saw a mighty angel
proclaiming in a loud voice,
"Who is worthy to break
the seals and open the
scroll?" 3 But no one in
heaven or on earth or under
the earth could open the
scroll or even look inside it.
4 I wept and wept because
no one was found who was
worthy to open the scroll or
look inside. 5 Then one of
the elders said to me, "Do
not weep! See, the Lion of

Judah, the Root of David,
has conquered, so that he
can open the scroll and its
seven seals."
6 Then I saw between
the throne and the four living creatures and among
the elders a Lamb standing
as if it had been slaugh-
tered, having seven horns
and seven eyes, which are
the seven spirits of God
sent out into all the earth.
7 He went and took the
scroll from the right hand of
the one who was seated on
the throne. 8 When he had
taken the scroll, the four
living creatures and the
twenty-four elders fell before the Lamb, each hold-
ing a harp and golden bowls
full of incense, which are
the prayers of the saints.
9 They sing a new song:
"You are worthy to
take the scroll
and to open its
seals,
for you were
slaughtered and
by your blood
you ransomed
for God
saints from[n] every
tribe and
language and
people
and nation;
10 you have made them
to be a kingdom
and priests
serving[o] our
God,
and they will reign
on earth."
11 Then I looked, and I
heard the voice of many angels surrounding the throne
and the living creatures and
the elders; they numbered
myriads of myriads and
thousands of thousands,
12 singing with full voice,
"Worthy is the Lamb
that was
slaughtered
to receive power and

ἐνίκησεν ὁ λέων ὁ ἐκ τῆς φυλῆς Ἰούδα,
[10]overcame [1]the [2]Lion – [3]of [4]the [5]tribe [6]Juda,

ἡ ῥίζα Δαυίδ, ἀνοῖξαι τὸ βιβλίον καὶ
[7]the [8]root [9]of David, to open the scroll and

τὰς ἑπτὰ σφραγῖδας αὐτοῦ. **6** Καὶ εἶδον
the seven seals of it. And I saw

ἐν μέσῳ τοῦ θρόνου καὶ τῶν τεσσάρων
in [the] midst of the throne and of the four

ζῴων καὶ ἐν μέσῳ τῶν πρεσβυτέρων
living creatures and in [the] midst of the elders

ἀρνίον ἑστηκὸς ὡς ἐσφαγμένον, ἔχων
a Lamb standing as having been slain, having

κέρατα ἑπτὰ καὶ ὀφθαλμοὺς ἑπτά, οἵ
[2]horns [1]seven and [2]eyes [1]seven, which

εἰσιν τὰ ἑπτὰ πνεύματα τοῦ θεοῦ
are the seven Spirits – of God

ἀπεσταλμένοι εἰς πᾶσαν τὴν γῆν. **7** καὶ
having been sent forth into all the earth. And

ἦλθεν καὶ εἴληφεν ἐκ τῆς δεξιᾶς τοῦ
he came and has taken out of the right [hand] of the

καθημένου ἐπὶ τοῦ θρόνου. **8** Καὶ ὅτε
[one] sitting on the throne. And when

ἔλαβεν τὸ βιβλίον, τὰ τέσσερα ζῷα
he took the scroll, the four living creatures

καὶ οἱ εἴκοσι τέσσαρες πρεσβύτεροι ἔπεσαν
and the twenty-four elders fell

ἐνώπιον τοῦ ἀρνίου, ἔχοντες ἕκαστος
before the Lamb, having each one

κιθάραν καὶ φιάλας χρυσᾶς γεμούσας
a harp and [2]bowls [1]golden *being* full

θυμιαμάτων, αἵ εἰσιν αἱ προσευχαὶ τῶν
of incense*s*, which are the prayers of the

ἁγίων. **9** καὶ ᾄδουσιν ᾠδὴν καινὴν
saints. And they sing [2]song [1]a new

λέγοντες· ἄξιος εἶ λαβεῖν τὸ βιβλίον
saying: Worthy art thou to receive the scroll

καὶ ἀνοῖξαι τὰς σφραγῖδας αὐτοῦ, ὅτι
and to open the seals of it, because

ἐσφάγης καὶ ἠγόρασας τῷ θεῷ ἐν τῷ
thou wast slain and didst purchase – to God by the

αἵματί σου ἐκ πάσης φυλῆς καὶ γλώσσης
blood of thee out of every tribe and tongue

καὶ λαοῦ καὶ ἔθνους, **10** καὶ ἐποίησας
and people and nation, and didst make

αὐτοὺς τῷ θεῷ ἡμῶν βασιλείαν καὶ
them to the God of us a kingdom and

ἱερεῖς, καὶ βασιλεύσουσιν ἐπὶ τῆς γῆς.
priests, and they will reign on(? over) the earth.

11 καὶ εἶδον, καὶ ἤκουσα φωνὴν ἀγγέλων
And I saw, and I heard a sound [2]angels

πολλῶν κύκλῳ τοῦ θρόνου καὶ τῶν
[1]of many round the throne and the

ζῴων καὶ τῶν πρεσβυτέρων, καὶ ἦν
living creatures and the elders, and [4]was

ὁ ἀριθμὸς αὐτῶν μυριάδες μυριάδων καὶ
[1]the [2]number [3]of them myriads of myriads and

χιλιάδες χιλιάδων, **12** λέγοντες φωνῇ
thousands of thousands, saying [2]voice

μεγάλῃ· ἄξιός ἐστιν τὸ ἀρνίον τὸ
[1]with a great (loud): Worthy is the Lamb –

ἐσφαγμένον λαβεῖν τὴν δύναμιν καὶ πλοῦτον
having been slain to receive the power and riches

the tribe of Judah, the Root
of David, has triumphed.
He is able to open the scroll
and its seven seals."
6 Then I saw a Lamb,
looking as if it had been
slain, standing in the center
of the throne, encircled by
the four living creatures
and the elders. He had sev-
en horns and seven eyes,
which are the seven spir-
its[i] of God sent out into all
the earth. 7 He came and
took the scroll from the
right hand of him who sat
on the throne. 8 And when
he had taken it, the four living creatures and the twenty-four elders fell down before the Lamb. Each one
had a harp and they were
holding golden bowls full of
incense, which are the
prayers of the saints. 9 And
they sang a new song:

"You are worthy to take
the scroll
and to open its seals,
because you were slain,
and with your blood
you purchased men
for God
from every tribe and
language and people
and nation.
10 You have made them to
be a kingdom and
priests to serve our
God,
and they will reign on
the earth."

11 Then I looked and
heard the voice of many angels, numbering thousands
upon thousands, and ten
thousand times ten thou-
sand. They encircled the
throne and the living creatures and the elders. 12 In a
loud voice they sang:

"Worthy is the Lamb,
who was slain,
to receive power and

[n] Gk *ransomed for God from*
[o] Gk *priests to*

[i] 6 Or *the sevenfold Spirit*

wealth and
wisdom and
might
and honor and glory
and blessing!"
13Then I heard every creature in heaven and on earth
and under the earth and in
the sea, and all that is in
them, singing,
"To the one seated on
the throne and
to the Lamb
be blessing and honor
and glory and
might
forever and ever!"
14And the four living creatures said, "Amen!" And
the elders fell down and
worshiped.

καὶ σοφίαν καὶ ἰσχὺν καὶ τιμὴν καὶ
and wisdom and strength and honour and
δόξαν καὶ εὐλογίαν. **13** καὶ πᾶν κτίσμα
glory and blessing. And every creature
ὃ ἐν τῷ οὐρανῷ καὶ ἐπὶ τῆς γῆς καὶ
which [2]in – [3]heaven [4]and [5]on [6]the [7]earth [8]and
ὑποκάτω τῆς γῆς καὶ ἐπὶ τῆς θαλάσσης
[9]underneath [10]the [11]earth [12]and [13]on [14]the [15]sea
[ἐστίν], καὶ τὰ ἐν αὐτοῖς πάντα, ἤκουσα
[1]is, and – [2]in [3]them [1]all things, I heard
λέγοντας· τῷ καθημένῳ ἐπὶ τῷ θρόνῳ
saying: To the [one] sitting on the throne
καὶ τῷ ἀρνίῳ ἡ εὐλογία καὶ ἡ τιμὴ
and to the Lamb the blessing and the honour
καὶ ἡ δόξα καὶ τὸ κράτος εἰς τοὺς
and the glory and the might unto the
αἰῶνας τῶν αἰώνων. **14** καὶ τὰ τέσσερα
ages of the ages. And the four
ζῷα ἔλεγον· ἀμήν, καὶ οἱ πρεσβύτεροι
living creatures said: Amen, and the elders
ἔπεσαν καὶ προσεκύνησαν.
fell and worshipped.

wealth and wisdom
and strength
and honor and glory and
praise!"
13Then I heard every
creature in heaven and on
earth and under the earth
and on the sea, and all that
is in them, singing:
"To him who sits on the
throne and to the
Lamb
be praise and honor and
glory and power,
for ever and ever!"
14The four living creatures
said, "Amen," and the el-
ders fell down and wor-
shiped.

Chapter 6

The Seven Seals

THEN I saw the Lamb
open one of the seven
seals, and I heard one of the
four living creatures call
out, as with a voice of thunder, "Come!"[p] 2I looked,
and there was a white
horse! Its rider had a bow;
a crown was given to him,
and he came out conquer-
ing and to conquer.
3 When he opened the
second seal, I heard the
second living creature call
out, "Come!"[p] 4And out
came[q] another horse,
bright red; its rider was permitted to take peace from
the earth, so that people
would slaughter one another; and he was given a great
sword.
5 When he opened the
third seal, I heard the third
living creature call out,
"Come!"[p] I looked, and
there was a black horse! Its
rider held a pair of scales in
his hand, 6and I heard what

6 Καὶ εἶδον ὅτε ἤνοιξεν τὸ ἀρνίον
And I saw when [3]opened [1]the [2]Lamb
μίαν ἐκ τῶν ἑπτὰ σφραγίδων, καὶ ἤκουσα
one of the seven seals, and I heard
ἑνὸς ἐκ τῶν τεσσάρων ζῴων λέγοντος
one of the four living creatures saying
ὡς φωνῇ βροντῆς· ἔρχου. **2** καὶ εἶδον,
as with a sound of thunder: Come. And I saw,
καὶ ἰδοὺ ἵππος λευκός, καὶ ὁ καθήμενος
and behold[,] [2]horse [1]a white, and the [one] sitting
ἐπ' αὐτὸν ἔχων τόξον, καὶ ἐδόθη αὐτῷ
on it having a bow, and [2]was given [3]to him
στέφανος, καὶ ἐξῆλθεν νικῶν καὶ ἵνα
[1]a crown, and he went forth overcoming and in order that
νικήσῃ. **3** Καὶ ὅτε ἤνοιξεν τὴν σφραγῖδα
he might overcome. And when he opened the [2]seal
τὴν δευτέραν, ἤκουσα τοῦ δευτέρου ζῴου
– [1]second, I heard the second living creature
λέγοντος· ἔρχου. **4** καὶ ἐξῆλθεν ἄλλος
saying: Come. And [4]went forth [1]another
ἵππος πυρρός, καὶ τῷ καθημένῳ ἐπ'
[2]horse[,] [3]red, and to the [one] sitting on
αὐτὸν ἐδόθη αὐτῷ λαβεῖν τὴν εἰρήνην
it was given *to him* to take – peace
ἐκ τῆς γῆς καὶ ἵνα ἀλλήλους σφάξουσιν,
out of the earth and *in order that* [2]one another [1]they shall slay,
καὶ ἐδόθη αὐτῷ μάχαιρα μεγάλη. **5** Καὶ
and [3]was given [4]to him [2]sword [1]a great. And
ὅτε ἤνοιξεν τὴν σφραγῖδα τὴν τρίτην,
when he opened the [2]seal – [1]third,
ἤκουσα τοῦ τρίτου ζῴου λέγοντος· ἔρχου.
I heard the third living creature saying: Come.
καὶ εἶδον, καὶ ἰδοὺ ἵππος μέλας, καὶ
And I saw, and behold[,] [2]horse [1]a black, and
ὁ καθήμενος ἐπ' αὐτὸν ἔχων ζυγὸν
the [one] sitting on it having a balance

Chapter 6

The Seals

I WATCHED as the
Lamb opened the first of
the seven seals. Then I
heard one of the four living
creatures say in a voice like
thunder, "Come!" 2I
looked, and there before
me was a white horse! Its
rider held a bow, and he
was given a crown, and he
rode out as a conqueror
bent on conquest.
3When the Lamb opened
the second seal, I heard the
second living creature say,
"Come!" 4Then another
horse came out, a fiery red
one. Its rider was given
power to take peace from
the earth and to make men
slay each other. To him
was given a large sword.
5When the Lamb opened
the third seal, I heard the
third living creature say,
"Come!" I looked, and
there before me was a black
horse! Its rider was holding

[p] Or "Go!"
[q] Or *went*

seemed to be a voice in the
midst of the four living
creatures saying, "A quart
of wheat for a day's pay,[r]
and three quarts of barley
for a day's pay,[r] but do not
damage the olive oil and the
wine!"
7 When he opened the
fourth seal, I heard the
voice of the fourth living
creature call out,
"Come!"[p] 8I looked and
there was a pale green
horse! Its rider's name was
Death, and Hades followed
with him; they were given
authority over a fourth of
the earth, to kill with
sword, famine, and pesti-
lence, and by the wild animals of the earth.
9 When he opened the
fifth seal, I saw under the
altar the souls of those who
had been slaughtered for
the word of God and for the
testimony they had given;
10they cried out with a loud
voice, "Sovereign Lord,
holy and true, how long will
it be before you judge and
avenge our blood on the inhabitants of the earth?"
11They were each given a
white robe and told to rest
a little longer, until the
number would be complete
both of their fellow ser-
vants[s] and of their brothers and sisters,[t] who were
soon to be killed as they
themselves had been killed.
12 When he opened the
sixth seal, I looked, and
there came a great earth-

ἐν τῇ χειρὶ αὐτοῦ. 6 καὶ ἤκουσα ὡς
in the hand of him. And I heard as

φωνὴν ἐν μέσῳ τῶν τεσσάρων ζῴων
a voice in [the] midst of the four living creatures

λέγουσαν· χοῖνιξ σίτου δηναρίου, καὶ τρεῖς
saying: A chœnix of wheat of(for) a denarius, and three

χοίνικες κριθῶν δηναρίου· καὶ τὸ ἔλαιον
chœnixes of barley of(for) a denarius; and [2]the [3]oil

καὶ τὸν οἶνον μὴ ἀδικήσῃς. 7 Καὶ
[4]and [5]the [6]wine [1]do not harm. And

ὅτε ἤνοιξεν τὴν σφραγῖδα τὴν τετάρτην,
when he opened the [2]seal – [1]fourth,

ἤκουσα φωνὴν τοῦ τετάρτου ζῴου λέγοντος·
I heard [the] voice of the fourth living creature saying:

ἔρχου. 8 καὶ εἶδον, καὶ ἰδοὺ ἵππος
Come. And I saw, and behold[,] [2]horse

χλωρός, καὶ ὁ καθήμενος ἐπάνω αὐτοῦ,
[1]a pale green, and the [one] sitting upon it,

ὄνομα αὐτῷ [ὁ] θάνατος, καὶ ὁ ᾅδης
name to him[c] – death, and – hades

ἠκολούθει μετ' αὐτοῦ, καὶ ἐδόθη αὐτοῖς
followed with him, and [3]was given [2]to them

ἐξουσία ἐπὶ τὸ τέταρτον τῆς γῆς,
[1]authority over the fourth [part] of the earth,

ἀποκτεῖναι ἐν ῥομφαίᾳ καὶ ἐν λιμῷ
to kill with sword and with famine

καὶ ἐν θανάτῳ καὶ ὑπὸ τῶν θηρίων
and with death and by the wild beasts

τῆς γῆς. 9 Καὶ ὅτε ἤνοιξεν τὴν πέμπτην
of the earth. And when he opened the fifth

σφραγῖδα, εἶδον ὑποκάτω τοῦ θυσιαστηρίου
seal, I saw underneath the altar

τὰς ψυχὰς τῶν ἐσφαγμένων διὰ τὸν
the souls of the [ones] having been slain on account of the

λόγον τοῦ θεοῦ καὶ διὰ τὴν μαρτυρίαν
word – of God and on account of the witness

ἣν εἶχον. 10 καὶ ἔκραξαν φωνῇ μεγάλῃ
which they had. And they cried [2]voice [1]with a great(loud)

λέγοντες· ἕως πότε, ὁ δεσπότης ὁ ἅγιος
saying: Until when, *the* Master – holy

καὶ ἀληθινός, οὐ κρίνεις καὶ ἐκδικεῖς
and true, judgest thou not and avengest

τὸ αἷμα ἡμῶν ἐκ τῶν κατοικούντων
the blood of us of the [ones] dwelling

ἐπὶ τῆς γῆς; 11 καὶ ἐδόθη αὐτοῖς ἑκάστῳ
on the earth? And [3]was given [4]to them [5]each one

στολὴ λευκή, καὶ ἐρρέθη αὐτοῖς ἵνα
[2]robe [1]a white, and it was said to them *in order* that

ἀναπαύσωνται ἔτι χρόνον μικρόν, ἕως
they should rest yet [2]time [1]a little, until

πληρωθῶσιν καὶ οἱ σύνδουλοι αὐτῶν καὶ
should be fulfilled also the fellow-slaves of them and

οἱ ἀδελφοὶ αὐτῶν οἱ μέλλοντες ἀποκτέν-
the brothers of them the [ones] *being* about to be

νεσθαι ὡς καὶ αὐτοί. 12 Καὶ εἶδον
killed as also they. And I saw

ὅτε ἤνοιξεν τὴν σφραγῖδα τὴν ἕκτην,
when he opened the [2]seal – [1]sixth,

καὶ σεισμὸς μέγας ἐγένετο, καὶ ὁ ἥλιος
and [2]earthquake [1]a great occurred, and the sun

a pair of scales in his hand.
6Then I heard what sound-
ed like a voice among the
four living creatures, saying, "A quart[j] of wheat for
a day's wages,[k] and three
quarts of barley for a day's
wages,[l] and do not damage
the oil and the wine!"
7When the Lamb opened
the fourth seal, I heard the
voice of the fourth living
creature say, "Come!" 8I
looked, and there before
me was a pale horse! Its rider was named Death, and
Hades was following close
behind him. They were giv-
en power over a fourth of
the earth to kill by sword,
famine and plague, and by
the wild beasts of the earth.
9When he opened the fifth
seal, I saw under the altar
the souls of those who had
been slain because of the
word of God and the testimony they had maintained.
10They called out in a loud
voice, "How long, Sover-
eign Lord, holy and true,
until you judge the inhabitants of the earth and
avenge our blood?" 11Then
each of them was given a
white robe, and they were
told to wait a little longer,
until the number of their
fellow servants and brothers who were to be killed as
they had been was com-
pleted.
12I watched as he opened
the sixth seal. There was a
great earthquake. The sun

[r] Gk *a denarius*
[s] Gk *slaves*
[t] Gk *brothers*

[j] 6 Greek *a choinix* (probably about a liter)
[k] 6 Greek *a denarius*
[l] 6 Greek *a denarius*

quake; the sun became
black as sackcloth, the full
moon became like blood,
[13]and the stars of the sky
fell to the earth as the fig
tree drops its winter fruit
when shaken by a gale.
[14]The sky vanished like a
scroll rolling itself up, and
every mountain and island
was removed from its
place. [15]Then the kings of
the earth and the magnates
and the generals and the
rich and the powerful, and
everyone, slave and free,
hid in the caves and among
the rocks of the mountains,
[16]calling to the mountains
and rocks, "Fall on us and
hide us from the face of the
one seated on the throne
and from the wrath of the
Lamb; [17]for the great day
of their wrath has come,
and who is able to stand?"

Chapter 7

The 144,000 of Israel Sealed

AFTER this I saw four
angels standing at the
four corners of the earth,
holding back the four winds
of the earth so that no wind
could blow on earth or sea
or against any tree. [2]I saw
another angel ascending
from the rising of the sun,
having the seal of the living
God, and he called with a
loud voice to the four angels who had been given
power to damage earth and
sea, [3]saying, "Do not damage the earth or the sea or

ἐγένετο μέλας ὡς σάκκος τρίχινος, καὶ
became black as sackcloth made of hair, and

ἡ σελήνη ὅλη ἐγένετο ὡς αἷμα, **13** καὶ
the [2]moon [1]whole became as blood, and

οἱ ἀστέρες τοῦ οὐρανοῦ ἔπεσαν εἰς τὴν
the stars – of heaven fell to the

γῆν, ὡς συκῆ βάλλει τοὺς ὀλύνθους
earth, as a fig-tree casts the unripe figs

αὐτῆς ὑπὸ ἀνέμου μεγάλου σειομένη,
of it [2]by [4]wind [3]a great(strong) [1]being shaken,

14 καὶ ὁ οὐρανὸς ἀπεχωρίσθη ὡς βιβλίον
and the heaven departed as a scroll

ἑλισσόμενον, καὶ πᾶν ὄρος καὶ νῆσος
being rolled up, and every mountain and island

ἐκ τῶν τόπων αὐτῶν ἐκινήθησαν. **15** καὶ
out of the places of them were moved. And

οἱ βασιλεῖς τῆς γῆς καὶ οἱ μεγιστᾶνες
the kings of the earth and the great men

καὶ οἱ χιλίαρχοι καὶ οἱ πλούσιοι καὶ
and the chiliarchs and the rich men and

οἱ ἰσχυροὶ καὶ πᾶς δοῦλος καὶ ἐλεύθερος
the strong men and every slave and free man

ἔκρυψαν ἑαυτοὺς εἰς τὰ σπήλαια καὶ
hid themselves in the caves and

εἰς τὰς πέτρας τῶν ὀρέων, **16** καὶ
in the rocks of the mountains, and

λέγουσιν τοῖς ὄρεσιν καὶ ταῖς πέτραις·
they say to the mountains and to the rocks:

πέσετε ἐφ᾽ ἡμᾶς καὶ κρύψατε ἡμᾶς
Fall ye on us and hide us

ἀπὸ προσώπου τοῦ καθημένου ἐπὶ τοῦ
from [the] face of the [one] sitting on the

θρόνου καὶ ἀπὸ τῆς ὀργῆς τοῦ ἀρνίου,
throne and from the wrath of the Lamb,

17 ὅτι ἦλθεν ἡ ἡμέρα ἡ μεγάλη τῆς
because [7]came [1]the [3]day – [2]great [4]of the

ὀργῆς αὐτῶν, καὶ τίς δύναται σταθῆναι;
[5]wrath [6]of them, and who can *to* stand ?

7 Μετὰ τοῦτο εἶδον τέσσαρας ἀγγέλους
After this I saw four angels

ἑστῶτας ἐπὶ τὰς τέσσαρας γωνίας τῆς
standing on the four corners of the

γῆς, κρατοῦντας τοὺς τέσσαρας ἀνέμους
earth, holding the four winds

τῆς γῆς, ἵνα μὴ πνέῃ ἄνεμος ἐπὶ τῆς
of the earth, in order that [3]not [2]should [4]blow [1]wind on the

γῆς μήτε ἐπὶ τῆς θαλάσσης μήτε ἐπὶ
earth nor on the sea nor on

πᾶν δένδρον. **2** καὶ εἶδον ἄλλον ἄγγελον
every(any) tree. And I saw another angel

ἀναβαίνοντα ἀπὸ ἀνατολῆς ἡλίου, ἔχοντα
coming up from [the] rising of [the] sun, having

σφραγῖδα θεοῦ ζῶντος, καὶ ἔκραξεν φωνῇ
a seal God of [the] living, and he cried [2]voice

μεγάλῃ τοῖς τέσσαρσιν ἀγγέλοις οἷς
[1]with a great(loud) to the four angels to whom

ἐδόθη αὐτοῖς ἀδικῆσαι τὴν γῆν καὶ
it was given *to them* to harm the earth and

τὴν θάλασσαν, **3** λέγων· μὴ ἀδικήσητε
the sea, saying: Do not harm

τὴν γῆν μήτε τὴν θάλασσαν μήτε τὰ
the earth nor the sea nor the

turned black like sackcloth
made of goat hair, the
whole moon turned blood
red, [13]and the stars in the
sky fell to earth, as late figs
drop from a fig tree when
shaken by a strong wind.
[14]The sky receded like a
scroll, rolling up, and every
mountain and island was
removed from its place.
[15]Then the kings of the
earth, the princes, the generals, the rich, the mighty,
and every slave and every
free man hid in caves and
among the rocks of the
mountains. [16]They called
to the mountains and the
rocks, "Fall on us and hide
us from the face of him who
sits on the throne and from
the wrath of the Lamb!
[17]For the great day of their
wrath has come, and who
can stand?"

Chapter 7

144,000 Sealed

AFTER this I saw four
angels standing at the
four corners of the earth,
holding back the four winds
of the earth to prevent any
wind from blowing on the
land or on the sea or on any
tree. [2]Then I saw another
angel coming up from the
east, having the seal of the
living God. He called out in
a loud voice to the four angels who had been given
power to harm the land and
the sea: [3]"Do not harm the
land or the sea or the trees

the trees, until we have
marked the servants[u] of
our God with a seal on their
foreheads."
4 And I heard the num-
ber of those who were
sealed, one hundred forty-
four thousand, sealed out
of every tribe of the people
of Israel:
5 From the tribe of Ju-
dah twelve thou-
sand sealed,
from the tribe of Reu-
ben twelve thou-
sand,
from the tribe of Gad
twelve thousand,
6 from the tribe of Ash-
er twelve thousand,
from the tribe of
Naphtali twelve
thousand,
from the tribe of Ma-
nasseh twelve thou-
sand,
7 from the tribe of Sime-
on twelve thou-
sand,
from the tribe of Levi
twelve thousand,
from the tribe of Issa-
char twelve thou-
sand,
8 from the tribe of Zebu-
lun twelve thou-
sand,
from the tribe of Jo-
seph twelve thou-
sand,
from the tribe of Ben-
jamin twelve thou-
sand sealed.

The Multitude from Every Nation

9 After this I looked,
and there was a great multitude that no one could
count, from every nation,
from all tribes and peoples
and languages, standing before the throne and before
the Lamb, robed in white,
with palm branches in their
hands. 10 They cried out in
a loud voice, saying,
"Salvation belongs to
our God who is
seated on the
throne, and to
the Lamb!"
11 And all the angels stood
around the throne and
around the elders and the
four living creatures, and
they fell on their faces before the throne and wor-
shiped God, 12 singing,
"Amen! Blessing and

[u] Gk *slaves*

δένδρα, ἄχρι σφραγίσωμεν τοὺς δούλους
trees, until we *may* seal the slaves
τοῦ θεοῦ ἡμῶν ἐπὶ τῶν μετώπων αὐτῶν.
of the God of us on the foreheads of them.
4 Καὶ ἤκουσα τὸν ἀριθμὸν τῶν ἐσφραγισ-
And I heard the number of the [ones] *having been*
μένων, ἑκατὸν τεσσεράκοντα τέσσαρες
sealed, a hundred [and] forty-four
χιλιάδες ἐσφραγισμένοι ἐκ πάσης φυλῆς
thousand*s* *having been* sealed out of every tribe
υἱῶν Ἰσραήλ· **5** ἐκ φυλῆς Ἰούδα δώδεκα
of sons of Israel: of [the] tribe Juda twelve
χιλιάδες ἐσφραγισμένοι, ἐκ φυλῆς Ῥουβὴν
thousand*s* *having been* sealed, of [the] tribe Reuben
δώδεκα χιλιάδες, ἐκ φυλῆς Γὰδ δώδεκα
twelve thousand*s*, of [the] tribe Gad twelve
χιλιάδες, **6** ἐκ φυλῆς Ἀσὴρ δώδεκα
thousand*s*, of [the] tribe Aser twelve
χιλιάδες, ἐκ φυλῆς Νεφθαλὶμ δώδεκα
thousand*s*, of [the] tribe Nephthalim twelve
χιλιάδες, ἐκ φυλῆς Μανασσῆ δώδεκα
thousand*s*, of [the] tribe Manasse twelve
χιλιάδες, **7** ἐκ φυλῆς Συμεὼν δώδεκα
thousand*s*, of [the] tribe Symeon twelve
χιλιάδες, ἐκ φυλῆς Λευὶ δώδεκα χιλιάδες,
thousand*s*, of [the] tribe Levi twelve thousand*s*,
ἐκ φυλῆς Ἰσσαχὰρ δώδεκα χιλιάδες,
of [the] tribe Issachar twelve thousand*s*,
8 ἐκ φυλῆς Ζαβουλὼν δώδεκα χιλιάδες,
of [the] tribe Zabulon twelve thousand*s*,
ἐκ φυλῆς Ἰωσὴφ δώδεκα χιλιάδες, ἐκ
of [the] tribe Joseph twelve thousand*s*, of
φυλῆς Βενιαμὶν δώδεκα χιλιάδες ἐσφραγισ-
[the] tribe Benjamin twelve thousand*s* *having been*
μένοι. **9** Μετὰ ταῦτα εἶδον, καὶ ἰδοὺ ὄχλος
sealed. After these things I saw, and behold[,] [2]crowd
πολύς, ὃν ἀριθμῆσαι αὐτὸν οὐδεὶς ἐδύνατο,
[1]a much (great), which [3]to number *it* [1]no one [2]was able,
ἐκ παντὸς ἔθνους καὶ φυλῶν καὶ λαῶν
out of every nation and tribe*s* and people*s*
καὶ γλωσσῶν, ἑστῶτες ἐνώπιον τοῦ θρόνου
and tongue*s*, standing before the throne
καὶ ἐνώπιον τοῦ ἀρνίου, περιβεβλημένους
and before the Lamb, *having been* clothed [with]
στολὰς λευκάς, καὶ φοίνικες ἐν ταῖς
[2]robes [1]white, and palms in the
χερσὶν αὐτῶν· **10** καὶ κράζουσιν φωνῇ
hands of them; and they cry [2]voice
μεγάλῃ λέγοντες· ἡ σωτηρία τῷ θεῷ
[1]with a great(loud) saying: – Salvation to the God[c]
ἡμῶν τῷ καθημένῳ ἐπὶ τῷ θρόνῳ καὶ
of us – sitting on the throne and
τῷ ἀρνίῳ. **11** καὶ πάντες οἱ ἄγγελοι
to the Lamb.[c] And all the angels
εἱστήκεισαν κύκλῳ τοῦ θρόνου καὶ τῶν
stood round the throne and the
πρεσβυτέρων καὶ τῶν τεσσάρων ζῴων,
elders and the four living creatures,
καὶ ἔπεσαν ἐνώπιον τοῦ θρόνου ἐπὶ
and fell before the throne on
τὰ πρόσωπα αὐτῶν καὶ προσεκύνησαν
the faces of them and worshipped
τῷ θεῷ, **12** λέγοντες· ἀμήν, ἡ εὐλογία
– God, saying: Amen, – blessing

until we put a seal on the
foreheads of the servants of
our God." 4Then I heard
the number of those who
were sealed: 144,000 from
all the tribes of Israel.

5From the tribe of Judah
12,000 were sealed,
from the tribe of Reu-
ben 12,000,
from the tribe of Gad
12,000,
6from the tribe of Asher
12,000,
from the tribe of Naph-
tali 12,000,
from the tribe of Manas-
seh 12,000,
7from the tribe of Sime-
on 12,000,
from the tribe of Levi
12,000,
from the tribe of Issa-
char 12,000,
8from the tribe of Zebu-
lun 12,000,
from the tribe of Joseph
12,000,
from the tribe of Benja-
min 12,000.

The Great Multitude in White Robes

9After this I looked and
there before me was a great
multitude that no one could
count, from every nation,
tribe, people and language,
standing before the throne
and in front of the Lamb.
They were wearing white
robes and were holding
palm branches in their
hands. 10And they cried out
in a loud voice:

"Salvation belongs to
our God,
who sits on the throne,
and to the Lamb."

11All the angels were standing around the throne and
around the elders and the
four living creatures. They
fell down on their faces before the throne and wor-
shiped God, 12saying:

"Amen!
Praise and glory

glory
and wisdom
and thanksgiving and
honor
and power and might
be to our God forever
and ever!
Amen."
13 Then one of the el-
ders addressed me, saying,
"Who are these, robed in
white, and where have they
come from?"
14 I said to
him, "Sir, you are the one
that knows." Then he said
to me, "These are they who
have come out of the great
ordeal; they have washed
their robes and made them
white in the blood of the
Lamb.
15 For this reason they
are before the
throne of God,
and worship him
day and night
within his
temple,
and the one who is
seated on the
throne will
shelter them.
16 They will hunger no
more, and thirst
no more;
the sun will not
strike them,
nor any scorching
heat;
17 for the Lamb at the
center of the
throne will be
their shepherd,
and he will guide
them to springs
of the water of
life,
and God will wipe
away every tear
from their
eyes."

Chapter 8

The Seventh Seal and the Golden Censer

WHEN the Lamb
opened the seventh
seal, there was silence in
heaven for about half an
hour.
2 And I saw the seven
angels who stand before
God, and seven trumpets
were given to them.
3 Another angel with a
golden censer came and
stood at the altar; he was
given a great quantity of incense to offer with the
prayers of all the saints on

καὶ ἡ δόξα καὶ ἡ σοφία καὶ ἡ εὐχαριστία
and – glory and – wisdom and – thanks
καὶ ἡ τιμὴ καὶ ἡ δύναμις καὶ ἡ ἰσχὺς
and – honour and – power and – strength
τῷ θεῷ ἡμῶν εἰς τοὺς αἰῶνας τῶν
to the God[e] of us unto the ages of the
αἰώνων· ἀμήν. 13 Καὶ ἀπεκρίθη εἷς
ages: Amen. And [6]answered [1]one
ἐκ τῶν πρεσβυτέρων λέγων μοι· οὗτοι
[2]of [3]the [4]elders saying to me: These
οἱ περιβεβλημένοι τὰς στολὰς τὰς
the [ones] *having been* clothed [with] the [2]robes –
λευκὰς τίνες εἰσὶν καὶ πόθεν ἦλθον;
[1]white who are they and whence came they?
14 καὶ εἴρηκα αὐτῷ· κύριέ μου, σὺ
And I *have* said to him: Lord of me, thou
οἶδας. καὶ εἶπέν μοι· οὗτοί εἰσιν οἱ
knowest. And he told me: These are the
ἐρχόμενοι ἐκ τῆς θλίψεως τῆς μεγάλης
[ones] coming out of the [2]affliction – [1]great
καὶ ἔπλυναν τὰς στολὰς αὐτῶν καὶ
and washed the robes of them and
ἐλεύκαναν αὐτὰς ἐν τῷ αἵματι τοῦ
whitened them in the blood of the
ἀρνίου. 15 διὰ τοῦτό εἰσιν ἐνώπιον τοῦ
Lamb. Therefore are they before the
θρόνου τοῦ θεοῦ, καὶ λατρεύουσιν αὐτῷ
throne – of God, and serve him
ἡμέρας καὶ νυκτὸς ἐν τῷ ναῷ αὐτοῦ,
day and night in the shrine of him,
καὶ ὁ καθήμενος ἐπὶ τοῦ θρόνου σκηνώσει
and the [one] sitting on the throne will spread [his] tent
ἐπ' αὐτούς. 16 οὐ πεινάσουσιν ἔτι οὐδὲ
over them. They will not hunger longer nor
διψήσουσιν ἔτι, οὐδὲ μὴ πέσῃ ἐπ' αὐτοὺς
will they thirst longer, neither *not* fall on them
ὁ ἥλιος οὐδὲ πᾶν καῦμα, 17 ὅτι τὸ
the sun nor every(any) heat, because the
ἀρνίον τὸ ἀνὰ μέσον τοῦ θρόνου ποιμανεῖ
Lamb – in the midst of the throne will shepherd
αὐτοὺς καὶ ὁδηγήσει αὐτοὺς ἐπὶ ζωῆς
them and will lead them upon [2]of life
πηγὰς ὑδάτων· καὶ ἐξαλείψει ὁ θεὸς
[1]fountains [3]of waters; and [2]will wipe off – [1]God
πᾶν δάκρυον ἐκ τῶν ὀφθαλμῶν αὐτῶν.
every tear out of the eyes of them.

8 Καὶ ὅταν ἤνοιξεν τὴν σφραγῖδα τὴν
And when*ever* he opened the [2]seal –
ἑβδόμην, ἐγένετο σιγὴ ἐν τῷ οὐρανῷ
[1]seventh, occurred a silence in – heaven
ὡς ἡμιώρον. 2 Καὶ εἶδον τοὺς ἑπτὰ
about a half-hour. And I saw the seven
ἀγγέλους οἳ ἐνώπιον τοῦ θεοῦ ἑστήκασιν,
angels who before – God stood,
καὶ ἐδόθησαν αὐτοῖς ἑπτὰ σάλπιγγες.
and there were given to them seven trumpets.
3 Καὶ ἄλλος ἄγγελος ἦλθεν καὶ ἐστάθη
And another angel came and stood
ἐπὶ τοῦ θυσιαστηρίου ἔχων λιβανωτὸν
on the altar having [2]censer
χρυσοῦν, καὶ ἐδόθη αὐτῷ θυμιάματα πολλά,
[1]a golden, and there was given to him incenses many (much),

and wisdom and thanks
and honor
and power and strength
be to our God for ever
and ever.
Amen!"
13Then one of the elders
asked me, "These in white
robes—who are they, and
where did they come
from?"
14I answered, "Sir, you
know."
And he said, "These are
they who have come out of
the great tribulation; they
have washed their robes
and made them white in the
blood of the Lamb.
15Therefore,

"they are before the
throne of God
and serve him day and
night in his temple;
and he who sits on the
throne will spread
his tent over them.
16Never again will they
hunger;
never again will they
thirst.
The sun will not beat
upon them,
nor any scorching heat.
17For the Lamb at the
center of the throne
will be their
shepherd;
he will lead them to
springs of living
water.
And God will wipe away
every tear from their
eyes."

Chapter 8

The Seventh Seal and the Golden Censer

WHEN he opened the
seventh seal, there
was silence in heaven for
about half an hour.
2And I saw the seven an-
gels who stand before God,
and to them were given
seven trumpets.
3Another angel, who had
a golden censer, came and
stood at the altar. He was
given much incense to of-

the golden altar that is before the throne. 4And the
smoke of the incense, with
the prayers of the saints,
rose before God from the
hand of the angel. 5Then
the angel took the censer
and filled it with fire from
the altar and threw it on the
earth; and there were peals
of thunder, rumblings,
flashes of lightning, and an
earthquake.

The Seven Trumpets

6 Now the seven angels
who had the seven trum-
pets made ready to blow
them.
7 The first angel blew
his trumpet, and there
came hail and fire, mixed
with blood, and they were
hurled to the earth; and a
third of the earth was
burned up, and a third of
the trees were burned up,
and all green grass was
burned up.
8 The second angel
blew his trumpet, and
something like a great
mountain, burning with
fire, was thrown into the
sea. 9A third of the sea became blood, a third of the
living creatures in the sea
died, and a third of the
ships were destroyed.
10 The third angel blew
his trumpet, and a great
star fell from heaven, blazing like a torch, and it fell
on a third of the rivers and
on the springs of water.
11The name of the star is
Wormwood. A third of the

ἵνα δώσει ταῖς προσευχαῖς τῶν ἁγίων
in order that he will give [it] with the prayers of [2]the [3]saints

πάντων ἐπὶ τὸ θυσιαστήριον τὸ χρυσοῦν
[1]all on the [2]altar – [1]golden

τὸ ἐνώπιον τοῦ θρόνου. 4 καὶ ἀνέβη
– before the throne. And went up

ὁ καπνὸς τῶν θυμιαμάτων ταῖς προσευχαῖς
the smoke of the incenses with the prayers

τῶν ἁγίων ἐκ χειρὸς τοῦ ἀγγέλου ἐνώπιον
of the saints out of [the] hand of the angel before

τοῦ θεοῦ. 5 καὶ εἴληφεν ὁ ἄγγελος
– God. And [3]has taken [1]the [2]angel

τὸν λιβανωτόν, καὶ ἐγέμισεν αὐτὸν ἐκ
the censer, and filled it from

τοῦ πυρὸς τοῦ θυσιαστηρίου καὶ ἔβαλεν
the fire of the altar and cast

εἰς τὴν γῆν· καὶ ἐγένοντο βρονταὶ καὶ
into the earth; and there occurred thunders and

φωναὶ καὶ ἀστραπαὶ καὶ σεισμός.
sounds and lightnings and an earthquake.

6 Καὶ οἱ ἑπτὰ ἄγγελοι οἱ ἔχοντες
And the seven angels – having

τὰς ἑπτὰ σάλπιγγας ἡτοίμασαν αὐτοὺς
the seven trumpets prepared themselves

ἵνα σαλπίσωσιν. 7 Καὶ ὁ πρῶτος
in order that they might trumpet. And the first

ἐσάλπισεν· καὶ ἐγένετο χάλαζα καὶ πῦρ
trumpeted; and there occurred hail and fire

μεμιγμένα ἐν αἵματι καὶ ἐβλήθη εἰς
having been mixed in (with) blood and it was cast to

τὴν γῆν· καὶ τὸ τρίτον τῆς γῆς
the earth; and the third [part] of the earth

κατεκάη, καὶ τὸ τρίτον τῶν δένδρων
was burnt down(up), and the third [part] of the trees

κατεκάη, καὶ πᾶς χόρτος χλωρὸς κατεκάη.
was burnt down(up), and all [2]grass [1]green was burnt down(up).

8 Καὶ ὁ δεύτερος ἄγγελος ἐσάλπισεν·
And the second angel trumpeted;

καὶ ὡς ὄρος μέγα πυρὶ καιόμενον ἐβλήθη
and as [2]mountain [1]a great [4]with fire [3]burning was cast

εἰς τὴν θάλασσαν· καὶ ἐγένετο τὸ τρίτον
into the sea; and [5]became [1]the [2]third [part]

τῆς θαλάσσης αἷμα, 9 καὶ ἀπέθανεν τὸ
[3]of the [4]sea [6]blood, and [10]died [1]the

τρίτον τῶν κτισμάτων τῶν ἐν τῇ θαλάσσῃ,
[2]third [part] [3]of the [4]creatures – [5]in [6]the [7]sea,

τὰ ἔχοντα ψυχάς, καὶ τὸ τρίτον τῶν
– [8]having [9]souls, and the third [part] of the

πλοίων διεφθάρησαν. 10 Καὶ ὁ τρίτος
ships were destroyed. And the third

ἄγγελος ἐσάλπισεν· καὶ ἔπεσεν ἐκ τοῦ
angel trumpeted; and fell out of –

οὐρανοῦ ἀστὴρ μέγας καιόμενος ὡς
heaven star a great burning as

λαμπάς, καὶ ἔπεσεν ἐπὶ τὸ τρίτον τῶν
a lamp, and it fell onto the third [part] of the

ποταμῶν καὶ ἐπὶ τὰς πηγὰς τῶν ὑδάτων.
rivers and onto the fountains of the waters.

11 καὶ τὸ ὄνομα τοῦ ἀστέρος λέγεται
And the name of the star is said(called)

fer, with the prayers of all
the saints, on the golden altar before the throne. 4The
smoke of the incense, to-
gether with the prayers of
the saints, went up before
God from the angel's hand.
5Then the angel took the
censer, filled it with fire
from the altar, and hurled it
on the earth; and there
came peals of thunder,
rumblings, flashes of lightning and an earthquake.

The Trumpets

6Then the seven angels
who had the seven trum-
pets prepared to sound
them.
7The first angel sounded
his trumpet, and there
came hail and fire mixed
with blood, and it was
hurled down upon the
earth. A third of the earth
was burned up, a third of
the trees were burned up,
and all the green grass was
burned up.
8The second angel sound-
ed his trumpet, and some-
thing like a huge mountain,
all ablaze, was thrown into
the sea. A third of the sea
turned into blood, 9a third
of the living creatures in the
sea died, and a third of the
ships were destroyed.
10The third angel sounded
his trumpet, and a great
star, blazing like a torch,
fell from the sky on a third
of the rivers and on the
springs of water— 11the
name of the star is Worm-

waters became worm-
wood, and many died from
the water, because it was
made bitter.
12 The fourth angel
blew his trumpet, and a
third of the sun was struck,
and a third of the moon,
and a third of the stars, so
that a third of their light
was darkened; a third of the
day was kept from shining,
and likewise the night.
13 Then I looked, and I
heard an eagle crying with a
loud voice as it flew in mid-
heaven, "Woe, woe, woe
to the inhabitants of the
earth, at the blasts of the
other trumpets that the
three angels are about to
blow!"

ὁ Ἄψινθος. καὶ ἐγένετο τὸ τρίτον τῶν
– Wormwood. And [5]became [1]the [2]third [part] [3]of the

ὑδάτων εἰς ἄψινθον, καὶ πολλοὶ τῶν
[4]waters *into* wormwood, and many of the

ἀνθρώπων ἀπέθανον ἐκ τῶν ὑδάτων ὅτι
men died from the waters because

ἐπικράνθησαν. 12 Καὶ ὁ τέταρτος ἄγγελος
they were made bitter. And the fourth angel

ἐσάλπισεν· καὶ ἐπλήγη τὸ τρίτον τοῦ
trumpeted; and [5]was struck [1]the [2]third [part] [3]of the

ἡλίου καὶ τὸ τρίτον τῆς σελήνης καὶ
[4]sun and the third [part] of the moon and

τὸ τρίτον τῶν ἀστέρων, ἵνα σκοτισθῇ
the third [part] of the stars, in order that [4]might be darkened

τὸ τρίτον αὐτῶν καὶ ἡ ἡμέρα μὴ φάνῃ
[1]the [2]third [part] [3]of them and the day might not appear

τὸ τρίτον αὐτῆς, καὶ ἡ νὺξ ὁμοίως.
the third [part] of it, and the night likewise.

13 Καὶ εἶδον, καὶ ἤκουσα ἑνὸς ἀετοῦ
And I saw, and I heard one eagle

πετομένου ἐν μεσουρανήματι λέγοντος φωνῇ
flying in mid-heaven saying [2]voice

μεγάλῃ· οὐαὶ οὐαὶ οὐαὶ τοὺς κατοικοῦν-
[1]with a great(loud): Woe[,] woe[,] woe to the [ones] dwell-

τας ἐπὶ τῆς γῆς ἐκ τῶν λοιπῶν φωνῶν
ing on the earth from the remaining voices

τῆς σάλπιγγος τῶν τριῶν ἀγγέλων τῶν
of the trumpet of the three angels –

μελλόντων σαλπίζειν.
being about to trumpet.

wood.[m] A third of the waters turned bitter, and
many people died from the
waters that had become bitter.
12The fourth angel sound-
ed his trumpet, and a third
of the sun was struck, a
third of the moon, and a
third of the stars, so that a
third of them turned dark.
A third of the day was without light, and also a third of
the night.
13As I watched, I heard
an eagle that was flying in
midair call out in a loud
voice: "Woe! Woe! Woe to
the inhabitants of the earth,
because of the trumpet
blasts about to be sounded
by the other three angels!"

Chapter 9

AND the fifth angel blew
his trumpet, and I
saw a star that had fallen
from heaven to earth, and
he was given the key to the
shaft of the bottomless pit;
2 he opened the shaft of the
bottomless pit, and from
the shaft rose smoke like
the smoke of a great fur-
nace, and the sun and the
air were darkened with the
smoke from the shaft.
3 Then from the smoke
came locusts on the earth,
and they were given au-
thority like the authority of
scorpions of the earth.
4 They were told not to
damage the grass of the
earth or any green growth
or any tree, but only those
people who do not have the

9 Καὶ ὁ πέμπτος ἄγγελος ἐσάλπισεν·
And the fifth angel trumpeted;

καὶ εἶδον ἀστέρα ἐκ τοῦ οὐρανοῦ πεπτω-
and I saw a star out of – heaven having

κότα εἰς τὴν γῆν, καὶ ἐδόθη αὐτῷ
fallen onto the earth, and was given to it

ἡ κλεὶς τοῦ φρέατος τῆς ἀβύσσου. 2 καὶ
the key of the shaft of the abyss. And

ἤνοιξεν τὸ φρέαρ τῆς ἀβύσσου· καὶ
he opened the shaft of the abyss; and

ἀνέβη καπνὸς ἐκ τοῦ φρέατος ὡς
went up a smoke out of the shaft as

καπνὸς καμίνου μεγάλης, καὶ ἐσκοτώθη
smoke [2]furnace [1]of a great, and [6]was darkened

ὁ ἥλιος καὶ ὁ ἀὴρ ἐκ τοῦ καπνοῦ
[1]the [2]sun [3]and [4]the [5]air by the smoke

τοῦ φρέατος. 3 καὶ ἐκ τοῦ καπνοῦ
of the shaft. And out of the smoke

ἐξῆλθον ἀκρίδες εἰς τὴν γῆν, καὶ ἐδόθη
came forth locusts to the earth, and [2]was given

αὐτοῖς ἐξουσία ὡς ἔχουσιν ἐξουσίαν οἱ
[3]to them [1]authority as [5]have [6]authority [1]the

σκορπίοι τῆς γῆς. 4 καὶ ἐρρέθη αὐτοῖς
[2]scorpions [3]of the [4]earth. And it was said to them

ἵνα μὴ ἀδικήσουσιν τὸν χόρτον τῆς
in order that they shall not harm the grass of the

γῆς οὐδὲ πᾶν χλωρὸν οὐδὲ πᾶν δένδρον,
earth nor every (any) greenstuff nor every (any) tree,

εἰ μὴ τοὺς ἀνθρώπους οἵτινες οὐκ ἔχουσιν
except the men who have not

Chapter 9

THE fifth angel sounded
his trumpet, and I saw
a star that had fallen from
the sky to the earth. The
star was given the key to
the shaft of the Abyss.
2When he opened the
Abyss, smoke rose from it
like the smoke from a gi-
gantic furnace. The sun and
sky were darkened by the
smoke from the Abyss.
3And out of the smoke lo-
custs came down upon the
earth and were given power
like that of scorpions of the
earth. 4They were told not
to harm the grass of the
earth or any plant or tree,
but only those people who

[m]11 That is, Bitterness

seal of God on their foreheads. 5 They were allowed
to torture them for five
months, but not to kill
them, and their torture was
like the torture of a scorpion when it stings someone.
6 And in those days people
will seek death but will not
find it; they will long to die,
but death will flee from
them.
7 In appearance the lo-
custs were like horses
equipped for battle. On
their heads were what
looked like crowns of gold;
their faces were like human
faces, 8 their hair like wom-
en's hair, and their teeth
like lions' teeth; 9 they had
scales like iron breast-
plates, and the noise of
their wings was like the
noise of many chariots with
horses rushing into battle.
10 They have tails like scorpions, with stingers, and in
their tails is their power to
harm people for five
months. 11 They have as
king over them the angel of
the bottomless pit; his
name in Hebrew is Abad-
don,[v] and in Greek he is
called Apollyon.[w]
12 The first woe has
passed. There are still two
woes to come.
13 Then the sixth angel
blew his trumpet, and I
heard a voice from the
four[x] horns of the golden
altar before God, 14 saying
to the sixth angel who had

τὴν σφραγῖδα τοῦ θεοῦ ἐπὶ τῶν μετώπων.
the seal – of God on the(ir) foreheads.

5 καὶ ἐδόθη αὐτοῖς ἵνα μὴ ἀποκτείνωσιν
And it was given to them *in order that* they should not kill

αὐτούς, ἀλλ' ἵνα βασανισθήσονται μῆνας
them, but *in order that* they shall be tormented [2]months

πέντε· καὶ ὁ βασανισμὸς αὐτῶν ὡς
[1]five; and the torment of them [is] as

βασανισμὸς σκορπίου, ὅταν παίσῃ ἄνθρωπον.
[the] torment of a scorpion, whenever it stings a man.

6 καὶ ἐν ταῖς ἡμέραις ἐκείναις ζητήσουσιν
And in those days [2]will seek

οἱ ἄνθρωποι τὸν θάνατον καὶ οὐ μὴ
– [1]men – death and by no means

εὑρήσουσιν αὐτόν, καὶ ἐπιθυμήσουσιν
will they find it, and they will long

ἀποθανεῖν καὶ φεύγει ὁ θάνατος ἀπ'
to die and [2]flees – [1]death from

αὐτῶν. **7** καὶ τὰ ὁμοιώματα τῶν ἀκρίδων
them. And the likenesses of the locusts

ὅμοιοι ἵπποις ἡτοιμασμένοις εἰς πόλεμον,
like *to* horses *having been* prepared for war,

καὶ ἐπὶ τὰς κεφαλὰς αὐτῶν ὡς στέφανοι
and on the heads of them as crowns

ὅμοιοι χρυσῷ, καὶ τὰ πρόσωπα αὐτῶν
like *to* gold, and the faces of them

ὡς πρόσωπα ἀνθρώπων, **8** καὶ εἶχον
as faces of men, and they had

τρίχας ὡς τρίχας γυναικῶν, καὶ οἱ
hairs as hairs of women, and the

ὀδόντες αὐτῶν ὡς λεόντων ἦσαν, **9** καὶ
teeth of them [2]as [3]of lions [1]were, and

εἶχον θώρακας ὡς θώρακας σιδηροῦς,
they had breastplates as [2]breastplates [1]iron,

καὶ ἡ φωνὴ τῶν πτερύγων αὐτῶν ὡς
and the sound of the wings of them as

φωνὴ ἁρμάτων ἵππων πολλῶν τρεχόντων
sound [3]chariots [2]of horses [1]of many running

εἰς πόλεμον. **10** καὶ ἔχουσιν οὐρὰς ὁμοίας
to war. And they have tails like

σκορπίοις καὶ κέντρα, καὶ ἐν ταῖς οὐραῖς
to scorpions and stings, and [6]with [7]the [8]tails

αὐτῶν ἡ ἐξουσία αὐτῶν ἀδικῆσαι τοὺς
[9]of them [1]the [2]authority [3]of them [4][is] to harm –

ἀνθρώπους μῆνας πέντε. **11** ἔχουσιν ἐπ'
[5]men [11]months [10]five. They have over

αὐτῶν βασιλέα τὸν ἄγγελον τῆς ἀβύσσου,
them a king the angel of the abyss,

ὄνομα αὐτῷ Ἑβραϊστὶ Ἀβαδδών, καὶ
name to him[e] in Hebrew Abaddon, and

ἐν τῇ Ἑλληνικῇ ὄνομα ἔχει Ἀπολλύων.
in the Greek [2][the] name [1]he has Apollyon.

12 Ἡ οὐαὶ ἡ μία ἀπῆλθεν· ἰδοὺ ἔρχεται
The [2]woe – [1]one(first) passed away; behold [4]comes

ἔτι δύο οὐαὶ μετὰ ταῦτα.
[1]yet [2]two [3]woes after these things.

13 Καὶ ὁ ἕκτος ἄγγελος ἐσάλπισεν·
And the sixth angel trumpeted;

καὶ ἤκουσα φωνὴν μίαν ἐκ τῶν τεσσάρων
and I heard [2]voice [1]one out of the four

κεράτων τοῦ θυσιαστηρίου τοῦ χρυσοῦ
horns of the [2]altar – [1]golden

τοῦ ἐνώπιον τοῦ θεοῦ, **14** λέγοντα τῷ
– before – God, saying to the

did not have the seal of God
on their foreheads. 5 They
were not given power to kill
them, but only to torture
them for five months. And
the agony they suffered
was like that of the sting of
a scorpion when it strikes a
man. 6 During those days
men will seek death, but
will not find it; they will
long to die, but death will
elude them.
7 The locusts looked like
horses prepared for battle.
On their heads they wore
something like crowns of
gold, and their faces resembled human faces. 8 Their
hair was like women's hair,
and their teeth were like lions' teeth. 9 They had
breastplates like breast-
plates of iron, and the
sound of their wings was
like the thundering of many
horses and chariots rushing
into battle. 10 They had tails
and stings like scorpions,
and in their tails they had
power to torment people
for five months. 11 They had
as king over them the angel
of the Abyss, whose name
in Hebrew is Abaddon, and
in Greek, Apollyon.[n]
12 The first woe is past;
two other woes are yet to
come.
13 The sixth angel sounded
his trumpet, and I heard a
voice coming from the
horns[o] of the golden altar
that is before God. 14 It said
to the sixth angel who had

[v] That is, *Destruction*
[w] That is, *Destroyer*
[x] Other ancient authorities lack *four*

[n] *11* *Abaddon* and *Apollyon* mean *Destroyer.*
[o] *13* That is, projections

the trumpet, "Release the four angels who are bound at the great river Euphrates." 15 So the four angels were released, who had been held ready for the hour, the day, the month, and the year, to kill a third of humankind. 16 The number of the troops of cavalry was two hundred million; I heard their number. 17 And this was how I saw the horses in my vision: the riders wore breastplates the color of fire and of sapphire[y] and of sulfur; the heads of the horses were like lions' heads, and fire and smoke and sulfur came out of their mouths. 18 By these three plagues a third of humankind was killed, by the fire and smoke and sulfur coming out of their mouths. 19 For the power of the horses is in their mouths and in their tails; their tails are like serpents, having heads; and with them they inflict harm.

20 The rest of humankind, who were not killed by these plagues, did not repent of the works of their hands or give up worshiping demons and idols of gold and silver and bronze and stone and wood, which cannot see or hear or walk.

ἕκτῳ ἀγγέλῳ, ὁ ἔχων τὴν σάλπιγγα·
sixth angel, – having the trumpet:

Λῦσον τοὺς τέσσαρας ἀγγέλους τοὺς
Loose the four angels –

δεδεμένους ἐπὶ τῷ ποταμῷ τῷ μεγάλῳ
having been bound at the [2]river – [1]great

Εὐφράτῃ. **15** καὶ ἐλύθησαν οἱ τέσσαρες
Euphrates. And were loosed the four

ἄγγελοι οἱ ἡτοιμασμένοι εἰς τὴν ὥραν
angels – *having been* prepared for the hour

καὶ ἡμέραν καὶ μῆνα καὶ ἐνιαυτόν,
and day and month and year,

ἵνα ἀποκτείνωσιν τὸ τρίτον τῶν ἀνθρώπων.
in order that they should kill the third [part] – of men.

16 καὶ ὁ ἀριθμὸς τῶν στρατευμάτων τοῦ
And the number of the bodies of soldiers of the

ἱππικοῦ δισμυριάδες μυριάδων· ἤκουσα τὸν
cavalry [was] two myriads of myriads; I heard the

ἀριθμὸν αὐτῶν. **17** καὶ οὕτως εἶδον
number of them. And thus I saw

τοὺς ἵππους ἐν τῇ ὁράσει καὶ τοὺς
the horses in the vision and the

καθημένους ἐπ' αὐτῶν, ἔχοντας θώρακας
[ones] sitting on them, having breastplates

πυρίνους καὶ ὑακινθίνους καὶ θειώδεις·
fire-coloured and dusky red and sulphurous;

καὶ αἱ κεφαλαὶ τῶν ἵππων ὡς κεφαλαὶ
and the heads of the horses as heads

λεόντων, καὶ ἐκ τῶν στομάτων αὐτῶν
of lions, and out of the mouths of them

ἐκπορεύεται πῦρ καὶ καπνὸς καὶ θεῖον.
proceeds fire and smoke and sulphur.

18 ἀπὸ τῶν τριῶν πληγῶν τούτων ἀπεκτάν-
From *the* [2]three [3]plagues [1]these were

θησαν τὸ τρίτον τῶν ἀνθρώπων, ἐκ
killed the third [part] – of men, by

τοῦ πυρὸς καὶ τοῦ καπνοῦ καὶ τοῦ
the fire and the smoke and the

θείου τοῦ ἐκπορευομένου ἐκ τῶν στομάτων
sulphur – proceeding out of the mouths

αὐτῶν. **19** ἡ γὰρ ἐξουσία τῶν ἵππων
of them. For the authority of the horses

ἐν τῷ στόματι αὐτῶν ἐστιν καὶ ἐν
[2]in [3]the [4]mouth [5]of them [1]is and in

ταῖς οὐραῖς αὐτῶν· αἱ γὰρ οὐραὶ αὐτῶν
the tails of them; for the tails of them

ὅμοιαι ὄφεσιν, ἔχουσαι κεφαλάς, καὶ ἐν
[are] like *to* serpents, having heads, and with

αὐταῖς ἀδικοῦσιν. **20** καὶ οἱ λοιποὶ τῶν
them they do harm. And the rest –

ἀνθρώπων, οἳ οὐκ ἀπεκτάνθησαν ἐν ταῖς
of men, who were not killed by –

πληγαῖς ταύταις, οὐδὲ μετενόησαν ἐκ
plagues these, not even repented of

τῶν ἔργων τῶν χειρῶν αὐτῶν, ἵνα μὴ
the works of the hands of them, in order that not

προσκυνήσουσιν τὰ δαιμόνια καὶ τὰ εἴδωλα
they will worship – demons and – idols

τὰ χρυσᾶ καὶ τὰ ἀργυρᾶ καὶ τὰ χαλκᾶ
– golden and – silver and – bronze

καὶ τὰ λίθινα καὶ τὰ ξύλινα, ἃ οὔτε
and – stone and – wooden, which [2]neither

βλέπειν δύνανται οὔτε ἀκούειν οὔτε
[3]*to* see [1]can nor *to* hear nor

the trumpet, "Release the four angels who are bound at the great river Euphrates." 15 And the four angels who had been kept ready for this very hour and day and month and year were released to kill a third of mankind. 16 The number of the mounted troops was two hundred million. I heard their number.

17 The horses and riders I saw in my vision looked like this: Their breastplates were fiery red, dark blue, and yellow as sulfur. The heads of the horses resembled the heads of lions, and out of their mouths came fire, smoke and sulfur. 18 A third of mankind was killed by the three plagues of fire, smoke and sulfur that came out of their mouths. 19 The power of the horses was in their mouths and in their tails; for their tails were like snakes, having heads with which they inflict injury.

20 The rest of mankind that were not killed by these plagues still did not repent of the work of their hands; they did not stop worshiping demons, and idols of gold, silver, bronze, stone and wood—idols that cannot see or

[y] Gk *hyacinth*

[21]And they did not repent
of their murders or their
sorceries or their fornication or their thefts.

Chapter 10

The Angel with the Little Scroll

AND I saw another
mighty angel coming
down from heaven,
wrapped in a cloud, with a
rainbow over his head; his
face was like the sun, and
his legs like pillars of fire.
[2]He held a little scroll open
in his hand. Setting his right
foot on the sea and his left
foot on the land, [3]he gave a
great shout, like a lion roaring. And when he shouted,
the seven thunders sound-
ed. [4]And when the seven
thunders had sounded, I
was about to write, but I
heard a voice from heaven
saying, "Seal up what the
seven thunders have said,
and do not write it down."
[5]Then the angel whom I
saw standing on the sea and
the land
raised his right hand
to heaven
6 and swore by him
who lives
forever and
ever,
who created heaven and
what is in it, the earth and
what is in it, and the sea
and what is in it: "There
will be no more delay, [7]but
in the days when the sev-
enth angel is to blow his
trumpet, the mystery of
God will be fulfilled, as he

περιπατεῖν, **21** καὶ οὐ μετενόησαν ἐκ τῶν
to walk, and they repented not of the

φόνων αὐτῶν οὔτε ἐκ τῶν φαρμακειῶν
murders of them nor of the sorceries

αὐτῶν οὔτε ἐκ τῆς πορνείας αὐτῶν
of them nor of the fornication of them

οὔτε ἐκ τῶν κλεμμάτων αὐτῶν.
nor of the thefts of them.

10 Καὶ εἶδον ἄλλον ἄγγελον ἰσχυρὸν
And I saw another [2]angel [1]strong

καταβαίνοντα ἐκ τοῦ οὐρανοῦ, περιβεβλημέ-
coming down out of – heaven, *having been* clothed

νον νεφέλην, καὶ ἡ ἶρις ἐπὶ τὴν κεφαλὴν
[with] a cloud, and the rainbow on the head

αὐτοῦ, καὶ τὸ πρόσωπον αὐτοῦ ὡς ὁ
of him, and the face of him as the

ἥλιος, καὶ οἱ πόδες αὐτοῦ ὡς στῦλοι
sun, and the feet of him as pillars

πυρός, **2** καὶ ἔχων ἐν τῇ χειρὶ αὐτοῦ
of fire, and having in the hand of him

βιβλαρίδιον ἠνεῳγμένον. καὶ ἔθηκεν τὸν
a little scroll *having been* opened. And he placed [1]the

πόδα αὐτοῦ τὸν δεξιὸν ἐπὶ τῆς θαλάσσης,
[3]foot [4]of him – [2]right on the sea,

τὸν δὲ εὐώνυμον ἐπὶ τῆς γῆς, **3** καὶ
and the left on the land, and

ἔκραξεν φωνῇ μεγάλῃ ὥσπερ λέων μυκᾶται.
cried [2]voice [1]with a great(loud) as a lion roars.

καὶ ὅτε ἔκραξεν, ἐλάλησαν αἱ ἑπτὰ
And when he cried, [4]spoke(uttered) [1]the [2]seven

βρονταὶ τὰς ἑαυτῶν φωνάς. **4** Καὶ ὅτε
[3]thunders [5]the [7]of them*selves* [6]voices. And when

ἐλάλησαν αἱ ἑπτὰ βρονταί, ἤμελλον
spoke the seven thunders, I was about

γράφειν· καὶ ἤκουσα φωνὴν ἐκ τοῦ
to write; and I heard a voice out of –

οὐρανοῦ λέγουσαν· σφράγισον ἃ ἐλάλησαν
heaven saying: Seal thou [the] things which [4]spoke

αἱ ἑπτὰ βρονταί, καὶ μὴ αὐτὰ γράψῃς.
[1]the [2]seven [3]thunders, and [3]not [2]them *thou mayest* [1]write.

5 Καὶ ὁ ἄγγελος, ὃν εἶδον ἑστῶτα
And the angel, whom I saw standing

ἐπὶ τῆς θαλάσσης καὶ ἐπὶ τῆς γῆς,
on the sea and on the land,

ἦρεν τὴν χεῖρα αὐτοῦ τὴν δεξιὰν εἰς
lifted [1]the [3]hand [4]of him – [2]right to

τὸν οὐρανόν, **6** καὶ ὤμοσεν ἐν τῷ ζῶντι
– heaven, and swore by the [one] living

εἰς τοὺς αἰῶνας τῶν αἰώνων, ὃς ἔκτισεν
unto the ages of the ages, who created

τὸν οὐρανὸν καὶ τὰ ἐν αὐτῷ καὶ τὴν
the heaven and the things in it and the

γῆν καὶ τὰ ἐν αὐτῇ καὶ τὴν θάλασσαν
earth and the things in it and the sea

καὶ τὰ ἐν αὐτῇ, ὅτι χρόνος οὐκέτι
and the things in it, that time [2]no longer

ἔσται, **7** ἀλλ' ἐν ταῖς ἡμέραις τῆς
[1]shall be, but in the days of the

φωνῆς τοῦ ἑβδόμου ἀγγέλου, ὅταν μέλλῃ
voice of the seventh angel, whenever he is about

σαλπίζειν, καὶ ἐτελέσθη τὸ μυστήριον
to trumpet, even was finished the mystery

hear or walk. [21]Nor did
they repent of their mur-
ders, their magic arts, their
sexual immorality or their
thefts.

Chapter 10

The Angel and the Little Scroll

THEN I saw another
mighty angel coming
down from heaven. He was
robed in a cloud, with a
rainbow above his head; his
face was like the sun, and
his legs were like fiery pillars. [2]He was holding a little scroll, which lay open in
his hand. He planted his
right foot on the sea and his
left foot on the land, [3]and
he gave a loud shout like
the roar of a lion. When he
shouted, the voices of the
seven thunders spoke.
[4]And when the seven thunders spoke, I was about to
write; but I heard a voice
from heaven say, "Seal up
what the seven thunders
have said and do not write
it down."
[5]Then the angel I had
seen standing on the sea
and on the land raised his
right hand to heaven. [6]And
he swore by him who lives
for ever and ever, who created the heavens and all
that is in them, the earth
and all that is in it, and the
sea and all that is in it, and
said, "There will be no
more delay! [7]But in the
days when the seventh an-
gel is about to sound his
trumpet, the mystery of

announced to his servants[z]
the prophets."
8 Then the voice that I
had heard from heaven
spoke to me again, saying,
"Go, take the scroll that is
open in the hand of the angel who is standing on the
sea and on the land." 9 So I
went to the angel and told
him to give me the little
scroll; and he said to me,
"Take it, and eat; it will be
bitter to your stomach, but
sweet as honey in your
mouth." 10 So I took the little scroll from the hand of
the angel and ate it; it was
sweet as honey in my
mouth, but when I had eat-
en it, my stomach was
made bitter.
11 Then they said to me,
"You must prophesy again
about many peoples and
nations and languages and
kings."

Chapter 11

The Two Witnesses

THEN I was given a
measuring rod like a
staff, and I was told,
"Come and measure the
temple of God and the altar
and those who worship
there, 2 but do not measure
the court outside the temple; leave that out, for it is
given over to the nations,
and they will trample over
the holy city for forty-two
months. 3 And I will grant
my two witnesses authority
to prophesy for one thou-
sand two hundred sixty
days, wearing sackcloth."
4 These are the two ol-
ive trees and the two lampstands that stand before the

[z] Gk *slaves*

τοῦ θεοῦ, ὡς εὐηγγέλισεν τοὺς ἑαυτοῦ
– of God, as he preached [to] the [2]of him*self*

δούλους τοὺς προφήτας. 8 Καὶ ἡ φωνὴ
[1]slaves the prophets. And the voice

ἣν ἤκουσα ἐκ τοῦ οὐρανοῦ, πάλιν
which I heard out of – heaven, again

λαλοῦσαν μετ' ἐμοῦ καὶ λέγουσαν· ὕπαγε
speaking with me and saying: Go thou

λάβε τὸ βιβλίον τὸ ἠνεῳγμένον ἐν τῇ
take the scroll – *having been* opened in the

χειρὶ τοῦ ἀγγέλου τοῦ ἑστῶτος ἐπὶ
hand of the angel – standing on

τῆς θαλάσσης καὶ ἐπὶ τῆς γῆς. 9 καὶ
the sea and on the land. And

ἀπῆλθα πρὸς τὸν ἄγγελον, λέγων αὐτῷ
I went away toward the angel, telling him

δοῦναί μοι τὸ βιβλαρίδιον. καὶ λέγει
to give me the little scroll. And he says

μοι· λάβε καὶ κατάφαγε αὐτό, καὶ
to me: Take and devour it, and

πικρανεῖ σου τὴν κοιλίαν, ἀλλ' ἐν τῷ
it will embitter [3]of thee [1]the [2]stomach, but in the

στόματί σου ἔσται γλυκὺ ὡς μέλι.
mouth of thee it will be sweet as honey.

10 καὶ ἔλαβον τὸ βιβλαρίδιον ἐκ τῆς
And I took the little scroll out of the

χειρὸς τοῦ ἀγγέλου καὶ κατέφαγον αὐτό,
hand of the angel and devoured it,

καὶ ἦν ἐν τῷ στόματί μου ὡς μέλι
and it was in the mouth of me as [2]honey

γλυκύ· καὶ ὅτε ἔφαγον αὐτό, ἐπικράνθη
[1]sweet; and when I ate it, [4]was made bitter

ἡ κοιλία μου. 11 καὶ λέγουσίν μοι·
[1]the [2]stomach [3]of me. And they say to me:

δεῖ σε πάλιν προφητεῦσαι ἐπὶ λαοῖς
It behoves thee again to prophesy before peoples

καὶ ἔθνεσιν καὶ γλώσσαις καὶ βασιλεῦσιν
and nations and tongues and [2]kings

πολλοῖς. 11 Καὶ ἐδόθη μοι κάλαμος ὅμοιος
[1]many. And was given to me a reed like

ῥάβδῳ, λέγων· ἔγειρε καὶ μέτρησον τὸν ναὸν
to a staff, saying: Rise and measure the shrine

τοῦ θεοῦ καὶ τὸ θυσιαστήριον καὶ τοὺς
of God and the altar and the

προσκυνοῦντας ἐν αὐτῷ. 2 καὶ τὴν
[ones] worshipping in it. And the

αὐλὴν τὴν ἔξωθεν τοῦ ναοῦ ἔκβαλε
[2]court – [1]outside of the shrine cast *out*

ἔξωθεν καὶ μὴ αὐτὴν μετρήσῃς, ὅτι
outside and [3]not [2]it *thou mayest* [1]measure, because

ἐδόθη τοῖς ἔθνεσιν, καὶ τὴν πόλιν τὴν
it was given to the nations, and the [2]city –

ἁγίαν πατήσουσιν μῆνας τεσσεράκοντα
[1]holy they will trample [3]months [1]forty-

[καὶ] δύο. 3 καὶ δώσω τοῖς δυσὶν
and [2]two. And I will give to the two

μάρτυσίν μου, καὶ προφητεύσουσιν ἡμέρας
witnesses of me, and they will prophesy [5]days

χιλίας διακοσίας ἑξήκοντα περιβεβλημένοι
[1]a thousand [2]two hundred [3][and] [4]sixty *having been* clothed

σάκκους. 4 οὗτοί εἰσιν αἱ δύο ἐλαῖαι
[in] sackclothes. These are the two olive-trees

καὶ αἱ δύο λυχνίαι αἱ ἐνώπιον τοῦ
and the two lampstands – [2]before [3]the

God will be accomplished,
just as he announced to his
servants the prophets."
8Then the voice that I had
heard from heaven spoke
to me once more: "Go,
take the scroll that lies
open in the hand of the angel who is standing on the
sea and on the land."
9So I went to the angel
and asked him to give me
the little scroll. He said to
me, "Take it and eat it. It
will turn your stomach
sour, but in your mouth it
will be as sweet as honey."
10I took the little scroll
from the angel's hand and
ate it. It tasted as sweet as
honey in my mouth, but
when I had eaten it, my
stomach turned sour.
11Then I was told, "You
must prophesy again about
many peoples, nations, languages and kings."

Chapter 11

The Two Witnesses

I WAS given a reed like a
measuring rod and was
told, "Go and measure the
temple of God and the al-
tar, and count the worshipers there. 2But exclude the
outer court; do not measure
it, because it has been giv-
en to the Gentiles. They
will trample on the holy
city for 42 months. 3And I
will give power to my two
witnesses, and they will
prophesy for 1,260 days,
clothed in sackcloth."
4These are the two olive
trees and the two lamp-
stands that stand before the

Lord of the earth. 5 And if
anyone wants to harm
them, fire pours from their
mouth and consumes their
foes; anyone who wants to
harm them must be killed in
this manner. 6 They have
authority to shut the sky,
so that no rain may fall during the days of their prophesying, and they have au-
thority over the waters to
turn them into blood, and
to strike the earth with every kind of plague, as often
as they desire.
7 When they have fin-
ished their testimony, the
beast that comes up from
the bottomless pit will
make war on them and con-
quer them and kill them,
8 and their dead bodies will
lie in the street of the great
city that is prophetically[a]
called Sodom and Egypt,
where also their Lord was
crucified. 9 For three and a
half days members of the
peoples and tribes and languages and nations will
gaze at their dead bodies
and refuse to let them be
placed in a tomb; 10 and the
inhabitants of the earth will
gloat over them and cele-
brate and exchange
presents, because these
two prophets had been a
torment to the inhabitants
of the earth.
11 But after the three
and a half days, the
breath[b] of life from God
entered them, and they
stood on their feet, and
those who saw them were

κυρίου τῆς γῆς ἑστῶτες. 5 καὶ εἴ τις
[3]Lord [2]of the [4]earth [1]standing. And if anyone

αὐτοὺς θέλει ἀδικῆσαι, πῦρ ἐκπορεύεται
[3]them [1]wishes [2]to harm, fire proceeds

ἐκ τοῦ στόματος αὐτῶν καὶ κατεσθίει
out of the mouth of them and devours

τοὺς ἐχθροὺς αὐτῶν· καὶ εἴ τις θελήσῃ
the enemies of them; and if anyone should wish

αὐτοὺς ἀδικῆσαι, οὕτως δεῖ αὐτὸν
[2]them [1]to harm, thus it behoves him

ἀποκτανθῆναι. 6 οὗτοι ἔχουσιν τὴν ἐξουσίαν
to be killed. These have the authority

κλεῖσαι τὸν οὐρανόν, ἵνα μὴ ὑετὸς
to shut – heaven, in order that [3]not [1]rain

βρέχῃ τὰς ἡμέρας τῆς προφητείας αὐτῶν,
[2]may [4]rain(fall) the days of the prophecy of them,

καὶ ἐξουσίαν ἔχουσιν ἐπὶ τῶν ὑδάτων
and authority they have over the waters

στρέφειν αὐτὰ εἰς αἷμα καὶ πατάξαι
to turn them into blood and to strike

τὴν γῆν ἐν πάσῃ πληγῇ ὁσάκις ἐὰν
the earth with every [kind of] plague as often as

θελήσωσιν. 7 Καὶ ὅταν τελέσωσιν τὴν
they may wish. And whenever they finish the

μαρτυρίαν αὐτῶν, τὸ θηρίον τὸ ἀναβαῖνον
witness of them, the beast – coming up

ἐκ τῆς ἀβύσσου ποιήσει μετ' αὐτῶν
out of the abyss [1]will make [3]with [4]them

πόλεμον καὶ νικήσει αὐτοὺς καὶ ἀποκτενεῖ
[2]war and will overcome them and will kill

αὐτούς. 8 καὶ τὸ πτῶμα αὐτῶν ἐπὶ
them. And the corpse of them on

τῆς πλατείας τῆς πόλεως τῆς μεγάλης,
the open street of the [2]city – [1]great,

ἥτις καλεῖται πνευματικῶς Σόδομα καὶ
which is called spiritually Sodom and

Αἴγυπτος, ὅπου καὶ ὁ κύριος αὐτῶν
Egypt, where indeed the Lord of them

ἐσταυρώθη. 9 καὶ βλέπουσιν ἐκ τῶν
was crucified. And [10]see [1][some] of [2]the

λαῶν καὶ φυλῶν καὶ γλωσσῶν καὶ
[3]peoples [4]and [5]tribes [6]and [7]tongues [8]and

ἐθνῶν τὸ πτῶμα αὐτῶν ἡμέρας τρεῖς
[9]nations the corpse of them [4]days [1]three

καὶ ἥμισυ, καὶ τὰ πτώματα αὐτῶν
[2]and [3]a half, and [2]the [3]corpses [4]of them

οὐκ ἀφίουσιν τεθῆναι εἰς μνῆμα. 10 καὶ
[1]they do not allow to be placed in a tomb. And

οἱ κατοικοῦντες ἐπὶ τῆς γῆς χαίρουσιν
the [ones] dwelling on the earth rejoice

ἐπ' αὐτοῖς καὶ εὐφραίνονται, καὶ δῶρα
over them and are glad, and [2]gifts

πέμψουσιν ἀλλήλοις, ὅτι οὗτοι οἱ δύο
[1]they will send to one another, because these – two

προφῆται ἐβασάνισαν τοὺς κατοικοῦντας
prophets tormented the [ones] dwelling

ἐπὶ τῆς γῆς. 11 Καὶ μετὰ [τὰς] τρεῖς
on the earth. And after the [1]three

ἡμέρας καὶ ἥμισυ πνεῦμα ζωῆς ἐκ τοῦ
[4]days [2]and [3]a half a spirit of life out of –

θεοῦ εἰσῆλθεν ἐν αὐτοῖς, καὶ ἔστησαν
God entered in[to] them, and they stood

ἐπὶ τοὺς πόδας αὐτῶν, καὶ φόβος μέγας
on the feet of them, and [2]fear [1]great

Lord of the earth. 5 If anyone tries to harm them, fire
comes from their mouths
and devours their enemies.
This is how anyone who
wants to harm them must
die. 6 These men have power to shut up the sky so that
it will not rain during the
time they are prophesying;
and they have power to
turn the waters into blood
and to strike the earth with
every kind of plague as often as they want.
7 Now when they have fin-
ished their testimony, the
beast that comes up from
the Abyss will attack them,
and overpower and kill
them. 8 Their bodies will lie
in the street of the great
city, which is figuratively
called Sodom and Egypt,
where also their Lord was
crucified. 9 For three and a
half days men from every
people, tribe, language and
nation will gaze on their
bodies and refuse them
burial. 10 The inhabitants of
the earth will gloat over
them and will celebrate by
sending each other gifts,
because these two prophets
had tormented those who
live on the earth.
11 But after the three and a
half days a breath of life
from God entered them,
and they stood on their
feet, and terror struck

[a] Or *allegorically*; Gk *spiritually*
[b] Or *the spirit*

terrified. 12 Then they[c] heard a loud voice from heaven saying to them, "Come up here!" And they went up to heaven in a cloud while their enemies watched them. 13 At that moment there was a great earthquake, and a tenth of the city fell; seven thousand people were killed in the earthquake, and the rest were terrified and gave glory to the God of heaven.

14 The second woe has passed. The third woe is coming very soon.

The Seventh Trumpet

15 Then the seventh angel blew his trumpet, and there were loud voices in heaven, saying,

"The kingdom of the world has become the kingdom of our Lord
and of his Messiah,[d]
and he will reign forever and ever."

16 Then the twenty-four elders who sit on their thrones before God fell on their faces and worshiped God, 17 singing,

"We give you thanks, Lord God Almighty,
who are and who were,
for you have taken your great power
and begun to reign.
18 The nations raged,
but your wrath has come,
and the time for judging the dead,
for rewarding your servants,[e] the prophets
and saints and all who fear your name,
both small and

[c] Other ancient authorities read *I*
[d] Gk *Christ*
[e] Gk *slaves*

ἐπέπεσεν ἐπὶ τοὺς θεωροῦντας αὐτούς.
fell *on* on the [ones] beholding them.

12 καὶ ἤκουσαν φωνῆς μεγάλης ἐκ τοῦ
And they heard [2]voice [1]a great(loud) out of –

οὐρανοῦ λεγούσης αὐτοῖς· ἀνάβατε ὧδε·
heaven saying to them: Come ye up here;

καὶ ἀνέβησαν εἰς τὸν οὐρανὸν ἐν τῇ
and they went up to – heaven in the

νεφέλῃ, καὶ ἐθεώρησαν αὐτοὺς οἱ ἐχθροὶ
cloud, and [4]beheld [5]them [1]the [2]enemies

αὐτῶν. **13** Καὶ ἐν ἐκείνῃ τῇ ὥρᾳ ἐγένετο
[3]of them. And in that – hour [2]occurred

σεισμὸς μέγας, καὶ τὸ δέκατον τῆς
[3]earthquake [1]a great, and the tenth [part] of the

πόλεως ἔπεσεν, καὶ ἀπεκτάνθησαν ἐν τῷ
city fell, and [5]were killed [6]in [7]the

σεισμῷ ὀνόματα ἀνθρώπων χιλιάδες ἑπτά,
[8]earthquake [3]names [4]of men [2]thousands [1]seven,

καὶ οἱ λοιποὶ ἔμφοβοι ἐγένοντο καὶ
and the rest [2]terrified [1]became and

ἔδωκαν δόξαν τῷ θεῷ τοῦ οὐρανοῦ.
gave glory to the God – of heaven.

14 Ἡ οὐαὶ ἡ δευτέρα ἀπῆλθεν· ἰδοὺ
The [2]woe – [1]second passed away; behold[,]

ἡ οὐαὶ ἡ τρίτη ἔρχεται ταχύ.
the [2]woe – [1]third is coming quickly.

15 Καὶ ὁ ἕβδομος ἄγγελος ἐσάλπισεν·
And the seventh angel trumpeted;

καὶ ἐγένοντο φωναὶ μεγάλαι ἐν τῷ
and there were voices great(loud) in –

οὐρανῷ, λέγοντες· ἐγένετο ἡ βασιλεία
heaven, saying: [6]became [1]The [2]kingdom

τοῦ κόσμου τοῦ κυρίου ἡμῶν καὶ τοῦ
[3]of the [4]world of the Lord of us and of the
[5][the kingdom]

χριστοῦ αὐτοῦ, καὶ βασιλεύσει εἰς τοὺς
Christ of him, and he shall reign unto the

αἰῶνας τῶν αἰώνων. **16** καὶ οἱ εἴκοσι
ages of the ages. And the twenty-

τέσσαρες πρεσβύτεροι, οἱ ἐνώπιον τοῦ
four elders, – [2]before –

θεοῦ καθήμενοι ἐπὶ τοὺς θρόνους αὐτῶν,
[3]God [1]sitting on the thrones of them,

ἔπεσαν ἐπὶ τὰ πρόσωπα αὐτῶν καὶ
fell on the faces of them and

προσεκύνησαν τῷ θεῷ, **17** λέγοντες·
worshipped – God, saying:

εὐχαριστοῦμέν σοι, κύριε ὁ θεὸς ὁ
We thank thee, [O] Lord – God the

παντοκράτωρ, ὁ ὢν καὶ ὁ ἦν, ὅτι
Almighty, the [one] being and the was, because
=the one who is [one who]

εἴληφας τὴν δύναμίν σου τὴν μεγάλην
thou hast taken [1]the [3]power [4]of thee – [2]great

καὶ ἐβασίλευσας· **18** καὶ τὰ ἔθνη ὠργίσ-
and didst reign; and the nations were

θησαν, καὶ ἦλθεν ἡ ὀργή σου καὶ ὁ
wrathful, and [4]came [1]the [2]wrath [3]of thee and the

καιρὸς τῶν νεκρῶν κριθῆναι καὶ δοῦναι
time of the dead to be judged and to give

τὸν μισθὸν τοῖς δούλοις σου τοῖς προφήταις
the reward to the slaves of thee *to* the prophets

καὶ τοῖς ἁγίοις καὶ τοῖς φοβουμένοις
and to the saints and to the [ones] fearing

τὸ ὄνομά σου, τοῖς μικροῖς καὶ τοῖς
the name of thee, to the small and to the

those who saw them. 12 Then they heard a loud voice from heaven saying to them, "Come up here." And they went up to heaven in a cloud, while their enemies looked on.

13 At that very hour there was a severe earthquake and a tenth of the city collapsed. Seven thousand people were killed in the earthquake, and the survivors were terrified and gave glory to the God of heaven.

14 The second woe has passed; the third woe is coming soon.

The Seventh Trumpet

15 The seventh angel sounded his trumpet, and there were loud voices in heaven, which said:

"The kingdom of the world has become the kingdom of our Lord and of his Christ,
and he will reign for ever and ever."

16 And the twenty-four elders, who were seated on their thrones before God, fell on their faces and worshiped God, 17 saying:

"We give thanks to you, Lord God Almighty,
the One who is and who was,
because you have taken your great power
and have begun to reign.
18 The nations were angry;
and your wrath has come.
The time has come for judging the dead,
and for rewarding your servants the prophets
and your saints and those who reverence your name,

great,
and for destroying
those who
destroy the
earth.”
19 Then God’s temple
in heaven was opened, and
the ark of his covenant was
seen within his temple; and
there were flashes of lightning, rumblings, peals of
thunder, an earthquake,
and heavy hail.

Chapter 12

The Woman and the Dragon

A great portent appeared
in heaven: a woman
clothed with the sun, with
the moon under her feet,
and on her head a crown of
twelve stars. 2 She was
pregnant and was crying
out in birthpangs, in the agony of giving birth. 3 Then
another portent appeared
in heaven: a great red dragon, with seven heads and
ten horns, and seven dia-
dems on his heads. 4 His tail
swept down a third of the
stars of heaven and threw
them to the earth. Then the
dragon stood before the
woman who was about to
bear a child, so that he
might devour her child as
soon as it was born. 5 And
she gave birth to a son, a
male child, who is to rule[f]
all the nations with a rod of
iron. But her child was
snatched away and taken to
God and to his throne; 6 and
the woman fled into the wilderness, where she has a
place prepared by God, so
that there she can be nourished for one thousand two
hundred sixty days.

[f]Or *to shepherd*

μεγάλοις, καὶ διαφθεῖραι τοὺς διαφθείροντας
great, and to destroy the [ones] destroying

τὴν γῆν. **19** καὶ ἠνοίγη ὁ ναὸς τοῦ
the earth. And was opened the shrine –

θεοῦ ὁ ἐν τῷ οὐρανῷ, καὶ ὤφθη ἡ
of God – in – heaven, and was seen the

κιβωτὸς τῆς διαθήκης αὐτοῦ ἐν τῷ
ark of the covenant of him in the

ναῷ αὐτοῦ, καὶ ἐγένοντο ἀστραπαὶ καὶ
shrine of him, and occurred lightnings and

φωναὶ καὶ βρονταὶ καὶ σεισμὸς καὶ
voices and thunders and an earthquake and

χάλαζα μεγάλη.
[2]hail [1]a great.

12 Καὶ σημεῖον μέγα ὤφθη ἐν τῷ
And [2]sign [1]a great was seen in –

οὐρανῷ, γυνὴ περιβεβλημένη τὸν ἥλιον,
heaven, a woman *having been* clothed [with] the sun,

καὶ ἡ σελήνη ὑποκάτω τῶν ποδῶν αὐτῆς,
and the moon underneath the feet of her,

καὶ ἐπὶ τῆς κεφαλῆς αὐτῆς στέφανος
and on the head of her a crown

ἀστέρων δώδεκα, **2** καὶ ἐν γαστρὶ ἔχουσα,
[2]stars [1]of twelve, and in womb having,
=being pregnant,

καὶ κράζει ὠδίνουσα καὶ βασανιζομένη
and she cries suffering birth-pains and being distressed

τεκεῖν. **3** καὶ ὤφθη ἄλλο σημεῖον
to bear. And was seen another sign

ἐν τῷ οὐρανῷ, καὶ ἰδοὺ δράκων μέγας
in – heaven, and behold[,] [3]dragon [1]a great

πυρρός, ἔχων κεφαλὰς ἑπτὰ καὶ κέρατα
[2]red, having [2]heads [1]seven and [4]horns

δέκα καὶ ἐπὶ τὰς κεφαλὰς αὐτοῦ ἑπτὰ
[3]ten and on the heads of him seven

διαδήματα, **4** καὶ ἡ οὐρὰ αὐτοῦ σύρει
diadems, and the tail of him draws

τὸ τρίτον τῶν ἀστέρων τοῦ οὐρανοῦ,
the third [part] of the stars – of heaven,

καὶ ἔβαλεν αὐτοὺς εἰς τὴν γῆν. Καὶ
and cast them to the earth. And

ὁ δράκων ἕστηκεν ἐνώπιον τῆς γυναικὸς
the dragon stood before the woman

τῆς μελλούσης τεκεῖν, ἵνα ὅταν τέκῃ
– *being* about to bear, in order that whenever she bears

τὸ τέκνον αὐτῆς καταφάγῃ. **5** καὶ
[2]the [3]child [4]of her [1]he might devour. And

ἔτεκεν υἱὸν ἄρσεν, ὃς μέλλει ποιμαίνειν
she bore a son[,] a male, who is about to shepherd

πάντα τὰ ἔθνη ἐν ῥάβδῳ σιδηρᾷ· καὶ
all the nations with [2]staff [1]an iron; and

ἡρπάσθη τὸ τέκνον αὐτῆς πρὸς τὸν
[4]was seized [1]the [2]child [3]of her to –

θεὸν καὶ πρὸς τὸν θρόνον αὐτοῦ. **6** καὶ
God and to the throne of him. And

ἡ γυνὴ ἔφυγεν εἰς τὴν ἔρημον, ὅπου
the woman fled into the desert, where

ἔχει ἐκεῖ τόπον ἡτοιμασμένον ἀπὸ
she has *there* a place *having been* prepared from

τοῦ θεοῦ, ἵνα ἐκεῖ τρέφωσιν αὐτὴν
– God, in order that there they might nourish her

ἡμέρας χιλίας διακοσίας ἑξήκοντα.
[5]days [1]a thousand [2]two hundred [3][and] [4]sixty.

both small and great—
and for destroying those
who destroy the
earth.”
19 Then God’s temple in
heaven was opened, and
within his temple was seen
the ark of his covenant.
And there came flashes of
lightning, rumblings, peals
of thunder, an earthquake
and a great hailstorm.

Chapter 12

The Woman and the Dragon

A GREAT and wondrous
sign appeared in heav-
en: a woman clothed with
the sun, with the moon under her feet and a crown of
twelve stars on her head.
2 She was pregnant and
cried out in pain as she was
about to give birth. 3 Then
another sign appeared in
heaven: an enormous red
dragon with seven heads
and ten horns and seven
crowns on his heads. 4 His
tail swept a third of the
stars out of the sky and
flung them to the earth. The
dragon stood in front of the
woman who was about to
give birth, so that he might
devour her child the mo-
ment it was born. 5 She gave
birth to a son, a male child,
who will rule all the nations
with an iron scepter. And
her child was snatched up
to God and to his throne.
6 The woman fled into the
desert to a place prepared
for her by God, where she
might be taken care of for
1,260 days.

Michael Defeats the Dragon

7 And war broke out in
heaven; Michael and his
angels fought against the
dragon. The dragon and his
angels fought back, 8but
they were defeated, and
there was no longer any
place for them in heaven.
9The great dragon was
thrown down, that ancient
serpent, who is called the
Devil and Satan, the de-
ceiver of the whole
world—he was thrown
down to the earth, and his
angels were thrown down
with him.
10 Then I heard a loud
voice in heaven, proclaiming,

"Now have come the
salvation and
the power
and the kingdom of
our God
and the authority of
his Messiah,[g]
for the accuser of our
comrades[h] has
been thrown
down,
who accuses them
day and night
before our God.
11 But they have
conquered him
by the blood of
the Lamb
and by the word of
their testimony,
for they did not cling
to life even in
the face of
death.
12 Rejoice then, you
heavens
and those who dwell
in them!
But woe to the earth
and the sea,
for the devil has
come down
to you
with great wrath,
because he knows
that his time
is short!"

The Dragon Fights Again on Earth

13 So when the dragon
saw that he had been
thrown down to the earth,
he pursued[i] the woman
who had given birth to the
male child. 14But the woman was given the two wings
of the great eagle, so that
she could fly from the serpent into the wilderness, to

[g] Gk *Christ*
[h] Gk *brothers*
[i] Or *persecuted*

7 Καὶ ἐγένετο πόλεμος ἐν τῷ οὐρανῷ,
And occurred war in – heaven,

ὁ Μιχαὴλ καὶ οἱ ἄγγελοι αὐτοῦ τοῦ
– Michael and the angels of him –

πολεμῆσαι μετὰ τοῦ δράκοντος. καὶ ὁ
to make war[d] with the dragon. And the

δράκων ἐπολέμησεν καὶ οἱ ἄγγελοι αὐτοῦ,
dragon warred and the angels of him,

8 καὶ οὐκ ἴσχυσεν, οὐδὲ τόπος εὑρέθη
and prevailed not, not even place was found

αὐτῶν ἔτι ἐν τῷ οὐρανῷ. 9 καὶ ἐβλήθη
of them still in – heaven. And *was cast*

ὁ δράκων ὁ μέγας, ὁ ὄφις ὁ ἀρχαῖος,
[1]the [3]dragon – [2]great, [4]the [6]serpent – [5]old,

ὁ καλούμενος Διάβολος καὶ ὁ Σατανᾶς,
– *being* called Devil and the Satan,

ὁ πλανῶν τὴν οἰκουμένην ὅλην, ἐβλήθη
the deceiving [one] the [2]inhabited [earth] [1]whole, was cast

εἰς τὴν γῆν, καὶ οἱ ἄγγελοι αὐτοῦ μετ'
to the earth, and the angels of him with

αὐτοῦ ἐβλήθησαν. 10 καὶ ἤκουσα φωνὴν
him were cast. And I heard [2]voice

μεγάλην ἐν τῷ οὐρανῷ λέγουσαν ἄρτι
[1]a great(loud) in – heaven saying: Now

ἐγένετο ἡ σωτηρία καὶ ἡ δύναμις καὶ
became the salvation and the power and

ἡ βασιλεία τοῦ θεοῦ ἡμῶν καὶ ἡ ἐξουσία
the kingdom of the God of us and the authority

τοῦ χριστοῦ αὐτοῦ, ὅτι ἐβλήθη ὁ κατήγωρ
of the Christ of him, because [3]was cast [1]the [2]accuser

τῶν ἀδελφῶν ἡμῶν, ὁ κατηγορῶν αὐτοὺς
[5]of the [4]brothers [6]of us, the [one] accusing them

ἐνώπιον τοῦ θεοῦ ἡμῶν ἡμέρας καὶ
before the God of us day and

νυκτός. 11 καὶ αὐτοὶ ἐνίκησαν αὐτὸν
night. And they overcame him

διὰ τὸ αἷμα τοῦ ἀρνίου καὶ διὰ τὸν
because of the blood of the Lamb and because of the

λόγον τῆς μαρτυρίας αὐτῶν, καὶ οὐκ
word of the witness of them, and not

ἠγάπησαν τὴν ψυχὴν αὐτῶν ἄχρι θανάτου.
they loved the life of them until death.

12 διὰ τοῦτο εὐφραίνεσθε, οὐρανοὶ καὶ
Therefore be ye glad, heavens and

οἱ ἐν αὐτοῖς σκηνοῦντες· οὐαὶ τὴν
the [ones] [2]in [3]them [1]tabernacling; woe [to] the

γῆν καὶ τὴν θάλασσαν, ὅτι κατέβη ὁ
earth and the sea, because [3]came down [1]the

διάβολος πρὸς ὑμᾶς ἔχων θυμὸν μέγαν,
[2]devil to you having [2]anger [1]great,

εἰδὼς ὅτι ὀλίγον καιρὸν ἔχει. 13 Καὶ
knowing that [2]few(short) [3]time [1]he has. And

ὅτε εἶδεν ὁ δράκων ὅτι ἐβλήθη εἰς
when [3]saw [1]the [2]dragon that he was cast to

τὴν γῆν, ἐδίωξεν τὴν γυναῖκα ἥτις
the earth, he pursued the woman who

ἔτεκεν τὸν ἄρσενα. 14 καὶ ἐδόθησαν
bore the male. And were given

τῇ γυναικὶ αἱ δύο πτέρυγες τοῦ ἀετοῦ
to the woman the two wings of the [2]eagle

τοῦ μεγάλου, ἵνα πέτηται εἰς τὴν ἔρημον
– [1]great, in order that she might fly to the desert

7And there was war in
heaven. Michael and his
angels fought against the
dragon, and the dragon and
his angels fought back.
8But he was not strong
enough, and they lost their
place in heaven. 9The great
dragon was hurled down—
that ancient serpent called
the devil, or Satan, who
leads the whole world
astray. He was hurled to
the earth, and his angels
with him.
10Then I heard a loud
voice in heaven say:

"Now have come the
salvation and the
power and the
kingdom of our
God,
and the authority of his
Christ.
For the accuser of our
brothers,
who accuses them
before our God day
and night,
has been hurled down.
11They overcame him
by the blood of the
Lamb
and by the word of
their testimony;
they did not love their
lives so much
as to shrink from
death.
12Therefore rejoice, you
heavens
and you who dwell in
them!
But woe to the earth and
the sea,
because the devil has
gone down to you!
He is filled with fury,
because he knows that
his time is short."

13When the dragon saw
that he had been hurled to
the earth, he pursued the
woman who had given birth
to the male child. 14The
woman was given the two
wings of a great eagle, so
that she might fly to the

her place where she is
nourished for a time, and
times, and half a time.
15 Then from his mouth the
serpent poured water like a
river after the woman, to
sweep her away with the
flood. 16 But the earth came
to the help of the woman; it
opened its mouth and swallowed the river that the
dragon had poured from his
mouth. 17 Then the dragon
was angry with the woman,
and went off to make war
on the rest of her children,
those who keep the com-
mandments of God and
hold the testimony of
Jesus.

The First Beast

18 Then the dragon[j]
took his stand on the sand
of the seashore. 1 And I saw
a beast rising out of the sea;
and on its horns were ten
diadems, and on its heads
were blasphemous names.
2 And the beast that I saw
was like a leopard, its feet
were like a bear's, and its
mouth was like a lion's
mouth. And the dragon
gave it his power and his
throne and great authority.
3 One of its heads seemed to
have received a death-
blow, but its mortal
wound[k] had been healed.
In amazement the whole
earth followed the beast.

εἰς τὸν τόπον αὐτῆς, ὅπου τρέφεται
to the place of her, where she is nourished

ἐκεῖ καιρὸν καὶ καιροὺς καὶ ἥμισυ καιροῦ
there a time and times and half of a time

ἀπὸ προσώπου τοῦ ὄφεως. **15** καὶ ἔβαλεν
from [the] face of the serpent. And [3]cast

ὁ ὄφις ἐκ τοῦ στόματος αὐτοῦ ὀπίσω
[1]the [2]serpent out of the mouth of him behind

τῆς γυναικὸς ὕδωρ ὡς ποταμόν, ἵνα
the woman water as a river, in order that

αὐτὴν ποταμοφόρητον ποιήσῃ. **16** καὶ
[2]her [3]carried off by [the] river [1]he might make. And

ἐβοήθησεν ἡ γῆ τῇ γυναικί, καὶ ἤνοιξεν
[3]helped [1]the [2]earth the woman, and [3]opened

ἡ γῆ τὸ στόμα αὐτῆς καὶ κατέπιεν
[1]the [2]earth the mouth of it and swallowed

τὸν ποταμὸν ὃν ἔβαλεν ὁ δράκων ἐκ
the river which [3]cast [1]the [2]dragon out of

τοῦ στόματος αὐτοῦ. **17** καὶ ὠργίσθη
the mouth of him. And [3]was enraged

ὁ δράκων ἐπὶ τῇ γυναικί, καὶ ἀπῆλθεν
[1]the [2]dragon over the woman, and went away

ποιῆσαι πόλεμον μετὰ τῶν λοιπῶν τοῦ
to make war with the rest of the

σπέρματος αὐτῆς, τῶν τηρούντων τὰς
seed of her, the [ones] keeping the

ἐντολὰς τοῦ θεοῦ καὶ ἐχόντων τὴν
commandments – of God and having the

μαρτυρίαν Ἰησοῦ· **(18)** καὶ ἐστάθη ἐπὶ τὴν
witness of Jesus; and he stood on the

ἄμμον τῆς θαλάσσης.
sand of the sea.

13 Καὶ εἶδον ἐκ τῆς θαλάσσης θηρίον
And I saw [3]out of [4]the [5]sea [1]a beast

ἀναβαῖνον, ἔχον κέρατα δέκα καὶ κεφαλὰς
[2]coming up, having [2]horns [1]ten and [2]heads

ἑπτά, καὶ ἐπὶ τῶν κεράτων αὐτοῦ δέκα
[1]seven, and on the horns of it* ten

διαδήματα, καὶ ἐπὶ τὰς κεφαλὰς αὐτοῦ
diadems, and on the heads of it

ὀνόματα βλασφημίας. **2** καὶ τὸ θηρίον
names of blasphemy. And the beast

ὃ εἶδον ἦν ὅμοιον παρδάλει, καὶ οἱ
which I saw was like *to* a leopard, and the

πόδες αὐτοῦ ὡς ἄρκου, καὶ τὸ στόμα
feet of it as of a bear, and the mouth

αὐτοῦ ὡς στόμα λέοντος. καὶ ἔδωκεν
of it as [the] mouth of a lion. And [3]gave

αὐτῷ ὁ δράκων τὴν δύναμιν αὐτοῦ καὶ
[4]to it [1]the [2]dragon the power of it and

τὸν θρόνον αὐτοῦ καὶ ἐξουσίαν μεγάλην.
the throne of it and [2]authority [1]great.

3 καὶ μίαν ἐκ τῶν κεφαλῶν αὐτοῦ ὡς
And one of the heads of it as

ἐσφαγμένην εἰς θάνατον, καὶ ἡ πληγὴ
having been slain to death, and the stroke

τοῦ θανάτου αὐτοῦ ἐθεραπεύθη. καὶ
of the death of it was healed. And

* αὐτοῦ, of course, may be neuter or masculine—"of it" or "of him". δράκων being masculine (=Satan), we have kept to the masculine. But θηρίον is neuter. Yet if it stands for a person, as ἀρνίον certainly does, it too should be treated, as to the pronoun, as a masculine. However, not to enter the province of interpretation, we have rendered αὐτοῦ by "of it", though it will be seen that αὐτόν (him) is used in ver. 8, τίς (who?) in ver. 4, and ὅς (who) in ver. 14. See also ch. 17. 11.

place prepared for her in
the desert, where she
would be taken care of for a
time, times and half a time,
out of the serpent's reach.
15 Then from his mouth the
serpent spewed water like a
river, to overtake the woman and sweep her away
with the torrent. 16 But the
earth helped the woman by
opening its mouth and
swallowing the river that
the dragon had spewed out
of his mouth. 17 Then the
dragon was enraged at the
woman and went off to
make war against the rest
of her offspring—those
who obey God's command-
ments and hold to the testimony of Jesus.

1 And the
dragon[p] stood on the shore
of the sea.

The Beast out of the Sea

And I saw a beast coming
out of the sea. He had ten
horns and seven heads,
with ten crowns on his
horns, and on each head a
blasphemous name. 2 The
beast I saw resembled a
leopard, but had feet like
those of a bear and a mouth
like that of a lion. The dragon gave the beast his power
and his throne and great authority. 3 One of the heads
of the beast seemed to have
had a fatal wound, but the
fatal wound had been
healed. The whole world

[j] Gk *Then he*; other ancient authorities read *Then I stood*
[k] Gk *the plague of its death*

[p] *1* Some late manuscripts *And I*

[4]They worshiped the dragon, for he had given his authority to the beast, and
they worshiped the beast,
saying, "Who is like the
beast, and who can fight
against it?"
5 The beast was given a
mouth uttering haughty and
blasphemous words, and it
was allowed to exercise authority for forty-two
months. [6]It opened its
mouth to utter blasphemies
against God, blaspheming
his name and his dwelling,
that is, those who dwell in
heaven. [7]Also it was allowed to make war on the
saints and to conquer
them.[l] It was given au-
thority over every tribe and
people and language and
nation, [8]and all the inhabitants of the earth will worship it, everyone whose
name has not been written
from the foundation of the
world in the book of life of
the Lamb that was slaugh-
tered.[m]
9 Let anyone who has
an ear listen:

10 If you are to be taken captive,
into captivity you go;
if you kill with the sword,
with the sword you must be killed.

Here is a call for the endurance and faith of the saints.

The Second Beast

11 Then I saw another
beast that rose out of the
earth; it had two horns like
a lamb and it spoke like a
dragon. [12]It exercises all
the authority of the first
beast on its behalf, and it

[l] Other ancient authorities lack this sentence

[m] Or *written in the book of life of the Lamb that was slaughtered from the foundation of the world*

ἐθαυμάσθη ὅλη ἡ γῆ ὀπίσω τοῦ θηρίου,
[4]wondered [1]all [2]the [3]earth after the beast,

4 καὶ προσεκύνησαν τῷ δράκοντι, ὅτι
and they worshipped the dragon, because

ἔδωκεν τὴν ἐξουσίαν τῷ θηρίῳ, καὶ
he gave the authority to the beast, and

προσεκύνησαν τῷ θηρίῳ λέγοντες· τίς
they worshipped the beast saying: Who

ὅμοιος τῷ θηρίῳ, καὶ τίς δύναται
[is] like *to* the beast, and who can

πολεμῆσαι μετ' αὐτοῦ; 5 καὶ ἐδόθη αὐτῷ
to make war with it? And was given to it

στόμα λαλοῦν μεγάλα καὶ βλασφημίας,
a mouth speaking great things and blasphemies,

καὶ ἐδόθη αὐτῷ ἐξουσία ποιῆσαι μῆνας
and was given to it authority to act [2]months

τεσσεράκοντα [καὶ] δύο. 6 καὶ ἤνοιξεν
[1]forty-two. And it opened

τὸ στόμα αὐτοῦ εἰς βλασφημίας πρὸς
the mouth of it in blasphemies against

τὸν θεόν, βλασφημῆσαι τὸ ὄνομα αὐτοῦ
– God, to blaspheme the name of him

καὶ τὴν σκηνὴν αὐτοῦ, τοὺς ἐν τῷ
and the tabernacle of him, [1]the [ones] [3]in –

οὐρανῷ σκηνοῦντας. 7 καὶ ἐδόθη αὐτῷ
[4]heaven [2]tabernacling. And it was given to it

ποιῆσαι πόλεμον μετὰ τῶν ἁγίων καὶ
to make war with the saints and

νικῆσαι αὐτούς, καὶ ἐδόθη αὐτῷ ἐξουσία
to overcome them, and [2]was given [3]to it [1]authority

ἐπὶ πᾶσαν φυλὴν καὶ λαὸν καὶ γλῶσσαν
over every tribe and people and tongue

καὶ ἔθνος. 8 καὶ προσκυνήσουσιν αὐτὸν
and nation. And [7]will worship [8]him

πάντες οἱ κατοικοῦντες ἐπὶ τῆς γῆς,
[1]all [2]the [ones] [3]dwelling [4]on [5]the [6]earth,

οὗ οὐ γέγραπται τὸ ὄνομα αὐτοῦ ἐν
[3]of whom [4]has not been written [1]the [2]name *of him* in

τῷ βιβλίῳ τῆς ζωῆς τοῦ ἀρνίου τοῦ
the scroll – of life of the Lamb –

ἐσφαγμένου ἀπὸ καταβολῆς κόσμου.
having been slain from [the] foundation of [the] world.

9 Εἴ τις ἔχει οὖς ἀκουσάτω. 10 εἴ
If anyone has an ear let him hear. If

τις εἰς αἰχμαλωσίαν, εἰς αἰχμαλωσίαν
anyone [is] for captivity, to captivity

ὑπάγει· εἴ τις ἐν μαχαίρῃ ἀποκτενεῖ,
he goes; if anyone by a sword will kill,

δεῖ αὐτὸν ἐν μαχαίρῃ ἀποκτανθῆναι.
it behoves him by a sword to be killed.

Ὧδέ ἐστιν ἡ ὑπομονὴ καὶ ἡ πίστις
Here is the endurance and the faith

τῶν ἁγίων.
of the saints.

11 Καὶ εἶδον ἄλλο θηρίον ἀναβαῖνον
And I saw another beast coming up

ἐκ τῆς γῆς, καὶ εἶχεν κέρατα δύο
out of the earth, and it had [2]horns [1]two

ὅμοια ἀρνίῳ, καὶ ἐλάλει ὡς δράκων.
like *to* a lamb, and spoke as a dragon.

12 καὶ τὴν ἐξουσίαν τοῦ πρώτου θηρίου
And [3]the [4]authority [5]of the [6]first [7]beast

πᾶσαν ποιεῖ ἐνώπιον αὐτοῦ. καὶ ποιεῖ
[2]all [1]it does(exercises) before it. And it makes

was astonished and fol-
lowed the beast. [4]Men worshiped the dragon because
he had given authority to
the beast, and they also
worshiped the beast and
asked, "Who is like the
beast? Who can make war
against him?"
[5]The beast was given a
mouth to utter proud words
and blasphemies and to exercise his authority for forty-two months. [6]He opened
his mouth to blaspheme
God, and to slander his
name and his dwelling
place and those who live in
heaven. [7]He was given
power to make war against
the saints and to conquer
them. And he was given authority over every tribe,
people, language and na-
tion. [8]All inhabitants of the
earth will worship the beast
—all whose names have
not been written in the
book of life belonging to the
Lamb that was slain from
the creation of the world.[q]
[9]He who has an ear, let
him hear.

[10]If anyone is to go into captivity,
into captivity he will go.
If anyone is to be killed[r] with the sword,
with the sword he will be killed.

This calls for patient endurance and faithfulness on
the part of the saints.

The Beast out of the Earth

[11]Then I saw another
beast, coming out of the
earth. He had two horns
like a lamb, but he spoke
like a dragon. [12]He exercised all the authority of the
first beast on his behalf,

[q]8 Or *written from the creation of the world in the book of life belonging to the Lamb that was slain*

[r]10 Some manuscripts *anyone kills*

makes the earth and its inhabitants worship the first
beast, whose mortal
wound[n] had been healed.
13 It performs great signs,
even making fire come
down from heaven to earth
in the sight of all; 14 and by
the signs that it is allowed
to perform on behalf of the
beast, it deceives the inhabitants of earth, telling
them to make an image for
the beast that had been
wounded by the sword[o]
and yet lived; 15 and it was
allowed to give breath[p] to
the image of the beast so
that the image of the beast
could even speak and cause
those who would not wor-
ship the image of the beast
to be killed. 16 Also it
causes all, both small and
great, both rich and poor,
both free and slave, to be
marked on the right hand or
the forehead, 17 so that no
one can buy or sell who
does not have the mark,
that is, the name of the
beast or the number of its
name. 18 This calls for wisdom: let anyone with un-
derstanding calculate the
number of the beast, for it
is the number of a person.
Its number is six hundred
sixty-six.[q]

τὴν γῆν καὶ τοὺς ἐν αὐτῇ κατοικοῦντας
the earth and [1]the [ones] [3]in [4]it [2]dwelling

ἵνα προσκυνήσουσιν τὸ θηρίον τὸ πρῶτον,
in order that they shall worship the [2]beast – [1]first,

οὗ ἐθεραπεύθη ἡ πληγὴ τοῦ θανάτου
of which [4]was healed [1]the [2]stroke – [3]of death

αὐτοῦ. 13 καὶ ποιεῖ σημεῖα μεγάλα,
of it. And it does [2]signs [1]great,

ἵνα καὶ πῦρ ποιῇ ἐκ τοῦ οὐρανοῦ
in order that [3]even [4]fire [1]it [2]makes [5]out of – [7]heaven

καταβαίνειν εἰς τὴν γῆν ἐνώπιον τῶν
[6]to come down onto the earth before –

ἀνθρώπων. 14 καὶ πλανᾷ τοὺς κατοι-
men. And it deceives the [ones] dwell-

κοῦντας ἐπὶ τῆς γῆς διὰ τὰ σημεῖα
ing on the earth because of the signs

ἃ ἐδόθη αὐτῷ ποιῆσαι ἐνώπιον τοῦ
which it was given to it to do before the

θηρίου, λέγων τοῖς κατοικοῦσιν ἐπὶ τῆς
beast, telling *to* the [ones] dwelling on the

γῆς ποιῆσαι εἰκόνα τῷ θηρίῳ, ὃς ἔχει
earth to make an image to the beast, who has

τὴν πληγὴν τῆς μαχαίρης καὶ ἔζησεν.
the stroke of the sword and lived [again].

15 καὶ ἐδόθη αὐτῷ δοῦναι πνεῦμα τῇ
And it was given to it to give spirit to the

εἰκόνι τοῦ θηρίου, ἵνα καὶ λαλήσῃ ἡ
image of the beast, in order that [6]even [5]might [7]speak [1]the

εἰκὼν τοῦ θηρίου, καὶ ποιήσῃ [ἵνα]
[2]image [3]of the [4]beast, and might make *in order that*

ὅσοι ἐὰν μὴ προσκυνήσωσιν τῇ εἰκόνι
as many as might not worship the image

τοῦ θηρίου ἀποκτανθῶσιν. 16 καὶ ποιεῖ
of the beast should be killed. And it makes

πάντας, τοὺς μικροὺς καὶ τοὺς μεγάλους,
all men, the small and the great,

καὶ τοὺς πλουσίους καὶ τοὺς πτωχούς,
both the rich and the poor,

καὶ τοὺς ἐλευθέρους καὶ τοὺς δούλους,
both the free men and the slaves,

ἵνα δῶσιν αὐτοῖς χάραγμα ἐπὶ τῆς
in order that they should give to them a mark on the

χειρὸς αὐτῶν τῆς δεξιᾶς ἢ ἐπὶ τὸ
[3]hand [2]of them – [1]right or on the

μέτωπον αὐτῶν, 17 [καὶ] ἵνα μή τις
forehead of them, and lest anyone

δύνηται ἀγοράσαι ἢ πωλῆσαι εἰ μὴ
could *to* buy or *to* sell except

ὁ ἔχων τὸ χάραγμα τὸ ὄνομα τοῦ
the [one] having the mark[,] the name of the

θηρίου ἢ τὸν ἀριθμὸν τοῦ ὀνόματος
beast or the number of the name

αὐτοῦ. 18 Ὧδε ἡ σοφία ἐστίν. ὁ ἔχων
of it. Here – [2]wisdom [1]is. The [one] having

νοῦν ψηφισάτω τὸν ἀριθμὸν τοῦ θηρίου·
reason let him count the number of the beast;

ἀριθμὸς γὰρ ἀνθρώπου ἐστίν. καὶ ὁ
for [2][the] [3]number [4]of a man [1]it is. And the

ἀριθμὸς αὐτοῦ ἑξακόσιοι ἑξήκοντα ἕξ.
number of it [is] six hundreds [and] sixty-six.

and made the earth and its
inhabitants worship the
first beast, whose fatal
wound had been healed.
13 And he performed great
and miraculous signs, even
causing fire to come down
from heaven to earth in full
view of men. 14 Because of
the signs he was given power to do on behalf of the
first beast, he deceived the
inhabitants of the earth. He
ordered them to set up an
image in honor of the beast
who was wounded by the
sword and yet lived. 15 He
was given power to give
breath to the image of the
first beast, so that it could
speak and cause all who refused to worship the image
to be killed. 16 He also
forced everyone, small and
great, rich and poor, free
and slave, to receive a
mark on his right hand or
on his forehead, 17 so that
no one could buy or sell unless he had the mark, which
is the name of the beast or
the number of his name.
18 This calls for wisdom. If
anyone has insight, let him
calculate the number of the
beast, for it is man's number. His number is 666.

[n] Gk *whose plague of its death*
[o] Or *that had received the plague of the sword*
[p] Or *spirit*
[q] Other ancient authorities read *six hundred sixteen*

Chapter 14

The Lamb and the 144,000

THEN I looked, and
there was the Lamb,
standing on Mount Zion!
And with him were one
hundred forty-four thou-
sand who had his name and
his Father's name written
on their foreheads. 2 And I
heard a voice from heaven
like the sound of many waters and like the sound of
loud thunder; the voice I
heard was like the sound of
harpists playing on their
harps, 3 and they sing a new
song before the throne and
before the four living creatures and before the elders.
No one could learn that
song except the one hun-
dred forty-four thousand
who have been redeemed
from the earth. 4 It is these
who have not defiled themselves with women, for
they are virgins; these follow the Lamb wherever he
goes. They have been re-
deemed from humankind as
first fruits for God and the
Lamb, 5 and in their mouth
no lie was found; they are
blameless.

The Messages of the Three Angels

6 Then I saw another
angel flying in midheaven,
with an eternal gospel to
proclaim to those who
live[r] on the earth—to every nation and tribe and
language and people. 7 He
said in a loud voice, "Fear
God and give him glory, for
the hour of his judgment
has come; and worship him
who made heaven and
earth, the sea and the
springs of water."

[r] Gk *sit*

14 Καὶ εἶδον, καὶ ἰδοὺ τὸ ἀρνίον
And I saw, and behold[,] the Lamb
ἑστὸς ἐπὶ τὸ ὄρος Σιών, καὶ μετ' αὐτοῦ
standing on the mount Sion, and with him
ἑκατὸν τεσσεράκοντα τέσσαρες χιλιάδες
a hundred [and] forty-four thousands
ἔχουσαι τὸ ὄνομα αὐτοῦ καὶ τὸ ὄνομα
having the name of him and the name
τοῦ πατρὸς αὐτοῦ γεγραμμένον ἐπὶ τῶν
of the Father of him *having been* written on the
μετώπων αὐτῶν. **2** καὶ ἤκουσα φωνὴν
foreheads of them. And I heard a sound
ἐκ τοῦ οὐρανοῦ ὡς φωνὴν ὑδάτων πολλῶν
out of – heaven as a sound ²waters ¹of many
καὶ ὡς φωνὴν βροντῆς μεγάλης, καὶ
and as a sound ²thunder ¹of great(loud), and
ἡ φωνὴ ἣν ἤκουσα ὡς κιθαρῳδῶν
the sound which I heard [was] as of harpers
κιθαριζόντων ἐν ταῖς κιθάραις αὐτῶν.
harping with the harps of them.
3 καὶ ᾄδουσιν ᾠδὴν καινὴν ἐνώπιον τοῦ
And they sing ²song ¹a new before the
θρόνου καὶ ἐνώπιον τῶν τεσσάρων ζῴων
throne and before the four living creatures
καὶ τῶν πρεσβυτέρων· καὶ οὐδεὶς ἐδύνατο
and the elders; and no man could
μαθεῖν τὴν ᾠδὴν εἰ μὴ αἱ ἑκατὸν
to learn the song except the hundred
τεσσεράκοντα τέσσαρες χιλιάδες, οἱ
[and] forty-four thousands, the
ἠγορασμένοι ἀπὸ τῆς γῆς. **4** οὗτοί εἰσιν
[ones] *having been* purchased from the earth. These are
οἳ μετὰ γυναικῶν οὐκ ἐμολύνθησαν·
[those] who ²with ³women ¹were not defiled;
παρθένοι γάρ εἰσιν. οὗτοι οἱ ἀκολουθοῦντες
for ²celibates ¹they are. These [are] the [ones] following
τῷ ἀρνίῳ ὅπου ἂν ὑπάγῃ. οὗτοι ἠγοράσ-
the Lamb wherever he may go. These were
θησαν ἀπὸ τῶν ἀνθρώπων ἀπαρχὴ τῷ
purchased from – men firstfruit –
θεῷ καὶ τῷ ἀρνίῳ, **5** καὶ ἐν τῷ στόματι
to God and to the Lamb, and in the mouth
αὐτῶν οὐχ εὑρέθη ψεῦδος· ἄμωμοί εἰσιν.
of them was not found a lie; ²unblemished ¹they are.
6 Καὶ εἶδον ἄλλον ἄγγελον πετόμενον
And I saw another angel flying
ἐν μεσουρανήματι, ἔχοντα εὐαγγέλιον
in mid-heaven, having ²gospel
αἰώνιον εὐαγγελίσαι ἐπὶ τοὺς καθημένους
¹an eternal to preach over the [ones] sitting
ἐπὶ τῆς γῆς καὶ ἐπὶ πᾶν ἔθνος καὶ
on the earth and over every nation and
φυλὴν καὶ γλῶσσαν καὶ λαόν, **7** λέγων
tribe and tongue and people, saying
ἐν φωνῇ μεγάλῃ· φοβήθητε τὸν θεὸν
in ²voice ¹a great(loud): Fear ye – God
καὶ δότε αὐτῷ δόξαν, ὅτι ἦλθεν ἡ ὥρα
and give ²to him ¹glory, because came the hour
τῆς κρίσεως αὐτοῦ, καὶ προσκυνήσατε
of the judgment of him, and worship
τῷ ποιήσαντι τὸν οὐρανὸν καὶ τὴν γῆν
the [one] having made the heaven and the earth
καὶ θάλασσαν καὶ πηγὰς ὑδάτων. **8** Καὶ
and sea and fountains of waters. And

Chapter 14

The Lamb and the 144,000

THEN I looked, and
there before me was
the Lamb, standing on
Mount Zion, and with him
144,000 who had his name
and his Father's name written on their foreheads.
2 And I heard a sound from
heaven like the roar of
rushing waters and like a
loud peal of thunder. The
sound I heard was like that
of harpists playing their
harps. 3 And they sang a
new song before the throne
and before the four living
creatures and the elders.
No one could learn the
song except the 144,000
who had been redeemed
from the earth. 4 These are
those who did not defile
themselves with women,
for they kept themselves
pure. They follow the
Lamb wherever he goes.
They were purchased from
among men and offered as
firstfruits to God and the
Lamb. 5 No lie was found in
their mouths; they are
blameless.

The Three Angels

6 Then I saw another angel
flying in midair, and he had
the eternal gospel to proclaim to those who live on
the earth—to every nation,
tribe, language and people.
7 He said in a loud voice,
"Fear God and give him
glory, because the hour of
his judgment has come.
Worship him who made the
heavens, the earth, the sea
and the springs of water."

8 Then another angel, a
second, followed, saying,
"Fallen, fallen is Babylon
the great! She has made all
nations drink of the wine of
the wrath of her fornica-
tion."
9 Then another angel, a
third, followed them, crying with a loud voice,
"Those who worship the
beast and its image, and receive a mark on their foreheads or on their hands,
10they will also drink the
wine of God's wrath,
poured unmixed into the
cup of his anger, and they
will be tormented with fire
and sulfur in the presence
of the holy angels and in the
presence of the Lamb.
11And the smoke of their
torment goes up forever
and ever. There is no rest
day or night for those who
worship the beast and its
image and for anyone who
receives the mark of its
name."
12 Here is a call for the
endurance of the saints,
those who keep the com-
mandments of God and
hold fast to the faith of[s]
Jesus.
13 And I heard a voice
from heaven saying, "Write
this: Blessed are the dead
who from now on die in the
Lord." "Yes," says the
Spirit, "they will rest from
their labors, for their deeds
follow them."

Reaping the Earth's Harvest

14 Then I looked, and
there was a white cloud,
and seated on the cloud
was one like the Son of
Man, with a golden crown
on his head, and a sharp

ἄλλος ἄγγελος δεύτερος ἠκολούθησεν λέγων·
another angel a second followed saying:
ἔπεσεν ἔπεσεν Βαβυλὼν ἡ μεγάλη, ἣ
Fell[,] fell Babylon the great, which
ἐκ τοῦ οἴνου τοῦ θυμοῦ τῆς πορνείας
of the wine of the anger of the fornication
αὐτῆς πεποτικεν πάντα τὰ ἔθνη. 9 Καὶ
of her has made to drink all the nations. And
ἄλλος ἄγγελος τρίτος ἠκολούθησεν αὐτοῖς
another angel a third followed them
λέγων ἐν φωνῇ μεγάλῃ· εἴ τις προσκυνεῖ
saying in [2]voice [1]a great(loud): If anyone worships
τὸ θηρίον καὶ τὴν εἰκόνα αὐτοῦ, καὶ
the beast and the image of it, and
λαμβάνει χάραγμα ἐπὶ τοῦ μετώπου αὐτοῦ
receives a mark on the forehead of him
ἢ ἐπὶ τὴν χεῖρα αὐτοῦ, 10 καὶ αὐτὸς
or on the hand of him, even he
πίεται ἐκ τοῦ οἴνου τοῦ θυμοῦ τοῦ
shall drink of the wine of the anger –
θεοῦ τοῦ κεκερασμένου ἀκράτου ἐν τῷ
of God – *having been* mixed undiluted in the
ποτηρίῳ τῆς ὀργῆς αὐτοῦ, καὶ βασανισθήσε-
cup of the wrath of him, and will be torment-
ται ἐν πυρὶ καὶ θείῳ ἐνώπιον ἀγγέλων
ed by fire and sulphur before [2]angels
ἁγίων καὶ ἐνώπιον τοῦ ἀρνίου. 11 καὶ
[1]holy and before the Lamb. And
ὁ καπνὸς τοῦ βασανισμοῦ αὐτῶν εἰς
the smoke of the torment of them unto
αἰῶνας αἰώνων ἀναβαίνει, καὶ οὐκ ἔχουσιν
ages of ages goes up, and they have not
ἀνάπαυσιν ἡμέρας καὶ νυκτὸς οἱ προσκυ-
rest day and night the [ones] wor-
νοῦντες τὸ θηρίον καὶ τὴν εἰκόνα αὐτοῦ,
shipping the beast and the image of it,
καὶ εἴ τις λαμβάνει τὸ χάραγμα τοῦ
and if anyone receives the mark of the
ὀνόματος αὐτοῦ. 12 Ὧδε ἡ ὑπομονὴ
name of it. [1]Here [3]the [4]endurance
τῶν ἁγίων ἐστίν, οἱ τηροῦντες τὰς
[5]of the [6]saints [2]is, the [ones] keeping the
ἐντολὰς τοῦ θεοῦ καὶ τὴν πίστιν Ἰησοῦ.
command-ments – of God and the faith of Jesus.
13 Καὶ ἤκουσα φωνῆς ἐκ τοῦ οὐρανοῦ
And I heard a voice out of – heaven
λεγούσης· γράψον· μακάριοι οἱ νεκροὶ
saying: Write thou: Blessed [are] the dead
οἱ ἐν κυρίῳ ἀποθνήσκοντες ἀπ' ἄρτι.
[1]the [ones] [3]in [4][the] Lord [2]dying from now.
ναί, λέγει τὸ πνεῦμα, ἵνα ἀναπαήσονται
Yes, says the Spirit, in order that they shall rest
ἐκ τῶν κόπων αὐτῶν· τὰ γὰρ ἔργα
from the labours of them; for the works
αὐτῶν ἀκολουθεῖ μετ' αὐτῶν.
of them follows with them.
14 Καὶ εἶδον, καὶ ἰδοὺ νεφέλη λευκή,
And I saw, and behold[,] [2]cloud [1]a white,
καὶ ἐπὶ τὴν νεφέλην καθήμενον ὅμοιον
and on the cloud [one] sitting like
υἱὸν ἀνθρώπου, ἔχων ἐπὶ τῆς κεφαλῆς
a son of man,* having on the head

8A second angel followed
and said, "Fallen! Fallen is
Babylon the Great, which
made all the nations drink
the maddening wine of her
adulteries."
9A third angel followed
them and said in a loud
voice: "If anyone worships
the beast and his image and
receives his mark on the
forehead or on the hand,
10he, too, will drink of the
wine of God's fury, which
has been poured full
strength into the cup of his
wrath. He will be tormented with burning sulfur in
the presence of the holy angels and of the Lamb.
11And the smoke of their
torment rises for ever and
ever. There is no rest day
or night for those who worship the beast and his image, or for anyone who receives the mark of his
name." 12This calls for patient endurance on the part
of the saints who obey
God's commandments and
remain faithful to Jesus.
13Then I heard a voice
from heaven say, "Write:
Blessed are the dead who
die in the Lord from now
on."
"Yes," says the Spirit,
"they will rest from their
labor, for their deeds will
follow them."

The Harvest of the Earth

14I looked, and there be-
fore me was a white cloud,
and seated on the cloud
was one "like a son of
man"[s] with a crown of
gold on his head and a

[s] Or *to their faith in*

* See also ch. 1. 13 and John 5. 27.

[s] *14* Daniel 7:13

sickle in his hand! 15 Another angel came out of the
temple, calling with a loud
voice to the one who sat on
the cloud, "Use your sickle
and reap, for the hour to
reap has come, because the
harvest of the earth is fully
ripe." 16 So the one who sat
on the cloud swung his
sickle over the earth, and
the earth was reaped.
17 Then another angel
came out of the temple in
heaven, and he too had a
sharp sickle. 18 Then another angel came out from the
altar, the angel who has authority over fire, and he
called with a loud voice to
him who had the sharp
sickle, "Use your sharp
sickle and gather the clusters of the vine of the earth,
for its grapes are ripe."
19 So the angel swung his
sickle over the earth and
gathered the vintage of the
earth, and he threw it into
the great wine press of the
wrath of God. 20 And the
wine press was trodden
outside the city, and blood
flowed from the wine
press, as high as a horse's
bridle, for a distance of
about two hundred miles.[t]

Chapter 15

The Angels with the Seven Last Plagues

THEN I saw another
portent in heaven,
great and amazing: seven
angels with seven plagues,
which are the last, for with
them the wrath of God is
ended.
2 And I saw what ap-
peared to be a sea of glass
mixed with fire, and those

[t] Gk *one thousand six hundred stadia*

αὐτοῦ στέφανον χρυσοῦν καὶ ἐν τῇ χειρὶ
of him crown a golden and in the hand
αὐτοῦ δρέπανον ὀξύ. 15 καὶ ἄλλος ἄγγελος
of him sickle a sharp. And another angel
ἐξῆλθεν ἐκ τοῦ ναοῦ, κράζων ἐν φωνῇ
went forth out of the shrine, crying in [2]voice
μεγάλῃ τῷ καθημένῳ ἐπὶ τῆς νεφέλης·
[1]a great (loud) to the [one] sitting on the cloud:
πέμψον τὸ δρέπανόν σου καὶ θέρισον,
Send(Thrust) the sickle of thee and reap thou,
ὅτι ἦλθεν ἡ ὥρα θερίσαι, ὅτι ἐξηράνθη
because came the hour to reap, because was dried
ὁ θερισμὸς τῆς γῆς. 16 καὶ ἔβαλεν
the harvest of the earth. And [6]thrust
ὁ καθήμενος ἐπὶ τῆς νεφέλης τὸ δρέπανον
[1]the [one] [2]sitting [3]on [4]the [5]cloud the sickle
αὐτοῦ ἐπὶ τὴν γῆν, καὶ ἐθερίσθη ἡ
of him over the earth, and [3]was reaped [1]the
γῆ. 17 Καὶ ἄλλος ἄγγελος ἐξῆλθεν ἐκ
[2]earth. And another angel went forth out of
τοῦ ναοῦ τοῦ ἐν τῷ οὐρανῷ, ἔχων καὶ
the shrine – in – heaven, [3]having [2]also
αὐτὸς δρέπανον ὀξύ. 18 καὶ ἄλλος ἄγγελος
[1]he [5]sickle [4]a sharp. And another angel
ἐξῆλθεν ἐκ τοῦ θυσιαστηρίου, [ὁ] ἔχων
went forth out of the altar, the [one] having
ἐξουσίαν ἐπὶ τοῦ πυρός, καὶ ἐφώνησεν
authority over the fire, and he spoke
φωνῇ μεγάλῃ τῷ ἔχοντι τὸ δρέπανον
[2]voice [1]in a great (loud) to the [one] having the [2]sickle
τὸ ὀξὺ λέγων· πέμψον σου τὸ δρέπανον
– [1]sharp saying: Send(Thrust) [4]of thee [1]the [3]sickle
τὸ ὀξὺ καὶ τρύγησον τοὺς βότρυας τῆς
– [2]sharp and gather the clusters of the
ἀμπέλου τῆς γῆς, ὅτι ἤκμασαν αἱ
vine of the earth, because [4]ripened [1]the
σταφυλαὶ αὐτῆς. 19 καὶ ἔβαλεν ὁ ἄγγελος
[2]grapes [3]of it. And [3]thrust [1]the [2]angel
τὸ δρέπανον αὐτοῦ εἰς τὴν γῆν, καὶ
the sickle of him into the earth, and
ἐτρύγησεν τὴν ἄμπελον τῆς γῆς καὶ
gathered the vine of the earth and
ἔβαλεν εἰς τὴν ληνὸν τοῦ θυμοῦ τοῦ
cast into the [2]winepress [3]of the [4]anger –
θεοῦ τὸν μέγαν. 20 καὶ ἐπατήθη ἡ
[5]of God – [1]great. And [3]was trodden [1]the
ληνὸς ἔξωθεν τῆς πόλεως, καὶ ἐξῆλθεν
winepress outside the city, and [2]went *out*
αἷμα ἐκ τῆς ληνοῦ ἄχρι τῶν χαλινῶν
[1]blood out of the winepress as far as the bridles
τῶν ἵππων, ἀπὸ σταδίων χιλίων ἑξακοσίων.
of the horses, from [3]furlongs [1]a thousand [2]six hundred.

15 Καὶ εἶδον ἄλλο σημεῖον ἐν τῷ
And I saw another sign in –
οὐρανῷ μέγα καὶ θαυμαστόν, ἀγγέλους
heaven[,] great and wonderful, [2]angels
ἑπτὰ ἔχοντας πληγὰς ἑπτὰ τὰς ἐσχάτας,
[1]seven having [2]plagues [1]seven the last,
ὅτι ἐν αὐταῖς ἐτελέσθη ὁ θυμὸς τοῦ
because in them [4]was finished [1]the [2]anger
θεοῦ. 2 Καὶ εἶδον ὡς θάλασσαν ὑαλίνην
[3]of God. And I saw as [2]sea [1]a glassy

sharp sickle in his hand.
15Then another angel came
out of the temple and called
in a loud voice to him who
was sitting on the cloud,
"Take your sickle and
reap, because the time to
reap has come, for the harvest of the earth is ripe."
16So he who was seated on
the cloud swung his sickle
over the earth, and the
earth was harvested.
17Another angel came out
of the temple in heaven,
and he too had a sharp sickle. 18Still another angel,
who had charge of the fire,
came from the altar and
called in a loud voice to him
who had the sharp sickle,
"Take your sharp sickle
and gather the clusters of
grapes from the earth's
vine, because its grapes are
ripe." 19The angel swung
his sickle on the earth,
gathered its grapes and
threw them into the great
winepress of God's wrath.
20They were trampled in
the winepress outside the
city, and blood flowed out
of the press, rising as high
as the horses' bridles for a
distance of 1,600 stadia.[t]

Chapter 15

Seven Angels With Seven Plagues

I SAW in heaven another
great and marvelous
sign: seven angels with the
seven last plagues—last,
because with them God's
wrath is completed. 2And I
saw what looked like a sea
of glass mixed with fire

[t]20 That is, about 180 miles (about 300 kilometers)

who had conquered the beast and its image and the number of its name, standing beside the sea of glass with harps of God in their hands. 3 And they sing the song of Moses, the servant[u] of God, and the song of the Lamb:

"Great and amazing
are your deeds,
Lord God the
Almighty!
Just and true are your
ways,
King of the
nations![v]
4 Lord, who will not
fear
and glorify your
name?
For you alone are
holy.
All nations will
come
and worship before
you,
for your judgments
have been
revealed."

5 After this I looked, and the temple of the tent[w] of witness in heaven was opened, 6 and out of the temple came the seven angels with the seven plagues, robed in pure bright linen,[x] with golden sashes across their chests. 7 Then one of the four living creatures gave the seven angels seven golden bowls full of the wrath of God, who lives forever and ever; 8 and the temple was filled with smoke from the glory of God and from his power, and no one could enter the temple until the seven plagues of the seven angels were ended.

Chapter 16

The Bowls of God's Wrath

THEN I heard a loud voice from the temple telling the seven angels, "Go and pour out on the earth the seven bowls of

[u] Gk *slave*
[v] Other ancient authorities read *the ages*
[w] Or *tabernacle*
[x] Other ancient authorities read *stone*

μεμιγμένην πυρί, καὶ τοὺς νικῶντας
having been mixed with fire, and the [ones] overcoming
ἐκ τοῦ θηρίου καὶ ἐκ τῆς εἰκόνος αὐτοῦ
of the beast and of the image of it
καὶ ἐκ τοῦ ἀριθμοῦ τοῦ ὀνόματος αὐτοῦ
and of the number of the name of it
ἑστῶτας ἐπὶ τὴν θάλασσαν τὴν ὑαλίνην,
standing on the ²sea – ¹glassy,
ἔχοντας κιθάρας τοῦ θεοῦ. 3 καὶ ᾄδουσιν
having harps – of God. And they sing
τὴν ᾠδὴν Μωϋσέως τοῦ δούλου τοῦ
the song of Moses the slave –
θεοῦ καὶ τὴν ᾠδὴν τοῦ ἀρνίου, λέγοντες·
of God and the song of the Lamb, saying:
μεγάλα καὶ θαυμαστὰ τὰ ἔργα σου,
Great and wonderful the works of thee,
κύριε ὁ θεὸς ὁ παντοκράτωρ· δίκαιαι
[O] Lord – God the Almighty; righteous
καὶ ἀληθιναὶ αἱ ὁδοί σου, ὁ βασιλεὺς
and true the ways of thee, the king
τῶν ἐθνῶν· 4 τίς οὐ μὴ φοβηθῇ, κύριε,
of the nations; who will not fear, [O] Lord,
καὶ δοξάσει τὸ ὄνομά σου; ὅτι μόνος
and *will* glorify the name of thee? because [thou] only
ὅσιος, ὅτι πάντα τὰ ἔθνη ἥξουσιν καὶ
[art] holy, because all the nations will come and
προσκυνήσουσιν ἐνώπιόν σου, ὅτι τὰ
will worship before thee, because the
δικαιώματά σου ἐφανερώθησαν. 5 Καὶ
ordinances of thee were made manifest. And
μετὰ ταῦτα εἶδον, καὶ ἠνοίγη ὁ ναὸς
after these things I saw, and was opened the shrine
τῆς σκηνῆς τοῦ μαρτυρίου ἐν τῷ οὐρανῷ,
of the tabernacle of the testimony in – heaven,
6 καὶ ἐξῆλθον οἱ ἑπτὰ ἄγγελοι οἱ ἔχοντες
and ⁴came forth ¹the ²seven ³angels – ⁴having
τὰς ἑπτὰ πληγὰς ἐκ τοῦ ναοῦ, ἐνδεδυμένοι
⁵the ⁶seven ⁷plagues out of the shrine, *having been* clothed [in]
λίνον καθαρὸν λαμπρὸν καὶ περιεζωσμένοι
³linen ¹clean ²bright and *having been* girdled
περὶ τὰ στήθη ζώνας χρυσᾶς. 7 καὶ
round the breasts [with] ²girdles ¹golden. And
ἓν ἐκ τῶν τεσσάρων ζῴων ἔδωκεν τοῖς
one of the four living creatures gave to the
ἑπτὰ ἀγγέλοις ἑπτὰ φιάλας χρυσᾶς
seven angels seven ²bowls ¹golden
γεμούσας τοῦ θυμοῦ τοῦ θεοῦ τοῦ ζῶντος
being filled of(with) the anger – of God – living
εἰς τοὺς αἰῶνας τῶν αἰώνων. 8 καὶ
unto the ages of the ages. And
ἐγεμίσθη ὁ ναὸς καπνοῦ ἐκ τῆς δόξης
was filled the shrine of(with) smoke of the glory
τοῦ θεοῦ καὶ ἐκ τῆς δυνάμεως αὐτοῦ,
— of God and of the power of him,
καὶ οὐδεὶς ἐδύνατο εἰσελθεῖν εἰς τὸν
and no one could *to* enter into the
ναὸν ἄχρι τελεσθῶσιν αἱ ἑπτὰ πληγαὶ
shrine until should be finished the seven plagues
τῶν ἑπτὰ ἀγγέλων. 16 Καὶ ἤκουσα
of the seven angels. And I heard
μεγάλης φωνῆς ἐκ τοῦ ναοῦ λεγούσης τοῖς
a great(loud) voice out of the shrine saying to the
ἑπτὰ ἀγγέλοις· ὑπάγετε καὶ ἐκχέετε τὰς ἑπτὰ
seven angels: Go ye and pour out the seven

and, standing beside the sea, those who had been victorious over the beast and his image and over the number of his name. They held harps given them by God 3 and sang the song of Moses the servant of God and the song of the Lamb:

"Great and marvelous
are your deeds,
Lord God Almighty.
Just and true are your
ways,
King of the ages.
4 Who will not fear you, O
Lord,
and bring glory to your
name?
For you alone are holy.
All nations will come
and worship before
you,
for your righteous acts
have been
revealed."

5 After this I looked and in heaven the temple, that is, the tabernacle of the Testimony, was opened. 6 Out of the temple came the seven angels with the seven plagues. They were dressed in clean, shining linen and wore golden sashes around their chests. 7 Then one of the four living creatures gave to the seven angels seven golden bowls filled with the wrath of God, who lives for ever and ever. 8 And the temple was filled with smoke from the glory of God and from his power, and no one could enter the temple until the seven plagues of the seven angels were completed.

Chapter 16

The Seven Bowls of God's Wrath

THEN I heard a loud voice from the temple saying to the seven angels, "Go, pour out the seven

the wrath of God."
2 So the first angel went
and poured his bowl on the
earth, and a foul and painful sore came on those who
had the mark of the beast
and who worshiped its im-
age.
3 The second angel
poured his bowl into the
sea, and it became like the
blood of a corpse, and every living thing in the sea
died.
4 The third angel
poured his bowl into the
rivers and the springs of
water, and they became
blood. 5 And I heard the angel of the waters say,
"You are just, O Holy
One, who are
and were,
for you have judged
these things;
6 because they shed the
blood of saints
and prophets,
you have given
them blood to
drink.
It is what they
deserve!"
7 And I heard the altar respond,
"Yes, O Lord God,
the Almighty,
your judgments are
true and just!"
8 The fourth angel
poured his bowl on the sun,
and it was allowed to
scorch them with fire;
9 they were scorched by the
fierce heat, but they cursed
the name of God, who had
authority over these
plagues, and they did not
repent and give him glory.
10 The fifth angel
poured his bowl on the
throne of the beast, and its
kingdom was plunged into

φιάλας τοῦ θυμοῦ τοῦ θεοῦ εἰς τὴν γῆν.
bowls of the anger – of God onto the earth.
2 Καὶ ἀπῆλθεν ὁ πρῶτος καὶ ἐξέχεεν τὴν
And [3]went away [1]the [2]first and poured out the
φιάλην αὐτοῦ εἰς τὴν γῆν· καὶ ἐγένετο
bowl of him onto the earth; and [5]came
ἕλκος κακὸν καὶ πονηρὸν ἐπὶ τοὺς ἀνθρώπους
[4]sore [1]a bad [2]and [3]evil on the men
τοὺς ἔχοντας τὸ χάραγμα τοῦ θηρίου καὶ
– having the mark of the beast and
τοὺς προσκυνοῦντας τῇ εἰκόνι αὐτοῦ. 3 Καὶ
– worshipping the image of it. And
ὁ δεύτερος ἐξέχεεν τὴν φιάλην αὐτοῦ
the second poured out the bowl of him
εἰς τὴν θάλασσαν· καὶ ἐγένετο αἷμα
onto the sea; and it became blood
ὡς νεκροῦ, καὶ πᾶσα ψυχὴ ζωῆς ἀπέθανεν,
as of a dead man, and every soul of life died,
τὰ ἐν τῇ θαλάσσῃ. 4 Καὶ ὁ τρίτος
the things in the sea. And the third
ἐξέχεεν τὴν φιάλην αὐτοῦ εἰς τοὺς
poured out the bowl of him onto the
ποταμοὺς καὶ τὰς πηγὰς τῶν ὑδάτων·
rivers and the fountains of the waters;
καὶ ἐγένετο αἷμα. 5 Καὶ ἤκουσα τοῦ
and it became blood. And I heard the
ἀγγέλου τῶν ὑδάτων λέγοντος· δίκαιος
angel of the waters saying: Righteous
εἶ, ὁ ὢν καὶ ὁ ἦν, ὁ ὅσιος, ὅτι
art thou, the [one] being and the [one who] was, the holy [one], because
=the one who is
ταῦτα ἔκρινας, 6 ὅτι αἷμα ἁγίων
[2]these things [1]thou judgedst, because [2][the] blood [3]of saints
καὶ προφητῶν ἐξέχεαν, καὶ αἷμα αὐτοῖς
[4]and [5]of prophets [1]they shed, and blood to them
δέδωκας πεῖν· ἄξιοί εἰσιν. 7 Καὶ ἤκουσα
thou hast given to drink; [2]worthy [1]they are. And I heard
τοῦ θυσιαστηρίου λέγοντος· ναί, κύριε
the altar saying: Yes, [O] Lord
ὁ θεὸς ὁ παντοκράτωρ, ἀληθιναὶ καὶ
– God the Almighty, true and
δίκαιαι αἱ κρίσεις σου. 8 Καὶ ὁ τέταρτος
righteous the judgments of thee. And the fourth
ἐξέχεεν τὴν φιάλην αὐτοῦ ἐπὶ τὸν ἥλιον·
poured out the bowl of him onto the sun;
καὶ ἐδόθη αὐτῷ καυματίσαι τοὺς
and it was given to him to burn –
ἀνθρώπους ἐν πυρί. 9 καὶ ἐκαυματίσθησαν
men with fire. And [2]were burnt [with]
οἱ ἄνθρωποι καῦμα μέγα, καὶ ἐβλασ-
– [1]men [4]heat [3]great, and they blas-
φήμησαν τὸ ὄνομα τοῦ θεοῦ τοῦ ἔχοντος
phemed the name – of God the [one] having
τὴν ἐξουσίαν ἐπὶ τὰς πληγὰς ταύτας,
the authority over these plagues,
καὶ οὐ μετενόησαν δοῦναι αὐτῷ δόξαν.
and they repented not to give [2]to him [1]glory.
10 Καὶ ὁ πέμπτος ἐξέχεεν τὴν φιάλην
And the fifth poured out the bowl
αὐτοῦ ἐπὶ τὸν θρόνον τοῦ θηρίου· καὶ
of him onto the throne of the beast; and
ἐγένετο ἡ βασιλεία αὐτοῦ ἐσκοτωμένη,
[4]became [1]the [2]kingdom [3]of it *having been* darkened,

bowls of God's wrath on
the earth."
2 The first angel went and
poured out his bowl on the
land, and ugly and painful
sores broke out on the people who had the mark of the
beast and worshiped his
image.
3 The second angel poured
out his bowl on the sea, and
it turned into blood like that
of a dead man, and every
living thing in the sea died.
4 The third angel poured
out his bowl on the rivers
and springs of water, and
they became blood. 5 Then I
heard the angel in charge of
the waters say:

"You are just in these
judgments,
you who are and who
were, the Holy One,
because you have so
judged;
6 for they have shed the
blood of your saints
and prophets,
and you have given
them blood to drink
as they deserve."

7 And I heard the altar respond:

"Yes, Lord God
Almighty,
true and just are your
judgments."

8 The fourth angel poured
out his bowl on the sun, and
the sun was given power to
scorch people with fire.
9 They were seared by the
intense heat and they
cursed the name of God,
who had control over these
plagues, but they refused to
repent and glorify him.
10 The fifth angel poured
out his bowl on the throne
of the beast, and his kingdom was plunged into dark-

darkness; people gnawed
their tongues in agony,
11 and cursed the God of
heaven because of their
pains and sores, and they
did not repent of their
deeds.
12 The sixth angel
poured his bowl on the
great river Euphrates, and
its water was dried up in
order to prepare the way
for the kings from the east.
13 And I saw three foul spirits like frogs coming from
the mouth of the dragon,
from the mouth of the
beast, and from the mouth
of the false prophet.
14 These are demonic spirits, performing signs, who
go abroad to the kings of
the whole world, to assemble them for battle on the
great day of God the Al-
mighty. 15 ("See, I am coming like a thief! Blessed is
the one who stays awake
and is clothed,[y] not going
about naked and exposed
to shame.") 16 And they assembled them at the place
that in Hebrew is called
Harmagedon.
17 The seventh angel
poured his bowl into the
air, and a loud voice came
out of the temple, from the
throne, saying, "It is
done!" 18 And there came
flashes of lightning, rumblings, peals of thunder,
and a violent earthquake,
such as had not occurred
since people were upon the
earth, so violent was that
earthquake. 19 The great
city was split into three
parts, and the cities of the

καὶ ἐμασῶντο τὰς γλώσσας αὐτῶν ἐκ
and they(men) gnawed the tongues of them from

τοῦ πόνου, 11 καὶ ἐβλασφήμησαν τὸν θεὸν
the pain, and *they* blasphemed the God

τοῦ οὐρανοῦ ἐκ τῶν πόνων αὐτῶν καὶ
– of heaven from the pains of them and

ἐκ τῶν ἑλκῶν αὐτῶν, καὶ οὐ μετενόησαν
from the sores of them, and they repented not

ἐκ τῶν ἔργων αὐτῶν. 12 Καὶ ὁ ἕκτος
of the works of them. And the sixth

ἐξέχεεν τὴν φιάλην αὐτοῦ ἐπὶ τὸν ποταμὸν
poured out the bowl of him onto the [2]river

τὸν μέγαν Εὐφράτην· καὶ ἐξηράνθη τὸ
– [1]great Euphrates; and [4]was dried [1]the

ὕδωρ αὐτοῦ, ἵνα ἑτοιμασθῇ ἡ ὁδὸς τῶν
[2]water [3]of it, in order that [8]might be prepared [1]the [2]way [3]of the

βασιλέων τῶν ἀπὸ ἀνατολῆς ἡλίου. 13 Καὶ
[4]kings – [5]from [6][the] rising [7]of [the] sun. And

εἶδον ἐκ τοῦ στόματος τοῦ δράκοντος
I saw out of the mouth of the dragon

καὶ ἐκ τοῦ στόματος τοῦ θηρίου καὶ
and out of the mouth of the beast and

ἐκ τοῦ στόματος τοῦ ψευδοπροφήτου
out of the mouth of the false prophet

πνεύματα τρία ἀκάθαρτα ὡς βάτραχοι·
[3]spirits [1]three [2]unclean [coming] as frogs;

14 εἰσὶν γὰρ πνεύματα δαιμονίων ποιοῦντα
for they are spirits of demons doing

σημεῖα, ἃ ἐκπορεύεται ἐπὶ τοὺς βασιλεῖς
signs, which go*es* forth unto the kings

τῆς οἰκουμένης ὅλης, συναγαγεῖν αὐτοὺς
of the [2]inhabited [earth] [1]whole, to assemble them

εἰς τὸν πόλεμον τῆς ἡμέρας τῆς μεγάλης
to the war of the [2]day – [1]great

τοῦ θεοῦ τοῦ παντοκράτορος. 15 Ἰδοὺ
– of God *of* the Almighty. Behold

ἔρχομαι ὡς κλέπτης· μακάριος ὁ γρηγορῶν
I am coming as a thief: blessed [is] the [one] watching

καὶ τηρῶν τὰ ἱμάτια αὐτοῦ, ἵνα μὴ
and keeping the garments of him, lest

γυμνὸς περιπατῇ καὶ βλέπωσιν τὴν
naked he walk and they(men) see the

ἀσχημοσύνην αὐτοῦ. 16 Καὶ συνήγαγεν
shame of him. And [t]he[y] assembled

αὐτοὺς εἰς τὸν τόπον τὸν καλούμενον
them in the place – *being* called

Ἑβραϊστὶ Ἁρμαγεδών. 17 Καὶ ὁ ἕβδομος
in Hebrew Harmagedon. And the seventh

ἐξέχεεν τὴν φιάλην αὐτοῦ ἐπὶ τὸν ἀέρα·
poured out the bowl of him on the air;

καὶ ἐξῆλθεν φωνὴ μεγάλη ἐκ τοῦ ναοῦ
and [3]came *out* [2]voice [1]a great(loud) out of the shrine

ἀπὸ τοῦ θρόνου λέγουσα· γέγονεν. 18 καὶ
from the throne saying: It has occurred. And

ἐγένοντο ἀστραπαὶ καὶ φωναὶ καὶ βρονταί,
there were lightnings and voices and thunders,

καὶ σεισμὸς ἐγένετο μέγας, οἷος οὐκ
and [2]earthquake [3]occurred [1]a great, such as not

ἐγένετο ἀφ' οὗ ἄνθρωπος ἐγένετο ἐπὶ
did occur from when† man was on

τῆς γῆς, τηλικοῦτος σεισμὸς οὕτω μέγας.
the earth, such an earthquake so great.

19 καὶ ἐγένετο ἡ πόλις ἡ μεγάλη εἰς
And [4]became [1]the [3]city – [2]great into

ness. Men gnawed their
tongues in agony 11 and
cursed the God of heaven
because of their pains and
their sores, but they re-
fused to repent of what
they had done.
12 The sixth angel poured
out his bowl on the great
river Euphrates, and its
water was dried up to prepare the way for the kings
from the East. 13 Then I saw
three evil[u] spirits that
looked like frogs; they
came out of the mouth of
the dragon, out of the
mouth of the beast and out
of the mouth of the false
prophet. 14 They are spirits
of demons performing mi-
raculous signs, and they go
out to the kings of the
whole world, to gather
them for the battle on the
great day of God Almighty.
15 "Behold, I come like a
thief! Blessed is he who
stays awake and keeps his
clothes with him, so that he
may not go naked and be
shamefully exposed."
16 Then they gathered the
kings together to the place
that in Hebrew is called Ar-
mageddon.
17 The seventh angel
poured out his bowl into
the air, and out of the temple came a loud voice from
the throne, saying, "It is
done!" 18 Then there came
flashes of lightning, rumblings, peals of thunder and
a severe earthquake. No
earthquake like it has ever
occurred since man has
been on earth, so tremen-
dous was the quake. 19 The
great city split into three

[y] Gk *and keeps his robes*

[u] 13 Greek *unclean*

nations fell. God remem-
bered great Babylon and
gave her the wine-cup of
the fury of his wrath. 20 And
every island fled away, and
no mountains were to be
found; 21 and huge hail-
stones, each weighing
about a hundred pounds,[z]
dropped from heaven on
people, until they cursed
God for the plague of the
hail, so fearful was that
plague.

τρία μέρη, καὶ αἱ πόλεις τῶν ἐθνῶν
three parts, and the cities of the nations
ἔπεσαν. καὶ Βαβυλὼν ἡ μεγάλη ἐμνήσθη
fell. And Babylon the great was remembered
ἐνώπιον τοῦ θεοῦ δοῦναι αὐτῇ τὸ ποτήριον
before – God to give to her/it* the cup
τοῦ οἴνου τοῦ θυμοῦ τῆς ὀργῆς αὐτοῦ.
of the wine of the anger of the wrath of him.
20 καὶ πᾶσα νῆσος ἔφυγεν, καὶ ὄρη
And every island fled, and mountains
οὐχ εὑρέθησαν. **21** καὶ χάλαζα μεγάλη
were not found. And [2]hail [1]a great
ὡς ταλαντιαία καταβαίνει ἐκ τοῦ οὐρανοῦ
as a talent in size comes down out of – heaven
ἐπὶ τοὺς ἀνθρώπους· καὶ ἐβλασφήμησαν
on – men; and [2]blasphemed
οἱ ἄνθρωποι τὸν θεὸν ἐκ τῆς πληγῆς
– [1]men – God from the plague
τῆς χαλάζης, ὅτι μεγάλη ἐστὶν ἡ πληγὴ
of the hail, because [5]great [4]is [1]the [2]plague
αὐτῆς σφόδρα.
[3]of it [6]exceeding.

parts, and the cities of the
nations collapsed. God remembered Babylon the
Great and gave her the cup
filled with the wine of the
fury of his wrath. 20 Every
island fled away and the
mountains could not be
found. 21 From the sky huge
hailstones of about a hundred pounds each fell upon
men. And they cursed God
on account of the plague of
hail, because the plague
was so terrible.

Chapter 17

The Great Whore and the Beast

THEN one of the seven
angels who had the
seven bowls came and said
to me, "Come, I will show
you the judgment of the
great whore who is seated
on many waters, 2 with
whom the kings of the earth
have committed fornica-
tion, and with the wine of
whose fornication the in-
habitants of the earth have
become drunk." 3 So he
carried me away in the spirit[a] into a wilderness, and I
saw a woman sitting on a
scarlet beast that was full of
blasphemous names, and it
had seven heads and ten
horns. 4 The woman was
clothed in purple and scarlet, and adorned with gold
and jewels and pearls,
holding in her hand a gold-
en cup full of abominations
and the impurities of her
fornication; 5 and on her
forehead was written a
name, a mystery: "Babylon

17 Καὶ ἦλθεν εἷς ἐκ τῶν ἑπτὰ ἀγγέλων
And came one of the seven angels
τῶν ἐχόντων τὰς ἑπτὰ φιάλας, καὶ
– having the seven bowls, and
ἐλάλησεν μετ' ἐμοῦ λέγων· δεῦρο, δείξω
spoke with me saying: Come, I will show
σοι τὸ κρίμα τῆς πόρνης τῆς μεγάλης
thee the judgment of the [2]harlot – [1]great
τῆς καθημένης ἐπὶ ὑδάτων πολλῶν, **2** μεθ'
– sitting on [2]waters [1]many, with
ἧς ἐπόρνευσαν οἱ βασιλεῖς τῆς γῆς,
whom [5]practised fornication [1]the [2]kings [3]of the [4]earth,
καὶ ἐμεθύσθησαν οἱ κατοικοῦντες τὴν γῆν
and [5]became drunk [1]the [2]dwelling [on] [ones] [3]the [4]earth
ἐκ τοῦ οἴνου τῆς πορνείας αὐτῆς. **3** καὶ
from the wine of the fornication of her. And
ἀπήνεγκέν με εἰς ἔρημον ἐν πνεύματι.
he carried away me into a desert in spirit.
καὶ εἶδον γυναῖκα καθημένην ἐπὶ θηρίον
And I saw a woman sitting on [2]beast
κόκκινον, γέμοντα ὀνόματα βλασφημίας,
[1]a scarlet, *being* filled [with] names of blasphemy,
ἔχοντα κεφαλὰς ἑπτὰ καὶ κέρατα δέκα.
having [2]heads [1]seven and [2]horns [1]ten.
4 καὶ ἡ γυνὴ ἦν περιβεβλημένη πορφυροῦν
And the woman was *having been* clothed [in] purple
καὶ κόκκινον, καὶ κεχρυσωμένη χρυσίῳ
and scarlet, and *having been* gilded with gold
καὶ λίθῳ τιμίῳ καὶ μαργαρίταις, ἔχουσα
and [2]stone [1]precious and pearls, having
ποτήριον χρυσοῦν ἐν τῇ χειρὶ αὐτῆς
[2]cup [1]a golden in the hand of her
γέμον βδελυγμάτων καὶ τὰ ἀκάθαρτα
being filled of(with) abominations and the unclean things
τῆς πορνείας αὐτῆς, **5** καὶ ἐπὶ τὸ
of the fornication of her, and on the
μέτωπον αὐτῆς ὄνομα γεγραμμένον,
forehead of her a name *having been* written,

Chapter 17

The Woman on the Beast

ONE of the seven angels
who had the seven
bowls came and said to me,
"Come, I will show you the
punishment of the great
prostitute, who sits on
many waters. 2 With her the
kings of the earth committed adultery and the inhabitants of the earth were in-
toxicated with the wine of
her adulteries."
3 Then the angel carried
me away in the Spirit into a
desert. There I saw a woman sitting on a scarlet beast
that was covered with blasphemous names and had
seven heads and ten horns.
4 The woman was dressed
in purple and scarlet, and
was glittering with gold,
precious stones and pearls.
She held a golden cup in her
hand, filled with abomina-
ble things and the filth of
her adulteries. 5 This title
was written on her fore-
head:

[z]Gk *weighing about a talent*
[a]Or *in the Spirit*

* Even in English a city is often personified as feminine.

the great, mother of whores
and of earth's abomina-
tions." 6And I saw that the
woman was drunk with the
blood of the saints and the
blood of the witnesses to
Jesus.
When I saw her, I was
greatly amazed. 7But the
angel said to me, "Why are
you so amazed? I will tell
you the mystery of the
woman, and of the beast
with seven heads and ten
horns that carries her. 8The
beast that you saw was,
and is not, and is about to
ascend from the bottomless
pit and go to destruction.
And the inhabitants of the
earth, whose names have
not been written in the
book of life from the foundation of the world, will be
amazed when they see the
beast, because it was and is
not and is to come.
9 "This calls for a mind
that has wisdom: the seven
heads are seven mountains
on which the woman is
seated; also, they are seven
kings, 10of whom five have
fallen, one is living, and the
other has not yet come; and
when he comes, he must remain only a little while.
11As for the beast that was
and is not, it is an eighth but
it belongs to the seven, and
it goes to destruction.
12And the ten horns that
you saw are ten kings who
have not yet received a
kingdom, but they are to receive authority as kings for
one hour, together with the

μυστήριον, ΒΑΒΥΛΩΝ Η ΜΕΓΑΛΗ,
a mystery, BABYLON THE GREAT,

Η ΜΗΤΗΡ ΤΩΝ ΠΟΡΝΩΝ ΚΑΙ
The Mother of the Harlots and

ΤΩΝ ΒΔΕΛΥΓΜΑΤΩΝ ΤΗΣ ΓΗΣ.
of the Abominations of the Earth.

6 καὶ εἶδον τὴν γυναῖκα μεθύουσαν ἐκ
And I saw the woman *being* drunk from

τοῦ αἵματος τῶν ἁγίων καὶ ἐκ τοῦ
the blood of the saints and from the

αἵματος τῶν μαρτύρων Ἰησοῦ. Καὶ
blood of the witnesses of Jesus. And

ἐθαύμασα ἰδὼν αὐτὴν θαῦμα μέγα. 7 καὶ
[2]I wondered [1]seeing [3]her [4][with] [6]wonder [5]a great. And

εἶπέν μοι ὁ ἄγγελος· διὰ τί ἐθαύμασας;
[3]said [4]to me [1]the [2]angel: Why didst thou wonder?

ἐγὼ ἐρῶ σοι τὸ μυστήριον τῆς γυναικὸς
I will tell thee the mystery of the woman

καὶ τοῦ θηρίου τοῦ βαστάζοντος αὐτὴν
and of the beast – carrying her

τοῦ ἔχοντος τὰς ἑπτὰ κεφαλὰς καὶ τὰ
– having the seven heads and the

δέκα κέρατα. 8 Τὸ θηρίον ὃ εἶδες ἦν
ten horns. The beast which thou sawest was

καὶ οὐκ ἔστιν, καὶ μέλλει ἀναβαίνειν
and is not, and is about to come up

ἐκ τῆς ἀβύσσου καὶ εἰς ἀπώλειαν ὑπάγει·
out of the abyss and [2]to [3]destruction [1]goes;

καὶ θαυμασθήσονται οἱ κατοικοῦντες ἐπὶ
and [4]will wonder [1]the [ones] [2]dwelling [3]on

τῆς γῆς, ὧν οὐ γέγραπται τὸ ὄνομα
[3]the [3]earth, of whom [3]has not been written [1]the [2]name

ἐπὶ τὸ βιβλίον τῆς ζωῆς ἀπὸ καταβολῆς
on the scroll – of life from [the] foundation

κόσμου, βλεπόντων τὸ θηρίον ὅτι ἦν
of [the] world, seeing the beast that it was

καὶ οὐκ ἔστιν καὶ παρέσται. 9 ὧδε
and is not and is present. Here [is]

ὁ νοῦς ὁ ἔχων σοφίαν. αἱ ἑπτὰ
the mind – having wisdom. The seven

κεφαλαὶ ἑπτὰ ὄρη εἰσίν, ὅπου ἡ γυνὴ
heads [2]seven [3]mountains [1]are, where the woman

κάθηται ἐπ' αὐτῶν, καὶ βασιλεῖς ἑπτά
sits on them, and [3]kings [2]seven

εἰσιν· 10 οἱ πέντε ἔπεσαν, ὁ εἷς ἔστιν,
[1]are: the five fell, the one is,

ὁ ἄλλος οὔπω ἦλθεν, καὶ ὅταν ἔλθῃ
the other not yet came, and whenever he comes

ὀλίγον αὐτὸν δεῖ μεῖναι. 11 καὶ τὸ
[4]a little [while] [2]him [1]it behoves [3]to remain. And the

θηρίον ὃ ἦν καὶ οὐκ ἔστιν, καὶ αὐτὸς
beast which was and is not, even he

ὄγδοός ἐστιν, καὶ ἐκ τῶν ἑπτά ἐστιν,
[2]an eighth [1]is, and [2]of [3]the [4]seven [1]is,

καὶ εἰς ἀπώλειαν ὑπάγει. 12 καὶ τὰ
and to destruction goes. And the

δέκα κέρατα ἃ εἶδες δέκα βασιλεῖς
ten horns which thou sawest [2]ten [3]kings

εἰσιν, οἵτινες βασιλείαν οὔπω ἔλαβον,
[1]are, who a kingdom not yet received,

ἀλλὰ ἐξουσίαν ὡς βασιλεῖς μίαν ὥραν
but [2]authority [3]as [4]kings [5]one [6]hour

λαμβάνουσιν μετὰ τοῦ θηρίου. 13 οὗτοι
[1]receive with the beast. These

MYSTERY
BABYLON THE GREAT
THE MOTHER OF PROSTITUTES
AND OF THE ABOMINATIONS
OF THE EARTH.

6I saw that the woman was
drunk with the blood of the
saints, the blood of those
who bore testimony to
Jesus.
When I saw her, I was
greatly astonished. 7Then
the angel said to me: "Why
are you astonished? I will
explain to you the mystery
of the woman and of the
beast she rides, which has
the seven heads and ten
horns. 8The beast, which
you saw, once was, now is
not, and will come up out of
the Abyss and go to his destruction. The inhabitants
of the earth whose names
have not been written in the
book of life from the creation of the world will be
astonished when they see
the beast, because he once
was, now is not, and yet
will come.
9"This calls for a mind
with wisdom. The seven
heads are seven hills on
which the woman sits.
10They are also seven
kings. Five have fallen, one
is, the other has not yet
come; but when he does
come, he must remain for a
little while. 11The beast
who once was, and now is
not, is an eighth king. He
belongs to the seven and is
going to his destruction.
12"The ten horns you saw
are ten kings who have not
yet received a kingdom,
but who for one hour will
receive authority as kings
along with the beast.

beast. 13 These are united in
yielding their power and
authority to the beast;
14 they will make war on the
Lamb, and the Lamb will
conquer them, for he is
Lord of lords and King of
kings, and those with him
are called and chosen and
faithful."
15 And he said to me,
"The waters that you saw,
where the whore is seated,
are peoples and multitudes
and nations and languages.
16 And the ten horns that
you saw, they and the beast
will hate the whore; they
will make her desolate and
naked; they will devour her
flesh and burn her up with
fire. 17 For God has put it
into their hearts to carry
out his purpose by agreeing
to give their kingdom to the
beast, until the words of
God will be fulfilled. 18 The
woman you saw is the great
city that rules over the
kings of the earth."

Chapter 18

The Fall of Babylon

AFTER this I saw anoth-
er angel coming down
from heaven, having great
authority; and the earth
was made bright with his
splendor. 2 He called out
with a mighty voice,

"Fallen, fallen is
Babylon the
great!
It has become a
dwelling place
of demons,
a haunt of every foul
and hateful bird,
a haunt of every
foul and
hateful beast.[b]
3 For all the nations
have drunk[c]
of the wine of the
wrath of her
fornication,

[b] Some ancient authorities lack *a haunt of every foul and hateful beast*
[c] Other ancient authorities read *she has made all nations drink*

μίαν γνώμην ἔχουσιν, καὶ τὴν δύναμιν
one mind have, and the power
καὶ ἐξουσίαν αὐτῶν τῷ θηρίῳ διδόασιν.
and authority of them to the beast they give.
14 οὗτοι μετὰ τοῦ ἀρνίου πολεμήσουσιν
These [2]with [3]the [4]Lamb [1]will make war
καὶ τὸ ἀρνίον νικήσει αὐτούς, ὅτι κύριος
and the Lamb will overcome them, because [3]Lord
κυρίων ἐστὶν καὶ βασιλεὺς βασιλέων, καὶ
[3]of lords [1]he is and King of kings, and
οἱ μετ' αὐτοῦ κλητοὶ καὶ ἐκλεκτοὶ καὶ
the [ones] with him [are] called and chosen and
πιστοί. 15 Καὶ λέγει μοι· τὰ ὕδατα
faithful. And he says to me: The waters
ἃ εἶδες, οὗ ἡ πόρνη κάθηται, λαοὶ
which thou sawest, where the harlot sits, peoples
καὶ ὄχλοι εἰσὶν καὶ ἔθνη καὶ γλῶσσαι.
and crowds are and nations and tongues.
16 καὶ τὰ δέκα κέρατα ἃ εἶδες καὶ
And the ten horns which thou sawest and
τὸ θηρίον, οὗτοι μισήσουσιν τὴν πόρνην,
the beast, these will hate the harlot,
καὶ ἠρημωμένην ποιήσουσιν αὐτὴν καὶ
and [3]*having been* desolated [1]will make [2]her and
γυμνήν, καὶ τὰς σάρκας αὐτῆς φάγονται,
naked, and [2]the [3]flesh*es* [4]of her [1]will eat,
καὶ αὐτὴν κατακαύσουσιν [ἐν] πυρί· 17 ὁ
and [2]her [1]will consume with fire; –
γὰρ θεὸς ἔδωκεν εἰς τὰς καρδίας αὐτῶν
for God gave into the hearts of them
ποιῆσαι τὴν γνώμην αὐτοῦ, καὶ ποιῆσαι
to do the mind of him, and to make
μίαν γνώμην καὶ δοῦναι τὴν βασιλείαν
one mind and to give the kingdom
αὐτῶν τῷ θηρίῳ, ἄχρι τελεσθήσονται οἱ
of them to the beast, until [4]shall be accomplished [1]the
λόγοι τοῦ θεοῦ. 18 καὶ ἡ γυνὴ ἣν
[2]words – [3]of God. And the woman whom
εἶδες ἔστιν ἡ πόλις ἡ μεγάλη ἡ ἔχουσα
thou sawest is the [2]city – [1]great – having
βασιλείαν ἐπὶ τῶν βασιλέων τῆς γῆς.
a kingdom over the kings of the earth.

18 Μετὰ ταῦτα εἶδον ἄλλον ἄγγελον
After these things I saw another angel
καταβαίνοντα ἐκ τοῦ οὐρανοῦ, ἔχοντα
coming down out of – heaven, having
ἐξουσίαν μεγάλην, καὶ ἡ γῆ ἐφωτίσθη
[2]authority [1]great, and the earth was enlightened
ἐκ τῆς δόξης αὐτοῦ. 2 καὶ ἔκραξεν
from the glory of him. And he cried
ἐν ἰσχυρᾷ φωνῇ λέγων· ἔπεσεν ἔπεσεν
in a strong voice saying: Fell[,] fell
Βαβυλὼν ἡ μεγάλη, καὶ ἐγένετο κατοικητή-
Babylon the great, and became a dwelling-
ριον δαιμονίων καὶ φυλακὴ παντὸς
place of demons and a prison of every
πνεύματος ἀκαθάρτου καὶ φυλακὴ παντὸς
[2]spirit [1]unclean and a prison of every
ὀρνέου ἀκαθάρτου καὶ μεμισημένου, 3 ὅτι
[4]bird [1]unclean [2]and [3]*having been* hated, because
ἐκ τοῦ οἴνου τοῦ θυμοῦ τῆς πορνείας
[8]of [9]the [7]wine [6]of the [5]anger [10]of the [11]fornication

13 They have one purpose
and will give their power
and authority to the beast.
14 They will make war
against the Lamb, but the
Lamb will overcome them
because he is Lord of lords
and King of kings—and
with him will be his called,
chosen and faithful followers."
15 Then the angel said to
me, "The waters you saw,
where the prostitute sits,
are peoples, multitudes,
nations and languages.
16 The beast and the ten
horns you saw will hate the
prostitute. They will bring
her to ruin and leave her
naked; they will eat her
flesh and burn her with fire.
17 For God has put it into
their hearts to accomplish
his purpose by agreeing to
give the beast their power
to rule, until God's words
are fulfilled. 18 The woman
you saw is the great city
that rules over the kings of
the earth."

Chapter 18

The Fall of Babylon

AFTER this I saw anoth-
er angel coming down
from heaven. He had great
authority, and the earth
was illuminated by his
splendor. 2 With a mighty
voice he shouted:

"Fallen! Fallen is
Babylon the Great!
She has become a
home for demons
and a haunt for every
evil[v] spirit,
a haunt for every
unclean and
detestable bird.
3 For all the nations have
drunk
the maddening wine of
her adulteries.

[v] 2 Greek *unclean*

and the kings of the
earth have
committed
fornication
with her,
and the merchants
of the earth
have grown rich
from the
power[d] of her
luxury."
4 Then I heard another
voice from heaven saying,
"Come out of her, my
people,
so that you do not
take part in her
sins,
and so that you do
not share
in her plagues;
5 for her sins are
heaped high
as heaven,
and God has
remembered
her iniquities.
6 Render to her as she
herself
has rendered,
and repay her
double for
her deeds;
mix a double
draught for her
in the cup she
mixed.
7 As she glorified
herself and lived
luxuriously,
so give her a like
measure of
torment and
grief.
Since in her heart she
says,
'I rule as a queen;
I am no widow,
and I will never see
grief,'
8 therefore her plagues
will come in a
single day—
pestilence and
mourning
and famine—
and she will be
burned with fire;
for mighty is the
Lord God who
judges her."
9 And the kings of the
earth, who committed for-
nication and lived in luxury
with her, will weep and
wail over her when they see
the smoke of her burning;
10 they will stand far off, in
fear of her torment, and
say,
"Alas, alas, the great
city,
Babylon, the mighty
city!
For in one hour your

[d] Or *resources*

αὐτῆς πέπωκαν πάντα τὰ ἔθνη, καὶ
[12]of her [4]have drunk [1]all [2]the [3]nations, and
οἱ βασιλεῖς τῆς γῆς μετ' αὐτῆς ἐπόρνευσαν,
the kings of the earth with her practised fornication,
καὶ οἱ ἔμποροι τῆς γῆς ἐκ τῆς δυνάμεως
and the merchants of the earth [2]from [3]the [4]power
τοῦ στρήνους αὐτῆς ἐπλούτησαν. 4 Καὶ
[5]of the [6]luxury [7]of her [1]became rich. And
ἤκουσα ἄλλην φωνὴν ἐκ τοῦ οὐρανοῦ
I heard another voice out of – heaven
λέγουσαν· ἐξέλθατε ὁ λαός μου ἐξ αὐτῆς,
saying: Come ye *out*[,] the people of me[,] out of her,
ἵνα μὴ συγκοινωνήσητε ταῖς ἁμαρτίαις
lest ye share in the sins
αὐτῆς, καὶ ἐκ τῶν πληγῶν αὐτῆς ἵνα
of her, and [3]of [4]the [5]plagues [6]of her [1]lest
μὴ λάβητε· 5 ὅτι ἐκολλήθησαν αὐτῆς αἱ
[2]ye receive; because [4]joined together [3]of her [1]the
ἁμαρτίαι ἄχρι τοῦ οὐρανοῦ, καὶ ἐμνημό-
[2]sins up to – heaven, and [2]remem-
νευσεν ὁ θεὸς τὰ ἀδικήματα αὐτῆς.
bered – [1]God the misdeeds of her.
6 ἀπόδοτε αὐτῇ ὡς καὶ αὐτὴ ἀπέδωκεν,
Give ye back to her as indeed she gave back,
καὶ διπλώσατε τὰ διπλᾶ κατὰ τὰ ἔργα
and double ye the double according to the works
αὐτῆς· ἐν τῷ ποτηρίῳ ᾧ ἐκέρασεν
of her; in the cup in which she mixed
κεράσατε αὐτῇ διπλοῦν· 7 ὅσα ἐδόξασεν
mix ye to her double; by what things she glorified
αὐτὴν καὶ ἐστρηνίασεν, τοσοῦτον δότε
her[self] and luxuriated, by so much give ye
αὐτῇ βασανισμὸν καὶ πένθος. ὅτι ἐν
to her torment and sorrow. Because in
τῇ καρδίᾳ αὐτῆς λέγει ὅτι κάθημαι
the heart of her she says[,] – I sit
βασίλισσα καὶ χήρα οὐκ εἰμὶ καὶ πένθος
a queen and a widow I am not and sorrow
οὐ μὴ ἴδω· 8 διὰ τοῦτο ἐν μιᾷ ἡμέρᾳ
by no means I see; therefore in one day
ἥξουσιν αἱ πληγαὶ αὐτῆς, θάνατος καὶ
will come the plagues of her, death and
πένθος καὶ λιμός, καὶ ἐν πυρὶ κατακαυ-
sorrow and famine, and with fire she will be
θήσεται· ὅτι ἰσχυρὸς κύριος ὁ θεὸς ὁ
consumed; because strong [is] [the] Lord – God the
κρίνας αὐτήν. 9 καὶ κλαύσουσιν καὶ
[one] judging her. And [5]will weep [6]and
κόψονται ἐπ' αὐτὴν οἱ βασιλεῖς τῆς
[7]wail [8]over [9]her [1]the [2]kings [3]of the
γῆς οἱ μετ' αὐτῆς πορνεύσαντες καὶ
[4]earth [10]the [ones] [12]with [13]her [11]having practised fornication and
στρηνιάσαντες, ὅταν βλέπωσιν τὸν καπνὸν
having luxuriated, when*ever* they see the smoke
τῆς πυρώσεως αὐτῆς, 10 ἀπὸ μακρόθεν
of the burning of her, [2]from [3]afar
ἑστηκότες διὰ τὸν φόβον τοῦ βασανισμοῦ
[1]standing because of the fear of the torment
αὐτῆς, λέγοντες· οὐαὶ οὐαί, ἡ πόλις
of her, saying: Woe[,] woe, the [2]city
ἡ μεγάλη, Βαβυλὼν ἡ πόλις ἡ ἰσχυρά,
– [1]great, Babylon the [2]city – [1]strong,

The kings of the earth
committed adultery
with her,
and the merchants of
the earth grew rich
from her excessive
luxuries."
4 Then I heard another
voice from heaven say:

"Come out of her, my
people,
so that you will not
share in her sins,
so that you will not
receive any of her
plagues;
5 for her sins are piled up
to heaven,
and God has
remembered her
crimes.
6 Give back to her as she
has given;
pay her back double
for what she has
done.
Mix her a double
portion from her
own cup.
7 Give her as much torture
and grief
as the glory and luxury
she gave herself.
In her heart she boasts,
'I sit as queen; I am not
a widow,
and I will never
mourn.'
8 Therefore in one day her
plagues will
overtake her:
death, mourning and
famine.
She will be consumed by
fire,
for mighty is the Lord
God who judges her.

9 "When the kings of the
earth who committed adul-
tery with her and shared
her luxury see the smoke of
her burning, they will weep
and mourn over her. 10 Terrified at her torment, they
will stand far off and cry:

" 'Woe! Woe, O great
city,
O Babylon, city of
power!

judgment
has come."
11 And the merchants
of the earth weep and
mourn for her, since no one
buys their cargo anymore,
12 cargo of gold, silver, jewels and pearls, fine linen,
purple, silk and scarlet, all
kinds of scented wood, all
articles of ivory, all articles
of costly wood, bronze,
iron, and marble, 13 cinnamon, spice, incense,
myrrh, frankincense, wine,
olive oil, choice flour and
wheat, cattle and sheep,
horses and chariots,
slaves—and human lives.[e]
14 "The fruit for which
your soul longed
has gone from you,
and all your dainties
and
your splendor
are lost to you,
never to be found
again!"
15 The merchants of these
wares, who gained wealth
from her, will stand far off,
in fear of her torment,
weeping and mourning
aloud,
16 "Alas, alas, the great
city,
clothed in fine linen,
in purple and
scarlet,
adorned with gold,
with jewels, and
with pearls!
17 For in one hour all
this wealth has
been laid
waste!"
And all shipmasters and
seafarers, sailors and all

ὅτι μιᾷ ὥρᾳ ἦλθεν ἡ κρίσις σου. 11 καὶ
be-cause in one hour came the judgment of thee. And

οἱ ἔμποροι τῆς γῆς κλαίουσιν καὶ
the merchants of the earth weep and

πενθοῦσιν ἐπ' αὐτήν, ὅτι τὸν γόμον
sorrow over her, because [4]the [5]cargo

αὐτῶν οὐδεὶς ἀγοράζει οὐκέτι, 12 γόμον
[6]of them [1]no one [3]buys [2]any more, cargo

χρυσοῦ καὶ ἀργύρου καὶ λίθου τιμίου
of gold and of silver and [2]stone [1]of valuable

καὶ μαργαριτῶν καὶ βυσσίνου καὶ πορφύρας
and of pearls and of fine linen and of purple

καὶ σηρικοῦ καὶ κοκκίνου, καὶ πᾶν
and of silk and of scarlet, and all

ξύλον θύϊνον καὶ πᾶν σκεῦος ἐλεφάντινον
[2]wood [1]thyine and every [2]vessel [1]ivory

καὶ πᾶν σκεῦος ἐκ ξύλου τιμιωτάτου
and every vessel of [2]wood [1]very valuable

καὶ χαλκοῦ καὶ σιδήρου καὶ μαρμάρου,
and of bronze and of iron and of marble,

13 καὶ κιννάμωμον καὶ ἄμωμον καὶ
and cinnamon and spice and

θυμιάματα καὶ μύρον καὶ λίβανον καὶ
incenses and ointment and frankincense and

οἶνον καὶ ἔλαιον καὶ σεμίδαλιν καὶ σῖτον
wine and oil and fine meal and corn

καὶ κτήνη καὶ πρόβατα, καὶ ἵππων
and beasts of burden and sheep, and of horses

καὶ ῥεδῶν καὶ σωμάτων, καὶ ψυχὰς
and of carriages and of bodies, and souls

ἀνθρώπων. 14 καὶ ἡ ὀπώρα σου τῆς
of men. And the fruit [5]of thee [1]of the

ἐπιθυμίας τῆς ψυχῆς ἀπῆλθεν ἀπὸ σοῦ,
[2]lust [3]of the [4]soul went away from thee,

καὶ πάντα τὰ λιπαρὰ καὶ τὰ λαμπρὰ
and all the sumptuous things and the bright things

ἀπώλετο ἀπὸ σοῦ, καὶ οὐκέτι οὐ μὴ
perished from thee, and no more by no(any) means

αὐτὰ εὑρήσουσιν. 15 οἱ ἔμποροι τούτων,
[2]them [1]shall they find. The merchants of these things,

οἱ πλουτήσαντες ἀπ' αὐτῆς, ἀπὸ μακρόθεν
the [ones] having been rich from her, [2]from [3]afar

στήσονται διὰ τὸν φόβον τοῦ βασανισμοῦ
[1]will stand because of the fear of the torment

αὐτῆς κλαίοντες καὶ πενθοῦντες, 16 λέγοντες·
of her weeping and sorrowing, saying:

οὐαὶ οὐαί, ἡ πόλις ἡ μεγάλη, ἡ περι-
Woe[,] woe, the [2]city – [1]great, – *having*

βεβλημένη βύσσινον καὶ πορφυροῦν καὶ
been clothed [with] fine linen and purple and

κόκκινον, καὶ κεχρυσωμένη ἐν χρυσίῳ
scarlet, and *having been* gilded with gold

καὶ λίθῳ τιμίῳ καὶ μαργαρίτῃ, 17 ὅτι
and [2]stone [1]valuable and pearl, because

μιᾷ ὥρᾳ ἠρημώθη ὁ τοσοῦτος πλοῦτος.
in one hour [3]was made desolate [1]such great [2]wealth.

καὶ πᾶς κυβερνήτης καὶ πᾶς ὁ ἐπὶ
And every steersman and [1]every [2]one [4]to

τόπον πλέων καὶ ναῦται καὶ ὅσοι τὴν
[5]a place [3]sailing and sailors and as many as [2]the

In one hour your doom
has come!'
11 "The merchants of the
earth will weep and mourn
over her because no one
buys their cargoes any
more—12 cargoes of gold,
silver, precious stones and
pearls; fine linen, purple,
silk and scarlet cloth; every
sort of citron wood, and articles of every kind made of
ivory, costly wood,
bronze, iron and marble;
13 cargoes of cinnamon and
spice, of incense, myrrh
and frankincense, of wine
and olive oil, of fine flour
and wheat; cattle and
sheep; horses and car-
riages; and bodies and
souls of men.
14 "They will say, 'The
fruit you longed for is gone
from you. All your riches
and splendor have van-
ished, never to be recov-
ered.' 15 The merchants
who sold these things and
gained their wealth from
her will stand far off, terrified at her torment. They
will weep and mourn 16 and
cry out:

" 'Woe! Woe, O great
city,
dressed in fine linen,
purple and scarlet,
and glittering with
gold, precious
stones and pearls!
17 In one hour such great
wealth has been
brought to ruin!'

"Every sea captain, and
all who travel by ship, the
sailors, and all who earn

[e] Or *chariots, and human bodies and souls*

whose trade is on the sea,
stood far off 18 and cried out
as they saw the smoke of
her burning,
"What city was like
the great city?"
19 And they threw dust on
their heads, as they wept
and mourned, crying out,
"Alas, alas, the great
city,
where all who had
ships at sea
grew rich by her
wealth!
For in one hour she
has been
laid waste.
20 Rejoice over her,
O heaven,
you saints and
apostles and
prophets!
For God has given
judgment for
you against
her."
21 Then a mighty angel
took up a stone like a great
millstone and threw it into
the sea, saying,
"With such violence
Babylon the
great city
will be thrown
down,
and will be found no
more;
22 and the sound of
harpists and
minstrels and of
flutists and
trumpeters
will be heard in you
no more;
and an artisan of any
trade
will be found in you
no more;
and the sound of the
millstone
will be heard in you
no more;
23 and the light of a
lamp
will shine in you no
more;
and the voice of
bridegroom
and bride
will be heard in you
no more;
for your merchants
were the
magnates of the
earth,
and all nations were
deceived by
your sorcery.
24 And in you[f] was
found the blood
of prophets and
of saints,
and of all who have
been slaughtered
on earth."

[f] Gk *her*

θάλασσαν ἐργάζονται, ἀπὸ μακρόθεν ἔστησαν
[2]sea [1]work. [2]from [3]afar [1]stood
18 καὶ ἔκραζον βλέποντες τὸν καπνὸν
and cried out seeing the smoke
τῆς πυρώσεως αὐτῆς λέγοντες· τίς ὁμοία
of the burning of her saying: Who(What) [is] like
τῇ πόλει τῇ μεγάλῃ; 19 καὶ ἔβαλον
to the [2]city – [1]great ? And they cast
χοῦν ἐπὶ τὰς κεφαλὰς αὐτῶν καὶ ἔκραζον
dust on the heads of them and cried out
κλαίοντες καὶ πενθοῦντες, λέγοντες· οὐαὶ
weeping and sorrowing, saying: Woe[,]
οὐαί, ἡ πόλις ἡ μεγάλη, ἐν ᾗ ἐπλούτησαν
woe, the [2]city – [1]great, by which [8]were rich
πάντες οἱ ἔχοντες τὰ πλοῖα ἐν τῇ
[1]all [2]the [ones] [3]having [4]the [5]ships [6]in [7]the
θαλάσσῃ ἐκ τῆς τιμιότητος αὐτῆς, ὅτι
[8]sea from the worth of her, because
μιᾷ ὥρᾳ ἠρημώθη. 20 Εὐφραίνου ἐπ'
in one hour she was made desolate. Be thou glad over
αὐτῇ, οὐρανὲ καὶ οἱ ἅγιοι καὶ οἱ ἀπό-
her, heaven and *the* saints and *the* apost-
στολοι καὶ οἱ προφῆται, ὅτι ἔκρινεν ὁ
les and *the* prophets, because [2]judged –
θεὸς τὸ κρίμα ὑμῶν ἐξ αὐτῆς. 21 Καὶ
[1]God the judgment of you by her. And
ἦρεν εἷς ἄγγελος ἰσχυρὸς λίθον ὡς
[4]lifted [1]one [3]angel [2]strong a stone as
μύλινον μέγαν, καὶ ἔβαλεν εἰς τὴν θά-
[2]millstone [1]a great, and threw into the sea
λασσαν λέγων· οὕτως ὁρμήματι βληθήσεται
saying: Thus with a rush [5]shall be thrown
Βαβυλὼν ἡ μεγάλη πόλις, καὶ οὐ μὴ
[1]Babylon [2]the [3]great [4]city, and by no means
εὑρεθῇ ἔτι. 22 καὶ φωνὴ κιθαρῳδῶν
[shall] be found longer. And sound of harpers
καὶ μουσικῶν καὶ αὐλητῶν καὶ σαλπιστῶν
and of musicians and of flutists and of trumpeters
οὐ μὴ ἀκουσθῇ ἐν σοὶ ἔτι, καὶ πᾶς
by no means [shall] be heard in thee longer, and every
τεχνίτης πάσης τέχνης οὐ μὴ εὑρεθῇ
craftsman of every craft by no means [shall] be found
ἐν σοὶ ἔτι, καὶ φωνὴ μύλου οὐ μὴ
in thee longer, and sound of a mill by no means
ἀκουσθῇ ἐν σοὶ ἔτι, 23 καὶ φῶς
[shall] be heard in thee longer, and light
λύχνου οὐ μὴ φάνῃ ἐν σοὶ ἔτι, καὶ
of a lamp by no means [shall] shine in thee longer, and
φωνὴ νυμφίου καὶ νύμφης οὐ μὴ
voice of bridegroom and of bride by no means
ἀκουσθῇ ἐν σοὶ ἔτι· ὅτι [οἱ] ἔμποροί
[shall] be heard in thee longer; because the merchants
σου ἦσαν οἱ μεγιστᾶνες τῆς γῆς, ὅτι
of thee were the great ones of the earth, because
ἐν τῇ φαρμακείᾳ σου ἐπλανήθησαν πάντα
by the sorcery of thee [4]were deceived [1]all
τὰ ἔθνη, 24 καὶ ἐν αὐτῇ αἷμα προφητῶν
[2]the [3]nations, and in her [2]blood [3]of prophets
καὶ ἁγίων εὑρέθη καὶ πάντων τῶν
[4]and [5]of saints [1]was found and of all the [ones]
ἐσφαγμένων ἐπὶ τῆς γῆς.
having been slain on the earth.

their living from the sea,
will stand far off. 18 When
they see the smoke of her
burning, they will exclaim,
'Was there ever a city like
this great city?' 19 They will
throw dust on their heads,
and with weeping and
mourning cry out:
" 'Woe! Woe, O great
city,
where all who had
ships on the sea
became rich through
her wealth!
In one hour she has been
brought to ruin!
20 Rejoice over her, O
heaven!
Rejoice, saints and
apostles and
prophets!
God has judged her for
the way she treated
you.' "
21 Then a mighty angel
picked up a boulder the size
of a large millstone and
threw it into the sea, and
said:
"With such violence
the great city of
Babylon will be
thrown down,
never to be found
again.
22 The music of harpists
and musicians, flute
players and
trumpeters,
will never be heard in
you again.
No workman of any
trade
will ever be found in
you again.
The sound of a millstone
will never be heard in
you again.
23 The light of a lamp
will never shine in you
again.
The voice of bridegroom
and bride
will never be heard in
you again.
Your merchants were
the world's great
men.
By your magic spell all
the nations were led
astray.
24 In her was found the
blood of prophets
and of the saints,
and of all who have
been killed on the
earth."

Chapter 19

The Rejoicing in Heaven

AFTER this I heard what seemed to be the loud voice of a great multitude in heaven, saying,
"Hallelujah!
Salvation and glory
and power
to our God,
2 for his judgments
are true
and just;
he has judged the
great whore
who corrupted the
earth with her
fornication,
and he has avenged
on her the blood
of his
servants."[g]
3 Once more they said,
"Hallelujah!
The smoke goes up
from her forever
and ever."
4 And the twenty-four elders and the four living creatures fell down and worshiped God who is seated on the throne, saying,
"Amen. Hallelujah!"
5 And from the throne came a voice saying,
"Praise our God,
all you his
servants,[g]
and all who fear him,
small and great."
6 Then I heard what seemed to be the voice of a great multitude, like the sound of many waters and like the sound of mighty thunderpeals, crying out,
"Hallelujah!
For the Lord our God
the Almighty reigns.
7 Let us rejoice and
exult
and give him the
glory,
for the marriage of the
Lamb has come,
and his bride has
made
herself ready;
8 to her it has been
granted to
be clothed
with fine linen,
bright and
pure"—
for the fine linen is the righteous deeds of the saints.
9 And the angel said[h] to me, "Write this: Blessed are those who are invited to

[g] Gk *slaves*
[h] Gk *he said*

19 Μετὰ ταῦτα ἤκουσα ὡς φωνὴν
After these things I heard as [3]voice
μεγάλην ὄχλου πολλοῦ ἐν τῷ οὐρανῷ
[1]a great (loud) [4]crowd [2]of a much (great) in – heaven
λεγόντων· ἀλληλουϊά· ἡ σωτηρία καὶ ἡ
saying: Halleluia: The salvation and the
δόξα καὶ ἡ δύναμις τοῦ θεοῦ ἡμῶν,
glory and the power of the God of us,
2 ὅτι ἀληθιναὶ καὶ δίκαιαι αἱ κρίσεις
because true and righteous the judgments
αὐτοῦ· ὅτι ἔκρινεν τὴν πόρνην τὴν
of him; because he judged the [2]harlot –
μεγάλην ἥτις ἔφθειρεν τὴν γῆν ἐν τῇ
[1]great who defiled the earth with the
πορνείᾳ αὐτῆς, καὶ ἐξεδίκησεν τὸ αἷμα
fornication of her, and *he* avenged the blood
τῶν δούλων αὐτοῦ ἐκ χειρὸς αὐτῆς.
of the slaves of him out of [the] hand of her.
3 καὶ δεύτερον εἴρηκαν· ἀλληλουϊά· καὶ
And secondly they *have* said: Halleluia; and
ὁ καπνὸς αὐτῆς ἀναβαίνει εἰς τοὺς
the smoke of her goes up unto the
αἰῶνας τῶν αἰώνων. **4** καὶ ἔπεσαν οἱ
ages of the ages. And [8]fell [1]the
πρεσβύτεροι οἱ εἴκοσι τέσσαρες καὶ τὰ
[3]elders – [2]twenty-four [4]and [5]the
τέσσερα ζῷα, καὶ προσεκύνησαν τῷ θεῷ
[6]four [7]living creatures, and worshipped – God
τῷ καθημένῳ ἐπὶ τῷ θρόνῳ λέγοντες·
sitting on the throne saying:
ἀμὴν ἀλληλουϊά. **5** καὶ φωνὴ ἀπὸ τοῦ
Amen[,] halleluia. And a voice [2]from [3]the
θρόνου ἐξῆλθεν λέγουσα· αἰνεῖτε τῷ θεῷ
[4]throne [1]came out saying: Praise ye the God
ἡμῶν, πάντες οἱ δοῦλοι αὐτοῦ, οἱ
of us, all the slaves of him, the
φοβούμενοι αὐτόν, οἱ μικροὶ καὶ οἱ
[ones] fearing him, the small and the
μεγάλοι. **6** Καὶ ἤκουσα ὡς φωνὴν ὄχλου
great. And I heard as a sound [3]crowd
πολλοῦ καὶ ὡς φωνὴν ὑδάτων πολλῶν
[2]of a much(great) and as a sound [2]waters [1]of many
καὶ ὡς φωνὴν βροντῶν ἰσχυρῶν, λεγόντων·
and as a sound [2]thunders [1]of strong (loud), saying:
ἀλληλουϊά, ὅτι ἐβασίλευσεν κύριος ὁ θεὸς
Halleluia, because [7]reigned [1][the] Lord [2]the [3]God
ἡμῶν ὁ παντοκράτωρ. **7** χαίρωμεν καὶ
[4]of us [5]the [6]Almighty. Let us rejoice and
ἀγαλλιῶμεν, καὶ δώσομεν τὴν δόξαν αὐτῷ,
let us exult, and we will give the glory to him,
ὅτι ἦλθεν ὁ γάμος τοῦ ἀρνίου, καὶ
because [5]came [1]the [2]marriage [3]of the [4]Lamb, and
ἡ γυνὴ αὐτοῦ ἡτοίμασεν ἑαυτήν, **8** καὶ
the wife of him prepared herself, and
ἐδόθη αὐτῇ ἵνα περιβάληται βύσσινον
it was given to her *in order* that she might be clothed [with] [3]fine linen
λαμπρὸν καθαρόν· τὸ γὰρ βύσσινον τὰ
[1]bright [2]clean; for the fine linen [3]the
δικαιώματα τῶν ἁγίων ἐστίν. **9** Καὶ
[4]righteous deeds [5]of the [6]saints [2]is. And
λέγει μοι· γράψον· μακάριοι οἱ εἰς τὸ
he tells me: Write thou; blessed [1]the [ones] [2]to [4]the

Chapter 19

Hallelujah!

AFTER this I heard what sounded like the roar of a great multitude in heaven shouting:

"Hallelujah!
Salvation and glory and
power belong to our
God,
2 for true and just are his
judgments.
He has condemned the
great prostitute
who corrupted the
earth by her
adulteries.
He has avenged on her
the blood of his
servants."

3 And again they shouted:

"Hallelujah!
The smoke from her
goes up for ever and
ever."

4 The twenty-four elders and the four living creatures fell down and worshiped God, who was seated on the throne. And they cried:

"Amen, Hallelujah!"

5 Then a voice came from the throne, saying:

"Praise our God,
all you his servants,
you who fear him,
both small and great!"

6 Then I heard what sounded like a great multitude, like the roar of rushing waters and like loud peals of thunder, shouting:

"Hallelujah!
For our Lord God
Almighty reigns.
7 Let us rejoice and be
glad
and give him glory!
For the wedding of the
Lamb has come,
and his bride has made
herself ready.
8 Fine linen, bright and
clean,
was given her to
wear."

(Fine linen stands for the righteous acts of the saints.)

9 Then the angel said to me, "Write: 'Blessed are

the marriage supper of the
Lamb." And he said to me,
"These are true words of
God." 10Then I fell down at
his feet to worship him, but
he said to me, "You must
not do that! I am a fellow
servant[i] with you and your
comrades[j] who hold the
testimony of Jesus.[k] Worship God! For the testimony of Jesus[k] is the spirit of
prophecy."

The Rider on the White Horse

11 Then I saw heaven
opened, and there was a
white horse! Its rider is
called Faithful and True,
and in righteousness he
judges and makes war.
12His eyes are like a flame
of fire, and on his head are
many diadems; and he has
a name inscribed that no
one knows but himself.
13He is clothed in a robe
dipped in[l] blood, and his
name is called The Word of
God. 14And the armies of
heaven, wearing fine linen,
white and pure, were fol-
lowing him on white
horses. 15From his mouth
comes a sharp sword with
which to strike down the
nations, and he will rule[m]
them with a rod of iron; he
will tread the winepress of
the fury of the wrath of God
the Almighty. 16On his
robe and on his thigh he has
a name inscribed, "King of
kings and Lord of lords."

[i] Gk *slave*
[j] Gk *brothers*
[k] Or *to Jesus*
[l] Other ancient authorities read *sprinkled with*
[m] Or *will shepherd*

δεῖπνον τοῦ γάμου τοῦ ἀρνίου κεκλημένοι.
[5]supper [6]of the [7]marriage [8]of the [9]Lamb [4]*having been* called.

καὶ λέγει μοι· οὗτοι οἱ λόγοι ἀληθινοὶ
And he says to me: [1]These – [2]words [5]true

τοῦ θεοῦ εἰσιν. **10** καὶ ἔπεσα ἔμπροσθεν
– [3]of God [4]are. And I fell before

τῶν ποδῶν αὐτοῦ προσκυνῆσαι αὐτῷ.
the feet of him to worship him.

καὶ λέγει μοι· ὅρα μή· σύνδουλός σού
And he says to me: See thou [do it] not; [2]a fellow-slave [3]of thee

εἰμι καὶ τῶν ἀδελφῶν σου τῶν ἐχόντων
[1]I am and of the brothers of thee – having

τὴν μαρτυρίαν Ἰησοῦ· τῷ θεῷ προσκύνησον.
the witness of Jesus; – [2]God [1]worship thou.

ἡ γὰρ μαρτυρία Ἰησοῦ ἐστιν τὸ πνεῦμα
For the witness of Jesus is the spirit

τῆς προφητείας.
– of prophecy.

11 Καὶ εἶδον τὸν οὐρανὸν ἠνεῳγμένον,
And I saw – heaven *having been* opened,

καὶ ἰδοὺ ἵππος λευκός, καὶ ὁ καθήμενος
and behold[,] [2]horse [1]a white, and the [one] sitting

ἐπ' αὐτὸν πιστὸς καλούμενος καὶ ἀληθινός,
on it [2]faithful [1]*being* called and true,

καὶ ἐν δικαιοσύνῃ κρίνει καὶ πολεμεῖ.
and in righteousness he judges and makes war.

12 οἱ δὲ ὀφθαλμοὶ αὐτοῦ φλὸξ πυρός,
And the eyes of him [are as] a flame of fire,

καὶ ἐπὶ τὴν κεφαλὴν αὐτοῦ διαδήματα
and on the head of him [2]diadems

πολλά, ἔχων ὄνομα γεγραμμένον ὃ οὐδεὶς
[1]many, having a name *having been* written which no one

οἶδεν εἰ μὴ αὐτός, **13** καὶ περιβεβλημένος
knows except [him]self, and *having been* clothed [with]

ἱμάτιον βεβαμμένον αἵματι, καὶ κέκληται
a garment *having been* dipped in blood, and [4]has been called

τὸ ὄνομα αὐτοῦ ὁ λόγος τοῦ θεοῦ.
[1]the [2]name [3]of him The Word – of God.

14 καὶ τὰ στρατεύματα τὰ ἐν τῷ οὐρανῷ
And the armies – in – heaven

ἠκολούθει αὐτῷ ἐφ' ἵπποις λευκοῖς, ἐνδεδυμένοι
followed him on [2]horses [1]white, *having been* dressed [in]

βύσσινον λευκὸν καθαρόν. **15** καὶ ἐκ
[3]fine linen [1]white [2]clean. And out of

τοῦ στόματος αὐτοῦ ἐκπορεύεται ῥομφαία
the mouth of him proceeds [2]sword

ὀξεῖα, ἵνα ἐν αὐτῇ πατάξῃ τὰ ἔθνη·
[1]a sharp, in order that with it he may smite the nations;

καὶ αὐτὸς ποιμανεῖ αὐτοὺς ἐν ῥάβδῳ
and he will shepherd them with [2]staff

σιδηρᾷ· καὶ αὐτὸς πατεῖ τὴν ληνὸν
[1]an iron; and he treads the winepress

τοῦ οἴνου τοῦ θυμοῦ τῆς ὀργῆς τοῦ
of the wine of the anger[,] of the wrath –

θεοῦ τοῦ παντοκράτορος. **16** καὶ ἔχει
of God *of* the Almighty. And he has

ἐπὶ τὸ ἱμάτιον καὶ ἐπὶ τὸν μηρὸν
on the garment and on the thigh

αὐτοῦ ὄνομα γεγραμμένον· ΒΑΣΙΛΕΥΣ
of him a name *having been* written: KING

ΒΑΣΙΛΕΩΝ ΚΑΙ ΚΥΡΙΟΣ ΚΥΡΙΩΝ.
OF KINGS AND LORD OF LORDS.

those who are invited to the
wedding supper of the
Lamb!'" And he added,
"These are the true words
of God."
10At this I fell at his feet to
worship him. But he said to
me, "Do not do it! I am a
fellow servant with you and
with your brothers who
hold to the testimony of
Jesus. Worship God! For
the testimony of Jesus is
the spirit of prophecy."

The Rider on the White Horse

11I saw heaven standing
open and there before me
was a white horse, whose
rider is called Faithful and
True. With justice he
judges and makes war.
12His eyes are like blazing
fire, and on his head are
many crowns. He has a
name written on him that
no one knows but he him-
self. 13He is dressed in a
robe dipped in blood, and
his name is the Word of
God. 14The armies of heav-
en were following him, riding on white horses and
dressed in fine linen, white
and clean. 15Out of his
mouth comes a sharp
sword with which to strike
down the nations. "He will
rule them with an iron scepter."[w] He treads the winepress of the fury of the
wrath of God Almighty.
16On his robe and on his
thigh he has this name written:

KING OF KINGS AND LORD OF LORDS.

[w] *15* Psalm 2:9

The Beast and Its Armies Defeated

17 Then I saw an angel
standing in the sun, and
with a loud voice he called
to all the birds that fly in
midheaven, "Come, gather
for the great supper of God,
18 to eat the flesh of kings,
the flesh of captains, the
flesh of the mighty, the
flesh of horses and their
riders—flesh of all, both
free and slave, both small
and great." 19 Then I saw
the beast and the kings of
the earth with their armies
gathered to make war
against the rider on the
horse and against his army.
20 And the beast was cap-
tured, and with it the false
prophet who had per-
formed in its presence the
signs by which he deceived
those who had received the
mark of the beast and those
who worshiped its image.
These two were thrown
alive into the lake of fire
that burns with sulfur.
21 And the rest were killed
by the sword of the rider on
the horse, the sword that
came from his mouth; and
all the birds were gorged
with their flesh.

17 Καὶ εἶδον ἕνα ἄγγελον ἑστῶτα ἐν
And I saw one angel standing in
τῷ ἡλίῳ, καὶ ἔκραξεν ἐν φωνῇ μεγάλῃ
the sun, and he cried out in [2]voice [1]a great (loud)
λέγων πᾶσιν τοῖς ὀρνέοις τοῖς πετομένοις
saying to all the birds – flying
ἐν μεσουρανήματι· δεῦτε συνάχθητε εἰς
in mid-heaven: Come *ye*[,] assemble ye to
τὸ δεῖπνον τὸ μέγα τοῦ θεοῦ, **18** ἵνα
the [2]supper – [1]great – of God, in order that
φάγητε σάρκας βασιλέων καὶ σάρκας
ye may eat flesh*es* of kings and flesh*es*
χιλιάρχων καὶ σάρκας ἰσχυρῶν καὶ σάρκας
of chiliarchs and flesh*es* of strong men and flesh*es*
ἵππων καὶ τῶν καθημένων ἐπ' αὐτῶν,
of horses and of the [ones] sitting on them,
καὶ σάρκας πάντων ἐλευθέρων τε καὶ
and flesh*es* of all [2]free men [1]both and
δούλων καὶ μικρῶν καὶ μεγάλων. **19** Καὶ
slaves both small and great. And
εἶδον τὸ θηρίον καὶ τοὺς βασιλεῖς τῆς
I saw the beast and the kings of the
γῆς καὶ τὰ στρατεύματα αὐτῶν συνηγμένα
earth and the armies of them *having been* assembled
ποιῆσαι τὸν πόλεμον μετὰ τοῦ καθημένου
to make the war with the [one] sitting
ἐπὶ τοῦ ἵππου καὶ μετὰ τοῦ στρατεύματος
on the horse and with the army
αὐτοῦ. **20** καὶ ἐπιάσθη τὸ θηρίον καὶ
of him. And [3]was seized [1]the [2]beast and
μετ' αὐτοῦ ὁ ψευδοπροφήτης ὁ ποιήσας
with it the false prophet the [one] having done
τὰ σημεῖα ἐνώπιον αὐτοῦ, ἐν οἷς ἐπλάνη-
the signs before it, by which he de-
σεν τοὺς λαβόντας τὸ χάραγμα τοῦ
ceived the [ones] having received the mark of the
θηρίου καὶ τοὺς προσκυνοῦντας τῇ εἰκόνι
beast and the [ones] worshipping the image
αὐτοῦ· ζῶντες ἐβλήθησαν οἱ δύο εἰς
of it; [4]living [3]were cast [1]the [2]two into
τὴν λίμνην τοῦ πυρὸς τῆς καιομένης
the lake – of fire – burning*
ἐν θείῳ. **21** καὶ οἱ λοιποὶ ἀπεκτάνθησαν
with sulphur. And the rest were killed
ἐν τῇ ῥομφαίᾳ τοῦ καθημένου ἐπὶ τοῦ
with the sword of the [one] sitting on the
ἵππου τῇ ἐξελθούσῃ ἐκ τοῦ στόματος
horse – proceeding§ out of the mouth
αὐτοῦ, καὶ πάντα τὰ ὄρνεα ἐχορτάσθησαν
of him, and all the birds were filled
ἐκ τῶν σαρκῶν αὐτῶν.
by the flesh*es* of them.

17 And I saw an angel
standing in the sun, who
cried in a loud voice to all
the birds flying in midair,
"Come, gather together for
the great supper of God,
18 so that you may eat the
flesh of kings, generals,
and mighty men, of horses
and their riders, and the
flesh of all people, free and
slave, small and great."
19 Then I saw the beast
and the kings of the earth
and their armies gathered
together to make war
against the rider on the
horse and his army. 20 But
the beast was captured,
and with him the false
prophet who had per-
formed the miraculous
signs on his behalf. With
these signs he had deluded
those who had received the
mark of the beast and worshiped his image. The two
of them were thrown alive
into the fiery lake of burning sulfur. 21 The rest of
them were killed with the
sword that came out of the
mouth of the rider on the
horse, and all the birds
gorged themselves on their
flesh.

Chapter 20

The Thousand Years

THEN I saw an angel
coming down from
heaven, holding in his hand
the key to the bottomless

20 Καὶ εἶδον ἄγγελον καταβαίνοντα ἐκ
And I saw an angel coming down out of
τοῦ οὐρανοῦ, ἔχοντα τὴν κλεῖν τῆς
– heaven, having the key of the
ἀβύσσου καὶ ἄλυσιν μεγάλην ἐπὶ τὴν χεῖρα
abyss and [2]chain [1]a great on the hand

Chapter 20

The Thousand Years

AND I saw an angel com-
ing down out of heav-
en, having the key to the
Abyss and holding in his
hand a great chain. 2He

* Feminine, agreeing with λίμνη, not with the neuter πῦρ.
§ Agreeing, of course, with ῥομφαίᾳ.

pit and a great chain. 2 He
seized the dragon, that ancient serpent, who is the
Devil and Satan, and bound
him for a thousand years,
3 and threw him into the pit,
and locked and sealed it
over him, so that he would
deceive the nations no
more, until the thousand
years were ended. After
that he must be let out for a
little while.
4 Then I saw thrones,
and those seated on them
were given authority to
judge. I also saw the souls
of those who had been be-
headed for their testimony
to Jesus[n] and for the word
of God. They had not wor-
shiped the beast or its image and had not received its
mark on their foreheads or
their hands. They came to
life and reigned with Christ
a thousand years. 5 (The
rest of the dead did not
come to life until the thousand years were ended.)
This is the first resurrection. 6 Blessed and holy are
those who share in the first
resurrection. Over these
the second death has no
power, but they will be
priests of God and of
Christ, and they will reign
with him a thousand years.

Satan's Doom

7 When the thousand
years are ended, Satan will
be released from his prison
8 and will come out to deceive the nations at the four
corners of the earth, Gog
and Magog, in order to
gather them for battle; they
are as numerous as the

[n] Or *for the testimony of Jesus*

αὐτοῦ. 2 καὶ ἐκράτησεν τὸν δράκοντα,
of him. And he laid hold [of] the dragon,
ὁ ὄφις ὁ ἀρχαῖος, ὅς ἐστιν Διάβολος
the [2]serpent – [1]old, who is Devil
καὶ ὁ Σατανᾶς, καὶ ἔδησεν αὐτὸν χίλια
and – Satan, and bound him a thousand
ἔτη, 3 καὶ ἔβαλεν αὐτὸν εἰς τὴν ἄβυσσον,
years, and cast him into the abyss,
καὶ ἔκλεισεν καὶ ἐσφράγισεν ἐπάνω αὐτοῦ,
and shut and sealed over him,
ἵνα μὴ πλανήσῃ ἔτι τὰ ἔθνη, ἄχρι
in order that he should not deceive longer the nations, until
τελεσθῇ τὰ χίλια ἔτη· μετὰ ταῦτα
[4]are finished [1]the [2]thousand [3]years; after these things
δεῖ λυθῆναι αὐτὸν μικρὸν χρόνον.
it behoves [2]to be loosed [1]him a little time.
4 Καὶ εἶδον θρόνους, καὶ ἐκάθισαν ἐπ'
And I saw thrones, and they sat on
αὐτούς, καὶ κρίμα ἐδόθη αὐτοῖς, καὶ
them, and judgment was given to them, and
τὰς ψυχὰς τῶν πεπελεκισμένων διὰ τὴν
the souls of the [ones] having been beheaded because of the
μαρτυρίαν Ἰησοῦ καὶ διὰ τὸν λόγον
witness of Jesus and because of the word
τοῦ θεοῦ, καὶ οἵτινες οὐ προσεκύνησαν
– of God, and who did not worship
τὸ θηρίον οὐδὲ τὴν εἰκόνα αὐτοῦ καὶ
the beast nor the image of it and
οὐκ ἔλαβον τὸ χάραγμα ἐπὶ τὸ μέτωπον
did not receive the mark on the forehead
καὶ ἐπὶ τὴν χεῖρα αὐτῶν· καὶ ἔζησαν
and on the hand of them; and they lived [again]
καὶ ἐβασίλευσαν μετὰ τοῦ Χριστοῦ χίλια
and reigned with – Christ a thousand
ἔτη. 5 οἱ λοιποὶ τῶν νεκρῶν οὐκ ἔζησαν
years. The rest of the dead did not live [again]
ἄχρι τελεσθῇ τὰ χίλια ἔτη. Αὕτη ἡ
until were finished the thousand years. This [is] the
ἀνάστασις ἡ πρώτη. 6 μακάριος καὶ
[2]resurrection – [1]first. Blessed and
ἅγιος ὁ ἔχων μέρος ἐν τῇ ἀναστάσει
holy [is] the [one] having part in the [2]resurrection
τῇ πρώτῃ· ἐπὶ τούτων ὁ δεύτερος θάνατος
– [1]first; over these the second death
οὐκ ἔχει ἐξουσίαν, ἀλλ' ἔσονται ἱερεῖς
has not authority, but they will be priests
τοῦ θεοῦ καὶ τοῦ Χριστοῦ, καὶ βασιλεύ-
– of God and – of Christ, and will
σουσιν μετ' αὐτοῦ [τὰ] χίλια ἔτη.
reign with him the thousand years.
7 Καὶ ὅταν τελεσθῇ τὰ χίλια ἔτη,
And when*ever* are finished the thousand years,
λυθήσεται ὁ σατανᾶς ἐκ τῆς φυλακῆς
[2]will be loosed – [1]Satan out of the prison
αὐτοῦ, 8 καὶ ἐξελεύσεται πλανῆσαι τὰ
of him, and will go forth to deceive the
ἔθνη τὰ ἐν ταῖς τέσσαρσιν γωνίαις τῆς
nations – in the four corners of the
γῆς, τὸν Γὼγ καὶ Μαγώγ, συναγαγεῖν
earth, – Gog and Magog, to assemble
αὐτοὺς εἰς τὸν πόλεμον, ὧν ὁ ἀριθμὸς
them to the war, of whom the number

seized the dragon, that ancient serpent, who is the
devil, or Satan, and bound
him for a thousand years.
3 He threw him into the
Abyss, and locked and
sealed it over him, to keep
him from deceiving the nations anymore until the
thousand years were end-
ed. After that, he must be
set free for a short time.
4 I saw thrones on which
were seated those who had
been given authority to
judge. And I saw the souls
of those who had been be-
headed because of their
testimony for Jesus and because of the word of God.
They had not worshiped
the beast or his image and
had not received his mark
on their foreheads or their
hands. They came to life
and reigned with Christ a
thousand years. 5 (The rest
of the dead did not come to
life until the thousand years
were ended.) This is the
first resurrection. 6 Blessed
and holy are those who
have part in the first resurrection. The second death
has no power over them,
but they will be priests of
God and of Christ and will
reign with him for a thousand years.

Satan's Doom

7 When the thousand
years are over, Satan will
be released from his prison
8 and will go out to deceive
the nations in the four corners of the earth—Gog and
Magog—to gather them for
battle. In number they are

sands of the sea. 9 They
marched up over the
breadth of the earth and
surrounded the camp of the
saints and the beloved city.
And fire came down from
heaven[o] and consumed
them. 10 And the devil who
had deceived them was
thrown into the lake of fire
and sulfur, where the beast
and the false prophet were,
and they will be tormented
day and night forever and
ever.

The Dead Are Judged

11 Then I saw a great
white throne and the one
who sat on it; the earth and
the heaven fled from his
presence, and no place was
found for them. 12 And I
saw the dead, great and
small, standing before the
throne, and books were
opened. Also another book
was opened, the book of
life. And the dead were
judged according to their
works, as recorded in the
books. 13 And the sea gave
up the dead that were in it,
Death and Hades gave up
the dead that were in them,
and all were judged according to what they had done.
14 Then Death and Hades
were thrown into the lake
of fire. This is the second
death, the lake of fire;
15 and anyone whose name
was not found written in
the book of life was thrown
into the lake of fire.

[o] Other ancient authorities read *from God, out of heaven,* or *out of heaven from God*

αὐτῶν˙ ὡς ἡ ἄμμος τῆς θαλάσσης. 9 καὶ
of them [is] as the sand of the sea. And

ἀνέβησαν ἐπὶ τὸ πλάτος τῆς γῆς, καὶ
they went up over the breadth of the land, and

ἐκύκλευσαν τὴν παρεμβολὴν τῶν ἁγίων
encircled the camp of the saints

καὶ τὴν πόλιν τὴν ἠγαπημένην· καὶ
and the [2]city – *having been* [1]loved; and

κατέβη πῦρ ἐκ τοῦ οὐρανοῦ καὶ κατέφαγεν
[2]came down [1]fire out of – heaven and devoured

αὐτούς· 10 καὶ ὁ διάβολος ὁ πλανῶν αὐτοὺς
them; and the Devil – deceiving them

ἐβλήθη εἰς τὴν λίμνην τοῦ πυρὸς καὶ
was cast into the lake – of fire and

θείου, ὅπου καὶ τὸ θηρίον καὶ ὁ
sulphur, where [were] also the beast and the

ψευδοπροφήτης, καὶ βασανισθήσονται ἡμέρας
false prophet, and they will be tormented day

καὶ νυκτὸς εἰς τοὺς αἰῶνας τῶν αἰώνων.
and night unto the ages of the ages.

11 Καὶ εἶδον θρόνον μέγαν λευκὸν καὶ
And I saw [3]throne [1]a great [2]white and

τὸν καθήμενον ἐπ' αὐτόν οὗ ἀπὸ τοῦ
the [one] sitting on it [4]of whom [1]from [2]the

προσώπου ἔφυγεν ἡ γῆ καὶ ὁ οὐρανός,
[3]face [6]fled [1]the [2]earth [3]and [4]the [5]heaven,

καὶ τόπος οὐχ εὑρέθη αὐτοῖς. 12 καὶ
and a place was not found for them. And

εἶδον τοὺς νεκρούς, τοὺς μεγάλους καὶ
I saw the dead, the great and

τοὺς μικρούς, ἑστῶτας ἐνώπιον τοῦ θρόνου,
the small, standing before the throne,

καὶ βιβλία ἠνοίχθησαν· καὶ ἄλλο βιβλίον
and scrolls were opened; and another scroll

ἠνοίχθη, ὅ ἐστιν τῆς ζωῆς· καὶ ἐκρίθησαν
was opened, which is [the scroll] – of life; and [3]were judged

οἱ νεκροὶ ἐκ τῶν γεγραμμένων ἐν τοῖς
[1]the [2]dead by the things *having been* written in the

βιβλίοις κατὰ τὰ ἔργα αὐτῶν. 13 καὶ
scrolls according to the works of them. And

ἔδωκεν ἡ θάλασσα τοὺς νεκροὺς τοὺς
[3]gave [1]the [2]sea the dead –

ἐν αὐτῇ, καὶ ὁ θάνατος καὶ ὁ ᾅδης
in it, and – death and – hades

ἔδωκαν τοὺς νεκροὺς τοὺς ἐν αὐτοῖς,
gave the dead – in them,

καὶ ἐκρίθησαν ἕκαστος κατὰ τὰ ἔργα
and they were judged each one according to the works

αὐτῶν. 14 καὶ ὁ θάνατος καὶ ὁ ᾅδης
of them. And – death and – hades

ἐβλήθησαν εἰς τὴν λίμνην τοῦ πυρός.
were cast into the lake – of fire.

οὗτος ὁ θάνατος ὁ δεύτερός ἐστιν, ἡ
This [2]the, [4]death – [3]second [1]is, the

λίμνη τοῦ πυρός. 15 καὶ εἴ τις οὐχ
lake – of fire. And if anyone not

εὑρέθη ἐν τῇ βίβλῳ τῆς ζωῆς γεγραμ-
was found [2]in [3]the [4]scroll – [5]of life [1]*having been*

μένος, ἐβλήθη εἰς τὴν λίμνην τοῦ πυρός.
written, he was cast into the lake – of fire.

like the sand on the sea-
shore. 9 They marched
across the breadth of the
earth and surrounded the
camp of God's people, the
city he loves. But fire came
down from heaven and de-
voured them. 10 And the
devil, who deceived them,
was thrown into the lake of
burning sulfur, where the
beast and the false prophet
had been thrown. They will
be tormented day and night
for ever and ever.

The Dead Are Judged

11 Then I saw a great white
throne and him who was
seated on it. Earth and sky
fled from his presence, and
there was no place for
them. 12 And I saw the
dead, great and small,
standing before the throne,
and books were opened.
Another book was opened,
which is the book of life.
The dead were judged ac-
cording to what they had
done as recorded in the
books. 13 The sea gave up
the dead that were in it, and
death and Hades gave up
the dead that were in them,
and each person was
judged according to what
he had done. 14 Then death
and Hades were thrown
into the lake of fire. The
lake of fire is the second
death. 15 If anyone's name
was not found written in
the book of life, he was
thrown into the lake of fire.

Chapter 21

The New Heaven and the New Earth

THEN I saw a new heav-
en and a new earth; for
the first heaven and the
first earth had passed
away, and the sea was no
more. 2 And I saw the holy
city, the new Jerusalem,
coming down out of heaven
from God, prepared as a
bride adorned for her husband. 3 And I heard a loud
voice from the throne saying,

"See, the home[p] of
God is
among mortals.
He will dwell[p] with
them as
their God;[q]
they will be his
peoples,[r]
and God himself will
be with them;[s]
4 he will wipe every
tear from
their eyes.
Death will be no
more;
mourning and crying
and pain will be
no more,
for the first things
have
passed away."

5 And the one who was
seated on the throne said,
"See, I am making all
things new." Also he said,
"Write this, for these
words are trustworthy and
true." 6 Then he said to me,
"It is done! I am the Alpha
and the Omega, the begin-
ning and the end. To the
thirsty I will give water as a
gift from the spring of the
water of life. 7 Those who
conquer will inherit these
things, and I will be their
God and they will be my
children. 8 But as for the
cowardly, the faithless,[t]
the polluted, the murder-
ers, the fornicators, the
sorcerers, the idolaters,
and all liars, their place will
be in the lake that burns
with fire and sulfur, which
is the second death."

[p] Gk *tabernacle*
[q] Other ancient authorities lack *as their God*
[r] Other ancient authorities read *people*
[s] Other ancient authorities add *and be their God*
[t] Or *the unbelieving*

21 Καὶ εἶδον οὐρανὸν καινὸν καὶ γῆν
And I saw [2]heaven [1]a new and [2]earth
καινήν· ὁ γὰρ πρῶτος οὐρανὸς καὶ ἡ
[1]a new; for the first heaven and the
πρώτη γῆ ἀπῆλθαν, καὶ ἡ θάλασσα
first earth passed away, and the sea
οὐκ ἔστιν ἔτι. **2** καὶ τὴν πόλιν τὴν
is not longer. And [3]the [4]city –
ἁγίαν Ἰερουσαλὴμ καινὴν εἶδον κατα-
[5]holy [6]Jerusalem [2]new [1]I saw coming
βαίνουσαν ἐκ τοῦ οὐρανοῦ ἀπὸ τοῦ θεοῦ,
down out of – heaven from – God,
ἡτοιμασμένην ὡς νύμφην κεκοσμημένην
having been prepared as a bride *having been* adorned
τῷ ἀνδρὶ αὐτῆς. **3** καὶ ἤκουσα φωνῆς
for the husband of her. And I heard [2]voice
μεγάλης ἐκ τοῦ θρόνου λεγούσης· ἰδοὺ
[1]a great(loud) out of the throne saying: Behold[,]
ἡ σκηνὴ τοῦ θεοῦ μετὰ τῶν ἀνθρώπων,
the tabernacle – of God [is] with – men,
καὶ σκηνώσει μετ' αὐτῶν, καὶ αὐτοὶ
and he will tabernacle with them, and they
λαοὶ αὐτοῦ ἔσονται, καὶ αὐτὸς ὁ θεὸς
[2]peoples [3]of him [1]will be, and [2][him]self – [1]God
μετ' αὐτῶν ἔσται, **4** καὶ ἐξαλείψει πᾶν
with them will be, and will wipe off every
δάκρυον ἐκ τῶν ὀφθαλμῶν αὐτῶν, καὶ
tear out of the eyes of them, and
ὁ θάνατος οὐκ ἔσται ἔτι, οὔτε πένθος
– death will not be longer, nor sorrow
οὔτε κραυγὴ οὔτε πόνος οὐκ ἔσται ἔτι·
nor clamour nor pain will *not* be longer;
ὅτι τὰ πρῶτα ἀπῆλθαν. **5** καὶ εἶπεν
because the first things passed away. And [6]said
ὁ καθήμενος ἐπὶ τῷ θρόνῳ· ἰδοὺ καινὰ
[1]the [one] [2]sitting [3]on [4]the [5]throne: Behold [2]new
ποιῶ πάντα. καὶ λέγει· γράψον, ὅτι
[1]I make [3]all things. And he says: Write thou, because
οὗτοι οἱ λόγοι πιστοὶ καὶ ἀληθινοί εἰσιν.
these – words faithful and true are.
6 καὶ εἶπέν μοι· γέγοναν. ἐγώ τὸ ἄλφα
And he said to me: It has occurred.* I [am] the alpha
καὶ τὸ ὦ, ἡ ἀρχὴ καὶ τὸ τέλος. ἐγὼ
and the omega, the beginning and the end. [3]I
τῷ διψῶντι δώσω ἐκ τῆς πηγῆς
[1]to the [one] [2]thirsting [4]will give out of the fountain
τοῦ ὕδατος τῆς ζωῆς δωρεάν. **7** ὁ νικῶν
of the water – of life freely. The over-[one] coming
κληρονομήσει ταῦτα, καὶ ἔσομαι αὐτῷ
shall inherit these things, and I will be to him
θεὸς καὶ αὐτὸς ἔσται μοι υἱός. **8** τοῖς δὲ
God and he shall be to me a son. But for the
δειλοῖς καὶ ἀπίστοις καὶ ἐβδελυγμένοις
cowardly and unbelieving and *having become* foul
καὶ φονεῦσιν καὶ πόρνοις καὶ φαρμακοῖς
and murderers and fornicators and sorcerers
καὶ εἰδωλολάτραις καὶ πᾶσιν τοῖς ψευδέσιν
and idolaters and all the false [ones]
τὸ μέρος αὐτῶν ἐν τῇ λίμνῃ τῇ καιομένῃ
the part of them in the lake – burning
πυρὶ καὶ θείῳ, ὅ ἐστιν ὁ θάνατος ὁ
with fire and *with* sulphur, which is the [2]death
δεύτερος.
[1]second [, shall be].

* Collective neuter plural; *cf.* ch. 16. 17.

Chapter 21

The New Jerusalem

THEN I saw a new heav-
en and a new earth, for
the first heaven and the
first earth had passed
away, and there was no
longer any sea. 2I saw the
Holy City, the new Jerusalem, coming down out of
heaven from God, prepared
as a bride beautifully
dressed for her husband.
3And I heard a loud voice
from the throne saying,
"Now the dwelling of God
is with men, and he will live
with them. They will be his
people, and God himself
will be with them and be
their God. 4He will wipe
every tear from their eyes.
There will be no more
death or mourning or cry-
ing or pain, for the old order of things has passed
away."
5He who was seated on
the throne said, "I am making everything new!" Then
he said, "Write this down,
for these words are trustworthy and true."
6He said to me: "It is
done. I am the Alpha and
the Omega, the Beginning
and the End. To him who is
thirsty I will give to drink
without cost from the
spring of the water of life.
7He who overcomes will inherit all this, and I will be
his God and he will be my
son. 8But the cowardly, the
unbelieving, the vile, the
murderers, the sexually immoral, those who practice
magic arts, the idolaters
and all liars—their place
will be in the fiery lake of
burning sulfur. This is the
second death."

Vision of the New Jerusalem

9 Then one of the seven
angels who had the seven
bowls full of the seven last
plagues came and said to
me, "Come, I will show
you the bride, the wife of
the Lamb." 10 And in the
spirit[u] he carried me away
to a great, high mountain
and showed me the holy
city Jerusalem coming
down out of heaven from
God. 11 It has the glory of
God and a radiance like a
very rare jewel, like jasper,
clear as crystal. 12 It has a
great, high wall with twelve
gates, and at the gates
twelve angels, and on the
gates are inscribed the
names of the twelve tribes
of the Israelites; 13 on the
east three gates, on the
north three gates, on the
south three gates, and on
the west three gates. 14 And
the wall of the city has
twelve foundations, and on
them are the twelve names
of the twelve apostles of
the Lamb.
15 The angel[v] who
talked to me had a measuring rod of gold to measure
the city and its gates and
walls. 16 The city lies four-
square, its length the same
as its width; and he mea-
sured the city with his rod,
fifteen hundred miles;[w] its
length and width and height
are equal. 17 He also measured its wall, one hundred

9 Καὶ ἦλθεν εἷς ἐκ τῶν ἑπτὰ ἀγγέλων
And came one of the seven angels
τῶν ἐχόντων τὰς ἑπτὰ φιάλας, τῶν
– having the seven bowls, –
γεμόντων τῶν ἑπτὰ πληγῶν τῶν ἐσχάτων,
being filled of(with) the seven [2]plagues – [1]last,
καὶ ἐλάλησεν μετ' ἐμοῦ λέγων· δεῦρο,
and spoke with me saying: Come,
δείξω σοι τὴν νύμφην τὴν γυναῖκα
I will show thee the bride[,] the wife
τοῦ ἀρνίου. 10 καὶ ἀπήνεγκέν με ἐν
of the Lamb. And he bore away me in
πνεύματι ἐπὶ ὄρος μέγα καὶ ὑψηλόν,
spirit onto [4]mountain [1]a great [2]and [3]high,
καὶ ἔδειξέν μοι τὴν πόλιν τὴν ἁγίαν
and showed me the [2]city – [1]holy
Ἰερουσαλὴμ καταβαίνουσαν ἐκ τοῦ οὐρανοῦ
Jerusalem coming down out of – heaven
ἀπὸ τοῦ θεοῦ, 11 ἔχουσαν τὴν δόξαν
from – God, having the glory
τοῦ θεοῦ· ὁ φωστὴρ αὐτῆς ὅμοιος λίθῳ
– of God; the light of it [was] like *to* a stone
τιμιωτάτῳ, ὡς λίθῳ ἰάσπιδι κρυσταλλίζοντι·
very valuable, as [2]stone [1]*to* a jasper *being* clear as crystal;
12 ἔχουσα τεῖχος μέγα καὶ ὑψηλόν,
having [4]wall [1]a great [2]and [3]high,
ἔχουσα πυλῶνας δώδεκα, καὶ ἐπὶ τοῖς
having [2]gates [1]twelve, and at the
πυλῶσιν ἀγγέλους δώδεκα, καὶ ὀνόματα
gates [2]angels [1]twelve, and names
ἐπιγεγραμμένα, ἅ ἐστιν τῶν δώδεκα
having been inscribed, which is(are) of the twelve
φυλῶν υἱῶν Ἰσραήλ. 13 ἀπὸ ἀνατολῆς
tribes of sons of Israel. From east
πυλῶνες τρεῖς, καὶ ἀπὸ βορρᾶ πυλῶνες
[2]gates [1]three, and from north [2]gates
τρεῖς, καὶ ἀπὸ νότου πυλῶνες τρεῖς,
[1]three, and from south [2]gates [1]three,
καὶ ἀπὸ δυσμῶν πυλῶνες τρεῖς. 14 καὶ
and from west [2]gates [1]three. And
τὸ τεῖχος τῆς πόλεως ἔχων θεμελίους
the wall of the city having [2]foundations
δώδεκα, καὶ ἐπ' αὐτῶν δώδεκα ὀνόματα
[1]twelve, and on them twelve names
τῶν δώδεκα ἀποστόλων τοῦ ἀρνίου. 15 Καὶ
of the twelve apostles of the Lamb. And
ὁ λαλῶν μετ' ἐμοῦ εἶχεν μέτρον κάλαμον
the [one] speaking with me had [3]measure [2]reed
χρυσοῦν, ἵνα μετρήσῃ τὴν πόλιν καὶ
[1]a golden, in order that he might measure the city and
τοὺς πυλῶνας αὐτῆς καὶ τὸ τεῖχος αὐτῆς.
the gates of it and the wall of it.
16 καὶ ἡ πόλις τετράγωνος κεῖται, καὶ
And the city [2]square [1]lies, and
τὸ μῆκος αὐτῆς ὅσον τὸ πλάτος. καὶ
the length of it [is] as much as the breadth. And
ἐμέτρησεν τὴν πόλιν τῷ καλάμῳ ἐπὶ
he measured the city with the reed at
σταδίων δώδεκα χιλιάδων· τὸ μῆκος καὶ
[2]furlongs [1]twelve [3]thousands; the length and
τὸ πλάτος καὶ τὸ ὕψος αὐτῆς ἴσα ἐστίν.
the breadth and the height of it [2]equal [1]is(are).
17 καὶ ἐμέτρησεν τὸ τεῖχος αὐτῆς ἑκατὸν
And he measured the wall of it *of* a hundred

9One of the seven angels
who had the seven bowls
full of the seven last
plagues came and said to
me, "Come, I will show
you the bride, the wife of
the Lamb." 10And he car-
ried me away in the Spirit
to a mountain great and
high, and showed me the
Holy City, Jerusalem, coming down out of heaven
from God. 11It shone with
the glory of God, and its
brilliance was like that of a
very precious jewel, like a
jasper, clear as crystal. 12It
had a great, high wall with
twelve gates, and with
twelve angels at the gates.
On the gates were written
the names of the twelve
tribes of Israel. 13There
were three gates on the
east, three on the north,
three on the south and
three on the west. 14The
wall of the city had twelve
foundations, and on them
were the names of the
twelve apostles of the
Lamb.
15The angel who talked
with me had a measuring
rod of gold to measure the
city, its gates and its walls.
16The city was laid out like
a square, as long as it was
wide. He measured the city
with the rod and found it to
be 12,000 stadia[x] in length,
and as wide and high as it is
long. 17He measured its

[u] Or *in the Spirit*
[v] Gk *He*
[w] Gk *twelve thousand stadia*

[x] *16* That is, about 1,400 miles (about 2,200 kilometers)

forty-four cubits[x] by human measurement, which the angel was using. 18 The wall is built of jasper, while the city is pure gold, clear as glass. 19 The foundations of the wall of the city are adorned with every jewel; the first was jasper, the second sapphire, the third agate, the fourth emerald, 20 the fifth onyx, the sixth carnelian, the seventh chrysolite, the eighth beryl, the ninth topaz, the tenth chrysoprase, the eleventh jacinth, the twelfth amethyst. 21 And the twelve gates are twelve pearls, each of the gates is a single pearl, and the street of the city is pure gold, transparent as glass.

22 I saw no temple in the city, for its temple is the Lord God the Almighty and the Lamb. 23 And the city has no need of sun or moon to shine on it, for the glory of God is its light, and its lamp is the Lamb. 24 The nations will walk by its light, and the kings of the earth will bring their glory into it. 25 Its gates will never be shut by day—and there will be no night there. 26 People will bring into it the glory and the honor of the nations. 27 But nothing unclean will enter it, nor

[x] That is, almost seventy-five yards

τεσσεράκοντα τεσσάρων πηχῶν, μέτρον
[and] forty-four cubits, a measure

ἀνθρώπου, ὅ ἐστιν ἀγγέλου. **18** καὶ
of a man, which is of an angel. And

ἡ ἐνδώμησις τοῦ τείχους αὐτῆς ἴασπις,
the coping of the wall of it [was] jasper,

καὶ ἡ πόλις χρυσίον καθαρὸν ὅμοιον
and the city [was] ^{2}gold ^{1}clean(pure) like

ὑάλῳ καθαρῷ. **19** οἱ θεμέλιοι τοῦ τείχους
^{2}glass ^{1}*to* clean(pure). The foundations of the wall

τῆς πόλεως παντὶ λίθῳ τιμίῳ κεκοσμημένοι·
of the city ^{3}with every ^{4}stone ^{2}precious ^{1}*having been* adorned;

ὁ θεμέλιος ὁ πρῶτος ἴασπις, ὁ δεύτερος
the foundation – first jasper, the second

σάπφιρος, ὁ τρίτος χαλκηδών, ὁ τέταρτος
sapphire, the third chalcedony, the fourth

σμάραγδος, **20** ὁ πέμπτος σαρδόνυξ, ὁ
emerald, the fifth sardonyx, the

ἕκτος σάρδιον, ὁ ἕβδομος χρυσόλιθος,
sixth sardius, the seventh chrysolite,

ὁ ὄγδοος βήρυλλος, ὁ ἔνατος τοπάζιον,
the eighth beryl, the ninth topaz,

ὁ δέκατος χρυσόπρασος, ὁ ἑνδέκατος
the tenth chrysoprasus, the eleventh

ὑάκινθος, ὁ δωδέκατος ἀμέθυστος. **21** καὶ
hyacinth, the twelfth amethyst. And

οἱ δώδεκα πυλῶνες δώδεκα μαργαρῖται·
the twelve gates [were] twelve pearls;

ἀνὰ εἷς ἕκαστος τῶν πυλώνων ἦν ἐξ
respectively† ^{2}one ^{1}each of the gates was of

ἑνὸς μαργαρίτου. καὶ ἡ πλατεῖα τῆς
one pearl. And the street of the

πόλεως χρυσίον καθαρὸν ὡς ὕαλος διαυγής.
city [was] ^{2}gold ^{1}clean(pure) as ^{2}glass ^{1}transparent.

22 Καὶ ναὸν οὐκ εἶδον ἐν αὐτῇ· ὁ γὰρ
And a shrine I saw not in it; for the

κύριος ὁ θεὸς ὁ παντοκράτωρ ναὸς αὐτῆς
Lord – God the Almighty shrine of it

ἐστιν, καὶ τὸ ἀρνίον. **23** καὶ ἡ πόλις
is, and the Lamb. And the city

οὐ χρείαν ἔχει τοῦ ἡλίου οὐδὲ τῆς
not need has of the sun nor of the

σελήνης, ἵνα φαίνωσιν αὐτῇ· ἡ γὰρ
moon, in order that they might shine in it; for the

δόξα τοῦ θεοῦ ἐφώτισεν αὐτήν, καὶ
glory – of God enlightened it, and

ὁ λύχνος αὐτῆς τὸ ἀρνίον. **24** καὶ
the lamp of it [is] the Lamb. And

περιπατήσουσιν τὰ ἔθνη διὰ τοῦ φωτὸς
^{3}shall walk about ^{1}the ^{2}nations through the light

αὐτῆς, καὶ οἱ βασιλεῖς τῆς γῆς φέρουσιν
of it, and the kings of the earth bring

τὴν δόξαν αὐτῶν εἰς αὐτήν· **25** καὶ οἱ
the glory of them into it; and the

πυλῶνες αὐτῆς οὐ μὴ κλεισθῶσιν ἡμέρας,
gates of it by no means may be shut by day,

νὺξ γὰρ οὐκ ἔσται ἐκεῖ· **26** καὶ οἴσουσιν
for night shall not be there; and they will bring

τὴν δόξαν καὶ τὴν τιμὴν τῶν ἐθνῶν
the glory and the honour of the nations

εἰς αὐτήν. **27** καὶ οὐ μὴ εἰσέλθῃ εἰς
into it. And by no means may enter into

wall and it was 144 cubits[y] thick,[z] by man's measurement, which the angel was using. 18 The wall was made of jasper, and the city of pure gold, as pure as glass. 19 The foundations of the city walls were decorated with every kind of precious stone. The first foundation was jasper, the second sapphire, the third chalcedony, the fourth emerald, 20 the fifth sardonyx, the sixth carnelian, the seventh chrysolite, the eighth beryl, the ninth topaz, the tenth chrysoprase, the eleventh jacinth, and the twelfth amethyst.[a] 21 The twelve gates were twelve pearls, each gate made of a single pearl. The great street of the city was of pure gold, like transparent glass.

22 I did not see a temple in the city, because the Lord God Almighty and the Lamb are its temple. 23 The city does not need the sun or the moon to shine on it, for the glory of God gives it light, and the Lamb is its lamp. 24 The nations will walk by its light, and the kings of the earth will bring their splendor into it. 25 On no day will its gates ever be shut, for there will be no night there. 26 The glory and honor of the nations will be brought into it. 27 Nothing impure will ever enter it,

[y] *17* That is, about 200 feet (about 65 meters)

[z] *17* Or *high*

[a] *20* The precise identification of some of these precious stones is uncertain.

anyone who practices abomination or falsehood, but only those who are written in the Lamb's book of life.

Chapter 22

The River of Life

THEN the angel[y] showed me the river of the water of life, bright as crystal, flowing from the throne of God and of the Lamb 2 through the middle of the street of the city. On either side of the river, is the tree of life[z] with its twelve kinds of fruit, producing its fruit each month; and the leaves of the tree are for the healing of the nations. 3 Nothing accursed will be found there any more. But the throne of God and of the Lamb will be in it, and his servants[a] will worship him; 4 they will see his face, and his name will be on their foreheads. 5 And there will be no more night; they need no light of lamp or sun, for the Lord God will be their light, and they will reign forever and ever.

6 And he said to me, "These words are trustworthy and true, for the Lord, the God of the spirits of the prophets, has sent his angel to show his servants[a] what must soon take place."

7 "See, I am coming soon! Blessed is the one who keeps the words of the prophecy of this book."

Epilogue and Benediction

8 I, John, am the one who heard and saw these

[y] Gk *he*
[z] Or *the Lamb. 2In the middle of the street of the city, and on either side of the river, is the tree of life*
[a] Gk *slaves*

αὐτὴν πᾶν κοινὸν καὶ [ὁ] ποιῶν
it every(any) profane thing and the [one] making
βδέλυγμα καὶ ψεῦδος, εἰ μὴ οἱ γεγραμ-
an abomination and a lie, except the [ones] *having been*
μένοι ἐν τῷ βιβλίῳ τῆς ζωῆς τοῦ ἀρνίου.
written in the scroll – of life of the Lamb.

22 Καὶ ἔδειξέν μοι ποταμὸν ὕδατος
And he showed me a river of water
ζωῆς λαμπρὸν ὡς κρύσταλλον, ἐκπορευόμε-
of life bright as crystal, proceed-
νον ἐκ τοῦ θρόνου τοῦ θεοῦ καὶ τοῦ
ing out of the throne – of God and of the
ἀρνίου. **2** ἐν μέσῳ τῆς πλατείας αὐτῆς
Lamb. In [the] midst of the street of it
καὶ τοῦ ποταμοῦ ἐντεῦθεν καὶ ἐκεῖθεν
and of the river hence and thence
ξύλον ζωῆς ποιοῦν καρποὺς δώδεκα,
a tree of life producing fruits twelve,
κατὰ μῆνα ἕκαστον ἀποδιδοῦν τὸν καρπὸν
according to ²month ¹each rendering the fruit
αὐτοῦ, καὶ τὰ φύλλα τοῦ ξύλου εἰς
of it, and the leaves of the tree [will be] for
θεραπείαν τῶν ἐθνῶν. **3** καὶ πᾶν κατάθεμα
healing of the nations. And every curse =no curse will be any
οὐκ ἔσται ἔτι. καὶ ὁ θρόνος τοῦ θεοῦ
will not be longer. longer. And the throne – of God
καὶ τοῦ ἀρνίου ἐν αὐτῇ ἔσται, καὶ οἱ
and of the Lamb ²in ³it ¹will be, and the
δοῦλοι αὐτοῦ λατρεύσουσιν αὐτῷ, **4** καὶ
slaves of him will do service to him, and
ὄψονται τὸ πρόσωπον αὐτοῦ, καὶ τὸ
they will see the face of him, and the
ὄνομα αὐτοῦ ἐπὶ τῶν μετώπων αὐτῶν.
name of him [will be] on the foreheads of them.
5 καὶ νὺξ οὐκ ἔσται ἔτι, καὶ οὐκ
And night will not be longer, and not
ἔχουσιν χρείαν φωτὸς λύχνου καὶ φωτὸς
they have need of light of lamp and of light
ἡλίου, ὅτι κύριος ὁ θεὸς φωτίσει ἐπ'
of sun, because [the] Lord – God will shed light on
αὐτούς, καὶ βασιλεύσουσιν εἰς τοὺς
them, and they will reign unto the
αἰῶνας τῶν αἰώνων.
ages of the ages.

6 Καὶ εἶπέν μοι· οὗτοι οἱ λόγοι πιστοὶ
And he said to me: These – words [are] faithful
καὶ ἀληθινοί, καὶ ὁ κύριος ὁ θεὸς τῶν
and true, and the Lord the God of the
πνευμάτων τῶν προφητῶν ἀπέστειλεν τὸν
spirits of the prophets sent the
ἄγγελον αὐτοῦ δεῖξαι τοῖς δούλοις αὐτοῦ
angel of him to show to the slaves of him
ἃ δεῖ γενέσθαι ἐν τάχει. **7** καὶ ἰδοὺ
things which it behoves to occur quickly. And behold
ἔρχομαι ταχύ. μακάριος ὁ τηρῶν τοὺς
I am coming quickly. Blessed [is] the [one] keeping the
λόγους τῆς προφητείας τοῦ βιβλίου τούτου.
words of the prophecy of this scroll.

8 Κἀγὼ Ἰωάννης ὁ ἀκούων καὶ βλέπων
And I John [am] the [one] hearing and seeing
ταῦτα. καὶ ὅτε ἤκουσα καὶ ἔβλεψα,
these things. And when I heard and *I saw*,

nor will anyone who does what is shameful or deceitful, but only those whose names are written in the Lamb's book of life.

Chapter 22

The River of Life

THEN the angel showed me the river of the water of life, as clear as crystal, flowing from the throne of God and of the Lamb 2down the middle of the great street of the city. On each side of the river stood the tree of life, bearing twelve crops of fruit, yielding its fruit every month. And the leaves of the tree are for the healing of the nations. 3No longer will there be any curse. The throne of God and of the Lamb will be in the city, and his servants will serve him. 4They will see his face, and his name will be on their foreheads. 5There will be no more night. They will not need the light of a lamp or the light of the sun, for the Lord God will give them light. And they will reign for ever and ever.

6The angel said to me, "These words are trustworthy and true. The Lord, the God of the spirits of the prophets, sent his angel to show his servants the things that must soon take place."

Jesus Is Coming

7"Behold, I am coming soon! Blessed is he who keeps the words of the prophecy in this book."

8I, John, am the one who heard and saw these things.

things. And when I heard
and saw them, I fell down
to worship at the feet of the
angel who showed them to
me; 9but he said to me,
"You must not do that! I am
a fellow servant[b] with you
and your comrades[c] the
prophets, and with those
who keep the words of this
book. Worship God!"
10 And he said to me,
"Do not seal up the words
of the prophecy of this
book, for the time is near.
11Let the evildoer still do
evil, and the filthy still be
filthy, and the righteous
still do right, and the holy
still be holy."

12 "See, I am coming
soon; my reward is with
me, to repay according to
everyone's work. 13I am
the Alpha and the Omega,
the first and the last, the beginning and the end."
14 Blessed are those
who wash their robes,[d] so
that they will have the right
to the tree of life and may
enter the city by the gates.
15Outside are the dogs and
sorcerers and fornicators
and murderers and idola-
ters, and everyone who
loves and practices falsehood.
16 "It is I, Jesus, who
sent my angel to you with
this testimony for the
churches. I am the root and
the descendant of David,
the bright morning star."
17 The Spirit and the
bride say,
"Come."
And let everyone who

[b] Gk *slave*
[c] Gk *brothers*
[d] Other ancient authorities read *do his commandments*

ἔπεσα προσκυνῆσαι ἔμπροσθεν τῶν ποδῶν
I fell to worship before the feet

τοῦ ἀγγέλου τοῦ δεικνύοντός μοι ταῦτα.
of the angel – showing me these things.

9 καὶ λέγει μοι· ὅρα μή· σύνδουλός
And he tells me: See thou [do] not; ³a fellow-slave

σού εἰμι καὶ τῶν ἀδελφῶν σου τῶν
⁴of thee ¹I am and of the brothers of thee the

προφητῶν καὶ τῶν τηρούντων τοὺς λόγους
prophets and of the [ones] keeping the words

τοῦ βιβλίου τούτου· τῷ θεῷ προσκύνησον.
of this scroll: – ²God ¹worship thou.

10 Καὶ λέγει μοι· μὴ σφραγίσῃς τοὺς
And he tells me: Seal not the

λόγους τῆς προφητείας τοῦ βιβλίου τούτου·
words of the prophecy of this scroll;

ὁ καιρὸς γὰρ ἐγγύς ἐστιν 11 ὁ ἀδικῶν
²the ³time ¹for ⁵near ⁴is. The [one] acting unjustly

ἀδικησάτω ἔτι, καὶ ὁ ῥυπαρὸς ῥυπανθήτω
let him act unjustly still, and the filthy [one] let him act filthily

ἔτι, καὶ ὁ δίκαιος δικαιοσύνην ποιησάτω
still, and the righteous [one] ²righteousness ¹let him do

ἔτι, καὶ ὁ ἅγιος ἁγιασθήτω ἔτι.
still, and the holy [one] let him be hallowed still.

12 Ἰδοὺ ἔρχομαι ταχύ, καὶ ὁ μισθός
Behold I am coming quickly, and the reward

μου μετ' ἐμοῦ, ἀποδοῦναι ἑκάστῳ ὡς
of me [is] with me, to render to each man as

τὸ ἔργον ἐστὶν αὐτοῦ. 13 ἐγὼ τὸ ἄλφα
the work ²is ¹of him. I [am] the alpha

καὶ τὸ ὦ, ὁ πρῶτος καὶ ὁ ἔσχατος,
and the omega, the first and the last,

ἡ ἀρχὴ καὶ τὸ τέλος. 14 μακάριοι οἱ
the beginning and the end. Blessed [are] the [ones]

πλύνοντες τὰς στολὰς αὐτῶν, ἵνα ἔσται
washing the robes of them, in order that ⁴will be

ἡ ἐξουσία αὐτῶν ἐπὶ τὸ ξύλον τῆς
¹the ²authority ³of them over the tree –

ζωῆς καὶ τοῖς πυλῶσιν εἰσέλθωσιν εἰς
of life and ³by the ³gates ¹they may enter into

τὴν πόλιν. 15 ἔξω οἱ κύνες καὶ οἱ φαρμακοὶ
the city. Outside [are] the dogs and the sorcerers

καὶ οἱ πόρνοι καὶ οἱ φονεῖς καὶ οἱ
and the fornicators and the murderers and the

εἰδωλολάτραι καὶ πᾶς φιλῶν καὶ ποιῶν
idolaters and everyone loving and making

ψεῦδος.
a lie.

16 Ἐγὼ Ἰησοῦς ἔπεμψα τὸν ἄγγελόν
I Jesus sent the angel

μου μαρτυρῆσαι ὑμῖν ταῦτα ἐπὶ ταῖς
of me to witness to you these things over(in) the

ἐκκλησίαις. ἐγώ εἰμι ἡ ῥίζα καὶ τὸ
churches. I am the root and the

γένος Δαυίδ, ὁ ἀστὴρ ὁ λαμπρὸς ὁ
offspring of David, the ³star – ¹bright –

πρωϊνός.
²morning.

17 Καὶ τὸ πνεῦμα καὶ ἡ νύμφη λέγουσιν·
And the Spirit and the bride say:

ἔρχου. καὶ ὁ ἀκούων εἰπάτω· ἔρχου.
Come. And the [one] hearing let him say: Come.

And when I had heard and
seen them, I fell down to
worship at the feet of the
angel who had been show-
ing them to me. 9But he
said to me, "Do not do it! I
am a fellow servant with
you and with your brothers
the prophets and of all who
keep the words of this
book. Worship God!"
10Then he told me, "Do
not seal up the words of the
prophecy of this book, because the time is near.
11Let him who does wrong
continue to do wrong; let
him who is vile continue to
be vile; let him who does
right continue to do right;
and let him who is holy continue to be holy."

12"Behold, I am coming
soon! My reward is with
me, and I will give to everyone according to what he
has done. 13I am the Alpha
and the Omega, the First
and the Last, the Beginning
and the End.
14"Blessed are those who
wash their robes, that they
may have the right to the
tree of life and may go
through the gates into the
city. 15Outside are the
dogs, those who practice
magic arts, the sexually immoral, the murderers, the
idolaters and everyone who
loves and practices falsehood.
16"I, Jesus, have sent my
angel to give you[b] this testimony for the churches. I
am the Root and the Off-
spring of David, and the
bright Morning Star."

17The Spirit and the bride
say, "Come!" And let him
who hears say, "Come!"

[b] *16* The Greek is plural.

hears say,
"Come."
And let everyone who
is thirsty come.
Let anyone who
wishes take the
water of life as
a gift.
18 I warn everyone who
hears the words of the
prophecy of this book: if
anyone adds to them, God
will add to that person the
plagues described in this
book; 19if anyone takes
away from the words of the
book of this prophecy, God
will take away that per-
son's share in the tree of
life and in the holy city,
which are described in this
book.
20 The one who testifies
to these things says, "Surely I am coming soon."
Amen. Come, Lord
Jesus!
21 The grace of the
Lord Jesus be with all the
saints. Amen.[e]

καὶ ὁ διψῶν ἐρχέσθω, ὁ θέλων λαβέτω
And the thirsting [one] let him come, the wishing [one] let him take

ὕδωρ ζωῆς δωρεάν.
[the] water of life freely.

18 Μαρτυρῶ ἐγὼ παντὶ τῷ ἀκούοντι
[2]witness [1]I to everyone hearing

τοὺς λόγους τῆς προφητείας τοῦ βιβλίου
the words of the prophecy – [3]scroll

τούτου· ἐάν τις ἐπιθῇ ἐπ' αὐτά, ἐπιθήσει
[4]of this: If anyone adds upon(to) them,* [2]will add

ὁ θεὸς ἐπ' αὐτὸν τὰς πληγὰς τὰς
– [1]God upon him the plagues –

γεγραμμένας ἐν τῷ βιβλίῳ τούτῳ· 19 καὶ
having been written in this scroll; and

ἐάν τις ἀφέλῃ ἀπὸ τῶν λόγων τοῦ
if anyone takes away from the words of the

βιβλίου τῆς προφητείας ταύτης, ἀφελεῖ
scroll of this prophecy, [2]will take away

ὁ θεὸς τὸ μέρος αὐτοῦ ἀπὸ τοῦ ξύλου
– [1]God the part of him from the tree

τῆς ζωῆς καὶ ἐκ τῆς πόλεως τῆς ἁγίας,
– of life and out of the [2]city – [1]holy,

τῶν γεγραμμένων ἐν τῷ βιβλίῳ τούτῳ.
of the things *having been* written in this scroll.

20 Λέγει ὁ μαρτυρῶν ταῦτα· ναί, ἔρχομαι
Says the [one] witnessing these things: Yes, I am coming

ταχύ. Ἀμήν, ἔρχου κύριε Ἰησοῦ.
quickly. Amen, come[,] Lord Jesus.

21 Ἡ χάρις τοῦ κυρίου Ἰησοῦ μετὰ
The grace of the Lord Jesus [be] with

πάντων.
all.

Whoever is thirsty, let him
come; and whoever wishes,
let him take the free gift of
the water of life.

18I warn everyone who
hears the words of the
prophecy of this book: If
anyone adds anything to
them, God will add to him
the plagues described in
this book. 19And if anyone
takes words away from this
book of prophecy, God will
take away from him his
share in the tree of life and
in the holy city, which are
described in this book.
20He who testifies to
these things says, "Yes, I
am coming soon."
Amen. Come, Lord
Jesus.
21The grace of the Lord
Jesus be with God's peo-
ple. Amen.

[e] Other ancient authorities lack *all*; others lack *the saints*; others lack *Amen*

* Neuter plural; see last clause of ver. 19.